1917
Bolshevik
Revolution
begins

1991
Soviet Union
dissolves

D0026116

1945
Nazism defeated

1989
Fall of Berlin Wall

1517
Luther's 95 Theses
posted

1242
Mongols withdraw
from the West

1914
Assassination of
Archduke Ferdinand
leads to World War I

1453
Ottomans capture
Constantinople

ca. 8000 B.C.
Agriculture
invented

ca. 4000 B.C.
First civilization
emerges

ca. 1400 B.C.
Phoenicians
develop alphabet

ca. 800 B.C.
Homer
compiles *Iliad*

1054
Orthodox and
Catholic
(Eastern and Western)
churches split

ca. 480–430 B.C.
Greek Golden Age
flourishes

1347
Death arrives
estern Europe

ca. 2680 B.C.
Great Pyramid of
Khufu built

ca. A.D. 30
Public ministry and
death of Jesus Christ

St. Petersburg
[Petrograd]

Moscow

RUSSIA

BELARUS

Minsk

KAZAKHSTAN

Volga R.

Don R.

Kiev

UKRAINE

Dnieper R.

Kishinev

Caspian Sea

Bucharest

Black Sea

GEORGIA

Tbilisi

Baku

AZERBAIJAN

ARMENIA

Yerevan

ULGARIA

ofia

je

Istanbul
[Constantinople]

Ankara

TURKEY

IRAN

ECE

Athens

IONIA

CYPRUS

[Fertile Crescent]

Antioch

SYRIA

Baghdad

IRAQ

[Sumer]

Crete

[PHOENICIA]

Beirut

Damascus

LEBANON

Amman

KUWAIT

Kuwait

Sea

Jerusalem

ISRAEL

JORDAN

Alexandria

EGYPT

Cairo

Gizah

SAUDI   ARABIA

The West Transformed

A HISTORY
OF WESTERN CIVILIZATION

The West Transformed

A HISTORY
OF WESTERN CIVILIZATION

C. Warren Hollister
University of California
Santa Barbara

J. Sears McGee
University of California
Santa Barbara

Gale Stokes
Rice University

HARCOURT COLLEGE PUBLISHERS
Fort Worth   Philadelphia   San Diego   New York   Orlando   Austin   San Antonio
Toronto   Montreal   London   Sydney   Tokyo

Publisher:	Earl McPeek
Executive Editor:	David C. Tatom
Developmental Editor:	steve Norder
Market Strategist:	Steve Drummond
Project Editor:	Travis Tyre
Production Manager:	Serena Barnett
Art Director:	Sue Hart

Cover: Lorrain, Claude (1600–1682). *Harbor at Sunset.* Louvre, Paris, France. Giraudon/Art Resource, NY.

ISBN: 0-15-508117-9
Library of Congress Catalog Card Number: 98-75625

Address for orders:
Harcourt, Inc., 6277 Sea Harbor Drive, Orlando, FL 32887-6777
1-800-782-4479

Address for international orders
International Customer Service
Harcourt, Inc., 6277 Sea Harbor Drive, Orlando, FL 32887-6777
407 345-3800
(fax) 407 345-4060

Address for editorial correspondence:
Harcourt College Publishers, 301 Commerce Street, Suite 3700, Fort Worth, TX 76102

Web site address:
http://www.harcourtcollege.com

Harcourt, Inc. will provide complimentary supplements or supplement packages to those adopters qualified under our adoption policy. Please contact your sales representative to learn how you qualify. If, as an adopter or potential user, you receive supplements you do not need, please return them to your sales representative or send them to:
Attn: Returns Department, Troy Warehouse, 465 South Lincoln Drive, Troy, MO 63379.

Printed in the United States of America

0 1 2 3 4 5 6 7 8   048   9 8 7 6 5 4 3 2

To the memory of
C. Warren Hollister,
a beloved friend
and a magnificent teacher of
the history of
Western civilization

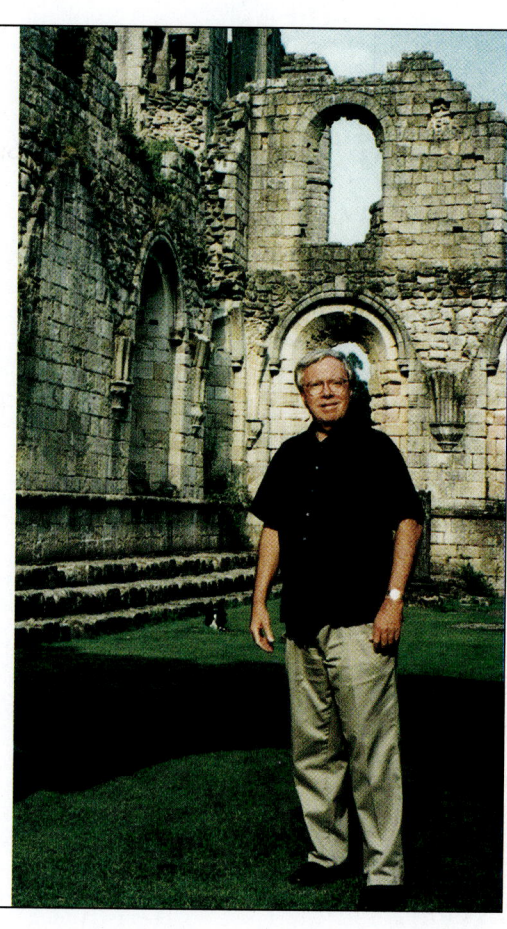

Your Authors

C. Warren Hollister (1931–1997) taught medieval European history and the history of Western civilization at the University of California from 1958 until his retirement in 1994. As the leading authority on the Norman Conquest of England, Professor Hollister's many books include *Anglo-Saxon Military Institutions on the Eve of the Norman Conquest* (Triennial Book Prize of the Conference on British Studies, 1962), *The Military Organization of Norman England* (1965), *Monarchy, Magnates, and Institutions in the Anglo-Norman World* (1986), *Medieval Europe* (Eighth edition, 1997), *The Making of England, 55 B.C. to A.D. 1399* (Seventh edition, 1996), and his forthcoming biography of Henry I. He has served in the presidencies of the Pacific Coast Conference on British Studies (1968–1970), the North American Conference on British Studies (1985–1987), the Charles Homer Haskins Society (1982–1990), the American Historical Association (Pacific Coast branch, 1990–1991), and the Medieval Academy of the Pacific. He was a fellow of the Medieval Academy of America and the Royal Historical Society (London), and he has received fellowships from Fulbright, Guggenheim, American Council of Learned Societies, and the National Endowment for the Humanities. He has written several musical comedies, coauthored a children's fantasy *(The Moons of Meer)*, and was an expert on the life of L. Frank Baum, the author of *The Wizard of Oz*. Professor Hollister received his B.A. from Harvard University and a Ph.D. from the University of California-Los Angeles and has served as departmental chair at the University of California-Santa Barbara (1967–68 and 1969–70).

J. Sears McGee has taught early modern European history and the history of Western civilization at the University of California since 1971. His research concerns religion and politics in seventeenth-century Britain. He is a fellow of the Royal Historical Society (London) and president (1998–2000) of the Pacific Coast Conference on British Studies. His books include *The Godly Man in Stuart England* (1971) and his edition of three of the early works of John Bunyan (*The Miscellaneous Works of John Bunyan*, vol. 3, 1987). He earned a B.A. from Rice University and a Ph.D. from Yale University. Professor McGee was department chair at the University of California-Santa Barbara from 1990 to 1995. The UCSB Academic Senate named him Outstanding Teacher in the Social Sciences in 1990, and in the same year, the student-led organization Mortar Board awarded him a top prize for teaching.

Gale Stokes is the Mary Gibbs Jones professor of history at Rice University. He has taught the introductory course in modern European history at Rice for more than thirty years and has won several university awards for his teaching. Stokes's primary field of research has been the history of eastern Europe, particularly the Balkans. He has been a fellow at the Woodrow Wilson International Center for Scholars in Washington, D.C. and has held many fellowships, including the Fulbright, Fulbright-Hays, American Council of Learned Societies, and the National Endowment for the Humanities. His book *The Walls Came Tumbling Down: The Collapse of Communism in Eastern Europe* won the 1994 Vucinich Award of the American Association for the Advancement of Slavic Studies. Other books published in the 1990s include *From Stalinism to Pluralism: A Documentary History of Eastern Europe, The Politics of Development: The Emergence of Political Parties in Nineteenth Century Serbia*, and *Three Eras of Political Change in Eastern Europe*. Professor Stokes has been chair of the history department at Rice since 1997.

Preface

Our title, *The West Transformed*, suggests our approach to the presentation of Western civilization to students and conveys our conviction that the past has created our present and is the source of our future. History, we believe, is the study of the tension between *continuity* and *change* in human affairs, and of how human beings respond to the transformations that always challenge and often threaten them. Although we consider the West a cultural tradition, we see it as undergoing constant transformation —geographically, as it expands out of its Near Eastern cradle to the Mediterranean, Europe, and the Atlantic basin; institutionally, as it evolves new forms of polity; religiously and philosophically, as countless generations of its people grapple with the meaning of life and encounter the worldviews of other civilizations; economically and socially, as human communities become more complex; and finally technologically and environmentally, as burgeoning populations exert ever more pressure on natural resources. How and why this never-ending process of transformation occurs is the stuff of history.

Our approach to Western civilization avoids the compartmentalized isolation of people, events, and movements that seems to afflict many textbooks as they dutifully attempt to "cover all the bases." Instead, we narrate the story of civilization in the West as a continuous series of transformations—cultural, technological, social, and political. This chain of changes stretches back to the Neolithic Revolution in the Near East. Frequently, we pause to emphasize the long lines of historical continuity: the Mesopotamian and Greek roots of the Old Paradigm that dominated Western science until the Scientific Revolution; the pervasive legacy of Judaism in the Western value system and how, in Christianity, this legacy both blends and clashes with the Hellenic tradition; and the ways in which Roman law and values live on in our institutions and the institutions themselves, which are rooted in the Middle Ages.

Equally, the discontinuities of history have a constant place in our story. Civilization itself, with its divisions of labor, its social hierarchies, its capacity to generate wealth, and its propensity toward exploitation, meant a jolting break from the way of life that pre-civilized peoples had known. The invention of agriculture; Bronze- and Iron-Age metallurgy; urbanization; the rise and fall of empires; the invention of more efficient (and more expensive) ways for armed forces to kill each other; the spiritual and social tensions that new religious and philosophical ideas have always unleashed; the conflicts that have resulted as increasingly diverse groups within societies sought dignity, equity, and a place in civil society; and the all-pervasive impact of the Scientific, Industrial, Energy, and Information Revolutions over the past few hundred years—these are only a few of the dramatic changes to which a presentation of Western history needs to speak. In writing each chapter, we have tried to keep such larger questions as these in mind and have tried to avoid letting the narrative get mired in narrow detail.

A major innovation in our approach is constantly to emphasize Western civilization's global context. Although the college course known as Western Civilization may have originated, several generations ago, in a triumphalist spirit, the day for such self-congratulation is clearly past. In writing our book, we have never forgotten that for long periods the societies that constitute the Western world were peripheral and backward compared to other parts of the globe. This focus is most apparent in the introductions to each of the six parts into which the book is divided. Each part introduction is designed to give not only a foretaste of the chapters that follow, but equally importantly to set a significant segment of the West's history in a global perspective. Likewise, each chapter frequently draws comparisons between Western and non-Western civilizations. And we neither celebrate the West's rise to global ascendancy as reflective of inherent superiority nor assume that such ascendancy will endure; rather, our approach is to analyze the forces that drove Westerners from the fifteenth century onward to press outward to meet their needs and thus to initiate a process of globalization that is apparently irreversible.

The West Transformed, like any work of historical synthesis, must be selective. Our book is designed to meet the requirements of most instructors in the Western Civilization or European Survey course, but we have chosen to emphasize certain key elements:

• *A lively, often vivid, writing style* We love history and find it endlessly fascinating. We have tried to express our love for the discipline and our respect for its literary tradition that goes back to Herodotus by trying to avoid a dry, "textbook" style. And although we think that jokes are more appropriately delivered in the lecture hall than in the textbook, we have written with an occasional light touch.

• *The interrelatedness of social, economic, cultural, and political history* We would not describe our approach as "driven" by preponderant attention to any one of these subjects; rather, we try throughout to show how all of these factors are constantly at work in producing historical change. A good example is our treatment of the Roman Republic (Chapter 4), in which we stress the crucial role of the Roman *familia* in maintaining traditional religious and cultural values, the transformation of the republic through war and conquest, and the Romans' attempts to adapt their institutions (culminating in those of the Principate) to conditions of uncertainty and instability. Chapter 8, which treats high medieval economic and religious history, uses the concept of a "Dual Revolution" to explain how the return of a money economy, the revitalization of towns, and the intensification of urban Christian piety resulted in both the emergence of papal leadership in the West and the challenge of religious heterodoxy. Chapter 14 gives equal weight to the beginnings of Western expansion in the global arena and the expansion of the Western economy during the "long sixteenth century," along with the social consequences of demographic growth supported by increasingly inadequate technology. Our treatment of the Enlightenment (Chapter 18) is preceded by a thorough discussion of the eighteenth-century society and economic structure on which the enterprise of the *philosophes* rested, and it ends with the discovery by some philosophes of envi-

ronmental problems. The concept of the Dual Revolution returns in a different guise in Chapters 20 and 21 to describe the two related but independent shaping forces of the Industrial and French revolutions. Chapter 22 (The Origin of Modern Ideology) approaches the emergence of liberalism, conservatism, socialism, and indeed the modern concept of *ideology* in the context of post-Revolutionary politics and the era's search for stability amid decidedly unstable social and economic conditions. And all of Part Five (The Century of Power) is organized around the concept of power in the modern world, especially how the Europeans' use of power led to, among other things, two catastrophic world wars.

• *Special focus on the history of science, technology, and the environment* Because we regard the Scientific Revolution and the Industrial (or Energy) Revolution as key factors in the shaping of Western civilization as it has come to exist, as well as world-transforming phenomena, we believe that a textbook for the Western civilization course ought to accord these processes sustained attention. We have also been mindful of how often Westerners' transformation of their world has had major implications for the environment in which they live.

In *The West Transformed*, both the Scientific Revolution and the Industrial Revolution are the subjects of entire chapters (Chapters 17 and 20). Moreover, in many other chapters we anticipate this emphasis by paying attention to science, technology, and environmental change. See, for example, the discussion in Chapter 1 of the importance first of agriculture and later of iron metallurgy in transforming the ancient world; in Chapter 3 the treatment of Greek science, which includes an analysis of why the Industrial Revolution had to wait seventeen hundred years after the impressive achievements of Hellenistic engineers and mathematicians; and in Chapters 10, 11, and 14 the sections on medieval and Renaissance science and technology. As we approach the modern period, this emphasis continues in Chapter 18's discussion of how environmental consciousness awakened during the Enlightenment, and Chapter 23 fully treats the spread of the Industrial Revolution to the Continent beginning in the 1820s. Chapter 26 shows how cultural modernism paralleled the reshaping of scientific paradigms in the era of Einstein and Freud, and Chapter 32 examines the rooting of contemporary history in the Information Revolution and weaves in global environmental concerns. Finally, the book gives more than cursory attention to important changes in military technology and their larger ramifications for societies, economies, and states: see in particular Chapter 1 (the impact of chariots and iron weaponry), Chapter 11 (gunpowder and gunnery), Chapters 12 and 16 (the Military Revolution as it unfolded in the Renaissance and in the seventeenth century), and Chapter 28 (World War I).

• *Close attention to the development of Western value systems and religious traditions* Our book takes very seriously the obligation of the Western civilization course to acquaint students with the evolution of Westerners' ideas of the sacred and human destiny. Thus Chapter 1 offers a full account of the emergence of ancient Judaism—probably the most thorough treatment of this subject in any Western civilization textbook. Chapter 3 gives extra attention to explaining Greek religion and classical philosophy, which are essential foundations to all that follows in the course. Chapter 5 provides a detailed explanation of the transformation of Greco-Roman paganism, the emergence of Christianity out of first-century Judaism, the sociology of early Christianity, and the beginnings of Christian theology. Chapter 6 includes early medieval Judaism among the heirs to the Greco-Roman legacy, alongside Byzantium, Islam, and the semi-barbarian West. Chapters 10 and 11 carefully explain high and late medieval philosophy, theology, and university life. In Chapter 12 we dispose of the myth of Renaissance "neopaganism," and in Chapter 13 we carefully examine both the vigor of late medieval popular piety at the beginning of the sixteenth century and the power of the Protestant and Catholic Reformations' challenges to that piety. The discussion of the Enlightenment in Chapter 18 grapples with the philosophes' attempts to construct an essentially post–Judeo-Christian worldview, and in Chapter 22 this story continues with a thorough discussion of modern ideologies. Chapter 26, which is devoted entirely to the emergence of modernism from the 1880s to 1914, offers an essential preparation for understanding the conflicted twentieth-century mentality.

• *Special focus on the shaping and reshaping of the family* One of the fundamental institutions in all cultures is the family, yet *The West Transformed* makes clear to students that family structures and gender roles are historically determined. Chapter 4, for example, shows that what the Romans meant by the familia was not the nuclear family of today; Chapter 7 discusses the wide-ranging importance of changes in women's diet and the emergence of the Western nuclear family around the year 1000; and Chapter 12 stresses how the famous individualism of the Renaissance was tempered by the pervasive power of kinship. Throughout the book, we emphasize how the status of women and conceptions of childhood reflect family relationships and socioeconomic structures. Chapters 14 and 18 make this clear in the case of early modern Europe, and Chapter 23 does the same for industrializing nineteenth-century Europe.

• *In treating traditional political history, an emphasis on analysis over detailed narrative* Our years of classroom teaching experience have convinced us that survey-level students can easily feel overwhelmed with detail when they read about wars, diplomacy, and high politics. We have tried to keep such narratives as concise and crisp as possible, paying greater attention to the changes that they wrought than to the (often literal) thrust-and-parry of events. See, for example, the ways in which we have dealt with the Peloponnesian War (Chapter 2), the Punic Wars and the Roman Revolution (Chapter 4), the Crusades (Chapter 9), the Hundred Years' War (Chapter 11), the Thirty Years' War (Chapter 15), eighteenth-century diplomacy and wars (Chapter 19), the French Revolutionary and Napoleonic wars (Chapter 21), and Italian and German unification (Chapter 24). But we have also taken the opportunity to demonstrate how wars and political upheavals can sometimes work to powerful effect. Examples include our treatment of the Norman Conquest (Chapter 9), England's "Glorious Revolution" of 1688 (Chapter 16), the coming of the French Revolution (Chapter 21), and the outbreak of World War I (Chapter 27).

• *Constant attention to the role of individuals in history* One of the longest-standing historical controversies revolves around the question of whether impersonal forces or outstanding individuals make history. We are equally skeptical of "great man" theories and of "inevitable" historical movements. Students, we believe, need to understand that individuals and the events in which they participate are shaped by myriad forces, which stretch over long spans and are perceptible only with historical hindsight, and that sometimes unpredictable consequences flow from flukes, chance, and personality. Individual men and women frequently appear in our narrative; sometimes they are faces in the crowd that give a human touch to great events, and sometimes they are great actors requiring deft characterization.

Each chapter, moreover, offers a pair of boxed essays called "The Human Experience" that generally focus on individuals whose lives embody the historical events under discussion in the surrounding text. In most chapters, the subject of one sketch is a famous man or woman, and the other is a lesser-known individual whose life nonetheless opens vistas on how the average person coped with the historical changes and continuities of the time.

• *An introduction to the use of historical evidence* Each chapter also contains numerous selections of source material called "The Historical Evidence." In most cases we give an extended extract, and in other cases we show several contrasting documents juxtaposed in a single box. The purpose of this feature is to show students the kind of evidence that the working historian must draw upon in order to make generalizations and judgments, and to ask them to stretch their critical faculties.

• *A thorough glossary that encourages repeated student use* Although we have avoided jargon wherever possible, there are terms in historical writing that beginning students need to grasp as part of their study. Many of these terms—*bourgeoisie* and *middle-class*, *feudalism* and *ideology*, *patronage* and *paradigm*, *revolution* and *liberalism* are some examples—may present conceptual problems to students when used without explanation. We have therefore applied **boldface type** to such potentially troubling words. Boldface is used on terms the first time they appear, inviting the student to turn to the glossary (at the end of the volume) for a discussion of the term's meaning, how historians use the term, and sometimes how the meaning of the term has changed over time or in different ideological contexts. (*Bourgeoisie* and *liberalism* are good examples.) We hope that students will develop the habit of turning to the glossary whenever they see a boldface term, whether or not they think they understand the word.

• *A fine collection of maps to which students should constantly refer* History cannot be studied without good maps, and we have taken special pains to ensure that the ones in this book are accurate, readable, and graphically appealing. The map program includes the annotated endpaper maps that indicate the places where several key events in the West's history occurred. These maps provide students with a geographic context in which to place events within both the European continent and the world.

• *Unique ways of both beginning and ending the book* Two unusual features of *The West Transformed* are the Prologue that begins it and the Epilogue/Prologue section that ends it. The Prologue offers a detailed look at the evolution of human beings and human societies before the advent of civilizations, subjects that in conventional textbooks get crowded into the first few pages of a chapter otherwise devoted to the ancient Near East. Our approach allows the instructor the option of asking students to ponder what it means to be human at the very beginning of their journey through the history of Western civilization or, alternatively, of beginning the course directly with the dawn of civilization in Mesopotamia and Egypt.

The Epilogue/Prologue similarly offers several creative options for closing the course. The usual textbook procedure is to turn the final chapter into a lengthy catalogue of contemporary events. We believe that the end of the Cold War and the collapse of the Soviet Union—the revolutions of 1989 and 1991—bring to a decisive close a number of historical eras, and that the 1990s are part of historical changes whose implications we cannot yet fully grasp. The Epilogue/Prologue uses the historically cloudy period through which we are now passing to take a long-range look at the road we have traveled and the paths that may well extend into the future. It considers a few events—notably the rocky road to European unity, the travails of the post-Communist world, and the Wars of Yugoslav Succession—as major developments worthy of analysis. But in other cases it resists the temptation to pile one current event upon the next, opting instead for a reflective consideration of how contemporary events—as well as the profound transformations being wrought by the Information Revolution, biotechnology, and environmental change—may fit into a long-run historical perspective.

HOW THE WEST TRANSFORMED CAME TO BE

The originator of this book was the late C. Warren Hollister, a prolific historian whose many books and articles on the Anglo-Norman empire and medieval Europe earned him great scholarly distinction and whose numerous former Ph.D. students are now making important contributions to the teaching and writing of medieval history at colleges and universities all over North America. But Warren Hollister was not a scholar who succumbed to the temptation of spending all of his teaching time with advanced students. During his long career at the University of California, Santa Barbara, he regularly taught the middle quarter of the three-quarter Western civilization sequence. When J. Sears McGee arrived in Santa Barbara in the mid-1970s, he teamed up with Professor Hollister. Together they taught the course annually for many years. Dr. Hollister was a stellar lecturer who mastered the art of presenting complex topics in ways that were accessible and engaging to beginning students. Together they worked closely with their teaching assistants in order to provide the mostly first-year students with an introduction to the history of Western civilization that was coherent, challenging, and enjoyable. Professor Hollister composed songs that he sang *a cappella* to emphasize key points, and McGee (having no singing ability) wrote limericks that performed the same task. They frequently sat in on discussion sections and did their best to keep the students' questions, difficulties, and level of understanding in mind. As they began working on this book, they planned and wrote it in the context provided by this close contact with students. When Gale Stokes joined the writing team, he brought to it thirty years of experience in teaching the introductory modern European history course at Rice University. Stokes has not sung songs to his students or written limericks, although he wishes he could, but his course has been formulated over the years to keep in the forefront those same skills of reading, writing, and thinking historically that all of us have seen as fundamental to the educational experience.

All three authors shared, in other words, a deep conviction about the importance of teaching beginning students. It is a conviction that we all have tried very hard to embody and reflect in *The West Transformed*.

FLEXIBLE ADOPTION

As instructors ourselves, we are very much aware that different schools operate on different schedules. Therefore, Harcourt College Publishers has provided for this textbook to be offered in four flexible formats:

- A complete, hardcover, single volume: *The West Transformed: A History of Western Civilization* (ISBN 0-15-508117-9).

- A two-volume paperback version for the two-semester or two-quarter course: *The West Transformed*, Volume I To 1715 (ISBN 0-15-508129-2) and *The West Transformed*, Volume II Since 1648 (ISBN 0-15-508130-6). Note that there is an overlap of chapters between the two volumes. Volume I runs through Chapter 17 (The Scientific Revolution), while Volume II begins with Chapter 16 (The Age of Louis XIV).

- A three-volume paperback version for the three-quarter course: *The West Transformed*, Volume A To 1500 (ISBN 0-15-508126-8), *The West Transformed*, Volume B 1300–1815 (ISBN 0-15-508127-6), and *The West Transformed*, Volume C Since 1789 (ISBN 0-15-508128-4). Again, there is overlap between volumes to provide the instructor with the most flexibility as possible in covering the material. Volume A ends with Chapter 11 (The Late Middle Ages: Crises and Transitions), Volume B starts with Chapter 11 and then ends with Chapter 21 (The French Revolution), and Volume C begins with Chapter 20 (The Industrial Revolution).

- For those course offerings concentrating on Europe from the Renaissance, there is a shortened paperback volume: *The West Transformed*, Since 1300 (ISBN 0-15-508131-4), which begins with Chapter 11 (The Late Middle Ages: Crises and Transitions).

SUPPLEMENTAL PACKAGES

While we believe *The West Transformed* is a very accessible text for students and instructors alike, we realize the importance of providing additional supplementary material to help enhance the learning and understanding of Western civilization.

Harcourt College Publishers offers a number of such supplements. Please contact your Harcourt sales representative for a full presentation of these materials and ordering information.

Test Bank

Prepared by a team of experienced instructors of the Western civilization course—Ellen Howell Myers (San Antonio College), Sylvia Sebesta (San Antonio College), and Bruce G. McNair (Campbell University)—the testing program features a variety of multiple-choice, true/false, and essay questions from which to choose. An answer key is provided for the multiple-choice and true/false questions. In addition to writing questions, E.H. Myers has capably reviewed and edited all the questions to ensure uniformity of style (ISBN 0-15-508119-5).

Computerized Test Banks

The test bank questions are offered on 3.5" floppy disks in three formats: MS Windows 95/98 (ISBN 0-15-508121-7), Macintosh (ISBN 0-15-508122-5), and DOS (ISBN 0-15-508120-9).

Study Guide

Eugene Larson (Los Angeles Pierce College) has prepared the student study guide. Split into two volumes to accompany Volume I and Volume II formats of the textbook (the most widely used version of Western civilization textbooks), the Study Guide features chapter learning objectives, which are tied to the objectives listed in the Instructor's Manual; chapter summaries; map exercises; reinforcing exercises for people, places, and events; questions on historical documents; and a self-test with answers. Volume I of the Study Guide (ISBN 0-15-508124-1) covers material through Chapter 17 of the textbook, while Volume II of the Study Guide (ISBN 0-15-508125-X) begins with Chapter 16.

Instructor's Manual

Kathleen M. Noonan (Diablo Valley College) and Joseph G. de Roulhac (University of California-Santa Barbara) have combined their skills to produce the Instructor's Manual (ISBN 0-15-508118-7). Each IM chapter consists of learning objectives and a chapter outline (the same as found in the student's Study Guide); additional teaching objectives; proposed class discussion (or essay) questions; questions relating to the Historical Evidence and Human Experience boxes and two short classroom quizzes.

Overhead Transparencies

The overhead transparency program has been split into two volumes. Volume I (ISBN 0-15-508123-3) contains overhead transparencies for the Prologue and Chapters 1–17. Volume II (consult your sales representative for the ISBN) covers Chapters 16–32 including the Epilogue/Prologue. Each set of some 50 transparencies includes many of the maps and some of the figures and tables found in the various volumes.

The West Transformed Web Site

This student-oriented Web site is an extension of the student's Study Guide. It reiterates chapter learning objectives and summarizes each chapter, provides Internet links related to the chapter's topics, is a virtual Study Hall for further exploration of the Internet so students can participate in critical thinking exercises, and contains a handy glossary of key terms.

A separate Instructor's Resources section (password protected) gives the instructor a list of chapter-relevant readings for class assignments and discussions and allows for online testing of your students.

You may access the Web site at

www.harcourtcollege.com

Western Civilization Videos/Films for the Humanities

You may choose from a wide variety of videos from the extensive Films for the Humanities history catalog. Contact your local Harcourt sales representative for a complete listing of available videos. Adoption requirements apply.

Arts & Entertainment History Videos

Many outstanding selections are available from the Arts & Entertainment video library that includes videos from A&E's extensive *Biography* collection. Contact your local Harcourt sales representative for a complete listing of available videos. Adoption requirements apply.

PBS Video Series

Several excellent videos are available from the Public Broadcasting Service video series written and narrated by David Macauley. Contact your local Harcourt sales representative for a complete listing of available videos. Adoption requirements apply.

The Western Civilization Videodisc

This disk provides instructors with a wide-ranging resource that is organized in a flexible format, making it easy to prepare illustrated lectures and tailor-made presentations. Adoption requirements apply.

Acknowledgments

Of course, no project of this size and scope can be created by a small circle of individuals. While we, as authors, take full responsibility for what you see on these pages, we do wish to affirm and acknowledge the help of many people.

In the early days of this project and again when the project came under Harcourt's auspices, James Miller made and continues to make exceptionally valuable contributions. His encouragement during our writing of the many drafts, his enthusiasm for pressing us to see both the big picture of Western civilization and the small picture of historical data, and his willingness to step up his involvement upon the loss of Warren Hollister have made this project the result of a rich cooperative effort.

Many of our colleagues in the scholarship and teaching of Western civilization also provided us with valuable and insightful suggestions. We are thankful to Lawrence Backlund (Montgomery County [Pennsylvania] Community College), Carolyn Conley (University of Alabama-Birmingham), Paul S. Cunningham (Community College of Baltimore County-Catonsville [Maryland]), Georgena Duncan (Arkansas Tech University), Lefflett T. Easley Jr. (Campbell University), Steven Fanning (University of Illinois-Chicago), Jerry L. Gaw (David Lipscomb University), Janine C. Hartman (University of Cincinnati), Shirley A. Hickson (North Greenville College), David Hudson (California State University-Fresno), James K. Kieswetter (Eastern Washington University), Wayne S. Knight (J. Sargeant Reynolds Community College [Virginia]), Richard D. Lewis (St. Cloud State University), Keith P. Luria (North Carolina State University), Paul Madden (Hardin-Simmons University), E. Deanne Malpass (Stephen F. Austin State University), Wendell R. Mauter (Quincy College), Dennis J. Mitchell (Jackson State University), Jeremy D. Popkin (University of Kentucky), Katherine K. Reist (University of Pittsburgh-Johnstown), Harry Ritter (Western Washington University), Aviel Roshwald (Georgetown University), Marian J. Rubchak (Valparaiso University), Richard L. Rudolph (University of Minnesota), Joanne Schneider (Rhode Island College), Marshall Schatz (University of Massachusetts-Boston), James Shedel (Georgetown University), Richard H. Silliman (Emory University), Elaine G. Spencer (Northern Illinois University), Carl Strikwerda (University of Kansas), Jack Thacker (Western Kentucky University), Spencer C. Tucker (Virginia Military Institute), and David Weinberg (Wayne State University).

In addition to those colleagues listed above, we want to offer a special thank you to H. A. Drake (University of California-Santa Barbara) and Joe W. Leedom (Hollins University). Both of these fine professors worked with or studied with Warren Hollister and know his work intimately. They both reviewed more polished versions of Dr. Hollister's early drafts to help ensure that Warren's spirit remained within the text.

There are other colleagues whom we would like to recognize, though they are mentioned elsewhere in the preface. They are the dedicated educators who have taken the time and effort to create the supplementary packages that support _The West Transformed_. Eugene Larson (Los Angeles Pierce College) has taken the formidable task of creating a usable student study guide. Kathleen M. Noonan (Diablo Valley College) and Joseph G. de Roulhac (University of California-Santa Barbara) agreed to provide additional information and insight for the Instructor's Manual. And Ellen Howell Myers (San Antonio College), Sylvia Sebesta (San Antonio College), and Bruce G. McNair (Campbell University) have lent their talents to writing the test bank questions. Thank you one and all.

Work on a project this size could not move beyond the manuscript stage without the fine help of the editorial and production teams at Harcourt College Publishers. Their many hours of up front support and behind the scenes effort have enhanced the finished product. Thanks go to steve Norder (developmental editor), Travis Tyre (project editor), Sue Hart (art director), Serena Barnett (production manager), Florence Fujimoto (art coordinator), and Shirley Webster (picture and rights coordinator). And a special thank you to David C. Tatom, executive editor, who believed enough in this project to ensure its resurrection and completion. Lili Weiner (photo researcher) and Marcy Luneta (permissions researcher) provided important professional help for which we are very grateful. The authors also heartily thank Lauren Johnson for her indispensable assistance at the early stages of this project.

Finally, a most warm thank you must go to the many students who have both endured and enjoyed our lectures. It is their desire to learn and understand our Western heritage and how its many transformations have contributed to our current civilization that led us to create _The West Transformed_.

J. S. M.
G. S.

Contents in Brief

Contents

Features

THE HISTORICAL EVIDENCE

MAPS

The West Transformed

A HISTORY
OF WESTERN CIVILIZATION

Neanderthal and Cro-Magnon Skulls   On the left is a Neanderthal skull about fifty thousand years old; on the right is a Cro-Magnon skull from (at most) thirty thousand years ago. Both were found at sites in France. Note the massive ridges above the eye sockets, the heavier jaws, and the protruding cheek-bones of the Neanderthal; the Cro-Magnon skull, by contrast, is anatomically close to that of a modern human being. There is little difference in these two individuals' cranial capacities. *John Reader/Science Photo Library.*

early humans could consume, accelerating intellectual development. (Uncooked, these foods cannot be digested by humans and thus are of no nutritional value.) A better diet, in turn, enabled *Homo erectus* to grow to 6 feet tall and develop a larger brain capacity. What level of intelligence this may have meant is uncertain. But finely crafted spears unearthed in 1995 from a German peat bog suggest that *Homo erectus* hunters four hundred thousand years ago could ambush big game in ways requiring better communication. Animal bones found in France from about three hundred thousand years ago were adorned with deliberately scratched designs. *Homo erectus* clearly enjoyed a long developmental span.

In Africa, perhaps four hundred thousand years ago, we—*Homo sapiens*, or "thinking man"—evolved from *erectus*, who by no means immediately disappeared from the scene. As the name implies, *Homo sapiens*'s most significant characteristic was the astonishing brain expansion that occurs in childhood. Mothers, then as now, were not physically able to deliver babies with heads large enough to accommodate adult brains; the fastest rate of skull growth and brain development must happen *after* birth. (Even so, the size of babies' heads relative to *Homo sapiens* mothers' pelvic openings suggests that childbirth was for the first time becoming prolonged, painful, and sometimes impossible without assistance.) After birth, children's prolonged dependency as the brain reached maturity demanded far longer and more intense parental attention to offspring. Larger brain capacity permitted *Homo sapiens* to improve their stone axes and other tools. They sought to explain

and tame nature's unpredictable forces by developing spiritual ideas.

Archaic *Homo sapiens* subspecies spread from Africa far and wide across Eurasia. Among these archaic *Homo sapiens* were the Neanderthals (or Neandertals), whose remains have turned up at Near Eastern and European sites ranging from more than 125,000 to 35,000 years old.

The Neanderthals' life span coincided with the two most recent glaciations of the Ice Age.[2] When the Neanderthals arrived in the Mediterranean world, the third (or Riss) glaciation still covered much of Europe, and they moved further into Europe during the subsequent Riss-Würm Interglacial. This warm period began about 127,000 years ago, when hippos inhabited the rivers of subtropical

---

[2] "Ice ages," during which major climatic change triggers large-scale advances of polar ice caps and mountain glaciers, are known to have recurred since the first and greatest one, which came during the Precambrian time, between six hundred million and a billion years ago. Over the past 730,000 years, eight advances and retreats of glaciation, spaced at approximately even intervals, have taken place.

Much less severe glacial stages, in which polar and high-altitude ice caps expand slightly and global temperatures drop, have occurred within historical memory, notably in late antiquity, in the late Middle Ages, and in the "Little Ice Age" of the seventeenth century. Since about 1700, the earth has been in a warming phase that modern environmental conditions are probably accentuating.

Scientific explanations for glaciations involve cyclic changes in the gravitational pull of other solar bodies, the earth's tilt, and the rate of its spin. Varying amounts of atmospheric carbon dioxide also play an important role in regulating periods of global warming and cooling, including glaciation.

Britain. But some ten thousand years later, a slow cooling trend set in, and by seventy thousand years ago European winters were long and harsh. By forty thousand years ago enough snow had accumulated to create a huge ice cap covering Scandinavia and the British Isles. Northern Asia, North America, and the southern regions of South America were similarly affected. Scientists call this, the fourth glaciation of geologically recent times, the Würm Glaciation. Conditions reached their coldest during the glaciation's later phases, when huge amounts of ocean water were transferred to the ice caps in the form of precipitation that neither melted nor evaporated. Finally, about thirteen thousand years ago, the climate warmed and glaciers began a rapid retreat. By 8,500 years ago, Britain was free of glaciers and was cut off from the European continent by rising seas.

That the Neanderthals survived the extreme climatic swing from the Riss-Würm Interglacial to the height of the Würm Glaciation testifies to their powerful physique and adaptability. Their stocky, extremely muscular bodies conserved heat, and their greater intelligence (compared to *Homo erectus*) helped them adjust to the tough conditions of life in subarctic Europe. Almost all known Neanderthal skeletons show traumatic injuries, probably sustained in encounters with large animals. Indeed, the sparseness of known fossil evidence for all early human beings underscores how small were populations and how precarious were lives. (For example, the longest-lived Neanderthal yet discovered was about 45, and one-armed, one-eyed, lame, and arthritic.) But the fact that many of the Neanderthals' injuries had healed shows that these people had mentally evolved to the point where they cared for (rather than just abandoning) injured kinfolk. Pollen from the flowers with which late-stage Neanderthals buried their dead hints at both compassion and spiritual beliefs. In short, the old cartoon image of Neanderthals as dim-witted, knuckle-dragging brutes needs considerable modification.

Recent and controversial application of DNA analysis to the study of human evolution suggests that sometime between eighty thousand and thirty thousand years ago, a *Homo sapiens* population explosion began. Since this period coincided with the Riss-Würm Glaciation, most of this demographic expansion must have taken place in tropical or temperate regions closer to the Equator. Previously distinct *Homo sapiens* subspecies, which had probably lived widely separated from each other, vanished. Did this winnowing result from a more efficient subspecies wiping out its rivals, interbreeding with them, or simply proving more efficient and resourceful? Theories abound, but there is no certainty. One factor that must have weighed heavily in the newcomers' favor was the likelihood that they alone, unlike Neanderthals and other archaic *Homo sapiens* subspecies, had become anatomically capable of complex speech. We do know that there emerged a lone surviving subspecies, *Homo sapiens sapiens*—human beings as we now

exist—who may have evolved in Africa as recently as fifty thousand years ago. Although anthropologists disagree as to whether all of modern humanity descends from this particular group or evolved by parallel processes in geographically separate strands, all recognize that humanity today constitutes a single, genetically close-knit family, in which ethnic or racial differences are recent and trivial.[3]

The Paleolithic

Long after the emergence of *Homo sapiens*, human life continued to depend on hunting, fishing, and gathering wild plants, and on tools and weapons crafted from stone or bone. Hence the era's name: the Old Stone Age, or **Paleolithic.** The Paleolithic represents by far the longest phase in human history, beginning with *Homo erectus*'s fashioning of chipped stone tools and giving way to a more recent historical era only around 10,000 B.C. (Even now, remnants of Paleolithic cultures survive in parts of New Guinea, Australia, and the Amazon.)

Paleolithic people were wanderers. Groups of about twenty to thirty people moved with the seasons, carrying with them their infant children and their few simple tools. In such bands, *Homo sapiens* spread throughout the **Old World,** including New Guinea and Australia (which they reached by rafts). They also crossed into the **New World** by way of the Siberia-Alaska "land bridge," at the latest around 12,000 B.C., but (as recent evidence suggests) maybe as early as 40,000 years ago.

Some authorities believe that Paleolithic peoples' reverence toward the earth and its myriad spiritual forces prompted them to seek prey only to satisfy the immediate needs of their communities—thereby preserving a delicate ecological balance. Others argue that Paleolithic hunting was limited less by awe for nature than by limitations in their hunting technology and by the ferocity of the animals they hunted. Whatever the case, most Paleolithic groups had to supplement hunting or scavenging by gathering vegetation, and if neither produced sufficient food for the group, starvation ensued. By our standards, life expectancy remained pathetically short.

Near the end of the Paleolithic, and as the glaciation was reaching its greatest intensity (about thirty-five thousand to ten thousand years ago), a *Homo sapiens* subspecies called the Cro-Magnons appeared in Europe. Anatomically

---

[3] The gene pool of the entire human race is far more homogeneous than that found among even small populations of other animals. There is a substantial but not universally-accepted body of evidence that all modern humans descended from an "African Eve" who lived perhaps 150,000–200,000 years ago; the chronology depends on the mutation rate of mitochondrial DNA that one assumes. (Mitochondrial DNA passes only from mother to offspring and mutates at a steady rate.) Such use of biochemical analysis in studying human evolution is a new technique that many paleoanthropologists are reluctant to embrace, and many findings attributed to it are undergoing continuous reevaluation.

A Paleolithic Tool Besides requiring a high degree of skill to make, Paleolithic stone tools and weapons such as this cutter were quite efficient. Present-day New Guineans have demonstrated that they can cut down a tree as quickly using their traditional tools as with a modern steel ax. They prefer modern tools, however, because they do not have to be made by hand and last longer. *Courtesy of The American Museum of Natural History.*

and radiocarbon dating[4] suggests an age of some thirty thousand years, far older than other known cave paintings.

The caverns in which the paintings appear were not permanently inhabited in Cro-Magnon times. We know from equally striking (and even older) rock paintings in southern Africa and Australia, where the tradition of making such images continued almost to the present, that they were used in casting spells before hunts. Analogous non-European paintings also show human figures, deliberately distorted and known to represent trance-like states. Such cave paintings occupy a unique place at the dawn of human art. The mastery of draftsmanship they display would remain unparalleled for thousands of years.

Small stone images of women, often with exaggerated breasts, buttocks, and genitals, have been found throughout the areas inhabited by Cro-Magnons. They are probably charms associated with fertility and birthing. One such figure from southwestern France holds a bison horn, shaped like a crescent moon and marked with thirteen lines. Similar groups of markings found on mammoth tusks, on rocks, on ivory staffs, and on animal bones suggest that late-Paleolithic peoples had developed a lunar calendar (with thirteen months per year) in order to plan their hunting and food gathering. They surely also noticed that lunar phases coincided fairly closely with the menstrual cycle. If indeed these markings were related to observed phases of the moon, the people who made them were trying to coordinate their activities according to predictable patterns, and certainly were speculating about cosmic mysteries.

they were very close to modern humans. The Cro-Magnons brought the art of hunting to new levels of efficiency. One Cro-Magnon site in France attests to the slaughter of ten thousand horses, and at another in the Czech Republic the bones of a thousand mammoths were piled up by generations of hunters. The bow and arrow (invented in Africa and eventually spread throughout much of the Old World) made hunting both easier and safer. At the other end of the inhabited world, the first Americans, with the help of climatic change, wiped out the New World's largest animals with similarly grim dispatch.

One of the dazzling achievements of Cro-Magnon culture was its cave paintings. Caverns such as those at Lascaux in France and Altamira in Spain blaze with boldly realistic portrayals of hunted animals, painted with assurance and a marvelous economy of line and enlivened with bright colors. In the recently discovered caverns of Chauvet, near Avignon in southern France, subterranean galleries depict cave bears, cave lions, bison, panthers, owls, hyenas, and herds of woolly rhinos. Undiscovered until the mid-1990s, the paintings of Chauvet are uniquely vivid,

The Chauvet Cave Paintings Now-extinct varieties of wild cattle and rhinocerous appear in this painting. *© Jean Clottes/ Ministere de la Culture/Sygma.*

---

[4] All living things absorb the isotope carbon-14 at a steady rate over time. By measuring the amount of carbon-14 in a fossil or something else that was once organic, scientists can estimate its age, give or take a few thousand years.

Despite various theories, we do not know how Cro-Magnons and Neanderthals interacted. Nor can we explain how the Cro-Magnons themselves vanished about twelve thousand years ago. We do know that their disappearance coincided with the beginning of the present period in the earth's natural history, the **Holocene.** Global warming rapidly ended the most recent glaciation. As the Northern Hemisphere's ice cap retreated into the Arctic and the high mountains, new *Homo sapiens sapiens* populations entered Europe. By about 8000 B.C., much of the ice was gone. Europe was warming, and North Africa and the Near East were experiencing the hot, drying conditions that produced the Sahara Desert. Reindeer retreated above the Arctic Circle; the woolly rhinoceros and mammoth died out. Thick coniferous forest blanketed northern Europe, and central and western Europe acquired today's temperate vegetation.

As early as 9000 B.C. the Near Eastern hunter-gatherer economy began changing dramatically. The increased fertility of a gradually warming and drying ecosystem enabled hitherto wandering communities to begin settling down. Adopting so-called "broad spectrum gathering," bands now ranged out from permanent communities to collect various foods, depending on the season—wild barley and wheat, fruits, fish, wild sheep and goats, pigs and cattle. Such settled communities first emerged in the fertile lowlands stretching inland from the eastern Mediterranean coast, and in the valleys and foothills of the Zagros Mountains between Iraq and Iran (see Map P-1).

The Neolithic Revolution

After a time, some of these permanent communities took the first steps toward the greatest revolution humanity has yet experienced: the development of agriculture. This shift may well have been a response to a rising population made possible by settled life, a growing scarcity of large game animals, and increasingly intense competition for plant and animal resources. It was almost certainly women (the "gatherers," in contrast to their hunting menfolk) who discovered how to use seed, probably while they were collecting edible plants near the settlement. As game became scarcer and a food supply based on the *cultivation*—rather than the chance gathering—of plants became more secure, ways of life changed dramatically. The stone tools used in early agriculture were familiar; for example, small sickles that cut stalks of grain had earlier been used in gathering. But new techniques for making these tools involved grinding and polishing rather than chipping, and archaeologists call the era in human history that now began the **Neolithic,** or New Stone Age.

By modern standards, the transition from Paleolithic to Neolithic was a very long process, stretching over centuries and even millennia. But compared to Paleolithic times, the shift from food *gathering* to food *production*, and all the social and technological changes that accompanied it, happened with jarring abruptness. It has aptly been termed the **Neolithic Revolution.**

As farming emerged, and as animals were concurrently domesticated for food, humans gradually gave up wandering. Increasingly, people now had relatively large, permanent communities, with substantial shelters and a controlled food supply: wheat, barley, vegetables, sheep, pigs, cattle, and goats. People continued to hunt and fish (as they still do), but the survival of the community no longer hinged on their success.

In some respects, settled villages made life safer. Larger families were possible now that infants and old people no longer had to be transported from one hunting site to the next (or left to die if food was short). Children's labor became more valuable to farming parents. Life became a little more secure for the very young and the very old.

But settled life also had heavy costs. Farming is hard, rather boring work compared to foraging and hunting.

A Paleolithic "Venus" "Venus" is a fanciful name suggesting the ancient Roman goddess of love. This figure holds a bison horn with thirteen marks. "Venus" figurines have been unearthed from Mexico to China. © *R. Sheridan/Ancient Art & Architecture Collection.*

MAP P-1

THE NEOLITHIC REVOLUTION IN THE NEAR EAST

Large permanent communities lost the relative egalitarianism of hunter-gatherers and became socially stratified, with better-off minorities coming to dominate poorer majorities. Neolithic communities faced new problems in health and sanitation. Epidemic diseases, rare among small nomadic bands, from now on would breed in crowded, unsanitary living conditions and would be spread by trade. And farmers growing a few different crops are more vulnerable than foragers to extreme weather—dry or wet spells, unseasonable freezes, floods, and storms. Some scholars claim that Paleolithic **nomads** were not only less socially and economically stratified but also much healthier than their Neolithic descendants. Others argue, more persuasively, that the Neolithic Revolution substantially lengthened life spans.

The Neolithic Revolution spread gradually through the Near East and then, slowly and unevenly, reached westward into Europe and eastward into India. Independently of Near Eastern influence, other Neolithic revolutions began in the eighth millennium B.C. in the African grassland south of the Sahara, in the sixth millennium B.C. in northern China, and in the fifth millennium B.C. in Mexico. But wherever and however they occurred, the advent of agriculture, animal domestication, and permanent settlements transformed human life.

Gradually Neolithic economies grew more diverse. The ability to store food was enormously enhanced when, about 6000 B.C., Old World people first learned to fashion pottery on a turning wheel. The invention of the potter's wheel dramatically accelerated the production of durable pottery, necessary for the conservation and transportation of grains and liquids, and it required a new group of specialists, the potters. Another such group, which may have consisted largely of women, specialized in the weaving of cloth from wool—a Neolithic invention roughly concurrent with the advent of pottery, and of similar importance. At some point, difficult to determine, Neolithic peoples began to construct crude wheeled carts, which allowed them to transport goods on a much larger scale and which, along with pottery, underlay the intensification of trade—sometimes across very large distances. The wheel may seem a perfectly obvious device, but it is not. It was unknown to Egyptian civilization during its formative centuries, and the sophisticated civilizations of the Americas never hit on the idea (because they had no domesticated animals large enough to pull wheeled carts).

Growing distinction between rich and poor resulted from the emergence of more complex social organizations in the Neolithic villages. Their inhabitants had to make rational plans to till the soil, breed and slaughter animals, ward off raiders, and appease moody gods. The increasing complexity of Neolithic economies and societies required centralized direction.

The simplest way to describe how this direction took shape is to say that, relying first on consensus and eventually on force, community leaders emerged. Thus there originated chiefs or "big men," supported by fighters, administrators, and priests. The fighters had the weapons; the administrators gave the orders; the priests supplicated the gods—and the others obeyed. But this oversimplifies enormously. For example, anthropologists know that in many so-called primitive cultures the king is killed as a periodic sacrifice to the community's well-being, or when his physical powers begin to wane. The line between "king" and "priest" is often indistinct. And administrators appeared late.

There is also a gender revolution to consider. Neolithic village life had a gendered division of labor. Women's work included not only weaving but also light farming and a great variety of domestic tasks; men's work encompassed most crafts, probably plowing, and certainly making war, hunting, and serving the gods in increasingly elaborate temples. Such gender distinctions were by no means universal, and our knowledge of illiterate societies such as the Neolithic villages can only be inferred from the social organization of similar societies today (and from a few dim archaeological clues). Anthropologists believe that in the earliest agricultural societies women, who supplied most of the community's caloric intake and knew the mysteries of growing things, wielded great power. Memories of female power survive in ritual and folklore. But economic specialization fostered a trend toward political and economic domination by males that has characterized subsequent civilizations. The power struggles that may have accompanied this trend are largely guesswork.

The earliest major Neolithic village thus far unearthed, at Jericho in Palestine, has been dated by carbon-14 analysis to around 7800 B.C. (Village sites recently discovered in Iran may be even older.) By the middle of the fifth millennium—that is, about 4500 B.C.—Neolithic villages dotted southwestern Asia, Egypt, and southeastern Europe. By about 3800 B.C. they had spread across the rest of Europe and China.

Neolithic villages were not necessarily small. The village on the 32-acre site now called Çatal Hüyük in southern Turkey, which was occupied from about 6500 to 5500 B.C., could well have been the largest human community on earth at its time, numbering ten thousand or more. Its inhabitants built mud-brick houses, wove wool into cloth, and ate a varied diet (peas, nuts, vegetable oil, apples, and honey, besides the usual grain cereals). They imported seed for some of these crops from considerable distances, and they irrigated their fields by diverting river water.

They also wielded formidable weapons: sharper flint spearheads and arrowheads, daggers, and lances. European villages were much smaller, but still they had acquired the essential characteristics of settled agriculture: regularly cultivated fields worked with plows, exchanges of some commodities with other peoples, and permanent dwellings—apparently "longhouses," which anthropologists associate with extended families descending through the female line. These villages probably looked much the same as the ones the Romans found when they invaded Gaul and Germany in the first century B.C.

Neolithic villages in the Near East and Europe disclose revolutionary technological and cultural changes. By modern standards the changes were slow. But judged by the rhythms of Paleolithic life, the invention of agriculture had sparked a rapid chain reaction: animal domestication, temples, pottery, weaving, craft specialization, fearsome new weapons, wheeled carts, rafts, and a gendered division of labor.

Across the fifth millennium B.C., the technology of the Near Eastern Neolithic villages moved ahead step by step. At Jarmo, in Iraq, twelve separate levels of settlement are piled on top of each other, its more recent levels attesting clearly to a more varied craftsmanship. Here and elsewhere, the presence of materials unavailable locally (such as obsidian) suggests the burgeoning of interregional commerce, often over vast distances. By 4000 B.C. some Neolithic villagers were beginning to fashion metal ornaments and tools.

Neolithic Jericho This stone wall was probably intended mainly for protection against floods. © R.Sheridan/Ancient Art & Architecture Collection.

We have now reached the threshold of civilization. The fourth millennium (4000–3000) B.C. would see the building of the world's first cities, the development of large-scale irrigation systems in Mesopotamia and Egypt, the invention of writing, the birth of the state, and the smelting of tin and copper into bronze, the most durable metal then known. Thenceforth, throughout most of the Near East, bronze gradually replaced stone for making weapons and tools.

CIVILIZATION

Civilization has been defined in various ways. The word derives from the Latin *civitas* ("city"), suggesting that urban life is a major component of what we consider as civilization. For although city dwellers constituted only a minority of the population in the ancient civilizations, urban elites dominated life. The new cities, walled communities numbering from several thousand to tens of thousands, became the focal points of political authority, religious ritual, tax collection, commerce, ideas, literature, and art. The wealthier and more powerful townspeople were thus a privileged group, freed from the burdens of gathering and producing food. They owed their comfortable existence partly

to the labors of their servants and slaves, but even more to rural agricultural abundance, which they siphoned off through taxes, tribute, and profitable commerce.

Another characteristic of the earliest civilizations was their use of metal weapons and tools. The birth of civilization more or less coincided with the dawn of the **Bronze Age.** The new bronze tools and, more importantly, bronze weapons (swords, daggers, and spearheads) retained their keen cutting edges far longer than copper or stone weapons and were therefore particularly prized. But since the smelting of bronze was a laborious process, its use was limited largely to the urban elites—thus contributing further to the social stratification of the emerging cities.

Writing, too, was a mark of civilization, and its advent constituted still another fundamental revolution in technology. Like bronze weapons, writing tended to be monopolized by an urban elite—in this case a small, highly trained scribal class serving priests, kings, and administrator-nobles. By about 3500 B.C., temple scribes in the flourishing Mesopotamian city of Uruk were keeping accounts in the first known pictograms—picture writing. Writing gave humanity the means of keeping track of its commercial affairs and of its past with vastly greater precision and reliability. Writing has been aptly described as

MAP P-2
EARLY CIVILIZATIONS

the most significant intellectual tool ever discovered. With it, the dim world of campfire legend brightened into the dawn of recorded history.

Mesopotamian influence is clear in the rise of civilization in Egypt and Iran, and through long-distance trade Mesopotamia also probably helped stimulate the earliest civilization in what is now Pakistan and India, along the Indus River and its tributaries. (The first irrigation systems there suggest a Mesopotamian model.) By about 2500 B.C., an impressive new Indus Valley civilization had emerged. Extending outward in small villages for about a thousand miles, it centered on the two large, well-planned cities of Harappa and Mohenjo-daro, with wide streets, drainage systems, and walls some 3 miles in circumference. The Shang civilization in China, arising some centuries thereafter along the Huang-Ho and Yangtze Rivers, was likewise based on irrigation that could control floods, most likely independent of Near Eastern influence. And the emergence of civilization in Mexico during the first millennium B.C. was obviously unaided by Old World precedents (despite far-fetched theories of transatlantic raft crossings or intervention by helpful aliens from outer space). Map P-2 on the previous page shows the locations of the world's early civilizations.

Similarly, as a result of a more meticulous application of the carbon-14 dating method, it is now clear that the inhabitants of central and western Europe independently developed copper and bronze metallurgy. Without Near Eastern guidance, they also built vast, astronomically oriented burial chambers and religious monuments, such as Stonehenge in southern England. Transalpine Europe cannot be described as a "civilization" until Roman times, because the earlier Europeans had neither cities nor writing. But from an extraordinary excavation of a cemetery at Varna on Bulgaria's Black Sea coast has come a treasure trove of copper and gold ornaments and tools dating to about 4600–4200 B.C., too early to reflect a diffusion of Near Eastern know-how.

Scholars are thus much less inclined than they once were to view the emergence of copper and bronze metallurgy, the clearing and diking of river valleys, the development of writing, and other attributes of civilization as simply a result of people picking up Mesopotamian ideas. They now tend to view civilizations throughout the world as independent responses, by widely separated Neolithic peoples, to a variety of environmental challenges.

One such challenge was that of irrigating a river valley. The periodic flooding of such great rivers as the Tigris-Euphrates, Nile, Indus, and Huang-Ho spread silt across their valleys, making them richly fertile. But these inundations were also dangerous to valley dwellers, as early Mesopotamian and Chinese myths of world-destroying floods surely attest. In Mesopotamia, for example, the valley could be permanently settled and cultivated only when the inhabitants learned to control the Tigris and Euphrates floods that came virtually every year around harvest time.

Stonehenge Stonehenge was built in three stages from about 3100 to 1100 B.C. Enormous labor and ingenuity were required to transport the huge stones (weighing up to 50 tons) from almost 250 miles away and then set them precisely in place. Stonehenge was used in religious rites by the succession of Neolithic peoples who occupied the site over a two-thousand-year history. One series of stones forms an axis that aligns with the sunrise at the summer solstice. Many theories have been suggested to explain Stonehenge's cultic significance, but none have gained general acceptance. One thing, though, is sure: Stonehenge was abandoned long before either the Celts (with their druid priests) or the Romans reached Britain. © R. Sheridan/Ancient Art & Architecture Collection.

Mesopotamia's River Valleys The reedy marshlands of present-day southern Iraq probably look much the same as the river valleys in which ancient Mesopotamian civilization began. Dwellings and boats such as these resemble depictions in ancient art. The build-up of silt brought downstream by the Tigris and Euphrates Rivers created hundreds of square miles of new land at the headwaters of the Persian Gulf. © *R. Sheridan/Ancient Art & Architecture Collection.*

They also had to learn to distribute water across wide arid areas by a system of canals and dikes, meticulously planned and constructed on a vast scale. Developing and maintaining such irrigation systems demanded a coordinated human effort well beyond the capacity of a Neolithic village society. It required, in short, a political authority capable of dominating a significant population and territory. The establishment of such authority produced the earliest city-states and the first civilizations.

Many explanations for the rise of civilizations have been advanced, although no single one suffices. Rather, we should see the emergence of civilizations in the conjunction of many factors—among them accelerating economic and social change, evolving environments, and opportunities that ambitious men saw to assert coercive power. Life was becoming complicated. It is with such complex societies and cultures that we will be occupied for the remainder of this book.

Selected Reading

New discoveries, as well as reevaluations of earlier finds, spur constant revisions in what is known about early human history. The interested general reader is advised to keep current with nontechnical articles that appear in such periodicals as *Scientific American* and *National Geographic*. But lay persons should also bear in mind that paleoanthropology is a highly contentious field.

Human Evolution

Campbell, Bernard G., and James D. Loy. *Humankind Emerging* (1997). The seventh edition of a standard textbook in physical anthropology, well written and illustrated.

Fagan, Brian M. *People of the Earth: An Introduction to World Prehistory*, 9th ed. (1998). A thorough, lively survey stressing similarities in prehistoric human behavior throughout the world.

Johanson, Donald C., and James Shreeve. *Lucy's Child: The Discovery of a Human Ancestor* (1989). The best general account. Johanson, one of the most famous living paleoanthropologists, discovered "Lucy."

Lewin, Roger. *Bones of Contention: Controversies in the Search for Human Origins*, 2nd ed. (1997). A fascinating account of the major controversies over human evolution that have embroiled paleoanthropologists, biochemists, and geologists, revealing how great scientists often see what they want to see in the data because of preconceived ideas and personal ambitions.

———. *Human Evolution: An Illustrated Introduction*, 3rd ed. (1993). A valuable recent account of the origins of humanity drawing on East African evidence.

Tattersall, Ian. *The Fossil Trail: How We Know What We Think We Know about Human Evolution* (1995). A comprehensive survey, written for general readers, by the curator of anthropology at the American Museum of Natural History, New York. In this and the next title, Tattersall argues that the hominids should be reclassified into a slightly larger number of species than are discussed in this Prologue.

————. *The Last Neanderthal: The Rise, Success, and Mysterious Extinction of Our Closest Human Relatives* (1995). Covering a much wider compass than the title suggests, this beautifully illustrated book traces human evolution from the earliest hominids to the Neanderthals.

The Neolithic and the Evolution of Civilization

Cohen, Mark Nathan. *Health and the Rise of Civilization* (1989). This meticulous study argues that the Neolithic Revolution and the emergence of civilization brought a decline in nutrition and health.

Cunliffe, Barry, ed. *The Oxford Illustrated Prehistory of Europe* (1994). A lavishly illustrated and authoritative collaborative work by outstanding scholars in the field. The book comes down to the beginnings of "barbarian" Europe after the transformation of the Roman Empire in the West.

Ehrenberg, Margaret. *Women in Prehistory* (1989). An important, controversial study of women's contribution to the agricultural revolution and their role in prehistoric Europe.

Mellaart, James. *The Neolithic of the Near East* (1975). Discusses archaeological investigations of Neolithic villages.

Renfrew, Colin. *Before Civilization: The Radiocarbon Revolution and Prehistoric Europe* (1979). A persuasive presentation of the view that Neolithic Europe developed independently of the Near East.

Trump, D. H. *The Prehistory of the Mediterranean* (1980). A comprehensive, judicious account.

PART ONE

THE BIRTH OF THE WEST

The year 2001 marks an epoch: the beginning of the third millennium of the Christian calendar, also frequently termed the Common Era. Being at a turn of the millennium may make us reflect on the meaning of history and the pace of historical change. And a moment's thought might bring to mind an even more startling realization. We are also embarking on the *sixth* millennium since the beginnings of Western civilization itself.

Why we should trace Western civilization back to the reedy marshes of Mesopotamia or the pyramids of Egypt is not self-evident. Are we thereby equating the history of the whole world with the history of "the West," or stretching the definition of "the West" beyond the breaking point by connecting it to the most ancient Near East? What, after all, does the history of peoples who believed in such divinities as Enlil, Osiris, Isis, and Innana—who devoted their greatest energies to building tombs for their kings or considered themselves slaves of their gods—have to do with our own world of instant global communications, with our concerns for human rights, self-government, and self-realization?

There are several good answers to these questions. One answer can be summed up briefly as *the interconnectedness of traditions*. Regardless of our ethnic background, we who are citizens of North America, Europe, or other countries that were settled by large numbers of Europeans are connected by innumerable ties with early modern and medieval England, France, Spain, Italy, Portugal, Germany, and other European societies. Our language, our political and economic institutions, our cultural and religious heritage, the ways we organize our society and look upon nature—all these have their roots in European civilization.[1]

And what is Europe? As we study Europe's medieval and early modern history, it becomes apparent that four

great taproots run back into ancient times—not just to the beginning of the Common Era, but much farther back still. The first of these taproots is the indigenous traditions of pre-Christian Europe, which survived long after the coming of Christianity, mainly in the form of folk culture and popular religion. The second was the institutions of Rome: its laws, its political structures, and the Christian church, which acquired its formal doctrines and organization after it became the official church of the Roman Empire. The third great taproot was the cultural heritage of ancient Greece: its basic philosophical ideas, its concepts of citizenship, its ideals of "the good life" and the pursuit of excellence. The fourth was the Judeo-Christian religion: the belief in a single God who cared intensely about the destiny of human beings, who controlled and directed history itself in a purposeful way, in whose image the human race had been created, and who (in the words of a famous African American spiritual) "has got the whole world in his hands." These four traditions do not necessarily harmonize nicely with each other; indeed, there are powerful tensions between them. But we cannot understand the European culture to which we are heirs unless we are aware of what these traditions are, and realize how they relate to each other.

By tracing our steps backward, we can see how the modern world grew out of earlier historical eras. Ultimately, we realize that ancient Rome, Greece, and Israel can only be explained as the end-products of civilized traditions that had been developing for three or four thousand years before the the Common Era—during the centuries and millennia that we conventionally designate "B.C."

Having made that journey backwards in time, we are ready to consider the second reason for beginning the story of Western civilization so far in the past. The mental exercise that we must now make involves considering what were the basic assumptions of ancient times and seeing the long-range patterns of thought that those assumptions set in motion. *Ideas have consequences*. Out of the great cultural matrix that constituted the ancient Near East and early Greece and Israel, a set of powerful beliefs took shape

---

[1] This is not meant to minimize the heritages that have come to the United States from Africa, East Asia, and other parts of the non-Western world. But these heritages have not played the *primary* shaping role in American or European culture and society that the Western tradition has.

that still influences most Western people's thinking, even though they may be unaware of it. One of these beliefs is, as we have already mentioned, the understanding of God as a unitary being who created the human race in his likeness and who holds men and women accountable for their behavior. Another of these great shaping assumptions is that ultimately "real" things actually exist—that they are not illusions. A third primary assumption is that history moves along a line, rather than in endlessly recurring cycles. A fourth one is the conviction that the earth belongs to humanity and that we have a right to dominate and transform nature (an idea, incidentally, that modern concerns about our environment's fragility are forcing us to reconsider). All these are ideas that distinguish the West and its cultural tradition from the world's other great cultural traditions: those of India and of East Asia, for example, or those that have a more direct intellectual link to the very old human cultural traditions that endow everything in nature with a soul and consciousness of its own. These primary Western cultural assumptions certainly did not emerge full-blown from the ancient Near East and Greece. But if we look carefully at our ancient historical roots, we can begin to grasp how they took shape, and we can appreciate their powerful hold on our own consciousness. That is another reason for seeking a holistic understanding of the West's history.

The approach that this book takes to the history of the West's transformation over time does not imply any narrowly chauvinistic judgment that the West and its values are "better" than those of other cultural traditions. (Nor does it make the equally naive argument that all the evils in history, or in today's world, are solely the West's fault.) We do not assume that the West's history forms an isolated compartment. On the contrary, we emphasize that the West's transformation is part of a still wider process of global history. The West has influenced other parts of the world, especially since about 1500; but it has often been influenced by other societies and other cultural traditions as well. If the West is today exerting a powerful influence on non-Western traditions, it is also being enriched by an unprecedented openness to those traditions. For long periods of its history, the West was undoubtedly less wealthy, less technologically advanced, less culturally sophisticated, and less efficiently governed than other parts of the world at the same time. If at the beginning of the third millennium of the Common Era the West's technology and insti-

tutions appear to be setting the standard for global development, this does not mean that Western ways have proven their superiority retroactively or will last for all time to come.

Part One of this book lays the foundations for understanding how the West took shape and transformed itself. It begins with the ancient Near East's emergence from prehistory, which happened gradually between about 4000 and 3000 B.C. Part One ends in the fourth and fifth centuries A.D., when imperial Rome had become the master of virtually all the "civilized" parts of the Western world (and of some of its fringe areas) and when the Christian church had completed its rise from a tiny, persecuted Jewish sect to equal partnership with the Roman emperors in governing the Mediterranean world.

We must not forget, however, that while the West was thus taking shape, so were other distinctive parts of the world. At the other end of Eurasia, the rise of Chinese civilization culminated in the Han Empire, which was in many ways comparable to imperial Rome in unifying enormous territories under a single government and a single cultural standard. India meanwhile developed two subtle philosophical and religious traditions, Buddhism and Hinduism, which differed profoundly from the West's Judeo-Christianity in many respects, but which—like Christianity—also set out to convert societies and cultures far from the land of their birth. Iran had, by the first centuries of the Common Era, developed into a major political power, able to contend militarily on equal terms with the Roman Empire; culturally, it served both as a watershed and a transmission belt between the ancient West and ancient India. In Africa below the Sahara, the vigorous, prolific, and technologically well-equipped Bantu people were making themselves masters of the continent. And in the Western Hemisphere, totally isolated from the rest of the world, the beginning of the Common Era saw the flowering of the "Classic" phase of Mexican civilization and the early stirrings of a complex society in the Peruvian Andes.

There is, in short, a global coherence to the story of the ancient West that we will tell in Part One. As you read Chapters 1 through 5, keep asking yourself what signs you see of your own cultural values emerging. They will be faint at the outset: You will have to look closely. But by the time you reach Chapter 5, you will for some time have felt yourself on familiar ground. ✺

CHAPTER *1*

THE ORIGINS OF WESTERN CIVILIZATION: THE ANCIENT NEAR EAST

Treasure from the Royal Cemetery of Ur
University Museum (neg T4-28 c.4),
University of Pennsylvania, Philadelphia.

MESOPOTAMIA		EGYPT		NEAR EAST	
ca. 5500	Settlement of Sumer begins	ca. 3150	Unification of Egypt by Menes	1450–1300	Hebrews enslaved in Egypt
ca. 4000	First city-states	3150–2700	Early Dynastic Period	?1300	Moses leads Hebrews out of Egypt
2600–2500	Royal tombs of Ur (First Dynasty)	2700–2200	Old Kingdom	?1250	Hebrews enter Canaan
2400–2250	Ebla flourishes	2400–2250	The First Pyramids	1200	Fall of Hittite kingdom; beginning of Iron Age
2370	Sargon unites Sumer and Akkad	2370–2215	Akkadian Empire	1020	King David creates a united Hebrew kingdom
2370–2215	Akkadian Empire	2200–2040	First Intermediate Period	922	Hebrew kingdom splits into Israel and Judah
2250	Akkadians sack Ebla	2040–1785	Middle Kingdom; pharaohs recover power	883–859	Reign of Ashur-nasir-pal II; revival of Assyria begins
2100–2000	Ur (Third Dynasty) flourishes	1785–1560	Second Intermediate Period; Hyksos rule Egypt	745–612	Assyrian Empire dominates Near East
2000	Amorites establish Old Babylonian Empire	1560–1070	New Kingdom (Empire)	612	Chaldeans destroy Assyria, establish New Babylonian Empire
1700	Hammurabi conquers Fertile Crescent, issues Law Code; Indo-European disruptions begin; origin of Hittite kingdom	1379–1361	Reign of Akhenaten	585–538	Hebrew Babylonian Captivity
1530–1100	Kassites dominate Mesopotamia			549–538	Cyrus the Great conquers the Near East, establishes Persian Empire
				521–486	Darius the Great rules Persian Empire
				330	Greeks, under Alexander the Great, conquer Persian Empire

All dates are B.C. and most are approximate.

For perhaps four thousand years it lay undisturbed, forgotten except for a dim biblical reference to "Ur of the Chaldees," from whence the Hebrew patriarch Abraham had set out on his journey to the land of Canaan. But it came to light in 1927 when archaeologist Leonard Woolley excavated ancient Ur in southern Iraq. Some of what Woolley uncovered is shown in the photograph (see previous page) from the University of Pennsylvania's University Museum in Philadelphia, where half the treasure is displayed. (The rest is in Iraq's National Museum.) It constitutes one of the most important archaeological finds of the twentieth century, for it helped restore to historical memory the beginnings of civilization in the delta of the Tigris and Euphrates Rivers—the land of Sumer.

Woolley called his discovery the Royal Tombs of Ur. One of many cities of Sumer, Ur, struggled ceaselessly for advantage. At the head of each stood a king and a temple with its priesthood. Woolley's discovery made it dramatically clear what wealth and what impressive art Ur possessed—and at an astonishingly early date. Scholars now believe that the Ur treasures went into the earth about 2600 B.C., roughly contemporary with the building of the great pyramids of Egypt. But only centuries of prior development can explain such sophisticated art, or the trade routes that brought to Sumer the gold, lapis lazuli, and other exotic materials from which the treasure was fashioned—none of them naturally occurring either in southern Iraq or nearby lands.

The story of how the Ur treasure came to be buried is as awesome as the treasure's splendor and artistry. There were two principal tombs, of which the upper was that of a woman, Shub-Ad. Woolley announced (but some experts now dispute it) that the tombs were those of a king and a queen. Most of the skeletons lay peacefully, accompanied by the remains of oxen and the carts that they had pulled. Apparently all the humans, including Shub-Ad and maybe even the presumed king, had died voluntarily, wearing their finest jewels and no doubt their most resplendent robes. The cups from which they had drunk a poison or a narcotic lay among their bones; the young female harpers had died playing their instruments, intoning solemn chants that accompanied the court into eternity.

The tombs of Ur bring us face-to-face with the impressive material culture of ancient Sumer, with the mysteries of life and death—and with some fundamental questions. By the middle of the third millennium, when the rulers of Ur led their courtiers into death, human sacrifice had mostly ended in Sumeria, as it was also ending in Egypt. Did earlier practices survive (or were they revived) at Ur around 2600 B.C.? The mentality revealed by such rites leads us back into the **Stone Age,** and to grisly practices observed in recent centuries among remote peoples in India and Africa. Were the presumed king and Shub-Ad incarnations of the god Dumuzi and his consort the earth-goddess Inanna—she who, like the divinities of early agricultural peoples everywhere, can ensure the earth's fertility only by descending into the land of death and being reborn? Was Shub-Ad, as queen or priestess, enacting such a ritual? Did the Sumerians, like other primitive people, piously slay their king with a priestess (or the queen) when he lost his vitality? Or did these worthies sacrifice *themselves,* promising immortality to those who went to death with them? We may never know.

This chapter traces some of Western civilization's deepest roots back to their origins in Mesopotamia and Egypt—the oldest civilized societies. About 4000 B.C. a complex human community began to develop in what is now Iraq, largely as the result of diking and channeling the parallel Tigris and Euphrates Rivers and clearing the great, fertile valley between them. A few centuries later the Egyptians built a similar irrigation system to make cultivation possible in the valley of the Nile. Comparable irrigation systems subsequently emerged in India's Indus Valley and still later along some of the rivers of China. The "hydraulic civilizations" that resulted from these great flood-control projects transformed human life in their respective regions for all time to come.

The early Mesopotamians drastically reshaped the Neolithic culture of western Eurasia by originating, among other things, kingship, urban life, bronze metallurgy, writing, record-keeping, law, mathematics, and the calendar. The Egyptians learned much from Mesopotamia, and added much: an altogether unique art, important contributions in medicine and applied mathematics, a distinctive monumental architecture, widely influential religious concepts, and a better calendar. In time, civilization spread northwestward from Mesopotamia into Anatolia (modern Turkey), and southwestward along the eastern coast of the Mediterranean Sea. There the Hebrews, or Israelites, established a strong but short-lived state and—more important—a new and deeply original **monotheism** that has contributed decisively to Western culture.

In time, the Near East fell under the control of a succession of great empires—Assyrian, Chaldean, and Persian. But it was not the great empires but rather the smaller Near Eastern states and peoples that produced some of the most significant cultural and technological innovations: the smelting of iron, coinage, and the alphabet. The **Iron Age,** which began about 1200 B.C., laid the basic technological and social foundations on which the world would rest for the next three thousand years—until the **Industrial Revolution** of modern times.

THE MESOPOTAMIAN ROOTS

The name "Mesopotamia" derives from the Greek words *mesos* ("middle") and *potamoi* ("rivers"). The birth of civilization in the Tigris-Euphrates Valley during the fourth millennium B.C. was made possible by Mesopotamia's geography and environment, and by the Neolithic Revolution, which had transformed its primeval culture.

For thousands of years the entire Near East had experienced decreasing rainfall. Grasslands slowly became deserts. The valleys of the Nile and the Tigris-Euphrates, once densely overgrown swamps, gradually became habitable. Many thousands of years ago, indeed, the Persian Gulf's shoreline lay some 200 miles inland of where it now is: The lower Tigris-Euphrates Valley was made by silt deposits during Neolithic times. The process may have survived in human memories, and perhaps coincides with the dating that archaeologists have established for the oldest pottery found in the Mesopotamian delta—about 5500 B.C. By 4000 B.C., Mesopotamia had become, as it remains today, a long strip of fertile lowlands, its alluvial soil continually enriched by the twin rivers as they flow into the Persian Gulf. To the northeast, toward the Zagros Mountains, is a highland region, and to the south is the Arabian Desert. The rich lowlands of the valley form the eastern part of a large semicircular region whose western extremity runs along the eastern Mediterranean coast. This **Fertile Crescent,** arcing northward from the Mediterranean and the Persian Gulf, throughout history lured peripheral hill and desert peoples alike (see Map 1-1).

The Sumerians and the Emergence of Civilization, ca. 4000–2350 b.c.

Most of Iraq's earliest Neolithic villages lay in the high country to the northeast, which had long been attracting settlers because of its fertile soil, adequate rainfall, and native grasses—wheat and barley. The Tigris-Euphrates Valley itself presented special problems. Its soil, replenished annually by flood-borne silt, was vastly more fertile

MAP 1-1
SUMER, MESOPOTAMIA, AND ADJACENT LANDS

than that of the neighboring hills, but its swamps had to be drained, its river water had to be distributed over the dry land, and above all its destructive floods had to be mastered. Once this program was initiated by organized community effort, the rich land produced a surplus, which enabled populations to proliferate and states to expand. No longer did everybody have to till the soil; other careers were now possible. The vast majority remained on the land (as they would throughout the world until very recent times), but a crucially important minority began to specialize in war, administration, handicrafts, trade, and service to the gods. This process had commenced, as we have seen, in the Neolithic villages; it accelerated significantly in the new Mesopotamian cities.

The Sumerians, who built Mesopotamia's original civilization, are the first known inhabitants of the Tigris-Euphrates delta. Who they were and where they came from is a mystery. Their language, unlike any other known to us, was the first human tongue to be expressed in writing, and

their culture, whose origins are equally obscure, became the nucleus of all later Mesopotamian civilization. (See Table 1-1.)

Sumerians and later Mesopotamians saw life and the world in deeply fatalistic terms that reflected their environment, in which nature seemed violent and unpredictable. They could never completely tame the floods. Weeks of blistering heat (as high as 120°F in midsummer) might be followed by torrential rains that turned field into marshland. Furious winds whipped up suffocating dust storms. Worse still, the fertile valley lay open to incessant raids and periodic conquests by envious tribes from the northern hills or the southern desert. The price of civilization in Mesopotamia was constant insecurity.

The Sumerians projected this ever-present anxiety onto their conceptions of humanity and its gods. Like all other early peoples, they tended to regard objects in the natural world as personalities with wills of their own. Mountains, trees, rivers, and springs were alive and conscious.

TABLE 1-1

PHASES OF EARLY MESOPOTAMIAN CULTURE AND POLITICS

All dates are B.C. and approximate.

8000–4000	Neolithic era
before 5500	Settlement of the delta (Sumer) begins
4000–2350	Civilization emerges; intercity wars
2600–2500	First Dynasty of Ur: royal tombs
2400–2250	Ebla flourishes
2370–2215	Akkadian Empire: Dynasty of Sargon
2100–2000	Sumerian Empire of Ur
2000–1530	Amorite Domination: Old Babylonian Empire
1700–1500	Emergence of Indo-European peoples
1530–1100	Kassites dominate Mesopotamia

Awed by nature, the Sumerians saw themselves as its playthings. They felt impotent before its invincible powers, as tragic figures subject to the whims of the gods. "Mere man—" one Sumerian mused, "his days are numbered; whatever he may do, he is but wind." The scanty allusions to an afterlife in Mesopotamian literature represent it as a state of darkness and gloom.

Sumerian religion's function was to explain the origin of the world and the present condition of human life. Placating the gods through sacrifices and rituals seemed a reasonable means of coping with the often unpredictable terrors of nature. With a technology and view of nature far simpler than ours, the Sumerians looked to their many gods to explain and grapple with the environment that surrounded, sustained, and intimidated them.

As agricultural people, the Sumerians recognized the regularity of nature, the daily sweep of the sun, and the annual procession of the seasons that governed the rhythm of planting and harvesting. They watched the stars closely, calculating the zodiac's return to its starting position (and perhaps noting its slight annual lag), and from these observations established a year of 360 days (corresponding

Sumerians at Prayer   Small statues like these (from early in the third millennium B.C.) must have been produced on a vast scale in ancient Sumer, for archaeologists have discovered so many. Sumerians placed them in temples to represent themselves before the gods, always with the same large staring eyes and humbly clasped hands. Gingerly looking up to inscrutable divinities, these figures are often held to symbolize the angst-ridden Mesopotamian psyche. But overinterpretation can be dangerous: Ordinary Sumerians surely did not spend all their time in fear and trembling; perhaps they left that job to these figures.   *Courtesy of the Oriental Institute, University of Chicago.*

to the 360 degrees of a circle),[1] with five days at the end for solemn festivals of renewal.

Three dramatic ceremonies marked the Sumerian new year. One was the king's ritual confession of his faults and his humiliation by the high priest—probably a softened version of the primitive ritual of actually sacrificing the king. Second was the king's sexual intercourse with a priestess representing the fertility goddess Inanna. Worship of an Earth Mother, whose earliest incarnation is no doubt the "Venus" figurines of late Paleolithic times, is part of the oldest cultural heritage of every agricultural people. In Mesopotamia, as in many other early societies, the Neolithic Revolution gave a new intensity to the Earth Mother's cult—as it also did to the veneration of sacred forces represented by the bull, which pulled plows, impregnated cows, and suggested with its horns the waxing and waning moon, and by extension, the menstrual cycle. Many scholars today believe that in the distant past, before there were writing systems to record rituals and before women lost their early leadership in agricultural communities, the Earth Mother had been the dominant partner in these rites, which involved sacrificing a male. The fact that in Sumerian myth Inanna alone returns each year from her sacrificial journey to the underworld, leaving behind her slain spouse Dumuzi, the shepherd, suggests that memories of female supremacy and male sacrifice lingered on.

The third essential new year's observance was a public recital of *Enuma Elish*, the creation myth. The world, as Sumerians and later Mesopotamians heard every time the priests intoned the epic, had once been a watery chaos—as could be seen by looking out over the Persian Gulf at dawn from the delta's marshy shore. Then, continued the epic, the sky god An had separated the heavens and the waters, and from the mingling of freshwater and saltwater the earth had been formed—as had actually happened when Tigris and Euphrates silt formed the delta and Sumer. Primeval earth and sea spirits had given life to the land and the ocean; they had warred; out of this war had emerged the wise Enki, who before retiring into splendid aloofness begot the vigorously male Enlil, the maker of the human race and capricious ruler of its destinies. Enlil, the god of storms, could be beneficent, bringing life-giving rain, but he also embodied destruction and wildness. Against the orderly sequence of crops and seasons, Enlil represented nature's terrifying, unpredictable side. Nevertheless, the point of annually reciting the *Enuma Elish*, which narrated all this cosmic drama, was to reaffirm order in the face of chaos.

Helpless before the wrath of the elements, Sumerians saw themselves as slaves of the gods. This theme of human bondage appears vividly in the *Enuma Elish*, where Enlil decrees, "Let man be burdened with the gods' toil, that the gods may freely breathe." The Sumerians honored the gods whom they served by building great temples in the centers of their cities, and obviously they hoped that the gods, like severe but occasionally indulgent parents or masters, could be wheedled into being gracious.

The Ziggurat at Ur The Third Dynasty rulers of Ur erected this ziggurat between about 2100 and 2000 B.C., and it was kept in repair by subsequent Mesopotamian rulers until the fall of Babylon to the Persians. This photograph shows a restoration. © *Richard Ashworth/Robert Harding Associates, London.*

---

[1]Their numerical system, based on multiples of 60, left its mark on our own reckoning of degrees in a circle and minutes in an hour.

Temple priests controlled part of the land and labor of the inhabitants. Indeed, it was in the service of the temples and their gods that the Sumerians made many of their most fundamental contributions to civilization. The temple buildings themselves constitute humanity's earliest efforts at monumental architecture. They were vast, terraced artificial mounds known as *ziggurats*, built of clay bricks often faced with colored and ornamented tiles. They housed not only places for worship and sacrificial offerings but also quarters for the priests, dormitories for their servants and slaves, and storage rooms for the vast amounts of foodstuffs that the temple received in taxes. The largest ziggurat rose as high as a twelve-story building.

The first Sumerian writing was done by temple scribes who began to keep accounts of the considerable economic resources of their temples. Such were the mundane origins of literacy. One expert has truly said that "history begins at Sumer"—for history, narrowly speaking, is the reconstruction of the past from written sources, and our first strictly historical evidence is Sumerian.

Mesopotamian writing consists of inscribing wedge-shaped marks on clay tablets with a reed stylus, a technique that later spread throughout much of the Near East. The script is called *cuneiform* after the Latin *cuneus*, meaning "wedge." The first cuneiform symbols, pictograms (little pictures), evolved in time into ideograms—conventionalized figures representing things or abstract concepts. Eventually scribes achieved greater flexibility by adding syllabic symbols, representing various sounds. Since the cuneiform symbols ran well into the hundreds, writing was a complex art that remained for many centuries the monopoly of a small, highly trained scribal class.

Sumerian mathematics seems also to have arisen from the needs of the temples. Their priests had to keep close account of the vast resources that flowed into their repositories in the form of taxes-in-kind, and they did so by compiling written inventories and ledgers. Besides their astronomical reckonings in units of 60, another basic numerical unit among the Sumerians (as among many other peoples) was 10, reflecting the natural impulse to count on the fingers. They understood addition and subtraction and could handle fractions. They established standard units of weight and measure and perfected a lunar calendar. All these achievements were the products of hard, practical necessity. All appear to have risen first from the needs of the temple community to better serve the gods.

The invention of writing was followed by the birth of literature. The Sumerians could now record on clay tablets the stories of their people, which they had previously communicated across the generations through chant and song. In these stories the gods again played a dominant role. The tragic and powerful *Epic of Gilgamesh* describes a Sumerian royal hero's courageous, fruitless search for immortality and includes an early version of the flood story that recurs in the Bible. Sumerian writing has a grave, solemn style that changed little from one generation to the next. Sumerian authors and poets saw no value in originality, preferring to follow earlier models

Sumerian Cuneiform Tablet   The clay tablet above records transactions from about 3000 B.C. and shows Sumerian cuneiform just emerging from pictographs. In the right tablet from a thousand years later, cuneiform has developed fully and is being used to describe geometrical exercises.   © *The British Museum.*

THE HISTORICAL EVIDENCE

Extract from *Gilgamesh*

ca. 2000 B.C.

The flood narrative that follows was originally probably an independent Sumerian story, but it was fitted into the Gilgamesh epic as a climax to the hero's fruitless search for immortality. Gilgamesh has met Utnapishtim, the guardian of the river that separates mortals from the gods, and Utnapishtim tells him how he, alone of all human beings, came to live forever. A just man, he was warned by Ea, the god of wisdom, that the storm god Enlil had decided to destroy humanity in a mighty flood. Ea instructed Utnapishtim to build an ark in which he, his family, and his animals could ride out the catastrophe. He obeyed. Then . . .

With the first light of dawn a black cloud came from the horizon; it thundered within where Adad [Enlil], lord of the storm was riding. . . . A stupor of despair went up to heaven when the god of the storm turned daylight to darkness, when he smashed the land like a cup. . . . Even the gods were terrified at the flood. . . . Then Ishtar* the sweet-voiced Queen of Heaven cried out like a woman in travail: "Alas the days of old are turned to dust because I commanded evil; why did I command this evil in the council of all the gods? I commanded wars to destroy the people, but are they not my people, for I brought them forth?" . . . The great gods of heaven and of hell wept, they covered their mouths.

For six days and six nights the winds blew, torrent and tempest and flood overwhelmed the world. . . . When the seventh day dawned the storm from the south subsided, the sea grew calm, the flood was stilled; I looked at the face of the world and there was silence, all mankind was turned to clay. . . . [Utnapishtim sent out birds, and eventually a raven found food. He landed on a mountaintop and poured out an offering to the gods.] Then, at last, Ishtar also came, she lifted her necklace with the jewels of heaven that once Anu [An] had made to please her. "O ye gods here present, by the lapis lazuli round my neck I shall remember these days. . . . Let all the gods gather round the sacrifice, except Enlil. He shall not approach this offering, for without reflection he brought thee."

[The other gods agree that Enlil went too far in wiping out the human race. Enlil himself repents, seeing that Utnapishtim and his wife were virtuous, and grants them immortality.]

---

*The surviving copies of *Gilgamesh* were made by the Babylonians and Assyrians and used the later versions of the gods' names. Scholars believe, however, that in its original version the gods had Sumerian names: Innana for Ishtar, An for Anu, and Enlil for Adad.

Source: From *The Epic of Gilgamesh*, trans. N. K. Sandars, rev. ed. (Harmondsworth, England: Penguin, 1972), pp. 109–112.

---

and preserve tradition. To do something differently was to do it incorrectly.

Many of these same qualities affected Sumerian sculpture. It too was almost exclusively religious, and much of it was devoted to the decoration of the temples. On a miniature scale, Sumerian sculpture achieved its greatest (and earliest) mastery in the beautifully carved cylinder seals, which the owner would roll across soft clay or wax to leave the equivalent of a signature. To some modern tastes Sumerian sculpture seems static, somber, and impersonal, and despite a gradual trend toward realism it was nearly as tradition-bound as Sumerian literature. Yet the statuettes, relief carvings, and seals of Sumerian artists also convey dignity. Altogether they give moving expression to the Sumerian religious outlook and take their place alongside the works of the poets and architects as the first expressions of a cultural tradition that would dominate southwestern Asia for thousands of years.

In historical times, the Sumerian city-states were dominated by a male hierarchy of kings, priests, administrator-nobles, and warriors; whatever struggles with powerful women had occurred lay in the prehistoric Neolithic past. Far beneath the dominant males in wealth and prestige were merchants and artisans, free workers and peasants. At the bottom were slaves, although they were not numerous in Mesopotamian society until much later. Among the enslaved population was a crucially important body of female textile workers—a group dating back to Neolithic times—who produced one of the cities' primary exports: wool cloth. These and other slaves in Sumerian cities, like those of subsequent ancient civilizations, were recruited largely from among prisoners of war but also from defaulting debtors and other "criminals," from paupers who accepted slavery in order to eat, and from the descendants of these groups. The war prisoners were products of the incessant intercity warfare that had afflicted Mesopotamia ever since the earliest days of urban life. Slavery was a product not of ethnicity but of misfortune.

Slaves and free peasants, who far outnumbered everyone else, were obliged to work the temple lands or the lands of kings or nobles, but they were often allowed to till their own fields as well and to sell their own surpluses. Most agrarian workers, however, remained impoverished, as would their counterparts worldwide for millennia to come.

By the beginning of recorded Sumerian history, women were already assuming the subordinate status characteristic of their roles in future societies. A Sumerian wife ordinarily had immediate charge of the upbringing of her children, and she usually oversaw the family's domestic servants (if any) and organized the affairs and maintenance of her residence, whether great or small, including the production of clothing and the preparation of meals. But she did so under the overall control of her husband, and it was he who participated in most economic and social affairs outside the home.

Because Mesopotamia is largely a treeless plain in which stone and metals are rare, the Sumerians depended on trade for many of their needs. Timber and metals had to be imported, so that Mesopotamian cities were built largely of clay bricks. The Sumerians developed large-scale commercial networks in which their exports—wool cloth, grain, vegetable oil, and metal weapons and tools—were carried in wheeled carts, river barges, and seagoing vessels as far away as India and the eastern Mediterranean. In return, the Sumerians imported not only metals, which their smiths fashioned into bronze weapons and similar goods, but also gems to be fabricated into jeweled orna-ments for both export and domestic use—to enhance the prestige of the wealthy and powerful, to demonstrate their superiority to others less fortunate, and sometimes to take into their tombs.

Most Sumerian cities appear to have been first governed by groups of priests and nobles. The practice developed, however, of appointing a temporary king to rule during military emergencies. In time such emergencies became more frequent, until monarchy was permanent and hereditary. The chief priest and the king were sometimes the same person, for kingship, like almost every other Sumerian institution, was primarily religious; but when they were not the same, the city submitted to the dual authority of temple and palace.

It was the king's task to lead the city's troops into battle and to experience the dreams and other portents from which priests might interpret the gods' will. But even he was merely the foremost slave of the city's chief god. The rise of monarchies stemmed largely from the growing tendency toward intercity warfare and the consequent need of central leadership to direct urban armies. The ultimate political unification of the region was long delayed by the fierce independence of cities bearing such poetic names as Ur, Lagash, Umma, and Uruk.

The Expansion of Sumer

As the struggles went on, Sumerian civilization spread northward along the Tigris-Euphrates Valley into a country called Akkad. This region was settled chiefly by Semitic-speaking peoples (a language group unrelated to Sumerian

Royal Standard of Ur   This scene is one of two panels on a small chest about 69 centimeters (19 inches) long, created with inlays of shell and lapis lazuli. It dates from around 2500 B.C. and was recovered from the Royal Cemetery at Ur. In this scene, a procession of soldiers gathers around the king (center of the top row). Notice the carts, which are among the oldest representations of wheels, and the asses (not horses) that draw them.   © *The British Museum.*

but including both modern Arabic and Hebrew), who had migrated from their original homeland in Arabia northward into Syria and then eastward into Mesopotamia. Under Sumerian influence, the inhabitants of Akkad built cities of their own and joined in the intercity battles, thus dividing Mesopotamia between the Semitic northern district of Akkad and Sumer to the south. But the relationships between Semites and Sumerians were exceedingly complex, and we must not view these peoples as two antagonistic blocs. The inhabitants of almost every city, Sumerian or Akkadian, came from both language groups.

As Mesopotamian civilization developed, it came into contact with city-states that were emerging far to the east and west of the Tigris-Euphrates Valley. The Neolithic village of Tepe Yahya in Iran, some 500 miles to the east of Mesopotamia, had evolved by about 3400 B.C. into a city-state whose scribes were recording commercial transactions on clay tablets. Tepe Yahya grew much larger after about 3200 B.C., by which time other Iranian cities were also keeping written records. The scribes at Tepe Yahya, as elsewhere in Iran, inscribed their tablets in a language altogether different from that of Mesopotamia: They wrote in the earliest known form of Old Persian. Tepe Yahya may well have been one of several way stations along a trade route that linked Mesopotamia to the Indus Valley, carrying products and ideas between the two civilizations.

In 1975, Italian archaeologists announced the discovery of a great city called Ebla, far to the west of Mesopotamia in northern Syria. In the "Palace of Ebla" they found thousands of clay tablets, the earliest dating back to about 2400 B.C. The tablets are inscribed in Mesopotamian cuneiform script, but in a Semitic language, not in Sumerian. The evidence suggests that Ebla (meaning perhaps "City of the White Stones") was the center of a flourishing kingdom in the third millennium B.C. and a potent military and commercial rival to the city-states of Mesopotamia. Its population may have reached forty thousand.

Ebla's writing, art, political structure and religion were all clearly Mesopotamian in inspiration. Like the cities of Mesopotamia, Ebla was ruled by kings. It exported textiles and fine metalware along a far-flung trade network that extended eastward past Mesopotamia into western Iran, southward into Palestine, and northwestward to Anatolia (Asia Minor, modern Turkey). At its height, around 2400–2250 B.C., Ebla appears to have controlled a considerable empire encompassing northern Syria, lower Anatolia, and at times part of northern Mesopotamia. After about 2250 B.C. it suffered several military reverses and was sacked, probably more than once, but it remained a factor in Near Eastern politics until about 1600 B.C.

The Unification of Mesopotamia

While Ebla flourished, the Akkadian conqueror Sargon (ca. 2370–2315 B.C.) was bringing all Mesopotamia under his rule. He subdued the Mesopotamian city-states after more than a millennium of turbulent independence and created the first empire to bind Akkad and Sumer into a single, durable unit. Sargon's daughter, the priestess Enheduanna, merits fame comparable to her father's as the first poet known by name, the author of poems honoring the goddess Inanna.

Sargon's descendants maintained uneasy control of the Tigris-Euphrates Valley for several generations. Around 2250 B.C. his grandson led an army into Syria and burned Ebla to the ground. Later its citizens rebuilt it, but Ebla thereafter never seriously contended in the political struggles of the Near East.

In time, invaders from the northeast destroyed Sargon's Akkadian Dynasty, ushering in another period of political upheaval. Around 2100 B.C., the Sumerian city of Ur rose to dominance. (Scholars call this "Third Dynasty Ur," to distinguish it from the earlier city-state of the Royal Tombs.) The new Ur built the largest of all ziggurats, and its kings, unlike earlier Sumerian monarchs, claimed to be divine. But after a century of fame and fortune, the empire of Ur fell victim to local revolts and invasions from Iran. With its collapse Sumerian political power came to a permanent end. The Sumerian cities were encompassed by larger empires under the control of Semitic-speaking peoples.

During the troubled era around 2000 B.C., several new Semitic peoples moved into the valley. One such group, the Amorites from Syria, occupied a number of Mesopotamian cities, including Babylon (near modern Baghdad). As the Amorites widened their dominion, Babylon evolved into a great imperial capital. Hammurabi (ca. 1700 B.C.), the most celebrated of the Amorite kings of Babylon, conquered all of Akkad and Sumer and eventually extended his sway across the entire Fertile Crescent from the Mediterranean Sea to the Persian Gulf. Building on Sumerian traditions that had been evolving for two thousand years, Hammurabi created a political structure of exceptional efficiency. His famous law code, based on earlier and shorter Sumerian codes and drawing heavily from Sumerian custom, proclaimed its purpose in its prologue:

> To cause justice to prevail in the land,
> To destroy the wicked and the evil,
> That the strong may not oppress the weak.

Hammurabi made no claim to personal divinity but assumed the more traditional role of steward of the gods. His code opens a window into Babylonian society, which like its Sumerian predecessors was stratified into nobles and priests, free commoners (merchants and workers), and slaves. The code's detailed mercantile regulations indicate an active, complex commercial life. Wives had rights that even their husbands must respect, and a wife with wealthy parents might receive and control an extensive **dowry** throughout her marriage and after her husband's death. But the Code of Hammurabi is in many respects harsher than its Sumerian predecessors, suggesting a heightened

THE HISTORICAL EVIDENCE

Hammurabi's Code

ca. 1700 B.C.

The following extracts from Hammurabi's long, detailed Code give some idea of how the king tried to uphold law and order in Babylon.

1: If a seignior* accused another seignior and brought a charge of murder against him, but has not proved it, his accuser shall be put to death.

2: If a seignior brought a charge of sorcery against another seignior, but has not proved it, upon going to the river shall throw himself in the river, and if the river has overpowered him, his accuser shall take over his estate; if the river has shown that seignior to be innocent and he has accordingly come forth safe, the one who brought the charge of sorcery against him shall be put to death, while the one who threw himself into the river shall take over the estate of his accuser.

22: If a seignior committed robbery and has been caught, that seignior shall be put to death.

23: If the robber has not been caught, the robbed seignior shall set forth the particulars regarding his lost property in the presence of god, and the city and governor, in whose territory and district the robbery was committed, shall make good to him his lost property.

88: If a merchant lent grain at interest, he shall receive sixty *qu* of grain per *kur* as interest. If he lent money at interest, he shall receive one-sixth shekel six *se* per shekel of silver as interest.†

142: If a woman so hated her husband that she has declared, "You may not have me," her record shall be investigated at her city council, and if she was careful and was not at fault, even though her husband has been going out and disparaging her greatly, that woman, without incurring any blame at all, may take her dowry and go off to her father's house.

143: If she was not careful, but was a gadabout, thus neglecting her house and humiliating her husband, they shall throw that woman into the water.

202: If a seignior has struck the cheek of a seignior who is superior to him, he shall be beaten sixty times with an oxtail whip in the assembly.

203: If a member of the aristocracy has struck the cheek of another member of the aristocracy who is of the same rank as himself, he shall pay one mina of silver.

204: If a commoner has struck the cheek of another commoner, he shall pay ten shekels of silver.

205: If a seignior's slave has struck the cheek of a member of the aristocracy, they shall cut off his ear.

---

*In this translation, the European word *seignior* is used to indicate the Babylonian equivalent of a free man of some social standing.

†In both cases, this amounts to 20 percent interest.

Source: Adapted from *Ancient Near Eastern Texts Relating to the Old Testament*, ed. James B. Pritchard, 3rd ed. (Princeton, NJ: Princeton University Press, 1969), pp. 166–175. Trans. Theophile J. Meek. Parentheses, indicating words extrapolated by the translator, have been omitted for the sake of readability.

---

authoritarianism. Capital punishment is frequent where it had once been rare, and the notion of retributive justice—"an eye for an eye"—is carried to macabre extremes: If a house collapses, killing its occupant, the builder is executed; if the occupant's son is killed, the builder's son must die; if a patient dies during an operation, the surgeon is executed; if the patient loses an eye, the surgeon loses his fingers—and with them, presumably, his career.

The Emergence of the Indo-European Peoples

Even when the Babylonian Empire was at its height, new peoples continued to move into the Fertile Crescent from the surrounding mountains and deserts. Many of them belonged to groups known collectively as **Indo-European,** for although they were ethnically diverse and politically disunited, their languages derived from a single Indo-European language core that has been traced back some five thousand years to the grassland north of the Black Sea. From there it spread eastward into India and westward across the Near East into Europe, fragmenting in the process into many dialects and separate languages. It is the ancestor of ancient Latin, Greek, Persian, and Sanskrit, and of the modern Slavic, Romance, Germanic, and Indian languages (see Figure 1-1).

Between about 1700 and 1500 B.C., Indo-European peoples and other newcomers, tempted by the riches of flourishing civilizations, disrupted the political and cultural continuity of not only the ancient Near East but other vast areas of the then civilized world. For example, after about

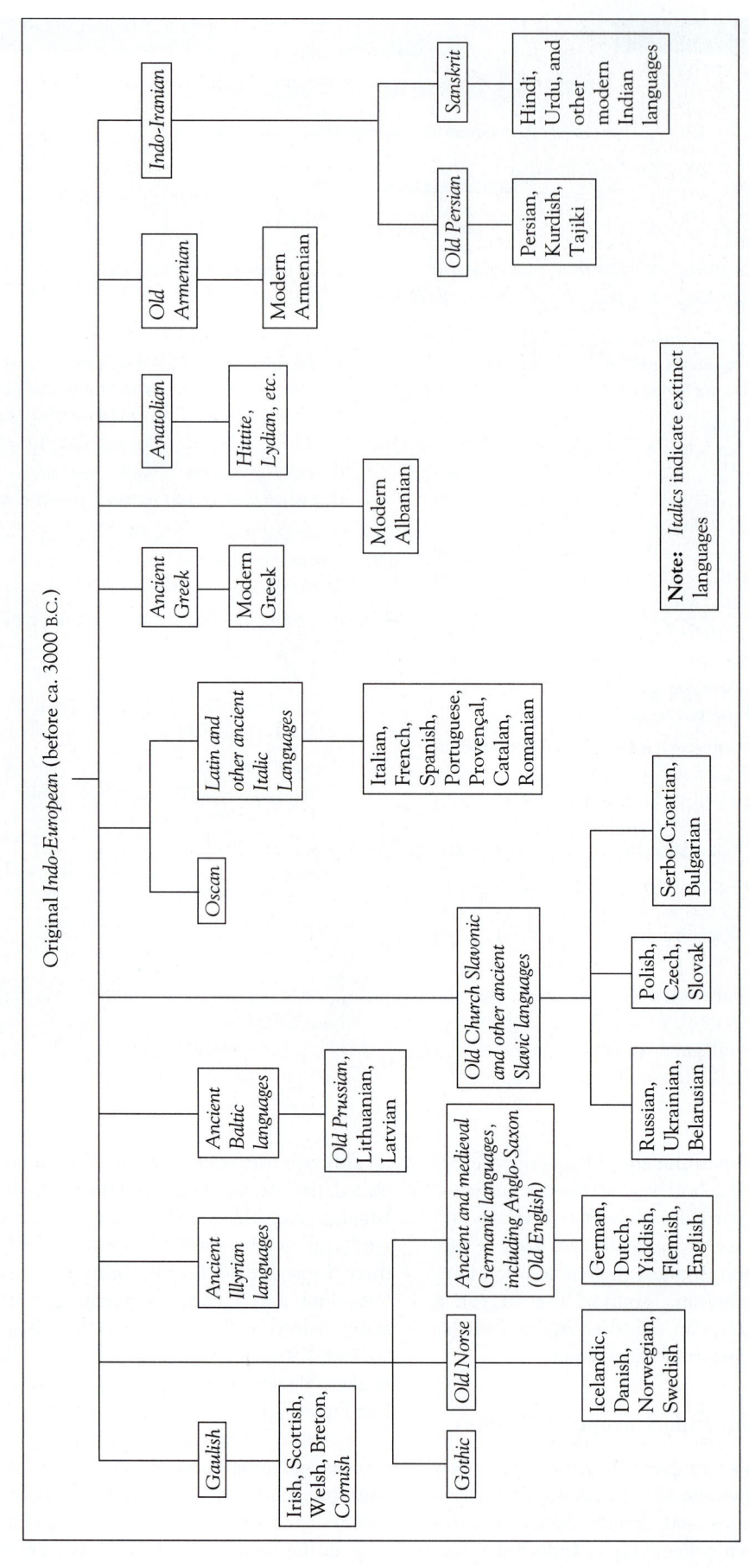

Original *Indo-European* (before ca. 3000 B.C.)

Note: *Italics* indicate extinct languages

FIGURE 1-1
THE INDO-EUROPEAN LANGUAGES

Chariotry This is one of the earliest depictions of chariots, which Indo-Europeans used to devastating effect in the middle of the second millennium B.C. Chariots must also have been great fun between the wars. This carved depiction of driver, archer, and horses chasing a stag comes from about 1400 B.C. and was made by the Hittites, one of the Indo-European peoples who forced their way into the ancient Near East. *Erich Lessing/Art Resource, NY.*

1600 B.C., Indo-European tribes known as Aryans, having moved southeastward into Iran, began descending into the Indus Valley. There, with their new horse-and-chariot military technology, they looted and ravaged whatever remained of the first Indian civilization.

Around 1530 B.C., Indo-European invaders from Iran, called Kassites, destroyed Hammurabi's dynasty in Babylon. Like other Indo-European peoples, the Kassites used horses and chariots to intimidate and conquer. The chariot seems probably (though not certainly) to have been previously unknown to civilized peoples of the Indus Valley and the Near East, and it carried Indo-European invaders to victory after victory. Kassite rulers lorded it over Mesopotamia for the next four centuries—not as gods or as agents of gods, but simply as a landed nobility with a monopoly on chariots.

But before looking further at the Semitic and Indo-European kingdoms of western Asia, let us turn to the valley of the Nile, many hundreds of miles to the west of the Tigris-Euphrates, where another great civilization had developed in relative isolation from Mesopotamia.

THE EGYPTIAN ROOTS

"Egypt is the gift of the Nile." The ancient Greek historian Herodotus first made this oft-repeated observation, but its truth had long been recognized by the Egyptians themselves. One of their most moving hymns opens: "Hail to you, O Nile, that issues from the earth and comes to keep Egypt alive!"

The valley of the Nile winds northward like a green serpent, many hundreds of miles long but no more than 8 miles wide, through the vast and barren Sahara Desert toward the Mediterranean. As the river approaches the sea, 4,000 miles from its origins in central Africa, the Nile

Valley spreads out into a broad, flat delta some 150 miles across. The narrow valley to the south and the delta to the north form two distinct regions known as Upper and Lower Egypt. (Since the two regions are named according to their location on the northward flowing Nile, Lower Egypt is shown above Upper Egypt on a modern map; see Map 1-2.) Ancient Egypt has thus been called "the Kingdom of the Two Lands."

Unification and the Early Dynastic Period

Ninety percent of present-day Egypt is a waterless desert; the Nile Valley is the great exception. Its remarkable fertility, greater even than that of the Tigris-Euphrates, results from the rich silt deposited by annual floods.[2] The Nile floods made the valley habitable despite the absence of rainfall and the searing heat.

The evolution from Neolithic culture to civilization in Egypt resembled the Mesopotamian pattern. By draining

MAP 1-2
ANCIENT EGYPT: THE OLD AND MIDDLE KINGDOMS

---

[2]The age-old flooding of the Nile ended in 1970 with the completion of the high dam at Aswan.

swamps, digging canals, and building dikes, the early Egyptians succeeded in exploiting the black soil of the Nile Valley and controlling the yearly floods. The influence of the slightly earlier Mesopotamian model is suggested by the presence of Sumerian artifacts and artistic motifs at the beginning of Egypt's formative period, but the extent of Sumerian influence on early Egypt remains a subject of heated scholarly debate.

Toward the close of the fourth millennium B.C., the Neolithic villages along the Nile had congealed into larger political units called nomes. Gradually the nomes formed two major kingdoms: Upper Egypt (the Nile Valley) and Lower Egypt (the Delta). Around 3100 B.C. a half-legendary conqueror from Upper Egypt named Narmer (or, as later Greek historians called him, Menes) unified the entire land and ruled it from his capital at Memphis—centrally located near the juncture of Upper and Lower Egypt (see Table 1-2). He is said to have ruled for sixty-two years before he was killed by a hippopotamus. Narmer thus became the first of Egypt's kings or, as they would later be called, pharaohs.[3]

The next 450 years, ca. 3150–ca. 2700 B.C., constitute an ill-recorded but uniquely creative epoch in Egyptian history. During this half millennium, as the early kings consolidated their hereditary authority, a culture was developing that would shape Egyptian life for two millennia to follow. The Egyptians expanded their irrigation system significantly. They developed an extensive knowledge of astronomy and used it to create a 365-day solar calendar, more accurate than the thirteen-month lunar calendar of the Mesopotamians. They were the first to divide the day into twenty-four hours and to subdivide it into two twelve-hour segments. Their work in physiology and medicine (especially surgery) would not be surpassed until Greek

times. They probably influenced the Greeks as well in practical mathematics, in which their scribes applied arithmetical and geometrical calculations to such official functions as the surveying of fields, the construction of buildings, the keeping of accounts, and the distribution of wages in kind (often in the form of grain and beer). Egyptian artists developed a graceful, majestic style, and architects demonstrated increasing skill in designing large structures of stone (although sometimes with shaky foundations).

Around the beginning of the Early Dynastic Period, Egyptians developed a form of writing that we know as **hieroglyphics** (from the Greek word for "sacred carving"). Like cuneiform writing, it combined pictograms and phonetic symbols, but in other respects the two systems of writing were altogether distinct (see Figure 1-2). Some experts contend that the Sumerians gave the Egyptians the fundamental concept of writing; others think that the Egyptians hit on it themselves. This is a good example of the ongoing scholarly debate over whether cultural changes radiate outward from a single source or develop independently.

The Egyptians first carved hieroglyphics onto relief sculptures and incorporated them into wall paintings. But eventually an Egyptian literature arose, including hymns, love poems, fables, guides to getting ahead in the world, even ghost stories. Like other aspects of Egyptian culture, hieroglyphic writing attained full development in early dynastic times and changed very little thereafter—apart from gradually expanding the original array of about seven hundred characters. Palace and temple scribes of later centuries saved time and effort by keeping their records in a cursive script known as hieratic—a simplified variant of hieroglyphics. Discovering how to make a paperlike substance from papyrus, a reed that grows along the Nile, immensely aided the creation of Egyptian literature.

The Early Dynastic Period was, in short, an exciting, adventurous age of artistic and cultural experimentation that set an indelible mark on all of ancient Egypt. When that era closed, about 2700 B.C., Egyptian civilization had matured.

The Egyptian Way

Although both Egypt and Mesopotamia arose out of the taming of river valleys, the two civilizations differed sharply in style and mood, in part because they differed in environment. The flooding Nile raged less savagely than the Tigris-Euphrates, and its inundations were much more predictable. (Significantly, Egyptian religion—unlike Mesopotamian or Chinese—produced no flood legend.) Egyptian winds blew less ferociously, the sky remained a brilliant blue, and the natural resources of the area usually proved more than sufficient to support the Nile Valley's relatively modest population. The surrounding Sahara Desert shielded early Egyptian civilization from invasions. There was an amiable regularity to life, and the forces of nature seemed friendlier and less menacing.

TABLE 1-2

PERIODS OF ANCIENT EGYPTIAN HISTORY

All dates are B.C. and approximate.

3150–2700	Early Dynastic Period
2700–2200	Old Kingdom
2200–2040	First Intermediate Period
2040–1785	Middle Kingdom
1785–1560	Second Intermediate Period, Age of the Hyksos
1560–1070	New Kingdom (or Empire)

---

[3]The word *pharaoh* means "great house." At around 1800 B.C., it became the name for Egyptian kings.

FIGURE 1-2
HEIROGLYPHICS

As this illustration shows, hieroglyphics began as simple picture-writing but evolved into a way of grammatically expressing complex ideas. The translation of this Twelfth Dynasty sentence reads: "It is my son who causes my name to live upon this stela."
Source: Adapted from Ancient Egypt, *Great Ages of Man Series (New York:* Time, *1965), pp. 154–155.*

Accordingly, the ancient Egyptians tended to be confident, pragmatic, and optimistic, convinced that nature had blessed them and would continue to do so. Of course individuals differ, and ancient Egypt must have had its pessimists, and Mesopotamia its optimists. Egypt was not immune to sandstorms, droughts, and crop failures, and the heat was fierce. By modern standards, ancient Egyptians did not enjoy good health or long lives—although one pharaoh (Pepi II, who came to the throne as a child) reigned more than ninety years. But the mood expressed in ancient Egyptian art, architecture, and literature exudes serenity and confidence—even joy and exuberance—a delight in the good things of this world and the pleasures of the moment.

These worldly attitudes might seem to conflict with the ancient Egyptian emphasis on death, as reflected in the great pyramids and in the ever-increasing opulence of the massive vaults in which pharaohs, great nobles, and officials lay entombed. But the abundance of grave goods inside these tombs—finely wrought furniture, robes, weapons, utensils, musical instruments, boats, toilet articles, along with frescoes depicting events from everyday life and colorful religious celebrations—makes it clear that upper-class Egyptians expected the afterlife to be an unbroken extension of the present. For similar reasons, their corpses were often mummified and thus preserved so that the spirit might reenter and reinhabit its earthly body. It became customary in later centuries to place beside the richly ornamented coffin of the mummified corpse numerous doll-like statuettes which, after the reanimation of the

dead spirit, would come to life, grow in size, and perform the various tasks of household servants in the "other world." (This practice is obviously much more benign than killing and entombing actual servants, which was done in predynastic Egypt.)

Once established, Egyptian culture and Egyptian society changed only very slowly over the centuries. The Egyptian spirit was sufficiently tolerant and undogmatic to accept such cultural adjustments as changing conditions might require; yet by the standards of later civilizations, Egypt was relatively static. Its inertia was in part a product of isolation but stemmed also from the attitude of the Egyptians themselves. Theirs seemed the best of all possible worlds, and they preferred to perpetuate it, not to change it.

The Egyptians viewed the universe as orderly and benevolent. The key concept in Egyptian religious thought is expressed in the word *ma'at*, which can be translated as "truth," "justice," "harmony," "balance," or "righteousness." Most of the Egyptian gods were not ferocious and arbitrary as in Mesopotamia, nor were the Egyptians their slaves. On the contrary, the gods cared about Egypt and favored it exceedingly. Indeed, the pharaoh himself was a living god and his rule was, at least ideally, a manifestation of ma'at. His word was law, and Egypt therefore produced no law codes. As it was said, "The law is in the pharaoh's mouth." Being a god, he expressed in his words and deeds the basic harmony of the cosmos. He was the victorious champion of the Egyptians against the forces of chaos and darkness.

THE HUMAN EXPERIENCE

Nakht, the Paleopathology Boy

Since history as recorded by ancient writers tends to dwell almost entirely on the deeds of emperors, kings, generals, and great religious prophets, it is extremely difficult to reconstruct the life of an ordinary person in antiquity. But the new science of paleopathology—the multidisciplinary analysis (or "autopsy") of corpses that have survived from antiquity—has cast precious light on the nutrition and health of ancient Egyptians, rich and poor alike. Such autopsies have made clear the widespread incidence among the people of ancient Egypt of malaria, tuberculosis, severe ear infection, a wide variety of intestinal worms and kindred parasites, silicosis (a lung disorder caused by inhaling sand over long stretches of time), and perhaps smallpox, polio, and gout. Paleopathological autopsies also disclose severe tooth loss, common to all classes in ancient Egypt, resulting from the infiltration of windblown sand into grain storehouses and kitchens. The teeth of pharaohs and commoners alike were steadily worn down, often nearly to the gums, leading to early tooth loss and to chronic tooth and gum infections that could in some cases be fatal. (Conversely, the bodies of ancient Egyptians contained only about 10 percent of the lead that is found in modern bodies, indicating a dramatic increase in lead pollution in more recent times.)

Beginning in 1974, the mummy of a young man from Upper Egypt was subjected to an autopsy of unprecedented thoroughness by a team of some forty specialists employing such sophisticated techniques as computerized X-ray scanning and electron microscopy. Written on his coffin is the young man's name, Nakht, and the fact that he was a weaver at a great temple at Thebes. Nakht died about 1200 B.C., during the era of the New Kingdom, roughly a century and a half after the death of the pharaoh Akhenaten. People of Nakht's modest social class were rarely mummified; the expense of his entombment and coffin would have been well beyond his means and must have been funded by his temple as a perquisite of his job. (Egyptians did, however, sometimes accord the honor of mummification to corpses other than those of kings and nobles: not only occasional commoners like Nakht but also highly revered animals, including crocodiles and cats.)

Nakht was about fifteen or sixteen years old when he died. He was roughly 5 feet 8 inches tall and weighed between 100 and 120 pounds. Judging from what we know of other Egyptian workers of his era, he would have lived in a small mudbrick house and would have been undernourished. This last guess is confirmed by his autopsy: A careful analysis of the growth patterns of his bones discloses recurring bouts of severe illness, probably associated with malnutrition, during the final years of his short life.

Nakht's bloodstream served as host to a particularly nasty tropical parasite known as schistosome, the eggs of which were discovered in his kidneys and liver. The resulting disease, known as schistosomiasis, had damaged his bladder and kidneys and had caused cirrhosis of the liver.

Indeed, Nakht's body was a hive of parasites. Tapeworm eggs were identified in his intestines, and tests of the tissue of his enlarged spleen suggest that, like many other Egyptians in antiquity, he suffered from malaria.

We know nothing of the day-to-day details of Nakht's life. He appears in no surviving written record except for the writing on his own coffin indicating his name and occupation. But his autopsy—conducted some 3,200 years after his death with the aid of remarkable new paleopathological techniques—suggests that he suffered many of the afflictions common to his fellow Egyptians, great and humble, during his very short life span.

Had Nakht lived on into early adulthood, he might very well have contracted such degenerative diseases as arteriosclerosis and arthritis. We tend today to associate these ailments with middle or old age, but they are often identified in autopsies of ancient Egyptians who died in young adulthood. And of course Nakht's teeth, in a few more years, would probably have been ground down to a painful level. Nakht's early death spared him the afflictions of adulthood, but his autopsy serves as a valuable reminder of the widespread incidence of debilitating diseases in even a highly civilized kingdom of the ancient Mediterranean world. The energy level of ancient Egyptian society, and of other Mediterranean societies of premodern times, must have been severely sapped by these afflictions. ❖

The whole of Egypt was the pharaoh's personal estate, and he controlled all Egyptian commerce and manufacturing. His warehouses sheltered vast stores of grain, including a surplus for distribution during times of drought and famine. There were no independent merchants or entrepreneurs in Egyptian society. The pharaoh dominated everything through his upper administrators, provincial governors, town magistrates, tax collectors, and miscellaneous lesser bureaucrats. A priestly class, relatively small at first, grew in numbers and power across the centuries of the

Old Kingdom. In the absence of significant social unrest or external military threats, the pharaoh's army remained during these early centuries little more than a militia. At the bottom of society were artisans, large numbers of peasant-farmers, and slaves. Egyptians of all ranks and conditions were subject to royal orders. All gave large portions of their produce to the royal treasury and could be drafted to work in the royal mines or on the royal tombs.

The god-king concept affected every aspect of Egyptian life. The great early works of monumental architecture were royal tombs rather than temples—although temple architecture became significant later. Most of the early sculpture and decorative art was associated with the tombs of the pharaohs. Yet in this king-centered system people of ability could rise and prosper in the pharaoh's service. One enthusiastic scholar even suggested that the pyramids themselves were vast public works projects, and in a sense they were. Apparently the god-king's rule was accepted gratefully, not sullenly. Much of the labor of building the pyramids occupied the flood season, when peasants could not cultivate their own land. Moreover, because there were few wars and therefore fewer prisoners, Egypt had fewer slaves than Mesopotamia. Egypt was united, and therefore its cities did not fight among themselves. Women, although barred from the formal education necessary for entry into the Egyptian bureaucracy or scribal class, were much freer than women in Mesopotamia to take part in public life—to own property, conduct business, pursue lawsuits, and participate in religious rituals. Under the absolute monarchy of their god-kings, Egyptians of both sexes were less rigidly stratified than the inhabitants of most other early civilizations. Nevertheless, aristocratic women, in Egypt as in Mesopotamia, were expected to focus their activities on home and household. Sheltered indoors, they were often portrayed by Egyptian artists as much lighter skinned than their sun-bronzed husbands.

Like most ancient peoples, the Egyptians crowded their universe with gods and spirits. Their greatest god, Re, personified the life-giving sun. He appeared in many guises and was often associated in divine partnership with some other god. Amon-Re became in middle and later Egyptian history the most illustrious of these twofold gods. During the New Kingdom, Amon-Re was god of victories, and his magnificent temple at Karnak amassed enormous wealth.

Osiris, another important deity, was thought to have once been a benevolent pharaoh who taught his people

Family Fun in Ancient Egypt   Scenes such as this were often shown in Egyptian tomb paintings; this one comes from Thebes, ca. 1400 B.C. There are two views of the father as he hunts birds in the marshes, surrounded by his wife (who holds him around the waist) and his two daughters.   *Erich Lessing/Art Resource, NY.*

agriculture. His sister-wife Isis, symbolic of the fertile earth (and counterpart of the Mesopotamian earth goddess Inanna), was believed by Egyptians to have been supremely wise and adept at magic. In later legend, Osiris was killed and dismembered by Set, his animal-headed brother. But afterwards, in response to Isis's lamentations and incantations, Osiris was miraculously restored to life. Isis bore her resurrected husband a son, Horus, and Osiris himself passed on into the next world to become the judge of souls. The Isis-Osiris cult contributed to the glorification of Egyptian kingship: Each living pharaoh was an incarnation of Horus, and each dead pharaoh was Osiris.

The theme of death and resurrection runs through all of ancient religious thought. All ancient cultures had mythological variants explaining the death of vegetation in winter and its regeneration in spring: the concept also symbolized the death of the sun each evening and its rebirth at dawn. Indeed, the Nile itself followed this same sequence; the low Nile of early spring, bringing the specter of famine to the land, gave way in the summer to a new, resurgent Nile that revivified the fields. And individual Egyptians might well hope that they too, like the sun and the river,

would conquer death. The Osiris-Isis myth eventually came to symbolize this hope of individual salvation and eternal life. It became one of the most important cults of Hellenistic and Roman times.

The Old, Middle, and New Kingdoms

Egyptian culture's coming-of-age was followed by a five-hundred-year period known as the Old Kingdom (ca. 2700–2200 B.C.), during which Egyptian culture flourished under the power of the pharaohs and the favor of the gods. The Old Kingdom constitutes Egypt's classical age. At no other time was Egypt so stable or so confident.

The authority and prestige of the pharaohs of this period receive dramatic testimony in the pyramids in which they were entombed. The largest pyramids were built during the Fourth Dynasty (ca. 2600–2450 B.C.) at Gizeh near the Nile, then at the desert's edge but now close to the urban sprawl of present-day Cairo. The Great Pyramid of Khufu (or Cheops, as ancient Greek tourists called him) rises some 480 feet, four times as high as the great ziggurat at Ur and almost as high as the Washington Monument. This immense mass of some 6 million tons of stone is fitted together with a precision that testifies not only to the skill and patience of its builders but also to their knowledge of practical mathematics. The pyramids were built without tackle, pulleys, cranes, or wheeled vehicles (the wheel had not yet come to Egypt). Large wooden ramps would have been used to move the great stones into their proper places. The cost in human labor was prodigious; a significant portion of the entire Egyptian workforce must have been engaged in pyramid building over generations of the Old Kingdom. The ancient Greek historian Herodotus (ca. 485–ca. 425 B.C.) reported that gangs of one hundred thousand men worked in rotation for some twenty years on the pyramid of Cheops, adding that the workers loathed their task of dragging the huge stones. Yet the pyramids need not be regarded as brutal monuments to the royal ego. As god-king, the pharaoh was the nexus of Egyptian religious thought, and his tomb was a monument important to virtually all Egyptians. The proper entombment of the dead pharaoh was essential, so Egyptians believed, to the perpetuation of ma'at and the continued prosperity of the kingdom.

The growing power of priests and nobles at the expense of the pharaoh marked the end of the Old Kingdom. The nomarchs, who served as the pharaoh's agents in the provinces or nomes, became increasingly autonomous, and their offices evolved gradually into hereditary lordships. By about 2200 B.C. the authority of the pharaoh had faded completely, and the nomarchs became the real masters of Egypt. The resulting era of unrest and political fragmentation is known as the First Intermediate Period (ca. 2200–2040 B.C.).

Horus and Pharaoh   This magnificent head of Khephren, the Old Kingdom king, over whom Horus hovers protectively, forms both an artistically appealing and a religiously symbolic union of what ancient Egyptians considered the dual nature of the god. Horus the eternal god is manifested as a falcon; the divine king, serenely majestic in this life, becomes Horus's father Osiris on his death.   *Hirmer Fotoarchiv.*

THE HISTORICAL EVIDENCE

Before the Judgment Seat

ca. 1500 B.C.

Ancient Egypt produced an immense number of "mortuary texts"—guides to what would happen after death, written on papyrus and deposited with the deceased in the tomb. By the sixteenth century B.C., when the following text was produced, Egyptians were being told that those who could truthfully avow their guiltlessness before the gods would enjoy immortality. This extract gives a good idea of what Egyptians regarded as righteous behavior.

What is said on reaching the Broad-Hall of the Two Justices, absolving X of every sin which he has committed, and seeing the faces of the gods . . .

I have not committed evil against men.
I have not mistreated cattle.
I have not committed sin in the place of truth [a temple].
I have not known that which is not [i.e., what is forbidden to know]. . . .
I have not blasphemed a god.
I have not done violence to a poor man. . . .
I have not defamed a slave to his superior.
I have not made anyone sick.
I have not made anyone weep.
I have not killed.
I have given no order to a killer.
I have not caused anyone suffering.

I have not cut down on the food-income in the temples.
I have not damaged the bread of the gods. . . .
I have not had sexual relations with a boy.
I have not defiled myself.
I have neither increased or diminished the grain-measure. . . .
I have not taken milk from the mouths of children. . . .

Hail to you, ye gods who are in this Broad-Hall of the Two Justices! I know you; I know your names. I shall not fall for dread of you. Ye have not reported guilt of mine up to this god in whose retinue ye are.

Source: From *Ancient Near Eastern Texts Relating to the Old Testament,* ed. James B. Pritchard, 2nd ed. (Princeton, NJ: Princeton University Press, 1955), pp. 34–35. Trans. John A. Wilson.

The breakdown was purely internal, brought about by excessive delegation of royal rights and by the ever-increasing burden of building and maintaining the stupendous royal tombs. There were no foreign invasions; isolation continued to shelter Egypt from external dangers.

The disintegration of royal authority, with the social upheaval that accompanied it, struck a devastating blow to Egyptian confidence. Writers of the age bemoaned the loss of ma'at. Some pondered the advantages of suicide; others abandoned themselves to debauchery. One writer complained of the end of Egypt's accustomed peace: "I show you the land topsy-turvy. That which never happened has happened. Men take up weapons of warfare, so that the land lives in confusion."

But the general reaction was neither cynicism nor despair. Rather, Egyptians made a serious effort to replace the materialism of the past with deeper spiritual and moral values. Eternal life had formerly been associated primarily with huge tombs and limited largely to the pharaoh and his family, officials, and servants. Now salvation came to depend more on an upright life than an appropriate tomb, and the possibility of an afterlife opened to all. The Egyp-

tians would never again build royal tombs on anything like the scale of the Fourth Dynasty pyramids. Not only were they immensely expensive, but they also served as conspicuous beacons to grave robbers—who abounded during times of disorder and were less interested in ma'at than in self-enrichment.

The new, more inclusive attitude toward life after death affected Egyptian thought and society in countless ways. A text from the First Intermediate Period has the creator god say, "I made the four winds that every man might breathe thereof. . . . I made the great inundation that the poor man might have rights therein like the great man. . . . I made every man like his fellow." For the first time in history, long before the age of the socially conscious Hebrew prophets (discussed later in this chapter), Egyptians envisioned universal human dignity and justice.

Gradually the Egyptian monarchy recovered something of its former self, and with this revival of centralized authority the Middle Kingdom commenced (ca. 2040–1785). The pharaohs now ruled from Thebes (present-day Luxor) in Upper Egypt. Under their direction, Egypt's confidence returned, and the old materialism and optimism

THE HUMAN EXPERIENCE

Akhenaten, Nefertiti, and Tiy

The pharaoh Akhenaten originally bore a traditional royal name, Amenhotep IV. Unusual for the son of a pharaoh (who usually married their sisters), his mother was an Egyptian commoner named Tiy. The young prince's scrawny body kept him from participating in the hunts and similar macho pursuits that his royal father enjoyed, but for some reason—perhaps it was his sharp mind—he was given the throne. Once in power, he revolutionized Egypt.

The solar disk, called Aten, had long been a minor Egyptian deity, but the new pharaoh decreed that this was the only god that he would worship. For emphasis, he changed his name to Akhenaten ("He who serves Aten"). Abandoning Thebes, with its ancient temples and temple priesthood dedicated to Amon-Re, Akhenaten and his wife Nefertiti built a new capital 300 miles to the north and named it Akhetaten ("the horizon of Aten"—the modern Amarna). There they devoted themselves to the worship of what Akhenaten regarded as the god of the universe, the ultimate source of ma'at, the creator of

the world. Akhenaten declared in his hymn to the god Aten:

> O sole god, like whom there is no other!
> Thou didst create the world according to thy desire,
> Whilst thou wert alone.

Akhenaten's revolution was born of the new imperial age. It was an attempt to destroy the ever-increasing power of the established priesthoods, especially that of Amon-Re. Moreover, Aten's universality reflected the new cosmopolitanism that was gripping even previously self-contained Egypt. The Egyptians' world was no longer just the valley of the Nile; they now knew that other nations worshiped other gods. The elegantly beautiful Nefertiti may have been a princess from the Indo-European kingdom of Mitanni, in present-day northern Syria, married to the pharaoh to cement an international alliance. If so, it is quite possible that she, as much as Akhenaten, was responsible for the new religion, to which she remained faithful even when he eventually

wavered. In the art associated with Akhenaten, Nefertiti, and their court, the naturalistic, even grotesque, style of the New Kingdom reached a crescendo.

Absorbed with his god, Akhenaten neglected his dull job of managing Egypt's empire. As trouble mounted and his mother intervened with practical advice, Nefertiti was sent away and Akhenaten made reluctant concessions to tradition. The worship of Aten scarcely survived Akhenaten's death, although the new artistic tendencies continued to flourish. Within a few years the bold heresy had been demolished, and Osiris and Amon-Re returned in triumph.

Why did Akhenaten fail? Perhaps the most significant reason was the nature of Aten—an abstract, distant deity, a god of the intellect rather than the emotions. Nor was it really the only god, for Akhenaten, like any Egyptian king, regarded himself as divine. In his system only the pharaoh and his family worshiped Aten. Everybody else worshiped him. "You are in my heart," said Akhenaten to his god, "and

reemerged, tempered by the social conscience that Egypt had newly acquired.

But the monarchy never recovered its absolute power or unquestioned moral authority. The nomarchs remained powerful during the Middle Kingdom, and the priesthood grew richer and stronger. Art and literature flourished once more, always within the framework of ideas and forms established during the first dynasties. Egyptian culture and commerce now spread far beyond the Nile Valley—southward into the Sudan and northward into Palestine and Syria. And tomb scenes show the same humor and love of life as before.

During the later 1700s B.C., at roughly the time that Indo-Europeans and other peoples were beginning to disrupt Mesopotamia, a group of invaders settled in Egypt. These newcomers, usually called Hyksos ("rulers of foreign

lands") after their kings, were a mixture of various peoples largely Semitic in language and culture. Some of the Hyksos came from what is today Israel and Palestine—a land in ancient times called Canaan. They had adopted the new Mesopotamian military technology, as yet unknown to the Egyptians, and introduced into the Nile Valley improved bronze weapons including daggers and scimitars, much more powerful bows, and horse-drawn chariots. Encouraged by renewed internal tensions within Egyptian politics and society, the Hyksos used their military edge to take over the Egyptian government and hold it for several generations. By remaining self-consciously separate from (and, they doubtless thought, superior to) the indigenous Egyptians, they earned the Egyptians' bitter enmity.

The Hyksos' ascendancy occurred during another period of internal division and strife known as the Second there is no other that knows you." Consequently Aten had no real impact on Egypt at large, even during Akhenaten's reign. The theory that Akhenaten's religious ideas influenced the Hebrews who were then slaves in Egypt, thereby propelling Israel toward monotheism, is altogether implausible. But whatever its weaknesses, Akhenaten's vision was of singular originality and scope. If he fell short of monotheism, he approached it more closely than anyone before him, with the possible exception of the Hebrews. ❖

Source: Translations by J. A. Wilson, in J. B. Pritchard, ed., *Ancient Near Eastern Texts Relating to the Old Testament*, 3rd ed. (Princeton, NJ: Princeton University Press, 1969), p. 370.

Akhenaten, Nefertiti, and the Solar Disk As part of his religious revolution, Akhenaten overturned all the conventions of how a pharaoh should be presented. Here, he and Nefertiti play with some of their six daughters under the protection of the Aten, its rays ending in outstretched hands. He is shown with a realism that accentuates his awkward physique. So is she, although another famous painted bust shows her as an elegantly beautiful woman. *Staatliche Museen, Berlin, Preussischer Kulturbesitz, Agyptisches Museum. Photo by Margarete Busing.*

Intermediate Period (ca. 1785–1560 B.C.). Although their impact on Egyptian life was limited chiefly to collecting tribute, they deflated Egypt's confidence and buoyancy. The continuity of Egyptian culture did not cease, but it was compromised. Thereafter, Egypt was never quite the same.

In time the Egyptians learned from their new masters how to wage war with horses and chariots, and they used the new military technology to oust the Hyksos from power. The result was the establishment of the last great creative era in ancient Egyptian history, the New Kingdom, or "Empire" (ca. 1560–1070 B.C.). After a period of consolidation, the pharaohs began for the first time to pursue a policy of aggressive imperialism, leading large companies of well-armed charioteers out of a land that had once known only small police forces and militia. The Egyptians quickly extended their military and commercial influence over an extensive region that included the rich provinces of Syria and Palestine, and the numbers of Egyptian slaves grew swiftly. Egypt's isolation was over, and the valley of the Nile was now open not only to new luxuries but also to new styles, ideas, and religions.

The intellectual and artistic currents of this cosmopolitan age transformed the Egyptian mood. The old serenity gave way to an exciting, fluid artistic style. The old idealized portraiture evolved into a new naturalism that at times bordered on caricature and an obsession with the grotesque. The newly expanded kingdom maintained itself only at the cost of constant watchfulness and ever-increasing tension, and the old sense of confidence and optimism, undermined by the Hyksos, did not return. Yet despite the new regimentation and sharp social stratification of this imperialistic society, the pharaoh was no longer simply a divine autocrat. His independence and authority were increasingly compromised by the rise of priestly power, and his wealth was rivaled by that of the god Amon-Re.

Etched against this fluctuating background stands the curious, perhaps tragic figure of the pharaoh Akhenaten (reigned 1379–1361 B.C.). Often described, not quite accurately, as humanity's first **monotheist,** Akhenaten rejected the many gods whom Egyptians had always worshiped. He defied the powerful priesthood of Amon-Re, suppressed the cult of Osiris, and chiseled the names of these and other gods from the temples. In their place Akhenaten established the god Aten, the solar disc with rays ending in hands. Akhenaten's bold religious initiative has fascinated historians of religion, but it was short-lived. Soon after the pharaoh's death, his god was rejected and forgotten; Osiris and Amon-Re returned in triumph.

Akhenaten's own son-in-law, the pharaoh Tutankhamen, restored the old priesthood that Akhenaten had dismissed. He renounced Akhenaten's **heresy** and welcomed the old gods home. We know very little about Tutankhamen: He died in his late teens, probably at the hands of an assassin, and is not known to have done anything of significance during his brief reign except to betray his father-in-law's principles. At his death, his name was wiped from the historical record. Yet "King Tut" is today perhaps the most celebrated personage of ancient Egypt because his tomb, and only his, was sufficiently well hidden deep underground in the Valley of the Kings to elude the plundering of grave robbers. The consequences of this fortunate circumstance are astonishing: The archaeologist who discovered the tomb, Howard Carter, on first entering it in 1922, was dumbfounded at the sight of gilded burial shrines and golden coffins, one inside another; of precious objects in great profusion and endless variety—a stunning collection of treasure and art from one of the great eras of Egyptian civilization, all now spectacularly displayed at the Egyptian Museum in Cairo.

Ancient Egypt had one more great king: Ramses II, whose reign encompassed most of the thirteenth century B.C. (1279–1213). A military man whose father may have been born a commoner, he emblazoned his exploits on his many monuments. (Once he turned a near-disaster of his own making into one more testimony to his all-conquering glory.) Ramses was a builder on a grand scale, but also something of a cosmopolitan. His favorite wife was a foreigner, whom he commemorated in a temple to the Near Eastern goddess Astarte (Inanna). Later Egyptians admired his memory. But after him, Egyptian kings would see themselves primarily as the heirs of a past greatness.

Egypt, Canaan, and the Hittites

Moving through Canaan—the ancient name for what is now Israel, Palestine, Lebanon, and Syria's Mediterranean coast—the Hyksos had entered and eventually taken over Egypt itself. At least some of the invaders' leaders seem to have been Canaanite princes. After expelling the Hyksos, Egypt's New Kingdom rulers not surprisingly decided that their country's future security demanded that Canaan be effectively controlled.

Canaan consists of a plain along the Mediterranean shoreline, narrowing until it reaches the formidable coastal mountains and sheltered harbors of Lebanon and Syria, and a hilly but fertile interior. To the south lies the Negeb Desert, an extension of the wasteland that covers the Sinai Peninsula. The Jordan River and the Dead Sea form Canaan's eastern boundary.

The ancient Canaanites spoke Semitic languages and had occupied the land since at least 3000 B.C. During the second millennium, the coast of northern Canaan was dotted with rich commercial cities. One of these, Ugarit (in modern Syria), not only kept its independence but also boasted a great royal palace and library. (The vast collection of clay tablets recently excavated from Ugarit's library

Tutankhamen Combining the restored conventions of the pharaoh's dignity with the naturalistic style of Akhenaten's cultural revolution, this is an exact likeness of the young King Tutankhamen. It is the funeral mask that covered his actual mummy, made of solid gold and inlaid with semiprecious stones. © *R. Sheridan/Ancient Art & Architecture Collection.*

shed much light on the making of the Old Testament, as we shall see a little later.) In the more primitive interior of Canaan, numerous small fortified hilltop towns, including Jerusalem, were ruled by local strongmen who fought each other relentlessly and probably participated in the Hyksos' rule of Egypt (ca. 1785–1560 B.C.). After the Hyksos' expulsion, New Kingdom Egypt's domination of Canaan meant the grudging submission, around 1500 B.C., of these princelings to the pharaoh's overlordship. If they paid their tribute, they could run their internal affairs and happily continue their feuds. Egypt's policy was to play the petty Canaanite lords off against each other, to maintain friendly relations with important cities like Ugarit, and to deal with the formidable kingdoms north of Cannaan either as allies or as enemies.

Two Indo-European kingdoms then dominated what is today northern Syria and Turkey. The first of these kingdoms, Mitanni, flourished from about 1500 to 1360 B.C., and for a time stretched its power into northern Iraq. At first a rival of imperial Egypt, Mitanni eventually became its ally (although relations soured when parsimonious Akhenaten once sent the Mitannian king a statue covered with gold foil instead of the promised solid gold). But in the end Mitanni fell to another rising state, the Hittite Empire. The Hittites had established a kingdom in Asia Minor (modern Turkey) around 1700 B.C. and reached the peak of their power about 1400–1200. While the Pharaoh Akhenaten was worshiping the solar disk and challenging the priests of Amon-Re, the Hittites were extending their authority in northern Syria at Egyptian expense.

The early Hittite state has been termed **feudal.** Powerful nobles controlled large chunks of the kingdom and forced the kings to bargain with them in meetings of the *pankus,* or general assembly. Such meetings were particularly important at the beginning of reigns, when the succession of a new king had to be ratified. Kings who could lead profitable conquering expeditions against neighbors, however, seem to have given the Hittite aristocracy what it wanted—and also increased their own autocratic power. By the time the Hittite Empire was at its height, the pankus no longer met.

In the thirteenth century B.C., Egypt and the Hittites finally came to blows. About 1265, Ramses II launched a military campaign against Hittite Syria. There, in a great battle at Qadesh, the Hittites fought the Egyptians to a standstill and forced Ramses to accept a treaty of "good peace and good brotherhood." Wealth flowed into the Hittite Empire, and its capital (near modern Ankara, Turkey) was embellished with handsome relief carvings, including hieroglyphics based on the Egyptian model. Scribes from Babylon composed numerous cuneiform texts in the Hittite language. The formidable new empire seemed destined for a long life.

While imperial Egypt and its rivals were contending for supremacy in the eastern Mediterranean, two of the

FIGURE 1-3
PROTO-SINAITIC INSCRIPTION (EARLY ALPHABETIC WRITING)

These letters were found inscribed on a sphinx. It is believed that they may be translated as "loved by Ba'alat [Baal]" and "votive offering for Ba'alat." Baal was the name of a Canaanite deity.
Source: Adapted from A. C. Moorhouse, The Triumph of the Alphabet: A History of Writing *(New York: Henry Schuman, 1953), p. 107, fig. 32.*

most significant innovations in human history were being developed. One was alphabetic writing.

Around 1700 B.C., someone in a Canaanite city—we do not know who or where—hit upon a quick way of learning to keep accounts. Instead of hundreds of syllabic signs, this clever Canaanite used twenty-nine symbols, derived from cuneiform, one for each consonant. During the next few centuries the alphabet was reduced to twenty-two letters, and eventually the Greeks would add vowels.[4] But even without these improvements the Canaanite alphabet constituted an enormous simplification and opened up the possibility of a vast expansion of literacy (see Figure 1-3). Writing was no longer a mysterious art, acquired only after years of study, and the monopoly of the old scribal class was broken. The invention of the alphabet extended the effects of civilization to a much larger segment of society than ever before.

THE IRON AGE AND THE DIFFUSION OF CIVILIZATION IN THE NEAR EAST

The second great technological change that occurred late in the second millennium B.C. was the spread of techniques for smelting iron. Historians once credited the Hittites with this breakthrough and thought that they monopolized iron metallurgy until about 1200 B.C. We now know, however, that low-carbon iron was being worked in the Near East and southeastern Europe much earlier to produce rings and ceremonial objects, too brittle for ordinary use. The date 1200 B.C. is now regarded as a significant milestone because by that time knowledge of iron metallurgy had become fairly widespread in the eastern Mediterranean. So important was

[4]The Hebrew alphabet, which is also derived from the ancient Canaanite writing system, retained its right-to-left progression and its absence of vowels.

this diffusion that historians still use this date to mark the end of the Bronze Age and the beginning of the Iron Age.

Iron makes up 5 percent of the earth's crust and is the most abundant of all metals—far more so than copper and tin, from which bronze is made. And iron produces stronger, harder, and sharper tools and weapons. But smelting it is much more difficult than making bronze. Pure iron melts at 1,540°C (about 2,800°F), a temperature that could not be achieved until the modern blast furnace was invented in the nineteenth century. However, ancient ironsmiths learned how to roast iron ore in a concentrated charcoal pit fire at 1,200°C (about 2,100°F), producing a "bloom"—a lump of solid iron, unburned charcoal, and slag (see Figure 1-4). When hammered and then quickly plunged into water, the result is a reasonably durable substance that a blacksmith can heat and reshape.

It is never possible permanently to prevent the spread of technology for making tools or weapons. The Hittite kings tried to do so, but failed. Ironsmiths were in demand everywhere; in ancient times people regarded them as practically magicians. The spread of iron smelting know-how was of enormous importance in history because with it deadly new weapons could be produced cheaply—and not necessarily under the control of the kings and aristocrats who had ruled Bronze Age societies. "Barbarian" peoples on the fringes, among whom ironsmiths settled, could compete on equal (or more than equal) terms with great, civilized kingdoms. When applied to toolmaking, the new iron technology made it possible to bring new land under cultivation, to cultivate more efficiently, and so to increase food production. Slowly displacing bronze making, iron-smelting technology spread throughout the Old World during a period of more than a thousand years after its discovery. Ultimately this benefited humanity immensely. But its first effects were destructive.

Sea People, Phoenicians, and Egypt's Decline

Between 1200 and 1180 B.C., the great city of Ugarit and the powerful Hittite Empire collapsed—never to rise again—amid upheavals and invasions that rocked the whole eastern Mediterranean world. Savagely destructive, the marauders wielded iron as well as bronze weaponry. The secret that the Hittite kings had tried to safeguard had been turned against them.

Egypt had been one of the fearsome new raiders' first targets, in the 1230s and again ca. 1200–1160 B.C. Egyptian sources called the attackers the Sea People, and from these sources we know that some of them spoke Indo-European languages. Probably they were organized in loose confederations of war bands. Some seem to have originated in southeastern Europe and the Aegean Sea region (see Map 1-3). Later, turmoil around 1200 B.C. profoundly reshaped the development of early Greek civilization. Almost certainly, the upheavals in Greece were directly connected with the movements of peoples and the spread of iron technology, which in turn helped destroy the Hittite Empire and shook Egypt to its foundations. Beyond that, these migrating, raiding people have kindled much debate over scraps of evidence about them.

Historians speak of the history of the Near East between roughly 1200 and 800 B.C. as a **dark age.** For the major societies in the Nile and Tigris-Euphrates Valleys that had dominated the Bronze Age, these were indeed disastrous times: impoverishment, violence, migrations of savage new populations, and cultural stagnation. But iron making also spread, so that by 800 B.C. iron tools and weapons had displaced bronze ones throughout the eastern Mediterranean. This technological revolution helped spark an economic and cultural revival.

The turmoil after 1200 B.C. also presented a unique opportunity to the Semitic peoples of the Near East. With Egypt temporarily eclipsed and the future empires of Assyria, Neo-Babylon, and Persia as yet unborn, the peoples of the eastern Mediterranean shore found their place in the sun (see Table 1-3 on page 28).

The Canaanite city-states suffered violent attacks between 1300 and 1000 B.C. First had come the Israelites (or Hebrews, later known as Jews), who had entered Canaan from east of the Jordan River, and whose story we will trace in the next section of this chapter. From the west, however, Canaan absorbed another devastating invasion,

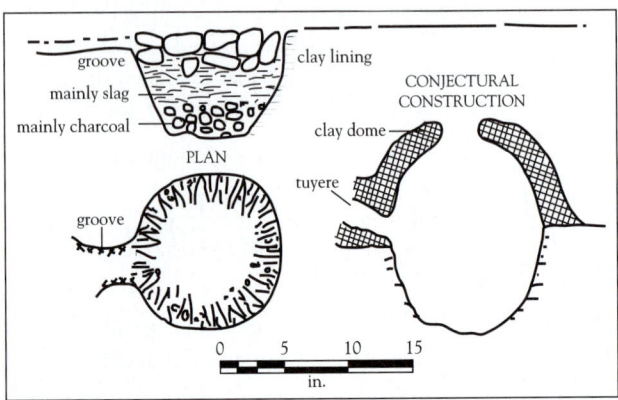

FIGURE 1-4
ANCIENT IRON SMELTING

This drawing shows how historians think ancient smiths smelted iron ore in a simple pit, covered with a clay dome. Air was pumped in through the tuyere with the help of a goatskin bellows. The bloom formed at the top, and after everything cooled the dome was broken to remove it. Then the bloom was reworked to make wrought iron implements. More efficient furnaces, which allowed the slag to flow out at the bottom, were developed in Roman times.
Source: Based on Theodore A. Wertime and James D. Mulhy, eds., The Coming of the Age of Iron (New Haven, CT: Yale University Press, 1980), p. 210, fig. 7.10.

MAP 1-3

THE SEA PEOPLE AND THE COLLAPSE OF THE BRONZE AGE

that of the iron-weaponed Philistines.[5] Archaeological and linguistic evidence now makes it fairly certain that the Philistines came from somewhere in the Aegean area—either the island of Crete or the Greek mainland. Theirs is the clearest known case of Sea People settling down where they had raided. Beginning about 1175 B.C., they made themselves masters of several towns on the Canaanite coast, including Gaza, from which neither Egyptians nor Israelites could dislodge them for at least two centuries.

Those coastal Canaanites who had survived or regrouped after the Sea People's invasions are known to history by the name the Greeks eventually gave them: the Phoenicians. Fanning out from the city of Tyre (in modern Lebanon), which had survived attack, Phoenicians rebuilt other devastated towns and founded new ones. From about 1100 to 600 B.C., they displayed a remarkable talent for navigation, commerce, and colonization. North Africa, Sicily and Sardinia, and Spain all saw the establishment of Phoenician cities and the development of mining and other export-oriented Phoenician enterprises. Phoenician ships sailed throughout the Mediterranean, carrying Near Eastern goods and ideas into southern Europe and North Africa, and bringing the raw materials of these newly opened lands to the ancient Near East (see Map 1-4 on page 29). Their artistic styles, their system of weights and measures, their alphabet, and perhaps even their preference

for living in compact city-states were all Phoenician legacies to the ancient Greeks. Our own alphabet comes from the Phoenicians, by way of the Greeks.

Merchants sailing westward from Phoenicia passed through the Straits of Gibraltar and out into the Atlantic. They may well have reached Britain and the Azores, and they made their way southward down the west coast of Africa at least as far as Cape Verde and perhaps farther. (Much is obscure about the Phoenicians' voyages because, fearing competitors, they kept secret what they learned about currents, winds, tides, routes, and anchorages.) The greatest of all Phoenician colonies was Carthage in modern Tunisia, founded by Tyre late in the eighth century B.C. and destined to be Rome's greatest, and deadliest, rival.

While the Philistines were establishing themselves in Canaan and the Phoenicians embarking on their wide-ranging voyages, Egypt was at last sinking into decline. Amid the turmoil of invasions by the Sea People and others, Egypt's profitable trade with the eastern Mediterranean ended. Worse, meteors provided Egypt's only significant source of iron. Paying exorbitantly to import larger quantities of iron, the Egyptian economy suffered. Inflation and all the demoralization that it produces stalked the land. Organized gangs (often with official connivance) committed the supreme sacrilege of systematically looting ancient tombs and unceremoniously dumping pharaohs' sacred mummies in the desert.

True, the Egyptian Empire endured for nearly three centuries after the deaths of Akhenaten and Ramses II; it even survived the Sea People and inflation. Ultimately, though, it could not prevent the rise of a strong Israelite kingdom around 1000 B.C., nor take advantage of the Israelites' subsequent political decline. Except for momentary fits of

---

[5]From whom the name *Palestine* comes. Because the Philistines are the "bad guys" of early biblical history, their name has also passed into modern European languages as proverbial beer-swilling boors—insensitive to all the finer things of life. This canard is quite unfortunate. For one thing, they drank wine. Also, they may well have been early Greeks.

TABLE 1-3

LATER NEAR EASTERN HISTORY

All dates are B.C.

1450–1300	Hebrews enslaved in Egypt
1379–1361	Reign of the pharaoh Akhenaten, who introduces the worship of the Aten
?1300	Moses leads Hebrews out of Egypt into the Sinai Desert
1265	Hittites battle Egyptians and force Ramses II to accept a compromise peace treaty
1200	Fall of the Hittite Kingdom; beginning of the Iron Age, which revolutionizes Middle Eastern technology
1250	Hebrews enter Palestine, defeat Canaanite city-states
1020	King David creates a united Hebrew kingdom
933	Hebrew kingdom splits: Israel and Judah
883–859	Reign of Ashur-nasir-pal II: revival of Assyria begins
745–612	Assyrian Empire dominates the Near East
612	Chaldeans establish the Neo-Babylonian Empire
585–538	Nebuchadrezzar conquers Judah; Hebrews undergo the Babylonian Captivity
549–538	Cyrus the Great conquers the Near East, establishes the Persian Empire
538	End of Babylonian Captivity; Hebrews return to Palestine
521–486	Darius the Great rules the Persian Empire
330	Greeks, under Alexander the Great, conquer the Persian Empire

the Greeks were honest enough to admit their debt to Egypt in science, medicine, and mathematics. Rome would absorb much of the Egyptian religious tradition. Above all it was the Egyptians, second only to the Sumerians, who created civilization itself in the western world. Israel and Persia, Greece and Rome, rose from their ruins.

Israel: The People of Yahweh

Israel's emergence as a nation and a faith might never have occurred had Canaan been controlled by those great empires that were so formidable in the middle of the second millennium B.C., or that would again be so powerful at the end of the Near East's "dark age." The Israelites were a tiny people, and Canaan was a small corner of the Near East. The story of Israel's sudden emergence, and of how during that fleeting moment the Israelites forged a religion that would sustain them during thousands of years of subsequent oppression and dispersal, and that would form a fundamental element in Western civilization, is truly amazing.

No other ancient people have a history so well documented. The Hebrew Bible, studied by scholars and believers through all the centuries of Western civilization, is the fountainhead of Judaism, Islam, and Christianity and thus crucial to the heritage of countless millions of people today. Especially when combined with archaeological evidence, it enables us to endow the dry bones of ancient Israel with flesh and life. Although some nineteenth-century researchers dismissed the Bible as mere myth, scholars now regard much biblical material as a relatively reliable—and enormously important—record of the past. Interpreting this biblical record, however, is fraught with controversies.

The Birth of Israel Genesis, the first book of the Bible, attests that at the beginning of time God created the heavens, the earth, and all living things including Adam (meaning "a man") and his spouse Eve. Having disobeyed God, this primeval couple was expelled from the Garden of Eden, became mortal, and henceforth had to earn their bread by the sweat of their brows and to bear children in pain. After many generations (whom Genesis meticulously named), humanity degenerated into such a state of wickedness that a furious God wiped it out in a universal flood, sparing only the righteous Noah, his family, and a single pair from every animal species.

Genesis further recorded that Hebrew history began when one of Noah's descendants, Abraham, entered into an agreement, or **Covenant,** with God. Abraham promised not to worship any other god, and in return he and his family received the special protection of this divinity, whose name Abraham knew as El. The Covenant was renewed by all succeeding generations of Abraham's clan and became a basic ingredient of Jewish religious thought. Abraham would doubtless have conceded the *existence* of other

energy, the ancient kingdom's rulers slipped into contentment at conserving what they had and passively admired past glories. After 600 B.C., Egypt succumbed to disintegration from within and attacks from without. Thereafter it was generally ruled by foreign dynasties or foreign peoples—Libyans, Assyrians, Persians, Greeks, and eventually Romans. At times, the Egyptians sought to recapture their earlier creativity, but it always eluded them.

The Egyptians failed to achieve the eternity for which they had hoped, but for two thousand years they came closer than most other people. And although their dynamism failed at last, their architecture and art, their science and medicine, even their religion, became the legacy of subsequent cultures. The Greek column is Egyptian in origin, and

MAP 1-4

THE PHOENICIANS IN THE MEDITERRANEAN

deities, but he differed from his Near Eastern contemporaries in that he *worshiped* only one. The existence of other gods was irrelevant to him. Thus, he practiced "monolatry" (the worship of one god among many) rather than true monotheism (the belief in one God).

How does this story, familiar to every Bible reader, fit into the history of the ancient Near East that modern archaeologists and historians have reconstructed? Probably the first Hebrews were nomadic Semites who (like many others) had wandered in and out of Mesopotamia and traced their descent from an ancestor named Abraham. (Some scholars believe that around 1500 B.C., perhaps in the wake of the Kassite invasion of Mesopotamia, the ancestors of the Hebrews migrated to Canaan.) Genesis's accounts of the Creation, the Garden of Eden, and the Flood all echo Mesopotamian traditions, and the biblical Tower of Babel[6] may recall an actual ziggurat. Linguistic evidence suggests that Genesis was actually written down between 950 and 700 B.C., weaving together two distinct strands from ancient oral traditions.[7] The mid-twentieth century discovery of the library at Ugarit shows, moreover, that much of Genesis contains traditions that the Hebrews

shared with other Canaanite peoples of the second millennium B.C., if not even earlier. El, for example, was a Canaanite god whose name survives in many Hebrew words, including *Isra-el* ("the Lord contends"). In the original Hebrew, one strand of what we now know as the Book of Genesis uses the name El (or Elohim, a plural understood in a singular sense) for God; the second strand calls the divinity *Yahweh* (often translated as "the Lord God").

And who were the Israelites, or Hebrews? Correspondence between the Egyptian government and the princes of second-millennium Canaan speaks of rural people called the *'apiru*. These people do not seem to have been an ethnic or religious group, but rather a generic category of outlaws. Nevertheless, their name may have later been applied (perhaps by enemies) to the Hebrews. We know that many Canaanites found their way into Egypt during the second millennium, voluntarily or involuntarily. The story in Genesis that they were driven into Egypt by famine is plausible. The migration to Egypt is said to have begun by Joseph, Abraham's great-grandson, who, after having risen from the dust to become the pharaoh's chief minister, was joined there by his father Jacob and eleven brothers. But the Hebrew community in Egypt clearly also included kindred folk and probably other Semitic people.

It was the policy of the Egyptian New Kingdom (remembering the Hyksos) to enslave all foreigners. No Egyptian sources mention the specific presence of Hebrews in their land, although there is plenty of evidence for "Asiatics"—mostly slaves, but some men who reached high positions. While performing forced labor for the pharaohs,

---

[6] The survivors of the Flood, Genesis tells us, tried to build the Tower of Babel so that they could escape future floods. To frustrate and rebuke this impious scheme, God caused the builders to speak mutually unintelligible languages. The tower remained unfinished, and the human race scattered in confusion.

[7] A third strand was added in the fifth or sixth centuries B.C.

the Hebrews may have extended their Covenant of Abraham to include greater numbers of oppressed people. In the meantime Egypt enriched itself from the profits of empire, and Akhenaten experimented with his solar religion. But the Hebrews, at the bottom of the Egyptian social order, remained unaffected.

Around 1300 B.C. (dating is uncertain and alternatives vary by centuries), Moses became the Hebrews' liberator and the vehicle through whom Yahweh revealed himself as their God. Egyptian sources make no mention of Moses or of any of the dramatic events in the biblical Book of Exodus, which narrates and interprets the Hebrews' deliverance and their new Covenant with Yahweh. Reconciling the scraps of verifiable information that we do have with the dramatic narrative of Exodus has puzzled and divided generations of scholars.

Exodus records that having killed an Egyptian for unjustly beating a Hebrew, Moses fled from Egypt. He found refuge among the Midianites, a Semitic people in the northwestern corner of what is now Saudi Arabia, and married the daughter of a Midianite priest. In the Land of Midian he heard God's voice from a burning bush, commanding him to return to Egypt and become Israel's deliverer. God called himself "I Am Who I Am," which in Hebrew is very close to *Yahweh*—the name of a divinity worshiped among Canaanites and Midianites. Moses obeyed, and, according to Exodus, God brought down a succession of disasters upon Egypt when Pharaoh refused to let the Hebrews go. Then, for a generation at least, Moses and his band wandered in a desert traditionally identified as the Sinai but more likely the Land of Midian.

In the wilderness, according to Exodus, Moses received a revelation commanding the Hebrews—the nation of Israel—to renew Abraham's Covenant. The new Covenant bound God to Israel, and in return promised them Canaan. Through Moses, God gave Israel its basic laws, summed up in the Ten Commandments, the first of which was to acknowledge no god but God. Moreover, the divinity whom Abraham had known as El (or Elohim) revealed to Moses that his name was YHWH (traditionally transliterated into English as Yahweh, or Jehovah). Hebrew law forbade making any image of God, lest people worship it as an idol; and it became custom to pronounce the word *Adonai* ("the Lord") where the text read "YHWH."

When the Hebrews emerged at last from the wilderness and invaded Canaan, Moses was dead and a new generation had arisen. Under the leadership of Joshua the Hebrews entered Palestine, perhaps around the mid-1200s B.C. The biblical account says that they won a series of victories over Canaanite cities and that ancient Jericho's walls came tumbling down. Archaeological evidence, however, reveals nothing so dramatic; rather, the invaders seem to have occupied the valleys between Canaan's hill towns and gradually taken over the latter. The struggle with the indigenous Canaanites continued for another two centuries, during which the Hebrews were deeply influenced by Canaanite culture. They adopted a Canaanite dialect and Canaanite alphabet, and some worshiped Canaanite gods. During these years the Hebrews organized themselves into twelve tribes under chieftains known as "judges." There was, as the Bible recorded, "no king in Israel"; Yahweh, the Hebrews believed, was their true ruler. Nor did they as yet have any written scriptures.

Kings and Prophets   About 1020 B.C. the priest Samuel anointed one of Israel's tribal chieftains, Saul, as the nation's first king. One reason that the Israelites accepted a monarchy was a manifest need to unite in the face of

Solomon's Temple Based on scanty archaeological evidence and primarily on the biblical description, this drawing shows how the Temple probably looked in Solomon's time. The interior—Yahweh's earthly home—was empty. Storage rooms for tribute and the king's palace stood adjacent. Animal sacrifices took place in the forecourt. Some believe that in place of the pillars stood the statues of two legendary giants. *Drawing by C. Stevens, based on specifications of W.F. Albright and G.E. Wright.*

growing pressure from the Philistines. But another reason was that the Israelite population was becoming so dense and quarrelsome that a central government was needed to keep order. Saul waged war against the Philistines with some success but was outshone by his able successor, David (reigned ca. 1000–960 B.C.), who is said to have demonstrated his prowess as a youth by slaying the gigantic Philistine Goliath with a slingshot.

Under David and his son Solomon (reigned 960–922 B.C.), Israel reached its political zenith, dominating much of Syria-Palestine and extending inland to the upper Euphrates. The Phoenician cities retained their independence only through a policy of submissive cooperation. This golden age etched itself on Israel's imagination for all time to come—the age that endless generations of Jews never despaired of recovering.

David made his capital in Jerusalem, a small city that he had conquered from its Canaanite ruler, and there he started building a permanent, central sanctuary for Yahweh. Solomon completed the Temple. But it would take centuries to become the sole focus of Yahwistic worship.

Solomon made Jerusalem the cosmopolitan capital of a wealthy empire (see Map 1-5), surrounding himself with all the trappings of Near Eastern monarchy, from bureaucrats to concubines. He worshiped not only Yahweh but also the Canaanite and other divinities of his numerous foreign wives. The earliest version of the Pentateuch, or **Torah**—the first five books of the Bible, hitherto preserved orally—was probably put into written form during Solomon's reign. But Solomon's subjects were obliged to pay for all this imperial glory and scholarship with heavy taxes and forced labor, and many concluded that the price was too high. On Solomon's death (922 B.C.), his realm broke in two: a larger northern kingdom known thenceforth as Israel, and a smaller, more compact southern kingdom of Judah, centering on Jerusalem.

Hebrew history is chronicled by a series of historical books in the Bible that make the half-millennium from ca. 1020 to 586 B.C. one of the best documented periods in ancient history. The Bible's historical books tell a story—which archaeological evidence supports—of the Hebrews and their kings tending to lapse into **polytheism** and of growing disparities of wealth within both kingdoms. According to the biblical books of the era of the divided monarchy, God was angered by these changes and constantly punished his people, yet never wholly abandoned them. Cumulatively, the biblical writers asserted that God was shaping human events for divine ends—a new vision of history that became a crucial part of the Judeo-Christian heritage. The chief articulators of this new vision were the **prophets.**

The prophetic tradition developed first in the turbulent northern kingdom, Israel. There, popular respect for centralizing royal authority was thin. Polytheistic tendencies, moreover, were strong as a result of royal marriages with neighboring non-Hebraic dynasties, producing such biblical villainesses as Queen Jezebel, a foreign consort who tried to supplant Yahweh with the Canaanite divinity Baal. The first prophets were spurred into action by resisting Jezebel. But prophecy in the northern kingdom was not just a matter of courageous men and women speaking out in Yahweh's cause. The prophets (who were mostly well-to-do rather than from among the downtrodden) gained a recognized place in society as the popular conscience: They were the human voices through which God spoke directly to his people. Their teachings rested on two fundamental concepts: (1) the overriding seriousness of the Covenant that God had made with the Hebrew people, and (2) the consequent obligation of God's people to treat one another justly. Law and ritual meant nothing without sincerity of purpose and personal righteousness. Shocked by the legal manipulations by which the rich deprived the poor of justice, the prophet Amos cried: "Let judgment run down as waters, and righteousness as a mighty stream" (5:24).[8] God, he threatened, would ensure Israel's downfall as punishment for its rulers' injustice:

> Therefore because you trample on the poor
> and take from them levies of grain,
> You have built houses of hewn stone,
> but you shall not live in them;

MAP 1-5
CANAAN AND THE LAND OF ISRAEL

Map legend:
- Judah
- Israel
- Approximate route of the Exodus

Labels on map: Cyprus; Ugarit; ANCIENT LAND OF CANAAN; Approximate limits of Solomon's Empire; Tyre; Jordan River; Jerusalem; Jericho; Dead Sea; PHILISTINES; Negeb Desert; EGYPT; Sinai Desert; MIDIAN; Arabian Desert; Mount Sinai

---

[8]This was the biblical verse that Dr. Martin Luther King Jr. chose to have inscribed on his tomb. This quotation is taken from the King James (Authorized) version of the Bible; other biblical quotations are from the *New Oxford Annotated Bible*.

You have planted pleasant vineyards,
but you shall not drink their wine. (5:11)

It hardly took a prophet to see how precarious was the independence of the two little Hebrew kingdoms in the face of the mighty new empire of Assyria, whose power was spreading relentlessly through the Near East in the late eighth and early seventh centuries B.C. (see the next section). But to the prophets, Assyria for all its frightening power was simply an instrument of God's purpose:

Indeed [continued Amos], I am raising up against you a
    nation,
O house of Israel, says the Lord, the God of hosts,
and they shall oppress you. (6:14)

In 722 the prophecy came true. Israel fell to Assyria's Sargon II, who applied the brutal practice that his kingdom meted out to most people it defeated. The Assyrians resettled much of Israel's population across the Near East and moved alien peoples into Israel. Absorbed into indigenous populations elsewhere, the people of Israel vanished from history, and ever since they have been known as the "ten lost tribes."

Judah, the southern kingdom, staved off conquest for a century and a half by adopting a generally subservient policy. These years were crucial for the development of Judaism. First, it was during these decades that the biblical books narrating the history of the united monarchy and its two successor kingdoms were compiled and edited, interpreting Hebrew history in the light of the rigorous new religious faith that was taking shape in Jerusalem. The original Torah text was expanded by incorporating a second oral tradition, which came to Jerusalem from the kingdom of Israel.[9] Under the influence of one reformer, the prophet Isaiah, King Hezekiah tried to purge Judea of polytheistic practices and supported the Jerusalem priesthood in concentrating worship at the Temple. Second, just as Israel was being conquered by Assyria, its prophetic tradition shifted to Jerusalem. Isaiah, who had direct access to Judah's kings, espoused the cause of the poor. God, Isaiah announced, was disgusted:

I have had enough of burnt offerings of rams
and the fat of fed beasts; . . .
Trample my courts no more. . . ;
incense is an abomination to me. . . .
Your new moons and your appointed festivals
my soul hates;
They have become a burden to me,
I am weary of bearing them. (1:11–14)

And with striking brevity, Isaiah's contemporary, the prophet Micah, announced God's moral purpose in history:

He has told you, O mortal, what is good;
and what does the Lord require of you . . .
but to do justice, and to love kindness,
and to walk humbly with your God? (6:8)

The prophetic vision of justice and righteousness did not extend to humanity at large, but as yet encompassed only the Hebrew community. Yet even with that important qualification it was a profound affirmation of human dignity and a formative step in creating Western civilization's tradition of social justice. The prophets of Judah offered a new vision of humanity's relationship with the divine. Never before had Near Eastern gods rejected proper rituals. For Isaiah, however, Yahweh was not just the lord of all the earth but also a divinity more interested in peace and justice than in ritual—a stern and angry but still loving father of his chosen people. Some day, Isaiah foretold, God would humble all the mighty nations of the world; then, peacefully accepting the religion of Isaac and Jacob:

They shall beat their swords into plowshares,
and their spears into pruning hooks;
nation shall not lift up sword against nation,
neither shall they learn war any more. (2:4)

The era of Isaiah also produced the Book of Job, the Hebrew Bible's searching exploration of that most difficult of questions: Why do the innocent suffer? Job, a pious man whom God has blessed with a large family, riches, and good health, suddenly loses everything, and is tempted to curse God for his misfortune, while his friends try to convince him that he is being punished for some secret sin. Job neither succumbs to despair nor blames God for his suffering, but continues to insist that divine justice works in mysterious ways. When God (speaking "out of the whirlwind") eventually challenges Job to acknowledge his overwhelming power, Job can only humbly admit that, as a human being, he is but dust—whereupon, in a further demonstration of divine omnipotence, Job is given back his wealth, more sons, and a healthy life span of 140 years. The question of undeserved evil is not resolved, but the fact that such questions were being asked shows how religious sensibilities had evolved. The fate of humanity as a whole, not merely of chosen peoples, was in divine hands: Individuals, too, had begun to ask what the divine majesty had in store for them.[10]

Distracted by more pressing wars and rebellions elsewhere, the Assyrians never took Judah. However, Assyrian

---

[9]The new strand is called by scholars the *Elohist,* taking its name from the designation *Elohim,* with which it names God. The older strand, whose earliest written form probably dates from Solomon's time, ca. 950 B.C., is designated the *Yahwist,* from its name for God.

[10]Similar questions were being asked in Mesopotamia in the fifteenth century B.C. in the text that scholars call "the Babylonian Job," but the answer seems more simplistic: The god Enlil restores the fortune of the sufferer who has prayed sufficiently long.

cultural influence, under which several of Hezekiah's successors fell, threatened Judah's monotheistic religious reforms for much of the seventh century B.C. But even as Assyria itself was crumbling before a new Near Eastern imperial power, Neo-Babylon, a second wave of religious reform gathered momentum in Jerusalem. Under King Josiah (reigned 639–609 B.C.), the priests of the Temple discovered a "book of law," authored by Moses himself; modern scholars think this was Deuteronomy (or a large part of it), the book of the Torah that sets forth in great detail the secular and religious laws of Judaism. Frightened by the sweeping curses that Deuteronomy threatens for noncompliance, and urged on by another great prophet, Jeremiah, the king took the lead in cleansing Judah of "idolatrous" worship, such as the old Canaanite custom of sacrificing in "high places" (on mountaintops).

Josiah's death left Judah wavering between policies favoring reliance on the two powers then contending for dominance in the Near East, Egypt and Neo-Babylon (also called Chaldea). Jeremiah urged submission to Neo-Babylon, a deeply unpopular stand since it meant paying a crushing tribute to which everyone in the land was forced to contribute. Unwisely, Judah's rulers turned toward Egypt, which proved to be a "broken reed." In 587–586 B.C., the Neo-Babylonian king, Nebuchadrezzar, conquered Jerusalem. He destroyed the Temple and had the last king of Judah blinded after witnessing his sons' executions. More than ten thousand Temple priests, skilled craftsmen, merchants, and others of the kingdom's elite were forcibly resettled near Babylon. Only "the poor of the people, which had nothing" (Jeremiah 39:10), remained.

The religion of Israel, however, had not perished. Among the exiles in Babylon it would be refined and enriched by contact with the great traditions of Near Eastern culture. Within less than a century, members of that Exile community would return to Jerusalem and there implant the religion that henceforth we should refer to as Judaism. But the Exile and the exiles' return are best understood after we have surveyed the history of those great empires that ruled the Near East during the centuries of Israel's rise, fall, and transformation.

The Rise of New Empires

Israel's expansion under David and Solomon in the eleventh and tenth centuries B.C. was possible only because no stronger power existed in the Near East to oppose them. As we have seen, this power vacuum did not last. Forty years after the Israelites split into two kingdoms in 922 B.C., the first of a series of mighty new empires, Assyria, began taking shape in what is today northern Iraq.[11] When

A Triumphant Assyrian King   The bas-relief on this obelisk shows King Shalmaneser III (reigned 858–842 B.C.) receiving tribute and homage from Jehu, a king of Israel.   © *The British Museum.*

Assyria eventually succumbed, Neo-Babylon took its place. Finally, Persia would become dominant. The heyday of these great states would end only with the conquest of Persia by Alexander the Great in 330 B.C. During these centuries Near Eastern imperialism reached its zenith.

Assyria on the March   The Assyrians, a Semitic-speaking people from northern Mesopotamia, employed innovative military tactics and outright terror to build the largest empire the Near East had yet known. Their rise dates from the reign of the brutal, masterful king Ashur-nasir-pal II (883–859 B.C.). At its height, in the late seventh century B.C., the Assyrian Empire dominated the civilized populations of the entire Fertile Crescent, and even Egypt.

The Assyrian kings carved out their empire with armies of unmatched effectiveness. They were the first to use iron weapons on a large scale, the first to employ military engineers routinely to assist in the destruction of enemy defenses by such devices as battering rams and siege towers. Whereas Near Eastern armies had previously consisted of ill-trained conscripts led by nobles, Assyrian armies, recruited from throughout the empire, were trained into professional units and led into battle by seasoned

THE HISTORICAL EVIDENCE

The Assyrian Siege of Jerusalem: Two Versions

701 B.C.

Assyria attacked Judah in 701 B.C., but the onslaught failed, probably because an epidemic swept through the army besieging Jerusalem. Upon Isaiah's advice, King Hezekiah of Judah resumed his vassal status. The Assyrian king Sennacherib collected his tribute and went home, boasting of his irresistible might. Some years later he was assassinated.

The first account of the siege is by the prophet Isaiah. Notice how Sennacherib's emissary (who is probably of Hebrew origin) tries to frighten the people of Jerusalem with the thought that Hezekiah's religious reform may have offended Yahweh.

In the fourteenth year of King Hezekiah, King Sennacherib of Assyria came up against all the fortified cities of Judah and captured them. The king of Assyria sent the Rabshakeh from Lachish* to King Hezekiah at Jerusalem, with a great army. . . . The Rabshakeh said to [Hezekiah's emissaries]: . . . "On what do you base this confidence of yours? . . . See, you are relying on Egypt, that broken reed of a staff. . . . But if you say to me, 'We rely on the Lord our God,' is it not he whose high places and altars Hezekiah has removed, saying to Judah and Jerusalem, 'You shall worship before this [the Temple] altar.'?" [The Rabshakeh also threatens a terrible siege, in which the people "are doomed . . . to eat their own dung and drink their own urine," but they refuse to surrender.]

When King Hezekiah heard it, he tore his clothes, covered himself with sackcloth, and went into the house of the Lord. . . . When the servants of King Hezekiah came to Isaiah, Isaiah said to them, "Say to your master, 'Thus says the Lord: Do not be afraid because of the words that you have said, with which the servants of the king of Assyria have reviled me. I myself will put a spirit in him, so that he shall hear a rumor, and return to his own land; I will cause him to fall by the sword in his own land.'"

[The Rabshakeh continues to mock Hezekiah's resistance, saying that other gods have failed to protect their kings from Sennacherib's might, and sends a letter to this effect to Hezekiah.] Hezekiah received the letter . . . and read it; then Hezekiah . . . spread it before the Lord. And Hezekiah prayed to the Lord, saying, "O Lord of hosts, God of Israel, who are enthroned above the cherubim, you are God, you alone of all the kingdoms of the earth, you have made heaven and earth. Incline your ear, O Lord, and hear; . . . hear all the words of Sennacherib, which he has sent to mock the living God. . . . So now, O Lord our God, save us from his hand, so that all the kingdoms of the earth may know that you alone are the Lord."

And here is the story that Sennacherib inscribed on a monument describing his ever-victorious campaign in the west, including Judah. (It is worth noting that Jerusalem's population at the time probably did not exceed a few thousand.)

As to Hezekiah the Jew, he did not submit to my yoke, [sic] I laid siege to 46 of his strong cities, walled forts and to the countless small villages in their vicinity, and conquered them by means of well-stamped earth-ramps, and battering-rams brought thus near to the walls combined with the attack by foot soldiers, using mines, breeches, as well as saper work. I drove out of them 200,150 people, young and old, male and female, horses, mules, donkeys, camels, big and small cattle beyond counting, and considered them booty. Himself I made a prisoner in Jerusalem, his royal residence, like a bird in a cage. . . . Thus I reduced his country, but I still increased the tribute . . . to be delivered annually. Hezekiah himself, whom the terror-inspiring splendor of my lordship had overwhelmed, . . . did send me, later, to Nineveh, . . . together with 30 talents of gold, 800 talents of silver, precious stones, antimony, large cuts of red stone, couches inlaid with ivory, . . . elephant hides, ebony wood, boxwood, and all kinds of valuable treasures, his own daughters, concubines, male and female musicians.

---

*A high official, who evidently spoke both Aramaic and Hebrew. Lachish was another city near Judah that had been conquered and devastated by the Assyrians.

Sources: Isaiah 36:1–2, 4–6; 37:1, 5–8, 14–20 (*New Oxford Annotated Bible*); James B. Pritchard, ed., *Ancient Near Eastern Texts Relating to the Old Testament,* 2nd ed. (Princeton, NJ: Princeton University Press, 1955), p. 288; trans. A. Lewis Oppenheim (parentheses indicating extrapolated words have been omitted in the interest of readability).

The Assyrians Attack Lachish   This relief, carved for the royal palace at Nineveh after Sennacherib returned from his campaign against Judah in 701 B.C., should be compared to the documents. It depicts the Assyrian war machine in operation: A battering ram hammers at the walls of Lachish as archers shoot at the defenders; in the center the defeated people file out on their way into exile, while in the lower right corner the city's leaders are impaled.   © *The British Museum.*

generals. Assyrian armies skillfully combined footsoldiers, charioteers, cavalrymen, and siege engineers under a single command. As a consequence of their superior military technology, the Assyrians won victory after victory. Their empire eventually extended from central Anatolia to southern Iraq, and from Egypt to the borders of Iran, which Assyrian armies repeatedly invaded (see Map 1-6).

From their capital at Nineveh on the Tigris, the Assyrian kings ruled through an officialdom much more highly centralized than any before it. The royal government kept administrative records on an unprecedented scale, and it maintained tight control of local governments through a series of inspectors ("messengers") who moved to and fro between Nineveh and the provinces. Provincial government was itself transformed, as the relative autonomy enjoyed by the outlying districts of previous empires came to a halt. Under the new order of things, imperial provinces passed under the strict control of Assyrian commanders, or governors absolutely devoted to the monarchy. The regime suppressed local autonomy utterly, to the point of routinely murdering or horribly mutilating former leaders of conquered regions and often—as we have already seen in the case of the kingdom of Israel—moving whole populations to remote locations. For the time being, the entire ancient world was united under a power that crushed insurrections with well-publicized ferocity. On his monuments, one Assyrian king boasted that he had punished rebels by tearing out their tongues, mashing the rebels to death, then feeding their corpses to pigs and vultures. The Assyrians passed on the idea of a highly centralized imperial administration to their successors—the Neo-Babylonians, the Persians, and eventually the Romans—but most later conquerors renounced their extreme brutality as counterproductive.

Assyrian culture derived its inspiration from Sumer and Babylon. Its gods were more warlike versions of the ancient Mesopotamian deities. Themes of war and conquest permeated Assyrian culture and society: The Assyrian kings saw themselves as servants of their god Assur—and saw rebels as the god's enemies, whom it was pious to crush ruthlessly. Assyrian art, such as the huge reliefs carved on the palace walls at Nineveh, glorified the monarchy and its conquests. A large library of cuneiform texts collected at Nineveh by the last Assyrian king consists

MAP 1-6
THE ASSYRIAN AND NEO-BABYLONIAN EMPIRES

chiefly of omens and astrological observations to guide him in his military campaigns. But the library also preserved much of the ancient cultural heritage of Sumeria and Akkad, which would have been lost forever without Assyrian royal patronage.

The bloodthirsty Assyrian militarism brought unity and a degree of peace to the long-troubled Near East. But once Assyrian leadership faltered, the empire collapsed under the rage of its subject peoples. A coalition of Indo-European Medes from western Iran and Semitic Chaldeans from Babylonia destroyed Assyria forever. Nineveh fell in 612 B.C., and its site is still desolate.

Assyria's Successors: The Anatolian Kingdoms, Neo-Babylon, and Persia

With the fall of Assyria, the Near East temporarily lacked a single master. Judah was able to play several stronger powers off against each other. Egypt recovered its independence, if not its cultural creativity. Anatolia passed to the Lydians, a people who produced what was probably the world's first coinage and whose kings Midas and Croesus were celebrated in Greek myths as monarchs of fabulous wealth. The core of Assyria itself, together with its northern and eastern provinces, became subject to the Medes. The southern and western provinces fell to the Chaldeans, who established the Neo-Babylonian Empire (see Map 1-6).

Neo-Babylon adapted much of the Assyrian administrative structure but also, as in restoring the Code of Hammurabi, drew upon Mesopotamia's ancient past. The city of Babylon was rebuilt with unprecedented splendor in glazed, colored tiles decorated with lions and dragons. The vast gardens—the "hanging gardens of Babylon"—with which the kings adorned their great city became a wonder of the world. At its height, Babylon covered some 500 acres and its population exceeded one hundred thousand. Its walls were so broad that, so it was said, two charioteers could ride on them abreast. It was into this wealthy and cosmopolitan city that the exiles from Jerusalem were deported.

Neo-Babylon's great contribution to Western civilization was its study of the stars. Chaldean wise men scrutinized the heavens from observatories atop the towers of their fascinating city. They mapped the stars, kept painstaking records of lunar eclipses and planetary movements, and, through meticulous observation and mathematical calculation, determined the exact length of the year. Their work—some of it of astonishing accuracy considering the instruments and clumsy arithmetic at their disposal—laid the foundations of astronomy in Greco-Roman times and throughout the medieval and early modern West. The practical application of this knowledge was, however, astrology, the effort to discern human fate and the will of the gods in the vast movements of the heavens. Most of the complex, highly deterministic astrological lore that would beguile the Western world until the rise of

modern science in the seventeenth and eighteenth centuries (and again haunts American supermarket tabloids) was of Neo-Babylonian origin.

Despite its brilliance, the Neo-Babylonian renaissance perished ingloriously. The regime collapsed in 538 B.C. when Persian armies overwhelmed Babylon. The city's name lives on (perhaps unfairly) in Judeo-Christian tradition as a synonym for decadence and wickedness. But it would never again be the capital and cultural center of an empire.

The Persians, like the Medes to whom they were closely related, were an Indo-European people who had settled on the Iranian plateau in the second millennium B.C. Their traditional subordination to the Medes ended in 549 B.C. when the Persian leader, Cyrus the Great, seized the Median crown and made himself ruler of both peoples. During the subsequent decade Cyrus conducted an astonishing series of military campaigns that won him an empire stretching from India through Mesopotamia to Lydia (western Turkey) and Syria-Palestine. With the conquest of Egypt shortly after his death, the Persians unified the entire Near East into a single empire, larger even than its Assyrian predecessor.

The Persian Empire represents the synthesis of Near Eastern political and cultural traditions under a government that achieved stability less through military terror than through a policy of toleration. Shrewdly employing calculated magnanimity and toleration, Cyrus proved himself one of the most creative leaders of antiquity. Not only, as we shall see, did he permit the Jews to return to their homeland and rebuild their Temple; the Persians allowed all the peoples of the empire a broad religious and cultural autonomy, so long as they remained docile, provided troops for the imperial army, and paid their taxes.

Although less brutal and repressive than their Assyrian and Neo-Babylonian predecessors,[12] the Persian kings consciously followed the Assyrian model in designing their administration. At its height under Darius the Great (reigned 521–486 B.C.), the Persian government, with its center at the great fortress-palace at Persepolis, formed an absolute hereditary monarchy. A central council of nobles assisted the king, and he was represented in the provinces by imperial governors, called satraps. Although the monarchy permitted the provinces to retain indigenous customs, it kept in touch with them through a network of imperial inspectors who saw to it that the satraps remained both honest and loyal. The regime stimulated commerce by an extensive network of roads and by the introduction of imperial coinage in the Lydian tradition. The Greek historian Herodotus commended the efficiency of the Persian postal service: "Neither snow nor rain nor heat nor gloom

---

[12]This generous estimate of the Persian kings diminishes over time; toward the end of the Persian Empire, its rulers tended to revert to the traditional brutality of other Near Eastern conquerors.

Homage to Darius the Great   Having usurped the Persian throne and defeated ten rivals, Darius had this mighty tribute to himself chiseled into a high mountainside at Bisitun (also called Behistun) in southwestern Iran about 520 B.C. The text beneath the carved figures is in three languages, including Akkadian. At great personal risk, the nineteenth-century British scholar Henry Rawlinson copied the text, and by 1849 deciphered the Akkadian cuneiform: the key breakthrough to modern understanding of the ancient Near East. *Deutsches Archaeologisches Institut.*

of night stays these couriers from the swift completion of their appointed rounds."

The culture of the Persian Empire is a summing up rather than a new departure. In most respects it is a development of age-old Mesopotamian concepts, although the use of tall stone columns gives Persian architecture a delicate elegance all its own. The Persian king refrained from claiming divinity and was satisfied merely to stress his divine appointment. Nevertheless, the pomp and ceremony surrounding him—the "king of kings," he called himself—was truly stupendous. He alone could dress in royal purple. Some fifteen thousand courtiers dined lavishly at his table every day while he himself remained hidden from their gaping stares. His servants covered their mouths while in his presence so as not to breathe his private air. A red carpet was rolled out for him (alone) to walk on—the origin of an age-long tradition of "red-carpet treatment."

And he was portrayed as a giant among ordinary mortals in the sculpture decorating his palace.

In the religious sphere the Persians showed their greatest originality. They, no less than the Jews, broke sharply with Near Eastern religious tradition. The almost legendary Persian prophet Zoroaster (or Zarathustra) proclaimed a highly intellectualized doctrine of ethical monotheism centering on the god Ahura Mazda ("the wise lord"). Adoption by Darius the Great and his successors ensured the faith's future, although Iran's ancient Indo-European religious traditions also lived on. In the centuries after Zoroaster's death, Zoroastrianism incorporated older Iranian gods as lesser deities and elevated the evil Ahriman to a position almost equal to that of Ahura Mazda. Zoroastrianism thus evolved into an intensely dualistic faith that stressed the universal struggle between good and evil. Ahura Mazda became the god of light, goodness, mind, and spirit; Ahriman represented darkness, evil, and base matter. The human body, along with much of the material world, came to be viewed as evil; the spiritual world and the human soul as good. Zoroastrianism, together with the other Iranian religious traditions, remained dominant in Persia and Mesopotamia until the Islamic conquests of the seventh century A.D.,[13] and its good-and-evil dualism influenced Jewish, Indian, Greco-Roman, and medieval Christian thought.

A decline in the quality and humanity of imperial leadership marred the Persian Empire's last century. Disputed successions, coups, and palace intrigues proliferated. The regime grew increasingly repressive, and efficiency gave way to corruption and civil strife. The consequent loss of confidence and alienation of subject peoples set the stage for the spectacular Greek victories under Alexander the Great that destroyed the Persian Empire in 330 B.C. and inaugurated still another act in the age-long drama of the ancient Near East (see Chapter 3).

Exile and Return: The Consolidation of Judaism

Exile in Babylon—"the Babylonian Captivity"—was a searing experience for pious Hebrews. Cut off from the Jerusalem Temple, the one place where for generations they had believed that Yahweh could legitimately be worshiped, the exiles' despair is captured in the opening lines of Psalm 137:

> By the rivers of Babylon—
> There we sat down, and there we wept,
> When we remembered Zion.[14]

Sketchy evidence about the Exile suggests that it was not oppression that bore hardest on the Hebrews transplanted to Babylon, but something more insidious: the temptation to assimilate into a rich and sophisticated world culture. Probably not a few Hebrew exiles, who had come from the top of Judah's society, succumbed; we know that many prospered. To stiffen the resistance of those who wished to cling to their ancestral faith, the Hebrew leaders modified the concept of "Israel"—from that of a nation inhabiting its God-given land and worshiping in Jerusalem's Temple to that of a dispersed community bound together by ritual and hope of divine deliverance. It was during the Babylonian Captivity that the Sabbath and dietary codes[15] of Judaism came into focus, as well as

the insistence on male circumcision and bans on marriage outside the faith. Cumulatively, these made household piety crucial for defining Judaism and discouraging apostasy. The Psalms, that magnificent collection of the 150 chants traditionally used in Temple worship, were assembled and edited during the Exile as a vehicle of household devotion.

The greatest prophet of the Exile—the nameless author whom scholars call the Second Isaiah[16]—affirmed Yahweh as the universal deity: "All the nations are as nothing before him; they are accounted by him as less than nothing and emptiness" (40:17). And although Yahweh had allowed Jerusalem's destruction as punishment for his chosen people's transgression, he now promised that a righteous "suffering servant," of whom the Second Isaiah spoke cryptically, would someday expiate Israel's guilt.

Babylon's fall to Cyrus in 538 B.C. seemed to religious Jews so literally Heaven-sent an event that the Second Isaiah hailed the Persian king as "the Lord's anointed" and a "redeemer." (Similarly, pious Babylonians regarded Cyrus as the restorer of the true worship of their god, Marduk, from whose traditional cult the last Chaldean monarch had strayed: proof of the Persian conqueror's shrewd strategy of conciliating his new subjects' diverse religious traditions.) Cyrus's plan was to restore to the Jews the Jerusalem Temple and to make it the focal point of Persian rule in Palestine, strategically important because it lay close to the route to Egypt.

Rebuilding of the Temple was finished in 515 B.C.; but, as the biblical record indicates, the work did not go smoothly, nor was it easy to reestablish a proper Jewish community. Many Jews now lived comfortably in Babylon and had little desire to return to backwater Jerusalem; those who did go clashed bitterly with Judah's "people of the land." The latter considered themselves Israelites, but they had been left leaderless during the Captivity and found some of the returning exiles' new religious views and practices alien. Nor did those who had remained appreciate being asked to restore the former exiles' property. For their part, those who experienced the Exile tended to consider themselves alone as "Israel" and regarded those who had remained in Judah as religiously suspect, if not un-Jewish. Indeed, the Hebrew language had given way in Judah to Aramaic, the Semitic language spoken by most ordinary people in the Near East.[17] When, some years later, the high priest Ezra returned to Jerusalem to assume leadership of the Temple (and ensure

---

[13]A small Zoroastrian sect survives to this day in Iran and Pakistan.

[14]Mt. Zion is a hill sacred to the Jews, just outside the walls of Old Jerusalem. The term later acquired broader meanings: the Heavenly City; the people of Israel.

[15]Some of these may have originated during the Hebrews' struggles with the pork-eating Philistines, but they were greatly elaborated during the Exile.

---

[16]"The Second Isaiah" is the anonymous author of chapters 40 through 55 of the Book of Isaiah, which clearly were written during the Exile and are distinct from the preceding chapters that record the preaching of the historical Isaiah in Jerusalem before the Chaldean conquest.

[17]Aramaic remained the common tongue of the Near East into the time of Jesus; it was the language in which he preached.

that taxes were paid to the Persians), interpreters had to translate into Aramaic as he read to the assembled populace the Hebrew text of the Jewish law.

It took several centuries to impose on Palestine the Judaism that had been born in the Exile. Unfortunately, little is clear about what happened during this period. We do know that the Samaritans—worshipers of Yahweh in the former northern kingdom of Israel, who clung to an older form of Hebraic worship that did not recognize the primacy of the Jerusalem Temple—never became Jews of the new type. Judah, however, eventually accepted the Jerusalem-oriented piety. How deep were the roots that the new Judaism struck there would be proven by the people's stubborn resistance when, in the second century B.C., Palestine's new Greek rulers attempted to uproot the Yahwist faith, and still later when Roman conquerors became lords of the land (see Chapter 3 and 5).

About 500 B.C., when the Jerusalem Temple had been newly restored and Ezra was defining what it meant to be a Jew, the Greeks stood on the verge of their classical age; Rome was an obscure little town, throwing off its foreign kings and just beginning to develop its fundamental institutions. In the chapters that follow, we shall trace the emergence first of Greece and then of Rome, and still later analyze the ways in which Greco-Roman traditions fused—or became uneasily juxtaposed—with the ancient Near Eastern and Jewish heritage, forming that creative yet tension-ridden amalgam that we call Western civilization.

CONCLUSION: WESTERN CIVILIZATION EMERGES

This chapter has covered an enormous time span—by far the longest of any chapter in this book. It has also encompassed an immense transformation of the human spirit. When civilization began in the Near East, gods were still thought to be manifestations of nature: the earth, the sea, the storm, and fertility. Kings were divine forces, too, and sometimes they were either sacrificed to the other earth spirits or took their own human victims with them when they returned to the ghostly realm of nature. When, about 500 B.C., the story of Near Eastern civilization that we have been tracing ended, gods and kings still sat on their thrones—but these were thrones that were now perceived as serving *human* needs. Gods and kings were becoming the saviors, not simply the awesome masters, of humanity. At different paces, and with differing local manifestations, the same transformations occurred in Egypt, in Mesopotamia, in Persia, and among the Hebrews.

Although the ancient Near Eastern empires collapsed politically, the civilization that they had fostered survived in spirit. As we shall see in Chapter 2, ancient Greece was indebted to the Near East and would remold this intellectual and cultural legacy in ways unimagined by its prede-

cessors. (With charming immodesty, one Greek writer emphasized the point: "Whatever the Greeks take over from foreigners, they transform by making it something finer.") Politically, first Alexander the Great and his successors, and then all-conquering Rome, would continue consolidating the Near East under authoritarian rule (see Chapters 3 and 4).

A second great transformation also occurred in the ancient Near East: the dawning of the Iron Age, about 1200 B.C. Although subsequent history would witness many refinements and technical improvements, the technology and society that grew out of the discovery of iron metallurgy would remain basically intact for three thousand years. Only around A.D. 1800, with the beginning of the Industrial (or **Energy**) Revolution, would there be another fundamental change in the way society produced its goods and organized itself.

Religion loomed large in the story that Chapter 1 has told, for two reasons. First, religion was the most important legacy of the ancient Near East to the later West. Second, religion gave these people the rock on which to build a worldview and give order to their lives. Mesopotamians and Egyptians wrestled with the same questions that still define the human condition: From what does life come? Who are we? What purpose does our existence serve? What is our destiny—collectively and individually? The Hebrews—who entered history when both Mesopotamia and Egypt had passed their creative peaks—absorbed much of their predecessors' cultural heritage and asked the same questions. Their impact on future civilization has been immense.

The Hebrew Bible, itself a majestic literary monument, has been of incalculable importance in shaping Western culture. The Hebrews' sense of history—as a dynamic, purposeful, morally significant process of human–divine interaction—went far beyond the historical concepts of other Near Eastern peoples and became a fundamental element in the historical vision of Western civilization. But at the core of everything lay the Hebrews' concept of ethical monotheism—the vision of a single God of infinite power who is also Lord of righteousness and mercy. The Hebrews confronted their universe in a new way. The myriad divine forces of tree, rock, and mountain dissolved before the unutterable holiness of the God of Israel. Yahweh became the King of kings, yet the Hebrews remained his chosen people. History itself could be understood only in terms of Israel's encounter with God. The Hebrews were unique among the peoples of the ancient Near East in their sensitivity toward history, for to them God's relations with humanity occurred in a historical dimension, and history itself was directed by God toward predetermined goals. Our modern sense of **progress**—our confidence (sometimes shaken) that change is for the best—is merely a secularized version of the ancient Hebrew faith.

Selected Reading

Sources

New Oxford Annotated Bible (1991/1994).

Pritchard, James B., ed. *Ancient Near Eastern Texts Relating to the Old Testament* (1969).

Sandars, N. K., trans. *The Epic of Gilgamesh*, rev. ed. (1972).

Simpson, William K., trans. *The Literature of Ancient Egypt: An Anthology of Stories, Instructions, and Poetry* (1973).

The Ancient Near East

Bottero, Jean. *Mesopotamia: Writing, Reasoning, and the Gods* (1992). Trans. Zainah Bahrani. A study of the ancient Near East between about 3000 and 300 B.C. that places particular emphasis on Assyrian studies.

Diakonoff, I. M., ed. *Early Antiquity* (1991). Trans. Alexander Kirjanov. An intriguing, up-to-date survey of ancient Near Eastern civilizations.

Frankfort, Henri. *The Birth of Civilization in the Near East* (1968). A classic interpretation, clearly written and well argued.

Frankfort, Henri, et al. *Before Philosophy: The Intellectual Adventure of Ancient Man: An Essay on Speculative Thought in the Near East* (1966). Still the best intellectual history of the ancient Near East.

Gadon, Elinor W. *The Once and Future Goddess: A Symbol for Our Time* (1989). A fascinating study of the role of the ancient earth goddess in history.

Knapp, A. Bernard. *The History and Culture of Ancient Western Asia and Egypt* (1988). A good, standard survey running to the fourth century B.C.

Nissen, Hans J. *The Early History of the Ancient Near East, 9000–2000 B.C.* (1988). Trans. Elizabeth Lutzeier, with Kenneth J. Northcott. This concise work of astute and somewhat unconventional scholarly synthesis stresses the elements of continuity linking Neolithic cultures with the early civilizations of Mesopotamia.

Mesopotamia

Algaze, Gulliermo. *The Uruk World System: The Dynamics of Expansion of Early Mesopotamian Civilization* (1993). This valuable new study of Mesopotamian politics and economics concludes that vigorous cross-cultural commerce gave rise to imperial expansion.

Kramer, Samuel N. *History Begins at Sumer*, 3rd ed. (1981). Gracefully written and adept in its use of Sumerian writings.

Lloyd, Seton. *The Archaeology of Mesopotamia: From the Stone Age to the Persian Conquest*, 2nd ed. (1984). An authoritative account of archaeology between the Tigris and the Euphrates, well illustrated.

Piggot, Stuart. *The Earliest Wheeled Transport from the Atlantic Coast to the Caspian Sea* (1983). The best study of the development of the wheel and of horse-drawn wheeled vehicles.

Roux, Georges. *Ancient Iraq*, 3rd ed. (1992). A comprehensive, engagingly written account of ancient Mesopotamia that uses contemporary writings with great skill.

Egypt

Aldred, Cyril. *The Egyptians*, rev. ed., with color plates (1987). A splendidly illustrated general account.

Baines, John, and Jaromir Malek. *Atlas of Ancient Egypt* (1980). A valuable, well-illustrated reference tool.

Desroches-Noblecourt, Christianne. *Tutankhamen* (1976). Stunning illustrations recreate the world of the New Kingdom pharaoh.

Grimal, Nicholas. *A History of Ancient Egypt* (1992). Trans. Ian Shaw. A lucidly presented political and economic history that makes adroit use of archaeological evidence.

Johnson, Paul. *The Civilization of Ancient Egypt*, paperback ed. (1994). An expert, well-written survey.

Kemp, Barry J. *Ancient Egypt: Anatomy of a Civilization* (1989). Highly original and idiosyncratic.

Nibbi, Alessandra. *The Sea Peoples and Egypt* (1975). A fascinating, controversial work of historical revisionism that makes expert use of archaeological evidence.

Redford, Donald B. *Akhenaten: The Heretic King* (1984). Authoritative and vividly written; the best study of the subject.

———. *Egypt, Canaan, and Israel in Ancient Times* (1992). Admirable scholarship, artfully presented.

Wilson, John A. *The Culture of Ancient Egypt* (1963; originally published as *The Burden of Egypt*, 1951). A pioneering work of reinterpretation, daring in its time, now widely accepted.

The Diffusion of Near Eastern Civilization

Collins, Robert J. *The Medes and the Persians: Conquerors and Diplomats* (1972). An excellent account.

Coogan, Michael, ed. *The Oxford History of the Biblical World* (1998). The most recent and comprehensive account of the history of Israel through the late Roman period, written by a team of experts and beautifully illustrated.

Ghirshman, Roman. *Iran from the Earliest Times to the Islamic Conquest*, rev. ed. (1978). A comprehensive study drawing on both documents and excavations.

Kaufmann, Yehezkel. *The Religion of Israel, from its Beginnings to the Babylonian Exile* (1960). This shortened version of a magisterial, multivolumed work has been translated and abridged by Moshe Greenberg.

Kristiansen, Kristian. *Europe before History: The European World in the First and Second Millennium* (1998). A fascinating account of European prehistory.

Macqueen, James G. *The Hittites and Their Contemporaries in Asia Minor*, rev. ed. (1986). A superb general account.

Martin, Henri Jean. *The History and Power of Writing* (1994). Trans. Lydia G. Cochrane. A learned and wide-ranging account of how systems of writing and the communication of the written word have shaped cultures and societies throughout history, from earliest times to the present.

Miles, Jack. *God: A Biography* (1995). An engrossing interpretation of God's actions and message as they evolved in the course of the Hebrew Scriptures.

Miller, J. Maxwell, and John H. Hayes. *A History of Ancient Israel and Judah* (1986). Covering the period from the early Hebrews to the sixth century B.C., this study is especially valuable in making clear the obstacles to our understanding of the accounts in Genesis.

Oates, Joan. *Babylon*, 2nd ed. (1986). An outstanding work of scholarship and exposition.

Pearlman, Moshe. *In the Footsteps of Moses* (1974). An evocative account of Moses and the Exodus from Egypt.

Russell, Jeffrey B. *The Devil: Perceptions of Evil from Antiquity to Primitive Christianity* (1977). Includes a valuable analysis of the origins and development of Persian dualism.

Sandars, N. K. *The Sea Peoples: Warriors of the Ancient Mediterranean, 1250–1150 B.C.*, rev. ed. (1985). Stresses the ambiguity of the evidence and the danger of overinterpreting it.

Van Seters, John. *Abraham in History and Tradition* (1975). An astute and successful effort to disentangle history and legend.

THE FOUNDATIONS OF ANCIENT GREECE

Odysseus and the Sirens © *Trustees of the British Museum.*

Third millennium	Emergence of Minoan civilization		**560–494**	Ionian poleis fall under Lydian and later Persian control
2000–1500	Minoan civilization at its height		**ca. 510–500**	Cleisthenes establishes democracy in Athens
1900 or 1600	Invasion of Greek mainland by Indo-European proto-Greeks		**490**	First Persian invasion repulsed at Marathon
1600–1200	Mycenaean civilization in Greece and later on Crete		**480–479**	Second Persian invasion; battles of Thermopylae, Salamis, and Plataea
ca. 1200	Trojan War (?); catastrophes overwhelm Greece and Aegean, initiating Greek dark age		**480–431**	"Golden Age" of Athenian culture
Eighth century	Homeric epics and poems of Hesiod written down		**477**	Athenian-led Delian League formed
776	First recorded date in Greek history: beginning of Olympic Games		**454**	Transformation of Delian League into de facto Athenian Empire
750–550	Greek colonization of Mediterranean and Black Sea coasts		**431–404**	Peloponnesian War
By 700	Monarchy largely replaced by aristocracy		**430–429**	Plagues at Athens; death of Pericles
700–500	Coinage, hoplite warfare, and social tensions spread		**416**	Athenians massacre Melos
Seventh century	Spartan regime comes into focus		**415–413**	Disastrous Athenian attempt to conquer Sicily fails
Sixth century	Many poleis succumb to tyrannies		**404**	Athens surrenders to Sparta
594	Solon's reforms in Athens		**399**	Trial and execution of Socrates
561–510	Athens ruled by Pisistratus and his sons		**359**	Philip seizes throne of Macedon
			338	Battle of Chaeronea: Macedonian victory effectively ends Greek independence

All dates are B.C.

Having filled his crew's ears with wax to muffle the sirens' seductive song, which lures to doom all who hear it, Odysseus insists that his men lash him to the mast with all his senses engaged.

> . . . then we die
> with our eyes open, if we are going to die,
> or know what death we baffle if we can.[1]

It was this scene from Homer's *Odyssey* that, several hundred years after the great Homeric epics were first written down, a Greek artist painted on the cup shown in the photograph (on page 43)—one of countless images from Homer's tales that Greeks loved to see decorating the pottery that they used on convivial occasions.

The *Odyssey*, one of world literature's great adventure stories, narrates the Greek chieftain Odysseus's perilous, ten-year-long voyage home from the Greek conquest of Troy, describes his final triumph over his enemies, and ends in his moving reunion with his faithful wife and son. Odysseus's wanderings and the other yarns that various characters tell in the course of the epic together encompass virtually all the eastern Mediterranean—Egypt, Phoenicia, Anatolia, Cyprus and Crete, and Sicily—and perhaps even lands farther west. Homer surely had not been to these places (indeed, tradition had it that he was blind). But Greeks of his time had heard of them. As a tale of a hero's triumph over the terrors of the sea, the *Odyssey* reflects a central quality of the Greek experience. For the Greeks were, above all, a seafaring people. Sailing out into the Aegean from their barren, mountainous homeland, within a few generations of Homer's time they would plant colonies far and wide. By the time the cup in our photograph was painted, Greeks dominated the commerce of the eastern Mediterranean. In the end the Greeks, like Odysseus, conquered the sea to win both fame and sorrow.

The story of Odysseus is more than a simple tale of dangers courageously overcome and foes shrewdly outwitted. At the very beginning of the *Odyssey*, Zeus, king of all Creation, pensively shakes his immortal head over humans' habit of blaming the gods for their fate:

> My word, how mortals take the gods to task!
> All their afflictions come from us, we hear.
> And what of their own failings? Greed and folly
> Double the suffering in the lot of man.[2]

---

[1] *The Odyssey*, trans. Robert Fitzgerald (Garden City, NY: Anchor, 1963), Book Twelve, lines 158–160.

[2] Ibid., Book One, lines 38–41.

Even Odysseus is not immune, careful as he might be to offer the gods proper reverence. It was his unwitting offense to the powerful sea god Poseidon that condemned him to his wanderings, and only other divinities' intervention allowed him at last to return. Homer, we should not forget, was the contemporary of the first Hebrew prophets, and like them he sought to translate the divine will into human values. Their message—as we saw in Chapter 1—emphasized human beings' ethical duties to one another, and taught that the God who ruled the universe was shaping history for his own purposes. Homer was more pessimistic: Gods, he said, often worked at cross-purposes; if one ordered a certain human action, another might take offense. But if human beings must submit to their will, at least let them do so with courage, grace, and a decent regard for social obligations appropriate to their status. These were lessons that ancient Greeks never forgot. Along with the very different message of prophetic Judaism, such ideas have passed into the common core of the Western value system.

Chapter 2 begins in the Aegean world of a millennium and more *before* Homer. It takes us through the fifth century B.C., when the Greek city of Athens dominated the lands around the Aegean, and it ends in the fourth century B.C., with the Greeks on the verge of being absorbed into the empire of Alexander the Great, who would go on to conquer most of the world known to the civilized peoples of the West. Chapter 3 will explore the culture of ancient Greece more closely, will tell the story of Alexander and his successors, and will end with the building of a *Hellenistic*—"Greek-like"—culture that would profoundly influence first Rome, later Europe, and eventually the Americas.

GREEK ORIGINS: LEGEND AND REALITY

By the time the two great Homeric epics, the *Iliad* and the *Odyssey*, were committed to writing in the eighth century B.C., Near Eastern civilization was reviving after several centuries of disruption—and it was already more than two thousand years old. In tracing the history of ancient Greece from its Aegean and Homeric roots, and in anticipating its future impact on societies far to the west of the Greek homeland, we must never forget that the Aegean world in which Homer lived was on the distant fringe of the still more ancient world of the great Near Eastern empires.

The Aegean Civilization

Homer's epics tell of the Greek conquest of Troy, a proud city on the coast of Anatolia. A little more than a century ago, this story seemed mere inspired fancy. But during the 1870s and 1880s Heinrich Schliemann, a retired German businessman and amateur archaeologist, confounded schol-

arly critics by excavating Troy and other Homeric sites, thereby giving reality to a supposedly imaginary civilization that had flourished eight centuries before the golden age of Athens. Troy, we now know, really existed, though who lived there remains a mystery. Trojans may very well have fought with invaders from the Greek mainland early in the twelfth century B.C.—about the time that Homer's heroes would have come there. Yet modern archaeology also demonstrates that such a war was probably just a pirate raid, and certainly not Homer's ten-year siege ending in Troy's final, fiery destruction.

Schliemann's digging up of Troy was not the only startling discovery from beneath ancient rubble that revealed the Greek peninsula's and the Aegean Sea's most ancient history. On the Greek mainland, Schliemann would later unearth Mycenae, a city from before Homer's time with strong fortifications and dazzling wealth in its royal tombs. Then, early in the twentieth century, archaeological excavations by Sir Arthur Evans on the island of Crete disclosed a civilization resembling that of Mycenae, but even older and more splendid.

From the ruins at Knossos and at the sites of other ancient palaces on Crete, archaeologists have recovered stone tablets containing writing in two scripts, now known as "Linear A," the earlier version, and "Linear B," which was also used at Mycenae and other sites on the Greek mainland. Linear A, despite many attempts, has not yet been deciphered, but in 1952 the English cryptographer Michael Ventris cracked Linear B. He found it to be an early form of Greek.

The work of Schliemann, Evans, Ventris, and other students of early cultures bordering the Aegean Sea has opened a vast new world, previously unknown. The study of these first sites of civilization in Europe—all of them in contact with the far older world of Egypt and Mesopotamia—remains exciting as long-accepted theories continue to fall victim to new discoveries.

The Kingdom of Minos   Memories of the early Aegean culture lingered in later Greek literature like a hazy dream. The civilization is known as "Minoan"—after Minos, a legendary king of Crete in Greek mythology, and perhaps the title of the Cretans' priest-kings. The Minoans were not Greeks, and their language bears no resemblance to Greek, yet they deeply influenced the later Greek way of life.

Minoan civilization emerged on the island of Crete during the third millennium B.C. and reached its height between—very approximately—2000 and 1500 B.C. (Minoan chronology remains much disputed.) Possibly the Minoans came to Crete from somewhere in the Near East. Certainly they derived their technological and artistic skills from Mesopotamia, Egypt, and Anatolia, as well as from a slightly earlier culture centering on islands in the Aegean Sea known as the Cyclades, which produced impressive works of decorative art in lead and silver, and an abundance of graceful marble grave statuettes.

Excavations on Crete have unearthed ruins of several great sprawling palaces, complete with plumbing systems and windows with glazed panes. These palace complexes were the center of Minoan civilization, and they seem to have served simultaneously as cult centers, residences, workshops, and warehouses. The excavations bear witness to severe earthquake damage, probably on more than one occasion during the centuries after about 2000 B.C., with a particularly devastating, islandwide earthquake around 1800 B.C. But the palaces were afterwards rebuilt on an even grander scale.

Light and flowing—that is the overwhelming impression that the Minoans have left us in the art on which we must depend heavily to interpret their culture. Plants, animals, marine life, and youths playing games are all portrayed with a confident flair and a stunning naturalism. Palace walls were decorated with vivacious paintings, and their rooms contained exquisite statuettes and polychromatic pottery (including gigantic storage jars) fashioned with consummate skill and taste. The Minoans' lively spirit is nowhere better illustrated than in their depictions of boxing matches, acrobatics, and bull-leaping. The last involved male and female athletes grabbing a charging bull by the horns while one of them would gracefully leap over his back. Curious scholars once asked an American cowboy how this might have been done; he told them curtly that it could not be done at all. Yet because bull-leaping scenes of striking realism occur in Minoan art—in statuettes as well as frescoes—we can only conclude that somehow it *was* done, perhaps through the joint efforts of superbly trained athletes and an unusually obliging bull, and with occasional gory mishaps.

Minoan religion has been a subject of much fascinating guesswork—but guesswork it remains in the absence of decipherable religious texts. Minoan statuettes of elegantly dressed, bare-breasted young women, often brandishing snakes, might represent a fertility goddess of the sort that abounded in prehistoric Europe and the Near East (the Sumerians' Innana, for example). The prominence of female divinities in Cretan religious imagery and the depiction of stylish women boldly assuming highly public roles in other Cretan works of art suggest that here women retained the strong position from which other early civilizations drove them. But we cannot be certain.

An absence of large freestanding temples in ancient Crete suggests that the Minoans, like the later Greeks, did not accord priesthoods the exalted prestige typical of Near Eastern societies. Some experts believe that priest-kings were young men, chosen for an eight-year term but either paralleling or subordinate to the authority of a priestess who represented the Cretans' supreme female deity. The prominence of bulls and bull-leaping rituals in Minoan imagery, along with the bare-breasted women (emphasizing both their sexuality and their nurturing capacity), suggests cults of divinities who ensure fertility, die, and are reborn. Such beliefs, as we have already seen, have deep roots in the Neolithic. A more somber side of Minoan religion also appears in the remains of damaged children's bones, hinting at human sacrifice.

The palaces and towns of the Minoan golden age lacked strong fortifications. Yet scenes of military conflict in recently discovered Minoan frescoes make it clear that the Minoans were not unaccustomed to warfare. More likely, the entire island of Crete was united under the kings of Knossos, and the Minoan fleet was usually able to protect it from foreign enemies.

Cretan Bull-Leaping   This depiction of the Cretans' favorite sport dates from about 1500 B.C. and is in the Palace of Knossos. *Erich Lessing/Art Resource, NY.*

Cretan Female Divinity Aristocratic women must have enjoyed a relatively high status in the Minoan world. They were not confined to the private sphere of hearth and home, as they had been in Mesopotamian society and as they would later be in Greek society, but are depicted in frescoes participating in public ceremonies and attending public functions alongside men. Statuettes and frescoes of the age show them with marvelously elaborate hairdos, and some—either priestesses or goddesses—are dressed in hooped skirts with tight-fitting bodices that leave the breasts exposed. The snake goddess here is clad in the height of aristocratic Minoan fashion. A mother goddess and other female deities, whose shrines have been found in some twenty-five caves throughout the island, clearly played a major role in Minoan religion. *Nimatallah/Art Resource, NY.*

The Minoans owed their success to their isolation and their ships. Isolation gave Crete a feeling of security, optimism, and lightheartedness reminiscent of early Egypt, but the lure of the sea resulted in a cultural dynamism that was distinctly un-Egyptian. Long before Phoenicians ventured into the Mediterranean, Minoan seafarers were trading with the Aegean islands, Anatolia, Syria, North Africa,

and even Spain (see Map 2-1). They imported tin and copper for the superb Minoan bronze armor that in turn became a chief item of export, along with delicate pottery fashioned by Minoan artisans.

Besides artisans and seafaring traders, the Minoan economy employed agricultural laborers, both free and enslaved, whose numbers must have far exceeded those of the artisans, merchant-sailors, and palace elites. The agrarian economy focused on the cultivation of vineyards, olive trees, and grain—the so-called "Mediterranean triad." From this the Minoans obtained the basic ingredients of their diet: wine, olive oil, and wheat and barley (which they made into bread, barley cakes, and porridge). This triad of grapes, olives, and grain, having established itself in the Aegean world around 3000 B.C., would dominate Mediterranean agriculture throughout the centuries of classical antiquity and, indeed, down to the present day.

Judging from the grandeur of Knossos and other Minoan palace complexes, with their vast storage rooms, the Minoan economy appears to have been highly centralized and largely under royal control—as in Egypt and Mesopotamia. The huge jars in the Minoan palaces, with capacities of up to a quarter-million gallons, were doubtless used to store the wine, grain, and olive oil that the palace bureaucracies collected as taxes-in-kind and afterwards redistributed to the populace or traded for the kings' profit. The Minoan economy was exceptionally prosperous during the golden age of Crete, enabling the Minoan palaces to grow ever larger and the aristocracy to live in style.

By about 1600 B.C., the palace economy had reached a level of complexity that required the keeping of extensive records, written on clay tablets in the as-yet indecipherable Linear A. This script, like its successor Linear B, ceased using pictograms early in its development and afterwards consisted entirely of characters representing syllables. In this regard, it was a more sophisticated form of writing than Sumerian cuneiform or Egyptian hieroglyphics, both of which used pictograms along with syllabic signs and other figures, but it had not yet achieved the simplicity and economy of the Phoenician alphabet. Since we cannot read Linear A, we must avoid overinterpreting the Minoan religion, economy, or political system. But it would be a reasonable guess that the information on Linear A tablets resembles that transcribed in Linear B: mostly accounts and inventories of goods in the king's possession, such as foodstuffs, armaments, ships, horses, and furniture.

No great literature has come down to us in Linear B, and we should not entertain high hopes for Linear A. The Minoans evidently transmitted their songs and stories orally. All of them have perished or blurred into Greek mythology. Many centuries later, the Greeks remembered "King Minos" as a just and benevolent lawgiver—but also as a horrible tyrant whose palace contained an immense labyrinth in which children were consumed as sacrificial offerings by a monster whom the Greeks called

MAP 2-1
THE AEGEAN WORLD
BEFORE 1200 B.C.

the Minotaur ("Minos's bull"). These contradictory myths may reflect the mainland Greeks' experiences with Cretan rulers at different times, and perhaps also two sides to the Cretans' religion.

The Mycenaean Greeks   A long-accepted view held that around 1900 B.C. the earliest Greeks, speaking an Indo-European language, migrated from the Balkans into what is now the Greek homeland, displacing or merging with earlier inhabitants. About 1580 B.C., this view asserts, these formerly simple pastoralists fell under the spell of Minoan culture. They created what is called the Mycenaean civilization, taking its name from the city of Mycenae, which lasted until it was overwhelmed by the catastrophes that befell the entire Near East around 1200 B.C.

But a controversial new view of ancient Greek origins has been recently advanced—one that is linked to the reevaluation of the Indo-European dispersal that we encountered in Chapter 1. According to this new view, Greece's pre-Greek population was overwhelmed by chariot-driving Indo-European conquerors from Anatolia about 1600 B.C.—about a century after the rise of the Hittite kingdom, and about the same time that the Indo-European Kassites were taking over Babylon and the Aryans were sacking ancient India. Although not all scholars are convinced, the new theory does clarify many issues in ancient Near Eastern and early Greek history.

The Mycenaean Greeks' culture differed radically from that of Crete. Their chief divinities were male; they glorified war; they built massive fortifications around their great palace complexes, whose ruins have been excavated at such sites in the Peloponnesus as Mycenae, Pylos, and Tiryns. But in crucial respects the Mycenaeans learned

from the Cretans. For example, they adapted the Minoan script (Linear A) to their Indo-European language. The result was Linear B, which used the Minoan syllabary to express early Greek words. Their art, architecture, and customs all betray strong Minoan influence; they even tried bull-leaping. And Mycenaean women began adopting Minoan dress, hairdos, and cosmetics.

Strife, domination, and the flaunting of wealth pervaded the Mycenaean warriors' world. From such fortresses as Mycenae and Tiryns, they lorded it over the surrounding country. If Homer's testimony centuries later is correct, eventually all the princes of southern Greece recognized a loose overlordship by the warrior-kings of Mycenae. Kings and their chieftains were buried in "shaft graves," unlike anything in Minoan tradition but comparable to the funeral customs of other early Indo-Europeans. When Schliemann turned from Troy to Mycenae, the great archaeologist found what he immediately declared was the tomb of the Homeric hero Agamemnon, crammed with magnificent treasures. Agamemnon's tomb it surely was not, but it clearly showed the Mycenaeans' ability to extract wealth.

Nor were the Mycenaeans simply a landed nobility. As seafarers they traded and plundered far and wide. Piracy brought an abundance of wealth and slaves back to the Greek mainland. Before long, Mycenaean seamen were challenging Cretan domination of the Aegean. Sometime during the sixteenth century B.C. a band of Mycenaean Greeks seems to have seized Knossos itself, for records there were henceforth kept in the Greek Linear B. About 1550 B.C., Minoan civilization was ravaged by an islandwide disaster, the precise nature of which remains uncertain. Many scholars once believed that the cause was an immense volcanic eruption—perhaps the greatest in human memory—on the island of Thera (now called Santorini), 90 miles north of Crete, accompanied by a monstrous tidal wave. More likely, however, the destruction resulted from a large-scale invasion of Crete, perhaps by Mycenaean Greeks. The eruption at Santorini buried its chief town beneath deep layers of pumice. Structures, implements, pottery, and frescoes were preserved much more perfectly in Akrotiri than in the Cretan palaces themselves, providing a vivid glimpse of the life and art of a Minoan town.

The exact date of the Santorini eruption remains in dispute (the most plausible current estimate is 1628 B.C.). But dating the artifacts relative to those at Knossos and the other palaces of Crete suggests that the eruption occurred more than a half-century before the destruction of the great palaces. Whatever the cause of the disaster on Crete, it left the centers of Minoan civilization in ruins. The palaces were never rebuilt on their previous scale, although Knossos was inhabited thereafter by Mycenaean kings.

The disintegration of the Minoan state opened the trade of the entire eastern Mediterranean to Mycenaean ships. Perhaps around 1200 B.C., according to Homer, King Agamemnon of Mycenae led the Greeks (Homer called them Achaeans) against Troy. But even at the time of the fabled Trojan War, the political stability of Mycenaean Greece was shaking; soon it would collapse.

Akrotiri Fresco This fresco reveals a rich and vibrant society on Santorini, associated with that of Minoan Crete–about which we know little more than what beautiful works of art like this can suggest. © *R. Sheridan/Ancient Art & Architecture Collection, Ltd.*

The "Agamemnon Mask" from Mycenae The solid gold death mask recovered from a Mycenaean tomb by Heinrich Schliemann is not, as its excited discoverer thought, the image of the legendary King Agamemnon, but it does testify to the wealth and haughty pride of the Mycenaean ruling class. #654.1803. *Athens, National Museum. Aus ders Burg von Mykenai. Sog. Agamemnon-Maske. Hirmer Fotoarchiv.*

The Dorians and the Greek Dark Age, ca. 1200–800 B.C.

On the testimony of the ancient Greek historian Thucydides, scholars long assumed that the destruction of Mycenaean civilization resulted from an invasion by so-called Dorian Greeks, whose movements were part of the widespread Near Eastern turmoil around 1200 B.C. (see Chapter 1). This assumption may be true, but it is by no means certain. The Mycenaeans did not record their disaster; Thucydides wrote seven hundred years afterwards; and the Dorians could not write at all.

The Mycenaeans' catastrophe coincided with a general disruption—and in some cases the collapse—of civilized life throughout the eastern Mediterranean world around 1200 B.C. But who were the Dorians, and was their onslaught against the Mycenaeans part of the crisis that gripped the entire region? Or was it a local matter, only coincidentally connected to the fate of the Hittites, the Egyptians, and other Near Eastern peoples? The Greek tradition that described the Dorians' takeover with an intriguing metaphor—"the return of the sons of Heracles"—sets the stage for a puzzling problem.

There is no scholarly agreement about who the Dorians were and what they did. Some historians connect the Mycenaean collapse and the end of the Bronze Age to the destructive fury of peoples (including Dorians?) from beyond the civilized world who wreaked havoc throughout the Near East. Other historians deny that there was a Dorian "invasion" of Greece at all, arguing that Mycenaeans fell victim to a massive revolt by the mainland's previously subjugated native population—people who were known later as the Dorians. Perhaps civil wars had weakened the Mycenaeans to the extent that they could not resist a revolt. (Inconveniently, there is no archaeological evidence for such weakening.) A controversial study asserts that changes in weaponry at the end of the Bronze Age permitted foot soldiers of the Mycenaean armies, recruited from the social or geographical fringes, to defeat aristocratic charioteers. Mycenaean refugees who escaped the carnage on the Greek mainland joined the restless wandering of other uprooted peoples. Many fled to strongholds on the coast of Anatolia; some, as we saw in Chapter 1, probably struck out farther afield and may have become the Philistines who settled in Canaan.

Whatever the cause of the disasters on the Greek mainland, the result was a sweeping away of the Mycenaean lords' domination. Into the vacuum flowed illiterate, uncivilized Greeks speaking a dialect called Dorian. Once apparently restricted to the northern region of Thessaly, several centuries later Dorian-speakers had settled throughout the Peloponnesus, Crete, and on some islands.

Dorian Greeks—whoever they were—knew nothing of Minoan-Mycenaean culture, and their displacement of the Mycenaeans was a historical calamity. The Mycenaean world vanished. Linear B tablets of this era, baked in the flames of their burning cities, bear silent witness to the catastrophe but leave the attackers unnamed. Knowledge of Linear B had been the monopoly of a small scribal class in Mycenaean society. No one remained who could read and write in it. As the Mycenaean cities were sacked and incinerated, the civilization that had begun in Crete and on the Greek mainland collapsed in ruins and faded into legend.

The disintegration of Mycenaean culture roughly coincided with the collapse of the Hittites and the decline of the Egyptian New Kingdom—indeed, with the whole "Time of Troubles" of the ancient Near East. The far-flung maritime activities of the Phoenicians in the following epoch were made possible not only by the troubles of the Near Eastern empires but also by the disruption of Mycenaean commerce.

Between Mycenaean and classical Greece lies a chasm of some four centuries known as the "dark age" of Hellenic history.[3] The Greeks lapsed into illiteracy, and when (centuries later) they began to write once again they no longer used Linear B but instead a much simplified script based on the Phoenician alphabet. The era would probably not have seemed noticeably "dark" to its own people; it is dark to us because so many of its secrets are hidden by the absence of written sources and substantial buildings.

As the post-Mycenaean Greeks withdrew from maritime commerce and piracy, their economy was forced back onto the stony Greek soil, and their society became more rustic and more localized. Their farms, worked by slaves and tenant farmers, continued producing grapes, olives, and grain—the "Mediterranean triad"—but seldom in abundance. Most farms had passed under the control of individual households, each headed by a patriarchal lord, the wealthier of whom might manage not only a large family but also a sizable coterie of servants, slaves, tenant farmers, shepherds, and hired hands. These agrarian households, great and small, became the basic social units of dark-age Greece. The Greek term for such a unit was *oikos*, and its management was called *oikonomia*, from which our words "economy" and "economics" come.

With the collapse of Mycenaean culture, most of the Peloponnesus was occupied by Dorian Greeks. The leadership of that area, once exercised by Mycenae, centuries later would pass to the Dorian-speaking people of Sparta. Some Mycenaean Greeks known as Ionians fled across the Aegean and settled along the western coast of Anatolia and its offshore islands (see Map 2-2). Thenceforth, that region was known as Ionia and became an integral part of Greek civilization.[4] Other Ionians gathered at Athens, still an obscure stronghold on the mainland, or on various Aegean islands. Throughout all subsequent ancient Greek history, there would be enmity between Dorians and the so-called Ionian Greeks of Athens, the islands, and Ionia.

In the chaotic conditions of dark-age Greece, political authority crumbled. The Greeks grouped themselves in tribes that, in turn, were subdivided into clans and finally into agrarian households under their individual lords or patriarchs. Each clan included a number of related families that shared a single religious cult. The powers once exercised by kings were assumed by the elders of the tribes and clans. Some royal dynasties survived the upheaval but with much diminished power—as military commanders and cult leaders. The collapse of the Mycenaean palace complexes put an end to domination of Greece by kings until the time of Philip of Macedon and his son Alexander the Great.

---

[3] Hellenic = Greek; Hellas = Greece.
[4] In ancient Greece, Ionia was a place (today the western coast of Turkey), but important communities of Greeks speaking the so-called Ionian dialect lived elsewhere as well. The most important Ionian city, Athens, was not in Ionia at all.

MAP 2-2
POST-MYCENAEAN GREECE

Hesiod, Homer, and the Gods

During the eighth century B.C. the darkness lifts and the silence ends. Literacy returns; actual voices, and not simply the silent testimony of grave goods and ruins, begin to speak—and the greatest voice that we hear is Homer's, the foremost of all epic poets and the first great creator in Greek and European literature.

But the ancient Greeks did not simply recover their voices and produce Homer miraculously. By Homer's time, the lands around the Aegean Sea were reestablishing their long-standing connection with the ancient Near East. It was this renewed contact, not just a spontaneous explosion of creativity, that started ancient Greece on its journey to civilization and laid the foundations of later European culture.

Even dark-age Greece had not been entirely cut off from the Near East. As early as the tenth century B.C., Phoenician merchants began visiting the Aegean to barter cloth and other commodities. By 800 B.C., Greek traders established an outpost in Phoenicia. Trading with the Phoenicians, they learned alphabetic writing; indeed, the very word *alphabet* (which we have inherited from the Greeks) is of Phoenician origin—*alpha* and *beta*, the first two Greek letters, are the Phoenicians' names for their first two letters, *aleph* and *beth*, which in turn are the Semitic pictographs for "ox" and "house." Without the Greeks having acquired this key technique, the Homeric epics could only have survived by oral transmission.

Commercial contact with the Near East also helped stimulate a highly distinctive Greek art. Dark-age Greek pottery was decorated in what art historians call geometric style: patterns of broad and narrow stripes, intricate linear designs, swirls, and stylized stick figures. Once Greek artisans and merchants found themselves competing in Near Eastern markets to sell wine and olive oil, the decorations on the pottery in which these wares were transported had to appeal to buyers. Eventually the Greeks fused their geometric style with the easterners' predilection for naturalism and fantastic animals and plants, creating what is called black-figure ware.[5] The emergence of this new style dates from between 725 and 700 B.C., and it soon displayed the determination to show real human beings (or human-looking gods) doing real things that would shape Greek art for many centuries. Almost simultaneously, the first alphabet with Greek (not Phoenician) letters appeared, painted on pottery.

Intellectual contact also helped stimulate the Greek spirit. Homer's fellow eighth-century Greek poet, Hesiod,[6] hardly compares as an artist to the maker of the *Iliad* and the *Odyssey*; nevertheless, he is important both for documenting Greek social history as the dark age was ending and for sorting out the complicated tangle of Greek divinities. In the latter sense his influence on later Greek life and culture was almost as great as Homer's. His long *Theogony*, while no masterpiece, in many details echoes the ancient

---

[5] "Black-figure" means that the pictures were painted on the clay before it was hardened in the kiln; the firing left the picture as a black silhouette against the reddish background. In the late sixth century B.C., so-called red-figure painting was developed, in which the background and tiny details of the figure were painted but the figure itself remained unpainted; this technique permitted a finer modeling of the image. See black-figure examples on pp. 54 and 64. See chapter-opening photo and the illustration on p. 80 for red-figure samples.

[6] Many authorities believe that "Hesiod" was several different poets.

A

The Evolution of Early Greek Style   These illustrations show
the evolution of Greek styles in painting and sculpture. The
geometric-style painting (A) is from Attica, and shows chariot-
riding warriors—evidence that chariots were still used in the
seventh century B.C. This was probably close in time to the
writing down of the Homeric epics, in which heroes are depicted
using chariots as "taxis" to get to and from the battlefield, where
they fight on foot. The pitcher (B) is an example of early
Corinthian export-oriented painting, ca. 650–625 B.C. and shows
a strong "orientalizing" influence in its depiction of birds. The
Cypriot votive figure (C) betrays strong Assyrian as well as
Egyptian influence ca. 500 B.C. From such figures later evolved
Kouroi, statues often 6 feet or taller that were made in great
abundance as memorials to the dead. They are idealized nude
depictions of male aristocrats in their prime, not portraits.

A   *Erich Lessing/Art Resource, NY.*
B   *Staatliche Antikensammlungen und Glyptothek. Photo by Studio
     Koppermann.*
C   *Kunsthistorisches Museum, Vienna.*

B

C

Sumerian creation epic *Enuma Elish*—which, incidentally,
was just then being written down by Assyrian scribes, and
so must have been "in the air" throughout the Near East.

Theogony reeks of incest, cannibalism, and mayhem.
The sky god Ouranos mates with the earth goddess Gaia,
begetting children whom he tries to destroy (by swallowing
them), but after vomiting them up he is vanquished by his
offspring: Kronos and the earth-dwelling Titans. Kronos
begets another generation of gods, headed by Zeus; eventually Zeus destroys Kronos and banishes the Titans—and

Zeus or Poseidon This magnificent bronze statue, recovered from an ancient shipwreck in the Aegean, was cast in the mid-fifth century B.C. It stands 6 feet 10 inches tall and spans the same distance. Scholars are uncertain whether it represents Zeus or Poseidon; more important, it illustrates vividly the anthropomorphic nature of the Olympian gods, to whom aristocrats were particularly devoted. Bronze was apparently used very frequently for Greek and Roman statuary, but examples now are rare; most of it was melted down in late antiquity or the Middle Ages. *Erich Lessing/Art Resource, NY.*

everything ends with Zeus and his divine relatives gloriously enthroned on Mount Olympus.[7] Modern scholars who study this gory "succession myth" see not only the direct influence of *Enuma Elish* but also Hesiod's attempt to reconcile several discordant religious traditions. In his saga, Hesiod weaves together, on the one hand, divinities of the ancient Near East, of the Minoans, and of the pre-Mycenaean cultures of the Greek mainland, and on the other hand the gods of the Indo-European Greeks, headed by Zeus. Begetting (with mortal partners) the familiar heroes of Greek mythology, Zeus and the other Olympian gods set the human race in motion and reign righteously. Hesiod's purpose was to justify the reign of the gods to humankind, and—to his satisfaction, at least—he achieved it.

How, where, and by whom the epics attributed to Homer were written down, no one knows. Both the *Iliad* and the *Odyssey* are the products of a long oral tradition that ran back to Mycenaean times. Wandering from one noble household to the next, and accompanying himself by plucking a stringed instrument, the *aidos* ("singer of tales"[8]) chanted sagas of heroic deeds that he had learned

from older practitioners of his craft. Using a large repertoire of recurrent phrases aided memorization. An aidos might embellish or combine his tales, but always within the framework of conventions. Homer was such an aidos. And although the Homeric tales are of Mycenaean times, the society that they actually describe, with its weak kingship and headstrong aristocracy, is really that of Homer's time—the Greek dark ages. Some scholars doubt that there is a common author of the *Iliad* and the *Odyssey*, which may have been committed to writing several decades apart and seem to reflect different moods. Others retort that a single person could well have been responsible for two poems over several decades, having changed moods in the interim. One scholar joked that the epics should not be attributed to Homer at all but to an entirely different person of the same name. The issue will probably never be resolved.

Both epics not only tell dramatic stories of battle, heroism, and adventure but also dwell on ultimate problems of human life. The point of the *Iliad*, for example, is the tragedy that flows from a quarrel between two touchy, hot-tempered Greek leaders, Agamemnon and Achilles, toward the end of the Trojan War:

> Divine Muse, sing of the ruinous wrath of Achilles, Peleus' son, which brought ten thousand sorrows to the Greeks, sent the souls of many brave heroes down to the world of the dead, and left their bodies to be eaten by dogs and birds: and the will of Zeus was fulfilled. Begin where they

---

[7] A snow-covered mountain in Thessaly.
[8] This term was coined by the American scholar Albert Lord, whose study of traditional oral poetry as practiced in the twentieth century in remote parts of Yugoslavia has reopened to us the world of the Homeric *aidos*. We now know that this art is found in preliterate societies throughout the world.

first quarreled, Agamemnon the King of Men, and great Achilles.[9]

Despite Homer's allusion here to the will of Zeus, and despite the repeated instances in the narrative of divine intervention, his characters are no mere puppets of the gods. Rather they are intensely—often violently—human, and they are doomed to suffer the consequences of their own choices and deeds. In this respect, as in others, Homer foreshadows the Greek tragic dramatists of the fifth century B.C.: Achilles' dazzling career with its harvest of ten thousand sorrows prefigures the fate of ancient Greece itself. The gods were said to have offered Achilles two alternatives: a long, tedious life or glory and an early death. His choice of the latter symbolizes the meteoric course of Hellenic history.

Whatever his identity, Homer has never been surpassed as an epic poet. The *Iliad* and the *Odyssey* were studied by young Greeks as models of personal conduct, and all later Greek writers and artists found them an inexhaustible source of inspiration. These poems set a standard for later Greeks in their rigorous organization around a single theme, their lucidity, their moments of tenderness that never slip into sentimentality—in short, their brilliant synthesis of heart and mind. Modern scholars still marvel at their terse power, their beautiful imagery ("rosy-fingered dawn," "wine-dark sea"), and their formal structure.

The gods of Mount Olympus, who dominate Homer's epics and Hesiod's *Theogony*, had diverse origins. Zeus, hurler of thunderbolts and ruler of Olympus, was Indo-European and Mycenaean. Poseidon, the sea god, was Minoan. Aphrodite, the fickle goddess of love and sexuality, was Innana and Ishtar, newly immigrated from Babylon. Apollo and others had been local deities long before they joined the assemblage on Olympus; Hesiod's stories (usually involving copulation) tell how each arrived there.

By Homer's and Hesiod's time these diverse gods had been arrayed in a hierarchy of interconnected deities familiar to all Greeks. The Olympian gods were **anthropomorphic;** that is, they were human in form and personality, capable of rage, lust, jealousy, and all the other traits of the warrior-hero (and even the rest of us). But they also possessed immortality and other superhuman attributes. No more than the ancient Sumerian hero Gilgamesh could Achilles, the greatest Homeric warrior, expect everlasting life. As a mortal, his glory alone would live.

The universality of the Olympic cult significantly counterbalanced the localism of Greek politics. It strengthened Greek cohesion through religious sanctuaries common to all Greeks—at Delos, Olympia, Delphi, and elsewhere—and through the Olympic Games, first recorded in 776 B.C. (see Chapter 3). Apollo's priests at Delphi, for example, were constantly consulted by anxious individuals and cities. The answers, supposedly from the god himself and uttered by the oracle in a trance, were famously cryptic but sometimes revealed good political sense.

Yet Greek religion also had its intensely private and local side. Each clan and each district also honored its special gods, many of whom, like Athena the patron goddess of Athens, also belonged to the Olympic pantheon. These local gods were propitiated in family devotions or regional and civic cults. Such gods concerned themselves chiefly with the well-being of groups rather than with the fate of the individual, and their worship was almost indistinguishable from patriotism. The Olympian gods appealed above all to aristocrats; ordinary people usually looked elsewhere for personal protection, solace, and hope.

Dionysus and His Female Worshipers The Dionysian cult appealed particularly to women. Perhaps this was one way in which women dealt psychologically with the repression they suffered in ancient Greek life; it is also possible that men, fearing "insatiable" female sexuality, greatly exaggerated the ferocity of Dionysian rites and tried to channel them into something "safe." But such psychological theorizing about the ancient past is always risky. Here, two of Dionysus's devotees (called Bacchants or Maenads) present him with animals that they have killed in their ecstatic revels. *Bibliothèque Nationale, Paris.*

---

[9] From *The Greeks*, rev. ed., trans. H. D. F. Kitto (Harmondsworth, Penguin, 1957), p. 45.

Ancient nature deities rivaled the Olympians in devotion and exceeded them in popular affection. Animism (the belief that material objects have living souls) persisted in all its numberless and exotic forms; the world of Greek households, like that of their Near Eastern neighbors, teemed with minor gods, ghosts, and every imaginable kind of spirit. Minoan divinities, either female or appealing strongly to women, lived on. Demeter the goddess of grain and Dionysus the god of wine—both largely ignored in the Homeric epics—were at least as important to most Greeks as the proud deities on Mount Olympus. Both offered their followers a hope of personal immortality absent from the Olympian religion.

Demeter's name means "Earth Mother," the Neolithic embodiment of fertility. Her cult at Eleusis, a small town near Athens, ran back to Minoan times, and the annual rites celebrated there, the Eleusinian Mysteries, dramatized the annual cycle of death and rebirth in nature. For the Athenians, these were the most solemn of all religious observances: The yearly return of life-giving crops depended on the favor of Demeter. In very different fashion Greeks honored Dionysus, the god of wine, with wild celebrations during which female worshipers would put on fawn skins and crowns of ivy, abandon their families, and dance through the night by torchlight to the music of flutes and drums, shouting the wild ritual cry "Euoi!" In early Greek history, and perhaps at later times in isolated mountain regions, any man they encountered in their frenzy was said to risk being literally torn limb from limb. But as Greek cities developed, they toned down the Dionysian cult into respectable civic rituals.

THE WORLD OF THE CITY-STATES

With the Mycenaean collapse, Greek kingship effectively perished. Emerging from the dark age, the Greeks had an unparalleled opportunity to make a fresh start, which they seized by adopting a radically different political and cultural outlook. They began to create an altogether new way of life—new to the Aegean world and, indeed, to the entire Near East. Instead of reestablishing palace cultures centering on a monarch of overwhelming wealth and power, they built a society based on human communities. Greek civilization was unique in emphasizing *public* space—the market, the theater, the public temple—over private space, whether a palace or simply a home. The homes of even the wealthiest Greeks remained simple and stark, in contrast to the surpassing beauty of the public temples that would soon be rising in the emerging Greek cities.

By Homer's time a relatively sophisticated Greek culture was coming into focus all around the Aegean Sea—in Ionia, on the Aegean islands, in Athens and its surrounding district of Attica, in the Peloponnesus, and elsewhere in mainland Greece. But the Greek peoples did not coalesce into a single pan-Hellenic state. Partly they were discouraged from doing so by the roughness of the coast, the abundance of settlements on offshore islands, and the mountains and inlets that divided the Greek peninsula into many separate districts.

Environment alone, however, cannot fully explain the independent city-states of ancient Greece, for some small states were separated by no geographical barriers whatever. (Several, for example, might share a single island.) The Greeks lived in city-states partly by necessity but mainly by choice. Classical Greek culture without the city-state would have been inconceivable.

The Polis

We have used the term *city-state* to describe what the Greeks called the *polis* (plural: *poleis*). Actually, "city-state" fails to convey the full meaning of the Greek word *polis*. In classical times the word was packed with emotional and intellectual content: Each polis had its own distinctive customs and its own gods and was an object of intense religious-patriotic devotion. More than a mere place, it was a community of citizens—the inhabitants of both city and surrounding district who enjoyed political rights and played a role in government. Words such as *political*, *politics*, and *policy* derive from this term. The Greek philosopher Aristotle is often quoted as saying, "Man is a political animal"; what he really meant was that men (not women) are creatures who belong in a polis.

The polis was the Greeks' answer to the perennial conflict between individual and community. Though there were exceptions (including Athens at its height), most poleis were small enough for their members to interact as individuals; the chief political virtue was participation, not obedience. Accordingly, the polis became the vessel of Greek creativity and the matrix of the Greek spirit. A unified pan-Hellenic state might have eliminated the intercity warfare that tormented classical Greece, but at the expense of the very institution that made classical Greece distinctive.

Still, there were drawbacks to the Greek system of independent, competing poleis. These tiny states could flourish only because no external kingdom—Assyria, for example—was close enough to be interested in attacking or exploiting Greece.

The chief threat to the Greeks of this era was the violence of their own people. Greek communities often responded to that threat by erecting, atop a central hill, a citadel called an *acropolis* ("high town"). The acropolis was at once the chief religious center and, in war, the population's refuge. With the quickening of local commerce, an *agora* ("marketplace") usually developed at the foot of the acropolis, and farmers whose fields lay nearby built houses around the market. Like agriculturalists in other ancient societies, they found it safer to live in cities than on outlying farms.

The Social Orders

In the course of the eighth century B.C., at about the time the polis was emerging, descendants of original tribal elders were becoming a hereditary aristocracy. An occasional polis might still have a king, but generally monarchy (where it lived on at all) withered into a ceremonial office. By 700 B.C. or shortly thereafter, most Greek kings had either been overthrown or shorn of all but their religious functions, leaving the aristocracy in full control.

Below the aristocracy stood free farmers who owned relatively small patches of land. They had no voice in public affairs, and their economic condition on the rocky Greek soil was always precarious. Although the large-scale cultivation of vines and olives usually brought prosperity and power to aristocrats, small farmers risked sinking from free status into a growing body of slaves.

Hesiod, himself a farmer, vividly portrayed the condition of the small free farmers of his time. In his *Works and Days*, Hesiod described a world that had declined from a primitive golden age to the present "age of iron," ruled by a corrupt nobility. For the common farmer, life was "bad in winter, cruel in summer—never good." Yet Hesiod insisted that righteousness would triumph in the end. In the meantime the farmer must work all the harder. "In the sweat of your face," he wrote, "shall you eat bread."[10] In an age in which the farmer's lot was declining, Hesiod proclaimed his faith in the ultimate victory of justice and the dignity of toil.

Colonization, ca. 750–550 B.C.

As Hesiod wrote *Works and Days* in the eighth century B.C., the population of the Greek world was rising rapidly, badly straining its agricultural technology. The boom may have been stimulated by a shift to more intensive farming, but this is by no means certain. Whatever its causes, the effects of the swelling population were potentially devastating to the small farmer, not to speak of the landless and the homeless. To relieve the pressure, indeed to avert starvation, Greek communities began sending colonists far and wide across the eastern and central Mediterranean.

By 750 B.C. the Greeks had taken to the sea—as pirates in search of booty or as merchants in search of copper and iron (rare in Greece) and the profits of trade. As in Mycenaean times, the same Greek crew might plunder one port and peacefully sell the loot in the next. Greek seafarers found many fertile districts ripe for colonization, and during the next two centuries (ca. 750 to ca. 550 B.C.) a vast movement of colonial expansion transformed not only Greece itself but the whole Mediterranean world.

Greek poleis, great and small, dispatched bands of colonists across the seas to found new communities on distant shores, often subduing hostile indigenous populations. In time, some colonies sent out colonists of their own to establish still more settlements until, by about 550 B.C., some two hundred Greek colonies dotted the Mediterranean and Black Sea coastlines from the Crimea to the Straits of Gibraltar. The typical colonial polis—although bound to its mother city by ties of kinship, sentiment, and commerce, and by a common patriotic cult—was politically independent. Greek cities were not building colonial empires; even the word *colony*, implying a "possession" of the homeland, can be misleading. The motives behind the colonial movement are to be found in the economic and social troubles afflicting mainland Greece, aggravated by the population surge.

Colonization meant new opportunities for those with little or no land. In the stark environment of the pioneer colony, hard work was more likely to bring its reward than in the Greece of Hesiod. Here were all the opportunities for rapid social and economic advancement that one associates with a frontier society. Colonization also provided community leaders with a useful safety valve to relieve population pressures and accumulating discontent. Adventurous, disaffected, or unpopular aristocrats could usually be found to lead the enterprise. On the other hand, the few sources that describe colonization suggest that only compulsion could uproot many colonists from their native soil, their household gods, and their family ties. One inscription recorded that recruits were chosen by lot, one son from each family, and it threatened curses or death for individual men who returned, or resisted going. (Only if the colony failed could the whole group come back.) Starvation and the threat of internal social upheaval were probably the main reasons why Greek communities resorted to the desperate expedient of sending its people as far away as Italy, the Black Sea, and Libya.

The spread of Greek settlements across vast reaches of the Mediterranean world was an astonishing development, comparable only to what the Phoenicians had begun a century or so earlier. (Greeks and Phoenicians tended to avoid planting colonies in the same areas; when they competed, as in Sicily, there could be violent clashes.) The Ionian polis of Miletus alone founded some eighty colonies. So many Greek settlements were established in southern Italy that the whole area became known as *Magna Graecia*—Great Greece. The small colonial polis of Byzantium, dominating the trade route between the Black

---

[10] This was exactly the sentence that Yahweh decreed for the disobedient Adam in the Book of Genesis, which had been put in writing in Israel about a century before Hesiod. There is, of course, no reason to believe that Hesiod was familiar with the Hebrew Scriptures. Recall from Chapter 1 that between the eighth and sixth centuries B.C., ancient Israel was also experiencing severe stress from population growth and social conflict, a major consequence of which had been the prophetic reshaping of Judaism into an intensely moralistic religion.

Sea and the Mediterranean, a millennium later became Constantinople, the capital of the Eastern Roman or "Byzantine" Empire. (Today it is Istanbul, Turkey). The Greek colony of Neapolis ("New Polis") in southern Italy became Napoli, or Naples; Nikaia ("Victory Town") became the modern French Riviera resort of Nice; Massilia became Marseille; Syracuse in Sicily remains one of the island's chief cities. Through the poleis of *Magna Graecia*, the Greek way of life was transmitted to half-civilized Etruscans and Romans of central Italy (see Chapter 4), another important episode in the diffusion of Greek civilization (see Map 2-3).

Colonizing profoundly affected the evolution of Greek society. The flourishing commerce that developed among the far-flung settlements brought renewed prosperity to Greece itself, which became an important source of wine, olive oil, and manufactured goods for the colonies. The needs of the new settlements stimulated the growth, back in the homeland, of artisan and commercial classes (smiths and potters, stevedores and sailors) and transformed many poleis from quiet farming or fishing towns into bustling mercantile centers. Coinage, which had been invented in the eighth century B.C. in western Anatolia, now entered the Greek world, where it became a welcome alternative to the cumbersome bartering of goods. Its introduction further stimulated commerce. The commercial surge created a new elite of merchants and manufacturers who gradually elbowed their way into the high society of the old landed nobility.

Athenian Coin   This coin comes from the fifth century B.C. The owl, stamped on all Athenian coins, was sacred to the goddess Athena. The rich lode of silver mined at the tip of Attica allowed Athens to issue vast numbers of these coins, which were used to pay for the imported grain and timber on which the city depended.   #13.0360. *Reverse of an Athenian silver tetradrachm (ca. 480–460 B.C.) Hirmer Fotoarchiv.*

Hoplites and Tyrants

The generations between about 700 and ca. 550 B.C. witnessed economic and political changes of the most fundamental significance. It was in this era, when commerce was quickened by the elixir of coinage, that the Ionian poet Pythermus wrote the golden line that alone of his works has survived: "There's nothing else that matters—only money."

Coinage, iron smelting, body armor, and the alphabet all passed into Greece from the Near East (and from the

MAP 2-3
GREEK COLONIZATION

Seventh-Century Hoplites About 650 B.C. these hoplites were painted, attacking in formation to a tune played by a piper behind them. They are outfitted in the latest equipment—helmet, breastplate, greaves to protect the shins, large circular shields, and thrusting spears. Battles consisted of these crunching attacks and ended when one side broke and ran. The vase on which this scene was painted was discovered in Italy, attesting to the wide spread of Greek colonization and trade. *591.2038. Rome, Villa Giulia. Sog. Chigi Kanne. Oinochoe. Protokorinthisch. 3. Viertal 7. Jahrhundert. oberer Streifen: Krieger schreiten zum Kampf. Hirmer Fotoarchiv.*

Etruscans in Italy, who were under Near Eastern influence), and all contributed to the transformation of Greek society. The Greek alphabet served as the vehicle not only of Homer's poems but also (as we will see in Chapter 3) of a remarkable literary flowering in Ionia during the seventh and sixth centuries B.C. And while the new coinage was stimulating the economy, the increasing abundance of iron enabled people of relatively modest means to purchase the armor that Greeks trading on the Phoenician coast first saw Assyrian soldiers wearing. By the early seventh century B.C., Greek cities were fielding armies of well-drilled, mailed foot soldiers called *hoplites*.

The new infantrymen wielded iron swords and 9-foot pikes, and they fought in a tight formation known as a *phalanx*, usually eight ranks deep. Each man's shield also covered the comrade on his left, making interdependence and mutual trust essential. With strict discipline and constant training, hoplites could defeat mounted warriors. No longer would everything depend on the hand-to-hand single combat in which aristocratic heroes (above all Homer's) had exulted; such derring-do survived only in the aristocratic cavalry arm that the Greeks still maintained but now used mainly for scouting or mopping-up operations. The advent of the hoplite coincided with important political changes within Greek society. Mounted aristocrats were losing their

preeminent military role and thus their claim to exclusive political leadership. Hoplites who fought for the polis began to demand a voice in running it.

By about 550 B.C. the best sites had been occupied and colonization was waning. The rise of new powers—Carthage in the west and Lydia and Persia in the east—blocked further expansion. As the safety valve closed, old pressures of economic and social discontent returned. One after another the poleis plunged into civil strife as ordinary people contended with the wealthy and privileged. In many instances these conflicts ended in the overthrow of aristocratic control by the tyrant who, like some of his modern counterparts, claimed to govern in the interests of "the people." One of the earliest and most important examples of **tyranny** arose in sixth-century Corinth, a flourishing commercial city that had taken an early lead in developing Greek pottery and painting, as well as in colonizing. Not surprisingly, the struggle of rich and poor was also intense in Corinth, and tyranny was its outcome.

To the Greeks a tyrant was not necessarily an evil ruler—just one who rose to power without hereditary or legal right. (The word probably came from the language of the Anatolian kingdom of Lydia, and meant "king.") Typically, tyrants did not smash the machinery of government but merely brought it under their control. Most tyrants were ambitious, disaffected aristocrats who were prepared to question the traditional aristocratic control of the polis for the sake of their personal advantage. Attuned to the currents of their age, they used the new coined money to hire hoplite mercenaries and manipulated social discontent to their own ends. Since most of them depended on the backing of commoners, they sought to capture mass support by canceling or scaling down debts, sponsoring impressive public works projects (temples, city walls, water and drainage systems), giving aristocratic lands to commoners, and shifting tax burdens from the poor to the wealthy.

In most Greek communities tyranny proved ephemeral. Some tyrants were overthrown by the older privileged classes. The early Corinthian tyranny, for example, lasted two generations before succumbing to a stable **oligarchy** that endured for centuries. Others succumbed to the middle and lower classes who, as they became increasingly self-confident, grew tired of being manipulated and sought to control politics directly. By the opening of the fifth century B.C., Greek political structure included every imaginable configuration of upper-, lower-, and middle-class rule.

Sparta

The two dominant poleis of the fifth century—Dorian Sparta and Ionian Athens—stood at opposite ends of the Greek political spectrum. Neither played an important role in colonization, for both controlled extensive territories in their own districts. Athens evolved through the traditional stages of monarchy, aristocracy, tyranny, and democracy, but Sparta developed a peculiarly mixed political system that discouraged commerce, cultural inventiveness, and the amenities of life for the sake of rigid discipline and military efficiency.

Back in the eighth and seventh centuries B.C., Sparta had undergone much the same political and social changes as other Greek city-states. It had displayed a lively culture, rich in poetry and pottery painting, and had played a vigorous role in the development of Greek civilization. Yet by 550 B.C. the Spartan spirit—always serious—had turned dour, and military concerns became central to Spartan life. The severity of its art and its Doric architecture contrasted sharply with the charming elegance of Ionia and the cultural dynamism of Attica. Politically, Sparta became rigidly conservative. The Spartans never relinquished their monarchy, but merely weakened it. With the rise of commoners, Sparta incorporated democratic features into its system, yet the monarchy and aristocracy endured. The Spartans could adapt cautiously to new conditions but found it impossible to forsake old institutions.

THE HISTORICAL EVIDENCE

The Excellence of a Hoplite

ca. 650 B.C.

The seventh-century B.C. poet Tyrtaeus, who may have been a Spartan and who certainly wrote poetry to inspire Spartan warriors during their all-out struggle to crush the Messenian rebels, composed these memorable verses on what it meant to fight for one's polis as a hoplite. (It should not be forgotten, of course, that the Spartans were fighting to keep the equally valiant Messenians enslaved.)

For no man ever proves himself a good man in war
  unless he can endure to face the blood and the slaughter,
  go close against the enemy and fight with his hands.
Here is courage, mankind's finest possession, here is
  the noblest prize that a young man can endeavor to win,
  and it is a good thing his city and all the people share with him
  when a man plants his feet and stands in the foremost spears
  relentlessly, all thought of foul flight completely forgotten,
  and has well trained his heart to be steadfast and to endure,
  and with words encourages the man who is stationed beside him.
Here is a man who proves himself to be valiant in war.
With a sudden rush he turns to fight the rugged battalions
  of the enemy, and sustains the beating waves of assault.
And he who so falls among the champions and loses his sweet life,

so blessing with honor his city, his father, and all his people,
  with wounds in his chest, where the spear that he was facing has transfixed
  that massive guard of his shield, and gone through his breastplate as well,
  why, such a man is lamented alike by the young and the elders,
  and all his city goes in mourning and grieves for his loss. . . .
But if he escapes the doom of death, the destroyer of bodies,
  and wins his battle, and bright renown for the work of his spear,
  all men give place to him alike, the youth and the elders,
  and much joy comes his way before he goes down to the dead. . . .
Thus a man should endeavor to reach this high place of courage
  with all his heart, and, so trying, never be backward in war.

Source: From *Greek Lyrics*, 2nd ed., trans. Richmond Lattimore (Chicago: University of Chicago Press, 1961), pp. 14–15.

Toward the end of the eighth century B.C., when other Greek poleis were beginning to relieve their social unrest and land hunger by colonization, Sparta conquered the fertile neighboring district of Messenia, appropriating large portions of the conquered land for its own citizens and reducing many Messenians to a state of slavery identical to that of the Spartans' own slaves back in their homeland—some of whom may have lost their freedom during the original Dorian settlements. The Spartans' slaves, now including the Messenians, were known as *helots*. A Spartan poet likened them to "asses worn down by intolerable loads," and a modern scholar described them as "little better off than farm animals." As Dorian Greeks, they were ethnically and linguistically identical to their Spartan masters, whom they outnumbered by more than 10 to 1. And they did not accept their servitude placidly. In the late seventh century B.C. they revolted, and the Spartans crushed them only after a desperate struggle. It became clear that Sparta could keep its helots enslaved only through massive military force and constant watchfulness. Accordingly, the Spartans transformed their polis into a garrison state whose citizens became a standing army. Culture declined to the level of the barracks; the good life meant endless boot camp.

Sparta thus became a tense, humorless society dedicated to perpetuating the status quo by force. Fear of helot rebellion grew into a collective obsession, as some nine thousand Spartan citizens assumed the never-ending task of keeping about one hundred thousand proud and restless Greek helots in permanent slavery. Young Spartans were sometimes permitted to kill helots as a military training exercise. Somewhat better off was a group of free noncitizens, the *perioikoi*, who were excluded from political participation but were indispensable because they engaged in commercial activities forbidden to Spartan citizens. The Spartan state divided its lands into lots, one for each citizen, and the helots who worked these lots relieved the citizens of all economic responsibility, freeing them to pursue military training and to serve in the army. Women were denied citizenship, but they were freer than in most other Greek cities. They could own land, manage farms, and engage in business. Public education was also provided for them, something Athens would never see fit to do, although Spartan girls were educated only to be the wives and mothers of soldiers. They, along with the perioikoi and the helots, were expected to preserve male citizens from all nonmilitary distractions.

Ancient writers credited the Spartan political system to a semilegendary, seventh-century lawgiver named Lycurgus, who could not possibly have done all the things attributed to him. Although it drew from earlier Spartan traditions, the system had such rigorous logical consistency as to suggest the hand of a single designer. Sparta had two kings, whose powers had been much reduced by the sixth century B.C. One or the other of them commanded every military campaign, but at home they shared authority with three political bodies: (1) an aristocratic council of elders consisting of twenty-eight men at least sixty years old, elected for life; (2) an executive board of five ephors, elected annually; and (3) an assembly of citizens, known as "equals," that included every eligible Spartan male over thirty. Since all Spartan citizens could vote in the assembly, Sparta was technically a democracy, but it could more accurately be described as an oligarchy, dominated by the twenty-eight elders and the two kings. The Spartan political system denied citizenship to many freemen, to all women, and of course to helots and perioikoi.

Moreover, the citizens' assembly was empowered to approve or disapprove questions of state only by acclamation, and its members were not permitted to debate the issues. The debating in the assembly was done by senior citizens of the oligarchy—not by brash young thirty-, forty-, and fifty-year-olds, who were expected to keep humbly silent. Accordingly, the assembly never became an arena of rough-and-tumble political conflict. In almost every instance, it either approved measures favored by the elders and kings or, less often, decided between evenly matched factions within the oligarchy. And it did not vote by a wimpy show of hands: The side that could shout the loudest carried the day.

The lives of Sparta's citizens were tended and guided by the polis from cradle to grave, always for the purpose of producing strong, courageous, highly disciplined soldiers. Spartans were famous for being "laconic"—for expressing what little they had to say with blunt brevity.[11] The introduction of alien styles, luxuries, and ideas was strongly discouraged. At a time when coinage was stimulating economic life elsewhere, Sparta continued to use cumbersome iron bars as its medium of exchange. Spartan citizens seldom left their homeland except on military expeditions, which rarely ventured beyond the Peloponnesus, and outsiders were discouraged from visiting Sparta. Puny or malformed infants were abandoned by order of state officials to die of exposure. (Such treatment of unwanted children was common in the ancient world, but it was usually the father's or some other male patriarch's decision, not the state's.) At the age of seven the Spartan boy left home for the barracks and spent his next thirteen years in a grueling program of military, physical, and psychological training: enduring hardships, terrorizing and killing helots for practice, and unquestioningly obeying the polis.

A boy was typically guided through this training program by a young adult citizen, who chose him as his lover. Often a powerful emotional bond would develop between the two. Once the youth reached adulthood he and his tutor would usually fight in the Spartan army side by side, as a team. Often, indeed, the citizen-tutor helped

---

[11] The word *laconic* refers to Lakonia, another name for Sparta and its surrounding region.

his protégé choose a wife. In Sparta, as throughout ancient Greece, homoerotic love was fully compatible with "manliness," marriage, and procreation.

Assuming that he had shaped up, the twenty-year-old Spartan entered the citizen army. This meant barracks life for another ten years. He might marry, but he could visit his wife only if he eluded the barracks guards (this seems to have been regarded as a test of skill). At thirty, if all went well, he became a full-fledged citizen. He could now live at home, but he ate his meals at a public mess to which he was obliged to contribute the produce of his assigned fields. The fare at these public messes was "spartan" in the extreme. Confessed one visitor, after trying to get down an infamous concoction called black broth (which contained a fair amount of animal blood): "Now I understand why the Spartans do not fear death."

The Spartan citizen had almost no individual existence; body and soul, he was dedicated to the polis. If the helot's life was hard, so was the citizen's. Life in Sparta might seem the absolute antithesis to the polis ideal of a free citizenry—yet many Greeks (who did not have to live under it) admired the Spartan regime. To them Sparta represented the ultimate in self-denial and commitment to a logical idea. The Greeks admired the ordered life, and nowhere was life more ordered than in Sparta. Greeks saw a crucial difference between the helot and the Spartan citizen: Helots endured hardships because they *had* to, citizens because they *chose* to. Nor did the Spartans use their military might to pursue imperialistic ambitions. Their superbly drilled hoplite armies were the finest in Greece, yet they employed them with restraint. To the accusation of artistic sterility a Spartan might reply that Sparta, with all its institutions directed toward the single aim of preserving its political order, was itself a work of art.

Athens

A settlement had existed on the site of Athens since Mycenaean times, but not until well past the dark age did it assume a leading role in Greek politics and culture. By about 700 B.C., Athenian kings had been deprived of political power by the aristocracy, which dominated affairs through a council of elders called the Areopagus. Early in its history, Athens had extended its authority over the entire district of Attica. But the free inhabitants of Attica became Athenian citizens, not Athenian slaves, and the district was held together by bonds of mutual allegiance. To be Attic was to be an Athenian.

The unification of Attica meant that the polis of Athens comprised a singularly extensive area, and consequently the Athenians suffered less severely from land hunger than many of their neighbors. Athens therefore sent out no colonists; yet lying only 4 miles from the coast, it was influenced by the revival of Greek commerce. Very slowly, new mercantile classes evolved. So did class ten-

sions—and in Athens, as in other Greek cities, the grievances of merchants and commoners, especially debt-ridden farmers, threatened aristocratic rule. But Athens avoided social revolution by gradually modifying its institutions, extending political participation first to smaller landowners, next to merchants and manufacturers, and finally to all citizens.

Solon and Pisistratus   In the early sixth century B.C. (the traditional date was 594) the Athenian polis granted extraordinary powers to an aristocrat named Solon to reform its laws. Solon's reforms left the preponderance of political power in the hands of the wealthy but nevertheless included measures of great benefit to farmers and urban commoners. His laws abolished enslavement for default of debts and freed all debtors who had previously been enslaved. He extended the right to Athenian citizenship significantly. And to give his new arrangements permanence, he described them in poetry—in this essentially oral culture, still the chief means for disseminating and remembering ideas.

Although he was the first Athenian reformer to challenge the aristocratic hold on government, Solon hardly qualifies as an idealistic benefactor. He came to power at a time of social turmoil, in which the poor evidently were threatening social revolution and the better-off were chafing under the rule of aristocrats who still excluded them from power. Solon's reforms ended the aristocrats' exclusive right to membership in the polis. Henceforth wealth—not ancestry—would be the basis for political participation, but even the poorest citizen would no longer fear enslavement for debt.

Solon's reforms divided Athenian citizens into four ranks, all of them defined by their wealth (based on agricultural production). Members of only the top two ranks could sit on the Areopagus, but men from the third rank down were included in the Council of Four Hundred—a new legislative body that had much less prestige than the Areopagus but exercised some control over it. Even the lowest rank of citizens could now participate in the popular Assembly—whose powers, however, were as yet limited. Solon also established popular courts whose judges were chosen by lot from among the entire citizenry without regard to wealth. For Athenians (who were always suspicious of rigged elections), selection by lot was simply a means of putting the choice into the hands of the gods. Its consequence was to raise to important offices men who were their own masters and owed nothing to wealthy and influential political backers.[12] On the whole, selection by

---

[12] Of course the system also produced a predictable quota of incompetents, but more recent history attests that the elective principle is by no means immune to that fault. Moreover, modern Americans still use a lottery system in choosing the juries that render verdicts on those accused of serious crimes.

THE HISTORICAL EVIDENCE

Solon Defends His Reforms

ca. 570s B.C.

In these verses Solon explains why he reformed the laws of Athens.

My purpose was to bring my scattered people back
    together. Where did I fall short of my design?
I call to witness at the judgment seat of time
    one who is noblest, mother of Olympian
    divinities, and greatest of them all, Black Earth.
I took away the mortgage stones stuck in her breast,
    and she, who was a slave before, is now set free.
    Into this sacred land, our Athens, I brought back
    a throng of those who had been sold, some by due
    law,
    though others wrongly; some by hardship pressed
    to escape
    the debts they owed; and some of these no longer
    spoke
Attic,* since they had drifted wide around the
    world,
    while those in the country had the shame of
    slavery
    upon them, and they served their masters' moods
    in fear.
These I set free; and I did this by strength of hand,
    welding right law with violence to a single whole.

So I have done, and carried through all that I
    pledged.
I have made laws, for the good man and the bad
    alike,
    and shaped a rule to suit each case, and set it
    down.
Had someone else not like myself taken the reins,
    some ill-advised or greedy person, he would not
    have held the people in. Had I agreed to do
    what pleased their adversaries at that time, or
    what
    they themselves planned to do against their
    enemies,
    our city would have been widowed of her men.
    Therefore,
I put myself on guard at every side, and turned
    among them like a wolf inside a pack of dogs.

---

*The Greek dialect of Attica, including Athens.

Source: From *Greek Lyrics*, 2nd ed., trans. Richmond Lattimore
(Chicago: University of Chicago Press, 1961), p. 22.

---

lot worked well in Athens and gradually became a characteristic feature of Athenian government.

Although Solon's laws did not transform Athens into
a democracy, they moved it in that direction by replacing
aristocratic control with timocracy—a political system in
which power is based on wealth rather than lineage. But
they did not go far enough for restless members of the
Athenian lower classes, who demanded an ever-increasing
degree of economic relief and political power. Their continued unrest plunged Athens into a brief bout of tyranny.

Between 561 and 527 B.C., a colorful and popular
tyrant named Pisistratus dominated the Athenian government. He was succeeded by two sons, who carried on their
father's policies of lavish building and giving jobs to the
poor, but with diminishing political popularity. A coalition
of exiled nobles, returning to Athens in 510 B.C. with a

Spartan army, drove the Pisistratid dynasty from power and
brought a permanent end to tyranny in Athens.

The Democratic Reforms of Cleisthenes   Some returning aristocrats sought to overturn the reforms of Pisistratus
and Solon and to reestablish aristocratic rule in all its
faded glory. Others, however, were willing to accept
diminished estates and popular rule in exchange for political stability. In the closing decade of the sixth century,
this more adaptable faction found its leader in the states-
manlike aristocrat Cleisthenes, who rose to power with
popular backing. Whether out of idealism or because he
needed popular support against his more conservative
rivals, Cleisthenes gave Athens a new, thoroughly democratic political system that became the foundation of the
Athenian "golden age."

Pisistratus and Sons

Like many tyrants, Pisistratus was nobly born and well liked. He was nevertheless a "tyrant," according to the ancient Greek definition of the word, because he seized power unconstitutionally. Twice he was expelled by rival aristocrats, but in 546 B.C. he returned from exile with an army and seized control of Athens for a third time. (This time, allegedly, he dressed the tallest woman he could find as the goddess Athena and claimed her special protection.) He remained in power until his death in 527, achieving the elusive goal of all despots: He died peacefully—in power and in bed.

Pisistratus was succeeded by his sons—Hipparchus, who was slain in a homosexual love quarrel in 514, and Hippias, who was overthrown and banished in 510 by an Athenian aristocratic faction with massive backing from Spartan troops. Pisistratus's luckless sons lacked their father's political skill, yet the general policies of all three Pisistratid tyrants were much the same. Although their dynasty came to power and remained in power without constitutional sanction, they otherwise retained most of Solon's laws. A number of aristocratic clans supported their regime with varying degrees of enthusiasm, but

the power of the Pisistratids rested ultimately on popular support.

Pisistratus actively courted the poorer people of Athens through a variety of measures. He granted them portions of the estates of exiled aristocratic rivals, thereby establishing Athenian agriculture on a much stabler and more democratic basis than before. He established Athenian commercial outposts on the waterway linking the Aegean and Black Seas, thereby taking the first crucial steps toward empire. He and his sons followed a cautious and restrained foreign policy and gave Athens peace, prosperity, and a degree of social and political harmony that it had long needed. By no later than 525 B.C., the dynasty had begun to coin the Athenian "owls" that were to become famous throughout the ancient world—silver coins with the head of Athena on one side and an owl symbolizing her wisdom on the other.

The Pisistratids were also great patrons of the arts. With their encouragement, poets and artists from throughout the Greek world flocked to Athens. Builders ornamented the Acropolis and the lower city alike with lavish new temples and other public buildings. Besides the aristocratic gods and goddesses of Olympus,

Pisistratus and his sons encouraged popular, non-Olympic cults such as the Eleusinian mysteries and the worship of the wine god Dionysus. It had become a tradition at the annual festival in the god's honor—the Dionysia—to include a dramatic performance by a chorus speaking in unison. In about 534, Pisistratus awarded a prize to the first tragic playwright who separated an actor from his chorus, thereby taking a giant step toward the great Greek dramas of the following century. The playwright's name, Thespis, survives in our own word *thespian*—an actor or, more specifically, an actor in a tragedy.

Pisistratus was thus the best of all possible tyrants. He made Athens a major artistic, religious, and commercial center. And he contributed significantly to the solution of the agrarian dilemma that had afflicted Attica for generations. Despite the moans and groans of some aristocratic families, the polis was at peace with itself at last. Although a dictator, he actually helped pave the way for the democratic regime that would arise within a generation of his death, in which ordinary people chose among policies presented to them by well-born orators. ❖

Until the time of Cleisthenes' reforms, loyalty to clan and tribe, and to their aristocratic leaders, had remained strong. But now Cleisthenes dealt a body blow to the tribes and clans by abolishing their military and political functions, preserving only their ceremonial roles. He also ended the participation in Athenian politics of traditional regions and localities, long centers of factional and aristocratic influence. He replaced them with new and artificial local units called *demes*, eventually numbering some 175, which were themselves clustered into ten new "tribes," replacing the traditional clan-dominated tribes of earlier times. Membership in the new tribes was no longer based on kinship. Each of them was made up of numerous demes scat-

tered throughout Attica. Consequently, members of every class—commercial, industrial, rural, and aristocratic—were more or less evenly divided among the ten tribes.

As in Sparta and elsewhere in Greece, political participation was limited to males, but in Athens it came to include every native-born freeman of eighteen years or over. (Citizenship was subsequently restricted to men whose parents were both Athenians.) The total politically active citizenry of mid-fifth century Athens has been estimated at about 55,000 men. Together with their wives, kinswomen, and children they would have numbered about 130,000. There were also some 70,000 free resident aliens called *metics* (including women and children), who often grew wealthy from the profits of commerce but who lacked all political rights. And there were nearly 100,000 slaves, many of them Greeks.

When we speak of Athenian democracy we must always remember that perhaps a quarter of the people living in Athens were enslaved, and that slaves, women, and metics had no voice in politics whatever. It is difficult but essential to understand that virtually *all* people in the ancient world accepted slavery as a necessary part of the natural order. People of good will urged that slaves be well treated; but since slavery was integral to the ancient economy, nobody proposed that it be abolished.

Scholars have disagreed sharply as to the degree to which Athens was democratic. Can *democracy* describe a society in which less than 20 percent of the population can vote and participate in government? On the other hand, political participation in Athens far exceeded that of any previous society in the ancient world, where slavery was also endemic and the concept of citizenship was unknown. Moreover, citizenship was far less exclusive in Athens than in Sparta; and with respect to the citizenry itself, Athens was more thoroughly democratic than any modern state. Citizens did not elect the legislators; they *were* the legislators.

Cleisthenes took bold steps toward the creation of a democratic regime by curtailing the powers of the Areopagus, opening the Council (now a Council of Five Hundred) to the participation of all ranks of citizens, and transforming the Assembly into a primary political force in the polis. Every matter of public policy was decided by the Assembly, whose membership included all Athenian citizens, from landless laborers to aristocrats. Although all citizens could participate in the Assembly, the somewhat smaller and more manageable Council of Five Hundred transacted day-to-day business.

Cleisthenes provided that every Athenian citizen over thirty was eligible for selection to the Council. It was made up of fifty men from each tribe, chosen annually by lot from a list of tribal nominees. Each of these fifty-man tribal groups served for one-tenth of a year. Their order of rotation was determined by a crude machine, which archaeologists have unearthed. It worked much like our modern bubble gum machines: A stone for each of the ten tribes was put in the machine, and each month one stone was released, preventing any tribe except the last from knowing in advance when its term would begin. Cleisthenes further provided that every day a different chairman for the fifty-man tribal panel be chosen by lot. His further provision that no man could serve on the Council more than twice led to the extraordinary result that between a quarter and a third of all male Athenian citizens had the experience of serving on the Council.

Selection by lot was an integral feature of the Athenian constitution, and as time went on it became more pervasive still. Most of the various magistrates and civil servants came to be selected by lot, for limited terms, and they were strictly responsible to the Council of Five Hundred and the Assembly. This was a citizen's government in every sense of the word—a government of amateurs rather than professional bureaucrats.

Neither Council nor Assembly could provide the long-range personal leadership essential to the well-being of the state. The Assembly was too unwieldy, the Council too circumscribed by rotation and lot. Consequently, Cleisthenes

Greek Workshop An Athenian black-figure vase painting dating from about 500 B.C. depicts a blacksmith and his helpers (slaves?) at work, with their finished products displayed as if for sale. *01.8035 Blacksmith's Shop. Black Figure Amphora, ca. 500–490 B.C. Greece, Athens. Ceramic H: 0.361 m. Diam: 0.259 m. Museum of Fine Arts, Boston, Henry Lillie Pierce Fund © Museum of Fine Arts, Boston. All rights reserved.*

provided for the annual election of a board of ten generals (*strategoi*), each of whom could stand for reelection repeatedly. Some scholars believe that the office of general was meant to be the chief office in the polis, and it soon became the *only* elected office. It was from this office that such celebrated leaders as Themistocles and Pericles directed Athenian affairs in the fifth century B.C.

The success of the Greek polis in achieving harmony between the individual and society was nowhere more complete than in Athens, the scene of man's first significant encounter with democracy (though not woman's). The great Athenian historian Thucydides celebrated this achievement in words he attributed, perhaps accurately, to Pericles, who was striving to rouse Athenian spirits at the outset of a daunting war with Sparta:

> Our constitution is called a democracy because it is in the hands not of the few but of the many. But our laws secure equal justice for all in their private disputes, not as a matter of privilege but as a reward of merit. . . . Alone of all states we regard a man who holds aloof from public life not as harmless but as useless. We deliberate in person all matters of policy, holding not that words and deeds go ill together but that acts are foredoomed to failure when undertaken undiscussed. . . . In short I say that Athens is the school of Hellas, and that her citizens yield to none, man for man, in independence of spirit, many-sidedness of attainment, and self-reliance in body and mind.[13]

Pericles and others who led democratic Athens until late in the fourth century B.C. were highly educated and wealthy men, often from the old aristocracy. How did they manage to retain the confidence of an Assembly that consisted overwhelmingly of ordinary Athenian artisans and farmers, who by majority vote made all the final decisions? Members of the Athenian elite had to be careful not to appear condescending or to flaunt their learning, just as rich Athenians had to avoid too public a display of their wealth. Wealthy men who failed to appear generous in footing the bill for civic festivals or architectural embellishments, or in making wartime contributions of money, risked becoming targets of lawsuits that could bankrupt them. Similarly, it was usually only well-trained orators of upper-class origin who addressed the Assembly, but if they advocated unpopular or unsuccessful policies they might well be fined or even exiled. Pursuing a political career, therefore, entailed a fair amount of risk, but men took it up in a spirit of aristocratic competition. Pericles was the boldest and most eloquent—and certainly the luckiest—of them all.

---

[13] From Pericles' Funeral Oration, in Thucydides, *History of the Peloponnesian War*. The translation follows that of Sir Alfred Zimmern with slight modifications.

CLASSICAL GREECE: ZENITH AND TRANSFORMATION

During the sixth century B.C., while Solon, Pisistratus, and Cleisthenes were transforming Athens into what eventually became a prosperous democracy, the cultural center of the Hellenic world was Ionia. There, on Anatolia's western shore, the Greeks were in direct contact with the ancient Near East. The results of this contact were fruitful indeed, for the Ionian Greeks adapted Near Eastern art, architecture, literature, and learning to their own distinctive outlook. They created a brilliant, elegant culture, more gracious and luxurious than any that existed in Greece itself. It was in this setting that Greek philosophy, science, and lyric poetry were born, which we will explore in Chapter 3. Ionian poleis underwent much the same political and economic developments as those of Greece, and by the sixth century B.C. the lower classes were attempting to diminish the control of aristocrats. In the Ionian city of Miletus, aristocrats and commoners went to the extreme of burning one another alive.

These social conflicts were affected drastically by the intervention of outside powers. During the 560s and 550s the coastal cities of Ionia fell one by one under Lydian control, and when Cyrus the Great conquered Lydia in 546 they passed into the Persian Empire. In 499 the Ionian cities rebelled against Persia and persuaded the Athenians to send twenty ships to aid them. But Athenian aid proved insufficient, and by 494 the Persians crushed the insurrection, punctuating their victory by sacking Miletus. Ionia's gamble for independence had failed, and Darius the Great of Persia swore vengeance on Athens. The Persian Wars, Herodotus observed, were precipitated by the sending of twenty ships.

The Persian Wars, 490–479 B.C.

In 490 B.C., Darius led an army across the Aegean to teach the Greeks a lesson. As was often the case, the Greeks, even in the face of this calamity, found it difficult to form a common front. The Spartans agreed to help Athens defend itself but delayed sending their army because of a religious observance. Athens had to face the Persians almost alone. The two armies met at Marathon in Attica, 26 miles from Athens (see Map 2-4), and the Athenian hoplites, fighting shoulder to shoulder for their homes and polis, won a brilliant victory: Sixty-four hundred Persians fell, whereas fewer than two hundred Greeks died. Legend has it that a Greek soldier, Philipides, ran back to Athens to announce the great victory, dropping dead of exhaustion as he delivered the news.

The Athenians did not win at Marathon by heroism alone. Although outnumbered, they were better armed (the Persians had shorter spears and wicker shields), and the Persian army lacked its accustomed cavalry. Nevertheless,

MAP 2-4
GREECE AT THE TIME OF THE PERSIAN WARS

the Athenian victory was a dazzling achievement. It won for Greece an invaluable ten-year postponement of the Persian threat and may indeed have helped preserve the world of the polis itself.

Understandably, the victory at Marathon generated in Athens a tremendous surge of pride and self-confidence—in its hoplites, its newly-minted democracy, and the superiority of its culture to that of "barbarians" (as the Greeks termed all non-Greeks).[14] The "king of kings," ruler of the world's greatest empire, had been humbled by a small army of free Athenian citizens. For such men, so it seemed, nothing was impossible. The epitaph attributed to the great Athenian dramatist Aeschylus includes no mention of his surpassing literary achievements but only the proud claim that he had fought at Marathon.

The buoyant optimism that filled Athens in the wake of Marathon was tempered by the sobering knowledge that the Persians were not good losers and were likely to return in far greater numbers. Darius spent his last years planning a devastating new attack against Greece, but when the second invasion came, in 480, it was led by his son and successor, Xerxes. A Persian army of some 180,000 fighting men, stupendous by the standards of the age, moved by land around the northern Aegean shore supported by a powerful armada.

Xerxes had paved his way into Greece by alliances with opportunistic Greek cities such as Argos and Thebes. In the meantime Athens had been preparing for the onslaught under the enterprising leadership of Themistocles, a statesman of great strategic imagination who saw

clearly that the one hope for Athens was to build a strong fleet and seize control of the Aegean from the Persian Empire. By the time Xerxes led his forces into Greece, Themistocles' fleet was ready.

Sparta had by now awakened to the danger of a Persian conquest and was perhaps also worried about Athens winning further prestige from another single-handed victory. During the sixth century, Sparta had established a regional defensive alliance known as the Peloponnesian League, and by the century's end nearly every state in the Peloponnesus had joined it, including the wealthy commercial polis of Corinth. Each member had one vote, but Sparta alone had the privilege of summoning and presiding over the league's assembly and was usually able to dominate it. Now, in the shadow of Xerxes' invasion, representatives of the Peloponnesian states met at Corinth with delegates from Athens and other poleis. Here they agreed to form a much larger organization—the Pan-Hellenic League—to coordinate the common defense.

As Xerxes moved southward through northern Greece, a small army of Spartans and other Greeks led by the Spartan king Leonidas opposed the Persians at Thermopylae, a narrow pass between sea and mountains through which Xerxes' host had to move before breaking into the south (refer again to Map 2-4). The Persians found that their immense numerical superiority was of little use on so restricted a battlefield and that man for man they could not match the Greek hoplites. But at length a Greek turncoat led a contingent of Persians along a poorly defended path through the mountains to the rear of the Greek position. Now completely surrounded, the Greeks continued to fight—and died to the last man.

Although the battle of Thermopylae was a defeat for the Spartans, it became a long-remembered symbol of their

---

[14] The Greek word *barbarian* alluded to the Greeks' belief that all foreign languages sounded like gibberish—"bar-bar." The modern English equivalent is "It's all Greek to me."

courage. The inscription that was later placed over their graves is a model of dignified understatement:

> Tell them the news in Sparta, passer by,
> That here, obedient to their words, we lie.[15]

Much delayed, Xerxes' army now moved on Athens. The Athenians, at Themistocles' bidding, evacuated Attica and took refuge elsewhere, some in the Peloponnesus, others on the island of Salamis just off the Attic coast. The refugees on the island had to sit by helplessly as the Persians plundered Athens and burned the temples on the Acropolis. But Themistocles' strategy was vindicated when the Greek and Persian fleets fought a decisive naval engagement in the Bay of Salamis. The bay provided insufficient room for the huge Persian armada to maneuver, and the smaller but heavier Greek fleet, with the new Athenian navy as its core, pulled alongside the Persian ships and overwhelmed their crews in hand-to-hand combat.

Xerxes, who witnessed the disaster from a rocky headland, ordered his army to withdraw to northern Greece for the winter. He himself departed for Asia, never to return. In the following spring (479) a pan-Hellenic army under Spartan command routed the Persians at Plataea on the northern frontier of Attica. And shortly afterwards the Greeks won a final victory over the war-torn remnants of the Persian army and fleet at Cape Mycale in Ionia. Now, one after another, the Ionian cities broke loose from Persian control. Hellas had preserved its independence and was free to pursue its own destiny.

Ironically, Themistocles fell victim to political infighting shortly after his triumph at Salamis and had to flee Athens. He ended his days in the service of the king of Persia.

The Athenian Empire

The Greek world in 479 B.C., lacking our hindsight, could not be certain that the Persian invasions were truly over. Consequently, a number of cities including Athens were reluctant to dissolve the wartime alliance of Greek poleis that had served them so well against the common enemy. Sparta, always fearful of a helot revolt and reluctant to keep its forces far from home, withdrew from the alliance, along with the other cities of the Peloponnesian League. But the Athenians were unwilling to lower their guard. They were convinced that a large fleet had to be kept in readiness for the defense of Greece, and such a fleet could not be maintained by Athens alone. In 477 a new alliance emerged under Athenian leadership that included most of the maritime poleis on the coasts and islands of the Aegean from Attica to Ionia.

The alliance is known as the Delian League because its headquarters and treasury were on the island of Delos, an ancient pan-Hellenic religious center in the Aegean Sea. Its goals were not only to defend Greece but also to attack the Persians, which it did with considerable success in subsequent years. Athens and a few other cities contributed ships to the Delian fleet; the remaining members contributed money. All were entitled to a voice and a vote in the affairs of the league, but Athens, with its superior wealth and power, gradually became the senior partner.

Slowly the Delian League evolved into an Athenian Empire. In 454 B.C. the league's treasury was transferred from Delos to Athens, where some of its funds were diverted to the welfare and adornment of Athens itself. The Athenians justified this financial wizardry with the argument that their fleet remained always vigilant and ready to protect league members from Persian attacks, and that Xerxes had, after all, burned their temples. These explanations were not always received sympathetically by other league members. A party of touring Ionians visiting Athens might well admire the magnificent new structures rising on the Acropolis, but their admiration would be chilled by the realization that their own cities were contributing to the building fund.

When some members tried to withdraw from the league, they quickly discovered that Athens regarded secession as illegal and was ready to enforce the continued membership of disillusioned poleis through military action. With the development of this policy in the 460s, and the relocation of the treasury in 454, the transformation from Delian League to Athenian Empire was complete.

The half-century between Salamis and the outbreak of the Peloponnesian War was the Athenian golden age (480–431 B.C.). The empire rose and flourished, bringing Athens unimagined wealth, not only from imperial assessments but also from the splendid commercial opportunities offered by Athenian domination of the Aegean. Athens was now the commercial hub of the eastern Mediterranean world and the great power in Greece.

The Golden Age

The economic and imperialistic foundations of Athens' golden age are important to us chiefly as a backdrop for the cultural explosion that has echoed through the millennia of Western civilization. Through a rare and elusive conjunction of circumstances, a group of some fifty-five thousand politically conscious Athenian citizens created in the decades after Salamis a unique, many-sided culture of superb taste and unsurpassed excellence. The culture of the golden age of Athens was anticipated in the sixth century B.C. and even earlier, and the creativity continued into the fourth century and beyond. But for many modern observers, the zenith of Greek culture occurred in imperial Athens around the time of Pericles, in the middle decades

---

[15] The probable author of this magnificent epigram, Simonides, was not a Spartan. Poets do not flourish in a barracks state.

Aspasia

In the male-dominated society of classical Greece, two of the most important careers open to women were those of priestess and prostitute, and these two careers could be closely intertwined. The most famous of all prostitutes (*hetairai*) in classical Greece was Aspasia, born around 470 B.C. to the wife of a citizen of the prosperous Ionian city of Miletus. Since Greek towns normally forbade free women to become prostitutes, it has been conjectured that Aspasia's parents dedicated her as a child to a temple of Aphrodite, goddess of love, to be trained to become a temple prostitute. Such a parental decision must be seen in the context of an age that would have regarded it as an act of piety, and in which unwanted infants—female ones in particular—might lawfully be abandoned by their parents to die of exposure or be found, raised, and sold by a slave dealer.

Temple prostitution was viewed as an honorable profession—indeed, a holy one. But the prostitutes were nevertheless slaves of their temples. At some point early in her career Aspasia gained her freedom, probably as a gift from an admirer, and set up her own practice. As a young woman of beauty and keen intelligence, she soon won the affection of some of Miletus's leading citizens. It was probably while she was still in her early or mid-twenties that Aspasia joined the growing flood of immigrants into imperial Athens, which was prospering enormously amid Pericles' great building program. In Athens she established an upper-class "house of assignation" and staffed it with young women carefully chosen for their beauty, wit, and charm. In time the house of Aspasia became celebrated throughout the Greek world—not only for the beauty of Aspasia and her girls but also for the distinction

of their clientele and the brilliance of the intellectual discourse between men and women that went on there. In classical Greek society such male-female meetings could occur in no other context. Aspasia's house became a favorite meeting place of Athens's leading politicians, artists, and playwrights. The elderly philosopher Socrates became a close friend of Aspasia's and dropped in often to converse with her.

Pericles himself fell deeply in love with Aspasia. He could not legally marry her because the law provided that Athenian citizens could marry only the daughters of citizens. But he divorced his wife and took Aspasia as his constant companion, and by 441 B.C. she had borne him a son and namesake. Her fame now reached new heights, but her position at Pericles' side also drew much hostile comment from citizens who suspected that the course of Athenian

of the fifth century. Chapter 3 will examine this extraordinary cultural flowering more closely.

Despite its dazzling achievements, the golden age of Athens was no **utopia.** The architecture and sculpture of the Acropolis, the tragic dramas, and the probing philosophical speculation were produced against the familiar human background of petty politics and commercial greed, and in a society based, like others of its time, on large-scale slavery. The status of women was as low or lower in Periclean Athens than at any other time or place in Greco-Roman antiquity. In Sparta and other Dorian cities women could own property; in Athens they could not.[16]

Pericles exercised authority in democratic Athens through his position on the board of generals, to which he was elected for fifteen consecutive years (and thirty times

altogether) between 461 and his death in 429. This official authority, which he shared with nine other *strategoi* on the board, was enhanced by his great personal popularity and prestige—as an aristocrat of the most noble lineage who was also a person of keen intelligence, iron integrity, and democratic views. And the fact that Athenian citizens accepted and endorsed his leadership for some three decades illustrates the remarkable equilibrium between aristocratic statesmanship and popular sovereignty achieved in the golden age. Even Pericles, however, was subject to the Athenian Assembly. He could exercise his authority only by persuasion or political manipulation.

Under the authority of Pericles, Athens became more thoroughly democratic than ever before. All public offices and council positions were opened to every adult male citizen. Pericles sponsored a law providing pay for members of juries, thereby enabling the poor to perform this important function. Because every judicial decision could be appealed to a popular court selected from an annual panel of jurors, this body too came to include citizens of all ranks. As a further expression of popular sovereignty, a

---

[16] Writing in the fourth century B.C. for an Athenian audience, the philosopher Aristotle criticized Sparta mainly for giving its women too much power. Aristotle, incidentally, offered no criticism of Sparta's treatment of its helots, and he forthrightly justified slavery.

polities was being influenced by a foreigner and, worse yet, a woman. The comic poet Cratinus, taking full advantage of Athens's freedom of speech, attacked Aspasia viciously as "Pericles' dog-eyed whore." Rumors circulated that Aspa-

#671.9204.   *Hirmer Fotoarchiv.*

sia was helping Pericles write his political speeches or even, as Plato later alleged, ghostwriting some of them for him. To the citizens of Periclean Athens, politics was a man's game, and women had no business writing speeches or pulling strings behind the scenes. Today it is quite impossible to sort fact from rumor; we will never know to what degree Aspasia influenced policies, diplomacy, and political oratory during the golden age of Athens.

Shortly after the onset of the Peloponnesian War in 431 B.C., a plague carried off both of Pericles' sons by his ex-wife, leaving only his son by Aspasia, to whom Athenian law denied citizenship. Pericles humbly pleaded with members of the Athenian Assembly to grant him a legal heir by extending citizenship to Aspasia's son and, pitying their bereaved leader, they did so. Pericles died

in 429, and in later years his son, also named Pericles, became a statesman and general.

Aspasia afterward became the companion of a wealthy wool dealer named Lysicles, who, perhaps not coincidentally, was one of the earliest non-noble merchants to strive for the political leadership of Athens. Aspasia and Lysicles presented a standing target for the barbs of comic poets, who could now give expression to their prejudices against both women and tradesmen in politics. How, they asked, could an unschooled merchant whose intellectual horizons had once been limited to sheep and wool suddenly become a great political orator? Aspasia, they said, was giving him a crash course in rhetoric. Perhaps she did.

Lysicles became an Athenian general and died fighting in Anatolia. After his death Aspasia drops from historical view, and we do not know how her life ended. Nevertheless, for a number of years she was a unique figure in classical Athens—a woman who exercised political power and influence, and not simply through her beauty, charm, and sex appeal.

procedure known as "ostracism," which was intended to discourage political strife and power-grabbing, had entered the Athenian political process not long before Pericles' ascendancy: Each year, any Athenian citizen might propose the name of a person whom he considered a threat to the well-being of the polis. If at least 6,000 votes were cast, the Assembly banished for ten years whoever received the most votes.

Pericles maintained the support alike of the Athenian citizen-merchants and of poorer Athenians by staunchly advocating empire building. Well-to-do Athenian citizens profited enormously from the empire's merchant trade, but humble citizens whose only asset was a strong back found steady employment and maybe even a little profit in serving as rowers in the Athenian fleet. Citizens at both ends of the economic spectrum could enjoy lording it over "foreigners"—the metics who came to Athens to work or make money, but who were forever barred from citizenship, as well as of those who were citizens merely of the Athenians' subordinate allies. Empire made every patriotic Athenian breast swell with pride.

On every other Greek, Athenian imperialism grated. Almost inevitably, it sparked the hostility of Sparta and its Peloponnesian League. Corinth, the league's second greatest power and Athens's chief mercantile rival, was especially alarmed. In 433 B.C. a complex dispute arose between Corinth and Athens, which in 431 escalated into all-out war between the Peloponnesian League and the Athenian Empire. It was a war that Pericles would have much preferred to avoid—a protracted, agonizing struggle that ultimately destroyed the Athenian Empire and shook the Greek political structure to its foundations.

The Peloponnesian War, 431–404 B.C.

For the most part the Peloponnesian War was a matter of a whale fighting a tiger. Athens was invincible by sea, Sparta by land. When the Spartans marched into Attica year after year to devastate the fields, the population would withdraw behind Athens's ramparts—which included a parallel pair of long and virtually impenetrable walls extending four miles overland to the port of Piraeus. These walls linked

A Trireme   Athenian ships, called triremes from their three decks of oars, required many rowers, as this modern replica shows. Manning these ships (which were used both for war and for trade) gave work to ordinary Athenian citizens, who eagerly supported imperialism. © *Mike Andrews/Ancient Art & Architecture Collection.*

Athens to its fleet and therefore to the commercial wealth of the eastern Mediterranean, so the Athenians could live indefinitely on imported foodstuffs.

Democratic Athens and regimented Sparta represented two contrary political systems, and each tended to reproduce its own political structure in the states dependent on it. Sparta encouraged oligarchy throughout the Peloponnesus, whereas Athens was inclined to favor democratic factions within the cities of its empire. Yet the Peloponnesian War was not so much an ideological conflict as a simple power struggle. The Athenians were bent on preserving and extending their empire, especially in Sicily; Sparta and its allies were determined to end the threat of Athenian imperialism. Athens was coming to be regarded as a despot among some of the states of its own empire; but the Athenian fleet that patrolled the Aegean discouraged rebellion. Paradoxically, the "mother of democracies" was driven to ever more repressive expedients to hold its empire together (see Map 2-5).

In 430 and 429 B.C., Athens, crowded with refugees from throughout Attica, was struck by a plague that wiped out perhaps a quarter of its population, including Pericles himself. The loss of this far-sighted statesman, combined with the terrible shock of the plague, led to a rapid deterioration in the quality of Athenian government. Leadership passed to hotheads, and the democracy acquired the worst characteristics of mob rule. A general who, through no fault of his own, failed to win some battle might be sent into exile. (Such was the experience of the great Athenian historian-general, Thucydides.) In 416 B.C. the Athenians seized the island of Melos, an innocent neutral in the struggle, and proceeded to slaughter all its men and enslave its women and children.

Pericles had confessed on the eve of the war that he was more afraid of Athens's mistakes than of Sparta's designs. His fear was well founded, for as the war progressed along its dreary course, Athenian strategy grew increasingly reckless. Most of the Athenian fleet was lost when two ill-planned expeditions against Syracuse—far to the west in Sicily—both ended in disaster. As Athens's grip on the Aegean loosened, its subject cities began to rebel, and at length a Peloponnesian fleet, financed in

MAP 2-5

THE ATHENIAN EMPIRE AND THE PELOPONNESIAN WAR

part by Persian gold, destroyed what was left of the Athenian navy and choked off the city's overseas food supply.

In 404 the Athenians surrendered—their wealth lost, their spirit broken, their empire in ruins. Although Athens remained the intellectual and cultural center of the Greek world—it even make an economic and political comeback—its years of imperial supremacy were over.

AFTERMATH: THE FOURTH CENTURY B.C. AND THE MACEDONIAN CONQUEST

In political terms, the sixty-six years between the end of the Peloponnesian War in 404 and the Macedonian conquest of Greece in 338 form a complicated era of chaos and anticlimax. (Culturally, as we shall see in Chapter 3, this was an age of brilliant achievement.) The end of the

THE HISTORICAL EVIDENCE

The Athenians' Sicilian Disaster

413 B.C.

The tragic climax to the historian Thucydides' great history of the Peloponnesian War is an analysis of the demagogic politics that induced the Athenians to attack Syracuse, and a harrowing account of their defeat in 413 B.C. The politicians who planned the attack had glibly claimed that they could easily turn Sicily into a permanent source of food and wealth for Athens. But few of the Athenian citizen-soldiers who went to Sicily ever came back. The following passage describes the trapped Athenian army's desperate attempt to escape after their siege of Syracuse failed and their ships were destroyed.

It was a lamentable scene, not merely from the single circumstance that they were retreating after having lost all their ships, their great hopes gone, and themselves and the state [Athens] in peril; but also in leaving the camp there were things most grievous for every eye and heart to contemplate. The dead lay unburied, and each man as he recognized a friend among them shuddered with grief and horror; while the living whom they were leaving behind, wounded or sick, were to the living far more shocking than the dead, and more to be pitied than those who had perished. These fell to entreating and bewailing until their friends knew not what to do, begging them to take them and loudly calling to each individual comrade or relative whom they could see, hanging upon the necks of their tent-fellows in the act of departure, and following as far as they could, and when their bodily strength failed them, calling again and again upon heaven and shrieking aloud as they were left behind. So that the whole army being filled with tears and distracted after this fashion found it not easy to go, even from an enemy's land, where they had already suffered evils too great for tears and in the unknown future before them feared to suffer more.

Dejection and self-condemnation were also rife among them. Indeed they could only be compared to a starved-out town, and that no small one, escaping; the whole multitude upon the march being not less than forty thousand men. All carried anything they could which might be of use, and the heavy infantry and troopers, contrary to their wont, while under arms carried their own victuals, in some

cases for want of servants, in others through not trusting them; as they had long been deserting and now did so in greater numbers than ever. Yet even thus they did not carry enough, as there was no longer food in the camp. Moreover their disgrace generally, and the universality of their sufferings, however to a certain extent alleviated by being borne in company, were still felt at the moment a heavy burden, especially when they contrasted the splendour and glory of their setting out [from Athens] with the humiliation in which it had ended.

For this was by far the greatest reverse that ever befell an Hellenic army. They had come to enslave others, and were departing in fear of being enslaved themselves: they had sailed out with prayers and paeans,* and now started to go back with omens directly contrary; travelling by land instead of by sea, and trusting not in their fleet but in their heavy infantry.

Sadly for the Athenians, their ultimate fate was even worse. Thucydides goes on to narrate how those who did not die in the retreat were killed after their surrender, enslaved, or perished of hunger and thirst while penned up as prisoners in a quarry.

---

*Exultant hymns of victory or praise.

Source: Thucydides, *The Peloponnesian War*, Section 75. Trans. Richard Crawley (London: J. M. Dent [Everyman's Library Edition], 1910), pp. 404–405.

Peloponnesian War left the polis system drained of vitality and demoralized by intercity warfare. Athens's surrender made Sparta dominant in the Greek world—but only for a generation. The victorious Spartan fleet had been built largely with Persian money, and Sparta paid its debt by allowing Persia to reoccupy Ionia. The Spartans were too unimaginative to be good imperialists, and their armies had shrunk after incurring enormous casualties in the Peloponnesian War. For a time they tried establishing oligarchic regimes throughout the former Athenian empire—indeed, a particularly nasty one ruled Athens itself—but they proved unable to give Hellas any leadership.

Fourth-century Greek political history is a bewildering period of military strife and shifting hegemonies. For a brief period Thebes rose to supremacy. Then Athens began to form a new Aegean league but was foiled by Persian intervention. In the middle decades of the fourth century B.C. power tended to shift between Sparta, Athens, and Thebes, while the Athenians' nemesis, Syracuse, dominated Sicily and southern Italy. Envoys from Persia, always well supplied with money, saw to it that no state became too powerful. A Greece divided and wracked by warfare could be no threat to the Persian Empire.

The oligarchy that the Spartans imposed on defeated Athens made itself infamous for its purges of democratic politicians (who had not given democracy a good name during the war's later stages), but it was soon overthrown. The Athenian democracy returned—one of its first actions being to execute the unpopular philosopher Socrates, whom people identified both with slick-talking intellectual radicals and with discredited oligarchs—and it flourished vigorously for most of the fourth century (see Chapter 3). This time no rich empire sustained it, proof that belief in democracy had penetrated deeply into the Athenians' political consciousness. But the quality of democratic politics had deteriorated badly. Oratorical competition between elite politicians degenerated into eloquent mud-slinging, each protesting that he alone was virtuous and that his rival was in the pay of some sinister special interest.

Ironically, Persia's diplomacy opened the way for an event that it had been determined at all costs to avoid: the establishment of hegemony over Greece by a single power. The debilitating intercity wars left Greece unprepared for the intervention of a new threat on its northern frontier. Macedon (or Macedonia) was a kingdom whose inhabitants, although ethnically Greek, lagged far behind other Greeks in political and cultural development. It was a warrior kingdom evoking the days of Homer's heroes. In 359 B.C. a talented opportunist named Philip grabbed the throne of Macedon by murdering all his rivals. With great political astuteness he tamed and unified the Macedonian tribes, secured his northern frontiers, and then began a patient and artful campaign to dominate Greece.

Having spent three years of his boyhood as a hostage in Thebes, Philip of Macedon had acquired a full appreciation of both Greek culture and Greek political instabil-

Philip of Macedon The mines of Macedonia kept Philip well supplied with gold, which he used liberally to hire mercenary soldiers and Greek intellectuals—and to bribe politicians in the Greek cities that he wished to control. This gold piece shows a fine likeness of the king, but not the eye that he lost in an assassination attempt. *#13.0564 V. Gold coin (observe) of Philip II. Hirmer Fotoarchiv.*

ity. He hired the great philosopher Aristotle to tutor his son Alexander. He fought, bluffed, and cajoled his way into the south, accompanying his conquests with repeated declarations of peaceful intentions. And when at last Athens and Thebes resolved their ancient rivalry and joined forces against him, it was too late. At Chaeronea in 338 B.C., Philip won the decisive battle and Greece lay at his mercy.

Philip allowed the Greek city-states to run their internal affairs, but he organized them into a league whose policies he manipulated. Distrusted by the Macedonians, Athenian democracy came to an inglorious end. With the subordination of Greek independence to the will of King Philip, the classical age of Greek history was over. The accession of Philip's illustrious son Alexander launched a new age that would spread Greek culture throughout the Near East and transform Greek life into something drastically different.

CONCLUSION: THE GREEK WAY OF LIFE

Ancient Greece produced a way of life that has never been attempted anywhere else in the history of the world. Its uniqueness lay not in its experiments with democracy, but in its combination of intimate scale and formidable power.

The Greek polis demanded a total commitment *from* its citizens, yet never (except Sparta) did such a demand translate into total control *over* the citizenry.

What saved the poleis from **totalitarianism** was the other essential characteristic of Greek life: its competitiveness. Instead of allowing the state to control him for its own ends, the Greek citizen vied with his fellow citizens in displaying his individual excellence for the community's benefit and admiration. This was true even in Sparta, and indeed can be considered that otherwise grim commonwealth's saving grace.

Some periods in the subsequent history of Western civilization—the eighteenth and nineteenth centuries, for example—accorded the ancient Greeks uncritical admira-

tion. That was a mistake. Ancient Greece was no paradise for slaves, women, or the victims of its frequent wars. Athenian democracy may have stimulated a brilliant culture during the fifth century B.C., but during the fourth century it decayed into a mixture of demagoguery, corruption, and indecisiveness, and not many mourned its passing. Nor did the polis system have that essential characteristic of an ideal—permanence. No one has ever succeeded in recreating the polis way of life; nor, as we embark on another millennium, does it seem to be the wave of any foreseeable future. The greatest significance of the ancient polis is that it was the setting in which classical Greek culture came into focus, and indeed was essential to that culture—to which we turn in Chapter 3.

Selected Reading

Sources

When reading Greek literature, history, and philosophy, find good, modern English translations. For Chapter 2, Homer, Herodotus, and Thucydides are the indispensable authors. Also of great value are:

Fornara, Charles W., ed. and trans. *Archaic Times to the End of the Peloponnesian War*, 2nd ed. (1983).

Lefkowitz, Mary R., and Maureen B. Frant, eds. and trans. *Women's Life in Greece and Rome*, 2nd ed. (1982).

Rhodes, P. J., ed. and trans. *The Greek City-States: A Source Book* (1986).

Sweet, Waldo E. *Sport and Recreation in Ancient Greece* (1987).

General and Reference Works

Boardman, John, Jasper Griffin, and Oswyn Murray, eds. *The Oxford History of the Classical World* (1986); the Greek chapters have been published as *The Oxford History of Greece and the Hellenistic World* (1991). More compact than *The New Cambridge Ancient History*, but stimulating and authoritative.

Cartledge, Paul. *The Greeks* (1993). Explores how Greeks attempted to differentiate themselves from others.

Fine, John V. A. *The Ancient Greeks* (1983). A splendid and fairly detailed history, emphasizing the rise of the polis.

Finley, Moses I. *The Ancient Greeks*, rev. ed. (1977). A masterful general history.

Green, Peter. *Ancient Greece: An Illustrated History* (1979). Masterful.

Kebric, Robert B. *Greek People* (1989). Interestingly unconventional social history.

Kitto, H. D. F. *The Greeks*, rev. ed. (1964). Elegant, witty, and wise; one of the best short introductions to ancient Greece ever written.

New Cambridge Ancient History, The (7 volumes to date, 1970 ff.). Immensely detailed and authoritative; to be consulted on specific topics.

Crete, Mycenae, and the Dark Age

Chadwick, John. *The Decipherment of Linear B*, 2nd ed. (1967). Discusses the achievement of Michael Ventris in cracking the code, and the new world that it disclosed.

———. *The Mycenaean World* (1976). A fine overview by a pioneering scholar, stressing social and economic history.

Drews, Robert. *The Coming of the Greeks: Indo-European Conquests in the Aegean and the Near East* (1988). A controversial approach that challenges traditional scholarship by locating the Indo-European homeland in Armenia and by dating the Indo-European entry into Greece to around 1600 B.C.

———. *The End of the Bronze Age: Changes in Warfare and the Catastrophe ca. 1200 B.C.* (1993). A similarly groundbreaking account of the downfall of the Mycenaean world and the onset of the ancient "dark age" in the eastern Mediterranean.

Finley, M. I. *The World of Odysseus*, 2nd ed. (1982). A penetrating work of synthesis, showing how much can be learned from Homer.

Fitton, J. Leslie. *The Discovery of the Greek Bronze Age* (1996). A vivid account of Schliemann and subsequent archaeologists and the significance of their discoveries; this intriguing book is at once impeccable in its scholarship and highly readable.

McDonald, William A., and Carol G. Thomas. *Progress into the Past: The Rediscovery of Mycenaean Civilization*, 2nd ed. (1990). An excellent summary of Mycenaean scholarship and archaeology.

Willetts, W. F. *The Civilization of Ancient Crete*, 2nd ed. (1991). The best comprehensive account, from the origins of Minoan civilization to the Roman conquest, making full use of archaeological evidence.

The World of the City-State

Andrewes, Antony. *The Greek Tyrants*, rev. ed. (1963). This relatively brief work is still the best account of its subject.

Forrest, W. G. *A History of Sparta, 950–192* B.C., 2nd ed. (1980). A short but exemplary history.

Graham, A. J. *Colony and Mother City in Ancient Greece*, 2nd ed. (1983). An expert treatment of the colonization movement.

Grant, Michael. *The Rise of the Greeks* (1987). An authoritative, stylishly written account of the history and archaeology of the early Greeks, 750–480 B.C.

Murray, Oswyn. *Early Greece*, 2nd ed. (1993). A social and economic history from the close of the Mycenaean era to the Persian Wars.

Snodgrass, Anthony. *Archaic Greece: The Age of Experiment* (1980). A crucial period of Greek development treated from an archaeological perspective.

Starr, Chester G. *The Economic and Social Growth of Early Greece, 800–500* B.C. (1977). An astute analysis that places Greece in its eastern Mediterranean setting; Starr's *Individual and Community: The Rise of the Polis, 800–500* B.C. (1986) is a companion volume on political development during the same period.

The Zenith and Transformation of Classical Greece

Blundell, Sue. *Women in Ancient Greece* (1995). The author deftly examines a great variety of evidence to illuminate the economic and legal position of Greek women and the nature of their daily lives.

Davies, John Kenyon. *Democracy and Classical Greece*, 2nd ed. (1993). A stimulating analysis and reinterpretation.

Dover, Kenneth J. *Greek Homosexuality*, rev. ed. (1989). The authoritative work on the topic.

Finley, Moses I. *Ancient Slavery and Modern Ideology* (1980). A short, hardheaded account of Greco-Roman slavery and modern misconceptions of it.

Garlan, Yvan. *Slavery in Ancient Greece* (1988). Trans. Janet Lloyd. The best general account of the subject.

Hornblower, Simon. *The Greek World, 479–323* B.C., rev. ed. (1991). The first volume in the Classical Civilizations Series, this work makes full use of archaeological evidence and inscriptions as well as the more traditional literary evidence (all extensively quoted) to reexamine in broader perspective the civilization of classical Greece.

Kagan, Donald. *Pericles of Athens and the Birth of Democracy* (1990). The best biography of Pericles, this sympathetic account places him at the core of fifth-century Athenian democracy.

Massey, Michael. *Women in Ancient Greece and Rome* (1988). An admirable work of scholarship; well written and absorbing.

Ober, Josiah. *Mass and Elite in Democratic Athens* (1989). A highly original sociological analysis of Athenian politics.

Rhodes, P. J. *The Athenian Empire* (1985). Brief but valuable.

Roberts, J. W. *City of Sokrates: An Introduction to Classical Athens* (1984). A meticulous study of the physical setting, society, constitutional arrangements, mentality, and culture of fifth-century B.C. Athens; the best such study in print.

Wycherley, R. E. *The Stones of Athens* (1978). Lively, nontechnical essays reconstructing the topography and buildings of Athens in the fifth and fourth centuries B.C.

HELLENISM AND ITS DIFFUSION

Prometheus *Scala/Art Resource, NY.*

ca. 600	Sappho, first great lyric poet, establishes a school at Lesbos
ca. 590	Thales, first important Greek philosopher, proposes a theory of the universe
ca. 582–507	Life span of Pythagoras, mathematician and mystic
ca. 550	Anaximander proposes an early evolutionary theory
ca. 525–456	Life span of Aeschylus, first great tragic dramatist
ca. 500	Heraclitus and Parmenides debate the nature of reality—eternal change vs. eternal stability
496–406	Life span of Sophocles, tragic dramatist and author of *Antigone*
485–406	Life span of Euripides, tragic dramatist of unparalleled realism
ca. 484–ca. 425	Life span of Heroditus, "father of history"
469–399	Life span of Socrates, examiner of "unexamined lives"
ca. 460–400	Life span of Thucydides, first critical historical scholar
ca. 460–370	Life span of Hippocrates, first major Greek medical writer
ca. 450–385	Life span of Aristophanes, greatest Greek comic playwright
ca. 440	Democratus proposes an early atomic theory

432	Completion of the Parthenon
427–347	Life span of Plato, revolutionizer of philosophy
384–322	Life span of Aristotle, who further revolutionizes philosophy
342–270	Life span of Zeno, founder of Stoicism
341–270	Life span of Epicurus, founder of Epicureanism
336–323	Reign of Alexander the Great, conqueror of Persia
323	Death of Diogenes
323 ff.	The Hellenistic Age
ca. 300	Euclid codifies the laws of geometry
ca. 280–264	Aristarchus of Samos proposes a heliocentric hypothesis
212	Death of Archimedes, greatest mathematician and engineer of antiquity
167–164	Jews revolt against Seleucid rule, climaxing but not ending with purification of the Jerusalem Temple
ca. 160–125	Hipparchus greatly advances geocentric astronomy
63	Roman general Pompey ends Jewish independence
A.D. 90–168	Life span of Claudius Ptolemy, mathematician who sums up the theory of a geocentric universe

All dates are B.C. except when noted otherwise.

*P*rometheus, the hero who has given humanity the knowledge of fire, hangs bound to a mountainside by order of Zeus. This myth, narrated in the Greek painting shown on page 75, is the subject of one of Greek literature's greatest masterpieces, Aeschylus's drama *Prometheus Bound*. The Promethean myth endures in Western civilization as a metaphor of humanity's striving to reach its potential.

The Athenian audiences witnessing *Prometheus Bound*, sometime between 470 and 460 B.C., would have fully understood its religious significance. The setting is the world soon after Zeus and the other Olympian gods have deposed their predecessor, Kronos (see Chapter 2). Zeus had seized power with the help of Prometheus, one of the Titans—a race of dull-witted giants whom Kronos had created, along with humanity. But Prometheus was different from the other Titans: His mother, Gaia (Earth), had secretly given him intelligence and a sympathy for human beings, the botched creatures whom Zeus intended to wipe

out. By stealing fire (the Olympians' monopoly) and bringing it to humanity, along with other useful knowledge, Prometheus forestalled Zeus's plans—hence his terrible punishment. Prometheus, however, has one secret that can save him: He alone knows how the Olympian gods might meet their doom; and he will defy Zeus, who is desperate to learn this secret, until the king of the gods relents.

Prometheus Bound is a drama of lofty poetry and breathtaking blasphemy:

In one word, I detest all gods who could repay
My benefits with such outrageous infamy.[1]

So Prometheus answers Zeus's messenger, the god Hermes, who has come to urge him to submit.

---

[1] Aeschylus, *Prometheus Bound*, trans. Philip Vellacott (Harmondsworth, England: Penguin Books, 1962), p. 49.

Thus ends *Prometheus Bound*—but not Aeschylus's story. Today, we possess only the first of three dramas; only fragments remain of the others. In them, apparently Zeus turns from reliance on brute force to justice, and the hero Heracles releases Prometheus. Zeus manages to evade his doom thanks to a prophecy that Prometheus reveals, and humanity achieves its destiny through reason rather than violence.

Prometheus Bound, and the conservative way in which Aeschylus resolved its rebellious heresies, aptly serves to introduce the ancient Greek cultural experience. As a young man, Aeschylus had fought at Marathon—for this alone he asked to be remembered in his epitaph—and he supported Athens's bold experiment in democratic government. The pride with which he shows Prometheus justifying humanity's rise from wretched ignorance to confident creativity reveals his own, and his Athenian audience's, awareness of the intellectual revolution transforming Greece in the sixth and fifth centuries B.C. The philosophy, cosmology, mathematics, architecture, sculpture, literature, and drama that flourished in Aeschylus's Athens shaped the course of Western civilization itself. But Aeschylus also understood the latent potential for violence and irrationalism to overwhelm human effort; hence his insistence that divine justice must play its part in ensuring the rule of reason and mercy.

Understanding the ancient Greek cultural achievement requires that we define the word *culture* broadly, to include not only great literature and the fine arts but also attitudes, customs, and everyday behavior. That is one of the purposes of Chapter 3. Its second purpose is to examine how Greek civilization changed across time, beginning with the time when the Greeks were supplementing older mythic understandings of the world with rational explanations, and extending down to the age of Alexander the Great's successors, who passed ancient Greece's legacy on to the Jews and Romans—and ultimtely to us.

THE HELLENIC MIND

In the first two chapters we traced the earliest attempts by Near Eastern cultures to comprehend the world and nature, and the beginnings of Greek thought in Homer's and Hesiod's time. The explanations that emerged from such efforts are termed *mythic* in that they rested on the supernatural. Divine forces permeated nature; things happened because they were somehow alive; myth unites the human and the supernatural experiences. The decisive break that ancient Greeks achieved, between the seventh and the fourth centuries B.C., was to supplement—but not wholly to supplant—a mythic with a rational understanding of nature.

Ancient Greeks rarely became irreligious. Their dramas, their civic festivals, their Olympic Games were all religious celebrations. Their public art and architecture were devoted largely to honoring the gods. Their generals sometimes altered strategy because of a divine portent. But their philosophers succeeded by and large in holding the gods at bay and untangling the natural from the supernatural. To the Greeks, as to other ancient peoples, the cosmos was awesome. But some Greeks possessed the open-mindedness and audacity to probe the cosmic mysteries with their intellects. The deeply religious Aeschylus celebrated this intellectual freedom so long as his fellow Greeks continued to regard their gods as the guardians of civilization and its values.

The Quest for Arete

To understand ancient Greek history, it is helpful to learn several Greek words. We have already considered *polis*, or city-state (as well as other words that have become part of the English language, such as *democracy* and *monarchy*). In this chapter, we shall encounter several key words whose meaning in ancient Greek cannot easily be summed up with a single English equivalent. One of them is *arete*.

"Excellence" is the most direct way to translate arete, but it did not mean simply getting an "A." When an ancient Greek spoke of something—or someone—as having arete, he or she meant that the thing or person possessed in correct balance all necessary "rightness." "Virtue" is another way of translating *arete*, but we have to be careful because in contemporary English the word *virtue* has taken on overtones absent from its original sense—that of possessing the inherent *value* of being right.[2] The word *arete* had strong moral overtones: Possessing arete meant that something was true to its nature, and should therefore be admired and emulated.

And how was arete to be determined? Here we encounter our second Greek word: *agon*, whose simplest translation is "contest." But the fact that such varied English words as "agony" and "antagonist" derive from it should tip us off to the broad meaning that *agon* had to an ancient Greek. It meant a competition to demonstrate excellence (arete), but no mismatch would do: Merely winning proved nothing. True arete would emerge only from a contest between equals, each making a supreme effort to demonstrate all-around excellence and goodness.

The earliest precise date in their history that the ancient Greeks recorded was (by the modern reckoning) 776 B.C. This was the year of the first Olympic Games; and from then until the end of ancient Greece itself, Greek people measured the passage of time by the four-year Olympic cycle. The importance that ancient Greeks accorded to this inter-polis athletic competition is a mark of how seriously they took arete and agon.

---

[2] *Virtue* is a Latin word that has its own interesting meanings, which we will explore when we encounter Roman and Renaissance history in later chapters.

Athletes Athletic competitions were a crucial part of aristocratic life in the sixth century B.C., when this painting was created. The Olympic Games, for example, included sprints, distance races (of about a mile), and races in heavy armor. (The marathon is a modern invention.) There were also javelin and discus throws, wrestling and boxing, and horse and chariot races. In the latter, the breeder of the winning horse, not the rider or driver, enjoyed the glory of victory. *Lee Boltin Picture Library.*

Homer's *Odyssey*, which probably passed into written form around the time those first Olympic Games were being held, provides a wonderful example. Odysseus has been shipwrecked alone on an island whose king welcomes him with exemplary hospitality, even hinting that his daughter (herself possessing the full arete appropriate for a young woman) would make a fine wife. Without even asking his guest's name, the king summons the young men of his island to hold an agon that will demonstrate their—and their island's—prowess. But when one winner, a boorish whippersnapper, hints that the stranger must have been the captain of some lowly scow peddling trinkets from island to island, the unknown man picks up a discus and hurls it farther than anyone else present—and adds that he could probably win a foot race if he had a little time to get back in shape. This demonstration of his arete leads into the scene in which Odysseus reveals his name and narrates his adventures.

The Olympic Games and similar competitions were religious ceremonies in which the athletes offered their arete to the gods. They were so sacred that any wars being fought between poleis had to be suspended for the duration. Only freeborn males could attend, let alone compete

(slaves or women who intruded could be put to death), and the honor of winning went not only to the champion but also to his polis. Some of the greatest fifth-century B.C. Greek poetry, the odes of Pindar, celebrated such victories and were sung by a chorus of friends welcoming the winner home.

The men who competed in the early Olympics and other games were aristocrats. (The word is related to *arete*, and means one of "the best.") Directly or indirectly, their whole lives were devoted to competition. Homer's heroes were all aristocrats, forever striving against one another to prove their mettle. Their competitiveness carried over into the world of the polis. There is no better introduction to the life and concerns of a sixth-century aristocrat than the poetry of Theognis, a gentleman from Megara (near Athens). Many of his verses grumble sourly but eloquently that nowadays no one values anything but money: True worth, he says, can never be bought. Such aristocrats lived most of their lives in each other's company. Since they did not learn an ordinary trade, their education took place in the gymnasium ("boys' place") and featured equal doses of athletic, military, and literary training; as young men and adults, they were expected to keep themselves fit and warlike by constant exercise naked in the gymnasium; to relax, they would spend the evening at a drinking party (*symposium*), competing in everything from singing their own songs to spitting wine at a target. Women, if present at all, served as flute-playing dancing girls, or as prostitutes who might also be intellectually cultivated; secluded at home, aristocrats' wives were trained only to bear children and manage the household. Male aristocrats' emotional attachments were often to each other. Homoerotic love, one of the great themes of Greek literature, was itself often highly competitive—and, as far as we can tell, overwhelmingly aristocratic. Theognis's verses, addressed to a variety of younger men for whom he was by turns mentor, confidante, and jealous lover, overflow with proud claims to having immortalized his beloved in verse, with complaints about how the aristocratic world is going to wrack and ruin, and with whines that the young ingrates have spurned him for a competitor.

The Lyric Poets of Ionia

Open-mindedness and audacity were nourished by the free and turbulent atmosphere of the polis. Greek rationalism grew out of Greek competitiveness, and among the first manifestations of this new spirit of self-awareness was the development of lyric poetry during the seventh and sixth centuries B.C. by the aristocrats of the poleis, principally in Ionia. At this time these cities were tormented by social and political strife.

The essence of Greek lyric poetry is the poet's *personal* expression of his own thoughts and emotions. (*Her* own thoughts, too: As we shall see, one of the greatest of all lyric poets was a woman.) Thus it differs from the epic poetry of Homer, and from the later dramatic poetry of the Athenian playwrights, which we will discuss later in this chapter. Lyric poetry was meant to be sung to the accompaniment of a lyre (hence "lyric") and was often embellished by dance. It originated as a choral song for religious festivals, but by the seventh century B.C. it was becoming a vehicle for intense personal expression, often at *symposia*. Intensely expressive as it was, Greek lyric poetry constituted a literary achievement of the highest importance, yet it transcends literature. The works of lyric poets such as Archilochus of Paros in the seventh century and Theognis of Megara and Sappho of Lesbos in the sixth century disclose a self-consciousness and an intensity of personal experience far exceeding anything previously recorded in literature. At a time when Spartan mothers were sending their sons to war with the stern command, "Return with your shield—or on it," the Ionian Archilochus jauntily expressed a more individualistic viewpoint:

> Some barbarian is waving my shield, since I was obliged to
> leave that perfectly good piece of equipment behind
> under a bush. But I got away, so what does it matter?
> Let the shield go; I can buy another one equally good.

With such lines as these, Archilochus of Paros ceases to be a mere name and emerges as a vivid, engaging personality—a social rebel who rejected the stern, honor-ridden morality of the Greek warrior-aristocrat. He was history's first articulate coward.[3]

The most deeply personal of the lyric poets was Sappho, who in sixth-century B.C. Lesbos directed a school for young women. She, like all other early Greek poets, was thoroughly aristocratic; and although we know little about the society of Lesbos, it appears that upper-class women there formed close-knit bonds paralleling but completely separate from those of their male kin. Sappho's beautiful and passionate love lyrics were addressed to her students. The people of antiquity saw Sappho as divinely inspired and the equal of Homer. Never before had the oscillating emotions of love been expressed with such intensity:

> O then the sweat streams down me and I tremble,
> In all my body. Pale as the grass I grow!
> And death itself, my strength and powers fading,
>   Seems to approach me.[4]

The Intellectual Revolution

The same surge of individualism that produced lyric poetry in the growing, strife-torn poleis of Ionia gave rise to humanity's first effort toward a rational, not a mythic,

"The Archaic Smile"   This enigmatic smile, which became stylized on most Greek sculpture of the sixth century B.C., is thought to have originated in Ionia, and some scholars associate it with the Ionian intellectual revolution. This female head (detached from the rest of a standing figure) is from Miletus, ca. 550 B.C. With some imagination, we might associate Sappho with the culture that created this image. *Staatliche Museen, Berlin Preussischer Kulturbesitz, Antikensammlung/SK 1631. Photo by Jürgen Liepe, 1991.*

understanding of the physical universe. So far as we know, the first philosopher and theoretical investigator of nature in Western history was a sixth-century Ionian, Thales of Miletus, who announced that water was the primal element of the universe. This hypothesis, crude though it may seem, constitutes a deeply significant effort to impose intellectual unity on the diversity of experience. The world was to be understood as a single physical substance. Presumably, solid objects were made of compressed water, air of rarefied water, and—one supposes—empty space of dehydrated water. Thales' "water hypothesis" did not convince his successors, but the crucial point is that Thales *had* successors. Others continued his attempt to explain the physical universe through natural rather than supernatural principles. Intellectual history had taken a bold new turn.

Ionian thinkers after Thales continued to speculate about the primal substance. One suggested air as the basic element. Another, Anaximander, set forth a primitive theory of evolution and declared that people were descended from fish. But these intellectual pioneers, their originality notwithstanding, disclose a basic weakness that characterized

---

[3] But he too had to prove his worth by living by his wits, and tradition has it that he died bravely fighting. Translation: Richmond Lattimore, *Greek Lyrics*, 2nd. ed. (Chicago: University of Chicago Press, 1960), p. 2.

[4] *Sappho of Lesbos: Her Works Restored,* trans. Beram Saklatvola (London: Charles Skilton Ltd., 1968), p. 55.

A Symposium The women shown on this fifth century B.C. painted cup are *hetaerae* entertaining men at a symposium. Upper-class men had many opportunities to form liaisons with such women, as well as with male lovers. *The Granger Collection, New York.*

Greek scientific thought throughout the classical age. They exhibited the all-too-human tendency to rush into sweeping generalizations on the basis of a grossly inadequate factual foundation. Beguiled by the potentialities of rational inquiry, they failed to appreciate how painfully difficult it is to arrive at sound conclusions. Consequently, the hypotheses of the Ionians were inspired guesses. Anaximander's theory of evolution, for example, was quickly forgotten because, unlike Darwin's, it rested on so little data.

The profoundest of the early Ionian thinkers was Heraclitus of Ephesus, who lived about 500 B.C. Interpreting his ideas is difficult because only fragments survive—isolated pronouncements that have the solemn authority of a prophet. The essence of these fragments is that the world is in constant flux. Nothing is stable or fixed. "You only step into a river once," because it always changes. Fire, everdestroying, was the only metaphor that captured the world's essence, and so was the one basic element. "Becoming," not "Being," defined the universe. Harmony lay in the interplay—the mutual attraction and repulsion—of opposites. Heraclitus called this harmony the *Logos*, a mystical concept that literally means "the word" but is better interpreted as "the Way."[5]

Heraclitus's teachings seemed to open the door to vast new intellectual and spiritual possibilities: mystical unities of opposites, cycles of "becoming," the identity of matter and spirit, of mind and body. Through just such a door

were passing Eastern thinkers roughly contemporary with Heraclitus: the nameless authors of the Upanishads in India, and the Chinese thinker traditionally known as Laozi (or Lao-tzu), the father of Daoism. (The Chinese concept of the *Dao*, and the Indian of *Dharma*, bear striking resemblances to Heraclitus's Logos.) Had the Greek world followed Heraclitus as its prophet, perhaps Western civilization would have unfolded along paths similar to those of South and East Asia. But it did not.

Heraclitus's philosophical ideas almost immediately begot their opposite. His contemporary Parmenides completely rejected Heraclitus's vision of a universe never at rest: He maintained that the "true" universe was perfect and immobile. This perfection he called "Being." In contrast, the constant change that we perceive is only that—a *perception* of our faulty human senses. The world of Spirit—Being, Thought, Mind—is eternal and unchanging. Only the everyday, humdrum world of Matter, or "body," is subject to change and disorder, to turmoil and upheaval, to decay and death.

Parmenides' ideas, like Heraclitus's, survive only as fragments. But between them, Heraclitus and Parmenides bequeathed to later Greek thinkers a disturbing choice between a universe that never stood still and a universe sharply separated into eternal Spirit and corruptible Matter.

Pythagoras (ca. 582–507 B.C.) had already opened still a third road. An Ionian by birth, he moved to southern Italy, where he founded a quasi-religious brotherhood. He drew heavily from the cults of Dionysus and Demeter and was influenced especially by Orphism, a salvation cult that was becoming popular throughout Greece in the sixth

---

[5] The word *Logos*, after the first century A.D., passed into Christian theology and became identified with Jesus Christ. See Chapter 5.

THE HISTORICAL EVIDENCE

Early Greek Philosophers

sixth–fifth centuries B.C.

The following extracts give a brief glimpse of what some of the founding fathers of Greek philosophy thought—or, in some cases, what later Greek writers claimed that they had said.

Heraclitus

This order, the same for all things, no one of gods or men has made, but it always was, and is, and ever shall be, an ever-living fire, kindling according to fixed measure, and extinguishing according to fixed measure. . . .

Hesiod is the teacher of most men; they supposed that his knowledge was very extensive, when in fact he did not know night and day, for they are one.

God is day and night, winter and summer, war and peace, satiety and hunger; but he assumes different forms, just as when incense is mixed with incense; every one gives him the name he pleases. . . .

You could not step twice in the same rivers; for other and yet other waters are ever flowing on. . . .

Opposition unites. From what draws apart results the most beautiful harmony. All things take place by strife.

Good and bad are the same. . . .

Upward, downward, the way is one and the same. . . .

All things are full of souls and of divine spirits.

Parmenides

There is left but this single path to tell thee of: namely, that being is. And on this path there are many proofs that being is without beginning and indestructible; it is universal, existing alone, immovable, and without end; nor ever was it nor will it be, since it now *is*, all together, one, and continuous. . . . From what did it grow, and how? I will not permit thee to say or to think that it came from non-being; for it is impossible to think or to say that non-being is.

Pythagoras (according to Aristotle)

The Pythagoreans, because they see many qualities of numbers in bodies perceived by sense, regard objects as numbers, not as separate numbers, but as derived from numbers. And why? Because the qualities of numbers exist in harmony both in the heaven and in many other things.

Democritus (according to Diogenes Laertius)

The first principles of the universe are atoms and empty space; everything else is merely thought to exist. The worlds are unlimited; they come into being and perish. . . . Further, the atoms are unlimited in size and number, and they are borne along in the whole universe in a vortex,* and thereby generate all composite things—fire, water, air, earth; for even these are conglomerations of given atoms. . . .

All things happen by virtue of necessity, the vortex being the cause of the creation of all things, and this he calls necessity. . . . In nature there is nothing but atoms and void space. These, then, are his opinions.

---

*The whirling of atoms around what Democritus thought was the universe's central axis.

Source: T. V. Smith, ed., *Philosophers Speak for Themselves: From Thales to Plato* (Chicago: University of Chicago Press, 1934), pp. 11–13, 16, 45, 57.

---

century B.C. Orphism stressed guilt and atonement, required various ascetic practices, and promised an afterlife of suffering or bliss depending on the purity of one's soul. This and similar cults appealed to those who found inadequate solace in the heroic, worldly gods of Olympus. Following Orphic beliefs, Pythagoras advocated a communal life and the doctrine of transmigration of souls—that is, immortality through reincarnation. Some historians believe that this idea may have reached the Greek world (by way of the Near East) from India, where it had an important place in the religious teachings of ancient Brahminism and still permeates Hinduism.

A fundamental Pythagorean idea—and for Western culture a profoundly significant one—was that nature's basic element was *number*. Thus Pythagoras rejected the Ionian philosophers' metaphors of water, air, and fire. The Pythagoreans studied the intervals between musical tones and worked out basic laws of harmony. Having demonstrated the relationship between music and mathematics, they applied these principles to the whole universe. Pythagoreans asserted that the cosmos obeyed the laws of harmony and, indeed, that the planets in their courses produced musical tones that harmonized into a cosmic rhapsody: the "music of the spheres." Implicit in these doctrines is the pregnant concept, fundamental to modern Western science, that nature is to be understood mathematically.

In Pythagorean mathematical thought, the number 10 was held in mystical reverence. This and other

Pythagorean teachings underlay various mystical beliefs of later times, some of which still flourish. The Pythagoreans also played a crucial role in the development of mathematics and mathematical science. They produced the Pythagorean theorem and the multiplication table, and a revival of their ideas helped stimulate the emergence of modern science in the sixteenth and seventeenth centuries. The Greeks were at their best in mathematics, for here they could reason deductively—applying self-evident concepts to specific cases—and their distaste for the slow, patient accumulation of data was no hindrance.

Mathematics became tremendously important to Greek thinkers after Pythagoras. To understand why, it is helpful to realize that Greek mathematics meant geometry—the most visual and tangible way of expressing numerical patterns. The Greeks had no algebra, and their arithmetic was gravely limited by a clumsy notation and the absence of a zero. (Zero would have meant nothingness, an abhorrent idea.) Geometry, however, encouraged their bent toward elegant, symmetrical representation, and it stimulated logical, abstract thought. It was both practical and beautiful, especially when applied to the design of everyday objects from a drinking bowl to a temple. And through it even an untutored slave boy could be brought step by step to understand profound truths, as the great teacher Socrates would later be shown doing in one of Plato's dialogues, the *Meno*. Geometry was the Greeks' metaphor for Truth.

Fifth-century B.C. Greek thinkers wrestled with the intellectual legacy of Heraclitus, Parmenides, and Pythagoras. The questions they confronted are among the central problems that have preoccupied philosophers ever since: whether the universe is in a state of flux or eternally changeless; whether or not its nature can be grasped by the reasoning mind; whether it is composed of one substance or of many. (Even the word *philosophy* was coined by Greeks at this time: It meant "the love of wisdom.")

Thus the Sicilian Greek philosopher Empedocles (ca. 494–432 B.C.) taught that the cosmos consisted not of a single element but of four: earth, air, fire, and water—a conception that would dominate chemical investigations until the late eighteenth century A.D. Empedocles further taught that change in the physical universe resulted from the interaction of tiny particles of these four elements as they alternately attracted and repelled each other. A man of diverse talents (Empedocles was also a statesman, physician, orator, and poet), he was revered by his contemporaries as godlike. According to an unlikely legend, he so convinced himself of his own divinity that he sought to prove it by jumping into the volcanic cone of Mount Etna, leaving behind nothing but a pair of golden slippers. Empedocles' emphasis on the interaction of particles, as well as Heraclitus's assertion that perpetual change defines the universe, may have influenced Democritus (ca. 440) to develop a doctrine of thoroughgoing materialism. Democritus's position anticipates modern science in several respects. He maintained that the universe consists of countless atoms in random configurations—that it has neither center nor edge but is much the same in one place as another. In short, our earth is in no way unique and the universe is infinite.

Like Anaximander's theory of evolution and Heraclitus's vision of a universe in constant flux, Democritus's atomic theory was essentially a philosophical assertion, not a scientific hypothesis based on extensive empirical evidence. And infinity—as well as the kindred concepts of nothingness and change—profoundly disturbed the ancient Greek mind. Consequently atomism was rejected by all but a few ancient and medieval thinkers. Not until the seventeenth century, when the Western world had entered that sweeping intellectual upheaval known as the **Scientific Revolution** (see Chapter 17), did Democritus's notion of an infinitely vast universe composed of infinitely small atoms get taken seriously. Evolution would not come into its own until the nineteenth century. And the power of Heraclitus's core idea—that change and "Becoming," not stability and "Being," define the cosmos—was not fully appreciated by Westerners until the advent of relativity and quantum theory in twentieth-century physics.

In medicine and history the Greeks of the fifth century B.C. resisted the lure of premature generalization and concentrated on the tiresome but essential task of accumulating accurate data. In medicine, Hippocrates (ca. 460–ca. 370 B.C.) and his followers recorded case histories with scrupulous care. Their painstaking clinical studies and their rejection of supernatural causation launched medicine on the course it still follows. Appropriately, modern physicians begin their careers by taking the Hippocratic Oath, which includes the eminently sensible rule, "Do no harm."

A similar reverence for the verifiable fact was demonstrated by the ancient Greek historians. History in the modern sense begins with Herodotus (ca. 484–ca. 425 B.C.). Born in Halicarnassus, on the border between Ionia and the Persian Empire, he moved to Athens and became one of its unabashed admirers. Herodotus was a person of boundless curiosity who, in the course of extensive travels through Greece and the Near East, accumulated a vast store of data for his brilliant and entertaining history of the Persian Wars. He is traditionally celebrated as the "father of history," but his cogent ethnographic comments on various peoples in the lands he visited make him, as well, the "father of anthropology." Herodotus made some effort to separate fact from fable, but he manifested a great fondness for a colorful story.[6] For instance, he tells of how King Croesus of Lydia consulted the Delphic oracle before starting a war with the Persians. The oracle told Croesus that he would destroy a great empire. So he blithely began the war—only to discover that the empire was his own.

---

[6] This fondness has caused some unkind people to call him "the father of lies."

THE HUMAN EXPERIENCE

Thucydides

Born of an aristocratic family around 460 B.C., Thucydides played an active role in Athenian politics during the closing years of the age of Pericles—whom he much admired. He served as a general in the Peloponnesian War until 424 B.C., when he was exiled for having failed to lead his troops to the relief of a city under attack by the Spartans. In the years that followed, Thucydides traveled widely to gather evidence for his great history of the Peloponnesian War. His history was not an effort at self-justification but an even-handed, brilliantly analytical study of politics and warfare during the first twenty years of the war. He left the history unfinished at his death, about 400 B.C.

Like the finest historians today, Thucydides took great pains to report history accurately. "Of the events of the war," he wrote, "I have described nothing but what I either saw myself or learned from others whom I questioned most carefully and specifically. The task was laborious, because eyewitnesses of the same events gave different accounts of them, as they remembered or were interested in the actions of one side or the other."

Thucydides approached history in a new way. The Hebrews viewed it as the unfolding of a divine plan; Thucydides' own Greek predecessors had believed that historical events could be foretold by oracles and omens and could be affected by the intervention of deities. To Thucydides, however, human events had no supernatural dimension. They were the outgrowth of political action on the part of statesmen and popular assemblies, whose plans were often thwarted by the winds of chance. Thucydides had no real interest in social or economic history; rather, his approach was political and psychological. He was above all fascinated by the motivations underlying political action, and a central theme of his work is the deleterious effect of prolonged warfare on political prudence. As he put it:

In peace and prosperity, poleis and individuals have better sentiments because they do not find themselves suddenly confronted with imperious necessities. But war takes away the easy supply of daily wants, and so proves a rough master that brings most men's characters to a level with their fortunes.

Thus as the Peloponnesian War dragged on, "Reckless audacity came to be considered the courage of a loyal ally; prudent hesitation, specious cowardice; moderation was held to be a cloak for unmanliness."

At the center of Thucydides' conception of history was the polis. Like no one before him, he subjected the political conflicts in the Greek poleis to keen, unsentimental analysis. To Thucydides, the polis was an endlessly fascinating arena of contending political views and interests, and since he tended to see political issues as the central problems of existence, he ascribed to the polis a dominating role in the dynamics of history. Here, as elsewhere, Thucydides' thought was characteristically Greek.❖

Herodotus's critical treatment of historical evidence was surpassed by a historian of the next generation, Thucydides, a disgraced Athenian general who wrote an account of the Peloponnesian War with unprecedented objectivity and an acute sense of historical criticism. Thucydides' penetrating analyses of political behavior influenced such later Western political theorists as Thomas Hobbes in the seventeenth century. Altogether, he ranks as the most perceptive of all ancient Greek historians.

The rationalism of early Greek thought has long appealed to the Western imagination—particularly in the eighteenth and nineteenth centuries, when the West's faith in reason and progress reached flood tide. But we must never forget that a strong current of irrationalism also lurked in Greek culture. The unpredictability of the gods and the frenzy with which divinities like Dionysus were worshiped; the inexorable workings of Fate and Chance, against which human reason had little defense; the passions that could be unleashed by humans acting on their emotional impulses; the pride that flawed and destroyed even the noblest character—all these the ancient Greeks keenly felt, and made room for in their art and literature. Classical culture was a defense against the irrational, but a fragile one. The twentieth century, which had its fill of rationalism and irrationalism alike, appreciated the Greeks' awareness of both.

THE CULTURE OF CLASSICAL GREECE

History has seldom seen anything quite like the creativity of fifth-century B.C. Athens. Virtually every surviving work of art, from the greatest temple to the simplest ornament, was made with taste and assurance. Emotions ran strong and deep, but they were controlled by a sure sense of form that neither permitted ostentation nor degenerated into formalism. The art of the period was an incarnation of the Greek maxim, "nothing in excess"—a perfect embodiment of the taut balance and controlled excitement that has been called "the classical spirit."

Classical Culture and the Polis

Classical Greek culture mirrored the liberty and dynamism of the polis. Compared to the societies of the Near East, the world of the polis was intense and fluid. Political systems, philosophical concepts, and artistic styles evolved at a furious pace. Aristocracies declined, tyrannies flourished, and democracies emerged in an atmosphere of social change and acute political awareness. The citizens of the Greek poleis knew that they were a people apart and that what separated them most fundamentally from their predecessors and contemporaries was their freedom. Herodotus describes Greeks as telling a Persian official: "A slave's life you understand, but never having tasted liberty you cannot tell whether it is sweet or not. Had you known what freedom is, you would have bidden us fight for it." The Persian Wars represent for Herodotus an epic struggle between slavery and freedom.

It is not difficult to understand how Greek citizens, whose freedom exceeded that of any previous civilized people, produced such a dynamic culture. It is less easy to explain the harmony and restraint of Greek classicism, for no people had ever before lived with more intensity and fervor. Herodotus tells us that even the barbaric Scythians

of the Black Sea coast lamented the Greek impulse toward frenzy, and an unfriendly Corinthian in Thucydides' history observes that the Athenians "were born into the world to take no rest themselves and to give none to others."

Perhaps the Greeks stressed moderation and restraint precisely because these were the qualities most needed by an immoderate, exuberant people. Cooperation and self-control were essential to the communal life of the polis, and civic devotion reined in rampant individualism. During the classical age the polis stimulated individual creativity but directed it toward the welfare of the community. Individualism and civic responsibility achieved a momentary, precarious balance.

Athenian Life

In Periclean Athens (see Map 3-1), individualism was strongly tempered by the citizen's obligations to the polis. One of the basic differences between the daily life of the Athenian in the fifth century B.C. and that of the modern American is the Athenian's willingness to give precedence to public over private affairs. The home lives of even the most affluent Athenian citizens were rigorously simple:

MAP 3-1
ANCIENT ATHENS AND ATTICA

Their clothing was plain, their homes were modest, their furniture was rudimentary. With the intensification of individualism in the fourth century B.C., private homes became more luxurious, but during the golden age the Athenian's private life was, by our standards, almost as frugal as the Spartan's.

The austerity of private life was counterbalanced, however, by the brilliant diversity of public life. Under Pericles, imperial Athens lavished its wealth and genius on its own adornment. The great works of art and architecture were dedicated to the polis and its gods. Life was enriched by the pageantry of civic religious festivals, by spirited conversation in the marketplace (the *agora*), by exercise in elaborate civic gymnasiums complete with baths and dressing rooms, and of course by participation in political affairs. The pursuit of excellence in body and mind, so typical of Greek culture, went on in a civic atmosphere. The good life was not the life of the individual but the life of the citizen. The very competitiveness of educated speakers in proposing courses of action to Athens's Assembly, which as we saw in Chapter 2 was the essence of the city's democracy, was the political embodiment of the pursuit of arete.

Nevertheless, most inhabitants of Periclean Athens were denied participation in political affairs. The wives, daughters, and underage sons of adult male citizens could neither vote nor hold political office; slaves and metics (resident foreigners) were excluded from citizenship altogether. And even though many metics prospered in business, many slaves were well treated, and some women doubtless had considerate husbands, only adult male citizens could participate fully in the life of the polis. The great philosopher Aristotle sought a rational justification for this arrangement by proving (to his own satisfaction) that slaves and women were by nature inferior beings.

The golden age of Pericles thus rested on economic foundations not only of imperial tribute but of slavery. Although precision is impossible, the best modern estimates suggest that the majority of Athenian slaves were of non-Greek origin. But Greeks also enslaved many fellow Greeks. As elsewhere in the Near East, slaves in Athens included prisoners of war or their descendants; others had fallen victim to pirate raids (as in the case of the philosopher Diogenes; see The Human Experience story of Diogenes later in this chapter); still others were simply noncitizens whose taxes had fallen excessively delinquent. Slaves might be personal servants or highly valued tutors. They might be permitted to work for artisans or even to follow a trade independently, turning over most of their earnings to their owner (who might allow them to save toward buying their freedom). Or they might be consigned to the often brutal toil of agricultural labor, or worked to death in Attica's silver mines, where conditions were truly appalling. All slaves, however, were under the absolute authority of their masters, who were free to beat them, chain them, or abuse them sexually. Many masters appear to have treated their slaves decently, and household slaves perhaps led tolerable lives. But lacking all legal rights, slaves were entirely dependent on their masters' whims—and could be sold to a brutal new master at any time. It must always be remembered that slavery was basic to most ancient economies. Periclean Athens, with its vast numbers of slaves and its powerless women, was no utopia.

The lives of "respectable" Athenian women were restricted largely to the home—and there, to the "women's quarters." A wife usually had heavy domestic duties and was legally under her husband's control; he could kill her if he caught her in adultery. Even more than in most other ancient civilizations, public life in Athens was an exclusively male realm. Like other Greek men, some Athenian males found homosexual love outside the home, and patronizing male or female prostitutes was no disgrace. (*Being* a male prostitute was, however, forbidden to citizens.) The parties and festive gatherings of the wealthier male citizens included no wives but were enlivened by *hetaerae* ("female companions")—high-class prostitutes of good education and free status.[7] The hetaerae were non-Athenians, often from Ionia, and were celebrated for their wit and charm. Notable among them was an Ionian woman named Aspasia, the mistress of Pericles, whom we met in

Fifth-Century Athenian Women   In contrast to the free-and-easy women of the symposium, the Athenian women in this fifth-century painting on a *lekythos*—a container for oils and ointments, probably kept in the women's quarters of a home—are shown performing all stages of cloth making, from spinning the wool to weaving a garment. Garments purchased outside the home were extremely expensive, which was one reason why most Athenians probably owned only one or two tunics. Respectable women such as these rarely ventured beyond the household and would never associate with males outside their own family. *The Metropolitan Museum of Art, Fletcher Fund, 1931. (31.11.10). Photograph ©1999.*

---

[7] Ordinary harlots with no pretension to culture were called *pornai*.

Chapter 2. Her name, appropriately, means "welcome." For wives, the age of Pericles was far from golden. "She knew that it was her job to be neither seen nor heard," said a fourth-century B.C. writer, referring to the young wife he had married. "What more could I want?"

The Periclean Achievement

The striking of a delicate balance between public and private life in Periclean Athens, during the fifth century B.C., forms a precious but fleeting episode in the evolution of the polis. Old-fashioned aristocratic conservatism was dying; ahead lay the ever-intensifying individualism of the fourth century, when Athens would be humbled first by defeat in the Peloponnesian War and then by the Macedonian conquest. In short, as Greek life was evolving from civic allegiance to individualism, from traditionalism to self-expression, from aristocracy to democracy, there came a moment when these opposites achieved equilibrium. That moment was immortalized in some of the finest works of architecture, sculpture, and drama the world has ever known.

The golden age of Greece was the golden age of Athens, for imperial wealth and Pericles' ambitious building program drew talent from throughout the Greek world. Periclean Athens had a long artistic tradition behind it—and a buoyant self-assurance that was born at Marathon, confirmed at Salamis, and heightened by successful imperialism. But the Athenian golden age was expensive to the rest of Greece in both money and talent. Indeed, the Greek polis at its cultural zenith had already evolved considerably from the original ideal of the independent self-contained state. Athens was not merely a polis; it was the heart of an empire. And although civic spirit vitalized Athenian culture, imperial trade and tribute paid the bills. The culture of the golden age is unquestionably a polis culture, but it is the culture of a polis that was losing its innocence.

The Athenian Dramatists The civic culture of the Athenian golden age achieved its most remarkable triumphs in drama, architecture, and sculpture. All three illustrate the public orientation of Greek cultural life. Athenian tragedy rose out of the worship of Dionysus, as the songs and dances of the worshipers gradually evolved into a formalized drama with actors and a chorus. The sixth-century B.C. Athenian **tyrant** Pisistratus gave enthusiastic support to the festival of Dionysus, and by the fifth century it had become a great civic institution. Wealthy citizens were expected to finance productions, and each year civic judges awarded prizes to the three best tragedies. Here again, competition encouraged excellence.

Performances were stark. The most important ones took place in the outdoor Theater of Dionysus that still stands on a slope of the Athenian acropolis. A modern visitor can mount its stone seats and, looking down, imagine dramas unfolding on its stage some twenty-five hundred years ago. The chorus sang and danced to a simple musical accompaniment and commented at intervals on unfolding drama. Behind the chorus were low, broad steps on which masked actors performed. There were never more than three actors on the stage at one time, and the sets were simple. Violence always happened offstage. The dramas were based on mythological or historical themes, often dealing with the legendary royal families of early Greece, but the playwrights went beyond the realm of historical narrative to probe fundamental problems of morality and religion.

The immense popularity of these uncompromisingly austere and profound productions testifies to the remarkable cultural elevation of fifth-century Athens. The citizens

The Theater of Dionysus, Athens This stage dates from the fourth century B.C., replacing the one on which the great Greek tragedies and comedies received their first performances. *©R. Sheridan/Ancient Art & Architecture Collection.*

Antigone This painting on an Athenian cup, from ca. 380–370 B.C., is taken from a scene in Sophocles' drama, but is not a depiction of a performance; actors would have been masked. *Archaeological Museum, Istanbul. Photo Archäologisches Institut, Istanbul.*

who flocked to the Theater of Dionysus formed a critical and sophisticated audience. Many had participated in the numerous dramas that were constantly being performed both in the city and in the surrounding Attic countryside. It has been estimated that each year some three thousand citizens had the experience of performing in a dramatic chorus, and thousands more had been trained, as a part of the normal Athenian curriculum, in singing, dancing, public speaking, and acting. Drama was never mere entertainment—it held a central and meaningful place in the life of the polis and serves as an added illustration of the versatility of Athenian citizens during the golden age.

The three great tragedians of fifth-century Athens were Aeschylus, who wrote during the first half of the century; Sophocles, whose productive period covered the middle decades of the century; and Euripides, a younger contemporary of Sophocles (and a friend of Socrates). All three exemplify the seriousness, order, and controlled tension that we identify as "classical," yet they also illustrate the changes that the classical spirit was undergoing.

Aeschylus, whose *Prometheus Bound* we have already encountered, honored traditional values. Deeply devoted to the polis and the Greek religious heritage, he probed with majestic dignity the fundamental relationships of humanity and its gods, the problem of injustice in a righteous universe, and the terrible consequences of overweening pride. His trilogy *The Oresteia*, which we have complete, is one of the greatest probings of the human condition in all literature: What happens when Right clashes with Right? In the myth that Aeschylus dramatizes (which everyone in the audience knew), a curse has haunted the royal house of Argos ever since one king committed the ghoulish crime of slaying his brother's sons and tricking the boys' father into eating them. The murderer's son—himself innocent of the crime—is Agamemnon, a proud leader in the Greeks' war against Troy. Impatient for glory, Agamemnon sacrifices his daughter to the goddess Artemis. His horrified wife Clytemnestra takes as her lover the sole survivor of the original cannibalistic murder and, when Agamemnon returns triumphant from Troy ten years later, slays him. Agamemnon's return and murder occupy the first drama; the second depicts the vengeance that his son Orestes is directed by Apollo to take by killing Clytemnestra and her lover. But then, Orestes is pursued by the Furies—earth spirits who relentlessly punish the inexcusable crime of matricide by making him an outcast. The third part of the trilogy shows Orestes fleeing to the sanctuary of Athena. There the Athenian Assembly ponders whether to punish Orestes; the vote is evenly split and Athena herself appears to cast the deciding vote for mercy. She persuades the Furies (belonging to the older generation of divinities, for whom the sole law is vengeance) to join her in protecting Athens: The old earth spirits may continue to punish impiety, but the new spirit of justice that Zeus and his daughter Athena uphold will also be honored. Thus Aeschylus—a firm democrat—unites tradition and modernity, justifying both.

Sophocles was less tradition-bound than Aeschylus and less intellectually rigorous. (Politically, however, he was more skeptical of democracy.) But he was a supreme dramatic artist with an unerring sense of plot structure and

Watercarriers (from the Parthenon Frieze) Magnificent reliefs, such as these watercarriers, once encircled the frieze of the Parthenon, the central building of the Athenian Acropolis. The entire set of reliefs depicts a great civic procession—an annual celebration in which a woman's garment is presented to the Virgin Athena by the people of the city. The sense of grace and flowing movement is apparent even in the most badly damaged of the figures. *Erich Lessing/Art Resource, NY.*

characterization. His plays, first presented during the golden age of Pericles, treat the most violent and agonizing emotional situations with restraint and sobriety. In Sophocles the classical equilibrium is fully achieved: intense passion under masterful control.

The depth and power of fifth-century tragedy is exemplified in Sophocles' *Antigone*, which explores the perennial conflict between individual conscience and public authority. Antigone's brother has disobeyed the king of Thebes and has been killed. The king, her uncle, refuses to permit her brother's burial even though burial was a sacred duty. Torn by a conflict between the royal decree and her sense of religious obligation, Antigone defies the king, buries her brother, and is condemned to death.

Aeschylus's characters were really types rather than individuals; in Sophocles the individual emerges with much greater clarity; but Euripides portrays his characters with unparalleled realism and psychological insight. With the tragedies of Euripides, the new age of individualism was dawning. The younger dramatist Euripides displays the logic, the skepticism, and the hard-headed rationalism of the sophists who were then the rage of Athens. One of his characters audaciously asserts, "There are no gods in heaven; no, not one!" And Euripides, far more than his predecessors, demonstrated a deep, sympathetic understanding of human nature—its hopes and fears, its unpredictability and irrationality, and above all its individuality

and its questioning of tradition. His last and greatest play, *The Bacchae*, written in his old age after he had fled from Athens because of threats to prosecute him for blasphemy,[8] offers a frightening vision of irrationality. A young king tries to stamp out the fanatical cult of Dionysus and is torn apart by a band of the god's female worshipers led by his own mother. The boy's tragedy is that he has brashly denied the place of the irrational, destructive element in the human soul, something (Euripides is telling us) that we disregard at our peril.

Spellbound for hours by the terrors and sublimity of a tragic trilogy, Athenian audiences released their tension with raucous comedy—the traditional culmination of religious drama. The supreme fifth-century Greek comic playwright was Aristophanes. Taking advantage of the freedom of the Athenian theater, he subjected his fellow citizens great and small to merciless ridicule as he exposed the pretensions and follies of imperial Athens during the Peloponnesian War. The aristocratic Aristophanes expressed his deep-rooted conservatism by lampooning Socrates and the sophists. Socrates appears in a comedy called *The Clouds* hanging from a basket suspended in midair so that

---

[8] A few years later, Euripides' friend Socrates would be executed on similar charges.

The Parthenon Pericles' aristocratic enemies complained that his building program was a boondoggle designed to keep the democratic masses employed and that the account books were intentionally altered. We do not know whether these charges were justified, but the result was one of the supreme architectural and sculptural ensembles in all history. The Parthenon was on a scale larger than almost any other temple in the Greek world—a monument to civic pride, like medieval cathedrals. Construction on the building projects begun in Pericles' day was never finished after the Peloponnesian War. *Scala/Art Resource, NY.*

he can contemplate the heavens at closer range, while his students below study geology, their noses in the earth and their rears upraised toward the sky. The sexual innuendo, slapstick buffoonery, and political in-jokes of the play must have made Athenian audiences roar with laughter.

The plays of Aristophanes reflect the political discontent of his audiences. He mocked Athens's wartime leaders with a frankness that modern democracies (at least before the 1960s) would scarcely tolerate. The audacity of his criticism illustrates the intellectual freedom of Periclean Athens. Yet his plays also betray a yearning for the dignity and traditionalism of former years and a disturbing conviction that all was not well.

Embellishing the Polis: Architecture and Sculpture The evolution of ancient Greek life from conservatism to classical balance to individualism can be illustrated in the stages of Greek art. A delicate, static, aristocratic elegance had marked the seventh and sixth centuries' "archaic style." Fifth-century art acquired a serious, balanced, but gracefully flowing "classical" style; that of the late-classical fourth century B.C. and the "postclassical" Hellenistic Age showed an accelerating trend toward individualism and naturalism. The works of the fifth-century sculptors were archetypes— idealized human beings. Later, in the fourth century, sculptors would abandon the archetype for the specific.

Every aspect of fifth-century Athenian culture displays the classical spirit of restrained excitement. We find it in Athenian drama, where the most violent deeds and passions are presented in an ordered framework. We find it in the history of Thucydides, who treats with calm analysis the impetuous, often brutal excesses of the Peloponnesian War. And we find it in the architecture and art of fifth-century Athens: deeply moving yet marvelously balanced and controlled. When Xerxes' Persian troops burned the Acropolis in 479, they handed the next generation of Athenians a challenge and an opportunity: to rebuild the temples in the new, classical style—to crown the polis with structures of such perfection as the world had never known. Athenian imperialism provided the money, and Pericles— overriding conservative critics—pursued a lavish policy of civic beautification as a part of his effort to make Athens the cultural center of Hellas. In effect, the city challenged the rest of Greece to a contest (agon) to prove arete. The age of Pericles was therefore a period of feverish public building, and its supreme architectural monument was the main temple on the reconstructed Acropolis—the Parthenon. This geometrically perfect structure, dedicated to the polis's divine protector Athena, is the ultimate expression of the classical ideal. It creates its effect not from a sense of fluidity and upward-reaching, as in twentieth-century skyscrapers, but from a superb harmony of proportions. Here indeed was "nothing in excess."

The genius of the architects was matched by that of the sculptors who decorated the temples and created the great statues that stood inside them. The most celebrated of fifth-century sculptors was Phidias, the master sculptor of the Parthenon, who was responsible either directly or through his assistants for the splendid relief sculptures of its friezes. Phidias created a majestic statue of Athena in ivory and gold for the interior of the Parthenon (a small copy survives). He made a still larger statue of the same goddess, also long gone, which could be seen by ships several miles out at sea—like the Statue of Liberty. The work of Phidias and his contemporaries comes at the great moment of classical balance. Their works portray human beings as

Phidias's *Athena* Inside the Parthenon stood a huge statue of Athena, in gold and ivory. This is a small Roman copy from the second century A.D. Our contemporary mental picture of classic Greek sculpture in pure white marble is misleading: In ancient times, the figures were painted in vivid, even garish, colors.
© *R. Sheridan/Ancient Art & Architecture Collection Ltd.*

THE HISTORICAL EVIDENCE

The Sophist Protagoras

ca. 450 B.C.

Protagoras was one of the most prominent sophists active in Periclean Athens. His opinions disturbed tradition-minded Athenians, and eventually they were suppressed; perhaps that is one reason why only isolated fragments of his writings survive, along with hostile accounts of them—among others, in one of Plato's dialogues. Protagoras's famous dictum that "man is the measure of all things" directly challenged traditional views of the omnipotence of the gods.

Protagoras's Own Account of His Teachings (fragments)

Man is the measure of all things, of things that are that they are, and of things that are not that they are not.

As to the gods, I have no means of knowing either that they exist or that they do not exist. For there are many obstacles that impede knowledge, both the obscurity of the question and the shortness of human life.

Education needs natural gifts and practice; a man must begin to learn in his youth; education does not sprout in the soul unless a great depth is reached.

Diogenes Laertius on Protagoras (in addition to repeating the first two statements)

Protagoras was the first to maintain that there are two sides to every question, opposed to each other, and he even argued in this fashion, being the first to do so. . . .

He used to say that the soul was nothing apart from the sense . . . and that everything is true. . . . For this* introduction to his book the Athenians expelled him; and they burned his works in the market-place, after sending round a herald to collect them from all who had copies in their possession.

He was the first to exact a fee of a hundred minae and the first to distinguish the tenses of verbs, to emphasize the importance of seizing the right moment, to institute contests in debating, and to teach rival pleaders the tricks of their trade. Furthermore, in his dialectic he neglected the meaning in favor of verbal quibbling. . . . He too first introduced the method of discussion which is called Socratic.

----

*"As to the gods, . . ." as quoted above.

Source: T. V. Smith, ed., *Philosophers Speak for Themselves: From Thales to Plato* (Chicago: University of Chicago Press, 1934), pp. 61–62.

----

types, without individual problems or cares, vigorous yet serene, ideally proportioned, and often in a state of controlled tension.

The architecture and sculpture of the Parthenon and its surrounding temples exemplify the synthesis of religious feeling, patriotic dedication, artistic genius, and intellectual freedom characteristic of the age of Pericles. It would be pleasant to think of the Athenians of this period enjoying the beauty of these temples that so perfectly express the mood of the age. But such was not the case. The Parthenon, the first of the new Acropolis structures to be completed, was not finished until 432 B.C. a scant year before the outbreak of the Peloponnesian War that ultimately brought Athens to its knees. By 432 the old civic-religious enthusiasm was already waning. For centuries thereafter, Greek art would be a living, creative force; indeed, some of its most celebrated masterpieces were products of these later centuries. But the balanced, confident spirit of Periclean Athens—the spirit that shaped the works of Sophocles and Phidias and inspired the Parthenon—could never quite be recovered.

Teaching and Questioning the Polis: The Sophists and Socrates In philosophy, history, and science, reason was winning its victories at the expense of the supernatural. The anthropomorphic gods of Olympus were especially susceptible to rational criticism. Few people influenced by Ionian philosophy or the new traditions of history and medicine, for example, could seriously believe that Zeus hurled thunderbolts or that Poseidon caused earthquakes. Some Greeks began to see Zeus as a transcendent god of the universe; others called him a metaphor; a few rejected him altogether. But anyone who doubted that Zeus tosses thunderbolts might also doubt that Athena protects Athens. And the rejection of Athena and other civic deities clearly threatened the traditional spirit of the polis, and exposed it to divine retribution. Skepticism was gradually undermining civic patriotism, and as skepticism advanced, patriotism receded. Once again we are confronted with the dynamic and paradoxical nature of the Greek experience: The polis produced the inquiring mind, but in time the inquiring mind eroded the most fundamental traditions of the polis.

Skepticism was nourished in fifth-century B.C. Athens by men known as sophists ("wisdom-ists"), a diverse group of professional teachers drawn from all over the Greek world by the wealth of the imperial city. Much of our information about the sophists comes from the hostile writings of Plato, who portrayed them as tricksters. In reality most of them were dedicated to reason and sound argument. But they were also professionals who charged high fees for their services and—in teaching well-to-do youths—went beyond traditional family-centered education, which had been limited to reading and reckoning, music, and athletics.

Unlike the Ionian philosophers, the sophists were more interested in human behavior than the cosmos. They investigated ethics, politics, history, and psychology, and professed to teach the ways of achieving arete—excellence in anything the student wanted. But in applying cold logic to these areas and teaching their students to do the same, they aroused the wrath of conservatives and encouraged irreverence toward tradition. (There is always a limit to the amount of skepticism and change that any social system can tolerate.) One teacher, a friend of Pericles, got thrown out of Athens for suggesting that the sun—traditionally considered divine—was merely a burning rock "as large as the Peloponnesus." Some sophists undoubtedly taught the tricks of debating and getting ahead, while questioning the traditional doctrines of religion, patriotism, and dedication to community welfare. By stressing rhetorical techniques, they invited the charge that they had no values—that they would teach you how to persuade an audience of anything, right or wrong. Plato accused one of claiming that "justice is the interest of the stronger"—that is, that Might makes Right. Collectively, the sophists' intellectual rigor stimulated (and responded to) "modern" Athenians' doubts, relativism, and questionings of tradition.

Socrates (469–399 B.C.), the patron saint of intellectuals, played a pivotal role in Western thought. He was, in a sense, a sophist himself, although he proclaimed himself their enemy. He differed sharply from them because he accepted no fees and confessed that he knew only how to ask questions. He also claimed to hear a divine voice that spoke to him alone, and had the habit of falling into mystic trances.

A native Athenian who had done his duty as a hoplite, and a stonecutter by trade, Socrates wandered the streets of Athens during the desperate later years of the Peloponnesian War encouraging his listeners to test their ethical beliefs and preconceptions with the tool of reason. "An unexamined life," he once said, "is scarcely worth living." Like the sophists, Socrates was interested in human rather than cosmic matters, but unlike many of them he was dissatisfied with merely tearing down traditional beliefs. Employing what later came to be known as the "Socratic method," he set the stage by posing seemingly innocent questions to his listeners that invariably entangled them in a hopeless maze of contradictions. Then, having demolished their opinions with relentless questioning,

Socrates   As he himself said, Socrates was anything but handsome. An ancient biographer claimed that, serving as a hoplite in the Peloponnesian War, he frightened off Spartan attackers by glaring fiercely at them. Apparently this allowed his comrades to escape from a dangerously exposed position. © *Trustees of the British Museum.*

he substituted closely reasoned conclusions of his own on the subject of ethics and the good life. Knowledge, he taught, was synonymous with virtue, for a person who knew the truth would act righteously. Driven by this optimistic conviction, he continued to attack cherished beliefs—to be a gadfly, as he put it.

Gadflies are never popular. The democrats of Athens, frightened by their defeat in the Peloponnesian War

THE HISTORICAL EVIDENCE

Socrates' Apology

399 B.C.

Socrates was put on trial for "corrupting the youth of Athens" after citizens like Anytus—referred to here—brought formal charges against him. His trial took place before 501 Athenians, who functioned as both judge and jury. After his execution, his disciple Plato wrote several narratives of the great gadfly's last days, including The Apology,* *supposedly the long speech that Socrates made in his own defense. The speech has always been regarded in Western civilization as a classic statement of intellectual integrity in the face of popular hysteria. But we must also keep in mind Plato's strong bias against democracy, and the connections that Athenians saw between Socrates' devastating logic, the decline of old-fashioned values, and the notorious behavior of some of Socrates' students at the end of the Peloponnesian War.*

Suppose, then that you acquit me. . . . Suppose that . . . you said to me "Socrates, on this occasion we shall disregard Anytus† and acquit you, but only on one condition, that you give up spending your time on this quest and stop philosophizing. If we catch you going on in the same way, you shall be put to death." Well, supposing, as I said, that you should offer to acquit me on these terms, I should reply, "Gentlemen, I am your very grateful and devoted servant, but I owe a greater obedience to God than to you; and as long as I draw breath and have my faculties, I shall never stop practicing philosophy and exhorting you and elucidating the truth for everyone that I meet. I shall go on saying, in my usual way, 'My very good friend, you are an Athenian and belong to a city which is the greatest and most famous in the world for its wisdom and strength. Are you not ashamed that you give your attention to acquiring as much money as possible, and give no attention or thought to truth and understanding and the perfection of your soul?' And if any of you disputes then and professes to care about these things, I shall not at once let him go or leave him; no, I shall question him and examine him and test him; and if it appears that in spite of his profession he has made no real progress toward goodness, I shall reprove him

for neglecting what is of supreme importance, and giving his attention to trivialities. I shall do this to everyone that I meet, young or old, foreigner or fellow-citizen; but especially to you my fellow-citizens, inasmuch as you are closer to me in kinship. This, I do assure you, is what my God commands; and it is my belief that no greater good has ever befallen you in this city than my service to my God; for I spend all my time going about trying to persuade you, young and old, to make your first and chief concern not for your bodies nor for your possessions, but for the highest welfare of your souls, proclaiming as I go 'Wealth does not bring goodness, but goodness brings wealth and every other blessing, both to the individual and to the State.' Now if I corrupt the young by this message, the message would seem to be harmful; but if anyone says that my message is different from this, he is talking nonsense."

---

*The Greek word *apologia* means "defense," not "apology" in the contemporary English sense.

†One of Socrates' accusers at his trial.

Source: Plato, *The Last Days of Socrates*, rev. ed., trans. Hugh Tredennick (Harmondsworth, England: Penguin, 1969), pp. 61–62.

(which was hastened by the treachery of one of Socrates' pupils), could bear him no longer. In 399 B.C., five years after their surrender to Sparta, they brought Socrates to trial for denying the gods and corrupting the young, and by a narrow majority they found him guilty. Under Athenian law, he had the right to propose his own punishment. He suggested jokingly that the Athenians punish him by giving him free meals at public expense for the rest of his life (the customary reward to a champion athlete). By refusing to take the business seriously, he was condemning himself to death. Declining an opportunity to escape into exile, he was executed by poison. He expired with the cheerful

observation that at last he had the opportunity of discovering for himself the truth about life after death.

Plato and Aristotle

Socrates would have failed as an American university professor: Although he was a splendid teacher, he did not publish. We know of his teachings largely through the graceful dialogues of his student Plato (427–347 B.C.), an Athenian aristocrat and one of history's supreme intellects.

In his *Republic*, Plato outlined the perfect polis. Its explicit purpose was to secure justice, to ensure that Might did not make Right. Ironically (as it must seem to us today), the philosopher rejected the democracy that he knew and described an ideal state more Spartan than Athenian. Plato's republic would wield total power over its inhabitants—all for good ends, of course. But farmers, workers, and merchants would have no political rights. A military-executive elite, trained with Spartan rigor, would defend and administer the state, under the direction of philosopher-kings, the wisest and most virtuous products of a state training program that consumed the better part of their lives. Women, if they met the exacting standards, could become philosopher-kings, too (and as a consistent feminist he admitted qualified women to his school). But Plato was equally radical in proposing that the republic's rulers should pair up ordinary men and women, just as a wise farmer breeds his animals. Culture would not be encouraged in Plato's republic. Dangerous and novel ideas would be forbidden, poets (even Homer) outlawed, and all music prohibited except martial, patriotic tunes.

What are we to make of a utopia that bans Mozart and whistles "Yankee Doodle," a polis that could never have produced a Plato? We must remember that democratic Athens was in decline when Plato wrote. He could not love the polis that had executed his master, nor was he blind to the selfish individualism and civic irresponsibility that afflicted fourth-century B.C. Greece. Plato had the wisdom to recognize that through the intensity of its creativity, and the freedom and breadth of its intellectual curiosity, the polis was burning itself out. Achilles had chosen a short but glorious life; Plato preferred longevity even at the cost of mediocrity, and he designed his republic to achieve that goal. There would be no sophists to erode civic virtue, no poets to exalt the individual over the community (or abandon their shields as they fled from battle). Plato's cavalier treatment of commerce represents a deliberate rejection of empire and money-making. Like a figure on a Grecian urn, his ideal polis would be rigid—and enduring. His was the first utopia in Western history: the first rational plan for a society designed to resolve all conflict and end all injustice. There would be many more in the nearly twenty-five hundred years that followed.

There remains the paradox that this intellectually static commonwealth was to be ruled by philosophers. We tend to think of philosophy as singularly disputatious, but Plato saw Truth as absolute and unchanging. He assumed that all true philosophers would agree with him. His assumption has proved to be resoundingly false, yet Plato nevertheless exerted an enormous influence on the development of thought.

Plato, like other thinkers of his time, faced two seemingly irreconcilable choices in defining the nature of the world. Heraclitus had claimed that the only thing "real" is constant change, or "Becoming"; Parmenides had insisted that only unchanging "Being" is real. Plato agreed with Parmenides: The "real" universe is perfect and unchanging;

Plato This bust, from Plato's time, may be an authentic portrait. His real name was Ariston; *Platon* was a nickname meaning "broad," probably a reference to his shoulders. (As a young man, Plato was well known as a wrestler.) *Staatliche Museen, Berlin Preussischer Kulturbesitz, Antikensammlung. Antike Portrats/Platon.*

what we experience in the visible universe is mere diversity and impermanence.[9] The objects that our senses perceive are only the pale, imperfect reflections of ideal models or archetypes that exist in a world invisible to us. For example, we observe numerous individual cats, some black, some yellow, some fat, some skinny. All are imperfect particularizations of the ideal cat, purring in the Platonic heaven. Again, we find in the world of the senses many examples of

---

[9] Modern physicists who delve into ancient philosophy find Heraclitus's theory of constant flux and "Becoming" a good metaphor for the behavior of subatomic particles, and they reject Plato's vision of ultimate reality as something stable and unchanging. To this Plato would doubtless retort that the things made up of molecules, atoms, and subatomic particles may indeed be ephemeral and "unreal," but their forms remain unchanging in the mind of God.

duality: lovers, twins, bookends, and so on. But they merely exemplify, more or less inadequately, the idea of "two," which in its pure state is invisible and intangible. We cannot see "two." We can only see two things. But—and this is all-important—we can conceive of "twoness" or abstract duality. Likewise, with sufficient effort, we can conceive of "catness,"—of the archetypal cat. If we could not, so Plato believed, we would have no basis for grouping individual cats into a single category.

In short, the world of phenomena is not the real world. The phenomenal world is variegated and dynamic—and illusory. But the *real* world—the world of archetypes—is not forever in flux, as Heraclitus had believed; it is clearcut and static, as Parmenides had declared. We can discover this real world through introspection, for knowledge of the archetypes is present in our minds from birth, dimly remembered from a previous existence. (Plato believed in a beforelife as well as in an afterlife.) So the philosopher studies reality not by observing but by thinking.

Plato illustrated this doctrine with a vivid metaphor. Imagine an underground cave whose inhabitants are chained so that they can never turn toward the sunlit opening but can see only shadows projected against an interior wall.[10] Then imagine that one inhabitant (the philosopher) breaks his chains, emerges from the cave, and sees the real, sunlit world for the first time. He will have no wish to return to his former shadow world, but he will nevertheless do so out of a sense of obligation to enlighten his chained companions. Similarly, the philosopher-kings rule the republic unwillingly, through a sense of duty. They would prefer to meditate undisturbed. Yet they alone can rule wisely, for they alone have seen the Truth.

Plato's doctrine of ideas has always been alluring to people who seek order and unity, stability and virtue, in a universe that appears fickle and chaotic. Plato declared that the greatest of the archetypes is the idea of the Good, and this notion has greatly appealed to people of religious temperament ever since. His theory of knowledge, which emphasizes contemplation over observation, is obviously hostile to the methods of experimental science. Yet Plato's archetypal world meshes perfectly with the mathematician's world—the world of pure numbers. "Let no one ignorant of mathematics enter" was carved over the entrance to his school, the Academy. Plato drew heavily from the Pythagorean tradition—"God is a mathematician," he once said—and Platonic thought, like Pythagorean thought, has contributed immensely to the development of mathematical science. As for philosophy, that discipline developed over the next two thousand years in the shadow of two giants. One was Plato; the other was Aristotle, Plato's greatest pupil at the Academy.

The son of a Greek physician in the service of King Philip of Macedon, Aristotle (384–322 B.C.) remained at the Academy for nearly two decades. Then he returned to Philip's court to tutor the future Alexander the Great. When Alexander, having come to power, had no more need of a tutor, Aristotle went back to Athens, founded a school of his own (the Lyceum), and wrote most of his books. At length the Athenians condemned him for "impiety." Unlike Socrates, Aristotle escaped into exile, explaining that he wished to spare Athens from committing a second sin against philosophy. He died shortly thereafter, in 322 B.C., a year after world-conquering Alexander had gone to his own early grave. Thus Aristotle's life spanned the final years of classical Greece and the dawn of the Hellenistic Age.

Aristotle was a universal scholar—a polymath. He wrote authoritatively on a great variety of topics: biology, politics, literature, ethics, logic, physics, and **metaphysics.** Like the physician Hippocrates and the historians Herodotus and Thucydides, but on a grander scale, Aristotle advocated the painstaking collection and analysis of data. His groundbreaking biological studies were based on

Aristotle This is a Roman copy of a Greek original from the fourth century B.C. By Roman times, this was the standard image of a Greek philosopher: bearded, wide-browed, serene, and with penetrating gaze. *Kunsthistorisches Museum, Vienna.*

---

[10] Today, Plato would doubtless show people chained to a television set.

careful observation and classification into genus and species.[11] In logic and metaphysics, he brought Plato's theory of ideas down to earth by asserting that the archetype exists in the particular—that one can best study the archetypal cat by observing and classifying individual cats. He thus gave observation a higher priority than had Plato. Although his political studies included the designing of an ideal commonwealth, he also investigated and classified the political systems of many existing poleis and demonstrated that several different types were conducive to the good life. In ethics, he advocated moderation in all behavior, arguing that emotions and actions (anger and love, eating and drinking) are themselves neither good nor evil; they should be neither suppressed nor carried to excess: Virtue is the avoidance of extremes, the "golden mean." His literary criticism is still admired for its penetrating analysis of tragedy, and at various times in Western history his notions of how a drama should be constructed stood as virtual law.[12]

For two thousand years Aristotle defined Western physics. His approach rested on three fundamental assertions. First, building on Plato's position that "true" reality is perfect and changeless, Aristotle insisted that motion is an unnatural state: Ideally, things are stable; if they move, something must be pushing them. Second, for Aristotle the organizing principle of the material universe—the world that we see about us—is *purpose*. That is, everything exists because it has a purpose to fulfill, which is unchanging and has been assigned by God.[13] Third, Aristotle defined things in terms of their qualitative rather than quantitative differences. For example: The heavenly bodies are perfect and eternal; objects on earth are "imperfect," "corruptible," changeable, and impermanent. Or take another example: Material objects fall because that is their nature; as corruptible, impermanent things, they belong to the earth and always return to it. (Fire and air naturally move upwards because they are incorruptible.)

Mathematics had no genuine role in Aristotle's system. Ultimately, modern science draws its experimental method from Aristotelian data-collecting and its mathematical analysis from Pythagorean-Platonic thought.

Altogether, Aristotle's explanation of how the world works was a massive intellectual achievement with a powerful internal logic. All the pieces fit together. Nothing in it contradicted common sense—that is, what an intelligent and diligent collector of data could see with his or her eyes. In the second century A.D. the astronomer and mathematician Ptolemy would complete Aristotle's world picture by constructing an elaborate mathematical scheme that accounted for the visible movements of heavenly bodies. Together, the Aristotelian-Ptolemaic synthesis would constitute what historians of science call the **Old Paradigm.** As such, it would dominate Western science until the sixteenth and seventeenth centuries, when it was overturned in successive steps by Copernicus, Galileo, and Newton (see Chapter 17).

Aristotle's physics and metaphysics powerfully shaped the direction of Western religious thought for many centuries to come. His account of physical reality rested on the concept of a single motive power behind the universe—the unmoved mover and the uncaused cause to which all motion and causation ultimately went back. Hence Aristotelianism later became a philosophical framework for Islamic and Christian monotheism, and during the Middle Ages it would give crucial inspiration to both faiths, as well as to Judaism. This is not to say that Aristotle fit comfortably with the Judeo-Christian and Islamic traditions. Aristotle's God had not created the eternal universe and would not destroy it; his sole function was just to get things moving. God took no interest in the fate of human beings, and did not give them immortality. As we shall see in Chapter 10, these were dimensions of Aristotle's thought that medieval monotheists—Muslim, Jewish, and Christian—either had to explain away or reject.

Plato and Aristotle stood at the apex of Greek philosophy. Both were religious men (indeed, monotheists), and both were dedicated to a life of reason. Building on a rationalizing heritage that had begun only two centuries before them, both produced philosophical systems of unparalleled sophistication and depth. Their thought climaxed the intellectual revolution that brought such glory and turmoil to Greece.

The Decline of the Polis

Plato and Aristotle alike were conservatives not only in their view of democracy—Plato condemned it, and Aristotle thought that it could work only if people were thoroughly virtuous—but also in their belief that the ideal polis should be kept as compact as possible. For Aristotle, this meant a city small enough for every citizen to know his fellow citizens well. If we compare his ideal polis to an academic setting, the analogy would be to a small liberal arts college (from which no one ever graduates). Fourth-century Athens was nothing of the sort: Its modern academic counterpart would be a huge state university campus.

---

[11] Not, however, the genus and species of modern biology, which originated with Carl Linnaeus in the eighteenth century.

[12] Aristotle's dramatic rules included an insistence on the unity of time and place: The drama must focus on a single incident that builds to a climax and is resolved. Shakespeare's plays, which sometimes sprawl over a long span of time or are set in different places, violate these rules; the dramas of seventeenth-century French classicism respect them carefully. Aristotle would have hated soap operas.

[13] *Teleology* is the technical name that philosophers use for the attempt to define the purpose of things; a *teleological* explanation for something is an explanation in terms of that object's purpose. Aristotle was the first great philosopher to use this approach.

THE HISTORICAL EVIDENCE

Aristotle on Democracy and Class Politics

ca. 320 B.C.

Aristotle's Politics *is a classic work of political philosophy and a gold mine of insights into the mentality of the polis. Much of his book strikes contemporary readers as objectionable—his contempt for manual labor, for example, or his assurance that women and slaves were inherently inferior and deserved not having any rights. It is also apparent that Aristotle hankered for old-fashioned polis life of the sort that had become completely obsolete by the late fourth century B.C. Aristotle did not reject democracy, but he contrasted it sharply with its degenerate form, "mob rule." The following passage is interesting for the light that it sheds on how democratic politics worked in the Athens of Aristotle's time, and what a pro-aristocratic thinker thought of it all.*

Popular leaders, in their endeavour to win the favor of the masses, make great use of the law-courts; by legal confiscations they augment the people's funds. Those who have the interests of the constitution at heart ought to resist these attempts. . . . For it is not their fellow democrats that they [the popular leaders] bring into court but men of wealth and distinction. This constitution like any other ought . . . to command the support of citizens of all classes. At least those who exercise government should not be regarded as enemies.

In these thorough-going democracies populations are large and attendance at meetings of the Assembly is difficult for people unless they are paid. And unless money for this is forthcoming from the revenues, there is hostility among the upper classes; for the money has then to be raised by taxation and confiscation and the improper use of law-suits—things which before now have caused democracies to fall. . . . On the other hand if revenues are available, do not do what popular leaders do—make a free distribution of the whole surplus. For the duty of the truly democratic politician is just to see that people are not destitute; for destitution is the cause of the deterioration of democracy. Every effort must therefore be made to perpetuate prosperity. And, since this is to the advantage of the rich as well as the poor, all that can be got from the revenues should be collected into a single fund and distributed to those in need, if possible enough for the purchase of a piece of land, but if not, enough to start a business or work on the land.

Source: Aristotle, *The Politics*, trans. J. A. Sinclair (Harmondsworth, England: Penguin, 1962), pp. 245–246.

The essential characteristic of the classical polis had been the participation of its citizens in the political and cultural life of their community. Citizens were expected to take care of their private business and at the same time attend the assembly, participate in decisions, serve in the administration, and fight in the army or navy. Statesmen such as Pericles were at once administrators, orators, and generals. The polis at its height was a community of well-rounded citizens with many interests and capabilities.

But as the fourth century progressed and gifted amateurism waned, professionals took over athletics. Military tactics became more intricate. Administrative procedures grew more complicated. Oratory demanded specialized study. Performance in the great Athenian dramas passed from ordinary citizens to professional actors and choruses. As these and other disciplines became more and more difficult to master, audiences became mere spectators. The polis of the later fourth century B.C. was filled with professional administrators, orators, scholars, bankers, actors, sailors, and merchants, whose demanding careers left them time for little else. Citizens were becoming absorbed in their private affairs, and political life was losing its allure. Citizen-soldiers gave way increasingly to mercenaries, partly because civic patriotism was running dry but also because fighting was now a full-time career and mercenaries were better at it. The precarious equilibrium achieved in the classical age between competence and versatility—between individual and community—would not last. As the celebrated scholar H. D. F. Kitto observed, "Progress broke the polis"; yet progress was a fundamental ingredient of the way of life that the polis created.

In short, the classical Greek polis bore the seeds of Western civilization, but also those of its own destruction. Like Homer's hero Achilles, the polis died an early death—but not before redirecting the course of history.

ALEXANDER AND THE DIFFUSION OF HELLENISM

In 336 B.C., barely two years after his climactic victory over the Greeks at Chaeronea, King Philip of Macedon suffered the fate of his own victims. He was murdered as a consequence of a palace intrigue and war, and he was succeeded by his son, Alexander, later to be called "the Great."[14] In his final months, Philip had been preparing a large-scale attack against the Persian Empire, hoping to transform the grudging obedience of the Greek city-states into enthusiastic support by leading a pan-Hellenic war of revenge against the traditional enemy. Alexander, during a dazzling reign of thirteen years, exceeded his father's most fantastic dreams. Leading his all-conquering armies from Greece through Persia to India, he changed the course of the ancient world's history.

With the rise of Alexander's world empire and of the somewhat more permanent kingdoms that his successors carved out of it, the political orientation of the ancient Greeks shifted decisively. Polis gave way to metropolis, and self-governing citizens devolved into subjects. The poleis survived throughout much of Greece as quasi-autonomous urban communities, but they were manipulated and dominated by Alexander's successors through local pro-Macedonian political factions, often backed by Macedonian garrisons in town citadels. One such garrison, small but intimidating, camped in the Athenian seaport of Piraeus through most of the third century B.C. Thus the enterprising spirit of the polis dimmed under the overshadowing authority of kings. Deprived of true political independence, the polis lost its dynamism and its cultural significance. Periclean democracy did not long survive Philip and Alexander.

Alexander's Conquest of Greece

Although he was only twenty when he inherited the throne, Alexander possessed in fullest measure the combination of physical attractiveness, athletic prowess, and intellectual distinction that had long been the Greek ideal. Here was a magnetic leader who inspired intense loyalty and admiration among his followers, a brilliant general who adapted his tactics and strategy to the most varied circumstances, and a champion of Hellenic culture and the Greek way of life. Two great teachers had schooled him: Aristotle the master philosopher, and King Philip himself, the best general and most adroit political opportunist of the age. Alexander acquired his generalship from his father and his Hellenism from his tutor. His turn of mind is epitomized by the two things that he kept beneath his pillow: the *Iliad* and a dagger.

Alexander the Great   This is thought to be a likeness from Alexander's lifetime, showing him as he liked to be depicted: as the hero Heracles. It is fascinating to try to speculate about what insights into Alexander's character and aims this portrait suggests. *Museum of Fine Arts, Boston; Otis Norcross Fund. All rights reserved.*

At first, the Greek poleis squirmed under Alexander's rule. He quelled their uprisings mercilessly; at rebellious Thebes, for instance, he killed all the men and sold the women and children into slavery. But his campaign against Persia evoked genuine support. In the spring of 334 B.C., he led a Greco-Macedonian army of some thirty thousand foot soldiers and five thousand cavalry into Anatolia and, during the next three and a half years, won a series of stunning victories over the loosely structured Persian Empire. Striking hard and swiftly, making skillful and effective use of hoplites, sometimes personally leading cavalry charges against Persian armies, he won the confidence and devotion of his men through his tactical genius, his charismatic leadership, and his audacious courage. He never abandoned a siege or lost a battle.

Alexander freed the Ionian cities from Persian domination (bringing them under his own authority) and conquered the imperial provinces of Syria and Egypt. Then,

---

[14] There is some reason for suspecting Alexander's participation in the assassination plot.

deep in the enemy's heartland, he won a decisive victory over the Persian army at Gaugamela on the Tigris in 331 B.C. The triumph at Gaugamela enabled Alexander to seize the vast imperial treasure at Persepolis, ascend the imperial throne, and bring an end to the dynasty of ancient Persia.

The Hellenization of the Near East

This was a glorious moment for the Greeks. The foe that had so long tormented Hellas was conquered. More than that, the ancient Near East now lay open to Greek enterprise, culture, and exploitation. Alexander's conquest of the Persian Empire set the stage for a new epoch—a period known as the *Hellenistic* Age, as distinct from the previous *Hellenic* Age—the age of the polis. The Greeks had now mastered the ancient Near East, and under them a great cosmopolitan culture developed, distinctly Greek in tradition yet transmuted by the influence of the subject Near Eastern civilizations, by the huge new cities that Greek kings ruled, and by the spacious new environment in which Greeks now lived. The new culture has thus been termed "Hellenistic"—not purely Greek (Hellenic) but "Greek-like."

The hellenization of the Near East was facilitated by Alexander's policy of founding cities in the wake of his

conquests and filling them with Greek settlers. These communities, although intended chiefly as military and commercial bases, became oases of the Greek way of life that often exerted a powerful pull on surrounding areas. Many were named, immodestly, after their founder. The greatest by far was Alexandria in Egypt, which Alexander established at the mouth of the Nile. Alexandria quickly outstripped the cities of Greece itself to become the commercial metropolis of the Hellenistic world. Before long it had developed a cultural and intellectual life that outshone contemporary Athens.

Once he ascended the throne of Persia, Alexander began preparations for further campaigns. He spent the final seven years of his life conquering the easternmost provinces of the Persian Empire and pushing into India. Impelled by a thirst for conquest and the lure of undiscovered lands, his spirit and ingenuity were taxed to the utmost by the rugged mountains of Afghanistan, hostile stretches of the Indus Valley, and Indian enemy armies with hundreds of war elephants. Despite all this he established hegemony over the Indus Valley, making a vassal of its king, and then pressed eastward. But at length his own army, its endurance exhausted, refused to go farther. It is the mark of a great leader, his generals told him, to know

MAP 3-2
ALEXANDER THE GREAT'S EMPIRE AND ITS SUCCESSORS

when to stop. Reluctantly, Alexander returned in 323 B.C. to Persia. On the way, he and his army almost died of thirst in southwestern Iran's desert.

The empire of Alexander (see Map 3-2) was the greatest that the world had ever seen—vaster even than the Persian Empire. Wherever he went Alexander adapted himself to the customs of the land. He ruled Egypt as a divine pharaoh and Persia as "king of kings," demanding that his subjects prostrate themselves in his presence. (His Greek followers objected vigorously.) He married the daughter of the last Persian king and urged his principal lieutenants to follow his example by taking wives from among the Persian aristocracy. His goal was apparently to make his rule palatable to indigenous elites. But his great plans and high hopes were dashed when, at his headquarters in Babylon, he suddenly died at thirty-two, perhaps of malaria—or, some suspect, of poison. He left behind him a sense of loss and bewilderment and a vast empire that only a second Alexander could have held together.

The Hellenistic Kingdoms

Alexander's followers fought ferociously over who would inherit his empire (which, dying, he bequeathed "to the strongest"). In the bloodbath, his wife, son, close kinfolk, and mother (who started it all) perished. After several decades the struggle ended with some of Alexander's leading generals dividing the empire between them. The result was a series of Macedonian royal dynasties that ruled Greece and most of the Near East. Other notable Hellenistic states had never been part of Alexander's empire (but were on his list for future conquest); of these, Syracuse was the most important. It flourished in the shadow of Carthage's western Mediterranean empire, dominating much of Sicily, until the Romans overwhelmed both in the late second century B.C. And a number of smaller states arose from the wreckage of Alexander's empire. But there were three main successor kingdoms—Ptolemaic Egypt, Seleucid Asia, and Antigonid Macedonia (which had control over mainland Greece)—and they endured until Rome swallowed them all up in the second and first centuries B.C.

Ptolemy, one of Alexander's ablest generals, established a dynasty that would rule Egypt until a Roman army deposed his descendant, the famous Cleopatra VII, in 30 B.C. From their magnificent capital of Alexandria, the Ptolemies ruled with all the pomp and authority of the pharaohs, enriching themselves through the tight control that pharaohs had traditionally imposed on the Egyptian economy. Alexandria was the wonder of the age, with its imposing public buildings, its superb library and museum[15]

for scholarly research, its far-flung commerce, and its population of a half-million or more—ethnic Greeks and "orientals" who learned Greek, including a significant community of Jews. But apart from this and a few other Greek settlements, Egypt remained essentially unchanged.

Ptolemaic Egypt was a bureaucrat's paradise. "No one has the right to do what he wants to do, but everything is regulated for the best," one edict proclaimed, and at first all this worked with considerable efficiency. Taxes were extremely heavy, keeping ordinary people impoverished even in good times. By the second and first centuries B.C., however, Egyptian resentment of Ptolemaic rule grew stronger, and the economy deteriorated.

The second important chunk that split off from Alexander's conquests was northern Syria, together with much of the rest of the old Persian Empire. This share fell to another of Alexander's generals, Seleucus, who founded the Seleucid dynasty. Its center was the city of Antioch on the eastern Mediterranean, second only to Alexandria in population and opulence. The kingdom of the Seleucids had a looser organization than that of the Ptolemies, and over time some of the Near Eastern peoples began to rebel against the Seleucid policy of imposing Greek culture on them. Resentment was strongest among the Persians and Jews, who had each produced powerful monotheistic religions and resented bitterly the influx of Greek religious thought. Farther to the east, the Parthians, a non-Persian people from the region of the Caspian Sea, had taken most of the Iranian plateau by the mid-third century B.C., establishing a powerful empire that even Rome could never conquer. (A Greek-ruled kingdom, Bactria, survived until about A.D. 1 at the farthest reaches of Alexander's former empire, in what is now Afghanistan.)

The third important successor state, Macedon, soon passed to a dynasty known as the Antigonids, whose authority extended southward across mainland Greece and into Anatolia. But their control of the Greek poleis was never very firm, and in the international politics of the Hellenistic world they were usually overshadowed by the Ptolemies and Seleucids. Eventually the Antigonids lost western Anatolia to other Greek-ruled kingdoms, notably Pergamum, that survived until the arrival of the empire-building Romans.

Some Hellenistic monarchs were capable, energetic, and hardworking men and women. (Some were also vicious or incompetent, and a few may have been mad.) Hellenistic kingship bore a far closer resemblance to the traditional monarchies of the ancient Near East, with their god-kings or kings who claimed to be the gods' stewards, than to the aristocratic or democratic self-government of the archaic and classical Greek poleis. Of course there was a dramatic contrast of scale, as the new monarchies sprawled over immense areas, which everyone agreed could be ruled only by an autocrat through his bureaucracy.

More striking still was the aura of divinity surrounding these autocrats. *Soter*—"savior"—was one of the most

---

[15] This was not, as we understand the word *museum*, an institution where works of art or scientific artifacts were shown, but rather a "think tank" that brought together a select group of notable scholars in residence. The name comes from the Muses—in Greek mythology, the guardian spirits of the arts.

frequent titles that they bore, formally or informally. One Seleucid king (an upstart of vicious character and little ability) gloried in the name Alexander I Theopator Euergetes Epiphanes Nicephorus—"Son of a Divine Father/ Benefactor/God-Manifest/Bringer of Victory."[16] Such extravagance was not simply a matter of kings arrogantly claiming to be gods; much of this "divinizing" welled up from below, encouraged partly by Greek traditions of seeing something divine in heroes like Heracles and Achilles, and partly because god-kings were an ancient Near Eastern tradition. The actual worship of rulers went farthest in Egypt, where the Ptolemies claimed to be successors to the pharaohs—and often adopted the pharaonic custom of marrying their sisters, which produced a number of masterful queens; Cleopatra VII was the last of them (far from marrying her half-brother, however, she killed him). Hellenistic kings were looked upon by their subjects half in fear and half in reverent awe, as divinely appointed bulwarks against the whims of Fortune. These royalty were one more symptom of an age of anxiety.

HELLENISTIC THOUGHT AND CULTURE

Thus the conquests of Philip and Alexander the Great transformed the ancient world. Huge kingdoms encompassing diverse peoples overshadowed the old city-states as the characteristic sovereign units of Hellenistic society. The entire Near East was becoming gradually hellenized as ambitious Greek settlers poured into the new cities of Seleucid Asia and Ptolemaic Egypt that Alexander had founded. The Greek language itself changed as the old dialects—Attic, Ionian, Doric, and others—got homogenized into a simpler, less polished vernacular that Greeks of many different origins shared, and that foreigners who needed to speak Greek could more readily learn. This *koine* ("common") Greek would be the main language in the eastern Mediterranean for centuries to come, in which the

---

[16] He died in 145 B.C. and was a usurper.

The Great Altar at Pergamum The Greek kings of Pergamum, a state on the northwestern coast of Anatolia that broke off from the Antigonid kingdom of Macedonia, built this magnificently elaborate altar between 175 and 150 B.C. It is one of the grandest surviving Hellenistic urban architectural ensembles and has been reconstructed in a museum in Berlin. *Staatliche Museen, Berlin Preussischer Kulturbesitz, Antikensammlung in Pergamenmuseum. Photo by Linde & Co., 1902.*

New Testament would be written and from which modern Greek descends.

The Greek immigrants who fanned out across the Near East tended to prosper in their new environment, planting in the societies of the ancient Near East a dominant Greek upper class of merchants, intellectuals, artists, and officials. And they introduced into their new surroundings such amenities of polis life as theaters, temples, and public buildings in the Greek style. Rather than blending Greek and Near Eastern cultures, the Hellenistic cities became islands of Greek life and transmitters of Greek ideas, customs, and styles into surrounding Near Eastern communities.

The Change in Mood

The new environment provided vast opportunities and encouraged a sense of the **cosmopolitan** that contrasted with the former provincialism and civic cohesion of the polis. This was an age of vigorous and profitable business activity, of successful careers in commerce and banking. Women's ties to the home loosened with the opening of new opportunities to hold and dispose of property and to engage in commercial enterprises. Some Greeks even came to believe that husbands and wives should be equal partners in marriage. Sculptors and writers treated womanhood with a sensitivity unknown in the classic period.

But as always, the good life was for the fortunate few. Slavery not only continued, but increased—in places like Sicily, on a massive scale. Peasants and urban commoners remained at an economic level of bare subsistence. Cities began to fill with impoverished day laborers, who often had been squeezed off the land. The typical agrarian unit was no longer the small or middle-sized farm but the huge plantation worked by gangs of slaves. Inflation, driven by the pressure of growing population on static resources, became a chronic problem. Ineradicable urban poverty baffled the governments of the day, and no one had good ideas of what to do about it. (The independent city-state of Rhodes, on the Aegean island of that name, came closest when it devised a system of public works and grain doles, but this mechanism functioned only as long as Rhodes remained a prosperous commercial center.) Usually the best solution was to appeal to the haphazard generosity of rich men, who generally preferred to underwrite civic beautification and elaborate public festivals.

The poleis of mainland Greece remained, but only as shells of their former selves. They lost most of their vitality as economic stagnation spread. Enterprising youths sought their fortunes in the Hellenistic cities overseas, lured by the glitter and bustle of Alexandria and Antioch as Greeks of an earlier generation had flocked to imperial Athens. No longer involved in political affairs (except as royal bureaucrats) or caught up in the intense life of a free community, overseas Greeks found themselves adrift in a

The Boxer Statuary of the Hellenistic Age ranks among the most famous of all Greek works of art, and some works are so familiar that they risk becoming clichés. This is unfortunate because they are masterpieces that speak eloquently of Hellenistic values. The tired pugilist shown here dates from 100—50 B.C. and is cast in bronze. Note the gloves—which made ancient boxing even more brutal than the modern version—and the man's broken nose. This is a copy of the original work, whose sculptor's name is unknown. *Scala/Art Resource, NY.*

wide and bewildering world over which they had little control.

The cosmopolitanism of the Hellenistic age gave rise to a sense of estrangement and alienation, uncertainty and loneliness. Fourth-century B.C. trends toward individualism, professionalism, and specialization accelerated. Writers and artists pushed realism and sentimentalism to their limits. Many Hellenistic artists turned to portraying the tragic and grotesque with powerfully effective results. Their work might lack the serenity and balance of the earlier period, but it surpassed classic art in psychological depth, virtuosity, and emotional impact. Painting flourished, and from literary descriptions and a few scraps of murals that

Ptolemy II Philadelphus and his Sister-Wife Arsinoe II   This is one of the great cameos from the Hellenistic world, 11.5 cm in diameter and carved from nine layers of hard stone. It dates from about 278 B.C. Ptolemy II's headdress combines Greek and Egyptian religious symbolism. Until her early death, Ptolemy II's sister, Arsinoe, was the dynamic partner in the marriage and the kingdom, and one of the great Hellenistic queens.
Kunsthistoriches Museum, Vienna.

have survived we can deduce that it achieved strikingly realistic effects, verging on the techniques of perspective. The more durable small-scale works of art created for rulers and the rich—medallions, cameos, coins, and jewelry— often bear witness to exquisite taste and skill.

Hellenistic literature is highly polished, and to judge from the large number of authors' names that we know, it must have produced a vast body of poetry, drama, and other writing. It also bred a host of professors and critics, to whom we are indebted for the editions we now possess of earlier classics. But relatively little of all this has been preserved, and the Hellenistic literature that we do have lacks the power of the surviving archaic and classical literature. A vital spark had gone out when the mass civic audiences (and performers) of polis-oriented drama and choral odes dried up, giving way to the diverse and widely scattered reading publics of the Hellenistic world, whose specialized tastes ran the gamut from racy trivia to ultra-sophisticated verse. Likewise the pointed civic consciousness of the fifth-century comic playwright Aristophanes gave way to the highly individualized realism of the Hellenistic drawing-room comedy and bedroom farce. From this point onward, Greek literature divides into "highbrow" and "middlebrow" categories. The highly individualistic quality of "highbrow" Hellenistic writing, which rejected the rugged grandeur

and vast themes of Homer and the classical dramatists, is summed up by one poet's sour remark that "a big book is a big nuisance."

Religion's Answers

Hellenic religion, with its traditional civic orientation, was all but transformed in this new age. Ancient bonds and loyalties faded, as many adventurous Greeks uprooted themselves from their poleis and struck out on their own. The result was an intense individualism, which found expression in a variety of religious and ethical ideas stressing personal fulfillment or personal salvation rather than family and community involvement. Individualism and cosmopolitanism went hand in hand; for as the Greeks retreated spiritually away from the polis and into themselves, they came to see all humanity as a multitude of individuals. In such an undifferentiated, universal community, intelligent Persians, Egyptians, and Jews seemed no worse than intelligent Greeks. The traditional contrast between Greek and "barbarian" faded. The free spirit of the polis had set the Greeks apart, but now the polis, in its traditional sense, was becoming an anachronism. Yet the concept of *cosmopolis* ("world-city"), the idea of a common humanity, was too abstract to provide the sense of involvement and orientation that the polis had formerly given. The rootless Greek tended to turn away from the old Olympic gods and seek solace in more personal religious concepts. Hellenistic religion meant a withdrawal from active social participation and a search for sanctuary in a restless, uncertain world.

The Hellenistic age soon was awash in mystery and salvation cults, such as Orphism and the worship of Dionysus and Demeter, which had always lurked around the fringes of Olympian religion, and which the poleis had tried to tame by making them civic cults. Now various Near Eastern mystery religions also found their avid Greek believers. Most of these centered on the death and resurrection of a god who promised personal salvation—freedom from Chance, pain, and death. From Egypt came the cult of Osiris who died, was reborn, and now sat in judgment on the dead. (Not only did many Greeks adopt aspects of Egyptian religion intact, but the Ptolemaic kings also invented the pseudo-Egyptian religion of a benign god called Sarapis, Isis's wealth-bestowing spouse, which became quite popular throughout the Greek-speaking world.) From Anatolia came Cybele, a slightly reworked version of the ancient Great Mother, the incarnation of fertility. From Persia, somewhat later, came the worship of Mithras, a variant of Zoroastrianism that incorporated the latter's vision of a cosmic struggle between good and evil with a savior-hero who redeemed his male worshipers. (Women looked elsewhere, usually to Isis, for salvation.)

Alongside these and other Near Eastern cults flourished a revival of neo-Babylonian astrology, of magic,

Sarapis Invented by Egypt's Ptolemaic rulers as a spouse for the traditional Egyptian goddess Isis, Sarapis was worshiped throughout the Greek-speaking world, but this seems to have made little impression on native Egyptians. The head shown here was copied from a huge, jewel-laden cult statue in Alexandria. The basket perched on his head symbolizes "plenty." In some of his temples, elaborate machinery and lighting effects allowed the god's statue to move dramatically among the worshipers, like an American politician holding a televised "town meeting." © *R. Sheridan/Ancient Art & Architecture Collection.*

witchcraft, and sorcery. The cult of the goddess Tyche (Fortune), who rewarded talent and ambition and brought her worshipers material well-being (or so they hoped), but who could also bring everything tumbling down in ruin, spread like wildfire through the Greek world. The Hellenistic world became a religious melting pot in which a single individual might be a devotee of several cults—many tried them all. More thoughtful people sometimes adopted "syn-

cretism," the notion that the gods of different peoples are actually various manifestations of the same god and that Zeus, Osiris, even Yahweh, all symbolize a single divine spirit. (As we shall see, strictly monotheistic Jews found this doctrine abominable.) Religious beliefs and attitudes throughout the Hellenistic world, with their emphasis on individual salvation and savior gods, were preparing fertile soil for the later emergence of Christianity. But they also betrayed Hellenistic Greeks' loss of confidence in their traditional divinities and ideals, their tense anxieties, and their growing taste for mumbo jumbo.

Philosophers' Answers: Skeptics, Cynics, Epicureans, and Stoics

The most sophisticated post-classical Greeks turned neither to the old Orphic and Dionysian cults nor to the salvation cults of the East, but adapted elements of the Hellenic intellectual tradition to the new conditions.

One group, the Skeptics, intensified the relativism of the sophists by denying the possibility of any knowledge at all, whether of people, gods, or nature. The human mind, they maintained, is incapable of apprehending reality (if, indeed, there is any such thing as "reality"), and all beliefs and statements of fact are equally unverifiable. In doubting everything, they carried rationalism to its ultimate, self-destructive limit—questioning reason itself—and thus reflected the profound uncertainty of the new age.

Another group, the Cynics, demonstrated in various forms of eccentric behavior their contempt for conventional piety and patriotism and their rebellion against the hypocrisy they detected in their contemporaries. Diogenes, the most famous of the Cynics, was a fourth-century dropout—one historian, not intending disrespect, has called him a beatnik—who sought integrity in a world of careerists and phonies.

The impulse to withdraw from society that fascinated Skeptics and Cynics was also evident in the two religio-ethical systems that emerged in the fourth century B.C. and influenced Western thought and conduct for centuries thereafter: Epicureanism and Stoicism. Both were philosophies of resignation that taught believers to fortify their souls against the buffets of life.

Epicurus (ca. 341–270 B.C.), after whom his school was named, taught that people should seek happiness. But happiness to the Epicureans was not the pursuit of thrills, nor even lavish eating and drinking—but a quiet, balanced life. The drunkard's life is saddened by countless hangovers, the libertine's by endless emotional complications. Happiness is achieved not by chasing pleasures that will never satisfy, but by living simply and unobtrusively, being kind and affectionate to one's friends, enduring pain when it comes, and avoiding needless fears. The Epicureans denied that life and the universe have meaning and a purpose. Rather,

THE HUMAN EXPERIENCE

Diogenes

Diogenes came as a young man to Athens from his native Ionia and became a pupil of a rather bizarre philosopher named Antisthenes, who had himself been a student and disciple of Socrates. Although Plato and Aristotle both regarded Antisthenes as badly educated and, indeed, stupid, Diogenes was captivated by his austere lifestyle and his strict avoidance of all conventional social courtesies or small talk. In time, Diogenes far surpassed his master in both reputation and personal austerity.

Diogenes was convinced that the times were out of joint. He asked to be buried face down when he died, "because before you know it, what's down will be up." He is said to have carried a lantern, by the light of which he said he was searching for an honest man but had never found one. He rejected all official and traditional religions, all participation in civic life, marriage, the public games, and the theater. He ridiculed the prestige associated with wealth, power, and reputation, and honored instead the simple life of courage, reason, honesty, and avoidance of all pretense. A life of virtue could best be attained

by rejecting civilization and returning to nature. The person of wisdom and integrity should live like a dog, without affections or worldly possessions. The term *Cynic* associated with Diogenes' school of thought originally meant "canine" or doglike.

Thus Diogenes wandered the streets begging for his food, homeless but free. His bedchamber was a large tub outside a temple of the Great Mother; his latrine was the public street, and there he made love to prostitutes, who generously waived their fees. He used to eat and drink from a single crude wooden bowl, until he saw a peasant boy drinking from the hollow of his hands, whereupon Diogenes promptly destroyed the bowl as a needless luxury.

It is reported that while on a voyage Diogenes was captured by pirates and sold as a slave to a rich Corinthian named Xeniades. When Xeniades asked him what he did for a living, Diogenes answered waggishly that the only trade he knew was that of governing others and that he therefore wished to be sold to someone who needed a master. He spent his remaining years in Corinth, tutor-

ing Xeniades' two sons and lecturing at public festivals on the subject of virtuous self-control.

Diogenes' growing fame brought him to the attention of the master of the known world, Alexander the Great. At their one recorded meeting, Alexander is said to have offered Diogenes any gift or favor he might choose. Diogenes replied that the single favor he wished was that Alexander would move over so as not to block the sunlight. Taking no offense, Alexander is said to have remarked, "If I were not Alexander, I would choose to be Diogenes." According to our most informative source, who might well be stretching matters, Diogenes died in Corinth in 323 B.C. on the very day that Alexander died in Babylon. Whether false or true, Diogenes had become, next to Alexander, the greatest celebrity of his generation.

We are not told whether Diogenes was buried face down. We do know that his many admirers in Corinth erected a pillar in his memory on top of which they set a marble dog. ❖

they revived the teachings of the atomists, viewing the universe not as a great hierarchy of cosmic spheres surrounding the earth but as a multiplicity of atoms, much the same one place as another. Our world is not the handiwork of God but a chance configuration. The gods, if any, care nothing for us, and we ought to draw from this the comforting conclusion that we needn't fear them.

Epicureanism was a philosophy of withdrawal. It was a serene teaching that sought to banish fear, curb passions, and dispel illusions. Its doctrine of happiness was too bland to stir the millions and convert empires, but it gave solace and direction, during the remaining centuries of antiquity, to a minority of intelligent and sensitive people.

Stoicism derives its name from an Athenian civic building, the "Painted Stoa," in which Zeno (342–270 B.C.), the founder of Stoic philosophy, taught his followers.

(Its ruins were excavated in the 1980s.) Zeno, like the Cynics, stressed the worthlessness of material possessions and advocated, as the central principle of his philosophy, the supreme importance of individual virtue. All people, whether rulers, nobles, artists, or peasants, should pursue their vocations honestly and seriously. The significant thing is not individual accomplishment but individual effort. Politics, art, and even farming are ultimately valueless, yet in working at them as best we can, we manifest our virtue. Since virtue is all-important, good Stoics are immune to the vicissitudes of life. They may lose their property; they may even be imprisoned and tortured; but except by their own will they cannot be deprived of their virtue—their one truly precious possession. By rejecting the world, Stoics created impenetrable fortresses within their own souls. Out of this doctrine there emerged a sense not only of individualism but of cosmopolitanism; the idea of the polis faded before the wider Stoic concept of an all-encompassing human community.

Ultimately the Stoic emphasis on virtue was rooted in a cosmic vision, contrasting sharply with Epicureanism, based on the Greek conception of a rational, orderly, purposeful—and thoroughly deterministic—universe. Zeno taught that the harmonious movements of heavenly bodies, the growth of complex plants from simple seeds, all point to the existence of a Divine Plan that is both intelligent and good. We humans are incapable of perceiving the details of the Plan as it works in our own lives, yet by living virtuously and doing our best, we are cooperating with it. The god of the universe, Zeno assured his followers, cares about humanity. This wise, compassionate doctrine survived until the end of classical antiquity. Like Epicureanism, it was incapable of drawing multitudes of converts, but it became a significant component in the religious life of Rome and deeply influenced the conduct of several Roman emperors. Its ethical norms and concept of human fellowship merged easily into early Christianity, but its cosmic determinism also meshed perfectly with astrology.

Hellenistic Science and Technology: A Dead End?

Greek science reached maturity in the Hellenistic age. The inspired guesswork of the earlier period gave way to a rigorous and highly creative professionalism. Hellenistic scientists followed and improved on Aristotle's example, collecting and sifting data with great thoroughness before framing their hypotheses.

Alexandria was the center of scientific thought in this age. Here the Ptolemies built and subsidized a great research center—the museum of Alexandria—and collected a library of unprecedented size and diversity containing some half-million papyrus rolls. At Alexandria and elsewhere, science and mathematics made rapid strides as Greek rationalism encountered the rich heritage of Near Eastern astrology, medical lore, and practical mathematics. The fruitful medical investigations of Hippocrates' school were carried on and expanded by Hellenistic physicians, particularly in Alexandria. Their pioneer work in the dissection of human bodies[17] enabled them to discover the nervous system, to learn a great deal about the brain, heart, and arteries, and to perform a variety of new surgical operations. In mathematics, Euclid (ca. 300 B.C.) summed up the two preceding centuries of Greek geometry by organizing it all into a systematic series of axioms and proofs that are still taught today.

The wide-ranging military campaigns of Alexander and the subsequent cultural interchange among large areas of the ancient world led to a vast increase in Greek geographical knowledge. Eratosthenes, the head of the Alexandrian library in the later third century B.C., produced the most accurate and thorough world maps that had yet been made, complete with lines of longitude and latitude (see Figure 3-1) and climatic zones. Recognizing that the earth was a sphere, he calculated its circumference with great accuracy.

Painstaking accuracy and occasional daring ingenuity also distinguished Hellenistic astronomy. In the mid-third century B.C., Aristarchus of Samos (who worked at Alexandria) suggested that the earth rotates daily on its axis and revolves yearly around the sun. This **heliocentric**

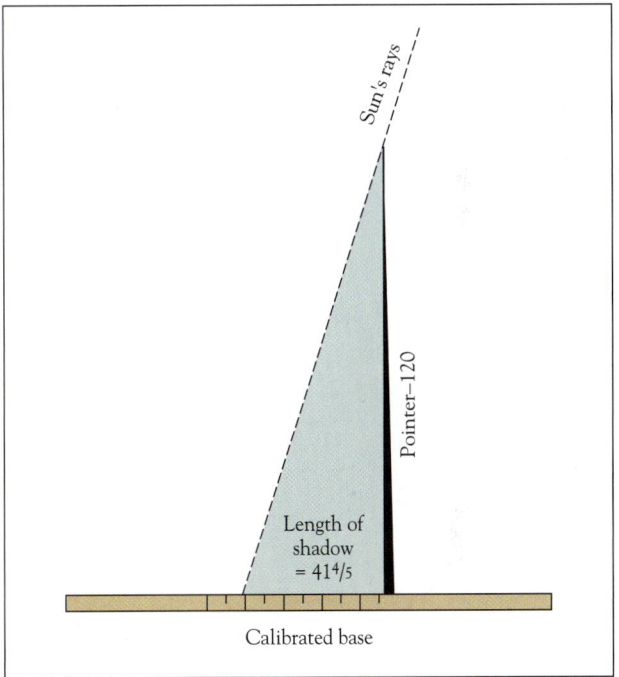

FIGURE 3-1
ERATOSTHENES' GNOMON

This simple device enabled Eratosthenes to measure the sun's shadow—and hence its elevation—at different latitudes, and from that to calculate the length of a single degree of latitude on the earth's surface. With that established, he could compute the earth's 360-degree circumference by simple multiplication. Exactly how accurate his figure was, we cannot say because we do not know which of several *stadia* (units of linear measurement) he was using. His measurements might have been as close as 0.7 percent or as far off as 17 percent. Eratosthenes had no way of knowing that the earth bulges slightly at the Equator. But whatever his result, it would have been more accurate than Christopher Columbus's estimate when he ventured out into the Atlantic in 1492. See Chapter 14.
Source: Frank Frost, Greek Society, 4th ed. (Lexington, MA: D.C. Heath, 1992), p. 139.

---

[17] The corpses were executed criminals, helpfully donated by the royal government. Such desecration of bodies—even those of criminals—would have been condemned under the old polis culture.

hypothesis dramatically anticipates modern astronomical knowledge, but in antiquity it remained merely brilliant guesswork and could not become the basis for further theorizing. Like Democritus's atomism, heliocentrism had frightening implications. One was obvious: The earth was no longer the center of everything. Another was that if the earth moved, it should be possible to detect changes in the stars' elevation during the year; yet since such changes are not visible to the naked eye, the stars must be immensely far away.[18] Thus the terrible idea of an infinite universe recurred.

Moreover, Aristarchus assumed that the earth follows a circular path around the sun. This characteristically Greek faith (fully shared by Plato and Aristotle) that only circular motion was "perfect" doomed Aristarchus's theory, because a circular orbit could not explain the precise astronomical observations being made at Alexandria.[19] The hallowed doctrine of an earth-centered universe of measurable

---

[18] Technically, this variation is called the *parallax*. With sophisticated equipment, modern astronomers can measure the parallax of nearby stars.

[19] The actual orbits of the earth and the other planets are elliptical, not circular. Hellenistic geometricians learned how to derive ellipses, but none suggested applying such motion to the heavens. Copernicus also believed in perfectly circular planetary orbits; elliptical orbits were established only by Kepler and Newton in the seventeenth century. See Chapter 17.

A

C

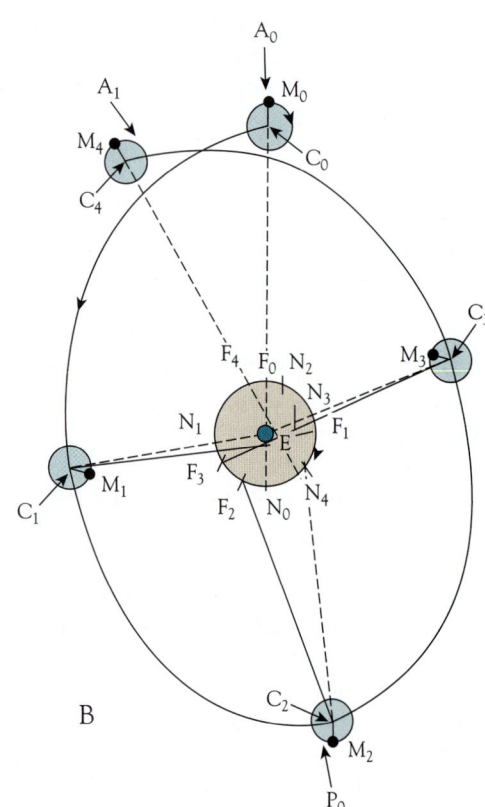

B

FIGURE 3-2
PTOLEMAIC ASTRONOMY

As these three modern diagrams indicate, Ptolemy's geometrical scheme explaining the apparent rotation of the sun, moon, planets, and stars around a stationary earth was staggeringly complex. A triumph of geometrical ingenuity, Ptolemy's system requires circles within circles to account for all known astronomical data. A gives the overall plan (omitting the moon); B shows the moon's special rotational pattern; C represents in greater detail the movements of the sun and Mars.
Source: W. M. O'Neil, Early Astronomy from Babylonia to Copernicus (Sydney, Australia: Sydney University Press, 1986), figures 6.1–6.3, pp. 86, 88–89.

size simply rested on "commonsense" observational data. Using this vast body of data, which incorporated centuries of Babylonian astronomical record-keeping, the great second century B.C. astronomer Hipparchus developed a system of circles and circles-within-circles centered on the earth that accounted exceedingly well for the observed motions of the sun and moon. His ingenious ideas were perfected by the Alexandrian astronomer Claudius Ptolemy (A.D. 90–168).

Hipparchus and Ptolemy were not necessarily interested in explaining the actual mechanics of the cosmos (see Figure 3-2). Their **geocentric** system was primarily a mathematical scheme that allowed the planets' positions in the starry sky to be predicted. As modern historians of science put it, they aimed to "save the appearances." It is not entirely clear whether all this was supposed by its inventors to have actual physical existence, although later the notion flourished that heavenly bodies were carried by solid but transparent crystal spheres. The Hipparchian-Ptolemaic theory fit in well with the best observations of ancient astronomy. It represented antiquity's final word on the subject, and until the sixteenth century A.D. would stand unchallenged. By increasing celestial predictability, it also powerfully supported astrology.

The greatest scientist and engineer of antiquity worked far from Alexandria. This was Archimedes of Syracuse (died 212 B.C.). He did brilliantly original work in both pure and applied mathematics: developing single-handedly the science of hydrostatics, experimenting successfully with levers and pulleys to lift tremendous weights, inventing a system for expressing large numbers, and coming very close to discovering integral calculus. The famous incident of his running home naked from the bath shouting *"Eureka!"* ("I've found it!") was occasioned by his sudden discovery of the principle of buoyancy: Something floats if it is buoyed up by a force equal to the weight of the water displaced. Another legend asserts that he was killed after Syracuse fell to a Roman army and a Roman soldier burst in upon him while he sat absorbed in drawing geometrical figures in the sand.

Archimedes' death, if the legend is true, underscores an essential point about Hellenistic science and technology. One of the few practical applications for this brilliant work was in the design of machines for besieging or defending cities. (Archimedes himself built many of the machines that Syracuse used in trying to fend off the Romans.) Tradition also credited Archimedes with inventing a large screw that lifted water for irrigation (see Figure 3-3). Astronomy, of course, had its practical applications, including navigation—but the chief one was astrology. Besides these, Hellenistic science remained theoretical and abstract, and one of technology's chief uses was to fashion clever toys. War and the piracy that made every voyage perilous kept the Hellenistic world so well provided with slaves that very little incentive existed to devise labor-saving

FIGURE 3-3
ARCHIMEDES' SCREW

This ingenious device had a practical application in the market-oriented agriculture of huge estates in Hellenistic Sicily and Egypt.

machinery. (In Ptolemaic Egypt, it is true, Greek engineers introduced more efficient irrigation and large-scale land reclamation. The Ptolemies had plenty of incentive to encourage such innovation because it increased the amount of land that could be profitably cultivated, but they had no reason to want to lessen the toil of their peasantry.) The philosophical and religious thinkers of the age, with few exceptions, scorned science as vain and technology as useless. Riches could be amassed from landowning, **tax farming,** money-lending, and slave-trading, but no one thought to invest capital in economically productive enterprises that might have profited from ingenious engineering. In conquering Archimedes' Syracuse and the rest of Sicily, the Romans gained only a province for vast plantation agriculture worked by slaves under the lash.

Hellenism and the Jews

Alexander the Great's conquests included Judea, which on his death passed to the Ptolemies. In the course of the Hellenistic world's complex international politics, Judea came under Seleucid control shortly before 200 B.C. The high priests of Jerusalem, whom the Hellenistic kings (like their Persian predecessors) appointed from among the traditional high-priestly families, were the actual rulers of Judea. Judaism long remained unmolested, although individual Jews began to take an interest in the Greek way of life.

Trouble first arose in connection with high-priestly politics. About 175 B.C. a certain Jason—note his hellenized name—bribed his way into being named the high priest and began pushing hellenization so far as to set up a gymnasium in Jerusalem, where he and like-minded Jews could cavort naked and otherwise outrage Jewish piety. Equally dangerous, the Seleucid kings had already learned of the considerable wealth of the Jerusalem Temple. King Antiochus IV Epiphanes ("God-Manifest," reigned

Antiochus IV Epiphanes Historians have never agreed what Antiochus IV had in mind when he tried to uproot Judaism. Most likely, he misunderstood the hellenizing enthusiasm of a small circle of Jerusalem insiders (including the high priest) and gravely underestimated how deep a hold Judaism had on its followers. This coin gives some idea of how a Hellenistic king like Antiochus advertised himself to his subjects; the reverse side shows Zeus, to whose worship he tried to rededicate the Jerusalem Temple. © *Trustees of the British Museum.*

175–164 B.C.) took the bait, accepting an even bigger bribe from another Jew who called himself by the Homeric name of Menelaus. A struggle broke out between Jason and Menelaus, with mutual slaughters of each other's supporters. Menelaus and his allies became heavily dependent on the Seleucids. Emboldened, in 167 B.C. Antiochus set up a Greek garrison in Jerusalem, imposed heavy new taxes on the Jews, and outlawed all distinctive Jewish customs and ceremonies. Torah scrolls were destroyed, the Temple was turned into a shrine to Zeus, and—supreme outrage!—a pig was sacrificed on its altar.

Antiochus thereby provoked a guerrilla rebellion of Jews who lived in or had fled to the countryside, led by a traditional priestly family called the Hasmoneans. The most charismatic of the family was Judah, who from his exploits gained the nickname Maccabee, or "Hammer." By 164 B.C., the rebels had regained the Temple and rededicated it to Yahweh, an occasion that Jews still celebrate in the joyous feast of Hanukkah.

But the struggle was not over—indeed, it took many tragic twists. Not for a long time were the Greek mercenaries driven from their garrison in Jerusalem. In the meantime Judah Maccabee died in battle, having already taken the fateful step of inviting the Romans to meddle in the

Jews' quarrel with the Seleucids. Bloody fighting broke out among the next two generations of Hasmoneans. Out of the turmoil eventually emerged a high priest named Alexander Janneus (103–76 B.C.), who made himself virtually a king. A ruthless and capable man whose exploits included the conquest of neighboring lands and the mass crucifixion of hundreds of rebels, Janneus walked a fine line between upholding Jewish tradition and encouraging hellenization. After he died, his sons continued the Hasmonean tradition of fighting each other, until in 63 B.C. the Roman general Pompey intervened decisively, ending Jewish independence.

The great Hellenistic city of Alexandria rivaled—indeed, surpassed—Jerusalem as a center of Jewish culture during these tumultuous centuries. The Ptolemies were tolerant of the Jews (partly because they never gave up hopes of regaining Judea) and protected the Alexandrian Jewish community against the city's not always friendly Greek majority. Koine Greek became the everyday speech of the Jews of Alexandria, as well as the numerous other cities around the eastern Mediterranean where Jews settled. With Hebrew becoming virtually a foreign language to these Jews, the first important translation of the Hebrew Bible, into Greek, was carried out at Alexandria in the third century B.C. This was the so-called *Septuagint.* Impressed by the intensity of Judaism's moral code, a few Greeks converted to faith in Yahweh, and more incorporated respect for the Jewish tradition into their own philosophical and religious beliefs. Moreover, with the linguistic—if not the cultural—hellenization of the Alexandrian and other **Diaspora** Jews, the way was being prepared for the efforts of deeply religious Jews in the first centuries B.C. and A.D. to attempt a reconciliation of Judaism's ethical monotheism with Hellenistic philosophy (see Chapter 5).

The Jews' delicate relationship with their Greek neighbors and the tumultuous history of Judea during the third to first centuries B.C. had important implications for Judaism. Some of the late books of the Hebrew Scriptures (including the books of Daniel, Esther, and Judith) take the form of Hellenistic novels, exploring how a pious Jew should behave in the midst of an alien culture.[20] The book of Ecclesiastes shows the deep imprint of deterministic Stoic philosophy: "All is vanity. . . . The thing that hath been, it is that which shall be, and that which is done is that which shall be done: and there is no new thing under the sun" (Eccl. 1:2, 9). Set against this somber vision were the concluding chapters of Daniel, with their terrifying and majestic vision of God sending "the son of man"—the Messiah—to blast into dust the kingdoms of this world and prepare the way for divine judgment over all Creation.

---

[20] Although all of these books are set in earlier periods of Near Eastern history, biblical scholars today agree that they were written in Hellenistic times.

Daniel culminates in the Hebrew Bible's only unequivocal promise of life after death: "And many of them that sleep in the dust of the earth shall awaken, some to everlasting life, and some to shame and everlasting contempt" (12:2).

The Book of Daniel (part of which was written in Greek) was a product of the Maccabean revolt, which undoubtedly kindled **apocalyptic** hopes among pious Jews who were resisting attempts by Antiochus IV and his Jewish collaborators to destroy their religion. During these same years the challenge to traditional piety posed by encroaching Hellenism and the Hasmonean high priest-kings set in motion at least three major Jewish **sectarian** movements, all of which would play important roles in Judaism and earliest Christianity during the first century A.D. The Sadducees seem to have regarded themselves as the defenders of high-priestly practices that the more worldly leaders of Judaism were abandoning or compromising, but they recognized as binding only the first five biblical books, the Torah. Thus they vigorously opposed the second sectarian movement, the Pharisees, who asserted belief in a divinely inspired oral tradition descending from Moses. One of these tenets was that God would bestow eternal life on the righteous and everlasting punishment on the wicked. The Pharisees—whose name is associated with the Hebrew verb for "to separate"—held that the Messiah would come and God's justice be done only when the Jewish people observed the Law with the utmost rigor. Despite persecution (Janneus crucified many of them), they set about trying to hasten the day of deliverance by setting an example of strictest piety. Of the third sectarian movement, that of the Essenes, tantalizingly little is known for certain. But it seems to have produced the famous collection of documents known as the Dead Sea Scrolls, discovered in a desert cave near the Dead Sea in 1947. These documents indicate a passionate rejection of the Jerusalem priesthood, apocalyptic expectations of Israel's imminent cleansing, and—like the Pharisees—faith in life after death.

Such Jewish apocalyptic movements (there were others about which almost nothing is known) simmered during the Hasmonean period and would explode in the first century A.D. This outburst would not only inspire Israel's final revolts against Roman rule but would also give birth to Christianity. They parallel the salvation cults of the Hellenistic Greeks, but differ in being driven not merely by a yearning for personal escape from death but also by a moral earnestness that no Hellenistic cult came close to matching. They were, in short, products of the ethical monotheism that had been taking shape for centuries in Judaism, and that was about to challenge the very different ethical and philosophical ideas of the Greco-Roman world.

The Hellenistic Legacy

Greek culture exerted an immense influence on the Roman Empire, on Byzantium and Islam, and on the medieval West, and it did so largely in its Hellenistic form. The conclusions of the Hellenistic philosophers and scholars tended to be accepted by the best minds of later ages, but the Hellenistic spirit of free inquiry and intellectual daring was not. There is something curiously modern about the Hellenistic world—its confident scientists, its cosmopolitanism, its materialism, its religious diversity, its trend toward specialization, its large-scale business activity, and its sense of drift and disorientation.

But the Hellenistic economic organization, regardless of superficial similarities, was vastly different from ours. Based on human slavery rather than machines, it benefited only a tiny fraction of the population. The great majority remained servile, illiterate, and impoverished.

Still, the upper classes throughout the Mediterranean world and the Near East were exposed to Greek culture and the Greek language. From Syria to southern Italy, a common culture was developing, which shared ideas and gods. The way was being paved for the political unification of the Mediterranean world under Rome and for its spiritual unification under the Christian church. Alexander's dream of a homogeneous world synthesizing Greek and Near Eastern cultures was gradually coming into being. But had Alexander foreseen the ultimate consequences of his handiwork—the conquest of Hellas by an Italian city and a Near Eastern faith—he might well have chosen to emulate Diogenes.

CONCLUSION: HELLENISM AND WESTERN CIVILIZATION

The intellectual achievement of the Greeks fundamentally shaped Western civilization. The cultures of the ancient Near East produced significant pioneer work in mathematics, engineering, and practical science, and the Hebrews developed a profound ethical system based on the revelation of the one Creator-God. The Greeks, however, first took the step of scrutinizing humanity and the cosmos with the tool of logic, looking at the universe as a natural phenomenon that rested on discoverable principles of cause and effect, not simply divine will. And it was they who first attempted to base morality and the good life on reason.

The Babylonians had studied the stars to discern the future; the Egyptians had mastered geometry to build tombs and chemistry to create mummies. The Greeks had much to learn from their predecessors, but they turned their investigation toward a new end: a rational understanding of humanity and the universe. This revolutionary change launched a process that, with many ups and downs, would shape the development of the natural and social sciences throughout Western civilization. The Greek achievement has been described, with only slight exaggeration, as "the discovery of the mind."

Ahead of us lie two chapters in which we will trace the rise of Rome to world power, and the beginnings of

Christianity. Rome, as we shall see, completed the work of Alexander and the Hellenistic kings in welding together the Mediterranean world and giving it a single system of law. But as a great Roman poet would put it, in conquering the Greeks, Rome itself fell captive to Greek civilization. Christianity, too, could only begin to convert the Mediter-ranean world when it ceased to be primarily a rural Jewish sect and adopted the language and addressed the troubles of Greek-speaking Hellenistic cities. Western civilization represents a synthesis of Hebrew and Greco-Roman values, to which the Greeks' contribution was indispensable.

Selected Reading

Sources

Austin, M. M., ed. and trans. *The Hellenistic World from Alexander to the Roman Conquest: A Selection of Ancient Sources in Translation* (1981).

Bowra, C. M., ed. *Landmarks in Greek Literature* (1966).

Buchanan, Scott, ed., and Benjamin Jowett, trans. *The Portable Plato* (1948).

Crawford, Michael, ed. and trans. *Archaic and Classical Greece: A Selection of Ancient Sources in Translation* (1983).

Crawley, Richard. Thucydides' *History of the Peloponnesian War* (1982, revised by T. E. Wick).

Edmonds, J. M., trans. *Lyra Graecia*, rev. ed., 3 vols. (1979).

Finley, Moses I., ed. and trans. *Greek Historians*, rev. ed. (1984).

Lattimore, Richmond, and David Grene, eds. and trans. *The Complete Greek Tragedies*, 7 vols. (1959).

Homer. *Iliad* and *Odyssey*. A study of Greek literature must begin with Homer's works, which have often been translated. Superb modern verse translations are by Richmond Lattimore, by Robert Fitzgerald, and by Robert Fagles and Bernard Knox.

Jowett, Benjamin, and Thomas Twining, trans. *Aristotle's Politics and Poetics* (1957).

Knox, Bernard, ed. *The Norton Book of Classical Literature* (1993).

Rayor, Diane J., trans. *Sappho's Lyre: Archaic Lyric and Women Poets of Ancient Greece* (1991).

Greek Art and Thought

Becatti, Giovanni. *The Art of Ancient Greece and Rome* (1967). A richly detailed account of art in classical antiquity, superbly illustrated.

Boardman, John. *Greek Art*, 3rd ed. (1985). A clearly presented survey by a noted scholar.

Burkert, Walter. *Greek Religion* (1985). The best introduction.

Cornford, F. M. *Before and after Socrates* (1932; rev. ed., 1979). A short, lucid account of Greek thought from the Ionians through Aristotle.

Goldhill, Simon. *Reading Greek Tragedy* (1986). A keenly intelligent and highly original work of interpretation.

Lawrence, A. W. *Greek Architecture*, 4th ed. (1983). A valuable, reliable introduction.

Pollitt, J. J. *Art and Experience in Classical Greece* (1972). A sympathetic, thought-provoking interpretation.

Williamson, Margaret. *Sappho's Immortal Daughters* (1995). An erudite, sensitive, wide ranging study of Sappho, her poetry, and her milieu.

Zimmermann, Bernhard. *Greek Tragedy: An Introduction* (1991). Trans. Thomas Marier. A succinct yet comprehensive and deeply intelligent account, the best on the subject.

Alexander and the Hellenistic Age

Bosworth, A. B. *Conquest and Empire* (1988). A thoughtful and persuasive biography of Alexander the Great.

Clagett, Marshall. *Greek Science in Antiquity*, rev. ed. (1966). An accomplished treatment by a major historian of science.

Grant, Michael. *From Alexander to Cleopatra: The Hellenistic World* (1982). A masterful survey of the Hellenistic kingdoms and of Hellenistic culture and philosophy.

Hamilton, J. R. *Alexander the Great* (1973). Sees Alexander as ruthlessly ambitious.

Long, A. A. *Hellenistic Philosophy: Stoics, Epicureans, Sceptics*, 2nd ed. (1986). The best general account.

Peters, F. E. *The Harvest of Hellenism: A History of the Near East from Alexander the Great to the Triumph of Christianity* (1970). A fine synthesis of the Hellenistic world, stressing cultural and religious history, including the Jewish and early Christian experiences.

Pollitt, J. J. *Art in the Hellenistic Age* (1986). An excellent, well-illustrated survey.

Renault, Mary. *The Nature of Alexander*, 2nd ed. (1976). A stylishly written and intelligently argued biography.

Samuel, Alan E. *The Shifting Sands of History: Interpretations of Ptolemaic Egypt* (1989). A valuable brief account of new interpretations, with a fine bibliography.

Walbank, F. W. *The Hellenistic World*, rev. ed. (1993). A short survey of Hellenistic politics and culture from the death of Alexander to the Roman conquest of Greece, arguing that Hellenistic civilization is best seen as an effort to hellenize Near Eastern culture rather than to synthesize the two.

Welles, C. Bradford. *Alexander and the Hellenistic World* (1970). An illuminating account that stresses social and economic history.

ROME: FROM REPUBLIC TO EMPIRE

The Roman Family
Scala/Art Resource, NY.

753	Traditional date for the founding of Rome
ca. 616–509	Etruscan kings rule Rome
494	Plebeians threaten to secede from Rome
458	Cincinnatus is made dictator, saves Rome, returns to his farm
ca. 450	Rome adopts the Twelve Tables, Rome's first law code
367	Plebeians become eligible for the consulship
287	Senate's veto power over plebescites lost, initiating joint patrician-plebeian rule of the Roman Republic
265	Rome controls all Italy south of the Po River
264–241	Rome defeats Carthage in the First Punic War
218–201	Rome defeats Carthage in the Second Punic War
149–146	Rome destroys Carthage in the Third Punic War
146	Macedonia becomes a Roman dependency
133	Tribunate and murder of Tiberius Gracchus; land reform fails

123–122	Tribunate of Gaius Gracchus; his assassination in 121 squelches land reform once again
107	Marius opens the army to the poor
83–80	Sulla reestablishes the republican constitution
60–44	Julius Caesar is a dominant figure in Roman politics
48	Julius Caesar assumes power in Rome
44	Julius Caesar is knifed to death in the Roman Senate
43	Murder of Cicero
31	Defeat of Antony and Cleopatra in battle of Actium; Octavian (Augustus) takes power
A.D. 14	Death of Augustus
A.D. 68–69	Overthrow of Nero; "year of the four emperors"
A.D. 69–79	Reign of Vespasian
A.D. 96–180	Age of the great second-century emperors: Nerva, Trajan, Hadrian, Antoninus Pius, and Marcus Aurelius

All dates are B.C., except when noted otherwise.

*T*he gentleman in the sculpture that opens this chapter, a Roman of the first century B.C., stands before us as he wished posterity to remember him. He is wrapped in a toga symbolizing membership in the Roman Senate, and he holds the death masks of two of his forefathers—wax images taken at the moment of death, which descendants thereafter preserved in the highest honor in their household shrine.

Most of the words that such men would have used to describe their values have entered our English vocabulary, albeit sometimes in altered form: *gravitas* ("weight," or seriousness of purpose), *pietas* ("piety," or respect for tradition and duty), *clementia* ("clemency," or willingness voluntarily not to insist on one's full due), *humanitas* ("humaneness," or recognition of one's own fellowship with others as human beings), and *virtus* ("manliness" or "virtue," a word that comes from the Latin noun *vir*, or "man"). Such were some of the qualities that, Romans believed, had rightfully made them masters of the world by the first century B.C. These would be the ideals familiar to George Washington's generation of Americans, and the qualities that classically educated British gentlemen down to the twentieth century would say fitted them to rule an empire on which the sun never set. The two-thousand-year reign of the ancient Romans' definition of dignity,

duty, and power attests to the impact that such values have had on Western civilization.

It is easy in our own time to dismiss Roman values as mere cant. For all the idealization that Romans accorded to women (often their own mothers), ancient Rome was a man's world in which women were honored only insofar as they measured up to masculine ideals. The same Romans who prided themselves on their *clementia* and their *humanitas* saw nothing unjust in slavery, felt nothing wrong with condemning a captured city to pillage and massacre, and believed nothing amiss in inflicting savage punishments on rebels fighting for their own freedom. *Pietas* did not stop Romans from indulging repeatedly in civil wars that cumulatively cost hundreds of thousands of lives. *Gravitas* did not prevent rich Romans from developing staggering appetites for food and luxury, nor any of them from cheering the cruelest sport human beings have ever turned into mass entertainment—fights to the death by gladiators in the arena.

All these excesses were as much a part of Roman history as were the values by which Romans judged themselves and asked posterity to judge them. To trace the evolution of their ideals and to account for their excesses is the historian's task. But to ask *why* such ideals and such excesses could coexist, apparently amicably, in the same culture is to plumb some of the deepest mysteries of the human condition. For better or worse, Rome is an essential link in the unfolding of Western civilization, and the ironies of Rome's history still haunt us.

Rome's rise from a small hilltop village to the capital of a vast empire is the supreme political success story of the ancient world. The very word *republic* is a Roman invention—its Latin form is *Res Publica,* or "the public thing"—and it more closely approximates our modern idea of a republican government than the ancient Greek concept of a *polis.* Not only did early Romans have to hammer out for themselves the structure of their republic, but they also faced a hard struggle at first for mere survival and then for ascendency over the neighboring villages of Latium—the area south of Rome along the Italian coast. Yet eventually Rome ruled an empire that encompassed the entire Mediterranean basin and stretched northward across Gaul to remote Britain. It was the greatest empire in the history of western Eurasia, matched at the time only by the similarly vast empire that the Han Dynasty was building in ancient China.

But Rome's overall success was not without its setbacks and failures. The Roman Republic was almost annihilated by the armies of its greatest rival, Carthage. And once the Romans had conquered the Carthaginians, they turned against one another in savage political power struggles. A society organized for war and captivated by military victories could be ruthlessly destructive to itself as well as to foreign enemies. Rome's internal conflicts abated for several generations with the emergence of powerful Roman emperors, who took unobtrusive control of the republican offices. But later, in the third century A.D., the empire was afflicted by anarchy even more murderous than before.

THE ROMAN REPUBLIC

Had Alexander the Great lived longer than his thirty-two years he probably would have led his conquering armies westward into North Africa, Sicily, and Italy. There he would have found three vigorous cultures: Carthage, a cluster of Greek city-states, and the growing republic of Rome.

Carthage, traditionally said to have been founded in 814 B.C. as a Phoenician commercial colony strategically located on the North African coast southwest of Sicily, developed an extensive commercial empire that far outstripped Phoenicia in power and wealth. Carthage established a number of commercial bases in western Sicily, which brought it face-to-face with the Greek city-states that dominated the eastern sections of the island.

The Greek poleis of southern Italy, a region known as Magna Graecia, were products of the age of Greek colonization in the eighth and seventh centuries B.C. They evolved much like the city-states in the Greek homeland, were convulsed by intercity conflict, and were caught up in the Peloponnesian War. Unification was delayed until the

Roman conquests of the third century B.C. brought these Greek cities under a common master.

Rome, which presumably would have been the third target of Alexander's new conquests, was in the fourth century B.C. already a well-established state. Rome traced its history back as far as most Greek poleis: By the modern reckoning, its traditional founding date had been 753 B.C. Since 509 B.C., Rome had been a republic, and by Alexander's death in 323 it was emerging as the dominant power in central and southern Italy.

Early Rome

The ascent of Rome was slow compared with the dazzling imperialistic careers of Persia and Macedon, but it proved more lasting. There was nothing meteoric about the serious, hardheaded Romans—they built slowly and well. Their great military virtue was not tactical brilliance but stubborn endurance. As the most celebrated historian of Rome, Edward Gibbon (1737–1794), pointed out, they lost many battles, but from their beginnings to the great days of the empire they never lost a war. Since it was they who ultimately provided the ancient world with an enduring, all-encompassing political framework, students of history have always been fascinated by the development of Roman political institutions. Among Rome's greatest contributions were its achievements in the realm of law, government, and imperial organization. In its grasp of political realities lay the secret of its triumphant career.

Italy, unlike Greece with its myriad islands and isolated valleys, is a land in which one region merges with another (see Map 4-1). The Apennine mountain range stretches across northern Italy to the south of the Po Valley, which was inhabited in ancient times by Celtic peoples whom the Romans called Gauls. The Apennines then turn southward to divide the peninsula. Geographically, Italy is thus less resistant to unification than Greece, and it was far easier for Rome to extend its power across neighboring lands than it had been, for example, for Athens.

Obscurity shrouds Rome's beginnings. As early as 1400 B.C. the site of Rome was inhabited, but it is uncertain whether the people living there were Indo-European ancestors of the Italic ethnic group, to which the Romans belonged. By the mid-eighth century B.C., when Romans believed their city was founded—and probably long before—Italic speakers were living in huts on the Palatine Hill near the Tiber River. Gradually, settlements developed on several neighboring hills. Around 625 B.C. these various settlements coalesced to form the city-state of Rome.

The strategic position of this cluster of hills, 15 miles inland on one of Italy's greatest rivers, was of enormous importance to Rome's future growth. Ancient Mediterranean ships could sail up the Tiber to Rome but no farther, and Rome was the first point where the river could be easily crossed—in the beginning by a ford, and soon afterward

MAP 4-1
EARLY ITALY

by bridges. Hence Rome was a key river crossing and road junction and also, at least potentially, a seaport. It was at the northern limit of fertile Latium, whose rustic inhabitants, the Latins, gave their name to the Latin language. North of Rome lay the district of Etruria (very roughly, modern Tuscany)—a more urbanized region whose inhabitants, the Etruscans, shaped the culture of early Rome.

Etruscan civilization flourished in central Italy between the eighth and fifth centuries B.C. in an assortment of independent hilltop towns and cities sharing a common culture. Scholars disagree as to whether the Etruscans had always lived in Italy or had migrated there from elsewhere. Their culture bears marks of Greek and Near Eastern influence, but it is highly distinctive nonetheless. They left no decipherable literature, and their non-Indo-European language differs so sharply from other languages of the ancient world that scholars are having great difficulty translating it.

The Etruscans were skilled engineers who equipped their cities with well-designed drainage systems. They grew wealthy from the abundance of metals in their hills—tin, copper, iron, gold—and wrought them into a wonderful variety of objects, from graceful bronze statues to dental braces. Their remarkable works of art—bronzes, decorated

urns, recumbent effigies, marvelous horses, and tomb frescoes with vividly colored scenes from mythology and daily life—disclose a vivacious, pleasure-loving civilization of striking originality.

It was in Etruscan form that Greek culture made its first impact on Rome. The Romans adopted the Greek alphabet in its Etruscan version, and perhaps through Etruscan inspiration they organized themselves into a city-state, thereby gaining an inestimable advantage over the numerous half-civilized tribes in the region between Etruria and Magna Graecia. From the Etruscans the Romans took some of their high gods (including Jupiter, the Zeus-like king of the Roman gods) and their belief that the future could be revealed by examining the intestines of sacrificial animals. Gladiatorial combats—originally a part of funeral rites and perhaps a vestige of human sacrifice—were another Etruscan legacy to the Romans. So, too, was that enduring symbol of Roman government, the fasces, a bundle of rods with a projecting axe head, signifying the right of legitimate political authority to punish wrongdoers by whipping or beheading them.

During much of the sixth century B.C., Rome was ruled by kings of Etruscan extraction known as the Tarquins,

Etruscan Funeral Monument Etruscans evidently thought of the afterlife in pleasant terms, for most of their tomb paintings and sculpture depict smiling, relaxed people. Here, a husband and wife recline on a couch to eat. This was the way that Romans, too, preferred to eat their main meal.   *© R. Sheridan/Ancient Art & Architecture Collection.*

whose talented and aggressive leadership made the Romans an important power in Latium. The community grew in strength and wealth, and an impressive temple to Jupiter was built in Etruscan style atop one of the hills.

About 509 B.C. the Romans overthrew their Tarquin dynasty of Etruscan kings, thereby transforming Rome into an aristocratic republic. The king was replaced by two magistrates, known as consuls, who were elected annually from the membership of the aristocratic Senate, and who governed with its advice. The consuls exercised their authority in the name of the Roman people but in the interests of Rome's landowning elite. This elite, the patricians, defended their prerogatives zealously against the encroachments of the lower orders—the plebeians or plebs. Plebeian-patrician intermarriage was prohibited, and for a time the plebeians were almost entirely without political rights and considered themselves oppressed by debt to the patricians. But step by step the plebeians improved their condition and expanded their role in the government.

"The Struggle of the Orders" is the traditional name of the conflict in which plebeians slowly wrested from patricians a significant share in the governance of Rome and relief from the abuses of indebtedness. The plebeians began in 494 B.C. by organizing themselves into a kind of private corporation known as the Council of Plebs. They elected representatives, called tribunes, to be their spokesmen and to represent their interests before the patrician-controlled Roman government. The tribunes acquired the remarkable power to veto, in the name of the plebeians,

measures issuing from any organ of government. Moreover, anyone violating the sanctity of a tribune's person (that is, murdering him or beating him up) was to be punished by death. Under the leadership of their tribunes the plebeians were able to act as a unit and to make their strength felt. On at least one occasion, in the midst of a military emergency, they seceded as a body from the Roman Republic (that is, they went on strike), leaving the patrician army officers with no troops to lead. This incident underscores an important parallel between early Greek and early Roman history: Italy, like Greece, had been profoundly transformed by the coming of hoplite warfare. Roman plebeians, like the ordinary men of Greek poleis, had a vital military role, and they could exact a political price for performing it.

About 450 B.C., under plebeian pressure, the Romans committed their legal customs to writing. The result was Rome's first law code—the Twelve Tables—which was displayed in the city's center. By later standards these laws were harsh: Defaulting debtors, for example, were executed or enslaved, and the basic principle of an-eye-for-an-eye justice hardly differed from the spirit of Hammurabi's Code (see Chapter 1). But the laws did protect individual plebeians from the capricious authority of the patrician consuls. The Twelve Tables are the first major landmark in the evolution of Roman law.

Having gained a measure of legal protection, the plebeians next sought additional farmlands. The Romans habitually annexed a portion of the territory of conquered peoples, and with such military successes as the capture of the rich Etruscan city of Veii early in the fourth century B.C., the Senate was persuaded to distribute this land to plebeians, both singly and in groups. By providing lands to a growing Roman population, this policy removed some of the economic basis of plebeian discontent.

In time, resolutions passed by the Council of Plebs (plebiscites) came to be accepted as law unless vetoed by the Senate. Intermarriage was now allowed between the two orders, the enslavement of Roman citizens for debt was abolished, and a law of 367 B.C. opened the consulship itself to plebeians. At the same time, or shortly afterwards, it was stipulated that at least one consul must always be a plebeian. In the years that followed, plebeians became eligible for all offices of state. Finally, by a law of 287 B.C., the Council of Plebs won the right to have its plebiscites binding on the entire state without being subject to senatorial veto.

Nevertheless, the rise of the plebs by no means transformed Rome into an egalitarian democracy. The most powerful of the Roman citizens continued to control their state through a client-patron system that dated back to Rome's earliest times. Like the bosses who used to control the politics of American cities, or like Mafia godfathers,[1] powerful Romans took large numbers of "clients" under their protection, supporting their economic and legal interests and receiving their political support in return. The reciprocal rules of clientage had the force of law: Under the Law of the Twelve Tables, for example, a patron who broke faith with his clients was outlawed.

Through their clients, powerful patrons exercised indirect control of Rome's many assemblies and offices, including the Council of Plebs itself. Historians have debated vigorously the degree of this control by wealthy Romans. It used to be thought that the client-patron system rendered Roman democracy largely a sham; more recently, however, some have argued that the client-patron system was limited in its effects and that the Roman Republic had true democratic elements.

Whatever the case, the traditional domination by the patricians had by now given way to a more subtle influence exerted by a new nobility of wealthy, office-holding plebeian and patrician families. According to Roman custom, a family became "noble" when one of its members was elected as a consul; so once the patricians lost their monopoly on the consulship, it became possible for politically active plebeians to enter the nobility. During the fifth and fourth centuries B.C., moreover, a number of plebeian families had accumulated large estates, and some of them began to rival patricians in wealth and political influence. Rich plebeians now became patrons themselves, with

clients of their own. More and more, the plebeian tribunes tended to be drawn from wealthy and noble families. By 287 B.C.—when plebiscites acquired the force of law—the old division between patrician and plebeian was no longer important. The new patrician-plebeian nobility had achieved political ascendency.

The machinery of Roman republican government was complex and changing. It included numerous civic officials with various titles and responsibilities, and several different legislative assemblies, the most important of which were the Centuriate Assembly and the Tribal Assembly—the latter an official body patterned after the plebeians' (unofficial) Council of Plebs. Both the Centuriate Assembly and the Tribal Assembly were made up of the entire Roman citizenry, but each had its own distinctive function and organization. In each the nobility had a highly audible voice.

The Centuriate Assembly was divided into 193 groups known as centuries, each with a single vote. These centuries were distributed according to socioeconomic class, with the richest interests controlling a majority of the centuries. Of the 193 centuries, 98 were allotted to citizens with considerable property, whereas the mass of citizens without any property whatever (the proles) were lumped into one century, with one vote. Since the richest centuries voted first, and since voting ceased as soon as a majority was reached, poorer men often had no say at all in the Centuriate Assembly.

The Tribal Assembly was likewise dominated by propertied families, though less directly. Its members were organized by districts known as tribes (the Roman citizenry had traditionally been divided into tribal groups: originally about twenty, later thirty-five). Each tribe had a single vote, and although the tribes consisted largely of poorer citizens, the noble families influenced the Tribal Assembly through their clients. Of the tribes, four were urban and thirty-one rural, and the difficulty of coming in from the countryside resulted in the rural votes being strongly influenced by the nobility and the clients they brought with them.

One of the most important functions of these assemblies was to manage the entrance of new generations into Rome's political system. In order to be eligible for office, a young Roman male first had to serve honorably in a series of military campaigns. Then, at age thirty, he began to run the *cursus honorum*, or "race of honors." This was a rigidly prescribed sequence of offices to which he was eligible for election by the assemblies. Support by noble patrons was essential. Competition, fierce to begin with, grew fiercer as a man attempted to move up the ever-narrowing pyramid of senior offices. To fail was to disgrace your family. The system, of course, rewarded talent and did not prevent the rise of "new men" who were the first of their family to attain office. But it also forced ambitious young Romans to adhere closely to traditional patterns of behavior—the first and foremost being military valor.

---

[1] The Italian word *padrone* descends directly from the Latin *patronus*, or "patron"—the man to whom clients pledged their support.

Brutus This magnificent bronze portrait bust is generally believed to date from the third century B.C. and to represent Lucius Junius Brutus, the patrician who killed Rome's last Etruscan king and helped found the Roman Republic. Some, however, maintain that the piece is from the first century B.C. and represents Marcus Portius Brutus, Caesar's assassin and a descendant of the "first" Brutus. Whatever the intended identity of the bust, it superbly conveys the stern self-discipline and self-confidence that the Roman aristocracy prized. *Alinari/Art Resource, NY.*

The nobility's primary instrument of power was the Senate. Originally composed of the heads of patrician families who advised the kings, the Senate under the Roman Republic evolved into an assembly of former holders of civic offices. The senators therefore constituted an impressive reservoir of political talent and experience. Strictly speaking, the Senate remained an advisory body, yet the prestige of its members gave it actual power far exceeding that of any other organ in the Roman state. Many wealthy plebeians entered the Senate once civic offices were opened to them, and thereafter an inner core of patrician-plebeian noble families dominated the Senate.

Thus the new nobility retained in practice a dominating influence over Roman politics. Nevertheless, there was no shortage of disputes inside the Senate and assemblies, since Romans seldom voted on purely economic grounds. And the inclusion of the lesser orders in Roman gover-

nance, however limited, stands as a tribute to Rome's political realism. Much Roman blood was spilled on battlefields but relatively little on the city's streets. The willingness to settle internal conflicts by compromise—the ability of the patricians to bend before the winds of social change—preserved a sense of cohesiveness and a spirit of civic commitment without which the Roman conquests would have been impossible.

"The Old Ways"

Conservatism—resistance to change, veneration for "the old ways"—was the essence of the Roman mentality. Like every human society, of course, Rome changed, but Romans never ceased to insist that in olden times things had been better. Romans took their conservatism with religious fervor, and indeed made a religion of it.

The family lay at the core of Roman society, the Roman state, and Roman religion, and by honoring "family values" the Romans expressed their pious conservatism. But by *familia* the Romans understood something different from our modern nuclear household of father, mother, and children; significantly, there is no Latin word for such a social unit. The Roman familia was an extended household headed by its patriarchial senior male, the *paterfamilias,* and embracing his brothers and unmarried sisters, his children (including adult married ones), cousins, and perhaps a venerable widowed grandmother—as well as slaves and other dependents. In its turn, the familia was part of a still larger unit, the *gens* (clan), stretching back to time immemorial and destined to live on forever—hopefully in honor, although an individual's disgrace could tarnish it. The Roman gentleman pictured at the beginning of this chapter was piously exhibiting the ancestors of his *gens*. Roman religion consisted significantly in propitiating the divinities that hovered around the familia and the gens. Clientage, or **patronage**—note its root in the word *pater,* or "father"—bound Roman families in ties of dependence and reciprocal obligation generation after generation. The Roman state was fundamentally a pyramid of families that obeyed a common core of laws, had a collective destiny, and acknowledged a reciprocal relationship with the same high gods.

By law, the paterfamilias was the master of his extended family, whether they lived under his roof or not. Unless he had legally emancipated his adult sons, they could do nothing—marry, for example, or buy or sell anything—without his consent. Legally he had power of life or death over the entire familia. Stories from the early republic told of stern patriarchs who executed their sons for disobedience, including failure to follow their military orders. To be sure, the paterfamilias was supposed to take such drastic action only after consulting a family council, and in the later years of the republic and empire fathers who claimed to be exercising their traditional authority could come under severe legal scrutiny. But not for several centuries after Rome had been Christianized did Roman patriarchs cease to wield life-or-death powers over their own (or their sons') newborn offspring. If the paterfamilias liked the baby's looks he let it remain in the familia; if the baby was scrawny or handicapped, or if he decided that the family already had enough children—particularly girls—the infant was taken from the home and abandoned. Some had the good fortune to be rescued by adults in need of children, but others simply died of exposure or were picked up and raised by slave traders.

The paterfamilias led the familia's religious devotions, ensuring the protection of the *lares* and *penetes,* the gods who safeguarded the household and its larder. In precisely the same spirit, the official cults of the Roman state were conducted by priests who were simply eminent citizens serving their term. Dignity—coupled in some cases with a willingness to do the messy work of poking through animal guts or to run through the streets at festival time clad only in a breechcloth—was the main requirement. Roman religion had no theology save traditional myths, and no morality beyond respect for "the old ways." Custom and the opinion of one's fellow Romans, not divine expectations, dictated what was "moral."[2] Formal religion's concern was with social cohesion. The Roman calendar brimmed with holidays on which it was unlucky to do any private business, including some whose original agricultural or civic purpose had long since been forgotten. On such occasions there would be impressive ceremonies, and ordinary Romans would get relief from their simple everyday fare in public feasting so extravagant that enormous quantities of uneaten food would get heaved into the Tiber. Omens ranging from comets and eclipses to the birth of two-headed calves were taken with the utmost seriousness as foretelling public troubles; generals were expected not to begin battles without favorable "signs." In these and many other ways the gods were firmly believed to communicate with Rome, and *pietas* ("piety") required everyone to listen and act respectfully. The same faithfulness to tradition united the household and the state, and the requirement that a man harden himself to bear the terrors of the battlefield on pain of everlasting disgrace buttressed the old-fashioned Roman family while helping make Roman armies in the long run practically invincible.

The Career of Conquest

The backbone of Old Rome was the small, independent farmer who intensively worked his small plot—about a half-acre was the minimum necessary for subsistence—while remaining always vigilant against raids by tribes from the surrounding hills. He consumed whatever he and his familia produced and had few wants.

Perhaps such stern resolution and rustic virtues were exaggerated by Roman moralists looking back nostalgically from a later, decadent age; but there can be little doubt that the tenacious spirit and astonishing military success of early republican Rome owed much to the steadfast discipline of these citizen-farmers. As triumph followed triumph, as military booty and enslaved war captives poured into Rome from far and wide, the character of its citizenry deteriorated. One of the great tragic themes of Roman history is the gradual erosion of social morality by wealth and power—and by the gradual expansion of huge slave-labor estates at the expense of small farmers.

The expulsion of the last Etruscan king around 509 B.C. was followed by a period of retrenchment during which the Romans fought for their lives against the attacks of neighboring tribes. In time an alliance was formed between Rome and the communities of Latium, in which Rome gradually became the senior partner. After 400 B.C. the Etruscan cities, unwilling to unite for their mutual defense, fell one by one under Roman domination.

The Romans were usually generous with the Italian peoples whom they conquered, allowing them a good measure of internal self-government, and were therefore generally successful in retaining their allegiance. In time, if a conquered people proved loyal, they might hope to be granted Roman citizenship. In this fashion Rome was able to construct an empire far more cohesive and durable than that of Periclean Athens. Gradually, the Roman conquests gained momentum. Battles were often lost—Rome was sacked in 387 B.C. by an army of Gauls from the Po Valley of northern Italy—but the Romans brushed off their defeats and pressed on. By 265 B.C. all Italy south of the Po Valley was under their control. Even the Greek cities of Sicily acknowledged Roman supremacy. Thus, midway through the third century B.C., Rome took its place, alongside Carthage and the three great Hellenistic successor states, among the leading powers of the Mediterranean world.

Carthage and Rome now squared off. In 264 B.C., a dispute over a Sicilian city sparked the first of three savage conflicts known as the Punic Wars (after *Poenus,* the Latin word for "Phoenician" or Carthaginian). Rome was forced to build a navy and take to the sea. The wars, especially the first two, were long and bitter (see Map 4-2). Rome lost numerous battles, scores of ships, and warriors and sailors by the hundreds of thousands. At the outset of the Second Punic War (218–201 B.C.), the troops and war elephants of the masterly Carthaginian general Hannibal crossed the Alps and swept Italy from end to end, winning victory after victory. At Cannae in 216 B.C., the encircled Roman army suffered its worst defeat in history. Only dogged Roman determination and the loyalty of Rome's subject-allies saved the state from extinction. But the Romans hung on,

---

[2] For instance, word that someone had shamed his familia spread like wildfire; a cowardly soldier might as well never come home.

THE HISTORICAL EVIDENCE

Cincinnatus

458 B.C.

The first-century B.C. historian Titus Livius (or Livy, as the English-speaking world knows him) filled his great account of the Roman past with edifying stories of the heroic deeds and exemplary conduct from the Republic's simple early days. One of the best known of these semilegendary events—for which Livy is our only source— occurred in 458 B.C. Cincinnatus was a former consul who had lost most of his property as a result of a lawsuit, but he was the man to whom Rome turned when it faced a deadly threat from its neighbors. Whatever the truth of this and many other of Livy's stories, they all had great power in forming Romans' and later generations of West- erners' ideas of political virtue.*

The city was thrown into a state of turmoil, and the general alarm was as great as if Rome herself were surrounded. Nautius was sent for, but it was quickly decided that he was not the man to inspire full confidence; the situation evidently called for a dictator, and with no dissentient voice, Lucius Quinctius Cincinnatus was named for the post.

Now I would solicit the particular attention of those numerous people who imagine that money is everything in this world, and that rank and ability are inseparable from wealth: let them observe that Cincinnatus, the one man in whom Rome reposed all her hope of survival, was at that moment working a little three-acre farm. . . . A mission from the city found him at work on his land—digging a ditch, maybe, or ploughing. Greetings were exchanged, and he was asked—with a prayer of God's blessing on himself and his country—to put on his toga and hear the Senate's instructions. This naturally surprised him, and, asking if all were well, he told his wife Racilia to run to their cottage and fetch his toga. The toga was brought, and wiping the grimy sweat from his hands and face he put it on; at once the envoys from the city saluted him, with congratulations, as Dictator, invited him to enter Rome, and informed him of the terrible danger of Minucius's army. . . . Preceded by his lictors [and by the senators] he was . . . escorted to his residence [in Rome] through streets lined with great crowds of common folk who, be it said, were by no means pleased to see the new Dictator, as they thought his power excessive and dreaded the way in which he was likely to use it. . . .

Cincinnatus directed the steps that were to be taken to defend the city, and the decisive battle took place, in which the Romans scored a smashing victory.

In Rome the Senate was convened by Quintus Fabius the City Prefect, and a decree was passed inviting Cincinnatus to enter in triumph with his troops. The chariot he rode in was preceded by the enemy commanders and the military standards, and followed by his army, loaded with spoils. We read in accounts of this great day that there was not a house in Rome but had a table spread with food before its door, for the entertainment of the soldiers who regaled themselves as they followed the triumphal chariot, singing and joking as befitted the occasion. . . .

Only the impending trial of Volscius for perjury prevented Cincinnatus from resigning immediately. The tribunes who were thoroughly in awe of him made no attempt to interfere with the proceedings, and Volscius was found guilty and went into exile. . . . Cincinnatus finally resigned after holding office for fifteen days, having originally accepted it for a period of six months.

---

*The story of Cincinnatus was much admired by the officers of the Continental Army after the American Revolution, who formed a society that pressured Congress for the payment of promised bonuses. Cincinnati, Ohio, was named in his—and their—honor.

Source: From Livy, *The Early History of Rome*, Books 1–5 of *The History of Rome from Its Foundation*, trans. Aubrey de Sélincourt (Harmondsworth, England: Penguin, 1960), pp. 197, 200.

---

managing to win the last battle. Fourteen years after Cannae, in 202 B.C., Rome's superior manpower resources and the superb generalship of Scipio Africanus[3] brought the Second Punic War to a victorious conclusion in the battle

of Zama. Victory gave Rome an extensive empire in Sicily, North Africa, and Spain.

Carthage was a worthy opponent that defended itself with skill and determination, and after the Second Punic War it threatened to make a comeback. Grimly the foremost defender of Rome's "old ways," Cato the Elder (234–149 B.C.), ended every Senate speech with the words, "And I say to you, Carthage must be destroyed." In the

---

[3] Publius Cornelius Scipio was given the honorary name Africanus to commemorate his victory over the Carthaginians in North Africa.

MAP 4-2
THE PUNIC WARS

Third Punic War (149–146 B.C.), he posthumously got his wish. Even the besieged Carthaginians' desperate attempt to appease their gods by throwing their children into a sacrificial fire failed. Rome reduced Carthage to smouldering ruins and enslaved and dispersed its population.

In the meantime Rome became involved in the rivalries among the Hellenistic kingdoms of the eastern Mediterranean. Ptolemaic Egypt, Seleucid Asia, Antigonid Macedon (Macedonia), and the smaller Greek states had long been at one another's throats; Rome's victories over Carthage made it stronger than any one of them. Greek states frequently sought Roman aid against their enemies, and more often than not the Romans gave the requested support so as to maintain the balance of power in the east.

The motives for Rome's expansion have been a subject of fierce debate. It has long been maintained that Rome entered the Greek world more as a pacifier and referee than as a conqueror, or because of a misguided fear of dangerous neighbors. Other historians have argued just as strongly that most Romans were no more reluctant to engage in empire building than Alexander the Great or Napoleon; on the contrary, the Romans were downright eager to acquire eastern riches. And the ultimate glory for which every Roman leader thirsted, that of holding a triumph in the streets of Rome, could be had only by waging a successful war.

Whatever their motives, the Romans gained control, directly or indirectly, of almost all the Hellenistic world in the course of the second century B.C. Rome won a decisive victory over the Seleucids in 189 B.C. and conquered

Macedon in 168 B.C. In 146 it demolished the ancient Peloponnesian city of Corinth and transformed Greece into a nominally independent satellite supervised by the Roman governor of Macedon. The remaining Hellenistic kingdoms were now overshadowed and had no choice but to bow to Rome's leadership. In time, they all became Roman provinces. As the second century drew to a close, Rome was the master of the Mediterranean world. There now arose the baffling problem of adapting a government designed to rule a city-state to the needs of an empire.

Social, Cultural, and Political Changes, 264–146 B.C.

Rome changed significantly during the Punic Wars and the republic's subsequent empire building in the Greek-speaking world. Partly this change was the intoxicating effect of unimagined wealth and military success, which gradually undermined the old civic virtue and encouraged arrogance and materialism, as well as social conflict and cultural disorganization.

Ancient Near Eastern religion, already familiar to Hellenistic Greeks, began to seep into Rome even before the wars with Carthage were over. Shortly before the end of the Second Punic War, Romans imported the Anatolian cult of Cybele, the Great Mother, and their victory (attributed to her) helped make her a permanent fixture in Roman religion. But a generation later, in 186 B.C., the Senate suppressed the Dionysian cult, recently arrived from Syria, when stories leaked out of secret sex orgies and disrespect for traditional authority among the sect's female and lower-class recruits.[4]

As Rome was conquering the Greek world it was falling increasingly under the spell of Hellenistic culture. Cato the Elder lamented that Roman soldiers were corrupted by the luxuries of eastern Mediterranean lands and scorned "the Greeklings" as double-talking degenerates. (His ire was particularly roused when a Greek philosopher, visiting Rome on a lecture tour, on his first day defended every conservative Roman value and on the next day demolished them all, sophist-fashion.) But Cato himself embodied the transformations that were permeating Roman life. A "new man" of plebeian origin, Cato fervently advocated investing in the purchase of slaves and the development of vast estates (*latifundia*) that were undermining the old-fashioned sturdy farmers whose values he eloquently championed.

Ultimately, Greece was perhaps the victor. The full tide of Hellenistic skepticism and individualism, which had earlier undermined allegiance to the Greek polis, now began its transforming work on Roman conservatism and civic patriotism. For all his sneers at "Greeklings," Cato read and spoke Greek well, and even sent his son to finish his education at Athens. Cato's political enemies, the Scipio family, championed Hellenic cultural values. With considerable encouragement from the Scipios, Greek literature and art flooded into Rome. In part this resulted from the pillaging of masterful works of sculpture from Periclean Athens for the homes of wealthy Romans, and in part from the new industry of fashioning exact copies of Greek statuary. Patronized by the Scipios as well, Roman authors began producing the first imaginative works of Latin literature—comedies and satires in the fashionable Hellenistic style. And a great Hellenistic historian, Polybius (ca. 200–120 B.C.), who had gone to Rome as a hostage but spent the rest of his life as an honored guest in the Scipios' circle, wrote a large-scale history of Rome's rise that gave classic expression to the idea that the republic's institutional strengths explained its success.

As in Greece, change had both positive and negative effects. While the numbers of slaves were increasing, the status of women was also improving. Whereas Roman women had previously been squarely under the control of their fathers, husbands, or adult male guardians, they could now own property, attend public games, and move freely about the city. This resulted not from changes in the laws but from less rigorous enforcement of them, and from the growing popularity of a new, less binding form of marriage—marriage "by *usus*," a kind of common-law marriage. Many male Romans liked the new arrangement because it ensured that a wealthy woman's dowry would not be lost to the familia into which she married and that unsatisfactory

(including childless) marriages could be terminated easily. The practical effect was to substantially increase the divorce rate and to give wives much greater freedom. As a man of the first century B.C. wrote: "Who among the Romans would be embarrassed to bring his wife to a dinner party? Or whose wife does not have first place at home or attend the public festivals?" By this time, upper-class Romans regarded as quaint the ancient Greek custom of secluding women in an inaccessible part of the home.

What later republican Rome lost in civic virtue it gained in cultural and intellectual depth; for prior to its hellenization, Rome was almost totally lacking in high culture. Moreover, the Stoic notion of universal brotherhood was a singularly appropriate philosophy for a great empire, and conquered peoples occasionally benefited as their Roman masters adopted Stoicism. But with Greek art, literature, and learning came the disquieting Hellenistic feeling of drift and alienation, aggravated by the decay of family farms in favor of plantations.

Traditionally Romans had regarded their soil as a sacred family trust and the farmer who worked his own land as the republic's unshakable foundation. Personally *cultivating* the land—not turning it over to gangs of slaves who would tend livestock on it—was the ideal. But things changed as Rome emerged triumphant from its wars. Both Carthage and the Hellenistic kingdoms had been dominated by large plantations rather than small independent farms, and as the Romans conquered them, they acquired something of their enemies' economic outlook. Conquests brought vast wealth and hordes of slaves into the hands of the Roman senatorial class, whose members regarded commerce and industry as sordid occupations and were constrained by the strongest of social pressures to invest only in land. (In 218 B.C. a law was passed barring senators from trade and moneylending.)

Accordingly, portions of central and southern Italy were now converted into extensive farms known as *latifundia*, worked by slaves and operated in accordance with the latest Carthaginian and Hellenistic techniques of large-scale farming. Cato's *De agricultura*, the oldest surviving work of Latin prose, shows full awareness of these trends, as well as a skinflint's determination to wring every last penny out of his slaves. (Old slaves, he advised, should be sold off, even for a pittance, to avoid having to feed them once they lost their usefulness.) Whereas the small farms had produced grain and other basic foodstuffs, the latifundia concentrated on the commercial production of wine and olive oil or sheep. The small farmers, whose energy and devotion had propelled Rome's expansion, were subjected to such heavy military demands that they found it increasingly difficult to maintain their farms. Their numbers were significantly reduced by continuous conscription for overseas conquests. Many of those who were not conscripted sold out to latifundia owners and moved into the cities, especially Rome itself, where they joined multitudes of penniless immigrant citizens (many of them descendants

---

[4] This reaction foreshadowed official and popular Roman response to Christianity in the first centuries A.D. See Chapter 5.

of ex-slaves from all over the Mediterranean area) and were transformed into a chronically underemployed mob. In later years the riots of this underclass terrorized the government, and their hunger and boredom could only be handled by subsidized food and free entertainment of an increasingly violent sort—the proverbial "bread and circuses."

During the Punic Wars important changes were occurring in the social structure of the Roman elite. With the acceleration of commerce, a new, non-noble class of merchants, landowners, and public contractors emerged and eventually acquired such wealth as to rival the old nobility. This new class came to be known as the equestrian order because the wealth of its members enabled them to serve in the Roman army as cavalry rather than infantry. The equestrian order was effectively excluded from the cursus honorum and therefore from eventually entering the Senate, but its members did not object. Fundamentally unpolitical except when their own interests were at stake, the equestrians were content to share with the nobility the rising living standards resulting from Roman military triumphs and increased contact with the Hellenistic world. Equestrians were free to engage in businesses, such as farming and moneylending, that raked in huge profits, and many Roman senators found ways to get around legal prohibitions against sullying their hands commercially by working through intermediaries—equestrians, or even clever slaves. As equestrians and nobles alike came to live in increasing luxury, the gap between rich and poor steadily widened, and social unrest began to threaten Rome's traditional stability.

Meanwhile the Roman government, which had earlier acted with restraint toward its subject allies in Italy, was proving incapable of governing justly its newly acquired territories overseas. Most of Rome's non-Italian holdings became provinces ruled by aristocratic Roman governors and exploited by Roman tax collectors. Governor and tax collector often worked in partnership to bleed the provinces for personal advantage. The grossest kinds of official corruption were tolerated by the Roman courts of law, whose noble judges hesitated to condemn dishonest officials of their own class for the sake of oppressed but alien provincials. After a time, some provincial governors began making it a practice to set aside a portion of their booty to bribe the courts. A joke of the time explained that a provincial governor had to make *three* fortunes—one to pay for his election, one for bribes when he went on trial for corruption, and one to enjoy in his retirement.

Violence and Revolution: The Last Century of the Republic

These deep-seated problems produced a century of violence and unrest (133–30 B.C.) that resulted ultimately in the downfall of the Roman Republic and the advent of a new, imperial government. The first steps toward revolution were taken by two reform-minded noblemen, the brothers Tiberius and Gaius Gracchus, who advocated a series of popular reform measures and thereby built up a powerful faction among the Roman commoners.

Tiberius Gracchus served as tribune in 133 B.C. and Gaius held the same office a decade later. Both recognized that the decline in able recruits for the Roman army and the deterioration of morale among the citizenry were caused by the virtual elimination of the small farm from central Italy. Their solution was to create new farms for the dispossessed out of the public lands owned by the Roman state. This was a courageous program, but the virtuous Roman farmer of yesteryear could not be conjured back into existence. Most of the public lands had fallen under the de facto control of powerful noble families. Exploiting state lands for their own profit, the nobles reacted frigidly to the proposal that they surrender portions of these lands to create small farms for the impoverished. In the bloodbaths that followed, both brothers were murdered at the nobles' instigation—Tiberius in 133, Gaius in 121. The nobility demonstrated that, despite past concessions, it was still in control. But it also betrayed its political and moral bankruptcy. The violence that was now unleashed would torment the republic for a century and finally demolish it.

For a generation, ordinary Romans continued to press for the Gracchan reforms. The landed nobility found itself pitted not only against the masses but sometimes against the equestrians as well. But the great political fact of the last republican century was the rise of individual adventurers who used successful military careers as springboards to political power.

In 107 B.C. a skillful and ambitious military commander named Marius abolished the long-standing property qualification for military service, opening the army to impoverished volunteers. The property qualification had been diminishing over the previous century in response to a decline in military manpower. Now the process was complete, and the jobless and homeless thronged into the legions. Military service became, for many, the avenue to economic security, since soldiers of a successful and politically influential general could often expect to receive on retirement a gift of land from the Senate. The army began to acquire a more professional outlook, and soldiers came to feel loyalty to their commanders rather than to the state. The opportunities for a ruthless general with a loyal army at his back became virtually limitless.

The subordination of the Roman Republic to the power of generals deepened during the decade of the eighties, amid a struggle between the two foremost commanders of the age, Marius and Sulla. As the architect of open recruitment, Marius drew much of his support from the poor, whereas Sulla tended to ally with the wealthier and more established. But personal ambition was the principal driving force.

In 88 B.C., Marius and Sulla competed for the command of a major military campaign. The Senate awarded the command to Sulla, but Marius, using terrorist tactics, forced a reversal of this decision and gained the command for himself. Sulla, part of his army already assembled, led it in an unprecedented march on Rome. The Senate was outraged, but Sulla nevertheless compelled it to restore his command and then departed for four years' campaigning in the eastern Mediterranean. With Sulla busy elsewhere, Marius and his followers resumed control of Rome and slaughtered their political rivals with Assyrian thoroughness. At length, in 83 B.C., Sulla returned and wrested control of the city from Marius's faction—Marius himself having meanwhile died.

Spectacularly breaching Roman tradition, in 82 B.C. Sulla made himself dictator of the Roman Republic. In times of grave crisis the republic had officially concentrated all power in the hands of a dictator, permitting him to exercise virtually unlimited jurisdiction—but only

for a maximum of six months. Sulla forced the Senate to vote him the dictatorship for an indefinite period, and he used his new power to settle old scores. He tortured and killed many of his enemies and dispossessed others, enriching himself from their confiscated fortunes. But Sulla had no intention of holding power forever. A conservative at heart, he employed his dictatorial prerogatives to establish a series of laws that confirmed and strengthened the power of the Senate, then retired in 79 B.C. to live in luxury on his country estate, leaving the republic to stagger on.

In the decade of the sixties, the great senatorial orator Marcus Tullius Cicero (106–43 B.C.) strove desperately to unite senators and equestrians against the growing threat of generals and riotous urban masses. Cicero's consummate Latin in his orations, essays, and letters would make him the model of literary style in many European languages through the eighteenth century. But his political talents proved inadequate to the task of saving the Roman Republic. His dream of reconciling the interests of senators and equestrians shattered upon the selfishness of each. And his

THE HISTORICAL EVIDENCE

Cicero on Duty

43 B.C.

In the last months of his life, after he had fled from Rome following Caesar's murder and Mark Antony's seizure of power, Cicero passed his time writing De Officiis *("On Duties"), setting forth his vision of the moral gentleman's duty to* humanitas. *Soon after finishing it, he was put to death on Antony's orders.* De Officiis *was mandatory reading—both as a model of Latin style and for its message of* noblesse oblige—*for aristocratic European men from the Renaissance through the eighteenth century.*

Just imagine if each of our limbs had its own consciousness and saw advantage for itself in appropriating the nearest limb's strength! Of course the whole body would inevitably collapse and die. In precisely the same way, a general seizure and appropriation of other people's property would cause the collapse of the human community, the brotherhood of man. Granted that there is nothing unnatural in a man preferring to earn a living for himself rather than for someone else, what nature forbids is that we should increase our own means, property, and resources by plundering others.

Indeed this idea . . . is not only natural law, an international valid principle: the same idea is also incorporated in the statutes which individual communities have framed for their national purposes. . . .

The same conclusion follows even more forcibly from nature's *rational principle*, the law that governs gods and

men alike. . . . For great-heartedness and heroism, and courtesy, and justice, and generosity are far more in conformity with nature than self-indulgence, or wealth, or even life itself. . . .

It is more truly natural to model oneself on Hercules and undergo the most terrible labours and troubles in order to help and save all the nations of the earth than (however superior you are in looks and strength) to live a secluded, untroubled life with plenty of money and pleasures. . . . That is to say, the finest and noblest characters prefer a life of dedication to a life of self-indulgence: and one may conclude that such men conform with nature and are therefore incapable of doing harm to their fellow-men.

Source: From Cicero, *De Officiis*, Book 3, in *Selected Works*, rev. ed., trans. Michael Grant (Harmondsworth, England: Penguin, 1971), pp. 166–167.

THE HUMAN EXPERIENCE

Catullus and Lesbia

Gaius Valerius Catullus (84–54 B.C.) is widely regarded as ancient Rome's foremost lyric poet. His life and poetry exhibit none of the somber old republican virtues, for Catullus was a young man of his times, sophisticated and up-to-date. He was sensitive to the current styles and literary fashions that were flooding into Italy just then from the Greek world—from Hellenistic Alexandria in particular. His 114 surviving poems were influenced not only by the Hellenistic poets but also, going back much further, by the great lyric poets of archaic Greece, above all, Sappho of Lesbos.

No contemporary biography of Catullus has survived; probably none was ever written. We must therefore piece together events in his life from passing references to him in the writings of others, and from internal evidence in his own poems. A native of Verona in northern Italy, Catullus moved with his family to Rome, which he much preferred to Verona. He remained in Rome for much of his life, living for at least a time in a villa of modest size. His father seems to have been relatively rich and politically well connected—indeed, a friend of Julius Caesar himself.

Although Catullus lived only thirty years, he lived them to the hilt. His brief lifetime was marked by the strongest of passions—intense loves and violent hatreds, directed in some cases toward the same person at different times. In his poetry he mentions such late-republican contemporaries as Cicero, Pompey, and Julius

Caesar, his father's friend. For reasons not altogether clear, Catullus absolutely despised Caesar and lampooned him scurrilously in his poetry, until Caesar, in an admirable display of diplomatic forbearance, invited the youth to dinner and managed to calm him down. Thereafter, Catullus and Caesar seem to have got along tolerably well.

Caesar's motive for undertaking to charm the young hothead was apparently an apprehension that Catullus, whose poetic gifts were winning him growing fame, could well damage Caesar's historical reputation. And although Catullus ceased his literary assaults against Caesar, he continued to heap scorn (and worse) on other, less celebrated contemporaries. His rapier wit and literary genius were beginning to strike fear in his enemies.

But Catullus loved just as intensely as he hated. He wrote most affectingly of a dead brother, whose grave he visited while on a journey to Anatolia (his one recorded trip abroad after settling in Rome). He wrote with flaming passion about his erotic loves—a homosexual love affair with a youth named Juventius, and, most notably, his adoration of a beautiful married woman whom he called "Lesbia" and who was evidently the great love of his life.

"Lesbia" has been identified, with a high degree of probability, as Clodia Pulchra—a beautiful patrician woman who was married to a prominent Roman politician named Metellus Celer. He had earlier governed

the district that included Catullus's native Verona, and it is likely that Catullus, while still a provincial youth, had fallen under Clodia's spell. Whatever the case, Catullus wrote no less than twenty-five poems about her, which collectively exhibit, with the greatest passion and clarity, the pathology of a love affair—from extreme ardor to disenchantment and a potent brew of love and loathing. Apparently Catullus, although clever in most respects, was evidently slow to realize what others knew very well: that Clodia Pulchra, his beloved "Lesbia," was an unsavory character from an unsavory family. Her brother was a crooked politician, and she herself—according to the contemporary testimony of Cicero and the account of the second-century A.D. biographer Plutarch—was flamboyantly licentious.

Thus Rome's greatest lyric poet, having soared to the heights, glided down into the depths. Having poured out his adoration, he ended the affair with a poetic dagger thrust:

> I hate and love, nor can the reason tell;
> But that I love and hate I know full well. . . .
> Farewell, my love, Catullus now is done;
> Set fast in stone against this thankless one.
> But Lesbia, can you abide the slight—
> To have no lover come to spend the night? ❖

efforts to perpetuate the traditional supremacy of the Senate were doomed by the Senate's own incapacity, by the smoldering unrest of the city mobs, and by the power hunger of the military commanders. It was Cicero's misfortune to be a conservative amid revolutionary turbulence—a man of words in an age of generals.

The Cultural Revolution of the Late Republic

Cicero was not an original thinker, but an eloquent writer who ranks among the most important transmitters of classical Greek culture to later ages. An admirer and popularizer of the Stoic philosophers, his ideal was *humanitas*—a well-meaning, well-educated, but rather nebulous reverence for the common decencies that unite all human beings. While no opponent of slavery, he did advocate the humane treatment of slaves; and although he made a fortune as an advocate for well-heeled clients facing legal trouble, few more eloquent foes of corruption have ever spoken out.

There was not only political revolution in the air in Cicero's Rome, but moral and cultural uncertainty as well. If Cicero sought in Stoic philosophy a means of reviving the Roman upper class's moral values and sense of political responsibility, spokesmen for other cultural viewpoints pointed out different paths. The great poet Lucretius (99–55 B.C.) popularized Epicureanism, a philosophy easily (and misleadingly) caricatured as "eat, drink, and be merry." Withdrawal from the active life, the avoidance of pain, and the realization that the gods—if they existed at all—cared nothing for human beings were the essence of Epicureanism (see Chapter 3). Lucretius revived Epicurus's original teaching that moral virtue, not selfish greed, was the key to avoiding pain. In his beautiful philosophical poem *De natura rerum* ("On the Nature of Things") he passionately denounced religion as a breeder of evil and explained how the physical universe emerged from the chance convergence of atoms whirling through an infinite void. Lucretius reportedly died insane, a victim of his wife's experiments with love potions. Another great poet, Catullus, needed no aphrodisiacs to enflame his libido or his verse. Catullus and his fellow first-century B.C. writers (who all knew each other) personified a new type of citizen; the independent, sophisticated, and flamboyantly extroverted man of letters for whom the sober, pious republican values were either to be rescued from decay or superseded with something new.

Growing material wealth and cultural sophistication undermined old family values by the second and first centuries B.C. Where once education had occurred in the household itself under the paterfamilias's watchful eye, now well-to-do youths routinely got a good schooling in Greek literature and philosophy and in the art of public speaking, climaxed by a "grand tour" through Greece. But the *content* of the philosophy they learned and the speeches they were trained to deliver could vary greatly. The rising frequency of easy divorces, coupled with a high death rate (from both natural causes and political violence) among adults in what we would today consider middle age, ensured that many young Romans grew up in broken or merged households. Under such conditions, the primary influence on their character was not a traditional paterfamilias but a mother or even a sophisticated slave teacher. (In their formative years, the Gracchus brothers and Julius Caesar, for example, received crucial elements of their upbringing from financially and intellectually independent mothers.) Children who survived the perils of infancy were evidently cherished and their deaths were deeply mourned, and close

A Baker's Shop, Pompeii   This baker's shop in Pompeii does a brisk trade.   *Museo Archeologico Nazinale, Naples, Italy/The Bridgeman Art Library International Ltd.*

emotional bonds sometimes even grew up between husbands and wives—but this was not a cultural expectation that Romans brought to marriage. Custom required husbands and wives to behave with frosty decorum in public—Cato said that he never embraced his wife unless there was a thunderstorm[5]—but womanizing or even overtly affectionate men were considered effeminate, just as were homosexuals. (Among the great politicians who fought for control of Rome after 60 B.C., Pompey lost face when he showed himself genuinely in love with his young wife, and the bisexual Caesar drew jeers for being "the wife of every man and the husband of every woman" in Rome.) Nobody made much fuss when men sought sexual satisfaction outside marriage, but so did powerful widowed, divorced, and even married women who felt secure in their wealth.

Rome in the first century B.C. had become an immense, turbulent city, with a population that modern estimates place as high as a million. If we exclude from our mental image any form of modern technology, Rome might well be compared to a swollen, multicultural American city like New York or Los Angeles, or to some Third World metropolis. People were pouring into Rome from all over

---

[5] And added that he was a happy man when it happened to thunder.

THE HISTORICAL EVIDENCE

A Gourmet's Table

first century B.C.

In the last days of the republic a rich Roman put on a banquet that a somewhat disapproving guest described in the following letter.

I will limit myself to an approximate account, so far as I can remember them, of the sorts and names and places of origin of the delicacies for which land and sea were scoured with tireless gluttony, as enumerated with such strong disapproval by Varro [another writer]. Here is the list: peacock from Samos, hazel hens from Phyrgia, cranes from Media, young kid from Ambracia, tunnyfish from Chalcedon (in Bithynia), oysters from Tartesus (in Spain), whitefish from Pessinus (in Phrygia), oysters from Tarentum, scallops from Chios, swordfish from Rhodes, parrot fish from Cilicia, nuts from Thasos, dates from Egypt, acorns from Iberia. Such greed of a palate which looks everywhere for rare delicacies brought from far countries, such a hunt for tidbits will be found the more disgusting the more we think of some verses of Euripides . . . that certain dainties are only concocted, not because they are necessary to sustain life but for sensual overindulgence disdaining anything easy to prepare and from exaggerated luxury.

Source: Aulus Gellius, *Noctes Atticae* VI, 16, 41 ff. Quoted in Karl Christ, *The Romans*, trans. Christopher Holme (London: Chatto & Windus, 1984), p. 108.

---

the Mediterranean: not just Italians, but also Greeks, Anatolians, North Africans, Egyptians, Syrians, and Jews. Many were solid artisans or small-scale merchants who operated tiny shops on the street side of their modest residences. But many others lived in squalid, flimsy three- to six-story apartment buildings called *insulae,* or "islands." Disconnected from traditional extended-family structures and living hand-to-mouth from day labor, petty crime, and government doles, these people presumably considered themselves transients to a more settled way of life; but many never reached it. Not all rootless Romans were desperately poor; some were the offspring of well-to-do families who had drifted to the city in search of opportunity and excitement. Both male and female desperadoes from such irregular backgrounds joined a half-baked conspiracy to seize power in Rome under the political adventurer Catiline in 63 B.C., but the plot was exposed by Cicero and the participants executed. The Roman mob, and the question of who should master it, remained a key factor in the equation of late-republican politics.

Food offers a significant indicator of Roman social and political history. In their days of subsistence on tiny independent farms, early Romans had eaten a simple diet of bacon, beans, garden vegetables, cheese, and garlic, all cooked in olive oil.[6] When Sicily became a grain-exporting Roman colony, bread became the staple of Romans' diets,

and both keeping the price of grain reasonable and supplying the unemployed with grain doles became important objectives of anyone who ruled the state. But for the Roman rich, gourmandizing became an obsession. Perhaps because the range of "normal" foods was relatively restricted—the "Columbian Exchange" that created the varied modern diet lay a millennium and a half in the future—the cooks serving the Roman elite explored every possibility for extracting novelty from what they had to work with, and no expense was spared in importing exotic delicacies to tickle jaded palates. Banqueting, in which guests reclined on comfortable couches while slaves brought course after course, consumed hours on end and provided ample opportunity for sexual dalliance.

About one-third of Rome's (and of Italy's) population were slaves, about the same proportion as in the pre–Civil War American South. The basic facts of slavery—the slave's utter lack of security or dignity and the master's total power—were constants in both societies. And Roman masters, like those in the slave South, lived with a constant undercurrent of dread that their slaves might flee, rebel, or, still worse, poison them. (The Roman answer to this problem was a rule that if a slave killed a master, *all* the slaves of that household were to be executed.) But there were important differences, too. No racial caste system underpinned Roman slavery: A few blacks can be documented among Rome's slaves, but they were exotic novelties, just like blond Germans and Slavs who might also find their way onto the slave market. As in Greece and the Hellenistic world, war, piracy, and networks of slavers reaching beyond Rome's borders dragged an endless stream of

---

[6] Tomatoes, the foundation of pasta sauce and pizzas that modern Americans associate with Italian cookery, were **New World** plants, unknown in Eurasia until after Columbus's voyages (see Chapter 14).

The Gladiatorial Show In A.D. 59 a riot broke out at the Pompeii arena during a gladiatorial show in which fans from neighboring Nuceria were killed. As punishment, the Senate in Rome shut down Pompeii's arena for ten years. *Erich Lessing/Art Resource, NY.*

wretches into slavery. The experience of slaves could vary enormously, from those condemned to an early death at underfed, backbreaking mine or agricultural labor to such specialists as tutors, office managers, and physicians. Some slaves ran city shops or plied skilled crafts and were indistinguishable on the street from ordinary free Romans. Manumission—the freeing of slaves—occurred on a considerable scale (laws prevented the *too* frequent granting of freedom), and freedmen and freedwomen occupied an important, honorable niche in Roman society. Legally, former slaves remained in a clientage relationship to their former masters. But for those slaves whose intelligence, training, and luck put them on a track leading to manumission, the prospect of eventual freedom might have mitigated the

terrors of their plight. Such slaves were tied to their masters in complex bonds of mutual expectation. A few freed slaves even managed to inherit their masters' property and marry their widows, or otherwise to amass great wealth; the racy *Satyricon* of the first-century A.D. Roman novelist Petronius drew an unforgettable picture of the fabulously wealthy and grossly vulgar freedman Trimalchio. In a handful of cases, reality did not lag far behind.

An entirely different dimension of Roman slavery was the enormously popular and lucrative business of supplying gladiators. Although gladiatorial combats had been held in Rome since Etruscan times, their explosive growth as mass entertainment seems to have coincided with the wars of the third century B.C., when uprooted populations eager for

THE HUMAN EXPERIENCE

Spartacus

Spartacus, a slave and gladiator, escaped captivity in 73 B.C. and for the next two years led a massive insurrection against the Roman Republic. His rebellion illustrates not only the political insecurity of the republic's last century but, more generally, the potential for local and regional violence that existed throughout the history of ancient Rome as a consequence of deep and widespread social discontent.

Only with difficulty can Spartacus's career be patched together from the hostile accounts of several Roman writers. A native of Thrace, he became a Roman soldier but then seems to have deserted. He was subsequently captured, enslaved, and assigned to become a gladiator. While training for his new career at a gladiatorial school in Capua, he and a band of fellow fighters made their escape. They took refuge near the top of the then-dormant volcano Mount Vesuvius, where Spartacus became the commander of an army of brigands.

Responding swiftly, Rome sent an army of three thousand legionaries to encircle the rebels and starve them out. But Spartacus and his men descended on the legionaries and routed them. As news of the successful insurrection spread, multitudes of paupers and runaway slaves swelled Spartacus's band into an army that could hold its own against the Romans on the battlefield. A second, larger Roman army, led by the commander Varinius, found Spartacus's ex-slaves entrenched in regular formation on the open plain. Prudently declining battle, Spartacus led his army off secretly, and when the Romans advanced they found his fortifications empty.

Varinius pursued the rebels across the length and breadth of the southern Italian countryside, to no avail. Spartacus defeated Varinius in several pitched battles and just missed taking him prisoner. The rebels plundered a number of cities and, in time, extended their control over most of southern Italy.

The Roman Senate now took serious alarm. It sent both consuls, each with his own army, against Spartacus, who routed each of the armies in turn. Spartacus then led his rebels northward toward the Alps in the hope of crossing into Gaul. Since Gaul had not yet been incorporated into the Roman Republic, it would have been a land of freedom for former Roman slaves.

But in an astonishing display of homesick sentimentality, the slaves refused to leave Italy. Spartacus had no choice but to turn back. His next move was to lead his men against the city of Rome itself, but his army's nerve seems to have failed again. The slaves drew back from attacking the city, and Spartacus led them into the south once more.

The Senate sent still another army against Spartacus led by a magistrate named Crassus, whose far-flung commercial enterprises—including the buying and selling of slaves on a very large scale—had made him the richest man in Rome. More fortunate than his predecessors, Crassus defeated Spartacus in battle. Spartacus thereupon withdrew southward to the toe of the Italian boot with the idea of crossing the narrow straits of Messina to the island of Sicily, where great numbers of restless slaves were eager to join his army. He made arrangements with pirates to ferry his

men across the straits; but as Crassus marched his army southward, the pirates betrayed and abandoned the rebels, leaving them trapped at the tip of the Italian toe.

Crassus tightened the trap by digging a ditch and building earthwork ramparts all the way across the tip of the peninsula. But Spartacus and his army burst through and took to the hills of southern Italy once again. The morale of the rebels had been shaken by recent events, however, and dissension was increasing among them. One band seceded from the main army, only to be annihilated by the Romans. And the determined Crassus continued his pursuit. Spartacus crushed the vanguard of the advancing Roman army, but his troops disobeyed his command to retreat after inflicting the blow. As a result, the rebels faced the full strength of Crassus's army, and in a fiercely fought battle Spartacus and most of his men perished. Spartacus himself is reported to have died still gripping his sword. Six thousand captured rebels were crucified along the road from Capua to Rome, their rotting bodies left hanging on their crosses as a warning.

Crassus's victory advanced his political career considerably. But even greater credit was given to another general, Pompey "the Great," who, curiously enough, had never faced Spartacus in battle. Pompey and his army were returning from Spain when they encountered and destroyed a band of rebels fleeing from the battle that had claimed Spartacus's life. Yet Pompey afterward boasted that he, and no other man, had ended the rebellion. ❖

Freed Couple This Roman couple from the first century A.D. had both been born slaves. As freed people, they had many clientage obligations to their former owners, but they obviously prospered enough to afford this handsome funeral monument. *71.AA.260, artist unknown; Funerary Relief with busts of Popillius and Calpurnia. Early 1st century A.D. Carrera marble, H: 63.5 cm; W: 89 cm; D: 20.3 cm. The J. Paul Getty Museum, Malibu, California.*

thrilling diversions swelled the city and captured enemies became plentiful. By the late republic, staging massive, bloody combats of men and beasts became expected of Rome's rich and powerful, and the strongest reaction that even basically humane men like Cicero could muster was bored disapproval. Gladiators were slaves highly trained to fight with unusual combinations of weapons—a typical event might pit a nimble man armed only with a net and trident against a heavily armored but cumbersome fighter—and they were expected to fight to the death, although the crowd might let a man who had put up a good battle live to entertain them again. Crowds howled, bands played, refreshments got hawked, bets were placed, fans debated the fine points of this or that champion as knowingly as modern Americans size up basketball stars, and women fell in love with swaggering winners. A few free Roman men (and even women) are known to have tried their luck against the enslaved pros. Sports and other entertainments reveal much about any society's values, and in Rome's case the gladiatorial shows and other "blood sports" of the arena suggest a fascination with violence that few other cultures have seen fit to unleash—but that, arguably, are latent in any society.

CAESAR AND THE PRINCIPATE

By 60 B.C. the Roman Republic was approaching its final days in an atmosphere of chaos and naked force. The dominant political figures of Cicero's generation were military commanders such as Pompey and Julius Caesar (100–44

B.C.), who bid against one another for the backing of the lower classes, seeking to convert mob support into political supremacy. The three great political figures of the age—Pompey, Cicero, and Caesar—were all murdered. The failure of republican government was now manifest, and the entire system of Roman rule seemed on the verge of collapse. But Rome emerged from this crisis transformed and strengthened, so much so that its empire endured for another five hundred years in the West and fifteen hundred years in the East. The resurrection of the Roman state out of the wreckage of the old order was one of antiquity's most stunning political achievements.

The new order, which saved Rome from the agonies of the late republic and brought a long era of peace and stability to the Mediterranean world, was chiefly the handiwork of two men: Julius Caesar and his grandnephew Augustus. For a time Caesar ruled with two colleagues, and after his death a similar coalition guided Rome for a few years. But a more centralized and lasting regime took shape under Augustus, who preferred the title of *princeps* ("first citizen") and whose new political system has thus been termed the Principate.

Julius Caesar and Augustus, 49 B.C.–A.D. 14

Julius Caesar was a man of many talents—a superb general, an astute politician, and an author whose lucid *Commentaries on the Gallic Wars* was a significant contribution to the great literary surge of the late Roman Republic. Above all, Caesar was a person of keen practical intelligence who

MAP 4-3
THE ROMAN REPUBLIC AFTER CAESAR'S CONQUEST OF GAUL

could probe to the core of any problem, work out a logical solution, and then carry his plan to realization.

A relative of Marius, Caesar rode the whirlwind of violence and ambition that was shattering Roman society during the mid-first century B.C. His political intuition and unswerving faith in himself catapulted him to increasingly important political and military offices during the turbulent sixties. Opposed and distrusted by the conservative Senate, he allied himself with Pompey, a disgruntled general, and Crassus, an ambitious millionaire. These three formed a coalition of political bosses, known to historians as the First Triumvirate,[7] which succeeded in dominating the Roman state.

Leaving Italy to his two colleagues, Caesar spent most of the following decade (58–50 B.C.) in Gaul. There he led his army on a spectacular series of campaigns that resulted in the conquest of what is now France and Belgium, and established his reputation as one of history's greatest military leaders. Caesar's conquest of Gaul pushed Roman civilization far northward from the Mediterranean basin into the heartland of western Europe. The long-range consequences of his conquest are immense, for in the centuries that followed, Gaul was thoroughly romanized. The Roman influence survived the later barbarian invasions to give France a Romance tongue (that is, a language that evolved from Latin), and to provide western Europe with an enduring Greco-Roman cultural heritage (see Map 4-3).

While Caesar was winning Gaul, his interests in Italy were suffering. His advocacy of land redistribution and of other policies dear to the hearts of the lower classes earned him the hostility of the Senate. And his stunning military successes threatened to thwart Pompey's own ambitions. Out of common fear of Caesar, Pompey and the Senate joined forces, and in 49 B.C. they declared Caesar a public enemy. His career and his life at stake, Caesar defied the Roman constitution by leading his army across the Rubicon River, which marked Italy's northern boundary. In a series of dazzling campaigns (49–48 B.C.), he defeated Pompey and the hostile senators. Pompey fled to Egypt and was murdered there, leaving the Senate with no choice but to come to terms with the man who towered unchallenged over Rome.

Caesar was a magnanimous victor. He restored his senatorial opponents to their former positions and ordered the execution of Pompey's murderer. He could afford to be generous, for he was now the unquestioned master of the state. Caesar assumed the office of dictator and held it not for the traditional six months or, like Sulla, with the intention of early retirement, but year after year. Ultimately he forced the Senate to grant him the dictatorship for life. He also assumed the key republican office of consul and retained the title of *pontifex maximus* ("supreme pontiff," or chief priest of the civic religion), which he had held for some years. In 44 B.C. he received the unprecedented honor of having a temple dedicated to his *genius* (the "spirit" of his clan), and the month of July was named in his honor. The political institutions of the republic survived, but they were

---

[7] *Triumvirate* means "three-man alliance."

now under his thumb. The whole Roman electorate had become his clients. He was officially called the *imperator*— the wielder of the *imperium*, or right to command—and although the term had not yet acquired all the connotations that we now associate with the word *emperor*, the whiff of monarchy was in the air.

Caesar used his power to reform the Roman Republic along logical, practical lines. He introduced a radically new "Julian" calendar that, with some adjustments, is in almost universal use today. He organized numerous distant colonies that drained off a considerable number of Rome's unemployed and halved the bread dole. He did much to reform Italian and provincial government and to purge the administration of abuses. In short, his regime resembled that of a talented Greek **tyrant** such as Pisistratus.

Caesar's reforms were immensely beneficial, but he went too far too fast. His disregard for hallowed republican institutions was too cavalier, and his assumption of the dictatorship for life alarmed powerful senators. On a major religious holiday, the Ides of March (March 15), 44 B.C., he was stabbed to death in the Senate by senatorial conspirators led by Brutus and Cassius. As they rushed from the Senate the assassins shouted, "Tyranny is dead!" They were wrong: it was the republic that was dead, and Rome now had only the choice between one-man rule and anarchy. By killing Caesar, they had given up the former for the latter.

Caesar's assassination meant fourteen more awful years of civil strife. The conservative party of Brutus and Cassius struggled against would-be heirs to Caesar, and the heirs

fought among themselves. In the complex maneuvers of this civil war some of the most famous figures in ancient history played out their roles and often lost their lives. Mark Antony, Caesar's trusted lieutenant, defeated Brutus and Cassius in battle, and they both committed suicide. The golden-tongued Cicero, Rome's supreme literary craftsman, was murdered for his hostility to Antony. And when the fortunes of war turned against Antony and his celebrated wife, Cleopatra VII of Egypt, they took their own lives.

The ultimate victor in these struggles was a young man virtually unknown at the time of Caesar's death. Octavian (later known as Augustus), Caesar's grandnephew and adopted son, was eighteen when Caesar died. Inferior to Caesar in generalship, Octavian was nevertheless Caesar's superior as a political realist. During his long, illustrious reign Octavian completed the transformation of the Roman state from republic to empire. But his reforms looked more traditionalist than Caesar's, and he succeeded—where Caesar had failed—in soothing the Senate. He reformed the Romans and made them accept it. And he died peacefully in his own bed.

The Augustan Age

In 31 B.C. Octavian's forces crushed those of Antony and Cleopatra at the decisive naval battle of Actium. A year later Octavian entered Alexandria as master of the Mediterranean world. He was then the same age as Alexander at the time of his death, and it might be supposed that the two world conquerors, both young, brilliant, and handsome, had much in common. But Octavian refused to visit Alexander's tomb in Alexandria, observing, so it was said, that true greatness lies not in conquest but in reconstruction. Appropriately, Octavian's historical reputation lies not in his military victories but in his accomplishments as peacemaker and architect of the Roman Empire.

The reformation of Rome, completed by Octavian, gave the Mediterranean world two centuries of almost uninterrupted peace during which classical culture developed and spread to the outermost reaches of the Roman Empire. In the turbulent centuries that followed, people looked back longingly at the almost legendary epoch of the *Pax Romana*, or "Roman Peace." Octavian accomplished the seemingly impossible task of reconciling the need for one-man rule with the republican traditions of Old Rome. He preserved the Senate; indeed, he increased its prestige. Making no attempt to become dictator, he manipulated the government in subtler ways. Thus he retained the elected republican magistracies but used his enormous patronage power to influence who won the elections. He controlled the army, and like Caesar he concentrated various key republican offices in his own person. Eventually he went beyond Caesar himself in being granted the power of a tribune (including the right to initiate legislation and the unlimited right of veto, which tribunes had originally

Julius Caesar   In 44 B.C. Caesar became the first *living* Roman to be depicted on a coin, although he issued this coin only after partisans of the dead Pompey had struck a coin showing their hero. This was an example of Caesar trampling on republican feelings. Putting one's head on a coin was a provocative action, smacking of monarchy. Soon after the coin appeared, his assassins struck.   © *R. Sheridan/Ancient Art & Architecture Collection.*

Augustus Caesar When this, probably the most famous statue of Augustus, was made, he was in his fifties (elderly by Roman standards), yet in his capacity as imperator the image that he always projected to the people of the Roman Empire was that of a virile, commanding young man. *Pater patriae* (the "Father of His Country"), a title formally conferred upon him by the Senate, was another attribute that he used on his coins and inscriptions to impress upon everyone that he had become the paterfamilias of the entire Roman world. The Emperor Augustus Addressing His Army. *Marble, originally painted, ca. 10* B.C. *Found in the Villa of Livia, wife of Augustus, at Prima Porta. Vatican, Rome.*

endar at the expense of luckless February. After his death he—like Caesar—was proclaimed a god, a posthumous distinction that would later be bestowed on all but the most disreputable of his successors.

Much as Augustus may have enjoyed these various honors, he cultivated an unostentatious public image. Calling himself simply *princeps* ("first citizen") suggested that he was the leading Roman—nothing more. He lived fairly modestly, associated freely with his fellow citizens, honored the dignity of the Senate, and dressed and ate simply. It has been said that the government of the Principate was the mirror opposite of the government of modern Britain—the former a monarchy masquerading as a republic, the latter a republic masquerading as a monarchy. But although the Principate was at heart a monarchy, it was by no means an arbitrary one. Augustus ruled with a keen sensitivity toward popular and senatorial opinion and a respect for tradition. Ancient Rome, like modern Britain, had no written constitution, but it had a venerable body of political customs—an unwritten constitution—that Augustus treated with cautious deference.

He had merely restored and improved the republic, Augustus claimed; actually, he was Rome's true master. Roman political liberty was the single great casualty of the Principate, but its loss was rendered less painful by the political deftness of the first princeps. In its place, Augustus provided peace, security, and justice—themes constantly reiterated in the Latin and Greek inscriptions that were carved in prominent public places everywhere in the Roman world, and on the coins that everybody used. The administration of the provinces was more closely regulated, and corruption and exploitation reduced. In Rome itself an efficient imperial bureaucracy developed that was responsible to the princeps alone. Although class distinction remained strong, it became easier for an able person from one of the lesser orders to rise in the government service; Augustus drew in particular upon the rich but hitherto politically disengaged equestrians.

Rather prudish in his private life and convinced that decay of "the old ways" had fatally corrupted the republic, Augustus set about reforming Roman morals. Adultery, for example, became a crime; men were expected to divorce licentious wives (but not the reverse); and a great army of snoops and informers set to work. Augustus banished his own daughter for promiscuity and exiled the great poet Ovid to what is today Romania for writing such charmingly naughty verses as *The Art of Love*. But in the end, the chief effect of the great morality campaign was to provide lucrative opportunities for blackmailers. Illicit carnality is not known to have diminished.

Despite his failure as a moral uplifter, Augustus's stable new regime, the promise of enduring peace, the policy of "careers open to talents," and the leadership of the imperator himself combined to evoke a surge of optimism, patriotism, and creative originality. As part of his policy of

exercised in behalf of the plebeian order). This power, with its great flexibility, was ideal for Octavian's needs and became a potent instrument of imperial control. Future emperors dated the beginning of their reign from the moment they received the tribunician power.

Octavian's authority closely resembled Julius Caesar's. He too was designated imperator, and altars were set up all over the Roman world at which people were expected to show their loyalty by burning incense before his statue. In 27 B.C. the Senate voted him the new name of Augustus, a term that carried with it no specific power but had a connotation of reverence—almost holiness. And like Caesar he arranged to have a month (August) named in his honor. The necessity that his month should have as many days as Caesar's July resulted in a permanent asymmetry in our calpromoting respect for Roman tradition, Augustus assiduously supported gifted writers and artists. In the arts and letters the Augustan Age stands at the apex of Roman creativity. Under Augustus, Roman artists and poets achieved a powerful synthesis of Greek and Roman elements. Roman architecture was obviously modeled on the Greek, yet expressed a distinctively Roman spirit. Roman temples often rose higher than those of classical Greece and conveyed a feeling that was less serene—more imposing and dynamic. Augustan poetry—the urbane and faultless lyrics of Horace, the worldly verses of Ovid, the majestic cadences of Vergil—all employed Greek models and ideas, but in original and characteristically Roman ways.

Rome's supreme poem, Vergil's *Aeneid*, is cast in the epic form of Homer and deals, as Homer's *Odyssey* does, with the voyage of an important figure in the Trojan War. But "pious Aeneas,"[8] Vergil's hero, was also the legendary founder of Rome, and the poem is shot through with patriotic prophecies about the destiny of the state that Aeneas was to found. Indeed, some readers have seen in Aeneas a symbol of Augustus himself. The *Aeneid* conveys the feeling of hope—that the Roman people, founded by Aeneas and now led by the great peacemaker Augustus, had at last fulfilled their mission to bring enduring concord and justice to the tormented world:

> Let it be your charge, O Roman,
>> To rule the nations in your empire;
> This shall be your art:
>> To ordain the law of peace,
>> To be merciful to the conquered.
>> To beat the haughty down.[9]

Imperial Leadership after Augustus, A.D. 14–180

Augustus died at the age of seventy-six in A.D. 14. During the decades following his death the Principate grew more centralized and more efficient. The imperial bureaucracy slowly expanded, but taxes remained relatively light and intelligently assessed, and the law became increasingly humane. The system that Augustus established proved sturdy enough to adapt and endure despite the relative incapacity or viciousness of many of his imperial successors.

The abilities of Augustus's immediate successors ranged from uninspired competence to (putting it charitably) mental incapacity. We encounter the psychopathic cruelty of Nero (reigned 54–68)—he who strummed his lyre while watching the Roman slums go up in flames and then organized a gruesome slaughter of early Christians to deflect rumors that he himself had set the fire[10]—and the insane antics of Caligula (reigned 37–41), who wallowed in the pleasure of watching his prisoners tortured to death. Caligula is reported to have allowed his favorite horse to dine at the imperial table during formal state dinners, consuming the finest food and wines from jeweled dishes and goblets. At Caligula's death (by assassination) he was on the point of raising the beast to the office of consul. Caligula and Nero were autocrats of the worst sort, and both were removed violently from power.

On the whole, however, the emperors of the early Principate retained the traditional attitudes exemplified by Augustus himself, even if most failed to match him in political wisdom. The most competent of Augustus's first-century successors was Vespasian (reigned 69–79), the general who became princeps at the end of a bloodbath known as "The Year of the Four Emperors" following Nero's overthrow in A.D. 68. A rough-hewn man from the provinces who made his mark by beginning the bloody work of crushing the great Jewish revolt in Judea (see Chapter 5), Vespasian gave Rome a decade of relatively honest and frugal government. (Characteristically, he established public restrooms in Rome where people could relieve themselves for a small fee; when his son and successor Titus objected that raising revenue this way was beneath the imperial dignity, Vespasian thrust a coin under his nose and asked, "Does it smell?") After assassinations and the occasional **coup d'état** that had ended the reigns of most of Augustus's successors, Vespasian's death from an ordinary illness portended a settling-down of imperial authority, and his deathbed quip deflates the pretension of the imperial cult: "Alas, I think I'm becoming a god."

The second century A.D. witnessed a more consistent improvement in imperial leadership. Rome's rulers between A.D. 96 and 180—Nerva, Trajan, Hadrian, Antoninus Pius, and Marcus Aurelius—have been traditionally called the "five good emperors." Their success can be attributed largely to the temporary solving of one of the knottiest dilemmas in the whole imperial system—the problem of succession. In theory the Senate chose the princeps, but in fact the succession usually fell to a close relative of the previous emperor and was often arranged by the emperor in advance. Too often this led to a disputed succession settled by violence and even civil war (which had brought Vespasian to power). But none of the second-century emperors—Trajan, Hadrian, Antoninus Pius, or Marcus Aurelius—came to the throne through normal hereditary succession. Each had been chosen by the previous emperor, who had legally adopted as his son and successor a younger man of outstanding ability.

---

[8] Vergil represents Aeneas as "pious" in the Roman sense of being respectful of tradition and duty.

[9] *Aeneid*, Book 6; adapted from *The Aeneid*, edited with introduction and commentary by J. W. Mackail (Oxford, England: Oxford University Press, 1930).

---

[10] For the persecution of the Christians, see Chapter 5.

This policy was intelligent, but also necessary: None of the "five good emperors" had sons of their own except Marcus Aurelius, the last of them. Yielding to a temptation that his four predecessors had not faced, Marcus chose his own son to succeed him—Commodus, who turned out to be incompetent and bloodthirsty. With Commodus's disastrous reign (A.D. 180–192), enlightened imperial rule came to an end. It was followed by a century of military despotism, assassinations, economic and administrative breakdown, cultural decay, and civil strife that—as we shall see in Chapter 5—nearly destroyed the Roman state.

The Empire under the Principate

In the two centuries from the rise of Augustus to the death of Marcus Aurelius (31 B.C.–A.D. 180), the Roman Empire expanded gradually to include a vast area encircling the Mediterranean Sea and bulging northward across present-day France and England. It extended about three thousand miles from east to west (about the breadth of the United States)—from the Tigris-Euphrates Valley to the Atlantic. According to the best scholarly guesses, its inhabitants numbered some 50 million—heavily concentrated in the eastern provinces, where commerce, urbanism, and civilization had been flourishing for thousands of years (see Map 4-4).

Augustus added considerable territory to the empire, and several later emperors, most notably Trajan, made significant conquests. But most emperors were content to guard the frontiers and preserve what had already been won. To the east, Rome's boundary demarcated a balance of power that had to be struck with the Parthian Empire and its aggressive third-century heir, the Persian Empire. Elsewhere Rome's expansion was halted only by deserts, mountains, wastelands, untamed forests, and the Atlantic. In short, the empire encompassed virtually all the lands that could be subdued by Roman armies and cultivated profitably by Roman landowners.

The burden of defending these frontiers rested on an imperial army of some three hundred thousand to five hundred thousand men, organized on principles laid down by Augustus. Infantry legions manned by Roman citizens on long-term enlistments were supplemented by auxiliary forces, both infantry and light cavalry, made up of non-Romans who were granted citizenship at the end of their extended terms of service. The army was concentrated

MAP 4-4

THE ROMAN EMPIRE AT ITS HEIGHT, UNDER TRAJAN

along the frontiers except for the small, privileged Praetorian Guard in Rome that served the princeps—and sometimes overthrew him and named his successor.

A high degree of military mobility was ensured by the superb system of roads that linked Rome with its remotest provinces. Paved with close-fitted stones and running in straight lines mile after mile, these roads were nearly as eternal as the city they served. They eased the flow of commerce as well as the movement of troops and remained in use many centuries after the Pax Romana was shattered.

The empire's greatest commercial artery, however, was not built of stone. It was the Mediterranean, completely surrounded by imperial territory and referred to affectionately by the Romans as *Mare Nostrum*, "our sea." Roman fleets patrolled the Mediterranean and cleared it of pirates for the first time in antiquity so that peaceful shipping could move safely between the many ports of the empire. Long-range trade in luxury goods earned lucrative profits for all the middlemen involved. The merchants of the empire's far-flung cities traded over enormous distances, even beyond the imperial borders: Roman coins have turned up in abundance along the Baltic shores of northeastern Europe, and a lively trade flourished between Rome and India. Romans and Chinese, although never in sustained contact, knew of each other's existence, mainly through the silk trade.

Roman institutions and classical culture spread far and wide across the empire under the canopy of the Pax Romana. As distant provinces became increasingly romanized, the meaning of *Rome* and *Roman* gradually changed. By the time of Augustus these terms embraced the greater part of Italy. Later, as the decades of the Pax Romana followed one another, citizenship was extended to more and more provincials until finally, in A.D. 212, every free inhabitant of the empire received citizenship. By then the emperors themselves often came from the provinces: The second-century emperor Trajan, for example, was a native of Spain. Centuries later, the terms *Rome* and *Roman* acquired a universal connotation: A Greek autocrat in Constantinople, a Frankish chieftain at Aachen, a Saxon king in Germany, a Habsburg dynast in Vienna would all, in later ages, refer to themselves as "Roman emperors."

Romans were imperialists in the starkest sense of that word. "When foreign peoples could safely be pardoned I have preferred to preserve rather than exterminate them"—chilling words, which Augustus included in the inscriptions celebrating his victories that he set up in cities throughout the empire. Those whom Roman armies conquered had

Defeated Germans
Tacitus's British chieftain might have had scenes like this in mind when he accused the Romans of making a desert and calling it peace. Here, German tribesmen who fought in vain against the imperial army are decapitated one by one. The scene appears on a second-century column that an emperor erected in Rome to commemorate a victory. *Mansell/Time Inc.*

fought tenaciously for their right to be left alone. "Harriers of the world," said a British chieftain of the Romans in eloquent words that the historian Tacitus imagined him saying: "To plunder, butcher, steal, these things they misname empire; they make a desolation and they call it peace." But with time, at least some subjects came to see benefits in the Pax Romana. "Wars have so far vanished as to be legendary affairs of the past," wrote a Greek man of letters about A.D. 150, continuing:

> A man simply travels from one country to another as though it were through his native land. We are no longer frightened by the Cilician pass [in the Anatolian mountains] or by the narrow tracks that lead from Arabia into

Egypt. We are not dismayed by the height of mountains, or by the vast breadth of rivers or by inhospitable tribes of barbarians. To be a Roman citizen, nay even one of your subjects is a sufficient guarantee of personal safety.

Presumably Augustus would have been pleased with so cooperative an attitude.

Life under the Pax Romana

The most conspicuous effect of romanization was the spread of cities. The city-state, the characteristic political unit of the Greco-Roman world, now extended to the outermost provinces—to Gaul, Spain, the lands along the

---

THE HISTORICAL EVIDENCE

Pliny the Younger as Benefactor

ca. A.D. 110

Early in the second century A.D. the wealthy Roman writer and senator Pliny the Younger had an inscription (the first selection presented below) carved at his native Verona, in northern Italy, detailing some of the bequests that he made to the city. (One sesterius—plural sesterce—the monetary unit referred to, would buy a large loaf of good bread in Pliny's time.) Such philanthropy was expected of all wealthy Romans, and in return they liked to advertise their generosity. In one of Pliny's letters (the second selection below), he commends a friend for another act of liberality: furnishing gladiators for the good people of Verona. The city's arena had a seating capacity of twenty thousand. Presumably the gladiators killed each other rather than the panthers, which did not arrive in time. It may seem odd that Pliny's friend put on the gladiatorial show in commemoration of his late wife, but educated Romans were aware that in Etruscan times gladiatorial combats were part of funeral rites—an offering, perhaps, to the gods of the underworld.

Gaius Plinius Caecelius Secondus . . . [a long list of his distinctions follows]. He left . . . [blank here] sesterces in his will for the construction of baths, with an additional 300,000 [plus?] sesterces for decoration, and in addition to that 200,000 sesterces for upkeep; and for the support of his freedmen, a hundred persons, he likewise bequeathed to the municipality 1,866,666 sesterces, the income from which he desired to have applied thereafter to an annual banquet for the public. In his lifetime he also gave 500,000 sesterces for the support of the boys and girls of the lower class, and also a library and 100,000 sesterces for the upkeep of the library.

Gaius Plinius to his dear Maximus, greeting.

You were right to promise a combat of gladiators to our good friends the people of Verona, by whom you have so long been loved, admired, and honored. It was from there, too, that you took your wife most dear and lovely, to whose

memory some monument or show was due, preferably this exhibition, which is especially appropriate for commemorating the dead. Besides, you were so unanimously pressed to do so, that to refuse would have seemed not constancy but obstinacy. It was a distinguished gesture, too, that you were so ready, so generous in providing them; for these, too, are the marks of a noble spirit. I am sorry the many African panthers you had purchased did not arrive in time; but even though they were delayed by bad weather and failed to appear, it was nevertheless understood, as you deserved, that it was not your fault that you did not exhibit them. Farewell.

Source: Naphthali Lewis and Meyer Rinehold, *Roman Civilization: A Sourcebook* (New York: Columbia University Press, 1951), vol. 2, pp. 349, 353–354.

A Chariot Race   Apart from the finish line, the most exciting part of a Roman chariot race was the turn at each end of the course (the Circus), where crashes were common and part of the thrill. Romans took their racing seriously: All over the empire there were two parties, the Greens and the Blues, that rooted for rival teams of racers (no doubt chanting the equivalent of "We're Number One!") and that often came to blows in the Circus or the streets outside. This wall painting is from a Pompeiian home.   *Art Resource, NY.*

Rhine and Danube, even remote Britain. The city still retained much local self-government and normally controlled the rural territories in its vicinity. In other words, the city was the key unit of local administration; the government of the Roman state remained fundamentally urban. Authority in these cities devolved upon the richest citizens, who in return for holding the reins of power were expected to dip deeply into their own coffers to fund the handsome public buildings and the periodic festival celebrations that were essential to the Roman way of life.

Paradoxically, the cities of the empire, especially in the west, were of only modest importance as commercial and manufacturing centers. Although small-scale urban industry often flourished, particularly in the east, the economy of the empire remained fundamentally agrarian. Many of the western cities, including Rome itself, consumed far more than they produced. Like modern Washington, D.C., these Roman cities were primarily administrative and military centers. During the first two centuries of the empire the economy could support them, but this would not always be the case. Later, when the cities began to decline, the whole political structure of the western Roman Empire was gripped by crisis, as we shall see in Chapter 5.

Roman cities at the height of the empire were probably as pleasant and exciting places to live as any premodern urban center could be. The rich, of course, lived luxuriously, and although the poor continued to crowd into ramshackle firetraps, there were compensations. Besides the inevitable gladiatorial fights, Roman city dwellers could also thrill to chariot races and the theater. (Lacking modern filmmakers' techniques of "special effects," Roman producers occasionally had to satisfy the public's craving for

"action" with the real thing: For example, in *The Death of Hercules* at the turn of the third century A.D., the actor in the starring role was burned to death on the stage.)

Vivid evidence of daily life in a Roman city survives beneath the volcanic pumice that buried Pompeii after poisonous fumes killed the inhabitants. But we must remember that Pompeii was a rich resort and retirement city, a Roman Malibu or Palm Beach. Like the inhabitants of upscale communities today, the Pompeiians demonstrated a keen interest in politics, and the slogans that they scribbled on their walls bear witness to an upcoming election: "His neighbors urge you to elect Lucius Statius as magistrate; he is worthy. Aemilius Celer, a neighbor wrote this. May you take sick if you maliciously erase this message." "If upright living is considered any recommendation, Lucretius Fronto is well worthy of the office." "I ask you to elect Marcus Cerrinius Vatia. . . . All the late drinkers support him." "The small working thieves support Vatia." "I ask you to elect Aulus Vettius Firmus. He is worthy of the municipality. I ask you to elect him, ballplayers. Elect him!" "I wonder, O wall, that you have not fallen in ruins from supporting the stupidities of so many scribblers." (And added a prostitute, "For two *asses* cash, I am yours.")[11]

As long as they prospered, Roman cities were graced by the engineering and architectural skills at which the Romans excelled. They were equipped with a good water supply and sewage disposal, which Romans (partly for religious reasons, for Jupiter disapproved of garbage in the

---

[11] For two *asses*, according to other advertisements on the wall, one could also buy a jug of better quality wine; ordinary wine sold for one *as*.

Upper-Class Pompeiian Home In this, one of the more luxurious houses of Pompeii, you are looking from the walled garden terrace toward an open-air dining room, embellished with mosaics. *Alinari/Art Resource, NY.*

streets) considered indispensable to civilized life. As far back as the fourth century B.C., Rome had built the first of the four great aqueducts that brought fresh water into the city, and some of these impressive engineering feats still survive in far-flung parts of the Roman world, such as Pont du Gard (southern France) and Segovia (Spain). Another essential part of Roman life was frequent bathing, which urban people of both sexes and all social classes enjoyed for hygiene, relaxation, and sociability. Every important Roman town had its baths, the grandest of which were the immense public baths that remain in Pompeii and Rome (see Figure 4-1 and Map 4-5).

By the first and second centuries A.D., the small farms of early republican Rome, on which extended families subsisted with their own labor, had given way across much of the empire to the great latifundia—owned by the wealthy and tilled by slaves or half-free peasants. Although the products of Roman farming varied widely from region to region, the principal crops of the empire were grain, grapes, and olives—the old "Mediterranean triad" that had dominated agriculture in the Mediterranean basin for countless generations. Grain (chiefly wheat and barley) and grapes were cultivated throughout most of the empire. (It may not be wholly accidental that the northern borders of the Roman Empire correspond rather closely to the northern limits of grape cultivation; beyond that line, Romans could not imagine civilization flourishing.) From these the Romans produced two of the basic staples of their diet in the imperial period: bread and wine. Olive trees also grew

Roman Aqueduct at Segovia, Spain One of the greatest Roman works of engineering, this 10-mile-long aqueduct was built of granite blocks without mortar. It was erected under Trajan and remained in use into the twentieth century. *AKG London.*

FIGURE 4-1
BATHS OF POMPEII

Pompeii's great public bath was well preserved by a blanket of volcanic ash. In the center, under an open sky, was a gymnasium (A) and swimming pool (B). Men entered the baths (at C), stripped and plunged into a cold bath (D), left their clothes (in E), got warmed up (in F), and sweated in the hot room (G). Women had an undressing room (H) and both a warm and a hot room (I, J) as well. Other services included a (presumably unisex) latrine (K) and individual hip baths (L).
Source: Adapted from Pompeii A.D. 79: Treasures from the National Archaeological Museum, Naples, and the Pompeii Antiquarium, *ed. John Ward-Perkins and Amanda Claridge (New York: Knopf, 1978), p. 57.*

through the rose-tinted spectacles of Edward Gibbon and his nineteenth-century successors, who considered it humanity's happiest age. Roman classical culture was impressive, but it was also narrowly limited, shared only by the empire's upper crust. And although everybody benefited from the Pax Romana, the great majority were impoverished and undernourished. Infanticide was one particularly brutal consequence of Rome's marginal economy: The empire—or, more precisely, the vast majority of its people, who were poor—could not afford excess mouths. Tomb inscriptions and such other scraps of evidence as we possess point to appalling rates of child mortality (even discounting infanticide) and suggest that adults were lucky if they survived past their thirties.

Such conditions persisted throughout the Principate and beyond, not as economic misfortunes that might be remedied by economic stimulus programs but as the means necessary for the functioning of great estates, mines, and wealthy households. And rich Romans' wealth could be immense: The fortunes of each of the two richest Roman senators of the first century A.D. had the value of 1.5 million tons of wheat; in modern American terms and allowing for price fluctuations, that would be at least $1.5 billion, untaxed.

The huge incomes and leisured lives of the empire's elite, and the very survival of the imperial economy, depended on the muscles of slaves and poor laborers, who constituted 80 to 90 percent of the total population. In the first century A.D. a Greek scientist named Hero of Alexandria reportedly designed a device that ran with a simple steam engine, and perhaps with a little more tinkering it might have been developed into a piston-driven machine. But the Industrial Revolution would have to wait 1,700 years. Revealingly, Vespasian rejected suggestions that

in abundance, though their vulnerability to cold restricted their cultivation to the frost-free lowlands around the Mediterranean Sea. The people of the Mediterranean basin used olive oil in place of butter, which was favored by the Germanic tribes to the north and east but turned rancid in the southern heat. Throughout much of Italy, grain production had given way to the raising of grapes, olives, sheep, and cattle. The fertile wheat-growing provinces of Egypt and North Africa had by now become the primary suppliers of bread for the teeming city of Rome.

In the early empire, as in the late republic, slaves played a crucial role in the economy, especially in agriculture. But as the frontiers stabilized and the flow of war captives dwindled, the chief source of slaves was cut off. Landowners now began to lease out major portions of their estates to sharecroppers called *coloni*, who sank into a semiservile status foreshadowing that of medieval serfs. Agricultural slavery persisted, however, far into the Middle Ages, dying out only in the years around A.D. 1000.

The condition of the slaves, coloni, and urban poor should warn us against viewing the Roman Principate

MAP 4-5
THE CITY OF ROME, C.A. A.D. 200

labor-saving mechanisms be encouraged: How, then, would enough work be found for the idle poor? Hero's contraption remained a toy.

The failure of an industrial revolution to begin in antiquity, despite the ingenuity of ancient engineers and the enormous wealth seemingly available for investment, underscores an important point. The Romans' economic values (like those of all other ancient peoples) were not those of the modern world. Moneymaking had several objectives—conspicuous consumption, winning political security, raising one's status—but apart from buying slaves, no one thought of investing money productively. In the traditional Roman value system, saving meant being a miser, which was no compliment. And what good would saving do? Better to spend what you have on the good things life has to offer—food, a splendid house or a country villa, art and books, slaves to wait on you hand and foot—and then demonstrate that you are a worthy citizen by liberally spending more money to beautify your city and entertain the crowds. Plowing money back into the economy was not something that could generate prosperity, either for yourself or others. Under such circumstances, true **capitalism** (as opposed to mere moneymaking, however hard-boiled) could not develop.

Nor was the Pax Romana, so widely and properly admired, as complete as one might suppose or as imperial propaganda proclaimed. Germanic tribes hammered repeatedly at Rome's frontiers and sometimes pierced them, while deep within the empire, towns and countryside suffered a degree of local violence and mayhem far exceeding that of European societies today. By modern standards, the provinces of the Roman Principate were woefully underpoliced and undergoverned.

Roman women, even the wealthiest, were barred from holding any political office. By long tradition they were expected to stay home and obey their husbands, but during the imperial era, as in the late republic, many Roman wives held property and most of them traveled freely within their cities. Indeed, in the empire's later centuries women acquired considerable independence with respect to marriage, divorce, and the holding of property, and many upper-class women were well educated. The poet Juvenal (ca. A.D. 55–ca. 130), who filled his satirical poems with devastating attacks on all "modernizing" trends that he believed were innundating old Roman ways with crass moneymaking and gross consumption, naturally despised the emancipated, out-of-line women of first-century Rome and lampooned them savagely. No responses from women thus caricatured have survived.

But virtually all ancient civilizations were afflicted by slavery, poverty, malnutrition, internal violence, the suppression of women, and the killing of unwanted infants (although the Jews' religion prohibited infanticide). In these respects Roman imperial civilization was no worse than the others, and in the larger cities, with their public baths and free bread, it was significantly better.

Fashionable Roman Woman This lady was probably a sister of Emperor Titus, and her hair is done in the height of fashion. The fashionable, emancipated women whom Juvenal pilloried probably strove for a similar look. *Alinari/Art Resource, NY.*

Under the second-century emperors, imperial policy professed to be humane. To a degree it really was compassionate, influenced by Stoic teachings about human brotherhood and social and political responsibility. Unlike Caligula and Nero, who used their power to indulge sadistic whims, emperors such as Hadrian, Antoninus Pius, and Marcus Aurelius viewed their authority as a trust—a commission to govern in the interests of their people, whether rich or poor. They funded charities, provided food to orphans and paupers, launched building programs, and assisted cities in financial distress. Hadrian won wide popularity by canceling all private debts to the imperial government. But given the nature of the Roman economy, such policies could effect no fundamental improvement. Roman life under the "good emperors" could be pleasant enough, but it helped to be male, adult, rich, and naturally immune to a host of epidemic diseases.

The Silver Age

The cultural epoch from approximately the death of Augustus to the death of Marcus Aurelius (A.D. 14–180) is known as Rome's "Silver Age." Less celebrated than the first century B.C.'s "Golden Age," it nevertheless produced literary, intellectual, and artistic works of the first order. Some critics have seen in Silver Age writers such as the Stoic Seneca and the essayist Pliny the Younger a decline in creative genius from predecessors such as Cicero, Catullus, Vergil, Ovid, and Horace. These critics have stressed the

THE HISTORICAL EVIDENCE

Marcus Aurelius on the Human Condition

ca. A.D. 175

Marcus Aurelius, the last of the "five good emperors," wrote these "Meditations" in Greek while he was on campaign against the German tribes pressing on Rome's Danube frontier. They are a moving expression of the Stoic philosophy that deepened and humanized much of the best thought of the era.

Begin the morning by saying to thyself, I shall meet with the busybody, the ungrateful, arrogant, deceitful, envious, unsocial. All these things happen to them by reason of their ignorance of what is good and evil. But I who have seen the nature of the good that it is beautiful, and of the bad that it is ugly, and the nature of him who does wrong, that it is akin to me, not only of the same blood or seed, but that it participates in the same intelligence and the same portion of the divinity, I can neither be injured by any of them, for no one can fix on me what is ugly, nor can I be angry with my kinsman, nor hate him. For we are made for co-operation, like feet, like hands, like eyelids, like the rows of the upper and lower teeth. To act against one another then is contrary to nature; and it is acting against one another to be vexed and to turn away. . . .

Every moment think steadily as a Roman and a man to do what thou hast in hand with perfect and simple dignity, and feeling of affection, and freedom, and justice; and to give thyself relief from all other thoughts. . . .

Since it is possible that thou mayest depart from this life this very moment, regulate every act and thought accordingly. But to go away from among men, if there are gods, is not a thing to be afraid of, for the gods will not involve thee in evil; but if indeed they do not exist, or if they have no concern about human affairs, what is it to me to live in a universe devoid of gods or devoid of Providence? But in truth they do exist, and they do care for human things, and they have put all the means in man's power to enable him not to fall into real evils. . . . Now that which does not make a man worse, how can it make a man's life worse? But neither through ignorance, nor having the knowledge, but not the power to guard against or correct these things, is it possible that the nature of the universe has overlooked them; nor is it possible that it has made so great a mistake . . . that good and evil should happen indiscriminately to the good and the bad. But death certainly, and life, honour and dishonour, pain and pleasure, all these things equally happen to good men and bad, being things which make us neither better nor worse. Therefore they are neither good nor evil.

Source: From Marcus Aurelius, *Meditations*, Book 2, sections 1, 5, 11, in *The Stoic and Epicurean Philosophers*, ed. Whitney J. Oates, trans. George Long (New York: Random House [Modern Library], 1940), pp. 497–99.

---

pretentious, ornate style of second-century literature and the stale conformity of first- and second-century art. And they have attributed these supposed shortcomings to the "homogenization" of imperial society and the dullness of peace and security. Such judgments are necessarily relative, and many sensitive people across the centuries have viewed writers of the Silver Age with enormous admiration.

But however one judges the originality of Silver Age literature, there can be no question but that it produced major works of synthesis. Plutarch (ca. 46–120), in his *Parallel Lives*, provided biographies of famous Romans along with notable figures from his native Greece. One of the most widely read works in antiquity, Plutarch's *Lives* undertook to educate youth in the nature of virtue as exemplified by models from both the Greek and Roman past.

Suetonius's *Lives of the Caesars* is less edifying. A compendium of court scandal, it educates its reader as much in the nature of vice as of virtue and portrays several Roman emperors and their wives as sex maniacs. More significant is

the work of Tacitus (ca. 55–120), whose histories trace the course of the early empire carefully and vividly—always with an old-fashioned republican bias. Tacitus also wrote an important study of the early Germanic peoples under the title *Germania* (see Chapters 5 and 6), and a biography of a Roman governor of Britain named Agricola, who was Tacitus's father-in-law. This last work is a source of fundamental importance for the history of Roman Britain.

Throughout the Silver Age, classical culture spread outward and downward. Remote provincial towns built temples and baths, theaters and triumphal arches in the Roman style; libraries and schools graced every significant city. Ordinary urban children got the rudiments of education from schoolmasters who, for a tiny per-pupil fee and aided by a liberal use of the stick, would pound into them the rudiments of reading and writing. (The many irreverent and obscene scribblings on the buildings of Pompeii attest to the extent of urban literacy.) Well-to-do young people could get a good education either from private tutors, often slaves, or from schools of rhetoric. Late in the first century A.D. a great teacher of rhetoric, the Spanish-born Quintilian (ca. 35–ca. 96), published his *Institutio oratoria* ("The Education of the Orator"), a wide-ranging treatise on education and all aspects of oratory. A sterling character and a broad cultural education, Quintilian insisted, were the keys to effective public speaking, and these could only be instilled by a careful educational program that developed each student's unique potentials. The day had already passed when the fearless, upright orator could aspire to shape public policy with eloquent reasoning, but Quintilian's book, rediscovered in the fifteenth century after centuries of neglect, constituted one of "Silver Age" Latin culture's greatest legacies to **Renaissance** Europe. Indeed, it is the foundation of all modern theories of education that stress persuasion and encouragement rather than intimidation in training young people. "Pupils, if rightly instructed, regard their teacher with affection and respect. And it is scarcely possible to say how much more willingly we imitate those we like."

Alexandria, the Hellenistic metropolis, retained its commercial and intellectual importance throughout the age of the Principate, producing brilliant Jewish and early Christian theologians as well as several distinguished scientists who developed and synthesized the achievements of their Hellenistic predecessors. As we have seen in Chapter 3, Ptolemy of Alexandria, who died about A.D. 180, molded Greek and Hellenistic astronomical knowledge into a sophisticated and comprehensive geocentric model of the universe that explained and predicted the movements of the sun, moon, and naked-eye planets with considerable (but not complete) accuracy. His dazzling intellectual achievement was altogether unique in human history up to its time and would not be superseded for more than a thousand years. Ptolemy also wrote the most complete geography of antiquity. And Galen (A.D. 131–201), a medical scientist from Hellenistic Pergamum, turned out a series of works on biology and medicine (often quite inaccurate) that dominated these fields for the next millennium.

In literature and art, science and philosophy, the Silver Age effortlessly blended Greek and Roman traditions. Its cosmopolitanism is echoed in the varied languages, religions, and homelands of its writers. Alongside Latin-speaking Romans such as Tacitus, Suetonius, and Seneca stand the Epicurean satirist Lucian from Syria, the Greek-speaking biographer Plutarch, and the Jewish historian Josephus—a Roman citizen who wrote in Greek. In the works of these and other Silver Age writers, the rich legacies of Greece, Rome, and the ancient Near East were summarized and fused.

Roman Law

Of all the achievements of this epoch perhaps the most far-reaching—certainly the most distinctively Roman—was the development of imperial law. The rigid code of the

Twelve Tables was gradually broadened and humanized by the magistrates of the later republic and early empire, by the great Roman lawyers of the second and third centuries A.D., and by the enlightened intervention of the emperors themselves. "Justice," wrote the second-century A.D. jurist Ulpian, "is the steadfast and unchanging will to give every man his due. The commandments of the law are these: to live honorably, not to injure one's fellow men, to give every man his due." Granted that ancient Romans with their hierarchical society would not have agreed with us that every man's (let alone every woman's) due should be equal, the basic idea that the state's function was to ensure justice was a fundamental legacy from the Roman world to the present.

As the Romans became acquainted with more and more peoples, each with its unique set of laws and customs, they gradually emancipated themselves from the peculiarities of their own law and strove to replace it with a body of fundamental principles drawn from the laws of all people. The *Ius Gentium* or "law of peoples" slowly transformed the Roman code into a legal system suitable to a vast, diverse empire.

Marcus Aurelius Philosopher-king Marcus Aurelius exemplifies all that was noble and also much that was fatally flawed in imperial Rome at the height of its grandeur. This bronze statue in the center of Rome, a technical masterpiece, would inspire emulation by some of the greatest sculptors of Renaissance and early modern Europe. © *R. Sheridan/Ancient Art & Architecture Collection.*

The evolution of Roman law into a universal system of jurisprudence owed something also to the Greek concept of the law of nature—the *Ius Naturale*—which played a prominent role in the later history of Western thought. More abstract than the *Ius Gentium*, the "law of nature" or "natural law" is based on the belief that in a divinely ordered world there are certain universal norms of human behavior that all people tend to follow, regardless of their own customs and traditions. All human societies, for example, have laws or taboos against murder, theft, and rape. Such ethical norms, based on general principles of political and social justice, served to rationalize and humanize the law of the empire and to provide it with a sturdy philosophical foundation. In this sense at least, the Romans gave practical expression to their professed but often fuzzy faith in humanitas.

Roman law, a product of the Latin practical political genius influenced by Greek speculative thought, gave substance to the Augustan ideal of justice. Codified with enormous effort by the sixth-century emperor Justinian (see Chapter 6), it has become a crucial part of the Western heritage—to this day the basis of the legal systems of practically the whole Western world (and many of the West's former colonies) except the United States and England.[12]

---

[12] For the roots of modern American and English law in the medieval English common law rather than in Roman law, see Chapter 9. Nevertheless, Roman law also left important marks on Anglo-American jurisprudence.

CONCLUSION: ROMAN VALUES

Rome, as noted at the beginning of this chapter, is one of the greatest success stories in the history of the Western world. Although force and violence played a significant role in building and maintaining the Roman Empire, these had also been decisive in the rise of every other imperial structure in antiquity. Rome's legacy was the longest lasting, and in some respects—notably its legal system and its vision of a state dedicated to justice and humanitas—it has never wholly perished. These were ideals, as were the values that Romans professed: seriousness of purpose, respect for tradition, courage, and incorruptibility. Of course, neither individual Romans nor their society always lived up to these ideals; but that does not invalidate them as foundations on which to build a society. The rise and flowering of imperial Rome was simultaneous with that of Han China (202 B.C.–A.D. 220), and in both cases a tradition of the rule of law was being built to which civilized people still look back with respect two thousand years later.

By Marcus Aurelius's death in A.D. 180, Roman civilization had developed into a vast, encompassing culture. Geographically, it embraced most of the territories where the ancient Latin, Greek, and Near Eastern ways of life held sway, and it was fusing the cultures of the Mesopotamians, Egyptians, Minoans, Greeks, and Jews into an immense empire that enjoyed political cohesion and relative peace. There were cracks in the Roman imperial facade, yet no previous empire had been as successful in providing its inhabitants with lives of comparable security or promise. But there was trouble ahead.

Selected Reading

Sources

Davenport, Basil, ed. *The Indispensable Roman Reader* (1951).

Knox, Bernard, ed. *The Norton Book of Classical Literature* (1993).

Lefkowitz, Mary R., and Maureen B. Fant, eds. *Women's Life in Greece and Rome* (1982).

Lewis, Naphtali, and Meyer Rinehold, eds. *Roman Civilization*, 2 vols., 3rd ed. (1990).

Mandelbaum, Allen. *The Aeneid of Vergil: A Verse Translation* (1982).

Shelton, Jo-Ann. *As the Romans Did: A Sourcebook in Roman Social History*, 2nd ed. (1988).

General Histories of Rome

Alföldy, Géza. *The Social History of Rome* (1988). Provides an adept blend of social history and politics.

Boardman, John, Jasper Griffin, and Oswyn Murray. *The Roman World* (1988). The Roman volume of the learned and well-illustrated series of essays, *The Oxford History of the Classical World*.

Crawford, Michael. *The Roman Republic,* 2nd ed. (1993). Perhaps the best introduction to the republican period.

Dixon, Suzanne. *The Roman Family* (1991). Makes adept use of comparative anthropology and literary sources.

Giardina, Andrea, ed. *The Romans* (1993). Trans. Lydia G. Cochrane. A collection of penetrating essays on typical Romans in a variety of vocations.

Le Glay, Marcel, Jean-Louis Voisin, and Yann Le Bohec. *A History of Rome* (1996). An important work of synthesis.

Matthews, John, and Tim Cornell. *Atlas of the Roman World* (1982). A useful, carefully executed reference tool.

Wells, Colin. *The Roman Empire,* 2nd ed. (1995). A companion volume to Michael Crawford's book, this is perhaps the best introduction to the empire period up to A.D. 235.

The Roman Republic and Early Empire

Badian, Ernst. *Publicans and Sinners* (1983); and *Roman Imperialism in the Late Republic*, 2nd ed. (1968). Rigorous studies of the acquisition and financial management of the Roman Empire.

Beard, Mary, and Michael Crawford. *Rome in the Late Republic* (1985). New perspectives on a much discussed topic.

Bradley, K. R. *Slaves and Masters in the Roman Empire: A Study in Social Control* (1984). A short, stimulating book that plausibly reconstructs Roman slavery as a repressive phenomenon cunningly perpetuated by a system of rewards and punishments.

Campbell, J. B. *The Empire and the Roman Army* (1984). A study of the army's role in both foreign conquests and domestic politics.

Duncan-Jones, Richard. *The Economy of the Roman Empire* (1984). A highly sophisticated economic analysis.

Dupont, Florence. *Daily Life in Ancient Rome* (1992). Trans. Christopher Woodall. The lives of Roman citizens in various callings cast fresh light on the culture and society of the Roman Republic.

Dyson, Stephen L. *The Creation of the Roman Frontier* (1985). This major study, covering the late republic and early empire, makes expert use of both documentary and archaeological evidence.

Garnsey, Peter, and Richard Saller. *The Roman Empire: Economy, Society, and Culture* (1987). A skillful, multifaceted account that paints a relatively dark picture of the effect of the economy on the lower levels of society.

Grant, Michael. *The Etruscans* (1980). An important study that stresses the marvels of Etruscan art, the immense Etruscan impact on Rome, and the inability of the Etruscan cities to unite against the Romans.

Greene, Kevin. *The Archaeology of the Roman Economy* (1986). An astute multidisciplinary study.

Gruen, Erich S. *The Hellenistic World and the Coming of Rome* (1984). A significant and persuasive work of reinterpretation and synthesis in which Rome's eastward expansion is seen in its Hellenistic context.

Harris, William V. *War and Imperialism in Republican Rome, 327–70 B.C.* (1970). An important and original work of scholarly analysis.

Luttwak, Edward N. *The Grand Strategy of the Roman Empire from the First Century A.D. to the Third* (1976). An expert on modern strategic defense presents a fresh, comprehensive analysis of Roman imperial military policy, showing similarities and contrasts to the role of the United States as a world power.

MacMullen, Ramsey. *Roman Social Relations, 50 B.C. to A.D. 294* (1974). Paints a more somber picture than the traditional one.

Meier, Christian. *Caesar* (1996). The best biography of Julius Caesar.

Rawson, Elizabeth. *Intellectual Life in the Late Roman Republic* (1985). In this landmark study of intellectual life in Rome during the 50s and 40s B.C., the author explores with impressive erudition the interaction of Greek and Italian intellectual elites and stresses the eagerness of Romans to assimilate Hellenistic culture.

Rousselle, Aline. *Pornea: On Desire and the Body in Antiquity* (1993). Trans. Felicia Pheasant. A social history of sexuality during the Roman imperial era.

Starr, Chester G. *The Beginnings of Imperial Rome in the Mid-Republic* (1980). A very short, challenging work of reinterpretation; it argues that Rome between 338 and 264 B.C. was larger and more active commercially than was previously thought.

———. *The Roman Empire, 27 B.C.–A.D. 476: A Study in Survival* (1982). A relatively brief, thought-provoking study of the imperial era and its challenges.

Syme, Ronald. *The Roman Revolution*, 2nd ed. (1960). A great pioneering work that downplays constitutional factors and stresses the political significance of families and factions in the late republic.

Talbert, Richard J. A. *The Senate of Imperial Rome* (1984). Detailed and comprehensive; the definitive account.

CHAPTER 5

RELIGION AND THE TRANSFORMATION OF THE ROMAN EMPIRE

The Good Shepherd *Scala/ Art Resource, NY.*

6–4 B.C.	Generally accepted birth date of Jesus of Nazareth
ca. A.D. 30	Crucifixion of Jesus, followed (in Christian belief) by his Resurrection
ca. 32–ca. 62	Conversion and missionary journeys of St. Paul, who preaches Christianity to both Jews and "Greeks"
64	First large persecution of Christians, at Rome under Nero
66–73	"Great Revolt" of Jews in Judea, ending in the destruction of the Temple and the fall of Masada
ca. 60–ca. 100	Gradual separation of Christians from Judaism; Gospels written; simultaneous rise of rabbinic Judaism
second century	Gnosticism at height of its influence among Christians
132–135	Last great Jewish uprising in ancient times, led by Simon Bar Kochba; Jews barred from Jerusalem
ca. 150	First Christian bishops
180	Death of Marcus Aurelius, last of the "good emperors"
185–254	Life span of Origen, first great Christian theologian
193–211	Reign of Septimius Severus; Roman army grows in power
205–270	Life span of Plotinus, great pagan philosopher and founder of Neoplatonism
235–284	Height of the Roman anarchy; barracks emperors
284–305	Reign of Diocletian; beginning of the "Dominate"
303–311	"Great Persecution" of Christians in Roman Empire
306–337	Reign of Constantine, Christian convert who establishes an imperial policy of religious toleration
325	Council of Nicaea: Trinitarian Christianity triumphs over Arianism
330	Constantine founds Constantinople
354–430	Life span of St. Augustine of Hippo, shaper of Christian theology for the next millennium
361–363	Reign of Julian the Apostate; his attempt to reverse Christianization of Roman Empire fails
376	Emperor Valens permits Visigoths to enter the Roman Empire
378	Battle of Adrianople: Visigoths defeat Romans, kill Valens
395	Emperor Theodosius I dies; eastern and western halves of the empire permanently divided; Christianity becomes the Roman Empire's state religion, and paganism is formally banned
406	Western Roman Empire recalls its legions from the Rhine frontier
408	Emperor Honorius cripples Rome's defense by killing Stilicho
410	Alaric and his Visigoths sack Rome
430	Death of St. Augustine; Vandals capture Hippo
433–453	Attila rules Huns, leads them against empire in the West
440–461	Pontificate of Leo I, defender of Rome against the Huns and advocate of papal authority
451	Huns defeated in Gaul
476	Odovacar deposes last Roman emperor, ending Roman Empire in the West
481–511	Clovis rules the Franks, conquers Gaul, and converts to Catholic Christianity
493–526	Theodoric, king of the Ostrogoths, rules Italy

All dates are A.D., except when noted otherwise.

"I am the good shepherd: the good shepherd giveth his life for the sheep." Remembering these comforting words of Jesus, second-century believers in him painted the picture, shown here, on the wall in the catacombs, a network of underground passageways just outside Rome. It is one of his earliest known images.

The catacombs were used primarily for burials both by Christians and Jews. Their existence was no secret. The oldest catacomb, containing this painting of the Good Shepherd, was first owned by a wealthy woman named Domitilla, the wife of Titus Flavius Clemens, a cousin to Emperor Domitian. In A.D. 95, Clemens was executed for "atheism"— the charge frequently brought against early Christians who denied Rome's gods. Domitilla was for a while exiled, but she kept her property and made it available to the city's Christians. They used it for hundreds of years as a burial ground, unhindered by the government. More than a quarter of a million Christians—many of them children—are believed to have been interred in this and other catacombs.

The painting is no masterpiece, but then its creator was almost certainly an amateur. Professional painters in second-century Rome were not likely converts to Christianity because most of their normal work involved mythological, pagan, or sexual images abhorrent to Christians. Yet whoever painted the Good Shepherd in Domitilla's catacomb doubtless took as a model the pastoral or mythological scenes that decorated public and private spaces in Rome—perhaps Orpheus, also a shepherd who promised his followers eternal life (see Chapter 3).

The fact that the second-century Christians made an *image* of Jesus Christ is significant. Despite the presence of a few aristocrats like Clemens and Domitilla, most Roman Christians were rather humble people drawn from a Jewish community that numbered some fifty thousand in the first and second centuries. Making "graven images"—particularly of God or of other sacred persons—was one of the worst offenses that a Jew could commit.

Doubtless for that reason, we have no representations of Jesus from the first century A.D. Even though Roman Christians remained conscious of their Jewish heritage for several hundred years, by the time this catacomb scene was painted the prohibition was beginning to weaken. Depictions of Christ as the Good Shepherd thereafter became fairly common—in fact, they were the favorite way in which early Christians visualized their savior.

In a religiously soaked atmosphere, Christians first parted ways with Jews and, by the fourth century, converted the Roman Empire. Some of the Christians' beliefs and practices resembled those of older and competing religions. Yet Christianity differed from pagan religions in two fundamental ways. First, its founder and savior was an actual historical personage; beside Jesus, such mythical idealizations as Isis and Mithras came to seem faint and unreal. Second, its God was not merely the best of many gods or an intellectual abstraction, but instead, the One God of the Hebrews, unique in all antiquity in his claims to exclusiveness and omnipotence.

While Roman Christians and Jews were using their catacombs, religion in the Roman Empire was fundamentally changing. Traditional pagan cults blended with Near Eastern mystery religions offering individual salvation. The ultimate beneficiary of this ferment was the Christian faith, which became the empire's official religion while a line of authoritarian soldier-emperors still ruled it, during the fourth century. In the Hellenistic east the Roman Empire would endure, in a Christian form, a thousand years more. In the west, the Roman Empire by A.D. 500 succumbed to Germanic rule; but even so it had become sufficiently Christianized to be the embryo from which medieval Western Christendom grew.

PAGAN, JEW, AND CHRISTIAN

Romans honored many gods. Like the Greek poleis, Rome had its official civic deities, who by the later years of the republic had been identified with parallel Greek Olym-

pians: Jupiter with Zeus, Minerva with Athena, Venus with Aphrodite—the list was long. Besides these high gods, innumerable local divinities and cults enjoyed official toleration and patronage. None claimed a monopoly on truth, and people might participate in many of them. The Principate added an important new element: the cult of the emperor. Augustus and his successors (with a few notorious exceptions) were deified by the Senate upon their deaths, being designated "Son of God."

Romans and provincials alike were expected to participate in formal ceremonies honoring the deified emperors and traditional gods who ensured Rome's safety. These observances, which Romans considered acts of patriotism and social solidarity, amounted to a collective investment in cosmic insurance. Few people either loved these gods or expected love from them, but they did hope that paying proper homage would avert trouble. Besides, sacrifices were joyous occasions—sacred barbecues that often meant lots of good eating and drinking. Non-Roman subjects of the empire were expected to join in to show their allegiance, and few objected to adding a handful of new deities to the divine crowd that they worshiped already.

Jews did object. "I am the Lord your God; you shall have no other gods before me" was the Jews' first commandment. Rome had long recognized Jews as a people apart and usually excused them from participation in the official cults; besides, the Temple priests at Jerusalem routinely prayed to Yahweh for Rome's prosperity. But in the late first century A.D. Romans learned that new Jewish sectarians were emerging, called Christians, who not only refused to worship the emperors and the empire's divine guardians but actually looked forward to a Judgment Day when Rome and all its hellish works would go down in flames. To Romans, this was atheism and treason. Almost alone of all the empire's religions, Christianity suffered serious persecution. But in an astonishing reversal, by A.D. 400 it would be Rome's official faith. How did this happen?

Pagans

Modern peoples' idea of ancient **paganism** has been shaped by lurid movies showing decadent priests and priestesses gyrating in weird rites. The reality is more interesting. When Romans "got religion," they turned to cults that offered hope and emotional release.

The forces that had bred rootlessness and disorientation in the Hellenistic world were now at work throughout the Roman Empire: cosmopolitanism, autocracy, and, for most people, grinding poverty and lost hope. In imperial Rome, the shift from civic god to savior god, from this world to the next, gained enormous momentum as the Pax Romana soured, turning the high hopes of classical humanism—a rational universe, an ideal republic, the good life—into cruel illusions.

One answer to this darkening mood was to cast trembling eyes toward astrology, sorcery, and Fate. We have already seen in Chapters 1 and 3 that Neo-Babylonian study of the night sky evolved into a complex lore about how the celestial bodies determined earthly events, and that Hellenistic Greeks not only accepted this avidly but turned "chance" into an inscrutable goddess. Chance did not remain a coy "lady luck"; by the second century A.D., people throughout the empire were more apt to see her as *Fortuna*—Fate—the ominous personification of what was written in the stars. A few sturdily old-fashioned Romans like Vespasian and the satirist Juvenal called it humbug, but from emperors to slum-dwellers, almost everyone else thought astrology plausible or convincing. Casters of horoscopes did a lucrative business—unless they cast secret

Roman Astrology This second-century A.D. statue shows Jupiter enthroned, surrounded by the twelve signs of the zodiac. Whether the god is meant to be seen as the master, the servant, or the embodiment of the astral system is not clear.   *Mansell/ Time Inc.*

horoscopes of the emperor, in which case they could be executed, for knowing what Fate had in store for him endangered public order. And what if you knew your own fate? Experts differed: Some said that the stars were infallible; others claimed that they merely indicated tendencies that you could still outwit. Of course, still other experts in dark mysteries were also available—sorcerers who, for a fee, would prepare a hair-raising curse, turning all the powers of nature against your enemy. Some of these have survived, engraved on metal plates: In one, a jilted girlfriend calls on the goddess of the underworld to smite her ex-lover with dreadful ills from his scalp to his toenails.

A few astrologers brazenly maintained that the only gods were astral deities manifested in the sun, moon, planets, and stars; but most people of the empire were not so intellectually rigorous. Cults were their answer. Jupiter and his colleagues, like the Greek denizens of Olympus, had long been asked to safeguard social and political *groups*; the gods of the new cults, often of eastern origin, increasingly were trusted to respond to *individuals*. The Greek cult of Dionysus (Bacchus to the Romans), banned from Rome as subversive and obscene in 186 B.C., became highly respectable, even fashionable, by the first century A.D. And besides Bacchus, the Egyptian Isis and the pseudo-Egyptian Serapis, the Persian Mithras, the Phrygian Great Mother, the Syrian sun god, and other exotic deities all offered individuals hope of redemption and eternal life that had never occurred to Rome's staid old gods.

Outwitting the stars and Fate, getting the occult powers of the universe on your side instead of against you—that was what the cults offered. If there was an afterlife (most people were unsure about it), religion offered insurance. And although peace of mind was expensive (most cults charged a high initiation fee), few forbade patronizing other cults. The result was that Roman cities resounded incessantly with the sounding horns and tinkling cymbals of the religious celebrations that packed the calendar. Patriotic, civic, and agricultural rites, usually involving the slaughter of animals, filled the air with bleats, smoke, and smells. Processions honoring Isis moved through the streets, her statue borne on worshipers' shoulders, flowers scattered in her path, and hastily scribbled prayers pinned on her robe. By the third century, men—no women were allowed—huddled in pits below a grate on which a bull was sacrificed, his blood drenching them as a sign that they had come under the protection of Mithras. Most spectacular of all were the annual celebrations of Cybele, the Great Mother: In her honor, chanting priests marched through the streets slashing their bodies and scattering blood to onlookers, while candidate-priests castrated themselves and threw their testicles at her statue.

But this holy gore was not all there was to paganism. For those who could afford it, pilgrimages to sacred groves and famous shrines were a favorite way of getting right with the gods. Generously endowed priesthoods, often devout,

THE HISTORICAL EVIDENCE

A Vision of Isis

ca. A.D. 200

Apuleius (ca. 125–ca. 200), a North African Latin author well educated in philosophy, was converted to the worship of Isis after having squandered most of his inheritance on wine, women, and cultic initiations. Later, having become a well-connected lawyer and marrying a rich widow, he had to fend off charges that he poisoned (or bewitched) his wife to gain her wealth. He survived all this to become a respected priest of Osiris, and wrote his famous novel The Golden Ass *as an allegory of his own transformation from dissolute youth to serene sage. The gist of the story is that young Lucius, through a love affair with a slave girl, dabbles in magic and is transformed into a donkey; from this literally asinine perspective he has many amusing adventures (which reveal much about second-century life and religious cults), but in the end he is graciously restored to humanity by Isis. In the extract that follows, Isis speaks to Lucius.*

"You see me here, Lucius, in answer to your prayer. I am Nature, the universal Mother, mistress of all the elements, primordial child of time, sovereign of all things spiritual, queen of the dead, queen also of the immortals, the single manifestation of all gods and goddesses that are. My nod governs the shining heights of Heaven, the wholesome sea-breezes, the lamentable silences of the world below. Though I am worshipped in many aspects, known by countless names, and propitiated with all manner of different rites, yet the whole round earth venerates me. The primeval Phrygians call me Pessinuntica, Mother of the gods; the Athenians, sprung from their own soil, call me Cecropian Artemis; for the islanders of Cyprus I am Paphian Aphrodite; for the archers of Crete I am Dictynna; for the trilingual Sicilians, Stygian Proserpine; and for the Eleusinians their ancient Mother of Corn.

"Some know me as Juno, some as Bellona of the Battles; others as Hecate, others again as Rhamnubia, but both races of Aethiopians, whose lands the morning sun first shines upon, and the Egyptians, who excel in ancient learning and worship me with ceremonies proper to my godhead, call me by my true name, namely, Queen Isis. I have come in pity of your plight, I have come to favour and aid you. Weep no more, lament no longer; the hour of deliverance, shone over by my watchful light, is at hand.

"Listen attentively to my orders."

Source: From *The Golden Ass: A New Translation by Robert Graves from Apuleius* (New York: Farrar, Straus & Giroux, 1951), pp. 264–265.

maintained these blessed spots, and to believers' anxious questions oracles offered answers inspired by the god himself, delivered in a trance amid impressive solemnity. (Sometimes the answer was, in effect, "don't ask too much.") And if going to an oracle was impossible, a believer could always dream. People constantly saw and conversed with the gods in fantasies and dreams, and experts wrote books telling readers what they meant. The collections of dream-narratives that survive—many brimming with sexual imagery—would profitably employ a modern psychoanalyst for a lifetime.

Ancient paganism was not dying in the second, third, and even fourth centuries A.D. Rather, it was changing—becoming both more diverse (incorporating gods from all over the Mediterranean and even India) and more uniform (synthesizing these cults into a comprehensive allegory for

natural forces). Intelligent, sensitive souls who practiced pious asceticism *did* believe in the pagan cults, *did* nourish hopes and convictions that the gods cared for people, and *did* turn to these deities and their oracles for guidance with life's perplexing problems. Unchecked, Greco-Roman paganism might well have followed an evolutionary path similar to what in India during the early centuries A.D. created Hinduism, still today a living, polytheistic religion that incorporates everything from primitive magic to austere philosophy.

The third century's dominant philosophical movement, Neoplatonism, contributed strongly to paganism's transformation. Neoplatonism, as the name implies, represented a powerful revival of Plato's metaphysical system of Forms, with perhaps a dab of Indian transcendentalism seeping in through the Near East. The philosopher Plotinus (A.D.

205–270), one of the most influential minds of the Roman imperial era, taught that there was a single divinity, "the One"—infinite, unknowable, impersonal, and approachable only through a mystical experience. The One was the ultimate source of everything. All existence, Plotinus implied (though he rarely said much about the here-and-now), could be likened to circles radiating outward from the One, diminishing in excellence and significance as they grew more distant from their divine source. Reason, exalted by classical Greeks, lost its fascination as the philosopher's mind rose to the One in a mystic trance.

Plotinus's system of thought is the most otherworldly philosophy ever developed by a major Western thinker. The ethical questions that Stoics and Epicureans had pondered never seem to have intruded on his lofty meditations.

Plotinus   This haunting bust is thought to represent Plotinus; if so, it beautifully captures the philosopher's absorption in otherworldly metaphysics; it pained him, he once said, to have to turn from his heavenly visions to the labor of writing down what he had witnessed. So little did he regard this humdrum world that he never bothered to say where he was born. He died, we are told, of a loathsome malady that he bore bravely but that drove away all his friends.   *Ostia Museum, Italy.*

He and the philosophers he influenced regarded the pagan deities as crude but useful symbols of the One and its vast chain of cosmic emanations. Neoplatonism gave the pagan cults new life, bringing them into line with the trend toward mysticism and monotheism. Neoplatonism's warm and fuzzy metaphysics steadily blurred the distinction between Jupiter and the eastern Mediterranian deities.

One deity that Greco-Romans occasionally approached was the Hebrews' God. Some converted. Many more—so-called "God-fearers"—clustered around the fringes of Jewish communities, impressed by Hebrew ethical monotheism but reluctant to commit themselves. Even statues depicting Yahweh were placed in pagan temples by anxious heathens who feared to risk leaving out any possible deity. But such idols were never made by Jews, for whom compromising God's oneness or worshiping God's image was a terrible sin. Ancient paganism's tendency to grow by absorbing new gods, rites, and philosophies wherever it found them crashed like an ocean wave against a rock when its current reached Jewish monotheism.

Romans and Jews

In 63 B.C. Pompey, conqueror of Judea, boldly strode into the Holy of Holies, the innermost sanctuary of the Jerusalem Temple, which only the Jewish high priest was permitted to enter, and that only on Yom Kippur, the Day of Atonement. There, Pompey was astonished to see nothing at all in what Jews revered as God's earthly dwelling.

Pompey's impious act signaled an appropriately ominous beginning for the dramatic and troubled relationship between Rome and Palestine, out of which would emerge world-transforming events. The Romans' opportunistic quisling, King Herod (reigned 37–4 B.C.), stayed in power by adroitly stepping through the minefield of revolutionary Roman politics and by cutting down any potential domestic challenger. Herod slightly dampened his Jewish subjects' hatred by sponsoring a spectacular enlargement of the Jerusalem Temple. Not only did he claim this as an act of piety toward Israel's God, but in this and other major building projects he also generated thousands of jobs.

Herod's successors were less able (if no less ruthless), and during the first century A.D. Palestine was subdivided into several small units. Jerusalem and surrounding Judea, for example, came under direct Roman rule, embodied by procurators like Pontius Pilate (A.D. 26–36). Even among Romans, Pilate gained a reputation for cruelty and greed, and he was recalled to Rome to answer for his abuses.

Palestine was not the only place where Romans and Jews met. Greek-speaking Diaspora Jews lived in cities all around the Mediterranean and may have constituted 10 to 15 percent of the empire's urban population. Rome itself during the first century A.D. was home to some fifty thousand Jews, mainly the freed descendants of slaves and hostages brought there by Pompey. Despite sometimes violent clashes with other ethnic and religious groups in these cities, the Diaspora Jews were prospering, and sometimes they even regarded Roman rule positively. Julius Caesar gave them important privileges, and Augustus paid for annual sacrifices in his behalf at the Temple.

Alexandria became a major center of Jewish culture. Here Jewish scholars—in particular a religious philosopher of the early first century A.D. called Philo Judaeus (Philo the Jew)—sought to interpret Jewish biblical revelation using Greek philosophy. Drawing on Aristotle, the Stoics, and above all Plato, these scholars developed a symbolic approach to the Hebrew Scriptures that would echo through Jewish and Christian thought across the centuries.

The Jews' situation in Palestine was particularly turbulent. Internal Jewish religious affairs (which touched virtually every aspect of daily life) were handled by the high priest, whom the Romans appointed, and a clerical council, the Sanhedrin. The Temple itself was the domain of a small Jewish priestly movement, the Sadducees. Another sectarian group, the Pharisees (numbering perhaps six thousand in the first century A.D.), was scattered throughout Palestine and some Diaspora communities, and it held itself up as the guardian of an ultra-rigorous approach to the Jewish Law. Still another movement, the Essenes, lived in monastic communities. All these groups clashed, sometimes venomously. The Pharisees venerated an oral tradition that, they said, paralleled and "completed" the Torah, the biblical books attributed to Moses. This oral tradition included belief in the resurrection of the righteous and in mysterious hierarchies of supernatural beings—holy angels and malevolent devils—permeating all Creation and every facet of earthly life. Hell, Satan's realm, awaited the ungodly. By contrast, the Sadducees rejected every religious idea not explicitly sanctioned by the Torah; thus they denied an afterlife for individual souls. Ranged against both were the Essenes, who denounced the Temple cult as corrupt and wicked, saw themselves as Sons of the Light, and anticipated eternal life.

Ordinary Jews' resentment of extortionate taxes, collected by corrupt and bitterly hated local collaborators called publicans, erupted in A.D. 6 in a revolt led by Judas the Galilean, which the Romans suppressed only with considerable bloodshed and the liberal use of crucifixion. Judas's followers went underground to form the revolutionary Zealot movement, whose many offshoots included terrorist bands that assassinated Jewish collaborators.

Apocalyptic visions of God's intervention into the world burned brightly amid Jews' everyday anxieties. Zealots and Essenes alike looked forward eagerly to the long-promised Messiah, and the Pharisees claimed that when all Israel followed their scrupulous observance of the Law, he would come. Observing the Law, however, was difficult because of the high moral and ethical code that it demanded and the minute requirements that it prescribed for daily life. "Possession by devils" explained illness or any abnormal behavior; for cures, people trusted to the many holy men (*hasidim*) wandering the land; and anyone who claimed to be a *hasid* had to prove it by working miracles. "Sinners" were everywhere, and included not just people of lax behavior but also individuals following a different interpretation of the Law. Any number of ritual defilements or violations of the Law could make a person unfit for "table fellowship," the sign of social bonding in Judaism and other ancient Near Eastern cultures. Hatred ran deep between Jews who worshiped at the Jerusalem Temple and the Samaritans of north-central Palestine, who rejected Temple worship. "Hellenists," or Greek-speaking Jews from the Diaspora, visited Jerusalem for Judaism's great festivals, but were suspected of harboring strange Greek ideas. Galileans, inhabitants of the fertile region north of Samaria, came more regularly to the Temple.

Out of Galilee, sometime in the late 20s A.D., emerged a wild-looking hermit preaching in the desert beyond the Jordan River. He may have had prior connections with the Essenes, but unlike that monkish brotherhood he took his message, directly and urgently, to the people. His message was that God's judgment would soon descend on the sinful world, and that the people of Israel must give up their evil ways before the Messiah arrived to separate the saved from the damned. Those who sincerely repented of their sins he forgave and baptized in the Jordan. His preaching attracted such large crowds that the Romans' puppet kinglet, Herod Antipas, had him beheaded. But executing John the Baptist (for so he was called) did not quiet Galilee. Soon John's cousin was stirring Galileans with such a mixture of hope, awe, and fear that Antipas thought John had risen from the grave. He had questionable associates (one with the dangerous-sounding name of Simon the Zealot), and Pilate found it prudent to crucify him around A.D. 30. About ten years later, a Zealot revolt broke out under Judas the Galilean's two sons, Jacob and Simon. Like their father, they ended their lives on Roman crosses.

Roman misgovernment and popular unrest came to a head in A.D. 66, producing what has become known as the Great Revolt, which battle-hardened Roman legions needed seven years to quell. Every religious faction and every social class in Palestine joined the struggle, although sometimes fighting fellow Jews as well as Romans. Starved into surrender, in A.D. 70 Jerusalem fell to the Roman general Titus.[1] Thousands of Jews were killed or sold as slaves, and the looted Temple was destroyed. In 73 came the tragic last act, when the Romans cornered some nine hundred Zealots in one of Herod's fortresses, Masada. Seeing their situation hopeless, the defenders killed their wives, their children, and themselves rather than be taken captive.

Judaism survived, however. The Temple was gone, but even before the revolt ended, the Romans permitted a

---

[1] Vespasian's son; Vespasian had begun suppressing the revolt but turned the job over to Titus after he himself became emperor in A.D. 69; Titus would eventually succeed him in 79–81.

The End of the Temple
When Titus's troops took Jerusalem they carried off enormous booty of gold objects, including the Menorah, or seven-branched candlestick, shown here. Titus's victory was celebrated in a great triumphal arch still standing in the Roman Forum, on which these scenes were carved.   *Foto Marburg / Art Resource, NY.*

Jewish council to meet in Jamnia (in Hebrew, Yavnah). Destruction of the Temple and the end of its sacrificial cult had effectively swept away the Sadducees' place in Jewish life, and Roman troops had dispersed or destroyed the Essenes. The Pharisees remained, and at Jamnia they began systematizing Judaism.

Between the second and sixth centuries A.D. a new Judaism came into focus. The center of its life was no longer the Temple—for whose rebuilding Jews slowly abandoned hope—but the synagogue. As its Greek meaning ("assembly of the people") suggests, the synagogue was originally a Diaspora institution dating from the second century B.C. Synagogues were controlled by their community, not by clergy, although scriptural readings, preaching, teaching, and disputations about the Law's application in daily life all took place in them. Teachers who gathered around the synagogues were known as rabbis. Courts that settled civil disputes among Jews also became largely the preserve of the rabbis, their decisions grounded in their understanding of the Law.

"Rabbinic Judaism" is the phrase often associated with the post-Temple religion and culture of Israel, but such a designation exaggerates its uniformity. The compilations of rabbinic wisdom that appeared included extensive debates and alternative interpretations. There were three main collections of this commentary. The *Mishnah* treated daily-life matters, but rarely with reference to the Bible, for scripturally based rumination on these matters was the substance of the two *Talmuds* (one of Palestinian origin and one originating among the Mesopotamian Jews). Finally, the *Midrashim* assembled a vast body of exegesis on the biblical books and on the "Oral Torah" which the rabbis eventually agreed was God's revelation.

Mystical oral tradition thus became an honored part of rabbinic Judaism. The Council of Jamnia had tried to limit revelation to the "written Torah"—that is, the biblical text—but mysticism and apocalyptic hopes exerted an irresistible pull on the Jewish community. Messianism may have figured in an uprising of Egyptian and North African Jews early in the second century. Then, in the period 132–135, still another massive revolt erupted in Judea under the charismatic Simon Bar Kochba ("Son of the Star"), whom some rabbis hailed as the Messiah but others rejected. As in the first century A.D., it took an all-out Roman military effort to crush the insurgents, and afterwards the Romans drove all Jews from Jerusalem and turned the city of David into a pagan colony called Aelia Capitolina. The searing, disillusioning experience of Bar Kochba's revolt divided Jews more than it united them, and its failure helped transform messianism from a burning hope of revolutionary deliverance into a mystical longing for spiritual regeneration.

Building an impregnable bastion around God's beleaguered people was the fundamental aim of the rabbis' centuries-long work of codifying the Law and its commentaries. Studying the Torah became a male Jew's holiest duty. Considered as a whole, and with all its myriad qualifications and alternatives, rabbinical wisdom defined what it meant to be a Jew. This synthesis was achieved only amid intense debate within the scattered Jewish communities—conflicts that involved drawing sharp lines and excluding heterodox sects. Hellenistic Judaism as represented by the Neoplatonist Philo Judaeus became heavily encrusted with the Pharisees' elaborate "angelology," and with occult fascinations that would culminate in the medieval *Cabala*, a compendium of magical lore. But through all this there also grew steadfast the commitment to ethical behavior that Jews recognized as their living legacy from Israel's ancient prophets. One of the rabbis who began the work of reconstructing Judaism after the Temple's destruction is said to have consoled a friend who wondered how, with atoning sacrifices ended, Israel now could be reconciled with God. By "deeds of loving-kindness," the rabbi replied.

Jesus

Challenged by someone to teach him the Torah while he stood on one foot, the rabbi Hillel of the first century B.C. answered: "Do not do to others what is hateful to you. That is the whole Law and the prophets; all the rest is commentary. Go and learn." Another rabbi, not long after, put it this way: "In everything do to others as you would have them do to you; for this is the law and the prophets" (Matthew 7:12). Hillel is revered today as one of the precursors of rabbinic Judaism. The virtual identity of his version of "the Golden Rule" to that of Jesus Christ—also quoted here—underscores the latter's roots in Jewish tradition.

Jesus of Nazareth (ca. 6 B.C.–ca. A.D. 30)[2] is the most mysterious of history's great figures. The earliest accounts of him, the Gospels, were written thirty to sixty years after his death, and are not biographies at all.[3] Rather, they are spiritual interpretations of his doings and sayings, intertwined with prophecies meant to show that he was the Messiah. Any attempt to extract from these accounts "the historical Jesus" is fraught with difficulties.

Nevertheless, most historians today agree that some things *can* be known about Jesus. He was a real person (skeptics once questioned this) and a monotheistic Jew. He probably came from a prosperous artisan family that could afford to educate him well. The Gospels show him preaching in synagogues and being called "rabbi." Steeped in Scripture and the apocalyptic currents of the time, he was deeply affected by the Second Isaiah's prophecy of Israel redeemed by a "Suffering Servant" and by the Book of Daniel's vision of God sending the "Son of Man" as the Messiah.[4] After John baptized him, he retired into the

wilderness to ponder the mission to which he felt God's call. The Gospels say that in the desert he rejected temptations to seek earthly glory.

Emerging from his ordeal, Jesus quickly attracted attention in Galilee as a hasid. As people demanded, he proved himself by healing the sick, exorcising devils, and performing miracles. His preaching was geared mainly toward simple rural folk, whose language he used in his parables. He dined with well-off "winebibbers," and the fishermen and other Galileans whom he recruited as his twelve apostles were not necessarily poor, but his followers were chiefly women, "sinners," the destitute, and the ritually outcast.

"The time is fulfilled, and the kingdom of God has come near; repent, and believe in the good news" (Mark 1:15). This was the heart of Jesus' message, differing radically from the warnings of John the Baptist and other sectarians that Jews must prepare for a *future* "Day of Yahweh." Jesus did not object to ritual as such, but only to ritual infected with pride and divorced from love of God and neighbor. He had come, he said, not to abolish the Law but to fulfill it; and unlike Judas the Galilean, Jesus opposed violence. Jews—*all* Jews, regardless of their sectarian allegiance or personal holiness, **heretical** Samaritans, outcast lepers, whores, and even tax collectors—were called to the Kingdom. They must trust God, their heavenly Father, with a childlike faith; they must repent of their evildoing and begin to treat one another with love and compassion, like brothers and sisters; they must understand that something apocalyptic was happening—that ordinary life must cease. Money, possessions, status, even the ties of marriage and kinship, now meant nothing, for the Kingdom of God had begun. Although the Gospels picture him as a warm, magnetic leader who miraculously healed the sick, raised the dead, and stilled the winds, he was also capable of furious outbursts. "Do not think that I have come to bring peace to the earth; I have come not to bring peace, but a sword. For I am come to set a man against his father, and a daughter against her mother. . . . Whoever loves father or mother more than me is not worthy of me" (Matthew 10:34-35, 37). "If you wish to be perfect, go, sell your possessions, and give the money to the poor, . . . then come, follow me. . . . It is easier for a camel to go through the eye of a needle than someone who is rich to enter the kingdom of God" (Matthew 19:21, 24). Hell awaited those who ignored him: "So shall it be at the end of the age. The angels will come out and separate the evil from the righteous and throw them into the furnace of fire, where there will be weeping and gnashing of teeth" (Matthew 13:49–50). And all this would come soon: "Truly I tell you, that there are some standing here who will not taste death until they see that the kingdom of God has come with power" (Mark 9:1).

The Gospels record that Jesus' own family and hometown thought him mad, and that even his disciples had

---

[2] Jesus' probable birth "B.C." results from computational errors by the seventh-century Christian creators of the dating system that we still use. Conflicting chronologies in the Gospel accounts make it impossible to determine exact dates.

[3] *Gospel* is an Old English word that means "good news" and is a direct translation of the Greek word *euanglion*. Four Gospels circulated by the end of the first century (others were composed, probably after A.D. 100, but they have not been regarded as valid by most Christians since ancient times). Three of the canonical Gospels—Mark, Matthew, and Luke—largely shared common underlying material; the fourth, John, grew out of very different traditions.

[4] For the Second Isaiah and the "Suffering Servant," see Chapter 1; for Daniel and the "Son of Man," see Chapter 3.

THE HISTORICAL EVIDENCE

Jesus' Sermon on the Mount

ca. A.D. 75

This distillation of Jesus' teaching, from the fifth chapter of the Gospel of Matthew, is inseparable from his "good news" that the Kingdom of God had begun.

Blessed are the poor in spirit, for theirs is the kingdom of heaven. Blessed are those who mourn, for they will be comforted. Blessed are the meek, for they will inherit the earth. Blessed are those who hunger and thirst for righteousness, for they will be filled. Blessed are the merciful, for they will receive mercy. Blessed are the pure in heart, for they will see God. Blessed are the peacemakers, for they will be called children of God. Blessed are those who are persecuted for righteousness' sake, for their's is the kingdom of heaven. Blessed are you when people revile you and persecute you and utter all kinds of evil against you falsely on my account. Rejoice and be glad, for your reward is great in heaven, for in the same way they persecuted the prophets who were before you. . . .

You have heard that it was said, "An eye for an eye and a tooth for a tooth." But I say to you, Do not resist an evildoer. But if anyone strikes you on the right cheek, turn the other also; and if anyone wants to sue you and take your coat, give your cloak as well; and if anyone forces you to go one mile,* go also the second mile. Give to anyone who begs from you, and do not refuse anyone who wants to borrow from you.

You have heard that it was said, "You shall love your neighbor and hate your enemy." But I say to you, Love your enemies and pray for those who persecute you, so that you may be children of your Father in heaven; for he makes his sun rise on the evil and on the good, and sends rain on the righteous and on the unrighteous. . . . Be perfect, therefore, as your heavenly Father is perfect.

---

*Probably a reference to the Roman army's right to requisition civilians to carry equipment.

Source: Matthew 5:3–11, 38–45, 48, from *The New Oxford Annotated Bible*.

---

difficulty grasping his incredible radicalism. When a crowd tried to seize him and acclaim him Israel's messianic king, he fled. Eventually his apostles (Peter taking the lead) declared that he was the Messiah—but Jesus told them to keep this secret; he was not the expected conquering hero. By then, Jesus knew that he would have to suffer and die as part of the work of inaugurating the Kingdom of God. Fatefully, he made a pious Jew's Passover journey to Jerusalem about A.D. 30.

Jesus had already angered the Sadducees by speaking with divine authority and attacking their complacency. His mass following also frightened them, for they knew from experience that any disturbance would provoke a savage Roman reprisal against all Jews. He had scandalized many (not all) of the Pharisees with his biting criticism of hypocrisy, and by his associations with disreputable people. He defiled himself by eating meals with the ungodly; and since many of his miracles involved touching ritually "unclean" persons—lepers, a hemorrhaging woman, corpses—how dare he then come into the Temple? The last straws were the popular enthusiasm accompanying Jesus' entrance into Jerusalem and his provocative chasing of swindling moneychangers from the Temple. The Jerusalem authorities accused him before Pilate of claiming to be king of the Jews—an act of treason. Pilate had him lashed and condemned to an ignoble death by crucifixion.

His followers fled, and on the cross he cried: "My God, my God, why have you forsaken me?"

The foundation of Christian faith is that on the third day after his crucifixion, Jesus rose from the dead. Those who believed that they saw him resurrected affirmed that he gave them solace and instructions to teach "all nations." Forty days after the Resurrection, he was said to ascend bodily into heaven with the promise to return soon to judge all souls and bring the world to an end.

The Earliest Churches

Convinced that Jesus had risen and was the Messiah, his apostles pooled all their property and formed a community to preach his gospel and await his glorious return. James, described in the Acts of the Apostles as "the Lord's brother," became the leader of this community but insisted that it adhere strictly to Jewish ritual and have nothing to do with gentiles. James apparently exercised a commanding influence over the Jerusalem-based and Temple-oriented "Jesus movement,"[5] displacing Jesus' own designated chief apostle, Peter, who was more willing to seek non-Jewish

---

[5] This is the term that scholars now use for the earliest Christians, particularly those who tried to remain within the Jewish tradition.

converts. In the year 62, James was killed. Jesus' rigorously ritualistic followers left the Temple before the Great Revolt, but other Jewish-Christian sects survived in Palestine until the fourth century.

It was a Greek-speaking Jew from the Anatolian city of Tarsus who, beginning in the mid-30s, transformed the Jesus movement into the core of a new world religion. His Hebrew name was Saul—or Paul in Greek—and next to Jesus himself, he must be regarded as the decisive figure in the emergence of Christianity and one of the pivotal individuals in world history.

Unlike Jesus, Paul left a full written record of his career, ideas, and personality. Educated as a Pharisee, Paul was in Jerusalem about the year 32, when he took part in the execution of one of Jesus' adherents. Soon after that he went to Damascus as the Temple's representative charged with rooting out Jesus' followers. On the way he had a blinding vision of Jesus, and became a convert. By the late 30s he turned up in Antioch. In that cosmopolitan city, where believers in Jesus had already come from Jerusalem, Paul began reaching out to Greek-speaking "God-fearers," people who despite their attraction to Judaism had not become full-fledged Jews. In Antioch the word *Christian* first came into use to describe Paul's disciples, God-fearers and Jewish alike. Followers of Jesus, Paul said, were not bound by Jewish rules of purity. It was more important that people, whoever they were, accept Jesus as their savior. Such notions horrified James's "Jesus movement" in

Jerusalem. Paul declared himself an independent apostle, directly inspired by Jesus and the Holy Spirit. As such, he traveled extensively in Anatolia and Greece (see Map 5-1), establishing Christian communities and developing his doctrines, which circulated as letters, or Epistles. Arrested in the late 50s, as a Roman citizen he claimed the right to be judged in Rome. He was sent there as a prisoner, spent several years loosely guarded, and was beheaded in 62.

Except for his vision on the road to Damascus and what Peter told him, Paul had no direct knowledge of Jesus. For Paul, the all-important thing was faith in Jesus' redeeming death and Resurrection. "And if Christ has not been raised, then our proclamation has been in vain, and your faith has also been in vain" (1 Cor. 15:14). Faith was a God-given gift, which Paul himself experienced—utterly undeservingly, he said, since he had persecuted believers. The Law of Moses, he held, had been given to the Jews by God, but try hard as they could, neither they nor any sinful people could ever fulfill the Law's spirit. Thus they deserved damnation. Jesus' sacrifice on the Cross had lifted this guilt from all men and women, be they Jew or "Greek." Infused with faith, believers in Jesus must open themselves to the working of the divine spirit in their souls, treat each other with love, and confidently await Jesus' return.

Quarrelsomeness and great physical stamina, epilepsy and ecstatic trances, a magnificently poetic vision of love transforming human relations—all this combined in Paul's genius as a religious prophet. Fluent in colloquial Greek, he

MAP 5-1
ST. PAUL'S MISSIONARY JOURNEYS

THE HISTORICAL EVIDENCE

Paul's Epistle to the Romans

A.D. 56

In the year 56 Paul wrote his epistle to the Romans, addressing a Christian community that already existed there. (According to the Roman historian Suetonius, the Roman Jews were banished around the year 49 because of a dispute caused by one "Chrestus." Suetonius probably meant that the Christians among the Roman Jews were expelled, but evidently they either filtered back or new ones appeared by 56.) This epistle is the culmination of Paul's teaching, and it would start Martin Luther down the road to the Protestant Reformation. In reading these extracts, it is important to understand that the Christians to whom Paul wrote were of Jewish origin. For him, faith replaces the Law, circumcision, and Jewish ritual as the seal of the Christian "New Israel."

I want you to know, brothers and sisters, that I have often intended to come to you (but thus far have been prevented), in order that I may reap some harvest among you as I have among the rest of the Gentiles. I am a debtor both to Greeks and to barbarians, both to the wise and to the foolish—hence my eagerness to proclaim the gospel to you also who are in Rome.

For I am not ashamed of the gospel; it is the power of God for salvation to everyone who has faith, to the Jew first and also to the Greek. For in it the righteousness of God is revealed through faith for faith; as it is written, "The one who is righteous will live by faith." . . .

Therefore you have no excuse, whoever you are, when you judge others; for in passing judgment on another you condemn yourself, because you, the judge, are doing the very same things. You say, "We know that God's judgment on those who do such things is in accordance with truth." Do you imagine, whoever you are, that when you judge those who do such things and yet do them yourselves, you will escape the judgment of God? Or do you despise the richness of his kindness and forbearance and patience? Do you not realize that God's kindness is meant to lead you to repentance? But by your hard and impenitent heart you are storing up wrath for yourself on the day of wrath, when God's righteous judgment will be revealed. . . . Therefore there will be anguish and distress for everyone who does evil, the Jew first and also the Greek, but glory and honor and peace for everyone who does good, the Jew first and also the Greek. For God shows no partiality.

All who have sinned apart from the [Jewish] law will also perish apart from the law, and all who have sinned under the law will be judged by the law. . . .

Then what advantage has the Jew? Or what is the value of circumcision? Much, in every way. For in the first place the Jews were entrusted with the oracles of God. . . .

What then? Are we [Jews] any better off? No, not at all; for we have already charged that all, both Jews and Greeks, are under the power of sin. . . .

Therefore, since we are justified by faith, we have peace with God through our Lord Jesus Christ, through whom we have obtained access to this grace in which we stand; and we boast in our faith of sharing the glory of God. And not only that, but we also boast in our sufferings, knowing that suffering produces endurance, and endurance produces character, and character produces hope, and hope does not disappoint us, because God's love has been poured into our hearts through the Holy Spirit that has been given to us. . . .

What then are we to say? Should we continue in sin in order that grace may abound? By no means! How can we who died to sin go on living in it? Do you not know that all of us who have been baptized unto Christ Jesus were baptized unto his death? Therefore we have been buried with him by baptism unto death, so that, just as Christ was raised from the dead by the glory of the Father, so we too might walk in newness of life.

Source: Romans 1:13–17; 2:1–5, 9–12; 3:1–2, 9; 5:1–5; 6:1–4, from *The New Oxford Annotated Bible*.

apparently cared nothing for classical culture; at Athens, he and the local Epicureans and Stoics completely misunderstood each other. Although his theology would eventually exert a tremendous influence on the Western mind, he was not an intellectual. Rather, he was intensely emotional, mystical, and charismatic. "Quench not the spirit," he said, and this included "speaking in tongues"—the practice, called *glossolalia*, of permitting the tongue to escape rational control and vocalize a stream of ecstatic syllables. But Paul also had common sense and formidable organizational skills: Outpourings of the spirit, he counseled, should be confined to private meetings of believers so as not to attract outsiders' ridicule.

Socially and politically, Paul was conservative. He admonished slaves to remain faithful to their masters, wives to submit to husbands, and all Christians to obey the Roman government.[6] Unmarried himself, he disliked sexuality and considered marriage a regrettable concession to "weakness of the flesh." Frequently his Epistles admonished Christians about their sexual activities (suggesting that some converts thought freedom from the Law liberated them from conventional behavior, or saw Christianity as a mystery cult that did not require inward moral change). And although he sought female converts, he tried to dampen outsiders' suspicion that Christianity drew women across conventional social boundaries. Apart from his own sense of the behavior appropriate for believers in Jesus, Paul needed to make Christianity seem respectable to the Romans.

Historians used to assume that the first Christian communities consisted almost exclusively of the poor, the dispossessed, and the slaves of Roman cities. Certainly the message of a savior who had worked with his hands, had surrounded himself with fishermen, ex-prostitutes, and similar riffraff, had been crucified by the imperial authorities, and had promised salvation to all who followed him—free or slave, man or woman—could resonate with the downtrodden of the first century A.D. But most modern scholars now believe that the earliest Christian communities embraced a broad spectrum of urban life, and that although people of meager or modest means predominated, well-to-do support was crucial. Many of the Christian community leaders named in Paul's Epistles were women, evidently prosperous ones, attesting to their important place in first-century Christianity. Significantly, Paul's first convert in Europe was a woman at Philippi named Lydia, who was not Jewish although she had worshiped at the synagogue; she was a well-to-do traveling merchant dealing in purple dye (a luxury item) and headed her household, perhaps after her husband had died. Paul made her household his base of operations while he lived and preached in Philippi.

Christians used the Greek word *ekklesia* to describe their religious communities, borrowing the familiar term for any social, cultural, or political assembly in the Greco-Roman world.[7] For most early Christians, the ekklesia had

Christian Woman at Prayer   Early Christians do not seem ordinarily to have prayed on their knees, hands clasped, but rather to have stood facing the east with arms extended, perhaps in imitation of their crucified savior. This image of a second-century praying woman comes from a catacomb.   *The Granger Collection, New York.*

to serve as a surrogate civic club and family, for they had to sever many normal social ties. Perhaps the easiest way to become a first-century Christian might be—as in the case of Lydia of Philippi—to transform one's entire household into a religious community dedicated to Jesus. But less well-off people faced more difficult situations. Slaves or other dependents who converted individually to Christianity would have to survive in their everyday world surrounded by pagan superiors, relying on a Christian ekklesia for moral support. Even the autonomous individuals in the big-city slums who became Christians had to limit ties to their own kin and to the myriad civic clubs that helped make Roman urban life bearable. And they had to abstain from the meat that was distributed at public sacrifices to the gods, often poor people's only opportunity to eat meat.

Because first-century Christians expected the world to end within their lifetimes, their communities were loosely organized, depending in the final analysis on recognition of spiritual gifts. (Only after about A.D. 100, as hope faded for Jesus' immediate return, did Christians begin to create a more hierarchical structure.) Within the community, early

---

[6] Some scholars believe that "most excellent Theophilus," the otherwise unidentified dignitary to whom both the Gospel of Luke and the Acts of the Apostles are dedicated, was a high Roman official who wanted to learn more about Christianity from Paul and his assistants. Both Luke and Acts seem to go out of their way to exonerate Roman officials, including Pontius Pilate, from responsibility for Jesus' execution and otherwise to portray Romans in a positive light.

[7] *Ekklesia* entered Latin as *ecclesia*, or "church," and from it we derive such words as *ecclesiastic*.

Christians looked after widows, orphans, and others worthy of charity.

First-century Christian communities worshiped in private homes. They met regularly for communal prayer, a sermon or the reading of a message from a teacher such as Paul, a meal at which they exchanged a kiss of peace (called *agape*), and a sharing of bread and wine called the Eucharist,[8] or Communion. Commemorating Jesus' final Passover meal with his friends before the Crucifixion, Christians viewed the Eucharist as an indispensable channel of divine grace through which the believer received the spirit of Christ. Another ceremony, baptism, initiated a believer into Christian fellowship, forgave past sins, and imparted the grace (moral strength) of the Holy Spirit. For Paul, baptism was the visible affirmation of faith, the Christian equivalent of circumcision. A person could be baptized only once, after a probation that could last for years. Early Christians often delayed baptism until the moment of death.

Paul's Epistles suggest that Christian communities needed constant hectoring. Transgressors were shamed and "shunned"—a complete cutting off from the ekklesia until they repented. Gaining forgiveness was no light matter: Months or even years of self-abasement might be required, and even then many offenses were provisionally forgiven (for God had the last word) only when the sinner lay dying or was martyred. Many second- and third-century Christians considered three sins unforgivable: murder, idolatry, and adultery.

Fear of hell and demons was intrinsic to early Christianity. Jesus' dire warnings of hell and the "casting out of demons" through which he healed testify to the place in his message of the terrors haunting the Judaism of his time. Early Christians inherited these fears. They, like all ancient people, felt a gnawing unease about nature's mysterious powers and Fate's uncanny propensity to plunge life into chaos. Pagans tried to ease worries by joining cults and sacrificing, but to the first Christians the pagan divinities were themselves demons. Dramatic exorcisms drew converts, and fear of hell kept them in line. Greco-Roman ideas of the afterlife ranged from assertions that it did not exist to vague notions of postmortem rewards and punishments, but few pagans conceived of eternal damnation. A yawning hell—deep, hot, endless, and escapable only through faith in Jesus—became one of Christianity's long-lasting legacies to Western civilization.

Christians today believe that Jesus is God, but it is not clear exactly what first-century Christians understood. Certainly all of them accepted Jesus as the Messiah (*Christos*, meaning "Anointed One," is a Greek translation of the Aramaic word *messiah*). But Christians of Jewish and of non-Jewish background might well have had different notions of messiahship. Incarnate gods and sons of gods were nothing new to Greco-Romans: Paul and his friend Barnabas once were hailed as Hermes and Zeus by a pagan crowd; the imperial cult revered emperors as "Son of God." Thus ex-pagan Christians could more readily think of Jesus, "the Son of God," as divine than could those of Jewish background who accepted him as the Messiah. Paul, a monotheist, taught simply that Jesus was the crucified and resurrected savior, through whom God worked. The Gospels of Mark, Luke, and Matthew (probably written between the 60s and the 80s) all declared Jesus to be the Messiah and Son of God. But none explicitly said what "Son of God" meant.

One of the earliest, but most profound, Christian attempts to describe Jesus was in the Gospel of John—the Fourth Gospel, which was composed using material quite different from that of the three others, probably in the 90s. John used a subtle Greek concept, *Logos*, with which Philo Judaeus (see above) had earlier described God. For John, the Logos was the eternal Light that had always been a part of God, which in Jesus had been made flesh and sent into the world (the Darkness) to be its redeemer.

From the beginning, therefore, Christianity had started down the path toward the sophisticated notion of a single divinity with three aspects—Father, Son/Logos, and Holy Spirit. In the centuries to come, working all this out would tax the skill of theologians, bring mobs into the streets, and send martyrs to their deaths. The problem arose out of Christianity's dual ancestry: Jewish monotheism with its messianic hopes, and Greek philosophy with its polytheistic memories. But it also gave Christians the unique advantage of a single, infinite God approachable through the lovable and human Jesus, while the Spirit of God remained among them to strengthen their faith.

Persecution and Entrenchment

Early Christians sometimes needed all the courage they could muster. Making one of the earliest references to Jesus and the Christians in a non-Christian source, the Roman historian Tacitus recorded at the beginning of the second century how Nero blamed them for the great fire that destroyed much of Rome in A.D. 64:

> Nero fastened the guilt and inflicted the most exquisite tortures on a class hated for their abominations, called Christians by the populace. Christus, from whom the name had its origins, suffered the extreme penalty during the reign of Tiberius at the hands of one of our procurators, Pontius Pilatus, and a most mischievous superstition, thus checked for the moment, again broke out not only in Judaea, the first source of the evil, but even in Rome, where all things hideous and shameful from every part of the world find their centre and become popular. Accordingly, an arrest

---

[8] The Greek word for *thanksgiving*.

THE HISTORICAL EVIDENCE

The Gospel of John

ca. A.D. 90

The Gospel of John is quite different in many respects from the three other accepted ("canonical") Gospels. The questions of who wrote the Gospel of John and what it means have always stirred scholarly debate. Many today think that the Gospel of John was written at the end of the first century, either by the then-aged apostle John or by someone claiming to be in his tradition; that it was written during an intense debate between Jewish Christians and Jews over Jesus' messiahship; and that its perspective on the nature of Jesus differs radically from that of Paul and the three other Gospels. This is the opening of the Gospel:

In the beginning was the Word [*Logos*], and the Word was with God, and the Word was God. He was in the beginning with God. All things came into being through him, and without him not one thing came into being. What has come into being in him was light, and the light was the light of all people. The light shines in the darkness, and the darkness did not overcome it.

There was a man sent from God, whose name was John.* He came as a witness to testify to the light, so that all might believe through him. He himself was not the light, but he came to testify to the light. The true light, which enlightens everyone, was coming into the world.

He [Jesus] was in the world, and the world came into being through him; yet the world did not know him. He came to what was his own, and his own people did not accept him. But to all who received him, who believed in his name, he gave power to become children of God, who were born, not of blood or of the will of the flesh or of the will of man, but of God.

And the Word became flesh and lived among us, and we have seen his glory, the glory as of a father's only son, full of grace and truth.

---

*John the Baptist.

Source: John 1:1–14, from *The New Oxford Annotated Bible*.

---

was first made of all who pleaded guilty; then, upon their information,[9] an immense multitude was convicted, not so much for the crime of firing the city, as of hatred against mankind. Mockery of every sort was added to their deaths. Covered with the skins of beasts, they were torn by dogs and perished, or were nailed to crosses, or were doomed to the flames and burnt, to serve as a nightly illumination, when daylight had expired.

Nero offered his gardens for the spectacle, and was exhibiting a show in the circus, while he mingled with the people in the dress of a charioteer or stood aloft in a car. Hence, even for criminals who deserved extreme and exemplary punishment, there arose a feeling of compassion, for it was not, as it seemed, for the public good, but to glut one man's cruelty, that they were being destroyed.

Martyrs   From the beginning the Christians—originally a term of disparagement—were a people apart. Mostly they kept to themselves and proselytized one-on-one. But convinced that they alone possessed the Truth that would one day triumph, they uncompromisingly rejected all other religions. "Atheists" was the label usually pinned on these people who avoided public baths, social clubs, civic rituals, the imperial cult, and anything else involving sacrifice. As we have seen, Romans and Hellenistic Greeks already made allowance for Jews' aloofness from such "respectable" behavior. But as pagans became more aware of the Christian movement (which at first had seemed an obscure Jewish sect), it struck them as dangerous. Snubbing the gods was serious: It might bring down the wrath of these capricious divinities upon any community that tolerated it. Disturbing rumors circulated about the Christians—that they went out of their way to recruit women, that their secret ceremonies involved orgies and cannibalism. (Early in the second century a Roman governor in Anatolia, Pliny the

---

[9] Doubtless obtained by torture, which was the accepted means of extracting information from slaves in any criminal investigation.

Marcus Aurelius Sacrificing
The philosopher-emperor
Marcus Aurelius believed it
his duty to uphold traditional
Roman religion. Here he is
shown offering devotions to
Jupiter and Minerva at one
of Rome's great temples.
With his toga drawn over his
head, he is exercising the old
republican office of *pontifex
maximus*, or supreme priest of
the Roman civic cult.
Mansell / Time Inc.

Younger, after torturing slave women who were church deacons, reported to Trajan that these stories were baseless. But gossip continued.) Above all, Christians openly said that Jesus would destroy the world and plunge nonbelievers into hellfire; indeed, they prayed that this cataclysm come quickly. Not surprisingly, they were unpopular.

It is more surprising how infrequently the first- and second-century emperors actually persecuted Christians. Nero had the excuse of needing to deflect blame for the great Roman fire; but, as Tacitus indicated, his sadism was counterproductive. Most later rulers cracked down on Christians reluctantly, as if fearing to unleash popular disturbances. About 110, the "good emperor" Trajan instructed his friend Pliny neither to hunt Christians down nor to heed anonymous accusations—these would be against "the spirit of the age." Christians were to be punished only if they were formally accused, tried, convicted, and still persisted in refusing to venerate the gods. Responding to local outrage against Christians, Marcus Aurelius ordered them thrown to the beasts in what is today Lyon, France. He disdained Christians as fanatical show-offs who were bent on subverting the empire and flouting society.

Persecutions of the first and second centuries thus tended to be local affairs, resulting primarily from popular hostility rather than systematic imperial policy. Droughts, earthquakes, epidemics, and other disasters attributable to

the gods' displeasure with the "atheists" triggered cries of "Christians to the lions!" So did rumors of cannibalism and incest. When emperors themselves attacked Christians, it was usually in connection with some imperial crisis. But these persecutions were neither sufficiently ruthless nor sufficiently sustained to exterminate the Christian community.[10]

The last book of the Christian Scriptures, the Book of Revelation (also called The Apocalypse), vividly shows how first-century Christians reacted to persecution. Revelation[11] describes a frightening vision of Jesus bringing vengeance on a sinful world, while comforting "the seven churches of Asia" for their steadfastness. The persecutions to which the Book of Revelation responded were typical local affairs. That is, in cities like Ephesus and Pergamum (among "the seven churches of Asia"), outraged mobs and city fathers put Christians to death for refusing to chip in to build temples grander than those of rival towns. Roman imperial officials were apparently not involved. Still,

---

[10] The pagan authorities might have learned much from the Christian inquisitors of the Late Middle Ages or sixteenth-century Spain on the subject of liquidating troublesome religious minorities.

[11] Traditionally attributed to the same John who wrote the Fourth Gospel, but striking differences in the two books' Greek grammar and style make it unlikely that the same person actually wrote both.

Revelation depicted Rome as "the Whore of Babylon," mounted on a scarlet beast with seven heads and ten horns.

Persecution affected Christians in different ways. Some fled; some got a slave or a pagan friend to sacrifice for them. Bribing the right officials often saved well-to-do Christians from the fatal choice between sacrificing at the risk of damnation or refusing to sacrifice at the cost of certain martyrdom. Christian accounts of martyrdoms often depict the Roman judge pleading that the accused sensibly save their lives by burning a pinch of incense. Condemned Christians, jailed until they could be dispatched in a gory public show, were often visited by fellow believers who brought them food and sought their blessing. One Christian account told of a man who decided to save himself by performing the sacrifice but got so drunk at his farewell prison gathering that he forgot to recant, and so was martyred with the rest.

Some Christians welcomed martyrdom. Dying for the faith was believed to ensure an instant crown of heavenly glory and to wipe out the martyr's guilt for sins. In 155 a pagan mob dragged into court the octogenarian St. Polycarp, the Christian leader in Smyrna (now Izmir, Turkey), and when he refused to deny his redeemer, he was dispatched to a bonfire. Another early leader, St. Ignatius of Antioch, was taken overland to Rome to be thrown to the beasts, but along the way he was greeted by admiring crowds, preached sermons, and discouraged attempts to have him rescued. About 150, a movement led by a certain Montanus appeared among rural Anatolian Christians, who claimed that direct inspiration by the Holy Spirit was the only valid source of religious truth. Many Montanists were women, apparently reclaiming the first-century tradition of female Christian prophecy that more conservative church leaders discouraged. An important part of the Montanist "New Prophecy" was the idea that Christians must witness their faith by courting martyrdom.

Montanism spread into North Africa, where ancient Carthaginian religious traditions involving human sacrifice (including, in extreme situations, oneself) lived on beneath an imposed Roman veneer. In 203, these ecstatic traditions inspired at Carthage one of the best-documented cases of Christian martyrdom—that of Saints Perpetua and Felicity. The daughter of a wealthy and respectable pagan, Perpetua was twenty-two and had just given birth to a child; Felicity, about the same age and also a new mother, was her slave and close friend. Jailed, Perpetua defied her father when he alternately threatened her and begged her to give up her disgraceful madness. Perpetua kept a prison diary of her dreams and visions, almost down to the moment when she and Felicity ecstatically died in the amphitheater before a howling crowd.

Roots of the Institutional Church There were several spasmodic imperial persecutions of Christians during the third century. But from 261 until the beginning of the fourth century, live-and-let-live toleration prevailed between Christians and the Roman authorities. Christians remained a very small minority; one well-informed modern authority guesses that they constituted 5 percent of the empire's population. Still, the churches were now recruiting members openly, building substantial public houses of worship, and providing relief for indigent members—which must have been especially welcome in these economically distressed times.[12] Christian authors began to offer comforting reassurances that Jesus' stark call to give away everything really meant that the wealthy should be generous. The churches were also acquiring considerable property by bequests from well-to-do members. Christianity was becoming respectable, if not widely followed.

As Christian documents become more common, for the second and especially the third centuries, the organization of the churches emerges more sharply. These documents disclose growing distinctions between those who governed the churches and administered the **Sacraments,** and the laity whom they served. One line of separation was gender: First-century churches may have accorded women substantial roles as deacons, but later on males assumed all the significant leadership posts. Until the late third century, however, a substantial majority of Christians seem to have been women.

Priests wielding mysterious powers were familiar in the pagan world, but a Christian priesthood developed only belatedly. Paul, having broken with the Jewish priesthood, insisted that all believers in Jesus were priests,[13] and this was the consensus of first-century Christianity. Only by the third century does it appear that Christians were moving back to the idea of a formally ordained clergy who alone could conduct religious services and administer sacraments. Sharpening disputes over doctrine, and concern that "correct" teaching prevail over heresy, explain much of the organizational tightening that occurred. The office appearing in the second century, a **bishop** (the martyr St. Polycarp was an early one) was normally chosen by acclamation or consensus among the urban community of which he was a spiritual leader. The most prominent bishops were the metropolitans or archbishops of the big cities, to whom bishops in surrounding smaller places looked up. Atop the hierarchy were the bishops, or patriarchs, of the three greatest cities of the empire—Rome, Alexandria, and Antioch—who exercised spiritual authority (usually theoretical) across vast areas. By the second and third centuries, Christians were using the Greek word *catholic* to refer to the "worldwide" community of all believers in Christ (see Map 5-2).

---

[12] The economic crisis of the third-century Roman Empire is discussed later in this chapter.

[13] This would become a crucial idea for Martin Luther and the other Protestant reformers in making their break with the Roman Catholic church. See Chapter 13.

MAP 5-2
CHRISTIAN CHURCHES IN THE ROMAN EMPIRE, CA. A.D. 300
The dots on this map locate the known Christian churches on the eve of the Great Persecution (303–311). Note the heavy concentration in the Near East, Egypt, Anatolia, Italy, and North Africa. In the independent kingdom of Armenia, Christianity was established as the state religion in the late third century. By contrast, no Christian communities are known in Britain in A.D. 300.

As early as the second century, bishops of Rome claimed preeminence.[14] One basis for this assertion was the tradition that St. Peter had been the first bishop of Rome and had been martyred there. (But although the evidence for Peter's presence in Rome during Nero's reign is strong, the office of bishop did not appear there until afterwards.) Another strength was the Roman church's ability to hold a middle position on the issue of who should be a Christian. On one side stood those (especially the North Africans) who saw the Christian movement as a sect open only to those meeting the most rigorous standards of purity; at the other extreme were those who were willing to relax discipline and make Christianity as inclusive as possible, a tendency more characteristic of the Greek-speaking east. Likewise, the Roman church and its bishops championed a

middle way in the great doctrinal controversies that convulsed the Christian movement beginning in the second century—a middle way that avoided both the North Africans' enthusiasm for personal revelation by the Holy Spirit and the easterners' predilection for philosophical disputes. Although establishing effective papal authority over even western Christendom would require many centuries, the Roman church was already staking out its ground.

Christianity between Judaism and Classical Culture

Down to the early fourth century, Jews outnumbered Christians in the Roman Empire. Their synagogues were handsome and well endowed; Jews held significant positions in some city governments. The Jewish population was rising, partly because of Jews' horror of the infanticide that pagans routinely practiced and partly because they were attracting converts. There is considerable evidence of a back-and-

---

[14] They called themselves popes, but *papa* in colloquial Latin meant exactly what it means in English, and was a title of affection and respect accorded to other bishops as well.

Third-Century Synagogue
This imposing synagogue in the city of Capernaum was built in the third century A.D., a time of prosperity for the Jews of Galilee. Note the Greco-Roman architectural style. *© R. Sheridan / Ancient Art & Architecture Collection.*

forth flow of adherents between the Christian and Jewish camps—especially women, who did not face the issue of circumcision. But as part of their effort to draw lines defining Judaism, the rabbis denounced Christians for deifying Christ alongside Yahweh.

The signs of Christian-Jewish separation were already clear in the late first century. Within Judaism, believers in Jesus as the Messiah were being excluded from the synagogues, along with other Jewish sectarians. Simultaneously, within the Christian movement, the progression of Gospel-writing (from Mark in the 60s to John near the century's end) shows both an evolving understanding of Jesus and a sharpening of the intra-Jewish quarrel over his message. The late first-century Epistle to the Hebrews, whose authorship is much debated, attests to the "pull" that Jewish Christians felt to return to their old religious allegiance. The writer vigorously opposed this reversion. Responding to what were probably rabbinical attacks on Christians' "polytheistic" worship of Jesus, he asserted that Christ, the Son of God and exalted above all the angels, had become human and established a new covenant, making Christians the "new Israel." About the same time, the Gospel of John directed a similar message to Jews and Jewish Christians: that believers in Jesus worshiped God not in temples or on hilltops, but "in spirit and truth," and that "God is spirit." Finally, the Book of Revelation, although rooted in the Jewish apocalyptic tradition, came closest of all first-century Christian writings to focusing actual *worship* on Jesus as God. These three books brought "the Jesus movement" almost to the breaking point with Judaism. But it took the conscious efforts of both Christian and Jewish leaders in the second and third centuries to snap the connection entirely.

Paul's welcoming of gentile converts and John's quasi-Greek presentation of Christ as God's eternal Logos had shifted the Jesus movement toward Greek cultural influence—that is, toward people whose pagan background allowed them readily to understand their savior as a divinity. In the second century, as ex-Jews started to be outnumbered in the churches by converted gentiles, Christian leaders faced trends that might have turned Christianity into a mystery cult—currents strongest among eastern Christians.

Historians use the word *gnosticism* (from the Greek *gnosis*, or "knowledge") to describe the second-century mingling of Christianity, Neoplatonism, Persian dualism, and Greek myth. All strands of gnosticism held that the material world was an evil illusion, and that God could not have degraded himself by assuming a flesh-and-blood body; Christ, then, was not truly human but only a divine phantom. (Some gnostics saw Yahweh as the evil creator of the material world.) Gnostics claimed apostolic origins, and a large collection of their writings turned up in 1945 in the form of papyrus rolls preserved in the Egyptian desert. To read these texts is to plunge into a dimly Christian version of the Hellenistic cults. Gnostics claimed that the full Christian message had been revealed only as *secret* wisdom accessible to those literally "in the know."

A premise that the world of things is unreal, that nothing is as it appears, and that the savior is a bridge to a world of unseen Spirit is a rickety foundation on which to build a mass religious movement. It is also very far from Judaism.

Second-century Christian thinkers who were still rooted in the flesh-and-blood traditions of Jewish Christianity, such as St. Justin Martyr (ca. 100–ca. 160) and St. Irenaeus (ca. 130–ca. 200), vehemently resisted gnosticism. By the year 200 the Christian Scriptures as we know them today (called the New Testament) had largely been agreed upon, eliminating the esoteric gnostic texts. It is in this context that the Latin-speaking theologian Tertullian thundered, in words that have often been quoted inaccurately as evidence of early Christians' ignorant contempt for Greek culture, "What has Athens to do with Jerusalem . . . ? What have heretics to do with Christians? . . . Away with all attempts to produce a Stoic [and] Platonic . . . Christianity!" Actually, Tertullian—a sophisticated Stoic before he converted to Christianity—was targeting Neoplatonic gnosticism.

In their arguments against both Judaism and gnosticism, the defenders of emerging Christian **orthodoxy** ("correct belief") confronted difficult issues. How could Christ be both God and man? How can the One God have three aspects? Christians assumed that wrong opinions about God were inspired by the devil, and hence heresy. "It behooves us," wrote Irenaeus sometime before A.D. 200, "to learn the truth from those who possess that succession of the Church which is from the apostles"—the basic premise of the medieval church. As questions were raised, solutions defined, and dissenters damned, Christian doctrine grew specific, elaborate—and, though it would have horrified Tertullian—dominated by the premises of Greek philosophy.

The anti-gnostics emphasized Jesus' humanity—yet pressing that point too hard risked underestimating or denying his divine quality, in which most Christians by now believed. During the third century, a majority of Christian leaders condemned assertions that Jesus was a man whom God had raised to divinity. The position that came to be defined as orthodox lay midway between this "heresy" and the equally abhorrent gnosticism: Christ was fully human *and* fully divine. As a coequal member of the Holy Trinity, he had always existed and always would, but at one moment in history he had assumed human form. As the man Jesus, he had walked the earth, resisted temptation, taught, suffered, and been crucified. In this way, both Greek inclinations to see Jesus as a savior god and Judaism's faith in a divinely sent but human Messiah were preserved. A Christian synthesis of matter and spirit emerged, bridged by Christ.

The intellectual advocates of early Christianity are known as "apologists," although "defenders" would be a better English version of the underlying Greek term. In reponding to pagan critics and internal "heretics," the apologists defined what became Christian doctrine on issues the apostles had never faced. It is of the highest significance that the apologists worked within a Greek philosophical framework. The greatest of them, Origen (d. 254), the son of a martyr and educated in Alexandria's best

schools, constructed an all-inclusive Christian philosophical system on Platonic foundations. Plato and other great Greek philosophers, he said, had been led toward truth by the Christian God. Several of Origen's major conclusions were rejected by later Christian orthodoxy,[15] and his arguments seldom impressed pagan intellectuals. But his and other theologians' defense of their faith in terms of Greek philosophy helped ensure that ancient philosophy became part of Christian European civilization.

As Christian theology became hellenized, pagan thought (as we have seen) grew otherworldly. Origen's greatest pagan contemporary—they had the same teacher—was the Neoplatonist Plotinus. With a transcendental outlook taking root throughout the ancient world, Christianity was coming into tune with the times; it appealed to an age hungry for personal redemption. Yet its triumph was by no means assured, for it faced other salvation religions such as Mithraism and the Isis cult—and Greco-Roman paganism in its new, Neoplatonic armor. Back in Marcus Aurelius's time the Neoplatonist Celsus had written the first philosophical attack on Christianity, which Origen answered almost a century later in his book *Against Celsus*. Plotinus dismissed Christianity as beneath contempt, and his student Porphyry (ca. 233–304) published a blistering polemic against it.[16] By allegorizing Greco-Roman myths about the gods and integrating natural phenomena into a wider world of spiritual forces, Neoplatonist philosophers emerged as some of Christianity's fiercest enemies, and in the fourth and fifth centuries would be among the last pagans to capitulate.

Still another threat to Christianity, as well as to the Greco-Roman tradition, appeared in the third century from beyond Rome's borders. This was the faith preached by a Mesopotamian prophet, crucified under Persian rule, named Mani (ca. 216–276). Mani saw himself as the creator of a new world religion, synthesizing and superseding earlier faiths. Manichaeanism drew heavily on Zoroastrian ideas about the unreality and evil of the material world and the inevitable triumph of spiritual forces. Living in Persia, Mani was aware of Buddhism, which during his time was spreading out of India to China (where it flourished) and Persia (where it withered). To Jews, Manichaeanism was preached as uncompromising monotheism, and among Christians the new religion inherited the old gnostic appeal. Aggressive missionaries spread the Manichaean word, requiring austere lives of the cult's elite but permitting converts to enjoy the good things of life almost until

---

[15] One was the hopeful idea that in the end everyone, even the devil, would be forgiven their sins and saved: Hell, he thought, was useful chiefly for frightening simple people into believing.

[16] After Christianity triumphed, all copies of Celsus's and Porphyry's books against it vanished, and their arguments can only be reconstructed from citations in the Christian books refuting them.

their dying day—perhaps a more attractive prospect than Christian leaders' harping on sin and self-denial.

Against these rivals Christianity could offer the human appeal of the historic Jesus, the growing profundity of its theology, the infinite majesty of its God, and the compassion and universalism of its message. Few social groups could ignore its attraction. By the third century some intellectuals were being drawn by its hellenized theology, prosperous townspeople by its mysticism, and bureaucrats by the ever-increasing effectiveness of its administrative hierarchy. For in administration no less than in theology, the emerging Christian church was learning from the Greco-Roman world.

THE THIRD-AND FOURTH-CENTURY CRISES: DISINTEGRATION AND AUTOCRACY

The empire-wide persecutions of the third and early fourth centuries were products of a crisis in Roman civilization, and were launched by the Roman government. The greatest imperial persecution, and the last, came at the opening of the fourth century under Emperor Diocletian. But Diocletian is not remembered only as a harrier of the Christians. He reigned at the end of a hundred years of trouble that had almost brought the Roman Empire to its knees. The reforms he introduced gave the empire centuries more in which to shore up its foundations and preserve ancient culture.

The Third-Century Anarchy

The turbulent third century—the era of Origen and Plotinus—meant catastrophic changes for the Roman Empire. The age of the "five good emperors" (A.D. 96–180) was followed by a hundred troubled years during which the swift rise and fall of emperors alternated with military despotism. With increased pressures from external peoples, imperial survival came to depend more than ever on military defense—and the Roman legions, well aware of that, made and unmade emperors. Roman armies battled one another repeatedly for control of the imperial office until (to exaggerate only slightly) a man might be a general one day, emperor the next, and dead the third. No less than nineteen emperors reigned during the calamitous half-century between 235 and 284, not to mention innumerable usurpers and pretenders whose plots worsened the general chaos. In this fifty-year period every emperor save one died by assassination, by suicide, or in battle. The Silver Age had given way to what one Roman historian described as an age "of iron and rust."

A crucial problem was that of the imperial succession, and all too often it was solved by force alone. As the power of the army increased and military rebellions became commonplace, the succession depended more and more on the whim of the troops. The period's most successful emperor,

Septimius Severus (reigned 193–211), stayed in power by expanding and pampering the army, opening its highest offices to every class, and broadening its recruitment. A military career became the logical springboard to high civil office, and the bureaucracy increasingly displayed a military cast of mind. The old ideals of the Republic and the Principate meant less to those now in power, many of whom rose from the bottom of society through successful army careers to positions of high political responsibility. These new administrators were often strong and able, but they were not the sort to admire old Roman political traditions. As emperors such as Septimius Severus raised taxes to replenish their treasuries and appease their troops, the civilian population grew powerless and impoverished. Septimius's dying words to his sons summed up his reign and the times: "Enrich the soldiers and scorn the world."

But Rome's troubles in the third century cannot be ascribed entirely to the problem of imperial succession. As early as the reign of Marcus Aurelius (161–180) a devastating plague struck the empire and then lingered for a generation, while Germanic tribes spilled across the Rhine-Danube frontier and rampaged as far as Italy. Marcus Aurelius, the philosopher-emperor, dutifully spent most of his reign fighting off invaders, and only by enormous effort did he succeed. He died at what is today Vienna, defending the Danube frontier. During the third century the Germans attacked repeatedly, penetrating the frontiers time and again,

Septimius Severus and Family Septimius Severus, Rome's first general-emperor of North African origin, married a forceful and politically well-connected wife, Julia Domna. In this painting he is shown with her and their son, the future emperor Caracalla, about 205. Their other son, Geta, has been obliterated from the painting; Caracalla had his brother killed when he took power. *Severus, Lucius Septimus 146–211 n. Chr. Original: Staatliche Museen zu Berlin. Bildarchiv Preussischer Kulturbesitz (bpk), Berlin Antikensammlung.*

forcing cities to erect protective walls, and threatening for a time to destroy the empire altogether. And the Germanic onslaught was accompanied by attacks from the east, where the Persian Empire had recently been reconstituted by able kings of the Sassanid dynasty (A.D. 226–651).

Rome's worst problems were internal. Third-century political chaos ran parallel to social and economic breakdown. The ever-rising exactions of a mushrooming bureaucracy and an insatiable army overwhelmed urban and rural people alike. The self-governing town—the bedrock of imperial administration and of Greco-Roman civilization itself—encountered grave financial difficulties. As one city after another turned to the emperor for financial aid, civic autonomy shrank. These problems arose partly from the unproductive nature of many of the Roman cities, partly from rising imperial taxes, and partly from economic stagnation. Long before the death of Marcus Aurelius, Rome had abandoned conquest in favor of consolidation. Now, when the influx of slaves and booty ceased, the empire had to become economically self-sufficient. For a while all seemed well, but as administrative and military expenses mounted without a corresponding growth in commerce and industry, the economy deteriorated. The army, once the provider of conquered riches, became a drain.

By the third century, if not before, plagues, hunger, and a sense of hopelessness resulted in a gradual decline in population, especially in the cities. While imperial expenses and taxes rose, the tax base contracted. Prosperity gave way to depression and desperation. Peasants fled their fields to escape the hated, venal tax collector, and urban artisans and professionals sank into demoralized poverty; those who stayed at their jobs were taxed all the more heavily. Beggars proliferated everywhere, pirates again roved the Mediterranean, and robbers haunted the Roman roads.

The western half of the empire suffered most. What industry there was had always been centered in the east, and money gradually flowed eastward to pay for luxury goods, some of which came from Persia, India, and China. In short, the empire as a whole, and its western part especially, suffered from an unfavorable balance of trade.

The ever more desperate financial circumstances of the third-century Roman Empire forced the emperors to debase the coinage—diluting the gold and silver in their coins with copper and lead. As always happens, devaluation produced only temporary relief. In the long run, a runaway inflation crippled the economy and hastened the decline of the commercial class. Between A.D. 256 and 280 the cost of living rose 1,000 percent.

The third-century anarchy climaxed during the 260s. By then the Roman economy lay in ruins. Germanic armies burst through the frontiers. Gaul, Britain, and much of Syria all broke loose from imperial control. Imperial collapse seemed imminent.

The empire survived, but only through the tremendous efforts of military leaders who seized power in the late third century. The third-century agonies, however, indelibly marked the empire. The new imperial structure that conjured order out of chaos was an autocracy undisguised by republican trappings.

The Reforms of Diocletian, 284–305

Even at the height of the anarchy, some emperors strove desperately to defend the Roman state. After 268 a series of able, tough emperor-generals from the Danubian provinces turned the tide. They restored the frontiers, smashed the invading armies of Germans and Persians, and recovered lost provinces in Gaul and in the east. At the same time, these emperors took measures to stem social and economic decay. Such policies were expanded and brought to fruition by Diocletian (reigned 284–305) and Constantine (reigned 306–337), to whom belong the credit and responsibility for reconstituting the empire along authoritarian lines that recalled the ancient Near Eastern and Hellenistic monarchies. No longer merely a *princeps*, or "first citizen," the emperor became *Dominus et Deus*—lord and god—and it is appropriate that the new despotic regime that replaced the Principate should be called the "Dominate."

Imperial Revival In the days of Augustus it had been necessary, so as not to offend republican sensibilities, to disguise the power of the emperor. In Diocletian's day the imperial title had for so long been abused that it seemed

Tax Collecting in the Third Century The ever-rising exactions of tax collectors, shown in relief from the Balkan provinces, were both a cause and a symptom of the crisis that gripped imperial Roman society in the third century A.D. *Alinari/Art Resource, NY.*

THE HISTORICAL EVIDENCE

A Thracian Village Appeals to the Emperor

A.D. 238

Gordian I, a general proclaimed emperor by his troops in A.D. 238, reigned for all of twenty-two days. Then he was shoved aside by another general and committed suicide. But during his ephemeral reign, he sent out a message inviting any subjects with grievances to inform him. This is the response of a village in Thrace (modern northeastern Greece and southern Bulgaria). Note the villagers' claim to trust that when the emperor knows the truth he will come to his people's aid. Such appeals to the government's self-interest in keeping taxpaying subjects from running away will be frequent in medieval and early modern Europe.

To the Emperor . . . Gordian . . . , petition from the villagers of Scaptopara and Geresa [?]. During the most fortunate and eternal time of your reign you have often stated in rescripts that the villages should be inhabited and improved instead of having the inhabitants driven from their homes. Such a policy is conducive to the security of your subjects and the advantage of your most sacred treasury. Wherefore we too convey a just supplication to your divinity.

We dwell in and are property owners in the aforementioned village, which is exposed to wanton damage because it possesses the advantage of hot springs and is situated between two of the army camps which is in your Thrace.

And in the past, as long as the inhabitants remained undisturbed and unharmed, they paid their tribute and other levies unexceptionably. But when certain parties began at times to proceed to insolence and employ violence, then indeed the village began to decline. A famous festival is celebrated two miles from our village, and those who visit there for fifteen days of the festival do not remain at the site but leave it and descend upon our village, forcing us to provide them with hospitality . . . without payment. In addition to these, soldiers too . . . come to us, and likewise compel us to provide them with hospitality and supplies and pay us no money. And the governors of the province and even your procurators for the most part

visit here for the benefit of the waters. We are continually entertaining the authorities . . . ; but, unable to bear the burden of others, we appealed repeatedly to the governors of Thrace, who in accordance with the divine ordinances gave orders that we should be left undisturbed. For we pointed out that we could no longer abide it, but actually had a mind to abandon even our ancestral hearths on account of the violence of those who descend upon us—and in truth we have declined from many home owners to a very few.

They again beg the emperor to order that things be put to right.

And if we are [still] oppressed, we will flee from our homes, and the treasury will be involved in very great loss. But pitied through your divine foresight, we will remain in our places and be able to provide the sacred tribute and other taxes. And this will come about for us in the most fortunate times of your reign, if you give orders for your divine letter to be inscribed on a stele and set up in public, so that we shall be able, if we obtain this, to acknowledge our thanks to your fortune.

Source: From Naphthali Lewis and Meyer Lewis, *Roman Civilization: A Sourcebook* (New York: Columbia University Press, 1951), vol. 2, pp. 439–440.

necessary to exalt it. Borrowing from Hellenistic and Persian court ceremonial, Diocletian and his successors employed every art of costume, makeup, and drama to look majestic. Everyone had to fall prostrate in the emperor's presence, and Constantine added the touch of wearing a sparkling diadem on his head.

The man who organized this pomp was a dour, hard-bitten, shrewd old soldier from the Balkans. Diocletian had made his career in the army and came to power in the usual military coup. Once in power, his most immediate task was

to survive—and in so doing he was able to end the turbulent era of short-lived "barracks emperors" and military usurpers. To neutralize challengers, stabilize the succession, and reduce the ever-growing burden of governing the empire, he decreed that there would thenceforth be two emperors—one in the east, the other in the west—who would work together. Each would have the title "Augustus," and each would adopt a younger colleague with the title "Caesar" to share his rule and ultimately succeed him. To do this, Diocletian reorganized the empire into four administrative districts, each under an Augustus or a Caesar (see Map 5-3). Aware of the increasing importance of the eastern over the western half of the empire, Diocletian made his capital in the east and did not set foot in the western capital, Rome, until the close of his reign. A usurper would now face the daunting task of overcoming four widely scattered rulers instead of one. The chances of military usurpation were further reduced by Diocletian's rigorous separation of civil and military authority. He enlarged the army, chiefly by incorporating Germanic forces who now assumed much of the burden of guarding the frontiers. But by restricting generals' jurisdiction over civilian districts, he shrank their power and enlarged his own.

Imperial control was the keynote of the new regime. Diocletian based his power not on the authority of the army but on that of the gods, closely associating himself with Jupiter. The Senate was now merely ornamental, and the emperor ruled through his obedient and ever-expanding bureaucracy, issuing edict after edict to regiment the state. He met the shortage of money by decreeing a new land tax in kind. Huge building projects soaked up unemployment, and the widespread flight from productive labor was countered by laws binding peasants, artisans, and merchants to their jobs. A system of hereditary social orders quickly developed—a caste system in which sons were required by law to take up their fathers' careers and

tax burdens. Peasants were tied to the land. Workers in the mines and quarries were literally branded.

This caste system was more theoretical than real, for such measures were hard to enforce. Nevertheless, the Dominate tangled everyday life in red tape. Economic collapse was temporarily averted, but at the cost of social petrification and blighted hopes. Once-autonomous cities lay in the grip of the imperial government. Loyalty to the empire waned rapidly among property-owning townspeople, formerly among its chief supporters but now crushed by taxes and (as one historian has put it) condemned for life to the Chamber of Commerce.

But it was Diocletian's mission to save the empire whatever the cost, and for every problem he offered a heavy-handed solution. A thoroughgoing currency reform retarded inflation but did not stop it, and so by edict he fixed the prices of most commodities. The usual effects followed: Thousands of bureaucrats got jobs giving orders and supervising markets, shortages appeared and black markets abounded, and stronger inflationary pressures built up.

The four-part division of the empire among two Augusti and two adopted Caesars was an imaginative political reform. But it worked effectively only while Diocletian was in charge. When he retired in 305, worn out and sick, a new struggle ensued, ending in Constantine I's victory over all rivals but one in 312.

MAP 5-3
THE ROMAN EMPIRE UNDER DIOCLETIAN

Emperor Diocletian   This gold coin shows Diocletian as he wanted his subjects to see him: indomitable.   *Spink & Son Ltd. / The Bridgeman Art Library.*

The Great Persecution   To counter the growing challenge of Christianity, Diocletian reluctantly agreed to launch a decade-long persecution of unprecedented severity. Imperial persecution proved no more successful than price control. But the very fact that both were attempted illustrates how far the emperor would go to revive the Roman state.

Various motives have been offered to explain this "Great Persecution"; the most plausible is Diocletian's fear that the gods would not bless the new imperial order until he uprooted "atheists" who outraged traditional Roman ways. (For the same reason, Diocletian tried to outlaw the "immoral" Egyptian practice of brother-sister marriages and persecuted Manichaeans.) In 303, imperial decrees ordered the destruction of Christian churches, the burning of Christian Scriptures, and the removal of Christians from high positions in the army and the government. Initially, Diocletian hoped to avoid making martyrs and shrewdly targeted only Christian leaders. Often he was successful: Many important Christians, including bishops, complied or evaded, which discredited them in their people's eyes. Apparently satisfied, Diocletian abdicated, forcing his co-Augustus to do likewise. Both turned power over to their respective Caesars.

The greatest violence came when in 305 Diocletian's successors ordered all Christians to sacrifice on pain of death. Ordinary Christians, often repudiating fainthearted leaders, defied the orders where the authorities attempted

to enforce them rigorously—especially in North Africa and Egypt. There the greatest numbers of martyrs perished, sometimes with sadistic tortures, but the price was high in terms of civil disruption. Often the pagan public sympathized with the Christians rather than their persecutors. The two persecuting co-rulers handed their potentially rival colleagues an excellent tactical weapon: the opportunity to win support by promising the Christians toleration.

By 311, it was obvious that persecution had not only failed to unite the empire under its old gods, but was abetting a civil war among the empire's would-be masters. The winner in the west was Constantine, one of the Caesars since 306. Constantine came to terms with his brother-in-law Licinius, ruler of the eastern provinces, and in early 313 the new pair of co-rulers issued the epochal Edict of Milan. Under it, all religions in the Roman Empire received equal rights, and the Christian church regained confiscated property. The Great Persecution had ended with Christianity legalized.

The Reign of Constantine, 306–337

In October 312, as his army approached Rome for a showdown battle, Constantine—so he said—saw in the sky a blazing cross and the Latin words *in hoc vinces* ("in this [sign] you will conquer"). That night, Christ himself appeared to Constantine in a dream. On the morrow, the day of the battle, Constantine ordered his soldiers to paint on their shields the letters *chi* and *rho* —in Greek, the first two letters of *Christos*—to form a cross: ☧. Constantine ascribed his victory in this, the Battle of the Milvian Bridge, to Christ. Having proved his power, Christ became Constantine's God.

Constantine's turn to Christ, as well as the steps that he and the unenthusiastic Licinius (a pagan) took the next year in legalizing Christianity, are among the most dramatic—and most debated—events in the history of Western civilization. Caesar and Christ had come to terms; the way was open for Christianity to become the established church of the Roman Empire and to begin its dominant role in Western society and culture. Yet we can only understand this sweeping transformation in the light of the larger patterns of Constantine's imperial ambitions and the fourth-century mentality.

Constantine's triumph marked the return to Rome of political stability and the consummation of Diocletian's economic and political reforms. A brutal autocrat, he never hesitated to shed blood when necessary (and often when not). In an edict of 332, Constantine tightened Diocletian's policy of freezing occupations and making them hereditary. He increased imperial authority and embellished imperial ceremony. But Constantine also moved in radical new directions. In place of the principle of adoption, Constantine founded a new imperial dynasty. For twelve years Constantine shared authority with Licinius, but in 324 he defeated him and had him strangled, and thereafter ruled alone. Nevertheless, the east-west division of power became common again after Constantine's death, and he himself contributed to this by building a magnificent eastern capital, Constantinople ("Constantine's City"), on the site of an ancient Greek polis, Byzantium.

Dedicated with impressive Christian ceremonies in 330, Constantinople was to be the second Rome. It had its own Senate, its own imposing palaces and public buildings, and its own hungry proletariat fed by the bread dole and diverted by chariot races in its enormous Hippodrome. A

Constantine the Great This head was once part of a monumental statue of the emperor at Rome, several times life-size. Such gigantic representations were seldom considered appropriate under the Roman Republic or the Principate, and they suggest the extent to which the late empire's rulers, from Diocletian to his Christian successors, felt they had to employ overkill to impress their subjects. *Alinari / Art Resource, NY.*

few decades after its foundation it even acquired its own Christian patriarch. Constantine plundered the Greco-Roman world of art treasures to adorn his new city and lavished vast resources on its construction. Commanding a superb strategic location, Constantinople would remain the capital of the Eastern Roman—or Byzantine—Empire for well over a thousand years, impregnable behind great landward and seaward walls, and controlling the rich commerce flowing between the Black Sea and the Mediterranean. (See Chapter 6, Map 6-1.)

Constantine's most momentous decision was to adopt Christianity and reverse imperial anti-Christian policies. Like many Christian laity, he put off baptism until his dying moment; that way he could be ruthless with a clearer conscience. But Constantine had been committed to Christianity ever since—as he saw it—Christ gave him victory in 312. Not only did he legalize Christianity and favor it in many none-too-subtle ways, but he intervened freely in church disputes over organization and doctrine. He built many churches—above all in Constantinople, Rome, and Jerusalem—with funds confiscated from pagan temples. But he did not attack Jews or pagans head-on. Pagans still constituted the majority of the Roman population, including the army, and Constantine tolerated their cults. The Christian God was his personal deity, but not until the end of the fourth century did his successors make Christianity the empire's official religion.

Various explanations have been offered for Constantine's conversion. But there is no reason to doubt that he was, in fourth-century terms, sincere. By his time the empire's mood was deeply religious, and we must not impose on him the mentality of a modern rationalist, skeptic, or cynic. There were no agnostics in the fourth century. Like Diocletian, Constantine based his rule on divine sanction; but since the Christians' God had proved the stronger, he replaced Jupiter.

FROM THE CHRISTIAN EMPIRE TO THE FALL OF ROME

Constantine's conversion made it possible for the church to grow rapidly under imperial protection. In the generations following Constantine's conversion, Christianity had the support of an almost unbroken line of Christian emperors. The Church of the Holy Sepulcher (over Jesus' tomb) in Jerusalem and several great churches in Rome were built at imperial expense. The crucifixion of criminals ceased (it seemed impious to punish lawbreakers by the same means that Jesus had redeemed the world), but malefactors were still thrown to wild animals in the arena. Fights to the death by gladiators gave way under Christian influence to the less bloodthirsty sport of chariot racing—but only at the end of the fourth century. And infanticide, now prohibited by law, became disreputable, although it did not

A Constantinian-Era Roman Church   Churches were an architectural innovation of the late third and early fourth centuries. Pagan temples had served mainly as a god's shrine, and worship took place outside it. Christian churches, like Jewish synagogues, had to accommodate large numbers for indoor worship. As a result, the imperial palace (basilica) was taken as a model. This photograph shows St. Sabina's, built in Constantine's time but greatly embellished in later centuries.   *Scala / Art Resource, NY.*

generally cease until around 500. Such a crude means of population control was as repugnant to Christians as it had always been to Jews, and it was losing much of its social utility in an era of declining population. Slavery continued, for the imperial economy could not survive without it. The church urged its members to free their slaves, but few, including clergy, complied: They would have suffered economic ruin.

In 312, perhaps 10 percent of the inhabitants of the empire were Christians, with a majority concentrated in the east; by the century's end, Christians were the majority. Rural areas held out longest, but even there the great Christian landowners (now including churches, bishops, and monasteries) used both persuasion and coercion to get their slaves and peasants to exchange pagan for Christian worship. In the cities, rich and poor—but especially the ambitious, thinking more of the imperial favor they would gain than of the salvation they might win[17]—flocked to the church.

No longer persecuted, Christianity became official, conventional, respectable—and the persecutor. Of course, it lost some of its former spiritual intensity in the process. Time-serving hypocrites abounded; aristocratic families

supplied most bishops and patriarchs. And as so often happens in human institutions, external victory enflamed internal disputes.

Doctrinal Wrangles and Christian Triumph

"No wild beasts are such enemies to mankind as are most Christians to each other," said one fourth-century historian. In theological controversies, as in so many other matters affecting the fourth-century church, the Christian emperors played a determining role. Some crucial doctrines that most Christians today take for granted owe their formulation to political decisions by fourth-century emperors.

In Constantine's day Christianity faced two great internal debates. One had grown directly out of the Great Persecution: What should be done about Christians—particularly priests and bishops—who had saved their lives by sacrificing to the pagan gods? In North Africa, that hotbed of puritanical, sectarian Christianity, the Donatist movement arose, demanding that backsliders be permanently banned from Christian fellowship and that baptism and the Eucharist administered by offending clergy be declared invalid.

Although most clergy agreed that substantial penances should be imposed on those who had denied Christ under persecution, the prevailing view in the church was that forgiveness should ultimately prevail. The alternative would raise the bar so high that only the most saintly would be

---

[17] In any culture, such people usually consider themselves important enough for the heavenly powers to look kindly upon them; getting their worldly due is what counts.

considered Christians. That, of course, is exactly what the Donatists wanted; but that was no way to run a church that Constantine intended to be a rock on which the Roman Empire rested. He unequivocally backed the mainstream clerics in condemning Donatism as a heresy, and until well into the fifth century (when they were finally either wiped out or driven underground) the Donatists felt the same persecuting zeal from their fellow Christians and the Roman state that they had suffered under Diocletian and his pagan successors.

The second great Constantinian-era debate focused on that elusive question raised but not settled during the third century: Exactly what was the relationship between God the Father and God the Son? Even while the Great Persecution raged, a priest in Alexandria named Arius had proposed that the Son was "of a similar substance" with the Father, but was not "of the same substance." (In Greek, the difference literally amounts to one letter—ι, or *iota*—in the spelling of the crucial word.) On this seemingly trivial matter hinged vast implications, for Arius held that the Son was subordinate to the Father—something less than fully God. To his opponents, Arius's belief in Christ's subordination to God the Father perverted the true doctrine of the Trinity: the equality and co-divinity of Father, Son, and Holy Spirit.

Within a few months after he had crushed his pagan co-emperor Licinius and reunited the Roman world under his direct rule, Constantine decided to heal the Arian-Trinitarian dispute. In 325, he personally presided over Christendom's first *ecumenical* ("universal") council of bishops at Nicaea, conveniently near his own residence. He did not fully understand the theological positions at stake, but advocates of the Trinitarian position managed to win his support. With imperial backing, a strongly anti-Arian creed was adopted almost unanimously. The three divine Persons of the Trinity were declared equal: Jesus Christ was "begotten, not made, of one substance with the Father."

But Constantine was no theologian. In later years he waffled, sometimes favoring Arians, sometimes condemning them, and imperial policy remained ambiguous throughout most of the fourth century. One of his successors embraced Arianism and, had he lived long enough, might have made it official doctrine. Arius himself died (reputedly by divine vengeance, in a public latrine) in 336, but battles between Arians and anti-Arians boiled incessantly in Alexandria, Constantinople, and other cities throughout the fourth century, with hungry mobs, demagogic preachers, and grasping politicians giving no quarter.

Only one of Constantine's fourth-century successors, Julian "the Apostate" (reigned 361–363), reverted to paganism. Julian had been raised a Christian, but his disgust with doctrinal infighting and his love of Neoplatonic philosophy induced him, on inheriting the crown, to reveal himself as the champion of Rome's old gods. An antiquarian pedant (people laughed at the philosopher's beard that

he grew and the learned books he read), Julian hoped to reinvigorate the pagan priesthoods with morality and charity—to show that they rather than the quarreling Christian priests represented true goodness. He did not persecute Christians (they were by now too strong), but he did favor anti-Christians in his appointments, and his sacrifices killed so many cattle that jokes circulated about the empire running out of livestock. He wrote a book against Christianity, admired Jews, and began to rebuild the Jerusalem Temple. But he reigned only two years. He died in battle against the Persians, reputedly sighing "You have conquered, O Galilean!" Except for one ephemeral usurper, all later emperors were Christian autocrats. Pressure on pagans, heretics, and Jews grew heavier.

The decisive blows fell in the last two decades of the fourth century. The sternly orthodox Theodosius I (reigned 378–395) banned the teachings of the Arians and broke their power, making orthodox Christianity the official religion of the empire. Theodosius outlawed paganism as well. By this time, decades of imperial disfavor had weakened paganism enough for a frontal assault to succeed. Just as Diocletian had done against the Christians at the beginning of the fourth century, so now pagan sacred writings were burned, pagan places of worship were destroyed, and pagan rites were banned. Mobs, usually whipped up by Christian monks and clergy, smashed "idols" (probably destroying some great works of art in the process), tore down temples and shrines, wrecked sacred groves, and tortured and lynched pagan priests and priestesses. When zealous Christians had done such things earlier in the fourth century, pagan mobs had fought back; now, defenders of the old ways could hardly resist, and the army, still not completely Christianized, had orders not to interfere.

As this desacralization raged from Gaul to Egypt, the heavens stayed quiet; the ground did not tremble. Far from answering insults to their power with cosmic rage, Rome's old gods meekly shuffled away. This was probably the key to the Christian triumph. Seeing Zeus and Dionysus, Venus, Mars, and the innumerable divinities of hearth and field succumb to Christian vandalism with hardly a whimper, ordinary Greeks and Romans drew the same conclusion that had occurred to Constantine at the beginning of the fourth century: The Christian God *must* be stronger.

The Price of Triumph

Yet the Christian triumph, won with political force backed by physical coercion, was not complete. Two significant non-Christian religious movements survived the death of the pagan gods. First was the still-expanding Manichaean faith, which had also seen the Greco-Roman divinities as its deadly foes. It remained an alternative to Christianity well into the fifth century, competing for the allegiance of the young St. Augustine, the man who became Latin-speaking Christianity's greatest spokesman—and, as we shall see in later chapters, would resurface in different guise to challenge medieval Christianity. Second, Judaism was not outlawed along with paganism, although Jews suffered legal discrimination. Conversions from Christianity to Judaism were forbidden, and Jews were barred from all but the most burdensome of municipal offices. Such laws foreshadowed the treatment Jews would receive in medieval Christendom and Islam. But they also attested to the wealth and internal strength that the Jewish community retained in the fourth-century Mediterranean world. The Temple remained a ruin amid Jerusalem's new Christian churches, but Judaism's consolidation around its synagogues and rabbis continued.

Another, more subtle, shadow lay across the Christian triumph. Fourth-century conversions tended to mean following the path of least resistance, and the new converts were usually a far cry from the earlier saints and martyrs. Former pagans might concede that Christian magic was greater than that of the old gods, but they still had to internalize Christian values and piety.

Despite Emperor Theodosius's best efforts at repression, enforcing orthodoxy proved difficult. Old heresies lingered, and vigorous new ones arose. Even Arianism survived—not among the citizens of the empire but among the Germanic peoples beyond Rome's frontier. For during the mid-fourth century, at a time when Arianism was still strong in the empire, several Germanic tribes had been converted to Christianity by Arian missionaries, and the trinitarian policies of Theodosius I had no effect on them. Consequently, when in time these tribes poured into the Western Roman Empire and established successor states on its ruins, they found themselves divided from their Roman subjects not only by language and custom but by a religious chasm as well.

Moreover, by accepting imperial support against paganism and heresy, the church sacrificed much of its moral freedom. As a Christian, Constantine could no longer claim divinity, but Christian writers invested him with an almost godly status. For Eusebius, a bishop who wrote *Life of Constantine* as well as a history of the early church that remains a major historical source, the converted emperor was the thirteenth apostle, the master of all churches, the divinely chosen ruler of the Roman people. His commanding position in ecclesiastical affairs was clear in his domination of the Council of Nicaea, and the ups and downs of Arianism in the following decades depended largely on the whims of his successors.

In the eastern part of the empire this glorification of the imperial office ripened into the notion that the emperor was God's agent on earth. Church and state tended to merge under the sacred authority of the emperors at Constantinople. Indeed, the Christianization and sanctification of the imperial office were potent forces in winning for the eastern emperors the allegiance and commitment of the masses of their subjects. Religious loyalty to the Chris-

tian emperor provided indispensable nourishment to the eastern Roman state over the ensuing centuries. Conversely, widespread hostility toward imperial orthodoxy in districts of the Near East dominated by heretical groups resulted in the alienation and eventual loss to Islam of several of Byzantium's wealthiest provinces (see Chapter 6).

Christian emperors got less veneration in the western provinces, where as the fifth century dawned the imperial system was visibly failing. Western churchmen were beginning to realize that Christianity was not irrevocably bound to the fortunes of Rome. Gradually the Western church began to assert its independence of state control—with the result that church and state in medieval western Europe never fused.

The Desert Saints

Many ardent Christians felt abandoned by a church that no longer challenged them to heroic self-sacrifice—one that embraced so many opportunists. In Egypt, even before the Great Persecution, a Christian peasant named Anthony (251–356) was either inspired or frightened by learning of Jesus' call to give up everything and follow him. Taking the Gospel literally, St. Anthony became the most famous hermit of his generation, and inspired many imitators. (Some felt driven to the desert not only by hope for salvation but also by hopelessness at struggling to wring a living from a minuscule plot of overtaxed land; following Christ also meant fleeing the tax collector.) Anthony, like most other "desert fathers," preferred to resist the devil and receive ecstatic visions alone. But the world did not leave such saints in solitude. As he grew older (he would live to 105), Anthony was sometimes persuaded to visit Alexandria as a preacher, and his advice was eagerly sought in theological disputes. So, too, St. Simeon Stylites (ca. 390–459), a Syrian hermit famous for living his last forty years atop a pillar 50 feet high, became a veritable Christian oracle, attracting crowds eager for his blessing and his advice. After his death a military honor guard conducted his remains in triumph to his tomb, where they continued to work miracles.

Not all these new saints were hermits in desolate fastnesses. Informal monastic communities also arose, their members inspiring each other (or competing?) in self-mortification. Women, as well, felt the call to austerity and solitude. The communities that they established grew and flourished, offering not only an opportunity to save their souls but also a freedom from male authority previously unknown to all but the most privileged women of the ancient world.

The New Art

In the era of the Christian empire, the Greco-Roman visual arts were transformed by a sense of otherworldliness

Fourth-Century Fresco Painting of Christ This painting, from the Roman catacombs, retains the naturalistic style of late Roman art, but it also takes on the otherworldly atmosphere that will dominate Byzantine and early medieval Western religious painting. Note the halo and the Alpha-Omega (A-ω) symbolism around Christ's head; halos were not used in earlier Christian art, and the A-ω image has its origin in the Gospel of John, where Jesus describes himself as "the Alpha and the Omega, the beginning and the end." *Pontificia Commisione di Archeologia Sacra.*

that had long been gathering momentum. Greek classicism had undergone important modifications in the Hellenistic age and again during the Principate. In the late empire, otherworldliness transformed the classical spirit.

There had always been a spiritual-mystical element in Greco-Roman culture, coexisting with the earthly and concrete. Now the mystical element grew far stronger. The better minds turned to religious thought, spiritual fulfillment, and individual salvation. Artists and their patrons grew less interested in showing physical perfection than in portraying the inner person. The new Christian art depicted slender, heavily robed figures with solemn faces and deep eyes—windows into the soul. Techniques of perspective, which the artists of classical antiquity had developed to a fine degree, mattered less to the artists of the late empire (as they have mattered less to twentieth-century artists). Minimizing physical realism, they embellished their works with rich, dazzling colors that stimulated in the beholder a sense of heavenly radiance and spiritual grandeur. Here was an art vastly different from that of Greek antiquity, with different techniques and different goals, yet just as successful as the art of the Athenian golden age, and more fundamentally original than anything the Roman Empire had done before.

Doctors of the Latin Church

Constantine's conversion hastened the fusion between Christianity and Greco-Roman culture. During the generations following his death, the process was brought to completion by three celebrated scholar-saints—Ambrose, Jerome, and Augustine—honored in later generations as the "Doctors of the Latin Church." Working when Christianization of the Roman state was far advanced but before the Western Roman Empire's intellectual vigor waned, they used their mastery of Greco-Roman thought to interpret the Christian faith. The writings of these three men exerted a commanding influence on succeeding generations of Latin-speaking Christians.

Although Ambrose, Jerome, and Augustine made their chief impact as thinkers, all three were immersed in political and ecclesiastical affairs. St. Ambrose (ca. 340–397) was bishop of Milan, which by the later fourth century had replaced Rome as the western imperial capital. He was famed for his eloquence and administrative skill, for his vigor in defending trinitarian orthodoxy against Arianism, and for the ease and mastery with which he adapted the literary traditions of Cicero and Vergil and the philosophy of Plato to Christian purposes. Significantly, he was the first major churchman to assert that in the realm of morality the emperor himself is accountable to the Christian priesthood. When Emperor Theodosius I massacred seven thousand rebellious inhabitants of Thessalonika in a single day, Ambrose barred him from the church in Milan until he had publicly and humiliatingly repented. Ambrose's bold stand and Theodosius's submission set a long-remembered precedent for the principle of ecclesiastical superiority in questions of faith and morals.

St. Jerome (ca. 340–420) was the most celebrated biblical scholar of his time. He was a restless, troubled man with a touch of acid in his tongue who once told an opponent, "You have the will to lie, good sir, but not the skill to lie." Rich enough to wander far and wide through the empire, he lived in Rome for a time, then fled the worldly city to found a monastery in Bethlehem. Jerome's monks devoted themselves to the copying of Latin manuscripts, a task that would be carried on by countless monks in the medieval centuries and that, in the long run, resulted in the preservation of important works of Greco-Roman antiquity that would otherwise have perished.

Jerome feared that his love of the classics might dilute his Christian fervor. In a dream, Jesus banished him from heaven thundering, "You are a Ciceronian, not a Christian!" For a time Jerome renounced all pagan writings, but he was much too smitten by the charms of classical literature to persevere. In the end he concluded that Greco-Roman literature might properly serve the Christian faith.

Jerome's supreme achievement lay in scriptural commentary and translation. It was he who produced the translation of the Bible from its original Hebrew and Greek into Latin. His version, called the Vulgate, would be the standard biblical text for medieval western Europe, although it contained substantial translation errors.

St. Augustine of Hippo (354–430) was the foremost Christian philosopher of Roman antiquity. As bishop of Hippo he was deeply involved in the political-religious problems of his age. Like Jerome, he worried about the dangers of pagan culture, finally concluding, much as Jerome did, that Greco-Roman learning, although not to be enjoyed for its own sake, might properly be used to elucidate the faith.

Augustine was the chief architect of medieval theology. Even more than his contemporaries he succeeded in fusing Christian doctrine with Greek thought—especially the philosophy of Plato and the Neoplatonists.

Plato had held that abstract ideas were more important than tangible things (see Chapter 3). The Neoplatonist Plotinus, as we have seen, taught that sparks of the divine One—true reality itself—showered down on human souls. As a young pagan intellectual, Augustine had been deeply impressed with Neoplatonism and had studied Plotinus in Latin. When he converted to Christianity, Augustine "baptized" Plato and Neoplatonism but combined them with the fierce moral intensity that had dominated North African Christianity since Tertullian at the beginning of the third century. As a Platonist, Augustine stressed the primacy of ideas or archetypes over material objects, but instead of locating these ideals in the abstract Platonic heaven or Plotinus's pagan One, he said that they were in the mind of God. The human mind had access to the archetypes through an act of God that Augustine called "divine illumination."

Augustine not only vigorously defended the Christian orthodoxy of his day; he virtually *defined* orthodoxy. The nature of the Trinity, the question of evil in a world created by God, the special character of the Christian priesthood, and the nature of free will and **predestination**—all received from him statements that the medieval Latin-speaking church would regard as divinely inspired.

The most influential of his vast outpouring of books, *The City of God*, was prompted by the barbarians' sack of Rome in 410, which pagans (still numerous) ascribed to Rome's desertion of its old gods. Augustine responded by advancing a Christian theory of history in which he interpreted human development not in political or economic terms but in moral terms. As the first Christian philosopher of history, Augustine drew heavily on the historical insights of the ancient Hebrews (see Chapter 1). Like the prophets, he asserted that kingdoms and empires rose and fell according to a divine plan that lay forever beyond human comprehension. Augustine rejected the idea, common in antiquity, that history was an endless series of cycles. He argued instead that history was moving toward a divinely appointed goal. Our modern "linear" view of history—the unfolding of progress—is simply a secularized reworking of Augustine's thought.

The salvation of individual souls, *The City of God* maintains, depends not on the fortunes of Rome but the grace of God. And, Augustine said, if we look at history from the moral standpoint—from the standpoint of souls—we see not the clash of armies or the rivalry of states but a far more fundamental struggle between good and evil, which has raged through history and rages even now in each soul. Humanity is divided into two classes: those who live in God's grace and those who do not. The former belong to Augustine's "City of God," the latter to "the Earthly City." Citizens of the two cities are hopelessly intermixed in this world, but they will be separated at death by eternal salvation or damnation. Only God could know what effect Rome's decline would have on the City of God. Perhaps the effect would be beneficial; perhaps even irrelevant.

Augustine set forth a doctrine of the priestly office's special sacramental power amid violent efforts by the North African church authorities to destroy the Donatist movement—efforts that he fully endorsed. The priestly office, he said, superseded the character of the individual priest, and the power that God had entrusted to the church was never affected by the sins of its clergy. Throughout the Middle Ages, this would be the church's retort to every heretic who claimed that corrupt priests could not validly administer the sacraments.

Augustine ranks with Paul as one of Christianity's seminal minds. His pronouncements on priestly power and church authority remain a keystone of Roman Catholicism. His Christian Platonism governed medieval Western theology until well into the twelfth century and remains influential in Christian thought today. His emphasis on divine grace and predestination, although softened considerably in medieval times, reemerged in the sixteenth century to dominate early Protestant doctrine. And his theory of the two cities, although often in simplified form, had an enormous influence on Western historical and political thought over the next millennium.

Ambrose, Jerome, and Augustine were at once synthesizers and innovators. The last great minds of the Western Roman Empire, they operated at a level of intellectual sophistication that Christian western Europe would not regain for seven hundred years. The strength of the classical tradition that underlies medieval Christianity and Western civilization owes much to the fact that these men, and others like them, found it possible to be both Christians and Ciceronians.

East and West, "Decline and Fall"

Ever since Diocletian, the Roman imperial office had usually been divided between a western and an eastern emperor, and by the close of the fourth century the split had become

THE HUMAN EXPERIENCE

St. Augustine of Hippo

In his *Confessions*—the first major autobiography ever written—Augustine (354–430) described his long intellectual and moral journey along a twisting path from youthful hedonism to Christian piety. He did so in the form of a long prayer—a confession to God—written in the hope that others, lost as he once was, might be led to Christianity.

Augustine told of his dissolute boyhood and early manhood in the North African portion of the Roman Empire. Despite the prayers and admonitions of his Christian mother, Monica, he rejected her faith. He took a mistress, who bore him a son. He studied philosophy and rhetoric. And he drifted from one creed to another. As a young student of the classics, he was an ardent pagan Neoplatonist. Finding this rarefied philosophy too abstract, he turned to the radical doubt of Skepticism. Then, for a while, Manichaeanism offered what seemed to be the most plausible answer to the question that tortured him most of his life: Why does God permit evil? Not until he was thirty-two years old did he convert to Christianity.

Augustine's conversion occurred in stages, while he was teaching rhetoric in Milan. Out of curiosity, he went to hear the preaching of Milan's eloquent and renowned Christian bishop, Ambrose, and he was profoundly moved. "I came to damn," Augustine said, "and stayed to praise."

Nevertheless, Augustine was not yet prepared to abandon his life of wine and women. While in Milan he became betrothed to a wealthy heiress not yet of marriageable age, and out of respect for his betrothal he parted from the mistress who had borne him a son. But as one of Augustine's mid-Victorian biographers discreetly remarks, "Neither the pain of this parting nor consideration for his not yet marriageable bride prevented him from forming a fresh connection

of the same kind." Augustine prayed to God to deliver him from his slavery to the pleasures of the flesh; but then added, "Let me wait a little longer."

But Ambrose's sermons and Augustine's own intellectual and spiritual quest were drawing him more and more deeply into the Christian religion, and the tension between his growing faith and the worldliness of his life was becoming unbearable. The great emotional crisis of his life occurred late in the summer of 386, when a friend told him about the development and spread of Christian monasticism, and how two young imperial officials, betrothed as Augustine was, had abandoned the world and the prospect of marriage to become monks. Profoundly moved, Augustine said to his friend, "What's the matter with us? What does this story mean? These two men have none of our education, yet they rise up and storm the gates of heaven while we, for all our learning, lie here wallowing in this world of flesh and blood."

Overcome, Augustine rushed from the house: "I now found myself driven by the torment in my breast to take refuge in the garden, where nobody could interrupt that fierce struggle, in which I was my own opponent, until it reached its conclusion." Augustine tore at his hair and beat his forehead. His past sins seemed to speak to him in tempting whispers: Did he really intend to renounce them forever? His conscience countered: "Close your ears to the unclean whispers of your body." Then, as Augustine reports, "a great storm broke within me, bringing with it a deluge of tears." He flung himself beneath a fig tree, continuing to weep, when he heard a child's voice repeating a phrase over and over again: "Take it and read, take it and read."

In the belief that those words were a divine command, Augustine

sought out his copy of Paul's Epistles, opened it at random, and read a passage from the Epistle to the Romans:

> No drunken orgies, no promiscuity or licentiousness, and no strife or jealousy. Let your armor be the Lord Jesus Christ, and forget about satisfying your bodies with all their lusts.

"I had neither the desire nor the need to read further," Augustine wrote. "As I finished the sentence, as though the light of peace had been poured into my heart, all the shadows of doubt dispersed."

Augustine gave up his wealthy bride-to-be, his sex life, and his teaching career. St. Ambrose baptized him in Milan the following Easter, A.D. 387, to the overwhelming joy of his mother Monica, who was at his side.

Subsequently returning to his native North Africa, Augustine formed a small religious community and headed it for a time. His writings were by now winning him fame throughout the Western Empire. In the 390s he was dragged unwillingly into church administration, being appointed bishop of the important North African port city of Hippo. There he produced a great quantity of literary and philosophical works of immeasurable importance, including the *Confessions* and, much later, the *City of God*.

As he wrote, Augustine was also occupied with the day-to-day cares of his diocese and his flock. His contribution to religious thought arises not from the dispassionate working out of an abstract system of theology but rather from his responses to the urgent issues of the moment. One such issue was the survival of the Roman Empire itself. And by strange coincidence, in A.D. 430, within months of the death of the man who wrote the *City of God*, the Vandals had sacked his episcopal city of Hippo. ❖

permanent. From then on, although the empire continued to be regarded as a single unit, one emperor ruled the eastern half from Constantinople while another presided over the western half—no longer from Rome but from some more strategically situated capital, first Milan, then Ravenna.

The political split reflected a cultural and linguistic division of long standing. Use of Latin had spread across the western provinces, but Greek had remained the major language in the east. (The educated elite throughout the empire were usually bilingual.) The eastern half of the empire had been civilized far longer than North Africa and Europe—far longer than Rome itself. The east contained the bulk of the population; its agriculture was dominated less by owners of vast plantations who, in the west, resisted imperial taxation and, to a degree, imperial authority. Eastern cities were larger, more numerous, and more commercially active than the newer ones of the west, which suffered from an unfavorable balance of trade.

During the fourth and fifth centuries, the west's balance of trade with the east grew worse than ever. In exchange for eastern silks, spices, jewels, and grain, the west had little to offer except slaves, hunting dogs, and a diminishing hoard of gold coins. Thus, with the coming of large-scale Germanic invasions in the fifth century, the Eastern Roman Empire managed to survive while the political superstructure of the western provinces disintegrated.

The catastrophic "decline and fall" of the Roman Empire has fascinated historians across the centuries, for it involves not only the collapse of one of humanity's most impressive and enduring states but also the twilight of Greco-Roman civilization itself. From his elitist and antireligious perspective in the eighteenth-century **Enlightenment,** the great historian Edward Gibbon saw Rome's fall as "the triumph of barbarism and religion." In the two centuries since Gibbon, many other reasons have been proposed (no less than 210 different causes according to a recent survey). They include climatic changes, diseases, bad ecological habits, sex orgies, slavery, Christianity—even too many hot baths (which supposedly destroyed sperm) and lead poisoning from Rome's water pipes. None of them makes much sense. Classical civilization began and ended with slavery, and it was rather less common in the late empire than in the Principate. Christianity had deeper roots in the east than in the west, yet the Eastern Roman Empire carried on for another millennium. Greeks and Romans had enjoyed hot baths for centuries, with no discernible effect on male abilities to beget children. As for orgies, the spectacular ones occurred under the pagan Principate: Christian conversion made them unstylish, and the fifth-century invasions came long after the age of orgies had passed. One historian bizarrely blamed the fall of Rome on homosexuality—which was much more accepted in fifth-century B.C. Greece than in fifth-century A.D. Rome, and which might more plausibly be associated with the rise than the demise of classical civilization.

The best explanation for Rome's collapse in the west involves the failure of the Roman economy to change or expand, and the parasitic nature of western cities. (All this may have been exacerbated by a global cooling trend during the third and fourth centuries A.D.—although the climate seems to have been warming again after about 400.) Then too, the fifth-century western emperors tended to be less competent than their eastern colleagues, and more open to the hazardous policy of filling their armies with Germanic troops under Germanic generals. The first-century Roman Empire had been sufficiently resilient to endure the likes of Caligula and Nero; the far weaker Western Roman Empire of the fifth century could not survive Honorius and Romulus Augustulus.

The riddle of Rome's "decline and fall" will never be solved to everyone's satisfaction; indeed, the question is misleading. For Rome did not literally "fall." Instead, it made an immense strategic withdrawal from its less productive western provinces to the wealthier, long-civilized eastern Mediterranean. Some historians consider the real mystery to be why the Western Roman Empire lasted as long as it did.

The political collapse culminated in the deposition of the last Western emperor in A.D. 476; but the true period of crisis was the chaotic third century, when the empire nearly disintegrated. Viewed against the background of the third-century anarchy, the work of reconstruction under Diocletian and Constantine seems a remarkable achievement. The strong imperial government that emerged at that time became the basis of the Byzantine state for centuries thereafter. But in the west the reforms succeeded only temporarily. The body politic's death was staved off, but its disease festered uncured.

During the generations after Constantine, the economic problems that had plagued the western provinces of the third-century empire intensified. Instead of buying manufactured objects from major urban centers, various regions of the empire tended to produce them locally, and therefore less efficiently. The aristocracy disdained business, preferring to draw their wealth from great plantations, their status from high public office, and their pleasure from the company of fellow aristocrats.

The Roman economy remained agrarian to the end, and farming techniques advanced very little during the imperial centuries. The Roman plow was adequate but rudimentary, windmills were unknown, and water mills were nowhere near as numerous as in eleventh-century England. Roman landowners, relying on their slaves and coloni, seemed uninterested in labor-saving devices. The horse could not be used as a draft animal because the Roman harness could strangle the animal under a heavy load. Oxen and servile human beings were responsible for powering Roman agriculture.

The economic exhaustion of the Western Roman Empire was accompanied by population decline, runaway inflation, deepening poverty, escalating bureaucracy, and

Late-Empire Roman Agriculture This mosaic from present-day Algeria shows Roman agriculture as it was practiced on a North African estate in the third century A.D., but the scene would have been similar in the fourth and fifth centuries as well. Notice that plows are simply bent sticks scratching the soil, pulled by oxen with ropes around their necks. *German Archaeological Institute, Rome. Neg. 64.737.*

taxation. Only the senatorial aristocracy, a small class of great landowners, managed to prosper. As early as the third century they were withdrawing from civic affairs. Abandoning their town houses and fortifying their country estates, they warded off bandits and tax collectors alike by assembling private armies. Having deserted the cities, the aristocracy would remain an agrarian class for the next thousand years.

The decline of the city wrecked the urbanized administrative structure of the Western Roman Empire. More than that, it crippled the civic culture of Greco-Roman antiquity. The civilizations of Athens, Alexandria, and Rome could not survive in the fields. It is in the decay of urban society that we find the crucial connecting link between political collapse and cultural transformation. In a very real sense Greco-Roman culture was dying long before the demise of the Western Roman Empire; the deposition of the last Western emperor in 476 was merely a delayed entombment. By then, the rational outlook of Greco-Roman classicism had been transformed. The army and even the civil government had become germanized as desperate emperors, faced with a growing shortage of people and resources, turned more and more to non-Romans to defend their frontiers and keep order. In the end, Germans abounded in the army, entire tribes patrolled the frontiers,

and Germanic military leaders assumed positions of high imperial authority. Survival depended on Germanic defenders holding off Germanic invaders.

Germans, Huns, and the Fall of Rome

Germanic peoples from central and southeastern Europe had long been knocking at the empire's gates.[18] But until the late fourth century, the Romans had always managed eventually to drive the invaders out or absorb them politically. Beginning in the 370s, however, an overtaxed empire faced powerful new Germanic pressures.

The Germanic tribes mostly saw the empire as something to enjoy, not destroy; but their age-long yearning for fair lands across the Roman frontier was suddenly made urgent by the westward thrust of a confederation of nomads that may originally have roamed north of the Great Wall of China. These Huns—for so they were called—were formidable mounted warriors. Sweeping out of the Eurasian plain, they conquered one Germanic tribe after another

---

[18] The evolution of Germanic society before and after the German tribes migrated into the Roman Empire is discussed in Chapter 6.

and turned them into satellites. They subdued the Ostrogoths and made them a subject people. Another Gothic group, known subsequently as the Visigoths, tried to save itself by appealing for sanctuary behind the empire's Danube frontier. The eastern emperor Valens, a devout Arian, sympathized with the Visigoths because they were converts to his brand of Christianity. In 376 he took the unprecedented step of permitting a multitude of Visigoths and associated peoples to cross peacefully into the empire.

Trouble began almost immediately. Crooked imperial officials cheated and abused the Visigoths, who retaliated by going on a rampage. At length Valens himself took the field against them, but his incompetence cost him his army and his life at the battle of Adrianople in 378. Valens's successor, Theodosius I, managed to pacify the Visigoths, but he could not expel them.

When Theodosius died in 395, imperial authority was split between his two young sons. Arcadius, barely eighteen, became emperor in the east; Honorius, a child of

eleven, assumed authority in the west. The two halves would never be rejoined under a single ruler. Not long after Theodosius's death, a new Visigothic leader named Alaric led his people on a second pillaging campaign that threatened Italy itself. In 406 the desperate Western emperor recalled most of his troops from the Rhine frontier to block Alaric's advance. The result was disastrous. In the dead of winter, 406, the Vandals and other Germanic tribes crossed the frozen, ill-guarded Rhine into Gaul. Shortly thereafter the Roman legions abandoned distant Britain, and the island was gradually overrun by Angles, Saxons, and other Germanic war bands (see Map 5-4).

In 408 Emperor Honorius engineered the murder of his ablest general, a man of Vandal ancestry named Stilicho. Honorius, by now in his mid-twenties, was probably mentally retarded. He and his handlers suspected, maybe with reason, that Stilicho's devotion to the imperial cause was less than fervent. But without Stilicho, Italy was virtually defenseless. Honorius and his court barricaded themselves

MAP 5-4
THE BARBARIAN INVASIONS

This or any map showing the movement of barbarian peoples around and into the Roman Empire tends to give an exaggerated impression of military invasions. Some onslaughts—particularly the Huns' and perhaps the Vandals'—are usefully depicted with the thrusting arrows characteristic of modern military actions, but in the case of many others the movements were more akin to migrations over broad expanses of terrain and fairly extended periods of time.

THE HUMAN EXPERIENCE

Attila the Hun, the "Scourge of God"

Attila, leader of the Huns during their invasions of the Roman Empire, is well known but not well loved. His atrocities, reported in hair-raising detail by contemporary Roman observers, were probably no worse than those of the Roman armies. One of the most terrifying things about the Huns was that, being Asian nomads from Mongolia, they did not look like Romans or Germans; they were therefore regarded by people of the West as hideously ugly—short, foul, skinny, low-browed, high-cheeked, and scar-faced. As one contemporary put it, "Their swarthy aspect was fearful and they had a kind of shapeless lump for a head, with pinholes rather than eyes."

Less biased contemporaries described Attila as brown-skinned and broad-chested, with deep eyes, an upturned nose, and hair prematurely gray. He ruled the Huns from 433 to 453, at first jointly with his brother (who vanished under mysterious circumstances). By about 440 he and his horsemen had made themselves virtually supreme over the Germanic tribes of central Europe and had frightened the Eastern Roman Empire into paying an annual tribute. Attila established his capital not far from modern Budapest. A report by an ambassadorial mission from Constantinople in 448 provides a vivid description of Attila and his court. He walked around the wooden buildings of his headquarters with a "dignified strut" and entertained the envoys from Constantinople in his large wooden banquet hall, where attendants served food and drink in silver plates and cups. Attila himself drank from a wooden cup typical of older, less elegant days. At nightfall "torches were lit and two barbarians approached Attila and sang songs they had composed celebrating his victories and brave deeds in war." Afterward Attila retired to his bed, on a raised platform in the same hall, to sleep under "linen sheets and jeweled coverlets." The ambassador's sense of cultural superiority over the newly rich Hun is dimmed by the fact that the mission from Constantinople had hired an assassin to murder Attila. Discovering the plot, he contemptuously sent the envoys home.

In 450 the Roman emperor discontinued making tribute payments to the Huns, but rather than seeking revenge on Constantinople, Attila turned to the vulnerable west. (Rome, too, had walls, but they could not compare to Constantinople's.) Accompanied by his Huns and tributary Germans, he crossed the Rhine in 451. He claimed that he was coming as a kind of Prince Charming to rescue the Roman princess Honoria, who had been put under house arrest for having an affair with a palace chamberlain. In a fit of anger, Honoria had sent her ring to Attila with the plea that he marry her and carry her off to freedom. Although Honoria is said to have been beautiful, Attila's chief motive for coming west was doubtless plunder. His army was met by an allied Roman-Visigothic force near Troyes in central Gaul, where, after a day of mutual carnage, Attila withdrew his warriors from the battlefield and led them home to Pannonia.

In the following year Attila descended on Italy, sacking and pillaging cities as he moved toward Rome. It was at this point that he was confronted by Pope Leo I at the head of a delegation of Roman senators. According to the best account, Pope Leo, "an old man of harmless simplicity, venerable in his gray hair and majestic clothing," was suddenly and miraculously joined by Saints Peter and Paul, swords in their hands and clad in bishops' robes. Whether because of this marvel or because his army was dying from heat and plague, Attila withdrew once again from the Western Roman Empire. He died in 453 during the night following a great banquet celebrating his marriage to a young Germanic woman named Ildico. Perhaps he had too much to drink at the banquet; perhaps Ildico was more than the middle-aged Hun could cope with. There were rumors of violence, but more probably his death was natural and (as one Victorian writer delicately put it) "due to his own intemperate habits." ❖

behind the impregnable marshes of Ravenna, leaving Rome to the mercies of Alaric. In 410 the Visigoths entered the city unopposed, and Alaric let them plunder it for three days.

The sack of Rome devastated imperial morale. "My tongue sticks to the roof of my mouth," wrote St. Jerome on hearing of the catastrophe, "and sobs choke my speech." But in historical perspective the event was merely a single milestone in the Western Roman Empire's disintegration. Leaving Rome to its witless emperor, the Visigoths moved on to southern Gaul and Spain. The kingdom they established there endured until the Muslim conquest in 711.

Meanwhile other Germanic peoples were carving out kingdoms. The Vandals swept through Gaul and Spain and across the Straits of Gibraltar into Africa. In 430, the year of St. Augustine's death, they captured his city, Hippo.

Establishing a North African kingdom, they took to the sea as buccaneers, devastating shipping and sacking coastal cities—including Rome in 455. The Vandal conquest of North Africa cost Rome much of its grain supply, while Vandal piracy shattered the peace of the Mediterranean and crippled what was left of the Western Roman Empire's commerce.

In the mid-fifth century the Huns themselves attacked the west, led by Attila, the "Scourge of God." Defeated by a Roman-Visigothic army in Gaul in 451, the Huns returned the next year, bearing down on Rome and leaving a path of devastation. The Western emperor left Rome undefended, but its bishop, Pope Leo I, somehow persuaded Attila to withdraw from Italy. When the Hunnish leader died soon thereafter, his "empire" collapsed and the Huns vanished from history. They were not mourned.

In its final years the Western Roman Empire, whose jurisdiction now scarcely extended beyond Italy, fell under the control of hard-bitten Germanic military adventurers. Emperors continued to reign for a time, but barbarian generals were the power behind the throne. In 476 the general Odovacar deposed the last emperor—a boy named Romulus Augustulus. Odovacar sent the emperor's crown and related paraphernalia to Constantinople and asserted his sovereignty over Italy by diverting one-third of the agrarian tax revenues to his Germanic troops. Odovacar claimed to rule as an agent of the Eastern emperor, but in fact he was on his own. A few years later the Ostrogoths, now free of Hunnish control and led by an astute king named Theodoric, advanced into Italy. Theodoric invited Odovacar to a peace conference, murdered him, and established his own rule over Italy.

Theodoric and Clovis

Theodoric reigned as king of Italy from 493 to 526. Although apparently illiterate, he respected Roman culture: Arian Ostrogoths and orthodox Romans worked together under his governance, repairing aqueducts, erecting new buildings, and bringing some prosperity back to the long-suffering peninsula. The improving political and economic climate permitted a modest intellectual revival that contributed to the transmission of Greco-Roman culture into the Middle Ages. At a time when the knowledge of Greek was dying out in the west, the philosopher Boethius, a high official in Theodoric's regime, produced Latin translations of Greek philosophical works that were read in western schools for the next five hundred years. Boethius wrote his masterpiece, *The Consolation of Philosophy*, when, fallen from favor, he sat in prison awaiting execution. The book's central theme is that earthly misfortunes cannot affect the inner life of a virtuous individual. Although such a notion is consistent with Christianity, Boethius drew his ideas primarily from Plato and the Sto-

ics. Boethius was a Christian, yet he never mentioned Christianity explicitly in his *Consolation*. Nevertheless, the work remained immensely popular throughout the Middle Ages.

Theodoric's secretary, Cassiodorus, was another scholar of distinction (though incorrigibly long-winded). A wealthy Roman aristocrat, Cassiodorus spent his later years as abbot of a monastery that he had built on his own lands in southern Italy. Like Jerome, he set his monks to copying and preserving the literary works of antiquity, both Christian and pagan.

While Theodoric ruled Ostrogothic Italy, another Germanic king, Clovis[19] (reigned 481–511), was carving out a Frankish kingdom in the former Roman province of Gaul. Although far less romanized than Theodoric, Clovis possessed a keen instinct for political survival. Going well beyond Theodoric, he adopted the straightforward policy of murdering all possible rivals. Gregory of Tours, a sixth-century bishop and historian, quotes him as saying, "Oh woe, for I travel among strangers and have none of my kinfolk to help me!" But Gregory adds, "He did not refer to their deaths out of grief, but craftily, to see if he could bring to light some new relative to kill."

It may seem odd that good Bishop Gregory approved wholeheartedly of Clovis's rule. That savage chieftain is pictured in Gregory's *History of the Franks* as one who "walked before God with an upright heart and did what was pleasing in his sight." The explanation is that Clovis, untouched by Arianism, was converted directly from Germanic paganism to orthodox Christianity. He respected and favored the churches, whereas other Germanic rulers were handing them over to the Arians. Clovis himself regarded Christianity as magic that helped him win battles (much as Constantine had done), but the church supported him as a hero of Christian orthodoxy. The French still admire him.

Another reason for Clovis's good press was that he maintained relatively warm relations with the old landholding aristocracy (to which Bishop Gregory belonged). Because of the depopulated condition of the countryside, there were adequate lands for Frank and Gallo-Roman alike. The great landowning families of Roman times generally remained in place to enjoy their fields and their bishoprics, and to serve the Frankish regime as high officials. For them, Clovis's victory was a mere coup d'état.

In succeeding generations Frankish and Gallo-Roman landowners, sharing a common religion, fused through intermarriage into a single aristocratic order. Slowly, the royal name "Clovis" evolved into "Louis," and "the Franks" became "the French." And friendship between the Frankish

---

[19]Clovis is the French form of his name. He called himself by the Germanic name Clodovic.

monarchy and the Christian church developed into a cornerstone of medieval European politics.

Europe in A.D. 500

As the sixth century dawned, the Western Roman Empire was only a memory. In its place was a group of Germanic successor states that vaguely prefigured the nations of modern western Europe. Theodoric headed an Ostrogothic-Arian regime in Italy. The orthodox Clovis, busy murdering his kinsmen, was completing the Frankish conquest of Gaul. The Arian Vandals lorded it over a restive orthodox Christian population in North Africa, seizing the wheat plantations and introducing former aristocratic landholders to the joys of field work. The Arian Visigoths were being driven from southern Gaul by the Franks, but they continued to lord it over Spain for the next two centuries. And Angles and Saxons began establishing the small pagan kingdoms in Britain that would one day coalesce into "Angle-Land," or England (see Map 5-5). (Legend had it that the last remnants of Celto-Roman civilization in Britain were defended by a local chieftain, "King Arthur.")

While Germanic kingdoms were establishing themselves in the west, the Roman papacy was beginning to play an important independent role in European society.

We have seen how Pope Leo I (reigned 440–461) assumed the task of protecting the city of Rome from the Huns, thereby winning the moral leadership of Italy. Leo and his successors declared that the Roman popes constituted the highest church authority, and, following the example of St. Ambrose, they insisted on church supremacy over the state in spiritual matters. In proclaiming papal supremacy and ecclesiastical independence, the papacy was wisely disengaging itself from the faltering western emperors. The mighty papacy of the twelfth and thirteenth centuries was yet far off, but it was already foreshadowed in the boldly independent stance of Leo I. The Western Roman Empire might be crumbling, but eternal Rome still claimed the world's allegiance.

CONCLUSION: LATE ANTIQUITY AND THE WESTERN SYNTHESIS

Notwithstanding the collapse of imperial government, the decline of cities, and the victory of a great Near Eastern religion, Greco-Roman culture never really died in the west. It profoundly influenced the fourth-century Christian theologians and, through them, medieval and modern Western thought. Even the Roman administration survived, through the Middle Ages and beyond, in the orga-

MAP 5-5
EUROPE AND THE MEDITERRANEAN WORLD IN A.D. 500

nizational structure of the church. Just as papal Rome echoed imperial Rome, so too did the ecclesiastical "dioceses" and "provinces" reflect imperial administrative units that had borne identical names. The bishops of the late empire had become deeply involved in imperial governance, participating in numerous civic functions and checking on the activities of Roman officials. When the imperial government perished, bishops filled the vacuum by assuming political control of their dioceses, maintaining food supplies and supervising the upkeep of fortifications. Since most bishops now came from the old senatorial aristocracy, such duties seemed natural.

The classical past was the source of repeated cultural revivals great and small down through the centuries: in the era of Charlemagne, in the High Middle Ages, in the Renaissance and the Reformation, and in Enlightenment neoclassicism. Directly or indirectly, Roman law shaped all of Western jurisprudence. Memories of democratic Athens and republican Rome haunted and inspired the framers of modern constitutions, including our own. Latin remained the language of educated west Europeans for well over a thousand years, evolved into the modern Romance languages, and gave structure, suppleness, and thousands of words to other European tongues, including English. The dream of recreating Rome's *imperium* would obsess empire builders from Charlemagne to Mussolini.

Before the Roman collapse in the west, Christianity absorbed and turned to its own purposes much of Rome's heritage, carrying on the Roman administrative and legal tradition into the medieval and modern worlds. The Christian empire based in Byzantium preserved its Roman and Hellenistic heritage almost intact, and long before it succumbed to the Muslim Ottomans it had passed on this heritage to at least a dozen nations in eastern Europe and the Caucasus. In the west, Rome's secular leadership gave way to the spiritual leadership of the Roman church. The pope assumed the old republican and imperial title of *pontifex maximus* ("supreme priest") and in the organizational sense the medieval church has been well described as a ghost of the Roman Empire. Yet it was far more than that, for the church gave the disfranchised majority a sense of individual worth—what Cicero had called *humanitas*—that the Roman Empire had never provided.

One baleful consequence of the story that this chapter has traced must be acknowledged: the bitter estrangement of Christians and Jews. As the Jewish Christians of the first century fused with their Greek- and Latin-speaking converts, and as Judaism reconstituted itself around the rabbis, mutual curses and hatreds deepened. And because Christians took over the secular power of the Roman state and its modern heirs, they gained the power to act on their religious prejudice.

Selected Reading

Sources

Bible. For early Christianity, the New Testament is indispensable.

Eusebius. *Ecclesiastical History*, trans. G. A. Williamson (1965).

Gregory of Tours. *History of the Franks*, trans. Ernest Bréhaut (1965).

Josephus. *The Jewish War* and *Jewish Antiquities*, trans. G. A. Williamson (1961). Josephus was a Jewish general who, during the Great Revolt, went over to the Romans. Later, he wrote these two important books, which are important for understanding first-century Judea, including the lifetime of Jesus. Josephus's accounts need to be read with caution, as can be done in these scholarly translations.

St. Augustine. *Confessions*, trans. Vernon J. Bourke (1953); and *City of God*, trans. Henry Bettenson (1984).

Roman Religion, Judaism, Early Christianity, and the Conversion of the Empire

Becker, Jürgen. *Paul: Apostle to the Gentiles* (1993). Trans. O. C. Dean Jr. The most recent authoritative study of this great, contradictory figure.

Bernstein, Alan E. *The Formation of Hell: Death and Retribution in the Ancient and Early Christian Worlds* (1993). A fascinating exploration of the idea of hell among ancient Jews and Greco-Romans and in early Christianity.

Brown, Peter. *Augustine of Hippo: A Biography* (1967). A wise and learned study, extraordinarily sensitive to Augustine and his world.

Chadwick, Henry. *Augustine* (1986). A brief, lucid introduction to Augustine's thought.

———. *Early Christian Thought and the Classical Tradition: Studies in Justin, Clement, and Origen* (1966; paperback, 1984); and *The Early Church* (1967). Illuminating accounts by a major scholar.

Daniélou, Jean, and Henri Marrou. *The First Six Hundred Years* (1964). Trans. Vincent Cronin. This major study, the first volume in The Christian Centuries Series, combines scholarly objectivity with a Roman Catholic perspective.

Dunn, James D. G. *The Parting of the Ways: Between Christianity and Judaism and Their Significance for the Character of Christianity* (1991). A learned study of how first-century Christianity separated from Judaism.

Ferguson, John. *The Religions of the Roman Empire* (1970). A valuable comprehensive study.

Frend, W. H. C. *The Rise of Christianity* (1984). A massive and detailed narrative from the time of Jesus through the establishment of the Christian empire—perhaps the best current account.

Grant, Michael. *Jesus: An Historian's Review of the Gospels* (1977). A scholarly reconstruction, with which not all will agree, stressing that Jesus was perceived as a failure by most of his contemporaries.

———. *The Jews in the Roman World* (1973). Thorough and judicious.

Lane Fox, Robin. *Pagans and Christians* (1986). A beautifully written, learned, stimulating, and highly original study of the mental worlds of pagans and Christians during the period between the second and fourth centuries A.D.

Liebeschuetz, J. H. W. G. *Continuity and Change in Roman Religion* (1979). Explores the shifts in religious sentiment from the late years of the Roman Republic to St. Augustine.

MacMullen, Ramsey. *Christianizing the Roman Empire, A.D. 100–400* (1984). A succinct survey, engagingly written.

McNamara, Jo Ann. *A New Song: Celibate Women in the First Three Christian Centuries* (1983). A perceptive study, arguing persuasively that the development of communal life for celibate Christian women constituted a dramatically new opportunity for women to adopt a lifestyle previously unavailable to them.

Meeks, Wayne A. *The First Urban Christians: The Social World of the Apostle Paul* (1983). A fascinating, groundbreaking study.

Neusner, Jacob. *Judaism in the Beginning of Christianity* (1984). A major study by one of the leading Jewish scholars of first-century Judaism.

Vermes, Geza. *Jesus the Jew*, 2nd ed. (1983); and *Jesus and the World of Judaism* (1983). Two important books by a major scholar, placing Jesus in the context of the Judaism of his time.

The Later Empire and the Germanic Invasions

Brown, Peter. *The Making of Late Antiquity* (1993). This work, complex yet approachable, amplifies and updates Brown's classic work, *The World of Late Antiquity: A.D. 150–750* (1971), which cast fresh light on social and cultural changes in eastern and western Europe and the Near East. These and others of Brown's works argue persuasively against the traditional notion of a fifth-century break separating the ancient from the medieval world.

Cameron, Averil. *The Later Roman Empire, A.D. 284–430* (1993); and *The Mediterranean World in Late-Antiquity, A.D. 395–600* (1993). Two superb works of original scholarly synthesis, cast in the mold of Peter Brown's concept of "Late Antiquity."

Ferrill, Arther. *The Fall of the Roman Empire: The Military Explanation* (1986). A convincing reexamination.

Gibbon, Edward. *The History of the Decline and Fall of the Roman Empire*, 7 vols., ed. J. B. Bury (1896–1900; repr. 1974). A shortened version of Gibbon's eighteenth-century masterpiece is the one-volume edition edited by D. M. Low (1960).

Goffart, Walter. *Barbarians and Romans, A.D. 418–584: The Techniques of Accommodation* (1980). A provocative work that argues strongly against the idea of the Western Roman Empire sinking under a barbarian deluge and stresses the separateness of individual Germanic groups.

Grant, Michael. *The Climax of Rome: The Final Achievement of the Ancient World, A.D. 161–337* (1968); and *The Fall of The Roman Empire*, 2nd ed. (1990). Two important works that provide revealing insights into Roman social development and change.

Heather, Peter. *Goths and Romans, A.D. 332–489* (1991). Revises older views on the Ostrogoths and Visigoths as distinct, coherent tribes long before their entry into the empire, and shows that the reality was far more complex.

Jones, A. H. M. *The Later Roman Empire, 284–602: A Social, Economic, and Administrative Survey* (1986). A major classic, building on a great body of this scholar's earlier work on the subject.

Krautheimer, Richard. *Three Christian Capitals: Topography and Politics* (1983). A penetrating and highly original study of architecture, society, and culture in late antique Rome, Constantinople, and Milan.

Todd, Malcolm. *The Early Germans* (1992). A readable, sophisticated archaeological and historical study of the Germanic peoples in their "preinvasion" setting, their movements into the empire, and the resulting cultural synthesis.

Van Dam, Raymond. *Leadership and Community in Late Antique Gaul* (1985). An original, persuasive interpretation of the receding imperial administration, the regional and local aristocracy, the evolution of Christian communities and heresies, and the growing social importance of the cult of saints and relics—St. Martin of Tours in particular—in late Roman and early medieval Gaul.

Williams, Stephen. *Diocletian and the Roman Recovery* (1985). An engagingly written portrayal of Diocletian as a masterful ruler who restored a faltering empire.

PART TWO

WESTERN EURASIA IN THE MIDDLE AGES

The "Middle Ages" is the historical label that European historians conventionally attach to the thousand-year period after the disappearance of the Western Roman Empire, from about A.D. 500 to A.D. 1500. When the term *middle ages* was coined several hundred years ago, the implication was clearly that this had been a stagnant period between the past glories of western antiquity and the coming glories of a Europe reborn to progress and achievement.

Chapters 6–10 should thoroughly demolish the notion of medieval European history as a Dark Age during which culture supposedly stagnated and "progress" ceased. This era was, on the contrary, one of the most creative periods in history—the seedbed of modern Western civilization. As we shall see in Chapters 6 and 7, during the early centuries of the Middle Ages, between about 500 and 1050, Europe found itself economically hard pressed, beset by invaders, and (except around the year 800) politically fragmented. However, Chapters 8, 9, and 10 will show how, at about the years 1000–1050, western Europe entered a new, more confident era of economic boom and urbanization. Christianity, whose hold on western Europeans was originally superficial, penetrated into their consciousness. The church became a cohesive international institution. Secular states gained political cohesion and Europe experienced a great literary, artistic, and intellectual flowering. By the twelfth and thirteenth centuries, Western civilization achieved a dynamism that could match any achievements of ancient times.

But from a global perspective, the term *Middle Ages* may beg the question: the middle of *what?* To gain a world-history perspective on the Middle Ages, we should think of western Europe[1] as lying within three concentric circles.

The first circle embraces the lands and peoples that we studied in Part One: the Near East and the Mediterranean

world. In Part One we described this region as the birthplace of Western civilization, whose evolution we traced from the earliest stirrings of civilized life in Mesopotamia and Egypt to the expansion of Roman rule and Greco-Roman culture. As Part Two will show, while the level of civilization in early medieval western Europe was declining sharply, civilization and a highly organized state continued in the Christian East Roman Empire. Over its thousand-year history (until 1453), the East Roman (or Byzantine) Empire experienced several intense crises, but for much of the Middle Ages it stood out as one of the wealthiest and most formidable states in all of Eurasia. It gave the Balkan Peninsula and Russia the distinctive version of Christianity that still sets these lands apart from western Europe. But meanwhile the Eastern Roman Empire suffered heavy losses with the meteoric rise of a vital new religion among the people of Arabia—Islam. Early in the seventh century Arabian armies, fervently united by Islam but also driven by a well-honed taste for plunder, seized control of Western civilization's birthplace—Mesopotamia, Egypt, and Syria-Palestine—and then swept through the huge Persian empire along the southern shore of the Mediterranean, and into Iberia. Only ephemerally, during the eleventh- and twelfth-century Crusades, would medieval Christians again rule in the Near East. In the centuries after the Arab invasion, the populations of the conquered lands became deeply attached to Islam, and Islamic thinkers absorbed and creatively built upon the Greco-Roman and Near Eastern cultural legacies to which they were heirs. There came into existence a wealthy and dynamic new cultural sphere, the Islamic world, so distinct from Christendom that it constituted a new civilization, expansively oriented toward Central and South Asia and toward sub-Saharan Africa.

Thus within the first of the global contexts that we have described, the Middle Ages is the era in which Western civilization shifts westward. Its ancient Near Eastern cradle is cut away, joining the heartland of the Islamic world. But at the same time Byzantine Christianity and East Roman institutions become firmly implanted in Russia and the Balkans, and Latin (West Roman) Christianity

---

[1] Defined as the British Isles, France and the Low Countries, Germany, Italy, Iberia, Scandinavia, and east-central Europe. As we shall see in Chapters 6–10, this geographical definition of western Europe corresponds to the countries that during the Middle Ages constituted Latin Christendom.

and institutions mature and flourish even in parts of western Europe where Rome had never ruled. Western civilization, in short, becomes a *European* cultural and political sphere, although it never loses touch with the Near Eastern and Mediterranean roots that it shares with the Islamic world.

The second concentric circle in which we are considering Western civilization's global context, is the great chain of civilizations across Eurasia, which had its origin in ancient times. By the second century A.D., these centers of civilized life formed almost an unbroken band. The Han Empire covered most of present-day China and reached as far west as Central Asia; India under the Gupta dynasty spread its cultural and economic influence into Southeast Asia; and the Sassanian Empire in Iran recovered almost all of ancient Persia's eastern provinces. At the western end of this chain of civilizations sprawled the Roman Empire, stretching from a bitterly contested frontier with Iran to the border of Scotland (where a Roman wall still stands).

Not long before the beginning of the period covered by Part Two of this book, this chain of civilizations temporarily broke. Barbarian attacks and internal discord brought down the Han Empire, just as they also gravely disrupted the Roman Empire. The East Roman (Byzantine) and Sassanian Empires fought each other so fiercely that by the 630s both lay dangerously vulnerable to the Arabian onslaught. India suffered no such disasters, but it experienced a profound religious transformation as Buddhism largely gave way to resurgent Hinduism. During the West's Middle Ages, Buddhism would be transplanted from its Indian birthplace to China and later to Japan, just as Christianity would become a dwindling minority faith in its original Near Eastern cradle but the foundation of a vigorous new center of civilization in Europe. Like the old East Roman Empire, so too China recovered from the crisis that had overwhelmed the Han. By the late 500s China was reunified, and from then until the late thirteenth century a series of powerful and wealthy dynasties ruled the mainland of East Asia: the Sui (581-618), the Tang (618-907), and the Sung (960-1279). And just as a resurgent Christian Byzantium exerted a powerful impact on half-barbaric early medieval western Europe and Russia, without actually ruling them, so during the seventh and eighth centuries imperial China became the irresistible model for Japan. During this so-called Nara period, Japan absorbed religious, philosophical, and political influences from China without falling under its direct control. But beginning about A.D. 800, Japan took its own road toward a more decentralized system of government and social organization that bears many uncanny parallels to feudalism in medieval western Europe.

In short, when we consider the European Middle Ages from the larger perspective of Eurasian history, the transition from what had been the Roman world into what became the European world follows a larger pattern of ancient civilizations being transformed. First came crisis and partial collapse, accompanied by the transplanting of religious traditions; then followed the rebuilding of a new chain of impressive centers of civilization. The richest and generally most efficiently governed of these was China.

Besides being decentralized societies, the west European and the Japanese ends of the Eurasian chain of civilizations enjoyed one incomparably important advantage: geographical security. By the thirteenth century, a savagely destructive and expansive new barbarian force was forming in the interior of Asia, the Mongol confederation. It overwhelmed Russia in the 1230s and conquered all of China by the 1270s. Meanwhile, between the late eleventh and the thirteenth centuries, a succession of Turkic invaders, also of Central Asian origin, overran much of India, Persia and the Arab caliphate (empire), and Byzantium; and although these Turkic conquerors converted to Islam, their attacks proved immensely destructive of both human beings and civilized institutions. Of all the advanced societies of Eurasia, only Japan and western Europe were spared devastation and alien rule, with fateful future consequences.

Finally, we can gain a third, and truly *global*, perspective on medieval Europe by viewing it in the context of parallel transformations in the Western Hemisphere, sub-Saharan Africa, and Oceania.[2] Of these lands Westerners knew nothing. A few Vikings planted precarious colonies in Greenland and northeastern North America shortly after the year 1000, but these settlements had virtually no contact with the rest of Christendom and eventually disappeared. Europeans were dimly aware that a Christian king ruled Ethiopia, but this realm of "Prester John" was shrouded in the mists of fairy tale. No Europeans crossed the Sahara, and sailing down the west coast of Africa was impossible because no medieval European ship could get back against winds that always blew southward. The handful of Westerners who read ancient geographical books knew that some kind of a landmass theoretically existed as ballast in the globe's southern hemisphere, but no one had ever been there. And how could they go to the "bottom" of the globe, where people would have to walk upside down?

Medieval Europeans had no inkling that in central Mexico and the Andes of South America a series of rich, powerful, and socially highly stratified empires were being built up, or that the Maya people of what is now southern Mexico and Guatemala were creating elaborate temple-cities and making precise astronomical calculations. They knew nothing of the spread of agriculture across most of North America or the rise of the city of Cahokia, near modern St. Louis, which around 1300 had a population as large as London's. Muslims, but not European Christians, were aware that south of the Sahara, where camel caravans from the Mediterranean reached West Africa's grasslands

---

[2] Australia, New Zealand, and the Pacific islands.

and river systems, black-skinned kings ruled a series of rich commercial empires: the pagan empire of tenth-century Ghana and the later Muslim states of Mali and Songhay. Nor did Europeans have any direct knowledge of the lively, Muslim-controlled seaborne commerce that traversed the Indian Ocean, linking Southwest Asia, India, and East Africa. Southeast Asia had only a theoretical existence for medieval Europeans—the last in a chain of buyers of exotic, high-priced condiments from the "Spice Islands" whose export was entirely in Muslim hands. And in the South Pacific, fabulous feats of navigation were being performed by Polynesian rowers who used their ability to "read" the stars and currents to settle one distant island group after another.

The story of how representatives of Christendom found their way to, and generally wreaked havoc upon, these distant cultures will not begin until Part Three. During its Middle Ages, the West was shielded but isolated at the western tip of Eurasia. Distance—and more than a little luck—kept it safe from the conquering hordes that at the end of the Middle Ages poured out of Central Asia to overwhelm almost all the rest of Eurasia. The stormy North Atlantic kept all but the Vikings pinned to the mainland and the closest offshore islands. Yet that same ocean brought to Europe's northerly latitudes plentiful rain and the warming Gulf Stream. These conditions created a climate in which even a relatively backward agricultural technology (unimpressive not only by modern standards but also in comparison to Chinese know-how of that time) could yield surpluses sufficient to sustain urbanization. Cities and the agriculture to feed them are, we have already seen, the foundations of civilizations. In Part Two we will see how the civilization that emerged in western Eurasia consolidated its distinctive version of Christianity and built the economic, religious, and political institutions that, after 1500, it would begin to carry around the globe.

AFTER ROME: BYZANTIUM, ISLAM, THE WEST, AND JEWS

Interior of Hagia Sophia, Istanbul *© R.F. Hoddinott/Ancient Art & Architecture Collection.*

98	Tacitus completes *Germania*
330	Constantine founds Constantinople
ca. 480–547	Life span of St. Benedict of Nursia, founder of the Benedictine order
481–511	Clovis rules the Franks, conquers Gaul, and converts to Catholic Christianity
493–526	Theodoric, king of the Ostrogoths, rules Italy
527–565	Emperor Justinian rules Byzantium, conquers North Africa and Italy, and instigates a compilation of Roman law
590–604	Pontificate of Gregory the Great, foremost of the early medieval popes
597	King Ethelbert of Kent converts to Christianity
622	The Hijra, initial date on the Muslim calendar: Muhammad flees Mecca for Medina, establishes the first Islamic community
632	Death of Muhammad
637	Arabs capture Persian capital Ctesiphon and conquer Persian Empire
680	Ecumenical Council of Constantinople: Orthodoxy triumphs over Monophysitism
711	Muslims invade Spain, destroy Visigothic kingdom

717–718	Muslim attack on Constantinople is turned back
726–843	Byzantine emperors generally pursue iconoclastic policies, stirring great dissension
732	Franks under Charles Martel defeat Muslims at Tours
735	Death of Bede, greatest historical scholar of early medieval Europe
750–1258	Abbasid dynasty of Islamic caliphs
786–809	Reign of Harun-al-Rashid, most celebrated Abbasid caliph
800	Pope Leo III crowns Charlemagne Roman emperor in the West
867–1056	Macedonian dynasty rules Byzantium; golden age of Byzantine culture and maximum restoration of Byzantine power
1055	Chief of Seljuk Turks conquers Baghdad and assumes title of "Grand Sultan"
1071	Battle of Manzikert
1258	Mongols take Baghdad and kill its eight hundred thousand inhabitants
1453	Constantinople falls to the Ottoman Turks

All dates are A.D.

On December 27, A.D. 537, Roman Emperor Justinian I for the first time entered Constantinople's Church of the Holy Wisdom (Hagia Sophia). In just five years, workers had created the enormous new church out of the ruins of an older one, which had been destroyed in a riot. Older Roman buildings had been pillaged for gold, silver, ivory, and dazzling mosaics to adorn its walls, and the vast central dome—107 feet across— seemed to float 181 feet above the floor. Justinian was stunned. "Glory to God who has judged me worthy of accomplishing such a work as this," he murmured. And then, thinking of the ancient Hebrew king who had built the first Temple at Jerusalem, he added proudly: "O Solomon, I have outdone you!"

Hagia Sophia's immense scale and the ingenuity with which its architects disguised the great dome's supports make it an engineering marvel. But its air of ethereal glory lifts it into the ranks of the world's supreme architectural masterpieces. Although today it is a museum, Hagia Sophia mentally takes back all who visit it to the intense spirituality of medieval Byzantine culture. "On entering this church to pray," wrote a contemporary of Justinian, "one feels at once that it is the work, not of man's effort or industry, but

in truth the work of the Divine Power; and the spirit, mounting to heaven, realizes that here God is very near and that He delights in this dwelling that He has chosen for Himself."

Hagia Sophia, like Constantinople, stands at a cultural and historical crossroads. In Justinian's time, Hagia Sophia's mosaics were apparently more floral—that is, Near Eastern—than pictorial. Classical harmony was abandoned in decorating the walls with dramatic polychrome marbles, a typically Persian touch. The plan preserves the rectangular layout of a Roman basilica, and its vast dome has both Roman and Persian models. Greek geometry was used to design the curved masonry supports for the dome. Hagia Sophia made the dome the central feature both of Byzantine church architecture and of medieval houses of worship from Christian Sicily to Muslim Jerusalem.

Justinian's reign marked a transition from antiquity to the Middle Ages. Three cultural traditions would soon come into focus—Byzantine, Islamic, and west European— that would inherit the legacy of the ancient West. Justinian was the last Roman emperor to attack ancient paganism; he closed the Athenian Academy, founded by Plato, in 529. But only six years after his death in 565, the

Prophet Muhammad was born. Justinian's native language was Latin, and he considered himself the restorer of the Roman Empire. His codification of ancient Roman law is the foundation of the legal systems of most modern Western states, but the Roman state he rebuilt would also survive for nine hundred years as a medieval Christian autocracy.

In Justinian's time, western Eurasia contained two great civilized powers: the Eastern Roman (or Byzantine) Empire and the Persian Empire under the Sassanid Dynasty. In eastern Eurasia lay two other ancient civilizations: India, then at its height under the Gupta emperors; and China, where the Tang Dynasty was beginning to preside over the wealthiest society of the age.

After Justinian's death, two new centers of civilization emerged in western Eurasia. First, in the seventh century Islamic armies inspired by Muhammad conquered Sassanid Persia and forced the Eastern Roman Empire to fight for its life—a struggle that would last until 1453, when triumphant Muslims turned Hagia Sophia into a mosque. Second, the sixth and seventh centuries saw Western Christendom gradually, painfully emerge from the wreckage of the Roman Empire. Christian monks carried their Mediterranean-born and Latin-speaking religion into the dank forests of Britain, Germany, and the Slavic lands, taming barbarism and laying modern Europe's foundations.

Inseparable from the birth of the medieval world's three great cultures is the history of another ancient people's survival. Medieval Jews remained scattered minorities everywhere. Yet the period between the decline of Rome and the eleventh century was crucial for Judaism, ensuring that Jews escaped absorption into the new world religions that were taking shape and extending their spheres.

THE SURVIVAL OF THE EASTERN ROMAN EMPIRE

By A.D. 500, the Western Roman Empire had split into Germanic kingdoms. But from Constantinople the eastern emperors still ruled an immense realm from the Balkans to Egypt. The eastern provinces had always outnumbered those in the west. Its civilization was far older and deeper-rooted, and it had more and bigger cities. Free landowning peasants, practically gone from the western provinces, were still numerous in the east. Commerce and industry had always been livelier there. There was a net drain of gold coins from western regions to pay for eastern imports. When invaders poured across the imperial frontiers in unprecedented numbers, the richer east proved far more resilient than the west.

The Eastern Roman (or, as it was later called, "Byzantine") Empire enjoyed important strategic advantages. Anatolia (the Asian part of modern Turkey) provided a great reservoir of laborers, soldiers, and money, all protected from Germanic incursions by the Black Sea and by Constantinople's walls. Its tough, loyal troops gave the

Eastern emperors an alternative to the dangers of becoming dependent on hired Germanic armies.

"God-defended" Constantinople held fast. Its command of the commerce flowing between the Black Sea and the Mediterranean made Constantine's city the economic and political heart of the Eastern Roman Empire. So long as its walls remained unbreached, the empire would endure (see Map 6-1).

The Eastern Roman Empire had the further advantage, during the crucial fifth century, of being better governed. While Roman rule in the western part of the empire was collapsing, able eastern rulers consolidated their position. Even so, the eastern emperors could have done little without their capital's superb strategic location and the commercial and human resources of the lands they ruled.

Byzantine Government and Eastern Christianity

The Byzantine Empire synthesized Roman government, Christian religion, and Hellenistic culture. From Rome came its legal system and its bureaucracy. Byzantine autocracy was a child of the exaltation that Diocletian and Constantine had demanded, and imperial control of the Byzantine church harked back to Constantine and Theodosius I. The heavy taxation of late Roman times continued, and for ordinary people life in Byzantium remained hard.

The Byzantine mood, like that of the late Roman Empire, stressed defense and self-preservation. Byzantines saw their state as the ark of Christian civilization, bobbing on an ocean of heathen barbarism, that must be preserved at all costs. Entrenchment was required, not expansion; caution, not daring.

This defensive mood revealed itself in both the Byzantine bureaucracy and the Byzantine army. The bureaucracy, like all officialdoms, abhorred change and risks. Sometimes resisting the initiatives of Byzantium's more vigorous and imaginative emperors, it provided cohesion during the reigns of incompetents. The small, highly trained Byzantine army also clung to low-risk strategies. Its generals practiced their art with cunning, acutely aware that the preservation of the empire depended on the survival of their troops. For the same reasons, imperial diplomats perfected tactics of statecraft that have given the word *byzantine* its overtones of subtle deviousness.

Byzantine Christianity was a direct outgrowth of the Christianity of the later years of the Roman Empire—its theology tightened and defined by the reaction to Arianism, its priestly hierarchy overshadowed by the power of the emperors. Continuing Constantine's precedent of dominating the Council of Nicaea in 325, Byzantine emperors tended to lord it over the patriarchs of Constantinople and, through them, the Orthodox church.

In turn, the Byzantine emperors drew strength from the loyalty of their Christian subjects. To Orthodox

MAP 6-1
CONSTANTINOPLE

This map shows the main lines of the city as designed by Constantine and rebuilt by Justinian. Between 413 and 447, Constantine's original wall was supplemented by a double outer wall; its ruins still stand, and it was breached only once in history, by the Ottoman Turks in 1453. The Golden Horn, off the Bosphorus, in wartime could be protected by a heavy chain across its mouth. Only a few architectural traces of Constantine's city now remain, but some of the great churches of the Byzantine period (such as Hagia Sophia) still stand.

Christians, the emperor was no mere secular sovereign. As God's vice regent, he had the decisive voice in all matters affecting Christian governance, practice, and doctrine. He was protector of the church, and his armies fought for God. The people understood this, and many Byzantine rulers enjoyed far more popular support than any pagan emperor had known.

Constantine's fourth-century turn to Christianity and the steady trend toward making it the empire's official religion may have almost overwhelmed the church with time-serving opportunists, but by the fifth and sixth centuries piety, especially in great cities like Constantinople, was becoming deep and genuine. Amid a tremendous outpouring of hymns and miracle-working icons, there came into focus in fifth-century Byzantium the cult of the Virgin Mary, which would later spread to the medieval West. "Second Eve," who by her humble obedience to God's will contrasted with the Eve of Genesis who had succumbed to temptation; Virgin Mother, through whom God Incarnate had come into the world; merciful intercessor for sinners before God—in all these aspects Mary was exalted by theologians, clergy, and popular devotion to a position only slightly below that of Jesus himself. Christ and the Virgin had become the protectors of all that Rome stood for.

But the emperor's dominating position in Byzantine Christianity was a source of weakness as well. Heresy became a threat to the state. The fourth through sixth centuries were singularly rich in doctrinal disputes, which in the end cost the empire dearly. Most important was the debate over Christ's nature, which by no means ended with the imposition of the Nicene Creed (see Chapter 5). The church's rejection of Arius's teaching (that Christ was a man raised to Godhood) called forth two new positions that also were eventually condemned as heresy. One was the view expressed by a patriarch of Constantinople named Nestorius (d. ca. 451), who objected to calling the Virgin Mary "God-Bearer": Applying that title to Jesus' mother, Nestorius said, detracted from the Savior's humanity. But so powerful was the upwelling cult of the Virgin that Nestorius was condemned by the Council of Ephesus in 431. His followers fled to Rome's archenemy Persia, where a Nestorian church flourished for many centuries and won converts as far east as China. (Even today, small Nestorian communities remain in the Middle East, India, and East Asia.)

The other heresy of this period—the most widespread and the one most dangerous to Byzantium—was Monophysitism. It arose in Egypt and spread into Syria and Palestine, intensifying hostility toward the Orthodox emperors. The Orthodox-Monophysite quarrel turned on whether Christ's manhood and Godhood constituted two separate natures (Orthodoxy) or were fused into one nature (Monophysitism). In the Monophysites' idea of Christ's single nature, his divinity tended to supersede his humanity. Thus Monophysitism harked back to ancient Near Eastern spiritualism, in which the physical world seemed either evil or unimportant.

The Orthodox-Monophysite struggle raged long and bitterly. Ordinary people in Constantinople and Alexandria

The Virgin as "God Bearer" This seventh-century mosaic from Cyprus escaped the destructive fury of Iconoclasm. Mosaics of this type, made by pressing tiny pieces of glass into plaster in such a way as to catch the light, magnificently captured Eastern Christians' passionate faith in the Virgin as the intercessor with Christ—a faith later shared by medieval Western Christians. *© Ancient Art & Architecture Collection Ltd.*

took sides passionately. The emperors were convinced that doctrinal correctness was essential to ensuring divine favor but were not always sure what the correct doctrine was. So sometimes they persecuted the Monophysites, sometimes they favored them, and sometimes they worked out compromises that satisfied no one. The controversy dragged on until the seventh century, when the disaffected Monophysite provinces were swallowed by conquering Islamic armies. Only then, at the Council of Constantinople in 680, did Orthodoxy win its final victory within what remained of the Byzantine Empire. (Monophysitism lives on as the faith of the Coptic Christians of Egypt, who today constitute about 10 percent of the population of that otherwise overwhelmingly Islamic country.)

Even apart from the disastrous conflicts of Orthodoxy with the Nestorians and the Monophysites, however, some

parts of what is often called Eastern Christendom were only sporadically—if at all—subject to the Byzantine emperors and church. In Armenia, long a buffer between Rome and Persia, the king was converted to Christianity in 287 (a generation before Constantine), and in 314 Christianity became the state religion. About 330 the ruler of Georgia (then called Iberia), in the Caucasus, also became a Christian. Christianity provided a strong basis for national identity in both countries against Persian and later Muslim domination, although the Armenian church's dissent against certain Orthodox views blocked the full imposition of Byzantine influence. Precariously balancing against powerful neighbors, Armenia would reach its greatest cultural flowering in the tenth century and Georgia in the twelfth; and in both lands national consciousness would be kept alive by priests and monks in later centuries of rule by Turks, Mongols, and Persians.

Christianity reached the East African land now called Ethiopia in the fourth century, when Syrian missionaries converted the king of Aksum, an important trading center between the Mediterranean and India. But the Ethiopian church accepted Monophysitism, and this theological divergence, as well as the seventh-century Islamic conquest of North Africa, almost entirely severed Ethiopia from the rest of Christendom for many centuries. A highly distinctive religion took root that combined Monophysite Christianity, Judaism, and African traditions.

Byzantine Culture

The Greek culture that Byzantium inherited was not the culture of classical Athens. That tradition had undergone many modifications, above all during the third and fourth centuries A.D.

There had always been a potent spiritual-mystical element in Greco-Roman culture, coexisting with the traditional classical concern with the earthly and concrete. Under the late empire the mystical element grew stronger. More and more, rigorous minds turned to theology, scriptural interpretation, and the quest for individual salvation. Both the pagan philosopher Plotinus and the Christian theologian St. Augustine, for example, had considered the physical sciences a waste of time. Although a strong classical tradition remained in the arts and crafts, in religiously oriented work (which included depictions of the emperor) artists were expected to suggest intense spirituality. Byzantine artistic conventions were developed and closely guarded in the great workshops of Constantinople, which were part of the imperial palace complex. Here highly trained and supervised artisans produced the mosaics and icons, the delicate ivories, enamelware, and jewelry, and the rich brocades and silks that not only enriched the Byzantine court and church but were also exported to the West, the Islamic world, and beyond.

It was in keeping with Byzantium's spirit that its artists were able to produce enduring masterpieces without ever forgetting that they were creating sacred objects. Here was an art vastly different from that of Greek antiquity, with different techniques and different goals, yet as valid and successful as the art of classical Athens. Once derided by critics as "static," Byzantine art's sophisticated abstract and symbolic qualities became more understandable to twentieth-century eyes, and today it is generally acknowledged as one of the great links in Western civilization's cultural tradition.

As Byzantine society and culture emerged out of the late Eastern-Roman world, much of the empire's Latin-Roman heritage fell away. Knowledge of Latin practically disappeared, though Byzantines never ceased to regard themselves as "Romans" and their state as the "Roman Empire." In this new, transcendental environment, the ancient Hellenic cultural tradition was thoroughly Christianized. Byzantine Greek deteriorated from the standards of ancient style, just as Latin became far less polished in western Europe. During the calamitous seventh and eighth centuries, a combination of economic, religious, and political crises almost wiped out Byzantium's educated classes and brought Eastern Christendom's cultural level almost as low as western Europe's. Yet most Byzantines never forgot their ancient Greek heritage, and standards revived impressively beginning in the ninth century.

The Byzantine Centuries

Drawing a line between the end of Roman antiquity and the onset of "medieval" Byzantine history cannot be done with precision. But most historians agree that sometime during the sixth century a crucial transition occurred. From then until it fell to Ottoman conquerors in 1453, Constantinople formed Christendom's bastion at the juncture of Europe and Asia (see Table 6-1).

The Age of Justinian The first major creative surge of Byzantine culture came during the reign of Justinian (527–565), in some respects the last of the ancient Roman emperors. He and his court spoke Latin, and he was obsessed with reviving the old Roman Empire by reconquering its lost western provinces. Under his direction the vast heritage of Roman law was assembled into a single, coherent code. But Justinian was a Byzantine no less than a Roman—and he would surely have perceived no distinction. His reign saw Byzantine art achieve its classic forms, and his regime defined the imperial-Christian autocracy that would typify the Byzantine state to the end of its days.

TABLE 6-1

BYZANTINE CHRONOLOGY

330	Constantine founds Constantinople	690s	Muslims conquer Byzantine North Africa
395	Final division of Eastern and Western Roman Empire	717–718	Great Muslim siege of Constantinople
527–565	Reign of Justinian I	717–741	Reign of Leo III the Issaurian; beginning of Iconoclasm
533–534	Conquest of Vandal North Africa	843	End of Iconoclasm
535–555	Gothic Wars; conquest of Italy	867–1056	Macedonian dynasty: Reconquest of Balkans; conversion of South Slavs and Russians; Byzantium at its apex
541–543	First great plague strikes Byzantium and the Mediterranean world	976–1025	Reign of Basil the Bulgar-Slayer
548	Death of Empress Theodora	ca. 980–1015	Reign of Prince Vladimir of Kiev, who converts to Byzantine Christianity
568	Lombards invade Italy	1071	Seljuk Turks rout Byzantines at Manzikert; loss of Anatolia
610–641	Reign of Heraclius; Byzantium defeats Persia but Islamic armies conquer Syria, Palestine, and Egypt	1453	Fall of Constantinople to Ottoman Turks
641–668	Reign of Constans II and introduction of theme system		
680	Council of Constantinople: Orthodoxy triumphs over Monophysitism in Byzantium's remaining provinces		

San Vitale Besides Hagia Sophia, the greatest Byzantine church that survives is San Vitale in Ravenna, built by Justinian. San Vitale's mosaics and other ornamentation can be seen today as they were in Justinian's time. This photograph shows the chancel, its wall decorated with a great mosaic of Justinian and his court (Theodora is shown on the opposite wall), and Christ with angels and saints in the vault above. *Scala/Art Resource, NY.*

Justinian owed his successes not only to his determination and ambition, but also to his predecessors' ability to fend off Germanic invasions and to accumulate a sizable treasury surplus. Justinian was also fortunate in that the western Germanic kingdoms, which he meant to conquer, were losing their early vigor. Theodoric, king of the Ostrogoths, died in 526, a year before Justinian ascended the throne, and the Vandal monarchy of North Africa was growing disorganized and corrupt.

Justinian was aided immeasurably by his wife and co-ruler, Empress Theodora, a woman no less ambitious than he and even more resolute. Formerly an entertainer, Theodora was gifted with great beauty and extraordinary

practical intelligence. Together, she and Justinian brought new energy to an old, conservative regime. But although the audacious policies of Justinian and Theodora were successful, they left the empire exhausted. Justinian applied his considerable knowledge of theology to the tangled problem of reconciling Orthodoxy and Monophysitism, but his complex compromise satisfied neither side. After a great urban uprising accompanied by an immense fire destroyed much of the city,[1] he spent prodigiously to rebuild Constantinople on an unprecedented scale, culminating in Hagia Sophia.

At Justinian's bidding a talented group of lawyers assembled the immense mass of legal precedents, juridical opinions, and imperial edicts constituting the legacy of Roman law. They systematized these materials into a vast collection known as the *Corpus Juris Civilis*—the "body of **civil law**." Justinian's code became not only the keystone of Byzantine jurisprudence but also the vehicle by which Roman law returned to western Europe in the twelfth century, with incalculable importance to the development of sophisticated and rational legal systems in the European states. But the importance of the *Corpus Juris Civilis* extended even farther. Roman law had once contained strong elements of popular sovereignty, but in Justinian's hand it acquired the autocratic flavor of the Byzantine state. Thus, in the late medieval and early modern West it tended to support the rise of royal absolutism, rejecting the limited-monarchy notions of Germanic legal tradition. Later European kings would find much to admire in Justinian's precept that the emperor's decree is law.

Historians often criticize Justinian for wasting limited resources trying to reconquer the West. True, the reconquest (and Constantinople's rebuilding) drained the treasury almost dry, and the victories of Justinian's western armies proved largely ephemeral. Yet Justinian, keenly sensitive to the Roman imperial tradition, could not rest until he had made one all-out attempt to recover the lost provinces. His small armies, led by the brilliant generals Belisarius and Narses, easily conquered Vandal North Africa in 533–534 and wrested a long strip of the Spanish Mediterranean coast from the Visigoths. Then for twenty years his troops battled the Ostrogoths in Italy, crushing them in 555 after enormous effort and expense. These "Gothic Wars" ravaged Italy, destroyed the Roman senatorial class, and left Rome in ruins (see Map 6-2). During his final years Justinian ruled almost the entire Mediterranean

---

[1] The so-called Nika riots (named for the cry "Nika!" meaning "Win!") began with a set-to between the Blues and the Greens, admirers of rival chariot-racing teams. In Byzantium, leagues of fanatical sports fans were patronized by opposing aristocratic factions and even by the imperial government. Religious controversies, too, were often divided along Blue-Green lines. It is as if the stability of the United States government rested on a balance of power between riotous NASCAR fans.

Theodora

About 497 there was born to a bear-keeper at the Hippodrome—Constantinople's equivalent of Madison Square Garden and the Indianapolis Speedway—a daughter named Theodora. Such were the beginnings of a woman who rose from the social depths to great political power.

We will never know the truth of the stories told about Theodora's younger days in the *Secret History* of Procopius, one of the great Byzantine historians but also a salacious puritan. As the title suggests, the *Secret History* was written "for the desk drawer" and did not circulate publicly until long after the people it described had died. Be that as it may, Procopius's book reads in part like the scenario of an X-rated film, graphically describing the escapades of a prostitute and stripteaser. It may be one of history's most audacious acts of character assassination.

It is, however, probably true that Theodora was forced into prostitution as a young girl, and it is certain that she later became an actress, a disreputable occupation because it could involve appearing on the stage nude or in sexually explicit situations. As an actress, she became the mistress of a high-ranking official, who took her to Alexandria but then discarded her. She returned to Constantinople, worked as a wool spinner, reestablished contact with the Blues (one of the capital's two great circus-fan factions), and became the lover of a prominent Blues supporter, the emperor's nephew Justinian.

Justinian was sufficiently smitten with the intelligent, beautiful, and sexy Theodora to want to marry her. His father was a peasant who had risen to the pinnacle of power through a military career, so Justinian (like his uncle, Emperor Justin) was a social upstart, unimpressed by stuffy notions of respectability. However, marrying an actress was legally forbidden to senators (such as he had become), and the law had to be changed to allow him to take a "repentant" actress as his wife. This he did in 525. By 527, Justin was dead, Justinian was emperor, and Theodora was empress.

No scandal touched her for the rest of her life, although she and Justinian were bitterly hated by the older aristocracy—men such as Procopius, who served the imperial couple as a high official while writing his *Secret History*. Not just social snobbery but also outrage that a woman (and such a woman!) should wield real power doubtless explains Procopius's motive. As empress, however, Theodora behaved with great dignity and consummate showmanship.

She also proved herself a woman of extraordinary courage and political intelligence. Most laws issued while she was empress bore her name as well as Justinian's, and she corresponded with foreign rulers and received their ambassadors—unheard-of innovations. Even before she met Justinian she had been converted to Monophysitism, and although she never managed to win over her husband, she did prevail on him to stop persecutions and attempt various theological compromises. When the Nika riots destroyed much of Constantinople in 532, she talked Justinian into making a bold stand in the capital rather than fleeing, but after its brutal suppression she also persuaded him that senatorial cliques had been the ultimate instigators of the turmoil, so that he should continue depending on social nobodies in staffing his regime. As his lawyers worked on the great codification project, she lobbied successfully for strong laws forbidding the sexual exploitation of young women and increasing women's rights in divorce cases—areas in which she had personally suffered.

Theodora died, probably of cancer, in 548. The famous mosaic of her at Ravenna, executed a few years before her death and shown here, is probably not a portrait from life, but still is a haunting image of one of history's extraordinary women. ❖

© R. Sheridan/Ancient Art & Architecture Collection.

MAP 6-2
JUSTINIAN'S
CONQUESTS

coastline, but his swollen empire was bankrupt, and Theodora's death in 548 left him demoralized and irresolute.

One of the lines that helps separate the ancient and medieval eras in the Western world was drawn in the years 541–543. A devastating plague—the worst since the time of the Peloponnesian War, a thousand years earlier—swept out of the Red Sea area and devastated Byzantium and much of Europe. Densely populated areas like Egypt and Constantinople were worst hit; the city may have lost more than 250,000 of its approximately 375,000 people. And this was just the beginning: Plagues recurred sporadically over the next two centuries, taking a fearful toll of lives, crippling the Byzantine economy, and forcing the pace of a host of changes that marked the emergence of a medieval society in the old Eastern Roman Empire. But even without the plague, Byzantium would have found it difficult to hold Justinian's conquests.

Invasions, Retrenchment, and Revival After Justinian, Byzantium found itself perpetually on guard against nomadic or seafaring "barbarians," whose onslaughts were another sign that the Eastern Roman Empire was entering its medieval environment. Germanic, Viking, Berber (North African), and Slavic peoples became an incessant threat, and even more dangerous were nomadic invaders from Inner Asia. Attila's fifth-century Huns had been only the beginning (see Chapter 5); recurring waves of steppe tribes would pour westward for nearly a millennium. In the early sixth century the Bulgars, a Turkic tribe, invaded the Balkans. Then, in 561 a new Asian conqueror, the Avars, subjugated both the Bulgars and the Slavs living along the Danube River. Byzantium now lay in the shadow of the Avar horde.

All these Asian invaders boasted ruthlessly efficient light cavalry. Their **nomadism** made them difficult to attack. Ultimately they would be absorbed by the larger settled populations that they overran, dispersed, or driven back to the steppes. But for centuries these people would bring terror to the great civilizations of Asia and Europe.

Justinian's western conquests did not last. In 568, three years after his death, the Germanic Lombards (Langobards or "Long Beards") burst into Italy, further devastating that tormented land and carving out a large kingdom in northern Italy centering on the Po Valley, a region still called Lombardy. Byzantium retained much of southern Italy and clung to Ravenna, Venice, and other Adriatic outposts, but its hold on the peninsula loosened. Shortly afterward, the Visigoths reconquered Byzantine lands in southern Spain. Eventually, in the 690s, Muslims overran Byzantine North Africa. In 751 the Lombards seized Ravenna, further reducing Byzantium's presence in Italy.

Justinian's successors had to abandon his ambitious western policies and gird themselves for survival. Not only did the Avars now control the Balkans, but the Persian Empire also pressed dangerously against Byzantium's eastern frontier.

The great crisis came under Emperor Heraclius (reigned 610–641). Persian armies occupied Syria, Palestine, and Egypt, and in 626 Constantinople just barely withstood a furious combined siege from Persians and Avars. But the indomitable Heraclius crushed the Persian army in 628 and regained everything that had been lost. He even recovered from the Persians the alleged True Cross on which Jesus had been crucified—the holiest of all Christian relics. At that moment, Heraclius was the greatest hero of Byzantine history.

But no sooner had Heraclius defeated the Persians than Muslim armies, inspired by their new religion of Islam, burst out of Arabia to wrest Syria, Palestine, and Egypt from the empire and put Constantinople once again in peril. The Muslims besieged the city several times, most determinedly in 717 and 718, on which occasion the dogged Byzantine defense may have prevented not only the empire but Europe from being absorbed into the Islamic world. The empire withstood Islam's powerful northward thrust, holding Constantinople, Asia Minor, and an unsteady hegemony in the Balkan peninsula. The division of medieval western Eurasia into three major cultural spheres—Byzantium, Islam, and Western Christendom—was beginning to gel.

Ruralization, Iconoclasm, and Recovery Byzantium had survived, but just barely. During the seventh and eighth centuries, in Anatolia and the Balkans alike, almost all the cities of the empire declined and were transformed. Continuous military threats caused them to be either abandoned or converted into fortified villages. In Athens, the populace withdrew to the fortified acropolis—the "hill town"—and much of the Greek countryside was settled by Slavs. Moreover, the Byzantines had lost to Islam such major cities as Damascus, Alexandria, Antioch, and Carthage, so that the empire became smaller and poorer. Yet it was now more homogeneously Greek and Orthodox, and more centered on Constantinople, the one great city remaining in an otherwise largely agrarian society.

That agrarian society also became a militarized one. The armies of Justinian and Heraclius had been barbarian mercenaries. But mercenaries have to be paid, and the empire's economic decline and loss of its rich Near Eastern provinces brought matters to a head. In the mid-seventh century Constans II (reigned 641—688) reorganized the empire into *themes*—large provinces, each with its territorial guard of peasant-soldiers with a lifetime obligation of military service. To offset a drastic pay cut, these warriors received from the state hereditary land allotments. The governor of each theme commanded the troops in wartime. Until the late eleventh century, the theme system remained the cornerstone of Byzantine defense policy, and as long as the troopers took their duties seriously (and governors did not rebel) they served the empire well.

Defeat and strategic withdrawal in the face of Islamic invasion, a decline of urban life, and the empire's ever-growing reliance on its simple peasant-soldiers all combined to produce a mood of harsh puritanism in eighth-century Byzantine life. Legal changes were one reflection of the emperors' solicitude for the country people. Thus the early eighth-century Farmer's Law protected smallholders against the loss of their land through debt. And since few Byzantines could read the Latin of Justinian's laws, a simplified new code, the Ecloga (739), was issued, softening certain harsh provisions that had borne heavily on ordinary people. So that criminals could repent rather than immediately face divine justice, the Ecloga also abolished capital punishment for many offenses (not, however, for homosexual acts). To modern sensibilities, perhaps, the "kinder" alternatives are not always palatable: blinding, slitting noses and tongues, and cutting off ears all came into common use as punishments that would remove offenders from public life but allow them to meditate in some monastery.

Nothing is more revealing of the crisis in core Byzantine values—and none had greater implications for Byzantium's relationship with the West—than the bitter eighth-century struggle over iconoclasm, or "breaking images."

The issue was whether Christians could offer devotion to statues and pictures of Christ, the Virgin, and the saints. Icons—the word in Greek means "image" or "picture"—had gradually come to assume an important role in Christian worship, especially in eastern monasteries. Most theologians held that Christians might honor (that is, "venerate") icons as *symbols*, but all agreed that to *worship* these depictions would violate God's commandment

Iconoclasm The monk who illuminated his manuscript with this scene, in which a mosaic of Christ is being whitewashed, was anti-iconoclast and writing after the veneration of icons had been restored. (On the same page, the lancing of Jesus on the cross is also illustrated, implying that this was an offense comparable to destroying his holy image.) Many attempts have been made to explain iconoclasm as a social, economic, or political movement, but the best explanation seems to be that its inspiration was religious: If old icons had failed to prevent Muslim victories, then God must be punishing Christians for idolatry; hence, the icons must be destroyed. *l'École Practique des Hautes Ètudes, Paris.*

forbidding idolatry. In fact, Byzantines tended to lavish such hopes on miracle-working icons that they came close to worshiping them as manifestations of divine power. Returning victoriously from the wars with Persia, for example, Heraclius's first act had been to prostrate himself before the icon of the Virgin in Hagia Sophia that had blessed his departing army. Churches and monasteries (usually located in towns) profited from throngs of pilgrims praying before these icons. On the other hand, the Anatolian peasant-soldiers who bore the brunt of Muslim onslaughts wondered whether their defeats might be divine punishment for idolatry; Islam, after all, vehemently rejected idol worship.

When a new dynasty of military-oriented emperors ascended the throne, beginning with Leo III (reigned 717–741), imperial policy adopted the puritanical sentiments of the Anatolian peasant-soldiery. (It was no coincidence that Leo also issued both the Farmer's Code and the Ecloga.) In 726 Leo forbade the worship of images by banning icons altogether. Wherever they could be found, icons were destroyed, and mosaics depicting Christ and the saints were smashed or plastered over. Cultural losses must have been huge, for little of what was undoubtedly Byzantium's rich pre-eighth-century religious art survives from areas ruled by the iconoclastic emperors. Not until 843 was the making and veneration of icons permanently legalized in Byzantium. From then on, icons again played an immensely important role in Byzantine religion and culture.

While it lasted, iconoclasm served the interests of the Byzantine emperors by weakening the enormously wealthy eastern monasteries. There was definitely an element of rural-urban antagonism at the heart of the struggle, for city-dwellers and their clergy (above all, the people of Constantinople) were fervently attached to the icons. Iconoclasm grievously offended many Byzantines. In western Europe, no one supported the eastern emperors in banning images. The popes condemned iconoclasm as heretical, directly challenging Constantinople over a major theological issue for the first time. (It would not be the last.) Although it ultimately failed in the Byzantine church, iconoclasm in the 750s aroused intense enmity between Rome and Constantinople—and, as we shall see in Chapter 7, caused a fundamental reorientation of papal policy, away from alliance with Byzantium and toward dependence on a rising new power in northwestern Europe.

The end of iconoclasm coincided with a period of recovery: a reversal of Byzantium's centuries-long retrenchment and ruralization. The disastrous cycle of plagues abated after the late eighth century, perhaps as unhealthy urban concentrations dispersed and survivors built up immunities. By the mid-ninth century, Byzantium's economic and social

A Macedonian Ivory One of the greatest genres of Byzantine art was the carving of ivory, in which beautiful precision was attained in a small space. This, the so-called Harbaville Triptych now in the Louvre (Paris), is a private altarpiece from the tenth century, depicting Christ enthroned. *Giraudon/Art Resource, NY.*

crisis was easing. Money flowed back into imperial coffers. Towns revived, and by the twelfth century Constantinople regained the population of 300,000– 400,000 that it had in Justinian's time, making it by far Europe's largest city.

The beneficiary of this resurgence was the Macedonian dynasty of emperors (867–1056), whose first member, the Balkan-born soldier Basil I, took power by murdering his predecessor. The Macedonians broke with tradition by energetically expanding Byzantium's borders in all directions.

The empire's reviving economy and enhanced security made possible an impressive artistic and literary revival, and an outpouring of missionary activity brought the Slavs of the Balkans and Russia into Christendom. The Macedonian era, in short, was Byzantium's "Golden Age."

Constantinople faced danger if a hostile power controlled the land at its doorstep—present-day Bulgaria. That was the case in the late seventh century, when the Bulgars threw off Avar rule and took control of what is today Bulgaria, Macedonia, and northern Greece. The Bulgars were Turkic, but most of the people whom they dominated were Slavs. Throughout the eighth century and well into the ninth, Byzantine emperors fought one war after another against the Bulgars, who at times threatened Constantinople itself. Only in 865 was a Bulgar khan, Boris, ready to

accept Christianity—and he drove a hard bargain, playing Byzantium off against the pope to gain an autonomous Bulgarian church under his control. By the time Boris converted, the Bulgars were fusing with the country's Slavic population, forming the Bulgarian people. The creation of a Slavic liturgy hastened this ethnic and cultural transformation. Nevertheless, the Byzantine emperors continued to find Bulgaria a serious problem, for its new Christian kings set their sights on nothing less than the imperial throne. The most celebrated Macedonian emperor, Basil II "the Bulgar-Slayer" (reigned 976–1025), campaigned year after year in the Balkans, finally demolishing the Bulgarian army in 1014. He blinded fifteen thousand prisoners, leaving one in each hundred one-eyed to lead his helpless comrades home; the Bulgarian king died of shock at the spectacle. Thus did Basil II break all resistance.

Bulgaria's conversion was part of a broader Byzantine effort to spread Christianity among the Slavs. Moravia, another Slavic proto-state, emerged in the early ninth century somewhere in Central Europe. (Most authorities locate it in present-day Slovakia, but some place it in Croatia.) Resisting pressure from recently converted but expansive Latin Christians in neighboring Bavaria, the Moravian rulers asked distant Byzantium to send missionaries who would set up a Christian society free of intrusive

MAP 6-3

BYZANTIUM AND THE RELIGIOUS DIVISION OF EUROPE

German influence. Saints Cyril and Methodius, highly educated brothers from Thessalonika who knew the language of the Balkan Slavs, were dispatched from Constantinople in 863 to spearhead the enterprise. They created the first Slavic alphabet (called Glagolitic) and translated the Bible and the liturgy into the language known as Old Church Slavonic. Moravia did not survive: In 907 new Asian invaders, the pagan Magyars (Hungarians), crushed it and permanently occupied the Danube basin. But Cyril and Methodius's work endured. The Cyrillic alphabet now used by Russians, Ukrainians, Bulgarians, and Serbs derives from Glagolitic, and Old Church Slavonic became the literary and ecclesiastical language of the medieval South and East Slavs. Thus a Slavic written language and Slavic Christianity came into being side by side. Macedonian-era evangelism had brought Russia and much of the Balkans into the Orthodox church and Byzantium's cultural sphere, whereas the Magyars and the western Slavs—Poles, Czechs, Slovaks, Slovenes, and Croats—would be converted to Latin Christianity. The line separating these spheres is still crucial in European affairs (see Map 6-3).

The Conversion of Russia The age of the Macedonian emperors coincided with the rise of Russia, far beyond the political boundaries of the empire. Ancient Greece and Byzantium always depended on grain imports from the shore of the Black Sea. In the ninth and tenth centuries, river-borne trade routes from the Black Sea to the Baltic linked Byzantium with the vigorous commerce of the Viking world (see Chapter 7). Numerous Byzantine coin hoards dating from this era have been unearthed in Scandinavia, and Byzantine armies hired Norse mercenaries. Swedish Vikings probed deep into Russia in the ninth century and established a dynasty in the north Russian trading center of Novgorod, ruling over the native Slavs and later intermarrying with them. In the tenth century a ruler of Novgorod captured the strategic Russian commercial town of Kiev, which became the nucleus of a new Russian state.

The Macedonian emperors maintained friendly relations with Kievan Russia. Basil the Bulgar-Slayer received crucial military aid from Prince Vladimir of Kiev and promised to give his sister to Vladimir in marriage. The result of this union was the conversion of Kievan Russia. Vladimir, on marrying his Byzantine princess, agreed to adopt Christianity, and his people quickly followed him. Kiev never submitted politically to the Byzantine emperors, but spiritually its people entered the Byzantine sphere.

Military Disaster and Cultural Survival The Macedonian dynasty died out in 1056, and with it ended an era of Byzantine grandeur. The theme system decayed, and military preparedness slumped. Fatefully, this downturn coincided with the westward migration of a powerful new Asian tribe, the Seljuk Turks, into the Middle East. Recently converted to Islam, the Seljuks had made a puppet of the Islamic ruler at Baghdad. In 1065 the Seljuks wrested

Armenia from Byzantium, and when an imperial army attempted to drive them from eastern Anatolia, the army was annihilated at Manzikert in 1071.

Manzikert is one of history's most decisive battles. Even though the Seljuks did not follow up their triumph, the disaster crippled Byzantium by breaking its hold on Anatolia. In the same fateful year of 1071, the Normans conquered the vital Byzantine Adriatic port of Bari, virtually driving Byzantium from western Europe. By now, Latin Christendom was acquiring the wealth and power of a great civilization, and prostrate Byzantium had to beg European aid. The century of Manzikert ended with the First Crusade and the fall of Jerusalem (1099)—not to the Byzantines but to Latin crusaders (see Chapter 9). Byzantium tottered on until 1453, but it was never again the same. Its years of expansion were over, and most of its energies were consumed in a struggle to survive.

Yet Byzantine culture long outlasted Manzikert. Art and learning continued to flourish through Byzantium's final centuries. When Constantinople fell in 1453, Byzantium was experiencing a classical revival that significantly influenced the Italian Renaissance (see Chapter 12).

To the end, Byzantium revered its classical heritage. As a custodian of Greco-Roman culture, the Eastern Roman Empire made a crucial contribution to Europe's emerging civilization. Roman law and Greek philosophy and literature were studied in Constantinople while they were virtually unknown in the West. Byzantine art's influence on medieval Western Christendom was, in the words of a modern historian, "far-flung and everywhere beneficial: and whatever else the West disliked and despised about the East, its mosaics and enamels, its textiles and ivories, its pearl and onyx, its painting and its gold work were eagerly coveted and jealously guarded in western treasuries."[2]

Yet Byzantium's government never transcended the rigid late Roman autocracy or the defensivness that engulfed the empire after Justinian's death. Byzantium's sometimes awesome creative impulses were tempered by its ancient and holy tradition. Its religious art was *sacred* art, which transmitted divine power to believers, and creating such art was an act of devotion. Byzantine artists and scholars—whose patrons were the imperial court and the church—were expected to preserve, not to innovate. The Byzantine church saw its mission as safeguarding a body of sacred truth already revealed and complete. Byzantine Christianity was more mystical than Western Christianity, but less open to change.

Byzantium contributed much to Europe. It was a military bastion and a cultural treasure chest, and its maritime trade stimulated the economic awakening of western commercial centers such as Venice, Genoa, and Pisa. But it was

---

[2] Romilly Jenkins, *Byzantium, The Imperial Centuries* (New York: Vintage Books, 1969), p.385.

THE HISTORICAL EVIDENCE

Prince Vladimir Converts Russia

ca. 988

The Primary Chronicle *(compiled by Russian Orthodox monks) is our major source for early Russian history. It recounts the story of how, when the Viking prince Vladimir of Kiev was looking for an appropriate new religion to adopt, he sent emissaries to observe Islamic Bulgars, Jewish Khazars, German Latin Christians, and Greek Orthodox at worship. Their reports on Islamic, Jewish, and Latin worship were all negative, but Orthodoxy was different:*

"The Greeks led us to the edifices where they worship their God, and we knew not whether we were in heaven or on earth. . . . We only know that God dwells there among men, and their service is fairer than the ceremonies of other nations."

Vladimir thereupon inclined to Orthodoxy, especially when it was pointed out to him that his grandmother Olga, "who was wiser than all other men," had been an Orthodox Christian. He captured the Greek city of Kherson, in the Crimea, and sent word to the Byzantine emperor that he would "deal with" Constantinople as he had with Kherson unless he was bought off with the emperor's sister as his wife. She was duly dispatched, but with the proviso that Vladimir must be baptized.

By divine agency, Vladimir was suffering at that moment from a disease of the eyes, and could see nothing, being in great distress. The Princess declared to him that if he desired to be relieved of this disease, he should be baptized with all speed, otherwise it could not be cured. When Vladimir heard her message, he said, "If this proves true, then of a surety is the God of the Christians great," and he gave orders that he should be baptized. The Bishop of Kherson, together with the Princess's priests, after announcing the tidings, baptized Vladimir, and as the Bishop laid his hand upon him, he straightway received his sight. Upon experiencing this miraculous cure, Vladimir glorified God, saying "I have now perceived the one true God." When his followers beheld this miracle, many of them were also baptized. . . .

After Vladimir was baptized, the priests explained to him the tenets of the Christian faith, urging him to avoid the deceits of heretics. . . .

When the Prince arrived at his capital [Kiev], he directed that the idols should be overthrown, and that some should be cut to pieces and others burned with fire.

Many people, as yet unconverted, objected, but Vladimir held firm.

Thereafter Vladimir sent heralds through the whole city to proclaim that if any inhabitant, rich or poor, did not betake himself to the river, he would risk the Prince's displeasure. When the people heard these words, they wept for joy, and exclaimed in their enthusiasm, "If this were not good, the Prince and his *boyars* [nobles] would not have accepted it." On the morrow, the Prince went forth to the Dnieper [River] with the priests of the Princess and those from Kherson, and a countless multitude assembled. They all went into the water; some stood up to their necks, others to their breasts, the younger near the bank, some of them holding children in their arms, while the adults waded farther out. The priests stood by and offered prayers.

Vladimir built Christian churches on the sites of pagan shrines, and enforced the baptism of his other subject cities.

He took the children of the best families, and sent them to schools for instruction in book-learning. The mothers of these children wept bitterly over them, for they were not yet strong in faith, but mourned for them as for the dead.

Vladimir also distributed alms to the poor on a lavish scale.

He is the new Constantine of mighty Rome, who baptized himself and his subjects. . . . Vladimir died in the orthodox faith. He effaced his sins by repentance and almsgiving, which is better than all things else.

Source: From *Harvard Studies and Notes in Philology and Literature*, vol. 12, by Samuel H. Cross. Copyright © 1930 by the President and Fellows of Harvard College. Reprinted by permission of Harvard University Press.

on the East and South Slavs that Byzantine culture left its deepest imprint. There, Orthodox Christianity remains powerful, and memories of Byzantium linger. The Soviet authorities controlled the church for seventy years; yet like Byzantium, Russian Orthodoxy displayed a remarkable capacity for survival. It survived communism, and will doubtless survive post-Soviet westernization.

ISLAM

The medieval Byzantine, Latin Christian, and Islamic cultures all played crucial roles in world history. The impact of Western Christendom on today's world is obvious enough. Byzantium shaped Russia and the Balkans. Islam remains a vital religion and way of life—from Indonesia to the Arab world and much of Africa, and with European outposts in Bosnia and Albania. This vast Islamic belt was created by a militant, compelling religion that appeared in seventh-century Arabia (see Table 6-2).

The Coming of Islam

Western Christendom remained for many centuries the most backward of western Eurasia's great cultures. It had much to learn not only from Byzantium, but also from Islam. The influence of these neighbors was impeded, however, by Europe's hostility toward "infidel" Muslims and "effete, treacherous" Byzantines. In the eighth and ninth centuries the West's contacts with Islam were limited largely to the battlefield. Only after A.D. 1000 did western Europeans begin to draw on the rich legacy of Muslim thought and civilization.

TABLE 6-2

ISLAMIC CHRONOLOGY

(Western Calendar Dates)

ca. 571–632	Life span of Muhammad
622	The Hijra (by the Islamic calendar: A.H. 1)
632–655	The first conquests: Syria, Persian Empire, Egypt
655–661	Civil war: Umayyads versus Ali
661–750	Umayyad dynasty; new conquests: North Africa, Spain
717–718	Arabs besiege Constantinople
732	Arabs defeated at Tours
750–1258	Abbasid dynasty at Baghdad
786–809	Harun-al-Rashid rules; zenith of Abbasid power

Muhammad, ca. 571–632 For countless centuries, nomadic tribes from the Arabian Peninsula had pushed northward into the Fertile Crescent. Many Semitic invaders and empire builders of the ancient Near East originally came from the Arabian Desert—Amorites, Chaldeans, Canaanites, and Hebrews. These peoples were quickly assimilated into the ancient Near Eastern civilization of the Fertile Crescent and developed it in new, creative ways. But their kinfolk who stayed in Arabia remained without a central government.

In the sixth century A.D. most Arabians were still nomadic and polytheistic, but new civilizing influences were being brought in by the caravan routes that crisscrossed the peninsula. Cities developed to serve the caravans. The greatest of these, Mecca, became a bustling commercial center that sent caravans north and south and grew wealthy. Meanwhile, new foreign ideas challenged old ways. In this cosmopolitan environment, Muhammad was born, around the year A.D. 571.

The future prophet of one of the world's great religions belonged to a lesser branch of one of Mecca's leading clans. With little formal education, he became a caravan trader. Through his travels and his contacts with Christian Arab tribes and Jewish merchants in Mecca, he encountered Judaism, Christianity, and Persian Zoroastrianism. A sensitive man with a powerful, winning personality, he had a mystical experience in his late thirties and began to preach his new faith. He won little support in Mecca apart from his wife and relatives and a few converts among the poor. The ruling merchants of Mecca ignored his teaching and feared that his new religion would discredit the Meccan temple with its great meteoric stone, the Kaaba, which was a profitable center of pagan pilgrimages. Mecca's hostility forced Muhammad to flee his native city in 622 and settle in the town of Medina, 280 miles northward on the caravan route.

The flight to Medina, known to Muslims as the *Hijra*, was so momentous a turning point for early Islam that it marks the first year of the Muslim calendar. Muhammad quickly won Medina to his faith and became its political as well as religious leader. Muhammad's concept of a sacred community (*umma*) combines the functions that in Christendom are divided between church and state. Medina became the model for later Islamic society worldwide.

The Medinans made war on Mecca, raiding its caravans and blockading its trade until, in 630, Mecca surrendered and was incorporated into the umma. During the two remaining years of his life Muhammad received the voluntary submission of many tribes in Arabia. By the time of his death in 632 he had united Arabia as never before into a coherent political-religious group, well organized, well armed, and inspired by a powerful new monotheistic religion. And because he sternly forbade warfare among believers, Muhammad turned the Arabs' restless energies toward foreign lands.

THE HISTORICAL EVIDENCE

The Qur'an

early seventh century

The Qur'an is perhaps the most widely read book in history. More than a book of worship, it is the text from which non-Arab Muslims learn Arabic. And as the supreme authority not only in religion but also in law, science, and the humanities, it became the standard text in Muslim schools for every imaginable subject. The following selection comes from the surah (chapter) called "Mary," and describes God's earlier revelations to the Jews and Christians. Here, as throughout the Qur'an (which means "Recital"), God speaks to Muhammad.

In the Name of Allah, the Compassionate, the Merciful

. . . To John [the Baptist] We said: "Observe the Scriptures with a firm resolve." We bestowed on him wisdom, grace, and purity while yet a child, and he grew up a righteous man; honouring his father and mother, and neither arrogant nor rebellious. Blessed was he on the day he was born and the day of his death; and may peace be on him when he is raised to life.

And you [Muhammad] shall recount in the Book the story of Mary: how she left her people and betook herself to a solitary place to the east.

We sent to her Our spirit in the semblance of a full-grown man. And when she saw him she said: "May the Merciful defend me from you! If you fear the Lord, leave me and go your way."

"I am the messenger of your Lord," he replied, "and have come to give you a holy son."

"How shall I bear a child," she answered, "when I am a virgin, untouched by a man?"

"Such is the will of your Lord," he replied. "That is no difficult thing for Him. 'He shall be a sign to mankind,' says the Lord, 'and a blessing from Ourself. This is Our decree.'"

Mary conceives Jesus and bears him alone.

. . . Carrying the child, she came to her people, who said to her: "This is indeed a strange thing! Sister of Aaron [i.e., virtuous woman], your father was never a whoremonger, nor was your mother a harlot."

She made a sign to them, pointing to the child. But they replied, "How can we speak with a babe in the cradle?"

Whereupon he spoke and said: "I am the servant of Allah. He has given me the Gospel and ordained me a prophet. His blessing is upon me wherever I go, and He has commanded me to be steadfast in prayer and to give alms to the poor as long as I shall live. He has exhorted me to honour my mother and has purged me of vanity and wickedness. I was blessed on the day I was born, and blessed I shall be on the day of my death; and may peace be upon me on the day when I shall be raised to life."

Such was Jesus, the son of Mary. That is the whole truth, which they are unwilling to accept. Allah forbid that He Himself should beget a son! When He decrees a thing He need only say: "Be," and it is.

Yet the Sects are divided concerning Jesus. But when the fateful day [of Judgment] arrives, woe to the unbelievers! . . .

Forewarn them of that dreadful day, when Our decrees shall be fulfilled whilst they heedlessly persist in unbelief. . . .

You shall also recount in the Book the story of Abraham:

He was a prophet and a saintly man. He said to his father: "How can you serve a worthless idol, a thing that can neither see nor hear?"

"Father, the truth has been revealed to me about many mysteries: therefore follow me, that I may guide you along an even path."

But Abraham's father refuses to abandon idolatry, and Abraham abandons his clan.

. . . These are the men to whom Allah has been gracious: the prophets from among the descendants of Adam and of those whom We carried in the Ark with Noah; the descendants of Abraham, of Israel, and of those whom We have guided and chosen. For when the revelations of the Merciful were recited to them they fell down on their knees in tears and adoration.

But the generations who succeeded them neglected their prayers and succumbed to temptations. These shall assuredly be lost. But those that repent and embrace the Faith and do what is right shall be admitted to Paradise and shall not be wronged. They shall enter the gardens of Eden, which the Merciful has promised His servants in reward for their faith. His promise shall be fulfilled.

Source: From *The Koran*, 4th rev. ed., trans. with notes by N. J. Dawood (Harmondsworth, England: Penguin, 1974), pp. 33–36.

The Islamic Religion   Faith was the cement with which Muhammad unified Arabia. The new faith was called *Islam*, Arabic for "submission." Muhammad taught that people must submit to the single, almighty God—in Arabic, *Allah*. Muhammad announced himself to be the last, "the seal" of a long line of prophets. Among his predecessors he honored Abraham, Moses, the Old Testament prophets, and Jesus.

Islam respected the Old and New Testaments. But the Muslims had a book of their own, the Qur'an, which superseded its predecessors. The Qur'an is the infallible bedrock of the Islamic faith: "All men and jinn[3] in collaboration," so it was said, "could not produce its like." Muslims regard it as the word of God, dictated to Muhammad by the angel Gabriel from an original "uncreated" book in heaven. Accordingly, its divine inspiration and authority extend not only to its precepts but also to its every letter, making any translation a species of heresy. Every Muslim must read the Qur'an in Arabic, and thus as Islam spread, Arabic spread with it.

Muhammad told believers that God would assure them eternal salvation if they led upright, sober lives and followed the precepts of Islam. Above all, they made a simple confession of faith: "There is no god but Allah, and Muhammad is his prophet." Making this confession of faith is the first of the "five pillars" of Islam, binding on every Muslim; the other four are the obligation to pray five times daily, to fast during the month of Ramadan, to give alms generously, and if possible to make at least one pilgrimage to Mecca. A sixth obligation (which many Muslims regard as equally binding) is to struggle devoutly toward the welfare and expansion of the sacred community—in Arabic, to engage in *jihad*. Such holy war was the supremely meritorious activity. (Actual warfare, however, was commanded only against pagan "idolaters.") Law in Islamic lands rested on the Qur'an and the large body of tradition and commentary that grew up around it, and the fusion of religion and politics that Muhammad created at Medina remained a fundamental characteristic of Islamic society. There was (and is) no Muslim priesthood, no Muslim "church" apart from the state: Muhammad's political heirs, the caliphs, were defenders of the faith and guardians of the faithful.[4] The tension between church and state that troubled and enlivened medieval Europe was thus unknown in the Muslim world.

The Islamic Empire

Immediately after Muhammad's death in 632, the explosive energy of the Arabs, harnessed by Islam, broke upon the world. The spectacular conquests resulted in part from the youthful vigor of Islam, in part from the weakness of its enemies. Persia and Byzantium had just exhausted each other in a long, desperate conflict. And the Monophysites of Syria and Egypt remained hostile to their Orthodox Byzantine masters.

The Arabs entered these tired, embittered lands afire with religious zeal. They did not seek converts to their new faith—Islam was regarded in its early generations as a religion for the Arab community only—nor did they have any master plan of conquest. Most of the early campaigns began as plundering expeditions, but with each victory the momentum grew.

Early Conquests   Striking into Syria in 636, the Arabs annihilated a huge Byzantine army, captured Damascus and Jerusalem, and by 640 had occupied the entire land, detaching it permanently from Byzantine control. In 637 they inflicted an overwhelming defeat on the Persian army and entered the Sassanid capital, Ctesiphon, gazing in wonder at its opulence. Within another decade they had subdued all Persia and reached the borders of India. In later years they would penetrate deeply into the Indian subcontinent and lay the religious foundations of the modern Muslim states of Pakistan and Bangladesh (see Map 6-4).

Eventually, most Persians came to accept the new faith, abandoning Zoroaster for Muhammad and thus assuming a great role in later Islamic politics and culture. Yet despite mass conversions to Islam during the 700s, the Persians retained important elements of their ancient culture. Iran's distinctiveness from the Arab world remains important today.

Meanwhile, Muslim armies pushed westward into Egypt, and in the 640s captured Alexandria. With Egypt and Syria in their hands, the Muslims sent navies (largely manned by Christian Egyptians and Syrians) to challenge Byzantine domination of the eastern Mediterranean. They captured Cyprus, raided ancient Rhodes, and won a major victory over the Byzantine fleet.

Civil War, 655–661   In 655 Islamic expansion paused while the succession to the caliphate was contested between the Umayyads, a leading family in the old Meccan commercial elite, and Ali, the cousin and son-in-law of Muhammad. Ali headed a faction that was to become exceedingly powerful in later centuries. His followers insisted that the leader of the Islamic community must be a direct descendant of the Prophet. Muhammad had no surviving sons and only one daughter, Fatima, who had married Ali.

In 661 the Umayyad forces defeated Ali and initiated the Umayyad Dynasty, which ruled the Islamic world from Damascus for nearly a century. But the faction that had once supported Ali remained a dedicated minority, evolving into a dissenting Islamic religious movement, Shi'ism. Opposing the orthodox, or Sunni, Muslims, Shi'ism became an occult underground doctrine that occasionally

---

[3] Jinns (or djinns), in Islam, are supernatural spirits who can be either beneficent or malevolent, and hence they are comparable to Judeo-Christian angels and demons.

[4] The word *caliph* means "successor" (that is, to Muhammad, God's messenger).

MAP 6-4
THE EXPANSION OF ISLAM

rose to the surface in civil insurrection. In the tenth century the Shi'ites gained control of Egypt and established the Fatimid Dynasty in Cairo. Shi'ism inspired a band of Muslim desperadoes known as the "Assassins." The Shi'ite movement survives to this day. It is, for example, the doctrine of the majority of Muslims in Iran and southern Iraq.

The Umayyad Dynasty, 661–750   The intermission in Muslim expansion ended with the Umayyad victory over Ali in 661. And even though the Islamic capital was now Damascus rather than Medina, the old Arabian aristocracy remained in ultimate control. Damascus itself gained a magnificent mosque built by Byzantine architects and embellished by Byzantine mosaic-setters.

Except for years when civil war preoccupied the Islamic side, the military struggle between Byzantium and the caliphate raged relentlessly across Anatolia. Constantinople was the chief military goal, but the great city repulsed a series of powerful Muslim attacks between 670 and 680. The Byzantine defense was aided by a secret weapon known as "Greek fire"—a napalm-like liquid containing quicklime that ignited on contact with water and could only be extinguished by vinegar or sand. In 717 and 718, Constantinople fought off a great Arab army and navy. This proved a turning point, although Byzantium remained on the defensive. Having expended their energies and resources without success, the Arabs abandoned efforts to take the city. Byzantium would bar Islam from southeastern Europe until late in the Middle Ages.

But Islam continued to win spectacular victories. From Egypt, Arab armies moved through North Africa, which its distant Byzantine rulers could not defend. In 711 they invaded Spain and crushed the Visigothic kingdom in a single battle, bringing Spanish Christians and Jews under their dominion and driving the Christian princes into the Pyrenees. Finally, Muslim Arabs and Berbers invaded southern Gaul and threatened the kingdom of the Merovingian Franks. In 732, a century after Muhammad's death, the Muslims were halted at the battle

of Tours by a Christian army led by the Frankish warrior Charles Martel.

The Muslim army that Charles Martel defeated, which had come to loot the shrine of St. Martin at Tours, was small and makeshift in comparison with the great host that besieged Constantinople in 717 and 718. But the two battles

The Mosque of Umayyad Damascus   Built about 715 on the site of a demolished Christian church (which in turn had been built over a Roman temple of Jupiter), the mosque at the Umayyad capital Damascus shows many Roman architectural features. Mosques, like Christian churches, needed a large interior space to accommodate throngs of worshipers.   © *R. Sheridan/ Ancient Art & Architecture Collection.*

ended the era of major Islamic expansion at the expense of the two Christian societies. The rest of the Middle Ages witnessed ongoing Christian-Islamic warfare and some territorial change—most of Spain, for example, reverted to Christian control by the middle of the thirteenth century, and the remainder in 1492. But by and large, Islam, Byzantium, and Western Christendom achieved equilibrium by the mid-700s and remained in uneasy balance for centuries.

For the rest of the Middle Ages, the three heirs of the Roman world tended to expand away from one another—Byzantium into the Balkans and Russia, Islam into Asia, and Western Christendom into central and northern Europe. The Crusades were only a minor exception to this generalization; the Christian reconquest of Spain and the victory of the Seljuk Turks over the Byzantines in Asia Minor were much more important exceptions. But not until the fourteenth century, when the Islamic Ottoman Turks swept into the Balkans, did the balance of the three powers collapse.

The Golden Age of the Abbasids

In 750, eighteen years after the battle of Tours, the Umayyads were overthrown. Their successors, the Abbasids (750–1258), were also of Arabian origin. But the Abbasid caliphs encouraged political participation by the highly civilized conquered peoples, now converting to Islam in large numbers. Above all the Abbasids favored the Islamicized Persian aristocracy, and shortly after the victory of the new dynasty, the Islamic capital was moved from Damascus to Baghdad on the Tigris River in present-day Iraq, near the old Persian capital of Ctesiphon and ancient Babylon. With this move Islam shifted its sights eastward, relieving some of the pressure against the Byzantines and the West. In 751 the Muslims

won a major victory over a Chinese army at the battle of Talas in Central Asia, and thereafter Islam expanded into India and the East Indies.

The new government at Baghdad was run by a medley of races and peoples, and individuals of humble origin could rise high in the service of the caliph. (As one disgruntled aristocrat growled, "Sons of concubines have become too numerous among us; O God, lead me to a land where I shall see no bastards.")

Baghdad became one of the world's great cities, the center of a vast commercial network. Silks, spices, and fragrant woods flowed to its river wharves from India, China, and Indonesia; furs, honey, and slaves came from Scandinavia; and gold, slaves, and ivory from tropical Africa. Baghdad was the hub of a far-flung banking system with branches in other cities across the Islamic world. A check could be drawn in Baghdad and cashed in Morocco, 4,000 miles to the west. The Abbasid imperial palace, occupying a third of the city, contained innumerable apartments and public rooms, quarters for eunuchs, harems, government offices, and a remarkable reception room complete with an artificial tree of gold and silver on whose branches mechanical birds chirped. (The imperial throne room in Constantinople boasted a similar toy.)

Baghdad reached its height under the Abbasid caliph Harun-al-Rashid (reigned 786–809), whose opulence and power became legendary. Harun was accustomed to receiving tribute from the Byzantine emperors. When the usurping Emperor Nicephorus refused to pay, Harun sent a peremptory note, along with a military campaign, which forced the luckless Nicephorus to resume payment.

His era was notable too for its vigorous intellectual life. Islamic scholars studied and synthesized the learning of

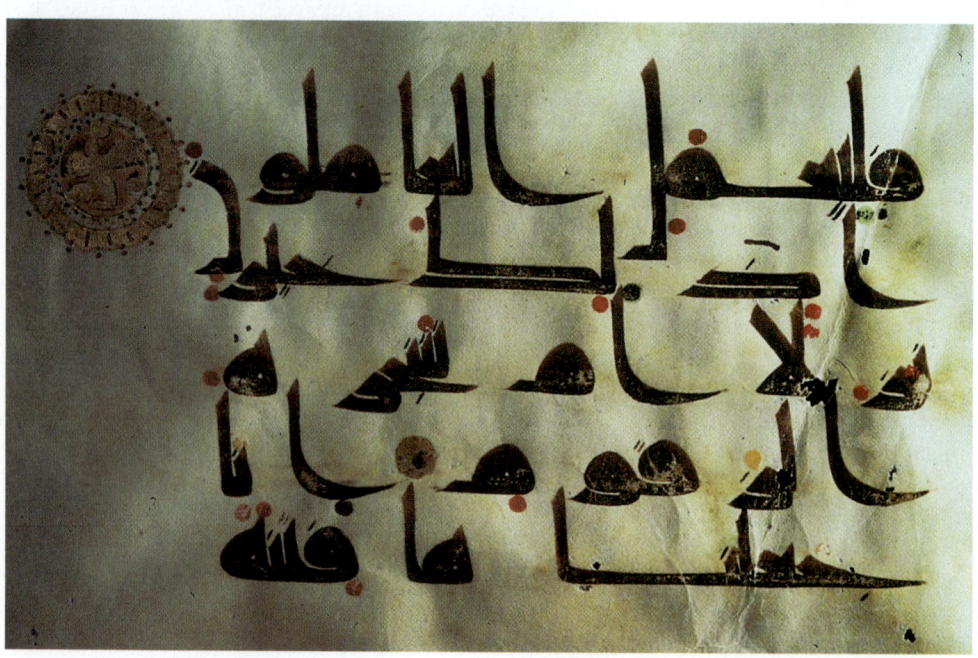

Islamic Calligraphy The Qur'an does not expressly forbid the representation of living things, but by the early eighth century Islamic practice rapidly embraced this prohibition. The ban was not universally observed in every subsequent Islamic society, but where it was in force, it constricted opportunities for visual art, so that calligraphy became an important focus for creative expression. The flowing lines of Arabic script make bold yet graceful handwriting a fine art. This is a fine example of Abbasid calligraphy. *Werner Forman/Art Resource, NY.*

Greece, Rome, Persia, and India. In Baghdad, Harun's son and successor founded the House of Wisdom—a great intellectual institute that was at once a library, a university, and a translation center. Here and elsewhere Islamic scholars pushed their learning far beyond what had been reached under the Umayyads. Drawing from various older traditions, Islamic culture came of age with remarkable speed. At a time when Charlemagne was struggling to civilize his rustic, illiterate Franks (see Chapter 7), Harun reigned over glittering Baghdad.

The Abbasid government drew heavily from the administrative routines of Byzantium and, especially, Persia. A sophisticated bureaucracy based in Baghdad kept in touch with the provinces through a host of tax-gatherers, judges, couriers, and spies. Although no more sensitive to social justice than other governments of its day, the Abbasid regime did increase the amount of land under cultivation by draining swamps and undertaking extensive irrigation works. The status of peasants and unskilled laborers was kept low by the competition of multitudes of slaves, many of them blacks from Africa.

The teachings of the Qur'an had tended to raise the status of Arab women above the level of pre-Islamic Arabia, with its male-dominated tribal culture and unrestrained **polygyny.** (Muhammad limited men to four wives.) But during the Abbasid era there was a spread of severely misogynistic customs, partly Persian in origin: the seclusion of women in private quarters such as harems, and the hiding of women's faces and bodies behind veils and voluminous draperies.

The Abbasid Decline

The Abbasids could not permanently maintain power across the vast reaches of the Islamic Empire. Local power could easily ripen into full autonomy. The Abbasid revolution of 750 was followed by a long process of political disintegration. Even in the palmy days of Harun-al-Rashid, the far western provinces—Spain, Morocco, and Tunisia—were ruled by independent local dynasties. (Islamic Spain, indeed, had never been under Abbasid control at all, but had its own Umayyad rulers.) And by the late ninth century the trend toward disintegration was gaining momentum as Egypt, Syria, and eastern Persia (Iran) broke free.

By then the Abbasid caliphs were slowly losing their grip on their own government in Baghdad, as ambitious army commanders gradually usurped power and the tax machinery. In the later tenth and eleventh centuries the Fatimid caliphate of Cairo extended its authority to Syria and even (briefly) to Baghdad. In 1055 the chief of the Seljuk Turks conquered Baghdad, assumed the title of "Grand Sultan," and routed the Byzantines at Manzikert in 1071.

The decline of Seljuk power in the twelfth century was followed by a period of further Islamic political disintegration coinciding with the Crusades (see Chapter 9). By the later twelfth century Islam recovered itself in Syria and Egypt, and during the thirteenth century the crusaders were driven out. But in that same century the emasculated Abbasid caliphate was destroyed. The Mongols took Baghdad in 1258, massacred its inhabitants (allegedly eight hundred thousand people), and ended the dynasty and the office that had ruled Baghdad for five centuries.

Economic Decline and Islamic Consolidation

The political troubles that the Abbasids endured from about 950 to 1258 accompanied a gradual economic decay, similar to what had occurred in the seventh and eighth centuries in Byzantium and in the fifth through eighth centuries in western Europe. Trade dried up, money became scarce, and Islamic rulers rewarded underlings with land or revenue rights rather than wages. Thus imperialism gave way to localism, and wealth tended increasingly to be identified with land rather than with commerce.

The general unrest of the period encouraged waves of popular protest—both socioeconomic and religious—that had the paradoxical effect of greatly strengthening Islam's attractiveness to non-Arabs. A quasi-heretical, mystical movement known as Sufism became immensely popular throughout the Islamic world. For centuries the Sufi movement, although never tightly coordinated, provided the chief impetus to missionary work among the infidel. Sufi mystics—often illiterate, always fervent—achieved the conversion of millions of people from Africa to China. It was they, rather than the orthodox Sunni religious scholars and lawyers, who could bring the hopeful message of Islam to ordinary people in times of trouble. Drawing on the Neoplatonic notion that reality rests in God alone, Sufis sought mystical union with the divine and stressed God's love, downplaying orthodox emphasis on God's stern authority. Many Islamic scholars vigorously opposed this mystical trend, but by the tenth century Sufism was the most powerful religious force in Islam. To this day, Sufism is one of the most potent elements in the piety of many Muslims.

Islamic Culture: Conversion and Diffusion

Throughout the era of political disintegration, the Muslim world remained united by a common culture and faith. By the reign of Harun-al-Rashid, most of the inhabitants of Syria, Egypt, and North Africa had converted to Islam, even though these lands had once supported well-organized Christian churches. Although there were exceptions, particularly in Spain, Muslims did not ordinarily persecute Jews and Christians. Rather, the Islamic authorities imposed discriminatory rules on nonbelievers (often avoidable for a price), and they taxed them. Some Muslim rulers discouraged the conversion of infidels out of fear of shrinking their tax base. (see Figure 6-1).

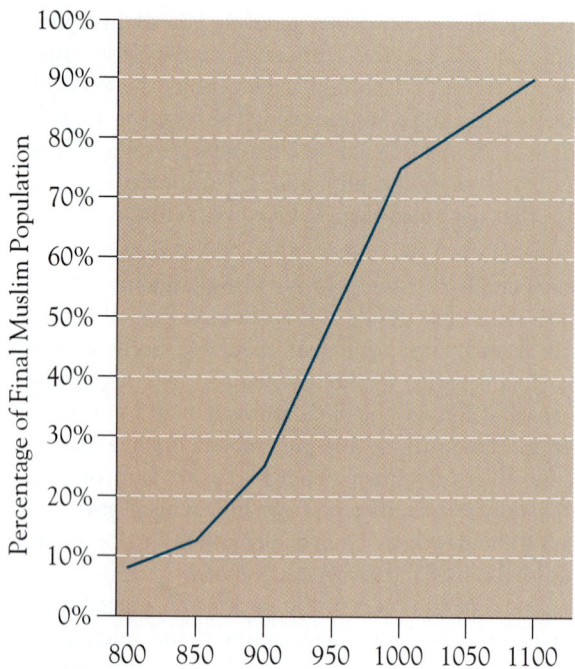

FIGURE 6-1

RATE OF SPANISH CHRISTIAN CONVERSIONS TO ISLAM

The intellectual awakening of Harun-al-Rashid's time continued for another four centuries. The untutored Arab from the desert became the cultural heir of Greece, Rome, Persia, and India, and within less than two centuries of the Prophet's death, Islam supported a mature, sophisticated civilization, highly attractive to the Christian populations it had conquered. Its astonishing rise attested to the Arabs' success in absorbing the great traditions of their conquered peoples and synthesizing these traditions in ways both new and unique. Islam borrowed, but never without digesting. What it drew from other cultures it made its own.

The political disintegration of the ninth and tenth centuries was accompanied by a diffusion of cultural activity throughout the Muslim world. During the tenth century, for example, Cordoba, the capital of Umayyad Spain, became the wealthy center of a brilliant cultural flowering. With a population of a half-million or more, Cordoba was another Baghdad. No city in western Europe was anything like it. It was the wonder of the age—with its mansions, mosques, synagogues, aqueducts, and baths, its bustling markets and shops, its efficient police force and sanitation service, its street lights, and its splendid, sprawling palace, sparkling with brightly colored tiles and surrounded by minarets and sparkling fountains.

All across the Islamic world, from Cordoba to Baghdad and far to the east, Muslim scholars and artists were developing the legacies of past civilizations. Muslim architects

were molding Greco-Roman forms into a graceful and distinctive new style. Philosophers were commenting on Plato and Aristotle, despite the hostility of orthodox Islamic theologians. Physicians were improving the ancient medical doctrines of Galen and his Greek predecessors, describing new symptoms, and identifying new drugs. Astronomers and astrologers were devising better instruments to make accurate observations, were refining Ptolemy's geocentric system, were preparing tables of planetary motion, and were giving the most visible stars Arabic names that are still used—Altair, Deneb, Aldebaran, and (alas) Zubenelgenubi and Zubeneschamali. The famous astronomer-poet of eleventh-century Persia, Omar Khayyam, devised a calendar of singular accuracy.

Perhaps the greatest achievement of Islamic learning was to synthesize ancient Greek and Indian mathematics. From Greece, Muslims learned geometry and trigonometry; from the Hindus, they took algebra (Arabic: *al Jabr*) and the so-called Arabic numerals—the decimal system, nine numerical symbols, and zero. Their understanding that geometry and algebra are two complementary problem-solving tools was a major intellectual breakthrough. Only when Westerners belatedly acquired quantitative skills from Islam, late in the Middle Ages, could they move beyond finger-counting—and the multiplication of XIV by LXXI.

Islamic literature excelled in both poetry and prose. Muslim poets endeavored to perfect individual verses rather than to create long, coherent poems. For example, the quatrains of Omar Khayyam's *Rubaiyat* seem to emphasize alphabetical sequence. The chapters of the Qur'an itself, never organized by Muhammad, were assembled shortly after his death in order of decreasing length, with no attempt at structural unity.

The Arab conquests during the century after Muhammad changed North Africa and Southwest Asia forever. Within its all-encompassing religious and linguistic framework, Arabic culture provided a new stimulus and a new orientation to the long-civilized peoples of former empires. With its manifold ingredients, the rich Islamic heritage eventually stimulated minds in the twelfth- and thirteenth-century West. Later, in 1453, Islamic armies would bring Byzantium to an end and make Constantinople (Istanbul to the Turks) the predominantly Muslim city that it remains. Later still, in the sixteenth and seventeenth centuries, their armies would besiege Vienna in the heart of Europe. Only in the nineteenth century was the Islamic world eclipsed by the West, militarily and politically—a subordination clearly ceasing today.

EARLY WESTERN CHRISTENDOM

The term *Middle Ages* was invented by historians several centuries ago to describe Western Europe between about A.D. 500 and 1500—from the collapse of the Western

Roman Empire to the eve of the Reformation. Since most of those bygone historians were Protestant admirers of ancient Rome, they tended to apply the label *Middle Ages* pejoratively. Some dismissed it all as "a thousand years of darkness." But now scholars regard the "Dark Age" label as drastically misleading, for Europe by the 1100s resembled "early modern" Europe much more than it resembled Europe in the 500s. Historians now generally subdivide medieval Western Europe into three periods:

Early Middle Ages	ca. 500–1050
High (or Central) Middle Ages	ca. 1050–1300
Late Middle Ages	ca. 1300–1500

Early medieval Europe was in no sense comparable in wealth or sophistication to the Byzantine and Arab worlds (although recent research has shown it to be much less primitive than was once believed). It deserves our attention less for its military, political, intellectual, and artistic achievements than for its having served as an incubator for some of the institutions, social relationships, and habits of mind that contributed to the emergence of a great civilization in the High Middle Ages—the nucleus of the West that, beginning shortly before 1500, would project its power, techniques, styles, and ideas around the globe.

The Land and Its People

Until recently, historians' mental image of transalpine western Europe in late Roman and early medieval times was a sparsely populated wilderness. But this traditional picture of post-Roman Europe—and of pre-Roman Europe as well—has now been discarded. Archaeological investigations have demonstrated that human settlement was far more widespread and complex than once suspected. Invading Romans found many large, flourishing agricultural villages. Hilltop forts protected well-organized communities, farmland tilled with heavy plows, and networks of fields, stock corrals, and homesteads. The lands north of the Alps that Romans conquered in the first centuries B.C. and A.D. had undergone many millennia of economic and cultural development from the Stone Age to the Bronze Age (ca. 3000–100 B.C.). By about 100 B.C., the Iron Age had spread throughout transalpine Europe. Finally, during the half-millennium of Roman occupation (ca. 100 B.C.–A.D. 400) there arose cities on the Greco-Roman model—Lyon, Paris, Cologne, Vienna, London, and many others.

Europe's weather is bracing but not intimidating. Northwestern Europe's dependable, year-round rainfall and the fertile soils of its numerous river valleys encourage agricultural productivity—so much so that a Greek geographer in the first century A.D. could describe the region as "producing in perfection all the fruits of the earth necessary for life." By the fifth century, Europe's climate was better still.

Between roughly A.D. 400 and 1200, Europe was less rainy and slightly warmer than it had previously been—or is now. The summer growing season was longer, and vineyards flourished some 300 miles farther north than they do today, reaching southern England, for example. Marshes and bogs receded, and the North Atlantic had less floating ice and milder storms.

The European heartlands form a vast plain that fans out from the Pyrenees and the Alps, stretches northeastward across France and Germany, and crosses eastern Europe to the Ural Mountains, where Siberia (and Asia) begins. In Roman and early medieval times, as in preceding millennia, this vast plain was the route of countless tribes migrating westward out of Siberia and Inner Asia. Interspersed on the plain are several low, mineral-rich mountain ranges, and it is crossed by a network of broad rivers fed by year-round rains.

Europe has been shaped and nourished by its rivers. They connect interior settlements with the sea and with each other. Most of Europe's major cities were built on riverbanks—Paris, London, Milan, Cologne, and many others—so that even though they lay far from the sea, they functioned as ports. A further stimulus to commerce is Europe's long, irregular coastline, with its huge bays and peninsulas, and accessible offshore islands such as Sicily and the British Isles. Together, Europe's climate, rich soils, rivers, and coastline offer an ideal environment for human habitation and productive enterprise.

Before the Roman conquests and long thereafter, most of Europe north of the Alps was dominated by Indo-European-speaking peoples, classified by modern linguists into four large groups: Celts, Germans, Slavs, and Balts (see Chapter 1, Figure 1-1). In successive waves, these peoples probably migrated into Europe early in the first millennium B.C. and slowly intermingled with, absorbed, or pushed aside indigenous pre-Indo-European-speakers.[5] Almost all that we know about them must be deduced from archaeology and from the writings of Greeks and Romans who met or heard of them.

Westernmost of the transalpine Indo-Europeans were the Celts, spreading over Britain and Ireland, Gaul, and western Germany.[6] They were skilled at music and poetry, metalwork and textile making. Romans laughed at their barbaric custom of wearing pants instead of tunics (*breeches* is a Celtic word). Most Celts were farmers, living in villages amid cultivated fields. Others conducted commerce across vast reaches of Europe north of the Alps. The Celts

---

[5] The Basque language, spoken in the Pyrennees, is the last surviving pre-Indo-European tongue in modern western Europe. In eastern and northern Europe, Finnish, Estonian, and Lapp are also pre-Indo-European survivals, and Magyar (Hungarian) and Turkish are later arrivals.

[6] And also the Po Valley in northern Italy, from whence they devastated Rome in the third century B.C. By the first century B.C., however, the Romans had conquered the Po Valley Celts.

built fortified towns along their trade routes, some of which became important provincial cities in Roman times. But the Celts were split into hundreds of independent tribes that united only occasionally, briefly, and grudgingly into larger confederations. They fought hard against the Romans, but in the long run could not match the military resources of that Mediterranean superpower.

Under the Roman conquerors, Celtic agricultural villages continued to function much as before. In time, most of these communities were incorporated into the great estates of the provincial Roman aristocracy (itself part Celtic through intermarriage). The farmer-villagers became unfree peasants and were forced to pay rents and dues to their lords. Some became slaves.

East of the Celts lived the Germanic peoples of what is now north-central and eastern Germany, as well as southern Scandinavia. The great Roman historian Tacitus's *Germania*, completed about A.D. 98, described in admiring tones the life and culture of the Germans, most of whom still lived east of the Roman frontier that ran along the Rhine and the upper Danube. It is doubtful whether Tacitus had much firsthand contact with Germans; mainly he drew on other writers whose books no longer exist. Like many subsequent accounts of "barbarian" life written by sophisticated critics of their own "degenerate," overcivilized societies, Tacitus's book aimed primarily to shame his compatriots with an image of noble savages. Germans, so Tacitus told his fellow Romans, were a nation of brave warriors and virtuous women. "With their virtue protected they live uncorrupted by the allurements of public shows or the stimulant of feastings," he claimed, wagging a finger at his readers. "No one in Germany laughs at vice, nor do they call it the fashion to corrupt and be corrupted." Modern scholarship confirms Tacitus on some points—such as the Germans' addiction to war, contempt for cowardice, and harshness toward female adultery—but mainly the reality that archaeology presents is more complex and somber.

"Germania" (as we may call the area beyond Rome's frontier) contained perhaps 3 million people by the fourth century A.D.—at best, one-tenth of the population of Rome's European provinces. Like the Celts before Rome conquered them, the Germans were fragmented into tribes and war bands that fused and dissolved repeatedly, and fought each other ferociously. Their religion was based on the deification of natural phenomena, personified by storm, thunder, war, and fertility divinities whom they worshiped in sacred groves and to whom they sacrificed animals and human beings. Germans, again like Celts, were agricultural rather than nomadic, and they developed plows more efficient than anything the Romans possessed—tools strong enough to break and turn over heavy north European turf, the direct forerunners of the medieval European peasant's wheeled plow. Their villages were substantial settlements, consisting of "long houses" designed for extended rather than nuclear families.

Tacitus's picture of the Germans' innocence of money is belied by the large hordes of Roman coins that have been found east of the Rhine. Commerce between Germania and Rome was intense. Romans exported to the Germans jewelry and other crafts (not to speak of an illegal trade in weapons), and from them bought salt, furs, slaves, and amber. Trade in all these commodities enriched the elites that were coalescing in ancient German society: headmen whose family compounds were increasingly set apart from the dwellings of other villagers, and chiefs of war bands and tribal confederacies. Such men sought opportunities to make money, whether by accepting service with the Romans or by plundering their outposts. By the third and fourth centuries A.D., Germans were achieving parity with Romans in the quality of their weapons, and leaders emerged who organized the larger confederacies— Ostrogoths, Visigoths, Vandals, Franks, Burgundians, Lombards, Angles, and Saxons—that broke into and took control of the Western Roman Empire

In the eastern part of what Romans called Germania lived other Indo-European-speakers, the Slavs and the Balts. The Slavs' earliest known European homeland was in eastern Poland and western Ukraine; the Balts settled the coasts of Latvia, Lithuania, and what used to be East Prussia (now the Kaliningrad area of Russia). These peoples' greater distance from the Roman world ensured that their agricultural way of life changed more slowly than did the Germans'. But change it did, and by the sixth and seventh centuries the Slavs followed the Germanic peoples in crossing into both the western and the eastern Roman worlds, while the Balts were prospering from the amber trade.

Post-Roman Europe

During the generations following the Germanic settlements of the fourth and fifth centuries A.D., western Europe lost much of the administrative structure of the Roman Empire. But the Christian church preserved a great deal of the classical legacy, and bishops exercised both spiritual and political authority across considerable areas. During the 600s and early 700s the municipal governments of Roman antiquity were disappearing north of the Alps, and archaeology has disclosed a process of urban economic collapse. Yet many Roman towns endured as small ecclesiastical centers—sites of bishops' cathedrals and headquarters of episcopal government over surrounding districts.

Some towns became important centers of pilgrimage, attracting Christians from far and wide. They venerated relics––the bodies or clothing of deceased saints––which were regarded as conduits of spiritual power and physical healing. The cathedral at Tours, for example, possessed the body of St. Martin (bishop of Tours, 372–397), which was

THE HISTORICAL EVIDENCE

St. Radegund, Queen and Nun

late sixth century

The daughter of a Thuringian king, Radegund (ca. 518–587) was captured as a prize of war and was married to the polygamous Frankish king Clothar I, who won her by fighting his brothers, all sons of Clovis. As one of her medieval biographers reported, she decided to leave Clothar when he ordered her brother's killing.

From the king she went directly to blessed Medard of Noyon, earnestly beseeching him to consecrate her to God once she changed her habit [i.e., put on a nun's habit]. Royal officials, however, embarrassed the blessed man to the extent of dragging him violently from the altar in the basilica so that he would not veil the king's wife. . . . When the saint [Radegund] perceived this, she entered the sacristy, put on the habit of a nun, and proceeded to the altar, where she addressed the blessed Medard, saying: "If you refuse to consecrate me, fearing more a man than God, you will be responsible for the soul of one of your sheep, O Pastor!" Shaken by her entreaty, as if he were struck by thunder, he laid his hands on her and consecrated her deaconess.

Through the intercession of St. Medard and another saintly clergyman, Clothar was eventually persuaded to release her from the marriage and to establish her as the abbess of a nunnery at Poitiers, over which she presided for the rest of her life. (Other women in her situation were not so lucky.) In another contemporary biography written by a nun named Baudovina, something of Radegund's character emerges:

When the lesson was read, with pious solicitude caring for our souls, she said, "If you do not understand what is read, it is because you do not ask solicitously for a mirror of the soul." Even when the least [of us] out of reverence took the liberty to question her, she did not cease with pious solicitude and maternal affection to expound what the lesson contained for the good of the soul.

Despite her marital break, she kept in touch with the Frankish kings and was distressed by their civil wars, and tried to mediate. Baudovina continues:

Because she loved all the kings, she prayed for the life of each and instructed us to pray without interruption for the stability [of their kingdoms]. Whenever she heard that they had turned against each other with hatred, she was greatly shaken and sent letters to the other and the other [imploring them] not to wage war and take up arms against each other but to conclude peace so that the country should not perish. In the same way, she sent great men to give salutary advice to the illustrious kings so that the country should be made more salubrious both for the king and the people. She imposed continuous vigils upon the congregation [of nuns] and instructed us with tears in her eyes to pray for the kings without interruption.

Source: From Suzanne Fonay Wemple, *Women in Frankish Society: Marriage and the Cloister 500 to 900* (Philadelphia: University of Pennsylvania Press, 1981), pp. 152, 184.

---

said to have healed many who touched the tomb. Holy men such as St. Martin had been revered in life as transmitters of God's power, wisdom, and love, and their remains retained this function after death. People wanted to be buried near these relics. Just as great lords were expected to protect living dependents who clustered around their strongholds, so the living and the dead alike were believed to come under the saints' spiritual protection against demons and the powers of darkness.

The urban bishoprics, with their relics and vast estates, played a major role in the economy of the post-Roman Germanic kingdoms. So, too, did the large monasteries (abbeys) with their surrounding fields, and often with wonder-working relics of their own. The abbey of St.-Denis near Paris, for example, housed the body of its renowned namesake, Dionysius or Denys, the first bishop of Paris (d. ca. 258) who after having his head chopped off by persecuting Romans was said to have picked it up so that he could see where he was going. St. Denis later became the patron saint of France.

Bishops and abbots were the social and economic equals of the lay aristocracy, to whom they often had close ties of kinship; together they formed the landholding elite of the post-Roman West. The great estates—whether lay, ecclesiastical, or royal—were tilled by slaves or by semiservile, rent-paying villagers in an economic

A Eighth-Century Reliquary   This small casket from Merovingian Francia bears the inscription "Teuderich the priest had this made in honor of St. Maurice." It is decorated with precious stones and an imitation Roman cameo. It contained a purported bone of St. Maurice, a third-century Roman soldier and Christian martyr, whose cult for centuries remained vital in medieval Switzerland and the Rhineland.   *Erich Lessing/Staatliche Museen, Berlin, Germany/Art Resource, NY.*

environment that was becoming increasingly localized and self-contained. A small-scale luxury trade persisted, but the agrarian communities of the sixth and seventh centuries produced most of what they needed. Since lives were meager, needs were few.

Germanic invasions and Germanic settlements had some effect on the ethnic character of western Europe, and a much greater impact on the region's social and cultural life. Because the Germanic newcomers were relatively few compared to the Latin-speaking populations of these provinces, no ethnic "germanization" took place. First in Gaul and then elsewhere, Germanic invaders gradually fused with the indigenous population. In the process, free Germanic farmers often dropped into the ranks of semiservile villagers, or even slaves. At the aristocratic level, the pattern of life was influenced by the Germanic warrior outlook, while the civility of Roman villa life diminished accordingly. The Germanic conquerors, as we have seen, took only portions of the old Roman estates (or taxed them) while establishing new estates for themselves. In the meantime, important churchmen were acquiring extensive lands through the accumulation of pious gifts. Whether under new lords or old, lay or ecclesiastical, villagers worked on.

On the other hand, the ideas of the late Roman Empire and Christianity gradually liberalized Germanic legal attitudes toward women, who rose steadily from their earlier legal status as perpetual minors under constant male control. The ancient Germans had valued women highly—in monetary terms, that is, as the breeders of children. (A man who killed or abducted a woman owed her male kins-

men a high monetary compensation, or *wergeld;* otherwise they would kill him in retaliation.) As individuals, however, women had virtually no rights under ancient Germanic custom. Wives were usually acquired by sale or abduction, and the line between the two was dim. Polygyny was permitted to any man who could afford it; and adulterous wives were dispatched by being drowned in a pond or a peat bog. Germanic peoples brought these folkways into the Roman lands that they occupied. But Christianity, as well as Roman law, gradually softened such attitudes. As they became Christianized and romanized, wealthy and powerful Germanic men found it more difficult (though not yet impossible) to maintain flocks of wives and concubines, or to divorce their spouses at will and kill them if necessary. Christianity also permitted some Germanic or Roman women, rather than submit to unwanted marriages arranged by their families, to find refuge in monastic life. Daughters could inherit lands, and widows could be guardians of their children and could exercise considerable power over their property. The blending of Roman and Germanic landholders into a single social order, combining elements from both cultures, produced the aristocracy of medieval Europe. And, at the bottom of the social scale, unfree peasant men (*coloni* or slaves) found that by marrying a free Germanic woman their children might inherit their mother's free status—a major factor, historians now believe, in undermining slavery in late antiquity.

The Germanic Kingdoms: Government and Intellectual Life

The century between A.D. 500 and 600 witnessed important changes throughout Western Christendom. In A.D. 500, as we saw in Chapter 5, Theodoric's Ostrogothic regime dominated Italy, the Vandals ruled North Africa, the Visigoths governed Spain, Clovis and his Franks were conquering Gaul, and the Anglo-Saxons were expanding their settlements in Britain. A century later, two of these states had fallen to Justinian's armies: North Africa was now Byzantine rather than Vandal, and the Ostrogothic kingdom of Italy collapsed.

By 600, pagan Anglo-Saxon tribes occupied much of Britain, dispossessing and enslaving many of the Celtic inhabitants and driving others into the hills of Cornwall, Wales, and southern Scotland. (The Welsh still speak their ancient Celtic language.) Anglo-Saxon Britain had become a patchwork of independent kingdoms in which Christian conversion was just beginning. Despite Roman trappings, the basis of government in the Germanic kingdoms was the war band. The king's job was to lead his warriors in extracting wealth from any source and to distribute loot according to his warriors' rank and prowess. A king who failed would fall to a rival or be defeated by an enemy.

Gaul—or "Francia," as it was becoming known—in 600 was thoroughly dominated by the Germanic Franks. Its rulers were the successors of Clovis, founder of the Merovingian Dynasty.[7] But Merovingian kings normally divided their kingdom among their sons, who usually fought it out until, as sometimes happened, one emerged as sole monarch of the Franks. On his death, the kingdom would be divided anew and the battles would start over.

Occasionally an able Merovingian king ruled effectively, if ruthlessly, over all or much of a united Frankish kingdom. The most celebrated later Merovingian, Dagobert I, received part of the kingdom in 622 from his father Clothar II—who himself had united Francia by seizing power from his elderly aunt, Queen Brunhilde (by having wild horses tear her apart). Dagobert took over the rest of Francia on Clothar's death in 629 and thereafter ruled vigorously over all the Franks until his death in 638. He was generous to the clergy; by allowing his favorite abbey of St.-Denis to hold an annual fair, he managed at one blow to stimulate commerce and please God. He issued Latin charters employing Roman legal formulas and had Latin law codes drawn up for Germanic people under his sway.

But Dagobert's reign was exceptional, and brief. His dynasty could never get out of the habit of murdering rivals—usually kinsmen. Over time, Merovingian kings became far less effective as their power and estates slipped into aristocratic hands. Yet the Merovingians hung on in Francia for 250 years—much longer than any other Germanic dynasty—giving way only in 751 to a new dynasty, the Carolingians (see Chapter 7).

The Arian kings of Visigothic Spain were more successful in retaining vestiges of the old Roman administration—particularly for levying and collecting taxes. At first, they lacked the Merovingians' crucial advantage of a shared faith with their Roman subjects. The problem was solved when King Reccared (586–601) converted from Arianism to Catholicism, bringing along most of the Visigothic aristocracy and Arian clergy. This holy stampede helped fuse Spain's Roman and Germanic landowners. Reccared then held a church council at Toledo, his capital, in 589, which outlawed Arianism. The monarchy scored another success in the 620s, reconquering the Mediterranean shore from Byzantium (then fighting for its life against Persia). But the Visigothic kings, like the Merovingians, allowed power and wealth to seep away to the nobles. As Gregory of Tours put it, the Visigoths "had adopted the reprehensible habit of murdering on the spot any king who displeased them and replacing him with someone they preferred." The regime fell to an Islamic army in 711.

The century since Theodoric's reign had been disastrous for Italy. The horrors of Justinian's Gothic wars gave way to those of the Lombard invasion. By 600 the peninsula was divided between the Byzantines in Ravenna in the south and the Lombards in the north. The papacy, under nominal Byzantine jurisdiction, dominated the lands around Rome and sought to preserve its fragile independence by playing Lombard against Byzantine. At critical moments, however, it looked to the Byzantines as its defenders.

Roman administration survived after a fashion in Europe—particularly in Ostrogothic Italy and Visigothic Spain, less so in the kingdom of the Franks. But long before the imperial collapse of the fifth century, Roman government in the West had been gradually disintegrating. All through the late imperial era, government and economic life were becoming ever more localized. Resistance to imperial taxes grew, and great landowners gathered private armies on their fortified estates. Germanic kings and the surviving Roman elite were by no means incompetent; they merely inherited administrative machinery already in need of repair. The unfavorable trade balance with the eastern Mediterranean persisted, making gold coins scarce; rural violence worsened; and aristocrats were to pay taxes to Germanic kings as to Roman emperors.

Although strong continuities linked late Roman and early medieval times, the shift was accompanied by widespread misery. The church could do little to help, particularly in troubled rural areas, because its organization was confined largely to the shrinking towns and walled monasteries. Only gradually, and much later on, was the **parish** organized. In the meantime peasants seldom saw a priest even once a year. Churchmen, like kings and nobles, were known to peasants more as grasping landlords than as guardians of justice.

Western intellectual life suffered accordingly. The culture of old Rome was fading, and a new phase of civilization in western Europe had scarcely begun. Books—mainly Scripture and the writings of Latin Fathers—were copied by monks and nuns. The leading scholars of the era were bishops, mostly Roman aristocrats. Bishop Gregory of Tours (d. 594; see Chapter 5) noted that "all but five of the bishops of the see [bishopric] of Tours have been connected with my family." Gregory's History of the Franks, our best source for the early Merovingians, is in some respects impressive. But it is written in ungrammatical Latin (for which he apologizes), displays blatant bias, and tends to dwell on improbable miracles and all too probable atrocities. Both the story that he tells and the way he tells it display the cultural decline in sixth-century Gaul.

Pope Gregory the Great (d. 604), another bishop of aristocratic Roman birth, was honored by Westerners as a Doctor of the Latin Church. Gregory's writings show great practical wisdom and psychological insight, but not the intellectual sophistication of the fourth-century Doctors. Gregory watered down Augustinian theology, overshadowing

---

[7] Named after Clovis's legendary ancestor Merovech.

Augustine's profound insights with a preoccupation with demons and relics.

Bishop Isidore of Seville (d. 636), the foremost Latin Christian scholar of his generation, aspired to collect all human knowledge in his *Etymologies*. A valuable work for its time, it was studied for centuries thereafter. But Isidore uncritically included every scrap of information he could find. In fairness, it should be said that he was victimized by the credulity of ancient Roman writers and by the weakness of the Latin scientific tradition. Nevertheless, the greatest mind of the age writes that "The Cynocephali are so called because they have dogs' heads and their very barking betrays them as beasts rather than men. These are born in India. The Cyclopses, too, hail from India, and they are so named because they have a single eye in the middle of their forehead." After describing similar marvels, Isidore concludes with a belated touch of skepticism that "other fabulous monstrosities of the human race are said to exist, but they do not; they are imaginary."

Western Monasticism

Encouraged by popes and supported by kings, monks were a potent transforming force in the early medieval West. Yet despite the role that they assumed as cultural transmitters, as landowners, and as custodians of relics, these tasks were not supposed to be their real function. At heart, monasteries were places of prayer, meditation, and service to God and humanity—places where aristocrats could give up war and live relatively undisturbed.

Monastic life is not unique to Christianity; a few intensely religious people of all faiths have always sought to withdraw from the world and devote themselves to uninterrupted communion with the divine. Among late Roman and medieval Christians this current was particularly strong, with monasticism becoming regarded as the most perfect form of the Christian life. As Christ had said: "Anyone who has forsaken home, brothers, sisters, father, mother, wife, children, or lands for my name's sake will be repaid a hundred times over and inherit everlasting life" (Matthew 19:29).

Among Christians, the impulse toward withdrawal and renunciation began in the third and fourth centuries, when St. Anthony fled to the Egyptian desert and St. Simeon Stylites mounted his pillar (see Chapter 5). But a more down-to-earth type of monasticism also developed. First in early fourth-century Egypt and then throughout the Eastern Roman Empire, male and female monastic communities, based on a cooperative rather than a hermit life, were attracting numerous Christians who found the post-Constantinian church too complacent. By the early fifth century these East-Roman ideas of ordered communal monasticism were being carried to Europe.

The Irish Monks   In Ireland, a new strain of Christian monasticism emerged. The Celts of Ireland had been con-

The Lindisfarne Gospel   Dating from the late seventh century, this is one page from a copy of the Gospels made by Irish monks at Lindisfarne, in Northumbria. The creation and contemplation of such intricate detail may have served as meditative exercises. *By permission of the British Library.*

verted to Christianity in the fifth century by St. Patrick and other missionaries from a still-romanized Britain; by 600 the Irish developed an astonishingly creative Celtic-Christian culture. Having never been part of the Roman Empire, Ireland had no cities and therefore lacked the urban-based substructure of episcopal organization that existed on the Continent. Instead, Irish Christianity developed a distinctive organizational structure based on great autonomous monasteries. Celtic bishops did not rule dioceses; their functions were spiritual and sacramental only. They had no administrative power and usually lived in monasteries under the authority of an abbot, who was invariably linked to the clan leaders who dominated Irish society.

Celtic monasticism became one of the great energizing forces of the age—in Ireland, in Scotland, on the Continent, and even among the English. Far from papal reach, it spawned a variety of unique customs. During the sixth and seventh centuries, Irish monks excelled in the rigor of their scholarship, the depth of their sanctity, the austerity of their lives, and the scope of their missionary work. Irish monastic schools were perhaps the best in western Europe at the time, and a rich Irish artistic tradition culminated in the illuminated manuscripts of the eighth century. Irish missionaries, striving to deepen and expand monastic life on the Continent, founded a number of important religious houses in Francia and northern Italy, and spread Christianity east of the Rhine. Frankish aristocratic abbey founders often adopted modified versions of Irish monastic customs for their own communities of monks.

St. Benedict and Pope Gregory the Great Early medieval western Christianity was primarily shaped not by Irish but by Benedictine monks and their papal patrons. The Benedictines were named for St. Benedict of Nursia (ca. 480–547), often called the father of western monasticism. That designation marginalizes the Irish and other early monastic movements in western Europe before Benedict's time. Benedict's great contribution was to synthesize earlier practices into a written rule (the Benedictine Rule) of monastic life. Thereafter, Pope Gregory I (Gregory the Great, reigned 590–604) and his successors gradually imposed the Benedictine Rule on Western Christendom.

Like other Christian leaders of his time, St. Benedict was an upper-class Roman. Born in Nursia, a province in the mountains of central Italy, he was sent to Rome for his education. But he fled the worldly city before completing his studies and took up a hermit's life in a cave near the ruins of Nero's country palace. In time, word of his saintliness circulated and disciples gathered around him. Benedict was more than a simple ascetic. He had keen psychological insight and was a superb organizer who learned from the varied experiences of his youth how the monastic life might best be lived. His tremendously influential monastic rule discloses not only his personal genius but also a sense of order that was characteristically Roman.

Benedict founded monasteries, attracting not only would-be saints but also ordinary people and the offspring of wealthy Roman families. At length he built his great monastery of Monte Cassino atop a mountain midway between Rome and Naples. His sister, St. Scholastica, established a nearby hermitage and visited him once a year to talk of spiritual matters. Scholastica became the patron saint of all Benedictine nunneries, while Monte Cassino remained for many centuries one of western Europe's chief centers of religious life.[8]

In its early years, the Benedictine movement very nearly perished. A generation after Benedict's death, Monte Cassino was pillaged by the Lombards, and its monks scattered. Some took refuge in Rome, where they came into contact with the future pope, Gregory the Great. Gregory was deeply impressed by their accounts of Benedict's holiness and by the Benedictine Rule. He wrote a biography of Benedict that achieved tremendous popularity and brought widespread attention and support for Benedictine monasticism. Most of the biography deals with Benedict's miracles, but Gregory also wrote admiringly of the Benedictine Rule.

"Conspicuous for its discretion" was how Gregory described the Benedictine Rule. Modern scholars have discovered that it derived from an earlier, anonymous monastic rule by a mysterious figure, "the Master." But St. Benedict improved on the "Rule of the Master" by giving it a novel quality: humane practicality. It provided for a busy, closely regulated life, simple but not ruthlessly austere. Although designed for communities of men, it was readily adaptable to nunneries. Benedictine monks and nuns were decently clothed, adequately fed, and seldom left to their own devices. Theirs was a life dedicated to God and the attainment of personal sanctity through prayer and service, yet it was also a life that any serious Christian could lead. Benedictine communities were even open to children, dedicated (unasked) to religious life by parents or guardians and then educated in a monastery school.

The monastic day was filled with carefully regulated activities: communal prayer, devotional reading, and work—labor in the fields, household chores, manuscript copying. Benedictine communities had priests to administer the Eucharist, but most monks were not priests. Monks and nuns alike took vows of poverty, chastity, and obedience, resisting the three great worldly temptations of personal possessions, sex, and ambition. Elected for life, the heads of Benedictine houses ruled their abbeys without questioning. But they were strictly responsible to God and were instructed to govern justly in accordance with the Benedictine Rule. Benedict cautioned abbots not to "sadden" or "overdrive" their monks nor give them cause for "just murmuring." Here especially is the quality of discretion to which Pope Gregory alluded and which was such a significant element in the Rule's success.

Within two or three centuries of Benedict's death, the Rule had spread throughout Western Christendom. There was no centralized monastic organization but rather a host of individual monasteries sharing a single way of life. Benedict had envisioned his monasteries as sanctuaries into which pious Christians might withdraw. But the vast estates collected by many abbeys, along with secular society's need to make use of the disciplined, literate monks, thrust the Benedictines deeply into early medieval politics.

In reality, therefore, the Benedictines enormously affected the world they renounced. Their schools produced most of the literate Europeans who kept reading and writing alive during the Early Middle Ages. They served as a cultural bridge, transcribing and preserving the writings of Latin antiquity in a largely nonliterate society. It was thanks in large part to Benedictines that early medieval Europe did not lapse into the illiteracy that virtually destroyed early Greek culture after the fall of Minoan-Mycenaean civilization (see Chapter 2).

Scribal work could be exhausting, as we learn from occasional scribbles on medieval manuscripts: "The art of

---

[8] Monte Cassino was destroyed during World War II. German defenders holed up in it, and it was blasted into ruins by Allied bombardment and an assault by ground troops.

writing is difficult; it tires the eyes, breaks the back and cramps the arms and legs." "The end has come; give me a pot of wine." "Give the poor scribe a pretty girl" (presumably a fleeting erotic fantasy, not to be taken too seriously).

Preserving a cultural lifeline to classical-Christian antiquity was by no means the Benedictines' only contribution to early western Europe. They spearheaded Christianity's penetration into heathen lands. They were scribes and advisers to princes and filled high ecclesiastical offices. Receiving gifts of land from pious donors over many generations, monasteries built up large estates, some of which were models of intelligent organization and technological innovation. For although the individual Benedictine vowed personal poverty, a Benedictine abbey might acquire immense wealth. With the coming of **feudalism** (see Chapter 7), Benedictine abbots became great vassals responsible for political and legal administration and military recruitment over large areas. Above all, as islands of learning and security in an ocean of ignorance and turbulence, the Benedictine monasteries were the spiritual and intellectual centers of the developing classical-Christian-Germanic synthesis that underlay civilization in Europe. In short, Benedictine monasticism became the supreme civilizing influence in the early Christian West.

We have already met Pope Gregory as a popularizer of Augustinian thought. His theology, although highly influential in subsequent centuries, failed to rise much above the intellectual level of his age. His real genius lay in his keen understanding of human nature and his ability as an organizer. His *Pastoral Care,* a treatise on the duties and obligations of a bishop, is a masterpiece of common sense. It answered a great need of the times and became one of the most widely read books in the Middle Ages.

Gregory loved monastic life and ascended the papal throne with genuine regret. Hearing of his election, he went into hiding and had to be dragged into St. Peter's basilica to be consecrated. But once resigned to his responsibilities, Gregory bent every energy to the extension of papal authority. He believed fervently that the pope, as successor of St. Peter, was the rightful ruler of the church. He reorganized the financial structure of the papal estates and gave their increased revenues to charities. His integrity, wisdom, and administrative ability won him an almost regal position in Rome and central Italy, as Lombards and Byzantines struggled for control of the peninsula. Reforming the Frankish church was beyond his immediate powers, but he set in motion a process that would one day also bring France and Germany into the papal fold when he dispatched a group of monks to convert the pagan Anglo-Saxons of England.

The Conversion of the Barbarian West

In the fourth and early fifth centuries, Jesus' command to "teach all nations" had been more theoretical than practical. Christianity was overwhelmingly the religion of the towns and of romanized—that is, Latin- or Greek-speaking—populations. The word *pagan* meant a country person, whose attachment to the traditional rituals of rural or forest life seemed an especially high barrier to receiving the Christian message. But gradually this identification of Christianity with *Romanitas* (the Roman way of life) began to change. This change owed much to the decay of cities and to the entrenchment of bishops and monks in rural strongholds, which brought them into constant contact with ordinary country folk. During the fifth and sixth centuries the hard work of converting these often-recalcitrant people came to be seen as religiously meritorious. Eventually the same motivation inspired earnest souls to carry the Gospel to distant heathen.

St. Patrick, a fifth-century romanized British Christian, was the earliest of these missionaries. As a boy he had been abducted to Ireland by pirates. He learned Irish, and eventually escaped to Gaul. Then, having become a bishop, he made his way back to Ireland, where he claimed to have converted thousands, laid the foundations for the distinctive Irish brand of Christianity, and became the focus of innumerable legends.

At the end of the sixth century, Patrick's example was taken up by Roman and Frankish churchmen who targeted Britain. During the sixth century Britain had been overrun by Angles and Saxons from northern Germany and Denmark. Although small pockets of Christianity may have remained, most of the island had been thoroughly paganized and de-romanized. The mission to England was led by the monk St. Augustine (not to be confused with St. Augustine of Hippo), with enthusiastic backing from Gregory the Great. In 597, Augustine and a large entourage arrived in the southeastern English kingdom of Kent and began their work. England then consisted of various independent Germanic kingdoms, of which Kent was briefly the most powerful. Augustine was assured a friendly reception because Queen Bertha, wife of Kent's King Ethelbert, was a Frankish Christian. With her support, conversion proceeded swiftly. In a mass ceremony, Ethelbert and thousands of his subjects were baptized. His chief town, Canterbury, became the headquarters of the new church, with Augustine as Canterbury's first archbishop. Under his influence Ethelbert issued the first laws written in Anglo-Saxon.

The fortunes of English Christianity rose and fell with the varying fortunes of the Anglo-Saxon kingdoms. Kent declined after Ethelbert's death, and by the mid-600s political power shifted to the northernmost Anglo-Saxon realm, Northumbria. This remote outpost became the scene of a deeply significant encounter between Irish-Celtic Christianity moving southward from its monasteries on the coasts of Scotland, and Roman Christianity spreading northward from Kent and influenced by the Benedictine Rule.

THE HUMAN EXPERIENCE

Bertha of Kent and Ethelberga of Northumbria: Two Germanic Christian Queens

In the conversion of pagan Germanic kingdoms to Christianity, royal women often played a crucial role. The conversion of Clovis and his Frankish people in the 490s, for example, owed much to the efforts of Clovis's Christian wife, Queen Clotilde, who served as the essential link between her pagan husband and the clergy of Gaul. The pattern was repeated a century later in England when Queen Bertha, a Merovingian princess and descendant of Clovis, provided crucial assistance in the conversion of her husband, King Ethelbert of Kent in 597.

Little is known of Bertha's early life; even the dates of her birth, marriage, and death are uncertain. Like all royal and aristocratic marriages of the time, Bertha's was arranged by her parents in negotiations with the bridegroom or his parents. The motive, as in all such marriages, was the advancement of family interests through a useful alliance. Bertha herself was probably not consulted. Indeed, until she crossed the English Channel to Kent for her wedding, Bertha had probably never met her future husband.

Because Bertha was a Christian princess about to marry the pagan king of a pagan people, Ethelbert had been made to agree that she could practice her religion freely and could

bring a Frankish bishop with her to serve as her chaplain. King Ethelbert gave his bride an abandoned Romano-British church, St. Martin's, Canterbury, which still stands. It is likely (though not certain) that Pope Gregory the Great was in touch with her on the subject of St. Augustine's coming mission to Kent. Whatever the case, Queen Bertha contributed significantly to its eventual success by instructing Ethelbert in the basic principles of her faith. According to Bede's *Ecclesiastical History*, when Augustine and his companions arrived in Kent, King Ethelbert "ordered that they should be provided with all necessities. . . . For he had already heard of the Christian religion, having a Christian wife of the Frankish royal house named Bertha." It was in Bertha's church of St. Martin's that Augustine and his monks worshiped and preached; and it was probably there that Ethelbert was baptized in 597.

A few years later, Pope Gregory wrote to Bertha that the fame of her learning and good works had spread as far as Rome, even Constantinople. While urging her to even greater efforts to strengthen her husband's faith, he declared that she, more than anyone else, was responsible for converting the English.

Bertha bore Ethelbert a son, who succeeded in time as king of Kent, and a daughter, Ethelberga, who was wed to a pagan king, Edwin of Northumbria. In important respects the marriage of Ethelberga and Edwin is a case of new actors playing a familiar script. The Christian Ethelberga was permitted to practice her faith in pagan Northumbria and to bring a bishop with her to serve as her chaplain. The pope wrote to King Edwin expressing hope for his conversion, "most especially as we understand that your gracious queen and true partner is already endowed with the gift of eternal life through Holy Baptism." And to Queen Ethelberga the pope wrote, "We have been much encouraged by God's goodness in granting you an opportunity to kindle a spark of the true religion in your husband. . . . Persist, illustrious daughter, in using every effort to melt the coldness of his heart by teaching him about the Holy Spirit, so that the warmth of divine faith may enlighten his mind through your constant encouragement."

Persuaded by Queen Ethelberga and her chaplain, Edwin became Northumbria's first Christian king. He received baptism, along with all his nobles and many of his lesser subjects, on Easter Sunday, 627. ❖

Although Irish and Roman Christianity shared a common faith, they had different cultural backgrounds, different kinds of monastic life, different church organizations, and different systems for calculating the date of Easter. (Exactly when Easter occurred was a matter of great importance in this age, believing as it did that the effectiveness of ritual depended on precise timing.) The Roman Easter date won official recognition at a synod convened in 664 at Whitby, atop a windy bluff overlooking the North Sea. Here the king of Northumbria chose Roman-Benedictine Christianity, assuring papal influence in England. Five

years later, in 669, the papacy sent a scholarly Greek, Theodore of Tarsus, to become archbishop of Canterbury and reorganize the English church into a system of bishops and dioceses. Northumbria's conversion and Archbishop Theodore's tireless efforts made England, only a century out of paganism, Europe's most vigorous and creative Christian society.

English churchmen led Western Christendom's next missionary campaign, beginning about 690, which was directed toward northern Germany and Denmark. Both lands were inhabited by people ethnically kin to the

Anglo-Saxon English, and the pattern of conversion resembled England's. Some local rulers accepted Christianity; others (like a certain Danish king) resisted and proved "fiercer than any wild beast and harder than stone." Success depended on these rulers' judgment calls: How impressive were the prophecies, cures, exorcisms, and miracles that missionaries performed? (For example, St. Boniface, the English "apostle to the Germans," chopped down a sacred oak without the Germanic gods immediately striking back.) Would rulers' war bands reject traditional cults? What could they gain by employing Christian churchmen as administrators and advisers? Not the least significant question was whether a Germanic leader saw the adoption of Christianity as a way of warding off the eastward-expanding power of the Frankish kingdom or, instead, viewed Christianity as an opening wedge for Frankish domination. Wherever they could, missionaries founded monasteries that would become the nuclei of civilizing influences in medieval central Europe. Besides his work in Germany, St. Boniface also reformed the church of Francia, infusing it with Benedictine idealism, systematizing its organization, and binding it more closely to the papacy despite constant protests from Frankish bishops who wanted a free hand for themselves in Germany. (He also brought nunneries under the more direct supervision of bishops and other male authority figures, dampening the independent spirit that nuns had hitherto often displayed.) In 754, beyond the Frankish kings' protection, Boniface was killed by pagan robbers on Germany's northwestern coast.

Barbarian Europe was converted top-down. Rulers, their kinfolk, and their great warriors accepted Christianity first. Ordinary people were baptized later, as monasteries, bishoprics, and parishes were founded. Last of all—generations or even centuries later—came the internalization of a Christian outlook among ordinary people. Christian churches were often converted pagan cult centers, sanitized by an exorcism and sanctified by saints' miraculous relics. But old pagan customs and beliefs lingered for centuries, blending into Christianity. Four days of the English week—Tuesday, Wednesday, Thursday, and Friday—preserve the names of Anglo-Saxon gods (Tiw, Wodan, Thor, and Frig),[9] and charms performed in England centuries after its conversion mixed Christian and pre-Christian remedies.

The Irish-Benedictine encounter in seventh-century Northumbria began a notable cultural awakening known as the Northumbrian Renaissance. The two traditions energized one another to such an extent that the evolving civilization of the Christian West reached a pinnacle in this remote land. Boldly executed manuscript illuminations of both Celtic and Germanic inspiration, a new script, a vig-

The Northumbrian Renaissance   This biblical illumination was copied from an Italian manuscript by a monk at Jarrow during Bede's lifetime. It shows the prophet Ezra writing, but it captures the spirit of intellectual life in Bede's Northumbria.   *Firenze, Biblioteca Medicea Laurenziana, Ms. Laur. Amiantino 1, c. v. Su concessione del Ministero per i beni e le attivitá culturali é vietata ogni ulterioire riproduzione con qualsiasi mezzo.*

orous vernacular epic poetry, an impressive architecture—all enriched Northumbrian culture in the late 600s and early 700s. The Northumbrian Renaissance centered on the monasteries founded by Irish and Benedictine missionaries, such as Jarrow, home of the supreme scholar of the age, the Venerable Bede.

Bede became a Benedictine at Jarrow as a child and remained there until he died in 735. The greatest of his many works, the *Ecclesiastical History* of England, displays a critical sense far above any other early medieval scholar's work. The *Ecclesiastical History*, our chief source for early English history, is the first major historical work to use the recently invented Christian calendar (A.D.—*Anno Domini*, the year of the Lord). Bede's chronological scheme reflects his deep sense of historical unity and purpose: the transformation of the world—and particularly of England—through the spread of the Gospel and the

---

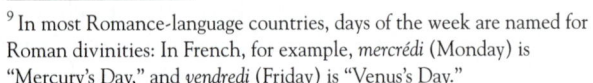

[9] In most Romance-language countries, days of the week are named for Roman divinities: In French, for example, *mercrédi* (Monday) is "Mercury's Day," and *vendredi* (Friday) is "Venus's Day."

THE HISTORICAL EVIDENCE

Bede on the Power of Relics

731

One of the constant themes of Bede's history is the power of miracles, performed through the saints who brought Christianity to the English people. Here is a typical account of a cure wrought by the relics of St. Cuthbert, a bishop whose remains were found uncorrupted eleven years after his death, when in 698 his tomb was opened.

In that monastery [Lindisfarne, in Northumbria] was a youth whose eyelid had a great swelling on it, which growing daily, threatened the loss of the eye. The surgeons applied their medicines to ripen it, but in vain. . . . The brother having long laboured under this malady, but that, on the contrary, it grew daily worse, was cured on a sudden through the Divine Goodness, by the relics of the holy father, Cuthbert; for the brethren, finding his body uncorrupted, . . . took some part of the hair, which they might, at the request of friends, give or show, in testimony of the miracle.

One of the priests of the monastery, named Thridred, who is now abbot there, had a small part of these relics with him at that time. One day in the church he opened the box of relics, to give some part to a friend that begged it, and it happened that the youth who had the distempered eye, was then in the church; the priest, having given his friend as much as he thought fit, delivered the rest to the youth to put into its place. Having received the hairs of the holy head, by some fortunate impulse, he clapped them to the sore eyelid, and endeavoured for some time, by the application of them, to soften and abate the swelling. Having done this, he again laid the relics into the box, as he had been ordered, believing that his eye would soon be cured by the hairs of the man of God, which had touched it; nor did his faith disappoint him. It was then, as he is wont to relate it, about the second hour of the day; but he, being busy about other things that belonged to that day, about the sixth hour of the same, touching his eye on a sudden, found it as sound with the lid, as if there never had been any swelling or deformity on it.

Source: From Bede, *Ecclesiastical History,* unnamed translator (London: J. M. Dent [Everyman's Library], 1910), p. 223.

monastic life. The *Ecclesiastical History* establishes Bede as the foremost Christian intellect since Augustine of Hippo. And the extent of classical-Germanic synthesis is made clear by the fact that Bede, unlike the scholars of the 500s and 600s, was not a well-born Roman but of Germanic ancestry.

By Bede's death in 735, the Northumbrian kings were declining and Northumbrian culture was fading. But Northumbrian learning was carried to the Continent during the eighth century by Anglo-Saxon Benedictine missionaries led by St. Boniface. By the end of the 700s, the cultural center of Christendom shifted southward again from England to the rising empire of the Frankish leader, Charlemagne (see Chapter 7). Charlemagne's leading scholar was Alcuin, a Northumbrian Benedictine and a student of one of Bede's pupils.

BETWEEN WORLDS: EARLY MEDIEVAL JEWS

The Jewish experience in what the Christian calendar reckoned as the first millennium A.D. intertwined with the history of all of Rome's heirs. Though Jewish populations remained relatively numerous, they dispersed widely—from the Germanic kingdoms to North Africa and throughout the Near East.

Rarely in late antiquity and the Early Middle Ages did Christians overtly attempt to wipe out Judaism. Constantine and most later Christian Roman emperors had imposed restrictions on Jews but did not force them to convert. Popes such as Gregory the Great agreed that involuntary conversions were futile. But at times when the danger of non-Christian conquest seemed acute, Heraclius and the iconoclastic emperors in Byzantium, as well as various Visigothic kings of Spain, did try to compel Jews to submit to baptism on pain of death. Appeasing divine wrath by extirpating "infidelity" was, of course, precisely the thinking of the Roman authorities who had martyred Christians. The results of persecution of Jews by beleaguered Christian rulers were similarly barren; indeed, it impelled Jews to turn to their persecutors' enemy. Under Heraclius, Jews sided with Persia (and were massacred by the counterattacking Byzantines), and in both the Near East and Spain they usually hoped that Islamic conquest would be to their benefit.

For many centuries before Muhammad, Jews had lived in Arabia, sometimes winning converts, and Jewish

St. Ildefonsus Debates with a Jew   Early medieval Christian persecution of Jews was fiercest in Visigothic Spain. The tide of Islamic conquest was coming closer by 657, and there are also indications that despite stern laws against it Jews were winning Christian converts by attacking the claim that Jesus had been the Messiah or by persuading Christians to adopt Jewish dietary rules. This manuscript illumination shows the archbishop of Toledo, St. Ildefonsus, debating with a Jew, probably a rabbi. Several Spanish polemics of Christian leaders against Judaism survive from the seventh and eighth centuries. Depictions of Jews from this period are very rare.   *Firenze, Biblioteca Medicea Laurenziana, Ms. Laur. Ashb. 17, c. 18, Su concessione del Ministero per i beni e le attività culturali é vietata ogni ulteriore riproduzione con qualsiasi mezzo.*

communities remained important in the new Islamic societies. Muhammad was probably educated by Jews and was bitterly disappointed when they later rejected him. Despite a massacre carried out under his orders during the conquest of the Arabian peninsula, the Qur'an's injunction to tolerate "the people of the book" usually shaped Muslims' policy toward Jews. Under Islamic rule, Jews were finally permitted to live legally in Jerusalem. Centuries of alien rule had made Jewish communities resistant both to persecution and to the lure of cosmopolitan cultures like Islam (temptations that Near Eastern and Spanish Christians found harder to

ignore). The Umayyad and Abbasid caliphs depended heavily on Jewish physicians, bankers, and officials. Baghdad, Cordoba, Alexandria, and Cairo all boasted thriving and well-taxed Jewish communities. Relations soured by the eleventh century, as Sufi proselytizers provoked popular anger against Jews and Christians who refused to convert. In Islamic Spain, the advance of Christian crusaders heightened Muslim militancy against all infidels. Overall, though, the Islamic "golden age" was relatively prosperous for Jews—and an era of notable achievements as Jewish scholars helped recover Greek philosophy and science (see Chapter 10).

In the West, the substitution of Germanic for Roman rule had less of an effect on Jews than did the era's economic decay and de-urbanization. Jews, like Romans, often moved into the countryside and came to terms with their new rulers. Ordinary Jews appear to have become peasants. Wealthier Jews, barred from intermarriage with Christians unless they converted, did not join the new aristocracy formed from the fusing of Germanic warriors and Gallo-Roman elite, but they did thrive as long-distance traders, royal administrators, and tax collectors.

In one improbable place medieval Jews ruled a state of their own—on the steppes of southern Russia, where around A.D. 740 the Turkic Khazars converted to Judaism. The Khazars (allies of the Byzantines against the Muslims) apparently decided that they could better safeguard their independence by choosing Judaism over Christianity. It is debatable how deeply Judaism penetrated into Khazar society, but the kingdom prospered and was militarily significant for two centuries. Then, in 965, the Khazars succumbed to simultaneous attacks by Russians and fierce new steppe marauders.

The crucial changes that created medieval Jewish culture dated from the first few centuries A.D.: loss of an autonomous Jewish state, destruction of the Temple, the assumption of leadership by the rabbis, and estrangement between Jews and Jewish Christians. Under these conditions, early medieval Jews had to concentrate on maintaining bonds between communities separated by vast distances. Committed to warding off persecution and assimilation, they survived by becoming introspective and defensive. The cultural and spiritual strength that they nurtured in the centuries after Imperial Rome's transformation prepared Jews for still greater trials from the eleventh century onward, when the Islamic and Byzantine societies that had tolerated them declined and Western Christendom grew more fervent in its faith—and less tolerant of the Jews in its midst.

CONCLUSION: *THE HEIRS OF ROME*

Rome's heirs—Byzantium, Islam, Western Christendom, and the medieval Jews—would remain in tension throughout and beyond the Middle Ages. Eventually, Byzantium would fall in 1453; western Europe would pull ahead of Islam militarily and economically; Judaism would face ghettos and pogroms. But in the long run Byzantium's faith, Eastern Orthodox Christianity, endures; Islam remains one of the most powerful forces of our contemporary global society; Judaism, from which the ethical monotheisms of Christianity and Islam alike have sprung, has become the West's conscience, a source of its basic moral values. The creative tension between these heirs of Rome continues to this day.

Early medieval Europe differed from Byzantium and the Islamic world in innumerable ways, the most obvious being its lower level of civilization. But just as important is the fact that in western Europe, the church was able to develop more or less independently of the state. True, church and state often worked hand in glove, but religion and secular politics never merged to the degree that they did in Constantinople, in Islam, and in ancient civilization. Early Western Christendom was marked by a separation between cultural leadership, which was ecclesiastical and monastic, and political power, which was in the hands of Germanic kings and Roman-Germanic aristocracies. This split contributed much to the fluidity, dynamism, and tendency toward change of Western culture. Like St. Augustine's two cities, the warrior culture of the Germanic kingdoms and the classical-Christian culture of church and monastery remained always in the process of fusion, yet never completely fused. Their tense interplay—indeed, their contradictions—shaped medieval civilization, as we shall see in the chapters that follow.

Selected Reading

Sources

Bede. *Ecclesiastical History*, trans. Leo Shirley-Price (1975).

Geanakoplos, Deno John, ed. *Byzantium: Church, State, and Civilization Seen through Contemporary Eyes* (1984).

The Koran, 4th rev. ed., trans. with notes by N. J. Dawood (1974). It is impossible to understand Islam without reading the Qur'an. Dawood's work is an excellent modern English translation, which rearranges the *surahs* into a topical order (while retaining the original numbers).

Lewis, Bernard, ed. *Islam: From the Prophet Muhammed to the Capture of Constantinople* (1987).

Byzantium

Browning, Robert. *The Byzantine Empire*, rev. ed. (1992). A sympathetic, chronological treatment of Byzantine politics, culture, literature, philosophy, and art.

Geanakoplos, Deno J. *Interaction of the "Sibling" Byzantine and Western Cultures in the Middle Ages and Italian Renaissance, 330–1600* (1976). A learned discussion of Byzantine-Western relations across thirteen centuries.

Jenkins, Romilly. *Byzantium: The Imperial Centuries*, A.D. *610–1071* (1966). A fine account of the period from Heraclius to the battle of Manzikert, particularly valuable on the age of the Macedonian emperors.

Mango, Cyril. *Byzantium: The Empire of New Rome* (1980). A lively and thought-provoking synthesis, stressing the earlier phases of Byzantine civilization.

Runciman, Steven. *The Byzantine Theocracy* (1977). A brief survey of relations between the Byzantine church and empire stressing the emperor's role as God's viceroy.

Treadgold, Warren. *The History of the Byzantine State and Society* (1997). A large-scale synthesis of the entire span of Byzantine history that, unlike earlier general histories, pays full attention to social history; likely to remain the standard work of its kind for many years.

Islam

Ahmed, Leila. *Women and Gender in Islam* (1992). Although this study runs up to the present, much of it provides a valuable treatment of women in medieval Islam.

Fletcher, Richard. *Moorish Spain* (1992). A highly readable account running from the Berber invasion of A.D. 711 to the early seventeenth century, this book views Islamic Spain without its usual silver lining: It was "not a tolerant and enlightened society even in its most cultivated epoch."

Grunebaum, G. E. von. *Medieval Islam: A Study in Cultural Orientation*, 2nd ed. (1956). A learned and original work, the best on the subject in the English language. A valuable shorter account by the same author is *Classical Islam: A History, 600–1258* (1970).

Hodgson, Marshall G. S. *The Venture of Islam: Conscience and History in a World Civilization*, 3 vols. (1974). A comprehensive, learned, and highly stimulating survey of Islamic civilization that is probably still the best introduction to the field.

Hourani, Albert H. *A History of the Arab Peoples* (1991). This comprehensive work, covering all of Arab history, provides an outstanding account of medieval Islam.

Humphries, R. Stephen. *Islamic History: A Framework for Inquiry* (1991). This, the best treatment of its kind, covers the period from the origins of Islam to the 1400s.

Lapidus, Ira M. *A History of Islamic Societies* (1988). A comprehensive, broad-gauged history.

The Early Medieval West

Campbell, James, ed. *The Anglo-Saxons* (1982). A splendid, beautifully illustrated survey with chapters by Patrick Wormald, Eric John, and the editor.

Collins, Roger. *Early Medieval Spain: Unity in Diversity, 400–1000* (1983). An outstanding, highly original account stressing regional diversity and rehabilitating, to a degree, the Visigothic monarchy.

Fletcher, Richard. *The Barbarian Conversion: From Paganism to Christianity* (1997). An ambitious, beautifully written synthesis that narrates the spread of Christianity into western and northern Europe; the author emphasizes how significant was the realization that Christianity need not mean "Romanness."

Geary, Patrick. *Before France and Germany* (1987). A brief survey incorporating recent historical interpretations and archaeological findings, which emphasizes the vitality and significance of the Merovingian era in Frankish history.

Grant, Michael. *Dawn of the Middle Ages* (1981). A lucid account of Western Europe between 476 and 816, splendidly illustrated.

Hodges, Richard, and David Whitehouse. *Mohammed, Charlemagne and the Origins of Europe: Archaeology and the Pirenne Thesis* (1983). A highly original and sometimes convincing reinterpretation of Henri Pirenne's thesis (see Pirenne entry below) on the basis of modern archaeological findings.

James, Edward. *The Franks* (1986). A highly readable work that employs historical and archaeological evidence to cast new light on the Franks from later Roman to Carolingian times.

Lasko, Peter. *The Kingdom of the Franks: Northwest Europe before Charlemagne* (1971). A splendidly illustrated account of the Merovingian Franks emphasizing Frankish art.

Pirenne, Henri. *Mohammed and Charlemagne* (1955 reprint). The firmest statement by the great Belgian scholar of his controversial thesis that Roman civilization endured in the West until the eighth century; should be read along with Hodges and Whitehead (see above).

Richards, Jeffrey. *The Popes and the Papacy in the Early Middle Ages, 476–752* (1979). A welcome effort to view the early medieval papacy without the distorting lens of later papal ideologies.

Riché, Pierre. *Education and Culture in the Barbarian West, Sixth through Eighth Centuries* (1976). Trans. John J. Contreni. An impressive, richly detailed work of interdisciplinary scholarship.

Wallace-Hadrill, J. M. *Early Germanic Kingship in England and on the Continent* (1971). Authoritative studies of kingship from the early Germanic tribes through Charlemagne and Alfred.

———. *The Frankish Church* (1983). An erudite, witty, and original study of the Church in Merovingian and Carolingian Francia.

Wemple, Suzanne Fonay. *Women in Frankish Society: Marriage and the Cloister, 500 to 900* (1981). A meticulously documented analysis of Frankish women in both the church and the family, arguing that their status declined between Merovingian and Carolingian times.

CHAPTER 7

THE WESTERN REVIVAL

Aachen, Imperial Chapel
E. T. Archive.

714–741 Rule of Charles Martel as mayor of the palace in Merovingian Francia

732 Charles Martel defeats the Muslims at Tours

741–768 Rule of Pepin the Short in Francia

751 Frankish-papal alliance sealed; Pepin crowned king of the Franks, beginning the Carolingian Dynasty

754 Death of St. Boniface, missionary to the Germans and organizer of the Frankish church; papal anointment of Pepin

768–814 Reign of Charlemagne (Charles the Great), conqueror of continental Western Christendom

772–804 Charlemagne conquers and converts the Saxons

774 Charlemagne conquers the Lombards in northern Italy

800 Pope Leo I crowns Charlemagne Roman Emperor in the West

814–840 Reign of Louis the Pious; beginning of Carolingian disintegration and of widespread Viking raids on western Europe

840–876 Louis the German rules East Francia

840–877 Charles the Bald rules West Francia

842 Louis the German and Charles the Bald seal an alliance with the bilingual Oaths of Strasbourg

843 Treaty of Verdun: the three sons of Louis the Pious divide the Carolingian Empire into East Francia, the Middle Kingdom, and West Francia

871–899 Alfred the Great, king of Wessex, rolls back Danish invasions and stabilizes Anglo-Saxon England

ca. 875–930 Norse settlement of Iceland

ca. 890–955 Magyars settle the Danube basin, raid western Europe

911 Vikings (Northmen, Normans) granted a territorial base in Normandy by King Charles the Simple

936–973 Reign of Otto I (the Great), German king and later Holy Roman emperor

955 Otto the Great defeats the Magyars at the Lechfeld, ending their raids

962 Otto I crowned Holy Roman emperor by pope

987 Hugh Capet replaces the last Carolingian kings of France, beginning the Capetian Dynasty

ca. 1000 Ottonian Renaissance in Germany; Vikings colonize North America; Hungary becomes a Christian kingdom

1017–1035 Danish king Canute rules England, Denmark, and Norway

1039–1056 Reign of Emperor Henry III

1042–1066 Reign of Edward the Confessor, last successful Anglo-Saxon king of England

1066 William the Conqueror defeats Anglo-Saxon forces at battle of Hastings, beginning Norman rule in England

The Germanic kings who ruled western Europe after the collapse of Roman power there seldom stayed put. For hundreds of years they traveled about their realms with as big a retinue as they could muster, consuming the food of one estate and moving on to the next, lugging their treasure along with them and doling out what they needed to maintain their followers' loyalty. It seemed the best way to keep an eye on what was happening, and it avoided the expense of setting up permanent headquarters. With towns shrinking, sometimes almost vanishing, who could even think of starting a real capital?

Charles the Great, king of the Franks, did. In 794 he established a permanent capital at Aachen in what is now the westernmost part of Germany. Charles the Great (or Charlemagne, to use the name by which he is better known to history) consciously aimed to create a Constantinople of his own. Aachen was called "New Rome," and an impressive palace-church was built in the Byzantine style—almost literally a poor man's Hagia Sophia. Though his "Mary Church" at Aachen was a far cry from Justinian's masterpiece, it was a marvel for its time and place. It made a powerful impact on contemporaries, and it remains impressive to this day, as is apparent from the photograph at the beginning of this chapter. Charlemagne's contemporary biographer described it as a beautiful basilica adorned with gold and silver lamps, with rails and doors of solid brass, and with columns and marbles from Rome and Ravenna. Organizing the transport of all this from Italy to the Rhineland was a major logistical effort on Charlemagne's part—an effort not only to create a beautiful church but also to imitate the Byzantines and impress his own Germanic subjects.

Charlemagne's building of a seat of government and a beautiful royal chapel—assembled, to be sure, out of pillaged materials—indicates that something unprecedented was afoot in the West around the year 800. As he established himself in Aachen, Charlemagne was in the throes of uniting all of Western Christendom (except England) into the single dominion that historians call "the Carolingian Empire." In Charlemagne's realm the various cultural ingredients—classical, Christian, and Germanic—that went into the making of European civilization achieved an unprecedented synthesis. Charlemagne was a Germanic king who surrounded himself with Germanic warrior-aristocrats and made war for an old-fashioned motive: plunder. But he also consorted with well-educated churchmen who were trained in classical scholarship, and he took seriously his role as protector of the Latin church. Although his realm was fundamentally Germanic, its intellectual life, limited though it was, drew heavily from the classical-Christian tradition. The fusion of these ingredients was evident in his beautiful chapel at Aachen, in the life of the Carolingian court, in the rising vigor of the Carolingian church, and in the person of Charlemagne himself.

Charlemagne's revived Roman Empire did not last, and it would not be the model for the future Western state. During the calamitous ninth and tenth centuries, western Europe was almost overwhelmed by new invaders: Magyars from the east, Muslims from the south, Vikings from the north. Besides sowing terror and creating enormous impoverishment, these invasions wrought significant changes in Europe's political and social organization. The political entities known as France, Germany, and England came into focus. In France, it is true, political authority crumbled into local units as unwieldy royal armies failed to cope with the Viking raids. But elsewhere the invasions had the effect of augmenting royal power. The German monarchy, after a period of relative weakness, underwent a spectacular recovery in the tenth century, while in England the hammer blows of the Danes ultimately unified the Anglo-Saxon states into a single kingdom. In general, Europeans submitted to whatever leadership could provide an effective defense—whether kings, territorial princes, or, as in northern Italy, urban bishops.

Many Europeans expected that the year 1000—marking, they thought, a millennium since the birth of Christ—would mean the end of the world. Instead, a recovery was under way. The invasions ceased. Cities and trade were reviving. Population began to grow, and peasants were clearing forestland for new settlements. Confidence began to gain ground. Western Europe was on the verge of the three hundred years of economic growth and cultural creativity that historians call the High Middle Ages. In 1003 one monk, who had anxiously anticipated the millennium, wrote with wonder and perhaps relief:

After the above mentioned year of the millennium, which is now about three years past, there occurred throughout the world, especially in Italy and Gaul, a rebuilding of church basilicas. Notwithstanding the greater number were already well established and not in the least need, nevertheless each Christian people strove against the others to erect nobler ones. It was as if the whole earth, having cast off the old by shaking itself, were clothing itself everywhere in the white robe of the church. Then, at last, all the faithful altered completely most of the episcopal seats [residences] for the better, and likewise, the monasteries of the various saints as well as the lesser places of prayer in the towns.[1]

A new millennium was dawning in which western Europe would slowly rise to global dominance.

THE CAROLINGIANS

If in the year 800 a visitor from the richest society on earth—that is, from China—had toured western Eurasia, he would not have been impressed when he passed from the Abbasid and Byzantine Empires to Charlemagne's Francia. Baghdad and Constantinople were great cities and centers of far-flung commerce. Charlemagne's kingdom had no cities worth the name, and his subjects were overwhelmingly impoverished rural people. But if the Chinese traveler had talked to Charlemagne's people carefully, he might have realized that it was dawning on a few of them that they were a people apart—"Europeans," agents of a new, distinctive civilization rooted in Athens and Jerusalem, Germany and Rome, and bound together, much as Byzantines, Muslims, and Chinese were, by a common faith, scholarly language, and cultural heritage.

The new Europe was spiritually and intellectually enlivened by the wide-ranging Benedictines, who disseminated a cultural tradition based on the Bible, the writings of the fourth- and fifth-century Latin Doctors, and the surviving masterpieces of Latin literature. Over this evolving culture presided a new dynasty of Frankish monarchs, the Carolingians.[2]

Although Charlemagne thought of himself as reviving the Western Roman Empire, his state differed profoundly from the empire of old. It was thoroughly agrarian in its economic organization, with its culture centered on the monastery, the cathedral, and the royal and noble courts instead of the urban marketplace. And although Charlemagne extended his rule into Italy, the focus of his activities remained northern Francia. In short, the new Europe

---

[1] A *Documentary History of Art*, ed. Elizabeth G. Holt (Princeton, NJ: Princeton University Press, 1957), vol. 1, p. 18.
[2] The Carolingians were named after their early leader Carolus, or Charles, Martel ("the Hammer," reigned 714–741).

no longer faced the Mediterranean; its center of gravity had shifted northward.

The Early Carolingians

The Merovingian Dynasty, founded by Clovis (see Chapter 5), had weakened during its final century. A fundamental problem was that the Merovingians, like all other early medieval monarchs, had to give away portions of their crown lands, generation after generation, to attract and keep loyal followers. By the later 600s, the Merovingians were impoverished, and power had passed to the landed aristocracy. Meanwhile, as a consequence of generations of strife among the kinsmen of deceased Merovingian kings, Francia had split into several distinct districts, the most important of which were Neustria (Paris and northwestern France), Austrasia (the heavily germanized northeast, including the Rhineland), and Burgundy in the southeast (see Map 7-1).

During the seventh century, there emerged from the landholding aristocracy of Austrasia the family known to historians as the Carolingians. Supported by a handful of allied and related families (and boasting at least one saint in their pedigree), the Carolingians managed to eliminate or assimilate rival families until they had achieved supremacy in Austrasia.

The Carolingians became "mayors" (from the Latin word for "greater") of the Austrasian royal household—that is, they held the chief administrative office in the Austrasian royal court. They made the post hereditary, and as the Merovingian kings became increasingly poor and powerless the Carolingians became Austrasia's real masters.

Carolingian mayors built up their power by collecting considerable numbers of trained warriors, in the tradition of the old Germanic war band. These men became "vassals" (from a Celtic word for "servant") of the Carolingians, placing themselves under the mayor's protection, accepting his food, shelter, and support, and pledging him their loyalty. Other aristocrats had similar private armies of vassals, but the Carolingians, with far the greatest number of followers, dominated the scene.

In 687 a Carolingian mayor named Pepin of Heristal led his Austrasian army to a decisive victory over the Neustrians, and the Carolingians thenceforth controlled both districts. With Neustria in their grip they were able to dominate Burgundy, and when Muslim raiders from Spain struck at Gaul in the early 730s, the Franks stood united against them under the Carolingian mayor Charles Martel—Pepin of Heristal's bastard son (see Figure 7-1).

Charles "the Hammer" (for so Martel translates) was an aptly named chieftain. Not only did he repel the Muslims at the battle of Tours (732), but he also won victory after victory over Muslims and Christians alike, consolidating his power over the Franks and extending the boundaries of the Frankish state. Charles Martel rewarded his military followers with estates in the conquered lands, and with further estates that he confiscated from the Frankish church. Although churchmen complained loudly, there was little they could do to oppose the hero of Tours and master of the Franks.

The Carolingians followed the same practice of dividing lands among male heirs that had weakened the Merovingians. But, by chance, the Carolingian rulers over several generations had only one long-surviving heir. Luck

MAP 7-1
FRANCIA

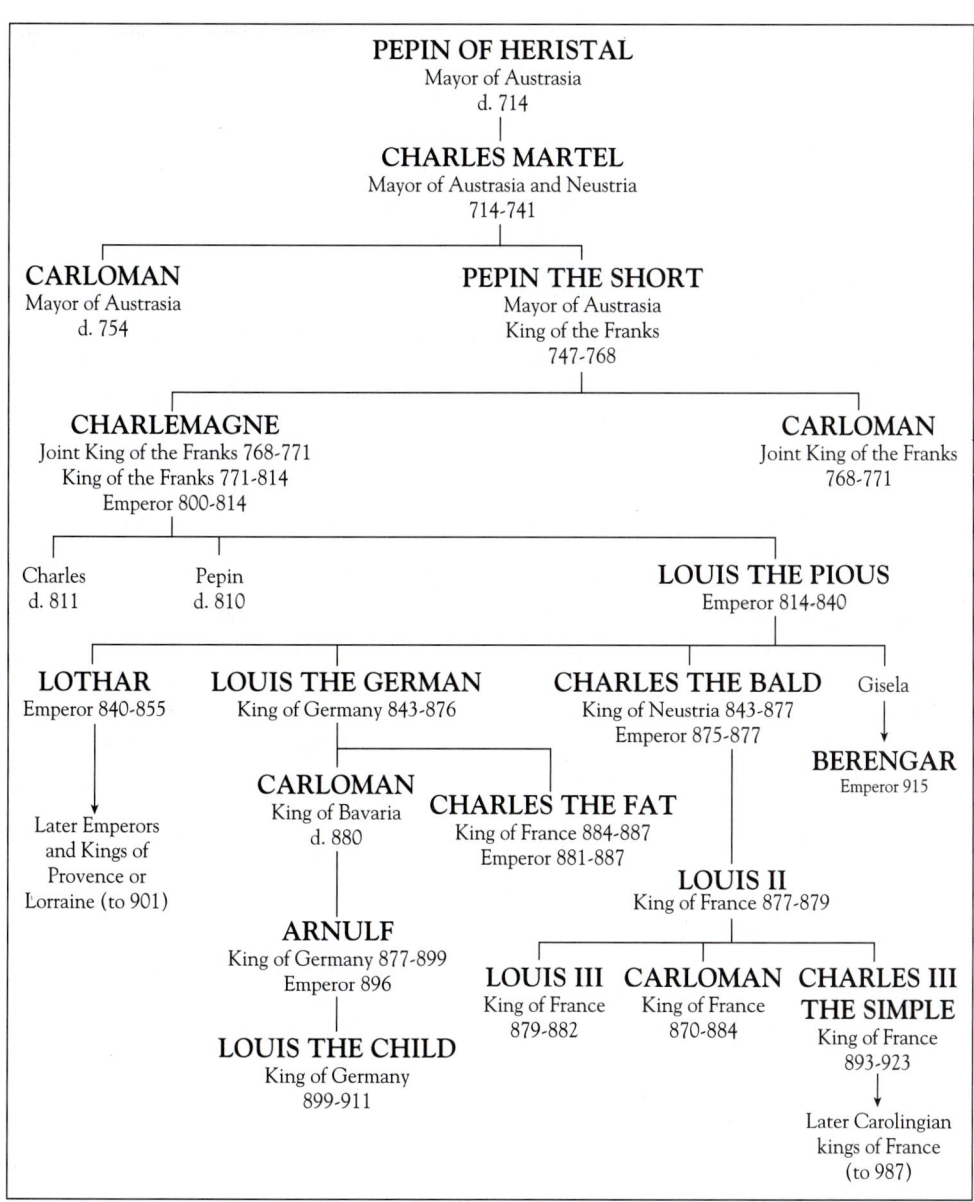

PEPIN OF HERISTAL
Mayor of Austrasia
d. 714

CHARLES MARTEL
Mayor of Austrasia and Neustria
714-741

CARLOMAN
Mayor of Austrasia
d. 754

PEPIN THE SHORT
Mayor of Austrasia
King of the Franks
747-768

CHARLEMAGNE
Joint King of the Franks 768-771
King of the Franks 771-814
Emperor 800-814

CARLOMAN
Joint King of the Franks
768-771

Charles
d. 811

Pepin
d. 810

LOUIS THE PIOUS
Emperor 814-840

LOTHAR
Emperor 840-855

LOUIS THE GERMAN
King of Germany 843-876

CHARLES THE BALD
King of Neustria 843-877
Emperor 875-877

Gisela

Later Emperors
and Kings of
Provence or
Lorraine (to 901)

BERENGAR
Emperor 915

CARLOMAN
King of Bavaria
d. 880

CHARLES THE FAT
King of France 884-887
Emperor 881-887

ARNULF
King of Germany 877-899
Emperor 896

LOUIS II
King of France 877-879

LOUIS THE CHILD
King of Germany
899-911

LOUIS III
King of France
879-882

CARLOMAN
King of France
870-884

**CHARLES III
THE SIMPLE**
King of France
893-923

Later Carolingian
kings of France
(to 987)

**FIGURE 7-1
THE CAROLINGIANS**

sustained Frankish unity. When Charles Martel died in 741, his lands and authority were apportioned to his sons, Carloman and Pepin the Short. But Carloman ruled only six years, in 747 retiring (voluntarily, so it appears) to the monastery of Monte Cassino—leaving the whole inheritance to his brother Pepin. Carloman represented a new kind of Germanic ruler, deeply affected by the spiritual currents of his age, whose piety foreshadowed that of numerous saint-kings of later centuries. Christian culture and Germanic political leadership were beginning to converge.

The Franco-Papal Alliance

As Charles Martel was hammering together a Carolingian realm and Pepin the Short was consolidating it, the Eng-

lish Benedictine St. Boniface was busy converting the Germanic peoples north and east of the Rhine to Christianity (see Chapter 6).

A man of commanding presence—well over 6 feet tall, which in his day made him seem almost a giant—Boniface had behind him papal authority. In 732 the papacy appointed him archbishop in Germany. Throughout his career he was a devoted representative of the Benedictine Rule and the papacy. As he put it, he strove "to hold fast the Catholic faith and unity, and to yield submission to the Church of Rome as long as life shall last for us."

Boniface also had the military backing of the Carolingian mayors—Charles Martel and his sons, Carloman and Pepin the Short. Armed with the Christian faith and the Benedictine Rule, and supported by England, Francia, and Rome, Boniface labored among the Germanic peoples in

Frisia, Thuringia, Hesse, and Bavaria. There he won converts, founded new Benedictine monasteries in the wilderness, and erected the organizational framework of a disciplined German church. He suffered moments of discouragement, as when he wrote to an English abbot, "Have pity upon an old man tried and tossed on all sides by the waves of a German sea." Yet Boniface accomplished much, and the monasteries that he established were to become centers of learning and evangelism that played a great role in civilizing the peoples of Germany.

During the decade following Charles Martel's death in 741, Boniface devoted much of his energy to Francia, where the church stood in urgent need of reform. Many areas had no clergy at all, most peasants were scarcely removed from paganism, and priests themselves reportedly hedged their bets by sacrificing animals to Germanic gods. Charles Martel, although willing enough to support Boniface's missionary endeavors among Germanic pagans, did not want reformers interfering with his own Frankish church and perhaps raising awkward questions about his policy toward church lands. Carloman and Pepin, however, encouraged Boniface to reform the Frankish church, and beginning in 742 he held a series of synods for that purpose. Working closely with the papacy, he remodeled the Frankish ecclesiastical organization on the disciplined pattern of England and papal Rome. He reformed Frankish monasteries by imposing the Benedictine Rule, saw to the establishment of monastic schools, encouraged the appointment of dedicated bishops and abbots, and developed a network of parish churches to bring the Gospel to the peasantry. Thus Boniface laid the groundwork for both the new church in Germany and the reformed church in Francia—and as such, was one of the chief architects of what would become the Carolingian cultural revival.

Boniface's introduction of Roman discipline and organization into the Frankish church was followed almost immediately by a political alliance between Rome and Francia. It may well have been at Boniface's prompting that the Carolingian mayor, Pepin the Short (reigned 741–768), sought papal support for his seizure of the Frankish crown. Although the Merovingian monarchs had become impoverished puppet-kings, they retained enormous prestige. If the Carolingians hoped to replace the Merovingians on the Frankish throne, they would have to call on the most potent spiritual sanction available to their age: papal consecration. In supporting Boniface and his fellow Benedictines, the Carolingian mayors had fostered papal influence in the Frankish church. Now, seeking papal blessing for a dynastic revolution, Pepin could reasonably expect a favorable response.

The popes, for their part, needed a strong, loyal ally in Italy. The Carolingians, who had supported the Benedictine missionaries and Boniface's reforms, must have seemed an ideal champion. And by the mid-eighth century a champion was badly needed. For many years the papacy had been trying to establish its own autonomous state in central Italy, the "Republic of St. Peter." Pursuing this goal, the popes had often turned to Byzantium for protection against the Germanic Lombards. Although Christian, the Lombards threatened papal independence. But by 750 the popes could no longer rely on Byzantine protection, for two reasons. First, the papacy abominated the policy of iconoclasm that the Byzantine emperors had recently embraced (see Chapter 6), and naturally it feared depending on the troops of a heretical emperor for its defense. Second, the Lombards were rapidly becoming so aggressive that, iconoclasm or no, Byzantine troops could no longer be counted on to defend the papacy.

By 750 the Lombards were on the march once again, menacing not only Byzantium's Italian holdings but also the territories of the pope himself. In 751 the Lombards captured Ravenna, which had long served as the Byzantines' Italian capital and, protected by marshes, was believed impregnable. With the fall of Ravenna, the papal position in Italy became more precarious than ever.

Accordingly, an epoch-making papal-Frankish alliance was struck. Pepin sent messengers to Rome with a far from theoretical query: "Is it right that a powerless ruler should continue to bear the title of king?" The pope answered that by the authority of the Apostle Peter, Pepin was henceforth to be king of the Franks, and ordered that he be anointed into his royal office by a papal representative. The anointing ceremony was duly performed at Soissons in 751. It had the purpose of buttressing the new Carolingian Dynasty with the strongest of spiritual sanctions. Not by force alone, but by the supernatural potency of anointment, was the new dynasty established on the Frankish throne. Appropriately, this ceremony—the symbolic junction of the power of Rome and Francia—was performed by the aged Boniface.

With Pepin's anointment, the last of the Merovingians was shorn of his long hair (a symbol of royalty) and sent to a monastery. Three years later, Boniface, now nearing eighty, returned to his missionary work in northern Germany and there met a martyr's death at the hands of marauders. In the same year, 754, the pope himself traveled northward to Francia where he personally anointed and crowned Pepin at the royal monastery of St.-Denis, thereby conferring every spiritual sanction at his disposal on the upstart Carolingian monarchy. At the same time he sought Pepin's military support against the Lombards.

Pepin obliged, leading his army into Italy, defeating the Lombards, and granting a large portion of central Italy to the papacy. This "Donation of Pepin" was of lasting historical significance. It had the immediate effect of relieving the popes of the ominous Lombard pressure and created the nucleus of the Papal States, the "Patrimony of St. Peter," which with only one significant break (under Napoleon) the popes would rule until 1870.[3] But despite the papacy's rescue from the Lombards, it remained to be seen whether the popes could prevent their new champion from becoming their master.

Pepin the Short, like all successful early medieval monarchs, was an able war leader. As the first Carolingian king, he followed in the warlike tradition of his father, Charles Martel. Besides smiting the Lombards in Italy, he drove the Muslims from Aquitaine and maintained domestic peace. He died in 768, leaving Francia larger, more powerful, and better organized than he had found it.

Charlemagne

Pepin the Short was a remarkably successful monarch, but he was overshadowed—literally and figuratively—by his son Charles the Great, or Charlemagne (reigned 768–814). A great military leader, a statesman of rare ability, and a friend of learning, Charlemagne exhibited a strong sense of responsibility for the welfare of the society over which he ruled. In this last respect he contributed much to the developing conception of Christian kingship.

Charlemagne was 6 feet 3½ inches tall,[4] thick-necked and pot-bellied, and majestic in bearing. Thanks to his able biographer, Einhard, who wrote his *Life of Charlemagne* a few years after the emperor's death, Charlemagne has come down to posterity as a three-dimensional figure. Einhard, a tiny man, wrote enthusiastically of his oversized hero. The Roman historian Suetonius was Einhard's model, and in fact he lifted whole passages from Suetonius's biography of the emperor Augustus in *Lives of the Twelve Caesars*. Yet much in Einhard's *Life* represents his own appraisal of Charlemagne's deeds and character. Reared at Boniface's monastery of Fulda, Germany, Einhard served for many years in Charlemagne's court and thereby gained an intimate knowledge of the emperor. Einhard's warm admiration of Charlemagne emerges clearly from the biography, yet the author saw his faults as well:

> Temperate in both eating and drinking, he hated drunkenness in anybody, particularly in himself and those of his household. But he found it difficult to abstain from food and often complained that fasts injured his health. . . . His meals usually consisted of four courses, not counting the roast, which his huntsmen used to bring in on the spit. He was fonder of this than of any other dish. While at the table he listened to reading or music. The readings were

Charlemagne This silver penny, minted between 806 and 814, is probably a reasonably authentic portrait of Charlemagne. It certainly fits Einhard's description of the great emperor. *Bildarchiv Preussischer Kulturbesitz (bpk), Berlin Photo: Karin Marz. Original: Staatliche Museen zu Berlin.*

stories and deeds of olden times; he was also fond of St. Augustine's books, especially of the one entitled *The City of God*. So moderate was he in the use of wine and all sorts of drink that he rarely allowed himself more than three cups in the course of a meal.[5]

Einhard comments at length on Charlemagne's military and political career, but the most fascinating passages in the biography deal with the emperor's way of life and personal idiosyncrasies that disclose him as a human being rather than as a shadowy hero of legend. For instance: "While he was dressing and putting on his shoes, he not only gave audience to his friends, but if the Count of the Household told him of any lawsuit in which his judgment was necessary, he had the parties brought before him then and there, considered the case, and gave his decision, just as if he were sitting on the judgment seat."

Einhard was also eager to show Charlemagne's thirst for learning. He portrays the emperor as a fluent speaker of Latin, a student of Greek, an orator of such skill that he might have passed for a teacher of rhetoric, a devotee of the liberal arts, and in particular a student of astronomy who learned to calculate the motions of the heavenly bodies. But Einhard's final tribute unwittingly discloses the

---

[3] In 1870 the recently united Kingdom of Italy seized Rome as its capital. In 1929, while Mussolini ruled Italy, the papacy was permitted to regain the territorial independence that it still holds in the form of 109-acre Vatican City.

[4] We know this because his tomb was opened in the nineteenth century and his bones measured.

[5] The size of the cup is not mentioned.

THE HISTORICAL EVIDENCE

Charlemagne's Missi Dominici

802

In 802 Charlemagne issued a general capitulary (law) outlining the responsibilities of his envoys, the missi dominici; what follows is the preamble of this lengthy document. Notice the moralistic tone. How effective were these missions likely to be in practice?

Therefore, the most serene and most Christian lord emperor Charles has chosen from his nobles the wisest and most prudent men, both archbishops and some of the other bishops also, and venerable abbots and pious laymen, and has sent them throughout his whole kingdom, and through them by all the following chapters has allowed men to live in accordance with the correct law. Moreover, where anything which is not right and just has been enacted in the law, he has ordered them to inquire into this most diligently and to inform him of it; he desires, God granting, to reform it.

And let no one, through his cleverness or astuteness, dare to oppose or thwart the written law, as many are wont to do, or the judicial sentence passed upon him, or to do injury to the churches of God or the poor or the widows or the wards or any Christian. But all shall live entirely in accordance with God's precept, justly and under a just rule, and each one shall be admonished to live in harmony with his fellows in his business or profession; the canonical clergy* ought to observe in every respect a canonical life without heeding base gain, nuns ought to keep diligent watch over their lives, laymen and the secular clergy† ought rightly to observe their laws without malicious fraud, and all ought to live in mutual charity and perfect peace.

And let the missi themselves make a diligent investigation whenever any man claims that an injustice has been done to him by any one, just as they desire to deserve the grace of omnipotent God and to keep their fidelity promised to Him, so that entirely in all cases everywhere, in accordance with the will and fear of God, they shall administer the law fully and faithfully in the case of the holy churches of God and of the poor, of wards and widows and of the whole people.

And if there shall be anything of such a nature that they, together with the provincial counts, are not able of themselves to correct it and do justice concerning it, they shall, without any ambiguity, refer this, together with their reports, to the judgment of the emperor; and the straight path of justice shall not be impeded by any one on account of flattery or gifts from any one, or on account of any relationship, or from fear of the powerful.

---

*Monks, whose lives were regulated by the "canonical" Rule of St. Benedict.

†Parish priests, who were not monks and who lived in "the world."

Source: From *University of Pennsylvania Translations and Reprints*, trans. D. C. Munro (Philadelphia: University of Pennsylvania, 1900), vol. 6, no. 5, pp. 11–12. Paragraphing has been changed for ease of reading.

---

emperor's limitations: "He also tried to write, and he used to keep tablets and blank pages in bed under his pillow so that in his leisure hours he might accustom his hand to form the letters; but as he did not begin his efforts at an early age but late in life, they met with poor success."[6]

Charlemagne could be warm and talkative, but also cruel and violent, and his subjects regarded him with both admiration and fear. He kept track of his regional administrators by sending out pairs of inspectors known as *missi dominici* ("envoys of the lord") to make certain that his orders were being obeyed and his revenues were not being pocketed. The missi dominici, consisting usually of one churchman and one layman, typified the **theocratic** trend

of Charlemagne's reign. They were moderately effective, but only because they represented a monarch who had (and used) the power to punish and reward.

Charlemagne's strong, if superficial, piety prompted him to build churches, collect relics, and struggle for a Christian cultural revival in Francia. But he also filled his court with concubines and various disreputable characters. In short, Charlemagne, despite his military and political genius, was a man of his age, in tune with the forces of change yet by no means removed from the past.

Expansion and the Imperial Coronation

Above all else Charlemagne was a warrior-king. He led his armies on yearly campaigns as a matter of course. When his magnates and their retainers rallied around him annually the question was not whether to go to war but whom to

---

[6] Some modern historians argue that Einhard overstated Charlemagne's inability to read and write.

fight. Only gradually did Charlemagne develop a coherent scheme of conquest built on a notion of Christian mission and addressed to the goal of unifying and systematically expanding the Christian West. At the behest of the papacy, he followed his father's footsteps into Italy. There he conquered the Lombards completely in 774, incorporated them into his growing state, and assumed for himself the Lombard crown. Thenceforth he employed the title "King of the Franks and the Lombards."

In 778 Charlemagne attacked the Spanish Muslims, but Islamic Spain was too strong to be beaten. He did manage eventually to establish a border district on the Spanish side of the Pyrenees Mountains known as the Spanish March (from an old Germanic word meaning "boundary" or "frontier"). A relatively minor military episode in Charlemagne's Spanish campaign of 778—an attack by a band of Christian Basques against the rear guard of Charlemagne's army as it was retreating across the Pyrenees—became the inspiration for one of the great epic poems of the eleventh and twelfth centuries: the *Song of Roland* (discussed on page 350 in Chapter 10). The epic's nameless author(s) transformed the Basques into Muslims and the skirmish into a heroic struggle between rival faiths. Charlemagne was described as an awesome conqueror, two hundred years old, and Roland, the warden of the Breton March and commander of the rear guard, acquired a fame far out of proportion to his actual historical importance.

Rebuffed in Spain, Charlemagne devoted much of his strength to extending his eastern frontier. In 787 he conquered and absorbed Bavaria, organizing its easternmost district into a forward defensive barrier. This East March, or "Ostmark," became the nucleus of a state later to be called Austria. In the 790s Charlemagne pushed still deeper into the southeast, destroying the nomadic, predatory Avars. For generations they had been plundering central Europe and extracting heavy tribute from Byzantium. Charlemagne seized a substantial portion of the Avar treasure: Fifteen four-ox wagons were required to transport the hoard of gold, silver, and jewels back to Francia. The Avar loot significantly swelled Charlemagne's treasury and helped fund his subsequent building program and patronage to scholars and churches. Such Avars as survived melted into surrounding ethnic groups.[7]

Charlemagne directed his most prolonged military effort against the **pagan** Saxons of northern Germany. With the twin goals of protecting the Frankish Rhineland and bringing new souls into Christendom, he campaigned for some thirty-two years, conquering the Saxons repeatedly and baptizing them by force, only to have them rebel when his armies withdrew. In a fit of savage

exasperation he ordered the execution of 4,500 backsliding Saxons in a single day in 782. At length Saxony submitted to the remorseless pressure of Charlemagne's soldiers and the Benedictine monks who followed them. By 804 Frankish control of Saxony was well established, and eventually Christianity seeped deeply into the Saxon soul. A century and a half later, Christian Saxons were governing the most powerful state in Europe and fostering a significant artistic and intellectual revival that enriched the culture of tenth-century Christendom (see Map 7-2).

By incorporating central Germany into Western civilization, Charlemagne's armies had succeeded where the legions of ancient Rome had failed. No longer a mere Frankish king, Charlemagne by the year 800 ruled Western Christendom, except for the Byzantine-oriented principalities of southern Italy and the Anglo-Saxon kingdoms in England. At Rome on Christmas Day 800, his accomplishment gained formal recognition when Pope Leo III placed a crown on his head and acclaimed him "Emperor of the Romans." In legal theory, this dramatic act reconstituted the Roman Empire in the West after a 324-year intermission. It was also the ultimate consummation of the Franco-papal alliance of 751.

Charlemagne's imperial coronation has evoked heated controversy among historians. Einhard claimed that Pope Leo took Charlemagne by surprise and bestowed on him an unwanted dignity. Many modern historians have been skeptical of Einhard's story, arguing that Charlemagne could certainly have prevented a coronation that he did not wish. Indeed, scholars in Charlemagne's court, beguiled by the dream of empire, may well have urged him on. Some historians have noted that Byzantium lacked an emperor in 800—a woman, Irene, was reigning—and that Charlemagne disclosed his interest in the Roman imperial crown by unsuccessfully proposing marriage to Irene. (She probably would not have made a good spouse, having seized the Byzantine throne by deposing and blinding her own son.) Some have also suggested that the coronation was largely a product of internal Roman politics during the years 799 and 800. In any event, the acclamation that Charlemagne received from the people of Rome immediately after his coronation had obviously been well rehearsed, and it is hard to believe that Charlemagne did not know what was afoot.

Most likely Charlemagne's imperial coronation of 800, like the royal coronation of Pepin the Short in 751, represents a blend of papal and Carolingian interests. For some years Charlemagne had been attempting to attain a status comparable to that of the Byzantine emperors. Establishing a permanent capital at Aachen, as we have already seen, had been one sign of this resolve. The coronation of 800 may well have been similarly imitative.

The papacy, on the other hand, may have regarded the coronation as an opportunity to regain some of the

---

[7] The destruction of the Avar horde cleared the way for the rise of the early Slavic kingdoms of Bulgaria and Moravia (see Chapter 6).

MAP 7-2

CHARLEMAGNE'S EMPIRE AT ITS HEIGHT, CA. 802

At its greatest extent, Charlemagne's empire ranged from the English Channel to beyond the Danube River. Farther to the east, Slavic tribes and subjects of the former Avar Confederation had been forced to pay tribute to Charlemagne's court.

initiative it had lost to the all-powerful Charlemagne. To be sure, the Carolingians had been promoted from kings to emperors, but their empire thenceforth bore a "Made in Rome" trademark. In later years the popes would insist that what they gave they could also take away. Indeed, the papal chancery had recently produced a famous forged document called the "Donation of Constantine"[8] in which the first Christian emperor allegedly gave to the pope the imperial diadem and governance over Rome, Italy, and all the West. The pope supposedly returned the diadem but kept the power. Later popes, drawing on the "Donation of Constantine," regarded Charlemagne's imperial successors as stewards exercising political authority by delegation from the papacy, wielding their power in the interests of the Roman church.

Charlemagne respected the papacy, but he never accepted the subordinate role that papal theory demanded of him. He was careful to retain the title "King of the Franks and the Lombards" alongside his new imperial title. When the time came to crown his son emperor, Charlemagne excluded the pope from the ceremony and did the honors himself. These maneuvers were the prologue to a long, bitter struggle over the correct relationship between empire and papacy—a struggle that reached its climax in the eleventh, twelfth, and thirteenth centuries (see Chapter 8). For the moment, Charlemagne's power was unrivaled and the popes were much too weak to resist him. The warm Carolingian-papal relations of Pepin's day continued, and the papacy was nearly smothered in Charlemagne's affectionate embrace.

Only in very recent years has a vastly different Europe peacefully approached the kind of unity that Charlemagne imposed. But never again would Western Christendom flirt so seriously with theocracy. The papal anointing of Pepin and Charlemagne gave the Carolingian monarchy a sacred, almost priestly quality. Charlemagne used his immense authority to govern not only the body politic but the imperial church as well. The laws and regulations of his reign, known as *capitularies*, dealt with both ecclesiastical and

---

[8] Probably sometime in the 740s. At the time, the popes regarded the "Donation" not as a blatant forgery but as a restoration of documentation for an arrangement that they were convinced had actually been concluded. Only in the fifteenth century was it established by linguistic analysis that the "Donation" dated from the eighth, not the fourth, century (see Chapter 12).

secular matters. At his Synod of Frankfurt in 796, he issued legislation on Christian doctrine. Driven by a sense of responsibility for systematizing church discipline, and by a need to incorporate dependable educated churchmen into the structure of Carolingian government, he was a far greater force in the church than was the pope. Indeed, the intellectual revival called the "Carolingian Renaissance" grew out of Charlemagne's concern for the welfare of the church and the perpetuation of ecclesiastical culture as essential buttresses of the Carolingian state.

The Carolingian Renaissance

The term *Carolingian Renaissance* can be misleading. Charlemagne's age produced little original philosophical or theological work. If we look for a renaissance in the sense of Renaissance Italy (see Chapter 12), we will be disappointed. The intellectual task of the Carolingian age was less exalted: to rescue the West's culture from the pit of ignorance into which it was sinking.

As with so many other aspects of the era, the Carolingian Renaissance bears the stamp of Charlemagne's will and initiative. He saw the desperate need for schools in his kingdom and sought to provide them. Charlemagne's schools taught just the basics, however; no institutions of higher learning existed north of the Alps, and none would

emerge for centuries. All that the Carolingians could do was to promote primary and secondary education, and this itself was immensely difficult. Francia had no professional teachers. The only hope for educational reform lay with the church, which had an almost complete monopoly on literacy. So Charlemagne tried to force the cathedrals and monasteries of his realm to operate schools that would preserve and spread the rudiments of classical-Christian culture. A capitulary of 789 commands that "In every episcopal see and in every monastery, instruction shall be given in the psalms, musical notation, chant, the computation of years and seasons, and grammar, and all books used shall be carefully corrected."

A curriculum of the sort proposed in this capitulary can hardly be described as sophisticated or demanding, yet many Carolingian monasteries and cathedrals fell far short of its modest standards. Still, Charlemagne succeeded in vastly improving the quantity and quality of schooling in his empire. There was even an attempt to make village priests provide free instruction in reading and writing (a skill often beyond them as well). Only a fraction of Charlemagne's subjects acquired literacy. But those few provided an all-important nucleus that kept knowledge alive and passed it on. It was, above all, in the monastic schools that learning flourished—in houses such as Fulda, Tours, and Reichenau. During the turbulent generations following

Reichenau Monastery On an island in the Rhine River between modern Germany and Switzerland, Reichenau was one of the great monasteries of Carolingian Europe. In this photograph of the monastery chapel's interior, the frescoes (dating from ca. 836) have been heavily restored. *Theo Keller.*

Charlemagne's death many of these monastic schools survived to become seedbeds of the much greater intellectual awakening of the eleventh and twelfth centuries.

As an integral part of his effort to raise the intellectual standards of his realm and sustain Christian culture, Charlemagne assembled scholars at his court from all over Europe. One such scholar was the emperor's biographer, Einhard, from eastern Francia. Another was the poet-historian Paul the Deacon, of the great Italian Benedictine house of Monte Cassino. Paul the Deacon's *History of the Lombards* provides an invaluable account of that Germanic tribe and its settlement in Italy. From Spain came Theodulf, later bishop of Orleans and abbot of Fleury, a tireless supporter of Charlemagne's educational reforms and a poet of considerable talent. The most important of these Carolingian scholars, however, was Alcuin of York, the last significant mind produced by the Northumbrian Renaissance (see Chapter 6). Alcuin, like his compatriot St. Boniface, linked the Christian cultural life of the Venerable Bede's Northumbria with the intellectual upsurge of Carolingian Francia.

Alcuin performed the essential task of preparing an accurate new edition of the Bible. He purged it of the scribal errors that had crept in over the centuries, thereby saving Christian culture from the confusion arising from the corruption of its most fundamental text. For many years the chief scholar in Charlemagne's court school, Alcuin spent his final years as abbot of the wealthy monastery of St. Martin of Tours. He was extraordinarily well educated for his period, and his approach to learning typified the whole philosophy of the Carolingian Renaissance: to produce accurate copies of important traditional texts, to encourage the establishment of schools, and in every way possible to cherish and transmit the classical-Christian cultural tradition, without, however, adding to it in any significant way. "There is nothing better for us," Alcuin wrote, "than to follow the teachings of the Apostles and the Gospels. We must follow these precepts instead of inventing new ones or propounding new doctrine or vainly seeking to increase our own fame by the discovery of new fangled ideas."

Alcuin and his fellow scholars were neither intellectual innovators nor men of conspicuous holiness. Drawn by Charlemagne's wealth and power and enriched by his patronage, they struggled to improve the scholarly level of the Carolingian church, but they showed little concern for deepening its devotional life or pursuing speculative thought. They had the talents and inclinations—and the limitations—of schoolteachers.

Accordingly, Alcuin and his colleagues regularized the liturgy of the church and encouraged the preaching of sermons. The haunting, hypnotic unison tones of Gregorian Chant—the earliest form of music for which we possess a readily decipherable notation—spread through west European churches and monasteries thanks to the Carolingian Renaissance. Carrying forward some of the monastic

reforms begun by Boniface, Alcuin's reformers persuaded Charlemagne to command that all monasteries establish schools and follow the Benedictine Rule. Although these commands were not everywhere obeyed, they did help preserve literacy and standardize monastic life, albeit at the cost of driving out Irish traditions and sometimes dampening the independent spirit of nunneries. A new official script was developed—the Carolingian minuscule—that derived in part from the Irish and Northumbrian scripts of the previous century, and from the scripts of certain Merovingian abbeys. Thenceforth the Carolingian minuscule superseded the often crabbed scripts earlier employed on the Continent. Its letters were clearly and separately formed (rather like modern printing, which derives from it), and capitals and lowercase were distinguished, unlike the Roman practice of RUNNINGWORDSTOGETHER. As a result, reading became much easier and gradually more widespread. Reliance on committing works to memory also diminished. (Alcuin, for example, had claimed to be able to memorize twenty pages at one sitting, a feat that was perhaps facilitated by reading aloud but certainly required enormous concentration.) Throughout the realm, monks set to copying manuscripts on an unprecedented scale. If classical-Christian culture was advanced very little by these activities, it was at least preserved. Above all, its

Merovingian and Carolingian Script   The example above is a typical Merovingian document from about 680. Below is Carolingian minuscule, from a document about 825. The Carolingian hand is ideally adapted for reading aloud at a measured pace (for example, to a group of monks), the normal way in which information was disseminated in the Early Middle Ages.   *Paris, National Archives.*

THE HUMAN EXPERIENCE

Walafrid Strabo

Although the Carolingian Renaissance could boast no thinkers of great originality, it did produce a considerable number of intelligent and productive scholars who merit respect. Among the most attractive of them was Walafrid Strabo (or Walafrid the Squint-Eyed, as he cheerfully called himself).

Born in southern Germany about 808, of impoverished parents, Walafrid was sent as an illiterate boy of eight to the nearby Benedictine monastery of Reichenau, an important center of Carolingian learning set on an island in the Rhine (see p. 233). An apt and enthusiastic pupil in the abbey school, he quickly learned Latin and then proceeded to master the Bible, the writings of the Latin Doctors, and the principles of the liberal arts. Like many well-educated men of his era, Walafrid enjoyed writing Latin poetry; unlike most of them, he did it well.

Walafrid had entered Reichenau as a child, dedicated by his parents. As was expected of him, he took lifetime monastic vows on coming of age. He did so happily, because he had by then developed a deep religious faith and a devotion to monasticism. Perhaps because he was genial by nature, or perhaps because he took very seriously Christ's injunction to "love your neighbor," Walafrid was the kindest and most loving of the Carolingian writers. He muted his criticisms and looked for the best in everyone, which made him an exception.

Because Reichenau was in close touch with other centers of Carolingian learning, news of Walafrid's intellectual precocity spread quickly. By the age of fifteen, at the urging of a teacher, he was sending his verses to imperial bishops, always with characteristic Benedictine humility. He addressed a verse to one bishop "as a mouse to a giant."

Walafrid also produced lives of the saints—one of the most popular literary genres of the Early Middle Ages. By the time he was eighteen he had written two such lives, both in verse. The second—a portent of disasters to come—was the life of an Irish saint who had been killed by Vikings.

Walafrid's abbot at Reichenau sent him at eighteen to study under one of the most eminent scholars of the age, Raban Maur, abbot of the great German monastery of Fulda, which St. Boniface had founded a century before. Raban Maur was in the midst of the immense and typically Carolingian labor of compiling biblical commentaries excerpted from the writings of the Latin Doctors. Walafrid was fascinated by Raban Maur's project and enthusiastically joined him in it. And Raban, who was himself a poet (to put it charitably), encouraged Walafrid's poetic gift. The two became lifelong friends.

Walafrid remained at Fulda for only three years. At twenty-one, he was summoned by Emperor Louis the Pious to his court at Aachen to tutor the emperor's youngest son, Charles (who, being only five years old, did not yet merit his future nickname, "the Bald"). Walafrid remained at court for nine years (829–838), tutoring, studying, writing, and, as always, winning friends. These were tumultuous years for the empire: From 829 onward, Charles's two older brothers, Lothar and Louis the German, waged intermittent war against their father, who was virtually imprisoned at Aachen in 832 and was forced by hostile bishops to abdicate temporarily in 833. "Alas, how plainly is Satan's honor served!" wrote Walafrid to a friend. "Peace is driven far from earth."

Throughout these upheavals Walafrid managed to turn Charles the Bald into the best educated of the Carolingian monarchs. In 838 Walafrid, now thirty, was rewarded by being appointed abbot of Reichenau. At the death of Louis the Pious in 840, the civil war between his sons intensified. Louis the German removed Walafrid as abbot and sent him into exile. Walafrid wrote to Raban Maur complaining of dire poverty and need; he lacked even sandals. Even so, he continued to write and study, and in 842 changing political winds brought Walafrid back to his abbey and to the royal favor.

Walafrid regretted the division of the empire at Verdun in 843, yet he now enjoyed the trust and favor of all three royal brothers and was sometimes at their courts. At Reichenau he restored with his own labor an abandoned herb and vegetable garden and wrote touching poems about the various plants. To an absent friend he wrote:

> When from on high the moon's pure
>   splendour shines,
> Stand then beneath the sky and
>   think, enthralled,
> Upon that glory's far-flung radiance;
> How its pure splendour holds
>   encircled those
> In body far apart, in love fast bound.
> If face can see no more the face that
>   cares,
> At least this light shall tell us of our
>   love.
> Abiding friendship sends these little
>   lines;
> If, too, in thee the chain of faith
>   stands firm,
> For thee I pray forever happiness.

In 848, about forty years old and (by the standards of the day) almost elderly, Walafrid represented Louis the German on a diplomatic mission to his old pupil Charles the Bald. Returning in 849, he drowned in a boating accident. He was buried at his beloved Reichenau, and his former teacher and grieving friend, Raban Maur, wrote his epitaph. ❖

Source: Verse translated by Eleanor Shipley Duckett from *Carolingian Portraits: A Study in the Ninth Century* (Ann Arbor, Mich.: University of Michigan Press, 1962), p. 160.

base was broadened. In the task they set themselves, the Carolingian scholars were eminently successful.

It was characteristic of the powerful theocratic tendencies of the age that this educational achievement was accomplished through royal rather than papal initiative. Germanic kingship and classical-Christian culture had joined hands at last. With the breakdown of European unity after Charlemagne's death, the momentary fusion of political and cultural energies dissolved, yet the intellectual revival continued. A deeply spiritual movement of monastic reform and moral regeneration began in Aquitaine under the leadership of the saintly Benedict of Aniane. Soon the influence of this movement took hold at

Gregory the Great with Carolingian Scribes   This beautiful late ninth-century ivory depicts Pope Gregory the Great, inspired by the Holy Spirit, composing part of the Mass while Carolingian scribes copy his words. Note the detailed architecture above Gregory: This gives an idea of the Roman-inspired building style that the Carolingians and their successors favored—a style that art historians call Romanesque.   *Kunsthistorisches Museum, A-10101 Wien Archivphoto-NR. I 18413.*

the court of Charlemagne's son and successor, Louis the Pious. Louis gave St. Benedict of Aniane the privilege of visiting any monastery in the empire and tightening its discipline to the chagrin of numerous abbots and monks. And in 817 a significantly expanded version of the Benedictine Rule, based on the strict monastic regulations of Benedict of Aniane, was promulgated for all the monasteries of the empire and given the weight of imperial law. Benedict of Aniane's reform represents a marked shift from the spiritually superficial monastic regulations of Charlemagne's day to a deep concern for the Christ-centered life. The elaborated Benedictine Rule of 817 lost its status as imperial law in 840, with the death of Louis the Pious, but it remained an inspiration to subsequent monastic reform movements in the centuries that followed.

While Carolingian spiritual life was deepening in the years after Charlemagne's death, Carolingian scholarship continued to flourish in the cathedral and monastic schools. In keeping with the Carolingian-era program of preserving the classical-Christian tradition, learned clergy of the Carolingian Renaissance's "second generation" devoted themselves to preparing encyclopedic accounts of existing knowledge. Although unoriginal, these works contributed significantly to cultural transmission. For example, Raban Maur (d. 856), abbot of Fulda, produced a learned compilation about all subjects that occurred to him, on the pattern of Isidore of Seville's *Etymologies*. Raban Maur also carried forward the Carolingian educational tradition by writing a handbook on the instruction of the clergy that had a great impact on the operation of monastic schools.

The intellectual revival sparked by Charlemagne echoed through subsequent generations. In the monasteries and cathedrals of the ninth and tenth centuries, particularly in the German districts of Charlemagne's old empire, documents continued to be copied, schools continued to operate, and commentaries and summaries of ancient texts continued to appear. By the eleventh century, Europe was ready to build on sturdy Carolingian foundations.

The Dynamics of Carolingian Expansion and Decline

The Carolingian Empire was ephemeral. Rising out of a chaotic past, it disintegrated in the turbulent era that followed. The Carolingians had achieved their early successes, under Pepin of Heristal and Charles Martel, not only because of strong leadership but also because of the sizable landed resources that the family came to control and the loyal, well-armed vassals and aristocratic supporters whom these resources could attract. Carolingian armies were better organized and better disciplined than those of all neighboring powers except the Umayyad Caliphate in Spain. No rival principality made such effective use of armored horsemen as did the Carolingians. And once Carolingian expansion was under way, it fed on its own

THE HISTORICAL EVIDENCE

A Carolingian Estate

ninth century

This inventory describes the estate (villa) of Villeneuve St. Georges, belonging to the great monastery of St.-Germain-des-Prés outside Paris, and was drawn up sometime between 806 and 829. As its name ("New Villa") indicates, this was a new settlement, and unusual for its time. Most dues are in kind or labor, but there is some evidence of money payments being substituted, probably reflecting the ability of peasants to sell some of their produce in Paris. The fact that "winter" and "spring" grains are mentioned may indicate that a three-field crop rotation has been introduced; the third field would lie fallow. (But it is also possible that the old two-field system was still in use because the "spring" grain is sown in half the amount of the land being used for the "winter" grain; in that case half of the "spring" field would be left fallow.) Note also the presence of both slaves and **serfs**, *or villeins (coloni). The former have unlimited labor obligations, but both are settled on holdings. Some of the households contain grown children. Slaves and coloni are intermarrying, and over time this will tend to erase the distinction.*

Sous and deniers *are small-denomination coins. There is uncertainty about exactly what some measures of land and volume were (they varied with locale), but an* arpent *was about one-third of an acre.*

There is a master's manse at Villeneuve with a dwelling and sufficient other buildings, 172 bonniers of arable land which can be sown to produce 88 muids. There are 91 arpents of vineyard where 1,000 muids can be harvested, 166 arpents of meadow, from which 166 waggons of hay can be gathered. There are three flour mills the rent of which brings in 450 muids of grain. Another one is not rented out. There is a league round where 500 swine can be fattened.

There is a well-constructed church with all its furniture, a dwelling house, and sufficient other buildings. Three manses are dependent on it. Divided between the priest and his men, there are 27 bonniers of arable land and one ansange, 17 arpents of vineyards, 25 arpents of meadow. This provides a horse, as a "gift." In the service of the master, nine perches and an ansange are ploughed, two perches for the spring grain, and four perches of meadow are enclosed.

Actard, villein *(colonus)*, and his wife, also a villein *(colona)*, named Elgilde, "men" of St. Germain, have with them six children called Aget, Teudo, Siméon, Adalside, Dieudonnée, Électard. They hold a manse containing five bonniers of arable land and two ansanges, four arpents of vineyard, 4½ arpents of meadow. They provide four silver sous for military service and the other year two sous for the livery of meat, and the third year, for the livery of fodder, a ewe with a lamb. Two muids of wine for the right of pannage, four deniers for the right of wood; for cartage a measure of wood, and 50 shingles.* They plough four perches for the winter grain, and two perches for the spring. Manual and animal services, as much as is required

of them. Three hens, 15 eggs. They enclose four perches of meadow. . . .

Adalgarius, slave of St. Germain, and his wife, a villein *(colona)*, named Hairbolde, "men" of St. Germain. This man holds a servile manse. Hadvoud, slave, and his wife, slave, named Guinigilde, "men" of St. Germain, have with them five children [named here]. These last hold a free manse containing one and a half bonniers of arable land, three-quarters of an arpent of vineyard, 5 1/2 arpents of meadow. They look after four arpents in the vineyard. They deliver for pannage three muids of wine, a setier of mustard, 50 withies,† three hens, 15 eggs. Manual service where they are ordered. And the female slave weaves serge with the master's wool, and feeds the poultry whenever she is ordered to do so.

Ermenold, villein *(colonus)* of St. Germain, and his wife, slave; Foucard, slave, and his wife, slave, named Ragentisme, "men" of St. Germain. These last two hold a servile manse containing two bonniers, one and a half ansanges of arable land, an arpent of vineyard, two and a half arpents of meadow. They owe the same as the preceding one. The female slave and her mother weave serge and feed the poultry whenever they are commanded to do so.

*These are in place of the various services named. Pannage is the right to fatten hogs in the forest.

†Withies are thin, flexible twigs used for tying bundles.

Source: From Georges Duby, *Rural Economy and Country Life in the Medieval West*, trans. Cynthia Post (London: Edward Arnold, 1968), pp. 368–369.

momentum. Conquests brought plunder and new lands with which the Carolingians could enrich themselves and reward their supporters. It became Carolingian policy to install loyal Franks, mostly Austrasians, as counts and dukes of the conquered provinces. Accordingly, the interests of the Frankish landholding aristocracy became ever more closely tied to the fortunes of the Carolingian family. As long as the Carolingians could bring in profits from military campaigns, they commanded the enthusiastic obedience of disciplined followers. A Frank would gladly obey Charlemagne if it meant a cut of the Avar treasure or a lordship in Italy or Saxony. Carolingian expansion was like a snowball: growing as it rolled, rolling as it grew.

This process typified the early medieval economy, in which lords and kings enriched themselves in part through trade but even more through plunder. Such wealth, won by war, yielded one of the primary economic transactions between a lord and his neighbors or followers: the exchange of gifts. Among aristocratic peers, "gifting" was a means of outdoing rivals and gaining prestige; it motivated the followers of a lord to serve him faithfully.[9] At the highest level, in the relationships between the Carolingian kings and their counts and vassals, it was the glue that held together the leadership of the empire.

Yet even at its height, Charlemagne's regime remained economically primitive and undergoverned. Towns were few, small, and scattered, and the roads that linked settled areas were miserably poor. There was some trade, most of it dependent on the river network: Carolingian villages often had to obtain their iron, salt, and wine from outside sources, and the great lay and clerical landholders imported luxury goods such as jewelry and precious fabrics from afar. Slave trading remained an important economic activity, with miserable columns of Germanic or Slavic captives regularly being marched out of east-central Europe, assembled at huge Frankish slave markets, and dispatched (sometimes having first been castrated) to the Mediterranean world. Slavery also remained an important source of labor on the great estates of Carolingian magnates, lay and clerical.

Charlemagne did what he could to encourage trade and economic development. He maintained a silver coinage of good quality, though most ordinary transactions continued to be based on barter. He concluded a reciprocal agreement with an Anglo-Saxon king guaranteeing merchants' safety; he encouraged the construction of roads, bridges, and lighthouses; and he even planned a canal between the Rhine and the Danube. But by Byzantine or Islamic standards, Carolingian commerce trickled rather than gushed.

Despite the plunder of conquests, Charlemagne had nowhere near the funds to support a salaried bureaucracy. Like his predecessors, he had to depend on the competence and loyalty of landholding regional officials: dukes, lords of the marches (margraves), and counts of the nearly three hundred counties of the empire. These men were royal officials, pledged to obey the king-emperor. But pledges are frail threads, and the Carolingian counts could act independently when loyalty no longer suited them. Many were drawn, of necessity, from aristocratic Frankish families with landed power bases of their own. Moreover, in place of salaries the counts were granted the use of extensive royal lands from which they could not easily be dislodged. And because of the vast distances and poor communications, they had to be entrusted with broad powers over the royal tribunals, taxation systems, and military recruiting arrangements in their counties. A count who owed his office to Charlemagne and whose authority over potentially troublesome provincials depended on Charlemagne's continued backing would respectfully receive his missi dominici. Local officials, however, obeyed royal commands and capitularies not out of patriotic allegiance to the Carolingian state but because of their devotion to Charlemagne's person—a devotion based on the bonds of common interest that linked the conquering monarch and his aristocracy.

These bonds had always been fragile. And when the Carolingian Empire ceased expanding, as it did after the final submission of Saxony in 804, bonds began to loosen. As the flow of lands and plunder dried up, aristocratic loyalty waned, and the empire started to disintegrate. Disaffection and rebellion clouded Charlemagne's last decade and brought chaos to the reign of his son, Louis the Pious. Once the snowball stopped rolling, it began to melt.

The Carolingian Empire, impressive though it was, lacked a vigorous commercial life and other necessary ingredients of a flourishing civilization. Its revenues were small and its administrative institutions grossly inadequate to the needs of a great state. But even though Charlemagne's "Roman Empire" was merely a shadow of its ancient namesake, one cannot help respecting its founder for doing so much with so little, for making such an effort to transcend his own primitive past.

AFTER CHARLEMAGNE

Ephemeral though it was, the Carolingian Empire might have evolved further had it not been for a series of new invasions. During the ninth and tenth centuries, Western Christendom was hammered from three directions: from the east by seminomadic Magyars (Hungarians), from the south by Muslims, and from the north by Vikings. Europe emerged from its ordeal with a political organization radically different from that of the Carolingian Empire.

---

[9] "Gifting" as social and political cement has a long history; it was central to the world of Odysseus, for example (see Chapter 2). It was also crucial in Native American cultures.

The Decline of the Empire

The fragmentation of Carolingian Europe was not entirely the result of attacks from outside. Charlemagne himself, in keeping with Frankish tradition, planned to divide his state among his sons. But the luck of the Carolingians was still running, for Charlemagne outlived all but one son. When the great conqueror died in 814, his realm passed intact to his single heir, Louis the Pious (reigned 814–840).

Louis was by no means incompetent. Indeed, he has been described as the most intelligent of the Carolingians. But he was less astute militarily and politically than his father Charlemagne, his grandfather Pepin the Short, and his great-grandfather Charles Martel. And because Carolingian expansion stopped a few years before his accession, Louis could not reward his aristocratic followers with gifts of land and treasure on the scale to which they had long been accustomed. During the generations of Carolingian expansion, the Frankish aristocracy had grown far richer and more powerful. Now, with access to new lands and booty cut off, many great landholders deserted the monarchy and looked to their own interests.

Louis the Pious was well nicknamed. He ran Charlemagne's minstrels and concubines out of the imperial court. He gave his wholehearted support to the monastic reforms of Benedict of Aniane. And far more than his hardheaded father, Louis committed himself to the dream of a unified Christian empire—a City of God brought down to earth. But dreams alone cannot sustain empires, and Louis lacked the resources necessary to maintain cohesion throughout the wide dominions that the Carolingians had won. He was the first of his line to conceive of bequeathing supreme political authority to his eldest son, thereby making the unity of the kingdom a matter of policy rather than luck. Ironically, though, he turned out to be the last Carolingian to rule an undivided Frankish realm. His bold plan for a single succession was foiled by the ambitions of his younger sons, who rebelled against him, vied with him for aristocratic support, and plunged the empire into civil war.

When Louis the Pious's troubled reign ended at his death in 840, his three surviving sons fought over the spoils. The eldest, Lothar, claimed the indivisible imperial title and supreme power over the whole realm. The other two sons, Louis the German and his half-brother Charles the Bald, fought to carve out independent royal authority in East and West Francia, respectively.

The battle among the brothers symbolized a fundamental tension within the empire between imperial unity and regionalism. The principle of unity, represented by Lothar, was more an abstraction than a reality, for even at its height the Carolingian Empire had been a loosely joined cluster of separate principalities, differing in language, culture, and administrative traditions. The empire's linguistic diversity was made vividly clear when Charles the Bald and Louis the German met at Strasbourg in 842 to seal their alliance against Lothar. Charles took his oath of allegiance in the German vernacular so that Louis's East Frankish army could understand him, whereas Louis for the same reason swore his loyalty in the Romance language of Charles's West Franks—the ancestor of modern French. The Oaths of Strasbourg show that the kingdoms claimed by Charles and Louis were not artificial creations but were rooted in separate cultural and linguistic traditions.

The battle for the succession was resolved by the Treaty of Verdun in 843. Lothar bowed to the combined might of his younger brothers, and the empire was divided permanently (see Map 7-3 on next page). The Treaty of Verdun, along with subsequent settlements, marked the disintegration of the Carolingian Empire into its component parts, which themselves dimly foreshadowed the political map of modern Europe. Lothar kept the imperial title but was denied any superior jurisdiction over the realms of Louis the German and Charles the Bald. Louis ruled East Francia, which became the nucleus of modern Germany. Charles the Bald became king of West Francia, which evolved into modern France. Lothar retained a long, narrow strip of territory that snaked for some thousand miles northward from Italy to the North Sea and incorporated slices of what are today western Germany and eastern France, as well as the Netherlands, Belgium, Switzerland, and northern Italy. This Middle Kingdom included the two "imperial capitals"—Rome and Aachen—but its frontiers were difficult to defend, and it lacked cohesion. At Lothar's death in 855 it was subdivided among his three sons, one of whom inherited Carolingian Italy along with the old Lombard crown and the now hollow imperial title. From the ninth century until World War II, fragments of Lothar's Middle Kingdom would be fought over between Germans and French.

The struggles among Charlemagne's grandsons occurred against a background of Viking, Magyar,[10] and Muslim invasions, which accelerated the political fragmentation already set in motion by internal weaknesses. As it turned out, even the more modest political units arising from the Treaty of Verdun were too large—too far removed from the desperate realities of the countryside—to cope with the onslaughts of seafaring Vikings or Magyar horsemen. During the ninth and tenth centuries Carolingian leadership was visibly failing. The ineffectiveness of the later Carolingians is apparent in the unflattering names their contemporaries gave them: Charles the Fat, Charles the Simple, Louis the Child, Louis the Blind, Louis the Stammerer.

---

[10] Properly pronounced "mód-jar," not "mag-yar."

MAP 7-3
THE TREATY OF VERDUN

The New Invasions

The Muslims, Hungarians, and Vikings who plundered the declining Carolingian world were in part drawn by its growing political instability and in part impelled by forces operating in their own homelands. Europe suffered much from their marauding, yet it was tough enough to survive and eventually absorb the invaders. And these invasions were the last that Western Christendom was destined to endure. From about A.D. 1000 to the present, western Europe has been uniquely able to develop on its own, sheltered from the alien attacks that disrupted or destroyed so many other civilizations during the past millennium. As the great French historian Marc Bloch once said, "It is surely not unreasonable to think that this extraordinary immunity, of which we have shared the privilege with scarcely any people but the Japanese, was one of the fundamental factors of European civilization."

Yet in the ninth and tenth centuries Europe's hard-pressed peoples had no way of knowing that the invasions would one day end. A Frankish writer of the mid-ninth century described the Viking attacks in these chilling words:

> The number of ships grows larger and larger; the great host of Northmen continually increases; on every hand Christians are the victims of massacres, looting, and arson—clear proof of which will remain as long as the world itself

endures. The Northmen capture every city they pass through, and none can withstand them.

In southern Gaul people prayed for divine protection against the Muslims: "Eternal Trinity, deliver thy Christian people from the oppression of the pagans." To the north they prayed: "From the savage nation of the Northmen, which lays waste our realms, deliver us, O God." And in northern Italy: "Against the arrows of the Hungarians be thou our protector."

Muslims and Magyars The Muslims of the ninth and tenth centuries, unlike their predecessors in the seventh and early eighth, came as raiders rather than conquerors and settlers. People of the Christian West referred to them insultingly as "Saracens" ("heathen nomads"). From their bases in Africa, Spain, and the Mediterranean islands they preyed on shipping, plundered coastal cities, and sailed up rivers to devastate far inland. Muslim gangs established bandit lairs on today's French Riviera, from which they raided the countryside and kidnapped pilgrims crossing the Alpine passes. Charlemagne never had much of a navy, and his successors were helpless to defend their coasts. In 846 Muslims fell on Rome itself, looting its churches. As late as 982 the German king Otto II was soundly whipped by a Muslim army in southern Italy. But by then the raids were tapering off. Southern Europe, now bristling with fortifications, had learned to defend itself and was even beginning to challenge Muslim domination of the western Mediterranean.

The Magyars—nomadic cavalry from the Asian steppes—settled in the central Danubian basin, overwhelming the Slavic Moravian state that had begun to form there (see Chapter 6). From the late 800s to 955 the Magyars terrorized Germany, northern Italy, and eastern and central France. Magyar raiding parties ranged across the land, seeking defenseless settlements to plunder, avoiding fortified towns, and outriding and outmaneuvering the armies mustered against them. In time, however, they became more sedentary, took up farming, and lost much of their nomadic mobility. In 955 King Otto the Great of Germany crushed a large Magyar army at the battle of the Lechfeld and brought the raids to an end at last. Within another half-century the Magyars established a Latin Chris-

tian kingdom, Hungary. By the turn of the millennium they were joining the community of Christian Europe. But they also formed a block of non-Indo-European-speakers in Slavic east-central Europe, with important consequences in the nineteenth and twentieth centuries.

Vikings The Vikings, or Norsemen, from Scandinavia were the most fearsome invaders of all. Then, as now, the Scandinavians were divided roughly into three groups: Danes, Swedes, and Norwegians. Only gradually did these groups jell into separate kingdoms; in the early years of Viking expansion Scandinavia was a patchwork of petty states. The population consisted of landowning aristocrats, free farmers, and slaves. As among other early Germanic peoples, women were subordinated to men, and some Viking lords had several wives. But mostly Viking women

A Viking Ship Now displayed in a museum in Oslo, this ship was built about 800 and was used for a royal burial (which made possible its survival). It is a superb work of naval architecture. Notice the very shallow draft, enabling Viking craft of this sort to navigate both the open, stormy sea and shallow rivers. A replica of this type of ship crossed the Atlantic in the late nineteenth century. *© Universitetets Oldsaksamling, Frederiksgt. 2, 0164 Oslo.*

enjoyed greater freedom of action than their counterparts in Western Christendom: They could own and pass on property, marry as they chose, and govern their family if their husbands were absent or dead. The Viking economy was based on grain growing and the raising of cattle and sheep, but good lands for farming and pasturing were limited largely to Denmark and southern Sweden. The land shortage and accompanying property disputes sparked incessant private warfare. Only a few small towns developed, as commercial centers for goods imported from the far-flung lands where Viking seafarers traded and plundered.

During the great age of Viking expansion in the ninth and tenth centuries the Danes, who were brought cheek by jowl with the Carolingian Empire by Charlemagne's conquest of Saxony, focused their attention on France and England. The Norwegians raided and settled in Scotland, Ireland, and Iceland. The Swedes concentrated on eastern Europe—the Baltic shores, Russia, and the Byzantine Empire. Yet the three Scandinavian peoples had much in common, and distinctions among them were not sharp. It is therefore proper to regard their raids, their astonishing explorations, and their vast commercial enterprises as a single great international movement (see Map 7-4).

Although the breakdown of Carolingian unity doubtless acted as a magnet to Viking marauders, their raids on the West began in Charlemagne's later years. The basic causes for their outward thrust must be sought in Scandinavia, where population had apparently increased by the later 700s to a level that the primitive Norse agriculture could not support. Overpopulation was probably aggravated by the growth of centralized royal power, which drove the more restless spirits among them to seek adventures and opportunities abroad. A third factor was the development of improved Viking ships—eminently seaworthy, propelled by both sail and oars, and capable of carrying crews of forty to a hundred warriors at speeds up to 10 knots. In these longships Viking warriors struck northern Europe at will. They sailed up rivers far into the interior,

MAP 7-4

THE INVASIONS OF EUROPE

plundering towns and monasteries and taking great numbers of captives, whom they sold as slaves in the markets of Spain and the Mediterranean. Sometimes they would steal horses and gallop across the countryside to spread their devastation still farther.

Europeans were accustomed enough to war, yet the Viking raids were new and terrifying. Carolingian armies were unused to naval warfare, whereas Scandinavians were marvelously skilled at building ships and navigating. Coming from a land of mountainous coasts and deep fjords, they had long used ships for traveling, fishing, fighting, and even entombment. Moreover, Christian warriors, fearful for their souls, tended to respect the sanctity of monasteries, which made them ideal targets for the pagan Vikings—at once wealthy and defenseless. The monastic chroniclers of the time, accustomed to peace within their walls, may have exaggerated the violence of the Viking age and the ferocity of Viking armies. Yet the Viking impact on northern France, England, and Russia was real, and it was lasting.

England was the first to suffer from Viking attacks. In 793 Norse brigands annihilated the Northumbrian monastery of Lindisfarne, and the next year they plundered Jarrow, where Bede had lived and died. Other major abbeys of Northumbria suffered a similar devastation. Thenceforth the Anglo-Saxon kingdoms were tormented by incessant Viking raids.

In 842 the Danes looted London. A few years later they began to establish winter bases in England, which freed them from having to return to Scandinavia after the raiding season. By the later 800s they had turned from piracy to large-scale occupation and permanent settlement. They overran the Anglo-Saxon kingdoms one after another, until by the 870s only the southern kingdom of Wessex remained precariously free of Danish control.

To the seaborne Vikings, the English Channel was a boulevard instead of a barrier, and their raiding parties attacked the English and French shores indiscriminately. They established permanent bases at the mouths of large rivers and sailed up stream to plunder monasteries and sack towns: Antwerp in 837, Rouen in 841, Hamburg and Paris in 845, Charlemagne's capital Aachen in 881.

But many European princes fought doggedly to protect their lands. King Alfred the Great of Wessex saved his kingdom from Danish conquest in the late 870s and began rolling back the Danish armies in England. King Arnulf of East Francia won a decisive victory over the Norsemen in 891 and thereby decreased the Viking pressure on Germany—although just then the Hungarian raids were beginning. West Francia continued to suffer, but in about 911 King Charles the Simple created a friendly Viking buffer state in northern France by concluding a treaty with a Norse chieftain named Rolf. The Vikings in Rolf's band had been conducting raids from their settlement at the mouth of the Seine River. Charles, less stupid than his name implies, reasoned that if he could make Rolf his ally, the Seine settlement might prove an effective barrier against further raids. Rolf became a Christian, married Charles the Simple's daughter, and recognized at least in some sense the overlordship of the French monarchy. Thus his state acquired a degree of legitimacy in the eyes of Western Christendom. Expanding gradually under Rolf and his successors, it became known as the land of the Northmen, or "Normandy." Over the next century and a half the Normans adopted French culture and the French language, built castles and founded monasteries, yet retained much of their former adventurousness and wanderlust. In the eleventh century Normandy was producing some of Europe's best warriors, administrators, monks, and thinkers.

France, England, and Germany formed only a part of the vast Viking world of the ninth and tenth centuries. By the mid-800s Norwegians and Danes had conquered the greater part of Ireland, and between 875 and 930 they settled remote, desolate, hitherto unpopulated Iceland. There a distinctive Norse culture arose, which for several centuries remained only slightly affected by the main currents of Western civilization. In Iceland the magnificent oral tradition of the Norse saga flourished and was eventually committed to writing, to provide epic entertainment during long, dark winters. The Norsemen of Iceland were perhaps the greatest sailors of all. They settled on the coast of Greenland in the late 900s, and about the year 1000 they established settlements in northeastern North America, certainly in Newfoundland and perhaps farther south as well, preceding Columbus by half a millennium. Indeed, the Greenland settlement hung on precariously until shortly before Columbus's first voyage, succumbing only then to colder temperatures and Eskimos.

To the east, Swedish Vikings overran Finland and seized control of European Russia's river network to trade with Constantinople and Baghdad. The Swedes attacked Constantinople three times between 860 and 941, as a result winning valuable trading privileges from the Byzantine emperors. Some Swedish Vikings took service in the Byzantine imperial guard.

In Russia, a Swedish dynasty established itself at Novgorod in the later ninth century, ruling over the indigenous Slavic population. "Varangians," these Vikings are called in Russian history. In the tenth century a Varangian prince of Novgorod captured the south Russian city of Kiev, which became the capital of the powerful, well-organized state of Kievan Russia. Gradually the Varangians intermarried with their Slavic subjects and adopted their language (as the Bulgars were doing in Bulgaria). As we saw in Chapter 6, the Kievan prince Vladimir—his name was a Slavicized version of the Germanic "Walter"—adopted Byzantine Christianity in 989 and opened Russia to the influence of Byzantine culture.

THE HISTORICAL EVIDENCE

A Woman of Iceland

late tenth century

The great Icelandic sagas, which were written down in the thirteenth century, pre-serve oral traditions going back to Viking times. One of the greatest is the Laxdæla Saga, *narrating the fortunes and feuds of related Norse settlers on the west coast of Iceland in the tenth and early eleventh centuries. One of the memorable characters is the beautiful and imperious Gudrun, daughter of Osvif, who is forced into the first of four marriages as a teenager. Later spurned by the man she loves, she avenges her-self on him, begetting other acts of bloody vengeance. Finally she becomes a nun and dies peacefully in her old age. This account of her first marriage demonstrates the power available to a strong-minded Viking woman, not long before the coming of Christianity.*

There was a man called Thorvald, who was the son of Halldor Garpsdale-Priest. He lived at Garpsdale, in Giljs-fjord. He was a wealthy man, but no hero. At the Alth-ing* he asked for the hand of Gudrun Osvif's-daughter, who was fifteen years old at the time. The proposal was received not unfavorably, but Osvif said that his terms would make it clear that Thorvald and Gudrun were not of equal standing. Thorvald spoke meekly, and said it was a wife he was asking for, not money. So Gudrun was betrothed to Thorvald, and Osvif alone decided the terms of the marriage contract: it was stipulated that Gudrun should be in charge of their money as soon as they were sharing the same bed, and be entitled to one half of all the estate, no matter how long or how little their marriage lasted. Thorvald was also to buy precious things for her, so that no woman of comparable wealth should own finer jewelry than Gudrun; but the value of the estate was not to be affected by such outlays.

People now rode home from the Althing. Gudrun was not consulted about all this, and she showed the strongest displeasure; but there the matter rested.

The wedding took place at Garpsdale in late summer. Gudrun had little love for Thorvald, and was hard to please in the buying of valuables. In all the Westfjords there were no jewels so costly that Gudrun did not consider them her due, and she repaid Thorvald with animosity if he failed to buy them, however expensive they might be.

Thord Ingunnarson made himself very friendly with Thorvald and Gudrun, and spent a lot of time with them, and there was much talk about an affair between Thord and Gudrun.

On one occasion Gudrun asked Thorvald to buy some gift for her. Thorvald said she showed no moderation, and slapped her on the face.

At that, Gudrun said, "You have not given me what every woman wants above all—good coloring; and you have taught me to stop bothering you for things."

That same evening, Thord arrived. Gudrun told him how she had been insulted, and asked him how she should repay it.

Thord smiled and said, "I have a good solution for this. Make him a shirt with such a wide neck-opening that by wearing it he gives you grounds for divorcing him."†

Gudrun raised no objection to this, and they dropped the subject. That same spring Gudrun declared herself divorced from Thorvald and went home to Laugar. After that there was a division of the whole estate, and Gudrun got half of it; it had increased in value by then. They had been together for two years.

---

*The assembly at which all adult Icelanders met to decide on their laws, settle disputes, and otherwise arrange their affairs. An organ of direct democracy, it survived for centuries.

†A wife could divorce her husband if he wore effeminate clothing, like this revealing "dress."

Source: *The Laxdæla Saga*, trans. Magnus Magnuson and Hermann Pálsson (Harmondsworth, England: Penguin, 1969), pp. 124–125.

SURVIVAL AND RECOVERY

The development of centralized monarchies in Denmark, Norway, and Sweden, which may well have been a factor in driving enterprising Norse seafarers to seek their fortunes elsewhere, ultimately tamed the Viking spirit. As Scandi-navia became increasingly civilized its kings discouraged roaming warrior bands, and its social environment pro-duced a more humdrum life. Far into the eleventh century, England continued to face Norse attacks, but these invaders were no longer pirate bands; instead, they were royal armies led by Scandinavian kings. The nature of the Scandina-vian threat had changed, and by the late eleventh century the threat had ceased altogether. Around the year 1000

Christianity was winning converts all across the Scandinavian world. In Normandy, in Iceland, in Russia—even in the kingdoms of Scandinavia itself—the Vikings were adopting the religion of the monks whom they had formerly terrorized. Scandinavians were joining Western civilization.

Even at the height of the invasions, the Vikings excelled at commerce as well as piracy. (The distinction was often faint.) They were the greatest seafarers of the age. They introduced Europe to the art of ocean navigation and enlarged the commercial horizons of Western Christendom. The scope of the Scandinavian trade network is suggested by the saga of a tenth-century merchant from Russia who sold an Irish princess to a wandering Icelandic farmer in a Norwegian town. Whether true or not, and disregarding the affront to Irish royalty, the tale reflects the cosmopolitanism and enterprise that Viking voyagers injected into the conservative, land-bound culture of Carolingian Europe. It also underscores the economic recovery that was spreading across all of Europe as the turn of the millennium approached.

England: Unification

In the later eighth century, on the eve of the Viking invasions, England was politically fragmented, as it had been ever since the Anglo-Saxons overran Roman Britain. But over the centuries the smaller kingdoms had gradually been amalgamated into four larger ones: Northumbria in the north, Mercia in the Midlands, East Anglia in the southeast, and Wessex in the southwest. The Danish attacks of the ninth century, by destroying the power of Wessex's rivals, cleared the field for the Wessex (West Saxon) monarchy and thereby hastened the trend toward consolidation that was already under way. But if the Danes were doing the Wessex monarchy a favor, neither side was aware of it during the troubled years of the later ninth century. For a time it appeared that the Danes might conquer Wessex itself (see Map 7-5).

At the moment of crisis a remarkable leader, Alfred the Great (reigned 871–899), rose to the West Saxon throne. Alfred did everything possible to save his kingdom from the Vikings, alternately fighting and bribing them. Finally, driven with a handful of companions into a remote swamp, he rallied his forces in the spring of 878 and smashed a Danish army at the battle of Edington. This victory turned the tide: The Danish chief agreed to adopt Christianity, to withdraw from Wessex, and to accept a "permanent" peace. When other Danes tried to continue the fighting, Alfred by 886 extended his own authority as far as London—even then England's chief town—and shortly thereafter concluded a peace that left him with most of southern and southwestern England. The rest of England—the "Danelaw"—remained independent of the Wessex monarchy, but virtually all of non-Danish England was now united under a single king.

MAP 7-5
ANGLO-SAXON ENGLAND, LATE NINTH CENTURY

Alfred was an able war leader. But more than that, he was an imaginative organizer who systematized military recruitment and built a navy, seeing clearly that Christian Europe could not drive back the Vikings without challenging them at sea. He lavished his resources on a crash program of fortifying and garrisoning towns, which thereafter served both as defensive strongholds and as places of sanctuary for the agrarian population in time of war. They served as commercial centers as well and provided a significant stimulus to English commerce long thereafter. And gradually, as the Danish tide ebbed, fortified centers were built to secure the territories newly reconquered. Alfred clarified and rationalized the laws of his people, issuing a new set of laws and enforcing them strictly. He ruled with an authority such as no Anglo-Saxon king had exercised before his time.

Alfred was also a scholar and patron of learning. His intellectual environment was even less promising than Charlemagne's. The great days of Bede were long gone, and by Alfred's time, Latin—the key to classical-Christian culture—was little known in England. Like Charlemagne, Alfred gathered scholars from far and wide[11] and set them to work teaching Latin and preparing Anglo-Saxon (Old English) translations of Latin works, to be available at the royal court and at episcopal centers throughout his kingdom.

---

[11] One of Alfred's scholars had the fascinating name "Werwulf."

Anglo-Saxon King with His Council   Anglo-Saxon kings ruled with the advice of an assembly of their chief nobles, called the *Witanagemot*. After 1066, William the Conqueror carried on the tradition by consulting with the royal council, or Curia Regis. Getting such advice helped kings make difficult decisions, such as (in the case shown here) imposing a death sentence.   *The British Library; A Saxon Witan. Neg. No. 28263 and 24233. Shelf mark/Man: Cott. Claud. B. IV page no./Folio: 59 min.*

Alfred himself helped to render into Anglo-Saxon such books as Boethius's *Consolation of Philosophy*, Gregory I's *Pastoral Care*, and Bede's *Ecclesiastical History*. In his translation of Boethius, Alfred added regretfully: "In those days one never heard of ships armed for war." And in his preface to the *Pastoral Care* he sadly recalled the days "before everything was ravaged and burned, when England's churches overflowed with treasures and books."

Even more than Charlemagne's, Alfred's cultural revival was a salvage operation in a desperate situation. The Viking pillaging of English monasteries and bishoprics threatened the survival of literacy and, indeed, of Christianity. The king was both modest and accurate when he described himself as one who wandered through a great forest collecting timber with which others could build.

Able successors in the early tenth century continued Alfred's reconquest and rebuilding. By the mid-900s all England was in their hands, and the kings of Wessex had become the kings of England. Many Danes remained in northern and eastern England, and melding Danish and English speech and customs would require many generations. But the creative response of the Wessex kings to the Danish threat had brought political unity to the Anglo-Saxon world. From the agony of invasions the English monarchy was born.

For a generation after the Anglo-Saxon conquest of the Danelaw, from about 955 to 980, England enjoyed relative peace and prosperity. English fleets patrolled the

shores, fortresses evolved into commercial centers, and churchmen, working closely with the monarchy, rebuilt and reformed monasteries. But the Danish inhabitants of northern and eastern England remained only half committed to the new English monarchy, and with the accession of a child-king, Ethelred "the Unready" (reigned 978–1016), the Danish invasions resumed.[12]

The new invasions evolved into a campaign of conquest directed by the Danish monarchy, which had recently become Christian. Incompetence, treason, and panic plagued the English defense. In 991 Ethelred began paying a tribute to the Danes, known thereafter as *danegeld*. Later, the danegeld evolved into a land tax that was exceedingly profitable to the English crown (when the Danes departed, the tax was pocketed by the English kings), but at the time, it meant a massive outflow of English wealth. In 1016 Ethelred died, and the next year King Canute of Denmark became the ruler of the English.

Canute, or Knut in his native Danish (reigned 1017–1035), was known to later generations as "Canute

---

[12] "Unready" is the traditional but incorrect translation of Ethelred's nickname. "Ethelred the Unred" is closer to the original but has the disadvantage of making absolutely no sense to those unacquainted with the Old English language. It was a kind of joke: The name "Ethelred" meant "noble counsel"; "Ethelred the Unred" meant "Noble Counsel the Uncounseled" or something of the sort and was perhaps more amusing in the tenth century than it is today.

the Great," and appropriately so. He conquered Norway as well as England, and joining these two lands to Denmark, he became the master of an empire centering on the North Sea, held together by the wealth of England. A product of the new civilizing forces at work in eleventh-century Scandinavia, Canute was no footloose Viking. He issued law codes, practiced Christianity, and generally kept the peace. Devoting much of his time to England, he cast himself as an Anglo-Saxon king in the old West Saxon mold. After first bloodily purging potential aristocratic troublemakers, he respected and upheld the ancient customs of the land and gave generously to monasteries.

But Canute's Danish-Norwegian-English empire was too unwieldy to survive his death in 1035. When the second of his two sons died in 1042, the English realm passed to Edward the Confessor, a member of the old Wessex dynasty who had grown up in exile in Normandy.

Edward the Confessor ruled England in relative peace. But his childless marriage ensured a disputed succession on his death in 1066 and set the stage for the Norman Conquest. When William the Conqueror, duke of Normandy, invaded England and won its crown in 1066, he inherited a prosperous kingdom with well-established political and legal traditions—a kingdom still divided by differences in custom but with a deep-seated respect for royal authority (see Chapter 9). With the timber that Alfred collected, his successors had built an ample and sturdy edifice.

France: Fragmentation

In England the Viking invasions resulted in royal unification; in France they encouraged a breakdown of political authority into more effective regional and local units. This difference can be explained in part by the fact that France, unlike England, was too large for the Vikings to conquer. Although many of them settled in Normandy, the chief Norse threat to France came in the form of plundering expeditions rather than conquering armies. Distances were too great, communications too primitive, the aristocracy too deeply entrenched, and the kingdom-wide army too slow-moving for the monarchy to take the lead in defending the realm. Military responsibility descended more and more to dukes, counts, and local nobles, who were better able to protect their regions from sudden Viking assaults.

As the monarchy waned, the dukes and counts evolved from Carolingian royal officials into territorial princes only loosely tied to the king. Their former custody of royal lands, tribunals, tax revenues, and military conscription ripened into hereditary authority. Lands and powers that they had once administered for the king they now administered for themselves, transforming France into a mosaic of largely independent duchies and counties.

The Carolingian kings of France became increasingly powerless until at length, in 987, the crown passed permanently from the Carolingians to the Capetian Dynasty (whose first king was an important territorial lord named Hugh Capet). Much later, during the twelfth and thirteenth centuries, the Capetian family would produce some of France's greatest kings, but for the time being the new dynasty was nearly as feeble as its predecessor. The Capetian power base lay in the region around Paris and Orléans —an area known as the Île de France, comparable in size and wealth to the other major French principalities of the period. In theory the Capetian monarch was king of all the French, but his limited jurisdiction and revenues made him merely one prince among many.

The disintegration did not stop at the duchy-county level. Within the principalities, and often between them, lay clusters of estates ruled by important lords who lacked the titles of duke or count but nevertheless wielded considerable authority and had large resources. Whether or not these lords supported their regional princes depended on the lord's interests and the prince's strength. Contemporary observers tended to regard the great landholders, whether dukes, counts, or untitled lords, as constituting a single class, the nobles. Mostly descended from powerful families of Carolingian times or before, nobles had the responsibility for maintaining peace and public order—and the capacity to wage war against Viking invaders and against each other.

Within each noble household was a group of military retainers—vassals—who by the late tenth century had come to be known as knights. Midway in status between the great noble families and the peasantry, the **knight** constituted the lower level of a two-tiered warrior aristocracy. Both nobles and knights were trained for mounted combat. They shared a common military vocation, were similarly equipped with arms, armor, and warhorses, and were exempt from agricultural labor. Indeed, great aristocrats came increasingly to describe themselves as "knight-nobles," higher in status than common knights, yet knights nonetheless. But whereas nobles possessed large estates, ordinary knights held few if any lands, and whereas nobles led armies into battle, knights followed and obeyed. Only later did it become common for knights to hold land and to marry into noble families.

The trend toward regional defense against invaders gave rise, during the tenth century, to a military innovation of surpassing importance: the castle. The earliest castles bore little resemblance to the great stone fortresses of the later Middle Ages; many were simply small, square wooden towers, planted on hilltops or artificial mounds and circled by wooden stockades. But when effectively garrisoned, they could be powerful instruments not only of defense but of territorial control as well. Many castles were built by nobles. Others were built (or seized) by ambitious men of less exalted status known as "castellans," who assembled knightly retinues of their own, brought surrounding territories under their control, and over time wriggled into the old nobility.

The coming of castles changed the character of the aristocracy by giving powerful families, old and new, a specifically located center of power. Soon they began identifying themselves by the name of their chief castle, their "family seat." Nobles previously known simply by their first names—Amaury, Geoffrey, Roger—now gloriously burst forth as Amaury de Montfort, Geoffrey de Mandeville, Roger de Beaumont, hereditary lords of the castles of Montfort, Mandeville, and Beaumont. Castles thus provided the nobility with a new sense of family identity. As the castle and lordship passed over generations from father to eldest son, the family tended increasingly to regard itself not simply as a group of relatives but as members of a hereditary line of descent. The result was a much clearer idea of family ancestry. When in time members of the knightly class began settling on estates, they too took the name of their estate as their family name and, like the nobility, evolved into a class of hereditary landholders.

Germany: Fragmentation, Reunification, and Renaissance

Invasions gave birth to unified monarchy in England while undermining it in France. Germany's response was different still: first the emergence of powerful, semi-independent duchies; then a resurgence of royal power.

Although East Francia (Germany) was subject to Viking attacks, the greater threat came from Magyars to the east. When the late-Carolingian kings of Germany proved unable to cope with the Magyar raids, authority descended, as in France, to the great regional officials of the realm: the dukes, who had formerly administered their duchies as agents of the monarchy.

Following their accustomed policy, the Carolingians had patterned their German duchies on earlier tribal divisions. During the turbulent years of the ninth century, these "tribal duchies" became virtually autonomous. Their dukes took direct control of royal lands and powers and dominated the churches within their districts. The process was all too familiar.

In the early tenth century Germany was dominated by five tribal duchies: Saxony, Swabia, Bavaria, Franconia, and Lorraine. The first three had been incorporated only quite recently into the Carolingian state, whereas the western duchies of Franconia and Lorraine were much more strongly Frankish in outlook and organization. The five "tribal" dukes might well have become the masters of Germany, but their ambitions were frustrated by two related factors. First, they failed to curb the Magyars. Second, an able new dynasty reinvigorated the German monarchy. The German Carolingian line sputtered out in 911 with the death of King Louis the Child. He was succeeded first by the duke of Franconia and then, in 919, by the duke of Saxony—the

first of an illustrious line of kings whose power was based on their domination of the powerful Saxon duchy.

The Saxon monarchy struggled hard to assert itself over the tribal duchies. Controlling their own duchy of Saxony, the Saxon kings quickly won direct control over Franconia and Lorraine, and imposed a protectorate on Lothar's old kingdom of Burgundy. But the semi-independent dukes of the two southern duchies, Swabia and Bavaria, presented greater problems. The monarchy's real victory occurred under the second and ablest of the Saxon kings, Otto I (reigned 936–973).

Otto I, "the Great," directed his considerable talents toward three goals and achieved them all. First was to defend Germany against the Magyar invasions; second was to recover royal lands and powers within the remaining tribal duchies; third was to extend German royal control to the crumbling, unstable Middle Kingdom that the Treaty of Verdun had assigned to Emperor Lothar back in 843.

We have already seen how this Middle Kingdom began to fall to pieces after Lothar's death. By the mid-tenth century it had become a shambles. Parts of it had been taken over by Germany and France, but its southern districts—Burgundy and Italy—retained a chaotic independence. The dukes of Swabia and Bavaria both hoped to seize these territories. Otto the Great, to forestall the rise of an unmanageable rival power to his south, led his armies into Italy in 951 and assumed the title "King of Italy."

From 951 onwards events unfolded rapidly. Otto the Great had to leave Italy in haste to put down a major uprising in Germany, and his triumph left him more strongly entrenched than ever. In 955 he won the crucial victory of his age when he crushed the Magyars at the battle of the Lechfeld, halting their raids at last. Otto's victory at the Lechfeld vividly demonstrated royal power: It vindicated the monarch's claim that he, not the dukes, was the true defender of Germany. With the Magyar menace ended, Germany's eastern frontier lay open to the gradual penetration of German-Christian culture. The tribal duchies were overshadowed, and the monarchy ruled supreme. Otto the Great seemed to his contemporaries the greatest monarch since Charlemagne.

Not long after his victory over the Magyars, Otto confronted still another crisis. Upon his departure from Italy, a Lombard magnate seized the Italian throne and began harassing the pope. In response to a papal appeal—which dovetailed with his own interests—Otto returned to Italy in force and recovered the Italian throne. In 962 the pope hailed Otto as "Roman Emperor" and placed the imperial crown on his head. This event, rather than the coronation of Charlemagne in 800, marks the true genesis of the medieval Holy Roman Empire.

Although the events of 962 are reminiscent of 800, Otto's empire was vastly different from Charlemagne's. Otto and his imperial successors exercised no jurisdiction over France or the remainder of Western Christendom.

Emperor Otto III Otto III's mother was a Byzantine princess, and she impressed on him a high consciousness of imperial dignity and duty. This illumination (ca. 998), which shows Otto receiving tribute from all parts of his empire, combines classical design with Germanic details, like the faces on the columns. *München, Bayerische Staatsbibliothek. Hirmer Fotoarchiv.*

The Holy Roman Empire had its roots in German soil, and most emperors subordinated imperial interests to those of the German monarchy. From its birth in 962 to its long-delayed death at Napoleon's hands in 1806, the Holy Roman Empire remained fundamentally a German phenomenon.[13]

The German orientation of Otto's empire is illustrated by the fact that neither he nor the majority of his successors over the next two centuries made any real effort to establish tight control in Italy. Only when they marched south of the Alps could they count on the obedience of the Italians; when they marched back to Germany, they left behind no real administrative structure but depended almost solely on the fickle allegiance of certain Italian magnates and bishops. The German emperors never successfully straddled the Alps.

In Germany things were quite different. There the coming of feudalism[14] was delayed for more than a century after Otto's imperial coronation. The great magnates became vassals of the king but normally had no vassals of their own. The chief tool that Otto and his successors used in governing their state was the church. Otto extended his power over the churches of the tribal duchies, making Germany's bishops and abbots the king's men. They were ideal royal officials, for they could not pass on their estates to legitimate heirs, and when one died, the king hand-picked

---

[13] The term *Holy Roman Empire* was not actually employed until the twelfth century. It is used here for convenience and with apologies to the purist. Tongue-in-cheek, one historian observed that the Holy Roman Empire was neither holy nor Roman nor an empire.

[14] Feudalism, which in the tenth and eleventh centuries was primarily a French phenomenon, is discussed more fully later in this chapter and in the glossary.

THE HUMAN EXPERIENCE

Roswitha of Gandersheim

A highly intelligent, well-educated nun of the Benedictine convent of Gandersheim in Ottonian Saxony, Roswitha (ca. 937–ca. 1004) was the earliest major female poet of the Middle Ages and the earliest post-Roman European playwright of either sex. Her birth into a Saxon noble family coincided roughly with the succession of Otto the Great—whom she came to admire greatly.

Like many other Benedictines of the Early Middle Ages, Roswitha (also spelled Hroswitha or Hrosvitha) was committed to the monastic life as a child and educated in her abbey. Gandersheim provided an excellent environment for learning. Founded by the duke of Saxony in 852, it was ruled by a series of abbesses of the highest nobility—most of them members of the Saxon royal house—and it therefore enjoyed both the prestige of a royal abbey and generous endowments from the royal family. Otto the Great's scholarly younger brother Brun, archbishop of Cologne (925–965), took a particular interest in Gandersheim and built it into a major intellectual and literary center. One of Roswitha's teachers, Gerberga II, abbess of Gandersheim—a woman deeply learned in classical Latin and Christian literature—was the niece of Emperor Otto I and Archbishop Brun.

Some details of Roswitha's life and education emerge from the various dedications with which she introduced her writings, and a smattering of further autobiographical information is to be found in the writings themselves. She received her early education from the nun Rikkardis, whom Roswitha later praised as "a most wise and beneficent teacher." She then proceeded to master many of the great works of Latin literature under the skillful tutelage of Abbess Gerberga. In short, Roswitha ought not to be regarded as being generations ahead of her time (always a misleading cliché); rather, she was one of the foremost talents of the Ottonian Renaissance, an outstanding yet not untypical product of tenth-century Germany.

Characteristically, then, Roswitha devoted the early years of her literary career to the writing of Latin religious poems (dedicated to her teacher Gerberga) on such subjects as the life and miracles of the Virgin Mary, the last words of Jesus, the deaths and transfigurations of Christian martyrs, and the lives of the saints. At the height of her literary powers, Roswitha turned to the far more original enterprise of writing plays—the first dramas to be written since the decline of the classical Roman theater, and the first ever to have been written in rhymed prose. Her plays thus constitute the emergence of a new literary form.

As Roswitha herself explained, she was inspired to become a playwright by reading the comedies of the early Roman playwright Terence. She was beguiled by the grace and refinement of his prose, and at times by his wit, but not at all by his subject matter, which dwelled on worldly pleasures and illicit loves. Quite consciously she employed Terence's literary form and style for purposes of Christian edification rather than pagan titillation.

Roswitha wrote six plays, in each of which she endeavored to dramatize Christian themes—holy love, the preservation of virginity against heavy odds, miraculous interventions at seemingly hopeless moments, the conversion and repentance of prostitutes, and the courage and joy of martyrdom. In Roswitha's play *Calimachus*, for example, the pagan Calimachus becomes passionately attracted to a young Christian married woman named Drusiana, who so desperately fears losing her virtue to him that she prays for death and is granted it. Calimachus approaches her tomb with the intention of ravishing her lifeless body, but Drusiana's virtue is preserved even in death when a snake strikes her assailant and poisons him. Then God miraculously restores them both to life, whereupon Calimachus becomes a convert to Christianity.

Later in life Roswitha turned to the writing of history in heroic verse. She celebrated the triumphs of Otto the Great in her *Deeds of Otto*, and she related the early history of her convent in her *Origins of the Abbey of Gandersheim*. Little is known of her final years, but the evidence suggests that she died quietly in her middle to late sixties, within a year or so of the death (in 1002), of the last Ottonian emperor, Otto III. Although her gifts as a dramatist are not to be compared with those of Sophocles, Shakespeare, or even Terence, her plays are still performed and admired. ❖

his successor. Thus the loyalty and political capacity of the king's administrator-churchmen were assured. After 962, German kings sometimes even named popes. There would come a time when independence-minded clergy would rebel, but under the Ottos that moment was still far off.

Otto's claim to rule the imperial church was supported by both tradition and theory. Otto was regarded as more than a mere secular monarch. He was *rex et sacerdos* ("king and priest"), sanctified by the holy anointing ceremony that accompanied his coronation. He was the vicar of God—the living symbol of Christ the King—the "natural" leader of the church in his empire. And he led it firmly and aggressively, reorganizing bishoprics, establishing new ones across the northern and eastern reaches of his empire, and defending them with his armies against hostile Danes and Slavs. Otto's religious foundations drew German churchmen and settlers far eastward into the lands of the Slavs, extending the German frontier to the boundaries of Poland. To forestall further German pressure Poland became a Christian kingdom in 966. The combined expansion of church and empire into pagan lands recalls Charlemagne's campaigns, generations earlier, against Otto's native Saxony.

Otto the Great's reign provided the impulse for an impressive intellectual revival that reached its culmination under his two successors, Otto II (reigned 973–983) and Otto III (reigned 983–1002). This "Ottonian Renaissance" produced able administrators and scholars, many of them bishops and other clergy associated with the royal court. Richly endowed abbeys and, in particular, nunneries, some of them headed by well-educated women from the royal family, became centers of learning and literary production.

The greatest Ottonian scholar was the monk Gerbert of Aurillac (d. 1003). Gerbert visited Spain and returned with a comprehensive knowledge of Islamic science. With this event the infiltration of Arab thought into Western Christendom began in earnest (discussed in Chapter 10). It was even rumored that Gerbert was a wizard in league with the devil—but the rumor was dampened (not ended) when he became Pope Sylvester II. Gerbert was no wizard but a harbinger of the intellectual awakening that Europe was about to undergo.

In 1024 the Saxon Dynasty died out and was replaced by a Franconian line known as the Salian Dynasty (1024–1125). Working hand-in-glove with the German church, the Salians improved and expanded the royal administration and ultimately came to wield even greater authority than Otto I. In the mid-eleventh century the strongest Salian emperor, Henry III (reigned 1039–1056), held sway over Germany and appointed popes almost as freely as he named his own bishops. In 1050, while the French monarchy still dozed, Emperor Henry III dominated central Europe and held the papacy in his palm (see Map 7-6).

Italy: Resurgence

When Charlemagne conquered Lombard Italy in 774, he was faced with the problem of reorganizing a kingdom much different from his own. For one thing, urban life had retained far more vitality in Italy than elsewhere in Western Christendom. For another, the Lombard royal administration that Charlemagne inherited differed sharply from the administration of Carolingian Francia. The Lombard kings had managed to exercise strong authority only in a region of northern Italy that came to be known as the Lombard Plain, or simply Lombardy—a rich, fertile region dominated by Milan and irrigated by the Po River. They ruled only loosely over the Lombard dukes of Friuli to the northeast (near Venice) and Spoleto to the south. Still farther south, below Rome, Lombard royal authority was nonexistent. Here a swarm of small powers waged incessant war with one another: independent duchies, coastal towns (Amalfi, Naples, Salerno), Muslim military settlements, and Byzantine enclaves left over from Justinian's conquests.

Characteristically, Charlemagne replaced Lombard royal officials with Frankish counts on the Lombard Plain, and in Friuli and Spoleto Lombard dukes gave way to new dukes drawn from Carolingian officialdom. Charlemagne never established his authority south of Rome, and even in Lombardy the new Carolingian order did not have time to solidify. Within a generation or two, Carolingian royal authority was faltering. And by the late 800s the north Italian crown had become the object of a brutal and confused power struggle involving various dukes of ambitious families.

None of these contending dynasties could hold the crown for long without establishing control over the Lombard Plain. Consequently, as one family after another seized the throne, it would place its own supporters in the controlling positions as counts in Lombardy. As a result of these policies, the old Carolingian aristocracy gave way throughout Lombardy to a new aristocracy dependent on one or another of the short-lived royal dynasties. Thus Lombardy, unlike France, experienced a nearly complete break with the Carolingian past. Whereas most of the principalities of France were ruled by descendants of Carolingian counts and dukes, the counties of Lombardy were not. And whereas the power of the French principalities was growing, that of the Lombard counties was diminishing for want of dynastic continuity.

ECONOMIC AND SOCIAL REBUILDING

The rise of new dynasties and the carving out of embryonic kingdoms in England, France, and Germany were not the only changes that were afoot between the 800s and about 1050. Quiet, sometimes almost imperceptible, change was also taking place in the way Europeans organized their society, earned their daily bread, and even constituted their families—changes that would cumulatively be of tremendous importance in shaping the West's medieval society, with consequences that still endure.

This section concerns itself with the reemergence of cities, primarily in Italy, and with the emergence of a cluster of political, social, and economic relationships that historians call *feudalism*, primarily in northern France. In both cases, these changes would later spread to much of western Europe. In addition, it considers the life of both peasants and nobles as **manorialism** and other aspects of medieval

MAP 7-6
EUROPE, CA. 1000

rural life took shape. As part of this transformation, one of the most fundamental changes in European life also came into focus: The nuclear family of father, mother, and children was replacing the older extended family and the clan as Western society's basic unit.

By the end of this period of transition and rebuilding, a new view of society emerged. According to this view, a well-ordered society had three elements: peasants who worked, nobles who fought, and clergy who prayed. Each had its God-given duty and dignity. But one group never quite fit into this famous scheme of the "Three Orders": the merchants and urban artisans who held everything together by making and selling things. Mere moneymaking continued to be regarded as greed—the soul-endangering pursuit of riches. This uneasiness would gnaw at European consciences until the eighteenth century.[15]

The Rebirth of the Italian Cities

As the Lombard counts weakened, the cities that they governed grew more independent. With the onset of the Muslim and Magyar invasions, the Italian cities, led by their bishops, became the chief centers of resistance. Contending Italian kings came to depend on their cities to repel the invaders and felt obliged to grant the urban bishops extensive powers and privileges—the right to build walls and fortified towers and the right to finance these projects by collecting tolls and public revenues. By the early 900s the cities had won full exemption from the counts' jurisdiction. The bishops controlled not only the cities' defenses but also their revenues and courts.

Throughout the 900s, the bishops remained firmly in power.[16] Ruling and defending their cities, they became the decisive force in northern Italian politics. The royal dynasties required their support, and more than once the opposition of bishops cost a monarch his crown. It was at the urging of a group of important Lombard bishops that Otto the Great intervened in the mid-900s, bringing an end to the royal dynastic squabbles by incorporating northern Italy into his empire.

Otto the Great and his imperial successors ruled northern Italy from a distance. Except on the rare occasions when they led their armies southward across the Alps, they based their authority on the support of the urban bishops, whose powers grew under German rule. Otto's conquest changed nothing, but it did furnish Italy the vitally

important benefits of relative peace and stability after a century of anarchy. The emperors helped relieve Italy of the Arab menace, both by leading armies against Muslim enclaves and by providing a settled environment that encouraged urban growth and commercial revival. By the late 900s, the north Italian ports of Genoa and Pisa were developing a vigorous and extensive Mediterranean trade and a growing merchant class. In the course of the next century, Genoa and Pisa seized the offensive from the Arabs, expelling them from the big Mediterranean islands of Sardinia and Corsica and launching raids against Muslim ports in Spain and North Africa. Southern coastal cities beyond the reach of the German emperor—Amalfi, Salerno, and Naples—had already taken to the sea. Most significant of all, the republic of Venice on the northern end of the Adriatic Sea emerged as a major economic and political power.

Long a Byzantine dependency, Venice achieved virtual independence by the ninth century but continued to send fleets to assist Byzantium in its wars. By carefully cultivating relations with both Constantinople and Islamic North Africa, Venice developed a flourishing triangular trade. During the 900s Venice evolved into Western Christendom's foremost commercial center. In a Europe that was overwhelmingly agrarian, the Venetians created the first medieval state to live by trade alone. Enriched by the exporting of salt from their lagoons and glass from their furnaces, and by the profits of commerce, they produced little food but purchased it instead in the markets of other north Italian towns. A Lombard remarked with astonishment that "These people neither plow nor sow nor gather grapes, [but] buy grain and wine in every market place."

Lucca: A Revived Roman City Aerial photography clearly reveals the origin of this square in the northern Italian port of Lucca: About the tenth century, the inhabitants turned a former Roman stadium into houses. Much of the original Roman structure is still preserved. *Archivo e Studio Folco Quilici, Rome.*

---

[15] As we shall see in the chaptrs on the Enlightenment and the Industrial Revolution, a major innovation in Western thought occurred in the eighteenth century, when economic enterprise and the amassing of wealth (traditionally condemned as a sin) came to be viewed as socially benign, and indeed beneficial. This intellectual reversal was a key step in the emergence of modern industrial capitalism.

[16] In the next century, the townspeople would challenge them. See Chapter 8.

In this respect Venice was unique, but other Italian ports—Genoa, Pisa, Amalfi—were following it into the lucrative Mediterranean trade. And their burgeoning commercial life stimulated the growth of inland cities such as Milan, Bologna, and Florence. Milan's population in A.D. 1000, although probably no more than about twenty thousand, made it the largest city in Lombardy and one of the most populous in Western Christendom. With the closing of the age of invasions, Italy had reversed two centuries-long historical trends: Its cities were growing once more, and its well-armed fleets were at last challenging the Byzantine and Muslim domination of Mediterranean commerce. As we shall see in Chapter 8, it was from urban-based commerce that a money economy revived in the West, and with it came changes of far-reaching consequence.

The Origins of French Feudalism

During the invasions and unrest of the ninth and tenth centuries, many knights and nobles of northern France came to hold estates on condition that they perform military and other service to a greater lord. An estate held on these terms was called a fief,[17] and the relationship of land-holding to service is known as feudalism (after *feudum*, the Medieval Latin word for "fief"). The holder of a fief became the vassal of his lord, rendering him loyal service in a solemn ceremony of homage. The granting of estates in exchange for loyal service was a convenient way for a lord to support a retinue of mounted warriors in an age of scarce money and abundant land.

Often such feudal arrangements would extend through several levels of lordship. In theory at least, the great territorial princes held their duchies and counties as fiefs of the king of France (though they did not always bother to render him homage, and they were as apt to fight against him as for him). Lesser nobles, in turn, might hold estates as vassals of counts or dukes, while granting smaller fiefs to vassals of their own. A single person might be both the vassal of a greater lord and the lord of lesser vassals.

The feudal concepts of vassalage and conditional land tenure were deeply rooted in the European past. One such root was the oath of fidelity and service that bound a warrior to his lord in Carolingian and Merovingian times. Another root was the late Roman and early medieval concept of granting an estate (a "benefice") in return for certain services. Charlemagne, as we have seen, permitted his magnates (counts and dukes) the use of royal estates in return for their military and administrative service, and the entire Carolingian political structure had been bound together by oaths of personal loyalty—to the king by his magnates and to the magnates by their own followers.

Only in the tenth and eleventh centuries, however, and only in portions of France, did these elements coalesce into the pattern of fiefs, lords, and vassals known to historians as feudalism. The term **feudal system**, so widely used in textbooks, conveys a misleading impression of order and universality. In reality feudal relationships coexisted with entirely different arrangements—lands held unconditionally, landless knights supported in noble households, political power based on public sovereign authority rather than on personal lordship over vassals, and loyalties based on kinship or wages rather than on homage. Even when relationships were feudal, they were not necessarily systematic. A single vassal, for example, might acquire several estates by swearing homage to several lords, who might well be mutual enemies. The resulting confusion of loyalties is suggested in this twelfth-century document:

> I, John of Toul, affirm that I am the vassal of the Lady Beatrice, countess of Troyes, and of her son Theobald, count of Champagne, against every creature living or dead, excepting my allegiance to Lord Enjourand of Coucy, Lord John of Arcis, and the count of Grandpré. If it should happen that the count of Grandpré should be at war with the countess and count of Champagne in his own quarrel, I will aid the count of Grandpré in my own person, and will aid the count and countess of Champagne by sending them the knights whose services I owe them from the fief which I hold of them.

Like much historical evidence, this document can be interpreted in more than one way. It suggests that feudal arrangements could be confused and complex, but it also represents an effort to bring order out of the chaos of multiple allegiances. In this last respect it typifies the tendency, beginning in the eleventh century and accelerating in the twelfth, to systematize feudal practices that had originally sprouted like dandelions on an ill-kept lawn.

Under the influence of strong territorial princes, feudal rights and obligations came to be defined with increasing precision (though the definitions varied from region to region). Typically, the vassal owed service in his lord's army—his own personal service and, often, that of additional knights from his household or estates. The vassal might also be obliged to join his lord's retinue on tours of the countryside (large retinues were status symbols), to serve in his lord's court of justice, to feed and house the lord and his retinue on their visits, to help raise a ransom should the lord be captured in battle, and to give the lord money on specified occasions—for example, the knighting of the lord's eldest son, the marriage of his eldest daughter, and the succession of a son to his father's fief. Early in its history the fief became hereditary, but the lord retained the right to confiscate it should his vassal die without heirs, to enjoy its revenues while rearing and training an orphan heir, and to veto the marriage

---

[17]Rhyming with "beef."

Homage   There are no visual representations of vassals doing homage in the Early Middle Ages. The pictures that we do have come from a later time, such as this from the thirteenth century. But although the armor changed, probably the ceremony did not greatly vary over the centuries. In it, the vassal knelt before his lord and placed his hands in his lord's. Then the lord would raise and embrace his man, completing the symbolism of acknowledging dependence and mutual trust.   *The British Museum.*

Because of its diversity, feudalism is difficult to define. Some scholars would abolish the word altogether;[18] others would prefer to speak of "feudalisms" rather than "feudalism." Feudalism is still a useful word if employed with caution. But if feudalism cannot be precisely defined, it can at least be described. Marc Bloch put it this way:

> A subject peasantry; widespread use of the service tenement (that is, the fief) instead of a salary, which was out of the question; the supremacy of a class of specialized warriors; ties of obedience and protection which bind man to man and, within the warrior class, assume the distinctive form called vassalage; fragmentation of authority—leading inevitably to disorder; and in the midst of all this, the survival of other forms of association, family and state. . . . Such then seem to be the fundamental features of European feudalism.[19]

Feudalism in Practice: The French Principalities

We have seen how Carolingian royal authority disintegrated into regional principalities and often still smaller units. As one historian has written: "Dirty, bloodstained, and exhausted lords surrounded by brutal warriors, making their way from primitive wooden castles to austere monastic refuges, must have been common sights on the West Frankish roads."[20] But as the invasions diminished, the disintegration was gradually reversed. New principalities emerged as ambitious noble families assembled groups of counties, through marriage and conquest, into large territorial blocs. By the early twelfth century the French principalities, old and new, were growing steadily in wealth and power. The dukes of Aquitaine and Normandy and the counts of Flanders, Anjou, Blois, Champagne, and Burgundy were in practice the equals of the king of France.

These great princes continued to base their power on the control of lands, of courts, and of public taxes and services that had formerly belonged to the Carolingian monarchy. The Carolingian system of government was not demolished but merely fragmented. Indeed, in some important respects it was improved. A number of territorial princes generated sufficient revenues to administer their dominions not through powerful regional landholders but through salaried officials who could be transferred or removed at will. The princes ruled not only as lords of fief-holding vassals but also through the exercise of public

of an heiress. Often, indeed, the lord chose the heiress's husband, sometimes charging him a stiff price for her hand and inheritance.

In return for these rights, the lord was duty-bound to protect his vassals, to deal with them justly, and to defend their fiefs against enemy attacks. In short, the lord-vassal relationship involved obligations in both directions. The essence of feudalism was the notion of reciprocal rights and duties. The relationship of a prince to his greater subjects resembled that of a lord to his vassals, and medieval aristocracies never permitted their rulers to forget that bad lordship justified the repudiation of homage.

---

[18] David Bates, in his *William the Conqueror* (London: Philip,1989, p. 14) describes *feudalism* and *feudal society* as "terms which have been invented in modern times to make the study of the Middle Ages more difficult."
[19] Marc Bloch, *Feudal Society* (Chicago: University of Chicago Press, 1961), vol. 2, p. 446.
[20] Jean Dunbabin, *France in the Making, 843–1180* (Oxford: Oxford University Press, 1985), p. 241.

authority and the control of increasingly efficient and flexible administrations. In time their governance became more effective than that of the old Carolingian Empire. They had the advantage of ruling compact territorial units and the further advantage of controlling a growing number of castles (increasingly now built of stone), which served as military and political power centers throughout their principalities. And as the eleventh century progressed, they benefited from an accelerating commercial revival.

The princes themselves contributed to this revival. They established new agricultural settlements on depopulated lands. They supported monastic reform (which usually brought marked improvement to the management of monastic estates) and encouraged the construction of water mills. They founded hundreds of new abbeys as centers of princely influence and agrarian development. And they opened up new lands for cultivation by clearing forests and draining bogs. The counts of Flanders organized and encouraged an elaborate program of dike building to reclaim land from the sea and convert it to sheep farming. The counts of Champagne (in northeastern France) sponsored a series of annual fairs for long-distance merchants and—for a price—guaranteed them safe passage through the county. Merchants from all over Europe (and above all from Italy) found that while trading in Champagne they could expect personal freedom, reasonable tolls, and fair justice.

The growth of agricultural productivity and the quickening of commerce increased princely revenues. With their new wealth, princes enlarged their administrations, armies, and networks of castles to the point where they could overawe their vassals, bring relative peace to their principalities, and protect the more helpless of their inhabitants from terror, robbery, and slaughter. In late eleventh-century Normandy and Flanders, no magnate could build a castle without permission, and the dukes of Normandy claimed the right to occupy a vassal's stronghold on demand.

The rise of strong principalities by no means stopped violence. Warfare was almost incessant—between rival princes and between lesser magnates within principalities or in the turbulent regions between them. Territorial princes in the south of France proved much less successful than those elsewhere in bringing order to their lands. But in central and northern France, for the first time since Roman antiquity, princely regimes were acquiring the administrative, military, and financial resources necessary for effective governance. As such, they mark a vital stage in the development of political cohesion from the loosely governed Carolingian Empire to the beginnings of the European state.

Villages, Manors, and Daily Life

During the tenth and eleventh centuries the commercial city remained a rarity except in Italy. Almost everywhere, wealth and power meant holding land, and throughout western Europe the vast majority of Europeans labored on the soil.

To discuss the typical medieval farm is as difficult as to discuss the typical American business, for medieval agriculture exhibited countless variations. Nevertheless some features of agrarian life recur throughout the more fertile and heavily populated portions of northwestern Europe. Certain generalizations can be made about medieval agrarian institutions, if we bear in mind that numerous exceptions can be found.

Any discussion of medieval rural life must begin by distinguishing between two fundamental institutions: the village and the **manor**. The village, the basic unit of the agrarian economy, consisted of a population nucleus ranging from about a dozen to several hundred peasant families, usually living in a cluster encircled by their fields. Where the soil was poor, peasant families might live in separate farms or hamlets, but across the fertile lowlands of northern France, England, and Germany, village life was the norm.

The manor, on the other hand, was an artificial unit—a unit of jurisdiction and economic exploitation controlled by a single lord. The lord might be a king or a great nobleman or churchman with numerous manors under his control. Or he might be a simple knight with only one or two manors at his disposal. The manor was often geographically identical with the village, but some manors embraced two or more villages, and an occasional large village might be divided into two or more manors. In any case, the agrarian routine of plowing, planting, and harvesting was based on the village organization, whereas the peasants' dues, obligations, and legal and political subordination were based on the manor.

The Village   The peasants of the Early Middle Ages, like the Romans and Celts before them, tended to live in agrarian settlements consisting of scattered individual farms or small clusters of them. The agricultural community, which had been an important element in the European landscape since prehistoric times, underwent fundamental changes between approximately the ninth and twelfth centuries, the chronology of this change varying from region to region. Before it occurred, rural communities were relatively impermanent, consisting of ramshackle cottages that lasted a lifetime at most and were easily abandoned if the villagers chose to relocate (as they often did). However, most early medieval villagers, historians now believe, were free property holders, and communities like those on the great Carolingian estates (see page 237) were not typical.

Around the turn of the millennium, the scattered, ephemeral settlements began to fuse into villages of the later medieval and modern type, with their houses set close together, often centered on a village green or a well or fish pond, and surrounded by great fields. Agrarian communities of this sort are known as "nucleated villages"—that is, a nucleus of houses encircled by fields. The causes of this process of village formation are not entirely clear. Perhaps a particularly large cluster of farms began to attract the inhabitants of the neighboring district through the power or initiative of a lord or through community consensus.

Village formation was stimulated by the emergence of castles and stone manor houses, as well as by the growth of monasteries, all of which served to anchor dependent agrarian communities. Another stimulus was the development of parishes—small ecclesiastical districts, centering on a local church that tended increasingly to be built of stone, becoming a second anchor. The social and religious life of villagers typically focused on parish churches, which provided the village community a sense of permanence.

At about this same period it became common for the village population to include a substantial group of artisans—wheelwrights, blacksmiths, carpenters, coopers, and joiners. With the help of these workers, peasant families began building larger and better-constructed cottages. In short, the traditional European village—with its church, its castle or manor house, its nucleus of sturdily built cottages surrounded by fields, and its organized community of artisans—was, around the year 1000, only a recent creation.

The lands around these villages would normally be divided into either two or three large fields. Two fields had been traditional and remained so throughout southern Europe. But the agrarian economy had been shifting in some districts of northern Europe from a two-field to a three-field system of crop rotation. The peasants of a three-field village would plant one field in the spring for fall harvesting, plant the second field in the fall for harvesting early in the next summer, and let the third field lie fallow throughout the year. The next year the fields would be rotated and the process repeated. Although three-field agriculture was becoming common in northern Europe, it was necessarily limited to areas where soil fertility was sufficient to sustain more intensive cultivation. Many villages continued to use only two fields, while others might have four, five, or even more, all subject to complex rotation arrangements.

The arable lands surrounding the village were known as "open fields" and were normally divided into unfenced strips, each about 220 yards long. Typically a single peasant family possessed several strips, scattered throughout the fields, from which it produced its own food for consumption, sale, or the payment of manorial and parish dues. But the village community pooled its plows, draft animals, and toil. Collective farming was necessary because plows were expensive and had to be shared, and because no one peasant owned sufficient oxen to make up the team of several beasts (often four) necessary to pull the heavy plow. The details of this collective process were usually worked out in the village council and were guided by custom.

Wheeled Plow and Horse Collar   The late medieval image (left) of a wheeled plow (developed centuries earlier) shows the heavy blade at the plow's front that sliced the turf, with the moldboard behind it turning the soil. Usually the pulling was done by four oxen with a rope tied around their necks. This would have choked a horse, and the horse collar (invented in the High Middle Ages) let horses plow and harrow (foreground). Plowing was difficult, and medieval farmers divided their plots into long strips. The aerial shot (above) shows these strips on medieval fields converted to pastureland two centuries ago. *(left) British Library, London/The Bridgeman Art Library. (right) Reprinted with the permission of Cambridge University Press.*

The need for cooperation in farming their open fields forced European villagers to learn how to regulate the inevitable disputes that would arise over boundaries and plowing rights. Villagers were under strong practical pressure to develop skill at carrying on their agrarian routine without the constant intervention of manorial lords or their bailiffs and without destructive community violence. It has been suggested (not all would agree) that these skills contributed to the later emergence of cooperative commercial enterprises and effective local government in medieval western Europe.

The shape, contour, and method of cultivation of the open fields varied with the topography of the region and the fertility of the soil. The length of the strips frequently depended on how far an ox team could pull the heavy plow without stopping to rest or turn. A group of four strips, which constituted the normal day's work of a plow team, became the basis of the modern English acre.

The open fields were fundamental to the village economy and, indeed, to the entire agrarian system of northern Europe. But there was more to the village community than a cluster of cottages and encircling fields. Besides their scattered strips in the fields, peasants ordinarily had small gardens next to their cottages where they raised vegetables and fruits and kept fowl to provide variety to their diet. The village also included a pasture where the plow animals grazed, and a meadow from which hay was cut to sustain the beasts over the winter. Some villages kept sheep and cattle on their pasture as a source of cheese, milk, and wool. Certain districts, particularly in Flanders and northern England, took up sheep raising on a scale so large as almost to exclude the growing of grains. They had to buy food with money earned from selling wool.

Attached to most village communities was a wooded area where fuel and building materials could be gathered. It also served as a forage for pigs, which provided most of the meat in the peasants' diet. There was commonly a stream or pond nearby that supplied the community with fish, a water mill for grinding grain, and a large oven that the community used for baking bread. By the eleventh century, some village communities were organized as parishes, with village churches and parish priests who were allotted lands of their own in the open fields. A single priest might collect the revenues of several village churches, living in style and delegating his priestly responsibilities to a vicar—often of peasant birth and barely literate.

The village community was economically self-sufficient only to a degree. There was always a certain amount of regional trade, and crucial items such as salt and metals often had to be imported from fairly distant sources. Thus villagers had incentive to produce food surpluses for trade. This incentive was intensified when the commercial revival of the eleventh and twelfth centuries vastly increased the market for grain.

The commercial revival and spread of a money economy (to be discussed in Chapter 8) were supported by the increased agricultural productivity brought about by early medieval innovations in agrarian organization and technology. Commercial expansion thus depended on food surpluses (as we have seen in the case of Venice) while also encouraging further surpluses. As towns and commerce grew, the village economy was integrated more and more into region-wide trade networks, and enterprising peasants acquired a means of making money by selling surplus grain. The expanding grain market in turn encouraged the creation of new fields from forests and marshes. By the mid-eleventh century the limited horizons of the early medieval village were visibly widening.

The Manor and Serfdom   Superimposed on the *economic* structure of the village was the *jurisdictional* structure of the manor. In the eleventh century throughout much of northern France, peasant villagers had become serfs bound to manorial lords. Soon thereafter, this manorial regime spread to southern France, to southern England, and to other parts of western Europe.

Historians disagree about how **serfdom** originated and when western Europe's rural social and economic system shifted from one based primarily on a mixture of slavery and free country folk to one resting primarily on serfdom. Documents shedding light on these questions are few, come from widely scattered places, and often are hard to interpret. At present, however, the picture appears to be as follows.

Rural slavery had been waning ever since the Roman world's great economic and social crisis of the third century A.D. As we saw in Chapter 5, many Roman landowners, faced with shrinking urban markets, gave up commercial farming and converted their slave gangs into semi-free, serf-like *coloni*, to whom they assigned plots. Slavery, however, did not disappear. During the Early Middle Ages many agrarian laborers were still outright slaves, especially on the great Carolingian manors for which documentation is fullest (see "A Carolingian Estate", p. 237). A few rural folk were landless laborers working for a wage, while others lived on holdings for which they owed various services. The majority of rural people, however, as late as the tenth century were apparently free. Beginning in tenth-century France, it was this great middle stratum of the peasantry who became serfs—people of unfree status, bound to their lords and usually also tied to their land. In return for their strips in the open fields, serfs owed various dues to their manorial lords, chiefly in kind, and were normally expected to toil for a certain number of days each week—often three—on the lord's fields. As these changes spread during the tenth and eleventh centuries, rural slavery correspondingly declined, and by 1100 it was becoming uncommon in western Europe.[21]

The insecure conditions of the invasion era prompted many free peasants to relinquish their freedom in exchange

---

[21] It was still found in some places.

for the protection of nearby lords, often bishops or abbots who could offer both military aid and the supernatural support of the saint whose sacred relics they guarded. Population increase—which meant that more mouths had to be fed and more heirs provided for on a holding of limited size—added to rural distress. So did the early stages of a developing money economy, becoming noticeable in the tenth century. A monastic land survey of around the year 900 records "fourteen freemen who have handed over their property to the abbey's manor, the condition being that each shall do one day's work a week." The great monastery at Cluny, in Burgundy, furnishes one of the best-documented cases of rural transformation around the year 1000. Here free peasants, sometimes in debt or finding that their holding could no longer support their family, and sometimes simply frightened by the violence of the times, exchanged their precarious independence for tenure as serfs on holdings that were grouped in villages over which monks were now the lords.

The lord—whether an individual nobleman or a church institution like a monastery—lived off the dues of enserfed peasants and from the produce of his own fields, which the serfs helped cultivate. Theoretically, the fields of the manor were divided into two categories: the lord's **demesne** (perhaps one-fourth to one-third of the total area) and the peasants' holdings (see Figure 7-2). But in actuality the demesne consisted of strips intermixed in the same fields with the peasants' strips. The demesne might be cultivated by slaves or hired hands, although by the eleventh century much of its workforce was serfs who also paid their lord a percentage of the produce of their own fields and fees for the use of the pasture, the woods, and his mill and oven. The use of water mills to grind grain had expanded very significantly during the Early Middle Ages. In Roman times such mills were relatively rare; in England in the mid-eleventh century, there were more than six thousand of them.

The lord also wielded significant authority over his peasants. The administrative center of the manor was the manorial court, usually held in the lord's castle or manor house. Here a rough, custom-based justice was meted out, disputes settled, misdeeds punished, and obligations enforced. Since most lords possessed more than one manor, authority over individual manors was usually exercised by an agent known as a "bailiff" or "steward" who supervised the manorial court, oversaw the farming of the demesne, and collected the peasants' dues. In addition to the peasants' demesne labor, the lord was entitled to certain payments deriving from his political and personal authority over his tenants. He might levy a tallage—a manorial tax that was theoretically unlimited in frequency and amount but was usually defined by custom. He was normally entitled to payments when a peasant's son inherited the holdings of his father and when a peasant's daughter married outside the manor.

FIGURE 7-2
A MEDIEVAL MANOR
This is a hypothetical sketch of how a "typical" three-field manor was laid out. Notice how, by mingling peasant strips and demesne strips, all members of the community, including the lord, would share in whatever good or bad luck would be visited upon an entire cultivated field—sufficient, insufficient, or excessive rainfall, for example. The lord and the peasants also shared access to pastures and forest.

In theory, serfs had no standing before the law, and some lords abused them pitilessly. But custom (and sometimes common sense) restrained most lords. Custom was strong in the Middle Ages and could protect serfs in many ways. They were by no means chattel slaves: They could not normally be sold away from their lands or families, and after paying their manorial dues they kept the remaining produce of their fields. At last resort they could flee to another lord, who might treat them better. The serfs' condition was hardly enviable, but it was better than that of ancient slaves.

Life in a Northern European Village By 1050, new social and economic conditions were transforming northern Europe's landscape. Forests dwindled and swamps were drained. There were gradual improvements in agrarian technology—notably the invention of the horse collar (see the illustration on p. 257), the development of the tandem harness, axled wagon wheels, the wider use of iron farm tools—all of which eased the task of clearing more lands for cultivation and producing more food for Europe's burgeoning population.

Let us not idealize things, however. The daily life of a high-medieval peasant was hard, almost beyond imagining. Village life might be in harmony with the seasons, but it was also vulnerable to nature's whims: droughts, floods, epidemics among humans and animals, crop diseases, summer's heat, and winter's chill. Today we are insulated from nature (and therefore romanticize it) by modern wonders: central heating, air-conditioning, a secure food supply, plumbing, deodorants, modern medicine, and many more, some of which may well be threatening our environment. We enjoy the protection of police and fire departments; we defy distance and terrain with our freeways and jets. Such things we take for granted, but in the Middle Ages, they would have seemed magical—or demonic.

By middle-class American standards, the peasant of 1050 lived in unspeakable filth and poverty. A typical peasant house, although perhaps more substantial than in Carolingian times, was a thatched roof resting on a timber framework, with the gaps between the framing filled with webbed branches covered with mud and straw. The houses of better-off peasants sometimes had two or three rooms, furnished with benches, a table, and perhaps a chest. Poorer peasants huddled in one-room cottages virtually bare of furniture.

The straw on which the family slept (all together) and procreated was apt to crawl with vermin. The stench of sweat and manure was ever-present and therefore largely unnoticed. Flies buzzed everywhere. The cottage might shelter not only a large family but chickens, dogs, geese, and occasionally cattle. Windows, if any, were small and few (and of course had no glass). The floor, usually of earth, froze in winter and turned oozy in spring. Arthritis and rheumatism were common, along with countless other ailments whose cure lay far in the future. A simple fire served for cooking and heating, but in the absence of chimneys the smoke filled the room before escaping through holes or cracks in the ceiling. Candles were luxuries; peasants relied on smoky, evil-smelling torches made of rushes soaked in fat, and stray sparks frequently set thatched roofs afire.

The daily routine of a family of village-dwelling serfs might begin with a predawn breakfast—perhaps coarse black bread and diluted ale for adults and children alike—after which the husband, wife, and post-toddling offspring would work until nightfall. Peasant work required close partnership between husband, wife, and children. Indeed, young peasant men were expected to marry before inheriting land, because women and children played essential roles in the peasant workforce. The father and sons did most of the heavy plowing. The wife and daughters took primary responsibility for the "inside work"—not only cooking and cleaning, but also making cheese and butter, spinning, and weaving cloth. They milked the cows, fed the livestock, tended the vegetable garden, and joined the men in haymaking, thatching, shearing the sheep, sowing

and reaping the grain, weeding the open fields, and sometimes plowing. In winter, the whole family might stay indoors making or repairing tools. The evening meal might be a pot of vegetable broth, more coarse black bread, more ale, and possibly an egg. Then it was early to bed, to rest for the next day's toil.

Even this somber picture is a bit idealized. Often one or more members of the peasant family would be immobilized by illness (for which there were no available physicians and few effective treatments) or tormented by parasites, infected injuries and wounds, and aches (no aspirin, just ale). Women endured one pregnancy after another; childbirth endangered mother and baby alike, and infant mortality was very high. Until modern times, well over a third of all children did not live out their first year, and about two-thirds died before age ten.

Occasionally villages might be decimated by famine. They might be pillaged or burned by their lord's enemy or might even become a battleground. From a twelfth-century French poem comes this chilling tale:

> They start to march. The scouts and the incendiaries lead. After them come the foragers who are to gather the spoils and load them into the great baggage train. The tumult begins. The peasants, having just come out to the fields, turn back uttering loud cries. The shepherds gather their flocks and drive them toward the neighboring woods in the hope of saving them. The incendiaries set the villages afire and foragers visit and plunder them. The distracted inhabitants are burned to death or led away with tied hands to be held for ransom. Everywhere alarm bells ring. Fear spreads from one side to another and becomes general. Everywhere one sees helmets shining, pennons floating, and horsemen covering the plain. Here money is seized; there cattle, donkeys, and flocks are taken. The smoke spreads; the flames rise; the terrified peasants and shepherds flee in all directions.

Such disasters were rare in the life of a single village, but when they occurred the helpless inhabitants had no choice but to rebuild, replant, and pray for survival through a cold, hungry winter.

In a typical peasant village the most substantial buildings were the lord's or bailiff's residence and the parish church. The lord's residence, the headquarters of the manor, was commonly surrounded by a walled enclosure that also contained a bakehouse, kitchen, barns, and other structures. To the manor house the peasants would bring portions of their produce, which they owed as customary dues. Here, too, they would bring their disputes to be settled in the lord's court. The parish church often stood at the center of the village. Its priest (assuming that it had one) was seldom well educated, although he might have learned the rudiments of reading and writing. He played a central role in the villagers' lives—baptizing infants, presiding at marriages and burials, and regularly celebrating **Mass.** The church was likely to be painted inside with scenes from the Bible or the life of the local patron saint; such paintings provided an elementary form of religious instruction to an illiterate congregation.

The church usually doubled as a village meeting hall, and on festival days it might be used for dancing, drinking, and revelry. The Christian feast days—Christmas, Easter, and many lesser holy days (holidays)—provided joyous relief from an otherwise grinding routine. In some districts the feast of Candlemas (February 2) was celebrated by a candlelight procession followed by a pancake dinner. On the eve of May Day the young men of some villages would cut branches in the forest and lay them at the doors of houses inhabited by young unmarried women. St. John's Day (the summer solstice, an ancient pagan celebration) brought bonfires and dancing. And throughout the year, time could be found for informal sports—wrestling, archery, cock fights, drinking contests, and a primitive form of soccer.

But for most of their days the medieval peasants labored to raise the food on which their families and communities depended for survival. An English writer of the late tenth century attributes these words to an imaginary serf:

> I work hard. I go out at daybreak, driving the oxen to the field, and then I yoke them to the plow. Be the winter ever so stark, I dare not linger at home for awe of my lord; but having yoked my oxen, and fastened plowshare and colter, every day I must plow a full acre or more. . . . I have a boy, driving the oxen with an iron goad, who is hoarse with cold and shouting. Mighty hard work it is, for I am not free.

Changes in Diet and Female Mortality The preceding paragraphs should banish any illusions about the happy medieval farmer—close to nature, living in rhythm with the seasons, free of urban anxieties—but they must not blind us to the fact that conditions were improving. The spread of iron or iron-tipped tools, better plows, better systems of crop rotation, water mills, and (beginning in the

twelfth century) windmills—such new devices contributed to the increase in food production and to gradual but significant improvements in diet. Food might have been monotonous, but it was basically nutritious, and becoming more so. The High Middle Ages saw a marked increase in the consumption of protein-rich and iron-rich foods—peas and beans (products of the new three-field rotation), cheese and eggs, fish and meat. Pork was beginning to appear more often on peasant tables, and the rabbit, introduced from Spain, reached France by late Carolingian times and England by the twelfth century. By the Late Middle Ages, Europe had become, in the words of one historian, "the most meat-eating culture in the world."

These dietary improvements seem to have produced a shift of enormous importance in the life expectancy of women. Scattered but fairly consistent evidence suggests that in Greco-Roman times and in the Early Middle Ages men outnumbered and outlived women. By the thirteenth and fourteenth centuries, however, writers speak of a surplus of women. The thirteenth-century scholar Albertus Magnus attributed women's greater longevity to the cleansing effect of menstruation and the fact that sexual intercourse drains the female less than the male. But this curious hypothesis fails to explain the basic shift: More males than females until the High Middle Ages; more females than males from then until now.

The explanation may lie in the increased consumption of iron-rich foods such as meat, beans, and other green vegetables. Menstruation, childbearing, and breast-feeding all drain iron from the body, so that women require much larger dietary intakes of iron than do men. The scarcity of iron in the diet of ordinary people of ancient and early medieval times probably resulted in most women becoming severely anemic by their early twenties, and therefore highly vulnerable to death from a variety of diseases. The improved diet of the High Middle Ages would have seriously reduced the high rate of female mortality resulting from iron-deficiency anemia. The whole population would

Peasant Woman and Children This mother seems to have her hands full trying to do the family cooking while keeping her children out of trouble and the fire. *The Bodleian Library, Oxford.*

live longer and more energetic lives than ever before, but the effect of the new foods on women would be particularly striking—altering the sex ratio in women's favor throughout European society to the present day.

The Coming of the Nuclear Family

Neither the Romans nor the early Germanic peoples had organized their families in ways that most of us would recognize. As we saw in Chapter 4, the Roman *familia* was headed by a senior male, who by custom and law wielded great power over his wife, offspring (including the grown ones), other relatives, clients, slaves, and miscellaneous dependents. Although some Romans, rich and poor, emancipated themselves from such domination, the alternatives seemed disreputable, unstable, and temporary. Meanwhile the Germans whom the Romans encountered (see Chapter 5) still lived in longhouses that were in effect large family compounds, often sheltering several wives and concubines, numerous offspring, a gaggle of other relatives, and slaves.

As Germanic and Roman societies slowly fused in the early medieval Western kingdoms, the extended families on which both elements rested continued to flourish. Women of Germanic origin did tend to gain slightly in status by marrying into families governed by Roman law. But we have also seen in Chapter 6 that polygyny (having multiple wives) endured among powerful Germanic men for several centuries after they became (nominally) Christian, allowing them to monopolize women whose wealth or other attractions rendered them desirable marriage partners. Germanic women also became attractive wives for men who under Roman law were unfree, because marriage to them would enable their children to gain freedom. Finally, women's shorter life expectancy relative to males made them a "commodity" in short supply. For all these reasons, women's economic value rose in the Early Middle Ages, embodied in the widespread custom of the husband giving his bride a rather substantial payment of money or property, called the bride-gift. Although extended families remained generally the rule, wives often kept control over the property they brought into their marriages. These relationships held true not only among the Germano-Roman elite, but apparently also among the peasantry, as occasional documents such as Carolingian-era estate inventories reveal.

The spread of a money economy, which began in the tenth century and gained momentum in the eleventh and twelfth (see Chapter 8), undermined the old-fashioned extended family and encouraged its substitution by the father-mother-children nuclear family. One reason was that by now nobles were finding plundering and gifting less lucrative and less reliable than collecting peasant dues and farming their demesne. Accordingly, they put a much higher value on their real estate holdings. As we have seen, nobles began to refer to these properties in giving them-

selves individual names ("Roger de Beaumont," for example) and looked for ways to consolidate their property rather than allow it to be dissipated. It thus became more common for fathers to bequeath all or most of their property to the eldest son, leaving the younger brothers to enter the church or shift for themselves as knights. Young knights were likely to join the entourage of some great lord, who might feed them at his table and refer to them as his "family"; but their objective was to amass enough money to woo a wife and establish a new nuclear family.

For the same reason, bestowal of the bride-gift became less common, until by the early thirteenth century it completely disappeared. Instead, wives' families were increasingly expected to provide a handsome **dowry**, whose control effectively passed into the husband's hands. Because women were living longer—and were more plentiful relative to the supply of prospective husbands—the balance of power in the matrimonial market shifted, enhancing the ability of fathers and husbands to keep property in a single "line." The spread of feudal relationships powerfully reinforced this tendency, as overlords tried to ensure that fiefs passed intact to a single new vassal—normally the eldest son.

These economic changes also encouraged peasants to substitute nuclear for extended households. Carolingian-era villagers tended to cluster, either around a great estate or in small, isolated clearings in Europe's immense virgin forest. But when, beginning in the late tenth century, monasteries and secular lords opened new settlements and created new villages, peasants saw the chance to gain full holdings for themselves. Granted, the peasants became serfs—but that gave the lords incentive to see that each nuclear-family unit had its own rent-paying holding. And because the peasants were serfs, their lords had the power to regulate how these holdings passed to heirs, just as feudal overlords could dictate who succeeded to a fief.

Finally, the formation and maintenance of nuclear families had the vigorous encouragement of the church. It had always condemned polygyny, and by the tenth century it was generally making its condemnation stick. The end of polygyny cut one of the props out from under the old-fashioned extended aristocratic family and provided more men with potential mates with whom to form separate households. At the same time the church forbade marriage within seven degrees of kinship (meaning that people with the same great-great grandparents could not marry) and with in-laws, such as a brother's widow.[22] These rules, which were often vigorously enforced, compelled everyone to be aware of family relationships and to seek marriage partners at a safe distance—another blow at complex

---

[22] In 1215 the Fourth Lateran Council (see Chapter 8) lowered the requirement to four degrees of kinship, but retained the prohibition against marrying in-laws and step-relations.

extended-family networks, which in the Early Middle Ages sometimes had a rather incestuous character.

Changes in the way tenth- and eleventh-century west Europeans organized something as basic and private as their family life were symptomatic of the ferment of the time. As the period called the High Middle Ages was beginning, roughly in the years 1000 to 1050, two developments of enormous importance were driving a host of other changes. First was the return of a money-based economic system, which had been in retreat ever since the crisis of third-century A.D. Rome. Second was the intensification of Christian faith among both the clergy and the laity of western Europe. The coming together of these two transformations constitutes medieval Europe's Dual Revolution, and it is the subject of Chapter 8.

CONCLUSION: EUROPE EMERGES

During the five or six centuries between the Western Roman Empire's transformation into Germanic kingdoms and the great resurgence of the later eleventh century, the foundations were laid on which arose the civilized life of western Europe. Kingdoms emerged that would play dominant roles in the history of the modern world—England, Germany, France—and distinctive customs and institutions were developing that would define and vitalize Europe throughout the next millennium. A classical-Christian cultural tradition was becoming absorbed, adapted, and fused with the customs of the Germanic peoples.

By the mid-eleventh century Europe's commerce was reviving, most strikingly in Italy, and everywhere the population was growing again. Indeed, the troubled era following the breakdown of Charlemagne's empire had a much livelier commerce than was once believed. Trade continued and even intensified during the post-Carolingian years along Europe's great river valleys—the Rhine, Seine, Po, Loire, Danube, Thames, and others. The growing wealth of the river valleys attracted Viking, Magyar, and Saracen raiders, and as the invaders were beaten back or absorbed, Europe's commerce surged. French princes, English kings, and German emperors alike encouraged markets and fairs and sought to control and systematize the minting of silver coins. The commerce of the Italian towns flourished under the Ottos and their successors, and when Otto the Great opened a rich silver mine at Rammelsberg in the 970s, a new wave of money flowed through northern Europe.

By 1050 both England and Germany were comparatively stable, well-organized kingdoms. The church was poised for a great movement of reform and centralization. The French monarchy was still weak, but by the end of the following century it would be on its way toward dominating France. Meanwhile, French principalities such as Champagne, Flanders, Normandy, and Anjou were well along the road to political coherence. Warfare was still commonplace, but it was beginning to lessen as Europe moved toward political stability. Above all, the invasions were over—the siege had ended. Hungary, Poland, the Czech kingdom of Bohemia, and Scandinavia were being absorbed into Western Christendom, as Russia and the Balkan Slavs were joining Eastern Christendom. Islam was by now on the defensive against the West. The return of prosperity, the increase in food production, the rise in population, the redefinition of the family, the quickening of commerce, the intensification of intellectual activity—all betokened the coming of a new age. Western civilization was on the verge of a creative explosion.

Selected Reading

Sources

Magnusson, Magnus, and Hermann Pálsson, trans. *Laxdæla Saga* (1969).

Turner, S. E., trans. *Einhard's Life of Charlemagne* (1960).

Wright, David, trans. *Beowulf* (1957).

Carolingian Europe

Blumenthal, Uta-Renate, ed. *Carolingian Essays* (1983). An excellent collection of scholarly essays on aspects of the Carolingian Renaissance, including biblical studies, philosophy and theology, liturgy, and canon law.

Ganshof, F. L. *Frankish Institutions under Charlemagne* (1968). A classic study of Carolingian institutional history.

James, Edward. *The Origins of France: From Clovis to the Capetians, 500–1000* (1982). Arranged around the ideas of authority and community, this is the best treatment of the social and economic history of the period.

McKitterick, Rosamond. *The Frankish Kingdoms under the Carolingians, 751–987* (1983). A comprehensive detailed history of the Carolingian Dynasty and Carolingian culture and religious life, arguing that Charlemagne differed from his luckless successors less in talent than in circumstances.

Nelson, Janet. *Charles the Bald* (1992). A brief, deeply learned, sympathetic study emphasizing the politics, economy, and institutions of ninth-century West Francia.

Riché, Pierre. *The Carolingians: A Family Who Forged Europe* (1993). Translated from the French edition of 1983, this is a richly detailed account of the first family of early medieval Francia.

The Vikings

Jones, Gwyn. *A History of the Vikings*, rev. ed. (1984). A valuable work of scholarly synthesis, stylishly written.

————. *The Norse Atlantic Saga*, 2nd ed. (1986). A vivid account of the Scandinavian discovery and settlement of Iceland, Greenland, and North America, followed by a generous sampling of translated Norse sources.

Loyn, H. R. *The Vikings in Britain* (1977). A brief, authoritative synthesis that treats a wide variety of evidence sensitively and clearly.

Europe after the Carolingians

Bachrach, Bernard S. *Fulk Nerra, the Neo-Roman Consul, 987–1040: A Political Biography of the Angevin Count* (1993). A skillfully researched, model biography of one of the great French princes of the tenth and eleventh centuries, emphasizing the sophistication of his administration and his castle building.

Bloch, Marc. *Feudal Society*, 2 vols. (1961; originally published 1940). A classic work, now outdated in part yet for its time boldly original in its scope, approaches, and conclusions. Bloch, one of the greatest historians of the twentieth century, served in the French Resistance during World War II and was killed by the Gestapo shortly before the Liberation.

————. *French Rural History* (1966). Trans. Janet Sondheimer. Originally published in French in 1931, this book changed our ways of looking at medieval Europe.

Bois, Guy. *The Transformation of the Year One Thousand: The Village of Lournand from Antiquity to Feudalism* (1992). Trans. Jean Birrell. Using the unusually rich documentation of Cluny monastery, the author argues that the late tenth and early eleventh centuries witnessed a profound transformation of the European economy and society. Compare this author's assessment of the meaning of Cluny's property transactions with that of Barbara Rosenwein, cited below.

Chapelot, Jean, and Robert Fossier. *The Village and the House in the Middle Ages* (1985). A pioneering reinterpretation, synthesizing history and archaeology.

Duby, Georges. *The Early Growth of the European Economy: Warriors and Peasants from the Seventh to the Twelfth Century* (1974). Trans. Howard B. Clarke. An impressive work of synthesis by the most innovative and influential living historian of medieval French economy and society.

Fichtenau, Heinrich. *Living in the Tenth Century: Mentalities and Social Orders* (1991). A highly original study of life, society, and popular thought in France during a period of social disorganization and fundamental change.

Koziol, Geoffrey. *Begging Pardon and Favor: Ritual and Political Order in Early Medieval France* (1992). The politics of tenth- and eleventh-century France are illuminated through a subtle analysis of rituals of supplication.

Leyser, Karl. *Communications and Power in Medieval Europe: The Carolingian and Ottonian Centuries* (1994). Ed. Timothy Reuter. A valuable anthology of the author's writings, most of them published previously in scholarly journals.

————. *Rule and Conflict in an Early Medieval Society: Ottonian Saxony* (1979). A work of impressive erudition that casts new light on Otto I, Saxon aristocratic women, and contemporary ideas of sacral kingship.

Loyn, H. R. *The Governance of Anglo-Saxon England* (1984). Clear and succinct—the best treatment of the subject.

Noble, Thomas F. X. *The Republic of St. Peter: The Birth of the Papal State, 680–825* (1984). This persuasive and highly original study argues that the eighth-century papacy was more than a leaf blown by the winds of Byzantine, Lombard, and Carolingian politics; it was consistently and purposefully striving to establish an independent papal state.

Poly, J. P., and Eric Bournazel. *The Feudal Transformation, 900–1200* (1991). This bold, provocative study of change in French society is quite persuasive yet has given rise to much controversy.

Reynolds, Susan. *Fiefs and Vassals: The Medieval Evidence Reinterpreted* (1994). A brilliant, meticulous, well-argued attack (with which we do not altogether agree) against the usefulness of the term *feudalism* in interpreting the Middle Ages.

Rosenwein, Barbara. *To Be the Neighbor of St. Peter: The Social Meaning of Cluny's Property, 909–1049* (1989). Skillfully applying the methods of social history and anthropology to an analysis of the property transactions between the abbey of Cluny and its neighbors, the author demonstrates that the significance of property was spiritual and symbolic no less than economic. This book should be read in conjunction with Guy Bois's analysis (cited above) of the economic and social transformations that Cluny's rearrangement of rural property entailed.

Smyth, Alfred P. *King Alfred the Great* (1995). This important book, the only recent biography of Alfred, has stirred intense scholarly controversy by rejecting as a later forgery the *Life of Alfred*, which previous scholars had attributed to Asser, Alfred's friend and court scholar.

Tobacco, Giovanni. *The Struggle for Power in Medieval Italy* (1989). This valuable account covers both the early and high-medieval periods.

Wickham, Chris. *Early Medieval Italy: Central Power and Local Society, 400–1000* (1981). A work of meticulous scholarship that focuses on social and economic history and makes adroit use of archaeological evidence.

CHAPTER 8

THE MEDIEVAL DUAL REVOLUTION: A MONEY ECONOMY AND RELIGIOUS REFORM

St. Francis of Assisi Renouncing His Father   *Scala/Art Resource, New York.*

910	Abbey of Cluny founded, fountainhead of church reform	1077	Henry IV obtains forgiveness from Gregory VII at Canossa	1173	Beginning of the Waldensian sect
1046	Emperor Henry III deposes three rival popes, inaugurating the papal reform movement	1084	Establishment of the reform monastic order of Carthusians; Henry IV crowned emperor	1176	Battle of Legnano: Lombard League and Pope Alexander III rout Emperor Frederick Barbarossa
1049	Papal reform begins in earnest with the accession of Pope Leo IX	1085	Gregory VII dies in exile	1198–1216	Pontificate of Innocent III
1056–1106	Reign of Henry IV as German king (later, 1084–1106, as emperor)	1095	Pope Urban II calls First Crusade	1210	Innocent III authorizes St. Francis's evangelical work
1059	Papal Election Decree transfers selection of popes from the emperor to the cardinal bishops	1098	Establishment of the reform monastic order of the Cistercians at Cîteaux	1214	Battle of Bouvines: Philip Augustus of France defeats King John of England
1073–1085	Pontificate of Gregory VII (Hildebrand)	1112–1153	Career of St. Bernard of Clairvaux as a Cistercian monk and evangelist	1215	Innocent III presides over Fourth Lateran Council
1075	Gregory VII prohibits lay investiture	1122	Pope Calixtus II and Emperor Henry V issue the Concordat of Worms resolving the Investiture Controversy	1216	Papacy sanctions the Dominican Rule
1076	Gregory VII excommunicates and deposes Henry IV	1152–1190	Reign of Emperor Frederick I Barbarossa	1226	Death of St. Francis of Assisi
				1233	Papacy establishes Roman Inquisition to combat heresy

"Repair my house, which, as you see, is well-nigh a ruin." Praying fervently before a crucifix, Francis of Assisi (ca. 1181–1226) believed that he heard Jesus speak these words to him. The son of a wealthy cloth merchant in a northern Italian town, Francis had enjoyed a boisterous, fun-loving adolescence but then found himself gripped by the profound spiritual crisis that had brought him to this prayerful moment. He went straight home, gathered up all of his own belongings and as much of his father's cloth as he could, and sold it—distributing the proceeds to the poor. Called to account by his father and the bishop of Assisi, he stripped off all his clothes and returned the garments to his father, saying that he now acknowledged only his Father in heaven. The bishop gave him a cloak so that, as a hermit, he could at least be decently clothed, and he went his way. That is the scene depicted at the beginning of this chapter, as painted many years later by the great artist Giotto (1266–1336). After living in solitude awhile, Francis devoted the rest of his life to the service of the poor and diseased. He built one of the medieval world's great religious orders, the Franciscan friars,[1] and inspired the formation of a similar women's order, the Poor Clares.

Widely regarded as Christianity's greatest saint—a man who tried to model his life on the actions and teachings of Jesus—Francis was a true product of the two revolutions that swept western Europe in the High Middle Ages: first, the revival of a money economy and the resurgence of urbanization; and second, the deep penetration of Christian teachings and church institutions into the population.

In subsequent chapters 19 and 20, this book will introduce the concept of the **Dual Revolution**—the intertwining of the Industrial Revolution and the French Revolution, which together ushered in the modern era in which we still live. But the notion of a dual revolution is an equally valid way of envisioning the changes that occurred in Europe between about 1050 and 1300, the High Middle Ages. The changes that western Europe experienced in this era were

---

[1] *Friar* means "brother" in Italian. Friars are not monks, for reasons that will be explained later in this chapter.

of such fundamental and enduring consequence that historians are increasingly coming to view the eleventh and twelfth centuries, rather than the later Renaissance and Reformation, as the primary turning point in the history of preindustrial Europe. By the High Middle Ages, Europe was no longer an impoverished, exclusively rural backwater on a distant fringe of Eurasia, as it had been in the days of Charlemagne. High-medieval Europe became a confidant, dynamic, and expansive center of civilization that could stand comparison with any society in the world of its time. It set a course of political, social, economic, technological, and cultural development that, with some modifications, continued along essentially the same trajectory until the next dual revolution, in the late eighteenth and early nineteenth centuries.

This chapter and the next two are devoted to various facets of high-medieval civilization—townspeople and clergy, kings and popes, writers and artists, teachers and students. In this chapter we explore the fundamental changes in economic and social structures that transformed high-medieval Europe, and the fundamental changes in religious attitudes, practices, and institutions that accompanied this transformation. In three words, its theme is "money and piety." Chapter 9 will deal with the third revolutionary change, which actually is an extension of the first two: the rise of the secular state, as embodied in high-medieval monarchy. Chapter 10 will pull these themes together by examining the high-medieval mind and imagination.

THE RETURN OF A MONEY ECONOMY

Money was never entirely absent from western Europe. Charlemagne had issued condemnations of **usury** (the illicit charging of interest) and of withholding grain from the market in times of shortage in the hope of profiting. He had also reformed the coinage, issuing good silver coins. We have seen evidence of money dues being collected on a Carolingian estate outside Paris in the early 800s and in the region around Cluny in the mid-900s, where debt was helping to transform free peasants into dependent serfs.

But money was often in short supply in medieval Europe, especially before the opening of new silver mines in tenth-century Saxony. Specie—that is, gold and silver coins—drained eastward, as in Roman times, and much gold also found its way into church ornaments. No gold coins were minted in western Europe from Merovingian times until the thirteenth century. The precious metal content of silver coins tended to drop from the Carolingian era through the rest of the Middle Ages, and for everyday needs small-denomination coins with a large copper content circulated. Barter remained important in local transactions throughout the Middle Ages.

What, then, does it mean to say that a money economy revived in western Europe in the tenth and eleventh centuries? It means that the pace of monetary-based economic transactions increased dramatically as Europeans repelled invaders and rebuilt their settlements, as settled church and state institutions took shape, and as the barbaric and early medieval social order built on plundering and "gifting" faded away. Money became necessary to settle accounts and acquire things that could not be produced or bartered for locally: iron tools and weapons; better quality cloth; wine, wherever grapes did not grow; salt, an essential preservative; and spices, used as medicine, to keep foods, and to disguise unsavory taste in food that had been preserved or had begun to go bad. Precise documentation, let alone statistical quantification, is impossible for early medieval Europe, and precision is often difficult to establish even in the High Middle Ages. Yet most historians agree that a line was crossed in the tenth and eleventh centuries, and that thereafter western Europeans were no longer thinking merely in terms of swapping things that they needed for bare subsistence, but were looking for opportunities to buy and sell things that could make life more enjoyable and work easier. By the late tenth century, as Cluny consolidated its holdings and as feudalism and serfdom came into focus, there are clear indications that a market economy was taking shape as well.

The clearing of fields and establishment of new crops went hand in hand with the quickening of commerce and the growth of towns. As commerce revived, old towns (usually of Roman origin) were revitalized and new ones emerged. Church, commerce, and urban government coexisted in a balanced relationship within the city's walls; but where trade was lively, merchants spilled outside the walls into new suburbs. Eventually new town walls had to be built, always a telltale sign of urban growth. The commerce of early post-Carolingian Europe owed much to the activities of Jewish merchants, who linked Western Christendom with the wealthier societies of Islam and Byzantium and conducted a regional and international trade in such commodities as cloth, grain, salt, slaves, and wine. During the eleventh and twelfth centuries Christians moved increasingly into commercial life, first in Italy, then to the north.

Towns, Fairs, and Commerce

As economic revitalization gathered momentum, settlements of merchants began springing up all across western Europe—sometimes as suburbs of older cathedral towns, sometimes outside the walls of monasteries, and often around one of the many fortresses that had risen in post-Carolingian Europe. These military strongholds were generally known by some form of the Germanic word *burgh*, and in time the term came to apply to the town itself rather than to the fortress that spawned it (much as Fort Pitt in western Pennsylvania became Pittsburgh). By the twelfth century a burgh, or borough, was an urban commercial center whose inhabitants—burghers (or burgesses)—constituted a new social group known later as the **bourgeoisie.**

The expansion of the Italian ports through which trade passed provides compelling evidence for Europe's commercial revival. The earliest important Italian commercial towns were in the southern part of the peninsula, such as Amalfi and Salerno, which lay closest to the Byzantine and Arab markets. But by the eleventh century, ports in northern Italy—closer to sources of European supply—took precedence and began growing rapidly. Pisa came first, then Genoa and Venice, and finally inland cities like Milan and Florence. During the High Middle Ages, Italian merchants dominated the Mediterranean, fetching eastern goods to the markets of Italy and then carrying them across the Alps into Germany, France, the Low Countries, and England. These commercial activities caused Milan's population to soar

A Medieval City The narrow streets of Assisi remain about as they were in St. Francis's time, although the city suffered earthquake damage in 1997, including the destruction of its basilica with Giotto's priceless frescoes depicting the life of St. Francis. This kind of scene would have been typical of prosperous cities in high-medieval Europe. As in modern New York or Hong Kong, space was at a premium in medieval cities, causing buildings to rise and streets to narrow. Because Assisi later became an economic backwater, its older buildings were not torn down to make way for new construction. *Gemeinnützige Stiftung Leonard von Matt.*

between the eleventh and early fourteenth centuries, from about twenty thousand to perhaps one hundred thousand. Venice, Florence, and Genoa reached comparable size.

Far to the north, the county of Flanders (roughly western Belgium) was also growing wealthy from commerce and manufacturing. Its trade extended through northern France and the British Isles, the Rhineland, and the shores of the Baltic Sea. Flanders had long been a great sheep-raising district, and its growing towns—Bourges, Ypres, St. Omer, Ghent, and others—became centers of woolen textile production. In time, international demand for Flemish cloth grew to the point where the Flemish wool supply was insufficient, and Flemish merchants began importing wool from England on an ever larger scale. Flemish textile making became the foremost manufacturing enterprise of the age, and the exporting of Flemish and Italian textiles to eastern Europe, the Middle East, and beyond was a crucial factor in slowing—perhaps at times reversing—Europe's age-long trade deficit.

The isolation of Europe's commercial centers first diminished and then evaporated as a network of commercial ties gradually connected them. The Flemish and northern Italian towns, for example, were becoming linked by a commercial axis running through the Rhine and Rhone Valleys. As other centers of production developed similar economic ties, much of western and central Europe came to be bound into a single network of commerce (see Map 8-1).

The growth of towns and their commercial links encouraged agricultural specialization. Money and merchants made it possible for local areas to concentrate on whatever they could produce most efficiently, using their profits to import other necessities. It is a basic principle of economics that such specialization, by enabling locales to exploit their comparative advantage, spurs trade, expands economies, and creates wealth. Thus the Paris basin exported grain, Scandinavia exported timber, Germany exported salt and fish, England exported wool and beer, Flanders exported cloth, and Burgundy exported wine. A thirteenth-century visitor to a Burgundian religious house reported that the surrounding lands were devoted exclusively to vineyards: "They send their wine to Paris, because they have a river at hand that flows there [the Seine], and they sell their wine for a good price from which they buy all their food and clothes." Throughout Western Christendom, commerce oiled the economy with an ever-increasing flow of money, inspiring the churchman-scholar Marbod of Rennes, around 1100, to burst into verse:

> Money! He's the whole world's master.
> His the voice that makes men run:
> Speak! Be quiet! Slower! Faster!
> Money orders—and it's done.

With the increasing abundance of money, princes could now collect taxes in silver coin rather than in goods, govern through salaried officials, and wage war with hired troops. Enterprising serfs could buy freedom and accumu-

MAP 8-1

MAJOR TRADE ROUTES IN TWELFTH- AND THIRTEENTH-CENTURY EUROPE

This map demonstrates how the Champagne fairs became the principal meeting place for traders from northern Europe and Italy and why the ports of northern Italy eventually gained control of the maritime trade between Europe and the southern and eastern Mediterranean. By the thirteenth century the trade routes in the Baltic area and eastward across Poland were also becoming important in the general European economy.

late tools and supplies. Aristocrats could pamper themselves with imported luxuries. And burghers, the chief beneficiaries of the new economy, could honor their civic saints (and express their civic pride) by building vast, richly decorated churches. Often, too, they honored themselves by building elaborate town halls, and the richest men built impressive stone houses where they dwelt in conspicuous elegance.

Urban Liberties

The new urban class was drawn primarily from the wealthier peasantry but also included vagabonds, runaway serfs, ambitious younger offspring of the lesser nobility, and, in general, the surplus of a burgeoning population. Early in the history of the medieval town, the custom became generally recognized that living within town walls for a year and a day qualified a person as a free burgher, whatever his or her origins. A famous German saying expressed this custom in a nutshell: *Stadtluft macht frei*—"town air makes [you] free."

At an early date traders began to form themselves into merchant **guilds** to protect themselves against exorbitant tolls and other exactions levied by the landed aristocracy. A town almost always lay within the territory of some lord—baron, bishop, count, duke, or king. And merchants found that only by forming guilds and acting in unison

could they win the privileges essential to their calling: freedom from servile dues, freedom of movement, freedom from tolls at every bridge or castle, and the rights to own town property, to be judged by the town court rather than the lord's court, to execute commercial contracts, and to buy and sell freely.

By the twelfth century, lords and kings were issuing charters to their towns that guaranteed many or all of these privileges. Some lords were forced to do so by urban riots and revolts; others did so voluntarily, recognizing the economic advantages of having flourishing commercial centers in their territories. Indeed, some farsighted lords began chartering new towns on their own initiative, laying out streets in a gridiron plan within the new walls and attracting commercial settlers by offering generous privileges (see Figure 8-1).

The first urban charters varied greatly, but in time it became common to pattern them after certain well-known models. Thus, the privileges that Henry I of England had granted to the burghers of Newcastle-on-Tyne, and those granted by Louis VI of France to the community of Lorris, were copied repeatedly throughout England and France. Magdeburg Law became the model for hundreds of so-called "German-law" towns established in eastern Germany and Poland during the High and Late Middle Ages—towns that often became the conduit for German speech

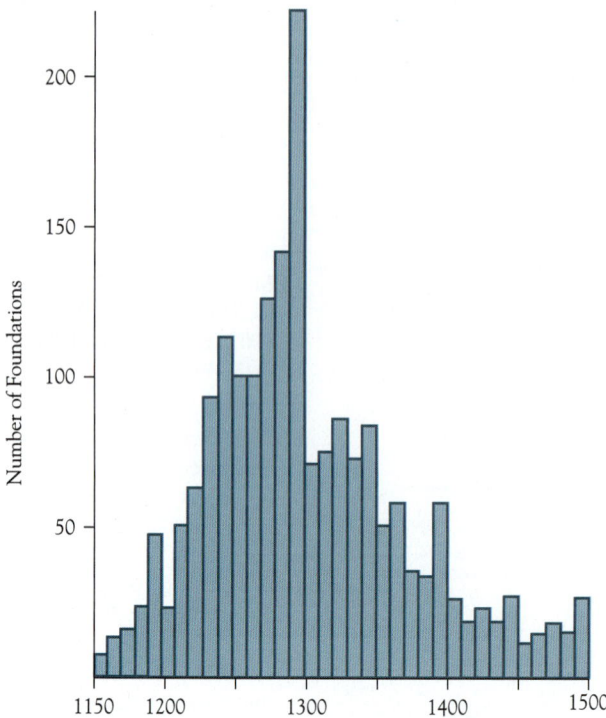

FIGURE 8-1

TOWN FOUNDATIONS IN CENTRAL EUROPE, 1150–1500

Source: Adapted from N. J. G. Pounds, An Economic History of Medieval Europe (London and New York: Longman, 1974), p. 100, fig. 3.1.

and customs in an otherwise Slavic-speaking countryside, and over the long run contributed to the eastward advance of cultural germanization.

Urban privileges created semiautonomous political and legal entities, each with its own local government, its own court, its own tax-collecting agencies, and its own customs. The merchants and artisans who inhabited these urban **communes** paid well for their charters and continued to render regular taxes to their lord. But—and this was all-important to town dwellers—they did so *collectively*, through their urban governments; they could handle their own affairs free of a lord's harassment. Townspeople enforced their own law in their own courts, collected their own taxes, and paid their dues to their lord in a lump sum. In short, they had won the invaluable privilege of handling their own affairs. And wise lords had no objection to simply gathering the golden eggs without administrative effort.

Prosperous merchants and master craftsmen profited the most from the urban charters, and it was they who came to control the town governments. Some towns witnessed the beginnings of a significant split between large-scale producers and wage-earning workers. Indeed, the medieval town is regarded by many economic historians as the birthplace of European capitalism. For as time progressed towns tended to become centers of industry as well as commerce. Manufacturing followed in the footsteps of

trade. And although most industrial production took place in small shops, some enterprising manufacturers employed considerable numbers of workers to produce goods, usually textiles, on a large scale. These workers labored not in a factory but instead in their own shops or homes. Since the entrepreneur sent raw materials out to them, this mode of production has been called the **putting out system.** Although quite different from the factory system, it was a crucial phase in the early history of capitalism.

Craft Guilds and Artisans

The more typical medieval manufacturers worked for themselves in their own shops, producing goods that they

Economic Activity in Medieval Paris This manuscript illumination shows the busy life of the Grand Pont, medieval Paris's main bridge over the Seine. Moneymaking included a trained bear doing its tricks before paying customers (top left), country men and women bringing in live animals for sale (center), and grain being delivered to the city's gristmills (bottom). Waterwheels such as these were a major technological innovation in medieval Europe. *Bibliothèque Nationale, Paris.*

THE HISTORICAL EVIDENCE

The Charter of St. Omer in Flanders

1137

Count William of Flanders granted this charter to the town of St. Omer in 1137. It served thereafter as a model charter for other Flemish towns.

1. First, that to every man I will show peace, and I will maintain and defend them as my own men without deceit. And I concede that their aldermen can make right judgment concerning all men, including myself. I grant liberty to those aldermen such as the most favored aldermen of my lands enjoy.

2. If any citizen of St. Omer lend money to anyone, and the borrower freely acknowledges this in the presence of lawful men who hold inheritances in the city, if the debt is unpaid on the agreed date, he or his goods may be detained until all is paid. If he is unwilling to pay, or denies the agreement, he shall be detained until he pays the debt, if he is convicted on the testimony of two aldermen or two sworn men.

3. If anyone is accused under the law of the Church, he need not leave St. Omer to do justice elsewhere, but may do what is right in the city, in the presence of the bishop or his archdeacon or his priest, and by the judgment of the clerics and aldermen. [Only persons charged with desecrating a church, assaulting a cleric, or raping a woman are to be tried in church courts; otherwise] the case should be heard in the presence of the [city] judges and my prévôt [representative].

4. [Citizens of St. Omer are not obliged to fight for the count], saving only if a hostile army invade Flanders. Then they must defend me and my land.

Other provisions either free citizens of St. Omer from certain taxes, tolls, and tariffs, or state exactly what it is that they owe.

8. In every market of Flanders, if anyone raises a complaint against them, they shall undergo the judgment of the aldermen concerning every complaint without a duel. They shall henceforth be free from the duel.

12. I command that their commune* remain undisturbed, just as they created it by oath. I shall let it be dissolved by no one. I concede to them all right and right justice, as it is best available in . . . Flanders. I shall ask of them no scot, no taille, and make no request for their money.

Subsequent provisions allow the citizens of St. Omer to coin a specified amount of money annually, retaining the profits for the town's benefit; grant the town the right to use a certain pasture; and permit the town to take official vengeance on people who injure them if the count fails to take action himself.

---

*The sworn oath of association, to which all citizens of the town were required to subscribe.

Source: From David Herlihy, ed. *Medieval Culture and Society* (New York: Harper & Row, 1968), pp. 181–184.

---

sold directly to the public. As early as the eleventh century, these artisans were organizing themselves into craft guilds, as distinct from merchant guilds. Over time, guilds proliferated and became increasingly specialized. But all guilds had many functions: they played a vital role in town governance, social interaction, and convivial drinking. They participated in charity work and religious observances, as well as ensured a decent funeral and prayers for each member's soul. They also had significant economic functions. To limit competition and ensure quality, craft guilds established strict admission requirements and stringent rules on prices, wages, standards of quality, and operating procedures. Young artisans learned their trade as apprentices in master's shops. After a specified period, sometimes as long as seven years, the apprenticeship ended. With good luck and well-off parents, the appren-

tice might then become a master. But young artisans normally had to work for years beyond their apprenticeship as day laborers—"journeymen" (the old French word for "day" is *journée*)—improving skills and saving money in the hope of someday establishing their own shop and becoming guild masters. Many never made it, and as time progressed and urban society crystallized, it became more common for artisans to spend their entire lives as wage earners. (For a guild document from the later Middle Ages, see Chapter 11.)

Throughout the High Middle Ages and beyond, women took an active part in town life. Since the master craftsman's shop was also his home, the modern distinction between home and workplace, between public and private spheres of activity, did not exist (nor did it in aristocrats' castles or peasants' cottages). This blurring of domestic and

THE HUMAN EXPERIENCE

Godric of Finchale, Merchant and Saint

The life of St. Godric of Finchale (ca. 1069–1170) provides a unique picture of the rags-to-riches business career of a native Englishman in the generations following the Norman Conquest. Godric had many contemporaries of humble birth who, like him, prospered greatly from the burgeoning commerce of the era. But writers of the time were not interested in such economic success stories. We know of Godric's rise to fortune only because he later rejected his worldly wealth to become a hermit-saint whose austere life of prayer and self-sacrifice came to be known and admired throughout western Europe. For that reason, he was the subject of no less than three pious biographies.

From these sources, we learn that Godric was born shortly after the Norman Conquest of England in a small town in Norfolk. His name marks him as one of the conquered English rather than the conquering Normans, and the names of his parents, Ailward and Aedwin, are similarly Anglo-Saxon. Godric was their first-born, and he remained at home with his parents and younger siblings throughout his boyhood and early adolescence.

At about the age of sixteen Godric left his family to seek his fortune. After four years as a wandering peddler, scavenging for lost or castoff goods and then selling them, he had prospered to the point that he could afford to make a pilgrimage to Rome—which he probably undertook not only for reasons of piety but also out of curiosity and a longing for adventure.

Godric then became a seafaring merchant, plying his wares in England, Flanders, Denmark, and Scotland. Soon he was able to buy a half-share in one merchant ship and a quarter-share in another. He became

an accomplished sea captain, steering his own ships from port to port and sometimes saving them from shipwreck (or so it was later said) by his uncanny skill at weather forecasting.

At this stage Godric was far from being the saint he would later become. In future years he bitterly repented the sins of lust and dishonesty that he had so often committed during his youth as a merchant and sailor. In 1101 he sailed to the Holy Land on what was said to have been a "pilgrimage to Jerusalem," and he doubtless set out on the voyage with a pious intent. Nevertheless, he probably did some trading and perhaps plundering along the way. It was probably he whom Crusade chronicles describe as "Godric the pirate from the kingdom of England," who rescued King Baldwin I of Jerusalem after the king had suffered a major defeat at the hands of Muslims. Godric in his early thirties is described by a friend as short, agile, and strong, with a broad forehead, sparkling gray eyes, and bushy eyebrows that almost met. He had an oval face, a long nose, a thick beard, and black hair that in later years would turn pure white.

On his return to England from Jerusalem, Godric seems to have been torn between resuming his worldly life and devoting himself to God. He served for a time as business manager for a rich nobleman but soon gave it up to undertake more pilgrimages—to Rome, to the shrine of St. Gilles in southern France, and to Rome again. Finally, in his mid-thirties, Godric abandoned his business career for good. He disposed of all his wealth and became a hermit, moving from place to place in the forests of northern England.

Eventually, after returning from one last penitential pilgrimage to Jerusalem, he settled down at a

lonely, beautiful site on the River Wear, just north of Durham, called Finchale (pronounced "finkle"). There Godric lived as a pious hermit for well over sixty years. Gradually his reputation for sanctity spread across England and Europe. He was visited by the great abbots and bishops of the north. He was venerated as a prophet of such potent gifts that some of the most celebrated leaders in Christendom—men such as Archbishop Thomas Becket and Pope Alexander III—sought his prayers and his counsel. He was also admired as a religious poet who set his verse to music, some of which still survives. His poetry is not for every taste, yet it represents something of a milestone in the history of English literature, constituting the earliest surviving Middle English verse. Godric was revered also for his love of animals—throughout the icy northern winters he would bring rabbits and field mice to his cottage to enjoy the warmth of his fire.

The evidence suggests that Godric lived to be at least one hundred years old. During his final illness he was nursed by the monks of Durham cathedral. After his death, in April 1170, the monks built a priory on the site of his hermitage at Finchale, the ruins of which remain to this day in an unspoiled vale alongside the River Wear.

Godric was only one of many holy men whose careers were subsequently recorded by admiring biographers. In his case, however, the record of his youthful years as a merchant and seafarer provides us with an unparalleled portrait of a self-made entrepreneur in an early phase of the medieval commercial transformation. ❖

THE HISTORICAL EVIDENCE

An Early Venetian Business Partnership

August 1073

In this document the partnership is called a collegantia; *other names for such arrangements include* commenda *and* societas.

In the name of the Lord God and our Savior, Jesus Christ. . . . I, Giovanni Lissado . . . together with my heirs, have received in *collegantia* from you, Sevasto Orefice . . . and your heirs, this [amount]: £200 [Venetian]. And I myself have invested £100 in it. And with this capital we have [acquired] two shares in the ship of which Gosmiro da Molino is captain. And I am under obligation to bring all of this with me in *taxegio* [a commercial voyage] to Thebes* in the ship in which the aforesaid Gosmiro da Malino sails as captain. Indeed, by this agreement and understanding of ours I promise to put to work this entire [capital] and to strive the best way I can. Then, if the capital is saved, we are to divide whatever profit the Lord may grant us from it by exact halves, without fraud and evil device. And whatever I can gain with those goods from any source, I am under obligation to invest all [of it] in the *collegantia*. And if all these goods are lost because of the sea or of [hostile] people, and this is proved—may this be averted—neither

party ought to ask any of them from the other; if, however, some of them remain, in proportion as we invested so shall we share. Let this *collegantia* exist between us so long as our wills are fully agreed.

But if I do not observe everything just as it is stated above, I, together with my heirs, then promise to give and to return to you and your heirs everything in the double, both capital and profit, out of my land and my house or out of anything that I am known to have in this world. . . .

[Signed by Giovanni Lissado with witnesses, including sea captain Gosmiro da Molino, and certified by a Venetian notary and cleric.]

———————————

*It is not clear which or where this particular Thebes is.

Source: From *Medieval Trade in the Mediterranean World: Illustrative Documents*, ed. and trans. Robert S. Lopez and Irving W. Raymond (New York: Columbia University Press, 1944), pp. 176–177.

---

business life worked to women's advantage: A master's wife and daughters could learn his skills just as his apprentices did—by observing and practicing. Indeed, master craftsmen and their wives normally shared authority over apprentices, on the assumption that the wife was well acquainted with her husband's craft. Widows commonly carried on the businesses of their deceased husbands, and the tendency for established businessmen in their late twenties or their thirties to marry women in their late teens produced, ten to twenty years later, an abundance of lively, prosperous widows. (A medieval man who survived past 45 or 50 was considered elderly.) Even while still married, women sometimes owned and operated their own businesses, distinct from those of their husbands. Town records show women collecting taxes, exchanging money, and engaging on their own in a wide variety of craft and merchant enterprises.

Economic Vitalization and Moral Worries

Significant numbers—never, of course, a majority—of burghers made their fortunes in commerce and manufacturing. Europe was astir with new life, and for someone who was clever and enterprising the possibilities were vast. In the

twelfth and thirteenth centuries, merchants were moving continuously along the roads and rivers of Europe. A regular circuit of fairs on the overland trade routes provided traders from northern and southern Europe with excellent opportunities to meet and trade—perhaps the greatest being the annual fairs sponsored very profitably by the counts of Champagne in northeastern France. Here they usually exchanged commodities directly, and as they were about to leave they settled up their debit-credit balances in cash.

Commerce was, of course, risky, and not just in the ways that businesses today routinely face. As the Mediterranean was cleared of pirates and Muslim raiders, sea voyages there became somewhat safer, but storms remained a danger (and even more so when ships ventured out into the Atlantic to reach northwestern Europe). Overland, merchants usually traveled in convoys for mutual protection, often following the ancient Roman roads. In the tenth and eleventh centuries they normally did business as individuals, and partnerships were uncommon. But such arrangements proliferated as trade—particularly maritime trade—increased in volume. Partnerships, often arranged for just a single trading journey, made it easier to spread risks and gave enterprising young men a chance to break into business by assuming the arduous job of traveling with

THE HISTORICAL EVIDENCE

Two Medieval Loan Contracts
late twelfth century

The first of the two contracts presented here openly calls for the payment of interest (at an annual rate of 20 percent) and would probably have been canceled had it been challenged in a church court. The second is a "bill of exchange" arrangement that probably fit the requirements of church law. In this one, Falzone is the banker who agrees in September to repay to Caviglia a debt contracted with Caviglia by Ottolino of San Martino and Rufino Belardengo; pledging their goods as security, they are hereby promising to give Falzone the necessary funds. Notice how the word loan *creeps into the contract, and note the precautions taken against currency debasement.*

Genoa: July 16, 1161

I, Embrone, have taken in loan from you, Salvo of Piacenza, £100 Genoese, for which I shall pay you or your messenger, personally or by my messenger, £120 within one year; but if I wish to pay you the aforesaid £100 and accrued interest before the next feast of the Purification, you must accept them. . . . If I do not so observe [these conditions], I promise you, making the stipulation, the penalty of the double. And on account of this I place in your power all my goods as security, so that if I do not so observe [these conditions], you may then enter [into possession] of whatever of my goods you want in consideration of the capital and the penalty. . . . [And I promise] not to deduct anything [from the debt], and I shall not claim release from its payment on account of the emperor* or of [any] discord which may exist between our city and yours, or of [interference from] any person. And for so long a time from then as you have that money with me, I shall protect it in your behalf against all men and I shall pay you whatever you ask. . . .

[Signed and witnessed]

Genoa: September 12, 1192

Oberto Falzone acknowledges that he shall give to Ricerio Caviglia £50 Genoese by the next octave of Saint Andrew

[December 7]. And if he does not pay then, he promises to give Provisine† [currency at the rate of] 12 [deniers] Provisine for every 15 [deniers] Genoese at the next fair of Lagny. And if [the coins] be deteriorated by alloy or by weight or be debased, he promises to give a mark of good silver for [every] 48 shillings up to the total of the entire debt. And [he promises to accept] the word of the creditor without oath in regard to expenses, losses, and [capital of the] loan, and he pledges his goods as security.

And Ottolino of San Martino and Rufino Belardengo [constitute themselves] as debtors and payers, and pledge, [both liable] for the whole amount, their goods as security, waiving [exemptions] under the legislation on joint liability and the legislation by which it is provided that the principal debtor be sued first. . . .

[Signed and witnessed]

---

*Emperor Frederick Barbarossa was at the time waging war in northern Italy; the contract thus barred wartime events from being construed as grounds for breaking the contract.

†Currency minted in Provins, a town in Champagne that was the scene of an annual fair.

Source: From *Medieval Trade in the Mediterranean World: Illustrative Documents*, ed. and trans. Robert S. Lopez and Irving W. Raymond (New York: Columbia University Press, 1944), pp. 158–159, 165–166.

---

the goods. Not, however, until the later Middle Ages would large-scale trading and banking firms become significant (see Chapter 11).

Credit is essential to growth in any economy because it allows someone to pursue an opportunity even though he or she is short of funds. In a market economy the price of capital (that is, the interest rate) is determined by supply and demand, weighing the borrower's creditworthiness against the lender's willingness to part with spare money. Medieval people were not so sure about all this: Lending at interest was the greatest moral issue connected with the

commercial revival. Usury was unequivocally condemned by the Judeo-Christian tradition.[2] But exactly what was usury? Theologians and church lawyers split hairs over this question throughout the Middle Ages. Essentially, the position

---

[2] Deuteronomy 23:19–20 (Authorized King James Version): "Thou shalt not lend upon usury to thy brother; usury of money, usury of victuals, usury of any thing that is lent upon usury. Unto a stranger thou mayst lend upon usury; but unto thy brother thou shalt not lend upon usury." Much debate has centered on the meaning of "thy brother" and "a stranger" in this passage.

that most of them reached was that charging interest was sinful if it represented a *sure* profit, but that interest could be asked in return for assuming a real business risk. Some church authorities also came to agree that what we would today call "opportunity cost"—forgoing a chance to use one's money for other purposes—made it morally acceptable to charge interest for a loan. Merchants who needed credit to finance a venture or who had profits to invest did enter into agreements openly stating that interest was being charged, but the risks were high because such contracts could be voided by church courts upon a would-be defaulter's proof that he was the victim of usury. Naturally, these difficulties tended to raise the price of credit, sometimes to loan-sharking levels. They also forced credit arrangements into complex subterfuges. The most frequent such device was the bill of exchange, a contract for payment of a sum at a specified date in a different currency. Since exchange rates varied with known patterns of market fluctuation, they were partly predictable but still dependent on a great variety of factors that contracting parties could not wholly control. The effect of such contortions was to make business transactions—by modern standards—cumbersome and costly. They also created moral quandaries that nagged at countless consciences. What gains had been "ill-gotten"? For centuries such worries produced deathbed confessions, restitutions, and charitable bequests.

Money, piety, and moral uneasiness blended in the new towns to vitalize the Christian culture of the High Middle Ages. It was money that built the great cathedrals, supported the Crusades, financed charities, and gave life and substance to the magnificent religious culture of the thirteenth century—money and, of course, an ardent faith. For townspeople, by and large, exhibited a piety that was more vibrant and intense than that of the peasantry and aristocracy. The surge of urban piety became a crucial factor in the development of high-medieval Christianity, spawning cathedrals and hospitals, universities and colleges, saints and heretics. The most celebrated saint of the era, Francis of Assisi, and the best known **heretic,** Peter Waldo (discussed later in this chapter), were both townsmen. In the electric atmosphere of the new cities, Christianity acquired an emotional content unknown to villages and manor houses.

At some point in the course of the medieval commercial transformation, perhaps toward the end of the twelfth century, commerce outdistanced agriculture to become the dominating force in the European economy that it has remained ever since. What occurred was more than a great economic boom: It was a permanent change, and of such fundamental historical magnitude that several distinguished scholars have described it as Europe's "economic takeoff." In centuries thereafter, Europe would endure depressions, plagues, and devastating wars, but it would never revert to the overwhelmingly agrarian economy of the Early Middle Ages.

City Life: Twelfth-Century London

With a population of about thirty thousand, late twelfth-century London was by far the largest city of its time in the British Isles and one of northwestern Europe's leading commercial centers. Many of England's bishops, abbots, and barons maintained townhouses there, and the king himself conducted much of his business at a palace—completed in 1099 and still standing—in London's western suburb of Westminster. Londoners were served by 139 churches, whose bells pealed across the city and its suburbs to mark the hours of the day.

London's narrow, unpaved streets were lined with houses and shops, most of them built of wood. Fire was an ever-present danger. During the day, people, dogs, horses, and pigs crowded the streets. (Half a century earlier a crown prince of France had been killed when his horse tripped over a pig in the streets of Paris.) But from the perspective of its twelfth-century inhabitants, London was a great, progressive metropolis. The old wooden bridge across the Thames River would soon be replaced by the new London Bridge, made entirely of stone. City sanitation workers cleared the streets of garbage. There was a sewer system—the only one in England—consisting of open drains down the centers of streets. There was even a public lavatory, established by Queen Edith-Matilda in the early twelfth century—the first of England's impressive network of "public conveniences." London was also well served with public bathhouses, at least until the early fourteenth century, when these "stews" were shut down as dens of fornication—perhaps to the benefit of the city's morals, but definitely to the detriment of public health (see Map 8-2).

By today's standards, London was a small, filthy, odoriferous firetrap. But twelfth-century Londoners were proud of their town. One of them, William fitz Stephen, writing around 1175, describes it as one of the world's most noble and celebrated cities, bristling with fortifications, and a hive of commercial activity:

> Those engaged in businesses of various kinds—sellers of merchandise, hirers of labor—go off every morning into their various districts according to their trade. Besides, there is [a] public cook shop in London, located on the riverbank in the district where wines are offered for sale in ships and in the cellars of the wine merchants. Each day, at this cook shop, you will find food according to the season—dishes of meat, roasted, fried, and boiled, large and small fish; coarser meats for the poor and more delicate for the rich, such as venison and large and small birds.

The delicacies offered by this medieval barbecue could be enjoyed not only by Londoners but also by visitors from afar:

> To this city merchants delight in bringing their trade by sea from every nation under heaven. The Arabian sends gold;

MAP 8-2
TWELFTH-CENTURY LONDON

This map shows the city about as it appeared in William fitz Stephen's time. Today this area is the business center of London.

the Sabaean, spice and incense.[3] The Scythian brings arms, and from the rich, fat lands of Babylon comes palm oil. The Nile sends precious stones; the Norwegians and Russians send furs and sables; nor is China absent with her purple silk, or France with its wines.

William fitz Stephen goes on to describe London's entertainments and sports—the miracle plays and the annual Carnival Day with its cock fights and athletic contests, when ball teams from London guilds and schools competed in the fields beyond the walls: "On feast days throughout the summer, the young men engage in the sports of archery, running, jumping, wrestling, slinging stones, hurling javelins beyond a certain mark, and fighting with sword and buckler."

Others, unimpressed by imported delicacies, feast days, and sports, disagreed with this high opinion of medieval London. A Jewish merchant from France is said to have warned a friend as follows:

If you go to London pass through it quickly. . . . Every evil or malicious thing that can be found anywhere on earth you will find in that one city. Steer clear of the crowds of pimps; don't mingle with the throngs in eating houses; avoid dice and gambling, the theater and the

tavern. You will meet with more braggarts there than in all of France. The number of parasites is infinite. Actors, jesters, smooth-skinned lads, Moors, flatterers, pretty boys, effeminates, degenerates, singing girls and dancing girls, quacks, belly dancers, sorceresses, extortioners, night wanderers, magicians, mimes, beggars, buffoons: all this tribe fill all the houses. So if you don't want to deal with evildoers, don't go to London.

These words are reinforced by present-day estimates of the annual murder rate in thirteenth-century London—8 homicides per 100,000 people—much higher than the per capita murder rate of modern Britain, although well below the current rates in many modern American cities. The violence of medieval London may be attributed in part to the presence (in 1309) of 354 taverns and more than thirteen hundred ale shops. Ale consumption seems to have been still more heroic in the medieval English countryside, where the murder rate was even higher than in the towns. Accident rates were also high in medieval life, in part at least attributable to the boozy state in which many people must have gone about their lives, fearing to drink water that they knew to be unhealthy.

The Landholding Aristocracy and the Money Economy

The commercial revival substantially affected medieval aristocratic life in the northern European countryside. For one thing, the much increased circulation of money gradually

---

[3] Saba (which the Bible called the kingdom of Sheba) was in southern Arabia, present-day Yemen. In the ancient and medieval worlds it was famous as a source of exotic spices and incense.

eroded early medieval lordship and vassalage. Rulers came to depend less on the military and administrative services that vassals performed in return for their fiefs, and resorted increasingly to mercenary troops and paid officials—first in England, and later on the Continent. Beginning in the twelfth century, English fief holders were often asked to pay a tax called scutage (literally, "shield money") in lieu of personal service in a royal campaign, and in time this practice spread to France and elsewhere.

Moreover, money and commerce made new luxuries available to the aristocracy: pepper, ginger, and cinnamon for baronial kitchens; finer and more colorful clothing; jewelry; fur coats for the cold winters (and to impress lesser folk); and carpets, tapestries, and better furniture to make dank castles more livable. These amenities, in turn, drove many nobles deeply into debt, thus increasing the business (and unpopularity) of lenders, who were often, but not always, Jews. Many aristocrats regarded overspending as a virtue—the mark of a generous spirit who did not necessarily have to be all that quick about repayment. (Such attitudes would persist among European aristocrats down to the twentieth century.)

In Chapter 7 we saw how one of the money economy's effects was to refocus the nobility on managing its property, and how this change from dependence on plunder helped create nuclear families in place of extended aristocratic lineages. Feudalism, with its emphasis on the orderly transfer of intact fiefs from one generation to the next, also reinforced this epoch-making trend. Another significant sign of

social and cultural transition within the upper class was the transformation of knights from dependent toughs to paladins of noble virtue.

The Flowering of Knighthood   The medieval aristocracy was, above all, a military class, trained from early youth in mounted combat. As we saw in Chapter 7, the aristocracy was two-tiered, divided between nobles (the great landholders) and knights (their followers). Over the generations, however, the social boundary between nobles and knights grew indistinct. The term *knight* gradually acquired high prestige: The church emphasized more and more the idea of Christian knighthood; the crusading movement (see Chapter 9) glamorized the "knights of Christ"; and fictional knights such as Roland, Tristan, Lancelot, and Parzival became heroes of high-medieval literature (see Chapter 10). In time even the grandest nobles were proud to be called "knights" and to share with less wealthy warriors a common code of knightly behavior known as chivalry (from *cheval*, the French word for "horse"). Common knights, in the meantime, were acquiring more extensive lands, building fortified dwellings on their estates, and marrying into old noble families. By the later thirteenth century, knights and nobles had blended into a single aristocratic order; they continued to vary greatly in wealth and power, but they shared a common chivalric **ideology** and knightly status.

For all the romantic images that today surround the medieval knight, he was, essentially, a warrior. Mounted on

Arming a Knight   As feudalism and courtly culture were refined, the mystique of knighthood deepened. Here, a king bestows sword and spurs on a young knight, who then (at right) dons chain mail and takes his shield and banner. Young knights often spent anxious years seeking their fortune, hoping to amass enough to marry and begin a family. Many did not survive youth, perishing in wars or tournaments.
© R. Sheridan/Ancient Art & Architecture.

a charger and clad in helmet and chain mail, he was a kind of military "machine"—the medieval equivalent of the modern tank. The analogy becomes still closer with the adoption, in the fourteenth century, of plate armor in place of chain mail, in response to the widespread use of the powerful and fearsome longbow.

Warfare was all too common in the High Middle Ages, not only among kings and great princes but also between neighboring barons. Fighting was what aristocrats had been trained for; it was the chief justification for their existence. Living off someone else's labor, indeed, was the essence of being a noble. In theory, nobles were the protectors of church and society, but most of them were interested primarily in defending and extending their own estates. And to some, nothing was more fulfilling than to do battle with the enemy—any enemy. As a twelfth-century French writer puts it:

I tell you that I never eat or sleep or drink so well as when I hear the cry, "Up and at 'em!" from both sides, and when I hear the neighing of riderless horses in the brush and hear shouts of "Help! Help!" and see men fall . . . and the dead pierced in the side by gaily-pennoned spears.

War could ravage the land, destroying farms and churches, and curbing it was a slow, painful process. Yet great battles were rare, and even when they occurred the knight was reasonably well protected by armor. Most medieval warfare consisted of castle sieges and the harrying of an enemy's peasants and property. (Wagons accompanied medieval armies, ready to carry off the loot.) For a knight, the great risk was to be taken captive, which obliged him to raise a large ransom. On the other hand, a skillful and lucky knight might take many captives and enrich himself from their ransoms. Whatever the case, high-medieval chivalry differed from previous aristocratic warfare in that it strongly discouraged the killing or maiming of fellow nobles, counts, dukes, or kings. The ideal was simply to hold them for ransom; harming them severely violated the chivalric ideology of a brotherhood in arms. And again the money economy

reared its head: Captives were to be ransomed for cash. War was becoming another form of business.

In peacetime, tournaments took the place of battles. The church legislated against tournaments, fruitlessly but with good reason: They often involved day-long mock battles among as many as a hundred knights, in the course of which a participant might be killed or taken for ransom. Purses and ransom money were lucrative, creating a class of knightly professionals who rode the circuit of tournaments like modern prizefighters. For a strong but impoverished young knight, it could yield a good living, and attract feminine admiration to boot.

Magnates had more sober tasks to perform as well. They presided at the castle court, gave counsel to their royal overlords, and managed their revenues and estates— a responsibility that they took more and more seriously as the commercial transformation increased the circulation of money and encouraged a profit mentality. For recreation, aristocrats went hunting or hawking in their private forests or hunting parks. Besides the sheer enjoyment of it, hunting cleared the forests of predators—wolves, bears, and wild boars—and provided tasty venison for the baronial table. (It also put fat on baronial bodies.) Lords and ladies alike avidly pursued falconry, a sport that consisted of releasing a trained falcon to soar upward, kill a wild bird in flight, and return it to earth uneaten. Both hunting and falconry were refined during the High Middle Ages into complex arts.

Indeed, the process of gradual refinement characterized high-medieval aristocratic life as a whole. It was much needed, but it cost money. Most baronial castles of the eleventh and early twelfth centuries were nothing more than square wooden hilltop towers surrounded by barracks, storehouses, stables, workshops, kitchen gardens, manure heaps, and perhaps a chapel—all enclosed, along with assorted livestock, within a moat or stockade. The tower (or "keep") was apt to be stuffy, smelly, leaky, smoky, gloomy, and cold. Since it was built for defense, not comfort, its windows were narrow slits for outgoing arrows, and

Falconry   In this high medieval drawing, aristocratic women enjoy the sport of falcony.   *From Queen Mary's Psalter.*

its few rooms had to accommodate not only the lord, his lady, and their children but also their servants, retainers, guests, and hangers-on—all of whom were collectively called the *familia*.[4] In this world of enforced togetherness, only the wealthiest of aristocratic couples could enjoy the luxury of a private bedchamber.

By the late thirteenth century, however, rich aristocrats were spending their money on more commodious dwellings, usually built of stone. Privacy remained rare, however, for great lords now commanded and fed larger retinues than before. But the sweaty, swashbuckling life of the eleventh-century baron had evolved by 1300 into a new, courtly lifestyle of good manners, troubadour songs, and (ideally at least) gentlemanly and ladylike behavior. In much of Christendom war had become less chronic, and the barracks atmosphere was softening. The old military elite was becoming "high society," increasingly conscious of itself as a **class.** Distinguished from lesser folk by its "good taste," the aristocracy became more exclusive and rigidly defined than in its earlier, less stylish days.

Aristocratic Women   It stands to reason that a society of landholding warriors would relegate women to supporting roles. Indeed women were subordinated to men in virtually all premodern societies—but less so in Western Christendom than, for example, in Islamic civilization, where the veil and harem flourished. We saw in Chapters 6 and 7 how late Roman and Christian influences softened the antifeminine attitudes embodied in early Germanic law codes. According to an early Anglo-Saxon law, for instance, "If a free man lies with another free man's wife, he shall pay the husband a sum of money and shall buy the husband another wife." By the tenth century, however, Anglo-Saxon women were holding property on a sizable scale and were bequeathing it to their sons and daughters, sometimes in equal portions. This was an extreme situation, for the trend in feudal Europe was toward consolidating property in the paternal line and passing it on through primogeniture. Nevertheless, circumstances continued to place considerable amounts of property in heiresses' hands. Practice was never altogether consistent with theory.

Christianity likewise could be highly inconsistent in its attitude toward women. St. Paul—at once a Christian evangelist and a Roman citizen—had injected a typically Roman antifeminine bias into the Christian mainstream. He conceded that in God's eyes there was no distinction between men and women or between slave and nonslave: "All are one in Christ." But this heavenly equality did not, in St. Paul's opinion, extend to earthly affairs: "Women should be silent in the churches," he wrote. "For they are not permitted to speak. . . . If there is anything they desire to know, let them ask their husbands at home" (1 Cor. 14:34–35).

Medieval Christianity echoed some of St. Paul's antifeminism. Women could not be priests; they could hold no church office except as an abbess or lesser official in a nunnery (though "double monasteries" admitting both men and women were occasionally presided over by abbesses). Holy men were apt to regard women as threats to male purity. The canons of a thirteenth-century priory expelled the nuns from their community on these grounds:

> Recognizing that the wickedness of women is greater than all the other wickedness in the world, and that there is no anger like that of a woman, and that the poison of snakes and dragons is easier to cure and less dangerous to men than associating with women, we and our whole community have unanimously decreed—for the preservation of our souls no less than of our bodies and property—that we will on no account receive any more nuns, to the increase of our damnation, but will avoid them as we would avoid poisonous beasts.

But many churchmen would have taken strong exception to this tirade. A thirteenth-century Dominican, for example, argued that God had favored women over men from the beginning:

> For God made man from the vile earth, but he made woman in Paradise. Man he formed of slime, but woman of man's rib. She wasn't formed of a lower limb of man—for example, of his foot—lest man should regard her as his servant, but of his midmost part, so that he should regard her as his fellow.

Geoffrey Chaucer, writing in the fourteenth century, tells the story of the oft-married Wife of Bath, whose late fifth husband persisted in reading aloud to her from a "book of wicked wives," recounting the evil deeds of innumerable wives from biblical, classical, and later times. As the Wife of Bath explained it:

> . . .when I saw that he would never stop
> Reading this cursed book, all night no doubt,
> I suddenly grabbed and tore three pages out
> Where he was reading, at the very place,
> And fisted such a buffet to his face
> That backwards down into our fire he fell.[5]

Alongside these diverse attitudes toward contemporary women, high-medieval Christianity idealized womanhood in its cult of the Virgin Mary (see Chapter 6). As the great symbol of maternal compassion, Mary became the subject of countless miracle stories. Sinners who trembled at the prospect of God's judgment would turn their prayers to Mary, confident that she could persuade Christ to forgive

---

[4] Despite the emergence of the nuclear family as the basis for the inheritance of aristocratic property, powerful men still maintained large entourages of dependents, both blood relatives and henchmen, to which the old Roman term *familia* was applied (see Chapters 4, 6, and 7.

---

[5] *The Canterbury Tales*, trans. Nevill Coghill (London: Penguin Books, 1952), p. 295.

The Virgin Nursing, ca. 1250 The image of the Virgin Mary nursing the infant Jesus was a favorite of medieval women, including mystics who had visions of nursing and playing with the holy child. The donor—the woman who commissioned this collection of the Psalms, probably an abbess—kneels at the lower left, beside a dog (symbolizing faithfulness) and a vanquished dragon (the devil). The Virgin's expression of tender delicacy epitomizes the love and trust with which both male and female Christians invested her by the thirteenth century. *Corbis/Bettmann.*

them—for what son could refuse his mother? Many of Europe's greatest cathedrals were dedicated to Mary ("Notre Dame," Our Lady).

The high-medieval troubadour songs and the rise of stylized courtesy in noble households resulted in still another kind of idealization. As romanticized fair ladies, women were placed on pedestals, from which they are only now descending. This idealization of women was itself a kind of dehumanizing process: High atop their pedestals, women remained objects still—although the pedestals tended to raise women from their former inferior status as threats to male purity, or objects of casual knightly seduction or rape, or victims of boorish, wife-beating husbands. Thus, the courtly lady remained an object, but a more revered object than before.

Medieval lords and ladies did not, of course, ordinarily behave like characters in some courtly romance. Wife beating persisted and, on a far lesser scale, husband beating as well (recall the Wife of Bath). Wives of all classes were immobilized for long periods by the bearing and nursing of numerous offspring, necessary for the preservation of family lines in an era of high infant mortality. Eleanor of Aquitaine, one of the great women of twelfth-century Europe and a patroness of troubadours, had eleven children but was survived by only two. She was imprisoned by her husband, King Henry II of England, for urging their sons to rebel and spent many years in comfortable captivity. Only at her husband's death was she released to live out her final years as a valued adviser to her royal sons and as a wealthy and independent grande dame of the realm.

Other medieval queens and noblewomen often served as regents, ruling in the absence of their husbands or sons. In the thirteenth century Blanche of Castile, mother of King Louis IX (St. Louis), ruled France for eight years in her son's name until he came of age and again when he was off crusading (see Chapter 9). A person of uncommon intelligence and resolution, Blanche put down a major baronial rebellion at the beginning of St. Louis's reign through an adroit blend of warfare and diplomacy. "To all intents and purposes," writes a modern French historian, "she may be counted among the kings of France."

Blanche and Eleanor were exceptional. In general, medieval society was a warrior's world, and women were not expected to fight in battle. True, even this convention could occasionally be defied: Isabel of Conches, the wife of a Norman baron of about the year 1100, was described approvingly by a contemporary monk-historian as generous, daring, and high-spirited: "In war she rode among the knights, dressed as a knight herself."

Isabel of Conches was a newsworthy exception to the male domination in warfare, but women could be influential in other ways as well. For if the aristocracy was a warrior class, it was also a class of hereditary landholders. In the absence of sons, a daughter might become a wealthy and coveted heiress; even if she had brothers, a well-born daughter might bring a large estate to her husband as a dowry and after his death retain some control over it. Women, married or single, could sometimes hold and grant fiefs, own goods, make contracts and wills, and litigate. A widow normally received a third of her husband's lands (their eldest son got the rest). And since wives were usually much younger than their husbands, landholding widows were commonplace.

A strong king might compel a wealthy maiden or widow to marry some royal favorite.[6] Indeed, the granting of an heiress in marriage to a loyal courtier could be an

---

[6] When this happened, it was despite the church's insistence that no marriage was valid if it was not voluntary on the part of both spouses. The church had better luck in enforcing this principle in the case of ordinary people.

important element in royal patronage—and a source of royal revenue as well. Many a family fortune was built on strategic unions, and it was not uncommon for aristocratic newlyweds to be in their young teens. (This was in marked contrast to the ages at which peasants married.) No noble family could afford the luxury of marriage for love; while there might be an occasional Romeo-and-Juliet situation in real life, it would have been a scandal, condemned by every respectable adult. Marriages based on family interests could sometimes, in time, become loving relationships; but they also encouraged the emphasis on extramarital romance in courtly literature—and certainly in reality as well. King Henry I of England had at least twenty-two illegitimate children. The church condemned adultery as a mortal sin, but aristocratic society winked at the escapades of well-born husbands. Their wives, however, were judged by a double standard that demanded wifely fidelity to ensure the legitimacy of family lines. A baron could sire illegitimate children across the countryside but expected his wife's children to be his own. This juxtaposition of male "wild-oat sowing" and female virtue is still prevalent today.

In feudal theory, wives were very much under their husbands' control; but in fact the wife might exercise a great deal of power. She usually governed the castle and barony when her husband was absent (as husbands often were, on wars or crusades). If the castle was attacked while the lord was away, his wife frequently commanded its defense. Even when the lord was home, the wife might enjoy considerable authority. In medieval marriages as in modern ones, some husbands were cruel and domineering, but others were ineffectual or senile—in which case, despite social and legal conventions, the wife ruled the castle.

Peasants and the Money Economy: Good Times and Bad

By the late eleventh and twelfth centuries, lords were under some pressure to improve the condition of their peasants, to keep them from migrating to towns or to newly cleared lands. Peasants were in demand, and noble or monastic land developers who were turning woods and marshes into fields competed for their services. As a consequence, the twelfth century witnessed the elevation of many peasants from servile status to freedom. Slavery, still fairly common in Carolingian times, was diminishing in the eleventh century and virtually disappeared from northern Europe in the course of the twelfth.

But even in the booming twelfth century these changes occurred slowly and unevenly. And by the thirteenth they were beginning to reverse, for population growth was gradually outstripping the increase in arable lands, raising land values, and creating a surplus of peasant labor. As land became more valuable than rural workers, lords throughout much of northern Europe began farming their **demesne** more intensively, often employing landless peasants at low wages or strictly enforcing the labor services of their remaining serfs.

Moreover, the thirteenth century witnessed a growth of legal consciousness and a hardening of custom that sharpened class divisions and made it much more difficult for serfs to gain freedom. In addition, free peasants might sink back into serfdom. It was the custom of some districts, for example, that a free man forfeited his freedom by marrying a servile woman, and a free woman suffered the same social descent if she married a serf. There are instances of landless free peasants of the thirteenth century submitting

Peasant Men and Women   For most of the year, peasant men and women worked at different tasks, but at harvest time they worked long hours side by side to bring in the harvest before rain, birds, or rot destroyed the precious grain. Yields were low—medieval farmers were doing well to harvest three or four grains for every one that they sowed—and on such tight margins survival was always precarious. *The British Library; Scything and binding grain. Neg. no. 93492 (HP). Shelfmark/Man: Add. 42130. Page no/Folio: 172 v Det (L).*

to serfdom in return for a plot of land. Quite apart from the matter of legal status, thirteenth-century peasants, lacking the leverage they had enjoyed in the earlier generations of land clearance and labor shortage, were subjected to heavy economic exploitation by their lords. They were burdened with higher rents and taxes, higher fines at the lord's court, higher charges for the use of his mill, wine press, and ovens. And a peasant who refused to pay could be replaced by someone else from among the growing body of landless laborers that the high-medieval population explosion produced. In short, western Europe still prospered for most of the thirteenth century, but the easy years of limitless land were passing, and for peasants there was trouble ahead.

The preceding paragraph has offered a large amount of generalization because haphazard medieval record keeping does not provide enough data for demographic historians to establish statistical trends for such key factors as the age of marriage, fertility, family size, and death rates. The evidence that we do have from the best-studied medieval country, England, suggests all male peasants married except the very poorest—the ones who lacked a holding large enough to support themselves and who made ends meet as hired laborers. Male villagers with decent economic prospects seem to have married at some point in their twenties, often before they had inherited land, because it was virtually impossible for a single man to work a normal holding by himself.[7] Peasant women whose fathers could give them a modest dowry married a few years younger than males, but rarely as teenagers. As soon as a peasant couple married, they began producing babies, at least half of whom would never live to adulthood. The better off a peasant family was, the larger its family tended to be: Probably its marginally better diet translated into higher survival rates for children and mothers. Poorer peasants, on the other hand, barely reproduced themselves—that is, rarely did more than two children survive their parents. But whatever their economic standing, and regardless of whether they were serfs or free, medieval English peasants preferred to live in conjugal units and seldom felt any obligations to cousins, uncles, or more distant kin. The nuclear family, in short, had come to stay.

One institution that had a great deal of influence on medieval family life was the church. We have already seen (Chapter 7) how church authorities strove—on the whole successfully—to prevent people of all social ranks from marrying close relatives. (Parish priests enforced these rules by posting "banns," which invited anyone with information disqualifying a marriage to come forward before the couple received the church's blessing, "or forever hold his

Giving Birth　Birthing was a common event in medieval life—as was the death of young children and of mothers giving birth. Male physicians rarely took part; even in aristocratic households like the one represented here, the mother giving birth was usually attended only by other women. This would have been the universal rule in humbler households.　*Bildarchiv der Österreichische Nationalbibliothek.*

peace." In communities where everyone seemed to know everybody, this was no mere formality.) And once married, couples never escaped priestly prying into their intimate lives. Sexual intercourse was forbidden on specific days of the week and on many special days during the year, and many varieties of "unnatural" sex were banned, including coitus interruptus (which the church ranked below father-daughter incest on the descending scale of wickedness). Priests were expected to cross-examine married men and women about such matters during confession, and given the lack of privacy in medieval life, they (and the neighbors) probably had a fair idea of what was going on. Under these circumstances, did medieval couples make any attempts at birth control? Some herbs were effective spermicides. Knowledge about them (as well as about many medicinal plants) certainly was passed along by midwives and "cunning women," and it may have been widely used in hard times or by the poor. In general, however, children were valuable to peasant families as a labor source, and given high childhood death rates parents had many incentives to keep producing offspring. Cases of abortion occasionally turned up in legal records—the most common way of terminating a pregnancy apparently was to "fall on" the

---

[7] It was uncommon for medieval people to live much beyond 50, so that if a man married at 25, his eldest son could expect to receive his inheritance at 25—about the time he in turn would normally marry and start begetting his own family.

fetus or take a drug in the hope of killing it—but social norms strongly opposed such acts. We have no way of knowing how often calculated neglect served as a crude form of family planning. Deliberate infanticide, however, was condemned both by the church and popular opinion as an abomination, and the relatively rare instances of mothers being prosecuted for killing their babies seem to have involved illegitimate pregnancies. If found guilty, the mother could expect to be put to death.

The close involvement of the church in the family affairs and sex lives of ordinary medieval people is striking evidence of how far Christianity had come by the eleventh and twelfth centuries in making its values, its rules, and its sanctions part of the fabric of life in western Europe. This is the subject we address in the rest of the chapter.

CHRISTIANIZING WESTERN SOCIETY

Western Europe, as we have seen, had largely been converted to Christianity during the Early Middle Ages (ca. 500–ca. 1050); but apart from the fervor of some—certainly not of all—monastic communities, this conversion had been rather superficial. For the great majority of western Europeans at this time, whether of high or low status, accepting Christianity entailed more a belief in its magical powers than an understanding of its ethical demands. The higher church authorities (abbots, bishops, and popes) were part of the ruling class, only exceptionally known for their piety; the lower clergy were usually ignorant and drawn from the peasantry, whose outlook they shared. Many peasants, indeed, rarely saw a priest. Clerical celibacy, though formally required, was often disregarded outside the monasteries. European society was Christian largely in name. Unlike the Byzantine world, Christian institutions and beliefs did not penetrate very deep into early medieval Europe.

By the tenth century, however, Christianity was beginning to strike deeper roots in western Europe, and change accelerated in the eleventh century. Two reasons for this development were the revival of towns and the spread of a money economy. Ancient Christianity had been almost exclusively an urban religion, and as towns and urban life reappeared in western Europe, Christian institutions came with them. So did Christian attitudes, for the greater impersonality of urban life, its competitiveness, and its obsession with moneymaking raised moral questions that peasant communities did not normally face. In some monastic communities, too, there was brewing a new religious fervor and a dissatisfaction with the condition of the church—particularly its dependence on the aristocracy. Cluny took the lead in articulating these new attitudes, and the spread of Benedictine monasteries on the Cluniac model helped spread the new religious intensity through much of Western Christendom. By the middle of the eleventh century, reforming zeal reached the papacy itself. Feeling a new fervor and religious

seriousness, popes began championing church reform and the spiritual regeneration of society.

The high-medieval papacy, as we shall see in this chapter, succeeded in some respects, but in other respects it fell short of its lofty aspirations. It defeated the German emperors, who in their way were also church reformers, yet whose notion of how the church should be governed resembled those of Byzantine autocrats. By 1300, Germany was fragmented and the emperors humbled. But by that time the papacy was falling victim to its own success. It had refashioned the Western church into a great hierarchical organization, reaching down to the parish level and defining right and wrong religious beliefs, but along the way it lost much of its ethical idealism. It stood, indeed, on the brink of a long crisis.

The changes discussed in the rest of this chapter can be summed up as the Christianization of high-medieval Western society. The church's institutions became deeply entrenched in everyday life, both in towns and the countryside. The sacraments, through which the church promised faithful Christians access to heaven, became the focus of intense personal piety. European laity of all social classes expected high standards of the clergy, and when the institutional church appeared to fall short, some of the laity veered off into heresy. In their newfound zeal, Christians both lay and clerical often gave in to an intense intolerance against "outsiders," above all the Jews living within Christendom and the Muslims beyond its borders. New religious orders arose, appealing primarily to urban concerns. And, as we shall see in Chapter 10, an impressive edifice of Christian-inspired art and thought arose. Latin Christianity, in short, became internalized—the focus of the distinctive west European way of life in this period, just as Eastern Orthodoxy had been internalized in Byzantium, and as Islam was in the lands it had conquered.

Christianization, therefore, was as central to the vitalization of high-medieval life as was the urban revival. It was the other half of the Dual Revolution of the Middle Ages.

The Church in 1050

The parish churches in eleventh-century villages that we encountered in Chapter 7 underscore the deeply significant fact that the long process of Christianizing Europe was under way by 1050. Whatever the intellectual and moral shortcomings of the village priests or vicars, they were at least representatives of the international church operating at the most immediate local levels throughout the European countryside.

At a more elevated level, Benedictine monasticism remained a potent force in European society. Benedictines offered continuous rounds of prayers for the welfare and salvation of their friends, neighbors, and benefactors—living and dead. They copied manuscripts, supplied knights from their estates to secular armies, and counseled princes. Perhaps even more than in Carolingian times, they played a major role in political life. This close association with

MAP 8-3

CLUNY AND THE SPREAD OF RELIGIOUS REFORM

The movement to free the church from lay control and to combat the abuses that had crept into its practices had its epicenter at Cluny Abbey in the tenth century and over the next 150 years spread to the Benedictine monasteries and bishoprics shown on this map. After Emperor Henry III placed a reform-minded pope on the papal throne in the early eleventh century, the movement spread to Rome.

secular politics sometimes resulted in abuses and corruption. Abbeys often found themselves under the direct "protection" of lay lords, who might pack monasteries or nunneries with their unmarriageable kinfolk, appoint cronies or younger siblings as abbots or abbesses, or even assume the abbatial function themselves. Aristocratic intervention in monastic affairs is understandable in view of the great wealth of the abbeys and the fact that many were founded by nobles as "family houses." But the results of such intervention on the Benedictine spiritual life were, at best, mixed.

Bishops and archbishops, too, were commonly appointed and controlled by lay lords. It was not unusual for a noble family to reserve a local bishopric, generation after generation, for its own junior members. Some bishops, on the other hand, wielded independent power over large districts, and there were times when bishops waged war against lay nobles. More often, however, bishops and nobles worked together in relative harmony, springing as they did from the same aristocratic milieu and sometimes the same family. All too frequently the interests and policies of such bishops were more worldly than spiritual and were directed more toward the advancement of their families than toward the welfare of the Christian community. These problems affected the mid-eleventh-century episcopacy from bottom to top—extending even to the papacy, which itself had become the grand prize of contending noble families in the city of Rome.

Abuses of these sorts gave rise throughout western Europe to powerful countermovements of church reform, typical of which was the reform movement centered on the Burgundian abbey of Cluny, whose place in tenth-century economic and social history was noted in Chapter 7. Founded in 910 by the duke of Burgundy, Cluny was free of local aristocratic and episcopal control and subject only to the pope, whose authority was feeble and remote, and it was blessed with a series of able and long-lived abbots. Cluny followed Benedict of Aniane's Carolingian-era modifications of the original Benedictine Rule (see Chapter 7). Its monks devoted themselves to an elaborate sequence of daily prayers, beautiful liturgical services, and a strict, godly life.[8] Richly endowed, holy, and seemingly incorruptible, Cluny was widely admired. Gradually it began to acquire daughter houses until, in time, it became the nucleus of a great congregation of reform monasteries extending across Europe—each of them headed by a prior who was subject to the abbot of Cluny (see Map 8-3). In the mid-eleventh century the congregation of Cluny was both powerful and wealthy, the recipient of countless gifts from the landed nobility from near and far, and its new abbey church,

---

[8] The monks of Cluny became obligated to offer so many daily prayers for the souls of those who had left bequests to the monastery that they gave up all the work that the Benedictine Rule required.

Emperor Henry III and His Bishops By freeing the papacy from control by the aristocracy of Rome, Emperor Henry III greatly advanced the cause of church reform. As this drawing in a contemporary manuscript makes clear, however, bishops were also dependent on the emperor. *Staatsbibliothek, Bremen.*

completed in the early twelfth century, was the largest and most splendid building of its time in all western Europe.

As the lay world became more and more exposed to Christianity, as kings such as Edward the Confessor in England and Henry III in Germany demonstrated their concern for the welfare of their churches, the church itself tended increasingly to come to terms with lay society. Through the ceremony of anointing, kings became virtual priest-kings. Indeed, contemporary political theory taught that the church and the world were one—a single, God-oriented organism in which clergy and lay lords each had appropriate roles to play.

Yet almost everywhere the church was under the control of lay aristocrats. Manorial lords appointed their priests; dukes and kings selected their bishops and abbots. The church played a vital role in the operation of tenth- and early eleventh-century states and society, but it was usually subordinate to the lay ruling class. From the lay standpoint it was an effective administrative tool, but from the spiritual standpoint it was sometimes inadequate and

even corrupt. Monasteries all too frequently ignored the strict Benedictine Rule. Some priests had concubines, and many had wives, despite the canonical requirement of priestly celibacy. Lay lords often sold important ecclesiastical offices to unworthy self-seekers who then recouped the purchase price by exploiting their tenants and subordinates. This commerce in ecclesiastical appointments was known as *simony*—after Simon the Magician, a New Testament character who tried to purchase the Holy Spirit. (Attempting to fly with diabolical aid, we are told in Acts of the Apostles, he plummeted to his death at a prayer from St. Peter.) Reformers regarded simony as shamefully corrupt. Traditionalists, however, defended it as an ecclesiastical version of a feudal inheritance tax. And to many bishops it was simply a shrewd investment. Archbishop Manasses of Rheims, who had paid handsomely for his office and then enriched himself from it, is supposed to have said, "The archbishopric of Rheims would be a good thing if only one didn't have to sing Mass because of it."

Before about 1050, a chasm divided the papal theory of Christian society and the realities of the contemporary church. Papal theory, based on a tradition running back to late Roman times, envisaged a sanctified Christian commonwealth in which lords and kings accepted the spiritual direction of priests and bishops, who, in turn, recognized the leadership of the papacy. The popes claimed to be the successors and representatives of St. Peter, who was thought to have been the first bishop of Rome—the first pope (see Chapter 5). Just as St. Peter was the chief of Christ's apostles, they argued, the pope was the monarch of the apostolic church. And as eternal salvation was more important than earthly prosperity—as the soul was more important than the body—so priestly power overshadowed that of secular lords, kings, and emperors. The properly ordered society, the truly Christian society, was one dominated by the church, which in turn was ruled by the pope. To many at the time, this view provided a persuasive justification for building a papal monarchy.

The Call for Reform

Such was the state of the Latin church as the mid-eleventh century approached. A church dominated by lay proprietors had long existed in Europe and had long been accepted. But with the surge of lay piety that accompanied the opening of the High Middle Ages, the comfortable relationship of church and lay leaders during the previous epoch was disturbing to some reformers and intolerable to others. Moderate reformers endeavored to curb these abuses; radicals set about transforming Western society into an international spiritual monarchy centering on the pope.

The struggle between papal monarchy and royal-imperial authority is often called a "conflict between church and state." But this is misleading. Many lay lords supported the reform papacy, and many churchmen opposed it. By and large, bishops had grown accustomed to

Pope Leo IX In this manuscript illumination from the late eleventh century, the first reforming pope, Leo IX, invests an abbot in Lorraine. Giving the pope unfettered authority to appoint abbots and bishops was a core principle of the eleventh-century church reform program, thought by its advocates to free the church from control by powerful lords. *Burgbibliothek, Bern.*

The ablest of Henry III's appointees, Pope Leo IX (reigned 1049–1054), waged a vigorous campaign against simony and clerical marriage. He held yearly synods at Rome, sent papal legates far and wide to enforce reform, and traveled constantly himself to preside over synods north of the Alps. Leo IX's pontificate opened dramatically when, at the Roman synod of 1049, the bishop of Sutri was condemned for simony and promptly dropped dead.

Leo IX's vigorous assertion of papal authority also aggravated the long and deepening hostility between the churches of Rome and Constantinople. In 1054 one of his legates placed a papal bull on the high altar of Hagia Sophia excommunicating the Eastern patriarch (who replied by excommunicating the pope), thus precipitating a split between Eastern and Western Christendom that has never been fully healed.[9]

More than anything else, Leo struggled to enforce church law and to purge the church of simony and clerical marriage. In most of his enterprises, he could count on the support of Emperor Henry III, for in these early years empire and papacy worked hand in glove to raise the moral level of the Latin church.

The Investiture Controversy

But there were those who felt that the real evil was lay supremacy over the church. To them Henry III's domination of papal appointments, however well intentioned, was the supreme example of that evil. A number of ardent reformers were to be found among the churchmen whom Pope Leo had gathered at his court. These newcomers, who dominated the reform papacy for the next several decades, came for the most part from monastic backgrounds and were influenced by the piety surging through the towns of eleventh-century northern Italy and Lorraine.

Hildebrand Becomes Gregory VII The most celebrated of these radicals was the Italian monk Hildebrand, a spellbinding leader and mover of events. Contemporaries described him as a small, ugly, pot-bellied man, but they also recognized that a fire burned inside him—a holy or unholy fire depending on one's point of view. For Hildebrand was the most controversial figure of his age. He was thought to have the power to read minds and may well have believed so himself. The ideal of a Christian society dominated by the church and a church dominated by the papacy consumed him.

Hildebrand served with prodigious vigor and determination under Leo IX and his successors. Then he became pope, taking the name Gregory VII (reigned 1073–1085).

their partnership with regional princes and had no desire to become the pawns of some overmighty pope. Conversely, a number of princes were advocates of at least moderate reform. Among these were French counts and dukes, English kings, and German emperors who had planted Cluniac and other reformed monasteries in their dominions and appointed staunch reformers to their bishoprics.

One such reformer, Emperor Henry III (reigned 1039–1056), led an army into Italy in 1046 to reform the papacy itself. Roman noble families had long viewed the papal office as a prize to be seized by the strongest among them. Roman family squabbles and complex maneuverings cast up three different men claiming to be pope in 1046, and Henry III proceeded to depose all three. He then drastically improved the quality of papal leadership by appointing the first of a series of reform popes.

---

[9] In the 1960s and 1970s a series of reconciliation gestures between the papacy and the Orthodox patriarch of Constantinople (Istanbul) included the mutual rescinding of these excommunications.

THE HISTORICAL EVIDENCE

Gregory VII: The *Dictatus Papae*

eleventh century

Gregory VII's program was a truly radical challenge to the status quo of eleventh-century Latin Christendom, as made clear by this famous summary of the prerogatives that he claimed in the papacy's behalf.

The Roman church was founded by God alone.

The Roman bishop alone is properly called universal.

He alone may depose bishops and reinstate them.

His legate, though of inferior grade, takes precedence, in a council, of all bishops and may render a decision of deposition against them.

He alone [the pope] may use the insignia of empire.

The pope is the only person whose feet are kissed by all princes.

His title is unique in the world.

He may depose emperors.

No [church] council may be regarded as a general one without his consent.

No book or chapter may be regarded as canonical without his authority.

A decree of his may be annulled by no one; he alone may annul the decrees of all.

He may be judged by no one.

No one shall dare to condemn one who appeals to the papal see.

The Roman church has never erred, nor ever, by the witness of Scripture, shall err to all eternity.

He may not be considered a Catholic who does not agree with the Roman church.

The pope may absolve the subjects of the unjust from their allegiance.

Source: From James Harvey Robinson, ed., *Readings in European History* (Boston: Ginn, 1904), vol. 1, pp. 274–275.

His pontificate would be one of the most violent and tragic of the Middle Ages.

As long as Henry III lived, radicals such as Hildebrand hovered in the background. But in 1056 the emperor died in the prime of life, leaving behind him a six-year-old heir, Henry IV, and a weak regency government. Henry III's death was a catastrophe for the empire and a godsend to the radicals who longed to wrest the papacy from imperial control. In 1059, under the influence of Hildebrand and other radicals, they issued a daring declaration of independence known as the Papal Election Decree, which ruled that thenceforth popes would be chosen by cardinals—the church's foremost bishops. The emperor and the Roman laity would merely give formal approval. This **revolutionary** proclamation was strongly challenged by both the emperor and the Roman aristocracy, but in the end the reformers won. The papacy had broken free of lay control; cardinals elected the pope, who designated the cardinals. The Roman Catholic church still uses this procedure.

The next step in the program of the radical reformers, the strict subordination of bishops and archbishops to the pope, was far more difficult. At a time when the church held perhaps a third of the land of Europe, the full realization of this vision of papal monarchy would cripple secular power and destroy episcopal autonomy. Nevertheless, Gregory boldly advanced his demands in a widely circulated statement called "The Dictate of the Pope" (*Dictatus Papae*).

One of the first arenas of conflict was the city of Milan, then in the grip of the new commercial revival and, like many of the new Lombard towns of the eleventh century, seething with activity. The Lombard bishops, who usually cooperated with the Holy Roman emperor and had the support of landholding nobles, opposed reform. But now, throughout Lombardy and in Milan in particular, their rule was being challenged by the growing class of merchants and artisans, backed by journeymen and peasants. In Milan and elsewhere, their enemies called these dissidents *patarenes* (ragpickers). Hostile to the traditional ruling group and fired by the new piety, the patarenes made common cause with the reform papacy against their bishops. The reformers in Rome had no sympathy for the archbishop of Milan, seeing him as an imperial agent who, by condoning simony and marriage among his clergy, symbolized the traditional church at its worst.

In 1059 the pope, with patarene support, brought formal charges against the archbishop of Milan, forcing him to confess his sins in public and promise to mend his unreformed ways. Over the next fifteen years, the patarenes continued their struggle against the noble-ecclesiastical

Henry IV and Gregory VII
Although Emperor Frederick Barbarossa's uncle, Otto of Freising, wrote this twelfth-century chronicle, this illustration from a copy of it is favorable to Gregory VII. It shows Henry IV, with his appointed "antipope" (a pope regarded by the church as illegitimately appointed or elected), driving Gregory VII into exile and death. *Foto Marburg/Art Resource, NY.*

ruling group, and the city was torn by murder and mob violence. When in 1072 the young Emperor Henry IV ordered an antireformer consecrated as archbishop of Milan, the patarenes rioted and the pope excommunicated Henry's counselors. The entire affair typifies the close alliance between radical urban piety and papal reform. Having placed themselves at the forefront of the new piety, the reformers were propelled by the revolutionary social-spiritual movement that was sweeping urban Europe. At odds with much of the traditional ecclesiastical establishment, they were in tune with the most vigorous forces of the age.

Going to Canossa: Gregory VII versus Henry IV The struggle over lay control of ecclesiastical appointments broke out in earnest in 1075 when Hildebrand, now Pope Gregory VII, issued a proclamation banning lay investiture. Traditionally, a newly chosen bishop or abbot was "invested" into office by receiving from his lay lord a ring and a pastoral staff, symbolic of his marriage to the church and his duty to be a good shepherd to his Christian flock. Gregory attacked this custom of lay investiture as the crucial symbol of lay authority over churchmen. By prohibiting the custom, Gregory was challenging the established social order and threatening the authority of every ruler in Christendom—none more than the Holy Roman emperor

himself. For the imperial system of administration was particularly dependent on the German and Lombard bishops.

By Gregory VII's time, Henry IV had grown to vigorous manhood and showed promise of becoming as strong a ruler as his father. When Gregory VII suspended a group of uncooperative, imperially appointed German bishops, Henry IV responded with a vehement letter of defiance. Backed by his bishops, he asserted his authority as a sovereign divinely appointed to lead the German church without papal interference and challenged Gregory's very right to the papacy. The letter was insultingly addressed to "Hildebrand, not pope but false monk," and concluded with a dramatic curse: "I, Henry, king by grace of God, with all my bishops, say to you: 'Come down, come down, and be damned throughout the ages.'"

Henry's letter was in effect a defense of the traditional social order of divinely ordained priest-kings, sanctified by the ceremony of holy consecration and anointment that accompanied their coronations, ruling as vicars of God over their lay subjects and their semiautonomous bishops.[10]

---

[10] The Byzantine emperors would have agreed with Henry's view of emperorship, if not with Henry's right to call himself an emperor.

Gregory's view of society was vastly different: He denied the priestly qualities of kings and emperors, suggested that most of them were gangsters destined for hell, and repudiated their right to question his status or his decrees. Emperors had no power to appoint churchmen, much less depose popes. But the pope, as the ultimate authority in Christendom, had the power to depose not only bishops but kings and emperors as well. Accordingly, Gregory responded to the letter with a startling exercise of his spiritual authority: In 1076 he excommunicated and deposed Henry IV. It was for the pope to judge whether or not the king was fit to rule, and Gregory had judged.

Radical though it was, the deposition was effective. Under the relatively placid surface of monarchical authority in Germany, aristocratic opposition had long been gathering force. Subdued during the reign of Henry III, local and regional princes asserted themselves during the long regency following his death, and Henry IV, on reaching maturity, had much ground to recover. Gregory VII's excommunication and deposition—awesome spiritual sanctions to the minds of eleventh-century Christians—unleashed in Germany all the latent hostility evoked by the centralizing policies of the Salian Dynasty (see Chapter 7). Excommunication meant that someone had been ejected from the church, and unless pardoned, was headed for hell and must be shunned by good Christians. Many Germans, churchmen and aristocrats alike, refused to serve an excommunicated sovereign. The German nobles took the revolutionary step of threatening to elect a new king in Henry's place, thereby challenging the ingrained German tradition of hereditary kingship. The elective principle, which would fatally weaken the late medieval and early modern German monarchy, had its real inception at this moment.

Desperate to keep his throne, Henry crossed the Alps into Italy to seek the pope's forgiveness. In January 1077, at the castle of Canossa in Tuscany, the two men met in what was perhaps medieval history's most dramatic encounter—Henry IV humble and barefoot in the snow, clothed in rough, penitential garments; Gregory VII torn between his priestly duty to forgive a repentant sinner and his conviction that Henry's change of heart was a mere political subterfuge. Finally Gregory lifted Henry's excommunication and the monarch, swearing to be good, returned to Germany to rebuild his authority.

Canossa was a long-remembered symbolic victory for the papacy,[11] but it also saved Henry IV's regime. Once his

throne was again secure, Henry resumed his struggle against papal reform. Amid the thunder of armed clashes and renewed excommunications and depositions, Gregory VII was obliged to call upon the Norman Robert Guiscard for help against an invading army of Henry IV (see Chapter 9). In the end Gregory fled Rome, and in 1085 he died in exile in Salerno. But there would be other popes who would fight, as Gregory had, for a papal monarchy over a free international church.

Papal Recovery and the Investiture Settlement   One of Gregory VII's ablest successors, Urban II (reigned 1088–1099), carried on the struggle for papal monarchy with much success. A former prior of Cluny, Urban adhered to the Gregorian ideology, but he was much more practical and diplomatic than his fiery predecessor. Urban rebuilt and expanded the papal administration, which had disintegrated during Gregory's final years, into an efficient bureaucracy suitable for a centralized papal government. In the long run, the power of the high-medieval papal monarchy probably owed more to its administration than to its excommunications.

Having gained tremendous moral authority for the papacy by calling the First Crusade in 1095 (see Chapter 9), Urban II continued to harass the unlucky Henry IV, stirring up rebellions in Germany that eroded his power. Urban's papal successors carried on these policies. At his death in 1106, Henry IV passed on a much weakened empire to his son, Henry V (reigned 1106–1125), who was himself in revolt when his father died. The new emperor enjoyed a happier reign, but only because he forsook his father's struggle to recover the fullness of imperial power as it had existed in 1050.

Toward the end of his reign, Henry V worked out a compromise settlement with the papacy that brought the Investiture Controversy to an end at last. (The issue had already been resolved in England and France, where the struggle had been considerably less bitter.) Over time, both papacy and empire tended to draw back from their extreme positions, and in 1122 they split their differences in the Concordat of Worms. Henry V agreed to give up lay investiture; Pope Calixtus II conceded to the emperor the important privilege of bestowing on the new bishop or abbot the symbols of his territorial and administrative jurisdiction (as distinct from his spiritual authority). Bishops and abbots were thenceforth to be elected according to the principles of canon (church) law, by the monks of a monastery or the priests of a cathedral,[12] but the emperor had the right to be present at such elections and to make the final decision in the event of a dispute. These reservations preserved a considerable degree of de facto imperial control over the appointment of important German churchmen. Royal control over a "canonical election" is

---

[11] In the 1870s, newly united Germany's chancellor Otto von Bismarck, locked in a struggle with Pope Pius IX, vowed not to submit with the ringing declaration: "We will not go to Canossa." At that time the eleventh-century papal-imperial struggle was seen by nationalists, Protestants, and anticlerical rationalists as a conflict between a reactionary church and a progressive nation-state. That misleading interpretation, fostered by textbooks, survived long into the twentieth century.

---

[12] Called the cathedral chapter, whose members were known as canons.

illustrated in the later twelfth century by a command of King Henry II of England to the monks at Winchester: "I order you to hold a free election, but nevertheless I forbid you to elect any one except Richard, my clerk, the archdeacon of Poitiers."

There was no real victor in the Investiture Controversy. The papacy had won its point—lay investiture was banned—but monarchs still exercised great control over their churches. The theory of papal monarchy over a reconstituted Christian society remained unrealized, and the old tradition of peaceful cooperation between kings and prelates was shaken but not destroyed. The papacy, however noble its intentions, had become politicized as never before. And by asserting its authority across Europe, it evoked hostile royalist propaganda and growing opposition.

Still, the papal-imperial balance of power had changed radically. The papacy was now a major political force, and the power of the emperor had diminished. During the chaotic half-century of this struggle, a mighty new aristocracy had emerged in Germany, bent on usurping royal rights. In northern Italy the Investiture Controversy crippled both imperial authority and episcopal autonomy. Burghers throughout Lombardy, under the banner of papal reform, rebelled against the control of nobles, bishops, and emperor alike and established quasi-independent city-states. By 1125, Milan and its sister cities were free urban communes, and imperial authority in Lombardy had become nominal.

In both Germany and Italy, imperial power was receding before the whirlwind of local particularism, fanned by the Investiture Controversy, the growth of towns, and the deepening of popular piety. Well before the Concordat of Worms, the decline of the medieval Holy Roman Empire had begun.

Renewed Papal-Imperial Struggle

For a quarter-century after Henry V's death, German nobles reverted to the elective principle asserted at the time of Canossa. Their choice always fell to a man of royal blood but not to the most direct heir. Between 1125 and 1152 a rivalry developed between two great families that had risen to power in the investiture era: the Welfs of Saxony and the Hohenstaufens of Swabia. In 1152 the princes elected as king a talented Hohenstaufen, Frederick I "Barbarossa" ("Red-Beard"), duke of Swabia, who took as his mission the reconstruction of the German monarchy.

The Age of Frederick Barbarossa Recognizing that the mighty imperial structure of Henry III was beyond recovery, Barbarossa strove to harness the new feudal forces of his age to royal advantage. He deliberately encouraged his great territorial princes to expand their power and privileges at the expense of lesser lords, while at the same time forcing the princes to recognize his own overlordship. Real-

Frederick Barbarossa In 1165 this striking portrait bust of Barbarossa was executed in gilded bronze. *Bildarchiv Preussischer Kulturbesitz (bpk). Berlin. Original Schloskirche Cappenberg.*

izing that the exercise of strong overlordship requires substantial material resources, Barbarossa set about to increase his revenues and extend the territories under his direct authority. A strong feudal monarchy required a substantial territorial core under exclusive royal control—an extensive royal demesne—to act as a counterweight to the great fiefs of the chief vassals. Frederick enlarged his demesne territories, most of which were concentrated in Swabia, by bringing many of the new monasteries and rising towns under imperial jurisdiction. The crux of his imaginative policy was the reassertion of imperial authority over the wealthy Lombard cities. With Lombardy under his control and its revenues pouring into the imperial treasury, no German lord could challenge him.

Barbarossa's Lombard policy earned him the hostility of the papacy, which had long opposed imperial power in Italy, and of the proudly independent Lombard cities. And should he become too deeply involved in Italy, Barbarossa opened himself to rebellion by the German nobility—in particular, the Welf family.

The papacy of the mid-twelfth century was having problems of its own. Pope Hadrian IV (reigned 1154–1159), who was to become one of Frederick Barbarossa's bitterest foes, was a gifted statesman of humble origins and the only Englishman ever to occupy the papal throne. Rome was turbulent during his years, for the patarene movement had reached the Holy City and had turned violently antipapal. The revolutionary social forces that had earlier allied with the papacy in breaking the power of an archbishop of Milan now generated rebellion against the pope's authority in Rome itself. The rebels decreed a revival of the ancient Roman republic, and Hadrian, forced into exile for a time, went so far as to lay the Holy City under interdict (suspending all church services and sacraments). By threatening Rome's lucrative pilgrim business, the interdict took the wind out of the rebellion. Republicanism collapsed, and Hadrian triumphed. But the movement persisted during the coming years as an anticlerical heresy—an early example of the opposition to ecclesiastical wealth and power that would soon find expression among the Waldensians and Albigensians (discussed later in this chapter).

The growing hostility between the papacy and the Roman townspeople was an ominous indication that papal leadership over urban reform movements was at an end. The papacy was no longer able to make common cause with the explosive forces of urban piety, as it had under Gregory VII, but was now beginning to suppress them. This split between papal leadership and popular piety was a factor of decisive importance in the ultimate decline of the papacy in the Late Middle Ages.

Hadrian IV and Frederick Barbarossa first met on the occasion of the imperial coronation in Rome in 1155. There, Hadrian insisted that Frederick follow "ancient tradition" and lead the papal mule.[13] At first Frederick refused to humble himself in such a manner, but when it appeared that there would be no coronation at all, he grudgingly submitted. This small conflict was a harbinger of far greater ones, for Hadrian and his successors proved to be implacable opponents of Frederick's drive to win control of the Lombard cities.

The Lombard struggle reached its height in the pontificate of Hadrian's successor, Alexander III (reigned 1159–1181). Shrewd and learned, Alexander was the first of a series of able popes trained in canon (church) law.[14] He allied the papacy with the Lombard cities, which had long engaged in inter-city warfare but now combined forces against the empire in a new confederation known as the Lombard League. Frederick intimidated and infuriated the Lombards by burning their great city of Milan to the ground. But in 1176 the Lombards retaliated by winning a decisive victory over Barbarossa at the battle of Legnano. Barbarossa responded to the military catastrophe at Legnano with as much good cheer as he could muster. Submitting to his triumphant enemies, he granted de facto independence to the Lombard cities in return for their admission of a vague imperial overlordship. Pope and emperor tearfully embraced. Barbarossa led Alexander's mule and promised to be a dutiful son of the Roman See.

But Barbarossa did not abandon his designs on Italy; he merely shifted his theater of operations to Tuscany, the rich province just to the north of the Papal States. At about the same time he arranged a marriage between his son and the future heiress of the Norman kingdom of southern Italy and Sicily. The marriage ultimately brought the great Norman kingdom into the imperial fold. Outmaneuvered and outwitted, the papacy faced the chilling prospect of imperial encirclement. After Alexander III's death in 1181 the papacy passed into feebler hands, and the farsighted emperor was at the height of his power when he died in 1190—drowning in a river when, clad in heavy armor, he fell from his horse while leading his army toward the Holy Land on the Third Crusade.

Prior to his death, Barbarossa had forced the princes to elect his eldest son, Henry VI, husband of the heiress of Sicily. In 1190 Henry succeeded his father without difficulty, and in 1194 he made good his claim to the kingdom of Sicily. The Papal States were now encircled by the Holy Roman Empire. But in an age in which the emperor had to remain always on the watch for regional rebellion, the imperial frontiers had become dangerously overextended. To make matters worse, Henry VI died prematurely in 1197, leaving an infant son, Frederick II. The problems the empire faced in 1197 would have taxed the ablest of leaders, yet at this moment imperial leadership failed. The papacy had its opportunity.

The Zenith of the Medieval Papacy: Innocent III

In the course of the twelfth century, the papacy had lost much of its former zealous reform spirit as it evolved into a huge, complex administrative institution with a large and growing bureaucracy. Taxes flowed into its treasury from all

---

[13] The tradition of the ceremonial leading of the papal mule seems to have originated in the eighth-century forgery, the "Donation of Constantine" (see Chapter 7).

[14] For the rise of canon law as a subject of professional specialization, see Chapter 10.

Pope Innocent III   A nearly contemporary fresco, this thirteenth-century depiction of Innocent III may well be a portrait. It emphasizes the great pope's youthfulness; he was only 38 years old when he was elected in 1198. He was a superb politician, diplomat, and lawyer.   *Scala/Art Resource, NY.*

Western Christendom; bishops traveled vast distances to make their spiritual submission to the Roman pontiff; the papal curia (the pope's council of highest officials) was the court of last appeal for an immense network of ecclesiastical tribunals across Christendom. Papal authority over the Latin church had increased immeasurably since the mid-eleventh century. And as the dream of papal monarchy came nearer realization, the traditional theory of papal supremacy over Christian society was increasingly magnified by canon lawyers. These subtle ecclesiastical scholars were beginning to dominate the papal curia and, like Alexander III, to occupy the papal throne itself.

Innocent III (reigned 1198—1216), the most powerful of all the lawyer-popes, began his pontificate in the year following Emperor Henry VI's death. Innocent was acutely intelligent, deeply pious, and one of the great preachers of his generation. He was also an imperious, self-confident aristocrat who held aloof from the surging religious emotionalism of humbler Christians.

Animated by the theory of papal monarchy in its most highly developed form, Innocent forced his will on the leading monarchs of Europe, playing off one ruler against another with consummate skill. He fought with the king of England over the appointment of an archbishop of Canterbury and with the king of France for divorcing his first wife, and he eventually forced both monarchs to submit. He launched the Fourth Crusade and initiated crusades against the Albigensians and the Spanish Moors (see Chapter 9). A mighty force in secular politics, Innocent also dominated the church more completely than any of his predecessors. In 1215 he summoned the Fourth Lateran Council, which produced a remarkable quantity of significant legislation: standardizing clerical dress, declaring a moratorium on new religious orders, requiring Jews to wear special badges, for-

bidding clerics to participate in the ancient Germanic legal procedure known as the ordeal,[15] banning fees for the administration of sacraments, ordering bishops to provide sermons at their services and schools in their dioceses, and requiring all Christians to receive the sacraments of penance and the Eucharist at least once a year.

But throughout Innocent III's pontificate one political issue took precedence over all others: the German imperial succession. It was a marvelously complex problem that taxed even Innocent's diplomatic skill. Involved were the questions of whether the kingdom of Sicily would remain in imperial hands, whether the imperial throne would pass to the Welfs or the Hohenstaufens, and whether an accommodation could be achieved between the hostile forces of papacy and empire. The German succession problem also touched the interests of the French and English monarchies: The Welf claimant, Otto of Brunswick, was a nephew and favorite of King John of England and could count on his support, whereas the Hohenstaufens enjoyed the friendship of the French king.

The direct Hohenstaufen heir, Henry VI's son Frederick, was an infant, so his uncle, Philip of Swabia, waged the campaign for the Hohenstaufens, while Otto of Brunswick (Otto IV) carried the Welf banner. Each faction elected its own candidate to the imperial office. Innocent claimed the right to intervene by virtue of the traditional papal privilege of crowning the emperor, but he delayed his decision

---

[15] *Ordeals* were physical tests that concerned issues under legal dispute. A person charged with a crime or facing a civil suit would have to prove his innocence by performing such feats as holding a red hot iron without receiving permanent scars, fighting his accuser, or otherwise allowing God to indicate who was in the right. See Chapter 9.

considerably, and in the meantime civil war raged in Germany. At length he settled on Otto, who had promised to support the papal interests in Germany and to loosen imperial control of the German church. Since a Welf emperor would presumably have no claim on the Hohenstaufen kingdom of Sicily, Otto's coronation would separate the two realms.

Yet civil war continued in Germany until Philip of Swabia's death in 1208. Otto was crowned emperor in 1209, but now he repudiated his promises, asserted his mastery over the German church, and even launched an invasion of southern Italy. Innocent responded by deposing Otto and throwing his support behind the young Frederick of Hohenstaufen.

From its inception the kingdom of Sicily had been, at least nominally, a papal vassal state (see Chapter 9), and Innocent claimed the overlord's privilege of being guardian of its underage king. But before backing Frederick, Innocent wrung promises from him: to abdicate as king of Sicily and sever the Sicilian kingdom from the empire, to lead a crusade, to follow the spiritual direction of the papacy, and in general to confirm the pledges that Otto of Brunswick had broken. The pope employed all his diplomatic skill and leverage to win over German nobles to Frederick II's cause. He was supported in part by King Philip Augustus of France, who was hostile to the English and their Welf allies.

The succession struggle reached its climax in 1214. England's King John invaded France from the west, while Otto of Brunswick led a powerful army against Philip Augustus from the east. But John's invasion bogged down and accomplished nothing, while Otto's army was routed by Philip Augustus at the battle of Bouvines. This decisive engagement changed the political face of Europe. As a result of Bouvines, Philip Augustus emerged as Europe's mightiest monarch, Otto's imperial dreams were dashed, and Frederick II became emperor in fact as well as in theory. The battle of Bouvines was a triumph not only for Philip Augustus and Frederick but also for Innocent III. His ward, now emperor-elect, was pledged to separate the kingdom of Sicily from Germany and free the German church of imperial control.

Germany itself was in chaos. The solid achievements of Frederick Barbarossa, which might have revived imperial power, had been demolished in long years of dynastic strife, during which the German princes usurped royal privileges and royal lands on a vast scale. By the time of Innocent's death in 1216, the imperial authority that Barbarossa had achieved was gone, almost beyond recovery. As we shall see in Chapter 9, Frederick II had to act like a secular king, not a medieval emperor, when he eventually threw off his early subservience and became the papacy's greatest foe.

The Medieval Latin Church at Its Prime

Innocent III seemed everywhere triumphant. Yet even at its height, papal authority remained limited in many

ways—by the growing power of the west European monarchies (see Chapter 9), by the fragility of royal promises, and by the longstanding difficulties in enforcing papal reform measures throughout Christendom.

Innocent's Fourth Lateran Council had decreed that all Christians must go to confession at least once a year, yet it is doubtful that the decree was enforceable. A study of late medieval Flanders has disclosed that a good many Flemings never confessed to a priest. Even in the area of international diplomacy, where Innocent achieved such conspicuous success, his successors could hardly be expected to carry on his juggling act indefinitely.

And it was becoming more and more difficult to view the papacy as a holy institution. Ultimately, papal power rested on spiritual prestige. But the thirteenth-century popes, despite their piety, their good intentions, and their continuing concern for ecclesiastical reform, were lawyers and diplomats rather than charismatic spiritual leaders. Although the papacy was a mighty force in the world of the thirteenth century, many pious Christians were coming to doubt that the papal government, with its bulging money chests and bureaucratic machinery, was the true spiritual center of the church and the citadel of Christ's kingdom on earth. Popes continued to dream of a regenerated Christian society led and inspired from Rome. But as time went on they dreamed less and plotted more.

The transformation of values that occurred during the High Middle Ages, resulting in part from economic-demographic expansion, the rise of cities, and the spreading web of money relations, produced fundamental changes in other areas as well. Scholars discovered new intellectual horizons; artists and writers expanded the dimensions of Western culture. Administrators pushed forward the art and science of government. And underlying all these changes (to be explored in the chapters that follow) was a deepening of the religious impulse that expressed itself in many different ways: devoutly orthodox, or anticlerical, or even openly heretical. Yet its basic institutional expression was the Catholic church,[16] and the most obvious characteristic that the vast majority of Latin Christians had in common was their Catholicism. A sense of allegiance to one's kingdom was only beginning to emerge, and the perspectives and loyalties of most Europeans tended to be at once local and international—the village and the Catholic church. In the twelfth and thirteenth centuries the majority of people were only vaguely aware of what was going on beyond their immediate surroundings. But despite their localism, they also knew that they belonged to something

---

[16] As explained in Chapter 5, *catholic* is a word of Greek derivation meaning "worldwide." By 1054, of course, the Eastern Orthodox churches were contesting the papacy's claim to be the supreme spiritual leader of the worldwide ("catholic") Christian movement. In the West, however, the papal-led church was everywhere accepted as being the "Catholic" church.

called Western Christendom—fragmented politically, but united by a common faith, by the growing power of the papacy, and by a shared enthusiasm for the Crusades.

The Catholic church in the High Middle Ages was a powerful unifying influence. It had made notable progress since the half-pagan pre-Carolingian era. A network of parishes now encompassed much of rural Europe, bringing the sacraments and basic Christian instruction to peasants. New bishoprics and archbishoprics were forming, and old ones were becoming steadily more active. The papacy never completely succeeded in breaking the control of kings and secular lords over their local bishops, but by the twelfth century it was coming to exercise a very real authority over bishops across much of western Europe. And the growing efficiency of the papal bureaucracy evoked the envy and imitation of the rising royal governments, whose emergence we will trace in the next chapter.

Sacraments and the New Piety

The buoyancy of high-medieval Europe is nowhere more evident than in the accelerating impact of Christian piety on European society. The sacraments of the church, which achieved their final development only in the twelfth and thirteenth centuries, introduced a significant religious dimension into the everyday life of ordinary Europeans. Their births were sanctified by the sacrament of baptism, in which they were cleansed of original sin[17] and initiated into the Christian fellowship. At puberty they received the sacrament of confirmation, which reaffirmed their membership in the church and gave them the additional grace to cope with the problems of adulthood. By the High Middle Ages, marriage had become a sacrament (with a corresponding refusal to allow divorce). If a man chose the calling of the Christian ministry, he was spiritually transformed into a priest and "married" to the church by the sacrament of holy orders. As death approached, the sacrament of extreme unction prepared the soul for its journey into the next world. And throughout their lives, Christians could receive forgiveness from the damning consequences of mortal sin by confessing and repenting transgressions and receiving the comforting sacrament of penance. Finally, they might partake of the central sacrament of the church—the Eucharist—receiving the body of Christ into their own bodies.

Thus the church through its seven sacraments brought God's grace to all its members, great and humble, at every critical juncture of their lives. The sacramental system gave comfort and reassurance: It made communion with God not merely the elusive goal of a few mystics but the recurrent experience of all believers. It also established the clergy as the link between God and humanity, and it made itself indispensable: "Outside the church there is no salva-

A Chalice from St.-Denis This magnificent chalice was fashioned out of solid sardonyx, a semiprecious stone, and embellished with gold and jewels. It forms part of the communion service made for St.-Denis Abbey at the order of Abbot Suger, who at the same time was establishing the Gothic style in architecture (see Chapter 10). At the time, laypeople were still permitted to receive communion under both species, although this would soon change. Notice the handles, so that the chalice can be held by the priest with less danger of spilling what the faithful believed was the blood of Christ. Communicants drank from the chalice through a small tube—the equivalent of a modern plastic straw. *Chalice of the Abbot Suger of Saint-Denis, Widener Collection, © 1998 Board of Trustees, National Gallery of Art, Washington D.C. 2/nd/1st Century B.C. (cup); 1137–1140 (mounting), sardonyx cup with heavily gilded silver mounting.*

tion." Only a priest—who must be male—could consecrate the bread and wine and thus, every time he said Mass, literally reenacted Jesus' sacrifice on Calvary. Only a priest could hear a penitent's confession and pronounce, on God's behalf, the words of forgiveness. The gulf between priests and other Christians, including nuns, thus widened immensely. The Latin church maintained this gulf by insisting, ever since the eleventh-century reform movement, that all of its clergy be celibate.[18] Popular sentiment not only endorsed this rule but also reserved special scorn for priests and monks who violated its spirit with illicit

---

[17] That is, the guilt that all human beings share with Adam and Eve.

[18] This was a major point of difference between the Latin and Greek churches. In Orthodoxy, celibacy is the rule for monks, out of whose ranks the higher clergy (bishops and patriarchs) are recruited, but parish priests are expected to be married.

relationships. There was widespread popular feeling that sinful priests could not validly consecrate the Eucharist or forgive sins, but this notion the church sternly resisted. Embracing St. Augustine's position (see Chapter 5), it held that the sacraments and the priesthood were sacred no matter what the failings of the individual priest. To have done otherwise would have destroyed the Western church as an institution and opened the floodgates to both heresy and hysteria—for then whom could the believer trust to impart God's gift of salvation?

Like clerical celibacy, the emergence of the Eucharist as the focal point of Western Christian piety had not been simply a matter of popes and theologians imposing dogma on believers. Indeed, testifying to the powerful roots that Christianity was developing in the western European consciousness, eucharistic theology tended to flow upward from the faithful. In early Christian times, the Eucharist had been a ceremony of fellowship, in which the breaking of Jesus' body and the shedding of his blood was recalled (see Chapter 5). Gradually the belief became so widespread among both Greek- and Latin-speaking Christians that Jesus was actually (not just symbolically) present in the Eucharist, but official church doctrine about exactly what this meant was slow to come into focus. Eleventh- and twelfth-century western theologians argued over the matter inconclusively. Popular sentiment and clerical preaching ran ahead of the philosophers and high churchmen, and by 1200 belief had become widespread in what was called in Latin **transubstantiation**: that when the priest said the consecrating words the bread and wine miraculously *became* Jesus' body and blood (the Host), leaving only the *appearance* of bread and wine. In 1215, Innocent III's Fourth Lateran Council merely ratified this belief when it allowed the word *transubstantiation* to be used in defining the Eucharist. Belief in transubstantiation was not yet mandatory—that would come only in the sixteenth century (see Chapter 13)—but it almost was. The Fourth Lateran Council also decreed that all Christians must confess their sins and receive the Eucharist (communion) once a year: an unenforceable rule, as we have seen, yet it was also a *minimum,* for devout believers were already eager to receive the Host as frequently as possible, and to see it honored with solemn public displays.

The twelfth and thirteenth centuries indeed witnessed a great surge of popular faith in the Eucharist. It became expected for the priest celebrating Mass to raise the Host and the chalice aloft after he pronounced the words of consecration. Some people rushed from church to church to see the Host being elevated as often as possible. Miracles wrought by and through the Eucharist were widely reported, often by popular preachers. And there were sinister rumors, too—that Jews vented their hatred of Christ and Christianity by stabbing the Host, making it bleed; or that witches and renegade priests cast diabolical spells by perverting the sacrament, for example by mumbling the words of consecration backwards at midnight.

There were other complications, too. Some sensitive souls quaked in terror that they had not confessed with sufficient sincerity to receive the Host. Others were bothered by the practice of allowing the priest alone to take communion "under both species"—that is, in both the wine (the Blood) and the bread (the Body); laypeople received only the consecrated bread, which they were told encompassed both species.[19] Finally, there began in the twelfth century the attempt of some devout women to give up eating entirely and live from the Eucharist alone, while simultaneously performing such other "austerities" as torturing themselves or licking pus from lepers' sores. Such practices were often combated by church authorities in the name of sensible moderation (although they could also merit postmortem canonization). They have attracted close scholarly attention in recent years because they were almost invariably manifestations of *female* piety and cast a larger light on the symbolism with which both men and women in the Middle Ages invested food, the body, and the need for nourishment. Moreover, such extreme devotion to the Eucharist became a vehicle for protest against clerical abuses: Some women, for example, claimed to be unable to swallow the Host if it was administered by a sinful priest.

In short, the intensification of popular piety had both a trickle-down and an upwelling dimension. The church's ever-increasing scope and its sophisticated theology were factors, but so was the rising religious self-awareness of the new age. The High Middle Ages witnessed a shift in religious attitude from the awe and mystery of earlier Christianity to a new emotionalism and dynamism. This shift is evident in ecclesiastical architecture, as the earthbound Romanesque style gave way during the twelfth century to the tense, upward-reaching Gothic (see Chapter 10). A parallel change is evident in devotional practice, as the divine Christ sternly sitting in judgment gave way to the tragic figure of Christ suffering on the Cross for the sins of humanity. A legend of the age told of the devil complaining to God that the tenderhearted Virgin Mary was cheating hell of its most promising candidates. Hell certainly lost none of its horror in the High Middle Ages. It grew, if anything, hotter and more terrifying as the popular imagination grappled with the eternal question of why there is so little justice in this life: Surely God must put things right in the next world to come. If they believed in the church and its sacraments, in the saints and the Blessed Virgin, good Christians could feel safe. Christianity became, as never before, a doctrine of love, hope, and com-

---

[19] This rule arose from fear that, in handing the chalice to laypeople, the Blood of Christ might be spilled; and there may also have been worry that enthusiastic believers would drink so frequently or deeply as to become inebriated. But the rule's effect was to open another gulf between the priest and the faithful. The Roman Catholic church abandoned this rule only in the late twentieth century.

Devils Leading the Damned into Hell   This lively scene was carved on the frieze around one of the doorways of Reims cathedral in the mid-thirteenth century and would have been noticed by every entering worshiper. Note the prominence of kings, bishops, monks, and wealthy laypeople.   *Giraudon/Art Resource, NY.*

passion. The God of justice was also the merciful, suffering God of love.

There was, however, a price to pay for this growing religious sensitivity. As people became increasingly devoted to their Christian faith, they also grew more intolerant toward those who deviated from its beliefs and practices, including homosexuals, witches, and magicians. The High Middle Ages also witnessed an intensification of hostility toward Jews and heretics (discussed a little later in this chapter), along with a heightening of crusading fervor (Chapter 9). The growth of spiritual self-awareness was thus accompanied by the emergence of what one historian has called "a persecuting society," aspects of which endure to this day.

Moreover, as much as the God of the high-medieval theologians was a God of love and reason, to the popular mind he became a divine magician who could shield his favorites from hunger, pain, disease, and sudden death. To the laity, religion offered four desperately needed things: the hope of eternal salvation from a harsh, threatening world in which sudden death was ever-present; an explanation for human suffering, as the spiritual discipline necessary for paradise; an expectation that God would balance the scales of cosmic justice by damning the wicked who seemingly flourished in this life; and the promise of a better life here and now.

Of course religion continues to offer these things, but in the Middle Ages, when human need was more intense and more immediate, the popular practice of the Christian

religion was quite unlike what it is today. There was, for example, a far greater emphasis on acquiring divine favor— wheedling or bribing God, as it were—through such mechanical means as ritualized prayers, charms, pilgrimages, holy images, and the relics of saints.

The most cherished relics of all were those associated with Jesus and the Virgin Mary. Since both were believed to have ascended bodily into heaven, relics of the usual sort were out of reach, but there remained pieces of their clothing, fragments of the True Cross, vials of Christ's blood and Mary's milk, Christ's umbilical cord, his baby teeth, and the foreskin removed at his circumcision. Reading Abbey, founded in southern England in the 1120s, had acquired hundreds of relics by the end of the twelfth century, including twenty-nine relics of Christ, six of the Virgin Mary, nineteen of the Old Testament patriarchs and prophets, and fourteen of the apostles. As a result of its avid collecting, Reading became a prosperous pilgrimage center, but it was merely one of many. Chartres still has the Virgin Mary's tunic. Until the Reformation, Canterbury had the body of St. Thomas Becket. Santiago de Compostela in northwestern Spain, to which one of the most popular routes of medieval pilgrimage led, housed the bones of St. James the Apostle.[20] Paris had acquired Christ's crown of thorns after it was taken from Constantinople following the Fourth Crusade. It was, indeed,

---

[20] Except for his arm, which was at Reading.

required that every parish church, as part of its consecration, have a relic sealed in its altar.

The cult of relics received innocent encouragement from ill-educated parish priests, as well as from bishops and abbots anxious to attract floods of pilgrims to their churches. It could be justified up to a point by the Catholic doctrine of the Communion of Saints—the caring fellowship of all Christians, whether in this world or the next. But in its obsession with the supernatural powers of material objects, popular belief carried a residue from the long-ago days of pagan magic.[21]

The high-medieval church suffered not only from popular credulity but from corruption as well. At the local level, it was not so much the ignorance of the parish clergy that angered laypeople (most of whom were equally unsophisticated), but instances of their lechery or greed. Unprincipled clergy were in evidence throughout the era—a result of the unfortunate necessity of staffing the church with human beings rather than angels. Some historians have delighted in cataloguing thieving bishops, gluttonous priests, and licentious nuns. But cases such as these were clearly exceptional. The great shortcoming of the high-medieval church was not gross corruption but rather a creeping complacency that sometimes resulted in a shallow, mechanical attitude toward Christian religious life and an obsession with ecclesiastical property. The medieval church had more than its share of saints, but among much of the clergy the profundity of the faith was often lost in the day-to-day affairs of the pastoral office, the management of large estates, disputes over land and privileges, and ecclesiastical status seeking. Anyone familiar with modern politicians, office workers, and academics will appreciate the problem.

Monasticism Old and New

The drift toward complacency has been a recurring trend in Christian monasticism. Again and again, the idealism of a monastic reform movement has been eroded and transformed by time and success until, at length, new reform movements gather to protest the growing worldliness of old ones. The first monks and hermits, like St. Anthony in the fourth century, were reacting against the complacency of Emperor Constantine's officially sponsored church, which no longer challenged Christians to suffer and die for their faith. The sixth-century Benedictine movement arose as a protest against the excesses and inadequacies of earlier monasticism. But despite Benedict's call to abandon the

world, his order quickly became involved in teaching, evangelism, and ecclesiastical reform, and by the tenth and eleventh centuries the whole Benedictine movement had become immersed in worldly affairs. Benedictine monasteries controlled extensive lands, operated Europe's best schools, supplied contingents of knights to secular princes, and worked closely with them in affairs of state. Then the monks of Cluny, beginning in 910, had rekindled the old Benedictine spirit across Europe. But by the twelfth century, the Cluniac houses were showing traces of the complacency against which they had originally rebelled. Prosperous, respected, and secure, Cluny was too content to give wholehearted backing to the radical reorientation of Christian spirituality for which many reformers now struggled.

Neither Cluny and its daughter houses nor other Benedictine monasteries could seriously claim any longer to be sanctuaries from worldly concerns. Nor was Benedictine monasticism any longer the unique force it had once been in Christianizing western Europe. The larger Benedictine monasteries and nunneries accepted novices only from the aristocracy and required a substantial "entrance gift" from the novice's family—usually a large estate. Aristocratic parents designated younger offspring for monastic careers at birth and sent them off to religious houses well before adolescence for education and training in the Benedictine life. The children themselves had little choice in the matter. Some indeed developed into devoted servants of God; others simply went through the motions.

Advocates of the new spirituality followed the two divergent roads of uncompromising withdrawal from society and ardent participation in the Christianization of society. The impulse toward withdrawal pervaded the Carthusian movement, which began in eastern France in 1084 and spread across Christendom during the twelfth century. Isolated from the outside world, the Carthusians lived in small groups, worshiping together in communal chapels but otherwise living as hermits in individual cells. This austere order exists to this day, and unlike most monastic movements, its severe spirituality has seldom waned. Yet even in the spiritually charged atmosphere of the twelfth century it was a small movement, offering a way of life for only a minority of heroically holy monks. Too ascetic for most, the Carthusians were widely admired but seldom joined.

The greatest monastic movement of the twelfth century was Cistercianism. Following a severely rigorous version of the Benedictine Rule, the Cistercian monks managed for a time to be both austere and popular. The motherhouse of this order, Cîteaux, was established in 1098 on an isolated site in eastern France. The Cistercian order grew slowly at first, then gradually acquired momentum. In 1115 it had four daughter houses; by the end of the century it had five hundred.

The spectacular success of the Cistercians demonstrates the immense appeal of the idea of withdrawal to

---

[21] A modern art historian has compared medieval saint cults with the contemporary American cult of Elvis Presley. The parallels are startling: worshipful biographies, miraculous cures, supernatural sightings, wonder-working relics (articles of clothing, locks of hair), and pious pilgrimages to a blessed shrine, in Elvis's case Graceland mansion. In the Middle Ages all this would have meant de facto sainthood, probably recognized eventually by the church.

Fountains Abbey: A Cistercian Monastery in Northern England   Much of Yorkshire was a wasteland in the twelfth century when this great Cistercian house was founded. This view shows the bell tower and, in the foreground, the chapel. After the destruction of English monasticism under Henry VIII in the sixteenth century, the monastery fell into ruins, as seen in this nineteenth-century depiction. *Victoria and Albert Museum, London/Art Resource, NY.*

the Christians of the twelfth century. Like Cîteaux, many (but not all) of the daughter houses were built in remote wilderness areas. The abbeys themselves were stark and austere, in dramatic contrast to the elaborate Cluniac architecture and sculpture. Cistercian life was austere, too—less severe than that of the Carthusians but far more so than that of the Cluniacs. The Cistercians sought to resurrect the strict, simple life of primitive Benedictinism, but in fact they were stricter than Benedict himself. The lands surrounding their abbeys were cleared and tilled by Cistercian monks and lay brothers, rather than by the ordinary serfs who worked the Benedictine fields. The numerous Cistercian houses were bound together tightly, not by the authority of a central abbot as at Cluny but by an annual council of all Cistercian abbots meeting at Cîteaux. Without such centralized control it is unlikely that the individual houses could have clung for long to the strict, ascetic ideals on which the order was founded.

The key figure in twelfth-century Cistercianism was St. Bernard. In 1112 Bernard joined the community of Cîteaux as a young man; three years later he became the founder and abbot of Clairvaux, one of Cîteaux's earliest daughter houses. St. Bernard became the most famous holy man of his generation—a mystic, and an unusually gifted

writer and preacher who stressed the loving rather than the stern side of Christ and the saints. This magnetic figure was crucial in the meteoric rise of the Cistercian order. Although the Cistercians sought withdrawal from the world, Bernard was drawn into the vortex of secular affairs. Indeed, as the twelfth century progressed, the entire Cistercian movement became increasingly involved in the world outside. And like the later Puritans and Quakers, the Cistercians discovered that their twin virtues of austere living and hard work resulted in an accumulation of wealth and, eventually, a corrosion of spiritual simplicity. Their efforts to clear fields around their often remote abbeys contributed to the advance of Europe's internal frontiers. They consolidated and managed their lands with considerable skill and introduced improvements in the breeding of horses, cattle, and sheep. As economic success brought ever-increasing wealth, Cistercian abbey churches became more elaborate, and the austerity of Cistercian life was progressively relaxed. In later years new offshoots emerged, such as the Trappists, who returned to the strict observance of the early Cistercians.

Some earnest Christians aspired to be nuns or monks without actually taking vows. By the end of the twelfth century upper-class women in the Netherlands were gathering informally for communal living, and in the thirteenth century the movement spread to northern France and Germany. It is quite likely that the high-medieval female "surplus," as well as the escalating cost of dowries, was creating a problem of what to do with marriageable women who could not be married off, a crisis to which women who chose a voluntary contemplative life were responding according to the values of their times. *Beguines*, these women were called, at first as a term of disparagement. Beguine communities supported themselves by doing needlework (a skill that all well-to-do girls were expected to master), performed good works, and spent much time in prayer. But because they had not taken vows they were free to leave their communities and return to their families. In time, many beguine communities established close ties with the Franciscans and Dominicans (discussed later in the chapter), whose mysticism they shared. Male counterparts of the beguines, called *beghards*, also arose in the thirteenth century, but they never achieved the beguines' prominence, probably because the great mendicant orders could absorb most men who inclined in this direction.

Enemies Within

The term *beguine* may be related to *Albigensian*, the name given to the most dangerous heresy confronting the Latin Christian church in the High Middle Ages, although there is no evidence of contact or sympathy between the two movements. Individual beguines, however, were condemned for heresy, most notably Marguerite Porete, one of the greatest mystical writers of medieval France, who was burned at the stake in Paris in 1310. Her tragic fate underscores the thin (often totally arbitrary) line that separated acceptable from unacceptable religious behavior. Communities of enthusiasts who were neither bound by vows nor supervised by churchmen of known orthodoxy were generally suspect in the eyes of the high-medieval church.

Thus, for all its glorious creativity and spiritual intensity, the High Middle Ages was also an increasingly intolerant era. Indeed, intolerance seemed to be spawned by the age's creativity and intensity, as if these qualities needed reining in by a church that was also acquiring organizational power and intellectual sophistication. By the twelfth and especially the thirteenth centuries, practices that earlier in the Middle Ages had never been acceptable to the church but still had not attracted extraordinary attention—such as homoeroticism and magic—were being forcefully condemned, and those found to be involved in them were harshly punished, often by death.

Meanwhile both the institutional church and the laity were beginning to mount fierce attacks on Jews and heretics. The reasons why the High Middle Ages should have been a time of such intense antisemitism, and why it produced both a rising tide of heresy and a savage repression of it, go to the heart of the era's powerful changes in social and religious life.

The Jews of Medieval Europe In a civilization whose values were defined by Christianity, and that was growing more fervently religious, members of a minority faith were apt to suffer. In most regions of Christian Europe, Jews had long been subjected to legal disabilities and popular bias. And their condition worsened in the High Middle Ages with the growth of Christian self-awareness, militancy, and popular devotion to the suffering Christ. Jesus, of course, was a Jew, and good Christian theology insists that he died for the sins of all humanity, but popular medieval sentiment often held that he was murdered by the Jews. And there were those who arrived at the grotesque conclusion that the "murder" should be avenged. The persecution of

Jews: The High-Medieval Christian View This thirteenth-century carving from Naumburg cathedral in central Germany shows Jews paying Judas thirty pieces of silver, the price of his betrayal of Jesus. They are wearing the conical hats that had become obligatory for them by the time this sculpture was made. Such representations both expressed and stirred up Christian hatred for the Jews in their midst. *Foto Marburg/Art Resource, NY.*

Jews—and of other dissenting groups—represents the dark underside of high-medieval Christian piety.

Jews had played a vital part in the earlier phases of medieval urban growth. They were active in the commercial life of Italian towns throughout the Early Middle Ages, and in 875 King Charles the Bald of France brought a community of Jews home with him from a visit to Italy and settled them in his kingdom. They spread into numerous cities of France and Germany, and finally into England in the wake of the Norman Conquest of 1066. Wherever they settled, they stimulated commerce through their mercantile expertise. Ever since the Christian conversion of the Roman Empire, however, Jews had been at best second-class citizens. A church council in 451 had prohibited Christians from marrying Jews, having dinner with them, or even going to Jewish physicians. Jews were not to hold Christian slaves, to take Christian oaths of fealty, or to be lords over Christians. Such rules were not strictly enforced in the Early Middle Ages, but by the late twelfth century, Jews were required to wear special badges or hats so that Christians might be warned to keep their distance; in 1215 the Fourth Lateran Council ratified this rule for both Jews and Muslims. The papacy was never a great friend of Jews, but it did endeavor to protect them from the violence of popular prejudice. An eleventh-century pope wrote to the bishops of Spain as follows:

> We are pleased with the account we have recently heard concerning the way you have protected the Jews who live among you from destruction by those who are setting out to fight the Saracens. For these warriors, moved by stupidity or perhaps blinded by avarice, wished to behave like savages, destroying those whom divine, fatherly love may well have intended for salvation. . . . Indeed, the cases of the Jews and Saracens are altogether distinct: warfare is rightful against the Saracens, who persecute Christians and drive them from their own towns and lands; but the Jews are everywhere ready to do service.

As the foregoing passage suggests, crusades against Islam could escalate Christian antisemitism to the point of bloodthirsty violence. Such was the effect of the First Crusade to the Holy Land in 1096 (see Chapter 9). It dawned on some crusaders that their mission to extend Christian power over infidels abroad might be prefaced (or satisfied) by slaughtering the "infidel" minority in Christendom itself. In the words of one Christian writer:

> They should have traveled their road for Christ, recalling the divine commands and holding to the discipline of the Gospel, while instead they turned to madness and shamefully, wantonly, cruelly cut down the Jewish people in the cities and towns through which they passed.

Massacres of Jews did not begin with the Crusades, but they became more frequent thereafter. Most were products of prejudice among common Christian town dwellers, whipped to a frenzy by rumors that Jews had stabbed the Host or ritually murdered Christian children (as they had allegedly killed Jesus). A pope decreed in 1272 that "Jews arrested on such an absurd pretext be freed from captivity."

Here again the papacy was assuming responsibility for protecting Jews from mindless grassroots savagery, a responsibility that popes shared with kings and emperors. But these enthroned guardians demanded much of the Jews in return for protection. Secular rulers borrowed heavily from Jewish burghers, milked them through arbitrary taxes, seized the property and loan accounts of Jews who died without heirs, and charged enormous sums for the rights to travel freely, receive a fair trial, and bequeath property. By the end of the thirteenth century, Jews were being expelled en masse from one west European kingdom after another by monarchs who coveted their wealth. Their services as moneylenders were no longer essential; Italian moneylenders had become an alternative source of credit. By 1400, many Jews in western and central Europe were confined to ghettos by a combination of Christian prejudice and Jewish desire for self-protection. Of those driven farther east, most settled in Poland, which at that time was relatively tolerant toward them. (Fourteenth- and fifteenth-century Polish kings and great nobles welcomed Jews for the same economic reasons that rulers of the underdeveloped western regions of Europe had once been willing to protect them.) Many Jews subsequently filtered back to western Europe or were invited to return when royal policy shifted. Bit by bit, however, patterns of antisemitism were accumulating that would have horrendous consequences, both during the Late Middle Ages and long after.

The Jews of the High Middle Ages have usually been associated almost exclusively with such activities as moneylending and commerce. But while it is true that Jews were excluded from Christian guilds and forbidden to be lords of Christian peasants, more recent scholarship suggests that many Jews, particularly in southern Europe, blended almost invisibly into the general urban society. In the south their activities were less strictly limited than in the north, and it is certain that, throughout Christendom, moneylending and commerce occupied only a small, highly visible minority of medieval Jews. Still, they differed from Christians in ways other than faith, for example, achieving a much higher literacy rate than their Christian contemporaries. Every substantial Jewish community had its own school, and the Jewish communities of medieval Europe produced such eminent thinkers as Rabbi Solomon ben Isaac (better known as Rashi) in France and the great Jewish philosopher from Spain, Moses Maimonides (1135–1204), who in his highly creative adaptation of Aristotle furthered the development of both Jewish and Christian thought in the thirteenth century (Chapter 10). These and other Jews contributed to medieval medicine, biblical scholarship, and philosophy all out of proportion to their numbers. In the areas of medicine and commerce, too, the contacts of European Jews with their co-religionists in Islam and Byzantium helped end Europe's isolation.

Heresies and the Inquisition The surge of popular piety also let loose a flood of criticism against the church, as the laity began to judge the clergy by more rigorous standards. Popular dissatisfaction spurred the rush toward the austere twelfth-century monastic orders. Yet the majority of Christians could not become monks or nuns, or even beguines, and for them certain heretical doctrines, old and new, began to exert a powerful appeal.

The heresies of the High Middle Ages flourished particularly in the rising towns of southern Europe. The eleventh-century urban revolution had caught the church unprepared. The new towns were becoming centers of a burgeoning lay piety, yet the church, with its roots in the older agrarian order, seemed unable to minister effectively to the vigorous and widely literate new burgher class. Too often the church failed to understand urban problems or to anticipate the growing suspicion of ecclesiastical wealth and power. Although most townspeople remained loyal to the church, a minority, particularly in the south, turned to new, anticlerical **sects.** In their denunciation of ecclesiastical wealth, these sects were doing nothing more than St. Bernard and the Cistercians had done. But many of the anticlerical sects crossed the narrow line between orthodox reformism and heresy by preaching without church approval. Far more important, they denied the exclusive right of the priesthood to administer sacraments. The church's response to this was always the answer that St. Augustine had given the fifth-century Donatists: The validity of the sacraments is guaranteed by God and resides in the institutional church; it does not depend on the worthiness of the individual priest (see Chapter 5).

One dissenting sect, the Waldensians, was founded by a Lyon merchant named Waldo. Around 1173 he gave all his possessions to the poor and began a life of apostolic poverty. He and his followers sought the church's permission to preach in the towns, but, after some confusion and delay, the church refused. It rejected preaching by untrained laypeople who, among the Waldensians, included women as well as men. The church preferred to leave religious instruction in the hands of ordained males. But Waldo and his followers continued preaching, and this act of defiance, along with their growing doubts about the special spiritual status of the priesthood, brought them condemnation by the church.

Similar groups, some orthodox, some heretical, arose in the cities of Lombardy. These groups, known as the Humiliati, proved troublesome to the local ecclesiastical hierarchies, but generally they escaped downright condemnation unless they denied the authority of the church. Many, however, did so, and by the opening of the thirteenth century heretical anticlerical sects were spreading across northern Italy and southern France, and into Spain and Germany.

The most popular heresy in southern France was associated with the group called the Cathari ("the Pure"), or Albigensians, after the town of Albi where they were particularly strong. The Albigensians fused two traditions: first, the anticlerical protest against ecclesiastical wealth and power; and second, a dualistic theology that may have had its roots in ancient Persia. The Albigensians recognized two gods: the god of good, who reigned over the universe of the spirit, and the god of evil, who ruled the world of matter. The Old Testament God, creator of the material universe, was their god of evil; Christ, whom they regarded as a purely spiritual being with a phantom body, was the god of good. The Albigensians believed in reincarnation, and their goal was to break free of the cycle of physical rebirth. Their morality stressed a rigorous rejection of all material things—of physical appetites, wealth, worldly vanities, and sexual intercourse—in the hope of one day escaping from the prison of the body and ascending to the realm of pure spirit. In reality this severe ethic was practiced only by a small elite of spiritual men and women known as *perfecti* ("perfect ones"); the rank and file normally ate well, made love, and participated only vicariously in the rejection of the material world by criticizing the affluence of the church. Indeed, their opponents accused them of gross licentiousness. (Romans had made similar charges against the early Christians; see Chapter 5.) And although such accusations were grotesquely exaggerated, it does seem likely that some nobles were attracted to the new teaching by the opportunity of appropriating church lands in good conscience.[22]

However this may be, the Albigensians were spreading rapidly as the thirteenth century dawned and were threatening the unity of Christendom and the authority of the church. Pope Innocent III, recognizing the gravity of the situation, tried with every means in his power to stifle Albigensianism. At length, in response to the assassination of a papal legate in Toulouse in 1208, he summoned a crusade against the Albigensians—the first crusade ever to be called against European dissenters.[23] The Albigensian

---

[22] Scholars debate what connection might exist between Albigensianism and the older, Persian-rooted Manichaean movement of late antiquity, as well as with a similar sect that swept through medieval Bulgaria and Bosnia, called the Bogomils. Whatever the connections, these traditions all shared common impulses that probably ran back to ancient Zoroastrianism, with its dualism of good and evil, and to Gnosticism, which distinguished between a spiritual universe of good and a physical universe of evil. For Zoroastrianism, see Chapter 1; for Manichaeanism and Gnosticism, see Chapter 5.

[23] Earlier, crusades had been preached against the Moors in Spain and the pagan Slavs and Balts of eastern Europe. These are discussed in Chapter 9. The Albigensian Crusade was different because its target was Europeans whose religious beliefs were formed in opposition to mainstream Christianity.

THE HUMAN EXPERIENCE

Pierre Clergue, the Priest of Montaillou

Records abound of the activities of popes and bishops during the High and Late Middle Ages, but only rarely do we catch a glimpse of an individual priest at the level of the village parish. One such person about whom we happen to know a great deal is Pierre Clergue, priest of the remote mountainside village of Montaillou in southern France, not far from the Spanish border. In the early fourteenth century, Montaillou was a village of about 200–250 inhabitants served by a single priest. It was not a typical village, nor was Pierre Clergue by any means a typical village priest. Montaillou was poor, backward, and influenced by the Albigensian heresy. Indeed, it was one of the last villages in France to cling to Albigensianism—not because its inhabitants were steadfast in their beliefs but because their community was so remote and unimportant that it was easily ignored.

Not until the early fourteenth century did Montaillou get the Inquisition's undivided attention. Between 1318 and 1325 Jacques Fournier, bishop of Pamiers (who later became the Avignonese pope Benedict XII), conducted a thorough and meticulously recorded inquest to identify and punish Albigensians in his diocese, and his records include many detailed interviews with the peasant inhabitants of Montaillou. From these records the modern French historian Emmanuel Le Roy Ladurie created a pioneering work of social history, *Montaillou: The Promised Land of Error,* which has been widely praised and widely maligned—incontestable signs of an interesting book. Le Roy Ladurie provides, among other things, a vivid word portrait of the priest Pierre Clergue.

Father Pierre was born of peasant stock, but his family was the most powerful and prosperous household in Montaillou. His brother Bernard Clergue was the bayle, or chief secular official of the village. Pierre himself was literate, articulate, assertive, and charming. He seems to have done his priestly duties conscientiously, saying Mass on Sundays and holy days, hearing confessions, attending councils of his diocesan bishop of Pamiers, and collecting tithes.

Like many of his parishioners, Pierre Clergue was neither a committed Albigensian nor a die-hard Catholic but a mixture of the two; he moved effortlessly between orthodoxy and heresy as it suited his interests. Sometimes he would behave as an Albigensian missionary, reading heretical doctrines to the people of Montaillou. On other occasions he would intimidate his enemies by threatening to accuse them of heresy before the Inquisition.

Pierre Clergue's abiding interest, however, was not religious doctrine but sex. Jacques Fournier's inquisitorial register provides the names of no less than a dozen of Father Pierre's mistresses, and the list is clearly incomplete. "He scattered his desires among his flock," Le Roy Ladurie writes, "as impartially as he gave his benediction." And his flock was

---

Crusade was a ruthless, savage affair that succeeded in its purpose, but only at the cost of spreading war across southern France. The French monarchy intervened in the crusade's final stages and thereby extended its sway to the Mediterranean. The Albigensian Crusade was an important event in the development of French royal power, and it reversed the trend toward heresy in southern Europe. It also disclosed the brutality of which the church was capable when it felt sufficiently threatened.

To ensure that southern France would remain staunchly orthodox, an institution emerged that exemplifies the medieval church at its most repressive: the Roman Inquisition. The Christian persecution of heretics dates back to the time of the Donatists and Arians in the late fourth century (Chapter 5), but it was not until the High Middle Ages that heterodox views presented a serious problem to European society. Traditionally the task of converting or punishing heretics had been handled at the local level. But in 1233 the papacy established a central tribunal for the purpose of standardizing procedures and increasing efficiency, staffed by well-educated inquisitors bound by religious vows and responsible to the pope himself. The procedures of the Inquisition included torture, secret testimony, conviction on the testimony of only two witnesses, the denial of legal counsel to the accused, and other practices that well exceeded the carefully defined limits of medieval church law. Many of these methods, including torture, were standard procedures in Roman law. In the context of the thirteenth century, they constituted a kind of martial law designed to cope with a dire emergency.

Most inquisitors—though not all—endeavored to act fairly, and their sentences were less severe than, for example, those of the sixteenth-century Spanish Inquisition. The great majority of persons whom the Roman inquisitors convicted received prison sentences or lesser penances (such as wearing crosses over their clothing). The inquisitors inflicted the death penalty only rarely. The Roman Inquisition cannot be justified, but like all historical astonishingly tolerant of his behavior. At least one woman of Montaillou, however, disapproved of Father Pierre's conduct and told him, "You are committing an enormous sin by sleeping with a married woman." "Not at all," he replied. "One woman is just like another. The sin is the same, whether she is married or not. Which is as much as to say that there is no sin about it at all."

> One summer about seven years ago [said an adolescent parishioner named Grazide] the priest Pierre Clergue came to my mother's house while she was out harvesting, and he was very persistent: "Allow me," he said, "to have sex with you." And I said, "All right." . . . I was a virgin at the time. I think I was fourteen or fifteen years old. . . . After that, in January, the priest gave me in marriage to my late husband, Pierre Lizier; and after he had given me to this man, the priest continued to have sex with me, frequently, during the remaining four years of my husband's life.

Grazide loved Pierre Clergue dearly and defended her own innocence with an argument straight out of the southern French troubadours (see Chapter 10): "A lady who sleeps with a true lover is purified of all sins." And she added, "With Pierre Clergue, I liked it. And so it could not displease God. It was not a sin." Father Pierre, in turn, declared, "I love you more than any woman in the world"—not only to Grazide but to his other sex partners as well.

Pierre Clergue's most serious love affair was with a widow of the lesser nobility named Beatrice de Planissoles. When Beatrice went to the parish church to confess her sins to Father Pierre, he cut her off with the words, "I prefer you to any other woman in the world" and embraced her passionately. Beatrice managed to elude this blatant sexual harassment and slip away, but after a courtship of several months she finally succumbed. Their relationship lasted some two years, and Beatrice, in her Inquisition transcript, tells of tender moments with Pierre: sitting beside him by the fire, or sometimes in bed, she would carefully remove all the lice from his body—a ritual known as "delousing" that was both hygienic and expressive of deep affection. She also reports that they committed the deliberate sacrilege of having intercourse in the parish church. In time, however, Beatrice remarried and moved from Montaillou.

The amorous priest's behavior is a reflection not of medieval society as a whole, but of life in an isolated, impoverished mountain village in which the church's teachings on monogamy and clerical celibacy had scarcely yet penetrated. "At an altitude of 1,300 meters," Le Roy Ladurie wryly observes, "rules of priestly celibacy ceased to apply." Nor did religion speak with one voice in Montaillou: Albigensians had an even stricter sexual code than Catholics, but the Albigensian teaching that all sex is wicked deprived many followers of a set of sexual standards to which they could realistically aspire.

Father Pierre served for some time as the official representative of the Inquisition in Montaillou. In this capacity he prosecuted some Albigensians but protected others. Eventually he himself was convicted by the Inquisition—not for licentiousness but for Albigensian leanings—and despite his family's efforts to obtain his release with lavish bribes, Father Pierre died in captivity. ❖

episodes it can be explained. To the medieval Catholic, heresy was a hateful thing, a betrayal of Christ, a cause for eternal damnation, a plague that could infect others. The Roman Inquisition was neither the first nor the last instance of human beings becoming unable to respond calmly to attacks on their deepest beliefs.

The Begging Friars: Dominicans, Franciscans, and Urban Christianity

The thirteenth century found an answer to the heretical drift that was much more compassionate and effective than the Inquisition. In the opening decades of the century two radically new orders emerged—the Dominicans and the Franciscans—whose members devoted themselves to lives of poverty, preaching, and charity. Rejecting the life of the cloister, they dedicated themselves to religious work in the world, particularly in the towns. Benedictines and Cistercians had traditionally taken vows of personal poverty, but the monastic orders themselves could and did acquire great corporate wealth. The Dominicans and Franciscans, on the contrary, were pledged to both personal and corporate poverty and were therefore known as mendicants (beggars). Capturing thirteenth-century Christendom's imagination, they drained urban heresy of much of its former support by demonstrating to townspeople that Christian orthodoxy could be both relevant and compelling.

St. Dominic (1170–1221), a Spaniard who preached in southern France against the Albigensians, conceived the idea of an order of men trained as theologians and preachers, vowed to poverty and the simple life, and dedicated to winning over heretics through argument, oratory, and example. Sanctioned by the papacy in 1216, the Dominicans expanded swiftly and by midcentury had spread across Christendom. Among the Dominican friars ("brothers") were some of the greatest philosophers and theologians of the age, including St. Thomas Aquinas, who saw their task

The Lord's Dogs   In Latin, *Dominicanes* ("Dominicans") can also be rendered as *Domini Canes* ("the Lord's dogs"), and that is the pun illustrated in this allegorical painting commissioned by Dominicans in fourteenth-century Florence. The hierarchy of Christendom here is depicted as the medieval papacy had envisioned, with the pope (center) assisted by the emperor on his left, wielding the sword of secular power. To the pope's right sit a cardinal, an archbishop, and an abbot; monks, friars, and a nun are at their feet. To the emperor's left are a king and a count, with nobles, burghers, and peasants gathered in increasingly humble postures in the lower right-hand corner. At the pope's feet are the lambs who symbolize the Christian faithful, guarded by a pair of the Lord's dogs. Well before this painting was made, the neat order of Christian society that it depicted had become obsolete.   *Erich Lessing/Art Resource, NY.*

as clarifying the doctrines that must be preached in order to save people from heresy.[24] Dominicans also participated actively in the Inquisition, but their most effective work was done through persuasion rather than force. In time, the Dominicans dropped their ideal of corporate poverty: They came to recognize that full-time scholars and teachers could not beg or do odd jobs or wonder where they would get their next meal. But long after they had modified their original mendicant ideals, the Dominicans remained faithful to their mission of championing orthodoxy by word and pen.

The order was immensely popular among women as well. In 1207 Dominic founded the first monastery of Dominican nuns for a group of followers that included a number of converted Albigensians, and he subsequently established two more female houses; by the beginning of the fourteenth century the number of Dominican nunneries had soared to more than 140. But unlike their male counterparts, the Dominican nuns led cloistered lives and were permitted no active ministry; they supported the preaching and teaching mission of the Dominican friars with their prayers and only in later centuries joined them in teaching and scholarship.

Dominic's contemporary, St. Francis (ca. 1182–1226), was the warm and appealing man whom we met in this chapter's introduction. Francis was firm, but he was anything but grim. His joyousness no less than his deep sanctity captivated his age. As disciples joined him, he wrote a simple rule for them based on the imitation of Christ through preaching, charitable activity in the world, total dedication to the work of God, and the absolute rejection of worldly goods. In 1210 he appealed to Innocent III for approval of his rule, and that mightiest of all popes, with some misgivings, authorized the new order. In the years that followed, the Franciscans expanded phenomenally. The personality of Francis himself was doubtless a crucial factor in his order's popularity, but it also owed much to the fact that Franciscan ideals appealed to the highest religious aspirations of the age. His native Italian town of Assisi had an influential Albigensian minority, but Francis's preaching

---

[24] Aquinas, whose work as a philosopher and theologian is discussed in Chapter 10, fully justified the execution of unrepentant heretics, whose errors threatened the souls of other Christians.

and example fatally undermined it. Across Europe urban heresy lost its allure as the cheerful, devoted Franciscans began pouring into Europe's cities, preaching in the crowded streets and setting a living example of Christian sanctity.

Pious people of other times have fled the world; the Albigensians renounced it as the epitome of evil. But Francis embraced it joyfully as the handiwork of God. In his "Song of Brother Sun," St. Francis expressed poetically his belief in the goodness of the physical universe—of Earth, Sky, Fire, Water, and Sun, "who brings us the day, and lends us his light"—all of which testify to divine bounty and love.

Francis and his followers humbly called themselves Friars Minor ("little brothers") and attempted to emulate the life of Christ. As the Franciscans proliferated, a female order was established by Francis's friend St. Clare of Assisi. Her followers were named the Poor Clares because they shared the Franciscan commitment to apostolic poverty. Like the Dominican nuns they did no public preaching, but they followed Francis's example by caring for the ill in hospitals and leper colonies. A third order of Franciscans, known as Tertiaries, took partial vows and dedicated themselves to the Franciscan way while continuing their former careers in the world. The Dominicans followed suit by developing a similar third order.

Early Franciscanism was too good to last. As the order expanded it outgrew its primitive ideals, and even before Francis's death in 1226 the papacy was obliged to authorize a more elaborate and practical rule for the order. In time, Franciscan friars began devoting themselves to scholarship and took their places alongside the Dominicans in Europe's universities. Indeed, Franciscan scholars such as Roger Bacon in thirteenth-century England played an important role in the revival of scientific investigation; and the minister-general of the Franciscan order in the third quarter of the thirteenth century, St. Bonaventure, was one of the finest theologians of the age (see Chapter 10). The very weight and complexity of the Franciscan organization forced it to compromise its original ideal of corporate poverty.

Although the order neither acquired nor sought the immense landed wealth of the Benedictines or Cistercians, it soon possessed sufficient means to sustain its members. In time, therefore, the Franciscans followed the course of earlier orders. Their primitive simplicity and enthusiasm were exhausted by time, popularity, and success. A dissenting group known as the Spiritual Franciscans sought to preserve the apostolic poverty and idealism of Francis himself, but most Franciscans were willing to meet reality halfway. They continued to serve society, but by the end of the thirteenth century they had ceased to inspire it.

The pattern of religious reform in the High Middle Ages is one of rhythmic ebb and flow. A reform movement is launched with high enthusiasm and lofty purpose; it galvanizes society for a time, then succumbs gradually to complacency and gives way to a new and different wave of reform. But with the passing of the High Middle Ages there was also a gradual waning of spiritual vigor within the established religious orders. Not until the sixteenth century did a new Catholic religious order (the Jesuits) attain the popularity and social impact of thirteenth-century Franciscanism. Popular piety remained strong, particularly in northern Europe, where succeeding centuries witnessed a significant surge of mysticism. But in the south a more secular attitude was emerging. Young people no longer flocked into monastic orders; soldiers no longer rushed off on Crusades in such great numbers; papal excommunications no longer wrought quite their former terror. An age was clearly ending.

CONCLUSION: DUAL REVOLUTION AND THE TRANSFORMATION OF WESTERN EUROPE

The two-pronged revolution that this chapter has traced transformed western Europe—those parts of Christendom that adhered to the Latin rather than the Greek church—from a besieged and impoverished backwater into a major center of civilization. Urban life, commerce, and a money economy revived. Feudalism, however we define it, helped give more coherence to social and political relationships. A hierarchical social order of clergy, nobles, and peasants was defined, alongside which arose a solid and economically indispensable class of townspeople (burghers), itself hierarchically structured. The papacy assumed effective leadership of the Western church and claimed headship over Christendom as a whole. Christianity became the internalized value system not necessarily the everyday behavior of the vast majority of Western Europeans. Outsiders—Jews, Muslims, and heretics—were firmly identified as enemies.

On the foundations laid by this dual revolution, western Europe erected an imposing political structure, the secular monarchy—in embryonic form, the model of the modern state. And Europeans embellished their new, more civilized way of life with works of art that are still immensely moving and with subtle philosophical speculations that still command great respect in the history of ideas. These political and cultural achievements—the subjects of the next two chapters—would have been impossible without the transforming energy of economic and religious changes that this chapter has examined.

The late thirteenth and fourteenth centuries would see the waning of high-medieval Europe's spiritual, economic, and territorial expansion. The spiritual energies of the mendicant religious orders diminished; the internal frontiers of forest and swamp had largely been won and the best farmlands reclaimed; and Europe's external expansion was everywhere ceasing or, as in the Holy Land, receding. This transformation—some, making a value judgment, would call it a decline—of Europe's high-medieval civilization will occupy our attention in Chapter 11. But the changes that Europe underwent during the high-medieval centuries altered Western civilization profoundly. They enriched its faith, expanded its boundaries, and urbanized its economy. These transformations would never be undone.

Selected Reading

Sources

Amt, Emiliee, ed. *Women's Lives in Medieval Europe* (1993).

Duby, Georges *Rural Economy and Country Life in the Medieval West* (1968), trans. Cynthia Postan. Almost half of this book consists of translated documents relating to rural history.

Geary, Patrick, ed. *Readings in Medieval History* (1989).

Emerton, Ephraim, trans. *The Correspondence of Pope Gregory VII*, (1933).

Lopez, Robert S. and Raymond, Irving W., ed. and trans. *Medieval Trade in the Mediterranean World* (1944).

Otto of Freising. *The Deeds of Frederick Barbarossa*, trans. Charles Christopher Mierow (1953).

Shirley-Price, Leo, trans. *The Writings of St. Francis* (1959).

General Works

Contamine, Phillippe. *War in the Middle Ages* (1984). Trans. Michael Jones. An extraordinarily wide-ranging study of warfare across a thousand years, including the tactics and strategy, political, social and economic implications, and cultural impact of the activity that was, according to Contamine, "the foundation and raison d'être of political power."

Le Goff, Jacques, ed. *Medieval Callings* (1990). Essays by scholarly specialists on medieval people in various walks of life.

———. *The Medieval Imagination* (1988). A model of the "new history," with essays on dreams, conceptions of time, space, the body, devils, and marvels across the medieval centuries.

Moore, R. I. *The Formation of a Persecuting Society: Power and Deviance in Western Europe, 950–1250* (1987). The author makes a case for an intriguingly somber reappraisal of the High Middle Ages and its impact on the future.

Murray, Alexander. *Reason and Society in the Middle Ages* (1978). Argues that a major increase in the circulation of money was accompanied by a shift in mental outlook and brought into power men skilled at reasoning and accounting.

Reynolds, Susan. *Kingdoms and Communities in Western Europe, 900–1300* (1984). A perceptive, highly original work stressing the horizontal bonds of association that affected medieval lay society, and challenging many traditional notions about medieval civilization.

Southern, R. W. *The Making of the Middle Ages* (1953). A brilliant, sympathetic interpretation of the eleventh and twelfth centuries.

Medieval Women

Atkinson, Clarissa W. *The Oldest Vocation: Christian Motherhood in the Middle Ages* (1991). Traces the evolution of Christian views of motherhood, including the speculations of male theologians and physicians.

Gies, Frances, and Joseph Gies. *Marriage and the Family in the Middle Ages* (1987). A comprehensive, well-written survey of the subject.

Gold, Penny Schine. *The Lady and the Virgin: Image, Attitude, and Experience in Twelfth-Century France* (1985). A fascinating study of how devotion to the Virgin Mary evolved in the High Middle Ages, taking into account attitudes toward women in medieval literature.

Klapisch-Zuler, Christiane, ed. *Silences of the Middle Ages*, vol. 2 of *A History of Women in the West*, ed. Georges Duby and Michelle Perrot (1992). A valuable survey by a leading German feminist historian.

Leyser, Henrietta. *Medieval Women: A Social History of Women in England, 450–1500* (1995). An excellent survey, including a generous selection of primary source materials translated into English.

Petroff, Elizabeth Alvilda. *Body and Soul: Essays on Medieval Women and Mysticism* (1994). Important studies of women's spiritual life in the Middle Ages.

Uitz, Erika. *Women in the Medieval Town* (1990). An excellent study that sets women in the context of high- and especially late-medieval urban life.

Town and Countryside

Bouchard, Constance B. *Holy Entrepreneurs: Cistercians, Knights, and Economic Exchange in Twelfth-Century Burgundy* (1991). An illuminating study based on extensive archival research.

Brooke, Christopher. *The Medieval Idea of Marriage* (1989). An intriguing, multidisciplinary study of marriage across the period 1000–1500, focusing on the High Middle Ages.

Duby, Georges. *The Knight, the Lady and the Priest: The Making of Modern Marriage in Medieval France* (1983). Clarifies the importance of marriage to the survival and advancement of aristocratic families and traces the conflict and reconciliation of the aristocratic and ecclesiastical models of marriage.

Fossier, Robert. *Peasant Life in the Medieval West* (1988). This engrossing study, translated from the French by Juliet Vale, uses historical, archaeological, and anthropological methods to investigate the high-medieval peasantry.

Genicot, Leopold. *Rural Communities in the Medieval World* (1990). An astute explanation of the rural community as a distinctive form of social organization, and of the reasons for its emergence in medieval western Europe.

Goetz, Hans-Werner. *Life in the Middle Ages: From the Seventh to the Thirteenth Century* (1993). A very readable study of medieval life among the several orders of society: peasants, townspeople, monks, and the ruling classes.

Hanawalt, Barbara A. *The Ties that Bound: Peasant Families in Medieval England* (1986). In this well-researched study the author argues persuasively—against traditional views—that all peasant families were nuclear, that most parents cherished their children (then as now), and that the legal distinction between serf and free had little discernible effect on daily life.

Herlihy, David. *Medieval Households* (1985). A tour de force of social history sweeping from Roman antiquity to the Italian Renaissance, this challenging, complex study maintains that households, as subsequently conceived, did not come into being until shortly before the advent of the High Middle Ages.

Lopez, Robert S. *The Commercial Revolution of the Middle Ages, 950–1350* (1971). Advances the thesis that the medieval commercial revolution was unique in world history and an essential precondition to later industrialization.

Mollat, Michel. *The Poor in the Middle Ages: An Essay in Social History* (1986). Translated from the French, this pioneering study of poverty and charity spans the whole of the Middle Ages.

Nicholas, David. *Medieval Flanders* (1992). A skillful, authoritative summary of Flemish history from Roman times through the fifteenth century by one of its major scholars.

Medieval Christianity

Bynum, Caroline Walker. *Holy Feast and Holy Fast: The Religious Significance of Food to Medieval Women* (1987). A brilliant, pathbreaking study that uses anthropological methods and feminist theory to demonstrate the central role of food and fasting in medieval women's religiosity, and to examine the place of the Eucharist in high- and late-medieval piety.

Hamilton, Bernard. *The Medieval Inquisition* (1981). Brief, clear, and balanced.

Lambert, Malcolm. *Medieval Heresy: Popular Movements from the Gregorian Reform to the Reformation*, 2nd ed. (1992). A learned, readable, thoughtfully original study; the best account of high- and late-medieval heresy.

Lawrence, C. H. *The Friars: The Impact of the Early Mendicant Movement on Western Society* (1994). This lucid and learned account shows how the Dominicans and Franciscans, with strong papal backing, extended their influ-

ence across Europe between the early thirteenth and mid-fourteenth centuries.

———. *Medieval Monasticism: Forms of Religious Life in Western Europe in the Middle Ages*, 2nd ed. (1989). A model survey, the best on the subject.

Le Roy Ladurie, Emmanuel. *Montaillou: The Promised Land of Error* (1975; English translation 1978). A great French historian's engrossing account of social, religious, and interpersonal life in an Albigensian community (from the early fourteenth century, but typical of the thirteenth century as well), based on the records of the Inquisition's investigations.

Lynch, Joseph H. *The Medieval Church: A Brief History* (1992). Succinct and judicious.

Russell, Jeffrey B. *Dissent and Order in the Middle Ages: The Search for Legitimate Authority* (1992). A valuable overview by the foremost scholar in the field.

Ward, Benedicta. *Miracles and the Medieval Mind* (1982). Meticulous studies of miracle accounts at Canterbury, Compostela, Rome, and Jerusalem demonstrate both change and continuity in attitudes toward miracles during the High Middle Ages.

Empire and Papacy

Arnold, Benjamin. *Princes and Territories in Medieval Germany* (1991). This impressive study centers on the question "Why did Germany evolve into a multiplicity of autonomous states?" and absolves the monarchy of a "failure" to unite the kingdom.

Blumenthal, Uta-Renate. *The Investiture Controversy: Church and Monarchy from the Ninth to the Twelfth Century* (1988). The best account of the Investiture Controversy in English.

Brentano, Robert. *Rome before Avignon: A Social History of Thirteenth-Century Rome*, rev. ed. (1990). A work of rigorous scholarship, gracefully written.

Haverkamp, Alfred. *Medieval Germany, 1056–1273*, 2nd ed. (1992). Trans. Helga Braun and Richard Mortimer. A multidisciplinary account providing particularly sympathetic treatments of Frederick Barbarossa and Rudolf of Habsburg.

Robinson, Ian S. *The Papacy, 1073–1198: Continuity and Innovation* (1990). A skillful study of the papacy's emergence as the primary force in ecclesiastical reform and of the rise of the papal monarchy.

Schimmelpfennig, Bernard. *The Papacy* (1992). Trans. James Stevert. A learned, beautifully written account running from the earliest times through the late Middle Ages.

Tellenbach, Gerd. *The Western Church from the Tenth to the Early Twelfth Century* (1993). This study casts brilliant light on the revolutionary changes that resulted from eleventh-century papal reform.

CRUSADERS AND KINGS IN THE HIGH MIDDLE AGES

St. Louis IX *The Granger Collection, New York.*

987	Beginning of the Capetian Dynasty of kings of France	1180–1223	Reign of Philip II Augustus in France	1272–1307	Reign of Edward I in England
1002	Breakup of the Spanish Caliphate of Cordova	1187	Muslims reconquer Jerusalem	1282–1302	War of the Sicilian Vespers ends French authority in Sicily
1060–1091	Normans conquer Muslim Sicily	1194	Emperor Henry VI becomes king of Sicily, uniting southern Italy and Sicily with the Holy Roman Empire	1285–1314	Reign of Philip IV "the Fair" in France
1066	Battle of Hastings; William, duke of Normandy, conquers England	1204	Fourth Crusade pillages Constantinople	1296	Pope Boniface VIII limits royal taxation of the clergy in *Clericis Laicos*, prompting strong resistance in France and England
1086	Domesday Book compiled in England	1212	Christian victory over the Spanish Muslims at Las Navas de Tolosa		
1087	William the Conqueror dies	1214	Philip Augustus defeats King John's allies at Bouvines	1302	Boniface VIII issues *Unam Sanctam*, an uncompromising assertion of papal authority over all the world
1095–1099	First Crusade, culminating in the capture of Jerusalem	1215	Barons force King John to agree on limitations of royal authority in Magna Carta		
1108–1137	Reign of Louis VI "the Fat" in France	1220–1250	Reign of Holy Roman Emperor and King of Sicily Frederick II	1303	Boniface VIII is captured and humiliated at Anagni by troops of King Philip IV of France and dies shortly thereafter
1130–1154	Reign of Roger the Great in Sicily	1226–1270	Reign of St. Louis (Louis IX) in France		
1152–1190	Reign of Holy Roman Emperor Frederick I Barbarossa	1236	Castile takes Cordova from Muslims	1309	Pope Clement V, moves the papacy from Rome to Avignon
1154–1189	Reign of Henry II of England, first of the Angevin kings	1254–1273	Interregnum in Germany, as imperial power disintegrates		
1176	Battle of Legnano: Lombard League and Pope rout Emperor Frederick Barbarossa				

In December 1244, the thirty-year-old king of France, Louis IX, solemnly swore to lead a crusade to wrest the Holy Land from Islam. His pious mother was aghast and tried to prevent him from going: Crusading, she and other intelligent people in the West had come to believe, was dangerous and futile. But go Louis did, in 1248. Two years later, his crusade ended in disaster in Egypt. Louis was captured. He may have been threatened with torture by the Muslims (and impressed them by showing no fear), but he returned home in 1254 only after a heavy ransom had been paid. Far from being disillusioned, Louis blamed the crusade's failure on his own sins, particularly the occasionally unscrupulous ways in which he had extracted money from his kingdom for his crusading army. He spent the rest of his reign doing penance, trying to rule France justly, and in the end making his kingdom the most efficiently governed monarchy in thirteenth-century Europe. The last action he undertook, however, was to make one last attempt at crusading, in 1269. And again he failed, getting no farther than what is today Tunisia, where he took sick and died the next year. With him, crusading itself virtually died. The French people acclaimed him a saint, and the papacy—with which as a living king he had frequently clashed—bowed to popular sentiment by canonizing him St. Louis in 1297. Today he is regarded as one of the greatest of French rulers, not merely for his ideals but also for his shrewdness and creativity as a statesman.

The sculpture shown at the beginning of the chapter was intended by its makers to represent St. Louis. But it is not an authentic portrait; none exists. Perhaps the king, who shunned royal garb and often dressed shabbily, refused out of humility to allow any artist to make his portrait. This figure was carved a century after Louis's death, and its features are thought to be those of the reigning French king of that time. But the statue was intended to *represent* St. Louis as the "Most Christian King," the title first applied to him by popular acclamation and borne by all his successors down to the ill-fated Louis XVI, who was guillotined in the French Revolution.

Louis IX epitomizes this chapter's two themes: first, the desire of high-medieval people to recover the Holy Land from Islam; and second, the rise of the high-medieval state. Both crusading and state-building involved the assertion of power and the question of what justifies the use of force. Neither enterprise should be judged in black-and-white terms. Crusading often involved anything but lofty ideals, and the building of states could stir idealism as well as provide numerous opportunities for furthering self-interest. And both cost untold innocent lives.

Historically, crusading proved largely a dead-end phenomenon. True, it represented an important event in medieval history. But only in the Iberian peninsula did it leave a long-lasting historical legacy, by helping to inspire later Spanish and Portuguese expansion overseas. Crusades against Islam eventually ground to a halt. St. Louis's two crusades were among the movement's last gasps.

The rise of the state, however, was anything but a dead-end: We still live with the result. The kingdoms that arose in high-medieval Europe were not predatory alliances for plunder, as the Germanic kingdoms of the Early Middle Ages had been. The new kingdoms were meant to safeguard law and order, justice, and the public peace, and they sometimes attracted principled loyalty. Reality often did not measure up to these ideals, which both recalled the principles of the ancient Greek polis and the Roman *res publica* as well as foreshadowed the modern state. The high-medieval monarchies may seem (and indeed are) far from modern representative democracies. But they are much closer to the modern state than were the early medieval kingdoms, whose primary purpose was to seek booty and engage in recreational warfare. And by the end of the thirteenth century, medieval kings had decisively shaken off attempts by the papacy to mastermind their policies. Although each new state in no way repudiated Christianity, it was not a **theocracy** nor agency of papal rule. The secular state was coming of age.

The economic and religious transformation of the eleventh through thirteenth centuries—the Dual Revolution that we studied in Chapter 8—was accompanied by far-reaching political changes. Like attempts to systematize feudalism, the rise of towns, and the development of commercial institutions, the creation of the medieval state represented an attempt to bring society under rational control. Papal and royal governments were rudimentary in 1050; by 1300 they had developed real bureaucracies. Surviving papal letters number about thirty-five per year in the years around 1100 but rise to thirty-six hundred per year by the early fourteenth century—and the same explosion of paperwork occurred at royal courts, reflecting similarly ballooning officialdoms. These statistics reflect the emergence of a new kind of papacy, capable of handling litigation and exercising authority throughout western Europe on a previously undreamed-of scale; and of monarchies that, for the first time, were beginning to display some of the administrative capabilities of early modern states.

During these 250 years England saw the beginnings of administrative and parliamentary monarchy. English politics were shaped by the growing concept that royal power must not transgress the rights of the nobility, the townspeople, and the church. This was the idea underlying Magna Carta, the "great charter" that the barons wrung from King John in 1215—and the idea of shared governance achieved its most significant embodiment in Parliament, which emerged a generation later.

The French monarchy also increased its power energetically. At the beginning of the thirteenth century one of its greatest kings, Philip Augustus, extended royal power across much of modern France, and in the middle of the century Louis IX strengthened both the power and the prestige of the French crown. By the century's end, the monarchy, less restrained by church and nobility than its English counterpart, dominated the French realm.

CRUSADING

In the eleventh, twelfth, and thirteenth centuries, western Europe's population boom produced abundant landless aristocratic younger sons who sought land and military glory on Christendom's frontiers. And the expanding peasant population provided a labor force for newly conquered lands. While the frontier warriors were carving out new estates for themselves, they were also (so they hoped) storing up treasures in heaven by pushing Western Christendom into Muslim Spain, Sicily, Syria, and the Slavic and Baltic regions of eastern Europe. Land, gold, and heaven—these were the alluring rewards of the medieval movement of expansion.

The great religious revival of high-medieval Europe also fueled territorial expansion. Christianity *did* matter to those who at the church's urging took up the cross as crusaders, whether to reclaim the Holy Land or Spain, or by the sword to extirpate heathendom in Prussia and Lithuania. Just as Muslim warriors thought of themselves as waging *jihad* in God's cause, so Christian knights expected a heavenly reward if they fell in battle for the sake of Christ, and whatever mundane rewards they might accrue in the righteous struggle were sanctified by their holy purpose. Crusading was one more way of giving life to Christian goals.

The Crusading Movement

A major political crisis in the Near East touched off European crusading. During the eleventh century a new warlike tribe from Central Asia, the Seljuk Turks, had swept into Persia, taken up the Islamic faith, and turned the Abbasid caliphs of Baghdad into their pawns. As we saw in Chapter 6, in 1071 the Seljuk Turks staggered the Byzantine Empire by smashing an imperial army at Manzikert and occupying parts of Anatolia. Stories (some of them probably true) of hair-raising Turkish atrocities against Christian pilgrims to Jerusalem began filtering westward, and when the desperate Byzantine emperor, Alexius Comnenus, swallowed his pride and appealed for Latin Christian help, Europe, under the leadership of a reinvigorated papacy, was ready to respond.

The Crusades fused three characteristic medieval impulses: piety, pugnacity, and greed. All three were essential. Without Christian idealism, the Crusades would have been inconceivable; yet the dream of reclaiming Jerusalem from the infidel was reinforced mightily by the lure of new lands and vast wealth. The crusaders seized the opportunity to devote their knightly skills to God's service—and to make their fortunes. It was to Pope Urban II (reigned 1088–1099) that Emperor Alexius sent his appeal for military aid, and Urban, a masterful reform pope, was quick to put the papacy at the forefront of an immense popular movement and grasp the moral leadership of Europe.

For more than a century, Western churchmen had been attempting to pacify Europe through a movement known as the "Peace of God," which prohibited military operations on lands of the church and the poor. The partial success of this effort inspired a similar movement called the "Truce of God," which sought to outlaw warfare on holy days and during holy seasons (including weekends, Friday through Sunday). The Crusades, strangely enough, were the climax of these earlier peace movements. For when Urban II proclaimed the First Crusade, he also proclaimed a peace throughout the Latin West, forbidding all warfare among Christians. Although Urban's peace was not everywhere honored, it did tend to protect their lordships the crusaders against stay-at-home enemies.

Crusading also contributed to peace within Christendom by directing aristocratic ferocity outward, against the Muslims. Knights who had previously been condemned by the church for violating the peace of Christendom were now lauded as soldiers of Christ. Thus Christian knighthood became a holy vocation, and knights were invited to achieve salvation through the exercise of their warlike prowess. Indeed, the church pictured crusading as an act of Christian love—toward persecuted fellow Christians in the East, and toward Christ himself, whose rightful lordship over the Holy Land had been usurped and polluted by nonbelievers. Just as a good vassal must help his lord recover a stolen lordship, so also must the Christian knight endeavor to restore Jerusalem to the Lord Christ.

The First Crusade In 1095 Urban II summoned Christian warriors to reconquer the Holy Land in an impassioned address to the Frankish aristocracy at Clermont-Ferrand in central France. He called on the French to avenge the Seljuk atrocities (which he described in bloodcurdling detail) by winning back the biblical "land of milk and honey" and driving the infidel from Jerusalem. To those who undertook the enterprise, he promised the highest of spiritual rewards: "Undertake this journey for the remission of your sins, with the assurance of the imperishable glory of the kingdom of Heaven."

With shouts of "God wills it!" French warriors poured into the crusading army. By 1096 an international military force—with a large nucleus of knights from central and southern France, Normandy, and Norman Sicily—swarmed across the Balkans to Constantinople. Charismatic preachers like Peter the Hermit stirred up a horde of ragged popular volunteers (whom the Muslims would eventually cut to pieces). Altogether, around twenty-five or thirty thousand knights went to the East, a relatively modest figure by modern standards but an immense host in the eyes of contemporaries.

Emperor Alexius was gravely disturbed. Having asked for military support, he had, as he put it, a barbarian invasion on his hands. The Byzantines wished only to recapture their lost provinces in Anatolia, whereas the crusaders were bent on nothing less than the conquest of the Holy Land. Soon the two sides were at odds. Going ahead alone (and abandoning Peter the Hermit's ragtag rabble), the knightly crusaders defeated the Muslims, captured Antioch after a long and complex siege, and in the summer of 1099 took Jerusalem itself, massacring many of its Muslim and Jewish inhabitants. With its capture, after only three years of campaigning, the goal of the First Crusade had been achieved.

No future crusade was to enjoy such success, and during the two centuries that followed, the original conquests gradually slipped away. For the moment, however, Europe rejoiced at the triumph of the crusaders. Some of them returned home to heroes' welcomes. Others settled down in Latin Syria to enjoy the fruits of their conquests. A long strip of territory along the eastern Mediterranean shore was now divided, according to feudal principles, among the crusader knights. These warriors consolidated their conquests by erecting elaborate castles, whose ruins survive to this day as tourist attractions and guerrilla hideouts.

The conquered lands were organized into four crusader states: the county of Edessa, the principality of Antioch, the county of Tripolis, and the kingdom of Jerusalem (see Map 9-1). This last was the most important, and the king of Jerusalem was theoretically the overlord of all the

THE HISTORICAL EVIDENCE

The First Crusade: The Liberation of Jerusalem

1099

Fulcher of Chartres was an eyewitness to the entire First Crusade, from Urban II's call for the delivery of Jerusalem from the infidel to the climactic siege and capture of the Holy City by the crusaders. He left a valuable chronicle describing what he saw—written, of course, from a staunchly Christian viewpoint. Here he narrates what happened when Jerusalem fell to the crusading army.

Then the Franks entered the city magnificently at the noonday hour on Friday, the day of the week when Christ redeemed the whole world on the cross. With trumpets sounding and with everything in an uproar, exclaiming: "Help, God!" they vigorously pushed into the city, and straightway raised the banner on the top of the wall. All the heathen, completely terrified, changed their boldness to swift flight through the narrow streets of the quarters. The more quickly they fled, the more quickly were they put to flight.

Count Raymond and his men, who were bravely assailing the city in another section, did not perceive this until they saw the Saracens jumping from the top of the wall. Seeing this, they joyfully ran to the city as quickly as they could, and helped the others pursue and kill the wicked enemy.

Then some, both Arabs and Ethiopians, fled into the Tower of David; others shut themselves in the Temple of the Lord and of Solomon,* where in the halls a very great attack was made on them. Nowhere was there a place where the Saracens could escape the swordsmen.

On the top of Solomon's Temple, to which they had climbed in fleeing, many were shot to death with arrows and cast down headlong from the roof. Within this Temple about ten thousand were beheaded. [Other sources say three hundred.] If you had been there, your feet would have been stained up to the ankles with the blood of the slain. What more shall I tell? Not one of them was allowed to live. They did not spare the women and children.

---

*Fulcher is probably referring to the Dome of the Rock, one of Islam's holiest shrines, built on the site of the Temple (which the Romans had destroyed in the first century A.D.; see Chapter 5).

Source: From The Chronicle of Fulcher of Chartres, translated by Martha E. McGinty. In *The First Crusade*: The Chronicle of Fulcher of Chartres *and Other Source Materials*, Second Edition, edited by Edward Peters. Copyright © 1971, 1988 University of Pennsylvania Press, pp. 68–69. Reprinted by permission of the publisher.

---

crusader territories. In fact, however, he had difficulty enforcing his authority, and the crusader states were tormented from the beginning by rivalries and dissension.

The Later Crusades   Gradually the Muslims began to recover their lands. One churchman attributed the crusaders' reverses to their wickedness: "They devoted themselves to all kinds of debauchery and allowed their womenfolk to spend whole nights at wild parties; they mixed with trashy people and drank the most delicious wines." Another offered this analysis: "It is no wonder that the Christians suffer losses from Saracens, rats, and locusts, when they neglect to pay their church dues properly." Whatever the reasons, the crusader county of Edessa succumbed to Islamic pressure in 1144. The resulting Second Crusade (1147–1148), launched to rescue Edessa, was a total disaster, the crusaders returning home shamefaced and empty-handed.

During the 1170s and 1180s a new, unified Islamic state arose in Egypt under the skillful leadership of the warrior-prince Saladin. Chivalrous and able, Saladin negotiated a truce with the crusader states; but the truce was broken by a Christian robber baron—a characteristic product of grass-roots feudal enterprise—who persisted in attacking Muslim caravans. The result was a great showdown battle between Christians and Muslims at Hattin, north of Jerusalem, on July 4, 1187. Saladin surrounded the crusader army and virtually annihilated it, and he afterwards conquered large portions of the crusader states without serious opposition. Three months after Hattin, Saladin captured Jerusalem in a two-week siege, but forbade his men to plunder it.

The catastrophe at Hattin and the fall of Jerusalem roused still another crusading effort. The Third Crusade (1189–1193) was led by three of medieval Europe's most illustrious monarchs: Emperor Frederick Barbarossa of Germany, King Philip Augustus of France, and King Richard the Lion-Hearted of England. But Barbarossa drowned on the way, and most of his army trudged back to Germany; Philip Augustus quarreled with King Richard and went home; and Richard, although he won some victories and captured the important port of Acre, failed to take Jerusalem. Worse yet, on his return journey Richard became the

MAP 9-1
THE CRUSADES

prisoner of Barbarossa's son, Emperor Henry VI, who released his royal captive only after England had paid the staggering sum of £100,000—quite literally, a king's ransom.

Although lacking distinguished royal leaders, the Fourth Crusade (1201–1204) had as its instigator the most powerful of the medieval popes, Innocent III. It was the oddest of the Crusades. It never reached the Holy Land, yet in its own tragic way was spectacularly successful. The crusaders resolved to avoid the perils of overland travel by crossing to the Holy Land in Venetian ships. Unfortunately, they contracted with the Venetians for many more ships than were necessary and at a far greater cost than they could afford. The doge of Venice nevertheless agreed to take what money the crusaders had and to transport them to the Holy Land if they would do him a favor on the way. They were to recapture for Venice the port of Zara (today Zadar, on Croatia's Dalmatian coast), which had recently come into the hands of the king of Hungary. Pope Innocent III was infuriated by this bargain, which diverted the crusading army against a king who was not only a Latin Christian but a papal vassal as well. He excommunicated the crusaders when they attacked Zara, and washed his hands of the whole business.

Undeterred, the warriors went doggedly on. After capturing Zara in 1202, they were again diverted, this time by a dispute in Constantinople over the Byzantine throne. In return for promises of wealth, aid against the Muslims, and union of the Eastern and Western churches under Rome, the crusaders agreed to help one of the claimants. They installed their new friend, but he was soon murdered by his own countrymen. So the crusaders, to get what they thought was due them, resolved to seize Constantinople.

Accordingly, in 1204 they took the great city by storm and subjected it to three long-remembered days of pillage and massacre. After nearly nine centuries, the impregnable Byzantine capital had fallen; the crusaders had succeeded where hordes of Goths, Persians, Arabs, Avars, Bulgars, and Vikings had failed. Count Baldwin IX of Flanders

Richard the Lion-Hearted at Acre In an appalling atrocity of the crusading era, Richard I is said to have ordered the mass beheading of 2,700 Muslim prisoners after he took Acre. Despite a well-publicized personal duel with the great Muslim sultan of Egypt (Saladin), Richard did not succeed in retaking Jerusalem. *Bibliothèque Nationale, Paris.*

became emperor, and he and his successors ruled in Constantinople for more than half a century. A nucleus of the old Byzantine state held out in Anatolia, nursing its grievances and gathering its strength, until in 1261 the Latin Empire was overthrown and Greek emperors reigned once again in Constantinople. But Byzantium had suffered a blow from which it never entirely recovered.

As a consequence of the Fourth Crusade, the Eastern and Western churches were temporarily reunited. Innocent III, who had absolved the crusaders from excommunication after the fall of Zara and excommunicated them anew for attacking Constantinople, recanted when he realized the "great blessings" that had befallen Latin Christendom with the capture of the schismatic city. The crusaders, for their part, forgot about the Holy Land and returned to Europe with immense booty from the Byzantine metropolis: precious gems, money, and gold. The greatest prize of all was an immense store of relics—bones, heads, and arms of saints, Jesus' crown of thorns, St. Thomas the Apostle's doubting finger, the "Shroud of Turin,"[1] and similar holy

---

[1] The Shroud of Turin is an authentic-looking fabric that appears to have been imprinted with an image of Christ's body while it was wrapped around him in the tomb after his crucifixion. It became a treasured relic in Europe after it was stolen from Constantinople. In modern times it baffled scientists until very recently, when bits of its fibers were removed and subjected to technical analysis. It now seems clear that the shroud and its image were skillfully fabricated in Byzantium sometime before 1204.

loot. Perhaps more important, the West acquired direct access to the intellectual legacy of Greek and Byzantine civilization. But the old hostility between Greeks and Latins was aggravated by the events of the Fourth Crusade into a virtually insurmountable wall of hatred.

Subsequent crusades were almost all unsuccessful, to say the least. In 1212 a visionary, ill-organized enterprise known as the Children's Crusade ended in tragedy. Thousands of boys and girls flocked into the ports of southern Europe, gripped by religious fervor and convinced that the Mediterranean would dry up and give them a miraculous pathway to the Holy Land. Many of them returned home sadder but wiser, and the rest were sold into Muslim slavery.

Western Christendom launched further crusades in the course of the thirteenth century—Louis IX's two crusades among them—and most ended disastrously. The only one to succeed was led by Emperor Frederick II, who negotiated with the Muslims a Christian occupation of Jerusalem in 1229 and crowned himself its king. But he had to return home to face a war with the pope, and in his absence the Holy City reverted to Islam in 1244. No Christian army would set foot in Jerusalem again until 1916, when the British drove out the Ottoman Turks during World War I.

By the end of the thirteenth century, crusading enthusiasm had understandably waned. In 1291 the fall of Acre—the last Christian bridgehead on the eastern Mediterranean coast—brought an end to the crusader

Knights of the Early Crusades These knights are armed and wearing chain mail, as were the warriors who fought in the First Crusade and in the crusading movement in medieval Spain. This illumination is from an early eleventh-century Spanish manuscript. *By permission of the British Library. Shelfmark/Man: Add. 11895 folio: 102 v.*

states in the Holy Land. The reigning pope described the catastrophe as "a doleful cup of bitterness."

But the Crusades were more than simply a romantic and bloody fiasco. Crusading held the imagination of Europe for two centuries, uniting Western Christendom in a vast effort that brought Christian rule to portions of the Holy Land for most of the High Middle Ages. At the same time, European merchants established themselves in the crusader states and enormously enlarged their role in international commerce. When the crusaders departed, the merchants remained, continuing their domination of the eastern Mediterranean and, after the capture of Constantinople, the Black Sea as well.

Crusading Orders The Crusades gave rise to several religious orders of Christian warriors, bound by monastic rules and dedicated to fighting the Muslims and advancing the crusading cause. One was the Knights Hospitalers, which drew chiefly on the French for its membership. Another was the Knights Templars, an international brotherhood that acquired great wealth through pious gifts and intelligent estate management and gradually became involved in far-flung banking activities. A third order, the Teutonic Knights, was composed chiefly of Germans. In the thirteenth century the Teutonic Knights transferred their activities from the Holy Land to the Baltic coast, where they assisted in the eastward thrust of German Christian culture against pagan Balts and Christian Poles.

Orders of a similar sort arose on other frontiers of Western Christendom. The Knights of Santiago de Compostela and the Order of Calatrava, for example, were dedicated to fighting the Muslims in Spain and furthering the Christian reconquest of the Iberian Peninsula. These crusading orders, bridging as they did the two great medieval institutions of monasticism and knighthood, represent the ultimate synthesis of the military and the Christian life. They were praised in their time for "going in war to fight, and returning in peace to rest and pray, so that they behave like knights in battle and like monks in convent."

The Reconquest of Spain

During the eleventh century, knightly adventurers from all over Christendom—but particularly from France—flocked over the Pyrenees to help take back Iberia from Islam. The caliphate of Cordova had broken up after 1002 into warring fragments, but the small Christian kingdoms of northern Iberia, often battling among themselves, were at first slow to take advantage of this opportunity. But in 1085 the Christian kingdom of Castile captured the great Muslim city of Toledo—which thereafter became a crucial contact point between Islamic and Christian culture. Early in the twelfth century a second Christian kingdom, Aragon, began an offensive against the Moors (see Map 9-2).

In 1140 Aragon was strengthened by its unification with the county of Barcelona—Charlemagne's old Spanish

MAP 9-2
IBERIA: "RECONQUISTA" AND PILGRIMAGE

This map shows the major links between Iberia and the rest of medieval western Europe. European (especially French) knights contributed significantly to the military manpower that began the rollback of Muslim territory. Over many generations, meanwhile, tens of thousands of Christians from all over Europe made the pilgrimage journey to Santiago de Campostela. A series of great cathedrals along the way attracted throngs of devotees of their relics, culminating in the shrine of St. James (Santiago) at Campostela. Pilgrims' contributions helped support the cost of crusading. Pilgrims identified themselves with (among other things) cockle shells attached to their hats; it is from this that comes the French term *coquilles St.-Jacques*, familiar to everyone who orders scallops in a French restaurant today.

March. And meanwhile still another Christian state, Portugal, was forming as an independent kingdom facing the Atlantic. But stiffening Muslim resistance, and continued bickering among Christian leaders, for a time brought the reconquest to a virtual halt.

Finally, in 1212, Innocent III proclaimed a crusade against the Spanish Muslims. The king of Castile advanced from Toledo with a pan-Iberian army and won a decisive victory at the battle of Las Navas de Tolosa. Thereafter, Moorish power was permanently crippled. Cordova itself fell to Castile in 1236, and by the late thirteenth century the Moors were confined to the small southern emirate of Granada. Castile now dominated central Spain, and the work of re-Christianization proceeded rapidly as Christian peasants were imported en masse into the newly conquered lands. Aragon meanwhile was overrunning the Muslim islands of the western Mediterranean and establishing a maritime empire.

The High Middle Ages thus witnessed the reconquest and Christianization of nearly all of the Iberian Peninsula and its organization into three major Christian kingdoms: Castile, Aragon, and Portugal. The effort was resumed at the end of the Late Middle Ages. In 1479, Castile and Aragon united to form the Kingdom of Spain, which in 1492 would finally overrun the Emirate of Granada, Islam's last Iberian outpost. By that time Spain, along with Portugal, was spearheading Europe's expansion into America, Africa, and the Far East (see Chapter 14).

The high-medieval *Reconquista* was not simply an essential precondition for these Atlantic ventures—the Iberians' expansion overseas was a direct continuation of the crusading zeal and lust for land born of the struggle with Islam. Christopher Columbus saw it as his ultimate objective to take Jerusalem by outflanking Islam from the east. He was truly the last of the crusaders.

The German "Push to the East"

Eastern Germany was the third sphere of medieval Europe's expansion. The German eastward drive was not a product of active royal or papal policy but rather a movement led by local aristocrats, in particular the dukes of Saxony. It was a gradual advance with a great deal of momentum behind it. What Germans call their *Drang nach Osten*, or "push to the east," dated back to the tenth century, when German princes and peasant settlers took over the Slavic-inhabited lands along the Elbe River and established such frontier outposts as Berlin. At that time the German advance prompted the pagan ruler of Poland to declare himself a Christian and a papal vassal, forestalling further pressure. But then, over a drawn-out period between about 1125 and 1350, the German advance resumed, pushing German-speaking settlements into Pomerania, Silesia, and Prussia, which Poland would not regain until after World War II (see Map 9-3).

German territorial gains, won through war and marriages between Saxon and local Slavic rulers, were consolidated by the creation of innumerable villages and massive migration of Germanic peasants. Thus the new areas were not only conquered; they were in large part Christianized and germanized.

The Teutonic Knights, who led the later phases of the German eastward push, established themselves in Prussia (then inhabited by a pagan Baltic people called the Old Prussians). A second German order (later merged with the Teutonic Knights), occupied what is now Latvia and Estonia and sought unsuccessfully to conquer the great Russian city-state of Novgorod and the huge pagan realm of Lithuania. Although during the fourteenth and fifteenth cen-

MAP 9-3
THE GERMAN "PUSH TO THE EAST"

Throughout the High Middle Ages, German, Dutch, and Flemish peasants moved into what is now eastern Germany, western Poland, and the Baltic states, attracted by the relatively favorable conditions under which they were invited to settle villages and towns. Over time, they gradually germanized the regions shown on this map. Military conquest by the German crusading orders and the tendency of native rulers (of Slavic ancestry) in Pomerania and Silesia to drift into the Holy Roman Empire's political orbit also promoted gradual germanization.

turies the German crusaders suffered some severe setbacks, much of the German acquisitions would endure until the defeat of Nazi Germany. Together with the crusaders' conquests in Iberia and in Sicily and southern Italy,[2] the great German advance enlarged the frontiers of Latin Christendom and helped expand its economy.

BUILDING THE ENGLISH AND FRENCH MONARCHIES

While empire and papacy were locked in their interminable struggles, and crusaders were battling the infidel in Palestine, Iberia, and the Baltic lands, England and France were evolving into centralized states. Strong monarchy came to England first, yet in the long run it was

---

[2] Norman conquests in southern Italy are discussed later in the chapter as an example of state-building.

THE HISTORICAL EVIDENCE

Flemish Peasants Settle the German East

1154

The following charter was given by the bishop of Neissen to the Flemish peasants settling the village of Kühren, in eastern Germany, in 1154. "Flemings" was a generic term for peasants from the Netherlands with a specialized knowledge of turning marshes into productive farmland. The document shows how the settlement of former Slavic lands in the Elbe basin was potentially profitable both to the new German landlords and to the German and Flemish peasants who created new villages there on favorable terms.

Gerungus, by the grace of God bishop of the church of Neissen, to all those present as well as future who invoke the name of God, perpetual grace and peace in the Lord. We desire that it shall be known by our congregation now and in the times to come how I have brought together and established in an uncultivated and almost uninhabited place energetic men coming from the province of Flanders, and how I have given in stable, eternal and hereditary possession to them and to all their descendants, the village called Kühren with the following rights. I have given these Flemings, in memory and as a sign of full possession, four marks [a sum of money, perhaps to cover the expenses of resettling], this village and 18 *manses* [a measure of land], with all the customs which exist now and which shall exist in the future, in the fields as well as in the woods, meadows, and pastures, in the waters and the mills as well as in the places for hunting and fishing. From these manses I have granted one to the church with all the tithes of the manse; I have given two of them to the mayor of the peasants whom they call *Schultheiss*,* but without title. The remaining manses, to the number of 15, pay every year 30 sous and 30 deniers for the right called *Zip*.† The said men give tithe on all their property except bees and flax, and they shall be responsible for the expenses of the "advocate" with a small escort three times a year for the pleas

which he must hold with them and where they live.‡ From what the "advocate" or the Schultheiss levies in these pleas, two-thirds shall be given to the bishop, and the third to the Schultheiss. Let our lands be free of tolls, except for what is sold to merchants. They can sell amongst themselves bread, barley beer and meat, but they must not establish a public market in the village. For all else, we enfranchise them from all exactions coming from the bishop, the advocate, the mayor, or any other man. And in order that these statutes shall not be violated in the future, we place them under our *ban* [authority], and we confirm them with our seal in the presence of witnesses.

---

*In German villages the Schultheiss was a hereditary mayor who was responsible for organizing the settlement. The modern surname Schultz derives from it.

†So-called "lower justice"—that is, the right of the village court to decide ordinary matters.

‡The advocate was an official dispatched by the bishop to settle major court cases and otherwise keep an eye on village affairs. Villagers were responsible for his expenses.

Source: From Georges Duby, *Rural Economy and Country Life in the Medieval West*, trans. Cynthia Postan (London: Edward Arnold, 1968), document 38, pp. 394–395.

the English who were more successful in limiting royal power. Early modern French **absolutism** and English parliamentary monarchy both have their roots in the High Middle Ages. More than that, the rise of effective royal administrative institutions was an early, crucial step in the evolution of the political environment that surrounds us today, one of the most fundamental medieval contributions to modern civilization.

England: The Birth of Representative Government

Worldwide, the year 1066 was memorable for the reappearance of Halley's Comet. In many cultures, it was feared that

the fiery apparition in the sky (said to have been visible even in daylight) presaged some awesome disaster. Among those who quaked, we are assured by the artisans who fashioned the famous Bayeux Tapestry, were the leaders of Anglo-Saxon England. Whether or not Halley's Comet had anything to do with it, the year indeed was epochal in English history. A complex chain of events began that would eventually produce not only the strongest monarchy in Europe, but also—and not entirely paradoxically—the foundations of modern representative government.

1066 and Its Implications Although the Anglo-Saxon kingdom had a strong foundation (see Chapter 7), it was in disarray when King Edward the Confessor died in January 1066. He left no son; indeed, the saintly ruler was said to have remained chaste throughout his married life. Dying, he gave his crown to England's ablest nobleman, Harold Godwinson, his wife's brother, and the council of leading men of the realm, the Witan, immediately ratified his choice.

Across the English Channel, Duke William of Normandy—"William the Bastard," as he was sometimes called on account of his illegitimate birth—objected. William claimed that in 1051 Edward had made *him* heir to the English crown. (He had dim claims through his great-aunt Emma, the widow of both Ethelred the Unready and King Canute.) Besides, he said, Harold Godwinson had a few years earlier sworn a mighty oath never to claim the crown. Now Harold appeared to be breaking his word—a serious charge in those days. To make matters worse for Harold, the king of Norway also entered the contest with his own claim to the throne. At that point, the pope decided to back William's claim and sent him a banner that he had personally blessed.

Both claimants got ready to enforce their demands that Harold surrender his new crown. Contrary winds forced the Normans to cool their heels during the summer—not the last time in history that the weather would affect a cross-Channel military operation. In September, the Norwegians landed in Yorkshire, and Harold rushed north in time to inflict on them a smashing defeat, in which the Norwegian king (a renowned warrior) lost his life. In the meantime William's Normans finally got across the Channel and built a defensive castle at Hastings. Harold had to regroup his exhausted troops, march back practically the whole length of England, and face William. The great battle was fought on October 14. The English defensive line inflicted heavy losses on the Norman cavalry. But at the end of the day a random Norman arrow struck Harold in the eye, killing him. His disheartened

men fled—and the duke of Normandy became William "the Conqueror." On Christmas Day, he was crowned King William I at Westminster Abbey.

There was nothing foreordained in the Norman victory. Until they lost their leader, the Anglo-Saxons had shown themselves the equal of the best warriors in Europe. Nor were Anglo-Saxon institutions wanting. William's victory, in which he probably owed much to chance, simply gave the Norman conquerors an opportunity to impose a new master on an already flourishing monarchical system.

William and his successors thereafter ruled wide dominions on both sides of the English Channel. As kings of England they were sovereign, but the French monarchy claimed overlordship of their possessions in France. England's continental involvement continued until the mid-fifteenth century and spawned generations of hostility between the two kingdoms, but it was also a source of power and wealth to the kings of England. When the English monarchy lost the bulk of its French dominions in 1204, the kings of France became the foremost monarchs of thirteenth-century Christendom (see Table 9-1).

England, in the meantime, developed a centralized monarchical regime of unprecedented power, based on a highly effective and increasingly elaborate royal administration. Tax collecting was enhanced by a sophisticated central accounting department; written royal commands in ever-increasing numbers poured from the royal chancery; and royal justice was administered by a growing number of judges, by an accelerating flood of professional lawyers, and by royal courts with varying and distinct jurisdictions. High-medieval France, although a half-century behind England, followed a similar path toward bureaucratic kingship. By the thirteenth century's end, both kingdoms had developed many of the basic institutions of the modern European nation-state.

The Battle of Hastings: A Norman View   The so-called Bayeux Tapestry, made in Normandy less than half a century after the Battle of Hastings, is a very important historical source for its accurate depiction of eleventh-century warfare. The Normans are the mounted warriors, and the English fight on foot.   *Musee de la Tapisserie, Bayeux, France/Bridgeman Art Library.*

TABLE 9-1

ENGLAND IN THE HIGH MIDDLE AGES

1066	Norman invasion of Anglo-Saxon England; battle of Hastings
1066–1087	Reign of William I "the Conqueror"
1087–1100	Reign of William II (William Rufus)
1100–1135	Reign of Henry I
1135–1154	Disputed succession: King Stephen
1154–1189	Reign of Henry II
1189–1199	Reign of Richard I "the Lion-Hearted"
1199–1216	Reign of John
1215	Magna Carta
1216–1272	Reign of Henry III
1272–1307	Reign of Edward I

England in 1066 had long been divided into shires (or counties), each with its own shire court and its own royal officer—the "shire reeve," or sheriff. It was the sheriff's responsibility to collect royal taxes and the revenues of royal estates, and to assemble the shire's military contingent when the king summoned the army. The sheriff presided over the shire court, whose members were drawn from important landholders of the district. The customs and procedures of the shire court were rooted in local traditions, and the sheriff was usually a local man whose sympathies were apt to be divided between his native shire and the king.

William the Conqueror came to England as a distant kinsman of Edward the Confessor. William promised to preserve the laws and customs of King Edward's day, many of which, in fact, were highly beneficial to the monarchy—including a smoothly functioning system of taxation and a configuration of shire courts unmatched elsewhere. But William added important new customs, many from Normandy, which made his government stronger than that of his Anglo-Saxon predecessors.

In the years immediately following the Norman Conquest, William effected a revolutionary change in England's aristocratic power structure by dispossessing virtually all major Anglo-Saxon landholders and replacing them with his own friends and military followers. The new aristocracy was French-speaking and accustomed to the Continental techniques of mounted combat. William established an aristocratic regime in England more or less on the Norman patterns but more systematically organized and more

The Anglo-Norman Monarchy The English kingdom that William the Conqueror won in 1066 was already centralized and relatively well governed. The chief officers in the Anglo-Saxon royal household were coming to assume important administrative responsibilities. Although the court was constantly on the move, traveling around the countryside from one royal manor to another, it remained in close touch with the king's regional and local officials.

A Motte-and-Bailey English Castle This is a modern scholarly reconstruction of the sort of castle most commonly built in England by William the Conqueror. Capturing such a castle with the resources available to a typical attacking force of the time was quite difficult. *W.L. Warren, Henry II, Berkeley, CA: University of California Press, 1973.*

THE HUMAN EXPERIENCE

Hugh, Earl of Chester

Although not the greatest English nobleman of his era, Hugh, Earl of Chester, nevertheless inherited considerable landed wealth and acquired far more in the course of his eventful career. His life was in some important respects typical of his age and class; in other respects, however, he emerges as a unique individual.

Hugh was born in Normandy about 1048, some eighteen years before the Norman Conquest of England. Like other Norman nobles, he was of Viking descent: His great-grandfather was a certain Ansfrid the Dane. But several generations in Normandy had transformed Ansfrid's descendants and those of his fellow Viking settlers into a French-speaking aristocracy.

Hugh's father was a wealthy Norman landholder and an important regional official—a viscount—of William, duke of Normandy, the future conqueror of England. Hugh inherited his father's estates and office of viscount. And as a result of the Norman Conquest of 1066, in which Hugh probably participated as

a teenaged commander of a large contingent of knights, he acquired lands and power in England far exceeding his inheritance in Normandy. King William the Conqueror showered wealth on his young vassal, granting him estates scattered across twenty shires and the prestigious title of earl (see The Historical Evidence, the "Domesday Book" on p. 323). It was Hugh's responsibility as earl to consolidate Norman power in the county of Cheshire on the frontier of Wales, and to expand Norman authority into the northern regions of that as yet unconquered land. To assist Hugh, the king gave him all the lands in Cheshire, except those belonging to the church, and granted him virtual kingly authority there: Hugh could summon all the Cheshire knights on his own authority, collect his own taxes, and appoint his own sheriff and lesser officials.

Hugh never abused these privileges. Unlike many of the great magnates of post-Conquest England, he remained steadfastly loyal to William the Conqueror and his royal succes-

sors. In the course of several baronial rebellions, Hugh gave the monarchy his total support—and he and his family consequently flourished.

Among the Welsh, however, Hugh was known as "Hugh the Wolf" because of his ruthless and savage military campaigns. The Normans were a conquering people, and Hugh was typical. He did not subdue all of northern Wales, but his men occupied large portions of it, slaughtering the Welsh in great numbers.

He was also called Hugh the Fat. Said a contemporary:

He was a great lover of the world and its pomp, which he regarded as the greatest blessing of the human lot. He was always in the forefront in battle, lavish to the point of prodigality, a lover of games and luxuries, actors, horses, dogs, and similar vanities. He was always surrounded by a huge following, noisy with swarms of boys of both high and low birth. Many honorable men, clerics and knights, were also in his entourage, and he cheerfully

directly subordinate to the royal will. Most English estates, both lay and ecclesiastical, were transformed into fiefs held by crown vassals in return for supplying a specified number of mounted knights and certain other feudal obligations. The king and his nobility secured their conquest by dotting the land with scores of castles. Most were simply square wooden towers built on earthen mounds and encircled by wooden palisades; only later were they rebuilt in stone.

The new magnates (great lords) tended to acquire their lands piecemeal as the kingdom passed progressively under William's control, with the result that their estates were scattered across various shires rather than coalescing into territorial blocs. This dispersion shaped England's political future, giving the baronage a kingdom-wide perspective at a time when France and Germany—segmented into regional princedoms—remained politically provincial. And William was careful to reserve for his own royal demesne about a sixth of the lands of England (similarly scattered), so that he and his successors would not be mere

nominal overlords like the early Capetian kings of France and the later Hohenstaufen emperors.

Drawing on the resources of their vast royal demesne, the Norman kings of England generally managed to keep their vassals on tight rein. Their commanding position atop the Anglo-Norman feudal structure owed much to the centralizing traditions of the Anglo-Saxon monarchy. The new barons established private courts, as had been their custom in Normandy, but alongside these baronial courts the older shire courts lived on. Baronial particularism was restrained by the Anglo-Saxon custom of general allegiance to the crown, which enabled the Norman kings to claim the direct and primary loyalty of every vassal and subvassal in England. A knight's allegiance to his immediate lord was now secondary to his allegiance to the king. The monarchy prohibited private war between vassals and permitted the building of private castles only by royal license. In brief, the new system of fiefs and vassals was molded by the powerful Anglo-Saxon tradition of royal

shared his riches with them. . . . He kept no check on what he gave or received [an interesting observation suggesting that contemporary magnates normally kept accounts of receipts and expenditures]. His hunting was a daily devastation of his lands, for he thought more highly of hawkers and hunters than of peasants or monks. A slave to gluttony, he staggered under a mountain of fat, scarcely able to move. He was given over to carnal lusts and sired a multitude of bastards by his concubines.

The author of these lines, an Anglo-Norman monk named Orderic Vitalis, probably got carried away in singling out Hugh. Innocent of our modern obsession with fitness, most medieval kings and nobles, who could afford to eat well, put on weight as they aged. All the French and English kings of Hugh's era were corpulent. (It was reported that William the Conqueror's corpse burst as it was being forced into its coffin.) Similarly, Hugh's enthusiasm for hunting and hawking was widely shared among his royal and aristocratic contemporaries, even if most of them pursued these sports with less abandon.

Set against Hugh's bacchanalian antics, one must bear in mind that he was also a faithful and trusted vassal of the kings of England and an extremely generous benefactor of the church. In Normandy, Hugh founded a great (and vastly expensive) Benedictine abbey, granting it extensive lands from his family estates scattered across the central and western districts of the Norman duchy. With his wife, Ermentrude, the daughter of a French count and countess, he founded a second, equally expensive Benedictine abbey in his English earldom: St. Werburg's, Chester. He established St. Werburg's in consultation with his close friend St. Anselm, abbot of Bec in Normandy and one of the wisest and holiest saints of the Middle Ages (see Chapter 10). Anselm and Hugh were an odd couple, to say the least, yet they accomplished much together. Under Anselm's guidance, Hugh filled his new abbey with pious and dedicated monks from Bec, and St. Werburg's became a center of ecclesiastical reform.

In 1101, while in his early fifties, Hugh fell gravely ill. (Perhaps overeating was taking its toll.) By July he knew that he was nearing death, and like other noble abbey patrons in similar situations, he took vows as a Benedictine monk and was welcomed into the austere monastic community of St. Werburg's. His timing could hardly have been better; after living as a monk for four pious days, he died.

From Orderic Vitalis's vivid description, Earl Hugh emerges as a festive, cheerfully disorganized man. From the broader viewpoint of Anglo-Norman warfare and diplomacy, his career was a dazzling success. He always managed to make the right moves; he thereby added an extraordinarily wealthy English earldom to his Norman estates and succeeded in holding both simultaneously throughout the later decades of his life. Perhaps most striking of all is the contrast between his ostentatious flouting of contemporary Christian moral principles—his savage campaigns against the Welsh, his unbridled gluttony and sexuality—and, on the other hand, his lavish generosity toward the church. But here again, the contradiction was not peculiar to Hugh; it was characteristic of the medieval aristocracy as a whole during the earlier generations of the High Middle Ages. ❖

supremacy, and by William the Conqueror's authority, into a tightly centralized regime.

On the Conqueror's death in 1087, his kingdom passed in turn to his two sons, William II (called Rufus for his red hair), who reigned from 1087 to 1100, and Henry I, who reigned from 1100 to 1135. Both were strong leaders, but Henry I was the abler. A skillful diplomat and administrative innovator, Henry rid England of rebellion and exploited the growing prosperity of his day through heavy taxes. By exiling troublemakers and winning baronial friends through his adroit use of royal patronage, Henry created a docile and strongly royalist aristocracy. In the words of one eyewitness observer, he gave his dominions "a peace such as no age remembers, such as his father himself was never able to achieve" (see Figure 9-1).

Under William the Conqueror and his sons, royal administrative institutions grew significantly. A unique survey of landholdings known as Domesday Book, the product of William the Conqueror's kingdom-wide census of 1086, bears witness to the administrative vigor of the new regime, which no contemporary kingdom in western Europe could have matched. By the close of Henry I's reign in 1135, royal justices were traveling all across England hearing cases in the shire courts, extending the king's jurisdiction throughout the land. Baronial courts and ecclesiastical courts still functioned, as did the ancient shire courts (under tightening royal control). But royal justice was on the march.

Administrative efficiency and royal centralization were the keynotes of Henry I's reign. Royal dues were collected systematically by sheriffs, who delivered their revenues to a new central auditing board known as the exchequer (so named because it did its accounting by moving counting pieces on a checkered cloth). The growing efficiency of the exchequer and the expansion of royal justice were both motivated in part by the king's desire for larger revenues—for the more cases the royal justices handled, the more fines went into the royal treasury; the more closely the sheriffs

FIGURE 9-1

THE NORMAN AND PLANTAGENET KINGS OF ENGLAND

church appointments. Indeed, he dominated the English church through pressure and patronage throughout his long reign. He continued to support decrees prohibiting simony and enforcing priestly chastity, but as the father of at least twenty-two bastards by a parade of mistresses, Henry's credentials as a moral reformer seemed a bit questionable.

Notwithstanding Henry's tireless romantic exploits, he had only a single surviving legitimate offspring—a daughter named Matilda, who was wed first to Emperor Henry V and then, on the latter's death, to Geoffrey Plantagenet, Count of Anjou in France. Matilda bore Geoffrey a son and named him after her father. Henry Plantagenet would ultimately rule widespread dominions. But at Henry I's death this child was only two years old, and Henry's nephew, Stephen of Blois (reigned 1135–1154), seized the crown. For nineteen troubled years, "Bad King Stephen" struggled with Matilda, her husband Geoffrey, and their growing son Henry to control the Anglo-Norman realm, while barons played one side against the other, built unlicensed castles, and fought for their own interests. England suffered vast economic hardship during this civil war, known as "Stephen's Anarchy."

The Zenith of the English Feudal Monarchy: Henry II, 1154–1189 Toward the end of Stephen's embattled reign, Henry Plantagenet was growing into vigorous manhood, his prospects brightened year by year. He became duke of Normandy in 1150 and inherited Anjou upon the death of his father in 1151. In 1152 he extended his dominion still farther by marrying Eleanor, heiress of the large southern French duchy of Aquitaine. In 1153 King Stephen was forced by his declining military fortunes to name Henry as his heir, and when Stephen died the following year, Henry peacefully assumed the throne as King Henry II of England. Henry Plantagenet now ruled an immense constellation of territories north and south of the English Channel, which historians have termed the Angevin Empire—"Angevin" because Henry II and his heirs were descended in the male line from the counts of Anjou. On the map, these Angevin dominions dwarf the modest territory controlled by the king of France (see Map 9-4). But Henry II and the sons who succeeded him had difficulty keeping order throughout these vast, diverse territories. The passing of all these districts into the control of one man destroyed for all time the system of medium-sized principalities that had previously shaped the political development of France.

Henry was an energetic, brilliant, exuberant man—short, burly, and red-headed. He was a literate monarch who liked scholars, encouraged the growth of towns, and presided over an economic boom. Under his rule, significant steps were taken toward the development of English **common law,** under the jurisdiction of royal courts, to supersede the various and complex jurisdictions of local and baronial courts. Generally speaking, legal actions relating

were supervised, the less likely it was that taxes would stick to their fingers. The Norman kings discovered that strong government was good business.

Henry I also became involved in the Investiture Controversy (see Chapter 8) when his archbishop, the great theologian St. Anselm,[3] adopted the papal position and refused to countenance the ceremony of royal investiture of prelates. Anselm's stance forced him into exile for a time, because Henry understandably declined to abandon the long-accepted practice. Not until 1107 did Henry, Anselm, and the papacy reach a compromise on the investiture issue, foreshadowing the 1122 Concordat of Worms between pope and emperor. Henry I relinquished lay investiture as such but retained much control over

[3] For Anselm's place in the history of medieval theology, see Chapter 10.

THE HISTORICAL EVIDENCE

Domesday Book

1086

Domesday Book got its name from the thoroughness with which William the Conqueror's officials compiled it. They were as relentless in pursuit of information about taxable property and the royal demesne, it was said, as God Almighty will be in ferreting out sin at the Last Judgment—Doomsday. The king not only intended the book to be a source of information for his government but also hoped that it would be a public reference showing who had a right to what property, forestalling legal disputes and personal feuds. The following extract gives an idea of the contents. It describes the holdings of Earl Hugh of Chester (see The Human Experience, "Hugh, Earl of Chester") in the western county of Wiltshire. Notice the continued presence of slaves attached to these manors, alongside serfs and peasants with small holdings. The value is the estimated annual revenue.

Earl Hugh holds RETMORE [manor] and William from him.* Before 1066 it paid tax of 1/2 hide.† Land for 3 ploughs. In lordship 1 plough with 1 slave.
1 villager, 3 small holders and 11 cottagers with 1 plough.
A mill which pays 14s [shillings]; meadow, 5 acres; pasture 3 furlongs long and 1 furlong wide; woodland 3 furlongs long and 2 furlongs wide.
The value was 50s [in 1066]; now 60s.

The Earl also holds:
WILSFORD. Haimo holds from him. Before 1066 it paid tax for 1 hide. Land for 1 plough; it is in lordship; 2 slaves; 3 cottagers.
Meadow, 6 acres; pasture 8 furlongs long and 1 furlong wide.
Value 40s.

HARTHAM. Edward holds from him. Before 1066 it paid tax for 2 hides. Land for 3 ploughs. Of this land 1 hide in lordship; 2 ploughs there; 2 slaves.
1 man-at-arms and 3 cottagers.
Meadow, 5 acres; woodland, 3 acres; pasture, 12 acres.
Value 40s.

BURCOMBE. Haimo holds from him. Before 1066 it paid tax for 4 hides. Land for 2 ploughs. Of this land 3 hides in lordship; 1 plough there, with 1 slave.
1 villager and 4 smallholders.

A mill at 10s; meadow, 6 acres; woodland, 10 acres; pasture, 20 acres.
The value was £3; now £4.

CADENHAM. William holds from him. Before 1066 it paid tax for 2 hides. Land for 2 ploughs. In lordship 1 hide of these; 1 plough; 2 slaves.
8 smallholders with 1 plough.
Meadow, 5 acres; woodland 2 furlongs long and 1 furlong wide.
The value was 30s; now 40s.
Before 1066 Ednoth the Steward held these five manors.

FISHERTON (Anger). Haimo holds from him. Godric held it before 1066; it paid tax for 3 hides. Land for 2 ploughs, in lordship 2 hides of this land; 1 plough there; 1 slave.
3 villagers and 5 smallholders.
A mill at 10s; meadow, 40 acres' pasture, 40 acres.
The value was and is £3.

---

*That is, William is Earl Hugh's feudal subvassal. Earl Hugh himself is a vassal of King William.

†A hide was a unit of land measure, 120 acres.

Source: From *Domesday Book*, vol. 6: *Wiltshire*. John Morris, general ed., Caroline Thorn and Frank Thorn, eds., from a draft translation prepared by Caroline Thorn (Chichester, England: Phillimore, 1979), pp. 68d–69a.

to the all-important subject of land tenure, whether involving disputes between the king's tenants-in-chief or their sub-tenants, passed under royal jurisdiction in Henry II's reign. The political unification of the Anglo-Saxon kings, beginning in the late ninth century, was now paralleled by a legal unification under the expanding jurisdiction of the twelfth-century royal courts.

Unless royal rights were involved, Henry's courts used sworn juries to collect evidence and return indictments, but did not try cases. Often the lords who presided over local justice welcomed royal courts' intervention, which spared them the thankless job of investigating crimes and unraveling lawsuits. In Henry II's time, trials were conducted by the local lords, typically through an ordeal in

MAP 9-4

THE "ANGEVIN EMPIRE" AND THE KINGDOM OF FRANCE

This map shows the actual possessions and the feudal claims of the two leading monarchies of western Europe in the mid-twelfth century.

which God was supposed to uphold the right. The defendant was tossed into water to see whether he floated, or was required to pick up a hot iron to see how quickly his burned hand healed. Sometimes the opposing parties fought it out (although Henry also demanded the outlawing of "notorious" offenders even if they won). Medieval kings in general distrusted ordeals but found their subjects unwilling to leave matters to a jury. The heaviest blow to "judgments of God" came in 1215, when the Fourth Lateran Council banned clerical participation, and during the thirteenth century reliance on ordeals waned. By then, the royal courts' more rational means of reaching verdicts[4] was making them more attractive to claimants than the old baronial or shire courts.

The development of common law, which Henry's royal courts used, was of immense long-range importance in the

later history of English-speaking peoples. Some of the most important principles that Americans today regard as essential rights have their origin in the common law: jury trials, open courts rather than closed-door inquests, the accused's right of access to incriminating evidence, a ban on evidence obtained under torture, and the presumption of innocence rather than guilt. Modern European and Scottish experience demonstrates that it is possible to guarantee defendants' rights under the civil (that is, Roman) law tradition as well—but in the Middle Ages and long after, the civil law seemed weighted on the side of the state. That the common law became well entrenched in England before the great revival of civil law took effect in Continental courts is a mark of the power and effectiveness of Henry II's government of England.

Predictably, Henry II sought to expand royal justice at the expense of the ecclesiastical courts, whose authority had also been increasing. The growing power of the international church was coming more and more to clash with the expanding administrations of England and other secular states. Royal and ecclesiastical governments were both growing in the twelfth century, and conflicts between them were bound to occur. The first great conflict, during Henry I's reign, had centered on Anselm; the second, under Henry II, swirled around Becket.

In 1162 Henry sought to bring the English church under strict royal control by appointing to the archbishopric of Canterbury his chancellor and good friend, Thomas Becket. But Henry had misjudged his man. As chancellor, Becket had been a devoted royal servant, but as archbishop of Canterbury he became a fervent defender of ecclesiastical independence and an implacable—some historians would say paranoid—royal enemy. Henry and Becket clashed heatedly over the issue of royal control of the English church and royal interference in the decisions of church courts. By 1164 their quarrel had become so violent that Becket fled to France. Finally, in 1170, the king and archbishop patched up a truce, and Becket returned to Canterbury. He then infuriated Henry once more by excommunicating a number of the king's supporters. Four of Henry's barons, overreacting to the royal anger, went to Canterbury cathedral and murdered Becket while he was praying at the altar.

This dramatic crime made a deep impact on the age. People in England and abroad regarded Becket as a martyr; tales spread of miracles at his tomb, and the papacy quickly proclaimed him a saint. For the remainder of the Middle Ages, Canterbury was a major pilgrimage center, and the cult of St. Thomas enjoyed immense popularity.[5] Henry, who had not ordered the killing but whose anger had prompted it, did penance by walking barefoot through the streets of Canterbury and submitting to a ceremonial

---

[4] The word *verdict* comes from two Latin words meaning "to speak the truth."

[5] His elaborate shrine was destroyed during the Reformation.

The Killing of Archbishop Becket Becket's brutal murder as he stood before his altar shocked all of Christendom, and public opinion immediately acclaimed him as a saint. Many depictions of the crime appear in contemporary chronicles. This illumination is from a manuscript of the Book of Psalms produced in an English abbey. Besides Becket and his killers, the other figures include saints Paul, Catherine, and Margaret, the bishop of York, and the abbey's founder. *By permission of the British Library. Shelfmark/ Man: Cott. Claud. B. 11 Folio: 341.*

flogging. Nevertheless, the king succeeded generally in arranging the appointments of churchmen friendly to the crown, and by the end of his reign royal justice had made significant inroads on the independence of the church and the authority of church courts. Here as elsewhere, Henry was steering England toward administrative and legal centralization.

Throughout his reign Henry divided his time between England and the French provinces of his "Angevin Empire," while the French monarchy did what it could to break up these dominions—encouraging rebellions on the part of Henry's sons and his estranged wife, Eleanor of Aquitaine. Henry put down the rebellions one by one, relegated Eleanor to comfortable captivity in a royal castle, and tried to placate his sons. It did him little good. The rebellions persisted, and as Henry lay dying in 1189 his two surviving sons, Richard and John, were both in arms against him. In the end the old king was outmaneuvered and defeated by his sons and the French. "Shame, shame on a conquered king," he reportedly murmured in dying.

John of Salisbury and the Obligations of Kingship While Henry II and Becket were contending, one of the greatest of English medieval scholars was at work in Becket's chancellery. John of Salisbury (ca. 1115–1180) was a gentle man, devoted to logic and to the restoration of the liberal arts, a student of Greek and a lover of classical literature. By serving Becket faithfully, he earned the royal enmity, and therefore had to spend much of his career beyond the reach of Angevin power—at Paris and at Chartres, where he eventually became bishop. While in Becket's service, his reading of Aristotle and other ancient philosophers set him to pondering how peace might be restored and justice ensured, and in 1159 he produced *Policraticus,* a major contribution to medieval political philosophy.

John was no apologist for theocracy. He acknowledged the divine nature of kingship but emphasized equally its responsibilities and limitations. The king draws his authority from God but is commissioned to rule for the good of his subjects rather than himself. He is bound to give his subjects peace and justice and to protect the church. If he abuses his commission and neglects his responsibilities, he loses his divine authority, ceases to be a rightful king, and becomes a tyrant. As such, he forfeits his subjects' allegiance and is no longer their lawful ruler. Under extreme circumstances, and if all else fails, John suggested tyrannicide. A good Christian subject, although obliged to obey his king, may, as a last resort, kill a tyrant. Henry II was not happy to learn about such theorizing.

Apart from the highly original doctrine of tyrannicide, (which John qualified so severely as virtually to rule it out), the views expressed in the *Policraticus* mirror the general political attitudes of the twelfth century: responsible limited monarchy and government in behalf of the governed. These theories, in turn, were idealized reflections of the actual monarchies of the day, whose power was held in check by the nobility, the church, and ancient custom. The day would come when the leading men of England would take practical action to impose such checks.

The Making of Magna Carta: Richard and John, 1189–1216

Although Henry II's final days were saddened by defeat, his Angevin dominions remained intact, passing into the hands of his eldest surviving son, Richard I, the Lion-Hearted (reigned 1189–1199). This warrior-king devoted himself chiefly to defending his French possessions and crusading against the Muslims.

Richard was a skillful soldier who not only won renown as a tournament champion and on the Third Crusade but also foiled every attempt of the French monarchy to reduce his Continental territories. During Richard's protracted absences, the bureaucracy established by his royal predecessors governed England satisfactorily for ten kingless years and even produced the huge ransom demanded by Emperor Henry VI, who had imprisoned Richard on his homeward journey from the Holy Land (see earlier). He died prematurely in battle against the French in 1099.

Richard the Lion-Hearted's younger brother, King John (reigned 1199–1216), is an enigmatic figure: brilliant in certain respects, a master of administrative detail, but suspicious, unscrupulous, and mistrusted. His crisis-prone career was sabotaged repeatedly by the halfheartedness with which his overtaxed vassals supported him, and by the energy with which some of them opposed him.

In Philip Augustus of France (reigned 1180–1223) John had a shrewd, unremitting antagonist. Taking full advantage of his position as overlord of John's Continental possessions, King Philip summoned John to the French royal court to answer charges brought against him by one of his own Aquitainian vassals. When John refused to come, Philip Augustus declared his French lands forfeited and invaded Normandy. In the chaos that followed, Philip Augustus was able to seize all of John's French dominions except portions of distant Aquitaine—most importantly, Gascony. King John had suffered a monstrous political and

military disaster. In the ten years after 1204, John wove a subtle web of alliances against King Philip, financed by the severe taxation of his English subjects. But his plans were shattered by Philip's decisive victory over John's Flemish and German allies at the battle of Bouvines in 1214. John's last hope of recovering Normandy and Anjou collapsed.

John also quarreled bitterly with Innocent III over the appointment of an archbishop of Canterbury. Here again, after a long struggle, John had to submit. In 1213 he accepted the pope's candidate for the archbishopric and indeed, in an effort to regain Innocent's diplomatic friendship, went so far as to concede to the papacy the overlordship of England and a substantial annual tribute to Rome.

Many of John's own barons were by then regarding him with hostility and contempt. The Bouvines disaster of 1214, on the heels of a long series of expensive and humiliating diplomatic setbacks, dimmed John's prestige still further. His diplomatic failures paved the way for the uprising of English barons that ended on the field of Runnymede in 1215, where they forced John to issue Magna Carta (the Great Charter). John had been taxing his subjects with grim efficiency to support his luckless military and diplomatic maneuvers, and he had proven himself much less adroit than his royal predecessors in winning the support of great magnates through favoritism and patronage. He also had a most regrettable habit of sexually harassing his barons' wives. His baronial enemies had good reason to hate him.

Magna Carta has been interpreted in contradictory ways—as the foundation stone of England's later constitutional monarchy, and as a backward-looking document designed to bolster the old aristocracy at the expense of the enlightened Angevin regime. Magna Carta was both. More to the point, its authors were looking neither forward nor backward but were contending with problems of the moment. Magna Carta's more important clauses were designed to keep the king within the bounds of popular sentiment and feudal custom. Royal taxes unsanctioned by custom, for example, were to be levied only with the consent of the great men of the kingdom. But implicit in the traditional doctrine that the lord had to respect the rights of his vassals and rule according to good custom was the constitutional principle of government under the law. In striving to make King John a good feudal lord, the barons in 1215 were groping toward constitutional monarchy. Thus Magna Carta expresses the notion that the king is bound by traditional legal constraints in his dealings with all classes of free English people. John of Salisbury would not have disagreed.

The chief constitutional problem in the years following Magna Carta was the question of how an unwilling king might be forced to stay within the bounds of law. Magna Carta itself relied on a watchdog committee of twenty-five barons who were empowered, should the king

THE HISTORICAL EVIDENCE

Magna Carta

1215

The "Great Charter" that the barons and high churchmen of England extracted from King John is a long document, and many of its clauses deal with specific offenses against feudal custom that John had been committing (and intended to keep on committing). Moreover, it applied only to the king's free subjects, at a time when as many as 80 percent of the English people were serfs. But scattered among Magna Carta's clauses were provisions that aim at ensuring a more sweeping respect for the rule of law. And as serfdom slowly disappeared in the generations that followed, the majority of people got the right to claim English liberties.

John, by the grace of God, king of England, lord of Ireland, duke of Normandy and Aquitaine, count of Anjou, to the archbishops, bishops, abbots, earls, barons, justiciars, foresters, sheriffs, reeves, servants, and all bailiffs, and his faithful people greeting. . . .

14. And for holding a common council of the kingdom concerning the assessment of an aid otherwise than in the three cases mentioned above, or concerning the assessment of a scutage* we shall cause to be summoned our archbishops . . . barons . . . [and other great lords]; and besides we shall cause to be summoned generally, by our sheriffs and bailiffs all those who hold from us in chief, for a certain day, that is at the end of forty days at least, and for a certain place; and in all the letters of that summons, we will express the cause of that summons, and when the summons has been given the business shall proceed on the appointed day, on the advice of those who shall be present, even if not all of those who were summoned have come.

21. Earls and barons shall only be fined by their peers, and only in proportion to their offence.

39. No free man shall be taken or imprisoned or dispossessed, or outlawed, or banished, or in any way destroyed, nor will we go upon him, nor send upon him, except by the legal judgment of his peers or by the law of the land.

40. To no one will we sell, to no one will we deny or delay, right or justice.

41. All merchants shall be safe and secure in going out from England and entering into England and in remaining and going through England, as well by land as by water, for buying and selling, free from all evil tolls, by the ancient and rightful customs, except in time of war, and if they are of a land at war with us; and if such are found in our land at the beginning of war, they shall be attached without injury to their bodies or goods, until it shall be known from us or from our principal justiciar in what way the merchants of our land are treated who shall then be found in the country which is at war with us; and if ours are safe there, the others shall be safe in our land.

52. If anyone shall have been dispossessed or removed by us without legal judgment of his peers, from his lands, castles, franchises, or his right we will restore them to him immediately; and if contention arises about this, then it shall be done according to the judgment of the twenty-five barons, of whom mention is made below concerning the security of the peace.[†]

---

*Earlier provisions had listed the fixed revenues ("aids") that the king was entitled to collect without consulting his subjects. For scutage, see Chapter 8.

[†]This refers to the watchdog committee established to ensure the king's compliance with his promises, as described in this chapter.

Source: From *University of Pennsylvania Translations and Reprints*, ed. and trans. E. P. Cheyney (Philadelphia: University of Pennsylvania, 1897), vol. 1, no. 6, pp. 6–16.

---

violate the charter, to call on the English people "to distrain and distress him in every possible way." The committee was not long idle, for John had no intention of carrying out his promises. He repudiated Magna Carta at the first opportunity, with the full backing of his papal overlord, Innocent III. The result was a full-scale revolt that ended only with John's death in 1216. The crown now passed, without objection, to his nine-year-old son, Henry III (reigned 1216–1272), supervised by a baronial council.

Barons, Bureaucrats, Common Law, and Parliament: From Henry III to Edward I, 1216–1307   In the course of Henry III's troubled fifty-six year reign, the English baronage attempted several major rebellions—not with the

Edward I's Stone Fortress in North Wales Contrast this stone fortress with the motte-and-bailey castle illustrated on p. 319. The greater resources that Edward I needed to command in order to build and provision strongholds such as this are readily apparent. © R. Sheridan/Ancient Art & Architecture Collection.

purpose of weakening the royal administration but, rather, in hopes of sharing in its control. The king, forced to recognize the demands of the magnates to participate more fully in the governance of the realm, gradually transformed the great baronial royal council—the Curia Regis—into Parliament. Henry III was lucky to survive defeat and temporary captivity at the hands of a large baronial coalition, and to die peacefully, still wearing his crown.

Henry III's son, Edward I, was a far abler monarch. The royal bureaucracy developed during his reign into a complex and efficient machine, and a system of royal courts was by then well established. Edward I completed the conquest of Wales and, to keep the turbulent Welsh in check, he built a series of enormous and elaborate stone castles, many of which stand to this day. He defended his remaining territories in southern France (Gascony) and came close to conquering Scotland.

By the beginning of Edward I's reign the power struggle between monarchy and baronage was largely resolved. Whenever the king issued a **statute** (that is, made a new law replacing custom or superseding an old law), proclaimed new taxes, or imposed unusual military demands on his subjects, he now did so "in parliament"—with the consent of the great barons and churchmen of the realm sitting with him in council. The soaring prosperity of town and countryside in the course of the thirteenth century resulted in the inclusion in the royal parliaments of representative townspeople, and members of the rural **gentry**— "knights of the shire." The composition of Edward I's parliaments varied, but by the close of the century they were coming to include all three classes of free laymen—barons, shire knights, and townspeople (with bishops and abbots meeting separately in "convocations"). In the course of the fourteenth century the townspeople and shire gentry split off into a separate House of Commons, which later got a grip on the royal purse strings.

Edward I completed the work of his predecessors by creating an effective and complex royal administrative system, bringing baronial justice under royal control, and building a comprehensive body of common law. Jury trials using common law (thus abolishing trial by ordeal) became compulsory under a royal statute in 1275. And the king nurtured the developing institution of Parliament, setting into motion forces that would have an immense impact on the future.

By Edward I's time, one other change was well under way in England as well, destined as much as Parliament and the common law to foster a sense of English nationhood. Ever since 1066, the spoken language of England's ruling class—the king and his court, the aristocracy, and high churchmen—had been Norman French. The Anglo-Saxon, or Old English, language was spoken by ordinary people. But during the thirteenth century, as English rule ended in many of the provinces of western France that had constituted Henry II's "Angevin Empire," the king's mighty men found themselves obliged to rely primarily on their English properties for their prosperity. Spending more time in England, they began speaking English more readily than French, although their version of English simplified the complex Germanic grammar of Anglo-Saxon and was heavily larded with words of French and Latin origin. The result was a linguistic mishmash known as Middle English, with a relatively streamlined grammar and a much expanded vocabulary. In 1295, the upper class was sufficiently proud of its linguistic independence that Edward I could warn that the consequence of a successful French

THE HISTORICAL EVIDENCE

Edward I Summons Parliament

1295

Facing an expensive war with Philip the Fair of France, in 1295 England's Edward I issued similar but separately addressed summonses to the bishops, barons, and representatives of shires and towns to meet with him in Parliament. Notice the king's overt appeal to English nationalism. The text of the king's summons to the archbishop of Canterbury is presented below; it is the longest and most rhetorical of all. Why does the king insist that representatives have "full and sufficient power"?

The king to the venerable father in Christ Robert, by the same grace archbishop of Canterbury, primate of all England, greeting. As a most just law, established by the careful providence of sacred princes, exhorts and decrees that what affects all, by all should be approved, so also, very evidently should common danger be met by means provided in common. You know sufficiently well, and it is now, as we believe, divulged through all regions of the world, how the king of France fraudulently and craftily deprives us of our land of Gascony, by withholding it most unjustly from us. Now, however, not satisfied with the before-mentioned fraud and injustice, having gathered together for the conquest of our kingdom a very great fleet, and an abounding multitude of warriors, with which he has made a hostile attack on our kingdom and the inhabitants of the same kingdom, he now proposes to destroy the English language altogether from the earth, if his power should correspond to the detestable proposition of the contemplated injustice, which God forbid. Because, therefore, darts seen beforehand do less injury, and your interest especially, as that of

the rest of the citizens of the same realm, is concerned in this affair, we command you, strictly enjoining you in fidelity and love in which you are bound to us, that upon the Lord's day next after the feast of St. Martin [in early November] in the approaching winter, you be present in person at Westminister; citing beforehand the dean and chapter of your church, the archdeacons and all the clergy of your diocese, causing the same dean and archdeacons in their own persons, and the said chapter by one suitable proctor, and the said clergy by two, to be present along with you, having full and sufficient power from the same chapter and clergy, to consider, ordain, and provide, along with us and the rest of the prelates and principal men and other inhabitants of our kingdom, how the dangers and threatened evils of this kind are to be met. Witness the king at Wangham, the thirtieth day of September.

Source: From *University of Pennsylvania Translations and Reprints*, ed. and trans. E. P. Cheney (Philadelphia: University of Pennsylvania, 1897), vol. 1, no. 6, pp. 33–35.

---

invasion would be the destruction of English speech.[6] In fact, as we shall see in Chapter 11, the dawning fourteenth century would see the writing of the supreme literary masterpiece in East Midlands dialect of Middle English, Geoffrey Chaucer's *Canterbury Tales*.

France: The Monarchy Triumphant

While William of Normandy was conquering England in 1066, his nominal feudal overlord, the king of France, was exercising unsteady control over a modest territory around

Paris and Orléans known as the Île de France. Beyond that, however, the French king was virtually powerless (refer again to Map 9-4). Although the French monarchy claimed the overlordship of great princes such as the dukes of Normandy and Aquitaine and the counts of Anjou, Flanders, and Champagne, only gradually did it acquire the power and prestige to make good this claim. From modest beginnings, the Capetians became the foremost dynasty in Christendom and headed a proto-modern bureaucracy comparable to England's.

The Early Capetian Kings
The Capetians (987–1328) had gained the throne originally by being elected by the magnates (great lords) of the realm. But from the first they sought to make their kingship hereditary. This they accomplished by producing male heirs at the right moment and by arranging for the new heir to be crowned before the old king died. Astonishingly, they sired male heirs for no less than eleven generations, across 341 years. And the stability of

---

[6] See above for "Edward I Summons Parliament". What he meant was that a French conquest might dispossess the Anglo-Norman ruling class, as William the Conqueror had expropriated the Anglo-Saxon nobility after 1066. The French of 1295 cannot be charged with planning to make every English peasant speak French (shortsighted as this might seem to modern French patriots).

their dynasty was further enhanced by the ability of Capetian younger sons to resist grasping at the crown through rebellion (see Figure 9-2).

In the early twelfth century the Capetians remained no stronger than several of their own princely vassals. While principalities such as Normandy and Anjou were becoming increasingly centralized, the Capetian Île de France, a fertile grain-growing district of great potential value to the monarchy, was still plagued with insubordinate barons. If the Capetians were to realize the potential of their royal title they had to deal with three great challenges: First, to master and pacify the Île de France; second,

to expand their political and economic base by bringing additional territories under direct royal authority; and third, to make their lordship over the great feudal principalities real rather than merely theoretical. Over the next two hundred years the Capetians achieved these goals so completely that by the close of the thirteenth century they controlled much of France, either directly or indirectly, and had built an efficient, sophisticated royal bureaucracy. This triumph, aided by both luck and ingenuity, was achieved by exploiting their powers as kings and overlords, by avoiding family squabbles, and by staying on comparatively good terms with the papacy.

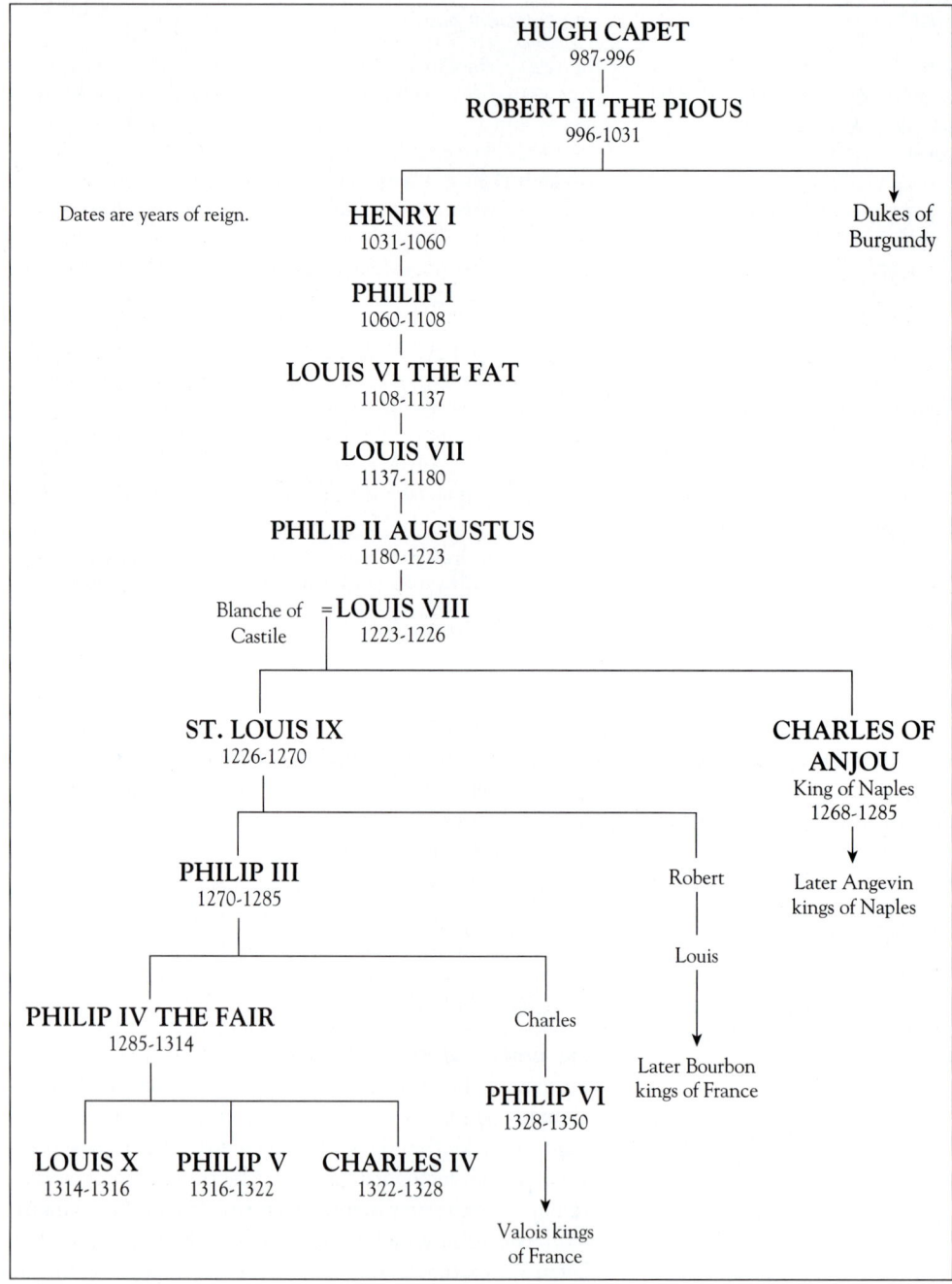

FIGURE 9-2
THE CAPETIAN KINGS OF FRANCE

Capitalizing on the enormous good fortune of an unbroken sequence of direct male heirs, the Capetians seldom overreached themselves and avoided grandiose schemes. They preferred to extend their power gradually and cautiously by entering into favorable marriages, by confiscating the fiefs of vassals who died without heirs, and by dispossessing vassals who violated their feudal obligations. Yet the majority of the Capetians had no desire to absorb the territories of all their vassals; rather they sought to build a kingdom with a substantial core of royal demesne lands surrounded by the fiefs of loyal, obedient magnates.

The first Capetian to work seriously toward consolidating royal control in the Île de France was King Philip I (reigned 1060–1108), a bloated hedonist who grasped the basic fact that the monarchy must make its home base secure (see Table 9-2.) Philip's realistic policy was pursued far more vigorously by his son, Louis VI "the Fat" (reigned 1108–1137)—gluttonous and mediocre, but blessed with an intelligent wife, Adelaide of Murienne. Encouraged by Queen Adelaide, Louis the Fat battled dissident barons year after year, until he could no longer find a horse with the strength to carry his ever-increasing weight. Yet by his death in 1137, the Île de France was orderly and prosperous, and the French monarchy was stronger than it had been since Carolingian times.

Louis the Fat received invaluable assistance in the later years of his reign from Abbot Suger of the great royal-sponsored monastery of St.-Denis near Paris. This gifted statesman served as chief royal adviser for some twenty years and labored hard and effectively to extend the king's sway and systematize the royal administration. The support of St.-Denis—the abbey and its patron saint—added much to the prestige of the Capetian house, whose support, in turn, enhanced the wealth and prestige of the royal abbey. Suger wrote an admiring biography of Louis VI—the first of

The Abbey of St.-Denis   As the traditional burial place of the kings and the shrine of the kingdom's patron saint, the abbey of St.-Denis had tremendous spiritual, cultural, and political significance for medieval France. In addition to his work as a statesman and historian, Abbot Suger set in motion the spread of the Gothic architectural style with the partial reconstruction of the abbey church. See pages 355–358 for more on Suger's activity as an architectural innovator. The photograph here shows how the abbey church appeared in the mid-thirteenth century, after extensive remodeling in the Gothic style.   *A. F. Kersting.*

TABLE 9-2	
FRANCE IN THE HIGH MIDDLE AGES	
987–1328	Rule of the Capetian Dynasty
1060–1108	Reign of Philip I
1108–1137	Reign of Louis VI "the Fat"
1137–1180	Reign of Louis VII
1180–1223	Reign of Philip II (Philip Augustus)
1223–1226	Reign of Louis VIII
1226–1270	Reign of Louis IX (St. Louis)
1270–1285	Reign of Philip III
1285–1314	Reign of Philip IV "the Fair"

a long series of French royal biographies written by monks of St.-Denis to glorify the Capetian kings.

Suger provided invaluable continuity between the reigns of Louis the Fat and his son, Louis VII (reigned 1137–1180). Pious and gentle, Louis VII was, in the words of one contemporary observer, "a very Christian king, if somewhat simple-minded." When Abbot Suger died in 1151, Louis was left to face unaided a formidable new threat to the French monarchy. The Angevin dominions were just then taking shape, and in 1154 the ominous configuration was completed when Henry Plantagenet, count of Anjou and duke of Normandy and Aquitaine, mounted the English throne as King Henry II. Louis VII sought to embarrass his mighty vassal by encouraging Henry's sons to rebel, but his efforts were too halfhearted to succeed.

Still, Louis's reign witnessed a significant extension of royal power. The great vassals of the crown, fearful of Henry II and respectful of Louis's impartiality and piety, began for the first time to bring cases to the court of their royal overlord and submit their disputes to his judgment. Churchmen and townspeople alike sought his support in their struggles with the nobility. These changes resulted not so much from royal initiative as from the fundamental trends of the age toward peace, order, and growing commercial activity. The French were turning increasingly to their genial, unassuming monarch for succor and justice. And the fertile Île de France, now well pacified, was providing more and more revenue for the Capetian treasury.

The Expansive King: Philip Augustus, 1180–1223

The French monarchy came of age under Louis VII's talented son, Philip (II) Augustus. By dexterous opportunism, Philip Augustus enlarged the royal territories enormously and tightened his overlordship of the remaining principalities.

Philip Augustus's great achievement was the destruction of the "Angevin Empire" and the establishment of royal jurisdiction over Normandy, Anjou, and their dependencies. For two decades he plotted against Henry II and Richard the Lion-Hearted; but it was not until the reign of King John of England (1199–1216) that Philip's efforts bore fruit. Against John's faithlessness, Philip was able to play the role of the just lord rightfully punishing a disobedient vassal. When Philip Augustus moved against Normandy during 1203 and 1204, John's unpopularity and remarkable inactivity played into the French king's hands. The prize that Philip had sought so long was now won with surprising ease. And once Normandy was conquered, John's remaining fiefs in northern France fell quickly. Ten years later, in 1214, Philip won his decisive victory over John at Bouvines (discussed earlier in the chapter). Settling for good the question of Normandy and Anjou, Bouvines was also a turning point in the power balance between France and Germany in the High Middle Ages. Thereafter the Capetian monarchy overshadowed the faltering kingdom of Germany and the much reduced territories of the kings of England. France became the great power in thirteenth-century Christendom.

Under Philip Augustus and his predecessors, significant improvements were occurring in royal administration. The royal court of justice (Curia Regis) had become the high feudal court of France and was proving an effective instrument for the assertion of royal rights. Hereditary noblemen who had traditionally served as local administrators in the royal territories were gradually replaced by salaried officials known as *baillis* (the French equivalent of the English word *bailiff*). These new officials, whose func-

tions were at once financial, judicial, military, and administrative, owed their positions to royal favor and were devoted to the crown. Throughout the thirteenth century the baillis worked tirelessly and often unscrupulously to erode the privileges of the aristocracy and extend the royal sway. This loyal and highly mobile bureaucracy, often lacking local roots, became in time a powerful instrument of royal absolutism. The baillis stood in sharp contrast to their English counterparts—the sheriffs and shire knights—who were usually drawn from the local gentry and had divided loyalties. Often, indeed, the baillis were not born nobles, but men of burgher origin. For many centuries to come, French kings would recruit their important officials from the bourgeoisie and offer them noble rank as a reward for faithful service.

Philip Augustus transformed Paris into the royal capital of France. Paris had previously been the largest city in France, with a population of perhaps twenty-five thousand, and was the major center of a royal government that, like the English, meandered constantly from place to place. Now, Philip kept his government more permanently in Paris, ruling from his royal palace at the west end of the island in the Seine, the Île de la Cité, which was also the site of the cathedral of Notre-Dame, nearing completion in King Philip's time. Philip erected great walls around the city, paved its major streets, and built a fortress, the Louvre, just outside the walls near the Seine as it flowed westward toward Normandy. (For centuries the Louvre served as a royal palace; today it is one of the world's great museums, and the recently discovered walls of Philip Augustus can be seen from an underground gallery beneath it.) In Philip Augustus's time, the population of Paris doubled to some fifty thousand—making it the largest city in Europe north of the Alps.

The closing years of Philip Augustus's reign coincided with the Albigensian Crusade, called by Pope Innocent III against the heretics of southern France (see Chapter 8). Philip Augustus personally stayed out of the crusade, but his son took an active part in it. And when the prince succeeded to his father's throne in 1223 as Louis VIII, he used all the resources of the monarchy to break the power of the Albigensians and extend Capetian royal authority southward to the Mediterranean.

It may seem surprising that Louis VIII, who inherited a vastly expanded royal jurisdiction and extended it still farther himself, gave out about a third of the hard-won royal territories as fiefs to junior members of his family. These family fiefs, carved out of the royal demesne, are known as *apanages*. Their creation should serve as a warning that the growth of the Capetian monarchy cannot be understood simply as a linear process of expanding the royal territories. The Capetians recognized the importance of keeping younger royal sons happy and did not hesitate to grant them counties and duchies. Indeed, given the limited transportation and communication facilities of twelfth- and thirteenth-century France, the kingdom was too large to be controlled directly by the king. At least for the time being the new vassals, bound to the crown by strong family ties, strengthened rather than weakened Capetian rule.

The Ideal King: St. Louis, 1226–1270   Louis VIII died prematurely in 1226, leaving the kingdom in the skillful hands of his pious Spanish widow, Blanche of Castile, who acted as regent for the boy-king Louis IX, the later St. Louis. Even after Louis came of age in 1234 he remained devoted to his mother, and Queen Blanche continued for years to play a dominant and highly capable role in the royal government.

St. Louis possessed both his mother's sanctity and her firmness. He was a strong monarch, determined to rule justly and to promote moral rectitude throughout the kingdom of France. His policy was to pursue peace at home while devoting every resource to crusading against the Muslims. Like earlier crusaders, he hated Judaism: He launched a major effort to "persuade" Jewish children to become Christians. But although clearly less tolerant of Jews than his contemporary, Emperor Frederick II, he protected his Jewish subjects from grassroots violence more effectively than, for example, Henry III in England.

St. Louis was content, in general, to maintain the royal rights established by his predecessors. His baillis and other officials were actually far more aggressive than he in extending royal power. Indeed, St. Louis established a system of itinerant royal inspectors known as *enquêteurs*, who reported local grievances and helped keep ambitious officials in check. Originally instituted to keep order during Louis's absence on the crusade, the enquêteurs labored through the remainder of the reign to restrain the abuses of other royal agents.

As we have seen, Louis's first crusade failed, and the king interpreted this outcome as a divine punishment for his sins. From his return in 1254 until his death in 1270 he dedicated himself to creating an ideal Christian monarchy. He opened the royal courts to all freemen (non-serfs) and did everything in his power to ensure that royal justice was fair and compassionate. He sponsored charitable works on an unprecedented scale. He instituted a new gold coinage of high quality, to the great benefit of French commerce. He labored to achieve peace throughout Christendom, arranging treaties with Henry III of England and with the king of Aragon that settled all outstanding disputes. He became a venerated peacemaker among Christians and was even called on to arbitrate between Henry III and his barons (who were chagrined when he decided solidly in favor of royal authority).

In St. Louis's France, medieval culture blossomed as never before. Towns and commerce flourished, and in the towns magnificent Gothic churches were rising. Louis's own palace chapel in Paris, La Ste.-Chapelle, built to house Jesus' crown of thorns, is one of the most beautiful

La Ste.-Chapelle, Paris   The walls of La Ste.-Chapelle consist primarily of glass, supported by buttresses on the outside. It is one of the greatest masterpieces of Gothic architecture (see Chapter 10).   *Scala/Art Resource, NY.*

buildings on earth. Under St. Louis the University of Paris became, even more plainly than before, Europe's foremost intellectual center, where some of the keenest minds of the age—Bonaventure, Albertus Magnus, Thomas Aquinas—were assembled (see Chapter 10).

Louis died while on a new crusade in 1270, victory still eluding him. His most cherished goal was never realized, but his policies at home won him the hearts of his Christian (not his Jewish) subjects. His reign brought enduring prestige and sanctity to the Capetian family and the French monarchy.

The Masterful King: Philip IV "the Fair," 1285–1314   St. Louis was loved and admired for keeping his ambitious officials in check. Under his successors the royal bureaucracy pursued centralization with little restraint. The saint-king was succeeded first by his son, Philip III (reigned 1270–1285), then by his grandson, Philip IV "the Fair" or "the Handsome" (reigned 1285–1314). Philip the Fair was a silent, enigmatic figure who fails to emerge from the

THE HUMAN EXPERIENCE

Blanche of Castile

Blanche of Castile, one of medieval Europe's most gifted rulers, was born in the south of Spain of royal parents in 1188. Her father was Alfonso VIII, king of the Spanish Christian kingdom of Castile. Her mother, Eleanor, was a daughter of Henry II of England and Eleanor of Aquitaine. If Eleanor of Aquitaine was the most celebrated queen of the High Middle Ages, her nearest rival was her granddaughter, Blanche of Castile.

As the result of a treaty concluded in 1200 between King John of England and King Philip Augustus of France, John's niece, Blanche of Castile, was married to King Philip's son, the future King Louis VIII. Blanche was twelve years old at the time, and her bridegroom was thirteen.

When King Philip Augustus died in 1223, full of years and triumphs, Blanche and Louis became the queen and king of France. Louis was reputed to be a gentle king, lacking his father's determination; but his regime benefited from his wife's keen intelligence and resolution. Louis devoted his final years to a successful military campaign against the Albigensian heretics and their allies in southern France, in the process of which the authority of the Capetian monarchy was established in Languedoc for the first time. But in 1226, at the age of 39, Louis died in the course of his campaigning, leaving his widow to rule France as regent for their twelve-

year-old eldest son, Louis IX—the future St. Louis.

In the years just following Louis's death, the great gains that the Capetian monarchy had achieved during the previous century were severely challenged. Rebellious coalitions of French nobles emerged to reclaim the power and independence they had lost to the boy-king's predecessors. These rebel alliances usually enjoyed the backing of King Henry III of England, who sought to regain the French principalities that his father King John had lost to Philip Augustus. The future of the Capetian monarchy hung in the balance, and the fact that it survived these troubled years and emerged with renewed strength is largely a product of Queen Blanche's statecraft.

In her young son's name, Blanche negotiated alliances, led armies, besieged castles, and in general overawed and outwitted her enemies through her astute and resolute leadership. She was celebrated not only for her skill in warfare and diplomacy but also for her deep piety, and she managed to transmit both these qualities to her son Louis, whose education she oversaw (see the accompanying illustration, from a contemporary manuscript). Altogether Blanche bore her husband twelve or thirteen children, but only six of them outlived their father. Louis, the eldest, was himself frail and afflicted with poor health, yet

Blanche is reported to have said that she would rather her son should die than that he should commit a mortal sin. For death could be a portal into paradise, whereas mortal sin, if unconfessed and unforgiven, doomed its perpetrator to eternal damnation.

Having been subdued by Blanche, some French nobles attacked her with ridicule. A proper sort of woman, they said, should not be leading armies or ruling kingdoms; such responsibilities should be exercised by men. Her enemies accused Blanche of being too haughty, of overspending, of having an affair with a papal legate, even of having conspired to bring about her late husband's death. Men sang comic songs about Blanche in the streets of Paris, portraying her as the she-wolf, "Dame Hersent," in the immensely popular set of fables about Reynard the Fox.

As one would expect, Blanche survived these petty attacks and overcame the threats against her son Louis. By the time Louis married in 1234, Blanche's policies as regent had succeeded in quelling all dissent and in restoring Capetian authority to its height. During the years that followed, the young king continued to rely heavily on his mother's wise advice, to the apparent annoyance of his queen, Margaret of Provence, whose political sense did not compare to that of Blanche.

Nevertheless, Blanche's continued role at court during the fourteen

records of his reign as a rounded personality, although he is important in French history. Lacking St. Louis's benevolent charm, he said little and listened much. One of his bishops observed, "He is neither a man nor a beast; he is a statue." Yet Philip was genuinely pious, intensely so after the death of his wife in 1305, and he was intelligent. He also had a flair for choosing skillful ministers.

Philip and his ministers held a lofty view of the rightful authority of the monarchy, a conception derived in part

from Roman law. They sought to advance royal power at the expense of the papacy, the nobility, and neighboring states. Philip waged an inconclusive war against Edward I of England over western Aquitaine. He made a serious effort to absorb Flanders but was thwarted by a bloody uprising of Flemish nobles and townspeople, who routed his army at the battle of Courtrai in 1302. More successful was his policy of nibbling aggression to the east against the faltering Holy Roman Empire.

years (1234–1248) between Louis's marriage and his departure on a crusade caused friction within the royal family. Predictably, a distinct coolness developed between Blanche and Queen Margaret along classic bride versus mother-in-law lines. And in 1244 a sharp split developed between the policies of mother and son when Louis, suffering from a nearly fatal illness, vowed to organize and lead a great crusade if he should live. Blanche was firmly opposed to such a spectacular and perhaps foolish stroke of militant piety, but Louis was determined to carry out his vow: In 1248 he embarked on an ill-fated crusade, which cost him vast treasure and, for a time, his freedom. He left Blanche to serve as regent of France once again.

Blanche did so, as before, with great distinction until her death in 1252. Even as a woman in her sixties, with her health failing, Blanche succeeded in providing powerful backing for the crusade that she had advised against. She negotiated special taxes from the church to support it; she consolidated Capetian control over the previously independent county of Toulouse; she completed the construction, begun by St. Louis, of a vast new crusade embarkation port on the Mediterranean; she carried on her son's reforms of the French royal administration; and she kept the peace. Her accomplishments were manifest and by now widely appreciated. The comic singers of Paris lapsed into silence; she was "Dame Hersent" no longer. A contemporary writer paid her what he meant to be the greatest possible compliment when he observed that she ruled as well as any man. ❖

Blanche Teaching Louis IX *The Pierport Morgan Library/Art Resource, NY.*

Like England's Edward I, Philip the Fair was constantly in need of money for his wars and was prepared to raise it by almost any means. In 1306 he arrested all the Jews in his kingdom, and after seizing their property and loan accounts, he expelled them from France. Edward I had treated English Jews in the same cruel fashion, and for similar reasons. Philip likewise despoiled his Lombard bankers. Another of his targets was the rich crusading order of Knights Templars, from whom he had been borrowing heavily. He darkened their reputation by a campaign of vituperative propaganda, much of which he may actually have believed. His preposterous charge that the Templars worshiped the devil was repeated by Edward II of England, and even by the papacy. Philip had more than fifty Templars burned at the stake as heretics, and their wealth found its way into the royal treasury. He launched a similar propaganda campaign against Pope Boniface VIII and, as we will discuss later in the chapter, sent his agents to arrest the proud old pope.

A Medieval French Coronation Medieval coronations were laden with spiritual symbolism. In this French miniature from the early fourteenth century, the new king has been anointed with holy oil and is being given the orb and scepter, signs of his authority to rule. *British Library, London, UK/The Bridgeman Art Lilbrary.*

Against his nobles, Philip pursued a strongly royalist policy, demanding direct allegiance and obedience from all the French within his overlordship, regardless of what duke or count might claim their loyalty. All these activities were manifestations of the prevailing political philosophy of his reign: that the French king was by right the secular and spiritual master of France and the dominating political figure in Western Christendom.

Throughout the thirteenth century the French royal bureaucracy had been developing steadily. The royal revenues came to be handled by a special accounting bureau, roughly parallel to the English exchequer, called the Chambre des Comptes. The king's judicial business became the responsibility of a high court known as the **Parlement** of Paris, which was to play a significant political role in later centuries.[7] Under Philip the Fair the bureaucracy became a refined and supple tool of the royal interest; its bourgeois officials, with their tenacious royalism, gave the king a degree of independence from the nobility unknown to contemporary England.

Still, the king could not rule without support from his subjects. Philip's victory over the papacy on the issue of royal taxation of the clergy and his attacks against the Jews and Knights Templars brought additional money into his

treasury. But the soaring expenses of government and warfare forced him to seek ever-new sources of revenue and, as in England, to secure his subjects' approval of extraordinary taxation. Instead of seeking such approval through kingdom-wide councils along the lines of the English parliaments, Philip usually negotiated individually with various taxpaying groups.

Nevertheless, it was under Philip the Fair that France's first kingdom-wide representative assemblies were summoned. Beginning in 1302, the Estates General was assembled from time to time, primarily to give formal support to the monarchy in moments of crisis—during the struggle with Pope Boniface VIII, for example, or in the midst of the Knights Templars controversy. The assembly included members of three great **estates:** the clergy, the nobility, and the townspeople. The Estates General continued to meet occasionally over the succeeding centuries, but it never became an integral organ of government as did Parliament in England. Its failure resulted in part from the fact that it had no real voice in royal taxation and was therefore not in a position to bargain with the king through increasing control of the purse strings. It was not, as in England, an evolutionary outgrowth of the royal council but an entirely separate body. There was no opportunity for burghers and gentry to join ranks, as in the English House of Commons; lacking the important responsibilities in local government that fell on English shire knights, the knights of France remained a subordinate part of the aristocratic order. Above all, the French nobility and bourgeoisie lagged behind the English in developing a national consciousness. Late thirteenth-

---

[7] The first step toward giving the Parlement of Paris an important place in the government of France had been taken under St. Louis, who began the practice of registering with this court the new laws that he promulgated. Far in the future, the Parlement would occasionally try to thwart the king by refusing to register new laws.

century France was too large, too segmented into cohesive principalities, and too recently brought under royal authority for its inhabitants to have acquired a strong sense of identification as a nation. Their outlook remained provincial.

Representative Assemblies

Despite the significant differences between the English Parliament and the French Estates General, the two institutions were kindred offspring of feudal monarchy. Both expressed the developing medieval concept of government by the consent of the realm. Similar representative institutions were emerging all over Western Christendom—in the kingdoms of Spain, in Italy under Frederick II, in the principalities of Germany, and in late-medieval Poland, Bohemia, Hungary, and Scandinavia. England's parliament was merely one expression of a broad and fundamental trend in medieval Europe.

In the opening years of the fourteenth century, the English Parliament was meeting regularly but the French Estates General only occasionally. The thirteenth-century conflicts between the English kings and nobility had resulted in a monarchy that routinely transacted its most important business in Parliament, with the assent of a nobility that was national in perspective. The outlines of modern England's parliamentary monarchy were already faintly visible in the thirteenth-century idea of a community of the realm.

In France, on the other hand, the crown had become the one great unifying concept. Originating in the cautious efforts of the twelfth-century Capetians, the concept was strengthened by Philip Augustus's military triumphs, reinforced still more by St. Louis's determination to create an ideal Christian monarchy, and given final shape by the royalist policy and propaganda of Philip the Fair.

In the course of the High Middle Ages, both monarchies developed effective royal administrations. Both

Edward I's Parliament
This stylized representation of Parliament (not necessarily a depiction of an actual session) shows the king enthroned at the upper center and flanked by his feudal subordinates: the king of Scotland, the prince of Wales (who in fact fought Edward), and England's two premier churchmen, the archbishops of Canterbury and York. On either side are seated the bishops (left) and barons (right). Royal judges sit in the center, on sacks of wool symbolizing England's dependence on the export of that commodity. Continuing this tradition, the chief justice of modern England still sits on a "woolsack." Representatives of the Commons are not depicted. *The Society of Antiquaries of London.*

tightened their control over baronial and ecclesiastical jurisdictions, although for centuries to come both would continue to share their sovereign authority (the right to tax, prosecute criminals, and adjudicate civil disputes) with their nobles, bishops, abbots, chartered towns, and rural communes. In 1300 the two regimes as yet had much in common. But with respect to the relationship between crown and community, their paths had clearly forked.

THE ROYAL-PAPAL STRUGGLE

In Chapter 8 we traced the clash of the reforming papacy with the medieval western emperors. This had been a struggle for the headship of Latin—indeed, of all—Christendom, and there were strongly theocratic claims on both sides. As we have seen, the conflict ended with the imperial power in western Europe shattered and its claims to religious leadership in tatters, and with the papacy the acknowledged spiritual overlord of Latin Christendom.

But while these titans fought it out, *royal* power, focused on individual kingdoms, had been striking deep roots in such lands as England, France, and Sicily. By and large, kings there were content to acknowledge the popes' spiritual headship, but they also strongly believed that God had given them a duty to look after their subjects' welfare in secular matters. When the high-medieval popes, who aimed at an all-encompassing leadership of all facets of Christian society, ran up against this conception of kingship, the results could be explosive.

The first place in which secular monarchy and the papacy collided was in the kingdom of Sicily, which had originated in the conquest of the island by Norman adventurers at about the same time that William the Conqueror was seizing England. Both Norman conquests had been blessed by the papacy, but in neither case did the Norman rulers accept permanent papal overlordship.

The Rise and Fall of the Kingdom of the Sun

One of the most militant forces in eleventh-century Europe was the ex-Viking aristocracy of Normandy, now Christian and increasingly French in culture. Driven by the pressure of population growth and the lure of lands and wealth, Norman knights waged war throughout Europe—in the reconquest of Spain, on the Crusades to the Holy Land, on the battlefields of England and France, and in southern Italy. In Sicily they built one of the most promising kingdoms of medieval Europe. Tragically but instructively, however, it ultimately failed.

The "Other" Norman Conquest The key figures in the Norman conquest of southern Italy were sons of a minor baron of northwest Normandy named Tancred de Hauteville. Tancred had twelve sons, and eight of them headed off to Italy in the 1030s and 1040s, poor in goods

but rich in ambition. In 1047 the most formidable of Tancred de Hauteville's sons, Robert Guiscard ("the Cunning"), arrived in southern Italy. The contemporary Byzantine princess Anna Comnena describes him as a man of tyrannical temper, cunning in mind, brave in action, tall and well-proportioned. His complexion was ruddy, his hair blond, his shoulders broad, and his eyes all but emitted sparks of fire. His bellow was loud enough to terrify armies—and he was ready to submit to nobody in all the world.

Robert Guiscard's wife, the Lombard princess Sichelgaita, was equally formidable and powerfully built, and she participated fully in the wars and politics of her era. Princess Anna Comnena was awed and terrified by Sichelgaita's military prowess: "When dressed in full armor, the woman was a fearsome sight."

Robert Guiscard began his Italian career as a bandit but gradually rose to become the leader of the southern Italian Normans. In 1059 his authority over southern Italy

Capella Palatina, Palermo The structural design of high nave and lower side aisles in the Capella Palatina derives from other churches of Western Christendom; the interior glitters with mosaics in the Byzantine style; and the decor of the vaulted ceiling suggests a Muslim paradise, inhabited by djinns instead of Christian angels. *Scala/Art Resource, NY.*

was recognized formally by the pope himself in the Treaty of Melfi, whereby Guiscard agreed to become a papal vassal and received in return the title of duke. Henceforth Robert Guiscard's conquests were "holy wars," and the papacy—which was becoming increasingly hostile toward the Holy Roman Empire to its north—came more and more to depend on Guiscard's support.

During the next quarter-century, Guiscard and his followers conquered all of southern Italy and the wealthy Muslim island of Sicily with its great port city of Palermo, one of the leading urban centers of the Islamic world. Palermo now became the largest and wealthiest city in Western Christendom, and its bustling harbor gave Guiscard the key to the central Mediterranean.

In the generations following Robert Guiscard's death in 1085, his Italian-Sicilian dominions became one of the wealthiest and best-governed states in medieval Europe. The lord-vassal structure of Norman feudalism was blended with the sophisticated administrative techniques of the South Italian Byzantines and the Sicilian Muslims. The mixing of cultures is vividly apparent in the Capella Palatina, built by Norman rulers of the twelfth century inside their palace at Palermo. The overall effect of the church, despite its diverse cultural ingredients, is one of great beauty and artistic unity—echoing the achievement of the southern Norman state in unifying peoples of many tongues and many pasts into a single, cohesive realm.

In the 1130s the papacy sanctioned the coronation of Guiscard's nephew, Roger the Great (d. 1154), as king of Sicily and southern Italy. Although officially known as the Kingdom of Sicily, the new Norman state, with the Sicilian metropolis of Palermo as its capital, included southern Italy as well. Roger the Great ruled strongly but tolerantly over the assorted peoples of his realm—Normans, Byzantines, Muslims, Jews, Italians, and Lombards—with their variety of faiths, customs, and languages. Palermo, with its superb

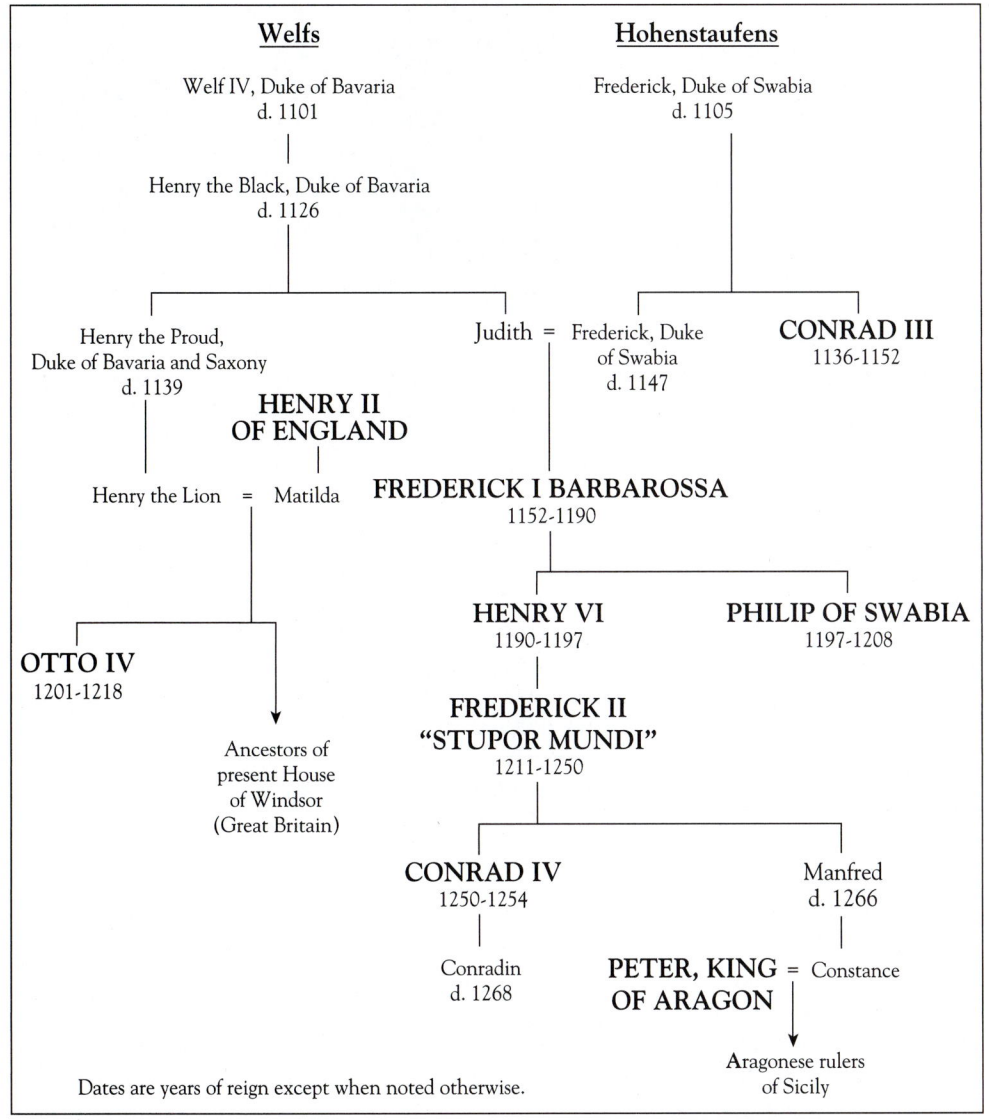

FIGURE 9-3
THE WELF AND HOHENSTAUFEN DYNASTIES

harbor and magnificent palace, its impressive public buildings and luxurious villas, was at once a great commercial center and a crucial point of cultural exchange. Known as the city of the threefold tongue, Palermo drew its administrators and scholars from the Latin, Byzantine, and Arabic traditions. The royal court was the hub of an efficient, centralized bureaucracy with special departments of justice and finance. The administration was staffed for the most part by non-noble professionals, devoted to the king and to bureaucratic efficiency. Drawing on the long experience of Byzantium and Islam, Roger's government was far in advance of most other states in Latin Christendom.

Under Roger and his successors the kingdom enjoyed a vital and diverse intellectual life. Sicily, like Spain, became a significant source of translations from Arabic and Greek into Latin. Sicilian translators provided western European scholars with a steady stream of texts from both classical Greek and Islamic sources, and these manuscripts, together with others reaching Europe from Spain, were the foundations of thirteenth-century Christendom's intellectual achievements.

In many ways Norman Sicily was western Europe's most interesting and fruitful frontier state. A center of intense interaction between Latin, Muslim, and Byzantine cultures, it demonstrated that the outer limits of Europe were not only advancing but also open. Europe besieged had given way to a new, expanding Europe, exposed to the invigorating influences of surrounding civilizations. And nowhere else except Spain was this cultural contact so intense as in Norman Sicily. East and West met in Roger the Great's sun-drenched realm and worked creatively side by side to make his kingdom the most sophisticated European state of its day.

As we saw in Chapter 8, Sicily and southern Italy eventually passed to imperial Germany's dynasty, the Hohenstaufens, when Frederick Barbarossa arranged the marriage of his son (the future Emperor Henry VI) to Princess Constance, heiress of the Norman realm. The son born of this marriage in 1194 was Frederick II, who grew up to become both Holy Roman emperor and king of Sicily (see Figure 9-3 on previous page).

"The Wonder of the World": Frederick II Brought up in Sicily, Frederick from childhood had been exposed to several religious traditions. He grew up to be a brilliant, anticlerical skeptic, more concerned with his harem and his exotic menagerie than with his soul. His dazzling career earned him the name *Stupor Mundi*, the "Wonder of the World." Pope Innocent III tried to mold the young prince into fulfilling a Sicilian king's nominal duties as a papal vassal, but once the great pope died in 1216, Frederick made it clear that he would ignore his youthful promises. Refusing to relinquish the kingdom of Sicily, he sought instead to bring all Italy within his empire. This policy won him the

Frederick II Among "the Wonder of the World's" numerous accomplishments was authoring a learned treatise on falconry. This illustration from an early manuscript of that book shows Frederick II as a monarch accompanied by one of his falcons. *Corbis/Bettman*.

implacable hatred of the papacy and prompted some churchmen to view him quite literally as the Antichrist.[8]

Frederick was a talented, many-sided man—perhaps the most flamboyant product of an intensely creative age. He was a writer of considerable skill and an amateur scientist, curious about the world around him. (According to a hostile account, one of his experiments involved sealing up a man in a barrel in order to find his soul after the man had starved to death. Frederick was said to have noted with

---

[8] In the Christian apocalyptic tradition, the Antichrist was the evil leader who was expected to arise just before the Second Coming of Jesus. Inspired by Satan, the Antichrist would gather under his banner all the forces of sin and seemingly take control of the world, only to be thwarted at the last minute by Jesus' return. Besides Frederick II, other prominent historical figures seen in the past as the Antichrist have included the popes (by the followers of Martin Luther), Martin Luther (by his Catholic enemies), Peter the Great (by traditionalists in Russia), and Napoleon.

MAP 9-5
EUROPE IN 1250

interest that no soul could be seen when the barrel was unsealed.) He ruled his kingdom of Sicily in the autocratic and systematic manner of a caliph: He established a uniform legal code, tightened and broadened the centralized administrative system of his Norman-Sicilian predecessors, encouraged agriculture, industry, and commerce, abolished internal tariffs and tolls, and founded a great university in Naples. (There were limits to his skepticism. Like all kings of his day, he regarded heresy as subversive, and decreed the death penalty for heretics.) Germany, however, he left largely to its princes, allowing imperial power to lapse. He had always preferred his urbane Sicilian homeland to the gloomy German north. Germany was important to him chiefly as a source of money and troops to carry out his policy of bringing all Italy under his rule. Frederick saw himself primarily as the secular king of Sicily (see Map 9-5).

This policy proved disastrous to the Holy Roman Empire. Frederick's aggressions in Italy evoked the opposition of a revived Lombard League and bitter papal hostility. The emperor gave up lands and royal rights in Germany in order to keep peace with the German princes and win their support for his persistent but inconclusive Italian campaigns. In the end, he was obliged to tax his beloved Sicily to the point of impoverishment in order to support his wars. Astute lawyer-popes such as Gregory IX (reigned 1227–1241) and Innocent IV (reigned 1243–1254) devoted all their diplomatic talents and spiritual sanctions to blocking Frederick's enterprises, building alliances to oppose him and hurling anathemas against him.[9]

In 1245 Innocent IV presided over a church council at Lyon, which condemned and excommunicated the emperor. Frederick was declared deposed, a rival emperor was elected in his place, and a crusade was called to rid Christendom of its ungodly tyrant. Revolts now broke out against Frederick throughout his dominions. The royal estates in Germany slipped from his grasp, and his Italian

_____
[9] An anathema is an excommunication in the form of a frighteningly dramatic ecclesiastical cursing ceremony.

holdings simmered with rebellion. Against this sad background Frederick II died in 1250, and his hopes and schemes died with him.

Exterminating the "Viper Brood" Frederick II's son succeeded him in Germany but died in 1254 after a brief reign. For the next nineteen years, Germany suffered a crippling interregnum (1254–1273), during which no recognized emperor held the throne. Castles rose like mushrooms from the German soil as princes and nobles, lacking a royal referee, undertook to defend and advance their interests on their own. Finally, in 1273, a vastly weakened Holy Roman Empire reemerged with papal blessing under Rudolf of Habsburg, the first emperor of a family that would play a central role in European history until 1918.

Rudolf attempted to rebuild the shattered royal demesne and shore up the foundations of imperial rule, but it was much too late. Any scheme to increase imperial power aroused the unremitting opposition of the German princes, who much preferred to extend their own principalities at the expense of the crown. Germany was now drifting toward the loose confederation of principalities and the anemic elective monarchy that characterized its constitutional structure from the fourteenth to the early nineteenth century. The failure of the medieval empire resulted in German political disunity for the next six hundred years. Whatever effective power existed in Germany was wielded at the level of territorial princes. They were, in effect, local kings.

The kingdom of Sicily, established by the Normans and cherished by the Hohenstaufens, passed shortly after Frederick II's death to his bastard son Manfred. The papacy, determined to rid Italy of Hohenstaufen rule (the "viper brood"), offered the Sicilian crown to Charles of Anjou, a younger brother of Louis IX of France. Charles, a cruel, ambitious man wholly unlike his saintly brother, defeated and killed Manfred in 1266 and established a French dynasty on the Sicilian throne.[10]

The inhabitants of the realm, particularly Sicilians, resented Charles and looked on his French soldiers as an army of occupation. When, on Easter Monday 1282, a French soldier molested a young married woman on her way to evening vesper services in Palermo, he was struck down, and on all sides arose the cry "Death to the French!" The incident resulted in a spontaneous uprising and a general massacre of Frenchmen throughout the island. When the French retaliated, the Sicilians offered the crown to King Peter III of Aragon, Manfred's son-in-law, who

claimed the Hohenstaufen inheritance and led an army to Sicily.

There ensued a long, bloody, indecisive struggle known by the romantic name of the War of the Sicilian Vespers. For twenty years Charles of Anjou and his successors, backed by the French monarchy and the papacy, battled the Sicilians and Aragonese. In the end, southern Italy remained under Charles of Anjou's heirs, who ruled it from Naples, while the island of Sicily passed under the control of the kings of Aragon. The dispute between France and Aragon (and the latter's heir, Spain) over southern Italy and Sicily dragged on for generations and precipitated a number of wars in early modern Europe.

Sicilian prosperity was wiped out as foreigners struggled to master the island. Once the breadbasket of ancient Carthage and Rome, and in the thirteenth century the wealthiest and most enlightened state in Italy, Sicily became pauperized and divided—a victim of international politics and of the ruthless papal-imperial struggle. Power lapsed into the hands of its territorial nobility, who introduced commercial sheep raising on a scale massive enough to destroy the island's ecology. By the eighteenth and early nineteenth centuries, the private armies that these nobles maintained to fight their interminable and bloody feuds made themselves the island's de facto masters. From them descended the modern mafias of Italy and the United States. Sicily has still not recovered its prosperity, and still struggles for law and order, a grim consequence of the failure of a firm government to survive past its promising youth in the days of the Normans and Frederick II.

The rest of Italy, too, emerged fragmented—but not impoverished—from the struggles of the High Middle Ages. The Papal States, straddling the peninsula, were torn with unrest and disaffection, and the papacy had trouble maintaining its authority over the inhabitants of Rome itself. North of the Papal States, Tuscany and Lombardy had become a mosaic of independent, warring city-states—Florence, Pisa, Siena, Venice, Milan, and many others—whose rivalries would form the political backdrop of the Italian Renaissance (see Chapter 12). Italy would enter the Renaissance era, extending from the late fourteenth through the sixteenth centuries, economically more prosperous than the rest of Europe, but politically fragmented and quarrelsome.

The Road to Anagni: Popes and Kings from Innocent III to Boniface VIII

To judge by the disintegration of the Holy Roman Empire, one might conclude that Innocent III and his thirteenth-century successors won an overwhelming victory. But as popes became increasingly absorbed in power politics, the papacy slowly lost its hold on the hearts of Christians. As the papacy became a great political power

---

[10] The last act of the tragedy came in 1268, when Charles had Manfred's nephew, Conradin, beheaded. In the nineteenth century, Manfred became the focus of romantic poetry and music depicting his mournful, futile career, and German nationalists demanded vengeance on France for Conradin's death.

THE HISTORICAL EVIDENCE

Unam Sanctam

1302

Boniface VIII's Unam Sanctam *(named, like most papal encyclicals, from the opening words of its Latin text) is the most sweeping assertion of papal authority in history, and the logical culmination of the reform movement as championed in the eleventh century by Gregory VII (see Chapter 8, The Historical Evidence, "The* Dictatus Papae*"). Unlike Innocent III, who had always based his far-reaching claims on canon law and the papacy's feudal rights, Boniface envisioned papal power over the secular world on the basis of his understanding of theological principles and his reading of the Bible. In politics, it is always dangerous to act on principles alone, as Boniface found to his sorrow when the very practical-minded King Philip the Fair disagreed with him.*

That there is one holy, Catholic and apostolic church we are bound to believe and to hold, our faith urging us, and this we do firmly believe and simply confess, and that outside this church there is no salvation or remission of sins, as her spouse [Christ] proclaims in the Canticles [the Song of Songs], "One is my dove, my perfect one. She is the only one of her mother, the chosen of her that bore her" (Canticles 6:8); which represents one mystical body whose head is Christ, while the head of Christ is God. . . .

We are taught by the words of the Gospel that in this church and in her power there are two swords, a spiritual one and a temporal [secular] one. . . . Certainly anyone who denies that the temporal sword is in the power of Peter has not paid heed to the words of the Lord when he said, "Put up thy sword into its sheath" (Matthew 26:52). Both then are in the power of the church, the material sword and the spiritual. But the one is exercised for the church, the other by the church, the one by the hand of the priest, the other by the hand of kings and soldiers, though at the will and sufferance of the priest. One sword ought to be under the other and the temporal authority subject to the spiritual power. . . . But that the spiritual power excels any earthly one in dignity and nobility we ought the more openly to confess in proportion as spiritual things excel temporal ones. Moreover we clearly perceive this from the giving of tithes, from benediction and sanctification, from the acceptance of this power and from the very governance of things. . . .

Therefore, if the earthly power errs, it shall be judged by the spiritual power, if a lesser spiritual power errs it shall be judged by its superior, but if the supreme spiritual power [the papacy] errs it can be judged only by God not by man. . . . Therefore we declare, state, define, and pronounce that it is altogether necessary to salvation for every human creature to be subject to the Roman Pontiff.

Source: From Brian Tierney, ed., *The Crisis of Church and State, 1050–1300* (Englewood Cliffs, NJ: Prentice-Hall, 1964), pp. 188–189.

and a big business, it found itself in need of ever more cash. By the end of the thirteenth century the papal tax system was so efficient that the papacy acquired an unsavory reputation for greed. As one contemporary complained, the supreme pastor was supposed to lead Christ's flock, not to fleece it. Ironically, the fiscal and political cast of the later medieval papacy resulted directly from its earlier dream of becoming the spiritual dynamo of a reformed Christendom.

The papacy humbled the empire only itself to be humbled by the rising power of the new centralized monarchies of northern Europe. By the end of the thirteenth century the kings of England and France were becoming less willing to tolerate within their realms a semi-independent, highly privileged, internationally controlled church. The issue of papal versus royal control of the church was an old one, but the ancient controversy now took a new form. The monarchies found themselves increasingly in need of money, particularly after 1294 when England and France became locked in a costly war. Both monarchies adopted the novel policy of systematically taxing their clergy, and Pope Boniface VIII (reigned 1294–1303) retaliated in 1296 with the papal bull, *Clericis Laicos*, expressly forbidding the practice.[11]

Boniface VIII was another lawyer-pope—proud, aged, and inflexible—whose visions of papal authority transcended even Innocent III's. He made it known that the pope is the "emperor sent from heaven" and "can do whatever God can do." But Boniface failed to grasp the implications of the

---

[11] A papal bull was an official decree sealed with a special seal, or *bulla*.

rise of centralized monarchies. His weakness was his inability to bend his stupendous concepts of papal power to the realities of European politics at the end of the thirteenth century.

In France's Philip the Fair, Boniface faced a dangerous antagonist. Ignoring *Clericis Laicos*, Philip continued to tax his clergy while setting his agents to work spreading scandalous rumors about the pope's morals. Boniface responded with the bull *Unam Sanctam* (1302), which uncompromisingly proclaimed universal papal rulership.

Philip now summoned a kingdom-wide assembly, and before it he accused Boniface of every imaginable crime, from murder to black magic to sodomy to keeping a pet demon. A small French military force crossed into Italy in 1303 and took Boniface prisoner at his palace at Anagni with the intention of bringing him to France for trial. Anagni, the antithesis of Canossa (see Chapter 8), symbolized the humiliation of the medieval papacy. The French plan failed—Boniface was freed by townspeople a couple of days later—but the proud old pope died shortly thereafter, outraged and chagrined that armed Frenchmen had dared to lay hands on his sacred person. Contemporaries found it significant that his burial was cut short by a furious electrical storm.

The high tide of papal monarchy now began to recede. In 1305 the cardinals elected a Frenchman to be Pope Clement V (reigned 1305–1314), who pursued a policy of cautious accommodation to the French throne. Clement submitted on the question of clerical taxation and publicly burned *Unam Sanctam*, conceding that Philip the Fair, in accusing Pope Boniface, had shown "praiseworthy zeal." In 1309, a few years after his election, Clement abandoned faction-ridden Rome[12] for a new papal capital at Avignon on the Rhone River, in southern France. There the papacy installed itself for several generations. The majestic papal palace still looms, fortresslike, over the walled city, the river, and the Pont d'Avignon. The papal administration continued to grow during the Avignon years, and papal spiritual prestige continued to dwindle. The town of Avignon belonged to the papacy, not to the French crown, yet France's enemies could never be confident of the papacy's political impartiality. The French kings were strong, and nearby.

It is easy to criticize Boniface VIII's inflexibility and Clement V's eagerness to please, but the waning of papal authority in the later Middle Ages did not result primarily from personal shortcomings. It stemmed from an ever-widening gulf between papal government and the spiritual thirst of ordinary Christians, combined with hostility to churchly internationalism by increasingly powerful centralized states such as England and France. It would be grossly unfair to describe the high-medieval papacy as "corrupt." Between 1050 and 1300 men of high purpose and great talent sat on the papal throne. Not satisfied merely to chide the society of their day by innocuous moralizing from the sidelines, they plunged into the world and struggled to sanctify it. Perhaps inevitably, they soiled their hands.

---

[12] But he did not give up his claim to rule the city and the Papal States.

The Coronation of Pope Clement V This manuscript illumination dates from the second half of the fourteenth century and so is not an authentic view of either the scene or the individuals involved. Yet it accurately and dramatically sums up what had happened. On the left stands Philip the Fair; on the right is Charles II of Naples, the son of Charles of Anjou. Between them, Clement appears to glance nervously at his French sponsors. The papacy had lost the independence for which most popes had been striving since the eleventh century. *The Granger Collection, New York.*

CONCLUSION: THE RISE OF THE STATE

Looking at the high-medieval church from the broadest possible perspective, we see a spiritual institution with a cohesion, independence, and political leverage unmatched in the history of the Western world. Although popes were never able to dominate kingdoms, at crucial moments they could wrestle with kings on even terms. The papacy was thus able to play a historically unprecedented role in inhibiting the rise of royal absolutism. Unlike the patriarchs of Constantinople, the popes acted independently of imperial control. And they fought tooth and claw to retain their independence against the threat of imperial encirclement—as Frederick II discovered to his sorrow.

Beneath the dust clouds of battles and high politics, the church sponsored the rise of universities, of schools and hospitals in vast number, of hostels for the poor and refuges for orphans and the handicapped. Under papal direction, church law and doctrine were developed and refined, and theological systems emerged that explored in rational terms the secrets of divine creation. In these and countless other ways the high-medieval church served and shaped the civilization of western Europe. Notwithstanding historical myths, the church did far more to stimulate European rationalism than to shackle it, to limit autocracy than to encourage it, to affirm human dignity than to diminish it. The impact of medieval Christianity on our modern world was too pervasive and complex to be precisely measured. But it may be significant that the civilization that has transformed the globe emerged from a society that possessed, in the words of the great British historian Sir Richard Southern, "the most elaborate and thoroughly integrated system of religious thought and practice the world has ever known."

But Europe's—and the West's—future was to be dominated not by a spiritual authority, but by the secular state. In hindsight, this was becoming clear by about 1300. By then the theocratic German monarchy or Holy Roman Empire had lost its Italian and Sicilian dominions and was becoming subordinated to the increasingly autonomous German princes. Its future was far from promising. The papacy was increasingly losing control of turbulent Rome. It would survive for most of the fourteenth century in Avignon, and even flourish at times, but the universal papal monarchy of Innocent III was dead.

The English and French monarchies, on the other hand, were solidly established and seemed to be growing in power. They would both face grave afflictions in the Late Middle Ages—the Hundred Years' War, lower-class rebellions, civil wars, the Black Death—yet the political future of Europe lay with these rising kingdoms moving inexorably toward nationhood. Still far in the future, in the nineteenth century, lay **revolution**, both violent and peaceful, that would transform these states into democracies. But their fundamental framework and rationale had been established in the High Middle Ages. Not until today, as a supranational European Community struggles (with uncertain prospects) to be born, would the territorially based sovereign secular state face serious challenge in Western civilization.

Selected Reading

Sources

Anna Comnena, *The Alexiad*, trans. E. R. A. Sewter (1969).

English Historical Documents, vol. 2, *1066–1189*, eds. and trans. D. C. Douglas and George Greenaway (1981), and vol. 3, *1189–1327*, ed. and trans. Harry Rothwell (1975).

Joinville. *Life of St. Louis*, trans. René Hague (1955).

Memoirs of the Crusades, trans. Frank T. Marzials (1958).

Peters, Edward, ed. *The First Crusade: The Chronicle of Fulcher of Chartres and Other Source Materials*, 2nd ed. (1998).

The Crusades

Bisson, Thomas N. *The Medieval Crown of Aragon: A Short History* (1986). Readable and erudite; the best history of medieval Aragon.

Christiansen, Eric. *The Northern Crusades: The Baltic and the Catholic Frontier, 1100–1525* (1980). The best study of the German advances and reversals in the northeast.

Douglas, David. *The Norman Achievement* (1969), and *The Norman Fate* (1976). Expert, readable studies of Norman activities in Normandy, Syria, Italy-Sicily, and England between 1050 and 1154.

Godfrey, John. *The Unholy Crusade* (1980). A careful study of the Fourth Crusade in its full historical context.

Housley, Norman. *The Italian Crusades: The Papal-Angevin Alliance and the Crusades against Christian Lay Powers, 1254–1343* (1982). Housley argues that these were proper crusades with useful and significant consequences.

Kedar, Benjamin Z. *Crusade and Mission: European Approaches toward the Muslims* (1984). Argues persuasively that, because Christian preaching was forbidden in Muslim lands, missions and crusades were seen as compatible; conquest must precede mission.

Lomax, Derek W. *The Reconquest of Spain* (1978). A detailed military-political narrative that portrays the reconquest as a conscious effort to reclaim for Christianity the lands lost to Islam in the early eighth century.

Matthew, Donald. *The Norman Kingdom of Sicily* (1992). A splendid introductory account.

Phillips, J. R. S. *The Medieval Expansion of Europe* (1988). Demonstrates that the expansion of Europe in the High and Late Middle Ages was built on classical geographical knowledge and was a precondition for the voyages of discovery.

Reilly, Bernard F. *The Medieval Spains* (1993). From a late-Roman province to the Spanish and Portuguese monarchies of ca. 1500, this succinct, lucidly written textbook emphasizes the effect of geography and repeated invasions on the development of the Iberian Peninsula in the Middle Ages.

Riley-Smith, Jonathan. *The Crusades: A Short History* (1987). Concise, lively, and authoritative.

———, ed. *The Oxford Illustrated History of the Crusades* (1995). This valuable and splendidly illustrated volume is the work of a dozen specialists working under the discerning editorship of Riley-Smith.

The Rise of the State

Abulafia, David. *Frederick II: A Medieval Emperor* (1988). This comprehensive study, the best of several accounts of Frederick II, portrays him as a ruler with traditional goals, less spectacularly innovative than previous historians have seen him.

Baldwin, John W. *The Government of Philip Augustus: Foundations of French Royal Power in the Middle Ages* (1986). This thoughtful and meticulous study shows that Philip's administration owed less than had been thought to Anglo-Norman influence.

Barlow, Frank. *Thomas Becket* (1986). In this biography of Becket—the best of many—Barlow demonstrates sympathy toward both king and archbishop but reverence toward neither.

Bates, David. *William the Conqueror* (1989). Although engagingly written, aimed at the general reader, and naked of footnotes, this work rests on an impressive body of scholarship and embodies important new interpretations.

Carpenter, D. A. *The Minority of Henry III* (1990). A path-breaking reinterpretation emphasizing politics and administration.

Chibnall, Marjorie. *Anglo-Norman England*, 2nd ed. (1992). The best survey.

———. *The Empress Matilda: Queen Consort, Queen Mother and Lady of the English* (1991). A superb biography of one of the most significant persons in Anglo-Norman history.

Clanchy, Michael T. *England and Its Rulers, 1066–1272: Foreign Lordship and National Identity* (1983). A stimulating interpretation of high-medieval England under Norman, then Angevin, and finally Poitevin and Savoyard influence.

Crouch, David. *The Image of Aristocracy in Britain, 1000–1300* (1992). A splendid, penetrating work of institutional and social history by one of the most gifted English medieval historians of his generation.

Duby, Georges. *France in the Middle Ages, 987–1460* (1991). Trans. Juliet Vale. A magisterial synthesis by France's most celebrated medievalist.

———.*The Legend of Bouvines: War, Religion and Culture in the Middle Ages* (1990). Trans. Catherine Tihanyi. Duby extrapolates from the most notable battle of thirteenth-century Europe to illuminate the history of Capetian France.

Dunbabin, Jean. *France in the Making, 843–1180* (1985). Concentrating on the period between the politically disastrous abdication of Emperor Charles the Fat in 887 and the accession of Philip Augustus to the firmly reestablished French throne in 1180, this excellent book achieves a balance between the ups and downs of kings, developments within the principalities and regions, and the evolution of aristocratic life.

Gillingham, John. *The Angevin Empire* (1984). A brief, expertly guided tour through Anglo-French history between 1144 and the early years of Henry III.

———. *Richard the Lionheart*, 2nd ed. (1989). An engagingly written biography portraying Richard not as an absentee king of England but as the effective ruler of his Anglo-Continental dominions.

Hallam, Elizabeth M. *Capetian France, 987–1328* (1980). Comprehensive and up-to-date, this study ably portrays the Capetian kings in their economic, social, religious, and cultural setting.

Hollister, C. Warren. *The Making of England, 55 B.C. to 1399*, 7th ed. (1996). The most widely used textbook on Roman and medieval Britain.

Holt, James C. *Magna Carta*, 2nd ed. (1992). The definitive study.

Jordan, William C. *Louis IX and the Challenge of the Crusade* (1979). Shows how St. Louis's piety and crusading zeal shaped his administrative policies and social reforms.

King, Edmund. *Medieval England, 1066–1485* (1988). A multidisciplinary history, gracefully written and lavishly illustrated.

LePatourel, John. *The Norman Empire* (1976). Stresses the unity of the Norman dominions in England and northern France to 1154.

Mortimer, Richard. *Angevin England, 1154–1258* (1994). A deft treatment of the politics, society, and culture of the first century of Angevin kingship.

Prestwich, Michael. *Edward I* (1988). The definitive biography.

Richard, Jean. *St. Louis: Crusader King of France* (1992). Trans. Jean Birrell. Translated from the French edition of 1985, this is the classic account of St. Louis in his full European and Near Eastern context.

Strayer, Joseph R. *The Reign of Philip the Fair* (1980). A prize-winning biography reflecting a lifetime of scholarship.

Warren, W. L. *Henry II* (1973). The most comprehensive scholarly account.

CHAPTER 10

THE MIND AND IMAGINATION OF THE HIGH MIDDLE AGES

Trinity in the Unity
Erich Lessing/Art Resource, NY.

ca. 1033–1109	Life span of Anselm, the first major philosopher of the High Middle Ages	ca. 1135–ca. 1202	Life span of Joachim of Fiore, mystic	1214–1294	Life span of Roger Bacon, advocate of experimental method
ca. 1071–1127	Life span of William IX, troubadour duke	1135–1204	Life span of Moses Maimonides, great Jewish philosopher	1221–1274	Life span of Bonaventure, philosopher and Platonist
ca. 1072–1144	Life span of Adelard of Bath, early English scientist	ca. 1140	Gratian completes his *Decretum*, definitive compilation and analysis of canon law	1225–1274	Life span of Thomas Aquinas, greatest philosopher of the High Middle Ages
ca. 1079–1142	Life span of Peter Abelard, philosopher, theologian, lover, and autobiographer	ca. 1144	Abbot Suger dedicates new church of St.-Denis, first true Gothic structure	ca. 1240–1282/1284	Life span of Siger of Brabant, theologian
1098–1179	Life span of Hildegard of Bingen, greatest woman theologian and composer of the Middle Ages	ca. 1170–1253	Life span of Robert Grosseteste, foremost scientist of his era	1265–1321	Life span of Dante, author of *Divine Comedy*
ca. 1100–1160	Life span of Peter Lombard, theologian	1193–1280	Life span of Albertus Magnus, philosopher, scientist, and teacher of Thomas Aquinas		

"hen I saw a bright light, and in this light the figure of a man the color of sapphire, which was all blazing with a gentle glowing fire. And that bright light bathed the whole of the glowing fire, and the glowing fire bathed the bright light, and the bright light and the flowing fire poured over the whole human figure, so that the three were one light in one power of potential. And again I heard the living Light . . ."

So the German Benedictine abbess St. Hildegard of Bingen (1098–1179) began an account of one of her visions in her long, intricately structured book of prophecy and commentary, *The Way of Knowing*, whose original manuscript version was adorned with vivid paintings (one of which is shown on the opening page of this chapter) executed under her direction by one of her nuns.[1] The

book culminated with a "mystery play" celebrating the ecstasy of redemption expressed not only in her verse but also her music, composed for performance by her nuns.

St. Hildegard was one of the most strikingly original and versatile minds of the High Middle Ages: mystical theologian and religious prophet; popular preacher and vivid writer; herbalist and holistic healer; dramatist and highly innovative composer whose work is among the most melodically appealing of all medieval music.

The youngest of ten children in an aristocratic German family, Hildegard was dedicated to God's service as a child and brought up by a female hermit. Eventually, she energetically administered her own abbey at Bingen, along the Rhine. In her forties she began publicly preaching, mostly to monks but sometimes also to laypeople, expounding the complex visions that she (and the churchmen who certified her orthodoxy) considered messages from God. Accepting conventional views of woman as "the weaker vessel," she nevertheless bitingly criticized male clergy for allowing the church (which she symbolized with a female image) to fall into corruption, and her kinsman Emperor Frederick Barbarossa for threatening schism.

---

[1] This illustration is based on a photocopy made after 1928 by a German nun, who colored it based on the original—fortunately so, for the only medieval manuscript containing St. Hildegard's mystical book and its illuminations was lost in the Allied firebombing of Dresden in February 1945.

Hildegard was not working in intellectual isolation. She admired the mystical thought of Bernard of Clairvaux, and he regarded her as an inspired prophet. She deeply impressed the philosopher and educator John of Salisbury. Her preoccupation with light and the soul's illumination belonged to a tradition of Augustinian Neoplatonism that permeated twelfth-century Christian thought. As a healer (she was responsible for the health of her nuns), she shared her era's interest in experimenting with herbal medicine. Her innovative compositions were part of a broader twelfth- and thirteenth-century evolution of music that included the development of a more sophisticated musical notation that we are now learning to read and perform and the assimilation of Islamic-influenced lyricism.

In St. Hildegard's lifetime, the revolutionary changes transforming high-medieval Europe's economic, religious, and political institutions were paralleled by major cultural and intellectual transformations. Europe in the High Middle Ages experienced an artistic and intellectual awakening that affected virtually all forms of expression.

High-medieval literature saw the flourishing of warlike epic poetry, the rebirth of lyric poetry, and the emergence of the romance. More sophisticated and sensitive than the epic, the romance was a new literary form concerned with such topics as the courtly deeds of the half-mythical King Arthur and his knights at Camelot, whose stories emerged from the songs and legends of the early medieval Welsh, and the adventures of clandestine lovers.

Architecture underwent similarly drastic changes as the massive Romanesque style evolved into the soaring and delicate Gothic style. With the advent of Gothic architecture in mid-twelfth-century France came a new sculptural style in which the characteristic Romanesque qualities of fantasy and symbolic distortion gave way to an idealized naturalism unmatched since classical antiquity. In frescoes and manuscript illuminations in jewel-like colors, the visual arts evolved both complex symbolism and elegant realism.

The High Middle Ages witnessed dramatic intellectual developments as well. Schools proliferated in towns and villages all across western Europe, and the first universities emerged—at Paris, Bologna, Salerno, Oxford, Cambridge, and elsewhere. Law and medicine became serious intellectual disciplines, the first glimmers of modern science appeared (more in the form of questions than of answers), and philosopher-theologians such as Thomas Aquinas produced vast, closely reasoned systems of thought that aspired to reconcile human reason and Christian faith.

HIGH-MEDIEVAL LITERATURE

The literature of the High Middle Ages was abundant and richly varied. Poets wrote both in Latin, the international language of medieval western Europe that all educated people not only read but also spoke, and in the vernacular lan-

guages of ordinary speech that had long been evolving in the various regions of Christendom. Christian piety found expression in a series of somber and majestic Latin hymns such as "Jerusalem the Golden" from the twelfth century:

> The world is very evil, the times are waxing late.
> Be sober and keep vigil, the judge is at the gate. . . .
> Brief life is here our measure; brief sorrow, short lived care.
> The life that knows no ending, the tearless life, is there.
>
> Jerusalem the golden, with milk and honey blessed,
> Beneath your contemplation sink heart and voice oppressed.
> I know not, O I know not what joys await us there,
> What radiancy of glory, what light beyond compare.

But one also encounters Latin poetry of quite a different sort, composed by young, wandering students and scholars,

The Wheel of Fortune   This illumination appears in the 1300 manuscript of the *Carmina Burana*, the great collection of student songs, once owned by and perhaps compiled at the Benedictine monastery of Benedictbeuern in Bavaria. The wheel of fortune illustrates a song on that subject. Its message, "Fortune Rules the World," goes back to pagan times, but too much should not be read into this. Affecting a devil-may-care attitude has been popular among students at all times.   *Bayerische Staatsbibliothek.*

and memorably set to music in a thirteenth-century collection of songs known as the *Carmina Burana:*[2]

> For on this my heart is set, when the hour is nigh me
> Let me in the tavern die, with my ale cup by me,
> While the angels, looking down, joyously sing o'er me . . .

These sentiments do not betoken a trend toward agnosticism but simply reflect the perennial student irreverence toward established institutions.

For all its originality, the Latin poetry of the High Middle Ages was outstripped both in quantity and in variety of expression by vernacular poetry. The drift toward emotionalism, which we have already noted in medieval piety, was paralleled by the evolution of vernacular literature from the martial epics of the eleventh century to the delicate, sensitive romances of the twelfth and thirteenth.

The Epic

The pre-Christian Teutonic north recorded its memories and fears in oral epics passed down generations by bards who resembled Homer in their exacting craft. But the first people to write down these sagas were monks. It was in this form that the moody and violent Old English masterpiece *Beowulf* comes down to us from the time of the Venerable Bede. Despite the monks' Christian veneer, the hero Beowulf is essentially pagan—a lonely figure who fights monsters, slays dragons, and pits his strength and courage against a wild, windswept wilderness.

The gradual refinement of the aristocracy in places like northern France by the eleventh and early twelfth centuries (see Chapter 8) created an appreciative audience for new vernacular epics known as *chansons de geste* ("songs of great deeds"). Sung by minstrels in the halls of castles, these chansons were heroic in mood. Like such modern film epics as *Star Wars* and *2001*, they were packed with action, and their heroes tended to steer clear of sentimental entanglements with women. The battle descriptions, often characterized by gory realism, tell of Christian knights fighting with almost superhuman strength against fantastic odds. The heroes of the chansons are not only proud and loyal to their lords but also capable of experiencing deep emotions—weeping at the deaths of their comrades and appealing to God to receive the souls of the fallen. In short, the chansons de geste mirror the warlike spirit and sense of military brotherhood that characterized

the knighthood of eleventh-century Europe. These qualities find vivid expression in the most famous chanson de geste, the *Song of Roland*, which tells of a bloody battle between a horde of Muslims and the detached rear guard of Charlemagne's army (led by Roland and including an armed bishop, Turpin) as it was withdrawing from Spain:

> Turpin of Reims, his horse beneath him slain,
> And with four lance wounds he himself in pain,
> Hastens to rise, brave lord, and stand erect.
> He looks on Roland, runs to him, and says
> Only one thing: "I am not beaten yet!
> True man fails not, while life in him is left."
> He draws Almace, his keen-edged steel-bright sword,
> And strikes a thousand strokes amid the press. . . .
> Count Roland never loved a recreant,
> Nor a false heart, nor yet a braggart jack,
> Nor knight that was not faithful to his lord.
> He cried to Turpin—churchman militant—
> "Sir, you're on foot, I'm on my horse's back.
> For love of you, here will I make my stand,
> And side by side we'll take both good and bad.
> I'll not leave you for any mortal man." . . .
> Now Roland feels that he is nearing death;
> Out of his ears the brain is running forth.
> So for his peers he prays God call them all,
> And for himself St. Gabriel's aid implores.

Roland, Turpin, and the rear guard are slain to a man, but the Lord Charlemagne returns to avenge them, and a furious battle ensues:

> Both French and Moors are fighting with a will.
> How many spears are shattered! lances split!
> Whoever saw those shields smashed all to bits,
> Heard the bright hauberks grind, the mail rings rip,
> Heard the harsh spear upon the helmet ring,
> Seen countless knights out of the saddle spilled,
> And all the earth with death and death-cries filled,
> Would long recall the face of suffering!

Charlemagne himself defeats the Moorish emir in single combat, avenging Roland:

> The Muslims fly, God will not have them stay.
> All's done, all's won, the French have gained the day.

No such battle actually occurred. Charlemagne's Spanish campaign was a fiasco, and it was left to the *Song of Roland* to supply the happy ending.

The Lyric

Alongside the martial epics of northern French literature, the middle and later twelfth century witnessed the influx of a new, more romantic poetry from southern France. In Provence, Toulouse, and Aquitaine a rich, colorful culture

---

[2] Not to be confused with the famous work of the same title and based on the same texts by the twentieth-century German composer Carl Orff. Interesting recordings exist of the medieval *Carmina Burana* based on recent musicological reconstructions of the old notation and performed by early-music groups that specialize in authentic techniques. These recordings reveal strongly accentuated rhythms and rollicking melodies that can appeal strongly to modern tastes.

THE HUMAN EXPERIENCE

Bernard of Ventadour

Bernard of Ventadour (ca. 1140–1190) was one of the twelfth century's most celebrated and imitated troubadours. Like other troubadours, Bernard was at once a composer and a poet; he created both the music and the lyrics for his songs.

The details of Bernard's life, provided in a biography in the Old Provençal vernacular, may well be embroidered and romanticized, but very little biographical information has survived apart from this one source. It reports that Bernard's mother and father were servants at the castle of the viscount of Ventadour in southern France. At an early age Bernard showed great talent as a poet and musician, and he was singled out by the viscount of Ventadour for training as a troubadour.

The happy days ended abruptly, so the vernacular biography relates, when Bernard's patron, the viscount, found the young man in bed with the viscountess. Bernard was banished from the castle and was obliged to seek his fortune elsewhere. Undaunted, he presented himself to the greatest artistic patron in western Europe: Eleanor, duchess of Aquitaine and queen of England.

Queen Eleanor was immediately impressed by Bernard's artistic gifts.

He spent a number of years at her court, composing and performing songs for the queen and her entourage. His songs earned him fame and fortune; they were immensely popular in their time and are performed to this day. No fewer than forty-four have survived.

Bernard's songs, like those of other troubadours of his time, celebrate the joys and heartaches of romantic love. One of his lyrics perfectly sums up his view of life:

> Singing isn't worth a thing
> If the heart sings not the song,
> And the heart can never sing
> If it brings not love along.

Another of Bernard's songs, "The Lark," available today in several recorded versions, is an evocation of one of the most frequently encountered themes in twelfth-century romantic poetry, the agony of unrequited love:

> When I see the lark beat its wings,
> Facing the sun's rays,
> Forgetting itself, letting itself sing
> Of the sweetness that enters its
>   heart—
> Ah! Such great longing enters me
> From the happiness I see,

> That only a miracle prevents my
>   heart
> From consuming itself with desire.
> Alas! I thought I knew so much of
>   love,
> And I know so little.
> For I can't help loving a lady
> Whom I cannot attain.
> She has all my heart,
> She has me entirely.
> She has left me nothing but desire,
> And a foolish heart.

His biographer reports—probably indulging in wishful thinking—that Bernard became Eleanor of Aquitaine's lover. Whatever the case, he accompanied the queen and her court on their travels through France, and the evidence suggests that he was in England on at least one occasion.

In later years, Bernard left Queen Eleanor's entourage to join the court of Raymond, count of Toulouse, whose name occurs in several of Bernard's songs. Like other worldly men and women—such as Hugh, Earl of Chester—Bernard ended his days in an abbey. He retired to the Cistercian monastery of Dalon in southern France and died there at the age of fifty. ❖

had been developing in the eleventh and twelfth centuries, and out of it came a lyric poetry of remarkable sensitivity and enduring value, written in the Romance language of southern France, Provençal. The lyric poets of the south were known as troubadours. Many of them were court minstrels, but some, including Duke William IX of Aquitaine (Eleanor's grandfather), came from the upper nobility. The art of the troubadours may well derive from the Islamic culture from across the Pyrenees in Spain: Experts detect elements of elegant Persian poetry in troubadour verse, and of the alternately languid and passionate styles of Arabic and Berber music in what can be reconstructed of troubadour

singing and rhythmic accompaniments. Echoes still linger in the haunting *flamenco* and *fado* music of modern Andalusia (southern Spain) and Portugal. But whatever its origins, the troubadour style proved infectiously popular in medieval Europe, and eventually spread far beyond southern France.

The wit, delicacy, and romanticism of the troubadour lyrics disclose a more genteel nobility than that of the north—a nobility that preferred songs of love to songs of war. Indeed, some historians have viewed medieval southern France as the source of the romantic-love tradition of Western civilization—usually heterosexual, but occasionally also homoerotic. It was from there that Europe derived such concepts as the idealization of women, the praise of male gallantry and courtesy, and the impulse to embroider relations between man and woman with agony and ecstasy. The favorite theme of the lyric poets was the hopeless, unrequited love between two people not married to each other:

> I die of wounds from blissful blows.
> And love's cruel stings dry out my flesh,
> My health is lost, my vigor goes,
> And nothing can my soul refresh.
> I never knew so sad a plight.
> It should not be, it is not right. . . .
> I'll never hold her near to me,
> My ardent joy she'll ever spurn.
> In her good grace I cannot be,
> Nor even hope, but only yearn.
> She tells me nothing, false or true,
> And neither will she ever do.

The author of these lines, Jaufre Rudel (flourished ca. 1148), unhappily and hopelessly in love, finds consolation in his poetic talents, of which he has an exceedingly high opinion. The poem concludes on a much more optimistic note:

> Make no mistake, my song is fair,
> With fitting words and apt design.
> My messenger would never dare
> To cut it short or change a line. . . .
> My song is fair, my song is good.
> 'Twill bring delight, as well it should.

Many such poems were written in twelfth-century southern France. Their recurring theme is the poet's passionate love for a woman. Occasionally, however, the pattern is reversed, as in this mid-twelfth-century lyric poem by Beatriz, Countess of Dia, one of twenty known female troubadours:

> I live in grave anxiety
> For one fair knight who loved me so.
> It would have made him glad to know
> I loved him too—but silently.
> I was mistaken, now I'm sure,
> When I withheld myself from him.
> My grief is deep, my days are dim,
> And life itself has no allure.
>
> I wish my knight might sleep with me
> And hold me naked to his breast,
> And on my body take his rest,
> And grieve no more, but joyous be.
> My love for him surpasses all
> The loves that famous lovers knew.
> My soul is his, my body, too,
> My heart, my life, are at his call.

> My most beloved, dearest friend,
> When will you fall into my power?
> That I might lie with you an hour,
> And love you 'till my life should end.
> My heart is filled with passion's fire.
> My well-loved knight, I grant thee grace
> To hold me in my husband's place,
> And do the things I so desire.

The Romance

Midway through the twelfth century, the southern troubadour tradition began to filter into northern France, England, and Germany. It brought with it a new aristocratic ideology of courtly manners, urbane speech, and romantic idealization. These, briefly, were the ideals of what has been called "courtly love." Their impact on the actual behavior of knights was limited, but their effect on the literature of northern Europe was revolutionary. Out of the convergence of vernacular epic and vernacular lyric there emerged a new literary form known as the romance.

Like the chanson de geste, the romance was a long narrative; like the southern lyric it was sentimental and concerned with love. It was commonly based on some theme from the remote past: the Trojan War, Alexander the Great, and above all, King Arthur—the half-legendary ruler of sixth-century Britain whose career had been popularized by the twelfth-century pseudo-historian Geoffrey of Monmouth. In Geoffrey's cunning hands, Arthur was transformed into an idealized twelfth-century monarch surrounded by charming ladies and chivalrous knights. His court at Camelot, as described by the late twelfth-century French poet Chrétien de Troyes, was a center of romantic love and refined religious sensibilities, where knights worshiped (but never married) their ladies and embarked on daring quests in a world of magic and fantasy.

In the chanson de geste, the great virtue was loyalty to one's lord; in the romance (and the lyric) it was love for one's lady. Several romances portray the old and new values in conflict. An important theme in both the Arthurian romances and the twelfth-century romance of Tristan and Iseult is a love affair between a vassal and his lord's wife. Love and feudal loyalty collide, and love wins out. Tristan loves Iseult, the wife of his lord, King Mark of Cornwall. King Arthur's beloved knight Lancelot loves Arthur's wife, Guinevere. In both stories the lovers are ruined by their love—yet love they must; they have no choice. And although the conduct of Tristan and Lancelot would have been regarded by earlier standards as nothing less than treason, both men are presented sympathetically in the romances. Love destroys the lovers in the end, yet their destruction is romantic—even glorious. Tristan and Iseult lie dead together, and in their very death their love achieves its deepest consummation.

A Noble Couple   This magnificent pair of sculptured portraits represents the Saxon Count Eckart and Countess Uta, who were honored among the patrons of Naumburg cathedral in Germany, ca. 1245. The couple's aristocratic pride and individuality are readily apparent.   *Foto Marburg/Art Resource, NY.*

erick II. The German poets, known as *minnesingers* ("love singers"), were influenced by the French lyric and romance but developed these literary forms along highly original lines. The minnesingers produced their own deeply sensitive and mystical versions of the Arthurian stories that, in their exalted symbolism and deep emotion, surpass even the works of Chrétien de Troyes and his French contemporaries.

As the thirteenth century drew to a close, the romance was becoming conventionalized and drained of inspiration. The love story *Aucassin et Nicolette*, which achieved much popularity, was actually a satirical romance in which the hero is much less heroic than heroes usually are, and a battle is depicted in which the opponents cast pieces of cheese at each other. Based on earlier Byzantine stories, *Aucassin et Nicolette* gives mortal love priority over salvation itself. Indeed, Aucassin scorns heaven:

> For into paradise go only such people as these: There go those aged priests and elderly cripples and maimed ones who day and night stoop before altars and in the crypts beneath the churches; those who go around in worn-out cloaks and shabby old habits; who are naked and shoeless and full of sores; who are dying of hunger and thirst, of cold and misery. Such folks as these enter Paradise, and I will have nothing to do with them. I will go to hell. For to hell go the fair clerics and handsome knights who are killed in tournaments and great wars, and the sturdy archer and the loyal vassal. I will go with them. There also go the fair and courteous ladies who have loving friends, two or three, together with their wedded lords. And there go the gold and silver, the ermine and all rich furs, the harpers and the minstrels, and the happy folk of the world. I will go with these, so long as I have Nicolette, my very sweet friend, at my side.

Another important product of thirteenth-century vernacular literature, the *Romance of the Rose*, was in fact not a romance in the ordinary sense but an allegory of the whole courtly love tradition, in which the thoughts and emotions of the lover and his lady are personified in actual characters such as Love, Reason, Jealousy, and Fair-Welcome. Begun by William of Lorris as an idealization of courtly love, the *Romance of the Rose* was completed after William's death by Jean de Meun, a man of bourgeois origin, whose contribution was long-winded, encyclopedic, and replete with passages vilifying women; Jean de Meun's antifeminine biases would be countered brilliantly, more than a century later, by Christine de Pisan (see Chapter 11).

Fabliaux and Fables

Neither epic, lyric, nor romance had much appeal below the level of the knightly aristocracy and upper clergy. The inhabitants of the rising towns had a vernacular literature all their own. From the bourgeoisie came the high-medieval

Alongside the theme of love in the romances is the theme of Christian purity and dedication. The rough-hewn knight of old, having been told to be courteous and loving, was now instructed to be holy as well. Lancelot was trapped in the meshes of a lawless love, but his son, Galahad, became the prototype of the Christian knight—worshipful and chaste. And Perceval (called Parzival in the German version), another knight of the Arthurian circle, quested not for a lost love but for the Holy Grail of Christ's Last Supper.

The romance flourished in twelfth- and thirteenth-century France and among the French-speaking nobility of Britain. It spread also into Italy and Spain and became a crucial factor in the evolution of vernacular literature in Germany during the age of Frederick Barbarossa and Fred-

fabliaux, short satirical poems filled with vigor and crude humor, devoted chiefly to ridiculing conventional morality. Priests and monks were portrayed as lechers, merchants' wives were easily and frequently seduced, and clever young men perpetually made fools of stuffy merchants. Medieval urban culture also produced the fable, or animal story, an allegory in the ancient Greek tradition of Aesop's fables in which various stock characters in medieval society are presented—thinly disguised—as animals. Most of the more popular fables dealt with Reynard the Fox and were known collectively as the Romance of Reynard. These tales ruthlessly parody chivalric ideals, in which the clever, unscrupulous Reynard outwits King Lion and his loyal, stupid vassals.

Dante

Vernacular poetry matured late in Italy, but in the works of Dante Alighieri (1265–1321) it achieved its loftiest expression. Dante wrote on a wide variety of subjects, sometimes in Latin, more often in the Tuscan vernacular. He composed a series of lyric poems celebrating his unconsummated love for the lady Beatrice—a Florentine teenager whom Dante worshiped from afar as the ideal of womanhood but probably never even spoke to before her marriage (to someone else) and early death. He assembled these poems, along with prose commentaries, in his *Vita Nuova* (the "New Life"). Dante's lyrics reflect a sense of joyous rebirth, and a more mystical and idealized love than that of the troubadours.

Convinced of the literary potential of the Tuscan vernacular, Dante urged its use in a Latin book addressed to scholars and writers who scorned the vulgar tongue. And he filled his own vernacular works with such magnificence, grace, and beauty as to convince by example those whom he could not persuade by argument. In his hands, the Tuscan vernacular became (and remains) the literary language of Italy.

Dante's masterpiece, the *Divine Comedy*, was written in the Tuscan vernacular.[3] Abounding in allegory and mystical symbolism, it encompasses in one majestic vision the entire medieval universe. Dante tells of his own midlife crisis in the form of a journey through hell, **purgatory,** and paradise, into the very presence of God. This device permitted the poet to make devastating comments on past and contemporary events by placing all those of whom he disapproved—from local politicians to popes—in various levels of hell. Vergil, the prototype of ancient rationalism, is Dante's guide through hell and purgatory; the lady Bea-

Dante in Hell In hell's bottommost pit, Dante and Virgil encounter Lucifer, imprisoned in ice, with three heads chewing the three worst traitors in history: Caesar's assassins Brutus and Cassius, and Judas. This illustration is part of a fifteenth-century manuscript of the *Divine Comedy. The Granger Collection, New York.*

trice, a symbol of purified love, guides him through the celestial spheres of paradise; and St. Bernard of Clairvaux, the epitome of medieval sanctity, leads him to the threshold of God. The poem closes with Dante alone in the divine presence:

> Eternal Light, thou in thyself alone
> Abidest, and alone thine essence knows,
> And loves, and smiles, self-knowing and self-known. . . .
> Here power gave way to high sublimity,
> But my desire and will were turned—as one—
> And as a wheel that turneth evenly,
> By Holy Love, that moves the stars and sun.

HIGH-MEDIEVAL ARCHITECTURE AND SCULPTURE

During the High Middle Ages, stone churches, abbeys, castles, hospitals, and town halls were built in prodigious numbers. More stone was quarried in high-medieval France

---

[3] In the Middle Ages a *comedy* was a vernacular narrative with a happy ending, but it was not necessarily funny.

alone than by the pyramid and temple builders across the three-thousand-year history of ancient Egypt. The most celebrated buildings of the High Middle Ages are the great cathedrals and abbeys: Chartres, Mont-Saint-Michel, Westminster Abbey, Notre-Dame Paris, Bourges, and many more. But it is nearly as impressive, driving through the European countryside, to see small stone churches of the twelfth and thirteenth centuries still in use in town after town.

Romanesque and Gothic

Two great architectural styles dominated the age. The Romanesque style flourished in the eleventh century and early twelfth, and as its name implies it was inspired by the study of surviving Roman architecture, with its skillful arches and massive piers. Beginning in the middle decades of the twelfth century, at least in France and areas influenced by French culture (but generally not Italy), Romanesque gave way gradually to the Gothic style. From about 1150 to the early 1300s the most famous of the Gothic cathedrals were built. Thereafter the Gothic builders, having worked out most of the architectural possibilities of their style, turned to decorative elaboration. At its height, Gothic architecture constituted one of humanity's most audacious and successful architectural experiments.

The evolution of high-medieval architecture was shaped by two fundamental trends in medieval civilization. First, the great cathedrals, Romanesque and Gothic alike, were products of the urban revolution—of rising wealth, civic pride, and intense urban piety (see Chapter 8). Second, the change from Romanesque to Gothic mirrors the shift in literature, piety, and aristocratic lifestyle toward emotional intensity and refinement. Romanesque architecture, although characterized by an exceeding diversity of expression, tended toward the solemnity of earlier Christian piety and the rough-hewn power of the chansons de geste. The Gothic style, although similarly diverse, is more dramatic, upward-reaching, aspiring. It embodies the heightened sensitivity that one finds in the romance, and the intellectual intricacy of scholastic philosophy (discussed later in this chapter).

The development from Romanesque to Gothic can be understood, too, as an evolution in structural engineering. The key architectural ingredient in the Romanesque churches was the rounded arch, which appears in portals, windows, arcades, and, often, in the stone vaulting of ceilings. The immense downward and outward thrusts of these heavy stone roofs required massive pillars and thick supporting walls.

Although some Romanesque churches, particularly in southern Europe, have wooden ceilings, Romanesque architects often vaulted their churches with stone, thereby creating buildings less susceptible to fire and, to some tastes, more artistically unified. In achieving this goal, the

Romanesque Architecture The massive structure and the rounded, Roman-style arches characteristic of Romanesque architecture are fully apparent in this convent church in the central German town of Quedlinburg, consecrated in 1129. Note as well the fanciful carvings, which frequently adorned Romanesque churches. The walls, today austerely white, were probably originally covered with bright frescoes. *Foto Marburg/Art Resource, NY.*

Romanesque builders constructed stone vaults far larger than ever before. The glittering mosaics and wooden roofs, which characterized the churches of late-Roman, Byzantine, and Carolingian times, gave way throughout much of northern Europe to stone as the key material in both Romanesque architecture and Romanesque sculpture. Indeed, the inventive religious sculpture of the age that ornamented the capitals of Romanesque columns and the semicircular area between the lintel and round arch of the portal (the tympanum) was totally architectonic, completely fused into the structure of the church itself. There were no freestanding statues.

The Romanesque interior is characterized by heavy walls and relatively small windows. Graceful and richly decorated in southern Europe, the style tends to become more severe as one moves northward. A church in the fully developed northern European Romanesque style conveys a

THE HISTORICAL EVIDENCE

Abbot Suger on the Rebuilding of St.-Denis Abbey

mid-twelfth century

In the following extract the great statesman Suger piously records the circumstances of repairing and enlarging the abbey church of St. Denis. Elsewhere in his lengthy account he describes in loving detail the beautiful and rich ornamentation of the church. The spirit in which the great building projects of the High Middle Ages were undertaken is readily apparent. The part of the church that Suger rebuilt became the stylistic model for Gothic architecture, first in the Île de France and later in many parts of Europe.

Through a fortunate circumstance attending this singular smallness—the number of the faithful growing and frequently gathering to seek the intercession of the Saints—the aforesaid basilica had come to suffer grave inconveniences. Often on feast days, completely filled, it disgorged through all its doors the excess of the crowds as they moved in opposite directions, and the outward pressure of the foremost ones not only prevented those attempting to enter from entering but also expelled those who had already entered. . . . Moreover the brethren who were showing the tokens [relics] of the Passion of Our Lord to the visitors had to yield to their anger and rioting and many a time, having no place to turn, escaped with the relics through the windows. When I was instructed by the brethren as a schoolboy I used to hear of this; in my youth I deplored it from without; in my mature years I zealously strove to have it corrected. . . .

Since in the front part, toward the north, at the main entrance with the main doors, the narrow hall was squeezed in on either side by twin towers neither high nor very sturdy but threatening ruin, we began, with the help of God, strenuously to work on this part, having laid very strong material foundations for a straight nave and twin towers, and most strong spiritual ones: *For other foundation can no man lay than that is laid, which is Jesus Christ. . . .* Through a gift of God a new quarry, yielding very strong stone, was discovered such as in quality and quantity had never been found in these regions. . . .

In carrying out such plans my first thought was for the concordance and harmony of the ancient [Merovingian-era] and modern work. By reflection, by inquiry, and by investigation through different regions of remote districts,

we endeavored to learn where we might obtain marble columns or columns the equivalent thereof. . . .

Suger considered salvaging ancient columns from the Baths of Caracalla in Rome and shipping them by sea. But then—Suger says—God revealed a nearby alternative.

For near Pontoise, a town adjacent to the confines of our territory, there [was found] a wonderful quarry [that] from ancient times had offered a deep chasm . . . to cutters of millstones for their livelihood. Having produced nothing remarkable thus far, it reserved, we thought, the beginning of so great a usefulness for so great and divine a building—a first offering, as it were, to God and the Holy Martyrs.

Suger goes on to relate a miracle by which St. Denis helped the workers pull up a prodigiously heavy load of stone, and then describes another act of divine intervention in which it was revealed where just enough timber for beams could be found.

Thus continually encouraged in so great enterprises by so great and manifest signs, we immediately hastened to the consecration of the aforesaid building. . . . [We] chanted in celebration of this ceremony a polyphonic praise amidst a great throng of diverse ecclesiastical personages and an enormous one of clergy and laity.

Source: From *A Documentary History of Art*, vol. 1, ed. Elizabeth Gilmore Holt (Garden City, N.Y.: Anchor, 1957), pp. 36–42.

sense of organic unity and solidity. Its sturdy arches, vaults, and walls, and its interior—today often stark but once covered with bright paintings—give an illusion of otherworldly mystery, yet suggest at the same time the steadfast power of the universal church and its symbolism.

During the first half of the twelfth century, new structural elements began to be employed in the building of

Romanesque churches: first, ribs of stone that crisscrossed the vaulting; next, pointed arches that permitted greater height in the vaults and arcades. Both these elements are to be found, for example, in the great Romanesque cathedral of Durham in northern England. By the middle of the century these novel features—vault rib and pointed arch—were providing the basis for an entirely new style of

St.-Denis Abbey: Early Gothic Style The choir of St.-Denis Abbey, rebuilt by Abbot Suger, is generally considered the first true work of Gothic architecture. This approach to church architecture spread through the Île de France and beyond, partly because of the royal associations of St. Denis and partly through the spiritual exhortations of St. Bernard of Clairvaux. For another view of the abbey at St.-Denis, dating from a later period and showing the full impact of the Gothic style, see Chapter 9, p. 331. *Anthony Scibilia/Art Resource, NY.*

architecture. They were employed with such effect by Abbot Suger in his new abbey church of St.-Denis near Paris around 1140, that St.-Denis is usually regarded as the first true Gothic church.[4]

French Gothic churches of the late twelfth century such as Notre-Dame (Paris) disclose the development of vault rib and pointed arch into a powerful, coherent style. During these exciting years, every decade brought new experiments and opened new possibilities in church building; yet Notre-Dame and the churches of its period and region retain some of the heaviness and solidity of the earlier Romanesque. Not until the 1190s were the full potentialities of Gothic architecture realized. The use of the vault rib and pointed arch, and of a third Gothic structural element—the flying buttress (first introduced at Notre-Dame)—made it possible to support weights and stresses in a new way. The traditional building, of roof supported by walls, was transformed into a radically new kind

Structural Elements of Gothic Architecture This diagram shows the structural elements used in constructing the wall of a Gothic cathedral. The way in which Gothic builders integrated highly visible structural supports into an overall design represents a brilliant solution to an aesthetic and engineering problem unmatched in later west European architecture until the rise of functionalism in the twentieth century. *From Gothic Art by Andrew Martindale, published by Thames and Hudson Inc., New York.*

---

[4] *Gothic* was a term never used in the Middle Ages and had nothing to do with the Ostrogoths and Visigoths of late antiquity. As applied to cultural history, the term was invented in the seventeenth century, and it had strongly negative implications at a time when high-medieval art and architecture seemed "barbarous" and "disorderly." Beginning in the nineteenth century, *Gothic* ceased to be a term of disapproval (except, perhaps, as it applied to popular novels, often with a medieval setting, that emphasized horror and gore).

of building—a skeleton—in which the stone vault rested not on walls but on slender columns and graceful exterior supports. The walls became mere screens, structurally unnecessary. They were replaced increasingly by huge windows of glass that flooded the church interior with light and color—for concurrent with the Gothic architectural revolution was the development, in twelfth-century Europe, of the new art of stained-glass making. The glowing windows created in the twelfth and thirteenth centuries, with episodes from the Bible, legends, and daily life depicted in shimmering blues and reds, have never been equaled.

The Gothic innovations of vault rib, pointed arch, and flying buttress created the breathtaking illusion of stone vaulting resting on walls of glass. The new churches rose upward in seeming defiance of gravity, losing their earthbound quality and reaching toward the heavens. By about the mid-thirteenth century all the basic structural possibilities of the Gothic skeleton design were fully realized, and in the towns of central and northern France there now rose churches of delicate, soaring stone with walls of lustrous glass. Never before in history had windows been so immense or buildings so lofty; and seldom since has European architecture been at once so daring and so assured.

The high Gothic style originated in the region around Paris in the late twelfth century, and the earliest of the great Gothic cathedrals are all in cities within about 150 miles of Paris. In scale alone, these buildings were unique in world architecture: The choir vaults of Beauvais cathedral, for example, rise some 156 feet above the floor; and when Beauvais's original vaults collapsed, intrepid architects and masons redid their calculations and rebuilt on the same scale. The vaults of Amiens and Reims almost match Beauvais's soaring height. No other buildings on earth come close. None, moreover, have comparably large windows, or make similar use of the dazzling new medium of stained glass. In later years the style spread, sometimes with little change, but elsewhere it varied with regional tastes. Gothic churches are much less upward-reaching throughout most of England, Germany, Spain, the Netherlands, and southern France. The Italians adopted the style only slowly and selectively.

Gothic sculpture, like Romanesque, was intimately related to architecture, yet the two styles differed markedly. Romanesque fantasy, exuberance, and distortion gave way to a serene, self-confident naturalism. Human figures were no longer crowded together on the capitals of pillars; often they stood as statues—great rows of them—in niches on the cathedral exteriors: saints, prophets, kings, and angels, Christ and the Virgin Mary, depicted as tall, slender figures, calm yet warmly human, often young and sometimes smiling. The greatest Gothic churches of thirteenth-century France—Bourges, Chartres, Amiens, Reims, La Ste.-Chapelle—are among the most impressive buildings on earth. They bring together many separate arts: architec-

The Gothic Statues of Chartres Dozens of elongated figures like these, individually modeled and gracefully integrated into the architectural ensemble, stand side by side in the portals of Chartres cathedral. They were carved about 1150. *Foto Marburg/Art Resource, NY.*

ture, sculpture, stained-glass, liturgical music—all directed to the single end of providing a majestic background for the central act of Christian worship, the great sacred drama of the Mass.

Cathedrals and Life in the Middle Ages

The cathedrals were normally built at the initiative of bishops, and their chapters[5] provided the institutional continuity necessary to sustain the work over decades or generations. They were designed by master architects, some of whose names have come down to us. Cathedral building represented an enormous investment: Chartres would cost at least $100 million to reproduce today. Revenues were raised in a variety of ways—through episcopal taxes and fund drives, and through donations by townspeople, guilds, regional lords, and great princes and kings. One of the rose

---

[5] The *chapter* was the body of clergymen (called the canons) who elected the bishop and shared with him responsibility for governing the diocese.

Stained Glass at Chartres
The art of stained-glass making came into its own in the era of Gothic cathedral-building and contributed stunning large-scale effects; yet the details are often impossible to see except close up. In this example from Chartres, masons are carefully laying stone with the help of a level. In the center, they are carving a statue. Masons were among the best-paid artisans who built the great medieval cathedrals. *Erich Lessing/Art Resource, NY.*

windows of Chartres displays the coats of arms of two of its benefactors, St. Louis and Blanche of Castile, his mother. Other Chartres windows depict the symbols of various contributing guilds—tailors, bakers, shoemakers, wheelwrights— and show the workers who did the actual building. St. Louis's stunning palace church, La Ste.-Chapelle, was well financed and was therefore completed in half a decade (see the photograph on p. 333). Conversely, Cologne cathedral, one of the greatest of Gothic structures, was never finished during the Middle Ages.[6]

Sometimes people objected violently to the heavy taxes that these projects required, and construction might be delayed or abandoned for want of funds. There are famous stories of townspeople and even noble men and women volunteering their labor, pulling carts from the stone quarry to the building site, or carrying food and wine to the workers. But these instances were not common, nor should it be overlooked that when unskilled volunteers did unpaid work they were preventing laborers from earning wages.

Cathedral-building, like other massive public works, required a hierarchy of skills. Unskilled workers, who might well be ex-peasants who had never learned an urban craft, hauled heavy loads. Many artisan enterprises sprang up around big building projects, including quarrymen, carpenters, and makers of mortar and plaster. Expert stonecutters and sculptors (the distinction was often blurred), masons, and glassmakers often migrated from one project

to another, and so did the architects, who themselves were often masons. These migrations helped spread building styles, and art historians can reconstruct such movements from the distinctive marks that stonecutters used to identify their work.

Stepping inside a medieval cathedral today, you enter an atmosphere of awesome hush that contrasts sharply with the bustle of the surrounding city. But in the Middle Ages, cathedrals were centers of urban life rather than refuges from it. The cathedral bells announced the hours of the business day, called university students to class, and proclaimed great public events—a victory in battle, the death of a famous person, the birth of a prince or princess. Townspeople flocked to their cathedral not for the Mass alone but for marriages, baptisms, funerals, civic and religious festivals, excommunications, and victory celebrations. On major feast days, such as Christmas and Easter, the cathedral would be ablaze with candles. Colorful processions would march noisily along its aisles and then out through its portals into the surrounding city.

A cathedral's relics might attract pilgrims from far and wide—many of them crippled or ill, desperate for a miraculous cure. At night, pilgrims might be found sleeping on the cathedral's straw-covered floor in company with local beggars and drunks. Abbot Suger, describing a boisterous multitude that pressed into his abbey church of St.-Denis, complained of "howling men" and of women who screamed "as though they were giving birth." The crowd of visitors, shoving and struggling to see the relics of St.-Denis, forced the abbey's monks "to flee through the windows, carrying the relics with them" (see The Historical Evidence, "Abbot Suger on the Rebuilding of St.-Denis Abbey" earlier).

---

[6] It was completed, in a burst of nationalist and Romantic enthusiasm, in nineteenth-century Germany.

Building a Cathedral   Although unskilled laborers were frequently hired to carry blocks of stone and other supplies up ramps and scaffolding, machinery was also used in cathedral construction, not only because of the vast scale of the work but also to control labor costs. This illustration from the second half of the thirteenth century shows a treadmill and pulley being used to raise stones, mortar, and workmen.   *Foto Marburg/Art Resource, NY.*

Even larger crowds flocked to Canterbury cathedral to visit the wonder-working tomb of St. Thomas Becket. If we could travel back in time, we would find ourselves overwhelmed by the ear-shattering cries of the mentally ill, and by the suffocating odor of poverty and disease. We would hear people shouting out their prayers in the half-darkness, or see them offering their pennies and homemade candles in desperate appeal for the saint's help. Someone might be boasting about his miraculous cure; someone else might be vomiting in a corner. Well-dressed nobles would be there, too, along with some high officials of the church; they would ignore the crowds of poor and diseased as they awaited their opportunity to present offerings of silver or gems.

Canterbury cathedral was a singularly popular pilgrimage center. Few holy relics were as famed for miraculous cures as those of St. Thomas Becket. But all across medieval Europe the cathedrals teemed with women and men from all social levels. One would encounter there the commotion and stench, the hopes and griefs, of a turbulent cross section of humanity.

UPBRINGING AND EDUCATION

One of the most significant developments in the High Middle Ages was a vast increase in the use of the written word. There was an enormous proliferation of government documents—written commands, property deeds, financial accounts, judicial transcripts—along with records of individual transactions (wills, business records, property transfers) and systematic treatises on philosophy, theology, law, and medicine. Works of literature were committed to writing rather than memorized and transmitted by oral recitation. Law came to be based less on local, long-remembered custom and more on coherent systems of secular and ecclesiastical jurisprudence. This entire process, which has been described as a shift "from memory to written record," resulted in basic changes in attitude and social organization. It encouraged a much more logical and systematic approach to every side of human experience, from the management of a business, farm, or kingdom to philosophical investigation. The ability to reason, read, and compute provided a direct avenue into the governmental institutions of church and state; it was becoming increasingly evident to ambitious youths that knowledge was power.

Accordingly, schools sprang up everywhere, and skilled teachers found themselves in great demand. The abbot Guibert of Nogent looked back from the early twelfth century to the earlier days of his youth, when "scarcely any teachers could be found in the towns and very few in the cities, and those who by good luck could be found didn't know much: they couldn't be compared with the traveling teachers of these days."

Medieval Childhood

Not many years ago, historians believed that medieval people had no conception of childhood as a distinct phase of human life, but regarded children simply as "little adults." Childhood thus had to be "invented" at some point in modern history (it was never clear exactly when). Subsequent research, however, has demolished this notion. For one thing, the revolutionary high-medieval changes in commerce and social organization required increasing numbers of well-trained specialists in a wide variety of vocations—trading, manufacturing, estate management, ecclesiastical and secular governance—and hence much greater emphasis than before on the rearing and training of children. To the old monastic schools were now added an abundance of urban schools and village schools. It has been estimated that about half the boys and girls of early fourteenth-century Florence were receiving at least a grammar-school education, in which they learned enough arithmetic and Latin to be able to meet the demands of adult society. Other medieval cities probably did not do as well (the statistics are lacking), and widespread illiteracy continued in the countryside until fairly recent times. But there can be no question that high-medieval society invested heavily in the education of its children.

Aristocratic and urban children, particularly boys, were usually sent away at an early age for training in another noble household or bourgeois business. This, of course, can be interpreted two ways: As parents palming off their children on someone else to rear, or as parents making careful, indeed loving, efforts to give their children a good start in life. (Children get sent to boarding schools today for a similar range of reasons.) And there is unmistakable evidence that many medieval parents were devoted to their children, whether at home or away. Despite the vexations of large families, and the emotional danger of lavishing affection on a child who might not survive infancy, parents could love their children dearly and care for them tenderly. Voices began to be raised against the age-long custom of child beating (which is still with us). The thirteenth-century writer Vincent of Beauvais cautioned that "children's minds break down under excessive severity of correction: They despair, they worry, and finally they hate. And this is most injurious, for where everything is feared, nothing is attempted."

Beginning in the twelfth century, books on the rearing and training of children began appearing in considerable number. One of the most popular of them, by the Spanish writer Raymond Lull, included sections on breast-feeding, weaning, early education, and the care and nourishment of children. "Every person," Raymond Lull observed, "must hold his child dear."

Actual child-rearing practices varied widely from family to family and class to class, and as in most ages they usually fell short of the social ideal. Warnings against excessive child beating show not only that it was frowned on but also that it continued. And although the practice of child abandonment, widespread in ancient societies, was now strictly forbidden, it was never eliminated. (Churches and various church institutions were often the recipients of children whom parents could not or did not wish to keep.) Nevertheless, whether judging by the proliferation of schools, the popularity of books on child rearing, or the sympathetic literary portrayals of childhood, Europeans of the High Middle Ages placed a large emotional and material investment in their children.

The Rise of the Universities

The greatest of the High Middle Ages' new schools, the universities, tended to be products of the growing cities. The urban revolution brought about the decline of the old monastic schools, which had done so much to preserve and enrich culture since Carolingian times. They were superseded north of the Alps by schools centering on nonmonastic churches, often cathedrals, and in Italy by semi-

secular municipal schools. Both cathedral and municipal schools had long existed, but only in the eleventh and twelfth centuries did they rise to prominence. Many now became centers of higher learning of a sort that Europe had not known for centuries. Their enrollments increased and their faculties grew until, in the twelfth century, some of them evolved into universities.

In the Middle Ages, *university* was a vague term denoting nothing more than a group of persons associated for any purpose. The word was commonly applied to the merchant and craft guilds of the rising towns. A **guild** or "university" of students and scholars engaged in the pursuit of higher learning was given the more specific Latin name, *studium generale*. When we speak of the medieval university, therefore, we are referring to an institution that would have been called a *studium generale* at the time. It differed from lower schools in that students drawn from many lands received instruction from a number of specialized scholars in a variety of disciplines. About the only requirement—apart from money enough to pay a modest matriculation fee and to cover room and board—was a fair fluency in Latin, the sole language of instruction. The studium generale offered a basic program of instruction in the traditional

MAP 10-1
MEDIEVAL UNIVERSITIES

Map legend:
Universities founded in the:
- 12th century
- 13th century
- 14th century
- 15th century

Cities labeled: St. Andrews, Oxford, Cambridge, Wittenberg, Erfurt, Prague, Cracow, Paris, Heidelberg, Vienna, Padua, Salamanca, Montpellier, Bologna, Salerno, Palermo "seven liberal arts": astronomy, geometry, arithmetic, music, Latin grammar, rhetoric, and logic. After completing the basic program, a student might specialize in one of the higher disciplines: medicine, civil or canon law, and philosophy or theology (the latter two often blended together).

Fundamentally, the medieval university was neither a campus nor a complex of buildings, but a guild—a chartered corporation of teachers (and sometimes of students) and an endowment of property to provide an income to meet expenses. With its classes normally held in rented rooms, it was a highly mobile institution, and on more than one occasion, when a university was dissatisfied with local conditions, it won important concessions from the townspeople simply by threatening to move elsewhere. Occasionally a university—like an American professional sports team—actually did move to another town.

In the thirteenth century, universities flourished at Paris, Bologna, Naples, Montpellier, Oxford, Cambridge, and elsewhere (see Map 10-1). Paris, Oxford, and a number of others were dominated by guilds of instructors in the liberal arts. Bologna, whose pattern was followed by other universities of southern Europe, was governed by a guild of students. The Bologna student guild managed to reduce the exorbitant local prices of food and lodgings by threatening to move collectively to another town, and it established strict rules of conduct for the instructors. Professors, for example, were placed under the outrageous obligation to begin and end their classes on time and to cover the prescribed curriculum. Since Bologna specialized in legal studies, its pupils were older professional students for the most part—students who had completed their liberal arts curriculum and were determined to secure sufficient training for successful careers in law.

Notwithstanding the enormous differences between medieval and modern university life, the modern university is a direct outgrowth of its high-medieval predecessor. We owe to the medieval university such customs as the formal teaching license, the practice—unknown to antiquity—of group instruction, the awarding of academic degrees, the notion of a liberal arts curriculum, and the tradition of honoring commencement day by dressing in caps and gowns, which are medieval clerical garb. (One custom that did not survive was the requirement that, on passing examinations, the student treated his professors to a banquet.)

Student Life at the University of Paris

Let us imagine ourselves at the University of Paris in the days of St. Louis. The intellectual environment hummed with philosophical disputes and passionate intellectual rivalries. And besides these battles of words, there were frequent tavern brawls, sometimes exploding into full-scale riots between students and townspeople, or among rival student gangs. New students were hazed unmercifully and imaginatively, while unpopular professors were hissed, shouted down, or, as a last resort, pelted with stones. Textbooks, which students either bought as manuscripts from booksellers or paid for the right to copy, drew complaints about high prices and inaccuracies.

A Medieval Professor and His Students "In a lecture, five things are required," wrote the high-medieval educator Vincent of Beauvais, "that it shall be clear, short, relevant, easy to listen to, and correctly measured and balanced." This relief from the tomb of a mid-fourteenth-century professor in an Italian university hints at such a level of professional competence. *Alinari/Art Resource, NY.*

THE HISTORICAL EVIDENCE

Rules of the University of Paris

1215

The following academic regulations give an idea of the teaching routines, degree of academic freedom, discipline problems, and relative status of professors (here called "masters") of the liberal arts and of theology that prevailed at the University of Paris in the thirteenth century. The trivium *and* quadrivium *together constituted the seven liberal arts in which undergraduates were instructed. (Our word* trivial *derives from the* trivium, *the three most basic liberal arts subjects: Latin grammar, rhetoric, and logic.) The four subjects of the* quadrivium—*astronomy, geometry, arithmetic, music—were more advanced, but sometimes got less attention.*

No one shall lecture in the arts at Paris before he is twenty-one years of age, and he shall have heard lectures for at least six years before he begins to lecture, and he shall promise to lecture for at least two years, unless a reasonable cause prevents. . . . He shall not be stained by any infamy, and when he is ready to lecture, he shall be examined according to the form which is contained in the writing of the lord bishop of Paris. . . . And [the liberal arts masters] shall lecture on the books of Aristotle on dialectic old and new in the schools ordinarily and not *ad cursum.** They shall also lecture on both Priscians ordinarily, or at least one.[†] They shall not lecture on feast days except on philosophers and rhetoric and the quadrivium and Barbarism and ethics, if it please them, and the fourth book of the *Topics.*[‡] They shall not lecture on the books of Aristotle on metaphysics and natural philosophy or on summaries of them or concerning the doctrine of master David of Dinant or the heretic Amaury or Mauritius of Spain. . . .[§]

The [masters of arts] may summon some friends or associates, but only a few. Donations of clothing or other things as has been customary, or more, we urge should be made, especially to the poor. None of the masters lecturing in arts shall have a cope [a hooded cape] except one round, black and reaching to the ankles, at least while it is new. . . . No one shall wear with the round cope shoes that are ornamented or with elongated pointed toes. If any scholar in arts or theology dies, half of the masters of arts shall attend the funeral at one time, the other half the next time, and no one shall leave until the sepulture [burial] is finished. . . .

Each master shall have jurisdiction over his scholar. No one shall occupy a classroom or house without asking the consent of the tenant, provided one has a chance to ask it. . . . Also, the masters and scholars can make both

between themselves and with other persons obligations and constitutions supported by oath or penalty in these cases: namely, the murder or mutilation of a scholar or atrocious injury done a scholar, if justice should not be forthcoming, arranging the prices of lodgings, costume, burial, lectures and disputations, so, however, that the university be not thereby dissolved or destroyed. . . .

As to the status of the theologians, we decree that no one shall lecture [on theology] at Paris before his thirty-fifth year and unless he has studied for eight years at least, and has heard the books faithfully and in classrooms, and has attended lectures in theology for five years before he gives lectures himself publicly. And none of these shall lecture before the third hour on days when masters lecture. No one shall be admitted at Paris to formal lectures or to preachings unless he shall be of approved life and science. No one shall be a scholar at Paris who has no definite master.

---

*Ad cursum refers to lecturing superficially on a text; "ordinarily" in this context means lecturing on it in painstaking detail. Aristotle's "books on dialectic old and new" were the basic texts in logic.

[†]Priscian was the standard textbook of Latin grammar. It was in two parts (hence "both Priscians").

[‡]These were subjects mostly regarded as of secondary importance in the basic liberal arts curriculum.

[§]These prohibitions barred teachers of the liberal arts from lecturing on Aristotelian texts reserved for professors at higher levels, or from discussing works or writers deemed heretical.

Source: From *University Records and Life in the Middle Ages,* ed. and trans. Lynn Thorndyke (New York: Columbia University Press, 1944), pp. 27–30.

Students flocked to the University of Paris from all over Western Christendom. Most were between fifteen and seventeen years old when they began their studies, and they tended to come from the middle social stratum of town dwellers and lesser landholders. Poor boys occasion-ally made it, when supported by wealthier patrons, but the sons of the high aristocracy did not pour in until a later era; university educations did not become fashionable in high society until the fourteenth century. And there were no female students at all.

The letters of medieval students to their parents or guardians have a curiously modern ring: "The city is expensive and makes many demands: I have to rent lodgings, buy necessities, and provide for many other things that I cannot specify. Therefore I beg your paternity that by the prompting of divine pity you may assist me, so that I may be able to complete what I have so well begun." And a father replies to his son: "I have recently learned that you live dissolutely, preferring play to work, and strumming your guitar while others are at their studies."

In the course of the thirteenth century, wealthy benefactors founded residential colleges at Paris where needy faculty members could receive room and board. Monks and friars on the faculty lived in houses built and supported by their orders. Most students, on the other hand, rented whatever rooms they could afford, and more than one student riot was inspired by the high cost of food and housing.

Students in thirteenth-century Paris began their day at five or six in the morning, when the bells of Notre-Dame cathedral summoned them to work. They would flock out of their rooms and boarding houses into the narrow, noisy streets and on to the lecture halls, which were scattered about the university quarter of the city. This district has been known ever since as the "Latin Quarter," for all lectures and examinations were in Latin, the universal scholarly and student language of medieval western Europe, making the university accessible to students from Spain to Poland. The lecture halls were bare and bitterly cold in the winter. Some had rough benches; in others, students had to sit on a straw-covered floor, using their knees to support the wax tablets on which they took their notes. The teacher mounted a platform at one end of the room and delivered a lecture that might run on all morning, unenlivened by visual aids.

In the afternoon, students would congregate in the meadows outside the city walls to join in various sports: races, long-jump contests, lawn bowling, swimming, ball games of different sorts, and free-for-all fights pitting students from one region of Europe against those from another. In the evenings, serious students retired to their rooms for study, while others gathered in Paris's numerous taverns and brothels. (In the same building, someone complained, there might be classrooms above and a whorehouse below.) Before graduating, however, all students faced long and difficult oral examinations.

THE PROFESSIONS

Most medieval students, like their modern counterparts, attended the university not because they thirsted to pursue pure knowledge (although a minority no doubt did), but primarily because they wanted to train for a well-paying profession: medicine, the law, or a comfortable position in the church. In this section and the next, we will first look at the medical and legal professions, and then consider philosophy and theology.

Medicine

The chief medical school of medieval Europe was the University of Salerno in southern Italy. Here, in a land of vigorous cultural intermingling, scholars were able to draw from the medical heritage of Islam, Byzantium, and antiquity. In general, medieval medical scholarship was a medley of observation, common sense, and superstition. We encounter the good advice that a person should eat and drink in moderation. But we are also instructed that onions will cure baldness, that the urine of a dog is an admirable antidote for warts, and that to prevent a woman from conceiving one must bind her head with a red ribbon.

Yet in the midst of all this, important progress was being made in medical science. The comprehensive medical writings of the ancient Greek scientist Galen were studied—and their errors gradually noted. So were the often more valuable works of Islamic medical scholars, once Latin translations became available. And to this invaluable body of knowledge, Europeans—including St. Hildegard of Bingen—were now making original contributions on such subjects as the curative properties of plants and the anatomy of the human body. It is probable that both animal and human dissections were performed by the scholars of twelfth-century Salerno. These doctors, primitive though their methods were, laid the foundations on which western European medical science was to rise.

Civil and Canon Law

Medieval legal scholarship addressed itself to two distinct bodies of material: civil law and canon law. The legal structure of early medieval society was largely Germanic in inspiration and custom-based, particularly in northern Europe, where Roman law had virtually disappeared. Customary law remained strong throughout the High Middle Ages: It governed the relationships among the aristocracy and determined the obligations of the peasantry. It limited the prerogatives of kings and underlay Magna Carta (see Chapter 9). But from the late eleventh century on, Roman law was studied in Bologna and other European universities. Christendom was now exposed to a distinctly different legal tradition—coherent and logical—that began to compete with Germanic law, to rationalize it, and in some instances to replace it.

The foundation of medieval Roman law was the *Corpus Juris Civilis* of Justinian (see Chapter 6), which was all but unknown in western Europe throughout the Early Middle Ages but reappeared at Bologna in the late eleventh century. Italy remained the center of Roman legal studies throughout the High Middle Ages. The traditions of Roman law had never entirely disappeared there, and the Italian peninsula therefore provided the most fertile soil for their revival.

From Italy, the study of Roman law spread northward. A great school of law emerged at Montpellier in southern

France, and others flourished at Orléans, Paris, and Oxford. But Bologna remained the foremost center of Roman legal studies. There, scholars known as glossators wrote analytical commentaries on the *Corpus Juris Civilis*, clarifying difficult points and reconciling apparent contradictions. Later on they began to produce textbooks and important original treatises on the *Corpus Juris Civilis* and to reorganize it into a coherent sequence of topics. Eventually such an extensive body of supplementary material existed that the glossators turned to the task of glossing the glosses—clarifying the clarifications. Around the mid-thirteenth century the work of the earlier glossators culminated in a comprehensive work by the Bolognese scholar Accursius—the *Glossa Ordinaria*—which synthesized all previous commentaries on the *Corpus Juris Civilis*. Thereafter, Accursius's *Glossa Ordinaria* became the authoritative supplement to the *Corpus Juris Civilis* in courts of Roman law.

The impact of the glossators was particularly strong in Italy and southern France—old Roman provinces, where elements of Roman law had survived in local custom. By the thirteenth century Roman law was beginning to make a significant impact outside Italy as well, for by then civil lawyers trained in the Roman tradition were achieving an increasingly dominant role in the courts of France, Germany, and Spain. These lawyers worked for kings and used their legal training to exalt their monarchs. Although the Roman legal tradition had originally contained a strong element of constitutionalism, it inherited from Justinian's era an autocratic cast that the court lawyers of the rising monarchies put to effective use. Thus Roman law tended to make the governments of continental Europe at once more systematic and more autocratic. The durability of England's parliamentary regime owed much to the fact that a strong monarchy, founded on the principles of Germanic law with its custom-based curbs on royal authority, was already well established before northern Europe experienced the full impact of Roman law.

Canon (church) law developed alongside Roman law and derived a great deal from it. Methods of scholarship were similar in the two fields—commentaries and glosses were common to both—and the ecclesiastical courts borrowed much from the principles and procedures of Roman law. But whereas Roman law was based on the single authority of Justinian's *Corpus Juris Civilis*, canon law drew from many sources: the Bible, the writings of the ancient Church Fathers, the canons (laws) issued by church councils, and the decrees of popes. The *Corpus Juris Civilis*, although susceptible to endless commentary, was fundamentally complete in itself. Popes and councils, on the other hand, continued to issue decrees, and canon law was therefore capable of unlimited development.

Canon law, like civil law, first became a serious scholarly discipline in eleventh-century Bologna and later spread to other centers of learning. The study of canon law was strongly stimulated by the Investiture Controversy and subsequent struggles between popes and kings (see Chapters 8 and 9), for the papacy looked to canon lawyers to support its claims with cogent, documented arguments and apt precedents. But the medieval scholars of canon law were more than mere papal propagandists. They were grappling with the formidable problem of systematizing their sources, explaining what was unclear, reconciling what seemed contradictory—in other words, imposing order on the immense variety of dicta, opinions, precedents, and existing canonical collections on which their discipline was based.

The essential goal of the canon lawyers was to assemble their diverse sources—the "canons"—into a single coherent work. It was up to them, in short, to accomplish the task that Emperor Justinian had performed for Roman law back in the sixth century (see Chapter 6). The civil lawyers had their *Corpus Juris Civilis*; it was up to the canon lawyers to create their own "*corpus juris canonici.*" The first attempts to produce comprehensive canonical collections date from the Early Middle Ages, but not until the eleventh-century revival at Bologna were serious scholarly standards applied to the task. The definitive collection was completed around 1140 by the great Bolognese canon lawyer Gratian. Originally entitled *The Concordance of Discordant Canons*, Gratian's work is known to posterity as the *Decretum*.

Gratian not only brought together an immense body of canons, he also framed them in a logical, topically organized scheme. Using methods that were just beginning to be employed by **scholastic** philosophers, he raised questions in logical sequence, quoted the relevant canons, and endeavored to reconcile contradictions. The result was an ordered body of general legal principles validated by passages from the Bible, the Church Fathers, and papal and church council decrees. The *Decretum* became the authoritative text in ecclesiastical tribunals and the basis of all future study in canon law.

As time passed, and new decrees were issued, it became necessary to supplement Gratian's *Decretum* by collecting the canons issued after 1140. Together, the *Decretum* and the supplementary collections were given the title *Corpus Juris Canonici* and became the ecclesiastical equivalent of Justinian's *Corpus Juris Civilis*. These two great compilations, ecclesiastical and civil, reflect the parallel growth of medieval Europe's two supreme sources of administrative and jurisdictional authority: church and monarchy. They further reflect the high-medieval shift toward elaborate intellectual systems, expressed in writing and shaped by rational analysis.

PATHS TO THE TRUTH: PHILOSOPHY, MYSTICISM, AND SCIENCE

Medieval philosophy, too, is marked by analytical system-building. Although most important philosophers in high-medieval western Europe were clerics of one sort or another, ecclesiastical authority did not stifle speculation or limit controversy. Catholic orthodoxy, which would harden noticeably after the Protestant challenge appeared during the Reformation (see Chapter 13), was still relatively flexible in the twelfth and thirteenth centuries, and philosophers were by no means timid apologists for official dogmas. If some of them were impelled to provide the Catholic faith with a logical substructure, others asserted that reason does not lead to the truth of Christian revelation. And among those who sought to harmonize faith and reason there was sharp disagreement as to how it should be done. Their shared faith did not limit their diversity or curb their spirit of intellectual adventure.

High-medieval theologians and philosophers did not consider their pursuit of understanding God as being in conflict with the goals of those who sought to investigate and explain nature. On the contrary, these intellectuals were pursuing parallel goals, and some (like St. Albert the Great) made significant contributions both to theology and to the study of nature. The real clash was between those who strove to comprehend God and nature through reason, and those who insisted that only mystical faith, transcending reason, could open the road to truth.

The Roots of Medieval Philosophy

The high-medieval philosophers drew nourishment from five earlier sources.

From the Greeks they inherited the philosophical systems of Plato and Aristotle. At first these two Greek masters were known in western Europe only through a handful of translations and commentaries dating from late Roman times. By the thirteenth century, however, new and far more complete translations were coming into Latin Christendom from Spain and Sicily, and Aristotelian philosophy became a matter of intense interest and controversy in Europe's universities.

From the Islamic world came a flood of Greek scientific and philosophical works that had long before been translated into Arabic and were now translated from that language into Latin. These works entered Europe accompanied by extensive commentaries and original writings of Muslim philosophers and scientists, for Islam came to grips with Greek learning long before the West did. Islamic thought made a particularly vital contribution to European science. In philosophy it was further enriched by the work of Jewish scholars such as the great Spanish philosopher Moses Maimonides (1135–1204), whose *Guide for the Perplexed*—a penetrating attempt to reconcile Aristotle and Jewish Scriptures—influenced the work of thirteenth-century Christian philosophers and theologians.

The fifth-century Church Fathers—particularly Ambrose, Jerome, and Augustine—had been a dominant intellectual force throughout the Early Middle Ages, and their authority remained strong in the twelfth and thirteenth centuries. St. Augustine retained his singular significance and was, indeed, the chief vessel of Platonic and Neoplatonic thought in the medieval universities.

Early medieval scholars themselves contributed significantly to the high-medieval intellectual revival. Writings by Gregory the Great, Isidore of Seville, Bede, Alcuin, and Gerbert of Aurillac were all studied in the new schools. The original intellectual contributions of these men were less important, however, than the fact that they and their contemporaries had kept classical learning alive, thus creating the intellectual climate that made possible the reawakening of philosophical speculation in the eleventh century.

Finally, the high-medieval philosophers looked back beyond the scholars of the Early Middle Ages, beyond the Church Fathers, to the Hebrew and early Christian religious traditions as recorded in the Scriptures. Among medieval theologians the Bible, the chief written source of divine revelation, was the fundamental text and the ultimate authority.

Such were the chief elements—Greek, Islamic-Jewish, patristic,[7] early medieval, and scriptural—that underlay the thought of the scholastic philosophers. Strictly defined, **scholasticism** is simply the philosophical movement associated with the high-medieval schools—the monastic and cathedral schools and later the universities. More interestingly, it was a movement concerned above all with exploring the relationship between reason and revelation. All medieval scholastics—for so the philosophers and theologians who taught in the universities were called—believed in God. All were committed, to some degree, to the life of reason. Many of them were immensely enthusiastic over the intellectual possibilities inherent in the careful application of Aristotelian logic to basic human and religious problems. Some believed that logic was the master key to a thousand doors and that, with sufficient methodological rigor, with sufficient exactness in the use of words, the potentialities of human reason were all but limitless.

The scholastics applied their logical method to a multitude of problems. They were concerned chiefly, however, with matters of basic significance to human existence: the nature of human beings, the purpose of human life, the existence and attributes of God, the fundamentals of human morality, the ethical imperatives of social and political life, the relationship between God and humanity. These questions in metaphysics are among the most profound questions that one can ask. Many philosophers and scientists of our own day, working with an entirely different set of intellectual tools, regard them as unanswerable. But

---

[7] The adjective *patristic* refers to the Church Fathers—the writings of Jerome, Ambrose, Augustine, and others.

THE HISTORICAL EVIDENCE

Errors Condemned

1270

Some of Aristotle's pronouncements on physics and metaphysics clashed head-on with Judeo-Christian (and Islamic) faith. Averroes and some Christian intellectuals could reconcile these Aristotelian positions with their religious tradition only by developing the idea of "double truth." The bishop of Paris condemned such attempts as heretical in 1270. His condemnation also extended to various denials of free will by the advocates of astral determinism—that is, astrology. The prohibitions had to be issued repeatedly, strongly suggesting that not all teachers at Paris obeyed.

These are the errors condemned and excommunicated with all who taught or asserted them knowingly by Stephen, bishop of Paris, in the year of the Lord 1270 . . .

The first article is: That the intellect of all men is one and the same in number.*

2. That this is false or inappropriate: Man understands.

3. That the will of man wills or chooses from necessity [i.e., that there is no free will].

4. That all things which are done here below depend upon the necessity of the celestial bodies.

5. That the world is eternal.

6. That there never was a first man.

7. That the soul, which is the form of man as a human being, is corrupted [i.e., dies and decays] when the body is corrupted.

8. That the soul separated after death does not suffer from corporal fire [i.e., hell].

9. That free will is a passive power, not active; and that it is moved necessarily by appetite [i.e., basic human drives].

10. That God does not know things in particular.

11. That God does not know other things than Himself.

12. That human actions are not ruled by divine Providence.

13. That God cannot give immortality or incorruptibility to a corruptible or mortal thing.

---

*Averroes held that all human beings shared a common, eternal mind, but did not have individual minds. The idea was derived from Aristotle as a way of reconciling individual mortality with a kind of collective immortality.

Source: From *University Records and Life in the Middle Ages*, ed. and trans. Lynn Thorndike (New York: Columbia University Press, 1944), pp. 80-81.

---

the scholastics, lacking the modern sense of disillusionment, were determined to make the attempt.

Faith and Reason

Among the diverse investigations and conflicting opinions of the medieval philosophers, two central issues deserve particular attention: the degree of interrelationship between faith and reason, and the relative merits of the Platonic-Augustinian and the Aristotelian intellectual traditions. The issue of faith versus reason was perhaps the more far-reaching. Ever since the time of the Christian writer Tertullian in the third century (see Chapter 5), some intelligent Christians had insisted that God so transcended reason that any attempt to approach him intellectually was useless and, indeed, blasphemous.

Tertullian had many followers in the Middle Ages. St. Bernard of Clairvaux rejected the intellectual road to God in favor of the mystical, insisting that God, whose power is limitless, cannot be bound or even approached by logic, and denouncing his rationalist contemporary Peter Abelard. Another great twelfth-century mystic, Joachim of Fiore (whom we shall consider in more detail a little later in the chapter), devoted his life to unraveling the clues to the future that, he believed, could be extracted by a prayerful struggle with the Bible's baffling obscurities. That good and humbly cheerful soul, St. Francis of Assisi, dismissed all intellectual speculation as irrelevant to salvation.

The contrary view was just as old. Third-century theologians such as Origen (see Chapter 5) had labored to provide Christianity with a sturdy philosophical foundation and did not hesitate to explain the faith by means of Greek—and particularly Platonic—thought. Ambrose, Jerome, and Augustine (see Chapter 5), had wrestled with the problem of whether a Christian might properly use elements from the pagan classical tradition in the service of the faith, and all three answered yes. As Augustine put it: "If those who are called philosophers, and especially the Platonists, have said anything that is true and in harmony with our faith, we must not only not shrink from it, but claim it for our own use from those who have unlawful possession of it."

Augustine's is the viewpoint that underlies most of high-medieval philosophy—that reason has a valuable role to play as a servant of revelation. St. Anselm, following Augustine, declared: "I believe so that I may know." Faith comes first, reason second; faith rules reason—but reason can perform the useful service of illuminating faith. Indeed, faith and reason are separate avenues to a single body of truth. By their very nature they cannot lead to contradictory conclusions, for truth is one. Should their conclusions ever appear to be contradictory, the philosopher can be sure that some flaw exists in his logic. Reason cannot err, but our use of it can, and revelation must therefore be the criterion against which reason is measured.

This, in general, became the position of the high-medieval scholastic philosophers. The intellectual system of St. Thomas Aquinas rested on the conviction that reason and faith were harmonious. Even that arch-rationalist of the twelfth century, Peter Abelard, wrote: "I do not wish to be Aristotle if it must separate me from Christ." Abelard believed that he could at once be a philosopher and a Christian, but his faith took priority.

Among some medieval philosophers the priorities were reversed. Averroes (1126–1198), a brilliant Muslim Aristotelian of twelfth-century Spain, boldly asserted the superiority of reason over faith. He affirmed the truth of several of Aristotle's conclusions that were directly contrary to Islamic and Christian doctrine: that the world had always existed and was therefore uncreated; that all human actions were predetermined; that there was no personal salvation but only the return of human raindrops to the divine ocean. In the fourteenth century there emerged a Christian philosophical school known as Latin Averroism, based in part on the writings of the Paris theologian Siger of Brabant (ca. 1240–1281 or 1284). Like Averroes, Siger accepted Aristotle's eternally existing world as "logically necessary" yet nevertheless believed firmly in the Christian doctrine of the creation.[8] Expanding on this dilemma, Latin Averroists of the fourteenth century held that reason and revelation produced radically different conclusions. Their position came to be called the doctrine of the "twofold truth."

---

[8] Both St. Bonaventure and St. Thomas Aquinas opposed Siger vigorously. His position was attacked but not officially condemned by the church, and he was stabbed to death by a cleric who was charged by the papal authorities with keeping him under surveillance. Dante, however, praised him highly. Today it is difficult to reconstruct exactly what positions he held on various important points because not all his writings have survived.

Platonism-Augustinianism versus Aristotelianism

The conflict between the intellectual systems of Plato-Augustine and Aristotle did not emerge clearly until the thirteenth century, when the full body of Aristotle's writings reached western Europe in Latin translations from Greek and Arabic. Until then, most efforts at applying reason to faith were based on the Platonic tradition transmuted and transmitted by Augustine to medieval Europe. Many thoughtful Christians were deeply suspicious of the newly recovered writings of Aristotle. They regarded his work as pagan in viewpoint and dangerous to the faith. Other thirteenth-century philosophers, such as St. Thomas Aquinas, were much too devoted to the goal of reconciling faith and reason to reject the works of a man whom they regarded as antiquity's greatest philosopher—"the Philosopher," he was usually called. St. Thomas sought to adapt Aristotle's teachings to Christianity much as Augustine had Christianized Plato and the pagan Neoplatonists. In the middle decades of the thirteenth century, the Platonic and Aristotelian traditions flourished side by side, and in the works of certain English scientific thinkers they achieved a singularly fruitful synthesis.

The contest between Plato and Aristotle gave rise to a serious philosophical debate over the nature of the Platonic "forms," or, as they were called in the Middle Ages, "universals." As we saw in Chapter 3, Plato had taught that terms such as *dog* or *cat* not only describe particular creatures but also are language symbols for things that have reality in themselves—that individual cats are imperfect reflections of a model cat, an archetypal or "universal" cat. Similarly, there are many examples of circles, squares, or triangles. Were we to measure these individual figures with sufficiently refined instruments, we would discover that they are all imperfect. No circle in this world is absolutely round. No square or triangle has perfectly straight sides. They are merely approximations of a perfect "idea." In heaven, Plato would say, the perfect triangle exists. This ideal triangle is the source of the concept of triangularity that lurks in our minds and of all the imperfect triangles that we see in the physical world. The heavenly triangle is not only perfect but real. The earthly triangles are less real, and less worthy of our attention. Or, to take still another example, we call certain acts "good" because they partake, imperfectly, of a universal good that exists in heaven. In short, these universals—cat, dog, circle, triangle, beauty, goodness—exist apart from the multitude of individual dogs, cats, circles, triangles, and beautiful and good things in this world. And the person who seeks knowledge ought to meditate on these universals rather than study the world of phenomena in which they are only imperfectly reflected.

St. Augustine had accepted Plato's theory of universals but amended it. Augustine taught that the archetypes exist in the mind of God instead of in Plato's abstract "heaven." And whereas Plato had ascribed our knowledge of the universals to dim memories from a prenatal existence, Augustine maintained that God puts a knowledge of universals directly into our minds by a process of "divine illumination." Plato and Augustine agreed, however, that the universal exists apart from the particular and, indeed, is more real than the particular. In the High Middle Ages, those who followed the Platonic-Augustinian approach to universals were known as *realists*; they believed that a universal was an actual "thing" (in Latin, *res*).

The Aristotelian tradition brought with it another viewpoint on universals: They exist, to be sure, but only in the particular. Only by studying particular things in the world of phenomena can we gain a knowledge of universals. The human mind draws its knowledge of the universal from its observation of the particular by a process of abstraction. The universals are real, but in a sense less real—or less independently real—than Plato and Augustine believed. Accordingly, philosophers who inclined toward the Aristotelian position have been called *moderate realists*.

But as early as the eleventh century a French logician rejected both these views, declaring that universals are not real at all. "Dog," "cat," and "triangle" are mere words—names that we have concocted for bunches of individual things that we have lumped into arbitrary categories. These categories, or "universals," have no objective existence whatever. Reality is not to be found in them, but rather in the multiplicity and variety of individual objects which we can see, touch, and smell in the world around us. Those who agreed with this view were known as *nominalists*: For them, the universals had no reality apart from their *nomina*—Latin for "name." Nominalism stayed in the intellectual background during the twelfth and thirteenth centuries, but it would surge to the forefront in the fourteenth. Many churchmen regarded it as a dangerous doctrine, since its emphasis on the particular over the universal suggested that the church was not a single universal body but rather a vast accumulation of individual Christians. We shall have more to say about nominalism in Chapter 11.

The scholastic philosophers first made their appearance in the later eleventh century as an aspect of Europe's intellectual reawakening. The earliest important figure was St. Anselm (ca. 1033–1109), a native of northern Italy who, journeying to Normandy, became a monk and then abbot of Bec and who later, as archbishop of Canterbury, brought the Investiture Controversy to England (see Chapter 9).

As an Augustinian, Anselm took the realist position on the problem of universals. From Augustine, too, he derived his attitude on the relationship of faith and reason. He taught that faith must precede reason but that reason can illuminate faith. His conviction that reason and faith are compatible made him a singularly important pioneer in the development of high-medieval rationalism. He worked out several proofs of God, based on abstract reasoning rather than observation. And in his important theological treatise, *Cur Deus Homo* ("Why God Became Man"), he subjected the doctrines of the incarnation of Christ and the atonement of humanity to rigorous logical analysis.

Anselm's emphasis on reason, employed within the framework of a firm Christian conviction, set the stage for the significant philosophical developments of the following generations. With Anselm, Western Christendom regained at last the intellectual level of the fourth- and fifth-century Latin Doctors.

Twelfth-century philosophers were intoxicated by the seemingly limitless possibilities of reason and logic. The most audacious of them all was Peter Abelard (ca. 1079–1142), a Norman nobleman who chose logic rather than fighting as his career and whose dazzling rise ended in tragedy and defeat. Abelard is perhaps best known for his love affair with his student Heloise. (The fact that a young woman like Heloise was allowed by her aristocratic family to study sophisticated philosophy with a brilliant young male teacher is in itself remarkable.) Their relationship ended abruptly when Heloise's enraged uncle, a churchman, hired thugs to castrate Abelard. The lovers had secretly married but now separated permanently, both taking monastic vows, and in later years Abelard wrote regretfully of the affair in his *History of My Calamities*. There followed a beautiful correspondence in which Heloise, now an abbess, confessed her enduring love—"I am tortured by passion and the fires of memory." Abelard could offer her spiritual consolation, but nothing more.

Abelard was the supreme logician of the twelfth century. Writing several decades before the great influx of Aristotelian thought in Latin translation, he anticipated Aristotle's position on the question of universals by advocating a theory similar to Aristotle's moderate realism. Universals, Abelard believed, have no separate existence; our knowledge of them is derived from particular things by a process of abstraction. In a famous work titled *Sic et Non* ("Yes and No"), Abelard collected opinions from the Bible, the Latin Doctors, the councils of the church, and the decrees of the papacy on a great variety of theological questions, demonstrating that these authorities disagreed on such issues as whether it is ever permissible to lie, whether anything happens by chance, and whether sin is pleasing to God. Abelard employed a method of inquiry that would be developed and perfected by canon lawyers and philosophers over the next several generations. We have already seen how the canonist Gratian, in his *Decretum*, lined up conflicting authorities and reconciled them. Similarly, Abelard's successors in theology sought to reconcile contradictions and arrive at conclusions. Abelard, however, had earned conservative enmity by leaving the issues unresolved (arguing that students should reason them out for themselves). Abelard was a devout Christian, if something of an intellectual show-off, but many regarded him as a budding skeptic. Thus he left himself open to attacks by St. Bernard, who was hostile to the Christian rationalist movement and called Abelard's theology a "foolology." The brilliant teacher was driven from one place to another until at length his opinions were condemned by an ecclesiastical council in 1141. Abelard retired to Cluny and died there in 1142. The abbot of Cluny wrote Heloise a touching letter praising Abelard's late-blooming humility and assuring her that they would be reunited on the day of the Lord's coming.

Twelfth-century rationalism was far more than a one-man affair, however, and attacks on Abelard failed to halt its growth. His student Peter Lombard (ca. 1100–1160) produced an important theological textbook, the *Book of Sentences,* which offered conflicting opinions on the pattern of the *Sic et Non,* but which, like Gratian's *Decretum,* took the further step of reconciling contradictory authorities. Lombard's *Book of Sentences* remained for centuries a fundamental textbook in schools of theology.

The System Builders

In the later twelfth and early thirteenth centuries the movement of Christian rationalism was powerfully reinforced by the arrival of vast quantities of Greek and Arabic writings in Latin translation. For the first time, significant portions of the philosophical and scientific legacy of ancient Greece and Islam became available to west European scholars. Above all, the full Aristotelian corpus became available through the labors of translators in Spain, Sicily, and the Latin empire of Constantinople (see Chapter 9).

These translations filled a deep hunger among Western thinkers for a fuller knowledge of classical philosophy and science. The introduction of certain new Aristotelian works provoked a crisis in Western Christendom, for they contained implications that seemed hostile to the faith. And with the works of Aristotle, as we have seen, came the skeptical and intellectually impressive commentaries of the Spanish Muslim Averroes and his doctrine of the "twofold truth"—one truth, that is, for simple believers, but a second and contradictory truth for philosophers. For a time it seemed as though reason and revelation were sundered, and the church reacted in panic by condemning certain of Aristotle's writings. It was one of the major goals of thirteenth-century thought to rescue Aristotle and, indeed, reason itself for Western Christianity.

The thirteenth century was preeminently an age of consolidation and synthesis. Its scholars digested the insights and conclusions of the past and cast them into comprehensive systems of thought, known as *summas,* which provided structure and unity to Christian theological speculation.

The thought of Aristotle loomed large in the thirteenth-century schools, but the Platonic-Augustinian tradition was well represented, too. There was a tendency for Dominican scholars to espouse Aristotle and for Franciscans to follow Plato and Augustine. Thus the outstanding thirteenth-century exponent of Platonism-Augustinianism was the Franciscan St. Bonaventure (1221–1274), an Italian of humble origin who rose to become a cardinal of the church and minister-general of the Franciscan order.

Bonaventure was at once a philosopher and a mystic. In the Augustinian tradition, he was a realist on the matter of universals and a rationalist who stressed the subordination of reason to faith. He visualized the whole physical universe as a multitude of symbols pointing to God and glorifying him, eternally striving upward toward the Divine Presence. Human beings, he believed, stand at the fulcrum of creation. Our bodies make us the kin of beasts; our souls give us kinship with the angels. We perceive the physical universe through our senses, but we know the spiritual world—the world of universals—through the grace of divine illumination. The road to God and to truth, therefore, lies in introspection and worship, not in observation and experiment. Indeed, in Bonaventure's philosophy rational speculation is scarcely distinguishable from worship.

While Bonaventure was bringing new dimensions to the Augustinian outlook, two great Dominican scholars, Albertus Magnus (St. Albert the Great, 1193–1280) and Thomas Aquinas (1225–1274), worked toward reconciling Aristotle's philosophy with Christianity. Albertus Magnus, a German, was a scholar of widely ranging interests who made important inquiries into what we would now call the natural sciences (especially biology), as well as major contributions to philosophy and theology. He was a master of Aristotelian thought and a *summa* writer, whose goal was to purge Aristotle of the heretical taint of Averroism and transform his philosophy into the intellectual foundation of Christian orthodoxy. But the full achievement of this goal was left to his gifted Italian student, Thomas Aquinas.

In his copious writings—particularly his *Summa Theologica*—Aquinas explored all the great questions of philosophy and theology, political theory and morality. He used Aristotle's logical method and Aristotle's categories of thought but arrived at conclusions that were in harmony with the Christian faith. Like Abelard, St. Thomas assembled every possible argument, pro and con, on every subject that he discussed; but unlike Abelard, he drew conclusions and defended them with cogent arguments. Few philosophers before or since have been so generous in presenting and exploring opinions contrary to their own, and none has been so systematic and exhaustive. St. Thomas created a vast, unified intellectual system, ranging from God to the natural world, logically supported at every step. His theological writings have none of the passion of St. Augustine, none of the literary elegance of Plato; rather, they have an intellectual elegance, an elegance of system and organization akin to that of Euclid's geometry. As in Euclidian geometry, so in Thomistic theology: Once

THE HUMAN EXPERIENCE

St. Thomas Aquinas

St. Thomas Aquinas, the most celebrated philosopher of the Middle Ages, was born of a Norman-Italian noble family in 1225. He was educated at Monte Cassino and later at the University of Naples, which had been recently founded by Emperor Frederick II—a kinsman of Thomas Aquinas's family. Since Thomas had six older brothers, he could not expect to inherit any of his family's lands. His parents intended him to become a Benedictine monk and to rise in due course to an influential abbacy. But in 1244 he shocked them by choosing a life of poverty in the fervent new Dominican order. The following year, he went to the University of Paris, and he spent the rest of his life traveling, teaching, and writing.

Unlike Augustine, Aquinas had no youthful follies to regret. Unlike Anselm and Bernard of Clairvaux, he played no great role in the political affairs of his day. But notwithstanding his placid exterior life, Aquinas was waging a great struggle—against intellectual opponents on all sides—to demonstrate that Christian revelation and human reason point, from different directions, to a single body of truth. Faith can disclose realities hidden from reason, but reason, by its very nature, cannot refute any article of faith. Working in an environment in which virtually everyone believed in God but many doubted the power of reason, Aquinas must be seen as not so much a defender of Catholicism as a champion of the potential of the human intellect.

Never before had any philosopher approached the great questions in such a comprehensive and systematic fashion. Aquinas's *Summa Theologica* is organized into an immense series of separate sections, each dealing with a particular philosophical question. In Part I of the *Summa,* for example, Question 2 takes up the problem of God's existence. The Question is subdivided into three Articles: (1) "Whether God's existence is self-evident" (St. Thomas concludes that it is not); (2) "Whether it can be demonstrated that God exists" (St. Thomas concludes that it can be logically demonstrated); and (3) "Whether God exists" (here St. Thomas endeavors to prove God's existence).

In each Article, St. Thomas takes up a specific problem and subjects it to rigorous formal analysis. He always begins with a series of Objections (Objection 1, Objection 2, and so forth), in which he sets forth as effectively as he possibly can all the arguments contrary to his final conclusion. For example, Question 2, Article 3, "Whether God exists," begins with two Objections purporting to demonstrate that God does not exist. One of them runs as follows:

> Objection 1. It seems that God does not exist, because if one of two contraries can be infinite, the other would be altogether destroyed. But the name "God" means that He is infinite goodness. Therefore, if God existed there would be no evil discoverable; but there is evil in the world. Therefore God does not exist.

Leaving the objections for the time being, Aquinas subjects the problem to his own logical scrutiny and concludes that "the existence of God can be proved in five ways." Here is one of them:

> The fifth way is taken from the governance of the world. We see that things which lack knowledge, such as natural bodies, act for an end, and this is evident from their acting always or nearly always in the same way, so as to obtain the best result. Hence it is clear that they achieve their end not only by chance but by design. Now whatever lacks knowledge cannot move toward an end unless it be directed by some being endowed with knowledge and intelligence, as the arrow is directed by the archer. Therefore some intelligent being exists by whom all natural things are directed to their end; and this being we call God.

The analysis concludes with refutations of the earlier Objections:

> Reply to Objection 1. As Augustine says, "Since God is the highest good, He would not allow an evil to exist in His works unless His omnipotence and goodness were such as to bring good even out of evil." This is part of the infinite goodness of God, that He should allow evil to exist, and out of it to produce good.

Having completed his analysis, St. Thomas then turns to the next Article or the next Question and subjects it to the same process of inquiry.

The *Summa Theologica* runs some twenty volumes in its published form, yet Aquinas left it unfinished. In his last years, until his death in 1274 at the age of forty-nine, he devoted himself to prayer and meditation. The priest who heard his deathbed confession is said to have described it as being as innocent as a five-year-old child's. ❖

Source: Quotations from *Introduction to Saint Thomas Aquinas,* ed. Anton C. Pegis (New York: Modern Library, 1948), pp. 24, 27.

a problem is settled, the conclusion can be used in solving subsequent problems. Thus the system grows, problem by problem, step by step, as St. Thomas's wide-ranging mind takes up such matters as the nature of God, the attributes of God, the nature and destiny of humanity, human morality, law, and political theory. The result is a comprehensive edifice of thought embracing all major theological issues.

St. Thomas distinguished carefully between revelation and reason but endeavored to prove that they could never contradict each other. Since human reason is a valid avenue to truth, since Christian revelation is authoritative, and since truth is one, then philosophy and Christian doctrine have to be compatible and complementary: "For faith rests upon infallible truth, and therefore its contrary cannot be demonstrated." This was the essence of St. Thomas's philosophical position. He emphasized the reality of the physical world as a world of things rather than symbols. Embracing the moderate realism of Aristotle, he declared that universals are to be found in the real, physical world and nowhere else—that knowledge comes from observation and analysis, not from divine illumination. He shared with St. Francis and others the notion that the physical world is deeply significant in itself.

Similarly the state, which previous Christian thinkers had commonly regarded as a necessary evil—an unfortunate but indispensable consequence of the Fall of Adam—was accepted by Aquinas as a good and natural outgrowth of humanity's social impulse. He echoed Aristotle's dictum that "man is a political creature" and regarded the justly governed state as a fitting part of the divine order. Like John of Salisbury (see Chapter 9), St. Thomas insisted that kings must govern in their subject's behalf and that a willful, unrestrained ruler who ignores God's moral imperatives is no king but a tyrant. Just as the human body can be corrupted by sin, the body politic can be corrupted by tyranny. But although the Christian must reject both sin and tyranny, he should nevertheless revere the body, the state, and indeed all physical creation as worthy products of God's will, inseparable from the world of spirit, and essential ingredients in the unity of existence.

Aquinas sought to encompass the totality of existence in a vast, overarching unity. At the center is God, the author of physical and spiritual creation, the maker of heaven and earth, who himself assumed human form and redeemed all humanity on the cross, who discloses portions of the truth to his followers through revelation, permits them to discover other portions through the operation of the intellect, and will lead them into all truth after death through salvation. Ultimately, God is truth, and it is our destiny, on reaching heaven, to stand unshielded in the Divine Presence—to love and to know. Thus the roads of St. Thomas, St. Bonaventure, St. Bernard, St. Hildegard, and Dante, although passing over very different terrain, arrive finally at the same destination.

Aquinas's thought has often been regarded as the embodiment of the medieval world view. Yet many of his own contemporaries rejected it in whole or in part. Franciscans such as Bonaventure were suspicious of the intellectual tour de force of this gifted Dominican. Bonaventure was a rationalist but a cautious one, and his Franciscan successors came increasingly to the opinion that reason is of little or no use in probing metaphysical problems. After his death, St. Thomas's bold attempts to approach God through reason would come under withering criticism by other Christian thinkers who denied that the doctrines of faith could ever be logically demonstrated (see Chapter 11). For a while it seemed that his approach and even his writings might be officially condemned.

In the Catholic Reformation of the sixteenth century, however, Aquinas's sturdy faith that reason could support doctrine came into its own, and he was enthusiastically embraced by theologians and ecclesiastical politicians eager for intellectual ammunition to fire at Protestantism (see Chapter 13). The early twentieth century, too—when Catholic intellectuals felt themselves under siege by scientists and quacks, rationalists and irrationalists, atheists and agnostics, Marxists and fascists—was another age in which Aquinas's thought flourished. An entire school of Catholic "Neo-Thomism" arose, and St. Thomas was declared the official philosopher of Roman Catholicism. Such, in large measure, he remains to this day.

Mysticism and Apocalypse

Attempts to circumvent rationality and achieve spiritual oneness with God had always been an element in medieval devotional life. St. Anselm and St. Bonaventure, as we have seen, defended the aspiration to encounter God face-to-face, and late in his life Aquinas declared that he had witnessed a mystical vision of God, compared with which all his books were rubbish. Thereafter he never returned to his logical studies.

Various well-known medieval mystics never seriously entered on the path of rationalism in the first place. One of the most formidable of these was the southern Italian monk Joachim of Fiore (ca. 1135–ca. 1202), a Cistercian abbot who found administrative routine so distracting to his contemplative leanings that he became a hermit. Even so, he attracted a flock of disciples, and in 1196, he received papal permission to form his own monastic order. After his death his writings exercised a powerful fascination over the Franciscans and Dominicans.

Joachim agonized throughout his long life over the darker, more perplexing passages of the Bible. Seeing both the Old and New Testaments as revelations of God's providential role in history, as revealed respectively by God the Father and by Jesus the Son of God, the symbolism of the Trinity led him to foresee a coming Third Age of the Holy Spirit (see Figure 10-1). For Joachim, the culminating stage

FIGURE 10-1

JOACHIM OF FIORE'S THREE CIRCLES OF THE TRINITY

Joachim circulated numerous drawings and diagrams to explain his visions. This diagram shows his three-era view of history, integrating Jesus (IEUE), the Old Testament and New Testament (Vetus Testamentum and Novum Testamentum), and the three ages (primus status, secundus status, and tertius status), which correspond to the overlapping circles governed successively by the Father (Pater), the Son (Filius), and the Holy Spirit (Sps Scs, or Spiritus Sanctus). Note how history begins with Adam and culminates with the end of the world (finis mundi). At the upper and lower left corners, other diagrams fit the name IEUE into the Greek letters alpha (A) and omega (ω), symbolizing Jesus.
Source: From Bernard McGinn, The Calabrian Abbot: Joachim of Fiore in the History of Western Thought (New York: Macmillan, 1985), fig. 7, p. 180.

of history would be ushered in with the defeat of the Antichrist and the fulfillment of every awesome **prophecy** of the Book of Revelation—that perennial fount of Christian apocalyptic hopes and fears.

St. Augustine, St. Jerome, and Pope Gregory the Great had laid down what would become the medieval Latin church's basic interpretation of the Apocalypse. There would be, they said, no literal thousand-year reign of Christ on earth before the Last Judgment; rather the Book of Revelation's apocalyptic vision must be interpreted symbolically, as foretelling the long period when Christians would be led by the institutional church. That period, still unfolding, would last until the end of the world, God alone knew when. Joachim of Fiore broke with the Latin Church Fathers by reviving the prophecy of a coming thousand-year period of bliss and justice. What role the papal-led church would play in this New Age he never made very clear. But Joachim rejected as presumptuous the theology of Abelard's pupil Peter Lombard, with its basic premise

that the human mind, guided by reason and in harmony with church teachings, could comprehend God.

Joachim's attack on Peter Lombard directly challenged the theology that the thirteenth-century church considered orthodox, and the Fourth Lateran Council in 1215 rejected Joachim's criticisms. The Calabrian mystic himself had died about a decade before, and his apocalyptic visions were not officially criticized. Thereafter his writings and symbolic drawings, as well as a growing body of prophesies attributed to him, were circulated by enthusiasts. Among them were Franciscans and Dominicans who shared his dreams of a dawning age of heightened spiritual inspiration. The institutional church regarded the burgeoning Joachimite tradition half with respect for the possibility that it was divinely inspired, and half with nervousness that Joachim and his admirers might be dupes of the devil. Joachimite prophesies of imminent apocalyptic happenings, mixed with impatience about the church's failings, burned brightly if often surreptitiously throughout the Late Middle

Notre-Dame Cathedral: *The Last Judgment* The Last Judgment was a favorite theme for preachers, and it was generally portrayed above the central portal leading into a medieval cathedral. In the mid-twelfth century the scene became standardized, as shown here. Appearing "in great power and majesty," Jesus raises his hands to reveal the wounds of his crucifixion, by which he has redeemed those who followed him in life. Although not sanctioned by the Gospel of Matthew, the medieval scene always included the Virgin Mary and St. John, on whom people relied to intercede with Jesus, now the stern judge. *Alinari/Art Resource, NY.*

Ages. The Reformation, as we shall see in Chapter 13, would have more than its share of apocalyptic visions. Even now, the Catholic church still accepts the Augustinian position on the Apocalypse, and it has still not decided whether Joachim of Fiore was a saint or a heretic.

Some of the most celebrated mystical visionaries of the High Middle Ages were women. As the authority of the clergy increased with the development of canon law and the growth of the church bureaucracy, religious women—who were denied the priestly authority to preach and consecrate the Eucharist—found an alternative and more immediate source of divine authorization in their mystical union with Christ. The divine revelations of St. Hildegard of Bingen impressed St. Bernard of Clairvaux so deeply that he addressed her as a "prophetess of God." John of Salisbury was of similar opinion. Widely regarded as a direct source of divine knowledge, Hildegard was consulted by theologians on thorny points of doctrine and by popes and emperors on questions of high politics. Unlike her slightly younger contemporary Joachim, she never veered off into apocalyptic speculation.

At the thirteenth-century abbey of Helfta in Saxony, Gertrude of Helfta (d. 1301/1302) and other nuns had visions of a Christ who was at once regal and lovingly approachable; their writings express what has aptly been called "a poised, self-confident, lyrical female mysticism."[9] Much of their imagery was a Christianized version of the love poetry of the German minnesingers, with which the nuns doubtless had become acquainted through their own aristocratic families. In turn, the nuns of Helfta may

[9] Caroline Walker Bynum, *Jesus as Mother: Studies in the Spirituality of the High Middle Ages* (Berkeley: University of California Press, 1982), p. 185.

THE HISTORICAL EVIDENCE

The Soul's Journey to the Heavenly Court

late thirteenth century

The vivid imagery of the beguine Mechthild of Magdeburg's The Flowing Light of the Godhead *was deeply influenced by the style and content of German courtly love literature, as this selection shows. It is titled "Of the Soul's Journey to Court, Where God Reveals Himself."*

When the poor soul comes to court, she is wise and courtly, and so she looks upon her God with joy. Ah, with what great love she is received there. She is silent, intensely longing that He should praise her. Then with great desire He shows her His divine heart: it is like reddish gold, burning in a large charcoal fire. Then He places her in His ardent heart so that the Noble Prince and the little servant girl embrace and are united, as water and wine. Then she is brought to nought and abandons herself, as if she had no strength left, while He is sick with love for her, as He has always been, for (in this desire) there can be neither growth nor lessening. Thus she speaks: "Lord, You are my consolation, my desire, my flowing fountain, my sun, and I am your mirror." Such is the journey to court of the loving soul, who cannot be without God.

Source: From Emilie Zum Brunn and Georgette Epiney-Burgard, eds., *Women Mystics in Medieval Europe*, trans. Sheila Hughes (New York: Paragon House, 1989), p. 57.

themselves have been influenced by the mystical writings of the beguines, whose loosely organized groups grew to considerable numbers during the thirteenth and early fourteenth centuries in the towns of Germany and the Netherlands (see Chapter 8). The beguines sought to follow St. Francis's example of loving service to others in imitation of Christ—a kind of evangelism that was denied to the strictly cloistered female Franciscans, the Poor Clares. Living by no papally sanctioned religious rule and taking no lifetime vows, the beguines were alternately praised and condemned by ecclesiastical authorities; but they continued to flourish into the Late Middle Ages, representing a kind of mystical lay piety that grew increasingly significant in the fourteenth and fifteenth centuries.

The goal of imitating Christ gave rise in many thirteenth-century beguine communities to powerful mystical experiences, expressed in vernacular prose and poetry of great immediacy and intensity. The aristocratic beguine Mechthild of Magdeburg (d. ca. 1282), whose *Flowing Light of the Godhead* is a vivid and deeply personal description of her experiences of divine union, ended her days at Helfta as a nun. Dante praised her in his *Divine Comedy*, and Mechthild probably helped inspire the outpouring of mystical writings at Helfta. Her orthodoxy, like St. Hildegard's, was never seriously called into question by the church authorities, but as we have already seen in the tragic case of Marguerite Porete, who was burned in 1310 (see Chapter 8), having mystical visions always carried the danger of being declared a heretic, deluded by the devil. Anyone, indeed, who claimed a personal revelation from God was dangerous, for the institutional church asserted (on St. Augustine's ever-formidable authority) that God had entrusted the keys to heaven to it alone. In an age that took seriously the idea that souls in this life were making a perilous pilgrimage to salvation, from which Satan was trying to divert them to hell, subjective notions of the Truth were highly suspicious.

The Investigation of Nature

Compared with attempting to read the mind of God and predict what the future held in store, plumbing nature's mysteries seemed to medieval Christians considerably less dangerous. Nature, the Bible taught, mirrored the glory and omnipotence of its divine Creator, and the more that it could be understood, the deeper would be the investigator's faith in—and awe of—God. The idea, common in some circles today, that theology and natural science are mutually incompatible would have shocked the vast majority of medieval thinkers.

Early medieval west Europeans had virtually forgotten Greek and Roman attempts to understand the natural world, and had fallen far behind contemporary Islamic efforts to preserve and even advance the heritage of ancient learning. Such ignorance began to dissipate just before the year 1000, when Gerbert of Aurillac visited Islamic Spain, familiarized himself with Islamic thought, and made his own modest contribution to natural knowledge. Gerbert built a simple "planetarium" of balls, rods, and bands to illustrate the rotation of the stars and the motions of the planets. He introduced the abacus and Arabic numerals to the West and, following the Greeks, Arabs, and earlier West European scholars, he taught that the earth was round. Although Gerbert—who would become Pope Sylvester II—was regarded by some of his Western contemporaries as a bit of a magician, he had helped bring Europe abreast of the latest advances in Islamic science.

Muslim investigations continued thereafter to inspire Western scholars, particularly in the late eleventh and twelfth centuries. Philosophers such as Adelard of Bath (ca. 1144) retraced Gerbert's journey into the Islamic lands and returned with a new respect for scientific inquiry—as well as an abundance of astrological texts. (Astrology, regarded as a serious science, staged an impressive intellectual resurgence in high-medieval and late medieval Europe. Some philosophers and theologians, however, criticized it as excessively deterministic.)

The twelfth-century translators made the great scientific works of Greece and Islam known to the West. Adelard's translations from Arabic into Latin included Euclid's *Elements* and an important Muslim work on arithmetic that used "Arabic" (actually Indian) numerals. Other translators contributed Aristotle's *Physics*, Ptolemy's *Almagest* (to give that astronomical treatise its Arabic title), Arabic books on algebra, astrology, and medicine, and many others. And Western scholars began to write scientific books of their own. Such works, however, were mere summaries of Greek and Arabic knowledge. The purely assimilative phase of Western investigations of the natural world continued until the thirteenth century.

Franciscans initiated serious medieval scientific inquiries, inspired both by their religious devotion and their reverence for nature. The mysticism of St. Bonaventure represented one pole of Franciscan thought; at the other stood a group of thinkers who, inspired perhaps by St. Francis's love of nature, applied their logical tools to the task of investigating the physical world. Thirteenth-century Oxford became Europe's chief center of inquiry into the workings of nature and the birthplace of the first creative work in what would become Western science.

The key figure in the development of medieval learning about the natural world was the English scholar Robert Grosseteste (ca. 1170–1253), a future bishop of Lincoln. Although not a friar, Grosseteste was chief lecturer to Franciscans studying at Oxford. Grosseteste had a comprehensive knowledge of Platonic and Neoplatonic philosophy, Aristotelian physics, and the scientific legacy of Islam. At bottom, he was a Platonist and an Augustinian, but he wrote major commentaries on the scientific works of Aristotle and could draw on both traditions.

From Plato, Grosseteste derived the notion that mathematics is a basic key to understanding the physical universe; the fundamental importance of numbers is very much in keeping with the Platonic realist interpretation of

universals, and Plato himself had asserted that "God is a mathematician." From Aristotle, Grosseteste learned the importance of abstracting knowledge from the world of phenomena by means of observation and experiment (see Chapter 3).

Thus, bridging the two ancient traditions, Grosseteste brought together the mathematical and experimental components that together helped open the way for modern science. More than that, drawing on the suggestive work of his Islamic predecessors he worked out a far more rigorous experimental procedure than is to be found in the pages of Aristotle. A pioneer in the development of scientific method, he outlined a system of observation, hypothesis, and experimental verification that was eventually elaborated into the methodology of modern science.

Grosseteste was better at formulating a methodology than in applying it to specific problems, and his explanations of heat, light, color, comets, and rainbows were rejected in later centuries. But the experimental method that he formulated became in time a powerful intellectual tool. The problem of the rainbow, for example, was largely solved in the fourteenth century by Theodoric of Freiburg, who employed a refined version of Grosseteste's experimental method.

Grosseteste's work was carried further by the Oxford Franciscan Roger Bacon (ca. 1214–1294). The author of a fascinating body of speculative work, Roger Bacon dabbled in alchemy, and his curiosity carried him along what may now seem to us strange roads. But he foreshadowed modern scientists in his criticism of the deductive logic and metaphysical speculations that so fascinated his scholastic contemporaries: "Reasoning," he wrote, "does not illuminate these matters; experiments are required, conducted on a large scale, performed with instruments and by various necessary means."

At his best, Roger Bacon was almost prophetic. "Experimental science," he claimed, "controls the conclusions of all other sciences. It reveals truths which reasoning from general principles would never have discovered. Finally, it starts us on the way to marvelous inventions which will change the face of the world."

We must understand high-medieval science in its historical context, neither overrating its achievements nor sneering at its dead ends. Medieval Islamic and Western science, like the earlier Greek and even Babylonian inquiries into the natural world, belonged to what modern historians of science call the Old Paradigm. According to this set of ideas, the earth was still the center of God's creation, and explanations of nature and natural phenomena still tended to be qualitative and moralistic, not quantitative and mechanistic. The great conceptual breakthroughs that would produce modern science still lay several hundred years ahead in the Scientific Revolution.

Yet the work of the medieval Islamic scholars, of Grosseteste and Bacon, and of other westerners whom there is not space here to mention, was important. By patient observation and record-keeping, particularly of the night sky, they were accumulating data that are still of value to researchers. Honestly recording what they saw, and noticing unpredicted discrepancies, they were beginning to raise uncomfortable questions about the explanations of natural phenomena that they had inherited from revered intellectual predecessors. The first serious questions about Aristotle's laws of motion were being asked: Was it indeed true that all things should "naturally" be at rest? What was the mysterious force that seemed to be imparted to moving bodies, which one Western investigator termed *impetus?*

No medieval thinkers were in a position to challenge the Old Paradigm head-on. More data—more discrepancies from the predictions of Aristotelian and Ptolemaic science—had to accumulate. Mathematical sophistication had to increase. Yet the seeds were being planted, especially in Grosseteste's formulation of the rules of scientific reasoning, in Bacon's fascination with empirical research, and in both men's hunch that nature's secrets had something to do with mathematical patterns.

A Rational Universe

Mysticism was and would remain a potent force in medieval culture, but it was suspect by the church precisely because it could not be subjected to rational analysis and institutional control. The quest for such order underlay the achievements of the high-medieval logicians, scientists, and system builders, whose attitude toward the world was in some basic respects changing.

Some of the best minds of the twelfth and thirteenth centuries were coming to view God's created universe as a natural order, functioning in accordance with consistent, divinely constituted laws and therefore open to rational inspection. Abelard was an early exponent of this new naturalism, but it is also to be found in the writings of many other philosophers of the twelfth and thirteenth centuries. The collapse of the central tower of Winchester cathedral in 1107 was attributed by some to the entombment of the blaspheming King William II beneath it; but the historian William of Malmesbury had his doubts: "The structure could have fallen because of faulty construction, even if the king had never been buried there."

In the view of the scholastics, a rational, loving God had created a world that was both intelligible and good. The goodness of nature found its most eloquent expression in St. Francis's "Song of Brother Sun"; it also inspired the idealized naturalism of the Gothic sculptors, Dante's poetry in praise of Beatrice, Thomas Aquinas's philosophy, and the stirrings of scientific curiosity in Robert Grosseteste and Roger Bacon.

Many medieval people would long continue to regard the world as threatening and unpredictable, gov-

A Rational Universe: God the Architect In this illumination from a mid-thirteenth-century French Old Testament, God uses calipers to design the universe, bringing order out of chaos. This image epitomizes the high-medieval faith that God's creation is good, knowable, and rationally delimited. *Corbis/Bettman.*

erned by supernatural forces and possessed by the devil. Such attitudes flourished long after the Middle Ages were over, and indeed they are alive today, as the headlines of the supermarket tabloids readily reveal. But during the cultural awakening of the High Middle Ages such pessimism was gradually diminishing among the best minds of western Europe as they sought to probe and comprehend their universe.

CONCLUSION: *THE HIGH-MEDIEVAL LEGACY*

The fundamental changes of the High Middle Ages—economic, territorial, religious, political-administrative, literary, artistic, and intellectual—gave the Europe of 1300 all the hallmarks of a great, highly distinctive civilization. As Chapters 8, 9, and 10 have made clear, high-medieval Europe was no utopia: It was beset by the violence, corruption, exploitation, cruelty, poverty, and ruthless ambition that, unfortunately, characterize all human societies, including our own. But it must also be credited with remarkable achievements.

Europe became urbanized, economically as well as culturally, during the High Middle Ages. Its towns and cities were the sites not only of buoyant commercial activity, largely independent of state monopolies, but also of vast cathedrals whose scale and design made them unique in the world. Some cities were also the sites of flourishing universities, the first establishments of their kind, whose goals and institutions would be imitated throughout the globe down to the present. Nowhere was this juxtaposition of architecture, sculpture, and intellectual vitality more evident than in Capetian Paris, with its illustrious university (whose faculty celebrities included Abelard, Bonaventure, and Thomas Aquinas) and its churches, which included two of the foremost examples of Gothic architecture and sculpture in all Christendom—the cathedral of Notre-Dame, and La Ste.-Chapelle.

The papacy was a similarly unique institution, both for the degree of its centralized religious authority and for its independence from the major secular regimes of its day. And although the European state bureaucracies of 1300 were exceeded in size and complexity by those of China, the kingdoms that they served were balanced between monarchs, aristocratic assemblies, and an international church in a way that would not be found elsewhere. Meanwhile, the kingdoms of western Europe were evolving toward the great world powers that they would become a few centuries later.

Territorial expansion was another significant factor in Europe's high-medieval transformation. At a time when European cities were still relatively small, knights were winning for the Latin West such wealthy metropolises as Palermo, Toledo, Cordova, Antioch, and Constantinople. Their capture, and the extension of European maritime dominion into the eastern Mediterranean and the Black and Baltic Seas, poured money and precious goods into the towns and river valleys of the European heartland. Not all of these cities were still in Europe's possession in 1300. But the transformation that resulted from their capture, and from the great advances in Europe's frontiers, would never be undone.

By 1300, stunning churches in the new Gothic style, ornamented by equally impressive works of naturalistic Gothic sculpture, had been rising throughout much of western Europe for 150 years. Gothic statues, arrayed against the facades of churches and sometimes ornamenting their interiors, exhibit an idealized naturalism clearly inspired by classical models. But they also displayed a spiritual serenity that is distinctly unclassical—and characteristically high-medieval.

Gothic boldness and naturalism were reflected in the new approach to nature adopted by high-medieval theologians and philosophers. As they built brave new theological systems on rational foundations—exhibiting perhaps an unprecedented intellectual hubris as they tried to explain the material and spiritual structures of the universe—they credited the human mind with greater intellectual powers than most predecessors or successors have found plausible. Many believed that, with just a little more time and effort, they could lay bare the secrets of the divinely created cosmos. Such optimism is rare in history; in Europe it scarcely survived the thirteenth century, and it is long gone today. It is a hope characteristic of its times, and one that sets high-medieval civilization apart from most other societies.

This same cosmic optimism is evident in Dante's *Divine Comedy*, the crowning glory of high-medieval literature. Dante's journey through hell and purgatory, and upward through the spheres of the heavens to the presence of God, traces an itinerary through the universe of the scholastic theologians—at once a physical and a spiritual order, and one that a person such as Dante could know and understand. Dante's God is both a creator and a loving father: He is "Holy Love, that moves the stars and sun," and the universe that he created is both coherent and fundamentally good. This idea would not last, but it is a vision that ignited European thought at the height of the medieval phase of Western civilization.

Selected Reading

Sources

Dante, *Divine Comedy*. There are many translations of Dante's work, but especially recommended is Allen Mandelbaum's translation in three volumes (1980–1982). Avoid older translations of medieval literature that attempt to reproduce "archaic" English. Highly recommended are *The Song of Roland* (trans. Glyn Burgess, 1990) and *The Complete Romances of Chretien de Troyes* (trans. David Staines, 1990). For excellent English translations of medieval lyric poetry from France, Italy, Germany, and Spain, sample Angel Flores, *An Anthology of Medieval Lyrics* (1962). St. Hildegard of Bingen's *Scivias* has been translated by Mother Columba Hart and Jane Bishop, with an illuminating introduction by Barbara J. Newman and a preface by Caroline Walker Bynum (1990).

Holt, Elizabeth G., ed. *A Documentary History of Art*, vol. 1 (1957).

Pegis, Anton C., ed. *Introduction to Saint Thomas Aquinas* (1948).

Shapiro, Herman, ed. *Medieval Philosophy* (1964).

Thorndyke, Lynn, ed. *University Records and Life in the Middle Ages* (1944).

Zum Brunn, Emilie, and Georgette Epiney-Burgard, eds. *Women Mystics in Medieval Europe* (1989).

Mentality, Upbringing, and Education

Chenu, M. D. *Nature, Man and Society in the Twelfth Century: Essays on New Theological Perspectives in the Latin West* (1968). Eds. and trans. Jerome Taylor and Lester K. Little. Essays translated from the French, exploring basic changes in mental outlook in twelfth-century theology.

Clanchy, M. T. *From Memory to Written Record: England, 1066–1307*, 2nd ed. (1992). A challenging, highly original study of the emergence of a literate mentality in high-medieval England.

Hanawalt, Barbara A. *Growing Up in Medieval London: The Experience of Childhood in History* (1993). Focusing on the fourteenth and fifteenth centuries, this carefully researched, well-written study shows, as against earlier views, that medieval people were keenly aware of and responsive to the stages of childhood and adolescence.

Jaeger, C. Stephen. *The Origins of Courtliness: Civilizing Trends and the Formation of Courtly Ideals, 939–1210* (1985). This book brilliantly traces ideals of courtly behavior to the training of future bishops at German cathedral schools and the royal chapel in principles derived from Cicero and other classical writers.

LeGoff, Jacques. *Intellectuals in the Middle Ages* (1993). Argues cogently for the emergence of a new intellectual class toward the beginning of the High Middle Ages.

Morris, Colin. *The Discovery of the Individual, 1050–1200* (1972). The fascinating, controversial thesis of this book is embedded in its title.

Pedersen, Olaf. *The First Universities: Studium Generale and the Origins of University Education in Europe* (1997). Traces the history of European higher education back to Rome and Byzantium, and provides an excellent survey of the rise of the medieval university.

Rashdall, Hastings. *The Universities of Europe in the Middle Ages*, 2nd ed., 3 vols., eds. F. M. Powicke and A. B. Emden (1936). Originally published in 1896 and heavily revised in 1936, this classic remains a gold mine of information about medieval universities, students, professors, and education, organized university-by-university. It is more to be sampled than read through.

Shahar, Shulamith. *Childhood in the Middle Ages* (1990). An excellent summary and review of recent research.

Stock, Brian. *The Implications of Literacy: Written Language and Models of Interpretation in the Eleventh and Twelfth Centuries* (1983). A challenging, complex work arguing that European intellectual life was profoundly stimulated and transformed by the growth of literacy and the emergence of "textual communities."

Symoens, Hilde De Ridder, ed. *Universities in the Middle Ages* (1992). Part of a projected four-volume history of European universities down to the present, this impressive book assembles authoritative essays by some of the leading European and British scholars in the field.

Literature, Art, and Thought

Berman, Harold J. *Law and Revolution: The Formation of the Western Legal Tradition* (1983). In this wide-ranging intellectual tour de force, the author argues that the Western legal tradition and other fundamental components of Western culture had their inception in the Investiture Controversy—or, as he aptly calls it, "the papal revolution."

Bony, Jean. *French Gothic Architecture of the Twelfth and Thirteenth Centuries* (1983). Scholarly excellence and visual beauty combine in this authoritative, superbly illustrated volume.

Bynum, Caroline Walker. *Jesus as Mother: Studies in the Spirituality of the High Middle Ages* (1982). Perceptive essays on the social history of spirituality, the discovery of the self, and mysticism among the nuns of Helfta.

Flanigan, Sabina. *Hildegard of Bingen, 1098–1179* (1989). A good, comprehensive study of Hildegard's life and writings.

Grant, Edward. *Physical Science in the Middle Ages* (1971). Stresses the impact of Aristotelian physical science on the medieval scientific outlook.

Haren, Michael. *Medieval Thought: The Western Intellectual Tradition from Antiquity to the Thirteenth Century*, 2nd ed. (1992). A clear, concise, well-organized survey from Plato through Aquinas and Siger of Brabant.

Haskins, Charles Homer. *The Renaissance of the Twelfth Century* (1927). A seminal work that has retained its value for generations; particularly strong on Latin literature.

Knowles, David. *The Evolution of Medieval Thought*, 2nd ed. (1988). A short, lucid survey by a great English scholar who was also a Benedictine monk.

McGinn, Bernard. *The Calabrian Abbot: Joachim of Fiore in the History of Western Thought* (1985). The best English-language treatment of Joachim.

Martindale, Andrew. *Gothic Art from the Twelfth to the Fifteenth Century* (1967). A beautifully illustrated survey of all forms of Gothic art—cathedral architecture, sculpture, painting, and manuscript illumination.

Newman, Barbara. *Sister of Wisdom: St. Hildegard's Theology of the Feminine* (1987). An important, subtle, deeply learned exploration of the theology of the great twelfth-century mystic.

Partner, Nancy F. *Serious Entertainments: The Writing of History in Twelfth-Century England* (1977). A gifted writer and scholar explores the spiritual and intellectual qualities of three major twelfth-century historians, and in the process casts fresh light on the mental outlook of their era.

Price, B. B. *Medieval Thought: An Introduction* (1992). Clear and up-to-date in its scholarship, the best survey of the topic.

Southern, R. W. *Robert Grosseteste: The Growth of an English Mind in Mediaeval Europe* (1986). A masterful although speculative reexamination of one of medieval England's most intelligent churchmen, whose complex blend of conservative and radical approaches to thirteenth-century Christian society made him "an enigma to his contemporaries."

———. *Saint Anselm: A Portrait in a Landscape* (1990). A series of wise second thoughts on Anselm's public and intellectual career, revising an earlier study.

Tierney, Brian. *Church Law and Constitutional Thought in the Middle Ages* (1979). A work of fundamental importance that finds the roots of modern constitutional ideas in the ecclesiastical reform movement of the twelfth century—elaborated in Tierney's *Religion, Law, and the Growth of Constitutional Thought, 1150–1650* (1982).

Weisheipl, James A. *Friar Thomas d'Aquino: His Life, Thought and Work*, new ed. (1983). A sympathetic, scholarly treatment of Aquinas's life in its historical setting.

PART THREE

AN AGE OF TRANSITION

Sometimes very distant events trigger major historical consequences. So it was in the late twelfth century when a tribal leader named Temüjin unified the nomadic peoples north of the Great Wall of China and sent his mounted warriors in all directions. His people acclaimed him as Genghis (or Chingiz) Khan—"great king." The Mongol Empire that he and his successors built in the thirteenth century stretched from Ukraine and Iraq to Korea and southern China. Sung China, the Abbasid Caliphate, and Kievan Russia all collapsed before irresistible Mongol onslaughts. Genghis Khan (ca. 1155–1227) and his successors ruled by far the largest concentration of territories and peoples ever unified up to that time.

Four societies that the Mongols set out to conquer escaped succumbing. One was Vietnam, which not for the last time in history held off the world's mightiest military machine. The second, Japan, was twice assaulted by seaborne Mongol forces, but both times tough Japanese warriors and storms that the islanders called *kamikaze* ("divine wind") turned back the invaders. The third was Egypt, whose Turkic rulers (the Mamluks) had earlier defeated the European crusaders. The fourth survivor was Europe; but it was not military prowess or exceptional unity or even nature that saved the West—just sheer luck. In 1241 and 1242, huge Mongol pincers swept across the Ukrainian steppe to invade Poland and Hungary. Using their customary tactics—surprise attacks coordinated over vast distances, and a terrifying ruthlessness that often involved the slaughter of whole cities—the Mongols rampaged through Hungary and may have killed half the population. At Legnica in Silesia, meanwhile, the Mongols crushed an army of Polish and German knights. The road into Europe lay open. Then word arrived that Genghis Khan's successor Ogodei had died, and the invaders went home to redivide the empire. They never came back. But for two centuries to come, Mongol (or Tatar, as they were locally known)[1] rulers entrenched themselves in Russia, organizing a state called the Golden Horde.

By the early fourteenth century, another nomadic confederacy also confronted Christendom. The Ottomans, one

of many Turkic peoples driven from their Central Asian homeland by the Mongols, fled into Anatolia and took service as mercenaries under the Seljuk Turks, who themselves in 1071 had seized a large part of the Byzantine Empire (see Chapter 6). When in 1243 the Mongols destroyed the Seljuks, the Ottomans hung on, wedged between the Mongols and Byzantines and fighting both. Their fierce brand of Islam attracted Muslim adherents to their confederacy from all over the region.

In 1354 the Ottomans invaded southeastern Europe. At first they bypassed what little was left of the Byzantine Empire—Constantinople and its immediate environs. Serbia went down to total defeat in 1389 in the battle of Kosovo, virtually the entire Serbian aristocracy perishing on St. Vitus's Day, still Serbia's national day of mourning.[2] The Ottomans' dominion now extended over the Balkans. By luck, they survived a rout in 1402 at the hands of the Tatar chieftain Timur the Lame (Tamerlane), one of history's great mass murderers: More interested in conquering India than the West, he did not follow up his victory.

Economically and demographically, by the fifteenth century Constantinople had shrunk to a shadow of its former glory, though its great walls remained intact. So desperate did the situation seem in 1439 that, at the Council of Florence, the Byzantine emperor and the patriarch of Constantinople capitulated to virtually all the papacy's terms for a reunion of the Eastern and Western churches, hoping in return for Western aid. But in 1444 the Turks

---

[1] *Tatar* refers to the Mongol and Turkic peoples who coalesced into new confederacies in southern Russia. The spelling *Tartar* is a European pun on the Latin word *Tartarus*, meaning the infernal regions: "Tartars" were men from hell.

[2] The anniversary of the battle—June 28—was ill-advisedly chosen for Austro-Hungarian Archduke Francis Ferdinand's visit to the Bosnian capital, Sarajevo, in 1914; his assassination on that occasion by a Serbian nationalist precipitated World War I. More recently, Serbia's attempt to "ethnically cleanse" the Kosovo province, where mostly Islamic Albanians now constitute about 90 percent of the population, underscores how crucial Kosovo is to Serbian nationalists.

wiped out an army of European crusaders in Bulgaria, while Constantinople's populace repudiated union with the hated "Franks," trusting that their "God-defended" city would miraculously survive. Meanwhile the Ottoman sultan Mohammed II had enveloped Constantinople and assembled the latest heavy artillery and Western gunners. On May 29, 1453, the final assault began after the city refused to surrender peacefully. Ottoman artillery blasted an opening in the walls, through which the Muslim army poured. The last Byzantine emperor, Constantine XI, died fighting, and the civilians who took refuge in Hagia Sophia, praying for a miracle, were massacred. After three days of slaughter and looting, Mohammed "the Conqueror" restored order and gave thanks to God in Hagia Sophia, now a mosque. Constantinople was quickly resettled with Muslims, who called the city by the name it still bears—Istanbul.

All Europe recognized that Mohammed II, by conquering Constantine's unconquerable city, had ended an era and brought an ominous, expansive, and utterly alien new power onto their threshold. Mohammed followed up his victory by seizing the coastal areas of Greece and Albania from Venice. In 1480 the Ottomans invaded the kingdom of Naples and held the port of Otranto for a year, massacring all the men and setting up a profitable business in Christian slaves. In the sixteenth century they would overwhelm Hungary and besiege Vienna. Not until the end of the seventeenth century would the West begin to roll back the Turks, and only in the nineteenth century did the Balkan Christians regain self-rule.

From the perspective of global history, Europe during the fourteenth and fifteenth centuries was a cluster of relatively small states isolated at the western tip of a Eurasia dominated by vast empires. As Chapter 11 will show, during much of this period Europe was also suffering terrible disasters: famine, a deadly plague epidemic called the Black Death, economic depression, insurrections and civil war, and chronic wars between its kings.

But civilization had taken root in high-medieval Europe (ca. 1050–1300), and European society proved resilient enough to survive its late medieval traumas. By the mid-fifteenth century, economic and demographic recovery was under way. Europeans were strengthening their political institutions; they were developing a new form of economic organization that historians call capitalism; they were evolving the new cultural standards of Renaissance humanism; and they were tinkering with ingenious new devices to keep time, magnify objects, disseminate information, and navigate the seas. All these creative forces came together by 1500 to produce a new outburst of energy.

The best contemporary parallel to the West's impressive recovery was China's eventual absorption of the Mongol invaders. By 1368 China regained self-rule under the Ming Dynasty, which would govern until 1644. In the early fifteenth century, the Chinese government sent into the Indian Ocean large maritime expeditions that reached the coast of East Africa. Ultimately, however, the Ming decided that there was not enough in the outside world to be worth a global projection of Chinese power.

Western Europeans looked at the outer world differently. Even while the Mongol Empire was at its height, European merchants like Marco Polo (1254–1324) and emissaries of thirteenth-century popes were trekking the immense distance to "Cathay," as Westerners called China. Polo, who spent twenty-five years in the service of the Mongols (they liked to employ pliable foreigners), brought back tales of the seemingly incredible riches of East Asia. Many dismissed Polo's account as a fantasy, and the Franciscan friars whom the papacy sent to the Mongol khans failed to convert them to Christianity. (The khans opted for Buddhism and Chinese culture instead.) Then the advent of the Ottoman Turks severed overland links between Europe and the East. The sea, however, remained a possible means by which Westerners could both outflank Islam and regain the Holy Land by the back door, and also tap Asian markets without having to deal with Muslim middlemen. The challenge of blazing this maritime route to the East was taken up first by two Genoese sea captains as early as 1291—but they disappeared somewhere beyond Gibraltar. Fourteenth- and fifteenth-century Portuguese sailors were more cautious, adapting from their Muslim rivals new ships and navigational equipment and slowly learning how to deal with the currents and winds of the Atlantic. Gradually they opened a route down the African coast and (this was crucial) learned how to sail back against the winds. By 1500, they made some fateful discoveries: that the Atlantic could be a highway for Europeans, not just a barrier; that trading in black African slaves and putting them to work on sugar plantations could be enormously profitable; and that it was possible to sail around Africa and reach India.

Even more dramatic global changes were already under way. Barred by Portugal from attempting similar voyages, the next-door kingdom of Castile struck out westward. In 1492, Queen Isabella of Castile[3] commissioned a Genoese navigator, Christopher Columbus, to try to reach East Asia by sailing directly west, around the globe. Columbus failed to reach Cathay; but he did accomplish the epoch-making "discovery" (from the European perspective) of the Western Hemisphere. Unlike the Norse voyages to Greenland and North America around the year 1000, which Europeans had either forgotten or never known about, Columbus's four transatlantic expeditions got triumphant publicity in Europe. And the Castilian authorities followed them up

---

[3] She and her spouse, King Ferdinand of Aragon, jointly ruled a newly united Spain. But ventures into the Atlantic were strictly Castile's business.

with an aggressive policy of conquest, colonization, and Christianization. The American empire-building pursued by sixteenth- and seventeenth-century Europeans—first Castilians and Portuguese, and later French, Dutch, and English—surpassed even the Mongols in the amount of new territory brought under imperial sway and outdid even the Black Death in wreaking demographic catastrophe. The microbes that European colonizers, their African slaves, and their Eurasian animals unwittingly brought across the Atlantic and passed to the Western Hemisphere's native population, which lacked immunity to these infections, reduced the population of the Americas by up to 90 percent. At such a fearful cost, the globe and its peoples were united in a single ecological community.

While Europeans were forging their transatlantic empire and creating a transatlantic slave trade, Europe's internal history during the sixteenth and seventeenth centuries, to which the chapters of Part Three will give much attention, can be summed up in a few words: religious fracturing, political conflict, social unrest, economic fluctuation, and cultural creativity. The Protestant Reformation ended forever the dream of Christendom united in spirit and led by a single church. Kings and their expensive armies battled for supremacy, but between 1648 and 1715 they learned to accept the principle of a balance of power, in which no one state could realistically hope to prevail over all the rest. Ordinary people generally acquiesced in being subordinated at the bottom of a complex hierarchy of political and economic power, but occasionally they erupted in revolutionary outbursts that were put down with great brutality; by 1700, Europe was no closer to embracing democratic values than it had been in 1300. The pressure of population on inadequate technologies, as well as a swelling of the money supply by New World silver, combined in the sixteenth century to produce a giddy inflation.

But for much of the seventeenth century, Europe suffered deflation and depression. There were important technological advances, but a "critical mass" of know-how did not accumulate sufficiently to ignite sustained economic expansion. Wealth was accumulating, which some (not all) historians attribute primarily to the exploitation of Europe's new empires. This wealth remained concentrated in a few hands, but it did pay for tremendous cultural achievements.

Older generations of historians tended to see Renaissance and Reformation Europe as the birthplace of modern Western civilization. Today, historians are not so sure. Many see the era that Part Three surveys in terms of long-range continuities that reach back to the collapse of antiquity and the birth of the Middle Ages. The real historical turning point, for these historians, will come with the changes that Part Four will discuss: the Scientific Revolution, which from the sixteenth through the eighteenth centuries will bring about a wholly different way of understanding the natural world; the Industrial Revolution, which in the eighteenth and nineteenth centuries will harness the energy and technology necessary for building a mass-production (and environment-threatening) modern economy; and the Democratic Revolution, which beginning in North America in 1776 and in France in 1789 will open the governance of Western societies to viable participation by ordinary people.

The authors of *The West Transformed* accept the interpretation that the fundamental break between pre-modernity and modernity comes between the seventeenth and the nineteenth centuries. Part Three, therefore, tells a story primarily of continuities and transitions, not of radical breaks. Yet the continuities that we will explore also contain and nurture the seeds of the culture and society that will come to fruition later—and with which we still live. 🌾

CHAPTER 11

THE LATE MIDDLE AGES: CRISES AND TRANSITIONS

Allegory of Bad Government   *Scala/Art Resource, NY.*

1237–1242	Mongols invade eastern Europe and conquer Russia
1270–1308	Life span of Duns Scotus, the "Subtle Doctor," critic of Aquinas's theory of knowledge
ca. 1285–ca. 1349	Life span of Franciscan philosopher William of Ockham
1300	Beginning of large-scale witch-hunts
1309	Pope Clement V moves papacy from Rome to Avignon
1328	Valois Dynasty begins in France with accession of Philip VI
1337–1453	Hundred Years' War between England and France
1346	Edward III of England routs French at Crécy
1347–1350	Black Death kills about one-third of population of Europe
1351	Parliament passes Statute of Laborers, attempts to freeze wages of English workers
1356	Golden Bull leaves choice of succession of Holy Roman emperors to majority votes of seven great German princes; English rout French at Poitiers
1357	The Great Ordinance: Étienne Marcel attempts to make French monarchy "constitutional"
1358	French peasant uprising (Jacquerie Rebellion) crushed; Great Ordinance fails
ca. 1375	Gerard Groote founds Brethren of the Common Life
1378	Ciompi uprising in Florence
1378–1415	Great Schism: rival popes in Rome and Avignon
1381	Peasants' Revolt in England
1384	Death of John Wycliffe, English religious rebel
1409	Council of Pisa: unsuccessful effort to heal Great Schism results in three popes instead of two

1410	Polish-Lithuanian army routs Teutonic Knights at Tannenberg
1414–1418	Council of Constance heals Great Schism and burns Jan Hus
1415	Henry V of England crushes French army at Agincourt
1420–1434	Hussite Bohemia repels repeated attacks by German crusaders
1431	Joan of Arc burned at the stake
ca. 1430	Death of feminist Christine de Pisan
1431–1449	Council of Basel: decline and fall of conciliar movement
1439	Council of Florence: Byzantine emperor and patriarch agree to union with Latin church in a bid for Western aid; agreement rejected by populace of Constantinople and by Russian Orthodox church
ca. 1440–1455	Development of printing from movable type
1453	Ottoman conquest of Constantinople
1455–1485	Wars of the Roses in England
1469	Ferdinand of Aragon marries Isabella of Castile, paving way for union of the two most powerful Spanish Christian kingdoms
1480	Ivan III (the Great) of Moscow discontinues Mongol tribute, establishing Russia's independence from Mongols and primacy of grand princes of Moscow
1485	Henry VII, first Tudor monarch, ascends English throne
1492	Ferdinand and Isabella complete the Reconquest by taking Granada, last Iberian Muslim state; Christopher Columbus reaches Western Hemisphere
1497–1499	Portuguese explorer Vasco de Gama rounds southern Africa and reaches India
1517	Martin Luther initiates Protestant Reformation

*I*n the council chamber of the town hall of Siena, a picturesque town in central Italy, visitors still admire the pair of frescoes (shown opposite) painted in the late 1330s by one of fourteenth-century Italy's greatest artists, Ambrogio Lorenzetti. The subject is appropriate for its setting. As they went about the business of governing Siena, the worthies of the city council were invited by Lorenzetti to contemplate the effects of good government and bad government. In one fresco, citizens cooperate peacefully and the city thrives; in the other—shown here—lying, cheating, quarreling, and contentiousness lead to chaos. The devil presides, and the the foreground slumps a neglected figure, generally thought to represent the Common Good.

Neglect of the Common Good was a constant refrain of reformers during the Late Middle Ages. Both these moralists and people who pursued their own interests had good reason to regard the present and the future with deep foreboding. Even more than most eras of human history, the fourteenth and fifteenth centuries were violent and unsettled. Gradually confidence ebbed in high-medieval values and assumptions—a thriving economy, advancing frontiers, and a strong international church embodying a common faith and a rich intellectual and artistic heritage. In late medieval Europe, prosperity succumbed to depression, confidence collapsed into disillusionment, and philosophers' dreams of fusing the worlds of matter and spirit faded. Social behavior ran to extremes—to rebellion, hedonism, witch-hunting, and flagellation (the penance of self-inflicted whipping). Some people certainly led quiet, happy lives during these centuries—but as usual, such lives did not attract much public notice and so have tended to go unrecorded in history. The forces of crisis and disintegration have attracted most attention, among both contemporary observers and modern historians.

Europe's economic decline bred a mood of pessimism that periodically erupted into rage or religious frenzy. Writers, artists, and their patrons were often preoccupied with death and dying. Then, on top of food shortages and civil strife, the catastrophic Black Death struck in the mid-fourteenth century. Ambrogio Lorenzetti was one of its innumerable victims. Plagues returned regularly for centuries thereafter, carrying off millions of victims and darkening the spirits of survivors. A surge of antisemitism made scapegoats of the Jews.

Contemporaries had good reason to think that Christendom was on the verge of collapse. Two frightening Asian invaders, Mongols in Russia and Turks in southeastern Europe, isolated much of eastern Europe. In western Europe, the high-medieval "Christian commonwealth"—kingdoms that had generally acknowledged papal prerogatives—gave way to a constellation of quarreling monarchies and city-states. And the Latin church almost disintegrated between 1378 and 1415, as first two and then three popes claimed to be Christ's only true representative on earth. Civil violence and incessant warfare racked the western kingdoms, whose towns and countrysides alike suffered from often-uncontrolled crime and turmoil. Outlaw bands pillaged portions of England; one such band, the notorious Coterel gang, ruled for a time the bustling port of Bristol, terrorizing its inhabitants. In France, unemployed professional troops plundered and killed almost at will. A mercenary captain in fourteenth-century Italy advertised himself as "the enemy of God, pity, and mercy." There were times when governments seemed on the verge of collapsing altogether. Little wonder that many expected the end of the world.

Yet during the final half-century of the period, strong monarchies reemerged in Spain, France, England, and Portugal. The first three of these states would play powerful roles in European politics far into the future, and in succeeding centuries all four would send explorers, warriors, and settlers around the globe. By 1500 the popes had become mired in local Italian politics, medieval Christendom was breaking into sovereign fragments, and throughout the West the sovereign state was claiming its subjects' highest allegiance.

ECONOMIC CONTRACTION AND COMMERCIAL REVOLUTION

In western Europe, and in much of eastern Europe as well, the fourteenth and fifteenth centuries were an era of severe economic problems. The shift from high-medieval prosperity to late medieval depression was gradual, uneven, and painful. Nevertheless, some managed to thrive. This was particularly true of merchants and bankers at the top of the economic scale.

Europeans' sense of unease was compounded by a sense of encirclement by alien aggressors, first the Mongols and then the Ottoman Turks. That God permitted such a devilish power to flourish could only be explained in terms of punishment for Christians' sins. Equally dark thoughts were stirred by the era's famines and pestilences.

The Fourteenth-Century Depression

The economy of western Europe was beginning to falter as early as 1250, and by the early fourteenth century there were clear signs of severe crisis. Several related trends—shrinking population, contracting international and domestic markets, an end to the long process of land reclamation, and a creeping mood of pessimism—resulted in a general slump and a deepening of social antagonisms.

West European agriculture had reached its technological limits. The land most recently brought under cultivation tended to be minimally productive and highly liable to crop failure. Further population growth could be sustained only by a lowering of the peasantry's standard of living, either by subdividing peasant holdings into tiny plots or by expanding cultivation into new but poorer lands. When bad weather produced inadequate harvests, grain prices would soar and food stocks would dwindle alarmingly.

Bad weather, indeed, became chronic. Although obviously there was nothing comparable to the four great Ice Ages of prehistoric times (see Prologue), evidence from tree rings, glacial cores, and seabed sedimentation suggests that between about 1300 and 1700 several episodes of significant global cooling took place, sometimes called "the Little Ice Age." Late medieval Europeans—and other peoples around the globe—faced severe difficulties in feeding themselves adequately and resisting epidemic diseases.

Environmental deterioration may have contributed to climate change and declining health. By the early fourteenth century, for example, western Europe's forest cover had been reduced even below its present-day level. Not only the constant clearing of new (and increasingly marginal) farmland was responsible, but also Europeans' voracious hunger for lumber, firewood, and charcoal to fuel the many rural ironworks. In just forty days a single smelter could consume the woods within a 1-kilometer radius. Loss of trees on this scale adversely affected both temperature and precipitation and caused severe erosion and the loss of topsoil. Especially in England, deforestation led to a major energy crisis, requiring the first large-scale mining of coal—a resource that parts of Britain have in abundance. However, coal extraction was largely of the open-pit variety, the cheapest and easiest way to get at coal but also the most environmentally destructive. The coal that could readily be mined had a high sulfur content, and when it was burned in cities like London the result was a devastating smog, recognized even then as terribly unhealthy. Water pollution, too, was a constant problem created by the casual dumping in streams of animal, human, and industrial wastes—created, for example, by the use of noxious chemicals in tanning hides to produce leather.

The first great disasters struck Europe in the years from 1315 to 1317. Unusual cold and extremely heavy rains destroyed grain harvests in many areas, triggering mass starvation in much of the northern part of the Continent. "So many people died every day," wrote a Flemish abbot in 1316, ". . . that the air seemed to be putrefied. . . . Miserable beggars died . . . in great numbers in the streets [and] on dunghills." England was further afflicted by a devastating cattle disease from 1319 to 1321 and by a widespread crop failure in the latter year.

Thus even before the onset of the Black Death in the mid-fourteenth century, Europe's population was leveling off or declining. Resistance to disease fell, and adverse agrarian conditions postponed marriages, discouraged large families, and depressed birth rates.

The Black Death

The devastating spread of plague across fourteenth-century Europe probably represented a return of the epidemic that had ravaged the same regions in the sixth and seventh centuries (see Chapter 6), and of the pestilence that had swept ancient Greece during the Peloponnesian War (Chapter 2). Awful as these earlier disasters had been, nothing was as virulent as the late medieval Black Death. It was one of the most appalling natural disasters in human history.

Plague had been endemic in parts of China since the tenth century, and its spread westward was facilitated by the Mongol conquest and by travelers. In 1347 Genoese troops holding a small trade outpost on the Black Sea coast became infected with plague by an early form of bacteriological warfare. Besieging Tatars catapulted plague-infected corpses into the town, with the desired result that the terrified Genoese fled home by sea, bringing the terrible pestilence with them.

The Black Death appears to have been a combination of two related diseases: bubonic plague, which is carried by black rats and transmitted to humans by flea bites, and pneumonic plague, in which the bacillus spreads human-to-human by coughing, sneezing, and spitting. When untreated by modern antibiotics, bubonic plague has a high mortality rate. Untreated pneumonic plague—a less common form of the disease—rapidly kills virtually everyone it infects. In both cases, death is typically accompanied by high fever, terrible thirst and pain, and delirium.

From the Mediterranean ports, the plague advanced across Europe with terrifying speed during 1348 and 1349, probably hastened by the brisk interregional trade in rat-infested grain. Death tolls cannot be determined with any precision. The best estimate is that, overall, about one-third of Europe's population perished. In many crowded towns the mortality rate exceeded 50 percent, whereas an isolated rural area might suffer much less, or even be bypassed. Consequently, the most enterprising and best-trained Europeans were hit hardest. Few urban families could have been spared altogether (see Map 11-1).

Europe was stunned by the plague. Fourteenth-century medicine was at a loss to explain or cure infection, which (as we now know) was facilitated by unsanitary and crowded urban conditions. One eyewitness spoke of ships floating on the Mediterranean with dead crews. Many people fled their towns. Others plunged into religious frenzy or orgies of eating, drinking, and sex; a few remained faithfully at their posts, trusting to divine protection. Some of the heaviest mortalities were in monastic communities, but in other cases clergy were reported to have been among the first to flee. An inhabitant of Siena provides this description of the social disintegration that the Black Death brought:

> Father abandoned child; wife, husband; one brother, another. For this illness seemed to strike through the breath and the sight. And so they died. And nobody could be found to bury the dead for money or for friendship. . . . And in many places in Siena huge pits were dug and piled deep with great heaps of the dead. . . . And I buried my five children with my own hands and many others did likewise. And there were many corpses about the city who were so sparsely covered with earth that dogs dragged them out and devoured their bodies.

At papal Avignon great religious processions were organized: "Among them many of both sexes were barefoot; some were in sack cloth, some covered with ashes, wailing as they walked, tearing their hair, and lashing themselves

MAP 11-1
THE BLACK DEATH

with whips until they were bloody." Sometimes—especially in Germany—these harrowing outbreaks of public flagellation precipitated mob attacks on those people who so frequently got blamed for Christendom's troubles: the Jews.

By the end of 1350 the Black Death had run its course in western Europe, leaving its survivors traumatized and grief-stricken but determined to rebuild their lives. There is evidence of unusually high numbers of marriages and births in the years just following, as survivors tried to preserve family lines, repopulated deserted lands and villages, and took over the homes, shops, and even clothing of the dead.

But in 1361 and 1362 outbreaks of plague returned, striking especially hard at young people born since the Black Death. This "children's plague" was only the first of a long series of revisitations: Plague epidemics returned in

1369, 1374–1375, 1379, 1390, 1407, and periodically throughout the fifteenth and sixteenth centuries; the last great western outbreak was in London in 1666. Although none of these subsequent plagues resulted in deaths on the scale of the original Black Death, the seemingly endless recurrences kept people in a state of permanent anxiety. And the population of western and central Europe, having dropped drastically in the wake of the plague's first onset, appears to have continued its decline for the next 100 or 150 years. Populations began rising again only toward the end of the fifteenth century. Not until about 1600 did the European population regain its pre-Black Death level.

The grief and terror brought about by the plagues cannot be measured, but we can observe its more tangible effects: great numbers of deserted villages; unoccupied and dilapidated districts within city walls; the halving of the

Flagellants The flagellants' procession shown in this Flemish manuscript illumination (dating from shortly after the Black Death) was no spur-of-the-moment affair. The flagellants, like people on a pilgrimage, have organized a confraternity (religious brotherhood) and wear an identifying robe, hood and hat. *De la part de la Bibliothèque Royale Albert I.*

population around Paris between 1348 and 1444; the temporary decline of the European wool market; the severe shortage of labor; and bitter social conflict as rich and poor fought over conflicting views of justice.

Rural Rebellion and the Decline of Serfdom

With grim efficiency, the Black Death provided a sudden, radical solution to agrarian overpopulation. There was now an abundance of arable land and an extreme shortage of cultivators.

With the services of the plague's peasant survivors much in demand, their economic condition improved markedly. There was a sudden upward trend in the wages of landless agrarian workers, and peasants could buy or lease land cheaply. Some enterprising peasants accumulated numerous estates, hired laborers to farm them, and prospered. Landlords responded by attempting to cut wages, either by collusion or by legislation. In England, for example, the Statute of Laborers of 1351, and similar legislation that followed, aimed at freezing post-plague wages. But such measures (like price controls) ultimately failed as landholders often paid illegally high wages.

Violence afflicted cities and countryside alike during the second half of the fourteenth century. In the generation following the 1358 Jacquerie Rebellion in France (discussed later in the chapter), similar popular uprisings occurred in Germany, Iberia, the Netherlands, and England. The 1381 Peasants' Revolt in England was both a tax rebellion and an effort to cast aside the last vestiges of **serfdom,** bearing witness to a society in crisis. During this confused and bloody affair, rioters carried the severed head of the archbishop of Canterbury around London on a stick. "When Adam delved [dug] and Eve span [spun]/Who was then the gentleman?" demanded a famous slogan. A radi-

calized priest named John Ball emerged as the spokesman of ordinary English people, and for a time the rebels forced King Richard II to submit to demands that Ball boldly articulated. Soon, however, the king found an opportunity to double-cross the peasants, while a counterattack of professional troops suppressed the uprising. Even so, the days of English serfdom were numbered, and during the fifteenth century the institution all but died.

The rising wages brought about by the labor shortage, coupled with a decline in the price of grain resulting from the population drop, caught landlords in a "price scissors." Landlords throughout much of northwestern Europe ceased cultivating their **demesne** fields directly and rented them out to peasants instead. Serfs were becoming tenant farmers, no longer subject to their lord's manorial court and no longer required to work half the week on his fields. The decline of the old **manorialism** regime occurred gradually and not without sporadic violence, but by 1500 its demise was evident.

Many peasants profited from these new conditions, but others found themselves dispossessed when landlords, instead of renting out their demesnes, converted them to the production of more profitable goods such as wool, meat, wine, and beer (from barley and hops). Recurrent plagues resulted in a highly unpredictable boom-and-bust economy. There was a fall in the numbers of urban consumers who, throughout the High Middle Ages, had constituted an ever-growing market for agrarian products. And while in much of northwestern Europe the labor shortage prompted lords to free serfs to keep them from leaving for better opportunities elsewhere, landlords in eastern Germany and northern Poland did just the opposite, tightening existing bonds of serfdom and exacting peasant labor services more rigorously. By 1500 these landlords were beginning to establish the large grain-exporting estates worked by serfs that would typify the Prussian and Polish agrarian systems of subsequent centuries.

Townspeople in the Late Middle Ages

Although the towns of western Europe declined sharply in population, they recovered from the Black Death more quickly than the countryside. Urban populations tended to be distinctly lower around 1500 than they had been around 1300 or 1348, but in the less populous world of fifteenth-century Europe, cities were becoming relatively more prominent than in the pre-plague era.

Commerce remained generally depressed, but not everywhere. Certain localities north of the Alps, profiting from favorable commercial situations or technological advances—particularly in processing cloth or in mining—became more prosperous. Bruges in Flanders remained throughout most of the Late Middle Ages a bustling center of commerce on the northern seas. Towns along the trade route from Augsburg and Nuremberg in Germany to Prague in Bohemia and Cracow in Poland entered their golden age of economic and cultural growth. The cities of central and northern Italy continued to be lively commercial and cultural centers populated by prosperous merchants who paid the bills. Florence, with its textile industry and international banking, became the cradle of Italian **Renaissance** culture (see Chapter 12).

Textiles were the dominant medieval industry. Although fabrics included fustian (a mixture of flax and imported Near Eastern cotton) and luxurious silk, woolens were the era's most important type of cloth. Depending on the quality of material used and the manner in which it was finished, there were innumerable grades and prices of woolen cloth, which constituted one of the largest commodities in trade—along with the raw wool, natural dyestuffs, and chemicals used in manufacturing it.

As usually happens in depressed times, strong pressures of protectionism and social control appeared in late medieval town life. Those who were in a strong position closed ranks, but simultaneously special interests arose to defend their economic and political stake. This defensiveness was particularly evident in the **guilds.**

In the thirteenth century—and even more so in the fourteenth and fifteenth—merchant-dominated guilds faced severe challenges from lower-status artisans. Sometimes violently or under threat of violence, artisan craft guilds seceded from the dominant merchant guilds and carved out a modest place in the urban hierarchy. The larger and more economically diverse the town, the more craft guilds were apt to appear.

Artisan production was overwhelmingly small-scale. Few masters had much capital or equipment. Most lived hand-to-mouth, dependent on merchants who sold them raw material and bought their output. This was the so-called **putting-out system,** one of the roots of early capi-

Medieval Textile Making   Textile making was a long and complicated process, involving many stages of production and a variety of crafts. In Florence, there were twenty-six separate operations, each performed by a different specialist. This Flemish illumination shows cloth being made in an upper-class household rather than in an industrial setting. The technology shown here remained basic to textile making down to the Industrial Revolution.   *British Library Roy 16GVf. 56/E. T. Archive.*

talism. As high-medieval economic expansion gave way to late medieval contraction, inheritance (or marriage to a widow) became the chief avenue to masterhood. Journeymen proliferated: masters' employees who had finished apprenticeship but had not established independent status as a master, and perhaps never would.

Late medieval craft guilds often clashed with the local nobility and the merchant elite, but in larger industrial towns they also faced an increasingly restive **proletariat**—that is, workers who had only their labor to sell, and whose sense of grievance grew as chances for upward mobility diminished or disappeared. The most dramatic of these

THE HISTORICAL EVIDENCE

Regulations of the London Spur-Makers

1345

The kind of controls that medieval guilds imposed on their members are well illustrated by these rules adopted by the London guild of spur-makers (spurriers) and accepted by the city's mayor.

In the first place, . . . no one of the trade of spurriers shall work longer than from the beginning of the day until the curfew rings out at the church of St. Sepulcher . . . ; by reason that no man can work so neatly by night as by day. And many persons of the said trade, who compass [scheme] how to practice deception in their work, desire to work by night rather than by day; and then they introduce false iron, and iron that has been cracked, for tin, and also they put gilt on false copper, cracked.

And further, many of the said trade are wandering about all day, without working at all at their trade; and then, when they have become drunk and frantic, they take to their work, to the annoyance of the sick, and all their neighborhood as well, by reason of the broils that arise between them and the strange folk who are dwelling among them. And then they blow up their fires so vigorously, that their forges begin all at once to blaze, to the great peril of themselves and of all the neighborhood around.

The mayor and the town watch are authorized to stop anyone they find working at night or on Sunday and fine them.

Also, . . . no one of the said trade shall hang his spurs out on Sundays, or on any other days that are double feasts [of the church]; but only a sign indicating his business and such spurs as they shall so sell, they are to show and sell within their shops, without exposing them without or opening the doors or windows of their shops, on the pain aforesaid [i.e., a fine]. . . .

Also, . . . no one of the said trade shall take an apprentice for a less term than seven years, and such apprentice shall be enrolled according to the usages of the said city.

Source: From James Harvey Robinson, ed., *Readings in European History* (Boston: Ginn, 1904), vol. I, pp. 409–411.

---

conflicts erupted in late fourteenth-century Florence. In the summer of 1378 the city was shattered by a large-scale workers' rebellion. Florentine society consisted of a small minority of wealthy merchant families (called the *popolo grosso*, or "fat people") who were organized in the *arte maggiore* ("major guilds") and the much more numerous *popolo minuto* ("little people") of the *arte minore* ("minor guilds"). Below both of these strata were the *ciompi*—wage laborers (named for their wooden clogs) who did menial jobs in the textile industry but had long been forbidden to organize a guild or to take part in governing the city. The rebellious ciompi joined the popolo minuto in setting up a more democratic regime that legalized their guild and gave them a fixed number of offices. Within just six weeks, however, worsening economic conditions and the popolo minuto's suspicion of the upstart ciompi caused an abrupt reversal. The ciompi were driven from power, never to return; their guild was banned, and authority reverted to the popolo grosso, who marginalized the popolo minuto. The **oligarchy** that took control of Florence in this counterrevolution would preside over the launching of Renaissance culture later.

Not all late medieval manufacturing was urban; in fact, this period marked the beginning of a ruralization of European industry that would continue until the **Industrial Revolution.** Many factors were involved, but the cumulative effect was to retard many towns' demographic recovery and to increase the concentration of economic power in the emerging **capitalist** elite. Seeking lower costs and a way around guild rules, fourteenth- and fifteenth-century entrepreneurs increasingly gave part-time rural workers—often peasants on plots too small to support a family—such basic jobs as cleaning and weaving wool. (Rural women had always held an important role in manufacturing by spinning thread, using the distaff and spindle, and later the spinning wheel.) Urban masters thus found themselves being restricted to the more skilled dying and finishing processes. There was also a technological reason for ruralization: the increasing reliance on water-driven mills in the crucial task of *fulling* (the processing of newly woven cloth by soaking, boiling, and pounding it until the fibers thicken, or "felt"). Rural labor, moreover, dominated the making of linen and fustian textiles. Thus appeared the so-called "new draperies" of the English countryside, for example, which specialized in manufacturing cheap wool cloth. On the other hand, the Flemish towns lost their high-medieval dominance of European cloth making. Except for high-priced luxury products, the future of the European textile industry would be dominated by cheaper, less durable cloth made by workforces that included a significant proportion of rural "cottage labor."

Commercial Revolution and Early Capitalism

Around 1300, there accelerated a series of far-reaching changes in business practices and organization that many historians call the **Commercial Revolution** and see as the precursor of modern capitalistic business. These developments paralleled and reinforced the growing dominance of manufacturing by merchants through the putting-out system.

The change was a matter partly of scale, partly of organization, and partly of attitude. Hitherto the typical European merchant had been a man like the young St. Godric of Finchale (see Chapter 8: The Human Experience, "Godric of Finchale, Merchant and Saint"), who traveled with his goods from fair to fair, did much of his business in the form of barter with other merchants, and carried only enough money to meet incidental expenses and settle final accounts. By the early fourteenth century, however, such "lone wolf" operators were giving way to the commercial firm that worked from a home base and maintained longer-term representatives or partners in widely separated cities. The change first appeared in Italy (where in turn it owed much to Near Eastern practices) and spread in the course of the fourteenth and fifteenth centuries across most of western Europe. The new system demanded long-range credit systems, complex partnerships, and more sophisticated bookkeeping. Its effect was to enhance the wealth and power of the leading merchants at the expense of small-scale traders.

Banking was the crucial institution of the Commercial Revolution. The Italian word *banca* means "bench" and originally referred to the table that money changers set up at fairs. As medieval trade gained in volume, the size and complexity of the financial dealings of money changers correspondingly grew. Much of their business involved bills of exchange, which as we saw in Chapter 8 were usually covert contracts for interest-bearing loans. Although interest rates are usually impossible to determine from these documents, the profits were apparently large. So were the dangers of default. By the thirteenth century, money changers frequently offered insurance (at high rates) to merchants dispatching goods on accident-prone voyages. Constantly needing to raise more capital, money changers accepted deposits, often with subterfuges disguising interest payments. By the early fourteenth century these operations had reached a scale at which Italian money changers—bankers, we should henceforth call them—were entering

long-distance commerce and setting up associates in distant towns to buy and sell merchandise and handle credit transactions. The contracts that linked merchant or banking "houses" with their branches were often long-term business undertakings, not the one-time partnerships of earlier medieval merchants. Involved as they were in both banking and trade, able to acquire the best possible information about market conditions, and capable of moving goods and capital fairly quickly, the big merchant houses enjoyed powerful advantages. They also employed more complex accounting systems. By the fifteenth century, larger business operations were using double-entry bookkeeping, in which each transaction is recorded twice (on the debit and the credit ledger) permitting more systematic profit-and-loss analysis. These advantages partly explain the paradox that large-scale business operations were growing and often thriving despite the fourteenth-century economic contraction.

Just as the earlier medieval urban revival had radiated outward from Italy, so the Commercial Revolution had its epicenter in northern and central Italy. By the fourteenth century Florence supplanted earlier rivals to become a nerve center that combined the importing of wool from England and Iberia, the manufacture and distribution of cloth, and the control of intricate financial operations reaching all over western Europe. Venice, the focal point of Europe's spice trade, paralleled Florence's success. Trade in expensive but easily transported commodities such as fine cloth and spices could generate handsome profits because the consumers of such goods were the affluent, not hard-pressed ordinary people who bore the brunt of economic contraction.

The profits these commercial houses earned tempted them to engage in the riskiest of all ventures: lending to kings. At the outbreak of the Hundred Years' War in 1337 (soon to be discussed), England's Edward III borrowed heavily from the two largest Florentine firms, the Bardi and the Peruzzi. However, fourteenth-century war was expensive, and in 1341 Edward simply declared himself unable to repay. Within two years, in 1343, the Peruzzi went bankrupt, and the Bardi likewise collapsed in 1346—disasters not only for these two banking families but also for all their partners and investors, who (unlike modern stockholders) were fully liable for all losses. Economic collapse on this scale had wide ripple effects, including unemployment and social unrest, that served as a fitting prelude to the Black Death.

Other major firms arose in Florence during the decades after the Black Death, but none could compare to the Bardi and Peruzzi in sheer size. Among these newcomers, the most notable was the House of Medici, which dominated Florence politically and culturally during the Renaissance (see Chapter 12). Like their predecessors, the Medici family made their fortune in the cloth trade and banking (including handling financial transactions for the papacy),

THE HISTORICAL EVIDENCE

A Mercantile Firm's Business

1393

This letter is one of thousands in the archive of Francesco di Marco Datini, a merchant whose headquarters was in the small city of Prato, near Florence. Datini's firm had many associates all over Italy, France, and Iberia, and he kept in constant touch with them. The letter excerpted here was written to Datini by his chief associate in Genoa, and it offers a glimpse of the firm's wide-ranging interests.

"In the name of God" was the conventional opening of business letters, just as ledgers often bore the pious notation "In the name of God and profit." The "little slave girl" referred to here would likely have been imported from the eastern Mediterranean and would have been put to work in the Datini household; in a postscript to this letter, Datini is told that a ship from "Romania" (that is, Constantinople) is expected soon in port, perhaps carrying a human cargo.

In the name of God. On May 23, 1393.

We have written you in these days all that was needed; and the last was on the twenty-first, and in it we told you all that was needed; [we assume] you will have received it and answered it. And then, today, we have three letters of yours, written on the twelfth, fifteenth, and seventeenth, and we answer by this letter what is needed. . . .

You will have received the cloth from Pisa, and you and Monna Margherita [Datini's wife] ought to be very pleased with it. We were awaiting an answer from you to learn how [well] you think we have served you—which we hope we have. We are informed of the arrival of Tieri there,* and that in a few days from now you will send him away on a journey to Provence. . . .

We were informed that you have had a test of the woad [a dyestuff] made. We suppose that you had it tested by Niccolò [a Datini relative in Prato] and you have informed us about results. We have sent to Pisa four sacks of another lot and told them to send two sacks to you; therefore you have this also tested at once and inform us.

You have been told the reason why Luca[†] has not left for Valencia. He will leave as soon as possible. It is very serious that there is no answer as yet from Catalonia about later development. May God send us the best news, and may the news be peace between the two peoples, and likewise among all Christians. Should there be anything new, you will learn it. . . .

Of the wool you have with you, we agree that you should do with it whatever can be done to close it out.

Hold it there: it is impossible that it will not receive soon a better offer there. . . .

You received the oranges; we are glad.

We are informed about the little slave girl you say you personally need, and about her features and age, and for what you want her. We are informed. We shall see if there is anyone we consider suitable and we shall get her, although at present we are badly supplied here; nevertheless so far as we are able you shall have one. . . .

From [our] people of Florence you will have been informed of the news that came yesterday from Marseilles, for we told them to inform you because at that time we could not write to you ourselves. As you will have heard from them, the three ships of the corsair [pirate] of Spain and likewise two Catalan ones were at Marseilles, close to the chain of the harbor, armed and fully ready to defend themselves against anyone. . . .

[Addressed on the cover to:] Francesco di Marco, in Prato.

[Annotation on the cover in another hand:] From Genoa, on May 29, 1393. Answered same day.

---

*That is, in Prato. Tieri worked for the Avignon branch of the firm.

[†]Datini's chief associate in Spain.

Source: From *Medieval Trade in the Mediterranean World: Illustrative Documents*, trans. and eds. Robert S. Lopez and Irving W. Raymond (New York: Columbia University Press, 1944), pp. 400–403.

and they maintained important commercial ties with cities in the Low Countries. As we shall see in the next chapter, the Medici would thrive as long as they focused on their business interests; they reached their peak in the first half of the fifteenth century, during the career of Cosimo de' Medici (1389–1464), the richest banker, the political boss, and the foremost cultural patron of Renaissance Florence. But when the later fifteenth-century Medici acted more as princes and less as bankers, their economic fortunes dimmed.

THE HISTORICAL EVIDENCE

The Fate of a Labor Organizer

1345

This document from the Florentine archives shows how the court of the "captain of the popolo"—one of the city's chief magistrates—dealt with Ciuto Brandini, "a man of low condition and evil reputation," who had tried to organize wool industry laborers. What does the document's tone reveal about Florentine social attitudes?

Together with many others who were seduced by him, he planned to organize an association . . . of carders, combers, and other laborers in the woolen cloth industry, in the largest number possible. . . . He organized meetings on several occasions . . . of many persons of lowly conditions. And among other things done in these meetings, Ciuto ordered that there should be a collection of money from those who attended these assemblies . . . so that they would be stronger and more durable in this wicked organization, and so that they could accomplish the above-mentioned outrages and in order that—with arguments, force, and other means—they could oppose those citizens of good condition who wished to prevent Ciuto [and his fellows] . . . from accomplishing . . . their iniquitous thoughts, decisions, and activities.

Moving from bad to worse, he sought . . . to accomplish similar and even worse things, seeking always

[to incite] noxious disorders, to the harm, opprobrium, danger, and destruction of the citizens of Florence, their persons and property, and of the stable regime of that city. And the above-mentioned illegal plots planned by him would have taken place, from which there would have arisen tumult, sedition, and disorder among the *popolani* and guildsmen of Florence, except that [Ciuto] was seized and detained by an official of the captain and his court.

Ciuto confessed and was hanged.

Source: From Gene Brucker, ed., *The Society of Renaissance Florence: A Documentary Study* (New York: Harper & Row, 1971), pp. 235–236.

The Medici had counterparts north of the Alps in such fifteenth-century figures as Jacques Coeur, the financier of French kings, and the Fuggers of Augsburg, bankers to the Holy Roman emperors. The Fuggers shrewdly took advantage of their imperial clients' financial need and political weakness to win control of profitable mining and other raw-materials enterprises in fifteenth-century Germany. Coeur's career was more spectacular—but ephemeral. He built the most luxurious house in the French city of Bourges and seemed on his way to manipulating the finances of the fifteenth-century French monarchy, but he was ruined when his debtor, Charles VII, had him arrested on probably trumped-up charges and confiscated the house and all his wealth.

The gap between rich and poor appears to have widened in the fourteenth and fifteenth centuries (see Figure 11-1). Often violent conflicts and harsh judicial punishments testify to the determination of late medieval urban elites to do everything possible to retain their positions. Many towns were torn by the conflicts of rival elite families and their factions. In general, however, rich mercantile families retained their privileged economic status in

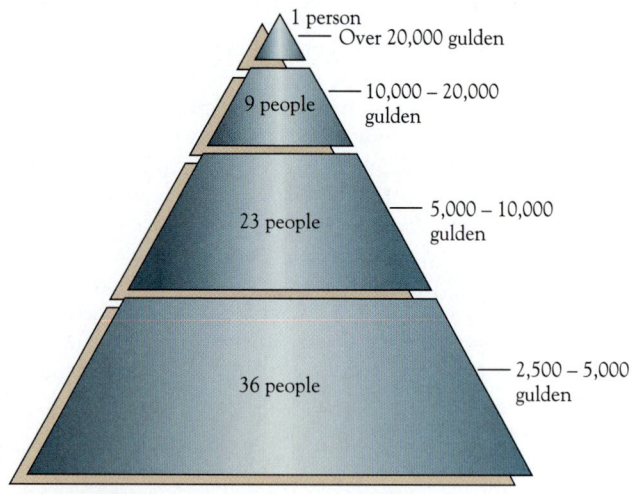

FIGURE 11-1

DISTRIBUTION OF WEALTH (BY HOUSEHOLDS) IN BASEL, 1405

This diagram reflects taxable wealth only; it omits the extremely large number of persons too poor to have any assessed wealth. *Source: Based on data from N. J. G. Pounds, An Economic History of Medieval Europe (London: Longman, 1974).*

the face of lower-class pressure by sharing their political authority with aristocrats or kings or, in Italy, by relinquishing it to despots.

POLITICAL CRISIS: WARRIORS AND KINGS IN THE LATE MIDDLE AGES

From the early fourteenth to the mid-fifteenth century, the high-medieval trend toward royal centralization went into reverse in most western countries. The major Iberian powers—Aragon, Castile, and Portugal—were tormented by sporadic upheavals. England and France were locked in the Hundred Years' War (1337–1453), driving England to bankruptcy and ravaging France's population. Central authority deteriorated further in Germany, and **tyranny** seized power in many Italian cities. Although east-central Europe stabilized in the fourteenth century, by the fifteenth century a pattern of decentralized aristocratic domination was becoming clear. Everywhere, this was an era of endemic, and increasingly professionalized, warfare.

Military Change in the Late Middle Ages

The landed aristocracy of late medieval Europe, forced by the "price scissors" to relinquish most of its demesne lands and its lordship over serfs, nevertheless developed chivalry to a pinnacle of refinement and splendor: shining armor, elaborate tournaments and feasts, knightly brotherhoods, and vivid banners emblazoned with noble coats-of-arms. The traditional **knight** retained much of his former military importance, and the nobility remained an elite of mounted, armored warriors.

But the dominance of mounted knights in warfare was being challenged by well-drilled infantry wielding longbows, crossbows, and cannon. Longbows and crossbows in particular were highly accurate and lethal. Perfected by English archers in border wars with the Welsh and Scots, the longbow could fire more shots per minute than the crossbow. Both weapons devastated knights and their horses despite ever-heavier plate armor.

Gunpowder was invented in China in the eighth or ninth century A.D., and not long afterward the Chinese were using it in bombs, rockets, and fireworks. By the late thirteenth or early fourteenth century they had adapted it to cannon, and around that time the new military technology appeared in Europe.

We do not know how gunpowder came west from China (perhaps the Mongols were involved), but it is virtually certain that Europeans were using gunpowder artillery in the 1320s—possibly earlier. By the later fourteenth and fifteenth centuries artillery was becoming important in European warfare. Cannon were awkward to haul, deploy, load, fire, and reload; they were not very accurate; and they could blow up. Thus they were more effective against fortifications or on shipboard than against mobile troops. Nevertheless, they forced a shift in defensive architecture from high, turreted castles to squat, thick-walled fortresses. The fifteenth century also witnessed the development of smaller firearms.

Monarchies had employed small permanent forces of salaried knights ever since the eleventh century, but by 1500 such forces were much more numerous and included large numbers of trained foot soldiers. The French king Louis XI (reigned 1461–1483) devoted some of his new tax revenues to maintaining a standing army of cavalry

Before a Tournament   Late medieval tournaments were great social events for aristocrats and were elaborately ritualized. This French illumination shows the preliminaries to a tournament—the display of contestants' helmets and standards, while the ladies of the court promenade past and select their "champions." The unarmored knights watch the proceedings (on left), and their squires stand behind the table. In the foreground stand four chamberlains who will perhaps serve as referees. *Livre des tournois du roi Rene; Bibliothèque Nationale.*

and infantry numbering up to twenty-five thousand men, which he could increase to several times that size by summoning reserves. Standing armies would mushroom during the next several centuries, but already they were beginning to assume some of the characteristics of early modern military organizations. The fifteenth-century reconsolidation of states stimulated the increased standardization and regimentation of their armed forces, exemplified by such innovations as collective training of both infantry and cavalry, soldiers marching in step, and a greater use of uniforms.

There was no decisive break between "medieval" and "modern" warfare. High-medieval military forces had often received regular wages, and had included archers, foot soldiers, and siege engineers as well as knights. Standing armies gradually increased, generation after generation, in size and technological sophistication, until by 1500 the monarchs of western Europe controlled military establishments of unprecedented size, expense, and destructive potential. The most formidable armies of all, however, remained those of the Ottoman Turks.

The Western Kingdoms

The **feudal** monarchies ruled at the beginning of the fourteenth century by Edward I in England and Philip IV ("the Fair") in France were formidable achievements, combining intricate networks of feudal obligations with proto-bureaucratic structures and early representative institutions (see Chapter 9).

In the final analysis, however, these states' vigor depended on the energy, intelligence, and ruthlessness of the king—qualities that Edward I and Philip the Fair possessed in abundance, but that many of their heirs lacked. If a king was underage, insane, or simply incompetent, power would lapse to the mightiest lords of the land; if he had no legitimate son, the realm could be torn apart in a war of succession or invaded by a foreign claimant. Moreover, royal finances were adequate only as long as the king stayed at peace. When he went to war, he immediately incurred the huge expense of hiring mercenaries. To pay his bills, he could tax his subjects—but that required concessions to a representative assembly. Or he could borrow from Italian bankers—but if he defaulted he could not expect ever to borrow again. Or he could tell his armies to live off the plundered enemy—but that would risk allowing successful commanders to become overmighty subjects, as well as turning unpaid troopers into dangerous marauders.

All these things that *could* go wrong in late medieval monarchies *did* go wrong for fourteenth- and fifteenth-century England and France. Several times France, with its pre-plague population of roughly 16 million, was governed so incompetently that England, with 2 million subjects, came close to conquering it. At other times, when its wars in France went badly, England lurched into civil war. Both countries experienced violent revolts of peasants and townspeople, goaded by the miseries of war and economic contraction. Both countries, in the end, longed for a return of strong kings who could keep order—but who would also avoid expensive foreign adventures and "live of their own" off regular royal revenues.

The Hundred Years' War Beginning in 1337, a series of Anglo-French clashes dragged on fitfully for 116 years, spates of savage warfare alternating with long truces. Historians call this series of campaigns the Hundred Years' War.

Broadly speaking, the conflict was a continuation of the Anglo-French rivalry that dated from the Norman Conquest. Since 1066, when William the Conqueror joined England to Normandy (see Chapter 9), English kings had ruled portions of France and battled French kings, their feudal overlords. In 1204 the Capetian crown had won the extensive northern French territories of the English kings' "Angevin Empire," but the English kings kept Gascony in the southwest. England's Gascon claim, cemented by a brisk commerce in English cloth and Bordeaux wine (for which the English developed a never-ending thirst), had provoked an expensive but inconclusive war (1294–1303) between Philip the Fair and Edward I (see Figure 11-2). Competing English and French claims to Gascony constituted one of several causes for the resumption of hostilities in 1337.

A second cause of the Hundred Years' War was the Anglo-French diplomatic struggle to control Flanders, today in western Belgium. French kings had long claimed lordship over the dukes of Flanders, whereas England and the Flemish towns had become tightly linked by a profitable wool trade.

Finally, the Hundred Years' War resulted from the protracted and repeated efforts of English kings to claim the crown of France itself. In 1328 the unbroken father-son succession of Capetian kings in France, which dated back to the tenth century, ended when King Charles IV died without a son. Edward III of England, whose mother was a daughter of Philip the Fair, at once laid claim to the French crown; but his claim was contested by Philip of Valois, son of Philip the Fair's younger brother. The French nobility, arguing unhistorically that the right to inherit cannot pass through a woman, raised Philip of Valois to the throne as Philip VI, the first of the Valois kings who would rule France until 1589. Edward III accepted the decision initially, but in 1337 he revived his claim.

None of these causes can be considered decisive, and war might yet have been avoided. But Edward III and Philip VI were both chivalrous, high-spirited monarchs who delighted in heroic clashes of arms. And not only had the nobles of both sides become infected by similar attitudes, but they also saw war—that is, looting towns and ransoming prisoners—as enormously profitable.

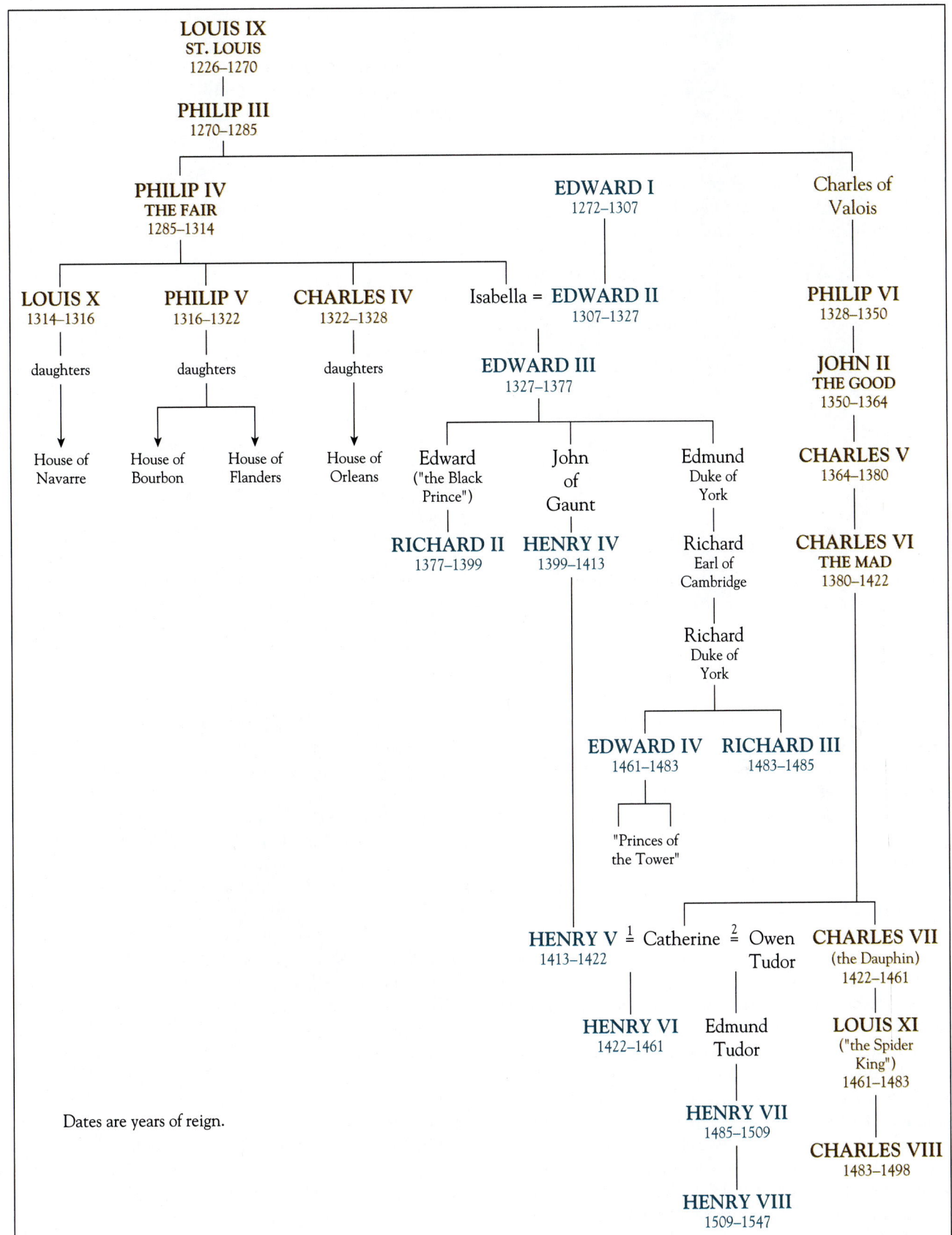

Dates are years of reign.

FIGURE 11-2
THE FRENCH AND ENGLISH SUCCESSIONS

Plate Armor   Armor like this—made for a fifteenth-century Italian commander—was worn in battle rather than on ceremonial occasions. Although heavy, a man could mount a strong horse (also armored) without having to be hoisted into the saddle. Still, the steel plate could be penetrated by an arrow shot from a powerful bow; armor thick enough to repel such a missile would have been too heavy to wear.   *Alinari/Art Resource, NY.*

French ardor cooled first. At Crécy in 1346, English longbowmen mowed down waves of recklessly charging, plate-armored French knights. For France, the nadir came under King John the Good—actually a very bad king, powerless to cope with the English or bring order to his demoralized, plague-stricken land. In 1356, his knights suffered a second crushing defeat at the battle of Poitiers, in which he was captured. The peace treaty (1360) left much of southwestern France in English hands (see Map 11-2).

The English admired Edward III so long as his armies were victorious; but they deposed and killed his effete grandson, Richard II, who preferred reducing the power of his nobles to fighting the French. By contrast, France acquired a competent and vigorous king, Charles V, whose armies avoided pitched battles, harassed the English unceasingly, and slowly drove them back. By his death the French monarchy was recovering. The English, reduced to small outposts around Bordeaux and Calais, virtually abandoned the war for a generation.

MAP 11-2

FRANCE AND THE HUNDRED YEARS' WAR.

These maps show lands ceded in 1360 (top) and as they looked in 1429 (bottom).

THE HUMAN EXPERIENCE

Joan of Arc

Joan of Arc (ca. 1412–1431), one of the most cherished heroes in the history of France, restored the morale and prestige of the Valois monarchy at the time of its lowest ebb and turned the tide of the Hundred Years' War.

Joan's brief but remarkable life began about 1412 in the village of Domrémy in eastern France—a region that had suffered gravely from the violence and plundering of the Hundred Years' War. Joan was one of five children of a fairly well-off farming couple. As a child she was lively and devout. Like most French people, she was saddened by the savagery of a conflict that dragged on endlessly and appeared to be drifting toward victory for the English and their Burgundian allies and away from the legitimate Valois kings of France.

In 1422, the Valois cause was feebly embodied in Charles the Mad's eldest son, the dauphin Charles. But the English and the Burgundians dominated northern France, while the dispirited dauphin fled to the south to preside falteringly over a government in exile. In 1428 the English and Burgundians laid siege to Orléans on the Loire, threatening to break through into the south if the city fell.

At the onset of adolescence, Joan began hearing the voices of angels and saints. They told her that the English had no right to be in France and that she must assume military leadership and drive them out. In 1429, at age seventeen, she persuaded the captain of a nearby Valois garrison to provide a small military escort to accompany her to the dauphin's court at the castle of Chinon.

The journey took eleven days, and the skeptical Charles kept her waiting another two. Finally he tested her by receiving her in disguise. She recognized him immediately and persuaded him that her voices were genuine and that she was sent by God to save the French monarchy. The dauphin's court spent the next three weeks investigating Joan's orthodoxy and chastity. Convinced that both were beyond doubt, Charles armed her, placed her in command of a large military force, and sent her off to relieve Orléans from its English besiegers.

Joan warned the English repeatedly to lift the siege. They laughed off the adolescent farm girl. Then she slipped through their lines with a sizable force to relieve the defenders and launched a series of successful counterattacks that eventually forced the English to lift the siege. Joan was triumphant, and she was forever after revered as the "Maid of Orléans." A month later Joan and the Valois troops routed their enemies at the battle of Patay.

Joan's victories shifted the momentum of the Hundred Years' War from the English to the French, who had now driven the enemy northward from the Loire Valley of central France. She continued to campaign until she made it possible for the dauphin to enter Reims cathedral—the traditional French royal coronation site—to be crowned in her presence on July 17, 1429, as King Charles VII. The Valois cause was triumphant, thanks to Joan.

But having saved the Valois dynasty, the Maid's luck turned. Charles, concluding that she was dangerously idealistic and unpredictable, no longer needed her. In September Joan was wounded in an assault on Paris for which Charles failed to provide adequate support. The following spring she led a force against the Burgundian siege of Compiègne and was captured while fighting bravely. King Charles, short of money, declined to ransom her, and the Burgundians sold her to the English to stand trial for heresy and sorcery in the English-occupied city of Rouen.

The trial was of course rigged. It was conducted by Pierre Cauchon, bishop of Beauvais, an ecclesiastical bureaucrat beholden to the English. The transcript survives, and Joan emerges as heroic, steadfast, and surprisingly articulate. Denied counsel, she defended herself against charges of dressing as a male warrior, her voices, and her unbelievable military success—all the more incriminating because it was against the English, who believed that God was on their side (and who now controlled the trial).

Isolated, mistreated, threatened with torture, and driven to illness, Joan submitted at last. She was given a life sentence. But she quickly reconsidered and defied her jailers by donning male clothing once again. She was thereupon condemned to be burned at the stake, and as she stood amid the flames, continuing to protest her innocence, she demanded that her executioner hold a cross before her eyes so that she could see it to the end. As he raised it she cried out, "Jesus!" and died. She was not yet twenty years old.

A quarter-century later, in 1456, the pope overturned Joan's sentence and declared her innocence. Pierre Cauchon, discredited and reviled, came to be known throughout France as "Bishop Pig." But Joan remained a subject of controversy for centuries and was canonized only in 1920, nearly half a millennium after her death. She is celebrated in France today as a legendary figure—a progenitor of French patriotism and savior of the Valois monarchy. Memorial figurines and plaques now mark the various points on her itinerary, and an armored statue of St. Joan stands in Reims cathedral, the scene of her most dazzling triumph. ❖

But Charles V was succeeded by the periodically insane Charles VI. His reign was dominated by a bloody feud between his younger brother, the duke of Orléans, and his uncle, the duke of Burgundy. In Capetian times, such powerful fief-holding members of the royal family had usually cooperated with the king; but now, with a mentally deficient ruler on the French throne, Burgundy and Orléans struggled for control of the kingdom. During the fifteenth century, the Orleanists became identified with the Valois cause, but Burgundy developed into a quasi-independent state between France and Germany.

The second phase of the Hundred Years' War erupted in the early fifteenth century when England's Henry V revived hostilities against a France ravaged by assassinations and civil strife. In 1415 Henry won an overwhelming victory at Agincourt. Following this triumph, the Burgundians joined forces with the English, and Charles the Mad was forced to allow a marriage between his daughter and Henry, and thus make the English king his heir. But both kings died in 1422, with Henry leaving his crowns to an infant son, Henry VI. Real power lapsed to England's high aristocracy and military contractors.

While Charles the Mad's son, the as-yet-uncrowned Charles VII, was carrying on a halfhearted resistance, the Burgundians and English divided northern France between them and prepared to crush what remained of the Valois monarchy. In desperation, Charles accepted the military services of Joan of Arc. Joan's victory at the siege of Orléans, her insistence on Charles's coronation in Reims cathedral, and her capture and death at the stake in 1431 have become legendary. The spirit that she kindled raised French hopes, and in the two decades following her death Charles VII's armies went from victory to victory. The conquest of France had always been beyond English resources, and early English successes in the Hundred Years' War had been largely a product of poor French leadership and internal divisions. When the French at length turned the tide, much of the credit went to their superior artillery, which battered down one English-held castle after another. Advanced, destructive, and expensive military technology made the difference.

By 1453, when the struggle was over at last, England had lost all of France except Calais on the English Channel. The age-long process of Anglo-French disentanglement was virtually completed, and Joan of Arc's vision was realized as Charles VII ruled France unopposed.

Kings, Rebels, and Representative Assemblies The
English Parliament developed significantly during these bloody years. During the fourteenth century, it changed from a body that met occasionally into a permanent institution, consisting of Lords and Commons. The House of Commons, representing townspeople and shire knights, bargained with a monarchy hard-pressed to pay for the Hundred Years' War. Commons traded its fiscal support for important political concessions, and by the fourteenth century's end it had gained the privilege of approving any taxation not sanctioned by custom. Gripping the royal purse strings, Commons exerted increasing influence on legislation. Adopting the motto "redress before supply," it refused to pass financial grants until the king had approved its petitions, and the king almost always acquiesced.

Yet the late medieval House of Commons was by no means the independent voice of a "rising **middle class.**" By and large, it was controlled with naked force or subtle manipulation by aristocrats. Elections could be rigged; representatives could be bribed or intimidated. And although Parliament deposed two English kings—Edward II in 1327 and Richard II in 1399—in both instances it was simply ratifying the results of aristocratic power struggles. It is significant that such parliamentary ratification should have seemed necessary, but Parliament had not yet become a free agent.

For France, the Hundred Years' War was a far worse agony than for England. All the battles took place on French soil, which mercenary companies continually pillaged, even when they were not actually fighting. When after the battle of Poitiers (1356) the French king John the Good was held by the English for ransom, the Estates General convened in Paris under the leadership of the Parisian cloth merchant Étienne Marcel and assumed the reins of government. This kingdom-wide assembly of churchmen, nobles, and townspeople had first been summoned in 1302 by Philip IV. Now, in 1357, the Estates General forced John's son, the young Dauphin (crown prince) Charles, to issue a radical constitutional statute known as the Great Ordinance. This statute embodied the demands of the burgher-dominated Estates General to join with the monarchy in the governance of France. The Estates General was thenceforth to meet regularly and to supervise the royal finances, courts, and administration through a small standing committee. Charles, deeply hostile to this infringement of royal authority, submitted for a time, then fled Paris to gather royalist support in the countryside.

By 1358 the horrors of plague, depression, and mercenary marauders drove the French peasantry into the so-called Jacquerie Rebellion.[1] The rebels and urban workers lacked coherent goals and effective leaders, but for two memorable weeks they managed to terrorize portions of the northern French countryside and to murder all the aristocrats they could lay hands on. They are reported to have forced a noble wife to eat her roasted husband, after which they raped and murdered her. At its beginning the

---

[1] The name derives from *Jacques* (James), the generic name personifying the French peasantry.

rebellion had enjoyed considerable support from townspeople, lesser nobles, **parish** clergy, and even some royal officials. But when the uprising began growing to dangerous proportions, the dauphin, backed by the upper aristocracy and urban elites, crushed it with a savagery worthy of the rebels themselves. The Jacquerie evoked a longing for law and order and a return to the ways of old. This conservative backlash doomed Étienne Marcel's constitutional movement in Paris. Marcel was murdered in midsummer 1358, and Charles returned to the city in triumph.

The Great Ordinance of 1357 became a dead letter after Marcel's murder, and in later centuries the French Estates General met less and less frequently. The dauphin, who in 1364 became the able King Charles V, instituted new tax measures that largely freed the monarchy from dependence on assemblies and made it potentially the richest in Europe.

The Estates General, unlike the English Parliament, failed to become an integral part of the government, and French kings reverted to their high-medieval practice of dealing with their subjects through local assemblies. There were **parlements** in France—outgrowths of the central and regional courts—but their functions remained primarily judicial; they neither granted taxes nor legislated. French national cohesion continued to lag behind that of England because France was much larger, more populous, and more culturally diverse. During the Late Middle Ages its great dukes still ruled whole provinces with little interference from Paris. In the absence of an articulate national parliament, only the king could claim to speak for all the French people.

Almost a century later, Charles VII—who by 1453 had cleared France of the English invaders—turned his attention to rebuilding the royal government. In this, he was aided by having obtained secure tax revenues, a standing army, and a growing bureaucracy, all of which allowed him to negotiate province-by-province for financial aid.

Although Burgundy failed to realize its early fifteenth-century potential for evolving into a "middle kingdom" between France and Germany, it figured significantly in the era's history. Burgundy's success under Duke Philip the Good (reigned 1419–1467) underscored the opportunities that a skillful, unscrupulous prince could exploit by playing off the English and French kings against each other, meanwhile collecting territories by shrewd marriages. By his death, a patchwork of Burgundian lands stretched from the border of Switzerland to Holland. The fact that within ten years, in 1477, all this came crashing down when Philip's son Charles the Rash died on the battlefield can be interpreted as one of history's numerous twists of fate. But the sudden end of Burgundy's bid for statehood also emphasizes the brittle artificiality of late medieval dynasticism: States held together by marriage and inheritance were like houses of cards. Local assemblies were strong in most of the Burgundian lands, but each focused on defending its interests against the others, as well as against the duke. No sense of national cohesion emerged; nor did the dukes ever quite decide whether they wanted

Philip the Good Receiving a Book Fashionably dressed (note the stylish footwear) and wearing the Golden Fleece, Philip the Good, duke of Burgundy, graciously receives the bulky chronicle of which this illumination is the frontispiece. Courtiers, also wearing the Fleece, look on, as does Nicholas Rolin, the powerful chancellor of Burgundy who is the bourgeois-looking man in blue behind Philip. He was a great patron of the arts in his own right and appears in several important Flemish paintings. *De la part de la Bibliothèque Royale Albert I.*

to be independent rulers or the dominant power within France.

Burgundy's chief legacy to European history was cultural. Its dukes, rich burghers, and clergy were generous patrons of the great Flemish painters and composers (discussed later in the chapter). The Burgundian court developed elaborate chivalric rituals, crowned by the most coveted of all honors, the Order of the Golden Fleece. All this rigmarole would long survive the downfall of fifteenth-century Burgundy, living on at the courts of the Burgundian dukes' Habsburg heirs until World War I.

The Holy Roman Empire: The Triumph of Localism

Fourteenth-century Germany also experienced radical regional splintering. Although local rulers within the Holy Roman Empire were not formally independent, those who ruled the larger or richer territories had virtually free rein to act as sovereign monarchs.

In Chapter 9, we saw that the fatal weakening of central government in the Holy Roman Empire had begun in the thirteenth century, when Emperor Frederick II bartered away power to Germany's princes in return for their support in making himself a strong king in Italy. Rudolf of Habsburg's election as Holy Roman emperor in 1273 did nothing to revive imperial authority. Rudolf used his position as emperor to bolster his dynasty's holdings in southern Germany and Austria—much to the alarm of the German princes who, after Rudolf's death in 1291, gave the imperial crown to less threatening dynasties.

Out of this welter arose the capable Charles IV (reigned 1347–1378) of the Luxembourg Dynasty, whose territorial base was the kingdom of Bohemia. As emperor, he formally sanctioned decentralization in 1356 in a document known as the Golden Bull.[2] This agreement between the emperor and the great secular and ecclesiastical princes of Germany excluded the papacy from the selection and coronation of emperors, who were to be chosen by seven designated German rulers. The electoral states themselves remained relatively stable, as did other large German principalities such as the Habsburg duchy of Austria. But the imperial office remained an empty honor. Emperors could exercise effective authority only by marshaling the strength and wealth of their hereditary lands (see Map 11-3).

Charles's first love was Bohemia, in the mid-fourteenth century an unusually prosperous country. The Czech lands had been converted to Christianity in the tenth century and had usually acknowledged overlordship by the medieval German emperors. At the beginning of the fourteenth century the native Czech dynasty died out and the Luxembourgers acquired Bohemia. Charles IV enhanced its wealth and profited greatly from its mines. His capital, Prague, gained some of the Late Middle Ages' most beautiful architecture, and in 1348 it became the seat of the first university in the Holy Roman Empire, still known as the Charles University. Charles gave much encouragement to

---

[2] The word *bull* refers to the seal (*bulla*) affixed to the charter by the emperor.

MAP 11-3

CENTRAL EUROPE IN 1378

This map shows the Holy Roman Empire at the death of Emperor Charles IV. Not every tiny statelet can be included.

Legend:
- Archbishop of Cologne
- Archbishop of Mainz
- Archbishop of Trier
- Bavaria
- Count-palatine of the Rhine
- Electorate of Brandenburg
- Electorate of Saxony
- Habsburg states
- Kingdom of Bohemia
- Luxembourg
- Swiss Confederation
- Teutonic Knights
- Holy Roman Empire

talented subjects of Czech origin, but as Germans moved into Bohemian cities and villages throughout the fourteenth century, the ground was being prepared for the German-Czech collision in the Hussite Revolution.

Suppressing revolutionary Bohemia, as we shall see later in this chapter, presented a formidable challenge to the Holy Roman Empire and emperor Sigismund (reigned in Germany 1410–1437), a younger son of Charles IV. A ruler whose chief attributes were his propensity for breaking his word and his chivalric swagger, Sigismund fell into financial straits so severe that he had to wear shabby, patched clothes in public. After his long-overdue exit from history in 1437, the German electors turned back to Habsburgs. The Habsburg Frederick III (reigned 1440–1493) was notable mainly for his long and dreary reign, for his chronic impoverishment and consequent political weakness—and for the matrimonial arrangements with which he laid the foundation for his dynasty's enormously important role in later European politics. Except for one (contested) election, Habsburgs would wear the Holy Roman

St. Vitus's Cathedral, Prague On the same hill with the royal castle, dramatically overlooking the Vltava (Moldau) River and the Old City of Prague, stands St. Vitus's cathedral. It is the masterpiece of architect Peter Parler, who directed its construction between 1353 and his death in 1399. Begun in the French Gothic style, St. Vitus's has many details that parallel similar innovations in late medieval England. Notice the clock: By the late fourteenth century, clocks were being added to public buildings in many European cities. *© Rafael Macia/Photo Researchers, Inc.*

Empire's crown until the end of the empire itself in 1806, and thereafter a Habsburg empire would sprawl across central Europe until 1918.

"Let others wage war; you, happy Austria, marry!" ran a fifteenth-century Habsburg slogan. Frederick III arranged for the marriage of his son Maximilian to the daughter of Duke Charles the Rash of Burgundy. When the latter perished in battle in 1477, Maximilian and his wife took over what is today Belgium, much of the Netherlands, and slices of western France, and later they inherited Austria and other chunks of southern Germany. Their son in turn married the daughter of the king and queen of Spain (see Chapter 13), laying the foundations of an immense European—and **New World**—empire.

Germany itself by 1500 had become a jigsaw puzzle of more than a hundred statelets, their boundaries shifting periodically through war, marriage, inheritance, and division. In many places "robber barons" flourished: imperial knights or petty princelings who controlled a single castle and extorted protection money from everyone passing by. There was talk of creating imperial institutions to put down lawbreakers, ensure justice, collect taxes, and raise armies—but no more than talk. Imperial authority in Italian politics was dead; so was papal authority in imperial elections. Germany and Italy were disentangled from each other at last, but both lands passed into more modern times divided internally and thus at a disadvantage in competing with the western monarchies.

Germans also tried to deal with fragmented sovereignty and chronic disorder during the fourteenth and fifteenth centuries by forming regional leagues and confederations. (There was even a league of peasants, the nucleus of what in the sixteenth century would become a revolutionary movement.) One league in the Rhineland, for example, was formed to combat local robber barons. It became as much a nuisance as the robbers themselves.

The largest interurban alliance was the Hanseatic League, which linked many towns in northern and eastern Germany and was led by the rich city of Lübeck. "The Hansa" achieved its greatest success in 1369 when it forced the king of Denmark to agree to its terms for conducting trade through the strategic straits that separate the Baltic Sea and the North Sea. At times the Hanseatic League regulated international commerce from Flanders to northwestern Russia. Yet by the end of the fifteenth century the Hansa, with no great power to back it up, was beginning to loose control of the Baltic trade to the English and the Dutch (see Map 11-4).

One of the late medieval Holy Roman Empire's many leagues still survives: the Swiss Confederation. It had its roots in a late thirteenth-century defensive compact of three tiny "forest cantons" around Lake Lucerne, whose self-governing peasants vowed to resist outside domination. In 1315 they defeated a Habsburg army (one of the heroes was the legendary archer William Tell), and in the fourteenth

MAP 11-4
THE HANSEATIC LEAGUE

Although membership in the Hanseatic League fluctuated, this map names the most important towns and locates less important ones that from time to time belonged. It also indicates the Hanseatic *Kontors*, which were settlements where merchants from member towns had the right to live, do business, and bring their legal disputes to a special court.

and fifteenth centuries the confederacy gained new members, including the cities of Zurich and Basel. Well-drilled Swiss pikemen were virtually invincible—and from this grew the temptation to hire out mercenary companies to neighboring states (even if it meant Swiss fighting Swiss). The crowning proof of Swiss military prowess came in 1477, when Duke Charles of Burgundy perished in a characteristically rash attempt to take them on. Until well into the sixteenth century, Swiss mercenaries would be the mainstay of many European kings. Even today, the papacy's colorful Swiss Guards keep this tradition alive.

Italy: The Changing Communes, 1250–1400

High-medieval Italy, at least north of Rome, was the land of **communes.** Although not legally independent, these were self-governing city-republics that had effectively freed themselves of outside control in the course of the epic struggle between Holy Roman emperors and popes during the eleventh and twelfth centuries (see Chapter 8).

The essence of the commune was the oath of association that its leaders and members swore. From its beginning, therefore, the medieval Italian commune faced the basic questions with which self-governing peoples, from ancient city-states to modern democracies, have wrestled: What is citizenship? Who should rule? Can law and order be justly maintained? What rights do political minorities have?

The communes were torn by internal struggles for political power. In the early twelfth century, control lay in the hands of wealthy merchants and landholding nobles who had moved into town and dominated the merchants' guilds. Before 1200 full citizenship in most communes was restricted by property qualifications, lengthy periods of res-

idence, guild membership, and other requirements. But in the thirteenth century, a group consisting largely of educated professional men, smaller merchants, and skilled craftsmen made serious efforts to enter political life. These *popolani* organized themselves into movements usually called the *popolo* (literally, "the people") and sought to break aristocratic strangleholds on city governments and law courts. Their efforts often meant bloody turmoil. Especially prominent among them were lawyers and notaries (men trained in Latin, the drafting of contracts, and the writing of letters but lacking university legal education). Immigrants, the poor, and the unskilled were excluded from the popolo, as we have already seen in the case of the Florentine ciompi in 1378.

In nearly all of these struggles, the popolani were divided. Some non-nobles supported the aristocrats; some nobles or knights led the popolo because they hated the dominant clique of the moment. The popolani sometimes excluded nobles from office by intimidation and violence. More frequently, however, they organized and lobbied to secure constitutional changes guaranteeing them a fixed number of places in government, or they elected a leader known as the captain of the people.

These developments allowed relatively large numbers of men (not women) to participate meaningfully in governing the Italian communes. Mid-thirteenth-century Siena, for example, had an adult male population of about five thousand and at least 860 public offices. Because terms were short, the percentages of males holding some sort of position was high. Councils with as many as a thousand members debated and resolved matters of the greatest importance—diplomacy, war, taxation, economic and social regulation, and the communal constitution. This participation in public life remained largely limited to the members of the guilds, and thus to men of middling rather than poor condition. Nevertheless, this political process involved more people in more important decisions than in high-medieval towns and was more open than anything before modern democracies emerged in the nineteenth and twentieth centuries. It strengthened an already powerful civic patriotism and an attachment to republican government and the ideal of independence from external authority (whether pope, emperor, noble, or neighboring city). As we shall see in Chapter 12, the republican ideal remained so powerful that Renaissance political thinkers continuously debated ways and means to reestablish it after it was gone.

Besides irrepressible factionalism, the other fact of life in the later medieval Italian commune was the rise of one-man rulers, or *signori* (lords). Like ancient Greek tyrants (see Chapter 2), thirteenth- and fourteenth-century Italian despots rode to power by exploiting factional strife and social conflict, promising to reestablish order and redress grievances. But they stayed in power by force, though some insisted that they still upheld republican liberty. Other signori were military men whom Emperor Frederick II and his fourteenth-century successors rewarded with pompous titles like "imperial vicar." The seemingly interminable wars in which early fourteenth-century Italy was a battleground for popes and would-be German emperors provided wonderful opportunities for plunder and coups by mercenary captains (*condottiere*). By all these means, durable signorial regimes arose in such important cities as Milan, Verona, and Padua. Milan, ruled by the often cruel and usually masterful Visconti family, steadily swallowed up other cities.

The despotisms of Milan and many other city-republics in northern Italy during the fourteenth century backed the imperial (or Ghibelline) cause; the hill country of central Italy was the land of the nominally pro-papal Guelf party. Once denoting the two sides in the high-medieval battles of emperors and popes (see Chapter 8), by the mid-fourteenth century the Guelf and Ghibelline labels lost ideological importance, becoming simply banners in a struggle for power. In many communes, rival Ghibelline and Guelf families battled for control. (The fictional Montagues and Capulets of Verona in Shakespeare's *Romeo and Juliet*, a retelling of an old Italian story, are a classic example.) Some cities, like Florence, were so dominated by one party (the Guelfs in Florence's case) that the other was exiled en masse, lurking as vengeful plotters in rival cities. Victorious parties themselves often split into implacable rivals. When this happened in Florence at the beginning of the fourteenth century, the great poet Dante was driven from his city on pain of death: No wonder that he filled hell with political enemies.

Although glorification of ancient republican traditions would not begin in Italy until the early Renaissance (see Chapter 12), the fourteenth-century Guelf communes that

escaped domination by signori were in fact republican regimes. The most important of these were the rival maritime city-republics of Venice and Genoa, and in Tuscany the similarly antagonistic cities of Florence and Siena.

The great city at the head of the Adriatic, Venice, traced its origins back to the collapse of Roman Italy, when refugees from Germanic invaders fled to offshore lagoons. By the eleventh century Venice's influence reached down the eastern coast of the Adriatic, and it shook free of Byzantine overlordship while holding the Holy Roman emperors at bay. Venice's notorious role in the Fourth Crusade (1204; see Chapter 9) not only ensured its ascendancy over the Adriatic but also won it lasting commercial concessions in the Byzantine world. But the Venetians had a serious maritime rival, Genoa. Never a significant power on the Italian mainland, Genoa made its fortune in the commerce of the western Mediterranean, in 1277 establishing the first regular seaborne link from Italy to England and Flanders. During the fourteenth century Genoa and Venice fought repeatedly to grab shares of each other's markets. Both succeeded. By 1400, Genoa held important outposts in the Aegean and Black Seas, while Venetian galleys were also carrying commerce to northwestern Europe (see Map 11-5).

Venice and Genoa presented stark political contrasts. Venice became famous in the Late Middle Ages and Renaissance for its political stability; Genoa, for its turbulence. This contrast mirrored the two republics' commercial styles: In Venice, trade was conducted in state-owned (and state-built) galleys, and state officials allocated each trader a share of the space and the profits; Genoese merchants were fiercely individualistic and competitive. But the contrast went further. Both republics were dominated by patrician elites who made their fortunes in long-range trade and finance, but Venice literally closed the book on new families entering the elite in 1297,[3] thereafter generally limiting access to the highest state offices to wealthy old families. Venice's incredibly complex government was designed both to minimize conflict within the elite and to facilitate emergency decision making. Over it all presided the *doge* (or duke), a dignitary chosen for life but generally a figurehead. (See Chapter 12 for a more detailed treatment.) Genoa also had an aristocratic council and a doge, but its politics were a violent free-for-all. The Venetian populace was generally content to allow the aristocracy to run things, especially because the city was prosperous and well-endowed with charitable institutions that looked after the poor. Genoese commoners were frequently courted by elite politicians, and frequently rioted on their patrons' behalf.

---

[3] After that year the Golden Book, in which were inscribed the names of Venice's aristocratic families, was not to include new names. Exceptions were made, but in general upstarts were not allowed to enter the ranks of the elite.

MAP 11-5
VENETIAN AND GENOESE TRADING NETWORKS

Fourteenth-century Florence and Siena resembled Venice in the complexity of their institutions and Genoa in their complex interactions of elite patricians and lower-status clients. There was more middle-class participation in both the Florentine and Sienese regimes, however, than in either Venice or Genoa—"middle-class" being defined as belonging to the popolo rather than the aristocracy. (Florence barred members of old aristocratic families from certain political functions.) Offices changed hands every few months, and often were selected by lot (much as jurors are chosen today in the United States). Despite this, both Florence and Siena were reasonably stable for much of the fourteenth century—the exception being during times of military challenge or severe economic distress, such as 1378, the year of the ciompi uprising.

Rome was always a unique city in medieval Europe. Its ruler, the pope, shared local power with turbulent nobles and their mobs. The city's only industry was the church—its pilgrimage shrines, its bureaucracy, its artisans and servants dependent on the aristocracy and the resident clergy. When the papacy abandoned Rome for Avignon in 1309 (see Chapter 9), the city went into a profound economic slump and became prey to its aristocrats' perpetual feuds. Out of this turmoil arose the fascinating figure of Cola di Rienzo, called Rienzi (ca. 1313–1354), a notary and the son of a tavern-keeper. Like many fourteenth-

century Italian notaries, Rienzi became a passionate admirer of ancient Rome; and like many religious seekers of the age, he also imbibed the **apocalyptic** visions of Joachim of Fiore (see Chapter 10). In 1343 he tried in vain to persuade the pope to return, and four years later, as tribune, he led a six-month insurrection. In 1354, after failing to interest Charles IV in bringing back a real Roman Empire, he made another attempt himself to restore the Roman Republic, which ended in his death at the hands of a mob.

Rienzi's meteoric rise and fall was symptomatic of several things: the distress and anxious expectations of fourteenth-century life, the frequent violence of communal life, and the power vacuum in Italy that the absence of popes and emperors had created. The "last of the tribunes" was a truly transitional figure: medieval in his Joachimite speculations about an imminent Millennium; proto-Renaissance in his reverence for the long-dead Roman Republic; and almost modern in his dream of a united Italy.

The story of Italy's political and cultural fortunes in the fifteenth century—the early Renaissance era—belongs to Chapter 12. As we shall see there, the political crazy quilt of late medieval Italy evolved into a delicate power balance between five major states: Milan, Venice, Florence, Naples, and the papacy. No less fateful would be the battle within the Italian soul between admiration for

Rome's imperial tradition and proud memories of Roman republicanism.

Europe's Eastern Borderlands

Like Italy and Germany, late medieval Poland, Lithuania, Hungary, and the Scandinavian states all experienced dynastic quarrels and endemic warfare. Most of the Balkans were overwhelmed by the Ottoman Turks. Only the Russians and Ottomans built strong and extensive territorial states, and both, by 1500, were uncompromisingly autocratic. Poland-Lithuania and Hungary followed the western European model of the state by developing parliaments, law codes, and political cultures that exalted aristocratic freedom. The consequences of this cultural and political westernization remain significant today, as do the autocratic Byzantine traditions of Russia and the Balkans. But Poland-Lithuania and Hungary (as well as Bohemia) also emerged from the Middle Ages with systems of serfdom that bore with increasing severity on their large peasant majorities.

The Ottoman Empire: The Ultimate Despotism

Long before Constantinople fell to Mohammed II "the Conqueror" in 1453 (see Part Three introduction), the Ottomans were adapting much of the old Byzantine and Abbasid bureaucratic traditions. The highly cultivated Mohammed spoke several western languages and considered himself the new Alexander the Great. But he was also the product of a cruel system under which—to prevent power struggles—all of an incoming sultan's half-brothers were routinely strangled.[4] Once, keeping his word that some Italian prisoners of war would not lose their heads, Mohammed had the men sawed in two. Ottoman armies usually sold their captives into slavery. The backbone of the Ottoman military was the elite janissary corps, recruited in a levy (the *devshirme*) whereby young Christian boys were taken from their families, brought up as Muslims, and turned into almost invincible warriors. Even the highest officials were the sultan's slaves and could be put to death at his pleasure. Although they considered themselves bound by the Qur'an and Islamic law, Ottoman sultans wielded power far more absolute than any western monarch could command.

Despite its cruelty and arbitrariness, many modern historians believe that the Ottoman empire was more efficiently and justly governed than most west European societies of the Late Middle Ages. As long as the empire was expanding, official rapacity could be satisfied at the expense of external victims of conquest. Christians and

Jews, as "people of the book," formed self-governing communities and practiced their faith relatively undisturbed as long as they paid their taxes. Many Greek merchants remained rich and influential under Ottoman rule, and there is evidence that (initially at least) Balkan Christian peasants found the Turkish yoke easier to bear than that of their native aristocracies. Important Jewish communities thrived in such cities as Thessalonika and Sarajevo. Large-scale voluntary conversions to Islam took place among the Albanians and the Bosnian Slavs. The Ottomans accepted as a compatriot anyone who professed Islam and adopted their way of life. Such attitudes, as well as the freedom that Muslim males enjoyed of maintaining (if they could afford it) four wives and unlimited concubines, facilitated ethnic mixing and brought many Christian renegades into the Ottoman service.

Poland-Lithuania and Hungary: Roots of Aristocratic Liberty

Poland became a Latin Christian kingdom in 966, but it fragmented in the twelfth century. The western borderlands gravitated into the German orbit, and the Teutonic Knights seized Poland's outlet to the Baltic (see Chapter 9). But in the early fourteenth century Poland's core territory was reunited. Under King Casimir the Great (reigned 1333–1370), the country enjoyed a prosperity unusual for the time and escaped the Black Death, thanks to its dispersed population. But after Casimir's death, the high aristocracy and bishops in 1386 married off his granddaughter to Prince Jagiełło of Lithuania (reigned 1377–1434), Europe's last **pagan** ruler, who along with the Lithuanian nobility accepted baptism. Thus was born the Polish-Lithuanian Commonwealth, the largest political unit wholly within Europe, stretching from the Baltic to the Black Sea and incorporating most of western Russia.

In both Poland and Lithuania, the great nobles predominated, and in Poland the crown became elective, though members of the Jagiellonian family were always chosen. The dual state humbled the Teutonic Knights in the battle of Tannenberg (1410) and by 1466 regained access to the Baltic. But the nobles cooperated only grudgingly with their rulers. The parliament (*Sejm*) that emerged during the fifteenth century was controlled by the high aristocracy (magnates), with burghers politically marginalized. By 1500 the peasantry was falling under harsher serfdom. Poland-Lithuania thus became a loosely governed elective monarchy in which the magnates held sway, sporadically challenged by the lesser **gentry.**

Medieval Hungary's history in many ways paralleled Poland's. It became a Latin Christian kingdom in the year 1000, and in the twelfth century united with neighboring Croatia. In the fourteenth century it had several capable monarchs drawn from the Angevin Dynasty, which also ruled Naples. Hungary's strongest king, Louis the Great (reigned 1342–1382), closely resembled Casimir the Great

---

[4] Ottoman sultans maintained large harems, where with a great many different women they begot numerous children. One son they would choose as their successor.

in aims and accomplishments, although he also played a large role in Italy's bloody politics.

Like Poland-Lithuania, Hungary had a powerful magnate class, which claimed supremacy after 1386 when the last Angevin king was killed. The magnates' elected king, Sigismund (reigned 1387–1437), who in 1433 was crowned Holy Roman emperor, squandered royal authority in his quest for opportunities elsewhere.

Unlike more distant Poland-Lithuania, Hungary faced a truly dangerous threat from the Ottomans. Knowing this, the Hungarian nobles elected a vigorous soldier-king, Matthias Corvinus (reigned 1458–1490), who established a strong monarchy. But the next two times the throne fell vacant, they chose weak Jagiellonian kings. As the fifteenth century ended, Hungary had a feeble government, a noble-dominated parliament, and a downtrodden peasantry,

which in 1512 would rise in a savage insurrection and be crushed with even more savage reprisals. Over it all, the Ottoman Turks threw a menacing shadow (see Map 11-6).

Russia: From Mongol Vassalage to the Tsardom of Moscow Medieval Russia took its Orthodox faith and the Byzantine basis of its civilization from Constantinople. Russia's spiritual as well as political center was Kiev. But by the early thirteenth century, Russia had split into many principalities as a result of its princes' habit of dividing their territory among their sons.

Kievan Russia perished in 1240 with the most devastating of all Mongol invasions. "When we passed through that land," wrote a papal representative who in 1245 and 1246 traveled to the Mongol headquarters, "we found lying in the field countless heads and bones of dead people; for

MAP 11-6

EASTERN EUROPE IN THE THIRTEENTH TO FIFTEENTH CENTURIES

[Kiev] had been extremely large and very populous, whereas now it has been reduced to nothing: barely two hundred houses stand there, and those people are held in the harshest slavery."

Even before the invasion, the center of gravity in Russian life had been shifting from Kiev to the forests of northern Russia, and the mid-thirteenth-century catastrophes accelerated the change. The city-state of Novgorod, which ruled much of northwestern Russia, escaped destruction by prudently submitting to overlordship by the Mongol khanate in Russia, the Golden Horde. Meanwhile Novgorod's prince, Alexander Nevskii (reigned 1236–1263), in 1240 repelled a Swedish invasion and in 1242 dealt the Teutonic Knights a crushing defeat. Dominated by a merchant oligarchy, Novgorod in some ways resembled the communal regimes of medieval Italy: The prince, for example, was elected by the city's assembly *(Veche)* and could be dismissed by it.

But in the long run, Russia's historical fate was shaped by the Byzantine-style autocracy of Moscow. Strategically located at the juncture of river routes, Moscow survived the Mongol invasion that wiped out some of the larger northeastern principalities. In the early fourteenth century the Golden Horde gave the Muscovite ruler Ivan Kalita (ca. 1328 or 1332–1341) the title of Grand Prince and the responsibility for collecting tribute from other Russian princes. *(Kalita* means "moneybag.") On occasion Moscow helped the Mongols crush other Russian rebels. Despite this, Ivan Kalita gained enormous prestige when he persuaded the metropolitan of Kiev—Russia's spiritual head—to relocate to what Russians thereafter called "Holy Moscow." When Ivan's descendant, Grand Prince Dmitrii Donskoi (reigned 1359–1389), won the first Russian victory over the Golden Horde on the Don River in 1380 *(Donskoi* means "of the Don"), Moscow's renown was further enhanced even though submission to the Mongols had to be renewed.

The emergence of what historians call "the tsardom of Moscow" culminated under Ivan III ("the Great," reigned 1462–1505), one of late medieval Europe's greatest monarchs. Ivan ceased paying tribute to the Horde and, throwing off all submission, defeated a Tatar-Lithuanian alliance in 1480. Meanwhile, between 1471 and 1478, he conquered and annexed Novgorod and destroyed its quasi-republican tradition. In 1493 Ivan proclaimed himself "Sovereign [*Gosudar*] of All the Russias," forcing all other Russian princes except those under Lithuanian rule to accept his supremacy. It would be only a short step in the sixteenth century for the Muscovite rulers to assume the title of *Tsar* (or caesar).

The Russian Orthodox church blessed the Moscow autocracy. In 1439 it had repudiated Byzantium's submission to the papacy (discussed earlier) and declared its independence of Constantinople. When Ivan married the niece of the last Byzantine emperor in 1472, he turned this dynastic connection into one more foundation stone for autocracy—for example, adopting the Byzantine double-headed eagle as Russia's emblem and introducing solemn Byzantine court rituals. By 1503, the Russian church was speaking of Moscow as the "Third Rome": The papal "First Rome" had lapsed into **heresy,** and Constantinople, the "Second Rome," had fallen to Islam—but the "Third Rome" would last until the end of the world.

The deep spirituality of late medieval Russia, like that of the Latin West in the same era, cannot be underestimated.

Rublev's *Old Testament Trinity* Many consider Andrey Rublev the supreme Russian icon painter and this his crowning work. It was painted for the iconostasis—the screen that separates the altar from the worshipers in Orthodox churches—of a church at Zagorsk, a large monastery near Moscow. According to an ancient church legend, three angels revealed to Abraham the mystery of the Trinity. Depicted with symbolism associated with the Father, Son, and Holy Spirit, the three angels are shown here with Abraham's house, the tree, and the rock signifying ascending gradations of Divine Knowledge. The austere design and luminous colors lend an aura of timeless serenity. It is believed that Rublev, a monk who was later canonized by the Orthodox church, painted this icon to support the church's position in a controversy over the Trinity. He and other Greek and Russian icon painters active around Moscow at the beginning of the fifteenth century are major figures in the development of Byzantine-influenced artistic and spiritual traditions, and are fully comparable to the great west European artists of the era. *Scala/Art Resource, NY.*

During these centuries the art of icon painting plumbed the depths of religious intensity. The mystical asceticism and profound faith of some Russian monks matched anything in the early Christian tradition. During the fifteenth century a movement arose within the Russian church insisting on the clergy's complete renunciation of political power and landed wealth, quite comparable to the spirit of St. Francis of Assisi and his followers. The stirrings of religious and intellectual reform in late Byzantine Christianity also touched the Russian church. But those in power in Russian Orthodoxy had a deep stake in the status quo—by 1500, it owned one-fourth of the land—and they stifled dissent. The church, even more than the autocracy, sealed off Russia from the Renaissance and Reformation movements of western Europe.

The Muscovite princes enjoyed popular support in their struggle against the Mongols, the Catholic Lithuanians, and the oligarchy of Novgorod, but their rule was autocratic to a degree worthy of Byzantine emperors and Mongol khans. Their state had no assemblies and no articulate middle class. At the top and the bottom of society, Russians were losing the mobility that had ensured a good measure of freedom during the Middle Ages. As the Moscow autocracy took hold, nobles (*boyars*) found their long-established right to change allegiance from one prince to another redefined as treason. Peasants groaned beneath heavy taxes and struggled to establish agriculture under difficult conditions in Russia's north, where many were migrating, just as their opportunity to leave their holdings was being cut back. They were not yet serfs, but serfdom was on the way.

By the time of Ivan the Great, Russia was beginning to acquire the attributes of a great power. Ivan continued Novgorod's practice of allowing in traders and technical experts from western Europe—but under conditions that kept outsiders secluded from the Russian population (who had religious and cultural reasons for being suspicious of them). The centuries, beginning with the Mongol conquest, during which Russia was isolated from the rest of Europe and plunged into oppressive poverty and backwardness could not be made up overnight.

SPIRITUAL CRISIS AND CULTURAL CHANGE

The late medieval West's drift away from a unitary concept of Christendom and toward the idea of a diversity of Christian nations was less a transformation than a shift in balance. Even during the High Middle Ages the ideal of a Christian commonwealth, guided by pope, **bishop,** and other clergy, had never truly been fulfilled. By the late thirteenth century the balance was tipping in favor of monarchs, and it tipped still more during the Late Middle Ages. Despite the troubles that afflicted late medieval kingdoms, by 1500 the papacy had become far weaker as an international force,

and the monarchies had grown stronger. The princely electors of Germany had long denied the papacy any role in imperial elections or coronations, and papal influence in the appointment of French, English, and Spanish bishops had ebbed. More important still, the Late Middle Ages witnessed a collapse of papal spiritual prestige and a widening chasm between Christian piety and the organized church.

The Changing Church

The late medieval trend toward secular sovereignty found powerful expression in the Italian lawyer Marsilius of Padua's book *Defensor Pacis* ("The Defender of Peace," 1324). Born about 1280, Marsilius taught at the University of Paris and served as a political adviser to pro-imperial signori in northern Italy. When his authorship of *Defensor Pacis* became known, he fled Italy and spent the rest of his life (he died about 1343) in the service of antipapal German kings.

Defensor Pacis created a scandal and earned its author a papal condemnation for heresy. What enraged the papacy was Marsilius's uncompromising argument that the clergy should be stripped of political authority, and that the state should wield sovereign power over all lay and clerical subjects alike. Thus the church, united in faith, would be divided politically into state churches obedient to their secular rulers and not to the pope. In his glorification of the sovereign state, Marsilius was deeply influenced by Aristotle's *Politics* (see Chapter 3), and he foreshadowed the evolution of late medieval and early modern politics.

Popes and Councils The late medieval papacy was vulnerable. Early in the fourteenth century, the popes had fled from faction-ridden Rome and settled in Avignon on the Rhone River, surrounded by French territory (see Chapter 9). There a series of able French pontiffs ruled from 1309 to 1376.

The Avignon popes were only occasionally subservient to the French crown; for the most part they were capable of strong, independent action. But their location suggested to France's enemies that they were no longer impartial. Attempts to return the papacy to Rome were foiled by the violent rivalries among the Roman aristocracy.

Meanwhile the Avignon popes carried the thirteenth-century trend toward administrative and fiscal efficiency to its ultimate degree. The large, finely tuned bureaucracy of papal Avignon provided revenues and personnel sufficient to make the papacy an even stronger international power than before. Pope John XXII (reigned 1316–1334), a man of austere life and administrative genius, launched a thoroughgoing reform of papal finances. He increased revenues significantly by attacking the long-standing custom of rake-offs at every level between the taxpayer and the papal treasury. But bureaucracy failed to inspire mystics and reformers, and France's neighbors resented the taxation and interference of what some mistakenly regarded as a tool of the French crown. Thus while the papacy was growing wealthier and more efficient, its spiritual capital was dwindling.

Lay protests against clerical wealth and power had been implicit in the thirteenth-century Franciscan movement, although St. Francis of Assisi had shown his devotion to apostolic poverty by living it rather than urging it on wealthy churchmen (see Chapter 8). The compromises of later Franciscanism produced a zealous protest group, the Spiritual Franciscans, whose insistence on universal ecclesiastical poverty turned them anticlerical and antipapal. John XXII saw fit in 1323 to denounce them as heretics, and during the rest of the fourteenth century numerous *Fraticelli*—Franciscan friars who believed themselves faithful to St. Francis's original ideals—were burned at stakes throughout Europe.

Only in 1376 did Pope Gregory XI respond to clamor from Europe's laity by moving back to Rome. Chagrined by the turbulence he found there, Gregory decided to return to France but died in 1378 before he could do so. Pressured by a Roman mob, the cardinals—most of them homesick Frenchmen—elected an Italian to the papal throne.

The new pope, Urban VI, had been a colorless ecclesiastical bureaucrat. Now, to everyone's surprise, he became a zealous reformer and began trimming the cardinals' revenues and influence. The cardinals fled Rome, canceled Urban's election on grounds of mob intimidation, and elected a French pope who returned with them to Avignon. In Rome, Urban VI appointed a new bench of cardinals, and for the next thirty-seven years the church was torn by the "Great Schism." When the rival popes died, their cardinals elected rival successors. Excommunications rocketed to and fro between Rome and Avignon, and the states of Europe chose sides according to their interests. Papal prestige was plunging into ruin, yet in the face of age-long papal claims to absolute spiritual authority, there seemed no power on earth that could arbitrate between two rival popes.

As the Great Schism dragged on, increasing numbers of Christians became convinced that the only solution was to convene a general church council. But since both popes argued that councils, being inferior to them, could not judge them, Christians were perplexed as to who, if not the popes, had the authority to summon a council. At length some of the cardinals themselves, in both camps, called the Council of Pisa, which in 1409 deposed both popes and elected a new one. But neither pope recognized the Council of Pisa or its action, so the two-way schism simply became a three-way schism. Each pope damned the other two and all who recognized them. This was not only scandalous; it was ludicrous. And meanwhile major challenges to the authority of the church itself (soon to be discussed) had arisen in England and Bohemia. Reformers in both countries no longer accepted the pope as the link connecting God and the Christian community.

Finally, the future Holy Roman emperor Sigismund arranged for the summoning of churchmen from all across Europe to the Council of Constance (1414–1418). Here at last the schism ended. Two popes were deposed, the third resigned, and Western Christendom was reunited by the election of Martin V (reigned 1417–1431).

To many thoughtful Christians, healing the Great Schism was not enough. The papacy stood discredited, and it was argued that future popes should be guided by general councils meeting regularly and automatically. Councils and assemblies were familiar enough in contemporary secular governments. Why shouldn't the church, too, be governed "constitutionally"? Such views had been argued by Marsilius of Padua in the fourteenth century and were revived in the fifteenth. They were widely accepted among the worthies at Constance, who made a genuine effort to reform the administration of the church along conciliar lines. The delegates affirmed the ultimate authority of councils in matters of doctrine and reform, they imposed a number of specific reforms, and they decreed that general councils would reconvene regularly.

All this met with intense opposition from Martin V and his successors, who insisted on absolute papal supremacy. The popes reluctantly summoned a council in 1423 and another in 1431, but undermined them. The last of the important medieval councils, the Council of Basel (1431–1449), drifted gradually into open schism with the papacy and petered out ingloriously. By then Europe's enthusiasm for councils was diminishing; the conciliar movement waned, and a single pope ruled unopposed once more in Rome. In 1461, Pius II gave conciliarism its deathblow by declaring it heresy to appeal against a pope's decision to a future council.

The popes between the dissolution of Basel (1449) and the beginning of the Protestant Reformation (1517) differed radically from their high-medieval predecessors. Abandoning much of their former jurisdiction over the international church, they devoted themselves to the beguiling culture and bitter local politics of Renaissance Italy (see Chapter 12). Struggling to hold the Papal States, they conceded to some northern monarchs extensive control over the church in their kingdoms in return for a formal recognition of papal authority and a sharing of church revenues between pope and king. French kings were so satisfied with this that in the Reformation era they would see no advantage in breaking with Rome and setting up a national church. English kings, however, got no such concessions.

Religious Rebels Uncertainty over who should lead the church and scandal about its moral condition exploded in the late fourteenth and early fifteenth centuries in a religious revolt—incipient in England and full-blown in Bohemia.

The precipitating figure of the late medieval religious revolt was the English clergyman John Wycliffe (d. 1384),

THE HUMAN EXPERIENCE

Jan Hus

To most modern Czechs, the fifteenth-century priest and martyr Jan Hus is their earliest national hero—the spiritual precursor of Tomaš G. Masaryk, the scholar-creator of post-World War I Czechoslovakia, and of Václav Havel, the dissident playwright under communism and now president of the Czech Republic.

Jan of Husinec, born about 1369, was a son of a poor artisan family from a small Bohemian town.* He got his education in Prague, where by 1396 the Charles University awarded him the degrees of master in arts and bachelor in theology.

The Prague of young Hus's day was electric with religious excitement. In the 1360s, Emperor Charles IV had encouraged eloquent reformers like the Austrian Conrad of Waldhausen and the latter's disciple Jan Milíč of Kroměříž to preach "religion of the heart" to the people of Prague. They attacked ritualism and superstition in religion, advocated frequent communion, demanded strict clerical morality, and downplayed church tradition and hierarchy. After Milíč died in 1391, two rich Prague burghers endowed Bethlehem Chapel, where preachers in Czech would keep alive his ideals. In 1402 Hus's gifts as a speaker and his earnest moralism brought him appointment to the chapel's pulpit. Hus, a master of the vernacular and author of the first book on Czech spelling, believed that addressing ordinary people in their own language was essential to their religious and moral improvement. At a time when the Bible had not been translated into Czech, Hus was urging the church to drop Latin and adopt the vernacular as the liturgical language.

Hus and the other Czech reformers had an English forefather in John Wycliffe, the inspirer of Lollardry and the first translator of the Bible into English. Wycliffe's ideas first arrived in Prague in the 1390s, brought back by Czech students who had traveled to Oxford on scholarships. A second great flood of Wycliffite writings, as well as a few Lollard preachers, reached the city in 1406 and 1407.

Although Hus's writings contain many passages taken almost verbatim from Wycliffe (a common practice in medieval scholarship), he was no plagiarist of Wycliffe's views. Hus jettisoned Wycliffe's teachings that were unpalatable to laypeople—like the denial of Christ's real presence in the Eucharist, and like **predestination,** the idea that God had already chosen the saved and the damned. But he found two of Wycliffe's teachings compelling: (1) that the "real church" is not a hierarchy led by the pope but the body of true Christians headed by Christ; and (2) that the ultimate source of Christian truth is Scripture, not churchly authority. He would defend these ideas with his life.

As the Czech religious reformers honed their message, a bitter struggle for power was unfolding in the university and the city. Germans, long the dominant urban minority, were being challenged by increasingly assertive Czech faculty and well-to-do burghers; disgruntled Czech artisans and poor Czech day laborers clashed with the city's German-speaking elite. Among the professors, seemingly esoteric philosophical ideas became a battleground, the Germans espousing nominalism and Ockhamism and the Czechs taking up realism—an approach whose most prominent recent advocate was Wycliffe. In 1409, when Charles IV's successor, King Václav, gave the Czech majority control of the university, the German professors and students moved to Leipzig, where they founded their own university.

Bent on revenge, the German academics told anyone in Europe who would listen that the Czechs were Wycliffite heretics. Many listened, including leaders of the conciliarist movement. The archbishop of Prague, hitherto sympathetic to the reformers, began to see them as a threat to church hierarchy. In 1410 he burned Wycliffe's writings and excommunicated Hus, and in 1412 he used the threat of an interdict on the city to drive Hus out of Prague. In Hus's absence, anticlerical and millenarian ideas far more radical than anything he advocated spread in Prague. Antireformist monks were beaten up, and relics destroyed as superstitious. Many Czechs began to take the communion cup, a departure from tradition that Hus came around to sanctioning.

Hus appealed against his excommunication to a future council—just what other critics of the papacy were doing. So when that council actually convened at Constance in 1414, he hardly could refuse to attend. Besides, King Sigismund gave him a safe-conduct, and Hus felt confident that he could defend what he saw as the truth. Immediately upon his arrival in November 1414, however, he was arrested. Although he was not physically tortured, his treatment was deplorable. Through it all, he insisted that he would recant only if his position could be proved contrary to Scripture. At the public hearings he finally got in June 1415, he was drowned out by catcalls. The verdict had already been prepared. On July 6, having been condemned for adhering to Wycliffe's heretical ideas (most of which he denied holding), he was stripped of his priesthood, consigned to the devil, and burned at the stake. When the news reached Prague, the result was a national revolt against the council, the pope, and Sigismund. The dress rehearsal for the Protestant Reformation had begun. ❖

_____

*The name _Hus_ is a pun on Husinec. It means "goose." Hus himself enjoyed the joke.

a master at the University of Oxford. He boldly struck at a thousand-year-old tradition of institutional authority by elevating Scripture over the pronouncements of popes and councils, anticipating what in the sixteenth century would be the Protestant position (see Chapter 13). Stretching the implications of contemporary mysticism to their limit, Wycliffe stressed the individual's inner spiritual journey toward God, questioned the real presence of Christ in the Holy Eucharist, de-emphasized the entire sacramental system, and denounced ecclesiastical wealth. Eventually his criticism became so dangerous to the established church that Wycliffe was stripped of his teaching position and convicted of heresy. But having powerful friends at court, and owing to the unpopularity of the papacy in fourteenth-century England, Wycliffe lived out his life as a free man. Only after his death were his bones dug up and burned and his followers, the Lollards,[5] hunted down ruthlessly by kings Henry IV and Henry V. By the early fifteenth century Lollardry was contained, but it had planted seeds of religious dissent that germinated until the Reformation.

English Lollardry represented an extreme expression of discontent with the church. Wycliffe's doctrines spread to distant Bohemia—the main conduits were intellectual ties between the universities of Oxford and Prague—where they were taken up by Czech critics such as Jan Hus (ca. 1369–1415).

The church in fourteenth-century Bohemia was as deeply in need of cleansing as any in western Europe. Recognizing this, Charles IV had encouraged Czech and German preachers of reform. But under his weak son, King Václav, religious reform became entangled with a Czech-German struggle for power within Prague and its university community, the German side accusing their Czech opponents of Wycliffite heresy. Hus and other Czech reformers embraced Wycliffe's anticlericalism—if not all his doctrines—more openly.

To get rid of their dangerous opponent and prove their orthodoxy, Václav's brother King Sigismund[6] and the Council of Constance in 1415 hit on the clever stratagem of luring Hus to Constance and burning him at the stake. But their treachery outraged the Czechs. When Sigismund succeeded Václav as king of Bohemia in 1419, the Bohemian diet (parliament) overwhelmingly rejected him.

From the Catholic perspective, Bohemian events spun out of control. Most Czechs abandoned the practice of barring the laity from the chalice at communion, which since the time of Innocent III had symbolized priests' unique position in the church (see Chapter 8). For the more conservative Utraquist party, led by the Czech nobility and the well-to-do burghers of Prague, the Eucharist "under both species" (that is, the consecrated wine as well as the bread) was the defining issue. But many Czechs—particularly artisans, peasants, and some of the lesser gentry—went much farther. Apocalyptic visions stirred these radical Hussites, inspiring religious hopes for Christ's imminent Second Coming and dreams of social leveling, even communism. The radical party, comprised of Táborites whose name came from the town that was their stronghold, separated from the Catholic church and elected their own bishop, although some rebels rejected priestly authority altogether.

On the issue of keeping Sigismund and his German crusaders out of Bohemia, conservative and radical Hussites stood together. In fact, the national cause desperately needed the radicals because one of their leaders was a military genius, Jan Žižka (d. 1424). Behind the shield of Žižka's Táborite army, control of the Bohemian church passed to the diet. In 1424 it proclaimed the Four Articles of Prague, an agreement across the Hussite spectrum that called for (1) freedom for priests to preach without ecclesiastical supervision; (2) communion for laypeople under both species; (3) abolition of excessive clerical wealth; and (4) secular punishment for all (including clergy) who committed mortal sins. Such a program, challenging the foundations of the hierarchical Western church, constituted a **revolutionary** message when the highly mobile Táborite troops struck deep into Germany and Poland during the 1420s. The challenge was all the more explosive when these "warriors of God" also spread radical appeals for social leveling.

In 1434, having repelled all external threats, Utraquists and Táborites turned on each other. The Utraquists prevailed, and in 1436 they came to terms with the Council of Basel (but not the pope), which recognized the Czechs' right to receive communion under both species. But the Táborite tradition survived in the Unity of Czech Brethren, a sect that exchanged radical social criticism for pacifism and mysticism. It endured long into the seventeenth century, and in the eighteenth century its heirs came to North America as the Moravian Church, which still exists.

Wycliffe, Hus, and their followers represented, in their opposition to the international church, a reconciliation of personal religious faith with national sovereignty. If Christianity was to be an individual matter, then the political claims of popes and bishops were hollow and secular rulers might govern without ecclesiastical interference. The anticlericalism of late medieval Christianity tended to support the growing concept of secular sovereignty, and the Bohemian diet's assertion of control over church policy foreshadowed the actions of secular authorities during the Reformation and the English Revolution of the sixteenth and seventeenth centuries (see Chapters 13 and 15).

Mystics Although passionate religious spirits such as Hus, Joan of Arc, and the leaders of the Czech Brethren

---

[5] *Lollard* is a Middle English word meaning "mumbler" (of prayers).
[6] Sigismund, a younger son of Emperor Charles IV, was already king of Hungary and "King of the Romans," a title borne by rulers who had not yet been crowned Holy Roman emperor—a dignity that he received only in 1433.

fused incipient **nationalism** with an individualist Christian mysticism, the wave of mysticism that swept across late medieval Europe was not always openly heretical or hostile toward the church. But by stressing the spiritual relationship between the individual and God, these heirs of Hildegard of Bingen and the Beguines (see Chapters 8 and 10) downplayed—even ignored—the ordained clergy and the sacraments as channels of divine grace. Although they believed in the Eucharist and could express their devotion to it in the most moving terms, they also dwelt on the indescribable ecstasy of a mystical union with God, for which no clergy, no popes, and no **sacraments** were needed.

Writing in the early fourteenth century, the Dominican Meister Eckhart (d. 1327) taught that humanity's true goal is utter separation from the world of the senses and absorption into the Divine Unknown. Eckhart had many followers, and during the fourteenth century other mystical communities emerged. St. Catherine of Siena (d. 1380), another Dominican mystic, attracted disciples of both sexes by her single-minded devotion to repentance and social reform as expressions of an all-consuming love of God. And around 1375 the highly influential Brethren of the Common Life was founded by the Flemish lay preacher Gerard Groote, a student of one of Eckhart's disciples and of the Czech reformers. The Brethren devoted themselves to simple lives of preaching, teaching, and charitable works. Their popularity in fifteenth-century northern Europe approached that of the Franciscans two centuries before, but like the Beguines the Brethren took no lifelong vows. Their schools were among Europe's finest and produced some of the leading mystics, humanists, and reformers of the fifteenth and sixteenth centuries.[7]

Supreme literary expression is given to late medieval mysticism in *The Imitation of Christ*, usually ascribed to a graduate of the Brethren schools, Thomas à Kempis (d. 1471). It typifies the mystical outlook in its emphasis on adoration over speculation, inner spiritual purity over external "good works," and direct experience of God over the sacramental avenues to divine grace. The *Imitation* remained within Catholic orthodoxy, yet it contained ideas that had great appeal to sixteenth-century Protestants. The emphasis on individual piety, common to all the mystics, tended to erode the medieval idea of a Christian commonwealth by viewing the church as a multitude of individual souls, each reaching out alone toward God.

Popular Piety   The religious ideas and practices of ordinary people differed radically from those of the mystics. Most Christians, if they could afford it, eagerly collected and venerated relics, visited local shrines where healing

The Master of Třeboň's *The Resurrection*, ca. 1385   The greatest Bohemian painter of the late Middle Ages, called the Master of Třeboň, is nameless and we do not know whether he was a German or a Czech. One of several panels of an altarpiece, this painting is notable for the contrast of the humble, awestruck features of the soldiers who are witnessing the Resurrection and the mystical, disembodied, yet elegant and serene figure of the risen Christ, all unified by a dramatically subdued color scheme. Some art historians detect a Byzantine influence. The growing mystical—and at the same time intensely realistic—trend in late medieval art and religion is quite apparent in works such as this. *Erich Lessing/Art Resource, NY.*

miracles were believed to occur, and went on pilgrimages to holy sites such as Jerusalem, Rome, Santiago de Compostela in Spain, or Becket's tomb at Canterbury. (One of the greatest works of late medieval literature, Geoffrey Chaucer's *Canterbury Tales*, is the story of such a pilgrimage.) In general, ordinary Christians practiced their religion much as they had done in previous generations, except that the plagues and disasters of the fourteenth and fifteenth centuries enhanced their apprehension of death. Wealthy people began founding chantry chapels in village churches and cathedrals, where they would one day be entombed and where priests, paid from their bequests,

---

[7] Two of the sixteenth century's preeminent spirits, Desiderius Erasmus and Martin Luther, were both products of the Brethren's schools.

would offer repeated Masses and prayers for their salvation. Less affluent Christians left bequests for candles to be lit in their memory and Masses to be offered for their souls. Books vividly illustrated with woodcuts circulated with titles like *Ars Moriendi* ("the art of dying").

In plague- and violence-ridden late medieval Europe, as in other times and places, God was the cherished protector of humankind in the face of a terrifying, unpredictable world that lacked effective police forces, weather services, and modern medicine. The saints shared with God the power of shielding Christians from harm and

The Art of Dying Perhaps the ultimate "how-to" books of all time, popular *Ars Moriendi* ("the art of dying") manuals counseled anxious men and women on how to prepare themselves for death, to fend off deathbed diabolical temptation, and to escape the fires of hell. This page is printed from a carved woodblock from about 1466. *The Granger Collection, New York.*

bringing well-being to them. Each trade honored its own saint, often in devotions organized by the guilds. Potters prayed to St. Gore, painters to St. Luke, horse doctors to St. Loy, dentists to St. Apolline. And for nearly every known disease, there was an appropriate saint. In southern France a cult developed around a blessed dog to whose shrine peasants brought their sick and deformed children in the hope of miraculous healing.

Such medieval beliefs may amuse or shock modern readers, who forget the startling cures announced every week in supermarket tabloids. For medieval people, the healing powers associated with saints satisfied a widespread longing for supernatural protection against dangers that seemed beyond comprehension. The doubts of the theologians were drowned out by the clamor of popular demand.

Black Arts: The Occult and Witchcraft Theologians, however, knew what they faced when it came to "traffic with the devil." Given our modern sense of **progress,** it may seem paradoxical that obsessions about magic and witchcraft climaxed not in the backward Early Middle Ages but rather in the period from 1300 to 1700. The best explanation is that late medieval and early modern theologians were, from their perspective, gaining a better understanding of how people could be manipulated by Satan—in whom Christians believed as firmly as they did in God and the saints.

Awe of the supernatural pervaded premodern life. Prevailing knowledge of the natural world fully accommodated beliefs (shared by ordinary people and elites) in ghosts, demons, and other mysterious phenomena. Folklore told of uncanny happenings; "cunning women," village seers, and often parish priests knew spells and herbal cures useful in dealing with the unseen world. (A fourteenth-century Czech reformer scolded those who "collect bones beneath the gallows or cut bits off the flesh of those who have been hanged; those who baptize frogs, mandagoras, or bones, or who consecrate mistletoe.") For the educated, biblical and classical learning explained nature in terms of a "great chain of being": God—angels—human beings—animals—plants, all hierarchically interlocked. Many educated people thought it possible to understand or even control extra-human natural forces. Hence the era's credence in astrology, which held that cosmic "intelligences" embodied in the planets and stars governed human destinies. Those who found astrology too deterministic tended to approach natural spirits through magic—*white* or *black*. White magic was benign; black magic meant invoking the devil.

Many saw no difference. In 1398 the theologians of the University of Paris condemned fellow faculty members who had been caught casting spells in hopes of finding hidden treasures; among the many errors that theologians denounced was the belief "that it is licit to use for a good end magic arts or other superstitions forbidden by God and the church." Undeterred, some of the great minds of the

Astrology and the Social Order The beautiful illuminations in the *Book of Hours* (a prayer book) of the duke of Berry, a member of the French royal family, are often used to illustrate daily life in the fifteenth century. Shown here are the routines of June. But although the work being done here reflects the gendered division of labor in the medieval village, these elegant figures are not real peasants—rather, they show what gentlemen like the duke of Berry wished rural life could be. Notice the zodiac signs at the top: Astrology seems to permeate the whole scene like a guarantee of peace, order, and harmony. The painting was executed in 1416 (a year after the battle of Agincourt) by the Limbourg brothers, miniature painters active in Paris at the beginning of the fifteenth century. The background shows the walls of Paris, the Louvre (royal palace), and La Ste.-Chapelle. *Giraudon.*

fifteenth-century Italian Renaissance continued to pursue such occult insights into nature's mysteries, sometimes with the help of the great medieval compendium of Jewish magical and mystical lore, the Cabala. Indeed, cabalistic studies were the chief intellectual meeting ground of fifteenth-century Christian and Jewish scholars—one more reason for Christian theologians to fear both occultism and Jews.

Such fascination (sometimes inquisitive, sometimes horrified) with the supernatural's place in everyday life helps explain one of the most notorious late medieval documents, the *Hammer of Witches*, published by two German Dominican inquisitors in 1486. Its compilers had diligently researched all that could be learned about the practices of people—mostly women, but also men—who allegedly had entered into diabolical pacts. There is little doubt that such practices went on in village and urban life; court records in fifteenth-century Florence, for example, describe trials for witchcraft involving women charged with invoking the devil's aid in concocting love potions or casting spells. (Specific details were not recorded lest others learn the evil secrets.) All manner of folk beliefs, suspicious behavior, or unexplained happenings could be interpreted as evidence of witchcraft. Moreover, some herbs and mushrooms used in folk cures and spell-casting produce hallucinogenic effects, as does the fungus *Claviceps purpurea* that grows on rye and is the natural source of LSD. By assembling this mass of material and describing the legal procedures (including torture) that could be used in obtaining confessions, the *Hammer* gave learned guidance to the church and secular courts that for more than two centuries would execute tens of thousands of suspected witches throughout the Western world (see Chapter 17).

Cultural Transformations

There was, to be sure, a strong sense of the new and "modern" among many creative Europeans of the fourteenth and fifteenth centuries, but the dominant temper of the era was to refine and perpetuate medieval ways, styles, and habits of thought. Often one encounters a sense of loss over the fading of medieval ideals and institutions, a conviction that civilization was declining. The Renaissance **humanist** Aeneas Sylvius Piccolomini—later Pope Pius II (d. 1464)—could look at the Ottoman threat and the strife among Christian states and conclude that nothing good was in prospect.

In this age of plague and depression, the thirteenth-century high-Gothic architectural principles of symmetry and balance gave way to a new emotionalism that lent dramatic intensity to late medieval art. An example was the evolution of Western music between the thirteenth and fifteenth centuries. In the age of the great scholastic philosophers, composers in Paris had written liturgical and secular music using simple three-part harmonies and no dissonances. But the so-called *Ars Nova* ("new art") style of the fourteenth century ventured into more complex rhythms and harmonies, suggesting spiritual agitation. By the fifteenth century, the Burgundian court was commissioning the most advanced music in Europe, attracting such masters as the Frenchman Guillaume Dufay and the Fleming Josquin des Prez. They used four-part harmony (that is, with a bass line) that greatly enhanced their work's aural

THE HISTORICAL EVIDENCE

Why Most Witches Are Women

1486

The authors of the Malleus Malificarum *(The Hammer of Witches), from which the following extracts are taken, assembled a large body of sworn testimony, legal and biblical texts, and citations from ancient and medieval authorities about the theory and practice of witchcraft and the ways to detect it. Here they answer the question of "Why Superstition Is Chiefly Found in Women." What explanation can you offer for their attitude toward women in general?*

As for the first question, why a greater number of witches is found in the fragile feminine sex than among men; it is indeed a fact that it were idle to contradict, since it is accredited by actual experience, apart from the verbal testimony of credible witnesses. . . .

For some learned men propound this reason; that there are three things in nature, the Tongue, an Ecclesiastic, and a Woman, which know no moderation in goodness or vice; and when they exceed the bounds of their condition they reach the greatest height and the lowest depths of goodness and vice. . . .

There follow many instances of goodness in the tongue, in ecclesiastics, and in women "when they are governed by a good spirit." Then the explanation continues:

Others again have propounded other reasons why there are more superstitious women found than men. And the first is, that they are more credulous; and since the chief aim of the devil is to corrupt faith, therefore he rather attacks them. . . .

The third reason is that they have slippery tongues, and are unable to conceal from their fellow-women those things which by evil arts they know; and, since they are weak, they find an easy and secret manner of vindicating themselves by witchcraft. . . .

For as regards intellect, or the understanding of spiritual things, they seem to be of a different nature from men; a fact which is vouched for by the logic of the authorities, backed by various examples from Scriptures. . . .

But the natural reason is that she is more carnal than a man, as is clear from her many carnal abominations. . . .

And as to her other mental quality, that is, her natural will; when she hates someone whom she formerly loved, then she seethes with anger and impatience in her whole soul, just as the tides of the sea are always heaving and boiling . . .

The authors go on to accuse women of weak faith, poor memory, seductive voice, vanity, and sundry other defects.

To conclude. All witchcraft comes from carnal lust, which is in women insatiable. . . . Wherefore for the sake of fulfilling their lusts they consort even with devils. . . . And blessed be the Highest Who has so far preserved the male sex from so great a crime: for since He was willing to be born and to suffer for us, therefore He has granted to men this privilege.

Source: From Alan C. Kors and Edward Peters, eds., *Witchcraft in Europe, 1100–1700: A Documentary History* (Philadelphia: University of Pennsylvania Press, 1972), pp. 114–115, 120–121, 127.

depth, and they willingly sacrificed the intelligibility of vocal lines to achieve verve, color, and contrasts of sound. From Burgundy, this intricate style spread to the courts of Italy—a reversal of the usual pattern of Renaissance Italy initiating a cultural trend and the rest of Europe following.

The drift away from the confidence and order of high medieval culture expressed itself in countless other ways—in the intensifying social conflict, in the architectural shift from high-Gothic symmetry to flamboyant late-Gothic decoration, in the evolution from Christian commonwealth to territorial states, and in the disintegration of Aquinas's fusion of faith and reason. The medieval search

for a rational cosmic order had reached its climax in Aquinas's hierarchical ordering and reconciliation of logic and revelation. The abandonment of the search is nowhere more evident than in the attacks of fourteenth-century philosophers on the Thomist system.

Questioning Reason St. Thomas's *Summa Theologica*, like the high-Gothic cathedral, reconciles religious aspiration and logical order with an omnipotent God who is both loving and rational. The fourteenth-century attack on this reconciliation was founded on two related propositions: (1) To ascribe rationality to God is to limit his omnipotence by the finite rules of human logic. (2) Although human reason can explore the universe that God chose to create for humankind (out of myriad possibilities), it can tell us nothing of God himself; logic and theology inhabit two separate, sealed-off worlds.

The first steps toward this concept of an incomprehensible God were taken by the Scottish Franciscan Duns Scotus (1270–1308), who produced a detailed but subtle critique of St. Thomas's theory of knowledge. He seriously doubted the validity of many of Thomas's arguments and proofs. Duns Scotus did not reject the possibility of explaining revealed truth through reason, but he was more cautious than Aquinas in his use of logic.

The Oxford Franciscan William of Ockham (ca. 1285–ca. 1349) attacked the Thomist synthesis more drastically. Ockham argued that God is utterly undemonstrable and must be accepted on faith alone. As a being of infinite power God can do anything that is not logically contradictory. He could have created an infinite variety of possible universes, each operating on different physical laws and ethical norms. But since he chose, for incomprehensible reasons, to create our particular universe, he made a pact with humanity that guaranteed the consistent and continued functioning of our physical laws and the moral order taught by the church and upheld by its sacraments. One can therefore depend on the rational functioning of the natural order and on the Christian teachings regarding the achievement of eternal salvation through moral rectitude and the sacraments. Nevertheless, human reason must be limited to these areas. The true nature of God is unfathomable. Ockham ruled out all speculations of **metaphysics** about ultimate reality. His principle that analytical categories are not to be multiplied beyond the necessary minimum, called "Ockham's razor," is still honored by philosophers and scientists as a basic premise of reasoning.

The Roots of Modern Science By severing the bonds between revelation and reason, William of Ockham blazed two paths into the future: mysticism unencumbered by logic, and science unencumbered by faith. Science, freed of its metaphysical underpinnings, could now proceed on its own (with the occult and the supernatural perhaps filling in the gaps). Thus Nicholas Oresme, a teacher at the University of Paris in the fourteenth century, attacked Aristotle's theory of motion and suggested that a rotating earth could explain the apparent daily movement of the sun and stars. Oresme's theories probably owed much more to thirteenth-century scholars such as Robert Grosseteste than to Ockham, but his willingness to challenge traditional explanations of the physical structure of God's universe is characteristic of an age in which speculation about the natural world was being severed from theology and metaphysics.

Many late medieval philosophers rejected Ockham's criticism, and some remained Thomists. But owing to the very comprehensiveness of Aquinas's achievement, his successors were reduced to detailed elaboration or minor repair work. Faced with a choice between the tedious niggling of late Thomism and Ockham's drastic limitations imposed on the scope of philosophical inquiry, many of Europe's finest minds shunned philosophy altogether for the more exciting fields of science, mathematics, classical learning—and magic. When the philosopher Jean Gerson (d. 1429), chancellor of the University of Paris and a leader at the Council of Constance, lectured against "vain curiosity in the matter of faith," the disintegration of the faith-reason synthesis was clearly evident.

The fifteenth century witnessed a revival of Platonism and Neoplatonism. The leading philosophers of the Italian Renaissance (see Chapter 12) were Platonists and drew from an extensive body of Plato's writings that had been unknown to high-medieval western Europe. Yet these Italians were amateur dabblers alongside their northern contemporary, Nicholas of Cusa (d. 1464), one of the great minds of Western philosophy.

Educated by the mystical Brethren of the Common Life, Nicholas began his career as a conciliarist but switched to the papal camp. He agreed, up to a point, with Ockham's view that human reason is limited to the disconnected phenomena of the physical universe. But he insisted that the contradictions and diversity of the material world were reconciled in an unknowable God. Nicholas of Cusa regarded God as approachable only through a mystical process that he termed "learned ignorance." Like Aquinas, he believed in an underlying universal order, but like Ockham he denied that any such order could be explained by human reason. Yet his concept of an unknowable God derived from a tradition far older than Ockhamism. It was rooted in the late-Roman Neoplatonism of the pagan Plotinus and his Christian followers (see Chapter 5), a tradition that had run as an undercurrent through the entire Middle Ages. Like the ancient Neoplatonists, Nicholas saw the universe as a ceaseless creative unfolding of the infinite God. But going far beyond them, he reasoned that a universe emanating from an infinite deity cannot be limited by human concepts of space and time. In short, God's created universe was potentially infinite, reconciling all that seemed contradictory to human reason. Even magic—in which Nicholas, like the Italian Renaissance Platonists, took a strong interest—was by no means implausible.

In his emphasis on mysticism and the limitation of human reason, Nicholas of Cusa was in tune with his age. In his vision of an ordered cosmos he echoed the thirteenth century. But in his bold conception of an infinite universe, vast enough to harmonize all that appears bafflingly contradictory to human reason, he anticipated some insights of modern philosophy and cosmology.

Late-Gothic Art and Architecture The change from high-medieval order to late medieval diversity is clearly evident in the field of art. The high-Gothic balance between upward aspiration and harmonic proportion—between the vertical and horizontal—was shifting in the cathedrals of the later thirteenth century toward an ever-greater emphasis on verticality. Formerly, elaborate capitals and horizontal decorative lines had balanced the soaring piers and pointed arches of the Gothic cathedrals, creating a tense equilibrium between heaven and earth. But during the Late Middle Ages, capitals disappeared and horizontal lines became discontinuous, leaving little to relieve the dramatic upward thrust from floor to vaulting. Late medieval churches achieved a fluid, uncompromising verticality, a sense of heavenly aspiration that bordered on the mystical.

By the mid-thirteenth century, the basic structural potentialities of Gothic style had been fully exploited. Windows were as large as they could possibly be, vaultings could be raised no higher without risking disaster, and flying buttresses reached maximum efficiency. The fundamental Gothic idea of a skeletal stone framework with walls of colored glass had been embodied in churches of incomparable nobility and beauty. During the Late Middle Ages, buildings changed in appearance as tastes changed, but the originality of post-thirteenth-century Gothic architects was inhibited by their devotion to a style that had already achieved complete structural development. Accordingly, the innovations of late-Gothic architecture consisted chiefly of new and more elaborate decoration, with the result that a number of late medieval churches are, to some modern tastes, overdecorated sculptural jungles. To other tastes, their decorative exuberance is a delight. Like Ockham's universe, the fourteenth- and fifteenth-century church became a fascinating miscellany of separate elements. Thus the "flamboyant Gothic" style emerged in late medieval France, while English churches were evolving from the "decorated Gothic" of the fourteenth century to the "perpendicular Gothic" of the fifteenth and sixteenth, with lace-like fan vaulting, sculptural profusion, and sweeping vertical lines. In the sixteenth century, Gothic architecture, having reached its limits, gave way throughout northern Europe to the classical Greco-Roman style of Renaissance Italy.

The serene, idealized humanity of thirteenth-century sculpture and painting gave way to heightened emotionalism and an emphasis on individual characteristics and peculiarities. Nothern painting reached a pinnacle in the mirrorlike realism of the Flemish school. Painters such as Jan van Eyck (d. 1440), pioneering in the use of oil paints, excelled in reproducing the natural world with a virtually photographic devotion to detail. Critics of the style claim that detail seems to compromise the unity of the total composition; but in a world viewed through Ockham's eyes, such naturalism is a virtue. In contrast, early Renaissance Italy developed a new artistic style in which naturalism was subordinated to a unifying idea (see Chapter 12).

Perpendicular Gothic Chapel   The chapel of King's College, Cambridge University, is a particularly striking example of the perpendicular Gothic style. Notice the elaborate fan vaulting. Construction of the chapel began in 1446.   *Art Resource, NY.*

Realism in Literature   Vernacular writing flourished in the Late Middle Ages, and not simply in the form of treatises on mysticism. Christine de Pisan (d. ca. 1430), Europe's first consciously feminist author, made adept use of French in writing on an astonishing diversity of topics and in many literary forms: lyric poems expressing her abiding love for her dead husband, who left her a widow at age twenty-five; an autobiography; a book of moral advice for women and a companion volume for men; a verse history running from the Creation to her own time; a study of great women of history; and her deservedly celebrated treatise *The Letter to the God of Love*, in which she very effectively rebuts the antifeminist diatribes in Jean de Meun's conclusion of the *Romance of the Rose* (see Chapter 10). *The Letter to the God of Love* was of groundbreaking importance—the first clear instance in European history of a woman writing, as a woman, against the slanders that women had so long endured. The treatise gave rise to a heated debate between Jean de Meun's sympathizers and Christine de Pisan's admirers—of whom there were many. None, however, could match Christine's eloquence as she responded to age-old allegations of the wickedness of women.

A number of late medieval writers turned to graphic realism. England's Geoffrey Chaucer (ca. 1335–1400), in his *Canterbury Tales*, combines rare psychological insight with a descriptive skill worthy of the Flemish painters and

Jan van Eyck's *The Marriage of Giovanni Arnolfini* This famous painting is signed "Jan van Eyck Was Here, 1434," as if witnessing his participation in the betrothal (or marriage) of the Luccese merchant Giovanni Arnolfini, resident in Bruges, to a young Italian woman. Detailed symbolism abounds: the faithful dog; the single lighted candle, signifying Christ's presence; the clogs Arnolfini has taken off because he stands on sacred ground; St. Margaret, the patroness of childbirth, carved on the chair by the bed. The mirror reveals an open doorway in which a man stands, presumably van Eyck himself. The pregnant condition of the bride is probably intended to be understood as expressing a hope for offspring. *Eyck, Jan van/Active 1422; died 1441. The Portrait of Giovanni (/) Arnolfini and his Wife Giovanna Cenami (?) (The Arnolfini Marriage). Oil on Wood. 81.8 × 59.7 cm. © The National Gallery, London.*

late-Gothic stone carvers. *The Canterbury Tales*, one of the foremost literary works of the Middle Ages, presents a series of stories told by a group of men and women on a pilgrimage to the shrine of St. Thomas Becket at Canterbury cathedral. We have already encountered one of Chaucer's Canterbury pilgrims, the oft-married Wife of Bath (see Chapter 8) who put an end to her husband's reading from the book of wicked wives. Chaucer describes another of the pilgrims, a corrupt friar, in these words:

Highly beloved and intimate was he
With country folk within his boundary,
And city dames of honour and possessions;
For he was qualified to hear confessions,
Or so he said, with more than priestly scope;
He had a special license from the Pope.
Sweetly he heard his penitents at shrift
With pleasant absolution, for a gift.[8]

François Villon (d. 1463), a brawling Parisian vagabond who barely escaped the gallows, expressed in his poems an anguished, sometimes brutal realism that vividly reflected the late medieval mood of insecurity:

The nostrils curl, the fingers clutch,
The hands are cold and moist as clay,
The flesh is clammy to the touch,
Death shakes the form, the face grows gray.[9]

To Villon, writing in a society of sharp status distinctions, death was the great democrat, the final leveler of all pretense.

TOWARD THE RENAISSANCE

Drawing sharp lines between historical periods is one of the most frustrating tasks a historian can attempt. No more contentious case exists than that of where the Middle Ages "ends" and the Renaissance "begins." Few if any historians today draw a sharp line.

However, most historians agree that important changes occurred during the fourteenth and fifteenth centuries, pointing to a new cultural, political, and economic environment in Europe. Some of these changes first appeared in Italy: a new literary style and pedagogical program called *humanism*; new approaches to painting and sculpture; new ways of thinking about the state and a new appreciation for the republican traditions of ancient Greece and Rome. And as later chapters will discuss, other epoch-making changes were under way in fifteenth-century Iberia, as mariners pushed out into the Atlantic and down the coast of Africa, equipped with the ships and navigational devices that would bring them to India and the Western Hemisphere by the year 1500.

In closing this chapter, we shall briefly consider three other trends that also point toward new conditions of life. These are a "bottoming-out" of the late medieval depression, the restoration of strong monarchical institutions, and—perhaps with the greatest long-range significance—the invention of clocks and printing, and a growing fascination with mechanical devices.

---

[8] Chaucer's *The Canterbury Tales*, trans. by Nevil Coghill (Harmondsworth, England: Penguin, 1952), p. 23.
[9] *The Testaments of François Villon*, trans. by John Heron Lepper (New York: Liveright, 1924), p.28.

Economic Revival and Technological Innovation

By the mid-fifteenth century, signs were multiplying that western Europe's long depression was giving way to a general economic upturn. Europe's population in 1500 was lower than in 1300, but it was rising. Commerce had been reviving since about 1460, and towns were growing again.

Whether Europeans invented them or adapted them from outsiders, a number of inventions had been crucial for the rise of medieval civilization. In the Early Middle Ages, these had included the wheeled plow for breaking heavy northern soil; the horse-collar, making it possible to harness horses to plows and wagons; stirrups, which gave a rider much more control over the horse and facilitated mounted warfare; water mills and windmills, for grinding grain into flour. Toward the close of the Middle Ages, in the fourteenth centuries, came other breakthroughs: the spinning wheel, which speeded up the women's work of making yarn; and gunpowder and firearms, which revolutionized late medieval warfare, making it both more expensive and more destructive.

But some of the most important late medieval technological innovations involved not the *invention* but the wider *use* of machinery. Thus water-driven fulling mills made wool production more efficient, water-driven pumps drained mines, and water-driven bellows proliferated in the small rural blast furnaces.

The new blast furnaces were one of the era's most important innovations. Using water-driven bellows and a new firebox, they generated far higher temperatures than the Roman-style iron smelters hitherto used by European smiths.[10] By increasing the amount of carbon that could be absorbed in the refining process, the blast furnace improved both the quality and quantity of iron that was produced. The result was cast iron, which could be used (for example) in making cannon. However, cast iron was not suitable for cutting tools because it was brittle and did not hold an edge; it had to be reworked into steel on the hearth.

Mining, like smithing, was rural-based. Iron ore was extracted from shallow pits or lake bottoms, and coal (as we saw earlier) was also dug from pits or strip-mined. Extracting gold, silver, tin, alum,[11] and rock salt, on the other hand, often required deep shafts; hence the importance of water-driven pumps and lifting equipment. Like smiths, miners regarded their lore as semi-magical. They formed secretive, highly skilled, close-knit communities, regulated by special privileges and "miners' laws." As the

economy recovered during the fifteenth century, some of them prospered: One such miner, who could afford to give his son an expensive university education in preparation for becoming a lawyer, was the father of Martin Luther.

The expanding mining industry enriched fifteenth-century kings, who claimed sovereign rights over riches beneath "their" soil. But usually they pledged these revenues to capitalists who lent them money. These capitalists, in turn, became the source for the significant investments needed to develop the mines, and they were the middlemen who supplied ore to the smiths and then sold refined metal. The Fuggers in central Europe and the Medici in Florence were the greatest examples of capitalists developing—and profiting mightily from—Europe's expanding mining and metallurgical industries in the fifteenth and sixteenth centuries.

The New Monarchies

By 1450, monarchies in western Europe were asserting their authority with greater consistency over the nobility and taking advantage of the economic and demographic revival. Historians sometimes use the term *new monarchies* in describing the regimes that emerged in England, France, and Iberia. But these regimes were "new" mainly by contrast to the crisis-ridden and depression-plagued kingdoms of fourteenth- and early fifteenth-century Europe. Western kings after 1450 were simply resuming trends that rulers like England's Henry II and Edward I or France's St. Louis IX and Philip the Fair had begun.

There were also new factors in late fifteenth-century public affairs. One was the ever-rising cost of warfare in an age of gunpowder and mercenaries. Another was a general public weariness with civil wars and rebellions precipitated by "overmighty" aristocrats and "insubordinate" lower classes. Still another was the growing presence in western Europe of educated laymen who served their rulers as professional bureaucrats. Finally, many people were coming to agree that "the state" was worthy of allegiance if it legitimately promoted law and order—that one could be a good Christian by obeying the church in matters of faith, but that God also sanctioned the secular authority of kings. The "new monarchies" responded to all these opportunities and challenges.

The Hundred Years' War had been over for scarcely two years when England plunged into an off-and-on civil war, the Wars of the Roses (1455–1485). The struggle pitted partisans of the reigning house of Lancaster (whose emblem was a red rose) against those who backed the rival duke of York (a white rose). The pathetic Lancastrian king Henry VI (reigned 1422–1461), by inheriting his grandfather Charles the Mad's incapacity rather than his father Henry V's prowess, proved to be one of the most incompetent of all English monarchs, and in the end he was killed by the Yorkists. Nobles and commoners alike grew tired of

---

[10] These were, in turn, an improvement on the ancient iron smelters developed in the first millennium B.C. and discussed in Chapter 1.

[11] Alum is the generic designation for two sulfates of aluminum. In the Middle Ages its use was crucial in processing raw wool and tanning leather.

endless bloodshed and longed for firm royal governance. They got it, to a degree, in the reign of the Yorkist Edward IV (reigned 1461–1483). Despite coming to the throne illegally[12] and being a drunkard, Edward was a competent ruler under whom significant administrative reforms were effected and the English monarchy's revenues substantially increased. (Kings who could "live of their own" were popular because this lessened their need to impose taxes.) But when Edward's able, unpopular brother succeeded him as Richard III (reigned 1483–1485), hostilities resumed. Enemies charged Richard with murdering two young Lancastrian princes in the Tower of London, but the mystery has never been solved. Richard's troubled reign ended on Bosworth Field in 1485, the battle in which he was killed and the Yorkist cause destroyed by a new claimant to the throne, Henry VII (reigned 1485–1509) of the house of Tudor.

Traditionally, the year 1485 separates medieval from early modern English history. This dividing line is particularly misleading because it gives the victorious Tudors all the credit for ending England's late medieval "anarchy"—credit that most historians now accord as much to Edward IV as to Henry VII. Both sought peace, a full treasury, and effective government, and by the late fifteenth century these goals were within reach. The economy was reviving, many of the more warlike nobles had perished in the Wars of the Roses, and the English were willing to exchange turmoil for obedience and peace. All that was needed now was strong royal leadership, and that was supplied in full measure by the willful, determined Tudors. Henry VII had the additional merit of being a skinflint who abstained from spending the considerable treasure amassed by his administrators. The pleasant role of royal spendthrift would fall to his flamboyant son, Henry VIII (see Chapter 13).

In France, centralization was carried much farther by Louis XI (reigned 1461–1483), known as "the Spider King" because of the political webs that he wove so dexterously for his enemies. Son and heir of Charles VII (whom he despised), Louis XI removed his rivals by clandestine murders, public beheadings, and sundry dirty tricks. However, he also took intelligent steps to stimulate the French economy—establishing new fairs to attract foreign merchants and their money, encouraging industries, and reducing internal tariffs. Siphoning off much of the resulting wealth with higher taxes, and living as cheaply as possible, Louis XI more than doubled royal revenues. To his delight, the Burgundian threat dissolved in 1477 when the last duke of Burgundy, the aptly nicknamed Charles the Rash, died fighting Louis's Swiss allies. The Spider King promptly confiscated half the duchy (the rest went to the Habsburgs). Scheming his way through a labyrinth of shifting alliances

and loyalties, he moved adroitly toward French unification and early modern **absolutism.**

By 1500 the French monarchy was ruling through a central administration of professional bureaucrats drawn from both the nobility and the bourgeoisie. The towns were flourishing once again; the English were gone for good; and French soldiers were carrying Valois claims into foreign lands.

The most clear-cut example of a "new monarchy" was the unification of Spain in the late fifteenth century. But the road to unity was neither easy nor straight.

When the high-medieval *Reconquista* (reconquest) of the Muslim states had ground to a halt around 1270, the Iberian Peninsula contained three strong Christian kingdoms—Castile, Aragon, and Portugal—along with little Navarre in the Pyrenees. Castile was the largest and Aragon the most urbanized. During the thirteenth and fourteenth centuries Aragonese kings conquered the Mediterranean islands of Majorca, Minorca, Sardinia, and Sicily, and Aragonese merchants began moving into international commerce. The emirate of Granada remained a Muslim stronghold.

Aragon and Castile were both plagued by civil turbulence. The Aragonese monarchy strove with only limited success to placate nobles and townspeople by granting significant concessions to the *cortes,* its regional representative assemblies. There was a prolonged urban revolt in the Aragonese province of Catalonia (eventually put down,

MAP 11-7
THE UNIFICATION OF SPAIN, 1469–1492

---

[12] So had the first Lancastrian king, Henry IV, in 1399, after Richard II's overthrow and murder.

with great difficulty, in 1472), while Castile was torn by constant aristocratic uprisings and disputed royal successions. Peace and strong government came within reach at last when Ferdinand of Aragon married Isabella of Castile in 1469. Isabella inherited her throne in 1474; Ferdinand inherited his in 1479.

The union of Castile and Aragon was *dynastic*—the marriage of two sovereigns. Cortes, tribunals, laws, and customs remained quite different in both lands, and localist sentiment and deep suspicions endured. Had Isabella opted for her other suitor, King John of Atlantic-oriented Portugal, Hispanic (and Latin American) history might have been very different. The kind of "Spain" that ultimately evolved thus depended crucially on the matrimonial politics of two fifteenth-century rulers, a reminder that chance and personal decisions often have enormous historical consequences (see Map 11-7).

In 1492 the united Spanish kingdom completed the Reconquista by overrunning Granada. The monarchy gave its Muslim and Jewish subjects a blunt choice: conversion or banishment. Many became nominal Christians, but ex-Jewish *conversos* and ex-Muslim *moriscos* were suspected by "pure-blooded" Spaniards of being insincere. The many Jews and Muslims who did not convert left, taking their wealth and talent to the Netherlands and the Ottoman Empire.

One of the fundamental institutions of the new Iberian monarchy was the Spanish Inquisition. Unlike the Roman Inquisition founded in the thirteenth century to combat Albigensianism (see Chapter 8), the Spanish Inquisition was an arm of the state—the only government institution that spanned both Castile and Aragon. Its main function at first was to root out backsliding ex-Jews and ex-Muslims, but in the sixteenth century it would also go after those suspected of "Lutheranism" (see Chapter 13). As an instrument of both political and doctrinal conformity, specializing in thought control, it brought the crown not only religious unity but also lucrative revenues.

The Castilian nobility concluded that its best interests lay in supporting the monarchy, and regional separatism diminished but did not disappear. With a measure of unity established and with immense wealth from the New World soon to be pouring in, Spain in 1500 stood on the theshold of rich cultural expression and international power.

Clocks, Paper, and Printed Books

Some of the technological innovations of the Late Middle Ages were profoundly significant not because they immediately began to increase European wealth, nor because they increased the destructiveness of warfare, nor even because they made possible global exploration and the conquest of distant continents—but because they had an immense, long-range impact on the Western mind.

The first of these inventions was the mechanical clock. Since ancient times, Europeans had measured time differently according to the season. The position of the sun determined what hour it was, with the summer day having longer hours than the winter day. Finer gradations of time were possible only by using such devices as a sandglass or a "water clock," which dripped water, but both needed vigilant human tenders. The twelfth-century Chinese were the first to hit upon building a machine whose gears moved at a steady pace, but such clocks did not survive the Mongol conquest, and the Chinese forgot the art of making them. Europeans seem to have invented mechanical clocks

Dondi's Clock, ca. 1350 Dondi's astronomical clock was not a device for telling daily time—other clocks were already being made for that purpose—but the machine's intricate movements predicted the yearly cycles of planets and fixed stars in the night sky. It also featured a perpetual calendar. By the sixteenth century it fell to pieces because no one knew how to maintain it, but Dondi left such precise drawings that this twentieth-century replica could be built. It is on display at the Smithsonian Institution in Washington. *© 1998 Smithsonian Institution.*

The Gutenberg Bible Gutenberg's Bible imitates the style of an elegant hand-copied parchment manuscript and even at the time of publication was a luxury purchase. Today, the few surviving Gutenberg Bibles are virtually priceless. *The British Library; Parabol (Bible). Neg No: H029777. Shelfmark/Man: C. 9. 0. 4 Page No/Folio: T/P. Parabola.*

expensive product, impractical for jotting things down—or on hard-to-store wax tablets. The first true paper was made in China and Japan, using the fibers of rice plants, which Europeans did not cultivate. Not until the fourteenth and fifteenth centuries did Europeans independently find a way of making paper—far more durable than the modern product—by pulping rags. Paper's invention in the Late Middle Ages was essential for the extension of literate culture to include the writing of letters and casual memoranda, as well as the printing of books and broadsides.

Printing was also invented in medieval East Asia. Westerners discovered it in the late fourteenth century, about the same time that papermaking began, but at first they applied the technique by laboriously carving a whole woodblock with the desired image and all words in reverse. The great breakthrough was the introduction of movable type in the mid-fifteenth century, a far more efficient way to print written material than woodblocks. Setting up as a printer required a large investment, and the first printers were often goldsmiths—men with capital, experienced in the precision casting of metals. Johann Gutenberg, an artisan in the German city of Mainz, claimed to have been the first to print from movable type, in the 1450s.

Although printing's effect on European culture was immense, the full impact was not felt until after 1500. During the fifteenth century, many Italian Renaissance humanists and wealthy collectors scorned printed books as cheap imitations of hand-copied manuscripts. Gutenberg's Bible, apparently the first important book to come off a European press, was printed on expensive parchment. But most early books, which used paper, were humbler fare—popular stories, religious tracts, almanacs, horoscopes, accounts of murders and miracles, and university textbooks. Printing from the beginning was a business, and like today's mass media, ephemeral reading matter far outnumbered "high culture" material.

All the breakthroughs we have been describing contributed enormously to the future course of Western civilization. Consider a few examples. Paper and printed books made literacy (and also numeracy) essential for all who wanted to get ahead. People did less reading aloud (as medieval scholars had done, a habit born of the need to communicate to nonreading listeners); silent, private, and thus more efficient reading now became common. Likewise, the making of the first reliable clocks facilitated the measurement of things by precise timing, without which modern science would have been impossible. Clocks were based on gears, and tinkering with geared machines that mechanically transmitted power suggested many a pregnant intellectual metaphor. As we shall see in later chapters, a mechanistic model of how the world works would gradually (in the sixteenth to eighteenth centuries) sweep away the **Old Paradigm**—an organic universe of innate qualities and chance events—and leave ever-shrinking space for the inexplicable and the uncanny.

independently, about 1320. One of the earliest such devices was an intricate machine for measuring the cycles of celestial bodies—sun, moon, planets, and stars—for which precise timings were essential, built around 1350 by an Italian craftsman named Giovanni de Dondi. As early as 1370, France's Charles V had several clocks installed in Paris and ordered the city's bells synchronized with the royal palace's clock so that citizens could regulate their daily lives. Within a few generations, every important town in Europe boasted public clocks, and by the late fifteenth century smaller timepieces were being made for the wealthy. Westerners were becoming time-conscious in ways human beings had never been before.

Paper may seem a humble product, but historically it cannot be taken for granted. The closest the ancient West got to a paperlike product was papyrus, made from reeds native to the Nile Valley. Medieval Europeans wrote on parchment—that is, calfskin, a durable but bulky and

Still, there were limits to the West's early love affair with machinery; indeed, those limitations serve as the defining characteristic of the medieval and early modern ages, as opposed to modern times. Medieval and early modern Europeans made no significant applications of machine-driven power to their most important industry, the weaving of textiles. Without the **Energy Revolution** born of steam power, there was no technological basis or economic incentive for trying to set up a factory system. Textile making remained a hand-labor industry, often carried on part-time in country cottages and largely controlled by merchant capitalists. Steam engines, factories, working classes in huge cities, industrial capitalism, and everything that flowed from these—including today's electronic marvels—all had to await the Industrial Revolution, which began in the late eighteenth century and is still unfolding.

CONCLUSION: FROM THE MIDDLE AGES TO THE RENAISSANCE

By 1500, commerce was thriving again all across Europe, and the population was growing. New inventions were changing the ways people lived. Although the papacy had dwindled from an international power to a local principality, the western European kingdoms had achieved stable governments, and small but rich states flourished in Italy. Advances in mining technology and metallurgy helped Europe increase its supply of silver and other metals essential to a recovering economy. Improvements in ship design and navigation opened the world's oceans to gold-seeking Europeans. In 1499, the first cargo of spices direct from India docked in Portugal. The late medieval economic crisis had passed. Europe had entered an era of economic growth and world expansion that would far outstrip its earlier surge in the High Middle Ages.

Why did Europe pull through? One obvious reason is that western Europe did not succumb to Mongol or Ottoman conquest. But let us also contrast the crises that afflicted western Europe in the fourth and fourteenth centuries. As we saw earlier the fourth-century crisis had led to the disintegration of Roman imperial government in western Europe. The fourteenth-century crisis, as we have seen in this chapter, left Europe's political and social institutions battered but intact. The difference can be explained by the tremendous changes that Europe had experienced between Roman and high-medieval times. Europe's urban life was far more vigorous in 1300 than in 300, and its agricultural productivity had also grown. During the High Middle Ages, Western civilization had become deeply rooted, and despite the late medieval crisis Europe remained a land of cities and agrarian villages, of governments, churches, guilds, hospitals, and universities. Whereas Roman Europe north of the Alps had lacked a vigorous urban and commercial life, the civilization that emerged in high-medieval Europe proved indestructible.

The early capitalism that emerged during the fourteenth and fifteenth centuries was an essential ingredient in future growth. Moneymaking had been going on for millennia. But early capitalism was different: It involved the systematic accumulation of power within the productive system by those who were amassing capital to invest. The evolution of banking and the business firm, the sophisticated manipulation of credit, and the growing control over production that the putting-out system entailed—all these concentrated economic power in the hands of merchant-bankers. Individual capitalists and their firms would rise and fall, but merchant-capitalism would endure. It brought efficiencies of scale and a strong measure of rationality to economic decision making. The price was paid by marginalized smaller traders, urban artisans, and rural cottage workers.

Three major aspects of the revitalization of Western civilization after 1350 remain to be discussed. First is the Renaissance, which got under way in Italy in the late fourteenth century. Second is the Reformation, in which many of the tensions of fourteenth- and fifteenth-century religion climaxed and new forms of worship emerged. And third is Europe's Age of Expansion, which began with the Iberian voyages of the fifteenth century. All three are in part late medieval phenomena, but they also helped usher in early modern times. To these, we now turn.

Selected Reading

Sources

Blakney, Raymond B., ed. *Meister Eckhart: A Modern Translation* (1941).

Froissart, Jean. *Chronicles.* Several editions.

Gray, Douglas, ed. *The Oxford Book of Late-Medieval Verse* (1985).

Thomas à Kempis. *The Imitation of Christ.* Many editions.

Morrison, Theodore, ed. *The Portable Chaucer* (1949).

Petroff, Elizabeth Alvilda, ed. *Medieval Women's Visionary Literature* (1986).

Christine de Pisan, *The Treasure of the City of Ladies, or The Book of the Three Virtues,* trans. and intro. Sarah Lawson (1985).

General

Hay, Denys. *Europe in the Fourteenth and Fifteenth Centuries,* 2nd ed. (1989). A good, succinct, general account.

Late Medieval Economic and Social History

Ashtor, Eliyahu. *Levant Trade in the Later Middle Ages* (1983). A richly detailed and comprehensive study of European (chiefly Italian) trade with the lands along the eastern Mediterranean, from the fall of Acre in 1291 to the end of the fifteenth century.

Dyer, Christopher. *Standards of Living in the Later Middle Ages: Social Change in England, c. 1200–1520* (1989). A perceptive, learned analysis concluding that the crisis of late medieval England brought very mixed consequences.

Langmuir, Gavin I. *History, Religion, and Antisemitism* (1990). A broadly ranging work of very great erudition.

McNeill, William H. *Plagues and Peoples* (1976). A brilliant book that treats epidemics as an important factor in global history.

Miskimin, Harry A. *The Economy of Early Renaissance Europe, 1300–1460* (1969). A brief, lucid, economically sophisticated account covering all of late medieval western Europe.

Nicholas, David. *The Domestic Life of a Medieval City: Women, Children, and the Family in Fourteenth-Century Ghent* (1985). A valuable, skillfully researched contribution to European family history, this work stresses the importance of the nuclear family and the simultaneous significance of larger bilateral kin groups.

Ward, Jennifer. *English Noblewomen in the Later Middle Ages* (1992). An admirable study, meticulously researched and lucid in style.

Late Medieval States

Bowsky, William M. *A Medieval Italian Commune: Siena under the Nine, 1287–1355* (1981). A major work of scholarship, well written and richly detailed, analyzing the cultural flowering and political stability of Siena under enlightened oligarchic rule.

Crummey, Robert O. *The Formation of Muscovy, 1304–1613* (1987). The best general study of medieval Russia.

Curry, Anne. *The Hundred Years War* (1993). A brief, skillful account that focuses on military and diplomatic history.

Du Boulay, F. R. H. *Germany in the Later Middle Ages* (1983). A succinct, well-crafted synthesis of recent scholarship.

Guenee, Bernard. *States and Rulers in Later Medieval Europe*, trans. Juliet Vale (1985; translated from the second French edition, 1981). A study of major importance showing the parallel growth of centralized administrative institutions and a sense of national identity in the states of Western Christendom during the fourteenth and fifteenth centuries.

Hillgarth, J. N. *The Spanish Kingdoms, 1250–1516*, vol. 2, *Castilian Hegemony* (1978). A masterful account of Spain in the period 1350–1516 with particular emphasis on Castile and Aragon.

Kaeuper, Richard W. *War, Justice, and Public Order: England and France in the Later Middle Ages* (1988). This important work of synthesis and reinterpretation explores the effects of war on the economy, social order, and governance of the two realms.

Ormrod, W. M. *The Reign of Edward III: Crown and Political Society in England, 1327–1377* (1990). A rich yet succinct biography that explores Edward's success in dealing with all sections of the active political elite.

Prestwich, Michael. *English Politics in the Fifteenth Century* (1990). A brief, introductory text.

Sumption, Jonathan. *The Hundred Years War: Trial by Battle* (1992). Concentrating on the war's early years, the author emphasizes the making of Edward III's military reputation and that of his subjects.

Waley, Daniel. *The Italian City Republics*, 3rd ed. (1988). An excellent introduction to the economic, social, and political history of the medieval communes in northern and central Italy.

Waugh, Scott. *England in the Reign of Edward III* (1991). This brief, lively account includes less on the Hundred Years' War and more on domestic problems and the growing power of Commons than is usual in studies of this period.

Late Medieval Christianity and the Church

Harvey, Barbara. *Living and Dying in England, 1100–1540: The Monastic Experience* (1993). This prize-winning work of social history examines daily life in English monastic communities, focusing on the evidence from Westminster Abbey.

Kaminsky, Howard. *A History of the Hussite Revolution* (1967). Still the most comprehensive modern account.

Kieckhefer, Richard. *Unquiet Souls: Fourteenth-Century Saints and Their Religious Milieu* (1984). A learned, well-written examination of the lives and values of fourteenth-century visionaries and mystics, female and male, with three case studies.

Peters, Edward. *Inquisition* (1989). This thoughtful, comprehensive study examines both the history and the myth of the Inquisition down to the present day.

Thompson, John A. F. *Popes and Princes, 1417–1517: Politics and Polity in the Late Medieval Church* (1980). A good, concise summary and analysis of the waning authority of the papacy between the Council of Constance and the Reformation.

Late Medieval Thought and Culture

Eisenstein, Elizabeth. *The Printing Revolution in Early Modern Europe* (1993). The latest work by a leading authority on the subject, offering a stimulating assessment of the effects of printing and print culture in shaping Western society, technology, and values.

Huizinga, Johan. *The Autumn of the Middle Ages* (1996). Concentrating on France and the Netherlands, this new translation of a classic work of cultural history stresses the fears and insecurities of the late medieval mood and leaves one rather depressed.

Kane, George. *Chaucer* (1984). A brief, illuminating biography.

Keen, Maurice. *Chivalry* (1984). An important, original book in which the author argues persuasively, against the historiographical grain, that late medieval chivalry was secular in origin, socially useful, and not simply decadent.

Ozment, Steven. *The Age of Reform, 1250–1550: An Intellectual and Religious History of Late-Medieval and Reformation Europe* (1980). A detailed study of the conflicts and interactions of religious ideologies from Aquinas to Calvin.

Swaan, Wim. *The Late Middle Ages: Art and Architecture from 1350 to the Advent of the Renaissance* (1977). A stylish, beautifully illustrated book that argues powerfully against the notion of artistic decline in late medieval Europe.

CHAPTER *12*

THE EUROPEAN RENAISSANCE

Judith and Holofernes
Scala/Art Resource, NY.

1264–1597	Este family dominates Italian city of Ferrara	1447–1455	Pontificate of Nicholas V	1501	Petrucci prints music using movable type, establishes a music printing house
1304–1374	Life span of Petrarch	1449–1492	Life span of Lorenzo de' Medici		
1323	Membership in Venetian Great Council made hereditary	1450–1466	Reign of Francesco Sforza in Milan	1503	Pope Julius II commissions Donato Bramante to design a new St. Peter's basilica
1343	New guild-based republic forms in Florence	1452–1519	Life span of Leonardo da Vinci	1508	Pope Julius II asks Michelangelo to paint the Sistine Chapel
1353	Boccaccio writes *The Decameron*	1454	Major Italian states sign Peace of Lodi	1512	Machiavelli writes *The Prince*
1389–1464	Life span of Cosimo de' Medici	1480	Botticelli paints *The Birth of Venus*	1514	Francis I leads a new French invasion of Italy
1395	Giangaleazzo Visconti buys title "Duke of Milan and Prince of the Empire" from Holy Roman emperor	1493	Aldus Manutius establishes Aldine Press, becomes first major publisher of "pocket" books	1516	Sir Thomas More writes *Utopia*
				1525	Battle of Pavia consolidates Spanish hold on Italy
		1494	Charles VIII leads first French invasion of Italy	1527	Charles V's Imperial forces sack Rome
1440	Valla publishes *Declaration Concerning the False Donation of Constantine*	1497–1498	Peak of Savonarola's power in Florence	1528	Castiglione publishes *The Book of the Courtier*
1447–1450	Ambrosian Republic in Milan	1499	Second French invasion of Italy	1546	Pope Paul III appoints Michelangelo supervising architect to complete St. Peter's

eath was close at hand in the fourteenth and fifteenth centuries, and few could ignore it. But from the same period there rose a vision of rebirth—or *renaissance*. The **Renaissance** introduced new styles and methods in education and the arts and new political ideas that redirected Western civilization and continue to inform it to this day. The concept of a "liberal arts education" emerged during the Renaissance. The Capitol building in Washington, D.C., follows Renaissance architectural models. Renaissance political thinkers were the first to grapple with the appearance of the secular and independent nation-state and the question of what acts can be justified to preserve its liberty. Donatello's *Judith and Holofernes,* shown opposite, celebrated the use of deception and violence to defend freedom.[1] The Renaissance is often treated as a historical period, but it was actually more a movement than an era. As such, it overlapped and influenced the Late Middle Ages and the Protestant and Catholic Reformations of the sixteenth century alike.

The Renaissance marked neither a sharp break with the Middle Ages nor the beginning of modern **civilization.** A nineteenth-century Swiss historian, Jakob Burckhardt, coined the term *Renaissance,* meaning "rebirth," and he argued that the era was the moment when the modern world began. For Burckhardt, the individualism and secularism that define Western culture started among Italians late in the fourteenth century. When reading Burckhardt, one can almost hear the trumpets echoing around the stone walls of Italian city-states announcing something "new." But people of the day did not think of themselves as "progressive." They spoke and wrote in terms of "recovery" of a lost culture, not the creation of a new one. Burckhardt's excessive enthusiasm notwithstanding, the Renaissance was less a wholly new beginning than an exciting transition, a many-faceted era of innovation, experimentation, stunning cultural achievement, and an astonishing harbinger of the shape of western Europe's political future.

---

[1] According to the biblical story, Judith, a beautiful widow, saved the Hebrew people from the wrath of the tyrant Nebuchadrezzar. She did it by making her way into the camp of the tyrant's army, which was commanded by a general named Holofernes. She enticed him to drink heavily and beheaded him while he slept in a stupor. In 1494, after Medici rule was overthrown and the Florentine republic reestablished, Donatello's gruesome but powerfully naturalistic sculpture of Judith and her victim—which is nearly eight feet tall—was taken from the Medici collection and placed in front of the Palazzo della Signoria (city hall)—along with Donatello's bronze *David*—as a warning to tyrants. In 1504, the *Judith* statue was replaced by Michelangelo's *David*, a less gory but no less potent statement that Florentines loved their liberty and would fight against any odds to preserve it, even if they were reduced to using a slingshot against a giant.

The Renaissance on the Italian peninsula passed through three phases: first, a fourteenth-century preparatory period dominated by the life and work of the founder of Renaissance **humanism,** Petrarch (Francesco Petrarca, 1304–1374); second, from Petrarch's death in 1374 until about 1450, three generations of Florentine leadership that linked humanistic endeavor with republicanism; and third, the period from 1450 to 1550, marked by wondrous artistic creativity in the service of princely courts in Ferrara, Mantua, Urbino, Milan, Naples, and, most spectacularly, Rome. The first two phases were characterized by optimism about what individuals could achieve in the public and civic arena, an optimism that faded during the third phase. By the sixteenth century this culture had spread into northern Europe—a different social and political milieu in which the focus shifted toward religious and moral reform. France had been Europe's leader in art and thought in the High Middle Ages and would be again by the seventeenth century. But from the fourteenth into the sixteenth centuries, Italy took over that role. We can best probe the question of what the Renaissance was by asking why it began in Italy.

THE UNIQUENESS OF ITALY, 1300–1500

Italy by no means escaped the troubles of the Late Middle Ages, but the Italian experience was different from that of other Europeans. Greater urbanization constituted part of that difference. In 1500, 12.4 percent of Italians lived in towns of ten thousand or more people, in contrast to 4.2 percent in France, 3.2 percent in Germany, and 3.1 percent in England and Wales. In the twelfth and thirteenth centuries, northern and central Italy became steadily more urbanized and enriched by industries, banking, and a flourishing commerce. Between two hundred and three hundred independent self-governing towns, known as communes, existed in Italy in 1200, and most of them grew rapidly during the thirteenth century. Much of this growth was due to immigration from the countryside by owners of land or small businesses, not landless peasants. By 1300 the largest commune, Milan, boasted 150,000 inhabitants; Venice had 120,000; Florence, 95,000; and Genoa, 60,000. In western Europe, only Paris had more people than Milan. Even as late as 1500, only six cities in Europe (Paris, Milan, Venice, Naples, Moscow, and Istanbul) were home to 100,000 or more inhabitants.

Yet Italy's differentness cannot be explained solely by its urbanization; in the Low Countries in 1500, for instance, 18.9 percent of the people lived in towns of more than ten thousand people—much more than the 12.4 percent of Italians. Indeed, the more prosperous urban families in northern Italy owned rural real estate, on which they relied for part of their food supply. So although the prominence of towns in Italy underlies the emergence of the Renaissance, Italy differed in political, cultural, and economic terms as well.

Self-Governing Cities

We can begin with political structure. Simply put, the towns and cities of Italy ruled the countryside—quite the opposite of the pattern elsewhere in Europe. Other European cities and towns had gained a measure of internal self-government, but the Italian communes became self-governing both internally and externally. By playing popes and Holy Roman emperors against each other during and after the Investiture Controversy (see Chapter 8), they gained autonomy from both. They thus had to make and conduct foreign policy in relation to other communes and states within Italy and to powers outside the Italian peninsula as well. Moreover, after 1200, many Italian cities had established republican forms of government. Usually after periods of internal political conflict, substantial numbers of merchants, skilled artisans, lawyers, and notaries exercised political power through election of councils and officials. Although by no means democratic, a novel republicanism pervaded civic life in northern Italy (see Chapter 11) in the twelfth and thirteenth centuries. The city-republics developed a political system based on citizen participation in decision making that retained great popularity and influence long after its practice had declined.

Marriage Patterns and Urban Life

Marriage patterns are another way in which the residents of Italian cities differed from many other Europeans. Northwestern Europe displayed a distinctive pattern of marriage in the early modern period: Women and men married late and at roughly similar ages of 23 to 24 and 26 to 27, respectively; a relatively high proportion (10 percent or more) never married. But in fifteenth-century Tuscany, the region around Florence, 90 percent of women were married or widowed by age fifteen (and 97 percent by age 25). Only 4.5 percent of Tuscan men remained bachelors. In 1427, Tuscan brides were most likely to be 16 years of age and their grooms at least six years older. In Florence itself, a dozen years separated the couple, and the age gap grew with wealth.[2]

In the countryside, a man with a wife and children benefited from their labor, but in the city a family was a hindrance for a man who was serving an apprenticeship or spending months and years trading abroad. Urban men therefore delayed marriage until they were well established financially. Late marriages increased the incidence of prostitution and sodomy, and punishments for adultery and fornication were mild. Even a rapist could evade chastisement by wedding his victim. Venetian courtesans' charms in particular gained wide fame; an English ambassador to Venice

---

[2] An extraordinarily detailed tax assessment was held in 1427 by the Florentine government, providing historians with a wealth of statistical information.

said of himself that "not being made of stone" he had better leave the city, and Shakespeare had Othello in his anger describe his wife Desdemona as "the cunning whore of Venice." Late male marriage also meant that many wives would outlive their husbands. Roughly 25 percent of adult Florentine women in 1427 were widows. Because the pool of men who lived long enough to marry was reduced by death, the value of a **dowry** rose so dramatically that many fathers could not afford one and forced their daughters into convents. In 1552, Florence's population of 59,000 included 2,786 nuns. Poor girls benefited from the growing practice of leaving money in wills to provide dowries so that they could marry, and charitable confraternities appeared that raised funds for this purpose. Yet in Venice at least (and probably elsewhere), the staggering dowries increased the power of the women from wealthy families who brought them to their marriages.

The escalation of the cost of dowries points to an important fact about the social scene in Renaissance Italy that harks back to its medieval and ancient roots. Despite Burckhardt's notion that "individualism" as we now comprehend it was a product of the Renaissance, most Renaissance-era individuals knew perfectly well that their families and the network of kinships—in which nuclear families functioned—held the key to their prospects, just as they had for many centuries. Leon Battista Alberti, one of the brightest stars in Burckhardt's constellation of individualists, owed part of his fame to *Della Famiglia (On the Family)*, a treatise that emphasized the importance of family loyalty and support (see page 436). Dowries for women, marriages to women with dowries that enabled men to sustain or increase their wealth, and access to apprenticeships (or, for those better off, partnerships in existing trading, banking, or manufacturing businesses) continued to rely heavily on family support and connections—just as in ancient Rome and medieval Europe. This was especially true at the higher end of the social scale, but it held for most ordinary people as well. Leading urban families kept dominating their neighborhoods and building and enhancing the palaces (*palazzi*) that served as their power bases. Marriage negotiations between the patriarchs of these families, such as the Medici and the Strozzi or the Rucellai in Florence, were no less complex and no less carefully considered and discussed than those between European monarchs. Then as now, "who you know" might affect a person's advancement, but a much more critical variable in the Renaissance was who were your kin.

Cultural Investment

Besides their more urbanized society, unique political autonomy, and distinctive marriage patterns, Italians differed from the rest of Europe culturally. In Italy, Romanesque tradition remained strong; the Gothic style in art and architecture was never prominent there. Unlike non-Mediterranean Europeans, Italians had only to open their eyes to see the abundant remains of classical Rome. Ruined temples, coliseums, arches, and aqueducts survived in many parts of Italy. Of course, France, Spain, and the Rhineland had some Roman ruins, but only Italy had them in abundance. Furthermore, high-medieval **scholastic** theology wielded less influence south of the Alps than elsewhere in Europe. The most prestigious discipline in Italian universities such as Bologna was law, not theology or philosophy as at Paris, Oxford, and Cambridge; the great Italian scholastic philosophers St. Bonaventure and St. Thomas Aquinas made their careers at Paris (see Chapter 10).

Economic Recovery

Finally, the Italian economy protected the communes from the worst aspects of the recession that gripped much of the rest of Europe in the fourteenth and fifteenth centuries. Nothing, of course, could save the Italians from the Black Death and later plague epidemics. In Venice, for example, plague struck every thirteen years on average between 1348 and 1630, killing horrendous numbers of people each time. In 1630 and 1631 alone, 46,000 out of 140,000 Venetians died—fully one-third of the population. But because the Italians continued, as they had in the High Middle Ages, to serve as Europe's bankers and to dominate the most active and lucrative zone of commerce—the Mediterranean—they maintained their grip on European trade. Silk, pepper, and spices from the East remained valuable commodities, and buyers throughout Europe continued to clamor for them, keeping Italian merchants and ships busy. Industry, in addition to finance and trade, also flourished in many Italian cities. During the fourteenth century, for instance, Florentine merchants, who earlier had bought cloth in northern Europe to sell to customers in the East, increasingly managed to market cloth manufactured within their own city. By the following century Venice, as well, achieved a sizable industrial sector.

In fact, Venice's success was the more spectacular. By 1400 it had surpassed its great rival Genoa and established a trading empire that stretched from Constantinople and the Islamic coasts to all of northern Europe. Venetian merchants fanned out into these regions via overland routes through the Alps to Germany and on fleets of merchant galleys to both Mediterranean and northern European ports. Early in the fifteenth century, the income of the Venetian state was half again as large as that of France, although Venice had only a tenth as many people.

Florence, Milan, Genoa, and Bologna at the same time had budgets as big as or bigger than Portugal's. Although depression and disease lowered overall output, per capita production increased during the Renaissance. Such growth was unevenly distributed and precariously maintained, and a small mercantile elite benefited the most. In Florence in 1427, for example, a mere one hundred families (about 1 percent of all families), had 25 percent of the city's huge wealth, and 31 percent had so little that they paid no taxes. Nevertheless, many "middling" families possessed considerable assets in land and other investments.

One chronicler wrote of Piacenza in 1390:

[The citizens] actually live in a clean and luxurious way, and in the houses are found utensils and crockery far superior to those of seventy years ago. . . . In a house one finds more fireplaces nowadays, while at one time, there was no fireplace at all. Fires were then made in the middle room, under the tiles, and all the inhabitants of the house gathered around the fire on which the food was cooked. I myself have seen this in many houses. In general, the people of Piacenza drink better wines nowadays than did their elders. [This] applies not only to the nobles and merchants but also to those who practice manual trades, who make reckless purchases, especially on clothes for themselves and their wives; employment seems to provide them with enough to support all this with honor.

Therefore, while the great territorial states outside Italy staggered during the long recession, many of the nimbler city-states prospered. Their citizens, like those of Piacenza, had the wealth not only to enjoy fine food and clothing but to turn their attention to art and culture. The relative prosperity of the Italians made the cultural Renaissance possible. Prominent among the beneficiaries were precisely the professional men and successful merchants of the communes to whom Renaissance humanism in its earlier forms would appeal. Soon, however, humanism moved beyond its civic origins to the courts of Italian princes and then to Europe as a whole. In the twentieth century, "humanism" has become associated with secularists, skeptics, and various antireligious groups. But its origins in the Renaissance had virtually nothing to do with such attitudes.

RENAISSANCE HUMANISM

Late medieval Italian devotees of the *studia humanitatis* (the "humanities") were called humanists. The word itself came from the Italian word *umanisti*, referring to teachers who employed classical texts with particular attention to the secular human condition. Most were editors and educators rather than philosophers or artists. Motivated by a passionate love of classical antiquity, they studied disciplines such as eloquence (rhetoric), history, poetry, and ethics (moral philosophy). These subjects had languished at the bottom rung of the curriculum of medieval universities; the things students had to struggle through before they could get to logic, law, and theology, which were the prestigious fields that led to the best jobs. The umanisti themselves upgraded their status by gradually establishing their claim to teach more valuable things, a claim easier to sustain in Italy than elsewhere because of the following they began to win among the nonacademic notaries and as teachers catering to the sons of rich families.

Because even the surviving literature of antiquity is vast, the humanists found in it much they could adapt to their own needs and tastes. Those who admired republican institutions, for example, emphasized the active public lives of the leaders of Republican Rome. Those employed by ambitious despots stressed the glory of Imperial Rome. Those pessimistic about public life tended toward the mysticism of Christianized Neoplatonic philosophy (see Chapters 10 and 11) or withdrew into narrowly antiquarian and literary pursuits. Either way, they did not advocate a secular, neo-pagan, or anti-Christian agenda. Northern or Christian humanism (to be discussed later) would focus on the literature of Christian antiquity—the Scriptures and writings of the Church Fathers, like St. Jerome and St. Augustine (see Chapter 5).

Nevertheless, Renaissance humanists shared several basic attitudes, one of the most important of which was their belief that moral and earthly concerns outweighed supernatural ones. They scorned medieval scholasticism's highly abstract philosophical questions and rigidly logical methods of answering them. Petrarch (1304–1374), the founder and guiding spirit of Renaissance humanism, put it this way: "The object of the will is to be good; that of the intellect is truth. It is better to will the good than to know the truth." Knowledge was useless unless it led to the good life; *good life* being understood in moral, not material, terms. Petrarch and his admirers believed that they would find the wisdom needed to reform and perfect individuals and society by searching diligently into classical literature and employing its methods of persuasion.

Classicism and a Sense of History

Petrarch and his successors scornfully—and unfairly—dismissed the Middle Ages as a cultural wilderness. Medieval Europe had in fact witnessed a series of classical revivals that culminated in the so-called Twelfth-Century Renaissance, a vital time during which scholars redeveloped the art of persuasion, or rhetoric, using classical texts (see Chapter 10). Although Petrarch must share credit with some medieval thinkers, and especially with a group of lawyers and notaries from fourteenth-century Padua, for beginning to restore the "purity" of classical texts, he is nevertheless rightly regarded as the originator of a new kind of humanism. Born near Florence, Petrarch grew up at Avignon during the fourteenth-century papacy's long residency there (see Chapter 11). His father, a notary, insisted that he study law. But his first love was classical literature, and he turned from law to literature after his father's death. He took great pains to achieve a style true to antique models in grammar, vocabulary, and spirit. He believed that he would be remembered for his Latin writings instead of what he thought of as the "trifles" he wrote in the vernacular. Ironically, his Latin epic, *Africa*, is deservedly forgotten while his "trifles" won him enormous admiration and were widely read.

THE HISTORICAL EVIDENCE

Peter Paul Vergerio on Liberal Education

1403

Peter Paul Vergerio (ca. 1368–1444) wrote the first authoritative theoretical statements about the new humanistic educational program. He summarized his thinking in a letter to a young prince, Ubertinus of Carrara, but his program applied equally to those aiming to serve a prince or a republic.

The . . . most important care which is due from father to son . . . is the duty of seeing that he be trained in sound learning. For no wealth, no possible security against the future, can be compared with the gift of an education in grave and liberal studies. By them a man may win distinction for the most modest name, and bring honor to the city of his birth however obscure it may be. . . . Children, although for the most part under the unwritten discipline of home, are not to be regarded as outside the control of public regulation. For the education of children is a matter of more than private interest; it concerns the State, which indeed regards the right training of the young as, in certain aspects, within its proper sphere. . . .

We call those studies liberal which are worthy of a free man; those studies by which we attain and practice virtue and wisdom; that education which calls forth, trains, and develops those highest gifts of body and of mind which ennoble men, and which are rightly judged to rank next in dignity to virtue only. . . . We come now to the consideration of the various subjects which may rightly be included under the name of "Liberal Studies." Amongst these I accord the first place to History, on the grounds of its attractiveness and of its utility, qualities which appeal equally to the scholar and to the statesman. Next in importance ranks Moral Philosophy, which indeed is, in a peculiar sense, a "liberal art," in that its purpose is to teach men the secret of true freedom. History, then, gives us the concrete examples of the precepts inculcated by Philosophy. The one shows what men should do, the other what men have said and done in the past, and what practical lessons we may draw therefrom for the present day. I would indi-

cate as the third main branch of study, Eloquence, which indeed holds a place of distinction amongst the refined arts. By philosophy we learn the essential truth of things, which by eloquence we so exhibit in orderly adornment as to bring conviction to differing minds.

The art of Letters [literature] . . . is a study adapted to all times and to all circumstances, to the investigation of fresh knowledge or to the recasting and application of old. Hence the importance of grammar and of the rules of composition must be recognized at the outset, as the foundation on which the whole study of Literature must rest; and closely associated with these rudiments, the art of Disputation or logical argument. The function of this is to enable us to discern fallacy from truth in discussion. . . .

After including logic, rhetoric, oratory, music, and arithmetic, Vergerio explains why he rejects "the three great professional disciplines: Medicine, Law, Theology":

Medicine, which is applied science, has undoubtedly much that makes it attractive to a student. But it cannot be described as a liberal study. Law, which is based upon moral philosophy, is undoubtedly held in high respect. Regarding Law as a subject of study, such respect is entirely deserved: but Law as practiced becomes a mere trade. Theology, on the other hand, treats of themes removed from our senses and attainable only by pure intelligence.

Source: From J. H. Hexter, ed., *The Traditions of the Western World* (Chicago: Rand McNally, 1967), pp. 293–297.

The most novel element in Petrarch's approach to the classics was his sense of history. Medieval scholars had studied the classics without fully realizing that the world that produced them had been supplanted by a substantially different world, and they taught Latin grammar by employing Aristotelian logic rather than the actual usage of classical writers. But Petrarch so immersed himself in the ancient world that he developed a strong sense for when things were depicted outside their correct historical context. His awareness of how words and phrases had been employed by classical writers led him to evaluate sources critically. For example, he analyzed a letter allegedly writ-

ten by Julius Caesar exempting Austria from his imperial jurisdiction. Petrarch correctly pointed out that, in addition to making other errors, the authors had Caesar using the imperial "we" and referring to himself as "Augustus" and "King." But Caesar had done none of these things, so the letter had to be a forgery.

Renaissance classicists differed from earlier classical revivalists not only in the sheer quantity of ancient literature they recovered and disseminated, but also in the way they used these materials. They sought to understand as fully as possible the culture that had produced the classics in order to reform their own culture and its institutions.

Petrarch   More than any other single individual, Francesco Petrarca (Petrarch) launched the fascination with classical culture that drove the Renaissance. Both poet and scholar, he collected Latin manuscripts until his library was the best in Europe.   *Alinari/Art Resource, NY.*

Petrarch's example was emulated by his younger contemporary, Giovanni Boccaccio (1313–1375), who, like Petrarch, wrote popular works in Italian. Boccaccio's most famous work, the *Decameron*, was a collection of amusing, earthy tales told in a realistic style by a group of Florentine ladies and gentlemen fleeing the Black Death in 1348. His book *Concerning Famous Women* contained an extensive review of renowned women from history that many other writers later drew from, despite the fact that Boccaccio praised mainly those women who displayed "masculine" qualities. He devoted himself primarily to searching for classical manuscripts and producing works on Greco-Roman antiquity, including a guide to classical geography and an encyclopedia of classical mythology. His discoveries generally occurred in monasteries where, as he wrote on one occasion, "these books were in fact not in the library, as they deserved to be, but in a sort of dark and gloomy prison at the base of a tower, of a type in which not even those condemned to death would be incarcerated." Usually, such finds occurred in monastic libraries, where the manuscripts

had long been ignored and forgotten, sometimes since Carolingian times.[3]

In the fifteenth century the humanists began to hunt for Greek manuscripts. Some texts were known in the medieval West, chiefly through translations into Latin. Now texts in the original Greek, many of them previously unknown, were added to the already formidable body of Latin materials—just as the printing press was coming into use in Italy. The high point of Greek studies came with the establishment of the Florentine Academy and Marsilio Ficino's Latin translation of Plato's *Dialogues* (1469). As we will see later in this chapter, Ficino's brand of Neoplatonism strongly influenced the direction of Renaissance thought, and his academy, a meeting place for humanist scholars and interested laymen, became a magnet for humanists visiting Florence from all over Europe. Some scholars of the late fifteenth century also took up the study of Hebrew, knowledge of which enabled them to undertake fresh analysis of the Old Testament—and also to delve into the mystical and magical lore of the Cabala (see Chapter 11).

All humanists, sometimes slavishly, imitated the classical Roman style, Cicero's especially. They wrote with the new critical attitude pioneered by Petrarch, who called Cicero "the great genius" of the ancient world. The work of the most famous Roman humanist, Lorenzo Valla (1407–1457), best exemplifies this approach. A linguist, grammarian, rhetorician, and master of both Latin and Greek, he produced a widely used handbook for humanists seeking to purge their writing style of the inelegancies and errors of Medieval Latin. In one treatise, Valla employed his brilliant critical techniques to correct errors in St. Jerome's Vulgate, the Latin translation of the Bible used by the medieval church (see Chapter 5). He described one of Jerome's choices as a "barbarous word" and denounced another passage as "crudely translated."

Even more audaciously, Valla went on to launch his most dramatic assault on traditional beliefs, his *Declaration Concerning the False Donation of Constantine* (1440), while working for the Neapolitan rulers who were then at odds with the papacy. Allegedly, the emperor Constantine had granted extensive power in the Western Roman Empire to Pope Sylvester I early in the fourth century. Others had questioned the authenticity of the document on which the papal claim rested, but Valla's argument that it had been forged was much more convincing. He noted, for example, that the document contains the term *satraps*, a word (meaning "ruler" or "official") not used by Romans. "What

---

[3] In no case were actual manuscripts from Greek or Roman times recovered. All the discoveries were of copies made by medieval monks. This underscores the importance of Gregorian, Carolingian, and Byzantine cultural preservations.

do satraps have to do with this?" he asked. "Stupid, Dumbbell! Do Caesars speak that way?" Valla, always sharp-tongued, concluded that Constantine had written no such document; rather, it came from "some fool of a priest who, stuffed and pudgy, knew neither what to say nor how to say it, and, gorged with eating and heated with wine, belched out these wordy sentences."[4]

Although high-medieval scholars had known and admired some classical literature, they did not adopt the historical perspective that permitted Renaissance humanists to study the literary legacy of Greece and Rome in its original context. For the medieval scholastics, such context was irrelevant because doctrinal truth was best perceived through philosophy and logic. Petrarch and Valla, however, believed that people would learn to understand and love Christianity and embody it in their deeds not through arid logic but through the rhetorical arts of persuasion. Powerful words (stories, poems, sermons, dramas) and visual images, they proclaimed, would instruct and inspire in ways that logical demonstrations never could, and those who wanted to master these arts had to master the culture of classical antiquity.

One of the most important finds was the complete manuscript of the rhetoric of Quintilian (see Chapter 4) in 1416 at the monastery of St. Gall. Quintilian, a great teacher in first-century A.D. Rome, had created a system of eloquence based on Cicero's ideas, and the umanisti made it the basis of their educational program. According to Lorenzo Valla, "Nobody can know Quintilian if he does not know Cicero. . . . Nor can one follow Cicero faithfully if he does not let himself be guided by Quintilian."

Education and Virtù

No aspect of the Italian Renaissance has proved more durable, and nothing expresses its spirit better, than its theory and practice of education. The ideal of the "Renaissance man" or *uomo universale* ("universal man") who knows about many different subjects and who can write and speak skillfully and pursuasively retains its appeal even today, as men and women enter into increasingly specialized professions. The Italian humanists looked mainly to Cicero for this concept; for him, attaining the highest state of human excellence was the purpose of education. Like Cicero himself in Republican Rome, these writers appealed to an audience of newly prosperous men who wanted a broad, nontechnical "liberal education." The acquisition of

professional skills in theology, medicine, and law—the highest goals of students at the medieval universities—did not impress the humanists. Rather, they advocated breadth of study, because, as one humanist put it, "We cannot rightly understand one subject unless we can perceive its relation to the rest."

The genuine Renaissance man possessed *virtus* (*virtù* in Italian); the word *virtù* comes from the Latin *vir* ("man"), so "manliness" is essential to its meaning (see Chapter 4). The possessor of *virtù* had wisdom, virtue, and a thirst for glorious achievement. He was modest and devout but not saintly, a witty conversationalist, a fine poet, a persuasive orator in both Latin and the vernacular, an elegant dancer, and a gentleman of excellent courtesy and beautiful manners who accepted good and ill fortune with equal grace. Such men embodied "true nobility" regardless of whether or not their family tree contained noble ancestors. A "noble" whose claim to nobility depended entirely on his lineage was a fraud, since, as one humanist put it, "nobility must be due to virtue alone." This new educational program, divorced from its urban context in Italy and adapted to the needs of princely courts and aristocrats, would spread across Europe by the late fifteenth century. Hostile to medieval specialization and the study of commentaries, the program emphasized the study of classical literature as the means to achieve *virtus*. (Nowhere did this approach take root more deeply than in England, where it remains the style of education for many who aspire to the highest ranks of government and business.)

Renaissance humanists, having used their energies to recover the literature of classical antiquity, required their students to devote much more time to the study of that literature than did their medieval predecessors. They urged students to learn grammar by analyzing the texts themselves rather than by memorizing rules or studying commentaries on the texts. The most famous schools of the Renaissance were those operated at the princely courts of Ferrara and Mantua. Here and elsewhere, students learned Latin, Greek, rhetoric, history, and moral philosophy from the actual classical texts, both pagan and Christian. The Mantuan school, La Casa Giocosa ("the Joyful House"), sought to create a pleasant setting in which students would not only study texts but also build virtuous characters as they enjoyed music, riding, swimming, and fencing.

Although La Casa Giocosa admitted some students from poor families, it primarily accepted the sons of princes, nobles, and wealthy merchants. No Florentine weaver or Venetian shipwright had the money or leisure to study Latin, much less Greek or rhetoric. Poor boys continued to attend universities and work their way up in the traditional professions and the church, but their careers were in institutions whose elevator of power was not likely to take them to the top floor.

La Casa Giacosa was also coeducational, a fact that on the surface suggests that the Renaissance would bring

---

[4] The eleventh-century papal officials who wrote the *Donation* believed that Constantine had actually made this bequest of power but that the document had been lost. They were wrong, of course. But they were acting on the basis of older medieval oral traditions—not, as Valla charged, stupidly concocting a lie.

THE HUMAN EXPERIENCE

Leon Battista Alberti, Architect and Theorist

In everything suitable to one born free and educated liberally, he was so trained from boyhood that among the leading young men of his age he was considered by no means the least. For, assiduous in the science and skill of dealing with arms and horses and musical instruments, as well in the pursuit of letters and the fine arts, he was devoted to the knowledge of the most strange and difficult things. And finally he embraced with zeal and free thought everything which pertained to fame. . . . His genius was so versatile that you might judge all the fine arts to be his.

So wrote Leon Battista Alberti (1404–1472) of himself, and the extraordinary thing is that he wrote the truth. According to Jacob Burckhardt, the nineteenth-century Swiss historian of the Renaissance, Alberti was the "first universal genius." Best known as a theoretician of art and architecture, he was also an engineer, mathematician, cryptographer, athlete, playwright, organist, city planner, and social thinker. He excelled in everything except humility.

The illegitimate son of a wealthy, noble Florentine wool trader and banker, Alberti was born in Genoa because his father had been banished from Florence during the harsh political struggles that wracked the city. He learned Greek and Latin at Padua, writing of himself that "letters [the literature of antiquity], in which he delighted so greatly, seemed sometimes like flowering and richly fragrant buds, so that hunger or sleep could scarcely distract him from his books." Afterwards he studied civil and canon law at Bologna and ancient sculpture and architecture at Rome, where he would later advise several popes. Back in Florence in the 1430s, he was closely associated with Brunelleschi while also serving

as a papal secretary. In his influential treatise *On Painting,* Alberti insisted that painting, architecture, and sculpture were liberal arts, appropriate pursuits for gentlemen. He improved and helped to popularize Brunelleschi's invention of scientific perspective, and he advocated a geometric grouping of figures into the harmonious whole appearing in many important Renaissance paintings (for example, Raphael's *School of Athens*).

Alberti's important work, *On Building,* performed a similar service for humanist architects. It was written in the 1440s, the years of his own emergence as a practicing architect, when Alberti was second in fame only to Brunelleschi. The facade of the Rucellai palace in Florence and the Tempio Malatestiano in Rimini (a classicizing marble exterior sheathing a medieval brick church, with proportions taken from the nearby Roman Arch of Augustus) remain as examples of his approach. The treatise revived the ideas of the Roman architect Vitruvius, arguing that designers of buildings should not merely imitate classical forms but embody their inner principles of geometric harmony. The plans of buildings and of whole cities should have these features in order to serve the needs of the people of the city-state. The church, for example, should be "the noblest ornament of a city and its beauty should surpass imagination. It is this staggering beauty which awakens sublime sensation, and arouses piety in the people."

Alberti viewed architecture as a social art, and he was also an important social thinker. His four-volume dialogue, *On the Family,* is a rich storehouse of humanistic thinking about the individual in relation to his family and his community. Writing in Italian, Alberti criticized the extravagance of aristocrats and praised the thrifty, hardworking citizen as the

best exemplar of civic virtue because he created wealth that could be used to defend the community when it was threatened. "Man is born to be useful to men," he proclaimed, and Alberti lived his creed. Further, he did it with a sense of humor. In his self-portrait he noted that "when his favorite dog died he wrote a funeral oration for him." ❖

Leon Battista Alberti's medallion displayed his portrait on one side and his emblem of a winged eye surrounded by a laurel wreath (the classical symbol for honor achieved by human actions) on the other. His motto, *Quid tum?* ("What next?"), celebrated his humanism and optimism. *British Museum.*

improvement to the status of women. Female literacy rates did rise in some urban environments. The fourteenth-century Florentine chronicler Giovanni Villani had estimated that eight to ten thousand boys and girls attended elementary schools in the 1320s, about 10 percent of the city's pre-Black Death population. For women of poor and middling families, however, there is no evidence that any gain occurred. In cities, the separation of home and workplace worked against the status and social power of women. Compared with rural women's work (such as raising chickens and helping with the harvest), the activities of many city women were entirely domestic and contributed no cash to their family budgets.

For aristocratic women, the matter is more complicated. Although feminist treatises written by both women and men appeared in the fifteenth and sixteenth centuries, the notion of "woman" did not notably change until around 1600. The Neoplatonist humanism of the late fifteenth century claimed that earthly love initiates the lover's movement toward mystical union with God. This meant that women might have positive spiritual value for men instead of being lustful snares who would jeopardize their struggle for eternal salvation. However exalting this new idea may have been for the female sex in theory, its practical value seems slight. Those humanists who thought that women should be well educated mainly sought to make them better company for Renaissance men—worthy objects of Neoplatonist admiration, perhaps, but certainly not persons with claims to careers outside the home, should they desire them.

Nevertheless, some aristocratic women became humanist writers, thereby confirming Christine de Pisan's views about female capacity for learning (see Chapter 11). During the fourteenth and fifteenth centuries, more than forty Italian men wrote treatises contending that women were no less able than men to learn the classical languages, master classical literature, and write in the classical style. Among the women who proved them right was Laura Cereta (1469–1499), whose father taught her Latin and Greek. Precocious and combative, she denounced women who disparaged learning in one of their sex: "These are the mushy faces who . . . spit tedious nothings from their tight little mouths." In another, she praised the work of both classical and contemporary women writers and asserted that "the free mind, not shirking effort, always soars zealously toward the good. . . . Nature has generously lavished its gifts upon all people, opening to all the doors of choice through which reason sends envoys to the will. . . . The will must choose to exercise the gift of reason." Criticized by churchmen for treading upon grounds suitable only for men, she published her Latin letters when she was eighteen and was never heard from again. Perhaps she wondered whether those male humanists really meant what they had written about female capacity for learning.

Secularism and the Active Life

Underlying the humanistic approach to education were a certain optimism about people's ability to shape their lives and environment and a new attitude toward striving for what Petrarch called "the glory which we may hope for here below." Despite the impressive creativity and energy of high-medieval civilization, its leading thinkers were uneasy about the pursuit of worldly success. The prevailing medieval outlook was Augustinian: that human beings, left to themselves, drift toward evil. St. Augustine had explicitly rejected the possibility that people could attain in this world the comprehensive excellence toward which the humanists were striving. Even Petrarch sometimes thought this way.

Many Italian humanists believed, on the other hand, that God had designed the world so that people might achieve their goals, and that not to reach for such success was to scorn the potential with which all were divinely endowed. Although important, this contrast between medieval pessimism and humanistic optimism must not be drawn too sharply. Petrarch's enjoyment of the worldly fame that his poetry brought him did not mean that he was uninterested in the salvation of his soul. His enjoyment and emulation of literature created by pagans did not lessen the fervor of his Christian belief. The humanists did not depart from the traditional Christian moral perspective. People should seek worldly fame, honor, and glory, the humanists felt, but not at the expense of justice, wisdom, temperance, and fortitude. Some of Petrarch's sharpest barbs were aimed at the medieval Averroists, for he agreed with Orthodox Christian theologians that these scholastic philosophers had pushed the claims of human reason much too far and were in danger of reviving Aristotle's denial of God's providence or the soul's immortality (for more detail, see Chapter 10 on "The Mind and Imagination of the High Middle Ages").

Scholars often associate Renaissance humanism with the growing secularism evident in the most urbanized areas where literacy rates were highest. This link is real, but its nature and implications are often misunderstood. Criticism of the church and churchmen, though nothing new, intensified in the Late Middle Ages (see Chapter 11). Lay institutions, such as monarchies and city-republics, increasingly gathered taxes from churchmen and otherwise governed churchmen. Fewer and fewer clerics served kings as advisers, administrators, and ambassadors; their places were taken by literate laymen. Although the universities continued to produce men for the law, medicine, and the church, they ceased to be the most significant centers of scholarly and philosophical activity in fifteenth-century Italy. Much of the new thinking proceeded in the courts of princes and the libraries and households of rich laymen. Yet the "decline of the church"—meaning the international Catholic church with its leadership of ordained, celibate men literate in Latin—by no means implies a decline in people's commitment to Christianity. As lay literacy grew in the fourteenth and fifteenth centuries, the church "declined," not because people lost interest in going to heaven, but because some felt more and more dissatisfied with the church's ability to help them get there. And since the increase in literacy occurred in cities and towns, where only a small minority of Europe's population lived, the church remained strong in rural areas and among the poorer urban groups. Among these people, indeed, devotion to the church and its traditional rituals deepened during the fifteenth century.

Renaissance humanists were turning away, not from Christian belief, but from certain medieval religious ideas and practices that they believed hindered people from behaving as God intended. For example, the church's insistence on St. Jerome's fourth-century Vulgate as the only valid translation of the Bible infuriated humanists who knew that it contained errors that formed a barrier between the reader and the ideas and actions of Christ and his apostles. The humanists chose as their main target scholastic learning, with its focus on metaphysical questions, the answers to which (in their opinion) were useless because they did nothing to encourage virtuous behavior. Humanists reevaluated traditional doctrines and arrived at a new vision of what God expected of humanity. They then used techniques of persuasion derived from classical literature to promulgate that vision. For many, the *studia humanitatis* was a way to renew Christian society through direct contact with the Bible, the writings of the early Church Fathers, and the pagan classics—all of which one could use to gain the persuasive power to inspire others to Christian behavior. The eloquence learned from Cicero and many other famous writers from antiquity could incite more action than any mere intellectual conviction so beloved by the scholastic philosophers.

This approach gave impetus to a new and powerful justification for secular activity and thereby modified medieval values. Some of the leading Italian humanists declared that a life spent in action in the secular world (*negotium*) was superior to a life spent in pure contemplation of theological subjects (*otium*). They said, in effect, that vigorous work in the economic and political arena of the city-state was more pleasing to God than solitary life in a monastery. This precisely reversed the medieval insistence that the monk's life of contemplation and prayer pleased God more than any other human calling. As with the contrast between medieval pessimism and Renaissance optimism, however, we must take care not to overdraw this distinction. Petrarch himself retained serious doubts about the value of *negotium*, and later humanists such as Pico della Mirandola criticized it (discussed more fully later in this chapter). Not all medieval writers encouraged withdrawal from the world, and humanists by no means denounced all contemplation. Nevertheless, the Renaissance tended to place a greater value on the active life—

most strikingly in Florence during the first half of the **quattrocento** (1400s). "Among the superior ones," wrote Florence's chancellor Coluccio Salutati (1331–1406), "there are more who dedicate themselves to the active life than occupy themselves solely with spiritual things, just as there are many more who save themselves in the active life than are chosen from the contemplative life." What Salutati called "the way of perfection" could be found by plunging into the service of one's family and state. To labor in such secular concerns, to reshape one's environment, and to achieve virtù *were* to come nearer to God. Work performed from this perspective was therefore not a penalty for sin but rather an ennobling activity.

This optimism about the value of secular activity did not last. After the mid-fifteenth century, Neoplatonism's growing popularity among humanists signaled a retreat from Salutati's more confident outlook. The reasons for this shift back toward contemplation lie in the political arena.

REPUBLICAN AND PRINCELY POLITICS IN RENAISSANCE ITALY

By 1300, as participation in political decision making by artisans, merchants and other non-elite citizens declined, the Italian city-states came to be ruled increasingly by oligarchies and princes. Over the next two centuries, regional and intercity warfare brought numerous smaller communes under the control of a few powerful states until, by the late fifteenth century, five major powers dominated Italy: the feudal kingdom of Naples in the south; the Papal States, a collection of territories ruled by the pope, in the center; and Milan, Florence, and Venice in the north (see Map 12-1). In 1494 France invaded Italy to reassert its claim to the kingdom of Naples, which had been seized by Aragon in 1442. A long struggle with Spain ensued as the two great European powers sought to control the peninsula. The Italian states, having created their own little empires, now became directly or indirectly subject to either France or Spain. After the middle of the sixteenth century, the Spaniards ejected the French from the peninsula and only Venice retained a substantial measure of independence. Papal Rome had only limited freedom of action after the Spanish victory.

If we add the hideous impact of the Black Death to the invasions, battles, sieges, exilings, conspiracies, betrayals, and heavy taxation that accompanied the buildup first of the major Italian political entities and then of the empires of France and Spain, the wonderful cultural creativity of the Italian Renaissance seems to have emerged in a dark and bloody milieu indeed. To find the real roots of the Renaissance, it is therefore important to return to the beginning of the **trecento** (1300s), when the medieval city-states enjoyed relative independence and the Black Death had not yet struck. We will first consider Florence and Venice, large communes where republican political

MAP 12-1
RENAISSANCE ITALY

On the eve of the French invasion in 1494, the "big five" states (Florence, Milan, Rome, Venice, and Naples) dominated the Italian peninsula, and only a few small enclaves still enjoyed a tenuous independence. Siena was conquered by Spain in 1555 and sold to Florence in 1557.

structures persisted. Florence and Venice made particularly massive contributions to Renaissance culture. No less important, the example of their republicanism continued to intrigue political thinkers as monarchical nation-states came to dominate most of Europe. We will then turn to examples of princely rule in Italy.

Florence: The Civic Humanist Moment

"What city, not merely in Italy, but in all the world," asked Salutati rhetorically in 1403, "is more securely placed within its circle of walls, more proud of its *palazzi*, more bedecked with churches, more beautiful in its architecture, . . . happier in its *palazzi*, wide streets, greater in its people . . . more inexhaustible in wealth, more fertile in its fields?" His answer was Florence, yet in 1200 Florence was merely a provincial town of fifty thousand people at most. It lacked a port and could not even offer a major route for pilgrims bound for Rome. During the trecento, however, Florentines replaced their Sienese rivals as bankers to the papacy and became the grain traders and bureaucrats of the Angevin kingdom of Naples. By 1300 its financial fame, along with its dynamic woolen-cloth industry, had drawn some hundred thousand people to Florence, making it the fifth most populous city in Europe. Florentine economic growth faltered in the recession years of the 1340s when several of the largest merchant-banking companies collapsed, followed by the deaths of forty thousand Florentines in the first onslaught of the bubonic plague—the so-called Black Death.

Florence's population level would remain depressed until the eighteenth century, when it finally regained its pre-plague numbers. Nevertheless, entrepreneurial and technical expertise brought relative prosperity to Florence during the century of economic contraction following the Black Death. Individuals and families rose and fell, but it was upon this solid, although no longer expanding, economic base that mercantile fortunes rested. These fortunes, often diversified in banking, cloth, public bonds, and real estate, built housing for immigrant labor, financed Florence's wars of territorial expansion across Tuscany, and patronized the artists and intellectuals who made Florence the single most important center of Renaissance creativity until supplanted by Rome after 1450.

Through the thirteenth and fourteenth centuries, more and more towns yielded to one-man rule. But the political structure of Florence remained republican, despite several attempts by ambitious men to gain control. A popular revolt that overthrew one would-be despot in 1343 gave birth to a complex **guild** regime, whose proponents, in the true spirit of the medieval commune, sought to diffuse decision making and prevent any **tyrant,** faction, or "mob" from dominating the city. As we saw in Chapter 11, this regime withstood a determined attempt by the poorest day-laborers, the ciompi, to impose something approaching mass democracy in 1378. The dominant guild system's executive arm, the Signoria, comprised nine officials called *priors* with two-month terms of office. A prior could not return to the Signoria and serve again until three years had passed. The members of the Signoria received advice from the Twelve officials, called *buonuomini*, or "good men" and the Sixteen *gonfalonieri*, the "standard bearers of justice". The *buonuomini* and the *gonfalonieri* held office for three and four months respectively. All legislation had to be proposed by the Signoria, and it could not take effect unless approved by two assemblies: the Council of the Popolo and the Council of the Commune, each of which had five hundred members who sat for six-month terms.

Although oligarchic rather than democratic, Florence's republican regime permitted broader participation in decision making than did any other state in Europe at that time. Although the Council of the Popolo and the Council of the Commune could not initiate laws, they had and used the important authority to veto measures they did not like (especially new taxes). The electorate for these assemblies and higher offices consisted of the members of twenty-one merchant and artisan guilds, some six thousand men. Landowning nobles (magnates), women, and laborers were excluded. But because a commission (the *scrutatores*) screened all nominees and favored members of the greater guilds (banking, wool, cloth) over those of the lesser guilds (carpenters, butchers, bakers), two-thirds of the guildsmen never held office. The names of those approved were placed in ballot bags and drawn by lot. The higher the office, the fewer names in the bags and the greater the wealth and social status of the men chosen. Nevertheless, around three thousand men held public office of one sort or another each year under the guild regime in Florence. Early in the fifteenth century, the population of adult men stood at about ten thousand. Neither in the ancient nor the modern world is it easy to find a constitution with power so widely diffused.

This guild-dominated administration lasted until the Ciompi revolt of 1378. Frightened by the tumult and continued economic crisis accompanying this brief worker's uprising, the city's lower-middle-class guildsmen turned to the patrician upper class—the members of families with wealth, experience in government, and generations of residence in Florence. As a result, the elite was soon back at the helm and the ciompi were thoroughly repressed, although the lower guilds managed to retain two seats in the Signoria. Florentine government, if oligarchic, was not entirely authoritarian, and political debate remained lively. Elsewhere on the Italian peninsula at this time, one-man rule increasingly triumphed over the republican institutions of the communes.

Until 1434, the year that Cosimo de' Medici began his subtle progress toward domination of the city's politics, a conservative patriciate of rich families ruled Florence. During this crucial interval, the city experienced both the

THE HISTORICAL EVIDENCE

Diary of Gregorio Dati

1412, 1421

Gregorio Dati's life falls into the "rags to riches" category. He came from an obscure Florentine family, yet he eventually was selected Standard-bearer of Justice in 1429, the highest office in the Florentine commune. From modest beginnings, he managed to build a considerable fortune in manufacturing and selling silk cloth. These excerpts from his diary illustrate his experience in the political arena. The "purses" were bags into which the names of all men eligible to hold particular offices were placed. Terms of office were short (two to four months), and only members of the city's twenty-one guilds could hold office. Both laborers and magnates were excluded. Although "new men" like Dati occasionally achieved office, the governing class at this time consisted of the male members of approximately one hundred families from a population of somewhere between fifty and seventy thousand.

3 May, 1412

On 28 April, my name was drawn as Standard-bearer of the Militia Company [one of the "colleges," an advisory body to the Signoria, Florence's ruling council; the Signoria's nine members, called priors, served two-month terms]. Up until then I had not been sure whether my name was in the purses for that office, although I was eager that it should be both for my own honor and that of my heirs. I recalled that my father Stagio had held a number of appointments in the course of his life, being frequently a consul of the Guild of Por Santa Maria, a member of the Merchants' Court and one of the officials in charge of gabelles [excise taxes] and the treasurers. Yet he was never drawn for one of the Colleges during his lifetime. . . . I recalled that I had aroused a great deal of animosity eight years ago because of my business in Catalonia, and that last year I only just escaped being arrested for debt by the Commune. On the very day my name was drawn for this office, only fifteen minutes before it was drawn, I had taken advantage of the reprieve granted by the new laws and finished paying off my debt to the Commune. That was a veritable inspiration from God, may His name be praised and blessed! Now that I can obtain other offices, it seems to me that, having had a great benefit, I should be content to know that I have sat once in the Colleges and should aspire no further. So, lest I should ungratefully give way to the insatiable appetites of those in whom success breeds renewed ambition, I have resolved and sworn to myself that I shall not henceforth invoke the aid of any or attempt to get myself elected to public offices or to have my name included in new purses. Rather, I shall let things take their course without interfering. I shall abide by God's will, accepting those offices of the guilds or Commune for which my name shall be drawn, and not refusing the labor but serving and doing what good I may. . . . And if I should depart from this resolve, I condemn myself each time to distribute two gold florins in alms within a month. I have taken this resolution in my fiftieth year. . . . Knowing my weakness in the face of sin, I make another resolve on the same day. In order to ensure the peace and good of my own conscience, I vowed that I would never accept any office, if my name should be drawn, wherein I would have power to wield the death penalty. If I should depart from this resolution, I condemn myself to give 25 gold florins in alms to the poor within three months for each such office that I have agreed to accept.

1421

My name was drawn to serve among the Twelve *buonuomini* ["Good Men," one of the two top advisory groups to the Signoria]. . . . My name was drawn to be Overseer for the Guild Hospital [the Foundling Home, on which construction under Brunelleschi's direction had begun in 1420] for one year. . . . My name was drawn to serve among the Lord Priors of the city of Florence for a term of two months, starting on 1 July and finishing on the last day of August 1425. . . . The war [with Milan] made our task extremely onerous but, by the grace of God, we left matters in a better way than we found them.

By the grace of God, I was Standard-bearer of Justice for two months from 1 March 1429. The priors serving with me were: Zanobi di Tommaso Bartoli, a feather-bed maker, Bianco d'Agnoli, a maker of wine glasses, as artisans of the quarter of S. Spirito; Riccardo di Niccolò Fagni and Berto di Lionardo Berti for S. Croce; . . . and Ser Iacopo Salvestri, our notary. By God's grace we worked harmoniously together and accomplished a number of good things.

Source: From Gene Brucker, ed., *Two Memoirs of Renaissance Florence: The Diaries of Buonaccorso Pitti and Gregorio Dati* (New York: Harper & Row, 1967), pp. 125–126, 133, 137.

Florence, ca. 1490 Clearly visible are the five miles of city walls, the Duomo (cathedral) with its huge dome (center), and the Palazzo della Signoria (city hall, right of center). The octagonal Baptistery is just in front of the entrance to the Duomo, and the three-story Medici palace is to the left of the Baptistery. *Scala/Art Resource, NY.*

greatest threats to its independence and the largest additions to its territory. One reason Florence sought to expand was to defend itself against the repeated invasions or threats of invasions from either Milan or Naples. These bitter, expensive wars evoked an important component of Renaissance thought: civic humanism, a self-conscious hearkening to Greek notions of the polis and to Ciceronian ideals of civic duty in the Roman Republic (see Chapters 2 and 4). Coluccio Salutati, chancellor[5] of Florence from 1375 until his death in 1406, and his disciple Leonardo Bruni (chancellor 1410–1414 and 1427–1444) built upon the political and legal theory of the medieval communes and the heritage of the Roman Republic to mount a thorough revival of the tradition of communal independence and republican institutions. Abandoning Petrarch's ambivalence, these leaders wholeheartedly urged the Florentine people to take pride in their city-state's great glory. A man should exercise his free will to create his own destiny, they declared, and in so doing serve both himself and his community. Whereas medieval writers had stressed the dangers of the pursuit of private interests, the civic humanists argued that individuals should work hard to build their personal fortunes—the community would benefit no less than they. By exalting the Roman republican tradition, Salutati, Bruni, and their supporters dethroned Caesar as the ideal ancient Roman and elevated his assassin, Brutus.

Civic humanism forms the central theme of Bruni's *History of the Florentine People*. In his view, the greatness of Florence, like that of the Roman Republic, lay in the fact that "the hope of rising to public honors, of building up a career by one's own efforts, is the same for everyone." Under one-man rule, only the flatterers of the prince could participate in decision making; in a republic, all citizens could develop their talents to the highest levels, thus better serving the community. The kind of intense loyalty to Florence engendered by civic humanism appears in an offer by one patrician in 1388 to donate all of his wealth to the city. "Our city is more important than our children," insisted another in 1413, "and for its welfare, everything possible should be done to preserve for posterity what we have received from our ancestors."

In addition to idealizing republican political institutions, Bruni's *History* offered a secular rather than a providential explanation for the rise and fall of states. Medieval chroniclers assumed that God's will, working in a linear fashion, guided events to Christ's return. Bruni did not explicitly reject **providentialism,** but he did ignore it in favor of a different dynamic. Bruni and other civic humanists saw in their own time a new cycle in which the long-lost culture of antiquity reappeared to inspire ever-higher achievements. This cyclical view, similar to that of

---

[5] Florence's chancellors directed the city-state's correspondence with other states, and both Salutati and Bruni used their office as chancellor to establish and advance the *studia humanitatis* as a means to increase Florence's power and standing. Giangaleazzo Visconti of Milan said that the persuasiveness of one of Salutati's letters was worth more than an army of a thousand men.

Aristotle and Cicero, became one basis for Renaissance optimism about human potential: Nothing is more invigorating than believing that one is riding the wave of the future. By the time of his death in 1444, Bruni had played an active role in Florence's political success and led in its splendid cultural advances as well, for the government and the guilds supported artists such as Brunelleschi, Masaccio, Donatello, and Ghiberti (all discussed later in this chapter). Their classicism, realism, and development of perspective paralleled in the visual arts the spirit that the civic humanists embodied in their histories, dialogues, orations, and letters.

By the 1440s, however, the fragile social balance that fostered civic humanism and republicanism had begun to collapse under the strain of wartime taxes. The defense of the medieval commune depended on citizens serving in the militia, but more and more, Florence trusted its defense to **condottieri,** generals who recruited and commanded soldiers. These men fought for pay, not love of the commune. Bruni had sharply criticized the use of mercenaries, praising instead the citizen who was both soldier and participant

in political life. But the growing cost of war pushed Florence toward centralized government and fiscal bureaucracy. While preserving the outward republican forms, Cosimo de' Medici (1389–1464) and his grandson Lorenzo (1449–1492) shrewdly employed their huge fortune from banking, commerce, mining, and industry to gain control of political life. They made allies through marriages, loans, and gifts of money and jobs (see Figure 12-1). Moreover, they reduced the random element of selection to public offices by manipulating the process of scrutinizing men for eligibility. Eventually, if one failed to join the Medici "party," one's name ceased to enter the ballot bags from which the names of officeholders would be drawn. Like American big-city political "bosses" and even in some respects like Mafia godfathers, they dangled carrots in the form of favors and wielded sticks of exclusion and even, in extreme cases, exile.

This narrowing of political participation had its effect upon culture and art. Public **patronage** of art and classical scholarship declined as wealth flowed more bounteously to the victorious "Mediceans," and aristocrats such as Lorenzo

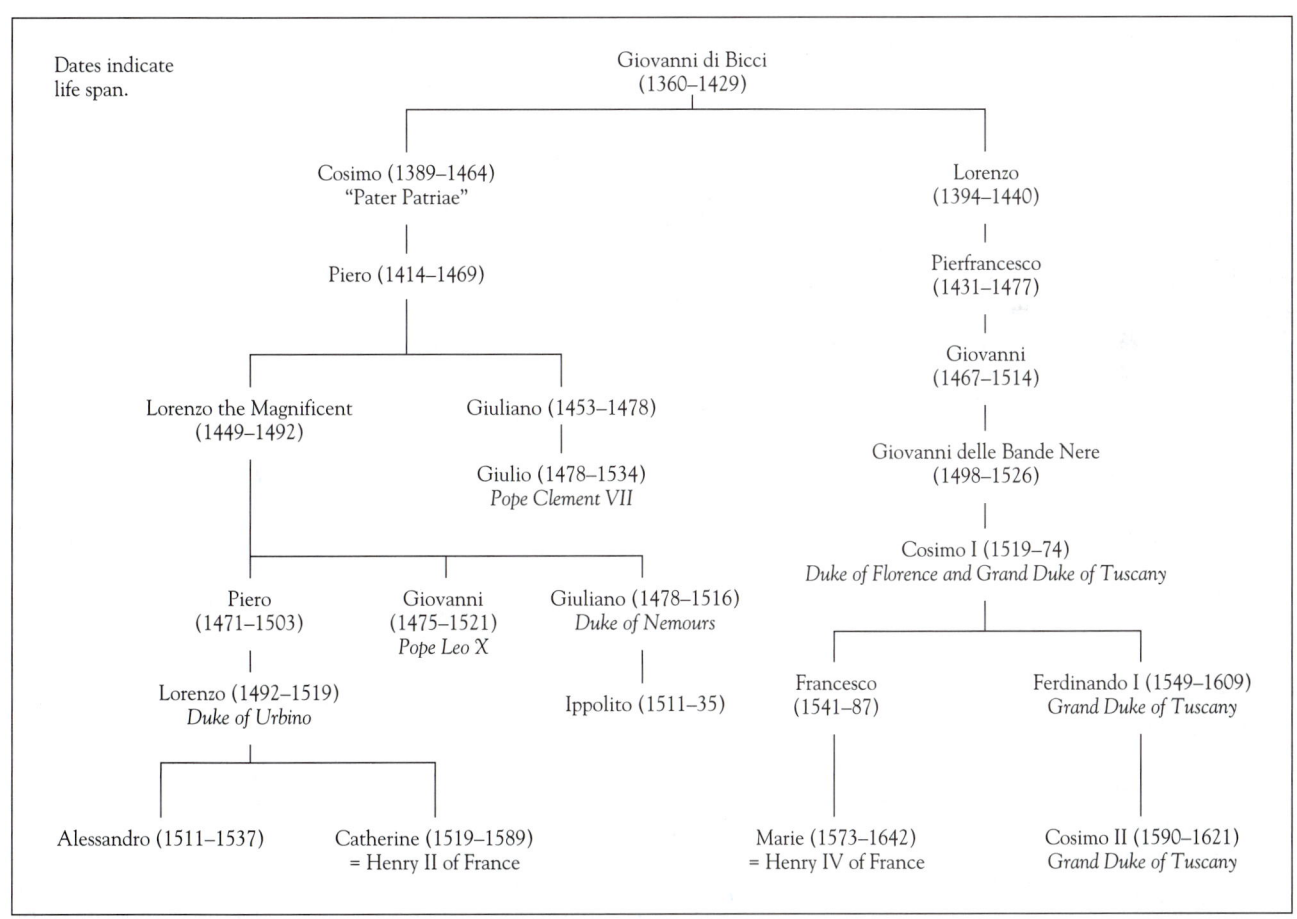

FIGURE 12-1
THE MEDICI FAMILY

Giovanni Pico della Mirandola On the reverse of Pico della Mirandola's portrait appeared the figures of Beauty, Love, and Pleasure—closely linked concepts in his philosophy. *Alinari/Art Resource, NY.*

became famous for their private collections of painting and sculpture. Lorenzo, in fact, gave more attention to his role as a Renaissance princeling than as a banker, a mistake his grandfather Cosimo had never made. After 1440 the major new architectural triumphs were the splendid *palazzi* (palaces) of the Medici and other patrician families. The open, public *loggias* (roofed galleries projecting from walls) that had symbolized the community-mindedness of earlier patricians gave way after midcentury to private courtyards in the new or newly remodeled *palazzi*.

A perfect example of the elitism and inwardness of late fifteenth-century Florentine culture is the shift of humanistic interest from Cicero to Plato—from questions of moral philosophy appropriate to public men in a republican environment toward the metaphysical and theological questions disputed by scholastic philosophers. A thread of Neoplatonic thinking had wound through Italian humanism from its beginning in Petrarch, but now it gained prominence. Central figures of the Florentine Neoplatonist school were philosophers Marsilio Ficino (1433–1499) and Count Giovanni Pico della Mirandola (1463–1494). Pico, a master of Hebrew and Greek despite his youth (he died at 31), criticized those who sought worldly fame or profit in his *Oration on the Dignity of Man*. He announced proudly that he had "relinquished all interest in affairs public and private" so that he could give all his time to philosophical contemplation. Pico almost certainly hoped to become famous for his brilliant intellectual achievements—but *otium* rather than *negotium* had the higher value for him. His goal was to show how the various and competing religious and philosophical systems actually represented an underlying (and overarching) unity. Pico coalesced Christ and Plato into a single and harmonious "truth."

Ficino, Pico, and their friends sought to harmonize Platonic and Neoplatonic thought with Christian doctrine. Patronized first by Cosimo de' Medici and later by Lorenzo, Ficino translated and published a large body of Greek writings unknown to the medieval West. To Ficino, ancient writers from Zoroaster and Hermes Trismegistus[6] to Plato were interpreters of the divine and anticipators of Christianity. This collection of Hermetic thought, made available to Europeans by Ficino, stressed the unimportance and fleeting nature of the human body and all physical things in contrast to the immortality of the soul, which Ficino equated with reason. People could achieve the good life only by withdrawal from worldly concerns into contemplation of reason itself: God. Thus the Florentine Neoplatonists reversed the values of the civic humanists; individuals no longer were to seek their highest excellence in a social setting. It is no coincidence that this change in values came about at the same time that careers in Florentine public life were open only to those who accepted the leadership of Lorenzo de' Medici. If high achievement in public life ceased to be an option for men of talent and intellect, we can hardly be surprised if lives of devotion to private contemplation seemed more attractive.

Venice: The Durable Republic

Yet as republican institutions yielded to Medicean dominance in Florence, they remained strong in Venice. The watery city of Venice had always been something of an exception in Italy. It had never bowed to popes or Holy Roman emperors. Scattered over islands, sandbars, and reclaimed land inside lagoons, the Venetians built no walls,

---

[6] Hermes Trismegistus supposedly was an Egyptian high priest in Moses' time (actually, he never existed). His purported writings were translated from Greek into Latin by Ficino and published after 1560. Hermetic writings center on the conviction that the human mind mirrors the entire universe. Thus an individual *magus* (a "natural" or "white" magician, see Chapter 11) can gain power over nature through understanding its secret principles. Although widely accepted as genuine and credible in the fifteenth and sixteenth centuries, the Hermetic writings were actually products of Gnosticism (second and third centuries A.D.), as a Protestant scholar demonstrated in 1614.

Venice, ca. 1500 In this view of Venice, the Arsenal can be seen on the right, above the two large round ships in the foreground. The Grand Canal snakes through the city like a backward "S" toward the left. The Rialto bridge crosses the canal at the right side of the curve. All major mercantile and financial matters, such as the fixing of interest rates and commodity prices, were conducted in the streets surrounding the bridge. A merchant who broke the rules might be denied access to the Rialto and thus participation in commerce. *Alinari/Art Resource, NY.*

yet they would remain unconquered until Napoleon Bonaparte's massive French armies swept across Europe at the end of the eighteenth century. The Venetians excelled in shipbuilding, trading, and seamanship, and by 1300 they had constructed a maritime and colonial empire unrivaled until the Portuguese and Spanish voyages of discovery to India and the New World. The population of Venice grew to 190,000 by 1570, and during the sixteenth century the city was regarded as the richest in the world. By that time, Venice wielded as much industrial as commercial power and was famous for fine glass, soaps, silk, wool cloth, and printed books. The Arsenal, where the government built ships and stored arms and equipment, covered 60 acres and employed two thousand men—5 percent of the city's workers. It was the largest industrial establishment in Europe, and perhaps in the entire world.

Venice's printing industry rivaled its trade and shipbuilding enterprises. Venetian printers made the first major attempts to put the new information technology to the service of scholarship by mass-producing well-edited versions of literary texts edited and proofread by qualified scholars. The city's best-known printer, Aldus Manutius, established his Aldine Press in 1493 and became the first important publisher of "pocket" books—reliable editions of Horace, Vergil, Catullus, Ovid, and other classical authors, as well as humanist works like Guarino's *Gram-*

mar, small enough to be easily carried. Their obvious utility undercut the snob appeal of owning elegant, hand-copied books. During the latter half of the sixteenth century Venetians published three and a half times as many books as did Milan, Florence, and Rome combined—hardly a surprising accomplishment, given that between 1489 and 1500 more than two hundred printing shops opened in Venice. Venice's extensive Mediterranean and northern European trade facilitated the distribution of these books and made the dramatic growth of the printing industry in Venice possible.

The Venetian maritime empire reflected pure state capitalism: The government built and owned the ships, decided where and when they would sail, chose the commanders, and rented cargo space to merchants. But Mediterranean pirates posed a constant threat, and Venice also faced stiff competition on the high seas from rival Italian cities. Following a series of hard-fought wars against Genoa between 1253 and 1431, the Venetian fleet was then forced to grapple with the growing naval might of the Ottoman Turks after the fall of Constantinople in 1453. In the long run, the profitability of Venetian commerce suffered more from the shift of long-distance trade from the Mediterranean to the Atlantic than from the progress of the Ottomans. During the fifteenth century, however, Venice had obtained control over substantial territory in northeastern Italy,[7] enabling investment in agriculture and industry on the mainland to offset at least some of the losses in overseas trade.

The unusual longevity of the Venetian republic fascinated political writers more and more as time passed. Venice's Byzantine heritage had contributed to a tradition of state supremacy over individuals and groups, including the church. The earliest *doges* (dukes) had been Byzantine officials, but Venetians ignored this fact, preferring to think of the doges as elected by "the people," meaning the General Assembly (a body dominated by families made powerful by trade and property). Following the assassination of an unpopular doge in 1172, a council of his advisers created a committee to nominate his successor. Doges continued to serve life terms and to exercise important political and ceremonial functions, but their power was progressively chiseled away by the solemn oaths required of each new doge and by an inquest of the former doge's accounts. Each doge's family now had to pay for any errors he had committed. The doges thus became tightly limited magistrates unable to take action without careful and systematic consultation.

From the fourteenth century until 1797, the Venetian constitution underwent surprisingly little change. The unwieldy General Assembly rarely met. Lawmaking, election of officials, and judicial authority lay in the hands of the Great Council. In 1297, the size of the Great Council was more than doubled—to include virtually all members of the established nobility and many commoners as well as immigrants of recent wealth—but its membership was also closed. Then in 1323 membership in the Great Council was made hereditary, thus restricting participation in Venetian politics to approximately one thousand men.

Several smaller groups were also important in Venetian government. The Council of Forty heard appeals from lower courts and reviewed legislation concerning financial issues. The Senate (about sixty members) debated and prepared legislation about commercial, diplomatic, and naval issues for consideration by the Great Council. The most powerful group comprised the Ducal Council (six members in 1178), the doge himself, and three leaders from the Council of Forty. This elite cluster, called the Signoria, conducted day-to-day business (including election to the higher offices). In the aftermath of a failed rebellion by frustrated nobles in 1310, a Council of Ten was appointed that soon became a strong force against any factional or other organized opposition to the government. As in many Italian communes, officials on these interlocking councils served short terms (two months to a year, except for the doge) and could not be reelected for two years.

Venice experienced the rumblings of political activity among guildsmen in the thirteenth century, but the *popolani*

failed to win the kinds of concessions achieved elsewhere.[8] One reason was that, although the popolani lacked political power, the government allowed guilds considerable latitude to organize and regulate their crafts, a policy that gave members meaningful control over their most immediate concerns. Another factor was the unity and homogeneity of the nobility—virtually all were merchants—freeing Venice of tensions between landowning aristocrats and urban magnates that commonly troubled other cities.

Aristocratic factionalism was further moderated by what seems an absurdly complicated method of choosing high officials. A nominating committee chosen by lot from members of the Great Council was reduced still further by lot, expanded by nomination, again reduced by lot, and so on through several stages that made manipulation by factions nearly impossible. To discourage campaigning by nominees, elections by secret ballot were held as soon as possible after the final nominating committee report. Under these procedures Medici-style manipulation of the electoral system was out of the question. Yet because they came from the Senate, in which membership was hereditary, nominees were not chosen truly at random. On the contrary, the same thirty or forty families controlled the top positions for centuries. Venetian society was more stratified than in Florence, but within the large aristocracy the nobles enjoyed greater equality of opportunity. Thus Venice remained an oligarchic republic long after the rest of Italy fell under the sway of princes.

The Princely Courts

Although civic humanists in republican city-states denounced one-man rule as tyrannical, dynastic rule had long dominated southern and central Italy and was increasingly common farther north. From our modern perspective, such regimes may seem inherently despotic, but the most successful Renaissance princes operated more through negotiation, patronage, and persuasion than harshness or violence. In many cases, ordinary people fared as well or better under despots as they did in oligarchic republics.

The House of Este (Ferrara)   Ferrara, for example, a city near the eastern end of the Po Valley in northeastern Italy, had operated under a communal government in the twelfth century. The rival Este and Torelli families, both powerful noble dynasties in the turbulent region, sought to dominate Ferrara, and members of each won election as *podestà* (magistrate) at different times. By the mid-thirteenth century, however, the Este defeated their rivals, and in 1264 Obizzo II, Marquess of Este, was elected *signore* (ruler) for life.

---

[7] Partly from the collapse of the Milanese empire of Giangaleazzo Visconti.

[8] Popolani, in medieval Italy, were leaders of the popolo— "the people," or citizens outside the established elite. They were not necessarily poor. As we saw in Chapter 11, popolani won a significant share of power in many medieval Italian communes.

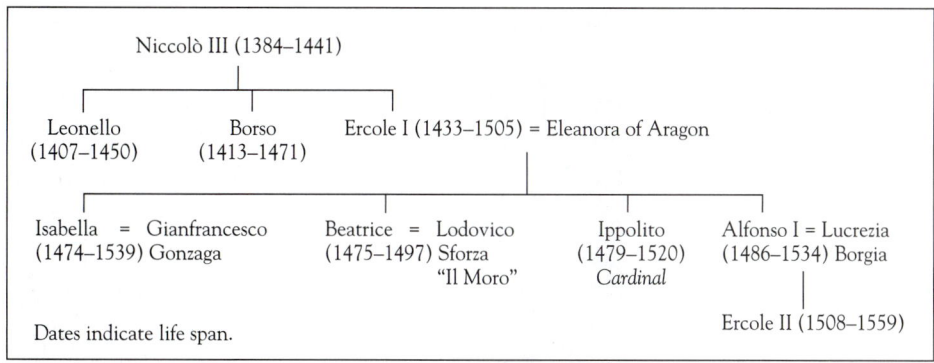

FIGURE 12-2
THE ESTE FAMILY

At first, Obizzo d'Este governed within the traditional communal system, but in 1287 he outlawed the guilds and soon gained the authority to choose his successor. While retaining the outward form of communal government, Obizzo skillfully gathered its legislative, judicial, and administrative powers into his own hands. He also brought new territory under Este control both by purchase and by accepting the requests of the feuding magnates of Modena and Reggio to rule their towns. When Obizzo died in 1293, quarreling among his sons resulted in the seizure of Ferrara by an invading army in 1310, and the establishment of a harsh regime directed from Naples. Yet only seven years later, the Ferrarese nobles and people rebelled, ousted the invaders, and elected three of Obizzo's grandsons to rule as *signori*.[9] The revolution of 1317 identified the house of Este with the cause of **liberty** from "foreigners" while confirming its authoritarian government within the city.

The Este family's reign in Ferrara continued without further interruption until 1597, when Duke Alfonso II died without a direct heir and the papacy successfully reasserted its old claim to rule Ferrara. But for nearly three centuries, a series of wily, strong-willed, colorful Este signori transformed a politically chaotic, mosquito-ridden, flood-prone city in the Po delta into a prosperous state with a court whose talented artists, scholars, and writers contributed significantly to Renaissance culture. The surviving evidence suggests that the Este princes enjoyed wide popular support, the Ferrarese apparently preferring the stability of Este leadership to the factionalism and strife they had experienced earlier. The only serious threats to Este hegemony came either from enemies outside Ferrara or from within the Este family itself.

The princes of the house of Este governed despotically and even, at times, brutally, but they understood the need to gain wide support for their regime by governing well. They levied heavy taxes, but they also spent huge sums from their own as well as the public coffers to benefit the people of Ferrara and its region. Niccolò III d'Este (reigned 1393–1441) brought a famous humanist and educator, Guarino da Verona (1374–1460), to Ferrara to serve as tutor to his son Leonello, teach at the university, and establish a school like Mantua's La Casa Giocosa. Niccolò's successors were his three sons, Leonello (reigned 1441–1450), Borso (reigned 1450–1471), and Ercole (reigned 1471–1505). Leonello, deeply influenced by Guarino, vigorously promoted humanistic activity in Ferrara and improved institutions for relief of the city's poor. Borso energetically assisted the growth of agricultural production through massive projects for flood control and land reclamation. He also spent liberally from his own funds to enhance the university, and the number of graduates increased fourfold as a result. Ercole gained admiration for his patronage of the arts and religious festivals, and his concern for the poor led him to initiate the *ventura,* an annual procession in which he and his attendants personally walked through the streets early in January soliciting food for the poor at the houses of better-off residents. All the Este princes strengthened their family's position by arranging marriages with ruling dynasties in Italy, France, and the German lands (see Figure 12-2). Their unusual longevity rested, however, on the care with which they rewarded their allies and servants in Ferrara with estates, offices, and honors.

The Milanese Despots Whereas Ferrara's commune never really had an active popolo movement, the great city of Milan was a genuine republic in the twelfth and thirteenth centuries. After 1212 the nobility and the popolo shared political power. But in 1278 Ottone Visconti, archbishop of Milan, became the first *signore* to have effective control of the city. In that year, he led an army of nobles and their men that seized the city and overthrew the popolo. From then until the mid-fifteenth century, the Visconti family dominated Milan.

Centrally located on major trade routes in the rich Po Valley, Milan had a full range of guilds, a powerful economy based on trade and manufacturing, and, like Florence, an elaborate structure of legislative assemblies and executive councils, controlled during the fourteenth century by various Visconti signori. One of them, Bernabò Visconti (reigned 1354–1385), revealed his arrogance when he crowed to the archbishop of Milan, "Do you not know, you fool, that here I am pope and emperor and lord in all my

---

[9] *Signori* is the plural of *signore.*

lands and that no one can do anything in my lands unless I permit it—no, not even God!" Bernabò tried to keep his nephew and successor, Giangaleazzo Visconti, under his thumb, but the young man responded by seizing and imprisoning him. According to some accounts, Bernabò's death in prison occurred on Giangaleazzo's orders. Giangaleazzo then extended Milan's power into Tuscany and had Florence surrounded when he died in 1402.

Giangaleazzo's career epitomizes the Visconti family's ambitions. His father arranged his marriage to a French princess, and in 1395 Giangaleazzo bought the title "Duke of Milan and Prince of the Empire" from the cash-strapped Holy Roman emperor, thereby becoming the first of Italy's Renaissance dukes. Humanists and writers from conquered city-republics such as Verona, Vicenza, and the old university city of Padua sought his patronage and hastily produced propaganda celebrating his victories. Had Giangaleazzo lived long enough to subdue Florence, Milan might have become the center of a group of Italian territories large enough to withstand the onslaughts of Spain and France in the sixteenth century. But after his death, the subject cities rebelled, forcing his successors to struggle to rebuild his empire.

When Giangaleazzo's unpopular son, Filippo Maria, died without a male heir in 1447, the Milanese proved beyond a doubt that the medieval republican tradition still lived. Many leading noblemen, judges, and lawyers, some of whom had been Filippo's counselors and ambassadors, agreed to recreate the medieval commune. A council of twenty-four men (four from each of Milan's six districts and named the "Captains and Defenders of the Liberty of the Commune") took over executive authority and nominated a new Council of Nine Hundred (150 men from each district), which would have legislative powers. This Ambrosian Republic (so-called after the city's patron saint, Ambrose) immediately began wrestling with debt, unpopular taxes, and revolt. Nearly all the subject cities rebelled, either installing republican governments of their own or seeking protection from cities such as Venice, Florence, and Naples, while ambitious *condottieri* jostled for pieces of the Visconti empire.[10]

The Ambrosian experiment failed when Francesco Sforza, a famous condottiere who was employed to fight Milan's enemies, betrayed the citizens' trust in him. He had married Filippo Maria's daughter and was known to covet his late father-in-law's position. Allying himself with Venice, Sforza blockaded food supplies into Milan and shrewdly exploited rifts among its leaders. He seized authority over the starving city in February 1450, reigning as duke until his death in 1466.

The Assassination of Galeazzo Maria Sforza Galeazzo Maria Sforza's ten-year reign in Milan demonstrated that a humanist education did not necessarily make a man genuinely humane. Cruel and tyrannical, he was murdered in a church, which enabled his brother Ludovico to seize control of the city. *Corbis/Bettmann*

Francesco Sforza's son (Galeazzo Maria) and then his grandson succeeded him, but real power lay in the hands of his wily younger son, Ludovico (known as "il Moro"—the Moor—nicknamed for his dark complexion). Ludovico and his wife, Beatrice d'Este, presided over the most opulent court in Italy, where they patronized both Donato Bramante (later the architect of the new St. Peter's in Rome) and Leonardo da Vinci. But Ludovico's success did not last. When the French captured Milan in 1499, he was imprisoned and spent the rest of his life in a French dungeon.

The bitter rivalry and costly warfare that characterized relations between Milan and Florence was one of many examples of the struggles among the numerous Italian states in the fourteenth and early fifteenth centuries. The signing of the Peace of Lodi (1454) initiated a forty-year era of peace among the five largest states (Florence, Milan, Venice, the Papal States, and the kingdom of Naples). This diplomatic achievement resulted partly from the spread of new techniques in international relations whereby, instead of dispatching men in the medieval manner on short-term missions with specific goals, governments permanently installed resident ambassadors in foreign capitals. The Italians pioneered this practice of employing resident diplomats and agents, and their numbers grew substantially in the second half of the fifteenth century. Florence, Venice, Naples, and Milan all had installed agents at each other's courts by 1458, and the larger powers outside Italy soon followed suit. In 1604 an English diplomat got into trouble with his monarch for this sly but revealing definition: "An ambassador is an honest man sent to lie abroad for the good of his country."

---

[10] *Condottieri* (singular *condottiere*) were the commanders who raised and led troops of mercenary soldiers, selling their services to the cities of medieval and Renaissance Italy.

Leonardo da Vinci's *The Last Supper* Leonardo painted his famed *Last Supper* on the wall of a Milanese church that Bramante was remodeling. Always experimenting, he tried using a new technique that failed; the oil-tempera medium he used began flaking away only a few years after it was finished. Enough remains, however, to confirm it as one of the masterpieces of the High Renaissance. *Santa Maria della Grazie, Milan, Italy/The Bridgeman Art Library.*

THE RISE OF ROME AND THE FALL OF ITALY

The papacy itself formed a princely regime, although of a unique kind because of its spiritual and ecclesiastical reach across all of Western Christendom. That the popes managed to play a key role in Renaissance cultural and political life is remarkable, given the damage done to papal authority during the fourteenth century. In the early 1400s Rome's condition was pitiable. The city's prosperity depended on the flow of pilgrims into the city, the payment of annates (clerical income taxes) into the papal treasury, and a large, free-spending papal court. But the popes and their enormous entourage of courtiers and bureaucrats had gone to Avignon in 1309. The attempt to return the papacy to Rome in 1376 led to the Great Schism, further weakening papal government (see Chapter 11). The long-standing papal goal of achieving territorial security and fiscal control of the Papal States seemed doomed to failure. Wild animals roamed within the walls of Rome itself, cows grazed on the ruined Forum, and sheep wandered over four of the famed seven hills. Papal recovery began when the Great Schism ended and the Council of Constance elected Martin V as pope in 1417. Yet the rise to greatness of papal Rome occurred against an increasingly somber political background. For many Italians, the later fifteenth and sixteenth centuries came to mean the loss of independence and subjection to foreign rule.

The Renaissance Papacy and Cultural Triumph

Pope Martin V returned to Rome in 1420, but rioting forced his successor, Eugenius IV, to flee to Florence in 1434 (see Table 12-1). Eugenius's recognition of Alfonso V of Aragon's Neapolitan claims brought him the support he needed to return to Rome in September 1443. By then, Eugenius's court was full of humanists, and the temporary recovery of the papacy became permanent.

Eugenius fired his old friend Cosimo de' Medici as papal banker, seized Medici property in Rome, and held to his alliance with Naples in a diplomatic revolution that reasserted papal authority in central Italy. Nicholas V used the security inherited from Eugenius to glorify the papacy through literature and architecture. An insatiable bookworm, Nicholas attracted many humanists into his service, planned the Vatican Library, and stressed the value of Greek texts (both pagan and early Christian), thus shifting scholarly emphasis from Latin to Greek antiquity. The best known humanist to join Nicholas's enterprise was Lorenzo Valla (introduced earlier in the chapter), a native of Rome who had long worked at the Aragonese court in Naples. The rapprochement between Alfonso and the popes enabled Valla to continue his campaign to reform the church along humanist lines. The result was that Rome outstripped Florence as the leading center of humanistic scholarship. The decline of republicanism in Florence and

TABLE 12-1

THE RENAISSANCE POPES

Martin V	(Colonna)	1417–1431
Eugenius IV	(Condulmaro)	1431–1447
Nicholas V	(Parentucelli)	1447–1455
Callistus III	(Borgia)	1455–1458
Pius II	(Piccolomini)	1458–1464
Paul II	(Barbo)	1464–1471
Sixtus IV	(della Rovere)	1471–1484
Innocent VIII	(Cibò)	1484–1492
Alexander VI	(Borgia)	1492–1503
Pius III	(Todeschini)	1503
Julius II	(della Rovere)	1503–1513
Leo X	(Medici)	1513–1521
Hadrian VI*	(Dedal)	1522–1523
Clement VII	(Medici)	1523–1534
Paul III	(Farnese)	1534–1549
Julius III	(Ciocchi del Monte)	1550–1555

The family name of each pope appears in parentheses, and the dates are those of each man's service as pope. During this period, popes averaged 8.8 years on the throne of St. Peter, predictably enough since young men had little chance of winning an election in the College of Cardinals.

*The last non-Italian (he was Dutch) to be elected pope until the Polish-born John Paul II was chosen in 1979.

elsewhere as one-man rule became the norm caused the civic spirit of Cicero to give way to the Neoplatonism that characterized the later Renaissance. In other words, *otium* took precedence over *negotium* as power contracted into the hands of popes, princes, and princes in all but name (such as Lorenzo de' Medici).

Pope Nicholas believed that learned men would be impressed by literary achievements, but, as he said on his deathbed:

> To create solid and stable convictions in the minds of the uncultured masses, there must be something which appeals to the eye; . . . if the authority of the Holy See were visibly displayed in majestic buildings, . . . belief would grow and strengthen from one generation to another, and all the world would accept and revere it.

Nicholas V's architectural counselor was Leon Battista Alberti (see The Human Experience, on page 436, for

more details), and it was probably Alberti who first suggested replacing Constantine's fourth-century papal basilica with a grander structure. Later, in 1503, Pope Julius II took the drastic step of beginning a new St. Peter's basilica. In so doing, however, Julius fulfilled the logic and expressed the power of the papal revival begun more than a half-century earlier.

In the interim Pope Sixtus IV, Julius's uncle, cleared streets, restored aqueducts and city walls, and employed artists to glorify his efforts. Sixtus also gave a powerful boost to urban development by permitting churchmen's heirs to retain property that had been purchased with clerical income. Because previously the church could confiscate such investments when the holder died, it is unlikely that wealthy clerics would have built their superb palaces without this policy change. Rome's beautification continued through the pontificates of two lavish patrons, Leo X and Clement VII, respectively the second son and the illegitimate nephew of Lorenzo de' Medici. Paul III built the magnificent Farnese palace, resumed the building of St. Peter's, and commissioned Michelangelo to complete the Sistine Chapel frescoes that he had worked on under both Julius II and Clement VII.

St. Peter's Basilica, Rome   Donato Bramante began to design the new St. Peter's, the largest church in Western Christendom, in 1506, employing concrete rather than the stone and brick employed by medieval architects. When he died in 1514, only a start had been made, and progress was slow until Michelangelo took over the task in 1546. *Alinari/Art Resource, NY.*

The immoral and acquisitive behavior of many Renaissance popes contrasts strangely with the sublime structures they paid for. It is tempting to conclude that the artistic giants of the High Renaissance were commissioned and paid by moral pygmies. For instance, Sixtus IV probably connived in the assassination plot directed at the Medici brothers on Easter Sunday in 1478. Innocent VIII belied his name by begetting no fewer than sixteen bastards before his ordination and by celebrating their marriages in the Vatican. Alexander VI made his illegitimate son, Cesare Borgia, a cardinal at age nineteen and helped the treacherous young man build his own principality in central Italy. Cesare was widely believed to have murdered both his elder half-brother and one of the husbands of his sister, Lucrezia. The bold, warlike Julius II led his armies in the field and commissioned Raphael and Michelangelo to portray him in armor astride a horse. The famous northern humanist, Desiderius Erasmus, imagined what St. Peter might have said when Julius II appeared at the entrance to heaven: "You have tens of thousands of men with you, and I do not perceive in so great a mob any one who so much as looks like a Christian. What I do see is a most foul conglomeration of men that smell of nothing but brothels, booze and gunpowder." Julius III was quite the opposite—an unprepossessing fellow, described as a rabbit by one visitor. He made the keeper of his pet monkey a cardinal.

Yet the Renaissance popes were by no means the first to sell positions, to profit from dispensations (licenses to exempt individuals from church laws) and from indulgences, and to exploit their powers to strengthen the positions of their families, friends, and clients. Ever since the eighth century, popes, like secular princes, had been deeply concerned with worldly power. When the dust of the French and Spanish invasions finally settled, the popes retained considerable authority, both in the wider church and in the Papal States (where they were themselves temporal princes). They exercised this authority from a city adorned by works of artistic genius. Once again, all roads led to Rome.

The Italian Political Tragedy

A new age in European diplomatic history was born in 1494 when the stupidly aggressive twenty-four-year-old king of France, Charles VIII, led his army of French cavalry, Swiss infantry, and a large artillery train (at least forty cannon) into Italy in an initially successful attempt to seize Naples from the Spanish. Charles's firepower encouraged the spread of the *trace italienne*, an expensive new style of fortification employing low, thick walls and raised gun towers to defend cities that could no longer rely on medieval curtain walls. Charles's invasion also initiated more than half a century of warfare in which the Italians steadily lost control of their peninsula to outsiders. Spain controlled both Milan in the north and Naples in the south by 1530, and for a time even Rome lay under under Spanish control. Complicated alliances took shape, dissolved, and formed again with bewildering rapidity.

Charles VIII's objective was to make good the old Angevin claim to the kingdom of Naples. He was encouraged in this wild adventure by Ludovico Sforza, the Milanese despot whose power was being undermined by Naples, the papacy, and Florence. Franco-Milanese collaboration succeeded in the short run, as Charles conquered the kingdom of Naples in 1494. On their way to Naples, the French marched through Pisa, Florence, and Rome without a fight. The first victim was Piero de' Medici, Lorenzo's heir, who barely escaped from the Florentines with his life when his craven surrender of Pisa provoked a fierce rebellion in Florence. The Florentine republic was swiftly restored under the influence of a charismatic Dominican friar, Girolamo Savonarola (1452–1498). For years Savonarola had prophesied the city's fall to a foreign king because of its worldliness and luxury, and events seemed to prove him divinely inspired. (Michelangelo said late in his life that he could still hear Savonarola's voice ringing in his ears long after the friar's death.)

In 1497 Savonarola convinced the Florentines to bring their jewelry, cosmetics, wigs, secular books, songbooks, pornographic pictures, musical instruments, and gaming tables to enormous bonfires in the "burning of the vanities." He thundered that Pope Alexander VI "is no Christian, he who, believing in no god, surpasses the bounds of all faithlessness and impiety." Alexander excommunicated him and forbade anyone to listen to his preaching. Savonarola's attempt to build a morally perfected Florentine commune, which he thought of as the New Jerusalem described in the New Testament, ended when factions opposed to him won civic elections in 1498.

Raphael's *The Mass at Bolsena*   For his patron, Pope Julius II, Raphael painted a series of frescoes in the Vatican that included this vivid affirmation of the church's central liturgical doctrine of transubstantiation. Julius kneels prayerfully at the right, as a young German priest at the altar who doubted whether Christ's body really appeared in the Mass is astonished to see the wafer bleeding.   *Scala/Art Resource, NY.*

The Execution of Savonarola Savonarola's refusal to obey an order from Pope Alexander VI to stop his preaching scared Florentines who feared papal excommunication if they continued to listen to the evangelist. After his arrest by the Signoria, he admitted under torture that his prophecies lacked divine sanction. On May 28, 1498, he was hanged and his body burned in front of a large crowd. Donatello's statue *Judith and Holofernes* oversaw the grim spectacle from its location just outside the Palazzo della Signoria. *Nicolo Orsi Battaglini/Art Resource, NY.*

Charged with heresy, he was hanged and his body was burned in the Palazzo della Signoria.

Meanwhile Charles VIII's adventure had ended in abject failure. The military effectiveness of his troops was undermined by syphilis (called "the Italian disease" in France and "the French disease" in Italy). King Ferdinand of Aragon's army forced the French out in 1495 and restored the Aragonese presence in Naples. Charles VIII died childless in 1498 after accidentally banging his head on a door frame. Thus the French invasion of 1494 served mainly to suck the Habsburg monarchs of Spain and the Holy Roman Empire into Italian politics permanently. Another French invasion in 1499 triggered a new round of musical-chair alliances, as Pope Julius II desperately sought to consolidate papal control of central Italy.

Led by Francis I, the French invaded yet again in 1514 and prospered temporarily. Then, at the battle of Pavia in 1525 the forces of the young Charles V—king of Spain from 1516 and Holy Roman emperor from 1519—finally defeated them and consolidated the Spanish hold on Italy. In 1527 Charles's unpaid troops sacked Rome. They stripped the rich city of food and valuables, and a contemporary wrote: "The stench of dead bodies is terrible; men and beasts have a common grave, and in the churches I have seen corpses that the dogs have gnawed." After a

short-lived revival of the Florentine republic from 1527 to 1530, partly inspired by memories of Savonarola's preaching about Florence's divinely ordained destiny, Charles V installed the Medici as dukes there in 1532 (see Figure 12-1), ending the Signoria's 250-year rule. The Florentine republic was finally dead.

The early sixteenth century thus became a calamitous era for Italy. True, the Italians' forebears had crossed new frontiers in thought, art, and statecraft and had created a richly varied and sophisticated cultural and political world. But the tenuous balance of power among their states, however brilliant the culture, crumbled before the much larger forces of newly invigorated and centralized monarchies.

The Italian response to this political chaos can be seen in the lives and writings of Baldassare Castiglione (1478–1529), Francesco Guicciardini (1483–1540), and Niccolò Machiavelli (1469–1527). Castiglione, author of *The Book of the Courtier* (1528), was born near Mantua and educated in Milan and afterwards served nobles and popes as a scholar, poet, and diplomat. Guicciardini, a Florentine from a leading patrician family, served the Medici rulers in a variety of posts until a falling out with his prince forced him into retirement. Machiavelli, a Florentine from a poor noble family who was elected second chancellor of Florence in 1498 and went on missions to the king of France, the Holy Roman emperor, and others. When the Florentine republic was overthrown in 1512, he began writing his famous little book titled *The Prince*—a vain attempt to win the favor of the restored Medici rulers. Castiglione, Guicciardini, and Machiavelli flew high on talent and humanistic education, moved among the powerful men of the age, and died disappointed politicians and prolific writers. Significantly, each wrote in Tuscan, the Florentine dialect that since Dante's time had served as the Italian literary language and had received such glorious use by Dante, Petrarch, and Boccaccio.

Castiglione's *Courtier* gave a wealth of specific information on how to become the perfect courtier. The book, above all, skillfully popularizes humanistic ideas about education, culture, and thought, drawing heavily on Cicero, Plutarch, and Ficino's Neoplatonism. "I would," Castiglione wrote, "have the courtier devote all his thought and strength of spirit to loving and almost adoring the prince he serves above all else, devoting his every desire and habit and manner to pleasing him." His ideal courtier is encouraged to use all of his polished skills to help his prince govern well and defend his state, but the book offers little realistic advice about politics. The courtier is told that monarchy is the best and most natural form of government and that he and his prince should embody all of the conventional virtues at all times: They must be honorable, prudent, temperate, just, magnanimous, and so on. Such behavior would bring tranquillity, a state that leaves no room for chaotic republican liberty. If the goddess Fortune defeats the prince, as is her wont, then he and his courtiers can still take pride in their honorable behavior and can happily contemplate eternal truths. Castiglione's calm acceptance of princely values helped *The Courtier* to achieve enormous popularity outside Italy, where readers neither experienced nor sympathized with republican government. Indeed, most of them regarded republican regimes much as one Italian aristocrat regarded the city-state of Siena: He scorned it as a place "governed by a hundred tyrants—stocking-makers, locksmiths and other low types—who behave like pigs, so that when one shouts the rest come running."

In sharp contrast, Machiavelli and Guicciardini refused to retreat into Neoplatonist disdain for the active, public life. Machiavelli's *The Prince* offers advice for the use of power in the real world rather than the world as moralists would like it to be. Machiavelli proclaimed that "a man who wishes to make a profession of goodness in everything must necessarily come to grief among so many who are not good." Like Castiglione, he urged the prince to display *virtù* by establishing and maintaining his state, but he thought it absurd to assume that adherence to traditional virtues would achieve those ends. Machiavelli's prince would always appear virtuous while actually performing whatever cruel, miserly, faithless, or deceptive deeds the situation required. *Virtù* for Machiavelli was not a quiver of good

qualities, but the bold and effective use of power to arm oneself against Fortune and win. Fortune would still triumph at times, but a prince could certainly improve the odds by doing unto others as they would probably do unto him if they could.

Machiavelli's younger friend Guicciardini shared in this pessimism about human nature and the rule of Fortune. His *History of Italy* covers the calamitous years from 1492 to 1534 and presents a shrewd and cynical study of the motives and actions of his contemporaries. Like Machiavelli, he believed that wealth had corrupted the Florentine citizenry's willingness to put the common good over private gain. They both hoped, nevertheless, that Italians would somehow reform their institutions and rebuild this essential public spirit, a collective *virtù* that would recreate the splendors of the Roman Republic. They differed, however, over the kinds of republics they admired. The more aristocratic Guicciardini praised the Venetian system with its elaborate devices to minimize the effects of factionalism and class tensions. Machiavelli preferred a more democratic republic, although he doubted that such an institution could actually be established amid the chaos of early sixteenth-century Italy. Nevertheless, in a sharp break with most humanist political thought, he held that the tensions between nobles and popolani would strengthen the commonwealth in the long run.

Machiavelli's *Discourses on Livy*, written after the Florentine republic he had served was overthrown, reveal his true political views. Rejected by the new Medici rulers, he advised citizens, rather than the prince, to behave as good Christians *except* when their liberty was threatened. By "liberty" Machiavelli meant freedom from foreign domination and freedom to maintain the republican institutions that enabled all to aspire to the highest offices and honors. He urged people to use whatever means, however bloody, unjust, or deceitful, to preserve this precious liberty. Advice of this sort earned Machiavelli an odious reputation because it seemed to deny all traditional morality. Moralists, preachers, and dramatists repeatedly denounced him as an emissary of the devil. For example, one French writer declared in 1576 that Machiavelli's ideas were "vicious and detestable in the highest degree." But few read him carefully enough to realize what he was really saying: that the end justifies the means only if that end, as it was for Judith against Holofernes, is the liberty of one's homeland and one's people.

More acutely than any of his contemporaries, Machiavelli anticipated the coming of the modern nation-state. His political analysis revealed his awareness that the older devotion to Christendom was yielding to a new, secular **ideology** of devotion to the state. The fierce local patriotism of the medieval and Renaissance city-states proved the forerunner of future loyalties—as reflected in the famous nineteenth-century American's toast: "Our country, right or wrong." Machiavelli ended his advice to the Medici prince with this heartfelt appeal to Italian patriotism: "This barbarian occupation stinks in all our nostrils! Let your illustrious house . . . take up this task with that courage and with that hope which suit a just enterprise; so that, under your banner, our country may become noble again."

THE ARTS AND TECHNOLOGY IN THE RENAISSANCE

In the Middle Ages the principal source of artistic patronage had been the church, but the commercial civilizations of high-medieval Italy and Flanders produced an increase in commissions from laypersons and secular institutions such as guilds and princely courts. During the Renaissance in Italy, the creation of music for secular purposes expanded significantly, especially with the emergence of new forms (frottola, villanella, madrigal) employing lively rhythms, vernacular texts, and four or five singers. In the heyday of city-republics, the values of the elite had militated against personal display of wealth and encouraged the exercise of patronage through government and guilds for the benefit of the community as a whole. But as communes fell increasingly under the control of princes and oligarchies, personal display grew more common. Demand for portraits rose, as well as the desire for grandiose private houses, chapels, and tombs.

THE HUMAN EXPERIENCE

Maso di Bartolommeo, Artisan and Businessman

The decorative arts formed a booming sector in the economy of Renaissance Florence. The guild that included masons, woodworkers, artists, and architects had more than nine hundred members in 1391, perhaps 20 percent of the total craft guild membership in the city. Art was big business, as the guilds themselves, the church, and rich private patrons commissioned grand structures and insisted that they be magnificently decorated. Behind the first rank of such famous men as Ghiberti, Donatello, and Brunelleschi stood others working in the same materials. One who did so successfully was a stonemason and metalworker named Maso di Bartolommeo (1406–1457).

The story of Maso's progress began 10 miles from Florence in the town of Prato. Michelozzo Michelozzi (1396–1472), later architect of the Medici palace and then in partnership with Donatello, hired Maso to assist them on a major project—the Prato cathedral's outdoor pulpit. At one point during the lengthy work on the Prato pulpit, Maso had to go to Florence to persuade Donatello to return to Prato to complete the work. The comment on the account of his expenses was blunt: "He made a fool of us." This resentment did not prevent Maso from producing bronze statuettes based on Donatello's bronze *David* that were popular because they celebrated Florence's victory over Milan. In Florence between 1443 and 1449, Maso and his brother Giovanni cast objects in bronze for the Duomo (cathedral): a staircase, several bells, and a grill. In his rented shop on Via Porta Rossa, Maso housed the equipment for this demanding work, which also included casting cannon for Florence and other cities. By no means was all of Maso's work subcontracted from Michelozzo. Maso employed workers as he needed them for bronze casting, quarrying, and stonecutting. He also kept up a good business in other objects such as coats of arms, candlesticks, chandeliers, gratings, church steps, fireplace mantels, and water basins. He worked on the palace of the Duke of Urbino and on the Medici palace itself.

Much is known about Maso's activities because he was an excellent bookkeeper. His *Libro di Ricordi* (account book) for 1448–1455 has survived. Thoroughly cross-referenced, the accounts show, for example, how Florentines could serve as each other's bankers. Maso's landlady, instead of receiving his rent payments, simply sent people to whom she owed money to him to collect cash. In the same way, well-established artisans might use debts owed them by their employers to pay their own debts. Maso frequently paid his employees in gold florins rather than in smaller silver and copper coins—yet he carefully noted the exchange value on that day in lire because the value of the lire (a money of account) tended to depreciate in relation to the florin. Maso's book reveals "a systematic approach to accounting that is in some respects superior to the way many great London merchants kept their account books as late as the seventeenth century."* With their thriving trade, thorough record-keeping, and careful craftsmanship, small businessmen like Maso contributed significantly to the maturation of the Florentine economy and the quality of the city's life. ❖

*From Richard A. Goldthwaite, *The Building of Renaissance Florence* (Baltimore: Johns Hopkins University Press, 1980), p. 314.

Both lay and clerical patrons made contracts with artists that spelled out the character of the artwork and the process of producing it in considerable detail. In 1485, for example, one painter agreed to paint a scene depicting the adoration of the Magi: "He is to color and paint the said panel all with his own hand in the manner shown in a drawing on paper with those figures and in that manner shown in it, in every particular according to what I, Fra Bernardo [the patron], think best." The contract specified the quality of the pigments and other materials, the date of completion, and the amount to be deducted if the deadline was missed. Fra Bernardo even insisted that if the piece did not seem worth the price of 115 florins after it was finished, the painter would "receive as much less as I . . . think right."

The spread of humanism stimulated artists to take an interest in classical subjects and grasp the opportunity to paint and sculpt them. Some of the most admired artists gained higher social status as the fine arts came to be regarded as appropriate pursuits for gentlemen with

Donatello's *David* Although fighting Goliath naked might seem foolhardy, Donatello's depiction was based on the biblical account in which David himself rejected the offer of armor. The implication, which favored Florentine chauvinism, was that David's true protection (like the city's) came from God's favor. This bronze statue was taken to join Donatello's *Judith and Holofernes* in front of the Palazzo della Signoria in 1495. *Scala/Art Resource, NY.*

Ghiberti's *The Sacrifice of Isaac* In 1401 Ghiberti entered a competition to create a pair of bronze doors for the Baptistery next to the Duomo in Florence. His winning proposal, *Sacrifice of Isaac*, placed foreground figures projecting farther out from the panel than those farther back, an important step in the development of perspective. *Scala/Art Resource, NY.*

humanistic educations. Readers of Castiglione's *Courtier* were reminded that the ancient Greeks "required boys of gentle birth to learn painting in school . . . and admitted it to first rank among the liberal arts" and that the Romans too had held it "in highest honor."

The church, however, remained the largest single patron, and by the latter part of the fifteenth century Rome replaced Florence as the artistic center of the Renaissance. Laypersons, too, continued to commission works on religious subjects. The trend toward more natural and realistic depictions did not necessarily indicate a decline of interest in religion. But whether a subject was religious or secular, the keynotes of the new style were realism (imitation of nature) and classicism (imitation of subjects, themes, and styles from classical antiquity), fused into a striving to express deep feelings about human life.

Donatello's *Herod's Feast* Donatello executed this gilt-bronze relief in the mid-1420s for the baptismal font of Siena's cathedral. As the head of John the Baptist is presented, the shocked expressions of Herod and his guests and the swirling figure of Salome closely observing her stepfather are vividly shown. Two children (to the left) flee from the horrible scene. *Scala/Art Resource, NY.*

The Arts in the Quattrocento

The influence of humanistic studies was felt upon all the arts. People interested in music, for example, debated ancient Greek theories about how emotion could best be expressed musically and experimented with ancient scale patterns. In 1501, Ottaviano Petrucci (1466–1539) discovered how to print music using movable type. Petrucci, who had received a humanist education at the court of Urbino, established a music publishing house in Venice that soon had imitators in Rome, Milan, and elsewhere.

But humanism's influence is nowhere more apparent than in the architectural and sculptural achievements of Renaissance Italy. Like writers and philosophers, artists made a conscious effort to imitate classical styles. An important Florentine guild, the finishers and dyers of wool cloth, in 1401 commissioned bronze doors for the Baptistery, a splendid Romanesque structure next to the still unfinished Duomo (Florence cathedral). The winner of the design competition was Lorenzo Ghiberti (ca. 1378–1455), whose panel depicting the sacrifice of Isaac combined the classical nude torso of the young victim with new realism in the handling of space.

Assisting Ghiberti was a young man who would eventually surpass him and become the greatest sculptor since classical times: Donatello (1386–1466), creator of the powerful *Judith and Holofernes* shown at the beginning of this chapter as well as the marble *David* that the Signoria com-

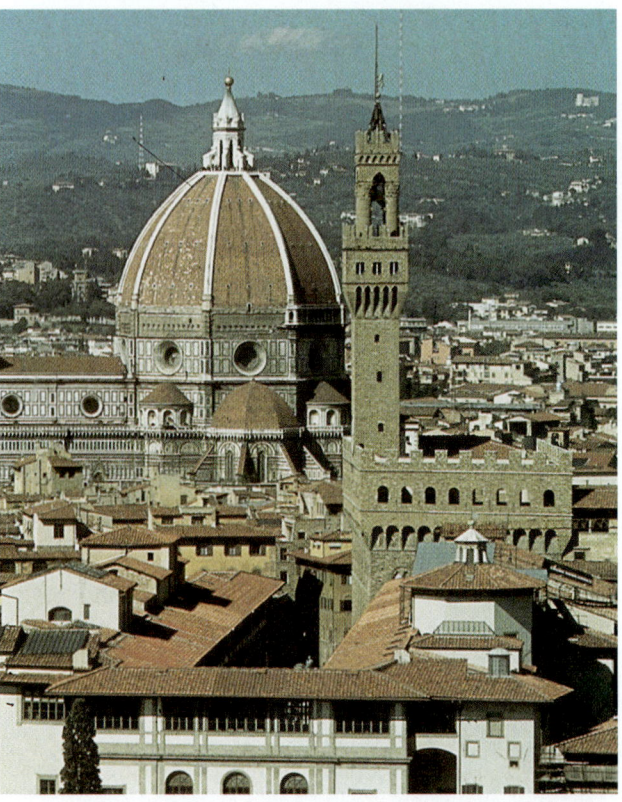

Brunelleschi's Dome Growing up in Florence, Michelangelo saw Brunelleschi's magnificent octagonal dome on the Duomo, and he described the one he designed, for St. Peter's in Rome, as the "sister" of the one in Florence: "I am going to make its sister, bigger, yes, but not any more beautiful." *Scala/Art Resource, NY.*

Constructing Brunelleschi's Dome This sketch, probably by one of Brunelleschi's assistants, shows how the Duomo scaffolding inside the dome looked, although exactly how the astonishing technical feat was accomplished remains unknown. *Museo dell' Opera del Duomo, Florence.*

Giotto's *The Kiss of Judas*
In this fresco in the Arena Chapel in Padua (ca. 1305), the landscape background Giotto painted lacks realism, but the figures draped in their cloaks are quite different. Judas's arm around Christ as he identifies him to his enemies with a kiss creates a dramatic, vivid moment. *Scrovegni (Arena) Chapel, Padua, Italy/The Bridgeman Art Library.*

missioned in 1416 to symbolize the city's defiance of Milan. Probably acting on a commission made soon after the victory of Anghiari in 1440, Donatello made a different *David,* which was "the first free-standing naked figure executed in bronze since antiquity."[11] The bronze David has long hair, wears a rustic hat, and stands with his foot proudly planted on Goliath's head. The statue thus celebrates another successful defense of Florence's independence. Donatello's works reflect the world as we see it, but they also dramatize it. One of his bronze reliefs for the Siena Baptistery, *Herod's Feast,* is a good example of both mathematical perspective and dramatization. Once, while working on the statue of a prophet, Donatello is said to have shouted, "Speak, speak, or the plague take you!"

One loser in the competition for the Baptistery doors in Florence was Filippo Brunelleschi (1377–1446). This son of a notary, initially trained (like Ghiberti) as a gold-

smith, turned his efforts from sculpture to architecture and is remembered as the first great Renaissance architect. His initial triumph was the completion of the Duomo commissioned by the wool guild of Florence. Begun in 1299, construction had proceeded slowly throughout the fourteenth century, as numerous architects failed to solve the problem of building a dome to cover the huge opening (140 feet in diameter) over the choir. Ghiberti had also proposed a solution, but this time Brunelleschi won. He built two interior shells rather than a solid mass, thereby lessening the weight, and he invented hoisting machines to raise materials, instead of using traditional ramps and scaffolds. Cosimo de' Medici reportedly recommended him to Pope Eugenius as "a man whose powers are so great that he could build a vault over the world."

Brunelleschi also displayed his astonishing technical ingenuity by inventing a method of drawing according to mathematical perspective—determining a vanishing point in relation to which the sizes of all objects in a picture are scientifically determined. Painters and sculptors quickly adapted this method to attain much greater realism. With his knowledge of mathematics and optics, neither of which

---

[11] John Pope-Hennessy, *Donatello, Sculptor* (New York: Abbeville Press, 1993), p. 147.

Masaccio's _Holy Trinity_ Masaccio pioneered the new technique of perspective, creating the illusion that the flat wall on which he painted this fresco had been punched through and a church built behind it. By inserting depth cues, he made the figures appear to be at different distances, as indicated in Figure 12-3. For example, the kneeling figures in the front are life-size, whereas the standing pair just inside the pillars are smaller (about 5 feet tall). The architectural setting is classical, a building that Alberti, Bramante, or Brunelleschi might have designed. _Santa Maria Novella, Florence, Italy/The Bridgeman Art Library._

had much interested humanists, Brunelleschi (together with Donatello) began a close study of the ruined buildings of classical Rome. He was soon designing buildings that embodied Greco-Roman principles of symmetry and regularity. He insisted on harmonious proportions in which the ratios between the height, length, and depth of spaces be expressible, like those of musical harmony, in whole numbers. These ratios, Brunelleschi believed, because they existed everywhere in the universe, must have come from God. The hallmarks of his elegant and thoroughly un-Gothic style—round-arched arcades, rounded roofs and ceilings (cupolas), flat walls simply adorned with ornamental columns (pilasters)—appear in Florence's foundling hospital (built for the silk guild, 1419–1424), the churches of San Lorenzo and Santo Spirito, and the Pazzi Chapel.

Early Renaissance painters, by contrast, could not imitate classical painting because so little of it had survived. They aspired, nevertheless, to create works of art in the classical and naturalistic manner, and they found in the frescoes of the late medieval artist Giotto (1276–1337) a major source of inspiration. A Florentine chronicler said at the beginning of the fifteenth century that Giotto's figures were so natural that they appeared "to speak, to weep, to rejoice" (see page 457). Yet Giotto himself had been influenced by Gothic statuary, and similar trends figure into the work of the first and most important early Renaissance painter, Masaccio (1401–1428). In his _Holy Trinity_ fresco in Santa Maria Novella, this young Florentine genius produced the first painting to use Brunelleschi's mathematical perspective (see Figure 12-3). In the recently cleaned Brancacci Chapel frescoes depicting the expulsion of Adam and Eve from the Garden of Eden, Masaccio achieved an amazing realism and dramatic impact. These new methods of depicting emotion and movement in paintings parallel Donatello's innovations in sculpture. And Masaccio pioneered _chiaroscuro_, the technique—available only to painters—of using light and shade to heighten the realism

FIGURE 12-3
PERSPECTIVE IN MASACCIO'S _HOLY TRINITY_ FRESCO

This two-dimensional architectural drawing shows how Masaccio used Brunelleschi's mathematical perspective theories for his fresco of the _Holy Trinity_ in the chapel in Santa Maria Novella.
Source: Adapted from Gene Brucker, _Florence: The Golden Age, 1138–1737_ (Berkeley and Los Angeles: University of California Press, 1998), p. 207.

Botticelli's *The Birth of Venus* Botticelli's ethereal, haunting figures in this painting do not, like those of Masaccio, have their feet firmly on the ground, nor do they have Donatello's solid, muscular strength and dynamic tension. They seem to float, as if yearning to escape to a higher, spiritual world. Lorenzo de' Medici and his friends particularly admired Botticelli's work.   *Galleria degli Uffizi, Florence, Italy/The Bridgeman Art Library.*

of his compositions. Not until Michelangelo painted the Sistine Chapel nearly a century later would Masaccio's work be equaled in these respects.

The mid-fifteenth-century shift in attitudes from civic to Neoplatonist humanism had parallels in the arts. The works of Sandro Botticelli (1444–1510) reflect this change. In his most famous painting, *The Birth of Venus*, the classical Roman goddess of love and beauty had, in Neoplatonist thought, a celestial counterpart—the Virgin Mary, representing divine love. The complex religious imagery of Botticelli's paintings could be understood only by a small coterie of men like Castiglione's courtiers, who spent their days in gracious pursuits and discussed such philosophical matters as the parallels between classical and biblical symbols.

The High Renaissance

Between 1495 when Leonardo da Vinci began work on his famous fresco, *The Last Supper,* and the sack of Rome in 1527 came the short but astonishingly creative High Renaissance. Leonardo (1452–1519), the illegitimate son of a Florentine lawyer, excelled as civil and military engi-

neer, architect, inventor, and scientist no less than as a painter and is often thought of as the perfect "Renaissance man." Yet he lacked the knowledge of classical languages and literature that was the core of a humanistic education. In any case, he was contemptuous of the humanists as bookworms and windbags. Like most artists of his day, he was apprenticed to a senior artist to learn his craft and therefore had little time for humanistic study. His voluminous notebooks are chock full of carefully drawn details of human and animal bodies and plants, as well as ideas and inventions far ahead of their time (among them: machine guns, armored military cars, helicopters, earth-moving machines, and diving helmets). In producing the first rigorously accurate botanical and anatomical drawings, Leonardo veered sharply from the interests of the earlier humanists, who had focused on humanity and society rather than nature. In applying science to art, he completed the trend begun when Brunelleschi combined optics and mathematics to invent perspective. Leonardo argued that the painter had to know anatomy so that he could portray motion by showing the muscles of a person or an animal performing particular movements. Otherwise, as he put it, the figures would "seem a sack full of nuts rather

Leonardo da Vinci's *War Machines* Whether serving princes or republics, many artists were called upon to exercise their imaginations on military as well as religious and other pursuits. Leonardo's idea for a chariot-like device with whirling blades was never realized, but his wheeled, armored, gun-carrying vehicle fore-shadowed the warhorse of modern battlefields: the tank. *British Museum, London, UK/The Bridgeman Art Library.*

Michelangelo's *The Pietà* In contrast to Leonardo, Raphael, and Titian, Michelangelo considered himself a sculptor above all else. His wet nurse was the wife of a stonecutter, and he later said that he acquired his fascination for marble "with my mother's milk." He sculpted his first *Pietà* when he was twenty-four. The youthful Virgin, with her tender expression, holds her dead son's body. He signed his name on the strap that crosses her shoulder. Michelangelo's ability to express human feeling in marble has never been surpassed. *St. Peter's Vatican, Rome, Italy/The Bridgeman Art Library.*

than the surface of a human being or indeed, a bundle of radishes rather than muscular nudes."

But Leonardo's genius was not restricted to technical mastery and scientifically observed detail. These techniques served a higher goal—the portrayal through gestures and movement of what he called "the intention of man's soul." Earlier painters had depicted the Last Supper, but none had captured the dramatic moment when Christ announced, "One of you shall betray me," while holding out his hands in a gesture of resignation. By placing the vanishing point directly behind Christ's head, Leonardo focused the viewer's attention on him (see page 449). Much better preserved than the fresco in Milan is his oil portrait, the *Mona Lisa*. Perhaps the most famous painting in Western art, it combines in perfect balance a real woman with the ideal of womanhood.

Like Leonardo, Donato Bramante (1444–1514) spent a large part of his career working for Ludovico Sforza, the despot of Milan. But in 1499 he moved to Rome, where he soon received commissions from Pope Julius II to design a new St. Peter's basilica and rebuild much of the Vatican. Bramante brought to Rome the humanist ideas about architecture initiated by Brunelleschi—classicism and a preference for circular plans, a style imitated ever since not only in churches and palaces but even in American legislative halls. Bramante's design for St. Peter's was boldly ambitious, but when he died in 1514 only the main piers of the new structure had been built. Shortage of money and political crises slowed progress until Michelangelo took

Michelangelo's *Last Judgment* Covering the entire east wall above the altar in the Sistine Chapel, this recently restored fresco conveyed ideas then circulating in Italy about the need for church reform. Immediately below Christ's left leg, St. Bartholomew holds a flayed skin representing the mode of his martyrdom, and on the skin is a grimly distorted self-portrait of the artist. *Vatican Museums and Galleries, Vatican City, Italy/ The Bridgeman Art Library.*

over in 1546. Michelangelo's completed version, although huge, is one-third smaller than Bramante's church would have been (see page 450).

The prolific Raphael (1483–1520) succeeded Bramante as architect of St. Peter's. Both hailed from Urbino, and both were bitter rivals of Michelangelo. Bramante used his prestige to promote Raphael's career while putting roadblocks in Michelangelo's way. Raphael was urbane, affable, easily successful. His art resulted from long study and an ability to synthesize into his own style the ideas of the great masters of his day. Raphael was famous for his superb Madonnas, and his frescoes in the Vatican's papal apartments are triumphs of color, realism, balance, and vivid narrative. Many combined a Bramantesque architec-

tural setting with the symmetry of Leonardo's *Last Supper* and the lively energy of Michelangelo's Sistine Chapel scenes. They suited well the Renaissance papacy's ambitious program to dramatize the church's theology and the power of its leadership (see page 451).

Michelangelo (1475–1564), quite unlike the cheery Raphael whom he disliked, was a moody, difficult, suspicious man. His father wanted him to become a merchant, but he stubbornly insisted on an artistic career. From 1490 to 1492 he lived in Lorenzo de' Medici's household, and, like Botticelli, was deeply impressed by the Neoplatonic Christianity of Ficino and the prophecy of Savonarola. In Rome, during the years between 1496 and 1500, he won instant fame by producing a life-sized *Pietà* expressing the

Neoplatonic idea that physical beauty reflects spiritual beauty.

In 1501 Michelangelo returned to Florence. Inspired by classical statues he had studied in Rome, he began his famous 17-foot-high marble *David*, commissioned by the reborn Florentine republic to celebrate its triumph over Piero de' Medici. In 1505 he was recalled to Rome by Pope Julius II to commence work on Julius's tomb. Three years later Julius urged him to turn his attention to painting the Sistine Chapel ceiling. Michelangelo protested that he was a sculptor, not a painter, but the pope persisted, and eventually Michelangelo set to work with furious energy so that he could return to his marble as soon as possible. He suspected that his enemy Bramante had talked the pope into giving him the task, expecting him to fail. To Michelangelo's supreme disappointment, his initial plan for the tomb was never fulfilled, but in less than four years he covered 5,800 square feet of Sistine ceiling with one of the greatest paintings in Western art. The nine central scenes from Genesis, prefiguring human salvation through Christ, were almost certainly suggested by the humanistically inclined theologians of Julius's court. The powerful figures, with their strength and vitality, are like huge painted sculptures, and the ceiling implies a calm confidence in God's protection of his creatures through infusions of the divine spirit.

Julius died in 1513, only four months after the ceiling was completed, and Michelangelo went back to his beloved Florence. There he worked mainly on architectural and sculptural commissions for the two Medici popes, Leo X and Clement VII. The Rome to which he returned in 1534 had been devastated physically by warfare and psychologically by the outbreak of the Protestant Reformation (see Chapter 13). It was therefore in a very different atmosphere that he undertook his later works—the completion of St. Peter's, the rebuilding of Rome's civic center (the Campidoglio), and the *Last Judgment* fresco on the altar wall of the Sistine Chapel.

The *Last Judgment* best reveals the changes of style and mood. Gone is the calm assurance and harmonious balance of the High Renaissance. The wrathful Christ at the center pronounces the terrible sentence on writhing figures—the saved seem almost as frightened as do the damned. It is no wonder that when Paul III first saw this awesome painting, he dropped to his knees to pray. Nor is it any wonder that a younger contemporary, Giorgio Vasari, in his *Lives of the Painters, Sculptors, and Architects,* wrote of Michelangelo that God had sent to earth "a spirit capable of supreme expression in all the arts, one able to give form to painting, perfection to sculpture, and grandeur to architecture." Although the Italians lost the political freedom that had helped inspire the Renaissance, their artists and thinkers created a culture of astonishing power and far-reaching influence.

THE RENAISSANCE IN THE NORTH

By the sixteenth century, humanism was thriving outside of Italy. Italian humanists traveled, lectured, and taught in other countries, and many Spaniards and northern Europeans studied in Italy, encountered the new learning at its source, and then took it back home. Henry VIII of England, Francis I of France, his sister Marguerite, queen of Navarre, and the Holy Roman emperor, Maximilian I, were among those princes who sought with considerable success to make their courts centers of humanistic creativity. Princely support frequently forced the conservative opponents of humanism on the defensive in their effort to preserve scholasticism's domination of university education. First in Spain and later across northern Europe during the sixteenth century, men could expect to achieve high government office only if they had mastered classical Latin and been educated in the Renaissance humanist curriculum. Increasingly, humanistically educated laymen made their way into government service. Spanish, French, English, German, and Polish translations of Castiglione's *Courtier*

Erasmus In 1523, Hans Holbein painted this portrait of Erasmus. Given the Dutch humanist's huge literary output, he must have spent most of his time with pen in hand, just as Holbein depicted him. *Louvre, Paris, France/The Bridgeman Art Library.*

demonstrated that a movement that had originated in Italian city-republics could prosper in monarchies beyond the Alps.

Christian Humanism and Erasmus

Around 1500, northern humanism underwent an important change of orientation best expressed in the terms *Christian humanism* and *biblical humanism*. Italian humanists had been primarily although by no means exclusively preoccupied with the literature and culture of pagan antiquity and with the application of its values and insights to secular issues and concerns. Although some Italian humanists had argued for religious reform, they had never enunciated a specific reformist program. However, the Frenchman Jacques Lefèvre d'E'taples (ca. 1455–1536) and the Dutchman Desiderius Erasmus (ca. 1466–1536) created just such a program. Appropriating the methods that Petrarch and his successors had used when they applied the ideas of Cicero and other pagan writers to the literature of Christian antiquity, these northern scholars applied those same techniques of discovering, editing, and criticizing to the texts of Christian antiquity. Both thought (like Petrarch) that loving God and living as a Christian were more important than knowing theological doctrines and arguing about them. Whereas the Italians sought social and moral reform of their communities through invigorating contact with classic literature, Christian humanists sought reform of the church through the inspiration provided by the wisdom of Christ, his apostles, and leaders of the ancient church. Lefèvre's *Fivefold Psalter* (1509), which placed different ancient texts of the Psalms side by side for comparison, and his commentary on St. Paul's epistles (1512) constituted pioneering contributions to the new biblical humanism.

Erasmus, the most prolific, brilliant, and famous Christian humanist, visited and corresponded with princes and popes while carefully maintaining his independence of them. All over Europe people read Erasmus's amazing output of translations, commentaries, treatises, dialogues, and satires. Erasmus worked to take the Bible and writings of the early Church Fathers out of the exclusive custody of scholastic theologians (whom he charged with completely misunderstanding them), to perfect them by correcting textual errors introduced by medieval writers who lacked command of the ancient languages, and to make them available to all. A superb writer who shrewdly burnished the image of himself and the movement he wished to present to the world, Erasmus understood the enormous power of the printing press. He made printing shops, rather than universities or princely courts, his base of operations. He used the critical methods developed most spectacularly by Lorenzo Valla to make the Scriptures available in everyday language so that many more people could read and understand them. Erasmus wrote that the result would be the emergence of "a genuine race of Christians everywhere, a people who would restore the philosophy of Christ not in ceremonies alone and syllogistic propositions but in the heart itself and the whole life."

Erasmus, the illegitimate son of a Dutch priest, placed the "philosophy of Christ" (as he called it) at the center of his program for individual and social reform. He contrasted the "finespun trifles" of scholastic philosophy with Christ's example of simple goodness, peace, and love. Individual salvation and moral reform could not, he insisted, be attained by praying to Christ for miraculous intervention against natural laws but by truly understanding Christ and imitating his moral example. Venerating relics and saints and making pilgrimages, then so popular, would disappear as people began to emulate the moral integrity of the saints instead of praying to their earthly remains.

Erasmus's most effective weapon was satire. His *Praise of Folly* (1511) ridiculed the long-winded debates of scholastic theologians over "whether God could have taken upon Himself the likeness of a woman? Or of a devil? Of an ass? Of a gourd? Of a piece of flint?" With devastating wit, *Folly* attacks clergymen of all types who mind their privileges and purses zealously while failing to attend to the spiritual needs of the people. Popes guilty of such worldliness, such as Julius II, did not escape Erasmus's censure. However, his purpose was reform of the church and its clergy, not their overthrow, and he was delighted when Pope Leo X accepted the dedication of his 1516 edition of the New Testament. Erasmus objected not to the church's theology but to the behavior of many of its clergymen.

Thomas More's Humanist Utopia

Erasmus's English friend, Sir Thomas More (1478–1535), in his famous book *Utopia* (1516), was more obliquely satirical. He coined the word **utopia** from Greek words that meant "no place," a signal that he was describing an imaginary commonwealth rather than one that actually existed or could exist. The work's first section, the "Dialogue of Counsel," wrestles with a question central to humanist thought: Is an educated person morally obligated to take part in public affairs (*negotium*)? Should a humanist stand aloof from the court, filled with people who flatter the prince in order to gain his favor, or should the humanist plunge into the struggle to get the prince's ear in order to convince him that, as More wrote, "it is the king's duty to take more care of his people's welfare than of his own?"

More's fictional narrator argues for the latter course of action because he claims to have had a lengthy sojourn on an island whose people have abolished private property and live peaceful, happy lives unmarred by the pride and greed so prevalent among Europeans. In the land of Utopia, "virtue has its own reward, yet everything is shared equally, and all men live in plenty." By imagining a place where people live charitably and amicably among themselves although they have never heard of Christianity, More attacked the moral and social evils of unreformed Christian Europe. The Utopians showed their disdain for gold by using it to make chamber pots and chains for prisoners; and they permitted no idleness, with the result that production was so high that no one had to work more than six hours a day. A man and a woman considering marriage had to display themselves to each other naked (chaperoned, of course, by discreet elders) to ensure against sexual disappointment, but marriage once entered into was generally inviolate. Adultery was punished by slavery. The Utopians dined communally and dressed simply and identically. Their highly regulated and austere utopian lives, somewhat reminiscent of the "philosopher-kings" in Plato's *Republic* (see Chapter 3) embody both the reformist and the repressive aspects of the humanist agenda.

CONCLUSION: THE RENAISSANCE AND THE COMING REFORMATION

The Renaissance began in Italy long before the new technology of printing existed, but by late in the fifteenth century Italian humanists such as Ficino and Pico employed it to disseminate their work. Early in the sixteenth century,

northern humanists such as Erasmus and his followers took full advantage of the new medium to spread their Christian humanist call for reform. Both the Italian and northern humanists had redirected the sophisticated culture of high-medieval Europe by rediscovering and reinterpreting the legacy of pagan and classical antiquity. The humanists deeply believed that the ancient Greeks and Romans who had lived before, during, and after the advent of Christianity had produced a body of texts that contained the solutions to all the religious, social, moral, and political problems that sixteenth-century Europe faced. In 1516—the year in which Erasmus published his New Testament, a nine-volume edition of the works of St. Jerome, as well as his edition of Seneca's works—the humanists' optimism about the future seemed fully justified. In the second decade of the sixteenth century, many educated Europeans expected that Christendom's ecclesiastical and political institutions were about to undergo gradual but steady improvement as Erasmian Christian humanism gained adherents.

They were wrong. Although methods and ideas created during the fifteenth-century Renaissance continued to shape all reforming movements during the sixteenth century and thereafter, Europe at the beginning of the sixteenth century lay on the brink not of peaceful reform, but of a century and a half of struggle and warfare between Protestants and Catholics.

Selected Reading

Sources

Brucker, Gene, ed. *Two Memoirs of Renaissance Florence* (1957).

Cassirer E., Kristeller P. O., and J. H. Randall, eds. *The Renaissance Philosophy of Man* (1948).

Erasmus, Desiderius. *The Praise of Folly*, trans. C. H. Miller (1979).

Machiavelli, Niccolò. *The Prince*, trans. R. M. Adams (1977).

The Portable Renaissance Reader, eds. J. B. Ross and M. M. McLaughlin (1953).

The Renaissance

Aston, Margaret, ed. *The Panorama of the Renaissance* (1996). Copiously illustrated overview of the major topics of the Renaissance era.

Burckhardt, Jacob. *Civilization of the Renaissance in Italy* (1990). A highly influential, if no longer wholly convincing, argument for the modernity of the Renaissance, first published in 1860.

Hale, J. R. *The Civilization of Europe in the Renaissance* (1993). A richly detailed, topically organized survey of "the long sixteenth century" (1450–1620), the interval during which "Europeans" first came to see themselves as an identifiable entity despite their many differences.

Hay, Denys, and John Law. *Italy in the Age of the Renaissance, 1380–1530* (1989). A clear and balanced survey that incorporates recent scholarship effectively.

Martines, Lauro. *Power and Imagination: City-States in Renaissance Italy* (1979). An ambitious study of the complex relationships between political, intellectual, moral, and aesthetic developments from the medieval communes to the High Renaissance.

Nauert, Charles G. Jr. *Humanism and the Culture of Renaissance Europe* (1995). Offers a brisk introduction to the humanist movement and its development through the late Renaissance; has an excellent bibliographical essay.

Rabil, Albert Jr., ed. *Renaissance Humanism*, 3 vols. (1988). A massive collective scholarly enterprise covering humanism's origins and development.

Skinner, Quentin. *The Foundations of Modern Political Thought*, vol. 1, *The Renaissance* (1979). Examines the minor as well as the major political writers of the Renaissance after an illuminating survey of selected themes in late medieval political thought.

The Renaissance States

Baron, Hans. *The Crisis of the Early Italian Renaissance* (1966). A revised edition of the most important study of Florentine civic humanism.

Brucker, Gene A. *Renaissance Florence* (1969). An excellent introduction to Florentine politics, society, culture, and the connections between them.

Gundersheimer, Werner L. *Ferrara: The Style of a Renaissance Despotism* (1973). A vivid and penetrating study of one of the first medieval communes to choose despotic rule.

Holmes, George. *The Florentine Enlightenment* (1969). A fine discussion of the linkage between philosophical, literary, and artistic developments in the first half of the fifteenth century, with emphasis on the connections between Florence and the papacy.

Lane, Frederick C. *Venice, a Maritime Republic* (1973). A splendid, comprehensive history of this unique, colorful city.

Stinger, Charles L. *The Renaissance in Rome* (1985). Argues for an ideological and cultural Renaissance in Rome (1443–1527) that differed significantly from the movement elsewhere and reached its apogee during the pontificates of Julius II and Leo X.

Renaissance Culture and Society

Baxandall, Michael. *Painting and Experience in Fifteenth-Century Italy*, 2nd ed. (1988). Thoughtful discussion of the relationship between Renaissance society and the style of the pictures its painters produced.

Burke, Peter. *The Italian Renaissance*, rev. ed. (1986). A stimulating exploration of the relationship between the creativity of Renaissance artists and their sociocultural milieu (how works of art were used, how people became artists and writers, their social position, patronage of the arts, and so on).

Goldthwaite, Richard A. *The Building of Renaissance Florence* (1980). Studies the construction industry and the people involved in it from patrons and famous artists through masons, stonecutters, wallers, kiln-men, and day-laborers.

Herlihy, David, and Christiane Klapisch-Zuber. *Tuscans and Their Families* (1985). Uses the Florentine *catasto* (an extensive census of the members and property of some sixty thousand households under the city's control) to produce an amazingly detailed and varied picture of the Florentine social world.

Kelly-Gadol, Joan. *Leon Battista Alberti* (1969). An excellent intellectual biography.

King, Margaret L. *Women of the Renaissance* (1990). Broad survey of women's roles in the family, the church, and the public sphere in Europe between 1350 and 1650.

Klapisch-Zuber, Christiane. *Women, Family, and Ritual in Renaissance Italy* (1985). Includes essays on childhood, marriage, wet-nursing, kinship relations, female celibacy, and related issues.

Smart, Alastair. *The Renaissance and Mannerism in Italy* (1971). A clear and brisk survey of the major painters and sculptors.

CHAPTER *13*

REFORMERS AND REFORMATIONS

Luther's Bible, 1534

1516	Erasmus publishes his Greek New Testament, the basis for vernacular translations all over Europe
1517	Martin Luther's Ninety-Five Theses initiate the Protestant Reformation
1521	Luther's refusal to obey Charles V's orders to recant at the Diet of Worms
1525	The German Peasants' War
1529	Luther and Zwingli's quarrel over the doctrine of the Mass foreshadows the Evangelical-Reformed split in the Protestant movement
1530	The Augsburg Confession
1531	Lutheran princes in Germany form Schmalkaldic League
1533–1534	Henry VIII's rejection of papal claims to jurisdiction in England; Parliament acknowledges Henry as the head of the church in England
1534–1535	Seizure of Münster by radical Anabaptists
1536	Calvin's *Institutes of the Christian Religion* published
1540	Pope Paul III's bull accepts Ignatius of Loyola's new religious order (Society of Jesus, or Jesuits)

1545–1563	Council of Trent meets to reform the Catholic church and address the Protestant challenge
1547	Schmalkaldic League's defeat at Mühlberg by Charles V
1555	Charles V agrees to the Peace of Augsburg; allows German princes to decide whether states will be Lutheran or Catholic
1558	Death of Mary I; succession by her Protestant half-sister, Elizabeth I
1562–1598	French civil wars of religion pit French Calvinists (Huguenots) against the Catholic League
1566	Second Helvetic Confession; revolt of the Netherlands against Philip II of Spain
1572	St. Bartholomew's Day massacre (3,000 Huguenots murdered)
1573	Confederation of Warsaw, a declaration of religious toleration
1588	Failure of Philip II and Spanish Armada to overthrow English and Dutch with a single blow
1598	Henry IV issues Edict of Nantes, allowing a qualified toleration to Huguenots in Catholic France

On June 15, 1520, Pope Leo X condemned a German friar named Martin Luther (1483–1546) and forty-one of his contentions, insisting that Luther retract his views or be excluded from the church. In December 1520, church officials in Cologne and other cities publicly burned Luther's books, and he retaliated by burning the books of his critics. At the Diet of Worms (Germany's imperial representative assembly) in 1521, Luther concluded his refusal to a final demand that he recant by saying, "Here I stand. I can do no other. God help me, Amen." The emperor Charles V's response was no less dramatic: "A single monk, led astray by private judgment, has set himself up against the faith held by all Christians for a thousand years and more, and impudently concludes that all Christians up till now have erred." Luther was told that if he persisted for three weeks in his obstinacy he would be "regarded as a convicted heretic. . . . No one is to harbor him. His followers also are to be condemned.

His books are to be eradicated from the memory of man." When Luther's German translation of the Bible appeared in 1534, it contained vivid woodcuts that displayed the fierce animosity between Luther and the papacy. In the image shown opposite, for example, the "whore of Babylon" rides a frightening beast, wears the papal tiara (a crown with three coronets), and in her left hand holds "the cup of abominations." No reader familiar with the New Testament's Book of Revelation (see Chapter 5) would have failed to recognize that this figure represented the devil, to whom the "kings of the earth" (on the left) were paying homage as she urged them to persecute the people of God. Luther's theological ideas and powerful preaching and writing triggered the Protestant Reformation. The ensuing Protestant-Catholic controversy sparked widespread warfare that afflicted much of Europe for more than a century, culminating in the Thirty Years' War (1618–1648). These "wars of religion" ended a thousand years of Western

Christian unity. Although fundamentally disputes over religious doctrines, they were also much more than that. As people in all walks of life struggled and fought over how to achieve eternal salvation, theological conflicts became intricately linked with cultural, social, political, and economic concerns.

Most Christians, who believed that there could be only one true church, assumed that allowing people to preach or practice false religion, or heresy, would anger God and that he would punish them with wars, rebellions, plagues, and famines. They knew, for example, that bad weather ruined crops, and since they thought that God directly controlled the weather, hunger was the result of divine anger. For many, everyday life consisted of a constant struggle for even a marginal existence. Therefore, people looked to religion to solve economic and social problems. Whereas today we seek reform by means of political parties, and party platforms are in turn shaped by larger ideologies such as **liberalism, socialism,** and communism, we often may not realize how these ideologies are affected by religious traditions. An ideology is an expression of hope about the future, a political program for improving life for one's own and succeeding generations. The still largely rural peoples of the sixteenth century depended primarily on churchmen for their education, their beliefs and traditions, and their reformist ideas. Reform movements in the past had swept through the church, modifying it without destroying its unity. This time, however, the outcome was different. Instead of containing reform internally, the church split into pieces.

POLITICS AND RELIGION ON THE EVE OF THE REFORMATION

Religion played a central role in public life in the sixteenth century, just as it had for medieval Europeans. Princes and magistrates saw themselves commissioned by God, and responsible to God, for keeping order in their territories. The church assisted them in that task by having its courts enforce moral laws (such as those regulating marriage), by educating the laity in its duty to obey the established political authorities, and by providing the only comprehensive means of communication. Indeed, the church was the only institution with an agent (the parish priest) who could speak to the people regularly and inform them of things the rulers wanted them to know. Sixteenth-century Europe experienced rapid rates of population growth and rampant inflation (see Chapter 14), and the potential for social unrest and political instability grew accordingly. When movements for religious reform erupted, the ruling powers could neither ignore them nor resist the urge to use them to meet their own needs.

The Great Powers of Europe at the Beginning of the Sixteenth Century

Europe's complex political structure in the early sixteenth century created the environment in which reformers had to work. France, England, and Spain, although nominally subject to single dynastic rulers, were by no means fully unified internally. Their late medieval kings (see Chapter 11) could not simply issue orders and expect automatic compliance from regions, powerful nobles, representative assemblies, judicial bodies, and urban governments. Even Philip II of Spain, for example, had to spend enormous amounts of time meeting with the *cortes* (assemblies) of his kingdoms. From March through August 1563, he negotiated with the Cortes of Castile in Madrid. In August, Philip left Madrid for the Cortes of Aragon, where the realms of Aragon, Valencia, and Catalonia met separately. Late on Christmas Eve, he ordered that his bed be brought in as a hint to the representatives to hasten matters. Nevertheless, these sessions did not end until 3 A.M. on January 23, 1564. Philip left for Barcelona later that morning.

The Holy Roman emperor, despite his grandiloquent title, exercised even less authority in the German-speaking lands than did his fellow princes in their territories to the west. Unlike them, he attained his office by election. Since 1273, the leading representative of the Habsburg Dynasty had often been elected emperor, and after 1438 he was always elected. The Habsburgs wanted to keep it that way, but it often took generous dispensation of patronage,

TABLE 13-1	
THE POPES OF THE REFORMATION ERA	
Leo X (Medici)	1513–1521
Hadrian VI (Dedal)	1522–1523
Clement VII (Medici)	1523–1534
Paul III (Farnese)	1534–1549
Julius III (del Monte)	1550–1555
Marcellus II (Cervini)	1555
Paul IV (Caraffa)	1555–1559
Pius IV (Medici)*	1559–1565
Pius V (Ghislieri)	1566–1572
Gregory XIII (Buoncampagni)	1572–1585
Sixtus V (Peretti)	1585–1590

* Not related to the Medici family of Florence, to which Leo X and Clement VII had belonged.

FIGURE 13-1
THE HABSBURG DYNASTY

promises, and hard cash to cinch the matter. Although each new emperor was chosen by four secular princes who each bore the title of "elector" (Brandenburg, Bavaria, Saxony, and the Palatinate) and three archbishop-electors (Mainz, Cologne, and Trier), the list of independent and quasi-independent entities with which he had to bargain for resources did not end with these seven powerful men. The representative assembly (Diet) of the empire, known

as the *Reichstag*, also included 30 more lay rulers, 120 bishops and abbots, and 65 cities and towns ("imperial cities") with the right of sending delegates. Germany's lesser nobility, the "imperial knights," although losing ground to cities and territorial princes and having little role in the Reichstag, still had the ability to resist imperial policy when they opposed it—as many often did. Nor could the obedience of German peasants be taken for granted; they rebelled

MAP 13-1
EUROPE IN THE AGE OF CHARLES V, CA. 1526

eighteen times between 1500 and 1524 over economic and legal issues.

When Emperor Maximilian I died in 1519, a Europe-wide political crisis ensued as the pope and the French, among others, opposed the selection of the ranking Habsburg candidate, Maximilian's grandson Charles. The French were horrified by the prospect of Charles assuming authority over so many territories because they feared Habsburg encirclement. Francis I (reigned 1515–1547) felt so threatened that he allied France at times with the Ottoman Turks to escape from what felt like a tightening Habsburg noose. Francis also made alliances with the Renaissance popes and other Italians who wanted to break the Spanish grip on their peninsula. The bitter dynastic rivalry between the Habsburgs and the Valois kings of France dominated European international relations throughout most of the sixteenth century (see Figure 13-1). Dynastic interests, which had dominated medieval politics, continued to far

outweigh national interests in European politics. Indeed, national feeling scarcely counted as a political factor, at least until late in the sixteenth century.

The new emperor, Charles V (1500–1558), was the grandson of Maximilian on one side and of Ferdinand of Aragon and Isabella of Castile on the other. Charles's mother Joanna (Juana), the daughter and sole heir of Ferdinand and Isabella, had married Philip "the Handsome," Archduke of Burgundy (the Netherlands), the son of the Habsburg Holy Roman emperor, Maximilian I. Charles inherited Spain from his mother in 1516, and from his father he inherited the Netherlands as well as a claim to Germany—a claim he made good when elected Holy Roman emperor in 1519. As his chief adviser told him in 1519, "God has set you on the path towards world monarchy"—an extraordinary challenge for a nineteen-year-old who had grown up in the Netherlands speaking Flemish and French. Loans from the Fuggers, a wealthy

Charles V, Holy Roman Emperor   Painted after Charles's victory over the Protestants at Mühlberg in 1547, this 1548 portrait by Titian (like his portrait of Paul III) embodies the Venetian tradition of rich color and subtle use of light and shadow.   *Scala / Art Resource, NY.*

Augsburg-based family of international bankers, enabled Charles to win the election. Jakob Fugger did not hesitate to remind Charles of his debt: "It is well known that Your Imperial Majesty could not have gained the Roman Crown save with my aid, and I can prove the same by the writings of Your Majesty's Agents given by their own hands." Charles's son Philip II later depended heavily on Genoese bankers, as did other monarchs. Although Europe's princes continued to be landowning aristocrats, capitalists involved in banking and commerce played a much more potent role than their counterparts in Mughal India, Ming China, or Tokugawa Japan.

Politics and religion intertwined during the sixteenth century, and Charles V spent most of his life struggling to defend his sprawling territories against the Turks, the French, and the Protestants. Maximilian had added Bohemia and Hungary to the Habsburgs' ancestral lands in Austria, with the result that Charles had to try to hold them, too, against the expanding Muslim empire of the Ottoman Turks. Although Ferdinand and Isabella had presided over the final expulsion of Muslim power from the Iberian Peninsula in 1492, the new Muslim threat posed by the Ottomans on the eastern side of Europe had grown throughout the fifteenth century. The Turks consolidated their grip on the Balkans (including present-day Greece, Bulgaria, Serbia, Bosnia, and Albania) by the 1430s. Ottoman armies led by Suleiman the Magnificent (reigned 1520–1566) conquered most of Hungary by smashing the

Grünewald's Isenheim Altarpiece   This altarpiece, painted between 1512 and 1516, consists of a series of hinged panels that were displayed in several configurations in a monastery in Germany that was devoted to the care of sick people. The panel shown here is a Nativity scene with angels (to the right) serenading the newborn child—but just above the viol-playing angel is a feathered figure representing a fallen angel, Lucifer, who looks in awe and astonishment up toward God. Lucifer's expulsion from heaven was central to the story of how sin had come into the world, which created the need for the penitential system of medieval Catholicism.   *Erich Lessing / Art Resource, NY.*

Hungarian armies at Mohács (1526) and besieged the Habsburg capital of Vienna in 1529 (see Map 13-1). Ottoman ships became increasingly active in the western Mediterranean after capturing Rhodes in 1522. Ironically, the Ottomans gave the Protestant movement invaluable assistance by forcing Charles to send money and troops he would otherwise have used against the heretics in Germany in the 1520s.

Religious Currents in the Early Sixteenth Century

In the decades around 1500, Europeans took pleasure in and received comfort from their religion, and they supported it with their time, energy, and resources. The popularity of religious guilds and confraternities—associations in which groups of people in the same craft or trade or with other common interests joined together to hear **Mass** and care for their poorer members—stood at its peak early in the sixteenth century. The church organized, with the vigorous support of whole communities, a plethora of processions, festivals, and plays throughout the year to honor Christ, his mother, and the saints. Most people participated in these religious activities and indeed helped shape them in ways that made them more satisfying. Wills provide one tangible indication of this satisfaction; in the first half of the sixteenth century in England, for example, nearly all testators made religious bequests, especially to parish churches.

Late medieval Christians embraced the church's doctrine that they could gain both divine favor in this life and eternal salvation in the next through the sacrament of penance. The penitential cycle required sincere confession of sins at least once a year to a priest and dutiful performance of the works (penances) he prescribed to remove the guilt that each sin imposed. Any sins left unexpiated by penance at the time of death had to be atoned for by sufferings the soul would undergo in purgatory, after which it would proceed to heaven. Anxiety about purgatory, however, was allayed by the church's offer of indulgences—papally authorized documents that penitent sinners could obtain by doing particular good works or purchase for themselves or deceased relatives or friends. Indulgences were coveted because they shortened sentences in purgatory. Pilgrimages to the shrines containing the relics of saints remained immensely popular everywhere with men and women from all walks of life. Indulgences came with visits to most shrines, and new shrines appeared, especially in Germany (Christ's robe at Trier, miracle-working images of the Virgin at Regensburg and Grimmenthal, and others). Prosperous townspeople, nobles, and princes also created endowments to fund the saying of numerous Masses for their souls in ever-growing numbers. Elector Frederick of Saxony, Luther's protector, had collected more than 17,443 relics by 1518, including milk from the Virgin Mary and parts of Jesus' swaddling clothes. Piously viewing these relics brought remission of 127,799 years and 116 days of suffering in purgatory. Frederick employed eighty-three priests to say Masses for his soul in 1520. Confraternities paid for Masses and prayers for the souls of their deceased members. Meeting the rising demand required more priests; in northern England, for example, the number of men ordained around 1500 was twice that of a hundred years earlier.

The proliferation of Masses for the dead, indulgence sales, relic cults, and the like demonstrates that traditional religion enjoyed good health on the eve of the Protestant Reformation. Late medieval heretics, such as the Lollards in England, the Hussites in Bohemia, and the Fraticelli in Italy and elsewhere, were in decline (see Chapter 11). The church had many critics, to be sure, and some of them had access to the new tool of the printing press. But they targeted the church's failings in areas other than its provision of religious services. Erasmus (see Chapter 12) and many others followed the tradition of medieval reformers in some respects. They assailed the papacy because the popes had become princes more interested in enhancing their political power in Italy than in tending to the spiritual needs of Christians. They attacked bishops and other members of the higher clergy who spent most of their time administering the church's estates, serving as officials in secular governments, or pursuing careers in the church's own swelling bureaucracy. Reformers charged that such clerical careerists relied on money siphoned away from the localities, so that

the priests who actually served their flocks lived in want while their distant superiors wallowed in luxury. In other words, the church was perceived as a grasping institution run by arrogant bureaucrats. It needed a thorough housecleaning, and indeed, many of the voices calling for reform came from the ranks of churchmen themselves. Yet as long as most people continued to believe in the church's system for saving souls—the sacrament of penance and the theology of faith and good works that underpinned it—there seemed no reason to doubt that Western Christendom would remain unified. Then Martin Luther challenged the validity of that system.

THE PROTESTANT REFORMATION BEGINS

Martin Luther's father, a hardworking and prosperous miner of peasant origin, wanted his brilliant son to be a lawyer. The boy obediently studied law after finishing his bachelor's degree at the University of Erfurt. On July 2, 1505, he was returning to Erfurt after visiting his parents when a thunderstorm suddenly struck and a lightning bolt knocked him off his horse. Terrified, he promised the patroness of miners, St. Anne, to become a monk if he should survive. On July 17, he fulfilled his vow by joining the **Observant** Augustinian order and was ordained a priest in 1507. The church's doctrine held that the monastic life afforded the best hope of salvation, and Luther performed his duties with the utmost seriousness. Many years later, he facetiously proclaimed, "If ever a monk got to heaven by his monkery it was I."

Yet, to his astonishment, Luther discovered that the penitential cycle intensified rather than quelled his fear that he was damned. In 1512 he completed his doctoral study in theology, and while preparing lectures in theology for his students at the new university of Wittenberg, Luther found the solution to his persistent, agonizing sense of sinfulness. He became convinced that forgiveness for sin resulted from faith alone, not—as the church taught—from a combination of faith and good works. No sinful act damns, no good act saves, he concluded. Only belief in Christ as the son of God saves, and the ability to believe comes from God. Luther concluded that Christ enters the lives of individuals out of divine mercy, not human merit. This change in a theological formula—from the conviction that believers are saved by faith alone rather than by faith and good works—proved to have revolutionary consequences not only for the church but for European politics, society, and culture.

Martin Luther: Salvation by Faith Alone

In 1517, Luther was thirty-four years old. He had no intention of destroying Christian unity. Throughout his life he maintained that he sought only to restore true Christian

THE HISTORICAL EVIDENCE

Luther's "Tower Experience"

ca. 1510

At several points later in his life, Martin Luther referred to a time when, in a study located in a tower in his monastery, he suddenly achieved a new understanding of "the justice of God," the key insight that underlay his mature theology. Scholars cannot agree about the dating of this "tower experience"; it could have been as early as 1508 or as late as 1519, or somewhere in between. Here is an account Luther wrote in 1545, the year before his death. He explained that he had become desperately anxious to grasp the meaning of a phrase in St. Paul's letter to the Romans (1:17): the "justice of God" (see Chapter 5: The Historical Evidence, "Paul's Epistle to the Romans").

I hated that phrase, "justice of God," which according to the usage and custom of all the teachers I had to understand as what they called the formal or active justice with which God himself is just and punishes unjust sinners. But for myself, even though I was living irreproachably as a monk, I felt that before God I was a sinner with an utterly disquieted conscience, and I could not believe that He was placated by my satisfactions [penances]. I did not love, indeed I hated, that God who punished sinners; and with a monstrous, silent, if not blasphemous, murmuring, I fumed against God, and said: "As if it is not enough that wretched sinners are eternally damned by original sin and crushed by every sort of calamity through the law of the decalogue [Ten Commandments], without having God add sorrow upon sorrow by the gospel, that the gospel too should threaten us with his justice and wrath!" Thus a fierce battle raged in my troubled conscience. Yet I knocked persistently upon Paul in this passage, most earnestly wanting to know what St. Paul intended. At last I meditated night and day, God had mercy on me. I realized the significance of the context, namely: "In it the justice of God is revealed, as it is written, 'He who through faith is just shall live.'" *

I began to understand that "the justice of God" meant that justice by which the just man lives through God's gift, namely by faith. This is what it means: the justice of God is revealed by the gospel, a passive justice with which the merciful God justifies us by faith, as it is written: "He who through faith is just shall live." Here I felt that I was altogether born again and had entered paradise itself through open gates. Immediately the whole face of Scripture was totally transformed for me. . . . Now I exalted in that sweetest phrase with as much love as I had previously hated the words "justice of God." So this verse in Paul was truly for me the gate to paradise.

***

Source: From Ian D. Kingston Siggins, ed., *Luther* (New York: Barnes & Noble, 1972), p. 77; ultimate source, Helmut Lehmann and Jaroslav Pelikan, trans. and eds., *Luther's Works* (St. Louis and Philadelphia: Concordia Publishing House, 1955).

*In the Chapter 5 Historical Evidence selection, this passage from Romans is translated: "For in it the righteousness of God is revealed through faith for faith: as it is written, 'The one who is righteous will live by faith'."

doctrine, meaning biblically based beliefs from which the church had strayed. Nevertheless, in November he took the first step on the road that soon led to the Protestant Reformation by circulating his Ninety-Five Theses, a list—written in Latin and thus originally intended for theologians—that addressed a series of points about which he believed the church's doctrine concerning indulgences was wrong. He was provoked by the activities of Johann Tetzel, a Dominican friar and seller of indulgences whose shady sales tactics attracted many critics in addition to Luther. Tetzel sold aggressively, as his jingle shows: "As soon as the coin in the coffer rings / A soul from purgatory's fire

springs." Pope Leo X, in need of cash to continue building the new St. Peter's, had authorized the sale, and Tetzel responded eagerly. He reportedly quipped that the indulgence was so potent that it would save even a man who had impregnated the Virgin Mary.

Luther angrily denounced the indulgence campaign, among other things, in his Ninety-Five Theses and, without his knowledge, the theses were translated into German and widely distributed. In Luther's view, because salvation depended on faith alone, neither the pope nor anyone else could sell it for money. When news of Luther's argument reached Leo, he allegedly scoffed, "Luther is a drunken

Protestant versus Catholic Christianity This colored version of a woodcut by Lucas Cranach the Elder also appeared widely in black and white. It demonstrated, as its caption said, "the difference between the true religion of Christ and the false idolatrous teaching of Antichrist." From his pulpit just left of the central pillar, Luther preaches about Christ's sacrifice, and two sacraments (baptism and Holy Communion) are celebrated. Note that laypersons receive both bread and wine, a break with Catholic practice limiting the wine to clergymen only. On the right a fat friar preaches words he receives from a devil, Catholic ceremonies are satirized (and rejected by God and St. Francis from above), and the pope (lower right) counts money. *AKG London.*

German. He will feel different when he is sober." In 1520, Leo X ordered Luther to recant; Luther responded by publicly burning the papal decree, whereupon the pope excommunicated him. In 1521, as described at the beginning of this chapter, Luther was called by imperial summons to appear before the Diet in the city of Worms. Although an earlier reformer, John Hus, had been burned at the stake by the Council of Constance in 1415 (see Chapter 11), this was not to be Luther's fate. Emperor Charles V, anxious about the threats from the Ottomans and the French, needed the support of the German princes and cities too much to violate the guarantee of safety Luther had been given.

Luther's attack on indulgences is highly significant because indulgences intersected with the doctrines of purgatory, clerical authority, and salvation. The popes claimed the authority to reduce or eliminate one's term in purgatory by means of indulgences. Indulgence selling was not new, nor was Luther the first to denounce it. In 1509, for example, Erasmus had written scathingly of the "businessman or

soldier or judge who, by laying down one single little coin from his huge plunder, thinks that the whole putrid bog of his life has been purified." But Luther's attack was based on a quite different understanding of vital doctrines. It led him, in time, to argue that the papacy itself should be abolished and the church radically transformed.

Luther held that because Christ's sacrifice on the Cross had already atoned for all human sin, one could not gain God's favor by going on pilgrimages, obtaining indulgences, joining monasteries or convents, venerating relics, praying to saints, confessing to a priest, or doing penance. All of these popular and time-honored "good works" were useless. Of the traditional seven sacraments, Luther rejected five as having no warrant in the Bible: ordination, confirmation, marriage, penance, and extreme unction (last rites). He reinterpreted the remaining two, baptism and Holy Communion (the Eucharist), making their effectiveness depend on the believer's faith instead of on the inherent power of the sacrament itself. He therefore denied that priests had the miraculous ability to transform bread and wine into the body and blood of Christ (**transubstantiation,** approved by the Lateran Council in 1215; see Chapter 8).

As Luther worked out the implications of his ideas, he concluded that the role of the clergy in society would have to change drastically. Catholic doctrine held that a priest, ordained by authority of the pope, had special powers not available to laypersons. In administering the sacrament of penance the priest absolved people of guilt for their sins; in the Mass he repeated Christ's sacrifice on Calvary. No layperson could hope to enter heaven without the priest's help. But for Protestants, the clergy ceased to be what it had been for more than a thousand years, a special group with authority and privileges available only to its members. Wherever Europe became Protestant, monasteries and convents were closed and their inhabitants required to rejoin lay society. Luther proclaimed that, in a sense, each Christian became a priest—a great responsibility but, for many laypersons, an exciting and liberating experience. Luther's doctrine of the priesthood of all believers meant that every person was called to a certain station in life—pastor, farmer, butcher, mother, baker—and no calling pleased God more than another. What was important was the spirit of love and obedience to God's will in which people performed their duties. Ideally, as Luther put it, the father caring for his infant child looks at diaper changing and such "lowly and distasteful and despised chores and knows that they are adorned with divine approval as with precious gold and silver . . . not because diapers are washed, but because this is done in faith."

Luther's reinterpretation of biblical conceptions of the correct role of the clergy did not mean that trained *pastors*, a word that Protestants preferred to *priest*, were no longer needed. But pastors should be chosen by the community, not by bishops. Nor was there any reason why pastors should not marry and have families. Each Christian had to try to understand the Bible, relying upon the pastor and the Christian community for guidance but knowing that salvation was in God's hands, beyond any clergyman's reach. This stress on the irrelevance of behavior to salvation quickly drew fire from Catholics who thought it would remove the pressure to live a moral life. If sinful people could achieve nothing toward salvation by good works, Catholics argued, then none would have any reason to discipline their lives, and violence, adultery, gluttony, and a host of other sins would multiply until society collapsed in an orgy of self-indulgence. Luther responded that the inward assurance of salvation by faith would free Christians from fear of damnation and give them the confidence to live morally and to love and help their neighbors.

Luther and his Catholic critics agreed that the Bible was the source of truth. But the great question remained: Who had the power to decide which interpretation of Scripture was correct? Catholics insisted that this power lay with councils and popes. In contrast to St. Thomas Aquinas's trust in human reason, Luther's ideas were rooted in late medieval nominalism, which conceived of God as beyond human comprehension and of overwhelming majesty (see Chapter 11). Human agencies could not share in that majesty or rewrite the Scriptures to suit their needs. Luther denounced the pope as the Antichrist prophesied in Scripture, the leader of a monstrous fraud designed to enrich churchmen while enslaving the laity. He believed that God had called him to restore Christianity's biblical foundations, one of which was the Christian's liberty from the tyrannical grasp of the traditional clerics.

Luther's campaign had unintended consequences in the countryside. Southern and central Germany were wracked by a series of uprisings known collectively as the Peasants' War (1524–1525). Goaded by increasing rents, demands for labor services, and incursions onto formerly common resources, mobs of peasants, miners, and artisans sacked towns and monasteries and attacked their noble landlords, destroying castles and massacring their garrisons. A widely circulated rebel manifesto discloses marked similarities between this uprising and the late medieval peasant rebellions. Taking Luther's Christian liberty to mean social liberty, the peasants made many demands: an end to serfdom; lower rents; restoration of common fields that landlords had taken over; rights to take fish, game, and firewood; and the freedom to choose their own pastors.

The theologian of this rebellion was an ex-Lutheran preacher, Thomas Müntzer. Believing that the end of the world was near, he declared that God had ordered him to instigate a great social rebellion, asking his peasant followers, "Why do you continue to let yourselves be led around by the nose? . . . The time has come for bloodshed to fall upon this impenitent and unbelieving world." Luther responded to the revolt with angry condemnations of both princes and peasants, the former for oppressing their laborers and the latter for the terrible sin of rebellion. After seventy thousand peasants died in the suppression of the revolts and Müntzer was captured and savagely put to death, Luther wrote: "I wanted to do two things: quiet the peasants and instruct the lords. The peasants were unwilling, and now they have their reward. The lords too will not hear, and they shall have their reward also." Since the lords maintained their powers, Luther meant that they would receive their "reward" after death in the form of reserved seats in hell.

The Protestant movement Luther initiated got its name at the Diet of Speyer in 1529, when six princes and fourteen cities responded with a strongly worded "Protest" against the majority's decision to outlaw Lutheranism. The attraction of secular authorities toward the Protestant program rested partly on religious conviction and partly on a shrewd appreciation for the fact that it enabled them to secularize church property and enhance their control over their subjects. In 1530 Luther and his followers stated their basic principles and fundamental doctrine in the Augsburg Confession, the authoritative summary of the Lutheran tradition that was

Iconoclasm in Zurich
Zwingli and his followers insisted on the removal of what they called "idols" from the churches (statues, carvings, paintings, stained glass, and other medieval artwork), a campaign that eventually extended far beyond Switzerland. The focal point of worship should be, they insisted, not the body and blood of Christ in the Mass but God's word read and explicated from the pulpit. After the elaborate medieval ornamentation was removed, many Protestants painted the walls of their churches white and made the pulpit larger and more prominent. *Zentralbibliothek, Zurich.*

spreading across Germany and Scandinavia. But other reformers began adopting quite different principles. And having rejected papal authority, the Protestant movement was left without an institutional mechanism capable of resolving its theological debates. Protestantism thus began breaking up into denominational fragments (Episcopalians, Presbyterians, Congregationalists, Baptists, and so on), a process that continues to this day.

Ulrich Zwingli: Reformation in a Civic Setting

This fragmentation began in the 1520s when the Swiss reformer Ulrich Zwingli (1484–1531), a former priest and an admirer of Erasmian humanism, disagreed with Luther. The Swiss Confederation at that time had six member states (cantons) long famous for the high quality of their soldiers and effectively independent of the Holy Roman Empire. Erasmus himself lived in Basel for many years, and his presence drew humanist scholars from all over Europe to the Swiss city. Basel's printers enjoyed international fame for printing his works and those of the early Church Fathers. The influence of Erasmian humanism powerfully influenced the Reformation among the Swiss, and nowhere less so than in Zurich, the city-state whose governing council called Zwingli to be the "People's Priest" at the principal church there in 1518. When the plague struck Zurich in 1519, he ministered to its victims and then himself caught the disease and nearly died. His recovery powerfully strengthened his sense of utter dependence upon God and of God's election of him to salvation.

Simplicity was at the heart of Zwingli's theology, an emphasis that owed much to his reading the Church

Fathers as well as Erasmus's 1516 edition of the New Testament in Greek. In such sources, he could find no trace of evidence that the worship services of the early Christians bore any resemblance to those of the late medieval church. He became convinced that the elaborate decoration of churches in the Middle Ages had led people into the sin of idolatry— the worship not of God but of statues and relics. Like Luther, he believed that salvation came from faith alone, but unlike Luther, Zwingli's interpretation of this doctrine led him to radical change in worship. He drew the distinction between sacred and profane things differently from both Luther and the traditionalists. Whereas Luther banished only nonbiblical images from churches and wrote hymns for his followers to sing, Zwingli insisted that all stained glass, singing, organs, and statues be banished so that people would concentrate solely on the Bible. "In Zurich," he said proudly, "we have churches which are absolutely luminous; the walls are beautifully white." He did not oppose music outside the churches; on the contrary, he sang, played numerous instruments, and composed music, but only for private entertainment. In public worship, he insisted, music distracted from the word of God and must therefore be banned.

In 1529 Luther and Zwingli met at Marburg in the German state of Hesse in the hope of forging a united front in the face of Catholic opposition. Their principal debate was over the nature of the Eucharist. They agreed that the priest had no special power to transform the bread and wine into Christ's body and blood. Although they concurred on what the Mass was *not*, they could not agree on what it *was*. Luther rejected the highly technical, orthodox teaching of transubstantiation but continued to believe that Christ's body was really present for the believing recipient in the consecrated bread and wine. This "real presence" doctrine means that, although the officiating priest does not actually convert the bread and wine into Christ's body, the latter coexists with the former through the faith of the Christian who receives them. Luther quoted Matthew 26:26—*Hoc est corpus meum* ("This is my body")—as proof of the real presence of Christ. To emphasize his unbudging insistence, he wrote the text in chalk on the table.

Not so, responded Zwingli, citing John 6:54, 63: "Those who eat my flesh and drink my blood have eternal life. . . .It is the spirit that gives life; the flesh is useless." In his view, nothing tangible could contain the divine spirit. The Last Supper (Zwingli's term for the Mass) was a memorial service, commemorating Christ's sacrifice but in itself conveying no grace. Heated words followed. Pointing again to John 6, Zwingli insisted "This text will break your neck." "Don't brag," replied Luther scornfully, adding, "Our necks don't break that fast. You are in Hesse now, not Switzerland."

In addition to simplicity in worship, Zwingli emphasized the necessity that the whole community had to be reformed and that the civic authorities had to serve as the leaders of the effort. For Zwingli, church and state had to be united and Christians had to be active citizens. Zwingli organized a series of public debates in 1522 and 1523 that helped convince Zurich's ruling council to abolish the Mass in favor of a ceremony commemorating the Last Supper. He was horrified when some fellow reformers began to question infant baptism and argue instead for its replacement with "believers' baptism," meaning baptism only of *adults* who truly believed in the Scriptures and behaved accordingly. These radical Protestants—despised and cruelly persecuted by both Catholics and mainstream Protestants—were called Anabaptists, meaning "rebaptizers." Because the first generation of Anabaptists had been baptized at birth (Catholic or orthodox Protestant), rebaptism was necessary; hence the derisive term coined by their enemies.

After a public discussion with the first Anabaptists in 1525, Zwingli and Zurich's council members agreed that infant baptism signified an individual's entry into church and community and must be retained. Zwingli encouraged the officials to persecute those who refused to conform to this policy. Dozens of converts to adult baptism were arrested, exiled, and, when they insisted on returning, imprisoned again. One of their leaders suffered execution by drowning, and others who refused to recant were expelled. Just as Luther sided with the princes against the peasants, so Zwingli aligned himself with the civic rulers against what seemed a threat to public order. Both reformers recognized that the fate of their reform program depended on alliances with secular rulers. Thus, the Lutheran form of worship and church organization became established in much of Germany and Scandinavia by the

middle of the sixteenth century. Zwingli died in battle while serving as a chaplain to Swiss Protestant forces in 1531, but his ideas had a powerful influence not only in Switzerland but in England, the Netherlands, and other parts of Europe.

Radical Opposition to the Magisterial Reformation

Luther's alliance with the princes against Müntzer and the peasants and Zwingli's insistence that religion must be a matter of public affirmation rather than private choice (the essence of the confrontation with the first Anabaptists) put both these reformers firmly on the side of the secular authorities. Luther, Zwingli, and others like them are called magisterial reformers because they worked with the support of the "magistrates," meaning princes, nobles, and municipal officials whose task it was to maintain public order. As magisterial reformers, Luther and Zwingli agreed that each church would serve a geographically defined area called a parish. Everyone living within the parish would be baptized into membership and would attend services, a system inherited from medieval practice. The small splinter group of radical Protestants who emerged initially in Zwingli's Zurich in the 1520s asked why geography alone should determine church membership. Why not limit membership only to those who demonstrated the Christian ideal in their lives? Since those who do not are bound for hell anyway, why hinder their journey?

The Anabaptists assumed that the state or any political authority was, by its very nature, ungodly, worldly, and wicked—and that it derived its powers from the devil. Ironically this first call for separation of church and state came from people who believed that the state and worldly society in general were evil, a far cry from the liberal idea of the eighteenth and nineteenth centuries that church and state should be separate so that each could prosper. Many Anabaptists held that the only course for a true Christian was separation from *both* state and society and withdrawal into underground congregations, not unlike those of early Christian times. The result, at least from the magisterial perspective, was to undermine the church as a social organization and as a means of social control. For Luther and Zwingli, the Anabaptist insistence that only the "righteous" should submit to baptism smacked of the Catholic idea that good works earned salvation from God.

A few Anabaptists attempted to launch a social **revolution** by interpreting the biblical **prophecy** of a thousand-year rule of the saints before the end of the world (millenarianism) as a mandate for apocalyptic overthrow of the established order. In February 1534 a group of Anabaptists took over the northern German town of Münster, driving away or murdering all the men who opposed them and seizing their wives, daughters, houses, and money. Jan Bockelson, a tailor from Leiden, ran naked through the streets, gathered sixteen wives (one of whom he ultimately beheaded), made himself king over ten thousand Münsterites, and lived in luxury until the former Roman Catholic bishop of Münster led an army and besieged the city. Before it finally fell on June 25, its residents were reduced to eating cats, mice, and even human corpses. "King Jan" was tortured to death with red-hot tongs, and the refugees returned to rebuild the traditional order.

The hideous disaster at Münster gave Anabaptists a terrible reputation, but King Jan and his friends by no means typified the group. Most Anabaptists were nonviolent people who interpreted the Scriptures literally. Many took Matthew 5:34 ("Do not swear at all") to mean no one should take an oath of any sort—to king, emperor, or magistrate. They would neither serve on juries nor accept public office. Some groups, such as the Hutterites, founded by Jakob Hutter in Moravia, rejected the holding of private property and lived communally on the model of the early Christians described in the New Testament (Acts 2:43–45). Many were pacifists, refusing to fight in armies or to resist their persecutors. Perhaps the most typical of the Anabaptist sects was led by a Dutchman and former Catholic priest, Menno Simons (1496–1561). To this day, the pacifist Mennonites live simply, spurn many modern inventions, and hold governmental authority (including public schools) suspect. Old Order Amish communities in Pennsylvania and elsewhere trace their origins back to the sixteenth-century Mennonites.

Anabaptism was largely a lower-class phenomenon without significant political impact—except that it frightened property owners half to death. Especially after Münster, the Anabaptists' image for many Europeans resembled that of murderous terrorists. Anabaptist objections to private property, routine judicial processes, and military service (had they become widespread) would clearly have damaged or even destroyed whole communities. Contemporaries failed to realize the extent to which Anabaptists were split into small groups, often holding widely differing views. Anabaptists gathered in voluntary, not geographical, congregations. These little groups, who considered themselves the only saved portion of humankind, created a sort of rigid Protestant monasticism—a retreat from an evil world.

THE VICTORY OF MAGISTERIAL REFORM

During the 1520s in Germany and elsewhere, large numbers of clergymen converted to Protestant views. The intelligentsia of Christendom, in astonishing numbers and with surprising speed, heard and read about salvation by faith alone and the sole authority of the Scriptures and began to preach about these new and exciting principles. All over Europe, the Protestant message convinced friars, monks, and priests who, in turn, set out to convert the laity. Experiences like that of Johannes Bugenhagen (1485–1558), a former monk, occurred many times. Handed a copy of one of Luther's works, he glanced through it and declared: "Since the days of Christ's passion many heretics have assailed the church, but none is so pernicious as the author of this book." After thorough study, however, Bugenhagen changed his mind completely and said, "The entire world is blind—this man alone sees the truth." He married in 1522, went to Wittenberg the next year, and helped lead victorious Protestantizing efforts in several German cities and provinces and finally in the kingdom of Denmark. Charles V and the popes doomed Protestant chances in Italy and Spain, but elsewhere the outcome seesawed back and forth. From the earliest days, the unavoidable fact was that without backing from princes and other secular authorities, Protestant reformers had no chance of success. With it, they rarely failed.

In Germany, Scandinavia, England, Scotland, and parts of the Netherlands, Switzerland, and eastern Europe, the Protestants carried the day, and at times they even seemed near to doing so in France as well. One important reason was that, having disallowed the special status and powers of churchmen and insisting on the sanctity of lay callings, they conceded to lay magistrates the authority to judge religious matters formerly reserved to the clergy alone. Especially in northern Europe, many rulers adopted the reforms and withdrew their allegiance from Rome. Their reasons varied. They stood to amass political power and wealth at the church's expense, but self-aggrandizement of this kind carried grave risks since they might have to defend their gains against rebels or Charles V's invading armies. Conscientious belief of the truth of the reformers' message was in many cases at least as important as calculations of gain.

Francis I and the French Reformers

In 1520 in Paris, "no books are more eagerly bought up than those of Luther. . . . Everywhere people speak highly of Luther," according to one of Zwingli's friends in a letter to him. Yet Protestantism in France under Francis I, which grew slowly at first and then more rapidly, had to contend with a monarch whose control over the church in France was already substantial. A strong tradition of "Gallican liberties" dating from the fifteenth century exempted the French church from papal jurisdiction. For example, the king had the right to block appeals to Rome in ecclesiastical court cases, a power that Henry VIII of England coveted. In 1516, Francis and Pope Leo X concluded the Concordat of Bologna, granting the king control over appointments to all the higher positions in the church. Francis, therefore, did not need Protestant reforms to strengthen himself in relation to the pope.

Reformers had some support in the French royal family. Francis's sister, Marguerite of Navarre, encouraged the work of the reform-minded bishop of Meaux in the 1520s. Some of the preachers he employed advocated Lutheran ideas, although the bishop himself was no Lutheran. In 1533, however, radical opponents of the Mass put up posters ridiculing it in Paris and other cities (the Affair of the Placards), angering the king. Executions of *sacramentaires* holding such views followed during the 1530s. Francis assisted German Protestants because they made life difficult for his Habsburg enemies; he discouraged Protestants at home after 1533, but he never undertook the kind of vigorous persecution that would have been needed to root out the movement altogether. In the 1540s and 1550s, leadership of French Protestants came increasingly from the free city of Geneva just over the border from France.

John Calvin: The Sovereignty of God

John Calvin (1509–1564) became the savior of Protestantism when the Catholic resurgence began in the 1550s. He was born and educated in France, where his father planned for him to be a lawyer. Like Luther, he received a heavy dose of scholastic training and, like Zwingli, he was strongly influenced by northern humanism. His genius lay in the creation of a religious apparatus suited to political and social realities. The militant Protestantism of the later 1500s was, for the most part, militant Calvinism. In the Low Countries, France, England, Scotland, Switzerland, and parts of the Rhineland and Bohemia, Calvinism became the characteristic form of Protestantism—and these were the most heavily populated areas in Europe outside of the Habsburg territories. Calvin's impact extended from eastern Europe to the New World, where the Puritan experiment in New England owed much to him.

Calvin's approach to Christian reform was above all systematic, and his talent is nowhere more evident than in his *Institutes of the Christian Religion*, first published in 1536 when he was only twenty-six years old. Clearly organized and lucidly written, this treatise was expanded greatly in subsequent editions and became the most widely used compendium of Protestant thought, admired even by those who disagreed with Calvin on some points. The central doctrine of Calvin's theology was the absolute sovereignty of God:

> Not only heaven and earth and inanimate creatures but also the plans and wills of men are governed so as to move precisely to the end destined by God. . . . Not only the Creator of all, . . . he is also everlasting Governor and Preserver. . . . He sustains, nourishes, and cares for, everything he has made, even to the least sparrow.

The *Institutes* is basically an analysis of God's purpose as revealed in Scripture. Calvin, trained in law, philosophy, and humanistic studies, was thoroughly logical and thus

IOANNES CALVINVS

John Calvin Friends and associates spoke well and often of his capacity for friendship, his deep feelings, his hot temper, and his loving relationship with his wife, but unlike Luther, Calvin never spoke about the spiritual experiences that transformed him from a lawyer and humanist to a Protestant theologian. The logical precision with which John Calvin developed his doctrine of God's overwhelming power has forever dominated his image in history, and this portrait probably portrays Calvin as being more grim than he actually was. *Museum Boijmas van Beuningen, Rotterdam.*

followed to logical conclusions the principles he found in the Bible.

The most famous of these conclusions is his doctrine of absolute predestination—what Calvin himself called "this horrible decree." Implied by Augustine, upheld by Luther and Zwingli, and made fully explicit by Calvin, predestination means that God has chosen some individuals, described as "the Elect," "the Saints," and "the godly," to receive forgiveness of their sins, the ability to believe in God, and therefore eternal life; others are forever damned. None of the fortunate have done anything to deserve or earn these gifts; they have simply been chosen by a merciful God for the sake of his Son. Calvin recognized that predestination seemed harsh, but his study of the Bible convinced him that it was indeed the divine message for all who hoped to enter heaven. Moreover, as an English formulation put it in 1563, "the godly consideration of predestination . . . is full of sweet, pleasant and unspeakable comfort to godly persons."

On the controversial subject of Holy Communion, Calvin compromised. He rejected Luther's "real presence" of Christ, yet thought the sacrament was more than a mere memorial service as Zwingli contended. The bread and wine, Calvin claimed, remained bread and wine but they conveyed spiritual benefit to the believing recipient. Thus Christ was present in spirit in the elements rather than in substance. Lutherans did not accept this compromise, but Heinrich Bullinger, Zwingli's successor at Zurich, did. The Zwinglian and Calvinist groups were thus united, most fully in the Second Helvetic Confession (1566). This creed proved an important milestone in the formation of the Reformed Protestant tradition, which was basically Calvinist, as distinguished from the Evangelical Protestantism of the Lutherans.

Calvin, in sharp contrast to Luther, believed that all Christians must do their best to reform themselves, their families, and others around them in order to establish the moral order dictated in the Scriptures and explicated by the *Institutes*. Today many assume that predestination would lead to fatalism and inaction. Why struggle to be virtuous if God has already decided one's fate? But many sixteenth-century Europeans embraced Calvin's stark theology wholeheartedly, wrote religious diaries, listened to complicated sermons, conferred with fellow "saints"—all in order to examine their lives for evidence of saving grace, for hints that they indeed were among the Elect. Thus belief in predestination led not to resignation or hedonism but to action, which meant living morally and performing deeds of charity and mercy to others. In short, Luther removed good works from the process of salvation. Calvin kept them out of the process theologically but reintroduced them psychologically. Instead of doing good works to earn salvation (the traditional approach that Luther attacked), Calvinists did them to gain assurance that they were *already* saved.

Calvin: The Reformer of Geneva

In 1536 Calvin joined a group of reformers in Geneva, an important commercial town of about seventeen thousand French-speaking inhabitants. At first, the town government rejected their program and forced them into exile. But following new elections, Calvin was asked to return, and in 1541 he set to work building in Geneva what the Scottish reformer John Knox called "the most perfect school of Christ that ever was on earth since the days of the Apostles." One could join the "reformed" church upon profession of faith, and infants were baptized into it. To ensure that the Word of God was preached correctly (meaning in accor-

dance with Protestant doctrine) and the sacraments administered rightly (meaning without Catholic ceremonialism), Calvin established a school for preachers in 1559. This Genevan Academy, a major source of preaching talent, became the cutting edge of international Protestantism in the latter half of the sixteenth century.

The central institution for the elaboration and enforcement of reform in Geneva was the Consistory. Composed of six pastors and twelve elders, it administered the "godly discipline," the hallmark of Calvin's ecclesiastical organization. The elders were laymen chosen by and from among members of Geneva's governing bodies; they came from different parts of the city, so that the Consistory's "eyes may be everywhere," as Calvin's instructions put it. The Consistory encouraged people to report any kind of misbehavior, such as adultery, fighting, dancing, card playing, gambling, and laughing in church. Everyone had to attend church, live an upright life, and forgo altars displaying images and prayers to the Virgin Mary. Backsliders faced public denunciation from the pulpit and admonition from the Consistory either to change their ways or be excommunicated.

Critics denounced Geneva as a place where informers and gossips tattled on their neighbors. A man was punished for naming his dog Calvin, another's tongue was pierced for "blasphemy against ministers," and some blasphemers and adulterers were executed. But for centuries Catholic courts, too, had imposed punishments for sinful behavior. And against the Genevan excesses of zeal must be balanced the fact that Geneva's educational system and its care for the sick and the aged were among the best in Europe. Calvin and the Consistory objected not to taking pleasure in things God created but to the abuse of those things. Eating, drinking, and singing were to be enjoyed, but gluttony, drunkenness, and lewd songs were offenses.

The crucial innovation at Geneva was giving laymen a voice in religious policy. The Consistory, with its large lay membership, fused long-separated temporal and spiritual authorities. Many of these laymen (lawyers, merchants, nobles) had hungered for more influence in church affairs; in fact, this yearning constituted one cause of the Reformation. Calvin's institutionalization of a union of laymen and churchmen, which helps to explain the success of Calvinism throughout northern and western Europe, became his most important contribution to the political and social practice of the Reformation. Whereas medieval churchmen had vigorously, if not always successfully, resisted lay participation in religious matters, Calvin created channels in which it could operate openly and legitimately.

Calvin's Geneva became the setting for a dramatic confrontation between the magisterial reformation and the antitrinitarians—intellectuals who reopened the great Christological debates of the fourth century (see Chapter 5). These evangelical rationalists were primarily Italians

THE HISTORICAL EVIDENCE

Geneva's Ecclesiastical Ordinances

1541

The church in Geneva under Calvin had four kinds of officers: pastors (who preached and administered the sacraments), doctors (meaning teachers of religious doctrine), elders, and deacons. The last two were laypersons, and their selection and function was specified in Geneva's Draft Ecclesiastical Ordinances. As described in the selections presented here, elders maintained moral discipline in their parts of the city, and deacons took care of the poor and the sick. In each case, the laity took over duties formerly in the hands of the clergy.

Concerning the third order . . . Elders

Their office is to have oversight of the life of everyone, to admonish amicably those whom they see to be erring or to be living a disordered life, and, where it is required, to enjoin fraternal corrections themselves and along with others. In the present condition of the church, it would be good to elect two of the Little Council, four of the Council of Sixty, and six of the Council of Two Hundred [Geneva's governing bodies], men of good and honest life, without reproach and beyond suspicion, and above all fearing God and possessing spiritual prudence. These should be so elected that there be some in every quarter of the city, to keep an eye on everybody.

The fourth order of ecclesiastical government . . . Deacons

There were always two kinds in the ancient church, the one deputed to receive, dispense and hold goods for the poor, not only daily alms, but also possessions, rents and pensions; the other to tend and care for the sick and administer allowances to the poor. This custom we follow again now for we have procurators and hospitallers. . . .

[Their] election . . . is to take place like that of the elders. . . . It will be their duty to watch diligently that the public hospital is well maintained, and that this be so both for the sick and the old people unable to work, widowed women, orphaned children and other poor creatures. The sick are always to be lodged in a set of rooms separate from the other people who are unable to work, old men, widowed women, orphaned children and the other poor.

Source: From John Dillenberger, ed. *John Calvin: Selections from His Writings* (Garden City, N.Y.: Anchor, 1971), pp. 235–236; ultimate source, *Calvin: Theological Treatises*, vol. 22, Library of Christian Classics Series, trans. with introductions and notes by J. K. S. Reid (Philadelphia: Westminster Press, 1954).

---

and Spaniards whose roots lay in Erasmian humanism. Many were either skeptical of or opposed to **orthodox** Christianity's most fundamental doctrine, Trinitarianism (the belief that God exists in three persons—Father, Son, and Holy Spirit). Their emphasis fell on Christ's humanity, not his divinity. Forced to flee their Catholic homelands, they found various havens. Perhaps the best known of the antitrinitarians was Michael Servetus (1511–1553), an eccentric and argumentative Spanish physician. His *Restoration of Christianity* (1553) contained his reasons for rejecting infant baptism and the divinity of Jesus, as well as a pioneer analysis of how blood circulates from the heart to the lungs and back again. Jailed by the Inquisition in France for heresy, and on the run from the Inquisition in Spain as well as France, Servetus escaped and fled to Geneva, where he was apprehended and imprisoned.

Actually, Servetus was reckless to come to Calvin's city: Eight years earlier he had written to Calvin and enclosed a few pages of his antitrinitarian arguments. Neither in jail after his arrest nor during his trial did Servetus recant his views. The judges, asserting that in his book he had called the Trinity "a diabolical monster with three heads," condemned him to be burned at the stake. Calvin favored beheading—then considered the most humane method of execution—but he was overruled (the lasting influence of the Genevan model of clerical and civic relations did not mean that elections in Geneva always produced councils that agreed with Calvin). Servetus was in fact the only heretic burned in Geneva. Other magisterial reformers defended the prosecution, and he probably would have suffered a similar end anywhere in western Europe. Driven from Switzerland, other antitrinitarian leaders went to Transylvania and Poland, where the authorities were unable or unwilling to persecute them and where they found numerous converts among the educated nobility and gentry. For example, Lelio Sozzini (1525–1562) and his nephew Fausto (1539–1604) left Siena and found their way to Raków in Poland, where they established Socinian churches and schools and were forebears of the modern Unitarian denomination.

Politics in the Lutheran Reformation

Charles V rightly perceived the greatest danger to his empire as coming from the Ottoman Turks, an enemy powerful enough to threaten Gibraltar and Moscow simultaneously. Charles's wars with the Ottomans and the French forced him to seek the cooperation of powerful German princes, both Protestant and Catholic. Even German Catholic princes proved troublesome because they opposed Charles's every effort to strengthen imperial authority. And in 1531 the German Protestant princes and cities formed the Schmalkaldic League to defend their cause with military force. By 1542, they controlled northern Germany. Charles, preoccupied by the Ottomans, could not gather the forces to challenge them until 1546. Then in 1547 he won a stunning victory over the league's army at Mühlberg. Briefly, it appeared that he would extinguish Protestantism in the Holy Roman Empire.

Fortunately for the Protestants, the Schmalkaldic League obtained French help, and Charles was forced to the bargaining table. By the Peace of Augsburg (1555), he agreed that the religion of each state in the empire would be determined by its prince, Catholic or Lutheran; those who disliked the prince's choice could move elsewhere. Church lands seized by Lutheran princes were to remain in their possession. Even though this compromise appalled those of doctrinaire outlook, it was a long way from genuine toleration because it excluded Calvinists, Anabaptists, and other religious dissidents.

The coexistence of Lutherans and Catholics agreed on at Augsburg did keep the peace in Germany until 1618, when a Protestant rebellion against the Habsburgs triggered what would become the Thirty Years' War and the last major attempt to unify the empire politically and make it wholly Catholic again. Charles himself, understandably exhausted, abdicated in 1556 and joined a monastery in Spain as a lay brother to await his death. It came only twenty-one months later. Having concluded that his political burdens were heavier than one ruler could bear, Charles divided his dominions. He granted Spain, the Netherlands, and Spanish Italy to his son, Philip II. His younger brother, Ferdinand, to whom he had given the reins of the Holy Roman Empire in 1553, was elected to succeed him as emperor in 1558. Over the next decades, the Spanish and Austrian branches of the Habsburg family remained allied but often pursued separate interests. The former ruled Spain until 1700; the latter governed Austria until the end of World War I.

Attempts to extend Lutheranism outside of Germany enjoyed their only important success in Scandinavia. Lutheran preachers worked in Denmark beginning early in the 1520s, while King Frederick I (reigned 1523–1533) protected them and seized property and authority from Catholic churchmen. A brief civil war in 1534 pitted conservative nobles and bishops against Frederick's son, Christian III (reigned 1534–1559). Victorious, Christian was elected king by the national assembly (Rigsrad). In 1536, Christian jailed the Catholic bishops and called another assembly that endorsed his progam to establish a Lutheran state church in Denmark. In Sweden, a comparable change occurred, although more slowly. In 1527 King Gustavus Vasa (reigned 1523–1560), backed by the national assembly (Riksdag), took over large amounts of church property and curtailed clerical jurisdiction. At the same time he initiated a reform process that produced an essentially Lutheran establishment by the 1540s. Since Sweden and Denmark then controlled Finland and Norway respectively, Scandinavia became thoroughly Lutheran mainly due to the efforts of kings allied with major portions of the lay nobility.

The Reformation in Eastern Europe: Successes and Failures

In Poland and Hungary, unlike Scandinavia, weak or divided royal power allowed Lutheranism and Calvinism to sweep in almost unopposed after 1525. Many powerful noblemen adopted Protestantism and won authority over religion in their lands from kings who could not afford to alienate them. By the early 1560s, antitrinitarian Italian radicals fled from Switzerland to Poland and Hungary after the burning of Servetus. Free from persecution, they won many gentry converts, although most Protestant nobles remained Calvinist. In 1569, a majority of the upper house of the Polish Sejm (Diet) were Protestants.

Proud of their political freedom, the Polish and Hungarian nobles demanded toleration even for radicals. In 1571 the diet of Transylvania (the part of Hungary not under Ottoman or Habsburg control) granted religious freedom to Catholics, Lutherans, Calvinists, and Unitarians (antitrinitarians). Then, in 1573, needing to elect a new king after the old dynasty had died out, the Polish nobility established Europe's most tolerant religious policy. In the assembly known as the Confederation of Warsaw, they declared that they would choose no king who would not swear to maintain religious freedom. Noting the "great discord" in their land over religion, they promised "that all of us differing in religion will keep the peace between ourselves and shed no blood." In both Poland and Hungary, however, the Protestant camp was too divided to prevent a resurgent Catholicism from regaining dominance (see Map 13-2).

MAP 13-2
THE RELIGIOUS DIVISION OF EUROPE, CA. 1572

Map legend:
- Reformed faith dominant
- Catholic; reformed faith growing
- Catholic; reformed faith in many locales
- Catholic; some penetration of reform
- Catholic
- Eastern Orthodoxy
- Some penetration of Antitrinitarianism
- Holy Roman Empire

REFORM IN THE CATHOLIC CHURCH

The Protestant Reformation resulted in part from the church's failure to respond effectively to repeated calls for reform from within its own ranks. Ever since the Great Schism, the papacy had been working against the conciliarists to restore its authority over the church (see Chapter 11). By the middle of the fifteenth century, the popes had regained firm control. After 1517, conservatives suspected that any Catholic who urged reform, such as Erasmus, was a secret Lutheran, even though Erasmus himself never accepted Protestant doctrine and eventually wrote against Luther. Because Luther, Zwingli, and many other leaders of what became the Protestant movement had in fact been clerics, conservatives could point to numerous examples to prove their argument that any call for "reform" was dangerous. For example, the production of Luther's German Bible and the other vernacular translations that rapidly proliferated depended heavily on the techniques pioneered by Renaissance humanists and most of all by Erasmus himself. Erasmus, said the conservatives, "laid the egg that Luther hatched."

Eventually, however, a powerful and creative campaign for reform within the church emerged, a campaign that employed the humanistic legacy no less effectively than the Protestants did. This effort benefited from the continuing affection many ordinary people held for familiar piety and ritual. Those who see Catholic renewal as a culmination of preexisting pressures—something that would have come about with or without the Protestant challenge—call this movement the Catholic Reformation. Those who view it primarily as a reaction against Protestantism, a counter-revolutionary crusade, speak of the Counter Reformation. It was both. Yet it is notable that nowhere did either the Protestant or Catholic Reformations take hold without the support and encouragement of those at the top.

The Papacy and Religious Reform

At first it seemed that for Catholic renewal to occur, it would have to do so in spite of the popes. Pope Leo X, the second son of Lorenzo the Magnificent of Florence (see Chapter 12), concentrated on further enriching and entrenching the Medici family and even went to war in an unsuccessful effort to establish his nephew as duke of Urbino. Clement VII, Leo's cousin, behaved in much the same way, and both men remained more interested in Italian politics than in the future of the church. In some respects, Paul III did not appear much of an improvement. Aged sixty-seven when installed in the chair of St. Peter, Paul owed his 1493 appointment as cardinal to the attractions of his sister, mistress of the notorious Pope Alexander VI. As a young man, Paul himself had a mistress who bore him four children, but in 1513 he ended his relationship with her, was ordained a priest in 1519,[1] and soon became a stalwart reformer. Like other Renaissance popes, Paul took care of his family, appointing two teenaged grandsons as cardinals and frequently advancing his relatives. But he also made cardinals of reform-minded humanists, appointed Michelangelo to complete the painting of the Sistine Chapel and the construction of the new St. Peter's (see Chapter 12), issued a bull in 1540 recognizing a militant new religious order (the Society of Jesus), and in 1545 convoked the Council of Trent.

At the northern Italian city of Trent, churchmen from throughout Catholic Europe met in three sessions (1545–1547, 1551–1552, 1561–1563) to address the problem of reform. Dominated by Italian and Spanish bishops who opposed the compromises with Protestants sought by German and French bishops, the council strongly reaffirmed and carefully restated traditional Catholic doctrines: salvation by faith *and* good works, the sanctity of all seven sacraments, the unique and essential role of priests, the celibacy of clergy, the existence of purgatory, the veneration of saints, the use of images, the authority of the pope, and the validity of transubstantiation, monasticism, pilgrimages, and indulgences. St. Thomas Aquinas was frequently cited at Trent, where his thought won an authority that it had never enjoyed during his lifetime (see Chapter 10). The council encouraged reforms such as the establishment of seminaries in every diocese to enable priests to teach the newly clarified doctrines of the church to the people and to explain why Protestant doctrines should be rejected. Papal, centralized control of the church was strengthened, against the desires of those who preferred a measure of local autonomy.

Meanwhile the establishment of the Roman Inquisition in 1542 created a powerful tool for enforcing these orthodox and explicitly anti-Lutheran positions in Italy. The inquisitor had authority to seek out and interrogate suspected heretics (using informers, secrecy, and torture). Those found guilty and unrepentant were publicly burned. Adapted from the thirteenth-century inquisition against the Waldensians and Albigensians (see Chapter 8), the Roman Inquisition was also modeled in part on the more

Pope Paul III Titian was the culminating figure in Renaissance painting in Venice. In this portrait, the aged little pope steals the show from his towering grandsons by sheer force of character. *Erich Lessing / Art Resource, NY.*

recent Spanish Inquisition. As one cardinal (who later became Pope Paul IV) said, "No one must debase himself by showing toleration towards heretics of any kind, above all towards Calvinists." Yet this new instrument was quite capable of leniency: In approximately 150,000 trials between 1550 and 1800 in Spain, Portugal, and Italy, the execution rate was only 1 in 50.

Because heretical ideas seemed no less threatening than the heretics themselves, books too had to be purged from the community by fire. In 1559 the papacy published the *Index of Prohibited Books*, a list (frequently updated) of books that no Catholic should read without explicit permission and only for purposes of refutation. Whenever the authorities could find such books, public burnings were held. The church maintained the *Index* until 1966, and in the sixteenth century it included not only Protestant books but Erasmus's works, Boccaccio's *Decameron*, and Machiavelli's *The Prince*. The enforcement of the *Index*, however, varied widely. Quite effective in Spain and Italy, it had little impact in France and many of the German-speaking territories. The Council of Trent also declared that the only valid Latin version of Scripture was St. Jerome's Vulgate (see Chapter 5), despite the numerous translation

---

[1] In the Renaissance church it was not considered necessary that a cardinal be an ordained priest.

THE HUMAN EXPERIENCE

Menocchio, Miller of Montereale

Domenico Scandella, known as Menocchio (1532–1599) lived nearly all of his life in Montereale, a little town in the Friuli region some sixty miles northeast of Venice. In Montereale, Menocchio married, fathered eleven children, served as mayor and church administrator, and earned his living primarily as a miller—although at one time or another he also worked as a carpenter, schoolteacher, mason, and guitar player at festivals. In his day Montereale had no school, so it is not certain where Menocchio learned to read and write. Convicted as a relapsed heretic in 1599, he was executed not long after his second trial.

Menocchio's crime was rare in the Friuli—only one other heretic was executed in the region. Nor was the Holy Office (Roman Inquisition) thirsty for Menocchio's blood. His first trial began on February 7, 1584, and involved lengthy interrogations before the sentence of life imprisonment was given on the following May 17. By 1586, however, Menocchio convinced the authorities of his repentance. He promised to wear the *habitello* (painted cross signifying his offense) over his clothing and refrain

from propagating the ideas that had got him into trouble.

In strictly legal terms the Holy Office acted precisely and fairly. Defendants had many opportunities to recant and could explain themselves fully. Every word uttered by the defendant had to be written down by the notary or his deputy. Thanks to this procedure, we have access to Menocchio's mind. He admitted that he had told fellow villagers that "if I had permission to go before the pope, or a king, or a prince who would listen to me, I would have a lot of things to say; and if he had me killed afterward, I would not care."

Menocchio talked about his opinions to anyone who wanted to listen and to many who did not. Some of his observations were simply anticlerical (for example, "Priests want us under their thumb, just to keep us quiet, while they have a good time"). But as he himself told his judges, "I have an artful mind, and I have wanted to seek out higher things about which I did not know." Of the origins of the world, he held that "all was chaos . . . and out of that bulk a mass formed—just as

cheese is made out of milk—and worms appeared in it, and these were the angels." He denied the doctrines of original sin and the Trinity, the divinity of Christ, the virginity of Jesus' mother, the immortality of the soul, and the validity of the sacraments ("You might as well go and confess to a tree as to priests and monks").

Menocchio was not a learned man, but somehow he had read and heard enough to fire his vivid imagination, steeped as it was in traditional oral culture, peasant experience, the books he had read, and his own truculence and curiosity. A victim of the Counter-Reformation's passion for theological uniformity, he thought of himself as "a philosopher, astrologer, and prophet" and affirmed his belief that "God is all things." If the miller of Montereale had kept his opinions to himself, he could have saved his life. Unfortunately for him, but fortunately for us, Menocchio failed to control his urge to proselytize, even when speaking to his judges. ❖

errors that Christian humanists had been detecting in it for more than a century.

Paul III and his immediate successors thought more in terms of restoring the church to its former glory than changing it into something new; they lived in the luxurious manner of Renaissance princes and did little to stamp out the nepotism that had long characterized papal patronage. A new era of post-Tridentine ("after Trent") Catholicism began with the papacy of Pius IV. Pius and his three successors (to 1590) overhauled the church's administration and put the reform program proposed by the Council of Trent into practice. The College of Cardinals lost influence when the pope created committees of cardinals (called "congregations," such as the Congregation of the Index), gave them responsi-

bility for seeing that particular reforms were carried out, and had them report directly back to him.

The life and work of St. Carlo Borromeo (1538–1584), cardinal and archbishop of Milan, exemplifies this post-Tridentine Catholicism. Instead of hunting, feasting, and jostling for political influence and money in Rome, he resided in his diocese (the first archbishop of Milan to do so in eighty years). He spent his time in prayer, fasting, preaching, and ceaseless pastoral labor on behalf of his flock (including personally ministering to the sick and dying during an attack of the plague in 1576). No respecter of persons, Borromeo excommunicated Spanish viceroys who got in his way. He founded and supervised numerous schools, hospitals, and charitable organizations, severely disciplined erring clergy, and visited every corner of his huge diocese (763 parishes). A carpenter recorded in his diary that the cardinal urged members of all the confraternities in the city to take Communion daily and encouraged them by personally dispensing it to thirteen hundred people. Working and fasting himself to exhaustion, he died at age forty-six, having set an example that was already being widely imitated in the ranks of the higher clergy.

The New Orders

If the characteristic of Protestantism was fragmentation, the hallmark of revived Catholicism was thirty new religious orders and organizations under firm papal direction. The most important was the Society of Jesus (the Jesuits), founded by an extraordinary Spaniard, St. Ignatius of Loyola (1491–1556). A courtier and soldier in the service of Charles V, Loyola suffered terribly when a French cannonball crushed one leg and wounded the other in 1521. During a slow and painful recuperation, Ignatius experienced a spiritual anguish reminiscent of Luther's. After putting aside his sword and dagger, he donned the clothing of a beggar and set out on a pilgrimage to Jerusalem. At Manresa, a town near Barcelona, he formulated a method for achieving self-discipline in one of the most influential books ever written, the *Spiritual Exercises*.

First published in 1548, Loyola's *Spiritual Exercises* prescribed a precise program of spiritual purification to be followed in every detail for four weeks. In vivid, sensuous images the reader was to contemplate the life and death of Christ. To grasp the implications of Christ's death, one had to begin by picturing one's own. Only after such meditation could the reader understand the meaning of Christ's Crucifixion and Resurrection. The purpose of this contemplation was to build workers for the faith who could, if necessary, be martyrs. Loyola had, in fact, invented a new religious institution, the "retreat," and the direction of retreats became an important Jesuit ministry. Against Lutheran and Calvinist doctrine, the Jesuits endorsed and stressed the freedom of the human will, and the retreats became means of strengthening the participants' belief in it and heightening their opposition to Protestants.

Becoming a full member of Loyola's order required great effort, much more than for other Catholic orders. Two probationary years were followed by seven years of intense study. Only strong, intelligent, energetic men[2] passed muster, and their impact was far out of proportion to their numbers—some two thousand in 1556 and thirteen thousand by 1615. In addition to the normal priestly vows of poverty, chastity, and obedience, the Jesuits took a special additional vow of personal obedience to the head of the

order and to the pope. Loyola wrote that every Jesuit "should be known by this very mark, that he looks not to the person to whom he yields obedience; but that he sees in him the Lord Christ, for whose sake that obedience is rendered. . . . Your own will lay down. . . . In doing so you do not lose it—you augment it and bring it to perfection."

Like the Calvinists, the Jesuits stressed reforming activity in the world, not withdrawal from it. Modern readers may have just as much difficulty understanding the appeal of Jesuit obedience as of Calvin's predestination. Nevertheless, Loyola's ideas undeniably appealed to men of the sixteenth century, attracting thousands of able adherents—so many, in fact that some had to be turned away for lack of resources to train them. This movement produced not slavish robots but men of imagination, courage, initiative, and confidence. Jesuits became the leading educators and missionaries of the Catholic cause and, as such, won back areas lost to the Protestants in Europe and spread Christianity into Asia and the Americas. Their hugely popular secondary schools (called "colleges"), which charged no tuition and numbered 144 by 1579 and 372 by 1615, combined instruction in the humanistic curriculum with Christian doctrine and such practical subjects as modern languages. They made extensive use of "school drama," and the plays and other presentations the students put on included poetry, oratory, and dancing. Although a grumpy Jesuit in Bologna complained that children in the streets cried "Here come the comedy priests," the Jesuit schools became so attractive that they helped win many members of the urban and landowning elites back to Catholicism.

The emergence of new religious orders such as the Jesuits occurred at the same time as the rejuvenation of several older orders. The Carmelites, for example, underwent reform and reinvigoration by the aristocratic Spanish mystic, St. Teresa of Ávila. Inspired by visions, St. Teresa set about restoring the "Primitive Rule" of her order and in 1562 founded the Discalced (meaning "shoeless") Carmelites. The "Descalzos" wore rope sandals, slept on straw, ate no meat, and lived on alms. Leading her followers in prayer and missionary work, St. Teresa spurned ritual and ceremony: "I am not," she stressed, "one of your sign-of-the-cross mongers." St. Teresa and St. Ignatius Loyola alike faced stormy opposition from Catholic conservatives, who suspected them of heresy or, at best, excessive enthusiasm and unseemly self-denial. Both were imprisoned for a time by the Inquisition.

Important though the work of reforming popes and bishops undoubtedly was, the success of the Catholic Reformation owed at least as much to new religious orders that set many skilled, devoted, and enthusiastic hands to the tasks of renewal. Through missionary campaigns, liturgical reforms (such as the advocacy of frequent Communion), preaching, writing and publishing works of instruction and devotion, catechizing, caring for the sick and the

---

[2] There were (and still are) no female Jesuits.

THE HISTORICAL EVIDENCE

From the Autobiography of St. Teresa

1588

St. Teresa experienced visions of heaven, but not all her visions were pleasurable ones. In Chapter 32 of her autobiography, first published in 1588, she described how God favored her by giving her a view of hell. After the experience recounted in the selection below, she began the campaign to reform the Carmelites that led the Roman Catholic church to declare her a saint in 1622, only forty-five years after her death. In 1814 she was declared the national saint of Spain.

Some long time after the Lord had bestowed on me many of the favours that I have described, together with others that were very great, one day when I was at prayer, I found myself, without knowing how, plunged, as I thought, into hell. I understood that the Lord wished me to see the place that the devils had ready for me there, and that I had earned by my sins. All this happened in the briefest second; but even if I should live for many years, I do not think I could possibly forget it. The entrance seemed to me like a very long, narrow passage, or a very low, dark, and constricted furnace. The ground appeared to be covered with a filthy wet mud, which smelt abominably and contained many wicked reptiles. At the end was a cavity scooped out of the wall, like a cupboard, and I found myself closely confined in it. But the sight of all this was pleasant compared with my feelings. . . .

I do not think that my feelings could possibly be exaggerated, nor would anyone understand them. I felt a fire inside my soul, the nature of which is beyond my powers of description, and my physical tortures were intolerable. I have endured the severest bodily pains in the course of my life, the worst, so the doctors say, that it is possible to suffer and live. . . . But none of them was in any way comparable to the pains I felt at that time, especially when I realized that they would be endless and unceasing. But even this was nothing to my agony of soul, an oppression, a suffocation, and an affliction so agonizing, and accompa-

nied by such a hopeless and distressing misery that no words I could find would adequately describe it. . . . I was terrified, and though this happened six years ago, I am still terrified as I write; even as I sit here my natural heat seems to be drained away by fear. . . .

[This vision] has benefited me very much. . . . Since that time . . . everything has seemed endurable to me in comparison with a single moment of the suffering that I had to bear then. . . . It was this vision that filled me with the very deep distress which I feel on account of the great number of souls who bring damnation on themselves—of the Lutherans in particular, since they were members of the church by baptism.* It has also given me a fervent desire to help other souls. Indeed I believe that if I could free a single one from these dreadful tortures, I would willingly suffer many deaths. . . .

I tried to think what I could do for God, and decided that the first thing was to follow the call to a religious life that the Lord had given me, by keeping my Rule with every possible perfection.

---

*In Spain, all heretics were called Lutherans, whether or not they were followers of Luther. In fact, few of them were.

Source: From J. M. Cohen, *The Life of Saint Teresa of Ávila by Herself* (London: Penguin, 1957), pp. 233–236.

poor (including the Jesuit ministry to prostitutes and their children), founding and staffing of schools and universities, and many other activities, these orders demonstrated Catholicism's vitality and enabled it to respond effectively to the new challenges of the sixteenth century.

Catholic Reform and State Power in Spain

Catholic reform in Spain, like Protestant reform in northern Europe, needed the help of the secular authorities to

succeed, and the church in Spain was more subject to the monarchy than in any other place. Late in the fifteenth century, Ferdinand and Isabella had negotiated control of ecclesiastical appointments away from the pope and also wangled his acquiescence to the creation of the Spanish Inquisition as an organization under royal rather than papal control. The Inquisition was directed initially against the *conversos* and *moriscos* (respectively, Iberian Jews and Muslims who had converted to Christianity but whose sincerity was doubted by many Spanish Catholics).

tually disappeared, and sixteenth-century Spaniards came to equate Catholicism with Spanishness.

A deeply devout Catholic, Philip II nevertheless understood that where the Protestant heresy had had time to develop and gain political support it could not be rooted out. He had lived in both England and Germany and had Protestant friends there. He knew that his father had signed the Peace of Augsburg. As the ruler of the Netherlands, where his father had been born, Philip faced his worst nightmare in the form of the rebellion that broke out in 1566. The fact that many, though by no means all, of the rebels were Calvinists made it worse still. He could see that Calvinist success in the Netherlands would encourage the growth of heresy in France, thus bringing danger to Spain's very borders. Because Philip had to quell the rebellion of his own subjects in the Netherlands, he found himself drawn into wars against Protestants that were still raging when he died in 1598. The potent mixture of rebellion and religion entangled Philip's kingdoms with French, English, and Scottish developments.

Bernini's *Ecstasy of St. Teresa* For a church in Rome, Gianlorenzo Bernini sculpted this vivid representation of the moment when an angel's arrow pierced St. Teresa's heart. She wrote that "the pain was so great that I screamed aloud; but at the same time I felt such infinite sweetness that I wished the pain to last forever. It was not physical but psychic pain. . . . It was the sweetest caressing of the soul by God." *Erich Lessing / Art Resource, NY.*

Spain had once welcomed the influence of Renaissance culture. Erasmus's works circulated widely early in the sixteenth century in Spain, and Charles V had patronized him. But the spread of Lutheran and other heretical ideas in the 1520s had roused the state to oppose virtually all "novelties." Servetus, after all, was a Spaniard who escaped the Spanish inquisitors' grasp. After centuries of crusading to oust the Muslims from the Iberian Peninsula, Spanish monarchs desperately wanted to maintain Catholic orthodoxy. Charles V did not want Spain to undergo the catastrophe he had witnessed in Germany, and he advised his son Philip to use the Inquisition vigorously to maintain unity. In 1559, ninety-six "Lutherans" (a generic term for heretics in Spain) died in flames, and twenty more followed them in 1562. Heresy in Spain vir-

El Greco's *The Dream of Philip II* El Greco depicted Philip (bottom center) seeing Christ's monogram (IHS) and angels adoring it. To the right, the jaws of hell threaten Christendom. *Erich Lessing / Art Resource, NY.*

THE ENGLISH AND SCOTTISH REFORMATIONS

The British Isles were no exception to the rule that Protestantism needed the support of princes or city councils to grow, but the situation here nevertheless proved unusual. Britain was home to two kingdoms and dynasties, the Tudors in England and Ireland and the Stuarts in Scotland. Early in the sixteenth century in England, adherents of the Lollard heresy (see Chapter 11) continued to criticize high-living clergymen and their sacramental system while reading the Bible in English among themselves. Yet Lollard numbers were few, and most people exhibited their devotion to traditional piety. In the 1520s, both Henry VIII (reigned 1509–1547) in England and James V (reigned 1513–1542) in Scotland took a dim view of the Lutheran ideas being cautiously circulated by a handful of university-educated preachers. In England, for example, Henry VIII wrote a treatise defending the traditional doctrine of the seven sacraments against Luther's objections. Pope Leo, deeply gratified, bestowed a new title, "Defender of the Faith," on the English monarch. William Tyndale (ca.1494–1536), an English humanist and Lutheran who made the first English translation of the New Testament to be printed, had to flee his native country in 1524. Condemned as a heretic in Flanders, he was strangled to death and his body burned. Reportedly his last words were, "Lord, open the king of England's eyes." Eventually, Protestantism won out in both countries. Ireland, however, was a different story. Although all of Ireland theoretically owed obedience to the English crown, until late in the sixteenth century effective English rule did not extend outside of the area around Dublin, known as "the Pale." Protestant evangelizing therefore had little success on an island where the majority of the people spoke only Gaelic and where to embrace Protestantism meant also to collaborate with the English invaders and their alien law and culture.

From Henry VIII to Bloody Mary

Henry VIII, ever a good Catholic, decided in the late 1520s that he must get the pope to annul his marriage to Catherine of Aragon. He had married Catherine, the widow of his older brother Arthur, in 1509. She had not given him a male heir, and he feared a disputed succession after his death or a struggle to determine a marriage partner for their daughter Mary. Either scenario would threaten England's domestic peace and internal unity, inviting intervention by foreigners.

In the past, monarchs with such problems had usually found popes willing to help—in return, of course, for some valuable recompense. Other kings had simply ignored papal objections. But Catherine was the aunt of the Holy Roman emperor, Charles V, who was at the peak of his

Henry VIII   This portrait (ca. 1537) is one of many that the German artist Hans Holbein painted of Henry VIII and members of his court. Henry greatly admired Holbein's skill, saying "I can make seven lords of seven ploughmen, but of seven lords I cannot make even one Holbein."   *Scala / Art Resource, NY.*

power in the late 1520s, and his troops, who had sacked Rome when he failed to pay them in 1527, still posed a threat to Pope Clement VII when Henry's request for an annulment arrived. Charles knew that if Henry had no son, Mary would succeed him, and England could easily be brought into the Habsburg orbit. Rather than reject Henry's request outright and drive England toward the Lutheran camp, Clement simply stalled. After six years of waiting in vain for the annulment, Henry acted unilaterally. Like many other princes during the Reformation, he used the precedent set by the Roman emperor Constantine to justify his claims to authority in religious matters (see Chapter 5). His shrewd, reform-minded adviser, Thomas Cromwell, guided an act through Parliament in 1533 declaring that the final appeal for ecclesiastical cases would no longer be Rome but the courts of the English archbishops. Clement VII had no choice but to excommunicate Henry, and the English Reformation was under way. Henry married Anne Boleyn, whom he had long loved, and she bore him a daughter, the future Queen Elizabeth I—but no son. Anne was beheaded in 1536 after Henry became

HENRY VII
(1485–1509)

Arthur = Catherine   1   HENRY VIII   3   Jane Seymour   Margaret = JAMES IV
(d. 1502) of Aragon   =   (1509–1547)   =   (d. 1537)   King of Scotland
           (d. 1535)   (1473–1513)

                                            2
                                            = Anne Boleyn

PHILIP II = MARY I   ELIZABETH I   EDWARD VI   JAMES V
King of Spain (1553–1558) (1558–1603) (1547–1553)   King of Scotland
                                                             (1513–1542)

                                                              MARY
                                                             Queen of Scots
                                                             (1542–1587)

All dates are regnal dates unless otherwise indicated.   JAMES VI/JAMES I
                                                             King of Scots
                                                             (1587–1625)
                                                             King of England
                                                             (1603–1625)

FIGURE 13-2 THE TUDOR DYNASTY

convinced of her adultery. Henry[3] then married Jane Seymour, who died after giving birth to the long-awaited son, Edward (see Figure 13-2).

The break with Rome required reorganization of the English church, and Henry put internal peace above doctrinal consistency. In the Act of Supremacy (1534), Parliament recognized the monarch as "Supreme Head" of the church in England, a role British monarchs still play. (They also kept the papal-granted title "Defender of the Faith.") To the delight of Protestant critics of monasticism, Henry then did what German Lutheran princes were doing: He confiscated the property of the English monasteries, which comprised more than a fourth of all the arable land in the country. Much of it he soon sold to members of the landowning classes, thus creating a powerful incentive not to return to the Catholic fold. James V, Henry's Scottish nephew, took careful note of his uncle's example in the 1530s. While remaining an orthodox Catholic, James helped himself to the lands of Scottish bishops and monks by means of excessive taxation rather than outright seizure. The churchmen had to sell land to pay the taxes, and many of its new lay owners would in due course find Protestantism attractive.

Henry's policy of elevating the needs of the state over the demand for doctrinal purity is evident in the Anglican church he established, neither fully Protestant nor fully Catholic but borrowing from both. The king replaced the pope, the Bible appeared in English, and the traditional seven sacraments gave way to only three (baptism, Holy Communion, and penance). The existence of purgatory was questioned, and indulgences were denounced. Protestants, though encouraged, had hoped for more changes. Catholics, while distressed, were relieved that Henry retained transubstantiation, worship services in Latin, and clerical celibacy. The changes stretched out across a dozen years, and Henry occasionally tacked back in the conservative direction, making it hard for those who disliked the changes to decide where and when to make a stand. Sir Thomas More (see Chapter 12), Henry's lord chancellor, suffered beheading in 1535 after refusing to accept the royal takeover of the church.[4] One major popular rebellion, the Pilgrimage of Grace, broke out in northern England in 1536. Henry quelled it forcibly and thereby survived the only serious internal threat to his new order in church and state. But heads rolled on both sides. In 1540, the conservative faction convinced the king that Cromwell was a

---

[3] Henry married three more times: Anne of Cleves, Catherine Howard, and Catherine Parr. The fates of his wives are neatly summed up in this little jingle: "Divorced, beheaded, died / Divorced, beheaded, survived."

[4] The Catholic church declared him St. Thomas More in 1935.

Title Page of Henry VIII's Great Bible Before 1539, possession of a copy of the Bible in English was illegal, but reformers convinced Henry VIII to encourage his subjects to read this new translation, which was based partly on William Tyndale's earlier work. The title page shows Henry at the top handing the Word of God (*Verbum Dei*) to Cromwell and Thomas Cranmer, Archbishop of Canterbury, who pass it down to the people. They, in turn, shout "*Vivat Rex*" ("Long live the king")—and even a prisoner in jail (lower right) joins the chorus. Henry later had second thoughts and tried to restrict Bible-reading, but the restrictions were unenforceable. *Stock Montage, Inc.*

heretic and a traitor, and the adviser who had engineered the break with Rome was beheaded (much to Henry's later regret).

During the six years following Henry's death in 1547, the doctrinaire reformers thoroughly Protestantized the Church of England. But in 1553, on the death of Henry's fifteen-year-old son and heir, Edward VI, the religious tide turned with the accession of the Catholic daughter of Henry VIII and Catherine of Aragon, Mary Tudor. After marrying Prince Philip of Spain (soon to become King Philip II), Mary set about to return England to Roman Catholicism. Hundreds of upper-class Protestants fled to

Edward VI's Protestant Revolution   This woodcut, published in John Foxe's popular *Book of Martyrs* in many editions during and after Elizabeth's reign, summarizes the thorough Protestantization of the English church that occurred during young King Edward VI's six-year reign (1547–1553). At the top, Catholic images have been taken from the church and are being burned or removed for shipment to Rome. A Protestant worship service, centered on preaching and retaining only baptism and Holy Communion as sacraments, is in progress. People listening to the sermon do so with their Bibles open, and a Communion table has replaced the altar.

centers of advanced reformist thought such as Calvin's Geneva. While in exile, their commitment to a more radical Protestantism grew, and their influence in England through the movement known as Puritanism was to be profound and long-lasting. Nearly three hundred Protestants who did not flee and would not recant were publicly burned as heretics—hence the queen's nickname, "Bloody Mary." The victims included Archbishop Cranmer and three Edwardian bishops, but the majority were relatively humble folk who could not afford to escape into exile. Mary's fondest hope had been to bear an heir who would keep England Catholic, but when she died childless in 1558 her Protestant half-sister Elizabeth came to the throne. What the English people thought of this series of changes in religion remains unclear because taking a position was so dangerous that relatively few did so.

Reform and Revolt in Scotland

When James V died in December 1542, his infant daughter Mary ("Mary, Queen of Scots" who reigned from 1542–1587) succeeded him, and a regency government took over in her name. After 1554, the regent was Mary's mother, the French princess Mary of Guise. In 1558 she arranged the marriage of her daughter to the French king's son and heir, Francis, creating the prospect of a union of the French and Scottish crowns and reaffirming the long-standing Franco-Scottish alliance against England. By the late 1550s, the reformist party in Scotland had become thoroughly Calvinist and led by pro-English aristocrats (called the "Lords of the Congregation") and a preacher named John Knox. Knox, who had been captured by French troops and spent nineteen months chained to an oar in a French galley, had assisted in the Protestant reform of the English church under Edward VI. He spent Bloody Mary's reign in exile in Calvin's Geneva (see page 481).

Mary Stuart, meanwhile, had grown up at the French court. She and her husband, the heir to the French throne, coveted the English throne as well. Mary's grandmother, Margaret—daughter of Henry VII and sister of Henry VIII—had married James IV, and their son was Mary's father. Because, from the Catholic point of view, Henry VIII's marriage to Anne Boleyn was bigamous and their daughter Elizabeth illegitimate, Mary Stuart called herself queen of England from the moment of Mary Tudor's death in 1558. Her husband Francis became king of France in July 1559, but her reign as his queen was brief. He died in December 1560, and she returned to Scotland in August 1561. In 1559, meanwhile, with help from Elizabeth of England, the rebellion of the Calvinist party had overthrown the French regency of Mary of Guise, expelled the regent and her army, ousted the Catholic clergy and worship, and installed a thoroughly Calvinist church, the "Kirk." Lacking military power, Mary Stuart had no choice but to bide her time, meanwhile cooperating with Knox and his friends. To strengthen her claim to the English crown, she married Henry Stuart, Lord Darnley, who was descended from the second marriage of her grandmother Margaret.

Although Mary and Darnley's son eventually became king James VI of Scotland and later James I of England, their marriage ended in catastrophe. Darnley helped murder a man he mistakenly thought was Mary's lover, and she in turn helped plot Darnley's murder at the hands of the man who became her next husband, the Earl of Bothwell. A rebellion forced her to flee to England in 1567, leaving her infant son and his regency in the hands of the Calvinist party. Mary's flight enabled the Calvinists to consolidate their earlier victory, at least in the Scottish Lowlands, where English was spoken. In the Gaelic-speaking Highlands, the new religion made only slow and patchy headway. The national reformation of Scotland was rare in that it overthrew the established regime, unlike the usual pattern in which the authorities used Protestantism to increase their power.

RELIGIOUS SETTLEMENTS IN AN AGE OF REFORMATION

The political and constitutional history of early modern Europe would have been totally different without such men as Luther, Zwingli, Calvin, and Loyola. None of them could abide "mixtures" of Catholic and Protestant doctrines or styles of worship. All wanted peace, but not at the expense of pure, true religion. To understand why their impact on politics was so substantial, we must recall the factors that shaped the governments of the Late Middle Ages: dynasties, land, and money. The Reformation added a fourth ingredient: religion. And because church and state were not yet separate, religious disputes fostered new and volatile situations—such as the fighting in the Holy Roman Empire preceding the Peace of Augsburg (discussed earlier), the French civil wars of religion, and the Dutch Revolt against Spain (described later in this section). Thus the Reformation affected politics, just as politics affected the Reformation. By the end of the wars of religion in 1648, the Catholic and Protestant churches had undergone great changes, and the hard-line, doctrinaire approach was clearly in decline on both sides. The most successful political leaders were those who took a *politique* approach, meaning a willingness to sacrifice doctrinal consistency to gain internal peace and guard themselves and their subjects against foreign enemies. In doing so the English, French, and Dutch eventually reached "mixed" religious settlements, to the despair of doctrinaire Catholics and Protestants alike. In these cases, the conflict triggered by the all-or-nothing attitude of doctrinaire zealots on both sides yielded to settlements, however fragile, imperfect, and temporary, crafted by politique leaders. In England, resolution came peacefully; in France and the Low Countries, it came only after lengthy and bloody warfare.

The Elizabethan Settlement

Elizabeth I was twenty-five years old when she became queen of England, reigning from 1558 to 1603. She was the archetypal politique, and although her compromise religious settlement angered both Catholic and Protestant diehards, it saved her country from civil war. Elizabeth and her first Parliament restored royal supremacy over the church and decreed that worship services be in English, a reform from Edward's day that stuck. But priests were clothed in traditional vestments again, ensuring that the service would still have a Catholic appearance. Elizabeth's rewording of the prayers in the Communion service allowed anyone who believed in the real presence of Christ's body to continue to do so, a retreat from the Zwinglian stance taken under Edward. But the official doctrine, the Thirty-Nine Articles (1563), enunciated central Protestant positions (salvation by faith alone, predestination, rejection of purgatory).

The result was a theological muddle, a mixture of Catholic liturgy and Protestant doctrine. Neither party was satisfied. Although only a handful of radicals were willing to risk the loss of everything by rebelling, these few extremists threatened to create serious problems. Some Catholics plotted to overthrow Elizabeth in favor of her Catholic cousin, Mary, Queen of Scots. They were executed as traitors, along with a good many others whose guilt remains doubtful. Mary herself was beheaded after her treason trial in 1587. And radical Protestants—called Puritans for their desire to "purify" the English church of its remaining Catholic elements—pressed Elizabeth hard both in her council and in Parliament. But Elizabeth stood firm, and the compromise held. Across the English Channel in France, attempts at a similar compromise did not succeed.

Civil War in France

At the end of the 1500s, France, home to more than 16 million people, was the most populous nation in western Europe but by no means the most powerful. France's troubles began immediately after the conclusion of a treaty ending the wars between the Habsburg Dynasty of Spain and the Valois Dynasty of France—the Treaty of Cateau-Cambrésis (1559). During a tournament held to celebrate the treaty, the French king Henry II, was fatally wounded when a splinter from a lance penetrated his eye.

Henry II's untimely death plunged France into four decades of internal conflict, vividly demonstrating the difficulty of governing a sixteenth-century kingdom when power passed to a minor or to a woman whom the nobility neither respected nor feared (see Figure 13-3). Henry's eldest son, the fifteen-year-old Francis II (husband of Mary, Queen of Scots), died after a reign of only eighteen months and was succeeded by his ten-year-old brother, Charles IX (reigned 1560–1574). A third brother, the childless Henry III (reigned 1574–1589), ruled until his assassination ended the Valois line. During the reigns of Francis and Charles, France's regent and real ruler was their mother, Catherine de' Medici (Lorenzo's great-granddaughter). As a woman, a regent, and a foreigner, her political position was precarious, and the uncertain succession made the religious divisions even more disruptive than they were in England.

Catherine, a Catholic, tried to pursue the kind of politique course in religious matters that Elizabeth I successfully followed in England. But she faced a daunting task. Huguenots (French Calvinists) were already numerous—perhaps 1.5 million strong, which made them almost 10 percent of the kingdom's population—and concentrated in the towns. Calvinism thrived among the nobles; by the 1560s nearly half the nobility was Protestant. Nobles, townspeople, and regional officials had lost many of their traditional rights to the centralizing monarchy, and all three groups sought to capitalize on royal weakness and

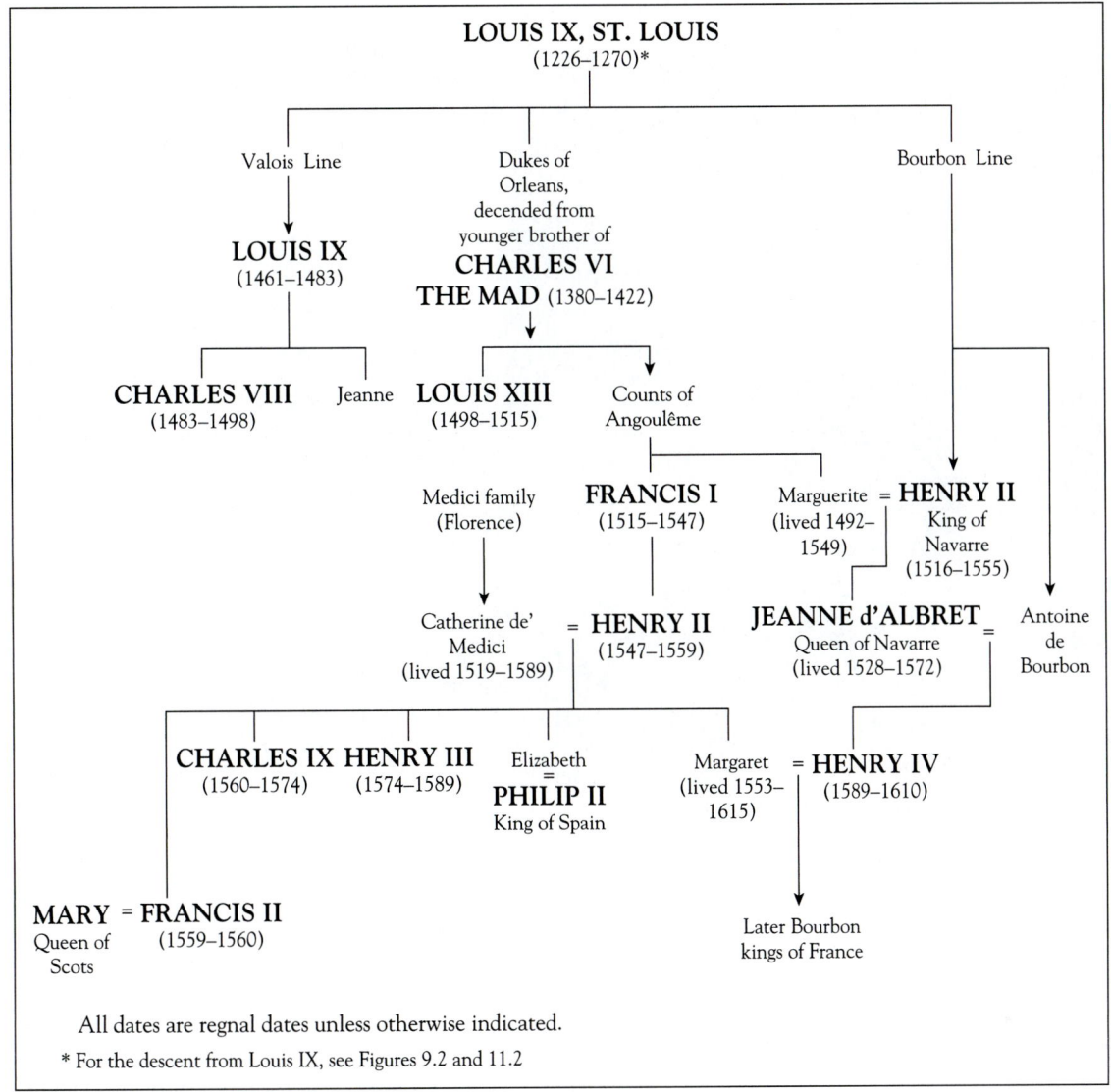

FIGURE 13-3
FRENCH KINGS IN THE SIXTEENTH CENTURY

Handwritten annotation in red:
LOUIS IX → LOUIS XI
LOUIS XIII → LOUIS XII

religious conflict to regain those liberties. For them, religious reform and political gain went hand in hand.

When, in 1562, Catherine tried to head off religious conflict by permitting the Huguenots to worship more freely, the hard-line Catholic party, led by the noble house of Guise, massacred a Huguenot congregation at Vassy. The killings initiated the first of a series of brutal Catholic-Huguenot wars. Countless religious riots demonstrated the deep commitment of people of all classes to belief in the filthy, diabolical, polluting nature of the other side's religion. Catholic crowds in Normandy killed Huguenots and crammed pages torn from their Bibles into their mouths, saying, "They preached the truth of their God. Let them call him to their aid." Huguenots in Paris murdered a Catholic who tried to keep them from desecrating the

holy-wafer box, asking, "Does your God of paste protect you now from the pains of death?"

The most ghastly incident was the St. Bartholomew's Day Massacre in 1572. Henry, Duke of Guise, led a group that murdered the Huguenot leader, Admiral Coligny, in his bed at 2 A.M., and Catholic mobs butchered three thousand Huguenots in Paris and more in the provinces. But instead of destroying the Huguenots, the tragedy galvanized them to obtain aid from foreign Protestants and fight back. The Guises, in turn, organized the Catholic League, supported by Spanish money and—by 1590—Spanish troops. A truce or a peace would be established from time to time, only to break down amid new warfare in which the stakes included control of the crown of France and the fate of great noble families in addition to religion.

The Massacre of St. Bartholomew's Day   This 1584 propaganda painting of the slaughter of Huguenots in Paris in 1572 had been preceded by woodcuts in books and pamphlets that circulated widely among Protestants in and outside France. The young king, Charles IX, examines the headless corpse of a Huguenot leader (right center), and his mother, Catherine de' Medici, views a pile of corpses (upper left). Both Charles IX and Pope Gregory XIII had medals struck to celebrate the event. Russia's Ivan the Terrible, however, considered it one more example of west European depravity.   *The Granger Collection, New York.*

The Revolt of the Netherlands

The Low Countries constituted a vital part of Philip II's inheritance, valued as a market for Spanish wool and wine and as a source of grain, armaments, textiles, and timber. The French coveted the region's wealth and strategic location. The English economy, heavily dependent on the export of wool cloth, would have collapsed without access to the market the Low Countries provided. Encompassing modern Belgium, Luxembourg, and the Netherlands, the region was divided in the sixteenth century into seventeen provinces, the most important of which were Holland in the north and Flanders in the south—the latter with its flourishing textile towns and its thriving trading and financial center of Antwerp. Each of the seventeen provinces remained a separate political entity, jealously guarding its own medieval customs and liberties, including the right to consent to taxes. Inevitably their governance would pose grave difficulties to Philip II's regents. (Map 13-3 illustrates the political and religious divisions of the time.)

When Philip's reign began, the Low Countries were still predominantly Catholic. Their Catholicism, however, consisted of a relatively tolerant Erasmian Catholicism rather than the rigid Counter-Reformation variety. Although the Catholics disliked the Calvinists, Anabaptists, and other Protestants, they despised Philip's high-handed attempts to impose without consultation a scheme of ecclesiastical reform. His centralizing plan not only wiped out ancient liberties; it also brought inquisitors to root out heresy. In Flanders alone between 1559 and 1564, some 1,350 heresy prosecutions occurred. In August 1566 the persecuted Protestants reacted with a wave of destructive attacks upon stained glass, images, and sacramental objects used in Roman Catholic worship. More than four hundred churches and convents in West Flanders alone suffered what the mobs considered "purification." Philip's regent in the Netherlands, his half-sister Margaret of Austria, used the words "defilements, abominations, sacrileges" to describe this iconoclastic campaign. Utterly horrified, Philip alienated Catholics and Protestants alike by sending in an army of ten thousand troops under a tough old general, the Duke of Alba. Ruling with the aid of a court of three Spaniards—the "Council of Troubles"—Alba beheaded two nobles in proceedings that were illegal under

THE HUMAN EXPERIENCE

Marguerite of Navarre, Jeanne d'Albret, and French Reform

The lives of two queens, Marguerite of Navarre (1492–1549) and her daughter Jeanne d'Albret (1528–1572), mirror the history of the reform movement in France. Marguerite was the beloved sister of Francis I and in her own right a leader of Christian humanism. Brilliant, thoroughly educated, and beautiful, she wrote voluminously in several genres. In the tradition of Boccaccio's *Decameron,* her popular *Heptameron* (1558), contained seventy stories about love. Her treatises and religious poetry show her interest in a mystical piety in the Neoplatonist tradition of Marsilio Ficino and his Florentine Academy. Like Erasmus, Marguerite died a Catholic, yet she wrote poems expressing sympathy with Protestant ideas such as predestination and justification by faith. She encouraged and protected such humanistic reformers as Jacques Lefèvre d'Étaples (1455–1536), a brilliant scholar who translated the New Testament and the Psalms into French, and Guillaume Briçonnet, bishop of Meaux, a mystic who worked to reform the sale of indulgences and excessive devotion to relics in his diocese. Thanks to her influence with her brother the king, Marguerite saved many reformers from prison and even from the stake. Her tolerance for more radical reformers sparked a quarrel with Calvin, but there can be little doubt that those she was able to protect laid the groundwork for the Huguenot movement that grew so rapidly after her death.

Jeanne d'Albret publicly announced her Calvinist faith late in 1560. Her husband, Antoine de Bourbon (d. 1563), was next in line for the French throne if the Valois line died out, and her son was Henry IV, the king who engineered France's recovery after the civil wars of religion (see Figure 13-3). Antoine adopted Calvinism mainly because he hoped the Calvinists would help him regain the southern portion of Navarre from Spain. The Catholics won him back by offering him Sardinia in 1562, an apostasy for which Jeanne never forgave him. "He planted a thorn not in my foot, but in my heart," she said, although she continued to love him.

In Navarre in 1561, Jeanne issued an edict placing Catholic and Reformed worship on an equal basis. Jeanne wanted to make Navarre Calvinist—without bloodshed, she hoped. Excessive zeal on both sides spoiled her hopes, but in Navarre and in the civil wars in France she showed herself a forceful contender. When the pope's ambassador tried to persuade her to withdraw her edict in Navarre, she responded:

> I am not planting a new religion but restoring an old one. . . . I have forced no one with death, imprisonment or condemnation. . . . Your feeble arguments do not dent my tough skull. I am serving God and He knows how to sustain His cause. . . . How much good did it do my husband to defect to Rome? . . . You have abandoned the holy walk of my mother for the humors of Rome. . . . If I err, I may be excused as a woman for my ignorance, but yours, as a cardinal, is shameful. I follow Beza, Calvin and others only in so far as they follow scripture.

To read Jeanne's letters is to see where her son got some of his drive and ability. She died only months before the St. Bartholomew's Day Massacre of Huguenots assembled for Henry of Navarre's wedding. She would not have approved of his ultimate reconversion to Catholicism, but his Edict of Nantes protected the faith she had done much to promote. ❖

Jeanne d' Albret   *The Granger Collection, New York.*

local law. Thousands of alleged heretics were tortured and killed, and their property seized. When Alba imposed a new 10 percent sales tax without consultation, he struck at the Low Countries' economy as well as their religion and constitution.

The Dutch rebellion took a major step forward in 1572 when rebels known as the Sea Beggars seized the little port of Brill and used it as a base to capture other coastal towns. They managed to shut off access to Antwerp from the sea, thus making it difficult for Alba to

MAP 13-3
RELIGIOUS CONFLICT IN THE AGE OF PHILIP II.

The inset shows the route of the Great Armada.

get supplies. In 1576 Spanish troops mutinied because they had not been paid and sacked Antwerp, killing some eight thousand people and unifying disparate rebel elements. By the late 1570s, Philip was faced with a full-scale rebellion that threatened to wrest the entire Netherlands from Spanish control.

The rebel leader, William "the Silent," Prince of Orange, hoped to lead all seventeen provinces into independent nationhood. A rich nobleman of politique outlook, William came closest to his goal at the signing of the Pacification of Ghent in 1576. Representatives from all seventeen provinces agreed to call for expulsion of Spanish troops and an end to heresy trials. But in 1578 Philip sent a new army into the Netherlands under a brilliant soldier and tactician, Alexander Farnese, Duke of Parma. Parma cleverly exploited potential divisions in William's unwieldy coalition and scored enough military victories to convince the Catholic nobility in the southern provinces to break their alliance with the Calvinists.

During the 1580s Parma retook most of the areas south of the Rhine, forcing Calvinists to flee northward. Their fortunes declined further when William the Silent was assassinated by a fanatical Catholic cabinetmaker in 1584. In 1585 Parma recaptured Antwerp and formed a union against the rebellious north. He continued to advance against the desperate rebels, but they still held vital ports and now were getting aid from England. Brooding in the Escorial, his vast palace outside Madrid, Philip II conceived a grandiose scheme to destroy two enemies with one crushing blow.

The Crisis of 1588 and Its Aftermath

By the mid-1580s Philip's conflicts with the Protestants of England, France, and the Low Countries had become inextricably intertwined, but his hopes for defeating them and regaining all the Dutch territory remained high. In 1571 his navy had won a tremendous victory over the Turks at Lepanto, the largest naval battle ever fought, involving 600 ships and more than 160,000 men. In 1580 he had acquired the crown of Portugal after the death of the young Portuguese king created a disputed succession. Combining

Bruegel's *Massacre of the Innocents* In this scene set in a frigid Netherlandish village, Bruegel compared the biblical story of Herod's murder of children with the brutality of Spanish soldiers (led by Alba in the center of the cavalry troop) as they enforced Philip II's policies during the winter of 1566–1567, the year the revolt began. *Erich Lessing / Art Resource, NY.*

diplomacy, bribery, and force, Philip made good his own claim. He thereby gained not only Portugal itself with its valuable Atlantic ports and large navy but an overseas empire stretching from Brazil to the Indian Ocean (see Chapter 14). Meanwhile a dramatic increase of silver from American mines provided funds for a bold strike against the heretics in the north. Philip's plan was to use Spanish and Portuguese ships to cover the movement of Parma's seasoned troops from the Netherlands to conquer England, thereby ending English assistance to French Huguenots and Dutch rebels. Philip could then reconquer the rest of the Netherlands and ensure the victory of the Catholic League in France.

The Spanish Armada of 130 ships and 28,000 men sailed on July 21, 1588, from Corunna, reaching the entrance to the English Channel on July 29. For nine days, English and Spanish ships fought artillery duels from beyond boarding range. The English, with their ships serving as platforms for heavy bronze guns, used tactics first sys-

tematically employed nearly a century before by the Portuguese against the numerically superior Muslim fleets in the Indian Ocean. Although the English navy had improved gun carriages that enabled more rapid firing of salvos, the Spaniards nevertheless held their defensive formation. They anchored, largely intact, off Calais to await Parma's army. The English countered by sending fireships—small ships loaded with flammable materials and set aflame—into the Spanish anchorage at night. Forced by the fireships to scatter, the onset of a fierce storm (called "the Protestant wind") prevented them from regaining their formation. The Armada then suffered major losses from both the English artillery and more bad weather. A third of its ships never got back to Spain.

The defeat of the Spanish Armada did wonders for Protestant morale. Immediately after the battle, a Huguenot leader wrote to one of Elizabeth's advisers: "In saving yourselves you will save the rest of us." Both the Huguenots and the Dutch rebels gained new enthusiasm

THE HISTORICAL EVIDENCE

Elizabeth I's Armada Speech
1588

Fortunately for the English, their fleet's weather-aided victory over the Armada meant that the troops being hastily prepared to defend England did not have to face Parma's veteran army. Before the outcome of the naval battle was known, Elizabeth herself visited her army's camp and made a speech designed to strengthen the men's morale. Always a brilliant speaker, Elizabeth sought to overcome the traditional assumption that women had no place on the battlefield. We have no way of knowing how many of the men who heard her were convinced by her rhetoric, but it is difficult to imagine any speech more effective at such a dire moment.

My Loving People: We have been persuaded by some that are careful of our safety, to take heed how we commit ourselves to armed multitudes, for fear of treachery; but I assure you, I do not desire to live to distrust my faithful and loving people.

Let tyrants fear; I have always so behaved myself, that, under God, I have placed my chiefest strength and safeguard in the loyal hearts and good will of my subjects, and therefore, I am come amongst you, as you see, at this time, not for my recreation and disport, but being resolved in the midst and heat of the battle, to live or die amongst you all, to lay down for my God, and for my kingdoms, and for my people, my honor and my blood, even in the dust.

I know I have the body but of a weak and feeble woman; but I have the heart and stomach of a king, and of a king of England too; and think foul scorn that Parma or Spain, or any prince of Europe should dare to invade the borders of my realm; to which rather than any dishonor shall grow by me, I myself will take up arms, I myself will be your general, judge, and rewarder of every one of your virtues in the field.

I know already, for your forwardness you have deserved rewards and crowns; and we do assure you in the word of a prince, they shall be duly paid you. In the meantime, my lieutenant-general shall be in my stead; not doubting but by your obedience to my general, by your concord in the camp, and your valor in the field, we shall shortly have a famous victory over those enemies of my God, of my kingdoms, and of my people.

Source: From Joseph M. Levine, ed., *Elizabeth I* (Englewood Cliffs, N.J.: Prentice-Hall, 1969), pp. 66–67.

---

and confidence. The English took it as evidence that England was God's chosen nation. The growing ebullience of English culture owed much to the victory. After 1588 Englishmen felt like David, who with a slingshot, had killed Goliath. In fact, the Spanish Goliath was far from dead. Spain remained a mighty power, albeit a power on the defensive.

The year 1588 also proved a turning point in France's bloody civil wars. Ever since the St. Bartholomew's Day Massacre of 1572, war had followed war, and atrocity had followed atrocity, while France's economy disintegrated and the people starved. In 1588 Henry III, angered by Guise usurpation of royal authority, arranged the murder of Henry, Duke of Guise, the leader of the Catholic League. Seven months later a Dominican friar killed the king in retaliation. With the last of the Valois dead, the Huguenot leader, Henry of Navarre—from a junior branch of the royal family—had the best hereditary claim to the throne. But his religion ensured the fierce opposition of many French Catholics and the continuation of civil war. The struggle became more international, as Elizabeth I sent more troops to serve under Henry in 1590, and at the same time Philip II ordered Parma to use his Spanish army to lift the Huguenot siege of Paris. Although the Spanish invasion ended the siege, Henry of Navarre nevertheless won in the end. He ascended the throne as Henry IV (reigned 1589–1610), the first king of the Bourbon Dynasty, which would rule until the French Revolution. He quieted his enemies by converting to Catholicism in July 1593. Although hard-line Catholics tried to damage him by claiming that he had said cynically that "Paris is worth a Mass," he was too clever to make such a gaffe publicly. Handsome, witty, and shrewd, Henry IV was one of France's ablest kings.

As a Huguenot turned Catholic, Henry IV adopted the policy of religious compromise urged by the politiques. Amid the bloodshed of the 1570s and 1580s, the politiques had developed into a third political force opposing the extremism of both Huguenots and Catholic Leaguers. Comprising mostly moderate Catholics, they advocated toleration on the practical ground that the cost of restoring religious unity was too high. Henry IV showed himself to be the perfect politique when in 1598 he issued the Edict of Nantes, granting the Huguenots liberty of conscience and limited freedom of worship. Huguenots could worship at specified places in each district; special courts were set up to try cases in which they were involved so that they need not fear judicial bias; they retained the right to hold office and receive educations. And to ensure their safety, Henry even gave them political and military control of a hundred fortified places. Neither the Huguenots nor the Leaguers were happy with the arrangement. As with the Elizabethan settlement, both parties wanted the whole loaf, and like the settlement in England, the edict caused trouble later. But it did restore domestic order and, for all its imperfections, was a major step toward religious toleration. For the first time, the government of a large European country accepted the coexistence of two religions. Although France remained a Catholic realm, the Huguenots were permitted to live and worship there, a significant defeat for the Counter-Reformation.

The Dutch rebellion, meanwhile, continued for two generations after the defeat of the Armada. Not until 1609 was a truce signed, and not until 1648 did Spain finally concede to the seven northern provinces their independence and their Calvinism. They came to be known as the United Provinces or the Dutch Republic. The ten southern provinces reconquered by Parma remained Catholic and Spanish,[5] but the economy of the Spanish Netherlands lay in ruins. By blocking Antwerp's access to the sea, Amsterdam in Protestant Holland reaped the rich benefits of the seventeenth-century Dutch Empire. The defeat of the Armada was a turning point in both naval and world history.

Neither for the first time nor for the last, politique leaders, willing to compromise, defeated doctrinaire extremists. Having forged religious settlements that "mixed" Catholicism and Protestantism in one way or another, they managed to make peace internally and focus energies and loyalties on their nations. The religious settlements differed from each other as much as the nations. Instead of the uniformity that both Geneva and Rome sought to impose universally, the religious settlements worked because they consisted of elements drawn from the differing cultures and experiences of each people. The religious policies of Elizabeth I, Henry IV, and William the Silent aimed to heighten national identity and unity; their honored places in their country's histories rest on the success of those policies.

---

[5] In 1830, this region would become the kingdom of Belgium.

THE REFORMATION, SOCIETY, AND CULTURE

Both Catholic and Protestant reformations profoundly altered European society and culture. Both relied upon the work of Renaissance humanism and its northern, Erasmian version. Many who began as Erasmians ended up as Protestants, while many others—like Erasmus himself and Thomas More—remained within the Catholic fold. The enormous popularity of Jesuit schools and universities, for example, derived largely from their humanist curriculum. Erasmus and Luther, both brilliant writers who understood the enormous power of the printing press, went beyond their medieval predecessors by striving to make the Scriptures available in everyday language so that many more people could read and understand them. Readers, they believed, would become doers of God's Word, and the result would be a massive renewal and reform of Christendom itself in every aspect of social, moral, economic, and political life. The Bible, which contained God's commandments and instructions concerning every aspect of human life, had been available to medieval Christians only in a corrupted Latin version. The pioneering textual work of Erasmus and his colleagues made possible a series of translations of the Bible into German (by Luther himself in 1522), English, French, and the other European languages. Thus, the perfected text of the Bible would at last be widely understood by churchmen and laypeople and available to them in print. It would at last be obeyed by popes and princes no less than peasants and artisans—or so the reformers hoped.

The Reformation and the People

Why did Protestantism initially spread so rapidly, and how did it affect European society? Certainly many thousands, even millions, abandoned saints and relics and joined the new faith. In Germany fifty of sixty-five imperial cities at one time or another switched, often permanently. Cutting across class lines, not only princes and nobles embraced the movement but scholars, town dwellers, and peasants. The popularity of early Protestantism has long been attributed to a reaction against clerical corruption and abuses and the late medieval obsession with the performance of rituals.

One clue to its success lay in the widespread use of pamphlets in German by Luther and his associates (see Table 13-2). Between 1517 and 1525, literally millions of pamphlets poured off the presses, each containing fifteen to forty pages, cleverly illustrated and couched in language common folk could understand. Unlike earlier heresies, Lutheranism employed the powerful new medium of the press to convey its revolutionary ideas. In promoting this abundant and captivating literature, the pamphleteers used fiery slogans like "the freedom of the Christian," "the certitude of salvation," and "the priesthood of all believers."

TABLE 13-2

PRINTING IN STRASBOURG

Protestant Publication by Subject Matter and Period

Subject Matter	1515–1548	1549–1569	1570–1599
Anti-Catholic polemic	294	26	37
Doctrine and theology	129	32	26
Biblical commentary: Latin	90	5	3
Biblical commentary: German	51	14	3
Sermons	84	10	14
Anabaptist doctrine	44	1	1
Polemic against Anabaptists	23	0	0
Devotionals and prayerbooks for lay use	20	8	15
Hymnals and devotional songs	18	58	8
Manuals and aids for the clergy	63	3	6

Breakdown of Protestant Publications

Subject Matter	1520–1525	1526–1530	1531–1535	1536–1540
Polemic by Luther	54	0	8	1
Polemic by Strasbourg reformers	25	4	0	0
Polemic by laymen (includes von Hutten)	58	2	4	2
Sermons by Luther in German (many polemic in nature)	49	2	1	2
Sermons by Luther in Latin	1	3	0	0
Doctrinal works on the Eucharist in German	10	6	1	0
Doctrinal works on the Eucharist in Latin	1	0	0	0
Other doctrinal works in German	40	6	0	1
Other doctrinal works in Latin	12	9	1	4

Strasbourg was a major center of Protestant evangelism and printing, and its printers produced a huge flood of pamphlets in German attacking Catholicism in the first half of the sixteenth century. This volume of polemical material is evidence of a propaganda campaign of unprecedented proportions. The writers included not only clergy but lay men and women.

Source: Adapted from Miriam Usher Chrisman, *Lay Culture, Learned Culture* (New Haven: Yale University Press, 1982), tables 12 and 13, pp. 156, 157.

They exploited the complaint that the church made unreasonable demands in the confessional. Luther's *Sermon on the Sacrament of Penance* (1519), in which he scoffed at the traditional role of confession as a tribunal where the priest was the judge, raced through fourteen editions in only three years. Luther and his followers further argued that the confessional had actually become a "school" for sin and a device for extorting money from the laity so that clerics could live in style. Believers had, in other words, been "duped" into thinking that their salvation depended on priestly intercessions when the Scriptures demanded only a sincere faith.

Early Protestantism offered a less ritualistic faith and a new ethic of service to others. In this sense, the Reformation has been seen as a release from a vast, burdensome machine that collected money while corrupting both lives

Earthy Lutheran Propaganda   In this woodcut from a 1545 pamphlet, the pope's tiara (compare to pictures on p. 466, 475) has been turned upside down and is being used as a latrine by a mercenary soldier, while two of his colleagues rearrange their clothing after preceding him in the same activity. The papal shield, beneath the tiara, does not bear the the usual keys to the kingdom of heaven, but rather a burglar's device to open locks and steal people's money. The German text says that the pope had used Christ's kingdom in the same way that the soldiers here are using the pope's kingdom and predicts that the papacy will soon fall.

and the Word of God. This is, obviously, an exaggerated picture. The medieval church was not nearly as corrupt as the pamphleteers claimed (or as many modern historians have assumed). Protestants overidealized the laity, just as Catholics had overidealized the clergy. But it is the nature of all revolutions to oversimplify the complexity of social institutions and to overlook the fact that reforms, while solving some problems, can create others.

Women, Families, and Religious Reform

The complex character of the intersection of Protestant ideas and social realities is exemplified in the impact of the Reformation upon women. While alleging that celibate priests, monks, and nuns were immoral and hypocritical, Protestants stressed the positive value of married life. One wrote, "It is better to make a home and teach the Word of God to one's family than to mutter frigid prayers alone in a sanctuary." Luther's marriage to Katherine von Bora, a former nun, was a happy partnership, and Luther crowed that "I would not give up my Katy for France or Venice." Some

Protestant noblewomen played prominent roles in the movement (see "Marguerite of Navarre, Jeanne d'Albret, and French Reform"), and there were women preachers among the Anabaptists. Leadership roles for women remained rare, but even the majority of wives who remained at home, subject to their husbands, gained some new legal advantages. Genevan law treated a husband's adultery as a crime equally as serious as a wife's, undermining—although by no means eliminating—the old double standard. The grounds for divorce and remarriage were extended in some areas. In Geneva, for example, a man who converted to Protestantism gained a divorce on the basis of "religious desertion," meaning that his wife refused to accept his new faith and would not come to Geneva with him. Augsburg's civic "Marriage Court" frequently awarded compensation to women who had been seduced or needed child support.

While the position of married Protestant women may have improved in certain respects, many unmarried women suffered. The closing of convents left few respectable havens for widows and spinsters and put enormous pressure on all women to marry for their own safety whether they wanted to or not. Those who did not were often isolated and became the most likely victims when the number of witchcraft persecutions soared in the sixteenth century (see Chapter 17). Before the Reformation, many German cities had sanctioned the operation of brothels, and thus prostitutes had benefited from public approval of their role in making cities safe for "respectable" females. But the reformers rejected the idea that the dangerous force of male sexuality ought to be controlled through prostitution. The new ideal became (preferably early) marriages in which both partners were virgins, an ideal that, since it was never fully realized, made the position of prostitutes more precarious.

Fundamentally, Protestantism was distinctly more patriarchal than Catholicism. Protestant women often showed great steadfastness in defending the religious ideas they had picked up from their reading and listening, but Protestants banned the cult of the Virgin Mary and condemned prayer to saints, many of whom were female. Neither women nor men were henceforth encouraged to emulate Saints Barbara, Catherine, or Bridget. Even in areas that remained Catholic, women who tried to participate in reform often ran into serious obstacles. In Milan, St. Carlo Borromeo insisted that women and men worship separately. In general, efforts of women to teach or otherwise work outside of cloistered convents failed to overcome patriarchal biases and were suppressed sooner or later by Catholic authorities.

The Reformers and Western Culture

Words or images? Did Protestants want to exclude the latter from worship and replace them with nothing but Bible readings and sermons? Did Catholics want to retain stained glass, crucifixes, paintings, and other religious artwork in worship while de-emphasizing the Scriptures? The Reformed wing of Protestantism that stemmed from Zwingli and Calvin did indeed regard most religious artwork as idolatrous and wanted these representations removed from the churches and the walls whitewashed. Biblical verses were painted on the walls, and their services concentrated heavily on preaching and hearing God's Word. This did not mean, however, that illustrations could not be used in the books and pamphlets that taught Reformed doctrine. The Lutheran position, here as in other matters, was less extreme. Lutherans purged their churches of art that represented "false" Catholic doctrines such as purgatory and papal authority, while allowing crucifixes and other images to stimulate devotion. Catholic reformers vigorously defended religious images, but they also worked hard to increase the number of educated preachers and teachers who could train the faithful in Catholic doctrine so they could defend themselves against the arguments of the heretics. In other words, they did not hesitate to fight fire with fire by printing materials defending their views and attacking the Protestants. In southern Germany, for example, "miracle books" addressed to pilgrims seeking knowledge of the stories and histories of local shrines appeared in huge numbers.

In religion and culture alike, diversity increased during the sixteenth century. The vernacular translations of the Bible and the swelling tide of printed books promoted the growth of literature in languages spoken by the people. The trend began in Renaissance Italy, where, ironically, a movement inspired by revival of interest in classical Latin and Greek also produced magnificent literature in Italian: Petrarch's sonnets, Boccaccio's *Decameron*, the works of Machiavelli, and many others. The educational needs of townspeople in an increasingly complex commercial economy grew at the same time that humanists, Protestants, and Catholic reformers were advocating literacy so that people could understand and support reformist goals. Thomas More wrote his *Utopia* in Latin, but many of his later works in English, including his harsh attacks on Protestants. Sometimes he was colloquial, sometimes even vulgar (he wrote that Luther was "shut up in the Devil's anus") as he strove to frighten his compatriots with the dangers of heresy.

Although scholars and diplomats would continue to use Latin for generations, the sixteenth century saw the proliferation of vernacular classics. Two examples are *Pantagruel* and *Gargantua* by François Rabelais (1494–1553), a worldly French monk, physician, and Christian humanist. Amid much learned word play, Rabelais's sprawling works are marked by bawdy humor, rollicking descriptions of gluttons and other sinners, and sharply satirical criticism of all social classes, churchmen in particular. The immensely popular *Essays* of the Catholic nobleman Michel de Montaigne (1533–1592) are rich in psychological insights. Writing during the French religious wars, Montaigne pre-

sented a powerful argument for tolerance based on skepticism about the certainty of human knowledge. "Man is quite insane," he wrote. "He wouldn't know how to create a maggot, and he creates Gods by the dozens."

The sixteenth century brought about profound change for ordinary people, as reformers—both Catholic and Protestant—tried to obliterate aspects of popular culture they opposed and replace them with theologically approved alternatives. They objected to practices they considered pagan, disorderly, superstitious, cruel, or immoral, such as magic, witchcraft, bearbaiting, folk dancing, bullfights, folktales, minstrels, and masks. Many of these beliefs and recreations found expression in the carnivals that had long been celebrated in the winter months between Christmas and the sober season of Lent. The carnivals reached their climax on the day before Lent began—*Mardi Gras* ("Fat Tuesday"). In England, for example, a poet wrote in 1630 that there was "such boiling and broiling, such roasting and toasting, such stewing and brewing, such baking, frying, mincing, cutting, carving, devouring and gorbellied gourmandising, that a man would think people did take in two month's provisions at once into their paunches, or that they did ballast their bellies with meat for a voyage to Constantinople, or the West Indies." The number of babies conceived during the carnival season was unusually high. Verbal and physical aggression, hidden beneath the masks people wore, characterized the festival, as did protests against the government, nobles, Jews, and other real or alleged enemies.

Opposition to such activities, with their focus on food, sex, and violence, was strong among Catholic reformers and especially strong among Calvinists. Catholics pruned the carnivals of their more objectionable features, and Calvinists often banned the celebrations altogether. In Milan, Borromeo denounced carnivals, stage plays, and taverns as ferociously as any "puritan" in Protestant territory. Meanwhile, Protestant leaders struggled vigorously to make the Bible the centerpiece of a reformed popular culture, a goal that the new vernacular translations made possible. Luther wrote hymns such as "A Mighty Fortress Is Our God" to displace the "love-ballads and carnal verses" he disliked. Psalm singing became a popular dimension of the developing Protestant tradition of church music, which would later culminate in the magnificent chorales of Johann Sebastian Bach (1685–1750).

Despite the reformers' emphasis upon God's written word and their suspicion of images, Protestant Europe in the sixteenth century produced a number of notable painters. Albrecht Dürer (1471–1528) of Nuremberg, a Christian humanist and admirer of Luther, adapted to his own distinctive style the High Renaissance themes of harmony, proportion and perspective. Dürer's numerous prints (for example, *Adam and Eve* and *The Four Horsemen of the Apocalypse*) enjoyed wide circulation. Perhaps the greatest portrait painter in northern Europe was Hans Holbein the

Dürer's *Four Horsemen of the Apocalypse* Issued in 1498, Albrecht Dürer's woodcut appeared in a book that was the first work entirely by a single artist. The "four horsemen" (war, famine, plague, and death), whose appearance signified the end of the world, cut down humanity under the hoofs of their powerful horses. By 1520, he had converted to Luther's doctrine and spent the last years of his life in the creation of a new Protestant art. *The Granger Collection, New York.*

the Virgin Mary in every possible way because Protestants disputed her Immaculate Conception. The Catholic Reformation reasserted the spiritual value of art, architecture, and music, but it certainly had its "puritan" side. In 1564, the Council of Trent insisted that loincloths be painted on the private parts of the nude figures in Michelangelo's *Last Judgment* in the Sistine Chapel.

The style of painting that flourished from the end of the High Renaissance (1520) until about 1600 is described by art historians as Mannerism. Less devoted to realism than their High Renaissance predecessors, Mannerist painters typically heightened the emotional impact of their compositions with exaggerated figures and lurid colors. Traces of the Mannerist style appear in Michelangelo's later paintings such as the *Last Judgment* fresco in the Sistine Chapel (see p. 461, and even in Raphael's later work. The Venetian painter Tintoretto (1518–1594) displayed it

Interior of St. Peter's Basilica The magnificent interior of the new St. Peter's in Rome was completed during the first half of the seventeenth century. With its towering marble columns and its profusion of light and glittering ornaments, the basilica exemplified the urge to represent visually the grandeur of the church's authority and the truth of its theology. *Saskia Ltd. / Art Resource, NY.*

Younger (1497–1543), a German whose ability to make his subjects real and human is especially evident in his portrayals of Erasmus (see p. 462) and of Henry VIII and his courtiers (see p. 490). Pieter Bruegel the Elder (1525/1530–1569) of Flanders displayed a very different kind of genius and was known primarily for his drawings and paintings of landscapes, biblical events, and peasant life. Bruegel memorably exposed the brutalities of the Spanish occupying army in *The Massacre of the Innocents* (see p. 499).

The Council of Trent denounced the Protestant attack on religious images, and Catholic reformers, after some hesitation, enrolled artists in their crusade. Paintings and statues were now commissioned for the specific purpose of defending doctrines that the Protestants had rejected. They showed saints doing good works because Protestants said that such behavior did not save the soul; they glorified

Tintoretto's *Last Supper*   Painted toward the end of Tintoretto's life for the church of S. Giorgio Maggiore in Venice, his *Last Supper* presents a busy room full of servants to the right and the apostles earnestly debating among themselves to the left of the long table. Angels hover while Christ himself administers the bread to a disciple, and a cat searches for leftovers in the foreground.   *Scala/Art Resource, NY.*

fully in his version of *The Last Supper* (1592–1594), a painting that contrasts with Leonardo da Vinci's famous fresco on the same theme (compare Tintoretto's depiction, to da Vinci's on p. 449). Instead of Leonardo's evenly lighted, frontal view of a calmly seated group of men with Christ at the center, Tintoretto depicts the scene from an angle with flickering, shifting light, bright colors, and a buzz of activity.

The last and best-known Mannerist painter was El Greco (1541–1614), a Greek (as his name implies) who studied in Venice, spent most of his life in Philip II's Spain, and practiced Loyola's spiritual exercises. His paintings feature strong, vivid colors, crowded compositions, and elongated, sinuous, distorted figures tortured by painful tension as they seek spiritual vision (see p. 489). These works, instead of the confidence in human capabilities and sense of human strength evident in the art of the High Renaissance, reflect strain, anxiety, intensity, and emotionalism. Philip II himself disliked El Greco's paintings, preferring instead the work of Titian with all its High Renaissance ideals. Philip yearned for a world that artists knew was gone.

CONCLUSION: THE REFORMATIONS AND THEIR AFTERMATH

Martin Luther and his fellow magisterial reformers sought to initiate not a new church but a revival of Christianity in what they thought was its pristine form, the church that Jesus Christ himself and his apostles had instituted. It would be a church that preached and practiced Christ's own doctrines, such as salvation by faith alone and the priesthood of all believers—not purgatory, monasticism, transubstantiation, papal monarchy, or any of the other corruptions that had been invented by wicked clergymen to line their pockets and sustain their worldly power. This revived, reformed, and unified Christian institution would, they believed, bring about a sweeping moral regeneration of individuals, families, communities, states, and empires. People would love and serve their neighbors, doing good works to thank God for the gift of salvation instead of feverishly struggling to earn it. Princes and other secular authorities would jump on the bandwagon, and a new era of peace and happiness would ensue.

Instead, the magisterial Protestants split into Evangelical and Reformed camps and still found themselves beset with enemies. On one side, Anabaptists and other more radical voices charged that their programs fell far short of the example that Jesus had set and that reliance on princes and politicians was a pact with the devil. On the other, Paul III, Loyola, and others spearheaded an ambitious reform of the Roman Catholic church and put the Protestants on the defensive. Instead of a new age of peace, bitter conflicts broke out within and among the states of Christendom. Doctrinaire Catholics and Protestants despised politiques no less than they hated each other. The growth of overseas empires exported these tensions around the world, and population growth within Europe itself exacerbated them. Insofar as princes gained authority over churches, as they did in both Catholic and Protestant states, their power grew. Yet as the sixteenth century waned, they found themselves forced to look for new tools to contain the destructive forces that the Reformations had unleashed.

Selected Reading

Sources

Cohen, J. M., trans. *The Life of Saint Teresa of Ávila by Herself* (1957).

Duke, Alastair, Gillian Lewis, and Andrew Pettegree, eds. *Calvinism in Europe, 1540–1610* (1992).

Englander, David, Diana Norman, Rosemary O'Day, and W. R. Owens, eds. *Culture and Belief in Europe, 1450–1600* (1990).

Hillerbrand, Hans J., ed. *The Protestant Reformation* (1968).

The Reformations

Cameron, Euan. *The European Reformation* (1991). The best one-volume account of the Reformation movements available, especially for its sensitive analysis of the complex relationship between the desires of the reformers and the political ambitions of the laity.

Eire, Carlos M. N. *War against the Idols* (1986). Demonstrates the importance of the Calvinist attack on idolatry for the Reformation as a whole.

Pettegree, Andrew, ed. *The Early Reformation in Europe* (1992). Essays on the first thirty years after 1517 in eastern and southern Europe as well as Germany and the north and west.

Skinner, Quentin. *The Foundations of Modern Political Thought*, vol. 2, *The Reformation* (1979). Companion volume to Skinner's study listed in Chapter 12—an excellent descriptive analysis of the developments in political thought during a period of extreme tension.

The Reformers

Collinson, Patrick. *Archbishop Grindal, 1519–1583* (1979). Important study of a leading English reformer who had the courage to refuse to obey Elizabeth I when her orders conflicted with his beliefs.

DeMolen, R. L., ed. *Leaders of the Reformation* (1985). Essays on Erasmus, Luther, Zwingli, Loyola, Calvin, and others.

Friesen, Abraham. *Thomas Müntzer: A Destroyer of the Godless* (1990). Penetrating study of the development of the thinking of one of the predominant figures among the radical reformers.

MacCulloch, Diarmaid. *Thomas Cranmer: A Life* (1996). Deeply researched and beautifully written biography of Henry VIII's archbishop of Canterbury, who led the Protestantizing of the Church of England under Edward VI and was burned at the stake under Mary.

Oberman, Heiko A. *Luther: Man between God and Devil* (1989). Lively portrayal of Luther's personality, thought, and experience.

O'Malley, John W. *The First Jesuits* (1993). A brilliant study of Loyola and his colleagues, covering the founding and direction of the Society of Jesus up to 1565.

Steinmetz, David. *Calvin in Context* (1995). An excellent introduction to Calvin's thought, which distinguishes the Genevan's original ideas from those he borrowed and adapted from a wide range of sources.

The Reformation and Politics

Dickens, A. G. *The English Reformation*, 2nd ed. (1989). A clear narrative shaped by the view that many in England welcomed the coming of Protestantism.

Haigh, Christopher. *English Reformations* (1993). Stresses the popularity of traditional Catholicism and argues that only political pressure from the ruling elite made England Protestant in the long run.

Kamen, Henry. *Philip II of Spain* (1997). A fine biography based on extensive research that dispels many myths that have swirled about this embattled monarch.

Kingdon, Robert M. *Myths about the St. Bartholomew's Day Massacres, 1572–1576* (1988). Shows how Protestants used the press to advance their cause by printing accounts of the deaths of the victims of the famous 1572 massacre of French Protestants.

Mattingly, Garrett. *The Armada* (1959). The classic and highly readable account of the Spanish Armada campaign of 1588 in its diplomatic and political as well as military aspects.

The Reformation, Society, and Culture

Burke, Peter. *Popular Culture in Early Modern Europe* (1978). A colorful survey of the culture of ordinary people in preindustrial Europe before and during the "reform" that began in the sixteenth century.

Cressy, David. *Birth, Marriage, and Death: Ritual, Religion, and the Life-Cycle in Tudor and Stuart England* (1997). Far-ranging study of the traditional rites of passage in their social and religious context.

Davis, Natalie Z. *Society and Culture in Early Modern France* (1975). Pioneering essays on the "little people" in sixteenth-century France, including artisans, tradesmen, urban women, religious riots, and the poor.

Duffy, Eamon. *The Stripping of the Altars* (1992). Detailed argument for the strength and vitality of late medieval Catholicism in England and the people's resistance to Protestant reform.

Ginzburg, Carlo. *The Cheese and the Worms: The Cosmos of a Sixteenth-Century Miller* (1982). Fascinating reconstruction of the life and thought of an unusual peasant.

Roper, Lyndal. *The Holy Household: Women and Morals in Reformation Augsburg* (1989). Argues that the morality taught by the urban reformers was based on a theology of gender and analyzes its impact on women in Augsburg.

Scribner, R. W. *For the Sake of Simple Folk*, 2nd ed. (1994). Examination of woodcuts and other visual material used to reach the "common people" of Reformation-era Germany.

Wiesner, Merry E. *Women and Gender in Early Modern Europe* (1993). Surveys a large body of recent scholarship on women in Europe from 1500 to 1750.

THE OLD WORLD AND THE NEW

The New World   *Photographed by Richard Hurley for the John Carter Brown Library at Brown University.*

1275–1292	Marco Polo visits the central Asian and Chinese empire of Kublai Khan, Genghis Khan's grandson		1499–1501	Amerigo Vespucci explores coastal South America
ca. 1300–1531	Inca Empire flourishes on the Pacific coast of South America		1500	Pedro Cabral makes the first known landing by Europeans in Brazil
ca. 1350–1519	Aztec Empire rises and dominates central Mexico		1513	Vasco de Balboa sights the Pacific Ocean after crossing the Isthmus of Panama
1360–1644	Ming Dynasty rules China after ousting the Mongols		1519	Hernán Cortés conquers the Aztec Empire
1405–1433	Chinese Admiral Zheng He explores the Indian Ocean		1519–1522	The first circumnavigation of the earth is made, initiated by Ferdinand Magellan
1487	Bartolomeu Dias rounds the Cape of Good Hope and enters the Indian Ocean		1531	Francisco Pizarro conquers the Inca Empire
1492	Christopher Columbus discovers the New World, thinking he has reached the outer islands of Japan		1542	Charles V issues the New Laws of the Indies, mandating humane treatment of the indigenous peoples in the New World
1497–1499	Vasco da Gama makes the first voyage from Europe to India		1556	Chinese authorities permit the Portuguese to establish a trading base at Macao
1497	John Cabot discovers Newfoundland and Nova Scotia		1577–1580	Francis Drake makes the second circumnavigation of the earth
			1600	The English-owned East India Company receives a charter
			1602	The Dutch East India Company is founded in Amsterdam

Battista Agnese, a Genoese cartographer who worked in Venice, drew the world map shown on page 509 in the mid-1540s, and its outline of North and South America—the "New World" to Europeans—was fairly accurate, more so than his outline of India, Southeast Asia, and China. Yet the Americas had been quite unknown to Europeans just a half-century before. Note the black line on the map, which Agnese included to show the approximate route of the first circumnavigation of the earth, made about thirty years earlier. He also indicated the route of the Spanish fleet that annually carried gold from Peru up through Central America and then across the Atlantic. In an astonishingly short time, in other words, Europeans had not only solved the riddle of ocean navigation but begun regularly to ship precious metals from the Americas. The Portuguese had pioneered the techniques for sailing the open oceans and made the first voyages into the Indian Ocean, and Christopher Columbus—an Italian sailing in Spain's service—mastered the Atlantic Ocean.

Columbus's earliest biographer portrayed in heroic terms the famous sailor's initial arrival in Portugal in 1476. Columbus (1451–1506), then a twenty-five year old Genoese seaman, was shipwrecked after a sea battle with Venetian galleys and, although wounded, managed to swim six miles to the coast of Portugal. This daring escape from disaster might have happened, but its veracity cannot be confirmed. Columbus did, however, live among the Portuguese for ten years after 1476, and in 1478 or 1479 he married a woman from a noble Portuguese family. He learned Portuguese methods of ocean sailing and navigating—the most advanced in the world. While in Portugal, he became convinced that he could gain access to the riches of East Asia by sailing west from Europe. In 1484 Columbus tried to get King John II of Portugal (reigned 1481–1495) to subsidize his planned voyage. The king was cordial but lost interest when the Portuguese explorer Bartolomeu Dias (ca. 1450–1500) sailed into Lisbon in 1488 from his voyage around the southern tip of Africa. With Dias's proven route into the Indian Ocean, John thought he no longer needed Columbus, whose "Enterprise of the Indies" also met with rejection by Henry VII of England, Charles VIII of France, and the Spanish co-monarchs Isabella of Castile and Ferdinand of Aragon.

But then, early in January 1492, Ferdinand and Isabella reconsidered. Perhaps Columbus's cause had benefited from his Portuguese wife's relationship to the part-Portuguese Isabella. Whatever their reasons, the Spanish rulers granted Columbus the ships and a little over half of the 2 million maravedís that he needed. They required the town of Palos to provide the two of the three ships; the rest came from Italian merchants and other sources. (At that time, 2 million maravedís was about the annual income of a lesser nobleman—not a staggering sum.) Ferdinand and Isabella also gave him the authority "to discover and acquire certain islands and mainlands in the Ocean Sea." If he succeeded, he would earn a nobleman's status, be named governor general over whatever new provinces he discovered, and glory in the title "Admiral of the Ocean Sea"—not bad for the son of a poor Genoese rope maker. Columbus embarked on August 2 on a southwesterly course for the Canary Islands, then Spain's only notable territory outside of Europe. Arriving there on August 9, he spent nearly three weeks repairing, refitting, and provisioning his little ships. On September 6, he sailed due west and left the world that Europeans knew.

Columbus's brilliant—or perhaps merely lucky—choice of the Canaries for his departure put the dependable easterly winds behind him and assured him a quick passage westward. Speedy or not, many of the crew of about ninety men feared by early October that they had traveled so far that their food and water would run out before they could get back to Spain. Some said that "it was a great madness . . . to risk their lives to further the mad schemes of a foreigner who was ready to die in the hope of making a great lord of himself." Some considered tossing Columbus overboard at night and pretending that he had fallen while making astronomical observations. Fortunately for him, on October 11 the men saw large quantities of flotsam, indicating the nearness of land. On October 12 Columbus's small fleet made its first landfall in the New World, on an island in the Bahamas.

The voyages of Dias into the Indian Ocean and of Columbus across the Atlantic opened broad new vistas and tantalizing opportunities, quickly seized by ambitious Europeans. In 1519 Ferdinand Magellan, a Portuguese in the service of Spain, sailed with five ships around South America and into the Pacific. He thus discovered the route to Asia that Columbus had sought, but only after terrible suffering by his crew. They were reduced to eating ox hides and rats for a time, and one survivor wrote that "rats were sold for one-half ducado apiece, and even then we could not get them. . . . The gums of both the lower and upper teeth of some of our men swelled, so that they could not eat under any circumstances and therefore died." After finally reaching the Philippines, Magellan died in a clash with the local people, but one of his lieutenants continued around the world, returning to Spain in 1522 with the one remaining ship and seventeen starving sailors. This voyage—the first known circumnavigation of the earth—was completed only thirty years after Columbus's initial discovery of the Americas. In 1492, the stormy Atlantic to the west and hostile empires on the Asian landmass to the east narrowly constrained Europeans. By 1522, the constraints were gone.

OVERSEAS EXPLORATION BEGINS

Renaissance humanists had thought that re-creating the "golden age" of Greco-Roman civilization would cure society's ills. But the discoveries of Dias, Columbus, Magellan,

and others weakened the widely held belief that the ancients had known everything worth knowing. The voyages unveiled new worlds unknown to antiquity and demonstrated the value of direct experience over the revival of ancient wisdom. They also supported the claims of those who believed that history was going somewhere, that it followed a divine plan and was more than just a series of kingdoms rising and falling until the world's end. In the long run, the age of discovery encouraged the idea of progress, a great social myth that helped bring our own world into being and still underlies the American dream.

Precursors

Columbus was not the first European to reach the Americas. Daring Vikings had made their way first to Iceland around A.D. 870 and then to southern Greenland about a century later (see Chapter 7). By 930 the Iceland colony had a population of perhaps twenty-five thousand, perhaps as much as 8 percent of the Norwegian people. Erik the Red led a fleet that established a colony in Greenland that lasted for about five hundred years and contained more than five thousand people in its prime. Erik's son Leif Eriksson and others reached the North American continent around the year 1000, and Leif called his discoveries "Markland" ("Forest Land") and "Vinland," probably in Labrador and Newfoundland. The indigenous people thwarted Norse efforts to settle there, driving them back to their base in Greenland. But the Norse continued to hunt, fish, cut timber, and trade with the Eskimos long after the initial contact.

By around 1500, the declining Norse colony in Greenland disappeared for reasons that remain somewhat mysterious. Its younger members may have joined an Anglo-Portuguese expedition to colonize the mainland (an expedition that failed, leaving few traces of its fate). In any case, the Norse colony had always been small, and another possibility is that bubonic plague, smallpox, or some other epidemic badly damaged its viability. Greenland lacked timber and iron, the short growing season severely limited agricultural output, and demand for North Atlantic products sagged in the Late Middle Ages. Even Iceland, the first sizable European colony overseas, suffered in a similar fashion. In any case, the resources that Portugal, Spain, France, England, and Holland could put behind their explorers and colonizers greatly exceeded those of Norway.

Methods

Important late medieval technological advances in shipbuilding and navigation instruments stimulated the wave of discoveries, although these developments represented the culmination of centuries of patient experimentation and innovation. The most significant advance was the marriage of the most useful features of northern European and Mediterranean ship design, construction, and rigging. The vessels of each region differed widely in response to unique maritime conditions. The Mediterranean experienced little tidal action and was thoroughly mapped. Merchants conducted their business along the coasts, and sailors usually slept on land or anchored within sight of it. Even when Venetian, Aragonese, and Genoese ships late in the thirteenth century began to travel around Iberia to Flanders, they reached the English Channel by hugging the coast. A ship's master knew little about navigation but much about piloting—maneuvering in and out of harbors and estuaries in light winds. By the eleventh century, Mediterranean ships no longer employed the square sails of Roman times; rather, they used the roughly triangular "lateen" sails used by Arabs to this day. The square sail works best when the wind is blowing from the stern—what sailors call "running before the wind." In the lake-like Mediterranean, the lateen rig afforded superb maneuverability. Sailors could easily beat to windward—that is, sail a zigzag course on a series of tacks against the wind—and thus navigate the irregular coasts of northern Africa and southern Europe.

Medieval ships on the Atlantic coast (called cogs) were built for rougher conditions—stronger tides, higher winds, and heavier seas. Round-hulled and buoyant, they lacked the clean, graceful lines and easy handling in light breezes of Mediterranean ships, and they needed the right wind and tide to get out of port. But they could carry more cargo with smaller crews. Trade was growing in bulky but low-priced commodities such as wheat, and the clumsy round ships could carry these goods cheaply. It took fifty seamen to man-

age a 250-ton lateen-rigged ship in the Mediterranean but only twenty in an Atlantic cog. This efficiency allowed cogs to invade the Mediterranean after 1300.

Using both square and lateen sails, ships of the early fifteenth century began to combine the best features of both traditions. These hybrids set the stage for the great age of oceangoing sailing ships. Columbus and those who followed him used lateen sails in light winds but raised square sails in the powerful, dependable trade winds that carried their ships across the long reaches of the open sea. The addition of artillery in the sixteenth century made these ships the most important new weapons platform since the chariot. With cannons, small crews could defend themselves while carrying more cargo and staying at sea longer.

Besides suitable ships and sails, sailors needed a means of navigating when out of sight of land for long periods. The marine compass, a device used to indicate a ship's course, was in use in European waters by the late 1200s. The Chinese had been navigating with the help of compasses since at least a century earlier, but whether Europeans learned of the device from China or developed it independently is unknown. Also widely used before Columbus were instruments such as the quadrant, astrolabe, and cross-staff. These enabled sailors to take readings on either the sun or the stars to determine their position (that is, their latitude) north or south of the Equator.[1] The Portuguese pioneered the technique of sailing north or south until they reached the degree of latitude they wanted and then sailing east to make landfall in Europe or Africa at the desired point. During the fourteenth and fifteenth centuries, European mariners (especially the Portuguese) had also learned much about seasonal wind patterns as they sailed back and forth to the island groups in the eastern Atlantic. They knew at which latitudes and in which months they could expect strong easterly or westerly winds. Columbus used the same techniques and knowledge but traveled west instead of east.

Motives

Early explorers used the prospect of winning souls for Christianity to persuade devout monarchs such as Isabella of Castile and other potential backers to underwrite part of the considerable cost of their activities. Stung by the Muslim overthrow of the medieval crusader states (see Chapter 9), Europeans dreamed of regaining the "Holy Land." Columbus's "grand design," as he called it, involved regaining Jerusalem with an attack on the Muslims from the rear.

Late Fifteenth-Century Caravel This model of a caravel has the lateen rig on three masts, just as Columbus's two caravels did on the journey from Spain to the Canary Islands. But such ships could easily be re-rigged with square sails on the main and foremasts, which is what Columbus did before sailing farther west. See the image on the facing page, where the model of a carrack is square-rigged. The carrack's hull type was similar to the older cog. *The Granger Collection, New York.*

---

[1] Not until the eighteenth century, however, could longitude (that is, distance east or west of an imaginary vertical line running from pole to pole) be measured precisely. The problem was solved only when clocks were built that withstood atmospheric conditions on the open sea in order to measure accurately the time it took to sail a known distance.

A Cosmographer in His Study A lodestone (magnet, used in a compass) is floating in water at lower left, and a quadrant lies flat on the corner of the table (above and slightly to the left of the lodestone). The cosmographer is measuring distances with a pair of dividers in the same way that a mariner at sea would use dividers on his chart. © R. Sheridan / Ancient Art & Architecture Collection.

He had dreamlike "visions" in which he thought he received instructions directly from God, and like many of his fellow Christians, he believed that the recapture of Jerusalem was the necessary prelude to the Second Coming of Jesus.

Although religious motives for their voyages certainly persisted, the letters and journals of most of the explorers suggest that crusading ideals influenced but by no means dominated their thinking. Religious zeal undoubtedly drove Columbus, but his ambition for power, wealth, and prestige was no less important. "We came here to serve God, and also to get rich," candidly wrote one of the Spaniards who went to Mexico early in the sixteenth century. Nor was the bold confidence in human ability allegedly inspired by Renaissance humanism a significant factor, for the explorers were practical men rather than learned Renaissance gentlemen. Most of the princes who encouraged and financed the voyages displayed a similar pragmatism; more trade meant more tax revenue, and more money enhanced the state's ability to deal with domestic and foreign enemies.

In most cases, the prime motive for exploration was profit. Explorers knew that commodities readily available in East Asia could be sold at steep prices in Europe. Columbus and Dias were not seeking new islands or continents, but merely new, shorter routes to Asia and its "Spice Islands." In a Europe lacking enough fodder to keep large herds of animals alive through the winter, an insatiable demand raged for seasonings (such as pepper) to improve the taste of meat from animals slaughtered in the autumn. Spices, silks, and other Asian luxuries had flowed across Arab lands into Europe in relative abundance during the High Middle Ages. Italian merchants such as Marco Polo in the thirteenth century helped sustain this old and important trade (see Part Three Introduction); Columbus's own copy of Polo's book survives with his comments scrawled in the margins. Thanks to the effort of many Italians like Polo, Asian spices and knowledge of the places where they originated proliferated in late medieval Europe. But the Mongol collapse and the conquest of the Ottoman Turks in and beyond the eastern Mediterranean drove the cost of commercial exchange sky-high by the late 1300s. Columbus and other explorers thus sought primarily to find safe, inexpensive routes to regions already known. Columbus, not knowing that the Mongol Empire had fallen in the middle of the fourteenth century and been replaced in China by the Ming Dynasty, carried a letter of introduction to the "Great Khan," whom he expected to find ruling "Cathay."[2]

Columbus had convinced himself that major errors permeated Europeans' conventional wisdom about the world's geography, and he was confident (indeed, arrogant) in asserting that he alone knew the truth, which urged him forward despite many setbacks. He did not have to convince anyone that the earth was round. (That people thought it was flat is a myth created by eighteenth-century anticlerical writers who loved to heap scorn on medieval churchmen.) Thanks to the recovery and

---

[2] It was written in Latin, which no one in Ming China could have read.

publication by Renaissance humanists of geographical texts by such ancient authorities as Ptolemy (ca. 85–165; see Chapter 3), Columbus could easily study their ideas and those of many other geographers. Ptolemy's *Geography*, for example, had been translated into Latin in 1410, and Columbus's copy was printed in Rome in 1478. In the margins he wrote that "every ocean can be navigated."

The Turning Point, ca. 1500

Long before Dias, Columbus, and Magellan sailed, Basque, Irish, and perhaps other sailors may have reached land in the Western Hemisphere—and the Norse certainly did. But the voyages around 1500 were a turning point in world history because the Europeans followed up their initial explorations with regular commercial contact and colonization. They established permanent naval bases, trading stations, and settlements in an effort to exploit their discoveries. These voyages, unlike earlier ones, led to the creation of the first seaborne empires and the first world economy. The stunning success of the Portuguese provoked attempts at emulation, first by the Spanish and then by the Dutch, English, and French. Yet an important question remains. Both the Chinese and the Arabs possessed the maritime technology to conquer the oceans before the Europeans did. Why did Europeans overtake civilizations more advanced than their own?

Because Columbus believed that he could reach China and Japan by sailing west, he relied heavily on writers (such as Marco Polo) who—we now know—exaggerated both the eastward extension of China and the distance between China and Japan. Columbus also preferred sources that minimized the width of a degree of longitude along the Equator, since a smaller circumference for the earth made his objective seem more plausible and therefore more appealing to the backers he so desperately needed. Columbus's calculations yielded a circumference that is too low by 32 percent. By selecting only authors whose ideas suited him, he concluded that the Canaries lay only 2,400 nautical miles from Japan instead of the 10,600 nautical miles that actually separate them. Luckily for Columbus and his men, they stumbled across Caribbean islands where they could obtain food and fresh water. If nothing but open ocean had been there, they would have died long before they got to Asia. Ironically, Ptolemy and most medieval scholars were closer to the truth about the size of the oceans and of the earth itself than Columbus was.[3]

In the Late Middle Ages Europe was an isolated cape at the northwestern tip of the great Eurasian-African landmass, hemmed in by a stormy, impassable sea on one side,

vast deserts and contrary winds on another side, and an aggressive, expansive, and populous Ottoman Empire on still another flank. The population and wealth of the Ottomans (who were themselves inferior in these respects to both Mughal India and Ming China) dwarfed the Europeans. How Europe emerged from a period of economic and demographic depression, burst out of these constricting boundaries, and mounted a worldwide drive to power is an astonishing story that must be grasped in order to understand the nature of Western civilization—its strengths as well as its flaws.

In terms of territorial growth, the Islamic empire of the Ottomans expanded explosively. Relying on massive armies, the Ottomans took Constantinople in 1453. By 1566 they had rolled west into Morocco, east to the borders of Persia, and north through the Balkans into central Europe. They besieged Vienna in 1529, inadvertently helping the Lutherans by forcing Charles V to defend the Habsburg capital rather than fight in Germany. The Turks stood again at the gates of Vienna in 1683. By contrast, the key to Europe's expansion lay in the conquest of the oceans. Columbus and his colleagues started a process that led to the domination of the world by European civilization. The **Scientific Revolution** of the seventeenth century and the Industrial Revolution of the late eighteenth and nineteenth centuries completed this expansion, transforming the world from a configuration of more or less independent civilizations to a global network woven together by European science and technology—the first "world civilization."

Around 1500 the civilizations of Asia were both older and technologically more sophisticated than that of Europe. Indeed, much of the technology that enabled the Europeans to explore the oceans was first deployed in Asian waters. The Chinese invented gunpowder and the magnetic compass, the Persians the astrolabe, the Arabs the lateen sail. In 1405 a huge Chinese expedition of 287 vessels, sixty-two of which were "treasure ships" between 370 and 440 feet long, set out under the command of the Grand Eunuch Zheng He and visited India. (Columbus's largest ship measured about 85 feet in length.) Six more Chinese expeditions followed, of which the last three reached eastern Africa. But after Zheng He's last voyage in 1433, no others occurred mainly because what little trading had been done had slight commercial value. Arab ships and sailors in the Indian Ocean regularly made long ocean crossings, and in the 1430s an Arab ship rounded the Cape of Good Hope at the southern tip of Africa and sailed far into the Atlantic.

Thus Arab and Chinese seamen were capable of entering the Atlantic and even crossing it long before Columbus did. Their wealthy, powerful governments could have financed global voyages more easily than Portugal or Spain. But the Arabs in East Africa and the Middle East did not sail around to West Africa because they could easily obtain its principal products (gold, ivory, and slaves) on the east

---

[3] In fact, the circumference of the earth had been calculated with much greater accuracy by the ancient Greek mathematician Eratosthenes in the third century B.C. (see Chapter 3).

coast. China, rich in resources, was largely self-sufficient; what it did not possess it could readily find in the Bay of Bengal and the South China Sea. The fact that Europeans were the first people to make these voyages can be explained not by superior technology but by their needs and their distinctive social psychology.

Europe's relative material poverty spurred Europeans into the age of discovery. Merchants and townspeople in Europe had greater influence on royal policy than did their counterparts in Asia, and in Europe more people had the freedom to seek their fortunes than in the centralized Asian societies. Western need for silks, spices, and other luxury goods forced Europeans, with their scarce material and human resources, into an unending quest for new inventions that would make human labor more effective and efficient. The Ottoman Turks, although they placed artillery on their ships, preferred to rely on the traditional (and labor-intensive) tactics of ramming and boarding. In 1509, they sent a large fleet with fifteen thousand men against a much smaller Portuguese squadron. The Portuguese artillery inflicted a heavy defeat, preventing the Muslims from getting close enough to use their superior manpower. Nevertheless, the Muslims clung to their obsolete naval tactics.

China's scholar-officials similarly preferred their established ways of doing things to experimentation with new ones. Like the Japanese, they considered merchants the lowliest social group. Their highest values were literary, not commercial or "practical." They had too much (justifiable) pride in their ancient culture to adopt Western methods. A perceptive Jesuit visitor to China in the seventeenth century described its ruling elite as unwilling "to make use of new instruments and leave their old ones without an especial order from the Emperor to that effect. They are more fond of the most defective piece of antiquity than of the most perfect of the modern, differing much in that from us who are in love with nothing but what is new." Europeans, relatively few in number and relatively poor in resources, could not afford such complacency.

The First Voyages

In 1291, two Genoese brothers sailed two ships past Gibraltar and down the coast of Africa; no one knows what happened to them. Theirs was the first documented effort to sail to India via the Atlantic, and it occurred in the same year that Acre, the crusaders' last foothold in the Holy Land, fell to the Muslims. Long before Columbus appeared on the scene, Portuguese and Spanish expeditions had reached out into the Atlantic. A map from 1339 shows the Canary Islands, and fourteenth-century Italian, Castilian, Aragonese, and French adventurers all took an interest in them. Both commercial and territorial rivalries meant that no one wanted an enemy to gain control of potentially useful new bases (see Map 14-1).

MAP 14-1
EUROPEAN EXPLORATION

THE HISTORICAL EVIDENCE

Prince Henry's Motives

mid-fifteenth century

Gomes Eannes de Azurara, who worked with Prince Henry in Portugal, wrote a chronicle of the long struggle by Portuguese mariners to explore the west coast of Africa. In this excerpt, he offers his view of the factors that had motivated Prince Henry (the "Lord Infant," so called because in Spanish and Portuguese the word infante *referred to a son of the king who was not in direct line to inherit the crown). What is the significance of the importance Azurara gives to astrology at the end of the document?*

And you should note well that the noble spirit of this Prince, by a sort of natural constraint, was ever urging him both to begin and to carry out very great deeds. For which reason, after the taking of Ceuta* he always kept ships well armed against the Infidel [the Muslims], both for war, and because he had also a wish to know the land that lay beyond the isles of Canary and that Cape called Bojador,† for that up to his time, neither by writings, nor by the memory of man, was known with any certainty the nature of the land beyond that Cape. Some said indeed that Saint Brandan had passed that way; and there was another tale of two galleys rounding the Cape, which never returned.‡ . . . And because the said Lord Infant wished to know the truth of this—since it seemed to him that if he or some other lord did not endeavour to gain that knowledge, no mariners or merchants would ever dare to attempt it (for it is clear that none of them ever trouble themselves to sail to a place where there is not a sure and certain hope of profit)—and seeing also that no other prince took any pains in this matter, he sent out his own ships against those parts, to have manifest certainty of them all. And to this he was stirred up by his zeal for the service of God and of the King Edward his Lord and brother, who then reigned.§ And this was the first reason of his action.

The second reason was that if there chanced to be in those lands some population of Christians, or some havens, into which it would be possible to sail without peril, many kinds of merchandise might be brought to this realm, which would find a ready market. . . .

The third reason was that, as it was said that the power of the Moors in that land of Africa was very much greater than was commonly supposed, and that there were no Christians among them, nor any other race of men . . . [therefore] every wise man is obliged by natural prudence to wish for a knowledge of the power of his enemy. . . .

The fourth reason was because during the one and thirty years that he had warred against the Moors, he had never found a Christian king, nor a lord outside this land, who for the love of our Lord Jesus Christ would aid him in the said war. Therefore he sought to know if there were in those parts any Christian princes, in whom the charity and the love of Christ were so ingrained that they would aid him against those enemies of the faith.

The fifth reason was his great desire to make increase in the faith of our Lord Jesus Christ and to bring to him all the souls that should be saved. . . .

But over and above these five reasons I have a sixth that would seem to be the root from which all the others proceeded: and this is the inclination of the heavenly wheels. . . . But here I wish to tell you how by the constraint of the influence of nature this glorious Prince was inclined to those actions of his. And that was because his ascendant was Aries, which is the house of Mars and exaltation of the sun, and his lord in the XIth house, in company of the sun. And because the said Mars was in Aquarius, which is the house of Saturn, and in the mansion of hope, it signified that this Lord should toil at high and mighty conquests, especially in seeking out things that were hidden from other men and secret, according to the nature of Saturn, in whose house he is.

---

* A port in Morocco that was Portugal's first territorial acquisition outside Europe. It still belongs to Spain.

† Cape Bojador is on the coast of what is today Western Sahara (a disputed territory ruled by Morocco), about 100 miles south of the Canary Islands. In the early fifteenth century this marked the southern limit of Europeans' knowledge of Africa's Atlantic coast.

‡ St. Brandan (or Brendan) was a sixth-century Irish abbot known for his voyages in the Hebrides and, in an eighth-century Irish epic later translated into Latin, was described as having voyaged to "blessed isles" in or across the Atlantic. As late as Columbus's time sailors were still claiming to have sighted "St. Brandan's Isle," likely having seen a mirage. The "two galleys" mentioned here are probably those of the Genoese brothers who disappeared into the Atlantic in 1291, mentioned earlier in this chapter.

§ Edward I, Prince Henry's elder brother (reigned 1433–1438).

Source: From Gomes Eannes de Azurara, *The Chronicle of the Discovery and Conquest of Guinea*, trans. R. Beazley and E. Prestage (London: The Hakluyt Society, 1896), pp. 27–30, 79–83.

In 1402, what became a long struggle to conquer the seven rugged islands of the Canary archipelago began. An expedition under Castilian control defeated some three hundred native Canarians (called *Guanches*) on one of the small eastern islands. Within a few years the Castilians seized two more islands, and several Portuguese efforts to oust them failed. By 1475, the Guanches retained only three islands; they fought tenaciously until the last and largest, Tenerife, fell in 1496. In the lowlands Spanish cavalry triumphed, but the Guanches retreated to the rugged highlands where their guerrilla tactics worked well. However, European diseases ran rampant among natives who had no resistance to them, as would happen later in the Americas. Many who survived disease suffered enslavement by the Spaniards, who introduced sugar plantations based on slave labor. By the end of the sixteenth century, the Guanches—who probably numbered about eighty thousand when the Castilians first arrived—had completely died out.

Portuguese voyages of discovery and colonization to the previously uninhabited Madeiras (ca. 1420) and Azores (1427) enjoyed backing from Prince Henry (1394–1460), one of five sons of the king of Portugal. Henry's nickname, "the Navigator," came not from his contemporaries but from nineteenth-century historians who argued that Henry established a scientifically oriented academy of navigation to find new methods to conquer the Atlantic. In actuality, no such institution existed anywhere in Portugal (or indeed in Europe), and Henry's main contributions to Portuguese exploration, though significant, came in the form of organization, finance, encouragement, and political support. The Portuguese push southward into Africa commenced in 1415 with the conquest of Ceuta, a Moroccan port immediately across the Strait of Gibraltar. A series of efforts to explore the African coast beyond Ceuta began around 1419, and by the time Henry died in 1460, Portuguese ships had reached what is today Sierra Leone. In *The Lusiads* (1572), Luis de Camoëns (1524–1580), Portugal's best-known poet, produced an epic that expressed his nation's pride in the exploits of its mariners:

Thus we went forth to break those oceans through,
Where none before had ever forced the way.
We saw the new isles and the climates new
Henry the Great discovered in his day.

The Encounter with Africa and the Beginning of the Slave Trade

The Portuguese explored the Atlantic coast of Africa primarily in search of two commodities: gold and slaves. Gold, scarce in medieval Europe (see Chapter 7), could be obtained from Muslim traders who brought it overland across the Sahara from West Africa, but direct Portuguese access would lower the price. The same was true for slaves,

who were needed for the sugar plantations that had been established in the Mediterranean and on several Atlantic islands in the Late Middle Ages. African societies had long relied on slaves—usually war captives, conquered peoples, criminals, and traitors. The use of forced labor in one form or another increased as African kingdoms became more powerful. Forced service as soldiers, artisans, farmers, and domestic workers was common, just as it had been among the serfs of medieval Europe.

As the fifteenth century progressed, the Portuguese pushed down the West African coast and established trading outposts along the way, often through peaceful negotiations with the indigenous authorities. Portuguese cloth, beads, and metal goods were exchanged for gold and slaves, reorienting much of the long-established trans-Saharan commerce to the coast. Spanish explorers and traders also joined the new African trade, pushing prices up and forcing the Portuguese to spend money to defend their position.

Along the Guinea coast of West Africa, the Europeans encountered a number of small but well-organized states quite able to defend themselves. The Portuguese reached Benin in 1475, a state whose people regarded their monarchs as divine and whose artisans produced superb bronze sculpture. The *obas* (kings) of Benin ruled a wealthy and durable state that lasted until 1897. Between 1482 and 1488, three Portuguese expeditions encountered another powerful kingdom, Kongo, which lay far to the south of Benin at the mouth of the Congo River. The king ruled through a network of chiefs and maintained tight control of trade, mining, and the monetary system. Like many other African rulers, he sold slaves to the Europeans just as he had sold (and continued to sell) them to Muslim traders.

Inland lay the great kingdoms of sub-Saharan Africa, of which the Portuguese and other Europeans remained largely ignorant. Some of these kingdoms commanded remarkable wealth and resources. Mansa Musa, king of Mali, entered Cairo in 1324 en route to Islam's holy city of Mecca, reportedly accompanied by more than eight thousand men, all splendidly dressed, followed by a baggage train of eighty camels, each bearing 300 pounds of gold dust. On his return he took with him a famous Arab architect who built new mosques in Timbuktu and other towns—the first brick buildings in West Africa. Mansa Musa also encouraged education, establishing universities at Timbuktu and Jenne that became famous for law and theology throughout the Islamic world. But though some of the sub-Saharan kingdoms remained potent, the advent and subsequent expansion of the Atlantic slave trade after the mid-fifteenth century brought a new element into Africa's power equation: the Europeans.

Slavery made possible a new, highly profitable market-oriented agriculture in areas that the late medieval Iberians dominated overseas. The Canaries under Spain and

The Portuguese Fort at Elmina Begun in 1482 and supplied with a garrison of 500 soldiers, this fort at Elmina remained the principal slaving port in West Africa for centuries, first under the Portuguese and then under the Dutch, who seized it in 1637. *The Granger Collection, New York.*

Madeira under Portugal provided not only the model for the large-scale sugar plantations that would eventually proliferate in Brazil and the Caribbean islands, but also the sugarcane plants themselves and the mills and other technology for processing sugar. Initially, most slaves on the Atlantic island plantations were the Guanches captured by Castilian raiders, but as they died out, enslaved North African Moors and blacks from sub-Saharan Africa were imported to replace them. Soon after 1600, the population of Madeira consisted of some two thousand slaves and approximately fifteen thousand Portuguese settlers. The Atlantic islands embodied a new kind of European exploitation in that considerable numbers of Iberians moved there to live and pursue commercial agricultural and mining activities relying on slave labor. Slavery there was designed almost exclusively for market production. This made Atlantic slavery fundamentally different from the largely household-oriented servile relationships with which Africans and Arabs were familiar.

On to India and East Asia

Dias's discovery of the route around the Cape of Good Hope opened the door to Portuguese advance into the Indian Ocean. He was followed in 1497–1498 by Vasco da Gama (ca. 1469–1524), a Portuguese nobleman who led four small ships on the first European oceanic voyage to East Africa and India. His mission was to make an alliance with Christian rulers who the Portuguese believed resided in East Africa and to bring back spices, gold, and precious jewels. A Christian kingdom had in fact survived inland in Ethiopia (see Chapter 6), but medieval rumors about a powerful African Christian emperor called Prester John proved greatly exaggerated. Departing from Lisbon in August 1497, da Gama spent ninety-three days on his outward journey without seeing land (nearly three times as long as Columbus). Making a wide eastern loop in order to reach the belt of westerly winds deep in the South Atlantic, he rounded the southern tip of Africa in mid-December. Da Gama worked his way up the eastern African coast and reached southwestern India, anchoring near Calicut on May 20, 1498. On May 28, after communicating with local authorities, he went ashore to negotiate for authorization to trade for spices.

Da Gama learned that there was no ready market for the commodities he had to offer (mainly woolens and hardware). By such experiences, the Portuguese soon realized how old, complex, and sophisticated was the trade carried on by the diverse mix of peoples who lived around the Indian Ocean. Muslim traders, well entrenched in many parts of the region, had good reason to resist the Portuguese incursion. With difficulty, da Gama managed to gather a cargo of pepper and cinnamon that sold at a high price when he finally got back to Lisbon in September 1499. In 1502, he returned with twenty-five ships and used their firepower to begin taking over the spice trade. This time he shipped back so much pepper to Lisbon that the price dropped to only 10 percent of what the Venetians paid for it in Egypt, yet the Portuguese profit margin remained substantial.

With astonishing speed, daring, and brutality, the Portuguese established fortified naval bases at outposts such as Mozambique (1507) in East Africa, Hormuz (1507) in the Persian Gulf, Goa (1510) in India, Malacca (1511) on the Malay Peninsula, and the Moluccas (1535) in the Spice Islands. From these bases, they controlled the existing trade for their own shipping and collected tolls from local ships. Short of manpower on both land and sea, the Portuguese maintained their widely dispersed bases by exploiting the quarrels among lesser Muslim or Hindu rulers and paying off more powerful ones. They also employed terror tactics such as massacres in towns and mutilation of captives. But in the Middle East, India, and China, Portugal and other European states had to face not just small, coastal states but centralized, powerful, heavily populated empires. The Europeans, although always squabbling with each other, could often manipulate the small states. They might even negotiate helpful alliances with the big ones, but they never had the resources to conquer them. A Portuguese ship docked in China for the first time in 1513, and in 1556 the Ming emperor's government permitted the Portuguese to build a warehouse at Macao (near Guangzhou) in order to trade for silk. In some places, the Portuguese hold proved highly durable: Macao reverted to China only in 1999, Mozambique and Angola successfully fought for independence by 1975, and India annexed Goa in 1961. Yet in some respects, Portugal's legacy is notable for its lack of longevity. With the important exception of Brazil, where plantation agriculture using slave labor was extensive and where the Portuguese language and major aspects of its culture persevere, much of the Portuguese trading empire in Africa and Asia was gobbled up in the seventeenth century by the Dutch and the English. Portugal enjoyed a head start due to its location and the experience and skill of its seafarers, but the greater human, political, and financial resources of its rivals eventually won out.

In the late fifteenth and sixteenth centuries, European knowledge of India and China was outdated and imprecise, but many centuries of contact through trade and travelers meant that these lands were, however inexactly, "known." Da Gama mistook a Hindu temple for a Christian church because he knew nothing about Hinduism. But he also took along men who knew Arabic, and their knowledge helped him communicate with people he encountered in eastern Africa and western India because Islam had expanded into those regions. Before da Gama went ashore in Calicut in 1498, the emissary who preceded him was amazed to meet a pair of Tunisian Muslims who spoke Castilian and Genoese. Huge crowds of Hindus in Calicut flocked to gaze upon their Portuguese visitors and called them "hat men" because of their bizarre headgear. Muslim writers, remembering the Crusades, referred to the Portuguese as "Franks," hardly an accurate term and yet one based on an earlier contact. However, in the New World,

the Europeans and the people they encountered there had no shared cultural experience on which to build their conceptions of each other. The utter lack of comprehension on either side would have tragic consequences.

BUILDING THE NEW WORLD EMPIRES

No one in fifteenth-century Europe thought in terms of a single Spanish nation. In 1469, Isabella, who became queen of Castile in 1474, married Ferdinand II of Aragon, who became king of Aragon in 1479. Together they were known as the "Catholic Kings," the title Pope Alexander VI (see Chapter 12) granted them in 1494; but their kingdoms retained their separate traditions, laws, and governing institutions. Castile had excellent Atlantic ports, and both Castile and Aragon had long traditions of seafaring in both the Mediterranean and the Atlantic. Ferdinand and Isabella ruled a population of 7.5 million early in the sixteenth century, more than seven times as many people as Portugal. Unlike the Spaniards, the Portuguese, ever scrambling for laborers, had to send paupers and convicts to man their bases abroad. Yet in 1479 the Portuguese won a maritime war that forced the Spaniards to yield their monopoly of West African trade. In the decades around 1500, the Spanish watched Portuguese successes in East Africa and the Indian Ocean with growing envy and alarm.

Ferdinand and Isabella approached the Atlantic enterprise cautiously because they had unfinished business at home. The Muslim invasion of the Iberian Peninsula that began in 711 established a powerful Islamic state, the caliphate of Cordova, that flowered in the ninth and tenth centuries (see Chapter 6). Its collapse into several smaller Moorish states after 1002 gave the resurgent Christians, themselves divided into several monarchies, a chance to reconquer Iberia. This Reconquista, battle after bloody battle, continued intermittently throughout the High Middle Ages until only the Moorish emirate of Granada remained at the time of Ferdinand and Isabella's marriage (see Chapters 9 and 11). So long as the war for Granada continued, the corulers repeatedly told Columbus they could not fund his enterprise. Late in 1491, however, when the royal court camped at Real de Santa Fé near the besieged city of Granada, the Muslims finally capitulated. The royal decision to support Columbus was made early in the new year and its terms signed in April 1492. The marital union of Castile and Aragon and the conquest of Granada advanced Spanish unification to the point that a wider expansion could be contemplated. What no one could have conceived as the "Catholic Kings" made their ceremonial entry into Granada in December 1491 was the huge size and unexpected nature of the "New Spain" that would emerge in the coming generation.

Ferdinand and Isabella's Entry into Granada   In the Chapel Royal of the cathedral in Granada, this carving (ca. 1521) celebrates the restoration of Christianity to southern Spain by depicting the entry of Ferdinand and Isabella to the city in December 1491 after a long and bitter siege. The final defeat of the Muslims enabled the Spaniards to invest in Columbus's ambitious and—many thought—impossible plan to sail west to Asia. *The Granger Collection, New York.*

Columbus and America

During his first voyage, Columbus found not only islands in the Bahamas but also the large islands of Hispaniola (now divided between Haiti and the Dominican Republic) and Cuba. Soon after he returned in March 1493, many editions of his report about his astonishing discoveries quickly found their way into print and circulated widely to amazed European readers. He wrote that the islands were "fertile to a limitless degree" with numerous harbors "beyond comparison with others which I know in Christendom," and he promised slaves, cotton, and spices "as much as their highnesses shall command," "great mines of gold and other metals," and "a thousand other things of value." A major surprise from the European perspective was Columbus's description of the innocence of the people he encountered: "All of them go around as naked as their mothers bore them. . . . They do not carry arms nor are they acquainted with them, because I showed them swords and they took them by the edge and through ignorance cut themselves. They have no iron." That Columbus brought back little gold in 1493 was disappointing, but he did bring seven "Indians" (Taínos, the indigenous people of the Bahamian archipelago), who fascinated all who met them.[4]

At their baptism as Christians at the royal court, the godparents were Queen Isabella and her son.

Intrigued by prospects that the ever-enthusiastic Columbus dangled before them, Ferdinand and Isabella quickly funded a second voyage for their "Admiral of the Ocean Sea." This ambitious expedition of seventeen ships and fifteen hundred men arrived off Hispaniola November 27, 1493. Columbus established a colony there, but he chose the site poorly. As he continued his Caribbean explorations, the colonists' rapacity alienated the previously friendly Taíno people. As a navigator, mariner, and publicist, Columbus possessed undoubted genius, but his managerial skills left much to be desired.

While Ferdinand and Isabella maneuvered to establish their claim to the lands Columbus had "found," the Portuguese asserted that the 1479–1480 agreement with Spain meant that any newly discovered lands south of the Canaries and west of Africa belonged to them. Eventually, in 1494, Spain and Portugal signed the Treaty of Tordesillas, which drew a line between the Portuguese and Castilian claims at approximately 1,400 miles west of the Azores. The treaty confirmed Portugal's right to African waters and trade (and thus its access to the Indian Ocean and, later, Brazil) in exchange for Castile's ownership of what would be its New World empire. In 1500 a fleet of thirteen Portuguese ships on its way to India and headed by Pedro Cabral (ca. 1467–ca. 1520) instead made the the first documented European landing in Brazil. After claiming Brazil

---

[4] Because the designation "Indian" is widely used today, we will use it on occasion in this discussion to refer to the native peoples of the New World.

Christopher Columbus   In the sixteenth century and later, artists who never saw Columbus made paintings and engravings that purported to represent him. This one has been attributed to a Genoese painter, Ridolfo del Ghirlandaio (ca. 1446–1506). Columbus's son Fernando wrote that his father was "of more than average stature, the face long, his body neither fat nor lean. . . . In youth his hair was blonde, but when he reached the age of thirty, it all turned white."   *The Granger Collection, New York.*

for his king and lingering for ten days, Cabral sailed on to India.[5]

Columbus made his third (1498–1500) and fourth (1502–1504) expeditions into Caribbean waters in hopes of proving that he had reached islands near Japan and China. He did indeed learn much more about the geography of the area, but he came no closer to East Asia. On the third voyage, his mismanagement of a dispute with Spanish colonists led to his arrest and return to Castile in chains, and on the fourth voyage he spent nearly a year ship-

wrecked on the coast of Jamaica before being rescued. Despite his troubles, Spanish efforts to colonize the Caribbean increased. By 1500, Hispaniola already had a European population of fifteen hundred, and soon Jamaica (1511) and Cuba (1511–1514) were brought under Spanish control. The Spaniards forced the conquered islanders to provide labor in the search for gold, not much of which was to be found. Like the Guanches of the Canary Islands, the Taínos soon began to die off, since they lacked immunity to European diseases. In the first decades of the sixteenth century, African slaves were replacing them and worked to produce agricultural products (sugar, brazilwood) and other natural resources (copper, pearls). European animals (cattle, pigs, sheep, goats) were imported, and between the livestock and the sugar the islands quickly came to resemble the Atlantic islands the Europeans had earlier conquered and remade in their image.

Columbus's example helped others to gain the support they needed to explore the western side of the Atlantic Ocean. In 1496, another Genoese mariner named Giovanni Cabotto (better known by the English version of his name: John Cabot) got England's Henry VII to commission him to lead an expedition across the North Atlantic. Probably hoping to find an alternative route to China, he "discovered" and claimed for England present-day Nova Scotia and perhaps Newfoundland (lands of whose existence English fishermen may have had prior knowledge). On a second voyage in 1499, he disappeared at sea. His and subsequent explorers' attempts to find a "northwest passage" to Asia were frustrated by arctic ice, and meanwhile the first reports of gold on the North American mainland proved false. Castilian-commissioned explorers therefore decided to concentrate their efforts on the Caribbean area. One of them, Amerigo Vespucci (1451–1512), a Florentine merchant who had settled in Seville, explored the coast of what is now Venezuela in 1499 and again in 1501. He insisted (correctly) that these new lands were not merely a part of Asia, as Columbus stubbornly maintained, but a new continent. Vespucci's vividly written letters describing what he called in Latin the *Novus Mundus* ("New World")—and pirated editions of the letters containing dubious additions by people who had never been there—so captured European imaginations that a mapmaker's decision to label the transatlantic region as "America" turned out to be decisive.

Exploration reached another milestone in 1513, when Vasco de Balboa (1475–1517), a Spaniard exploring the Isthmus of Panama for gold, became the first European to see the Pacific Ocean.

Indian Empires, Spanish Conquistadores

The peaceful, relatively isolated island communities of Taínos fell quickly to the Spaniards, but in Mexico and Peru there were rich and culturally impressive Indian

---

[5] Some historians think that Portuguese mariners, blown off course as they sailed down the African coast, had found their way to Brazil even before Columbus's first voyage, but that this knowledge was kept secret in order to block Castilian interlopers. If true, that would explain Portugal's insistence, when negotiating the Treaty of Tordesillas, on moving the mid-ocean partition line far enough west to encompass Brazil, and it would suggest that Cabral's landfall in 1500 represented a decision to "go public" with Portugal's claim to American territory.

THE HISTORICAL EVIDENCE

The Naming of America

1507

Why "America" rather than "Columbia," since Columbus and not Amerigo Vespucci first "found" the New World? Martin Waldseemüller, a German geographer and map-maker, argued for "America" on the grounds that Vespucci had reached the continent of South America a year before Columbus. After learning more about Columbus's voyages, Waldseemüller changed his mind and removed the name America from the map he published in 1516. But the name nevertheless had already caught on. Here is the reasoning he offered for his initial decision in 1507.

It is clear from astronomical demonstrations that the whole earth is a point in comparison with the entire extent of the heavens; so that if the earth's circumference be compared to the size of the celestial globe,* it may be considered to have absolutely no extent. There is about a fourth part of this small region in the world which was known to Ptolemy and is inhabited by living beings like ourselves. Hitherto it has been divided into three parts, Europe, Africa, and Asia. . . .

Europe is so called after Europa, the daugher of King Agenor. While with a girl's enthusiasm she was playing on the sea-shore accompanied by her Tyrian maidens and was gathering flowers in baskets, she is believed to have been carried off by Jupiter, who assumed the form of a snow-white bull, and after being brought over the seas to Crete seated upon his back to have given her name to the land lying opposite.

Africa is bounded on the west side by the Atlantic Ocean. . . . It is called Africa because it is free from the severity of the cold.

Asia, which far surpasses the other divisions in size and in resources, is separated from Europe by the river Tanais (Don [in southern Russia]) and from Africa by the Isthmus [the Sinai Peninsula]. . . . Asia is so called after a queen of that name.

Now, these parts of the earth have been more extensively explored and a fourth part has been discovered by Amerigo Vespucci (as will be set forth in what follows). Inasmuch as both Europe and Asia received their names from women, I see no reason why any one should justly object to calling this part Amerige, i.e., the land of Amerigo, or America, after Amerigo, its discoverer, a man of great ability.

---

* In Ptolemaic astronomy (which Waldseemüller accepted), the universe, or "celestial globe," had as its outer edge the sphere of fixed stars.

Source: From Martin Waldseemüller, *Cosmographiae Introductio*, trans. Joseph Fischer and Franz von Wieser (Ann Arbor: University Microfilms, 1966), pp. 68–70; reprinted in Herbert H. Rowen and Carl J. Ekberg, eds., *Early Modern Europe: A Book of Source Readings* (Itasca, Ill.: Peacock, 1973), pp. 109–110.

---

civilizations that, in theory, should have proved tougher nuts to crack (see Map 14-2). By conquering them, Spain could acquire instant empires. The Aztecs, who centered in the valley of Mexico with their capital Tenochtitlán (on the site of modern Mexico City) and the Incas, who settled in the central Andes mountains with their capital Cuzco, based their civilizations on agriculture: the Aztec on maize (in U.S. usage, corn) and the Inca on varieties of the potato. Maize, considered a goddess by Aztecs, was so easy to grow that Mexican peasants had to work their fields only fifty days a year, even though they possessed neither plows, wheels, horses, nor metal implements. They were therefore able to devote much effort to the massive building programs demanded by their priests and kings.

The Aztec Empire that the Spaniards encountered had grown out of a Mexican civilization stretching far back in history. Independently of the Old World's **Neolithic Revolution,** agriculture had been discovered in central Mexico during the fifth millennium B.C. Around the time of the birth of Christ, Mexican society became highly complex and sophisticated; historians label this the period of "Classic" Mexican civilization, in which many of the enduring religious, political, and cultural elements of Mesoamerican life came into focus.[6] One of the principal heirs of Classic

---

[6] *Mesoamerican* refers to the geographical region, people, and cultures of Mexico and Central America.

Inca Territory, ca. 1250–1438
Inca Conquests, 1438–1527
Inca roads

Aztec Territory, ca. 1440
Aztec Conquests, 1440–1520
Maya States and Culture

MAP 14-2
THE AMERINDIAN EMPIRES

Mexico, the Maya civilization of Yucatán, Guatemala, and Honduras, took shape about A.D. 100 and reached its peak between 600 and 900. Creating a way of life vaguely like that of ancient Egypt and Mesopotamia, the Maya built great ceremonial centers with colossal stone platforms and pyramids arranged around courtyards and approached by causeways. Carvings, wall paintings, and **hieroglyphics** (which scholars are only beginning to decipher) disclose the Maya's remarkable knowledge of mathematics and astronomy. Driven by a need to understand grand cosmic cycles and mundane weather patterns alike, Mayan priests measured the solar year with greater accuracy than the Hellenistic Greeks and the medieval Arabs and Europeans could manage. The Maya were overthrown around A.D. 900 by invaders from central Mexico, the Toltecs—themselves successors to a series of heirs of the Classic civilization. In their turn, the Toltecs succumbed to other Mexican peoples, the latest of which were the warlike Aztecs, who founded their empire around 1350 and conquered much of central Mexico. When Hernán Cortés arrived, the Aztecs were still extending their imperial sway and showing few signs of decline.

The Aztecs excelled as warriors, organizers, and builders. They incorporated many features of Maya and Toltec culture, including the custom of human sacrifice. Believing that the sun god Huitzilopochtli could keep making his daily journeys across the sky only with the help of human blood, the Aztecs made regular sacrifices of captured enemies and slaves. To celebrate the dedication of the Great Temple at Tenochtitlán, celibate priests, trained in the elaborate rhythm of the calendar-regulated liturgy, cut out the hearts of 20,000 people. With more than 200,000 inhabitants, and with gardens, palaces, and canals supplied with fresh water by a large aqueduct, Tenochtitlán was larger than any contemporary city in western Europe. Yet in 1519 the Spanish *conquistador* ("conqueror") Hernán Cortés overthrew the Aztec Empire with only 1,200 soldiers and sixteen horses. In large part, Cortés did this by exploiting the grievances of the Aztecs' subject peoples, who paid heavy tributes in maize and many other commodities to the Aztec emperor and who understandably looked to Spaniards to deliver them from their tyrannical ruler. To great psychological effect, Cortés carefully deployed his horsemen and firearms, weapons the Aztec

The Rising of Venus and Aztec Theology   This is a sheet from a "Venus calendar," a section of a type of manuscript that was in Aztec temples and religious seminaries. Aztecs worshipped the "morning star" (the planet Venus), and they believed that when Venus rose ahead of the sun many dangers lay in store. Here Venus is the figure on the left.   *Werner Forman/Art Resource, NY.*

soldiers had had never seen before. The emperor, Moctezuma II (reigned 1502–1520), used his absolute authority to permit Cortés and his men to enter the capital. It was a fatal mistake.

Similar flaws doomed the Incas of Peru, the most politically advanced people in the New World. Like the Aztecs, the Incas were heirs to cultures dating back many centuries. A highland tribe, they began to expand by force around the time that William the Conqueror was invading England (1066). At its peak, their empire stretched nearly 2,000 miles, from modern Ecuador to central Chile and east across the Bolivian plateau. Although virtually preliterate,[7] Inca culture was advanced in mathematics, engineering, and surgical techniques. Inca craftsmens' skill in stone construction and working soft metals (gold, silver, copper, and bronze) struck awe in the Spaniards gazing upon the splendor of the imperial capital, Cuzco.

The Inca Empire was thoroughly autocratic, an administrator's paradise, with a huge army that stood ready to quash rebellion and a population of around 7 million—nearly as many as Spain. A superb road system, boasting 10,000 miles of roads and numerous bridges, tunnels, and causeways, all leading to Cuzco, accommodated only foot and llama traffic. (Like the Aztecs, the Incas lacked large beasts of burden and hence the wheel.) Of this system, a Spaniard wrote, "Should our great emperor wish a similar thing, we could not build it." Relays of trained men rushed messages (and occasionally fresh fish) at a speed of 125 to 150 miles a day. There was no private property or trade; the state owned and allocated all property and even determined the age at which people had to marry.

It was precisely the centralized and despotic character of the Inca Empire that enabled the Spanish conquistador Francisco Pizarro (1475–1541) to conquer it. Illiterate, illegitimate, brutal, greedy, and treacherous, Pizarro exemplified the worst of Western society of his day, as well as cunning and reckless courage. Setting out from Panama in 1531 with only 180 men and twenty-seven horses, he had the good fortune to reach Peru while the Incas were embroiled in a civil war between two half-brothers contending for the throne. One of them, Atahualpa, welcomed the Spaniards with great ceremony. But the visitors suddenly killed Atahualpa's attendants and took him captive—just as Cortés had done away with Moctezuma. Without Atahualpa's leadership, the Inca administrative

---

[7] The Inca communicated some information by means of knots on cords. But their ability to build a relatively sophisticated civilization without the aid of a writing system was almost unique in world history.

Hernán Cortés, the Greatest Conquistador

Hernán Cortés (1485–1547) was the son of an impoverished Castilian noble. His father required him to study law at the University of Salamanca, but in 1504, like many other adventurers, he made his way to the New World. There, he fought in the conquest of Cuba (1511–1513) under its governor, Diego Velásquez. In 1519 Velásquez provided Cortés, who had been serving as his secretary, with a fleet of eleven ships, six hundred volunteers, sixteen horses, and a few artillery pieces and muskets. His mission was to explore the coast of Mexico and Yucatán. Upon arriving in Mexico and hearing reports of an empire rich in gold to the west, Cortés used his legal knowledge to free himself from Velásquez's authority. This elaborate charade included founding the *pueblo* (town) of Vera Cruz and its *cabildo* (council) whose "citizens" commissioned Cortés as their captain-general. After leaving a garrison in Vera Cruz and dispatching a letter requesting Charles V to confirm his regime, Cortés burned the remainder of his ships, made soldiers of his sailors, and set out to build his own province.

A shrewd psychologist and diplomat, Cortés cleverly used the grievances of the subject tribes to get their help as interpreters, guides, porters, and allies against the Aztec emperor, Moctezuma. A monarch who took his role as religious leader seriously, Moctezuma, who was expecting the return of the great god Quetzalcóatl, may have mistaken Cortés for the white-skinned, bearded god whose arrival had been prophesied. He welcomed the conquistadores into Tenochtitlán. Cortés soon made Moctezuma his captive and attempted to rule through him. No one will know how long it might have worked, because Cortés had to return to the coast to deal with a force Velásquez had sent to arrest him. Always the manipulator, Cortés talked most of the men from Cuba into joining his own force, but his lieutenants back in the capital had provoked the Aztecs there into a rebellion in which at least half of the Spaniards were killed. Moctezuma died—he was either stoned to death by his people or murdered by the Spaniards, depending on how one interprets the sources. Cortés, who had returned from Vera Cruz, had to fight for three months to regain the capital. With the help of allies from among former subject tribes, he managed to retake Tenochtitlán in August 1521. He was also assisted by a catastrophic outbreak of smallpox that killed the new emperor and half the population of the huge city.

The conquistadores reduced Tenochtitlán to rubble, doubtless to the great glee of those Indians who had been forced to supply tribute and victims for human sacrifice. In 1522 Charles V appointed Cortés governor and captain-general of New Spain. With Indian labor, Cortés quickly rebuilt the city in the Spanish architectural style. He handed out groups of native villages (*encomiendas*) to his lieutenants and retained even bigger ones for himself and the emperor. The *encomenderos* thus stepped into the places of the Aztec overlords, living off tribute and labor services paid by their villages. Although the Indians were not slaves and retained their land, Charles V and his advisers worried that the *encomenderos* might become a New Spanish nobility that could threaten royal power, just as the old Spanish nobles had done before Ferdinand and Isabella tamed them. In 1535 he replaced Cortés with a viceroy and strengthened royal control over the territory the conquistadores had won. Cortés returned to Spain in 1539 and died there, rich but bored and powerless. He could never be what Charles V wanted—a bureaucrat. ❖

Cortés and Malintzin   An Aztec artist drew Cortés and a woman named Malintzin (also known as Malinche and called Doña Marina by the Spaniards), who had earlier been sold into slavery by allies of the Aztecs. Malintzin, who later became Cortés's mistress and mother to his son, spoke both Nahuatl and Maya. Through her, he gained a tremendous advantage: the ability to communicate with nearly all of the indigenous groups in the region.   *Document sur l'Apperreamiento, ca. 1540, ms. mex. 374, courtesy of the Bibliothèque Nationale, Paris.*

machine was too paralyzed to prevent Pizarro's tiny force from taking Cuzco, seizing its gold, and establishing a new Spanish capital at Lima. Unlike Mexico, the conquered Inca Empire proved difficult for the Spaniards to dominate. A major revolt in 1536 was only the first of several Inca insurrections. Pizarro himself was murdered in 1541, one of several Spanish leaders to die violently in Peru.

The New World Empires of Spain and Portugal

For most of the sixteenth century, only one European country rivaled Portugal in the quest for overseas riches: Spain (see Map 14-3). The heart of Spain's empire lay in the Caribbean islands and from Mexico to South America (excluding Brazil). After Columbus had claimed the big Caribbean islands and the swashbuckling conquistadores had conquered Mexico and Peru, Ferdinand and Isabella's successor and grandson Charles V replaced these adventurers as colonial governors with lawyers and clerics from Spain. Having tamed proud magnates at home, the Spanish monarchs had no intention of permitting a new aristocratic threat to develop overseas. As members of appellate

MAP 14-3

SPANISH AND PORTUGUESE CONQUESTS BEFORE 1600

courts (*audiencias*), the bureaucrats governed the new territories and made sure that the Castilian crown's financial interests were protected. (Aragon and its subjects were given no role in ruling America.) All trade was routed through Seville and carefully regulated by another Castilian royal agency, the Casa de Contratación (House of Trade).

The treatment of the indigenous peoples became a vexing problem for the crown. The conquistadores had installed the *encomienda* system, which permitted settlers to require Indian villagers to work for them. Spanish law acknowledged Indian property rights, and the *encomendero* received not land ownership but the use of Indian labor. Nevertheless, in practice the result was often tantamount to enslavement. Thus the Indians, formerly forced to grow food for Aztec and Inca overlords, now had new masters to feed. The Spanish brought horses, mules, sheep, and cattle to provide transport, hides, wool, and beef, and the combination of farming and ranching gradually yielded the capital to establish towns, industries, and mines. For the crown, the mines became the most important New World resources; 20 percent of the gold and silver went to Spain to support the Habsburg wars against Frenchmen, Protestant **heretics,** and other enemies (see Chapter 13).

Spanish mistreatment of the American Indians provoked loud outcries from churchmen trained in the humanist tradition, such as the Dominican friar Bartolomé de Las Casas, whose efforts to protect the natives met with at least partial success. Las Casas and his supporters scored their greatest victory with the "New Laws of the Indies" issued by Charles V at Burgos in 1542. These laws stated that Indians were free people who deserved payment for their labor, and who were fully capable of understanding Christianity and so should be convinced to adopt it by persuasion rather than compulsion. Although later amendments and ineffective enforcement in many areas undermined the impact of these humanitarian decrees, they nevertheless constituted Europe's first official attempt to protect the native peoples of the New World.

Spanish policy emphasized the establishment of towns, each arranged around a central square. These towns served as centers for governmental authority in the surrounding region. Mexico City (built on the ruins of Aztec Tenochtitlán) and Lima in Peru grew into large cities, but the size of other Spanish towns varied enormously. Spanish colonists gained the means to purchase expensive luxuries from Europe after the discovery of fabulously rich silver deposits at Potosí in Peru (modern Bolivia, 1545) and Zacatecas in northern Mexico (1546). So lucrative were these mines that the cliché "worth a Peru" endured in several European languages for centuries as the equivalent of "rolling in money." For the native Americans forced to work in them, however, the mines generally meant harsh exploitation and short lives.

THE HISTORICAL EVIDENCE

The Devastation of the Indies

ca. 1541

Bartolomé de Las Casas (1474–1566) arrived in the West Indies in 1502 as a layman to serve as a legal adviser to Spanish officials, and he received an encomienda soon afterwards. Appalled, however, by the way the Indians were being treated by other Spaniards, he gave up his grant, became a Dominican, and spent the rest of his life in a campaign to protect the native Americans. Although at first he concurred with those who wanted to bring African slaves to New Spain to replace the dying Indians, he came to oppose slavery, too. His most famous work, The Devastation of the Indies: A Brief Relation, *was a plea to Charles V that Spain's enemies later gleefully quarried for their anti-Spanish propaganda.*

The Indies were discovered in the year one thousand four hundred and ninety-two. In the following year a great many Spaniards went there with the intention of settling the land. Thus, forty-nine years have passed since the first settlers penetrated the land, the first so-claimed being the large and most happy isle called Hispaniola, which is six hundred leagues in circumference. Around it in all directions are many other islands, some very big, others very small, and all of them were, as we saw with our own eyes, densely populated with native peoples called Indians. . . .

And of all the infinite universe of humanity, these people are the most guileless, the most devoid of wickedness and duplicity, the most obedient and faithful to their native masters and to the Spanish Christians whom they serve. They are by nature the most humble, patient, and peaceable, holding no grudges, free from embroilments, neither excitable nor quarrelsome. These people are the most devoid of rancours, hatreds, or desire for vengeance of any people in the world. And because they are so weak and complaisant, they are less able to endure heavy labor and soon die of no matter what malady. . . . They are also poor people, for they not only possess little but have no desire to possess worldly goods. For this reason they are not arrogant, embittered, or greedy. Their repasts are such that the food of the holy fathers in the desert* can scarcely be more parsimonious, scanty, and poor. . . . They are very clean in their persons, with alert, intelligent minds, docile and open to doctrine, very apt to receive our holy Catholic faith, to be endowed with virtuous customs, and to behave in a godly fashion. . . .

Yet into this sheepfold, into this land of meek outcasts there came some Spaniards who immediately behaved like ravening wild beasts, wolves, tigers, or lions that had been starved for many days. And Spaniards have behaved in no other way during the past forty years, down to the present time, for they are still acting like ravening beasts, killing, terrorizing, afflicting, torturing, and destroying the native peoples, doing all this with the strangest and most varied new methods of cruelty, never seen or heard of before, and to such a degree that this Island of Hispaniola, once so populous (having a population that I estimated to be more than three million), has now a population of barely two hundred persons. . . .

As for the vast mainland, which is ten times larger than all Spain, even including Aragon and Portugal . . . we are sure that our Spaniards, with their cruel and abominable acts, have devastated the land and exterminated the rational people who fully inhabited it. . . .

Their reasons for killing and destroying such an infinite number of souls is that the Christians have an ultimate aim, which is to acquire gold, and to swell themselves with riches in a very brief time and thus rise to a high estate [social status] disproportionate to their merits.

---

* Las Casas here is referring to the fifth-century Christian hermits in the Egyptian desert, such as St. Anthony. (See Chapter 5.)

Source: From Bartolomé de Las Casas, *The Devastation of the Indies: A Brief Account*, trans. Herma Briffault (New York: Seabury, 1974; reprinted Baltimore: Johns Hopkins University Press, 1992), pp. 27–31.

Colonial policy encouraged the emigration of prospective wives from Spain to the New World, and women were aboard Columbus's ships on his 1498 voyage. Approximately one-third of the Europeans coming to "New Spain" by the 1570s were women. The presence of Spanish wives and daughters reduced the influence of indigenous women on the character of colonial society and enhanced the growth of a white colonial aristocracy in Spanish America. By contrast, few Portuguese women emigrated, and Portuguese men in the colonial outposts in Brazil, Africa, and around the Indian Ocean usually married or made mistresses of local women.

The Cathedral of Mexico City On the site of the main Aztec temple, the Spaniards built this magnificent cathedral in the classical style pioneered in Renaissance Italy and favored during the reign of Philip II. It was finished in 1667 except for the towers, which were added later. Many churches that were started later display the Baroque architecture of seventeenth-century Europe, but a distinctive "colonial Baroque" version emerged as highly skilled local craftsmen executed elaborate, decorative embellishments. This nineteenth-century engraving captures the setting better than modern photographs, which show it engulfed in dense traffic and pollution. *Courtesy of S. L. Cline.*

Unlike the Spanish in Mexico and Peru, the Portuguese in Brazil found no reason to make their way inland from the Atlantic coast. The initial attraction was what Europeans called "brazilwood," a commodity much in demand in the textile industry for its red dye, and coastal trading posts emerged to which natives brought brazilwood in return for shirts, mirrors, and other trade goods from Portugal. In 1534, the Portuguese king granted broad hereditary privileges to *donatorios* (mostly gentry or prosperous merchants) who would develop Brazil without the kind of supervision on the use of native labor that Charles V sought to impose in New Spain. The early efforts of the donatorios to produce sugar using the indigenous Tupí as labor had failed, since they rebelled, killed themselves, fled into the interior, or died of European diseases. But by around 1550, African slaves were being imported to work on sugar plantations, and in 1600 at least sixty thousand were at work in Portuguese Brazil. Many thousands more unwillingly arrived in the seventeenth century. The lack of Portuguese women and the relatively small number of Portuguese males who emigrated ensured that the Brazilian population and culture became a mixture of African, Indian, and Portuguese elements.

By 1600, approximately 275,000 blacks had been shipped to the Atlantic islands, America and Europe—just the beginning of the African **diaspora,** for the number of enslaved and uprooted black people would rise sharply for two more centuries. Because European diseases killed off the Amerindians, whom the Europeans had initially expected would provide labor to exploit the New World, Africans, many of them skilled in tropical agriculture, took their place. The result was a triangle of trade: European wares (cloth, firearms, gunpowder) to Africa; slaves to the Americas in return for sugar, tobacco, and cotton; and these latter commodities to Europe for cash. (Africans, moreover, brought some of their own crops to the Western Hemisphere, augmenting the ecological revolution that was taking place.)

The Columbian Exchange

Columbus's arrival in the New World initiated a lengthy and complex interchange of plants, animals, diseases, and technologies between the Old World and the New, which historians call the Columbian Exchange. Columbus and the conquistadores who followed him to the Americas had obvious technological advantages when they fought indigenous people: sailing ships, horses, wagons, steel weapons, and gunpowder. Not only the relatively primitive and isolated Taínos and Tupís, but the skilled and organized Aztecs and Incas suffered massive defeats despite their huge edge in numbers. But the actual role played by European technology should not be overrated, nor should the native Americans' ability to adapt to and adopt many of these innovations be underrated. In the Canary Islands, the Guanches quickly learned to avoid Spanish cavalrymen and to fight away from open, flat land where mounted men had the advantage. The Taínos' fearsome (and allegedly cannibalistic) enemies, the Caribs, resisted would-be European conquerors and retained considerable autonomy in their islands until late in the seventeenth century. The Araucanians in Chile defeated Spanish horsemen and used captured Spanish firearms so adeptly that they outlasted Spanish power in South America. By the early seventeenth century, many native North Americans were gaining mastery of horses and guns and used them to make the acquisition of their land both costly and deadly, as U.S. General George Armstrong Custer (in the nineteenth century) and others would discover. The Plains Indians, for example, obtained horses through a long chain of sales (illegal, because the Spaniards tried to prohibit them), thefts, and escapes of Spanish animals. By 1600, the transition of Plains culture from a pedestrian to a mounted one was under way.

The successes of the Europeans' conquest of the New World owed more to the germs, animals, and plants they brought with them than to their military skills and equipment. In the Mexican case, the deadly smallpox outbreak that killed half the Aztec defenders of Tenochtitlán while Cortés besieged it also killed Moctezuma's imperial successor. The defense of the city was tenacious and heroic, but according to a contemporary Spanish writer, after seventy-five days of siege and smallpox, "the streets, squares, houses, and courts were filled with bodies, so that it was almost impossible to pass. Even Cortés was sick from the stench in his nostrils." According to one recent estimate, the native population in Mexico alone plummeted from 11 million in 1519 to 2.5 million in 1597. (Table 14-1 documents the effect of smallpox on one Inca village.)

Cortés's Indian allies, no less devastated by smallpox than the Aztecs, noticed that the Spaniards seemed immune to the disease. In Europe, 80 percent of smallpox victims were children under age ten; most of those who escaped it as children had a degree of immunity resulting from their exposure. But the indigenous peoples of the Americas, like those of Australia and New Zealand, were subject to what scientists call virgin soil epidemics.[8] The ancestors of the Indians had crossed into North America over the **land bridge** across the Bering Strait between Siberia and Alaska at least fourteen thousand years ago (and possibly earlier; see Prologue). When the melting at the end of the Ice Age raised ocean levels, the bridge disappeared, initiating an almost total isolation until 1492. The native Americans' extreme vulnerability to smallpox, measles, diphtheria, bubonic and pneumonic plague, malaria, typhus, and yellow fever—diseases long endemic in many parts of Eurasia—demonstrated itself powerfully. Many Eurasian and African diseases came from human interaction with cattle, sheep, and other herd animals that

---

[8] Demographic catastrophes occurred in the eighteenth and nineteenth centuries in the Pacific region for the same reasons as in the Americas in the sixteenth and seventeenth centuries.

A European View of the Indians This woodcut (printed in Augsburg in 1505) depicts Caribbeans based on European literary traditions rather than on real knowledge of the New World. The caption states that "no one has anything of his own, but all things are common. And the men who have wives that please them make no distinction whether it is their mother or sister or friend. They fight with each other. They also eat one another and they hang and smoke the flesh of those killed. They live to 150 and have no government." Both cannibalism and lust are illustrated in the image. *North Wind Picture Archives.*

TABLE 14-1

SMALLPOX IN AN INCA VILLAGE

In the Peruvian highland village of Aymaya, the number of burials each year in the 1580s was in the twenties, but when the smallpox hit in 1590, 194 people died (more than 10 percent of the estimated population). The table shows the ages of the 147 male victims.

Age Group	Number of Deaths
0–4	36
5–9	30
10–14	5
15–19	7
20–24	24
25–29	23
30–34	12
35–39	6
40–44	0
45–49	1
50–79	0
80 +	3
Total	147

Source: Adapted from Noble David Cook's table from Brian Evans's chapter "Death in Aymaya of Upper Peru" in Noble David Cook and W. George Lovell, eds., *The Secret Judgments of God: Native Peoples and Old World Disease in Colonial Spanish America* (Norman: University of Oklahoma Press, 1992), pp. 144–160.

portion was a little less. . . . They died in heaps, like bedbugs." The conquistadores neither desired nor intended such a consequence; indeed, they wanted and needed the labor of the natives. Friars like Las Casas concerned for the Indians' souls could do no more than the *encomenderos* concerned for their bodily strength. The invaders had no way of understanding that they were conducting, in effect, biological warfare, and they lacked the power to hinder it once the microbes they carried in their bodies and the bodies of their animals were unleashed. Indeed, the diseases raced ahead of the Spaniards, and the Inca civil war that Pizarro exploited was triggered by smallpox. The Inca emperor Huayna Capac and the officers of his army died, "their faces being covered with scabs," and his death and that of his designated successor led to the succession dispute between Atahualpa and his half-brother that gave Pizarro his opening.

If their microbes constituted an army of unexpected but potent weapons that enabled Europeans to overwhelm the Indians' defenses, European plants and domesticated animals (horses, cattle, pigs, sheep, goats) helped them consolidate their gains and feed their growing colonial empires. In the pre-Columbian Americas, farmers had highly developed agricultural skills alongside limited pastoral opportunities. Only dogs and llamas were available to domesticate, but neither had much utility as a food source or beast of burden. Beginning with the Neolithic Revolution, however, Europe and Asia had a wide variety of animals capable of domestication, and horses, cattle, goats, and pigs had long been just as important as crops in sustaining Old World life. Countless farmers tended flocks and herds that supplied power to pull plows and carts, yielded wool and hides that could be made into clothing, and converted grasses that humans could not eat into meat that they did consume.

Columbus brought animals, seeds, seedlings, and cuttings on his second voyage in 1493, and others soon brought more. Animals and plants (such as bananas, oranges, melons, onions, peaches, sugarcane, wheat, rice) that quickly came to dominate American soil were imported and began a process that within a century revolutionized the flora and fauna of the New World. Rain forests on Caribbean islands gave way to sugarcane fields. Herds of cattle and horses from Spain proliferated rapidly as they devoured the grasslands that stretched from Mexico into Canada in the north and across the pampas of Argentina and Uruguay in the south. At the end of the century, a Spaniard in Argentina wrote that the number of wild horses was such "that they cover the face of the earth and when they cross the road it is necessary for travelers to wait and let them pass, for a whole day or more." As early as 1550 in Mexico, anyone who wanted a horse merely had to rope one, and thirty years later in northern Mexico even a poor rancher possessed a herd of twenty thousand cattle. The surviving indigenous people knew a good thing when

did not exist in the New World. People in the Old World, long exposed to these ills, often had some immunity or genetic resistance to them; the Indians had none. The only disease that may have gone from the Americas back to Europe was syphilis, although scientists have not yet determined its origins with certainty.

The first epidemic, probably of smallpox, seems to have struck late in 1518 or early 1519 in Hispaniola, the first Spanish colony. From there it quickly spread to Yucatán, central Mexico, and beyond. Wholly unprotected regardless of age, Amerindian communities lost 50 to 100 percent of their people. In the 150 years after Columbus arrived, a series of epidemics produced the most horrific human mortality in recorded history. One Spaniard in Mexico wrote that in many provinces "more than one half of the population died; in others the pro-they tasted it and became fine pastoralists at the earliest opportunity. Overgrazing destroyed native grasses, and hardier (sometimes noxious) Old World plants took their place. The numbers of native animals (llamas, alpacas) declined sharply as Eurasian animal diseases assaulted them. Not only did European colonists (and their African slaves) come and multiply; so did the plants and animals they brought with them. Horses, hogs, rats, rabbits, bees, daisies, dandelions, and innumerable weeds—no less than Europeans—thrived in the Americas (as they would later in Australia and New Zealand).

The plants native to the Americas that succeeded in the **Old World** are fewer, but their contribution to Old World diets proved critical. The most important have been maize (corn), beans,[9] sweet potatoes and yams, potatoes, and manioc (cassava), but many others (such as peanut, squash, pumpkin, pineapple, tomato, chile pepper, cocoa) are significant. The American imports became established in different parts of Europe, and in Africa and Asia as well, depending on soil and climate: maize in southern France, Iberia, Italy, the Balkans, and southern Russia; potatoes in the British Isles (especially Ireland), northern Europe, and all parts of Russia; manioc and yams in western sub-Saharan Africa; and beans nearly everywhere. The American plants added to food supplies without replacing established staples such as wheat, barley, rye, and (in Asia) rice. Indeed, their value was that many would grow on soils previously thought useless or during seasons when traditional crops would not grow. European agriculture gained in variety. But unlike the New World, in Europe there were few sweeping ecological transformations.[10]

Strange New Worlds

European responses to the news that flowed in about black Africa, the Americas, India, the "Spice Islands," China, and Japan ran the gamut from fear and incomprehension to admiration and fascination. Most reactions concentrated on what European Christendom could gain from the "discoveries," rather than on comprehending these new places and peoples in their own terms. Many Christians tried to square the new information with inherited mental pictures by interpreting its strangeness as really just a version of things already known. Assimilating new information was somewhat easier for Westerners in the case of the Islamic

states around the Indian Ocean, and even of India and China, because Europeans had earlier traveled overland to those places. Even sub-Saharan Africa, which Europeans had not visited, was vaguely familiar because a relatively few black slaves had been brought to the medieval Mediterranean by Arab traders. Thus Europeans knew something, even if much of what they "knew" was outdated and inaccurate, about Africa and Asia.

The Americas, however, were wholly novel. The very fact of their newness forced Europeans to ransack their cultural traditions to find categories, concepts, and words to comprehend it. For some observers, whether eyewitnesses or readers of their reports, the previously unknown places represented horrible heathen savagery; for others, they seemed paradises where the Amerindians, without benefit of Christianity, lived in just and humane societies. Columbus—who could have had a splendid career writing real estate advertisements had he lived today—usually emphasized the positive aspects. His accounts of his first voyage, which never mention mosquitoes, glowingly describe the lushness and beauty of the islands, the richness of the soil, and the excellence of the rivers and harbors. He stressed the friendliness, curiosity, and gentleness of the "Indians," as he named them. Building upon Columbus's letters, in 1505 a Spanish humanist said that the Indians "seem to live in that golden world of which old writers speak so much, wherein men lived simply and innocently, without enforcement of laws, without quarreling, judges and libels, content only to satisfy nature."

Yet the naked, painted bodies of the Indians shocked Columbus, and their material poverty disappointed him. He also mentioned what they told him about islands farther west in which there "were people who had one eye in the forehead, and others whom they called 'cannibals.' Of these last they showed great fear . . . because these people ate them and . . . are very warlike." Columbus displayed some skepticism, but he nevertheless related what he was told. Since a taste for human flesh had been associated with "savages" for many centuries, many European readers had no difficulty equating Indians and savagery. While Columbus downplayed the strangeness of the peoples he encountered, his friend Vespucci emphasized it. For him, the nakedness of the people signified not innocence but sinfulness: polygamy, incest, sodomy, fornication, bestiality, and cannibalism. When in 1503 Queen Isabella issued an order against enslaving Indians, she made an exception of "a certain people called Cannibals." Eyewitness accounts of Aztec blood sacrifices reinforced negative stereotypes. In 1547, a Spanish humanist thundered against Las Casas's defense of the Indians, asking "How can we doubt that these people—so uncivilized, so barbaric, contaminated with so many impieties and obscenities—have been justly conquered by a nation so humane and excelling in every virtue?" Then, as now, observers reached different conclusions about what the "facts" were, and their conflicting

---

[9] A few species of beans were indigenous to Europe and had been mainstays of Roman and medieval diets, but the addition of American species greatly increased the range of these nutritious foodstuffs available for consumption.

[10] The most significant ecological change that occurred during this period in Europe was the destruction of cropland by herds of sheep in Sicily and southern Italy (as already noted in Chapter 9), and also in Spain. The importing of sheep there had exactly the same effect as it did in Mexico.

reports allowed readers to choose which "facts" they believed genuine depending on their own preferences and prejudices.

DEMOGRAPHIC RECOVERY AND ECONOMIC GROWTH IN EUROPE'S "LONG SIXTEENTH CENTURY," 1450–1620

The tremendous long-range global consequences of the European seafarers' and empire-builders' work are obvious enough. Eventually, millions of people both near and far from Europe found themselves under the authority of European colonial governors. The discoveries set in motion a process that led, by the nineteenth and early twentieth centuries, to European domination of the world's economic system and much of its population. Yet it would be a mistake to attribute too much too quickly to the overseas discoveries. They did not immediately revolutionize the Old World's economy or society. The daily lives of Europeans were no more changed by the conquest of the oceans than our lives have been by pioneering into outer space. Only in the Americas did Europeans establish political domination before the eighteenth century, and even there it was incomplete. In the Old World during the sixteenth and seventeenth centuries, numerous African, Islamic, and Asian states continued much as before. Overseas exploration brought Europe both advantages and disadvantages. The latter included new expenses for government and new causes of conflict, such as wars over colonies and trading posts; the former included commodities that could be eaten (maize, potatoes, tomatoes, beans, chocolate), made into clothing (hides, dyestuffs, cotton), used to build ships (timber), or turned into jewelry or coins (precious stones, gold, silver).

During the sixteenth century, major demographic, economic and social change swept through the West, much of which would have happened even if Europeans had not discovered how to navigate the oceans. The increase in Europe's population was substantial enough in itself to fuel considerable economic growth. In general, overseas expansion accelerated trends already under way, such as growth of the money supply and increases in trade and population, rather than initiating new trends. These demographic and economic changes caused profound disruptions of the late medieval social fabric and created the background against which the religious unity of Christendom fragmented and the nation-state emerged as a new political entity in the sixteenth and early seventeenth centuries.

Population

For the understanding of some kinds of changes, hundred-year segments make awkward intervals. For example, economic historians today speak of the period from around 1450 to around 1620 as "the long sixteenth century." (Both the starting and ending points came twenty or thirty years later in some regions because economic changes did not occur uniformly.) Generally, however, in the mid-fifteenth century the European population stabilized and began to grow after a century of decline due to plague, wars, and famine (see Chapter 11). Beginning roughly in 1450, the "long sixteenth century" saw sustained demographic and economic growth—growth being defined in quantitative rather than per capita terms. Except in a few areas near the North Sea, this growth occurred without accompanying structural reorganization of agricultural and manufacturing activities along capitalistic lines.

Only after the middle of the twentieth century did historians apply themselves systematically to the important subject of demography. Fifteenth- and sixteenth-century Europeans did not share the modern world's lust for demographic data. The first census in the United States occurred in 1790, repeated in 1800.[11] The first national census in Europe was not conducted until such a count was made for England and Wales in 1801. By contrast, Chinese imperial officials began taking a census once every three years in the seventh century A.D. Ancient, medieval, and early modern governments in the West, unlike the Chinese bureaucrats, felt no need to know how many people lived within their borders, and seldom had very accurate ideas of the matter. Modern historians have nevertheless managed to interpret records originally compiled for other purposes to arrive at estimates of population change. For example, beginning in 1538 every parish in England was required to keep a register of baptisms, marriages, and deaths; parishes in Catholic Europe were told do so in 1563. Not all followed orders, and only a minority of these registers have survived. From those that are available, however, counting and sampling techniques can yield plausible estimates of populations, age and frequency of marriage, fertility, life span, mortality, and even sexual misconduct.

The population of Europe, which had grown rapidly in the eleventh, twelfth, and thirteenth centuries, had begun to level off before the Black Death struck in 1347, initiating a century of stagnation. After 1450, however, a substantial population increase began, and it was part of a worldwide surge. Between 1450 and 1600, Europe's population rose from 45 million to 78 million—almost but not quite regaining pre–Black Death levels. In the seventeenth century, population declined slightly before 1650, after which the increase resumed and became another gigantic surge after 1700. The sixteenth-century demographic surge is not easy to explain. It started long before New World foods had much impact. Better hygiene and water supplies had contributed to some improvement in urban mortality

---

[11] A national census every ten years is prescribed by the U.S. Constitution, to the delight of economic and social historians.

Peasant Wedding Feast, ca. 1565 Pieter Bruegel the Elder, a highly educated and well-traveled man, painted many vivid scenes of peasants going about their lives. In this wedding feast picture, bagpipers play while guests eat at the diagonal table (like the one in Tintoretto's *Last Supper*—see p. 506). A man fills pots of ale, a child licks a bowl (lower left), and guests continue to arrive (upper left). The sixteenth-century population explosion meant that scenes like this one were increasingly numerous. *The Granger Collection, New York.*

rates, but child mortality remained high in both town and countryside.

In explaining Europe's recovery, a factor that was probably more decisive than the slight decline in mortality rates was the rising birth rate. A distinctive feature of marriage in western Europe—as compared to eastern Europe and to other civilizations—was late marriage and a relatively high proportion (10 to 20 percent) of women who never married. The west European pattern of marriage came into focus around the year 1000, along with the substitution of nuclear for extended families as the basic social unit (see Chapter 7). In medieval and early modern western Europe, a woman who did marry generally delayed doing so until she and her husband could afford to live apart from their parents—assuming that the parents were still alive; often they were not. On average, women married at between 24.5 and 26.5 years of age, and men two to three years later. Illegitimate births being rare (because of strong com-

munity disapproval), the effect was to limit family size by narrowing women's childbearing years. Late marriage, in effect, served as a contraceptive device in a society determined not to have more mouths than its agricultural resources could feed. Even a small departure for a limited period in the direction of earlier marriage could cause population growth, and for a few areas, evidence suggests this is what happened. Between about 1550 and 1570 in upper Normandy, for example, women married three or four years younger than did their counterparts earlier and later. Data for the eighteenth-century population surge confirm that changes in marriage patterns made a large contribution to that increase. The sixteenth-century data are limited, but a similar dynamic probably operated.

The fact that population grew worldwide in the sixteenth century suggests another factor: climatic change. Temperatures colder than modern norms prevailed in the Northern Hemisphere during both the fourteenth century

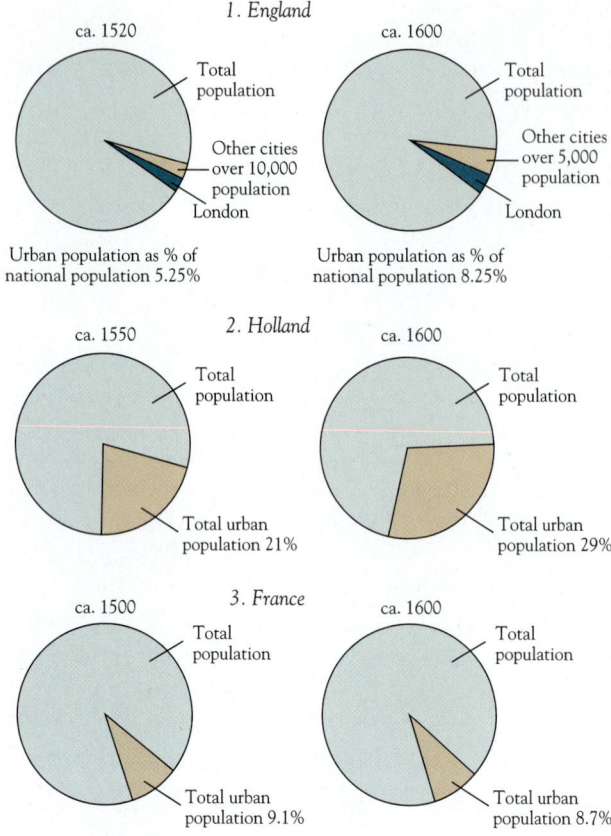

1. England

ca. 1520
Total population
Other cities over 10,000 population
London

Urban population as % of national population 5.25%

ca. 1600
Total population
Other cities over 5,000 population
London

Urban population as % of national population 8.25%

2. Holland

ca. 1550
Total population
Total urban population 21%

ca. 1600
Total population
Total urban population 29%

3. France

ca. 1500
Total population
Total urban population 9.1%

ca. 1600
Total population
Total urban population 8.7%

FIGURE 14-1

POPULATION GROWTH AND URBANIZATION IN SIXTEENTH-CENTURY ENGLAND, HOLLAND, AND FRANCE

In these graphs, "England" means England and Wales; "Holland" is the province of Holland (the most urbanized part of the Netherlands, which included such major cities as Amsterdam, Leiden, Haarlem, and The Hague); and "France" refers to the present-day territory of France, thus including areas that in the sixteenth century were part of the Holy Roman Empire. The urban population comprises towns of more than 10,000 inhabitants. *Source: Based on data from E. A. Wrigley, People, Cities, and Wealth (Oxford: Basil Blackwell, 1987), pp. 162, 182, 184.*

and the late seventeenth century (called a "Little Ice Age"; the 1690s represented the coldest decade in seven centuries).[12] Much of the world's population lives north of the Equator. The warmer weather in the "long sixteenth century" provided longer growing seasons, which in turn meant an expanded supply of food. Perhaps the farmers in upper Normandy and some other regions married younger because their land and labor produced more.

Although most early modern Europeans continued to work on the land, more people moved to the towns and cities, with the result that urban population went up faster than the population as a whole. Appalling as urban mortality rates were, migration from the countryside kept many towns growing. Some of these centers continued to flourish even after the general decline began (see Chapter 11). The proportion of rural to urban dwellers changed little, however, because more people lived in fewer cities. The number of cities with populations over 80,000 rose from four in 1500 to eight in 1600. London, for example, had around 40,000 people in 1500 and 200,000 in 1600, making it second only to Paris (which grew from 100,000 to 220,000 in the same period) among west European cities. Cities specializing in administration or international trade or

both—such as Lisbon, London, Moscow, Antwerp, Seville, Amsterdam, Madrid, and Istanbul (Constantinople)—grew most dramatically (see Figure 14-1).

The increase and shifts in population yielded complex results that benefited some individuals, groups, and regions, while harming others. For example, peasants enjoying long leases at fixed rents could become rich, especially if they lived close enough to supply the booming urban markets. Peasants less happily situated might be forced off the land altogether and into the expanding mass of vagabonds roaming the roads or migrating to towns and cities begging for work. These shocking and unsettling changes ultimately aggravated the political and religious conflicts that rocked early modern Europe.

Agriculture and the Price Revolution

The sixteenth-century population explosion sharply increased demand for all agricultural products. And because prices rise when demand outruns supply, nearly all goods—but especially those for food, fiber, and fuel[13]—became more

---

[12] Evidence for this comes from the study of glacial ice, tree rings, and similar material that can be subjected to sophisticated scientific analysis.

[13] Economists call the price of such indispensable goods *inelastic*. People have to buy them, whatever the cost. They tend to buy luxuries only when they have sufficient "discretionary income," and so the price of luxury goods is more *elastic*.

expensive. Although hands stood ready to work land that lay unused or had never been broken to the plow, agricultural technology showed only minimal innovation, and fertile new land could not be brought into production fast enough to restrain price rises. Inflation rates varied across Europe: In Spain, prices increased fourfold between 1500 and 1600; elsewhere, they doubled or tripled.

Another contributor to inflation was large increases in the money supply. At first these increases came mostly from within Europe itself, and were necessary to supply the currency required by a growing economy. In the first half of the century, production in the south German and Bohemian silver mines grew substantially as rural landlords and urban capitalists invested in them.[14] Central European silver made the Fugger family in Augsburg as rich and powerful in Charles V's day as the Medici had been in the fifteenth century. But by Charles V's reign, the ever-rising cost of war was causing governments to spend beyond their means. Often they tried to offset deficits by debasing their coinages—that is, reducing the silver or gold content without changing the face value of the coin. Such cheating did not fool merchants and creditors: It simply caused prices to rise. Several governments financed wartime expenditures by selling bonds, again swelling the money supply faster than economic productivity required. Then, in the mid-1540s, Spaniards found enormous silver deposits at Potosí and Zacatecas. By the 1560s, thanks to a new refining process, the flood of American silver into Europe began in earnest. By 1660 Europe's stock of silver was three times what it had been around 1500, and the New World had also begun supplying large amounts of gold (first from plundered Indian states and later from Portuguese mines in Brazil). Because economic growth nowhere matched this flood of money, the result was raging inflation (see Figure 14-2).

We can best understand the impact of population growth and price increases on rural life in terms of the control of land. More expensive food worsened the poverty of those who neither owned land nor had a legally secure right to use it at a reasonable rent, and throughout northern Europe the number of landless paupers grew alarmingly. Population growth, which occurred at the highest rates in northwestern Europe, unleashed a demand for grain that landowners in eastern Europe could profitably satisfy. In Poland and other countries east of the Elbe River, where kings were weak, landowning nobles powerful, and legal protection for peasant rights largely absent, a harsher form of serfdom—sometimes called *neoserfdom*—emerged. Lords forced peasants to work three days a week (or even more)

on the lord's demesne to produce grain that was shipped to western Europe by way of the Baltic Sea. In northern and central Europe west of the Elbe, the late medieval trend running against serfdom continued (see Chapter 11). Most peasants were no longer tied to the land, but whether their living standards improved depended on circumstances. Those with strong legal claims to the land they worked could sell their output easily as prices rose, while others (probably the majority) became wage laborers, an unhappy situation to be in when prices were rising faster than wages.

In France, a series of strong royal governments protected peasant tenants who paid legally specified rents. Many of those peasants who enjoyed terms negotiated during the post–Black Death labor shortage became rich: Their rents remained low while inflation raised the prices of whatever they produced. Some landowners, impoverished by having to accept rents unadjusted for inflation, saved themselves by taking royal offices or military commissions. In England, small farmers with secure tenure or agreements that protected them from eviction or excessive rents could sometimes buy more land and launch their heirs into the gentry. Nevertheless, numerous landowners in both countries found legal ways to raise rents or otherwise make themselves the prime beneficiaries of the higher prices for agrarian commodities, while reducing many peasants to wage laborers or sharecroppers. In Spain, 3 percent of the population owned 97 percent of the land, a much higher concentration than in England or France.

Landowners and peasants fared best in England, France, and the Dutch Republic, where a higher rate of urbanization—fueled by rising domestic and foreign trade, industry, finance, and commerce—created bigger markets for agricultural output. Proximity to a big city or town or access to a waterway promoted crop diversification and encouraged investment in projects to increase output, such as Dutch drainage schemes using canals, dikes, and windmills. In such cases, the relatively self-sufficient medieval villages, producing in their large open fields much of what they consumed, gave way to enclosed farms specializing in dairy products, fruits, vegetables, tulips, and dyecrops (plants that yielded dyes used in the finishing of wool cloth). Many farmers in such locations came to specialize in one or a few such crops produced entirely for the market instead of keeping to the older pattern of consuming much of what they grew and selling only the surplus in the market. In this way, more and more agricultural land both east and west of the Elbe was devoted to production for the market, as its owners sought to use the resources they controlled—capital, labor, and land—to earn a profit. In England, a key component of the drive to increase food production was **enclosure,** the transformation of the large open fields and commons of the typical medieval **manor** into fenced or hedged fields under single ownership that could be devoted to either grazing animals

---

[14] The word *dollar* comes from the German word *Thaler* (pronounced "tahler"), which in turn refers to coins minted from silver mined in the Joachimsthal ("Joachim's Valley") in Bohemia. Eventually, "dollars" identical in silver content with the Joachimsthal coins were minted as far away as Mexico.

Spanish Imports of Silver and Gold, 1503-1660

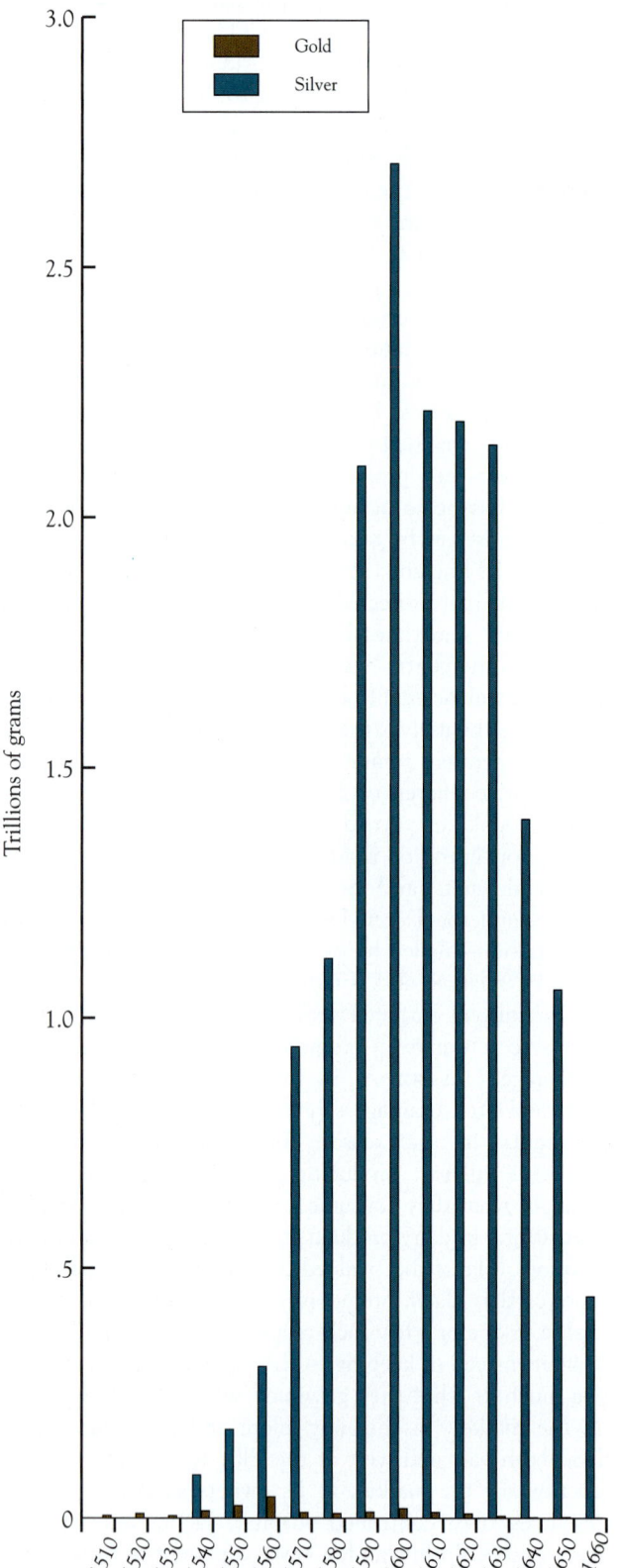

FIGURE 14-2
THE PRICE REVOLUTION

The chart on the left shows silver and gold imports into Spain. Imports of gold surged as Spanish conquistadores pillaged the Indian peoples or exploited readily discoverable natural sources. As these dwindled, so did the import of gold. Later in the sixteenth century, Portugal supplied considerable amounts of gold from newly discovered mines in Brazil. Imports of silver, on the other hand, reflect the discovery and subsequent working of the Spanish colonial mines of Zacatecas and Potosí. The graph below is a wage-price index (not adjusted for inflation). *Adapted from data in Earl J. Hamilton,* American Treasure and the Price Revolution in Spain, 1501–1650 *(Cambridge: Harvard University Press, 1934; reprinted New York: Octagon Books, 1965), table 3 (left), chart 18 (right), pp. 42, 273.*

Index of Wages and Prices in Spain, 1501-1650
Base = 1571-1580

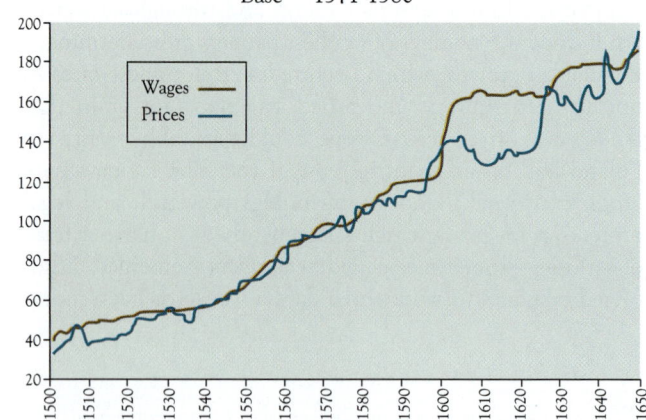

or to newer crops and methods of arable farming. About 25 percent of English peasants had "freehold" tenure that made them safe from enclosing landlords, but the rest were more vulnerable. Although social reformers denounced enclosure as a cause of rural poverty and migration to urban areas, the fact is that less than 10 percent of farmland in England underwent enclosure in the sixteenth century, with the majority of it in one region. Enclosure undoubtedly damaged many poorer peasants, but its beneficiaries included richer peasants (often called *yeomen*) as well as gentry.

Increased agricultural production paved the way for greater industrial activity in rural areas, where manufacturing was based on the "domestic" or "putting-out" system (see Chapter 11). This system, introduced primarily in Italy and the Low Countries in the Middle Ages, became much more pervasive and involved more products during and after the sixteenth century. Medieval cities had functioned as manufacturing centers, but by late in the fifteenth century Spain was the only country where the textile industry (Europe's largest) was still urban. Merchant capitalists, escaping expensive **guild** labor, hired rural men and women to transform raw wool into cloth, but each operation in the process (spinning, weaving, dyeing) was performed by different workers. Since many of them also did some farming and could grow some of their own food, their industrial labor was part-time and could more easily be attuned to the fluctuating demand for cloth.

The Spread of Capitalism

From the fifteenth century on, the story of the European economy is one of an uneven but nevertheless steady transformation of the processes of producing both agricultural and industrial goods. The spread of capitalism changed the way that relations between entrepreneurs and laborers functioned. In most parts of medieval Europe, producers and buyers conducted most commerce by meeting face-to-face at a market stall or shop. Craftsmen brought to market what they produced with their own hands and tools. Peasants sold only the surplus they did not eat or save as seed. The amounts of capital investment involved (such as weavers' looms or shoemakers' tools) were small, and relatively few items reached the point of sale from any great distance. The contrast with modern commerce is striking: The shelves of our supermarkets, shops, and department stores contain very few items produced in the region where they are sold, and many come from the other side of the globe. The transition from medieval markets to almost modern ones constitutes the Commercial Revolution (see Chapter 11), a long, slow, but tremendously important process stretching from the High Middle Ages to around 1800.

Over this period, commerce involved more and more people in one stage or another of a series of transactions in regional, national, and international markets. The greater the distance and the greater the time required to get from raw materials to finished products at the point of sale, the greater the role of middlemen who supplied the planning and the capital needed to sustain the chain of transactions. Conversely, the role of each worker in the process became smaller and his dependence on others greater. In modern-day business, the rise of multinational corporations has added yet another layer to the commercial system, but these new institutions operate on principles quite similar to the late medieval merchant capitalists who moved production into the countryside to lower their costs. (Present-day telecommuting, outsourcing, and the shifting of jobs to developing countries are not all that different from sixteenth-century "putting out.") Market pressure always drives producers to find the lowest prices for materials, labor, credit, and transportation.

The transition toward modern commerce began with the revival of towns and the growth of long-distance trade and urban industry in the High Middle Ages. Medieval capitalism achieved its fullest momentum in Flanders and northern Italy. In these regions, merchant-capitalists managed the efforts of an ever more specialized labor force while developing sophisticated methods of extending credit and arranging for settlement of accounts using paper (bills of exchange and letters of credit) instead of making payments in relatively scarce gold and silver. The commercial and financial skills needed to organize this trade were complex. Merchant bankers such as the Medici honed them to a high level, exercising great political power because of their wealth.

In medieval cities, a sharp division emerged between the merchants, who bought raw materials and arranged for the sale of finished products, and the artisans, who made the products from the raw materials. As industry grew more complex, the artisans, who formerly had sold their goods directly to local consumers, began to depend on the merchants. Some crafts lent themselves to this new system more rapidly than others. Textiles, especially, showed a pronounced shift to commercialization. In this burgeoning industry, production costs dropped as labor became more and more specialized. In Florence, for example, twenty different kinds of workers (including washers, combers, carders, spinners, weavers, dyers, stretchers, and fullers) transformed wool purchased from Spain and England into finished cloth. Artisans possessed their skills and their looms or dyeing vats and perhaps their houses, but they depended heavily on the merchants who supplied raw materials and paid them when their part in the process was complete. By the sixteenth century, textiles increasingly were produced by the putting-out system in rural areas, not only in Italy but in the Netherlands, Germany, France, and England. And in rural industry, it was not uncommon for the merchant to own the loom and the cottage in which the workers toiled, thus further reducing their independence.

THE HISTORICAL EVIDENCE

Change in the English Countryside: Two Views

1600, 1560s

Thomas Wilson, a minor official in Elizabeth I's government and a younger son of a gentleman, saw little to admire in the inflation-driven agricultural changes of the sixteenth century. In his view, the peasants (especially the richer ones, the yeomen) prospered at the expense of gentlemen. In the second selection, we see a quite different picture from the pen of William Harrison, who wrote his Description of England *in the 1560s. He thought that the position of the poorer farmers (copyholders) was worsening and that their landlords were to blame.*

Thomas Wilson's View

The cause that hath made the yeomanry in England so great [in times past] I cannot rightly call a policy, because it was no matter [in no way] invented and set down by authority for the bettering of that state of people, but rather by the subtlety [cleverness] of them and simplicity [foolishness] of gentlemen; for the yeomanry and mean [socially inferior] people being servants and vassals to the gents, who are the possessors and lord[s] of the lands and lordships and could not occupy all their lands themselves but placed farmers* therein at a time when by reason of the great wars† money was scarce and all things else cheap, and so lands let [rented] at a small rent. . . . The gentlemen, improvident of what should come after, and glad to have money in hands, did let unto said farmers all their lands and lordships (saving their dwelling) after the rate aforesaid, some for 30, some 40 and some 50, some 200 years. Soon after, the king [Henry VIII], by reason of the want of money, altered the coin and caused that which was before but 6d. [6 pence] to go for 12d. and after that again lessened it [the coinage] as much more, so that he that was wont [accustomed] to pay but 3d. which though it were all one in value yet hereby it came to pass that he which paid before 1 pound weight in silver for his farm, paid now but a quarter.

William Harrison's View

The inhabitants of many places of our country are devoured and eaten up and their houses either altogether pulled down or suffered [allowed] to decay by little and little, although sometime a poor man peradventure [perhaps] doth dwell in one of them, who, not being able to repair it, suffereth it to fall down and thereto thinketh himself very friendly dealt withal, if he may have an acre of ground

assigned unto him whereon to keep a cow or wherein to set cabbages, radishes, parsnips, carrots, melons, pompons [pumpkins], or suchlike stuff, by which he and his poor household liveth as by their principal food, sith [since] they can do no better. And as for wheaten bread, they eat it when they can reach unto the price of it, contenting themselves in the meantime with bread made of oats or barley: a poor estate [situation], God wot [knows]! . . .

Three things . . . are grown to be very grievous unto them, to wit: the enhancing of rents; . . . the daily oppression of copyholders, whose lords seek to bring their poor tenants almost into plain servitude and misery, daily devising new means and seeking up all the old how to cut them shorter and shorter, doubling, trebling and now and then seven times increasing their fines [annual dues], driving them also for every trifle to lose and forfeit their tenures (by whom the greatest part of the realm doth stand and is maintained) to the end they may fleece them yet more, which is a lamentable hearing. The third thing they talk of is usury,‡ a trade brought in by the Jews, now perfectly practised almost by every Christian and so commonly that he is accounted but for a fool that doth lend his money for nothing.

---

* In early modern England a farmer was a tenant—someone who rented ("farmed") land from a landowner.

† Wilson is probably referring to the Hundred Years' War and the Wars of the Roses (see Chapter 11).

‡ That is, lending money at interest (see Chapter 11).

Source: From Joel Hurstfield and Alan G. R. Smith, eds., *Elizabethan People: State and Society* (London: Edward Arnold, 1972; reprinted New York: St. Martin's, 1972), pp. 49, 50–51.

William Stumpe, Clothier of Malmesbury

Malmesbury Abbey in the southern English county of Wiltshire was founded in the seventh century. The abbey walls enclosed a church that once boasted a spire higher than that of Salisbury cathedral, as well as a large house for the abbot, a guest house, chapter house, and cloisters. Gardens, dovecotes, fishponds, meadows, and water mills graced the splendid property. When Henry VIII dissolved the monasteries, he sold Malmesbury Abbey for the considerable sum of £1,517 to a local clothier, William Stumpe.

The son of a humble weaver, William somehow managed to become a clothier, a capitalist who employed others to perform the various operations required to turn raw wool into Wiltshire's famed broadcloth. Clothiers invested the money to supply wool to weavers, often even owning the looms. In the putting-out system, the artisans typically worked in their own cottages, whether they owned the looms or not. Using pack-horses, the clothier moved the wool from carders to spinners and weavers and then to the fulling mill for cleansing, thickening, and softening before storing it in his warehouse until the right time to sell it.

Stumpe had succeeded so brilliantly as a clothier that, as early as 1524 he was among Malmesbury's wealthiest citizens. After buying the abbey in 1543, he carried out a plan that created what may have been the earliest example of a factory in England. He placed looms in every corner of the buildings formerly used by monks and employed weavers on his own premises. The town's annual output of three thousand cloths, much of which came from Stumpe's "factory," was impressive—in the 1470s an entire county could rarely produce more than four thousand. (A cloth was supposed to be at least 63 inches wide and 26 to 28 yards long.)

How many workers Stumpe employed in the old abbey is not known, but the scale of his plans for a similar enterprise shows that he had big ideas. In 1546 he negotiated with Oxford's town government to use the buildings at Osney Abbey for cloth production by two thousand employees. Nothing came of the Oxford project, but Stumpe's Malmesbury operation kept growing. A sizeable chunk of his profits went to buy land in Wiltshire and neighboring Gloucestershire. Stumpe built himself a mansion—on the abbey grounds. He held a variety of public offices and served as a member for Malmesbury in the Reformation Parliament (see Chapter 13). He reportedly once provided a meal to Henry VIII and his huntsmen. Stumpe's eldest son was knighted and later served as sheriff of Wiltshire. His fortune descended to his granddaughter and enabled her three daughters to marry earls. As the founder of a factory, William Stumpe was unique in his day. As a merchant whose heirs joined the English landed aristocracy, he was one of many. ❖

William Stumpe's New House
Stumpe's house, on the former abbey grounds in the heart of the town of Malmesbury, is a typical Tudor mansion, its architecture unaffected by the classicism that dominated Italy at the time. The house is still standing and, ironically, it is now a residence for nuns.
Courtesy of J. Sears McGee.

Whether rural or urban, the more production became commercialized, the greater the likelihood that men would gain income and status while women would see theirs diminish. In England before 1350, for example, nearly all ale brewing was done at home, and women frequently sold their ale in the community. Ale, which went sour quickly and thus was made frequently in small batches, had largely given way to beer by 1600. Beer lasted longer, so it could be more easily stored and transported. Because beer was brewed in much larger quantities, its production required managerial authority and access to capital that only men had. Women lost what had earlier been for many a lucrative sideline and for others a major source of revenue. Furthermore, girls generally received less education and training, and so they were more likely to get low paying, low skilled work. After 1500, the lines between male and female work increasingly hardened, and the jobs allocated to women became more menial. In 1570 in England's second largest city, Norwich, 80 percent of the girls between ages six and twelve were working, while only 33 percent of the boys were. Another one-third of the boys were in school.

During the "long sixteenth century," most capitalistic activities continued to operate on a relatively small scale, but there were exceptions. The best example of a large-scale capitalistic enterprise in early sixteenth-century Europe was the Venetian Arsenal, the huge shipbuilding and repairing factory owned and operated by the Venetian state. State capitalism of this sort can also be found in the Muslim world and elsewhere,[15] but in Europe, private businessmen carried on most capitalistic activity. These entrepreneurs faced considerable risks, but some who succeeded became rich enough to lend money at high interest rates to great princes. Borrowing from the Fugger family of Augsburg, for example, enabled Charles V to win the election as Holy Roman emperor (see Ch.13). Charles's son, Philip II of Spain (see Chapter 15) depended heavily on Genoese bankers, as did other monarchs.

The Fuggers and other entrepreneurs were not "free traders." They relied heavily on princely grants of monopolies and other protections against their rivals. Spanish rulers, for example, gave monopolies in colonial markets to Castilian (not Aragonese) producers, and English monarchs gave the Company of Merchant Adventurers control

---

[15] It also would flourish in Peter the Great's Russia (see Chapter 16).

The Royal Exchange, London.   Elizabeth I's financial adviser, Sir Thomas Gresham, was troubled that traders in London were forced to "walk in the rain when it raineth, more like pedlars[sic] than merchants." In 1565, he donated money to build the structure, similar to centers for commerce in Antwerp and Venice. Elizabeth proclaimed it the "Royal Exchange" in 1570.   *North Wind Picture Archives.*

over exports of wool to Flanders. Although Europe's princes continued to be landowning aristocrats, capitalists involved in banking and commerce played a much more powerful role than their counterparts in India, Ming China, or Japan. In Europe, rich merchants could gain the ear of princes and talk them into giving them special privileges—always, of course, in return for financial considerations such as customs duties and other taxes. Toward the end of the "long sixteenth century," ambitious merchants in England and the Dutch Republic convinced their governments to charter the first large **joint-stock companies** with monopolies over certain colonial commerce. In England, the East India Company began in 1600. With ten times as much capital, the Dutch East India Company started operation two years later. These ingenious new institutions, by spreading the risks among the owners and pooling the invested funds for use over time rather than restricting them to a single venture, greatly increased the willingness of individuals to invest.

Traditional moralists were horrified by the spread of capitalism, with its profit motive and its insistence on "efficiency." To most people of the age—ranging from judges, clergy, and intellectuals to ordinary folk—the emerging capitalist system meant the beggaring of the many for the benefit of the few. Protestant leaders like Martin Luther and John Calvin took the lead in condemning those who devoted their lives to the selfish pursuit of "mammon." Behind such vehement protests lay the ethical attitudes of Judeo-Christian religion and of ancient Greek philosophy—in other words, the whole tradition of

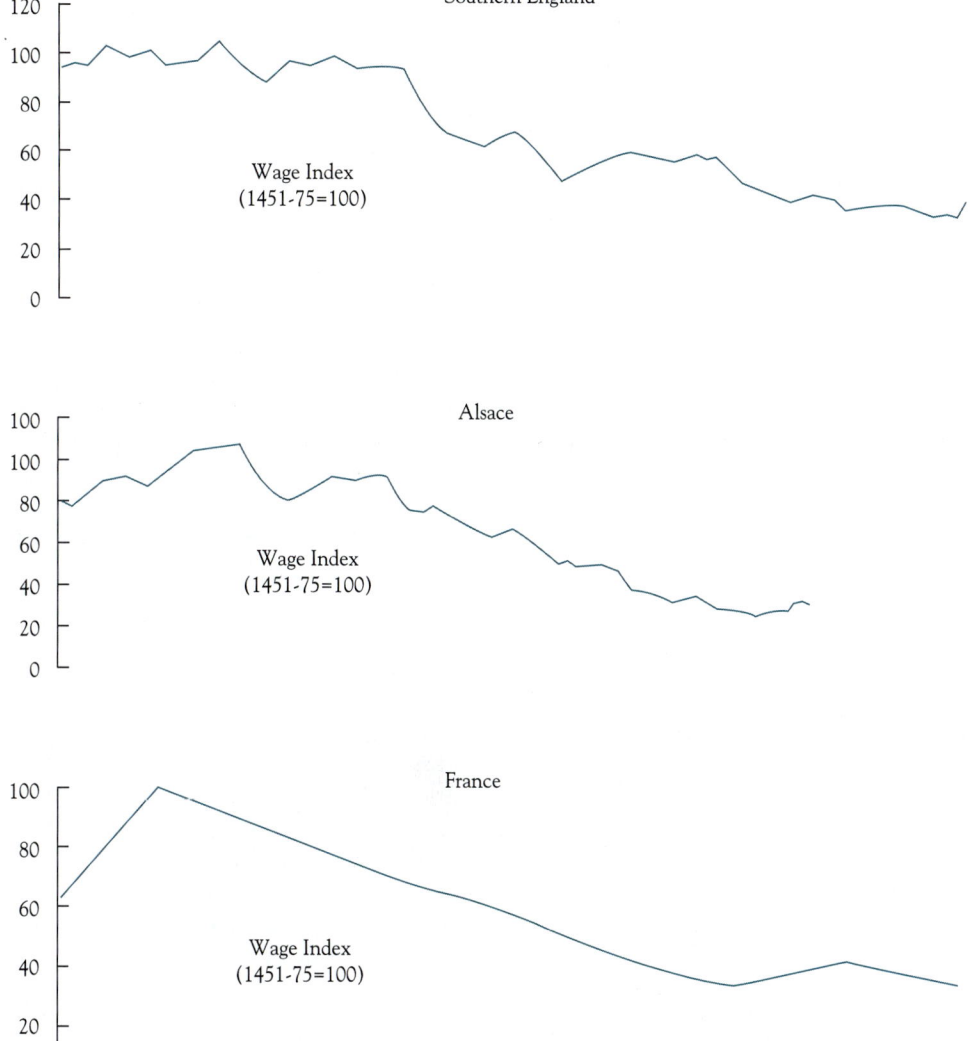

FIGURE 14-3
FALLING BUYING POWER

Reconstruction of the buying power of wages paid to workers for three regions: southern England, Alsace, and France between 1440 and 1640. Real wages peaked around 1480 and then began a long, downward slide. *Source: Adapted from data in Carlo Cipolla,* Before the Industrial Revolution: European Society and Economy, 1000–1700 *(New York: Norton, 1976), figure 8-2, p. 203.*

Western civilization. And the moralists were right when they weighed the human cost of early modern economic change.[16]

The staggering increase in prices, combined with the downward pressure of capitalist competition on wages, drastically reduced the buying power—or **real wages,** the amount of money corrected for inflation—of laboring families over the course of the sixteenth century (see Figure 14-3). An early warning came from the English humanist and traditional Catholic Sir Thomas More, whose famous book *Utopia* (1516) denounced landowners who put profit over Christian ethics by replacing farmers with sheep: "Your sheep, that were wont to be so meek and tame, and so small eaters, now, as I hear say, be become so great devourers, and so wild, that they eat up and swallow down the very men themselves." To More, and to most of his Catholic and Protestant contemporaries, the selfishness of greedy men caused inflation, and the solution was not economic or technological but moral and religious. To put private profit ahead of the common good—which is what More and other traditionalists thought was happening—seemed monstrously evil.

A quite different attitude appeared in *Jack of Newbury* (1596), a best-selling tale by an English silk weaver and ballad writer, Thomas Deloney (ca. 1543–ca. 1600). "Jack," a Berkshire weaver who gained a fortune by marrying his master's widow, after her death woos a comely maid. When he "opened his mind to her and craved her good will, . . . she took this motion kindly," but (as was expected of a dutiful daughter) she said that her parents would have to agree. Jack gave her father a tour of his splendid house and his large and busy workshop filled with men, women, and children happily making cloth. "Sir," the maid's father replies, "I see that you're 'bominable rich, and I'm content that you shall have my daughter, and God's blessing and mine light on you both."

Jack of Newbury and his proto-factory were fictional. Despite the real-life William Stumpe's pioneering venture along these lines (see The Human Experience, "William Stumpe, Clothier of Malmesbury," earlier in this chapter), such establishments generally were not economically or technologically practical until huge increases in energy production, generated by steam engines, touched off the Industrial Revolution in the mid-eighteenth century (see Chapter 20). Nevertheless, the dawning idea that a capitalist entrepreneur like Jack of Newbury could be " 'bominable rich" and still morally acceptable was prophetic—indeed, revolutionary. Over the next two centuries, the people of Europe and the Americas would grapple with this idea and, despite qualms that still persist, slowly accept it.

CONCLUSION: ENCOUNTERS AND EMPIRES

In his *Utopia*, Sir Thomas More also described a fantasy—an island where the people valued learning and each other more than gold, which they used to make chamberpots and toys. Although they had never heard of Christianity, the Utopians' system was designed to overcome pride and hold material things in common rather than as private property. They lived orderly, humane, honest, and peaceful lives. They were polar opposites to the restless, warlike, mendacious, greedy, cruel people in the Christendom that More himself inhabited and whom he wrote his book to criticize. Columbus's descriptions of the innocent Caribbean islanders he met in 1492 had similarities with More's fictional Utopians. More, like many social critics who would come later, cleverly exploited the device of an imagined place—a utopia—where individuals and institutions managed to escape all the flaws that beset the benighted Europeans.

Like Columbus, Vespucci, and other travelers, the stay-at-home More projected his own hopes and worries onto previously unknown people. But at least the Utopians were fictional and could not contract smallpox. The indigenous peoples of the Americas had been cut off from contact with the rest of the human race for many thousands of years, and Columbus revolutionized—and devastated—their world by restoring that connection. He had no way of knowing that Eurasian diseases would wipe out the vast majority of the Amerindian population within 150 years or so, no more than he could understand that he had not reached East Asia, but rather new continents that would be parts of European empires for a time and independent nations eventually.[17] The Amerindians paid a horrible price for their lengthy isolation. Indeed, the European presence took its toll elsewhere as well. Sub-Saharan Africa also paid a high price—a massive expansion of the trade in African slaves because Europeans demanded their labor to replace that of the native Americans who died.

Meanwhile the Portuguese navigated their way around southern Africa and on to India, China, and Japan. In the

---

[16] Historians today generally reject the view, once widely held, that the Reformation and Protestantism spurred the rise of capitalism. This notion, often called the Weber Thesis because it was put forward by the great German social scientist Max Weber early in the twentieth century, argued that Protestantism's emphasis on attending to one's "calling" (that is, one's everyday occupation) fostered the habits of thrift and enterprise that are central to the "spirit of capitalism." Advocates of this hypothesis also tended to claim that Calvinism dropped older prohibitions against usury and encouraged believers to consider themselves among God's elect if they prospered materially. More recent research has thoroughly demolished most of the alleged links between capitalism and Protestantism, at least in their sixteenth- and seventeenth-century manifestations.

[17] By the time Columbus died in 1509, he was almost alone among knowledgeable people in continuing to insist that he had reached the doorstep of Japan. He never thought of himself as the "discoverer" of the "New World."

Indian Ocean and the China seas, the Europeans met people who could withstand their germs but not necessarily their ship-borne artillery. Although initially forced to settle for coastal fortresses and trading bases, the Europeans brought Asians into a network of trade that for the first time in human history linked all the continents. In the long term, the effect of the daring seamanship of Dias, da Gama, Columbus, and their successors was to initiate construction of the global culture—and its global environmental concerns—in which we now live.

Ironically, as western Europeans united the world, at least in commerce and communications, they lost the historic institution that had long united them among themselves: the Christian church. Columbus had hoped that his efforts would culminate in the conquest of Islam by Christians and, in turn, clear the way for the end of the world and the apocalyptic return of Jesus Christ. Instead, Christendom split into Protestant and Catholic camps. Religious warfare within Europe raged for a century and a half, consuming many of the profits of colonial trade. By the end of the seventeenth century, Europeans would be preparing for a war that would determine the fate of Spain and its global empire.

Selected Reading

Sources

Briffault, Herma, trans. *Bartolomé de las Casas: The Devastation of the Indies* (1992).

Calloway, Colin G., ed. *The World Turned Upside Down: Indian Voices from Early America* (1994).

Dunn, Oliver, and James E. Kelley Jr., eds. and trans. *The "Diario" of Christopher Columbus's First Voyage to America* (1989).

León-Portilla, Miguel. *Pre-Columbian Literatures of Mexico* (1969).

Exploration and Empire

Fernández-Armesto, Felipe. *Columbus* (1991). A biography that separates the verifiable facts from the many myths about Columbus and his career.

Liss, Peggy K. *Isabel the Queen: Life and Times* (1992). An engaging and reliable biography of "Isabel the Catholic," the queen of Castile who was one of the founders of the Spanish monarchy and the Spanish Empire.

Parry, J. H. *The Age of Reconnaissance* (1969). Examination of discovery, exploration, and settlement from 1450 to 1650.

Russell, Jeffrey Burton. *Inventing the Flat Earth* (1991). Traces the origins of the myth that medieval people did not know the earth was round.

Scammell, G. V. *The World Encompassed* (1981). Comparative survey of European maritime empires from the Norse, the Hanseatic cities, and the Italians in the Middle Ages to the Portuguese, Spanish, Dutch, French, and English in the early modern period.

Seaver, Kirsten A. *The Frozen Echo* (1996). Uses archeological, textual, and other evidence to describe the Norse colony in Greenland and Norse explorations of North America from 1000 to 1500.

Subrahmanyam, Sanjay. *The Career and Legend of Vasco Da Gama* (1997). Sets the explorer's work in a richly detailed context of Portuguese courtly factions and complex trading, political, and cultural patterns around the Indian Ocean.

Encounters and Exchanges

Cook, Noble David. *Born to Die* (1998). Surveys the tragic impact of European diseases in the New World from 1492 to 1650.

Crosby, Alfred W. *Ecological Imperialism* (1986). A broad-ranging account of Europe's biological expansion to "New Europes" in the Americas and Australasia.

Elliott, J. H. *The Old World and the New* (1970). Four thoughtful essays on the intellectual, economic, and social impact of the discovery of America on early modern Europe.

Fagan, Brian M. *Kingdoms of Gold, Kingdoms of Jade* (1991). An anthropologist's well-illustrated introduction to pre-Columbian cultures in the Americas.

Grafton, Anthony. *New Worlds, Ancient Texts* (1992). Excellent study of how the Old World tried to comprehend the New World.

Hulme, Peter. *Colonial Encounters* (1986). Intriguing analyses of major texts concerning European perception of the Caribbean islands and islanders from 1492 to 1797.

Kupperman, Karen Ordahl. *America in European Consciousness, 1493–1750* (1995). Essays examining the varied ways in which America was incorporated into European thinking.

Lockhart, James. *The Nahuas after the Conquest* (1992). A sociocultural study of the Indians of central Mexico after the Spanish conquest, based on documents in the Indian language of that region, Nahuatl, which demonstrates the astonishing complexity of the relations between the "conquered" and the "conquerors."

Manning, Patrick, ed. *Slave Trades, 1500–1800: Globalization of Forced Labor* (1996). Articles reflecting recent scholarship on the rise and transformation of the slave trades in the three centuries after the European conquest of the oceans in the decades around 1500.

Pagden, Anthony. *The Fall of Natural Man* (1986). Describes the intellectual world within which Europeans comprehended the indigenous peoples of the New World.

Schwartz, Stuart. *Implicit Understandings* (1994). Twenty essays examining the ways that Europeans and non-Europeans tried to understand each other between 1450 and 1800.

Population, Economy, and Society

Bennett, Judith M. *Ale, Beer, and Brewsters in England* (1996). A thorough and engaging analysis of the reasons for the declining role of women in brewing from 1350–1600.

Braudel, Fernand. *The Structures of Everyday Life* (1981). A far-ranging and fascinating volume that ignores political history and has chapters on population, daily bread, food and drink, houses, clothes, fashion, technology, money, and towns and cities from 1400 to 1800. Although the primary focus is on Europe, stimulating comparisons with other civilizations abound.

Duplessis, Robert. *Transitions to Capitalism in Early Modern Europe* (1997). A broad-ranging analysis of the course and consequences of economic change in early modern Europe.

Kamen, Henry. *European Society, 1500–1700* (1984). Broad survey of social structures and social change emphasizing the experience of ordinary Europeans.

Laslett, Peter. *The World We Have Lost* (3d ed., 1983). The pioneering analysis of England's historical demography.

CHAPTER *15*

STRIVING FOR THE ABSOLUTIST STATE: THE EARLY SEVENTEENTH CENTURY

Henry IV Entrusting the Regency to the Queen
The Granger Collection.

WESTERN EUROPE

1610	Assassination of Henry IV of France
1609–1614	Expulsion of the *moriscos* from Spain
1614–1615	Last meeting of the French Estates General before 1789
1619	Orangists overthrow Republicans in Dutch Republic
1621–1643	Ascendancy of Olivares as chief minister to Philip IV in Spain
1624–1642	Ascendancy of Richelieu as chief minister to Louis XIII in France
1634	Frederick Henry establishes Secret Council in the Dutch Republic
1629–1640	Charles I's "Personal Rule" in England
1640	Rebellions in Catalonia and Portugal against Philip IV of Spain
1642–1645	English Civil War
1648–1653	Fronde rebellion in France
1649	Execution of Charles I
1649–1660	The English Republic and Cromwellian rule

CENTRAL, NORTHERN, AND EASTERN EUROPE

1533–1584	Reign of Ivan the Terrible in Russia
1587–1632	Reign of Sigismund III in Poland-Lithuania
1598–1613	Time of Troubles in Russia
1609	Letter of Majesty (Austrian monarchy)
1611–1632	Reign of Gustavus Adolphus in Sweden
1613	Election of Tsar Michael (Romanov) in Russia
1618	Defenestration of Prague
1619	Election of Ferdinand II as Holy Roman emperor
1652–1660	"Deluge" in Poland-Lithuania

THE EUROPEAN WARS

1620	Battle of White Mountain
1621	Dutch-Spanish truce ends
1618–1648	Thirty Years' War
1648	Peace of Westphalia
1655–1660	Little Northern War
1659	Peace of the Pyrenees
1660	Peace of Oliva

In Peter Paul Rubens's allegorical painting (previous page), the assassinated Henry IV of France hands the reins of government to his widow, Marie de' Medici, in trust for his nine-year old son Louis XIII. Although a regency was always a dangerous time for a country, the reigns of Henry IV and Louis XIII saw rapid progress toward the construction of the sovereign nation-state in France. Such a state possesses the power to inflict death by war or capital punishment and to impose taxes more or less at will. Political authorities had always possessed these and other powers, but we can best understand the political and constitutional history of seventeenth-century Europe in terms of seeking a centralized monopoly of these powers—a striving for **absolutism.** The various heads of state were aiming at more power than ever over the people who lived within their borders.

All across Europe, in the territorial units that we know as the modern nations (or at least their ancestors), emperors, kings, tsars, dukes, stadholders, electors, and the like tried to initiate or extend the process by which a unified, centralized, increasingly bureaucratic state controlled its people. The extent of their success varied widely, but everywhere the process went on. The French bureaucracy tripled in size in the century after 1600, and Prussians and Russians began to deal with bureaucrats for the first time. Local governors everywhere saw their authority wane while that of central authorities in the distant capital waxed. Even where the striving for royal absolutism failed, as in England and the Dutch Republic, central governments grew in size and authority. Although the powers of these governments were hardly impressive by twentieth-century standards, those who lost power knew well enough that a new order was emerging.

The burgeoning of "big government" and the concurrent weakening of local authorities—churchmen, landowners, mayors, aldermen, judges, guild officials, and members of representative assemblies—were two sides of the same coin, and they embody a sharp reversal of the medieval polity. Medieval political thought and practice had been constitutionalist rather than absolutist, meaning that power within the state was normally shared rather than focused in one individual or one council. In the High Middle Ages, many individuals and groups living within a kingdom exercised force, made law, and handed down binding judicial decisions without consulting the king. Many had the power to stop the king from doing what he wanted to do. Many nobles had what in effect were private armies of knights, and in their manor courts they judged numerous disputes. Elected town officials operated under royal charters, which gave them extensive rights of self-government in return for taxes that they paid the king.

Medieval representative assemblies could deny the king certain forms of revenue if they felt dissatisfied with his response to their requests for redress of grievances. The structure and powers of these assemblies varied, but they were numerous. National assemblies included the Estates General (France), the Imperial Diet (Holy Roman Empire), the Sejm (Poland), Parliament (England), the States-General (Dutch Republic), and the Riksdag (Sweden). Regional assemblies often existed as well (for example, the Cortes of Catalonia, Aragon, Castile, and Valencia in Spain). Outside western Europe's kingdoms, popes and cardinals also made decisions that affected the rulers' subjects, as did the Holy Roman emperor.

From the tenth century on, individuals and groups accumulated customary rights and privileges, to which their successors clung fiercely. In this constitutionalist environment, people thought not of liberty in the abstract sense but of the "liberties" legally guaranteed to particular social ranks and institutions. Thus it is a mistake to think of the development of political institutions in Western civilization as a slow but inexorable progress from the rule of one man toward republicanism and democracy. The story is much more complicated.

Ideas favoring absolutism arose in the late sixteenth and seventeenth centuries as a powerful ideology of opposition toward the constitutionalist assumptions inherited from medieval theory and practice. This new ideology aimed at clearing away the heavy underbrush of rights and privileges that constrained royal power. In the Middle Ages, all political rights had divine sanction—those of nobles, burghers, churchmen, and others no less than the king's. Absolutist thinkers rejected this idea, asserting that the monarch and his "divine right" overrode other rights. They argued that all law and force should be monopolized by the sovereign state and that no one could exercise any force or hand down any justice except at the king's command. They defined absolute sovereignty as the essence of the state, not to be overridden by popes, emperors, representative assemblies, judges, or municipal authorities. They insisted that the monarch had to be able to extract the tax monies required to defend the state, even if representative assemblies resisted him. Without such sovereignty, the absolutist thinkers warned, no political entity deserved the name of a state, nor could it long survive. Outmoded constitutionalist polities, they said, would fall to neighboring states that had understood and accepted the inevitable logic of absolute sovereignty; only absolutist methods could create and sustain the horrendously expensive military forces that the situation required. The seemingly endless Thirty Years' War (1618–1648), although fought in central Europe, involved forces and expenditure from all over Europe. Its huge cost, the absolutists maintained, could only be met by their methods.

THE TREND TOWARD ABSOLUTISM

From the tenth century until the sixteenth, Europe west of the Byzantine Empire had functioned with diffused political authority. But by late in the sixteenth century, many influential political thinkers as well as princes and their advisers became convinced that absolutism held the only hope for the future. Pressures toward absolutism came from three needs experienced by heads of state and their advisers: (1) to bring an end to religious discord; (2) to surmount the problems created by changes in the European economy; and (3) to enable their military forces to compete successfully in warfare transformed by gunpowder weapons. Without soldiers and sailors trained and equipped to employ these weapons effectively, they could neither defend their territory nor protect their people or their interests.

Religious Discord

The conflicting religious ideologies of the sixteenth century nearly destroyed France and sparked murderous conflict in the Netherlands and Germany. Many feared that Europe was becoming ungovernable. Radical Calvinist theorists justified active resistance to a ruler who enforced Catholicism, and radical Catholics responded in kind, going so far as to justify even assassination of **heretical** leaders. Huguenot writers opposed tyrannicide in all but the most extreme conditions, but they nevertheless developed a potent theory of resistance and revolution (see next page for "The Defense of Liberty against Tyrants"). According to them, France's Catholic kings, by mandating false worship, were requiring their people to commit the sin of idolatry. They should be overthrown by force, if necessary. For zealous Catholics, on the other hand, the possibility that the Protestant Henry of Navarre might become king of France (see Chapter 13) led to the conclusion that the power to overthrow and even murder a Protestant "tyrant" lay in the hands of the people.

THE HISTORICAL EVIDENCE

The Defense of Liberty against Tyrants

1579

The Defense of Liberty against Tyrants, a book first published anonymously in 1579, was written by Philippe Duplessis-Mornay (1549–1623), a French noble and a Huguenot who entered the service of Henry of Navarre and became his chief adviser by 1573. The Defense was the first Huguenot tract that clearly and explicitly justified resistance to lawful authority, and as such represents a landmark in the history of resistance theory. In one section, Mornay contended that kings should be resisted who required "impious rites," by which he and other Calvinists meant the "idolatrous" Catholic Mass. In the excerpt below, he considered resistance to "tyranny" of a different kind. Huguenots, because they formed a minority, sought to frame their arguments so as to attract support outside their own faction.

A king, . . . is someone who has obtained the kingdom in due form, either by descent or by election, and who rules and governs in accordance with the law. Since a tyrant is the opposite of a king, it follows that he has seized authority by force or fraud, or that he is a king who rules a kingdom freely given him in a manner contrary to equity and justice and persists in that misrule in violation of the laws and compacts to which he took a solemn oath. A single person can, of course, be both of these at once. . . .

The next question is whether a tyrant may be lawfully resisted and, if so, by whom and what means. . . . In the first place, nature instructs us to defend our lives and also our liberty, without which life is hardly life at all. If this is the instinct of nature implanted in dogs against the wolf, in bulls against the lion, in pigeons against the falcon, and in chickens against the hawk, how much stronger must it be in man against another man who has become a wolf to man. . . . Next, there is the law of peoples which distinguishes countries and boundaries that everyone is obligated to defend against any person whatsoever. . . . Last and most important is the civil law, which is the legislation that societies establish for their particular needs, so that here is one and there another kind of government. . . . If anyone tries to break this law through force or fraud, resistance is incumbent upon all of us, because the criminal does violence to that association to which we owe everything we have. . . . Thus the law of nature, the law of peoples, and civil law command us to take arms against tyrants without title, nor is there any legal scruple to detain us—no oath or compact whatsoever, entered into either publicly or privately. Therefore, when this kind of tyranny occurs, anyone may act to drive it out, including private individuals.

Source: From "A Huguenot Leader Justifies Resistance to Tyranny," in Julian H. Franklin, *Constitutionalism and Resistance in the Sixteenth Century* (New York: Pegasus, 1969), pp. 185–197.

The assassinations of the Catholic Henry III of France (1589), the Protestant William the Silent of the Dutch Republic (1584), and the Protestant-turned-Catholic Henry IV of France (in 1610, after nineteen failed attempts), as well as countless massacres and wars provoked by religious differences, impelled the *politique* approach. In France, where the term *politique* was coined, this meant acceptance of religious diversity so long as the peace of the community remained unbroken. The most influential statement of this view came in the *Six Books of the Commonweal* (1576) by Jean Bodin (1530–1596), a Frenchman who learned to fear anarchy firsthand when his life was threatened in the St. Bartholomew's Day Massacre (1572; see Chapter 13). Bodin originated the modern theory of sovereignty when he argued that "the first and chief mark of a sovereign prince"—the power upon which all other powers depend—was that he must be able to make law without consulting anyone else. His legislative authority must be subject to no one on earth—not to popes, emperors, customs, courts, or assemblies. Medieval "liberties" had to yield to the order that he imposed. He is not even limited by laws that he himself made. Although Bodin's theory gave at least some protection to the property rights of subjects, it vigorously asserted that *someone* in France had to wield enough power to maintain public order, or the nation would continue to tear itself apart in religious civil wars until there were no pieces left that were big enough to tear apart.

Hobbes's *Leviathan* The title page of Hobbes's *Leviathan* (1651) implies the book's argument—the need for an absolute monarch who could tower over the competing parties. His tunic is made up of his subjects, all looking upward at him. The symbols of secular and ecclesiastical authority appear on the sides below the king, a far cry from the medieval assumption that power in spiritual matters belonged only to churchmen. © *R. Sheridan/ Ancient Art & Architecture Collection.*

The other major theorist of absolutism was Englishman Thomas Hobbes (1588–1679). He wrote immediately after the civil wars in England in the 1640s, conflicts that partly stemmed from religious factionalism. Hobbes took his title *Leviathan* from biblical references to a "piercing" and "crooked" sea-monster of that name who devoured everything in his path and could not be controlled by men. This passionate desire for a Leviathan, a state so powerful that the monarch could not be restrained by any human authority, seems nearly as incomprehensible to us now as belief in Calvinistic predestination (see Chapter 13). Hobbes insisted that without a sovereign power, no one could be safe; therefore all persons had "to submit their wills, every one to his will, and their judgments, to his judgment." Otherwise they would have to exist in a state of nature in which they were perpetually at war with each other, and their lives would necessarily be "solitary, poor, nasty, brutish, and short." As with predestination, we can understand the attractiveness of a Leviathan only by putting it in historical context. Absolutism appeared to Bodin, Hobbes, and many others to offer the only workable solution to the religious divisions that exposed people to such anarchy as to render everyday human life impossible.

Absolutism provided a strategy for survival in a frightening political world, just as predestination served as a rock of certainty in an uncertain spiritual world.

Economic Change and State Power

The demographic and economic changes described in Chapter 14 had important political consequences. The European population expanded steadily during the sixteenth century, and growth continued in some regions into the seventeenth. The great inflation of the sixteenth century, which dragged on until 1630, has been called a price revolution. Between 1500 and 1650, the prices of many goods increased fivefold or sixfold. Yet kings found that many of their sources of income were fixed by laws and customs stretching back into the Middle Ages; royal revenues thus became less adequate as each inflationary year passed. Similarly, because rents were often fixed during long leases, the monarch's income from his demesne bought less and less. As another major source of income, he collected taxes from agricultural producers. Yet these taxes were assessed on incomes that grew more slowly than the government's expenses. In France, for example, royal revenue came mainly came from a direct tax on agricultural income called the *taille*. Nobles in France, Spain, and many other countries were exempt from direct taxation, which meant that the taille fell more and more on the peasantry. By the late fifteenth century, the French kings began to collect the taille without the approval of the Estates General. The yield increased from 1.5 million livres in 1500 to 6 million annually in the 1550s, but the government's debt kept swelling relentlessly.

Theoretically, a monarch was expected to "live of his own," meaning that he paid his personal expenses and those of government out of his ordinary income from the royal demesne and other sources. Additional income became available from direct taxation only in wartime and only after representative assemblies voted their approval. But even in peacetime, inflation and the growth of government rendered this medieval fiscal system inadequate. Supposedly temporary expedients, such as the sale of municipal, legal, and fiscal offices, tended to become permanent.

The sale of offices (**venalité**) became such an important source of revenue in France that attempts to reform it rarely succeeded for long. The practice of venalité allowed the king to gain income from social groups not subject to the taille. New courts were created or old ones enlarged to carry out judicial or administrative functions, and those who bought positions in them recouped their lump-sum outlays over time through fees that they charged for their services. Purchasers, mostly from the **bourgeoisie,** also gained status because as officials they joined the *noblesse de robe* ("nobility of the robe," referring to the gown worn by the officeholder). Henry IV's financial minister initiated the *paulette,* an annual payment that officials made in order to ensure their sons' inheritance of the offices they had purchased. Yet even such expedients proved insufficient as costs continued to rise faster than income. Between 1599 and 1648, as expensive wars erupted, the Spanish government declared bankruptcy three times; the French, twice. Absolutist theory addressed the problem directly by opposing the right of representative assemblies to consent to taxation on the grounds of the security of the state.

The Horrendous Cost of War

Although many factors contributed, the single most important reason for the enormous increase in royal expenses was the cost of war. As absolutist principles gained adherents, princes found more and more avenues into their subjects' pocketbooks, usually by undermining medieval "liberties." Wars also came to cost more than before because of changes in the ways military operations were carried out on both land and sea. It is tempting—but wrong—to attribute the progression entirely to technological change such as the introduction of gunpowder weapons: "One must always be wary of the temptation to attribute everything to a simple new entity. Technology can help to explain much, but it cannot explain everything."[1] A complex challenge-response relationship existed. On one hand, government had to respond to purely technological challenges: for example, changes in the accuracy, range, and rapidity of cannon and small arms in relation to older weapons; the portability of heavy siege artillery; and the cost of gunpowder and the difficulty of making gunpowder that would stay dry enough to be effective. On the other hand, government responses involved a varied array of nontechnological issues. Some of these included the resources available to, and the ambitions of, individual princes and entire dynasties; the presence or absence of men trained as civilians with particular weapons, such as the longbow in England but not elsewhere; and the decline in workers' real wages during the sixteenth century, which made military service an attractive alternative.

Did the increasing cost of war force states toward absolutist methods of obtaining money? Or did the emergence of more integrated, better unified, more absolutist states enable them to raise the money for larger military forces? To what extent did technological changes drive the tendency for armies to grow in size and cost? Clearly, the mere introduction of gunpowder weapons did not revolutionize European warfare (see Chapter 11). They first appeared in the 1320s, but their slow rate of fire, unwieldiness, and unreliability made them nearly useless in pitched battles between mobile armies. By late in the fourteenth century, however, large, heavy cannon were being used to smash the

An Arquebusier Arquebusiers carried the first shoulder-mounted firearm, a forerunner of the musket. By around 1600, gunpowder weapons carried by individual soldiers had been in use for well over a century, but their short effective range and time-consuming loading and firing process limited their impact in battles. *North Wind Picture Archives.*

walls of castles and cities during sieges. That is why groups of cannon are called "batteries"—they batter. Nevertheless, armored heavy cavalrymen, the successors of medieval knights, continued to have an important role until the introduction of wheel-lock pistols late in the sixteenth century reduced their usefulness. Even so, cavalrymen did not finally disappear from battlefields until after World War I, not least because of the persistent linkage between horsemanship and membership in the upper social class.[2]

Both in field and siege warfare, old weapons and tactics continued in use alongside the new guns, and the latter had to find a niche in which they could be effective. For example, the arquebus grew more common in warfare after its first appearance around 1450, and the musket came somewhat later. But even a skilled arquebusier or musketeer had to stand up to reload his cumbersome weapon through the muzzle; thus he required protection from either pikemen or some kind of fortification, lest he be cut down by cavalrymen after getting off only one or two shots.

---

[1] Bert S. Hall, *Weapons and Warfare in Renaissance Europe* (Baltimore: Johns Hopkins University Press, 1997), p. 3.

[2] The last important use of cavalry in European military operations was in the Russian Civil War of 1918–1921 and in the Russo-Polish War of 1920–1921. The Polish army and the Red Army both retained cavalry arms (for potential use against each other) in the 1920s and 1930s. The gallant and hopeless charges of Polish cavalry against Hitler's tanks in 1939 marked the death knell of mounted warfare.

Although deadly at close range, the round ball fired by a musket soon lost much of its velocity and accuracy as it encountered air resistance. The chances of hitting a man 100 meters or more away was less than 50 percent. A charging horseman with light body armor was reasonably safe until he got within 25 to 30 meters of the musketeer. Therefore officers told troops not to fire until they could see "the whites of their eyes." The small arms' short effective range, as well as their slow rate of fire, rendered them ineffective for attacking purposes until new tactics were created late in the sixteenth century.

At certain moments, technological change did produce major alterations in patterns of warfare. Mobile siege artillery of the kind the French developed in the mid-fifteenth century and brought to Italy in 1494 (see Chapters 11 and 12) gave the offensive side a huge advantage against the high, thin medieval walls of cities that had never faced such weapons. The Italian diplomat and historian Francesco Guicciardini was amazed that the French artillery could travel as fast as the army and be put in position so quickly. Still worse, he wrote, "so little time elapsed between one shot and another and the shots were so frequent and so violent . . . that in a few hours they could accomplish what previously in Italy used to require many days." But that advantage was soon offset by the spread of the *trace italienne*, a new style of fortification made of low, thick bastions arranged in zigzag fashion to enable defenders to fire on attackers from two or more directions. Expensive, lengthy sieges were required to conquer towns so defended, although the cost of building the trace italienne was so enormous that only large and prosperous urban centers could afford it.

The transformation of siege warfare due to mobile artillery and the trace italienne occurred early in the sixteenth century, but dramatic changes in the tactics of field warfare came later. Until the 1590s, battles were dominated by Spanish *tercios*. In these three-thousand-man massive formations, pikemen stood on the outside of a square so as to defend musketeers on the inside against charging enemy horsemen. Powerful but unwieldy, the tercio began to give way to the new tactics that the Dutch under Maurice of Nassau developed in their struggle for independence. The size of the basic unit dropped from three thousand to thirty, and the troops were deployed into ten lines of musketeers in order to fire in volleys. As one line fired, the others fell back to reload, then moved up for another volley. Rapid rotation of ranks overcame the slow reloading rate that had always hampered the musket's effectiveness. Maurice's troops also used paper cartridges that combined pre-measured amounts of gunpowder with the ball, further speeding up the rate of fire.

Although the Dutch themselves employed the new linear formations mainly in defense, in the 1630s the Swedes under Gustavus Adolphus attacked by moving each rank forward to fire its volley. Gustavus reduced the ranks from ten to six, and he personally demonstrated to new soldiers the techniques for firing muskets standing, kneeling, or lying down. He also employed the "double salvo," in which three lines of musketeers fired simultaneously: one on their knees, another crouching, and the third standing. The purpose, as one observer put it, was "to pour as much lead into your enemies' bosom at one time [as possible] . . . and thereby you do them more mischief . . . for one long and continuated crack of thunder is more terrifying to mortals than ten

The Siege of Breisach, 1638
Breisach (left center) had strong defensive bastions that prevented a direct assault, but the besieging French forces built an impressive set of siege works on both sides of the town that enabled them to stand firm against a strong army (upper right) sent by the Imperialists. The men, reduced to eating rats, leather, and corpses, were starved into submission and surrendered on September 14, 1638. The capture of Breisach gave the French their first foothold across the Rhine and blocked the "Spanish road" to the Netherlands. *The Newberry Library, Chicago.*

interrupted and several ones." Gustavus completed the tactical shift by adding light field artillery (four per regiment) to support both infantry and cavalry.

The soldier in a tercio needed little training, but the many small units using the new tactics had to be drilled to respond quickly to commands. They also needed many more officers than the older formations. Drill speeded up musket reloading, thus increasing firepower and allowing smaller units. The army had to be highly trained to operate not with the brute strength of a bull but with the agility of a fox. The higher level of training in turn made soldiering a year-round business. Instead of mercenaries hired for part of a year for a campaign, kings had to pay the troops all year to maintain the necessary skill and discipline. In turn, this required barracks to house the men and a bureaucracy to supply them. Although the size of armies did not escalate sharply until after 1660, the need for standing armies more or less continuously in training sharply increased military budgets after about 1590.

At about the same time, ship-borne artillery transformed naval warfare and warships became much larger, heavier, and costlier. The ships of the Spanish Armada averaged nineteen guns each in 1588, but in 1665 Dutch warships averaged sixty-two. Charles I of England's flagship, the *Sovereign of the Seas*, was launched in 1637 carrying 104 guns, which constituted 10 percent of the overall weight of this monster of a ship. Fighting on both land and sea had grown much more expensive.

ABSOLUTISTS VERSUS CONSTITUTIONALISTS

The military innovations, religious discord, and inflationary pressures put monarchs on a collision course with the traditional "liberties" of some subjects, most notably with the representative assemblies that had emerged in medieval Europe (see Chapter 9). Ironically, the assemblies had won their powers over taxation through the military needs of late medieval kings. In England, for example, repeated royal requests for money to fight the Hundred Years' War in France strengthened Parliament's grip on taxation (see Chapter 11). The various German diets had developed similarly.

By the seventeenth century, however, many of these assemblies were no longer as cooperative, and in some cases, religious dissenters tried to use the assembly to pursue their own agendas. Even without religious dissent, the assemblies tended to defend local interests, especially those of the large landowners. From the king's point of view, his opponents were holding the kingdom's safety hostage to their private interests. Absolutist political theory spoke directly to the problem by justifying either the abolition or the emasculation of the assemblies so that they could not prevent the collection of taxes needed to perform these ever more expensive tasks.

The seventeenth century was therefore an age of conflict, much of it violent, between absolutists and constitutionalists. Royal absolutism garnered the most success in Roman Catholic countries, whereas constitutionalism scored its biggest victories in Protestant states. Nevertheless, events in Germany and Sweden showed that Protestantism and absolutism were not incompatible, and the Catholic Poles showed that they could defy their Catholic kings' impulses toward absolutism. Louis XIV of France, the most famous absolutist, never managed to get rid of the **Parlement** of Paris or of all the provincial assemblies, as we shall see in Chapter 16. Moreover, by 1700 the English Parliament ranked as the most powerful in Europe, yet the monarch retained considerable power and influence. The problem everywhere centered on constructing a political and fiscal system that could maintain order, promote prosperity, and defend national interests. Advocates of absolutism pointed to the decline of political entities that continued to preserve medieval liberties vigorously (such as the Holy Roman Empire and the Polish-Lithuanian Commonwealth). These examples seemed to prove the unworkability of constitutionalism, and in central and eastern Europe constitutionalism indeed was disastrous. There, newer and more absolute powers arose—the monarchies of Austria, Russia, and Prussia. Their success came at the expense of constitutionalist neighbors, whose territory they seized in large chunks during the eighteenth century.

All over Europe, it became apparent that not only the expansion but even the survival of states depended on the creation of a bureaucratic regime that could act decisively. This had to be done, and done well, whether by absolutist or constitutionalist means. The pressure would have been much less intense if the internal struggles had found resolution without the strain of financing warfare. The first two decades of the century enjoyed relative peace, though the Holy Roman emperor's war with the Ottomans ground on until 1607. But from 1618 to 1648, the Thirty Years' War wracked central Europe, the Spanish effort to regain the Dutch Republic raged after 1621, the French entered the Thirty Years' War in 1635 (finally making peace with Spain in 1659), and a series of conflicts scourged eastern Europe. As one Spanish general noted, war became "a sort of traffic or commerce, in which he who has the most money wins."

Before we consider the wars in which the European states became embroiled, we must look at the striving for absolutism that unfolded within these states. The outcome of this effort determined the military success or failure of each.

The Spanish Dominions: Disillusion and Decline

Although in retrospect Spanish power clearly peaked under Philip II, contemporaries remained very much afraid of Spain for two more generations. Spain continued to control most of Italy and a huge overseas empire, but its internal weaknesses gradually became evident. The Spanish population, always relatively small, was shrinking, and the economy suffered from this loss of numbers combined with a lack of industry, growing colonial manufactures, the declining value of wool exports, and interloping foreign traders and pirates. Finally, although the central administration in Madrid could tax Castile at will, it faced constitutionalist barriers to the resources of other provinces.

Philip II had shared power with no one, but his son Philip III (reigned 1598–1621) began the practice, emulated by his successors, of delegating vast authority to a favorite (called the *privado* or *valido*). Often a favorite enriched himself and his clients while ignoring the cries of concerned Spaniards for economic and social reform. The royal household and those of the upper level of the aristocracy grew rapidly, wasting the energies of people in unproductive tasks while peasants paid heavy taxes avoided by landowners. The expulsion of 275,000 *moriscos* between 1609 and 1614 on the grounds (probably true) that they were secret Muslims deprived Valencia and Aragon of some of their most productive farmers and silk weavers.

Spain was therefore in steep decline when Philip IV (reigned 1621–1665) inherited the throne. The first part of his reign saw a major drive toward strengthening the central government and the monarchy owing to his choice of the incorruptible, indefatigable, and imaginative Count-Duke of Olivares (1587–1645) as privado. While the king alternated between his many mistresses and spells of repentance about them, Olivares worked to rebuild Spanish armies and navies in order to regain control over the Netherlands, defend Spain's overseas empire, and assist Philip's Austrian Habsburg cousins in the Thirty Years' War. Besides trying to tax the upper classes, the privado announced the Union of Arms, a scheme to get provinces other than Castile to pay what he calculated was an appropriate share of the cost of defending the empire. The cortes (representative assemblies) of Aragon, Valencia, and Catalonia resisted the Union of Arms, and the eruption of war with France in 1635 denied Olivares the time he needed to accomplish his reforms.

A French invasion of Catalonia in 1638 prompted Olivares to override the traditional liberties of that province by billeting soldiers on the population. The unpaid soldiers seized what they needed, and early in 1640 the Catalans rebelled and proclaimed a republic. The Portuguese also rebelled,[3] and other provinces followed suit. Olivares's enemies united against him and persuaded the king to fire him in 1643. Thus the constitutionalists in Spain and its dominions claimed victory, but they failed to make it last. The privado's successors managed to restore Spanish rule

The Count-Duke of Olivares   Diego de Velázquez, court painter to Philip IV and one of the finest painters of the age, created this magnificent equestrian portrait of Olivares with riding whip in hand. Yet Olivares's health was deteriorating, and in 1633 he wrote to a friend that "when I tried to mount a horse the other day I couldn't manage it. This is the worst thing that could happen to me, because I always used to recover my spirits and vitality once I was on horseback."   *Scala/Art Resource, NY.*

everywhere except Portugal, which permanently regained its independence. Yet the new order was nothing like the centralized one that Olivares had sought. The Catalans did not return to the fold until 1652, after a promise from the king to respect their traditional privileges. After Philip IV's death in 1665, the great power that had once terrified all Europe frightened no one, and the Spanish Empire drifted along until its European holdings were dismembered in the wars of the eighteenth century.

France: Rebuilding toward Greatness

In the 1590s, France appeared to be as poor a candidate for absolutism as Spain seemed a good one. But Henry IV, who achieved a religious settlement that worked, the Edict of Nantes (see Chapter 13), also pursued policies that laid the groundwork for a powerful and prosperous French state. A good judge of character, he appointed conscientious advisers who established effective systems of administration and justice after the chaos of the religious civil wars. He

---

[3] Since 1580, Portugal had been under the rule of the Spanish king, although it retained its separate institutions (see Chapter 13).

encouraged economic recovery as well. The royal debt stood at 300 million livres in 1593; by Henry's death in 1610 the treasury boasted a surplus of 15 million. Nor was it only the treasury that recovered. "I hope to make France so prosperous," Henry vowed, "that every peasant will have a chicken in his pot on Sunday." Although this admirable goal may not have been achieved, progress toward it certainly ensued.

Henry IV's measures marked the beginning of **mercantilism** in France. In mercantilism, the old ideal of economic self-sufficiency was applied to the modern nation-state. Just as Hobbes and Bodin felt that the state should be politically self-sufficient (that is, no pope or emperor must overrule the monarch), so **mercantilist** economic thinkers argued for an economic ideal of self-sufficiency. A nation should have a favorable balance of trade, they insisted, meaning that it sells to foreigners more than it buys from them and hence accumulates gold and silver. We can see the means to this happy end in the policies employed under Henry IV and more fully later in the seventeenth century. Protective tariffs shielded native industries from foreign competition, and detailed regulation of the quality of manufactured goods aimed at getting high prices in international trade. Mercantilists called for monopolies and subsidies for strategically desirable manufactures (weapons, ships, and so on) and urged the construction of roads, canals, and bridges to facilitate trade.

The theory of mercantilism required an active governmental role in the economy and assumed that expansion of the nation's economy could occur only at the expense of its rivals. Mercantilism provides impressive evidence of the strength of tradition in human thought, for it reveals the assumption that the total of trade and the wealth derived from it was somehow fixed (like everything else in the medieval order of things). But it also partakes of the new Machiavellian and Hobbesian notions that human actions are basically egoistic and self-centered—that individual energies need to be controlled by the state in order to achieve the common good. Further, this control was to emanate from a single authority; as Henry and his ministers went about their work of reconstruction, it is notable that not even once did they summon the Estates General, France's national representative body.

Henry IV was stabbed to death by a fanatical Catholic in 1610. His widow, Marie de' Medici, assumed control of a regency government that ruled in the name of the nine-year-old royal son and heir, Louis XIII. Henry himself said that he had married Marie for her money, and her use of power as queen regent failed to reveal any hidden talent for leadership. From 1610 to the emergence in 1624 of Armand-Jean du Plessis de Richelieu (1585–1642) as Louis XIII's chief minister, France again suffered revolts of Huguenots and some of the greater nobles. Marie called the Estates General in 1614 in the hope of stopping the drift toward anarchy, but her action achieved nothing. Few were

disturbed when she dismissed it in 1615. It would not meet again until the eve of the French Revolution in 1789.

Unlike thoroughly Catholic Spain, France had a large and powerful religious minority, the Huguenots. Although the Estates General no longer functioned as a barrier against absolutism in France, the Huguenots and those nobles who had resisted the centralizing policies of Henry IV's government certainly stood in its path. Richelieu, made a cardinal in 1622, determined to tame them both. By 1629 he had taken back the fortified towns granted to the Huguenots in the Edict of Nantes, including, after a fourteen-month siege, the formidable fortress of La Rochelle with its trace italienne. Of La Rochelle's population of forty-five thousand, more than eight thousand had died of starvation. But Richelieu shrewdly left them their religious rights, knowing that if he tried to enforce Catholicism on them the cost of suppressing the rebellions that were sure to follow would be too high. Richelieu's handling of the Huguenots, like his alliances with Protestant powers against the Catholic Habsburgs in the Thirty Years' War, demonstrates his secularism. He acted in the interests of the French state, and if, as they often did, his decisions damaged the Catholic church, he nevertheless let them stand.

Cardinal Richelieu   In this portrait by Philippe de Champaigne, Richelieu radiates steely determination. Always driven more by political than religious considerations, Richelieu also built an enormous personal fortune. Champaigne finally received the 500 livres owed him for this portrait from the cardinal's estate after Richelieu died.   *The Granger Collection, New York.*

THE HISTORICAL EVIDENCE

The Rebellion of the Nu-Pieds

1639

In 1639, the Nu-Pieds (the "barefooted" salt panners on the Norman coast) rebelled against the rising taxes extracted by Richelieu and Louis XIII to pay for the war against the Habsburgs. Despite the ringing rhetoric of this poem, royal troops suppressed the rebels, hanged some of them, and suspended the parlement of Rouen.

Fair Normandy, rise and rebel.
For what is it they give to you
In payment for long service true?
They give the harsh *gabelle* [salt tax].
Is this the hoped-for recompense
For loyalty to the Kings of France,
For fighting to preserve in peace
Their royal crown, their fleur-de-lys,
Defending them, time and again,
From England and from hostile Spain?

It is time to show posterity
By feats of arms and martial skill
Duke William [the Conqueror] is with us still. . . .

But could it be that it's too late?
The cardinal and armies take
Our riches, goods, all we possess,
And leave us in profound distress. . . .

Come, cowardly commissioners,
Come and indict us who dares.
Boidrot, Les Sablons, brave *nu-pieds*,
Despise you and your musketeers.
They mock your orders and your writs,
They thumb the nose at your edicts;
Our general, too, gives not a fig,
So, come, judge him without appeal.
Then come and see the grave he's dug
For you, alongside Poupinel [a hated tax collector].

Source: From *Diarie ou Journal du Voyage du Chancelier Séguier en Normandie après la Sédition des Nu-Pieds (1639–1640)*, (Paris: A. Floquet, 1842), pp. 415–417. Trans. Angela Scholar, in Margaret Lucille Kekewich, ed., *Princes and Peoples: France and the British Isles, 1620–1714: An Anthology of Primary Sources* (New York: Manchester University Press, 1994), pp. 199–201.

Great nobles such as Henry de Bourbon, Prince of Condé (1588–1646), participated in several plots against Richelieu. Employing an extensive spy network, the cardinal foiled these conspiracies while carefully strengthening the central government. In the long run, the key to defeating men like Condé lay in undermining their provincial power bases by establishing a bureaucratic administration under firm royal control. In medieval times, officials known as *intendants* had been sent out from Paris as occasional troubleshooters (see Chapter 9), but in the 1630s the intendants became the king's men in the provinces on a regular basis. Unlike the many officials who had bought their positions and could not be fired, the intendants depended heavily on the king because their office was revocable. They were regularly moved so that they would not develop local loyalties conflicting with royal priorities.

The intendants primarily served as tax officers. A striking measure of their effectiveness is the fact that by the early 1630s, Louis XIII's income was eleven times greater than that of Charles I of England, even though French population was only four times greater. The intendants also quickly gained military authority as well because they commanded troops intended to put down frequent tax rebellions caused by the mounting weight of wartime taxation. The intendants reported to a series of royal councils, and the councils issued instructions to them. The councillors usually came from the noblesse de robe rather than the *noblesse d'épée* (the old "aristocracy of the sword"). By 1640 Richelieu had constructed a centralized administration that was to underlie the absolutism of Louis XIV's reign and make France the most powerful nation in Europe.

With nobles and Huguenots under control, the remaining barriers to absolutism were the provincial parlements and the Parlement of Paris. As regional supreme courts, they had to register royal edicts before they could be enforced, and they could object to provisions that they deemed harmful. Richelieu and Louis XIII weakened these bodies, first by allowing royal councils to override their decrees and then by limiting their authority to protest royal edicts. In 1641, the members of the parlements were told that they could not discuss affairs of state at all and must register edicts concerning governmental matters without any debate. With this last constitutional means of protest gone, only rebellion could halt the progress of absolutism.

The rebellion that could have reversed France's direction came during the tenure of Richelieu's successor, Cardinal Mazarin (1602–1661). The rebels consisted of all the enemies of the centralizing policies that the French kings had pursued. Richelieu died in December 1642, and Louis XIII followed him to the grave five months later. France was thus forced to undergo yet another regency because the new king, Louis XIV, was only four years old. His mother, Anne of Austria, became the regent. She relied on Mazarin not only politically but personally, as a reading of her love letters to him demonstrates. Mazarin, an Italian educated in Spain, continued Richelieu's policies of centralization at home and war against the Habsburgs on all fronts.

Mazarin ignored warnings that the increased taxation required to finance the war would trigger rebellion. Immediately after the Thirty Years' War ended in 1648, a large-scale revolt known as the Fronde broke out (1648–1653) under the leadership of the parlements, especially the Parlement of Paris. The word *fronde* refers to a slingshot used by Parisian boys to hurl rocks, sometimes playfully and sometimes maliciously. The Fronde was a tax revolt, but its protagonists sought more than mere tax relief. Initial demands included not only shutting off revenues for the war effort, but abolishing the positions of many of the intendants and the very mechanisms of war finance. The *frondeurs* forced Mazarin and Anne to accept a group of fundamental political reforms that, had they lasted, would have transformed France from an absolute to a constitutional monarchy with the Parlement of Paris playing a role similar to that of the English Parliament.

Although led by members of the elite, the resistance to the regency government had widespread popular support. The arrest of one of the leading judges of the Parlement of Paris led quickly to the "Day of the Barricades" (August 27, 1648) as Parisians by the thousands rioted in support of the judge, blocking the streets with carts and barrels filled with paving stones to stop royal troops from entering the city. According to one observer, no less than 1,260 barricades appeared within a short time. A compromise between the judges and Anne of Austria led to the release of the imprisoned leader, and the barricades came down. Nevertheless, strong popular support for the frondeurs had been demonstrated in the capital, and numerous provincial outbreaks also occurred. The most radical antitax movement, the Ormée, seized control of the important southwestern city of Bordeaux in the summer of 1652 and held it for a year. Named after a square surrounded by elms where the rebels met, the partisans of the Ormée rejected the authority of the parlement no less than that of Mazarin and Anne. It took a blockade by the royal navy and a sizable royal army, plus numerous bribes, before Mazarin could regain Bordeaux.

Leaders of the noblesse d'épée saw in the Fronde an opportunity to regain the independence that they had once enjoyed. Paris fell to Condé's army in 1652, and the accompanying pitched battles, riotous mobs, murders, and plunderings roused fears that the French nation-state would again tear itself apart. The noblesse de robe and the middle and lower classes soon realized that a strong monarchy, even if it had arbitrary taxing and legislative powers, was preferable to aristocratic anarchy. The Fronde thus degenerated into a last, futile rebellion of the noblesse d'épée. Mazarin and Anne regained control, and absolutism in France escaped from the direst threat it had ever faced. The constitutionalist opponents of French absolutism were too much at odds with each other to make lasting common cause, and the government narrowly avoided the catastrophe that befell Olivares's efforts in Spain. When Louis XIV took over the reins of government in 1661, the work done by Richelieu and Mazarin to wrest military power from Huguenots and feudal nobles had strengthened the foundation on which he could complete the construction of an absolutist system in France (see Chapter 16).

The Austrian Monarchy and the Holy Roman Empire: The Habsburg Dilemma

In central and eastern Europe, the Habsburg family ruled a varied group of lands with a complicated political structure, and like their rivals, the Bourbon kings of France, they sought to master the Protestants within their borders. The core of their power lay in territories that they ruled on a hereditary basis, but they also sought to increase their control over the areas they held as elected rulers, such as the Holy Roman Empire and the kingdom of Bohemia (the modern Czech Republic plus the province of Silesia). Some Habsburg regions were governed directly by the emperor and others by kinsmen who at times acted in opposition to his wishes. The Habsburgs worked toward absolutism by trying to overcome the limitations placed on them by representative assemblies and municipal governments. For the most part, they also sought religious unity by championing the goals of the Counter-Reformation.

They had to move cautiously, however, for they needed Protestant support in their struggle with the Ottoman Turks on their southeastern frontiers. As late as 1570, some 70 percent of the people of the Holy Roman Empire were Protestants. Protestant nobles, even in the hereditary Habsburg dominions (such as Austria itself), used their power as members of the provincial **Estates** (diets) to defend their religious and constitutional privileges. In the 1570s, they extracted guarantees of religious toleration from the Habsburg emperor Maximilian II (reigned 1562–1576).

But the Spanish-educated Rudolf II (reigned 1576–1612) reversed his father's policy of toleration. With Jesuit and Spanish support, he drove Protestant preachers out of his hereditary lands and began depriving Protestants of offices and lands. Hungarian Protestant nobles rebelled in 1604, and rebellion threatened in Austria and Moravia. Melancholy and frequently deranged, Rudolf shut himself up in his palace (the Hradčany) in Prague after 1600, collected Mannerist art (see p. 505), and patronized alchemists and astrologers. In 1606 his relatives forced him to abdicate the Austrian throne in favor of his brother, Archduke Mathias. In an effort to soften Rudolf's unpopular policies, Mathias granted toleration in Protestant Hungary, a concession that Protestants in the Austrian and Bohemian Estates quickly demanded for themselves. In 1609 Mathias gave the Bohemian and Silesian Estates his Letter of Majesty, which guaranteed them freedom of worship and the right to meet whenever they liked.

The successes of the Protestant-led Estates in the Austrian monarchy deeply alarmed the Spaniards. The Spanish ambassador was at the center of negotiations that, on Mathias's death in 1619, led to the choice of Archduke Ferdinand of Styria as Holy Roman emperor. As Ferdinand II, this devout, Jesuit-educated Catholic fiercely opposed Protestants and constitutionalists in his Habsburg provinces throughout Europe. His chubby appearance and his talkative, amiable manner seemed at odds with his single-minded pursuit of Catholic and absolutist policies. Yet so feared was he by Protestant leaders that one of them said he would have preferred to see the devil or a Turk chosen as emperor. The fundamental principle that had settled the initial round of religious warfare in Germany in 1555 (Peace of Augsburg; see Chapter 13) was that the ruler had the right to decide whether his state would be Protestant or Catholic. In effect, Ferdinand set out to make the Holy Roman Empire and the Habsburg lands fully Catholic once again.

Ferdinand, who had been king of Bohemia since 1617, refused to abide by his promises to uphold Matthias's Letter of Majesty and revoked the privileges of the Bohemian Protestants. The nobles responded by throwing two imperial officials and their secretary out of a window in the Hradčany palace in May 1618. This event, the Defenestration of Prague, intentionally copied the initiation of the Hussite revolt two hundred years before.[4] One Protestant shouted, "See if your Virgin Mary will help you now" as they dropped. Seldom has such a farcical incident triggered such a huge disaster. The Defenestration set off the Thirty Years' War and will be discussed in the section on the European wars, later in this chapter.

Within the Holy Roman Empire, the outbreak of the Thirty Years' War at first gave the Habsburgs a golden opportunity to impose absolutism on Bohemia. Ferdinand ruthlessly crushed the Bohemian rebels in 1620, aided by the pope as well as his Spanish cousins and by another wealthy cousin, Duke Maximilian of Bavaria. He executed twenty-seven rebels and confiscated their lands—which amounted to half the estates in Bohemia. Moravia lost 30 percent of its population and Bohemia 50 percent as Protestants fled and invading troops spread disease. Ferdinand installed a new non-native Catholic nobility[5] while

---

[4] The defenestrees of 1421 were tossed from the window of Prague's town hall and landed on a mass of upthrust pikes, with fatal results.
[5] Its members included Spaniards, Italians, and even Irish.

The Defenestration of Prague Victims fell 60 feet but were uninjured. The secretary was rewarded with a title: Freiherr von Hohenfall (Lord of the Long Fall). Catholic accounts stated the men were carried to the ground by angels; Protestants contended that they escaped death by landing on a pile of manure. © *Ancient Art & Architecture Collection.*

suppressing traditional representative assemblies. His actions prompted economic and cultural collapse in a hitherto rich kingdom, a price that Ferdinand willingly paid to achieve religious conformity.

Ferdinand's initial victories whetted his appetite. He set out to do in the Holy Roman Empire what he had done in Bohemia and Austria. With the support of Duke Maximilian, he defeated the German Protestant princes and carried the standard of the Counter-Reformation all the way to the shores of the Baltic. Intoxicated by his success, Ferdinand issued the Edict of Restitution in 1629, requiring the restoration to the Roman Catholic church of all the land taken from it since 1552. But this unconstitutional redistribution of land angered both Catholic and Protestant princes and nobles. In the 1630s, their resistance, and the intervention of Swedish forces backed by France, put Ferdinand on the defensive. He died in 1637, his dream of a centralized Holy Roman Empire shattered.

The Thirty Years' War came to an end with the Treaty of Westphalia in 1648. By signing the treaty, Ferdinand III (reigned 1637–1657) had to accept a new constitution that all but destroyed the Holy Roman Empire. Its three hundred member states reasserted the traditional imperial constitution in which each was a sovereign power, collecting its own taxes and conducting its own diplomacy. No soldiers could be recruited nor monies raised without the unanimous consent of all member states, a condition impossible to achieve. The Austrian Habsburgs continued to hold the imperial title, but after 1648 little power came with it. The striving for an imperial government with enhanced authority had failed. Within Germany, the future lay with those states large enough to build potent central governments of their own: Brandenburg-Prussia, Saxony, and Bavaria. German unification (like Italian) was delayed for more than two centuries.

Sweden: The Lion of the North

A British historian of Sweden has noted that anyone "who finds Swedish history dull had better not read history at all."[6] In the sixteenth and seventeenth centuries, Sweden was embroiled with Denmark, Poland, Muscovy (Russia), and the more advanced western states in a long and complex struggle to control the Baltic Sea, with its increasingly valuable trade in timber, fish, grain, and metals. As elsewhere in Europe, states in the Baltic region were wrestling with the problems that created pressures toward absolutism. By comparison with states farther west, Sweden looked unimpressive. Sweden had less than a million people in the middle of the seventeenth century, many of whom paid taxes to the king in kind (copper, iron, fish, pelts, butter, tar). No one would have predicted that Gustavus Adolphus's thunderous

entry into the Thirty Years' War in 1630 would suddenly make his nation a major European power.

From the fourteenth through the eighteenth centuries, a struggle between kings and nobles dominated Sweden's tumultuous history. The kings sought absolute power, while the nobles tried to make the king a constitutional monarch under their control. The long union (1396–1523) of Sweden and Denmark (which then included Finland and Norway, respectively) ended with a Swedish rebellion led by the founder of the Vasa Dynasty, Gustavus I (reigned 1523–1560). Late medieval Swedish kings had been elected by the Riksråd, a council dominated by the aristocracy. The Riksråd required each new king to swear a coronation oath promising to uphold the traditional constitution with its protections of the legal rights of all subjects. The king could legislate and levy taxes only with the consent of the Riksdag, a national assembly composed of the four "estates": nobles, clergy, townsmen, and peasants. (No other European peasants had such direct political influence.) The monarch was hemmed in between the Riksråd and the Riksdag.

Gustavus I overthrew aristocratic constitutionalism (for which he said he did not "give two blueberries") by allying himself with the Riksdag against the Riksråd. In 1544 the Riksdag made the monarchy hereditary, thus denying the Riksråd the right of extracting concessions as conditions of electing new kings. When Gustavus died, it appeared that the political philosophy of the high aristocracy perished too. But in the late 1500s, the Catholicizing policies of several Swedish kings revived the corpse of constitutionalism, forcing the Vasa monarchs to reestablish their alliance with the Riksdag against the high nobility early in the seventeenth century. Gustavus Adolphus (reigned 1611–1632), as zealous a Lutheran as Ferdinand II was a Catholic, took enormous pride in the warrior-kings far back in Sweden's past and showed a keen interest not only in ancient Roman military writers but also in the innovations of Maurice of Nassau. Gustavus carried the political evolution still further by involving the Riksdag in major decisions. At the same time that ambitious rulers elsewhere were scheming to undermine the independence of their representative institutions, Gustavus took the opposite tack. He strengthened the estates by making them his partners in a program of administrative reform, economic development, and imperialistic expansion. The nobles became heads of government departments called "colleges," the core of a bureaucratic system that continued to function effectively long after Gustavus Adolphus's death. He created Sweden's first national army, recruited by conscription and armed with the best and newest weapons and tactics. In wars against Poland and Russia, Sweden took almost all the territory on the eastern and southern shores of the Baltic and thereby gained the ability to tax Poland's huge grain exports. When Ferdinand II's Habsburg armies threatened Swedish gains in the Thirty Years' War, Gustavus, dubbed the "Lion of the North," drove them back in brilliant campaigns that saved Protestantism in northern Europe and for a time established a

---

[6] Michael Roberts, *Essays in Swedish History* (Minneapolis: University of Minnesota Press, 1967), p. 13.

strong Swedish empire in Germany. When Gustavus was killed leading a cavalry charge, the seesaw struggle between monarchs and aristocrats resumed, and its final outcome still lay far in the future.

Poland-Lithuania: A Constitutionalist Catastrophe

Geographically, sixteenth-century Poland-Lithuania was the largest state in Europe except for Muscovy, and until 1588 it was religiously the most tolerant. Its numerous landowning nobility (10 percent of the population, the highest proportion in Europe) benefited from western Europe's growing demand for grain. In tumultuous mass meetings, the nobles elected the king every time the throne fell vacant. By 1572 the choice was further complicated by religious divisions. Lutherans, Calvinists, Anabaptists, antitrinitarians of various kinds, and Bohemian Brethren (an offshoot of the fifteenth-century Hussites) had all gained adherents among the nobility while quarreling with each other, and the Counter-Reformation had worked since the late 1560s to restore Catholic dominance.

In 1587 a grandson of Sweden's Gustavus I was elected King Sigismund III of Poland (reigned 1587–1632, and as king of Sweden 1592–1599). Sigismund, like Emperor Ferdinand II, was Jesuit-educated, and so eager was he to reconvert all his realms to Catholicism that he was called the "Polish Philip II." The Protestant Swedes deposed him in 1599. But Poland-Lithuania could not get rid of him despite the strong opposition he provoked by his intolerance, his adventurous foreign policy (he tried to become tsar of Russia as well as to retake Sweden), and his efforts to strengthen the crown at the expense of Poland-Lithuania's aristocratic liberties. The Polish Sejm (pronounced "same"), a body composed of a Senate of magnates and a Chamber of Deputies of gentry (but not burghers), in theory required unanimous consent to taxation. Such a rule posed an impossible barrier to a strong government, let alone absolutism. In 1606 Sigismund tried vainly to force the Sejm to accept the principle of majority rule and to give him a standing army and regular taxes. His efforts triggered a rebellion and a decisive defeat for his program.

Instead of becoming a supporter of the state, as did the Swedish Riksdag, the Sejm stymied the kings as its members defended their pocketbooks and their power over the **serfs.** In 1652 the Sejm for the first time exercised a *liberum veto,* meaning that its meetings were ended by a single negative vote in the Chamber of Deputies without any laws having been passed or taxes levied.[7] Gentry representatives invariably acted at the instigation of some magnate-led party, so the liberum veto actually served as a vehicle for magnate domination. Between 1652 and 1764, the liberum veto was cast no fewer than fifty-three times. This was liberty run wild, and its result was virtual anarchy. "With a single word, God created the world," reflected one rueful Pole, and "with a single word, we destroy Poland." Polish nobles used the veto to prevent the crown from raising sufficient forces to defend the country. During the 1650s and 1660s (years of "the Deluge" to Poles), Swedish, Russian, and other outsiders captured large pieces of Poland-Lithuania, and cossacks—Ukrainian warriors whose main occupation was fighting with Tatars in the southeastern borderlands—rampaged through the heart of the country. Although only the territorial losses to Russia proved permanent, the real damage was a vast destruction of material wealth, widespread massacres (pogroms) of Jews, devastation of the towns, and the ruin of the gentry as a force that might offset magnate power. Late eighteenth-century Poland was still recovering from this disaster when the commonwealth was partitioned among Russia, Prussia, and Austria (see Chapter 19).

From the point of view of a supporter of absolutism, the Poles got exactly what they deserved. Having chosen to defend their "golden liberty" and having blocked the creation of a strong centralized government, they lost their country to invading forces led by absolute monarchs.

Russia: The Rise of the Tsars

About 1350 the princes of Muscovy ruled only 600 square miles around Moscow. But under a line of able and energetic rulers of the Rurik Dynasty, Muscovite territory steadily expanded in all directions in what is called the "gathering of Russian lands." Like Sweden and Poland, Muscovy was dominated by a powerful hereditary aristocracy of princes and nobles, or *boyars.* Ivan IV, "the Terrible"[8] (reigned 1533–1584), was the first to use the title of "Tsar" (derived from "caesar"), but the ground for his tsardom had been prepared by Ivan III (d. 1503), who called himself *"Gosudar* [sovereign lord] of all the Russias" (see Chapter 11). Early in his reign, Ivan the Terrible encouraged constitutionalism. In 1549 he called the first *Zemskii Sobor,* a national assembly that included members of the boyars' council, churchmen, and merchants. However, he later unleashed a reign of terror against the boyars, torturing and executing many and exiling others in order to eradicate their power. He used their confiscated estates to strengthen the new service nobility (*dvoryanstvo*) that he was creating—men whose sons could take over their father's lands only so long as they continued to serve the

---

[7] The action in 1652 was taken to block a proposal to restructure the Polish-Lithuanian commonwealth by granting political equality to the Ukrainian provinces. Rebuffed, Ukrainian cossacks began a rebellion that escalated into the series of foreign invasions known as "the Deluge."

[8] "The Terrible" is the traditional English translation of the Russian adjective *groznii,* but a more accurate rendition would be "the Dread" or "the Awesome."

tsar. By humbling the boyars, Ivan crushed the only class that might have blocked the establishment of a centralized monarchy. During the 1500s, formerly free peasants living on the estates of the *dvoryane* (service nobles) were becoming serfs, a development that Ivan encouraged in order to support his service nobility.

In a fit of perhaps insane rage in 1581, Ivan killed his eldest son, leaving the throne to his feebleminded second son, Fyodor I (reigned 1584–1598), who preferred ringing church bells to ruling the state. Fyodor was the last of the Rurik Dynasty, and after his death Russia plunged into the "Time of Troubles" (1598–1613). Some boyar families attempted a comeback by supporting various pretenders to the throne against a background of terrible famine, rebellion, and interventions by foreign forces bent on taking advantage of the succession crisis. Muscovy's population declined by 25 percent, and various Russian pretenders, boyar politicians, and Polish and Swedish kings vied for the throne.

Finally in 1613, a new Sobor with representatives from the common people chose a member of an old boyar family, Mikhail Romanov (Michael I, reigned 1613–1645), as the tsar. The assembly required Michael to govern with its advice, thus making Russia a constitutional monarchy. Gradually, however, the power of the Sobor declined as

fewer members were elected and more were nominated by the tsar. The assembly became a rubber stamp for decisions that Michael had already made. No Sobor was called when the next tsar came to the throne—or ever again.

Unlike the assemblies farther west, the Zemskii Sobor had no deep roots in collective political experience. When the Time of Troubles ended, Russia reverted to its absolutist tradition under the tsars who were thought of as heirs of Caesar and Byzantium, rulers of the "Third Rome" (see Chapters 6 and 11). In 1649 the Romanov regime imposed a comprehensive new law code called the *Ulozhenie*. Its more than a thousand articles fixed the tsar's subjects firmly in their occupational and geographical categories and strengthened the state's power over them. Townspeople had to stay in their towns, and the authority of landowners (especially the service nobles) over peasants grew to the point that villagers became mere chattels. Whereas in 1500 the majority of peasants had been free, by around 1700 all but 7 percent were serfs who could be sold without any land changing hands. Provisions of the Ulozhenie accelerated this trend, for example, by abolishing the time limit on the recapture of escaped serfs. Brutal suppression of resistance to the code left Russian society solidly in the mold that it would have until the Russian Revolution of 1917.

Palm Sunday in Moscow Travelers' accounts of Russia, such as this one from a German source in the mid-seventeenth century, depicted a country that seemed strange to many Europeans. St. Basil's cathedral (upper left, mislabeled "Kremlin") was begun on the orders of Ivan IV to commemorate one of his conquests. De Wicquefort's *Voyages* by Leydon (1719).

The Dutch Republic: Orangists, Republicans, and an Economic Miracle

Although the Dutch and the English would develop constitutionalist systems capable of defending national interests effectively, they experienced the same striving for absolutism that occurred elsewhere, and it was by no means obvious that it would fail. Dutch politics were turbulent: One leading statesman was executed in 1619 and another was torn to pieces by a mob in 1672. Yet amid all these troubles, the Dutch nation protected itself against the military might first of Spain, then of England, and finally of France.

The Dutch rebellion had begun in 1566 as a defense of the medieval constitution of the Netherlandish provinces against the centralizing policies of Philip II of Spain (see Chapter 13). Although the Spaniards reconquered the southern provinces in 1584, leadership of the northern provinces fell in 1584 to Maurice of Nassau (1567–1625), the young son of the Dutch revolt's assassinated leader, William the Silent. A better general than his father, Maurice's innovative tactics defended the new Dutch state with great success until a twelve-year truce with Spain was signed in 1609. The Dutch economy boomed as Dutch ships moved into the vast empires of Spain and Portugal and achieved a near monopoly of the rich Baltic trade.

Dutch economic progress did not bring political stability, however. Throughout the 1600s, periods of predominance by Orangists and Republicans alternated. The Orangists supported the dynasty of the revolt's martyr, William the Silent. They wanted to move the Dutch Republic (the United Provinces) toward a more centralized polity under the authority of the noble house of Orange. Their opponents, the Republicans, struggled to maintain the medieval constitution, with its high level of provincial autonomy for each of the seven provincial assemblies as well as the States-General.

Up to 1619, the Republicans proved the more successful. Foreign affairs and defense lay firmly under the control of the national assembly, the States-General, composed of delegations from the provincial assemblies (States). In no instance was the choice of delegates democratic. Real power lay with an upper middle class known as the regents, who formed a closed society of wealthy merchants. Interconnected by marriage, the regents were in practice a hereditary ruling class, having shouldered aside the landowning nobility. Each delegation voted as a unit, and on any important matter unanimity was required. Thus each delegation had what in Poland would be called the liberum veto and what state delegations in the Continental Congress would have under the Articles of Confederation during and after the American Revolution. The States-General selected a new presiding officer every week by a process of rotation. Military organization was equally decentralized: Each province had an officer called the stadholder in charge of its troops and ships. The States-General chose a national military leader, usually the stadholder of Holland, the richest and most populous province.

This fragmented political structure in part explains why the Spaniards agreed to a truce in 1609. They quite reasonably thought that the Dutch "nation" would collapse without the artificial pressure applied by war. On paper, at least, the Dutch chances of evading conquest looked no better than those of the Poles. Fortunately for the Dutch, their system had unifying forces at work beneath the surface. Holland, contributing more than half of the Dutch military budget, enjoyed enormous influence over the other provinces. Moreover, the Calvinist burghers who formed the oligarchies throughout the United Provinces were merchants who understood the necessity of cooperation. Unlike the Polish nobles, separated by many miles between their vast estates, the regents knew that only the compromise and cooperation that had won their independence from Spain could preserve it. Another unifying influence came from an official known as the advocate, or grand pensionary, of Holland. Originally merely a legal adviser and spokesman, this official gradually became a sort of prime minister for Holland. Because Holland was the most powerful province, the grand pensionary functioned as a leader of the Dutch nation.

From 1588 to 1598, the stadholder, Maurice of Nassau, and the pensionary of Holland, Johann van Oldenbarnevelt, worked together effectively. But by 1618, the Dutch Republic's unity had collapsed during a major conflict between Protestant religious factions, the Gomarists (the rigid Calvinists) and the Arminians (who rejected the Calvinist doctrine of predestination). Maurice of Nassau risked civil war by backing the Gomarists and marching his army into Holland, but his coup succeeded. He purged Arminian regents from office and installed Orangists in their places. After an unfair trial, Oldenbarnevelt was executed for treason in 1619. As in Sweden, the monarchists allied with the more democratically minded enemies of the aristocratic constitutionalism embodied in the regents.

When Maurice of Nassau died in 1625, he was succeeded as leader of the Orange cause by his brother Frederick Henry (1584–1647). Capitalizing on popular acclaim for his victories over Spain, Frederick Henry persuaded the States of several provinces to make the stadholderate hereditary, a sharp break with the elective principle. At The Hague, he built up a court as splendid as that of many kings and began to have himself addressed as "Highness" instead of "Excellency," the form that had satisfied his predecessors. He arranged for the marriage of his heir to an English princess, thus further emphasizing the royalist ambitions of the house of Orange. And when, in 1634, he pushed the States-General to set up a foreign affairs committee under his control, the "Secret Council," his dominance of the government advanced to the point where the Dutch Republic seemed about to give way to an absolute monarchy. Frederick Henry's son and successor, William II (reigned 1647–1650), planned a coup to overthrow the last barrier to Orangist ascendancy, the States of Holland. But before he could complete it, he died of smallpox at age twenty-four, eight days before the birth of his only son.

With the house of Orange leaderless and news of William II's conspiracy spreading, regent constitutionalism suddenly took on new life. Led by a shrewd regent, Johann de Witt (1625–1672), the Dutch entered another age of republicanism. Only twenty-seven years old when he became the grand pensionary of Holland in 1653, de Witt and the regents pursued a policy of toleration towards Catholics, Anabaptists, and Jews. Persecution interrupted trade, they realized, and trade was the lifeblood of the Dutch Republic. Religious refugees—Jews from Spain, Calvinists from France and the southern Netherlands, and many others—brought capital, business talent, and craft skills that helped to make the Dutch nation the economic miracle of seventeenth-century Europe and Amsterdam the trading and financial center of the world. Yet the question as to which side would win the struggle between Orangist royalism or regent constitutionalism would remain unanswered until after William III reached adulthood.

England: Cavaliers, Roundheads, and a Regicide

The Tudor Dynasty ended with the death of Elizabeth I in 1603. James I (reigned 1603–1625), Elizabeth's cousin and a great-grandson of Henry VII, succeeded her. James, who already occupied the Scottish throne as James VI, became the first of a line of Stuart monarchs who would rule England and Scotland until 1714 (with one interruption from 1649 to 1660; see Figure 16-4 in the next chapter). Until 1707, when a controversial parliamentary union occurred, England and Scotland were separate kingdoms with the same rulers. After 1707, the union formed the kingdom of Great Britain.[9]

The English spent most of the seventeenth century in internal political struggles, beheading one king in 1649 after a civil war and kicking out another king in 1688. Few could have predicted that Britain would become a world power of the first rank by the early eighteenth century. A number of favorable omens for advocates of absolutism existed in Britain. England had long been a united and relatively centralized state, much more so than the Dutch Republic or France (see Chapter 9). It had no provincial assemblies and boasted a national legal system that the Stuarts found helpful as they sought to strengthen their position. English monarchs also had the right to call and dismiss sessions of Parliament whenever they chose. More-

over, the Stuart kings all came to the throne as mature men; there were none of the regencies that endangered absolutist progress in France and the Dutch Republic.

Two major barriers to absolutism—Parliament and the machinery of local government—nevertheless proved too stout for the Stuarts, although their own political ineptitude repeatedly assisted their constitutionalist opponents. The taxes that Parliament voted were essentially taxes on landed income. The noblemen who by hereditary right sat in the House of Lords and the gentlemen elected to the House of Commons by property owners came from and represented the classes who paid a significant proportion of royal expenses (unlike France and Spain, where noble income was tax exempt). By contrast with the Estates General of France, Parliament was a firmly established part of the English constitution. Having developed its procedures of election, debate, and legislation, the assembly was

Charles I Opening Parliament in 1625   Following tradition, Charles I called Parliament at the outset of his reign. With his councillors seated near him, the king would have seen the bishops to his right and the secular lords to his left. Members of the House of Commons (foreground) look on. The ceremonial opening of the British Parliament follows the same form to this day. *Mansell/Time Inc.*

---

[9] Britain's current government is implementing a "devolution" of certain powers to a new Scottish assembly, considered by some as a step toward the breakup of the union of 1707.

widely regarded as the proper place for the presentation of subjects' complaints and for communication between the landowning classes on the one hand and the monarch and his officials on the other. Furthermore, many members increasingly came to see Parliament as the place to defend both the principle of taxation only by consent and the English **common law** with its due process and trial by jury.

In local government, too, the contrast with France is notable. In England, unpaid amateurs called justices of the peace (JPs)—not paid, professional bureaucrats—did the most important work of local administration. Most JPs were substantial landowners. They wanted to maintain favor with the king, since his patronage enhanced their prestige and could lead to high office and other benefits for ambitious men. But if his demands seemed excessive or illegal, they could and did cease to cooperate without serious damage to their livelihoods. If the king could not get Parliament to pass a law or a tax, he thus had little chance of going around that body and imposing his will by demanding that local officials such as the JPs enforce his will arbitrarily. In any case, the Stuarts lacked the money for either a paid local bureaucracy or a standing army to impose their will by force.

Throughout most of the seventeenth century, many members of Parliament deeply opposed the foreign and religious policies of the Stuarts. They suspected—with more justification on some occasions than others—that the king wanted to overthrow the established Protestant religion at home and ally with Catholic powers abroad. In the 1620s and 1630s, the patronizing of "Arminian" clergymen such as William Laud by Charles I (reigned 1625–1649) provided the main cause of Protestant (especially Calvinist and Puritan) concern. Laud, made archbishop of Canterbury in 1633, was an Anglican whose liturgical changes emphasized ritual and ceremony in worship. To many Protestants, this looked like an attempt to bring back Roman Catholicism. Laud, who stated that "a greater reverence is due to the body than to the word of the Lord," tried to force parishes to replace their communion tables with Catholic-style altars set behind rails. He claimed that his aim was merely "to prevent dogs from pissing on them, or worse," but even non-Puritan Protestants often objected to this change, which seemed to imply that the service was a sacrificial Mass rather than a communion of the congregation. Many Puritan preachers lost their positions for refusing to perform the ceremonies, and some of them emigrated to Massachusetts with their followers. Others fled to the more tolerant Dutch Republic. Charles's failure to offer effective financial or military assistance to fellow Protestants on the European continent after the Thirty Years' War broke out deepened the suspicions of zealous Protestants about his ultimate religious goals. If, they wondered, his Arminian friends are not Catholics in sheeps' clothing, why did he fail to help Protestants in central Europe as they underwent a hammering by the armies of the Habsburgs?

Laud's religious policy had the dangerous effect of linking constitutional and religious grievances. It increased fears that Charles aimed to prepare the way for both arbitrary taxation and alteration of the national church that the Tudor monarchs had established with Parliament's active participation and support. Angered by the failure of the Parliaments of 1625 and 1626 to vote sufficient taxes for his military campaigns, he levied a forced loan on those landowners who would have paid the taxes and imprisoned many who refused to pay. Although the 1628 Parliament forced him to disavow such illegal taxation and imprisonment, he dismissed it in 1629 and called no parliaments in the 1630s. His most vigorous critics thought he wished to do away with Parliament altogether, although the odds are

John Lilburne, the Leveller Leader Frequently imprisoned after 1645 for his "seditious" behavior, John Lilburne made ingenious use of the printing press to trumpet his cause and make his personal struggles resonate with those of the people outside the political elite. To dramatize his imprisonment, he had bars added to an earlier portrait. *The Granger Collection, New York.*

THE HISTORICAL EVIDENCE

The Putney Debates

July 1647

Thomas Rainsborough's historic call for universal male suffrage occurred in a series of debates between senior officers of the New Model Army (including Oliver Cromwell) and Leveller spokesmen held at Putney, a town on the Thames River west of London, in July 1647. Many officers favored an extension of the franchise beyond wealthy landowners, but the question in their minds was how far extending the vote was compatible with the preservation of property. Would it lead to social "leveling," ending all hierarchical distinctions of status, wealth, and power? Responding to Rainsborough's call for universal adult male suffrage, one of the colonels at Putney, quoted here, explained the danger he foresaw if voters included men with no "permanent interest" (meaning the ownership of land). Do you think his fears were justified? How would you have answered him?

You have five to one in this kingdom that have no permanent interest. Some men [have] ten, some twenty servants, some more, some less. If the master and servant shall be equal electors, then clearly those that have no interest in the kingdom will make it their interest to choose those that have no interest. It may happen, that the majority may by law, not in a confusion, destroy property; there may be a law enacted, that there shall be an equality of goods and estate. . . . But there may be a more equitable division and distribution than that he that hath nothing should have an equal voice; and certainly there may be some other way thought of, that there may be a representative of the poor as well as the rich, and not to exclude all. I remember that there were many workings and revolutions, as we have heard, in the Roman Senate; and there

was never a confusion that did appear (and that indeed *was* come to) till the state came to know this kind of distribution of election. That is how the people's voices were bought and sold, and that by the poor; and thence it came that he that was the richest man, and [a man] of some considerable power among the soldiers, made himself a perpetual dictator. And if we strain too far to avoid monarchy in kings [let us take heed] that we do not call for emperors to deliver us from more than one tyrant.

Source: From *Puritanism and Liberty: Being the Army Debates (1647–1649) from the Clarke Manuscripts with Supplementary Documents,* ed. A. S. P. Woodhouse (London: J. M. Dent, 1938), pp. 63–64.

that he was hoping that a new generation of landowners would take a more sympathetic view of his policies.

Charles's "Personal Rule," as the decade of the 1630s was called, formed a critical period in the striving for absolutism in England. If the king had succeeded in raising enough revenue from customs surcharges, "ship money" (a levy based on precedents in which the monarch could conscript ships for defense in emergencies), and other nonparliamentary devices, he might have managed to govern indefinitely without the nuisance of Parliament. Initially, Charles enjoyed considerable success as ship money brought in £200,000 a year. But by 1637, large numbers of landowners were refusing to pay his controversial "ship money" levy, and without intendants or a standing army, Charles could not collect the money. In 1639, only 20 percent of the expected yield of the ship money tax reached his coffers. In effect, a tax rebellion succeeded.

These tense circumstances led to the revolutionary series of events starting with a major rebellion in Scotland in 1637 against the government's enforcement of Laud's liturgical program. The Presbyterians, who dominated Scotland and its "kirk," furiously denounced the new worship as "popish in its frame and forms"; one nobleman called it "the brood of the bowels of the whore of Babel." Its imposition without consultation with either the Scottish parliament or church assembly seemed no less objectionable. Needing an army to suppress the rebellious Scots, Charles could not resist the Long Parliament (1640–1660) when it dismantled the absolutist system that he had constructed. He was unable to prevent Parliament's impeachment of Laud and other advisers. He also signed bills requiring that Parliament meet at least once very three years and that he not dismiss it without its consent. Although a few years later the French frondeurs would

The Indomitable Katherine Chidley

In the raging political conflicts of the seventeenth century, princes were opposed by nobles, gentlemen, professionals, and urban oligarchs—all of whom saw themselves as conservatives protecting the old order against centralizing innovations. Constitutionalists tended to hail from the upper classes and had "liberties" to defend and established institutions in which to work (representative assemblies, courts, municipal governments). Yet the disorder created by their struggles occasionally permitted the emergence of genuinely popular movements fired by radical ideas.

In England, the Levellers formed one such movement. It produced a huge volume of printed pamphlets advocating its revolutionary program. Its contributors included Katherine Chidley, the wife of a Shrewsbury haberdasher. The Chidleys moved to London with their seven children in 1630 and joined an Independent congregation—a group of dissenters who considered the Church of England invalid, illegally formed their own church, and chose their minister.

In 1641 Katherine Chidley published *The Justification of the Independent Churches of Christ*. The work attacked Catholic, Anglican, and Presbyterian insistence on an established state church with authority over individual congregations and ministers. Supporting the right of Christians to found congregations and pick preachers, she asked, "Who hath a greater measure of the Spirit than believers? . . . And who hath greater authority upon earth than they that are visible saints?" She also asserted a wife's independence of her husband in spiritual matters: "I pray you tell me what authority the unbelieving husband hath over the conscience of his believing wife, it is true he hath authority over her in bodily and civil respects, but not to be a lord over her conscience." Thomas Edwards, the Presbyterian minister whose writings were criticized in Katherine Chidley's first book, described her as "a brazen-faced, audacious old woman." Undaunted, Chidley wrote additional pamphlets against his views and challenged him to a public debate on the topic of Independency. He declined. She also acted on her principles, helping to found an Independent church at Bury St. Edmunds and standing up in a church near London during the worship service to denounce ministers who disagreed with her.

Katherine Chidley also vigorously supported the Leveller leader, John Lilburne. In June 1653, she led a group of twelve women who tried to present a petition to the House of Commons opposing Lilburne's trial. She probably wrote the petition, which six thousand women signed, and its fiery language exemplifies her style. Katherine Chidley and her friends "boldly knocked at the door," but a member came out and told them that "the House could not take cognizance of their petition, they being women." They replied that the members of Parliament ought to "look to themselves, and not to persecute that man of God [Lilburne] lest they were also destroyed, as the late king" had been. Her last recorded appearance on the public stage came in July 1653, and it was characteristic of her. From a London pulpit, she "preached to the people very much in Lilburne's behalf." ❖

attempt comparable changes and fail, in England the constitutionalist faction won out, at least in the short run.

Charles's opponents, led by the brilliant parliamentarian John Pym (1584–1643), began to fear that the king was merely playing for time, waiting until he had an army that he could use to repudiate the legislation he had signed, collect taxes arbitrarily, and overthrow Protestantism. A new rebellion in Ireland in 1641 heightened the urgency of funding an army, and Charles's failed attempt to arrest Pym and four other opposition leaders in January 1642 confirmed fears about his trustworthiness. A bloody civil war broke out between Royalists (Cavaliers) and Parliamentarians (Roundheads), ending in the defeat of the royal armies in 1645 and the capture of the king in 1646. The key to victory was the Long Parliament's New Model Army, a truly national army funded and led from London instead of controlled by regionally based groups interested mainly in self defense against the Cavaliers.

The civil war unleashed a genuine democratic movement. Within and outside the Roundhead army, a group known as the Levellers agitated for extending the vote in parliamentary elections to include most adult males. In a debate with the leading officers of the New Model Army in 1647, one Leveller speaker, Colonel Thomas Rainsborough, made the first public and prominent case for universal manhood suffrage in human history:

For really I think that the poorest he that is in England hath a life to live as the greatest he; . . . I think it's clear, that every man that is to live under a government ought first by his own consent to put himself under that government; and I do think that the poorest man in England is not at all bound in a strict sense to that government that he hath not had a voice [vote] to put himself under.

Rainsborough was murdered in his lodgings by royalists in 1648, but huge crowds turned out in London for his funeral wearing Leveller colors.

The Levellers skillfully employed the printing press and based their arguments on natural rights rather than inherited "liberties" limited to particular groups. They wanted a republic in which a reformed and more democratically chosen Parliament would meet annually, with constituencies based on the distribution of the population and consisting of paid members so that working people as well as gentlemen could serve. Unsurprisingly, the Levellers felt common cause with the Ormée and in 1651 sent one of their spokesmen to stiffen the opposition to the French government in Bordeaux. Although the Leveller program was too radical to succeed in war-torn England, its contribution to the stock of political ideas was nevertheless important, and its supporters included women as well as men.

After a second civil war in 1648, the victorious Parliamentarian general Oliver Cromwell (1599–1658) concluded that Charles would have to be tried for making war on his own people. The army leaders purged the Long Parliament of their political enemies and set up a special court that convicted him of treason. Charles was publicly beheaded in London on January 30, 1649. Kings had been overthrown and killed before, but usually on the pretext that they had usurped someone else's right to rule. No one in England, however, questioned Charles's claim to the throne. His execution in the name of the people horrified all of Europe and indeed most English people. It was particularly offensive to the Orangists in the Dutch Republic. A greater perversion of the supposedly fixed natural order could hardly be imagined.

Ironically, the period after the king's execution was the only time during which the English lived under a government with the kind of authority absolutists craved—a military dictatorship led by Cromwell. Although he wanted to restore civilian government, Cromwell found himself forced to dismiss the remnant of the Long Parliament left after the purge of 1649, seize control of local government, and maintain the powerful, professional, and expensive New Model Army that had triumphed over all comers. He instituted a relatively tolerant ecclesiastical settlement, but he died before he could establish an effective alternative to the Stuart monarchy. In the absence of Cromwell's towering figure, factional bickering intensified until the Long Parliament was recalled and invited Charles II (reigned 1660–1685) to return from exile. With his return, the monarchy and the Anglican church were reestablished, and the striving for absolutism resumed.

THE EUROPEAN WARS, 1600–1660

Throughout the first six decades of the seventeenth century, the struggle between absolutists and constitutionalists continued inside states throughout Europe, and in 1660 the outcome remained in doubt nearly everywhere (see Map 15-1).

The Royal Oak of Britain
This savage critique of Oliver Cromwell came not from a Cavalier but from a Presbyterian writer to whom Cromwell's tolerant religious policy was reprehensible. Presbyterians had supported the Parliamentarian side in the civil war but could not abide the religious and secular radicalism that came in its wake. Cromwell is shown inspired by the devil and directing the destruction of English liberties (Magna Carta, the common law) and religion ("Biblia Sacra"). His underlings (i.e., Levellers) vigorously work in the hope of carrying away the spoils.

MAP 15-1

THE WARS IN CENTRAL EUROPE, 1618–1660

The domestic infighting, although driven partly by political, religious, and economic forces, had been aggravated by the prevalence of war. Even the English, who had ceased active military involvement in the Thirty Years' War by 1628, continued to have their politics complicated by the military and diplomatic conflicts on the Continent.

By 1660 war had settled some important questions while exacerbating domestic tensions. In 1600 two major diplomatic problems had confronted western Europe: the fate of the Netherlands, and the old Franco-Spanish rivalry. In central Europe, the primary question was whether the Holy Roman Empire's Ferdinand II and his son could establish confessional and political absolutism over the Protestants and German princes who in 1608 had formed the evangelical union. In northeastern Europe, control of the Baltic coastline constituted the major, although not the only, source of conflict.

The wars spawned by such issues frequently overlapped. Gustavus Adolphus remarked that "all the wars that are on foot in Europe are fused together and become one war." He was exaggerating, but he had a good point. At one time or another, the Protestant states—England, Sweden, Denmark, and the Dutch Republic—entered the battles of the empire.

Desire to help their coreligionists in part motivated these interventions, but no such purpose motivated the French in their support for the massive Swedish invasion that for a time threatened the Catholic cause with destruction in the mid-1630s. Cardinal Richelieu based his policy on "reason of state"—the French need to prevent encirclement by the Spanish and Austrian Habsburgs.

The twelve-year truce between Spain and the Dutch Republic ended in 1621, and many thought the two sides would renew the agreement. But with Maurice's triumph over Oldenbarnevelt, the anti-Spanish hard-liners triumphed in the Dutch provinces at the same time that the anti-Dutch hard-liners in Madrid insisted on conditions that even Oldenbarnevelt would have rejected (including an end to Dutch commerce with America). Revived war thus brought the Dutch in on the Protestant side in the Thirty Years' War.

The Thirty Years' War in central Europe, a titanic struggle, began in May 1618 with the Defenestration of Prague. Soon the Bohemian Estates boldly voted to depose Ferdinand as their king and elected in his place the Calvinist son-in-law of James I of Britain, the elector palatine, Frederick V (1596–1632). Not the least of the Habsburg worries was that if Frederick managed to retain Bohemia, he would have two of the seven votes needed to elect the next emperor. His votes, combined with those of Saxony and Brandenburg, would yield a 4-to-3 Protestant majority.

Ignoring advice from all sides against accepting the Bohemians' offer, the ambitious Frederick V traveled to Prague and was crowned king in November 1619. A year later, the army of the Catholic League (an alliance of German Catholic princes formed in 1609), crushed the Bohemians at the battle of White Mountain, just outside Prague. The Imperialists also had assistance from John George, elector of Saxony (reigned 1611–1656), a devout Lutheran who hated the Calvinists enough to assist Ferdinand II. Then in 1621 Spanish forces invaded Frederick's homeland, the Rhenish Palatinate. Its capital, Heidelberg, fell in 1622, and the priceless library of its university, long a center of Protestant scholarship and teaching, was sent to the pope. With the capture of the Palatinate, a critical stretch of the "Spanish road," the string of territories used

to move men and supplies overland between Spain and the Netherlands, now came under Catholic control.

After the defeat of the Protestants of Bohemia, Austria, Moravia, and the Palatinate (the so-called Bohemian-Palatinate phase of the conflict), the Thirty Years' War proceeded through three more phases: Danish (1624–1629), Swedish (1630–1635), and Franco-Habsburg (1635–1648) (see Figure 15-1). In the Danish phase, Christian IV of Denmark (reigned 1588–1648) led the Protestant forces. Christian initiated a major offensive, but in 1626 he suffered defeat by the Catholic League's army and a new player in the game, a Bohemian noble and military contractor named Count Albrecht von Wallenstein. Ferdinand had placed Wallenstein in charge of his forces in 1625, and by 1629 Wallenstein controlled most of Bohemia, Friedland, and the Baltic provinces of Pomerania and Mecklenburg. Olivares and Philip IV were plotting to join Wallenstein's power with that of the Spanish Netherlands to seize the rich Baltic shipping industry. If they had succeeded, the economy of the

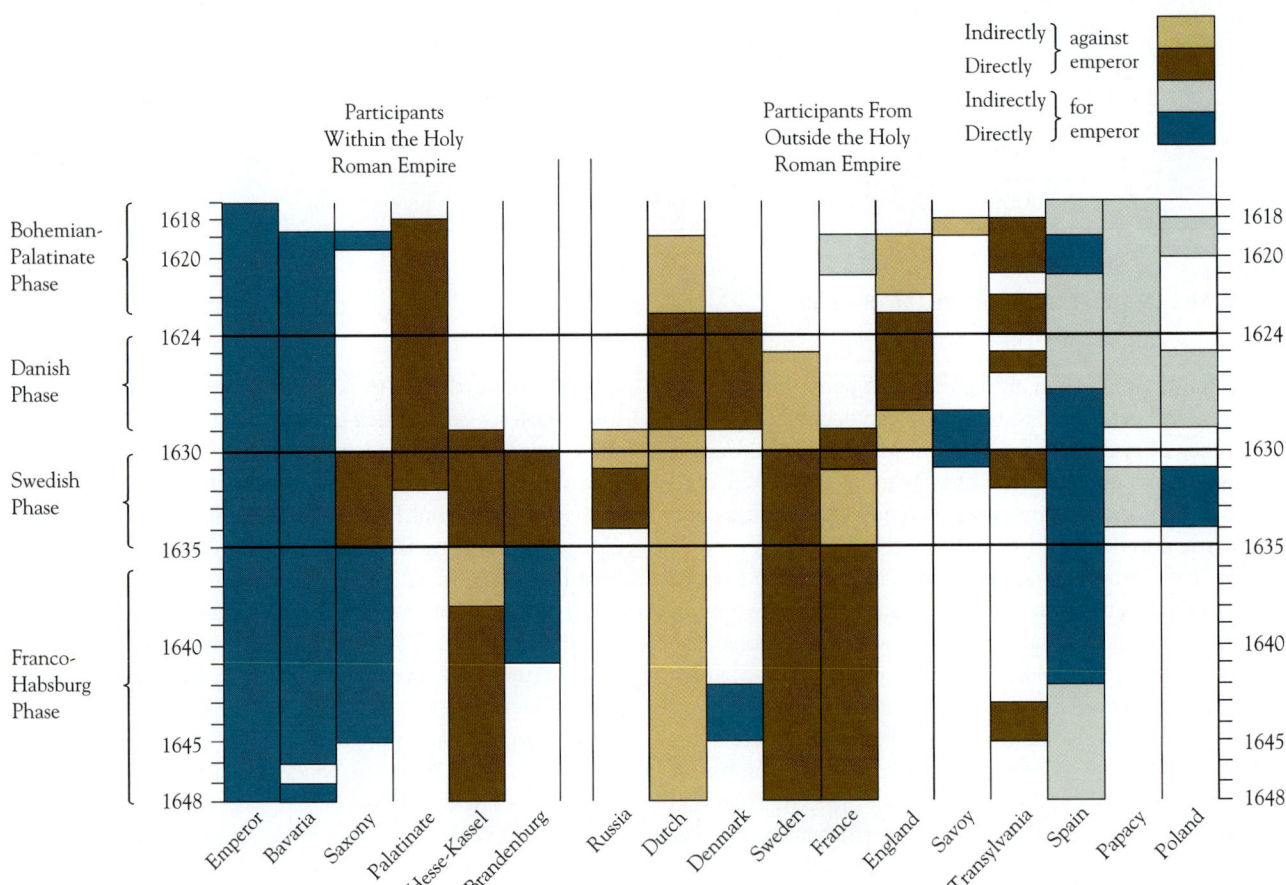

FIGURE 15-1
PARTICIPATION IN THE THIRTY YEARS' WAR

This chart shows which states fought during the Thirty Years' War and the periods of time that they took part, both directly (with troops in the field) and indirectly (financial and diplomatic contributions). Sweden, for example, initially contributed troops to help defend the Pomeranian town of Stralsund from Wallenstein in 1628, but Sweden did not actually go to war against Ferdinand until July 1630. Note that several states changed sides (for example, Saxony and Brandenburg). *Source: Adapted from Geoffrey Parker, ed., The Thirty Years' War, 2nd ed. (London and New York: Routledge, 1997), p. 139.*

Dutch Republic would have been wrecked and Spain could have reconquered the Dutch people.

By 1629 Ferdinand felt strong enough to issue the Edict of Restitution, but this uncompromisingly ultra-Catholic measure produced the backlash described earlier in the chapter and gravely weakened Ferdinand's position. More disasters engulfed the Imperialists when the Swedish king Gustavus Adolphus, subsidized by France, invaded northern Germany in 1630. The "Lion of the North," as Gustavus was called by his numerous Protestant admirers, moved so rapidly that he overshot the territory covered by his maps. Joined by the electors of Saxony and Brandenburg, the Swedish army moved to conquer Bavaria and Bohemia. The Swedish victory at Breitenfeld (September 17, 1631) pitted the new against the old pattern of warfare in that the Imperialists aligned their infantry in "thick" formations thirty men deep

while the Protestants employed Maurice of Nassau's "thin" linear battle order six ranks deep. The latter's overwhelming firepower, employing musket salvos and numerous field artillery pieces, killed 7,600 men in a few hours and put the rest of the Catholics into a headlong flight during which 9,000 were captured and more killed during the retreat. Only a third of the Imperialist army, which had formerly won all its battles, remained after Breitenfeld. The desperate Ferdinand turned again to Wallenstein, but Gustavus defeated him as well at Lützen (November 16, 1632). Catastrophically for the Protestants, however, the Swedish king died on the battlefield, and the Habsburgs regrouped sufficiently to defeat the Protestant forces at Nördlingen in 1634 (see Map 15-1).

Yet in retrospect it is clear that Ferdinand had been at the peak of his power in 1629. By dismissing Wallenstein in 1630, Ferdinand lost his last chance to build a unified

MAP 15-2
CENTRAL EUROPE AFTER THE PEACE OF WESTPHALIA, 1648

This map greatly simplifies the jigsaw puzzle of tiny states—principalities, bishoprics, free cities, and domains of imperial knights—within the Holy Roman Empire. They were strewn with especially bewildering complexity in central and southern Germany. The principal territorial changes imposed by the Peace of Westphalia included the transfer to France of strategic areas along the empire's western boundary, Sweden's annexation of western Pomerania, and enlargements of Brandenburg, Saxony, and Bavaria. The independence of Switzerland and the United Provinces (the Dutch Republic) was also formally acknowledged, although these countries had long been independent de facto. The most important result of all, however, was the defeat of Habsburg attempts to turn the Holy Roman Empire into a centrally directed, Catholic monarchy. In blocking this, France and many of the small states within the Holy Roman Empire had won a major victory. The pope declared the treaty "null and void," but no one heeded his protests.

THE HUMAN EXPERIENCE

Count Albrecht von Wallenstein, the Warrior Businessman

Up to a point, Wallenstein's story resembles that of Francesco Sforza, the Renaissance Italian who began as a condottiere hired by the Visconti despots of Milan and who ended as the ruler of the city. Wallenstein was born to an impoverished but noble Czech Protestant family in 1583. He converted to Catholicism in 1608 and married a rich widow whose estates in Moravia served as the first step on his stairway to power. He raised troops and fought for Emperor Ferdinand in the Bohemian revolt (1618–1620). Duly rewarded with the governorship of Bohemia, Wallenstein reaped windfall profits by debasing the coinage in the conquered provinces, profits that he used to purchase the confiscated lands of exiled Protestants. By 1623 he owned a fourth of Bohemia, lived in princely fashion in his castles, and indulged his fascination for astrology. Whereas Katherine Chidley seized the opportunity offered by war to express herself (see page 565), Wallenstein used it to enrich himself.

In 1625 Ferdinand, who wanted an alternative to depending on the Catholic League's army, accepted Wallenstein's offer to raise and command an army in his service. Ferdinand also made the entrepreneur duke of Friedland, a region north of

Bohemia owned mostly by the new duke and his many associates. As commander-in-chief of the imperial army, Wallenstein supplied the troops with food from his estates at prices that he fixed, and he brought skilled German and Italian artisans to Friedland, turning it into a major supplier of armaments. Like Gustavus Adolphus in Sweden, he excelled at exploiting the resources of relatively backward areas to build a military machine that, at its peak, stood as the most powerful in the Holy Roman Empire. He carefully regulated economic affairs in Friedland. Residents even had to drink beer from his breweries, and his private hangman executed the criminals convicted by his private judicial system.

Wallenstein treated Friedlanders and peasants on his estates generously and maintained sufficient discipline in his armies to keep them from plundering his civilians. But civilians off his turf fared badly. As his armies marched up and down Germany, they demanded "contributions" from everyone within reach. Local authorities anxiously read newsletters, trying to guess where the armies were headed so that they could protect themselves by building up stocks of food, fodder, and cash. Indeed, the

early seventeenth century saw the first regularly published newspapers (called corantos, or newsbooks), and this anxiety is one reason for their success. Wallenstein's forces lived quite efficiently off the areas through which they passed: "A more complete and grandiose merger of private commercial and military enterprise had never been seen before—nor since."*

The evidence is too contradictory to permit a firm conclusion about Wallenstein's ultimate goals, or about whether he even had any beyond self-aggrandizement. Some hoped—and many feared—that he would use his military power to unite Germany under his own leadership or at least force a general peace on the emperor. A group of Ferdinand's advisers certainly feared Wallenstein, and they convinced him that the general's negotiations with the Swedes and others were treasonous. Acting on secret orders, mercenaries stabbed Wallenstein to death in 1634. His body was pulled from the room "by the heels, his head knocking upon every stair." ❖

---

* W. H. McNeill, *The Pursuit of Plunder* (Chicago: University of Chicago Press, 1982), p. 121.

Germany by force of arms. Although he regained the support of the Saxon elector, John George, and of other German states by suspending the hated Edict of Restitution, the suspension marked the abandonment of his primary goal of destroying the Protestants in Germany. John George's and Ferdinand's 1635 agreement, the Treaty of Prague, settled the important political and religious issues within the empire. Ferdinand reluctantly retreated from the ultra-Catholic position and thereby signaled his willingness to give up on the reclamation of former church lands that had been taken over by Lutherans and Catholics alike. His more pragmatic advisers had won out over the

zealous Catholics who believed that the "holy war" against the Protestants was winnable. But the related struggle of the French and Dutch against the Spanish and Austrian Habsburgs continued. The Habsburg lands were wracked by war as French and Swedish armies moved into Bavaria and the Swedes threatened Prague and Vienna. Prague was under siege by a Swedish army in 1648 when news arrived of the signing at Münster of the Peace of Westphalia, ending the Thirty Years' War (see Map 15-2).

The presence of a Swedish army around Prague was proof that the Habsburg cause lay in financial ruins. In the 1640s, a series of defeats at Swedish and French hands

Eigentliche Vorbildung vnd Bericht, welcher gestalt der Keyserische General, Hertzog von Friedland, beneben etlich anderen Obristen vnd Officieeren zu Eger Hingerichtet worden, den 15. Febr: 1634.

ALBERTI DVCIS FRIDLANDINI, MILITIÆ CÆSAREANÆ, GENERALISSIMI, ET ALIORVM QVORVNDAM DVCVM ET OFFICIARIORVM cædes, Egræ die 15 Februar anni 1634. patrata.

M. Merian fecit

The Death of Wallenstein   Numerous contemporary broadsheets, such as this one by Matthäus Merian, depicted Wallenstein's murder. They were early "comic strips" telling a story about an event as a series of discrete steps: First the anti-Wallenstein officers sneak into his headquarters at night; then they massacre the pro-Wallenstein officers; then they force their way into Wallenstein's bedchamber and kill him; then they drag his body out. The recognizable forerunner of "the newspaper" appears in these broadsheets.   *The Granger Collection, New York.*

left Habsburg armies and strongholds on the defensive and Habsburg negotiators at Westphalia on the shakiest of grounds. The Westphalia treaty confirmed and extended the "liberties" of the German principalities, thereby ending Habsburg efforts to make Germany Roman Catholic in religion and more centralized in government. But it did more. Ferdinand III, who succeeded his father as Holy Roman emperor upon the latter's death in 1637, understood that the price of peace was compromise with the Protestants. At Westphalia, Calvinists received the same rights as Lutherans, and the Calvinist elector of Brandenburg emerged as an important power. The negotiators at

Westphalia ignored papal threats that Catholic princes who agreed to any cession of church property risked damnation; the treaty even stated that the pope's protests were meaningless. Richelieu and Mazarin had put the secular interests of France above religious dogma, and others followed suit. France made gains in the Rhineland that bolstered its freedom from Habsburg encirclement. This change, and the establishment of the independence of the Swiss cantons (districts) from the empire, cut the "Spanish road" to the Netherlands. The Habsburgs, after eighty years of war, even conceded independence to the Dutch Republic. France and Spain did not finally bury the

Callot's Miséres   Jacques Callot (1592–1635), a French artist, sought to dissuade his countrymen from entering the Thirty Years' War by issuing a series of engravings in 1632 and 1633 depicting the atrocities already suffered in central Europe. In this one, drunken soldiers loot an inn, rape women, and torture people to get them to reveal where they have hidden money and food. Nevertheless, in 1635, the year of Callot's death, Richelieu and Louis XIII entered the fray.   *The Granger Collection, New York.*

hatchet until 1659, however, when the Peace of the Pyrenees completed the dismantling of Spanish power in western Europe.

After Westphalia, Sweden controlled a substantial part of the lands on the Baltic's southern shore, but its neighbors grumbled. In the Little Northern War (1655–1660), Sweden and Brandenburg successfully invaded Poland and captured Warsaw easily. It appeared that Sweden's Charles X would be another "Lion of the North." But the Swedes were stopped by a coalition including Denmark, Russia, and Brandenburg (which switched allegiance), and countries farther away began to take sides. Europe staved off a massive sequel to the Thirty Years' War when the western powers engineered the Peace of Oliva (1660), in which Sweden obtained the remaining Danish provinces in southern Sweden but gave up its efforts to control the entire Baltic. The duchy of (East) Prussia, ruled by the same Hohenzollerns who also were electors of Brandenburg, was freed from Polish overlordship and permanently united with Brandenburg, further strengthening that emerging power. Poland-Lithuania survived largely because of its usefulness as a buffer state between Sweden, Brandenburg-Prussia, and Russia.

The economic and social impact of the Thirty Years' War is difficult to assess. Whether the Thirty Years' War wrought more destruction in human and economic terms than the French civil wars of religion or the first generation of the Dutch revolt is debatable; all these struggles spawned horrendous misery. Regions of strategic importance were hardest hit, yet cities such as Hamburg benefited from high levels of trade in food, uniforms, and armaments. Where armies were most active, civilian populations suffered badly, for troops frequently got out of control. Recruited with promises of bonuses and regular pay, soldiers found that commanders often failed to keep these promises. When on the move, armies looted, living off the land by seizing what they needed or wanted. Many peasants and townspeople lost all they had. When armies were encamped for lengthy periods, the surrounding population had to supply their needs, or have the supplies taken by force. As one historian has noted: "The self-sufficient military world portrayed in the novels of Hans Jakob Christoffel von Grimmelshausen, in which civilians appear almost as visitors from outer space, was created by the imperfect development of the modern state: strong enough to create a modern army, it was still too poor to finance it and too weak to control it."[10] The region around Rothenburg is a good example. In approximately 100 villages that had boasted 1,504 peasant households in 1618, only 447 still existed in 1641. Some of the villages lost all their population. The prewar level of peasant households in the Rothenburg area was not regained until 1700.

CULTURE AND THE STRIVING FOR ABSOLUTISM

Two of the greatest writers of the age, William Shakespeare (1564–1616) and Miguel de Cervantes (1547–1616), died within ten days of each other. They wrote works that fascinated both ordinary people and the educated elite of their

---

[10] Geoffrey Parker, *Europe in Crisis, 1598–1648* (Ithaca, N.Y.: Cornell University Press, 1969), p. 75.

THE HISTORICAL EVIDENCE

The Adventurous Simplicissimus

1669

In 1669, Hans Jakob Christofel von Grimmelshausen (1621–1676) published a novel called The Adventurous Simplicissimus. *His long service in various armies during the Thirty Years' War provided the experience that is recounted in the book. In this episode, the hero Simplicissimus explains how he had set out to find a genial parson whose advice he desired when he came upon a violent scene of a kind that occurred repeatedly in villages all over central Europe during the war.*

I walked toward the village, and when I got there I saw it in flames; a troop of cavalry had just plundered and set it on fire, killed some of the peasants, run off many and captured a few, among them the parson. Oh, my God! How full of trials and tribulations is a man's life?! One misfortune hardly stops before another overtakes us.

The cavalrymen were about to leave, and the parson was led by a rope like a poor sinner and slave. Some were screaming, "Shoot the bastard!" Others wanted money from him. He raised his hands and begged them, for the sake of their souls, to spare him and treat him with Christian mercy—in vain, for one of them rode roughshod over him and hit him with such a wallop over the head that blood trickled down; he collapsed, commended his soul to God, and lay there like a dead dog. The captured peasants didn't fare much better.

When it looked as if these horsemen had lost their minds in their tyrannical cruelty, an armed gang of peasants like an angry swarm of yellow jackets came charging out of the woods. They raised such a ghastly war whoop, attacked so furiously, and fired so savagely that my hair stood on end, for I had never attended this kind of a free-for-all. Nobody's likely to make monkeys out of our peasants from the Spessart or the Vogelsberg region—not the ones from Hesse, Sauerland, or the Black Forest! The horsemen made tracks, not only leaving the stolen cattle behind, but also throwing away the loot as they ran, giving up their prey lest they fall prey to the peasants. Still, a few were captured.

This introductory entertainment almost spoiled my desire to see the world; I thought if this is the way things are, the wilderness is far more attractive. Still, I wanted to hear the parson's explanations, but he was rather faint from his injuries and the beating he had received. He admonished me that he couldn't help or advise me because at present he had been reduced to such a condition, he would soon have to eke out a living as a beggar, and even if I wanted to stay in the woods, he wouldn't be able to give me any help, because, as I could see, his church and parsonage were at that very moment going up in smoke.

Source: From Hans Jakob Christofel von Grimmelshausen, *The Adventures of Simplicius Simplicissimus*, trans. George Schulz-Behrend, 2nd ed. (Columbia, SC.: Camden House, 1993), pp. 21–22.

---

day and have been widely read ever since in translations that carried them far beyond England and Spain. Cervantes, a poor apothecary's son who soldiered for Spain, fought against the Turks at Lepanto in 1571 (see Chapter 13), suffering a wound that cost him the use of his left hand for the rest of his life. Captured by pirates on his way home, he spent nine years in prison awaiting the ransom that permitted his release. His *Don Quixote* (part 1 published 1603, part 2 in 1615) has been called the first modern novel. Don Quixote, a tall, skinny, crazy, but engaging old knight, read chivalric tales so avidly that he came to believe the medieval world still existed. Among his many adventures, he attacked windmills thinking that they were giants and treated prostitutes as fine ladies. His short, fat, and very down-to-earth servant, Sancho Panza, knew real-

ity from illusion but nevertheless attended his master faithfully. Cervantes repeatedly contrasts illusion and reality at the same time that many Spaniards were beginning to face the possibility that their imperial success was itself a fading illusion.

Shakespeare, who grew up in the country town of Stratford-on-Avon in England's midlands, was the son of a maker and seller of gloves, purses, and other soft leather goods. Shakespeare went to London to act and later became part owner of the acting company for which he wrote plays. His characters—such as King Lear, Hamlet, Othello, and Macbeth—and their stories and speeches are among the most vivid and affecting ever told in English. Shakespeare's plays, brimming with hilarious comedy and awesome tragedy, made him wealthy in a country still basking in the glow of the Armada victory, whereas Cervantes died impoverished in a nation in decline. But, no less than that of Cervantes, Shakespeare's power as a dramatist and the durability of his appeal rest on the complex interplay between illusion and reality and the acuteness and profundity of his exploration of human psychology.

Cervantes and Shakespeare died two years before the Thirty Years' War began. Other leading writers during the first half of the seventeenth century had to confront a world torn by even more extensive and intrusive violence—but by no means did all literature concern war. Spain's leading playwright, Pedro Calderón de la Barca (1600–1681), received patronage from the court as well as popular acclaim; many of his plays revolve around traditional values of devotion to the monarch and the church. In 1625, he wrote a play celebrating the capture of Breda, one of Spain's last military victories in the war against the Dutch. Yet one of his best-known plays, *Life Is a Dream* (1635), portrays a prince imprisoned and denied knowledge of his identity because of a prophecy that he would overthrow his father. Despite a happy ending in which the young man convinces his father to restore his liberty and position, the play explores the tension between dreams and reality, illusion and truth, and death and life. Nor did Calderón avoid the consequences of war entirely. The hero of *The Mayor of Zalamea* (1642) is a prosperous peasant who sees his village brutally oppressed by the unruly soldiers billeted there and orders the hanging of their captain.

Opera—a new art form that began around 1600 as an entertainment for monarchs and nobles—even presented some stories in which unsavory characters triumphed. Claudio Monteverdi (1567–1643) began writing his operas for aristocratic courts, but toward the end of his life opera houses open to a paying public emerged in Venice. In his last work, *The Coronation of Poppaea* (1643), Nero and his ambitious lover Poppaea defeat Nero's virtuous wife Octavia and the wise philosopher Seneca, and Poppaea is crowned empress of Rome. Monteverdi and his librettist may well have had a satirical intent, and audiences would certainly have known that Nero and Poppaea later came to bad ends. Nevertheless, evil won out in the short run, a disturbing outcome for conservative moralists no matter how sumptuous and sensuous the music was.

CONCLUSION: BAROQUE ART AND THE EXPERIENCE OF WAR

The early seventeenth century saw the peak of the Baroque style in the arts, a style characterized by exuberant energy and love of dramatic moments pinpointed by vivid use of light and color. Large paintings by Peter Paul Rubens (1577–1640), mostly done for Catholic patrons (see chapter opening illustration) provide good examples. So do many early works by Rembrandt (1606–1669), who worked in Protestant Amsterdam. By 1660 the passions heightened by zeal for religious doctrine had begun to ebb. The declining ideological content of warfare itself partly stemmed from the horrific destruction that characterized the Thirty Years' War. We can detect a changing attitude toward war in the work of such a renowned court painter as Rubens.

Rembrandt's *Blinding of Samson*   In this work painted in the 1630s, Rembrandt illustrated the precise and violent moment when the Philistines blinded Samson. Since the biblical account says nothing about how the deed was done, Rembrandt was free to imagine the scene: a dagger, a soldier gripping a chain around his right wrist, and several others holding him down. The burst of light flooding into the dark tent evokes the stunning visual surprises produced by the designers of operas and plays in the seventeenth century. *1636. Oil on canvas. 79 × 9'11 (2.4 × 3 m). Stadelsches Kunstinstitut, Frankfurt.*

Rubens's *The Horrors of War* This painting reflects the changing attitude toward warfare that was evolving as a reaction to the Thirty Years' War. *Nimattalah/Art Resource, NY.*

Before about 1630, Rubens turned out many examples of the usual paintings showing monarchs and nobles on magnificent warhorses. His work glorified war and celebrated victories. But in 1636, he executed a painting titled *The Horrors of War*, and his description of the work expresses the point eloquently:

> The principle figure is Mars [the god of war], who . . . rushes forth with shield and blood-stained sword, threatening the people with great disaster. He pays little heed to Venus, his mistress, who . . . strives with caresses and embraces to hold him. . . . On the ground, turning her back, lies a woman with a broken lute, representing Harmony, which is incompatible with the discord of War. . . . That grief-stricken woman, clothed in black . . . is the unfortunate Europe, who, for so many years now, has suffered plunder, outrage and misery, which are so injurious to everyone that it is not necessary to go into detail.

Rubens, a Catholic from the southern Netherlands, had served for years not only as a painter but an ambassador for the Habsburg cause. He was not the only person who, as the Thirty Years' War seemed to proceed with no end in view and no outcome except disaster for everyone, began to realize that the cost of religious uniformity might be too high.

The striving for absolutism was nevertheless far from over, and the nation-states emerging from that struggle headed for conflict on a worldwide scale. Spain had a huge overseas empire, but Spain was politically and economically exhausted by the failed effort to regain the United Provinces while supporting the Austrian Habsburg drive to re-Catholicize Germany in the first half of the seventeenth century. Which powers would, in the longer term, be the winners as the struggle for hegemony continued? Would France, having surmounted religious civil wars and laid the foundations of an absolute monarchy, consolidate its position after Louis XIV seized the reins of leadership in 1661? Or would some nations find a way to defend themselves and their national interests without turning over all authority to an absolute monarch? In the aftermath of the treaties of Westphalia and Oliva, the absolutists appeared to be ascending. Was their ascent inevitable, or was there an alternative in the wings?

Selected Reading

Sources

Bonney, Richard, ed. *Society and Government in France under Richelieu and Mazarin, 1624–1661* (1988).

von Grimmelshausen, H. J. C. *Simplicius Simplicissimus*, 2nd ed., trans. G. S. Behrend (1993; original work first published in 1668).

Hobbes, Thomas. *Leviathan*, ed. C. B. MacPherson (1968; original work published in 1651).

Wolfe, Don, ed. *Leveller Manifestoes of the Puritan Revolution* (1944).

General Works

Bonney, Richard. *The European Dynastic States, 1494–1660* (1991). A detailed and up-to-date survey emphasizing the persistence of dynasticism in an era of state-building.

Dickens, A. G., ed. *The Courts of Europe: Politics, Patronage and Royalty, 1400–1800* (1979). Lavishly illustrated essays on the courts of the Austrian Habsburgs, Philip IV of Spain, Charles I of England, and others.

Munck, Thomas. *Seventeenth-Century Europe: State, Conflict and the Social Order in Europe, 1598–1700* (1990). A good survey that covers Scandinavia and east-central and southern Europe as well as the western states.

Parker, Geoffrey. *Europe in Crisis, 1598–1648* (1979). Concise narrative and lucid analysis of political history with an interesting concluding chapter on cultural developments.

Rabb, T. K. *The Struggle for Stability in Early Modern Europe* (1975). An overview of the "general crisis" debate that integrates cultural and intellectual factors into an explanation of the transition from turmoil to tranquillity after 1660.

Topical Studies

Aylmer, G. E. *The Levellers* (1975). A short, clear introduction (with documentary excerpts) to the first democratic political movement in modern history.

Elliott, J. H. *The Count-Duke of Olivares: The Statesman in an Age of Decline* (1988). A masterly biography of a complex man that throws new light not only on Spain but all of western Europe.

———. *Richelieu and Olivares* (1984). A very readable essay that depicts contemporary perceptions of these famous statesmen and analyzes the series of political problems they faced and the choices that they made.

Fraser, Antonia. *The Weaker Vessel* (1984). A detailed description of women's lives in seventeenth-century England.

Hall, Bert S. *Weapons and Warfare in Renaissance Europe* (1997). Analysis of the impact of gunpowder weapons from 1300 to 1600 that stresses the limits as well as the strengths of smooth-bore artillery and small arms.

Ingrao, Charles. *The Habsburg Monarchy, 1618–1815* (1994). Fine brief overview of the growth of Austrian-Habsburg military and cultural power in the early modern period.

Parker, Geoffrey. *The Military Revolution*, 2nd ed. (1996). Explains how western Europe, small and weak at the beginning of the sixteenth century, created the first worldwide empires by 1750.

———. *The Thirty Years' War*, 2nd ed. (1997). Brings together the work of a group of scholars to describe and analyze the huge conflict.

Ranum, Orest. *The Fronde* (1993). A narrative account that treats the Fronde as a revolution.

Roberts, Michael. *Gustavus Adolphus*, 2nd ed. (1992). An engaging short biography of the "Lion of the North" by a leading historian of Sweden.

Rowen, H. H. *The Princes of Orange* (1988). Examines the stadholderate in the Dutch Republic through studies of each of the holders of this important but unusual office from William the Silent to William V at the end of the eighteenth century.

Russell, Conrad. *The Causes of the English Civil War* (1990). A penetrating analysis that emphasized the centrality of the religious views of the members of the political nation in the outbreak of civil war.

Sharpe, Kevin. *The Personal Rule of Charles I* (1992). A richly detailed and sympathetic depiction of the royal reform program of the 1630s and the reasons for its failure in the aftermath of the Scottish rebellion of 1637.

Schama, Simon. *The Embarrassment of Riches* (1987). An innovative and invigorating study of the Dutch people and their culture in the era in which they achieved staggering wealth and power that presented them with acute moral dilemmas.

Treasure, Geoffrey. *Mazarin* (1995). A biography of the statesman who managed to sustain the movement toward absolutism in France during its greatest crisis—the Fronde and the minority of Louis XIV.

Underdown, David. *A Freeborn People* (1996). Stimulating essays on the linkages between popular and elite politics in early Stuart England.

PART FOUR

THE AGE OF REVOLUTION

The era between 1650 and 1850 was a time of revolutionary change. The cumulative impact was more sweeping than anything since the emergence of **civilization** itself (around 4000 B.C.) If today we could step into a time machine that would take us back to 1850 and place us in cities such as Manchester in England, Essen in Germany, or Lyon in France, not to mention London, Berlin, or Paris, we would immediately recognize a world that, although certainly different from our own, was nevertheless recognizably "modern." We would see iron mills, textile factories, railroad stations, daily newspapers, lending libraries, postal stamps, political parties, standing armies clothed in matching uniforms, and well-to-do men sporting another kind of uniform—the dark business suit. Not only would this environment seem familiar to us, we would recognize ideas that frequently came up in discussions of politics, economics, and society: Ideologies such as liberalism, nationalism, and socialism were all hotly debated topics. We would even recognize the idea of revolution itself, which by 1850 had taken on its modern connotation of fundamental social or political upheaval and change.

If our time machine were to take us back to 1650, on the other hand, we would be considerably less familiar with the world we found. If we encountered the idea of revolution at all, it would probably refer to the turning of a wheel back to its previous position, or it would be a metaphor for things being restored to their previous condition. We would meet people who considered themselves subjects of a monarch, not citizens of a nation. Instead of finding ourselves in a culture that espoused the potential equality of people, we would find society stratified into legally defined elements, of which the aristocracy would be politically the most important. In 1650, the term *citizen* referred to certain residents of cities and towns who, as members of recognized and established guilds, had gained the right to trade in clearly defined commodities or to manufacture specific goods. If they ever had occasion to vote, these citizens participated only in the municipal arena, because kings, princes, and noblemen monopolized authority in the great matters of state. The notion of equality, or widespread par-

ticipation in the public sphere, simply did not exist. Recall that in the late 1640s, a group known as the Levellers had asserted in England that ordinary people deserved votes in parliamentary elections, but these ideas seemed so dangerous to contemporaries that the movement was crushed.

The world as it existed in 1650 had changed in many details from what our time machine would have revealed had it taken us back to the beginning of civilization, around 4000 B.C., but in the broadest terms things would still have been comparable. The complex societies of Louis XIV's time, with their villages and cities, their kings and places of worship, and their hierarchy of wealth and status, had their roots in the discovery of agriculture some ten thousand years ago and had come into focus with the ensuing rise of civilization in the ancient Near East. With this Neolithic Revolution had come a sweeping transformation of human society, as people discovered how to extract energy systematically from living things—that is, from plants and animals. Later they learned to make tools and weapons out of a succession of metals—first copper, then bronze (an alloy of copper and tin), and finally iron. But iron metallurgy, which spread throughout Europe, Africa, and Asia beginning about 1200 B.C. (that is, at the start of the Iron Age), represented the last basic technological breakthrough that the world would see for almost three thousand years.

In 1650 (when Part Four begins), the young king of France, Louis XIV, was just starting the longest recorded reign in European history (1643–1715). The French monarchy that he headed was facing a challenge from rebellious nobles and townspeople who were bent on restoring the traditional rights and privileges they believed the state was eroding. The French monarchy faced down this challenge, and when in 1661 Louis became old enough to assert personal control over his government, the effective power of the French state increased again. Even so, compared to the intrusive capacities of modern governments (even democratic ones), Louis XIV's regime had little day-to-day influence over the lives of subjects. His government collected taxes, maintained courts of law, prescribed what religion its subjects could legally practice, and raised armies that were frequently sent to war against Louis's enemies abroad. But the vast majority of the people—in France as well as throughout Europe—still lived in rural villages, worked on the land, and had relatively little to do with a market economy. Kings like Louis XIV had few expectations of them other than paying their taxes and not making trouble.

From the late seventeenth century onward, however, population in Europe (and throughout the world) began to increase, and a more complex economic structure gradually emerged. Fundamental to this economic and social leap was the Industrial Revolution, which began in Great Britain around 1750. This broad group of innovations matched the significance of the Neolithic Revolution. During the Industrial Revolution, humans discovered how to extract vast new amounts of energy from nonliving things, such as coal. The availability of phenomenally rich new sources of energy began a profound transformation of all aspects of society that was clearly visible by 1850 and is still under way. During the era covered by Part Four, urban artisans and former peasants found themselves forced to become wage earners subjected to the discipline of machines and clocks, and a new working class began to emerge that eventually demanded attention in the political process. Women, who had formerly participated in rural and urban household production, also found their lives changed in basic ways.

These changes undermined the traditional social hierarchy, and members of the elite began to react to the challenges threatening their authority and status. Late in the eighteenth century these challenges culminated in the French Revolution, which established the new meaning of the term *revolution*—that of fundamental change rather than of a restoration of things to what they had been. By the time the French Revolution and the ensuing Napoleonic period were over in 1815, the power of most European monarchs and their supporting aristocracies had not been broken—but the French Revolution, along with the American Revolution, put ideas such as popular sovereignty, civil rights, equality of opportunity, and constitutionalism into public discussion. These and related notions eventually changed the way we think about politics just as thoroughly as the Industrial Revolution transformed the way we live and work.

Intellectually, a momentous and radical rethinking of the relationship between humans and the natural world also took place during this period. Earlier, in medieval Europe, intelligent people perceived the world around them as a "Great Chain of Being" that began with God in heaven and extended down through a hierarchy of living things to inanimate stones on the ground. The universe was earth-centered, and nature was regarded as comprehensible through common sense. Spiritual forces and innate qualities had explained how things happened. But

during the sixteenth and seventeenth centuries, beginning with Nicholas Copernicus's assertion that (contrary to appearances) the sun and not the earth was the center around which all the heavenly bodies revolved, a small group of Europeans were rethinking the way the world worked. In the course of this Scientific Revolution, the mental framework or paradigm that European thinkers used to explain natural processes shifted from one based on the abstract "quality" of things to one based on "quantity"—properties that could be analyzed and described using mathematics. This momentous mental shift culminated in the 1680s, when Sir Isaac Newton elaborated the laws of motion and universal gravitation. Newton's work and that of his precursors offered a model for the experimental and mathematical approach to natural phenomena that underlies modern science.

Newton's success in bringing order to the natural world began a new train of thought focused on progress and the future. Change, in other words, was ceasing to be rejected by the intellectual elite as something unnatural, undesirable, and fearful; educated Westerners were coming to embrace change as something normal, beneficial, and hopeful. Although humans had long sought moral and social improvement, heretofore they had usually looked to the past for inspiration. In sixteenth- and seventeenth-century Europe, the perfect and no longer approachable ideal world was perceived to have existed in mythical "golden ages," in the Greek city-states, in the Roman Empire at its peak, or in the early Christian communities. The new view—that science and technology might allow human beings to "conquer" nature—kindled hope that continuing material advance would permit society to create a better world in the future. During the eighteenth century, Western thinkers associated with the movement known as the Enlightenment turned Newton's method into wide-ranging proposals for achieving a perfected society. By 1850, many people—even those who did not belong to the cultural, social, and political elite—had begun to think of ways that such a society might be achieved.

Of course not everyone agreed with the aggressive rationalism of the Enlightenment thinkers. In the early nineteenth century, the Romantic movement sought to revive and defend the roles of feeling and emotion in human life. Nevertheless, the focus on a better future became and has remained a significant aspect of nineteenth- and twentieth-century modernization.

The period from 1650 to 1850 also saw a decisive shift in the West's relationship with societies elsewhere in the world. Europeans had begun exploring the Atlantic coast of Africa in the fifteenth century, and during the sixteenth century they found their way to Asia and the Americas. In the Americas, Spanish and Portuguese conquerors created large colonial empires, in part by unconsciously introducing infectious diseases that decimated the local populations. But in Africa and Asia, Europeans initially were not

able to create similar holdings; instead they entered into already existing trading networks. In the eighteenth and early nineteenth centuries, however, European technological advances—as well as the development of market mechanisms, the creation of profitable Caribbean colonies based on slavery, the profits of the slave trade itself, and the steady advance of mercantile interests in Asia—made the Atlantic-facing states of Europe the world's most powerful force for imperial domination. An indication of this shift was the worldwide character of two major eighteenth-century wars: the War of the Spanish Succession and the Seven Years' War. These wars were fought not only on the continent of Europe, but in Asia, in India, and on the seas of the world. By 1850, the British had almost completed their control of India, Russians and Americans had fulfilled their "manifest destiny" by expanding across Siberia and western North America, the French had established themselves in Indochina, and the Europeans had extracted the first of many humiliating trade and other political concessions from China. Only Japan stood aloof from the expansion of European political and economic intrusions, albeit on the eve of successfully adopting many aspects of the Industrial Revolution.

Part Four brings together a number of details from this period that are of intrinsic interest in their own right—the rule of Louis XIV, for example; the invention of the steam engine; Catherine the Great's enlightened leadership; and the revolt of the silkworkers of Lyon. But behind details such as these lies the cumulative and interlocking impact of the French and Industrial Revolutions. Prepared for by centuries of European developments, enriched by spreading European contacts with the rest of the world, and innovative in their structural and ideological contributions, these Dual Revolutions and the vast number of events that surrounded them, transformed the West. By 1850 an enormous family of changes had already gone a long way toward transmuting the world of 1650 into the world in which we now live.

Hall of Mirrors at Versailles   *Giraudon/Art Resource, NY.*

1661	Louis XIV takes over personal direction of France	1678	John Bunyan's *The Pilgrim's Progress* published	1688	Death of Frederick William, the Great Elector (Brandenburg-Prussia)
1664	Presentation at Louis XIV's court of Molière's *Tartuffe*	1679–1681	The Exclusion Crisis in England	1688	The Glorious Revolution overthrows James II in England
1667	Publication of John Milton's *Paradise Lost*	1682–1725	Peter the Great's reign as tsar of Russia	1697	Peace of Ryswick ends the Nine Years' War
1667–1668	Louis XIV's War of Devolution	1682	Completion of the French court's move to Louis XIV's new palace at Versailles	1700–1721	Great Northern War
1670	Aphra Behn's first play performed in London			1701–1714	War of the Spanish Succession
1672	Fall of Johann de Witt's constitutionalist regime in the Dutch Republic	1683	Ottoman Turks' siege of Vienna	1704	Battle of Blenheim
		1685	Louis XIV revokes the Edict of Nantes	1709	Battle of Poltava

The strivings toward **absolutism** that had dominated European politics since the sixteenth century reached their climax in the years 1660 to 1715. Nowhere was the absolutist ideal more fully realized than in Louis XIV's France. Although even Louis had to compromise with his most influential subjects, his success proved so great that only a huge coalition of his enemies blocked France from dominating Europe. To confirm his dazzling success, Louis built a palace at Versailles outside Paris whose splendor symbolized his political goal, and he styled himself as *Le Roi Soleil* ("the Sun King"). His luminous grandeur was architecturally embodied in the 250-foot-long and 30-foot-wide Hall of Mirrors (shown opposite). Mirrors along the walls opposite the windows projected dazzling light onto the ceiling, decorated with paintings by the great Baroque artist Charles Le Brun depicting the king's achievements heroically as the Labors of Hercules.

A sharp distinction must be drawn between **totalitarianism** of the twentieth century, such as with Adolf Hitler, and seventeenth-century absolutism in Louis XIV. Both exemplify forms of one-man rule, but modern police states have tools (such as radios, telephones, recording devices, and computers) and vast bureaucracies to deploy them that Louis XIV and his counterparts lacked. Dictators can now assert their power at the grassroots level in ways that no one in the seventeenth century could have imagined. The rulers of Prussia and Russia had no bureaucracy at all until the seventeenth century, and the number of French bureaucrats was small at the end of the sixteenth century.

Another way of explaining the difference is to point out that political authority in late medieval Europe was widely dispersed and that central governments were relatively weak. They could not, for example, collect the most lucrative forms of taxation without approval from their representative assemblies (either regional or national). These assemblies, which went under many names (Parliament in England, cortes in Spain, diets in the German-speaking lands, estates in France, and so on), not only controlled direct taxation but usually participated in the making of law. By no means democratic, they consisted for the most part of substantial landowners who had strong incentives to keep their privileges and to represent themselves and their interests, whether or not it suited the monarch and his central government. The problem was that religious, demographic, economic, and military changes occurred in the sixteenth century that placed enormous strain on the ability of governments to maintain internal concord and national security so long as so much power rested in the localities.

The attraction that absolutism held for many Europeans was that it would master the forces that had destroyed the peace of nations and communities since early in the sixteenth century. Surging population growth during the 1500s had caused huge price increases for food, fiber, and fuel, exacerbating social tensions that further complicated the impact of the Protestant Reformation. Germany, France, and the Low Countries suffered religious civil wars, and the same fate was avoided only narrowly in the England of Elizabeth I. Inflation and new kinds of military tactics and organization vastly increased the cost of warfare. Absolutist political theorists argued that the medieval practice of diffusing and localizing the power to make laws, collect revenue, and exercise force was ruinous because it allowed religious minorities and opponents of taxation to prevent the monarch from doing his (or occasionally her) job.

States everywhere either became more centralized or fell victim to the large, professional armies of their more centralized and absolutized neighbors. As central administrations grew stronger, internal order improved. Although local risings broke out, nothing comparable to such major rebellions as those of the Huguenots and Catalans occurred. During the Thirty Years' War (1618–1648), armies had rolled about like loose cannons on a deck, endangering their creators as much as their enemies. But after 1660, they were increasingly brought under control. Medieval constitutionalism, with its fragmented political structure, for the most part gave way to unified states controlled by one man, at least so far as decision making about war and peace and other aspects of high policy were concerned. Except in England and the Dutch Republic, the medieval representative assemblies that survived did so with their powers substantially reduced. The heavy strains that the sixteenth-century changes imposed on the medieval framework convinced many Europeans that unitary sovereignty under an absolute king provided the only solution.

FRANCE: THE ARCHETYPE OF ABSOLUTISM

During the half-century between the deaths of Henry IV (1610) and Cardinal Mazarin (1661), France was led by a

series of royal favorites. But at 7:00 A.M. on the day after Mazarin died, Louis XIV (see Figure 16-1), the twenty-two-year-old king, restored into his own hands the powers long delegated to others. With his 20 million subjects, Louis ruled nearly as many people as lived in England and Wales, the Low Countries, and Germany combined. A century of domestic struggles had undermined the power that should have accompanied the nation's wealth and strength, but Louis meant to rebuild and extend French power and influence. He called the councillors into his presence and told them that henceforward they should do nothing "except by my orders, or without consulting me, unless a secretary of state has brought the documents to be sealed." He then turned to the secretaries of state and said, "I order you to sign nothing, not even a letter of protection or a passport, without my command; to render your accounts to me personally each day; and to show favor to no one in your monthly reports. . . . The scene has changed."

It is one thing to announce a dramatic change of scene and another to effect it, but Louis, with his tremendous energy and confidence, proved a man of his word. Equally important, the work of Henry IV, Richelieu, Mazarin, and

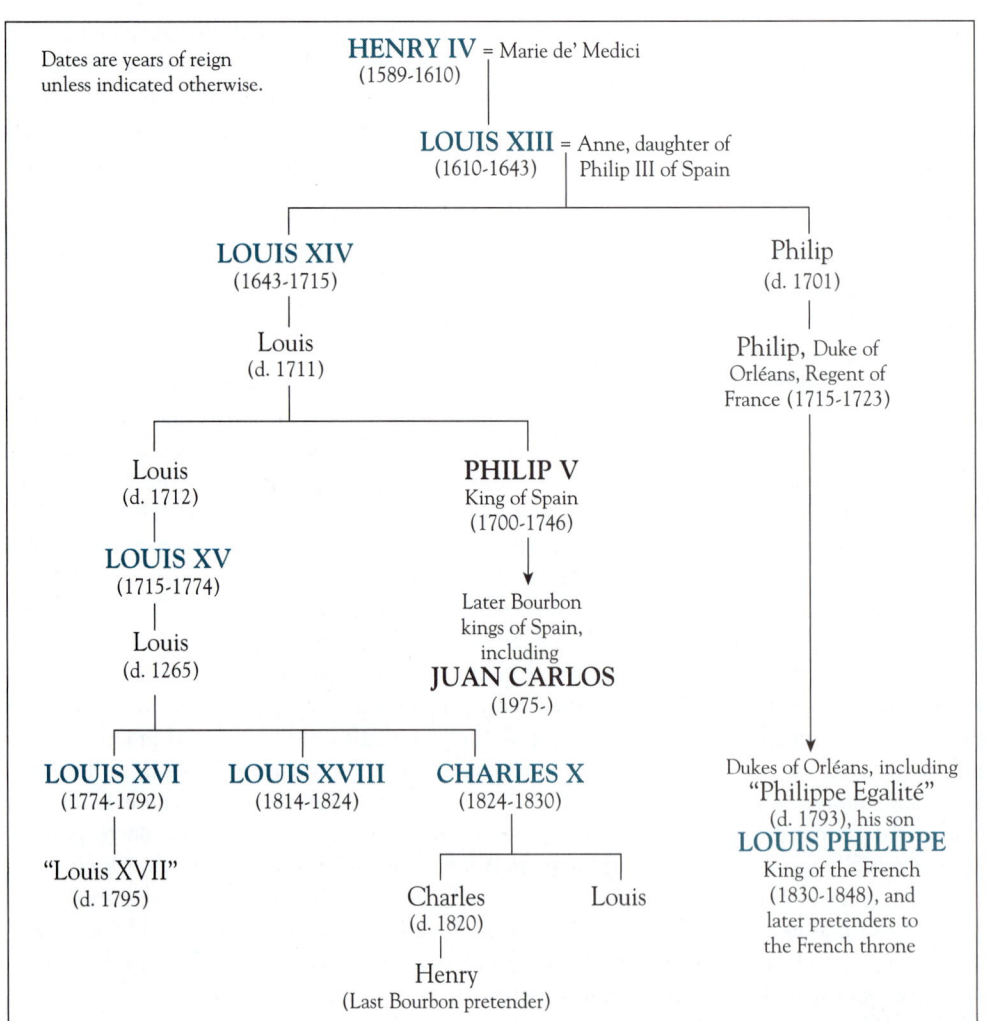

FIGURE 16-1
THE BOURBON DYNASTY

others had given him the necessary tools. Like Philip II of Spain, Louis had the stamina and will to work long, hard days on matters of state, but he devoted himself to the greatness of the French state, not to the success of the Catholic Reformation. Mazarin, Louis's tutor in statecraft, wrote to him that "God has given you all the qualities of greatness. . . . You must put them to use. . . . You owe your God and your *Gloire* [glory, fame]." Louis did his best, and it cannot be denied that he put his stamp not only upon France but upon Europe as a whole.

Warfare in the Age of Absolutism

Military weapons, tactics, and organization underwent an enormously expensive transformation in the latter half of seventeenth-century Europe, a transformation that shaped Louis XIV's state-building enterprise. What Louis did in France would, in turn, become the model for the rest of Europe. One part of the change was army size. At Rocroi in 1643, a big battle for its time, a total of 60,000 French and Spanish troops fought each other. At Malplaquet in 1709, however, 80,000 Frenchmen resisted 110,000 opponents. Gustavus Adolphus's entire army consisted of 30,000 men in 1631, whereas his successor Charles XII commanded 111,000 (5 percent of Sweden's population). As early as the 1660s, Louis XIV had an army larger than any in Europe since that of the Roman Empire. Yet these striking increases in army size occurred during a period when European population remained stagnant.

Between 1660 and 1720, however, the increase in the size of military forces was merely one change among many in the nature of warfare. After the Middle Ages, in the years between 1470 and 1530, warfare in Europe underwent its first period of dramatic innovation when gunpowder weapons were introduced to armies and navies and a new style of fortification, the *trace italienne*, spread widely (see Chapter 12). Although important tactical developments occurred after 1530, the next group of substantial changes came between 1660 and 1720. Louis XIV's innovations included standardized uniforms beginning in 1670, one of several ways in which greater uniformity in training and equipment was pursued. The standard weaponry of soldiers came to include three important novelties: flintlock muskets, pre-packaged cartridges, and socket bayonets.

Flintlocks were more expensive, but they were light enough to fire without the rest (stand) that heavy matchlock muskets had required. When used with cartridges packed in advance with premeasured portions of gunpowder, flintlocks could be fired nearly twice as fast as matchlocks. Well-trained men could get off three rounds a minute. Moreover, the introduction of the bayonet meant that infantry could consist entirely of musketeers, instead of a mixture of musketeers and pikemen (whose job was to protect the musketeers while they were reloading). With their bayonets, soldiers could fight against either cavalry or other infantry in close action. Pikemen disappeared from European armies in the decades around 1700, and the cavalry's part in battles began to decline as well.

Battle of Scheveningen
The Dutch and English navies fought each other in a series of three naval wars, the first of which raged from 1652–1654. This painting by W. W. Van de Velde depicts the fight off Scheveningen in August, 1653, in which the Dutch commander was killed and eleven ships and four thousand men were lost. At this time, the English navy had fourteen first-rates (warships mounting one hundred or more cannon) that had the same or greater firepower than the best-armed Dutch naval vessel. Defeats during this war forced the Dutch to undertake a costly naval building campaign.
National Maritime Museum, Greenwich, England.

The proportion of infantrymen and the artillerymen who supported them went up, and the number of cavalrymen went down. Because even the new muskets were not very accurate, training and tactics sought to maximize impact through the firing of volleys by men standing close together.

Increase in numbers and concentrated firepower also characterized the innovations in European navies after 1660. For example, the French navy had 760 cannon in 1661 and nearly 9,000 in 1700. Merchant ships, usually armed with relatively light artillery and widely used in naval warfare before the 1670s, gave way to increasing numbers of two-decker ships-of-the-line with cast-iron cannon able to fire balls more than twice as heavy. The Dutch, quickly followed by the English in the middle of the seventeenth century, introduced "line-ahead tactics" to European waters, meaning that they sailed in single file to engage the enemy. This maximized their firepower, as opposed to the older melee in which they might be able to use only some of their guns in order to avoid hitting their compatriots. For both armies and navies, the period witnessed greater professionalization of military men and training and the disappearance of forces not in the pay and under the control of the state. In other words, Louis XIV and his counterparts elsewhere controlled appointments of army and navy officers to a much greater extent than their predecessors had.

More firepower and heavy artillery on land and on sea required massive investment not only in the weapons themselves but also in the training of men to make effective use of them—and the ability of princes to find the money to make such enormous investments was the key to

military success after the mid-seventeenth century. Behind the changes in technology, tactics, and strategy lay a vital sociopolitical shift. Since the Reformation, European states had been divided internally no less than externally by religious discord and efforts by aristocrats to retain their traditional "liberties." But historian Jeremy Black has contended that "the seventeenth century witnessed a reknitting of the relationship" between monarchs and "significant sections of the elite across much of Europe," a reconciliation that brought "new political stability to many states, including, crucially, France, Austria and, from 1689, England."[1] Political stability, in other words, explains changes in the nature of warfare, not technology considered as an independent variable.

Versailles and the Royal Image

Absolutist monarchs fully appreciated the need for awe-inspiring settings in which to impress subjects and foreigners. The most celebrated example of this architectural trumpeting of power is Louis XIV's vast palace, built on the site of an old royal hunting lodge at Versailles. The "Sun King" could not be satisfied with the dwellings of his predecessors. In the 1670s, he employed thirty thousand workers to create at Versailles a magnificent chateau surrounded by enormous formal gardens. Fountains and buildings formed a carefully planned Baroque masterpiece of

[1] From Jeremy Black, *European Warfare* (New Haven: Yale University Press, 1994), p. 89.

The Salon of Mars at Versailles The Salon of Mars (the Roman god of war) was the largest of the suite of rooms known as the "Grand Apartments of the King." Over the fireplace, the sculpture of Louis XIV (in Roman dress like Julius Caesar) is titled "Louis XIV Victorious Over the Enemies of France." Louis's contemporaries clearly perceived the political statement being made. So powerful a king needed no such defenses as moats and fortifications. He opened the Gardens at Versailles and other residences to the public so long as they were "decently dressed." *Giraudon/Art Resource, NY.*

THE HUMAN EXPERIENCE

Madame de Sévigné, Passionate Letter Writer

Marie de Rabutin-Chantal (1626–1696), who became the Marquise de Sévigné when she married Henri de Sévigné in 1644, was an aristocrat born in Paris in a house in the fashionable Place des Vosges. Seven years after their marriage, her husband died following a duel over one of several women he had spent much of his time chasing. Although intelligent, warm-hearted, beautiful, and wealthy, Madame de Sévigné never remarried. She was devoted to her son and especially her daughter, Françoise-Marguerite, who married a Provençal nobleman, the Comte de Grignan, in 1669. It is to his appointment as governor of Provence that we owe her massive correspondence. Although the comtesse, her daughter, remained in Paris until after the birth of her first child in 1671, she then joined her husband in his distant province. This was the first of many lengthy separations, and Madame de Sévigné spent the rest of her life writing the vivid letters that eased the pain of distance between her and her beloved daughter.

Madame de Sévigné wrote about everything that she saw and felt, and her 1,372 letters offer fascinating insights into the age of Louis XIV from the point of view of a well-educated and well-connected noblewoman. She knew the king personally, as well as his family, his mistresses, and his courtiers. Although she did not live at the royal court, she visited frequently, socialized with many who did live

there, and on at least one occasion danced with Louis himself. She admired the king but nevertheless passed on a great deal of gossip. She took wry pleasure in describing the humorous side of courtly life. At one solemn ceremony at Versailles, for example, she told how one participant could not seem to get his wig on straight, while two others "got caught up in each other so furiously—swords, ribbons, lace, all the tinsel, everything got so mixed up, tangled, involved, all the little hooks were so perfectly hooked up with each other that no human hand could separate them. . . . In short, the whole ceremony, all the bowings, the whole performance having come to a halt, they had to be torn apart, and the strongest won."

Madame de Sévigné reported the latest rumors about Louis's love affairs, as well as other news. When the king permitted the Chevalier de Lorraine, the lover of his homosexual brother ("Monsieur"), to return to the court, she noted that "feelings vary in Monsieur's circle. Some have faces half a foot long, others equally shortened." After Louis's nineteen-year-old son ("Monsieur Le Dauphin") initially failed to consummate his marriage, she wrote that the king "instructed Monsieur Le Dauphin about everything he had to do, and gave him a sort of geography lesson with which he highly diverted the courtiers." Those and other stories were for amusement: "Take care not to answer all this gossip," wrote

Madame de Sévigné. "Alas, dear child, in three weeks time I shall have forgotten all about it myself."

Madame de Sévigné's close friends included such writers as La Rochefoucauld and Madeleine de Scudéry. When she described the touching love of one of Louis's illegitimate daughters for a young nobleman, a relationship that Louis encouraged and delighted in, she said "They are in love like characters in a novel." She saw plays, read continuously in classical and modern authors (Pascal, Montaigne, Rabelais, Corneille, Racine, Molière), and made shrewd comments on what she read. Her letters contain thoughtful reflections on people, religion, truth, friendship, life, death, and the passage of time. When her daughter mentioned that she was "frightened of great minds," Madame de Sévigné responded, "Alas, my dear, if you realized how awkward they sometimes are, you would soon cut them down to a reasonable size." She knew herself: "God wills that there must be some periods difficult to live through; one must try by submitting to His will to atone for an excessive regard for others than Him. Nobody could be more guilty of that than I am." She was thinking of her adoration of her daughter, which even she described as idolatrous. She ended her letters with endearments such as "Good-bye, sweet child." Yet her love for the comtesse led her to create a timeless literary monument. ❖

arches, colonnades, apartments, and huge reception halls lavishly decorated with chandeliers, tapestries, and huge mirrors. To Versailles, 10 miles distant from the crowds and noise of Paris, Louis moved most of his government offices and the entire royal court.

It used to be thought that Versailles was Louis's means to keep the great nobles under his eye and his control. The

Duke of Saint-Simon (1675–1755), himself a courtier who knew Versailles well, described how Louis strolled through the palace and gardens, systematically noticing "the absences of those who were always at court. . . . It was a demerit . . . for all those who were the most distinguished, not to make the court their habitual residence." If a noble who failed to show such dedication was proposed for an

THE HISTORICAL EVIDENCE

Bishop Bossuet on the Divine Right of Kings

1679

Jacques-Bénigne Bossuet (1627–1704), a famous preacher appointed by Louis XIV to direct his heir's education, wrote extensively on theological issues and did not hesitate to confront Louis himself about such moral lapses as his marital infidelities. The following excerpts are from his influential discussion of the origins and nature of royal authority. Note that although he held that kings held their office by divine right, they should use their powers to benefit their subjects. The king's government, he insisted, must be absolute but not arbitrary.

Monarchy is the most common, the most ancient and also the most natural form of government. The children of Israel spontaneously adopted the kingship, as being the form of government universally accepted. . . . Moreover this form of government was so much the most natural, that it was the earliest found in every nation. . . . Men are all born subjects: and paternal authority, which accustoms them to obedience, at the same time teaches them to have but one head. . . . Monarchical government is the best form. If it is the most natural, it is therefore the most enduring, and in consequence the strongest form of government. It is also the best defense against division, which is the deadliest disease of states, and the most certain cause of their downfall. . . . Kings should respect their powers and only employ them for the general good. Since their power comes from above, . . . they should not believe that they are masters of it and may use it just as they please; they should exercise it with fear and restraint, as a thing conferred on them by God, for which they are answerable to Him. . . . Kings should therefore tremble to exercise the power which God has given to them, and remember how terrible a sacrilege it is to abuse the power which comes from God. . . . What blasphemy and presumption it is for an unjust ruler to occupy the throne of God and give judgments contrary to His law, to wield the sword which He has placed in their hands to oppress and destroy his Children! They should therefore have regard for their power, for it is not theirs, but God's, to be used righteously and in fear. . . . [They should govern] as God himself governs, nobly, impartially, benevolently; in a word, divinely.

Source: From Andrew Lossky, ed., *The Seventeenth Century*, vol. 7, *Sources in Western Civilization* (New York: Free Press, 1967), pp. 221, 224, 225.

office or favor, Louis always rejected him. However, the king had achieved his conquest of the magnates before 1682, the year that the move to the new palace was completed. Versailles was not so much a device for controlling rebellious nobles as a symbol of an already completed victory over them.

Versailles provided a fitting context for Louis XIV, who wrote that "as the king is of a rank superior to all other men, he sees things more perfectly than they do, and he ought to trust rather to the inner light than to information which reaches him from the outside. . . . Occupying, so to speak, the place of God, we seem to be sharers of His knowledge as well as of his authority." Louis understood fully, however, that his decision-making process required information from worldly sources. He advised his son about the necessity of "keeping an eye on the whole earth, of constantly learning the news of all the provinces and of all the nations, the secrets of all the courts, . . . of being informed of an infinite number of things that we are pre-

sumed to ignore, of seeing around us what is hidden from us with the greatest care." In theory, then, Louis wanted to know everything, and he also believed that he owned everything. He wrote that "kings are absolute lords, and from their nature we have full and free disposal of all property both secular and ecclesiastical," but the cost of Versailles nevertheless so horrified him that he had the architect's accounts burned.

In building Versailles, Louis sought primarily to display his own glory rather than ensure the comfort of the thousands of people cooped up there. When an architect mentioned that some of the chimneys were so short that the fireplaces would smoke, Louis replied that they would have to smoke, for he would not have the chimneys seen from the gardens. The etiquette expected of courtiers was as precise as it was stifling. The day began and ended in the royal bedchamber, strategically located at the center of the palace. Courtiers attended the king with elaborate ceremony from the moment he was awakened at 8:30 A.M. until he returned to bed at 12:30 or 1:00 A.M. To hand him his shirt or hold a candle for him was a great honor. His chamber pot was removed by two sword-carrying gentlemen dressed in black velvet. People not only were forbidden to turn their backs on Louis, they could not even turn their backs on his portrait. Courtiers and servants had to bow low to the king's dinner if they encountered it being carried from the kitchens, and woe to the person who sat down in the presence of any unseated courtier of higher rank. Louis had an eagle eye for any breach of etiquette. When his brother helped himself to a dish before the king had done so, Louis intoned, "I perceive that you are no better able to control your hands than your tongue." Despite his ceremonial and work schedule, Louis nevertheless managed to carry on numerous love affairs, and he took good care of the children his mistresses bore by legitimizing them and

Louis XIV At a height of 5 feet 3 inches, Louis benefited from his wig and the high heels that he wore along with his coronation robes in this portrait, painted around 1700. The ballet-like pose recalls the king's famed skill as a dancer, and the aging face contrasts with youthful legs. He wears the medieval sword of justice, but carries his scepter more like a gentleman's cane than a regal symbol. Louis liked this painting by Hyacinthe Rigaud so much that he had several copies of it made. *Scala/Art Resource, NY.*

advancing their careers. Of the eight children borne by one mistress, for example, three of the four who reached adulthood married into princely families.

In the chapel, noted one observer, "the great persons of the nation assemble each day . . . their backs turned to the priest and the holy mysteries, their faces lifted towards their king who is seen kneeling in a gallery." Only Louis faced the altar, as if while he was worshiping God, the assembled throng was to worship him. The elaborate court ceremonies and the etiquette that accompanied them formed a vital part of an **ideology** of royal power, an ideology that distanced the king from his subjects and displayed his authority in everyday behavior no less than in the high councils where law was made and war and diplomacy planned and directed. Louis's calculated "magnificence," as historian Peter Burke has written, was thought by contemporaries "to be impressive, in the literal sense of leaving an 'impression' on the viewers like a stamp on a piece of wax."[2]

Louis enlisted the arts to advertise his power, and he took enormous interest in all forms of visual and textual propaganda. Throughout his long reign, a veritable army of writers, artists, and artisans produced medals, statues, coins, plays, speeches, sermons, poems, engravings, books, periodicals, dances, pageants, tapestries, paintings, sculptures, music, buildings, gardens, and even scientific experiments and demonstrations to project the image of Louis that he wanted both his subjects and foreigners to see and accept. These productions identified him with the heroic monarchs of antiquity (Alexander, Augustus, Constantine, Justinian), the church (Solomon, Theodosius), and medieval France (Charlemagne, Clovis, St. Louis). More than three hundred statutes and paintings of Louis still exist, although many of the statues were destroyed during the French Revolution. One equestrian statue was so huge that twenty men ate lunch inside the horse while it was being placed in the Place Louis-le-Grand in Paris. To be sure, monarchs had long sought to impress people in these ways, but Louis went about it more lavishly, ambitiously, and systematically than anyone before him.

The Machinery of Centralization

Louis XIV clearly had the personal qualities and the exalted sense of his own role to play the part of absolute monarch to perfection. Even the waspish Saint-Simon regularly praised the king's skill in such matters: "Louis made everything precious by discernment and stateliness. . . . Never was a man so naturally polite. . . . His bows . . . had an incomparable grace . . . down to his very manner of getting halfway up at the supper table" at the arrival of each lady entitled to sit in his presence. Louis could not,

---

[2] From Peter Burke, *The Fabrication of Louis XIV* (New Haven, Conn.: Yale University Press, 1992), p. 5.

however, have succeeded if Henry IV, Richelieu, and Mazarin had not established the monarch's power to raise taxes arbitrarily, the administrative machinery to collect the taxes, and a dependable army to enforce the collection of taxes.

In the early part of his reign, antitax rebellions broke out, requiring Louis to dispatch soldiers that he would rather have used on foreign campaigns. Nevertheless, he always succeeded in squelching resisters to his taxes and to his other harsh measures. The last and most serious of the tax rebellions exploded in Brittany in 1675, where rebels protested new charges on tobacco, pewter, and stamped paper (required for certain documents), as well as the long-established tax on salt. One group of the rebels produced a "Peasant Code" that included such demands as "that it is forbidden, on pain of being hanged from a gibbet, to give shelter to the salt-tax collector and to his children, and to provide them with food or any other goods; on the contrary, it is prescribed that they be tormented as if by a mad dog." Madame de Sévigné, a court lady whose voluminous letters are a major source for the period, described the government's punishment of one of the leading rebels: He was "broken on the wheel . . . quartered after his death, and his four quarters were displayed at the four quarters of the town."

One reason for Louis's success in these matters was that he managed to pay his soldiers—no French version of Wallenstein (see Chapter 15) broke loose on the deck of Louis's ship of state. Those provincial estates that still functioned voted the taxes that Louis demanded, although at times the government had to banish recalcitrant representatives to some faraway corner of France in order to get the money. In 1673 Louis ordered a still tighter restriction of the power of the **parlements** to delay enforcement of royal legislation; they could, he decided, remonstrate *after* registering his edicts, not, as had been the case, *before*. Provincial and central authority in France—and elsewhere—seesawed. When the royal government was weak, the regions grew strong. Louis's predecessors had tipped the balance toward the center, and during his reign the centralizing process advanced farther than ever before.

In the provinces, one of the keys to the new administrative order were the intendants (see Chapter 15). By the 1680s, all of France was broken into districts (*généralités*), each with an intendant and his steadily expanding staff. Unlike most officeholders, the intendants had not purchased their posts and could be removed if their performance disappointed the monarch. They could not ignore traditional local authorities, and much of their work proceeded through negotiations with provincial governors, nobles, town councillors, judges, and others. But the intendants had broad (if vaguely defined) powers over such vital matters as justice, tax assessment and collection, maintenance of public order, and military organization. As a result, they usually negotiated from a position of strength.

In what nostalgic nobles and burghers fondly remembered as the "good old days," the efforts of an arrogant royal official in a province could often be thwarted by direct appeal to the king's court. Louis XIV, however, streamlined the central administration to which the intendants reported. His High Council (*Conseil d'en Haut*) consisted of only three to five members, most of whom served for long periods. This body supervised several smaller councils, and its powerful ministers ensured that the policies were carried out. Louis's chancellor and controller-general oversaw judicial and financial matters, while four secretaries of state looked after war, the royal household, the navy, and foreign relations.

The army provides the best example of what could be achieved under a more centralized administration. Not only did it expand dramatically (thirty thousand in 1659; 97,000 in 1666; 400,000 in 1705), but it was also transformed into a standing, permanent force thoroughly under royal control. Before this transformation, most European armies combined mercenary units with other soldiers recruited, equipped, and led by nobles. Such armies were poorly coordinated and difficult to control both on and off the battlefield. Michel LeTellier (1603–1685) and his son the Marquis of Louvois (1641–1691), who succeeded him as secretary of state for war, carried out the basic reforms. Paying meticulous attention to detail, they constructed a civilian bureaucracy that handled virtually all logistical matters (supply, housing, uniforms, weapons, and pay). Private armies, like that of the Prince de Condé, which had opposed the monarchy during the Fronde, ceased to exist. With them went the political independence of the nobility, at least for the duration of Louis's reign.

Colbert: The Money Man

The work of LeTellier and Louvois made Louis XIV more powerful than his predecessors, but wartime levels of taxation had to be kept high to pay for this power even in peacetime. Jean-Baptiste Colbert (1619–1683) served as Louis's chief adviser in economic and financial matters. Between 1560 and 1690, the yield of taxes in France, after adjustment for inflation, quadrupled, and Colbert's contribution to this increase was significant. As controller-general, he managed, amazingly, to double net royal income between 1661 and 1672.

Colbert, like advocates of **mercantilism** before him, attempted to use the government's regulatory powers to promote trade, especially overseas trade, and economic development generally. He sponsored efforts to explore and establish colonial settlements in North America (French Canada—Quebec and Montreal—and the Mississippi Valley). In 1682, a French explorer made his way south from Quebec and claimed for his king the huge territory that he named Louisiana. Colbert pursued mercantilist policies with great diligence and thoroughness: more

THE HISTORICAL EVIDENCE

The Recruitment of Soldiers in France

1711

A French priest who wrote extensively on the details of life in his town of Angers in northwestern France described the methods used to find soldiers for Louis XIV's armies during the War of the Spanish Succession.

On 9 March the parishes brought their militiamen to the Town Hall. These militiamen were unmarried youths from each parish in the diocese. . . . Those who drew the lot were obliged to go to war on behalf of all the lads in their parish, and they each received a bounty [small cash payment] from the other lads, . . . depending on the numbers. The larger parishes furnished two, three, even four men. You have never seen greater sorrow in the parishes given the treatment which is meted out to them on the march. They are bound and chained like veritable animals, and treated even more shamefully. They are chained two by two, four by four and, when they arrive in each town or village, they are housed in barns and stables, sleep on straw, still chained, and guarded by armed townsmen. They die in considerable numbers, or desert when the opportunity presents itself. . . . The families of these young men are dev-

astated, but also responsible for their sons who they must hand over to the captains dead or alive. It is this which empties the parishes of young men and which makes cultivation difficult since, at the time of the [selection of militiamen], the young men take flight and wander here and there. But their fathers and mothers remain responsible, and this results in their having to purchase militiamen in the absence of the sons. . . . You never see so many peasants marry as in time of war, so as to escape the army.

Source: From René Lehoreau, *Cérémonial de l'Église d'Angers 1692–1721*, ed. F. Lebrun (Paris, 1967, p. 205), trans. Clive Emsley, in Margaret Lucille Kekewich, ed., *Princes and Peoples: France and the British Isles, 1620–1714: An Anthology of Primary Sources* (Manchester, England: Manchester University Press, 1994), selection 43.

public works, improved transportation, more subsidies for selected industries, creation of monopolistic overseas trading companies, reduction of internal customs, high tariffs against foreign competitors, closely detailed regulation of the quantity and quality of manufactured goods, and strong government support for the expansion of both the merchant marine and the navy. Indeed, Colbert made France a leading naval power. Henry IV's navy had consisted of a dozen galleys in the Mediterranean; at the time of Colbert's death in 1683, France had 176 warships in service and more under construction. Commercially, Colbert strove to increase the value of French exports while discouraging imports of manufactured goods, and, more basically, to strengthen the economy so that taxation would yield more revenue to the king. "Commerce," Colbert averred, "is a perpetual and peaceable war of wit and energy among all nations."

Colbert's efforts did help to establish French products in international markets and to burnish the reputation of its luxury goods—fine tapestries, silks, lace, carpets, and glassware. He set up a bureaucracy of inspectors to maintain and enhance quality in these products, a useful innovation at a time when such goods were produced by hand rather than by machine. The government inspector's seal signified excellence to distant buyers. Yet this system had

disadvantages. The inspectorate was financed by fees paid by producers. To pay the fees, they had to raise their prices, thus becoming less competitive. Some paid bribes to get substandard goods approved and thus undermined confidence in the seal of excellence.

Colbert's emphasis on luxury goods had limited value in the long run because the market for them was relatively small. What the French economy most needed was to invest in the improvement of agricultural production. The vast majority of French people worked on the land; heightened production would increase their incomes, and in turn demand for manufacturers and tax revenues would grow. Yet government policy discouraged the only people who possessed capital from investing in land. Nobles and churchmen were exempt from the taille, a direct tax on agricultural income paid mainly by peasants. Wealthy merchants frequently purchased offices in order to get the noble status and exemption from the taille that came with it. Because the taille was the principal source of royal revenue, the government wanted to leave as much land as possible in the hands of people who had to pay the tax. This system encouraged the preservation of small, inefficient farms, a problem in French agriculture even today. In England and Holland, by contrast, landowners paid direct taxes, and they bought and improved land.

Louis XIV Visiting the Gobelins Factory
Tapestries helped control the draftiness of palatial dwellings of the wealthy in northern Europe. With his goal of encouraging the manufacture of luxury products within France, Colbert in 1663 made Charles Le Brun director of French tapestrymaking at the Hôtel des Gobelins, after Louis XIV had named Le Brun his "First Painter." Here, Le Brun's design shows the king visiting the factory, which produced not only tapestries but furniture, mirrors, engravings, carpets, and other decorative products. *Giraudon/Art Resource, NY.*

Colbert attempted to control expenses and to reform the financial system. He tried unsuccessfully to dissuade Louis from building Versailles on the grounds that "it is much more concerned with Your Majesty's pleasure and diversion than with your glory." Recognizing that peasants were overtaxed, Colbert lowered the taille by 15 percent and raised indirect taxes on salt, wine, soap, tobacco, and other items. He also tried to reduce the corruption that siphoned off tax money into private pockets before it reached the king. Entrenched privilege, however, prevented Colbert from doing much more than nibbling at the edge of noble tax exemptions. Under the pressure of war his successors went further, introducing an emergency poll tax paid by all Frenchmen in 1695. The peasantry nevertheless remained the most heavily taxed social group. Colbert also recognized that the sale of offices presented a major barrier to the extension of royal power. A man who owned his office was not sufficiently obligated to the king. One of Colbert's most ambitious proposals was a plan to abolish the paulette (see Chapter 15) and repurchase many venal (purchased) offices. Although this reform too fell victim to the expense of war, Colbert's fiscal work underlay all of Louis XIV's achievements.

From the point of view of poorer people in France, the cost of establishing Louis's glory was excessive, as the series of tax revolts demonstrates. In 1715, a humble **parish** priest probably represented many others when he wrote that "Louis XIV, King of France and Navarre, died on September 1st of this year, scarcely regretted by his whole kingdom, on account of the exorbitant sums and heavy taxes he levied on all his subjects. . . . It is not permissible to repeat all the verses, all the songs, or all the unfavorable comments which have been written or said against his memory. . . . Only the moneylenders and tax-collectors were at peace, living joyfully with all of the money of the kingdom in their possession."

Huguenots and Jansenists

If centralization was the goal of Louis's absolutism on the administrative front, uniformity became the goal in religious matters. Although he quarreled repeatedly with the popes, Louis was a devout Catholic, the more so after 1680 as he came increasingly under the influence of his deeply pious mistress (and eventual wife) Madame de Maintenon and her Jesuit friends. With his Edict of Fontainebleau (1685), he revoked the Edict of Nantes (1598), which had guaranteed the Huguenots liberty of worship (see Chapter 13). Stigmatized as adherents of the "so-called Reformed Religion," the Huguenots now suffered official persecution. Their pastors were driven into exile and their worship prohibited. Some intendants pressed the Huguenots to convert by requiring them to house dragoons (mounted musketeers), whose brutal behavior often produced the desired results. Others gave Huguenot women the choice of converting to Catholicism or being consigned to Catholic convents. One intendant reported that "the women and girls of the pretended reformed religion feared the convents more than the dragoons, and many whom the latter had not been able to convert were now converted because they could not overcome their aversion to convents." More than two hundred thousand Huguenots emigrated to the Dutch Republic, Brandenburg-Prussia, England, Scandinavia, and the New World (including South Carolina and

Le Nain's *The Forge* Louis Le Nain (1593–1648) was one of three brothers, all of whom painted realistic scenes that depicted French peasants and artisans with gravity and compassion. The peasants, although poor, are neither sick nor hungry, and they seem dignified rather than demoralized by their toil. *Giraudon/Art Resource, NY.*

Pennsylvania), taking with them skills that strengthened the economies of France's rivals.

Disputes within France's Catholic majority were more dangerous to Louis than Huguenot opposition. In the 1680s, Louis locked horns with the papacy itself, climaxing a long-simmering feud over the right to collect revenues from vacant bishoprics. This right, known as the *régale*, had long belonged to the crown in some parts of France but not others, and the pope had been resisting Louis's attempt to extend it to all of France. In 1682 Louis pressed the Assembly of the Clergy to approve four articles that weakened the pope's power over the church in France. The pope responded by refusing to promote any clergy who had participated in the assembly, while the king refused to put up for promotion any who had not. Although both sides backed down and compromised in order to combine forces against Jansenism, the issue nevertheless remained potent long after Louis's death.

The Jansenists, an influential group among the Catholics to whom Blaise Pascal had belonged (see Chapter 17), presented a different challenge. Like Calvin and like St. Augustine, they emphasized the omnipotence of God, the sinfulness of humankind, and the need for special grace from God to overcome sin and live uprightly. Their acceptance of **predestination**, their sharp criticism of the laxity of Jesuit moral teaching, and their sympathy for the ideals of the Fronde angered Louis. During the last decade of his reign, he joined forces with the pope to suppress the

Jansenists and their ideas, a campaign that provoked a bitter argument with dissident churchmen and the Parlement of Paris. Although Louis's quest for religious uniformity succeeded in suppressing Protestantism, at the same time it exacerbated differences among French Catholics.

The Limits of Absolutism

Although Louis XIV sometimes wrote as if he thought he could know everything and dispose of the property of all his subjects, even he knew better. As he told a foreign ambassador in 1698, "There are certain things I can never do." The persistence of venal office holding, the entrenched privilege of tax-exempt groups, and the continued existence of parlements and some provincial assemblies revealed the limits of Louis XIV's "absolute" power.

In Louis's view, a despot was free of any limitations on his power—and Louis denied that he was a despot, noting his obligation to rule according to God's law. At least implicitly, he acknowledged constitutional limitations on his authority when he did not confiscate private property (such as venal offices) or attempt to abolish parlements and provincial assemblies, however much he might circumscribe their power or apply pressure to make them obey. Infuriated by the resistance of the Parlement of Paris to one of his demands in 1714, Louis cried that he would "make them crawl on their bellies" if they persisted in their dissent. Thousands of troops were billeted in Brittany in 1675 to suppress the antitax rebellion mentioned earlier and to encourage the **Estates** to grant taxes, a repressive measure that quickly produced 3 million livres. The mere threat of billeting achieved similar results in Provence in 1676. It was cheaper to pay what the king asked than be forced to stand by as soldiers seized what they wanted. Violence or the threat of it remained, however, a rarely used last resort.

However "absolute" Louis XIV's government might have appeared to his nervous neighbors, it still relied heavily on traditional mechanisms of **patronage** and the negotiations with privileged groups that patronage entailed. The highest ranking noblemen at court received over half their income from royal offices and payments; they had been not so much tamed as bought. The story in the provinces is similar. In Languedoc in 1677, for example, about a third of the royal taxes collected remained in the hands of the local rulers. French bureaucracy, despite its growth in the seventeenth century, remained too small to get all the work done, and many of its members, because they owned their offices, were imperfect instruments at best. If France had remained at peace Colbert might have been able to repurchase more of the venal offices and make the bureaucracy more effective. But military expenses grew from 30 percent to 70 percent of the budget in wartime, so more money had to be raised by lobbying assemblies, selling offices, raising old taxes and instituting new ones.

Colbert's reforms, such as buying back offices and reducing the tax burden on peasants, could not survive under the pressure of wartime finance, and France was at war almost continuously after 1672. By late in Louis's reign, aristocratic political power was reviving and administrative centralization was unraveling. But the weaknesses and limits of French-style absolutism in the seventeenth century are more apparent to modern historians than they were to most of Louis XIV's fellow princes. In a variety of ways, they tried to follow his example while also making their own innovative efforts to increase their freedom from vested interests. Absolutism was in some ways a will-o'-the-wisp, a system of government always in the making and never completed, although Louis XIV came closer than everyone else except Peter the Great in Russia.

ABSOLUTISTS TO THE EAST

Early in the seventeenth century, Poland-Lithuania and the Ottoman and Holy Roman Empires sprawled over much of central and eastern Europe, but by 1700 these huge, unwieldy entities were losing out to rising dynasties that stayed in power until World War I: the Hohenzollerns of Brandenburg-Prussia, the Austrian Habsburgs, and the Romanovs of Russia. The older powers failed to solve the problems spawned by religious conflict and economic and military change. Their failure created opportunities that their new, more centralized rivals exploited.

East and West differed fundamentally in socioeconomic terms. If one divides Europe by an imaginary line along the Elbe River and down to the Adriatic Sea, the contrast is striking. West of the line, most peasants were free, either working for wages or renting land that they farmed; cities and towns proliferated and commercial activity and productivity thrived. East of the line, peasants were or were becoming serfs, required to work several days a week on the lord's **demesne** to produce grain that he sold in western markets for his own profit. Only a few substantial towns existed. Noblemen and gentlemen, with their vast estates, profited from grain sales to western Europe and were well placed to resist the centralizing efforts of princes. In France the political independence of the nobility slipped during the seventeenth century, but everywhere in eastern Europe except Poland-Lithuania the aristocrats became partners in the construction of absolutist governments.

The Hohenzollerns and the Rise of Prussia

The key to the emergence of Prussia as the most powerful state in northern Germany was the army created by Frederick William, the "Great Elector" (reigned 1640–1688), and enhanced by his talented successors in the Hohenzollern Dynasty. Frederick William inherited the duchies of Brandenburg and Prussia (united only since 1618), but his state consisted of a disjointed cluster of territories. Brandenburg-Prussia, badly mauled in the Thirty Years' War, was virtually landlocked, abysmally poor, and wholly rural. Berlin

THE HISTORICAL EVIDENCE

Brandenburg's Readmission of the Jews

1671

In 1573, Jews in Brandenburg had been forced to leave, such expulsions there as elsewhere in the Holy Roman Empire being a consequence of Luther's attitude toward the Jews as well as continuing hostility from medieval times. The Great Elector, a Calvinist who was educated in Holland, understood the value of expanding trade and issued this edict dated May 21, 1671, which laid out the terms for the return of "fifty families of protected Jews."

We, Friedrich Wilhelm, by Grace of God Margrave in Brandenburg, High Chamberlain and Elector of the Holy Roman Empire, etc., hereby make public announcement and graciously notify all whom it may concern that We . . . have, for the furtherance of trade and traffic, decided to admit a number, to wit, fifty families of Jews from other places into Our Land of Electoral and Mark Brandenburg and most graciously to extend to them Our special protection. We hereby do this, under the following conditions:

1. We declare the admission of the said fifty Jewish families . . . in the following fashion: that they are authorized to settle in the places and towns most convenient to them, and there to hire, buy, or build rooms or whole houses and residences. . . .

2. These Jewish families shall be free to trade and traffic, conformably with Our Edicts, in the whole Land of this Our Electorate . . . to keep open stalls and booths, to sell cloths and similar wares . . . to slaughter in their houses and to sell what is above their needs or forbidden to them by their religion, and finally to seek their subsistence in any place where they live, and . . . like other inhabitants of this Land . . . to sell their wares at the annual and weekly markets. . . .

5. They must submit themselves in civil cases to the jurisdiction of the Burgomaster in charge of each place. . . . But should criminal cases arise among them, these are to be brought immediately to Us. . . .

6. They are not to be permitted to have synagogues of their own, but they may meet in one of their houses and there conduct their prayers and ceremonies, . . . and they are hereby permitted to keep a slaughterer, and a schoolmaster to instruct their children. . . .

9. Insofar now as the above Jews fulfill all the requirements made of them, as above, . . . We will afford them Our gracious protection and patronage for twenty years from the above date, and We also graciously promise, in Our Name and that of Our heirs, if We think fit, to continue this also after the expiration of the said period.

Source: From Mylius, *Corpus Constitutionum Marchiacarum*, vol. 5, chapter 3, trans. C. A. Macartney; in C. A. Macartney, ed., *The Habsburg and Hohenzollern Dynasties in the Seventeenth and Eighteenth Centuries* (New York: Walker, 1970), pp. 259, 260, 261.

had only six thousand people. All that the territories had in common was their ruler, and his authority was strictly limited by local diets dominated by Junkers (lesser nobles). There was no central government.

To rule this unpromising collection of provinces came the twenty-year-old Frederick William, a towering, powerful Calvinist educated in Holland. He had the good fortune to take over at a time when Swedish power was overextended and the Habsburg effort to centralize the Holy Roman Empire was on the verge of defeat. He sought to capitalize on this situation by creating a strong army and using it to defend and extend his lands. But he could not do so without the support of the provincial assemblies with their power over taxation. He persuaded the Junkers to vote him taxes by granting them greater authority over their peasants. The Junkers agreed as well to serve as offi-

cers in his army in return for permission to continue converting their peasants into **serfs.** This alliance with the nobles became the centerpiece of Hohenzollern policy: In return for virtually absolute authority in the countryside, the Junkers cooperated with the ruler's initiatives.

Enserfment of the peasants was Frederick William's carrot, but he also wielded a heavy stick. Using the taxes to build a standing army of eight thousand by 1648 (and thirty thousand by 1688), he was able to suppress any assembly's attempt to withhold taxes. In 1669, he had a young nobleman kidnapped, tortured, and executed, quite against Prussian law, for speaking out against a grant of taxes in the assembly. In Brandenburg, the diet of 1653 made the mistake of giving the elector the right to collect taxes on his own, and it was never summoned again. Urban tax protests were also overridden with the threat of military force, and eventually taxes on townsmen grew even heavier as the Junkers shifted the burden away from their agrarian and industrial activities in rural areas.

Frederick William's success rested on more than the application of force to achieve internal control. He fostered economic growth by encouraging religious refugees—Polish Jews and French Huguenots with their capital and skills—to settle in his dominions, where they enjoyed toleration of their worship (although the Jews had to conduct their services privately and could not build synagogues). The elector established an excellent postal system to link his territories and built a canal that made Berlin an inland port. His wife, who ran an estate that he gave her, introduced the potato to Brandenburg, while he pressed his subjects to pursue his own hobby, tending orchards. Indeed, he decreed that no couple should be allowed to marry before they had grafted branches on six fruit trees and planted six seedlings.

The Great Elector's biggest achievement was his construction of a powerful military system that attracted the energies and services of the landed class. His civilian bureaucracy—created to recruit and supply his army—ultimately became a central administration that ran all his territories. The highest posts in it were reserved for Junkers, and burghers settled for the middle and lower positions. The Junkers, therefore, became partners in the Prussian state, developing a strong loyalty to it that remained an important factor in German history into the twentieth century. At the end of the Great Elector's reign, the standing army contained 3 percent of the population, twice the proportion achieved in Louis XIV's France. As in other absolutist states, ordinary people had to shoulder a tremendous tax burden to maintain the system. But at least they were assured that foreign armies would not lay siege to their towns and burn their villages. They had to work hard, but they could work in peace. And after the horrific destruction of the Thirty Years' War in Germany, this security was a notable improvement.

Although the Great Elector declined to live in the luxurious style set by Louis XIV, his son Frederick I made Berlin into a capital worthy of a renowned monarch. He built chateaux and decorated them in the manner of Versailles, and he established state-supported academies of arts and sciences. Berliners, who numbered some sixty thousand by the early 1700s, began to call their city the Athens on the Spree and swelled with pride in its educational, intellectual, and artistic advances. In 1701, in return for allying with Emperor Leopold I in the War of the Spanish Succession, Frederick was rewarded with the right to crown himself king *in* Prussia—symbolic recognition of the growing prestige of the new state and the Hohenzollern family at its head. Amid all this cultural activity, however, Frederick did not forget his father's first love—the military. In the course of Frederick's reign, the standing army grew from thirty thousand to fifty thousand men.

The Austrian Habsburg Monarchy and the Conquest of the Turks

The Great Elector's counterpart in Austria was Leopold I. A gifted musician, he was Louis XIV's contemporary and bitter enemy, and in 1685, at Schönbrunn outside Vienna, he began building a palace to rival Versailles. Although he and his successor continued to be the Holy Roman emperors, the Thirty Years' War had shown that the empire could be neither centralized nor re-Catholicized. Leopold inherited the family's lands in Austria, Bohemia, and Habsburg Hungary (the small western strip of Hungary not under the Ottomans), and he devoted himself to strengthening his control over and extending them. The diets of his ancestral territories had power over taxes, obvious barriers to centralization.

Although Leopold's predecessors had crushed Protestantism in Austria and Bohemia, Protestants were still numerous in Hungary and determined to defend their

The Siege of Vienna   When the Christian army of 68,000 Polish, Bavarian, Saxon, and Imperial troops commanded by Sobieski arrived, the Ottomans had already made breaches in the walls of Vienna and were on the verge of taking the city. The Christians attacked early on the morning of September 12, 1683. As they poured out of the hills, they looked, wrote one Turk, like "a stream of black pitch." After a day of heavy fighting, the Turks were routed.   *Erich Lessing/Art Resource, NY.*

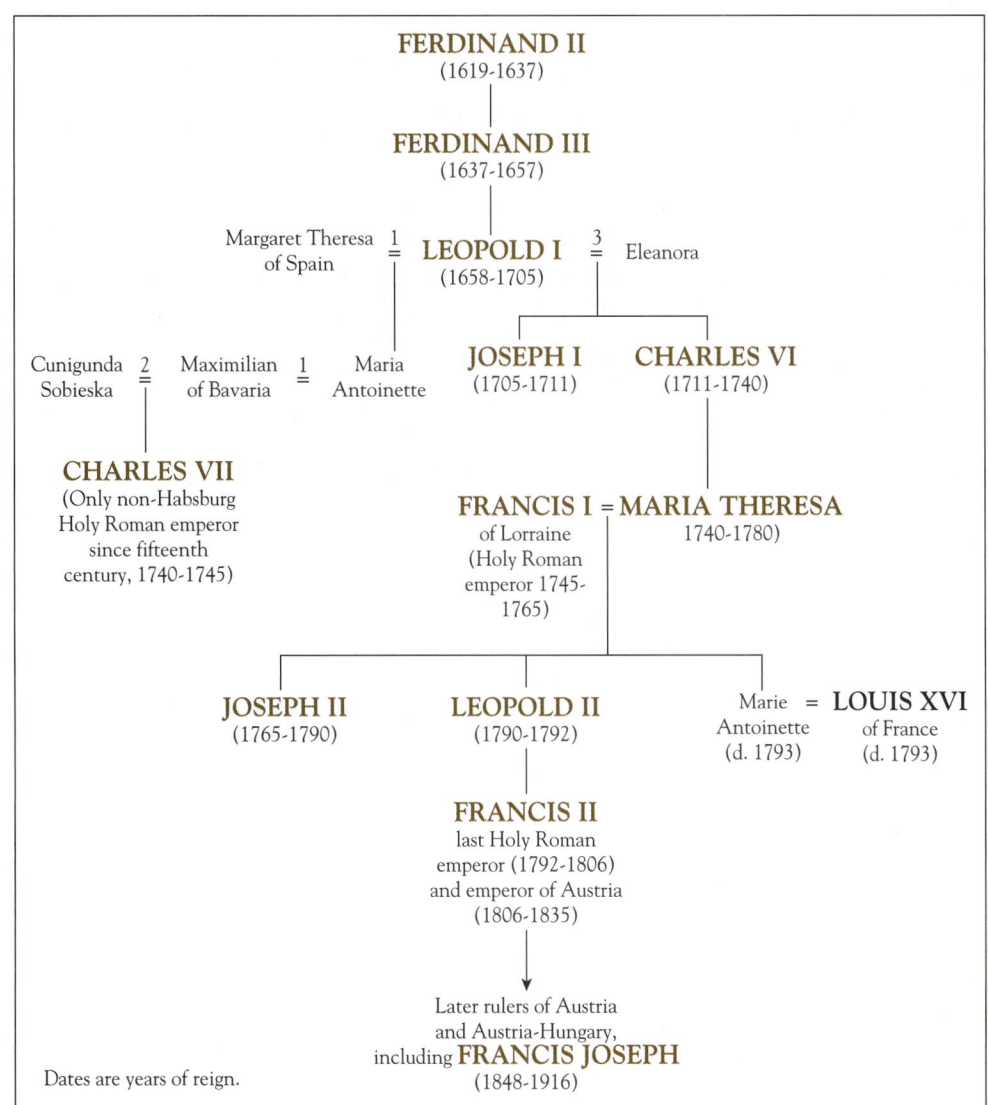

FERDINAND II
(1619-1637)

FERDINAND III
(1637-1657)

Margaret Theresa   1   **LEOPOLD I**   3   Eleanora
of Spain   =   (1658-1705)   =

Cunigunda   2   Maximilian   1   Maria   **JOSEPH I**   **CHARLES VI**
Sobieska   =   of Bavaria   =   Antoinette   (1705-1711)   (1711-1740)

CHARLES VII
(Only non-Habsburg
Holy Roman emperor
since fifteenth
century, 1740-1745)

FRANCIS I = MARIA THERESA
of Lorraine   1740-1780)
(Holy Roman
emperor 1745-
1765)

JOSEPH II   **LEOPOLD II**   Marie   =   **LOUIS XVI**
(1765-1790)   (1790-1792)   Antoinette   of France
                                           (d. 1793)   (d. 1793)

FRANCIS II
last Holy Roman
emperor (1792-1806)
and emperor of Austria
(1806-1835)

Later rulers of Austria
and Austria-Hungary,
including **FRANCIS JOSEPH**
(1848-1916)

Dates are years of reign.

FIGURE 16-2
THE HABSBURG
DYNASTY

liberties, including their religion. Like Louis XIV, Leopold believed in the necessity of religious uniformity. When elected emperor in 1658, Leopold had vowed to uphold religious liberty. After 1670, however, he repressed Protestants in the Habsburg lands by persecuting their pastors, offering them a choice between conversion to Catholicism or enslavement on his galleys. A resulting Protestant rebellion in Hungary, led by Count Imre Thököly, a Calvinist nobleman, forced Leopold to acknowledge traditional constitutional liberties and religious freedom for Protestants in 1681. Unfortunately for the Hungarian Protestants, Thököly then decided to ally with the Ottomans, and their defeat became his as well. Leopold insisted that the Hungarians accept the hereditary succession of the Habsburgs in Hungary and thus yield their centuries-old right to elect their king.

The turning point of Leopold's reign came in 1683. The Ottoman Turks had been pushing the Austrians northward toward Vienna for centuries, and a rapid Ottoman advance forced Leopold to flee Vienna in July. While 100,000 Ottoman troops besieged the capital, Leopold struggled to gather a relief force. The siege itself was brutal: The Austrian commander burned the suburbs in order to deny the enemies cover; the Turks massacred their Christian captives; the Austrians flayed and beheaded the captured Turks. Leopold gained the assistance of Louis XIV's former ally, Jan Sobieski, king of Poland-Lithuania (reigned 1674–1696) and a professional soldier, who led the decisive attack that ended the siege. Using new weaponry, especially the flintlock musket and the bayonet, the Austrians drove the Ottomans out of most of Hungary. After further Austrian victories, spearheaded by Leopold's brilliant general, Prince Eugène of Savoy, the Ottoman government acknowledged the Austrian reconquest of the Danube basin in the Peace of Karlowitz (1699). The goal of one of Leopold's favorite advisers was to "first render Hungary obedient, then destitute, and finally Catholic." Although Leopold never quite succeeded in abolishing Protestantism completely, the land claims of the mostly Protestant Hungarians in the recovered territories were denied and the land turned over to German Catholics, Orthodox Serbs, and other Balkan refugees. These population transfers helped create the tinder for ethnic conflicts that still persist.

For all of his military success, Leopold was never able to govern his subjects in a fully absolutist style. Although he established a centralized civil service at Vienna, the aristocracies of Leopold's ethnically diverse provinces remained powerful. The Habsburgs did not do away with the landowner-dominated diets but reduced their independence, partly by ceding greater control over the peasants to the landowners as the Great Elector had done in Prussia. This heterogeneous assemblage of kingdoms and duchies stayed connected only as a personal union under Leopold and his heirs. The Austrian Empire remained highly cosmopolitan down to the twentieth century, eventually including not only Austrians, Czechs, and Hungarians, but Croats, Serbs, Poles, Romanians, and Italians as well. Not until the end of World War I did most of the nationalities under Habsburg rule achieve independence.

Peter the Great and the Europeanization of Russia

Next to the austere, Calvinist-educated Great Elector and the pious, cautious, Jesuit-educated Leopold I, Peter the Great of Russia presents a sharp contrast. Illiterate until his teens and standing a gigantic 6 feet 7 inches,[3] he was boundlessly energetic, pitilessly cruel, childishly curious, hotheaded, frequently drunk, and always flamboyant. Hating ceremony (especially religious ceremony), he parodied it by forming what he called his "all drunken, maddest and all joking synod." This "synod" had its own prince and pope and was devoted to inebriated rituals performed both privately and publicly. Peter created modern Russia by forcing it to "westernize," and he acquired for his country a prominence in European affairs that it never lost. Even today, Russians remain deeply divided over whether to idealize Peter for turning their country westward or to curse

---

[3] In premodern times when the children of ordinary folk—and often the elites as well—lived on inadequate diets, human growth must have been by our standards severely stunted. (Recall that Louis XIV's adult height was 5 feet 3 inches.) Records of conscripted soldiers from the late seventeenth and early eighteenth centuries suggest that grown men 6 feet tall were uncommon; Peter the Great would have seemed enormous.

FIGURE 16-3
THE ROMANOV DYNASTY

MICHAEL ROMANOV
first Romanov tsar
(1613-1645)

Maria $\overset{1}{=}$ **ALEXEI** $\overset{2}{=}$ Natalia Nareshkin
(1645-1676)

Sophia, Regent of Russia, (1682-1689)

FEODOR III (1676-1682)

IVAN V (1682-1689) (co-tsar with Peter I)

PETER I THE GREAT (co-tsar with Ivan V, 1682-1689; sole tsar 1689-1725)

$\overset{1}{=}$ Eudoxia

$\overset{2}{=}$ **CATHERINE I** (1725-1727)

Catherine

ANNA (1730-1740)

Alexei (executed 1718)

Anna

ELIZABETH (1741-1762)

Anna

IVAN VI (1740-1741)

PETER II (1727-1730)

PETER III (1762) $\overset{?}{=}$ **CATHERINE II THE GREAT** (1762-1796)

PAUL I (1796-1801)

Later tsars of Russia

Dates are years of reign.

him for tearing his country's roots out of native soil. European visitors to seventeenth-century Russia were alternately fascinated and appalled by an exotic, barbarous place that had no literary language. A soldier of fortune from Scotland who later became a general in Peter's army first traveled from Prussia into Russia in 1661, and he was shocked at the contrast between the two countries. In Russian towns, he noted, the streets were "so dirty, and everywhere such nastiness, the people being so morose, and the houses so decayed."

The Russian people, cut off from Europe by the lack of an ice-free port, enormous overland distances, and profound cultural and religious differences, were deeply suspicious of all things foreign. Peter's father Alexei had decreed in 1675 that no man should cut his hair short, shave his beard, or dress in Western style. Peter, whose admiration

Peter the Great's Westernization Program In this woodcut by a folk artist, an Old Believer loses his beard to Peter himself (barber). In Russian Orthodox thinking, God was bearded and men were superior to women; shaving was therefore both sacrilegious and effeminate. Peter began his campaign against beards on the day after he returned from his "Grand Embassy" in 1698 by personally wielding clippers on influential subjects who turned out to welcome him back. One old carpenter hid his severed whiskers and said he intended to be buried with them. Peter also required Russians to replace traditional garments (such as high fur hats and long caftans) with "German" or other Western clothing. *Russian Folk Illustrations, 1881.*

for Western science and technology was as passionate as all his enthusiasms, decreed the opposite and taxed those who would not comply. During an eighteen-month "Grand Embassy" to western Europe, he spent so much time in Dutch and English dockyards that an English **bishop** wrote that "he is mechanically turned and seems designed by nature rather to be a ship-carpenter than a great prince." Indeed, at Zaandam, where Dutch East India Company ships were built, he spent four months working as a carpenter each day and drinking through the night in taverns with workers. He brought back seven hundred craftsmen to teach Russians to build the navy that Peter planned to use against the Swedes in the Baltic and the Ottomans in the Black Sea. He always liked working with his own hands, building ships, pulling teeth, plastering houses, clipping the beards of his courtiers—and torturing and executing traitors. Using the forced labor of forty thousand men, Peter built a new city on a barren, watery site near the Baltic and made it his capital. Because Russia had no wheelbarrows, all the earth had to be carried in bags or in the hems of the workers' clothes. St. Petersburg was Peter's "window on the West," representing the new nation that he had determined to build. He adored it just as much as most of the residents hated it.

Late medieval Russia had been ruled by Tatar khans, successors of Genghis Khan's Mongol Empire. Overthrowing them had required a new tradition of absolute obedience and devotion to the tsar. Peter manipulated the power that this tradition gave him to break down old ways and beliefs. He continued his predecessor's persecution of the Old Believers, dissidents who fiercely opposed liturgical reforms instituted in the 1650s. (Some twenty thousand burned themselves to death rather than participate in rituals in which the priests made the sign of the cross with two fingers rather than three.) He also destroyed the last vestige of the Russian Orthodox church's independence; when the patriarch died in 1700, Peter named no successor and placed the church under a civilian official. Nevertheless, the number of Old Believers continued to grow, reaching perhaps 20 percent of the population during the eighteenth century.

When a Swedish army of eight thousand smashed Peter's forty-thousand-man force at Narva in 1700, Peter set to work assembling an army fully modern in its training, weaponry, and administration. He lured German, Scottish, and other foreign officers by offering them lavish salaries; he introduced conscription to provide manpower; and he used serf labor in monopolistic industries to provide uniforms and weapons. **Serfdom** in Russia became an industrial as well as an agrarian institution, but industries were creatures of the state rather than of private enterprise. At Poltava in 1709, the tsar had his revenge when his army routed the invading Swedes under Charles XII. Toward the close of his reign, he had more than three hundred thousand soldiers, and he spent 85 percent of his revenue on his military forces. He tripled revenues in order to pay for his enormously expensive military program by expanding state monopolies and by raising old taxes and adding new ones on beards, hot baths, horse collars, weddings of non-Christians, and beehives, among other things. Peter redesigned administrative structures along Swedish lines to collect and spend the money. The new "colleges" (offices) answered to his Senate, a council that replaced the old Duma composed of aristocrats (boyars). The old national assembly (Zemskii Sobor) never met during Peter's time or afterwards, but the bureaucracy he put in place continued to grow under both tsarist and Soviet rule.

Peter's attitude toward his new administrative council was far from respectful. Indeed, the body existed solely to see that his endless stream of orders was carried out. In 1707 he ordered the members to keep minutes of their meetings, and he insisted that each sign his vote on every resolution. "No resolution to be taken without this," Peter wrote, "so that the stupidity of each shall be evident." The tsar allowed no one to stand in the way of his revolutionary program. In 1721 he replaced the boyars with a class of nobles whose privileges were based on service rather than birth. He promulgated a "Table of Ranks" that defined fourteen ascending and parallel grades of military and civil careers; nobility was awarded to those who reached the higher ranks. Boyars, like others, had to begin at the bottom and serve from age fifteen until death. Foreigners, especially Germans, were prominent in this service nobility, itself an extension of the *dvoryanstvo* (service nobility) founded by Ivan the Terrible (see Chapter 15).

The vast majority of Russians remained serfs, their condition in some ways worse than that of their Austrian or Prussian counterparts. Unlike the latter, Russian peasants could be and sometimes were sold apart from the land or their families, making them virtually indistinguishable from chattel slaves. Occasional prohibitions on the sale of serfs were unenforceable. Peter's absolutism rested on the subjection of all his people. Nobles continued to owe service to the state until 1762; serfdom was not abolished until 1861. Nor would Peter allow any turning back toward old ways, although some of his successors were less resolute. In 1718 he grew fearful that opponents of his westernizing policies were conspiring against him with the help of his son. The young man and the alleged conspirators, guilty of nothing more than disliking the tsar's policies, underwent arrest, torture, and execution. Rumors abounded that Peter himself tortured his son to death, and even if the rumors were false, Peter certainly gave the orders. Yet he died after contracting a chill from jumping into a wintry sea to save a drowning sailor.

THE EMBATTLED CONSTITUTIONALISTS

Throughout Louis XIV's long reign, absolutism looked more and more like a necessity to many intelligent Euro-

peans. One of these was the Polish-Lithuanian king, Jan Sobieski, whose counterattack saved Vienna in 1683, but his attempt to strengthen his native land's monarchy was thwarted by noble opposition. The Stuart, Orange, and Vasa Dynasties in England, the Dutch Republic, and Sweden continued to strive for greater power over legislation and taxation against their constitutionally minded opponents. Defenders of absolutism pointed to Sweden's decline and Poland-Lithuania's prostration as evidence of the unworkability of constitutional systems, but the Dutch and English experiences showed that such systems could be adapted to new challenges and conditions.

Sweden: Vasa Kings and the Riksdag

Sweden oscillated between absolutism and constitutionalism from the sixteenth century through the eighteenth. Charles XI (reigned 1660–1697), after coming of age in 1672, successfully undermined the authority of the old aristocracy by seizing much of the land that they had obtained earlier from the crown. In 1693 the Riksdag (the kingdom's representative assembly) declared Charles "an absolute sovereign king, whose commands are binding upon all, and who is responsible to no one on earth for his actions." The non-noble estates[4] in the assembly had joined with the king to complete the conquest of the nobility.

The conquest, however, was short-lived. Charles XII (reigned 1697–1718) was fourteen years old when his father died, and some observers were troubled when the crown slipped from his head at his coronation. A brilliant but rash general, he yearned to establish a huge Swedish empire in the manner of Gustavus Adolphus (see Chapter 15). His father had tried to keep Sweden out of war, recognizing that its population of 1.5 million was too small and its resources too limited for such dreams, but Charles XII was bent on conquest. Despite his early victories, he overextended his kingdom's military capabilities and took absolutism in Sweden down with him when he perished fighting the Danes. The fifty years after 1720, called the Age of Liberty in Swedish history, saw the revival of constitutionalism. A reinvigorated Riksdag and its "Secret Committee" ruled eighteenth-century Sweden with the king as its puppet.

But Sweden was no longer a great power, having been eclipsed by Russia, and the Baltic was no longer a "Swedish lake." Admirers of absolutism could still claim that constitutionalism led to national impotence. But the experience of England and the Dutch Republic would prove them wrong. These two maritime states were to lead the coalition that would defeat Louis XIV in the War of the Spanish Succession (1701–1714), and England would go on to

---

[4] These non-noble estates included representatives of the peasantry, who—uniquely in Europe—exercised a genuine political role.

amass a world empire in the eighteenth century. In these countries, constitutionalism not only survived—it thrived.

The Dutch Republic: Orangists and Republicans

In the 1650s and 1660s, the Dutch constitutionalists, led by the grand pensionary Johann de Witt (see Chapter 15), benefited from the long minority of William III, leader of the house of Orange. By the late 1660s, both the Dutch and the English had to worry about the growing power of Louis XIV. This was bad news for de Witt and his Republicans and good news for the Orangists. The shock that toppled the constitutionalist regime came with a forceful French invasion in 1672. By this time, William III was twenty-two years old and eager to assume leadership of his party. The French seized three provinces, and de Witt's

army could not stop them. De Witt resigned, but a hysterical mob in The Hague was not satisfied. He and his brother were brutally murdered, their bodies hung in a public square, and their fingers hacked off as souvenirs.

William had not tried to stop the mobs, but he did move quickly to take advantage of the collapse of the Republican regime. Appointed stadholder and captain-general by the States-General, he halted the French forces within sight of Rotterdam and, during the next two years, drove the enemy from the Dutch Republic. His military success helped him to establish regents who supported Orangist policies in Holland and the other provinces. He did not attempt to overthrow or alter the traditional constitutional framework with its powerful representative provincial and national assemblies. He settled for Orangist regents operating within the old structure, knowing that any attempt to destroy the power of the regents as a class

A Young Woman Standing at a Virginal Although violence repeatedly put seventeenth-century Dutch politics into turmoil, this painting is one of many that celebrates the daily lives of the growing numbers of increasingly well-to-do bourgeois families who could afford to fill their homes with art, musical instruments, and other comforts. In this example, Johannes Vermeer (1632–1675) hints at the world beyond the home with the landscapes on the wall. The hopes of the young woman with the alert gaze and elegant dress may be reflected by the cupid who grasps a letter—perhaps a love letter from her young man. *The Granger Collection.*

would risk civil disruptions that would have made the Dutch easy prey for Louis XIV.

William led his country through two long wars—from 1672 to 1678 and again from 1689 to 1697. King of England as well as stadholder after 1689, he spent the last years of his life preparing the broad alliance that would fight France a third time, from 1701 to 1714. Although he was never averse to strengthening the house of Orange, his highest priority was to maintain Dutch freedom from French domination. Even if he had been as keen to establish absolutist government as his short-lived father, he would have been starting too late. Earlier in the century, the Orangists had failed in their attempt to undermine the regent **oligarchies** that controlled the town governments, the provincial states, and the States-General. The Orangist failure had occurred at about the same time that the absolutist regime Richelieu had constructed in France withstood the challenge of the Fronde (see Chapter 15).

Tax collection, public order, justice, and all other important functions continued to be the responsibility of local authorities, and in the highly urbanized Dutch state these were municipal authorities. Although William never had the power to raise taxes without the consent of the States-General, the explosive growth of Louis XIV's mili-tary power presented such an obvious threat that taxes and loans were forthcoming. William never thought the monies sufficient. Nevertheless, the old constitution was made to function under pressure of the danger to national survival.

England: Restoration and Revolution

A hearty welcome awaited Charles II when he returned from exile in 1660, ushering in the period in English history known as the Restoration. Unhappy memories of the Cromwellian regime lingered, and the handsome, witty, cynical young king enjoyed widespread support. The 1660s proved difficult: The last major attack of the plague killed seventy thousand Londoners in 1665 (14 percent of the population), the Great Fire of 1666 destroyed most of the city's houses, and in 1667 the Dutch sailed up the Thames to launch a devastating raid on England's biggest naval base.

Through all the reverses, Charles remained personally popular, continuing to benefit from the memory of his late father as a martyr for the Anglican church. After Parliament blocked his attempt to suspend laws penalizing Roman Catholics and Dissenters (heirs of the Puritans) in 1673, Charles realized that the best way to increase his authority lay in using his patronage. He granted sinecures,

FIGURE 16-4
THE STUART DYNASTY AND THE BRITISH SUCCESSION

Dates are years of reign unless otherwise noted.

pensions, and bribes to build up a "court party" that he could depend on to vote his way in the House of Commons. Between 1678 and 1681, the government narrowly survived the major political conflict of the reign: the question of who should succeed to the throne on Charles's death. The king, who produced numerous bastards by his bevy of mistresses, was married to a Portuguese princess who remained childless. The heir-apparent was therefore his brother James, Duke of York.[5]

Many English Protestants suspected that James, who had converted to Roman Catholicism in 1667, would try to return England to the old faith and install continental-style absolutism backed by a standing army. In 1678 a clever liar named Titus Oates took advantage of these fears. Oates announced that, by pretending to be a Jesuit, he had penetrated the secrets of a group of plotters who were planning to murder Charles II in order to hasten his brother's accession to the throne. Parliament was horrified by the alleged "Popish Plot" and hastened to pay Oates a generous salary while he invented more details to heighten the tension.

Hysteria about the Popish Plot helped to create the circumstances in which the first English political parties were formed. The Whig party, led by Anthony Ashley-Cooper, Earl of Shaftesbury (1621–1683), emerged to spearhead the passage of a bill excluding the Duke of York from the throne, and the resulting political uproar is called the Exclusion Crisis. The Tory party coalesced to defend hereditary succession, but most of its members were Protestants who hoped that James would keep his religion a private matter when he became king. Fears of renewed civil war and suspicions that Shaftesbury was aiming to make himself the power behind the throne helped Charles and the Tories to defeat the Whigs by 1681. Several Whig leaders were tried for treason, and Shaftesbury—accompanied by his secretary, the philosopher John Locke—escaped into exile in Holland. The town governments that chose most of the members of the House of Commons were purged of Whigs and packed with Tories.

When he assumed the throne upon his brother's death in 1685, James II soon managed to alienate even his most loyal supporters. Louis XIV's decision to revoke the Edict of Nantes in the same year horrified Protestants in England, exacerbating their fears of James's intentions. James soon replaced his Anglican Tory advisers with Catholics, and he dismissed Parliament for questioning the appointment of Catholic officers in his steadily expanding army. Next he fired judges who objected to his power to "dispense" with laws against appointing non-Anglican officers. Then he installed Catholics and Dissenters in all kinds of positions, including the justices of the peace who governed the countryside. His Declaration of Indulgence (1688) extended religious toleration to Catholics and Dissenters, but Anglicans believed this was only a temporary measure that would soon give way to the persecution of all Protestants. The Anglican landowners, who had tenaciously clung to their control of local government, fumed, but so long as James's successor was Protestant they held to their principle of loyalty to the king. Until 1688, James's Protestant daughters occupied the next two positions in the line of succession (refer again to Figure 16-4). The eldest, Mary (wife of William of Orange), would follow him, and if she were to die without giving birth to a child, her sister Anne (wife of Prince George of Denmark) would ascend the throne. Mary and Anne had been born before James's conversion, and their mother, who had died in 1671, was the daughter of a leading Anglican politician.

But in January 1688, the pregnancy of Mary of Modena, whom James had married in 1673, was publicly announced. On June 10, she gave birth to a son, and suddenly there was a Catholic heir to take precedence over his Protestant half-sisters. From the outset, charges circulated that the pregnancy was a fraud, one nobleman having written on January 15 that "the Queen's great belly is everywhere ridiculed, as if scarce anybody believed it to be true." In March, Princess Anne wrote to her sister that many in England doubted that their stepmother was really pregnant. Anne thought that the queen should disprove the charges by making "either me, or some of my friends, feel her belly." Since the queen took no such precaution, rumors spread that some other infant had been smuggled into the royal chamber in a warming pan and presented as the new Prince of Wales. Belief in "the warming pan myth" spread widely among Anglicans, since it put James in the wrong for attempting to alter the legitimate succession.

On June 30, a small group of aristocrats from both parties wrote to James's son-in-law, William of Orange, asking him to come to England to save "the liberties of England and the Protestant religion." Of the alleged royal child, they asserted that "not one in a thousand believes [him] to be the Queen's." William, taking the greatest gamble of his career, sailed for England with an army, landing on the southwest coast early in November 1688. If, as Louis XIV expected, William got bogged down in a civil war in England, the Dutch Republic would be easy prey for the French. But no English civil war ensued. Support for James melted away, units of his army deserted to William, and James fled with his family into exile in France. The most important of the deserters was John Churchill, later to be named Duke of Marlborough for his victories over France[6] (discussed later in the chapter).

A hastily convened Parliament in effect deposed James and placed William and Mary on the throne as joint

---

[5] New York was named after him because it was during the last trade war with the Dutch that New Amsterdam became an English colony.

[6] He was the direct ancestor of Sir Winston Churchill, Great Britain's World War II prime minister.

England's Memorial
In this print, the eye of Providence (top right) protects the orange tree that symbolizes the house of Orange, from which William came. While Louis XIV brutalizes his subjects (left), an orange is falling from the tree and knocking James II's crown off while he and his wife and son flee to France. A ray from the eye of Providence also soothes the tottering Church of England, and a crowd of "Papists and Jesuits" scuttles away "from the hand of Justice" (lower right). Such prints were in effect "editorial cartoons," and they proliferated in both England and in the Dutch Republic in the second half of the seventeenth century. *British Museum, Catalogue of Prints and Drawings.*

sovereigns; William of Orange became King William III of England while remaining the Dutch stadholder. William and Mary agreed to abide by the Bill of Rights, a lengthy document in which Parliament declared that no Catholic could ever be the monarch and condemned the "dispensing power" and other devices by which Charles II and James II had sought to subvert "the liberties of England." This was the "Glorious Revolution" of 1688, accomplished with scarcely a shot fired in anger. The classes represented in Parliament had altered the hereditary succession, reclaimed their control over local government, and blocked efforts to make Parliament a royal rubber stamp.

The Glorious Revolution was conservative in its aims: preserving the Anglican church, the traditional institutions of Parliament, and decentralized local government. But the method—deposition of a legitimate, reigning monarch—indeed constituted a **revolution.** The Tories insisted that there was nothing "revolutionary" about the Glorious Revolution. It was an act of divine providence: God had intervened to protect the Protestant cause by placing William and Mary on the throne. The Whig view appeared in John Locke's *Two Treatises of Government,* published in 1690 but based on Locke's reflections about the Exclusion Crisis of the late 1670s. Locke contended that the events of 1688 validated two vital principles: first, that there was a contract between the government and the people who formed the community; and second, that the people had a right to resist **tyrants** who violated that contract. The Stuart kings, having invaded the people's property and their liberties (including religious liberty), had been rightly

deposed, and Locke argued that the same fate should befall any government that failed to protect the people's rights, which were due to them by natural law. Locke's political philosophy enjoyed enormous influence, not only in Britain but also in continental Europe and in North America. Its secularism and rationalism appealed strongly to the thinkers and writers of the Enlightenment in the eighteenth century (see Chapter 18).

After the Glorious Revolution

By his bold stroke, the Dutch stadholder ascended the English throne and created an alliance of the two main constitutionalist states. For their refusal to support James II, the Dissenters were rewarded with the Toleration Act, permitting them to worship as they pleased although still denying them political rights. Yet an important question lay unanswered. If the landowning classes had halted the progress of absolutism, what was to stop England from degenerating into the kind of aristocratic anarchy that prevented the central government from organizing to defend national interests and even the nation itself? As in the Dutch Republic, part of the answer lay in the well-established tradition of cooperation between monarch and aristocracy in the pursuit of shared national goals (such as independence from the papacy and Spain), which originated in the sixteenth century. The English and Dutch ruling classes well knew the benefits of naval and colonial activities in which the state had to take the lead. In the eighteenth century, Poland-Lithuania would be dismembered by Prussia, Russia, and

THE HISTORICAL EVIDENCE

John Locke's Anti-Absolutist Political Theory

1690

*Although Locke's political theory came to be seen as a theoretical defense of the Glo-
rious Revolution after his* Two Treatises on Government *appeared in print in 1690, he
had developed much of his political thought in the context created by the Exclusion
Crisis. In the years 1679 to 1681, no less than in 1688, the goal was the same: limiting the Stuart government's power. Locke wrote that in "the state of nature" (that is,
before communities were formed), all men were born in "perfect freedom." By the law
of nature, each man has power "to preserve his property, that is his life, liberty and
estate." Because differing abilities and judgments led to conflict, at some point in the
distant past men established a social contract by which they formed a community with
a government entrusted with the power to protect them and their rights (which
included religious liberty). A government consisted of the "legislative" (in England,
Parliament) and the "executive" (the king), and in these passages he gave examples
in which the tyrannical behavior of the latter effectively "altered" or "dissolved" the former, broke the contract, and entitled the people to establish a new government. In
other words, a right of rebellion remained in their hands. When Locke mentioned "the
people," was he leaning toward an oligarchic or a democratic conception? Scholars
continue to debate this topic.*

When such a single person or prince sets up his own arbitrary will in place of the laws, which are the will of the
society, declared by the legislative, then the legislative is
changed. . . . Whoever introduces new laws, not being
thereunto authorized by the fundamental appointment of
the society, or subverts the old, disowns and overturns the
power by which they were made. . . . When the prince
hinders the legislative assembling in its due time, or from
acting freely pursuant to those ends for which it was constituted, the legislative is altered. . . . When by the arbitrary power of the prince the electors or ways of election
are altered, without the consent and contrary to the common interest of the people, there also the legislative is
altered. For if others than those whom the society has
authorized thereunto do choose, or in another way than
what the society hath prescribed, those chosen are not the
legislative appointed by the people. . . . In these and the
like cases, when the government is dissolved the people are
at liberty to provide for themselves by erecting a new legislative, differing from the other by the change of persons,
or form, or both as they shall find it most for their safety
and good. For the society can never, by the fault of
another, lose the native and original right it has to preserve
itself, which can only be done by a settled legislative, and
a fair and impartial execution of the laws made by it. To
tell people they may provide for themselves by erecting a
new legislative when, by oppression, artifice, or being
delivered over to a foreign power, their old one is gone, is
only to tell them they may expect relief when it is too late,
and the evil is past cure. This is in effect no more than to
bid them first be slaves, and then to take care of their liberty; and when their chains are on, tell them they may act
like free men. . . . Men can never be secure from tyranny
if there be no means to escape it till they are perfectly
under it: and therefore it is that they have not only a right
to get out of it, but to prevent it.

Source: From David Wootton, ed., *John Locke: Political Writings* (New
York: Mentor, 1993), pp. 371, 373.

Austria because its aristocrats, isolated on their enormous
estates, failed to grasp the need to yield some of their independence to enable a national government to be effective.
In Poland-Lithuania, the question was whether there would
be *any* meaningful central authority; in the two maritime
nations, it was who would control that authority.

No less important, however, England still warily eyed
the danger of French ships and soldiers just across the English Channel. After 1688 the survival of England's traditional institutions depended on the success of William and
Mary. If Parliament did not vote taxes, French support
might restore James II, and all who had opposed him would

THE HISTORICAL EVIDENCE

Celia Fiennes Visits London

ca. 1702

Celia Fiennes (1662–1741), an indefatigable traveler and meticulous chronicler of her journeys, was born in her father's manor house near Salisbury, a country town 60 miles southwest of London. Her grandfather, a nobleman, and her father and uncles all fought in the Parliamentary cause during the 1640s, and her father also held high office in Cromwell's government. Between 1685 and 1703, on horseback and accompanied only by a few servants, she made her way over all of England and kept notes of what she did, saw, ate, heard, and thought. She was curious about everything: the quality of local beers and ales, the healing powers of spa waters, the variety of bird songs, the methods of local manufactures, the decoration of houses, the workings of government, and much else. Her elaborate descriptions of her trips were unknown until published in 1888, and the following excerpts are from her visit to London at the beginning of the eighteenth century. After depicting the coronation of Queen Anne in 1702, which she witnessed, Fiennes's Whig and Dissenting sympathies appear in her account of the English political system.

Our Kingdom is governed by Laws made and established pursuant to the first Constitutions and Magna Carta. . . . These Laws are made and are not truly authentic if not enacted and passed by our three States which is King, Lords and Commons, which can make Laws for all cases . . . which Constitution is by all the world esteemed the best, if kept to each one's basis, a triple foundation, and when the King exerts not his prerogative beyond its limits to the oppressing his people's privileges, nor the people exorbitant and tumultuous in the standing or running up their power and privileges to cloud and bind up the hands of the prince; . . . but alas! it's too sadly to be bemoaned, the best and sweetest wine turns soonest sour, so we by folly, faction, and wickedness have endeavored our own ruin, and were it not for God's providential care and miraculous works we should at this day been a people left to utter despair. . . . It is in the King's prerogative thus to call and dissolve parliaments, to declare war or peace . . . but the King ought not nor do rightly undertake any such thing but by the advice of his standing Privy Council, . . . to which he joins the Great Council of the nation which is

his two Houses of Parliament, . . . when great matters are in agitation as that of peace or war, . . . and strengthened by this, that the sinews of war is in the people, for without them no money is to be had. . . . There was also at the same time an Act to settle the succession in the Protestant Line [Act of Settlement, 1701], and just before our Hero [King William] resigned his life crown and throne he passed an Act to secure us more firmly against any Popish successor or pretended heirs to the Crown. . . . This was a great pleasure to our dying King to leave us with all the security possible to enjoy what he came to save us in, and give us, and what he had fought to obtain for us, Liberty in religion and privileges. I pray God we do not by our provoking sins move his anger not only to take from us our Benefactor and Deliverer, but also our said valuable blessings and privileges, the Gospel Light and being a Free Nation.

Source: From Christopher Morris, ed., *The Journeys of Celia Fiennes* (London: The Crescent Press, 1949), pp. 314–315, 320–322.

be treated as traitors. The Stuarts and Oranges had done their utmost to gain the kind of power that Louis XIV enjoyed in France, but by late in the seventeenth century William recognized that it was too late to try again. He had to find a means of working with Parliament and the States-General—but their members also had to cooperate with him. If they did not, the institutions and privileges that they had maintained at staggering cost might fall victim to Bourbon France.

Thus, a new political system emerged in England during the long wars with Louis XIV. The monarch—first William and then, since he died childless, his sister-in-law Anne (reigned 1702–1714)—increasingly found it necessary to choose ministers from the ranks of politicians who controlled blocks of votes in Parliament. Earlier English kings and absolutist monarchs everywhere would have been horrified that the outcome of elections to representative assemblies should directly or indirectly force the appointment of men to high office who might not be the king's choices. But the tremendous growth of royal patronage in wartime allowed the government to gain considerable influence in Parliament by giving jobs and other rewards to those who proffered their votes.

The result was a makeshift system in which the king was still in charge but had to rely on a cabinet composed of leading politicians who were more or less dependent upon sentiment in Parliament. The cabinet replaced the Privy

English Coffee House   Europe's first coffee house opened in Venice in 1647, and the first in England opened its doors in Oxford in the 1650s. Taste for the new beverage spread rapidly, and by 1739 London boasted 551 coffee houses whose customers used them to hear and read news and discuss and debate topics of all kinds (including cartoons such as on p. 602). Charles II and James II condemned them as places filled with "the most seditious, indecent and scandalous discourses" and tried—unsuccessfully—to outlaw them. That many of them were patronized by enemies of Stuart rule is certain, and their existence and increasing popularity helps demonstrate the growth of a literate public that was keenly interested in political events. *Corbis/Bettmann.*

Council, and through it the ruling classes gained a degree of influence over policy. This new influence encouraged a willingness to vote for and to pay the taxes needed to implement policy. Taxes on income from land reached annual levels of 20 percent during the wars with France. No less vital, wealthy individuals in England and the Dutch Republic willingly lent money to the government. The Bank of England was founded in 1694, largely to establish a source of credit for the government, and the bank's stock sold well because parliamentary control of taxation assured investors that interest would be paid and capital protected. The Bank of Amsterdam (founded in 1609) also offered cheap credit. By 1700, the Dutch government owed 250 million florins, against an annual revenue of only 13 million. Nevertheless people with money lent it because they had a say in the policies of those who spent it—people like themselves.

Colbert, fully aware of the need for credit, founded a state bank in France in 1674, but it lasted only nine years. Louis XIV had bought his freedom from the influence of his wealthier subjects by granting them tax exemptions, but in so doing, he lost the power to mobilize the resources of his country fully. In England and the Dutch Republic, the well-to-do paid taxes and influenced policy through assemblies. Nothing comparable to Versailles or St. Petersburg was built in either country. William III had—and needed—a monumental ego, but no one built him a monumental palace. He had to settle for a new wing added to the Tudor palace of Hampton Court. The absolutist system gave the king freedom of action, but the constitutionalist systems—awkward and decentralized though they were—enabled the monarch to tap wealth much more effectively. In 1700, France boasted a population of 20 million. England and Wales had 6 million; the Dutch Republic, just over 2 million. Notwithstanding, Louis spent the last decade of his reign on the defensive against those smaller enemies. Ironically, the English and the Dutch systems of public finance could not have been created without the survival of the Parliament and the States-General. These medieval representative institutions, heavily modified to suit the conditions of the brave new world in which they found themselves, retained the authority to negotiate with kings and stadholders the terms on which they would pay taxes.

DIPLOMACY AND INTERNATIONAL RELATIONS, 1660–1721

Monarchs and republics pursued their foreign policy goals, as they always had, through diplomacy and war. Just as warfare underwent major changes in the late seventeenth and early eighteenth centuries, so did diplomacy, which during this period attained its modern form. Permanent embassies in foreign capitals, unusual in 1600, became commonplace by 1700. As one measure of Louis XIV's impact, by 1715 French replaced Latin as the language of diplomacy. To the permanent army was added the permanent embassy. Diplomacy was therefore one of the many functions that underwent professionalization in the seventeenth century—another step up the ladder to "big government." Despite the growing sums spent on diplomats, however, the lion's share of governmental revenues went to armies and navies.

When we compare the international relations of this period with those of the first half of the century, three important points emerge. First, after 1659 Bourbon France gained the dominance in Europe that had formerly belonged to the Habsburgs. For nearly two centuries, France had been struggling to break free of Habsburg encirclement, and by 1659 it had succeeded. By 1660 the Spanish and Holy Roman Empires were in decline, and Leopold I was to demonstrate that, after 1683, the Ottoman Empire could be defeated by modern European armies. The rising powers were tantalized by opportunities to seize parts of the older empires and pieces of the worldwide trading empire that the Dutch had built (mostly at the expense of the Portuguese).

Second, the role earlier played by religion as a cause of international conflict was being replaced by secular considerations: dynastic, national, and commercial gain. These motives had never disappeared during the wars of religion, but religious concerns had given the struggles a peculiar bitterness. With more worldly motives coming to the fore, negotiations were more likely to succeed. Compromises were easier to attain when the stakes were land and money rather than eternal salvation.

Third, the new armies of centralized states—France providing the model—operated under more effective civilian control. There was no repetition of the horrors of the Thirty Years' War, in which armies had turned on civilian populations and supported themselves by brutal intimidation and theft. The tax burden required to pay for the new armies was painful, but at least taxpayers did not face the sudden loss of everything they possessed to marauding soldiers.

The galvanizing impact of Louis XIV's foreign policy on others came in stages. He enjoyed an almost unbroken string of successes until the mid-1680s, after which he maneuvered to defend his gains. One consistent goal was to make France's eastern borders more defensible by closing the invasion routes likely to be chosen by enemies. This required annexing most of the Spanish Netherlands and parts of the Holy Roman Empire and building elaborate fortifications to hold them. Louis's second goal was to protect the Bourbon Dynasty's claim to the vast Spanish inheritance when the childless Charles II of Spain died. Whereas initially the Dutch and later the English felt particularly threatened by the first goal, they and many others—notably the Austrian Habsburgs—feared that if Louis achieved his second goal, the tenuous **balance of power** would be destroyed and the widely feared "universal

monarchy" of France would come to pass. Significantly, the phrase *balance of power* came into use in this period.

French Expansion

Although France and the Dutch Republic had long been allied against the Habsburgs, Louis XIV despised the Dutch. Even if their republicanism and Protestantism had not been enough to exasperate him, their control of much of French trade affronted his theories no less than Colbert's. Louis invaded several parts of the southern (and still Spanish) Netherlands[7] and the Franche-Comté in 1667 and 1668 (see Map 16-1). This War of Devolution has also been called the War of the Queen's Rights because Louis claimed the lands he invaded as rightfully due to his wife by inheritance. His legal claim was dubious, but that hardly mattered since, as one of his counselors put it, "No judges are more equitable than cannons." His success horrified the Dutch because it brought French armies close to their southern border.

After arranging an alliance with Charles II's England, Louis invaded Dutch territory in the spring of 1672 with more than 130,000 troops, four times as many as the Dutch army had. The invasion initiated the Franco-Dutch War (1672–1678) and provoked the fall of the Republican Johann de Witt, an opening that William of Orange quickly exploited, as we have already seen. For the Dutch Republic, 1672 was a military, economic, and political catastrophe. The invaders seized more than half its territory by late in the summer, coming within 21 miles of Amsterdam. Louis accumulated additional conquests in the southern Netherlands and the Rhineland, building fortifications and strengthening his borders. William, only twenty-two years old, calmly ordered the dikes cut to make a "waterline" or moat and saved the rest of the country (including Amsterdam, Rotterdam, and The Hague). Joined by both branches of the Habsburgs in 1673, William pushed the French back out of Dutch lands in 1674. By the time the Peace of Nijmegen ended the war in 1679, Louis had failed to conquer the Spanish Netherlands, but he retained some of his gains there and in the Rhineland. He proudly wrote: "I was overjoyed at my good fortune and my good conduct, which had made me profit from every occasion to extend the limits of my kingdom at the expense of my enemies." Moreover, his ambitious program of fortification strengthened his defenses against invasion from the east.

The ink was scarcely dry on the Nijmegen treaty when Louis began a new series of land grabs by the legalistic device of "reunion." Tribunals, called Chambers of Reunion, staffed by Frenchmen in Flanders, Alsace, Metz, and the Franche-Comté predictably ruled that various pieces of

---

[7] Today, Belgium.

MAP 16-1

FRENCH TERRITORIAL ACQUISITIONS, 1643–1715

nearby land belonged to France. The French army enforced the rulings, seizing Luxembourg from the Spaniards and Strasbourg and Alsace (among other places) from the Holy Roman Empire. The Habsburgs signed the Truce of Ratisbon in 1684, agreeing to French retention of these gains for twenty years. In retrospect it is clear that Ratisbon was the high-water mark of Louis's foreign policy. France's vulnerable frontiers seemed secure at last, yet Louis would spend the rest of his life struggling, with only partial success, to hold what he had won.

When Louis began his campaign of "reunion" in the Holy Roman Empire, Leopold was too busy defending Vienna to resist it. However, the lifting of the siege of Vienna and the ensuing rollback enabled him to confront Louis, and he did not have to go it alone. Louis's revocation of the Edict of Nantes so angered the Great Elector of Brandenburg-Prussia that he changed sides and joined the emperor, the Dutch, and others in an anti-French alliance known as the League of Augsburg. During the Nine Years' War (1688–1697), Louis fought against centralized states able to field armies as good as the French forces. By 1689 English resources were also arrayed against him. At La Hogue in 1692, the combined English and Dutch fleets

defeated the powerful navy that Colbert had built, and in the Peace of Ryswick (1697) Louis was forced to give up much of the territory that he had won through the "reunions" and to recognize William as king of England. Momentarily, at least, the balance of power stood. France had not been forced back into its pre-1659 borders, but Louis yielded land that he had seized. In the huge war that soon followed, the anti-French alliance led by William and Leopold ultimately prevailed, but at enormous cost to all participants.

The War of the Spanish Succession

When Philip IV of Spain died in 1665, his heir was Charles II (born 1661, reigned 1665–1700), the pitiful result of many generations of Habsburg intermarriage. He was probably mentally retarded and certainly feeble and dyspeptic; his "Habsburg jaw" protruded so far that he could scarcely speak intelligibly or chew his food, and he also proved unable to sire an heir by either of his wives. In 1686, the papal nuncio noted that Charles had "a melancholic and faintly surprised look" and was "indolent, seeming to be stupefied." Yet he ruled, if in name only, the largest empire in the world: Spain itself, the Spanish Netherlands, southern Italy, Sicily, Sardinia, and the duchy of Milan in Europe, as well as the Philippines and much of the Americas. As he grew older and weaker, courtiers and diplomats schemed feverishly over the succession. The problem had long been foreseen. A secret treaty partitioning the Spanish Empire between Bourbons and Habsburgs was signed as early as 1668. New partition treaties made by William and Louis in 1698 and 1700 had the aim of avoiding war. Charles himself, however, was a Spanish patriot and wanted to maintain the unity of the empire. When he died, he left it all to his nephew, Philip of Anjou, who was Louis's second grandson (and thus not in direct line for succession to the French throne; refer again to Figure 16-1 earlier in this chapter).

When Philip of Anjou became Philip V, king of Spain, French troops moved into the Spanish Netherlands, and French merchants were given trading rights formerly enjoyed by the English in the Spanish Empire. The War of the Spanish Succession (1701–1714) could no longer be avoided because France's rivals believed they could not afford to let Louis XIV gain so much new strength. This was the first "world war" because the stakes included the globe-spanning Spanish Empire. The war was fought in Europe, Asia, and North America (where English colonists called it Queen Anne's War)—and the winners would gain territory in the Americas and Asia as well as in Europe.

France and Spain were allied against all the enemies that France had faced earlier, in the War of the League of Augsburg (Nine Years' War). William III did not live to see the outcome. He died early in 1702 as a result of a fall when his horse stumbled on a molehill. Though his enemies drank toasts to the mole, his anti-French coalition ultimately prevailed. The military turning point came early (see Map 16-2). In 1704 a French army was in position to threaten Vienna and thereby remove Leopold from the war. John Churchill, Duke of Marlborough, marched his troops 600 miles in six weeks to join forces with Leopold's commander, Prince Eugène of Savoy. Marlborough maintained secrecy so carefully that even his officers did not know their destination. This ploy enabled them to surprise the French at the Bavarian village of Blenheim (August 13, 1704) and shatter their proud army; thirty thousand of Louis's men were killed or captured. Before Blenheim, even old men could not recall a French defeat, but Louis's reputation for invincibility was destroyed and Marlborough's created in a single day.

After Blenheim, France continued to lose both battles and ground. Marlborough led allied forces into France itself during 1708 and 1709, and Louis offered major concessions to achieve a peace. Leopold and the Dutch, however, insisted on a policy of "No peace without Spain," meaning that they wanted Louis to assist them in a campaign to oust Philip from Spain. Louis refused, saying bitterly that "since I have to make war, I would rather fight against my own enemies than against my own children." He managed to hold out until the alliance of his enemies began to crack under the strain of the long struggle. In the treaties of Utrecht (1713) and Rastadt (1714), the Bourbon Dynasty held onto Spain and the overseas empire, but the Spanish Netherlands and Italian holdings went to the Austrians. France lost its conquests east of the Rhine, and the Dutch

MAP 16-2

THE WAR OF THE SPANISH SUCCESSION (1701–1714) AND THE GREAT NORTHERN WAR (1700–1721)

got a series of barrier fortresses in the now-Austrian Netherlands. The Dutch, however, were exhausted by the war and never regained their former prominence. The English got Gibraltar, Minorca, Nova Scotia, Newfoundland, and Hudson's Bay, as well as the immensely profitable right to transport slaves into Spanish America. By the time Louis XIV died in 1715, Great Britain[8] had risen to **great power** status.

The Great Northern War

Just as the War of the Spanish Succession prompted the partitioning of Spain's empire, so the Great Northern War (1700–1721) led to the fragmenting of Sweden's. At the turn of the century, Sweden still controlled most of the Baltic's shores, greatly to the resentment of the Russians, Danes, and Poles. In the early stages of the Great Northern War, Sweden seemed triumphant as Charles XII's vigor and military genius knocked all but the Russians from the conflict. Louis XIV's enemies worried that Charles would attack the Austrians from the north, perhaps fatally weakening the newly forged alliance against France and Spain. Instead, Charles marched deep into Russia in 1707 and then, after his defeat at Poltava in 1709, spent five years in exile in Turkey before returning to Sweden. Continuing to fight—almost insanely, most of his subjects thought—he perished on a Norwegian battlefield in 1718.

Following Charles's death in 1718, the aristocrat-dominated Swedish government yielded the eastern and southern Baltic provinces to Russia, Prussia, and Hanover (Treaty of Nystad, 1721). The days of Sweden's imperial power had ended, and Peter the Great had made Russia the predominant force in the Baltic. Russia became part of the European power structure, never again to recede into isolation.

CULTURE IN THE AGE OF ABSOLUTISM

A week before he died, Louis XIV reputedly told his five-year-old heir to "avoid, as far as is possible, making war. It is the ruin of the people. Do not follow the bad example which I have set you. I have often gone to war too lightly and pursued it for vanity's sake." Although toward the end Louis's enemies manage to deny him some of his military objectives, his early successes had induced many to try to replicate what they could of his political and administrative methods. Europeans also paid homage to French achievements in the arts by attempting to copy them. During Louis's reign, French culture won admiration and

inspired imitation everywhere. French replaced Latin as the language of diplomacy, and French neoclassicism in the arts became the preferred style across the Continent. Leopold I and other princes built their own versions of Versailles, and French manners, gardens, cooking, clothing, writing, and thinking were taken up by Europe's elite. Partly because of the chaos into which the Thirty Years' War propelled Europe, itself a product of the continuing polarization between the Protestant Reformation and the Catholic Reformation, the highest goal increasingly appeared to be the restoration of order. Louis XIV's France seemed to many to be a model for that order in cultural no less than political terms.

The French Model

As with political, military, and administrative matters, Louis's greatest achievements came before Versailles was finally completed in 1682. In the 1660s and 1670s, he moved nomadically about, while encouraging artists of all kinds, even dancing in ballets himself. Jean-Baptiste Lully (1632–1687), an Italian dancer and composer who was appointed Superintendent of the King's Music in 1661, was the absolute ruler of musical matters at the French court. Louis's government founded the *Académie Royale des Sciences* (Royal Academy of Sciences) along with academies of painting and dance, while the *Académie Français* (French Academy) was charged with the task of "purifying" the language by producing an official dictionary. The steady expansion of the printing industry accompanied a continuing "linguistic nationalism" that spread widely not only among the French but also among the Germans, the Dutch, and others who took intense interest and pride in the development of their literary languages.

The cultural scene of seventeenth-century France boasted one important institution not prominent anywhere else: the *salon*. The first opened in 1608, and they proliferated in the 1640s and 1650s, remaining influential until 1789. Salons, invariably conducted by aristocratic women in their Paris houses, served as meeting places for witty conversations among aristocrats and writers. Salon society nurtured some feminist ideas, especially on the subject of the traditional system of arranged marriages. For instance, the heroine in Madeleine de Scudéry's novel, *Le Grand Cyrus* (1649–1653), considers marriage "a lengthy slavery." Although she recognizes that there are "worthy men . . . as soon as I think of them as husbands, I see them as masters so likely to turn into tyrants that I cannot help hating them there and then and thank the gods for giving me an inclination totally opposed to marriage." Salon members became arbiters in linguistic and literary matters. Their goal was refinement, meaning rejection of archaic, vulgar, or plebeian words. As one result of their power, the vocabulary available to writers, at least in such "higher" genres as tragedies, odes, and epic poems, narrowed.

---

[8] In 1707, the kingdoms of England and Scotland were joined by the Act of Union, forming the United Kingdom, or Great Britain (see Chapter 19).

THE HUMAN EXPERIENCE

Aphra Behn, Playwright and Novelist

Aphra Behn, the first woman to earn her living as a writer, lived a life as adventurous as her career was unprecedented. She was probably born in 1640 in or near Canterbury in southeastern England. Her original surname is uncertain. As the daughter of a barber and a wet nurse, her social origins were humble, but she became a snobbish critic of people with origins like hers. Little is certain about her early life or her education. Although denied instruction in Latin—later a source of deep regret for her—she learned to read and write, to speak French, and to play the flute. Her knowledge of French enabled her to read Madeleine de Scudéry's *Le Grand Cyrus* and other novels admired in Louis XIV's France.

Behn may have served as a spy in the late 1650s for the royalists who were trying to overthrow Oliver Cromwell's regime. At some point, perhaps as a spy, she probably went to Surinam, a colony on the northern coast of South America (and one that Charles II would give up in return for another colony, later named New York). Behn returned to London from Surinam in the spring of 1664, and at some point during that year she married a man of either

Dutch or German ancestry—Mr. Behn. He died, perhaps in the terrible plague of 1665, apparently leaving her little or nothing. In July 1666, the widow Behn sailed to Antwerp to spy on the Dutch, with whom the English were at war. Her code name was "Astrea," and she was "Agent 160" in the government's cipher. Sir William Killigrew, Charles II's Groom of the Bedchamber, recruited her for this service. Her task was to reestablish contact with William Scot, a man she had known in Surinam and who, as a former spy for Oliver Cromwell, was involved in anti-Stuart plots in Holland. Although her reports included a warning about Dutch plans for an attack on the Thames—which were ignored with catastrophic results—she was not paid adequately for her expenses or her work. Her ship sank within sight of land on her return, but she escaped that danger only to find herself threatened with debtor's prison late in 1668.

The records are not clear as to whether she actually went to prison, and it is possible that instead she went to Italy for a time. But it is certain that she was back in England in 1669 and that her first play, a romantic tragicomedy, was performed by the

Duke's Company on September 20, 1670. The prologue daringly announced that the author was female, and the play's theme is set forth in the title: *The Forced Marriage; or, The Jealous Bridegroom*. Sixteen more of her plays were staged, and only John Dryden, the Poet Laureate, was more prolific during the 1670s and 1680s. Her narrative, *Oroonoko* (1688), is the vivid story of an African prince tricked into slavery who leads a slave rebellion. Based on the life of a slave she might have met in Surinam, it was frequently reprinted in England and France in the eighteenth century.

Behn needed to earn a living, and her bawdy, melodramatic plays matched the tastes of her Restoration audiences. In *The Town Fop* (1676), Sir Timothy Tawdrey tells his friends, Sham and Sharp, of his coming marriage: "The wench I never saw yet, but they say she's handsome—But no matter for that, there's money, my boys . . . or she were not for me. . . . My whole design is . . . with part of her portion [dowry] to set up my Miss [mistress] Betty Flauntit, which by the way, is the main end of my marrying." Nearly all her plays attacked the double standard and the existing practice of marriage for

---

Among the most popular writers in Louis XIV's France were a group of moralists whose witty collections of character sketches, fables, and sayings reflected the more secular sensibility of the salons with their delight in gossip and social satire. The *Maxims* of the cynical Duc de La Rochefoucauld (1613–1680), for example, include these:

"In order to succeed in the world, people do their utmost to appear successful."

"We all have strength to endure the troubles of others."

"The evil we do brings less persecution and hatred upon us than our good qualities."

Two of the finest dramatists in European history were favorites of Louis XIV: Molière (1622–1673) and Racine (1639–1699). Molière's wonderfully satirical comedies poked fun at religious hypocrites (*Tartuffe*), misers (*L'Avare*), and hypochondriacs (*Le Malade Imaginaire*). In *Le Bourgeois Gentilhomme*, his target was another familiar social type, the newly rich townsman, "Monsieur Jourdain." An anxious social climber, Jourdain puts on airs by hiring a professor of philosophy to give himself a veneer of education. He is childishly delighted to discover that he has been speaking prose all his life without knowing it. Molière's audiences included upwardly mobile members of the **bourgeoisie** who would have recognized that he targeted their vices. His popularity guaranteed an audience—and money. To the horror of her critics, Behn even asserted a woman's right to sexual freedom and pleasure. Although in politics she was thoroughly royalist, Aphra Behn took a revolutionary stance against a social system that denied women intellectual and personal fulfillment. Behn's last play appeared in 1687 just two years before her death (April 16, 1689). She was buried in Westminster Abbey, but in an exterior location rather than the interior; her tombstone has an epigraph that she herself may have written: "Here lies a Proof that Wit can never be/Defense enough against Mortality." ❖

From *The Widow Ranter,* 1688   Although it was the first play to have a British colony in North America as its setting, *The Widow Ranter* embodies Behn's conservative politics and her support of James II. Its hero, a colonial governor, dies deeply regretting his disrespect for the king. But the play's other central figure is the widow of a religious rebel; she smokes tobacco, drinks potent punch all day, and dresses and rides like a man. Always cheerful and open-hearted, she wanted to remarry but would not kowtow to men, asking "Why should I sigh and whine, and make my self an Ass, and him conceited?"   *The Granger Collection.*

he must have appreciated the irony that the socially insecure bourgeoisie would feel compelled to attend his plays and laugh at themselves, since being seen at fashionable plays wearing fashionable clothing was a demonstration of one's status.

Molière's friend, Jean Racine, ceased writing for the stage in 1677 when, at thirty-eight, he became Historian to the King. Missing a siege that same year, he adroitly explained, "Sire, before my tailor had finished my country clothes, Your Majesty had finished the siege." His tragedies, in carefully balanced rhymed verse, gained enormous success. An exponent of the neoclassicism visible in Versailles's architecture, he kept closely to the restrictive classical "dramatic unities" of time, action, and location. Yet he conveyed intense feeling—especially romantic love—within these narrow limits. In his masterpiece, *Phèdre,* his doomed protagonist expresses her incestuous love for her stepson with these words: "It is no longer a passion hidden in my veins: it is the goddess Venus herself fastened on her prey." Racine's Jansenist education asserted itself in the way that the woman at the center of each play struggles futilely against her tragic fate. Louis XIV, in his drive for religious uniformity, had persecuted the Jansenists, but their values continued to find expression in Racine's plays. Madame de Sévigné attended one of them in Louis's presence, and when he asked her opinion, she said, "Sire, I am charmed, and what I feel is beyond words." Many of her contemporaries reacted the same way.

Molière's *Tartuffe* Tartuffe, the religious hypocrite, wangles his way into a rich nobleman's house with his pious speeches and begins to pursue his host's wife ("God, it is true, does some delights condemn,/But 'tis not hard to come to terms with Him"). Louis paid Molière a salary of 1,000 livres a year, enjoyed his plays, and often had them presented at his court, as he did *Tartuffe* in 1664. Nevertheless, *Tartuffe* did not appear on the public stage until 1669. Churchmen were not amused, and the king had to intervene personally to make them give Molière a Christian funeral. *Corbis/Bettmann.*

Echoes of English Revolutions

Cultural expression in England was intimately connected with the violent struggles that brought down Charles I and James II. John Milton (1608–1674), England's greatest seventeenth-century poet, wrote pamphlets supporting the Roundhead cause and served as Latin secretary in the republican government that beheaded Charles I. Angered by Stuart censorship in the 1630s, his *Areopagitica* (1644) is a forceful defense of freedom of the press: "Though all the winds of doctrine were let loose upon the earth, so Truth be in the field, we do injuriously by licensing and prohibiting to misdoubt her strength. Let her and Falsehood grapple; who ever knew Truth put to the worse, in a free and open encounter?" Another pamphlet defending the execution of Charles I placed him on the list of men that Charles II's government sought to execute, but friends in Parliament

spared him this fate. Milton's epic poem, *Paradise Lost* (1667), written after he went blind and after the restoration of the monarchy that he despised, is a profound exploration of the problems of evil and human free will. Drawing heavily on his extensive knowledge of classical literature, Milton memorably depicts the pride of Satan, who says, "To reign is worth ambition though in hell: Better to reign in hell, than serve in heaven." And he describes the Garden of Eden as beautiful, with "flowers of all hue, and without thorn the rose."

The Restoration period is famous for the anti-Puritan bawdiness of writers such as the royalist Aphra Behn. But the values that Restoration rakes espoused did not go unchallenged. John Bunyan (1628–1688) was a new kind of literary genius—a Puritan thinker, New Model Army soldier, and preacher. A poor man without formal education, he drew on the Bible, a vivid imagination, personal experience, and a knack for storytelling. He wrote, he said, what he "smartingly did feel," and many of his works were composed during a twelve-year imprisonment for his refusal to desist from unlicensed preaching. *The Pilgrim's Progress* (1678), an immediate bestseller, is the allegory of the soul's progress toward heaven. Filled with dramatic incidents (for example, Christian's arrest and trial at Vanity Fair) and lively characterizations (Mr. Worldly-wiseman, Madame Bubble, Lord Hate-good), it has been translated into more languages than any book except the Bible and remains a classic.

Although Bunyan knew little about it, the dominant literary temper of the English upper classes after 1660 was the neoclassicism of writers like John Dryden (1631–1700) and Alexander Pope (1688–1744). Like Racine and others in France, these men exemplified a far-reaching European reaction against the religious, political, and intellectual conflict, confusion, and turmoil that had characterized the seventeenth century. Affected by the rise of modern science (see Chapter 17) and fearful of emotionalism and religious zealotry, they preferred calm, order, reason, simplicity, and clarity. In their lexicon, the words "*enthusiasm*" and "*fanaticism*" were interchangeable and applied to Puritans like Bunyan. Dryden satirized the enemies of Charles II and his brother James in *Absalom and Achitophel* (1681), condemning Shaftesbury, for example, as "Restless, unfixed in principles and place;/In power unpleas'd, impatient of disgrace./A fiery soul which, working out its way,/Fretted the pigmy body to decay." Pope's *Essay on Man* (1733) denounced political and religious activism: "For forms of government let fools contest; What'er is best administered is best:/For modes of faith let graceless zealots fight; His can't be wrong whose life is in the right."

The Triumph of Order

If exuberant theatricality struck the dominant note in the baroque culture of the earlier seventeenth century, it was giving way to a different note after about 1660. In the visual arts as in literature, the desperate search for and discovery of order is the underlying theme. A good example is a French painter who worked mostly in Italy, Nicholas Poussin (1594–1665). He was guided by antique sculpture and displays the more restrained classicism that characterized the later seventeenth century. His controlled compositions (for example, *The Holy Family on the Steps*, 1648) are serious and contemplative rather than explosively energetic.

This subdued approach gained strength as emotionalism lost out to the calm, confident, rule-seeking rationalism of the mechanical philosophers and to the admiration of increasingly powerful governments that could restore stability. The greatest visual expression of this late baroque classicism was Versailles; and the architect, painter, and interior designer who contributed much to its success was Charles Le Brun (1619–1690). Having studied in Rome, where he came under Poussin's influence, Le Brun was employed by Colbert to direct the Royal Academy of Painting and Sculpture. There, young artists and craftsmen were trained to follow Greek and Roman models and their more recent admirers, such as Raphael and Poussin. Le Brun's interiors at Versailles (see the chapter's opening picture) created the grandest imaginable setting for the Sun King, combining classical solemnity with elegant opulence.

Many princes in the Holy Roman Empire built their own versions of Versailles—the new palaces at Würzburg, Mannheim, Munich, and Dresden were the most spectacular. But it was the capital city of the Habsburg rulers that underwent the most extensive transformation in the German-speaking lands. Not only the emperors themselves but the Austrian aristocracy as a whole gained wealth and confidence after the siege of Vienna, and the city was rebuilt with astonishing speed into a showcase of monumental baroque palaces, churches, and squares. J. B. Fischer von Erlach (1668–1745), who had studied in Rome, was the leading architect. His

stately library wing for the Hofburg and the imaginative and graceful Karlskirche were among his important additions to the city. Fischer collaborated with Lukas von Hildebrandt (1668–1745) on Prince Eugène's Winter Palace, an elegant setting for Marlborough's fellow commander in the long struggle against France. Hildebrandt's splendid masterpiece, the fanciful Belvedere Palace (1721–1722), became Eugène's summer residence.

England, perhaps predictably, lacked a well-organized official architectural establishment like the Academy in France, but the Great Fire of London created a splendid opportunity for the construction of new buildings and churches after 1666. As these structures emerged, it became clear that neoclassical regularity and proportions would dominate the English skyline no less than they did across the English Channel. Sir Christopher Wren (1632–1723), a mathematician and scientist as well as an architect, drew on French and many other sources for such magnificent buildings as St. Paul's Cathedral, Greenwich Hospital, and the new wing at Hampton Court built for William and Mary. Yet the most grandiose new structure, Blenheim Palace, was designed by Wren's rival, Sir John Vanbrugh (1664–1726). Vanbrugh taunted the French by making a massive stone statement honoring not the monarch but a subject—John Churchill, the Duke of Marlborough, whose victory in distant Bavaria turned the tide of war against Louis XIV and shifted Europe's balance of power. Atop one column, a stone English lion munches on the French eagle, and everywhere battle flags, drums, and cannons carved in stone celebrate the battle of Blenheim. Gazing at it, one understands the wag who wrote a satirical epitaph for the architect's gravestone:

Under this stone, reader, survey
Dead Sir John Vanbrugh's house of clay.
Lie heavy on him, earth! for he
Laid many heavy loads on thee.

Blenheim Palace, Oxfordshire Parliament, in the name of the people of England, rewarded the Duke of Marlborough for his defeat of France by building this huge palace for him and his family. His descendants still live there, and Sir Winston Churchill was born on the site. *Courtesy of J. Sears McGee.*

CONCLUSION: LOUIS XIV AND THE EIGHTEENTH CENTURY

The glittering court that Louis XIV established at Versailles astounded many of his subjects and most foreigners who visited it or heard about it. Many who never viewed Versailles saw the statues, medals, coins, engravings, and countless other representations of the Sun King. Indeed, before photography, film, television, and the Internet, his image may well have circulated more widely than any other monarch in Europe's history. On the foundation erected by Richelieu and many others, Louis built the most powerful state in Europe, and other princes tried to emulate his example. He chipped away at the ability of nobles, judges, officials, churchmen, and others to say no to him, and he thus moved France toward an absolutist way of making political decisions. To an unprecedented extent, he centralized administration in France and sought religious uniformity as the logical companion to his administrative machine. He built up military forces so powerful that only a mighty alliance of his enemies could stop him from achieving all of his ambitious foreign policy goals. If his "absolutism" was incomplete and imperfect, it nevertheless advanced farther than most.

Paradoxically, however, Louis's many successes, impressive though they were to his contemporaries, could not altogether hide the fragility of the structure that had been built. His power over the wealth (such as it was) of peasants may have been absolute, but he had to negotiate with nobles and many others. The resulting compromises put the pocketbooks of his wealthier subjects beyond his reach, weakened the French economy, and divided French society. The parlements and the remaining provincial assemblies, although intimidated and weakened, still existed. The enormous cost of his foreign policy meant that such essential domestic changes as the reform of venal office holding and aristocratic privilege could not go forward.

Meanwhile, the English and the Dutch, forced to resist his diplomats, propaganda, troops, and sailors, managed to find means of extracting a greater proportion of their national wealth in taxes and loans for the war effort than Louis could in France. The English Parliament and the Dutch States-General had sufficient political influence over the Stuarts and the Oranges to reassure investors that interest owed them would be paid and that the loans would not be wasted. With the help of the Austrian Habsburgs, they maintained the balance of power, although France remained Europe's greatest power even after the Peace of Utrecht.

What Louis XIV did not comprehend was that the intellectual foundations of the traditional European world picture had undergone a vigorous shaking during his long reign. Although he patronized the arts and sciences in a lavish and yet manipulative manner, the new ideas that would radically reshape Europeans and their institutions in the eighteenth century came not from Frenchmen but from two Englishmen: John Locke and Isaac Newton. Louis would have understood eighteenth-century politics, but the spread of a new kind of scientific thought and practice created an intellectual and cultural world that he would scarcely have recognized.

Selected Reading

Sources

Locke, John. *Two Treatises of Government*, ed. Peter Laslett (1960).

Mettam, Roger, ed. *Government and Society in Louis XIV's France* (1977).

Ranum, Orest, and Patricia Ranum, eds. *The Century of Louis XIV* (1972).

Sévigné, Madame de. *Madame de Sévigné: Selected Letters*, trans. Leonard Tancock (1982).

General Surveys

Black, Jeremy. *European Warfare, 1660–1815* (1994). A wide-ranging study of military changes that considers both technological change and the relationship between military organization and society.

Hatton, R. M. *Europe in the Age of Louis XIV* (1969). An illustrated overview, organized along topical lines.

Ranum, Orest, ed. *National Consciousness, History and Political Culture in Early Modern Europe* (1975). Includes essays about Italy, France, Germany, England, Russia, and Spain.

Absolutist States

Beik, William. *Absolutism and Society in Seventeenth-Century France* (1985). Uses the province of Languedoc to explain how Louis XIV dealt with aristocrats more successfully than Richelieu and Mazarin did.

Bluche, François. *Louis XIV* (1990). A thorough biography that attempts to defend Louis against his critics without ignoring his failings.

Burke, Peter. *The Fabrication of Louis XIV* (1992). An engrossing essay on the relationship between art and power by a leading historian of culture.

Goubert, Pierre. *Louis XIV and Twenty Million Frenchmen* (1970). An innovative effort to write the history of

Louis's France in terms of its people rather than the "Sun King."

Hatton, R. M., ed. *Louis XIV and Absolutism* (1976). Includes essays on the nature of French absolutism and on religious, economic, and financial matters.

Hughes, Lindsey. *Russia in the Age of Peter the Great* (1998). A broad-ranging and richly detailed survey of Peter and his era in Russia.

Parker, David. *The Making of French Absolutism* (1983). Sets Louis's regime in a broad historical context, describing absolutism as a tendency rather than a program and stressing its limits in practice.

Sonnino, Paul. *Louis XIV and the Origins of the Dutch War* (1988). An engagingly written and deeply researched study of the interactions between Louis and his leading councillors from 1667 to 1672.

Spielman, John P. *Leopold I of Austria* (1977). A brisk, clearly written biography.

The Constitutionalist States

Harris, Tim. *Politics under the Later Stuarts* (1993). Studies the origins and development of political parties in England from 1660 to 1715, with stress on the roles of both constitutional and religious concerns.

Israel, Jonathan I., ed. *The Anglo-Dutch Moment* (1991). Authoritative essays on the impact of the Glorious Revolution within Europe and around the world.

——. *The Dutch Republic: Its Rise, Greatness and Fall, 1477–1806* (1995). A magnificent survey set in a broad context and packed with fresh insights.

Rowen, H. H. *John DeWitt, Grand Pensionary of Holland, 1625–1672* (1978). The definitive biography in English, richly detailed.

Schwoerer, Lois G., ed. *The Revolution of 1688–89: Changing Perspectives* (1992). Essays exploring a wide variety of issues concerning the "Glorious Revolution," including literature, law, and women's history, as well as religious and political aspects.

Speck, W. A. *Reluctant Revolutionaries* (1989). An excellent descriptive and analytical study of the Glorious Revolution in England.

Culture and Society

Armitage, David, Armand Himy, and Quentin Skinner, eds. *Milton and Republicanism* (1995). Essays exploring John Milton's political ideas and goals in their historical context.

Todd, Janet. *The Secret Life of Aphra Behn* (1996). An ingenious effort to describe Aphra Behn's life by relying on her works to provide additional insights beyond the skimpy biographical record.

Ranum, Orest. *Artisans of Glory* (1980). Focuses on historians in the service of the French monarchy, including Racine.

THE SCIENTIFIC REVOLUTION

Sight *Erich Lessing/Art Resource, NY.*

1473–1543	Life span of Nicholas Copernicus, astronomer and mathematician (*De Revolutionibus*, 1543)
1493–1541	Life span of Paracelsus (Theophrastus Bombastus von Hohenheim), doctor and chemist
1514–1564	Life span of Andreas Vesalius, anatomist (*De Fabrica*, 1543)
1544–1603	Life span of William Gilbert, physician and scientist (*De Magnete*, 1600)
1546–1601	Life span of Tycho Brahe, astronomer
1561–1626	Life span of Francis Bacon, theorist of science (*Novum Organum*, 1620)
1564–1642	Life span of Galileo Galilei, astronomer and physicist (*Sidereus Nuncius*, 1610; *Dialogue Concerning the Two Chief World Systems*, 1632)
1571–1630	Life span of Johannes Kepler, astronomer
1578–1657	Life span of William Harvey, anatomist (*De Motu Cordis*, 1628)
1588–1679	Life span of Thomas Hobbes, political philosopher (*Leviathan*, 1651)
ca. 1590–1600	Construction of the first microscope and the first telescope by Dutch lens grinders

1596–1650	Life span of René Descartes, mathematician and philosopher (*Discourse on Method*, 1637)
1620–1674	Life span of John Graunt, statistician (*Natural and Political Observations Made upon the Bills of Mortality*, 1662)
1623–1662	Life span of Blaise Pascal, mathematician and philosopher
1627–1691	Life span of Robert Boyle, physicist (published Boyle's Law 1662)
1628–1694	Life span of Marcello Malpighi, biologist
1632–1704	Life span of John Locke, educational psychologist and political philosopher (*Essay on Human Understanding* and *Two Treatises on Government*, 1690)
1632–1723	Life span of Anthony van Leeuwenhoek, biologist
1642–1727	Life span of Isaac Newton, mathematician and physicist (*Principia Mathematica*, 1687)
1662	Chartering of the Royal Society of London by Charles II (first issue of its *Philosophical Transactions* published 1665)
1666	Founding of the Académie Royale des Sciences by Louis XIV

By early in the seventeenth century, when Jan Brueghel's series of paintings on the senses included this one (*Sight*), a gentleman was expected to be accomplished in the study of nature no less than the Greek and Roman texts and the arts so prized during the **Renaissance.** This collector's room is filled to overflowing with busts of classical heroes and contemporary paintings, so his interest in the humanist agenda is evident. But a telescope, an astrolabe, a sextant, and other scientific instruments are also prominent (center foreground). Watches dangle from the table, and a globe stands ready for use (center left). Brueghel's collector has clearly moved away from the tendency of many early humanists to reject the **scholastic** philosophers' interest in observing nature and theorizing about the cause of natural events.

Although the word *science* was not used as a professional term until the nineteenth century, historians consider that the **Scientific Revolution** began in the sixteenth and seventeenth centuries. During that era, the term *natural philosophers* was used to describe individuals who applied themselves to the study of nature. They sought primarily to gain greater awareness of God's creation in order to better understand and admire God himself. Nature, for them, was God's "second book," packed with insights as valuable as those in God's first book, the Bible. From hindsight we know that their efforts laid the groundwork for an important new concept: the idea that knowledge of nature could yield power over nature for humankind.

Earlier hopes for **progress** envisioned moral and social improvement or expanded religious insight, but the Scientific Revolution dramatically changed Europeans' ideas about nature and their philosophy, religion, art, and literature as well. It gave birth to a belief in the possibility of continuing *material* progress, a kind of progress never envisioned before. Today, societies that reject many Western political and religious ideas and cultural forms nevertheless aspire to participate in the continuing development of science and technology and to enjoy their fruits. Thus the Scientific Revolution initiated a transformation not only of Western civilization but the entire world. We are troubled by the weapons of mass destruction and the environmental damage that modern science has made possible, but we have no enthusiasm for returning to a world without airplanes, anesthesia, antibiotics, or automobiles.

The essence of modern science is a quantifying and experimental approach that aims to discover the laws explaining phenomena. To be accepted, these laws—the fewer and the simpler the better—must be verifiable by controlled and repeatable experiments. Modern science does not *prove* anything—it hypothesizes and theorizes, accepting a theory as valid as long as no facts emerge to force rejection or modification of the theory. By contrast, medieval natural philosophers and their heirs in the sixteenth and seventeenth centuries believed they could determine immutable "first principles" and find ultimate truths. Since God was eternal, they assumed, so must be the "laws" governing the behavior of natural phenomena that he had built into the world he created. The very word *science* (*scientia* in Latin) meant *certain* knowledge, and it applied in both moral and natural philosophy. A key part of the story of the Scientific Revolution is the story of how, mainly in the seventeenth century, many came to think that certitude about natural phenomena was unattainable. Only probability lay within human grasp.

THE BACKDROP TO THE SCIENTIFIC REVOLUTION

The belief that human intelligence should be employed to make rational or empirical inquiry into natural phenomena is deeply rooted in the history of Western civilization. This belief, especially prominent among the ancient Greeks, flowered again when their thought was reintroduced in high-medieval Europe (see Chapters 3 and 10). It stimulated the development of universities where thinkers came to believe that the universe worked according to natural rules. A few scholars proposed an experimental approach in the twelfth and thirteenth centuries, but not until the seventeenth did it begin to take hold among natural philosophers.

Witchcraft and Sorcery

The spread of a probabilistic approach to the search for the laws of nature occurred only among the social elite in the seventeenth century, and initially only among a minority there. Attitudes toward sorcery and witchcraft afford good evidence of the growing divergence between learned and popular culture. Until about the mid-seventeenth century, belief in what we now dismiss as magic and superstition pervaded the entire social order. Such beliefs were not irrational in the context of the traditional worldview, and doubtless many modern beliefs will look very strange indeed a century or two from now when viewed from the perspective of whatever intellectual framework succeeds ours.

Practice and belief in the form of magic known as sorcery has been virtually universal in human communities from the earliest times. Scholars have documented an enormous variation in types of sorcery. They range from

simple, such as having sexual intercourse in planted fields to increase the soil's fertility, to complex, such as elaborate rituals invoking the help of the ghosts of ancestors or other benign spirits. Sorcery could be employed either to beneficial or malign ends, and religion served as "good magic."

Magical beliefs from Europe, Africa, America, and Asia show numerous similarities. An obvious kinship exists, for example, between the methods of the African witch doctors, the *curanderos* (healers) of Mexico and the southwestern United States, and the "cunning men" and "wise women" of mid-seventeenth century England who, to cite one instance, attempted to cure headaches by boiling locks of their clients' hair in their own urine, then throwing it in the fire. Folk remedies are sometimes helpful, whether physically or psychologically, and few of them could have done as much damage as many of the treatments prescribed throughout this period by university-trained physicians, such as bleeding and violent purges. Use of "magical" techniques and devices was by no means limited to the lower classes. Elizabeth I's lord chancellor gave her a ring as a defense against the plague, and a leading English natural philosopher wore a rabbit's foot to cure his colic. Jean Bodin, one of the sixteenth-century's most widely read and influential political philosophers, wrote a book vigorously denouncing the assertion that alleged witches were mentally disturbed old women who could really do no harm. Magical beliefs performed—and still perform—important social functions, as people sought protection from harm and revenge against the causes of their sufferings.

Greco-Roman and Hebrew ideas strongly influenced the development of the concept of witchcraft in Europe. Many Greeks and Romans came to connect sorcery with the invocation of evil spirits and the nocturnal orgies of gluttony, drunkenness, and sex allegedly practiced by the Dionysians and even early Christians. Jewish **apocalyptic** writings after 200 B.C. developed the idea of Satan, the powerful spirit who sought to seduce the Hebrews away from true worship and who united in his own person all that is evil. Like the Jews, the early Christians feared Satan and assumed that persons who thought they could invoke and direct spirits were in fact seeking help from the devil and serving as his agents. Sorcery could no longer be either beneficial or even a harmless activity, and this link between sorcery and diabolism underlay all European witchcraft (see Chapters 3 and 5).

As Christianity spread throughout the Roman Empire and beyond to the Celtic and Teutonic north, the concept of witchcraft acquired new elements derived from **pagan** religion. In the Early Middle Ages, sorcerers were required to do lengthy penance. The church viewed them as faithless, deluded persons who merely fantasized that they could travel around at night on broomsticks in order to sacrifice and devour children and participate in orgies. Harsh persecution of witchcraft did not occur until people came to

THE HISTORICAL EVIDENCE

Bodin on Witchcraft

1580

Jean Bodin's De la Démonomanie des Sorcieres *(Of the Demon-worship of Witches) was quite popular; it appeared in fifteen editions in four languages after its initial publication in 1580. He wrote it to refute the skepticism of Johann Weyer, a physician whose book arguing against the persecution of witches because witchcraft was impossible was first published in 1563. Witches, said Weyer, suffered from "melancholy," a form of mental illness that made them delusional. To Bodin, Weyer's position was contradicted by evidence and was dangerous to the state.*

If it is thus true that the demons by a just permission of God have the power to separate the soul from the body, why would they not have the power to transport them corporeally [bodily]? . . . And beyond the authority of so many persons* we have the ordinary experience of an infinity of [witchcraft] trials, where the testimony, verifications, confrontations, conventions and confessions at the point of death can be seen. So it is not stubbornness on Weyer's part to maintain the contrary, but impiety, and a desire on his part to increase the kingdom of Satan.

For we have proof of Witches absent at night who have confessed the truth and the cause for their absence. We know that those newly arrived at such assemblies, calling God to their aid or simply afraid and horrified at what they saw, suddenly found themselves a hundred or fifty leagues away from their house, and took days to return from the place where Satan had transported them in a fraction of an hour. I remember recently the examples of Loches, Lyon, Le Mans, Poitiers, Chateauroux, Longny, and very many others. Just read the authors whom I have listed, who cut through all of Weyer's arguments that Witches are melancholics. . . . It is thus extreme folly for

Weyer to confess that Simon the Sorcerer flew through the air,[†] and to maintain that the other Sorcerers deceive themselves in thinking they are transported through the air to their assemblies. Has Satan less power than he had then, which was after the death of Jesus Christ? Even Weyer says that in Germany he has seen a Sorcerer-mountebank who rose into the heavens before an audience in broad daylight, and when his wife caught hold of his legs she was carried away, and the maid clung to her mistress and was also carried away, and they remained a fairly long time like that in the air.

---

* Bodin has been quoting authorities ranging from ancient philosophers and medieval Christian theologians down to the Dominican authors of the *Malleus Maleficarum* (see Chapter 11).

† Bodin is referring to a story in the Acts of the Apostles in which a magician tried to buy the power of the Holy Spirit, but was struck dead at a prayer by St. Peter.

Source: From E. William Monter, trans. and ed., *European Witchcraft* (New York: Wiley, 1969), pp. 52–53.

---

believe that witches really *did* such things. The scholastic theologians thought that sorcery involved an actual or implied pact with the devil, an act of free will that made it easier to justify persecuting alleged sorcerers and witches (see Chapter 11).

Although the theoretical and legal basis for the suppression of witchcraft was established by 1300, the number of witches prosecuted remained small until late in the fifteenth century. The great witch craze therefore occurred during the Renaissance and Reformation rather than the Middle Ages. Not only Bodin but other leading intellectuals such as Francis Bacon and Johannes Kepler (both discussed later in this chapter) accepted the reality of witchcraft. If God could intervene in nature, they reasoned, so could the devil. The advent of printing facilitated the

spread of the conviction that witchcraft threatened society. The first and most widely read of many books against witches was the *Malleus Maleficarum* (The Hammer of Witches), and it went through sixteen German and eleven French editions by 1700. Its first edition in 1486 included an endorsement from Pope Innocent VIII (reigned 1484–1492), who had already issued a bull (1484) requiring the German Inquisition to act firmly against witchcraft (see "Why Most Witches Are Women" in Chapter 11).

Written by Jakob Sprenger and Heinrich Kramer, both German Dominicans who spent most of their careers hunting witches, the *Malleus* explained that witches were heretics who made pacts with the devil. They wrote that "this heresy, witchcraft, is unlike other heresies because the witch's pact is not tacit . . . [rather it is an implicit]

The Witches' Sabbath   An early and widely imitated representation of witchcraft, Hans Baldung Grien's woodcut appeared in 1510. A scary old hag shouts instructions to younger witches, one of whom is preparing a potion to harm their intended victims. Above, flying backwards on a goat (symbolizing lust), another witch sets off on an evil mission. Their nakedness signifies an idea emerging in the decades around 1500 that witches were sexual deviants in league with the Devil. Indeed, the most savage persecution of alleged witches occurred not during the Middle Ages, but in the century after 1560.   *The Granger Collection, New York.*

compact, but . . . a compact exactly defined and expressed," and therefore, "blasphemes the Creator and endeavours to the utmost to profane Him and to harm His creatures." Witches supposedly had intercourse with Satan and each other in orgiastic "sabbaths" while their neighbors slept. Sprenger and Kramer contended that witches sacrificed children to the devil and practiced a variety of harmful tricks on ordinary people. The belief that witches killed children and boiled their bodies to make magic salves rendered midwives particularly vulnerable to accusations. Arson and magical spells causing illness and death were the kinds of evils for which powerless persons—often old, lonely women—could easily be blamed. Overall, women constituted about 75 percent of the persons executed as

witches (see Table 17-1). Yet as in so many dimensions of witchcraft accusations, regional variation was wide. In parts of France, for example, the majority of the accused were male. The *Malleus* and similar handbooks became guides for judicial practice. Judges thought that they were not only protecting their communities but also affording witches the only opportunity to save their souls by recanting before being executed.

The witch craze peaked between 1560 and 1660, as rapid inflation and extensive and destructive religious warfare heightened the social distress that stimulated witchcraft accusations (see Chapters 14 and 15). The Holy Roman Empire experienced the most witch trials, but France, Poland, Hungary, Switzerland, the British Isles, and Scandinavia also had substantial numbers (see Map 17-1).

TABLE 17-1
SEX OF ACCUSED WITCHES

Region	Years	Male	Female	%Female
Namur, County of	1509–1646	29	337	92
Luxembourg	1519–1623	130	417	76
Finland	1520–1699	316	325	51
Estonia	1520–1729	116	77	40
Hungary	1520–1777	160	1,482	90
Geneva	1537–1662	74	240	76
Castile	1540–1685	132	324	71
Nord, Dept. of the	1542–1679	54	232	81
Venice	1550–1650	224	490	69
Franche-Comté	1559-1667	49	153	76
Essex, County of	1560–1675	23	290	93
Southwestern Germany	1562–1684	238	1,050	82
Basel, Bishopric of	1571–1670	9	181	95
Pays de Vaud	1581–1620	325	624	66
Toul, City of	1584–1623	14	53	79
Aragon	1600–1650	69	90	57
New England	1620–1725	75	267	78
Russia	1622–1700	93	43	32

Source: From Brian P. Levack, *The Witch-Hunt in Early Modern Europe*, 2nd ed. (London: Longman, 1995), table 3, p. 134.

Some of the most shocking cases happened in German Catholic states, which had the highest incidence of "chain reaction" witch-hunts: The alleged witches initially arrested would name numerous accomplices who were then seized as well. In Trier, for example, around three hundred accused witches named five colleagues apiece, resulting in about fifteen hundred trials. In only seven years in Bamberg, some three hundred witches were burned early in the seventeenth century. On balance, however, Protestant and Catholic areas were equally affected. Yet the variation within such areas is striking. In Protestant Scotland, for example, three times as many witches suffered execution as in England (with four times the population). Differences in legal systems and procedures could affect outcomes dramatically. Scottish law permitted confessions after torture, whereas English law did so only rarely. In Scotland trials carried out entirely by local authorities ended in conviction 91 percent of the time; central authorities were much more lenient.

Some of the highest levels of persecution occurred in areas where religious authority was under threat from either the Protestant or the Catholic side. Since witchcraft was considered a form of **heresy,** a religious enemy could be destroyed with such an accusation. The witch craze even reached the New World, where it culminated in the famous trials at Salem, Massachusetts, in 1692, and the execution of nineteen people. A precise count is impossible, but the best estimates indicate that approximately 110,000 people underwent trial and 60,000 of them suffered death for practicing witchcraft between 1450 and 1660, nearly twenty times the number of heretics executed by the Spanish Inquisition. According to one witch-hunter, however, the authorities were not doing nearly enough to protect people from witches. "Witches by the thousands everywhere," he wrote, were "multiplying upon the earth even as worms in a garden." The decline in witch-hunting after the middle of the seventeenth century had many causes, but one was the growth of a more skeptical view in the ruling classes concerning the validity of claims against witches. This skepticism also had various sources, but one was rising interest in new approaches to natural philosophy.

The Old Cosmology

The greatest achievement of the Scientific Revolution came in the field of astronomy. It replaced an earth-centered with a sun-centered conception of the universe, a universe in which the movement of heavenly bodies is governed by the law of gravity. Ironically, in view of all the material benefits that have flowed from modern science, this achievement yielded as a practical benefit only a more accurate calendar. When St. Paul urged the early Christians not to let the sun go down upon their wrath, he was reflecting the long-held belief that the earth lay at the center of the universe. People continued to think in these **geocentric** terms for a millennium and a half. But by the eighteenth century, sunrise and sunset were known to be figures of speech for the movement of the earth, not the sun. To fully appreciate the ramifications of this shift in ideas, we must compare the old cosmology with the system that replaced it and then survey the forces that undermined it.

A cosmology is a theory that seeks to explain the structure of the universe. All human communities created (and modified) cosmologies by which they understood their own place in relation to the world around them and above them. Whether simple or complex, the theories provided the answers that people require as to why things happen the way they do.

During the High and Late Middle Ages, the final authority on most scientific matters in Western civilization was the ancient Greek philosopher Aristotle. His cosmology was also referred to as the Ptolemaic system after Claudius Ptolemy (ca. A.D. 90–168), the most famous astronomer and geographer of antiquity, who put Aristotle's beliefs about the universe into geometrical form (see Chapter 3). The Aristotelian-Ptolemaic system in the form it had achieved by 1500 had certain central and interrelated

MAP 17-1
GEOGRAPHY OF WITCHCRAFT PERSECUTION

concepts. The earth was a sphere (not flat) lying at the center of the universe. Solid, unmoving, and unmoved, it was surrounded by a series of spheres. Some of Ptolemy's successors explained celestial mechanics by concluding that these spheres were made of a crystalline substance, which enabled them to carry the moon, sun, planets, and fixed stars. The heavenly bodies, in other words, were set like jewels in the invisible but quite real substance that formed the spheres. The motion of the spheres was perfectly circular, and each sphere proceeded at a fixed speed, neither accelerating nor decelerating. Beyond the outer sphere, that of the prime mover, lay heaven, the home of God and the angels. God supplied the force that moved the spheres.[1] Everything above the earth was made of an incorruptible material that did not exist on earth.

The system also explained sublunary motion, or movement on the earth side of the moon. On earth, the rules governing motion and matter differed from those ruling the spheres, for here all things were corruptible and subject to change. Objects on earth were made of a mixture of two or more of four basic elements—earth, water, air, and fire. Earth and water contained a principle of gravity (heaviness), whereas air and fire embodied a principle of levity (ability to rise). The former tried to move downwards and the latter upwards. A rock would seek to move towards the center of the earth, even if it were taken to Mars or Jupiter. Thus the "natural" motion of sublunary things was not circular but straight up or down.[2] Motion on earth resulted either from the continuing struggle of the four elements to return to their proper stations or from the application of force—what Aristotle called "violent motion."

This traditional system was thoroughly value-laden, meaning that it stemmed from abstract "qualities" such as "levity" and "gravity." Physical quantities such as weight and velocity played no explanatory role, which meant that mathematics were relatively unimportant.[3] God was the highest being, and his residence is the highest sphere above the earth. Downward from God ranged everything that he had created in an ordered hierarchy—the "Great Chain of Being." From the angels just below God to snails, trees, and rocks on earth, everything had a specified place and prescribed value. Only human beings could, by God's grace (so

Christianity proclaimed), escape death and deterioration. They could advance from the earthly sphere, where all things were subject to decay, to another world utterly free of corruption if they obeyed God's commandments.

Hierarchy in church and state was no less a part of God's plan. The king and the pope, mirroring God, stood atop the earthly order. Nobles and higher clergy corresponded to angels, and so on down to the lowliest peasant. Each kind of person had a place and was expected to remain there. (Peasants, for example, were the "feet" on which the rest of the social order "stood.") In the heavens, in nature beneath the heavens, and in human society, a divinely created order gave function and purpose to everything, all arranged by hierarchical "degree" (rank). An attack on one part of this elaborate system could logically appear as an attack on it all. "Take but degree away, untune that string,/And hark, what discord follows!" is what Shakespeare's character Ulysses declares in *Troilus and Cressida*, expounding the traditional European view in the midst of a long, eloquent speech ranging over the entire social hierarchy.

The old cosmology that Aristotle, Ptolemy, and many others had developed had extraordinary longevity because it was comprehensive and could be confirmed by common sense. It was thoroughly satisfying because it explained why the sun, moon, stars, and planets behaved as they did. Closely parallel mechanical and biological theories explained why objects on earth moved as they did and why the human body functioned as it did. The system was rational; unlike the myths that preceded it (see Chapters 1 and 3), it rested on human reason as applied to the facts observed in nature. The renowned scholars of the medieval church (especially St. Thomas Aquinas) further bolstered the cosmology's authority by harmonizing ancient Greek science with Christian doctrine (see Chapter 10). The traditional cosmology and the theories connected with it constituted a **paradigm,** meaning a model that provided the interpretive pattern for practitioners as they worked to improve their understanding of the causes of natural phenomena. When an anomaly was observed, something that did not seem consistent with the paradigm, practitioners worked to harmonize the new information with the paradigm. Occasionally, however, anomalies might provoke a crisis that would destroy the old paradigm and produce a new one. The Scientific Revolution perfectly illustrates just such a paradigm shift.

Scholastics, Humanists, and Magicians

Why did the Scientific Revolution occur at all, and why did it occur when it did? In theory, the old paradigm, so persuasive and so long dominant, could have held sway indefinitely. Medieval scholasticism and Renaissance humanism contained strands of both support and opposition to new approaches to the natural world. Many scholastic

---

[1] This force was interpreted as "holy love" in the *Divine Comedy* by the great medieval poet Dante. Indeed, Dante's classic rests upon a Ptolemaic view of the universe. See Chapter 10.

[2] *Sublunar* means "below the moon"—"below" in the Aristotelian and Ptolemaic sense of occupying the space between the earth and the moon, its nearest celestial neighbor. In Aristotelian physics, all change, "corruption," and irregular motion took place in the sublunar part of the universe. On the moon and all heavenly bodies "beyond" it, everything was perfect and unchanging.

[3] Geometry was, of course, important, as it had been in ancient Greece and the Hellenistic world (see Chapter 3). Geometry's function, however, was static—to explain, for example, the "perfect" and unchanging nature of circular motion in the geocentric universe.

philosophers, especially those at such universities as Oxford, Paris, and Padua, saw their task as perfecting the old cosmology, or, to put it another way, defending the established paradigm (see Chapter 11). A few, however, while studying anomalies, proposed solutions that foreshadowed aspects of the new paradigm that would appear during the Scientific Revolution. For example, to explain the movement of sublunary bodies, Jean Buridan (ca. 1295–1358) developed the concept of "impetus." Impetus was a mysterious quality added to a material object when it was thrown, which caused it to move forward rather than immediately fall to the ground. His theory provided a step toward Galileo's thoroughly mathematical solution of the problem, discussed later in this chapter. Nicholas Oresme (ca. 1320–1382), Buridan's student at Paris, did pioneering work, as did a group of Oxford scholars, on the analysis of motion using mathematical techniques. Their methods also underlay Galileo's achievement.

In some respects, Renaissance **humanism** resisted the emergence of the new science. For Petrarch and many other humanists, the scholastic quest for the ultimate causes of things was useless because such things were unknowable and merely took time away from the really important goals of moral and civic improvement. The initial humanist emphasis on literary and historical studies left little time for scientific and mathematical interests. Several Renaissance educational reformers also opposed mathematical study because its abstract character drew the mind away from practical matters and from the pursuit of moral perfection.

In important ways, however, humanists did contribute to the new science, most importantly by discovering, translating, and publishing texts from classical antiquity. For example, fragmentary texts by some ancient Greek philosophers contained arguments in favor of the movement of the earth rather than the sun.[4] But this reverence for the wisdom of antiquity had complex results. As we saw in Chapter 12, many humanists became convinced that the wisdom of the ancients, lost for so long, contained the Hermetic and Neoplatonic keys to magical manipulation of nature ("natural magic"). Whereas witches tapped into the world of spirits in order to do harm by means of a compact with the devil, well-intentioned scholars could tap into the same world for benign purposes through gaining "secret knowledge" of hidden forces. They often directed their energies into astrology and alchemy (where they sought to transform base metals such as lead into gold). One technique came from Pythagorean number mysticism. The

ancient Greek thinker Pythagoras (ca. 560–480 B.C.; see Chapter 3) had believed that "the principles of all things" could be found in numbers, especially prime numbers (whole numbers such as 3, 5, and 7 that are divisible only by themselves and 1). For Pythagoras's followers, numbers and their unchanging relationships to each other embodied the divine. Through the study of Plato and Pythagoras, mathematics returned to later humanist thought after having been banished earlier (see Chapter 3). Late in the fifteenth century, the school of Florentine Neoplatonists led by Marsilio Ficino contributed powerfully to a growing ascendancy of Platonic over Aristotelian ways of thinking during the Renaissance. One of Plato's attractions for humanists was that he was "new," in the sense that few of his works had been known to the medieval scholastics.

Some who claimed the ability to work wonders astrologically and alchemically were charlatans. For example, John Dee (1527–1608), Elizabeth I's famed mathematician,

Stradano's *The Alchemist* This detail from a late sixteenth-century painting depicts a bespectacled and scholarly alchemist directing the work of his assistants in his laboratory in the struggle to purge base metals of their impurities and—so they hoped—achieve their purified and perfected state: gold. For Tycho Brahe (among others), study of the heavens and of earthly metals were related. He wrote that he made "with much care alchemical investigations or chemical experiments. . . . The substances treated are somewhat analogous to the celestial bodies and their influences, for which reason I usually call this science terrestrial Astronomy." *Scala/Art Resource, NY.*

---

[4] As we saw in Chapter 3, the Greek mathematician Aristarchus of Samos (second century B.C.) argued for a sun-centered universe. But his theory, like the early theory of atoms advanced by Democritus (ca. 440 B.C.), ran counter to the worldview developed by Aristotle, and so was not followed up by other ancient investigators.

astronomer, astrologer, and consultant on navigation, greatly admired Edward Kelly's skill as a "skryer" (a "medium" able to conjure up spirits using a crystal ball). Kelly traveled to the court of Emperor Rudolf II at Prague and convinced him that he could make gold and silver (see Chapter 15). Kelly lived comfortably at Rudolf's expense for years, but when his fraud was finally discovered he was tossed into the dungeon where he later died. Dee himself, who advised Elizabeth's sailors on navigation and geography, found that a mob ravaged his house and library because he was suspected of communicating with the devil. Tricksters like Kelly notwithstanding, however, such important figures of the Scientific Revolution as Nicholas Copernicus, Paracelsus, William Gilbert, Tycho Brahe, Johannes Kepler, and Isaac Newton, all of whom will be discussed here, showed keen interest in one or more facets of the Renaissance tradition of natural magic.

THE NEW SCIENCE IN THE SIXTEENTH AND SEVENTEENTH CENTURIES

Contributions toward a different way of understanding the natural world came from many other sources as well. The successful efforts of Gothic sculptors and Renaissance artists to portray their subjects realistically rather than symbolically encouraged close observation of nature. The development of mathematical perspective in Renaissance art stimulated the measuring, quantifying approach to nature that characterizes modern science. Influences also stemmed from other fields that utilized mathematical skills, such as banking, navigation, printing, and surveying. Clearly, the ocean-conquering explorers, such as Columbus and Da Gama (see Chapter 14), demonstrated that the ancients had not known all that there was to know about the world, and their success stimulated others who had doubts about traditional ideas. But no single "cause" satisfactorily explains the initiation of the Scientific Revolution of the sixteenth and seventeenth centuries. Influences flowed in from too many directions for any one of them to be the sole or even the primary factor. One point is incontestable: Nearly all the new scientists had university educations, and no other **civilization** at the time had institutions comparable to the medieval universities of Europe. The universities of Paris, Oxford, Padua, Bologna, and others varied widely in courses and procedures. Open debate had limits where religion was concerned, but ample space existed for free discussion of ideas concerning nature. Despite Galileo's famous difficulties (discussed a little later), university men (including churchmen such as Copernicus) made good use of that space.

The Scientific Revolution can be considered in two phases. During the sixteenth century, significant new approaches to cosmology and the human body emerged,

but these innovations received little attention outside a relatively small group of specialists. Early in the seventeenth century, however, the attack on traditional ideas about both the heavens and human anatomy and physiology continued—and this time gained the attention of most literate Europeans. Organizations also appeared to promote and extend the findings of the new scientists. By around 1700 learned advocates of the old understanding of nature were hard to find.

Sixteenth-Century Science

The first major assault upon the old cosmology came from Nicholas Copernicus (1473–1543), a cleric and astronomer whose method was more mathematical than observational. Born in Poland, he studied there and at the universities of Bologna and Padua before returning to take up a post as canon of a cathedral[5] near the Baltic Sea in what was then Polish territory. A conservative man, Copernicus had no intention of starting any kind of revolution. He dedicated his book, *De Revolutionibus Orbium Coelestium* (On the Revolutions of the Heavenly Spheres, 1543), to Pope Paul III. In it, he argued that the earth rotated around the sun in an annual orbit like that of the planets and that it revolved on its axis every twenty-four hours. These ideas were not completely new. An ancient Greek thinker had proposed such a **heliocentric** view (see Chapter 3), but the more commonsensical Aristotelian geocentrism had long prevailed.

Astronomical observers had long been aware that the apparently irregular motion of the planets created problems for the geocentric system. Observed night after night against the background of the stars, the planets appeared to stop and go backwards for a time, thereby exhibiting what was called retrograde motion. Astronomers solved the puzzle by postulating the existence of additional spheres, so that a given planet's motion derived from the movement of several spheres riding upon each other. Ptolemy had added several different circles in order to explain mathematically the more detailed and accurate observations that had been made (see Figure 3-2). Copernicus particularly disliked the untidiness of these complications. He believed that God would have done things more simply. Placing the sun near the center of the universe, Copernicus showed that at least some of Ptolemy's circles could be omitted without losing any of the old data.

Notice that Copernicus's theory did not dispense with the spheres, those tireless crystalline teamsters of the heavenly highways. He never doubted that they were there, as the title of his book suggests by referring to "heavenly

---

[5] A canon was one of the clergymen who formed the governing (or, more accurately, advisory) body of a diocese. They elected the bishop and helped him administer the diocese and its lands.

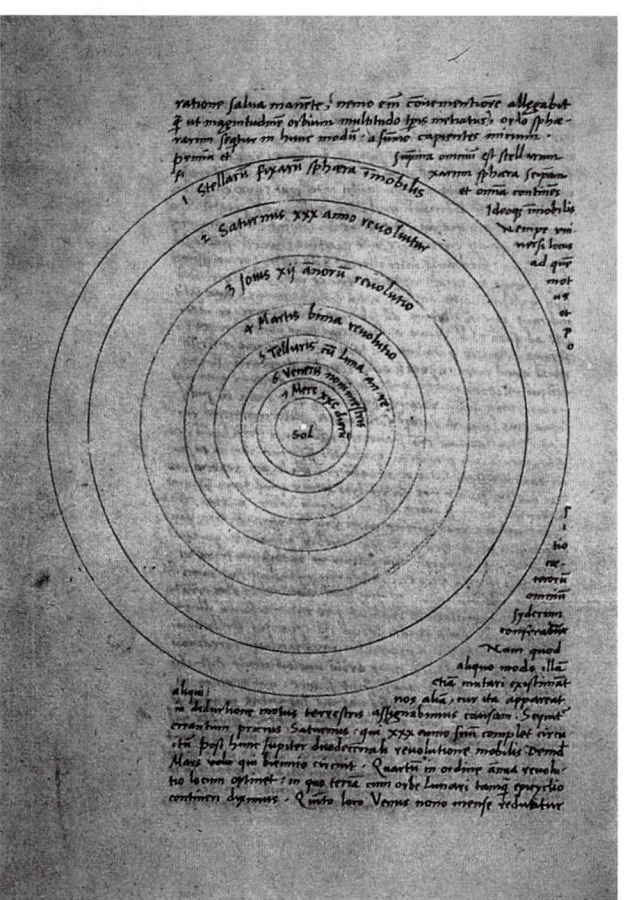

Copernicus's Heliocentric System Fearful of public ridicule, that he would be, as he wrote, "hissed off the stage," Copernicus resisted publishing his heliocentric hypothesis, knowing as he did that only fellow devotees of Hermetic and Pythagorean writings would welcome it. A tradition holds that he did not see his *De Revolutionibus* until he was on his deathbed, and it did in fact reach print in the year of his death. *The Granger Collection, New York.*

spheres," not heavenly bodies. Indeed, his work depended little on actual observation of nature and much on mathematical and philosophical ideas. For example, Copernicus clung to Aristotle's idea that the motion of the spheres was perfectly circular, and he argued that his theory did nothing to change the traditional understanding of motion on earth. His initial urge to "reform" Ptolemy may have been stimulated by his involvement in efforts (ca. 1509) to improve upon the Julian calendar. Because calendar reform would establish the true date for Easter, it was important to the Roman Catholic church and for all Christians. When in 1585 Pope Gregory XIII imposed the "New Style" calendar—which we still use, called the Gregorian calendar in his honor—most Protestant and Orthodox countries rejected it until the eighteenth century, and indeed Russia used the Julian calendar until 1918.

William Gilbert (1544–1603), an English physician, was no mathematician and took a much more experimental approach. Whereas Copernicus studded his argument with allusions to ancient authorities, Gilbert proudly proclaimed that his work was "almost a new thing unheard of before. . . . Therefore we do not at all quote the ancients and the Greeks as our supporters." He based his treatise on magnetism (*De Magnete*, 1600) on careful observations of the behavior of little magnets floating in water. From these he speculated (correctly) that the earth itself is an enormous magnet, rotating daily. Gilbert rejected Copernicus's view that the earth orbited the sun. But his projection of the force of magnetism throughout the universe contained the idea of action at a distance—no spheres were needed to explain movement; no divine Mover turned the spheres. Each magnet, he wrote, possesses an "invisible orb of virtue" around it. Gilbert thought of magnetism as an occult force, something ultimately unknowable and accessible only through magic. His work mixed experimentalism and the Hermetic theories of Renaissance natural magic.

Another brilliant observer and experimentalist, the flamboyant Danish nobleman Tycho Brahe (1546–1601), directed a team of assistants laboring at an observatory he built on a Danish island given him for this purpose by the king. Called *Uraniborg* ("City of the Heavens"), the observatory was the first structure in Europe built solely for scientific research, and Brahe designed the best instruments yet made to fill it. Having lost part of his nose in a duel, he installed a gold and silver replacement and at one point almost gave up astronomy for alchemy. Like Gilbert, he rejected heliocentrism, and instead postulated that the planets revolved around the sun and the sun around the earth (such was the power of the ancient idea of an unmoving earth). His demonstration that comets did not move between the earth and the moon, as had been thought, but wandered in the heavens, dealt a powerful blow against the concept of crystalline spheres. (Comets beyond the moon would obviously smash through those spheres.) Brahe was most famous for his naked-eye astronomical observations—the most thorough, precise, accurate, and sustained measurements made before the invention of the telescope. Every night he and his team observed and recorded the movements of the heavenly bodies, assembling the massive body of data that enabled Kepler to make the next great advance in astronomical theory.

The New Cosmology

Johannes Kepler (1571–1630) came from a troubled family in southwest Germany. His mother was accused of witchcraft, and his father narrowly escaped death by hanging. Despite having run afoul of the authorities, his parents intended that their son become a Lutheran minister. Kepler did study divinity at the Protestant university of Tübingen but then became a teacher of mathematics and astronomy in the Austrian town of Graz. When the forces of the Counter-Reformation ousted Protestant pastors and teachers from Graz in 1597, only Kepler was allowed to stay. By 1600, with the pressure for conformity mounting, he moved to Prague to become an assistant to the new imperial mathematician, Tycho Brahe. Upon Brahe's death in 1601, Kepler got his post and the task of casting Emperor Rudolf II's horoscopes (see Chapter 15). Kepler's brief partnership with Brahe had not been harmonious, partly because Kepler was already a convert to Copernican heliocentrism and his boss was not. But on the Dane's death, the young Kepler gained access to Brahe's astronomical papers, a veritable treasure trove.

From Brahe's data, Kepler derived his laws of planetary motion and presented them in a series of books published between 1609 and 1629. His laws required enormously complex computations without the benefit of calculus or any calculating device. The first two laws demonstrated (1) that the orbits of planets were not circular but elliptical, with the sun at one of the two foci of the ellipse; and (2) that the rate of the planets' movement was not uniform, although it was predictable. These two laws constituted a dramatic rejection of the traditional notions, taught

Galileo Offering His Telescope to the Muses Although Galileo gestures toward a sun-centered system, the muses (daughters of Zeus who represent the liberal arts) seem fascinated by his telescope. Astronomy was the responsibility of one of the muses, Urania (probably the central figure here with the stars in her crown).

by Aristotle and accepted by Copernicus. Kepler's third law showed that there was a consistent mathematical relationship between the times taken by the planets as they traveled around the sun and their distances from the sun. This law underlies Newton's later law of universal gravitation.

Unlike Brahe, Kepler surmised that if there were no spheres, then some other mechanism must be found to explain why the planets remain in their orbits. Influenced by Gilbert's theory of magnetism, Kepler suggested that the bodies forming the solar system were huge magnets, each possessing the "virtue" of magnetism as a motive force or soul. Kepler's laws were embedded in extraordinarily complicated Pythagorean numerical calculations purporting to discover the mystical harmonies of the universe. He believed himself to be the first man to hear the music of the spheres and see the intricate beauty of God's craftsmanship. At one point, he even admitted that a century might pass before his work would be understood. Kepler considered the wait reasonable, however, since, as he wrote, "God himself has waited six thousand years for his work to be seen."

Neither Copernicus nor Kepler experimented or observed; rather, they were primarily mathematicians seeking to account for data compiled by others. Galileo Galilei (1564–1642), a witty, engaging writer and a successful popularizer of Copernicanism, did both brilliantly. Like Kepler, Galileo was vain and touchy. Both men refuted the myth of the calm, rational scientist who relies solely on facts and has no ego. Born in Pisa, Italy, Galileo attended a Jesuit school and then the university of Pisa, where he wanted to study mathematics. His practical-minded father urged him to go into medicine so that he would make more money, but Galileo persevered and became a professor of mathematics, first at Pisa and then at the famous university of Padua.

Although Dutch lens grinders invented the telescope around 1600, Galileo was the first to turn it toward the heavens and to publicize his findings. His *Sidereus Nuncius* (Starry Messenger) appeared in March 1610 and caused tremendous excitement that brought him fame all over Europe. Whereas ancient Greek wisdom held that the moon and other heavenly bodies must be unsullied and uncorruptible, Galileo saw that the surface of the moon was not smooth at all—rather, he wrote, "it is full of irregularities, uneven, . . . just like the surface of the earth itself, which is varied everywhere by lofty mountains and deep valleys." This finding, along with his observation of sunspots, undermined the idea that the heavens were made of a specially incorruptible material. Moreover, Galileo's discovery of Jupiter's satellites showed that not all heavenly bodies rotate around the earth. His findings convinced most astronomers of the validity of heliocentrism.

Galileo's telescopic astronomy was exciting and easily understood, but in the long run his work in mechanics had equal importance. His concept of inertia revolutionized the physical sciences, and his experimental method transformed

THE HISTORICAL EVIDENCE

Galileo Attacks the Aristotelian Theory of an Immovable Earth

1632

Galileo's Dialogue Concerning the Two Chief World Systems, *from which the following excerpt is taken, contrasts the theories of Ptolemy and Copernicus in a debate between two fictional experts: Salviati, a Copernican, and Simplicio, an Aristotelian defender of Ptolemy. The book's accessibility to the educated public infuriated theologians and academic Aristotelians. Here, Salviati speaks for Galileo in advocating the Copernican hypothesis, and Sagredo is the open-minded layman who gradually accepts Copernicanism. Simplicio (who does not speak in this excerpt) does little more than repeat Aristotle's and Ptolemy's arguments.*

Salviati: Then let the beginning of our reflections be the consideration that whatever motion comes to be attributed to the earth must necessarily remain imperceptible to us. . . . So the true method of investigating whether any motion can be attributed to the earth, and if so what it may be, is to observe and consider whether bodies separated from the earth exhibit some appearance of motion which belongs equally to all. For a motion which is perceived only, for example, in the moon, and which does not affect Venus or Jupiter or the other stars, cannot in any way be the earth's or anything but the moon's.

Now there is one motion which is most general and supreme over all, and it is that by which the sun, moon, and all other planets and fixed stars—in a word, the whole universe, the earth alone excepted—appear to be moved as a unit from east to west in the space of twenty-four hours. This, in so far as first appearances are concerned, may just as logically belong to the earth alone as to the rest of the universe. . . . Thus it is that Aristotle and Ptolemy, who thoroughly understood this consideration, in their attempt to prove the earth immovable do not argue against any other motion than this diurnal [daily] one. . . .

Sagredo: I am quite convinced of the force of your argument, but it raises a question for me . . . : Copernicus attributed to the earth another motion than the diurnal.[*] By the rule just affirmed, this ought to remain imperceptible to all observations on the earth, but be visible in the rest of the universe. It seems to me that one may deduce as a necessary consequence either that he was grossly mistaken in assigning to the earth a motion corresponding to no appearance in the heavens generally, or that if the correspondent motion does exist, then Ptolemy was equally at fault in not explaining it away, as he explained away the other.

Salviati: This is very reasonably questioned, and when we come to treat of the other movement you will see how greatly Copernicus surpassed Ptolemy in acuteness and

penetration of mind. . . . But let us postpone this for the present and return to the first consideration, with respect to which I shall set forth, commencing with the most general things, those reasons which seem to favor the earth's motion, so that we may then hear their refutation from Simplicio.

First, let us consider only the immense bulk of the starry sphere in contrast with the smallness of the terrestrial globe, which is contained in the former so many millions of times. Now if we think of the velocity of motion required to make a complete rotation in a single day and night, I cannot persuade myself anyone could be found who would think it the more reasonable and credible thing that it was the celestial sphere which did the turning, and the terrestrial globe which remained fixed.

Sagredo: . . . I should think that anyone who considered it more reasonable for the whole universe to move in order to let the earth remain fixed would be more irrational than one who should climb to the top of your cupola just to get a view of the city and its environs, and then demand that the whole countryside should revolve around him so that he would not have to take the trouble to turn his head. Doubtless there are many and great advantages to be drawn from the new theory and not from the previous one (which to my mind is comparable with or even surpasses the above in absurdity), making the former more credible than the latter. But perhaps Aristotle, Ptolemy, and Simplicio ought to marshal their advantages against us and set them forth, too, if such there are; otherwise it will be clear to me that there are none and cannot be any.

---

[*] That is, the annual revolution of the earth around the sun.

Source: From Galileo Galilei, *Dialogue Concerning the Two Chief World Systems,* trans. Stillman Drake, 2nd ed. (Berkeley: University of California Press, 1967), pp. 114–115.

all science. Previously scientists had tried to explain the *cause* of sublunary motion—hence the idea that bodies moved in order to reach their "natural" locations. Galileo stated that motion is no less "natural" than rest and that the task of "natural philosophy" is to find mathematical formulas for changes in rates of motion. Unlike medieval natural philosophers, he did not care if the causes were innate qualities—such as "gravity" and "levity." And unlike Gilbert and Kepler, he did not care whether these changes stemmed from an occult "virtue"—such as magnetism.

Theorizing that all falling bodies accelerate downwards at the same rate, Galileo devised experiments to test his theory. "In such experiments, repeated a full hundred times," he wrote, "we always found that the spaces traversed were to each other as the squares of the times." His patient experimentation led to the discovery of mathematically predictable regularities in sublunary motion just as Kepler used Tycho's data to find regularities in heavenly motion. Galileo's method was as revolutionary as his law of uniform acceleration. Precisely measuring distances and times, he pioneered the modern scientific method. Not content merely to observe nature, he created experiments under controlled conditions that forced nature to reveal itself. And he did so to answer questions about "how much" and "at what rate"—not "why."

Some Protestant and Catholic churchmen welcomed Copernicanism, especially after Galileo demonstrated its physical reality and published his engaging books supporting it. But many others resisted. Ironically, Pope Urban VIII initially admired Galileo. In 1624 Galileo planned a trip to Rome but had to delay it because of poor health. A friend reported to him that the pope longed to see Galileo but urged him not to come until he was well, saying that "one should do whatever possible so that great men like you lived as long as possible." When Galileo finally arrived, Urban gave him six audiences in as many weeks and numerous presents and favors.

Unfortunately for Galileo, his early friendship with Urban ended in tragedy. By 1632, the pope was embroiled in a political crisis arising out of the Thirty Years' War and needed to demonstrate toughness against heretics. Claiming that Galileo had betrayed him by publishing a book (*Dialogue Concerning the Two Chief World Systems*, 1632) in which Galileo put the best arguments in the mouth of a defender of the physical reality of the Copernican system, Urban permitted the Roman Inquisition to try his former friend for heresy. In 1633 the Inquisition condemned Galileo for having broken an earlier promise not to "hold, teach, or defend" the Copernican theory. Aristotelian philosophers, angry at Galileo for having made them look foolish, successfully urged the Inquisition to muzzle Galileo. The conservative Inquisitors, worried that Galileo's defense of heliocentrism would undermine the infallibility of the Bible, seized the opportunity. Imprisoned briefly, Galileo then lived out the rest of his life under house arrest, mostly in his villa near Florence. There he continued to work and

write, although several of his later works had to be published in Holland. A devout Catholic, he consistently held that the church should not take a position one way or another on scientific questions.

Although Galileo broke with most of the tenets of the old cosmology, he retained a belief in the perfect circularity of inertial and planetary motion. An Englishman, Sir Isaac Newton (1642–1727), completed the break with the old cosmological apparatus. Born prematurely on Christmas Day in the year of Galileo's death, Newton was, according to members of his family, "so little they could put him into a quart pot and so weakly that he was forced to have a bolster all round his neck to keep it on his shoulders." Nevertheless, he survived his shaky start and went on to study at Cambridge. In 1669 the professor of mathematics there resigned his position in favor of the brilliant

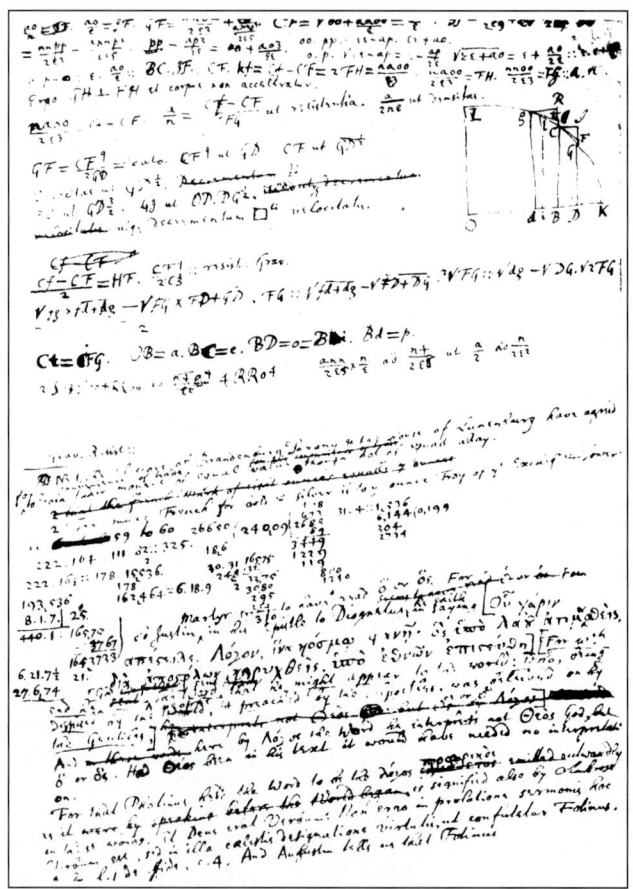

Newton's Interests At the top of this page from one of Newton's notebooks are some of his equations concerning motion in a resisting medium. This is the kind of work on which his fame is based. Immediately below them are calculations on currency values in France and Brandenburg. At the bottom are notes (in Greek, Latin, and English) from the Church Fathers (including Ambrose and Augustine) and other sources. His interest in theology was at times so intense that he complained that correspondence about optical and mathematical topics took too much time away from his theological reading. *The Granger Collection, New York.*

THE HISTORICAL EVIDENCE

Newton's Laws

1687

Newton published these famous laws, which revolutionized the conception of all motion in the universe, in his Principia Mathematica. *Although the mathematics he employed were too advanced for all but a handful of his contemporaries, the laws themselves were simple and straightforward. They underlay the universal law of gravitation that completed his description of the solar system as a huge machine.*

Law I. Every body perseveres in its state of rest, or of uniform motion in a right [straight] line, unless it is compelled to change that state by forces impressed thereon. . . .

Law II. The alteration of motion is ever proportional to the motive force impressed; and is made in the direction of the right line in which that force is impressed. . . .

Law III. To every action there is always opposed an equal reaction; or the mutual actions of two bodies upon each other are always equal, and directed to contrary parts. . . .

Source: From Marie Boas Hall, ed., *Nature and Nature's Laws: Documents of the Scientific Revolution* (New York: Harper & Row, 1970), pp. 271–272.

---

young man, an act of unusual perceptiveness and humility.[6] Newton's most famous book, the *Principia Mathematica*—the fully translated title is *Mathematical Principles of Natural Philosophy*—appeared in 1687. After 1687 he experienced periods of depression and suffered a nervous breakdown in 1693. In 1696 he was appointed Warden of the Mint and later became its Master, where he applied his computational skills to the monetary difficulties generated by England's long struggle with Louis XIV (see Chapter 16). Knighted by Queen Anne in 1705, he died in 1727 at age eighty-four. He was the first scientist buried in Westminster Abbey, an extraordinary honor.

Strange, aloof, suspicious, and secretive, Newton pursued a wide array of interests. He devoted much attention to alchemy, theology, and biblical chronology. His amazing ability to concentrate for days on a problem made him the archetype of the absent-minded professor. Once in his youth, he was leading a horse that escaped from its bridle, but Newton strolled home, not noticing that the horse was missing. An astronomer who knew him well wrote that if he were not reminded, he would go out "very carelessly, with his shoes down at heels, stockings untied, surplice [ecclesiastical garment] on, and his head scarcely combed."

Newton's system is so familiar to us that the achievement of the imagination that it represents must be placed against the Aristotelian cosmology if we are to understand its radically original character. He created a new paradigm, and it held firm until the work of Albert Einstein in the

early twentieth century (see Chapter 26).[7] The pieces of the jigsaw puzzle that he completed came from many sources—prominent among them were Copernicus's heliocentrism, Gilbert's magnetic attraction, Kepler's planetary laws, and Galileo's inertial physics. Newton's three laws of motion and the law of universal gravitation summarize the new synthesis.

Newton realized, as Galileo had not, that there need be no distinction between terrestrial and celestial motion. In the Newtonian system, the earth, like all the heavenly bodies, was floating in space. Every body—whether as large as the sun or as small as a speck of dust—attracts every other body with a force that depends on its mass and varies inversely as the square of the distance between them. The planets were prevented from continuing their motion in a straight line because gravity pulled them into the elliptical orbits that Kepler had visualized, just as it pulls a cannonball or an arrow to earth on a curved path. The force that holds the moon in orbit around the earth also pulls an apple to the ground from a tree. Moving bodies on earth obey the same laws as heavenly bodies. Neither crystalline spheres carrying bodies nor occult forces animating them are needed to explain movement of bodies anywhere in the universe. Gilbert's "virtue" of magnetism was something

---

[6] This is the same endowed chair that is now held by the famous cosmologist Stephen Hawking.

[7] Einstein's relativity theory, as well as the other great breakthrough in twentieth-century physics, quantum theory, does not invalidate Newton's work. But Newtonian physics now applies only to the "special case" of objects that are neither extremely large (where relativity prevails) nor minutely small (the domain of quantum mechanics). In the "special case," relativity and quantum effects are so small as to be virtually negligible.

alive, a kind of world soul or spirit, but Newton's gravity was a force working mechanically and behaving in a mathematically predictable way. He did not try to explain *why* gravity existed, nor could he say with precision what it was. Even now, scientists struggle to find out what it is, and a Nobel Prize–winning physicist has said that "the only difference" between our understanding of gravity and the medieval concept is that "the angels sit in a different direction and their wings push inward." Nevertheless, the mathematization of the study of nature lay at the center of the Scientific Revolution and found its culmination in Newton's laws. British poet Alexander Pope's 1730 couplet described the achievement:

> Nature and Nature's laws lay hid in night:
> God said, Let Newton be! And all was light.

Method and the Mechanical Philosophy

By example and sometimes by explicit commentary, the pioneers of the new science proposed a new methodology, and other thinkers quickly joined the discussion. An Englishman and a Frenchman—Sir Francis Bacon (1561–1626) and René Descartes (1596–1650)—stand out in this respect. Bacon issued an influential and elegantly written rationale for the inductive method in his *Novum Organum* (New Instrument, 1620). A lawyer and statesman who served both Elizabeth and James I, Bacon criticized natural philosophers who relied on inherited authority, occult properties, and abstract reasoning instead of planned experimentation. Induction, by contrast, avoided theorizing at the outset. Induction, Bacon wrote, "derives axioms from the senses and particulars, rising by a gradual and unbroken ascent, so that it arrives at the most general axioms last of all. This is the true way but as yet untried." Citing newly "found" regions of the earth, he envisioned modern scientists seeing farther not because they were smarter than Aristotle but because they could stand on his shoulders.

In *The New Atlantis* (1627), Bacon imagined a **utopia** for scientists, a research organization with state support and teams of workers. They would carry out systematic experimentation that would yield sure knowledge which, in turn, would improve the quality of human life. Their goal, Bacon wrote, was "the enlarging of the bounds of human empire, to the effecting of all things possible." Distrustful of abstract systems, he emphasized the importance of experiments as a means of obtaining proof, and as a lawyer he thought of proof in terms of establishing "facts" (evidence) that would satisfy a judge. Like alchemists and astrologers, Bacon asserted, scientists should seek power over nature to achieve what he called the "benefit and use of men" and "the relief of man's estate." Not a leading scientist himself—he preferred Brahe's cosmology to Copernicus's—Bacon nevertheless practiced what he preached, with unfortunate personal consequences. While testing the power of cold to preserve meat, he contracted pneumonia and died.

Although the empiricism of Bacon's program would have enormous influence on English science and inform the method of the Royal Society (discussed a little later), it had an important flaw: Bacon disliked mathematics because of its abstract, theoretical character. René Descartes, a distinguished mathematician, rejected Baconian induction in favor of the deductive method. Descartes located the error of earlier science not in its theorizing tendencies but in its excessive dependence on the evidence of the senses. Each philosopher, he thought, had built a world system on his own perceptions. But all qualities—blueness and greenness, hardness and softness, warmth and coldness, staleness and freshness—differed from one person to another, Descartes observed. Like Luther (see Chapter 13), Descartes found that everything he had been taught merely intensified his doubts. In his *Discourse on Method* (1637), Descartes explained that he had decided to reject everything he had learned from his senses and from books and to see whether there was anything of which he could be certain. The one fact that he discovered he could not doubt was the operation of his own mind. "*Cogito ergo sum*—I think, therefore, I am," he concluded. Confident of his own existence because he thought—even though most of his thinking consisted of

Descartes Writing His *Discourse on Method* Descartes had a dream in 1619 in which he believed he had been told by God to establish a new method of learning based on mathematics, a method that would overthrow all its predecessors. That meant overthrowing Aristotle—and here Descartes, in his study, pens his *Discourse* while resting his foot on a volume by Aristotle. Descartes wrote this work during the winter of 1635–1636 in Amsterdam.

doubting—Descartes reasoned that the ability to think must have come from "a Nature which was in reality more perfect than mine, and which possessed within itself all the perfections of which I could form any idea; that is to say, . . . God."

Having decided that the existence of God was as certain as the geometrical demonstration of the equidistance of all points on a sphere's surface from its center, Descartes asked himself what he could be sure of in nature. Because it was impossible to achieve certainty about qualities like color or occult forces such as Gilbert's magnetism, he decided, science should concern itself only with what he called "extension." A body occupies space that may be mathematically described in terms of its length, height, and depth. Only "extension," meaning occupancy of space, is certain, and all motion occurs as bodies press upon each other. Mind and matter are sharply distinguished, and the matter composing the universe (and our own bodies) is indifferent to our thoughts. Reasoning without much attention to experimental testing, Descartes constructed an elaborate theory of nature. The first such theory to be as comprehensive as Aristotle's, it rejected not only Aristotelianism but also the Renaissance magicians' belief in occult forces that caused movement and change. By late in the seventeenth century, the Cartesian approach to natural philosophy had triumphed in learned circles in France, where the Jesuits were numbered among its strongest defenders. Indeed, Jesuit educators fought the introduction of Newtonianism and helped delay its triumph in France until the middle of the eighteenth century.

The spirit of Cartesian rationalism opposed Baconian empiricism in methodological terms. Underlying them both, however, was the belief that scientists should work toward a mechanical explanation of natural phenomena, not one that relied on the occult forces of the natural magicians of the sixteenth century. Galileo's work partook of both methods, as did Newton's. The Newtonian system was thoroughly mathematical, but it also rested crucially on precise measurement of physical reality. Many Cartesians at first rejected Newton's concept of gravity because it seemed to them just the kind of occult force that could not be explained in purely mechanical terms. Newton was satisfied, as Descartes was not, to discover *how* nature behaves even when he could not be certain *why*. The tension between the differing methods was fruitful, as either one alone could be carried to excess. The fact is that the modern scientific method requires both inductive and deductive abilities in the effort to achieve, not certainty, but a highly probable confirmation of each hypothesis.

The Human Body

Although the most dramatic advances of the Scientific Revolution occurred in physics and astronomy, understanding of the human body also deepened. Before the sixteenth century, the reigning authority was the work of Galen, a Greek physician who, like Ptolemy, lived in Alexandria in the second century A.D. Galen postulated two kinds of blood, one flowing in the veins and the other in the arteries. Arterial blood directed the muscles and venous blood the digestive organs. Originating in the liver, all blood received vital spirits after passing through pores between the heart's ventricles. Like all things on earth, blood moved upwards and downwards, circular motion being found only in the heavens. Paralleling Aristotle's four elements—earth, water, air, fire—were four bodily "humors"—blood, phlegm, yellow bile, black bile—and all illness resulted from imbalance among humors. Physicians studied the color and smell of urine to determine which humor was in excess. Hence doctors were sometimes called "piss-prophets." Bloodletting, powerful laxatives, and herbal remedies were prescribed to rid the body of excess humors. Sometimes the patient recovered, thereby seeming to confirm the diagnosis.

Galen had based his system on the dissection of small animals. Although late medieval anatomists dissected human cadavers, Galen's authority went unchallenged until Andreas Vesalius (1514–1564) published his carefully illustrated *De Humani Corporis Fabrica* (On the Fabric of the Human Body) in 1543—the same year that Copernicus's *De Revolutionibus* appeared. The printing of Vesalius's book with plates made from drawings by artists skilled in the Renaissance's realistic techniques marked a dramatic improvement over hand-copied medieval books and drawings. Observers everywhere could suddenly compare their findings with each other's. Vesalius did not break with Galen's theory of vital spirits, but he could not find any pores in the wall between the ventricles. "Not long ago," he wrote, "I would not have dared to turn even a hair's breadth aside from Galen. But it seems to me that the septum of the heart is as thick, dense and compact as the rest of the heart. I do not see, therefore, how even the smallest particle can be transferred from the right to the left ventricle."

Meanwhile, an assault on the Aristotelian-Galenic system came from another quarter. Theophrastus Bombastus von Hohenheim, better known as Paracelsus (1493–1541), was born near Zurich. He studied under a famed alchemist and served as a military surgeon. Surgery was then a craft, usually performed by men of meager education and low social standing (such as barbers). To university-educated physicians, who rarely practiced surgery, the confident Paracelsus wrote that "every little hair on my neck knows more than you and all your scribes, and my shoe-buckles are more learned than your Galen." Rejecting the humoral theory of disease, he believed that disease came when forces attacked the body's organs. Diseases, Paracelsus insisted, should be treated with chemicals drawn from minerals rather than the herbs favored by Galenists, and experiments were needed to find new drugs and to determine their precise dosages.

Paracelsus based his ideas on the Neoplatonic and Hermetic theories that had informed the tradition of Renaissance magic. To Aristotle's four elements, he added

Vesalius's *De Fabrica* This is the title page (1543), and it shows Vesalius dissecting a corpse while surrounded by a fascinated audience. Like Copernicus, Vesalius was cautious. He approached the established Galenic verities with respect, but when his own observations could not confirm the master's views, he dissented respectfully—but firmly. *The Granger Collection, New York.*

The life sciences overall advanced dramatically in the seventeenth century. Natural philosophers developed novel means of classifying plants and animals, partly stimulated by new species found in the recently discovered regions of the world. The microscope, invented early in the period, found its most brilliant users in Holland's Anthony van Leeuwenhoek (1632–1723) and Italy's Marcello Malpighi (1628–1694). Malpighi published studies of silkworm eggs showing the "preformed" insects with all their organs in the eggs. "Preformationism" therefore held that all life was encapsulated in eggs. Moreover, because females produced eggs, the role of the female in generation seemed critical. But then in 1677, Leeuwenhoek, who also discovered bacteria and red corpuscles in blood, found male spermatozoa in semen. He called them "animalcules." A furious debate ensued between "preformationism" and "animalculism," with proponents of the latter holding that the organism was encapsulated in the male rather than the female contribution.

The discovery of the circulation of the blood, however, was the single most important physiological discovery of the age. English physician William Harvey (1578–1657) announced it in his book, *De Motu Cordis* (On the Motion of the Heart and Blood, 1628), but the idea did not win acceptance until Malpighi observed the capillaries in a frog's lung with his microscope in 1659. Capillaries provided the link between arteries and veins that Harvey believed must exist but that he had not been able to observe. Harvey had studied at Cambridge and Padua and later served as physician to James I and Charles I. At Padua, Vesalius had correctly described the heart's structure, and one of his successors there who taught Harvey had found the valves in veins. Several writers had speculated that blood from the heart traveled to the lungs to be mixed with air or some vital spirit, thus contradicting Galen's view that the lungs merely cooled heated blood. Others had theorized about the possible correspondence between a circular blood flow and the circularity of movement in the heavens—the microcosm-macrocosm analogy that had intrigued Paracelsus and others.

Harvey, somewhat like Newton, synthesized existing ideas and his own inductive work. He observed vivisections of small animals and decided that the critical element in the heart's motion was its contraction (systole) rather than its expansion (diastole) as Galen thought. Then he measured the capacity of the left ventricle and multiplied the quantity of blood expelled by the number of pulse beats. He calculated some 50 pounds of blood per hour in an animal whose body contained only a few pounds of blood. The conclusion that the same blood circulated throughout the body continuously was inescapable. Noting also that the valves were so constructed that they permitted movement in only one direction throughout the body, Harvey compared the heart to a water pump.

the triad of salt, sulfur, and mercury, partly because of their parallel with the Holy Trinity. Paracelsus's followers later elaborated a theory of the divine creation of the universe as an unfolding of nature in chemical terms. Paracelsus thought of the human body as a microcosmic reproduction of the chemical changes occurring in the entire universe— the macrocosm. Some Paracelsians therefore came to oppose bloodletting as a medical treatment because it drained the body of the *spiritus mundi*—the life force that coursed through the universe. Although the use of mercury and other poisonous metals probably killed as many patients as the older treatments, the "new medicine" came to rival the old. One reason that people found it attractive (and even survived it) may well have been that the Paracelsians emphasized observation of patients and their symptoms, where as Galenic physicians often theorized about medicine rather than actually see patients regularly.

Although Descartes used the pump analogy to incorporate Harvey's discovery into his mechanical philosophy, Harvey himself had more interest in the mystical implications of his work. He wrote that "the heart is the sun of the microcosm, even as the sun in his turn might well be designated the heart of the world; . . . it is the household divinity which, discharging its function, nourishes, cherishes and quickens the whole body, and is indeed the foundation of life, the source of all action." Harvey praised Charles I in terms of the traditional KING = SUN = HEART analogy derived from the Great Chain of Being. He thought of blood as a spiritual fluid, calling it "celestial, . . . the inmate of the spirit, . . . something analogous to heaven, the instrument of heaven, vicarious of heaven." Harvey was fundamentally an Aristotelian, for it was Aristotle who had insisted on the primacy of the heart—rather than the liver—in the body. And in discovering the circularity of blood flow, Harvey introduced into physiology the "perfect motion" that in the old cosmology was found only in the heavens. Ironically, he brought the perfection of the circle into scientific thinking about the human body only nineteen years after Kepler banished it from the solar system.

Patrons and Institutions

New methods and new ideas, about nature or anything else, require support if they are to survive and prosper. Individual thinkers, no matter how brilliant, innovative, or persistent, cannot create movements by themselves. They need financial support, and they need colleagues and followers who will carry forward the work they have begun. Copernicus, a Polish humanist who had studied law and medicine at Italian universities, held a church position that enabled him to pursue his lifelong astronomical research. In the late sixteenth and early seventeenth centuries, the patronage of princes (including princes of the church such as popes, bishops, and cardinals) was critical, not least because their endorsement could help to legitimize the new ideas in the eyes of contemporary intellectuals. A major barrier to the acceptance of the Copernican hypothesis had been its mathematical character. Philosophers, in the medieval scheme of things, explained the *causes* of phenomena, whereas mathematicians were mere technicians. In the same way, physicians far outranked anatomists, for physicians dealt with the underlying causes of illness. Philosophy and medicine were, in other words, cognitively superior to mathematics and anatomy, and their practitioners were socially and academically superior.

Although Galileo held university posts early in his career, he concluded that the legitimation of Copernicanism would require changes in the hierarchy of disciplines. Around 1600, he began diligently pursuing the patronage of the Medici dukes of Tuscany. Through his telescope in 1610, Galileo saw the four satellites of Jupiter, and he christened them the "Medicean Stars" and dedicated his discovery to the Medici family. Later that year, Duke Cosimo II appointed Galileo his Mathematician and Philosopher, and began paying him a salary. The grant of the title of "philosopher" by an absolute prince, coming as it did with other marks of favor, definitely raised Galileo's social status and strengthened his claims for the upgrading of mathematics and astronomy within the hierarchy of academic disciplines. At the same time, the Medicean Stars brought new local and European prestige to the Tuscan dynasty because of the fame of Galileo's telescopic findings as reported in his *Sidereus Nuncius*. Later Galileo tried to play the same courtly game with Pope Urban VIII, an effort that, as we have seen, began happily but ended disastrously.

In the sixteenth century, most natural philosophers discussed their work and corresponded about it among themselves. By early in the seventeenth century, however, informal groups began meeting regularly in a number of cities and towns to exchange ideas. In Florence, for example, the *Accademia del Cimento* (Academy of Experiments) met under the leadership and patronage of the duke's brother, Prince Leopold de' Medici, from 1657 to 1667. Lacking a charter, it collapsed after Leopold moved to Rome, but a volume summarizing its work appeared in 1667. At different times, groups composed of men interested in the new science met in Paris, London, Oxford, Bologna, Naples, Caen, Rouen, Castres, and Montpellier, among others. During the 1630s and 1640s, a Parisian friar, Marin Mersenne (1588–1648), conducted an enormous correspondence in which he summarized reports of new scientific work for people all over Europe. In these rather informal ways, something like a scientific community of international scope came into existence. By no means did all of its members have deep knowledge or technical expertise. Many were simply country gentleman, clerics, physicians, and lawyers who read books by Galileo and other leading natural philosophers; collected fossils, plants, insects, or animals; and took pleasure in discussing their interests with like-minded individuals. By such means, the new science crept into the consciousness of the educated elite in Europe during the seventeenth century.

During the 1660s, official government action registered the respectability and popularity of the new science in France and England. In 1666 in Paris, King Louis XIV established the *Académie Royale des Sciences* (Royal Academy of Sciences). Louis himself had no interest in science and visited it only once; the impetus for the establishment came from Jean-Baptiste Colbert as part of his plan for making the king the patron and focus of all creative activity in France (see Chapter 16). The goal, in other words, was the greater glory of the monarchy, as it had been when the Medici dukes patronized Galileo. The number of fellows was limited to around twenty of the brightest men whom Colbert could find, and their salaries and the money for equipment came from the state. King Charles II chartered the Royal Society of London in 1662, but this simply

The Académie Royale des Sciences, 1698 This representation of the activities of the members of the scientific academy established in Paris by Louis XIV is fanciful in that they appear in Greco-Roman garb in a temple-like architectural milieu that was no less classical. But their work in physics, astronomy, and mathematics does characterize what natural philosophers concentrated on late in the seventeenth century. The theological library (upper right) and the display of heraldic shields (center foreground) reinforced the idea that the study of nature in this mode strengthened rather than threatened the established religious, social, and political order. *Mary Evans Picture Library.*

gave the adjective *royal* to a group that already existed. In fact, most of its members had been meeting in Oxford and London for many years, and all the royal charter did was offer moral support. An Italian scientist who visited London in 1667 was saddened when he heard that the king was "accustomed to call his academicians by no other name than *mes fous* (my jesters)."[8] The Royal Society's funds came not from the state but from subscriptions paid by its numerous members, nearly half of whom were noblemen and gentlemen inspired by Baconian rhetoric. The first issue of the *Philosophical Transactions*, a model scientific journal, was published in 1665, and it continues to this day under the Royal Society's direction. During the eighteenth century, comparable national institutions emerged in Germany (Berlin, 1700), Russia (St. Petersburg, 1724) and North America (Philadelphia, 1769). As the scientific societies and their publications grew, information spread

faster, and scientific ideas could be tested and challenged more easily.

Although the growing volume of scientific publication promoted an international awareness of the new science and a sense of membership in an international community among experimenters, national differences can be observed in the way that scientists worked and thought. In Italy, Galileo succeeded by entertaining and exciting courtiers and princes with slashing attacks against his Aristotelian critics. In England, however, a nation devastated by civil war, the founders of the Royal Society studiously avoided personal attacks because they caused antagonism and disorder. English scientists placed heavy emphasis on the discovery of "matters of fact" that had been proven by repeated experiments observed publicly by many members.

In England the goal was to avoid argument, not encourage it. Sir Robert Boyle (1627–1691), a wealthy gentleman and a leader in the Royal Society, provided an influential model. Writing in the late 1650s, he explained to his colleagues that he had avoided close study of the works of Descartes or other creators of systems "that I might not be

---

[8] His father, Charles I, was the last English king to carry on his payroll an official royal fool.

Huygens's Air Pump at the Académie Royale, 1668
The study of atmospheric pressures was a major preoccupation of natural philosophers all over Europe in the second half of the seventeenth century. Huygens demonstrated his improved device at the *Académie Royale* in 1668, and he argued that his device was superior to those being used at the Royal Society in London by Sir Robert Boyle and others. Then as now, rivalry and competition among scientists was intense and sometimes quite bitter. *Edinburgh University Library*.

prepossessed with any theory or principles, till I had spent some time in trying what things themselves would incline me to think." Since hasty theorizing led to quarrels, the English style was to concentrate on the "things themselves," meaning observation and experiment in the Baconian manner. The English experimenters also maintained that, in physical matters, certainty depended on the degree of *probability* of a hypothesis. Since hypotheses about nature could be revised, the apparent certainty that mathematical demonstration yielded could never be achieved. In France, by contrast, the tradition of state support produced a more centralized approach to the scientific enterprise. Although Descartes's mechanistic system had few admirers in France before his death in 1650, by late in the seventeenth century the small group of elite scientists who made up the Académie Royale had all converted to it. Because science in France became focused on the prestigious Académie, Cartesianism became the reigning orthodoxy, not to be overthrown by the Newtonian paradigm until the middle of the eighteenth century.

Instruments, Techniques, and Technology

The seventeenth century also saw rich innovation in scientific instruments. Arabic numerals became widely used in place of cumbersome Roman numerals, and analytical geometry, calculus, and logarithms were invented.[9] Telescopes, microscopes, thermometers, barometers, air pumps,

slide rules, and precise pendulum clocks were introduced—most of which remain in extensive use today. Without such instruments, several major discoveries of the era would have been impossible. Robert Boyle, for instance, a tireless experimenter, used the barometer and air pump to discover the relationship between air pressure and volume (Boyle's law). An older invention, the printing press (see Chapter 11), underlay much of the new work in science, for it was essential for the dissemination of findings. Maps, diagrams, charts, tables of equations, and mathematical data accompanied the printed word, enabling scientists to check and build on each other's work on an unprecedented scale and with a newfound precision.

The new science's mathematizing spirit encouraged the spread of a more statistical outlook, which led people to expect a cycle of good and ill fortune. Such cycles did not need to be explained by supernatural influences. John Graunt (1620–1674), more than any other individual, laid the basis for the modern insurance business by founding the disciplines of statistics and demography. Graunt, a London draper and the only active tradesman to become a member of the Royal Society, studied lists of the numbers of christenings and deaths in each ward of London. More than a century earlier, the keeping of registers of births, marriages, and deaths had been mandated by Henry VIII's government, but Graunt was the first to analyze the information. In his *Natural and Political Observations Made upon the Bills of Mortality* (1662), he demonstrated, among other things, the numerical regularity of births and deaths and the likelihood of death from any particular cause. Medieval Italian moneylenders had insured ships and cargoes as a sideline (see Chapter 8), but not until after 1650 did specialized private businesses offer fire, marine, or life insurance. They could do so because the work of Graunt and others, with its delight in quantification, made it possible

---

[9] Newton claimed the credit for having discovered calculus, and his work in physics would have been almost impossible without it. Nevertheless, Newton's claim to priority was bitterly contested by another genius of the late seventeenth century, the German philosopher Gottfried Wilhelm Leibnitz (1646–1716).

THE HUMAN EXPERIENCE

W. J. Blaeu, Astronomer and Cartographer

Willem Janszoon Blaeu's father and grandfather were herring packers. For a time, it appeared that Willem (1571–1638) would stay in the herring business, for he spent several years clerking for a herring merchant. But in 1596 he traveled to the Danish island of Hven, where the famous astronomer Tycho Brahe worked in his observatory at Uraniborg. Brahe, in whose notebook Willem appears as "Vilhelmius Batavius" (William the Dutchman), took him on as an assistant and pupil. Blaeu must already have shown proficiency in geography, astronomy, and scientific instrument making because students were not admitted to Uraniborg except by Tycho's invitation. Blaeu took pride in the honor, as evidenced by the legend on a celestial globe that he later made, which read that the positions of the stars were "taken from the most accurate observations of Master Tycho Brahe, my former teacher."

In 1596 Blaeu moved to Alkmaar, near Amsterdam. He married Maertgen Cornelis and soon celebrated the birth of the first of their seven children. After moving to Amsterdam in 1599, he borrowed money to buy a house and began to make and sell maps, terrestrial and celestial globes, and scientific and navigational instruments (sextants, quadrants, and so on). By 1605 he had a new shop under the sign of a golden sundial in a street (now the fashionable Damrak) then lined by many booksellers and mapmakers.

Blaeu began to publish maps in 1604. His first sea atlas, *The Light of Navigation* (1608), scored a huge success and was frequently reprinted and published in England and France. As he put it, the book contained "what knowledge of Astronomy is necessary for the seafaring man," followed by charts precisely depicting coastlines (especially harbors and channels). Blaeu asked "all intelligent and observant pilots and those who are interested in navigation" to report errors to him for correction in subsequent editions. In 1623 the authorities gave him a ten-year copyright for his *Zeespieghel*, a group of tables listing the declinations of the sun and stars from which a navigator could calculate his position. In this way the astronomer-turned-publisher joined his manifold skills to assist seafarers.

Blaeu also made a good living from his publications. A shrewd businessman, he cleverly brought out his edition of Copernicus's *De Revolutionibus* just after the Catholic church denounced it in 1616. Blaeu's atlases kept expanding, and in 1636 he paid eleven thousand guilders for a building that he turned into a large, technically advanced printing plant. He designed a new press that embodied the first substantial improvements since Gutenberg's day (see Chapter 11). Blaeu died in 1638, less than a year after Maertgen. But his eldest son, John, who earned a doctorate in law from the University of Leiden, had entered his father's business in 1630 and continued and expanded it. His magnificent twelve-volume *Atlas Major* (1662), with its six hundred hand-colored, gold-leaf trimmed maps and splendid bindings, was the costliest book available late in the seventeenth century. The Dutch government even presented copies of the work to the Ottoman sultan and the Holy Roman emperor on state occasions. Ironically, however, W. J. Blaeu's inexpensive little *Light of Navigation* was a much more practical book, regularly used by many more people than the gorgeous atlas. ❖

to calculate the probability of losses—and therefore the appropriate premiums to charge. In this way, the Scientific Revolution in the physical sciences helped spawn a new "social science," which began to yield practical benefits late in the seventeenth century.

By late in the seventeenth century, some governments had begun to apply policies influenced by this new mentality. One of Louis XIV's advisers, for example, proposed basing taxation on the notion of people as numerical units rather than as members of social ranks—that is, on quantities rather than qualities. Louis XIV's army was modern in the sense that its units were all the same size and were recruited, supplied, and controlled from the center rather than by nobles who had regional power bases. From the state's point of view, the potential utility of the new science was greatest in the areas of agricultural, commercial, industrial and military development. But in many instances, the practical benefits that rulers like Louis XIV and the subscription-paying members of the Royal Society hoped to get in return for the money they invested in science lay in the distant future.

Practical applications of Europeans' growing knowledge of nature occurred throughout the Scientific Revolution. For example, in sixteenth-century Germany a series of important treatises on mining and especially the chemistry involved in extracting and refining minerals were published. In seventeenth-century England, enormous effort went into techniques for increasing agricultural output by improving techniques for surveying and draining land, breeding animals, growing new crops for animal fodder, and so on. John Evelyn (1620–1706), a country gentleman and a member of the Royal Society, crusaded for reforesting

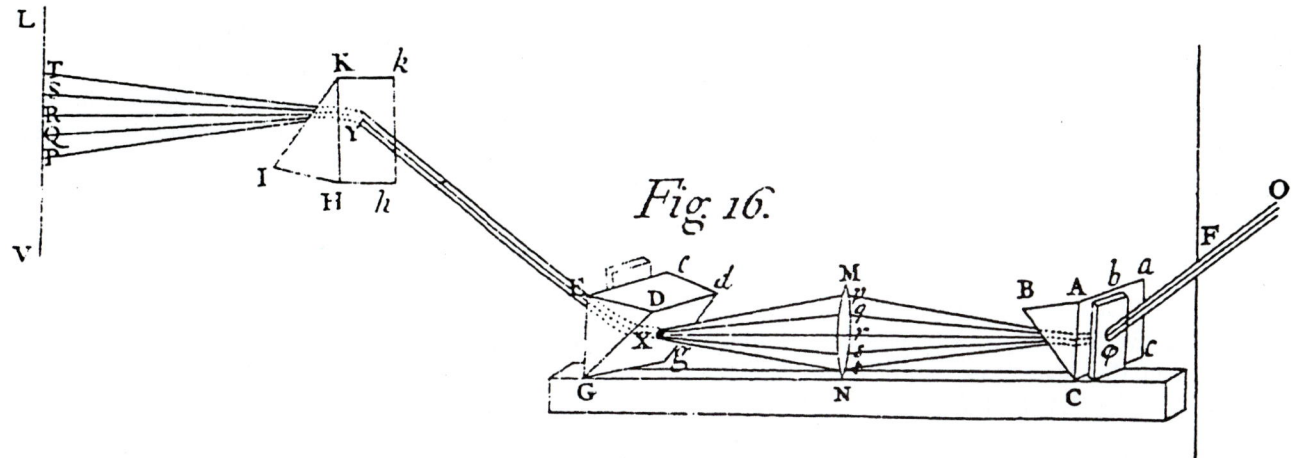

Diagram from Newton's *Opticks* (1704) Although Newton did his pioneering work on light in the late 1660s and early 1670s, he did not publish a full account until 1704. Using a laboratory built just outside his rooms in Trinity College, Cambridge, he performed experiments that perfectly exemplify the new methodology of the Scientific Revolution. Using prisms, he showed that white light is composed of the whole spectrum of colors. His wave theory of light is still influential. *The Granger Collection, New York.*

England because the medieval and early modern iron and shipbuilding industries had used up massive quantities of the nation's once-extensive forests. The success of the tiny Dutch nation rested on seaborne trade rather than agriculture. Accordingly Dutch scientists and craftsmen led the world in the development of telescopes, binoculars, and scientific instruments. Many scientists, including Newton, worked on ways to improve ship design and to find out how to determine longitude, the biggest unsolved problem facing navigators of both trading and naval vessels on the high seas. Galileo, for example, tried to use his observations of Jupiter's moons (the Medicean Stars) to determine longitude. One of the leading members of the Académie in Paris, the Dutchman Christian Huygens (1629–1695), discovered around 1675 that atmospheric pressure could produce energy if an enclosed fluid was heated and then cooled. He found, in other words, the operating principle of the steam engine—the basis of the **Industrial Revolution** (see Chapter 20).

THE SCIENTIFIC REVOLUTION: IMPACT ON SOCIETY AND CULTURE

The rise of modern science initiated a revolution that is still going on. The computer, especially because of its number-crunching capacity and its ability to store enormous amounts of data, is the most powerful tool yet developed for doing the work that scientists such as Copernicus, Kepler, Galileo, Bacon, Descartes, Harvey, and Newton launched. The fascination with quantification and experimentation that characterizes today's society sprang directly from the new way of knowing that these thinkers developed. Gradually, educated people came to believe that beneath the bewildering variety of things that we perceive with our senses lies a unified order that we can analyze with mathematics. Such an enormous conceptual change inevitably had consequences for social thinking and practice and for cultural expression in Europe. Some embraced and welcomed these consequences while others abhorred and opposed them, but literate people could scarcely avoid at least acquaintance with the new ideas.

At the end of the sixteenth century, Copernicanism had few advocates. In 1594 a well-educated English gentleman wrote that Copernicus was wrong and the ancient philosophers right to regard the universe as geocentric, "proving the same with many most strong reasons not needful here to be rehearsed, because I think few or none do doubt thereof." But in the next generation, Galileo's findings so shook this certainty that the English poet John Donne (1571–1631) lamented the loss of the familiar, comfortable Aristotelian cosmology:

> And new philosophy calls all in doubt,
> The element of fire is quite put out;
> The sun is lost, and th' earth, and no man's wit
> Can well direct him where to look for it. . . .
> 'Tis all in pieces, all coherence gone . . .

As the seventeenth century progressed, more and more educated people accepted the new kind of coherence supplied by the mechanical philosophy. But despite its seductive ability to answer difficult questions about the functioning of nature, it presented many new problems. Theology, ethics, morals, politics, literature, and art were all profoundly affected by the new worldview.

The merging of the new science with technology, so obvious today, did not become effective right away. Seventeenth-century scientists were members of a social and intellectual elite, and many sought knowledge more for its own sake than for practical advantages. Although Sir Francis Bacon had presented a rosy picture of the material improvements that would flow from the linkage of science and technology, this connection proved weak at first. The new understanding of motion in the universe and the motion of blood in the human body made no immediate difference to peasants toiling behind their plows, or to weavers laboring at their looms, or even to most members of the elite. Some landlords benefited from more scientific methods for surveying and draining their estates, and merchants involved in long-distance trade gained from advancements in mapmaking and navigational techniques. But because the vast majority of the population continued to work the land, their lives changed little between 1500 and the Industrial Revolution of the eighteenth century. Initially then, the Scientific Revolution helped to make some of the rich richer, and it widened the intellectual gap between the small, educated minority and the large, illiterate majority. Nevertheless, it did not not visibly transform Europe immediately.

Fading Fears of Witchcraft

After the mid-seventeenth century, the number of accused witches executed by the public authorities began to decline, particularly owing to changes in the opinions of the men who ran the machinery of prosecution—lawyers, clergymen, and judges. Many educated people who continued to believe in the possibility of witchcraft grew increasingly skeptical about whether it had been proved in particular cases. The leading Massachusetts Puritan preacher, Increase Mather (1639–1723), for example, had a change of heart on the subject of witchcraft after the Salem trials began in 1692. He continued to believe in witchcraft but concluded that courts of law could not detect it. Satan, he decided, manipulated evidence to convict innocent people. Today, scholars have come to doubt whether the gradual spread of the "mechanical philosophy" contributed to the new skepticism: Judges and juries were growing reluctant to indict and convict accused witches even before the new cosmology had won wide acceptance. But clearly the spread of Cartesian and Newtonian ideas after the mid-seventeenth century made it unlikely that ruling elites would ever allow another "witch craze" to erupt. The discovery of laws that explained some phenomena formerly attributed to God's or the devil's direct action, and the spreading conviction that sooner or later other laws would emerge to explain the remaining phenomena, made a critical attitude toward charges of witchcraft more plausible. As one English preacher wrote in 1677, "It is . . . simply impossible for either the Devil or witches to change or alter the course that God hath set in nature." But the illiterate masses knew nothing of the new science. Peasants whose lives depended on favorable weather and healthy animals continued to use "good magic" and to fear witches. In rural areas, lynchings of suspected witches occurred as late as the nineteenth century.

Science, Philosophy, and Religion

Nearly all the natural philosophers of the seventeenth century thought of themselves as devoutly religious men. Newton, for example, found proof of God's existence in nature. He asked:

> Can it be by accident . . . that all birds, beasts, and men have their right side and left side alike shaped; and just two eyes, and no more, on either side of the face; and just two ears on either side of the head; and a nose with two holes; . . . Whence arises this uniformity in all their outward shapes but from the counsel and contrivance of an Author?

Newton and his colleagues thought that their work should strengthen people's faith in God as the Creator of such an ingenious and intricate machine as the universe. Churchmen (including Increase Mather's son Cotton Mather) were active in the Royal Society and in other such groups elsewhere. To study nature was to investigate God's "other book," just as clergymen studied God's revealed word in the Bible. Each step taken toward fuller understanding of nature, wrote Newton, though it "brings us not immediately to the knowledge of the First Cause, yet it brings us nearer to it, and on that account is to be highly valued." Descartes's seventeenth-century proof of God's existence is reminiscent of St. Anselm's in the eleventh century (see Chapter 10), for each began with the fact of human imperfection and required that there be a source of the very concept of perfection, which could only be God.

Nevertheless, Descartes's method required that nothing be admitted as true unless it could be clearly demonstrated by human reason. By radically separating matter and spirit, Cartesian rationalism raised difficulties for traditional religious beliefs. If nature were governed entirely by laws that the human intellect could and would discover, the traditionally intimate relation between God and individuals was harder to conceive. Why pray to a Deity, however grand, who would not break his own laws occasionally to save people from suffering? French mathematician Blaise Pascal (1623–1662), himself a brilliant scientist, tackled the dilemma by condemning Cartesian rationalism and insisting on the necessity of personal religious experience. While rejecting Descartes's contention that God must exist, Pascal quite literally bet on God's existence and urged others to make the same wager: "Let us weigh the gain and the loss in wagering that God is. . . . If you gain, you gain all; if you lose, you lose nothing. Wager, then, without hesitation that He is."

Pietists in Germany, Quietists in France, and Quakers in England embodied a new mysticism that emphasized religious experience over reason. Denounced as "Enthusiasts" by the authorities who persecuted them, these people spoke of being inspired by an "inner light" whose source was God. George Fox (1624–1691), who founded the Society of

Blaise Pascal, Scientist and Mystic

Blaise Pascal (1623–1662) was a mathematician and scientist of rare originality and genius. His father was a high-ranking official in south-central France when Blaise was born, but the family moved to Paris when the boy was seven. Schooled by his father at home, Pascal soon showed extraordinary intellectual powers. His work as a mathematician prepared the way for the development of the differential calculus. His study of conic sections—finished before he turned sixteen—informs the modern handling of the subject. A pioneer in the development of the mathematical theory of probability, he also invented one of the earliest machines to perform simple arithmetical calculations—a forebear of adding machines and mechanical calculators. Pascal was an early member of the *Académie Royale des Sciences*, and, along with Galileo, a founder of hydrodynamics. Using the newly invented barometer, he became the first to demonstrate that air pressure decreases with an increase in altitude with an experiment at Puy-le-Dôme in 1648.

Despite his scientific prowess, Pascal's discomfort with the mechanical philosophy grew. "I cannot forgive Descartes," he wrote. "He would have preferred, in all his philosophy, to do without God; but he could not help allowing him to give a flick of the fingers to set the universe in motion. After that, he has nothing further for God to do." Pascal was drawn toward Jansenism. The Jansenists—so called after Cornelius Jansen (1585–1638; see Chapter 15)—defended St. Augustine's doctrine of the bondage of the will to sin without special grace from God, and they rejected the more optimistic outlook of the Jesuits. In 1651 Pascal's sister Jacqueline joined the Jansenist community at Port-Royal (near Paris). He visited her frequently and lived there for the last four years of his life.

Pascal's conversion experience came on November 23, 1654, and he thereafter wore his private "memorial" of the event sown into his clothing. It read in part: "God of Abraham, God of Isaac, God of Jacob, not of the philosophers and scholars. Certainty, certainty, feeling, joy, peace. God of Jesus Christ . . . He can only be found by the ways taught in the Gospel." Rejecting skepticism, the "reasonableness" of Christianity, and the rationalizing ethical theory of the Jesuits (which he saw as aimed at making faith too easy to attain), Pascal wrote in the *Pensées* published after his death: "The heart has its reasons which the reason does not know. . . . It is the heart that feels God, and not the reason." The moral message of Christianity was so fundamentally opposed to humankind's lustful, selfish nature, Pascal avowed, that the mere presence of faithful Christians in every generation proved the reality of the God of Scripture. Whether God exists or not, people's lives will be enormously improved morally and psychologically if they wager that he does. Pascal urged people to take the risk of belief—it was a bet that they could not lose. Still, his concept of Christian faith had moved far from the rational certainty of the high-medieval scholastic philosophers. ❖

Pascal's Calculating Machine
At age nineteen, Pascal made an early version of the computer that demonstrated both his mathematical genius and his devotion in the early part of his life to the mechanistic natural philosophy of Descartes. Although Pascal later criticized the Cartesian system and turned away from natural philosophy, the brilliance of his youthful contributions cannot be erased. *Corbis/Bettmann.*

Friends (Quakers) in England in the 1650s, discovered truth only after he realized that it was not to be had from books or preachers. After reaching this conclusion, he wrote, "I heard a voice which said, 'There is one, even Christ Jesus, that can speak to thy condition.' And when I heard it my heart did leap for joy." The religion of the Enthusiasts was emotional, and its mystical emphasis on direct divine inspiration sometimes had socially and politically subversive results. Some Quakers, for example, ran naked in the streets, disrupted the church services of others, and refused to perform military service. Because of the biblical injunction against swearing oaths, they also refused to serve on juries.

The authorities were as troubled by philosophical critics of traditional religion as they were by Enthusiasts. When missionaries and travelers began to publish their accounts of the customs of the Chinese and other peoples around the world, Europeans were forced to consider the possibility that other conceptions of the Supreme Being might be as valid as Christianity. Confident European assumptions about the superiority of European culture began to waver not long after the earth lost its position as the center of the universe. The writer whose massive *Historical and Critical Dictionary* (1697) became the principal source for this skepticism was Pierre Bayle (1647–1706). A Frenchman who fled France and lived and published in the tolerant Dutch Republic, Bayle believed in the existence of God but stressed that "morals and religion, far from being inseparable, are completely independent of each other. A man can be moral without being religious. An atheist who lives a virtuous life is not a creature of wonder, something outside the natural order, a freak. There is nothing more extraordinary about an atheist living a virtuous life, than there is about a Christian leading a wicked one."

The pantheism of Baruch Spinoza (1632–1677) proved fully as shocking as Bayle's skepticism. A lens grinder by profession, Spinoza grew up in the Jewish community of Amsterdam but was later expelled from the synagogue for his unorthodox teachings. His important works—which, among other things, rejected miracles and the divine inspiration of the Bible—were not published until after his death. In Spinoza's philosophy, God literally *is* the infinite universe, and everything in the universe operates out of the laws of necessity ordained by him. People, Spinoza argued, were wasting their time when they prayed to God to make exceptions to his laws. God cannot alter anything—to do so would deny the perfection that is the principal attribute of divinity. Human beings will find peace with each other and with themselves only when they overcome their passions[10] and accept, love, and understand God's perfection.

Like Spinoza, Thomas Hobbes (1588–1679) hated political turmoil, was influenced by Descartes's mechanical philosophy, and was denounced as an atheist. But Hobbes's materialism differed sharply from Spinoza's pantheism. Assistant to Sir Francis Bacon, exiled during the civil wars in the British Isles, and tutor to King Charles II, Hobbes was the first philosopher to build a systematic theory of human behavior on natural science. His view of human nature and the human condition was deeply pessimistic and psychologically acute. Individuals are merely matter in motion, he asserted, machines seeking to have pleasure and avoid pain. Without a sovereign power "to keep them all in awe," he wrote in his *Leviathan* (1651), "they are in that condition which is called war; and such a war as is of every man against every man." They live in "continual fear and danger of violent death," and their lives are "solitary, poor, nasty, brutish and short." Natural law dictates the only possible way out of this horrible condition. People joined together contractually to create the Leviathan of sovereign authority, an absolute government empowered to make law and punish criminals, thus providing the peace and security that permit agriculture, industry, and culture. Religion served as a source of pressure upon citizens to obey the law, and Hobbes had no patience with anyone who argued that religious ideology could ever justify rebellion. Once created, the government held power unconditionally. In theory, the Leviathan might be a representative assembly rather than a monarch, but Hobbes thought of one-man rule as the form of government most likely to function well in practice. The conclusion echoes Bodin's (see Chapter 15), and both men were driven to their conclusions by the chaos created by civil wars in their homelands.

Because his outlook was optimistic, English political theorist John Locke (1632–1704) gained a larger following than the grimly pessimistic Hobbes. In *An Essay on Human Understanding* (1690), Locke presented his opposition to the determinism of the mechanical philosophy. Rejecting Descartes's insistence on the unreliability of the senses, Locke argued that human beings could achieve a a reasonable certainty based on sense experience and reflection upon that experience. The human mind begins as an empty slate, he explained, a "white paper, void of all characters, without any ideas"—not even the innate idea of perfection. Wrong ideas and wicked behavior come from poor environment and education. Progressive reform of society and its institutions and therefore of human behavior, in Locke's view, was fully as possible as the scientific progress being made by his good friend Isaac Newton. As for religion, Locke stressed "the reasonableness of Christianity," especially the doctrine of moral responsibility, and he argued that scriptural revelation confirmed truths reasonable in themselves.

Locke's benign view of human nature and potential for self-government is evident in his political thought. Against Hobbes's monarchical absolutism, Locke provided a rationale for parliamentary sovereignty in his *Two Treatises of*

---

[10] Spinoza admired Johann de Witt and was horrified when de Witt's regime was overthrown in the Dutch Republic in 1672 and de Witt himself lynched by a mob (see Chapter 16). Spinoza's attack on indulgence in human "passion" in part reflected his dislike of political disorder and popular unrest, which Jewish communities even in tolerant Holland had ample reason to fear.

Government (published in 1690 but written in the late 1670s and early 1680s). He drew upon a tradition of constitutionalist thought originating in medieval political theory and practice (see Chapters 9 and 16). The Lockean state of nature was a much pleasanter place than the Hobbesian, for Locke thought that most people were inherently reasonable and ready to look out for each other's wellbeing. Nevertheless, they could protect themselves more effectively by entering into a contract to set up a government. But they did not make such a power absolute—they retained the right to resist a government that repeatedly abused their lives, liberty, and property.

Locke's ideas exerted a strong influence not only in England but on the Continent and in colonial North America. The second of the *Two Treatises* had seven French editions before 1789, as well as editions in Italy, Germany, and Sweden. At a time when absolutism was triumphing everywhere except in England, Poland-Lithuania, and the Dutch Republic (see Chapter 16), Locke modernized constitutionalism and gave it a powerful boost. Although not as philosophically precise or profound as the thought of Descartes or Hobbes, Locke's philosophy of common sense and reasonableness appealed successfully to the hopes of future generations and helped stimulate the optimism that would pervade the eighteenth-century **Enlightenment.**

Science and the Seventeenth-Century Imagination

The impact of the new science upon literature was no less striking than upon religion and philosophy. Earlier writers knew that their readers understood the Ptolemaic cosmology and its correspondence between the universe, nature, and human society, and their work brimmed with metaphors and images based on that cosmology. Shakespeare, for example, has Richard II's enemy Bolingbroke say, as the king approaches, "Be he the fire, I'll be the yielding water." The king's arrival is described: "See, see King Richard doth himself appear/As doth the blushing discontented sun . . . looks he like a king: behold his eye/As bright as is the eagle's." This may strike us as a fancy way of saying that the king is on his way and that Bolingbroke intends to behave submissively. But fire, sun, king, and eagle were primary in their categories—elements, planets, human society, and birds. The drama intensifies with the allusive, evocative use of familiar correspondences in the Great Chain of Being. Shakespeare's audiences sensed a power that we must discover intellectually and feel imperfectly because our cosmology lacks these correspondences between categories, such as fire among the elements, the sun among the planets, and so on. The rise of modern science narrowed the range of literary possibilities, introduced mechanical and mathematical concepts in place of the colorful imagery of the old cosmology, and created a preference for a simple, clear, economical writing style that remains the modern ideal for expository prose. A lab report,

for example, just tells the facts; it should not be flowery or use any more words than are necessary to describe the experiment. Sir Robert Boyle urged his fellow scientists to employ a "naked way of writing" in which the statements were "clear and significant" rather than "curiously adorned. . . . Our design is only to inform readers, not to delight or persuade them."

In the arts, the seventeenth century became the age of the Baroque style, a fusion of diverse influences on the rich heritage from the High Renaissance and Mannerism. From the new science came a preoccupation with movement, light, and time; from politics, an urge to express the power of absolutist monarchs; and from the Catholic Reformation, a passion to assert the power of popes and saints against the Protestant heretics. Instead of the idealized, serene figures and the balanced, evenly lighted, self-contained compositions of the High Renaissance, Baroque painters such as Caravaggio (Italian, 1573–1610) and Peter Paul Rubens (Flemish, 1577–1640), explored the emotional, dramatic content of the scenes they depicted, heightening it with exuberant motion that simultaneously moves outside the picture's frame and draws the viewer into it. But unlike those of a Mannerist like El Greco (see Chapter 13), the Baroque artists' human forms are intensely realistic. *The Calling of St. Matthew*, painted by Caravaggio in Rome at the turn of the seventeenth century, uses the shaft of light flooding through the window of a lowly Roman tavern to focus on the perplexity of the rich tax collector, whom Christ beckons with a gesture like that of God to Adam on Michelangelo's Sistine Chapel ceiling (see Chapter 12).

The same dynamism appears in the work of the Italian sculptor-architect Gianlorenzo Bernini (1598–1680). His *David* (1623), toes hooked over the edge of the base of the statue, is like a coiled spring as he hurls the stone at Goliath's head, and the viewer feels compelled to duck so as to avoid the missile. Bernini completed the interior decoration of St. Peter's with the enormous canopy and chair of St. Peter, each as dramatic in its impact as his gripping sculpture of St. Theresa's ecstasy as the angel pierces her heart with exquisite pain (see Chapter 13). Bernini also designed the vast colonnade that forms the approach to the great basilica and that perfectly expresses the majestic grandeur of the church. The theatricality of Bernini's style, with its marriage of sculptural and architectural forms and its vivid color, found a musical counterpart. Opera—combining music and drama with elaborate sets and costumes—was introduced in Rome and Venice in the seventeenth century.

The greatest Baroque painters of northern Europe were Rubens and Rembrandt van Rijn (1606–1665). Rubens, a well-traveled, worldly, and prolific gentleman, served as the court painter to the regents of the Spanish Netherlands. His religious paintings express Jesuit spirituality, and many of his works mix history and allegory, as in the swirling energy of *The Horrors of War*, which is pictured at the end of Chapter 15. Rembrandt's earlier works include such gripping scenes as the *Blinding of Samson* (1636), also in

THIS HISTORICAL EVIDENCE

Fontenelle's "Science for the Ladies"

1686

Bernard le Bovier de Fontenelle (1657–1757), the secretary of the Académie des Sciences from 1699 to 1741, helped to explain and popularize the new paradigm in his Conversations on the Plurality of the Worlds *(1686). He deliberately wrote so as to make the Scientific Revolution as engaging to elite women as the novels they delighted in, and the popularity of his book suggests that he enjoyed considerable success. In this passage, he explains the proposition "that the fixed stars are so many suns, each of which enlighten other worlds."*

Fontenelle's popularization expresses the view that traditional Christian theologians feared would emerge from the heliocentric theory and from speculations about an infinite universe: that other suns had other worlds. If this were true, were these other worlds inhabited by human-like creatures—and had they too been saved by Christ's sacrifice on earth? There were no easy answers to this question.

The Marchioness expressed great impatience to know what would become of the fixed stars. Shall they be inhabited as the planets are? said she. Or shall they not be inhabited? In short, what do you make of them?

You will guess, perhaps, if you have a great desire to know, answered I. The fixed stars cannot be less distant from the Earth than twenty-seven thousand six hundred and fifty times the distance from hence to the Sun, which is thirty-three millions of leagues, and if you displease an astronomer, he will place them yet farther off. . . . Their light as we see is lively and bright enough. If they receive it from the Sun, they must receive it very weak, after passing so far. . . . They are therefore luminous of themselves, and all of them, in one word, so many suns.

If I am not deceived, said the Marchioness, I already see to what you are leading. You are going to say, the fixed stars are so many suns, our Sun is the centre of a vortex, which turns round him, for why therefore shall not each fixed star be also the centre of a vortex, which shall have a motion around it? Our Sun hath planets that he enlightens, for why therefore should not each fixed star have planets that he enlightens?

I have not anything to answer, said I to her, than that which Phaedrus said to Enone, *It is thee who hath named it.*

But replied she, I see the universe so great that I am lost in it: I no longer know where I am. . . . Shall all this immense space, which comprehends our Sun and our planets, be only a little parcel of the universe? . . . This confounds me, troubles me, frightens me.

And as for me, I answered, I am very easy about it. When the heavens appeared to me as only a blue vault, where the stars were fixed like nails, the universe appeared little and confined within narrow bounds, I seemed oppressed: presently they give an infinite extent and profundity to this blue vault, in dividing it into a thousand and a thousand vortexes, it now seems to me that I breathe with more liberty, that I am in a much greater extent of air, and that the universe is far more magnificent. Nature hath not spared anything in producing it, she hath everywhere shown a profusion of riches, wholly worthy of her. . . . The other worlds render ours small, but they cannot destroy fine eyes, or a beautiful mouth, the value of these will always be the same, in spite of every world that can possibly exist.

This love is a strange thing, replied she, laughing; it is always safe, there is not any system whatever can hurt it.

Source: From Crane Brinton, ed., *The Portable Age of Reason Reader* (New York: Viking, 1957), pp. 308–311.

Chapter 15, although he is better known for the deeply introspective paintings and etchings of his later years. With great tenderness and deep humanity, he used light to reveal moods, emotion, and character.

If exuberant theatricality dominated the Baroque era, Rembrandt's later work shows that it was not the only note. Nicholas Poussin (1594–1665), a French painter who worked mostly in Italy, represents the classical side of seventeenth-century artistic sensibility. His restrained compositions are serious and contemplative rather than explosively energetic. This more subdued approach gained strength in the later decades of the century as emotionalism lost out to the calm, confident, rule-seeking rationalism of the mechanical philosophers and the admirers of

Caravaggio's *Calling of St. Matthew* This work heralded the new Baroque style of painting that emerged around the end of the sixteenth century. Like his Mannerist predecessors, Caravaggio focused on a dramatic moment (Christ's call to Saint Matthew to follow Him), and his subjects' faces and bodies express their feelings. But the scene's realism breaks with Mannerism's exaggerated colors and distorted forms. *Scala/Art Resource, NY.*

Louis XIV's absolutist state. The most impressive visual expression of this late Baroque classicism came with Louis XIV's palace at Versailles, designed by Charles Le Brun (see Chapter 16), Poussin's most successful disciple.

No single word can describe the rich tapestry of seventeenth-century culture: Newton's paradigm-creating imagination, Hobbes's pessimistic materialism, Locke's optimistic rationalism, Pascal's tortured wagering, Rubens's outwardly exploding energy, Rembrandt's inwardly looking sensitivity, Poussin's cool classicism—all were facets of the seventeenth-century temperament. The new science touched all artists and thinkers. Its touch, however, produced not sterile uniformity but a vigorous profusion of creativity.

CONCLUSION: ON TO THE ENLIGHTENMENT

The Scientific Revolution began in the middle of the sixteenth century with the publication of two books that questioned the traditional and long-established Aristotelian-Ptolemaic cosmology and the Galenic physiology associ-ated with it. Neither Nicholas Copernicus nor Andreas Vesalius intended to start a revolution, but the former's doubts about the immovability of the earth and the latter's doubts about the porosity of the wall between the heart's ventricles initiated an avalanche that would eventually bury not only the traditional understanding of the natural world but the methods for trying to understand it. Newton's laws described a new cosmology, and they did so in quantitative rather than qualitative terms. The observation, experimentation, and precise measurement required by this mathematical approach characterized Harvey's circulatory system, Kepler's planetary orbits, Galileo's mechanics, and the new science generally. Its success inspired the people who would later be called "social scientists" to look for quantitative data and laws to interpret the data on the model provided by Newton. No category of human expression and endeavor, from philosophy and religion to literature and the arts, could avoid confronting such an enormous change in the way Europeans understood the world and their place in it. They began to have a sense that nature might be mastered, might be made to serve humanity rather than being humanity's unpredictable (and occasionally cruel) master. The discovery that achieving a degree of mastery over nature might have unwanted consequences—such as environmental degradation—lay farther ahead.

The Enlightenment, an intellectual and cultural movement that pervaded the eighteenth century, stemmed directly from the Scientific Revolution.

Selected Reading

Sources

Cohen, I. Bernard, and R. S. Westfall, eds. *Newton* (1995).

Drake, Stillman, ed. *Discourses and Opinions of Galileo* (1957).

Hall, Marie Boas, ed. *Nature and Nature's Laws* (1970).

Pascal, Blaise. *Penseés*, trans. A. J. Krailsheimer (1966).

Sprat, Thomas. *History of the Royal Society*, eds. Jackson I. Cope and H. W. Jones, (1959).

The Rise of Science

Biagioli, Mario. *Galileo, Courtier* (1993). A penetrating and vivid depiction of Galileo's life and career in the context of sixteenth-century court culture.

Boas, Marie. *The Scientific Renaissance, 1450–1630* (1962). A survey treatment from Renaissance humanism and Copernicanism to Galileo and Kepler.

Debus, Allen G. *Man and Nature in the Renaissance* (1978). Relates developments in particular fields of sixteenth- and early seventeenth-century science to the broader intellectual context with stress on Hermetic and occult influences.

Frank, Robert G. Jr. *Harvey and the Oxford Physiologists* (1980). Close analysis of the work of the group of men who built upon Harvey's discovery of the circulation of blood for a new understanding of physiology.

Hall, A. Rupert. *The Revolution in Science, 1599–1750* (1983). A clearly written, one-volume survey—nicely detailed and thoughtful.

Kuhn, Thomas S. *The Copernican Revolution* (1957). A classic analysis of developments in planetary astronomy, which sensitively portrays the complexity and relative suddenness of the process of shifting from one paradigm to another. Kuhn initiated the widely accepted concept of paradigmatic shift in explaining scientific revolutions.

Lindberg, David C., and Robert S. Westman, eds. *Reappraisals of the Scientific Revolution* (1990). Essays questioning the validity of the standard picture of the "Scientific Revolution" of the sixteenth and seventeenth centuries.

Martin, Julian. *Francis Bacon, the State and the Reform of Natural Philosophy* (1991). Shows how Bacon applied his varied career as a lawyer, statesman, and scientist to the finding of facts and the making of rules.

Porter, Roy, and Mikulas Teich, eds. *The Scientific Revolution in National Context* (1992). Essays on the new science in Italy, France, England, the German nations, the Low Countries, Poland, Bohemia, and other places.

Shapin, Steven, and Simon Schaffer. *Leviathan and the Air-Pump* (1985). Focuses on Boyle's arguments in favor of experimentalism and Hobbes's arguments against it in England in the 1660s; an exploration of the sociology of scientific knowledge.

Vickers, Brian, ed. *Occult and Scientific Mentalities in the Renaissance* (1984). Papers on the way "magic" and "science" influenced each other (for example, Newton's alchemical work, Kepler's astrological interests, witchcraft in Lorraine) during the period from 1580 to 1640.

Westfall, Richard S. *The Construction of Modern Science* (1971). A survey of seventeenth-century science in terms of the interplay between mathematical and mechanical conceptions.

———. *The Life of Sir Isaac Newton* (1993). Condensed from Westfall's massive and definitive biography, this is an excellent and readable introduction to Newton as scientist and person.

Science, Society, and Culture

Briggs, Robin. *Witches and Neighbors* (1996). Approaches the subject of witchcraft through analysis of the experiences and beliefs of ordinary people and concentrates on the social, cultural, and psychological context of witchcraft accusations.

Hunter, Michael. *Science and Society in Restoration England* (1981). Studies the social relations of science in the era of Newton and Boyle, including support facilities, hindrances, and motivations for scientific activity.

Kroll, Richard, Richard Ashcraft, and Perez Zagorin, eds. *Philosophy, Science, and Religion in England, 1640–1700* (1992). Essays examining the cultural context of the new science in England, with particular emphasis on the Latitudinarians and John Locke.

Levack, Brian P. *The Witch-Hunt in Early Modern Europe*, 2nd ed. (1987). An excellent introduction to the enormous literature on this controversial subject.

Shapiro, Barbara J. *Probability and Certainty in Seventeenth-Century England* (1983). Analysis of the development of a new approach to the achievement of certainty in philosophy, science, religion, history, law, and literature in England, primarily between 1630 and 1690.

Thomas, Keith. *Religion and the Decline of Magic* (1971). A classic account of systems of belief in England (including astrology, witchcraft, magical healing, and others) from 1500 to 1700.

CHAPTER 18

THE AGE OF ENLIGHTENMENT

The First Balloon Crossing of the English Channel   *Cabinet des Estampes, Bibliothèque Nationale.*

1720	The Mississippi and South Sea Bubbles: Stock prices soar, only to crash later		1762	Rousseau's *The Social Contract* published
1721	First European inoculation for smallpox administered in England; Montesquieu's *Persian Letters* published		1764	Beccaria's *Essay on Crimes and Punishments* published
1733	Publication of Pope's *Essay on Man*, Voltaire's *Philosophical Letters on the English*		1751–1772	Diderot and others publish their monumental *Encyclopedia*
1738	John Wesley's conversion		1770–1827	Life span of Ludwig van Beethoven
1748	Publication of Montesquieu's *Spirit of the Laws*, Hume's *Enquiry Concerning Human Understanding*		1774	Goethe's *The Sorrows of Young Werther* published
1756–1791	Life span of Wolfgang Amadeus Mozart		1776	Adam Smith's *The Wealth of Nations* published
1759	Voltaire's *Candide* published		1781	Kant's *Critique of Pure Reason* published
			1788	Kant's *Critique of Practical Reason* published
			1808	Goethe's *Faust, Part One* published

The word *Enlightenment* connotes progress and optimism, and the first balloon crossing of the English Channel in 1785 (on previous page) celebrated the human achievement of flight—an advance that people had dreamed of for millennia. This Channel crossing occurred only two years after the first hot-air balloon flight and exemplified the fascination with the combination of science and technology that characterized much of the movement known as the Enlightenment. The eighteenth century certainly had its share of people who hoped that when the goals of the Enlightenment were realized, the lives of Europeans would improve dramatically in every way.

Firm believers in progress and the power of human reason, the **philosophes** (the word used to describe the intellectual leaders of the Enlightenment) called for rational analysis of society and its practices and institutions instead of blind acceptance of inherited traditions and authorities. They particularly questioned Europe's long-established hierarchical social system, a system that provided privileges and responsibilities not to individuals but to groups: nobles, clergy, townsmen, even peasants. One's "rights" or **"liberties"** came from one's membership in a group, and each of these groups consisted of many subgroups. Rights were corporate and collective rather than individual, meaning that there was no conception of universal or "human" rights. This was *Ancien Régime* (Old Regime) Europe, old because society had been organized along these lines for many centuries.

A new approach emerged with the revolutions in 1776 in North America and 1789 in France in what one distinguished scholar, R. R. Palmer, has named "the Age of Democratic Revolution." Western civilization changed from a monarchic and aristocratic ideal that assumed human inequality to a democratic ideal that proclaimed political equality (at least among propertied males). This revolutionary change could come about through violence and war, as it did in France and British North America. But it did not necessarily require violence. Whereas Europeans in preceding centuries had feared innovation and justified change only when they could represent it as a return to a past "golden age," such as the classical world or early Christianity, many eighteenth-century people began to think that the best might lie in the future. The reformist schemes that emanated from the Enlightenment helped to create a sense that change could not and should not be avoided. And some rulers, the "enlightened absolutists" (who will be considered in Chapter 19) were themselves leaders in the cause of reform.

PEOPLE AND PRODUCTION

The Enlightenment went forward in a context of far-reaching demographic and economic changes that would have occurred even if there had been no Enlightenment. By the eighteenth century, a genuine global economy had emerged, to which the dynamic sectors of economic growth in Europe owed much of their impetus. In certain parts of Europe, the "Agricultural Revolution" raised yields considerably, freeing many hands for work in manufacturing and industrial enterprises. In this way, agriculture helped prepare the way for the Industrial Revolution (see Chapter 20). Nevertheless, the overwhelming majority of the people continued to live and work on the land within the context of the traditional, hierarchical social and political order. Yet both inside Europe and elsewhere (most strikingly in British North America), a new wave of population growth led to novel opportunities, problems, and social strains.[1]

---

[1] The eighteenth century also saw a great demographic surge in China, but that hitherto prosperous society did not develop the technological innovation to respond to increasing demand. The result was nineteenth-century impoverishment and political decline.

THE HISTORICAL EVIDENCE

Immanuel Kant Defines Enlightenment

1784

Immanuel Kant (1724–1804) taught logic, metaphysics, and indeed practically the whole curriculum at the university in Königsberg (Prussia), where he was born and lived his entire life. In a series of important books, Kant offered penetrating philosophical analyses of such fundamental questions as how can we achieve certain knowledge and how can we behave ethically. This excerpt from an essay he published in 1784 contains some of his thoughts on the nature of the cultural era in which he lived. What kind of "tutelage" does Kant appear to have in mind?

Enlightenment is man's release from his self-incurred tutelage. Tutelage is man's inability to make use of his understanding without direction from others. Self-incurred is this tutelage when its cause lies not in lack of reason but in lack of resolution and courage to use it without direction from another. *Sapere aude!* "Have courage to use your own reason!"—that is the motto of enlightenment.

Laziness and cowardice are the reasons why so great a portion of mankind, after nature has long since discharged them from external direction, . . . nevertheless remains under lifelong tutelage, and why it is easy for others to set themselves up as their guardians. It is so easy not to be of age. If I have a book which understands for me, a pastor who has a conscience for me, a physician who decides my diet, and so forth, I need not trouble myself. I need not think, if I can pay—others will readily undertake the irksome work for me. . . .

For this enlightenment, however, nothing is required but freedom, and indeed the most harmless among all the things to which this term can properly be applied. It is the freedom to make public one's reason at every point. But I hear on all sides, "Do not argue!" The officer says: "Do not argue but drill!" The tax collector: "Do not argue but pay!" The cleric: "Do not argue but believe!" . . . Everywhere there is restriction on freedom. . . .

If we are asked, "Do we now live in an *enlightened age?*" the answer is, "No," but we do live in an *age of enlightenment*. As things now stand, much is lacking which prevents men from being, or easily becoming, capable of correctly using their own reason in religious matters with assurance and free from outside direction. But, on the other hand, we have clear indications that the field has now been opened wherein men may freely deal with these things and that the obstacles to general enlightenment or release from self-imposed tutelage are gradually being reduced. In this respect, this is the age of enlightenment.

Source: From Crane Brinton, ed., *The Portable Age of Reason Reader* (New York: Viking, 1956), pp. 298–299, 300–301, 305.

The Social Hierarchy

At first glance, the social structure of eighteenth-century Europe might seem to have changed little since the Middle Ages. As we saw in Chapter 8, medieval people conceived of society as composed of those who fought (nobility), those who prayed (clergy), and those who worked (peasants). This structure ignored townspeople, but their numbers remained relatively small, at least until the high-medieval surge in population and commerce increased them substantially. In the eighteenth century, monarchs still stood atop the social ladder, with the landowning aristocracy—successors to the medieval **knights**—on the rung immediately beneath them. Below the large landowners came the members of the "middling sort" of professionals (lawyers, physicians), better-off merchants, master craftsmen in the towns, and successful farmers in the countryside. On the lower rungs stood a wide variety of workers, and the poor occupied the lowest positions of all. The metaphor of the Great Chain of Being (see Chapter 17) continued to justify the social hierarchy for most people. Yet this apparent continuity with the past concealed many changes in the way its component groups actually lived. People on all the different rungs of the ladder of social hierarchy now had to change in order to maintain or advance their positions in the context provided by new demographic, economic, military, political, and intellectual developments.

For the aristocracy, the advance of military technology created new challenges. Historians once described the seventeenth and eighteenth centuries as a period of decline for nobles, but recent research emphasizes that the keynote was not so much decline as adaptation. The fundamental fact is that nobles continued to dominate the European scene long after the heavily armed cavalry that justified their high status in the Middle Ages had disappeared from battlefields. Eighteenth-century armies consisted mostly of infantry and artillery, not cavalry. In theory, there should have been no place for nobles who did not fight. Because the social and political position that had accompanied their essential military function had been undermined by the proliferation of gunpowder weapons, they should have shriveled into relative insignificance.

In practice, shrewd nobles adapted by insisting that their sons gain the skills needed to serve monarchs who focused on building more powerful, more centralized administrations. Instead of decline, what occurred was the rise of a new "administrative nobility," as many elite families used their patronage and wealth to ensure that their heirs got the education required by princes who needed bureaucrats, not armor-wearing wielders of lances and swords. Money was also needed to purchase the royal offices that put young aristocrats on the road to eminence. To be sure, not all nobles got the message, and those who did not indeed did decline. After 1600, the absolute numbers of aristocrats decreased noticeably in many countries. In Venetian territory, for example, the nobility in 1550 represented 1.6 percent of the population; in 1797 it was 0.8 percent. In France, about 1 percent of the population was

noble around 1450, but by the eve of the French Revolution in 1789 the percentage had dropped to barely more than 0.5 percent.

The decline in absolute numbers masks an actual rise in the numbers of members of the *high* nobility. England had 62 members of the House of Lords in 1559 and 204 in 1760. France had 17 *ducs et pairs* (dukes and peers) in 1610 and 52 in 1723. In essence, the nobility shrank in size, but the smaller numbers consisted of people with more wealth, power, and influence. Some served as commanders of royal armies and navies and others as high-ranking diplomats and administrators. They had preserved their places at the top of the social order by making themselves useful to the kings who needed help to run their newly centralized states. By late in the seventeenth century, although the tax exemptions long enjoyed by aristocrats were disappearing, the high nobility could afford to lose the exemptions whereas lesser lords could not. Tensions between rich and poor nobles usually ended at the latter's expense. Most of Spain's four hundred thousand nobles were impecunious *hidalgos*, who in 1773 received orders to perform manual work. At about the same time, Spain had nearly seven

The Yew Tree Ball at Versailles   In 1745, the famous Hall of Mirrors at Versailles was the scene of a splendid party at which French aristocrats celebrated the marriage of the Dauphin, the heir to Louis XV's throne. At this ball, Louis XV, dressed as one of the yew trees, met Madame de Pompadour. She soon became his mistress and dominated the court until her death in 1764.   *Giraudon/Art Resource, NY.*

hundred titled nobles (*grandes de España* and *titulos*), most of whom were thriving.

One reason for the continuing strength of the nobility was the success with which it recruited new members. Noble status was, after all, the goal of bright and upwardly mobile **gentry,** lawyers, officials, and merchants everywhere. Kings rewarded their most effective ministers with grants of nobility, and at any given moment the nobility of a country included many men whose ancestors had not been aristocrats. Another reason was the speed with which many ambitious people came to understand that land could be treated as a commodity. In the Middle Ages, nobles lived in fortified castles surrounded by lands that supported their retinues of armed men. They had little privacy because they were continuously surrounded by their subordinates in the large rooms that made up their residences. They thought of their land as a source of power more than a source of money.

By the eighteenth century in many cases, **feudal** attitudes toward land had given way to **capitalist** attitudes. The greater internal security afforded by rising nation-states meant that rural acreage was prized for the rents it yielded, and country residences could be houses rather than forts. Instead of venues for the display of local power, they could be retreats for gracious living for their owners—who had to spend more and more time at the royal court or capital rather than at home in the country. Elite status that had once depended mainly on local clout now depended more on royal favor. Country house architecture reflected these changed needs and priorities, and large halls for accommodating crowds of people were replaced by smaller dining and sitting rooms to enable their owners to have a level of privacy unknown to their predecessors in the sixteenth century and earlier. Then, a nobleman was unlikely even to urinate or defecate without being surrounded by retainers, and Erasmus merely advised that good manners required that no one initiate a conversation while his lord was so engaged. By the eighteenth century, noblemen also became more urbanized, as their business required them to be in London, Vienna, Madrid, or other capital cities for a larger portion of each year. They built and decorated townhouses that took as much or more of their money and attention as their country houses did.

The continuing political, social, and cultural predominance of the nobility during the eighteenth century must be viewed alongside another important development: urbanization. The fact that Europe was the center of an expanding global economy dramatically affected the growth or decline of urban areas. The spectacular population growth between 1700 and 1800 of port cities involved in trade with the Indies demonstrates this phenomenon. The population of Marseilles, for example, leaped from 20,000 to 100,000; of Bristol, from 20,000 to 64,000; and of Glasgow, from 13,000 to 84,000. Capital cities also burgeoned, as did a handful of industrial centers such as Man-

chester and Birmingham, although many inland towns stagnated or declined. London, both port and capital, nearly doubled its numbers, from 500,000 in 1700 to 900,000 in 1800. Liverpool, a mere village in 1650, ranked second only to London as a port and as home to 84,000 people by 1800. This growth reflects the drastically changed relationship between Europe and the world that Columbus and Da Gama had "found" three centuries before (see Chapter 14). We need to remember, in today's intensively urbanized world, that around 1800 only 5 percent of the world's population lived in cities of ten thousand people or more. Nevertheless, the urbanizing process certainly accelerated during the eighteenth century, and in Europe the urban percentage was probably 10 percent—double that for the world as a whole. Yet in Europe the regional variation was wide, ranging from 20 percent in Britain to perhaps as low as 3 percent in Russia.

In urban areas, whether booming or declining, the existing social and political institutions had medieval origins. Most towns had received royal charters in the Middle Ages that allowed them to govern themselves in most respects, and long-established merchant and craft **guilds** controlled the route to civil office (see Chapter 8). The mayor and the aldermen formed an oligarchy that governed the town by punishing crime and regulating commerce, but they kept a wary eye on nearby members of the landowning elite and the royal court as well in order to maintain good relations with authorities—who, if offended, might intervene and upset traditional ways of doing things.

Although urban societies in Europe were no less socially stratified than rural ones, the wealth that flowed from booming global commerce and domestic economic growth, especially after 1750, enriched the upper and to some extent the middling social strata in many cities and towns. At the top of each urban community, a rather small number of families comprising the richest merchants, professionals (lawyers and physicians), and officials (administrators and judges, as well as high-ranking clergy) formed the bourgeoisie whose members constituted the ruling oligarchy. In 1766 in Chartres, a town southwest of Paris, bourgeois households made up 8.3 percent of the total; for a large group of Hungarian towns in 1782, some 5.7 percent had similar status. In England, it has been estimated that the bourgeoisie increased from 9 to 15 percent of the population between 1688 and 1803.

Social and political conservatism permeated the outlook of the bourgeoisie everywhere—and they tended to imitate noble culture and, whenever possible, to reach out for noble status themselves. Arranging for their daughters to marry the sons of aristocrats, buying land and living in part off the rents (like many aristocrats), and holding certain offices were among the means to climb the social ladder. Aristocrats sometimes derided bourgeois pretensions, but, as already indicated, most aristocracies not only permitted but needed and welcomed new blood (and money) from time to time. There was nothing novel about this; Henry VIII's second queen, Anne Boleyn, had in her family tree a fifteenth-century lord mayor of London, himself descended from tenant farmers. The social barrier between aristocrats and burghers, although its exact nature varied widely from place to place, was rarely so high that it could not be vaulted over. The expansion of nonagricultural ways to get rich during the eighteenth century probably made the top of the barrier more attainable to more burghers than ever before. At the same time, the fact that many nobles built townhouses and spent more of their time in them merely increased the opportunities for social contacts across the barrier.

Artisans occupied the rung beneath the bourgeois upper crust. They and their families made up a much larger percentage of the population, but had little political power in their towns. Like their social superiors, they usually opposed change. For example, they tried to prevent immigration in order to minimize competition over labor and skills. Through their guilds, which were numerous, they tried to protect the sometimes precarious positions they had achieved, and except in England, guilds remained prevalent during the eighteenth century. No one could legally practice a trade without being a member of the appropriate guild, so high fees and other measures to limit entry were common. When, in 1774, a reform-minded royal adviser in France tried to introduce free-market principles and to abolish the guilds (see Chapter 19), the thunderous outcry led the king to fire him within four months. Guilds often opposed the introduction of labor-saving machinery, and in 1789 a member of "the Hatmakers, Fur-Skin Dealers, and Furriers of Rouen" was quite candid about the rationale for prohibiting machines: "It is unfortunate that, if the machines are done away with, French goods will be somewhat more expensive than foreign ones; but . . . if there is no competition, then there will be no worry about a home market." In other words, within France, consumers will pay the higher prices in order to preserve employment for their neighbors who will do the work with their hands.

Those urban workers who failed to get into a guild because their families lacked the money to buy them apprenticeships had to depend on occasional day labor. Many of them lived at or near the poverty line. In one sampling of urban communities around Europe at various points in the eighteenth century, the number of households receiving poor relief varied from a high of 20 percent to a low of 5 percent. In Grenoble in southeastern France in 1735, slightly more than 37 percent of households paid no taxes because officials thought they were too poor. For Lille, in northeastern France, the rate was 45 percent in 1740. In Paris in 1772, 40 percent of the children baptized were orphans, many abandoned by parents who lacked the means to care for them. Almost certainly, many were borne by prostitutes. Arriving at precise estimates of poverty rates

is impossible, but it seems clear that in many parts of Europe a large minority and perhaps at times a majority of town dwellers lived dangerously. If work grew scarce, or if bread prices suddenly increased, they might have no choice but to steal or beg in order to survive. In some instances, they became so desperate that they rioted against high prices, or even the fear that prices might rise. The "Flour War," a group of violent protests in and around Paris in 1775, is an example. Bread rioters in Bordeaux in 1773 said, according to an observer, that "we prefer to die on a gibbet rather than die of hunger, it's shorter."

For centuries, poor relief had in most places been a task for clergy, but the eighteenth century witnessed an ambitious array of proposals for government action on social welfare. By no means were all of them implemented, but on both the municipal and national levels significant efforts were made. The authorities frequently tried to intervene to push down the price of grain, although in the 1770s especially the results of their activity were disappointing. Workhouses in which poor people were taught simple crafts in the hope that they would be able to support themselves became fairly widespread. In Spain in 1774, for example, King Charles III mandated the creation of schools in certain provinces to teach people how to make linen. With rare exceptions, these and similar programs were underfunded because governments continued to put more money into preparation for war than into social expenditures.

Despite the urbanizing trend, the vast majority of Europeans were still peasants working the land outside— and in some areas far outside—the towns. Serfdom no longer existed in England and could be found only in a few places in western Europe. Eastern Europe was a different story. In Poland-Lithuania, for example, only 11 percent of the population were free peasants and nearly 70 percent were serfs.[2] Serfs had to perform labor services for their landlords (and sometimes for the community and the monarch as well), although the amount of time these required varied considerably. In Hesse-Cassel, a German state, it amounted to nearly half of the peasant's working time. In one Austrian province, peasants owed only fourteen days each year, while in another they were subject to 104 days. This did not mean that all eastern European peasants were worse off than their western counterparts. Some Polish peasants, for example, made enough money from the land they farmed for themselves to hire poorer men to do the work owed to the landlord. Yet most serfs suffered from the arbitrariness with which landlords could increase their obligations. It is a powerful comment on the burden they bore that when, in 1775, the Austrian Habsburg regime defined the working day as ten hours, the

---

[2] At least 10 percent of the population were nobles, some of whom were scarcely distinguishable from peasants in their manner of life.

An English Rural Scene, 1727 Although fanciful in its crowding together of many kinds of rural production, this engraving suggests the diversified character of the advanced agricultural regimes in England, the Dutch Republic, and a few regions elsewhere. The lord of the manor's grand house in the background overlooks the beginning of the grain harvest and the tending of sheep and cattle. A windmill and a water mill (foreground) provide labor-saving power. *Barnaby's Picture Library.*

effect was to reduce the amount of time many serfs had to work for their lords.

Just as central governments tried to improve the lot of the urban poor, they made efforts to improve the position of the peasantry. In some cases, especially where royal lands were involved, mandates to reduce labor services and other obligations had some positive results. But other landowners resisted royal initiatives that would have increased the cost of rural labor, and for the most part their resistance succeeded. Some peasants resisted by negotiating or by pursuing their grievances through the legal system—occasionally with success. When labor services seemed excessive, other

options were to run away, to do poor work, or to sabotage the landowner by arson, maiming his animals, or poaching his deer or other game. "To work as you do on the demesne" became a proverbial description of inattention and laziness in Poland and Russia—a counterpart to the modern phrase "good enough for government work." The last, and most dangerous, resort, was rebellion. Peasant risings such as the Great Fear (France, 1789), the "Golden Charter" revolt in Poland (1768), Pugachev's Rebellion (Russia, 1773–1774), and others punctuated the eighteenth century.

The Population Surge

The story of European population before 1700 is one of alternation between expansion and contraction. The massive sixteenth-century surge in population had, like its predecessors in the High Middle Ages, reached a plateau in some areas and actual decline in others. Europeans had long faced subsistence crises: Several poor harvests in a row would drive up the price of bread alarmingly; agricultural workers lost income with less grain to harvest; artisans lost revenue as consumers had to devote more of their family income to food; death rates rose because underfed people were more vulnerable to disease; birthrates fell as marriages were broken by death and as malnourishment impaired fertility.

This age-old cycle ended in the eighteenth century. The expansion that had begun in the sixteenth century had ended in the middle of the seventeenth, and a period of stagnation followed. After the first third of the eighteenth century, however, an era of population growth began that continues to this day and that will probably go on if the human race can avoid nuclear war or ecological disaster. We now think in terms of gaining control of the *rate* of population increase—we do not expect that world population will decline, even though it frequently did so before the eighteenth century. The two decades on either side of 1700 witnessed the last major subsistence crisis in Europe. Europe's population stood at about 120 million in 1700, but it ballooned to 187 million by 1800, a 64 percent jump. The rates of increase far exceeded those experienced during the sixteenth-century expansion, and they varied widely among countries. In western Europe between 1680 and 1820, England had the highest rate of growth—133 percent—compared to 39 percent for France and more than 50 percent for Spain, Italy, and Germany (see Figure 18-1).

Explaining why this unprecedented population surge happened is not easy. Broadly speaking, two obvious possibilities are that the fertility rate increased (so that more babies were born) and that the mortality rate decreased (so that fewer infants and children as well as adults died). Historical demography is a relatively new field of study, and its practitioners must make ambitious national and regional estimates using the relatively small number of parish registers and other kinds of data that have survived. However,

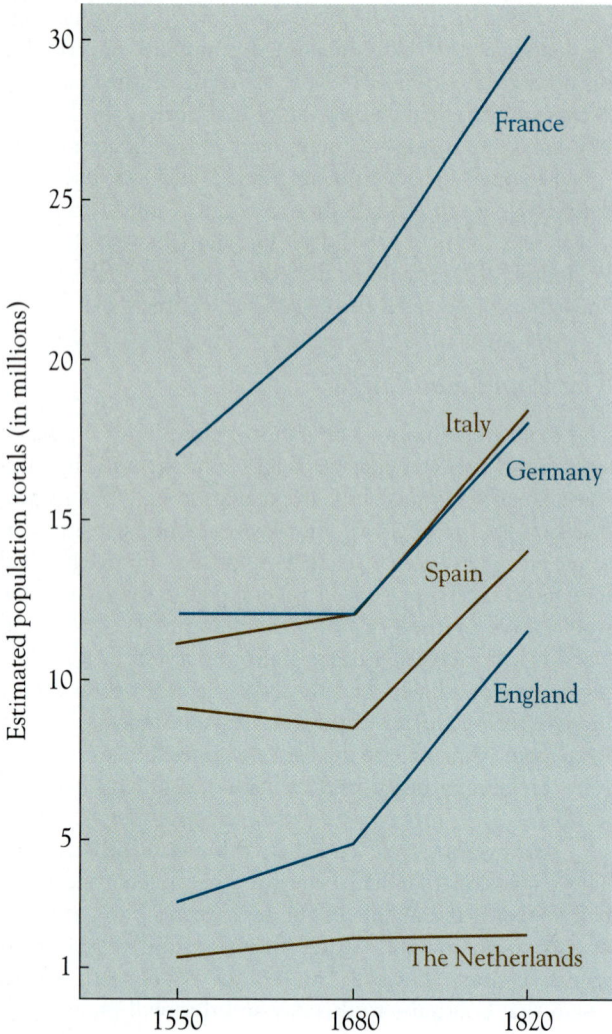

FIGURE 18-1
POPULATION GROWTH, 1550–1820
Source: Adapted from E. A. Wrigley, People, Cities and Wealth:
The Transformation of Traditional Society *(Oxford, England: Basil Blackwell, 1987), table 9.1, p. 216.*

ily size) seems to have been falling. In most countries the mean age of marriage for women remained fairly stable or actually rose (in Scandinavia, for example, from 26.7 years before 1750 to nearly 30 years in the decades around 1800). In France, the most thoroughly documented case, women's average reproductive period (the interval between the births of the first and the last child) dropped 37 percent. The most likely explanation is that in France a trend toward conscious use of birth control techniques in order to space children more widely was in place by mid-century—a full century ahead of the rest of Europe.

These national averages concealed wide variations from one locality to another. In rural villages where the spinning and weaving of textiles or the production of other manufactured products predominated, peasants tended to marry younger and have more children than in agrarian villages where marriage had to await access to acres. Wherever rural industries became established, the marriage age for women dropped. In one English county during the eighteenth century, for example, farmers married women between ages 27 and 29, whereas the brides of weavers and other artisans averaged 22.6 years old. Between the 1630s and 1790s, the population of the Swiss city of Zurich increased 80 percent, while in the nearby countryside a textile-producing district grew 300 percent.

Despite a higher birthrate in industrializing rural districts, a sinking death rate was the most significant contributor to Europe's accelerating population. Infant mortality declined dramatically nearly everywhere, and larger numbers of children continued to survive into their teens. In France and Switzerland before 1750, for example, only about half of the children born alive were still living at age fifteen; between 1780 and 1820, the incidence had risen to almost 60 percent in France and 70 percent in Switzerland.

Furthermore, changes involving armies, disease, nutrition, and transportation must be combined to explain why mortality rates declined enough to enable Europe to escape the age-old population pattern of advance followed by retreat. Within Europe at least, the demographic damage wrought by the movement of armies lessened. Before 1792, when the series of great wars stemming from the French Revolution erupted (see Chapter 21), Europe had enjoyed seventy years of relative freedom from the carnage wrought by military operations. Wars still scourged the countryside, but they were fought by smaller, better disciplined armies operating on a smaller scale than had been the case in the seventeenth century. Armies after the Thirty Years' War were more professional, and military hygiene was one of the main concerns of officers who more and more worked to keep their soldiers healthy so they could fight more effectively. Healthier and better trained soldiers, often living in barracks and camps rather than amid the general population, transmitted disease less often. As central governments grew more powerful, they could devote more attention and resources to the health of the people paying

enough evidence has been collected and analyzed to show that the contribution made by greater fertility was less significant than the decline in mortality. In other words, the surge was due mainly to the fact that people lived longer, rather than that more were born. Some interesting changes have been discovered, even if they tell us little about why overall population exploded. Illegitimacy rates, for example, certainly increased between the early eighteenth century and 1820. Before 1750 in England, out of every hundred babies born alive, 2.6 were born to unmarried mothers; in the forty years after 1780, that rate rose to 5.9 (see Table 18-1). Across the same span of time, the number of babies conceived before marriage doubled in France and nearly doubled in England and Germany. Nevertheless, except in Belgium, marital fertility (and therefore fam-

TABLE 18-1

ILLEGITIMATE BIRTHS AND PREMARITAL CONCEPTIONS

Country	Years	Illegitimate Births		Premarital Conceptions	
		*Reconstitutions	No. per 100 Live Births	Reconstitutions	No. per 100 First Births
England	pre-1750	24	2.6	14	19.7
	1740–1790	24	4.3	3	37.3
	1780–1820	24	5.9	2	34.5
France	pre-1750	8	2.9	9	6.2
	1740–1790	12	4.1	9	10.1
	1780–1820	6	4.7	6	13.7
Germany	pre-1750	11	2.5	12	13.4
	1740–1790	15	3.9	15	18.5
	1780–1820	8	11.9	8	23.8
Scandinavia	pre-1750	2 parishes	3.8	—	—
	1740–1790	3 countries	2.5	—	—
	1780–1820	4 countries	6.8	—	—
Spain	pre-1750	3	5.4	—	—
	1740–1790	2	5.1	—	—
	1780–1820	1	6.5	—	—

Although historians do not have enough information to make judgments concerning entire countries, there are limited figures from some European *reconstitutions** indicating increasing numbers of illegitimate births and premarital conceptions from 1750 to 1820. The number of illegitimate births is per 100 live births among the total population; the number of births from premarital conception is per 100 first births within eight months of marriage.

*Reconstitution refers to the technique historical demographers use to calculate vital statistics by extracting from parish registers the births, marriages, and deaths of individuals within a parish or group of parishes and then combining the data to identify demographic patterns.

Source: Adapted from data in Michael W. Flinn, *The European Demographic System, 1500–1820* (Baltimore, Md.: The Johns Hopkins University Press, 1981), tables 6.1 and 6.2, p. 82.

taxes to them and protect those people from predatory armies.

The eighteenth century also witnessed an improvement in public health. Bubonic plague virtually disappeared, at least from Europe.[3] Smallpox, however, continued to claim millions of victims and particularly devastated small children. The first European inoculation for smallpox occurred in England in 1721, when news of the procedure was brought back from Turkey by Lady Mary Wortley Montagu (1689–1762), the wife of an English ambassador to the Ottoman Empire. She had herself been scarred by the disease, but nevertheless courageously took the risk of having her second child inoculated. Opponents condemned the practice because it obstructed God's will, but members of the Royal Society used new methods to conduct statistical studies that supported its effectiveness. It became widespread in England by the 1740s and spread to other countries gradually. The French resisted inoculation until Louis XV died from smallpox in 1774. An English country doctor, Edward Jenner (1749–1823), having observed that milkmaids never contracted smallpox, published the results of his procedure for vaccinating people with cowpox in 1798. Because it carried even less risk than inoculation, Jenner's vaccination procedure soon became the favored defense against smallpox. By early in the nineteenth century, Spanish authorities were working hard to extend this newly available protection to Indians who had escaped the devastation wrought by smallpox in the New World (see Chapter 14).

Nutrition was another contributor to the population boom. Crops introduced from America came into widespread use. The Irish population, for example, increased

---

[3] Plague still occurs in remote parts of the Third World, but it can be controlled by modern antibiotics.

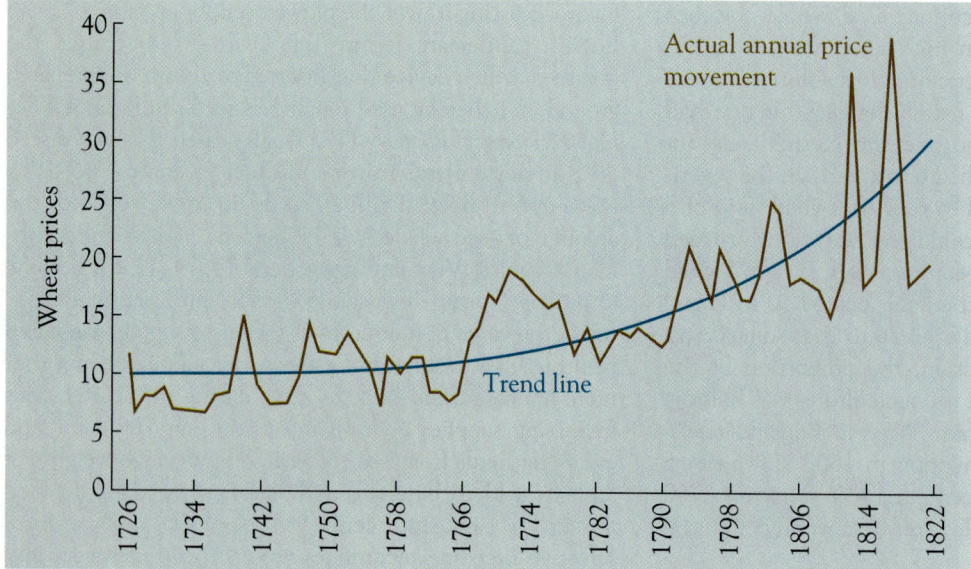

FIGURE 18-2

WHEAT PRICES IN EIGHTEENTH-CENTURY FRANCE

This graph shows the upward movement of annual average wheat prices in France (in livres per hectoliter, 1726–1819) and the trend line of these prices. Note how the price oscillations become more extreme over time, but that the general trend moves steadily upward. *Source: Adapted from David Hackett Fischer,* The Great Wave: Price Revolutions and the Rhythm of History *(New York: Oxford University Press, 1996), figure 3.02, p. 122.*

landowners and better-off peasants. Those who could afford such investment reaped the profits that flowed from growing demand and higher prices.

Few of the techniques fueling the "Agricultural Revolution" were entirely new. Convertible husbandry, for example, had been employed in the Low Countries since the Late Middle Ages. In the bourgeois-dominated Dutch Republic, political and social affairs lay in the hands of merchants rather than landowners. As a result, the Dutch were the first to treat agriculture as a business investment rather than a way of life. Urban merchants bought land and livestock and invested in land reclamation. Scarce Dutch land produced high-value butter, cheese, and meat, and the prosperous Dutch could afford to import grain from eastern Europe and later from England.

Technical improvements of the kinds that the Dutch pioneered were hard to make in countries where land was still divided into strips cultivated by different families, or where many small farms had emerged owing to the repeated division of holdings among numerous heirs. In England, **enclosure** of common fields to produce large farms of 100 to 300 acres advanced steadily until, by 1800, few cultivated open fields remained. The farmers[4] who either owned or leased these large farms pioneered the application of the new farming techniques that constituted the Agricultural Revolution. The system of primogeniture, in which all land went to the oldest son, was strengthened in England and enhanced the incentive and the ability to invest in enclosure and improvements. Landlords leased the farms to tenants who hired laborers for wages to work

the land, many of them descendants of peasants who had agreed to enclosure, been coerced into it, or who had sold their land because they could not produce as cheaply as the larger farmers. The residents of London, Amsterdam, and other cities formed huge and growing national markets, accessible by water for many producers. Population growth stimulated demand for food and in turn incentives for investing in agricultural production. Brisk demand, transportation, primogeniture, enclosure, and capital were as necessary as technical improvements to the transformation of agriculture.

Preconditions for the Industrial Revolution

In the High Middle Ages, industrial production had been largely centered in towns, where textiles formed the largest industry (see Chapter 8). Some of it remained there, but since the Late Middle Ages, more and more industrial activity had been carried on in the countryside through the **putting out system** (see Chapters 11 and 14). Textiles, Europe's most important manufactured commodity, were made primarily by rural workers using hand-operated spinning wheels and looms. During the eighteenth century, so many people in some regions supported themselves by producing in this way for distant markets that economic historians describe such regions as undergoing a process called **proto-industrialization.** In Flanders, for example, almost 50 percent of the population manufactured linen cloth in their cottages. Since they had only small amounts of land, they relied on industrial activity to yield the additional income they needed in order to survive. The entrepreneurs who supplied their raw materials benefited from their relatively cheap labor, since their small holdings allowed them to grow at least some of their food. Such districts could sustain more population than would have been possible

---

[4] The word *farmer* originally meant someone who rented rather than owned or held long-term title to his land. (Consider the expression "to farm out.") "Farming" was a profit-oriented business.

An English Rural Scene, 1727   Although fanciful in its crowding together of many kinds of rural production, this engraving suggests the diversified character of the advanced agricultural regimes in England, the Dutch Republic, and a few regions elsewhere. The lord of the manor's grand house in the background overlooks the beginning of the grain harvest and the tending of sheep and cattle. A windmill and a water mill (foreground) provide labor-saving power.   *Barnaby's Picture Library.*

effect was to reduce the amount of time many serfs had to work for their lords.

Just as central governments tried to improve the lot of the urban poor, they made efforts to improve the position of the peasantry. In some cases, especially where royal lands were involved, mandates to reduce labor services and other obligations had some positive results. But other landowners resisted royal initiatives that would have increased the cost of rural labor, and for the most part their resistance succeeded. Some peasants resisted by negotiating or by pursuing their grievances through the legal system—occasionally with success. When labor services seemed excessive, other

options were to run away, to do poor work, or to sabotage the landowner by arson, maiming his animals, or poaching his deer or other game. "To work as you do on the demesne" became a proverbial description of inattention and laziness in Poland and Russia—a counterpart to the modern phrase "good enough for government work." The last, and most dangerous, resort, was rebellion. Peasant risings such as the Great Fear (France, 1789), the "Golden Charter" revolt in Poland (1768), Pugachev's Rebellion (Russia, 1773–1774), and others punctuated the eighteenth century.

The Population Surge

The story of European population before 1700 is one of alternation between expansion and contraction. The massive sixteenth-century surge in population had, like its predecessors in the High Middle Ages, reached a plateau in some areas and actual decline in others. Europeans had long faced subsistence crises: Several poor harvests in a row would drive up the price of bread alarmingly; agricultural workers lost income with less grain to harvest; artisans lost revenue as consumers had to devote more of their family income to food; death rates rose because underfed people were more vulnerable to disease; birthrates fell as marriages were broken by death and as malnourishment impaired fertility.

This age-old cycle ended in the eighteenth century. The expansion that had begun in the sixteenth century had ended in the middle of the seventeenth, and a period of stagnation followed. After the first third of the eighteenth century, however, an era of population growth began that continues to this day and that will probably go on if the human race can avoid nuclear war or ecological disaster. We now think in terms of gaining control of the *rate* of population increase—we do not expect that world population will decline, even though it frequently did so before the eighteenth century. The two decades on either side of 1700 witnessed the last major subsistence crisis in Europe. Europe's population stood at about 120 million in 1700, but it ballooned to 187 million by 1800, a 64 percent jump. The rates of increase far exceeded those experienced during the sixteenth-century expansion, and they varied widely among countries. In western Europe between 1680 and 1820, England had the highest rate of growth—133 percent—compared to 39 percent for France and more than 50 percent for Spain, Italy, and Germany (see Figure 18-1).

Explaining why this unprecedented population surge happened is not easy. Broadly speaking, two obvious possibilities are that the fertility rate increased (so that more babies were born) and that the mortality rate decreased (so that fewer infants and children as well as adults died). Historical demography is a relatively new field of study, and its practitioners must make ambitious national and regional estimates using the relatively small number of parish registers and other kinds of data that have survived. However,

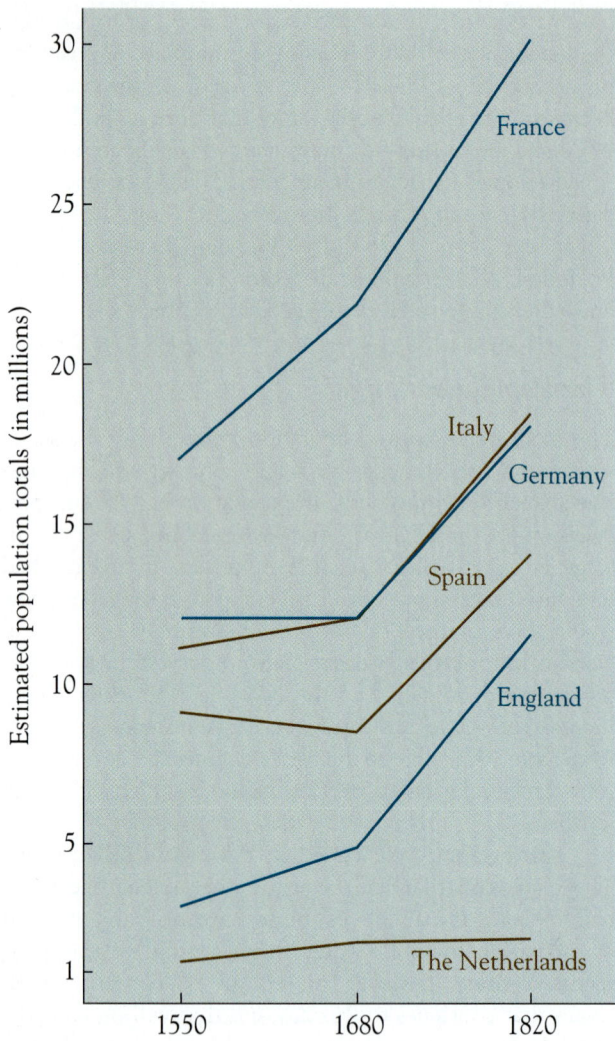

FIGURE 18-1
POPULATION GROWTH, 1550–1820
Source: Adapted from E. A. Wrigley, People, Cities and Wealth:
The Transformation of Traditional Society *(Oxford, England: Basil
Blackwell, 1987), table 9.1, p. 216.*

ily size) seems to have been falling. In most countries the mean age of marriage for women remained fairly stable or actually rose (in Scandinavia, for example, from 26.7 years before 1750 to nearly 30 years in the decades around 1800). In France, the most thoroughly documented case, women's average reproductive period (the interval between the births of the first and the last child) dropped 37 percent. The most likely explanation is that in France a trend toward conscious use of birth control techniques in order to space children more widely was in place by midcentury—a full century ahead of the rest of Europe.

These national averages concealed wide variations from one locality to another. In rural villages where the spinning and weaving of textiles or the production of other manufactured products predominated, peasants tended to marry younger and have more children than in agrarian villages where marriage had to await access to acres. Wherever rural industries became established, the marriage age for women dropped. In one English county during the eighteenth century, for example, farmers married women between ages 27 and 29, whereas the brides of weavers and other artisans averaged 22.6 years old. Between the 1630s and 1790s, the population of the Swiss city of Zurich increased 80 percent, while in the nearby countryside a textile-producing district grew 300 percent.

Despite a higher birthrate in industrializing rural districts, a sinking death rate was the most significant contributor to Europe's accelerating population. Infant mortality declined dramatically nearly everywhere, and larger numbers of children continued to survive into their teens. In France and Switzerland before 1750, for example, only about half of the children born alive were still living at age fifteen; between 1780 and 1820, the incidence had risen to almost 60 percent in France and 70 percent in Switzerland.

Furthermore, changes involving armies, disease, nutrition, and transportation must be combined to explain why mortality rates declined enough to enable Europe to escape the age-old population pattern of advance followed by retreat. Within Europe at least, the demographic damage wrought by the movement of armies lessened. Before 1792, when the series of great wars stemming from the French Revolution erupted (see Chapter 21), Europe had enjoyed seventy years of relative freedom from the carnage wrought by military operations. Wars still scourged the countryside, but they were fought by smaller, better disciplined armies operating on a smaller scale than had been the case in the seventeenth century. Armies after the Thirty Years' War were more professional, and military hygiene was one of the main concerns of officers who more and more worked to keep their soldiers healthy so they could fight more effectively. Healthier and better trained soldiers, often living in barracks and camps rather than amid the general population, transmitted disease less often. As central governments grew more powerful, they could devote more attention and resources to the health of the people paying

enough evidence has been collected and analyzed to show that the contribution made by greater fertility was less significant than the decline in mortality. In other words, the surge was due mainly to the fact that people lived longer, rather than that more were born. Some interesting changes have been discovered, even if they tell us little about why overall population exploded. Illegitimacy rates, for example, certainly increased between the early eighteenth century and 1820. Before 1750 in England, out of every hundred babies born alive, 2.6 were born to unmarried mothers; in the forty years after 1780, that rate rose to 5.9 (see Table 18-1). Across the same span of time, the number of babies conceived before marriage doubled in France and nearly doubled in England and Germany. Nevertheless, except in Belgium, marital fertility (and therefore fam-

Although European agriculture as a whole was not technically "revolutionized" in the eighteenth century, in some regions there was an "Agricultural Revolution" in the century after 1750. Like any major change, this one had earlier beginnings. In England and the Netherlands, for example, yield ratios had reached 6 to 1 early in the seventeenth century and continued to rise. At a yield ratio of 8 to 1, each peasant household could produce enough to feed not only itself but ten other people as well. By 1750, yield ratios in England and the Netherlands neared 10 to 1, and they would soon rise to 15 and even 20 to 1 for some crops. Despite the increased production, the proportion of the population directly involved in agriculture was falling. According to one estimate, farm labor in England represented 70 percent of the population in 1600, down to 55 percent in 1700, and 36 percent in 1800. Between 1700 and 1800, the productivity of English farm workers went up 41 percent.

Many factors coalesced to make such extraordinary jumps in productivity occur. Some were technical, as in the case of sowing methods. Traditionally, seed had been sown by broadcasting it over the plowed soil. Soon after 1700 an English gentleman, Jethro Tull (1674–1741) crafted the first seed drill, a device that inserted seed into the prepared ground and thereby used much less seed. Tull's book, *The Horse Hoeing Husbandry* (1733) advocated the use of seed drills to place plants in rows in order to control weeds by horse-drawn hoes. Drilling seeds in rows reduced the amount of seed needed by 70 percent. Another Englishman, Charles, Viscount Townshend (1674–1738), became known as "Turnip Townshend" for his enthusiastic preaching of the value of root crops as fodder to support large and healthier livestock herds. Better fodder supplies meant that more animals could be kept alive during the winter, thus increasing supplies of fresh meat and dairy products and enlarging herds from year to year. The average weights of animals sold to butchers in London more than doubled during the eighteenth century through the application of selective breeding techniques to oxen, cattle, sheep, and pigs that had long been used with horses. Other nitrogen-fixing fodder crops such as peas, beans, and clover were introduced, enriching the soil no less than the manure of the animals that grazed on them.

Farmers who practiced the "improving" gospel of Tull, Townshend, and others gave up medieval field rotations that left half or one-third of the land fallow at all times (see Chapters 7 and 14). The new patterns of crop rotation—called alternate and convertible husbandry—involved complex cycles that kept all the land in production. These methods also achieved a balance between grain and livestock farming and allowed farmers a more flexible response to changing prices of grain and meat. Agriculture was becoming more scientific and more commercial, at least in some regions. But progress was slow and uneven, and the sharp increases in agricultural productivity that occurred in England, the Low Countries, and some other places were by no means the norm.

Steeply increasing population after midcentury caused food prices to rise, especially in the 1760s and 1780s (see Figure 18-2). More expensive grain, the main foodstuff, made life harder for ordinary people. Governments had long tried to regulate prices and maintain supplies of grain for use in times of shortage in order to avoid violent protests by both urban and rural consumers. The growth of national and international markets, however, gave landlords the opportunity to ship their production to where it would bring the best price, and food riots protesting local shortages and high prices ensued. In France's "Flour War" (1775), for example, people seized grain from farmers and merchants and bread from bakers. The rioters, who usually paid what they considered a "fair price" for what they took, believed they had a right to subsistence that the authorities should protect. Yet the government used soldiers to reestablish order and hanged the ringleaders of the protests. Rising prices, although they made life harder for many, also stimulated investment in agricultural improvement by

Agricultural Methods in Diderot's *Encyclopedia* The philosophes who wrote the articles in the most ambitious publishing project of the Enlightenment era, *The Encyclopedia*, enthusiastically preached the gospel of new technology. This plate illustrates the older method of sowing seed by broadcasting (like the worker at left center above the plow), and also shows the new seed drill (right center) being used by a woman. *Corbis/Bettmann*.

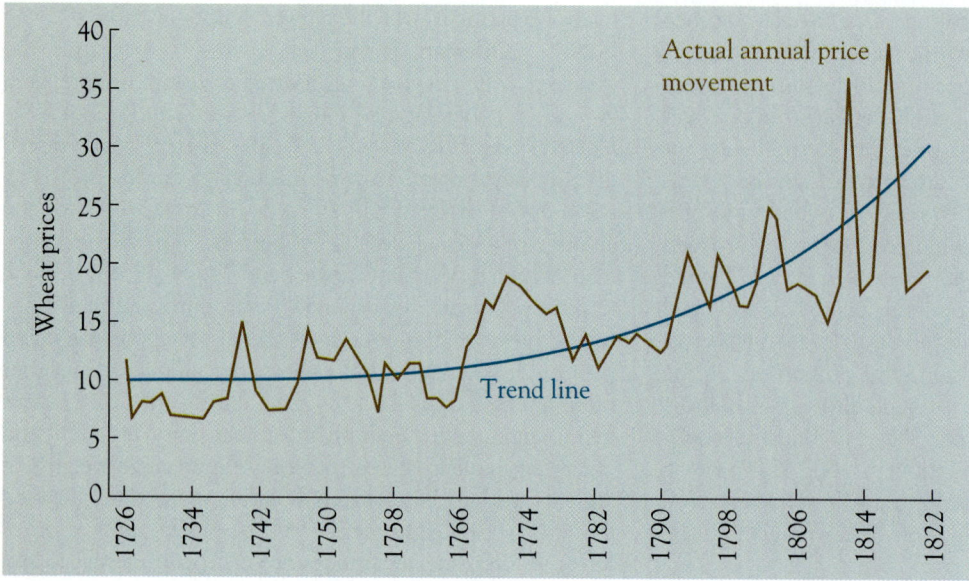

FIGURE 18-2

WHEAT PRICES IN EIGHTEENTH-CENTURY FRANCE

This graph shows the upward movement of annual average wheat prices in France (in livres per hectoliter, 1726–1819) and the trend line of these prices. Note how the price oscillations become more extreme over time, but that the general trend moves steadily upward. *Source: Adapted from David Hackett Fischer,* The Great Wave: Price Revolutions and the Rhythm of History *(New York: Oxford University Press, 1996), figure 3.02, p. 122.*

landowners and better-off peasants. Those who could afford such investment reaped the profits that flowed from growing demand and higher prices.

Few of the techniques fueling the "Agricultural Revolution" were entirely new. Convertible husbandry, for example, had been employed in the Low Countries since the Late Middle Ages. In the bourgeois-dominated Dutch Republic, political and social affairs lay in the hands of merchants rather than landowners. As a result, the Dutch were the first to treat agriculture as a business investment rather than a way of life. Urban merchants bought land and livestock and invested in land reclamation. Scarce Dutch land produced high-value butter, cheese, and meat, and the prosperous Dutch could afford to import grain from eastern Europe and later from England.

Technical improvements of the kinds that the Dutch pioneered were hard to make in countries where land was still divided into strips cultivated by different families, or where many small farms had emerged owing to the repeated division of holdings among numerous heirs. In England, **enclosure** of common fields to produce large farms of 100 to 300 acres advanced steadily until, by 1800, few cultivated open fields remained. The farmers[4] who either owned or leased these large farms pioneered the application of the new farming techniques that constituted the Agricultural Revolution. The system of primogeniture, in which all land went to the oldest son, was strengthened in England and enhanced the incentive and the ability to invest in enclosure and improvements. Landlords leased the farms to tenants who hired laborers for wages to work

the land, many of them descendants of peasants who had agreed to enclosure, been coerced into it, or who had sold their land because they could not produce as cheaply as the larger farmers. The residents of London, Amsterdam, and other cities formed huge and growing national markets, accessible by water for many producers. Population growth stimulated demand for food and in turn incentives for investing in agricultural production. Brisk demand, transportation, primogeniture, enclosure, and capital were as necessary as technical improvements to the transformation of agriculture.

Preconditions for the Industrial Revolution

In the High Middle Ages, industrial production had been largely centered in towns, where textiles formed the largest industry (see Chapter 8). Some of it remained there, but since the Late Middle Ages, more and more industrial activity had been carried on in the countryside through the **putting out system** (see Chapters 11 and 14). Textiles, Europe's most important manufactured commodity, were made primarily by rural workers using hand-operated spinning wheels and looms. During the eighteenth century, so many people in some regions supported themselves by producing in this way for distant markets that economic historians describe such regions as undergoing a process called **proto-industrialization.** In Flanders, for example, almost 50 percent of the population manufactured linen cloth in their cottages. Since they had only small amounts of land, they relied on industrial activity to yield the additional income they needed in order to survive. The entrepreneurs who supplied their raw materials benefited from their relatively cheap labor, since their small holdings allowed them to grow at least some of their food. Such districts could sustain more population than would have been possible

---

[4] The word *farmer* originally meant someone who rented rather than owned or held long-term title to his land. (Consider the expression "to farm out.") "Farming" was a profit-oriented business.

without proto-industrialization. Yet these workers lived precariously, always at risk when bread prices rose or demand for their products fell.

Beginning about 1760, the Industrial Revolution would utterly transform society by drawing workers away from their rural cottages into new cities where giant factories utilized energy from running water and fossil fuels. In the factories, they lost the freedom they had enjoyed in the countryside to decide when they would work and when they would stop. Instead of being masters of their looms and other tools, they became servants to large machines—a pattern that would persevere for some two centuries, until the emergence of the computer and advanced telecommunications once again enabled workers to perform highly skilled tasks at home. The numerous technological innovations and the factory system form the heart of the Industrial Revolution, which hit its full stride after 1800. The preconditions for the Industrial Revolution, which precipitated an enormous unprecedented and sustained increase in economic growth, may be considered in three interrelated categories: demand, transportation, and finance.

First and most important was the increase of both home and foreign demand (especially from the North American colonies) for industrial products. Eighteenth-century population growth heightened demand for food. The agricultural transformation described earlier produced that food at relatively low prices while also supplying wool and other materials and releasing labor to industry. People therefore had more disposable income, money that could be spent on manufactured goods or saved and invested. New levels of demand inspired investors and entrepreneurs to look for ways to increase production, most notably of cotton textiles, iron, and coal.

Better transportation was one reason that the huge increase in industrial output occurred in England. It meant lower costs for transactions, lower prices, and more demand. England already had 1,400 miles of waterways and canalized rivers when the great canal-building age began in the 1760s; Germany had only 300 miles. By 1802 English private investment had added more than 600 miles of canals, many of them connecting the rivers and improving linkages with ports on an island where no point is more than 70 miles from the sea. The effect on the cost of bulk transport was substantial. A packhorse carried 250 pounds; a horse on a towpath pulling a barge moved 50 tons. The Duke of Bridgewater's canal, carrying coal from his mines to Manchester, tripled the city's population by 1801. British private investors also financed, through turnpike trusts, improvements in overland transport. The London-Bristol stagecoach run, for example, took two days in 1754 and only sixteen hours in 1784. The pace of canal-building and road-building accelerated after the Industrial Revolution began, to be sure—but access to markets was relatively good even in the earliest stages.

Canals and Locks in the *Encyclopedia*   Canal building, although very expensive, occurred on a large scale during the eighteenth century. This plate from the *Encyclopedia* demonstrated how locks worked. Emperor Joseph II, after seeing a new canal in France, said, "I am proud to be a man when I see that one of my fellow-creatures has dared to imagine and execute so bold and vast a work." *The Granger Collection, New York.*

Improvements in agriculture and transportation required capital. Before the eighteenth century and during it in many countries, wealth was consumed or invested relatively less productively. Kings and aristocrats who owned the main source of wealth—land—spent what their acres yielded on wars, palaces and palatial houses, rich clothing and furnishings, fast horses, and countless servants. Frenchmen who got rich tended to buy land and lend money to the government rather than speculate in commerce, industry, or improving agriculture. They also bought offices that conveyed aristocratic status and tax exemption (see Chapter 19). A successful bourgeois in Spain or northern Italy was likely to follow a similar path; both social ambition and the shortage of alternative uses for mercantile profits suggested it.

British and Dutch landowners and merchants provide a partial exception to this general picture of low rates of investment in agricultural, commercial, and industrial activity. The contrast must not be overdrawn, as the grand country and town houses they built show them perfectly capable of conspicuous consumption. Nevertheless both nations had developed more sophisticated national money markets than existed elsewhere in eighteenth-century Europe. The contrasting experiences with state banking in Britain and France help to explain why.

Attempts were made to establish state banks in many countries in the eighteenth century. The shortage of coin and the great financial needs of governments forced experimentation with paper money (banknotes). In France a Scottish financier named John Law was the mastermind behind the *Banque Royale* (1720) and a **joint-stock company,** the Mississippi Company. Share prices soared as a frenzy of speculative buying (the "Mississippi Bubble") swept the country at the same time that a similar mania (the "South Sea Bubble") inflated the value of the shares of another company in Britain. When it became obvious that the revenues of these companies would not support the absurd levels that stock prices had reached, the "bubbles" burst and investors lost heavily. Law's plan for a state bank never recovered from the resulting loss of public confidence, and he was forced to flee into exile. But confidence in the Bank of England (which had been chartered with private capital in 1694) survived the crash of 1720 after Parliament stepped in to regulate the formation of new

companies. Despite the crash, banknotes issued by London and provincial banks circulated successfully. By 1793, four hundred country banks were operating when there had been only a dozen in 1755. And public confidence in a financial system based on parliamentary control of government policy underlay Britain's military and diplomatic success in the wars with France, success that paid off in access to world markets.

The relationship of the joint-stock companies like the Bank of England and other banks to industrialization was indirect. Early industrialists did not, on the whole, depend on banks for long-term credit. They often financed the construction of their factories and mills by their own revenues and using their own labor. Their books often showed large balances owed to mercantile firms for operating capital and raw materials, balances on which they paid interest for long periods. Their capital, therefore, did not come from banks or even from the growing market in mortgages, stocks, and bonds. Nevertheless the short-term credit available from banks did help support the whole system, which, in its complexity and relative stability, allowed a vital shift of capital resources from commerce and agriculture into industry.

Living the Good Life

Those who had the good fortune to be in a position to reap the benefits of economic growth and the political developments that accompanied it—meaning, as we have seen, the more alert and forward-looking members of the landowning aristocracy and their counterparts among the

Hogarth's *The South Sea Bubble* In his 1721 representation, William Hogarth shows the conniving directors of the South Sea Company trying to distract attention from the consequences of their wild speculation. "Honesty" (foreground) is broken on the wheel; "Honor" (right) is flogged by "Villainy," who has removed his mask; and "Trade" is rendered senseless (foreground, at right). A priest, a rabbi, and a Dissenting preacher gamble (lower left) while women (left) seek husbands who made fortunes by selling before prices crashed. *North Wind Picture Archives.*

bourgeoisie—were lucky in another way. They had the means and the leisure to spend time in the forerunners of modern resorts, then called "watering places." These were seaside and spa towns where, fashionable people thought, one could maintain or rebuild one's health by bathing in or "taking" (drinking) the "waters." In the spas, natural springs gushed water saturated with sulphur or other minerals believed to be beneficial. The most famous such town in Britain was Bath, where the population soared from three thousand in 1700 to thirty-five thousand in 1800. Obviously, the visitors could not spend all their time in the sulfurous water, so a sizable array of concerts, dances, and other entertainments emerged to keep them in Bath spending their money. Sitting for a portrait while in Bath became so common a pastime that a small army of artists stayed busy there.

Tourism, however, also became international. During much of the sixteenth and seventeenth centuries, Europe had been divided by religious conflict, and Protestants stayed away from Catholic areas and vice versa. The cooling down, although not the complete cessation, of those religious animosities after the middle of the seventeenth century had opened the door to an activity not much seen since the Middle Ages—tourism. In medieval Europe, the common mantle of Christendom sheltered pilgrims and scholars who moved about quite freely. During the eighteenth century, a new kind of "pilgrimage" developed called the "Grand Tour."

Although particularly associated with wealthy Britons, many Poles, Scandinavians, Germans, and Russians also made the Grand Tour. Paris and such Italian cultural magnets as Rome, Florence, Naples, Milan, and Venice were mainstays, but itineraries might also include stays in Geneva, Berlin, and Amsterdam. Many of the tourists were young aristocrats and would-be aristocrats for whom the Grand Tour flourished as an important part of their education. Visits to operas, especially in Italy where this relatively new art form was highly developed, and to collections of paintings and other artworks were deemed essential. Predictably, some of these young gallants found their way to gambling dens and prostitutes as well as art galleries. All travelers faced obstacles now largely vanquished, such as pirates in the Mediterranean, bedbugs in inns, arduous journeys through Alpine passes, and the formidable stench of all big cities. (It was reported, for example, that Berlin could be smelled 6 miles away. A visitor to Edinburgh in 1705 complained that he and his friends had to "take care where we trod for fear of disobliging our shoes" in human excrement and to "walk in the middle at night for fear of an accident to our heads.") Despite these inconveniences, the Grand Tour continued to thrive until tourism was cut short by the French Revolution and the Napoleonic wars at the end of the century. As one waggish poet put it, "How much a dunce, that has been sent to roam,/Excels a dunce, that has been kept at home." Exposure to the culture and thought of the Enlightenment outweighed the difficulties that travelers encountered.

Zoffany's Cognoscenti in the Uffizi In 1780, Zoffany produced this busy scene in the Tribuna Room (Uffizi Gallery) in Florence. Men and boys on the Grand Tour view Greek sculptures and paintings by Titian, Raphael, Rubens, Michelangelo, Rembrandt, Van Dyck, and others. Titian's *Venus of Urbino* is held by a museum official (center foreground), and Rubens's *Horrors of War* is on the back wall (center, middle level). England's diplomatic representative in Florence stands in his dark coat and red sash (right of Titian's painting). *Royal Collection, Windsor, Photo A. C. Cooper, Colour, Ltd. Copyright reserved; reproduced by gracious permission of Her Majesty the Queen.*

THE ENLIGHTENMENT: REASON ENTHRONED

Until the seventeenth century, European thought was dominated by traditions inherited from biblical and classical texts. Medieval thinkers, such as St. Thomas Aquinas, had built their ideas on pagan and Christian sources, and both the Renaissance and the Reformation had reinforced their authority (see Chapters 10, 12, and 13). The Christian doctrine of original sin held that human reason and moral capacity were seriously flawed.[5] People believed that humanity's greatest achievements lay in the past, and the most that could be hoped for was recovery of past glories. Many thought even that possibility unlikely and held that the world was decaying as it approached its end. Fifteenth- and sixteenth-century Europeans' encounters with lands unknown to the ancients shook this pessimism somewhat, but belief that human reason could advance civilization to new heights—the idea of progress—did not emerge until late in the seventeenth century.

From the Scientific Revolution to the Enlightenment

The Enlightenment was an extension and popularization of seventeenth-century scientific and philosophical advances (see Chapter 17) that produced the idea of progress. Newton's discovery of the law of gravity showed that human reason could reveal the inner workings of nature. Locke's psychology, which saw ideas in the human mind not as inborn but as results of interaction with the environment via the senses, suggested that moral values could be reformed through new systems of education. By Newton's method, nature could be controlled to benefit humanity, and by Locke's, society itself could be rationally reordered. The former would lead to freedom from the often-destructive forces of nature; the latter, to freedom from evil people and institutions. The Enlightenment's confidence in progress through reason and its rejection of traditional authorities rested on these foundations.

During the eighteenth century, the experimental, quantitative approach to understanding nature that was pioneered during the Scientific Revolution continued and indeed still continues. Once started, it never really ended. Established scientific societies continued to develop, and new ones emerged. In France, for example, provincial academies in Bordeaux, Dijon, and other towns that had earlier concentrated on issues of literary style were by midcentury emphasizing scientific efforts and providing libraries and laboratories in which to pursue them. Forty-three percent of the more than six thousand members of these provincial academies were nobles, meaning that the majority of members who were bourgeois associated in an egalitarian fashion in the work of scientific and practical improvement.

Although advances occurred in astronomy, botany, zoology, geology, electricity, and other areas of scientific inquiry during the eighteenth century, the most dramatic came in chemistry and particularly in the chemistry of gases. After the middle of the seventeenth century, various experimenters began to find what they called "airs," meaning vapors that had chemical properties different from ordinary air. In the early 1770s, the Frenchman Antoine Lavoisier (1743–1794) and the English Dissenter Joseph Priestley (1733–1804) independently identified oxygen (a word coined by Lavoisier). Lavoisier went on to propose a new theory of combustion and an entire new terminology for chemistry, which enabled the new science to escape its old association with alchemy. Priestley also discovered other gases, and both men created new instruments and techniques for studying gases. Lavoisier also undertook chemical analysis of spa waters, and other chemists worked to improve industrial processes such as dyeing and bleaching textiles.

The Scientific Revolution promised both material improvement and a better understanding of the ingenuity and beauty of God's creation through the use of human powers of observation and reasoning, and the literate people of eighteenth-century Europe responded enthusiastically. Booksellers worked to meet the demand for textbooks on scientific topics, and popularizers of science such as Bernard de Fontenelle ("Fontenelle's 'Science for the Ladies'," see p. 642) saw their books go through numerous editions. An Italian counterpart to Fontenelle's "Science for the Ladies" (titled *Newtonianismo per le Dame*) appeared in 1737, and Sir James Ferguson's 1757 book explaining Newton's astronomy in terms that laypersons could understand appeared in German and Swedish translations. In Britain, *The Newtonian System of Philosophy Adapted to the Capacities of Young Gentlemen and Ladies* was an instant best-seller; it went through no less than ten editions between 1771 and 1800. In its 126 pages, "Tom Telescope" presents six lectures discussing matter and motion, the solar system, optics, and other topics in thoroughly Newtonian and Lockeian terms. "Tom" also sternly warns his young readers against cruelty to animals—especially stealing a mother bird's eggs. Tom Telescope's sales quickly spurred numerous imitators, such as *Mr. Telltruth's Natural History of Birds and Animals* (1776), into the burgeoning market for science for children. Fascination with the Scientific Revolution within the elite public grew throughout the eighteenth century and underlay the appeal of the Enlightenment.

The Philosophes and Their Public

The leaders of the Enlightenment were called by the French word for "philosopher"—*philosophe*. Only a few of

---

[5] Original sin was the teaching that all human beings have inherited their sinful nature from Adam and Eve, and that humanity's inherently sinful condition explains the evil that flourishes in this world.

Astronomy for Amateurs
This English print (ca. 1750) satirized the gentry's interest in science by showing them peering through the wrong ends of telescopes and otherwise making fools of themselves with scientific instruments. Although satirists enjoyed poking fun at the well-heeled amateurs for their pell-mell rush into astronomy, botany, chemistry, and other fields, elite interest in science was invaluable in winning political and financial support for research and experimentation. *Museum of the History of Science, Oxford.*

the philosophes were philosophers in the usual sense of the word. Most were men of letters, propagandists, and publicists rather than original thinkers. They devoted themselves to spreading the gospel of Enlightenment through a torrent of essays, books, dictionaries, encyclopedias, pamphlets, poems, plays, and novels. Britons, Germans, Italians, Iberians, and Americans made important contributions to the movement, although as an intellectual phenomenon it developed most fully in France. The philosophes wrote for members of what came to be described as the "Republic of Letters," such as members of the literary and scientific societies and academies whose numbers grew exponentially during the eighteenth century. Such groups funded prizes for the best essays written by philosophes and anxiously struggled to keep abreast of the latest ideas.

The philosophes aimed at a radical reshaping of public opinion, and they sought to achieve it primarily through the printing press. By the eighteenth century, a new, large reading public had appeared and served as their potential audience. Some 2.5 million newspapers were sold in England in 1713, only eleven years after the first successful daily appeared. By 1753, the total was 7 million newspapers, and the tally skyrocketed to 16 million by 1801. Daily newspapers were common by late in the period, not only in capital cities but also in provincial towns. Germany already had fifty-seven newspapers in 1701. Parisian cafes, most of which received copies of newspapers, numbered 380 in

1723 and 6,000 in 1788. Literary journals and other periodicals proliferated, including circulating libraries, and attracted many subscribers. London alone had 122 by 1800, and 268 more operated elsewhere in England. Printers were more numerous and busier than ever before. These trends materialized earlier and more vigorously in western Europe but gradually spread to the east. Most, but not all, readers lived in cities and towns, while the majority of the population was still rural. Nevertheless, as both the availability of printed material and the number of readers grew, so did the importance of public opinion.

The Enlightenment was no more a unified, disciplined movement than the Renaissance or the Reformation had been, and like them, it shifted its outlook over time. Until around 1750, many philosophes felt confident that a benign providence directed human affairs and that, by nature, people wished to be good. Rejecting the doctrine of original sin, they thought that evil stemmed from inherited traditions and institutions. Later, this optimism broke down as many came to see nature as hostile or at best indifferent to human affairs. Although the philosophes scathingly criticized established religion, only a few went so far as to proclaim themselves atheists and materialists. All of them deplored existing institutions, but they differed widely as to how those institutions ought to be changed.

The philosophes nevertheless had much in common. They assumed that people everywhere were fundamentally

THE HISTORICAL EVIDENCE

Joseph Addison Addresses His Readers

1711

Joseph Addison (1672–1719) gained fame as a poet, essayist, and editor of English literary journals that disseminated Enlightenment ideas in a gentle, witty, and readable manner. His publications brought him wide popularity and stimulated imitations in many other countries. Journals like those that Addison helped create and for which he wrote copiously were new in the eighteenth century, and their success demonstrates the existence of an expanded readership and of a struggle to influence a relatively new phenomenon: public opinion. This extract comes from the March 12, 1711, issue of Addison's newspaper, The Spectator.

It is with much satisfaction that I hear this great city inquiring day by day after these my papers, and receiving my morning lectures [essays] with a becoming seriousness and attention. My publisher tells me that there are already three thousand of them distributed every day, so that if I allow twenty readers to every paper, which I look upon as a modest computation,* I may reckon about threescore thousand disciples in London and Westminster,[†] who, I hope, will take care to distinguish themselves from the thoughtless herd of their ignorant and inattentive brethren. Since I have raised to myself so great an audience, I shall spare no pains to make their instruction agreeable, and their diversion useful, for which reasons I shall endeavour to enliven morality with wit, and to temper wit with morality, that my readers may, if possible, both ways find their account in the speculation of the day. And to the end that their virtue and discretion may not be short, transient, intermitting starts of thought, I have resolved to refresh their memories from day to day, till I have recovered them out of that desperate state of vice and folly into which the age is fallen. The mind that lies fallow but a single day sprouts up in follies that are only to be killed by a constant and assiduous culture. It was said of Socrates that he brought philosophy down from heaven to inhabit among men; and I shall be ambitious to have it said of me that I have brought philosophy out of closets [private rooms] and libraries, schools and colleges, to dwell in clubs and assemblies, at tea-tables and in coffee-houses.

I would therefore in a very particular manner recommend these my speculations to all well-regulated families that set apart an hour in every morning for tea and bread and butter, and would earnestly advise them for their good to order this paper to be punctually served up, and to be looked upon as a part of the tea equipage. . . .

But there are none to whom this paper will be more useful than to the female world. I have often thought there has not been sufficient pains taken in finding out proper employments and diversions for the fair ones. Their amusements seem contrived for them rather as they are women than as they are reasonable creatures, and are more adapted to the sex than to the species. . . . Their more serious occupations are sewing and embroidery, and their greatest drudgery the preparation of jellies and sweetmeats. This, I say, is the state of ordinary women; though I know there are multitudes of those of a more elevated life and conversation, that move in an exalted sphere of knowledge and virtue, that join all the beauties of the mind to the ornaments of dress, and inspire a kind of awe and respect, as well as love, in their male beholders. I hope to increase the number of these by publishing this daily paper, which I shall always endeavour to make an innocent if not an improving entertainment, and by that means at least divert the minds of my female readers from greater trifles.

---

*Notice that Addison expects that *The Spectator* will be passed hand to hand and read aloud—not only in well-to-do private homes but also in coffee houses, then a new institution in London.

[†]Westminster was then a suburb of London, where the houses of Parliament were located. Today it is a neighborhood in the heart of London, akin to Capitol Hill in Washington, D.C. In addressing himself to readers in London and Westminster, Addison is writing for the political and social elite of early eighteenth-century Britain.

Source: From Peter Gay, ed., *The Enlightenment: A Comprehensive Anthology* (New York: Simon & Schuster, 1973), pp.276–278; from *Foundations of the Metaphysics of Morals, What is Enlightenment?* trans. Lewis White Beck, 1950. Reprinted by permission of Caroline H. Beck.

---

rational and capable of seeking freedom and happiness, if only inherited follies could be swept away. As more information about other cultures became available, philosophes used it to argue that Europe was neither morally nor culturally superior to the others; some even argued that Europe

was inferior. They opposed censorship and demanded intellectual freedom, so that humanity's greatest faculty—reason—could have full play. Press censorship was lax in the Dutch Republic and essentially ended in England in 1695, when the Licensing Act of 1662 was not renewed. In

France and in most other countries, however, governments continued to monitor printers and booksellers carefully in order to police both political and religious opinion. In Catholic states, Protestant books were often banned, although enforcement varied widely. In France, clandestine printing, smuggling, and circulation of the works of the philosophes was widespread and profitable for publishers willing to take risks to supply the demand from interested readers. In 1783 alone, one French bookseller obtained a thousand volumes of what officials considered "undesirable books" for his customers. After 1750, however, the better known philosophes only rarely had to worry about the authorities, censorship in France having become a game that all the players understood.

The major joint endeavor of the philosophes, the massive twenty-eight-volume *Encyclopedia, or Rational Dictionary of the Sciences, Arts, and Trades* (1751–1772), was a bold attempt to survey all knowledge. The goal of the work was stated by its editor, Denis Diderot (1713–1784), as follows:

> . . . to gather together the knowledge scattered over the surface of the earth, to explain its general system to the men with whom we live, and to transmit it to the men who shall come after us, . . . so that our descendents, becoming better informed, shall become at the same time more virtuous and happier, and so that we do not die without having deserved well of the human race.

Although it might seem that the motives of the philosophes who contributed to the *Encyclopedia* were wholly benign, that is not how they were perceived by conservatives or intended by some of the contributors. The *Encyclopedia* described improvements in the technology of building ships and canals, printing books, manufacturing iron, coal, textiles, and other products. But it also contained statements that deeply disturbed churchmen and devout laypeople, who fought hard against its publication. Diderot, who had been imprisoned for several months in 1749 for what his enemies perceived as his antireligious ideas, held a materialist view of the origins and function of natural phenomena that did not require a God who created all things. The *Encyclopedia*, although a richly detailed compendium of information about arts and crafts, also campaigned against established churches and for religious toleration. In the eighteenth century, as earlier, one could not discuss nature without discussing religion and politics.

The Philosophes and God

The archetypal philosophe was François-Marie Arouet, known by his famous pen name: Voltaire (1694–1778). In his witty, sarcastic, and forceful writings, he railed against intolerance and "superstition," by which he meant established religion—its dogmas and clergy no less than its rites and rituals. The Christian church, in his view, was the enemy of all progress because the preservation of its power required that people be kept ignorant of science and reason. "Theology," he announced, "amuses me; that's where we find the madness of the human spirit in all its plenitude." Voltaire's popular *Philosophical Letters on the English* (1733) pointedly contrasts England's relative intellectual and religious freedom to France's censorship and persecution of Protestants. He defined the Inquisition as a "wholly Christian invention to make the pope and the monks more powerful and turn a whole kingdom into hypocrites."

"Écrasez l'infâme" ("Crush the infamous thing") became Voltaire's battle cry, and for him the infamous thing was the inhumanity that stemmed from religious bigotry. He first used the slogan against the Catholic magistrates of Toulouse, who in 1761 brutally executed a Huguenot shopkeeper named Jean Calas by ordering his body broken on the wheel. Calas had been convicted of killing his son to prevent the young man from converting to Catholicism, but in fact he had either committed suicide or been murdered by parties unknown. Voltaire crusaded vigorously to establish Calas's innocence and to condemn the persecuting spirit that had demanded his agonizing death. Voltaire's advocacy of the cause of the Calas family in print succeeded so brilliantly that in 1763 the **Parlement** of Toulouse reversed itself and admitted that Jean Calas had been innocent of his son's death.

The anticlericalism that Voltaire shared with many philosophes implied the necessity of religious toleration. In the *Encyclopedia*, Diderot denounced the intolerant man as "an evil man, a bad Christian, a dangerous subject, a bad politician and a bad citizen." Toleration was essential because, as Voltaire wrote, "we are all formed of weakness and error: let us pardon reciprocally each other's folly. That is the first law of nature." Newton, the idol of the philosophes, had concluded that scientists could never know the ultimate reason of things; they could only deal in the probabilities that could be derived from careful observation and experiment. The philosophes in turn concluded that persecution could never be justified because certainty about **metaphysics** could never be achieved.

Enlightenment anticlericalism was not the same as atheism, although a few philosophes became atheists. Baron d'Holbach (1723–1789), in his *System of Nature* (1770), insisted that the universe consists of matter and motion, both of which have existed forever and needed no Creator. Further, he said, human beings are soulless machines whose actions are determined by forces beyond their control. But Voltaire and others disagreed with d'Holbach's stand. Voltaire and most of his colleagues were deists. **Deism** was "natural religion," by which the philosophes meant belief in a supremely intelligent, impersonal being who created the world, gave humanity the divine gift of reason, and expected people to treat each other with justice and charity. Anything beyond this they scorned as "revealed religion," meaning acceptance of the authority of the Christians' Bible, the Jews' **Torah,** the Muslims' Qur'an, or any other compendium of alleged divine revelation that

LE DÉJEUNÉ DE FERNEY.

De son d'après Nature à Ferney le 4 Juillet 1775   Gravé par Née et Masquelier même Anneé

Voltaire at Ferney Ejected from Prussia by Frederick the Great and refused re-entry to France by Louis XV, in 1757 Voltaire bought an estate in Swiss territory at Ferney. Near the French border and thus accessible to the many admirers who visited, Ferney remained Voltaire's home for the rest of his life. In this 1775 engraving, he is shown breakfasting in bed with his friends around him. *Corbis/Bettmann.*

was really a crafty device dreamed up by greedy priests. No clergyman, whether Christian, Jewish, or Muslim, could be trusted, and Voltaire's denunciation of Judaism was no less harsh than his criticism of Christianity. The English poet Alexander Pope (1688–1744), whose *Essay on Man* (1733) summed up much of what the philosophes thought, put it this way:

> For Modes of Faith let graceless zealots fight;
> He can't be wrong whose life is in the right.

Miracles were also suspect because they required suspension of the natural laws that human reason was discovering. The Scottish philosophe David Hume (1711–1776) perfectly expressed the Enlightenment view: "We may conclude that the Christian religion not only was at first attended with miracles, but even at this day cannot be believed by any reasonable person without one." Anything that was not reasonable, the philosophes argued, could not be true religion. The millions who had suffered and died in religious wars were victims of superstition and ignorance. The hero of Voltaire's highly popular short novel *Candide* (1759) repeatedly witnesses episodes of such inhumanity and spends much of his time on the run from the Inquisition.

According to the philosophes, underlying all the "revealed" religions was a "natural" core of simplicity and

humanity to which priests had added unnecessary mystifications and distortions in order to maintain their power. With characteristic sarcasm toward mystical aspects of religion, Diderot suggested in the *Encyclopedia* that France could save 4 million livres a year if Christians would stop consuming bread in the **Mass.** After all, he wrote, "bread does not carry more of a blessing than the water used to bless it, and consequently, one could be satisfied with just the water, which costs nothing." Such skepticism also informed the best known work of history produced during the eighteenth century, *The Decline and Fall of the Roman Empire,* written by the English philosophe Edward Gibbon (1737–1794). Gibbon related the "succession of bishops, of saints, of martyrs, and of miracles" to "the progress of superstition." In Gibbon's account, the barbarians defeated the Romans because the spread of Christianity had engendered what he called "an unresisting softness of temper" that proved fatal to their empire. In yielding to Christian revelation, the Romans lost the power of reason and the ability to defend themselves.

Enlightenment rejection of "revealed" religion did not mean a complete rejection of ritual. On the contrary, Voltaire, Montesquieu, Condorcet, Benjamin Franklin, and many other deists took part in a new movement called Freemasonry—a kind of deistic religion—which grew rapidly beginning in the 1730s. Organized in lodges in most

THE HISTORICAL EVIDENCE

Ben Franklin, Deist

1790

The career and thought of Benjamin Franklin (1706–1790) demonstrate that the British colonies in North America contained men who became fully engaged with the Enlightenment ideas that were gaining support in Europe. In this letter (dated March 9, 1790) to Dr. Ezra Stiles, the staunchly Calvinist president of Yale College, Franklin briefly characterized his religious position. His belief in a Supreme Being to whom honor was due and his reservations about the divinity of Jesus exemplify the opposition of many philosophes to "revealed religion" and their preference for "natural religion."

Reverend and Dear Sir,

    You desire to know something of my Religion. It is the first time I have been questioned upon it. But I cannot take your curiosity amiss, and shall endeavour in a few words to gratify it. Here is my creed. I believe in one God, Creator of the universe. That he governs it by his Providence. That he ought to be worshipped. That the most acceptable service we render to him is doing good to his other children. That the soul of Man is immortal, and will be treated with justice in another life respecting its conduct in this. These I take to be the fundamental principles of all sound religion, and I regard them as you do in whatever sect I meet with them.

    As to Jesus of Nazareth, my opinion of whom you particularly desire, I think the system of morals and his religion, as he left them to us, the best the world ever saw or is likely to see; but I apprehend it has received various corrupting changes, and I have, with most of the present dissenters in England, some doubts as to his divinity; tho' it is a question I do not dogmatize upon, having never studied it, and think it needless to busy myself with it now, when I

expect soon an opportunity of knowing the truth with less trouble. I see no harm, however, in its being believed, if that belief has the good consequence, as probably it has, of making his doctrines more respected and better observed; especially as I do not perceive that the Supreme takes it amiss, by distinguishing the unbelievers in his government of the world with any peculiar marks of his displeasure.

    P.S. . . . I confide that you will not expose me to criticism and censure by publishing any part of this communication to you. I have ever let others enjoy their religious sentiments, without reflecting on them for those that appeared to me unsupportable and even absurd. All sects here, and we have a great variety, have experienced my good will in assisting them with subscriptions for building their new places of worship; and, as I have never opposed any of their doctrines, I hope to go out of the world in peace with them all.

Source: From Crane Brinton, ed., *The Portable Age of Reason Reader* (New York: Viking, 1956), pp. 377–379.

---

cities and large towns, the Masons were most numerous in Britain and France but could also be found in Germany, Italy, Holland, Poland, Russia, and North America. Their thoroughly non-Christian rituals, the details of which they kept secret, celebrated the values the philosophes advocated: religious toleration, human reason and human brotherhood, progress, and philanthropy. Monarchs including Louis XV of France and Frederick the Great of Prussia; prominent political figures such as British prime minister Robert Walpole, Montesquieu, and George Washington; such musicians and writers as Wolfgang Amadeus Mozart, Joseph Haydn, and Johann Wolfgang von Goethe; and many other eminent men became Freemasons. Although they functioned as convivial social clubs for the members, many lodges also created and supported educational activities, such as lectures and reading clubs, that were open to

anyone who was interested, thereby serving as a means of disseminating Enlightenment ideas and values to the wider public. Despite papal decrees condemning Freemasonry in 1738 and 1751, the movement continued to grow and to attract Catholic laymen, and even priests, as members.

The Philosophes and the State

The philosophes strove to create an enlightened society, but they could not agree on the political means to achieve it. Charles de Secondat, Baron de Montesquieu (1689–1755), the most influential political thinker of the age, first made his mark on the movement with the *Persian Letters* (1721). This brilliant critique of European society took the form of the letters written by two fictional Persian visitors traveling through France, describing what they saw.

They left no sacred cow unkicked. The pope was called "an old idol worshipped out of habit," and religion was "less a matter of holiness than an excuse for dispute, open to everyone." The "Persians" also made one of the earliest French attacks on slavery and the slave trade.

Montesquieu was merely one of many philosophes who used the allegedly superior example set by foreign civilizations; Qing China, then at the height of its wealth and power, was a favorite. With its mandarin elite of bureaucrats, chosen after candidates had completed an extensive education and passed a rigorous examination, China's government seemed much more "rational" than patronage-obsessed France, with its venal officeholders and noble privileges. In 1721, a German philosophe was fired from his university position because he paralleled the teachings of Confucius and Christ. According to Voltaire, the Chinese empire was "powerful and wise" because it practiced religious toleration and altogether lacked "a college of priests, who ever controlled their laws"—an obvious swipe at Christian Europe. Voltaire warmly praised Confucius because the ancient Chinese sage had resisted the opportunity to form a religion when he could have made himself powerful by doing so. Confucius, Voltaire wrote, "rather chose to instruct men, than to govern them," the ambition that the philosophes claimed for themselves.

Montesquieu's greatest work was *The Spirit of the Laws* (1748), a long, rambling book that launched modern political sociology. In it, he argued that material factors such as geography and climate shaped political and moral systems. For example, he wrote that mountain people tended to enjoy more political liberty: "They defend themselves easily; they are attacked with difficulty," and so they did not need the all-powerful governments required to defend people in fertile regions. Because these systems were molded by their varied environments, no single constitution could function successfully everywhere. Taken to its logical extreme, Montesquieu's theory implied that environments determined constitutions, laws, and customs. But Montesquieu did not push his thinking this far. Rather, he asserted that, within limits, human beliefs also shaped political systems. As a lover of political freedom, Montesquieu admired the way in which medieval constitutionalism had circumscribed the power of kings (see Chapter 16). Like Voltaire, he also extolled the British constitution and drew, not always accurately, on the British example for his theory of the separation and balance of executive, legislative, and judicial powers. These powers had to be separated, he explained, in order to serve as checks on each other. Only thus could individual liberty be preserved. Montesquieu's doctrine of the separation of powers greatly influenced the framing of the Constitution of the United States in 1787, although he thought republican institutions would succeed only in small territories such as city-states or the Swiss cantons. In the *Federalist Papers* (1788), James Madison would reject the Frenchman's doctrine on this point. In Montesquieu's thinking, the aristocracy served as a vital bulwark against royal absolutism, and as a member of the parlement of Bordeaux, he gained practical experience that underlay his theories.

Voltaire was skeptical of the aristocrats whom Montesquieu favored. The tolerant and liberty-loving society

The Philosophes at Supper
This engraving conveys the vigor and intensity of the discussions when the philosophes got together. Here, Voltaire raises his arm to emphasize a point. Diderot is to his left, and Condorcet sits across from Voltaire with his back to the viewer. All seem to be listening intently, except the waiter carrying away a laden tray. *The Granger Collection, New York.*

for which Voltaire fought would most likely come about through the leadership of enlightened monarchs, he believed. They would have to be powerful enough to override all the entrenched defenders of the old order, such as aristocrats and churchmen. Except for a period late in his life during which he befriended the democratic side in Genevan politics, Voltaire advocated enlightened monarchy. He carried on a lengthy correspondence with the Russian empress Catherine the Great and spent three years at the court of Frederick the Great of Prussia. The Prussian stay began well enough, as Voltaire wrote, "ordinarily, we men of letters flatter kings; this one praised me from head to toe." But by 1752 they were quarreling, and Frederick referred to him as a "used orange." When Voltaire tried to leave the court for Frankfurt, Frederick put him under house arrest for several weeks.

By contrast, Jean-Jacques Rousseau (1712–1778) expected little from either aristocrats or kings: "Man is born free; and everywhere he is in chains." So began *The Social Contract* (1762), Rousseau's complex analysis of the tension between the rights of the individual and those of the larger community. Some readers and subsequent interpreters saw in the work a powerful argument for genuine democracy, but others in the twentieth century have perceived it as justification for totalitarian dictatorship.

Rousseau, a Swiss-born writer of humble social origins, was a democrat. He stated clearly that the people were sovereign and that government officials served merely as their delegates. But he also contended that to take part in society, people must subject their individual wills to the "general will." The "general will" was not necessarily determined by majority vote. It was what was truly best for the community, and it took precedence over the selfish, shortsighted desires of particular individuals. Freedom consisted of the subjection of individuals to laws dictated by this "general will"; indeed, Rousseau wrote that people might have to be "forced to be free." It is this last point that Rousseau's modern opponents have seized.

In his political theory, as in other aspects of his thought, Rousseau was both a man of the Enlightenment and one of its critics. *The Social Contract* received little attention during his lifetime, but ultimately it became his most famous work. His vision of a participatory democracy in which the community became a force for the moral development of all its citizens has provoked endless controversy. Neither Voltaire's enlightened monarchs nor Montesquieu's enlightened aristocrats have a place in Rousseau's community, for he believed that no such community could arise amid extremes of wealth and poverty. Liberty could not exist without equality, he averred. To be sure, Rousseau did not mean perfect economic equality, but he wrote that "no citizen shall ever be wealthy enough to buy another, and poor enough to be forced to sell himself." The kind of freedom that he dreamed of could not be imposed on the people by kings and nobles.

Jean-Jacques Rousseau Rousseau's disgust with life in princely courts and teeming cities led him to prefer long forest walks and a simple life in the country. In this sketch, he sits in contemplation beside a rushing current with his dog for company. *The Granger Collection, New York.*

The Philosophes and Society

The pervasive secularism of Enlightenment thought represented a major shift away from the traditional emphasis on life in this world as a pilgrimage to a better life in the next. On the contrary, the philosophes saw the purpose of life as fulfilled in human society, and they judged behavior in terms of social utility. By agitating for toleration and freedom of thought and expression, they hoped to reform society through the discovery of moral laws that were as universal as Newton's law of gravity, thereby founding modern social science. They thought of their vigorous criticism of the existing order as the work that had to be done before a truly rational society could emerge, a society devoted to "life, liberty, and the pursuit of happiness" in the words of American philosophe Thomas Jefferson. Jefferson and Benjamin Franklin epitomize the Enlightenment's insistence that knowledge be *useful* to humankind and that useless knowledge was worthless. They helped found the

THE HUMAN EXPERIENCE

Marquis de Condorcet, Social Scientist and Revolutionary

Marie-Jean-Antoine-Nicolas Caritat, Marquis de Condorcet, was born in 1743 into a noble family that had strong Huguenot convictions during the sixteenth century. Well before his birth, however, his ancestors had yielded to Louis XIV's pressure and converted to Roman Catholicism. His father died in battle when Condorcet was young, and the boy was raised by his devoutly Catholic mother (hence his first Christian name, Marie), who kept him in white dresses until he was eight years old. Although he was educated at the Jesuit Collège de Navarre, he soon vigorously rejected Catholic doctrine and became as anticlerical as his mentor and friend, Voltaire. Rejecting the military career planned by his family, in 1758 Condorcet went to Paris to apply himself to mathematics. A brilliant paper on integral calculus brought him entry to the Académie des Sciences in 1765, and he served as that important body's perpetual secretary from 1775 until 1793. His wife, Sophie de Grouchy (1764–1822), conducted one of the most admired salons of the era, providing the setting in which he and other philosophes could discuss their ideas for reform of finance, government, and education.

Condorcet sought to apply mathematics to social and political issues, and in doing so he helped pioneer the development of "social science." Indeed, the first use of the phrase came in a letter to Condorcet from one of his friends. He believed that the historical moment had arrived at which humanity was entering a new age of freedom to improve individuals and institutions by rational means. Condorcet depicted priests from the very earliest human civilizations as men who developed "the art of deceiving men in order to plunder them." He argued (erroneously) that ancient Greek "preachers" had brought down Socrates because he was teaching men to use their reason on their own, thus creating a dangerous threat to the ability of religious institutions to control them. For Condorcet, the rise of Christianity did not represent progress at all; rather, the Christian era was a long dark night of superstition and fanaticism from which Europe was at last awakening.

Politically active, Condorcet joined revolutionary clubs during the early years of the French Revolution, and in 1790 he published an essay in support of the rights of citizenship for women. After his election to the Legislative Assembly in 1791, he devoted much of his attention to plans for an ambitious program of public education. As a member of the National Convention, he voted in favor of declaring King Louis XVI guilty of treason in December 1792. But he did not agree with the more zealous revolutionaries who insisted on executing the king and installing the constitution proposed by the Jacobins. They soon turned on Condorcet and others who had urged a less radical course, and he decided to flee in July 1793. While in hiding, he wrote the *Sketch for a Historical Picture of the Progress of the Human Mind* (1795), his most famous work. Imprisoned by his enemies, he robbed them of the pleasure of executing him on the guillotine by taking a fatal dose of poison on March 29, 1794.

The optimism of Condorcet's *Sketch* is even more astonishing in the light of the dire circumstances under which he wrote it. Nevertheless, he predicted continuing progress on many different fronts. For example, he thought that "the improvement of medical practice, which will become more efficacious with the progress of reason and of the social order," would lead to increasingly long life for all who did not suffer death in "extraordinary accidents." Ever the mathematician, he said that longer lives "can be represented with some accuracy in figures or on a graph." Moreover, he considered it reasonable to hope for profound improvement for "the intellectual and moral faculties" through education. Condorcet, in other words, believed in the possibility and indeed the probability of the achievement of human perfection. He embodied the Enlightenment in its most idealistic form. ❖

American Philosophical Society, an organization that continues to this day to support humanitarian research.

The philosophes' humanitarianism was not limited to their campaign against intolerance. An Italian nobleman, Cesare Beccaria (1739–1794), in his *Essay on Crimes and Punishments* (1764) advocated rational reform of the administration of justice. This widely translated and read work—hailed by Voltaire as the product of a philosopher working "in behalf of reason and humanity"—called for a uniform system of penalties for crimes, regardless of the social rank of the criminal. Beccaria denounced torture, inhumane conditions in insane asylums and prisons, and penalties aimed at vengeance rather than deterrence. Noting that the death penalty even for petty thieving encouraged thieves to kill witnesses, Beccaria argued that punishments should be calibrated to the magnitude of the harm done to society by each

THE HISTORICAL EVIDENCE

Condorcet's Optimism

1794

One of the last of the philosophes, the Marquis de Condorcet (1743–1794), wrote his Sketch for a Historical Picture of the Progress of the Human Mind *in the imminent expectation of his own arrest and execution. Its praise for the Scientific Revolution and the application of its methods to society represent the central themes of Enlightenment thinking. But it should be noted that Condorcet, although expecting progress, recognized that a long road still lay ahead.*

Turning now our attention to the human race in general, we shall show how the discovery of the correct method of procedure in the sciences, the growth of scientific theories, their application to every part of the natural world, to the subject of every human need, the lines of communication established between one science and another, the great number of men who cultivate the sciences, and most important of all, the spread of printing, how together all these advances ensure that no science will ever fall below the point it has reached. We shall point out that the principles of philosophy, the slogans of liberty, the recognition of the true rights of man and his real interests, have spread through far too great a number of nations, and now direct in each of them the opinions of far too great a number of educated men, for us to fear that they will ever be allowed to relapse into oblivion. And indeed what reason could we have to fear, when we consider that the languages most widely spoken are the languages of the two peoples [the French and the English] who enjoy liberty to the fullest extent and who best understand its principles, and that no league of tyrants, no political intrigues, could prevent the resolute defence, in these two languages, of the rights of reason and of liberty?

But although everything tells us that the human race will never relapse into its former state of barbarism, although everything combines to reassure us against that corrupt and cowardly political theory which would condemn it to oscillate forever between truth and error, liberty and servitude, nevertheless we still see the forces of enlightenment in possession of no more than a very small portion of the globe, and the truly enlightened vastly outnumbered by the great mass of men who are still given over to ignorance and prejudice. . . . We observe that the labours of recent ages have done much for the progress of the human mind, but little for the perfection of the human race; that they have done much for the honour of man, something for his liberty, but so far almost nothing for his happiness. At a few points our eyes are dazzled with a brilliant light; but thick darkness still covers an immense stretch of the horizon. There are a few circumstances from which the philosopher can take consolation; but he is still afflicted by the spectacle of the stupidity, slavery, barbarism and extravagance of mankind; and the friend of humanity can find unmixed pleasure only in tasting the sweet delights of hope for the future.

Source: From Antoine-Nicolas de Condorcet, *Sketch for a Historical Picture of the Progress of the Human Mind*, trans. June Barraclough (London: George Weidenfeld and Nicholson, 1955), pp. 167–169, 173–176, 196–202; as appears in Peter Gay, ed., *The Enlightenment: A Comprehensive Anthology* (New York: Simon & Schuster, 1973), pp. 802–803.

---

kind of crime. Society would gain more by prevention of crime than by brutal treatment of the few criminals who got caught.

Some philosophes carried their quest for freedom from traditional ideas into the realm of economics. They questioned the **mercantilist** principles that had governed economic thinking for centuries. Instead of rigid state regulation of economic activities, they called for abolition of controls and a **laissez-faire** ("let things alone") or free-market economy. These philosophes, called physiocrats, freed economics from its former subservience to political thought into an independent science. Led in France by François Quesnay (1694–1774), the physiocrats perceived a

natural economic order that would, if given free play, bring prosperity to all. They believed that agricultural countries, such as France and England, could grow wealthy only if their farms became more productive, whereas trading nations like Holland could increase wealth only by restraining consumption. Food production should be encouraged and luxuries like sugar and tobacco discouraged. In economics, as in other areas explored by philosophes, the cry was "back to nature."

A Scottish philosophe, Adam Smith (1723–1790), published the most influential exposition of laissez-faire thinking, *The Wealth of Nations* (1776). Against the mercantilist assumption that a nation's wealth consisted of its amassed treasure of bullion, he argued that wealth depended on labor. Freed from governmental meddling, human nature would enable people to concentrate on what they did best, and the consequence would be greater wealth and prosperity for all. Each individual, Smith insisted, by advancing his own personal and, in a sense, selfish interest, increased his productivity and thus benefited the whole society. The individual, as he wrote, is "led by an invisible hand to promote an end which was no part of his intention." Although later interpreters have thought otherwise, Smith did not endorse low wages for laborers. The happiest countries, he believed, would have highly paid workers. Smith advocated freedom from monopolistic distortions of trade, not freedom for merchants and manufacturers to exploit labor.

Yet for all their talk of liberation from tradition and oppression, the philosophes gave little attention to the position of women. In Parisian salons, where ladies were no less active and powerful in the eighteenth century than they had been in the seventeenth (see Chapter 16), writers discussed their ideas in the company of intelligent, upper-

Self-Portrait of Elizabeth Vigée-Le Brun (1781) Although elite women participated in the philosophes' enterprise by leading salons and in other ways, few achieved public careers. One who did was the talented French painter whose work typifies the Rococo style, Elizabeth Vigée-Le Brun (1755–1842). She painted Louis XVI's queen Marie Antoinette and noble ladies not only in France but also in Germany, England, Italy, and Russia. *Kimbell Art Museum, Fort Worth, Texas.*

class women. The important difference was that in the eighteenth century the royal court no longer provided the dominant influence; rather, intellectual leadership had passed outside of the monarch's control. Montesquieu said that men's "power over women is mere tyranny" and that "among the most civilized nations wives have always had authority over their husbands." David Hume wrote that marriage should be "an engagement entered into by mutual consent" and denounced the "male tyranny" that obliterated the "equality, which nature has established between the sexes."

Yet Enlightenment feminism had definite limits. Articles in the *Encyclopedia*, while opposing legal disabilities burdening women, nevertheless pictured the ideal woman as a thrifty and obedient housewife. Rousseau, furthermore, flatly rejected the notion that women were intellectually equal to men or that they deserved any place in public life. In his novel on education (*Émile*, 1762), he described a program that would make Émile a perfect citizen in a democratic community. But for Sophie, his wife-to-be, education had two quite different goals: pleasing her husband and bearing his children. So influential was Rousseau's idolization of motherhood that breast-feeding, which he praised, became highly popular in aristocratic circles. The education of children, he argued, should proceed with the greatest sensitivity to their ages and capabilities. Therefore he denounced rote learning and too much emphasis on words instead of things. Ironically, however, Rousseau, who articulated the modern concept of childhood, placed his own five children in foundling homes. Although, as orphans, their chances of survival were poor, Rousseau claimed that he could not afford to raise them. And just as few philosophes genuinely included women in their arguments about the universality of "human rights," neither did they include peasants, most of whom were still illiterate. The philosophes in their voluminous writings addressed an expanded but largely urban audience of literate professionals, merchants, and artisans. They had no interest in and at times showed contempt for the majority that could not yet read.

The Philosophes and Their Critics

Conservatives all over Europe reacted with horror to most of the ideas of the philosophes and did their best to suppress them. As mentioned earlier, only the Dutch Republic and Great Britain permitted substantial freedom of the press. Protestant authorities in Geneva burned Rousseau's works, and Catholic authorities in France burned Voltaire's. Yet not all of the most damaging criticism of the Enlightenment came from conservatives. Opposition to some of its basic tenets arose among the philosophes themselves. David Hume's extreme skepticism about the possibility of certain knowledge of the existence of either natural law or the abstract God of the deists undermined the philosophical basis of the Enlightenment and at the same time

THE HISTORICAL EVIDENCE

The Roots of Rousseau's Romanticism

ca. 1766

Rousseau came to hate the citified (and, he thought, artificial) world of Parisian salons and the cultural style that the philosophes had created. The self-revelatory frankness of his Confessions, *written about 1766 while he was living with David Hume in England and published posthumously in 1781, shocked readers. This excerpt concerns his recollection of the circumstances in 1753 in which he came to write his* Discourse on Inequality *(published in 1754). It displays his growing sense that "civilization" corrupted rather than improved people because it overrode the "primitive" and "natural" emotions and ideas that enable us to act freely, humanely, and morally.*

In order to think this great matter [of inequality] out at my leisure, I went to Saint-Germain for some seven or eight days with Thérèse* and our landlady, who was a decent woman, and a woman friend of hers. I think of this trip as one of the most pleasant in my life. The weather was very fine; those good women undertook all the trouble and expense; Thérèse amused herself in their company; and I, without a care in the world, came in at meal-times and was unrestrainedly gay over table. For all the rest of the day, wandering deep into the forest, I sought and I found the vision of those primitive times, the history of which I proudly traced. I demolished the petty lies of mankind; I dared to strip man's nature naked, to follow the progress of time, and trace the things which have distorted it; and by comparing man as he had made himself with man as he is by nature I showed him in his pretended perfection the true source of his misery. Exalted by these sublime meditations, my soul soared towards the Divinity; and from that height I looked down on my fellow men pursuing the blind path of their prejudices, of their errors, of their misfortunes and their crimes. Then I cried to them in a feeble voice which they could not hear, "Madmen who ceaselessly complain of Nature, learn that all your misfortunes arise from yourselves!" . . .

The trip and the occupation improved my health and my humour. Several years before I had been so tortured by my retention of urine that I had put myself entirely into the doctors' hands. They had not alleviated my complaint, but had exhausted my strength and ruined my constitution. On returning from Saint-Germain I found that I had more strength and felt a great deal better. I acted on this discovery and decided to recover or die without physicians or drugs. So I said good-bye to them for ever, and started to live from day to day, staying quiet when I could not move and walking as soon as I had the strength. Paris life among pretentious people was so little to my taste; the cabals of men of letters, their shameful quarrels, the lack of honesty in their books, and the important airs they assumed in the world were so disgusting and antipathetic to me; I found so little gentleness, openheartedness, or sincerity even in the company of my friends, that in my disgust for that turbulent life I began to long ardently to live in the country.

---

* The woman he later married and the mother of his five children.

Source: From *The Confessions of Jean-Jacques Rousseau*, trans. J. M. Cohen (Harmondsworth, England: Penguin, 1953), pp. 362–363.

---

questioned Descartes's sharp mind-body distinction. Rousseau's exploration of irrational, intuitional, and emotional aspects of the human psyche ate away at confidence in the power of reason. His work underlay the rise of Romanticism, the philosophical outlook that succeeded the Enlightenment (see Chapter 22). He believed that we all possess an "inner voice" that comes from our feelings, not from education. In other words, our heart tells us what is right, not our reason. Rousseau thus returned, in a sense, to the notion of "innate ideas" that Locke and most of the philosophes had rejected.

Immanuel Kant, a Prussian philosophy professor, was another important thinker who represented the Enlighten-

ment and yet also went beyond it. In his *Critique of Pure Reason* (1781), he argued (like Hume) that the human mind cannot know the ultimate causes of things, but it *can* discover patterns of cause and effect. While denying that science could comprehend final truth, he upheld the value of science. In his *Critique of Practical Reason* (1788), Kant held that the human will is free, and its decisions, although influenced by material stimuli, are not necessarily determined by them, as Baron d'Holbach had thought. Kant called his most famous principle of egalitarian moral philosophy the "categorical imperative": "Act only on that maxim whereby thou canst at the same time will that it should become a universal law." In other words, do nothing

Chodowiecki's *The Happy Marriage*   The shift, signaled by Rousseau, from the assumption that truth is arrived at by reason to the notion that "feeling" (meaning the reasons of the heart, not the mind) should be trusted helped to engender a new emphasis on sentiment. Family feeling and the new enthusiasm for breastfeeding by mothers rather than by wet-nurses is portrayed here by the German engraver Daniel Chodowiecki. Although a time would come when this sentimentality seemed excessive and cloying, many people in late eighteenth-century Europe were drawn to it as an antidote to what had come to be perceived as the chilly rationalism of Enlightenment.   *The Granger Collection, New York.*

you would not urge all others to do. It was Rousseau's general will in a new form and, in another sense, a restatement of the "Golden Rule" of Christianity (see Chapter 5).

Ironically, the deism of the philosophes helped to trigger a religious revival. The Supreme Being of deistic "nat-ural religion" left many Europeans cold. Instead of this impersonal and distant deity, who never intervened in human affairs, the revivalists thirsted for spiritual rebirth in a direct, personal communion with God. The forms of revival varied markedly—Pietism in Germany, the Great Awakening in North America, Methodism in England, Hasidism among certain East European Jews. In mid-eighteenth-century Poland, for example, the Hasidic **sect** broke away from the intellectualism and formalism of the rabbis in favor of ecstatic prayer and the "omnipresence of God" in daily life.[6] Especially attractive to the many poor and illiterate Jews cut off from Talmudic scholarship, Hasidism eventually won the devotion of nearly half of Europe's Jews. German Pietism, initiated in the 1670s, stressed the need for a deep sense of sin and close study of the Bible, which would lead to one's "second birth," or faith in Christ as personal savior. In the eighteenth century, some Pietists demonstrated their rejection of the philosophes' confidence in reason by making decisions through randomly opening the Bible and acting on whatever verse their eyes happened to fall upon. Some Methodists did the same.

John Wesley (1703–1791), an Anglican minister, encountered Pietist doctrines and was influenced by them while traveling to Georgia as a missionary.[7] After he returned from America, he founded Methodism, a movement that grew within the established church but broke away from it in the 1790s. Methodism appealed strongly to workers who were caught up in the turmoil of Britain's Industrial Revolution after 1760. These people were unmoved by Anglican ritualism and its upper-class leaders, many of whom were deists. Hostile to Newton's cosmology and the Enlightenment, Wesley preached at least two sermons a day for more than fifty years to enormous audiences, often in open fields. He called on his listeners to repent their sinful lives and undergo a conversion like the one he had experienced in 1738: "I felt I did trust in Christ alone for salvation, and an assurance was given me, that He had taken away my sins, even mine, and saved me from the law of sin and death. I felt my heart strangely warmed."

THE CULTURES OF THE AGE OF REASON

In theory the philosophes asserted the brotherhood of all men and the universality of "reason," but in practice most of them assumed that the peasants and the urban poor were beyond their reach. Ever since the Scientific Revolution

---

[6] The word *hasid* is of Hebrew origin, and as early as the third century B.C. it meant a holy man or a member of a sectarian movement. See also Chapter 5.

[7] The British colony of Georgia was founded by philanthropists in the 1720s as a refuge for debtors and other victims of misfortune. Its founders tried to bar alcohol and slavery from the colony and to treat its Native American population fairly. None of these well-intentioned efforts succeeded.

that the Enlightenment thinkers strove to popularize, the gap between "low" and "high" cultures had been widening. For example, in the sixteenth century, the fear of witches and the readiness to persecute them pervaded European society from top to bottom. Growing doubts among the elite about the credibility of witchcraft accusations during the seventeenth century eventually ended the witch-hunt craze (see Chapter 17). But the newfound reluctance of upper-class magistrates to convict witches had not been accompanied by a reduction in ordinary people's concerns about witches. "Science for the ladies" and "Tom Telescope's" child-oriented explanation of the new understanding of nature and nature's laws informed the outlook of some better-off Europeans; the masses remained committed to older assumptions. Traditional religious attitudes continued to hold the allegiance of the majority of the population, living as they did in close proximity to their parish churches and depending on God's favor to protect their crops, their animals, and their health from the devil and his allies. The deism of the philosophes made headway among the educated elites, although its conquest was by no means complete even there. The "superstition" against which Voltaire and his ilk railed so furiously was the folk religion and popular piety of the day, and the persistence and venom that the philosophes brought to their task suggests that they knew it.

Popular Culture

Another telling instance of the sharpening cultural divide appears in a popular public event in Paris that was celebrated by people from the highest to the lowest social ranks—the Midsummer Day ritual. Part of the merriment included the burning of a sack of howling cats suspended on a scaffold over a huge bonfire, and in the sixteenth century members of the royal court usually participated in the event. Indeed, the king himself had the honor of setting the bonfire aflame. By the eighteenth century, however, only young artisans continued this cruel practice, and the elite refused to have anything to do with it.

Blood sports had long attracted all sorts of people. Queen Elizabeth I and her courtiers delighted in watching the hounds kill the deer they pursued. With her crossbow, the Queen personally shot deer enclosed in a pen. Bull-baiting, in which dogs attacked tethered bulls and tore off ears and pieces of skin while the bull fought back as best he could, is another example. Bear-baiting, cock-fighting, and similar entertainments also proliferated in medieval and early modern Europe not only during the carnival season but throughout the year. In 1694, an English writer stated that bull-baiting "is a sport the English much delight in; and not only the baser sort, but the greatest ladies." A cockfight in London in 1663 drew enthusiastic members of Parliament no less than "the poorest prentices, bakers, brewers, butchers, draymen and what not . . . all fellows one with another in swearing, cursing, and betting," according

to one observer. But the elite outlook was beginning to change, and English tourists in Spain and Portugal, if they attended bullfights at all, went only once. One such traveler wrote, "I was highly disgusted with the spectacle. It set my nerves on edge and I seemed to feel cuts and slashes the rest of the evening." Another called it "a damnable sport." Beginning in the 1740s, an outpouring of essays, tracts, and poems against cruelty to animals transformed the attitudes of those more prosperous folk who could read them.

Yet the notion of a growing division between elite and popular cultures must not be overstated. Neither culture was static or uniform, and neither was entirely sealed off from the other. Overall literacy rates began to rise during the sixteenth century, although from a very low starting point: Around 1500, only 5 percent of men and very few women could read. Literacy grew much more significantly in towns than in the countryside and among some social groups and occupations more than others. Printers, merchants, goldsmiths, and barber-surgeons, for example, attained literacy to a much greater extent than bakers, butchers, carpenters, and day laborers. Everywhere, non-elite women lagged because of the expectation that most would be housewives with no need to read in order to make a living. In mid-seventeenth-century Madrid, for example, 31 percent of men could not read, while 74 percent of women could not.

Important steps toward mass literacy occurred in the eighteenth century as municipal governments and local churches and charities devoted more resources to education for "the middling sort" and for workers. In London in the 1750s, some 92 percent of the men who married could sign their names, as could 75 percent of their brides. Rates were lower in small provincial towns and lower still in rural villages, although variations within different parts of the same town and between regions could be wide, and a unknown proportion could read but not write. (Nor does an ability to sign one's name necessarily mean an ability or inclination to read and write with ease.) However, interaction between the new literate culture and traditional oral culture was common and continuous, and the two cultures should not be seen as mutually exclusive. Much reading was still done aloud, both by literate persons to each other and to illiterate friends and neighbors. Our modern sense that reading is normally a solitary activity must be contrasted with the fact that it was a social and communal experience for many early modern Europeans.

One measure of the trend toward greater literacy, admittedly imprecise but nevertheless indicative, is the enormous increase in the amount and variety of material flowing from printing presses in the seventeenth and eighteenth centuries aimed at a socially varied readership. The percentage of titles printed in Latin dropped steadily, while the proportion of vernacular titles zoomed. In 1640, books in Latin made up 71 percent of those sold at two large German book fairs, the rest being in German. By 1700, the Latin proportion was 38 percent, and by 1800 it was only 4

THE HUMAN EXPERIENCE

Nicholas Contat, Printer and Joker

Nicholas Contat (ca. 1718–1768)—a printer, printer's foreman, engraver, and later wine merchant—wrote one of the few surviving accounts of a workingman's life in the eighteenth century. Before the nineteenth century, people who earned their living working with their hands were rarely literate. But compositors (the workers who set type in printing shops) had to be able to read and write. In 1737 in Paris, Contat began his four-year apprenticeship to Jacques Vincent, who like many other master printers had his establishment on the left bank of the Seine near the Sorbonne. The difficult lives of the apprentices and journeymen and the importance of their *chapelles* (worker's associations) form the central themes of Contat's *Anecdotes Typographiques* (written in 1762 but not published until 1980).

The hero of the *Anecdotes Typographiques* is "Jerome," a young man who obviously represents Contat. As apprentices, Jerome and his friend Léveillé live a miserable existence. The food they are given in the master's kitchen is disgusting, the room they sleep in is dirty and cold, and they must get up by 4 A.M. to begin the menial tasks they will face all day. Even the journeymen treat them badly, resenting the apprentices because they will add to the competition for the few opportunities to

become masters. Journeymen and apprentices, however, united in their resentment of the master and his wife, a resentment that boiled over into "the great cat massacre."

Mme. Vincent loved cats, and especially loved *La Grise* ("the Gray One"). But Jerome and Léveillé grew furious at the nocturnal howling of alley cats on the roof over their room. Léveillé, an excellent mimic, counterattacked by climbing to a spot near the Vincents' bedroom and howling like the alley cats. The hoped-for order came to the apprentices—clear out the alley cats, but do not harm La Grise. When the master and mistress were out, the apprentices and journeymen proceeded to kill every cat they could find, including La Grise, whose body they hid. Some they smashed with broom handles and metal bars; others they captured in sacks, held a mock trial, and hanged on a gallows. The men, wrote Contat, "are beside themselves with joy." Moreover, they proceeded to reenact the triumph in the shop for days afterwards, screaming with laughter and beating on everything in sight with their mallets and composing sticks to add to the fun.

Why was this wanton cruelty such a hilarious joke? Clearly, the cat massacre expressed exploited workers' anger against their boss. But why cats? Early modern European art and

literature frequently depict the torturing of animals, usually cats. In folktales, superstitions, and proverbs, cats were linked to witches and devils. Cats often appeared as witches' "familiars," wicked agents sent to trigger illness or misfortune for whoever the witch disliked. To maim them was to protect oneself. Cats also symbolized female sexuality by hinting at seductions and orgies. These animals therefore suited the workers' purposes perfectly. Léveillé tricked the boss into ordering the massacre, so he could not punish them. The joke's extraordinary success depended on the clever way the workers exploited a well-known collection of symbols, and they acted out a "script" that contemporaries would have understood perfectly. Destroying La Grise asserted simultaneously that the master was a cuckolded fool and his wife an unfaithful witch. What may appear to us as gratuitious violence against animals would not have been understood that way by Jerome and his buddies. Although the elite had by the eighteenth century turned away from participation in rituals of popular culture that abused cats or other animals (under certain circumstances), the older traditions on which the workers' drama depended were still alive and well in popular culture. ❖

percent. Religious works had dominated sixteenth-century printing, but, although they remained popular, many other genres flourished. The shelves of booksellers' shops and the packs of itinerant peddlers must have strained under the weight of it all. Broadsheets, pamphlets, ballads, and chapbooks (short books such as romances, fables, joke collections, and almanacs that were cheap enough to be bought even by workers and servants) proliferated. Many chapbooks contained versions of stories derived from oral traditions. The printing totals for one popular English almanac are astonishing: 107,000 in 1768; 220,000 in 1789; and 353,000 in 1800. Benjamin Franklin in North America made his for-

tune as the publisher of *Poor Richard's Almanack*, published annually and filled with Enlightenment exhortations to thrift and diligence. Chapbooks frequently appear in the library lists that have survived from the estates of wealthy households, further evidence that popular and elite culture continued to overlap in various ways.

Elites and the High Culture

In the realm of the arts, the eighteenth century defies the one-word classification (Romanesque, Gothic, Renaissance, Mannerist, Baroque) that described, with qualifications, earlier eras. In architecture, the Baroque style persisted, but particularly in France and England it was combined with or replaced by a classical or Palladian element. Early eighteenth-century France was also the birthplace of the sensuous, highly decorative style called Rococo, which spread to southern Germany and Austria. Rococo furniture and interiors were often embellished with Chinese motifs, and Chinese lacquer work, silks, and especially porcelain

enjoyed wide popularity that was hardly surprising in view of the philosophes' admiration for Chinese political and social institutions. Beginning in the 1740s, new archaeological work in Greece and Rome and the publication of precise drawings of ancient buildings stimulated yet another wave of enthusiasm for classical antiquity all over Europe. The resulting neoclassicism influenced not only architecture but interior decoration, furniture, pottery, and painting.

Rococo Architecture: Church of the Fourteen Saints Built between 1743 and 1772, this Rococo church by the architect Balthasar Neumann (1687–1753) is at Vierzehnheiligen in southern Germany. Its restrained exterior does nothing to prepare the visitor for its astonishing interior: white stucco, pastel colors, sinuous forms, and theatrical lighting. Vierzehnheiligen was one of several places that became popular pilgrimage sites during the Catholic renewal of the seventeenth and eighteenth centuries. *Anthony Kersting.*

A significant change in music as in the other arts can be identified in the midcentury period. In the early decades, composers produced stylish, ornate music in the later Baroque or Rococo manner, pleasing and harmonically complex but lacking in melody and often insubstantial. The towering exception to this generalization is the enormous body of work by J. S. Bach. The change that began in the 1740s can be heard in the symphonies of Franz Joseph Haydn (1732–1809). His first works followed the older style, but he helped to found the classical style that his younger contemporaries, Wolfgang Amadeus Mozart (1756–1791) and Ludwig van Beethoven (1770–1827), carried to its apogee. Mozart's opera *The Magic Flute* expressed his commitment to Freemasonry and the Enlightenment values of universal humanity and brotherhood that it represented. In the opera, the philosopher-king Sarastro symbolizes enlightened reason, while the hysterical Queen of the Night represents the Roman Catholic ritualism that philosophes and Freemasons despised. These renowned composers emphasized melody and harmonic simplicity. Classical operas were more realistic than their Baroque predecessors, were often socially satirical, and appealed to a growing, increasingly prosperous, and literate propertied class. New instruments (piano, flute, violin, clarinet) and new musical forms (symphony, string quartet, ballad, and comic opera) and the orchestra in its modern form all made their first appearance in the eighteenth century. The careers of these classical musicians also illustrate the continuing importance of royal or noble patronage, as it was not yet possible to make a living simply by writing music. Haydn, for example, played in and directed a rich Hungarian noble family's orchestra while writing music for it at the rate of two symphonies or concertos a week. Mozart served as organist and concertmaster for an Austrian archbishop for many years.

Experiment and innovation in many styles and genres also characterized literature. At the outset, French was the language of all who aspired to high culture: Frederick II of Prussia called his native German a "semi-barbarous tongue," used it only to speak to his servants, and delighted in Voltaire's jibe that "German was for soldiers and horses." Although the most admired poetry and drama early in the century was classical in form, governed by rigid rules promulgated by French writers, the dominance of classicism was undercut by several developments. One was the rise in literacy mentioned earlier, which greatly expanded the market for prose and especially prose fiction. Daniel Defoe's tales (*Robinson Crusoe*, 1719, with highly successful French and German translations in 1720; *Moll Flanders*, 1722) sold well and cleared the way for a new literary genre, the novel. Defoe also published numerous pamphlets and satires on a wide range of issues, including some savage verses against slave-traders (1702) and a proposal for academies to educate young women (1697). "I have often thought of it," he wrote, "as one of the most barbarous customs in the world, . . . that we deny the advantages of learning to women."

Samuel Richardson's *Pamela, or Virtue Rewarded* (1740), the first blockbuster novel, is told through the emotion-filled letters of a female servant whose employer's lust for her body was transmuted into admiration for her morals and the offer of marriage. Sentimental and preachy, Richardson nevertheless portrayed people and their feelings in realistic social settings. *Pamela's* enormous popularity called forth other novelists, most notably Henry Fielding. His *Joseph Andrews* (1742) satirized *Pamela*, and his *Tom Jones* (1749) was a boisterous, comic, bawdy, but fundamentally moralistic masterpiece. The novel, unburdened by classical rules, had arrived, and its practitioners soon spread across Europe, earning their livings from the sales of their works rather than the patronage of aristocrats.

The rise of the popular novel in England exemplifies the decline of French domination of European culture by the 1740s. National literatures developed where they had scarcely existed before (in Scandinavia, Russia) or where they had been eclipsed by the Sun King's shadow (in Germany, Britain). The shift was due partly to the expanding reading public and partly to the new emphasis on the emotions. One of those emotions—national feeling—promoted a fascination with "folklore," the orally transmitted poems, folk songs, and stories told among ordinary people in Germany, France, England, and other linguistic groups whether unified under national governments or not. As such material began to be collected and published after 1765, Johann Gottfried Herder (1744–1803), found that new terms had to be invented to describe it. He called collections of songs he made *Volkslieder* (folksongs), and he coined *Volksmärchen* and *Volkssage* as labels for fairy tales and folktales. Artisans, small farmers, and laborers must have been astonished when well-educated and well-dressed people showed up on their doorsteps asking them to sing their inherited songs and tell their old stories so they could finally be recorded and preserved.

Herder stressed the importance of native literatures for the people who created them and believed that nations grew organically over time just as individuals do. Enlightenment cosmopolitanism and rationalism came under attack from Herder and others who emphasized national distinctiveness and the importance of irrational but nonetheless deep and real emotions that arose out of a sense of connection with ethnic roots. Instead of emphasizing, as the philosophes did, what members of the human race had in common, the new tendency was to stress the differences that distinguished linguistic, geographical, and cultural communities. The middle decades of the eighteenth century witnessed numerous new patriotic endeavors, such as the establishment of organizations (both public and private) to celebrate national cultures. Human brotherhood began to take a backseat to human particularity. It is no accident that the famous collectors of tales like

"Little Red Riding Hood," "Rumpelstiltskin," and "Snow White" were keen German nationalists, the brothers Grimm—Jakob (1785–1863) and Wilhelm (1786–1859). The Grimms hoped to recapture an original German culture uncorrupted by what they perceived as the "foreign" artificiality of the Enlightenment. In their view, the superiority of the poetry of *das Volk* (the German-speaking peoples) was precisely that it had no known author and had emerged from a collective, uniquely German consciousness distilled over time.

The greatest German writer of the age, Johann Wolfgang von Goethe (1749–1832), said of the man who initiated this trend in Germany: "Herder taught us to think of poetry as the common property of all mankind, not as the private possession of a few refined, cultured individuals." Goethe's early novel, *The Sorrows of Young Werther* (1774), typified the *Sturm und Drang* ("storm and stress") literary movement of the 1770s in Germany. Goethe and other young writers rebelled against the French neoclassical principles, dominant in Europe since the reign of Louis XIV. *Werther* is a *Bildungsroman*, a "coming-of-age" novel about the education of a sensitive youth who, despondent over a failed romance, shoots and kills himself. The central message about the power of feeling and emotion and the psychological penetration of the story made it famous and spawned an epidemic of imitative suicides.

Goethe's masterpiece, the huge verse drama *Faust* (published in two parts, 1808 and 1832), retold the sixteenth-century legend of an aging magician who sells his soul to the devil in return for youth and power. Goethe's version of the tale exalts Enlightenment values. A deistic God calmly allows the devil to tempt Dr. Faust with earthly delights on condition that as long as he strives for greater knowledge and deeper experience, rather than becoming self-satisfied, hell cannot claim him. "Striving" and seeking human betterment (whatever the cost to actual human beings) apparently justify the rejuvenated professor's shabby treatment of Gretchen, the girl whom he loves and betrays. In the end, his soul soars to heaven—instead of sinking into hell, as in the original legend. Comparable in scale to Dante's *Divine Comedy* (see Chapter 10), but reflecting a post-Christian worldview, *Faust* is an Enlightenment-era allegory of Western man's drive for mastery, inspired (as the last line proclaims) by "the eternal feminine." *Faust* exerted a tremendous influence on nineteenth- and early twentieth-century European, and above all German, culture. Goethe's statement in 1815 that "Nature is a grand organ on which our Lord God plays and the Devil blows the bellows" hints at the philosophical issues he tackled in *Faust* and at his return to classicism later in his long and influential career. Goethe's work contributed powerfully to the emergence of German as a great literary language.

The emergence of novels and uplifting patriotic literature designed for a wide readership was accompanied by a no less significant expansion of the production of political and social reporting, satire, and criticism. Although technically illegal, the publication of the content of parliamentary debates in England began in the late 1770s in most newspapers not only in London but in the provinces. Foreign travelers displayed amazement at the knowledge of politics displayed by ordinary people. The humiliating details of George III's mental illness in 1788 appeared, shockingly, in the press and evoked pity that redounded to the king's credit after his recovery. In France, booksellers sold political pamphlets known as *libelles* in large numbers whenever they thought the police were not looking. These often contained slanderous attacks on members of the royal family and leading politicians. King Louis XVI of France, for example, was represented in libelles of the 1780s as impotent and his queen Marie Antoinette as an enthusiastic participant in orgies. A police official thought that such slanders "caused great harm to domestic tranquility" and undermined the public's belief in the legitimacy and sacral character of kingship. If so, the possibility that the monarchy and the established hierarchy deserved to be overthrown and replaced by a different social and political system became more imaginable.

The World and the European Imagination

Although undoubtedly important, colonies and trade formed only part of the interaction between Europeans and the wider world in the eighteenth century. In the decades around 1500, Columbus, Da Gama, and other seafarers had encountered places and peoples previously unknown in Europe (see Chapter 14). As European states built up empires of colonies and trading bases, interest in information about all aspects of these "new" places—not only their geography, climate, plants, and animals but the customs and characteristics of their societies—grew rapidly. In eighteenth-century Britain, for example, travel literature became the most popular genre. Europeans, having created a global economy, found themselves forced to deal with people who differed significantly from themselves. This presented a major conceptual problem for the philosophes who, in theory, agreed with Thomas Jefferson's famous assertion that "all men are created equal."

Among Enlightenment thinkers common responses to the problem of difference included inconsistency and ambivalence. Jefferson, for example, despite his ringing declaration about equality, owned slaves and made one of them his mistress. The most influential writer on colonialism, the French philosophe Abbé Guillaume Raynal (1713–1796), criticized the use of sugar, tobacco, and coffee as unnecessary luxuries whose production depended on the unjust practice of slavery. However, Raynal also opposed ending slavery too abruptly on the grounds that freeing slaves would endanger both them and society. Georges-Louis Buffon (1707–1788), the leading French naturalist of the period and the director of the royal gardens in Paris, argued for the common humanity of people everywhere and explained differing appearances as the result of climatic and other factors. Buffon also contended, however, that plants, animals, and human beings in Europe represented the highest forms and that their American versions represented degenerated versions. Others, such as Jefferson and Rousseau, angrily disagreed, regarding American species as superior.

Many Enlightenment writers imagined faraway islands as utopian paradises and admired indigenous peoples because they seemed to live in greater harmony with their environments and to be freer of the corruptions that philosophes assailed in Europe. Others, and sometimes the same writers in different contexts, justified colonial enterprise as an extension of "civilization" to savages. During the eighteenth century, the three voyages of an Englishman, Captain James Cook (1728–1779), completed the mapping of the world beyond Europe that had commenced in the fifteenth century. Cook sailed around New Zealand and charted the eastern coast of Australia, and in his last voyage (1776–1780) he traced the northwestern coast of North America and found the Hawaiian Islands. Although he was killed in a skirmish with Hawaiians in 1779, his work made the geography of the Pacific Ocean known to Europeans for the first time. With him sailed a botanist, Sir Joseph Banks (1734–1820), who brought back a huge collection of botanical specimens to the newly established royal gardens at Kew, west of London. As a friend of King George III, director of the gardens (and thus Buffon's English counterpart), and president of the Royal Society from 1778 until his death, Banks functioned as the principal scientific adviser to the British government. He used his position to shield both French and English scientists during the French Revolution and the wars that followed it.

A few philosophes managed to combine a love of Eden-like exotic islands with hardheaded empirical reasoning about preserving them from the ravages of uncontrolled capitalism. Pierre Poivre (1710–1786), a French naturalist and colonial administrator who served as intendant of the island of Mauritius in the Indian Ocean from 1767 to 1772, affords the best example of the group of concerns that we now call "environmentalism." Before taking up his post there, he had spent two years in China and much time traveling throughout the East Indies paying particularly close attention to Chinese, Indian, and Dutch agriculture, forestry, and water management. His reading, observation, and experimentation convinced him that deforestation led to erosion, altered rainfall patterns, and caused rivers and harbors to silt up. He used his authority on Mauritius to stop the widespread practice of burning or cutting down entire forests to clear land for plantations. "Reckless and ignorant men," he thundered in a public speech delivered soon after arriving on Mauritius, "thinking of nothing but themselves, have ravaged the island, destroying the trees by fire to make a fortune at the expense of the colony." His innovative conservation ordinance (1769) established reserves on high slopes and along streams that could not be logged or, if they had been logged, had to be replanted with trees at the planter's expense. The pioneering environmentalism of Poivre and his colleagues on Mauritius, with its concern about the damage human activity could do to nature, demonstrated that at least some Europeans had the ability to put humanity's long-term interest ahead of short-term profit.

Deforestation and the Disappearing Dodo of Mauritius This 1677 drawing, by one of Pierre Poivre's predecessors on Mauritius, shows how the logging of lowland ebony forests destroyed the habitats of dodoes, the gigantic, flightless birds indigenous to the island. By the time Poivre arrived on Mauritius, the dodo was extinct. *Drawing by Isaac Lamotius in the Algeneen Staatsarchief, The Hague.*

CONCLUSION: THE ENLIGHTENMENT PARADOX

Any attempt to assess the Enlightenment must recognize its paradoxical character. The philosophes proudly trumpeted equality and brotherhood among men and insisted that human reason, properly liberated and cultivated, could banish social ills and perfect individuals and society. They believed that if they could make the achievements of the Scientific Revolution and the consequences that flowed from it plainly evident to all, all would be well. Newton had discovered the universe's laws of motion, and his approach opened the door to continuing material progress through the conquest of nature. Locke, Newton's friend, had opened the other formerly closed door to continuing social progress through the correct nurturing of youth.

True, the leaders of the Renaissance and the Reformation had dreamed of "progress" of rather different kinds, but it had not happened. From the Enlightenment perspective, the Protestant and Catholic Reformations had made things worse, not better. The outcome of the Enlightenment, the philosophes believed, would be different. Few of them lived to see that, just around the corner, there lurked a future none of them foresaw and few of them would have welcomed. The French Revolution ushered in an age of fervent nationalism that brought not brotherhood and peace but warfare on an unprecedented scale. The Industrial Revolution created new wealth, but at the price of unprecedented urbanization, class consciousness, and environmental damage. Instead of amicable relations with "noble savages" and with long-established and admired civilizations in Asia came an era of colonialism.

Selected Reading

Sources

Crocker, Lester G., ed. *The Age of Enlightenment* (1969).

Foster, Robert, and Elborg Foster, eds. *European Society in the Eighteenth Century* (1969).

Gay, Peter, ed. *The Enlightenment* (1973).

Ménétra, Jacques-Louis. *Journal of My Life* (1986).

Redman, Ben Ray, ed. *The Portable Voltaire* (1977).

General Works

Black, Jeremy. *Eighteenth-Century Europe, 1700–1789* (1990). A lively and nicely detailed survey organized thematically.

Hufton, Olwen. *Europe: Privilege and Protest, 1730–1789* (1980). Especially informative and perceptive on the relations between social structure and political development.

Woloch, Isser. *Eighteenth-Century Europe: Tradition and Progress, 1715–1789* (1982). A broad-ranging account with some particularly interesting sections on social, religious, and cultural history.

Population, Economy, and the World outside Europe

Berg, Maxine. *The Age of Manufactures, 1700–1820* (1986). Explores the continuing importance of small-scale artisanal and domestic production in the textile and metal industries.

Blum, Jerome. *The End of the Old Order in Rural Europe* (1978). Thorough analysis of the condition of the peasantry and efforts at agrarian reform.

Deane, Phyllis. *The First Industrial Revolution*, 2nd ed. (1979). Lectures focusing on the changes that made Great Britain the world's first industrialized nation.

Flinn, Michael W. *The European Demographic System, 1500–1820* (1981). An excellent, clear summary of many specialized demographic studies.

Grove, Richard H. *Green Imperialism* (1995). Traces the early history of environmentalism in the context of European colonial expansion from 1600 to 1860.

Jones, E. L. *The European Miracle*, 2nd ed. (1987). Compares the economic histories of Europe with the Ottoman Empire, India, and China from 1400 to 1800.

Overton, Mark. *Agricultural Revolution in England* (1996). Contends that England's Agricultural Revolution occurred between 1750 and 1850 and was spearheaded by smaller farmers (both tenants and owner-occupiers) rather than owners of vast estates.

The Age of Reason

Darnton, Robert. *The Business of Enlightenment* (1979). The publishing history of Diderot's *Encyclopedia* carefully studied to reveal not only the minds of the entrepreneurs who made money from the century's best-seller but also the way the ideas of the philosophes made their way beyond the wealthy few to ordinary readers.

Gay, Peter. *The Enlightenment: An Interpretation* (1966, 1969). An admiring, comprehensive study of the philosophes.

Hampson, Norman. *The Enlightenment* (1968). The best brief introduction to the major themes of Enlightenment thought and the relationship of intellectual and social history in the eighteenth century.

Outram, Dorinda. *The Enlightenment* (1995). Explores the contradictions and tensions in the thought of the philosophes.

Porter, Roy, and Mikulas Teich, eds. *The Enlightenment in National Context* (1981). Essays stressing the varied forms the Enlightenment took in different countries.

Culture and Society in the Eighteenth Century

Darnton, Robert. *Forbidden Best-Sellers in Pre-Revolutionary France* (1995). Examines the huge volume of illegal literature, including libelles, broadsides, pornography, and much else and assesses its impact on politics and society.
———. *The Great Cat Massacre* (1984). Fascinating essays on eighteenth-century France combining anthropological and historical insights.

DeWald, Jonathan. *The European Nobility, 1400–1800* (1996). Argues that Europe's nobles adapted ingeniously and effectively to the massive changes that affected Europe during the early modern period.
Goodman, Dena. *The Republic of Letters* (1994). Demonstrates the central role played by the women who directed the Parisian salons in shaping the Enlightenment and its ideology.
Houston, R. A. *Literacy in Early Modern Europe* (1988). A lucid and brisk introduction surveying developments in education and print culture from 1500 to 1800.

CHAPTER 19

THE EIGHTEENTH-CENTURY STATE: GLOBAL EMPIRES AND THE BALANCE OF POWER

First-Rate Taking in Stores *Cecil Higgins Art Gallery, Bedford.*

We now use the phrase *first-rate* to mean something of the highest quality, but its initial use in 1666 described "twelve new ships, all of the first-rate" in the navy of England's King Charles II. "Rate," in this sense, referred to the number of heavy cannons. In 1793, the British navy had 5 "first-rates" (one hundred or more guns), 19 "second-rates" (ninety to ninety-eight guns), 114 "third-rates" (sixty-four to eighty guns), and so on down through "sixth-rates" (twenty to thirty-two guns). When both rated and unrated ships are counted, George III's navy on the eve of the revolutionary wars with France totaled nearly four hundred ships, and when the wars ended they added up to more than nine hundred.

In 1818, J. M. W. Turner painted *First-Rate Taking in Stores* (on previous page). The ship in this painting had a complement of more than a thousand officers and men. Even when engaged in the peaceful task of taking on food, water, and other supplies, its guns, deployed on three decks, proclaim an unmistakable threat. Turner's angle of vision from near the waterline conveys the stunning size and power of these floating fortresses. Ships of this kind defended trade and communication with overseas colonies and were used to acquire new colonies through war or the threat of war. Even more than armies, navies composed of such ships represented the ability of the eighteenth-century state to project power through technology, and they made possible European participation in global markets on favorable terms. During the eighteenth century, the states that built and maintained these potent military machines used them against each other, and they used them to establish colonial empires. However, no single state possessed enough troops and ships to defeat all the others. Their rivalries produced not one dominant power but a series of shifting alliances aimed at achieving a balance of power.

Although many rulers sympathized with the Enlightenment's campaign for peace, reform, and humanitarianism, they parted company with the philosophes when *raison d'état* ("reason of state") seemed to require the risk of war. Frederick the Great of Prussia enticed Voltaire to his court, and Catherine the Great of Russia corresponded at length with Diderot—but neither monarch is remembered as a peacemaker. In his *Philosophical Dictionary* (1764), Voltaire viciously satirizes an unnamed monarch who, in order to take over a province to which he has some dubious dynastic claim, dresses up "a large number of enthusiastic desperadoes" in blue uniforms and hats with white trim and "makes them turn right and left and marches them off to glory" in his quest to rule people who neither know him nor want his intervention. Why, Voltaire asked, should "a half-a-pound of lead fired from six hundred feet away" subject young men to agonizing deaths within sight of the towns where they were born, towns undergoing destruction "by sword and fire" at the hands of this aggressive monarch's troops? In 1773, Frederick responded to Voltaire in a letter: "Personally, I renounce war, lest I be excommunicated by the philosophes." How, Frederick asked, could he dress his men in "blue cloth and hats with white fringes" and make them "turn right and left . . . [and] march them off to glory without deserving the honorable title of bandit chief?" Clearly, Frederick understood that he and princes like himself were the targets of Voltaire's criticism, but Frederick had his escape route carefully planned. "There are, however, some just wars," he dryly added; "those necessitated by self-defense are undoubtedly of this kind." Unfortunately, the world has never lacked aggressors who claimed—and indeed often believed themselves to be—acting in self-defense. This is why the effort to maintain a balance of power proved so difficult and so tenuous.

Early in the sixteenth century, Christian **humanists** such as Erasmus had espoused pacifism and hoped that a world without war was near at hand. Similarly, the philosophes of the Enlightenment hoped that banishing religious dogmatism and superstition and establishing a society driven by rational pursuit of "life, liberty, and the pursuit of happiness" would signal the end of the destructive and wasteful warmongering that had so long plagued humankind. Yet European states in the eighteenth century waged not only the kind of dynastic and territorial warfare that had long been endemic, but also a newer kind of struggle for overseas trade and dominion. Geography dictated that Prussia, Austria, and Russia would be preoccupied with land warfare in and near Europe. The Atlantic states of France and Britain, however, while involved with those conflicts, also fought for land and commerce in North America and India. During these campaigns, a sharp distinction developed between the states that could put sufficiently large and professional armies into the field and navies onto the high seas, and those that would not or could not. Britain, France, Prussia, Austria, and Russia emerged as "first-rate" in the political sense, and former notable powers, such as Sweden, Portugal, Spain, the Dutch Republic, and the Polish-Lithuanian Commonwealth, found themselves pushed into "second-rate" status. Indeed, in the political sense, Poland-Lithuania disappeared from the map, partitioned by Prussia, Austria, and Russia.

EUROPE AND THE WORLD IN THE EIGHTEENTH CENTURY

Most eighteenth-century Europeans thought of their homelands as situated in relation to the "East Indies" and the "West Indies." Oceanic access to the former had been discovered by Vasco da Gama and to the latter by Christopher Columbus at the end of the fifteenth century. Those Europeans who could afford luxuries had long enjoyed silks and spices from the East Indies, and all knew of the silver and gold that had begun to flow from Mexican, Peruvian, and Brazilian mines in the New World during the sixteenth century. Not until the late seventeenth and eighteenth centuries, however, did commodities from the Indies reach European people in quantities sufficiently large and at prices sufficiently low as to affect their habits of consumption significantly.

Mercantilism and the Global Economy

The original steps toward the creation of a system of global trade had been taken in the fifteenth and sixteenth centuries by Portugal and Spain. In the seventeenth century, however, the Dutch, the French, and the English took over and expanded much of what their Iberian predecessors had constructed. When Philip II was crowned king of Portugal in 1580, the far-flung Portuguese Empire was suddenly fair game for Spain's enemies. The governments of England (in 1600) and the Dutch Republic (in 1602) issued charters to joint-stock companies that granted them monopolies over commerce with the East Indies. France, Sweden, Denmark, and other states also attempted to establish monopolistic overseas trading companies in good mercantilist fashion.

Lord Macartney's Mission to China   In 1793, Lord Macartney led a delegation to Beijing to lift narrow restrictions on the British East India Company. According to James Gillray's satirical cartoon, the Chinese emperor and his courtiers were unimpressed by Macartney's presents (a jackdaw in a cage, a mousetrap, and a copy of the works of Shakespeare—in English, of course). His refusal to perform the customary *kowtow* (a full prostration before the emperor) also gave offense. Although Macartney's effort failed, the volume of British global trade was already enormous, and before long even the fabled and long admired Chinese empire would bow to British military and commercial power. *British Museum.*

The Dutch East India Company ousted the English from the Southeast Asian trade (executing ten English merchants at Amboina in 1623), just as they had earlier pushed aside the Portuguese with a combination of more and better ships, more efficient management, and more alert diplomacy. Local Muslim rulers initially welcomed them as counterweights to the Portuguese, but the Dutch soon seized control of what became known as the Dutch East Indies (since 1949, the Republic of Indonesia). By sailing directly east from the Cape of Good Hope, instead of going to India on the way out and back as the Portuguese had done, the Dutch revised the patterns of Indian Ocean trade and achieved a virtual spice monopoly. In 1652 they established their only African colony (now the Republic of South Africa) at the Cape of Good Hope, where the company's ships could stop for supplies before the long trip to the Indies. A Dutchman, Abel Tasman, discovered New Zealand and Tasmania in 1642; and Dutch ships also became the first to reach the Australian coasts.

Although the Spice Islands (the Moluccas) in the East Indies remained the most profitable component of the Dutch Empire, its vessels also kept busy in the Atlantic. They wrested the West African slave trade from the Portuguese and held it for a generation. They chartered the Dutch West India Company in 1621 to exploit the Caribbean, and in 1628 one of its admirals, Piet Hein, pulled off the most lucrative naval escapade of the century by capturing the Spanish silver fleet on its annual journey from Mexico and Peru to Seville—a heavy blow to Spanish credit and prestige. The company also gained access to the fur trade of the Hudson River Valley in North America by establishing a settlement at New Amsterdam, a colony the English seized in 1664 and renamed New York.

Although English and French explorers continued to search unsuccessfully for a northwest passage around Canada and a northeast passage around Russia, the future lay farther south. From the late sixteenth century on, Dutch, English, and French adventurers busily made quasi-piratical incursions into the Spanish colonies. Preoccupied with the Dutch intervention in the Caribbean, Spain failed to prevent the English and French from establishing colonies in North America. By claiming virtually all the Americas except eastern Brazil, the Spaniards had bitten off more than they could chew (see Chapter 14). Northern Europeans managed to smuggle and trade in the region in spite of Spanish prohibitions. These scraps under the Spanish table nourished the northerners, who in time grew strong enough to establish themselves openly.

MAP 19-1

A GLOBAL VIEW OF EIGHTEENTH-CENTURY TRADE

When the eighteenth century began, Spanish, Portuguese, French, Dutch, and British traders all had substantial pieces of the action, although the Iberian states' share was declining while that of the northern Europeans grew. By 1800, the British were dominant, but all the others still had roles to play. This map shows the European colonial holdings at the end of the Seven Years' War (1763). Red lines show the routes of exports to and from Europe, and the direction and volume of the slave trade is indicated in the white lines.

By 1682 René-Robert de La Salle had traveled from French Canada across the Great Lakes and down the Mississippi to the Gulf of Mexico, thereby demonstrating the possibility of a vast empire of French settlements in the valley of North America's greatest river. The French government subsidized these efforts to build "New France," in contrast to the complicated and largely private financing of the various English settlements from "New England" down to Georgia on the Atlantic seaboard. Whereas the French tried—rather unsuccessfully—to attract the "better sort" to settle in America, the English settlers included many religious dissidents, criminals, and poor people. Lacking the native labor supply the Spaniards found, the English imported their own countrymen using the indenture system, a device adapted from medieval guilds whereby people came and worked, usually for four years, to pay for their passage, after which they were free. By 1700 more than a quarter-million people lived in the English colonies on the mainland, nearly twenty times the total for "New France" (see Map 19-1).

By late in the seventeenth century, commodities from around the world transformed Europeans' consumption patterns. Tobacco and chocolate from the New World, coffee from Arabia, and tea from China, all formerly unknown in Europe, achieved enormous popularity during the eighteenth century. European tea consumption did not take off until the 1720s, but in 1766, some 7,500 tons of tea left China for Europe—3,000 on English ships and 2,250 on Dutch ships. In 1787, France alone imported 38,000 tons of coffee, which workers as well as aristocrats drank as avidly as their counterparts in England drank tea. In 1725, the inventories of Parisians of modest means indicate that nearly 20 percent owned tea and coffee accessories; by 1745, more than 45 percent had them. Tobacco proved even more successful than coffee and tea. Cotton, initially imported from Egypt and India, came into widespread use. Sugar, formerly an expensive luxury used mainly as a medicine, boomed. After 1680, production on Caribbean islands such as Santo Domingo, Martinique, and Guadeloupe shot up, and in England, for example, consumption increased by a factor of fifteen during the eighteenth century. The South Sea Bubble in England and the Mississippi Bubble in France, both speculative crazes of the year 1720, swelled with investors' giddy expectations of the riches to be gained from trade with faraway places. The South Sea Bubble, for example, inflated on unrealistic hopes about the profitability of the trade in slaves that Britain had acquired in the Peace of Utrecht (1713), which had ended the War of the Spanish Succession. Even though these bubbles burst, leaving countless speculators bankrupt, the potential for wealth from overseas trade was still quite real, and it made many eighteenth-century investors rich.

Until the late seventeenth century, Europeans used gold and silver from their own mines and those in the **New**

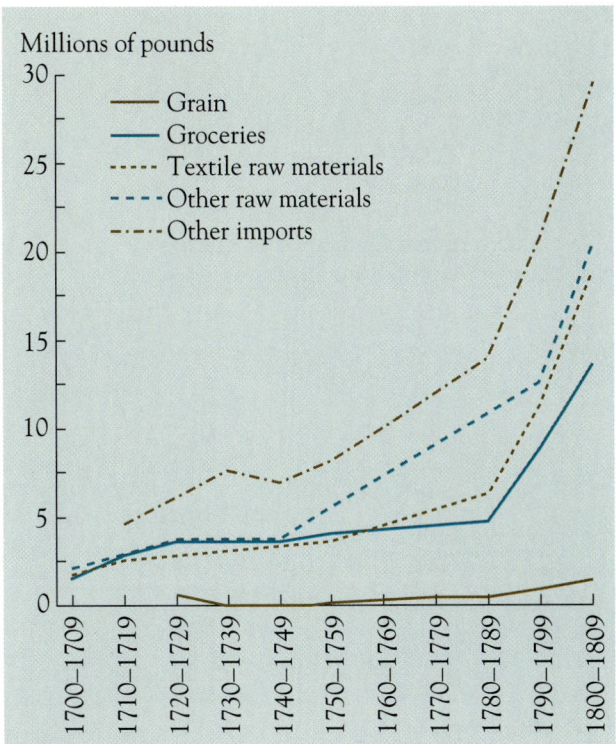

FIGURE 19-1
BRITISH IMPORTS, 1700–1800

Imports into Britain grew dramatically, as did exports (see Figure 19-2) during the eighteenth century and the first third of the nineteenth century. From slightly less than £5 million sterling in the decade after 1700, the total value was approaching £40 million a century later. Growth occurred in all categories. Some of the "groceries" (which included sugar, tea, chocolate, and coffee) and "raw materials" (such as raw cotton) were consumed in Britain, and some underwent processing and were re-exported. *Source: Adapted from Peter Mathias, The First Industrial Nation: An Economic History of Britain, 1700–1914, 2nd ed. (New York: Routledge, 1983), figure 11, p. 283, which is based on B. R. Mitchell, Abstract of British Historical Statistics (Cambridge, England: Cambridge University Press, 1962), pp. 279–281, 285–290.*

World to buy silks, pepper, calicoes, spices, coffee, and tea from Asia. The world *outside* Europe supplied things for Europeans to consume. By 1800, however, all this changed. The world had become a market for products manufactured in Europe or processed and re-exported by European merchants (for example, see Figures 19-1 and 19-2). India, for example, long a source of cotton cloth (the highest grade called "calico," the name taken from the Indian city of Calicut), saw its textile industry undercut by mechanized British production. Calico and other cotton fabrics from the mills of Manchester and Birmingham came to clothe people in India and the rest of the world. In Holland (blue and white "delftware") and Germany (Meissen "china"), industries thrived by imitating Chinese and Japanese

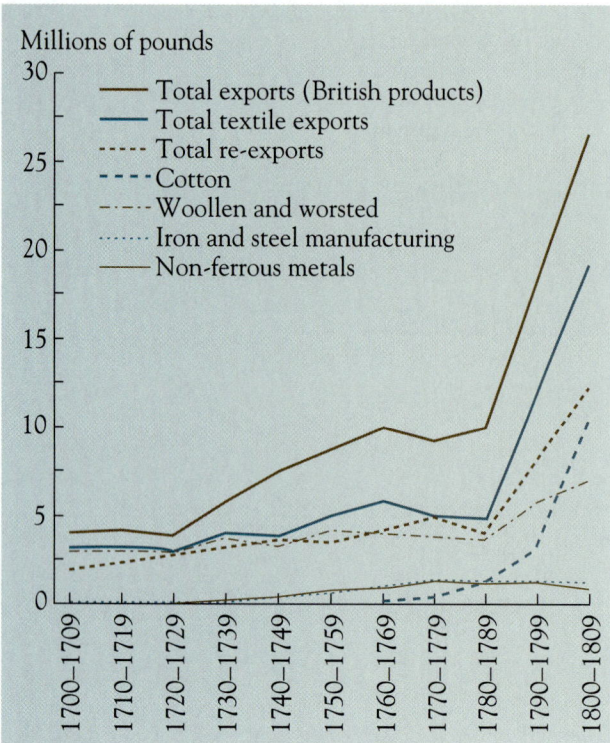

FIGURE 19-2
BRITISH EXPORTS, 1700–1800

Like imports, exports from Britain boomed, and the totals indicated here do not include "invisible exports," meaning the money Britons made from shipping, insurance, and financial services in their global trade network.
Source: Adapted from Peter Mathias, The First Industrial Nation: An Economic History of Britain, 1700–1914, *2nd ed. (New York: Routledge, 1983), figure 10, p. 281.*

porcelain. Because East Asian artisans closely guarded the secrets of making these wares, Europeans did not figure out how to match their quality until the mid-eighteenth century. The flourishing population of settlers in the Americas also formed important markets for European traders who were exporting such goods.

Although trade within Europe expanded and remained extremely important, the overseas portion of total commerce grew faster. In France, for example, overall foreign trade increased more than fourfold between 1716 and 1789, while colonial trade grew more than tenfold. Britain sold 80 percent of its exports to European buyers and bought an even higher portion of its imports from continental Europe in the first half of the eighteenth century. However, nearly all of the *growth* in British exports during the same interval went to Asia and America. Without the markets outside Europe, in other words, Britain's exports would have gained only slightly. Benjamin Franklin nicely summarized the assumption that he shared with most of his contemporaries: "No nation is ever ruined by trade."

The African Slave Trade

The brutal trade in African slaves taken to labor in the Americas had been initiated by the Portuguese in the fifteenth century (see Chapter 14), but in the seventeenth century English, French, and Dutch ships became heavily involved as well. Most of the slaves came from the west coast of Africa. Because the area had few good harbors, African states had tended to develop deep within the continent, often on rivers navigable only by canoe. Many kingdoms rose and fell in the interior both before and after the Europeans established their fortified coastal bases, and the inner regions remained unexplored by Europeans until the nineteenth century. Except for the colonists in Angola and the Dutch Cape Colony, Europeans did not settle in Africa. Inevitably, the slave trade destabilized and demoralized the African kingdoms as their leaders found it necessary to trade their captured enemies for European guns and other goods. Nevertheless, such West African states as Benin and Dahomey and the rich Asante Empire thrived in the eighteenth century by building strong political and cultural institutions.

Most of the more than 6 million slaves shipped in the 1700s went to Brazil, the Caribbean islands, and, later in the period, English-speaking North America. They endured a painful and dangerous passage—tightly packed below deck, chained and unable to stand, and with little or no opportunity for exercise. The trip required one to two months, and if the winds permitted a rapid voyage, 95 percent might survive the ordeal. But many voyages took longer, and as supplies ran low, 30 to 40 percent of the prisoners might perish. Sold to plantation owners, they were worked hard to grow, harvest, and process sugarcane and tobacco. Cotton did not become a major North American crop until the 1790s, thanks mainly to Eli Whitney's invention of the cotton gin in 1793. Rather, in the first part of the eighteenth century sugar was the most important commodity as European consumption of the product skyrocketed—from 13,400 tons in 1730 to 23,300 tons only twenty-six years later. As a result, West Indian planters made great fortunes and used part of their wealth to wield political influence back in Europe.

Between 1741 and 1810, when the slave trade reached its peak, English slavers carried as many slaves as their French and Portuguese rivals combined (see Figure 19-3). This fact may help to explain why the growing crusade to abolish the slave trade was most effective in England. The first vigorous opponents of the institution of slavery were the Quakers, who, beginning in the 1770s, ejected from their **sect** anyone who owned slaves. The English

Diagram of a Slaving Ship   This diagram was one of a number of exhibits prepared by opponents of the slave trade during debates held in the British Parliament in 1806 and 1807. They were not conjectural, for they were based on actual measurements of ships used in the slave trade. Advocates of abolition thoroughly researched the economic and other arguments of their opponents and criticized them systematically.   *North Wind Picture Archives.*

abolitionists, led by William Wilberforce (1759–1833), shrewdly recognized that the inhumanity of the trade was more vulnerable to criticism than the institution itself. On May 12, 1789, Wilberforce's speech opening the debate on abolition in the House of Commons vividly described conditions on a slaving ship: "So much misery condensed in so little room is more than the human imagination had ever before conceived." The abolitionists' long campaign passed a milestone in 1807 when Parliament abolished the slave

trade in the British Empire. If not for the "sugar lobby" backed by West Indian planters, the bill would have passed much sooner. After 1815 British naval vessels stopped slavers whenever they could find them. On July 31, 1833, a month after Wilberforce's death, Parliament finally passed a bill abolishing slavery itself. Emancipation elsewhere came slowly: in the French and Danish colonies, 1848; the Dutch colonies, 1863; the United States, 1863–1865; Cuba, 1886; and Brazil, 1888.

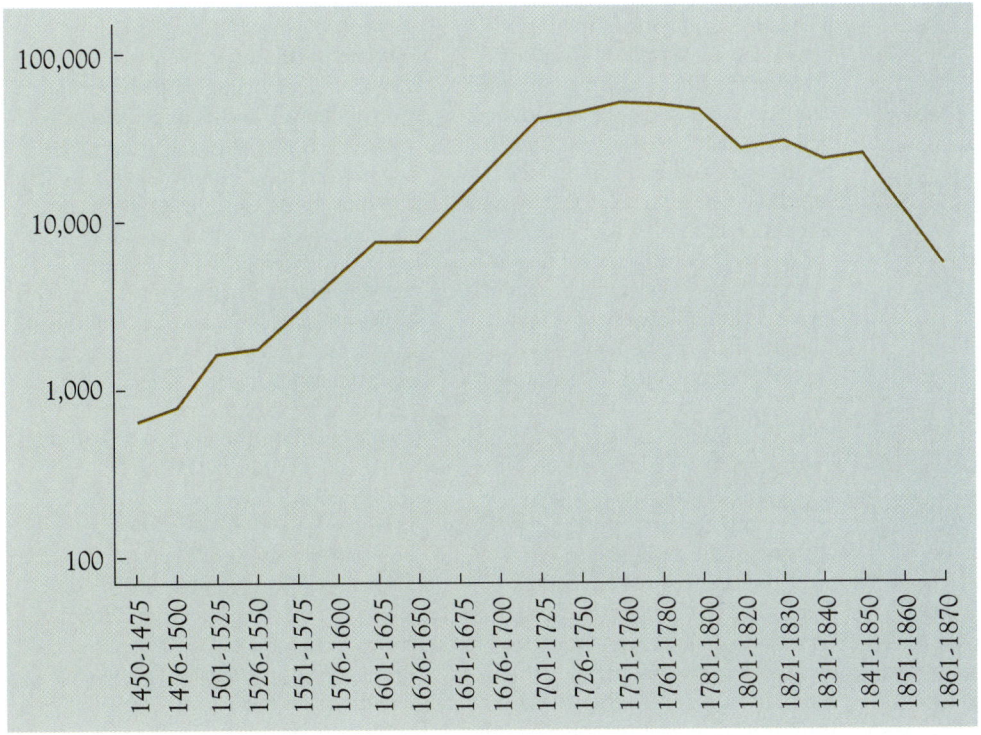

FIGURE 19-3
THE ATLANTIC SLAVE TRADE
The vertical axis shows the number of slaves shipped across the Atlantic in twenty-five-year segments of time. The scale is logarithmic rather than arithmetic.
Source: Adapted from Philip D. Curtin, The Atlantic Slave Trade: A Census *(Madison: University of Wisconsin Press, 1969), p. 266.*

THE HUMAN EXPERIENCE

Olaudah Equiano, Slave and Abolitionist

Born in 1745 in what is now northern Nigeria, Olaudah Equiano (or Ekwuno, a common Ibo name) grew up enjoying his place as the youngest son in an aristocratic family that possessed "many slaves," as he later wrote. When he was eleven, however, he and his sister were kidnapped from their home, taken on a long journey to the coast, separated from each other, and sold into slavery. Equiano's first view of white men came as he boarded the ship, and he was terrified that "those white men

with horrible looks, red faces, and loose hair" intended to kill and eat him. Frightened by the ocean and horrified by "the loathsomeness of the stench" inside the ship, he refused to eat and was punished by being tied to the windlass and flogged. Yet his spirits improved after he found some other victims on board who spoke his language and told him he would not be eaten but put to work in another country.

Equiano was taken first to Barbados and then Virginia, where a British naval officer bought him and gave him a new name, Gustavus Vassa. He served his master during the Seven Years' War in Canadian waters and elsewhere. Some families in England enabled him to get some schooling during stays there between voyages. After the war, Robert King, a Quaker merchant of Philadelphia who owned ships trading in the Caribbean, purchased him. Admiring the varied skills that Equiano had picked up (including barbering, arithmetic, and navigation), King made him an aide to Thomas Farmer, the captain of one of his ships. Farmer helped Equiano to do some trading on his own, and by 1766 he had saved the £40 he needed to buy himself out of slavery: "I who had been a slave in the morning, trembling at the will of another, now became my own master and completely free. I thought this was the happiest day I had ever experienced." For the next twenty-two years he alternated between working in London and on voyages to the Mediterranean, New England, Central America, and Greenland. He survived a shipwreck and dangerous encounters with white men who enjoyed terrorizing black men, whether slave or free. The Greenland episode was an attempt to discover a northwestern route to India through the Arctic, and a young officer named Horatio Nelson

(later Britain's greatest naval hero for his defeats of Napoleon's navy) was also on board. In 1787, the British government appointed Equiano to the post of Commissary of Provisions and Stores for the Black Poor to Sierra Leone, an effort to repatriate former slaves back to Africa.

The reason we know about Equiano's extraordinary life is that in 1789 he published his autobiography in London, the first by an African to appear in English. Equiano had been in contact with leaders of the anti-slavery movement since the mid-1780s and wrote the book to help this cause. His firsthand account of the sufferings of slaves on the Atlantic crossing, one of the few in existence by an African, gave potent ammunition to the abolitionists in their battle for public and parliamentary support. Titled *The Interesting Narrative of Olaudah Equiano, or Gustavus Vassa, the African, Written by Himself*, the vividly written memoir went through an astonishing nine editions within only five years. Dutch, Russian, and German translations followed, and Equiano shrewdly retained the copyright. During speaking tours around Britain on behalf of the movement to abolish slavery, he also sold copies of his book, and when he died in 1797 his estate was valued at close to a thousand pounds. Through his talents and accomplishments as a craftsman, a businessman, a writer, and a speaker, Equiano gave telling proof that proslavery arguments based on the alleged inferiority of Africans were utterly false. Near the end of his book, he expressed a hope "to have the satisfaction of seeing the renovation of liberty and justice resting on the British government, to vindicate the honor of our common nature" by abolishing slavery. Although he did not live to see it happen, his contribution was significant. ❖

This portrait appeared opposite the title page of Olaudah Equiano's best-selling autobiography. It portrayed him dressed as an English gentleman; doubtless this was his own choice as he had converted to devout Calvinistic Christianity. "My heart was still fixed on London," he wrote at one point, and in this image he holds his Bible open to Acts 4:12, which reads "Neither is there salvation in any name other [than Jesus Christ]." *The Granger Collection, New York.*

MAP 19-2

IMPERIAL RIVALRIES IN NORTH AMERICA AND THE CARIBBEAN BEFORE 1763

Although the prodigious ability of the islands of the Caribbean to produce sugar made them the most attractive to Europeans eager for quick profits, the rivalry between the British, French, and Spanish for North America proved more critical in the long run. Before the British conquest of Canada was completed by 1763, the holdings of the major powers seemed reasonably balanced.

The Last Century of Colonialism in the Americas

The economies of Spanish colonies in Central and South America and the Portuguese colony of Brazil continued to prosper during the eighteenth century (see Map 19-2). All of Spain's vast territories contained more than 14 million people by 1800, only 2 million of them Spaniards. In the decade after 1815, Spanish and Portuguese settlers would gain independence from their mother countries, whose governments, armies, and navies were becoming less able to restrain interloping British and French traders. Except among slaves on the sugar-producing islands in the Caribbean, however, neither the Spanish nor French colonies experienced anything like the amazing population explosion of the British colonies on the east coast of North America.

Large-scale immigration, a high birthrate, the relative abundance of land, and the relatively high price of labor helped push the population of the thirteen British colonies to a whopping 2.6 million in 1776, a tenfold increase from 1700. Four million people lived in the new nation when its first census was taken in 1790, of whom 750,000 were black.[1] Among the immigrants, the English were most numerous, but Germans, Swiss, Huguenots, Swedes, and Scotch-Irish (Scots who had previously settled in northern Ireland) populated the colonies as well. Along the Atlantic coast, a string of towns from Boston to Savannah prospered as centers of government and trade.

Also unlike the other European newcomers to the Americas, the English had placed a high value on private initiative and self-government. The first colonial assembly had met in Virginia in 1619, as the English there set out to replicate the political and social institutions that they had

---

[1] Mandated by the U.S. Constitution of 1787, this was the first nationwide census conducted in the Western world.

Charleston Harbor   The availability of fine natural harbors such as Charleston, Philadelphia, New York, and Boston in British North America facilitated trade and communication, making it easier for colonial promoters to recruit settlers and investors.   *North Wind Picture Archives.*

known in England. Although property qualifications limited the right to vote in all the colonies, men who met the qualifications were much more numerous than in England. In Massachusetts, for example, almost all adult males could vote, whereas in England in 1760 only about one-fourth were eligible. Like Parliament, the colonial assemblies controlled taxation and thus wielded considerable bargaining power with the governor, who was usually a royal appointee. The colonists sometimes quarreled with the commercial regulations imposed by Britain (such as the Navigation Acts that required them to move their goods in British or colonial ships and to send certain goods directly to Britain) and evaded them when they could—which was often. Smuggling was a major occupation. But until the 1760s, the colonists remained loyal to Britain and proud of their English heritage. They shared in the sense that, as British people, they enjoyed certain rights that their forebears had defended against a Stuart monarchy bent on establishing a French-style absolutism (see Chapter 16).

THE EIGHTEENTH-CENTURY STATE

During the seventeenth century, the balance of political power within many European states had swung away from assemblies and aristocracies toward monarchs inclined to absolutism. The remaining institutions of high-medieval constitutionalism, such as representative assemblies, were emasculated by men like Louis XIV. Where the older system survived, it generally displayed severe political weakness, as in Poland and the Holy Roman Empire; England and the Dutch Republic were exceptions. But during the early eighteenth century, nobles struggled, often successfully, to regain their position in the national political arena. In all the major states except Prussia, conditions favored aristocratic assertiveness rather than absolutist

ambitions. For example, in France after 1715, the nobility managed to claw back some of the ground that Louis XIV had taken from them because the Sun King's heir was his five-year-old great-grandson, Louis XV. Similarly, in Russia, a confused succession after Peter the Great's death in 1725 weakened the tsar's power until the middle of the eighteenth century.

Between the end of the War of the Spanish Succession in 1714 (see Chapter 16) and 1740, western Europe enjoyed a period of relative peace; leading statesmen concerned themselves more with domestic than international problems. A pair of major wars between 1740 and 1763 (the War of the Austrian Succession and the Seven Years' War) created a new political situation in which monarchs—the so-called "enlightened absolutists" or "enlightened despots"—again pushed for administrative centralization at the expense of aristocratic privileges. The most dangerous international rivalries arose between states that had centralized enough to field modern military forces. The Atlantic nations, France and England, fought mainly for overseas colonies and markets, but they also became entangled in the Austro-Prussian struggle over central European territory. These hostilities, although in some ways less destructive and less bitter than the religious conflicts had been or the nationalistic wars after 1789 would be, nevertheless had important consequences for the political, social, and international order.

Armies and Navies

Major changes in the weaponry and tactics of European armies and navies had occurred in the late seventeenth century (see Chapter 16). The introduction of flintlock muskets with packaged cartridges and bayonets increased infantry firepower and further diminished the role of cavalry. Warships built solely for naval use and crafted to carry heavy artillery replaced merchant ships temporarily armed for war. Line-ahead tactics, introduced to maximize firepower, made European navies the most powerful in the world. Indeed, no non-European navy would defeat a European one until the Japanese victory over the Russians in the war of 1904–1905.

Ships-of-the-line continued to grow in size and power, and during the eighteenth century the French succeeded at applying scientific methods to building warships and made their fleet the most technically advanced in Europe. Although less accomplished as naval architects, the British made two important innovations in the late 1770s. They covered the hulls of all their ships-of-the-line with copper to prevent damage by the "shipworm," an elongated marine clam (an aquatic termite of sorts that ruined oak beams with amazing speed). With copper bottoms, British ships could remain on blockade stations or out at sea for longer periods, so fewer ships had to be built. The British also introduced a shorter, lighter type of cannon, called a carronade after the Carron Iron Works that produced it in Scotland, to supplement the traditional long cannon. The carronade's range was shorter than the long cannon, but required only two men to fire it (the other needed eleven or twelve men). Moreover, they could reload and fire it twice as fast. Its effectiveness at short range led Napoleon himself to write in 1805 that the carronades "have done us great harm" and to urge his naval men "to perfect their system" for making and using the new British weapon.

In addition to the foregoing developments, there was some experimentation with completely new weapons. The French used hot-air balloons in the early 1790s to view enemy positions and convey messages, and an American inventor, David Bushnell (1740–1824), built the first functioning submarine in 1775. The *Turtle*, as Bushnell named his 7-foot-long wooden device, tried unsuccessfully to blow up British ships in New York harbor in 1776. These pioneering efforts to go both above and below the enemy would pay off in the twentieth century, but had little impact during the eighteenth. Instead, most military men concentrated on increasing the effectiveness of existing weapons. In 1747, for example, the Prussians began to utilize a novel type of screw-elevation that perfected their aim with artillery, and the Austrians adopted the same mechanism soon afterwards. Yet weapons continued to be made by hand. The mass manufacturing of muskets with interchangeable parts would have to wait until 1798, when Eli Whitney (already the father of the cotton gin) invented machines to make gun parts that could then be rapidly assembled by a worker. Soon clocks, sewing machines, and other products were being made the same way—and thus, as often happens, military technology was adapted to civilian purposes. The Internet, a product of the Cold War, stands in a long tradition.

The increasing size and professionalization of military establishments earlier initiated by Louis XIV continued during the eighteenth century—most dramatically in Prussia. The cost of standing armies whose soldiers were trained by continuous drilling to be ready to deliver maximum firepower on a battlefield obscured by smoke and confusion was enormous; such a cost could be borne only by highly organized bureaucratic states with extensive taxing powers. By 1740, the Prussian military was one of the three or four strongest in Europe, although Prussia stood thirteenth in population. In 1763, some 4 percent of Prussia's population served in the army, whereas at its peak the French army comprised 1.5 percent of France's people. Except sometimes in the artillery, men from the landed nobility and gentry still dominated the officer corps everywhere, but states tightened their control over training, supply, recruitment, and military administration generally. In Austria, the shock of defeat by Prussia in 1740 led to a policy of shrinking the military role of the higher aristocracy, expanding that of the lesser nobility, and upgrading the attractiveness and rewards of service as an army officer. A 1757 decree allowed commoners who had been officers for thirty years to be ennobled automatically as part of a conscious program of linking nobility to service, not birth. The Prussian victory over a larger French army at the battle of Rossbach (1757) triggered a drive for military reform in France. The French moved to reduce the sale of military offices in infantry regiments in 1763, and in 1776 a plan to eliminate the sale of military offices entirely was put in place. The nobleman who led the effort identified the problem succinctly: "Money confers neither talent nor merit; and the military calling demands a great deal of both." Russians adapted so successfully to Prussian innovations in the use of infantry and artillery that their victories in 1760 and 1761 threatened Prussia's very existence.

Some soldiers and sailors responded voluntarily to recruitment efforts, but many were conscripted. Exiles were welcomed as well, such as Irish Catholics in the French army or French Protestants (Huguenots) in the armies of Europe's Protestant states. Press-gangs forcibly conscripted seamen for Britain's navy, and compulsory military service in one form or another was widespread. In Prussia beginning in 1727, each regiment was given an area surrounding its garrison town that would supply its draftees. Some smaller German states came to specialize in supplying soldiers that were available for hire; Hesse-Cassel, for example, had nearly 10 percent of its population in arms in 1730, and the "Hessians" spent much of their time fighting for Britain. When George Washington led his men across the frigid Delaware River on Christmas night 1776, they defeated Hessian mercenaries serving in the British army. On land and sea, the penalties for insubordination or desertion were harsh and included flogging or facing the invariably lethal firing squad. A flogging might include the use of the knout (a Russian whip with a metal flail at the end) that would cause the death of most men who suffered it. In 1711, a Prussian decree sentenced deserters to the

The Well-Drilled Eighteenth-Century Army A new and distinctive feature of European armies beginning late in the seventeenth century was the prevalence of drilling. They practiced marching in step and changing directions in response to shouted commands by officers until the movements were virtually automatic. Whole regiments could take up and change positions smoothly under the stress of combat. The more "automatic" units were, the better they could deliver the continuous volleys of musket fire that won battles. *The Granger Collection, New York.*

amputation of their noses and ears and a life sentence at hard labor. Life in the armed services was dangerous; during the Seven Years' War, fourteen out of fifteen Prussian soldiers died. Yet many officers fully understood that success in battle depended on readiness, morale, and discipline under fire, and their paternalistic efforts to see that their men were properly fed, paid, equipped, and trained was central to their own professionalism. Beginning in 1765, France paid pensions to ex-soldiers, and in 1786, the number of French naval hospitals and doctors and surgeons was increased. Savage discipline, rampant disease, and violent death formed one side of the eighteenth-century story, but the other side was an enhanced humanitarian concern for soldiers and sailors.

Fading Absolutism

A seesaw struggle between absolutists and constitutionalists dominated seventeenth-century politics (see Chapters 15 and 16), and eighteenth-century rulers proved no less keen than their predecessors at maintaining and, if possible, increasing their ability to erode or abolish privileges such as tax exemptions that nobles and other groups vigorously tried to retain. But in some cases the eighteenth-century defenders of these privileges regained ground they had lost. The French monarchy remained the model of absolutism, but—despite the undeniable successes of his centralizing policies—Louis XIV had not so much defeated the nobles, *parlementaires*, churchmen, judges, and town governments as he had temporarily neutralized them. The traditions and institutions they represented did not disappear; they merely hibernated and then seized the opportunity that presented itself during the long reign (1715–1774) of Louis XV. Just like his great-grandfather Louis XIV, he came to the throne at the age of five. This meant a regency—always a dangerous time for royal authority.

The regency was first in the hands of Louis XV's uncle Philippe, Duke of Orléans (until his death while in his mistress's embrace in 1723), and then under another uncle until Louis took over in 1726. The hard-drinking, lascivious Philippe nevertheless possessed a fine intellect and considerable political shrewdness. As a concession to the old aristocracy that Louis XIV had excluded from power, he appointed councils headed by leading nobles who advised the regency council. In order to gain approval of his regental powers, he restored powers to remonstrate against royal edicts to the parlements, powers that Louis XIV had suspended. Philippe demonstrated his understanding of the need for financial reform in 1716 by his support for John Law's plan for a central bank that could issue paper money, but the wave of speculation that surrounded the bank and Law's Mississippi Company (see Chapter 18) doomed the attempt in France to establish the kind of financial system that already existed in Britain and the Dutch Republic. The British and Dutch governments could usually borrow money at interest rates that were half of what the French government had to pay—a premium that sharply narrowed France's freedom to maneuver despite its position as the richest and most populous state in Europe.

When the regency ended, Louis XV put his trust in his old tutor, Cardinal Fleury (1652–1743), commencing the last of the French regimes led by statesmen-churchmen such as Richelieu and Mazarin. Fleury, a devout and conservative man, took an authoritarian line against the Jansenists and the secularist ideas emanating from the philosophes. But he tried to avoid war, and he minimized expenditure when war could not be avoided, a policy the philosophes ought to have admired despite his censorship of them. The French economy gained strength throughout

THE HISTORICAL EVIDENCE

A Bureaucrat's View of Louis XV

1747

Louis XV frequently fired ministers and appointed others. The Marquis d'Argenson's memoirs reveal how he felt about being replaced in 1747 by the Comte de Maurepas and what he thought of Louis XV. D'Argenson, a schoolmate and lifelong friend of Voltaire, served as minister of foreign affairs from 1744 to 1747. Sour grapes certainly motivated some of his venom, but his story about how the king's dream was bruited about "in public" is more ominous, however unlikely it is that Louis actually had such a dream.

Monsieur de Maurepas increases in favor with the king, while I have been dismissed from my ministry because, showing with sincerity the necessity of peace (however made), I brought forward the means of doing so, while others retrograded. I formed for the king a strong party in Germany, both for the present moment and for that succeeding the peace; I smoothed his enemies; I preserved and inspired his friends; above all, I showed by my conduct that confidence could be placed in our sincerity.

M. de Maurepas is inexcusable in allowing our navy to run down; the parsimony of the late cardinal [Fleury] is no valid excuse; a zealous and intelligent man manages to do the little he has to do the best he can. Has he yet ever made a journey to the ports? He prefers an idle, intriguing life in Paris to all that urgent duty suggests for so essential a minister.

They tell an amusing tale in public of how the king dreamed the other night about cats; he saw four of them fighting: one thin, one fat, one blind of an eye, one blind in both eyes. A faithful valet explained to him his dream thus: "The thin cat is your people; the fat cat is the financiers [investors in tax collection syndicates]; the one-eyed cat is your council; and the blind cat is your Majesty, who does not choose to see anything."

Source: From Leonard W. Cowie, *Documents and Descriptions in European History, 1714–1815* (Oxford University Press, 1967), pp. 77–78. His source: Katherine Prescott Wormeley, *Journal and Memoirs of the Marquis d'Argenson*, (1901) 2 vols. (1905), vol. 2, pp. 4–5.

most of the eighteenth century. Foreign trade increased by 300 percent between 1726 and 1774, and population grew by about one-third during the eighteenth century. Had Fleury's cautious policies been sustained, Louis XV's successor might not have died on the guillotine. Louis's failings, however, ensnared his nation in ever-deeper troubles.

It did not help matters that the king's sexual behavior damaged the reputation of the monarchy in the relatively new but rapidly growing arena of public opinion. Madame de Pompadour, the most durable of Louis's numerous mistresses and a woman of ambition, energy, and intelligence, recognized the seriousness of the political situation. It was she, in a letter to Louis after the massive defeat of the French army by the Prussians at Rossbach, who wrote *"Après nous le déluge"* ("After us the flood").[2] Even before Pompadour's death in 1764, Louis was indulging his pen-

chant for sexual liaisons with his social inferiors. His last mistress had been an expensive prostitute. In the 1770s, a huge flood of books attacking his sexual and political behavior began to pour from the presses and continued to flow throughout the reign of his successor. The wave "of politico-pornographic publications which swamped Paris and elsewhere in unprecedented quantities," as one historian has written, "would finally sink the sexually faithful Louis XVI through the entirely mythical public persona created for his wife Marie Antoinette."[3]

After Fleury's death in 1743, Louis ruled personally rather than through a chief minister. Even if his private behavior had been impeccable, his laziness and lack of political courage, skill, and judgment would have done serious harm. Absolute power in incompetent hands is dangerous: He repeatedly cut short the careers of men who

[2] This famous and prophetic remark has often but wrongly been attributed to Louis XV and held to encapsulate his complacent willingness to tolerate entrenched abuses rather than exert himself to reform them.

[3] Emmanuel Le Roy Ladurie, *The Ancien Régime: A History of France, 1610-1774* (Oxford, England: Blackwell, 1996), p. 327.

Madame de Pompadour
Beautiful and witty, Madame de Pompadour's influence with Louis XV lasted until 1757, long after her sexual relationship with the king waned. Frederick the Great referred to her as "Her Petticoat Majesty." She produced and acted in theatrical productions at Versailles, and she had tickets printed so as to control access to the favored few. In this painting, made for her residence, she appears (on the right) in one of her roles. Her brother thought this (and a companion painting not shown here) to among the best likenesses of her. *Musee des arts decoratifs, Paris. Photo: Laurent-Sully Jaulmes. All rights reserved.*

knew much better than he what kinds of fiscal and financial reform were desperately needed and what foreign and domestic policies would benefit rather than weaken the nation. French involvement in the midcentury wars (discussed in detail a little later) brought heavy taxation, excessive debt, military defeats, and huge losses in North America, the Caribbean, Africa, and India. The need for revenue dictated an assault on noble exemptions from direct taxation and on the powers of the parlements to block the implementation of royal legislation. To this end, Louis XV appointed an eminent lawyer, René-Nicolas de Maupeou (1714–1792), as his chancellor. In 1771, Maupeou dissolved the parlements, sent many of their members into exile, and abolished the sale of judicial offices. He then appointed new courts with judges who received salaries, unlike their predecessors who owned their offices and paid themselves by collecting fees from litigants. A revision of tax assessments that sharply limited the old privileges soon followed. For once, Louis XV stood by his ministers, and it appeared that fiscal reform had been achieved. Then Louis died of smallpox in 1774.

The outcry against Maupeou's reforms gained such momentum that the new king, Louis XVI, reinstated the traditional parlements. Many philosophes were delighted when the king appointed one of the leading **physiocrats,** Baron Turgot (1727–1781), as controller-general of finance. True to his principles, Turgot instituted an ambi-

tious program that included abolishing most trade and craft guilds, ending price controls over grain and flour, and banishing the *corvée* (forced peasant labor for road maintenance) in order to advance the laissez-faire philosophy of economic liberty. Unfortunately, a bad harvest drove bread prices up, and the "Flour War" of 1775 (see Chapter 18) was blamed on Turgot. Turgot's dismissal in 1776 and the countermanding of his measures that followed ended the first of a series of failed attempts to cope with mounting fiscal problems. The royal deficit, which had stood at 40 million livres in 1774, zoomed to 112 million livres in 1786. The horrific increase in the deficit was due to the decision to assist the American rebels against Britain, a decision driven mainly by desire to avenge the humiliations of defeat in the Seven Years' War. The expense of assisting the American Revolution led to yet another attempt to tax the nobility, and the resulting protest opened the door to the French Revolution in 1789.

In Sweden and Poland, as well as France, aristocrats reasserted themselves during the eighteenth century. Sweden had amassed an astonishingly large empire in the seventeenth century, but Russia's decisive defeat of Charles XII's army at Poltava (1709) ended Sweden's domination of northeastern Europe (see Chapter 16). After Charles's death in 1718, Swedish nobles initiated what was called the "Age of Liberty"—meaning liberty from royal absolutism—in that nation's history. As in Poland, however,

THE HISTORICAL EVIDENCE

Voltaire, Diderot, and Catherine the Great

1773, 1778

Catherine the Great proclaimed herself a great admirer of the Enlightenment, and she took pleasure in her correspondence with such luminaries as Voltaire and Diderot. In a letter written on October 1, 1778, she described her feelings about Voltaire.

He was my master; it was he, or rather his works, that formed my way of thinking. I have told you more than once, I think: I am his pupil; when I was younger, I loved to please him; when I did something, it had to be worthy of telling him about it for it to please me, and then he was told of it straightaway; he was so well used to this that he used to scold me if I left out any news and [he] learned it from elsewhere. My meticulousness on this point slackened in recent years because of pressure of events. . . . And because of the enormous work which I have taken on, I have got out of the habit of letter-writing. . . . The famous writing-desk adorns my hermitage, and also the two busts of Voltaire; I prefer the bust without the wig.

In a memorandum that Diderot wrote for Catherine's use in 1773, he offered his view of a draft of her proposal for a new law code. From his perspective, the new code seemed a good start, but one that did not go far enough. In time, she might be able to perfect it, and he both flattered and chided her. His remarks also show his attraction to physiocratic ideas about agriculture and national wealth.

I see in Her Imperial Majesty's *Instruction* a plan for an excellent code of laws, but not a word on how to ensure the maintenance of this code. I see the name of despot renounced, but the essence retained, and despotism called monarchy. I see no proposal for the enfranchisement of the mass of the nation. Now without enfranchisement or liberty, there is no property; without property there is no agriculture; without agriculture there is no strength, greatness, riches, or prosperity. But the Empress has magnanimity, penetration, intelligence, enormous talent, justice, goodness, patience, and firmness. And, to use her own words, the tree which she cannot throw down by wrestling with it, she can cause to fall by cutting away at its roots little by little. She is magnificent, without being spendthrift, she enjoys good health, she is forty-four years old, and she has promised to live to eighty. There is nothing which one cannot complete with time and such a rare combination of excellent qualities.

Source: From A. Lentin, *Enlightened Absolutism (1760–1790): A Documentary Sourcebook* (Newcastle-upon-Tyne, England: Avero, 1985), pp. 38, 42.

---

the nobles' liberty also meant Sweden's vulnerability to the ambitions of other states. Between 1718 and 1772, the aristocratic party in the Swedish Riksdag (the "Hats") and the alliance of burghers and peasants (the "Caps") jockeyed for position and received support from neighboring powers who sought to influence the outcome according to their differing preferences. Until 1772, when French support helped Gustavus III overcome his opponents and attempt to restore absolutist rule, aristocrats dominated the monarchs. His program, like that of Joseph II of Austria (discussed in a moment), included Enlightenment-inspired reforms. But frustrated nobles mortally wounded Gustavus at a masked ball in 1792, and his country was swept into the maelstrom created by the revolution in France. In Poland-Lithuania, nobles preserved their "liberty"—by which they meant their freedom from any central government that would tax them to support a modernized army capable of defending their country—but magnate supremacy

barely masked the fact that Poland-Lithuania was a Russian satellite until the First Partition of 1772.

Enlightened Absolutism

The decline of absolutism in some states did not mean that absolutism was doomed. On the contrary, the experience of assertive oligarchies in France, Sweden, and Poland-Lithuania was quite different from developments in Prussia, Austria, and Russia and, in a different way, from those in Great Britain. Prussia's Frederick II ("the Great"), who liked to call himself "the first servant of the state," received Voltaire's accolade as "a philosopher who will make men happy." Voltaire spent several years at Frederick's court at Potsdam. Catherine the Great had long, private conversations with Diderot when he accepted her invitation to visit St. Petersburg in 1773. The Habsburg emperor Joseph II boasted in his will that, like Frederick, he had "lived as a

THE HUMAN EXPERIENCE

Catherine the Great, the Enlightened Empress

"Figchen" was her nickname as a child, Sophia her name at her christening in 1729, and Catherine the name she took after her conversion from Lutheranism to the Russian Orthodox faith in 1744. Daughter of a minor German princely family, she was chosen by the Russian empress Elizabeth (reigned 1744–1761) to marry her heir, Grand Duke Peter. He was seventeen, she fifteen, when they wed in 1745 amid a great whirl of balls and festivities in St. Petersburg. Peter, a childish, unbalanced young man who preferred playing with dolls to his wife's company, was unable to consummate the marriage. Catherine, a vigorous, sensual woman, in 1752 took the first of her twenty-one known lovers, who was almost certainly the father of the son who eventually succeeded her on the throne. The twenty-first lover was twenty-nine years old when Catherine died in 1796 at the age of sixty-seven.

On Christmas Day in 1761, the empress Elizabeth died, a wonderful present for Prussia. Catherine's husband, Peter III, immediately withdrew from the war against Prussia, saving Frederick the Great from defeat in the Seven Years' War, as discussed later in the chapter. Peter treated aged courtiers with public shows of contempt such as making them play hopscotch and encouraging his friends to kick and trip them. His policies, no less than his behavior, angered powerful officials and churchmen. Catherine's current lover, a dashing artillery captain named Grigory Orlov, and his brothers were prominent among the plotters who

engineered the coup d'état that overthrew Peter in 1762. They proclaimed Catherine the new ruler and arrested Peter. He was soon murdered, although it was publicly announced that he had died a natural death.

Catherine's expansionist foreign policy showed a similar bold opportunism, and she expended large sums to build up Russia's military forces. She expanded Russia's borders against the Turks to the south and the Poles to the west, bringing most of Ukraine under Russian rule. Besides large chunks of Poland-Lithuania, she annexed the Crimea and important parts of the Black Sea coast, gaining access to Constantinople and the Mediterranean. Her armies brought 200,000 square miles and 7 million people under Russian rule.

Despite the bloody beginning of her reign and the brutality of her foreign policy, Catherine attempted to introduce a new humanitarianism and civility to her backward empire, at least until Russia was rocked by a massive Cossack rebellion in 1773. A diligent reader of the works of Montesquieu, Voltaire, Diderot, Beccaria, and other philosophes, she was a person of warmth, energy, and intelligence. She convened the Legislative Commission in 1767 with the goal of introducing elements of consultation and consent into government. Although the commission itself achieved little, Catherine's subsequent legislation embodied positive steps to accomplish these goals. Surprisingly, her budgets showed a decreasing percentage of funds devoted to the military and an

increase in spending on such civilian activities as education, legal and judicial reform, road and canal building, the care of orphans, and the development of a salaried civil service. Torture was virtually eliminated and corporal punishment reduced and regulated. Peter III had freed nobles of the obligation to serve the state (see Chapter 16), and Catherine did not reinstate it. By and large, nobles kept serving— but out of choice rather than compulsion.

Although Catherine did take some steps to protect serfs against abuses by landlords, her reign proved to be the nadir of the Russian peasantry. The geographical extent of serfdom increased when it was extended into the eastern Ukraine for the first time. The sale of serfs apart from their land and sometimes as individuals separated from the rest of their family continued and even increased in the second half of the eighteenth century. Many of these sales were arranged to settle the gambling debts of landlords. Catherine's reputation as an enlightened ruler suffered further when, in 1793, she decreed strict press censorship. Aleksandr Radishchev, who had published a book criticizing Russian serfdom, was imprisoned on her orders and exiled to Siberia. Catherine certainly possessed the skills required to make herself appear to be an "enlightened despot," at least to readers of newspapers in western Europe during the earlier part of her reign. Whether her subjects experienced much improvement in their lives remains highly debatable. ❖

servant of the state," and he wrote in 1785 that "no constitution should exist if it is contrary to the principles of natural and social justice." Both a meritocrat and an egalitarian, Joseph stated his intention "to humble and impoverish the grandees" by destroying their privileges. He was

delighted when others described him as "the revolutionary emperor."

Charles III of Spain appointed a series of reforming advisers who angered nobles, churchmen, and other groups with their innovations, some of which were inspired by the works of the philosophes. Charles, Joseph, Catherine, Frederick, and Gustavus were prominent among the monarchs long described as "enlightened despots" or "enlightened absolutists," rulers who claimed to use their power to improve the lives of their subjects by employing the ideas of Enlightenment thinkers. These and other princes and their bureaucrats worked to impose reforms from the top down after 1740, but the philosophes provided only one source among many for the programs of enlightened absolutists.

Although the growth of armies pushed Austria, Russia, and Prussia toward becoming military autocracies, Prussia most clearly exemplifies the extent to which this process could be carried out by determined rulers. Continuing the trend initiated after the Thirty Years' War, King Frederick William I (reigned 1713–1740) poured his energy and resources into the army and increased its size from 50,000 men in 1713 to 83,000 in 1740. One Prussian in twenty-five was in uniform (whereas, for example, the French ratio was 1 in 250), and the Prussian system of training and equipping soldiers ranked at the top. Called the "Sergeant King," Frederick William was pious, frugal, and boorish, hating intellectuals and artists. He was the complete opposite of his skeptical, flute-playing, philosophe-courting son, Frederick the Great who, his father sneered, was "an effeminate chap who has no manly leanings . . . [and] wears his hair long and curled like a fool." The father relaxed by drinking beer and smoking a pipe with friends; the son, by writing symphonies and concertos. But they shared a deep devotion to the Prussian army, and both wore their blue uniform coats every day. In 1789, three years after Frederick the Great's death, the army contained 163,000 men. As one bureaucrat wrote, Prussia was "not a country with an army but an army with a country." Army officers, most from the nobility, outranked their counterparts in the civilian administration, and conscripted peasants made up the rank and file. No eighteenth-century state could outdo Prussia for militarism.

The tremendous cost of the midcentury wars prompted governments to struggle more energetically than ever to increase revenues. They frequently expropriated parts of the church's wealth, a policy applauded by philosophes, for whom the clergy represented bigotry and intolerance. Maria Theresa (reigned 1740–1780) and her son Joseph II (co-ruler with his mother from 1765 and sole ruler 1780–1790) banned the Jesuits in 1773 and used their wealth to initiate a system of primary schools. Joseph abolished many restrictions on the Jews, such as the requirements that they have beards and dress distinctively, and he expanded educational opportunities for them. Joseph's Edict of Toleration for Protestants and Orthodox Christians made Austria more hospitable to religious minorities than any other Catholic nation, but it was bitterly opposed by his Catholic subjects. Jesuits were ousted all over Catholic Europe during the mid-eighteenth century (Portugal, 1759; France, 1763; Spain, 1767). Joseph II's Edict on Idle Institutions (1781) went even farther, suppressing nearly a third of all monastic houses. In Protestant Prussia, Frederick established religious freedom, mainly because he wanted to encourage immigration and thereby enlarge the labor supply.

Frederick the Great "My people and I have come to an agreement which satisfies us both," said Frederick the Great. "They are to say what they please, and I am to do what I please." Amid his officers and on a white horse, Frederick appeared in this painting, as he usually did, in his blue uniform coat (which had numerous bullet holes that had been repaired). His nephew and successor, Frederick William II, is on a black horse behind him, but all eyes are on Frederick. *The Granger Collection, New York.*

The motive behind this religious and educational innovation was less theoretical than pragmatic, aiming at bolstering the wealth of the state. The goal was often power more than intellectual and religious freedom. The Jesuits' critics complained that the order's policy of strict obedience to their head, usually an Italian, meant that they posed a political danger. Assassination plots against the kings of France and Portugal were alleged, on dubious evidence, to have had Jesuit participants, and there were claims that Jesuits fomented riots in Spanish cities in 1766. Relentless pressure from the Bourbon kings of France and Spain forced the pope to abolish the Jesuit order in 1773.[4] Besides seizing the church's wealth, regimes tried to reduce or abolish tax exemptions for nobles and others, with the results in France mentioned earlier in this chapter. A similar struggle over taxation between rulers and the local assemblies of aristocrats erupted in the Austrian domains and led to open rebellion in Hungary and the Austrian Netherlands (now Belgium) in 1789.

In addition to their military, religious, and social policies, the enlightened absolutists saw clearly that their states needed fundamental agrarian reforms to increase production and the revenue that could be drawn from it. Especially in the German-speaking lands, the ideas of the **cameralists** exerted more influence than those of the French physiocrats (see Chapter 18). Cameralists, like the followers of mercantilism before them, perceived in economic development the means to strengthen the state, and—in sharp contrast to the physiocrats—they assumed that change had to come from the top down. They criticized oppression of peasants and advocated offering them greater personal and economic freedom as incentives for working harder. Yet cameralism assumed that the initiative lay with the king and that the king, using the science of administration that the cameralists developed, would regulate and stimulate the economy in order to meet the society's needs. The expected surplus would go to the state for use by the prince. The laissez-faire or free-market philosophy of the physiocrats had little appeal for the cameralists, for whom society was rigidly divided into **estates** in which all initiatives came from above. Frederick the Great, like others, would have liked to abolish serfdom, but to do so would have alienated the landowning aristocracy (the Junkers) from whom he drew his army officers and civil servants. Like Maria Theresa and Joseph II, he used his crown estates to experiment with limiting labor services and strengthening peasant tenure. But he did nothing to weaken the hammerlock of the Junkers on their peasants. Indeed, villagers' tax burdens grew heavier, not lighter, and the Prussian law code maintained the rigid social hierarchy that kept the peasants on the bottom. With the partial and short-lived exception of Joseph II's empire, the experience of the peasantry in central and eastern Europe (including Russia) proved similarly bleak.

Joseph II carried out the most radically progressive agrarian reforms, going much farther than the limitation of labor service (*robot*) to the three days a week decreed by his mother. In 1781 he freed the serfs from restrictions on movement and marriage. He took his boldest step in 1789, when he announced that on All Saints' Day, 1790, forced labor would be abolished throughout Habsburg lands and that peasants would pay no more than 30 percent of their income in taxes and rents. "Oh, what rapture among the people of our villages," wrote a Czech official after Joseph's decree.

When Joseph died in 1790, his effort to centralize the Habsburg monarchy into a unified state was in turmoil, and his successor rescinded most of the reform program. Even the peasants whom Joseph had tried to help were deeply angered by his efforts to remove what he regarded as "superstition" from the religion of the people. "Here lies a prince whose intentions were pure," wrote Joseph for his own epitaph, "but who had the misfortune to see all his plans collapse." His reign demonstrated the paradox of enlightened despotism: Reform could go forward so long as it did not radically threaten the position of the nobility, for the Ancien Régime governments required cooperation between rulers and aristocrats.

Ironically, in a number of smaller states (Tuscany, Lombardy, Mainz, Baden, Hesse-Cassel) rulers did manage to institute reforms. Because they were able to avoid the ruinously expensive wars that the big powers fought, these rulers were less desperate for revenue. They did not have to push innovation as fast or as far, and thus they were less likely to encounter resistance. But in larger states, amid tumultuous military and colonial competition, rulers rushed ahead because they believed that they were defending essential dynastic and national interests. As a result, their policies collided with the interests of precisely those members of the landowning elites whose support they most needed for successful government.

The New British State

Throughout the sixteenth and seventeenth centuries, the British played a peripheral role in international relations. They fought a series of naval wars with the Dutch in the second half of the seventeenth century that brought them New York (formerly New Amsterdam), and their commerce benefited from Dutch decline during the eighteenth century. Although Amsterdam continued to rival London

---

[4] The order was revived in the early nineteenth century as part of the massive Catholic backlash against the French Revolution and all its works, and the Jesuits resumed—and to this day maintain—their place among the intellectual elite of the Roman Catholic clergy.

THE HISTORICAL EVIDENCE

An Attack on Walpole

1727

Although Sir Robert Walpole ("Robin") was, after King George I, the most powerful man in England, his enemies had no difficulty publishing satirical pieces against him. This street ballad calling for George II to dismiss him—titled "Robin Will Be Out at Last"—is one of many examples and demonstrates the vigor of political polemics in Georgian Britain. French observers admired Britain's relative press freedom and compared it unfavorably to their government's policy, however erratic it was in practice. "Bubbles" referred to charges that Walpole had illicitly protected highly placed friends from the consequences of their involvement in the scandal of the South Sea Bubble (1720). "Jobbing" was used both of dealing in the stock market and of influence peddling in return for government jobs.

Good People draw near
And a Tale you shall hear,
A Story concerning one *Robin*,
Who, from not worth a Groat,
A vast Fortune has got,
By Politicks, Bubbles, and Jobbing.

But a few Years ago,
As we very well know,
He scarce had a Guinea his Fob in;
But by bribing of Friends,
To serve his dark Ends,
Now worth a full Million is *Robin*. . . .

As oft hath he said,
That our Debts should be paid,
And the Nation be eas'd of her Throbbing;

Yet on tick [credit] we still run,
For the true Sinking Fund
Is the bottomless Pocket of *Robin*. . . .

Come then let a full Glass
Round to King and Queen pass,
Who will ease our disconsolate Sobbing,
For if rightly I ween,
Such a good King and Queen,
Will give no Protection to *Robin*.

Source: From H. T. Dickinson, ed., *Politics and Literature in the Eighteenth Century* (London: J. M. Dent, 1974), pp. 72–74.

as a banking center and capital market, Dutch manufacturing and trade slid downward. A telling indicator is that in 1730 the Dutch controlled almost two-thirds of the trade in Baltic timber, so essential for shipbuilding; fifty years later they had only one-third. Britain's stunning successes in the War of the Spanish Succession and the Seven Years' War confirmed the island nation's status as a transcontinental world power. British traders roamed the globe under the effective protection of Europe's most potent navy, and victories on numerous battlefields demonstrated that British armies also had to be feared. This sudden transformation from an also-ran to one of the front-runners surprised many contemporary observers, and it contradicted the widespread belief that national or imperial power required an absolute ruler who could act quickly and decisively without having to consult a representative assembly.

British triumphs did not surprise such philosophes as Montesquieu and Voltaire, whose admiration of Britain's relative liberty of press, speech, and religion led them to an uncritical and poorly informed understanding of how the British government actually worked. In deeply Protestant Britain itself, many people would have agreed with one of their bishops when he said in 1715 that "a Protestant country can never have stable times under a Popish prince, any more than a flock of sheep can have quiet when a wolf is their shepherd." Having finally thrown off the Stuarts, with their Catholic leanings and absolutist hankerings (see Figure 16-4 in Chapter 16), the British—so the Protestant argument went—could bask in religious and political freedom and pursue progress with divine assistance.

Britain's swift ascent to **Great Power** status dated mainly from the Glorious Revolution of 1688 and its consequences, some of them unintended (see Chapter 16). After replacing his father-in-law, the Catholic James II, on the English throne, William III and the members of the ruling elite in England and Scotland who had endorsed his invasion had to fight for their survival against Louis XIV. Louis supported the restoration of the Catholic Stuarts to the British throne, and the remaining backers of the Stuart cause in Britain became known as "Jacobites" (from the Latin *Jacobus,* "James"). William's marriage to Mary had been childless, so when he died in 1702, Mary's sister Anne came to the throne. Anne had five children, but all of them predeceased her. Anne's death in 1714 therefore ended the Stuart line, and the successor kings were cousins from the German state of Hanover, brought over to preserve the Protestant tradition and the ascendancy of Parliament that had been the goals of the backers of the Glorious Revolution (refer again to Figure 16-4). From 1688 until 1745, however, when the last rebellion aimed at restoring the Catholic Stuarts failed, the specter of Jacobitism haunted Protestants in Britain.

Increasingly, executive authority lay in the hands of groups of members of Parliament who formed the Cabinet, the successor to the Privy Council (see Chapter 16). For most of George I's reign (1714–1727) and part of George II's (1727–1760), Sir Robert Walpole, Britain's first prime minister, maintained Whig domination of the government. Through the institutions of Parliament and Cabinet, Whig politicians dictated policy, and the disinterest of non-English-speaking George I and his son (and their devotion to their German subjects in Hanover) made the task easier. Walpole, who rose to power by extricating the country from the South Sea Bubble crisis, kept Britain out of war until 1739. In 1734, he proudly announced to the queen, "Madam, there are fifty thousand men slain this year in Europe, and not one Englishman." This feat enabled him to reduce the rate of land taxation, thereby undermining his Tory opponents in the struggle to appeal to the interests of the country gentlemen whose electoral clout shaped the House of Commons. He also tarred the Tories with the brush of Jacobitism, a shrewd method for keeping them out of office.

A brilliant politician, Walpole declined the royal offer of a peerage in 1721 in order to stay in the House of Commons. He manipulated patronage more thoroughly than any of his predecessors in order to garner parliamentary votes, and his enemies savagely attacked the allegedly corrupt methods he employed. Political satirists called his regime the "Robinocracy" and produced staggering amounts of propaganda against him—yet he maintained his grip on power for twenty years. Walpole's popularity suffered from his attempt to further reduce the land tax by introducing new excise taxes on tea, coffee, cocoa, and chocolate in 1734. London mobs burned him in effigy, and his critics forced him to withdraw his excise scheme. What

finally brought him down, however, was the war with Spain that began in 1739. The War of Jenkins's Ear earned its name from the Spanish coastal guards in American waters who tied Captain Robert Jenkins to the mast of his merchant ship and sliced off his ear while searching for contraband. This was just one of several incidents in which English sailors suffered rough handling by Spaniards. Jenkins pickled his ear in brandy and presented it to the House of Commons in a mahogany box when he appeared before that body in 1738. By 1739, English merchants active in the West Indies, helped by politicians who saw a chance to damage Walpole, had succeeded in whipping up a thirst for revenge among people in England. So popular had the commodities from overseas become at home that a war that might enhance trade had many supporters. Forced to go to war against Spain in 1739, Walpole mismanaged the effort and continued to lose support in Parliament. The military failures in the Caribbean stimulated a major expansion of the English fleet that soon had shipyards in both Britain and North America hard at work building the heavily armed ships-of-the-line that would soon dominate the world's commerce.

The growing power of the House of Commons was demonstrated in 1742 when Walpole resigned after losing a vote by a small margin. His fall offered powerful evidence that royal ministers owed accountability not simply to the king but to the entire House of Commons. In the midst of the major political crisis of the reign of George III (1760–1820), a crisis created by the rebellion of the colonies in North America, this doctrine of ministerial responsibility received further confirmation. George's minister Lord North, who resigned in 1782, bluntly told the king the political facts of life: "Your Majesty is well apprized that, in this country, the Prince on the Throne, cannot, with prudence, oppose the deliberate resolution of the House of Commons." The eighteenth-century British state was indeed absolute, but this ultimate power now resided in Parliament, not the monarch.

The political crisis of 1782–1784 came as George III's government, so overwhelmingly successful in the Seven Years' War, faced the traumatic loss of its North American colonies. Britain went from triumph to catastrophe in two decades. Yet by 1815 the loss of Britain's first empire in North America had been wholly overcome, and Britain had led the coalition that defeated Napoleonic France and gone on to build a new empire, larger than the first—an empire that ruled 200 million people (more than 25 percent of the world's population). Behind this imperial resurgence lay not only the agricultural advances that made British farmers exporters of grain by 1780, but a complex conjunction of economic, cultural, and political developments as well. Eighteenth-century Britain was in many ways a new state, one that had overcome some of the ancient animosities between the Scots and the English,

Hogarth's *Calais Gate, or The Roast Beef of Old England* Hogarth's popular 1749 engraving captured British scorn for the French. Lean French soldiers who survive on meager soup are mesmerized by a fat leg of English beef being taken to a hotel for Englishmen in Calais. The only well-fed Frenchman in the picture is the gluttonous priest, and the lean and tattered soldiers and barefoot nuns represent not only the poverty of the French, but their enslavement to a despotic king and a corrupt church. Angered over a brief arrest as a suspected spy on a trip to Calais in 1747, Hogarth (at left putting pen to sketch pad) represented the scene through the arch of a prison that symbolizes France itself. *The Granger Collection, New York.*

forged a potent alliance of landed aristocrats and middling property owners in town and countryside, and created a uniquely effective mechanism for public finance. Paradoxically, the very "weakness" of the state in relation to the propertied class (from whom, through Parliament, the government had to obtain approval of taxation) was the bedrock on which rested the state's credit and thus its demonstrable commercial, military, and diplomatic strength against European rivals.

To illustrate these changes in Britain's status, first consider the relationship between England and Scotland. From the Middle Ages to the eighteenth century, English efforts to defend their interests had been repeatedly hamstrung by the Scots. France, usually England's enemy, allied with Scotland and encouraged Scottish incursions across the border into England. In 1707, however, Scottish and English politicians negotiated a parliamentary union to bring together the two formerly separate kingdoms, thereby creating the United Kingdom, or Great Britain, and enabling Scots to trade freely in England and its colonies. When the highland Scots who backed the Jacobite cause rebelled and suffered a crushing defeat in 1745, a door opened to a more meaningful union, a door that widened when Scots in Britain's military forces fought gallantly during the Seven Years' War. Although ethnic stereotypes and tensions persisted (and do

to the present day) and many Scots resisted the loss of their legislature, a large step was taken toward the construction of a genuinely "British" national identity. "Born and educated in this country," announced George III in 1760, "I glory in the name of Briton." His appointments showed that he meant what he said. Scots increasingly held high positions in the central government in London and in colonial governments, as well as in the professions and in commercial institutions. Nor was it only the king who welcomed Scots. Sixty Scots served as members of Parliament (MPs) for *English* constituencies between 1760 and 1790, and that number grew to 130 between 1790 and 1820.

Second, although eighteenth-century British society has often been described as aristocratic, it was in fact neither an oligarchy nor a democracy but something in between. During the eighteenth century, political decision making in Britain became a matter for the propertied "middling sort," whether their property consisted of rural acreage, ownership of trading companies, or other businesses. The increasingly wealthy members of this group whose money came from farming, trade, or professional services aped the landed aristocracy, and many attained the coveted status of "gentleman." By midcentury, one contemporary novelist asserted that anyone who presented himself "in a clean shirt and powdered wig" would be addressed as "Sir" and "your Honor." Another suggested that "everyone is flying from his inferiors, in pursuit of his superiors who fly from him with equal alacrity." However much wits satirized the search for status, the search went on, and many achieved their goals. Moreover, most members of the traditional aristocracy understood that their own interests benefited from a thriving domestic, colonial, and European trade and that navies and armies were required to defend and expand that trade. Increasing trade enhanced revenue from excise taxes, enabling the government to ease the burden of the land tax. The economic growth that ensued from these policies (see Figure 19-4) improved the condition of ordinary people, most of whom

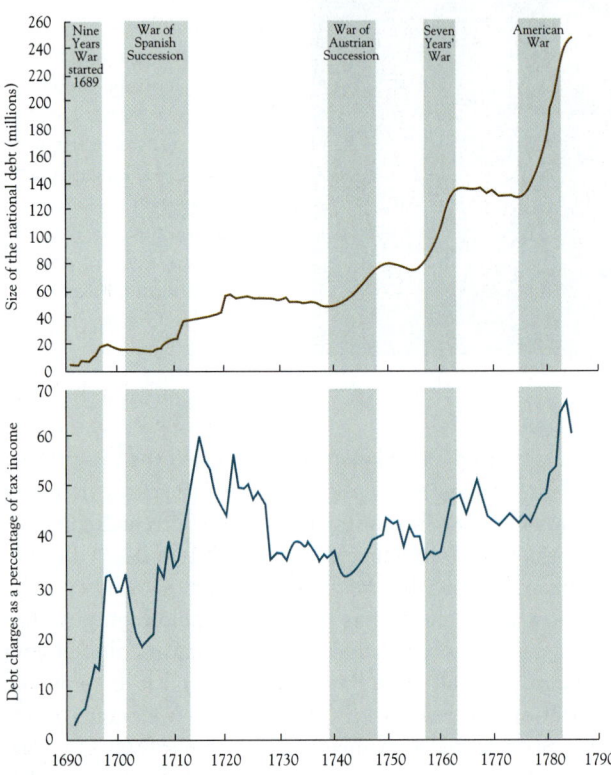

FIGURE 19-4
BRITAIN'S PUBLIC FINANCE

Although one might think that the huge increase in Britain's national debt and the sharp rise in the portion of revenue required to pay interest on it indicate a nation in serious distress, the opposite is true. British economic growth during the eighteenth century enabled successive regimes to pay the interest, and confidence that the interest would be paid encouraged people to lend to the state. The "unfunded" portion of the debt fell as the total debt rose, evidence that the politicians understood that designating particular tax revenues for debt service would permit the system to continue. The lack of a comparable confidence in France meant that government borrowing cost much more. *Source: Adapted from John Brewer, The Sinews of Power: War, Money and the English State, 1688–1783 (Cambridge, Mass.: Harvard University Press, 1990), figures 4.6 (p. 115), 4.7 (p. 117).*

became thoroughly patriotic and took pleasure in thinking themselves better off than the hated priest-ridden French with their tyrannical kings.

Third, the consensus among the propertied classes who controlled local government underpinned the creation of a British fiscal-military state, an institution that fought wars on public credit managed by the Bank of England. The following figures for the national debt (in millions of pounds) tell the story:

1697 £ 16.7
1720 £ 50.0
1748 £ 76.0
1763 £133.0
1783 £245.0

For much of this period, interest payments consumed 30 to 40 percent of annual revenue, rising to more than 50 percent (and at one point 66 percent) during the war with the Americans. The development of a financial market in London during the first half of the century enabled owners of government debt to raise cash if they needed it by selling securities. Because Parliament voted taxes that were earmarked to service the debt, its purchasers knew that it would be paid, and Parliament also funded the creation of a huge bureaucracy of excise agents to make sure that the money was indeed collected. The number of excise agents grew 405 percent between 1690 and 1782, by which time 14,000 of them raised sums that made Britain the most heavily taxed nation in Europe. Unlike France, where the sale of offices was the norm, in Britain it was rare; this meant that most of the revenue actually reached the treasury instead of being siphoned off by venal officers. The accountability of the king's ministers to Parliament meant that corruption and waste would not go unchallenged. Elaborate parliamentary inquiries in the 1780s and 1790s showed that "corruption" cost the British taxpayer about 2.4 percent of national revenue, less than a fourth of what the French paid to the tax farmers. The proven effectiveness of Britain's military forces depended on this relatively efficient system of credit and taxation.

The British faith in and devotion to Parliament did not mean that everyone agreed that Parliament itself had the ideal form or structure. Only a minority of adult men (around 14 percent) had the right to vote in parliamentary elections, and seats in the House of Commons were distributed with little reference to population patterns. The 8 million residents of London and its environs, for example, elected only eight MPs, whereas the remote county of Cornwall had forty-two members representing a hundred thousand people. Such rapidly expanding northern cities as Birmingham, Manchester, and Leeds elected none. John Wilkes (1725-1797), a radical journalist and savage critic of George III's government in the 1760s and 1770s,

Hogarth's *Canvassing for Votes* Here Hogarth criticized the use of bribes to gain votes in parliamentary elections. Representing the Whig and Tory parties, the hosts of two inns shower money on a farmer (center) in return for his vote. A banner depicts money flowing from government buildings to the countryside where Punch flings it at voters. Down the street, a riotous crowd assaults the Excise Office. A hostess (right) sits on the British lion (a figurehead from a navy ship) as the lion prepares to consume the French lily. A porter (kneeling to the left of the lion) prepares to distribute political pamphlets from bundles in front of him. *North Wind Picture Archives.*

cunningly employed the press in his campaign against what he and his allies believed was excessive influence in Parliament exercised by the king's ministers. The cry of "Wilkes and Liberty" rang through the streets as huge crowds demonstrated against the government's insistence on expelling Wilkes from his seat in Parliament after his conviction for libel, and more than fifty thousand voters signed petitions on his behalf. Many Wilkesites also argued that voters should be able to issue "instructions" to control the way their representatives voted on legislation. The electors at Bristol ousted their MP, the Irish political thinker and statesman Edmund Burke (1729–1797), because he insisted on the more traditional view. As he put it in a speech, "Parliament is not a congress of ambassadors from different and hostile interests . . . but . . . a deliberative assembly of one nation, with one interest, that of the whole." Burke found another constituency and continued to sit in Parliament until 1794.

Burke's argument prevailed. Especially in the 1780s, but unsuccessfully, parliamentary reformers promoted bills aimed at making representation more democratic and rational. Their campaign, reminiscent of the similar one of the Levellers in the 1640s (see Chapter 15), bore little fruit until 1832. In practice, however, Parliament was fully open to influence from the propertied classes because many small constituencies elected nonresident politicians who understood the needs of whole regions. Birmingham, Manchester, Leeds, Sheffield, and other unrepresented new industrial

cities did not submit petitions for reform in the early 1780s because they had never experienced difficulty in getting their concerns attended to by the legislature. Since more than fifty members of Parliament resided permanently in London and looked out for the capital city energetically, complaints arose that London had too much representation even though it actually elected only eight MPs. In a variety of informal ways, the British legislature served the nation much more effectively than its outward form would suggest. Many who did not vote had effective "virtual representation" in the sense that their interests received attention. Virtual representation did not, however, satisfy the British colonists in North America.

THE STRUGGLE FOR POWER

During the political agitation that resulted in the War of Jenkins's Ear, one member of the House of Lords denounced the Spaniards for their insistence on the right to search British ships. "No search," he thundered, "is a cry that runs from the sailor to the merchant, from the merchant to the parliament, and from parliament it ought to reach the throne." Eighteenth-century international politics was a ruthless struggle for commercial advantage and dynastic rights; ideology, whether religious or political, took a backseat. Coalitions of roughly equal strength grappled with each other. In central and eastern Europe, monarchs wanted either to gain land or hold the land they

Legend:
- France
- Lorraine (Ruled by ex-king of Poland 1735–1766; thereafter by France)
- Great Britain
- Habsburg Lands
- Prussia
- Silesia
- Russia
- Holy Roman Empire

MAP 19-3
EUROPE IN 1763

had. For the maritime powers the stakes also included overseas trading bases and territory, especially in India. By 1763—the end of the Seven Years' War—Great Britain had emerged as the supreme European imperial power and the arbiter of the balance of power on the Continent (see Map 19-3). But the equilibrium after 1763 was unstable, and it was upset from a completely unexpected quarter: Britain's North American colonies.

Midcentury Wars and the Diplomatic Revolution

Prussia's "Sergeant-King," Frederick William I, adored his army, but like his contemporaries Cardinal Fleury in France and Sir Robert Walpole in England, he avoided war. He used his precious troops only once in a short campaign against Sweden in 1715. In December 1740, not quite seven months after his father's death, Frederick II shocked all of Europe by attacking the Austrians. An Austrian diplomat had reported in 1736 that the young prince in Berlin could be expected to begin his reign with "a startling stroke," a prophetic remark indeed. Frederick invaded and conquered the large and wealthy province of Silesia on his southern border in only six weeks. Its coal and iron reserves

later supported Prussian industrialization. He thereby made Prussia a great power, but he had launched his kingdom into two major wars, the War of the Austrian Succession (1740–1748) and the Seven Years' War (1756–1763). Hanging on to Silesia against the Austrians and their allies proved to be fiendishly difficult.

Thus began the War of the Austrian Succession, for Frederick's victim was Maria Theresa, the twenty-three-year old Habsburg ruler of Austria. Her father, the Holy Roman emperor Charles VI (reigned 1711–1740), lacked a male heir, and he had put much of his energy into pressing other powers and the states that formed his empire into recognizing the Pragmatic Sanction, an agreement that legitimated Maria Theresa's succession. Since his father had agreed to the Pragmatic Sanction, Frederick had to find an excuse for his invasion. When an adviser fabricated a justification, Frederick praised him in these terms: "Bravo! This is the work of an excellent charlatan." When Maria Theresa offered him a portion of the Austrian Netherlands for the return of Silesia, he responded with contempt: "Let those who want peace give me what I want; or let them fight me again and be beaten."

Maria Theresa was soon beset not only by Frederick, but also by a Franco-Bavarian invasion of Upper Austria and Bohemia. Charles Albert, elector of Bavaria, who had refused to accept the Pragmatic Sanction, was asserting his claim to Maria Theresa's imperial crown with Frederick's encouragement. Maria Theresa's army had not been paid from 1738 to 1740 because her father did not have the money. Her position appeared so weak that one French general said a campaign against her would "resemble an occupation rather than a war." In the autumn of 1741, authorities in Vienna began preparing for the siege that they expected their enemies would soon begin. In January 1742, a diet held in Frankfurt unanimously elected Charles Albert as the new Holy Roman emperor, the first non-Habsburg since 1437.

Just when the Austrian cause appeared doomed, Maria Theresa, with her infant son in her arms, made a desperate appeal for help before the Hungarian diet. The chivalrous Hungarian nobles shouted, "We dedicate our lives and our blood," and promised a hundred thousand troops. In fact, however, after the enthusiasm of the moment waned, they actually sent 20,600—and they used the situation to strengthen noble control of taxation (and their own exemption from taxes) in Hungary. Although one adviser said that she would be better off trusting "the devil than the Hungarians," Maria Theresa nevertheless managed to recapture Austria and Bohemia. Her British allies, by then at war with France and Spain, won a series of victories in America and India that forced the French to the peace table. Her own armies, in combination with British forces under George II, pushed back her enemies on several fronts. In 1745 the empress had the satisfaction of seeing Charles Albert forced to renounce his claim to her throne. In the Treaty of Aix-la-Chapelle (1748), Maria Theresa, although unable to regain Silesia, prevented further partition of the Habsburg lands that her enemies had craved. The Habsburg monarchy survived the biggest threat it would face until World War I. Frederick the Great, the real winner, doubled Prussian population and revenue by keeping Silesia.

The Great War for Empire and the Partitions of Poland

During the second half of the seventeenth century, Russia and Austria kept expanding at the expense of their neighbors, as did Prussia after miraculously surviving a near-death experience in the Seven Years' War. The French, however, lost much of their overseas empire, and the Poles, the biggest losers, saw their nation disappear from the map.

Poland-Lithuania was still a Russian satellite in 1764, when Catherine the Great engineered the election of a discarded lover, the nobleman Stanisław August Poniatowski (1732–1798), to the Polish throne. In 1772, Prussia, Russia, and Austria carried out the First Partition of Poland (see Map 19-4), a shock that energized an Enlightenment-influenced reform movement among educated nobles and burghers who sought to strengthen the monarchy and reassert national independence. Reform culminated in 1791 when reformers and Poniatowski proclaimed a new constitution with a somewhat stronger, hereditary monarchy and abolition of the infamous liberum veto (see Chapter 15) that had allowed a single parliamentary deputy to block a bill. The attempt to restore Poland-Lithuania as a significant power galvanized Prussia and Russia into effecting the Second Partition of Poland in 1792 and restoring magnate domination in what was left of the country. When nationalists and radical reformers rebelled, the remainder of the commonwealth was gobbled up by Russia, Prussia, and Austria in the Third Partition of 1795.

The Seven Years' War held enormous danger for Prussia. Aix-la-Chapelle was more truce than treaty, as Austria was no more resigned to the loss of Silesia than France was to its defeats by Britain. Another dance of death was on the way, but in what is called the "diplomatic revolution,"

MAP 19-4

THE PARTITIONS OF POLAND AND THE EXPANSION OF RUSSIA

During the eighteenth century, the expansion of Russia to the south occurred at the expense of the Ottomans and to the east primarily at the expense of the Poles. But the Poles also lost territory to the Austrians and the Prussians.

THE HISTORICAL EVIDENCE

Maria Theresa and the First Partition of Poland

February 1772

The Empress Maria Theresa, a devout, humane, and amiable woman, demonstrated a deeply maternal approach to her tasks—perhaps not surprisingly since during the nineteen years of her marriage she had sixteen children. When her husband died in 1765, her son Joseph succeeded him as co-regent. Although Joseph's advocacy of Austrian participation in the First Partition of Poland carried the day in Vienna, Maria Theresa opposed it. Some of her reasons appear in this memorandum.

The easiest course would certainly be to accept the offer made to us of participating in the partition of Poland. But where is the justice in robbing an innocent party which we have always prided ourselves on defending and supporting? To what purpose are all these vast and costly preparations, all these loud, threatening affirmations of our determination to preserve the balance in northern Europe? The single motive of interest, that we should not remain alone between the two other Powers [Prussia and Russia] without securing any advantage, does not seem to me a sufficient or even an honorable pretext for joining in with two unjust usurpers, with the purpose of thrusting a third still further down, without any legal title.

I do not understand a policy which, when two use their superior strength to oppress an innocent victim, allows and enjoins a third to imitate them and commit the same injustice, as a simple precaution for the future and out of present expediency. . . . A Prince has no more rights

than any other mortal; the greatness and support of his State will not avail him when the day comes on which we must all give account for our actions. . . . I will even go so far as to say that to do no man injustice is not an act of magnanimity but an effect of true principles. . . . What would France, Spain, England say if we were now suddenly to ally ourselves with those whom we have tried so hard to keep in check and whose conduct we have declared to be unjust? This . . . would be a denial of all that has been done during thirty years of my reign. Let us try rather to reduce the pretensions of others than think of sharing with them under conditions so unequal; let us be held weak rather than dishonorable.

_____

Source: From C. A. Macartney, ed., *The Habsburg and Hohenzollern Dynasties in the Seventeenth and Eighteenth Centuries* (New York: Walker, 1970), pp. 190–191.

The First Partition of Poland In this cartoon (July 1772), King George III snoozes (far right) as Britain's role in the "balance of power" is outweighed by that of the Austrians, Russians, and Prussians. They eagerly carve up Poland, having tied the Polish king's hands behind his back (left). *British Museum Print Room.*

THE HISTORICAL EVIDENCE

Frederick the Great's Political Testament

1752

In 1752, Frederick, a prolific author who, unlike his father, always wrote in French rather than German, prepared a memorandum of advice for his successor that yields interesting insights into his mentality. It also shows that although he wrote a treatise refuting Machiavelli, he had learned from the Italian master.

You will perhaps ask how I advise you to act in the event of all these changes that I foresee? I am not rash enough to give you advice about distant and uncertain events. . . . I content myself with repeating what I have already said to you in more detail. Keep a prudent control over your finances, so as to have money when you need it; make no alliances except with those who have exactly the same interests as yours; never make treaties binding you to act in contingencies which are remote, but wait for the case to arise before deciding on your line and acting accordingly; take good care not to place your trust in the number and good faith of your allies; count only on yourself; then you will never deceive yourself. . . .

The policy of small princes is a tissue of cheatings; that of great princes consists of much prudence, of dissimulation, and of love of glory. It is a great mistake for a statesman to cheat always; he is soon seen through, and despised. Keen-sighted spirits reckon on a consistent conduct; that is why one must, as much as one can, change one's game, disguise it and turn oneself into a

Proteus, appearing now lively, now slow, now warlike, and now pacific. This is the way to confuse one's enemies and to make them circumspect in the designs they entertain against you. It is not only good to vary one's conduct: it must, above all, be framed to fit the situation of the moment, the time, the place, and the persons with whom one is dealing. Never threaten your enemies: a barking dog does not bite. Put pleasantness into your negotiations: soften down haughty or offensive expressions; never carry small disputes too far; count your own pride for nothing and the interest of the State for everything; be discreet in your business, and dissimulate in your designs. If the glory of the State obliges you to draw the sword, see that the thunder and the lightning fall on your enemies simultaneously.

Source: From C. A. Macartney, ed., *The Habsburg and Hohenzollern Dynasties in the Seventeenth and Eighteenth Centuries* (New York: Walker, 1970), p. 345.

---

the dancers changed partners. The Habsburgs of Austria joined their ancient enemies, the Bourbons of France, and Austria's former ally, Britain, joined Prussia. The Austrians also persuaded Russia to enter their campaign to dismember Prussia. Frederick the Great, who led his allies in trying to dismantle Maria Theresa's empire, suddenly faced the destruction of his own state.

Frederick, at times in such despair that he contemplated suicide, fought a series of brilliant campaigns against his larger enemies. His dominions were devastated, and after a defeat by Austrian and Russian armies in 1759 he wrote: "Of an army of forty-eight thousand I have less than three thousand men left. . . . Berlin must look to its own safety. This is a terrible event and I shall not survive it." Yet he regrouped, raised new forces, and won more victories. Late in 1761, however, enemy forces occupied much of Prussia and Silesia, and he seemed at the edge of final defeat. But he held out just long enough to be saved by a stroke of luck. The Russian ruler died, and the new tsar, Peter III (see Table 19-1), slavishly admired Frederick.

Peter took Russia out of the war, thereby presenting Frederick with what contemporaries called "the miracle of the House of Brandenburg." Although at enormous cost in lives and money, the Prussian ruler had held Silesia and avoided the dismemberment of Brandenburg-Prussia. Without the "miracle," militaristic Prussia would not have survived to lead the unification of Germany in the next century.

France and Britain, although involved alongside allies in land warfare in Europe itself, also fought on other continents and on the high seas. One theater of conflict was India. The Mughal rulers of India, whose splendor had awed European visitors, began to lose their grip on power early in the eighteenth century. India began reverting to its pre-Mughal form—a collection of independent, bickering kingdoms. Through making deals with Indian rulers, Europeans had established bases and trading stations in India. As the Mughals' ability to maintain order collapsed, European chartered companies that monopolized their homelands' trade in Asian goods found themselves drawn into

TABLE 19-1

THE ROMANOV SUCCESSION IN RUSSIA

Ruler	Reigned
Peter I	1682–1725
Catherine I	1725–1727
Peter II	1727–1730
Anna	1730–1740
Elizabeth	1741–1762
Peter III	1762
Catherine II	1762–1796
Paul	1796–1801

asserting direct rule, fortifying their bases, and governing the area around them. When the War of the Austrian Succession broke out in Europe in 1740, the representatives of the French and British East India Companies on the eastern coast of India organized forces and fought for control of the bases from which the lucrative trade in "India" goods was conducted. They allied with feuding local rulers, offering European firepower and the know-how to use it, which often proved decisive over larger Indian armies (see Map 19-5).

Early success went to the French when their ally, the *nawab* (prince) of Bengal, captured the British company's base at Calcutta in 1756. The nawab's men imprisoned the British garrison in a tiny dungeon, the stifling "Black Hole" of Calcutta, and many of the captives died during the night. Officials of the British East India Company (called "John Company") at Madras chose a junior officer of their small army, Robert Clive, to lead a counterattack. With help from Hindus opposed to their ruler, Clive's tiny force of fewer than three thousand men defeated the nawab's fifty-thousand-man army at Plassey on June 23, 1757. Clive completed the ouster of the French after installing his Indian ally as the new nawab of Bengal and accepting £200,000 and other gifts from him. In the long run, English naval strength provided the crucial factor in their defeat of the French.

Clive was a good example of a "nabob," as they came to be called back in England: men who amassed huge personal fortunes while employed by John Company in the disordered scene in India. Like the Spanish conquistadores who had enriched themselves by exploiting rifts in Aztec and Inca society (see Chapter 14), nabobs profited from the animosities that stemmed from conflicts between Muslims and Hindus in India. Although the French recouped some of their losses at the peace table in 1763, their days in India were numbered. In succeeding decades, the nabobs' self-

aggrandizing activities and misgovernment of Bengal forced the British government increasingly into the ill-managed affairs of John Company and eventually into establishing direct British rule in India.

France and Britain also battled in North America. Even before the Seven Years' War, France had made plain its intention to defend "New France" against the westward-moving British settlers. At Louisbourg on Cape Breton Island, the French built a massive fortress to defend

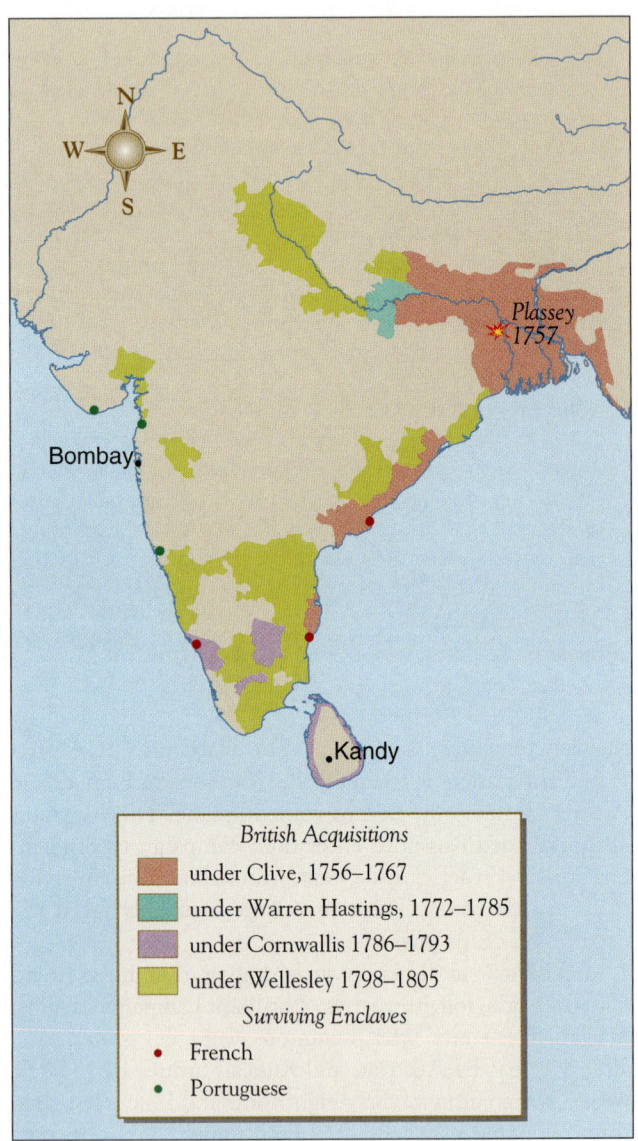

MAP 19-5
IMPERIALISM IN INDIA

As in North America, the story in southern Asia beginning in the mid-eighteenth century was one of British advance and French retreat. Although the French managed to retain several footholds in India, India's future proved to be one of increasing British dominance until the twentieth century.

Benjamin West's *The Death of General Wolfe* Painted by a North American artist in 1770, this portrait of Wolfe's death quickly became a best-seller. George III himself commissioned a copy. The details were not accurate, because the only Native Americans who were at the battle fought for the French. Other officers depicted were not present when Wolfe actually died. By putting Wolfe in military uniform instead of the usual toga or medieval armor and celebrating the heroic moment of victory and death, West glorified British military men in their new imperial setting. *Clements Library, University of Michigan.*

Canada by controlling access to the St. Lawrence River. During the War of the Austrian Succession, four thousand militia from New England managed to capture Louisbourg, but the French retrieved it at the peace table in 1748. The French were few in number (only seventy thousand in Canada in 1763), but they had explored the Ohio and Mississippi Valleys in the seventeenth century and built up a lucrative fur trade with the Indians. A string of French forts protected their claims, but the British disputed their ownership of some of the land. In 1754 a young Virginian militia officer named George Washington led an unsuccessful attempt to dislodge the French from one of these forts (Fort Duquesne, on the site of present-day Pittsburgh). A British army sent to capture Fort Duquesne in 1755 suffered defeat and the commanding general was killed.

The battles that began Washington's military education made up part of what the colonists called the French and Indian War, which in turn became a segment of the Seven Years' War. Despite the early French victories, British naval strength turned the tide in 1758 when Louisbourg fell to a British assault. This defeat cut off supplies and reinforcements from France to Canada. The small population of French settlers could not produce enough food to supply the army, and Fort Duquesne, along with several other forts, fell to the British. In 1759, British forces under General James Wolfe seized Quebec in a battle in which both he and the French commander, Louis-Joseph Montcalm, died. By the next year, the British had completed their conquest of Canada and the territory between their coastal colonies and the Mississippi River.

"New France" in North America was no more, and the French role in India was sharply reduced. British forces also captured the rich French sugar islands, Guadeloupe and Martinique, although they were restored to France in the Peace of Paris (1763). The political architect of the sweeping British victory over France in both India and America was William Pitt, the Elder (1708–1778). A brilliant orator who both envisioned and founded Britain's first empire, Pitt began his political career by attacking Walpole for defending Hanover while neglecting the needs of the colonies and the commerce that they represented. "When trade is at stake," he exclaimed, "you must defend it or perish." In 1757 his strategy was "to win Canada on the banks of the Elbe." This meant funding the Prussians in order to keep French forces busy in Germany while concentrating British energies on naval and amphibious campaigns overseas. Successful though Pitt's "blue-water" policy was, the tremendous expense of the war forced London to look to the American colonists for new tax revenues. After 1763, however, the colonists no longer had to fear that the French would block their westward progress. Ironically, at the moment of its greatest victory, the British Empire in North America was less than a generation away from collapse.

The American Revolution and European Politics

The first major **revolution** in what proved to be a wave of revolutions sweeping the Western world stemmed from a dispute about paying for armies and navies. The colonial assemblies in British North America began their protests against the London government's 1765 plan to raise revenues by levying a stamp tax on newspapers and public documents. The colonists objected less to the money involved than to what seemed to them a violation of constitutional principle. Like their fellow subjects of George III, they believed that there should be "no taxation without representation" in Parliament. Like the members of national and regional assemblies and other constituted bodies in Europe, the colonists wanted to retain their privilege of consent to taxation. From the British government's point of view, justification of the stamp tax was easy. Six million taxpayers in Britain were paying £2 million a year to service the debt from the Seven Years' War, a conflict that had greatly benefited the colonists. Britons were to pay a further £3.5 million for defense of the empire. It hardly seemed excessive to ask 1.5 million Americans to contribute the £150,000 that the stamp duty was expected to yield. In any case, British politicians could brook no challenge to parliamentary sovereignty, the central achievement of the Glorious Revolution of 1688.

Although the colonists wanted representation in Parliament, they also shared the original Whig ideology of suspicion toward excessive royal power and the corruption that invariably accompanied it. Like those Scots who chafed at the loss of home rule under the union of 1707, many colonists (and especially those who comprised the emerging elite dominating society and politics in North America) fiercely resisted the stamp tax. Surprised by the protest, London withdrew the Stamp Act but soon imposed a new set of charges on tea and several other imports to the colonies. By the time further protests forced the suspension of these duties (except for the tea duty, retained to symbolize Parliament's right to levy taxes), British leaders were growing convinced that a faction of Americans was conspiring for independence and therefore the destruction of the empire on which British defense against France depended. Conversely, many previously loyal colonists feared that a faction of politicians in London was plotting to enslave them.

When a group of Bostonians protested the remaining tax by tossing the East India Company's tea chests into the harbor (the "Boston Tea Party") just before Christmas in 1773, Parliament responded with the Coercive Acts, replacing the Massachusetts government with a military governor and closing the port of Boston. In 1775, fighting broke out near Boston when British troops and the Massachusetts militia skirmished at the towns of Lexington and Concord. The Americans declared their independence in 1776 and, with substantial French help, won it in the ensuing war that lasted until 1783. In North America, only Canada remained British, its population boosted by loyalists from the rebellious colonies.

The American rebels had won their independence as a collection of colonies loosely connected to each other and lacking a strong central authority to fund and direct the war effort. Victory over British forces by no means ended the revolutionary effort to establish a new republic that could function successfully as a unified nation instead of a confederation of states. If, for example, the model of the Continental Congress had persisted, executive authority would have been in the hands of the presiding officer of the national Congress rather than a popularly elected

The Colonies Reduced In 1765 Ben Franklin devised this image and had it printed on cards for his personal use. It shows Britannia with her limbs (labeled Virginia, Pennsylvania, New York, and New England) amputated—predicting Britain's eventual loss of her colonies. In the distance, British ships sail away. *The Granger Collection, New York.*

THE HISTORICAL EVIDENCE

The Declaration of Independence and Federalist, No. 51

1776, 1788

The Declaration of Independence, drafted by Thomas Jefferson, was proclaimed by the Continental Congress on July 4, 1776. (The actual vote had occurred two days earlier.) Anchored in universalistic Enlightenment philosophy, it also rested on distinctively British political assumptions.

When in the course of human events, it becomes necessary for one people to dissolve the political bands which have connected them with another, and to assume among the powers of the earth, the separate and equal station to which the laws of nature and nature's God entitle them, a decent respect to the opinions of mankind requires that they should declare the causes which impel them to the separation.

We hold these truths to be self-evident, that all men are created equal, that they are endowed by their Creator with certain unalienable rights, that among these are life, liberty, and the pursuit of happiness—that to secure these rights, governments are instituted among men, deriving their just powers from the consent of the governed, that whenever any form of government becomes destructive of these ends, it is the right of the people to alter or to abolish it, and to institute new government, laying its foundation on such principles, and organizing its powers in such form, as to them shall seem most likely to effect their safety and happiness. . . . The history of the present King of Great Britain is a history of repeated injuries and usurpations, all having in direct object the establishment of an absolute tyranny over these states. To prove this, let facts be submitted to a candid world. . . .

After independence was won, however, many influential Americans found themselves confronting what seemed an excess of liberty. Uncontrolled by a firm central government, the individual and sovereign states were falling victim to factionalism, including dangerous confrontations between creditors and debtors. The framing of the federal constitution and the successful drive to get it ratified by special state conventions represented a vigorous response to this perceived crisis. James Madison, the brilliant young political theorist whose vision of a strong federal system lay at the heart of the new constitutional order, co-authored with two other Founding Fathers the set of essays known as The Federalist *to advocate ratification of the Constitution by the New York convention. In Number Fifty-One of these essays, Madison broke entirely new ground in Western political thought by arguing that the safety of the state depended on dividing, not consolidating, sovereignty and that liberty rested not on virtue but on self-interest.*

To what expedient, then, shall we finally resort, for maintaining in practice the necessary partition of power among the several departments,* as laid down in the Constitution? The only answer that can be given is, that as all these exterior provisions are found to be inadequate, the defect must be supplied, by so contriving the interior structure of the government as that its several constituent parts may, by their mutual relations, be the means of keeping each other in their proper place. . . .

In order to lay a due foundation for that separate and distinct exercise of the different powers of government, which to a certain extent is admitted on all hands to be essential to the preservation of liberty, it is evident that each department should have a will of its own; and consequently should be so constituted that the members of each should have as little agency as possible in the appointment of members of the others. . . .

But the great security against a gradual concentration of the several powers in the same department, consists in giving to those who administer each department the necessary constitutional means and personal motives to resist encroachments of the others. The provisions for defence must in this, as in all other cases, be made commensurate to the danger of attack. Ambition must be made to counteract ambition. The interest of the man must be connected with the constitutional rights of the place. It may be a reflection on human nature, that such devices should be necessary to control the abuses of government. But what is government itself, but the greatest of all reflections on human nature? If men were angels, no government would be necessary. If angels were to govern men, neither external nor internal controls on government would be necessary. In framing a government which is to be administered by men over men, the great difficulty lies in this: you must first enable the government to control the governed; and in the next place oblige it to control itself. A dependence on the people is, no doubt, the primary control on the government; but experience has taught mankind the necessity of auxiliary precautions. . . .

---

* By the "departments" of government Madison means what Americans now call the "branches"—executive, legislative, and judicial.

president, and Congress could not have approved a treaty without the approval of state legislatures. Yet in Philadelphia in 1787, delegates to the constitutional convention created what the nineteenth-century British statesman William Gladstone described as the "most wonderful work ever struck off at a given time by the brain and purpose of man." The Founding Fathers, as they were later called, averaged forty-four years of age.

A Virginian, James Madison (then thirty-six years old), was the principal drafter of the Constitution of the United States, and in the *Federalist* essays he made his political philosophy crystal clear. By advocating a strong federal government but reserving certain powers to the states, he broke with more than two thousand years of political tradition by arguing that large, not small, republics have a better chance of survival and that citizens' self interest, not their virtue, would keep liberty safe. Montesquieu had thought that a large republic would become corrupt because of the distance of the rulers from the people, but Madison argued that the very diversity of interests and factions would act as "checks" upon each other and thus prevent the emergence of a single despotic power. Madison led the effort to pass the Bill of Rights (the first ten constitutional amendments), protecting individual freedoms from the central government that the Constitution established. Madison also worked vigorously for the separation of church and state, and state churches disappeared everywhere except in New England early in the nineteenth century. The last to go were the Congregationalists in Massachusetts and Connecticut in 1831–1833.

The American Revolution helped to trigger the final collapse of several governments in Europe. A series of revolutionary movements arose out of local conditions, and with wide variations in aims, composition, and degrees of success. The "Patriots" in the Dutch Netherlands worked against the Orangists and tried to loosen the regents' grip on power. The "Volunteers" in Ireland struggled to gain economic and legislative independence from England. The "Vonckists" in the Austrian Netherlands (Belgium) were radical opponents of Joseph II. The Third Estate in France resisted the attempt of the king and nobles to halt the French Revolution after it got under way. The revolutionaries, however different, shared Enlightenment ideals, including a desire to establish liberty (against political oppression), equality (against inherited privilege), and the sovereignty of the people (against monopolization of political power by kings and elite groups). They admired and emulated the American example of a bill of rights and a written constitution designed to define the distribution of power in government. Their notion of "democracy" did not include the vote for women nor even for all adult males— but these movements did aim to change governments and societies by greatly widening the circle of participation in political life.

The governments that fell in the Austrian Netherlands, British North America, and France did not do so because of the work of these democratic revolutionaries. The governments fell because they had failed to resolve their structural dilemma: an inability to finance military activities without alienating elite groups. The reaction of the elites brought the governments to their knees, and the democratic revolutionaries came forward in the confusion and disorder that ensued.

CONCLUSION: THE ENLIGHTENMENT AND THE DUAL REVOLUTION

France was Europe's most populous and most powerful state. French intellectuals had been the most numerous although by no means the only contributors to the Enlightenment. Despite the ancient Franco-British political rivalry, French philosophes lavishly admired British political institutions and the achievements of British scientists (especially Newton) and social thinkers (especially Locke). Historians have long debated whether Enlightenment thought and its dissemination to an increasingly literate and interested public triggered the French Revolution that began in 1789 and the other revolutionary movements of the late eighteenth century. The question is difficult in part because Enlightenment political and social thought lacked unity. Voltaire praised monarchy; Montesquieu favored aristocrats as the essential bulwark against royal tyranny; and Rousseau's "general will" (see Chapter 18) could be interpreted in either democratic or authoritarian directions. In fact the ideologies that drove political change, whether in France, North America, Britain, or elsewhere, employed not only the ideas of the philosophes but other ideas as well. Thomas Jefferson, for example, took his notion of equality from the Enlightenment, but he and those who joined the rebellion against George III also drew upon much older convictions about the "rights of Englishmen" to be taxed only with the approval of elected assemblies. An intellectual movement, the Enlightenment, moved forward at the same time as extraordinary population and economic growth, the establishment of overseas colonies and trading empires, and the burgeoning of the wealth and cultural and political influence of classes outside of the charmed circle of aristocrats. No single one of these developments "caused" the political upheaval, but all of them played a role in shaping the kind of upheaval that occurred.

The Enlightenment's passion for practicality and its fascination with technology, so evident in the pages of the magnificent *Encyclopedia* that Diderot and his friends created and in the careers of philosophes like Benjamin Franklin and Joseph Priestley, link it to the enterprises of the early Industrial Revolution. Provincial academies in Europe and North America were filled with men driven by a passion for "improvement" and convinced of the superiority of science and reason over inherited doctrines, traditions, and assumptions. This is not to say that all of the inventors of the machines and the founders of the factories during the Industrial Revolution were philosophes.

But the Enlightenment certainly contributed to the establishment of a greater openness to and thirst for pragmatic solutions and for new ideas, whether political, social, cultural, scientific, or technological. The roots of the **Dual Revolution**—French and Industrial—grew in soil that the Enlightenment helped to prepare.

Selected Reading

Sources

Equiano, Olaudah. *The Interesting Narrative and Other Writings* (1995). Ed. Vincent Carretta.

Lentin, A., ed. *Enlightened Absolutism, 1760–1790* (1985).

Macartney, C. A., ed. *The Habsburg and Hohenzollern Dynasties in the Seventeenth and Eighteenth Centuries* (1970).

Sonnino, Paul, ed. *Frederick of Prussia: Anti-Machiavel* (1981).

General Works

Black, Jeremy. *The Rise of the European Powers, 1679–1793* (1990). A very good overview of international relations in the period.

Doyle, William. *The Old European Order, 1660–1800,* 2nd ed. (1992). The best one-volume history of the period.

Langford, Paul. *A Polite and Commercial People: England, 1727–1783* (1992). A readable and broad-ranging survey that emphasizes the central role of the commercial middle class in British society and politics.

Treasure, Geoffrey. *The Making of Modern Europe, 1648–1780* (1985). A well-written overview with good bibliographical essays after each chapter; emphasizes the histories of the major political entities.

Global Empires

Curtin, Philip D. *The Atlantic Slave Trade: A Census* (1969). A careful analysis of the volume of the slave trade and fluctuations within it.

Miller, Joseph C. *Way of Death* (1988). A deeply researched and thorough study of the Angolan slave trade in Portugal's trading and colonial empire from 1730 to 1830.

Parry, J. H. *Trade and Dominion* (1971). Clear and readable account of European overseas empires in the eighteenth century.

Solow, Barbara L., ed. *Slavery and the Rise of the Atlantic System* (1991). Valuable essays by experts on various aspects of slavery in the early modern period.

Tracy, James D., ed. *The Political Economy of Merchant Empires* (1991). Essays analyzing the reasons for the success of Europeans at long-distance trade from 1350 to 1750.

Walvin, James. *An African's Life: The Life and Times of Olaudah Equiano* (1998). A biography of the extraordinary slave who gained his freedom and considerable wealth from his writing of the first autobiography of an African to be published in Europe.

Politics, War, and Revolution in the Age of Reason

Alexander, John T. *Catherine the Great* (1989). A carefully researched biography that examines not only Catherine's life but the legends that surround her.

Anderson, M. S. *The War of the Austrian Succession, 1740–1748* (1995). Concise introduction to a many-sided struggle in which dynastic ambitions played a powerful role.

Blanning, T. C. W. *Joseph II* (1994). An acute analysis of this ambitious and enlightened reformer and the reasons for his failures.

Brewer, John. *Sinews of Empire* (1990). A penetrating examination of Britain's rise to world power status from 1688 to 1783.

Christie, Ian R., and B. W. Labaree. *Empire or Independence* (1976). Two historians—one British, one American—describe the developments that led to the Declaration of Independence.

Colley, Linda. *Britons: Forging the Nation, 1707–1837* (1992). Stimulating and lively study of the emergence of a new "British" identity during the eighteenth century.

Doyle, William. *Venality* (1996). A thorough study of what the author calls "a French addiction," the sale of offices in its eighteenth-century phase.

Ingrao, Charles. *The Habsburg Monarchy, 1618–1815* (1994). Balanced introduction to the Habsburg drive to create a distinctive identity despite the diversity of peoples and cultures.

Palmer, R. R. *The Age of Democratic Revolution* (1959). An important interpretation that stresses the similarities among the movements for reform and revolution at the end of the eighteenth century.

Scott, H. M., ed. *Enlightened Absolutism* (1990). A collection of well-informed essays on rulers inspired by Enlightenment ideas in both large and small states.

Venturi, Franco. *The End of the Old Regime in Europe, 1768–1776* (1989). Explores movements opposing the traditional order on Europe's fringes (including Poland, Russia, Scandinavia, Bohemia, Greece) and the rise of public opinion in Europe (especially in Italy) in the period.

Wilson, Kathleen. *The Sense of the People* (1998). An exploration of the emergence of a popular political culture in eighteenth-century English towns in the context created by imperial expansion and war in North America.

CHAPTER 20

THE INDUSTRIAL REVOLUTION

Iron and Coal   *National Trust/Art Resource, NY.*

1630	First cotton cloth produced in England	**1776**	Publication of Adam Smith's *The Wealth of Nations*	**1817**	Publication of David Ricardo's *Principles of Political Economy and Taxation*
1698	Thomas Savery's fire engine pump	**1779**	First iron bridge, at Coalbrookdale	**1833**	Parliament passes first Factory Act regulating child labor
1712	Thomas Newcomen's steam engine	**1798**	Publication of Thomas Robert Malthus's *Essays on Population*	**1834**	New poor law replaces most outdoor relief with workhouses
1733	John Kay's flying shuttle	**1798**	Eli Whitney invents the cotton gin	**1851**	Crystal Palace exhibition
1764	James Hargreaves's spinning jenny	**1804**	First steam locomotive		
1769	James Watt's first steam engine	**1811–1812**	Artisans (Luddites) organize to destroy mechanized knitting frames		
1774	Chlorine production simplified				

The term **revolution**, which appears a number of times in this book, has several meanings. It can refer to political and social upheavals such as the French and American Revolutions, which occupied a few years and unfolded primarily in a single geographical location, or it can describe vast historical changes such as the **Scientific Revolution** or the **Industrial Revolution,** which occurred over long periods of time in many different places. Traditionally, historians have held that the Industrial Revolution took place in Britain roughly between 1780 and 1830, the approximate chronology used in this chapter. But many important technological, political, and social developments associated with the Industrial Revolution occurred before 1780; and by 1830 most of the changes that created the world we live in today were yet to come. Moreover, although the Industrial Revolution did emerge primarily in Britain, many of the forces that gave rise to it came from outside Britain, either from Europe or from the larger Atlantic community of North and South America, the Caribbean, and Africa. Thus it is difficult to pin down the chronology and geography of this pivotal development.

We also face a problem with the phrase *Industrial Revolution* itself. Because the discovery of how to extract large amounts of energy from coal was a key innovation of the revolution, we might just as easily use the term **Energy Revolution.** The sudden leap in the amount of energy made available by the steam engine and its successors had an impact on human lives as sweeping as did the discovery of agriculture and animal husbandry during the Neolithic Revolution, ten thousand years earlier. The **Neolithic Revolution** put so much portable, storable energy in the hands of agricultural societies that they pushed the older hunting-and-gathering cultures virtually off the face of the earth. After the Energy Revolution, industrial societies have been overwhelming agricultural civilizations in much the same way. The world is in turmoil in good measure because we are still grappling with the momentous transition from relatively modest levels of energy use to an energy-rich environment.

Yet the term *Energy Revolution* overlooks a second key development of the Industrial Revolution: the factory system. With its standardization, its routinized tasks, and its harsh discipline, the factory system became the worldwide norm for production. The factory served as a model for schools, jails, and hospitals, as well as the basis for identifying **social** classes, most notably "the working class." Until more than halfway through the twentieth century, factory chimneys and railroad locomotives, both of them belching clouds of smoke and steam, stood as the universal symbols of modernity and **progress.** William Bell Scott painted *Iron and Coal,* shown at the beginning of this chapter, about 1860. It is an idealized portrait of the bustling city of Newcastle and gives an idea of how positively the publicists of the Industrial Revolution felt about the changes taking place.

The factory and the steam engine, and their successors, transformed the way we live. The innovations of the early Industrial (or Energy) Revolution were the most fundamental technological changes that the world had seen since the beginning of the **Iron Age,** about 1200 B.C. In medieval Europe—still basically an Iron Age society—approximately 95 percent of the population worked the soil to provide the surplus on which the other 5 percent lived. In industrial societies today the proportions are almost exactly reversed. In North America, less than 2 percent of the population grows the food that Americans and Canadians eat, while more than 98 percent of the population survives through commerce, manufacturing, or services, usually in huge urban agglomerations. This shift, most of which has taken place over the last two hundred years, could come only through the application of massive amounts of energy to production. After almost three thousand years, the Iron Age had given way to what we can term the Industrial Age, or the Modern Age. That is why the global spread of industrialization is sometimes called **modernization,** for without it we cannot imagine modern life.

The Industrial Revolution also transformed social relationships. In agriculturally based societies, the landowning elites argued that their control over land justified their exclusive right to conduct public affairs and to receive deference from their social inferiors. Peasants and workers were willing to grant this respect, but in return they expected protection in hard times. Industrialization cut these threads of mutual obligation that tied agricultural societies together. **Middle-class** merchants and factory owners adopted an individualistic ethic based on the theories of classical economists such as Adam Smith, and workers came to see themselves as being in conflict with factory owners. Social relations became competitive, often conceived in terms of a struggle among antagonistic classes rather than as a relationship of obligation and deference.

Not only did it change the physical and social worlds, but the Industrial Revolution altered the focus of dreams as well. Early modern writers and philosophers looked back to classical models. The perfection of Athenian and Roman societies was to be remembered, admired, and emulated—but never again achieved. During the **Renaissance,** this notion began to change, and with the Scientific Revolution and the **Enlightenment** an optimistic sense of progress toward a better future emerged. The Industrial Revolution reinforced this tendency, opening up the hope that humans might suddenly have found the resources to solve the ancient problems of poverty and disharmony. Despite the urban blight, pollution, and discord that accompanied the Industrial Revolution, since its inception we have dreamed of the future as a place where perfection might lie. This sense of possibility and progress is perhaps what has distinguished modern Western civilization not only from other civilizations but from its earlier self. Human perfection may still elude us, but for the past two hundred years the hope that a better life hovers just over the horizon has invigorated us almost as much as the Energy Revolution itself.

WHY BRITAIN?

The Industrial Revolution was not inevitable, but it unfolded first in Great Britain for several good reasons. In the eighteenth century Britain was a rich country with capital resources at its disposal. Its political institutions, social relations, physical attributes, economic structure, legal system, and colonial successes all proved favorable to innovation.

A Favorable Political Climate

An open aristocracy based on property and **patronage** dominated eighteenth-century Britain. Entry into the British upper classes was relatively unrestricted, at least compared to the aristocracies on the Continent. It required one fundamental asset: landed property. If a man became rich through a fortunate marriage, by successfully practicing law, through trade, or from exemplary service to the king, he translated that wealth into a landed estate and entered the upper reaches of English society. To maintain his position he established a network of family, friends, and associates who mutually supported one another. Status was measured not only by property but by the number of "friends" whom a person could "oblige," and on whom one could call for appropriate reciprocal favors. In local affairs, the landowner felt a paternalistic obligation toward his **parish,** his village, and his tenants. In return he expected his social inferiors to show deference toward him. But the links of obligation of the most important families extended far beyond the local parish to political supporters and eventually to anyone who could provide service or help.

The British Parliament ran on an engine of patronage dispensed through these client networks. Fewer than two thousand prominent landowning families had access to Parliament, either directly or through family members or associates. They used that access to seek advantage for themselves, their families, and their friends, squabbling over government contracts or ways to improve their landholdings. Parliament's most characteristic gift to these landowners was permitting them to make **enclosures** of the common lands. Medieval and early modern manors and villages customarily set aside meadows and woodlands that all residents could use to graze their cattle or sheep and from which they could harvest hay and collect firewood. As the population grew, many marginal and poor peasants came to rely on the commons for basic sustenance. Gradually, however, local **gentry** succeeded in closing off some or all of this formerly community property with rows of hedges and fences, putting the poor peasants under great stress. The gentry needed parliamentary approval for enclosing such land for their own use, and because members of Parliament were all landowners themselves, they almost always granted their colleagues' petitions.

By the end of the seventeenth century, more than 70 percent of English land had been collected in farms of over 100 acres. In England, unlike many places on the Continent, land had always been bought and sold freely. As well-to-do owners consolidated their farms, they began to use their holdings as income-producing capital. Typically they rented their land to a tenant who employed workers and farmed for a profit. People dislocated from the **subsistence economy** by this process did not necessarily migrate to the cities, because enclosed estates often needed more farm workers than the commons had used. Indeed, during the eighteenth century the number of people working the land in Britain actually rose. But in these years the relationship among landlords, tenants, and workers increasingly became regulated by the laws of supply and demand. Landlords charged their tenants rents that the market would bear, and tenants took advantage of a surplus of local labor to drive down farm wages. France did not develop the same kind of capitalist relations in the countryside. There, where the king and the aristocracy competed for peasant resources, villagers often were able to obtain charters that guaranteed their traditional access to land and protected them from agricultural capitalists. Thus, even before the Industrial Revolution, British agricultural practices prepared the way for the transformation into **capitalism.**

Favoring landlords, Parliament also conducted a twofold policy that benefited commerce, although probably by default rather than by conscious design. The British government taxed its people heavily by the standards of the day. But it did so indirectly, through duties on imports and a wide variety of excise taxes, similar to today's taxes on cigarettes or gasoline. Local taxes aimed primarily to support the indigent. Tax revenues increased about four times as fast as economic growth during the Industrial Revolution. Nevertheless, because the size of the pie was increasing, and because everyone paid at least some taxes, the British people perceived the system as fair.

Parliament conducted a **mercantilist** policy of protecting traditional producers against innovation and competition from abroad. Nevertheless, it retained a strong belief in individualism, and its regulations were far less restrictive than those on the Continent. Investors and property owners had more or less a free hand to accumulate wealth. This was especially true because the local justices of the peace were precisely those landlords who wished to keep the government out of their business. Ironically, therefore, landlords' successful efforts to control their own affairs left commercial innovators free to build their fortunes.

If Parliament's **mercantilism** was relatively passive compared to that on the Continent, its policies abroad were correspondingly vigorous. Britain interfered—sometimes waging war—to protect its merchants and businessmen around the globe. During the eighteenth century, in fact, Great Britain was almost constantly embroiled in overseas conflict, although not always for reasons of trade. From Ireland to India and at many points in between, it established, protected, and expanded its colonial empire. Over these years, British commerce thus operated in the best of all possible worlds. At home the government remained passive toward business, unlike continental mercantilists, who regulated every aspect of production in an effort to control quality and maintain social harmony. Abroad, however, the government took an aggressive position. British traders could anticipate that their navy would protect them even in far-off ports.

The government that conducted these affairs, although well organized, was far from the centralized, mili-tarized state of a country like Prussia. On the Continent, where borders were difficult to defend, strong states arose protected by large standing armies. Continental monarchs drained their national resources by using these armies in dynastic struggles and in efforts to suppress locally based centers of power. By contrast, Britain concentrated its armed might in its navy. A navy has a number of political and economic advantages over an army. It fights far from home, so that its officers do not present the same political danger as army officers sometimes do. It is useful in protecting colonial trade, whereas an army is not. Finally, its troops do not trample valuable farmland and crops on local campaigns. Even the limited standing army that Britain did possess in the eighteenth century fought on the Continent, in North America, in India, and in Ireland, but not (except for an occasional Scottish rebellion) in Britain itself.

If the navy supported British trade by fighting abroad, its procurement of ships, weapons, and supplies stimulated the economy at home as well. Naval construction was the cutting edge of eighteenth-century technology, especially in armaments. Coastal towns traditionally supported the navy, because in less developed economies they benefited most from defense and commerce. But during the eighteenth century, the state took on more and more of the burden of paying for the navy, in part because naval procurement offered wonderful opportunities for graft and contracts to members of Parliament. More important, the navy stimulated the economy, especially in metals, because of the large amounts of money involved and the high level of technological skill required to build a major fighting ship. Investments in naval goods rippled through the economy. By these means, the British often turned potentially destructive wars abroad into growth at home.

Material and Human Resources

Two other sources of British wealth were its large and easily accessible coal and iron deposits, and its highly developed transportation network. Coal is very heavy, but England's island status made it relatively easy to ship along the coast and then inland by means of the country's extensive river system. During the eighteenth century a surge of canal building linked up many of the rivers and made shipping even easier (see Map 20-1). Road building expanded as well. When the innovations of the Industrial Revolution appeared, Britain already possessed a comprehensive network of internal transportation.

Compared with continental countries, Britain enjoyed relatively widespread prosperity. Because the British monarchs usually had been content to tax commerce rather than to participate in it directly, the wealth produced by the sugar islands in the Caribbean, the slave trade, and the extensive trade with North America and India found its way into a broad spectrum of private hands. The breadth of England's wealth continually astonished visitors. In the 1720s, one Dutch immigrant marveled that

MAP 20-1
ENGLAND'S RIVERS AND CANALS, 1840s

England "produces of itself all that can really conduce either to the Necessities and Convenience or the Pleasures and Satisfaction of Life." A Swiss tourist in 1790 remarked that "although the English labourer is better clothed, better fed and better lodged than the French, he does not work so hard."

England remained prosperous even though the population of England and Wales jumped from about 5 million in 1700 to almost 18 million by 1850. The Agricultural Revolution (see Chapter 19) made it possible to sustain this growing population. Britain still experienced poverty, injustice, and indifference, but in the eighteenth century it succeeded in feeding its growing numbers and enlarging its nascent middle class.

In sum, then, eighteenth-century Great Britain possessed unique characteristics that made it fertile ground for the Industrial Revolution. Its stable government was well attuned to commercial interests, both home and abroad, and an expanding colonial empire provided markets and raw materials. The Agricultural Revolution supported a rapidly growing population, many of whom constituted a potentially mobile labor force. Britain was blessed with rich stores of coal and iron ore, had developed a widespread system of river and canal transportation, and had a large, unrestricted internal market. A prosperous class of successful merchants and tradesmen assumed increasing importance. These advantages did not cause the Industrial

Revolution to take place in Britain, but they did provide a solid basis for its birth.

LAUNCHING THE INDUSTRIAL REVOLUTION

The steam engine and the cotton mill were such dramatically different technologies that even contemporaries considered them special. Looking back on the eighteenth and early nineteenth centuries today, however, one is impressed with the breadth of technological and social change. The Industrial Revolution taken as a whole consists of a slow but steady accumulation of thousands of innovations produced by the skill, industriousness, and inventiveness of British artisans. Innovations occurred in scores of specialties and varied considerably in their impact from region to region and from group to group. Some historians have even argued how unrevolutionary the process was, since it took place so gradually in so many crafts with such mixed results. Nevertheless, if we compare the way people in industrialized countries live today with how they lived three hundred years ago, it is clear that something momentous happened in the interim. In stressing the innovations in textiles and the invention of the steam engine, we try to capture a few key changes that cast long shadows down the future rather than the continuities that accompanied them.

The Advent of Cotton

Wool has always been a British speciality. In the twelfth and thirteenth centuries, England supplied this essential fiber to the weavers of Flanders (modern-day Belgium). In the sixteenth century, when sheep probably outnumbered people in England, statesman and writer Thomas More quipped that the sheep were eating the people rather than vice versa. (He meant that so many landowners were enclosing the commons to raise sheep that the poor peasants were becoming destitute.) By the eighteenth century, the so-called **putting-out system** of woolen production had become highly developed. Local factors, as the entrepreneurs were called, gathered raw materials or semifinished products such as thread or newly woven fabrics and supplied them to individual craftsmen, who performed specialized tasks such as spinning, weaving, fulling, and shearing.[1] The factors gathered up the finished products and sold them at a centralized market, such as the Cloth Hall in London.

This system of manufacturing goods is often called **proto-industrialization.** Although it was more highly

---

[1] *Fulling* is the process whereby woven material is cleaned of its grease, dried, stretched, and roughed up to raise the nap, which the shearer trims off to produce a smooth surface on the finished cloth. Water-driven triphammers had been employed in the cleaning stage of fulling since medieval times. See Chapter 11.

organized than subsistence farming and craftwork, and although it had links to distant markets, proto-industrialism had not yet made the transition to factory production. This did not preclude large operations. As early as 1736, for example, one textile enterprise had three thousand weavers working six hundred looms. Around 1750 a large sailcloth maker employed five thousand persons. But this was not typical. Usually proto-industrial artisans plied their individual specialties at home, where tasks often were differentiated by gender. Typically women would do the spinning (sometimes they were called spinsters), and men would do the weaving. Women bleached; men did fulling and shearing. Children also participated, helping their parents with the routine tasks of preparation and cleanup.

Mechanization came to the woolen trade, and even to the silk industry, before it came to cotton. The technology of linen and fustian production had been advancing incrementally since the Middle Ages and it continued to do so in the eighteenth century.[2] But it was in cotton that a series of ingenious innovations launched the Industrial Revolution proper. Cotton offers many advantages over wool. It is a tough and homogeneous fiber that lends itself to working by machine better than wool. Cotton produces a cloth that is washable and easily dyed, but at the same time durable. And cotton is comfortable. Until cotton became common, most people did not wear undergarments. Only the very rich could afford the soft, silk underwear of the aristocracy. Everyone else wore hot, scratchy woolen clothing with little or nothing underneath. The supply of cotton fiber was also readily expandable. When demand increased, farmers just planted more cotton, whereas the supply of wool depended on the time-consuming breeding cycle of sheep.

The fact that advances in textile production occurred in cotton suggests how important it is to place the Industrial Revolution in the context of larger developments. Cotton does not grow in Britain's cool, damp climate. Therefore a cotton textile industry was not possible on any scale until the development of Atlantic and world trade. Indeed, the first known cotton production facility in England dates only from about 1630. The British originally colonized India for its spices and the West Indies for their sugar, cocoa, and tobacco. By the eighteenth century, both regions were supplying English mills with large quantities of raw cotton (see Figure 20-1). The American South became a major supplier only after 1798, when Eli Whitney invented the cotton gin, a machine that removed the pesky seeds from the raw cotton that grows inland in North America.

Spinning and weaving are the two most basic operations that go into producing a piece of cloth (see Chapter 11). First the raw material—cotton, wool, silk, or linen—is

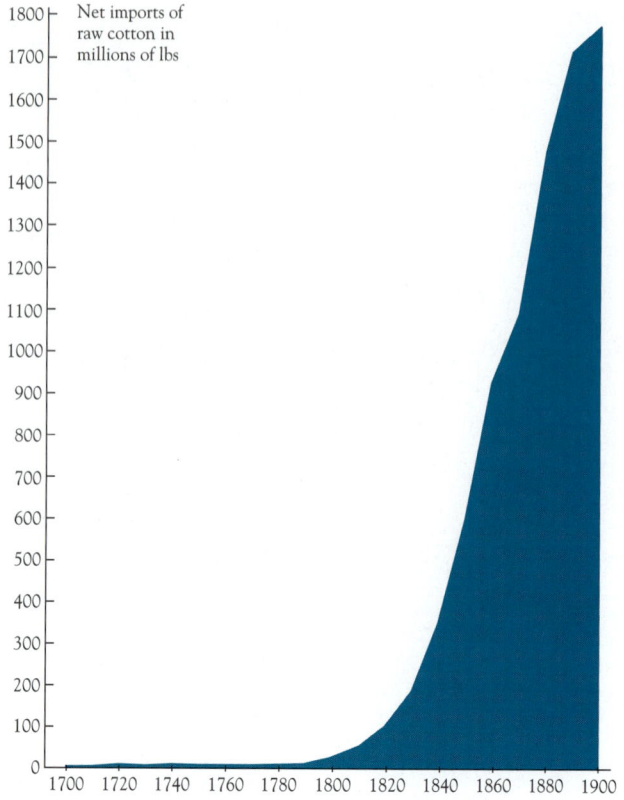

FIGURE 20-1

GROWTH OF IMPORTATION OF RAW COTTON, 1700–1899

The Industrial Revolution in textiles was highly dependent upon the import of cotton. Compare the steep rise in imported raw cotton with the equally steep rise in the number of power looms as shown in Figure 20-2, p. 722.

stripped of its seeds and other foreign matter, cleaned, combed out (or carded), and spun into thread. Then the threads are woven into a piece of material, which goes through a variety of finishing processes before becoming marketable cloth. The spinning process involves taking a clump of wool or raw cotton and pulling it out with one's fingers while turning it, so that a thin strand of twisted material results. The spinning wheel, which was invented before 1500, helps the spinner to pull and twist the thread evenly. The threads thus produced are woven together on a loom, a device that lets the weaver intertwine the threads into a piece of cloth. First the weaver arranges threads on a frame in such a way that every other thread going in one direction can be lifted in alternate actions of the mechanism. This creates a V-shaped gap (the shed) through which the weaver passes a thread attached to a piece of wood called a shuttle. The weaver then moves the loom so that the lower threads move upward and the upper threads downward, capturing the crosswise thread and setting up a new gap, through which he passes the shuttle again, and so on. Bit by bit, the cloth is created.

---

[2] *Fustian* is a coarse fabric made of cotton and flax.

Spinning During the Middle Ages thread was made by drawing carded wool from a distaff, held in the right hand, and spinning the strands with the left hand onto a spindle. This work became easier from the thirteenth century onwards with the invention of the spinning wheel (shown above). *Mary Evans Picture Library.*

In this process, the most time-consuming work was spinning. It took from three to five spinners to provide enough threads to occupy one weaver. Clearly, if someone could find a way to spin thread faster, production could grow. Unsuccessful spinning machines first appeared in the 1730s, and in 1761 the Royal Society offered a reward for the best invention capable of spinning six threads at once. In 1764 James Hargreaves, independently of the Royal Society's offer, made the device that finally performed this feat: the spinning jenny.[3] The hand-operated jenny could spin many more than six threads, and because of the precision of its mechanism it produced more uniform work than hand spinners. Only a few years later, in 1769, Richard Arkwright rigged a spinning jenny to a water mill, and within ten years Samuel Crompton had yoked several jennies to one large water mill. Thread production increased enormously.

---

[3] The term *jenny* comes from the female name Jane, for which Jenny is a nickname, such as Jack is for John. The machine was thought of as a kind of superwoman, able to spin many threads at once.

Weaving Cloth is constructed by interweaving threads, usually at 90 degrees to one another. The loom permits the weaver to raise up half the threads at each pass of the shuttle. The weaver then resets the loom with the treadle, raising the other half of the lengthwise threads, and passing the shuttle through the shed again, as this weaver is shown doing with his right hand. Doing this repeatedly slowly builds up a piece of cloth. *B. T. Batsford, Ltd., London.*

The Improved Spinning Jenny Hand-driven spinning jennies like this one vastly increased the amount of thread being produced and had the immediate effect of increasing the demand for weavers. *The Granger Collection.*

The logical next step—mechanizing weaving—was difficult because of the tension applied to the warp (lengthwise) threads and the abrasion that resulted as the weft (crosswise) threads passed through the shed. In 1733 John Kay invented a simple frame that permitted the weaver to flick the shuttle through the gap. Despite this invention—dubbed the flying shuttle—the technical problems were so difficult that not until the end of the century did inventors devise workable mechanized looms. Even then, these machines were inefficient. Power looms became practical only in the first quarter of the nineteenth century, when inventors found ways to apply water power and then steam power to the weaving process. At this point textile production—both woolen and cotton—exploded. Only a few dozen power looms existed in 1800, but by 1833 one hundred thousand such looms were humming away in Britain (see Figure 20-2). The value of cotton manufactured goods climbed from just over £5 million in 1800 to £40 million in 1833. And this was just the beginning.

The inventors of these and hundreds of other technical improvements often came from humble backgrounds. Richard Arkwright started as a barber and wig maker; Samuel Crompton was a weaver; and James Hargreaves was a carpenter and weaver. Some of them made fortunes, but almost all of them experienced various disasters. Rioters burned Arkwright's new mill at Chorley to the ground in 1779, although he recovered to become wealthy. Crompton, on the other hand, grew so frustrated with competitors trying to steal his invention that he gave it away and ended his life dependent on the fund-raising efforts of friends. A mob of fearful spinners destroyed Hargreaves's house, and he proved unable to protect his patent for the spinning jenny in court.

But the aggressive entrepreneur had many reasons to try cotton. Ingenious artisans continually improved on the early technology—and for those who could not, the unscrupulous could always steal someone else's innovation.

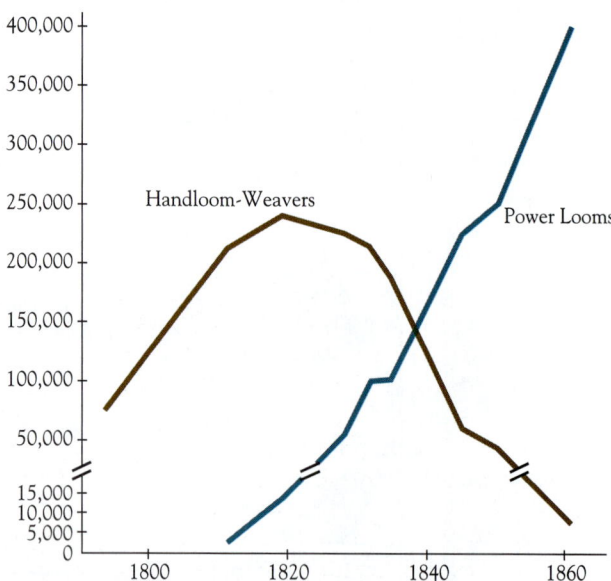

FIGURE 20-2

POWER LOOMS AND HANDLOOM WEAVERS IN THE BRITISH COTTON INDUSTRY, 1795–1861

Using steam to power spinning machines initially increased the need for hand weavers, but when power looms became common after about 1830, the hand weavers were doomed.

Source: Data from François Crouzet, The Victorian Economy *(New York: Columbia University Press, 1982), p. 199.*

Industrial espionage is not only a twentieth-century phenomenon. Labor was cheap and the equipment itself was relatively inexpensive. Poor people could not afford to establish mills, of course, but hundreds of well-to-do families managed to find the capital. Indeed, in these early days of industrialization, the main source of capital was private—individual families, not banks or the state, provided the start-up money for these enterprises. Britain's colonial successes had created much of that wealth, and it also ensured both a supply of raw cotton and a limitless market. Social costs, such as environmental protection and worker benefits, were almost nil. With cheap entry, inexpensive labor and raw materials, available private capital, a huge potential market, high profits, and little governmental interference, it is no wonder that cotton-cloth making was booming in Britain by the end of the eighteenth century.

The Energy Revolution in Steam

Water power, and even air power (in the form of windmills), had been used since the Middle Ages throughout Europe. Employing water mills to run cotton spinning machines, as well as fulling machines in the woolen industry and throwing machines in silk production, was a natural extension of that technology. But water power had serious limitations. The mills had to be near streams or rivers, which often required placing them in remote areas where the supply of workers was limited. The invention of the steam engine, which freed the factory from geographical limitations, provided the breakthrough that made the industrial age different in kind from the eras in which water mills, windmills, and sails were the main supplements to muscle power.

The steam engine emerged primarily in response to a serious fuel shortage. Like all agricultural societies, medieval people in Britain traditionally had used wood for heating and small-scale manufacturing, such as brewing and porcelain making. But by the sixteenth century Britain was running out of forests. To meet the shortage of wood, people turned increasingly to coal. Fortunately, coal was abundant in England, some of it very close to the earth's surface. By 1700, however, the most easily accessible coal was gone and Britain faced an energy crisis. When mines were sunk ever deeper into the earth in search of more coal, the shafts began penetrating the water table. Early efforts to control the resultant flooding sometimes used as many as five hundred horses pulling cables strung with buckets. Even this enormous effort could not contain large flows of water.

In 1698 Thomas Savery, a military engineer from a mining district in Devon, invented the "fire engine" pump in an effort to surmount the flooding problem. This grossly inefficient device relied on the principle that steam enclosed in a container will condense when cooled. If this cooling happens suddenly, a partial vacuum will result in the container. Savery boiled water by burning coal under a boiler and let some of the steam into a container con-

nected to the flooded mine. When he dashed the container with cold water, the steam inside condensed and pressure within the container fell. As a result, outside air pressure pushed water up the line and into the container. By a simple system of valves, Savery then introduced steam into the container under pressure, thus forcing the water up and out a pipe. "Raising water by fire," as people called it at the time, worked, but very badly. For one thing, the engine had to be no more than 20 feet above the water level for the atmospheric pressure to be effective. For another, the metal-fabricating techniques of Savery's day were not precise enough to contain steam under much pressure and this limited the vertical lift of the device. The Savery engine was only about one-twentieth as efficient as horses or men, but it had one fundamental advantage: It ran on coal, not horses. That is, it transformed the potential energy of coal into useful work.

In 1712 Thomas Newcomen, a talented blacksmith also from Devon, vastly improved on Savery's design. Newcomen added a piston. Now when the steam condensed in the cylindrical container, it did not pull up the water directly. Rather, the vacuum created by the condensation permitted atmospheric pressure to push a piston down. The weight of the pump apparatus then restored the piston to its original position. These alternating forces moved the piston up and down. This motion was transferred mechanically to a pump, the principles of which were well known, and water was evacuated nicely from the mine.

Newcomen's ingenious engine found quick, if limited, use. By 1734 perhaps sixty of them were at work in Britain, and a few even found their way to the Continent. Everyone who encountered the new device pronounced it wondrous. As the Reverend John Dalton gushed in 1755:

> Sagacious Savery![4] Taught by thee
> Discordant elements agree,
> Fire, water, air, heat, cold unite,
> And listed in one service fight,
> Pure streams to thirsty cities send,
> Or deepest mines from floods defend.
> Man's richest gift thy work will shine;
> Rome's aqueducts were poor to thine!

But the Newcomen engine had one serious flaw. The alternate heating and cooling of the cylinder into which the steam was admitted wasted considerable energy. Not until sixty-five years later did James Watt find a solution: Watt separated the cooling cylinder (the condenser) from the main cylinder. Watt's invention depended in part on insights derived from the Scientific Revolution, such as the measurement of atmospheric pressure and the concept of

---

[4] Newcomen worked with Savery, so that despite the fundamental improvements Newcomen made, Savery's name remained attached to the new device.

THE HUMAN EXPERIENCE

James Watt, Eighteenth-Century Engineer

James Watt (1736–1819), acknowledged by his contemporaries as the greatest engineer and inventor of the eighteenth century, was born in a small seaport in Scotland, the fourth of five children, three of whom died in infancy. He was a precocious child, although he did not do well in school, and when his father's carpentry business began to fail and his mother died, he managed through friends of his mother to obtain a one-year apprenticeship to a maker of scientific instruments in London. After a year of grueling training (he worked until nine every night, except Saturday, and often went hungry), Watt returned at the age of twenty-one to Glasgow. That city boasted one of the best universities in the British Isles. (Adam Smith was a professor there.) By good luck and skill, Watt soon became a mathematical instrument maker for the university. He proved so successful at this job that he was able to set himself up in private business and became renowned around Glasgow as a man who could build or fix anything.

In 1763 Watt was asked to overhaul the university's small working model of a Newcomen engine. When he failed to get it to work immediately, Watt began investigating the engine's properties and those of steam in general. In particular, he wondered why the Newcomen engine wasted so much of the steam's latent energy. Watt was thoroughly familiar with the scientific investigations into the properties of steam going on at Glasgow, and after some practical research of his own, he realized that heating and cooling the same cylinder was enormously inefficient. "I then saw," he recalled later, "that I must get quit of the condensed stream and injection water. . . . I had not walked further than the Golf House when the whole thing was arranged in my mind."

Having concluded that he needed to add a separate condenser, Watt found a sponsor in John Roebuck, owner of a local ironworks. In return for backing Watt in his experiments toward constructing a working steam engine, this eighteenth-century venture capitalist was to receive two-thirds of any profits. But almost as soon as the work had started, Roebuck began to fail financially. Watt, faced with the necessity of earning a living, found it increasingly difficult to keep working on the engine.

In 1774, however, Matthew Boulton, a wealthy, Birmingham manufacturer of iron products, took over Roebuck's interest in the steam engine in payment for his debts. Roebuck's other creditors did not object. As Watt put it, none of them "value the engine at a farthing." But Boulton had great confidence in the future of the steam engine and in Watt. He established Watt in a shop in Birmingham and paid him a stipend so that he could work exclusively on building a commercially viable engine. Watt achieved this goal almost immediately. Boulton and Watt were on their way not only to enormous commercial success but to transforming energy production across the world. ❖

latent heat. As instrument maker for the university in Glasgow, Watt was familiar with this work, but he was primarily a craftsman, not a scientist. He became the most famous of a new breed of specialist that combined science and craftsmanship: the engineer.

In Watt's machine, steam entered both the cylinder and a second container connected by a pipe. This second container, the condenser, remained cool. Steam entering it condensed immediately, and pressure dropped, thus operating the piston. Because the main cylinder stayed hot, Watt's engine was twice as efficient as the Newcomen engine. It used half as much coal for the same output and quickly became the standard for all steam engines. Watt made many improvements to his engine. He introduced steam at both ends of the cylinder, so that the piston became double-acting. Once the piston was exerting power in both directions, instead of only one, he found a way through the sun-and-planet gear mechanism to translate the up-and-down motion of the piston to the circular motion necessary to run machinery. He produced a fly-ball governor that used the principle of feedback to regulate the speed of the engine. If the engine rotated too rapidly, a weighted set of balls flew away from the flywheel, causing levers to close the steam valve.

Watt's engines worked well, but they were huge, suitable mainly for large industrial enterprises. Around 1800 inventors in both Great Britain and North America introduced the high-pressure engine. It dispensed with the condenser and abandoned the principle of producing pressure differentials by condensation. The new engine introduced steam under pressure, thus pushing the piston instead of drawing it with a vacuum. When a system of valves admitted steam under pressure at the proper moment at alternate ends of a cylinder, an enormous amount of power could be generated by an engine much smaller than the massive Watt engines.

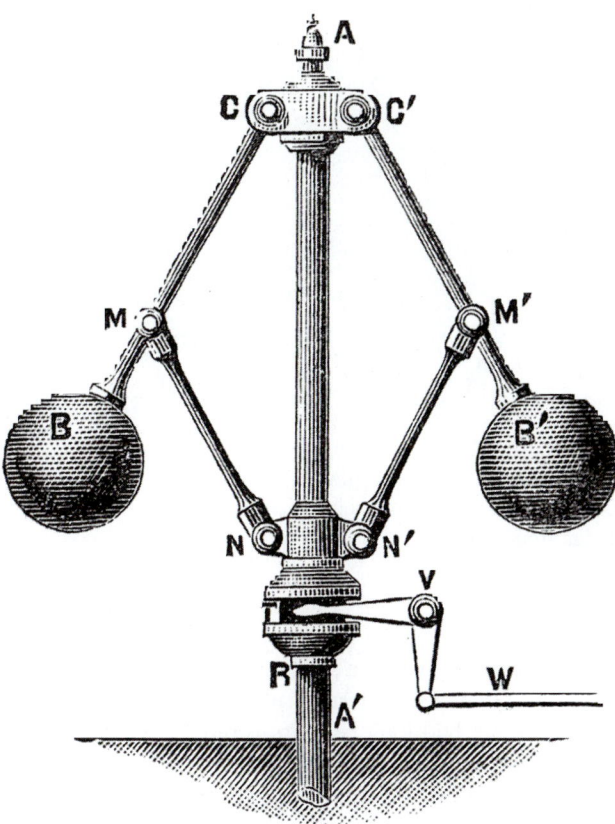

The Fly-Ball Governor A key improvement to the steam engine came with the invention of the fly-ball governor in 1787. As the speed of the rotation of a flywheel increased, centrifugal force pushed the balls out, thus pulling the mechanism down and closing the steam valve. The device could be adjusted to keep the engine running at a constant speed. The principle of feedback used here later proved fundamental in the invention of computers. *Mary Evans Picture Library.*

Steam engines powered only a minuscule part of the British economy in 1800, but their long-term impact was momentous. Watt's inventions, and those of his successors, transformed the steam engine from a water pump with limited applicability into a power source for an almost unlimited number of machines. In the course of the next hundred years, steam came to dominate the industries of Europe, making factories, railroads, and steamships possible. This vast new source of energy encouraged inventors to develop even more powerful energy-producing technologies, such as the internal combustion gasoline engine and commercial electricity.[5] Today, few steam engines remain at work, but their heirs generate the power without which our modern society would be unimaginable.

---

[5] The steam engine is an external combustion engine, because the heat is not generated inside the cylinder itself.

Iron and Chemicals: The Revolution Broadens

The innovations in textiles and in steam engines were inseparable from an enormous number of related discoveries and inventions. The precise tolerances that steam engines required, for example, depended on dramatic improvements in metals technology. Newcomen's early engines were made of expensive brass or bronze, because ironworking technology could not withstand the hot, pressurized containers of steam engines. Early Iron Age technology had involved smelting the ore in a simple charcoal pit in the ground (see Chapter 1). By Roman times, smelting evolved into stacking iron ore, limestone, and charcoal in a funnel shape about 30 feet high, setting the mound afire, blowing air through the burning mass with a bellows in order to reach the high heat required, and then removing a lump of iron (the "bloom") after the whole thing had cooled off. The bloom then had to be reheated, rolled, and hammered to remove some of the impurities, producing wrought iron. By the eighteenth century, iron makers had progressed to drawing off the molten product into small containers (called *pigs*, because they reminded people still close to the countryside of suckling piglets). This pig iron, also called cast iron, was then broken up into small pieces and roasted with an oxidizer such as iron oxide. The oxidizer combined with the carbon as carbon dioxide and left pure, or wrought, iron.

Coal was not used to fuel this process because it contains sulfur and other impurities that ruin iron. Early in the eighteenth century, the Darby ironworks at Coalbrookdale near Birmingham discovered that the coal of their region could be coked, or purified, by burning it in an oxygen-starved atmosphere. Coke burns hotter than charcoal and, given the shortage of wood, was both cheaper and more readily available than charcoal. In 1784 Henry Cort patented a process of purifying pig iron using coke and a new method of blowing large amounts of oxygen through the molten metal. When steam engines were harnessed to the bellows used in the Cort process, to the rolling mills that processed the iron, and to the forge hammers that shaped it, iron production took off.

The increased availability of affordable iron led inventors to use iron instead of wood to make windmill shafts and other structures; the first cast iron bridge appeared at Coalbrookdale in 1779. The greater precision that these new uses demanded prompted improvements in machine tools, such as cutting machines and lathes. By 1775 John Wilkinson's foundry could bore a cylinder with an accuracy of 0.001 inch per inch of cylinder diameter, a wholly new level of precision without which Watt's engine would have been impossible.

Advances in chemistry proved a particular boon to the textile industry. Traditionally, urine had been used to cut the natural grease that permeates raw wool, and the traditional method of bleaching fabrics had required soaking them in buttermilk and laying them out on bleaching fields in the sun. Because the process was repeated many times, whitening fine linens might take as long as six months. The discovery of an efficient technique for extracting chlorine in 1774 and recognition of its bleaching and degreasing powers by 1785 greatly enhanced the British capacity to make fine cloth.

Plentiful chlorine was not the only chemical bounty of the eighteenth century. The traditional sources of alkalies, needed to make glass, soap, and saltpeter (for gunpowder), were wood ash and potash. The first was expensive to produce in large quantities, and the second was not extensively mined in the eighteenth century. In the 1780s, the discovery of an inexpensive way to produce soda from salt dramatically lowered the cost of that alkali. Sulfuric acid, known then as oil of vitriol, also had proven difficult to produce. In 1700 this basic industrial product cost about two shillings an ounce. When in 1746 inventors found a way to make it in large quantities, the price plummeted. By 1800 it cost only half a shilling a pound.

Cotton production and the steam engine were the most significant inventions of the Industrial Revolution, but the changes in ironworking and in chemistry played a major role too, inspiring a sense of progress among industrial innovators.

The Birth of the Railroads

The inventions of the eighteenth century culminated in the railroad. The high-pressure reciprocating steam engine reduced the size of cylinders so radically from the 6-foot

Early Railcar, 1826 Very often when a new technology appears, users continue to think in old terms for some time. Early railcars, like this one, clearly derived their inappropriate design from earlier forms of transportation. *Mansell Collection & Time, Inc.*

bores common in Watt's engines that inventors realized almost immediately that a steam engine could drive a ship, or maybe a cart of some kind. Rail carts hauled by horses or human beings had long been in use in mines, so it was a short leap to placing a steam engine on a carriage and running it down a line. Inventors tried using steam engines on all sorts of conveyances, and by 1802 a steam-powered tug was already working the Forth and Clyde Canal in Scotland. The first steam locomotive followed in 1804.

Building a railroad necessitated a different approach than starting a textile mill. It demanded high investment, was risky, and paid off slowly—which made railroads

A View in the Whitechapel Road, 1831 Almost as soon as the steam engine became useful for locomotion, city dwellers feared the pollution that would result. In 1828, G. Cruikshank predicted what the streets of London would look like three years later. His vehicles were not very realistic, but over time the smoke proved all too accurate. *British Museum Print Room.*

Malvern Hill, Warwickshire, 1809 Huge country homes set in spacious lawns and gardens were the peak of social desirability for the wealthy in Britain, whether their riches derived from old land holdings or new entrepreneurial success. *The British Library.*

difficult to finance through personal fortunes, as textiles had been. In countries that developed later, investment capital was usually scarce, but England's position as the first industrializing country allowed it to grow rich before competition could arise. As industrialization proceeded, Britain's banking system grew increasingly sophisticated. The Bank of England issued large amounts of sound government bonds with ease, even during the expensive Napoleonic wars (see Chapter 22). Economic demands in those years also promoted a rapid growth of local banking, so that when railroad building became technically possible the financial infrastructure that could provide the necessary capital was in place.

By the 1820s, British entrepreneurs had huge profits on their hands. In traditional societies, the rich often spend their money in ostentation and conspicuous consumption. As a visit to the great English country mansions would reveal, not a few Englishmen spent their money extravagantly. But if entrepreneurs are to accumulate wealth, they must reinvest their profits, not spend them, and this is what many British industrialists did. Because early nineteenth-century Britain enjoyed only a relatively limited array of investment opportunities, capitalists with surpluses had few places to put their money. They fell for all sorts of schemes, such as spending heavily on the Greek Revolution of 1821 (see Chapter 22). Some of them, searching for a surer way to turn a pound, began to build and invest in railroads, even economically unwise ones.

The first commercially successful railroads were built in the 1820s, but the real boom came in the 1830s and 1840s,

when speculators and construction gangs laid down more than 6,000 miles of track, forming the basis of the British rail system. At its peak, this tremendous effort employed some 200,000 persons, stimulated a 40 percent expansion in mining and metallurgy industries, and absorbed an incredible £200 million of investment. This was industrialism on a scale beyond eighteenth-century imagination. By 1850 the railroads made Great Britain not just wealthy but strong. The first and therefore unique industrializing country, Britain opened a new era of human possibility.

The Climax: The Crystal Palace Exhibition

The climax of the Industrial Revolution came in 1851, at the Great Exhibition of the Works of Industry of All Nations held in Hyde Park, London. From its first stirrings, industrialization had evoked the awe of those who grasped its significance. In 1814 urban reformer Patrick Colquhoun wrote:

> It is impossible to contemplate the progress of manufactures in Great Britain within the last thirty years without wonder and astonishment. Its rapidity . . . exceeds all credibility. The improvement in steam engines, but above all the facilities afforded to the great branches of the woolen and cotton manufactories by ingenious machinery, invigorated by capital and skill, are beyond all calculation.

By the 1840s, this awe had spread widely. Late in that decade, the Royal Society of the Arts, with the support of the young Queen Victoria's husband, Prince Albert,

Interior of the Crystal Palace, 1851   The Crystal Palace in London pioneered modular architecture, which characterized modernism a good fifty years before that movement emerged. The structure burned in 1936, and the remnants were finally taken down during World War II so that German bombers could not use them as a landmark.

decided to hold an exhibition of modern technology, the first world's fair. The exhibition opened on May 1, 1851, and displayed thousands of objects from around the world, including an impressive 2-ton piece of cast steel from the Krupp foundry in Germany. The most famous exhibit was the building itself, the Crystal Palace. The original plans for the hall specified a brick building topped by a huge, cast iron dome. Public dissatisfaction with the design, however, led Joseph Paxton, the inventive superintendent of gardens for the Duke of Devonshire, to propose an entirely different kind of structure loosely modeled on the idea of a greenhouse. Paxton's building consisted of a prefabricated framework of 3,300 cast iron columns supported by 2,224 principal girders, onto which were fitted 900,000 square feet of sheet glass panes (which would have constituted one-third of English glass production in 1840). Thanks to standardized parts, a simple design, and clever engineering, Paxton was able to erect the enormous building—it covered 19 acres—in only thirty-nine weeks from the signing of the contract. Contemporaries were dazzled. Novelist William Makepeace Thackeray called it "a palace for a fairy prince," and a German visitor declared, "We cannot tell if this structure towers a hundred or a thousand

feet above us. . . . All materiality is blended into the atmosphere." Today architects admire the Crystal Palace for its functional characteristics, which prefigured **modernist** architecture and twentieth-century skyscraper construction techniques.

The rhetoric surrounding the opening of the Crystal Palace Exhibition suggests how broadly the Industrial Revolution expanded human dreams. As the *Economist* put it in 1851:

> Too many of us are disposed to place our Golden Age in the past. . . . Nearly everybody agrees by common consent to undervalue and abuse the present. We confess that we can not share their disappointment, nor echo their complaints. We look upon the past with respect and affection as a series of stepping-stones to that high and advanced position which we actually hold, and from the Future we hope for the realization of those dreams almost of perfectibility, which a comparison of the Past with the Present entitles us to indulge in.

"Gentlemen," rhapsodized Prince Albert, "the Exhibition of 1851 is to give us a true test and a living picture of the point of development at which the whole of mankind has arrived in this great task, and a new starting point from which all nations will be able to direct their further exertions." The *Economist* concluded: "All who have read, and can think, must now have full confidence that the 'endless progression,' ever increasing in rapidity, of which the poet sang, is the destined lot of the human race."

THE IMPACT OF INDUSTRY

From the success of the Crystal Palace Exhibition and the acceleration of technological change described in the preceding section, we might conclude that Britain suddenly changed into a thriving industrial landscape. But this was not so. Although techniques had improved almost across the board in the eighteenth century, most work was still done by hand. About 240,000 handloom cotton weavers remained in England in 1820, about twice as many as the number of factory workers in cotton at that time. In some crafts, industrialization even led to an *expansion* of hand

work during the first half of the nineteenth century. In Sheffield, for example, the number of cutlers and file makers, all small-scale artisans, climbed from six thousand to fifty thousand. Among garment makers, who used the vast amounts of textiles pouring out of the mills, shops employing fewer than ten workers remained the norm. There were about 750,000 English men and women engaged in making clothing and shoes by hand in 1851, including seamstresses, milliners, tailors, and shoemakers.

The Clash of Regions

The vigor of these trades suggests that industrial development varied among regions, as it did among segments of the population. Iron and coal production tended to concentrate in places where nature had conveniently placed those two minerals close together, such as the northeast area of the River Tyne near Newcastle, in Wales, and in the West Midlands near Birmingham (see Map 20-2). The

MAP 20-2
ENGLISH INDUSTRIALIZATION

latter city achieved renown particularly for the production of metal products, including nails, tools, brassware, enameled and plated goods, buttons, buckles, and, most important, guns. Birmingham became a bustling example of capitalism's variety and interdependence.

Textiles flourished as the main industry in the northern areas, with Yorkshire most noted for its woolens and Lancashire for cotton.[6] In Yorkshire, relatively independent yeoman farmers had developed a strong putting-out system that employed many small producers. In the long run, textile mills threatened this proto-industry, but for a time the early mills actually spurred its expansion. Benjamin Gott's woolen mill in Leeds, for example, founded in 1792, used a Watt steam engine for carding and fulling, yet Gott hired both factory and domestic workers to run jennies and looms by hand. Indeed, the growth in spinning capacity that power-operated jennies made possible initially led to an increase in the number of weavers. Only in the 1820s did their numbers start to decline with the introduction of steam-driven power looms, although their wages had begun to fall already in the 1790s.

Lancashire excelled in cotton-cloth production, as well as other economic activities. In Manchester, the region's main city, investors sank more money into warehouses and taverns than into cotton factories. Nevertheless, in the early 1830s Manchester boasted seven cotton mills employing more than a thousand workers, thirty mills with more than five hundred, and forty-six employing over two hundred workers. No wonder it was called the "cottonopolis" of England.

As these regions changed and grew, others declined. Kent, southwest of London, had served as a center of early modern industry. But owing to its closeness to London, and perhaps to its strong ties to the Anglican church, its merchants tended to involve themselves in projects of national scope rather than of local interest. As a result, the region failed to make the transition from proto-industry to modern industrialization. Instead of gravitating toward the industrializing sectors, farmworkers there were forced to subsist on seasonal employment and support from their parishes through what were termed the "poor laws." In general, the Industrial Revolution benefited areas close to iron and coal resources, regions that turned to cotton production, and cities that generated varied local economies. Regions far from natural resources, those in which proto-industries failed to adapt, and most rural areas suffered decline. Another factor appears to be religious affiliation. A significant number of successful industrialists were Dissenters (that is, those not willing to swear allegiance to the official Anglican church). Excluded from politics, tradi-

tional economies, and the universities, Dissenters seemed to take to business more readily than Anglicans, much in the manner of other excluded groups, such as the Jews and Russia's Old Believers.

Workers' New Lives

Two questions have long challenged analysts of the Industrial Revolution: How beneficial was it to workers, and how did it affect economic growth? No one disputes that the British economy grew rapidly in the second half of the nineteenth century and that **real wages** rose during that time. But the picture in the early years is much more murky. A generation ago, critics of capitalism argued that real wages actually declined during the Industrial Revolution; recently a more optimistic school of historians has held that a modest increase took place. A definitive answer is probably not possible, owing to the scarcity of hard data, the variety of work conditions included in the statistics that do exist, the extreme difficulty in pinning down just what constitutes worker satisfaction (is it only wages, or does it include work conditions, job satisfaction, or family situation?), and the political implications of one's position (the left emphasizes workers' difficulties; the right emphasizes production efficiencies).

What is certain is that the transfer of work out of the home and into factories profoundly altered laborers' lives. Domestic work, which characterized agricultural society and proto-industrialism, was a family affair. In the idealized artisan household, all members of the family worked under the supervision of the father. Children, considered an economic asset by families, performed light labor from the time they were five or six years old. Wives not only managed the household but produced income. All income went toward the family's collective use. By the time children became teenagers, they were full-time workers, often trained in the skills possessed by their parents. Even if they held jobs outside the household as day laborers or servants, they were expected to contribute to the family welfare. It was not until the twentieth century that resources began to flow from parents to children rather than vice versa.

Under industrialization the pressures on family life increased. Indeed, the picture of the idealized artisanal household is only a snapshot; in real life families grow, mature, and even collapse. When a factory weaver and spinner married and had children, the family faced constantly changing needs. If the wife, who might have held a job outside the home since she was sixteen or younger, stopped work to care for the children, her husband's wage often would not support the family. Women sometimes took in washing or sewing to supplement the family income. Yet, because women were chronically underpaid, even those who returned to factory work might not make enough money to cover the expense of caring for young children.

---

[6] Yorkshire is divided into three regions, called *ridings*: the North Riding, the South Riding, and the West Riding. In this chapter, the term *Yorkshire* refers to the West Riding.

THE HUMAN EXPERIENCE

A Birmingham Working Family about 1800

The following selection is adapted from an anonymous autobiography of a button maker published in 1850:

My father was a metal button turner. My mother was in the same business in the same shop. My father was of age when he married, and that was all. He had no money to buy furniture. His wages were about a pound a week, and my mother's about eight shillings or nine shillings at the very utmost. They procured furniture on credit, and never got rid of their furniture debt as long as they lived. My mother had eleven children, of whom I was the eldest. She was employed in the button manufacture all that time. Often till the day before her confinement she was at the lathe, and often returned to her work within three weeks. It was my business, as the eldest child, to nurse the younger ones. I was put to work at the buttons at seven years of age, and I thought myself very fortunate in being relieved from the disagreeable labor of nursing the baby. We had a wretched place to live in. My mother ran home daily at one o'clock to get a hasty dinner for my father. She had no time for cooking anything. Bread and treacle [sugar syrup], or bread and butter, was our usual fare, except on Sundays, when we got a joint of meat, and had it cooked at the public oven. My mother was a perfect slave. She could not read or write. She was naturally a clever woman. My father could read and write but he took no pains to let his children have the same advantages. He never sent any of us to school, but sent us all to work as soon as it was possible, that we could earn even as little as sixpence a week. He was always in debt, and fond of drink, and became latterly quite reckless. He spent his earnings in liquor, and trusted my mother to feed the children somehow or other—he did not care how. My mother did double work—in the shop and at home. I have known her to sit up till three or four o'clock in the morning, after a hard day's work, washing and mending our wretched clothes. When four of her children were ill at one time of the small pox, she had to go to the shop to work, or we should have starved. During her long years of misery she several times tried to do without the shop, and make the labor of her husband and children support us all. My father's earning were so small, and his drinking habits so inveterate, that very little found its way into my mother's possession. Her attempts to stay at home were in vain. She had always to go back to the shop. We have often been without fire and food in the winter, and exposed to distress and suffering of the most deplorable kind. When I was apprenticed I could not write my name. My sister, who was also sent to the button trade as soon as she could earn a penny a day, was never taught to read, nor to write, nor to use the needle, nor to cook, nor to wash. The whole of us were equally ignorant. My father worked at the lathe till within a week of his death. He died of a complication of diseases, brought on by intemperance. My mother died in childbed of her eleventh child, a few years before my father. Sorrow, privation, and hard work ruined her constitution. ❖

Source: Reprinted by permission from P. E. Razzell and R. W. Wainwright, *The Victorian Working Class: Selections from Letters to the Morning Chronicle.* Published by Frank Cass & Company, Ltd., 890–900 Eastern Avenue, Ilford, Essex, England, 1973.

As children matured and began to earn a pittance, the family could perhaps obtain slightly better housing. Parents who lived long enough expected their children eventually to care for them (see Table 20-1). If that prospect failed, the elderly might spend their last days in the workhouse established by the local parish for the indigent, as did many widows and orphans. Personality also influenced family life. Some adults proved better managers than others; some abused their children. Illness, accidents, or death sometimes upset the best of plans, and alcoholism ruined many a family.

Housing standards differed as well. To country people, many of whom lived in single smoke-filled rooms with earthen floors, slept on beds of vermin-infested straw, got only a dim light through murky oil-paper windows, and owned almost no furniture, virtually anything in the city looked good. At its best, the industrial city vastly improved on these conditions. In Manchester, developers constructed solid working-family residences by the thousands. The best of these consisted of two rooms about 15 feet square, each with glass windows at the front. Today these quarters would seem cramped to a modern Western family of four, but in 1820 such a house appeared spacious and healthy to families of six or even ten persons. In Birmingham, most independent artisans had their own homes. Rude clay huts clustered on the outskirts of town, but the center of the city was free of teeming tenements.

TABLE 20-1

AVERAGE AGES OF DEATH IN 1842

	Gentry	Tradesmen	Laborers
Liverpool	35	22	15
Manchester	38	20	17
Leeds	44	27	19
Truro	40	33	28
Rutland	52	41	38

Average life expectancies were lowered due to the high rate of death among young children. The last two locations listed in the table are rural areas.

Source: John Rule, *The Labouring Classes in Early Industrial England, 1750–1850* (London: Longman, 1986), p. 89.

socialist author Friedrich Engels estimated that 350,000 working people lived in Manchester, "almost all of them in wretched, damp, filthy cottages." A visitor to Leeds shortly thereafter described the city as a perfect "wilderness of foulness" built on a "slimy bog."

The problems of Manchester and Leeds were not untypical of the environmental damage characteristic of the early Industrial Revolution. Factory owners took no precautions whatsoever with their toxic wastes (if they even knew them to be toxic), simply dumping them into the nearest watercourse. Waste treatment plants did not exist. When raw filth did not just accumulate on streets, it found its way into the streams and rivers from which people took their drinking water, causing constant scourges of debilitating disease. Smoke from coal-burning steam engines added to the smoke already produced by tens of thousands of soft coal–burning stoves used in homes for heating, creating air so polluted that it occasionally killed the weak and infirm.

On the other hand, in many industrial cities, including Manchester, huge families dressed in rags often crowded into dank cellar apartments. Garbage-filled gutters, streams choked with rotting refuse, and polluted drinking water shocked middle-class investigators. In 1844 the future

BRITAIN REACTS

Human beings find ways to survive, even in extreme conditions such as those described in the preceding section. Unlike many other species, we can adjust to changes in our environment without perishing. We resist. The Industrial Revolution brought changes of such magnitude that those

The Impact of Industrialization on the Countryside   Despite impinging upon the primarily agricultural landscape, the presence of factories and belching smoke was often considered to be "progress." Note, too, the early steamship at the right of this painting. *Mansell/Time, Inc.*

affected vigorously struggled against them. For their part, early factory owners tried to organize their mills so as to reinforce the sense of order, deference, and paternalism that characterized English country life. Richard Arkwright, for example, built a small community to house and feed his workers in the tradition of paternalistic concern for his parish members. The first mills often were integrated operations in which owners used powered machinery only for some processes while contracting out most of the work to local artisans.

Nevertheless, over time factories undermined the status of skilled artisans. Traditionally, artisans were free to contract for work as they saw fit, to set their own schedules, and to come and go as they pleased. They had their own elaborate hierarchy that differentiated among high-status skills (for example, painting the carriages of the great and wealthy), those of middling status (painting ordinary carriages), and lower status jobs (journeyman painter), with accompanying variations in pay. But hired workers, even those earning more money than low-status artisans, comprised a different category. A factory owner dictated their hours, and machinery that in theory could run twenty-four hours a day regulated their pace of work. No longer at home or in a small shop, factory workers tended their machines six days a week, twelve to fourteen hours a day. Worse, their status declined. Some factory jobs required skill, but trained artisans rarely took the new jobs. Instead, jobs in textile factories often, although not exclusively, went to women, in part because the tasks were considered unskilled. Because of society's long-standing male orientation, sometimes the mere entry of women into a line of work lowered the status of a job from skilled to unskilled labor. Resistance to the factory system, therefore, did not center solely on the question of income, for factory workers often made more money and enjoyed greater job security than farm workers. Threatened artisans protested the subversion of an entire way of life, including their place of work, the character of their work, and, most important, their status.

Worker Resistance

Workers adopted several strategies, including machine breaking, to protect their livelihoods. As early as 1776, a mob destroyed an experimental spinning machine set up in a workhouse in Shepton Mallet. When an entrepreneur built a mill in Manchester in 1791 that was to hold four hundred looms, irate weavers burned it to the ground. But it would be a mistake to assess these early manifestations—there were literally hundreds of them—as unfocused outbursts of backward-looking rage. They often entailed conscious planning and organization. During the eighteenth century, working people united to enhance their bargaining power, to enforce apprenticeship rules, and to

seek higher wages or better working conditions. Although small, these organizations employed several devices of the modern labor union: strikes, pickets, and punishment of scabs, or strikebreakers.

In the centuries before the Industrial Revolution, artisans had enjoyed protection from both Parliament and local justices of the peace. Rules governing apprenticeship, prohibitions on fulling machines, and requirements that wool shrouds be used for burial only hint at the vast extent of codes that shielded artisans. Such rules made sense in a society in which the upper classes acted as the patrons of those whom they considered their social inferiors and in which master craftsmen controlled craft production. Many artisans thus deemed the introduction of new machines not only immoral—for it threatened their status, their way of life, and their livelihood—but inconsistent with British law. Consequently artisans went beyond breaking machines and organizing work stoppages, and appealed to the law. Throughout the 1790s, weavers, knitters, and shearers, among others, sent a steady stream of petitions to their local justices of the peace and even to Parliament. They based their appeals on centuries-old, even if sometimes poorly enforced, laws.

The debates sponsored by the select committee of Parliament to investigate woolen manufacturing in 1806 illustrate the issues and arguments used. The most pressing problem in woolens concerned the plight of shearers in Yorkshire. Because poor shearing technique could ruin a piece of cloth, the five thousand Yorkshire shearers were the aristocracy of the woolen workers, earning relatively high pay. But the introduction of the clipping frame, a mechanized device that turned an exacting, highly skilled technique into a routine, semiskilled task, pushed the shearers into action. During the 1790s, despite harassment, they organized, destroyed a number of shearing mills, raised a thousand pounds, and began to lobby Parliament to reinforce the old laws of apprenticeship and the ban on fulling machines. In response, the mill owners formed an association to prosecute the shearmen for conspiracy and to persuade Parliament to repeal the old rules. Parliament suspended the old laws, but before making the repeal permanent, it conducted an investigation into the woolen industry's problems.

The investigating committee's meetings provide an excellent case study in what was at stake during the Industrial Revolution. On one side of the debate stood the merchants, gentlemen clothiers, and the larger master clothiers. On the other were the artisans, primarily shearers, who were losing their jobs and who felt demeaned by the new machinery. The manufacturers made arguments that are still familiar today. According to the merchants and clothiers, unless factory owners were allowed to cast off the "impolitic antiquated shackles" supported by the organized workers, such as the apprentice laws, they would not

Shearing The man at the right is raising the nap on a piece of cloth so that the shearers on the left can cut it off very precisely with their massive shears, thus producing a smooth, fine cloth. Shearing was a skilled craft that required a sure touch and a good tool. *Mansell/Time, Inc.*

be able to compete. England would fall behind, and the textile trade would collapse. Economic efficiency demanded that productivity be stepped up, and this acceleration required displacing traditional craftsmen with new technology.

The shearers, basing their case on custom and justice, not on efficiency, argued from a moral basis. Apprenticeship was not only a useful training mechanism, they pointed out, it was "a moral and political institution" that served to "check and prevent early licentiousness." Factories were "nurseries always of vice and corruption, and often of disease, discontent and disloyalty," the shearers claimed. Machinery could not produce cloth of the same quality as hand workers. Such cloth was "deceitfully made," and the idea that machinery made for progress was a "foul imposition." The manufacturers demanded that the restrictions be repealed in order to break the shearers' monopoly over their craft. The shearers urged keeping the laws to prevent the innovators from creating a monopoly of control over production.

The shearers lost this struggle, and by 1809 all legislation protecting artisans in the wool industry had been repealed. At the same time, trade suffered when Napoleon's Continental Plan hindered access to the continental market. Furthermore, in 1811, as part of England's economic war against Napoleon, Orders of Council closed the American market as well, precipitating the War of 1812 with the United States. These events hit the stocking knitters of Nottinghamshire particularly hard. Parliament, having just repealed the regulations on woolens, was not about to institute new help for the stocking makers. To

protest their plight, bands of men began breaking up mechanized knitting frames. In the winter of 1811–1812, the shearers of Yorkshire and the cotton weavers of Lancashire joined in, called to action by handbills signed by the fictitious Ned Ludd:

> We will never lay down Arms [until] The House of Commons passes an Act to put down all Machinery hurtful to Commonality, and repeal that to hang Frame Breakers. But We. We petition no more—that won't do—fighting must.
>
> Signed by the General of the Army of Redressers
>
> Ned Ludd, Clerk
>
> Redressers for ever Amen

For the Luddites, as they were called, a way of life was at stake, but the government saw their protests as an insurrection. It made frame breaking a capital crime and brought in troops that temporarily suppressed the unrest and even hanged a number of unfortunate shearers. The Luddites launched new protests again in 1816 and later, but ultimately they could not stop the encroachment of machines into British society.

The Luddites and the organized working people who preceded them were not ignorant obstructers of progress, as the factory owners portrayed them. They were frustrated, skilled workers being displaced by the greatest revolution in textile production that the world had seen to date. Industrialism's strength is that it produces new levels of organization and efficiency. But those who have to bear the burden of change by losing their jobs and their status understandably have fought against it. For these workers, who like all of us have only one life to live, the future efficiencies of the free market were an abstraction for which they did not wish to sacrifice their dignity and their survival.

The Intellectual Response: Classical Economics

The manufacturers who successfully lobbied Parliament for repeal of the old laws protecting artisans based their arguments on the ideas of Adam Smith, the thinker most universally associated with the idea of a free market. The epitome of the absent-minded professor, who once allegedly walked into a tanning pit while conversing with a friend, Smith was nevertheless a close observer of economic behavior. A brilliant student, he received a scholarship to Oxford, and by age twenty-eight he had accepted the Chair of Moral Philosophy at the University of Glasgow. His first book, *The Theory of Moral Sentiments* (1759), made him famous. In it Smith did not ask the usual question of the Christian tradition: Why are human beings evil? Instead, he wondered why human beings were sometimes good. Given the passions that drive us toward self-aggrandizement, how is it that people can and do form moral judgments that inhibit them from unscrupulous behavior? Smith's answer was that although pursuit of our interests pits us against each other, our capacity for sympathy, imagination, reason, and reflection permits us to create institutions that turn antagonisms toward the common good.

The success of Smith's book brought him a well-paying job as tutor to an English nobleman during that young man's traditional year of travel through Europe. Over two years, Smith met numerous French intellectuals, including the physiocrat François Quesnay. Physiocrats argued that national wealth was not measured solely in gold and other specie, as mercantilists believed, but in the economy's production, which the physiocrats associated with agriculture rather than industry. They claimed that manufacturing and mercantile activities merely reshaped or redistributed the assets produced by agriculture and mining. Smith was impressed with Quesney's idea of **laissez-faire,** or "let [the producers] be," which went against the mercantilist and cameralist ideas of the time, but he could not believe that the only products of value to society came from agriculture and mining. On the contrary, the true wealth of nations, Smith decided, lay in their overall production, including industry and distribution.

Smith's *The Wealth of Nations*, perhaps the most famous treatise on economics ever written, appeared in 1776.[7] A unruly book of a thousand pages, it presented the

first and most enduring description of what we now call the market. The market in this sense is not a place or a thing but an abstraction that describes how societies produce and allocate goods. Given the luxuriant variety of cultures that human beings have created, it is surprising to learn from economists that in theory there are only three ways to produce and distribute goods: the traditional method, the command method, and the market. In real life, of course, every society uses a mix of these methods as shaped by its own historical trajectory.

As the name implies, traditional ways of resource allocation are passed down from parent to child. Peasant children till their land and manage their households in the way their parents teach them, wear clothes that are produced in an age-old manner, and eat a simple diet of food that they themselves grow. A person living in such a society is part of a network of blood and community relationships that determine his or her status. The question is not "What are you?" (Are you a student, doctor, or merchant?) but "Who are you?" (What parents, clan, or community do you belong to?). Money has little importance in this system, and land usage rights, status, and obligation have more weight than the private ownership of property. One uses resources rather than owning them. Such communities allow for little mobility and innovation, but they tend to be self-sufficient and stable.

In a command economy, someone directs how things are going to be produced and distributed. Historically, economic systems have combined traditional and command elements. Laboring people have lived in a traditional economy, and the upper classes have extracted resources from them for redistribution among themselves on the basis of strength or status. The most primitive command method uses naked force. Slavery is an obvious example. A more sophisticated method of command is not to seize resources but to issue minute instructions regulating their use. In their internal workings, medieval **guilds** tightly controlled their production while ensuring small-scale regional monopolies for the master craftsmen. Louis XIV's minister of finance, Jean Baptiste Colbert, issued extremely detailed regulations on every step of cloth production in an effort to stimulate the French economy. Command economies are considerably more sophisticated than traditional ones and have operated even in recent times, such as in the Soviet Union after 1917 and in several democracies during the national emergencies of the world wars.

The economy of early eighteenth-century Britain used a combination of traditional and command methods. These were what the Yorkshire shearers were defending in 1806—the traditions of the proto-industrial family and the command restrictions on new methods and machinery. Their defeat signaled the decline of these principles and the rise of the idea of the market, an important outcome of the Industrial Revolution.

---

[7] Its main competitor for this distinction is Karl Marx's *Das Kapital*, published in 1867. See Chapter 25.

As originally put forward by Adam Smith, market theory postulates the following basic law: If society guarantees the property rights of its citizens (such as the right to enforce contracts in court, the right to a patent or copyright, or the right against unlawful seizure), then the forces of supply and demand will ensure that everything society requires will be produced and distributed efficiently. There will be no need for tradition to define roles or for the state to control production. If demand for a certain product grows beyond the available supply, then the price of the product will rise. New people will be attracted to producing it, which in turn will lower the price. Theoretically, countless workings of this "unseen hand" in all sectors of the economy will produce a harmonious society in which everything that is needed is produced, distributed, and consumed.

The term *laissez faire* has become associated with these ideas of Adam Smith. The concept seems to imply that the market works best without any government interference. Actually, as Adam Smith himself recognized, the market cannot work at all without government intervention in at least two areas. First, only the government can prevent the formation of monopolies, in which one entity controls such a dominant portion of production that it can disregard the laws of supply and demand. Second, government must protect property rights. If individuals are not secure in their property, if contracts are not enforceable in court, if fraud is not prosecuted, and if the money is unstable, then the market cannot work. It is a misconception, therefore, to claim that Adam Smith advocates that the government do nothing. In fact, capitalism, or the free-market system (which is actually a mixed system), absolutely depends on proper government. Indeed, the Industrial Revolution could occur in Britain only because the state protected its citizens' property rights more firmly than governments in many other parts of the world.

In Adam Smith's optimistic view, market economies would grow, and this growth would benefit even the poor. In other words, a rising tide would lift all ships. Smith's idea of growth proved very congenial to the merchants of the Industrial Revolution. From that day to this, those who have sought to restructure an enterprise or an economy have justified their acts with the need for growth, and have placed the benefits of this growth in the future. Growth has become not just an academic abstraction, but a political necessity. Today, if a company's profits do not rise steadily, it becomes a takeover target. If a nation's economy does not expand, the politicians in power lose elections. Adam Smith's ideas contributed to the change in sensibility that made the drive toward a better future one of the commonplaces of industrialized society.

Two other famous economic thinkers complemented the work of Smith. The first of these was Thomas Robert Malthus, an English clergyman whose main ideas on population growth are still alive today. At the beginning of the eighteenth century, British men and women worried that their numbers were not growing fast enough to compete with the country's larger continental rivals. In 1696 Gregory King, the first person to analyze census data systematically, had calculated that it would take England and Wales until the year 2300 to double its population and until the year 3500 to reach a population of 22 million (it actually reached 22 million in approximately 1875). Writing a hundred years after King, by which time the English population had already doubled, Malthus disagreed. In his *Essay on Population* (1798), he estimated that population tended to double about every twenty-five years. Obviously the land available to produce food could not also double every twenty-five years. Even with increases in production, Malthus calculated, the rapidly growing numbers would soon run out of food. He postulated that population rises at a geometric rate (2, 4, 8, 16, 64, and so on), whereas food supplies expand at only an arithmetic rate (1, 2, 3, 4, 5). Although we can see now that Malthus's calculations were not correct—despite an explosion in world population, agricultural production has expanded more or less enough to support that population, at least for now—there is merit in his premise that overpopulation represents a real concern.

Britain avoided "the Malthusian trap" of overpopulation not only because improvements in agricultural technology stimulated food production, but because in broad terms industrialization seems to lower the birthrate. Agricultural societies have high birthrates but they also have high death rates. When industrialization creates prosperity among the middle classes in a society, the death rate drops rapidly. Then, a generation or so later, the birthrate follows suit. The decreasing death rate seems to be associated with the better average nutrition and housing that the middle classes can afford. The decline in birthrates may be associated with the lessened economic utility of children in industrial societies and the higher probability that they will not die in childhood. Malthus, an Anglican parson, believed that the best way to stop population growth was through the moral education of the prolific lower classes and by raising the age of marriage, thus limiting the time available for procreation.

The third member of the famous trio of classical economists was David Ricardo, a sophisticated financier and skilled orator. Retiring in his forties with the huge fortune that he had made in the financial markets, Ricardo entered the House of Commons, where he became something of a teacher of basic economics to the members of Parliament. Whereas Smith and Malthus were primarily moral philosophers who believed in human perfectibility through education, Ricardo was a technical economist. His primary work, *Principles of Political Economy and Taxation* (1817), was a theoretical discourse that established a number of basic ideas that Karl Marx later used. Two of the most important of these ideas were the labor theory of value and the iron law of wages. The labor theory of value was first put forward in the late seventeenth century by John Locke, who pointed out that acorns lying on the ground have no value until someone collects them and takes them to market. All goods, Locke extrapolated, attain value only through the labor that has been expended in making them available to consumers. This idea, elaborated by Ricardo, dominated economic thought in the nineteenth century, although it does not permit the accurate mathematical modeling that economists use today.[8]

The iron law of wages held that labor was a commodity and was therefore subject to the laws of supply and demand. Because factory owners faced constant pressure to keep profits up, they would strive to keep workers' wages as low as possible. If we couple this idea—that workers always would live near the subsistence level—with Malthus's belief that abstinence was the best form of birth control for the lower classes, we get an idea of why **classical economics** was called "the dismal science."

Stirrings of Humanitarianism

Despite Adam Smith's assertion to the contrary, the rising tide of industrialization did not lift all ships. The living conditions of the poorest members of the British working class shocked parliamentary investigators in the first third of the nineteenth century. Nothing provoked greater outrage than child labor, with its horrifying tales of cruelty, stunted growth, lack of education, and sexual abuse. The most damning depiction of child labor showed a girl stripped to the waist crawling on her hands and knees, dragging a cart laden with coal through a mine shaft. Stories of young lace makers strapped into frames that permanently bent their spines, or of boys cleaning machinery on Sundays, supposedly their day off, inflamed public opinion in the 1820s and 1830s. By the 1820s, the employment of

young children in textiles and mining had become a national disgrace. Exclaimed one contemporary:

> Poor infants! ye are indeed sacrificed at the shrine of avarice. . . . Ye are compelled to work as long as the necessity of your needy parents may require, or the cold blooded avarice of your worse than barbarian masters may demand! . . . Ye are doomed to labour from morning to night for one who cares not how soon your weak and tender frames are stretched to breaking!

In 1832 the *Report of the Select Committee on the Bill for the Regulation of Factories* presented this aspect of the factory system in such a bad light that it led to the Factory Act of 1833. The law forbade employing children under nine years of age and restricted children under thirteen to eight hours a day, two of which had to be spent in education. Not very advanced for our day, this Factory Act nevertheless began the process of regulating the employment of children in factories.

Criticism of child labor was an aspect of the humanitarian sensibility that emerged in Britain in the eighteenth century. This movement's adherents concerned themselves first and foremost with slavery, and persuaded Parliament in 1807 to prohibit British participation in the slave trade. They then moved on to other issues, such as education, treatment of the insane, and prison reform. Reformers' interest in the welfare of human beings far removed from them, whether slaves suffering in far-off parts of the world or prisoners moldering in British jails, was new. Slavery had always been considered an unfortunate but ordinary part of human society, and the fate of the insane or of prisoners usually met with indifference.

The new humanitarian concerns of the Industrial Revolution seem paradoxical, because they contradicted the notion of self-interest, which Adam Smith used as his first principle. Why should one care about others, especially those neither geographically nor socially close, when the laissez-faire system prospered through the pursuit of self-interest? Christian concern for others provides one clue; much of the humanitarian impetus came from evangelical

---

[8] Few if any economists (except Marxists) accept the labor theory of value today.

A Child Mineworker This drawing, included in an 1842 report to the British Parliament, shocked Victorian England. A 37-year old mother described the work: ". . . a belt round my waist . . . a chain between my legs, and I go on my hands and feet. The road is very steep . . . [and] we are in a family way." Note the absence of rails for the wheels. © *The British Library.*

movements, such as the Clapham Sect. But Christians had not always opposed slavery. What motivated them now? One answer proposed recently is that humanitarianism provided an effective method of social control in industrial society. By improving prisons, as the modern French philosopher Michel Foucault has put it, society sought not "to punish less, but to punish better"—that is, "to punish with more universality and necessity; to insert the power to punish more deeply into the social body." In this interpretation, humanitarianism was the industrial class's effort to impose its vision of the world on society with more power and penetration than preindustrial rulers had been able to do. Humanitarianism, in other words, was just another form of self-interest.

A less cynical explanation, and one that credits the sincerity of the humanitarians, suggests that the Industrial Revolution created a new level of sophistication. In medieval Europe, life was uncertain, but richly explicable. The local priest, fortune teller, wise man, or tavern keeper provided explanations for disturbing events that, if not accurate, at least were psychologically satisfying. As the worldwide market system emerged, however, the economy became more interdependent. People began to realize how much distant events affected their lives. As Britain's economic horizons broadened, some people began to feel that the well-being of persons far from them was part of their own moral responsibility.

As consciousness expanded, the means for intervening on behalf of others proliferated. Colonial holdings put English and Scottish people in direct contact with ethical problems they would not have encountered at home. (For example: Should members of slave families be sold separately?) The increased role of Parliament in English politics gave reformers a platform, and the successes of the Industrial Revolution bolstered their confidence that a better future was possible. The vast number of eighteenth-century sermons, homilies, and tracts concerning slavery and other social ills spread to a new interest in the welfare of the lower classes. The Factory Act of 1833, prohibiting child labor, was one of the first applications of this interest to industry.

Class Conflict

The term **class** came into common use in the eighteenth century, but it was used in a way characteristic of traditional society. Landed property was supposed to free its owners from the hurly-burly of commerce and allow them to consider the interests of the entire nation in a reasoned, objective way. Secure in their income, it was believed, the landed class did not need to defend and advocate partial interests, as did those with less stable livelihoods. Adam Smith himself held this point of view. In reality, of course, landlords did everything they could to further their particular interests, but the claim of being above petty concerns supported their assertion that landed wealth imposed special obligations and required deference.

Workers, too, perceived themselves as part of a structured society. As they saw it, they shared an honest position that the upper classes by rights should protect. In return, they accepted the obligation to show deference to their betters. Even when they rebelled, as in the case of the shearers, they based their arguments on moral claims characteristic of traditional society rather than on self-interest. Bread riots by "the mob" might erupt, and some "unmasterly" employers might ignore their obligations to their employees, but these events were seen as aberrations in a system of mutual obligation between employer and employee.

This view of the special position of landed wealth and of mutual obligation had begun to erode by the end of the eighteenth century. During the wars that raged across Europe from the 1790s until the defeat of Napoleon in 1815 (see Chapters 21 and 22), a combination of patriotic feelings and governmental repression maintained a superficial calm in Britain, despite the Luddite outbursts. But when the wars stopped, government expenditures on arms, uniforms, and other war supplies ceased, and an economic depression set in. Simultaneously, steam engines came into widespread use. Factories moved into cities, drawing thousands of workers into similar conditions of work and life. In this stressful atmosphere, the idea that employers were exploiting workers took hold. The new radicalism rejected the ideal of a harmonious society and insisted that workers had their own interests that were in competition with those of the employers.

This was the other side of the laissez-faire coin. Adam Smith had argued that the pursuit of self-interest would create a stable society. Employers had used his arguments to help destroy the old rules that protected artisans. Now factory workers also began to abandon the eighteenth-century ideal and to pursue their interests as a class. Although the problems peculiar to the early postwar years soon evaporated, the image of workers standing on one side of a barrier and capitalists on the other endured.

One important signpost of this breakdown was the decline in church membership and attendance. In 1750 more than 90 percent of the English were members of the Anglican church (the official Church of England), although many members did not attend church regularly. By 1850, however, the number of members had declined to 50 percent. Many workers were not religious and did not attend church. But the drop in adherence to the state church coincided with the successes of the Old Dissenters, the Methodists, the Baptists, the Catholics, and dozens of **sects**. Enthusiastic preaching, relevant messages, and warm services attracted people who found Anglicanism too formal, too rigid, and too upper-class. The emotional appeals of John Wesley, in particular, drew working-class people to Methodism, which exploded from about thirty-eight thousand members in 1781 to half a million by the 1850s. The landed elites correctly interpreted these changes as an erosion of the culture of deference.

The sense of being linked to other laborers created a distinctly new working-class ideal, despite the infinitely varied classifications of workers. Ironically, David Ricardo inspired this shift. Ricardo, in direct contrast to the eighteenth-century physiocrats, saw landowners as the parasites of society, skimming off increasing rents as the rest of the economy grew by the labor of workers and capitalists. This view led some Ricardians to argue that capitalists also

were profiting unfairly and that the workers were being deprived of the fruits of their labor. Karl Marx eventually would consolidate these ideas into a powerful and coherent system, but the accusation that the Industrial Revolution had brought oppression to workers was already afoot in the 1820s.

Just as the working class developed a separate sense of identity in the early nineteenth century, so did the landholding elite and the new middle class (see Table 20-2). Landowners revived a new form of the traditional ideal. They set themselves off as the maintainers of the genteel

TABLE 20-2
DISTRIBUTION OF ENGLISH NATIONAL INCOME, 1806

		Number of Families	Income per Family (pounds/year)	Aggregate Income (thousands of pounds/year)
Aristocracy	Sovereign	1	200,000	200
	Peers	287	8,000	2,296
	Other ranks	906	1,500–4,000	2,249
	Esquires	3,000	1,500	9,000
	Gentlemen	12,000	700	14,000
Middle Ranks	Top merchants	2,000	2,600	5,200
	Merchants	13,000	800	10,400
	Manufacturers	25,000	800	20,000
	Government officials	2,000	800	1,600
	Shipowners	5,000	500	2,500
	Freeholders	180,000	90–200	18,800
	Bureaucrats	10,500	200	2,100
	Local clergy	10,000	120	1,200
	Naval officers	3,000	150	450
	Innkeepers	50,000	100	5,000
Lower Orders (the working poor)	Artisans	450,000	55	24,750
	Peddlers	800	40	32
	Laborers	340,000	30	10,200
	Cottagers	400,000	15	6,000

		Families	Income
Percentage Distribution	Aristocracy	1.4	15.7
	Middle Ranks	31.6	59.4
	Lower Orders	67.0	24.9

Although consisting of less than a third of the English population, the "middle ranks" earned almost two-thirds of national income. The "lower ranks" received only a fourth of the income, with the small aristocratic ranks receiving the rest. Note: Only selected occupations are shown; some figures rounded slightly.

Source: Adapted from Patrick Colquhoun, *A Treatise on Indigence* (1806), as reproduced in Harold Perkin, *The Origins of Modern English Society, 1780-1880* (London: Routledge & Kegan Paul, 1969), pp. 20–21.

THE HISTORICAL EVIDENCE

The New Gruel Shops

(1834)

The poor saw the new poor law of 1834 as forcing them into unpleasant workhouses, where they would be fed on thin gruel. The following ballad appeared shortly after the act became law. Note: The phrase "feathers nearly two yards long" refers to horsehair, and "skilly gruel" is prison gruel.

Good people all I pray draw near that in this country
    dwell;
Concerning these new workhouses the truth to you
    I'll tell.
Now no relief they give the poor if out of work they
    drop,
For by this Act, off they are packed to those new
    gruel shops.

Chorus
May Providence protect the poor while on the earth
    they stop,
That none of them may have to go to these new
    gruel shops.
In England now like mushrooms they spring up from
    the ground,
And they will cost poor Johnny Bull full many a
    thousand pound;

He'll find this bill a bitter pill—it'll punch his belly
    through—
It'll cost him many a thousand pound for making
    water gruel.
The bedsteads there I do declare are made of iron
    strong;
The beds are filled with feathers fine, they're nearly
    two yards long.
No grates are there I do declare or smoke your eyes
    to torture;
For all the rooms are to be warmed by a pot of
    boiling water.

Each morning for their breakfast they're to have
    skilly gruel;
Poor women will not be allowed to have a cup of tea.
Men from their wives will parted be, indeed it is no
    joke;

---

tradition, which they contrasted with what they considered the coarse and grubby entrepreneurial ambitions of the middle class. For its part, the middle class began to develop standards of appropriate behavior. The emergence of class identities, therefore, did not derive solely from the working class's move to separate itself from the rest of society. The landowning class also redesigned its justifications in order to retain its genteel position, and the middle class purposefully divorced itself from the traditional ethic. Thus the Industrial Revolution was not only a technological and economic event. It was also a social and intellectual event that changed the way people thought about how they related to each other.

Repeal of the Poor Laws

One of the most significant signs of the change in social relationships was passage of the poor law of 1834. Since the time of Elizabeth I, local parishes had cared for their poor members, who were primarily agricultural workers. Anyone born or married in a parish and therefore appearing in its formal register qualified for aid. If workers moved out of the parish in which they were registered to find work elsewhere, their home parish retained responsibility for them. By the early nineteenth century, perhaps 50 percent of the working class of England was not living in the parish in which it was registered. The system had grown antiquated.

Poor relief came in two varieties: indoor and outdoor. The term *indoor relief* referred to workhouses, in which the poor were set to work carding, spinning, and weaving for paltry wages, in return for room and board. These institutions were filled mostly with the aged and infirm, widows, orphans, and single mothers with dependent children. Able-bodied but unemployed workers typically received *outdoor relief*, which guaranteed a family a minimum income and left the worker free to obtain employment even at substandard wages. In the allowance system, as one common form of outdoor relief was called, the parish determined an amount that would permit a worker and his family to survive and adjusted it periodically in relation to the price of bread. If the family's income dropped below that

Good peo-ple all I pray draw near that In this coun-try dwell:——— Con-cern-ing these now Work-hous-es the truth to you I'll tell——— Now no re-lief they give the poor if out of work they drop, For by this Act, off they are packed to those new gru-el shops.——— May Pro-vi-dence pro-tect the poor while on the earth they stop, That none of them may have to go to these new gru-el shops.

And no snuff must the women take, men neither
chew nor smoke.

For building these new workhouses some people did
agree
Because they thought from poor rates the law would
set them free;
But now they find out their mistake they scratch
their wooden blocks
They do repent they did consent to build these new
gruel shops.

Now to conclude and likewise end these lines which
I have penned,
I hope there's no one present here my song it might
offend.
Be kind unto the labouring poor who for your wealth
do toil;
The Lord will surely bless you with the widow's cruse
of oil.

Source: Adapted from Trevor May, *Economic and Social History of Britain 1760–1970.* (New York: Longman, 1987), p. 219.

amount, the parish would pay a supplement to bring it back up. Although this device had been in use since the mid-eighteenth century, the most famous such regulations were those established by the magistrates of Speenhamland in 1795. This form of support therefore was often called the Speenhamland system. It aimed not to carry the unemployed indefinitely but to tide over seasonal workers during the winter and other slack periods.

Malthus objected strenuously to traditional methods of poor relief. By guaranteeing a living wage to agricultural workers, he argued, the poor laws encouraged people to marry too early. If relief was abolished, then indigent young persons would have to wait until they had established themselves financially before marrying. The birthrate would drop, and the rate of population growth would slow. Naturally, Malthus opposed child allowances, which only increased the likelihood that the poor would procreate. Malthus also argued that the old poor laws drove wages down. Because the parish paid workers when their wages were low, it was in the interest of individual farmers to drop their wages. They could thereby save more on their wage

bill than they would have to pay in taxes. In Malthus's view, the poor laws created the very poverty that they aimed to remedy. In the long run, Malthus claimed, the abolition of poor relief would benefit workers. It would promote thrift, discourage population growth, and foster better work habits.

By the 1820s, the growing body of successful entrepreneurs had embraced Malthus's ideas. In 1832 the government formed a royal commission of inquiry, which concluded that the taxes used to support the poor were cutting into profits and rents. Two years later, in 1834, Parliament adopted a new poor law that by the 1840s replaced much outdoor relief with workhouses. Although the law did not ultimately transform the living standards of rural workers (in part because of its many loopholes), it did lower the amounts spent on relief. How well the new poor law worked, however, is not at issue. The point is that an entirely new way of thinking had staked its claim. The ideal of the hardworking, self-interested individual was muscling aside the image of a community of patronage and deference.

CONCLUSION: OPENING THE FUTURE'S POSSIBILITIES

The discovery of how to put the energy available in coal to widespread industrial use constitutes the heart of the Industrial Revolution. The explosion in production that came from this tapping of the latent energy of coal raised economic activity in Britain to new heights. The first effects were regional, with cotton mills congregating in Manchester, for example. But once the potential benefits of the new production methods became widely understood, it was only a matter of time before industrialization spread throughout Britain and eventually the world.

By 1830, the Industrial Revolution had not yet transformed either Britain or the world, but all the elements were in place. The marriage of the steam engine to the textile industries, particularly cotton, gave birth to a new kind of urban factory. These factories not only churned out enormous quantities of cotton and woolen goods, but they completely altered the lives of those who worked in them and those who ran them. Instead of growing food for their own use or performing artisanal work in their own homes, ordinary people now toiled in factories regulated by machinery and directed by owners. Unhappy workers organized themselves, broke machines, and appealed to the law, but they were unable to hold back the changes that overwhelmed them. A new sense of working-class solidarity against factory owners began to replace the old habits of deference.

The middle class, which flourished on the profits of the new economic activity, also drew back from the communal ideals of the patriarchal society, although the landed aristocracy tried to preserve those ideals. The classical economists—Smith, Malthus, and Ricardo—most eloquently expressed the middle class's new outlook. These writers argued that business, commerce, and production created the nation's wealth, not solely agriculture and mining. Moreover, if everyone pursued his or her self-interest, economic growth would result. To those who marveled at the increases in English productivity, these ideas were not only self-evident and congenial; they pointed the way to a prosperous future. In preindustrial societies, the educated had revered the classical past, and the ordinary citizen had lived in a restricted present; in industrial societies, almost everyone—educated, uneducated, middle class, and worker—came to believe in the possibilities of the future. Today we increasingly see that we cannot conquer nature. We must live within it. But for the past two hundred years, the power unleashed by the Industrial Revolution made the dream of a better future intoxicating.

Selected Reading

General Histories

Gutmann, Myron P. *Toward the Modern Economy: Early Industry in Europe 1500–1800* (1988). Excellent brief survey of the long history of industrial change that prepared the way for the mechanized Industrial Revolution.

Hudson, Pat. *The Industrial Revolution* (1992). Useful text that clearly lays out the various historical controversies concerning the Industrial Revolution.

Technology and the Industrial Revolution

Berg, Maxine. *The Age of Manufactures, 1700–1820*, 2nd ed. (1994). Revisionist account finding the key to the Industrial Revolution in technological creativity and the structures of industrial communities.

Chaloner, W. H., and A. E. Musson. *Industry and Technology* (1963). Many thoroughly annotated pictures.

Koditschek, Theodore. *Class Formation and Urban Industrial Society: Bradford, 1750–1850* (1990). Concentrates on one city but produces a broad analysis of middle and working class formation.

Kranzberg, Melvin, and Carroll W. Pursell Jr. *Technology in Western Civilization: The Emergence of Modern Industrial Society: Earliest Times to 1900* (1967). Thorough discus-sion of the technology of the Industrial Revolution that goes far beyond the spheres mentioned in this chapter.

Landes, David S. *Prometheus Unbound: Technological Change and Industrial Development in Western Europe from 1750 to the Present* (1970). Influential study of how the Industrial Revolution occurred in Britain and then swept over the Continent. A basic work.

The Social Impact

Braün, Rudolf. *Industrialisation and Everyday Life* (1990). Fascinating discussion of the putting-out system and its impact around Zurich in the seventeenth and eighteenth centuries.

Chambers, J. D., and G. E. Mingary. *The Agricultural Revolution, 1750–1880* (1966). Argues that the Industrial Revolution was not a disaster for rural England.

Himmelfarb, Gertrude. *The Idea of Poverty: England in the Early Industrial Age* (1984). The idea of poverty as the master theme of early industrialization. Critical of class analysis.

Mantoux, Paul. *The Industrial Revolution in the Eighteenth Century: An Outline of the Beginnings of the Modern Factory System in England* (1983). First published in 1905, this remains the classic account of the changes that produced the factory system.

Perkin, Harold. *The Origins of Modern English Society, 1780–1880* (1969). A well-written, well-organized, convincing social history.

Rule, John. *The Labouring Classes in Early Industrial England, 1750–1850* (1986). Substantial social history that summarizes a great deal of information.

Stone, Lawrence, and Jeanne C. F. Stone. *An Open Elite? England 1540–1880* (1984). Controversial argument that the English upper class was not as open as others, such as Perkin suggests (see Perkin's work cited above).

Thompson, E. P. *The Making of the English Working Class* (1964). Pathbreaking, influential study that set the terms of debate about the working class in English history for a generation. Emphasizes self-activization of workers.

Personalities

Hart, Ivor B. *James Watt and the History of Steam Power* (1949). Easy-to-read biography that shows how Watt relates to the science and technology of his day.

Heilbroner, Robert L. *The Worldly Philosophers*, 3rd ed. (1967). Extremely readable discussion of the great economists, including Smith, Malthus, and Ricardo.

CHAPTER 21

THE FRENCH REVOLUTION

The Tennis Court Oath   *Giraudon / Art Resource, NY.*

1774	Louis XVI's reign begins	**1795**	New, moderate revolutionary regime begins as the Directory	**1810**	Alexander I breaks with Napoleon
1778	France begins to aid the American Revolution, eventually leading to bankruptcy	**1799**	Napoleon Bonaparte seizes power and establishes Consulate	**1812**	Napoleon's invasion of Russia ends in disaster
1787	Assembly of Notables rejects Calonne's reform program	**1802**	Pope recognizes revolutionary changes in France (Concordat); Napoleon becomes Consul for Life	**1813**	Allied armies defeat Napoleon (Battle of the Nations)
1788	Estates General summoned			**1814**	Napoleon abdicates and is exiled to Elba; French monarchy restored
1789	Estates General turns into the National (Constituent) Assembly; the Revolution gathers steam	**1804**	Napoleon becomes emperor; *Code Napoléon* issued	**1815**	Napoleon returns from Elba but is defeated after 100 days (battle of Waterloo) and permanently exiled to St. Helena; Congress of Vienna completes peace settlement
1791	New constitution proclaimed	**1805–1806**	Napoleon defeats Austria, Prussia, and Russia		
1792	"Second revolution"; monarchy suspended and king put on trial	**1807**	Napoleon and Alexander I of Russia meet at Tilsit to divide Europe	**1821**	Napoleon dies on St. Helena
1793	Louis XVI executed; Reign of Terror begins under Committee of Public Safety				
1794	Reign of Terror ends with fall of Robespierre (Thermidor)				

*I*f the Industrial Revolution transformed the environment in which we live, the French Revolution changed the way we think. Almost every human society before the eighteenth century organized itself around the obvious fact that human beings differ from one another in intelligence, social status, wealth, gender, strength, and hundreds of other qualities. For this reason, it had always seemed perfectly natural that societies should be arranged hierarchically. In France, as in every European country, each member of society held a particular place in the hierarchy, which the French laid out with great care and understood in infinite detail. A good deal of social and political life centered on getting and keeping the signs of status that showed the world where one stood on this elaborate ladder.

The French Revolution fatally undermined this ancient assumption that societies should organize themselves hierarchically. The American Declaration of Independence of 1776 was the first political document to state that "all men are created equal," and the French Revolution injected the idea of equality directly into European politics. The famous painting shown opposite, *The Tennis Court Oath* by Jacques-Louis David, dramatically depicts the moment at which a few members of the formerly dominant social orders—the clergy and the aristocracy—joined with representatives of the rest of the French society to demand that all French citizens have an equal voice in making their country's laws.

People today remain just as unequal as ever in their physical characteristics and wealth, and organizations still require a hierarchy to operate effectively, but equality before the law and equality of access to civil rights has become a fundamental principle of all modern democracies. The word **equity** (a synonym for fairness) expresses the essence of this kind of equality. No one living three hundred years ago could have conceived of the campaigns for fair treatment that feminists, civil rights activists, and the disabled make in North America today. But because of the unfolding of events that the French Revolution made possible, claims for equal treatment by such groups now seem to reflect basic premises of Western civilization.

Equality in one's civil rights, or fairness, is the revolutionary era's most important contribution to Western civilization. Yet the Revolution gave birth to other concepts of almost equal impact. **Popular sovereignty**—the idea that the ultimate political authority resides in "the people"—was a product of the late eighteenth century that the French and American Revolutions popularized. It took several generations to work out just who counted as "the people," but the French Revolution established the principle that we have been refining for the past two hundred years.

Whoever "the people" were, they had a natural, inborn right to freedom, or **liberty.** In medieval and early modern Europe, the term *liberty* referred to a specific right granted by the ruler, such as freedom from having to pay a certain tax. "The liberties" of the French nobility actually meant their special privileges. Before and during the French Revolution, liberty came to refer to the underlying purpose of society—to provide the context in which each individual can be free to choose his or her own life course.

The third term in the revolutionary slogan of *"Liberté! Égalité! Fraternité!"* was brotherhood.[1] This word, too, has many meanings, but one of them suggests **nationalism.** Mobilization of the entire French nation during the revolutionary wars was one of the first instances of nationalism in a modern sense, and a German backlash against the French led to the development of nationalism in central Europe. Because nationalism also owes a debt to the notions of fairness and popular sovereignty, we often understand it, too, as an invention of the French Revolution. In fact, the modern meaning of revolution itself took shape in these pivotal years. In the seventeenth century, the term had meant a return to tried and true old ways, as a mill wheel revolves to its starting point. For example, England's "Glorious Revolution" of 1688 had allegedly meant a return to the good old days of limited, Protestant monarchy. After the French and American Revolutions, however, the term *revolution* came to mean a dramatic upheaval that ushers in something new. The dream that properly motivated people could overhaul a society has inspired revolutionaries from that day to this. Paradoxically, whereas the French Revolution made a theory of revolution against the state possible, it also *strengthened the state*. Despite all the clamors of the revolutionary period, the French bureaucracy emerged from the Napoleonic wars better organized and more entrenched than it had ever been under the Old Regime (*Ancien Régime*)—quite close, in fact, to its position in modern France.

The list of legacies continues—metric weights and measures; the Napoleonic Codes; universal male conscription for military service; the seizure of the extensive properties of the Catholic church and the turning of priests into state employees—but the point is clear: The French Revolution constitutes as important a political and ideological event as the Industrial Revolution was an economic and social one. For this reason, historians sometimes refer to these upheavals as the **"Dual Revolution."**

THE FRENCH REVOLUTION

The French Revolution may have transformed the way we think about politics, but in the years before it occurred no one anticipated the strength and depth of the changes it evoked. Enlightened thinkers introduced new definitions of liberty, despotism, and sovereignty into public use, but the French economy remained traditional, the aristocratic classes considered their privileges sacrosanct, and the Catholic church rested secure in its ancient social role.

When the upheaval burst on France and on Europe— unplanned and unexpected—it broke entirely new ground.

Prelude to Upheaval

If one word could sum up the social system of prerevolutionary France, that word would be *privilege*. In France, everyone from the brother of the king to the lowliest goatherd occupied a social position defined by tradition, family position, and a complex of rules, customs, and requirements passed down from the distant past or imposed by powerful contemporaries. In the case of artisans, noblemen, members of the **bourgeoisie,** seigneurs (landlords who had the right to dispense justice to their social inferiors), and many others, this position was a matter of law, specified in legal ways authorized by the king. The bourgeoisie of Paris, for example, were not a vague sort of middle class but persons who fulfilled specific definitions, such as living in Paris for a year and a day, maintaining a principal residence there for at least six months of the year, and contributing to community expenses. A man who met these requirements earned the designation *bourgeois gentilhomme* and had the right to exercise guardianship (an important privilege in an era when parents often died young, leaving wealthy minor heirs), to be exempt from the fee for buying a fief, and to seize the property of non-Parisians for debt. The term *bourgeois* thus described well-defined status held by specific individuals who owned clearly delineated rights and privileges. A *bourgeois gentilhomme* was not the social equivalent of a modern middle-class person. He probably lived on interest or rents, or he might hold a job as a royal official, a small shopkeeper, or an artisan. His status hinged solely on privilege, not on income, occupation, or what today we call social class.

Seigneurial rights owned by landlords were another important kind of privilege. These forced the peasant to pay fees for such services as milling, brewing, or crossing a river, to submit to the landowner's judicial court, and to provide various forms of unpaid service. The peasant who owed fewer eggs to his seigneur at Easter than did his neighbor also owned a privilege, as did the nobleman who had the exclusive right to place a weather vane on his barn. In the town processions in Montpellier, court presidents could not wear the ermine hoods signifying the rank of magistrate or even the plain hoods worn by bailiffs, but they proudly donned their scarlet robes to contrast themselves with the lower court officials, who were permitted only black robes, which could, however, be made of satin. The cutlers, engravers, and gilders of iron and steel in Rouen had an exclusive privilege to manufacture and sell 113 specific items in their town. And so it went, almost everyone in France participating in one way or another in an intricate web of privileges, the whole of which constituted society itself.

---

[1] Note that whereas this phrase accurately represents basic principles of the French Revolution, it was not actually used as a republican slogan in France until 1848, although the Batavian (Dutch) Republic did use it in 1795.

Privilege made France a corporate society, one organized around an infinitude of legally protected groups and thus difficult to rule. Other differences also created cleavages in France. Two separate dialects of French divided the northern and southern regions of the country. As late as 1870, some 40 percent of the citizens of France did not even speak standard French as their native tongue. In much of southern France, Roman law provided the basis of legal procedure, whereas in the northern areas the legal system grew primarily out of medieval customary law. Since the Reformation, the Huguenots—or French Calvinists— proved hard for the predominantly Catholic country to digest. French Catholicism itself was riven by Jansenism, a reformist movement, and other divergent tendencies. Moreover, a bewildering array of local weights and measures stood ready to confuse the merchant.

The king ruled over this mosaic kingdom with the help of his council, representatives in local regions, and a small bureaucracy. His primary ally in theory was the nobility, but in practice king and lords were in constant conflict. The higher (but not highest) reaches of the aristocracy ran the courts called **parlements** (not to be confused with the English Parliament), which they used to pressure the king. France contained twelve separate parlements and three sovereign councils, but by far the most important of these was the Parlement of Paris, which had jurisdiction over more than half of France. The power of the parlements lay in their authority to register laws; without registration, the laws could not be legally enforced. In theory, the king's right to promulgate laws was absolute, but in practice, foot dragging and even outright refusal to register a law could thwart the king's intentions. In such cases, the king could resort to his ultimate legal step, a *lit de justice*, in which he personally appeared before the parlement and ordered it to register his law. The king's natural reluctance, not to say irritation, when pushed to this extreme allowed the French courts to obstruct the king's will more freely than could English courts, which were bound to enforce the law in any event.

Financing the operation of the French state was difficult; France, unlike England, lacked a central bank as well as a banking system. Through an agreement reached in the fourteenth century, the French nobility had permitted the king to tax the non-noble residents of France in return for his promise not to tax them. Nobles did not pay the taille, the main direct tax on land, and considered this one of their most important privileges. But the king still needed money, and he constantly tried to find new sources. Since 1695 every adult male was supposed to pay the *capitation*, or head tax, on the basis of his position in twenty-two status groups called *états*, but this system provided many opportunities for cheating. Then there was the temporary *dixième* of 1710 (one-tenth of certain income), the *vingtième* of 1749 (one-twentieth), and an additional allegedly temporary tax that was periodically renewed, or

even doubled and tripled. Indirect taxes on necessities such as salt and wine, the unseen tax imposed by inflation, "loans" extorted from the wealthy by the king, and the periodic sale of offices completed the picture.

The citizens of France, not surprisingly, found the tax system confusing as well as unfair, not only because the nobility escaped the taille and found ways to evade the rest, but because private entrepreneurs collected the indirect taxes by **tax farming.** The government sold the right to collect such taxes at a discount to private businessmen, who then went out and collected the levies as a profit-making enterprise. It was impossible to get rid of these financiers, as they were called in France, because the king and his ministers themselves owned shares in the tax farms, and because the financiers supplied the state with most of its loans.

France's fiscal stability, always somewhat shaky, started to unravel in the 1780s, even though France was the strongest country on the Continent. Its economy grew during the eighteenth century almost as much as England's; with a population of 28 million, it could put more soldiers in the field than any other single country; and it retained its influential voice in international affairs. But the conflicts of midcentury had stretched the French economy, and the general economic downturn of the 1770s strained it further. The final straw came with France's support of the American Revolution. Louis XVI and his ministers were no revolutionaries, but they decided to support the Americans so as to damage England, France's traditional rival. The government had raised taxes or imposed new ones in 1749, 1756, 1760, 1763, and 1783, but these proved inadequate to the need. By 1787 French debt had ballooned to the point that paying interest on it ate up more than half the state's budget. There was only one way to solve the problem: reform the tax system. Several royal ministers had tried to do just that, but they had always had to retreat in the face of opposition from entrenched interests.

The French minister of finance (*contrôleur-général*) in 1786 was Charles-Alexandre de Calonne, whom a contemporary described as having "the vivacity of a young colonel, the elegance of a man of means, the pedantry of the magistrate, and some of the gaucheness of the provincial." Calonne was sympathetic to those who opposed change. He helped his friends with extensive financing schemes of public works, assisted indebted noblemen, and in general acted as a treasurer of last resort to the traditional moneyed classes. Nevertheless, he understood the need for fiscal change. Building on a century of French debates over the matter and on earlier schemes put forward by his predecessors, he proposed a broad reform plan in 1786. The centerpiece of his program was a land tax to replace the *vingtièmes*. The tax would fall on all landowners, noble and commoner alike. Local assemblies of landowners would assess the actual amounts.

Calonne's proposal threatened the ancient rights of the nobility in two ways: It removed their exemption from the land tax, and it brought commoners and nobles together in local administrative assemblies. The *contrôleur-général* knew that the Parlement of Paris, which represented the interests of the administrative aristocracy, the so-called Nobles of the Robe, would not register such a law.[2] He therefore persuaded Louis XVI to convene an Assembly of Notables, the first time such an advisory body to the king had gathered since 1626.

Calonne anticipated that the assembly's approval would lend such weight to his proposals that the parlements would have to accept them. However, contrary to Calonne's hopes, when the 144 persons selected by the crown met from February 22 to May 25, 1787, they refused to rubber-stamp his proposals. Instead, the assembly demanded an accounting of the deficit, criticized Calonne for his favoritism toward the financiers, rejected the tax on land as favoring the tax farmers, and decried the proliferating bankruptcies. Resistance to the royal reforms by the Assembly of Notables marked the real beginning of the French Revolution. It put the king on notice that if he wished to solve his fiscal problem by taxing the nobility, he would have to listen to them in a more formal and organized way.

Aristocratic opposition represented the culmination of long-simmering resentments. Nobles found the growth of a wealthy stratum of commoners threatening, the king's unwillingness to take them into his trust frustrating, and the methods by which new taxes were being proposed irritating. The new taxes could not be levied by local assemblies, they argued, and if the new taxes were to be permanent, only an Estates General consisting of representatives of the entire realm could authorize it.

The Parlement of Paris sought to use the Estates General, historically France's most representative institution, to gain a political voice. The aristocracy was not totally unwilling to be taxed equitably, but in return it sought a written constitution that would establish its dominant position in French politics. Over the next year and a half the king and the Parlement were locked in a struggle of wills over this issue. When the recalcitrant Parlement refused to authorize issuance of any more government bonds to salvage the government's financial position, Louis first banished it, then recalled it, and then suspended all parlements. But in the end, facing bankruptcy, Louis had no choice but to adopt the Parlement's solution. He called an Estates General for the spring of 1789.

---

[2] Nobles of the Robe were administrators, primarily judges. They may be contrasted to Nobles of the Sword—military officers. The latter claimed higher status, but by the 1780s the French nobility was so varied that this difference in dignity was no longer of great importance.

The Estates General

At this point, no one had the slightest idea that France was on the verge of cataclysmic changes. The parlements thought that they were defending their privileges and seeking a reform that would benefit them; the king was hunting for a way out of the financial impasse while giving up as little authority as possible. But this tug-of-war between king and lords, which had characterized every European country since the Middle Ages, unfolded in a France that had evolved markedly since the death of Louis XV in 1774. More than half the people in northern France, and almost all politically active persons, were literate. Despite the efforts of the king's agents to censor critical writings, the country had never seen so much public discussion of political events. The first daily newspaper made its appearance in Paris in 1777. During the 1780s, hundreds of pamphlets and articles circulated in both Paris and the provinces. Full of the idea of popular sovereignty made current by Rousseau, they also contained discussions of the American Revolution and cries of alarm about the dangers of arbitrary rule, or despotism, as the pamphleteers liked to call it. Even urban illiterates were beginning to hear such rhetoric, through public readings. With many losing confidence in a system that seemed increasingly archaic, the call for an Estates General found widespread support. But no one advocated revolution, no one called for a republic, and very few overtly opposed the privileges of the nobility. Unwittingly, however, the French were developing a new kind of vocabulary about politics that fatally threatened the old order.

The fact that Louis convened an Estates General rather than taking some other step shows how traditional the thinking of the contending parties remained. The Estates General was a medieval institution that had lain moribund since 1614. It was so forgotten that once Louis decided to call one, archivists had to scurry about to determine who should attend and how the delegates were to be selected. The term *Estates General* itself meant "a general gathering of the estates of the realm." In this context, the word *Estates* referred to the three broadest social categories in France: the clergy (the First Estate, about 240,000 persons); the nobility (the Second Estate, about 400,000 persons); and the *roturier*, or everyone else (the Third Estate, about 27 million persons).

Once the announcement came for the meeting of the Estates General, French political writers launched themselves into the election campaign, the first ever held in France, with a furious volley of pamphlets, speeches, and discussions. The most famous of these was the pamphlet *What Is the Third Estate?* by the Abbé Sieyès. "What is the Third Estate?" Sieyès asked. "Everything. What has it been until now? Nothing. What does it want? To be something!" For the Third Estate to be something, however, it had to change the traditional method of voting in the Estates

General. The Parlement of Paris had ruled that voting would be by estates, but the "patriots," as the supporters of the Third Estate styled themselves—after the love that they claimed for the *patrie* (fatherland)—vigorously opposed voting by estate, for that method would give the upper categories a 2-to-1 majority. They sought voting by head instead. But because each estate would consist of equal numbers of delegates, even this method would not help the Third Estate unless the number of delegates for the Third Estate was at least equal to the sum of those for the other two estates. In December 1788, the King's Council agreed to "the doubling of the Third," and decreed that there should be six hundred delegates to the Third Estate, and only three hundred each to the other two. However, it left in place the Parlement of Paris's decision that voting be by estate, thus seemingly negating this concession.

Agitated by the rhetoric of the pamphlets, the delegates to the Estates General began streaming into Versailles in May 1789. They had been elected through complex rules that varied for each estate and each region, but in general the clergy and the nobility were compact enough to meet separately in each district and elect their representatives. The Third Estate used a three-part voting system. Males over age twenty-five who paid taxes equivalent to three days' wages were eligible to vote for electors, somewhat more affluent men whose taxes were equal to ten days' wages. The electors in turn chose the delegates, who had to be landowners and possess significant wealth. The

persons ultimately chosen to represent the Third Estate were therefore all citizens of means. Nearly half of them were officeholders or officials, and another quarter were lawyers or notaries. The arriving delegates brought with them about thirty thousand suggestions, complaints, and petitions, the so-called *cahiers des plaintes et doléances* (reports of complaints and grievances), from their constituents. Couched in traditional terms, a large number of the cahiers naively held that the king, once he learned the truth about how France was being run, would right all wrongs. Virtually none of them called for the kinds of revolutionary changes that were about to sweep France.

After the king ceremonially opened the session, the first two estates got busy electing presiding officers and forming committees, but the Third Estate held back. Its leaders, which included Sieyès, still wanted the estates to meet together and vote by head. May passed into June, and still the Third Estate gave no sign of beginning its formal sessions. Stimulated by increasingly fervid discussions, the delegates began to conclude that their main task should be writing a constitution for France that would go far beyond what the aristocrats had sought.

Finally, on June 12 members of the Third Estate invited the other estates to join them in creating a constitutional assembly. A joint roll call was held, but only a few dissident members of the lower clergy showed up. In the following days, however, more and more clergy came over, and on June 17 the question was put: Should those

Agitation at the Palais Royale The Duc d'Orleans, a distant cousin of Louis XVI who supported the Revolution, opened the grounds of his Palais Royal to political debates. Centrally located in Paris (see Map 21-1), the Palais became a forum for some of the most radical oratory of the Revolution. Here, an agitator harangues the crowd two days before the fall of the Bastille. *AKG London.*

meeting with the Third Estate declare themselves a new and separate assembly to represent the entire nation? The resolution passed 491 to 89, and the National Assembly was born. The destruction of hierarchy as the social basis of government began.

Even the feckless Louis XVI could recognize a challenge of this magnitude. On June 19, realizing a dramatic concession was needed, he decided to grant a limited constitution. Before he could convene the Estates General to do so, however, the delegates of the National Assembly gathered for a meeting on June 20 only to find that the king's guard had locked their meeting hall. Furious at what they interpreted as the king's effort to prevent them from writing a constitution, but at the same time exhilarated, they scouted out a nearby vacant building, which happened to be the king's indoor tennis court. There they met and took a solemn oath "never to disperse: and to foregather wherever circumstances require until the kingdom's constitution be established and fixed on sound foundations." The painter Jacques-Louis David, whose depiction of the tennis court oath opens this chapter, felt that only the grandest style was adequate to represent this dramatic moment.

On June 23, Louis, distracted since June 14 by the death of his son, finally convened a royal session of the Estates General consisting of all three estates. Trying to be firm, he declared the National Assembly illegitimate. At the same time, he conceded the right of the Estates General to consent to taxes and to allocate other funds. "Never

has a king done so much for any nation," Louis boasted. The clergy and the nobility agreed and, after the king and his ministers had departed the hall, rose to leave. But the members of the National Assembly remained seated. Concessions that they would have welcomed a year earlier no longer sufficed. Louis had agreed to be a constitutional monarch, but he had not mentioned privilege. Now, with the bit in their mouths, the leaders of the Third Estate would be satisfied only with an attack on hierarchy. Louis hesitated. Should he clear the hall? Should he insist on his prerogatives by force? "Oh, well," he sighed, "the hell with it. Let them stay" (*"Eh bien, foutre! qu'ils restent!"*). With unrest in Paris growing and crowds gathering even in Versailles, on June 27 Louis commanded the nobles to sit with the Third Estate.[3] Although no real legislation or discussion of issues had yet taken place, the aristocracy, which had wanted an Estates General to assert its right to govern in return for permitting itself to be taxed, was already outflanked and defeated.

Popular Revolt

Paris was a huge city by the standards of its day—600,000 to 650,000 people—and most of France's richest citizens lived there (see Map 21-1). So did a vast army of the

---

[3] After August 7, the National Assembly began calling itself the National Constituent Assembly, but for clarity, we will continue to call it simply the National Assembly.

MAP 21-1
REVOLUTIONARY PARIS

In 1789, Paris and its neighbors were cities with narrow, twisting medieval streets, not the broad boulevards of today.

poor—perhaps 100,000 Parisians composed a floating population of migrant workers and homeless unfortunates. Between these extremes lived a variety of middling sorts, most prominently the approximately 100,000 craftsmen who belonged to the various guilds. The center of French culture, Paris was also a focal point of political intrigue. Political clubs that had formed during the crisis of 1788 introduced the educated to the open discussion of political issues. Already restless, Paris became especially volatile in 1789 because crop failures after a harsh winter had driven the price of bread to its highest level in thirty years. In April false rumors that wages might be cut led to riots in which troops killed or wounded fifty persons. To maintain order, Louis strengthened his guard inside Paris from four thousand to seventeen thousand. By July 12 he had brought in thirty thousand more troops from the north and east to camps outside the city.

The phlegmatic Louis XVI wanted the best for his subjects and usually proved open to compromise. But these not unattractive traits made him seem weak in comparison to his grandfather, Louis XV. He also suffered from the public's ridicule of his wife, Marie Antoinette, the daughter of Habsburg ruler Maria Theresa. Marie Antoinette had married Louis in 1770 at the age of fifteen; he was sixteen. She wanted to live a freer and more open life than was considered proper for a French queen, but her casual style led to allegations of sexual impropriety. The charge was not true, but because Marie Antoinette's close links with Vienna also stirred suspicion that she was an Austrian spy, scurrilous and pornographic pamphlets about her had found wide circulation for many years and undermined both her reputation and the king's, well before 1789.

On July 11, 1789, the king attempted to assert his control over the mounting chaos by dismissing his main minister, Jacques Necker. Even though Necker was a Swiss German, a Protestant, and a commoner, he had risen to the top of Catholic France through his successes as a banker, financier, and author—as well as through the success of his wife's salon.[4] He had made himself wildly popular with the people of Paris by importing grain into the city at a

---

[4] Upper-class hostesses periodically invited the wittiest, most intelligent, and most powerful men they could find to discuss matters of public interest. Through these salons, women such as Madame Necker exercised an important political and intellectual influence. Her daughter, Germaine de Staël, also maintained a famous salon.

Marie Antoinette   The portrait painter Elisabeth Vigée-Lebrun portrayed Marie Antoinette before the Revolution as a dutiful mother with her children in the nursery, as shown in the left photo. However, that is not how most French subjects felt about their foreign-born queen, even if she never did say "Let them eat cake" on hearing that people had no bread. Others saw her as the "The Austrian Hen." *(left) Marie Antoinette in the Nursery; painting by Elisabeth Vigée-Lebrun, Chateau de Versailles et de Trianon. © Photo RMN-Girard Blot. (right) © Phototheque de Musées de la Ville de Paris, Cliche; Habouzit, Musée Carnavalet.*

time of hunger and high prices. Parisians saw him as the guarantor of the city's bread supplies and the protector of the people's cause.

News of Necker's dismissal arrived in the capital about noon on July 12, a pleasant Sunday that found most people outside enjoying their day off. Agitators immediately began claiming that the king, whom they already deeply suspected, had purposely insulted the people of Paris. Soon six thousand persons carrying a bust of Necker marched to the Tuileries, the king's nearby castle along the Seine. The German cavalry regiment defending the king's property tried to disperse the demonstrators, causing some injuries, but when the crowd retreated at nightfall, the commanders withdrew their troops.

The next day, panicked by the bloodshed, fear of the king's troops, soaring bread prices, and Necker's ouster, crowds of Parisians ranged through the city looking for weapons with which to defend themselves. Others took to looting grain and bread storage points. The electors of Paris, who had been chosen to pick the Parisian delegates to the Estates General, met to figure out how to restore order. Late that evening, they decided to organize an armed force of citizens to protect the city. This National Guard soon came under the leadership of General Lafayette, the hero of the American Revolution.

The new force, which existed at first primarily on paper, lacked arms. On the morning of July 14, a crowd of twenty to thirty thousand entered the Invalides, a military garrison and hospital not far from the Tuileries, where they seized guns but no powder. Early that afternoon, artisans in search of gunpowder converged on the Bastille, the fortress and prison that many had come to consider a symbol of royal despotism. The crowd demanded that the commander withdraw his artillery, which they feared would set the neighborhood on fire. He did so, but when they demanded his weapons as well, he refused. After confused negotiations, some daring attackers cut the chains to the fortress's drawbridge, and the mob spilled into the prison courtyard. At about five that afternoon, four cannons taken from the Invalides arrived. When the Bastille commander surrendered under a pledge of protection, the crowd seized the luckless fellow from his guards, cut off his head, stuck it on a pike, and paraded with it, along with the head of another official, to city hall.

Within a few days, the Paris electors formed a new government and formalized the National Guard. In response, the first wave of aristocratic emigrés fled the city to begin twenty-five years of bitter wandering through Europe. Having opposed royal power for centuries, in the face of popular revolt they became staunch royalists. As the startling news of the fall of the Bastille spread across France, fresh uprisings broke out in most major cities. Representatives of the Third Estate, usually the electors who had participated in the second stage of the elections, seized power throughout the country. Within a few weeks, the authority of the king had given way to newly formed municipal governments and national guards almost everywhere in France.

The Storming of the Bastille
This painting is considered the most authentic depiction of the attack on the Bastille. Soon after its capture by Parisians in 1789, the new government dismantled the prison-fortress. A monument to the regeneration of the republic occupied the space during the Revolution. Today it is the site of the new Paris opera house. *Musée Carnavalet, Paris. Photo: AKG London.*

Nor did the peasantry remain unmoved. The poor harvest of the previous year, skyrocketing prices coupled with speculation, an alarming number of vagabonds and beggars coursing over the land, and rising hopes fueled by the elections of the spring agitated and unnerved the countryside. In the spring and early summer of 1789, angry peasants had burned records and toppled weather vanes (a sign of nobility, as explained earlier). About a week after the storming of the Bastille, rumors spread that the aristocracy had initiated a scheme to take revenge for the events in Paris, that the peasants' misery revealed a plot to starve the people, and that "brigands" were about to attack. Quickly these and other rumors took on a life of their own. "The Great Fear," as the French know it, swept like wildfire across the countryside. By early August, peasants in many regions of France were in revolt.

More than two hundred years later, France still celebrates July 14, the storming of the Bastille, as its national holiday. It inspired the seizure of power by electors in cities throughout France and sparked the upheaval among the peasantry that left the king powerless. Louis himself recognized this when he visited his capital a few days after the fall of the Bastille wearing the tricolored cockade symbolizing the city's autonomy.[5] But France was fortunate that the National Assembly was in session when royal power collapsed, for it provided a focal point for legitimizing and institutionalizing change. It would be an exaggeration to say that July 14, 1789, was the moment when the Old Regime of kingly power was overthrown in favor of *Liberté, Egalité, et Fraternité*. It took two years to write a constitution, twenty-five years for the events of the Revolution to play themselves out, and eighty-five years before the principles of the Revolution took firm root in French institutions. But tradition has made that day the symbolic dividing line between what came to be called the Old Regime and modernity. It reminds us that ultimately the French Revolution transformed the way we think about society and politics. (see Table 21-1.)

The Revolution of the Moderates

The National Assembly at Versailles reacted to the Great Fear by what is known in French history as "the night of August 4." Frightened by the violence in the countryside, and hoping to save what they could while putting into effect some of their egalitarian principles, a group of radical delegates persuaded a few noblemen to renounce their privileges. Suddenly one delegate after another, including representatives of the clergy, of towns, and of provinces, jumped up to abandon his seigneurial rights. By the end of the evening, many who had arrived with no intention of relinquishing their privileges got caught up in the enthusiasm of the moment and found themselves abolishing the purchase of offices, eliminating noble immunities and privileges, and establishing equality of taxation.

The next day, when the National Assembly realized the extent of what it had done, the delegates backpedaled from their early enthusiasm by deciding that peasants would have to pay an indemnity over twenty-five years for the abolished dues. But soon the peasants simply stopped paying, and in 1793 the payments were revoked. The final decree of August 13, 1789, summed up what the night of August 4 and its aftermath had accomplished: "The **feudal** regime is entirely abolished."

August 4, 1789, illustrates a significant dynamic of the French Revolution: its growing radicalism as events pressured inexperienced politicians to make decisions in an organizational vacuum. The delegates who arrived in Versailles in May did not come to make a revolution, although most of them, including the nobility, thought that France should have a constitution. Educated and secure citizens, they were familiar with the ideas of the Enlightenment, feared despotism, and hoped to settle France's affairs. But the more they debated, the farther they wanted to go. Indeed, their aims soon went beyond what most French citizens would have been willing to accept in 1789. But, already elected, the National Assembly no longer had to ask the nation's opinion. Once the king had proven unwilling to clear out the delegates by force, the National Assembly faced no serious countervailing power. Having finally drawn up its rules of procedure by the end of July, the Assembly spent the next two years redesigning the governance and society of France.

As one of its first acts, the Assembly adopted the Declaration of the Rights of Man and of the Citizen. "Men are born and remain free and equal in rights," the delegates proclaimed. Natural law, the framers of the declaration believed, held that all persons were equal in their possession of the rights of liberty, security, resistance to oppression, and property. In addition, because all persons have the right to resist oppression, it followed that the nation as a whole was sovereign, not the king. In 1766 Louis XV had asserted, "It is only in my person that the sovereign authority resides. . . . The whole public order derives from me; I am its supreme guardian. My people exist only in their union with me." In 1789 the Declaration of the Rights of Man stated simply: "Sovereignty resides in the nation." No longer would the people be subjects of a king. They had become citizens of a nation.

Meanwhile, in Paris, the headlong flight of many nobility and the beginnings of their counterrevolutionary activities abroad led agitators to suspect an "aristocratic plot" was being hatched against them. The yellow press, led by the vitriolic journalist Jean-Paul Marat, editor of the paper *Ami du Peuple* ("Friend of the People"), fanned the flames of this rumor, as did the political clubs that were springing up throughout the city. The most radical of these

---

[5] A cockade is a ribbon or rosette of ribbons worn in the hat as a symbol of party allegiance.

TABLE 21-1

The French Revolution, 1789–1795

First Phase: The Fall of the Old Regime

1789	May: Estates General convenes
	June: Tennis Court Oath (June 17); Third Estate proclaims itself the National Assembly; king reluctantly agrees
	July: Dismissal of Necker (July 11); fall of the Bastille (July 14)
	August: "Great Fear" sweeps countryside; abolition of the feudal regime by National Assembly (August 4–13); Declaration of the Rights of Man and of the Citizen (August 26)
	October: Women's march on Versailles; king and queen forced to return to Paris; Jacobin club organized

Second Phase: "The Regeneration of France"

1789	November: National Assembly confiscates church property
1790	April: Bonds issued on security of confiscated church land *(assignats)* become legal tender
	June: Nobility abolished
	July: Civil Constitution of the Clergy adopted
	August: Jacobin clubs proliferate throughout France
	November: Burke's *Reflections on the Revolution in France* published in London
1791	June: King and queen flee Paris but are discovered in Varennes and brought back; Le Chapelier law bans unions and strikes
	September: Louis XVI promulgates constitution; Jews admitted to citizenship
1792	June: Military defeats and dismissal of Girondin ministers provokes popular outrage in Paris
	July: Duke of Brunswick threatens Paris with destruction if Louis XVI is harmed

Third Phase: The Radical Revolution

1792	August: Uprising in Paris (August 10); establishment of Paris Commune; installation of National Convention
	September: "September Massacres" of suspected antirevolutionaries; National Convention proclaims republic (September 21)
	December: Louis XVI put on trial for treason
1793	January: Execution of Louis XVI (January 21)
	April: Convention establishes Committee of Public Safety
	August: Mass mobilization *(levée en masse)* decreed
	September: Under pressure from *sans-culottes,* Convention agrees to fix prices and unleash terror against "enemies of the people"
	October: Execution of Marie Antoinette; execution of Girondin leaders
1793–1794	Counterrevolutionary revolts in Lyon, Marseilles, Toulon, and the Vendée region
1794	June: Festival of the Supreme Being climaxes de-Christianization

Beginning of the Fourth Phase (lasting until 1815): Consolidation

1794	July: Overthrow of Robespierre and Committee of Public Safety (July 27; 9 Thermidor); moderate revolutionaries return to power
1795	August: Establishment of the Directory under new constitution

THE HISTORICAL EVIDENCE

Equality and Rights: From the Old Regime to the French Revolution

1666–1791

From a book on the social orders by the lawyer Charles Loyseau, 1666:

The order to which this book is dedicated is a species of dignity, or honorable quality. In France it is particularly called Estate. Inasmuch as order is a species of dignity, the Third Estate of France is not properly an order, [since] this would imply that all the people of France without exception were in dignity.

From the Remonstrance of the Paris Parlement, *1776:*

Any system tending under the guise of humanity and benevolence to establish an equality of duties between men would soon lead to disorder. The result would be the overthrow of civil society, the harmony of which is maintained only by [a] hierarchy of powers, authorities, preeminences, and distinctions which keeps each man in his place.

From a decree of the National Assembly, August 11, 1789:

The National Assembly entirely destroys the feudal regime.

From The Declaration of the Rights of Man and of the Citizen, *August 27, 1789:*

Men are born and remain free and equal in rights. Social distinctions can be based only upon the general good. . . . Liberty consists in the freedom to do everything which injures no one else; hence the exercise of the natural rights of each man has no limits except those which assure to the other members of the society the enjoyment of the same rights. These limits can only be determined by law. . . . No one shall be disquieted on account of his opinons, including his religious views, provided that their manifestation does not disturb the public order established by law.

From Marie-Olympe de Gouges, Declaration of the Rights of Woman, *1791:*

Woman is born free and lives equal to man in her rights. Social distinctions can be based only on the common utility.

From the Le Chapelier Law, enacted by the National Assembly in June 1791:

Since the abolition of all kinds of corporations of citizens of the same occupation and profession is one of the fundamental bases of the French Constitution, re-establishment thereof under any pretext or form whatsoever is forbidden. All assemblies composed of artisans, workers, journeymen, [or] day laborers shall be considered as seditious assemblies.

Sources: Quotation from *Rights of Man* is from James Harvey Robinson, ed., *Readings in European History* (Boston: Ginn, 1904), vol. 2, pp. 409–411. Other quotes are from Keith Michael Baker, ed., *The Old Regime and the French Revolution* (Chicago: University of Chicago Press, 1987), pp. 15, 22, 27,119–120, 263, 248–249.

---

clubs was the group of politicians who met at the Cordeliers monastery. The Cordeliers and the press determined not to let the people of Paris forget that the price of bread remained high, despite good weather, and that Louis XVI had not yet signed either the abolition of feudalism or the Declaration of the Rights of Man and the Citizen.

In this heated atmosphere, a rumor reached Paris on October 3 that a regiment of guards had trampled the tricolor, by now the revolutionary flag, with the approval of Marie Antoinette. Outraged at what they took as a calculated insult to the Revolution and to Paris, and frustrated by the cost of bread, several thousand women decided to act. On October 5, they set out from City Hall for Versailles to demand bread from the king. A few hours later an equally agitated National Guard followed. The king agreed

to meet with the women, and when a seventeen-year-old girl fainted before him with the word "bread" on her lips, he promised Paris provisions. He also consented to sign the August decrees. But once again, concessions that would have inspired joy earlier were not enough. The women refused to disperse, and representatives of the National Guard demanded that the king return to Paris. At the urging of Lafayette, the commander of the National Guard, Louis agreed. "My friends," he said, "I will go to Paris with my wife and children. To the love of my good and loyal subjects I entrust what I hold most precious." A few days later the Assembly moved to the capital city as well.

Once in Paris, the king found himself virtually under house arrest in his palace at the Tuileries. In April 1791, for example, when he sought to hear **Mass** in St. Cloud

Parisian Women March on Versailles   This contemporary print shows the women of Paris pulling one of their two cannons in their march on Versailles to ask the king for bread. Since as "passive citizens" they were not permitted to carry firearms or join the National Guard, their other weapons included pikes, brooms, and kitchen tools.   *Bibliothèque Nationale, Paris.*

from a priest who did not support the Revolution, the Paris crowds saw the king's attempt as an antirevolutionary act and blocked him. Cooped up with the queen, the king became more and more opposed to the Revolution. He entered into a secret correspondence with Count Mirabeau, who, despite his title, had emerged from a tumultuous life of debauchery, debt, and prison to become one of the most inventive of the revolutionaries. Marie Antoinette also attempted various schemes, but to no avail.

The pair's most famous adventure was their attempt to flee France on the night of June 20–21, 1791. Dressed in none-too-convincing disguises, carried by a heavy and sumptuous carriage, and guarded by sympathetic troops pre-positioned along their route, the royal couple escaped out the only door of the Tuileries left unguarded and set out for the Austrian Netherlands. But the attempt was ill-starred from the beginning. The couple left two hours late; consequently, their supporting troops had returned to their camps; and their carriage was too obvious. Detained at Varennes, only a few miles from the border, the humiliated Louis and Marie Antoinette were brought back to the Tuileries through Paris streets packed with silent crowds.

For many contemporaries the most profound revolutionary act—and a key step in the breakdown of revolutionary consensus—was the assault on that seemingly impregnable bastion of privilege, the church. The Revolution lurched into motion originally because of the king's

need for money. Naturally, the National Assembly remained just as insolvent as the king's old government had been. To meet public obligations, the new men had to find a source of income. The anticlerical tenor of Enlightenment thought and the delegates' increasing antagonism to privilege led to the idea of confiscating the church properties, which constituted as much as 10 percent of the revenue-producing land in France. In November 1789, the Assembly decreed that all church lands were henceforth the property of the nation, and in April 1790 the bonds (*assignats*) issued using those lands as security became legal tender, a form of paper money. Even more significant, in July 1790 the Assembly enacted the Civil Constitution of the Clergy, which made all clergymen salaried employees of the state, thereby abolishing the traditional church hierarchy and ending the age-old independence of the church.

About half of the church leaders refused to take the oath of allegiance that the new state now required of them. These non-juring priests became adamant opponents of the Revolution. The Civil Constitution of the Clergy thus worsened the internal divisions that wracked France during the revolutionary period. During the nineteenth century, many French saw the Revolution primarily as a battle between the republic and the Catholic church. Some historians and opponents of women suffrage even went so far as to blame women for the survival of priestly influence, arguing that women were prone to defend the church,

The Royal Couple's Failed Flight Nothing more thoroughly discredited the king in the eyes of the nation than his attempt to flee the country with his wife and children. Following his arrest at Varennes, he was escorted back to Paris. Cheap prints of the scene were widely distributed. *AKG London/Jerome da Cunha.*

especially in the bedroom to their husbands, because their allegedly more emotional character made it difficult for them to give up the mysteries of the church in favor of the rationality of the Revolution. But support of the church and opposition to the Revolution did not depend on any nefarious female support of priests, but on the cultural shock, social disruption, and emotional impact of the revolutionary assault, which exerted their influences irrespective of gender and engaged French passions for decades.

Despite the drama of the events of 1789 to 1791, these years are known today as the "moderate period" of the Revolution. By any standard, however, the moderates accomplished startling changes. Besides negating seigneurial rights and secularizing the clergy, the National Assembly, heavily influenced by laissez-faire economic theory, abolished the guilds in favor of free entry into trades. In order to reinforce freedom of trade and prevent the recurrence of special corporate groups, it prohibited the creation of labor unions too. The Assembly also paved the way for abolishing the patchwork of local laws, customs, and regional

authorities by reorganizing France into eighty-three departments, which still form the basis of French government (see Map 21-2).

The Assembly crowned its efforts with the Constitution of 1791, promulgated with Louis XVI's grudging consent on September 14 of that year. The new basic law retained a single legislature, the Legislative Assembly, rather than creating an upper house, which royalists had wanted, and granted the king only a suspensive rather than an absolute veto (he could delay legislation, but not reject it completely). To relieve itself of potential charges of self-interest, the Assembly enacted a self-denying ordinance that excluded any of its members from participating in the new Legislative Assembly created by the constitution, a step that almost certainly increased the radicalism of later legislatures by barring moderates with political experience.

The new constitution based voting on property holdings, dividing the electorate into taxpaying "active citizens" and non-taxpaying "passive citizens," but it did not extend these rights to women. The few female delegates to

MAP 21-2
FROM PROVINCES TO DEPARTMENTS

During the *Ancien Régime,* the Parlement of Paris had jurisdiction over about half of France. In the regions making up this area, called the *pays d' élections,* taxes were collected by officials appointed by the king or by those who had purchased their offices. The rest of France consisted of regions, called *pays d' état,* in which local assemblies, each with their own bureaucracies, annually voted payments to the king. The variety of arrangements of the Old Regime defies easy generalization. The Revolution wiped the slate clean of those arrangements, and created eighty-three more or less equally sized departments headed by prefects appointed from Paris.

the constitutional assembly had argued vigorously that equity demanded that all property owners, irrespective of gender, should have the vote, but without success. One of the most famous revolutionary feminists, although she remained a monarchist, was Marie-Olympe de Gouges, who in 1791 published the *Declaration of the Rights of Woman.* In advocating equal political rights for both men and women—"A woman has the right to mount the scaffold; she must also have the right to mount the tribune"— Gouges argued that men debase themselves when they subjugate women. In 1793, the National Convention sent Gouges to the guillotine for sedition, and as the official journal put it, "for having forgotten the virtues which befit her sex."

Echoes Abroad

The French Revolution frightened foreign monarchs, of course. Catherine the Great of Russia had been a most enlightened autocrat, but after the Revolution began she stopped protecting indigent philosophes and supported royalist emigrés instead. In Vienna, the death of reformer Joseph II had brought another reformer, Leopold, to the throne, but his demise in March 1792 elevated the young, impetuous, and none-too-bright Francis II to power. The new Habsburg leader became a staunch opponent of the Revolution, eventually eliminating Jacobin-like conspiracies in both Vienna and Budapest.

The country that suffered the most from these turns to the right by the central and eastern European monarchs more successful revolutionary movements in some western regions. In Belgium, for example, which was under Habsburg rule in the 1780s, disgruntled local leaders rebelled against the reforms introduced by Joseph II, only to be put down by their democratic opponents and in 1792 to be defeated by a French invasion. A Dutch patriotic movement from the 1760s reached fruition in 1795 with the creation of the Batavian Republic, while in 1798 a Helvetic Republic came into being under French protection in what is today Switzerland.

In the Germanies, on the other hand, the impact of the French Revolution was quite the opposite. In the political arena, the revolutionary period, including the era of Napoleonic conquests, provoked significant, if short-lasting, political and military changes in Prussia. Aristocratic reformers created a centralized cabinet and introduced modest laissez-faire changes in the economy, while military officers opened the officer corps to careers of talent. The purpose of these and related reforms, according to one of their architects, was "a revolution in the positive sense, one leading to the ennoblement of mankind, to be made not through violent impulses from below or

The Revolution as Nurturing Mother Drawing on ideas popularized by Jean-Jacques Rousseau before the Revolution, men of the revolutionary generation idealized women as mothers, whose proper role was to raise children, not stain themselves in the public arena. In this print, with the legend "The French Republic Offers Her Breast to All Frenchmen," the Revolution itself has become a mother. *Bibliothèque Nationale, Paris.*

was Poland. Russia, Prussia, and Austria had already seized a significant part of Poland in 1772. When the Poles promulgated a liberal constitution in May 1791, Austria and Russia took another piece. In 1794 and 1795, an abortive Polish revolution under the leadership of a hero of the American Revolution, General Tadeusz Kościuszko, induced the three eastern powers to divide the remainder of Poland among themselves. This last of the three partitions of Poland, as they are called, removed Poland from the map as an independent entity for more than one hundred years (see Map 21-3).

As conservative forces consolidated themselves in central and eastern Europe, the French Revolution evoked

MAP 21-3

THE PARTITIONS OF POLAND

The three central and east European autocracies started cutting off pieces of Poland for themselves as early as 1772, but the outbreak of the French Revolution accelerated both Polish efforts to stay independent, and Russian, Austrian, and Prussian efforts to keep Poland down. By 1796, the three powers had completely absorbed the old Polish-Lithuanian Commonwealth.

Mary Wollstonecraft: English Feminist

The most important theorist of women's rights that the French Revolution inspired was not French, but English. Her work is today considered the most powerful contemporary assertion of how the principles of the Revolution could be expanded beyond what was then thought proper for women.

Mary Wollstonecraft was born into a poor but not destitute family near London in 1759. Despite a meager education, she developed a passion for writing as a teenager and left home at age nineteen seeking her independence. At twenty-four she and her sisters started a school for teachers in a community of religious dissenters. The school failed within a few years, but Wollstonecraft matured intellectually under the influence of the philosophically inclined dis-

Tate Gallery, London / Art Resource, NY.

senters. Her first book, on the education of young girls, appeared in 1785 and was soon followed by a novel about a rebellious but high-spirited heroine who refused to swear obedience in marriage. Wollstonecraft became a professional writer, no mean feat for an eighteenth-century woman, and wrote for Samuel Johnson's journal, *The Analytic Review.* When Edmund Burke published his famous critique of the French Revolution, *Reflections on the Revolution in France*, in 1790, Wollstonecraft responded immediately with a defense of the Revolution, *Vindication of the Rights of Man.* The companion volume, *Vindication of the Rights of Woman*, appeared two years later.

Vindication of the Rights of Woman is the first sustained argument for the rights of women based on natural-law philosophy. In the eighteenth century, women were encouraged to be passive, submissive, and dependent because they were considered the "weaker vessel." But there is nothing natural about women's being dependent, Wollstonecraft argued. Women learned to discount reason because they grew up in an environment that encouraged submissiveness. As Wollstonecraft pointed out, it went against natural law and reason to believe that a just God would have made women less

valuable than men by denying them the ability to reason. That view exists only because the arbitrary authority of the army, the aristocracy, and the church sustains it, she argued, and women will assert their natural equality only when those authorities are overcome. Such an overturning would be good for all, she asserted, because those who exercise power against the weak are themselves corrupted by that process. Wollstonecraft thought that women should be physically strong and should be permitted privacy for contemplation. It was doubly important that women use this contemplation to educate themselves, she believed, because most women will become mothers and will need to imbue their children with ideas of equality and purpose.

The Girondin Jacques-Pierre Brissot and his circle welcomed Wollstonecraft when she visited Paris in 1792, although she had little impact on the course of the Revolution itself. Despite its later fame, her book had almost no impact in England either, except to expose her to attacks from the establishment as one of the "impious Amazons of Republican France," and "a hyena in petticoat." By contrast, William Godwin, one of England's most celebrated free thinkers, admired her greatly. After reading one of her books, he declared that "if ever a book [was] calculated to make a man in love with its author, this appears to me to be the book." After a friendship marked by mutual respect and warmth, Wollstonecraft and Godwin married in 1797, but she died in childbirth that same year. The daughter who survived that birth, Mary, married the poet Percy Bysshe Shelley and wrote the novel *Frankenstein.* ❖

THE HISTORICAL EVIDENCE

Burke, Paine, and Wollstonecraft Debate Social Conventions, Human Rights, and the Foundations of Government

1790–1792

How do our conventions of social behavior relate to ways in which we govern our-selves? Edmund Burke, Thomas Paine, and Mary Wollstonecraft considered this question from three very different perspectives in their polemics over the French Revolution.

From Edmund Burke, English, Reflections on the Revolution in France, *1790:*

If civil society be the offspring of convention, that convention must be its law. That convention must limit and modify all the descriptions of constitution which are formed under it. . . . Government is not made in virtue of natural rights, which may and do exist in total independence of it. . . . Society requires not only that the passions of individuals should be subjected, but that even in the mass and body as well as in the individuals, the inclinations of men should frequently be thwarted. . . . But now [in the name of abstract principles] all is to be changed. All the pleasing illusions . . . are to be dissolved by this new conquering empire of light and reason. . . . All homage paid to the sex [i.e., women] in general as such . . . is to be regarded as romance and folly. . . . The murder of a king, or a queen, or a bishop, or a father, are only common homicide; and if the people are by any chance, or in any way gainers by it, sort of homicide much the more pardonable.

From Thomas Paine, American, The Rights of Man, *1791–1792:*

Hitherto we have spoken . . . of the natural rights of man. We have now to consider the civil rights of man, and to show how the one originates from the other. Man did not enter into society to become *worse* than he was before, nor to have fewer rights than he had before, but to have those rights better secured. His natural rights are the foundation of all his civil rights. . . . Natural rights are those which appertain to man in right of his existence. Of this kind are all the intellectual rights, or rights of the mind, and also all those rights of acting as an individual for his own comfort and happiness, which are not injurious to the natural rights of others. Civil rights are those which appertain to man in right of his being a member of society.

From Mary Wollstonecraft, English, Vindication of the Rights of Women, *1792:*

I earnestly wish to point out in what true dignity and human happiness consists—I wish to persuade women to endeavor to acquire strength, both of mind and body, and to convince them that the soft phrases, susceptibility of heart, delicacy of sentiment, and refinement of taste, are almost synonymous with epithets of weakness, and that those beings who are only the objects of pity will soon become objects of contempt.

Sources: Edmund Burke, from *Reflections on the Revolution in France* (Garden City, N.Y.: Doubleday [Dolphin Books], 1961), pp. 72, 90; Thomas Paine, from *The Rights of Man* (Garden City, N.Y.: Doubleday [Dolphin Books], 1961), pp. 305–306; Mary Wollstonecraft, from *A Vindication of the Rights of Women*, ed. Carol H. Poston (New York: Norton, 1975), p. 9.

outside, but through the wisdom of the government." At the same time, some German writers began to contrast what they considered the solid (or perhaps mystical) virtues of German *Kultur* with what they called the superficial rationalizations of French *Civilisation.* As we shall see in the next chapter, these responses had the important effect of beginning the development of German and European nationalism.

In Ireland, a revolt inspired by the French Revolution and provoked in part by a cruel British occupation eventually broke out in 1798. Undisciplined British troops brutally put down the uprising and, to prevent any further outbreaks of republicanism in Ireland, Parliament passed the Act of Union, which brought Ireland into Great Britain until after World War I. In England itself, the French Revolution elicited initial support and found a number of sympathizers—notably the scientist Joseph Priestly, the poet William Wordsworth, the activist Thomas Paine, and the feminist Mary Wollstonecraft—but British radicalism never was able to achieve more than rhetorical successes. Instead, Britain became revolutionary France's most vigorous and consistent antagonist. The philosophical politician Edmund Burke emerged as the Revolution's most sophisticated opponent. In *Reflections on the Revolution in France* (1790), Burke argued that speculative and abstract theories of natural rights evoked a moral fervor that devalued tradition and thoughtlessly destroyed the hard-won material and spiritual resources of society. Change was desirable, but only when it built on the positive values already embedded in society, not when it was based on abstract ideas of democracy and popular sovereignty that undermined the leavening role of the hereditary aristocracy. To imagine that political action could create an ideal society was not only idle, but pernicious, Burke argued, because it destroyed the good in the old as well as the evil.

Having fled from France, Louis XVI's two brothers strove to organize resistance to the Revolution, but their monumental incompetence and absurd program earned them little success. As the great nineteenth-century historian Alexis de Tocqueville put it later, they dreamed of "an Ancien Régime even more odious than the one that had been destroyed." A few months after the abortive Varennes adventure, however, the Austrian and Prussian rulers publicly expressed their interest in maintaining the monarchical principle in France, and in February 1792 the two entered into an alliance to defend the European monarchies against revolution. When the Austrians began to press some relatively trivial property claims against France, firebrands in the Legislative Assembly insisted that France stand up to them. Carried along by strident rhetoric, the Assembly declared war on Austria April 20, 1792, with only seven dissenting votes (including that of Robespierre). From that moment until 1815, France remained almost constantly at war with Europe.

A Meeting at the Jacobin Club   Political meetings in the Jacobin club drew throngs of spectators. By the time of this engraving, January 1792, most moderates had resigned from the club and the debates were becoming increasingly radicalized.   *Bibliothèque Nationale, Paris.*

The Second Revolution: August 10, 1792

Shrill debate in the Legislative Assembly preceded the outbreak of war. Exaggerated tirades of the most bellicose deputies under the leadership of Jacques-Pierre Brissot had led the Assembly in November 1791 to define as traitors all those who had left the country and not returned by January 1, 1792. The Girondins, as Brissot's group came to be called (because many of its leaders came from the Gironde district of France), advocated war as a way of uniting the French nation and spreading the doctrine of popular sovereignty to other parts of Europe. They argued that in contrast to their moderate opponents, who favored constitutional monarchy, they represented the will of the people, not the interests of the discredited king and the "aristocratic plot." They turned to the streets of Paris, where their program of abolishing the distinction between active and passive citizens generated enthusiastic support.

Most of the Girondins belonged to the Jacobin club. The most famous political club in history, the Jacobins are indelibly associated with the use of violence as a revolutionary weapon. Delegates to the Estates General from Brittany in northwest France had established the club in May 1789 to conduct private discussions of political strategy. From the beginning, however, the club did not limit itself to Bretons or to delegates. The open, often stirring discussions at the club attracted many of the most articulate and daring advocates of revolution. When the National Assembly moved to Paris in October, the club moved with it and began meeting at the former residence of a religious order, the Jacobins, from which its name derives.[6] (Few recall that the formal name was the Society of Friends of the Constitution.) By then the club was frequented by all of the most famous revolutionaries, including moderates like Lafayette, soldiers of fortune such as Count Mirabeau, and radicals like Maximilien Robespierre. Socially, its membership resembled that of the National Guard, including professionals, master craftsmen, writers, journalists, and merchants. The club also accepted applications for affiliation from regional groups, so that already by August 1790 some 150 Jacobin clubs had sprung up throughout France. The Jacobins thus became the first extensive revolutionary organization in Europe.

After Varennes, about three hundred of the more moderate Jacobins resigned their membership and began meeting at the convent of the Feuillants under the leadership of General Lafayette. Although most regional affiliates were more sympathetic to the constitutional monarchism of the Feuillants than they were to the republicanism of the remaining Jacobins, the latter successfully used populist arguments, such as advocacy of universal male suffrage and

appeals for unity, to keep the affiliates in line. From this time on, the Jacobins changed from a political discussion society to a revolutionary organization that actively sought to overthrow the king and establish a popular republic. Jacobins united many radical elements, including the Girondins, and they became the center from which Brissot coordinated his agitation for war.

The war that the Legislative Assembly had launched so enthusiastically in the spring of 1792 went badly for the French. The army had lost a sizable number of officers to emigration, it lacked arms, and it was not up to strength. By the summer of 1792, its defeats in the Austrian Netherlands and elsewhere had unleashed a torrent of outrage among the Girondins and other patriots, always ready to smell an "aristocratic plot" in every misstep. In June, the dismissal of some Girondin ministers brought eight thousand well-organized supporters onto the streets. A delegation of the demonstrators petitioned the Assembly in person for abolition of the king's suspensive veto and for erasure of the distinction between active and passive citizens (that is, between those eligible to vote and those eligible to serve in office). The petitioners especially opposed the rule that only active citizens could participate in the National Guard and bear firearms, whereas passive citizens could carry only pikes.

The Assembly declined to act on these recommendations, even though military reverses led it to declare the nation in danger on July 11. The Duke of Brunswick, the Prussian commander-in-chief, heightened the tension with a manifesto of July 25, in which he proclaimed that the European allies were invading France to restore the king's authority. The manifesto threatened the city of Paris with "total destruction" if harm came to the king. Alarmed by this crude threat, and unnerved by Jacobin and Cordeliers agitation, Parisian municipal authorities decided in late in July to distribute arms to all citizens, even passive ones. Two weeks later, the citizens of Paris used these weapons to destroy not the foreign invader, but the constitutional monarchy.

The revolt began on August 10, 1792, when insurgents massacred most of the six hundred Swiss Guards who were protecting the king. By nightfall the rebels took control of Paris and declared a new revolutionary government of the city, the Paris Commune. The Commune, whose members comprised a cross section of the Paris working class along with some radical orators, imprisoned the king and launched a vindictive purge of their moderate enemies. The Girondins and their allies in the Legislative Assembly, many of whom had not favored a popular uprising of this magnitude, nonetheless quickly took advantage of it.

Because moderates had fled the Assembly in fear of their lives, the radicals had no difficulty conducting an election for a new legislature, this one called the National

---

[6] *Jacobin* is a French term for the Dominican order.

Convention. Elected on the basis of universal manhood suffrage (except for servants), the Convention would write a new, more democratic constitution for France, decide what to do with the king, and deal with the multitude of enemies of the people, both foreign and domestic.

The Revolution of the Radicals

The government of Paris and of many cities across France now lay in the hands of radical democrats who aimed to complete the abolition of social distinctions, extend the Revolution to all of humanity, and purify France. First, however, they had to face the immediate problem of the advancing European armies, which by September 2 had taken Verdun, only about 100 miles east of Paris. Massive efforts to mobilize troops and supplies yielded a French victory at Valmy on September 20. Within the year, revolutionary armies, justifying themselves on the basis of France's need to advance to its "natural frontiers" and their right to spread the message of popular sovereignty to the benighted peoples of Europe, annexed or occupied Savoy, Nice, Belgium, and the German-speaking territory west of the Rhine. If this were not enough, the National Convention declared war on England, the Dutch Netherlands, and Spain.

Victory abroad did not bring stability at home. Executions of purported enemies of the Revolution started almost immediately after August 10. The most senseless and barbaric killings occurred in the first week of September, when vigilante crowds obsessed with "punishing the guilty" swept through the prisons of Paris. Without orders or direction, the mobs killed about 1,400 suspected enemies of the Revolution, some of them aristocrats or nonjuring priests but most simply poor jailbirds.

The most important symbolic—and perhaps actual—enemy of the Revolution remained the king. On September 21, the newly convened Convention abolished the monarchy and established a republic. In December it decided to try the king for treason. The trial brought to a head the power struggle between the Girondins and the so-called Mountain, the most radical faction of the Jacobins that sat in the top leftmost seats in the legislature.[7] The Mountain had succeeded in expelling Brissot and his Girondist allies from the Jacobin club in October 1792. At the king's trial, the animosities between the two groups took a bitter and personal turn. Despite the Girondins' vociferous support of revolutionary war and of universal male suffrage, the Jacobins had replaced the Girondins as the party of the people of Paris. The Jacobins never achieved a majority in the Convention, but this support of the Paris Commune brought them overwhelming influence. The Girondins believed that Louis XVI should be tried as a citizen for treason, and, if found guilty, punished. The Jacobins, partly as a way of getting at the Girondins, claimed that the people had already condemned the king by the "second revolution" of August 10 and that he should be executed forthwith. "I can see no mean," argued Louis-Antoine Leon de Saint-Just, the youngest and most extreme of the Jacobins. "This man must reign or die."

---

[7] Because the moderates sat on the right side of the legislature, from that day until this conservatives have been designed the *right* and their opponents (liberals, radicals, socialists) the *left*.

Execution of Louis XVI
This popular print, considered reasonably historically accurate, shows the executioner's son holding up Louis XVI's head to the crowd. Prints like this circulated in large numbers during the Revolution. *Bibliothèque Nationale, Paris.*

Sans-Culottes Debate
Political clubs and section meetings seem to have occupied most of the leisure hours of the politically active Parisian artisans. This drawing dates from 1793. A few of the participants wear knee-britches, but most are dressed in ordinary working clothes. None seem to look or behave like "gentlemen," and all appear to be male. Compare these debaters with those shown in the engraving of the Jacobin club meeting earlier. *Bibliothèque Nationale, Paris.*

The guilty verdict was never in doubt, but the Girondins hesitated to take such a momentous step as killing the king without submitting the verdict to the people. The Mountain had no intention of asking the people what they wanted. They had convinced themselves that their beliefs reflected the popular will. They interpreted the Girondin proposal for a referendum as an effort to save the king and destroy the Revolution. The Girondin motion lost overwhelmingly, and in mid-January 1793 the Convention voted by a small but absolute majority to execute the king immediately.[8] On January 21, after a vote for a reprieve failed, Louis XVI rode through the packed streets of Paris to the guillotine. "I die innocent," he said on the platform. "I pardon my enemies and I hope that my blood will be useful to the French." When the blade swiped off his head, the son of the executioner held it up triumphantly. "Long live the Republic! Long live liberty! Long live equality!" the massive crowd roared. Then it surged toward the platform to soak handkerchiefs in the king's blood and to bid on the pieces of Louis's clothing that were cut up and immediately auctioned off.[9]

The revolutionary people of Paris who supported the Mountain and the Paris Commune during the two years of the radical revolution are known as the *sans-culottes* (those "without britches"), because they wore the long, straight pants characteristic of artisans rather than the knee-length satin britches of the aristocracy (and also of their servants). They were the bedrock of the neighborhood political councils (sections) on which Parisian revolutionary democracy rested. When mobilized, they comprised tens of thousands of artisans and shopkeepers. Two or three thousand of their deeply committed and vigorous activists radicalized the Revolution through their pressure on the Convention. Here is how one of them responded in April 1793 to the question of what defines a *sans-culotte*:

A sans-culottes, you stuck-up bastards? He is a being who always goes on foot, who has no millions, . . . no castle, no valets to serve him, and who lives simply with his wife and children, if he has any, on the fourth or fifth floor. He is useful, because he knows how to plow a field, to forge, to saw, to file, to roof a building, to make shoes and to spill out the last drop of his blood for the salvation of the republic. . . . In the evening, he attends his section, not powdered, perfumed, and booted in the hope of catching the attention of the female citizens at the tribune, but to support good motions with all his force and to pulverize those which come from the abominable faction of the men of estate. (Baker, 1987, p. 331)

[8] It is usually said that the decision to put the king to death was decided by one vote, and indeed 361 out of 721 voters did vote for death without conditions. However, 34 others also voted for death, but with conditions, such as that all Bourbons would have to leave France.

[9] Marie Antoinette met a similar fate. She was charged with treason, tried, found guilty, and sent to the guillotine on October 16, 1793.

With this kind of passion behind them, members of the Mountain, despite the group's minority status in the Convention, seized control of the Revolution. The Committee of General Security, supported by some 20,000 revolutionary committees throughout France, undertook to root out treason and subversion. When this police network uncovered hoarders, aristocrats, Feuillants, and other counterrevolutionaries, it turned them over to revolutionary tribunals, which "tried" the accused, found them guilty, and executed them, usually by the guillotine, the newly invented, egalitarian, and supposedly humane killing machine.[10] In April 1793, the Convention authorized the creation of the Committee of Public Safety, which, despite the approval of an extremely democratic constitution by a referendum in June 1793, soon assumed dictatorial control over the country.

The increasingly radical acts had destroyed whatever unity still existed in France. Counterrevolutionary revolts broke out in cities across the country, including Lyon, Marseilles, and Toulon (see Map 21-4). In western France, in the region known as the Vendée, a widespread peasant uprising provoked by conscription of recruits and fanned by non-juring priests pitted the revolutionary republic against peasant forces demanding the return of their traditional church. When the Convention failed to defeat the Vendée uprising immediately, it adopted a policy of devastating the region. Over the next year, it burned villages and killed all their inhabitants. The resulting ill will between Catholics and revolutionary democrats has plagued France ever since. To make matters worse, foreign armies now pressed France on several fronts.

To meet these threats, the Committee of Public Safety decided on mass mobilization. "Henceforth," it declared on August 23, 1793, "until the enemies have been driven from the territory of the Republic, the French people are in permanent requisition for army service." The decree ordered: "The young men shall go to battle. The married men shall forge arms and transport provisions; the women shall make tents and clothes and shall serve in the hospitals; the children shall turn old linen into lint; [and] the old men shall repair to the public places to stimulate the courage of the warriors."[11]

This **levée en masse** inaugurated a new era of war making that would reach a terrible fruition in the twentieth century. Heretofore in the eighteenth century, professional armies had fought set pieces in which commanders tried not to lose their valuable assets. The public was not deeply involved in these battles, which took place in relatively

---

[10] In the Old Regime, common criminals were hanged. Only the nobility had the right of beheading. Thus, in a bizarre way, the guillotine symbolized the Revolution's egalitarian thrust, as well as its interest in modern technologies.

[11] Despite the general mobilization, women were specifically forbidden to serve in the army, although a few managed to do so surreptitiously.

MAP 21-4
RESISTANCE AND COUNTERREVOLUTION

In assessing the contributions of the French Revolution, we often forget how much opposition it engendered. The Vendée uprising and the Terror are two important moments in which the revolutionary government defeated and even massacred its opponents.

confined locations. But now, for the first time, a country had called an entire nation to arms. The levée generated considerable revolutionary and even nationalistic fervor from a divided nation. This passion imbued French armies with a spirit that made them a formidable military force throughout the years of fighting that lay ahead. Headlong attacks by massed columns, rapid movement and efficient logistics, and the maximum use of artillery replaced the precision training of the Old Regime. But the very enthusiasm and involvement of the French public foreshadowed a horrible new kind of warfare in which not just armies, but entire populations strained every sinew in the war effort, and in which civilians too became military targets.

The Terror

The final stage in the revolution's radical phase started in September 1793. The sans-culottes lacked an explicit program, but their complaints were crystal clear: shortages of soap and sugar, high prices for bread, and profiteering. Kept in a state of anxiety by the popular press, they were also cultivated by radical political competitors of the Mountain, such as the *enragés* ("the wild ones") and the Hébertists from the Cordeliers club. The enragés put forward a simple program: Fix prices at a maximum level and guillotine the speculators. One of their leaders, Claire Lacombe, came onto the floor of the National Convention in May 1793 and beat delegate Théroigne de Méricourt almost to death with a whip. Under the influence of such extreme groups, an agitated delegation of sans-culottes surged into the Convention on September 5, 1793. "It is time that equality pass the scythe over every head," their spokesman declaimed. "It is time to terrorize all conspirators. Well then! Legislators, make terror the order of the day. Let the blade of law hang over all who are guilty!" The Convention agreed and in short order not only legalized the elimination of all enemies of the people but also met the sans-culottes' demand to fix prices. By the end of the year, dictatorial authority for conducting these policies passed completely into the hands of the Committee of Public Safety, whose most fanatical leader, Saint-Just, exhorted the people "to punish not only the traitors, but even those who are indifferent; you have to punish whoever is passive in the republic, and who does nothing for it."

Under the direction of the Committee of Public Safety and its chief spokesman, Maximilien Robespierre, almost half a million persons suffered arrest throughout France during the climax of revolutionary fervor, and more than fifteen thousand were guillotined.[12] The Terror, as this era became known, might have been justified at first as an effort to control the civil and foreign wars tearing at France in the summer of 1793. But when the season of crisis passed, the executions actually increased. Terror became more than a way to cleanse and regenerate a revolution in danger; it was now a method of rule wielded by an increasingly isolated group surrounding Robespierre.

Many of the Terror's most important victims were revolutionaries who lost out in factional struggles with Robespierre. In June 1793, the sans-culottes had forced the Convention to expel about twenty Girondin critics of the Mountain, and in October these men, including Brissot, went to their deaths, accused of mindless warmongering and self-interest. The leaders of the enragés, who fomented the September 1793 agitations, were its first victims, and the Hébertists went to the guillotine in March 1794. The final major sacrifice was Georges Jacques Danton, who had been the dominant figure on the Committee of Public Safety in mid-1793 and whose booming voice and unpredictable speaking style made him one of the Revolution's

most popular orators. Accused of "indulgence" toward the enemies of the Revolution for trying to moderate the Terror, he and his allies mounted the guillotine on April 5, 1794. The cool last words of Danton, who had an unusually large and none-too-handsome head, became famous. Addressing the executioner, he said, "Above all, don't forget to show my head to the people: it's worth seeing."

Robespierre and his colleagues felt justified in using terror, believing that they were substituting a new society based on reason and equality to replace the old society of faith and privilege. Only if the Old Regime could be destroyed root and branch, they felt, could the fragile new growth take hold. One of the most curious rationalizing reforms was the revolutionary calendar. To emphasize the significance of the Revolution, which the revolutionaries deemed greater than the birth of Jesus, the National Convention began numbering the years from the establishment of the republic on September 22, 1792. They divided the year into twelve months of thirty days each, each month consisting of three ten-day weeks. The months had names that suggested the time of year and the qualities of each month, such as *Nivôse* (Snow) and *Germinal* (Budding). To

Danton on His Way to the Guillotine   Georges Jacques Danton was one of the Revolution's great orators. "Audacity, again audacity, always audacity!" he once cried out at a critical moment. He went to his death with a proud gleam in his eye. *Drawing by Wille. Musée Carnavelet, Paris / E. T. Archive.*

---

[12] All in all, more than 30,000 persons died in the Terror, mostly in areas of rebellion. Of these only about 9 percent were noble—two-thirds were ordinary people.

THE HISTORICAL EVIDENCE

The Republic of Virtue

1793–1794

By the spring of 1793, the French Revolution moved into its most radical phase under the leadership of Maximilien Robespierre and the other members of the Committee of Public Safety. Their goal was not only to establish a new political regime to replace the now defunct monarchy, but also to restructure the entire French society. Every aspect of life would be changed, from what people called the days of the week and months of the year to what religion they followed. That new society, Robespierre told the Convention in 1793, would be based on the ideals of democratic virtue.

In our land we want to substitute morality for egotism, integrity for formal codes of honor, [and] love of glory for the love of money. Now, what is the fundamental principle of popular or democratic government, that is to say, the essential mainspring which sustains it and makes it move? It is virtue.

Robespierre's remaking of society reached its high point in June 1794 with the Festival of the Supreme Being, a pageant he, as president, spent much time in planning.

The president, armed with the Flame of Truth, will descend from the amphitheater and approach a monument raised on a circular basin, representing the monster, Atheism. From the middle of this monument, which the president will set on fire, the figure of Wisdom will appear. After this ceremony, the president will return to the rostrum and speak again to the people, who will answer him with songs and cries of joy.

The show did not occur exactly as planned: Wisdom emerged from the smoke badly smudged.

Source: From Keith Michael Baker, ed., *The Old Regime and the French Revolution* (Chicago: University of Chicago Press, 1987), pp. 370–377, 387.

Festival of the Supreme Being This engraving suggests the great effort that went into staging the revolutionary Festival of the Supreme Being in June 1794, over which Robespierre presided only six weeks before his arrest and execution. Painter Jacques-Louis David designed the event's centerpiece. Liberty sits on her throne to the right, along with a tree of liberty, while a classical urn to the left almost suggests a pagan offering. *Bibliothèque Nationale, Paris.*

accommodate 365 days, they added the *sanculottides*, or five holidays at the end of each year, entitled *Virtue, Genius, Work, Opinion,* and *Reward.* Every day was to be divided into ten hours of one hundred minutes, and each minute into one hundred seconds. The calendar reform was only one aspect of a violent campaign of de-Christianization, which led to the destruction of countless monasteries, convents, and churches throughout France. Robespierre and others tried to substitute a Republic of Virtue, complete with elaborate ceremonials, but in the long run tradition won out. Napoleon finally abandoned the revolutionary calendar in 1805.

A much more successful adoption was the metric system of measurement. No one outside of France adopted the revolutionary calendar, but by the end of the nineteenth century the metric system had replaced the scores of local measuring schemes that had flourished on the Continent since the Middle Ages. Today, except in the United States, it is the world standard.

Such dramatic changes proved difficult to sustain. The Terror itself proved too emotional, its promises too hollow, its aims too remote. By mid-1794, the French had endured five years of revolution and moral lectures, each more harrowing than the one before. Human beings can sustain this kind of tension for only so long. On the ninth day of the revolutionary month of Thermidor, Year II (July 27, 1794), after a now isolated Robespierre had demanded yet another purge of the Convention, a coalition of his extremist and more moderate opponents rose against him and sent the Puritan of natural reason to the guillotine. Since that time, the term *Thermidor* has been synonymous with reaction against revolutionary extremes.

NAPOLEON

With the fall of Robespierre, moderate revolutionaries returned to power. In 1795 they adopted yet another constitution. Five directors and a bicameral legislature elected by only twenty thousand property owners established a nervous, unstable regime. The Directory was designed as a liberal republic, but when threats appeared the directors resorted to coups. In 1797 they annulled an election of royalists, and in 1798 they refused to seat many elected candidates who came from the Jacobin left. Such behavior cost the Directory the respect of the French electorate. The Directory nevertheless had some solid successes. Facing a disastrous economic situation, it replaced the worthless paper currency, the assignats, with metallic currency, rationalized the tax structure, and consolidated the government debt. These measures provoked short-term distress, causing the Directory to lose even more public support, but they laid the foundations for later economic reconstruction. As dissatisfaction grew, a new phenomenon appeared: "the man on horseback," the military leader who vowed to save France, and, if permitted, all of Europe.

From Obscurity to Emperor

Napoleon Bonaparte was born in Corsica only one year after that poverty-stricken island became part of France. The son of a modestly noble family, Napoleon was so aggressive and energetic as a child that his father sent him at the age of nine to military school in France. There he proved a disciplined and hardworking student, although he excelled only in mathematics. Otherwise he remained a loner acutely aware of his Italian origins. He nevertheless mastered French and won a scholarship to the royal military academy in Paris, from which he emerged a second lieutenant of artillery in 1785. Napoleon became an adequate artillery officer, but he spent much of his early career in Corsica, where he dallied with nationalist and revolutionary politics. By chance, he happened to be in Paris on August 10, 1792, during the "second revolution." Already sympathetic to republicanism, he became a supporter of Robespierre.

By 1793 Napoleon was only a captain. Without the Revolution, he probably never would have advanced much higher, for he was not French, he lacked contacts at court, and the artillery branch normally produced few generals. But revolutions pave the way for talent, and Napoleon's success from this year on was nothing short of phenomenal. He made his first mark at Toulon, the major French naval base on the Mediterranean. In July 1793, the French navy there had revolted against the revolutionary Convention and formed a military alliance with the British navy. Napoleon managed to attach himself to the republic's forces besieging Toulon, whereupon he badgered, cajoled, and bulldozed the revolutionary leadership to accept his plan for capture of the city. It succeeded, and on December 22, 1793, Bonaparte won promotion to brigadier general, an impossible leap in less troubled times.

In 1795 Napoleon secured his position with what a later historian called "a whiff of grapeshot." In the spring of that year, the sans-culottes remained as dissatisfied as they had been a year before. Food was still scarce, prices high, and speculation rife. In April 1795, and again in May, the sans-culottes rioted, demanding bread and a return to the radical Constitution of 1793, but the Thermidorean Convention suppressed them without bloodshed. In October, royalists tried to raise the Paris Commune against the constitution that established the Directory. This time the government, following the urging of a member who knew Napoleon from Toulon, gave Bonaparte the task of defending it. Napoleon rushed cannons filled with grapeshot, links of chain, nails, and scrap metal into the approach to the Tuileries and fired them at the crowds point-blank, defeating the coup, pacifying Paris, and permitting the Directory to begin functioning. The grateful directors made Napoleon commander of the Army of the Interior and soon of the Army in Italy. He was twenty-six years old.

By mid-1795, France had made peace with all its enemies except Austria and England. For a year and a half beginning in 1796 the new commander attacked the Austrian armies in northern Italy. Inspiring his older, skeptical, but highly competent commanders, and motivating his troops by finding ways to pay them in gold rather than paper money, Napoleon marched from victory to victory until the Austrians surrendered. By the Peace of Campo Formio (1797), the Austrians confirmed the French conquests of Belgium and the west bank of the Rhine, as well as other acquisitions (see Map 21-5).

A master tactician who extracted just the right data from the tremendous confusion that surrounds a battlefield commander, Napoleon had the decisiveness to act as soon as he was aware of the true situation. Unlike the old-school generals whom he faced in Italy, he was a scrambler who applied constant pressure. He was willing to fight on Sundays, at night, during holidays, and in any kind of weather. He never asked for a truce, refused to brood over past mistakes, slept little, and pressed his enemies relentlessly. His

MAP 21-5
THE EXPANSION OF REPUBLICAN FRANCE, 1791–1799

Even before Napoleon, French revolutionaries began annexing neighboring territories, but under Napoleon metropolitan France extended down the boot of Italy and even into the Balkans.

troops and officers loved him because he paid them regularly and gave them victories. The directors in Paris liked him for the same reason—he won, and then he sent money and priceless art treasures home. Napoleon reportedly said once that the quality he admired most in a general was good luck, but his own victories were not the result of chance. A painstaking analyst, he stored everything he learned in a precise memory. He once described his mind as a vast file cabinet: When he chose to open one of the drawers, all the facts were still there. "A commander," he advised, "must ask himself many times a day what he would do if he were to come under attack at that moment. If he is embarrassed or wrong, he must make changes immediately." Napoleon's apparent good luck came from thorough knowledge and overwhelming energy, as well as from his willingness to place confidence in capable subordinate commanders. "Chance," he knew, "cannot bring success."

After Napoleon's victories in Italy, the directors began to fear that he might develop political ambitions. In part to get him out of their way, in 1798 they approved his outlandish plan to damage the British by invading Egypt and cutting the trade route to India. Napoleon's army reached Egypt, accompanied by scholars who began the modern discipline of Egyptology. But when the British navy destroyed the French fleet at Abukir Bay, Napoleon discovered that he had no way to supply his troops or return them to France. He found a typically daring solution: He abandoned his army and slipped into Paris before news of the Egyptian disaster could reach the Continent.

Napoleon's return to Paris in mid-October 1799 came at a propitious moment. The Directory was suffering military defeats again and as part of its fiscal reforms had repudiated debts greater than those of Louis XVI's government. Revolt had resurfaced in the Vendée, and resurgent Jacobins held a strong position in the legislature. To counter these threats, Abbé Sieyès, who had reappeared in French politics with his appointment as a director in 1799, had put together a political alliance willing to try yet another **coup d'état**, but he needed a military leader. Bonaparte arrived just in time to fill that slot.

Sieyès got more than he bargained for. The plan required him to trump up an emergency, call the bicameral legislature into session outside Paris in St. Cloud, and get the directors to resign. A new constitution appointing Sieyès, Napoleon, and a third person as "consuls" would then be adopted. (Note Napoleonic France's fondness for ancient Roman titles.) The upper house agreed to the scheme on November 9 (18 Brumaire in the revolutionary calendar), but when the lower house hesitated the next day, Napoleon appeared personally and demanded special powers to save the government. Hostile legislators challenged him, even struck him, and his guards had to carry him to safety. Ominously, the legislators began shouting "Outside the law!"—the chant that had accompanied Robespierre's downfall. But at the decisive moment, Lucien

The Napoleonic Legend
One of Napoleon Bonaparte's most spectacular accomplishments was leading his army across the Alps so that it could surprise the enemy in northern Italy. The painter Jacques-Louis David, a Jacobin turned enthusiast for Bonaparte, created this classic expression of the Napoleonic legend. Note the rock on which Bonaparte has inscribed his name next to those of Charlemagne and Hannibal. In David's conception, Bonaparte, his horse, and his indomitable will have become veritable forces of nature.
Giraudon/Art Resource, NY.

Bonaparte, Napoleon's brother and the president of the lower chamber, rallied the troops outside the hall. When the soldiers entered the assembly with bayonets fixed, the legislators fled, many of them out the windows. Lucien gathered enough compliant legislators to decree a temporary government that included Sieyès and Napoleon. Over the next month, Napoleon outmaneuvered Sieyès to become First Consul, the position from which he began his fifteen-year rule over France (see Table 21-2).

In seeking special powers, Napoleon had promised to end civil conflict, stabilize finances, codify the law, and terminate France's foreign wars. His efforts to fulfill these promises proved just as vigorous and sweeping as the promises themselves. He replaced locally elected officials with centrally appointed bureaucrats, called prefects, whose office persists in France to this day. He further rationalized taxation and streamlined collections. France was the most highly taxed country in Europe during his reign, but it also had the most stable currency, the least corruption, and one of the highest levels of tax compliance. To stabilize finances, Napoleon chartered the Bank of France. These steps, built on the earlier reforms of the Directory, helped the French economy prosper and even grow during his rule. Napoleon believed that secondary education should be based on merit. The lycées (secondary schools) and the baccalaureate examination that he instituted are still in use in France today. These innovations furthered the Revolution's secularizing impact, because they kept secondary education primarily in the hands of the state rather than the Catholic church.

TABLE 21-2

NAPOLEON BONAPARTE

1769	Born in Corsica
1793	December: Helps revolutionary army take Toulon
1795	October: Subdues Paris crowd with "whiff of grapeshot"
1797	Defeats Austrians and Russians in Italy
1799	October: Returns to Paris after Egyptian fiasco
	November: Coup of 18 Brumaire
	December: First Consul
1804	Crowns himself as emperor
1805–1806	Defeats Austria (battles of Ulm and Austerlitz), Prussia (battles of Jena and Auerstadt), Russia (battle of Friedland)
1805	Navy suffers defeat by British Admiral Nelson at Trafalgar
1807	Meets Alexander I of Russia at Tilsit; dominates the Continent
1812	June: Invades Russia
	October–December: Retreat from Moscow
1813	October: Defeated at Leipzig (Battle of the Nations)
1814	January–March: Allied armies invade France, seize Paris
	April: Napoleon abdicates; sent to the Island of Elba
	May: Louis XVIII (brother of Louis XVI) set on French throne
1815	March: Napoleon leaves Elba, lands on the southern coast of France; marches north; Louis XVIII flees
	June: Meets British and Prussian armies south of Waterloo and is defeated
	July: Exiled to the British island of St. Helena in the South Atlantic
1821	Dies on St. Helena

Napoleon brought new equilibrium to the realm by working out a concordat with the pope that came into effect in 1802. In return for a declaration that Roman Catholicism was the majority religion of France, the pope accepted the permanence of the church's losses during the Revolution. Priests remained state employees; divorce was permitted; and marriage became a civil contract rather than solely one of the **sacraments.** The agreement put to rest one of the most divisive conflicts of the revolutionary years. In an equally audacious secularizing innovation, Napoleon called together an assembly of Jewish notables to assess their loyalty to France. Assured by what he saw, he granted Jews full citizenship. Thus France became the first country in Europe to recognize Jews as full and equal citizens.

In many other spheres, Napoleon brought to fruition projects introduced by previous revolutionary regimes. He fully implemented the metric system, assisting in its spread throughout Europe and eventually the world. The National Library took its place as one of France's most esteemed institutions under Napoleon, the Louvre blossomed as the national museum, and the Great Schools—the elite institutions that still train France's governmental and business leaders—became permanent. His engineers constructed 50,000 miles of roads, built the Arc de Triomphe, and reconstructed Paris's sewer system.

Finally, and most importantly, Napoleon brought to life the revolutionary promise of equality through the promulgation of seven law codes. The civil code (*Code Napoléon*) of 1804, which Napoleon took a personal hand in writing, declared the principle of equality before the law, although it would not meet today's standards for equity, for it placed women in an inferior but protected position in order to meet Napoleon's concern for stabilizing the family. The criminal code, also based on the principle of equality before the law, introduced trial by jury and forbade arbitrary arrest. Napoleon's law codes rooted the principle of equality firmly in French legal practice, thus laying the groundwork for women and other excluded groups later to claim their rights.

Because all of these reforms not only outlasted Napoleon but have formed the fabric of French society ever since, it is fair to say that Napoleon completed the work of the French Revolution. Indeed, Napoleon saw himself that way, as the enlightened ruler bringing reason and good government first to France and then to Europe. But his accomplishments had a seamy underside. Revolutionary political theory insisted on popular sovereignty, and Napoleon professed to believe in this principle. But he did not hold ordinary elections (although one could argue that his popularity did reflect the general will). His contribution was the plebiscite, a yes-or-no vote on a specific issue. When he became First Consul in 1799, he asked the voters only one question: Do you approve of my becoming First Consul? The answer: 3,011,007 yes; 1,562 no. The fact that voters had to announce their votes aloud rather than drop ballots in a box may well explain the lopsided result. Such an electoral farce debased the notion of popular sovereignty.

Napoleon also kept close control over the press, suppressed free speech when it suited him, and had no compunctions about imprisoning and even executing opponents. Despite the principle of equality before the law, officers enjoyed special privileges. Under Napoleon's watchful eye—he worked fifteen hours a day, six days a week when in Paris—France was a dictatorship, whatever other principles it might have bequeathed the West. In 1802 Napoleon had himself appointed Consul for Life (the plebiscite voted 3,568,885 to 8,374 in favor of that decision), and in 1804 he elevated himself to emperor. In an elaborate ceremony in Notre Dame, he placed the crown blessed by the pope on his head with one hand, while with the other he grasped the sword of Charlemagne. The French dutifully approved, 3,572,329 to 2,567.

Abroad, Napoleon kept his promise to bring peace, at least for the moment. By the year 1802, France was free of war for the first and last time between 1792 and 1815. But Napoleon remained restless. He chafed at the idea of limits, and he had rarely failed at anything. Having risen from obscurity to rule over the most powerful state in Europe at the tender age of thirty, he naturally assumed that nothing lay beyond his grasp. He continued, as he put it, to follow his star.

From Emperor to Exile

In 1803 Napoleon set out to dismantle the Holy Roman Empire. Two years later, the major states of Europe combined to stop him, but they found the French emperor at the peak of his form. In 1805, at the battle of Ulm, he defeated the Habsburgs, and when their Russian allies came to their aid, he crushed them both at Austerlitz. In 1806, when Napoleon formally declared the Holy Roman Empire at an end, King Frederick William III of Prussia ordered Napoleon's troops to leave German soil by October 9. Instead of marching westward back to France, Napoleon marshaled his forces and moved east. On October 14, he humbled the Prussians at Jena and Auerstadt, reaching

Napoleon Crowns Himself
Jacques-Louis David's sketch made in preparation for his huge painting of Napoleon's coronation as emperor in Notre Dame Cathedral suggests much better than the painting itself the arrogance of Napoleon as he grasps his sword to his heart and places the crown on his head before a passive and supine Pope Pius VII. After crowning himself, Napoleon crowned his wife Josephine, who knelt before him. *Napoleon se couronnant-Etude pour la Sacre. David, Jacques-Louis (1748–1825). Louvre.* © *Photo RMN-Gerard Blot.*

Berlin from the Rhine River in only eighteen days. The Russians once more rushed to the rescue, and again Napoleon defeated them handily at Friedland in East Prussia. Frederick William fled to the medieval Baltic city of Königsberg (now Kaliningrad, Russia) to lick his wounds, and in 1807 Tsar Alexander I of Russia personally met Napoleon at nearby Tilsit and agreed to become France's ally in dividing Europe.

Napoleon's dizzying series of victories, which made him master of Europe, ranks among the most remarkable in the history of warfare. Ulm, Austerlitz, Jena/Auerstadt, and Friedland are still studied by strategists throughout the world as classic examples of effective warfare. Napoleon's understanding of the importance of supply ("an army marches on its stomach"), his strategy of overwhelming the enemy with massive force rather than maneuvering smaller, trained professional armies around, his sustained use of artillery, and his mobilization of the "nation in arms" all had their legacies in the wars of mass destruction that characterized the first half of the twentieth century.

By 1807 Napoleon dominated Europe (see Map 21-6). He directly administered only metropolitan France, but he had expanded its definition to include such un-French areas as the Netherlands, Milan, and, later, even the Illyrian Provinces, in today's Croatia and Slovenia. To the satellite states bordering France, he usually granted a constitution to accompany one of his friends or relatives as ruler. Some German states fell into this category, as did Naples and other Italian regions. The so-called independent allies—Austria, Prussia, and the Grand Duchy of Warsaw—he tried to control by indirect means.

Napoleon's success was not complete, however. Two countries continued to elude his influence. One, Russia, he temporarily neutralized at Tilsit, but the other, Great Britain, he could never overcome. Realizing that Britain's strength rested on its commercial power, Napoleon made every effort to destroy his rival's trade. But after Admiral Horatio Nelson sank the French fleet off Trafalgar in 1805, the French had no means to attack British commerce decisively or to sustain an invasion of the British Isles (although he made three abortive attempts). In 1806, therefore, Napoleon declared all European trade with Britain illegal. By creating this "Continental System," Napoleon hoped both to weaken England financially and

MAP 21-6

NAPOLEON'S EMPIRE AT ITS HEIGHT

¿Por Qué? Spanish painter Francisco José de Goya y Lucientes made an unforgettable series of etchings depicting the horrors and tragedies of the Peninsular War as they were experienced by ordinary people. Here, French soldiers hang a Spanish guerrilla by hauling on his legs. The etching is simply titled *Why? AKG London*.

to strengthen France commercially. To some extent, the policy worked. In the Rhineland, for example, textiles boomed without British competition, and in Britain itself the disruption to trade spawned social unrest. But by 1811, smuggling had grown so rife that Napoleon deemed it advisable to establish an agency just to tax the vast amount of illegally entering goods.

France and Britain came into direct military conflict in Spain and Portugal. In 1808 Napoleon had forced the none-too-competent Charles IV and his son Ferdinand to renounce the Spanish throne in favor of luxurious exile in France. Joseph Bonaparte, Napoleon's brother, became king of Spain. But Napoleon overestimated Spain's resources and underestimated the power of anti-French feeling there. Instead of finding a satisfied middle class favoring his reforms, he quickly confronted a country in revolt. The term *guerrillas* ("little wars") first came into use in Napoleonic Spain to describe armed bands that fought a regular army from the hills with hit-and-run tactics. Seeing an opportunity to hurt France, the British landed their own force in Portugal in 1809. The Peninsular War, as the ensuing struggle was called, proved brutal, as the etchings of the Spanish painter Goya show. Despite the constant efforts of Joseph, Napoleon, and all their generals, they never could pacify the Spanish or push out the British.

At the other end of Europe, Tsar Alexander I had always been a reluctant partner to Napoleon. On the last day of 1810 he finally withdrew from the Continental System, which had been damaging Russian trade, and began preparing for war. Napoleon more than reciprocated. On June 25, 1812, accompanied by more than 600,000 men,

the most immense army that Europe had yet seen in one campaign, he crossed the Polish border into Russia. Napoleon's forte was the major engagement, in which his powers of analysis, his daring and able commanders, his disciplined troops, and his decisiveness brought victory. But the Russians, not necessarily by design, refused to engage in a decisive battle, choosing instead many smaller engagements in which French losses mounted. Led eventually by the aged General Kutuzov (whom Tolstoy depicts in *War and Peace* as falling asleep in staff meetings to contrast him with Napoleon), the Russians slowly retreated into the vast spaces of the Russian plain. By fall, when the French had penetrated almost to Moscow, they reluctantly turned and fought at Borodino. After a bloody but inconclusive battle, the bulk of the Russian army once more withdrew, and on September 14, 1812, a greatly reduced French army entered a deserted Moscow.

Having occupied the ancient capital of Russia, Napoleon confidently awaited an offer of capitulation from Tsar Alexander I. But no such message arrived. After languishing for about six weeks in the empty and sometimes burning city, and with supplies, especially for the horses, running low, the French decided to move to winter quarters near Smolensk. Now the Russians began to make Napoleon pay. Once again withholding a major engagement, they harassed his army's flanks and forced his troops to retreat over the same devastated and barren route by which they had invaded. Winter struck, delivering temperatures of 20 degrees below zero, winds of 30 and 40 miles per hour, and driving snow. Desperate soldiers stole the clothing off the backs of weakened comrades and left them

THE HUMAN EXPERIENCE

Jakob Walter, Napoleonic Soldier in Russia

The following are condensed excerpts from the account of Jakob Walter, a soldier who survived Napoleon's invasion of Russia in 1812. In the first selection, Walter describes the first few days of the invasion:

On June 25 the army went over the bridges. We now believed that, once in Russia, we need do nothing but forage—which, however, proved to be an illusion. The town of Poniemon was already stripped before we could enter, and so were all the villages. Here and there a hog ran around and then was beaten with clubs, chopped with sabers, and stabbed with bayonets; and, often still living, it would be cut and torn to pieces. Several times I succeeded in cutting off something; but I had to chew it and eat it uncooked, since my hunger could not wait for a chance to boil the meat. The worst torture was the march, because the closed ranks forced all to go in columns; the heat and the dust flared up into our eyes as if from smoking coal heaps. The march proceeded day and night. [A few days later] it rained ceaselessly for several days, and the rain was cold. Bodily warmth was our only salvation from freezing to death. I had on only one pair of blue linen trousers, since I had thrown away my underwear because of the former heat. I could

not see at night and slid in every direction on account of the clay soil. Indeed, the soldiers fell about me so incessantly that most of them were completely covered with mud and some were left lying behind. During the third night a halt was made in a field which was trampled into a swamp. Here we were ordered to camp and to make fires, since neither village nor forest could be seen and the rain continued without end. Finally an estate was found off to one side. I with assistance built a little shelter. I lay in the tent shelter, hungry and wet. The comrades, however, who came in and lay down upon me served as a warm cover.

In the second selection, Walter describes his retreat across the Beresina River at the conclusion of the disastrous campaign:

One could not see the bridges because of the crowd of people, horses, and wagons. From morning to night we stood unprotected from cannonballs and grenades which the Russians hurled at us from two sides. At each blow from three to five men were struck to the ground. Only by the filling up of the space where a cannonball made room could one make a little progress forward. I had a horse to ride and one to lead. The horse I led I was soon forced to let

go, and I had to kneel on the one which I rode in order not to have my feet crushed off. To be on foot was to lose all hope. Everyone was screaming under the feet of the horses, and everywhere was the cry, "Shoot me or stab me to death!" The fallen horses struck off their feet many of those still standing. I frequently caused my horse to rear up, whereby he came down again about one foot further forward. Thousands swam into the river with horses, but no one ever came out again; thousands of others who were near the water were pushed in, and the stream was like a sheep dip where the heads of men and horses bobbed up and down and disappeared. Finally, when it was almost dark, I came to the bridge. Now it is with horror, but at the same time it was with a dull, indifferent feeling, that I looked at the masses of horses and people which lay dead, piled high upon the bridge. Indeed, one must say that the weight of the dead bodies was the salvation of those riding across, for without their load, the cannon would have caused the destruction of the bridge too soon. ❖

Source: From Jakob Walter, *The Diary of a Napoleonic Foot Soldier*, ed. Marc Raeff (New York: Bantam Doubleday Dell, 1991), pp. 41–42, 85–87.

---

to perish in the bitter cold; those who failed to find firewood or to fight their way to a fire froze; and foragers who wandered too far were picked off by the ever-present Cossacks (an elite Russian cavalry). Out of Napoleon's Central Army Group, which at its peak numbered 455,000 combatants, a mere 25,000 straggled back into Poland.

Both Napoleon and Tsar Alexander pondered their next moves. Kutuzov, having thrown the French out of his homeland, wanted to stop at the Polish border. But Alexander saw an opportunity to win renown as the liberator of Europe, and the Russians marched on. After tortu-

ous negotiations, Austria and Prussia joined them, and near Leipzig, in 1813 the allies crushed the French army. Eight months later, Alexander I triumphantly entered Paris itself. The victorious allies packed the captured Napoleon off to be sovereign of the island of Elba, just off the Italian coast. Next, they installed Louis XVIII, the younger brother of Louis XVI, on the French throne, restoring the gloating nobility that had surrounded his court in exile. And finally, after working out a text with the remaining Napoleonic officials, they persuaded Louis to "grant" a Charter, or conservative constitution, as a "gift" to the

French people "in the nineteenth year of our reign," as Louis put it.[13] Having learned nothing and forgotten nothing, as a witticism of the time put it, the Bourbons returned for one last try at ruling France. The allies repaired to Vienna to restore, they hoped, the old ways.

Before Europe could settle on how to end twenty-five years of upheaval, Napoleon pulled one more surprise out of his always resourceful sleeve. In March 1815, the deposed emperor suddenly showed up in southern France. The enthusiastic French, forgetting the decades of war that had just ended, rallied to his banner. Marching northward and raising a new army as he went, Napoleon forced Louis XVIII to flee and make way for a restored empire. His brash return instantly restored the allies' frayed unity. On June 18, 1815, an Anglo-Dutch army under the command of the Duke of Wellington met Napoleon's forces at Waterloo, near Brussels. It was a close match, and Napoleon demonstrated some brilliant maneuvering; nevertheless, he at last went down to final defeat. Recaptured, he was shipped off to the remote island of St. Helena, which sits alone in the middle of the South Atlantic, halfway between Africa and South America. He died there in 1821.

THE LEGACY OF THE FRENCH REVOLUTION

How big a break with the past was the French Revolution? The terms *Old Regime* and *Revolution* introduced at the time suggest that the revolutionaries themselves believed that they had embarked on an entirely new adventure. Indeed, this has been the main interpretation of the Revolution ever since. But have we simply taken the revolutionaries' word for it? What exactly did the French Revolution accomplish?

One of the Revolution's achievements was to strengthen the French state. Since the High Middle Ages, kings and their ministers had enhanced the power of the political center and chipped away at the influence of local entities. But the kings had to work through an encrusted mosaic of overlapping jurisdictions, laws, customs, and regulations. The revolutionaries simply swept these structures away. Napoleon appointed the prefects of the departments directly, and they are still appointed from Paris today. The Revolution also created the core of the modern French tax structure, its police forces, and its centralized educational system. But none of these innovations were entirely new. They were important steps in the centuries-long process of consolidating the ability of the state to govern, but a similar process unfolded in countries such as Prussia and Russia without revolution.

The Revolution's impact on the Catholic church in France also lay in the mainstream of European develop-

ments. The process of secularization had been going on from at least the sixteenth century, and in some places it continues today. For example, the practice of civil marriage, established during the French Revolution, only recently became the norm in the heavily Catholic country of Italy. In England the state seized monasteries and their income-producing lands in the sixteenth century, whereas the Russians secularized their church lands only in the twentieth.

The seizure of the church's wealth made up part of the overall process whereby the notion of sovereignty itself became secularized. Medieval Europeans had assumed that God reigned as the true sovereign over human affairs. In the sixteenth century, the idea emerged that the king's ability to make law identified him as the sovereign. Since the French Revolution, Europeans have considered the nation sovereign. In this centuries-long migration of the locus of sovereignty from the holy and divine to the secular and popular, the French Revolution was a fundamental, but not an isolated or unique, milestone.

French historians after World War II understood the French Revolution primarily as a struggle between classes. On the victorious side stood the capitalist bourgeoisie; the losers were the feudal lords. The working masses, or sans-culottes, were the most progressive element in this interpretation, but they failed to achieve their democratic and egalitarian goals. Nevertheless, in the Marxist view of many postwar French intellectuals, the Revolution was ultimately progressive, because it abolished feudalism and cleared the way for the bourgeoisie to develop capitalism—thus setting the stage for history's climactic struggle between capitalists and workers.

Critics of this interpretation have argued that the Revolution was not a class phenomenon in the modern sense, but simply a struggle over power. For example, the terms *sans-culotte* and *aristocrat* were political terms. In the years between 1789 and 1794, the word *aristocrat* came to mean "enemy of the Revolution," and *sans-culotte* signified "Parisian populist friend of the Revolution." The victors were not middle-class capitalists, but government officials, lawyers, people who lived off rents and interest from bonds, and small landowners. Old-fashioned categories such as rich versus poor seemed to work equally well as class terms in describing the Revolution.

Yet we do not designate a series of events as revolutionary merely for being a set of milestones in a family of long-term historical processes. What, then, was so revolutionary about the French Revolution? We find a clue in the vocabulary and ideas that the revolutionaries used in their struggles for power. When the revolutionaries debated questions such as "What is the Third Estate?" and "Who represents the nation?" and "What does equality mean?"—they were not engaged in philosophical discussions. They were trying to justify themselves in a struggle for power. In doing so, they invented a new way to talk and think about politics. It took another century for the ideas with which the revolutionaries explained their policies to become the

---

[13] Dating, that is, from the reported death in prison of Louis XVI's young son ("Louis XVII") in 1795. Thereafter, Louis's brother claimed to have "reigned" as Louis XVIII.

standard discourse of European politics. But today, few people in modern democracies question the ideas of liberty, equality, and nation. In other words, it is not the social or political results of the French Revolution, important though they may have been, that made the event unique, but the symbolic results. We can never again think about politics without using the ideas that the revolutionaries made popular.

CONCLUSION: FOUR PHASES OF THE FRENCH REVOLUTION

In the spring of 1789, the French kingdom would have been recognizable to someone alive in 1589—or even in 1189. It had a king anointed by God, aristocrats and clergy staunchly defending ancestral privileges, a hodgepodge of provinces with a jumble of written and unwritten laws, and institutionalized inequality of subjects (not citizens). A peasant revolt was brewing against hunger, taxes, landlords, and strangers; high prices and low food reserves had Paris rumbling on the verge of explosion. But much in French society had changed, too. New elites were emerging—not only an aristocracy gaining in wealth and self-assurance, but also upper-middle and professional classes that were doing the same thing. Neither elite would tolerate rule by an absolute king, or by the other elite.

During the summer of 1789 France's old political order collapsed with astonishing swiftness, for three reasons. First, the royal government had run out of money and had to ask its subjects for help. Second, it could not contain a series of artisan and peasant revolts. Third, once the National Assembly came into being, its members stepped out far ahead of the country in its enthusiasm for change. With France's traditional regime swept away, the first phase of the Revolution was over before the end of 1789.

The Revolution's second phase ran from late 1789 through 1792. The National Assembly wrote a constitution, attempted to control the church, and reformed landholding patterns. But divisions were hardening. The king did not accept his loss of authority. Many people were deeply offended by the reformers' plans to turn the Catholic church into just another state agency. The well-to-do and the pro-

fessionals—France's new elite—split into factions, and most aristocrats refused to merge into it. Peasants were satisfied with the Revolution's destruction of aristocratic power over them, but city people suffered miserably from inflation and unemployment. A war, foolishly begun, went badly.

These divisions came to a head in August and September of 1792, ushering in the bloody third phase of the Revolution. In fear of invading armies and roused by radical politicians, the mass of Parisians swept aside the empty shell of constitutional monarchy. Soon the king and his wife had been guillotined, and until the summer of 1794 terror was the order of the day. The Terror, however, was no simple-minded attempt to exterminate the aristocracy. Rather, it struck down anyone who broke the new rules of the revolutionary state: by "profiteering," evading the draft, rejecting the official religion, or joining the wrong political faction. Eventually, the tension became insufferable. In the summer of 1794, the revolutionary elite mustered enough unity to destroy the terrorists and suppress the Parisian masses.

Everything that happened during the Revolution's long fourth phase, 1794 to 1815, can be summed up in one word: consolidation. The powerful state that the Revolution had built from the wreckage of the medieval monarchy grew stronger still when a charismatic military and administrative genius, Napoleon Bonaparte, forced his way to the top in late 1799. He and the Revolution's elite of businessmen, lawyers, bureaucrats, military officers, and large landowners (including aristocrats who accepted the new order of things) ruled in a manner not too different from that of their noble predecessors—but they did so in a completely transformed state and with at least pretensions toward equity and enlightenment. The Catholic church grudgingly made its peace with the new French state, which now saw it as a guarantor of order.

Ultimately, the Revolution won on every front but one. It could not conquer all of Europe. The further spread of French revolutionary ideas and institutions would have to take the slower, but surer, path of example and emulation rather than imposition by naked force. It is to that spread, as well as to the Continent-wide expansion of the other half of the Dual Revolution—industrialization—that we turn to in the next two chapters.

Selected Reading

Sources

Baker, Keith Michael, ed. *The Old Regime and the French Revolution*, volume 7 of *University of Chicago Readings in Western Civilization* (1987).

Wollstonecraft, Mary. *Vindication of the Rights of Woman*, ed. Miriam Brody Kramnick (1985).

Overviews and References

Bosher, J. F. *The French Revolution* (1988). Post-Marxist narrative stressing the violence of the Revolution.

Doyle, William. *The Oxford History of the French Revolution* (1990). Well-written, up-to-date, and thorough history emphasizing the initial unpopularity of the Revolution and regional events.

Furet, François. *Interpreting the French Revolution* (1981). Influential interpretation by the dean of French historians of the French Revolution, emphasizing revolution in discourse.

————. *Revolutionary France, 1770–1870* (1992). A comprehensive analysis of the Revolution showing how long it took for its principles to become firmly established in French political institutions.

Furet, François, and Mona Ozouf, eds. *A Critical Dictionary of the French Revolution* (1989). Fascinating and authoritative articles on most of the important people, ideas, events, and historians of the French Revolution.

Hunt, Lynn. *Politics, Culture, and Class in the French Revolution* (1979). Discusses the French Revolution in terms of Furet's and Ozouf's work.

Palmer, Robert R. *The Age of the Democratic Revolution: A Political History of Europe and America, 1760–1800*, 2 vols. (1959–1964). A exceptionally broad-ranging study that links together the related events of the late eighteenth century.

Schama, Simon. *Citizens: A Chronicle of the French Revolution* (1989). Vivid descriptions of the major events through Thermidor. Transmits the excitement of the times.

Scott, Samuel F., and Barry Rothaus. *Historical Dictionary of the French Revolution, 1789–1799*, 2 vols. (1985). Provides hundreds of brief but authoritative articles on personalities and events. Excellent reference source.

Soboul, Albert. *A Short History of the French Revolution, 1789–1799* (1977). A brief explication of the Marxist view by the historian of the sans-culottes.

Tocqueville, Alexis de. *The Old Regime and the French Revolution* (English translation, 1855). The most important nineteenth-century interpretation; still exerts a strong influence.

Origins

Doyle, William. *Origins of the French Revolution*, 2nd ed. (1988). Excellent synthesis of recent research. Includes very informative historiographic essay.

Hardman, John. *Louis XVI* (1993). Revisionist biography of a king whom the author calls "fairly intelligent and fairly hard-working."

Lefebvre, Georges. *The Coming of the French Revolution* (English translation, 1947). This classic study, originally published in French in 1939, influenced all future class-based interpretations of the Revolution.

Sewell, William H. Jr. *A Rhetoric of Bourgeois Revolution: The Abbé Sieyès and What Is the Third Estate?* (1994).

Explores the techniques by which Sieyès influenced the rhetoric of the Revolution and thus shaped its most important contribution.

Climax and Napoleon

Chandler, David. *The Campaigns of Napoleon*, 2 vols. (1991). The definitive study of Napoleon's campaigns. Perfect for the military history buff.

Connelly, Owen. *Blundering to Glory: Napoleon's Military Campaigns* (1987). Succinct revisionist discussion of Napoleon's campaigns.

————. *Historical Dictionary of Napoleonic France, 1799–1815* (1985). Useful reference tool with brief articles on major persons and events.

Geyl, Peter. *Napoleon, For and Against* (1964). Tour de force that analyzes Napoleon by discussing what historians have said about him over the years.

Hampson, Norman. *Danton* (1988). One of the best biographies of the revolutionary leaders.

Jordan, David P. *The King's Trial: Louis XVI vs. the French Revolution* (1979). Lively, detailed, and broader than the title suggests.

Ozouf, Mona. *Festivals and the French Revolution* (1988). Serious study of the symbolism of the Revolution that goes beyond politics.

Palmer, Robert A. *Twelve Who Ruled: The Year of the Terror in the French Revolution*, new ed. (1989). A collective biography and history of the Committee of Public Safety.

Rudé, George. *The Crowd in the French Revolution* (1986; originally published 1959). Influential study of revolutionary riots showing social composition of the crowds and how aims were related to bread prices.

Revolutionary Women

Gutwirth, Madelyn. *The Twilight of the Goddesses: Women and Representation in the French Revolutionary Era* (1992). Illustrated study of gender interactions before and during the French Revolution, especially as revealed in visual representations.

Hufton, Olwen H. *Women and the Limits of Citizenship in the French Revolution* (1992). Sophisticated but readable set of essays on the role of women in the French Revolution.

Melzer, Sara E., and Leslie W. Rabine, eds. *Rebel Daughters: Women and the French Revolution* (1992). Collection of articles arguing that gender definitions did not exclude women politically from the Revolution as much as has usually been claimed.

CHAPTER 22

THE ORIGIN OF MODERN IDEOLOGY

Liberty Leading the People   Delacroix, Eugène 1830. Louvre © Photo RMN-Hervé Lewandowski.

1804	First Serbian Uprising	1830	Revolutions in France, Belgium, and Poland	1845–1846	Potato blight in Ireland (and elsewhere)
1815	Congress of Vienna	1832	Great Reform Bill passes in Britain after popular upheaval	1846	Corn Laws suspended and never reinstated
1816	British Corn Laws protect domestic grains				
1821	Beginning of Greek Revolution	1839	Belgium's independence and neutrality guaranteed by the Great Powers		
1825	Decembrist revolt in St. Petersburg				

*E*ugène Delacroix's painting of *Liberty Leading the People* (shown opposite) is perhaps the most famous and arresting image from the early post-Napoleonic period. A conservative reaction overtook Europe in the 1820s, but the ideas of popular sovereignty, nation, and freedom continued to bubble beneath the surface, as revolts and revolutions inspired by the French Revolution burst out in many places across Europe. In this painting, Delacroix symbolizes one of these outbreaks: the brief but dramatic July Revolution of 1830. Liberty, shown as a robust woman who is at the same time *la belle France*, leads "the people," shown in a beret, cap, and top hat to symbolize the unity of patriots of all classes.

Delacroix's painting does not show many hints of the Industrial Revolution, which took place more or less simultaneously with the French Revolution, because at first these two events were not directly related. The Industrial Revolution was well under way by the time the French Revolution prompted Europe to rethink its political and social organization, and the French Revolution unfolded without significantly stimulating industrialization in France. Yet over the course of the nineteenth century, the deeply intertwined interactions of this Dual Revolution reshaped the world. The flowering of the Industrial Revolution through technological and commercial innovation has almost completely changed the social reality in which we live—our settlement patterns, our work habits, and our relations with each other. At the same time the ideas that the French Revolution brought into the public sphere—**liberalism,** democracy, popular sovereignty, and constitutionalism—have altered the way we think about politics. Agricultural society has given way to industrial society; autocrats have been replaced by limited governments; and, as Delacroix's painting suggests, the social norm of hierarchy has been superseded by the ideal of establishing fairness and equity.

After Napoleon's final defeat, many Europeans hoped to return to the secure autocratic systems of the eighteenth century. In some ways they were successful, but in the long run it proved impossible to restore the old order. The generation that came of age after 1815 had no choice but to react to both challenges of the Dual Revolution: new ideas and a shifting economic environment. In Chapter 23, we will turn to the spread of the Industrial Revolution to the European continent and to the social and political problems that this development posed. In this chapter, we focus on the tensions that sprang from the new ideas generated by the French Revolution.

The relatively stable international system established at the Congress of Vienna provided the framework of post-Napoleonic politics. The negotiators at Vienna, after having fought each other through most of the eighteenth century, found new ways to contain the passions of state rivalry. A similarly unexpected creativity marked conservative thinking in the period. Despite a powerful autocratic reaction against the French Revolution between 1815 and 1848, conservatives reformulated their ideas in new terms. In other spheres, creativity took the form of **Romanticism,** a cultural movement that colored many aspects of life in the first half of the nineteenth century. All of these developments, which are discussed in the first third of this chapter, testify to the profound impact of the French Revolution—it moved even its opponents to new positions.

Those who generally favored the achievements of the French Revolution provided the most fruitful responses to it in the period between 1815 and 1848. These reactions—in the form of the ideologies of liberalism, nationalism, **socialism,** and revolution—have suffused European politics ever since. An **ideology** is a set of ideas that drives political activism. Prior to the French Revolution, ideologies were frequently cast in religious terms, or at least had religious overtones: Papalism in the High Middle Ages and Lutheranism, Calvinism, or Puritanism in the sixteenth and seventeenth centuries are often considered examples of premodern ideological thinking. So are the *politique* ideas of Europe's religious wars, **absolutism** during the period of Louis XIV, and republicanism in the American Revolution. After the French Revolution, however, when new elements such as the middle class and the working class entered society, their supporters created sets of ideas, often based on aspects of the French Revolution itself, to justify their claims and their programs. These sets of ideas constitute the modern ideologies that still motivate political action in today's world. Socialists, for example, based their arguments on the insight that human beings are social animals, whereas liberals argued on the basis of human individuality. Conservatives, on the other hand, understood society as an organism that grows and matures. Ideological arguments may also be cast in class terms, with socialism serving as the ideology of the working class, liberalism as the banner of the middle class, and **conservatism** as the outlook of aristocrats and landlords. Within each major ideology many shades of differences exist, but political competition based on ideological justifications is characteristic of the world following the French Revolution. In the last two-thirds of the chapter, we look at the origins and practices of the important new ideologies spawned by the French Revolution.

THE CONGRESS OF VIENNA

As the French armies retreated across the borders of their homeland in the winter of early 1814, the four powers that had put them to flight contemplated a future without Napoleon. After twenty-five years of revolution and warfare, the leaders of Russia, Austria, Prussia, and Great Britain made European stability a priority in their plans for peace. In February 1814, while still pursuing Bonaparte, they agreed to conduct a peace conference "as [envoys] entitled to treat for peace with France in the name of Europe, which is but a single entity." After restoring the Bourbons to the throne in the person of Louis XVIII and forcing the new king to accept a constitutional law called the Charter, the four victorious allies invited "all the Powers engaged on either side in the present war" to assemble in Vienna on October 1 to tie up the final details of the peace. Despite this open invitation, the main allies secretly reserved for themselves the right to make all the decisions concerning the reestablishment of equilibrium in Europe.

Intent on influencing the peacemaking, an outpouring of delegates, representatives, and claimants from every principality, subjugated nation, and ambitious prince in Europe converged on the Austrian capital. The city of 200,000 residents burst its seams under the flood of visitors. Among the arrivals were the representatives of the four victorious powers: the main ministers of Prussia, Britain, and Austria, along with Tsar Alexander I of Russia, who now called himself "the Tsar Liberator" for his role in defeating Napoleon. At first these four had no intention of inviting the French representative, Charles-Maurice, duc de Talleyrand-Périgord, to join their deliberations, although they did intend to ensure France's return to international respectability. Certainly they had no desire to include the hundreds of other delegations that thronged the sumptuous balls and private dinners that overwhelmed Vienna that winter. But when Alexander and his three colleagues tried to present France with an ultimatum the day before the congress was to open, Talleyrand cowed them with a brilliant display of arrogance and righteous indignation. If the Vienna Congress was to make decisions on the future of all of Europe, he argued, then all eight countries

that had formally agreed to end the Napoleonic wars in May 1814, including France, by rights must participate. Once the embarrassed powers admitted France to their discussions, Talleyrand abandoned his arguments on behalf of the other allies. In fact, despite the name "Congress of Vienna," the representatives of the rulers and republics that crowded into Vienna never met together in plenary session. When the five **Great Powers**—defined here as such for the first time—finally agreed on the text of an agreement in June 1815, they simply invited the rest of Europe to adhere. Except for the Ottoman sultan and the pope, all of the European continent's other sovereign rulers complied.

Three eighteenth-century principles, none of which had their origins in the French Revolution, are often said to underlie the decisions of the Congress of Vienna. These were legitimacy, **balance of power,** and compensation. Legitimacy referred to the principle that sovereigns who were born to their thrones should be restored as the legitimate rulers of their countries. The concept of a balance of power implied that stability could be achieved in Europe if power, measured in terms of territory and prestige, was evenly distributed among the main countries so that no single state, or combination of states, could threaten any other state's security. To ensure this balance, any increase in the territorial holdings of one power called for compensations to the other powers at the expense of the small states.

The most contentious geopolitical issue in which these principles came into play involved Poland and Saxony. Between 1772 and 1795, Russia, Prussia, and Austria had divided Poland among themselves. Napoleon had created a new entity, the Grand Duchy of Warsaw, and the Poles hoped to expand it into an independent state. But Tsar Alexander I meant to rule Poland himself. The difficulty was that Prussia had occupied Warsaw in 1795. If it had to give up the Polish capital, it demanded compensation in Saxony, whose king had supported Napoleon (thereby, in the eyes of some, forfeiting his legitimacy). And if the Prussians were to get Saxony, the Austrians insisted on receiving a balancing compensation. The powers ultimately created a small, autonomous Polish state with its capital at Warsaw, making the Russian tsar its king. Prussia gave to this "Congress Kingdom" part of the land it had taken in the partitions of Poland, but in return received part of Saxony, as well as territory along the west bank of the Rhine River. Austria also surrendered part of its Polish booty and took its compensation in northern Italy. These compensating changes in borders took no account of the principle of popular sovereignty that the French Revolution and Napoleon had spread through Europe, and therefore sowed the seeds for eventual conflicts over nationalism (see Map 22-1).

If we confine our examination of the Congress of Vienna to negotiations of this type, however, we will miss

MAP 22-1
EUROPE AFTER THE CONGRESS OF VIENNA

the settlement's main thrust, which was to abandon many eighteenth-century rules of international politics including the way in which the balance among powerful states worked. In the final two years of the wars against Napoleon, the allied powers had concluded that Europe needed a new perspective. Napoleon's sudden reappearance from Elba in the spring of 1815 only confirmed that view. The main goal of the Vienna Congress became to create

European-wide mechanisms for sustaining the integrity of the major powers. Whereas each Great Power pursued its own interests with vigor and skill, even threatening war on occasion, the goal of European stability remained uppermost in the negotiators' minds.

This may seem a wise and obvious principle following years of destructive and divisive war, but Great Power integrity in fact had not been a primary goal of eighteenth-century diplomats. In the century before the French Revolution, the most powerful states, claiming always to be pursuing a balance of power, had tried their best to undermine their enemies, seize territory, and regain previous losses. By contrast, the Congress of Vienna guaranteed the existence of the Great Powers and secured the borders of the smaller states. In other words, the powers abandoned the principle of balance of power maintained by destructive competition and adopted the idea of equilibrium based on mutual interests, consensus, and law. Instead of restoring the rules of the eighteenth-century balance-of-power game, which had always led to conflict, the Congress of Vienna created new rules by which the Great Powers guaranteed each other's rights, security, and independence.

This success was not an accident, but a specific goal of the negotiators. They did not demand that France be despoiled, as normal eighteenth-century practice would have required; therefore France brought little resentment of its defeat into future international relations. Equally important, the Vienna Congress created a group of relatively stable buffer states, such as Switzerland and the German Confederation, where the Great Powers could interact and compete without provoking armed conflict among themselves. The congress did balance the power of the main states through compensations, but the rules of the game by which this balance would operate in the future changed fundamentally.

Two other decisions helped to knit Europe more closely together than previously, and one "nondecision" lessened international tension for almost a century. In the first instance, Alexander I, who had fallen under the influence of a German mystic, persuaded the reluctant monarchs of central Europe to agree henceforward to base their relations "upon the sublime truths which the Holy Religion of Our Savior teaches." Alexander naively believed that if his royal colleagues adhered to this Holy Alliance, their unification into a "true and indissoluble fraternity" of rulers would ensure peace. Alexander's pious initiative remained a dead letter in international law, but it did launch an era of cooperation among the three conservative empires of east-central Europe—Prussia, Russia, and Austria—that lasted until after midcentury.

The decision was more important. In November, after leaving Vienna, the practical yet idealistic British foreign minister, Lord Castlereagh, persuaded the Great Powers to create a "concert of Europe." The signatories to this second, secular effort to construct a united Europe did not envision a "league of nations" or a "united nations." Those concepts would not emerge until the twentieth century. In fact the conferees did not understand or accept the idea of "nation," and in any event had no intention of permitting smaller states a voice in their deliberations. The **Concert of Europe** was merely an agreement among the Great Powers to negotiate about common policies at times of crisis. It

had no headquarters, no staff, no permanent residence, and no set procedures. When a crisis came up, such as revolt in Naples, one or another of the Great Powers would simply invite the others to a meeting in order to work out the steps needed to maintain order.

The Concert of Europe, too, soon collapsed, although Great Power representatives met in 1818, 1821, and 1822 to grapple with unrest across Europe. Without a common opponent such as Napoleon, the powers, which held differing political principles and pursued diverse objectives, found it difficult to agree on joint action. Nevertheless, from 1815 onward, the notion that the Great Powers had a duty to sustain the integrity of Europe never totally left European political thought. The Concert of Europe therefore stands as an important milestone in the centuries-long process that led from the joint recognition of state sovereignty in the Treaty of Westphalia in 1648 (see Chapter 15) to the system of sovereign states and international organizations within which we operate today.

The nondecision made at Vienna centered on avoiding involvement in the worldwide ambitions of either of the flanking powers—Britain and Russia. From the beginning of the age of exploration (see Chapter 14) until the time of Napoleon, Europeans had brought roughly a quarter of the earth's surface under their control as colonies and clients. Over the next hundred years they colonized another 50 percent of the world. During the eighteenth century, competition between colonial states often turned into wars that spread to Europe, and vice versa. The Congress of Vienna tacitly ignored British control of the seas and Russian ambitions in Central Asia—the conferees had little choice, given Russian remoteness and British success in dominating the Indian and Atlantic Oceans. But in so doing the continental powers isolated themselves from foreign conflict, even though they continued their colonizing efforts. By minimizing the chance of colonial competition spreading to the Continent itself, they created a powerful support for European stability.

These decisions became of prime importance in the Western Hemisphere, where shortly after the Napoleonic wars Latin American countries began winning their independence from Spain. Britain supported these ultimately successful wars, but they did not produce a full-blown European confrontation. In the United States, then becoming the only democratically governed nation in the world, the Monroe Doctrine (1823) declared that Europeans—whom Americans considered corrupt and despotic—should not interfere in the affairs of the Western Hemisphere. Had the powers been inclined to do so, as they had been in the eighteenth century, neither Europe nor the **New World** would have been as stable as they were for the hundred years that followed the Vienna Congress.

The negotiators at the Congress of Vienna did not announce their decisions widely; they faced no elections at home (except in the case of Castlereagh's government);

and they ignored the principles of equity and popular sovereignty. They redrew borders, paid little attention to smaller claimants, and acted primarily in pursuit of their own interests. But by recognizing that those interests lay primarily in an international order of mutual security rather than in the short-term pursuit of temporary gains, they created a system that endured for forty years. The idea of concert, the building of buffer states, and the insulation of Europe from foreign conflicts prevented major wars among the Great Powers for a hundred years, one of the most stable periods in European history.

THE CONSERVATIVE REACTION

Many members of the first post-Napoleonic generation recoiled from the ideals and practices of the French Revolution. Politically, autocratic regimes tried to negate the impact of the Revolution. Intellectually, conservatives found new ways to justify traditional arrangements.

The Autocratic Regimes

The most prominent advocate of autocracy in the first postrevolutionary generation was Clemens von Metternich, the exquisitely polite state chancellor of the Habsburg Empire. Metternich, whose marriage to Countess Kaunitz in 1795 not only made his fortune but connected him to the highest levels of Austrian society, dominated the diplomacy of the years of Napoleon's defeat and the Congress of Vienna. Shut out of domestic politics by a powerful rival and constrained by the reactionary views of his monarch, to whom he always deferred, Metternich used the German Confederation as a vehicle for pursuing the principles of monarchy, order, and stability. The German Confederation united the thirty-nine German states that survived the collapse of the Holy Roman Empire into a weak confederation that included both Prussia and the Austrian crownlands. Because each constituent state retained its own army, tax system, bureaucracy, and independence, the new entity possessed little actual power. But the confederation's Diet (legislature of state-appointed delegates), which met regularly in Frankfurt, provided an arena in which Austria and Prussia could compete without waging war. Austria occupied the permanent chair of the Diet; thus Metternich became the most powerful German political actor, "the coachman of Europe," as one wit called him.

Metternich feared that an international revolutionary conspiracy on behalf of popular sovereignty and constitutionalism would undermine the principles of religion, family, and authority in Europe. The reformist enthusiasms of some German students lent credence to these fears. As young men returned from the Napoleonic wars and took up their university studies again, the more nationalistic among them formed patriotic student societies to sustain and

Clemens von Metternich   This splendid portrait elegantly captures Metternich's stylish, proud, dominant, and rather disdainful personality. He wears the medallion of the Order of the Golden Fleece, which Habsburg rulers had been bestowing as their highest decoration since the fifteenth century.   *Painting, 1815, by Thomas Lawrence (1769–1830) Photo: AKG London.*

nourish love of the German fatherland (as opposed to loyalty to Saxony, Bavaria, or some other German state). In October 1817, almost five hundred members of these societies gathered in the Wartburg, the castle in which Martin Luther had translated the Bible. They celebrated the three hundredth anniversary of the moment that Luther had launched the Reformation. Their patriotic songs, fiery speeches, and grand bonfires struck a powerful chord among young Germans—and unnerved Metternich.[1] When in 1819 a mentally unbalanced student murdered a conservative playwright who was also a Russian informant, Metternich hurriedly persuaded the Diet to issue the Carlsbad Decrees. These rules called for every German state to

---

[1] The German students were not solely interested in patriotic songs and liberal ideals. They also burned the books they did not like and disrupted the classes of professors they considered reactionary—not unlike radicals in the United States during the 1960s.

institute strict censorship, to ban student organizations, and to submit all universities to the ultimate supervision of the confederation.

But Germany was not the most reactionary region in Europe. Naples, where the chief minister of Ferdinand I held that "the first servant of the crown should be the executioner," probably deserves that honor, or perhaps Spain. Upon his return to the latter country in 1814, King Ferdinand VII expressed his views clearly: "Not only do I refuse to swear to observe the Constitution, or to recognize any decrees of the Cortes [legislature], but I declare Constitution and decrees alike null and void, today and forever."

In France, by contrast, the Bourbon king, Louis XVIII, showed remarkable restraint in the face of determined agitation from extreme reactionaries. The Ultras, as these were called, so hated the king's acceptance of the Charter in 1814 that they called him "the crowned Jacobin." But the phlegmatic Louis remained steadfast in his conservative moderation. In 1820, just when his dignified policies

Louis XVIII Despite the attacks by republicans on the left and Ultras on the right, Louis XVIII was a better king than usually supposed. Exile had taught this brother of Louis XVI that compromise is the essence of politics—a lesson his younger brother and fellow emigré, the future Charles X, never learned. *Corbis / Bettman.*

had restored a stable political atmosphere, an assassin cut down the king's nephew. The Ultras used the event to claim that a revival of liberalizing revolution was about to hit France. "I saw [the assassin's] dagger," one of them said, "and it was a liberal idea." Voted into power a few years later by the tiny handful of eligible voters, the Ultras passed a new law on general security that permitted holding prisoners for three months without trial and that tightened restrictions on the press. The Ultras increased the power of the church, passed a law against sacrilege, and compensated emigrés who had fled during the revolutionary and Napoleonic periods.

Perhaps the most interesting reactionary monarch of the era was Nicholas I of Russia, who acceded to the throne in 1825 after the death of his older brother Alexander I. A rigid and intellectually limited man, Nicholas saw life as "merely service." He served his country, and he expected everyone else to serve him. "Orthodoxy, Autocracy, and Nationality" became the slogan of his regime, but obscurantism, arbitrariness, and negation better describe his leadership style. Nicholas stifled even the most oblique expressions of spontaneity or criticism. As one example, he sent the young Alexander Herzen, a renowned stylist of the Russian language and later the country's first prominent socialist, into exile because Herzen was a friend of some young men who had sung mildly critical songs at a party. (Not only had Herzen not sung the songs, he had not even been present at the party.) In another case, Nicholas declared the writer Peter Chaadaev insane when Chaadaev wrote that Russia did not belong to any of the great families of humanity. "Placed, as it were, outside of time," Chaadaev had written, "we have not been touched by the universal education of the human race."

Nicholas's reign stands as the apogee of Russian autocracy, the moment when the principles of obedience, loyalty, and servility coalesced in their most extreme forms. "In Russia," observed a conservative French visitor in 1839, "everything that meets your eye, everything that goes on around you is of a frightening regularity; . . . the government dominates everything and gives life to nothing. In this vast Empire, the people, if they are not tranquil, are silent; death hovers over all heads and strikes them capriciously. . . . There man has two coffins—the cradle and the tomb."

The New Conservatives

Not all conservatives were as single-minded as the reactionary rulers of postrevolutionary Europe. Between 1815 and 1850, many conservative thinkers went beyond mere rejection of new ideas and attempted to accommodate themselves to constitutionalism and popular representation. In their view, society formed an organic whole, a living entity that had developed over time, sustained by Christian faith. Efforts by French revolutionaries and later radicals to introduce sudden change based on abstract and secular ideas could only damage society's complex fabric and undermine the religious basis of morality, they argued. The new conservatives favored monarchy, of course, but some among them also opposed bureaucracy, which they believed laid the groundwork for despotism.

The most famous early statement of the view that tradition forms the basis of **civil society** was Edmund Burke's *Reflections on the Revolution in France* (1790; see Chapter 21). Constitutions could not be written by presumptuous men in the heat of passionate upheaval, Burke argued. A constitution was "no simple, no superficial thing," but "the result of the thoughts of many minds in many ages." Burke opposed despotism, but he also believed that to disrupt a functioning social order was akin to an ignorant man's taking a clock apart—neither society nor the clock would ever work properly again.

In Germany, too, conservative theorists such as Karl Friedrich von Savigny and Ludwig von Haller maintained that societies were organic wholes. No universal natural laws applied to all human experience, as eighteenth-century rationalists claimed, because each society is unique. Savigny's Historical School of Jurisprudence dismissed systems of law built on the principles of universality and abstract rights, such as the Napoleonic Codes, as abstractions without a foundation in the experience of any society. Yet German states were not without law. Quite the contrary. Even though reform had virtually stopped in Prussia after 1815, for example, Prussians prided themselves on maintaining a *Rechtsstaat,* or a state based on law. By apply-

ing legal standards derived from the German experience, the Prussians believed they could combine order and stability with fairness and equity.

The idea that every society was bound by its own experience became the conservative answer to reformers who stressed natural law and reason. To counter the threat that the principle of equality posed to hierarchical social organization, conservatives developed the theory of paternalism. In Prussia especially, the relationship of landowners to their peasants had long been a personal one in which the landlord thought of himself as the father of his estate family. He expected obedience from his peasants but also was obliged to sustain them in hard times. When the Industrial Revolution spread to the Continent and began to undermine this relationship, theorists extended this local ideal into a political theory, perhaps in an effort to justify the landlords' continued social dominance. The prince, they wrote, should serve as the strict but loving father to his people, who should produce for the good of the national family and obey the wise injunctions of the head of the family. Inequality, argued Haller, was a fact of life: The weak depend on the strong in society, just as they do in the family. The prince, therefore, was the bulwark of the social order, because his power alone permitted society to function for the happiness of all. In the early nineteenth century, these ideas reflected the social reality in which the husband and father dominated the family.

The new conservatives believed that religion confirmed their views. Protestant and Catholic conservatives alike considered state-supported religions, which championed

Ingres's *Apotheosis of Homer* In this 1827 painting of Winged Victory about to crown the epic Greek poet Homer, Jean-Auguste-Dominique Ingres includes about forty realistically rendered painters, sculptors, and writers from both ancient and more recent times. Besides the obvious classical temple, note the symmetrical, triangular composition of the canvas. *Louvre © Photo RMN.*

THE HUMAN EXPERIENCE

Eugène Delacroix, Romantic Painter

In 1830, when he had already won fame as France's foremost Romantic painter, Eugène Delacroix (1798–1863) responded to a critic by saying, "I am a pure classicist." Delacroix was bright, energetic, and handsome, but his comment suggests that he was also a bit contrary. "The wickedness of my expression," he boasted at the age of twenty, "almost frightens me." Delacroix was born to a prominent and wealthy family, although rumor and circumstantial evidence suggest that his real father may have been the ubiquitous Talleyrand. When Delacroix was only seven, his father died, leaving him an estate so encumbered with debts and doubtful titles that it dwindled away by the time he was about twenty-five.

Delacroix had always liked drawing, and at the age of fifteen he entered the studio of a Parisian painter. There his work, although still amateurish and imitative, came to the attention of Theodore Gericault. Delacroix participated in the creation of Gericault's greatest painting, *The Raft of the Medusa*. This painting depicted a scandalous shipwreck that had brought the corruption and incompetence of the French navy to light. Its implicit criticism of the government defied the tradition of glorifying the military that characterized the Napoleonic period. From Gericault, Delacroix learned of the enormous planning and research that goes into a huge painting (*Medusa* took up 378 square feet of canvas). Soon he produced his own raft painting: *The Bark of Dante*. Classical in theme, and therefore uncontroversial, it nevertheless gave viewers their first glimpse of the young painter's power.

French artists submitted their work to the government, which held a competition each year and displayed the winners in an exhibition called the Salon. When *The Bark of Dante* was accepted in 1822, Delacroix became an instant celebrity. Between then and 1831, more than twenty of his paintings were selected for the Salon. Today several of them are considered among the greatest masterpieces of the Romantic genre.

One of Delacroix's themes was the Greek struggle for independence, which gave the artist a chance to play to anti-Turk feeling while at the same time displaying richly colored clothing and the pathos of death, always a subject of Romantic yearnings. *The Death of Sardanapalus*, shown here, became one of the most notorious paintings of this aspect of Romanticism. In this work, the Assyrian king, having tired of the world, gathers all his belongings—his gold, his horses, and his women—and has them all destroyed before he himself commits suicide.

By 1830 Delacroix tired of the great canvases, and after a trip to Morocco in 1832 he turned his attention to architecture and mural paintings. Having solved his financial problems, he nevertheless continued to paint furiously, not even venturing

---

both ruler and nobility, as the backbone of society. Opposed to the new secular faiths of republicanism, nationalism, and socialism, all of which were inventing their own secular rituals, they wanted the official state church to conduct public education and to supervise public morality. The established churches of Europe agreed. The main state religions tended to support autocracy and traditional social values, and the devout members of these faiths usually proved to be politically conservative.

ROMANTICISM

If supporters of autocracy restored strong, repressive regimes in the post-Napoleonic period, and the new conservatives justified them, it was the Romantics who provided the emotional vigor of Europe's reaction against eighteenth-century rationalism. Romanticism refers to the school of thought that emphasizes feeling and emotion over calculation and rationality. This emphasis has always played a role in human affairs. If some thinkers and artists have been cool, balanced, and reasonable in their search for understanding, others have acted passionately and spontaneously. Romanticism had taken root before the French Revolution, around 1780. After the revolutionary interlude, it dominated European sensibilities until about 1850, even longer in music and painting.

Romanticism was not necessarily a conservative way of thinking; it appealed to people of all political persuasions. But in one sense Romantics were similar to the new conservatives: They spurned abstract rationality. What, they asked, had reason, experiment, natural law, education, and progress—the bywords of the eighteenth century—created? Twenty-five years of pain and turmoil, they answered. In their view, human reason was inadequate for comprehending the vast mystery of nature and the God of eternity who stood behind it. Understanding did not come through spiritless rationality but through creating imaginative works of art out of the enigmatic forces of life. God provided nature

The Death of Sardanapalus, 1830
Louvre © Photo RMN-Hervé Lewandowski.

into the streets to watch the Revolution of 1848. When he died in 1863, he left some six thousand works of wide variety. The Romantic genre that stressed the emotional impact of grand historical moments died with him. Nevertheless, his strong use of color and his innovative technique provided a bridge to the next generation of artists, the Impressionists. ❖

for human beings to experience directly, not to manipulate with scientific experiments.

In the arts, Romanticism flourished primarily in painting and in literature, especially poetry. Romantic artists rebelled against what they deemed the abstract, lifeless style of neoclassicism, the artistic style that had dominated the revolutionary and Napoleonic periods. They also resented the tendency of neoclassicism to support those in power. Neoclassicism was so named because it constituted a new approach to the themes of ancient Greece and Rome. Enlightenment thinkers valued classical literature for what they saw as its order and harmony, as well as for its secularism, and Napoleon supported neoclassicism because it reminded people of the imperial traditions of Rome that he imitated. Artists painting during the revolutionary era organized the visual space within their paintings carefully and rendered figures precisely.

Eugène Delacroix, the most famous French Romantic painter, moved away from the flawless renderings of his neoclassical predecessors to highly vivid representations. He rejected subjects from classical mythology in favor of poignant scenes calculated to touch the emotions. The exotic and the foreign, as well as the moving and even heartbreaking, became his subjects. His scenes from the Greek Revolution against the Ottoman Empire (discussed later in this chapter) evoked intense sympathy for the embattled Greeks. On the other hand, his lush Turkish paintings gave a sensual thrill to a public that had little opportunity to indulge in the exotic.

To the Romantics, nature was not a beneficent mechanism that humans could master, as rationalists conceived of it. Nature was a violent, unpredictable force that dwarfed human pretensions. Delacroix's passionate rendering of animals reflected this sensibility, but the two most famous Romantic painters who stood in awe before the overwhelming power of nature were the German Caspar David Friedrich and the Englishman Joseph Mallord William Turner. In Turner's paintings of storms, shipwrecks,

Slave Ship J. M. W. Turner's style was to blur the boundaries of form and color such as in his 1840 painting *Slavers Throwing Overboard the Dead and Dying—Typhoon Coming On*. English, 1775–1851. Oil on canvas. 90.8 x 122.6 cm (35¾ x 48¼ in.) *Henry Lillie Pierce Fund. Courtesy Museum of Fine Art, Boston.*

and disasters at sea, the wind and water merge into one overpowering force, while the battered, man-made ships almost disappear into insignificance.

Friedrich approached nature's wonders differently, often painting scenes of overwhelming natural phenomena that dwarf tiny human beings. Friedrich also incorporated a second aspect of the Romantic sensibility into his art: reverence for a mysterious past. Romantics believed that the powerful faith and mystery of the medieval age, particularly the Gothic era, had since been lost. "The more remote these times the more magical they appeared," pronounced the French religious writer François de Chateaubriand. Ancient oak forests in which puny human beings found their faith appealed to Romantics, and Gothic churches provided the concrete representation of the awe that they associated with divinity. Ruins such as Tintern Abbey, which inspired Wordsworth's poem, or the dilapidated remains in Friedrich's painting *Abbey in the Oakwood*, powerfully combined the ingredients of faith and nostalgia.

That Romanticism should be portrayed primarily in works of the creative arts was in itself an aspect of Romantic thought. The goal of the German poet Friedrich Schiller, for example, was to demonstrate the importance of art and creativity in human culture. Like many sensitive men before and after him, Schiller feared that the violence, division, and fragmentation cultivated by political struggle threatened civilization. The true accomplishments of humanity, he argued, lie not in the political blusterings of the powerful but in the creative capacities of the human spirit. "If man is ever to solve the problem of politics in

practice," he wrote, "he will have to approach it through the problem of the aesthetic, because it is only through beauty that man makes his way to freedom."

Many Romantics believed that the freedom Schiller hoped to find was best achieved through music, for music is of all the arts the most abstract and yet can exert the most direct appeal to the emotions. Ludwig van Beethoven enormously expanded the concept of the symphony by including a choral setting of Schiller's "Ode to Joy" (which would have been known as the "Ode to Freedom" had not censors insisted on the change) in his Ninth Symphony. Beethoven virtually invented the concept of musical Romanticism, but the Austrian Franz Schubert became the archetypical Romantic composer. His song cycles, written in the 1820s, vividly express Romanticism's simultaneous yearning for love and fascination with death.

For indeed, while part of Romanticism emphasized beauty as an immortal truth in its own right, another side of it fixated on human mortality. Perhaps it was this that prompted one of the late eighteenth-century founders of Romanticism, the poet Johann Wolfgang von Goethe (see Chapter 18), in his old age to denounce the movement as "all that is sick." The English poet John Keats, for example, believed that what the imagination seizes as beauty must be true. At the same time, Keats, who died at the age of twenty-six, played with the idea of decline and death, "the weariness, the fever, and the fret, where youth grows pale, and spectre-thin, and dies." The English writer Mary Shelley took the interest in death to an extreme in her novel *The Last Man*, in which the protagonist becomes

Friedrich's *Chalk Cliffs on Rügen* Romantic painter Caspar David Friedrich often painted contemplative but relatively insignificant human beings, here dressed in stylish middle-class fashion and overwhelmed by the immense force and structures of nature. *Courtesy of The Winterthur Library's Printed Book and Periodical Collection.*

the sole human survivor of a devastating plague. William Wordsworth was less interested than his peers in either beauty or death. He saw Romanticism as a form of modernity with more access to truth than "disemboweled rationality." As a young man, Wordsworth hoped to carry on the French Revolution by means of poetry. As he grew older, however, he adopted a nostalgia for faith, yet another characteristic of Romanticism. "Trailing clouds of glory do we come / From God, who is our home," he wrote in *Ode: Intimations of Immortality from Recollections of Early Childhood*.

The most popular English Romantic poet was George Gordon, Lord Byron. Born to a title and wealth, Lord Byron reflected the melancholy, brooding aspect of Romanticism. Byron could never reconcile his ideals of love, beauty, and faith with the banality of real life. In his view, human beings were "half dust, half deity, alike unfit to sink or soar." Exiled from England on account of sexual scandals, he

ended up in Greece, where he died an appropriately Romantic death trying to aid the Greek Revolution.

Romanticism's impact went far beyond the arts, however. It penetrated many areas of life in the post-Napoleonic years and affected many strata of the population. Religious thinkers such as Friedrich Schleiermacher understood the tendency of modern man to calculate and explain to be the true enemies of faith. "*Explaining* knows nothing of illuminating truth," he said. Our inborn religious feeling must be allowed to contemplate the infinite without rational restraints, Schleiermacher believed. Popular movements that stressed the emotional release of religious fervor attracted many working-class people. In Britain, a wave of Methodism, inspired by the vivid preacher John Wesley, attracted hundreds of thousands of working people in the first half of the nineteenth century, while in Germany Pietism performed a similar function. The emotional appeal of these revivalist faiths contrasted

THE HISTORICAL EVIDENCE

Romanticism

early 1800s

Bettina Brentano von Arnim met the composer Ludwig van Beethoven in 1810. Suffused with youthful romantic enthusiasm, she wrote to the poet Goethe of what Beethoven had told her about his art. The following statement is almost surely not what Beethoven said, but it gives a good sense of the confused but exalted prose that some Romantics found meaningful:

We do not know what knowledge brings us. The encased seed needs the moist, electrically warm soil to sprout, to think, to express itself. Music is the electrical soil in which the mind thinks, lives, feels. Philosophy is a precipitate of the mind's electrical essence; its needs which seek a basis in a primeval principle are elevated by it, and although the mind is not supreme over what it generates through it, it is yet happy in the process. Thus every real creation of art is independent, more powerful than the artist himself and returns to the divine through its manifestation. It is one with man only in this, that it bears testimony of the mediation of the divine in him.

German philosophy had a strong impact in Russia in the 1830s, introducing a philosophical romanticism characterized by Alexander Herzen:

Nobody at the time would have disowned a sentence like this: the concrescence of abstract ideas in the sphere of the plastic represents that phase of the self-questing spirit in which it, defining itself for itself, is potentialized from natural immanence into the harmonious sphere of formal consciousness in beauty. A man who went for a walk went not just for a walk, but in order to surrender himself to the pantheistic feeling of his identification with the cosmos. If on

the way he met a tipsy soldier or a peasant woman who tried to strike up a conversation, the philosopher did not simply talk with them, he determined the substantiality of the popular element, both in its immediate and its accidental manifestation.

John Keats (1795–1821) was a poetic genius who died young. The following letter, written hurriedly and therefore not entirely grammatical, suggests the intensity with which the Romantics turned away from Enlightenment rationalism:

I am certain of nothing but of the holiness of the Heart's affections and the truth of Imagination—What the imagination seizes as Beauty must be truth—whether it existed before or not, for I have the same Idea of all our Passions as of Love they are all in their sublime, creative of essential Beauty. O for a Life of Sensations rather than Thoughts.

Sources: Beethoven, from O. G. Sonneck, ed., *Beethoven: Impressions by his Contemporaries* (New York: Dover, 1954), pp. 80–81; Herzen, quoted by Martin Malia, *Alexander Herzen and the Birth of Russian Socialism* (New York: Grosset and Dunlap, 1965), p. 203; John Keats, letter to Benjamin Bailey, from *The Norton Anthology of English Literature*, 4th ed. (New York: Norton, 1979), vol. 2, p. 864.

---

with the formalistic and dry styles of the Anglican and Lutheran churches.

In architecture, Romantic styles were the order of the day. When the British government rebuilt Parliament after the great fire of 1834, it chose to do so in the Gothic style. John Nash built a famous pavilion in Brighton, England, that featured bulbous turrets and mosaics based on Ottoman models that the public considered exotic. Countless songs, stories, and prints sentimentalized the cozy, secure life of the middle-class family. Even in popular amusements, a new sensuality emerged in the waltz, which scandalized some Europeans: For the first time, men and women danced face-to-face while holding one another.

The phenomenon of the waltz suggests that Romanticism had an impact on how society conceived of women, too. In one sense, nationalistic Romantics exalted the ideal

of woman to express the ideal of the nation, which was often depicted as a nurturing female. "Marianne," "Germania," "The Daughters of Slava," and even Delacroix's *Liberty Leading the People* portrayed the nation symbolically as a powerful woman whose task was to ensure the health and fecundity of the realm. On the other hand, Romantics often relegated women to a subsidiary role as the physically and psychologically weak helpmates of the dynamic and intellectually superior male. Some Romantics feared female sexuality, which they considered dangerous and in need of containment. The Romantic vision of women paralleled that of the Catholic church, which either exalted women in the form of Mary, mother of God, or denigrated them as Eve, who brought about humanity's fall from grace.

In the final analysis, Romanticism was a way of thinking—an approach or emphasis, not a political ideology.

The Waltz   Like most dances, the waltz originated in peasant culture, but it became a craze among the nineteenth-century elite. One of its attractions was the suggestive nature of men and women dancing facing each other, as this comic scene of the lust unleashed by the dance suggests. Many crucial events in great nineteenth-century novels, such as Leo Tolstoy's *War and Peace* and *Anna Karenina*, took place in ballrooms.   *Victoria & Albert Museum, London / Art Resource, NY.*

Politically conservative Romantics, such as Burke, could find their inspiration in religion and the past, while politically liberal Romantics, like Byron, could understand it as liberating them on behalf of stirring political programs. Eventually even nationalists, who might be either liberal or conservative, found in Romanticism a rich source of symbolism and rhetoric. But, like many a passionate moment, Romanticism could not sustain its intensity. By the 1840s, social change, political upheaval, and economic pressure led to a new hardness and to a renewed interest in the rational methodologies of science (see Chapter 26).

THE RISE OF LIBERALISM

The ideas of freedom and liberty have existed in Western thought since ancient times, but they began to have widespread political implications only after the Enlightenment and the French Revolution. Constitutional monarchists fighting Napoleon in Spain in 1812 first used the term liberalism, but by midcentury it had become a common description for political movements that stressed constitutional government, an expanded electorate, and civil rights. The term *liberal* was also used to describe the economic principles of laissez-faire that emphasized free markets (see Chapter 20). Liberals based their politics, which in practice varied considerably, on the conviction that individual liberty was a fundamental value. In this way they matched the emphasis on individual creativity that was characteristic of Romanticism. In contrast to conserv-

atives of the era, who talked about governmental responsibility for social well-being, nineteenth-century liberals advocated reducing the powers and responsibility of the state to the minimum compatible with public order.[2] They saw in the self-control of liberated, responsible individuals the primary guarantee that society would continue to operate in a morally acceptable way. Engaged liberals achieved freedom of religion, freedom of the press, and freedom of association through the political process rather than resorting to violence or revolution. For this reason, liberalism could grow strong only in states that already permitted the public at least some participation in the political process.

Liberalism proved most effective in Britain, France, and Germany, although it also had an impact in Italy, Spain, Belgium, and elsewhere. In Britain, liberalism took two main forms: a political movement that expanded the electorate and reformed Parliament; and an economic movement that advocated free trade. These successes provided Europe with an example of how the principles of the French Revolution could be introduced into the political structure of a society without resorting to violent upheaval. In France, liberalism was narrowly conceived, less coherent, and less successful. German liberalism had close links with nationalism, a key ideology in its own right.

---

[2] Note how this relationship has been reversed in today's North America, where conservatives propose limiting government while liberals advocate using the powers of the state to achieve social equity.

Liberal Reform and Social Unrest in Britain

After Napoleon's defeat at Waterloo, Britain underwent a political reaction uncharacteristic of that usually open society. The demobilization of thousands of troops and the loss of the lucrative war-materials market led to economic depression and unemployment, thus adding to the social unrest already created by the Industrial Revolution. At the same time, the landed gentry who controlled Parliament feared that a wave of cheap grain produced by servile labor in eastern Europe would flood the country, undercutting the expensive grain that they produced under less favorable climatic conditions. Accordingly, in 1816 they pushed a law through Parliament prohibiting imports of grain into Britain and Ireland unless the price should rise above a figure at which they were certain to make a profit. These Corn Laws protected the gentry's profits, but they hurt ordinary people, who had to pay higher prices for bread, and factory owners, who had to keep wages up so that workers could afford the bread.[3]

These and other measures, coupled with the postwar depression, ignited serious unrest that thoroughly frightened the gentry. When an assassin attacked the heir to the throne, seemingly threatening revolution, the Tory (conservative) government suspended **habeas corpus,** which prohibits jailing someone without providing justification in court, and forbade public meetings. Nevertheless, in 1819 a crowd of fifty thousand gathered at St. Peter's Fields in Manchester to demand repeal of the Corn Laws. They insisted on radical political reforms as well, such as universal male suffrage and annual parliamentary elections instead of elections every seven years. When the local constables moved in, the crowd surged and the main speaker had to be rescued by mounted cavalry. In the process, the excited police killed eleven persons and wounded four hundred others. The opposition dubbed the disaster the Peterloo Massacre, in derisive reference to the role of Tory leader Wellington, victor at Waterloo.

The British government, as fearful of a renewed outbreak of revolution as any continental autocrat, struck back by promulgating the Six Acts. Among other things, these new laws prohibited blasphemous literature, slapped a heavy tax on newspapers, authorized searches of homes, and curtailed the right to hold public meetings. Like the Germanies, where Metternich introduced the Carlsbad Decrees, and France, where the Ultras dominated, England entered the 1820s by introducing reactionary measures on the heels of an assassination attempt.

But unlike Germany, France, and Russia, England's parliamentary system provided a mechanism for relieving the political strain. During the 1820s, the Whig party, the first English political grouping to be deemed "liberal,"

began to revive the eighteenth-century issue of parliamentary reform. English electoral districts, or boroughs, had remained unchanged from the seventeenth century, despite significant economic and demographic changes. Voting rules and representation varied wildly among districts. The extreme cases were Preston, in which every adult male had the vote, and Old Sarum, where no one lived at all. (Old Sarum's representatives were chosen by the Earl of Caledon, who owned the property there.) In many boroughs, elections consisted of the leading gentry gathering for dinner and announcing their choice for Parliament to those assembled for free beer outside. All in all, not more than a third of Parliament was chosen in a free, competitive election. The same class of landowning country gentlemen who took over Parliament in the seventeenth century still controlled it. The middle classes and the working classes had no direct representation.

In proposing parliamentary reform, the Whigs were not acting as democrats. Upper-middle class themselves, they had no intention of permitting ordinary people to participate in politics. For them the purpose of the commonwealth, as Locke had said, was the protection of property, by which he had meant land. Someone who did not own land had no stake in society and therefore had no reason to desire stability and order. The Whigs agreed, but they argued that other sorts of property should confer political rights too. Changing times required that entrepreneurs, indeed all upper-middle-class males, should also have the vote. Therefore, besides demanding that the electoral districts be drawn more equitably, they proposed extending the franchise to male householders who paid at least £10 rent a year, and to various other categories of substantial citizens. This policy, they believed, would bring into Parliament representatives of all the "responsible" classes previously excluded.

By today's standards, the Whig proposals were not earth shattering. They did not include women, for example, even though unmarried women could own property and some women presumably paid £10 annual rent. Nevertheless, in the late 1820s, the Whig program caused a sensation. The Tories, the conservative party still in control of the government, vigorously opposed it, fearing an unruly democratic future. But the Whig proposals appealed to the growing British middle class and in 1830 the liberals managed to assume power, not by revolution as in France, but by winning an election. The reform bill they quickly introduced passed a second reading in the House of Commons by the razor-thin margin of 302 to 301 but with amendments unacceptable to the Whigs. They called new elections and won a sizable majority that passed the bill in Commons again, 367 to 231. Now the House of Lords, the upper house of the English Parliament and a Tory stronghold, rejected the bill.

At this point, Britain teetered on the brink of revolution. The reform discussions had brought increasing

---

[3] In Britain, *corn* is what Americans call *grain*.

numbers of ordinary citizens into the debate throughout the country, sometimes inflamed by radical oratory and programs. When the reform bill faltered, talk spread in Birmingham of forming a national guard, the armed force of an aroused middle class. Crowds took to the London streets, and a mob controlled Bristol for two days. In desperation, King William IV returned the government again to Wellington and the Tories. But after a week of trying to form a cabinet, Wellington realized that he could not stop the force of a mobilized public. The Whigs finally broke the impasse by persuading the king to appoint fifty reform-minded men as new peers to the House of Lords. Intimidated, the Lords agreed to a bill acceptable to the Whigs, and in 1832 the Great Reform became law.

The new mandate went a long way toward equalizing electoral districts and slightly expanded the British electorate, to about 20 percent of the adult males. Despite the small size of this increase, the bill wrought a fundamental change in English politics. During the eighteenth century, the British king still actively participated in parliamentary affairs. Wellington's failure in 1832 showed that the monarch no longer could appoint a government that did not enjoy the support of a majority in the House of Commons. The threat of appointing fifty sympathetic new peers proved that Lords, too, could not deny Commons. The Great Reform solidified the cabinet system, by which the party that can muster a majority in the House of Commons controls the government. In this sense, it finally completed the Glorious Revolution of 1688, by which Parliament had

established its precedence over the king by threat of revolution. The Great Reform also showed that the British system could change without revolution. Violence and unrest had not overthrown the state but instead had produced reform. As the nineteenth century wore on, adjustments extending the Great Reform moved Britain in the direction of modern democracy.

Precisely because the Great Reform brought only a small increase in the franchise, and not full democracy, a broad alliance of artisans and skilled workers, building on the substantial tradition of artisanal activism outlined in Chapter 20, mobilized to advocate more political clout for all working males. After the government failed to take ameliorative steps during the severe depression of 1837–1838, a coalition of craftsmen put together a petition called the People's Charter. The Charter aimed to democratize British politics. It advocated universal manhood suffrage, vote by secret ballot rather than public balloting, and a salary for members of Parliament, so that poorer people could serve. In other words, the Chartists specifically wanted to expand the notion of "the people" to include all working males in the electorate and not restrict it just to property owners.

Enthusiasts stumping the country on behalf of these proposals gathered more than a million signatures to the People's Charter, which they presented to Parliament in 1839. Parliament, dominated by gentry landlords, summarily rejected the petition. During a second economic downturn a few years later, the Chartists gained more than three

Hayden's *Meeting of the Unions* Crowds of workers gathered throughout Britain to discuss the reform bills of 1832. This scene takes place in Manchester, where stormy meetings almost led to revolution. *City Museum and Art Gallery, Birmingham, United Kingdom.*

million signatures to a second version of the document. Once again, however, Parliament refused to consider it. After 1848 the Chartist movement collapsed, but the image of masses of workers uniting behind common demands for political inclusion remained a powerful memory among the British working class for decades.

Parliament adopted one other major reform before 1848, repeal of the Corn Laws. This was a success not of political liberalism, but of economic liberalism. Adam Smith's ideas, often called classical economics or *liberal economics*, lived on in early nineteenth-century Britain in the writings of Malthus and Ricardo, but not until the 1830s did these notions gain political importance.

Liberal economists favored free trade, arguing that restrictions on trade raise prices, introduce inefficiency, and hurt ordinary citizens. In the 1830s, two authors from Manchester, John Bright and Richard Cobden, began to attack the Corn Laws on this basis. Factory owners applauded the arguments of the Anti-Corn League that Bright and Cobden established, for if the Corn Laws were repealed and bread prices dropped, factory owners could lower wages and increase profits.

Following the economic depression in the second half of the 1830s that had produced the Chartist movement, Bright and Cobden denounced the landlords who profited from the Corn Laws as "a bread-taxing oligarchy," "power-proud plunderers," and "blood-sucking vampires." Abolishing the Corn Laws, as well as all tariffs, they argued, would not only lower prices and improve the health of the working classes, but it would also enhance the ability of British producers to buy and sell products abroad, thereby spurring economic growth at home. Theorists who followed this line of thought, called the Manchester School, grasped the relationship between free trade and general prosperity. More than a hundred years later, after World War II, this idea formed the basis of the postwar international trading system under which global commerce has boomed.

The Manchester School helped to raise the industrial middle class against the landowning gentry, but ironically it was the Tory prime minister Robert Peel who put its ideas into practice. Taking office in 1841, Peel realized that because about 40 percent of the government's revenue came from tariffs, abolishing them would deprive the government of a major source of income. In 1842, against a backdrop of economic crisis and deepening government debt, Parliament adopted his answer to the problem: an income tax. With the increased revenues that this tax produced, Peel was able to forgo the income from import duties, which he systematically reduced.

Peel's crowning achievement, repeal of the Corn Laws, was precipitated by an external event: a devastating potato blight in Ireland in 1845. Since 1801, Ireland had been an integral part of the United Kingdom of Great Britain and Ireland. The vast majority of the Catholic Irish labored as poor tenant farmers, because until 1829 only Protestants were allowed to own land in Ireland. Widespread poverty among these farmers had led them to cultivate potatoes. When served with milk, the potato provides all the necessary ingredients of a healthy diet. Furthermore, it is a prolific plant. A 1-acre plot, which could be cultivated by a single person, could provide enough food for a family of ten for an entire year. Most of the Irish poor lived almost exclusively on potatoes. Working men ate more than 10 pounds of them every day, and even in the poorhouse the

The Irish Famine One of the most dramatic examples of European emigration in the nineteenth century, when millions came to the new world, took place in the wake of the terrible Irish potato famine of 1848. Here hundreds of Irish lucky enough to be escaping starvation crowd the decks as they set off on their journey to the New World. *Image Select / Art Resource, NY.*

daily ration was a hefty 7 pounds. In 1845, however, the blight hit Ireland, and by 1846 it had destroyed the entire crop. Already scourged by poverty and evictions, millions of Irish faced famine.

Peel realized that only heavy imports of cheap grain would avert widespread starvation. Early in 1846, he got Parliament to suspend the Corn Laws "temporarily," and famine relief began immediately. At their peak, relief workers in Ireland served 3 million meals a day. Despite these efforts, which to this day Irish patriots claim were too little and too late, about a million Irish died. Another million and a half, out of a population of 8 to 9 million, emigrated—most of them to the United States. Ireland's population has not regained its pre-famine level even today.

The suspended Corn Laws were never reinstated. By midcentury the United Kingdom had become the first country in Europe to fully adopt Adam Smith's ideas about the free mobility of goods in international trade.

The Revolutions of 1830

On the Continent, liberalism had a different flavor from that in England. In 1830, the year the Whigs first achieved electoral success in Britain, Europe experienced three liberal revolts—in Poland, Belgium, and France.

In Poland, noblemen incensed at increasing Russian domination took the occasion of rioting against high prices to revolt against their new king—the Russian tsar, Nicholas I. After a short but bitter war, Nicholas's army crushed the insurgents. Legally, "Congress Poland," as the post-1815 arrangement was called, existed for another thirty-five years, but in practical terms Poland became simply another province of Russia. Many members of the Polish aristocracy fled to France, where they nurtured the flame of Polish nationalism for the rest of the century.

Belgium was the site of a second revolt in 1830, this one by liberal nationalists who rejected the rule of a Dutch king. Unlike the case of Poland, where the Great Powers did not intervene, Britain convened a conference in London that assured the Belgians their independence. The subsequent Belgian constitution, written in the 1830s, was the most liberal in Europe and served as a model for the Balkan countries when they became independent later in the century. By the treaty imposed on the Dutch king in 1839, the Great Powers guaranteed not only Belgium's independence, but also its "perpetual neutrality," a point that was to become important in 1914 when Germany invaded France through Belgium.

The most dramatic revolution of 1830 took place in Paris. From the time of the restoration of the Bourbons until 1830, the political struggle in France pitted the Ultras, or reactionaries, against the "doctrinaires," or liberals. The Ultras, made up primarily of landed aristocrats, hated the constitution that France had been forced to

Louis Philippe This contemporary cartoon ridicules the corruption and commercialism of Louis Philippe's era. The hawklike figure to the king's left is his liberal minister François Guizot. *Mansell / Time, Inc.*

THE HISTORICAL EVIDENCE

Tocqueville

1835, 1856

Alexis de Tocqueville (1805–1859) was one of the most acute political analysts of his day. His studies of the French Revolution (volume 1 first published in 1856) and of democracy in America (first published in 1835) are still read today. The two selections here, one regarding France and one regarding the United States, show his intense interest in freedom and equality.

On France

[The French people had two ruling passions:] One of these, the more deeply rooted and long-standing, was an intense, indomitable hatred of inequality. The other ruling passion, more recent and less deeply rooted, was a desire to live not only on an equal footing, but also as free men. At the time [of the French Revolution] the French believed they could reconcile freedom with equality. But when the virile generation which had launched the Revolution had perished the ideal of freedom lost much of its appeal, and the nation, at a loss where to turn, began to cast round for a master.

On the United States

The principle of equality, which makes [Americans] independent of each other, gives them a habit and a taste for following in their private actions no other guide than their own will. This complete independence tends to make them look upon all authority with a jealous eye and speedily sug-

gests to them the notion and the love of political freedom. This love of independence is the first to strike the observing and to alarm the timid, for as soon as the supreme power of the nation fails, which kept [the citizens] in their several stations, it would seem that disorder must instantly reach its utmost pitch and that the fabric of society must at once crumble away. Far from finding fault with equality because it inspires a spirit of independence, I admire it because it lodges in the very depths of each man's mind and heart that indefinable feeling, the instinctive inclination for political independence, and thus prepares the remedy for the ill which it engenders.

Sources: From Alexis de Tocqueville, *The Old Régime and the French Revolution*, trans. Stuart Gilbert (Garden City, N.Y.: Doubleday, 1955), pp. 207–209; and Alexis de Tocqueville, *Democracy in America*, the Harry Reeve text as revised by Francis Bowen and further corrected and edited by Phillips Bradley (New York: Knopf, 1946), vol. 2, pp. 287–288.

---

adopt and painted the "doctrinaires" as the revolutionary heirs to the Terror of 1793–1794. French liberals, consisting of members of the upper bourgeoisie, found the moderate Charter congenial, but they were far from revolutionary. They approved limiting the franchise to the wealthy, and most of them favored protective tariffs rather than free trade. French liberalism before 1830 was not a political program so much as a rejection of the Ultras' excesses during the 1820s.

When Louis XVIII died in 1824, his brother Charles X ascended the throne. Already sixty-seven years old and never particularly flexible, Charles lacked the dignity that had made Louis regal at least in demeanor. Charles despised representative government, but the Charter forced him to hold elections for the Chamber of Deputies. In 1827, despite official attempts to skew the results, liberals won as many seats as the moderate royalists, with the Ultras coming in third. When the royalist prime minister found it impossible to govern and resigned, Charles should have appointed a moderate or even liberal cabinet. But in these early days of parliamentary practice, the principle

that a government must reflect the makeup of the legislature had not yet been firmly established. Instead of turning to the moderates, Charles appointed a government made up exclusively of Ultras.

Charles X and the Ultras in 1830 were not as astute as Wellington would be in Britain in 1832. Wellington realized in only one week that Tories could not govern in opposition to a Whig Parliament. In France, however, Charles X lost his throne because he did not come to a similar conclusion. Early in 1830, the Chamber of Deputies voted no confidence in the new government, the first time that this maneuver had been used in France. When the resultant election produced a big liberal victory, Charles struck back by suspending the limited freedom of the press. He then dissolved the just-elected Chamber of Deputies and reduced the already small electorate to a minuscule 23,000 wealthy males.

The king's intransigence prompted just what English accommodation had avoided: a renewal of popular revolt. Parisian artisans, especially printers and members of the building trades, whom the liberals had successfully courted in the late 1820s, poured into the streets, erected barricades out of paving stones, and scuffled with authorities. The culmination of the July Revolution of 1830, as it is known, came when liberal leaders, including the elderly Lafayette and the ancient but always available Talleyrand, deposed Charles and called Louis Philippe, Duke of Orleans, to the throne. Louis Philippe was a Bourbon, but from the junior branch of the family. He descended from Louis XIII through Philippe Égalité, the radical aristocrat who had voted in favor of killing Louis XVI in 1793 and who had lost his own head to the guillotine shortly thereafter (see Chapter 21). Louis Philippe's victory in the Revolution of 1830 therefore infuriated the legitimists, who considered him an upstart, and pleased the liberals, who now came to power. Refusing to dress in military costume, Louis styled himself "the Citizen King." He walked the streets of Paris dressed in a business suit and carrying an umbrella, a sign at that time of bourgeois wealth. Louis Philippe's behavior so annoyed Nicholas I of Russia that he refused to address him as "My Brother," the customary salutation among monarchs.

Louis Philippe's victory did not pacify France, either. The artisans who had fought for three days in Paris had a different understanding of liberty from that of the upper bourgeoisie who assumed power. Under pressure from the beginnings of industrialization described in the next chapter, they understood liberty to mean the freedom to practice the trades in which they had trained. For the next two years, therefore, Paris and many other cities in France experienced violent incidents of machine breaking and impassioned demands that the new government ban the use of labor-saving machinery. The new regime, steeped in liberal economic doctrines, had difficulty understanding the artisans' pleas and feared their violence and rage. It ignored their protests and put down their demonstrations by force.

Artisan agitation did not move the French liberals to change France's electoral system, even to the extent the British liberals did in 1832. They loosened the property requirements for voting somewhat, but still only the wealthiest could vote—about five in every thousand, a figure far below that in England after 1832. Because of this high property requirement, critics of the regime, such as the writer Honoré de Balzac, denounced it as a "democracy of the rich." The liberals disagreed. They called it a regime of the *juste milieu*, or the Golden Mean. In Enlightenment fashion, they believed that government should be run by the rational elements of society, but instead of defining rationality as intelligence, they adopted the view that possession of property provided a rough demonstration of rationality. Louis Philippe's most important liberal minister, François Guizot, summed up this view with his famous advice to those who complained about not being able to participate in public life: "*Enrichessez-vous*," or, "If you want to participate, prove your ability by getting rich." By 1848 this cavalier attitude so discredited Louis Philippe and Guizot that they faced a revolution of their own.

Liberalism and Nationalism in Germany

Liberalism pervaded German politics in this period as well, but once again with its own flavor. Napoleon's defeat of Prussia in 1806 had inspired some of the kingdom's leading civil servants and army officers to sponsor serious reforms. When the Napoleonic threat receded, Prussian King Frederick William III turned away from reform. But the French occupation had generated a new spirit among some Germans, particularly among professionals. Lawyers and professors in particular were inspired by anger and resentment toward France, and their own inferior social position in countries dominated by kings and aristocrats frustrated them even more. They favored constitutions, civil liberties, and the other platforms of European liberalism, which they hoped would bring them some of the political clout they believed their intelligence and importance to society warranted, but some of them went further. These dreamers envisioned the consolidation of heterogeneous Germany into a single German state.

Romanticism influenced these German liberals, as it did everyone else at this time. Looking into the German past for meaning, especially for some unifying element that the present did not offer, they discovered *das Volk*. The noun *Volk* translates in English as "people." For Germans, however, the word has deeper and more emotional overtones than the term *people* has for English-speakers. It evokes a history of development from the oak forests of the original Germanic migrations through medieval and Gothic eras to the present. *Volk* began to achieve its modern meaning in the second half of the eighteenth century, particularly in the writing of philosopher Johann Gottfried Herder (see Chapter 18). For Herder, the Volk was a culturally coherent, historically developing community, "the invisible, hidden medium that links minds through ideas, hearts through inclinations and impulses, the sense through impressions and forms, civil society through laws and institutions, [and] generations through examples, modes of living and education."

A Romantic vision of the untutored Volk as the unspoiled bearer of true culture inspired scholars throughout Europe in the last third of the eighteenth century. Interest flowered in the study of language, which every normal person learned with ease and which seemed to link communities together. Educated in the Roman and Greek classics, scholars were astonished and thrilled to find oral folk poetry of almost Homeric quality among some of the less developed peoples of Europe, such as the Finns and the Serbs. Some Romantic writers decided that the essence of the national character lay in language, folklore, and other creations of ordinary people.

The turn toward the Volk marked the beginning of a new kind of answer to the question "Who are the people?" The French Revolution had introduced the idea that the people are sovereign, but it did not address the issue of just who "the people" were. That is, it did not specify which groups or individuals should have political rights. Today everyone is considered one of "the people," but this was not so in the early nineteenth century. British and French liberals proposed that "the people"—those who made up civil society and deserved political rights—were those who owned property. The Chartists went further, suggesting that every male should be able to participate in the political process. German liberals sided with their French and British colleagues on the question of property, although they also sometimes advocated the vote for those with professional qualifications as well. At the same time, however, they sympathized with the idea that "the people" consisted of every German who descended from the primeval German Volk. In other words, German liberals harbored a strong tendency toward ethnic nationalism.

Of course, liberals were not the only Germans who favored nationalism. Its roots in ethnic lineage, links with Romanticism, and usefulness in justifying political choices made nationalism popular with conservatives, too. Those who believed in the ideal of *Rechtsstaat* (a state run by law) could also appreciate arguments made on behalf of the nation. Nationalism's appeal to people who otherwise differed in their political ideologies helps to explain its staying power in central Europe.

THE CONTOURS OF NATIONALISM

Nationalism is so pervasive and so seemingly natural in today's world that it is difficult to conceive of it as having emerged rather recently, especially since patriotism, or the love of one's homeland, is a common phenomenon in history. But nationalism, which implies that the nation constitutes the basis for state and society, arose primarily in the nineteenth century. Its adherents claim that because the French Revolution established the principle that the people are sovereign, each unique collectivity of people—each nation—has the right to regulate its own affairs by organizing and controlling a sovereign state.

Two elements are involved here: the state and the nation. The deepest roots of the secular European state go back to the high-medieval monarchies, such as England and France, that successfully warded off papal control (see Chapter 9). The modern state system began to take shape during the religious wars of the sixteenth and seventeenth centuries and received its first formal recognition in the Treaty of Westphalia in 1648 (see Chapter 15). By 1815 sovereign states had become the basic units of European politics, as they are of world politics today. Therefore, when the French Revolution made popular sovereignty a practical possibility, the state system already existed.

The development of a consciousness of belonging to a unique nation is much harder to trace. Part of the reason is that the nation is an abstract entity and therefore difficult to grasp. A nation is usually defined as a group of people who speak the same language, share a past, and perhaps have the same religious background. There are many objections and exceptions to this generalization, but the main point is that people of the same nation recognize each other as members of the same group. They do not necessarily have to belong to one state, and this discrepancy has created many problems in the last two hundred years. Scholars debate whether national consciousness is primordial—part of a fundamental human need for community— or constructed—created by intellectuals, writers, and politicians. Probably it is both. Over the last two hundred years politicians, educators, and public figures of all kinds created—invented, even—the powerful unifying ideology of the nation-state. Today people learn they are part of a certain nation not only from their parents, but from school, from politics, and from public rituals that have been invented for the purpose (such as playing the national anthem at sporting events).

The first people who explicitly spoke of themselves as a political nation were the English, as early as the time of Shakespeare and Queen Elizabeth. "Good Queen Bess" used annual fire making and bell ringing to draw local communities behind her rule of "this blessed plot, this earth, this realm, this England" (Shakespeare). During the seventeenth century such celebrations commemorated an increasing number of historical moments, giving people in every village the feeling that English history was in fact theirs. The King James version of the Bible, published in 1611, helped link the English in a cultural unity. Because of a long history of individualism, and because of the importance of Parliament and the principle of representation, the English understood their nation as a collectivity of individual English citizens. The English form of nationalism, in which individuals constitute the nation, is sometimes called civic nationalism.

France developed an idea of national or popular sovereignty late in the eighteenth century, but the notion remained far more abstract than in England. The French Revolution lent a new concreteness to the idea, but French nationalism retained its elusive quality into the nineteenth century. The French defined *la nation* as a reservoir of dignity from which the people draw their personality. In England the idea of nation drew its meaning from the individuals who made it up, but in France individuals attained their nationality from the collective idea. Still, the French did not base nationality primarily on birth or ethnic background. In principle, at least, anyone who chooses to adopt French culture can become a citizen and join the French nation.

The type of nationalism that developed first in Germany and then throughout central and eastern Europe differs from the French and English models and is sometimes referred to as "ethnic nationalism." In other words, to be German one must have German ancestors, not just accept German citizenship. Like many nationalist movements that came later, German nationalism was based in good measure on resentment of another people. Napoleon's victories on behalf of the French nation inspired an anti-French reaction. If the French Enlightenment had emphasized revolutionary reason, the Germans would extol the mystical spirit of the Volk. The new nationalists rejected Herder's idea that every nation had an equal obligation to be true to its own culture, and instead favored the superiority of *German* culture. The philosopher Johann Gottfried Fichte argued that the special German mission was to redeem humanity from French rationalism. The extremist Ernst Moritz Arndt went so far as to claim (erroneously) that the Volk was uniquely pure because it had never been "bastardized" by foreign peoples. "Only the German," Fichte agreed, "is capable of real and rational love for his nation." The Romantic political theorist Adam von Müller put it this way: "Everything great, thorough, and lasting in all European institutions is German."

These aggressive statements are not peculiar to Germans—they are the common currency of nationalists everywhere—and they had only a modest influence in their own day. But the rejection of a perceived enemy, the emphasis on the uniqueness and purity of one's own language and culture, and the confinement of virtue to those born into the nation all characterize later forms of ethnic nationalism.

The French and the English, each in their own ways, could afford a civic nationalism, because they lived in well-established states. But the peoples of central Europe, the Balkans, and Italy found themselves either split into many states, as in Germany and Italy, or living in the multiethnic Habsburg, Ottoman, and Russian Empires. These divisions gave the nationalists in these regions a more revolutionary task than their counterparts faced in France and Britain and encouraged them to adopt forms of ethnic nationalism rather than civic nationalism. To realize their dreams, they would have to unite their divided people or to destroy the great empires. Either of these solutions would fundamentally restructure the face of Europe.

The most famous nationalist who promoted this restructuring was the Italian Giuseppe Mazzini. At the Congress of Vienna, the Great Powers had reorganized Italy into several conservative, even reactionary, kingdoms, most of them under the control or heavy influence of Austria and Metternich. The Papal States covering central Italy were ruled by the pope; Venetia and Lombardy (Milan) belonged to the Austrian Habsburgs; Sardinia and Piedmont (Turin) formed a kingdom in the north; and the Kingdom of the Two Sicilies (Naples) under a restored Bourbon king dominated the south (refer again to Map 22-1). Underground, however, the ideals introduced by

Guiseppe Mazzini of Italy   *Art Resource, NY.*

Napoleon and his relatives lived on, especially in small groups of rebels called the Carbonari.[4]

Founded in Naples in 1810, the Carbonari boasted tens of thousands of members throughout Italy by 1820, usually drawn from the young, educated members of the professional classes. They had no central organization, although Metternich thought that they did, and beyond an incipient nationalism they had no common program, for some of them were republicans and others were liberal monarchists. Early in the 1820s, the Carbonari fomented some unsuccessful revolts in Italy, but later in the decade, under constant persecution, they declined in numbers and in importance. When revolts in smaller Italian states, such as Modena and Parma, failed in the early 1830s, the movement sputtered out of existence.

Mazzini graduated from law school in his native Genoa in 1827 and almost immediately joined the Carbonari. Authorities promptly arrested him and sent him into exile in France. There, frustrated by the collapse of the movement, he formed a conspiratorial nationalist organization called Young Italy. The name did not refer to the age of the

---

[4] Named after charcoal makers, who, because of the isolation of their craft and the black charcoal dust that covered them, were considered both secretive and outcast.

members, although they tended to be young, but to the youth of the Italian nation, which, Mazzini thought, was about to enter adolescent growth and eventually attain complete adulthood. Through education and insurrection, Mazzini hoped, Young Italy would bring the moral values of progress, duty, and sacrifice to all the classes of Italy. Out of the peninsula's backward monarchies would come a liberal republic that would permit the full flowering of the Italian genius. When Young Italy's inexperienced efforts at revolution failed, Mazzini fled to London. There his dramatic appearance—flashing eyes, olive skin, white hair—his charisma, and the massive correspondence that he maintained with his agents and supporters throughout Europe made him that continent's most notorious revolutionary until his death in 1872.

THE EARLY SOCIALISTS

Both liberalism and nationalism were ideologies of the middle class. Liberals fought the entrenched position of the landowning classes in order to carve out a political role for themselves. In principle, nationalism had no such class basis, but in fact most of its early theorists and practitioners were relatively indifferent to social issues as long as politics and culture merged in one authentic myth.[5] Each ideology had its own way of defining the principle of equity and of specifying who constituted "the people." Liberalism defined equity in political terms and argued that only property owners had the right to participate in politics. Nationalism defined equity in terms of solidarities and, in its ethnic form, treated the people as a homogeneous cultural mass. These limitations left the door open for the socialists to provide a third interpretation: to extend the principle of equity into the economic sphere and to argue for the inclusion of women and workers in the concept of "the people."

The first radical socialist to go beyond the narrowly political promises of the French Revolution was France's Gracchus Babeuf, leader of a minuscule group called the Conspiracy of Equals that surfaced about 1796. Upset by the deterioration of the French economy that had slashed the value of the franc and filled Paris with a half-million persons on relief, Babeuf carried the revolutionary demand for equality to its logical conclusion. Adopting Rousseau's view that property lay at the root of evil, he called for "a great national community of goods." "The perpetual cause of the enslavement of peoples is nothing but inequality," Babeuf argued, "and as long as it exists the assertion of national rights will be illusory as far as the masses are concerned, sunk as they are beneath the level of human dignity." He wanted the state "to seize upon the new-born individual, watch over his early moments, guarantee the

milk and care of his mother and bring him to the *maison nationale* [national home], where he would acquire the virtue and enlightenment of a true citizen." In 1797 a French court tried Babeuf for treason and sentenced him to death.

Babeuf, a radical egalitarian, had naively assumed that depriving the rich would uplift the poor. His French successors in the 1820s and 1830s followed a more sophisticated approach. Henri Comte de Saint-Simon, who died in 1825, believed that industrialists, through their success in business, had come to understand proper methods of social organization. These producers, he argued, should reorganize the state along businesslike lines. The positive underlying forces of sentiment and religion would prompt entrepreneurs to see the benefits of a fair society, which Saint-Simon believed were clearly deducible from the study of history.

Saint-Simon scarcely discussed the position of women in his ideal society, but his followers, who created a strong Saint-Simonian movement in the early 1830s, attracted many women with their search for a new social role for women. Enlightenment thinkers had generally assigned women a subordinate role in society, as had Catholic tradition. The Napoleonic Code (see Chapter 21) set this subordination in law by decreeing that wives owed their husbands obedience, that they had no other domicile except with their husbands, that there would be no divorce, and that husbands would administer all their wives' personal property. The followers of Saint-Simon challenged this subordination, basing their argument on the dual nature of the sexes. Because males and females had different natures, their argument went, only a household consisting of both a male and a female operating on an equal basis could constitute a social entity. Conflicts among the Saint-Simonians in the 1830s pushed this idea in many directions, some defending indissoluble marriage, others favoring divorce, or "regulated mobility," and still others advocating free love.

The key to socialist thought such as that of the Saint-Simonians was to find a way of harmonious living. The pursuit of self-interest, made increasingly manifest by the coming of industrialization, was merely selfishness, they argued, a justification of the domination by male property owners, not the basis of a stable society. Instead of competition among isolated individuals regulated by the impersonal laws of supply and demand, the early socialists emphasized cooperation among equal partners to create a harmonious society.

One of the most influential thinkers of this kind was the strange Charles Fourier (1772–1837), who made his living as a traveling salesman. Believing that the repression of the passions was civilization's most damaging characteristic and poverty its most permanent vice, Fourier propounded the principle of "passionate attraction." He identified what he considered to be the twelve basic human

---

[5] An exception was Mazzini, who was passionately interested in elevating the working class.

Fourierist Utopia Charles Fourier never actually formed an ideal community (phalanstery) himself, but others tried to do so, and many other people dreamed of it. Jules Arnoult's imaginary rendition is one of the first to take into account industrialization. Note the the railroad line (center). *The Granger Collection, New York*

passions. By combining and recombining these, Fourier concluded that there were 810 possible human character types. Multiplying this figure by 2 (for men and women), he deduced that an ideal community would consist of 1,620 individuals. In this phalanstery, as he called it, the free play of human emotion would permit all to work at whatever they wanted. Women would enjoy full equality, and children would be brought up communally.

Despite the fantastical element in Fourier's calculations (he believed that each soul made 810 trips between earth and the planets and had 1,619 "other existences"), his vision of a richer, more abundant life struck a chord, especially among women. Fourier was the founder of the feminist tradition in French socialism. "The extension of the privilege of women is the greatest principle of all social progress," Fourier believed. Women in his utopian community would be fully free, although he believed that their special qualities of "sentiment" would lead them naturally toward certain roles. Nevertheless, these roles were to be voluntarily assumed, not imposed by dominant males.

The most vigorous French feminist influenced by the Saint-Simonians and Fourier was Flora Tristan. Having experienced rejection and poverty as a child, she compensated by pushing the idea of woman's special qualities to the opposite conclusion of that reached by conventional French society in the 1830s. Whereas doctors and others justified male domination by emphasizing woman's physical and psychological weaknesses, Tristan argued that women's moral qualities, such as love, altruism, and integrity were in fact those qualities that made women superior to men. Agreeing with Fourier (and the Romantic Schiller, mentioned earlier) that progress was not violence, competition, and force, she argued that increasing the presence of the feminine aspects of God's infinite personality would make for a better world of cooperation rather than one of oppression. For Tristan, progress consisted of freeing women to influence the course of social development.

French socialists tended toward abstract debate rather than practical action. By the mid-1830s the Saint-Simonian movement was faltering, and few phalansteries were established in France—although Americans such as Margaret Fuller, Nathaniel Hawthorne, and Ralph Waldo Emerson became involved in the short-lived Fourierist community of Brook Farm near Boston. Early socialism in Britain had a more practical bent, primarily through the efforts of Robert Owen. The self-made owner of a remarkable cotton mill at New Lanark, Scotland, Owen achieved great financial success by improving his employees' lives. He reduced the workday to ten and a half hours and forbade labor on Sundays. Owen refused to employ children younger than ten and instead provided them with free primary education. In addition, he insisted on hygienic work conditions and built solid, clean housing. The result flew in the face of liberal economics: Owen's satisfied workers produced enormous profits for him. Convinced that environment shapes personality, he became a fanatical advocate of an education plan that would yield social harmony by stressing love of community and rationality. Owen could not persuade the British government to implement his plans, however, so he authorized the establishment of short-lived ideal communities in America. New Harmony, Indiana, was the most famous of these.

Before 1850, the term *socialist* in Britain referred to a follower of Robert Owen. Owenites were not ordinary workers themselves, and they did not represent working-class opinion. Typically they were skilled artisans or disaffected members of the lower-middle class—intellectuals, we might call them today. Like the early French socialists, they too were interested in a new kind of sexual politics. They took the ideal of communal living to mean the elimination of individual families, and advocated equality for women. Even outside of communal societies, Owenite men and women ate together at the same table, unheard of at middle- and upper-class public dinners before 1850. At gatherings leaders called alternatively on men and women for comments, and Owenite clubs provided adult education opportunities for women. One of the most ardent Owenites was Emma Martin (1812–1851). Conventionally religious as a young woman, Martin became disillusioned and rejected Christianity for socialist activism. A good speaker, she drew unprecedented crowds of two and three thousand, even more when she spoke on "Marriage and Divorce." The hysterical reaction of Anglican clerics and sometimes of unruly crowds indicated how dangerous her ideas seemed to the conventional society of her time. Ill with tuberculosis, Martin spent the final few years of her life as a midwife, trying to break the male dominance of obstetrics.

Early socialists understood better than liberals that the ideal of equity needed to be translated into spheres other than politics, and they grasped the needs of working people and women better than the nationalists did. But their schemes for communal living, although they tapped a long utopian tradition in Western civilization that went back to Thomas More, medieval monasticism, and Plato, were not suited to complex, secular societies, and their radical free-thinking alienated much of ordinary society. Most of them advocated small, ideal communities, walled off from the difficulties inherent in conducting large-scale affairs. Despite their sympathy for workers and for women, early socialists found it difficult to create a viable political plan for helping them.

THE BUBBLING OF REVOLT

One final contribution of the French Revolution was the idea of revolution itself. Revolutions differ from revolts, peasant uprisings, or rebellions in that they are undertaken on behalf of an ideology. Before the French Revolution, one could assassinate a ruler or seize power from an elite, but the goal was simply to gain power. Peasant revolts had even less purpose. They were primarily outbursts of rage, usually put down with great bloodshed. Revolutionaries seek power, of course, and they are often full of rage, but they act in the name of a higher cause and seek to reorganize society. The post–French revolutionary generation was the first to dip its toe into these turbulent waters. In the thirty years after 1815, dozens of rebellions popped up all around Europe, most of them inspired by the new ideologies of liberalism and nationalism.

Weak New Nation-States

The conflict between restored monarchs and the representatives of new ideas provided a major theme of European history between 1815 and 1835. In southeastern Europe, however, Napoleon had left the Ottoman Empire unconquered; therefore, few new ideas penetrated and no restoration was needed. Nevertheless, the Ottoman Empire had

been declining since the sixteenth century. Economically it could no longer keep pace with the increasingly dynamic West, and politically it suffered from a breakdown of its administrative and military institutions. The impending death of what Nicholas I gloatingly termed "the Sick Man of Europe" opened the so-called Eastern Question: Who would get the Ottoman lands in the Balkans when the empire collapsed? Rivalry over which Great Power would pick up the Balkan pieces pervaded nineteenth-century diplomacy.

In 1804 a revolt in Serbia offered a new answer to the Eastern Question: Nationalist states run by native peoples, rather than imperial powers, might replace the Ottomans (see Map 22-2). The First Serbian Uprising was not a nationalist movement, because such ideas had scarcely begun to penetrate the Balkans. As the power of Istanbul (Constantinople) to control the far reaches of its empire withered, local strongmen and renegade military forces created their own quasi-independent regimes in the Balkans. To protest the brutal methods of one of these groups, frustrated Serbian merchants and peasants rose up under their leader Karadjordje ("Black George"). As long as the Ottomans preoccupied themselves with larger issues, such as relations with Napoleon and Russia, the Serbs held out. But when the Russians made peace with the Ottomans in 1812 to clear the decks for resisting Napoleon's invasion, the Ottomans crushed the Serbian rebels.

In 1815 a new revolt under a new leader broke out. Miloš Obrenović proved craftier than Karadjordje. He

MAP 22-2

THE BALKANS IN THE EARLY NINETEENTH CENTURY

Vuk Stefanović Karadžić, Serbian Linguist, Writer, and Folklorist

Among the peoples of central and eastern Europe, national consciousness emerged first in the minds of writers and linguists. These men, inspired by the French Revolution and particularly by the philosopher Herder, began to write histories of their own people, to study and codify their languages, and to define their special characteristics. Leopold von Ranke wrote German history "as it really happened"; Noah Webster compiled a dictionary in the United States to differentiate American English from the king's English; and the Grimm brothers helped to define the German Volk by collecting folktales.

Vuk Stefanović Karadžić (1787–1864) of Serbia was one of these early awakeners. Vuk, as he is known among the Serbs, was a sickly peasant child whose left leg was withered below the knee. When he was very young, a relative mixed gunpowder with water to make ink and taught Vuk the letters that he wrote on cartridge-paper. Vuk attended a monastery school off and on for three years and begged lessons from visitors to his village. Learning to read in this way, he entered into the service of the First Serbian Uprising, which lacked literate persons. When the Ottomans retook Belgrade, Vuk fled to Austria. Asked at the border what he had to declare, he answered "only my memory," which turned out to be prodigious.

In Vienna, linguist Jernej Kopitar, the official censor for Slavic books, quickly recognized Vuk's genius. Kopitar helped Vuk to publish his first grammar of spoken Serbian and his first songbook, in which he printed some of the remarkable oral epics that blind singers had sung to their peasant audiences in Serbia over the centuries. With this beginning, Vuk embarked on a long, contentious, and poverty-ridden career of publication. Over the years, he created a reformed alphabet for the Serbian language, wrote the first and most famous Serbian dictionary, worked out the details of Serbian grammar, published hundreds of epic poems taken from the oral tradition, and, with Ranke, wrote a history of the Serbian Revolution.

Vuk's main linguistic principle was to "write as you speak." This guideline may seem obvious, but anyone who has struggled with English spelling knows that the rules governing written languages can prove quite haphazard. This was true of the written Serbian of Vuk's day. The language included words, spellings, and structures that came from archaic church languages and from Russian.

For years, vigorous opposition from Orthodox church leaders prevented the adoption of Vuk's simplified alphabet and style. In Greece a similar battle raged between those who thought that the literary language should combine the best elements of classical and Byzantine Greek and those who believed, as Vuk did, that popular speech should provide the basis of the written language. In Greece the issue was never resolved, so that today there are two forms of modern Greek, *demotiki*, or the spoken language, and *katarevousa*, or the educated language. In Serbia, however, Vuk's reforms eventually prevailed, and written Serbian today accurately reflects spoken Serbian both phonetically and structurally.

Similar efforts to codify and standardize their written languages arose simultaneously among the Poles, Czechs, Hungarians, Romanians, and others. Language is such a natural phenomenon that it became perhaps the most important foundation for ethnic differentiation in central and eastern Europe. ❖

flattered the Ottomans, agreed to collect their taxes for them, and maintained order. By 1830 he had not only made himself the richest man in the Balkans, but he had won autonomy for his tiny and utterly backward country of peasant landowners. This seemingly insignificant beginning of the Serbian nation-state would eventually hold important consequences for the rest of Europe.

Events that more clearly deserve the name *revolution* broke out in Greece at about the same time. This small country, also under Ottoman rule, was much more diverse than Serbia. Rich and powerful Greek families wielded great influence in the Ottoman capital of Istanbul (medieval Constantinople); Greeks dominated the hierarchy of the Orthodox church, which the Muslim Ottomans permitted to operate in the Balkans; Greek shipbuilders had grown wealthy exploiting the Black Sea grain trade during the Napoleonic wars; a Greek **diaspora** around the Mediterranean put educated Greeks in contact with European ideas; and even poor Greeks were divided between mountain people and valley people. In addition to this social diversity, Greece boasted a unique past. Because every educated European was familiar with classical Greece and had heard of the Byzantine Empire, which modern Greeks also claimed as their heritage, westerners became much more interested in the Greek revolution than in the remote Serbian uprising.

In 1821 a group of Greek liberals and nationalists, the Philike Eteria (Society of Friends), touched off a Greek revolt against the Ottomans. Thwarted by Greece's rugged topography, Ottoman forces failed to put down the revolt after five years of vicious warfare. In 1826, however, the Sultan's Egyptian vassal, Mehmed Ali, entered the war, tipping the balance in favor of the Ottomans.[6] The Europeans promptly joined the conflict on the side of the Greeks. Indeed, the Greek Revolution generated enormous enthusiasm in western Europe. In France, Germany, and especially Britain, supporters known as philhellenes (or "lovers of the Greeks") rushed to the Greeks' defense, both financially and morally. A liberal Romantic vision of heroic defenders of ancient culture standing up against the Muslim Turk filled artists' canvases, inspired Romantic poets, and emptied the purses of sympathetic businessmen.

When enthusiastic volunteers like Lord Byron arrived in Greece, however, they found a poverty-stricken population divided into bitterly competing clans. The Greeks, it turned out, had little notion of constitutional ideals or classical culture, and behaved just as brutally as their Ottoman opponents. Undeterred, a conference of foreign ministers met in London in 1826 and decided that Mehmed Ali should not be allowed into Greece. The following year, the

British navy sank the entire Egyptian fleet at Navarino. From that moment on, the question was not whether the Greeks would win, but how the combatants would work out the final arrangements. In 1830 the Great Powers reconvened in London and agreed to recognize the independence of a small Greece. The Ottomans, whom the Russians had defeated in war in the meantime, had no choice but to accept the arrangement.

By 1830, therefore, the first new national states since the introduction of the idea of popular sovereignty came into existence in Europe. Serbia, only an autonomous region, had carved out its own place and was ruled by a native prince. Greece was an independent state, but because foreign intervention had made its creation possible, the Europeans imposed a German prince to govern the new entity. Otto of Bavaria was chosen, and he and his entourage ruled in Athens for thirty years. Small, weak, and prey to the European powers, neither Serbia nor Greece carried any weight in the international arena, but their birth presaged enormous changes. They were the first in a long line of new nation-states that over the next hundred years redrew the map of Europe.

Military Revolts

The Greek and Serbian uprisings were popular revolts by Christians against the Islamic empire. They had nationalist overtones, and they created new states. Most of the revolts during the first fifteen years of postrevolutionary Europe were not as successful. One of the sources of these revolts was the inspiration that the liberating mission of Napoleon's armies, as the French interpreted it at least, gave to forward-looking military officers. In 1820 Spain experienced a kind of revolt that would become common over the next century and a half in other parts of the world: the mutiny by junior officers on behalf of a revolutionary ideology, in this case, liberalism. In Naples too, a group of officers, inspired by the Spanish example, imposed a constitution on their reactionary monarch.

But such conflagrations were exactly what the Holy Alliance, not to mention the Concert of Europe, had been formed to prevent. Under the leadership of Metternich, the Great Powers authorized Austria to send troops to Naples in 1820 to quell the revolt there, and in 1823 they authorized France to do the same in Spain.

Russia too experienced a revolt by a handful of military officers, inspired by their experiences during the wars against Napoleon. A small group of aristocratic officers who considered Alexander I's draconian discipline dishonorable and believed that unrestrained autocracy destroyed social order tried to prevent Nicholas I, Alexander's youngest brother, from ascending the throne when Alexander died unexpectedly in December 1825. Unbeknownst to the plotters, or anyone else, the heir apparent to the throne, Constantine, at this time viceroy of Poland, earlier

---

[6] The fact that Mehmed Ali was an Albanian Muslim—that is, ethnically neither Turkish nor Egyptian—illustrates how unimportant nationality (as opposed to religion) was to the Ottomans.

THE HISTORICAL EVIDENCE

"Message to Siberia"

1827

Russians consider Alexander Pushkin (1799–1837) not only their greatest poet but also the founder of their modern literature. The formidable literary output of this St. Petersburg dandy included novels, short stories, lyric poetry, dramas, retellings of folktales and ancient epics, and a long, Byronic "novel in verse," Eugene Onegin. *His short life was Romantic to the hilt, crammed with love affairs, gambling, and feverish bouts of writing, and ending in a fatal duel with another man over the society woman Pushkin had recently married.*

Pushkin sympathized with the Decembrists, and knew some of them. His verses from 1827, titled "Message to Siberia," helped fix in Russians' memory these upper-class rebels whom Nicholas I exiled to labor camps.

Deep in the Siberian mine,
Keep your patience proud;
The bitter toil shall not be lost,
The rebel thought unbowed.

The sister of misfortune, Hope,
In the under-darkness dumb
Speaks joyful courage to your heart;
The day desired will come.

And love and friendship pour to you
Across the darkened doors,

Even as round your galley-beds
My free music pours.

The heavy-hanging chains will fall,
The walls will crumble at a word;
And Freedom greet you in the light,
And brothers give you back the sword.

Source: From *The Poems, Prose, and Plays of Alexander Pushkin*, trans. Max Eastman, ed. Avraham Yarmolinsky (New York: Modern Library, 1936), pp. 62–63.

---

had secretly agreed to give way to Nicholas. The new tsar was able to suppress the comic opera coup almost instantly. Having brought out his troops to stand in the palace square in St. Petersburg and shout "Constantine and Constitution!" to show opposition to Nicholas, the revolt's commander got "a frightful headache" and went home. The man whom the conspirators had named dictator spent the day wandering the streets before seeking asylum in the Austrian embassy. The troops themselves were completely ignorant of their mission. Some of them thought that "Constitution" was Constantine's wife.

The Decembrist revolt, so-called because it took place on December 14, had no chance of success, but it exerted a profound influence both on Nicholas and on the Russian mythology of revolution. Nicholas interviewed all the arrested conspirators personally and, after hanging five of them, sent more than a hundred others to Siberia. The trauma of revolt on his first day in office convinced him of the need for vigilance, and his secret police became notorious for their efficiency in rooting out disaffection. On the other hand, the heroism of the Decembrist exiles and their wives, who lived on in Siberia for another twenty to forty

years, inspired many later Russian revolutionaries. By creating martyrs, Nicholas inadvertently launched a long tradition of revolutionary valor in autocratic Russia.

The military coup d'état in Spain and Naples, as well as the Decembrist revolt, could hardly be called revolutions. Their protagonists failed to generate support among the masses, and they succumbed to foreign intervention. But neither were they simply revolts, for the officers sought to replace reactionary regimes with liberal constitutional governments, an outcome that would have revolutionized those states had they succeeded.

CONCLUSION: CONFRONTING CHANGE

The first post–French revolutionary generation confronted a number of unsettling new ideas. People react in several ways to the threat of change, whether they are politicians or ordinary citizens. Some simply ignore new ideas; by pursuing a business-as-usual policy, they hope that the innovations will go away so that they can continue their former lives. This was the reaction of rulers such as Ferdinand VII of Spain and Ferdinand I of Naples to the challenges posed by their liberal military officers. Others try to avoid the stress of change by suppressing the new ideas. Metternich was the most able European statesman to follow this strategy. Alternatively, one can resist change creatively by reinventing old ideas, as did many conservative thinkers when they cultivated notions of organic society and paternalism.

Those who found change exciting reacted in differing ways, too. Reformers in nonabsolutist states, like British and French liberals, tried to work within the system to change it, while revolutionaries, like liberals in autocratic states and some nationalists, wanted to destroy the old structures in order to install new ones. Romantics and utopian socialists took a different tack. Utopians proposed abandoning normal society for small, ideal communities, while Romantics, whether reformist, reactionary, or revolutionary, turned to innovations in painting, poetry, and architecture, not so much ignoring the new ideas—many of them were active in politics—as transforming them into a different medium. Early socialists criticized the subordinate position of women and began the lengthy process of creating a position for women in society that matched the French Revolution's promise of equity.

These varying responses might have led to serious conflicts in Europe. But for thirty years, the Congress of Vienna—by assuring the sovereignty of the Great Powers in international law, by creating buffer areas, and by not permitting events outside of Europe to draw them into conflict—created a relatively stable international system that maintained an uneasy peace. Underneath the surface, however, economic and social change percolated, adding dangerous new elements to the mixture. In 1848 the dam burst in the most serious, but last, general European revolution.

Selected Reading

General Histories

Hobsbawm, Eric J. *The Age of Revolution, 1789–1848* (1962). First volume of a magnificent three-volume history of the nineteenth century by one of Britain's foremost social historians. Uses the concept of Dual Revolution (French and Industrial).

Jardin, André, and André-Jean Tudesq. *Restoration and Reaction, 1815–1848* (1983). This rich study of France is divided into two sections: (1) a detailed historical narrative of national affairs, and (2) individual studies of France's greatly varied regions.

Johnson, Paul. *The Birth of the Modern: World Society, 1815–1830* (1991). A huge, broad-ranging book full of details, anecdotes, and stories. Johnson argues that "the matrix of the modern world was largely formed" in this period.

Pilbeam, Pamela M. *The 1830 Revolution in France* (1991). Actually a history of France from 1820 to 1835, this study investigates the extent to which the revolution of 1830 can be understood as bourgeois, liberal, artisanal, or anticlerical.

Salaman, Redcliffe N. *The History and Social Influence of the Potato* (1949; with new introduction and corrections, 1985). Everything you wanted to know about the impact of the potato, including a thorough discussion of its importance to Ireland in the nineteenth century.

Sheehan, James J. *German History, 1770–1866* (1989). An outstanding political, cultural, intellectual, and social history of the Germanies in the century prior to unification.

Ideologies and Political Movements

Nationalism

Anderson, Benedict. *Imagined Communities: Reflection on the Origin and Spread of Nationalism*, 2nd ed. (1991). Highly original and influential book, the title of which instantly entered into the vocabulary of nationalism studies.

Gellner, Ernest. *Nations and Nationalism* (1983). Witty and influential study that presents nationalism as the logical organizing principle of industrial societies.

Greenfeld, Liah. *Nationalism: Five Roads to Modernity* (1992). Controversial but useful book that makes modernization the product of nationalism, rather than vice versa. Stresses the difference between civic and ethnic nationalism.

Mack Smith, Denis. *Mazzini* (1994). Argues that Mazzini was more an idealistic patriot than a nationalist.

Riasanovsky, Nicholas V. *Nicholas I and Official Nationality in Russia, 1825–1855* (1967). Remains a fascinating study of the brutal and narrow-minded regime, which its propagandists called "the astonishment of the ages."

Wilson, Duncan. *The Life and Times of Vuk Stefanović Karadžić, 1787–1864: Literacy, Literature, and National Independence in Serbia* (1970). Surprisingly accessible biography of the great Serbian linguist and folklorist that also provides a good introduction to early modern Balkan and Central European life.

Socialism

Beecher, Jonathan. *Charles Fourier: The Visionary and His World* (1986). Scholarly biography arguing that the peculiarities of Fourier's grandiose schemes are integral to his insights as a social critic and understandable in light of the modernist belief that humans can reshape the world.

Grogan, Susan K. *French Socialism and Sexual Difference: Women and the New Society, 1803–1844* (1992). Excellent discussion of the feminism of the early French socialists: Henri Comte de Saint-Simon, Charles Fourier, and Flora Tristan.

Taylor, Barbara. *Eve and the New Jerusalem: Socialism and Feminism in the Nineteenth Century* (1983). Fascinating discussion of women supporters of Robert Owen's ideal of human emancipation.

Conservatism

Berdahl, Robert. *The Politics of the Prussian Nobility: The Development of a Conservative Ideology, 1770–1848* (1988). Shows how the Prussian nobility "euphemized" its domination of the peasantry by means of an ideology of paternalism.

Epstein, Klaus. *The Genesis of German Conservatism* (1966). Discusses three kinds of German conservatism (status quo, reform, and reactionary) as responses to the Enlightenment. Excellent historical background.

Liberalism

Brock, Michael. *The Great Reform Act* (1973). A detailed and authoritative account of the Reform Act of 1832 that started Britain on its pathway to democracy.

Sheehan, James J. *German Liberalism in the Nineteenth Century* (1978). Sees German liberalism as developing in an hostile environment, but not solely as a middle-class movement.

Romanticism

Eisler, Benita. *Byron: Child of Passion, Fool of Fame* (1999). A massive, vivid, and revealing portrait of the unpleasant man who was the greatest Romantic poet.

Halsted, John B., ed. *Romanticism* (1969). A collection of thirty texts by the most illustrious Romantics of the first half of the nineteenth century.

International Affairs

Kissinger, Henry. *Diplomacy* (1994). The former secretary of state's most complete history of modern European diplomacy argues that the balance of power was the mainspring of post-1815 stability.

Schroeder, Paul W. *Metternich's Diplomacy at Its Zenith, 1820–1823* (1962). Argues, in contrast to Kissinger, that Metternich was not a constructive European statesman, but rather a repressive Austrian diplomat who approached diplomacy cleverly but cynically on the basis of his desire to prevent change.

———. "The Nineteenth-Century International System: Changes in the Structure," *World Politics* 39, no. 1 (1986). Excellent summary argument that nineteenth-century European stability was based on guarantees of territorial integrity, the existence of buffers, and the acceptance of British sea power.

———. *The Transformation of European Politics, 1763–1848* (1994). A major reinterpretation of European interactions, especially the impact of the Congress of Vienna. Massive and detailed, but very important.

CHAPTER 23

INDUSTRIALIZATION AND REVOLUTION

Attack on the Pantheon   Phototheque des Musée de la Ville De Paris / Joffre-Musée Carnavalet.

*I*n one sense, industrialization spread through Europe very rapidly—in only a handful of generations it extended from Britain to Russia's Ural Mountains. But looked at from the viewpoint of a single lifetime, the process was far more leisurely than our imagination usually perceives it. Mentally it is easy to jump from the supposedly idyllic life of the healthy peasant to the grim, regimented, and polluted living conditions of European cities at the height of the Industrial Revolution and then on to the well-educated skilled laborer of today in two fictional leaps. But no country, including Great Britain, industrialized evenly or all at once.

The first societies that began to industrialize were those geographically or culturally closest to Britain: northern and western Europe, and North America. Industrialization began to affect these countries in earnest during the first generation after the Congress of Vienna. Its impact included not only the establishment of innovative textile and metallurgical factories, but also, paradoxically, the arrival both of laissez-faire ideas and of governmental intervention into the economy. The transition to wage earning, rather than production at home, began to change the relationship between men and women and dealt a fatal blow to artisans and their guilds. Nevertheless, by 1848 most people in Europe still lived on the land, and industrialization had not yet raised the standard of living of the manual laborer, the casual worker, or the marginal poor. These lower ranks of society crowded into the increasingly foul slums of industrial cities, which began growing at an explosive rate.

These seemingly inexorable changes, which we discuss in the first part of this chapter, may have been fundamental, but they were not the most stirring events of the first post-Napoleonic generation. In 1848 the most general outburst of popular revolt Europe ever experienced broke out all across the continent, dramatically closing sixty years of ferment that the French Revolution had begun in 1789. The revolutions of 1848 brought all the ingredients of Europe's initial confrontation with the Dual Revolution (French and Industrial) into play at once. The new ideologies of the early nineteenth century—liberalism, socialism, and nationalism, as well as the powerful cultural attitude known as Romanticism—all motivated professionals among the middle class to attempt to seize political power. Artisans displaced by the Industrial Revolution, and in some cases the urban poor that industrialization had not yet helped, provided the physical force that temporarily overthrew governments in almost every part of Europe except Russia.

N. A. Gabe's painting at the beginning of this chapter shows republican troops in revolutionary Paris settling accounts with an uprising of dissatisfied workers in June 1848. The painting suggests that the revolutions of 1848 failed when resurgent reaction overcame the original goals of socialism, liberalism, and nationalism. But 1848 was a failure only in the short run. As the last gasp of the traditional guild artisans, they cleared the decks for the creation of a working-class culture. A new sexual division of labor became established. Wage labor became reserved for men and poorly paid or unpaid domestic tasks became the conventional work for women. After 1848, socialism, nationalism, and liberalism, which Metternich and the conservatives had tried to contain, became the ideological bases of modern politics, while Romanticism lost its political significance. Conservatives became more flexible, adopting some of the political mechanisms of their opponents, such as universal manhood suffrage, as they adapted to industrialization. And industrialization itself took off with a vengeance. The climactic coming together in 1848 of several strands of the Dual Revolution set the stage for the next phase of European development, the Century of Power.

INDUSTRIALIZATION COMES TO THE CONTINENT

Once the initial steps of industrialization took place in Britain, they spread rapidly to the European continent, and in a similar sequence: the mechanization of textile production, followed by, or concurrently with, the development of an iron and steel industry and the construction of railroads. As late as the second half of the twentieth century, one of the most important symbols of modernity to developing countries, even in Europe, remained the steel mill. But continental industrialization was not purely imitative. The style of work it required, the mobilization of resources it demanded, and the scale of enterprise it encouraged all stimulated an accelerated pace of innovation that changed the world more in the last two hundred years than in any similar time period in human history.

A Rising Population

The Industrial Revolution came to Europe fitfully and with significant regional variations. But one phenomenon was common to the continent as a whole: a marked rise in population. European population fluctuated dramatically between the twelfth and the eighteenth centuries, but on average it grew at a rate of only about 0.14 percent per year. During the eighteenth century, however, it began to expand steadily, even spectacularly in places like Ukraine and England. Estimates vary, because governments in those days did not conduct censuses, but scholars calculate that from a figure of about 115 million in 1700, European population reached 188 million in 1800 and 266 million in 1850—a compound rate of growth of about 0.56 percent per year. This may not sound like much, given the rates of growth common in some parts of the world today. However, assuming that European population had stood at 42 million in the year 1000, a steady growth rate of only 0.56 percent per year would have pushed it to about 4.8 billion in 1850 rather than the actual figure of 266 million (see Figure 23-1).

No simple explanation can encompass such a broad increase in population, but it is clear that medical advances contributed very little. The only significant new medical technique of the eighteenth century was the smallpox vaccine, which was first developed in India. The slow spread of inoculation in Europe and its limited use made it only a minor factor in stimulating population growth. We can also discount new sanitation measures, because only after 1850 did European cities begin introducing modern sewer and water systems in earnest.

Shifting patterns of disease and new farming techniques may have played more important roles. Europeans adapted to some previously devastating diseases, like syphilis, and changing patterns of land development lessened the incidence of certain others. The mosquito that carries the malaria virus likes the blood of cows, for instance, but the virus cannot live in cows. Therefore, an increase in the size of cattle herds in Mediterranean countries had a tendency to lower the rate of malaria infection in humans while at the same time bolstering protein consumption. The introduction of crops from the New World, such as the potato and maize (corn), raised the calories

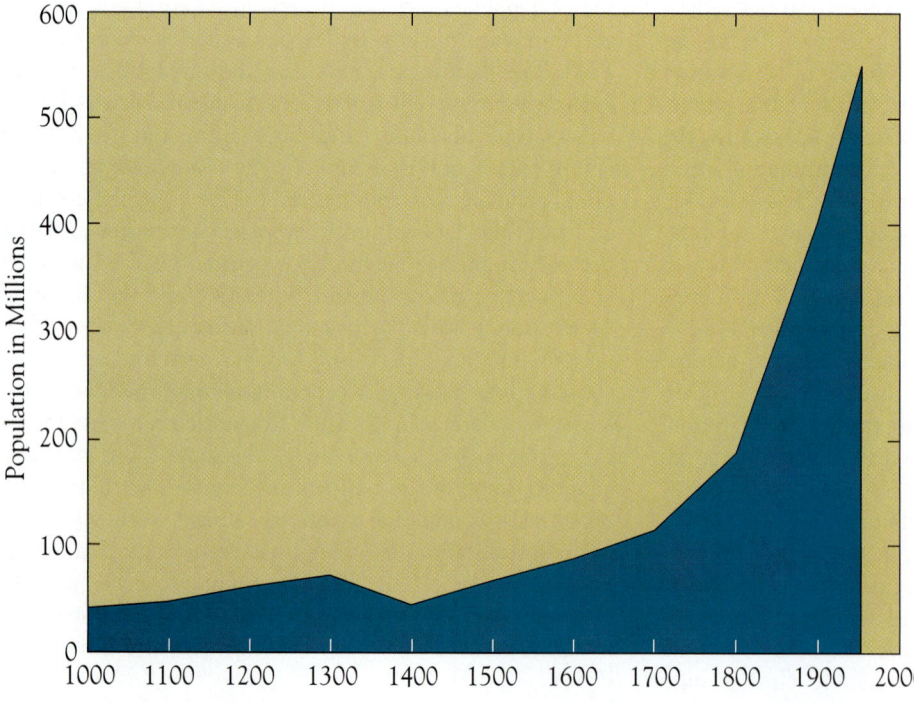

FIGURE 23-1
EUROPEAN POPULATION GROWTH

European population grew slowly, and not always steadily, from the year 1000 to 1700. In the early years of the Industrial Revolution between 1700 and 1850, however, the rate of growth increased dramatically.

Sketch of Krupp Foundry   In 1832 Alfred Krupp made this sketch of a bellows for his foundry. The objects on the right are ovens. Note that Krupp does not envision the use of steam power to run his bellows at this early stage.   *Historiches Archiv Krupp.*

A whole range of other inventions accompanied the frenzy of railroad construction. The steamship, for example, preceded the railroad in improving transportation, and by the 1840s had cut two-thirds off the time required to travel between New York and Liverpool. The telegraph became the device that permitted regulation of train traffic, but proved to have widespread other uses as well. In the eighteenth century France had built a series of semaphores that could transmit messages by setting levers in certain ways. An operator with a telescope would look at a semaphore on a hilltop 4 to 6 miles away and set his semaphore to the proper configuration. France had a system of more than five hundred such towers. But the discovery of electricity led to a series of inventions that culminated in the ability to send signals across wires electrically. By the 1840s, telegraph lines were appearing not only along railway lines to regulate train traffic, but as vehicles of news gathering. The Associated Press, founded in the United States in 1848, and Reuters (Paris, 1849), were two of the first modern news agencies. With the laying of underwater cables—the first transatlantic cable was completed in 1866—news that in 1830 might take weeks or even months to travel from the New World to Europe now made the journey in minutes.

More prosaic, but just as widespread in its impact, was the invention of the postage stamp, which spread rapidly from its introduction in England in 1840. Previously, mail carriers had collected postage from the recipient on the basis of how far the mail had traveled. In England, however, postal reformer Rowland Hill discovered that the actual cost of sending the mail did not vary, however far the letter was sent. To overcome all the difficulties of collection upon delivery, he conceived of charging the sender a small amount by selling stamped letter paper. But then he realized that educated middle- and upper-class people might write a letter on an ordinary piece of paper. When

Mail for the Masses   The first postage stamps, a one-penny black and a two-penny blue, went on sale May 6 and 7, 1840. The idea spread rapidly around the world. Because artificial dyes were not invented until almost twenty years later, the first stamps were printed in black or other basic colors. An unused example of the "penny black" in top condition is worth about $3,000 today. *National Postage Museum, Smithsonian Institution.*

they sent their servant to the post office, the letter would have to be copied onto the stamped paper—but because the servant was likely to be illiterate and unable to copy the letter, Hill, almost as an afterthought, conceived of an adhesive postage stamp. Thus did Britain's class and educational structure contribute to the dawn of the information age.

Friedrich List and the Zollverein

The early experiences of the Belgian iron industry in Germany illustrate how the principles of free trade and nationalism can come into conflict. Belgium's success in exploiting Germany's low tariff on pig iron benefited Belgium and European industrial development, but it hurt the inefficient German producers. In response to the problem, the German economist and publicist Friedrich List produced the first nationalistic theory of economic development. Ironically, at the same time the German states joined in a free-trade zone to increase their mutual trade.

The idea of a free-trade zone, or customs union (known as the *Zollverein*), had percolated through Germany for a number of years. In 1818 Prussia had dropped all internal trade barriers so as to link the new territories it had received at the Congress of Vienna more closely with its traditional lands, and by 1828 several of Prussia's smaller neighbors had joined them. Meanwhile, in southern Germany, Bavaria and Württemberg reached a similar agreement. On January 1, 1834, these two alliance systems combined in the Zollverein, which greatly lowered tariffs among them. Over the

next twenty years, most of the remaining German states joined the union, with the notable exception of Austria, and trade among them flourished.

Friedrich List was one of the most ardent supporters of the Zollverein. Unlike the many German nationalists who distrusted industrialization, fearing that it would corrupt the German Volk, List welcomed it. As early as 1819 he wrote a memorandum encouraging the creation of a German customs union. Shortly thereafter, when a court convicted him of subversive activities, he fled to America, where he participated in the tariff debates during Andrew Jackson's presidency and published his first book on political economy. In 1834 he returned to Germany as an American consul (he had taken out American citizenship) and became a vigorous, not to say obnoxious, champion of railroad construction. List supported free trade, but as a German nationalist he also realized that Britain's enormous economic head start put Germany at a severe disadvantage. He advocated tariffs that would permit Germany's "infant industries" to survive the early stages of industrialization and become competitive. Later, he argued, when these enterprises had become viable, the tariffs could be lowered. List himself was never successful. His passion and bluntness alienated all he met. "Whoever has seen him never forgets him," wrote one acquaintance. "His eyes flash, a storm always hovers around his broad brow, and his mouth always flames like the crater of a volcano." List eventually committed suicide from despair. Nevertheless, his combination of industrialization and nationalism provided a powerful theory of development, and his book on the subject, *The National System of Political Economy*, published in 1841, exerted a powerful influence for the rest of the century.

THE DISRUPTIVE IMPACT OF INDUSTRIALIZATION

The potential social impact of industrialization did not escape contemporary observers, particularly when they contemplated that fiery new invention, the railroad. In 1837 one German writer predicted that the railroad would have the same historical significance as the invention of printing, and another called it the Hercules that would "deliver nations from the plague of war, inflation, famine, national hatreds, unemployment and ignorance." Metternich also believed the railroad would have dramatic effects, but he limited himself to the generalization that it would transform politics and social conditions. As often was the case, Metternich's evaluation proved the more sober and the more accurate.

But even Metternich could not grasp the extent of the psychological change that the railroad provoked. Builders thought at first that trains would carry primarily freight, but it quickly became apparent that passenger traffic would be important, too. Cheap excursion tickets opened up tourism, previously the privilege of the wealthy, to ordinary people. During the second half of the century, the face of every city in Europe changed, as boosters constructed vast new railroad stations, cutting their tracks through residential areas to the center of the city. Time became important, because railroads ran on a schedule, and by the end of the century Europeans had adopted a standard time. For a hundred years, from about 1850 to 1950, the steam locomotive embodied power and adventure. Its plaintive whistle in the distance evoked excitement, energy, and a sense of possibility.

Industrial Work and Working Families

Everyone fell under the spell of these changes, but not everyone profited from them, especially in the early days. Some working people prospered under early industrialization, particularly those finding employment in mechanized spinning and weaving, railroads, mining, and iron manufacture. But in the years before 1848 even these favored groups faced harsh working conditions and unemployment in times of depression. The mining industry often paid its wages in credits, for example, which miners could use only in company stores. Periodically an economic collapse would follow a period of prosperity, and laid-off factory workers enjoyed no social safety net to protect them from hard times.

But factory hands and miners at least labored in expanding industries with potential for growth. Many

workers were not so lucky. When steamships began plying the Rhine River in the 1830s, for example, the men who for years had hauled barges up the river soon found themselves out of work. At first weavers prospered with the introduction of new spinning machines, but when weaving machines hit Europe the weavers suffered as much as their British counterparts had from declining wages and lost jobs. Peasants freed in some parts of Germany from their servile obligations had to borrow money and mortgage their crops. Having traded the landlord for the moneylender, they discovered that the moneylender felt none of the paternal responsibility for them that some traditional landowners had.

The coming of industrialization had a particularly powerful impact on the position of women, in both the middle class and the working class. In early modern Europe, the primary unit of production had been the family. Women and men—as well as children—worked together in the household. The same was true in the early days of industrialization. When small-scale producers lived in or near their factories, women often took over many of the aspects of running the business. But when factories became larger and moved physically away from the home, middle-class women found themselves relegated to a new position. Mine owners, textile mill operators, and other risk-taking and gain-seeking entrepreneurs spent almost all of their time away from the home. They assigned their wives the task of maintaining the household as a separate

Popularity of the Railroad   This French engraving from 1837 suggests how from the very beginning railroads attracted passenger traffic, astonishing and pleasing the public with dizzying speeds of around 20 miles per hour.   *Bibliothèque Nationale de France.* Photo:AKG London.

THE HISTORICAL EVIDENCE

Middle-Class Domesticity and Working-Class Life

1830s

By the 1830s and 1840s, middle-class women in Great Britain and other countries of western Europe were being told that they should dedicate their lives to service, both to their families and to those less fortunate. The lives of even relatively well-off working women were rather different.

In 1838, Mrs. Sarah Stickney Ellis addressed herself to other women of her social class.

It is from the class of [middle-class] females . . . that we naturally look for the highest tone of moral feeling, because they are at the same time removed from the pressing necessities of absolute poverty, and admitted to the intellectual privileges of the great: and thus, while they enjoy every facility in the way of acquiring knowledge, it is their still higher privilege not to be exempt from the domestic duties which call forth the best energies of the female character. . . .

It is not to be presumed that women possess more moral power than men; but happily for them, such are their early impressions, associations, and general position in the world, that their moral feelings are less liable to be impaired by the pecuniary objects which too often constitute the chief end of man, and which, even under the limitations of better principle, necessarily engage a large portion of his thoughts.

And in 1833 this is what parliamentary inquirers found out about how the unnamed wife of an English cotton spinner—forty years old, married for twenty-five years, the mother of five living children, and who "staid at

home" since her first child was born—made do on her husband's weekly income of £1, 5 shillings. After paying for food, rent, and coal, 6 shillings and 11 pence remained "for clothing, sickness of seven persons, schooling, etc." (The oldest daughter helped her father at work, and did not complain of fatigue or not sleeping. As the woman acknowledged, these conditions were quite good for a working family.)

Breakfast is generally porridge, bread, and milk, lined with flour or oatmeal. On Sunday, a sup of tea and bread and butter. Dinner, on week days, potatoes and bacon, and bread, which is generally white. On a Sunday, a little flesh meat; no butter, egg, or pudding. . . . Now and then buys eggs when they are as low as a halfpenny each. . . .

They never taste any other vegetables than potatoes; never use any beer or spirits; now and then may take a gill [a quarter of a pint] of beer when ill, which costs a penny. . . . The house consists of four rooms, two on each floor; the furniture consists of two beds in the same room, one for themselves, the other for the children; have four chairs, one table in the house, boxes to put clothes in, no chest of drawers, two pans and a tea kettle for boiling, a gridiron and frying-pan, half-a-dozen large and small

world. The women of this new middle class focused on reproduction—having and bringing up children—and on maintaining a haven away from the cutthroat world in which their husbands operated. Often, therefore, they were psychologically far removed from their market-oriented husbands. Centered in what modern historians call the cult of domesticity, they focused on religious service, charitable works, and moral uprightness.

The separation of male and female spheres under the impact of industrialization characterized working women's lives too. Early textile mills and mines employed thousands of young women, but over time a distinct sexual division of labor took place. Just as middle-class men began to consider themselves the producers of society, relegating their

wives to the "unproductive"—or reproductive—realm of the household, so wage labor came increasingly to be considered a male prerogative. In central Europe, for example, women sewing products at home for sale instead of for family consumption caused artisans to complain bitterly. They insisted that women had no right to produce for the market because being a housewife was the true and only appropriate occupation for women. They were supported in this by the Romantics, who put forward a theory of "proper" women's roles based on what they considered to be the "natural" functions of the sexes. Jobs that seemed associated with household tasks—washing or sewing—came to be considered women's work when done in the home, whereas similar tasks performed for wages—fulling or plates, four pairs of knives and forks, several pewter spoons. They subscribe 1d. [1 penny] a week for each child to a funeral society for the children [which will bury them if they die]. Two of the children go to school at 3d. a week each; they are taught reading for this, but not writing. Have a few books, such as a Bible, hymn-book,

and several small books that the children have got as prizes at the Sunday School.

Source: Both documents are taken from Walter Arnstein, ed., *The Past Speaks*, 2nd ed. (Lexington, MA: Heath, 1993), vol. 2, pp. 172, 175, 178.

Begas's *The Artist's Family*, 1826 The ideal of early 1800s German middle-class domestic life is vividly brought to life in this painting by Karl Begas. *Wallraf-Richartz Museum, Cologne.* WRM 1556.

tailoring—came to be considered men's work. A new sexual division of labor became characteristic of industrializing societies.

Industrialization damaged the positions of guild artisans most severely. The elimination of craft guilds and the laws that protected artisans evolved differently on the Continent than in Britain. As we saw in Chapter 21, French revolutionaries abolished all corporate bodies, such as guilds and trade unions, that could come between a free citizen and the state. The Chapelier Law of 1791 abolished the right of guilds to restrict entry into a trade, prohibited workers from forming associations to protect their interests, and outlawed strikes. The French Penal Code of 1810 took this principle even further by prohibiting all associations of

more than twenty persons for any purpose whatsoever. Prussia did not abolish guilds formally until 1845, but in the thirty years before that the Prussian government stopped enforcing many of the restrictions on trade called for by guild regulations.

Pressure on the traditional ways of production sparked protests from artisans ranging from petitions and complaints to strikes, machine breaking, and riots. Nineteenth-century liberals dismissed these expressions of despair as outbursts of irrational fury by an uneducated mob rebelling against progress. In actuality, as we saw in the case of the English shearers discussed in Chapter 20, many protests were well-organized movements that sought specific, limited remedies. Often it was trigger-happy government troops who ignited the violence that erupted at numerous demonstrations. The revolts of the silkworkers of Lyon, France, in 1831 and 1834 provide a specific example of the resentments and reactions characteristic of the tensions that stalked Europe in the 1830s under the pressure of industrialization. The Lyon case also shows that unrest sprang not only from technological change, but also from the spread of market ideas and practices.

The Revolts of the Lyon Silkworkers

Silks produced at Lyon constituted about one-third of the value of all French exports, making that city one of the most important manufacturing centers in the world. Silk making was less affected by new technologies than cotton spinning and weaving. The introduction of a semimechanical loom in 1804 had boosted productivity, but in 1830 most of the twenty-five thousand looms in Lyon were still hand-operated wooden devices. Some spinning was mechanical, but weaving remained in the hands of master weavers, who owned from one to four looms and worked at home with their families and one or two journeymen. By 1830 urban growth had forced many Lyon weavers to move their looms to cheaper locations outside the center of the city. This change reinforced the social division between the merchants living in the center of town, who supplied the raw material and sold the finished goods, and the weavers living in the suburbs, who produced the cloth.

The French Revolution removed restrictions on the silk trade. Anyone who could buy or rent a loom could become a weaver, and anyone who could put together the necessary raw materials could become a merchant. Between 1810 and 1830, therefore, entrepreneurs flooded the profitable silk trade. The number of merchants in Lyon jumped tenfold, while the value of Lyon's silk products only doubled. It was not new technology, therefore, that provoked social conflict in Lyon. Instead, a new, laissez-faire business climate put enormous pressure on merchants to keep weavers' salaries low and encouraged weavers to accept those salaries just to survive.

The merchants, themselves under pressure, constantly harried the weavers for faster work, lower wages, and higher quality. The weavers concluded that the root of their distress lay in the merchants' hard-hearted practices. Most weavers were literate, and their newspapers, an innovation for workers in 1830, harshly criticized the merchants. The weavers also discussed their grievances in secret societies, which they organized in a pyramid structure to evade the twenty-member limit on associations. In 1831 the weavers created a mutual aid society in an effort to take over the supply and sales functions themselves, cutting the merchants out. That same year, they persuaded the Lyon city government to establish a minimum fee for each type of silk weaving. When the merchants complained to

Paris about these threats to their livelihood, the central government—which strongly supported business and the upper-middle class—invalidated the minimum-fee agreement. Four days later, the weavers marched on the city center, and local authorities called out the National Guard. When shots rang out and several workers fell dead, the weavers stormed City Hall and seized control of the city. Cooler heads ultimately prevailed, and when the army arrived a few days later the uprising ended peacefully.

Frightened by the potential for violence that worker unrest posed, Louis Philippe's liberal government authorized the police to suppress the weavers' associations. In response, the silkworkers rose again in February 1834. "Live working or die fighting!" cried the journeymen. The government, run by an upper-middle class thoroughly frightened by what it considered the irrational fury of the mob, wrongly decided that this second uprising was part of a nationwide conspiracy of republicans bent on revolution. When the French army subdued the weavers after six days of fighting, it arrested thousands of surviving protesters.

The revolt of 1834 was the last gasp of the silk weavers. By 1850 mechanized production techniques had displaced them completely. The Lyon silkworkers' strikes and their brutal suppression entered the mythology of the French working class and aggravated the class hatreds that poisoned nineteenth-century (and later) French history. These workers embodied the frustrations and fate of traditional craftsmen throughout Europe in the face of new technologies and business methods.

The Hungry Forties

Despite such tensions, the everyday life of many city dwellers improved in the early 1840s. The textile revolution made clothing cheap and plentiful, so that even the poor began to wear underwear and to benefit from changes of clothing and bed linens. In Paris the first department store opened, and meat consumption rose. But in the early stages of industrialization, cycles of boom and bust struck with frightening regularity. Sometimes downturns were only local or regional, but the depression of 1835 affected most of Europe. The late 1830s saw a recovery, and some regions enjoyed a boom in the early 1840s, but in 1845 the agricultural cycle turned down. The potato blight hit, threatening peasants with mass starvation, and in 1846 a hot, dry summer led to the worst grain harvest in generations. The repeal of the Corn Laws in England stimulated international competition for grain and pushed the price up 50 percent between 1845 and 1847. For the poor, who spent almost all of their income on food, an increase of that magnitude spelled disaster.

These boom-and-bust **business cycles** were one of the socialists' primary complaints about the **capitalist** system. When times were good, optimistic manufacturers expanded

The Menacing Unemployed   In the "Hungry Forties" unemployed workers terrified the countryside as well as the industrial cities. This group consisted of railroad laborers who had been discharged from their jobs far out in rural France. Trying to live off the land, such wandering bands seemed (and sometimes actually were) a menace. They could be rounded up and deported to Algeria.   *Musée de l'Histoire de France. Centre Historique des Archives Nationales, Atelier de Photographie.*

and produced as much as they could, thus outrunning demand. Suddenly, sales could not sustain production and they had to cut back, laying off workers. Now pessimistic, they tended to overshoot on the low side as much as they had on the high side, reducing production so much that shortages developed even while masses of people were out of work. But shortages produced their own incentives, and the cycle began again. Manufacturers got rich and went broke in these vicious ups and downs, but workers suffered even more because they lived much closer to the edge of subsistence than did the manufacturers.

Between 1844 and 1847, Europe fell into one of its periodic economic contractions. During those years, for example, exports of bleached linens from the Zollverein dropped 40 percent. Collapses such as this put enormous numbers of people out of work. In Germany, one-third of the population of the large cities depended on public charity in 1847. Food riots broke out repeatedly. In April 1847, rioting in Berlin took regular army troops four days to suppress. The most serious revolt erupted in Silesia in 1844, just before the depression hit. Destitute weavers tried to enforce their demands for pay by attacking factory owners, but troops bloodily crushed their pitiable efforts. Between 1844 and the revolutions of 1848, an estimated fifty thousand Silesians died from famine-related diseases.

The widespread privation brought the term *pauperism* into common use for the first time. This word referred not to ordinary poverty, which had always existed, but to chronic destitution among people willing and able to work. Pauperism seemed related to industrialization and was therefore more pervasive and threatening than traditional poverty. Some social critics argued that only revolutionary changes could ease the problem, and many middle-class people feared that the anger of the underclass was about to boil over. A veteran conservative agreed: "I am not a prophet," the seventy-four-year-old Metternich said in 1847, "but I am an old physician and can distinguish between temporary and fatal diseases. We now face one of the latter." In January 1848, the French historian Alexis de Tocqueville put it this way to French legislators: "Can you not sense . . . that the earth is again trembling in Europe? Do you not feel—how shall I put it? the wind of revolution in the air?"

THE REVOLUTIONS OF 1848

Both Metternich and Tocqueville were right. In 1848 Europe experienced the most widespread outbreak of revolutionary activity in its history. In hundreds of towns and cities, disgruntled artisans and other citizens, urged on by "the party of movement"—liberals, republicans, nationalists, and, in France, even socialists—toppled governments and wrote constitutions. These revolutions were the final act in a sixty-year age of revolution that began in 1789.

THE HISTORICAL EVIDENCE

Tocqueville on Louis Philippe
1848

The revolution of 1848 in Paris resulted in part from outrage at the corruption of the business-oriented liberal regime of Louis Philippe. Here is Alexis de Tocqueville's characterization of that regime.

In 1830 the triumph of the middle class had been definite and so thorough that all political power, every franchise, every prerogative, and the whole government was confined and, as it were, heaped up within the narrow limits of this one class, to the statutory exclusion of all beneath them and the actual exclusion of all above. It entrenched itself in every vacant place, prodigiously augmented the number of places and accustomed itself to live almost as much upon the Treasury as upon its own industry. Posterity, which sees none but the more dazzling crimes, and which loses sight, in general, of mere vices, will never, perhaps, know to what extent the government of that day, towards its close, assumed the ways of an industrial enterprise, which conducts all its transactions with a view to the profits accruing to the shareholders.

Source: From *The Recollections of Alexis de Tocqueville*, trans. Alexander Taxeira de Mattos, ed. J. P. Mayer (London: Harvill Press, 1948), pp. 2–4.

(See Map 23-2.) In almost every instance the political leaders of the revolutions—those who assumed power or challenged for power—were not the middle-class industrialists who had begun multiplying in the 1830s. For the most part, these industrialists were politically indifferent, except insofar as good connections could assist them in receiving contracts or other benefits. Instead, the revolutionary leaders were a special stratum of the middle class, the educated professionals. Professors, lawyers, teachers, government bureaucrats, and journalists were the ones who best understood the new ideologies brought onto the political stage by the French Revolution and who most keenly felt the condescension of the aristocracy and the newly rich.

Just as the leaders of the revolutions of 1848 were not industrialists, the crowds that surged through the streets of European cities were not factory workers. The high cost of property in the center of the European capitals meant that most new factories had been placed in suburbs, or even in places far from the political center. At this early stage of industrialism, factory workers often were illiterate and almost untouched by the new ideologies. But two other groups did live in the centers of the capital cities: traditional artisans, who had lived there for generations, and the poor, many of them recently arrived. Artisans, distressed and under pressure from the new technologies, typically provided the initial surge of muscle for the revolutions. The poor, hungry and without political protectors, provided the bulk of the crowds.

Facing the professionals, artisans, and the poor were a variety of governments that had lost touch with their populations. They ranged from Louis Philippe's fragile regime of upper-class liberals through Prussia's patriarchal king, and from the well-meaning but confused pope to the arch-reactionary king of Naples. These rulers were almost as much under the spell of the French Revolution as were their opponents, in the sense that they felt they were in a revolutionary age. When outbursts took place their initial reaction was to succumb to what seemed yet another emanation of the inevitable.

A complete discussion of the revolutions of 1848 would take us from Sicily to the farthest reaches of the Austrian Empire, and beyond. But the main ideologies that motivated the revolutionaries provide a good organizing concept with which to make sense out of the main sites of revolution. In France, the purpose of revolution was to supplant the brittle liberalism of Louis Philippe with a broader sort of liberalism that included more of the nation in political affairs. France also experienced the only serious socialist experimentation of 1848. Nationalism drove the revolutions in the Habsburg Empire, particularly in Hungary. There Hungarian nationalists sought to separate themselves from Viennese domination while simultaneously dominating the other peoples that lived under their rule. In Germany, parliamentary constitutionalism became the main goal of the lawyers and teachers who led the revolution there, although nationalism also played a role. Finally, in Italy, all of the elements of radicalism,

MAP 23-2
1848 REVOLUTIONS

nationalism, and constitutionalism came together in a dis-jointed set of rapid-fire developments.

France: Liberals Defeat the Left and Succumb to the Right

France was not the first place through which the wind of revolution blew in 1848. That honor went to a flare-up in Sicily in January. But Paris remained the cultural center of Europe, and when news spread in February that Louis Philippe's regime had collapsed, fifty-odd uprisings followed across Europe within a few weeks. Louis Philippe suffered from a serious disability that had little to do with his per-sonality or his talents: He lacked legitimacy. Because he had replaced the centuries-old Bourbon dynasty with his own junior branch of the family, the Orleans line, Louis never won the respect of either the European princes or the conservative French monarchists.

Political parties did not exist in France, because of the law that prohibited associations of more than twenty per-sons. The opposition therefore consisted of many small

groups of varying persuasions. Two major camps—the repub-licans and the socialists—proved important in 1848, although many varieties of each existed and they overlapped considerably. All republicans favored eliminating the monarchy, but only a few advocated revolution. The most famous socialist was Louis Blanc, who came to the attention of the French public in 1840 with the publication of two best-sellers: *The Organization of Work* and *History of Ten Years, 1830–1840*. In his first book, Blanc proposed universal suffrage, control of key industries by the state, and a reorga-nization of production based on the principle of association (that is, cooperation rather than profit). His second, highly popular work was a witty critique of Louis Philippe's reign, or the regime of the bourgeoisie, as Blanc dismissively charac-terized it. (Already the words *bourgeois* and *bourgeoisie* tended to be uttered with either amusement or contempt by left-wing French intellectuals, as they still are.)

In 1847 various elements of the opposition began to hold political banquets around France. At these allegedly nonpolitical events, speakers rose between the fruit and the cheese courses to denounce the regime's considerable cor-ruption and to call for reform. As these banquets became more popular, they grew more daring. Radical republicans and socialists reminded diners of France's revolutionary past and of the hardships that the business downturn had imposed on workers.

The climax of the movement came when organizers tried to schedule a large banquet in Paris for February 22, 1848. After some dithering, the government banned the occasion on the grounds that widespread publicity and the organizers' decision to sell tickets to workers and students at reduced prices threatened violence. But on the appointed day, disgruntled artisans and students, disappointed at the banquet's cancellation, gathered anyway. In a city steeped in revolutionary memories, this was enough to bring excited crowds of artisans and journeymen onto the streets on the next day.

In 1848, Paris was not the city of long, straight boulevards that we know today. It retained a medieval layout, full of narrow, twisting alleys that an angered public could easily block with piles of large cobblestones and furniture, as they had done for the first time in 1830 (see Map 21-1). Surprised by the sudden appearance of these barricades, and unable to control the crowds with the small number of troops on hand, Louis Philippe called in the National Guard. But the guard consisted of middle-class men, many of whom also found the liberal regime of François Guizot too restrictive. When they confronted demonstrators shouting "Long live reform," and "Down with Guizot," they refused to fire, actually preventing the army from clearing the streets. Louis Philippe tried to save the situation by sacking Guizot, but on February 24 he had to acknowledge defeat and flee to England, just as his predecessor had.

No conspiracy underlay this spontaneous revolution, and no shadow government waited in the wings. When crowds occupied City Hall and the Tuileries, leading republicans gathered and announced themselves as the new government. Its dominant faction comprised upper-middle-class republicans—lawyers and writers—who sought primarily to open the restrictive regime to a broader range of property owners. Unlike the British Whigs, who had prevented revolution in Britain in 1832 by passing the Great Reform Bill, the liberal government immediately acceded to the demands of the Parisian crowd that had put them in office and introduced universal manhood suffrage, a demand of the sans-culottes as far back as 1792. Other than this paradoxical step, however, moderation was the byword of the February revolution. So great was the contrast between the inflamed rhetoric and the moderate actions of the republicans' main leader, the Romantic poet Alphonse de Lamartine, that the writer Honoré de Balzac called him an arsonist turned fireman.

From the beginning, the leaders of the new regime did their best to ignore the socialists, whom they saw as agents of the unruly mob and a threat to property. They fobbed off Louis Blanc with the title of "secretary" and asked him to set up a commission to study working conditions. The Luxembourg Commission, as Blanc's agency was called, consisted of several hundred representatives from the main industries and trades of Paris. It conducted spirited and serious debates on social issues for several months and eventually submitted a thorough report advocating a form of state socialism. But the commission's proposals stood no chance of acceptance by the republican government. Louis Blanc never exercised the influence on the revolution that his initial popularity had promised, although he foreshadowed the demand for activist government that social democrats and liberals would advocate in the twentieth century.

During the first days of revolutionary enthusiasm, the new leaders also created what at first seemed a radical answer to the needs of destitute Parisians: the national workshops. The government agreed either to find a job for every person who registered with the workshop, or to pay

"Liberty—Equality—Fraternity," 1848 The French slogan *"Liberté! Égalité! Fraternité!"* became widespread only in 1848. Here, shortly after the creation of the republic in the enthusiastic early days of the Parisian revolution of 1848, representatives of the National Guard, the workers, and the army clasp hands in brotherhood in front of a street barricade from the uprising. The unity would not last long. *"L'Union fait la force." Lithographie de Ch. Devrits, avril 1848. Bibliothèque Nationale Estampes.*

him a daily cash subsidy. In Marseilles, the workshops were fairly successful because local officials set the registrants to work on a much-needed canal. But in Paris, the appointment of an opponent of Blanc to administer the workshops virtually guaranteed their failure. Officials repeatedly denied the Parisian workshops permission to pursue useful projects, either employing the registrants in meaningless projects or paying them to remain idle. Understandably, the middle class and its republican government soon denounced the workshops as make-work giveaways.

Hostilities between the economically pressed artisans and the ruling middle-class professionals came to a head in the "June Days." By June 1848 the initial 10,000 enrollees in the national workshops had swelled to 120,000 persons. Both the workers and the middle class found the situation more and more outrageous, the workers because they received few jobs and late subsidy payments, the middle class because of what they considered the parasitic indolence of the poor. After an election in April that strengthened the middle-class element in the legislature, the government had decided that the workshops must go. Pleas for delay put off the decision, but on June 21 a decree removed all men between ages eighteen and twenty-five from the rolls unless they enlisted in the army. The decree also abolished pay by the day and organized brigades of workers to be sent to the provinces. The next day thousands of workers marched through Paris chanting "We will not go; we will not go!"

On June 23, the workers blockaded Paris's narrow streets with barricades again. Perhaps 40 percent of those who revolted in the June Days had been in the workshops, but among the rest were members of the many working-class societies that had sprung up since February, mostly employees from large firms, particularly furniture makers and metalworkers. By this time, most working people in Paris had concluded that the liberals were not going to give them what they wanted—jobs, food, and respect. But they found not just the Parisian National Guard arrayed against them but the entire nation. Members of the provincial middle class in particular resented the Parisian workers' tendency toward revolt and determined to put an end to what they considered the workers' chronic insurgency. The new railroads quickly brought National Guard forces to Paris from throughout France to participate in the short but brutal class war. Despite the workers' heroic resistance, government troops crushed the June uprising in a matter of hours, killing about 1,500 persons and deporting thousands more to Algeria. By defining the workers' demands as barbarism and treating the insurgents accordingly, the republican regime of 1848 widened the rift between the social classes that plagued nineteenth-century France.

In the French Revolution, the moderates of 1789 gave way to radicals in 1792, reaction in 1794, and "the man on horseback" in 1799. In 1848 the pattern was different.

Moderate republicans did not get replaced by radicals, whom they defeated in the June Days, and they imposed their own reaction. In the end, however, they, too, found themselves outflanked by "a man on horseback."

One of the main disputes in writing a new constitution in 1848 centered on how to elect the president. Early electoral reform had enfranchised almost all adult males, raising the electorate to more than 9 million. Should this vast new body of voters choose the president directly, or should the legislature, presumably in the hands of responsible elements, elect him? Liberals considered the second option safer, but despite their fear of the lower classes, most felt that only a popular vote could restore public confidence in the state. The republicans had come to power, after all, because the previous regime had failed to take the people adequately into account. Several candidates put themselves forward for the December 1848 election, among them Lamartine, poet and foreign minister of the February regime, and General Eugène Cavaignac, the suppressor of the June Days. But the winning candidate was Louis-Napoleon Bonaparte, the nephew of Napoleon I.

As a young man, Louis had joined the Carbonari and participated in an unsuccessful revolt. In 1836 and again in 1840, he tried to stage an uprising against Louis Philippe but succeeded only in landing in jail. There, he wrote a pamphlet titled "The Extinction of Poverty," which called for workers to farm untilled tracts of land communally. His own dreams he outlined in "Napoleonic Ideas," published before he entered prison. "Great men have this in common with divinity," he wrote. "They never die completely. The Napoleonic idea has sprung from the tomb of St. Helena as the Gospel rose triumphant despite the torment of Calvary." As one historian remarked, Louis-Napoleon may have been only Bonaparte's nephew, but he was the son of the Napoleonic tradition.

The February uprising found Louis-Napoleon in exile in London, where he had gone after escaping from prison by posing as a mason. When he returned to Paris in September 1848, after his election to the constituent assembly, his reputation for incompetence and lackluster intellectual accomplishments marked him as a man without a future—except for one thing. If there was a name that every French peasant recognized, it was Napoleon. The well-intentioned expansion of the franchise to include most adult males, therefore, played directly into Louis-Napoleon's hands, as did the widespread underestimation of his talents. The December election gave him almost 5.5 million votes, 4 million more than his nearest opponent. Lamartine received fewer than eighteen thousand.

It would be hard to imagine a more depressing failure for liberal republicans and socialists than the French revolution of 1848. Louis-Napoleon became president of the second republic in December 1848. Almost exactly three years later, this strange combination of liberal, pleasure-lover, and autocrat seized power in a bloody coup d'état,

Louis-Napoleon Bonaparte (Napoleon III) This representation of Napoleon III captures the tired, cynical, worldly character of the emperor in his mature years. *Photo: AKG London.*

and a year later, in 1852, he declared himself Emperor Napoleon III. Liberal republicans who thought that they could reform France politically while keeping the property-less at bay, and socialists who represented those property-less, seemed merely to have paved the way for the restoration of autocracy.

Austria: Nationalist Revolt

Unlike Louis Philippe, Ferdinand I, emperor of Austria, did not suffer from uncertain claims to legitimacy. The Habsburg Dynasty that he headed dated from the thirteenth century and ranked first in honor in Europe. But Ferdinand had other disabilities. Good-natured and loved by his people, he was also feebleminded and subject to fits. "I'm the emperor, and I want noodles," he is alleged to have cried

out at a state dinner. The Habsburg holdings, which included some dozen separate nationalities, did not make up a centralized state, despite the many agencies in Vienna that governed their various affairs. Rather, the empire remained a collection of entities accumulated over time. The widely varying arrangements governing each region served adequately in medieval and early modern Europe, but the legacies of the French Revolution had begun to erode the foundations of the traditional arrangements.

The Austrian bureaucracy stifled debate and censored printed material, stimulating the interest of writers, students, lawyers, and authors in the principle of free speech, one of liberalism's most important elements. But the regime also encouraged industry, including a modest launching of railroad construction. By 1848 Austria boasted more than four hundred stationary steam engines and almost three hundred steam locomotives for its new railroads. As elsewhere, this push toward mechanization put a great strain on the masters and journeymen. To make matters worse, the depression of 1845–1847 hit even the fledgling working class. In 1847 alone, factory owners dismissed some ten thousand workers from the new industries that had gathered in the Viennese suburbs.

Industrialization created grievances in Vienna and some other urban centers, but most of the population had other concerns, for the countryside remained primarily agricultural. In the eighteenth century, Maria Theresa and Joseph II had regulated the size of peasant holdings, limited the amount of labor that peasants had to perform, and prohibited use of the term *serf*. But peasants nevertheless continued to pay dues (usually in kind—such as butter and milk). They also provided labor services, paid a tithe to the church, transported goods, and served in the military, sometimes for life. Not all peasants had hard lives. Those who held large allotments of land were quite comfortable, and some families living in the proto-industrial areas like Bohemia adopted a profitable strategy of combining farming and industrial work. Nevertheless, all peasants chafed under the discrepancy between their technical freedom and the actual limitations on their lives. In particular, they wanted to abolish their remaining labor obligations and to obtain clear title to their land.

Despite these tensions among Austrian workers and peasants, the revolution of 1848 did not begin in Vienna but in Hungary. The medieval kingdom of Hungary had come under Habsburg control in the course of the sixteenth and seventeenth centuries. The Lands of the Crown of St. Stephen, as the Hungarians called their kingdom, consisted not just of the relatively compact group of Magyar-speakers living on the plain around Budapest. They included Transylvania, the counties that now make up Slovakia, Croatia, the so-called Military Frontier (lands bordering the Ottoman Empire), and the northern part of today's Serbia. In short, Hungary was just as multiethnic as the rest of the Habsburg lands (see Map 27-5).

Two political classes dominated Hungary: the great nobility and the lesser nobility. The several hundred magnate families enjoyed astounding wealth. The branches of the Esterházy family, for example, controlled more than a million acres of land containing over a hundred villages, forty towns or markets, and thirty castles and palaces. Families such as this occupied the highest offices of the realm, attended the upper house of the Hungarian Diet (the medieval noble legislature), and moved in the highest reaches of Viennese court society. In contrast, several thousand families of ordinary nobility, wealthy but unable to control the grand affairs of state, concentrated their power in the counties, which in Hungarian law were self-governing, and in the lower house of the Diet. The magnates, the county nobility, and a large number of poor nobility, some of whom did not live as well as the most prosperous peasants, constituted the *natio Hungarica*, or the "Hungarian nation." Before 1848, this term referred only to the noble 5 percent of the population. No one else had any political rights.

The twenty years before the revolution of 1848 was an era of reform in Hungary. István Széchenyi, a wealthy magnate who hoped to develop Hungary intellectually and politically, created an academy of sciences with his own money, organized Hungary's first political club, and connected the cities of Buda and Pest by building the first permanent bridge between them over the Danube River. By the 1840s, however, an upstart provincial nobleman of far lower rank, Lajos Kossuth, had eclipsed Széchenyi. Kossuth had little money and made his way as a lawyer, but his obsession was politics. In 1832, as a substitute member of the Diet's lower house, he began to write extensive reports on the sessions. Never before had the Diet's sessions been publicly reported, and the authorities found Kossuth's lively narratives so disturbing that they sent him to jail for three years. In 1841 Metternich tried to draw Kossuth into the imperial establishment by creating a newspaper for him to edit, but this only increased the lawyer's visibility among the Hungarian political class. In the elections to the 1847 Diet (only nobles could vote), Kossuth assembled a liberal program that called for freedom of the press, religion, and assembly; responsible government; and the final abolition of serfdom. When the Diet convened in November, Kossuth was the most popular politician in Hungary, and his liberal gentry allies dominated the lower house.

Unlike the men who deposed Louis Philippe in France, Kossuth was neither a republican nor a socialist. He anticipated that Hungary would retain its Habsburg king, and he had no intention of threatening the nobility's position of power. Kossuth was primarily an ethnic nationalist of the classic central European type. In his view, the Lands of the Crown of St. Stephen should constitute a centralized Hungarian state, a goal that he hoped to achieve by imposing Magyar (Hungarian) as the country's sole administrative and cultural language. As for the other languages spoken in Hungary, such as Romanian, Serbian,

Croatian, and Slovak, Kossuth sniffed, "Let these people cultivate their quaint customs and language, as long as they recognize that there is only one nation under the Holy Crown: the Magyar."

News of the fall of Louis Philippe reached Vienna on February 29, one week after the event. It hit Bratislava (then known by its Hungarian name of Pozsony), the seat of the Hungarian Diet and only 40 miles from Vienna, the next day. Two days later, Kossuth delivered a fiery speech to the Diet demanding a constitutional regime for Hungary. Hungary could not continue, he vowed, as long as "a corrupting puff of wind that benumbs our senses and paralyzes the flight of our spirit comes to us from the charnel house of the cabinet of Vienna."

Kossuth's speech, immediately translated into German and distributed in Vienna, set off enthusiastic demonstrations there. Petitions and demands from groups as varied as booksellers and medical students rained down on the imperial regime. When enthusiastic mobs took to the streets of Vienna on March 13, Metternich needed only two days to decamp for London. Trying to stem the tide, Ferdinand promised to create a national guard and to promulgate a constitution. Meanwhile, on March 15 the Hungarian Diet adopted Kossuth's entire program, thus establishing the framework for a liberal and nationalist regime in Hungary.

But just as the French Revolution did not end on July 14, 1789, neither were the Hungarian and Austrian revolutions over on March 15, 1848. In fact the struggle had just begun. It took the forces of the imperial regime a few months to regain their balance, because other parts of the empire also burst into revolt. In Italy, five days of revolution ejected the Austrian army from Milan; Venice declared itself a republic; and King Charles Albert of Savoy invaded Lombardy in response to an appeal from the revolutionaries in Milan. Elsewhere, between March and May the Serbs, Slovaks, Czechs, Romanians, and Transylvanian Germans all demanded various reforms. In June a congress of Slavic intellectuals from all across the empire convened in Prague to discuss whether their future lay with the Habsburgs.

But the imperial forces recovered. Under the leadership of generals Count Joseph Radetzky and Prince Alfred Windischgrätz, the Austrian military regrouped to defeat Charles Albert in Italy, disperse the Slav Congress from Prague, and surround Vienna. In September 1848, a third general, Count Josip Jelačić, *ban* (administrator) of Croatia, invaded Hungary. Jelačić's invasion brought events to a head. In Vienna the liberals had not actually taken power, relying on the emperor's promise of reform. The main fruit of their faith came on September 7, when the emperor finally approved the abolition of all peasant obligations, a step that the Hungarians had already taken in March. With this accomplishment, the middle-class revolutionaries felt that they had accomplished their goal of bringing freedom to the empire. The satisfied peasantry retired from further participation in the revolution. Both groups had enough of upheaval and now looked forward to a restoration of order.

The grievances of the working classes of Vienna, however, had not yet been resolved. Make-work projects like road building had only drawn thousands of workers to the capital, where the same sort of conflict developed between them and the middle class that had led to the June Days in Paris. Vienna had a less violent version of the same class confrontation in August, but the main workers' revolt came in October. Encouraged by radicals who admired the liberal Hungarians and resented Jelačić's invasion of Hungary, workers from the Viennese suburbs revolted again on October 6. But the revolt fell flat. Jelačić and Windischgrätz converged on the city and put down the workers by force. Deliberations on a new constitution continued in the Moravian town of Kroměříž (its German name was Kremsier). But in fact the Viennese revolution was over. On December 2, the victorious military leaders eased Ferdinand I into retirement and crowned his eighteen-year-old nephew Francis Joseph as the new emperor. Francis Joseph would not be bound by the constitutional oaths extracted from the befuddled Ferdinand.

The Hungarians, at war with the Austrians since September, refused to accept Francis Joseph as their king. To persuade them to change their minds, Windischgrätz occupied Buda and Pest.[2] This preemptive strike only solidified Hungarian resistance to the Austrians and their Romanian, Serb, and Croat allies. In April 1849, the Hungarians decided in desperation to declare their independence, but by this time their strength was ebbing. The final blow came in June, when Francis Joseph requested aid from fellow emperor Nicholas I of Russia. Once the Russians crossed the Carpathians, the Hungarians were finished. By August, the revolutionary army surrendered, and in October 1849 the last rebel fortress capitulated.

Very much as in France, the revolutions of 1848 in east-central Europe served mainly to restore autocracy. During the 1850s, Francis Joseph's chief minister Alexander Bach, a moderate turned efficiency-minded bureaucrat, abolished jury trials, introduced corporal punishment, and placed education in the hands of the Catholic church, permitting church authorities to ensure that no teaching in secular subjects conflicted with the teachings of the church. The peasants, freed from labor obligations and able to own land, benefited from the revolution, but the working class, the liberals, and the nationalists did not.

The most difficult issue that the revolution did not resolve was the position of the Slavic peoples. Most Slavs ended up fighting on the Austrian side against the Hungar-

ian bid for independence, but they did not benefit from Austrian victory. Croats complained that they received as a reward the same kind of repression that the Hungarians received as punishment. Unlike the Hungarians, the

Ruler of Many Lands   Emperor Francis Joseph, who ruled the Habsburg lands in one of the longest reigns of European history (1848–1916), is usually shown in his old age with characteristic muttonchop whiskers and a bald head. But Austrian painter Friedrich Johann Lieder painted him in 1851 as a youth of 21. Francis Joseph's full title gives some idea of the multinational empire over which he presided so long and of the Habsburg claims that reached far back into the Middle Ages: "We, . . . by God's grace, Emperor of Austria; King of Hungary, of Bohemia, of Dalmatia, Croatia, Slavonia, Galicia, Lodomeria, and Illyria; King of Jerusalem, etc.; Archduke of Austria; Grand Duke of Tuscany and Cracow; Duke of Lothringia, of Salzburg, Styria, Carinthia, Carniola and Bukovina; Grand Duke of Transylvania, Margrave of Moravia; Duke of Upper and Lower Silesia, of Modena, Parma, Piacenza, and Guastella, of Auschwitz and Sator, of Teschen, Friaul, Ragusa, and Zara; Princely Count of Habsburg and Tyrol, of Kyburg, Görz and Gradiska; Duke of Trient and Brixen; Margrave of Upper and Lower Lausitz and in Istria; Count of Hohenembs, Feldkirch, Bregenz, Sonnenberg, etc.; Lord of Trieste, of Cattaro and above the Windisch Mark; Great Vojvod of the Vojvodina, Serbia, etc., etc." *Gift of Herbert Mayer, 1929, The Picker Art Gallery, Colgate University, Hamilton, New York.*

---

[2] Then two cities on opposite banks of the Danube. They were combined into the single city of Budapest in 1872.

THE HISTORICAL EVIDENCE

Palacký's Rebuke to the Frankfurt Invitation

1848

The Frankfurt Parliament invited František Palacký, a prominent historian from Bohemia, to join them. Many Germans had long considered Bohemia as a culturally German province. Here is a condensed version of Palacký's reply, a powerful statement of the nationalist point of view that motivated the revolutions of 1848 in central and eastern Europe.

I am unable, gentlemen, to accept your invitation. The object of your assembly is to establish a federation of the German nation in place of the existing federation of princes, and in this manner expand the power and strength of the German Reich. Although I respect such effort, I cannot, precisely for the reason that I respect it, participate in any manner whatsoever. I am not a German—at least I do not feel myself to be one—and you would assuredly not desire to call me in to join you as a mere assentor, a "yes-man" without a mind or will of his own. I am a Czech of Slavonic blood, and with all the little I possess and all the little I can do, I have devoted myself for all time to the service of my nation. That nation is a small one, it is true, but from time immemorial it has been a nation of itself and based upon its own strength.

The second reason which prevents me from taking part in your deliberations is the fact that it is your irrevocable desire and purpose to undermine Austria, an empire whose preservation, integrity and consolidation is, and must be a great and important matter not only for my own nation but also for the whole of Europe, indeed, for humanity and civilization itself [in order to prevent the creation of a universal state under Russia]. Why is it, however, that we have seen [Austria] almost devoid of counsel in the fact of an advancing storm? It is because Austria has long failed to recognize the real juridical and moral basis of her existence, and has denied it; the fundamental rule, that is, that all the nationalities and all the religions under her scepter should enjoy complete equality of rights and respect in common. The rights of nations are in truth the rights of Nature. I am convinced that even now it is not too late for this fundamental rule of justice to be publicly and sincerely proclaimed in the Austrian Empire.

Source: From "Letter Sent by František Palacký to Frankfurt," *Slavonic and East European Review* 26 (1948): 303–308.

Habsburg Slavs had not sought full independence. František Palacký, the most prominent Czech nationalist of the period, perceived that small, ethnically based nations would find themselves easy prey for either German or Russian expansionism without the protection of a great power like Austria. Palacký advocated Austro-Slavism, by which he meant living under the umbrella of the Habsburgs as culturally distinct and recognized peoples. If the Habsburg state did not exist, he said, it would be "in the interests of Europe and indeed of humanity . . . to create it as soon as possible." The constitutional assembly at Kroměříž, which continued its work through the thick of the wars, backed the kind of cultural autonomy that Palacký advocated in a document it submitted in March 1849, but the newly ascendant aristocrats in Vienna rejected the proposed constitution out of hand. Some historians argue that in doing so they let slip the last chance of saving the medieval Austrian state.

Germany: Constitutional Debate

When news of Louis Philippe's overthrow filtered into southwest Germany in late February and early March 1848, demonstrations, petitions, and demands swept through the German states. Hearing shortly thereafter that even Metternich had fallen, most of the shaken rulers hurried to grant reforms and even constitutions to their agitated peoples. Developments varied according to the personalities, social structures, and chronology of events in each state. Almost any generalization about the German revolutions of 1848 and 1849 has counterexamples somewhere among the welter of events. But in the long run, the outcome hinged on what happened in Germany's strongest state, Prussia.

King Frederick William IV of Prussia was not a decisive man, and he actually rejoiced at the fall of the upstart Louis Philippe. But when unrest began stalking Berlin in

March 1848, he proved himself tactically astute. On March 17, after ten days of waffling, he decided to grant freedom of the press—which always headed the list of liberal demands—to recall the legislature into session, and to grant a constitution. The next day, however, when Berliners began celebrating the generosity of their king, some troops brought into the city to maintain order fired on the celebrants, and the city erupted in rage. The uprising shocked Frederick William. "It can't be," he allegedly lamented, "my people love me." Rather than continuing the bloodshed, as his military commanders wished, he ordered the main body of troops to withdraw from the city. On March 19, he stood in review while the bodies of almost three hundred dead insurgents, mostly journeymen between the ages of twenty and thirty-five, were carried past. The king appointed a new and moderately liberal government, which initiated what it hoped would become widespread political reform.

Journeymen aggrieved by the pressures of industrialization typically provided the manpower for the violence that characterized the revolutions of 1848, and this was particu-larly true of Germany. Religious differences between the Protestant north and the Catholic south served as another axis of confrontation. The traditional classes, especially the landholding aristocracy whose male members constituted the officer corps of the Prussian and other armies, resisted any diminution of their position. The educated classes—the lawyers, civil servants, teachers, and professors—saw the revolution as a chance to gain new status. Despite the passionate and sometimes violent conflicts that these cross-cutting interests provoked throughout Germany, the revolution there was primarily political rather than social (as in France) or national (as in Austria).

Even before the March days in Vienna, Hungary, and Berlin, the Diet of the German Confederation called on its members to send delegates to Frankfurt to discuss the possibility of a constitution. This pre-Parliament agreed that Germany needed a new constitution and authorized a constituent assembly to write one. Every German state thereupon held an election under its own rules and customs, and in May 1848 almost eight hundred delegates convened in the St. Paul's Church in Frankfurt. The delegates to this

Frederick William IV Honoring the Berlin Dead
When Prussian troops killed a number of rebellious artisans in Berlin at the outbreak of the revolution of 1848, King Frederick William IV took the politically calming step of bowing before the funeral cortege of the victims. *Holzstich, April 1848. Bildarchiv Preussischer Kulturbesitz (bpk), Berlin.*

The Liberals on a Teeter-Totter As this sarcastic German cartoon from 1848 suggests, many issues divided the Frankfurt Parliament and its earnest but inexperienced members. Territorial questions were among the most intractable.

Frankfurt Parliament comprised primarily government bureaucrats, court officials, teachers, professors, lawyers, writers, physicians, and officers. Only a few landowners, and no representatives of the working class or peasants, were present.

The Frankfurt Parliament's social homogeneity did not imply uniformity of opinion, however. Lacking political parties and experience in an open political atmosphere, the delegates understandably spent a good deal of time arguing basic issues. For example, they had difficulty in agreeing what constituted "Germany." Did it include the Poznań area, which Prussia had taken from Poland in the eighteenth century, where two-thirds of the residents were Polish speakers? What about Schleswig-Holstein, which the Danish king claimed? Was Austria to be part of the united Germany, and if so, what would happen to its associated non-German regions? The conflict between the ideas of a large Germany (including Austria) and a small Germany (excluding Austria) bedeviled German nationalism for another century.

Finding solutions to such thorny issues took time. In the case of Poznań, the delegates finally decided to divide the region into its predominantly German-speaking and Polish-speaking portions, but they left the exact borders of that division to later. The Schleswig-Holstein issue could not be put off, because a succession crisis there had led to a Danish invasion of Holstein in March 1848. Prussia responded to the Holsteiners' requests for help, but the del-

egates in Frankfurt were outraged that Frederick William had not consulted them. When they tried to negate the truce that Frederick William had negotiated, crowds attacked their meeting place, St. Paul's Church. Troops under the control of the confederation had to restore order. Finally, Austria itself decided not to give up its independent role in central Europe, thus thwarting the majority of delegates who thought that it should join the new Germany. The unsatisfactory resolution of these issues showed how few levers of power the Frankfurt Parliament controlled.

The Parliament might have asserted itself if it had satisfied the demands of the urban demonstrators. But after months of work, the assembly's economics committee utterly failed to produce any useful proposals. The attack on Parliament over the Schleswig-Holstein affair frightened the liberals and revealed the frustration of the German journeymen with them. Unwillingness—or inability—to find ways to satisfy the newly restive working class proved one of the liberals' greatest weakness everywhere in 1848. Russian essayist Alexander Herzen described their point of view dramatically:

The popular hurricane swept [the liberals] up to the top of a high steeple. . . . Glancing down at the abyss that opened before their eyes . . . they saw that what was crumbling was not only what they had considered prejudice, but also everything else. They were so terrified that some clutched at the falling walls, while others stopped, repentant, and began to swear to all passers-by that this was not at all what they had wanted.

The liberal failure should not be exaggerated, however. For one thing, no consensus existed on what would constitute a solution to the workers' problems. It is superficial to criticize German liberals for alleged mistakes made at the dawn of industrialization when we ourselves have yet to agree on approaches to welfare and unemployment.

Despite all the obstacles, the delegates in Frankfurt pushed on. Almost one year after the initial outbreaks of March 1848, they completed work on their constitution to the joyful peal of church bells throughout Germany. But what to do with the document? In the intervening year, it had become obvious that a united Germany was impossible without its most powerful state, Prussia. As elsewhere, the traditional elites in Prussia had recovered. Late in 1848, one of Frederick William's cleverest advisers had convinced his monarch that he could split the liberal and democratic forces by offering the Prussians their own constitution. By enacting universal suffrage for the lower house of the legislature, the king's advisers bet that the peasantry would remain conservative, as it did in France. Their instincts were on target. Despite some radical electoral victories in urban areas, especially Berlin, when the new Prussian legislature (the Landtag) convened in February 1849 it had a comfortable conservative and royalist majority.

In spite of this ominous development, the Frankfurt Parliament saw no alternative but to offer the crown of their united Germany to Frederick William. Its delegates did so early in April after a triumphant trip across Germany to Berlin. Twenty-nine German states adopted the Frankfurt constitution, and even the new Prussian Landtag approved it. But Frederick William refused to do so. He received the delegates politely, but rejected their constitution firmly. As he said in a letter later, "This so-called crown is not really a crown at all, but actually a dog-collar, with which they want to leash me to the revolution of 1848." When it heard the news of Frederick William's rejection, the Frankfurt Parliament started to disintegrate. Eventually the remnants of the delegates gathered in Stuttgart, but their efforts to raise the standard of revolt collapsed. In mid-July 1849, the last revolutionary garrison surrendered.

Italy: Composite Failure

Italy in the 1840s was even less united than Germany, and it contained even fewer nationalists. The collapse of the Carbonari revolts in the 1820s left Italy a collection of small states under the protection of Metternich's Austria. In the north, the Austrians occupied Lombardy and Venetia, in the center the pope prevailed in his role as a secular ruler, and in the south a reactionary Bourbon regime controlled Naples and Sicily. The only ruler with any possibility of opposing Austrian claims in Italy was Charles Albert, king of Piedmont. Nevertheless, a number of liberals, nationalists, and republicans maintained links with each other, primarily through their association with the exiled Giuseppe Mazzini, who kept up a prodigious correspondence with his co-believers from London. The enormously popular operas of Giuseppe Verdi, with their transparently national and political themes, helped inflame popular feelings. Finally, even though Italy had barely begun to industrialize, the artisans gathered in its major cities faced the same pressures as their counterparts elsewhere with the economic downturn of the 1840s.

The initial spark that ignited this flammable brew came from two sources, one expected and one unexpected. No one was surprised that Austrian occupation of the city of Ferrara in 1847 inflamed anti-Austrian feeling in Italy. The surprise was the unexpected behavior of the pope. In 1846 Pius IX ascended the throne of St. Peter and achieved instant popularity by granting amnesty to the political prisoners in the Papal States. Over the next year and a half, he enhanced his liberal reputation by forming a council of state to advise him. He even assembled a national guard, a traditional middle-class goal from the time of the French Revolution. Enthusiastic liberals began pressing King Charles Albert of Piedmont to follow suit.

Revolts in Naples and Sicily early in 1848 caused the corrupt Ferdinand II to grant his realm a constitution. Inspired, Charles Albert and the pope followed suit with their own basic laws. Animated by these concessions, and inflamed by the news that Vienna had risen in revolt, the citizens of Milan—the capital of Lombardy and Italy's most industrialized city—took to the streets. When Field Marshal Radetzky withdrew his troops, Charles Albert immediately invaded Lombardy from Piedmont, and in Venice revolutionaries declared a republic. As in other European revolts that year, the Italian successes of March 1848 were misleading. Charles Albert's forces were poorly armed and badly led. The revolutionaries in Milan found it impossible to agree on an appropriate organization for defense. And as soon as Radetzky launched his counterattack, both the pope and Ferdinand II withdrew their promised support from Charles Albert. In July 1848, Radetzky pushed the Piedmontese army out of Lombardy, and in March 1849 he crushed it so completely that Charles Albert had to abdicate in favor of his eldest son, Victor Emmanuel. In Venice, the republicans held out against an Austrian siege until August 1849. After a terrible bombardment that lasted more than a month and that rained more than thirty thousand shells on its defenses, Venice too surrendered to the force of Austrian arms.

In Rome, the pope initially tried to maintain political control by appointing a moderate liberal to head the council of state, but when an assassin cut this leader down, the pontiff decreed a democratic government and fled to Naples for protection. Now Rome experienced the closest thing to a social revolution of any of the European disorders of 1848. The new government extended the franchise to all adult males, conducted an election, and in February 1849 declared Rome a republic. Moreover, it abolished the tax on flour, gave unemployed artists and tailors work through government contracts, and distributed church lands to the peasantry. Much of this program was the work of Mazzini, who returned to share leadership of the Roman revolution with Italy's great general of revolution, Giuseppe Garibaldi (see Chapter 24).

The new Roman republic did not last. At first, Mazzini had thought that France, which had also declared itself a republic, would support him. But Louis-Napoleon had more interest in appeasing French Catholics by restoring the pope than he did in helping revolutionaries. In the spring of 1848 Napoleon sent a military force to Rome, and by the end of June, Mazzini and Garibaldi had to abandon the city to the French. Pius IX, disabused of all liberal tendencies, returned the next year, and the French kept their troops in Rome for twenty years. By 1850 all the earlier rulers of Italy had been restored, and reaction set in. The exception was Piedmont, where Victor Emmanuel appointed the liberal Count Emilio Cavour as prime minister in 1852.

AFTER THE REVOLUTIONS

One of the most memorable characterizations of the revolutions of 1848 was British historian A. J. P. Taylor's quip that they were a turning point in history that did not turn. Taylor was referring primarily to Germany, where in place of progressive new regimes based on the principles of responsible government, civil liberties, and destruction of the old order, Europe suffered a reaction that inexorably led to complete breakdown—World War I. In this view, the failures of 1848 constituted the end of Enlightenment dreams and the beginning of modern disasters.

In some ways, this is a powerful interpretation. After 1848 it was impossible to believe the Romantic view that revolutionaries could create a constitution on the basis of reason. One Frankfurt delegate identified the new sensibility: "The road to power is the only one that will satisfy and appease our yearning for freedom."

The Turning Point That Turned

But Taylor's witticism is too clever. By saying that 1848 was not a turning point, he creates the false impression that the post-1848 world resembled the pre-1848 world. In actuality, the economic changes that provoked the unrest of 1848 continued apace and indeed accelerated. The period

between 1850 and 1872 proved one of the two most dramatic eras of economic growth that Europe has ever experienced. Similarly, the ideas that shaped the thinking of the middle-class revolutionaries—liberalism, nationalism, and socialism—did not sink out of sight but grew in strength and penetrated deeper into society.

In the sphere of social relations, the revolutions finally liberated the peasantry of central Europe. Daily life did not necessarily improve in the countryside, but a long chapter of legal inequality closed. Both in France and Prussia, the peasantry entered political life for the first time as electors. In the future no politician could afford to ignore them. In the cities, the revolutions of 1848 ended the political aspirations of the artisans, at least as traditional craftsmen. After 1848 they became wage earners, and a new element, the working class, emerged. This redefinition of work increased pressure on women. Middle-class women found themselves consigned to the culture of domesticity, whereas working-class women were relegated to low-status jobs linked in some way to "feminine" household tasks. The demands of working people in 1848, however, foreshadowed their imminent entry into active public life.

In a backhanded way, the failures of 1848 furthered social stability, because they discredited the idea of revolution. Despite some inflamed rhetoric, the brief episode of the Paris Commune in 1870–1871 (see Chapter 24), and a few local insurrections immediately after World War I, 1848 saw the last revolutions in central and western Europe. We can gauge the importance of this fact by observing developments in Russia, which escaped revolution in 1848. Undeterred by negative memories of failed hopes, the Russian **intelligentsia** nurtured a stronger, more consistent revolutionary tradition than could exist elsewhere in Europe. This powerful tradition led directly to the Bolshevik Revolution of 1917.

The memory of 1848 may have been its most important legacy. The revolutions contained so many elements capable of such diverse interpretation that, together, they became what some have called a cover memory. The future that 1848 previewed—class conflict, nationalism, social dislocation, new political vocabularies—permitted later generations to reinterpret the revolutions in light of their own aspirations, and to project their goals onto this one dramatized historical moment. The French liberal leader Lamartine said that 1848 was the product of "a moral idea, of reason, logic, sentiment—of a desire for a better order in society." In the immediate aftermath of 1848, such a view seemed hopelessly naive, or in the eyes of later socialists, downright pernicious. But the desire for a better order did not die. The power of the new ideas inspired by the French Revolution and the additional social pressures activated by industrialization continued to eat away at the foundations of the old order, reinstalled by 1850, but shaken, significantly modified, and newly defensive.

THE HUMAN EXPERIENCE

Alexander Ivanovich Herzen, Socialist Russian Essayist

Alexander Herzen (1812–1870) was the illegitimate son of a reclusive and misanthropic Russian nobleman and a sixteen-year-old German girl. Brought up in his father's household speaking French, Russian, and German, Herzen received a good education and graduated from Moscow University. There, as a participant in a circle of idealistic young intellectuals, he received his introduction to socialist ideas by reading Saint-Simon (discussed in Chapter 22).

Exiled to the provinces by Nicholas I for his independent opinions, Herzen experienced the backwardness and ignorance of the Russian countryside firsthand. But eventually his father's influence made it possible for him to return to Moscow. There, after a second exile, he became the leading figure in a group known as the "Westernizers." This handful of thinkers admired European experience as they understood it through reading German philosophers such as G. W. F. Hegel and French socialists like Louis Blanc and Charles Fourier. The Westerniz-

ers stood in opposition to the "Slavophiles," who admired the special character of the Russian past and advanced theories of the mystical Russian spirit. Finally despairing of Nicholas's stifling regime, and having inherited his father's substantial fortune, Herzen left Russia in 1847.

The revolutions of 1848, which Herzen observed in Paris, convinced him that liberals were completely out of touch with the needs of ordinary people. The masses do not seek freedom, he said, "[They] want to stay the hand which impudently snatches from them the bread which they have earned." Nor are the people interested in abstractions such as the nation, he argued. The submission of people to such ideas, Herzen wrote, "is a continuation of human sacrifice, . . . the crucifixion of the innocent for the guilty. The individual . . . has always been sacrificed to some general concept, some collective noun, some banner or other."

Restless, rootless, remorseful, and seeing little hope for change, Herzen's spirits lifted after 1848 when he dis-

covered the self-governing peasant commune. As serfs, Russian peasants did not own land. Indeed, the very concept of ownership was foreign to them. Instead, elected elders administered the land that villagers used, redistributing it periodically to families on the basis of need. Believing that property lay at the root of modern evils, Herzen saw in this communal form of ownership a model for creating a new socialist society that would bypass capitalism. Russia's very backwardness gave it the opportunity to leapfrog directly to a modern, socialist system, he thought.

Herzen's autobiography, *My Past and Thoughts*, is one of the great works of Russian prose. Herzen advocated social reform, including the abolition of serfdom, and he wrote lucidly about issues of human dignity. But most of all, he despised despotism. "No, I shall not be silent," he wrote. "My words shall avenge those unhappy lives crushed by Russian absolutism, that infernal regime which brings men to moral prostration and to a deadly debility." ❖

The 1850s: A New Kind of Restoration

A. J. P. Taylor could make his judgment on the revolutions of 1848 in part because we often interpret the 1850s as a decade of reaction. Repressive regimes regained power in every country that revolution had touched and kept control where it had not. In Italy, the end of the revolutions in Sicily, Rome, Florence, Milan, and Venice brought severe repression. In central Europe, bureaucratic centralization was the byword of the 1850s. Spain, unaffected by 1848, continued on its conservative Catholic path only lightly touched by industrialization. And until 1855, Russia remained under the deadening hand of Nicholas I.

In the Germanies, conservative Prussian reformers tried to displace Austria, the traditionally dominant German state, by creating a new German union with Prussia at its head. Austrian objections almost led to war in 1850, but

at the last minute a compromise, the Punctuation of Olmütz, reinstated the German Confederation with Austria as the senior partner. The new Diet of the confederation responded by reviving the repressive laws of the Metternich era, which had been nullified during 1848.

Despite these signs of reaction, however, the restoration of the 1850s differed markedly from the restoration of the 1820s. After defeating Napoleon Bonaparte, restored aristocrats had felt pride in their return and confident that they could reestablish the old ways. Little or no industrialization disturbed their sleep, and the notion of democracy struck most of them as an absurdity not worth discussing. After 1848, however, conservatives faced a new world. They had brushed off the liberals, put down the nationalists, and repressed the socialists, but the ground beneath them continued to tremble. Railroads, urbanization, telegraphs, and claims from a suddenly more active society

The Autocrats Clean Up
This German caricature captures the failures of the revolutions of 1848. Dated August 1849, the caricature shows the returned autocrats (including French President Bonaparte sporting a Napoleonic hat) sweeping up the revolutionaries. Note the British lion sticking out its tongue at Europe. *The Granger Collection, New York.*

were only the most obvious new forces that threatened their position. Generations of textbooks that spoke of "the rise of the middle class" have led to the widespread impression that the upper classes of Europe, when confronted with industrialization, simply faded away. Nothing could be further from the truth. They responded with considerable imagination to the new threats. And they proved willing to use the novel tools that changing conditions made available to them, such as highly organized bureaucracies. Unable to hold back the economic growth that began to take off in the 1850s—although they tried—many conservative governments turned to managing the industrialization process in order to lessen the dangers that it posed. Men who had every interest in retaining their class position by denying the political rights of the masses even found ways to incorporate nationalism—which by its nature has a mass appeal—into their strategies.

Prussia's three-class voting system, installed in 1850 for elections to the lower house of the legislature, shows how conservative rulers put new ideas to use. This voting mechanism divided the electorate into three groups according to the proportion of direct taxes they paid. The first group, which paid one-third of the taxes, constituted about 5 percent of the male population; the second group, also paying one-third of the taxes, equaled about 12 percent of the population; and the final group contained the remaining 83 percent of the population. This system obviously favored the wealthy, who controlled two-thirds of the legislature. Public voting and indirect election enhanced their power

further. At election time, the first group of voters would come to the meeting place, declare their votes, and depart. Then the second group would do the same, and finally the third. No one voted directly for a candidate. Instead, voters selected electors, who then chose the legislative delegates. Rather than crudely abolishing constitutions, as Spanish and Neapolitan kings had done, or restricting the right to vote, as did Louis Philippe, the Prussians turned an ostensibly democratic procedure—universal male suffrage—into a method for maintaining the political authority of the traditional classes.

Another device that the Prussians adapted from the liberal repertoire was responsible government. However, by making the cabinet responsible to the king instead of to the legislature, they ensured that the legislature would remain a junior partner in governing. Having introduced these innovations, the Prussian king kept the loyalty of the landed aristocracy by retaining full authority over the army, especially over the appointment of officers.

Louis-Napoleon's France provides the most contradictory example of the post-1848 restoration. On the negative side, Napoleon III has evoked as much passionate hatred as any French ruler. "Napoleon the Little," French writer Victor Hugo called him. After World War II, many historians saw him as a nineteenth-century predecessor of twentieth-century dictators. The critics had substantial reason to hate the emperor. First, Napoleon seized power with blood on his hands. Painting himself as a staunch supporter of the second republic, he not only destroyed it, but he did so brutally, arresting some 28,000 persons and transporting 10,000 of them to Algeria. Second, Napoleon offended many with his autocratic style. Once he decided on a course of action, he insisted that it be carried out regardless of regulations. Liberal historians, not to mention those further to the left, considered him the betrayer of the best traditions of the French Revolution. Third, and perhaps most objectionable in a Napoleon, his countrymen perceived the emperor as vacillating and weak. The perception may have originated with his occasional leniency to his enemies or his apparent indecision in times of war, or even with the facade of imperial strength that he put up. (He wore rouge to cover physical debilitation caused by arthritis, hemorrhoids, gout, bladder stones, and kidney disease.) Finally, and not the least of Napoleon III's historical burdens, France suffered a mortifying defeat at the end of his reign in the Franco-Prussian War of 1870–1871. The loss humiliated the French and embittered Franco-German relations for seventy-five years.

More positively, by most standards Napoleon III accomplished a great deal. During the Second Empire, the French economy grew 2 percent per year, resulting in rising real wages for working people. To support this growth, a modern banking system emerged. Louis-Napoleon did not believe in state-owned enterprises, and in 1860 he reached a free-trade agreement with the United Kingdom that stimulated the French economy. But he did think that the state should help business, and under his paternalistic patronage confidence flowered. The great expositions of 1855 and 1867 were the French equivalents of England's Crystal Palace Exhibition of 1851, and they provided equally impressive displays of French technical and economic progress.

Napoleon III also took a strong personal interest in urban development, particularly in modernizing Paris. In 1853 he appointed Baron Georges Haussmann prefect of Paris and gave him a free hand to rebuild the capital city. Haussmann responded with energy and originality. He replaced the medieval streets of central Paris with straight boulevards and plentiful squares and parks. At the same time, the engineer Eugène Belgrand expanded and modernized the Paris sewer and water systems. Indeed, throughout Europe, the 1850s saw a vast effort to bring clean water into cities and to flush waste out, and Belgrand was one of the most vigorous of these reformers. Linked with the effort to improve public health was Napoleon III's support of scientist Louis Pasteur, for whom the emperor created a laboratory of physiological chemistry in 1867. Pasteur proved that microorganisms cause disease and devised a method of destroying them through heating, the process today known as pasteurization.

Critics point out that Haussmann built straight thoroughfares in part to make it easier for troops to control crowds and that Belgrand's sewers simply carried untreated natural wastes directly into the Seine 20 miles downstream.

Reconstruction also uprooted thousands of unwilling poor from the center of the city and moved them to the outskirts of town. Nevertheless, no one who visits Paris today can doubt that ultimately Haussmann and Belgrand created a wonderfully livable city.

LOOKING AHEAD: TOCQUEVILLE AND MILL

Only three political analysts from the period 1830 to 1860 are still widely read today: Karl Marx (whom we will discuss in Chapter 25), Alexis de Tocqueville, and John Stuart Mill. The reason that Tocqueville and Mill still have an audience is that they identified tendencies in their own time that are important for us today.

Tocqueville, a frail and anxious man, came from an aristocratic but relatively liberal family. Like Voltaire before him, he had an intense interest in the British system. In the early 1830s, he also took an extended trip through the United States, which formed the basis for his two-volume *Democracy in America*. "Nothing struck me more forcibly," Tocqueville wrote, "than the general equality of conditions [in America]," adding that "the influence of this fact extends far beyond the political character and the laws of the country: it creates opinions, engenders sentiments, suggests the ordinary practices of life, and modifies whatever it does not produce." Tocqueville did not find the same level of equality in Europe or in France, but he did argue that equality, and the democratic forms that might be associated with it, were an almost inevitable force that were on the rise there.

John Stuart Mill was a child prodigy whose stern father (the well-known philosopher James Mill) had him reading the ancient Greek historian Herodotus in the original at the age of eight. Mill's father trained him to follow in the footsteps of his close friend Jeremy Bentham, who had developed the philosophy of utilitarianism. According to this notion, public policies should be designed to create the greatest good for the greatest number of people. The younger Mill did develop his own utilitarian arguments, but went far beyond Bentham in working out a theory of individual liberty and in contemplating the tensions between freedom and organization.

Tocqueville's books on America greatly impressed Mill. He too was interested in democracy, but a more structured form than the one Tocqueville described in the United States. Mill favored a system in which voters chose representatives who then acted on the basis of their understanding of the national good, rather than on the basis of public opinion. Tocqueville described a direct democracy in which the opinion of the majority dominated public life, not only in the political sphere, but in mob action, repression of minorities, and religious intolerance. Mill wrote passionately about freedom as the necessary ingredient of individual development. As he saw it, one of the main threats to that individual liberty was rampant majority opinion such as Tocqueville described in America. The tyranny of the majority, Mill wrote, is a more serious threat to individual liberty in democracies than the acts of public officials and the law.

Later in his life, Tocqueville wrote a second important book, *The Old Regime and the French Revolution*. Tocqueville understood the French Revolution as an important break with the past, but he understood far better than most observers the high degree of continuity in the changes that it had brought to Europe. All French history from 1789 is one revolutionary event, he thought, "of which our fathers witnessed the beginning, and of which we, in all probability, shall not live to see the end." The centralizing state was the great continuity from the past that stood in the way of the democratization he saw as in the end inevitable. For two or three generations after his death in 1859, Tocqueville's writings dropped out of sight, increasingly forgotten. But in the twentieth century, when political movements like **totalitarianism** threatened democratic regimes, his defense of liberty in public life made him one of the most read, or at least most cited, nineteenth-century analysts.

Mill, too, wrote a book later in life that has proven almost as lasting as his book on individual liberty: *The Subjection of Women*. As a believer in equality, freedom, and representative government, and as the lover and then husband of a vigorous feminist, Mill became one of the first men to join with radical women to advocate woman's suffrage. He also argued that women must compete with men for jobs and that they should be equal partners in marriage. These views, published at a time when women had few legal rights, made this work his most controversial when it appeared in 1869. Today, with the revolution in women's position that has taken place in the past generation, those very arguments have made *The Subjection of Women* one of his most widely read books.

CONCLUSION: 1848, AN END AND A BEGINNING

The generation that elapsed between the end of the Napoleonic wars and the revolutions of 1848 was an unusually formative one for Europe. The unsettling confrontation with both aspects of the Dual Revolution—new ideas and new technology—produced original ways of thinking about politics, transformed social and gender relations, and foreshadowed the century that followed. Early in the period, it seemed possible to restore the old regimes in traditional relationships, but the Congress of Vienna instead established a new international system based on the willingness of the great powers to guarantee the security of all states. In the sense that this system prevented Europe-wide warfare, it was stable. But the Vienna accords could not prevent the underlying instability caused by the elaboration of new ideologies and the penetration of new technologies. The post-Napoleonic generation was not yet suffused with ideology, as the twentieth century became, but many of the ideas that remain standard political fare today originated at this time. Nationalism, liberalism, socialism, and conservatism all took root in the years between 1818 and 1848. Simultaneously, early industrialization introduced Europeans to the advantages of new technologies—cheap clothing and railroads, primarily—and to the pain of social dislocation—destruction of old trades and habits. When crops failed and the business cycle turned down, a disoriented Europe erupted in revolution.

In a sense, the revolutions of 1848 looked backward. They were an effort by a new group of property holders—the middle class as represented by the professionals—to put the ideas of the French Revolution into effect through political reform. The inability of the Frankfurt and Kroměříž conventions to put their constitutions into effect represented a failure of the Enlightenment hope that rational beings, gathered in peaceful concert, could put natural law into concrete political form and create a regulated and harmonious society.

In another sense, the revolutions looked forward. The middle class after all formed a new political element, as did the disgruntled journeymen who provided the urban push for revolution. The forces that drove the revolutionaries, from ideology to economic transformation, dominated the next century. Inspired by new notions of power politics, national advantage, and racial superiority, and backed by the hitherto unimaginable strength of the Industrial and Energy Revolutions, Europe drove itself both to the peak of its world power, and then to the utter catastrophe of World War II. The revolutions of 1848 looked back to dreams of the past, but they also foretold the nightmares of the Century of Power that now began.

Selected Reading

Sources

Pinkney, David H. *Decisive Years in France, 1840–1847* (1986). Intelligent, clear, and authoritative essay on the Guizot era.

Rudé, George. *Debate on Europe: 1815–1850* (1972). A somewhat dated but still very valuable discussion of how historians have interpreted the first half of the nineteenth century.

Industrial Development and Social Issues

Bezucha, Robert J. "The 'Preindustrial' Worker Movement: The *Canuts* of Lyon," in his *Modern European Social History*, pp. 93–123 (1972). Brief but very informative article on the uprisings of the Lyon silkworkers.

Blum, Jerome. *The End of the Old Order in Rural Europe* (1978). Fascinating narrative and analysis of the European peasantry from the eighteenth century up to emancipation in the mid-nineteenth century. A fundamental study.

Dobbin, Frank. *Forging Industrial Policy: The United States, Britain, and France in the Railway Age* (1994). Compares three national approaches to railroad building.

Good, David F. *The Economic Rise of the Habsburg Empire, 1750–1914* (1984). The standard account of Austro-Hungarian industrialization. Good research and excellent statistics, but quite readable.

Smith, Bonnie G. *Ladies of the Leisure Class: The Bourgeoises of Northern France in the Nineteenth Century* (1981). Fascinating study of domesticity among the wives of some of France's most successful entrepreneurs.

Personalities

Carr, Edward Hallett. *The Romantic Exiles: A Nineteenth Century Portrait Gallery* (1961). Lives, loves, tragedies, and joys in the bohemian lives of Russian radicals in exile, including Alexander Herzen and his family.

Echard, William E. *Napoléon III and the Concert of Europe* (1983). Scholarly history of Napoleon III's foreign policy.

Howarth, T. E. B. *Citizen-King: The Life of Louis-Philippe, King of the French* (1961). A standard biography, with considerable attention to politics.

Johnson, Douglas W. J. *Guizot: Aspects of French History, 1787–1874* (1975). Sympathetic, scholarly biography. Particularly good on foreign policy.

Jordan, David P. *Transforming Paris: The Life and Labors of Baron Haussmann* (1995). Excellent biographical treatment.

Pinkney, David H. *Napoleon III and the Rebuilding of Paris* (1972). Describes the complex issues surrounding Baron Haussmann's reconstruction of the center of Paris.

Williams, Roger L. *Gaslight and Shadow: The World of Napoleon III, 1851–1870* (1977). Ten biographies of figures of the Second Empire that together illuminate the era.

———. *The Mortal Napoleon III* (1971). Fascinating discussion of the many diseases suffered by Napoleon III, and a positive assessment of the man.

The Revolutions of 1848

Deák, István. *The Lawful Revolution: Louis Kossuth and the Hungarians, 1848–1849* (1979). Scholarly but readable history of the Hungarian revolution, particularly of its inspirational leader.

———. "The Revolution and the War of Independence, 1848–1849," in Peter Sugar, ed., *A History of Hungary*, pp. 209–234 (1990). A superb, succinct discussion of the Hungarian revolution of 1848 by a master of the subject.

Hamerow, Theodore S. *Restoration, Revolution, Reaction: Economics and Politics in Germany, 1815–1871* (1958). Classic study of the impact of social dynamics on the revolution of 1848 in Germany. Still widely used in courses.

Namier, Lewis. *1848: The Revolution of the Intellectuals* (1946). Brief interpretation emphasizing the Frankfurt Parliament and the contrast between dynastic property and national sovereignty.

Rath, R. John. *The Viennese Revolution of 1848* (1957). Particularly valuable for its wealth of translated documents.

Robertson, Priscilla. *Revolutions of 1848: A Social History* (1952). Dated, but still useful. Contains excellent anecdotal material and is quite readable.

Sperber, Jonathan. *Rhineland Radicals: The Democratic Movement and the Revolution of 1848–1849* (1991). Original and challenging history of the revolution in the most liberal part of the Germanies. Discusses subjects, such as religion, not well covered elsewhere.

———. *The European Revolutions, 1848–1851* (1994). A superb study of the revolutions of 1848 stressing the variety of the experiences. This is now the standard book on these events.

Stearns, Peter N. *1848: The Revolutionary Tide in Europe* (1974). A readable history of the revolutions emphasizing social issues.

PART FIVE

THE CENTURY OF POWER

In the century following the European revolutions of 1848, the globe came under the domination of a single civilization to an extent greater than at any other time in history. In part, this control took the shape of the vast European and American colonial empires that reached their maximum territorial span by the turn of the twentieth century and turned about one-third of the earth's land area into colonies. Perhaps even more impressive, and of more enduring significance, Western economic enterprise, technology, science, and ideologies spread throughout the world. Even non-Western societies that escaped European or American colonial rule had to adopt aspects of the Western way of life voluntarily, as did Japan and Turkey, or have these ways thrust upon them involuntarily, as was the experience of China and Persia. Latin America, having largely freed itself from colonial political control early in the nineteenth century, found itself economically bound to the industrialized economies of Europe and the United States in ways that often resembled colonial domination. World history from the mid-nineteenth to the mid-twentieth centuries is, in broadest terms, the story of how Western countries imposed their ecomonic, political, and cultural standards on much of the world, and of how non-Western peoples either temporarily succumbed to that imposition (albeit often only after stubborn resistance) or used Western models to build industrial, militaristic, nationalistic, or imperialistic states of their own.

During that almost hundred-year span, Europeans and Americans became fascinated with the actuality, psychology, and politics of power. The unprecedented spread of the Industrial and Energy Revolutions put more concrete physical strength in Western hands than ever before. Electricity, the internal combustion engine, plastics, machine guns, airplanes, radio, and steamships all came into common use between 1848 and 1945. A vast, interlocking network of industries and commerce produced, advertised, and sold these products. Sheer economic strength lay behind the final and most violent phase of European expansion.

Europeans justified their aggressive behavior, both in Europe and abroad, by arguing that international affairs represented a struggle for survival among competing nations. Transforming Charles Darwin's theory of evolution into a pseudo-scientific creed, Europeans described colonial expansion as a justifiable victory of the fit over the weak. The ideology of power found further echoes in new ideas of racial superiority and of the inferior position of women.

In politics, *Realpolitik*, or politics based on power relationships, became the dominant theory of international affairs. By the judicious application of force, Otto von Bismarck united Germany and destroyed the Concert of Europe. Bismarck dominated European politics by making central Europe strong and France weak. When World War I temporarily destroyed Germany, the French tried to apply their own principles of Realpolitik. Reversing Bismarck's strategy, they surrounded Germany with French allies and attempted to keep it economically weak.

Despite World War I's horrendous cost—almost 9 million soldiers lost their lives—it did not, as the American president Woodrow Wilson hoped, "make the world safe for democracy." Not only did nationalism, imperialism, and Realpolitik survive almost intact, but two brutal regimes pushed the notion that power was a value in itself to new levels. In Russia, communist dictator Joseph Stalin sent millions of his countrymen to their deaths in an effort to transform the Soviet Union by force. In Germany, Adolf Hitler, unrestrained by constitution, parliament, or civil society, brought the Century of Power to its catastrophic conclusion by instigating World War II and exterminating millions of Jews. Europe's utter collapse in 1945 suggested the bankruptcy of a politics unrestrained by the concepts of equity or accommodation.

The Century of Power, however, was not just an era when Europeans drove themselves to cataclysm; it was also a period of accomplishment and progress. Irreversible positive achievements marked the age. Democracy expanded in several of the most advanced industrial states. By 1945 the entire adult population of most European democracies participated in the political process. Real wages increased not only for the upper classes, but for the growing middle class and for the working class as well. In some of the smaller European countries, such as Sweden and the Netherlands, socially concerned governments created extensive welfare programs to ameliorate their citizens' worst economic uncertainties. For one of the few times in history, poverty actually declined. Bourgeois culture, including private philanthropy for the arts, replaced the aristocratic ethic as society's dominant aesthetic norm, offsetting to an important degree the conspicuous consumption that often went with new wealth. Advances in nutrition, health, and sanitation doubled the life span of the average person in developed countries. It was only during the Century of Power, with all its sacrifice of human life, that the three score and ten years promised by tradition came to pass for most members of developed societies.

The long-term contributions to human welfare of these accomplishments undoubtedly will surpass the devastation unleashed by demonic forces during the Century of Power. They constitute an important part of the seven chapters that follow. Nevertheless, a major theme of these chapters is how the allure of unrestrained power brought Europe low. Chapters 24, 25, and 26 discuss the implications of power politics, the development of economic strength, and the elaboration of cultural reactions. Chapters 27 and 28 show how the convergence of strength, ideology, and fear led to the Great War, while Chapters 29 and 30 delineate the consequences of failing to learn from that war that power used for its own sake leads to disaster. 🔥

POWER AND THE NATION-STATE

Negotiating   *Bildarchiv Preussischer Kulturbesitz.*

*I*t does not take a degree in art history to know who is dominating whom in the picture on page 843, showing Prussian leader Otto von Bismarck "negotiating" with leaders of the defeated French in 1871. Without even reading this chapter, one knows that it is the German armies who have just overwhelmed France, and not vice versa. Bismarck is not negotiating, he is dictating the conditions of peace, not only to France but perhaps even to Europe itself.

But fifteen years earlier, when the Great Powers gathered in Paris to settle accounts after the Crimean War, it would not have been possible to predict the outcome suggested in this picture. In fact, in 1856 the political configuration of Europe bore a much more striking resemblance to that of 1648 at the close of the Thirty Years' War than it did to the moment depicted in the painting of Bismarck's triumph. True, Poland and several small Italian and German states had disappeared in the two hundred years following Westphalia. Russia had expanded its boundaries to the Baltic and Black Seas, and Austria had forced the Ottomans out of Hungary.[1] But only two small states were entirely new (Belgium and Greece) and, despite the French Revolution, the only significant republic in Europe at the time was the Swiss Confederation. More than thirty German states filled central Europe, Italy remained broken up into many regions under diverse rulers, as it had since Roman times, and the Ottoman Empire retained formal control over the entire Balkans except Greece. Nationalism had not become the primary ideology of any state, and liberalism seemed in decline.

By the time our picture was painted, however, Europe's face had changed dramatically. Germany and Italy had unified into national states; France was a republic again; several new nation-states existed in the Balkans; and reforms had swept not only England and western Europe, but Austria and, to a degree, even Russia. These remarkable innovations did not all come peacefully. They were often the result of the application of calculation and power, the combination often referred to as **Realpolitik.** But neither did they evoke the turmoil and chaos that marked the Napoleonic wars or World War I. They constituted the third stage of political movement—from the era of enlightened monarchy, which characterized the late eighteenth century, to the era of the nation-state, which defined the twentieth century. The first stage in this transition was the French Revolution itself. The confrontation between revolutionary ideas and the forces of order from 1815 to 1856, discussed in Chapters 22 and 23, comprised the second stage. In this chapter we discuss the third stage: the era of liberal reform and the creation of new national states. More specifically, we look at how the European political balance changed between the Treaty of Paris in 1856 and Bismarck's retirement in 1890.

THE CRIMEAN WAR AND THE BREAKDOWN OF EUROPEAN STABILITY

Despite the many upheavals that stirred Europe between the Congress of Vienna in 1815 and the revolutions of 1848, the Vienna settlements had prevented the outbreak of any major international wars. But when Louis-Napoleon Bonaparte became president of the French Republic in 1848, he believed that the 1815 arrangements unduly restricted France's freedom of action and put too much power in the hands of Russia and Austria; this attitude persisted after he declared himself Emperor Napoleon III in 1852. Throughout his career, Napoleon's motivations were often unclear and his rhetoric notoriously imprecise. In turning his attention to the Balkans, which he did in 1850, he spoke vaguely of his sympathy for nationalism. But

---

[1] The Ottoman Empire was a multinational state whose administrators and soldiers consisted of many ethnic groups, including Turks. To retain this multiethnic sense, this book refers to those persons as *Ottomans* rather than as *Ottoman Turks* or the even more anachronistic term *Turks.*

British 8th Hussars in the Crimea The Mexican-American War (1846–1848) and the Crimean War were the first recorded by cameras, thus becoming, in a sense, the first media wars. However, early cameras required a long exposure time, so photographers could not get action pictures. They had to settle for posed shots, such as this one of British officers on duty in the Crimea. *Gernheim Collection, Harry Ransom Humanities Research Center, University of Texas at Austin.*

Austria and Russia were competing for influence in the lands of the declining Ottoman Empire (the "Eastern Question"), and he probably also thought the Balkans a good place to put Russia and Austria at odds.

The unlikely wedge that accomplished this end was Russian religious pride. The Ottomans were Muslim, but they respected the religious rights of Christians and permitted them some control over holy places in Jerusalem. Over the years, the Russians had succeeded in increasing the influence of Orthodox clergy over some of these places. In 1850 Louis-Napoleon protested to the Ottomans that Catholic clergy were being excluded from their rights in Jerusalem.

Napoleon's complaint launched a complex series of events over the next three years that drew in Great Britain and Russia. Eventually the Ottoman sultan felt sufficiently provoked by the Russians and encouraged by the British to declare war against Russia in 1853, whereupon the Russian navy promptly sank the entire Ottoman fleet in one horrendous battle. Britain, pushed by an aggressive and loosely controlled minister in Istanbul and driven by a raucous anti-Russian press campaign at home, entered the war on the side of the Ottomans, and France followed suit. Prussia and Austria, Russia's conservative partners in the Holy Alliance, did not want to come to their ally's aid, but Austria, happy to see its Russian rival in the Balkans getting a comeuppance, decided to occupy the Romanian principalities of Moldavia and Wallachia, territories the Russians had dominated for twenty years. The Austrian occupation, coming so soon after Tsar Nicholas I had sent troops to

help Francis Joseph put down the Hungarian revolution of 1848, embittered the Russians and poisoned Russo-Austrian relations for years (refer to Map 24-3).

The main problem facing the allies—which included Britain, France, and the Ottomans, along with the Kingdom of Sardinia—was where to fight the Russians. With the British and French fleets already in the Black Sea, they finally decided to take the war to the Russian mainland by invading the Crimea. One might think that the Russians could fight off invaders on their own soil. But their army, which relied on masses of manpower, proved no organizational or technological match for the forces of the industrializing West. The war proved exceptionally bloody, with losses on both sides totaling half a million men. For the first time in a major war, the European public could follow the battles and the casualties closely through reports transmitted by telegraph. It was also the first major war recorded by the newly invented photographic camera, and the first in which women participated as semiprofessionals. Florence Nightingale became a heroic figure to the British public—a "ministering angel without any exaggeration," as the *Illustrated London News* put it—for her pathbreaking innovations in nursing. Finally, after a lengthy siege, Sevastopol, the main city of the Crimea, capitulated, and Russia had to come to the negotiating table.

The peace conference took place in Paris in 1856. The allies forced some relatively minor concessions on defeated Russia, but the main outcome of the Treaty of Paris was to call into question the stability of European international relations. By detaching Russia from Austria, Napoleon III threw what remained of the Concert of Europe off balance and freed France from what he considered the restrictions of the Congress of Vienna. But Napoleon was not a careful strategic thinker. In freeing France from constraints, he had also freed others. Over the next fifteen years, he discovered that the beneficiary of that new freedom would not be France, but Prussia.

POWER POLITICS AND NATIONAL UNIFICATION

Napoleon III sympathized with national movements in southeastern Europe and even in Italy, but he did not grasp the implications of nationalism for France's position in Europe. Between 1859 and 1871, two hitherto divided peoples, the Italians and the Germans, united into single states and transformed European politics. Ironically, the liberal nationalists who had advocated the unification of Italy and Germany for a generation had very little to do with this achievement. Instead, conservative monarchists using diplomatic devices and sheer force expanded the authority of their own states over their neighbors. By playing the game of power politics with consummate skill, Camillo Cavour created an Italian state on the model of his native Piedmont, and Otto von Bismarck built a German empire dominated by Prussia. At first appalled by the crude militarism of these processes, Italian and German liberals ultimately found unification so intoxicating that they not only accepted it but became enthusiastic supporters of the politics of power.

In southeastern Europe, newly self-conscious nationalities also found the Italian and German examples inspiring. Facing a weakened Ottoman Empire, they too were able to establish new nation-states.

"Resurgence": Cavour and the Creation of Italy

In the Late Middle Ages, Italy had boasted the highest level of culture in Europe, and Rome reigned as the dominant city of Christendom. But in the sixteenth century, when European sailors, merchants, and slave traders opened the seas of the world, the Mediterranean—and Italy—declined in importance. By 1815 Italy consisted of eight diverse states. The largest of these was Naples, which included Sicily and the southern boot of Italy. The Papal States encompassed central Italy and were ruled by the pope. Tuscany, with its magnificent capital of Florence, lay just north of the Papal States. After 1815, Austria occupied Venetia, the remnants of the fabled maritime city-state of Venice, and Lombardy, where Milan was the main city. Piedmont, the most northwesterly region of today's Italy, fell under the Kingdom of Sardinia, as did the city of Nice. The House of Savoy, the oldest dynasty in Europe, ruled Sardinia-Piedmont from its capital in Turin.

Disunited politically, Italy also suffered from social and economic underdevelopment. Its nobility, which had never solidified into a unified class like the Prussian Junkers, was in decline, and its poverty-stricken peasantry, by far the largest part of the population, produced so little food that imports were needed to sustain the population. Industrialization had barely begun by the time of the 1848 revolutions. On top of this, the Catholic church infused Italian cultural and social life with a conservative worldview that discouraged change.

Yet Italy had not remained completely isolated from the great ideas of the French Revolution, as the activities of the Carbonari in the 1820s demonstrated. As elsewhere in Europe, standardization of a literary language had begun. The works of the exiled Giuseppe Mazzini were widely known among the educated, although his republicanism and his inclination toward revolution frightened many.

Besides Mazzini, mid-nineteenth-century Italians revered another patriot who transcended regionalism: Giuseppe Garibaldi, perhaps Italy's finest general. Direct and striking, Garibaldi had made his reputation as a guerrilla fighter in Uruguay in the 1830s. In 1848, in league with Mazzini, he returned to Italy to overthrow the pope's state and to create a Roman republic. When this effort collapsed in 1849, Garibaldi fled across the swamps of coastal Italy, carrying his dying wife in his arms. This romantic figure commanded respect throughout Europe for his honesty, his simple life, and his complete lack of personal ambition. He sought no gain. All he wanted was to unite Italy into one nation (see Map 24-1).

The man most responsible for that unification, however, was Count Camillo di Cavour, prime minister of Piedmont in the 1850s. Cavour had grown up as the second son of a well-to-do, French-speaking nobleman. A moderately rebellious youth, he found the military life assigned him as younger son boring and futile. In compensation, he read widely, particularly the liberal French historian and politician François Guizot and such English writers as Smith, Ricardo, and Malthus. Cavour embraced the idea of civil liberty and the theories of classical economics, but he did not turn to republicanism or revolution. Like his models, he believed in the regime of the *juste milieu* (Guizot's "golden mean") and in the political mission of the landowning class. Most of all, he believed in his own ability to shape the direction of Italian development.

Leaving the military, Cavour undertook management of a family estate north of Turin. By introducing subsoil drainage, crop rotation, and modern accounting methods, he made the property prosper, turning it into the basis of his eventual wealth. Cavour entered public life in 1847 as editor of a new newspaper, *Risorgimento*, or "Resurgence," the name now given to the entire movement that led to Italy's unification. Elected to parliament, he became minister of finance by 1850, and in 1852 he found himself prime minister of Piedmont. Cavour knew more about the

MAP 24-1
ITALIAN UNIFICATION

workings of parliaments and about economics than any other Piedmontese politician. He worked compulsively, and he possessed a remarkable memory. In only a few years, these skills permitted him to reform Piedmontese legal codes, restrict the immunities of the church, facilitate the publication of books, reduce tariffs, and encourage railroad building. The formerly backward Piedmont emerged in the 1850s as a liberal state with great-power aspirations.

A special motivation lay behind Cavour's reforms: He wanted to demonstrate that Italians could rule themselves without Austrian tutelage. Cavour had donated fifteen thousand troops to the anti-Russian coalition during the Crimean War so that he could raise the question of Italian unification at the peace conference, which he did without result.

Happily for Cavour, he found an enthusiastic ally in Napoleon III. Napoleon, although fearing radical Italians like Mazzini, thought he saw in Cavour a reliable tool for hurting Austria, which he successfully had separated from Russia in the Crimean War. The French emperor calculated that the creation of a northern Italian confederation under Piedmont would deprive Austria of Lombardy and Venetia. Early in 1858, Napoleon III survived a bloody assassination attempt at the hand of an Italian nationalist.

Determined to forestall extremists by encouraging moderates, and perhaps seeking a little personal glory for himself, he arranged to meet with Cavour. In July 1858, at Plombières near the Swiss border, the French emperor agreed to support Piedmont in a war to obtain Lombardy and Venetia, if Cavour could get Austria to attack first. Such an attack would make Napoleon's intervention plausible to the French public and to the other Great Powers.

Cavour began dropping hints that he wanted war, provoking Austria, and gathering volunteers. When Austria, supported by Britain, stood firm, Napoleon lost his nerve and told Cavour to back off. In April 1859, compliant Piedmont began to demobilize. The Austrians, thinking that the loss of Napoleon's support had fatally weakened Piedmont, decided to end Cavour's provocations for good by attacking. Having forced Cavour to back down, the Austrians ended up doing just what Napoleon and Cavour originally had wanted them to do. French armies, traveling on newly constructed railroads, arrived in northern Italy in record time and quickly defeated the Austrians in June at the battles of Magenta and Solferino.[2] From this victory Piedmont eventually obtained Lombardy. In compensation, and after plebiscites, France received Savoy and Nice.

Not satisfied with the partial result of obtaining only Lombardy, in 1860 Cavour persuaded his supporters in Tuscany and the former papal state of Romagna to hold fraudulent plebiscites uniting those territories with Piedmont. With momentum building toward the unification of all of northern Italy under the House of Savoy, the retired Garibaldi reentered the scene. Supported by King Victor Emmanuel of Piedmont, he gathered just over a thousand students, craftsmen, and writers, gave them red shirts as uniforms, and set sail to conquer Sicily on behalf of the new Italy. Armed with only smooth-bore, converted flintlock rifles for which he lacked ammunition, Garibaldi's "thousand" nevertheless found a tumultuous welcome in Sicily. The entire populace rose up against the government, and soon the general's preposterous band of freebooters had seized control of the island. Their victory constitutes one of the most remarkable military feats in European history. Evading the naval forces sent to keep him on Sicily, Garibaldi soon crossed over to the mainland and launched a triumphal march up the boot of Italy toward Naples.

Garibaldi's success posed a serious problem for Cavour, for Garibaldi was a republican, and Cavour had not contributed to his victory. But Garibaldi's greatness derived in part from his total lack of personal ambition. After touchy negotiations, he agreed to hand over Naples and Sicily to Victor Emmanuel and to retire again to his island retreat.

---

[2] Peace may have come quickly because both Francis Joseph and Napoleon III were physically sickened at the slaughter they personally witnessed at Solferino.

Giuseppe Garibaldi   Garibaldi was just over five feet tall, had bright red hair, and projected a calm but commanding presence. *Hulton Getty/Liason Agency.*

On October 21, 1860, a plebiscite allegedly registered 99 percent approval of southern Italy's accession to Piedmont, even though few understood what was involved or really wanted to join the north. One observer found that a crowd he thought was cheering "Long live the king and the constitution," was actually shouting "Long live the king and his uniform."[3]

In fact, southern Italy did not benefit greatly from its union with Piedmont. The Piedmontese, who contrasted the commercially developed cities of Turin and Milan with the poor and almost feudal Naples, considered the southerners backward, corrupt, and ignorant. Accordingly, even though the liberal Cavour claimed to favor representative government, he imposed Piedmontese law and administrative practice on Naples and Sicily directly, without their consent. When locals proved unable to understand the new system or protested by resorting to

brigandage, he declared martial law and ordered the execution of malcontents.

In 1861, Cavour died, weakened by six bleedings taken to counter an attack of malaria. He was just fifty-one. Cavour left as his legacy a new political entity: the kingdom of Italy, ruled by King Victor Emmanuel I. At the time of his death, Venetia remained in Austrian hands, and the pope, backed by French troops, retained control of the central part of the peninsula. But his work was soon completed. In 1866, in connection with the wars of German unification, Venetia joined Italy, and in 1871, for the same reason, all the papal lands did also, with the exception of the Vatican palace itself. For more than fifty years, the pope remained what outraged Catholics called "a prisoner of the Vatican," confined to its roughly two-tenths of a square mile, the sole remaining territory over which he ruled directly.[4]

Piedmont, developed by Cavour into the most modern part of Italy, had united the disparate Italian peoples into one state with all the external trappings of constitutional government. But neither Cavour nor Garibaldi had created a unified country. In the 1860s, only about 2 percent of Italians spoke the Tuscan literary dialect that today we call "Italian" (even Cavour had a shaky command of it), and regional differences along the peninsula remained enormous. The educated elites who assumed power had little knowledge of—and scant interest in—Italy's true social and economic conditions. For the rest of the nineteenth century, Italy remained weak and disunited, despite an expanding bureaucracy and a growing international presence.

"Blood and Iron": Bismarck and the Unification of Germany

The drama of Italian unification astonished Europeans. After all, Italy had lain in fragments since Roman times. Nevertheless, Cavour's accomplishment was not the biggest political sensation of the 1860s. The unification of Germany far overshadowed Italian developments in its consequences for the future. Since far back in the Middle Ages, the Holy Roman Empire had loosely tied the German lands together. The Austrian Habsburgs dominated that empire, as they did the German Confederation created in the Napoleonic period. But proud and ancient rulers in Bavaria, Saxony, Württemberg, and elsewhere successfully resisted Habsburg efforts to create a centralized state. With the Punctuation of Olmütz in 1850, which reestablished the German Confederation after its brief demise in 1848, the Habsburgs retained their preeminence. King Frederick William IV of Prussia did not object. For reasons of family connections and tradition, he believed that the Habsburg

---

[3] Compare this with the Russian soldiers in the 1825 Decembrist revolt, who thought that "Constitution" was Constantine Romanov's wife (see Chapter 22). Some of those shouting *"Viva Italia"* when Victor Emmanuel came to Naples apparently thought they were cheering his wife.

[4] In 1929, Mussolini's Italy finally reached an agreement with the papacy by which Vatican City became an independent state ruled by the pope.

emperor should retain his place of honor in Germany. But not all Prussians agreed. The liberals did not, for instance, and neither did Otto von Bismarck.

Bismarck was neither a nationalist, a liberal, nor a democrat. An aristocrat with a massive ego, he had expensive tastes, boundless energy, outlandish ambition, and enormous ability. On the other hand he was also a hypochondriac, an insomniac, and a glutton. Late in life he estimated he had smoked not fewer than one hundred thousand cigars and had drunk ten thousand bottles of champagne. One historian listed the cost to Bismarck of his excesses: "neuralgia, rheumatism, gout, migraine headaches, gall stones, and varicose veins, as well as . . . bouts of grippe, jaundice, shingles, hemorrhoids, gastric disturbances, constipation, and stomach aches and cramps." These problems neither improved Bismarck's temper nor lessened his passion. He once complained to his steward, "I could not sleep the whole night. I hated throughout the whole night."

As a Junker, one of the landed aristocracy that the rulers of Brandenburg had tamed in the seventeenth and eighteenth centuries, Bismarck belonged to the military

The Iron Chancellor This 1864 picture captures some of the brooding strength of Otto von Bismarck. One can almost see him preparing to browbeat his advisers, cajole his king, and impose his will on the Prussian Landtag. *Bildarchiv Preussischer Kulturbesitz (bpk), Berlin.*

and bureaucratic elite of Prussia. His early career was ordinary and indolent, shot through with the reactionary commonplaces of his caste. He raised one of these conventional views—the superiority of Prussia to all other European states, particularly to the Catholic and economically backward southern German states, and especially to Austria—to the central theme of his political philosophy. Appointed ambassador to the German Confederation in Frankfurt in 1851, Bismarck opposed everything that Austria proposed and strove to convince the other German states that Prussian interests defined the interests of Germany as a whole. He honed his talent for "deceptive frankness" and cultivated his ability "to choose in each fleeting moment of the situation that which is least harmful or most opportune." Agile at spotting such occasions, and aggressive in pushing any advantage, Bismarck pursued a cold and realistic policy for Prussia. "In politics," he said, "no one does anything for another, unless he also finds it in his own interest to do so."

Realpolitik, the German word for this strategy, does not mean just power politics, which were old hat in European history. Realpolitik involved harnessing the new forces of the age, especially industrial might and nationalism, to achieve state-power goals through the application of unsentimental, and generally unprincipled, tactics. It stands in contrast to the constitutional discussions of the Frankfurt Parliament, for example, or the romantic strivings of Garibaldi. Realpolitik is the political hallmark of the Century of Power. Many practiced it, but none succeeded as well as Bismarck, the era's most able politician.

Bismarck remained as ambassador in Frankfurt as long as King Frederick William IV retained power. But in 1857, when the king became incapacitated due to a stroke, all of Bismarck's skills of analysis, bonhomie, and calculation did not prevent the new regent, Prince William, from packing him off to St. Petersburg into a sort of exile. Bismarck had never made the slightest attempt to curry favor with William, and had even spread scurrilous rumors about his wife. But when William I took the throne in his own right in 1861, he soon discovered that this offensive but uncommonly talented man was the only one who could help him rule in an increasingly difficult political situation.

Reform-minded liberals had won control of the Prussian Landtag in 1858, and sparks immediately flew between the legislators and their conservative, divine-right monarch. The issue was military reform. William, advised by the Prussian general staff, wanted to double the size of the army, diminish the role of the militia, and institute compulsory military service for all young men. Liberals favored a strong military, but feared compulsory military service and the prospect of more power for the elite officer corps. When the Landtag went so far as to defeat the military budget in 1862, Prussian politics reached an impasse. Would civilian parliamentary controls be able to limit the king and his army? Some militarist hotheads contemplated a coup d'état. William himself floated the idea of abdicating in favor of his son, the Crown Prince Frederick, a liberal Anglophile known to favor the British parliamentary system. The solution was provided by Bismarck, whom William invited to become Prussian minister-president (prime minister) in September 1862.

Unpleasant as Bismarck could be personally, he had one quality that the king's other advisers lacked: a keen eye for fundamentals. Always keeping in mind the possibility, indeed the eventual necessity, of compromise with the Landtag, and at the same time setting in motion the wheels that would bring on the showdown that he sought with Austria, Bismarck began his almost thirty years in office by first winning the confidence of the king. He became more monarchist than William himself, completely rejecting the principles of 1848. In an early speech to the legislature's budget committee, he made his total

antipathy to the liberal viewpoint brutally clear. "The great questions of our time," he said, "will not be decided by speeches and majorities—that was the error of 1848— but by blood and iron."[5]

Finding ways to humiliate the legislators whenever possible, the "Iron Chancellor" ordered his bureaucrats to ignore the Landtag's failure to pass a budget and to continue tax collections and military reorganization anyway. He argued that the king had the right to rule by decree when conflicts between the government and the legislature make action impossible. In such cases, he contended, "conflicts become a question of power. Whoever holds the power then proceeds according to his own will, for the life

---

[5] In this famous speech, Bismarck actually said "iron and blood," but the reversed version has become the standard way of expressing it.

MAP 24-2
GERMAN UNIFICATION

Legend:
— German Empire, 1871
— German Confederation, 1815–1866
--- North German Confederation, 1867–1871
Austrian Empire (Austria–Hungary after 1867)
Territories annexed by Prussia, 1866
Prussia before 1866
Italian territory lost by Austria, 1859–1866
Alsace-Lorraine annexed by Germany 1871

Minor German states
Saxony
Hanover (annexed by Prussia)
Schleswig-Holstein (annexed by Prussia)
Elect. of Hesse (annexed by Prussia)
Baden
Württemberg
Bavaria

of the state cannot remain still even for a second." To make his point, he purged the bureaucracy, firing those connected with the liberal opposition. The legislature fumed but found itself helpless to resist as the bureaucracy fell in line and the army pushed ahead with its reforms.

In 1864 Bismarck took his first step toward achieving Prussian dominance over Austria by contriving to draw the German Confederation into a war with Denmark over the two disputed areas of Schleswig and Holstein (see Map 24-2). He aimed not so much to recover these two provinces for Germany—although that proved a popular goal—but to embroil Austria in the dispute. In the two years that followed the Austro-Prussian victory over the stubborn Danes, Bismarck found countless occasions to irritate the Austrians over occupation and border arrangements. His plan was to goad Austria into war, much as Cavour had done a few years earlier. Meanwhile he prepared the diplomatic ground by working out an agreement with Italy (which got Venetia for its troubles) and buying off Napoleon III with vague promises. Overcoming the obstruction of William I, who feared a fratricidal German war, Bismarck finally succeeded in pushing Prussia into war against Austria in the spring of 1866.

When the conflict broke out, most informed persons in Europe foresaw a lengthy struggle in which Austria's highly respected army and large reserves of manpower would prevail. Bismarck knew that he was rolling the dice, but he believed that the military reforms of the past few years would bring victory. Habsburg fiscal difficulties had mounted and the Hungarians had undermined the monarchy's unity by pushing hard for concessions. Prussia, on the other hand, had prospered economically and spent lavishly on its army. Under the leadership of the able minister of war, Albrecht von Roon, and a brilliant new chief of staff, Helmuth von Moltke, the Prussians had assembled a highly mobile and efficient fighting force. They had built their railroads not only for economic reasons but to speed troops to possible fronts. The General Staff had supplied Prussian

Prussian Infantrymen at Work   One of the most momentous changes in military technology of the 1850s and 1860s was the introduction of breech-loading rifles. Here Prussian infantry take advantage of their new weapon against the Austrians in 1866.   *AKG London.*

infantry with a new breech-loading rifle that could fire three times as fast as anything the Austrians had and that could be loaded and fired from a prone position. The Austrian muzzle-loaders simply could not compete. Finally, the Prussian officer corps received much more thorough training than its Austrian counterpart. Austrian staff work was almost nonexistent, its mobilization plan cumbersome, and its officer corps poorly educated.

Thanks to these advantages, the Prussians scored a complete and stunning victory. The decisive battle—at Königgrätz (called Sadowa by the defeated Austrians)—came only seven weeks after the start of the war. The humiliated Austrians were in no position to resist anything Bismarck wished to propose. But understanding that in the long run Austria and Germany would have similar interests, Bismarck strove to respect the honor of the Habsburg crown. Despite heavy pressure from his jubilant army, which hungered for a triumphal march through Vienna, and his king, who wanted to annex territory, Bismarck focused on the essential point. He persuaded William to impose no territorial demands or economic sanctions on Austria. Instead, Francis Joseph had to accept Prussian annexation of extensive northern German territories and to recognize a new, Prussian-dominated North German Confederation that excluded Austria. In other words, the only thing that Bismarck made Austria give up was its five-hundred-year primacy in central Europe.

Until 1866 Bismarck had ruled without the support of the Landtag, where the liberals continued their obstruction and opposition. But the victory at Königgrätz swept the liberals away in a wave of national enthusiasm. Bismarck astutely gave them a graceful exit: He persuaded William to admit in his January 1867 address from the throne that the government had acted unconstitutionally since 1862. In return, the mollified liberals agreed to a bill that retroactively approved Bismarck's actions for the past four years and agreed to support his foreign policy. This reconciliation proved that in the combination of liberalism and nationalism characteristic of German liberal politicians, nationalism carried the most weight. That Bismarck had established Prussian dominance over Austria by means of an aristocratic officer corps completely outside of parliamentary control—indeed, utterly hostile to the very idea of parliament—seemed less important than the success itself. As one representative of the moderate liberals said, "No one may be criticized for giving precedence to the issue of power at this time and maintaining that the issues of freedom can wait."

Victory over Austria had not fully unified Germany yet, for the southern German states, such as Bavaria and Württemberg, remained independent and heartily suspicious of Prussia. Bismarck tried several expedients for drawing these states closer to Prussia, but without success. France was even more wary of Bismarck. Napoleon III had never been a friend of the Habsburgs, but when Austria was humbled he suddenly realized that the European balance of power had shifted toward Prussia.

Neither Napoleon nor Bismarck actively sought war, but in 1869 a chance event, manipulated by Bismarck, led to confrontation. In 1868, after the queen of Spain had been deposed, the Spanish invited Prince Leopold of Hohenzollern Sigmaringen (a Catholic branch of the Prussian royal family) to accept the vacant throne. At first the prince refused, but with Bismarck's undercover urging, in June 1869 he accepted. Naturally, the Spanish invitation outraged the French, who saw themselves in danger of being encircled by German monarchs, much as they had been in the sixteenth and seventeenth centuries when Habsburg monarchs ruled in both Spain and the Holy Roman Empire. The French foreign minister immediately released a statement declaring that if Leopold did not withdraw his candidacy, France would "know how to fulfill its duty." Embarrassed, Leopold withdrew, but the impetuous foreign minister was not satisfied. The next day he sent his ambassador to the central European resort of Ems to ask vacationing King William to guarantee that Leopold's candidacy would not be renewed. The king politely refused to comply and informed Bismarck of the visit. Seeing an opportunity to wave "a red rag in front of the Gallic bull," as he put it, the wily minister-president edited the dispatch from Ems to make the ambassador's approach appear more insulting than it was, and William's response more abrupt. He then released the revised report to the press and sent it to German embassies around Europe with instructions to inform their governments of its contents.

The importance of the Ems dispatch in launching the Franco-Prussian War has probably been exaggerated, because the French government had already decided that it needed to humble Prussia to restore the balance of power. After the contents of the dispatch became public, however, Napoleon III—who knew that the French were not prepared—could no longer restrain his government, which imprudently declared war on July 19, 1870. The French declaration instantly fired the patriotic feelings of the southern German states, and they joined the Prussian offensive. Just as in the Seven Weeks' War almost four years earlier, the mobile and well-armed German forces swiftly overwhelmed their opponent. The French defeat at the pivotal battle of Sedan on September 2, 1870, was so complete that Napoleon III himself fell into German hands. By the spring of 1871, a hastily elected French assembly meeting in Bordeaux authorized a new government to accept humiliating peace terms.

Bismarck's martial success united the south German kingdoms around Prussia. In January 1871, in a militaristic coronation ceremony conducted in Louis XIV's Hall of Mirrors in Versailles (so as to humiliate the French), William I, king of Prussia, became William I, German emperor. Prussia dominated the new federally organized empire (the German term is *Reich*), but the south German

THE HISTORICAL EVIDENCE

The Ems Dispatch

July 13, 1870

On July 13, 1870, Bismarck dined with his generals Albrecht von Roon and Helmuth von Moltke. The three were depressed because their efforts to put a Hohenzollern prince on the vacant throne of Spain seemed to have failed. At that moment, a dispatch arrived from William I, who had been approached by the French ambassador at the resort of Ems. Bismarck reworked the information and sent it out to his embassies in an effort to inflame French opinion. The Ems dispatch, so-called because the events described took place at the resort of Ems, did not actually cause the ensuing war between Germany and France, but Bismarck's self-congratulatory story of how he reworked the information he received from Ems created a lasting legend of his diplomatic craft.

William I

Count Benedetti [the French ambassador] spoke to me on the promenade in order to demand from me, finally in a very importunate manner, that I should authorize him to telegraph at once that I bound myself in all future time never again to give my consent if the Hohenzollerns should renew their candidature. I refused at last somewhat sternly, as it is neither right nor possible to undertake engagements of this kind [forever].

William I's Aide

His Majesty has decided, with reference to the above demand, not to receive Count Benedetti [the French ambassador] again, but only to let him be informed by an aide-de-camp: That his Majesty had now received from the Prince confirmation of the news which Benedetti had already received from Paris [i.e., that the prince would not accept the throne], and had nothing further to say to the ambassador.

Bismarck's Comments

I put a few questions to Moltke as to the extent of his confidence in the state of our preparations. He answered that if there was to be war he expected no advantage to us by deferring its outbreak. In view of the attitude of France, our national sense of honor compelled us, in my opinion, to go to war.

Bismarck's Reworked Dispatch to His Embassies

After the news of the renunciation of the hereditary Prince of Hohenzollern had been officially communicated to the imperial government of France by the royal government of Spain, the French Ambassador at Ems further demanded of his Majesty the King that he would authorize him to telegraph to Paris that his Majesty the King bound himself for all future time never again to give his consent if the Hohenzollerns should renew their candidature. His Majesty the King thereupon decided not to receive the French Ambassador again, and sent to tell him through the aide-de-camp on duty that his Majesty had nothing further to communicate to the ambassador.

Moltke's Comment

Now it has a different ring; it sounded before like a parley; now it is like a flourish in answer to a challenge.

Source: From Otto von Bismarck, *The Memoirs*, (New York: Howard Fertig, 1966; reprinting the 1899 translation of A. J. Butler), vol. 2, pp. 97–101.

---

monarchs received special rights to discuss foreign affairs. They kept command of their armies in peacetime, and they retained considerable regional autonomy in the collection of taxes and other affairs. They even kept their own flags.

These arrangements made Germany difficult to govern as the century wore on, but Bismarck, in his new office of Chancellor, did not consider this too high a price to pay. He made one uncharacteristic mistake, however, although one that he could hardly have avoided. Enthusiastic

nationalists insisted on annexing the German-speaking but French-minded border region of Alsace-Lorraine. "The alienated children [of Alsace] must feel our fist," one of them ranted. "Love will follow the disciplining, and it will make them Germans again." The loss of these two provinces remained a bone in the throat of the French for the next forty years.

The unifications of Germany and Italy accomplished the dream of the liberal nationalists, but in a way that seemed to condemn the liberal philosophy. The liberals always linked national unification to constitutionalism, equality before the law, and civil liberties. But Cavour and Bismarck had united their countries on behalf of the old dynasties of Savoy and Hohenzollern. The new states were dominated not by new principles, but by extensions of old ones. Despite parliamentary forms, the social structure of the old societies lived on in the new. Despite middle-class and working-class inroads that came with German industrial development, the Junkers still ran the army in the aristocratic style to which they were accustomed. Victories over Austria and France only increased their prestige and confidence. The militarization of German society on the old Prussian model contrasted starkly with what the liberals and nationalists of 1848 had in mind. Cavour was more moderate, and the Italians adopted a constitution that seemed very liberal on the surface. In fact, however, Italian reality changed little. The landowning patrons of the south kept their peasants in quasi-serfdom, while the urban magnates of the north continued to dominate the Italian cities, adapting their ways to the new industrialism. The German and Italian cases showed that nationalism did not have to mean social or political revolution; it could be turned to support a traditional social system as well.

New States in Southeastern Europe

Further proof that nation-states did not have to be socially or even economically developed emerged in the 1870s in southeastern Europe. Unlike the German Empire, the Ottoman Empire was not in its ascendancy. In 1856 the Treaty of Paris recognized it as one of the great powers, but this condescending gift could not hide the fact that the medieval Muslim state was in decline. Ottoman rulers acknowledged their weaknesses and during the nineteenth century took vigorous steps to rectify them. A reform movement begun in the 1840s, the so-called Tanzimat era, aimed to introduce some Western elements into Ottoman practice. Tanzimat reforms created advisory councils in some Balkan regions, adjusted taxation to modern standards, and by 1856 had even introduced a constitution. But these measures could not eradicate the aging empire's primary political problem: the growth of national consciousness. By 1830 Serbia and Greece had already carved out their autonomy and independence, and in the 1840s both Bulgarians and Romanians began their national renascences.[6]

The Romanian provinces of Moldavia and Wallachia had been vassal states of the Ottoman Empire in the eighteenth century, but in the 1820s they had come under Russian control. At about the same time, some Romanian churchmen began to argue that because the Romanians spoke a romance language similar to French and Italian, they had existed as a people since Roman times. Romanian boyars (noblemen), rather than sending their children to school in Russia or Germany, began educating them in Paris. During the Crimean War, Russia had initially occupied Moldavia and Wallachia, but the Austrians had forced the Russians to withdraw. The conferees at Paris in 1856 did not want to give the regions to either Russia or Austria, but neither did they want to create a new national state of Romania. As a compromise, they agreed to let the two regions elect their own princes, who would remain vassals of the Ottomans. The conferees failed to anticipate the obvious Romanian counterploy. In 1859 both Moldavia and Wallachia elected the same person as prince, in effect uniting the two provinces. In 1878 the outwitted Europeans recognized Romania as an independent country.

The Bulgarian awakening had started in the 1840s but took a more religious turn than the other national movements. In 1870 Bulgarians living in Istanbul persuaded the ecumenical patriarch to grant the Bulgarian Orthodox church special status. The Bulgarian Exarchate, as it was called, received the right to add to its membership any diocese in the Balkans that voted to become Bulgarian Orthodox. Bulgarian churchmen fanned out into the Balkans and quickly added a sizable number of parishes to the fold. Most of these were in Macedonia. In this way, the Bulgarians created a territorial claim that has disrupted the politics of southeastern Europe ever since.

The Eastern Crisis of 1875–1878 affected all the Balkan peoples (see Map 24-3). In the spring of 1875 a peasant revolt broke out in Bosnia and Herzegovina, the most Muslim of the Ottoman provinces in southeastern Europe. A year later, a similar revolt erupted in Bulgaria. The Ottomans found it difficult to resolve the Bosnian crisis, but they put down the Bulgarian revolt by force. Their repression caught the eye of Britain's former prime minister William Gladstone, whose pamphlet *The Bulgarian Horrors* mobilized anti-Ottoman feeling in England. The uprisings also excited the Serbs, who hoped to ignite the entire Balkan peasantry in revolt against the Ottomans. Eventually carried away by their enthusiasm, the Serbs declared war on the Ottomans in 1876, their forces boosted by ardent volunteers from Russia. Contrary to Serbian expectations, the Balkan peasantry did not rise in revolt. The poorly trained and badly led Serbian army escaped utter disaster only through the diplomatic intervention of Russia. The Russians had attempted to maintain a sphere of influence in the Orthodox Christian portions of the Balkans from the time of Peter the Great early in the eighteenth century. Now, in 1877, they decided again, as they had in

---

[6] The term *renascence*, which is used in Bulgaria, suggests one of the most common ingredients of the nationalist myth throughout Europe: that the nation had existed since ancient times and was experiencing a "rebirth" in the nineteenth century. The Italian *risorgimento* is another such term. This idea has been called the Cinderella version of history: The beautiful nation rises from its long slumber when kissed by nineteenth-century liberalism.

Legend	
✶ Revolts, 1875–1876	▨ Romania before 1878
S E R Recognized as independent 1878	▨ Ceded by Romania to Russian Empire, 1878
E A S Autonomous 1878	▨ Annexed by Romania, 1878
– – Bulgarian boundary by Treaty of San Stefano (annulled)	▨ Montenegro before 1878
▨ Serbia before 1878	▨ Annexed by Montenegro, 1878
▨ Annexed by Serbia, 1878	▨ Greece before 1878
▨ Bulgaria by Treaty of Berlin, 1878	▨ Annexed by Greece, 1881
▨ Eastern Rumelia by Treaty of Berlin, 1878; annexed by Bulgaria, 1885	▨ Austria-Hungary before 1878
	▨ Occupied by Austria-Hungary

MAP 24-3

THE BALKANS IN THE MID-NINETEENTH CENTURY

1829 and 1853, to go to war. Breaking through stubborn Ottoman resistance early in 1878, Tsar Alexander II imposed a peace settlement at San Stefano, just outside Istanbul.

Not surprisingly, these dramatic events aroused the interest of all the European powers, especially Austria-Hungary.[7] In order to secure Habsburg neutrality, the Russians had agreed to permit the Dual Monarchy to occupy Bosnia and Herzegovina at the conclusion of the war. Francis Joseph coveted this territory not so much for its military or strategic value, but because Bismarck had blocked Austria-Hungary from asserting its Great Power status in Germany. Unable to exert its traditional influence to the north, the Habsburgs turned southward.

When the Austrians heard the terms of the Treaty of San Stefano, they were dismayed. If the treaty terms held firm, Bulgaria, presumably a grateful client of Russia, would stretch from the Black Sea almost to the Adriatic,

---

[7] In 1867 the Habsburg Empire split into two portions—Austria and Hungary—thus creating the Dual Monarchy (see discussion later in this chapter).

The "Bloody Turk" Tradition Gladstone was the author of a famous pamphlet called "The Bulgarian Horrors," but as this German-illustrated paper shows, depictions of Ottoman troops attacking Bulgarian women and children in 1876 were used to create anti-Ottoman feeling throughout Europe. *AKG London.*

encompassing all of Macedonia and cutting off further Austrian expansion in the direction of the Aegean Sea. Great Britain too adamantly rejected San Stefano, which threatened the commercial interests of British traders.

Into this volatile situation stepped Bismarck, who offered himself as an "honest broker" to adjudicate the controversy. The Treaty of Berlin, which the powers negotiated in the summer of 1878, deprived Bulgaria of Macedonia and split the fledgling state in two. The northern portion was recognized as an independent state, and the southern portion became an autonomous Ottoman province. The Treaty of Berlin also recognized the independence of Serbia, Romania, and Montenegro, but imposed certain obligations on them. Romania was to eliminate restrictions on Jews, an obligation the Romanians never fulfilled. Serbia had to reach a commercial agreement with Austria and to

build a railroad on Austrian terms. The Treaty of Berlin undid the Russian gains in the Balkans, gave over Bosnia and Herzegovina to Austrian administration, permanently embittered the Bulgarians, who felt that Macedonia was rightfully theirs, and turned Serbia into a client state of Austria-Hungary.

During the 1870s and 1880s, the new states of southeastern Europe used their independence to install Western political forms. All of them, including Greece, wrote constitutions, often on the model of the Belgian constitution of 1831, in which they adopted the trappings of Western constitutional monarchy: legislatures, political parties, elections, bureaucracies, and European-style legal systems. But little economic or social development underlay these new institutions. The economies of all the Balkan countries, with some regional exceptions in Greece, remained thoroughly grounded in peasant agriculture. In Bulgaria, Romania, and Serbia the most important economic element remained the state itself, incomparably richer and more powerful than any combination of private interests. Desirous of earning the respect of the developed West, which they now emulated, and proud of their success in throwing off the Ottoman yoke, the Balkan countries nevertheless remained small, backward, and easily dominated by the Great Powers. If the unifications of Italy and Germany proved that nationalism could work in traditional societies, the formation of the Balkan states proved that nationalism could succeed even in undeveloped economies and relatively undifferentiated social systems.

THE POLITICS OF CIVIL SOCIETY

The consolidation of new nation-states implied two things: that somehow "the nation" should participate in public affairs; and that "the state" should become strong. During the 1870s and 1880s, a complementary family of political reforms that simultaneously involved society in the political process and strengthened state apparatuses took place throughout Europe. Secularization of education spread, as states wrested education from the church and taught their citizens loyalty to the nation, and the electorate expanded. The creation of a republic in France foreshadowed the eventual end of monarchs as a vital political force. In central Europe, the Habsburgs experimented with a dual system of government that let the Hungarian and German halves of the empire govern themselves. In Russia, Tsar Alexander II freed the serfs, reformed his army, and introduced new legal norms. As varied as these efforts at change may seem, together they constituted a remarkable set of liberalizing and secularizing reforms that implied the existence of a civil society. The reforms of the period encouraged private associations, fostered public consciousness, and increased citizen participation in governance. The aristocratic classes did not disappear, nor was their influence significantly impaired. Indeed, the state itself became more efficient and more effective in intervening in public affairs. Nevertheless, by the end of the 1880s, many Europeans sensed that something new was happening, that they were making—in the catchword of the day—progress.

France's Lasting Republic

German liberals had rallied to Bismarck's program of national unification, but this did not mean that political parties of movement, as they were called, collapsed, either in Germany or elsewhere. In France, for example, a turn against Napoleon III and toward liberalism already had begun during the Second Empire. Many Catholics in France resented Napoleon's intervention in northern Italy in 1859 because of the pressure that it placed on the pope, and ordinary citizens begrudged the added costs of the war against Austria. In addition, in 1860 Napoleon irritated some business interests by signing a free-trade agreement with England.

To counter growing disenchantment, Napoleon began opening up the political process. He agreed to publish the debates in the National Assembly and to give that body the right to approve increases in public debt, thus making it less of a rubber stamp organization. These steps augmented public interest in politics and prompted an electoral swing toward opposition legislators. When the election of 1869 returned the largest liberal majority yet, Napoleon appointed Émile Ollivier, a leading liberal, as prime minister. Early in 1870, a plebiscite enthusiastically endorsed a new constitution that created "the liberal empire." It seemed that a solid parliamentary monarchy had arisen in France.

Events proved otherwise. Only months after the adoption of the new constitution, the Franco-Prussian War broke out. German troops brushed aside the French armies and captured Napoleon. When the mortally ill emperor abdicated early in September 1870, crowds took to the Paris streets, and for the third time in French history, revolutionaries declared a republic. Soon the Germans surrounded Paris, besieging the city for nineteen weeks until food ran out and starvation threatened. Forced to capitulate in February 1871, the temporary republican government held elections to create a legislature authorized to make peace with the Germans.

The new legislature, which met in far-away Bordeaux, was heavily monarchist, because the provincial and rural areas remained antirepublican. Nevertheless, the three royalist factions (Bourbon, Orleanist, and Bonapartist) could not agree on a candidate for the throne. As a temporary expedient, the new legislature chose Louis-Adolphe Thiers as prime minister. Thiers was a liberal, but not a republican, so the monarchists believed that he could rally broad support at a time of crisis. Once a proper king could be selected, they calculated, Thiers would be replaced with a monarchist prime minister. In May 1871, Thiers's government signed the Treaty of Frankfurt, whereby it gave up Alsace and Lorraine and agreed to German occupation of parts of France until reparations of 5 billion francs had been paid.

In March 1871, when the legislature moved from Bordeaux to Versailles, Thiers found Paris in a state of agitation. From the pronouncement of the republic in September 1870, radical forces gathered strength there. After the hardships brought on by the long German siege, Jacobin-style revolutionaries had replaced the relatively moderate democrats and socialists in the Paris city government (the **Commune**). Rather than reading the unrest as a sign of serious social dysfunction brought on by war, siege, and stress, Thiers interpreted it as rebellion against the middle-class order he sought to restore. Almost as soon as Thiers returned to Versailles, he ended the wartime moratorium on debt payments, which had benefited the lower classes, and stopped payments to National Guard members, who by 1871 consisted mostly of artisans and other working people. These measures were unpopular enough, but when Thiers attempted to disarm the National Guard, a spontaneous outburst of rage convulsed Paris.

The brief but vicious civil war that ensued between the Paris Commune and the national government was the most tragic event in modern French history. Karl Marx understood the Commune as a model of working-class government, and a generation later Lenin used Marx's interpretation of the Commune to shape his ideas about the communist state. Thus the Paris Commune had enormous symbolic importance in the history of European socialism. In reality, however, the communards were a heterogeneous group, most of whom had little notion of European socialism. Their revolt was driven by immediate goals, such as curbing inflation and disarming the National Guard, and not by socialist theories. The two months in 1871 during which the Commune fought for its existence brimmed with enthusiasm and experimentation, but the government held an overwhelming preponderance of force. Unable to defeat the Germans, the French army had little difficulty in massacring twenty thousand communards and imprisoning or transporting another ten thousand to colonial jails.

With memories of the suppression of the Lyon silkworkers in the 1830s and the June Days of 1848 still fresh, the quashing of the Commune struck some French citizens as final proof that middle-class liberals would prefer to kill workers than listen to their grievances. The French left never forgot or forgave the crushing of the Commune. Because of it and other nineteenth-century conflicts, class hostility in that country has always had a particularly sharp edge.

Destroying the Commune solved none of France's pressing political problems. A republic had been established, but it was the only large one in Europe.[8] Everyone believed that restoration of the monarchy was only a matter of time. While the Bourbon, Orléanist, and Bonapartist factions squabbled over such weighty matters as what flag they would fly when they came to power, conservative politicians found a way to replace Thiers with a less liberal prime minister. They waited until 1873, when Thiers—remarkably—had completed reparations payments and got the German occupying forces out of France, and then forced him out of office in favor of Marshal Maurice MacMahon, who commanded the forces that had put down the Commune.

Despite a seeming political consensus that monarchy was the proper form of government, the ideas of the French Revolution had penetrated deeply into French public life. Little question remained that the lower house of the legislature should be elected by universal manhood suffrage, or that the president should be chosen by the National Assembly for a seven-year term. The National Assembly wrote both of these principles into law in 1875. Under the new rules, the president appointed the government, but—

and this was a key innovation—the government answered to the legislature rather than to the president. The word *republic* appeared only once in these laws, which most people at the time did not see as permanent. Nevertheless, they formed the basis of a republican system that lasted until World War II.

The Third Republic, as it was called, inspired increased public confidence in the late 1870s. The elections of 1876 and 1878 returned solid republican majorities, despite gross interference in the process by MacMahon's government. Early in 1879, when MacMahon decided to resign, the republicans took power and put many of their most cherished reforms into effect. Over the next two or three years, they firmly established freedom of assembly; authorized freedom of the press; permitted the selling of newspapers on the streets; reintroduced divorce, which had been banned since 1816; and established July 14, Bastille Day, as the French national holiday. Under the leadership of Jules Ferry, the central government expelled the Jesuits and expanded control over all French schools, requiring a state license for teaching. Ferry finally turned Napoleon Bonaparte's vague ideas about universal education into reality by declaring elementary education compulsory and free. Monarchists and conservatives did not disappear from France, of course. Early in 1889 they even sought to reclaim control through urging the popular but feckless

---

[8] It is worth recalling that as of 1871, only one significant government in the world functioned as a republic and a democracy: the United States. Switzerland was also a republic, and it became effectively democratic in 1874.

Manet's *The Firing Squad*
The creation of the Commune by the working people of Paris in the wake of French defeat in 1871 panicked middle-class and rural France. The newspaper *Le Figaro* demanded that "the people of Paris must submit to the laws of war. Mercy is madness." Edouard Manet shows how this attitude sealed the fate of the captured communards. *Museum Folkwang, Essen.*

General Georges Boulanger to seize power. The general declined, spending the crucial night with his mistress instead. During the 1880s, the French achieved a significant portion of the century-old revolutionary dream of establishing a secular nation-state embracing civil liberties and market economics.

Gladstone and Disraeli Reform England

In roughly the same period that France made the transition to republican government, Great Britain opened its doors to reform as well. During the 1860s, two leaders emerged from long public careers to galvanize British politics. Benjamin Disraeli, later Earl of Beaconsfield, operated under the eth-

nic disadvantage of being the baptized son of a well-to-do Jewish mercantile family. A flamboyant youth who dropped out of school at age fifteen to become a novelist and a rake, Disraeli proved a brilliant Conservative party leader once he entered the House of Commons. Nationalistic and intensely interested in Britain's prestige abroad, as well as in expanding the empire, Disraeli was also an astute parliamentary strategist who understood the political value of personal charm. By treating Queen Victoria privately as a person rather than an institution, while at the same time remaking the monarchy into a genuinely popular institution, he became the queen's favorite politician. After a dissipated youth, Disraeli turned in middle age toward a defense of the monarch, of the House of Lords, and of the church.

Young Gentlemen's Reforms
In nineteenth-century French schools, discipline and dress were rigidly prescribed, and authority was very hierarchical. This satirical cartoon suggests how French schoolboys might have wished to "reform" the schools. Needless to say, no such reforms took place. *E.T. Archive.*

William Ewart Gladstone, the leader of the Liberals, was Disraeli's opposite in almost every way. The second son of a wealthy merchant, and educated in England's most exclusive upper-class institutions—Eton and Oxford—Gladstone nevertheless was broadly humanitarian in his impulses, widely learned, and enormously industrious. Entering Parliament as a Tory at age twenty-three, he became a junior minister just two years later. Gladstone was not entirely popular with his colleagues, and eventually he joined the Liberals. Moral almost to a fault, Gladstone lacked judgment in human relations, almost always expecting others to follow the ethical path. His subtle mind often found every possible reason to postpone action. On the other hand, once he became convinced of the rightness of a position he pursued it with obstinate vigor. Queen Victoria found him quite insufferable.

In the 1860s and 1870s, Disraeli and Gladstone alternated as prime minister, providing Britain not only with able leadership, but with the most entertaining political theater of the nineteenth century. Disraeli, a witty and dynamic speaker, confined his speeches to the House of Commons and similar official moments, but his pointed shafts often hit their mark. Gladstone's pontifications bored a cynical House, but his ethical messages were popular among his constituencies. In his old age, he became the first European politician to take his message directly to the people. Much to Queen Victoria's horror, he delivered rambling but stirring speeches from train platforms to excited crowds.

Disraeli's primary interest lay in foreign affairs. He acquired the Suez Canal for Britain in 1875 and in the next year had Victoria crowned Empress of India. Gladstone was more interested in domestic affairs, especially relations with Ireland. But both men proved responsive to the public interest in reform that characterized the 1870s and 1880s. By the 1860s, rapid economic growth had made some of the electoral districts created by the Great Reform Act of 1832 obsolete. In 1865 the Liberal leadership introduced a moderate reform bill that would redistribute seats in the House of Commons. The national debate and political crisis that this proposal ignited were almost as stirring as those of 1831 and 1832, and they yielded similar results. Conservatives at first defeated Gladstone's measure, and even some Liberals feared broadening the suffrage, but the public responded with such outrage that they had to retreat. Disraeli himself reintroduced a revised reform bill. After utterly defeating opposition leader Gladstone in skirmish after skirmish, Disraeli nevertheless permitted the Liberals to broaden the reform, and it became law in August 1867. By taking this "leap in the dark," as one conservative figure called it, Disraeli added about a million working males to the voting polls. In later years Gladstone added even more, so that by the end of Gladstone's last ministry in 1894 most British working males had the vote.

Gladstone came to power for the first time in 1868. Much like the republicans when they took the reins of gov-

Benjamin Disraeli: "The Mystery Man"   Disraeli was a far more colorful person than his rival Gladstone, and the British satirical journal *Punch* liked taking potshots at him. This cartoon suggests the many guises in which Disraeli appeared, including novelist, wit, bon vivant, and scholar, not to mention arrogant and ambitious (and very able) political figure.   *From the cartoon in* Punch.

ernment in France ten years later, Gladstone's Liberals generated a burst of legislation. They reformed the civil service, stimulated elementary education, made religious instruction optional, restructured the army, and introduced the secret ballot. Surprisingly, when Disraeli replaced Gladstone in 1874, the pace of reform not only did not slacken, it accelerated. The Liberals, who traditionally defended the rights of property, hesitated to pass laws that reined in business. Disraeli, on the other hand, believed that a strong state should act vigorously for the public good.[9] Under his leadership, the Conservative party began to regulate the purity of food and drugs, to oversee the quality of artisan dwellings, and to undertake public health

---

[9] Note that in the nineteenth century it was liberals who wished to restrict the state and conservatives who pursued a paternalistic interest in the welfare of the people. In late twentieth-century North America, this situation is reversed.

measures. They also tempered the regulations on unions and, in 1880, made elementary education compulsory. Other reform measures of the 1870s and 1880s included the creation of public parks, establishment of public libraries, and provision of assistance to the mentally ill and the disabled. "Tory Democracy," Disraeli called it. The Gladstone/Disraeli period pushed England a long way down the path toward a democratic political culture and toward a state dedicated to "progress."

The Failure of Home Rule for Ireland

In southeastern Europe, new Balkan states had won their independence from the weakened Ottoman Empire, but in the United Kingdom the Irish could not achieve the same goal from a powerful Britain. By the terms of the union of 1801, Ireland sent about a hundred members to the House of Commons. These members strongly influenced the repeal of the political restrictions on Catholics in 1829. In the second half of the century, the moderation of the early Irish members of Parliament gave way to more aggressive tactics. A nationalist movement called Young Ireland on the Mazzinian model tried to foment a revolt in 1848, but it failed. In 1867, an uprising led by the Irish Republican Brotherhood, or Fenians, miscarried as well.

Gladstone was one of the few British politicians willing to confront Ireland's relationship with England directly. As early as 1845 he had said,

> Ireland! Ireland! That cloud in the West! That coming storm! That minister of God's retribution upon cruel, inveterate, and but half-atoned injustice! Ireland forces upon us these great social and great religious questions. God grant that we may have the courage to look them in the face!

When he came to power in 1868, Gladstone sought to alleviate some of the Irish disabilities. The social situation in Ireland had not changed significantly since the famine of 1845–1847. Not only did the vast majority of the Irish labor as poor farmers, but economic depression in Ireland had led many struggling landlords to evict their tenants. Sometimes the landlords, most of whom were Protestant, even demolished the evicted tenant's house to prevent squatters from moving in. The state continued to collect a tithe to support the Protestant Church of Ireland. Because most Irish were Catholics, Gladstone thought this arrangement particularly unfair. In 1869 he put through legislation that deprived the church of its special rights, including the collection of the tithe. In 1870, he also pushed through a land act to protect Irish tenants from arbitrary eviction.

That same year, Irish patriots, including some members of Parliament, established the Home Rule League to seek autonomy in a less revolutionary way than Young Ireland or the Fenians. Charles Stewart Parnell became the leader of this movement in Parliament. He and his allies

began to obstruct the work of the House of Commons, even on bills that had nothing to do with Ireland. Gladstone did not care for these tactics, nor for the violence that Irish revolutionaries initiated on the streets, and he never found a way to cooperate with Parnell. Nonetheless, in 1886 he decided to stake his government and his reputation on passing Home Rule for Ireland. Combining the moral with the practical, Gladstone argued that Home Rule was not only right, but that it would save England money and improve Ireland's economic health as well.

In the showdown, a surge of English nationalism sent Gladstone's bill down to defeat. Many members of his own party split off to form the Liberal Union, which favored keeping the status quo. Gladstone returned to power one more time in 1892, but after he got a Second Home Rule Bill through the House of Commons, the House of Lords decisively defeated it.

Gladstone was not a liberal in the twentieth-century sense. He had a deep suspicion of the state, and he was not enthusiastic about social spending. But his willingness, representing the stronger side, to offer autonomy to the Irish, the weaker side, marks him as one of the towering statesmen of the nineteenth century—and one completely out of step with the Century of Power.

Germanizing Germany: The Kulturkampf

The republicans in France and the reformers in England did not have to concern themselves overly with the Catholic church. In France Catholicism remained strong, but its political power was confined to the monarchist elements who lost out in the 1870s. In England Catholics had been excluded from public life from the time of Elizabeth I until 1829. Despite a revival of interest in Catholicism among English intellectuals in the 1840s, Catholicism entered British politics primarily in relation to the Irish question.

In most of continental Europe, however, the Catholic church remained a powerful and generally reactionary force. Pius IX, who became pope in 1846, had launched his reign with a number of reforms. But the revolutions of 1848, which had forced him to flee the Eternal City, turned Pius IX into a reactionary. Resentful of liberal anticlericalism and doubtful that industrialization would produce a better life, he promulgated an encyclical condemning modernity in 1864. The accompanying *Syllabus of Errors* listed eighty specific errors that believers must reject, including rationalism, state-sponsored secular education, socialism, and communism. The eightieth error was to suppose that "the Roman Pontiff can and should reconcile and harmonize himself with progress, with liberalism, and with recent civilization."

Pius IX also supervised the formalization of two medieval traditions of the church: the immaculate conception of the Virgin Mary (in 1854), and papal infallibility

THE HUMAN EXPERIENCE

Charles Stewart Parnell, Irish Politician and Nationalist

Charles Parnell (1846–1891) was an unlikely Irish nationalist. A Protestant landowner, he spoke with an English rather than an Irish accent, was reserved and secretive, and sought an industrialized and modernized Ireland, rather than one based on ancient Irish traditions. And yet, in a meteoric political career that lasted only about fifteen years, he became "the uncrowned king of Ireland," remembered by the Irish with more affection and even passion than any Irish patriot of modern times.

Parnell's personal life is little known because he did not keep a diary and left no personal papers. His well-to-do family sent him to school in England at the age of seven, and at thirteen he inherited the family estate. At nineteen he entered Cambridge, but when he was suspended in his fourth year, he never came back to take a degree. After a lengthy tour of the United States, he returned to his estate to take up the public life that was the usual avocation of men of his class. He lost a bid for office in 1874, but in 1875 he succeeded and entered Parliament.

Irish patriots were already aware of Parnell's potential. In 1870 they had formed the Home Rule League, which aimed at winning political autonomy for Ireland. In 1874 the league invited Parnell to join its executive committee. Parnell was not a particularly gifted speaker, but he had earnestness, believability, principle, and humor—a "sweet seriousness," one admirer called it—that attracted followers. By 1877 he became president of the home rule movement, and in the 1880s the Irish national movement generally acknowledged him as its leader.

Parnell usually stuck to legal procedures and opposed violence. His parliamentary faction primarily relied on filibusters and manipulation of the rules to disrupt the work of Parliament. To hold the radical and moderate wings of the Irish movement together, Parnell developed a strategy of giving radical speeches and encouraging obstruction while at the same time acting in ways that would advance moderate reform. For example, Parnell declined to advocate an Irish boycott of Parliament after it ejected thirty-six Irish members and passed the Coercion Act of 1881, which gave the English viceroy in Ireland wide powers of arrest. On the other hand, at the passage of the Land Act of 1881, which established security of tenure and fair rents for Irish farmers, and which Gladstone had labored hard to pass, Parnell called the prime minister "this masquerading knight-errant, this pretending champion of the rights of every nation except those of the Irish nation."

During the 1880s, Parnell was Ireland's most prominent personality, but not necessarily the most successful. Personality conflicts and short-term political infighting prevented Parnell and Gladstone from cooperating to pass a home rule bill in 1885–1886. Then in 1889, a Captain O'Shea, a political trimmer who for twenty years had unsuccessfully sought a cabinet post while living off his wife's income, sued for divorce, naming Parnell as the corespondent. Because Mrs. O'Shea had been Parnell's mistress since 1880 and had borne him two children, and because of Captain O'Shea's own philandering, the divorce was uncontested. In an age when divorce in itself was considered a scandal, moralizing critics fell on Parnell. Infuriated by the hypocrisy of the media campaign, Parnell refused to resign as head of the Irish party, despite the succinct advice of the imperialist Cecil Rhodes: "Resign-marry-return." When Parnell died suddenly shortly thereafter, having married Mrs. O'Shea in the interim, Irish political unity disintegrated until World War I. ❖

(in 1870). The former dogma held that from the moment of her conception, Mary was miraculously free of original sin. This condition made it possible for her to bear the son of God, who by definition also was free of sin. According to the doctrine of papal infallibility, when the pope speaks *ex cathedra* (officially) on matters of faith and morals, he "is possessed of that infallibility with which the divine Redeemer willed his Church, . . . and therefore such definitions of the Roman Pontiff are irreformable of themselves."

Not well understood even by many Catholics, these two doctrines struck non-Catholics as the last straw in Pius IX's rejection of the modern world, particularly in Germany. Bismarck's new empire was not a unified state. Its component parts had kept many of their own traditions, currencies, and customs. In particular, northern Germany remained primarily Lutheran, whereas southern Germany and the Rhineland were primarily Catholic. In the 1870s, Bismarck strove to make a whole out of these disparate entities. His main political partners were liberals, particularly the National Liberals, the strongest party in the imperial legislature (the Reichstag).[10] In just a few years, they restructured both the criminal and civil courts, produced a new commercial code suitable for Germany's expanding capitalism, established a uniform coinage, created an imperial bank, and introduced dozens of other laws to promote the centralization of authority. The liberals did not achieve all they wanted—Bismarck did not support freedom of the press, for example, and he opposed plans to grant more autonomy to provincial and local governments. Most important, he remained responsible only to the emperor, not to the Reichstag. But with a stretch of the imagination, the National Liberals could see themselves as pursuing reforms equivalent to those associated with Gladstone in England or even the republicans in France.

The National Liberals' primary opponent was the Center party, founded in 1870 to advocate the rights of German Catholics. The Center party was socially conservative but not insensitive to changing conditions in Germany. It supported self-help agencies to aid the poor, for example. Moreover, many Catholic intellectuals and clergy refused to accept the Vatican decrees of 1870, preferring excommunication to a rejection of modernity. Nevertheless, the formation of a Catholic party just at the peak of Pius IX's reactionary policies infuriated many German Protestants. "The Church of Rome is a vampire draining the vital energies of the German spirit," thundered historian Heinrich von Treitschke.

As a Prussian Lutheran, Bismarck had always been suspicious of Catholics. As early as the 1850s he had concluded that a "militant, insatiable, and irreconcilable spirit" was driving the conservative part of the Catholic church to dominate Protestant sovereigns. In the period from 1866 to 1870, the Catholic caucus confirmed Bismarck's suspicions by repeatedly voting against his program. In 1871 it even opposed the government's draft of the empire's new constitution.

In the spring and summer of 1871, several related church-state issues came to a head, and Bismarck went on the attack. With widespread support from non-Catholic Germans, and with the enthusiastic backing of the National Liberals—who were happy to see the conservative Bismarck do their secularizing work for them—he took priests off the state payroll, eliminated church supervision of schools, and made civil marriage obligatory. When priests and **bishops** protested, he removed them from office and sometimes even imprisoned them. Liberals presented this campaign (the *Kulturkampf*) as "a great struggle for civ-

ilization in the interest of humanity" against a Catholic effort to push Europe back to the Middle Ages.

Bismarck had hoped to use the National Liberal party to unify his diverse new empire. But the Kulturkampf demonstrated the difficulty of that task, as Catholics and the Center party only grew stronger under adversity. When the Center party won a significant number of seats in the election of 1877 and Pius IX died a year later, the Iron Chancellor decided to repair relations with the Catholics, abandoning his erstwhile liberal allies.

The Kulturkampf produced some lasting reforms, such as civil marriage, but its most telling residue lay in the way Bismarck managed it. His main purpose in the 1870s was to unify the new German Empire—to Germanize it. By this he did not mean to make it ethnically homogeneous (Germany contained millions of Poles, Danes, Alsatians, and even south Germans who resented Prussian domination), but instead to convince his subjects that the new empire was a real country, a nation as any other, requiring their patriotic loyalty above any allegiance to its constituent regions. To achieve this goal, he did not try to bring people together. He set them against one another. Bismarck exercised the power at his disposal ruthlessly, attacked opponents as *Reichsfeinde* (enemies of the empire) when it suited the needs of the moment, and cast aside allies when the situation changed. As long as he maintained the confidence of William I, a policy that he followed assiduously, Bismarck remained the lodestone of German politics. When William I died in 1888, Bismarck could not bring himself to adopt a sufficiently servile demeanor before the young, impetuous, and none-too-bright William II. Only then—in 1890—did the Iron Chancellor have to resign.

Central Europe's Experiment in Dualism

Catholicism ran strong in the Habsburg lands, too, but the political situation there differed fundamentally from that in Germany. Rather than trying to unite a varied but single people into a new state, Francis Joseph faced the problem of keeping many peoples from splitting an already existing state apart. Austrian Germans were the most powerful of these nationalities; Hungarians the second. Despite bitter memories from the Hungarian revolution of 1848, Francis Joseph realized early in the 1860s that the empire's financial and military strength depended on an accommodation between these two peoples. Even before the Austro-Prussian war of 1866, negotiations for a settlement had begun. The crushing defeat at Königgrätz seemingly opened an opportunity for the Hungarians to take advantage of imperial weakness. But when Francis Joseph asked the main Hungarian negotiator to define his new conditions for a settlement, the Hungarian answered, "No more after Königgrätz than before, sire." With such a cooperative attitude, it took only a few months to work out an arrangement.

---

[10] Note that the Prussian legislature retained the title *Landtag*, from the ancient tradition of German "lands," whereas the imperial legislature became the *Reichstag* (from Reich, or "empire"). Even in Germany today, regions are still called "lands" (*Länder*).

THE HUMAN EXPERIENCE

Gersten Bleichröder, Bismarck's Banker

In 1803 Samuel Bleichröder opened a money exchange in Berlin. By the 1820s, he had become so successful at expanding into other banking fields that the Rothschilds selected him as one of their agents. The five sons of Meyer Amschel Rothschild had established branches in London, Paris, Vienna, Naples, and Frankfurt that made them the richest banking house in Europe. From the time Gersten Bleichröder (1822–1893) entered his father's business in 1839 until he assumed full control in 1855, one of his most important tasks was to maintain his link with this eminent banking family. Gersten proved an able banker, and German industrialization opened many opportunities to expand his business. By the early 1860s, the Bleichröder Bank had become one of the most important in Berlin.

When Bismarck transferred from Frankfurt to St. Petersburg in 1858, he asked Meyer Carl Rothschild whom he could recommend as a banker in Berlin, and Rothschild suggested Bleichröder. At first Bleichröder simply kept track of Bismarck's personal finances, but when Bismarck came to power in 1862, Bleichröder became deeply involved in his political life as well. During the crisis of 1866, for example, Bleichröder's machinations kept Bismarck and Prussia financially afloat during the difficult months when Bismarck

sought war, a feat that Bismarck later said "compels gratitude."

In 1871, at the peak of Bismarck's triumphs, William I presented his chancellor with an estate of more than 17,000 acres and elevated him to the rank of prince. Bleichröder's task was to make Bismarck rich enough so that he could afford the honor. The concept "conflict of interest" did not exist yet in Germany, and neither Bleichröder nor Bismarck were averse to trading on the basis of political information at their mutual disposal. But Bleichröder never involved Bismarck in shady projects. His investments combined safety and yield well enough to make Bismarck a millionaire several times over by the time of his death.

Bleichröder's Jewishness complicated his relationship with Bismarck. Even though the banker was perhaps the richest man in Germany when he died in 1893, the confidant of kings, the savior of princely fortunes, and the recipient of countless awards, he could never escape snide remarks and antisemitic insinuations. Bismarck respected and admired Bleichröder, and retained him to the end. Bismarck was also instrumental in removing the last impediments to the full legal equality of Jews in 1869. Yet he revealed a belittling attitude toward Bleichröder that was characteristic of many Germans, even when they fully appreciated the scope of

Jewish contributions to their own well-being and to Germany's greatness. "Pomeranian estate owners have always had their House Jew," Bismarck said. "I am a Pomeranian estate owner and have Bleichröder."

Both Bismarck and Bleichröder had to endure nasty antisemitic attacks on their relationship, and in his old age Bleichröder faced a determined effort by an embittered woman to blackmail him. The obtuse and insensitive Bleichröder probably did not suffer greatly from these attacks, but the vulnerability of a man of his contributions and stature cast a shadow across Germany that proved particularly dark for the future. ❖

Bildarchiv Preussischer Kulturbesitz (bpk), Berlin.

The Compromise of 1867, or *Ausgleich,* divided the Habsburg realm into two parts, creating Austria-Hungary, or the Dual Monarchy. The Hungarian portion, with its capital in Budapest, consisted of traditional lands of the Hungarian crown, such as Slovakia and Croatia, and several other ethnically mixed lands, such as Transylvania. The Austrian half comprised the ancient Habsburg crown lands of upper and lower Austria, Styria, and Carniola (today's Slovenia), including the capital Vienna, as well as Bohemia and Moravia (now the Czech Republic), and

other areas. Each partner had full control over all state functions in its territory, with the exception of three spheres: foreign policy, military affairs, and the financial arrangements necessary to sustain the two common activities. Both Austria and Hungary had their own governments, legislatures, and law codes—no common Austro-Hungarian parliament or government existed. The imperial ministers for foreign affairs, finance, and army—along with Francis Joseph himself—were the only joint governmental officials. These ministries were influential, but in the end, Francis Joseph and his circle of advisers made the most important imperial decisions over the next half-century.

The Dual Monarchy was ethnically complex, historically diverse, and linguistically incompatible. The Hungarians, restored almost to the level of independence that they had failed to win in 1848, quickly fell victim to creeping nationalism. In 1868 they granted the Croats autonomy and passed the Nationalities Law. On the surface these appeared to be models of cultural and ethnic toleration. In fact, however, the Croats never became an equal partner with the Hungarians, and within a few years the Nationalities Law was a dead letter. By the 1870s, the Hungarians were actively pursuing a policy of Magyarization.[11] "What we expect from them," said one Hungarian politician in referring to the other peoples in Hungary, "is not only that they speak the Magyar vernacular but that they start to feel like Magyars themselves."

---

[11] The Hungarian language is Magyar, which is a notoriously difficult language for non-Hungarians to learn. As a result of the education law of 1907, for example, about eighteen of the twenty-two hours of normal weekly class time in non-Magyar primary schools had to be devoted to teaching the Magyar language. Such is the human cost of linguistic chauvinism.

Most ethnic groups resented this attitude, but one group, the Jews, made good use of the situation. Jews had entered Hungary in increasing numbers from the second half of the eighteenth century, when they were expelled from Austrian lands, through the nineteenth century, when they fled the Russian Empire and Austrian Galicia. By the 1880s, more than 900,000 Jews lived in Hungary. By the end of the nineteenth century, some Jews, especially in Budapest, had risen to positions of wealth and social prominence. Rather than rejecting the Jewish presence, as did the Romanians, for example, the Hungarian aristocracy found ways to integrate the most successful Jews. Jews became an accepted and important part of Hungarian cultural and economic life.

Hungary did not lack for improvements in the 1870s. Much like liberals elsewhere in this decade, reformers regularized governmental procedures and reorganized the school system. But in contrast to other countries, the social class that dominated Hungarian liberalism was the aristocracy, not a mercantile middle class. Kálmán Tisza, a member of one of Hungary's oldest and richest families, founded the Liberal party in 1875. By manipulating elections and controlling the bureaucracy, Tisza and his upper-class allies maintained control of national politics until the end of the century. Lower-ranking country gentry found their niche in

The Hungarian Parliament   This magnificent neo-Gothic building was erected on the left bank of the Danube River in Budapest late in the nineteenth century and, like the British parliament building in London, is still in use today. Its lavish scale suggests the growing wealth of nineteenth-century Hungary.   *Hungarian Tourist Board.*

the bureaucracy, which provided them prestige and income without forcing them to engage in trade.

In Austria, the nationalities question had a much more political cast than in Hungary, because the legislature contained representatives from each traditional territory. Technically, "Austria" did not exist as a legal entity. It consisted only of lands, such as upper Austria, Bohemia, and Carniola, that recognized Francis Joseph as their ruler and were represented in the legislature (the *Reichsrat*). Because each land had its own legislative agenda, Austrian politics tended to be confrontational. The Czech representatives from Bohemia, for example, boycotted the Reichsrat through the 1870s after a deal to grant them relative autonomy fell through in 1871. On the other hand, aristocratic Polish representatives from Galicia, who ruled harshly over their Ukrainian peasants, were easily bought off with concessions and became strong government supporters.

In this confusing multinational patchwork, German-speaking liberals dominated Austrian politics in the 1870s. Representing the urban middle classes of the German-speaking portions of Austria, they advocated the traditional liberal program, including freedom of religion and secular education. Austria had concluded a concordat with the Vatican in 1855, but the German-speaking liberals used their outrage at the *Syllabus of Errors* to attack the arrangement. In 1870 Austria repudiated the concordat, and in 1873 the state took over supervision of church affairs. The liberals legalized civil marriage, removed schools from church control, made all Christian faiths equal, provided for compulsory free education (on paper at least), introduced jury trials for alleged violations of the press laws, and abolished many restrictions on Jews. In fact, Viennese Jews became one of the chief pillars of Austrian liberalism and capitalism in the 1860s and 1870s. In Germany, less thoroughgoing measures had provoked sharp conflict. In Austria, however, Catholic ecclesiastics disliked the changes, but they accepted them because reformers permitted the church to retain its prodigious wealth and numerous monasteries. Despite the secularizing tendency of the German-speaking liberals, therefore, Austria remained a devoutly Catholic country. As for the liberals, the decade of the 1870s proved, as it did elsewhere, to be their swan song. During the 1880s the Austrian half of the Dual Monarchy came under the control of a conservative coalition of aristocrats, clerics, and Slavic legislators.

Opposition and Reform in Autocratic Russia

The farther east that reform ideas penetrated, the more diffuse they became and the more obstacles they met. Republicans had succeeded in France, while both the Liberal and Conservative parties moved toward democracy in England. Belgium also followed English practice closely. In Germany, Austria, and Hungary, liberals faced an entrenched aristocracy and a strong Catholic church but still managed to implement secularizing and rationalizing reforms. In Russia, however, reform ran into almost insuperable barriers. In the first half of the nineteenth century, the repressive regime of Tsar Nicholas I had prevented any public discussion of change. Russia did not even have a middle class, because industrialization did not start in earnest until late in the century. In compensation, the Russians "invented" a new social stratum: the intelligentsia. This term, of Russian origin, refers to that relatively small group of educated persons who understand their function to be analyzing social and political relations.

The early intelligentsia tended to consist of dissident noblemen or the sons of priests who had managed to get a university education. These men saw themselves as occupying the social space between the autocrat—traditionally the sole political force—and the people, who were still barely conscious of their potential public role. During Nicholas I's reign (1825–1855), this new stratum reacted to the arbitrariness of Russian life with arcane discussions of Hegelian philosophy or with literary analysis. Two main schools of thought developed, the Western and the Slavophiles. More than mere copiers of Western thought, the Westerners were rationalists who, through their study of German philosophy and the early French socialists, concluded that humanity's active participation in real life constituted the true subject matter of history. The Russian past was not simply a story of the tsar's activities or of God's providence, they believed, but a tale of individuals who had put their thoughts into action and had shaped the Russian experience. This abstract idea could not bring its advocates into the political process in autocratic Russia, because the tsar offered no space in which a civil society might develop. But the Westerners did contribute a rationalistic tone to reformist ideology that characterized Russian revolutionary thought through the rest of the century.

Slavophiles were not unfamiliar with Western thought, but they adhered to the conservative position that society develops like an organism in nature. Rational individualism, in their view, produced an unfeeling society in which each person remained alone, uncomforted by family, nation, and faith. According to the Slavophiles, Russia's advantage over the West was that it had never stressed rationality and had never emphasized property rights. For these Romantics, Russia was not an impersonal, juridical, and competitive marketplace, but a harmonious community where universal belief gave spiritual expression to an indissoluble unity.

Yet it was Russia's defeat in the Crimean War, not these ideas, that initiated change. When Nicholas I died in 1855 in the midst of that conflict, his son, Alexander II, succeeded him. Many educated and progressive members of Nicholas's upper bureaucracy had understood that Russia's ramshackle autocracy needed reforming. Some of them even believed that modern conditions required that the government open itself to regular consultations with society. The Crimean defeat gave impetus to these

THE HISTORICAL EVIDENCE

The Russian Commune

1843

In the mid-nineteenth century, the discovery by the Russian intelligentsia of the peasant commune, primarily through the work of a German traveler and essayist named Baron August von Haxthausen, had a profound effect both on government policy and on oppositionists. For many, the commune seemed to exemplify the best characteristics of Russian life. When Alexander II freed the serfs, for example, he decreed that they must remain in the commune, while oppositionists like Nikolai Chernyshevsky used the idea of the commune to propagate ideas about a socialist Russia. Here is a key passage from von Haxthausen's book, with the original punctuation.

The principle is, that the whole of the land (tillage, meadows, pasture, woods, streams, etc.) belongs to the population regarded as a unity, and every male inhabitant has a right to an equal share. This share is therefore constantly changing; for the birth of every boy creates a new claim and the shares of those who die revert to the Commune. The woods, pasture, hunting-grounds, and fisheries remain undivided, and free to all the inhabitants; but the arable land and meadows are divided, according to their value, amongst the males. This equal division is of course difficult, as the soil differs in quality, and portions of it may be distant or inconveniently situated. There are however in each Commune skilful [sic] land-surveyors, without any educa-tion but what has been acquired from the traditional habits of the place, who execute the work to the satisfaction of all. The land is first divided, according to its quality, position, or general value, into sections, each possessing on the whole equal advantages; the sections are then divided into as many portions, in long strips, as there are shares required, and these are taken by lot. . . . The allotment takes place in an assembly of the whole Commune, including the women and children.

Source: Baron August Ludwig Maria von Haxthausen, *The Russian Empire, Its People, Institutions, and Resources,* trans. Robert Farie (London: Chapman and Hall, 1856), p. 119.

reforming bureaucrats, especially when the tsar himself agreed that Russia's weakness lay in the relationship of serfdom to the army.

Russia had not changed its military recruitment system since the time of Peter the Great. Rather than organizing a small professional army and supplementing it with a large reserve, as Prussia did, for example, the Russians maintained a huge army. The normal tour of duty for recruits was twenty-five years. This method was both expensive and ineffective, as the Crimean War proved. The tsars had always rejected the idea of a reserve force, because it would mean sending trained men back to serfdom in the villages—back, the tsars thought, to revolt. Alexander, advised by an able minister of war, concluded that in order to build a modern army, he needed free citizens, not serfs.

In 1856, only one year after his accession to power, Alexander announced his plans to an astonished meeting of the Moscow nobility: "You yourselves understand that the present condition of the serfs cannot remain unchanged. [They understood no such thing.] It is better to begin to abolish serfdom from above than to wait until it begins to abolish itself from below." Alexander's initiative set off a chaotic process of negotiation and regulation-writing. In March 1861, the tsar was able to promulgate an emancipation proclamation affecting 52 million serfs. The enormous set of new laws did away with serfdom, but they did not grant peasants equality with other citizens. Unless the former serfs accepted the so-called "pauper's plot," which was too small to sustain a family, they were obligated to make redemption payments to the state for forty-nine years. In many places, the land was not given to individual peasants, but to the peasant village commune.

In the Russian communes, serfs had worked the land of their lords, but for subsistence they had farmed small plots near their communities. Peasants did not own these plots. Instead the elected elder would parcel them out to families on the basis of the qualities of the land, such as fertility and access to water, and in accordance with need. Each family would receive several parcels, or strips. A widow with one able-bodied son might get less land, or lower quality strips, than a large family with several sons and grandchildren. Families often cultivated five or ten strips assigned in this way, sometimes miles away from each other. In some

Russian Villagers   Russian peasants lived difficult lives, but not always completely abject ones. Here peasants gather at a local market to stock up on essentials and to socialize. *Sovfoto/Eastfoto.*

regions, elders periodically redistributed the strips when family configurations changed.

All Russians were familiar with this system, but not until the 1850s did government officials and intellectuals become aware of its uniqueness. They quickly came to take pride in an institution that differed dramatically from those found in western Europe but that seemed essentially democratic, even socialistic. The commune appeared to embody the specifically Russian characteristic of *sobornost,* or quasi-religious "togetherness." When the tsar's reformers wrote the laws freeing the peasants, therefore, they kept the peasants administratively attached to their communes. Even if peasants moved to town, they still were accountable to their village and paid taxes through it.

For emancipated serfs to form the basis of a new Russian society, reforming bureaucrats realized that many other changes were needed. Hoping to create a society based on law, they reformed the legal system and introduced Western institutions such as trial by jury. Educational reforms, reorganization of the military, improvements in government finance, and limited forms of local administration all aimed at transforming the old Russian society of classes

(landlord, merchant, serf) into a modern society of citizens. Reshaping such a huge, encrusted structure proved more difficult than anyone had imagined, but at least the reformers had made a start.

The public discussion stimulated by the freeing of the serfs and Alexander's other reforms generated interest in "the people" among Russian intellectuals. As we have seen, since the French Revolution Europeans had struggled to clarify the meaning of that term. English liberals defined it in political terms—property owners with a stake in society were the sovereign "people." German nationalists invented a more emotional concept, the *Volk.* Western socialists began claiming that "the people" included the working class, and by the 1860s some European feminists began to assert that the expression, when used in a political sense, should include women too. In the 1860s Russian intellectuals devised their own variation of the idea of the Volk: they identified the peasantry—the *narod*—as the true bearer of Russian tradition.[12]

Most populists, as they were called, considered themselves socialists. One of these, Nikolai Chernyshevsky, wrote, "A vast revolution is occurring in the West, but it is terrible to think . . . how much suffering and loss it has already cost and how much more it will still cost." Chernyshevsky saw the peasant commune as a primitive form of cooperative, which in time could develop into a modern agricultural collective. By this means, he hoped, Russia might be able to jump directly from backwardness to socialism, thus skipping the problems of capitalism. Other thinkers in this second generation of the Russian revolutionary tradition maintained a wide range of views. Some were outright revolutionaries—"there is only one way out of this terrible oppressive situation: revolution, a bloody and inexorable revolution"—while others were thoughtful reformers who believed that the educated elites had a moral obligation to instruct the masses and prepare them for the future.

Whatever their coloration—Slavophile, Westerner, populist, or conservative—almost all members of the Russian intelligentsia were also nationalists. This became abundantly clear when in January 1863 demonstrations in Warsaw led to another Polish uprising. This one took the Russian army fifteen months to subdue, after which the occupiers destroyed the possibility of an independent Poland for another fifty years through executions, confiscations, and deportations. The European left, including Russian socialist exile Alexander Herzen, vigorously supported the Poles, whom they saw as struggling for national liberation from tsarist oppression. But no foreign government did, and inside Russia public figures of all persuasions united against their Catholic Polish neighbors. Much like the German liberals who succumbed to Bismarck's successes,

---

[12] In Russian, the word *narod* means both "the people" and "the nation."

Russian Realism In Russia, painters of the nationalist school, who were called "The Wanderers," created works of art in a realistic style based on history and on the lives of ordinary people. This art often provided not-so-subtle social commentary on the state of the Russian government, society, and the people. In *They Did Not Expect Him*, Ilya Repin hints that the young man returning home may have been a revolutionary returning from a prison sentence. *Tretyakov Gallery, Moscow, Russia/The Bridgeman Art Library*

nationalism rallied the Russian intelligentsia behind a tsarist regime that many of them hated.

The climax of the populist period came in the summer of 1874, when hundreds of enthusiastic students decided to "go to the people." They fanned out from the universities to villages with their message that the peasantry represented the true spirit of Russia and that the commune contained the hope of the future. But the peasants did not understand the populist message. Annoyed with rhetoric incomprehensible to them, distrustful of city folk, and loyal to the tsar, whom they thought of as "the little father," the peasants stoned the students and turned them over to the police. A few frustrated radicals undertook more extreme measures. In 1881 a small terrorist group called the "People's Will" assassinated Alexander II, bringing the populist era to an ignominious close.

Despite the reforms that Alexander II had introduced, the authority of the tsar remained unlimited. Russia still had no constitution, no legislature, and no political parties. Repression and the lack of institutions in which a politics

of accommodation or a civil society could grow radicalized a certain element of the intelligentsia. Just as likely to be exiled to Siberia for a trivial offense as a major one, revolutionaries emerged who sought to solve all of Russia's problems with one stroke. But the populists labored under a severe handicap: The peasants were not revolutionary. They did not blame the tsar for their problems, and they spurned the commune, which they abandoned whenever they could. The populists could not understand this behavior, and when they finally had gone to the villages, they were dismayed to find the peasant dirtier, smellier, greedier, and more violent than they had ever imagined. Populist disillusionment, which lasted through the 1880s, nevertheless prepared some members of the Russian intelligentsia for the appearance in the 1890s of a new candidate for bearer of the Russian future, the urban working class. One reason that Marxism took hold in Russia late in the nineteenth century was that Russian intellectuals, already radicalized by repression, had been searching for a social group to replace the peasantry as the revolutionary class.

CONCLUSION: NATION-BUILDING AND THE DECLINE OF LIBERALISM

The two most important political events of the 1860s and the 1870s were the unifications of Italy and Germany. Not only did two large, potentially powerful, and entirely new states come into being, but their unification encouraged nationalists in central and southeastern Europe to dream of having their own independent states. Serbia in particular began to think of itself as the Piedmont of the Balkans. Neither Cavour nor Bismarck were primarily nationalists, although Bismarck thoroughly mastered the patriotic idiom. They were both power brokers who imposed Piedmontese and Prussian standards on their Italian and German neighbors. Their success, and the policies that they and their successors followed after unification, began to build coherent national identities for their people.

National identity is not a natural phenomenon. It is imparted by the process of socialization through which one acquires a sense of belonging. During the 1860s, 1870s, and 1880s, many European peoples were moving to new levels of national consciousness. In the 1830s only intellectual and political elites had made nationalist arguments. Almost half the population of France did not speak French at home;[13] most Germans, immersed in their regional affiliations, had difficulty conceiving of a large German state; Italy, except for a few Carbonari and Mazzinians, remained primarily a geographic term; and in eastern Europe peasants thought of themselves in terms of religion rather than ethnicity. By the end of the nineteenth century, however, many Europeans had come to accept the idea that they were members of a specific nation.

The state educational systems introduced and enhanced throughout Europe in the second half of the nineteenth century provided a primary mechanism of inculcating national consciousness. Most European states strengthened their commitment to secular education in the 1860s and 1870s, taking education out of the control of the church and placing it in the hands of teachers trained and certified by the state. Secularized schools began teaching loyalty to the country and state rather than religious values. In multinational states like Austria-Hungary, one of the most insistent demands of nationalists was that schooling be conducted in local languages, so as to preserve and strengthen the feeling of ethnic unity.

The army served as another nationalizing device. In the 1860s and 1870s, most European states adopted conscription. Under this system, almost all young men spent two or three years in the army for training before returning to civilian life as members of the reserves. Recruits learned not just military arts but also new levels of cleanliness, nutrition, discipline, loyalty, and fluency in the standard tongue. For many peasant boys, the army opened a wider world in which knowledge of standard French or proper Romanian came to be seen as an asset, a doorway to a better life.

The introduction of political life to a growing proportion of the population also stimulated a sense of nationhood. Public figures found that by appealing to nationalist arguments they could attract votes, and ordinary voters found themselves increasingly confronted with issues that transcended local concerns. The gradual loosening of restrictions on the press, as well as the publication of debates that took place in national or imperial legislatures, encouraged a new civic awareness and formed a civil society prepared to take its place in the public sphere.

This civil society did not yet exert a powerful political impact, however. In Germany, for example, Bismarck organized the German Empire to maximize the power of the state and to minimize the effect of the vigorous political parties. The Reich, he maintained, was a gift of the various sovereigns of Germany, not a construct of popular sovereignty. Instead of a nation-state, Bismarck conceived of Germany as a "state-nation."

In southern Europe, where popular sovereignty allegedly formed the basis of the state, governments operated in a high-handed and arbitrary way. In all of these countries, politicians from ostensibly opposing parties strove to get into a position of power and stay there. In Italy the operative principle was *transformismo* ("transformism"), in which a small group of political figures simply changed places with each other every few years. In Bulgaria, *partisanstvo* was the rule. Every time a new party came into power, it immediately swept aside all appointees of the previous administration, down to the local policeman, and set about fixing elections so as to keep themselves at the public trough. In Spain, the conservative Don Antonio Canovas de Castillo, who ardently admired the British parliamentary system and became prime minister on the basis of a new constitution adopted in 1875, achieved stability in the 1870s and 1880 by letting the bureaucracy, church, and army loot the national treasury. In almost every formally constitutional and parliamentary country in southern Europe, bureaucracies grew at appalling rates, and liberalism became a byword for corruption and cynicism.

In countries where liberalism had a constructive influence, such as Britain, France, Germany, and Austria-Hungary, liberal momentum was slowing by the end of the 1880s. In Germany Bismarck abandoned the National Liberals in 1879, while that same year Francis Joseph supported a coalition of conservative forces that soon achieved the apt nickname of "the iron ring." Gladstone's last two ministries foundered on the issue of Home Rule for Ireland. In Russia Alexander II's assassination brought the considerably more reactionary Alexander III to the throne, while in

---

[13] Forty percent of the French people in 1870 spoke languages such as German, Occitan, Catalan, Basque, and Breton, or one of a vast array of mutually unintelligible local dialects.

Italy the 1880s saw the rise of Francesco Crispi, a former revolutionary who by the time he achieved power had turned into an arbitrary autocrat. Free trade had defined the economic policy of the 1860s, with both Germany and France following England's lead, but by the 1880s both countries reinstalled tariffs in order to protect their new industries.

The underlying dream of the liberals was fading as well. Liberals had hoped that rational human beings, gathered together in pursuit of the general good, would be able, without war and bloodshed, to safeguard property and individual rights while at the same time promoting the general welfare. By the 1880s, such aspirations not only seemed hopelessly naive, but the numerous failures of liberals to live up to their own principles fatally undercut their credibility. The example of Bismarck, bestriding an increasingly powerful Germany, appeared to show that in politics what counted was not good intentions, but sheer power. The viciousness of open political life hinted that men of good will might *not* be able to agree on appropriate courses, or, as some cynics argued, that maybe not all men were of good will. Realpolitik, or the politics of power, both in international affairs and in the fractious electoral and parliamentary life, became the order of the day. The humanistic ideals of liberalism came to be perceived as old-fashioned and ineffective.

Liberalism declined not only because of its own failings and the inevitable generational change as its practitioners aged but also because new forces were on the move as the Century of Power matured. Galloping industrialization greatly increased European might and dramatically changed the material and social environment. Chemicals, electricity, and motorcars were only the most important of these changes. A newly confident middle class and a newly self-conscious working class confronted each other in a changing economic atmosphere. Social Darwinism provided a novel ideology of power, leading to new forms of racism and gender differentiation. The ideal of limiting the state through political means did not disappear, of course, but during the last decades of the nineteenth century both the economic sinews of power and an ideology of power took central stage in the European experience.

Selected Reading

Biographies

Blake, Robert. *Disraeli* (1967). Standard biography of the conservative leader.

Crankshaw, Edward. *Bismarck* (1981). This popular biography is less solid than Gall or Pflanze (listed below), but it tells the story in an engaging and even controversial way.

Gall, Lothar. *Bismarck, the White Revolutionary*, 2 vols. (1986). Major biography emphasizing the preunification years. Gall sees Bismarck as instrumental in radically changing Germany despite his conservatism.

Jenkins, Roy. *Gladstone: A Biography* (1997). Wonderfully readable exposition of Gladstone's career and character by a British politician turned historian.

Mack Smith, Denis. *Cavour* (1985). Standard biography by the most important English-language historian of Italy. One could also consult with profit other biographies by the same author: *Cavour and the Unification of Italy; Victor Emmanuel, Cavour and the Risorgimento; Cavour and Garibaldi, 1860;* and *Mazzini.*

Pflanze, Otto. *Bismarck and the Development of Germany*, 3 vols. (1991). Balanced and judicious, and well researched, this is the best English-language biography of Bismarck now available.

Stern, Fritz. *Gold and Iron: Bismarck, Bleichröder, and the Building of the German Empire* (1977). Detailed history of the relationship between Bismarck and his banker, the interest of which transcends the personal.

Trevelyan, G. M. *Garibaldi and the Thousand* (1909); and *Garibaldi and the Making of Italy* (1911). Despite their age, these books provide some of the most stirring historical accounts ever written. Modern scholarship has called a number of Trevelyan's interpretations into question, however.

National and Regional Histories

Coppa, Frank J. *The Origins of the Italian Wars of Independence* (1992). Excellent textbook discussion of the period from 1848 to 1870, emphasizing military aspects, but not exclusively.

Craig, Gordon A. *The Battle of Königgrätz: Prussia's Victory over Austria, 1866* (1964). Fascinating study including technological and military aspects of the battle that achieved Prussian dominance in Germany.

_____. *Germany, 1866–1945* (1978). Craig is the preeminent interpreter of modern German history in the United States. This one-volume treatment emphasizes political events.

Croce, Benedetto. *A History of Italy, 1871–1915* (1963). The classic liberal interpretation of post-unification Italy. Argues that World War I destroyed a positive and promising system. Dated, but very influential.

Davis, John A. "Remapping Italy's Path to the Twentieth Century," *Journal of Modern History* 66 (1994): 291–320. Scholarly review of Italian revisionist historiography. Valuable especially for those who do not read Italian.

Jelavich, Barbara. *History of the Balkans*, 2 vols. (1983). Well organized and well written, this standard history also contains good maps.

Mack Smith, Denis. *The Making of Italy, 1796–1870* (1968); and *Italy: A Modern History*, 2nd ed.(1969). Influential accounts critical of liberalism's course in Italy, seeing it as a precursor to fascism. Contrasts with Croce's interpretation (listed above).

McCagg, William O. Jr. *A History of Habsburg Jews, 1670–1918* (1989). A complete survey of Jewish life in Habsburg lands, which were second only to the Russian Empire in the size of their Jewish population.

Read, Donald. *England, 1868–1914* (1979). Schematic, and therefore easy to use for reference, history of various aspects of British history.

Riasanovsky, Nicholas V. *A History of Russia*, 5th ed. (1993). The most widely used textbook of Russian history.

Social History

Edwards, Stewart. *The Paris Commune, 1871* (1973). Balanced, illustrated study of the Commune that sees it as patriotic, popular, innovative, and intense. Gives a good account of its repression.

Gleason, Abbott. *Young Russia: The Genesis of Russian Radicalism in the 1860s* (1980). A successful effort to make the Russian populists more accessible to serious students.

Hamerow, Theodore. *The Social Foundations of German Unification*, 2 vols. (1969). Emphasizes industrialization and social change as instrumental in German unification and in the growth of German nationalism.

Marx, Karl. *Civil War in France: The Paris Commune*, 2nd ed. (1888). Portrays the Commune as a proletarian revolution. Flawed, but extremely influential. Should be considered a document rather than a scholarly study.

Venturi, Franco. *Roots of Revolution: A History of the Populist and Socialist Movements in Nineteenth Century Russia* (1960). A positive early assessment of Russian socialism and populism that greatly influenced Western scholarship for a generation.

Zola, Émile, *The Debacle* (1870–1871). This novel about the Paris Commune has overtones interesting for France in the 1930s.

CHAPTER 25

THE ECONOMICS AND IDEOLOGY OF POWER

Gare Saint-Lazare   Fogg Art Museum, Harvard University Art Museums. Bequest from the Collection of Maurice Wertheim, Class of 1906.
Photo: David Matthews.

1848	Marx and Engels publish *The Communist Manifesto*	1869	Groundbreaking for Bon Marché department store	1895	*Confederation Général du Travail* established in France
1857–1859	First worldwide economic crisis	1873	Banking crisis in Austro-Hungarian Empire	1896	Herzl publishes *The Jewish State*
1859	Darwin publishes *On the Origins of Species by Means of Natural Selection*	1874	German Social Democratic party founded	1903, 1907	Pogroms kill hundreds of Russian Jews
1863	First organized group tour of France led by Thomas Cook	1881	First public power station opens in England	1906	Labour Party launched in Britain
1868	Trades Union Congress founded in Britain	1883	First social insurance law passed in Germany		

*I*t is said that artist Claude Monet asked the stationmaster at the Saint-Lazare railway station in Paris to run the steam locomotives in and out of the station many times so he could capture their power in different lighting conditions. He actually made seven paintings of the scene, one of which is reproduced on the preceding page. Monet's fascination with steam and power was typical during the unprecedented economic boom that transformed Europe from the middle of the nineteenth century until the eruption of World War I.

The Industrial Revolution not only caught on, it expanded and proliferated in unexpected and dynamic ways. Germany became the most industrialized country in Europe, and even Russia began a modernization process that made it the world's fifth largest industrial power by 1914. Heavy industries based on coal and steel transformed formerly pastoral regions; railroads penetrated every major European town; and the ironclad steamship came to dominate the seas, both commercially and militarily. The invention of the rifled bore and of smokeless powder made huge new artillery pieces and deadly machine guns feasible. Entirely new industries sprang up and flourished: chemistry, electricity, petroleum, and, by the end of the period, motorized vehicles, both on land and in the air. Millions of European peasants moved to cities—or to the United States—to take advantage of the new employment opportunities.

Such massive new developments unsettled European society. In general, the conservative landowning aristocracy managed to maintain its hold on power until World War I. But underneath the aristocracy, the middle class grew in size and influence, and a newly self-conscious working class came into being. Leisure time, previously the exclusive possession of the aristocracy, penetrated to both the middle class and the working class, creating a tourist industry and professional sports teams. Attitudes toward women and the family changed, as did work identities. National education systems improved literacy rates dramat-ically, and advances in paper-making and printing technologies put newspapers into the hands of millions of newly aware citizens.

Under these conditions, socialism emerged as a new political force. Inspired especially by the writings of Karl Marx, socialist critiques of disruption, unfairness, and imbalance found a broad response among the working classes of Europe. By World War I, socialist parties had become an integral part of European politics.

The strength that economic growth placed in each nation's hands backed up the new power politics discussed in the preceding chapter. At the same time, nationalists and racists seeking theoretical justifications of the untrammeled use of power found what they were looking for in the scientific work of Charles Darwin. They took Darwin's idea of evolution and turned it into an argument defending might over right, a survival of the fittest nations and races. **Social Darwinism** even claimed to justify women's subordinate place in society. If Realpolitik provided the conventional political wisdom of the Century of Power, economic growth provided its muscle and Social Darwinism its ideology.

THE INDUSTRIAL REVOLUTION MATURES

It is difficult to present the sweep of European economic growth during the period from 1850 to 1914 convincingly, because the story tends to bog down in statistics. After reading that British steel production increased from 334,000 metric tons in 1871 to 6,476,000 metric tons in 1910, that German production of sulfuric acid rose from 43,000 metric tons in 1870 to 1,381,000 metric tons in 1910, and that the capacity of Russian steam engines rose from 70,000 horsepower in 1850 to 3,100,000 horsepower in 1891, the mind starts to turn off, despite the extraordinary changes that those figures imply. The data

* Information for Austria-Hungary is for the entire empire. Information for Austria alone is for half the empire.

FIGURE 25-1
EUROPEAN ECONOMIC GROWTH, 1870–1910

Source: B. R. Mitchell, International Historical Statistics. Europe, 1750–1993, 4th ed. (New York: Stockton Press, 1998), pp. 3–8, 74–76, 466–467, 572–580, 673–677, 873–879, 895–896, 906–913.

are best presented in figures and graphs, as we have done in Figure 25-1.

Many things can be learned from Figure 25-1. For example, we can clearly see that population growth continued to play a significant role in economic expansion, as it had in earlier stages of the Industrial Revolution. The figures are even more remarkable when we take into account that millions of Europeans emigrated across the Atlantic in this period. The explosion in production of steel and sulfuric acid demonstrates Germany's sudden arrival as an industrial power. Far behind the United Kingdom in 1870 in both areas, Germany had leaped ahead of all its European competitors by 1910. Germany's leadership in education suggests one possible reason for this success. In the case of Russia, the figures show that country more industrialized than some have supposed when the Bolshevik revolution hit in 1917. Russia's leadership in length of railroad lines (of course, Russia is a huge country) implies that its heavy industry had well advanced by 1910. We can also detect Italy's failure to keep up, as evidenced by its low production levels and by Rome's inability to match the massive size of the other European capitals.

The economic surge during the second half of the nineteenth century that lies behind these figures breaks down into three broad periods. From 1850 to 1873 Europe experienced rapid growth in production and in world trade. Then, in 1873, a banking crisis in Vienna set off a deflationary period that lasted until the mid-1890s. From that point until World War I, economic growth revived.

Within each of these three periods, moments occurred that contradicted the era's generally expansionist character. For example, during the initial period of growth, the first worldwide financial crisis struck. In August 1857, a run on railroad securities in New York provoked a suspension of payments by banks in London and then in Hamburg. By November a panic gripped the Paris stock exchange. Although the crisis quickly passed and growth resumed, the rapid spread of the disaster revealed how interdependent the developing economies were becoming.

During the second period, the accumulated efficiencies of successful industrialization over the course of the century drove down the price of goods and services. This drop in prices put pressure on manufacturers but benefited workers, whose real wages rose. Despite the general deflationary character of the years between 1873 and 1895, European economies continued to grow, although at a slower rate than before. In some places, growth actually accelerated (see Map 25-1). In the Austro-Hungarian Empire, for example, the banking collapse in 1873 encouraged Austrian investors to move from risky industrial ventures into safe Hungarian state bonds, which the Hungarians used to foster processing industries related to agriculture. By the end of the century, Budapest had become second only to Milwaukee as a world center for flour milling.

MAP 25-1

EUROPEAN INDUSTRY AND COALFIELDS IN 1875

By 1875, heavy industry (especially clothmaking and metallurgy) was well established in Britain and much of western Europe, and it was developing in parts of Spain, Italy, Austria-Hungary, and Russia. Proximity to coal fields was important in inciting industry. But huge areas remained untouched by industry.

Germany's First Economic Miracle

The fastest growing European economy between 1850 and 1914 was Germany's. The initial spurt took place in the smelting industry, when the extent of the coal and iron resources of the Ruhr became apparent in the 1850s. Between 1851 and 1871, for example, the city of Dortmund increased its production of pig iron by thirty-five times, producing twice as much in 1871 as all of Germany had produced in 1850. Technological improvements made it possible to manufacture better and cheaper steel. In the 1850s English inventor Henry Bessemer discovered a fast way to refine pig iron by blowing air through molten metal, thus purifying it of its carbon content. Other inventions for saving fuel (the Siemens-Martin regenerative principle) and for removing impurities (the Thomas-Gilchrest method of phosphorous reduction) drove the price of steel down 80 to 90 percent by the mid-1890s, much in the way that innovation in the electronics industry drove down computer prices in the 1990s.

The British may have created many of these technological innovations, but it was the Germans who made the most of them. Paradoxically, they could do so in part because of their late start. British entrepreneurs, well established as the industrial leaders of Europe by 1851, became set in their ways, confident of their success, and resistant to change. The Germans, on the other hand, working from a modest base, introduced the most modern techniques available. They built large units of production, vertically integrated them (that is, included all aspects of creating a product, from raw material to sales, in one organization), and even introduced early forms of automation. By 1900 the German steel industry ranked as the most efficient in Europe, and Britain had lost its competitive edge.

Germany's most extraordinary industrial achievements, however, were not in the traditional fields of textiles and steel—although in 1900 its textile industry was the largest in Europe—but in organic chemistry and electricity. It is here that German superiority in education came into play: Unlike textile mills or steel production, where early technological changes often were introduced by tinkerers and inspired amateurs, the new fields of chemistry and electricity required trained scientists and engineers. In industrial chemistry, for instance, the basic discoveries had occurred primarily in England, where the first chemical dye—the color mauve—was synthesized in 1856. But in the 1860s, innovation shifted to Germany. German progress in creating artificial dyes led to the very colorful clothing we wear today, vastly more varied than could be imagined in 1850. Systematic research in organic chemistry at university and industrial centers opened other new worlds of chemically derived products. Nitroglycerin, paint lacquer, photographic film, artificial fabrics, cellophane, and plastics were only a few of them. By 1900 the German chemical industry controlled 90 percent of the European market in these previously nonexistent products.

Electricity constituted the third great breakthrough in Europe's centuries-long Energy Revolution. Europeans had used the chemical energy of gunpowder to conquer the world's sea-lanes in the sixteenth century, and in the

German Industrial Might
This photograph from about 1900 of German workers producing huge dynamos suggests how advanced the German electrical industry was by this time.
Heliogravure; Georg Buxentstein & Co. um 1900/Bildarchiv Preussischer Kulturbesitz (bpk), Berlin.

eighteenth century the British had tapped the potential energy of coal with the steam engine. Electricity has two enormous advantages over these methods of creating energy: It can be delivered anywhere, and it is flexible. Electricity can be used in small devices, such as sewing machines, or in huge manufacturing processes, like steel rolling mills. It can power massive public services like a subway or a trolley line, or it can light a single bulb in a home kitchen. Electricity eventually brought the power of the Energy Revolution into every business and household in the developed world.

Commercial production of electrical devices took off with the invention of the telegraph in the 1840s. By the 1860s, the German firm of Siemens already mass-produced cables and had invented the dynamo, which turns mechanical energy into electrical energy. In the United States, Thomas Edison's invention of the lightbulb in 1879 set off another wave of commercial development. Until then, electrical power had seemed useful only in individual factories that could generate their own power. But with Edison's invention, an explosion of demand for electrical lighting called forth rapid developments in central power stations and transmission techniques. The first public power station began operation in 1881 in England, and the first transmission of high-voltage power over a long distance took place in Switzerland in 1891. But once again, it was the Germans who pushed the technology to its furthest commercial possibilities, crisscrossing the Rhine Valley with production facilities and transmission lines. Germany's largest producer of electricity increased its output from 2.7 million kilowatt hours in 1900 to 388 million just fifteen years later. In 1913 the Siemens firm employed more than eighty thousand persons, and Germany produced more electricity than France and the United Kingdom combined. Cities throughout Europe began to sparkle with thousands of lights, and the urban experience of night changed forever.

Why Germany?

What explains Germany's rise to economic leadership in Europe during the second half of the nineteenth century? Before turning to that issue, a prior question needs answering: What factors favored European industrialization in general? The answer has several parts. First, Europe consisted of relatively stable political units, several of which were large enough to serve as effective market areas in the early stages of capitalism. Second, the British had already achieved a high level of production and a vigorous international trade. These first two factors acted as spurs to British competitors and as general models for development. European emulators did not copy the British example directly—each country evolved its own unique economic style—but the British model stimulated their efforts.

A third factor favoring European industrialization was that, unlike other parts of the world when they later began industrializing, Europe did not lack investment capital. New banking methods systematically tapped the resources of both British industrial success and the high level of traditional prosperity in countries like France, Belgium, the Netherlands, and Austria. Fourth, because of the efforts of both the Catholic and Protestant churches to educate their flocks, Europe boasted a high rate of literacy. Its labor pool could meet the relatively sophisticated demands of the new industries. Fifth, the destruction of the guilds by the mid-nineteenth century, along with the elimination of serfdom in central and eastern Europe, enhanced the mobility of labor. Peasants and artisans were freer than ever to take advantage of new employment possibilities.

Sixth, Europeans enjoyed stable currencies throughout the developmental period. Starting from the early 1870s, the major European currencies (and the U.S. dollar) were on the gold standard. Holders of paper money could exchange it for gold coins whenever they wished. The discovery of gold in California and Australia in 1848 and 1850, and in South Africa and Alaska after 1880, roughly tripled the world supply of this precious metal. Thus the European money supply kept pace with economic development, preventing inflation and facilitating growth. In contrast to the sixteenth century, when Spain frittered away its horde of New World silver (see Chapter 14), in the second half of the nineteenth century newfound gold went into productive investment.

Finally, in every country in Europe the state entered increasingly into economic affairs. The state had always played an important role in the development of capitalism. For an economy to grow, the legal system must enforce commercial contracts and other property rights, innovation needs to be rewarded through patent laws, the currency and the banking system should be stable, and taxation cannot eat up so much profit as to discourage investment.

Despite the dominance of the laissez-faire ideology of classical economics, every European state actively interfered in economic activity in the second half of the nineteenth century. Instead of relying on the so-called invisible hand of supply and demand to regulate the economy, continental governments turned more and more to "the visible hand," as one historian calls it. Most European public services were state owned, so that the enormous expansion of government-subsidized highways, railroads, telegraph lines, and eventually telephone systems lifted the whole economy. So did the vast increase in education, which required the training and hiring of tens of thousands of teachers, and improvements in social services, which demanded specialized bureaucracies to administer them.

Each state looked after its country's economy in its own way. In the 1880s France invested heavily in a network of secondary roads in an effort to draw rural regions into the web of market mechanisms. That same decade, the Italian government subsidized the young Italian steel industry and gave local bidders priority over foreign ones in railroad contracts. After the crash of 1873, the Austrians turned away from market principles and instead supported monopolies (called cartels). The most dramatic example of government intervention took place in Russia, where in the 1890s a vigorous minister of finance revamped Russian finances, put the country on the gold standard, attracted foreign investment, and stimulated heavy industry by building the Trans-Siberian railroad.

As liberalism declined and nationalism intensified, the abandonment of free trade provided the most obvious example of government's increased willingness to tinker with economic relations. During the 1880s, almost every continental country introduced protective tariffs. Bitter political struggles attended these changes. Often the tariffs sought primarily to placate powerful agricultural interests threatened by the huge influx of cheap North American grains in the 1870s. But the abandonment of free trade—along with Bismarck's social programs (discussed in a moment)—constituted a milestone of activist capitalism. Today, after two world wars during which governments strained every economic sinew for victory, the state's responsibility for furthering economic growth is a political commonplace.

But why did Germany race ahead of other countries, when these developments characterized most of Europe in similar fashion? Several possibilities exist. The extent and location of Germany's coal and iron ore deposits were ideal for developing a steel industry, for example, and the addition of Alsace in 1871 brought some of France's most advanced industries to the Reich. The German banking system was one of the most sophisticated in Europe, so that lack of capital never throttled development. Moreover, the Germans encouraged the creation of cartels, cooperative agreements among the largest enterprises in steel and chemicals that spread research costs and other expenses, thus allowing them to dominate world markets. In the United States under the Sherman Antitrust Act of 1890, cartels would have been illegal as monopolies, but for the Germans they protected markets and made economies of scale possible.

The superiority of German higher education also explains the explosion of its productivity. In both organic chemistry and electricity, the Germans forged ahead because of outstanding scientific and engineering abilities. In Britain, elites still imbued with the ethic of the gentlemanly amateur frowned on engineering as a career. The best universities there concentrated on training young men in religion and the classics rather than the sciences. In Germany (and in Italy), no such bias existed. As early as 1871, the University of Munich had fifty graduate students studying organic chemistry, whereas the entire United Kingdom could not boast a single university chair in that field.

Each European country had unique political and social characteristics that either fostered or hindered economic health. In Germany, the investment in education coupled with many other factors to produce sustained growth. Some small countries also enjoyed circumstances congenial to economic vitality; Belgium, Denmark, Switzerland, and the Netherlands all prospered in the second half of the nineteenth century. But in other countries, historical factors

Chemistry for the Common Man The Bayer Company of Germany was the largest company in the world in 1900. It advertised aspirin all over the globe. Heroin was also synthesized by Bayer chemists and marketed as a cough medicine (only later was it recognized as a dangerous narcotic). Ads like this one appeared in many prewar American newspapers. After the United States entered World War I, Bayer's U.S. assets were seized as enemy property, and ownership was transferred to an American firm. *The Granger Collection, New York.*

slowed the rate of growth. Laissez-faire traditions, for example, inhibited British liberals like Gladstone from intervening adequately to help business. Britain's pattern of small factories in which workers learned trades by practical experience, as well as an upper-class ethic of genteel living that did not esteem science and engineering, also limited that nation's ability to innovate. France's defeat in the Franco-Prussian war, along with Bismarck's successful efforts to isolate it diplomatically in the 1870s and 1880s, slowed the French growth rate. Backwardness in agriculture and a paternalistic approach among its entrepreneurs had the same effect. Italy experienced "modernization without growth." The market system penetrated Italy and forced its landlords and merchants to change their methods of doing business, but growth did not result until the 1890s, and then only in the north. Southern Italy, like Asturias, Slovakia, Bavaria, and many other regions of Europe, stayed undeveloped.

Some countries grew faster than others, and some got a late start. Industries clustered in favorable areas, leaving some regions behind, and attitudes changed slowly. But these variations do not obscure the main trend: From 1850 to 1914, the national economies of Europe grew and innovated at historically unprecedented rates.

THE SOCIAL IMPACTS OF ECONOMIC CHANGE

The economic explosion of the second half of the nineteenth century triggered major social change. For example, the growing prestige and power of industry led Europeans to redefine themselves. In medieval Europe, people had sized each other up on the basis of information about family, village, estate, or clan identification. Today we care less about these attributes. Typically we ask a new acquaintance, "What do you do?" by which we really mean, "What is your job?" From the answer to this simple question we get a rough idea of education, status, wealth, suitability for marriage, and many other things. In industrial societies a fundamental part of our self-assessment, as well as our assessment of others, comes from our job.

The multiplying links among national, European, and world economies had another consequence: the rise of professions. In medieval Europe events had been unpredictable but richly explicable. Peasants did not know why they experienced lean years, but in their own community they could find many possible clues. Proverbs, the local priest, witchcraft, horoscopes, and fate provided "explanations." The more interconnected economies became, however, the more impact remote events had on local affairs. Sicilian peasants, for example, might discover that their fruit was no longer exportable because of a stock market crash in New York.

To meet the need for explaining such faraway influences, specialists emerged who claimed to provide answers, usually on the basis of formal education or training. The trend toward analysis authenticated by training happened in all fields, not just in economics. By the end of the nineteenth century, historians, physicians, lawyers, and others began to band together in associations to certify their expertise and to regulate admission to their ranks. They became the professionals who provide the complex, secular—and allegedly reliable, scientific, and proven—explanations that we take for granted today.

Economic development also led to monetization. Tasks previously done as part of a family or community obligation became jobs undertaken for money. Road repair provides a good example. In early modern Europe, the local peasantry had repaired roads as part of their feudal obligations. Then, when engineers discovered how to make durable, all-weather roads by systematically laying stones—as did John Loudon McAdam early in the nineteenth century—the job became too specialized for local labor. The community or the state had to hire engineers to do it. Another example is urban trash removal. In the seventeenth century, urban dwellers simply threw their garbage, including human wastes, into the street. By the nineteenth century, cities built sewer systems and hired garbage collectors. These and many other examples suggest that one of capitalism's enduring tendencies is to measure more and more aspects of life in monetary terms.

The Rise of the Middle Class

Few phrases have claimed such widespread application in historical explanations as "the rise of the middle class." This lighter-than-air phenomenon has allegedly occurred at many points in the European past. But it was not until the nineteenth century that classes in the contemporary sense solidified. The industrialization process created two major groups that had not existed in their modern form under the old regime: the middle class and the working class. Poor and rich were ancient concepts, as were aristocrat and peasant. But the idea of giving a name to a class of people based primarily on where they stood in relation to industrialization was new.

The term *middle class* is easy to use, but hard to define precisely. In North America, sociologists tell us that the overwhelming majority of people consider themselves part of the middle class; a designation that includes almost everyone has to be used with caution. The term came into English usage in the nineteenth century, at the same time that analogous terms achieved their modern meaning in other European languages (*bourgeoisie* in French; *Bürgertum*, among others, in German; *ceti medi* in Italian). As the German and French terms suggest (*bourg* or *burg* meant "city"), the phrase originally identified privileged city dwellers who did not belong to the landed nobility. In the nineteenth century, the term expanded to mean citizens

Middle-Class Respectability
The idealized middle-class setting: children happily playing and learning under mother's watchful eye; father at home, but involved in important matters; pets, flowers, classical busts, and all the comforts of home.
Corbis/Bettmann.

with sufficient incomes to live in an independent, or "respectable," manner.

For the middle class, to be respectable meant to demonstrate one's freedom from physical work. Thus if schoolteachers and clerks in retail stores wore the right clothing, adopted certain habits of cleanliness, displayed "good" manners, and aspired to self-improvement, they could present themselves as middle class even if their incomes fell below that of skilled workers. At these lower strata of the middle class, lack of money often made it difficult to sustain respectability. In England the capacity to hire at least one servant, which required an income of about £200 a year, was perceived as a minimum requirement for respectable living in the second half of the nineteenth century, but junior clerks and schoolteachers earned only about £100 a year. In Italy, with its oversupply of trained lawyers, an underemployed attorney could find himself spending most of his income maintaining a formal guest room and decent clothing for public display. In this way, he retained his middle-class standing while living in cramped and disheveled back rooms. Similar conditions faced the swelling ranks of the lower bureaucracy throughout southern and eastern Europe.

The upper end of the spectrum, the *haute bourgeoisie* (as they were called in France), consisted of the wealthiest nonnoble landowners, bankers, and investors whose lives differed very little from the aristocrats whom they emulated. This was the middle class that appears in the nineteenth-century novel, or, in a more contemporary medium, in

English domestic dramas shown on public television. Their lives revolved around the country home, to which they repaired for house parties and weekends; the London social season in the spring and early summer; clubs where men met for dinner and port; and hunting parties, at which participants sometimes slaughtered thousands of birds in a single day.

In between these wealthiest citizens and the petty clerks came the ordinary middle class—doctors, lawyers, clergy, midlevel church and government officials, landlords, investors, merchants, and small factory owners. They measured their status by how many servants they had, what sort of horse and carriage they maintained, and the rectitude of their public behavior.

The middle class of the late nineteenth century made up a small part of the population. A typical estimate for France and England placed it somewhere between 20 and 25 percent of the populace, whereas in Italy the figure might have been as low as 10 percent. Of these, only a handful of the richest had any real hope of influencing politics. By World War I, upper-middle-class politicians had achieved overt power only in England, France, and Italy, and even there traditional values retained their grip. Throughout Europe kings co-opted the wealthy bourgeoisie into the ranks of the traditional aristocracy by giving them titles, while the well-to-do bought country estates and adopted aristocratic habits.

Despite the upper bourgeoisie's natural aspiration to the aristocratic life, middle-class values fundamentally

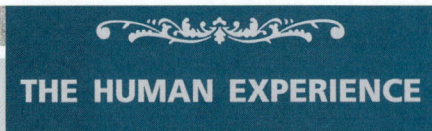

THE HUMAN EXPERIENCE

Aristide Boucicaut, Founder of the Bon Marché Department Store

The vast new quantities of products created by the expanding European economy in the second half of the nineteenth century allowed innovators to introduce a new kind of merchandising. In the 1850s, dry-goods stores in Paris began to expand by introducing new departments that offered furs, umbrellas, and similar items that went far beyond traditional clothing and fabrics. In 1852 when Aristide Boucicaut became involved with one of these stores, the Bon Marché, the left-bank firm consisted of four departments, employed twelve persons, and did about 450,000 francs of business a year, a sizable trade.

Boucicaut was forty-two at the time. The son of a hatter from Normandy, he had left home at the age of eighteen to become an itinerant peddler. Apparently successful at that trade, he settled in Paris in 1835 and married. Starting as a sales clerk in a prominent Paris shop, he quickly moved up to department head. By 1852 he managed to acquire 50,000 francs, with which he and a partner purchased Bon Marché. In 1863 Boucicaut bought out his partner, and in 1869 he laid the cornerstone for the enormous new building that made Bon Marché the most famous department store in France. By the time he died in 1877, Boucicaut headed the largest retail enterprise in the world with 1,788 employees and a sales volume of 73 million francs a year.

Very little is known about the personal details of Boucicaut's life, but a good deal is known about his store. Bon Marché's success rested on low prices and high turnover, as well as a new style of sales organization. Boucicaut and his successors invented an entire ethic for his employees. The firm rarely hired people older than thirty, although it required its new employees to have sales experience. Once employed, they had to be perfectly well behaved, courteous, accurate, and honest. If they slipped, their department head had the authority to fire them on the spot. In order to increase turnover and to keep track of the vast number of small purchases characteristic of a retail store, Boucicaut created a complex and rigid set of procedures that worked with almost military discipline. To stimulate sales, Bon Marché introduced mail orders, which led to the production of catalogues; vigorously advertised its merchandise throughout France and abroad; and even built its own workshops to produce a large portion of the goods that it sold.

This kind of rationalization of retail sales was an innovation, but Boucicaut and his wife were staunch bourgeois owners who maintained a paternalistic concern for the health, character, and even amusements of their employees. They formed a music group to play at company functions, introduced a more or less compulsory company picnic, and provided heavily supervised housing on the top floor of the store. The combination of paternalistic concern—a powerful tradition in French commerce—and modern merchandising methods made Bon Marché one of the most successful businesses of its day. ❖

ESCALIER CENTRAL : VUE INTÉRIEURE

Bon Marché The number and variety of goods offered in this massive store were unprecedented in Europe. Although large department stores also emerged in the United States at the time, it was not until the late twentieth century that shopping malls and superstores began to bankrupt small shop owners. *Mary Evans Picture Library.*

contradicted those of the traditional classes. The middle-class ethic held that an individual's place in society rested on merit alone, not on birth. Only ambition and effort should limit success. Individualism, hard work, and freedom of choice also ranked high. If one worked hard, planned ahead, and acted honestly and prudently, one would succeed in life and deserve whatever benefits society might provide. The "rags-to-riches" novels written by the American writer Horatio Alger—wildly popular in the nineteenth century—reflected this belief. In each of Alger's tales, a poor boy would succeed in becoming a wealthy business magnate by dint of his own abilities and hard work. In truth, not many made the leap from poverty to wealth, but just enough did to make the dream plausible.

For middle-class women, life was centered in the home and the family. Industrialization created this emphasis. For many centuries, most work took place in the home, either on the farm or in the artisanal shop. But with the advent of factories, the home and the place of work separated. Middle-class men left the home to work, leaving their wives to run the household. There the tasks of domesticity were suffused with the woman's reproductive role. She became the bearer of children, the keeper of the family, and the creator of a secure, comfortable haven of controlled, chaste regularity.

In England, the paragon of the style of chaste domesticity was, paradoxically, Queen Victoria, who gave her name to the age. Victoria had ascended the throne in 1837 at the age of eighteen and ruled until her death in 1901. She married for love—unlike most monarchs of the time—and when her husband Albert died in 1861 she lived in dignified widowhood for the rest of her days. Even though she found pregnancy depressing and disliked babies, Victoria bore nine children and at her death left thirty-seven grandchildren. Intense despite her small size—she was barely 5 feet tall—and sometimes hot tempered, Victoria nevertheless provided a model of restrained living on which genteel English bourgeois families based their notions of respectability. Her opinions were so predictably middle-class that after her death a close adviser remarked that "when I knew what the Queen thought, I knew pretty certainly what views her subjects would take."

In central Europe, the middle-class ideal became known early in the nineteenth century as the *Biedermeier* style. This term referred not only to a specific type of furniture—more rounded, more substantial, and more comfortable than eighteenth-century furnishings, and yet of pleasing line—but to the entire household into which the furniture was placed. The Biedermeier home was a refuge of comfort and commodious family living, solid but not ostentatious. The living room, the focus of family life, typified the middle class. Here one found comfortable chairs and tables arranged for family sociability, perhaps some children's toys piled in the corner, ancestors' portraits on the walls, and, at the right time of year, a Christmas tree twinkling by the hearth. Indeed, the nineteenth-century middle

The Middle-Class Queen   Decoration of a Christmas tree became popular in middle-class families in the nineteenth century in part because that paragon of middle-class virtue, Queen Victoria, celebrated in that way. This engraving shows her family in front of the tree.   *Corbis/Bettmann.*

class invented elaborate family Christmas celebrations as a way to solidify and amplify the importance of the family and the home.

The centrality of the home in the middle-class ethic implied a particular role for women. It was their task to create a family refuge where the weary male could find respite from the world of commerce. "When it storms in the world outside," said one Austrian writer, "when one despairs of strength and courage, what more remains to the best of men than confident association with his household happiness, intimate contact with his noble wife, with her kindness and quiet goodness."

Creating this retreat was not easy. In an age totally lacking in labor-saving devices—in which water often had to be hauled by hand, sanitation facilities were primitive, and fabrics were heavy—merely keeping the house and its inhabitants clean required enormous effort. Not surprisingly, cleanliness became an important middle-class virtue, for being clean signified that one had the requisite resources and time for it. Indeed, one of the motivating forces behind the remarkable drive in the second half of the nineteenth century to provide clean water, build urban sanitation systems, and erect better housing for the poor was not only the idea that these projects would improve public health, but also the middle-class notion that cleanliness in itself was a positive value. In the home, the comforts of middle-class domesticity depended heavily on the poorly paid labor of female domestics, chambermaids, seamstresses, hat-makers, and so forth, all of them in plentiful supply as the countryside poured its surplus population into the urban world. Working-class women were rarely in a position to live according to bourgeois notions of domestic propriety. In middle-class residences, however, it was the wife who was responsible for organizing her sometimes formidable workforce and turning the house into a home.

The ideal of a separate sphere of domesticity dominated middle-class womanhood in the nineteenth century. Businessmen of the time considered women ill-suited for the hurly-burly of commerce or for employment of any kind. Female responsibilities centered on reproduction—which included not only bearing children but seeing to their education—and on the uplifting moral, cultural, and religious domains. The gender separation between the male commercial sphere and the female family sphere was so pronounced that in some middle-class families, fathers rarely even spoke to their children.

Emphasizing the domestic space as the domain of women and the family, middle-class men went on to create new forms of public space for the edification of the public at large: parks, museums, and libraries. As cities expanded, local governments under the control of industrialists began to set aside areas as parks to retain some of the benefits of nature in the crowded urban environment. Philanthropists, both individual and corporate, created parks as well, often in return for having them named after themselves or a relative. Arboretums, botanical gardens, and zoological gardens provided pleasurable enclaves in these parks where the public could learn about exotic plants and animals.

Galleries for the pleasure of the knowledgeable and rich were common enough in the eighteenth century, but public museums were a nineteenth-century phenomenon. The first public museums drew heavily on the great royal and aristocratic collections. In 1793 the revolutionary Convention had opened the Louvre, the king's palace in Paris, as a public museum. The postrevolutionary French state so believed in the educational and moral function of art that it began to purchase and distribute new paintings to provincial museums. Whereas in the first half of the nineteenth century only one building was constructed in Europe specifically to house an art collection, the Alte Pinakothek in Munich, after 1850 the prosperous bourgeoisie in city after city constructed special buildings just for this purpose. A similar philanthropic venture was the public library, which found a wide response among an increasingly literate public.

In an age of declining working-class church attendance, many middle-class reformers saw these institutions as filling a gap in the public's ethical, moral, and aesthetic education. If each person was to succeed primarily on the basis of work and talent, fairness dictated that everyone should start from a reasonably equal point, which education would provide. Public education therefore had an important place in the middle-class political agenda, and schoolteaching became one of the earliest occupations to which women of this social stratum could aspire.

Of course, middle-class philanthropy was not always motivated solely by the desire to accomplish good works and educate the public. Equally important was the hope of gaining status by means of a conspicuous display of wealth, of gaining entry to the upper reaches of society, and of appearing cultivated and educated after a rough-and-tumble business career.

The belief in education and in the value of self-help gave the middle-class ethic an improving tone and led to a new way of forming and expressing public opinion. Voluntary associations proliferated in industrializing Europe. Some independent societies devoted their efforts to amusements, such as shooting clubs; or to culture, such as musical societies; or to religion, such as missionary societies. Others had sporting, educational, or political aims. But the most characteristic institutions of middle-class virtue were the reforming societies: the temperance unions, the societies for hospital construction, the society for the prevention to cruelty to animals, and even one association that encouraged the poor to cultivate potatoes. These associations became the social counterpart to the market economy. If competition among those pursuing economic self-interest acted as the engine of the laissez-faire economy, why should not the free competition of ideas pursued by persons organized in associations become the engine of civil society? In fact, voluntary organizations *were* middle-class civil society. They comprised a new public, not directly political, through which the middle class expressed its opinions and shaped the public mind.

Museums and parks became a popular bourgeois cultural institution in the late nineteenth century also because of an increase in leisure time. Aristocrats never concerned themselves with leisure, for they did no "work." But as the middle class began to amass wealth, its members found new ways to take advantage of the spare time that their affluence afforded them. Tourism attracted them, for example. The railroad made travel cheap and quick, gold coins were accepted everywhere, and border formalities were minimal. Already in 1841, Thomas Cook had advertised his first excursion train. After establishing a thriving travel and vacation business in England, Cook undertook his first group tour of France in 1863. Soon he began organizing trips to Switzerland, and in 1871 he even put together visits to Paris so that vacationers could view the public buildings burned out during the struggle over the Paris Commune and shudder at the "collapse of French civilization." Cook negotiated coupon deals with European railroads, snapped up hotels, and brought in his own food. He also learned that earnest middle-class tourists wanted not simply new sights but uplifting ones as well. Cook coupled historical tours and museum visits with visits to the mountains or the seashore to widen the horizons of those able to afford his services. Guide books, such as the Baedeker series, offered assistance to tourists and made fortunes for their publishers.

Perhaps the most visible expression of middle-class culture was its clothing. In the old regime, aristocratic men had dressed for display. They wore makeup, perfumes, lace, lavish colors, powdered wigs, and stockings to show off their legs. In an implicit criticism of such ostentation, middle-class men's styles evolved toward trousers (shapeless pants), a white shirt with a stiff collar and dark tie, and a dark jacket, the ancestors of today's business suit.

Women's clothing took a different turn. Bourgeois prudery prevented the open display of breasts common in the late eighteenth-century upper classes, but women's clothing nevertheless developed in a way that emphasized female reproductive and nourishing functions. By mid-century, the cumbersome crinoline hoop replaced the many-layered underskirts, and by the 1870s the hoop gave way to the bustle. Well-dressed middle-class women squeezed themselves into corsets that constricted their waists to as little as 18 inches, sometimes with serious damage to their health. The different pathways of male and female fashion clearly suggested the sharp differentiation that the nineteenth-century middle class made in gender roles. Moreover, they so clearly distinguished this class from its aristocratic predecessors that, in self-defense, the aristocrats themselves began to adopt middle-class fashions.

Karl Marx and Class

Categorizing people by class was a new form of social assessment characteristic of industrialized society. One of the first persons to use the idea systematically was Karl Marx. Marx assigned specific roles in history to the middle class, which he usually called the bourgeoisie, and to the working class, which he named the **proletariat.** Because his ideas were extremely influential, we now take a brief excursion into the views of this great thinker and into the development of socialist politics. We will then discuss the emergence of the working class.

Marx was born in 1818, the son of a lawyer. Radicalized while studying philosophy in Berlin, he earned a Ph.D., a degree actually granted by the university in Jena, and he began editing a German periodical. When the authorities found the journal too subversive, Marx fled to Paris, where he began a lifelong collaboration with Friedrich Engels, the son of a wealthy manufacturing family. During the 1840s, Marx wrote a number of essays and studies, many of which did not become known until the twentieth century, on subjects such as alienation and civil society. Early in 1848, he and Engels published *The Communist Manifesto*, which outlined a program of revolutionary action on behalf of the working class. The *Manifesto* ended with the famous call to action: "Workers of the world, unite! You have nothing to lose but your chains."[1]

---

[1] A literal translation of Marx's words is: "The proletarians have nothing to lose but their chains. They have a world to win. WORKING MEN OF ALL COUNTRIES, UNITE!"

En Route to Upper-Class Adulthood In England, even today, elite private schools were called public schools and enforced elaborate and expensive dress codes. For example, in these schools, knickers were appropriate for upper-class boys, but only when accompanied by a proper jacket. *The Granger Collection, New York.*

THE HISTORICAL EVIDENCE

The Philosophy of Karl Marx

1859

The Communist Manifesto of 1848 is not the most succinct outline of Karl Marx's philosophy. The best brief picture is the very short piece titled "Preface to A Contribution to the Critique of Political Economy." This selection is an excerpt from that preface.

In the social production of their life, men enter into definite relations that are indispensable and independent of their will, relations of production which correspond to a definite stage of development of their material productive forces. The sum total of these relations of production constitutes the economic structure of society, the real foundation on which rises a legal and political superstructure and to which correspond definite forms of social consciousness. It is not the consciousness of men that determines their being, but, on the contrary, their social being that determines their consciousness. At a certain stage of their development, the material productive forces in society come in conflict with the existing relations of production, or—what is but a legal expression for the same thing—with the property relations within which they have been at work hitherto. From forms of development of the productive forces these relations turn into their fetters. Then begins an epoch of social revolution. In considering such transformations a distinction should always be made between the material transformation of the economic conditions of production, which can be determined with the precision of natural science, and the legal, political, religious, aesthetic or philosophic—in short, ideological forms in which men become conscious of this conflict and fight it out. Just as our opinion of an individual is not based on what he thinks of himself, so we can not judge of such a period of transformation by its own consciousness; on the contrary, this consciousness must be explained rather from the contradictions of material life. No social order ever perishes before all the productive forces for which there is room in it have developed; and new, higher relations of production never appear before the material conditions of their existence have matured in the womb of the old society itself. Therefore mankind always sets itself only such tasks as it can solve; since, looking at the matter more closely, it will always be found that the task itself arises only when the material conditions for its solution already exist or are at least in the process of formation.

Source: Translation and edition published by *Foreign Languages Publishing House* in the Soviet Union (Moscow).

Marx believed that revolution was imminent, due to the pressure on workers created by industrialization. When the revolutions of 1848 failed, he went into exile in England, where he remained until his death in 1883. Marx lived a bohemian but happily married life in London, spending most of the rest of his days writing *Das Kapital,* his famous critique of capitalism.

Three influences shaped Marx's work: **utopian** socialism, liberal economics, and German philosophy. In utopian socialism, he found support for his desire for change, but not the clear thinking that he demanded. In liberal economics, he found the scientific discipline with which he could buttress his analysis of capitalism. But it was in German philosophy that Marx discovered the key to his thought. As a Ph.D. candidate in Berlin in the 1830s, Marx, like many German students of his day, fell under the influence of Georg Wilhelm Friedrich Hegel (1770–1831), the master German philosopher of the era.

Hegel believed that thought is differentiation. In other words, it is impossible to think about something without knowing that it is not something else. A cat is not a dog; a dog is not a mouse; A is not B. If we have an idea in our minds, such as the letter A, then the very existence of that idea means there must be things that are not A. Otherwise we could not even think A. In this way, Hegel asserted, every idea is self-contradictory; each notion carries within itself its own contradiction. We gain knowledge, Hegel argued, by uncovering all the negations inherent in an idea until we comprehend the whole idea in its contradictory entirety. Having done that, however, we then must subject the new, more complete notion to the same process, for it too contains its own negations. As this process continues, reality is revealed to us in its full complexity. Hegel's method is called the dialectic, a technique in logic that originated in classical Greece.

In one sense, Hegel's dialectic was radical and hopeful. It suggested that humanity was always transcending the limitations of earlier generations. In another sense, however, his ideas were quite conservative. If we are always transcending our past, then what we have today could be considered the culmination of history, the best of all possible worlds. Originally an admirer of the French Revolution, Hegel became a political conservative after 1815. For that reason, many students who admired his work were also his critics, Marx among them. Not satisfied with the abstract quality of Hegel's philosophy, Marx argued that the important thing was not to think about the world but to change it. Convinced that the dialectical process had power, he argued that its true content was not abstract philosophy, but human activity in a material world. Marx proposed to set Hegel on his feet, as he put it.

But what constitutes real human activity? In other words, what makes men and women human? Marx proposed that we are human because we produce. No other animal self-consciously perceives its own needs and then produces objects to meet those needs. This unique activity is what has made human beings a particularly successful species. Early humans produced food and tools to survive, but as soon as they met one need, new needs arose. Because no one can produce anything alone, men and women entered into social relations, at first in the family, then in warrior bands, and later in slave societies. These structures enabled production to flourish—indeed, created **civilization**—but at the same time they introduced a division of labor, or specialization. In the family, for example, men hunted and women farmed. With division of labor, the idea of property arose as well. Stronger or more able members of the group seized some of the group's production for themselves and then used the power that this gave them to secure special rights for themselves. In this way, according to Marx, classes took shape: those who owned the means of producing goods (the capitalists, or in the modern world, the bourgeoisie), and those who worked to turn out the goods (the workers, or in Marx's terminology, the proletariat).

Marx's point in these speculations was to show that the unique nature of human beings—their propensity to produce—leads inevitably to complex societies and to social classes. Therefore, he believed, class struggle was inherent in the historical process. But why could classes not live in harmony as liberals believed they could? Because, as Marx explained, the owning class will inevitably use its power to accumulate more at the expense of the producing class. They will thus go against the principle of equity established by the French Revolution. The producers, however, eventually will recognize that they are being exploited. In the end, the proletariat will see that it can alter its inferior position only by smashing the system constructed by the dominant class to protect itself. Such an upheaval brings on the next stages of historical development—socialism and, eventually, communism.

By building his idea of historical development on what he considered the most essential human attribute—production and how human beings stand in relation to the means of production—Marx claimed that he was being scientific, materialistic, and dialectical. He was scientific in that he spurned abstractions; he was materialistic because he rooted the historical process in productive relations; and he was dialectical because in his view the contradictions inherent in each historical stage inevitably produced a more sophisticated and productive successor.

Marx was quite specific in how he thought the dialectic of history would transform the structure of property. As entrepreneurs strove to keep their level of profits high by seeking cheap supplies of raw materials and labor, capitalism would spread throughout the world, and ever-larger firms would crowd out smaller ones. Eventually, global society would consist of only two classes: capitalists and proletarians. But this process, especially the gathering of masses of workers in large factories where they would learn the benefits of social cooperation, would itself educate the proletarians. They would come to see that their real interests lay not with their nation or their state, but with all other workers. They would develop a revolutionary class consciousness that would drive them toward the final seizure of power from the capitalists. At some point, perhaps during one of the periods of economic depression in the expected cycle of boom and bust, the exploited would "expropriate the expropriators," as Marx put it. In one giant upheaval, the working class of the world would seize the means of production for itself. After a brief period of consolidation, it would divide the value of production among all the workers. Class conflict would disappear, true democracy

Karl Marx and his Wife Karl Marx sits with his aristocratic wife, Jenny (ca. 1860). The two fell in love as youths and remained in love throughout their lives. Their marriage was turbulent and had its share of pain, but the couple always remained together. Jenny was an excellent writer in her own right. © *Stock Montage.*

would arise, and a wholly new era of human existence would dawn.

Marx's scheme was so grand, so hopeful, and so powerful in its logic that for one hundred years after his death in 1883 it attracted a large proportion of the world's intelligentsia. Today, after the collapse of Marxist regimes in Eastern Europe and the former Soviet Union, the flaws in his logic, his erroneous predictions, and the limitations of his examples are easy enough to pick out. For instance, if the dialectical process is inherent in human development, then it cannot stop with the creation of communism, as Marx said it would. But if the dialectical process is not inevitable, then no justification exists for Marx's dialectical theory of history. Marx was clearly wrong when he postulated that the working class would become more and more miserable. And, unfortunately for Marx, the twentieth-century socialist societies formed in his name (although not always in accordance with his ideas) proved economic and political failures.

Yet by stressing these and other objections to Marx's thought, it is easy to lose sight of its enormous power. Marx identified villains and heroes and provided for an inevitable happy ending, albeit not without struggle and loss. For Marx, poverty and misery were not merely moral failings to be laid at the feet of a feckless working class, as Malthus had thought, or ethical issues that could be corrected by proper Christian virtue, as Saint-Simon had thought, but unavoidable weaknesses of capitalism as a system. Humanity's hope actually rested with the dispossessed of this system, not with the beneficence of property owners. Socialism would succeed not through the formation of a few ideal communities as the utopian socialists had hoped, but through dialectical inevitability. The evils of the world *would* be solved. The optimistic tone of Marx's ideas, their originality, their appeal to the oppressed, their seemingly scientific nature, and their incisiveness inspired millions.

Workers' Organizations and Ideologies

Marx lived at a time when industrial workers throughout Europe had begun to organize themselves for economic and political goals. In 1864 Marx himself delivered the inaugural address at the organizational meeting of the First International Working Men's Association, a group of socialists and anarchists whose efforts to draw Europe's working classes together proved premature. Associations of working people were not new. They had existed in some form from the first stirrings of industrialization in every European country. In France, for example, secret mutual aid societies among artisans dated from at least the eighteenth century. In the nineteenth century, despite restrictive laws and vigorous opposition from industrialists, hundreds of small unions formed across Europe to protect entry into specific crafts and to seek better wages and working conditions. Strikes gave workers leverage, and sometimes the need to organize them inspired the creation of a union.

Before the 1870s, the union movement was small and weak. Germany, for example, had only about fifty thousand unionized workers in the mid-1870s. But from that point on, unions—and the strike—secured increasing legal recognition. In 1895 the *Confederation Général du Travail* (CGT; in English, the General Confederation of Labor) merged seventy workers' organizations in France. In England, the Trades Union Congress (TUC), founded in 1868, opened its doors to unskilled workers in 1889. In 1906 one faction of the British labor movement renamed itself the Labour Party and entered politics directly. In Germany, with the abandonment of the antisocialist laws in 1890, social democratic unions prospered. Despite enormous legal and political difficulties, by the turn of the century German union activity had begun to improve working conditions in many industries, even though unions probably represented no more than 10 percent of the country's industrialized labor force.

The main political advocates of working-class interests came not from unions but from socialist political parties, although they too enrolled only a relatively small proportion of the working population. The tenor of socialism varied across Europe with the political conditions in which it matured. The two extremes were England, where Marxian socialism never took root, and Russia, where the reactionary tsarist regime bred the most violent strains of revolutionary Marxism.[2] The Fabian Society, the most famous English socialist movement, came into being in 1884 as a small group of upper-middle-class intellectuals devoted to reconstructing society on the highest moral principles. The Fabians rejected violence and revolution. Because of the brilliance of its small membership, the society attracted considerable attention, but in practice it exerted little influence.

In France, politicians identifying themselves as socialist began to achieve local electoral success in the early 1890s, and in 1899 socialist parties received more than 20 percent of the votes cast for the National Assembly. A nationwide socialist party did not come into existence, however, until 1901. By World War I, it had only ninety thousand members out of a trade-union population of more than a million and out of a working-class population of many millions. Perhaps one reason for this disparity was that in France socialists used a different ideology from the union movement. The socialists spoke the Marxist rhetoric of proletarian revolution, whereas the union movement adhered to revolutionary syndicalism. The central notion of revolutionary syndicalism was the general strike. According to this idea, daily struggle with employers would create a strong sense of mutual affiliation that would eventually lead workers in every industry to strike at the same time, thus provoking the collapse of capitalism. The illusory

---

[2] For Russian socialism, see the discussion of the Russian Revolution in Chapter 28.

hope that a general strike could solve all their problems in one fell swoop proved inspirational to French workers, but it failed to achieve specific aims.

In Germany, two socialist groups formed in the 1860s: the relatively accommodating General German Workmen's Union in the north, and an amalgamation of Marxist workingmen's educational associations in the south. Because the German Empire founded in 1871 enjoyed universal male suffrage, these parties could compete in elections to the Reichstag. In 1874 they received 350,000 votes and took nine seats. Enthusiastic about their prospects, the two main groups consolidated into the German Social Democratic party in 1874.

The party's platform, which advocated republicanism, atheism, and revolution, unnerved Bismarck. He used two assassination attempts on William I, one of which seriously wounded the emperor, to inflame antisocialist feeling, even though the socialists had had nothing to do with either attempt. Riding the antisocialist fever that he had whipped up, Bismarck called for new elections and easily pushed a bill outlawing socialist activities through the new Reichstag. The draconian law closed down 127 newspapers and 237 other publications, crushed the weak new trade unions, and expelled leading socialists from urban areas.

Simultaneously, Bismarck began pressing for social reforms, in part to undermine the socialists, but also because many business leaders sought change. Conservative businessmen held the patriarchal view that employers should care for their workers even outside the workplace, and they advocated a nationwide social safety net. Laissez-faire advocates, such as Bismarck's National Liberal allies in the Kulturkampf, opposed welfare plans, but in 1879 Bismarck abandoned the National Liberals, freeing himself to push through a sickness insurance bill in 1883. This plan promised to pay half of a worker's wage for up to thirteen weeks in case of illness. In 1884 the Reichstag passed an accident insurance law, and in 1889 it added an old-age insurance law, which granted workers a pension at age seventy-one. A combination of employer, employee, and state contributions financed these plans.

Bismarck's remarkable insurance laws were the first of their kind in Europe. By the end of the century, several countries had adopted similar laws, and by World War I almost every European country had some social insurance program on the books.[3] Implementing these plans had several unanticipated consequences. To cover everyone in the country, the state had to take on an unprecedented degree of control over ordinary life. Accounting practices had to be upgraded to process the millions of participants, and old statistical methods had to be improved and new ones invented. The banking system had to innovate and expand

to facilitate payments, and currency stability became more important than ever.

Neither Bismarck's stick of repression nor his carrot of social benefits destroyed the Social Democrats, however. Instead, the state's hostility to socialist initiatives and its paternalistic attitude toward working people pushed German workers into the arms of the Social Democrats. During the 1880s, the percentage of voters supporting Social Democratic candidates actually rose, despite repression. When conflicts with William II and an electoral loss in 1890 forced Bismarck to retire, the antisocialist laws were not renewed and the Social Democrats returned to legality.

From 1890 until World War I, the Social Democrats were the largest political party in Germany, although the leadership's unwillingness to give up its obsolete revolutionary rhetoric prevented the party from achieving political power. Nevertheless, Social Democratic hospitals, day care centers, lunch programs, unions, unemployment assistance, pension schemes, and funeral insurance made it possible for a party member to spend his or her entire life secure within the fold of the party. This all-encompassing network of associations made German socialism the most cohesive such movement in Europe.

Working-Class Life

The variety of European socialisms belied Marx's belief that worker solidarity would create a proletarian internationalism uniting workers everywhere against capitalism. In 1889 representatives of several European socialist movements created a second international workingmen's association in an effort to put some muscle behind the idea of proletarian internationalism. But the Second International turned out to be a fragmented organization of socialist parties from various nations, not a unified voice for socialism. Even in the most developed countries, socialist parties, which had to compete with Catholic parties for the workers' political allegiance, found it difficult to enroll more than a portion of the working class. In Germany the Social Democratic party, through its many newspapers and associations as well as its continued participation in the electoral process, actually drew the working class away from militancy and toward middle-class political behavior. In France, the socialist party's newspaper, *L'Humanité*, was too scholarly and arid to attract more than about twelve thousand readers, at a time when two Paris tabloids boasted a circulation of about a million readers each. Most appalling to Marxist analysts, both the workers and the socialist parties proved far more loyal to their respective nations than to the international proletariat.

Until recently, much of the research into the history of the working class tried to explain these failures of the proletariat to develop an "appropriate" class consciousness. Early scholarship also assumed that studying unions and socialist political parties was tantamount to studying the working class itself. Over the last twenty years, however,

---

[3] Such programs did not begin in the United States until Franklin D. Roosevelt's New Deal in the 1930s, and not even today has the United States enacted a comprehensive public health insurance system.

Floor Planers at Work   This realistic painting by Gustave Caillebotte (1875) gives an idea of the sort of manual labor that supported the elegance of upper- and middle-class life late in the nineteenth century. The Salon rejected it for its mundane subject and unusual point of view, but the impressionists liked the heroic quality of the workers.   *The Granger Collection, New York.*

most social historians have abandoned both these efforts. Social historians in Germany, following the example of French advocates of a more total history, began investigating what they called "the history of everyday life." Instead of looking at political events, or seeking reasons why reality did not match theory, they began to document how workers actually lived. They investigated housing patterns, family arrangements, the role of women in the working-class family, speech patterns, clubs, drinking habits, leisure activities—in short all those things that make up the matrix of daily life.

This new style of research has revealed something that common sense should have told us earlier: Working-class life differed across as wide a spectrum as did middle-class life. Highly skilled workers in large plants whose parents had held similar positions constituted the *haut proletariat* (upper proletariat). These elite workers did not consider themselves middle-class, but they did aspire to respectability and were recognized by middle-class observers as "solid." The upper end of the working class also included the leaders of the social democratic parties. These persons, usually

not of working-class origin themselves, tended to be educated and sophisticated, able to work well with their middle-class and aristocratic opponents. At the other end of the ladder were the unskilled, vagrant day-workers, along with the semiemployed poor. Inarticulate, these people were unable to maintain bourgeois standards of hygiene and were too poor to keep up appearances. In times of crisis, they tended to express themselves through violence.

One place that working-class life differed greatly from middle-class life was in the position of children. Nineteenth-century working-class children did not stay home to be nurtured and educated, but went immediately into the workforce. The German-language memoir literature is full of pathetic stories of the barrenness of their early lives. "All that brightens a child's life—fairy tales and storybooks, toys and things like that—were foreign to us," says one such memoir. "No bright moment, no sunbeam, no hint of a comfortable home where motherly love and care could shape my childhood, were ever known to me," says another. "Whenever the other kids were running around in the streets in their childish high spirits, and I would direct my

THE HISTORICAL EVIDENCE

Work as a Domestic Servant

1888

One of the most common jobs for women between puberty and marriage during the period of industrialization was domestic service. Doris Viersbeck came to Hamburg in 1888 at about age 19 to such work, and, as so many others like her, left after a few years to get married. Here she describes being summoned to attend on her employers.

If the bell rang once, it was for me; twice was for the maid; and three short rings meant the manservant was wanted. When they rang for me, I was allowed first to ask at the speaking tube what they wanted; the maid and manservant had to rush right upstairs, and often for a trifle. At the speaking tube I had to say, "What do you wish?" If there was no answer, I had to run upstairs. Now, frequently I had something on the stove that couldn't be left for long. At the very least I had to take it off to make sure that it wouldn't boil over or burn. But this took too long for the ladies, so they rang again, loud and long, and when possible a third time, before I got upstairs. I was received crossly with mean looks. "My God, where have you been?"—that was the usual beginning. My apologies were not accepted. "Empty excuses," they called them.

The master didn't give us any peace down in the basement either. There was a hand bell over his bed that rang downstairs; it was there for him to use when he woke up at noon in order to call the manservant if he happened to be downstairs at the time. Sometimes he'd ring the bell constantly during the night. I complained to Frau Sparr about it and asked her to disconnect the bell for the night because we needed to get some sleep. But what did she reply to me? "What are you talking about? The bell is there to be rung, not to be turned off. If the master rings he has some wishes, and they must be respected at all times."

Source: From *The German Worker: Working-Class Autobiographies from the Age of Industrialization*, ed. and trans. Alfred Kelly (Berkeley: University of California Press, 1987), pp. 140–141.

gaze longingly out the window, I would be reminded by a slap from my mother that I had work to do," relates a third.

Working-class ways of life were not bourgeois modes written in rougher language. They were original reactions to the difficult situations in which workers found themselves. Pilfering, street gangs, drinking, illegitimacy, and even strikes—all of which middle-class observers feared as dangerous, disruptive, antisocial and, in short, not respectable—were responses to particular social pressures and followed their own norms. For example, pilfering from dock owners was considered acceptable, but stealing from other dockworkers was not. The rate of illegitimate births may have been high, but so were the number of marriages that followed such births. Street gangs attacked their enemies but upheld their internal codes of honor. These aspects of working-class life might not meet middle-class standards of decorum, but the people involved were not devoid of standards.

Working people found their own ways to adapt to new work patterns and to leisure time. Males and females did so in different ways. Men spent a good deal of their leisure time outside of the home in pubs or *Bierstuben*, one of the few places where they could freely gather, or in playing or watching football (called soccer in North America).

Drinking together always provided an important way for men to establish friendships, but playing sports together was new to the late nineteenth century. Meanwhile, women had the responsibility of keeping the home, sometimes with little financial help from the husbands. Some women had to take in boarders, sew piecework, or do laundry to make ends meet. Despite this constant struggle to put food on the table, working-class women, influenced by the newly popular self-help magazines that promulgated middle-class values, often adopted stringent standards of housekeeping and took pride in their ability to maintain the family's dignity.

When middle-class observers looked at working-class life, they did not see a creative culture, high standards, or aspirations. They tended to notice only drunkenness, poverty, sexual immorality, violence, and poor health. Reform associations began to intrude into workers' lives and governments began to pass legislation regulating housing, women's work, and health conditions. Investigators probed all aspects of working-class life with an eye to using social-science insights to "improve" working-class ways. Governments hired public health doctors to check up on children, established clinics for infants, and sent nurses on home visits to ensure that poor mothers were feeding their babies correctly. German schoolchildren were required to wear clothes of a certain standard, and were sent home if they did not meet it. Governments began to regulate prostitution, despite feminists' protests that prostitution really stemmed from poverty and men's predilections rather than the immorality of the prostitutes. By the end of the nineteenth century, middle-class activists and governments had insinuated themselves into the life of the working class far more actively than ever before—an important aspect of the general growth of government during the Century of Power.

THE IDEOLOGY OF POWER: RACE AND GENDER

The notion of class came into widespread use at the end of the nineteenth century, but it was far from the only social category that the Century of Power produced. Two other ways of differentiating people assumed importance as well: race and gender. Despite the seemingly obvious physical differences that distinguish people of different races or genders, the actual roles that race and sex play are socially constructed—that is, certain customs and ways of thinking dictate how people feel about themselves and about each other and what sorts of interactions are considered appropriate. For example, the ideal of domesticity characterized the middle class in the nineteenth century, but not the working class in the seventeenth century. Late in the nineteenth century, race and gender became increasingly sharply defined in a way that reflected the enormous growth in European power and strength. These sharpened definitions grew out of the ideas and practices associated with Social Darwinism, or the translation of Charles Darwin's scientific ideas on evolution into political rhetoric.

Darwinism: Scientific and Social

Charles Darwin was born in 1809 to a well-to-do family. His father was a successful doctor, and his mother came from the Wedgwood family, famous for its porcelain works. This wealth and that of Charles's wife, who was also a Wedgwood, assured a secure income for Darwin throughout his life. His father wanted him to become a doctor, but Darwin became nauseated during operations that he observed and showed no enthusiasm for his studies. So his frustrated father sent him off to Cambridge University to become a clergyman. "You care for nothing but shooting, dogs, and rat-catching," the elder Darwin admonished, "and you will be a disgrace to yourself and all your family."

At Cambridge, Darwin was a listless student of theology, but he became an avid amateur botanist and a frequent visitor to the home of John Stevens Henslow, a prominent scientist. When the organizers of a round-the-world expedition asked Henslow to recommend a botanist to accompany their voyage, he suggested Darwin. Only

twenty-two years old and reluctant to take up a parish, Darwin signed on. He spent the next five years observing the geology and plant life of South America and the South Pacific as part of the crew of HMS *Beagle*. He proved to be not only an indefatigable fact-finder but a keen observer and original analyst as well. Even before he returned to England, the letters he sent back to Henslow contained enough original geological research to win him admittance to the Royal Society.

Darwin had speculated about evolution during his voyages, but the idea that made him famous did not occur to him until after his return. The notion of evolution was in the air in the 1820s and 1830s, but it was not widely accepted. No one had yet proposed how it might work. The standard view held that species had fixed characteristics. Any variations were deemed the work of "the Supreme Intellect." From his observations, Darwin expressed doubts that nature was fixed. The 1830 study of Charles Lyell, *Principles of Geology*, the founding book of modern geology that Darwin took with him on the *Beagle*, reinforced his suspicions. Lyell taught Darwin that the world was constantly changing through volcanic action, earthquakes, and erosion. Lyell also held two other crucial notions

MR. BERGH TO THE RESCUE.

THE DEFRAUDED GORILLA. "That *Man* wants to claim my Pedigree. He says he is one of my Descendants."

Mr. BERGH. "Now, Mr. DARWIN, how could you insult him so?"

Popular Reaction to Darwinian Evolution Popularized interpretations of Darwin's theories quickly spread to the United States, where cartoonist Thomas Nast ridiculed the idea of descent from primates. Others latched on to the notion of "survival of the fittest" to support conservative social policies. *The Granger Collection, New York.*

uncommon in his day: (1) that the laws of nature remain constant over time and (2) that changes in nature take place over a very long time. These ideas encouraged Darwin to speculate that even species might undergo gradual but constant change.

In 1838, only two years after his trip, Darwin was reading Malthus when the mechanism of evolution popped into his mind. In an instant, he put together three ordinary facts and two conclusions to round out his idea. First, he knew that all organisms produce far more offspring than that grow to be adults, and second that species nevertheless remain roughly constant in population. He concluded that offspring must compete for survival. The third fact, confirmed by five years of acute observation, was that individuals within each species vary considerably. Therefore, he reasoned, some variations must be more advantageous than others in the fight for survival. In October 1838, he summed up his conclusions in his diary, "Under the struggle for life, favorable variations would tend to be preserved and unfavorable ones to be destroyed. The result of this would be the formation of a new species. Here, then, I had at last a theory by which to work."

Darwin understood that his idea posed a threat to the conventional religious view that God created each species individually. Fearing not just controversy but even a blasphemy suit, he spent the next twenty years publishing the data from the *Beagle* voyage and working on other problems, while at the same time perfecting his ideas. In 1858, however, British naturalist Alfred Russel Wallace sent Darwin a paper he was about to publish that put forward a theory similar to Darwin's. In 1859 Darwin rushed out his own volume, *On the Origin of Species by Means of Natural Selection, or the Preservation of Favoured Races in the Struggle for Life*. The work proved to be one of the most influential books ever published in the English language.

Today the scientific heirs of Darwin's theory of natural selection are as well established as those of Newton's theory of gravity. But the idea of individuals struggling for survival struck a chord that had nothing to do with science. The English sociologist and philosopher Herbert Spencer coined the phrase "the survival of the fittest," which Darwin incorporated in later editions of his book. Middle-class English society looked on Darwin's theory as scientific proof that those who prospered were, by definition, more intelligent, able, and ambitious—in short, more fit—than those who did not do well. Darwin's theory seemed to prove that poverty was the fault of the poor. Some of the cruelest among the Social Darwinists even began to assert that perhaps it would be better for society if those who could not succeed were left alone to die off.

In Germany, Social Darwinism did not catch on quickly among the middle class, and working-class politicians despised it as another way for the rich to justify their domination over the poor. But Darwin did influence intellectuals there. The biologist Ernst Haeckel played a key role in making Darwin's ideas available to the German public. Haeckel was a respectable scientist, but he also advocated an extreme form of Social Darwinism. He brought the ideas of Romanticism and materialism together into a powerful claim of German racial superiority.

On the face of things, Romanticism and materialism appear contradictory. Romanticism stressed intuition over reason, whereas materialism favored science over metaphysics. In the latter part of the nineteenth century, both tendencies had their supporters in Germany. Romantics believed that the customs of the *Volk* linked the German people in an emotional affinity, a depth of feeling, and a wealth of creativity that industrializing society could not match.[4] The German sociologist Ferdinand Tönnies gave Romantic nationalists fuel for this argument when he claimed that two ideal types of cultures existed: the natural, spontaneous, and intuitive *Gemeinschaft*, or community, and the impersonal, bureaucratic, and rational *Gesellschaft*, or society. Tönnies's countryman, the historian Wilhelm Heinrich Riehl, indicated which type of culture the Romantics preferred in the title of his multivolume work, *The Natural History of the Volk as the Foundation of a Germanic Sociopolitical System*.

On the other hand, the prestige of science rose in the 1860s and 1870s to a new high. Advances especially in chemistry led many young men to become materialists and to reject Romanticism and metaphysics. The contribution, if one could call it that, of Haeckel and those who thought like him lay in giving the Romantic vision a scientific cast. They argued that the allegedly superior culture of the German *Volk* resulted from evolution and therefore could be scientifically demonstrated. In this way, they transmuted German cultural pretensions into a pseudoscientific claim.

Already in 1853, the French writer Count Arthur de Gobineau had argued in *The Inequality of Human Races* that an allegedly separate race whom he called Aryans were superior beings not only in Europe but across the world. Gobineau feared that this race of superior beings would decline, as had all past superior races, because of intermarriage with inferior stock. Even more sinister was the work of Houston Stewart Chamberlain. An Englishman, Chamberlain nevertheless fell in love with German culture, married composer Richard Wagner's daughter, and wrote, in German, a book called *The Foundations of the Nineteenth Century*. This witch's brew of nationalistic, racist, and Romantic claptrap became a best-seller in Germany and later greatly influenced Adolf Hitler. In Chamberlain's view, Aryans would not decline if Germans could win the struggle for survival against racial contamination from within—Jews—and racial threats from without—the French. In such ways, European racial theorists of the late nineteenth century transformed Darwin's neutral scientific

---

[4] For a discussion of the term *Volk*, see Chapter 22.

idea into a justification for antisemitism, racial prejudice, and virulent nationalism.

The Scourge of Antisemitism

Hatred of Jews has plagued European history since the Middle Ages. Many medieval countries expelled their Jews, and even great reformers such as Martin Luther and Voltaire wrote anti-Jewish polemics. Expelled Jews found refuge chiefly in three places in medieval and early modern Europe: The Netherlands, the Ottoman Empire, and Poland. Jews driven from Spain and Portugal in the fifteenth and sixteenth centuries often settled in Dutch cities like Amsterdam, where they faced little religious harassment and often became quite prosperous. The Ottomans considered Jews "people of the book" (the Old Testament) and did not persecute them. The exodus from Spain in the fifteenth century created vibrant Jewish communities in cities like Thessalonika and Sarajevo, where they prospered into the twentieth century. The medieval Polish nobility also welcomed Jews, primarily as a middle stratum of estate managers and traders. Despite some terrible moments—such as the mid-seventeenth-century "Deluge," in which Ukrainian rebels and Polish troops massacred tens of thousands of Jews—by the end of the eighteenth century Poland was home to the largest Jewish community in the world. When Russia, Austria, and Prussia divided Poland at the end of that century, a significant portion of European Jewry ended up in Russia. Catherine the Great

banned Jews from residing outside regions in which they had significant population, which was known as the Pale of Settlement. This restriction continued into the nineteenth century, along with constraints on university entrance and other discriminatory practices. (Map 25-2 shows the cities and rural areas that had large Jewish populations in early twentieth-century Europe.)

The legal position of Jews changed in France when Napoleon accepted them as citizens liable to taxation, required to do military service, and eligible for government positions like all other citizens. Even when Jews were granted equal civil rights, as they were in most European countries by the end of the century, antisemitism persisted, but in a new form. In medieval times, Jews could erase the "stain" that Christians claimed infected them by converting to Christianity. But once racism became an evolutionary "science," Judaism, or any other supposedly ethnic quality, became genetic, incapable of change. This vicious new twist to antisemitism laid the theoretical basis for the Holocaust in the twentieth century.

The new racial views spread like wildfire among the European middle class in the 1870s and 1880s. The first overtly antisemitic political parties arose in Germany in 1878, in Austria in 1881, and in Hungary in 1882. They appeared at this time because some felt that Jews had played too important a role in the Congress of Berlin (1878), which had required Romania and Serbia to abolish their restrictions on Jews. The assassination of Tsar Alexander II (1881) set off a wave of *pogroms* (anti-Jewish

**MAP 25-2
EUROPE'S JEWISH
POPULATION, EARLY
TWENTIETH CENTURY**

riots and massacres) in Russia, and various scandals implicated Jewish bankers in Vienna and elsewhere.

Political antisemitism was most successful in Austria, where the lapsed liberal Georg von Schönerer advocated "the removal of Jewish influence from all sections of public life." Schönerer himself collapsed into madness, but Karl Lueger, one of the few lower-middle-class political figures to achieve renown in the Habsburg lands, used an antisemitic campaign to get himself elected mayor of Vienna in 1894. Francis Joseph refused to sanction Lueger's election, but eventually, in 1897, the emperor conceded and Lueger served in the post until his death in 1910. It was in the rural Lower Austria of Schönerer and the Vienna of Lueger that Adolf Hitler learned his antisemitism before World War I.

Jews in central Europe adopted three basic strategies to combat antisemitic threats: cultural creativity, assimilation, and Zionism. Culturally, Judaism in Europe had taken two different pathways in the eighteenth century: hasidism and haskala. Hasidism was a fundamentalist turn toward piety, simplicity, and populist wisdom, whereas the haskala represented a shift toward enlightenment, rationality, and secularism. By the nineteenth century, hasidism had prevailed in the villages of eastern Europe, but the haskala predominated in central European commercial centers and in Berlin.

As a second strategy undertaken to avoid antisemitism, some Jews assimilated to the culture of the country in which they lived, particularly in Germany, Austria, and Hungary. The most successful assimilation came in Hungary. Whereas in neighboring Romania middle-class liberals were virulently antisemitic, in Hungary aristocratic rulers co-opted successful Jews into their upper class. In the nineteenth and twentieth centuries, Francis Joseph ennobled 346 Hungarian Jewish families, 220 of these in the fifteen years before World War I. By 1910 more than 75 percent of Hungarian Jews listed Magyar as their native tongue, and almost none listed **Yiddish,** the predominant language of rural eastern European Jews.

Zionism, or Jewish ethnic nationalism, was a third device adopted by some Jews. Theodor Herzl, the originator of Zionism, reasoned that if Jews were going to be rejected for being rootless, then they needed a homeland. His book *The Jewish State*, published in 1896, gave birth to the political movement that led to the creation of Israel.

But the foregoing strategies did not always succeed in combating antisemitic reactions. The most dramatic intrusion of antisemitism into European politics in the years preceding World War I was the Dreyfus case in France. In 1894 a military court convicted Captain Alfred Dreyfus, one of the few Jews to serve on the French General Staff, of selling military secrets to the Germans, and sentenced him to life imprisonment on Devil's Island, a penal colony in French Guiana (northern South America). Two years later, a new chief of intelligence reopened the case and concluded that in fact another officer was the guilty party. But when the chief sought to exonerate Dreyfus and charge the other officer, he found himself transferred to

Antisemitism This Austrian cartoon from 1900 plays on the allegedly Jewish characteristic of exploiting workers. The text reads: "Automobile—patent Schmul. Cheapest operation! Completely safe!" Antisemitism was politically powerful, in Vienna in particular, despite the cultured life of upper-class Viennese Jews and their loyalty to the empire. *J. Rahr. Der Scherer. Innsbruck, 1900.*

193. J. Rahr. Der Scherer. Innsbruck. 1900

LE TRAITRE
Dégradation d Alfred Dreyfus

Humiliation of Captain Dreyfus Convicted of treason, Alfred Dreyfus was stripped of his military rank and sent to Devil's Island. Here a contemporary journal depicts the breaking of his officer's sword, the symbolic completion of his humiliation. Dreyfus was later proven to be the victim of a plot and restored to his rank, but the affair, with its overtones of antisemitism, bitterly divided the French public. *The Granger Collection, New York.*

Algeria. Thus began one of the most difficult episodes of the French Third Republic. Republicans and socialists, hitherto opponents, allied to charge the army with falsifying evidence and with conspiracy. Conservative and Catholic nationalists, as well as French antisemites, leaped to the army's defense and resisted reopening the case with every weapon at their disposal, including obstructionism and falsely sworn evidence. In 1899, however, the truth emerged. The guilty officer fled to England, and Dreyfus was returned to France. In 1906, he was finally cleared and even inducted into the Legion of Honor. The Dreyfus case starkly revealed the corruption, selfishness, and sheer wrong-headedness of the aristocratic and rigidly Catholic French officer corps. But its emotional charge sprang from Dreyfus's Jewishness.

The most serious antisemitic outbursts erupted in Russia, which suffered worse domestic turmoil than any other part of the continent. Pogroms there killed hundreds of

Jews in 1903 and in 1907. The Russian secret service even went so far as to concoct *The Protocols of the Elders of Zion,* a specious document alleging to prove a Jewish conspiracy to rule the world. Racists continue to use this forgery today. Finally, in 1913 Mendel Beiliss, a Jewish brickmaker from Kiev, was charged with ritual murder. The accusation revived the ancient calumny that Jews sacrificed Christian blood. Despite Nicholas II's active interest in convicting Beiliss of this outrageous charge, the jury acquitted him. All those who had conspired to accuse and try him, however, received promotions and advancement.

Gender and Race

Pseudoscientific ideas of race could prosper late in the nineteenth century because they seemed to explain the sudden burst of imperial expansion that had brought most of the world under European domination by the beginning of World War I.[5] Prosperity, economic development, expansion of colonies, technological progress—all suggested to Europeans that they had reached a unique stage of civilization that placed them on a vastly higher level than people in the rest of the world. For the middle class, this superiority implied a moral responsibility to help the inferior races, to "take up the white man's burden" as the British poet Rudyard Kipling put it. One believer at the time wrote that imperialism was "a conquest of virgin nature and the heathen races, a peaceful crusade bringing millions into the Empire of civilization, helping to raise them bit by bit to our level."

Ideas about the subservient place of women had close links with these condescending justifications of power and of racial superiority. According to a popular book by Max Nordau, significantly entitled *Degeneracy* (1893), evolution from asexual single-cell plants had produced two differentiated sexes. One, the male, had qualities of creativity, imagination, and reason. The other, the female, had qualities of fecundity, procreation, and nurturing. Because evolution must develop these qualities, Nordau argued, a creative woman was actually an evolutionary regression. Otto Weininger's hugely popular work, *Sex and Character* (1903), expressed even more surprising views. "There is not a single woman in the history of thought," declared Weininger, "not even the most man-like, who can be truthfully compared with men of sixth-rate genius."

In support of these misogynist notions, the popular middle-class art of the late nineteenth century portrayed the true womanly state as vacancy. Thousands of paintings showed ill or consumptive women, or women looking in a

---

[5] For imperialism, see Chapter 27.
[6] Schopenhauer never married, and despite his genius could not maintain normal relationships with anyone, male or female.

The New Woman   While popular bourgeois art often depicted turn-of-the-century women as "vacant," merely reflecting themselves in mirrors, women like Maria Montessori (the first Italian female medical doctor and professor of medicine) were disproving the myth and making their professional marks. In the case of Maria Montessori, her greatest contribution was to the education of children.

mirror and reflecting nothing, or women as children. As the philosopher Arthur Schopenhauer had asserted earlier in the century, "Women are childish, frivolous, and short-sighted, in a word, they are big children all their life long."[6] These ideas were not just the crackpot notions of a few cranks, but conventional wisdom in the upper reaches of middle-class society in the late nineteenth century.

Worse, some theorists concluded that because men were evolutionarily justified in their exercise of power over women, evolution also had provided women with a desire to be dominated. Thus, in their view, rape occurred because women wanted it. Richard von Kraft Ebbing, a German pioneer in the investigation of sexual perversions, said that masochism was a true perversion only among men, given that women had an instinctive desire to be

subjugated to men. Cesare Lombroso and Gugliemo Ferraro, two Italian investigators of female offenders, said that "the normal woman is naturally less sensitive to pain than a man."

These ideas of male superiority had close connections to ideas of racial superiority. According to Carl Vogt, every indication of evolutionary science led to the conclusion that "the grown up negro partakes, as regards his intellectual faculties, of the nature of the child, the female, and the senile white." The "degenerate" races, Weininger said, had become feminized, especially the Jews, whose faith was "saturated with femininity."

Women Fight for Equity

If powerful assertions of the superiority of males over females characterized the late nineteenth century, so did the feminist movement that challenged those ideas. In these years, women particularly earned success in writing novels, although some of the best novelists, like George Sand and George Eliot, chose to use male pseudonyms. Women did well in this field perhaps because they were not permitted to attend prep schools or universities; unless their parents taught them privately, they escaped the rigors of classical studies. This freedom from conventional forms may have permitted them to write with the humane touch that characterizes the best nineteenth-century novels.

In most spheres, however, women faced severe restrictions, both social and legal. The "Woman Movement" that began to chip away at those restrictions ran strongest in England, where the middle-class ethic permitted women to engage in philanthropic activities. Some women pushed these activities beyond merely helping the poor. In the 1830s, for example, Caroline Norton attacked the law that gave custody of all children to the father in case of divorce or separation. She succeeded in getting the Infant Custody Act of 1839 passed, which gave the mother custody of the children until age seven.

The Woman Movement coalesced in the 1850s under the influence of Florence Nightingale. This remarkable Englishwoman rejected the ideal of domesticity pressed on her by her wealthy middle-class family. Against the strong objections of her parents, who could not understand her desire to "lower" herself, she took up nursing, a hitherto male occupation then regarded (for women) on a level with prostitution. During the Crimean War, she formed a medical unit with her own funds. Her successes there made her a national hero and transformed nursing into a profession of high standards and prestige. Encouraged by Nightingale's success, in the 1850s activists began to attack the law that gave husbands complete control of their wives' wealth. The British Parliament eventually acted, and in 1878 married women obtained control over their earnings.

THE HUMAN EXPERIENCE

Ellen Key, Swedish Feminist

Dramatic campaigns for woman's suffrage and militant socialist advocacy left the strongest impressions of late nineteenth and early twentieth-century feminism. But these movements constituted only the melodramatic tip of the feminist iceberg. The word *feminism* itself, taken from the French, was a product of the 1890s. Thousands of women in all European countries, from Italy to Scandinavia, pursued new careers, transformed educational practices, and advocated new relationships between the sexes. Ellen Key (1849–1926) was one of these.

Brought up in a well-to-do and politically active family—her father was speaker of the Swedish parliament—Key experienced an austere childhood. Until age sixteen, she and her siblings ate breakfast and supper standing at a counter at which only milk and bread were served. At the age of twenty, she began spending her winters in Stockholm, where she continued her education and learned to write while acting as a secretary for her father. She spent her twenties reading, studying Scandinavian education, and traveling. When she was thirty, however, her father went

bankrupt and she had to earn a living. She took up teaching in one of Scandinavia's first coeducational schools and lectured at the People's Institute, a school formed in 1880 to educate workers.

Personally shy, Key nevertheless found that she had a talent for oratory. Soon her classes at the institute were overflowing and she began lecturing throughout Sweden. Already prominent, in 1890 she became controversial when she came to the defense of four young men who had been convicted of blasphemy for their overt advocacy of Darwinism. Sharply criticized for this defense, she entered into a period of intense writing in which she published book after book expressing her views on women's position in society.

Key believed strongly in individualism, in the need of every person to freely develop his or her personality within ethical and even altruistic bounds. For women, this freedom meant not only learning a trade, because all women must be in a position to live independently if they wished, but also undertaking their social function as mothers. "For most women," she wrote, "it ought still to

be the dream of happiness, some time in their lives, to have fulfilled the mission of motherhood." Key believed that freedom from "the inferior duties" of the household would lead most women not to higher callings but to "monotonous labor in factory, store, and office."

Key, who never married, held that the state should actively support motherhood. She advocated state pensions for mothers and proposed a year of social service for women. During this year, which she saw as equivalent to the military service required of all young men, women would study child psychology, education, the economics of the household, the physiology of birth, and techniques of mothering.

Key's work was very popular, even in the United States, although her view that women should experience sexual pleasure in marriage scandalized many. Her emphasis on self-fulfillment and motherhood, rather than on political gains or revolution, demonstrates the richness and variety of early twentieth-century feminism. ❖

In 1882 they won the right to keep the property that they brought to a marriage in their own name. In the 1860s, the first advocates of woman's suffrage demanded that the word *male*, introduced to the election codes by the Great Reform Act of 1832 (see Chapter 21), be changed to *person*, and the suffrage movement began to gain momentum.

The argument for women's rights in Britain had a strong basis in liberalism: If all are equal under the law, and if the people are sovereign, why should women not be considered part of "the people" and treated equally? John Stuart Mill, England's greatest liberal theorist, agreed. Influenced in part by his wife, the forceful feminist author Harriet Taylor, Mill supported property rights for women in Parliament. In 1869 his essay *On the Subjection of Women*

contended that equality built a stronger foundation for family life than what he called the **tyrant**-slave relationship. When shocked opponents argued that male domination was only natural, Mill answered, "Was there ever any domination which did not appear natural to those who possessed it?"

The woman's suffrage movement had limited success in Britain until the last few years before World War I. Two strategies dominated the struggle. Millicent Garrett Fawcett, founder of the National Union of Women's Suffrage Societies, urged education, lobbying, and other nonviolent forms of advocacy. "Let us prove ourselves worthy of citizenship," she advised. Emmeline Goulden Pankhurst, on the other hand, sought confrontation. The suffragists of her

Woman's Social and Political Union broke windows, poured paint into mailboxes, and slashed museum paintings. One of Pankhurst's followers even threw herself to her death beneath the hooves of the king's horse as it ran in the annual Derby in an effort to bring attention to the cause. Prison sentences followed by hunger strikes heightened the tension provoked by Pankhurst's tactics. Nevertheless, women did not get the vote in Britain until after World War I.

On the Continent, the women's movement concerned itself less with obtaining individual rights than with ensuring that men and women cooperated on the basis of equality. Continental feminism had two strands, the socialist and the nonsocialist. Socialists held that once capitalism had been overturned and socialism introduced, all problems of inequity would fall away. In France, feminist initiatives tended to get swallowed up in the larger movement of socialism. In Germany, however, the Social Democratic party created a separate woman's organization and named prominent women activists as "spokespersons" to the party at large.[7] The popular newspaper *Die Gleichheit* ("Equality"), edited by a woman, expounded the social equality of women for twenty-five years. By 1914, one in six members of the German Social Democratic party was a woman, which, because of the large size of the party, meant that Germany had more female socialists than France had socialists of both sexes.

The nonsocialist strand of late nineteenth-century continental feminism emphasized the cohesion of the community and the complementary mutual relationships between men and women. These "relational feminists," as they have been called, stressed "an ethic of care over an ethic of competition." Reformers in Italy, France, and Scandinavia sought improvements in legal codes, education, child care, and working conditions. Late in the nineteenth century, relational feminists countered Nordau and Weininger with arguments that proved almost equally as popular. For example, the popular Swedish author Ellen Key accepted the unique role that motherhood plays both for women and for society but insisted that women had a right to self-fulfillment as well. Thus, Key believed, society at large should support mothers while they stayed at home to bring up their children. In France, Nelly Roussel agreed on the unique social value of motherhood and on the state's responsibility to support it but argued strongly for the right of women to control their own fertility through contraception. By beginning to redefine the relations between the genders and between the state and its female citizens, the work of these and other activists shows how

deeply the social change produced by the industrial surge of the second half of the nineteenth century cut.

CONCLUSION: THE CONFIDENCE OF POWER

Power politics and increasingly shrill assertions of national self-righteousness set the political tone of the Century of Power (1848–1945). Unprecedented economic growth provided states with the actual power that undergirded Realpolitik. Entirely new industries sprang up, while older industries expanded at a rapid pace. The social group that reaped the most benefits from this economic boom was the middle class, which grew to constitute approximately a quarter of the population in developed countries. Norms of respectable living as defined by the members of this class spread widely, as did new forms of leisure and travel. Changing economic conditions also bred an awareness among many working people that they constituted a special class. Newly formed socialist political parties and unions encouraged this view, but most workers continued to function outside these organizations. At the higher end of the working class, women in particular tried to maintain standards of respectability on a middle-class model, but in many other ways working-class life differed significantly from middle-class norms. For this reason, middle-class reformers judged them deviant and set out to "clean up" working-class life.

Social Darwinism offered a pseudoscientific explanation for why Europe attained such enormous power in the nineteenth century: Evolution had made Europeans more civilized than other peoples and therefore more powerful in the struggle for survival. This idea spawned notions of racism, inflamed antisemitism, and assigned women an inferior position in society. Yet many rejected such fables, and by the turn of the twentieth century vigorous movements for improving women's lot were under way.

By the end of the nineteenth century, power politics backed by real economic strength and supported by Social Darwinism produced in Europeans a high degree of confidence in the progress of their civilization. The French referred to the period as *la belle epoch* ("the beautiful time"). And yet, doubts simmered beneath the surface. Not only had economic development unleashed new energies and dissatisfactions among the working class and among women, but the very height of European success bred a sense of dizziness. The term *fin de siècle* ("end of the century") captured this sense of foreboding. Never had things looked so good; but could they last? A widespread feeling that an epoch was ending and that potent dangers lay ahead led to a devil-may-care attitude about amusements and life. Fin-de-siècle forebodings showed up particularly vividly in the world of culture, to which we now turn.

---

[7] They actually used the term *spokesperson* because German, in which every noun has a gender designation, has no feminine equivalent to "spokesman."

Selected Reading

Sources

Appleman, Philip, ed. *Darwin*, from the Norton Critical Edition Series (1970).

Pool, Daniel. *What Jane Austen Ate and Charles Dickens Knew: From Fox Hunting to Whist—The Facts of Daily Life in Nineteenth-Century England* (1993). A fascinating collection of well-told factual details about everyday life.

Tucker, Robert, ed. *The Marx-Engels Reader* (1978). The best anthology of the work of the fathers of dialectical materialism.

Economic History

Gerschenkron, Alexander. *Economic Backwardness in Historical Perspective* (1962). One of the most influential studies of European economic development ever written.

Good, David F. *The Economic Rise of the Habsburg Empire, 1750–1914* (1984). Detailed argument that the Habsburg Empire was not an economic failure.

Miller, Michael. *The Bon Marché: Bourgeois Culture and the Department Store, 1869–1920* (1981). Interesting monograph on the French department store in which many innovations created a new culture of retail trade.

Milward, Alan S., and S. B. Saul. *The Development of the Economies of Continental Europe, 1850–1914* (1977). A reliable textbook.

Labor and Social History

Berlanstein, Lenard R. *Rethinking Labor History* (1993). A thoughtful collection of articles debating the linguistic turn in labor history: Is socially constructed discourse the real basis of labor history or is it a revised form of class analysis?

Evans, Richard J. *The German Working Class, 1888–1933. The Politics of Everyday Life* (1982). Argues that real working-class life consists in good measure of rebellious acts of rejection, not copying middle-class values.

Katznelson, Ira, and Aristide R. Zolberg, eds. *Working-Class Formation: Nineteenth-Century Patterns in Western Europe and the United States* (1986). This collection of seminal articles attacks the notion that the working class "failed" to achieve a revolutionary class consciousness. It concludes that working-class formation varied in every country according to structure, culture, disposition, and collective action.

Kocka, Jürgen. "The Middle Classes in Europe," *The Journal of Modern History* 67 (1995): 783–806. Superb brief explication of the concept of *middle class*.

Thompson, F. M. L. *The Rise of Respectable Society: A Social History of Victorian Britain, 1830–1900* (1988). A readable survey of marriage, childhood, play, homes, and other elements of social intercourse in Victorian England.

Marx

Kolakowski, Leszek. *Main Currents of Marxism*, 3 vols. (1978). The *Times Education Supplement* called this book "the most commanding, the most decisive, the most properly passionate and yet also the most accessible account of Marxism that we now have."

Tucker, Robert, ed. *Philosophy and Myth in Karl Marx* (1961). Argues forcefully that the early Hegelian influence on Marx can be traced even through his later work, which was not scientific or materialistic, as Marx claimed, but mythic.

Women's History

Boxer, Marilyn, and Jean Quataert. *Socialist Women: Socialist Feminism in the Nineteenth and Twentieth Centuries* (1978). Covers the relationship between socialism and feminism across all of Europe.

Bridenthal, Renate, Claudia Koonze, and Susan Stuard, eds. *Becoming Visible: Women in European History*, 2nd ed. (1987). A collection of essays surveying women's position in society throughout history. Good suggestions for further reading.

Dijkstra, Bram. *Idols of Perversity: Fantasies of Feminine Evil in Fin-de-Siècle Culture* (1986). Vivid analysis of the extreme ideas of female incapacity and vacancy, particularly as shown in painting. Profusely illustrated.

Smith, Bonnie G. *Changing Lives: Women in European History Since 1700* (1989). An excellent textbook.

Stites, Richard. *The Women's Liberation Movement in Russia: Feminism, Nihilism, and Bolshevism, 1860–1930* (1978). Shows how Russian feminism was a variant of European feminism that was transformed by the Bolshevik movement and revolution.

Jewish History

Johnson, Douglas. *France and the Dreyfus Affair* (1966). A standard work on this fascinating event, showing why it had such an impact.

Lindemann, Albert S. *The Jew Accused: Three Antisemitic Affairs (Dreyfus, Beiliss, Frank), 1894–1915* (1991). A sophisticated account of the cases of three wrongly accused Jews showing not only comparative levels of antisemitism prior to World War I, but some countervailing factors as well.

McCagg, William O. Jr. *A History of Habsburg Jews, 1670–1918* (1989). The standard work.

Mosse, George L. *Toward the Final Solution: A History of European Racism* (1978). A readable account of how seemingly scientific ideas of the eighteenth and nineteenth centuries contributed to the eventual killing of 6 million Jews.

The Victorian Era

Weintraub, Stanley. *Victoria: An Intimate Biography* (1987). Thorough, sympathetic biography of the queen who gave her name to an era.

Wiener, Martin. *English Culture and the Decline of the Industrial Spirit* (1981). Argues that English culture, despite its ostensible middle-class orientation, was not suitable for valuing and sustaining industrial growth.

THE BIRTH OF MODERNISM

Picasso's *Les Demoiselles d'Avignon* *Painted June–July 1907. Oil on canvas, 8' x 7'8" (243.9 x 233.7cm.). Acquired through the Lillie P. Bliss Bequest. Photo © 2000. The Museum of Modern Art, New York/Art Resource.*

1840	Liebig's *Organic Chemistry* revolutionizes the science of plants	1899	Freud publishes *The Interpretation of Dreams*
1847	Gustave Courbet paints *Burial at Ornans*	1897	Klimt leads the Vienna Secession artistic movement
1857	Flaubert publishes *Madame Bovary*	1903	First performance of Schoenberg's *Transfigured Night*
1863	Exhibition of The Rejected (including Manet's *Luncheon on the Grass*)	1905	Einstein's publishes his papers on relativity and other subjects
1871–1872	George Eliot publishes *Middlemarch*	1907	Picasso paints *Les Demoiselles d'Avignon*
1872	Nietzsche publishes *The Birth of Tragedy*	1913	*The Rite of Spring* opens in Paris
1881	Le Chat Noir cabaret opens in Paris		

*L*ate in the nineteenth century, in part because of European imperial expansion into Africa, European artists discovered the vitality of African art, particularly ritual masks. Pablo Picasso (1881–1973) was attracted to a similar style of art that he found in his native Catalonia. In 1905 the Autumn Salon in Paris exhibited a number of colorful canvases inspired by these influences. One critic was so taken aback by these works that he called the artists who had created them *fauves*, or wild beasts. At this time Picasso was in his "rose period," when his paintings had a reddish tint. But he was deeply moved by what he called "Negro art." It made him realize that "painting is not an aesthetic operation; it is a form of magic designed as a mediator between this strange, hostile world and us, a way of seizing the power by giving form to our terrors as well as our desires." Picasso painted *Les Demoiselles d'Avignon* ("The Young Ladies of Avignon," 1907), one of the most influential works of the twentieth century, in this mood.[1] This work, shown opposite, was not a casual piece undertaken in a creative fury, although the actual painting took only a few days. Picasso prepared more than thirty preliminary drawings, not counting scores of smaller sketches of portions of the painting.

When, after months of labor, Picasso showed the canvas to his friends, they were appalled. His colleagues were not philistines—they were among the most innovative and experimental artists and writers of their time. Still, they were unprepared for the complete destruction of all the rules of art that this picture represented. Picasso broke the human body into pieces and refit them together in strange ways. The faces of two of the figures are masks, and the planes of the bodies have little rounding. Worse, the painting had no background, no perspective. Its figures did not seem to reside in rational space. Leo Stein, one of Picasso's most fervent collectors and admirers, exclaimed, not in praise, "You've been trying to paint the fourth dimension. How amusing." Stein was right. Picasso was breaking the mold of static representation into a realm of imagination that went beyond ordinary experience, a realm more unsettling than the traditional forms of Western art because it presented terrors as well as desires.

Today we consider Picasso's painting one of the milestones in the development of modern art. The word *modern* has been used since the sixteenth century to mean "of this time." The term implies the idea of change, especially of progress. To assert that one is modern is to claim that one lives in a time in which life is fuller and richer than would have been possible earlier. The claim may be disputable, but it emerges from ancient biblical sources that made it part and parcel of the Western tradition. Instead of blending past and present or believing in a cyclical return of the past, Christians projected a one-way development of history from the Creation through the appearance of Jesus to the Second Coming. About the sixteenth century, the view that time moves in a direction in which the present supersedes the past had became widespread in Europe.

At the end of the nineteenth century, most Europeans considered themselves very modern in this sense of being at the apex of a progressive development of civilization. The phenomena discussed in the preceding chapter—vast economic growth, the power of railroads and electricity, new kinds of leisure—underlay this confidence. Scientific knowledge seemed secure and solid, so that all that remained to do was gather up sufficient facts to fill in the remaining holes.

But the very accomplishments of the industrialization that created this assurance also increased anxiety. In science, disturbing irregularities threatened the most basic understandings of the physical world. The character of time itself was changing, even in everyday life. Because railroads ran on a schedule, for example, they needed to rely on standard time. But timekeeping was not standard in the nineteenth century. Each region, even each town, kept time according to its own location. Not until 1884 did an

---

[1] The painting received its name only years later. Avignon refers not to the French city but to a street in the red-light district of Barcelona. The French word *demoiselle* also means "prostitute."

international convention divide the earth into twenty-four time zones and establish Greenwich as the zero meridian[2]—and even then years passed before the system took hold. By the turn of the century, the watch had become a prized possession, and a new pressure—the management of time—became the concern of all educated citizens.

Many other changes in ordinary life created anxieties as well. The spread of the metric system (see Chapter 20) did away with comfortable but confusing local weights and measures. Today English miles, feet, ounces, and pounds are all that remain. Standardized literary languages displaced the richly diverse mosaic of dialects and local languages; widely distributed newspapers homogenized public opinion into a relatively few categories; and factory schedules regimented working lives.

The scientists, writers, and artists we call modernists reacted against the tensions these standardizations produced. They questioned whether science really understood the physical world, whether progress was in fact being made, and whether conformity to middle-class values was actually a virtue. In their view, bourgeois culture, which they saw as dominating their era, was crass, dedicated to making money and exercising domination without any leavening balance of sensibility or ethics. To these critics—themselves products of the middle class—the virtues of conventional living seemed stultifying, naturalist paintings cloying, popular novels insubstantial, and consumerism demeaning. Modernists—impelled by radical individualism, or the idea of untrammeled personality freed from restriction—wanted to throw off all restraints on their right to interpret the world. This impulse to individualism, innovation, and criticism transformed Western culture as radically as it had ever been in such a short period of time and laid the cultural foundations for a disjointed, confused, and troubled twentieth century.

Given the individualistic nature of the modernist assessment and the pluralism of its techniques, no single philosophy could lie behind it. Nevertheless, developments in physics, psychology, and philosophy so fundamentally undermined nineteenth-century ideas that the first section of this chapter is devoted to these three areas. First we discuss the destruction of classical mechanics—the path from eighteenth-century natural philosophy through positivism to relativity theory. Next—at least as important in its impact on the popular mind—we explore Sigmund Freud's theory of the unconscious. Finally, we examine the corrosive philosophy of Friedrich Nietzsche. In the remainder of the chapter, we turn to artistic developments—first discussing the transformation of the novel, and then visiting the cultural specifics of a few representative cities.

---

[2] Greenwich is a suburb of London. The line of longitude that runs through it is the *zero meridian*, and all other places on the globe have their longitude defined in terms of degrees east or west of Greenwich.

DISTURBERS OF THE WORLD'S SLEEP

One of the most unexpected challenges to the nineteenth-century worldview was the dethroning of classical mechanics, the backbone of the exact sciences. Classical mechanics assumed that space was three dimensional and that forces operated according to Newton's laws. In the nineteenth century, these assumptions seemed as solid as the earth itself. Scientists believed that the fundamental laws of nature were known or knowable. They needed only to detail the exact mechanisms of a given phenomenon through precise observation. This mechanistic, materialist philosophy was called **positivism.**

Positivism

One of the main themes of nineteenth-century thought recapitulated an ancient question of Western philosophy: How can we know things about the world around us? (The study of how we obtain knowledge is called *epistemology*.) From the age of the ancient Greeks, two main approaches to this question have animated philosophers. The first, introduced to Greek philosophy even before the time of Plato, stipulates that we learn about the world through sensation (see Chapter 4). We see, feel, taste, smell, and hear, and therefore we know the reality around us. Over time, this general position has been elaborated in several specific philosophical movements, including nineteenth-century positivism. According to positivism, only the observation of verifiable facts provides accurate knowledge.

The second general approach is more abstract, interweaving both secular and religious threads. Plato had said that merely sensing material objects is not adequate because objects are temporary and changeable. A wood sculpture can be reduced to ashes by burning, but the idea of the sculpture remains intact. For Plato, ideas were eternal and unchanging, and therefore constituted the true reality. Christians also believed that reality could be found outside the material world, in the presence of God's creative will. Both of these latter points of view held that our experience involves something meaningful and real that is beyond the reach of mere sensation.

In the eighteenth century, the British philosopher David Hume demonstrated that there is no *necessary* connection between sensation and the ideas on which we base our actions. We learn by experience, by convention, and by habit, Hume agreed, but he showed that we can never prove causation absolutely. If that is the case, asked German philosopher Immanuel Kant late in the eighteenth century, how do we have what seems to be certain knowledge, such as that time only goes in one direction, or that objects occupy space? Kant agreed with Hume's contention that we can never know the essence of anything from observation. But, he said, notions of time and space are not products of sense experience or observation. They are simply the way the mind works. They are inherent categories of human thought. Causation also is not derived from observation, but from the interaction of categories of thought inherent to the mind. Kant did not want to rely solely on the science of his day, which he believed incapable of explaining ethics; but by suggesting that the mind contained its own mechanisms for creating understanding, he hoped to reassert the possibility of knowledge in the face of Hume's skeptical attack. Kant was engaged in what philosophers call **metaphysics,** or the investigation of first principles as the ultimate grounding of reality.

Kant's position that there were important things to be known beyond mere observation came to be called, in German, *Naturphilosophie* ("the philosophy of nature"). Naturphilosophie differed from what we think of today as science because it was primarily metaphysical. It postulated that the way to understand the world was to organize perception on the basis of a few basic principles, some of which were inherent in the organism and not susceptible to direct observation. One of the first great scientists to undermine this approach was Justus von Liebig (1803–1873), the father of organic chemistry. In the eighteenth century, persons whom we would call scientists today often had no institutional affiliation and were either wealthy or were supported by friends and patrons. In the nineteenth century, however, universities began to serve as the primary home of scientific investigation, especially in Germany. Liebig established a laboratory at the University of Giessen in 1824 to study the chemistry of plant life. In 1840 he published *Organic Chemistry in Its Application to Agriculture and Physiology*, which revolutionized the science of agriculture. Liebig argued that plants did not directly consume carbon from the decayed vegetable matter in soil (humus), as the natural philosophers held, but absorbed carbon from the air in the form of carbon dioxide and took from the humus only the chemicals created by its decomposition. Liebig proved a superb propagandist for his own work, which, despite his abilities as a chemist, often was riddled with errors and dogmatic assertions. The success of his book, his talent at self-promotion, and his abilities as a teacher of brilliant students generated broad enthusiasm for the notion that life could be understood as a chemical process for which no spiritual or metaphysical references were needed.

One problem Liebig grappled with through his experimental methods was animal heat. He asked, "Why are animals warm?" Under the laboratory conditions of the day, the total heat produced by an animal seemed more than the sum of the chemical reactions that experimenters found. Naturphilosophie could explain this by saying that there was an extra vital element at work not susceptible to measurement. Another German professor, Herman Ludwig Ferdinand von Helmholtz, disproved this claim. In a paper published in 1847, Helmholtz used mathematical and phys-

ical analysis to demonstrate the law of conservation of energy—that energy can be neither created nor destroyed, although it can change form. This breakthrough at the level of theory reinforced the conviction that no imponderable forces existed in the world and thus fortified enthusiasm for explanations that relied on observations of the material world rather than on metaphysics. In his subsequent career, Helmholtz did fundamental work on the physiology of the eye (he invented the ophthalmoscope, the device used today in eye examinations), the response time of nerves, and electrochemistry. This work firmly convinced him that all physical phenomena could be reduced to the laws of classical mechanics as originally put forward by Newton. His position was vigorously anti-metaphysical. The mind did not contain inherent notions of space, as Kant had claimed. All knowledge, in Helmholtz's view, was the product of interaction with the material world.

The work of Liebig and Helmholtz, among others, evoked great enthusiasm for materialism in central Europe. Ludwig Büchner's elaboration of an entire worldview based solely on material interactions, *Force and Matter* (1854), proved so popular that by 1884 the book had gone through seventeen German and twenty-two foreign editions. Büchner was a monist—"force and matter are fundamentally the same thing, contemplated from different standpoints"—and a determinist—"all human knowledge is necessarily and indissolubly interwoven with science." Near the end of the nineteenth century, another popular monist and Social Darwinist, Ernst Haeckel, summed up the self-satisfied materialist view: "Let us leave then the fruitless brooding over an ideal phantom to the 'pure metaphysician' and let us instead, as 'real physicists' rejoice in the immense progress which has actually been made by our monistic philosophy of nature."

The radical rejection of Naturphilosophie and metaphysics spread from the hard sciences into many other fields. The German historian Leopold von Ranke, for example, dismissed the use of abstract, universal principles, which he felt characterized the French Revolution, in favor of histories written according to the specific characteristics of each people. The basis of our understanding is not reason, he claimed, but historical continuity. Ranke created the idea of "scientific" history, or history written solely on the basis of detailed and accurate reading of primary documents. He believed that this method would enable historians to write about the past "as it actually was" (*wie es eigentlich gewesen*, one of the most famous phrases of the nineteenth century).

German scholars in economics and law seized on this idea and developed the notion that all phenomena in their fields were historically determined. They insisted on an empirical approach that would investigate how the total experience of a society, including its organic structures such as community and nation, had led to certain economic or legal results. Their approach is called **historicism.**

Its practitioners indulged in detailed, pedantic gathering of factual material in the hope that generalizations would somehow emerge from the accumulation of massive amounts of data.

Nineteenth-century materialism and historicism were in good measure German phenomena, but the inventor of the name that we use to describe their style of thought—positivism—was a Frenchman, Auguste Comte (1798–1857). This brilliant but fuzzy thinker started his career as secretary to the socialist Saint-Simon and ended as an advocate of strange visions of ecstatic Christianity. Between these two stages he produced several multivolume studies of what he called positive philosophy. Comte argued that philosophy had passed through three stages of development in its progress to true understanding. The first was the theological stage, in which speculation about reality concerned itself with supernatural and miraculous powers; the second was the metaphysical stage of the eighteenth century, in which first principles and Naturphilosophie formed the basis of investigation; the third and final stage was positive science, through which the nineteenth century was correcting the errors of the first two stages.

Comte held that all knowledge came from applying mathematically expressed natural laws to the objectively observed "positive data of experience." Metaphysics could never penetrate beneath surface appearances, in Comte's opinion. Neither could it provide a constructive blueprint for change, because it was primarily a method of speculation. Comte wanted not only to think about the world, but to change it. "Science whence comes prediction; prediction whence comes action," was one of his mottoes. The culminating science, in Comte's opinion, was sociology, the science of society. Underlying sociology were the material sciences of physics and chemistry, supported by mathematics, but only an all-encompassing science of society, in Comte's view, could understand the complexity of human interactions.

The founders of sociology as we know it today, who were writing at the turn of the century, went beyond Comte. Unlike the positivists, they introduced general notions that attempted to explain explicit theoretical frameworks. Émile Durkheim (1858–1917), the French scholar who is considered the father of modern sociology, could be just as indefatigable in his search for factual materials as any positivist, as his investigations of the rising rate of suicide in industrializing societies showed. But Durkheim did not let the facts speak for themselves. Dissatisfied with conventional explanations, he created an entire theory of how individuals internalized and used the conventional standards of their day. He pointed out, for example, that by observing an event, the observer actually becomes part of that event. The boundary between "society" and "the individual," therefore, was much more blurred than previous thinkers had claimed. Thus, Durkheim argued, it is not possible to obtain a static, or "objective," view of social relations, but only one that takes into account the continued interaction of individuals within a social system.

The German social thinker Max Weber (1864–1920) also suggested the necessity of conceptual frameworks, especially when comparing societies. He argued that to analyze human religious behavior across cultures, it was necessary to develop "ideal types," or generalized, purposefully incomplete concepts that go beyond the data itself while still permitting comparative statements to be made. His ability to theorize from a wide range of data permitted him to make observations about the relationship of the Protestant ethic and the spirit of capitalism that still evoke interest and controversy, and to create powerful theories about why people obey their governments. Together, Durkheim and Weber began to dismantle positivism in the social sciences.

Positivism Destroyed: Mach and Einstein

But dismantling was not destroying. During the course of the nineteenth century, positivism—invented by philosophers like Comte, supported by scientists like Helmholtz, and advocated by writers like Büchner—had replaced Naturphilosophie as the dominant scientific viewpoint. And it was in the hard sciences, which the positivists believed was their bedrock, that positivism reached its peak as well as its turning point late in the nineteenth century. Ernst Mach, who spent most of his career as a professor of physics at the Charles University in Prague, was a key transitional figure. Mach believed that verification through rigorous observation constituted the only admissible argument in natural science. He helped to found the school of thought called *empiriocriticism*, which held that all theories are only intellectual fictions that prove helpful in organizing data. Mach considered even the absolute view of time and space required by Newtonian physics to be an intellectual fiction. But his study of the propagation of waves led him to conclude that inertia, or the tendency of a moving body to continue in motion, could only be understood in relation to all other bodies in the universe. That is, motion was always relative. Although a gifted scientist, Mach's empiricism prevented him from pushing this insight to its logical conclusion. That task fell to Albert Einstein (1879–1955).

Einstein was not a precocious youth (he did not learn to talk until he was three), and his family was not considered particularly intellectual. He disliked high school and had trouble finishing it, but his mathematical abilities earned him admission to a technical school in Switzerland. There he received excellent training. Despite this inauspicious beginning, Einstein grew fascinated with physics, which he pursued with a determined passion. When he graduated, he could not find an academic job, in good measure because he was Jewish, so he went to work as an evaluator of patent applications in Bern. (He had become a

Swiss citizen, although born in Germany.) From the time he entered technical school at age sixteen until he published his famous set of four papers in 1905 at twenty-six, Einstein worked more or less alone, learning physics from reading the classic studies and wrestling with the contradictions that he found in them.

Forty years before the publication of Einstein's papers, British researcher James Clerk Maxwell had shown that light took the form of an electromagnetic wave. Classical mechanics understood wave propagation but held that the vibrations constituting the waves could be transmitted only through a medium, such as water. What medium transmitted light? Nineteenth-century physicists suggested that the entire universe was pervaded with an "ether," and that vibrations of this ether caused us to perceive light. The qualities of the ether were formidable—it had to be ubiquitous, rigid, and yet infinitely flexible. But the analogy of a fish in water seemed applicable. Just as one can imagine that a fish does not perceive that it is swimming in water, we might not perceive that we are living in ether. If an ether existed, however, it should be possible to detect its effect on the speed of light, which should move faster when propagated in the same direction that the ether was

flowing, and slower in the other direction. Then, in a famous series of experiments, the most important of which was conducted in 1887, the American scientists Albert Abraham Michelson and Edward Williams Morley proved, contrary to expectations, that light moved at the same speed in every direction. In other words, the supposed ether had absolutely no effect on the speed of light. It was undetectable. Nevertheless, only a few years after the Michelson-Morley experiment, Lord Kelvin, one of the world's most famous physicists, maintained that "one thing we are sure of, and that is the reality and substantiality of the luminiferous ether."

Einstein knew of the Michelson-Morley experiments, but he came to his insights primarily by contemplating the work of Maxwell and Mach. One of his key findings, published in 1905, was that light did not travel exclusively in a wave pattern, but also in packets of energy, later called photons. This concept disposed of the necessity for the ether. In another paper published in the same year, Einstein asked what would be the logical consequences of the fact that light moves at the same speed everywhere. Newton's assumption, fully accepted until Einstein, was that time and space were absolute and the speed of light varied.

The Speed of Light Albert Abraham Michelson poses in the lab in which he and Edward Williams Morley proved that light moves at the same speed in every direction. The two American scientists demonstrated in 1887 that the speed of light was constant and not affected by the hypothetical luminiferous ether. Their result helped lead Einstein to his theory of relativity. *AP/Wide World Photos.*

But Einstein knew that the speed of light did not vary—it was absolute. Therefore, contrary to what Newton held, time and space must vary according to the position from which we observe them. In other words, time and space are inextricably intertwined. The world is not three-dimensional, as the ancient Greek mathematician Euclid had held (see Chapter 4), nor is space uniform, as Kant speculated. Rather, the world is at least four-dimensional, with time as the fourth dimension, and it varies with the position of the observer. Just as Newton had created a new **paradigm** for classical mechanics, Einstein introduced another paradigm for twentieth century physics.[3]

In 1916 Einstein went further, modifying Newton's view of gravity. Gravity proved to be not a force, but "a curved field in the space-time continuum." On the basis of this understanding, Einstein made predictions, such as that light bends when it passes a massive body in space, that were confirmed by observation only many years later. Einstein also confirmed in mathematical terms the equivalency of mass and energy—$E = mc^2$, or the energy of an object is equal to its mass times the speed of light squared—a key concept in making the release of atomic energy possible. The laws of classical mechanics were no longer absolute. But for Einstein's effects to become noticeable, bodies had to be moving at a velocity close to the speed of light. In ordinary life, or even in the motion of planets, the effects were so small as to be virtually undetectable. Nevertheless, the development of physics in the twentieth century has amply demonstrated the correctness of Einstein's insights, making him, as one colleague called him, "the Copernicus of the twentieth century."

One of the first prominent scientists to champion Einstein's work was Max Planck, professor of theoretical physics at Berlin. In 1900, Planck explained many of the experimental anomalies that had been bedeviling physics in the previous decade by showing that the frequency of electromagnetic radiation had a constant relationship to its energy (Planck's Constant) and that this energy could be received only in discrete amounts, or quanta. The implications of Planck's work was similar to that of Einstein's, but at a different scale. Whereas Einstein showed that Newtonian physics does not accurately describe very large and very fast phenomena, Planck discovered that it did not accurately describe the workings of very small phenomena either, the interior of the atoms themselves.

Einstein and Planck, along with the other physicists who created the new quantum mechanics of relativity, were not modernists in the artistic or literary sense. But their work brought into question the capacities of ordinary perception. Space was flexible; time was relative; absolute proofs were impossible. Many writers and artists found these concepts exciting. Indeed, in the years preceding World War I so many of them challenged positivistic modes of thought that by the outbreak of World War I a small but critical element in society—the participants in high culture—no longer believed in the optimistic certainties of the nineteenth century. The *fin-de-siècle* ("end of the century") sense of foreboding that underlay the otherwise ebullient mood of progress fueled by economic advances and imperial successes had its source in these challenges.

The Relativity of Consciousness: Bergson and Freud

Henri Bergson is little read today, but in the years before World War I he was France's most influential and popular philosopher. Bergson was a lucid stylist and an inspired teacher. As a brilliant student in the 1880s, he adhered entirely to the positivist view that all reality could be described through the laws of classical mechanics. But in his mid-twenties, his views began to change, particularly when he contemplated the problem of consciousness. Psychological facts, Bergson observed, are not like physical facts. Contrary to what the positivists claimed, consciousness could not be explained through classical mechanics. It seemed to Bergson that consciousness flowed in waves that did not exist in space at all and that were not measurable by the rigid units of time used by science. The problem with the mechanistic view of the universe, Bergson concluded, was that it could not account for the changes brought on by the creativity of consciousness. The law of conservation of energy, for example, held that energy could never be created; it merely changed form under different circumstances. But to Bergson this theory implied that nothing truly new could ever occur. Because new ideas *had* emerged, the law of conservation of energy could not completely explain human experience. Some element not susceptible to the explanations of classical mechanics had to exist.

Bergson's ideas were part of a movement called *vitalism*. Vitalists could not accept Darwin's assertion that evolution proceeded by random changes enhanced by differential survival over time. This process seemed to deprive human beings of free will. Bergson gave vitalism its most famous slogan in the title of his book *Creative Evolution* (1907). He argued that Social Darwinists and materialists attributed qualities to evolution that were too mechanical and inevitable. Evolution did not march lockstep to some predetermined end, he wrote, but moved forward in a creative way, driven by what he called *élan vital* ("vital impulse"). Science was only one way of knowing, he said. Another way, superior in discerning the essence of reality, was intuition, which reached into the heart directly and with sympathy. In the work of Bergson and the vitalists, the pendulum swung from positivism back toward Naturphilosophie.

---

[3] For a discussion of paradigms in the Scientific Revolution, see Chapter 17.

Freud's Consulting Room
Freud and his Viennese patients were firmly established in the upper middle class. Freud's interest in African art is apparent, an exotic passion for the middle class. Notice the couch (on right) on which the patient reclined during a consultation. *Freud Museum/Sigmund Freud Copyright.*

Despite Bergson's popularity, his ideas had only a short-term impact after the shock of World War I displaced public concerns. The experience of Sigmund Freud (1856–1939) proved almost exactly the opposite. Obscure as a young man, his ideas about consciousness exerted an enormous impact over time. As a high school student, Freud found Darwin inspiring and Goethe stimulating, but when he entered medical school in 1873 at the age of seventeen he adhered to the positivist view. He trained in neurology under a strong supporter of Helmholtz's materialism. Yet, by the time he was thirty, Freud began to change his mind. He became increasingly interested in psychological disorders. Lengthy discussions with a colleague who had noticed that a patient's symptoms of hysteria lessened if she talked directly about them led Freud to develop the technique of *free association*.[4] Following a visit in 1885 to Paris, where he observed France's greatest neurologist induce tremors or paralysis in subjects by hypnosis, Freud hypnotized his patients to start them talking about their anxieties. By 1890 he found that he got better results by simply asking them to discuss whatever seemed related to their feelings. Patients let their thoughts and emotions move freely without hints from the analyst. Some modernist authors, such as James Joyce, later adopted a similar technique in their fiction, calling it *stream of consciousness*.

Listening to these confessions, Freud noticed that much of his patients' hysteria had links with childhood sexual experiences. He was astonished at the apparently large number of traumatic seductions that his patients related, but soon he hypothesized that these were fantasies born of wanting something forbidden (wish fulfillment) or of seeking the power of a dominant person (role reversal).[5] This insight revealed to him the complexity of an unconscious realm in which imagination assumes a presence more compelling than reality.

Freud's insistence on treating hysteria as a medical problem and his increasing interest in sexuality began to estrange him from his medical colleagues, but he persisted. When his scientific papers received a cold reception he said, "I understood that from now onward I belonged to those who have 'troubled the sleep of the world.' . . . I made up my mind that . . . I was prepared to accept the fate that sometimes accompanies such discoveries." In 1897, near the end of a period of considerable personal stress, he began to analyze himself, and in part on the basis of the results, he published his most original and powerful work, *The Interpretation of Dreams* (1899).

---

[4] *Hysteria*, which derives from the Greek word for "womb," was a nineteenth-century term for depression, particularly among women.

[5] Later investigations have suggested that in fact the women Freud interviewed were probably telling the truth about being molested.

Dreams, Freud argued, are not nonsense, as the positivist Helmholtz school of medicine believed, but glimpses into repressed infantile experiences, especially those surrounding sexuality. The manifest content of the dream—how it appears to us—hides its latent content, the shaping impulses of our personalities that we have repressed because they are too frightening. One of the most common of these impulses, he argued, was the ambivalent desires of children toward their parents. One particular such desire, the urge of the son to kill his father in order to possess his mother, which Freud called the Oedipus complex, became his central metaphor of the unconscious. Dreams, like slips of the tongue and neurotic symptoms, are a method of releasing these subterranean desires and relieving the anxiety that repression has caused us.

The Interpretation of Dreams attracted absurdly small sales at first. After a negative review in the German newspaper *Die Zeit*, it took eight years to sell the first edition of six hundred copies. Nevertheless, Freud's reputation as the discoverer of the unconscious eventually grew to worldwide proportions. Until his death in 1939, he continued to elaborate, develop, and enrich his understanding of the human mind. Today, even though the study of mental disturbances has taken a biochemical direction (as Freud himself suggested it would), and even though psychoanalysis has become a relatively exotic therapy compared with cheaper and more effective approaches, Freud's fundamental insight that the human consciousness conceals as much as it reveals, and maybe more, has become a modern truism.

The Great Underminer: Friedrich Nietzsche

Like Freud, the German philosopher Friedrich Nietzsche (1844–1900) believed that ordinary human consciousness conceals more than it reveals, but his attack in the nineteenth century differed markedly from Einstein's or Freud's. The young Nietzsche was appointed associate professor of philology (the study of language) at the University of Basel at the age of twenty-four, even before he had finished his doctoral dissertation—unheard of in German-speaking universities. When he did begin to publish, he did not write works in his specialty, ancient Greek literature. He hated the whole "molish business [of philology], the full cheek pouches and blind eyes, the delight at having caught a worm, and indifference toward the true and urgent problems of life."

For Nietzsche, the true and urgent problem was to escape from the nihilism (meaninglessness) that he thought characterized the age. The disgusting thing about nineteenth-century life, in Nietzsche's view, was that its apparent decency and compassion concealed a nauseating falseness and a conformist banality. The Bismarckian state, far from being the shining embodiment of German genius, as German nationalists held, was actually a bombastic inflator of false values and a cynical destroyer of aesthetics.

Friedrich Nietzsche   This portrait was drawn by a friend after Nietzsche had gone insane, probably as a consequence of syphilis. *The Granger Collection, New York.*

Christ may have been a perfect bearer of the good news of God's sympathy for man, but Christianity had replaced strong pagan values with weak admonitions to turn the other cheek. Nietzsche believed that unproductive smugness, intellectual snobbery, and facile condescension blocked the search for real values. He encapsulated these views in his famous epigram "God is dead." This was a tragedy, but it was human beings themselves who had corrupted and destroyed the true values of religion, art, and philosophy, he lamented. It is we ourselves, with our positivistic science and our materialism, who have killed God, Nietzsche insisted, and he feared what would happen to Western civilization when the reality of God's death reached the broad masses.

Nietzsche's first attack along these lines, *The Birth of Tragedy* (1872), remains one of his most widely read works. Ostensibly about Greek tragedy, the book actually argues that the interaction of two human motivations has been the wellspring of all culture. The Apollonian instinct, which he named after Apollo, the Greek god of music and poetry, is the rational drive to create order, beauty, and harmony, not only in art, but in one's own personality. The Apollonian strives toward individuation and uniqueness. The Dionysian drive, named after Dionysus, the Greek god

THE HISTORICAL EVIDENCE

Thus Spake Zarathustra: Friedrich Nietzsche and the Death of God

1883

Nietzsche chose the ancient Persian prophet Zoroaster (referred to as Zarathustra in this selection) to be his protagonist in part because he did not represent an omnipotent god such as Christians believed in. In fact, in this prologue, Nietzsche has Zarathustra proclaim the death of God. What he meant was that humans could no longer rely on a supernatural being to save them, but had to achieve meaning through their own efforts.

After spending ten years in the mountains, Zarathustra returns to human habitation, whereupon he meets an old saint in the forest. The two talk.

"Do not go to man [says the saint]. Stay in the forest! Go rather even to the animals! Why do you not want to be as I am—a bear among bears, a bird among birds?"

"And what is the saint doing in the forest?" asked Zarathustra.

The saint answered: "I make songs and sing them; and when I make songs, I laugh, cry, and hum: thus I praise God. With singing, crying, laughing, and humming, I praise the god who is my god. But what do you bring us as a gift?"

When Zarathustra had heard these words he bade the saint farewell and said: "What could I give you? But let me go quickly lest I take something from you!" And thus they separated, the old one and the man, laughing as two boys laugh.

But when Zarathustra was alone he spoke thus to his heart: "Could it be possible? This old saint in the forest has not yet heard anything of this, that *God is dead!*"

Source: From *The Portable Nietzsche*, ed. and trans. Walter Kaufmann (New York: Viking, 1954), pp. 123–24.

---

of wine and inspiration, is the human lust for physicality, the desire to exceed norms, to lash out, to get drunk, and to destroy. In unleashing passion, the Dionysian loses individuality and merges with the whole, replacing personality with ecstasy. The genius of Greek tragedy, Nietzsche thought, was to tame the Dionysian impulses with Apollonian forms. Abstract as this analysis may sound, *The Birth of Tragedy* constituted a bitter assault on the predominant academic view of Nietzsche's day that the Greeks—and by extension all human beings—were essentially virtuous and rational. Nietzsche wanted to reveal the passionate underside of human character, which he believed the hypocrisies of Victorian culture obscured.[6]

As he grew older, Nietzsche found an even more fundamental drive underlying human actions—the will to power. Every human being sought power, but not necessarily in the sense of political power. For Nietzsche, power lay

in the final accomplishment of combining the Apollonian and Dionysian drives into one personality. The superior being recognized and accepted his or her own passions and yet, seeking ultimate satisfaction, found the strength to integrate them into a single personality. Through this integration, one experienced the uniqueness of one's nature while simultaneously grasping the vastness of the world. This is what Nietzsche meant by power—the feeling that everything was right and that nothing needed to be added or subtracted from the moment. For power politics, he had only contempt.

Not everyone can put the will to power to its most exalted use. Nietzsche accepted the scientific validity of Darwin's theory of evolution, but in his mind human beings had not necessarily evolved to the top of the animal kingdom, as Social Darwinists held. To him, the theory of evolution implied that ordinary human beings are essentially beasts. Everyone has the potential to use the will to power to create a whole character, but only superior people—artists, philosophers, and saints—succeeded. Nietzsche called this superior person the *Übermensch*, or "overman." Such a person, by relying on his or her own insights rather than on conventional wisdom, rises above

---

[6] Nietzsche's analysis eventually had a profound impact upon scholars in the field of ancient history and literature. It opened their eyes to the importance of the irrational and pre-rational in classical culture. See Chapters 3 and 4.

the limitations of culture and personality, and achieves a plateau of understanding far above the uncomprehending masses. In other words, the Übermensch becomes free.

From this brief sketch of some of Nietzsche's most important ideas, it is easy to see how his work later exerted a baleful influence. No nineteenth-century philosopher was more dedicated to the painful uncovering of truth. Nietzsche questioned every presupposition and challenged every assumption. He passionately opposed systems of thought that confined the possibility of investigation. And yet the implications of expressions like "the blond beast" who asserted a "will to power," the concept of "overman" (which was transformed by the Irish playwright George Bernard Shaw into "superman"), Nietzsche's transformation of the Christian values of *good* and *bad* into *strong* (master) and *weak* (slave), and the ease with which his aphorisms can be taken out of context led to his appropriation by the Nazis as the justifier of their cause. Nietzsche's sister—who took control of his papers when the philosopher went insane and who was a committed antisemite— aided and abetted this process. She rearranged his notes, suppressed documents, made up anecdotes, and generally turned Nietzsche from a corrosive critic of all existing norms into a proto-Nazi. In actuality, of course, Nietzsche was contemptuous of antisemitism and nationalism. His sister's important aberration aside, Nietzsche's aphoristic style, his ability to penetrate deeply beneath the surface satisfactions of the late nineteenth century, and his interest in aesthetics made him perhaps the most characteristic early progenitor of modernism.

WRITING IN A NEW KEY: LITERARY MODERNISM

The earthquakes rumbling outward from Einstein, Freud, Nietzsche, and others opened a chasm at the feet of the twentieth century. The relativity of time, the vastness of the unconscious, and the passion underlying the human condition all undermined Victorian confidence. Moreover, all three areas of investigation were essentially international phenomena. It was immaterial, for example, that Dmitri Mendeleyev, the discoverer of the table of elements, was Russian; that Marie Curie, the discoverer of radioactivity, was Polish; or that Michelson and Morley were Americans. Their research quickly entered the international network of science. Freud's findings, although the product of a particular Viennese culture, seemed to apply to all human beings. And although Nietzsche attacked his own German society, his passionate denial of pretense and superficiality had a powerful impact on intellectuals in every country.

Literature and the visual arts have universal aspirations also, and the greatest nineteenth-century works can be appreciated by all. But literature, and to some degree art, has such close ties to the specific culture in which

Marie and Pierre Curie Marie Curie was born in Poland, studied physics in Paris, discovered two new elements (polonium and radium), found that beta rays consisted of negative particles, won two Nobel prizes, was the first woman professor at the Sorbonne, and had a daughter, Irene (shown here in not too good a mood) who was also a Nobel laureate. *Corbis.*

it arises that each country's literature is unique. The nineteenth-century English novel often reflected the Victorian ethic, whereas in France the genre had several distinct styles such as naturalism and realism. Russian novels, among the most powerful works of the nineteenth century, strongly reflected specifically Russian conditions. Nevertheless, in the few years before World War I and the decade that followed, the modernist impulse transformed all European literatures.

The Nineteenth-Century Novel

Although poetry and the short story flourished in the nineteenth century, the novel became the characteristic form of European literature in the Victorian era. Several explanations have been offered for this dominance. Novels, which were essentially extended stories, often centered on what the nineteenth century considered the woman's sphere— family life, courtship, and romance. When rising prosperity offered middle-class women more leisure time than ever, they took to reading novels.

But in an industrializing age, novels were not the literature solely of middle-class women. Broadened educational opportunities, technological improvements in papermaking and printing, and the spread of railroads all played their role in popularizing this literary form. Most of the best nineteenth-century novels were written as serial publications appearing weekly or monthly. This accounts for their stirring narrative style—novels were entertainment, and authors had to keep their readers' interest up. Writers often ended episodes with tantalizing hints of what was to come, much as television soap operas do today. With the advent of railroads, booksellers began offering novels in both serial and book form in railway stations, and sales climbed. Lending libraries and reading rooms cropped up, not only in the developed countries like Great Britain but also in small, poor ones, such as Serbia and Bulgaria. For a nominal annual fee, members could borrow books rather than buy them. The success of these enterprises led to the creation of public libraries, supported by government, where books could be borrowed freely. In 1870 the popularity of the novel moved English author Anthony Trollope to comment, "Novels are in the hands of us all; from the Prime Minister down to the last appointed scullery-maid." Indeed, Prime Minister Benjamin Disraeli himself had been a successful novelist in his youth.

Novels may have been entertainment, but the best of them were also works of art that probed human emotions and immersed the reader in timeless issues of ethical choice. Often, novelists provided social criticism along with their narratives, sometimes overtly moralizing, as in the case of Charles Dickens, and sometimes criticizing social pretensions more subtly, as in the case of Gustave Flaubert. Romanticism had a major impact on the novelists of the first half of the nineteenth century, but authors like Dickens, Honoré de Balzac, and Victor Hugo moved beyond romanticism to describe the life of ordinary people in a way that provided both a critique of social injustice and an uplifting moral message. In the second half of the century, authors like Ivan Turgenev, George Eliot, and Gustave Flaubert also described the lives of ordinary people, but with crisper prose and more realistic narratives. Devoid of the implausible coincidences characteristic of Dickens and the florid style typical of Balzac, these realists nevertheless had substantial aesthetic concerns. Finally, Émile Zola pushed beyond realism to naturalism, a pessimistic and determinist approach he alleged was scientific. Zola saw life as beyond human control, driven by the chance of random evolution.

Whatever the novelist's style or national tradition, the novel's omniscient narrator told a story extending over several years about families and their various complexities. Romance, or at least courtship, usually made up part of the story, although authors left physical sexuality to the imagination. Midcentury novels could contain evil characters, but on balance the outcomes had to be edifying. All in all, the novel provided a moral foil to the Victorian ethic, a mirror that reflected its fascination with science, and a critical lance to its pretensions.

In England many of the best novelists were women. Jane Austen, and Charlotte and Emily Brontë from the early part of the century, and George Eliot (the pen name of Mary Ann Evans) from midcentury, join Charles Dickens, William Thackeray, Thomas Hardy, and American-born Henry James on the short list of the finest English prose writers. Even lesser writers of social novels, gothic romances, and "potboilers" were often women. "No restrictions can shut women out from the materials of fiction,"

said George Eliot, "and there is no species of art which is so free from rigid requirements."

Nineteenth-century English novelists were inspired storytellers. The most popular among them in the first two-thirds of the century was Charles Dickens, whose publishing career spanned thirty years beginning in 1836. A masterful creator of comic characters, Dickens was also a reporter and social critic of the first order. Dickens often used the innocence of children to emphasize the crushing weight that industrial society imposes on the natural goodness of individuals. Few scenes in literature are more famous—or more pitiful—than the moment when the young orphan Oliver Twist, mistreated and half-starved, approaches the master of his orphanage and asks for more gruel. After the stupefied astonishment that this unprecedented request provokes, the horrified board of the orphanage throws Oliver into solitary confinement and offers five pounds sterling to anyone who will take him off their hands. In the end, of course, after many travails, Oliver's good nature—and the improbable discovery at the end of the novel of his genteel lineage—carries him through.

Dickens was a moralist, as were most nineteenth-century novelists. More than most, Dickens batters the

Dickens's Social Commentary What!? More gruel? Dickens's ability to draw affecting word portraits of social injustice made him one of the most powerful writers of his day. *The Granger Collection, New York.*

reader with insistent messages, especially in his later, more pessimistic novels. In *Bleak House,* for example, he used the overwhelming pettiness of the interminable inheritance case of Jarndyce and Jarndyce to ridicule lawyers and their court system. *Hard Times* describes a hardscrabble industrial town ("Coketown") where narrow educators use harsh methods to teach only facts. These caricatures of utilitarianism and classical economics deprive the human spirit of any breathing room. The Coketown manufacturers suck the life out of all those around them for their own petty gain.

George Eliot, the best English author of the 1860s and 1870s, was considerably more subtle. Her most renowned novel, *Middlemarch,* interweaves many themes—social change, the nature of science, the politics of the Great Reform, misreadings of personality—but its power lies in its nuanced and yet uplifting penetration into the personalities of its characters. Middlemarch is a provincial community in which people mistake each other's motives, misunderstand their own needs, and aspire to unattainable goals. And yet Eliot shows that growth is possible if one has the will to pursue real interests rather than those derived from others. Not only does her main character, who is a woman, survive a barren marriage to fashion a useful life, but even characters such as the local farm family prove capable of integrity.

Whether overt or subtle in their moral message, all English novels reflected the Victorian age's aggressive prudery concerning sex. The double standard of the day permitted middle- and upper-class men to satisfy their sexual desires through prostitutes and "fallen women," while married women were forced to remain modest and pure. English novels were therefore full of chaste women. If they flouted this norm, they suffered the consequences. The social pressure on writers to omit any hint of physical contact between the sexes was enormous. In one of the most famous instances, the late nineteenth-century author Thomas Hardy had to change a scene from the serialized version of *Tess of the d'Urbervilles.* His publishers refused to let Hardy have his hero carry milkmaids across a flooded road to safety. They insisted that Hardy provide a wheelbarrow, so that readers would not envision a man carrying a woman in his arms.

Women writers played an important role in France also; George Sand (pen name of Aurore Dupin) was one of the most successful French authors of mid-century. In the two decades before 1850, however, Victor Hugo and Honoré de Balzac filled the role in France that Charles Dickens did in England—although Hugo focused much more on politics than Dickens did, and Balzac moralized with a lighter touch. Both Hugo and Balzac broke with the romantics, who tended to write about the upper classes, and filled their novels with unrealistic and dramatic plot turns. The two men wrote about ordinary people in a direct way, but despite this verisimilitude, their works retained a romantic flavor.

Hugo, always politically engaged and furiously writing, started as a monarchist and ended as an exiled opponent of Napoleon III. His last novel, *Les Misérables* (1862), betrayed his romantic beginnings. In this vast and robust work, the hero sacrifices his fortune and his health to protect his family after being unjustly pursued for a youthful crime—a noble gesture reminiscent of the Romantic poets. The real inventor of the French novel, however, was Balzac. Flamboyant in his personal life, Balzac was driven, like Hugo, by an insatiable need to write. He would start with a simple story and then keep adding elements until he had a book. Using this method, he put together a set of about ninety novels and stories that he hoped would encompass all of French society. *The Human Comedy,* as he called this collection, culminated twenty years of literary effort and contained almost 2,500 named characters. Many of them came and went in smaller or larger roles until the reader grasped each character's personality by seeing it from various vantage points. Balzac established the convention in which an omniscient observer narrates a logically coherent and linearly developed story.[7]

Positivism and Darwinism had a strong impact in French writing, as the flamboyant style of Hugo and Balzac gave way to the straightforward realism of Gustave Flaubert. His *Madame Bovary* (1857) is not only a beautifully written dissection of middle-class aspirations and provincial vanities, but a profound critique of the limitations placed on women in nineteenth-century France. In it, the vivacious and able Emma Bovary marries a provincial doctor in order to escape her family. When her husband proves obtuse and inept, Emma, prevented by social convention from even conceiving of a career, is drawn to the excitement of affairs with impossible lovers. The realist Flaubert places a good part of the blame for Emma's illusions on her reading of romantic novels. Unhappiness at her inability to find satisfaction in her empty life eventually drives her to suicide.

Madame Bovary was considered so scandalous when it first appeared that Flaubert was indicted for "glorifying the poetry of adultery." He was acquitted, but the judge castigated Flaubert for his vulgar and shocking realism, which the judge took to be inadmissible in literature. Flaubert's crystal-clear descriptions of the situations that drove Emma's personality were not an accident, but the result of the extreme care that he took in composition. He sometimes spent an entire day polishing a single paragraph.

Realists had aesthetic intentions as well as social agendas, but naturalists, the most important of which was Émile Zola (1840–1902), were more concerned with science than art. They believed in the ability of classical mechanics to explain all aspects of life, even emotion. The French historian Hippolyte Taine put their creed this way: "There is a

---

[7] *Linear development* means the story proceeds from an earlier time to a later one in a straight line, without significant diversions.

THE HUMAN EXPERIENCE

Charles Baudelaire, Bohemian Precursor to Modernism

Charles Baudelaire (1821–1867) was not a modernist in the strict sense, for he lived in the first part of the nineteenth century and did not participate in the modernist movement as such. In many ways, however, he was a modernist before the term came into use. He experimented with form; he emphasized the dreamlike aspects of personality; he did not refrain from erotic subjects; and he understood himself as alienated from society. Most important, he attacked the nineteenth-century confidence that freedom leads necessarily to good. It is no wonder, then, that during his lifetime, and even after, his name was associated with depravity and dissolution. Baudelaire adopted a bohemian lifestyle that flew in the face of the ascendant middle class he purposefully alienated himself from. Addicted to opium and hashish, convicted of contravening public morals, debilitated by venereal disease, and crushed under a mountain of debt, he died almost in obscurity. Nevertheless, critics today consider him the greatest nineteenth-century French poet.

Baudelaire was born to a woman of twenty-eight and a man of sixty-two who promptly died, leaving him a substantial estate. His mother show-ered the boy with affection but remarried a military man who sent him off to military school. Baudelaire seemed to enjoy the experience, but in high school he developed a strong sense of independence and a powerful desire to become a writer. As soon as he graduated from high school, he left home and took up the dissolute life common to many wealthy young gentlemen of his day. His stepfather and mother tried to break him of his profligate ways by sending him on a lengthy trip to Asia, but he returned more independent and rebellious than ever. When he came into his fortune at the age of twenty-one, he moved into luxurious quarters, dressed in the finest clothes, and within two years had squandered a substantial part of his inheritance.

It was difficult to support oneself by writing alone in the mid-nineteenth century, but Baudelaire tried. In his twenties, he began writing art criticism—but with a new approach unlike anyone else's. Instead of simply describing the Salon, for example, and adding a few comments, Baudelaire used the shows as the basis for expounding his developing theory of art. Unlike the emerging realists, Baudelaire believed that imagination, aided by reverie and dream, was the only way to decipher nature's "forest of symbols" and to avoid the vice of banality.

In 1857 Baudelaire published many of the poems that he had written over the preceding fifteen years in a volume titled *The Flowers of Evil*. In Baudelaire's collection, unlike most other Victorian works, good did not triumph over evil. Quite the contrary. "Descend, descend, lamentable victims," he wrote. "Descend the road to eternal hell." The love poems are sometimes sensual and erotic ("And her arm and her leg, and her thigh and her loins/Polished like oil, undulating like a swan/Passed before my eyes"), and at other times macabre and depressing ("I am like a cemetery abhorred by the moon"). "The Thirst for Nothingness," "Obsession," and "The Self-Torturer" are a few titles from the section "Spleen and Ideal." In Baudelaire's vision, it is death—not progress—that awaits. Suffused with bizarre, drug-induced qualities and exuding contempt for conventional values, *The Flowers of Evil* could almost have been written by the equally bohemian Beat poets of the 1950s. ❖

cause for ambition, for courage, for truth, as there is for digestion, for muscular movement, for animal heat. Vice and virtue are products, like vitriol and sugar." Naturalists, like positivists, did not allow for the creative capacity of human beings. They were determinists: Heredity and environment alone defined one's fate.

Zola tended to portray simple characters with strong emotions and had a predilection for the social losers in the industrialization process, those whose lives the upper classes found sordid and dreary. The subjects of his novels included alcoholism, prostitution, and the grim experiences of coal miners. His *Nana* (1880) created a scandal with its description of the painful life of a prostitute, a theme that prompted conservatives to condemn Zola as a pornographer. In England, Zola's translator even went to prison. Zola had the most extreme faith in science of any nineteenth-century writer. In an essay titled "The Experimental Novel," published in 1880, he claimed that the novelist used his imaginary characters to conduct experiments capable of producing insights into the nature of personality, particularly crime and violence. Novelists do provide insights, of course, but Zola's faith that this was a scientific endeavor much like physics confused the methodologies of art and science. The latter operates in the systematic and linear realm of logic and system, whereas the former investigates inchoate sensibilities that often are difficult to express in rigorous form. Realists like Flaubert understood this better than naturalists like Zola.

Russian authors came under the influence of similar intellectual currents as did writers elsewhere in Europe, but this influence was diffused through the lens of Russia's unique political and social circumstances. Ivan Turgenev, for example, who spent much of his productive life in Paris, wrote a realist novel, *Fathers and Sons* (1862), that introduced the term *nihilism* and criticized the mutual incomprehension of Russia's two main social elements, the landowning nobility and the peasantry.

Yet Russia's two most powerful novelists rebelled against positivism. Fyodor Dostoevsky did not believe that human beings were "piano keys" to be played upon by evolution, but participants in their own lives, even though they often acted against their own self-interest. In *Crime and Punishment* (1867), Dostoevsky not only described the squalid murders committed by a highly intelligent student, but followed the murderer's entire thought process—the decision to kill, the carrying out of the crime, his ensuing guilt, and his confession. Raskolnikov, the murderer, believes that the extraordinary men of history were criminals. He kills a miserly old woman to determine whether he is such a person, but accidentally kills her innocent relative at the same time, thus muddying his purpose and throwing him into an anguish of guilt. The disturbing questions that Dostoevsky raised about human psychology established his long-term reputation in western Europe, for one finds in him hints of Freud, Nietzsche, and the twentieth-century philosophy of existentialism.

Dostoevsky immersed himself deeply in the controversies of his day, both as a novelist and as a journalistic writer. Nicholas I once sentenced him to death for participating in a mildly subversive philosophical discussion group. (The sentence was commuted to exile in Siberia as he was about to face the firing squad.) Count Leo Nikolaevich Tolstoy, on the other hand, spent most of his adult life living on his estate, running a school for peasant children, and writing. *War and Peace* (1869), Tolstoy's lengthy historical novel—the novelist Henry James called novels like it "baggy monsters"—follows the fortunes of several Russian aristocratic families during the Napoleonic period. Tolstoy sought, among other things, to disprove the positivist historical assertion that the direction of historical events was determined. He believed that pivotal events derived from the acts of ordinary individuals or families, not from great men and certainly not from rational calculation. His *Anna Karenina* (1875), on the other hand, typified the nineteenth-century novel in that it chronicled the downfall and eventual suicide of an elegant and able woman, criticized the emptiness of high society, and damned the nineteenth-century commonplaces—capitalism, industrialism, science, liberalism, and the railroad.

The Modernist Transformation: Joyce, Proust, and Kafka

Nineteenth-century novelists often were social critics as well as artists, but they presented coherent narratives, made their ethical position clear, kept the narrator aloof, and restrained themselves from overt sexuality. Modernist writers undermined all these conventions. Most important, the modernists experimented with form. Their texts no longer moved from one event to its logical successor, and their narrators often found themselves confused. Ambiguity and uncertainty, rather than fixed rational or moral positions, were the hallmarks of the modernists, as were increasingly explicit excursions into sexual behavior.

Joseph Conrad's *Heart of Darkness* (published in 1902) was a transitional work that expressed modernist ideas and had some stylistic affinities with modernism. Conrad (1854–1924) was a Polish merchant seaman who began to write in English relatively late in life. Perhaps because of this unusual background, *Heart of Darkness* did not explore romance and edification but the darkness of the human soul, including the unconscious. The narrator in this story, who travels up a turbulent river into Africa, is far from omniscient; he struggles with fears and terrors. Conrad confronted racism, rapacity, violence, and cruelty in a newly direct way, yet the novel contains so much ambiguity that it remains open to a wide variety of interpretations. *Heart of Darkness* contains no comforting happy ending.

Three of the most acclaimed modernist writers of the early twentieth century—James Joyce (1882–1941), Marcel Proust (1871–1922), and Franz Kafka (1883–1924)—all wrote their initial modernist work just prior to World War I and their most important major works just after the war. Joyce's *Dubliners*, which contains his most famous short story, "The Dead," appeared in 1914, and his *Ulysses* came out in 1922. The first volume of Proust's *Remembrance of Things Past* appeared in 1913, with the rest of the massive work appearing at intervals even after Proust's death in 1922. Kafka wrote his well-known story "Metamorphosis" in 1912.

An aversion to absolutes underlay the stylistic innovations of the modernists. Realists, like positivists, believed that they could portray the reality that they criticized. Modernists did not abandon criticism, but they understood reality in a far more complex way that went beyond social comment. Just as Einstein rejected the absolute nature of time, so modernist writers rejected the linear flow of causation. Both Joyce and Proust present their tale in digressions, diversions, and dislocations. As the critic Walter Benjamin said of Proust, he "snatched in passing the most astounding confidences of a declining age." Instead of clarity and flow, modernists provided depth and complexity. They portrayed ordinary experience as discontinuous, full of unexpected interruptions and wanderings of the mind. Events in modernist works are never complete in themselves. They are always in a state of becoming—there are no neat solutions.

In Kafka's work, cause and effect seem not to operate at all. Kafka's main character in *The Trial*, who is known only as Joseph K., can find no reason for his arrest, no

THE HISTORICAL EVIDENCE

Three Modernist First Lines from Kafka, Joyce, and Proust

1912, 1916, 1913

The best way to get a feel for modernist authors is to read their novels. To give an idea of how substantial their changes in style were, here are the first sentences of three works by authors discussed in this chapter. Of these three, only Proust starts out in a way that might be expected in a traditional narrative.

Franz Kafka

As Gregor Samsa awoke one morning from uneasy dreams he found himself transformed in his bed into a gigantic insect.

James Joyce

Once upon a time and a very good time it was there was a moocow coming down the road and this moocow that was coming down the road met a nicens little boy named baby tuckoo.

Marcel Proust

For a long time I used to go to bed early.

Sources: From Franz Kafka, "The Metamorphosis," *Selected Short Stories of Franz Kafka*, trans. Edwin Muir (New York: Modern Library, 1952), p. 19; James Joyce, *Portrait of the Artist as a Young Man* (New York: Viking, 1968), p. 7; Marcel Proust, *Remembrance of Things Past*, trans. C. K. Scott Moncrieff (New York: Random House, 1934), p. 3.

coherence in the mysterious accusations against him, and no logic in his judgment. For Kafka, Joseph K. is both guilty and innocent, unable to comprehend the world even at the moment of his casual execution. Proust's vision of time is equally unsettling. The ostensible theme of *Remembrance of Things Past* is the narrator's decision to write the novel that the reader is actually reading, which gives the novel a circular, and at the same time endless, feeling. The last part of the work is called *Time Regained,* and the last word in that last volume is *time*. The narrator, after endless digressions, prepares to write the novel that the reader has already read.

Joyce, Proust, and Kafka all probe the unconscious in ways unavailable to the nineteenth century. Indeed, Proust considered himself a novelist of the unconscious. He used what he called "involuntary memory." In the most famous scene in *Remembrance of Things Past*, the taste of a madeleine (a small piece of pound cake shaped like a seashell) dipped in weak tea suddenly unlocks the happy memories of the narrator's childhood and leads to the rest of the story. Joyce's similar device, especially in his early writing, is the small event or unexpected observation that provides a sudden sense of spiritual wholeness, not unlike the satisfaction that Nietzsche's overman experiences when he finally integrates his personality.

Joyce and Proust portrayed sex in new ways. Leopold Bloom, the Jewish outsider in Dublin whose experiences over the course of one day provides the subject of *Ulysses*, recalls masturbating as a youth. The final episode of the book details the semicoherent and passionate inner thoughts of his wife Molly during adulterous intercourse. These overt depictions of sexuality, while not pornographic by today's standards, prevented *Ulysses*'s publication in England until 1939. Proust wrote skillfully about love too, but unlike nineteenth-century authors he acknowledged homosexual as well as heterosexual attachments.

All three authors experimented with language. Joyce made up words, presented fragmented sentences, and relished puns, allusions, and obscure references. He wrote different sections of *Ulysses* in different ways; one chapter, for example, consists of 309 questions with answers. Proust, considered a talented narrative innovator, wrote in different voices, although readers often recall mainly the length of his sentences, some of which extend for more than a page. Both writers used stream of consciousness, or interior monologue. In this device, the author follows the not-entirely-random thoughts of a character, much in the way that Freud used free association. Proust opens *Remembrance of Things Past*, for example, with a thirty-page discussion of a man rolling over before he falls asleep. The point is to penetrate into the man's unconscious sensibilities while he lies in that half-world of not quite sleep—the night life of the mind, as Joyce called it. Kafka's prose was sparser (he admired Flaubert hugely) but the flatness of his narration contrasts with the originality of his situations. In the story "Metamorphosis," Gregor Samsa wakes up transformed into a huge beetle, utterly alienated from the world of humans. In "The Hunger Artist," the protagonist becomes the greatest practitioner of his trade, thereby starving himself to death while at the same time failing to achieve recognition for his talent. The mole in "The Burrow" finds comfort and security in an endless shuttling back and forth underground and out of sight.

These three authors were not the only ones experimenting around the turn of the century. French and Russian poets in particular pursued a new approach, which they called *symbolism*. Symbolists experimented with language in an effort to find an inner reality that ordinary prose could not capture. They believed that prose could never capture the "forest of signals," as the German poet Rainer Maria Rilke put it, that surrounds us. Instead they relied on allusion, metaphor, association, and analogies presented in innovative linguistic patterns. Popular particularly in the 1890s, symbolist poetry was yet another manifestation of the modernist sensibility.

THE URBAN IMPACT: MODERNISM IN THE ARTS

Cultural innovations as dramatic as modernism do not unfold in isolation or in only one field such as literature. At the turn of the twentieth century, every artist, writer, musician, philosopher, and critic reflected the breakdown of nineteenth-century certainties in their creative lives. Nev-

ertheless, the modernist thrust did not penetrate into the countryside, did not immediately undermine the power of the haute bourgeoisie or the aristocratic landowners, and did not have an immediate impact on religious faith. In the early twentieth century, modernism was an urban phenomenon. For that reason, we turn now to modernism as manifested in some of the great cities of Europe. We cannot discuss them all—Barcelona, Warsaw, Amsterdam, Cracow, Munich, Budapest, Prague, and many others were vital centers of ferment and innovation. Yet a close look at Paris and Vienna, and a glance at Moscow and St. Petersburg, should suggest how modernism transformed urban life across Europe.

Paris: Capital of the Nineteenth Century

Walter Benjamin, the German-Jewish critic, called Paris the capital of the nineteenth century. All the arts flourished in Paris, especially music, opera, and theater. In the 1890s, half a million people attended a theatrical production of some kind in Paris every week. Spectacular shows produced in huge halls and lit by limelight (calcium oxide—quicklime—heated to incandescence) were the rage. With the advent of electric lighting, tinsel, sequins, and foil provided glitter and sparkle that drew the public in droves.

This kind of popular theater irritated serious artists, who objected to its surface showiness, its lack of confrontation

*Courbet's *Burial at Ornans*,* 1847   The jury of the annual exhibition of paintings in Paris rejected Gustave Courbet's painting of a country funeral because it fell outside the conventions of its day. It was about ordinary events, it was painted in dull browns, and it was monotonous, as well as not uplifting. Not sold during Courbet's lifetime, it is today recognized as an important beginning of modern art. *Giraudon/Art Resource, NY.*

Manet's *Luncheon on the Grass,* 1863   Édouard Manet gives Courbet's realism a shocking twist by including a naked woman in an otherwise conventional middle-class scene. Also refused for the annual Salon, this painting was featured in the "Salon des Refusés" ("Exhibition of the Rejected").   *Erich Lessing/ Art Resource, NY.*

with the dark side of industrialization, and its motivation in profit. Some of the most serious challenges to mindless entertainment came from outside France. The Norwegian playwright Henrik Ibsen shocked and mesmerized audiences with his exposés of the psychological devastation that Victorian morality wrought on women, for example, and the plays of the Russian Anton Chekhov captured the despair and triviality of the lives of an exhausted Russian nobility. Both Ibsen and Chekhov used the traditional theater stage, wrote in normal language, and hoped to appeal to ordinary audiences, although they abandoned many conventions of nineteenth-century theater. In Paris, however, the reaction against popular spectacle took place offstage—in cabarets. The first cabarets were not nightclubs as we think of them today, but intimate gathering places at which avant-garde artists could meet, have a drink, and present their views to a sympathetic audience. Experimental artists called themselves avant-garde because they considered themselves harbingers of change, the advance scouts of a new and fuller life.

The first and most famous Parisian cabaret was le Chat Noir ("The Black Cat"), which opened its doors on November 18, 1881. Le Chat Noir was the exact opposite of popular theater. It was small, intended primarily for poets, painters, writers, and the like rather than the general public, and devoted to the small arts, such as poetry and singing. The poets who frequented le Chat Noir presented light, witty verse that mocked convention, but it was the singers who gave cabaret its character. The 1880s saw a

revival of the *chanson,* or traditional French song. In variety shows chansons tended to be sentimental, patriotic, and slightly vulgar. Cabaret chansonniers, on the other hand, performed biting songs of social protest that criticized philistinism and were often antiauthoritarian. "The Christmas Eve Revel of Beggars" was one such song:

> In icy Paris the church bells
> Ring, at the stroke of midnight, the song of Christmas,
> And the Vagabonds, without bread and without coats,
> Pass by shivering and cursing the heavens.
> Pale and muzzling the hunger besieging him
> The vagabond tells himself he will not go any further,
> And, far from the cops, stretching out on the snow,
> He'll kick the bucket in a corner like a mangy dog. . . .
> Fat bourgeois, fill yourself up, have a good time, kick up your heels!
> We, the paupers, are going to rouse ourselves!
> Alongside a bright hearth, vagrants without a sou or a stitch,
> We shall come one day to eat those chestnuts![8]

This mocking style scored such a success that within a year le Chat Noir was publishing its own newspaper and spawning imitations throughout Paris. By World War I, cabarets had spread throughout Europe.

---

[8] From Harold B. Segel, *Turn-of-the-Century Cabaret* (New York: Columbia University Press, 1987), pp. 38–39.

Painters also gathered in cabarets. Paris was Europe's most influential center for painting, for from the time of Louis XIV, the French government had put on a large annual show (the Salon) of works painted by members of the Academy of Fine Arts. The French revolutionary governments opened the Salon to nonmembers of the academy and began purchasing art for distribution to the provinces. The goal was educational—to raise the levels of taste and aesthetics and to instruct the nation in its historical and cultural heritage. By midcentury the selection jury for the Salon was receiving three to four thousand paintings for consideration each year. From this wealth, the jury, as well as the state purchasers, chose canvases that they considered most edifying for public morals, often limiting their selections to large conventional paintings with classical, romantic, or historical themes. Because the private market in art was quite limited until late in the nineteenth century, the Salons set the public—which meant middle- and upper-class—taste in art.

In the 1850s, several painters challenged conventional standards with works that paralleled the realist tendency in literature. Both the literary and the artistic move toward realism may have been influenced by the invention of photography, which presented an undeniably realistic, if often static, view of a scene. Gustave Courbet was one of the first realist painters. Rather than showing beautifully rounded, thinly disguised surrogates of ancient gods, Courbet's painting *Burial at Ornans* (1847, p. 918) depicts ordinary country people assembled for the burial of an unidentified person. Like Flaubert in *Madame Bovary*, Courbet accumulated factual details about his subject without telling the viewer what to think about it. This does not mean a painting like *Burial at Ornans* had no allegorical meaning: It clearly explores the aloneness of individuals facing their mortality. But the subject matter, the brownish palette that accurately portrayed earthy drabness, and the lack of a clear sign of how they should interpret the work shocked viewers.

Rouen Cathedral: Two Monet Impressions, 1894 Impressionists were sensitive to how changing light changed perceptions. Claude Monet painted the cathedral at Rouen from the same vantage point twenty times, in each instance portraying a different sense of its facade. *The Metropolitan Museum of Art, Theodore M. Davis Collection, Bequest 1915. (30.95.25.) Photograph © 1996 The Metropolitan Museum of Art; Erich Lessing/Art Resource, NY.*

David's *Death of Marat*, 1793 and Picasso's *Woman with Stiletto*, 1927   Comparison of these two pictures suggests what modernism means in art. On the top is David's famous portrait of the French Revolutionary journalist Marat, who has just been killed by Charlotte Corday. Of Picasso's painting on bottom, careful observation shows that it is modeled on David's painting, but in an exaggerated style. It shows an inflated Marat grasping for air after being attacked by a raging, screaming woman. Blood fills the tub and spills onto the floor. Not only a different image, it has a much more disturbing tone.   *Erich Lessing/Art Resource, NY (above); Musée Picasso, Paris. Droits d'autuer; Picasso Administration, Photo RMN-R. G. Ojeda. (below).*

Although today the originality of this painting is fully recognized, the Salon did not accept it and the work did not sell until after Courbet's death.

In 1863 the Salon rejected paintings from a number of young painters, including Edouard Manet. Manet had submitted a work titled *Luncheon on the Grass* (p. 919) depicting a naked woman picnicking in the woods with two fully dressed, proper-looking young men. Unclothed women had been a commonplace of European art for centuries, but Manet's figure was no classical nude. She was a contemporary woman staring out at the viewer, naked. Commentators called the painting "a shameful open sore," but the outcry from artists led Napoleon III to permit Manet and other rejected artists to hold an auxiliary exhibit. Crowds surged into the Salon des Refusés ("Salon of the Rejected"), but mostly to jeer and laugh. With the exception of Flaubert, who defended Manet, critics ignored the exhibit. Nevertheless, as the painter Paul Gauguin said later, "[Modern] painting begins with Manet."

The school of painting to which Manet belonged is called *impressionism*. Impressionists interested themselves in reality as much as the realists did, but they had a completely different view of what it constituted. They did not seek to portray "real life," which often implied social

Duchamps: Transition to Cubism   These three paintings show how cubism overtook Marcel Duchamps during a three-year period between 1910 and 1912. Although all three are about chess, each displays a unique and remarkable evolution. Top left, painted in 1910 and titled *The Chess Players* is a conventional painting of players. Bottom left, painted in 1911 and titled *Portrait of Chess Players* is of a similar scene but has become far more abstract. Finally, bottom right, painted in 1912 and titled *King and Queen Traversed by Swift Nudes* has Duchamps completely in the cubist style.
(*top left*) Acc #50-134-82, *Philadelphia Museum of Art*; (*bottom left*) Acc #50-134-56, *Philadelphia Museum of Art*; (*bottom right*) Acc #50-134-1102, *Philadelphia Museum of Art*.

criticism, but portrayed light, color, and air. "One does not paint a landscape, a seascape, a figure," said Claude Monet. "One paints an impression of an hour of the day." Impressionists transmitted their vision of these qualities with such vivacity that they remain today among the best known and most loved painters of the Western tradition. Edgar Degas, Paul Cézanne, Pierre Renoir, and Claude Monet were only the most renowned among them.

No sooner had impressionism begun to achieve some minimal recognition than younger artists pushed further. The postimpressionists went beyond recording the light and color that reached their senses to create entirely new perspectives. Vincent van Gogh laid thick swaths of brilliant color on his canvases to create distorted and yet intensely moving shapes. Paul Gauguin took a different route toward a similar end. Fascinated by primitive art, Gauguin left Paris to spend the most creative part of his career in the South Pacific, where his paintings of native

women and vegetation, sometimes in exotic and "unrealistic" colors, created their own vital world. Finally, the mature Paul Cézanne painted still lifes in which he depicted objects in the same painting from different angles, distorting perspective to offer the viewer illuminating interpretations of simple objects.

The postimpressionists undermined three-dimensional vision and attacked conventional ideas of color. But still, at least their art remained representational: Figures and scenes were recognizable, although presented in new and unsettling ways. Then, early in the twentieth century, artists from several countries completely recast the idea of representation. The greatest of these was Pablo Picasso, among the most prolific painters who ever lived and certainly the most influential in the twentieth century.

Picasso was born in southern Spain in 1881. His family quickly recognized him as a prodigy in art. When they moved to Barcelona in 1895, Picasso entered the bohemian

Kadinsky's *Improvisation No. 30, 1913* Not all innovation took place in Paris. Vasili Kandinsky, who in the 1920s and 1930s became noted for his completely abstract paintings, worked prior to World War I in Munich. This "improvisation" shows Kandinsky in transition from representational painting to his mature style. *Oil on canvas, 109.2 × 109.9 cm. Arthur Jerome Eddy Memorial Collection, 1931.511. Photograph © 1999. Art Institute of Chicago.*

life of Spain's most cosmopolitan city, becoming a regular at The Four Cats, a cabaret modeled after le Chat Noir. At the age of 19, he traveled to Paris and fell in love with the city. His art quickly found buyers, and by 1904 he settled in the French capital permanently.

After his great painting *Les Demoiselles d'Avignon,* discussed at the beginning of this chapter, Picasso moved on to a new level of abstraction, *cubism.* In 1908 he began a brief but fertile collaboration with Georges Braques that led to paintings that almost, but not quite, dispensed with representation altogether. But even cubism did not make the jump into total abstraction. That leap came not in Paris, but in Zurich, where during the decade of World War I the Russian painter Vasili Kandinsky abandoned any references to objects and began to paint pure abstractions. Kandinsky completed the line of development that led from the great storytellers of the early nineteenth century, both in literature and painting, through the realists and impressionists, to Picasso and the twentieth century. After Picasso and Kandinsky, the possibilities for presenting images in paint and other media opened to infinity.

Vienna 1900

The atmosphere in fin-de-siècle Vienna was heavier than in Paris. Not that Vienna was not exuberant. The light operas of Franz Lehár (*The Merry Widow*) and the waltzes of Johann Strauss ("The Blue Danube") kept the middle and upper classes of Vienna amused. But by 1900, the overwhelming formality and dignity of Emperor Francis Joseph, whose reign began in 1848 and ended in 1916, set a rigid tone that penetrated the mind-set of every Viennese. The writer Robert Musil called Austria-Hungary "Kakania." This play on words derived from the phrase *Kaiserlich und Königlich* ("imperial and royal"), which appeared everywhere in its abbreviated form as *K. und K.* (pronounced "kah unt kah"). Of course, *Kaka* is also a German baby word for excrement. In Kakania, Musil wrote,[9]

---

[9] From Robert Musil, *The Man without Qualities,* copyright © 1953 by Coward-McCann, Inc., taken from Perigee paperback edition published by G. P. Putnam Sons, 1980, p. 32.

Of course cars also drove along [the] roads; but not too many cars. The conquest of the air begun here too; but not too intensively. Now and then a ship was sent off to South America or the Far East; but not too often. There was some display of luxury; but it was not, of course, as over sophisticated as that of the French. One went in for sport; but not in madly Anglo-Saxon fashion. One spent tremendous sums on the army; but only just enough to assure one of remaining the second weakest among the great powers.

In the varied and multiethnic Austro-Hungarian Empire, Bosnians, Romanians, Slovaks, Italians, Czechs, and above all Jews—among others—competed with Germans for jobs in Vienna. Vast working-class neighborhoods surrounded an imposing administrative center. Francis Joseph had rebuilt the center of his capital in much the same way Napoleon III had rebuilt Paris. But instead of constructing straight boulevards, Francis Joseph had commissioned massive government buildings in a semicircle around the ancient medieval center of the city. The Ring, as it was called, created an impressive but overbearing style of architecture that spread throughout central and southeast Europe. In the army officer's club in Bucharest (Romania), or the national theaters in Belgrade (Serbia) or Zagreb (Croatia), one could almost imagine being in Vienna.

By the 1890s, many of Vienna's avant-garde had come to detest the Ring buildings. They considered them falsely traditional and stultifyingly nonfunctional. For this reason, some of the most important monuments of Viennese modernism took the form of buildings; modernist architects created designs based on function instead of on imperial grandeur. "Nothing impractical can ever be beautiful," architect Otto Wagner proclaimed in 1895. Wagner went on to build a savings bank and a chapel for an insane asylum in which all the corners of the pews were rounded to prevent the patients from injuring themselves.

Otto Wagner and his modernist colleagues argued that buildings should not only reflect the needs that they fulfill, but they should also exhibit a consistent style characteristic of the era: "To the age its art," they proclaimed. In cooperation with painters and craftsmen, they cultivated a decorative style to embellish their practical buildings that emphasized graceful curves and intricate designs. *Jugendstil*, as it was called in Vienna, is better known today by its French name, *Art Nouveau*.

Just as in Paris fifty years earlier, painters in the 1880s and 1890s associated with the state-sponsored Institute of Fine Arts dominated the Viennese art world. Their canvases reflected the grand, heavy, and yet cluttered buildings of the Ring. In 1897, just as in the Salon of the Rejected in Paris in 1863, a handful of artists seceded from the Art Institute to form their own movement. The creator of the Secession, as the group called itself, was Gustav Klimt. An academic painter in his youth, Klimt dazzled viewers with gold leaf, visions of sexuality, and haughty portraiture. But

Panorama von Wien.

The Ringstrasse, Vienna
Francis Joseph's rebuilding of Vienna compares with Napoleon III's restructuring of Paris, except that in Vienna the emphasis was on massive public buildings surrounding the medieval center of the city. The concentric Ringstrasse boulevards replaced older fortifications. Young Adolf Hitler, who came to Vienna in the 1890s hoping to study architecture, admired the grandiose style of the Ringstrasse buildings. *The Granger Collection, New York.*

**Klimt's *Pallas Athene*,
1898** Gustav Klimt, a
leader of the Viennese
Secession, tweaks the
Viennese establishment with
this painting. The city of
Vienna had adopted Athena,
the Greek goddess of
practical wisdom, as its icon
late in the nineteenth
century. Klimt shows Athena
with a pendant of Silenus,
Dionysus's drunken sidekick,
around her neck, holding not
justice but a naked woman in
her right hand.   *Erich
Lessing/Art Resource, NY.*

the Secession did not limit itself to painting. Its members, influenced by composer Richard Wagner's ideal of the Total Art Work, believed that all aspects of life should benefit from the enhanced perceptions made possible by high-quality decorative art.[10] Thus they maintained close links with architects, who brought Jugendstil even to tramway stops, and with the Vienna Workshop, which produced furniture, chinaware, serving dishes, and numerous other exquisite objects of daily use. Graphic art also prospered, as some of the most original of the Secessionists created placards for their shows and for their favorite cabaret, Die Fledermaus ("The Bat").

The Secession did not undermine the visual arts with the same thoroughness with which Einstein upended Newtonian physics or Joyce subverted traditional prose. In Vienna, the realm of music provided the most radical modernist innovation. Vienna has always been a city of music. Haydn, Mozart, and Beethoven all spent major portions of their careers there. In the late nineteenth century, Viennese musicians were split between followers of Richard Wagner and Johannes Brahms. Wagner's music, with its lush harmonies that stretched traditional tonality to the limits, attracted many followers, and his desire to create Total Art Works combining all the art forms into one grand presentation of emotion and insight inspired the Secessionists. Musical traditionalists favored Brahms, an upholder of classical forms who had the genius to use them creatively.

---

[10] Wagner (1813–1883), one of the most powerful composers of the nineteenth century, wrote massive operas primarily on subjects drawn from German myth and history. In addition to composing the music, he also wrote the words to his "music dramas" (his preferred term) and demanded elaborate sets and lighting. He even built his own theatre, hence his claim to be the creator of the Total Art Work.

Gustav Mahler (1860–1911) and Arnold Schoenberg (1874–1951) broke through both of these musical styles into new territory. For ten years Mahler directed the Vienna Court Opera. Mahler criticized as "slovenly" the undisciplined musicians he inherited and elevated them to a new standard of performance. He revitalized stage design with Secessionist artists and introduced the best new works of his era (including his own massive symphonies) to doubtful audiences. But as a German-speaking Jew from Bohemia, Mahler suffered from the perpetual feeling that he was an outsider. He reflected this sense in his symphonies by pushing traditional forms almost to the breaking point. For centuries, Western music had been written using a harmonic system based on a single tone. Works were written in a key based on that tone, and the relationships among the sounds were well known and thoroughly worked out. Mahler developed the idea of progressive tonality pioneered by Wagner by often ending a work in a different key from which he started. He also dissolved traditional tonalities by use of harmonies not belonging to the signature key.

If Mahler pushed musical tradition, Schoenberg destroyed it. Mahler is analogous to the postimpressionists in painting—a vivid innovator and a transitional figure. Arnold Schoenberg can be compared to Picasso—the ulti-mate disrupter. Critics jeered, hooted, and walked out of the first performance of one of Schoenberg's earliest works, "Verklärte Nachte" ("Transfigured Night"), when it was first performed in 1903, so experimental were the harmonies that he attempted. But "Transfigured Night" was at least written in a key. In 1907 and 1908 Schoenberg began dispensing with tonal organization altogether, and in 1909 he wrote his first composition with no tonal center. Any harmonic or melodic combination became acceptable. Much like James Joyce, whose first experimental writings came before World War I but who published *Ulysses* after the war, in 1922 Schoenberg, now living in Berlin, created a twelve-tone system of music to replace the eight-tone harmonic system that hitherto had formed the basis of Western music. Relatively few other composers adopted the twelve-tone system, although Schoenberg wrote in it the rest of his life, but his dissolution of tonality was as fundamental to restructuring the possibilities of musical creation in the twentieth century as Joyce's novels and Picasso's paintings.

The Moscow-St. Petersburg Variant

Historians have described the history of Russia as the history of three cities: Kiev, the mother; Moscow, the heart;

Vrubel's *Six-Winged Seraph*, 1904   Mikhail Aleksandrovich Vrubel was a Russian symbolist with links to the Art Nouveau style. This somewhat bizarre painting is typical of his demonic style and characteristic of the tremendous outflowing of Russian creativity in the first two decades of the twentieth century. *Scala/Art Resource, NY.*

THE HUMAN EXPERIENCE

Isadora Duncan, Dancer

Ballet was a highly developed art form in Europe, having begun in early modern times as a form of aristocratic amusement. In the egalitarian United States, however, ballet was little known in the nineteenth century, and popular dancing, such as reels, square dances, and vaudeville, were considered artistic contemptable. Victorian America considered female dancers tantamount to prostitutes; a woman could not get a job as a sales clerk if she had ever performed as a dancer. Late in the century, however, a handful of remarkable women, driven both by artistic needs and a desire to reform female health, invented a new kind of movement performance. Unable to find adequate inspiration in the United States, the most original of these women traveled to Europe. The Europeans stared, fascinated at Loie Fuller's dramatic lighting effects and swirling skirts, and they came out in droves to see Ruth St. Denis, who later returned to America to found modern dance.

The most influential of these women, at least in Europe, was Isadora Duncan (1877–1927). Daughter of a vigorous and reformist single mother who introduced her to music and other arts, Isadora moved to London in 1900 with her mother and brother, there to immerse herself in classical and Renaissance art. She translated these experiences into movements reminiscent of Greek statuary and began a performance career that lasted until her death in 1927.

In 1904 Duncan gave her first performances in St. Petersburg, to which she repeatedly returned. The World of Art group was transfixed. Not only did Duncan's flowing and yet fully centered movement fascinate them, but they were astounded that she used music originally written for the concert hall. Her interpretation of Chopin, Brahms, Beethoven, and others seemed to her audiences to flow organically from the music.

For the next twenty years, Duncan toured the world, established schools, had many tempestuous love affairs, bore three children, and brought her audiences to their feet, cheering. She combined the intensity of Stanislavsky to create an emotional bond with her material and the physical ability of Nijinsky to translate that bond into simple yet compelling movement. One of her associates, using modernist language herself, described a performance in Berlin in 1905:

Gliding, swaying she achieved an almost unearthly lightness. At times her movements had the quasi, unreal flowing continuity of dissolving into an endless horizon . . . vanishing into the periphery of unheard sounds and unseen movements suspended, dissolving with infinite gentleness . . . beyond the sphere of musical imagination.

European intellectuals revered Isadora Duncan as one of the most original artists of her time. But the general public rejected her as a proponent of free love and an underminer of public morality. Duncan restlessly sought magical moments. She was willing to throw over everything in an instant if she felt on the verge of finding them. After World War I, she thrilled to the artistic freedom that briefly prevailed in Bolshevik Russia, where she married the radical poet Sergei Esenin. When he beat her and eventually committed suicide, Duncan turned increasingly to alcohol. Her death, when a long scarf that she had worn in a famous performance accidentally caught in the spokes of a car wheel and strangled her, was as dramatic as her starburst career. ❖

The Granger Collection, New York.

and St. Petersburg, the head. Kiev was home to a Slavic state in the Middle Ages; Moscow the center of the late medieval tsardom and of Russian Orthodoxy; and St. Petersburg the rational city that Peter the Great built to face westward (see Chapter 16). During the nineteenth century, all three cities grew dramatically, but Moscow and St. Petersburg became particularly strong cultural and artistic centers. In drama the St. Petersburg Maryinsky theater and the Moscow Art Theater were counted among Europe's finest. In the latter, the director Konstantin Stanislavsky abandoned the stylistic conventions of nineteenth-century theater. He trained actors to adopt an intense inner identification with their characters. The Stanislavsky method, in which the actor internalizes the character's emotions and yet at the same time subordinates his or her individuality to the needs of the production as a whole, came to dominate the twentieth-century approach of stage and film acting. Today his technique is known simply as "The Method."[11]

In St. Petersburg, the most influential cultural movement at the turn of the century was the World of Art, named after a journal of the same name that first appeared in 1898. Serge Diaghilev, the guiding genius of this movement, was neither performer, musician, nor artist, but he could recognize talent and he brought artists together in new ways. In St. Petersburg, he became particularly interested in dance, one of the most established of the Russian arts. In 1906, Diaghilev left St. Petersburg for Paris, where he founded a new ensemble called the Ballet Russe, which soon became the world's most renowned ballet company. Diaghilev brought together not only great dancers and choreographers but powerful artists to design sets (Pablo Picasso, among others) and brilliant musicians to write scores. Diaghilev commissioned Igor Stravinsky, for example, to write *The Firebird* (1910), *Petrouchka* (1911), and *The Rite of Spring* (1913). The last of these dissonant but dramatic and exciting ballets particularly outraged its Paris audience, in part because of the primitive emotionality of the dance.

For Vaslav Nijinski, a prodigious dancer and the choreographer of *The Rite of Spring*, primitiveness did not derive from the African art that had interested Picasso, but from the modernist impulse to reject tradition, undercut pretension, and plumb new depths of the human personality. At the opening of *The Rite of Spring*, he and Stravinsky achieved this goal so successfully that people hissed, while others slapped the hissers. The composer himself shouted for the "sluts" in the audience to "shut up"; an outraged member of the audience called composer Maurice Ravel "a

dirty Jew" when he tried to defend the production. *The Rite of Spring* showed fewer than a dozen times in Paris and London before World War I. Nevertheless, its break with the past made it among the most influential ballets ever produced. When the war concluded, the Ballet Russe went on to perform throughout the world. Many of its productions remain part of the standard repertoire today.

The Rite of Spring marked the birth of modernism in ballet, but it was not performed in Russia. There, modernism took hold primarily in poetry and painting. In poetry influence flowed not from Russia to France, as in the case of ballet, but from France to Russia, as French symbolist poets provided the model for Russian symbolism. In painting, a handful of remarkable collectors maintained links between the European art world and Russia. They amassed and showed collections of impressionist and postimpressionist art. With the outbreak of World War I and the Russian Revolution of 1917, the floodgates of creativity burst open, realizing movements such as rayonism (in which paintings portrayed light in the form of rays of light) and constructivism (in which sculptures used the techniques of construction and reflected the dream of constructing a new society). For almost a decade after the Russian Revolution, Russian artists flourished, until Joseph Stalin's drive to total power suffocated them.

CONCLUSION: TOWARD THE TWENTIETH CENTURY

Some historians have written that World War I determined the course of the twentieth century, and in the next two chapters we discuss that pivotal event. But the Great War, as it was called at the time, came when European writers, artists, philosophers, and scientists had already begun to dismantle the cultural certainties of the nineteenth century. The modernists broke open the mold of conformity and tradition. They were only the most artistic, or intellectual, or insightful of those who pushed the pendulum in a new direction, since many ordinary people found their own ways to react against the pressures of the industrializing age. But the demonstrations that time and space are relative to each other, that a vast unknown lurks in the human unconscious, that human experience can be understood as fragmentary rather than coherent, that sexuality and aggression lie close beneath the surface of ordinary life, and that the terrors of the unknown are always with us set the stage for the anxieties of the twentieth century. In the nineteenth century, people felt confident in the certainties of progress. In the twentieth century, buffeted by two great world wars, a crushing economic depression, and the tension of nuclear confrontation, we have had to live with the uncertainties of ambiguity. This was the contribution, if it be such, of modernism.

---

[11] Method acting is exemplified in twentieth-century theatre and film by such stars as Marlon Brando and Robert De Niro.

Selected Reading

Sources

Bradbury, Malcolm, and James McFarlane, eds. *Modernism: 1890–1930* (1976).

Duncan, Isadora. *My Life* (1927).

Roberts, Michael Andrew. *The Novel: From Its Origins to the Present Day* (1993).

Romein, Jan. *The Watershed of Two Eras: Europe in 1900* (1978).

Sproccati, Sandro. *Guide to Art* (1992).

Positivism and Relativity

Bernstein, Jeremy. *Einstein* (1973). One of the clearest expositions of Einstein's contribution.

Bryant, Christopher G. A. *Positivism in Social Theory and Research* (1985). A brief but serious account of the development of positivism.

Pascal, Roy. *From Naturalism to Expressionism: German Literature and Society, 1880–1918* (1973). Solid coverage of a subject not discussed in this chapter.

Penrose, Roger. *Shadows of the Mind: A Search for the Missing Science of Consciousness* (1994). A contemporary rendering by a famous mathematician and physicist of the argument of *Naturphilosophie* and Bergson that consciousness cannot be reduced to any set of scientific rules. Difficult but fascinating.

Arts and Society

Bowlt, John E. *The Silver Age: Russia's Art of the Early Twentieth Century and the "World of Art" Group* (1979). Integrated discussion of the various artistic elements that made up Russia's Silver Age of art, music, and literature.

Mainardi, Patricia. *The End of the Salon: Art and the State in the Early Third Republic* (1993). A study of the resistance to change and the collapse of the traditional Salon in France.

Schorske, Carl E. *Fin-de-Siècle Vienna: Politics and Culture* (1981). Sophisticated and influential set of essays. Includes discussions of Freud, Klimt, Schoenberg, and others, as well as the architecture of the Ringstrasse.

Segel, Harold B. *Turn of the Century Cabaret* (1987). Covers the invention and spread of cabaret in nine European cities, including many direct quotations of works performed.

Shattuck, Roger. *The Banquet Years: The Origins of the Avant Garde in France, 1885 to World War I* (1968). A sophisticated cultural historian analyzes the birth of modernism in France.

Weber, Eugen. *France: Fin de Siècle* (1986). Theater, bicycling, daily life, sins, crazes, decadence, tourism, and more—it is all in this small gem describing life in France at the end of the nineteenth century.

Personalities

Everdell, William R. *The First Moderns: Profiles in the Origins of Twentieth Century Thought* (1997). Full of personal stories and factual evidence.

Fischer-Dieskau, Dietrich. *Wagner and Nietzsche* (1978). Readable narrative of the relationship between two brilliant, creative, and flawed men; written not by an academic scholar but by a great singer.

Friedrich, Otto. *Olympia: Paris in the Age of Manet* (1992). Manners and morals in Parisian artistic and other worlds during the time of the impressionists and realists.

Jones, Ernest. *The Life and Work of Sigmund Freud*, 3 vols. (1953). The basic biography of Freud, written by a long-time associate and colleague (also available in an abridged version edited by Lionel Trilling and Steven Marcus).

Kaufman, Walter. *Nietzsche: Philosopher, Psychologist, Antichrist*, 3rd ed. (1968). One of the best interpretive studies.

Millington, Barry. *Wagner*, rev. ed. (1992). Half the book consists of a reliable and balanced biography, the other half of a discussion of Wagner's music. Especially good for those with some musical training.

Pawel, Ernst. *The Nightmare of Reason: A Life of Franz Kafka* (1985). The standard biography of "the rare power of the unamplified human voice" of Franz Kafka.

Penrose, Roland. *Picasso: His Life and Work*, 3rd ed. (1981). A reliable biography of the great painter.

Pickering, Mary. *August Comte: An Intellectual Biography*, vol. 1 (1993). Clear, straightforward, thorough, almost positivist account of Comte's early years.

Robb, Graham. *Balzac: A Life* (1994). Entertaining discussion of Balzac's driven life. "What a man Balzac would have been," Flaubert commented, "had he known how to write!"

CHAPTER 27

IMPERIALISM AND THE COMING OF WORLD WAR I

Archduke Francis Ferdinand's Bloody Tunic *Erich Lessing/Art Resource, NY.*

1858	Britain suppresses the Great Mutiny and establishes direct control over India	1890	Bismarck replaced; Maxim machine gun invented	1908	Austria annexes Bosnia and Herzegovina; Young Turk revolt seeks to modernize Ottoman government
1856–1860	Second Opium War: Britain occupies Beijing	1890s	Russians construct Trans-Siberian railroad	1910	Creation of the Union of South Africa (final outcome of Boer War)
1867	Diamonds discovered in South Africa	1894	Franco-Russian alliance		
		1894–1895	Sino-Japanese War	1911	Revolution in China
1869	Suez Canal opens	1899	Boxer Rebellion in China		
1870s	Beginning of the Age of Imperialism	1904–1905	Russo-Japanese War	1912–1913	First and Second Balkan Wars
		1905	Revolution in Russia		
1882	Triple Alliance established (Germany, Austria-Hungary, Italy)	1907	Triple Entente (Britain, France, Russia)	1914	Assassination of Francis Ferdinand; World War I begins

A little after noon, on June 28, 1914, in the Bosnian city of Sarajevo, a 19-year-old Serbian nationalist who believed his plot to assassinate Archduke Francis Ferdinand, heir to the Habsburg throne, had failed, unexpectedly saw the archduke's car pull up and stop right in front of him. Gavrilo Princip pulled out his pistol, fired two shots, and killed both the archduke and his wife, Sophia. The archduke's blood-stained tunic, now on display in Vienna, is evidence of a personal tragedy—"Sophie dear! Sophie dear! Don't die! Stay alive for our children!" were among the archduke's last words—but the chain of events that followed the shooting were a tragedy for all of Europe, and indeed, for the world.

World War I is a watershed in the history of Western civilization. It led directly to the temporary but devastating triumph of two antidemocratic forces that dominated much of the twentieth century: communism and Nazism. Failure to resolve, or even to address, many of the problems that caused the war led to World War II, so that in a thirty-year period upwards of 50 million Europeans lost their lives, including most of Europe's Jewish population in the Holocaust. Short-range consequences of the Great War (as it was called before World War II) included the replacement of four traditional empires (Ottoman, Austrian, Russian, and German) with new nation-states in central Europe, a vastly increased role for government, and the final end, after more than a thousand years, of kings and emperors as viable political actors. Long-term results included the political collapse of Europe, the end of colonial empires, and the rise of the United States and the Soviet Union as the two superpowers of the second half of the century.

Clearly, then, World War I requires some explanation. The predominant approach for two generations was to assign blame. Was Germany's grab for world power the main cause, or perhaps Austrian fears of nationalism, or Russian and British blundering? We will discuss these questions briefly, but our main purpose will not be to accuse. Instead, over the next two chapters we will lay out a narrative explanation of the road to war, its course, and its outcome. But before we get to these subjects, we need to analyze a related series of events: the final climactic burst of Europe's four-hundred-year explosion into the rest of the world known as the "Age of Imperialism." Some historians have understood World War I to have been an aspect of **imperialism.** It is true that both imperialism and World War I were, in their own ways, outcomes of a marriage of Realpolitik, economic competition, and Social Darwinism, the three pillars of the Century of Power discussed in Chapters 24 and 25. But imperialism, despite its significance both for European countries and for the world outside of Europe, was not the fundamental cause of the Great War, as we shall see in the first half of this chapter.

In the second half of the chapter, we discuss the origins of the war. Here we need to take care not to fall into some inviting traps. Because we all believe in causation, it is legitimate to seek the causes of World War I. Having uncovered these causes, however, we might be tempted to jump to two illegitimate conclusions. First, it would be easy to believe that the series of events put forward constitutes its sole and sufficient explanation. But the pathways from the past to the present are infinite, and many satisfying interpretations exist. In this chapter we will stress the political, economic, and ideological factors, but someone interested in the history of daily life, for example, could write an equally valid but utterly different history of the prewar period.

Second, we must not jump from our narrative to the conclusion that World War I was inevitable, although certainly the grounds for it had been well prepared. At some point, the freight train running toward disaster lost control, but revealing a plausible set of causes for the war is not a valid argument that it was indeed inevitable. Human beings always retain agency or free will; that is, the ability to act independently and with originality, and chance often plays a very large part in shaping events. It is easy to practice the history of "What if?" and identify hundreds of moments when another decision, a piece of luck, or a changed circumstance could have shifted the direction of events. We offer one narrative, but we must remember that history is a mansion with many rooms and that outcomes are not foreordained.

THE CLIMAX OF IMPERIALISM

One reason for Europe's relative stability during the first three-quarters of the nineteenth century was that the Great Powers agreed at the Congress of Vienna to leave control of the seas to Britain and not to interfere with Russia's expansion into central Asia. Around 1870, however, the long-standing European interest in world trade and colonies intensified into the era called the Age of Imperialism. Europeans grew acutely conscious of their colonial holdings and competed vigorously for political control over African and other territories. Influenced by Social Darwinism, colonialists portrayed their conquests as a great step forward in civilization, the survival of the most advanced peoples—the fittest—over the inferior cultures of the world.

But European expansion was not solely a late nineteenth-century phenomenon. From the mid-fifteenth century, when Portuguese ships first sailed down the west coast of Africa, European ability to dominate the seas of the world with advanced sailing ships and sophisticated guns forced every culture in the world to react to European intrusions (see Chapter 14). In general, two kinds of relationships resulted: those in which European settlers seized control from technologically weaker indigenous populations; and those in which European traders established enclaves from which they conducted mercantile activities. The Western Hemisphere, including both North and South America, along with Australia, New Zealand, and South Africa, experienced the first kind of relationship, while the European presence in Africa, the Near East, India, and Asia was of the second kind. In South America, Spanish colonial administrators seeking precious metals maintained close ties to Spain and Portugal and dominated an indigenous population conquered by military force and decimated by disease. In North America, British colonists subdued a more thinly spread native population and established increasingly independent regimes. The Catholic faith predominated in South America and Protestantism in British North America, but the importation of African slaves played a major role in both regions.

The European presence in other parts of the world differed markedly from the American patterns. The main goal of the sixteenth-century explorers of Africa and the Pacific had been trade, not settlement nor conquest. In Asia, the French, Portuguese, Dutch, and English worked out commercial arrangements with local rulers, set up small coastal settlements, and generated intra-Asian trade for their own benefit. They shaped events in the immediate area within which they operated, but at first they were merely several among the many players in the complicated game of South Asian politics. In Africa, the European presence was even spottier. Africa's climate and disease pool hindered European penetration into the interior of the continent, as did the relatively high level of defensive organization of the African coastal states. Dutch settlers arrived in the Cape of Good Hope in the seventeenth century, but elsewhere Europeans took an interest in Africa primarily for the slaves it provided.

From Informal Empire to Imperialism

During the seventeenth and eighteenth centuries the British wrested control of the world's seas from their rivals. In the seventeenth century, they overcame Dutch and Portuguese traders, and in the eighteenth century they subdued the French and the Spanish. Despite the loss of the American colonies, by the end of the eighteenth century Britannia ruled the world's seas and a good deal of its trade. The British had not deliberately set out to create a colonial empire nor to dominate others culturally, but once the outward movement began, pride, hope of gain, confidence that British ways were vastly superior to those of the rest of the world, and pressure from British citizens who lived in the colonies combined to push British governments toward consciously imperial policies.

The conquest of India provides a good example of what one historian meant when he said that Britain acquired its empire in a fit of absence of mind. When the European voyages of discovery began, the Mughal Empire ruled India, but by the beginning of the eighteenth century this Muslim state had collapsed under a series of blows from Hindu and other rivals. Both the British and French had formed East India companies to promote trade, but these state monopolies operated from small territories on the Indian coast, scarcely more than flyspecks on the giant Indian subcontinent. The directors of the East India companies were interested in profits, not politics. Yet the homeland was far away—it took two years for a message from England to reach India and for a reply to return—and local officials sometimes developed their own political ambitions that went significantly beyond commerce.

During the eighteenth century, both the British and the French began to fish in the troubled Indian waters, making alliances and supporting one or another ruler in hopes of stabilizing a risky situation, bolstering revenues, or getting rich. During the Seven Years' War (1756–1763)—which was fought not only in Europe but in North America and South Asia as well—the British navy established its dominance in the Indian Ocean, and French influence declined (see Chapter 19). In the second half of the eighteenth century, aggressive East India Company representatives expanded British commitments beyond commercial needs. Parliament responded by creating a court system for British citizens in India, naming a governor general, and establishing a cabinet position for Indian affairs. During the Napoleonic wars, the British destroyed the last great French fleet, seized way stations on the route to India, and continued to extend their control over the Indian subcontinent. These expansionary moves may have been temporary reactions to various crises rather than a grand imperial policy, but the results were the same: imposition of British rule over what amounted to conquered peoples.

Victorians liked to boast that the sun never set on the British flag. Nevertheless, during the late eighteenth and early nineteenth centuries, few people outside of the colonial administrations themselves, in Britain or elsewhere, nurtured any great enthusiasm for colonies. Mercantilist theory of the seventeenth and eighteenth centuries had favored colonies as sources of raw materials for the mother country, but free-trade theory, just coming into its own, did not require colonies. According to classical liberalism, economies would grow if a region produced goods in which it had a competitive advantage and traded them freely. As early as 1748, the French economist Jacques Turgot argued that colonies were a waste of resources, because they eventually would turn on the mother country and become independent. He compared colonies to fruit, which "cling to the tree until they have received sufficient nourishment" and then drop away, "germinate, and produce new trees."

But the nineteenth century was a century of ideology, and soon after the Napoleonic wars popular politics and national pride entered the colonial equation. Early in 1830, Charles X of France, trying to regain some of the popularity that his antiliberal politics had cost him, decided to send French troops across the Mediterranean into Algeria, allegedly to avenge a slight to a French diplomat. In truth, he hoped that a military success would rally France behind him. The invasion did not help him politically—the July Revolution of 1830 overthrew him only a few days after the initial French victories—but once the French entered Algeria, subsequent governments found it impossible to withdraw. Soon French colonists began moving to Algeria, until they constituted some 10 percent of the population. From the initial invasion until 1962, when Charles de Gaulle finally got them out of Algeria, the French stubbornly clung to their North African colony. Despite crushing countless bloody revolts and expending enormous sums of money, they never managed to digest Algeria's Muslim population. Like Britain, France did not pursue a logical plan, although it developed many enthusiastic imperialists, but it nevertheless brutally imposed itself on the Algerians for more than a hundred years for reasons of national pride, great power dreams, and plain stubbornness.

As the British experiences in India and the French involvement in Algeria suggest, the traditional method of dating the Age of Imperialism from 1870, is somewhat artificial. In fact, Europeans added about one-third of their eventual acquisitions in each of three distinct periods: the years prior to 1800; between 1800 and 1870; and between 1870 to 1914.

The growth of the United States to its present configuration by 1870 was not a result of imperialism as such, but it did involve the dispossession of indigenous populations and the use of force to settle international disputes in favor of the United States. Around 1800, Spain, France, Russia, and Britain had important—even massive—claims on North American territory. Starting with the Louisiana Purchase in 1803 and ending with the defeat of Mexico and the Oregon settlement of the late 1840s, the United States rid itself of these foreign encumbrances. Rough treatment of Native Americans characterized the process as well. In the late 1830s, for example, the U.S. Army herded some fifteen thousand Cherokees from their ancestral homes in the southeast to reservations across the Mississippi. The discovery of gold in California in 1848 and the availability of cheap or even free land motivated settlers to undertake the hazardous westward trek. Advocates of expansion to the Pacific, sounding very much like the Social Darwinists of the later era of imperialism, argued as early as the 1840s that the superiority of American institutions and white culture made it America's "manifest destiny" to fill out the continent.

Russia, in a similar manner, had been expanding eastward since the time of Ivan the Terrible in the sixteenth century, reaching the Pacific Ocean by the mid-seventeenth century. In the nineteenth century, its expansion took on more of an imperialist tone as it invaded independent countries and foreign cultures to the south. During the period of the Napoleonic wars and just after, Russia conquered or annexed what are today Georgia, Armenia, and Azerbaijan, although the area, known as the Caucasus, remained one of the most turbulent regions of the Russian Empire. Then, in the 1860s, a reckless frontier general leading what he called "a handful of tireless, intrepid warriors" began to expand into Turkestan; by World War I this process had gained Russia a territory twice the size of France containing millions of Muslim peoples. Some British analysts saw this expansion as a threat to British influence in Afghanistan and to India, thus giving Russia another card to play in its European diplomacy. Others saw commercial interests behind the conquest. In the end, however, the expansion probably had no purpose beyond expressing the arrogance of a strong state taking advantage of weaker ones. "Motivated by a sincere desire not to be

Shanghai Cricket Match
When the Europeans came to China, they made little effort to interact with Chinese culture. Nevertheless, this Chinese artist has given a distinctly Chinese look to his rendition of a British cricket match in Shanghai in the 1880s.

drawn into making new acquisitions," the Russian foreign minister lamented to Tsar Alexander II in 1864, "we have had to obey willy-nilly the attraction of inexorable necessity. A strictly peaceful policy is impossible for a powerful and civilized state bordering upon half-wild tribes."

One final area of European imperial ambition needs to be mentioned: China. British efforts in China were not purposeless, because British interests controlled substantial trade there. But the British pushed into the Middle Kingdom without much thought of the consequences. Until 1833 the East India Company held a monopoly of foreign commerce with China. It used its privileged position to force opium on the Chinese, in return for which the company took tea for export to Britain. When Parliament abolished the company's monopoly with China in that year, private traders flocked to the new opportunities. These newcomers greatly extended the opium trade and addicted tens of thousands of Chinese, provoking the Chinese to try to stop the trafficking in opium. The British defended their merchants with force. The First Opium War (1839–1842) brought Britain the island of Hong Kong, while the Second Opium War (1856–1860) led to the occupation of Beijing by British and French troops in 1860.[1] The victorious

Europeans forced the Chinese to grant them special trading rights in certain Chinese ports. Among the Chinese concessions was the right of extraterritoriality, or the right of foreigners to be tried by their own courts, even if they committed a crime against a Chinese citizen. This humiliating provision provoked long-standing resentments in Asia.

Invisible Empires

As these examples suggest, Europeans exerted a constant expansionist pressure in all parts of the world into which they ventured. But the nineteenth century presented at least two new problems for colonizing countries. First, the regions in which Europeans had permanently settled achieved independence, or at least an increased level of autonomy. Canada, for example, achieved self-government in 1848 and dominion status as a federal state in 1867. Second, the sudden jump in economic strength of continental powers in the second half of the century increased competition for colonies.

The American Revolution was the first instance of European colonies successfully rebelling against their mother country and establishing their independence. Within fifty years, national revolts in South America freed that continent from Spanish and Portuguese control as well. Later in the century, Australia, New Zealand, and the Cape Colony in South Africa joined Canada in loosening their dependence on the crown. Britain could not maintain

---

[1] The British leased the New Territories, without which Hong Kong was not viable, in 1898. Both the island of Hong Kong and the New Territories reverted to China in 1997.

its economic domination over the large and well-endowed United States, but the British did manage to retain significant economic influence in the English-speaking dominions. In Latin America, the British overpowered the declining Spanish and Portuguese to establish a powerful commercial and financial presence by the end of the century, especially in Argentina. British trade with Latin America tripled between 1865 and 1913, and capital investment grew by a factor of almost 15. By 1913 fully one-quarter of all British publicly traded overseas assets were invested in Latin America.

The Industrial Revolution brought a new level of complexity to colonial relations as well. As the first industrial country, Britain reaped rich benefits from its exports of cotton goods during the first half of the nineteenth century (see Chapter 20). Some observers have called British success the imperialism of free trade. Of course Britain favored free trade, this interpretation argues, because Britain's industrial head start enabled it to outcompete all comers. But by the end of the century, as European countries, particularly Germany, began to catch up and even surpass the British in such fields as chemicals and electrical equipment (see Chapter 25), British preeminence in the trade of physical goods declined. "Gentlemanly capitalists," operating out of the financial center of London known as "the City," more than offset this threat by vastly expanding the shipping, insurance, and banking industries. During the period between 1851 and 1913, Britain imported far more goods than it exported, but its earnings from service industries increased so rapidly that its balance of payments surplus quadrupled. The real profits of British imperialism in the period before World War I were not in manufacturing, the original source of its industrial wealth, but in much less visible capital transfers.

Up until about 1870, these British investors usually had made loans to foreign governments, but after that date they increasingly placed them with private concerns, especially railroads, and even with local municipalities. By the end of the century, scarcely a country in the world had not felt the impact of British investment, and the pound sterling became the standard of international finance. Britain's informal empire—its commercial domination in places that were not actually colonies—proved at least as fundamental to its power as its formal empire in which it exercised direct political control (see Figure 27-1).

Growth of the British service industries reflected the success of the English landholding upper class in maintaining control of the main sources of British wealth. Through their command of banking, insurance, and shipping, a handful of families at the apex of British society and court life continued to dominate British politics, despite the declining importance of landed wealth in an industrial society, the rising affluence of industrialists, and the increasing democratization of English electoral politics. Financiers, who despised the "vile and mechanical" world

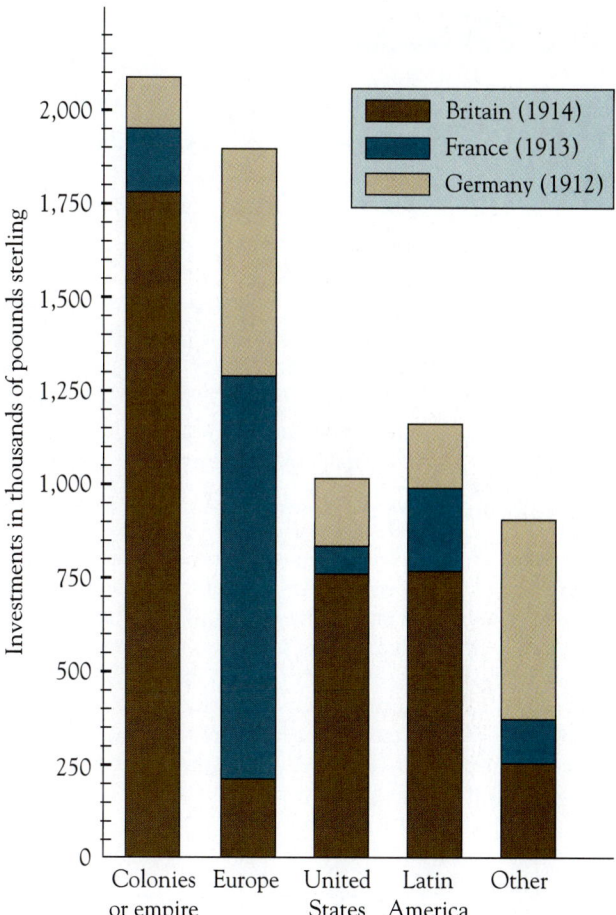

FIGURE 27-1

FOREIGN INVESTMENTS PRIOR TO WORLD WAR I

This chart shows that European investors generally preferred to invest in stable markets rather than in risky colonies. Britain is the exception, but even there more than half of the investment in the empire went to Canada, Australia, and New Zealand, with very little going to Africa and China.

Source: Based on data from Herbert Feis, Europe the World's Banker, 1870–1914 *(New York: Norton, 1965), pp. 23, 51, 74; sources for converting amounts to pounds in B. R. Mitchell,* British Historical Statistics *(Cambridge, England: Cambridge University Press, 1988), p. 703.*

of industry and who had attended the best private schools and universities, maintained their control of the City and the Colonial Office, especially in Indian affairs.

French and German banks also expanded their activities in the fifty years before World War I. By 1914, for example, Germany held more than 50 percent of the Ottoman debt, which the British had backed away from as increasingly risky after 1876. The French were the primary investors in Russia and in the Balkan countries. Europeans exerted influence over areas that were not actually colonies by lending to weak states that lacked the capacity

THE HISTORICAL EVIDENCE

Diaries of European Imperialists in the Congo

1890s

In 1890, John Dunlop invented the pneumatic tire. Demand for the rubber that went into bicycle and automobile tires created powerful incentives for Europeans to force natives in Peru, Brazil, the Congo, and elsewhere to gather rubber from tropical trees and vines. The result in the Congo was the "Rubber Terror." The following selections are chilling entries from two diaries during that period. The first is by a missionary describing what a French corporal told him, and the other is by a French officer.

The Missionary's Diary

Each time the corporal goes out to get rubber, cartridges are given to him. He must bring back all not used; and for every one used he must bring back a right hand! . . . As to the extent to which this is carried on, [Roi] informed me that in six months they, the State, on the Momboyo River had used 6,000 cartridges, which means that 6,000 people are killed or mutilated. It means more than 6,000, for the people have told me repeatedly that the soldiers kill children with the butt of their guns.

The Officer's Diary

28 March 1891: . . . The village of Bokanga was burned.

4 April 1891: A stop at Bolébo. . . . Since they wanted to meet us only with spears and guns, the village was burned. One native killed. . . .

12 April 1891: Attack on the Ikengo villages. . . . The big chief Ekélé of Etchimanjindou was killed and thrown in the water. . . .

14 June 1891: Expedition against the Loliva who refuse to come to the station. Dreadful weather; attack made in driving rain. The group of villages was large; couldn't destroy them all. Around 15 blacks killed. . . .

14 June 1891: At 5 A.M. sent the Zanzibari Metchoudi with about 40 men . . . to burn Nkolé. . . . The operation was successful and everything was burned. . . .

4 September 1891: At 4 A.M. preparations for attacking Ipéko. . . . The whole village was burned and the banana trees cut down. . . .

13 July 1892: The Bompopo villages were attacked 7 July by Lieutenant Sarrazijn; 20 natives killed; 13 women and children taken prisoner.

Source: From Adam Hochschild, *King Leopold's Ghost: A Story of Greed, Terror, and Heroism in Colonial Africa* (Boston: Houghton Mifflin, 1998), pp. 226–228.

to repay. When these governments defaulted, a consortium of European financial officers, often British and French, would take over administration of the local revenue sources to ensure repayment. By 1914, for example, the Ottoman Debt Administration, established in 1879 and headed by Europeans, had seven hundred offices and nine thousand employees throughout the Ottoman realm. The Debt Administration had a hand in almost every Ottoman decision of economic importance, thereby turning the formally sovereign Ottoman state into essentially a money-producing device for European bondholders. Europeans installed similar administrative mechanisms in Serbia, Greece, Bulgaria, Egypt, and China.

The Scramble for Formal Empire

The informal financial empires created by British, French, and German bankers were relatively invisible. They generated unprecedented amounts of capital by selling bonds to

thousands—perhaps millions—of well-to-do individuals in stock markets such as the Paris Bourse, but these activities only made headlines in the case of fraud or spectacular bankruptcies. When, as one author put it, "in the stillness of some distant, uninhabited valley the steam shovels and pneumatic drills pound out the path for steel rails and the locomotive," the source of the funding and the process by which it was transmuted into power remained shrouded in mystery. In the 1870s, however, a new, feverish quality entered into the colonial balance. Suddenly it seemed that informal empire was not enough. Now only direct political control, especially in Africa and China, seemed adequate to the needs of empire.

White Europeans had never before been able to penetrate the interior of Africa, primarily because of their susceptibility to local diseases, especially malaria. For most Europeans, the African interior remained a huge blank spot on the map: unknown territory. In the 1870s, press reports about men who were exploring this great

The "Rubber Terror"   Somber assistants of a missionary in the Congo display hands of other Congolese that were cut off by troops of the Anglo-Belgian India Rubber Company, probably in retribution for not fulfilling a rubber collection quota.   *Anti-Slavery International.*

unknown, particularly the humanitarian Dr. David Livingstone, excited newspaper readers. Adventurers such as the Anglo-American reporter Henry Stanley and the German imperialist Karl Peters began putting together private companies for the purpose of staking out claims to the African interior.

The most ruthless exploiter of Africa was King Leopold I of Belgium. In 1878 he formed a private company with Stanley, who had "discovered" the Congo River. By 1885 Leopold, Stanley, and their investors had created the Congo Free State, which was essentially Leopold's personal property. With scant regard either for the ecology of the region or for the lives of the Africans, whom his brutal overseers worked literally to death (the population of the Congo dropped from between 20 and 30 million to about 8 million during Leopold's administration), Leopold extracted enormous sums from his private colony. He spent the money on luxurious living, but he could not make the colony turn a profit. International outrage finally forced

Leopold to turn over administration of the Congo to the Belgian state in 1908.

Men like Leopold, Peters, and Stanley considered Africa to be without civilization, disorganized, and primitive. Claiming to represent a higher culture, they asserted the right to take control of whatever they could by any means. Peters—who concentrated on East Africa on behalf of German interests—introduced the technique of standard treaties with blank spaces for local leaders to fill in their names. According to one such treaty, the signer agreed to "cede to the Royal Niger Company, for ever, the whole of our territory, . . . the full power to mine, farm, and build in any portion of our country . . . [and the right to] settle all native disputes arising from any cause whatsoever." Although the Africans had no tradition of written contracts, the Europeans insisted on the legality of these pieces of paper and on their right to bind the Africans permanently.

The Europeans were not correct in assuming that the Africans were disorganized and backward. In West Africa, for example, the Ashanti had already begun a path of commercialization that was introducing capitalism and creating a mercantile middle class. A high Muslim civilization had existed for centuries in the area immediately to the south of the Sahara Desert. But the Europeans were blind to the nuances of African life. Certain of the superiority of their ways, they considered the subjugation of Africans not only justified, but beneficial to the "cheaper peoples."

Britain's interest in Africa centered on Egypt and South Africa. Intensifying involvement in Indian affairs had an important impact on Britain's interest in Egypt. In 1858 the British put down a massive revolt known as the Great Mutiny in India, abolished the East India Company, and took over direct political control of most of the Indian subcontinent. These events, and the advent of steamships, gave new currency to the old idea of building a canal from the Mediterranean to the Red Sea. Such a canal would cut weeks off the voyage between Europe and India. In 1854 the Egyptian ruler (known as the khedive), independent of Ottoman rule since 1841, granted a French concern the concession to build the canal, and in 1859 the work began. The scale of the project—more than 100 million cubic yards of dirt and sand had to be excavated—excited the imagination of all Europe. The party celebrating its opening in 1869 alone cost £1.3 million.

The Suez Canal Company was a private firm, owned primarily by the khedive and French investors, with some British participation. By 1875, however, the khedive had so squandered his resources that to avoid bankruptcy he had to sell his shares, which the British prime minister Benjamin Disraeli happily snapped up. The next year, still hopelessly indebted to European bondholders, the khedive surrendered control of his ministry of finance to joint British-French control, and by 1878 an Englishman became minister of finance and a Frenchman became minister of public works. These impositions sparked a nationalist backlash in Egypt against the khedive, whom his subjects increasingly saw as a tool of the West. To control this unrest, Britain simply occupied Egypt in 1882 and appointed a consul-general to administer it, allegedly in the khedive's name. The British prime minister at the time was William Gladstone. An opponent of imperialism, although he had 37 percent of his personal investment portfolio in Egyptian stock, Gladstone promised to withdraw "as soon as the

MAP 27-1

THE EUROPEAN PARTITION OF AFRICA

country and the organization of the proper means for the maintenance of Khedival authority will admit of it." Not until the completely transformed conditions of 1952 did the British finally fulfill that promise[2] (see Map 27-1).

The British and the Belgians were not the only ones scrambling for colonies in Africa. Almost every great European power (and several second-rate ones) infiltrated African regions, seized African colonies, or expanded earlier holdings: the French in Morocco and Gabon, the Germans in East Africa, the Italians in Tripoli and Somalia, the Spanish in the western Sahara, and the Portuguese in

Mozambique and Angola. International conferences in 1885 and 1889 failed to prevent the land rush, and by the 1890s disputes broke out. The most dramatic of these was the Fashoda crisis of 1898, in which the British threatened the French with war over control of the Sudan. The British public took an avid interest in African affairs, especially after a Muslim force killed the brutal English general Charles "Chinese" Gordon and his garrison at Khartoum in 1885. Under the lash of a sensationalist press, this "massacre," which was minor compared to the havoc that European forces wreaked on African armies, inflamed British public opinion.

A scramble for concessions in China soon followed the African tumult (see Map 27-2). During the nineteenth century the Dutch greatly expanded their control in what

---

[2] In 1956, the nationalist Egyptian govermnent seized control of the Suez Canal.

MAP 27-2

IMPERIALISM IN EAST ASIA, 1900–1910

is now called Indonesia, while the French established themselves in Indochina and the British in Burma. In 1854 an American fleet became the first foreign military vessels to enter a Japanese port. The Americans and Europeans spoke of "opening Japan," but the Japanese, alone among the peoples threatened by Western pressure, refused to submit. Instead, during the 1860s, they reformed their state and undertook to industrialize. In only a single generation, the Japanese made themselves the most industrialized country in Asia.

Europeans woke up to this fact when a war between China and Japan erupted over control of Korea in 1894. At first European journalists covering the war were condescending in the extreme to the upstart Japanese. But when the Japanese delivered well-armed and well-trained troops to Korea by steam-powered vessels and utterly defeated the Chinese, the correspondents changed their tune and extended their highest compliment: The Japanese, they marveled, seemed very much like Europeans. The Sino-Japanese war exposed China's weakness, and Europeans, already ensconced in their treaty ports, rushed to extract new concessions from China from the debilitated empire.

At this point, the United States entered the ranks of the active imperial powers. In 1898, after a series of incidents connected with the Cuban struggle for independence from Spain, and incited by a sensationalist and nationalistic press, the United States crushed the Spanish forces in the brief Spanish-American War, asserting its domination of Cuba and receiving Puerto Rico, Guam, and the Philippines for its troubles. At the same time, the United States annexed Hawaii. Now a Pacific power, and late to the Chinese buffet, the Americans declared (in the Open Door Note of 1899) that those who held spheres of influence in China should not charge discriminatory tariffs against the goods of others. Their hope was to open markets that the European enclaves now dominated to American goods.

The Europeans did not react to this American ploy, but a Chinese nationalist group, the Order of Literary Patriotic Harmonious Fists (Boxers), did. In 1899 they revolted against the European encroachments. When they killed a few Europeans and besieged foreign embassies in Beijing, the Europeans, joined by Japan and the United States, sent an expeditionary force to the capital, put down the Boxer Rebellion, and imposed a harsh peace on the Chinese. By 1902 the Germans, French, Italians, British, and Japanese all had seized chunks of the Chinese coastline; the Russians had occupied Manchuria; and all had forced large indemnities on China, taking control of custom duty collection to ensure payment. These blows fatally weakened the ancient empire, which in 1911 collapsed in revolution.

Two other violent episodes of the frenzied phase of imperialism deserve mention: the Boer War and the Russo-Japanese War. After the Napoleonic wars had brought the Cape Colony in South Africa under British control, English missionaries, settlers, and adventurers began pouring in. In 1835, the opposition of the South African Dutch population (known as the Boers) to Parliament's 1833 abolition of slavery in British colonies led some twelve to fourteen thousand Boers to migrate north to Transvaal, a new republic that they organized. In 1867, when prospectors discovered diamonds on the Orange River, and in 1886, when large gold deposits were unearthed near Johannesburg, foreigners surged into Transvaal and tensions between the Boers and the British exploded. The president of Transvaal, Paul Krueger, stoutly defended the independence of his country, while the main British imperialist in Cape Town, Cecil Rhodes,

A French Comment on British Prison Camps in the Boer War During the Boer War in South Africa, the British established the first concentration camps. This French political cartoon sarcastically compliments the British for creating the most humane way of bringing Boer prisoners rest and calm in the healthy outdoors: an electrified metal fence. © Topham Picturepoint/The Image Works.

strove to undermine it. Rhodes—who controlled 90 percent of the world's production of diamonds through the De Beers Mining Company and much of Africa's gold production through the Consolidated Gold Fields Company—wanted to set up a South African state under British control. He supported freebooting raids on Transvaal, pushed the British in Transvaal who did not have voting rights to petition Queen Victoria for redress, and accused Krueger of scheming to control British interests in South Africa. In fact, Rhodes was plotting to seize Krueger's country. These tactics backed Krueger into a corner. When he presented an ultimatum to the British in 1899, they responded with war.

The Boer War was bitter and dirty. After a slow start, the British hamstrung the Boer forces by bringing in 300,000 troops from India and England. When the Boers resorted to guerrilla warfare, the British bludgeoned them into submission by stringing hundreds of miles of barbed wire, constructing block houses, conducting massive sweeps, burning Boer farms, exiling captured guerrillas, and confining some 120,000 Boer women and children in concentration camps, where 20,000 of them died. Through this harsh process, the Union of South Africa under the king of England became a reality in 1910. Throughout the entire ordeal, of course, the Europeans paid scant attention to African needs. And although some 12,000 Africans perished in the war, the Boer War and the creation of the Union of South Africa were European affairs.

The Russo-Japanese War of 1904–1905 occasioned the most startling imperialist venture in Asia. In the 1890s construction of the Trans-Siberian railway had opened the Russian East. By 1900 the Russians had seized Manchuria and parts of Mongolia. About the same time, however, Russian moderates, who favored working out a sphere-of-influence arrangement with Japan, lost control of Russia's Asian policy to a group that wanted to expand Russia's influence into Korea. In 1904, after the Russians had rebuffed their repeated efforts at negotiation, the Japanese attacked the Russian naval base at Port Arthur in China.

The Russians fell into this war blindly overconfident, poorly led, and inadequately prepared diplomatically. Indeed, Nicholas II's minister of the interior thought that Russia needed "a little victorious war" to quiet social unrest at home. The tsar spoke contemptuously of "the little apes" and cavalierly promised that the white caps of Russian soldiers would snow the Japanese under. But the Japanese bottled up the Russian warships, sank the motley rescue fleet that Nicholas sent around the world from the Baltic, and crushed the tsar's armies on land (see Map 27-2). In 1905 U.S. President Theodore Roosevelt finally brought the competing parties together in Portsmouth, New Hampshire, where they signed a peace treaty that granted Japan full control over Korea. Once again, the interests of the Koreans themselves played no role in the conflict or in its resolution.

Why Imperialism?

How are we to explain these last great spasms of European expansion? Vladimir Ilich Lenin, the leader of the 1917 Bolshevik Revolution in Russia, offered an influential explanation.[3] Lenin based his analysis on Marx's assertion that capitalists were always pressured to improve profits. To do so, Lenin believed, they constantly had to seek cheap inputs from colonies. As capitalism developed, its leadership became concentrated in cartels and a handful of major banks, as in Germany. Not only were colonies essential to keep profits up, therefore, but they also provided vital places to absorb investment. Lenin thought that these two needs were so fundamental that they would eventually lead the major capitalist powers to war. Imperialism was the highest stage of capitalism, the one that immediately preceded its collapse, which Lenin thought imminent. For Lenin, World War I was the imperialist war through which the capitalist states would destroy themselves.

A related explanation, although not necessarily Marxist, argues that imperialism papered over cracks in society created by economic and political difficulties. Some German historians have claimed that this purpose drove Bismarck's belated and none-too-enthusiastic gestures at imperialism in the 1880s, although many other reasons lay behind Bismarck's policies. In England, liberal imperialists, and even some conservatives, most notably Joseph Chamberlain, believed that imperialism bolstered the working class, both psychologically through patriotism and economically by stimulating exports and thereby providing work. Nevertheless, however useful the idea of "social imperialism" may be as a justification, most imperial acquisitions came before this explanation became popular.

These more extreme economic and social explanations of imperialism have not endured. In particular, Lenin's Marxist explanation relied too heavily on class analysis. Finance and other service activities were fundamental to Europe's increasing control of the rest of the world, but they remained primarily in the hands of old elites, not the new manufacturing class, as Marx had predicted. Neither do these analyses explain why the creation of formal colonies seemed so important, especially in Africa, if informal control sufficed to generate profits. Formal colonies cost far more than they produced in trade. For every French citizen who settled in Algeria, four others lost their lives and two stood guard as soldiers. Moreover, investors preferred to place their money in economies with a high degree of safety rather than in the risky, unstable colonies

[3] Lenin's thinking was not particularly original. He derived his book, published in 1916, from the work of British and Austrian writers. Because of his later success as the leader of the Bolshevik Revolution, however, the influence of Lenin's book far exceeded that of his sources.

Joseph Chamberlain, British Entrepreneur and Politician

The overwhelming majority of influential public officials in Britain up until 1914 were upper-class men educated in exclusive secondary schools and trained at Cambridge or Oxford University. Joseph Chamberlain (1836–1914) was a remarkable exception. In the 1850s, his father, a successful shoe manufacturer, realized that the mechanization of screw-making would open a new market for standardized screws. Joseph entered that business at the age of eighteen without attending college. By the time he was in his mid-thirties, his financial acumen and aggressive sales techniques, especially on the Continent, made him and his partner the "Screw Kings" of the United Kingdom.

Chamberlain's family was Unitarian, and thus it combined strong ethical practice with distaste for the rigidities of the Anglican church and the landowning class that supported it. Concerned about the needs of the ordinary worker, Chamberlain entered politics and in 1873 was elected mayor of Birmingham. In his new post, he devoted his efforts to making "the cottage of the labouring man less of a hovel and more of a home." His innovative policies of slum clearance, educational reform, and municipalization of the city's water and natural gas supplies quickly earned him a national reputation as the "gas-and-water socialist."

In 1876, having sold his business, Chamberlain ran successfully for Parliament as a Liberal. In London he continued to pursue a relatively radical social agenda, but increasingly he turned toward imperial affairs. In 1895 he joined a Conservative government as secretary of state for colonial affairs, where he became Britain's leading imperialist. He believed that colonial success would bring workers prosperity. For that reason, he is sometimes called a social imperialist. By the time of the Boer War, however, Chamberlain had become much more interested in Britain's deteriorating international position than in social reform.

The Boer War disclosed Britain's lack of allies in Europe and its military weakness. Characteristically, Chamberlain devised an innovative plan for solving this problem. He proposed drawing the self-governing colonies together in a common market, with low internal tariffs and high protective tariffs against outside competition. Because this idea contradicted Britain's strong free-trade tradition, Chamberlain failed to persuade either the politicians or the public to adopt it. Instead he turned to his first love, education. He founded the University of Birming-

ham, inducing his wealthy friends and associates to support the new institution. He wanted the university to create schools for "railway engineering, electric lighting, railway management, and every large trade in the town" rather than provide a classical education for gentlemen.

The first industrialist to rise to high political position in a state dominated by landed and financial elites, Chamberlain is best remembered today as an imperialist. His greatest contribution, however, was to the ideal of a well-regulated urban life for all classes in his hometown of Birmingham. ❖

Hulton Getty/Liaison Agency.

seized in the last thirty years of the nineteenth century. Almost 75 percent of British foreign investment in 1914 went to six presumably safe places—the long-established colonies of Canada, Australia, South Africa, and India, as well as the United States and Argentina—whereas only 5 percent was invested in recent acquisitions in Egypt and China. As of 1914, only about 12 percent of German investment capital had gone to Africa and Asia, whereas almost 70 percent was in Europe and the United States.

Three characteristics of the Century of Power (1848–1945) came together to create the imperialist frenzy. The first of these was the increased prestige of the politics of power after the failures of the revolutions of 1848. The greatest practitioner of Realpolitik was Otto von Bismarck, whose successes provided an example of how one achieved national greatness. Diplomats continued to seek ways to cooperate, conferring on disarmament, colonialism, and various specific controversies. But Bismarck's enormous prestige, and his apparent success in lifting a Prussianized Germany to the top of continental politics, made exercising power a more important goal than maintaining equilibrium.

Social Darwinism and the intensified nationalism that accompanied it was the second characteristic that reinforced the idealization of power. Imperialists viewed their countries as locked in a struggle for survival with each other and with the "lesser" peoples of the world. In the competition among the imperial powers, fears of losing and a desire for advantage struck a rough balance. But in the battle with other peoples, the Europeans harbored no doubts about the superiority of their civilization and culture. "A single shelf of a good European library," sniffed British historian Thomas Babington Macauley in 1835, "was worth the whole native literature of India and Arabia." In 1908 English imperialist Douglas Sladen intoned, "To hear the Egyptian talk, you would imagine that his one desire was to improve his mind. . . . As a matter of fact, the Egyptian has no mind. . . . He is not a white man." The outcome of the confrontation between Europeans and such people, the Europeans thought, was obvious. "Can anyone doubt that the result of this competition of races will be the 'survival of the fittest?'" asked the American Josiah Strong.

Arrogant and condescending as these ideas may be, many practitioners of imperialism did not see themselves as merely dominating inferior peoples. They considered themselves engaged in what one author claimed was "a peaceful crusade, bringing millions into the Empire of civilization, helping to raise them bit by bit to our level." "In Central Asia," counseled one Russian bureaucrat, "we alone must be the masters so that with time through us civilization can penetrate there and improve the lives of those unfortunate offspring of the human race." **Chauvinist** patriots rejoiced as they saw increasingly large parts of the world map colored in "their" color (English red, German blue, for example).

Views of this sort struck a powerful chord with the growing electorate. With universal manhood suffrage already adopted by France and Germany and on the agenda

Britain's Worldwide Empire This Canadian postage stamp from 1898, with the British Empire shown in red, clearly expresses the statement "The Sun Never Sets on the British Empire." The slogan on the stamp is equally haughty: "We hold a vaster empire than has been."

in most other countries, politicians found that nationalism had strong public appeal. Supported by the yellow press—and even by some distinguished newspapers like *The Times* (London)—politicians began indulging in nationalist and imperialist rhetoric, described by one practitioner as "fireworks that do not warm and that leave nothing after them, but which for the moment sizzle, throw off brilliant sparks, and glow—and the world likes it, runs over, and looks."

Nationalists were arrogant and aggressive in part because they possessed not only an ethic of power politics and an ideology of struggle, but also the third characteristic of the Century of Power: the physical ability to impose themselves on others. The explosion of the Industrial and Energy Revolutions put more sheer strength in European hands than the world had ever known. Not only could Europeans outtrade traditional artisans with their textiles, metals, and chemicals, but entirely new technologies made military conquest easier than ever. Invulnerable gunboats powered by steam cruised up Chinese, Brazilian, and African rivers. The discovery of quinine, which prevented malaria, made it possible after about the 1840s for whites to penetrate hitherto inaccessible places. Before quinine, two of every three British soldiers stationed in the Cape Colony died of disease. When daily doses of quinine became routine, the death rate dropped to fewer than one in ten.

Improvements in guns were even more important. The invention of a reliable breech-loading mechanism and the percussion cap eliminated the necessity to ram ammunition down the barrel. Rifling the bore, or incising the interior of a barrel so as to impart spin to the bullet, greatly improved accuracy. In 1825 a soldier could fire only about once every two minutes, had to stand to load, and boasted an effective range of about 80 yards. Just fifty years later, an infantryman could fire several rounds a minute, load while lying down, and count on an effective range of more than 500 yards. The invention by a French chemist in 1884 of smokeless powder, which left no obscuring cloud of smoke and freed soldiers from having to clean weapons constantly, led to a further refinement: the machine gun. By 1890 the Maxim gun, which used the recoil from firing one shell to actuate the firing of the next one, could get off six hundred rounds a minute. Even more remarkable, the muscular European economies could turn out millions of the new weapons on demand. Vastly improved methods of steelmaking and the American invention of interchangeable parts contributed to this success.

These new armaments led to the most lopsided military confrontations since the Mongols swept into Europe in the thirteenth century (see Chapter 11). In 1897, for example, 32 Europeans supported by 507 African soldiers using machine guns defeated the 31,000-man army of the Nupe Emirate of Sokoto in what is today northwest Nigeria. Europeans simply mowed down their opponents, crushing not only their armies but their spirit, their culture, and their future.

THE HISTORICAL EVIDENCE

The Triple Alliance

1882

The fundamental basis of the alliance system that replaced the Concert of Europe was the alliance between Austria and Germany, which Bismarck completed in 1879. International affairs from that moment onward unwound from this central European linkage. The treaty text here is from 1882, when Italy was added to form what became known as the Triple Alliance (see Map 27-3). Note that Article III calls for joint efforts if any of the parties is attacked, a point that became crucial in 1914, and that Article VI makes the agreement secret, a tendency that became important as World War I neared its end.

Article I

The High Contracting Parties mutually promise peace and friendship, and will enter into no alliance or engagement directed against any one of their State.

Article II

In case Italy, without direct provocation on her part, should be attacked by France for any reason whatsoever, the two other Contracting Parties shall be bound to lend help and assistance with all their forces to the Party attacked.

The same obligation shall devolve upon Italy in case of any aggression without direct provocation by France against Germany.

Article III

If one, or two, of the High Contracting Parties, without direct provocation on their part, should chance to be attacked and to be engaged in a war with two or more Great Powers nonsignatory to the present Treaty, the *casus foederis* will arise simultaneously for all the High Contracting Parties (that is, the provisions of the treaty will come into effect).

Article IV

In case a Great Power nonsignatory to the present Treaty should threaten the security of the states of one of the High Contracting Parties, and the threatened Party should find itself forced on that account to make war against it,

---

The Age of Imperialism capped four centuries of European expansion into the world. The desire to proselytize the world for Christianity played an important role in this endeavor, even in the nineteenth century. Economic interests also had always played a role, especially in the creation of informal empires, and so did the necessity to react to events abroad. But the climactic surge toward formal empire in the forty years preceding World War I emerged from a conjuncture of Realpolitik, Social Darwinist pretensions, the appeal of nationalism to the growing electorate, economic strength, and technological advances.

The forces that provoked the imperialist frenzy were much the same factors that brought Europe to war by 1914, and imperial rivalries helped poison the political atmo-sphere. Germany in particular felt hemmed in by

Britain, unable to exercise its industrial strength around the world in the manner it considered fitting for a great power. Imperialist competition, therefore, played an important role in heightening European tensions prior to 1914. Nevertheless, imperialism was not the main cause of World War I. Despite Lenin's view that colonies were fundamental to capitalist economies, and despite exceptions such as the Fashoda crisis, only one war pitted two imperialist powers against each other: the Russo-Japanese war. The ten years preceding World War I saw many crises over colonial interests, but in the end no European state, not even Germany, decided that those interests were so vital that protecting them required a general war. Germany did feel profoundly threatened during the period, and so did Austro-Hungary, but not by imperialism.

the two others bind themselves to observe towards their Ally a benevolent neutrality. Each of them reserves to itself, in this case, the right to take part in the war, if it should see fit, to make common cause with its Ally.

Article V

If the peace of any of the High Contracting Parties should chance to be threatened under the circumstances foreseen by the preceding Articles, the High Contracting Parties shall take counsel together in ample time as to the military measures to be taken with a view to eventual coöperation.

They engage henceforward, in all cases of common participation in a war, to conclude neither armistice, nor peace, nor treaty, except by common agreement among themselves.

Article VI

The High Contracting Parties mutually promise secrecy as to the contents and existence of the present Treaty.

Source: From William Henry Cooke and Edith Pierpont Stickney, eds. *Readings in European International Relations* (New York: Harper & Row, 1931), pp. 8–9.

MAP 27-3

ALLIANCES, ALIGNMENTS, AND ANTAGONISMS

Austria and Germany first signed a treaty of alliance in 1879 and Italy joined in 1882, cementing the Triple Alliance. Shortly after William II of Germany "dropped the pilot," France and Russia signed an agreement (1894), and alignment between Britain and France in 1907 completed the Triple Entente. The two antagonistic camps entered into a vigorous competition that led to world war.

German leaders believed that hostile powers were encircling it, thwarting their country's aspirations to world power, while the Austria-Hungarian elites feared that nationalism threatened the very existence of their multinational Habsburg realm.

THE FAILURE TO CONTAIN POWER

When Napoleon III drove a wedge between Austria and Russia during the Crimean War, he had anticipated that it would benefit France. The Crimean War was indeed the first major crack in the post-1815 system, but as the stability of Europe unraveled in the second half of the nineteenth century the primary beneficiary—as well as the primary motivator—was not France, but Germany. Since the Peace of Westphalia in 1648 (see Chapter 15), the political and military energy of the Germanies had been dispersed in the Holy Roman Empire and the German Confederation. In 1871, unification under Prussian leadership replaced this central European power vacuum with a large, economically strong, and ably led state. This development in itself would have been enough to disturb the Vienna arrangements, but Bismarck's foreign policy, although often defensive and conservative, laid the groundwork for the emergence of two competing alliances. Whereas the idea of the Vienna settlement in 1815 had been for the five Great Powers jointly to maintain European stability, by 1914 two new groups of powers faced each other in what they both felt was a fateful competition.

The Alliance System

Bismarck's goal was to maintain European stability, but by means of his own actions, not through give and take with other Great Powers. Keenly aware that Germany lay between two potential enemies, France to the west and Russia to the east, he sought equilibrium by forging an alliance with Austria, keeping France isolated, and forestalling any possible Russo-Austrian combination with various expedients and assurances. The centerpiece of this policy was the German-Austrian Treaty of 1879, which sealed the demotion of Austria from the dominant German power to Prussia's junior partner. In 1882 Bismarck expanded the Austrian alliance to include Italy in what became known as the Triple Alliance. The Italian connection was never fundamental, but by linking Austria and Germany firmly together, Bismarck put to rest the long-standing rivalry between Austria and Prussia that had threatened stability in central Europe since the early eighteenth century.

Having forged the Triple Alliance, Bismarck mainly feared that Russia would combine with France. To prevent this, in 1881 he had brought the Russian emperor into the Three Emperors' League (Germany, Austria, and Russia) to support the status quo in the Ottoman Empire. In 1887, by means of the Reinsurance Treaty, he also conceded Russia's preponderance in Bulgaria in return for its neutrality in war, except if Germany should attack France.

As this last provision of the Reinsurance Treaty suggests, Russia remained susceptible to overtures from France. But as long as Bismarck was in power, he found ways to prevent the two countries from reaching an agreement. In 1890, however, a young and impetuous William II, who had acceded to the throne two years earlier, fired his overbearing chancellor. The new German government, calculating that Bismarck had given away too much in the Reinsurance Treaty, decided not to renew it, thus discarding the policy of keeping Russia friendly. Within months a French naval squadron visited St. Petersburg, and negotiations between France and Russia began. By mid-1892 the two governments had negotiated a military agreement, and in 1894 they formally agreed that if either were attacked by the Triple Alliance the other would come to its partner's aid. France quickly became the prime supplier of capital for Russia's industrialization.

Great Britain was not a party to either the Triple Alliance or the Russo-French agreement. Its nineteenth-century diplomatic stance was one of "splendid isolation," as the late Victorians called it. When Britain felt its interests challenged, as by Russia in Afghanistan or by France at Suez, it could and did react. But it stayed aloof from any standing commitments to continental affairs. One German government after another understood that an agreement with Britain was fundamental to Germany's safety, but their sometimes heavy-handed diplomacy could never find

PUNCH, OR THE LONDON CHARIVARI.—MARCH 29, 1890.

DROPPING THE PILOT.

"Dropping the Pilot" This cartoon from the British humorous magazine *Punch*, which shows Bismarck leaving office while a bemused William II looks on, has served as a model for countless cartoons since. It is still possible today to see occasional references to it in contemporary political cartoons. *From* Punch, 1890.

an appropriate formula. Instead, the British, feeling threatened by German economic competition by the turn of the twentieth century, began considering how to counter German power. Despite the antagonisms produced by the Fashoda crisis, for example, the French and British were able to reach a settlement of their outstanding controversies in 1904. The French conceded British control of Egypt, while the British recognized French interests in Morocco. In 1907 the Russians and the English also reconciled their differences by dividing up spheres of influence in Persia (Iran), Afghanistan, and elsewhere. These agreements, though not military treaties, completed formation of the Triple Entente (*entente* is French for "agreement") among Russia, France, and Great Britain.

While he was in office, Bismarck maintained European peace, despite many alarms and excursions. However, he did it not by mutual agreement with the Great Powers, but through manipulations from Berlin. When he left the scene, his less talented successors permitted the system he created to collapse, with the unintended result of creating two opposing alliance systems in place of the long-defunct Concert of Europe. The Triple Alliance and the Triple Entente, facing each other evenly matched and increasingly hostile, now turned every international incident into a test of strength. Germany continually negotiated with Britain; Italy often hinted its unreliability in the Triple Alliance; and Russia on occasion sought agreement with Austria. Now, instead of resolving crises by offering territorial compensations on the Continent itself, as the powers did in the eighteenth century, they offered compensations from their colonial holdings. In a way, imperialism had provided the Europeans the wherewithal to abandon the Concert of Europe without threatening the integrity of existing European states. As long as they could keep control over their colonies, they had cards to play. Stability in Europe now depended on the ability of the leaders of the two alliance systems to limit their competition to peripheral encounters.

Russia in Crisis

In the thirty years prior to 1914, Russia developed very rapidly economically, as we saw in Chapter 25. Its alliance with France in 1894, which opened the gates to French and Belgian capital, coupled with the astute management of its minister of finance Sergei Witte, brought the Industrial Revolution to Russia with a vengeance. At the same time, however, Russian political mechanisms did not change appreciably. Up until 1905, the tsar banned the very existence of political parties, and virtually no **civil society** existed outside the bureaucracy and court circles. Despite the emergence of a middle class, a working class, and a brilliant cluster of artists, writers, dancers, and critics, the Russian autocracy did not change. Nor did the government expend much energy on Russia's serious problems, such as nationalism, antisemitism, rural poverty, and societal frustration. As a consequence, Russia was the home to numerous underground movements, all of which had as their primary goal overthrowing the tsarist regime.

The Russian Revolutionary Tradition As we saw in Chapter 24, early in the nineteenth century some educated men—usually noblemen but sometimes the sons of priests—began to think critically about Russian political culture. This intelligentsia held an independent social position somewhere between the autocrat and the people. In the 1840s, the Slavophiles found sustenance in the autocratic tradition—its history, its strength, and its Christianity. The Westerners based their social critique on Western models and were more critical of Russian traditions.

In the 1860s, the next generation of activists, the populists, were the first in Russia to ask the question posed elsewhere in Europe during the nineteenth century: Who are the people? During the decade in which Tsar Alexander II freed the serfs, reformed the army, and introduced the jury trial, the populists decided that in Russia "the people" were the peasantry. But when these writers and students left their urban garrets and actually went into the countryside, as they did in the great "going to the people" movement of 1874, they found to their dismay the typical Russian peasant was dirty, venal, and narrow-minded, opposing neither capitalism nor the tsar.

A third generation of Russian revolutionaries began to emerge in the 1890s. Many in this generation based their critique of tsarist autocracy on the ideas of Karl Marx. To the Social Democrats, who founded an underground party in 1898, it seemed obvious that the new working class—the living, breathing harbinger of a better future—was a logical substitute for the backward peasantry as Russia's progressive class. Even the Social Revolutionaries, who founded an underground party in the tradition of the populists of the 1860s and 1870s, were heavily influenced by Marxian ideas. Not all Russian revolutionaries were devotees of Marx. Some were anarchists, for example, and even constitutional liberals, but by the beginning of the twentieth century, a significant portion of the Russian opposition had fallen to a greater or lesser degree under the influence of Marxism.

It seems paradoxical that Marxism should have had so much appeal in peasant Russia, because Marx had designed his revolutionary ideology for highly industrialized countries. Several reasons may explain why Russian intellectuals found Marxism so appealing. Unlike liberalism, Marxism was a complete and intellectually satisfying system that seemed to explain the modern world rationally. Its dialectical style, with roots in German philosophy, was familiar to Russian intellectuals from the beginning of the revolutionary tradition, and its claim to be scientific attracted the late nineteenth-century mind. In a repressive system, in which small-scale liberal reform faced almost insuperable obstacles and free speech was not an accepted principle, Marxism's promise to transform everything simultaneously in one mighty revolutionary upheaval had great appeal. Faced with exile or imprisonment for even moderate suggestions (Nicholas II called proposals for an advisory assembly "senseless dreams," for example), critics had nothing to lose by adopting ever more extreme ideas. Facing an immense and unmovable Russian autocracy, revolutionary cataclysm seemed a more realistic option than piecemeal reform.

Marxism also fascinated many Russians because of their love-hate relationship with the West, a trait they had in common with many other peoples under the impact of industrialization. The power and autonomy of the West was enormously attractive. Most of those who experienced

THE HISTORICAL EVIDENCE

Bloody Sunday in St. Petersburg

January 1905

In January 1905, after a series of dismissals and crises in 1904, and with workers in St. Petersburg on general strike, Father Georgi Gapon, a radical Orthodox priest, led a march on the Winter Palace to petition the tsar for redress. The crowd, which included women and children, was unarmed and carried Orthodox crosses and icons. Nevertheless, tsarist troops opened fire and killed more than a hundred demonstrators. By the end of 1905, Nicholas II had to relent and promise a constitution. The selections below include a portion of Gapon's petition, actually written by leftist advisers, and his pained response to the shootings.

Father Gapon's Petition

Sire: We, workingmen and inhabitants of St. Petersburg of various classes, our wives and our children and our helpless old parents, come to Thee, Sire, to seek for truth and defense. We have become beggars: we have been oppressed: we are burdened by toil beyond our powers: we are scoffed at: we are not recognized as human beings: we are treated as slaves who must suffer their bitter fate and who must keep silence. We suffered, but we are pushed farther into the den of beggary, lawlessness, and ignorance. We are choked by despotism and irresponsibility, and we are breathless. We have no more power, Sire: the limit of patience has been reached. There has arrived for us that tremendous moment when death is better than the continuation of intolerable tortures. We have left off working, and we have declared to the masters that we shall not begin to work until they comply with our demands. We beg but little: we desire only that without which life is not life, but hard labor and eternal torture. The first request which we made was that our masters should discuss our needs with us; but this they refused, on the ground that no right to make this request is recognized by law. They also declared to be illegal our requests to diminish the working hours to eight hours daily, to agree with us about the prices for our work, to consider our misunderstandings with inferior administration of the mills, to increase the wages for the labor of women and of general laborers, so that the minimum daily wage should be one ruble per day, to abolish overtime work, to give us medical attention without insulting us, to arrange the workshops so that it might be possible to work there, and not find in them death from awful draughts and from rain and snow. All these requests appeared to be, in the opinion of our masters and of the factory and mill administrations, illegal. Every one of our requests was a crime, and the desire to improve our condition was regarded by them as impertinence and as offensive to them.

---

the material benefits of the Energy and Industrial Revolutions, from the smallest sewing machine to the largest battleship, desired these gains for themselves and their country. But aspiring peoples also wanted the self-confidence that power makes possible. To be overwhelmed, dismissed, and dominated was humiliating. Russian thinkers hated the arrogance, the domination, and the pretensions that the West brought along with its technology. Democracy, parliaments, even Christianity sometimes seemed to be mere covers for imperialism rather than inherently valuable institutions.

Marxism provided the perfect vehicle for such mixed sentiments. Marx praised capitalism as the most productive economic system ever achieved. But he also said that it was false, unjust, and doomed to be replaced by an even more productive system: socialism. In this way, Marxism allowed Russian intellectuals, as well as revolutionaries in other parts of the world, to dream of doing away with the things they hated about the West—its culture of domination—while appropriating the things they loved, such as its strength and power.

Modernizing Russia and the Revolution of 1905 Socialism could come to Russia in the 1890s because Russian industrialization took off in that decade, creating a significant urban working class. In the twenty-five years preceding World War I, the Russians tried two main strategies of economic development: the "pull from the top" plan (investment driven) and the "push from the bottom" idea (demand driven). Sergei Witte, Russia's minister of finance in the 1890s, was the author of the first of these. Witte pushed construction of the Trans-Siberian railroad and encouraged foreign investment, particularly from Russia's new ally France. In contrast to some colonial areas, in Russia foreign investment did not create enclave industries where only the foreign investors profited. Russians, not

"How the Tsar Deals with Complaints" A dramatic rendering of Bloody Sunday. *Mary Evans Picture Library.*

Russia is too great. Its necessities are too various and numerous for officials alone to rule. National representation is indispensable. It is indispensable that people should assist and should rule themselves. To them only are known their real necessities. Do not reject their assistance, accept it, order immediately the convocation of representatives of the Russian land from all ranks, including representatives from the workingmen.

Father Gapon's Response to the Massacre

With naive belief in thee as father of thy people, I was going peacefully to thee with the children of these very people. Thou must have known, thou didst know this. The innocent blood of workers, their wives and children, lies forever between thee, O soul destroyer, and the Russian people. Moral connection between thee and them may never be any more. The mighty river during its overflowing thou art already unable to stem by any half measures, even by Zemskii Sobor [Popular Assembly]. Bombs and dynamite, the terror of individuals and by masses, against thy breed and against the robbers of rightless people—all this must be and shall absolutely be. A sea of blood—unexampled—will be shed. Because of thee, because of thy whole family, Russia may perish. Once and for all, understand this and remember, better soon with all thy family abdicate the throne of Russia and give thyself up to the Russian people for trial. Pity thy children and the Russian lands, O thou offerer of peace for other countries and blood drunkard for thine own!

Source: From A. J. Sack, *Birth of Russian Democracy* (New York: Russian Information Bureau, 1918), pp. 99–101, 103–104.

foreigners, administered Russian heavy industry. Witte's broadly conceived policies produced solid economic growth. In the 1890s, the Russian economy expanded at impressive annual rates of between 6.7 and 8.1 percent.

In the ten years preceding World War I, another government minister, Peter Stolypin, put into effect the push-from-the-bottom strategy by introducing agricultural reforms. Stolypin wanted to create a sturdy peasantry, whose prosperity would generate demand and drive light industrial growth. Russian peasants were no longer **serfs,** but most families still lived in village communes in which land was owned collectively and farmed in many small strips distributed around the village. Technically, as of 1900 they were still supposed to be paying redemption payments for the land they had received forty years earlier (see Chapter 25). Stolypin wanted to consolidate the strips into individual farms and to make peasants the private owners of these consolidated holdings. His "wager on the strong," as

he called it, was less successful than Witte's program, in part because of the enormous complexity of peasant land-holding laws. By the time of the 1917 revolutions the Stolypin reforms had affected fewer than one-tenth of the peasant holdings.

Witte and Stolypin governed a country that faced enormous problems at the turn of the twentieth century. The growing peasant population was increasingly impoverished. A famine in 1891 showed how antiquated the countryside remained. New factory workers, often peasants just arrived from the village, made up a restless urban population that responded readily to union organizers and socialists. Strikes became a common feature of city life. Moreover, Russia was a multinational empire in which a narrow-minded russification policy on the part of the last two tsars stirred restlessness among the non-Russians. About 5 million Jews lived in Russia—about half the Jews in the world—and antisemitism, with its accompanying pogroms (massacres and destruction of Jewish quarters), was widespread. Finally, Russian leadership was totally inept. Tsar Nicholas II (reigned 1894–1917) continued to depend on the four-centuries-old pillars of autocracy: the nobility, the army, the bureaucracy, and the church. His modest intellectual endowments did not accommodate such modern realities as workers or independent professionals. The nonpolitical urban elites known in Russia as "society" treated the ruler and his bureaucracy with contempt. These problems combined with the normal social tensions characteristic of industrialization to evoke a series of riots and unrest. By 1904 the tsar's reactionary government had imposed martial law in almost every Russian city and more than half of the provinces.

With Russia in the midst of a disastrous war with Japan, the need for reform had become so obvious that late in 1904 the regime finally agreed at least to discuss it. But Russia had no public forums for such negotiations. The government therefore legalized private associations to formulate proposals, and for the first time a public debate on Russia's future began. Crushing defeat by the Japanese in 1905 only aggravated the unrest these discussions occasioned, as did a mutiny on a Russian Black Sea battleship, the *Potemkin*. In August 1905, the government tried to calm the uproar by promising to create a Duma, or legislature, albeit only with advisory powers. The public dismissed the proposal as too little and too late. In September most of the workers in Moscow went out on strike, and in October a general strike of all workers shut down St. Petersburg.

Sergei Witte, called back to meet the emergency, advised the tsar to grant a constitution. On October 17, 1905, Nicholas issued a manifesto guaranteeing civil rights, establishing a Duma that would have to pass on legislation, and assuring that all classes would be represented in the Duma. The workers, by this time thoroughly aroused, tossed this concession aside and called for the end of the monarchy. But this final convulsion of popular enthusiasm failed. During 1906 and 1907, the government savagely repressed further outbursts of opposition. The hangman's noose became known as a "Stolypin necktie." Finally, after the tsar dismissed the first two Dumas for demands he considered too radical, Stolypin, by changing the electoral laws, managed to get a Duma that satisfied him in 1907. This "third Duma" served its full term until 1912.

The Autocracy in Decay   The revolution of 1905 accomplished a great deal. The establishment of a Duma, even one with less power than liberals might have wished, marked a significant break with Russia's autocratic past. The opening of debate, not only in the Duma but in newspapers and other public venues as well, enriched Russian political life considerably. Finland gained its autonomy, as did the universities, and peasant payments still due from the 1861 freeing of the serfs were canceled.

Nevertheless, liberals and socialists alike considered the revolution a failure. Instead of being satisfied with rel-

ative gains, they continued to dream of a true revolution, one that would sweep aside everything related to the old autocracy. For these dreamers, the revolution of 1905 held two lessons. First, as Leon Trotsky, later a prime mover in the Bolshevik revolution of 1917, pointed out, a Marxist working-class revolution might well succeed in Russia, despite its still strongly peasant character, because the workers were concentrated in the administrative centers of the empire, Moscow and St. Petersburg. Control of the workers in those cities therefore became vital to revolutionary strategy. Second, during the revolution of 1905, workers' councils, called *soviets* in Russian, had sprung up spontaneously and had effectively turned worker's passions to political use. Russian revolutionaries began to see soviets as the embodiment of the workers' ability to exercise political power. In 1917, when the soviets formed again, they seemed the appropriate location for revolutionaries to begin their struggle for political power.

Between the years 1907 and 1912 Russia resumed its economic growth, but starting in about 1912, with the

Nicholas II and Alexandra   Nicholas's rigid determination to safeguard the autocratic power he had inherited made him fatally ill-suited to govern Russia in an era of accelerating change. His wife, Tsarina Alexandra, the Danish-born granddaughter of Queen Victoria, was equally limited intellectually and reinforced her husband's inclination toward aloof autocracy. *Corbis.*

massacre of several hundred Siberian gold miners, the government's authority began again to decline. One cause was the incredibly incompetent leadership provided by Tsar Nicholas II. A handsome but limited man, Nicholas understood his main duty to be passing on his autocratic power intact to his son. With little or no understanding of the vast changes going on in Russia, he took advice only from a narrow circle of none-too-competent advisers, and from his wife, Alexandra. For example, one small but significantly ill-advised action led to the excommunication and vilification of Leo Tolstoy, the great author who had by the turn of the century become one of the world's most famous pacifists and a symbol of opposition to the tsar. Instead of honoring one of the great men of Russian culture, the tsar's ineptitude only confirmed to the world the narrow, stultifying quality of his regime.

Unfortunately, the son to whom Nicholas hoped to pass his autocratic power was a hemophiliac. When a charlatan wandering priest named Rasputin somehow found a way to stop the tsarevich's bleeding, Alexandra became attached to him to the extent that she valued his advice over all the government ministers and other advisers. But Rasputin was a drunken lecher, with no more idea of politics than a village dogcatcher. His scandalous behavior (such as taking off his clothes and swearing drunkenly at a St. Petersburg cafe), and the tsar's unwillingness to part with him, only provided the last proof to many in Russian society that the tsar neither cared about or was able to resolve any of the problems Russia faced. With conflict between the two alliance systems intense during the first years of the twentieth century, the center of the Russian political system seemed dangerously empty.

Imperial Germany and the Road to War

Many conflicts stoked the competition between the Triple Alliance and the Triple Entente, but Germany's active military and foreign policies played a prominent role in exacerbating tensions. As we have seen, German industrial growth in the second half of the nineteenth century outstripped that of the rest of Europe. Expanding German trade throughout the world inevitably brought it face-to-face with Great Britain. Disparaging remarks about products "made in Germany" became common in the British press, especially when in some fields, such as armor plating and chemicals, the Germans were producing better products than the British. Nevertheless, Germany faced a problem similar to Russia's: an autocratic leadership in an industrializing society. Unlike Russia, however, Germany took dramatic and far-reaching steps to preserve and even expand the position these leaders believed Germany deserved in the world.

Social Democracy and the Marriage of Rye and Iron

The social cleavages that came with industrialization were the main cause of tension in Germany. The German working-class movement reemerged after Bismarck's fall in the form

The Russian Imperial Home   As this Russian cartoon suggests, Nicholas and Alexandra (notoriously inept judges of character) are puppets manipulated by the "dark Rasputin." The wildly irreverent and lecherous monk held an almost hypnotic power over the royal family, which contributed to the destruction of the monarchy.   © *Stock Montage*.

of a strong Social Democratic political party and a large union movement. At a party conference in 1891, the Social Democrats reaffirmed their faith in the doctrines of Karl Marx, whose vocabulary of revolution they used for the next forty years. Despite its rhetoric, however, the Social Democratic party grew increasingly moderate. While it steadfastly opposed projects that it considered detrimental to the working class—such as raising tariffs in 1902—its opposition became more and more confined to the normal political parameters of a parliamentary state, and less and less revolutionary. By the turn of the century, the Social Democrats had become the foremost advocates of democratic reform in Germany. The trade-union movement, whose reach extended far beyond that of the Social Democrats, was even less revolutionary, concentrated almost entirely on obtaining benefits for its members.

Social Democratic advocacy of working-class interests, criticism of private property, demands for democratic reform, and success in elections turned the ruling elements in German society—the aristocrats, the military, and the industrialists—vigorously against the socialists. They aroused the intense hostility of Emperor William II (reigned 1888–1918). The Kaiser, although clever, utterly lacked practical sense. Undisciplined, constantly on the move, and self-indulgent, he compensated for a natural softness of character by an obsession with the military. He always appeared in uniform and delighted in leading dress parades. Surrounding himself with aristocratic, high-ranking army officers, he larded his conversation and speeches with phrases like Germany's "mailed fist," its "glistening coat of armor," and "the good German sword." William believed that Germany required its "place in the sun," and when he sent soldiers off to China to help quell the Boxer Rebellion, he told them to follow the example of Attila the Hun: "May the German name become known in such a manner in China that no Chinese will ever again dare to look askance at a German."

Not surprisingly, the Kaiser hated the Reichstag (the imperial legislature), which he called "a troop of monkeys and a collection of blockheads and sleep-walkers." He barely considered socialists his subjects at all, constantly berating them as disloyal, untrustworthy, and even traitorous. His view was that unless Germany was able to exercise its power around the world—*Weltmacht*—the nation would collapse. Given the increasing mastery that imperial Germany was displaying as an industrial and commercial giant, this obsession with alleged German weakness was ridiculous, but at the same time, it was symptomatic of the prewar atmosphere in Germany. Had William II been a figurehead, his spontaneous decisionmaking and bombastic

statements would have been merely embarrassing. But because the imperial constitution made the government responsible to William II and put him in control of the military, his capricious militarism wove its way into the very fabric of German society.

The emperor enjoyed the support of several key social groups, most importantly the Prussian Junkers (see Chapters 16 and 24). These noble landowners of northeastern Germany made up a significant proportion of the army officers and strongly supported the aristocratic and militaristic tone of William II's court. The Junkers' economic interest lay primarily in protecting the profitability of agriculture, particularly rye, which grew more easily than wheat or oats in the sandy soil and cool climate of the Baltic region. They fully concurred with William II's judgment about socialists. Many of them had the added trait of being antisemitic.

Besides the Social Democrats, the aristocrats, and the military, industrialists constituted a fourth significant political element in Germany. Growing in size and wealth, the industrial class formed associations of manufacturers in the 1880s to lobby for the interests of industry and business. Industrialists supported the imperial regime through nationalistic organizations such as the Pan-German League, the Colonial League, and the Naval League, but their economic interests diverged from those of the Junkers. In a manner reminiscent of the British factory owners at the time of the Corn Laws (see Chapter 22), heavy industrialists in particular supported low agricultural tariffs because they kept the price of food down, thus permitting business owners to maintain low wages. The Junkers, on the other hand, favored high tariffs on grain to

The "Yellow Peril" In this painting (1895), personally designed by William II, the Archangel Michael, considered a symbol for Germany, urges the other European states to beware of the threat from Asia, signified by a distant Buddha. Exaggerated fears of Asia were an aspect of late nineteenth-century racism and imperialism. The armed women on the left personify France, Germany, Britain, Russia, and others whom the Kaiser believed would rally to his aid. *Bildarchiv Preussischer Kulturbesitz.*

protect their farms, which faced formidable competition from the wheat fields of Russia's Ukraine, the United States, and Canada.

The first post-Bismarckian government, under the leadership of Chancellor Leo von Caprivi, leaned toward the industrialists. To achieve trade agreements abroad, Caprivi lowered agricultural tariffs, recognizing that the balance of economic strength had shifted in industry's favor. But this reasonable policy exacted a high price: the undying enmity of the Junkers, who grew increasingly nationalistic and antisemitic in the 1890s.

Caprivi's successors found a way to bring the Junkers and the industrialists together by playing on their mutual distrust of the socialists. Promising the industrialists antisocialist policies and commercial agreements, and the agriculturists higher tariffs, the government put together a "community of interests" that supported its conservative policies. This policy did not work in practice as smoothly as its originators had hoped, for the participants remained at each other's political throats. Nevertheless, by the turn of the century, this marriage of rye and iron had become a fixture of German political life.

The Naval Program   The second momentous German policy undertaken at the end of the nineteenth century was to vigorously build up its navy. Situated in the center of Europe, German states had always relied primarily on their armies. United Germany, however, organized torpedo-boat squadrons for attacking commercial shipping and developed an interest in ports abroad, particularly in China. The man most associated with these interests was Admiral Alfred von Tirpitz, who returned from East Asia early in 1897 to head the Imperial Naval Office. Tirpitz accepted the teachings of the American naval strategist Alfred Thayer Mahan, who argued that "command of the sea" was the key to national power. Mahan rejected the view that the inexpensive torpedo boats that Germany was building could take the place of battleships, and Tirpitz was won over.

Tirpitz believed that Germany never could take its rightful place of preeminence among the world powers—that is, exercise Weltmacht—unless it could challenge British naval superiority. Immediately upon becoming naval chief, he began courting public opinion through a sophisticated propaganda campaign. With the help of industrialist Friedrich Krupp (who prudently had purchased the Kiel shipyards in 1896) he formed the Naval League, which quickly enrolled one hundred thousand members and became a strident supporter of a naval buildup. Most important, Tirpitz convinced William II, already a fan of Mahan and a lover of the sea, that only a strong navy could turn Germany from a European power to a world power. "We must take the trident in our fist," William blustered.

In 1898 Tirpitz succeeded in pushing a naval bill through the Reichstag to build nineteen battleships and the destroyers, cruisers, and other ships needed to support them. Two years later, a supplemental bill doubled the number of battleships and accelerated construction. Tirpitz's goal was not to match the British navy ship for ship but to threaten the British navy in the North Sea. He calculated that even though the British would still be able to defeat the German fleet, they would be so weakened if they did so that they would become vulnerable to attack from others and would therefore not risk attack.

Tirpitz's naval program appealed to William II and his government for several reasons. First, in an era of imperialism and intense Social Darwinist nationalism, it seemed to offer Germany a powerful new weapon in the worldwide struggle for survival. A strong navy would permit Germany to challenge Britain for commercial domination and would free it from continental confinement between France and Russia.

Second, by making ship-replacement schedules automatic, authorizing expenditures for several years at once, and by creating new administrative organs, the naval bill and its supplements removed much control of the military budget from the Reichstag and placed it in the hands of the emperor and his officers. In other words, the naval program assisted William II and his advisers in keeping the Reichstag, which they profoundly hated, out of military affairs.

Third, the naval program provided a multifaceted device for papering over the deep divisions in German society. The new policy attracted industrialists because it poured enormous resources into their businesses. Krupp himself built forty-seven ships over the next fifteen years, taking a 100 percent profit on the armor that he supplied for battleship construction. The Junkers liked the nationalistic aspect of the program, but they resented its implication that international commerce was the goal of government policy. They believed that German values were rooted deeply in the land and in the traditions that surrounded their control of it. The government's willingness to raise tariffs, which it did in 1902, calmed them.

The architects of the plan also believed that the sight of technologically advanced German ships sailing the seas of the world and challenging the British would win the loyalties of the working class. They hoped the vision would raise "the masses to higher levels of moral conduct and wealth."

In the eyes of the aristocrats, the naval buildup offered yet another benefit: It would leave the exclusiveness of the army officer corps unchallenged. From the time of the Great Elector in the seventeenth century, the Prussian nobility had cherished its control of the officer corps and the special access to the crown that it provided (see Chapter 16). In 1900 almost half of the army officer corps, especially line officers, was noble, and at the highest ranks the proportion reached virtually 100 percent. These aristocratic leaders had hesitated to expand the army because it would not only mean commissioning more middle-class officers, but because it might mean bringing more democratic-minded proletarians into the ranks. The navy, a newer service, was less fastidious about the social background of its officer corps, at least at the middle levels.

Finally, the naval program was glamorous, the space program of its day. The ships were expensive and grand, pulsating with power and perched on the cutting edge of technology—"floating manifestations of German *Kultur.*"

For all these reasons, Tirpitz and William believed the naval program offered a many-layered solution to both their social and their foreign policy problems. Unfortunately for Germany and for Europe, they were wrong. On the domestic front, the naval buildup neither lessened social tensions nor subdued the Social Democrats. The program's enormous expense created severe financial difficulties that only sharpened political tensions, even among the conservative forces. In Germany's federal system, the central government raised money through indirect taxes and by imposing contributions on the individual states. At the federal level, the Social Democrats vigorously opposed increasing indirect taxes, which bore heaviest on the working class. At the local level, conservatives resisted raising contributions to the center because this implied higher property taxes. Far from fusing Germany's political cracks, therefore, the naval program actually split the conservatives and enhanced the popularity of the Social Democrats. In 1912 the Social Democrats became the largest party in the Reichstag, capturing more than one-third of the votes cast in the election of that year.

The naval program failed to work miracles in the foreign arena as well. The British, supported by an overheated public opinion and believing that the seas of the world were theirs by right, reacted strongly to the German naval program. The Triple Entente provided a diplomatic response, but its military rejoinder was more direct. In 1905 Britain laid the keel of the first of a new class of battleships, the *Dreadnought.* The technological marvel of its day, the *Dreadnought* was the first major ship to use steam turbine engines rather than reciprocating engines, permitting it to run for long periods at its top speed of 21 knots. It boasted ten 12-inch guns, up from the four 12-inch guns hitherto standard on battleships. Moreover, it took only one year to build, in contrast to the earlier record of thirty-one months. Faster and with longer range and more firepower than anything the Germans could mount, the *Dreadnought* threatened the entire German fleet.

So far, the Germans had competed on the basis of fleet size. Now they had to decide whether to match the new technological level as well. When they did so in the naval bill of 1906, the Liberal government in Britain, which had been elected in 1905 on a platform of reducing arms expenditures, changed its mind and approved a substantial increase in British naval construction. Still richer than Germany, more technologically advanced, committed to its worldwide empire, and more and more emotionally anti-German, the British entered enthusiastically into an escalating arms race (see Figure 27-2).

HMS *Dreadnought* The British *Dreadnought* was at the cutting edge of military technology when it was launched in 1906. Powered by a turbine engine, the ship was able to travel indefinitely at 21 knots without the terrible noise and vibrations of earlier ships. It proved an effective counterstroke to the German naval-building program. *Science Museum.*

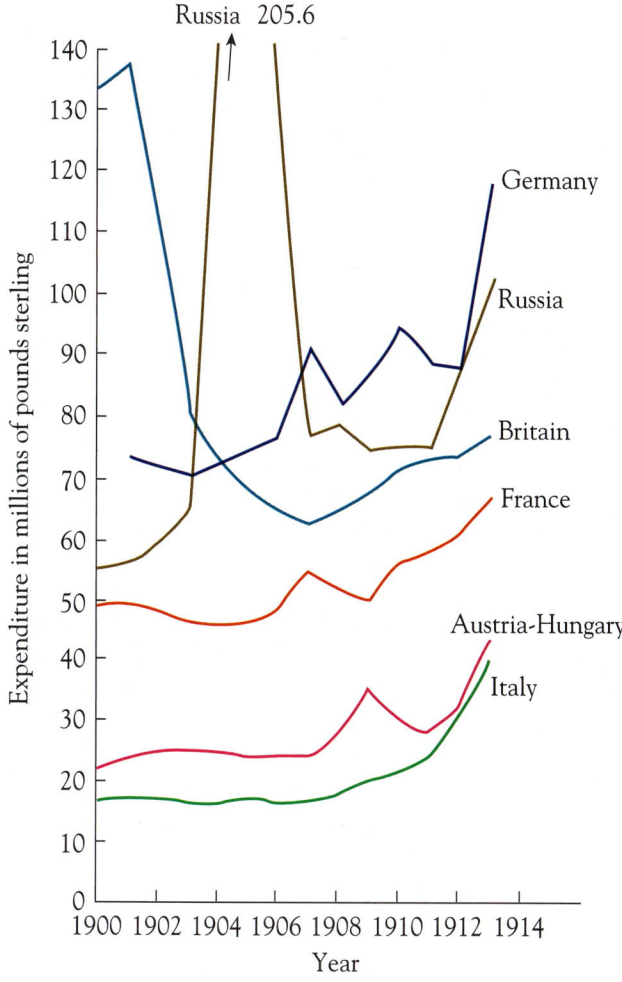

Russia 205.6

Expenditure in millions of pounds sterling

FIGURE 27-2

THE ARMS RACE: EUROPEAN MILITARY EXPENDITURES PRIOR TO THE GREAT WAR

Military expenditures for all the major powers were on the upswing by 1914, although they did not exceed 5.1 percent of any country's net national product, a fairly sustainable proportion by historical standards. In 1913, the expenditures of the Central Powers on arms approximately equaled those of the Triple Entente, as measured in constant pounds sterling.
Source: Figure based on David Stevenson, Armaments and the Coming of War: Europe, 1904–1914 *(Oxford, England: Clarendon, 1996), p. 2.*

The British naval acceleration made Tirpitz's program more expensive and less financially supportable than ever. Successful diplomatic negotiations between Berlin and London helped calm the situation, but the German General Staff sounded an alarm: If war were to come it would have to be won primarily on land, not at sea, ignoring William II's earlier assertion that "our future is on the water." The General Staff worried that the Russians, who were initiating substantial military reforms that the Germans estimated would be complete by 1917, would only get stronger. Naval power, they knew, would be of no use in a

war against the Russians. In the fall of 1911, these arguments prevailed. Naval construction continued, but at a slower pace, and the army received renewed emphasis. Germany's future—its "Africa," as Bismarck had put it—lay not in Weltmacht, colonies, and world trade, but in central Europe.

The Schlieffen Plan The German reemphasis on its ground forces stimulated the other European powers to build up their armies as well. In 1913 France raised its term of conscription from two to three years, so that by 1914 it had almost eight hundred thousand men under arms, slightly more than the Germans. "It would be a crime against civilization if we let our country fall into decadence," the French president argued in defending the buildup. At the end of 1913 the Russians adopted a vast military program that added half a million reserves to its standing army of 1.3 million. In May 1914, Colonel Edward M. House, President Woodrow Wilson's personal emissary to Europe, commented to Wilson that "the situation is extraordinary. It is militarism run stark mad. . . . There is some day to be an awful cataclysm."

Neither economic success nor the naval program, therefore, had solved Germany's basic geopolitical problem: the certainty that in the case of a continental war, Germany would face enemies on two fronts, east and west. Around the turn of the century, the chief of the General Staff, General Alfred von Schlieffen, had devised a solution to this problem. Schlieffen feared that an extended war in the east would bog down German troops and he had no desire to confront France's strong defensive alignment along the western German border. His innovation was to strike at France through Belgium and Luxembourg (see Map 27-4). The **Schlieffen Plan,** as revised by General Helmuth von Moltke after 1906, envisioned holding firm on the southern Franco-German border while sending a mass of troops through undefended Belgium in a huge pivoting movement, attacking the French forces from the rear and driving them against the Swiss frontier.[4] Schlieffen calculated that with the proper manning, the advantage of surprise, and a lightning-fast strike, he could knock France out of the war in a few weeks. The German army would then be free to turn its attention to the sluggish Russians.

The Schlieffen Plan was militarily brilliant, but it contained grave political flaws. It disregarded the neutrality of Belgium, guaranteed by the Treaty of London 1839, and thus put Germany at a severe diplomatic disadvantage. When war finally came, the violation of Belgium's neutrality roused British enthusiasm for retaliation. The plan's requirement of rapid mobilization and attack locked the government into a single, inflexible strategy. The fact that

---

[4] Moltke was the nephew of Bismarck's famous chief of staff of the same name.

Map legend:

German attacks according to original Schlieffen Plan (attack through Netherlands later abandoned)

Anticipated offensive of French forces

Climactic battle in eastern France according to Schlieffen Plan

MAP 27-4
THE SCHLIEFFEN PLAN

the Germans had only one military response, a massive attack, ensured that any war that broke out would spread quickly across Europe. Finally, the Schlieffen Plan put control of Germany's fate almost completely in the hands of the military. The plan attained such prestige in official circles that by 1910 it was beyond debate. In the years leading up to 1914, civilian leaders never participated—not even once—in discussions of military strategy. Once World War I erupted, therefore, the empire's fate hung on a single roll of the dice designed by Schlieffen and Moltke.

William II's capriciousness, the naval buildup, the efforts of the Junkers and industrialists to keep the socialists at bay, and the military's success in resisting civilian control all resonated with the nationalist rhetoric of German academics and publicists. Heinrich von Treitschke provided a unifying national history designed for *Weltpolitik*. Originally a liberal, Treitschke became a Bismarckian in 1866. A vigorous writer and speaker despite his deafness, Treitschke passionately glorified the Hohenzollern dynasty, the Prussian army, and the right of Germany, under Prussian leadership, to dominate the inferior peoples of Europe and the world. Many intellectuals shared Treitschke's ideas and spread them throughout Germany. The sociologist Max Weber, for example, who was considered a moderate,

said the following in 1895: "We must understand that the unification of Germany was [merely] a youthful folly . . . if it should be the conclusion and not the starting point for a German policy of Weltmacht." Some members of the extreme right went considerably further. As one example, in 1911 General Friedrich von Bernhardi, in a book titled *The Next War*, wrote:

> We must rouse in our people the unanimous wish for power . . . together with the determination to sacrifice on the altar of patriotism, not only life and property, but also private views and preferences. . . . Then alone shall we discharge our great duties of the future, grow into a World Power, and stamp a great part of humanity with the impress of the German spirit.

These overheated viewpoints, which were matched in only somewhat lesser degree in other countries, corroded European stability. By dismissing democratic parliaments as beneath the contempt of good Germans and glorifying the anti-Catholic, antisocialist, and antisemitic ideas of the German right, Treitschke and the others sustained the aristocratic and militaristic tone of German public life. Emphasizing Germany's "need" for world power, claiming that enemies encircled Germany, and insisting on a test of blood, German intellectuals fostered a volatile, even frenzied atmosphere that by 1914 made poor decisions almost unavoidable.

Austria-Hungary and the Outbreak of War

Poor decisions were not the sole prerogative of Germany, of course. Austria's declaration of war on Serbia in August 1914, which was intended to contain Serbian nationalism, proved to be not merely a misjudgment but a fatal error. The multinational character of Austria-Hungary, as the state was called after the Compromise of 1867, had not been a problem during the centuries over which the Habsburg monarchs had accumulated their lands (see Map 27-5). In medieval and early modern Europe, nationality made no political difference because each state organized itself on religion and the principle of loyalty to its prince. By the time of the unifications of Italy and Germany, however, many educated people in the empire had decided that loyalty to one's nation was almost as important as loyalty to the emperor. Few subjects went so far as to deny Francis Joseph's authority, but a great many began to think that their national group should be able to use its own language in dealing with the state (in court, for example), run its own schools, and publish its own books. Despite the relative mildness of nineteenth-century cultural nationalism, the contradiction between it and the medieval principle of loyalty to the ruler—the principle that united the Habsburg realm—was fundamental. As nationalism matured, its cultural aspirations inevitably spawned political demands, the most successful of which led to the creation of small nation-states in the Balkans, as we saw in Chapter 24. In

MAP 27-5
AUSTRIA-HUNGARY: THE DUAL MONARCHY

central Europe, new states could come to life only over the corpse of the Habsburg Empire.

Unrest in the Balkans   The conflict between nationalism and the medieval principle of loyalty to the emperor took concrete form as a struggle between Serbia and Austria-Hungary. The resolution of the Eastern Crisis of 1875–1878, discussed in Chapter 24, set the stage for the series of misfortunes leading to World War I. The Ottomans had retained control of Macedonia, but now each of the surrounding countries began maneuvering to eject the Ottomans and to acquire the region. Serbia, frustrated by Austro-Hungarian occupation of Bosnia and Herzegovina, also turned southward. The Serbian king decided to accept Austria's seizure of Bosnia and to put his foreign policy under Austria's wing, in return for which Austria agreed not to oppose Serbian ambitions in Macedonia. Bulgaria, frustrated because the Treaty of Berlin had deprived it of the region, sent teachers and armed bands into Macedonia to counter the Serb bands. The Greeks, who gained nothing from the Eastern Crisis, began to assert claims as well. By 1900 Macedonia had become the most explosive political problem in Europe.

From 1878 to 1903, Serbia was Austria's client, but in 1903 a group of Serbian military conspirators, convinced of the utter incompetence of their king, forced him to pay what they considered the appropriate penalty—they stabbed him forty-seven times and threw him out of his palace window. The new king, Peter Karadjordjević, who had translated John Stuart Mill as a young man and remained something of a liberal, favored Russia and wanted to end Serbia's subservience to Austria. Attempting to break Austrian domination of Serbia's trade, he signed a free-trade agreement with Bulgaria. The Austrians retaliated by shutting their borders to the importation of Serbian pigs. Because Serbia was an undeveloped country whose sole significant trade was exporting live pigs to Austria-Hungary, the Vienna government thought the prohibition would bring Serbia into line. But the Serbs struck back, building meatpacking plants and entering the international market for packaged meats. Much to everyone's surprise, the Austrians lost this Tariff War, as the Serbs call it (the Austrians called it the Pig War). By 1912 Vienna had to admit that the Serbs had not only survived, but prospered.

During the tensions created by the Tariff War, Austria pushed the Serbs over the edge when in 1908 it announced that it had annexed Bosnia and Herzegovina, which until then had remained technically part of the Ottoman realm. The Austrian foreign minister believed that he had received assurances from the Russian foreign minister that this move would be acceptable to the international community. He was mistaken. The annexation aroused an international furor. In Serbia, the latent but still potent hopes for adding Serbian territory in Bosnia (hopes still alive today) resurfaced, and outraged crowds took to the streets to protest the Austrian annexation. Newspapers shrilly criticized Austria, and the Belgrade government refused to recognize the annexation. To force the Serbs to acquiesce, the Austrians turned to their German allies, who in turn told the Russians that if they did not force the Serbs to accept the annexation, war between Germany and Russia was likely. Under heavy pressure, the Serbian government finally backed down, but with intense bitterness. Militant Serbs formed a nationalist society to keep their frustration on the surface of public life, and two years later a group of military officers organized Union or Death, a society known also as the Black Hand. This secret organization devoted itself to the nationalistic goal of incorporating all Serb lands, both in Bosnia and Herzegovina and elsewhere, into one greater Serbian state. In some ways, the annexation crisis of 1908 and 1909 provided a preview of the 1914 crisis, with the vital exception that in this case the Serbs backed down and the Austrians accepted their grudging apology.

The Two Emperors of Central Europe at Military Maneuvers
One indication of the growing militarist pall over public life in the years preceding World War I was the universal practice of European monarchs appearing in military uniform. Here William II and Francis Joseph, surrounded by their elegant staff, salute at a military review, while wearing the uniforms of each other's armies. *Corbis/Bettman.*

The annexation crisis and the Tariff War, along with a series of other incidents, greatly increased the hostility between Austria and Serbia, but Serbia refused to buckle. As Count Ottokar Czernin, a close friend of Francis Ferdinand, the heir to the Habsburg throne, lamented in 1913:

> We did not find the strength to crush Serbia . . . or the greatness to enlist them as our friends. We did not prevent their military development, but economically and commercially, by a policy of pin-pricks, we drove them to desperation. We closed our frontiers to them and all we have achieved thereby is that they have grown strong, they hate us, and for all that [they are] not afraid of us.

A stronger indictment of Austrian policy is hard to imagine.

The Mediterranean and Balkans in Crisis, 1911–1913

During the period between 1911 and 1914 Europe stumbled through one crisis after another in the Mediterranean and the Balkans, each leaving one or more of the powers convinced that they were being left behind or failing in some way. In the spring of 1911, the French moved to consolidate their interests in Morocco, violating a previous agreement with Germany. When the Germans sent a gunboat to protest, war threatened. Eventually the Germans retreated when the French offered them a portion of the French Congo, but many German observers felt that once again the Triple Entente had thwarted them.

The Italians, acutely aware of being the least of the great powers, had engaged in African colonialism for some years, but with only partial success. In 1911, with the other powers preoccupied by the Moroccan crisis, they decided to attempt to seize the Ottoman provinces of Tripolitana and Cyrenaica (modern Libya), which set off war with the Ottoman Empire. Italy poured one hundred thousand troops into North Africa and forced the Ottomans to give up Libya.

The Ottoman Empire itself had been in turmoil since 1908, when a group of army officers had forced the sultan to restore the relatively liberal constitution of 1876. The "Young Turks," as these officers were called, sought to modernize and centralize the Ottoman government, and they pushed through reforms in education based on Turkish nationalism rather than Ottoman and Islamic multiculturalism. But their own internal divisions—they did not consolidate their power until 1913—only undermined the ability of the Ottomans to put their house in order.

On top of these problems, in 1912 serious hostilities broke out in the Balkans, the outcome of Russian efforts to reconcile Serbia and Bulgaria after the annexation crisis of 1908. Though weakened by their defeat in the Russo-Japanese war and by their inability to support Serbia in 1909, Russian leaders stubbornly decided to reinvigorate their country by getting involved in Balkan affairs. From the time of Nicholas I (reigned 1825–1855), Russia had fought three wars more or less on behalf of the Balkan peoples, who in each instance had rejected Russia's heavy-handed benevolence. Russian interest in the Balkans had little to do with economic advantage, a drive for a warm water port, or redressing the balance of power. Russian tsars operated by principles that were far more personal and old-fashioned, reminiscent of the seventeenth rather than the nineteenth century. Every Russian tsar in the nineteenth century, and especially Nicholas II, devoted himself to the principles of honor and duty. For them, international treaties were not tools of state policy, but sacrosanct pledges of honor to their faith and to their Slavic brethren. They considered it their obligation to defend the Orthodox faith, which dominated most of the Balkans. Instead of dreaming of world missions and hatching grand designs, Russian tsars labored under the more mundane masters of duty and responsibility.

One of those responsibilities, strongly supported by vigorous groups of Slavophiles among the Russian public, was to lend fraternal support to the Orthodox Slavs of the Balkans. But in 1912, Russian diplomacy lost control of matters. After allying themselves under Russian tutelage, Serbia and Bulgaria forged a military pact with Greece, Montenegro, and Romania and attacked the Ottomans. In this First Balkan War, the five allies quickly achieved their goal of pushing the Ottomans almost completely out of southeastern Europe. But the victors could not agree on how to divide the spoils: Macedonia. Serbia even continued fighting in an effort to obtain access to the Adriatic Sea through Albania. In the Second Balkan War (1913), the four allies turned on Bulgaria and portioned out Macedonia for themselves. With Bulgaria's defeat, Greece took a little

MAP 27-6

THE FIRST AND SECOND BALKAN WARS, 1912–1913

Legend:
- Annexed by Serbia after first and second Balkan Wars
- Annexed by Montenegro after first and second Balkan Wars
- Annexed by Greece after first and second Balkan Wars
- Annexed by Greece, 1908
- Annexed by Bulgaria after first and second Balkan Wars
- Bosnia-Herzegovina, annexed by Austria-Hungary, 1908
- Albania, created out of Ottoman territory, 1912
- Territory contested by Bulgaria vs. Serbia/Greece after first Balkan War
- Territory sought unsuccessfully by Serbia after first Balkan War

over half of Macedonia and Serbia about a third, leaving only a small fraction for Bulgaria. The Serbian effort to gain access to the sea failed: Austria and Italy cut the Serbs off by creating a new state, Albania (see Map 27-6).

Sarajevo and War The spark that ignited this tinderbox of mutual antagonisms and anxieties struck in 1914 in Sarajevo, the capital of the recently annexed provinces of Bosnia and Herzegovina. On June 28, 1914, the most sacred Serbian holiday, Francis Ferdinand, the fifty-four-year-old heir to the Habsburg crown, visited Sarajevo.[5] He traveled to Bosnia and Herzegovina despite warnings from his advisers partly in order to honor his wife, Sophia. Because she was not of sufficiently high social rank, their marriage was morganatic; that is, Sophia was Francis Ferdinand's legal spouse, but she did not have the right to inherit or to receive certain honors that would otherwise be due her. Yet owing to the special legal status of Bosnia (it was part of neither Austria nor Hungary, and was administered separately), she could receive full honors there. Francis Ferdinand was an irascible and none-too-able man, but he dearly loved Sophia, and he planned this trip for her.

Unfortunately for the imperial couple, a group of six Bosnian Serbs, all under twenty years of age, decided that Francis Ferdinand would make a powerful symbolic sacrifice to the Serbian cause. These inexperienced nationalists had no plan in mind for following up the assassination; they sought only to commit a spectacular act expressing Serbian rage at Austria. They almost failed. When the royal caravan entered Sarajevo, driving along its well-advertised route beside the river, the second of the assassins in line threw a bomb. The device bounced off the rear hood of the car carrying the royal couple and instead exploded under a following car, injuring staff personnel but missing its main target. After attending to the wounded, Francis Ferdinand continued to the town hall for a strained reception. The thwarted assassins wandered aimlessly around town.

After the reception, the imperial pair climbed back into their open car. For safety reasons, security officials decided that instead of following the intended parade route through the center of the city, the caravan would drive rapidly out of town by a direct route. For some reason, the general in charge neglected to inform Francis Ferdinand's driver of this change in routing. When the driver started turning onto the street that was now to be avoided, alarmed officers told him to stop, back up, and continue straight. At that moment, as described briefly at the beginning of this chapter, Gavrilo Princip, one of the conspira-

tors, was standing on that very street corner, idly wondering what to do with his weapon. Suddenly, up drove Francis Ferdinand's car and stopped about 8 feet in front of him. Reacting almost instinctively, Princip pulled out his pistol and fired two shots. Princip was an inexperienced marksman, and he had none too good a weapon, but somehow those two almost random shots managed to kill both the archduke and his consort.

World reactions to the assassination assumed conventional forms of shock and surprise but they did not reflect any sense of special urgency. Indeed, one English headline read "To Hell with Serbia." Most of the diplomats of Europe left for their holidays confident that yet one more squabble in the Balkans would be ironed out somehow. Habsburg royalty and aristocracy accepted the death of the unloved Francis Ferdinand in an almost relieved way.

But some political and military leaders in Austria saw the incident differently. They seized on it as an excuse for "solving the Serbian question." Conrad von Hötzendorf, the belligerent Austrian chief of staff who believed that the struggle for existence was "the only real and rational basis for policy making," had unsuccessfully proposed war against Serbia at least nine times between 1908 and 1914. In January 1909, for example, he had pleaded with Francis Joseph: "The hour is struck. War is inevitable. Our blood throbs in our veins, we strain at the leash. Sire! Give us the signal!" After the assassination, Hötzendorf received a sympathetic ear from Count Leopold Berchtold, head of the government.

Both Berchtold and Hötzendorf well knew, as did the other less committed members of the State Council, that Austria could not undertake a military strike against Serbia without Germany's backing, for Russia now supported Serbia more resolutely than it had in 1908 and 1909. Early in July, the Austrian ambassador cautiously asked William II what position the Germans might take if the Austrians reacted strongly to the assassination. The Kaiser's response reflected the mood of a council of war held the previous day: Austria "might in this case, as in all others, rely upon Germany's full support." The ambassador reported that it was the emperor's "opinion that this action [against Serbia] must not be delayed." "Tread hard on the heels of the rabble," was William's more characteristic private comment.

It was clear to the Austrian and German leadership at the time, and it is clear today, that the German "blank check" transformed a Balkan quarrel into a world war. The German government—convinced that Germany was "encircled," thwarted in its drive for Weltmacht, bedeviled by social cleavages, believing in an inevitable Darwinian struggle between Teuton and Slav, and confident that in any test of blood the German sword would triumph— agreed with William that the time had come to act.

During July 1914, the other powers were not aware of Austria's plan to put an ultimatum to Serbia, nor did they realize Germany had decided on a course for war. In order

---

[5] On June 28, 1389, the Ottomans defeated an army of medieval Serbian knights in Kosovo, thus establishing Muslim control over Serbia that lasted about five hundred years. Oral poetry and national traditions sustained the memory of that defeat, turning it into the most emotional symbol of Serbian national renewal. The war in Kosovo in 1999 showed how powerful these feelings endure.

THE HISTORICAL EVIDENCE

The Blank Check

July 5, 1914

While Austria was considering its actions after the assassination of Franz Ferdinand, it sought the opinion of William II. His response is given below, relayed in a telegram from the Austrian ambassador to Germany to the Austrian foreign minister. Because William's unconditional assurances of support encouraged Austria to go ahead with its plan to "teach the Serbs a lesson," historians have called William's answer "a blank check." When Austria was not satisfied with the Serbian response to an ultimatum it proposed, despite Serbia's almost complete compliance with its demands, it declared war. Within a week the Great War had begun.

Telegram 237   Berlin, 5 July 1914
Strictly confidential   D. 7.35 P.M.
Ö.D. 10058   R. 10.00 P.M.

When I had informed Kaiser Wilhelm that I had an autograph letter from His Imp. and Roy. Apostolic Majesty [Francis Joseph], which Count Hoyos had just brought and which I was to give to him, I received an invitation to lunch with Their Majesties at noon in the Neues Palais. I gave the autograph letter and the enclosed memoir into the hands of His Majesty. In my presence the Kaiser read both with the greatest attention. The first thing he assured me was that he had expected some serious step on our part towards Serbia, but that at the same time he must confess that the detailed statement of His Majesty made him regard a serious European complication possible and that he could give no definite answer before having taken counsel with the Imperial chancellor.

After lunch, when I again called attention to the seriousness of the situation, the Kaiser authorised me to inform our gracious Majesty that we might in this case, as in all others, rely upon Germany's full support. He must, as he said before, first hear what the Imperial Chancellor has to say, but he did not doubt in the least that Herr von Bethmann Hollweg would agree with him. Especially as far as our action against Serbia was concerned. But it was his (Kaiser Wilhelm's) opinion that this action must not be delayed. Russia's attitude will no doubt be hostile, but to this he had been for years prepared, and should a war between Austria-Hungary and Russia be unavoidable, we might be convinced that Germany, our old faithful ally, would stand at our side. Russia at the present time was in no way prepared for war, and would think twice before it appealed to arms. But it will certainly set other powers on to the Triple Alliance and add fuel to the fire in the Balkans. He understands perfectly well that His Apostolic Majesty in his well-known love of peace would be reluctant to march into Serbia; but if we had really recognised the necessity of warlike action against Serbia, he (Kaiser Wilhelm) would regret if we did not make use of the present moment, which is all in our favour. As to Roumania he would take care that King Carol and his councillors would observe a correct attitude. He cannot sympathise with the idea of concluding an alliance with Bulgaria; he never trusted King Ferdinand and does not trust him now, nor his former or present councillors. Still he would make no objections to a treaty between the monarchy and Bulgaria, but this treaty must contain nothing to offend Roumania and it must—as the memoir proposes—be communicated to Roumania. Kaiser Wilhelm intends leaving to-morrow morning for Kiel, whence he starts for his northern tour; but before leaving, His Majesty will discourse with the Imperial Chancellor on the subject in question. For this purpose he has sent him to Hohenfinow, and will see him in the Neues Palais this evening. I shall certainly have an opportunity of seeing the Imperial Chancellor in the course of to-morrow.

Source: From Imanuel Geiss, ed., *July 1914, The Outbreak of the First World War: Selected Documents* (New York: Norton, 1967), pp. 76–77.

---

to mask their intentions, the Germans sent officials on their normal vacations, and William II set out on his annual yachting cruise from Kiel. But at 6:00 P.M., July 23, when the Austrian representative in Belgrade handed the Serbian government a lengthy ultimatum and demanded an answer within forty-eight hours, the chancelleries of Europe erupted into panicked activity. Literally thousands of telegrams flowed back and forth as diplomats frantically sought to find a way to restrain Austria or allay German fears. Two days later the Serbs almost completely capitulated to the Austrian demands, making only one or two technical exceptions. When William II read the Serb response later, he commented, "But this removes all cause for war." Nevertheless, when the Austrian representative

THE HUMAN EXPERIENCE

Theobald von Bethmann Hollweg, German Chancellor in 1914

The debate over Germany's responsibility for World War I sometimes focuses on the responsibility of one man, Theobald von Bethmann Hollweg (1856–1920), chancellor of Germany from 1909 to 1917. An honorable man, Bethmann accepted responsibility for his decisions. But historians have wondered ever since whether he was a clever manipulator or merely a bungler.

After enjoying a placid childhood on his family's 7,500-acre estate thirty miles from Berlin, Bethmann took a degree in law. But service in the Prussian court system made him feel as if he had "been looking at life like a cow at a new gate." Instead of switching to the glamorous foreign service, Bethmann entered the lowest rung of domestic administration, taking his father's former position as local commissioner.

From the beginning, Bethmann had two major assets. First, he was intelligent, controlled, and hardworking. He passed his entry tests with distinction, wrote his four-hundred-page thesis in six weeks, and impressed his superiors with his industry and ability. Second, he made an important early connection with

William II. In 1877 the crown prince visited the family estate for a hunt. William's right arm was crippled, but Bethmann nevertheless contrived the hunt in such a way that William shot his first deer. When Bethmann eventually became chancellor, William continued to feel warmth for him.

Bethmann's choice of domestic service proved a good one. An honest man as well as a highly gifted administrator, he quickly moved up the ladder—from administrator of Potsdam, to the governorship of Brandenburg (the youngest governor in Prussia at the time of his appointment), to Prussian Minister of the Interior by 1905. Finally, in 1909, retiring chancellor von Bülow persuaded William II to appoint Bethmann as his successor. The choice well suited the management of Germany's internal problems in the conservative, antiparliamentary style that William II wanted.

In July 1914, Bethmann fully supported William II's decision to grant the blank check to Austria. The chancellor believed the war could be limited; he maintained the vain hope that England would remain neutral; and he gave himself over to

dreams of Weltmacht and the Schlieffen plan. In these views he reflected the hopes and prejudices of German elites. On the other hand, Bethmann was not optimistic about Germany's position. He disapproved of the cant and rhetoric of William's court, and believed he was trying honestly to achieve peace. These contradictions have made it impossible to achieve consensus on Bethmann's role. Von Bülow called him "a good plowhorse," while his secretary said, "In breadth and independence of mind, he is a great man." Was Bethmann then a "political sleep-walker" and a "headless chancellor," or was he a "cool and calculating Machiavellian statesman whose bumbling moderation was a mere front for sinister aims"?

The likely answer is neither. Bethmann Hollweg's contradictions reflect the fact that humans are complex beings who do not always act consistently or make the right choices. The experience of the enigmatic chancellor, as one historian calls him, testifies to the ability of highly intelligent but nevertheless fallible human beings to make decisions that have tragic consequences. ❖

---

saw that the complex Serbian document was not a simple acceptance of the Austrian conditions, he rejected it out of hand. Within a few days, Austrian shells were falling on Serbian soil.

Historians have traced the international commotion that these acts produced literally minute by minute. The problem was that if Russia came to Serbia's defense, the treaty arrangements among the Triple Alliance and the Triple Entente would instantly draw all the main powers into war. The Germans had no desire to postpone hostilities. For the Schlieffen plan to work, they had to strike first. But for Germany to maintain the fiction that the war was the fault of encircling enemies, someone else had to appear to make the initial move. The German goal in the week after the Austrian ultimatum to Serbia, therefore, was

to dupe Russia into mobilizing its forces, an act that could be regarded as tantamount to a declaration of war. After a flurry of false starts and international exchanges of schemes to solve the crisis, the Russians took the Germans' false bait and mobilized. Claiming they were about to be attacked, the Germans acted. At 4:00 A.M. on the morning of August 4, 1914, streams of blue-uniformed German troops crossed the border into neutral Belgium, and the Great War was on.

CONCLUSION: WHY?

In the 1920s, an Austrian newspaper ran a contest to see who could write the best headline. The winner: "Francis Ferdinand Found Alive: Great War Fought in Vain." The joke, of course, lies in the absurdity of the premise: World War I was not about Francis Ferdinand. After reviewing the origins of the war, can we say what it was about? Definitely not imperial claims. In fact, if anything, the explosion into Africa and China at the end of the nineteenth century lessened the likelihood of a continental war. In the eighteenth century, each major power had to be compensated when any of its rivals gained territory or whenever it performed services for an ally. The Congress of Vienna changed that rule, so that the most significant territorial exchange to take place in the hundred years after 1815 was the German seizure of Alsace and Lorraine in 1871. When a system of competing alliances replaced the Concert of Europe, however, international politics reverted to some of the balance-of-power practices. But this time the territorial bickerings and compensations took place in the colonial world rather than on the European continent itself. Far from pushing Europe toward general war, colonial deals permitted the Europeans to avoid major conflicts. Early in 1914, for example, Germany and Britain settled their differences over the so-called Berlin-to-Baghdad railroad, a typically imperialist adventure in the Ottoman Empire. Damaging as imperialism was to the dominated peoples, and much as it produced tensions and frustrations, particularly for Germany, it was at least not the primary cause of the Great War.

Two more major problems were at the root of the conflict. The first was the economic explosion of the second half of the nineteenth century that put Germany at odds with the other European powers, particularly with France and Britain. As German economic strength grew and the Germans became more aggressive economically and militarily, they called forth equivalent reactions from the other powers, who began building up their armies and navies. A wave of armed militarism swept Europe. The emergence of a mass press amplified tensions. Daily newspapers, read by millions of urban dwellers by the first decade of the twentieth century, found they could attract readers with nationalistic diatribes and inflammatory rhetoric. Public reaction fueled by yellow journalism put increased pressure on politicians, particularly as the franchise expanded. Social Darwinism exacerbated strains by convincing some public figures that the only way to solve the problem of competition among two or more strong countries was for one of them to "win the struggle for survival." Despite the growth of liberal government in republican France, the expansion of a democratic franchise in Britain, the coming of a legislature (the Duma) to Russia, and other similar evidences of the value of the politics of accommodation in an industrial society, no mechanisms of liberal government arose in the international arena. It seemed that no one could conceive of any way for several powerful entities to interact except through a military triumph of one over the others.

The related second problem was the threat that intensifying nationalism posed for the Ottoman and, especially, the Habsburg Empires. Because it was weak, because it was Muslim, and because Europeans saw it as a field for their own predations rather than a state that on principle should be supported, the Ottomans lost their European holdings to small nation-states by 1914. Austria actually gained territory through that process, but it justly feared the potential consequences of the nationalism virus. For the Habsburgs, nationalism was potentially fatal. The conservative and aristocratic ideologies of the day offered Austria no clear way to deal with this paramount threat except violence—a last resort that could never permanently solve its problems.

World War I, then, while not inevitable in the form it took, was nevertheless the result of Europe's inability to resolve the massive tensions created by the march of the Dual Revolution (Industrial and French). New ideas of equity had undermined the stubborn and still powerful old classes, and economic change had brought new elements into the political equation. But economic development had also put unprecedented tools of aggression into the hands of governments that increasingly felt that only violence would solve their problems. When the war began in August 1914, both sides welcomed it in the belief that they would emerge victorious and whole within a few months.

Selected Reading

Sources

Geiss, Imanuel, ed. *July 1914, the Outbreak of the First World War: Selected Documents* (1974).

Snyder, Louis L. *The Imperialism Reader* (1962).

Origins of World War I

Albertini, Luigi. *The Origins of the War of 1914*, 3 vols. (1952–1957). Exhaustive and authoritative study.

Berghahn, Volker R. *Germany and the Approach of War in 1914* (1973). Widely used. Asserts primary German responsibility for World War I.

Dedijer, Vladimir. *The Road to Sarajevo* (1966). Detailed discussion of the Balkan background to the assassination of Francis Ferdinand.

Fischer, Fritz. *Germany's Aims in the First World War* (1967). The breakthrough book in post–World War I studies. It deals primarily with the elaboration of war aims during the course of the war.

———. *War of Illusions: German Policies from 1911 to 1914* (1975). Complex study arguing that German ruling classes sought war in 1914 to preserve their hegemony.

Herrmann, David G. *The Arming of Europe and the Making of the First World War* (1996). This book and Stevenson's work, listed below, present two illuminating accounts of the arms race preceding World War I.

Kennedy, Paul. *The Rise of the Anglo-German Antagonism, 1860–1914* (1980). Shows how antagonisms dominated the relationship, despite continual efforts to lessen tensions.

LaFore, Laurence. *The Long Fuse: An Interpretation of the Origins of World War I* (1965). Emphasizes the Balkan component and de-emphasizes German responsibility. Well written and widely used in classrooms.

Massie, Robert K. *Dreadnought: Britain, Germany, and the Coming of the Great War* (1991). Massive popular history with many anecdotes and colorful biographical sketches.

Mayer, Arno J. *The Persistence of the Old Regime: Europe to the Great War* (1981). A powerful corrective to the view that the middle classes rose to political dominance in the nineteenth century.

Remak, Joachim. *Sarajevo, the Story of a Political Murder* (1959). Detailed discussion of the assassination of Francis Ferdinand, showing the importance of chance in history.

Stevenson, David. *Armaments and the Coming of the War: Europe, 1904–1914* (1996). Together with Herrmann, cited above, provides an enlightening perspective on the pre–World War I arms race.

Wehler, Hans-Ulrich. *The German Empire 1871–1918* (1985). Very influential study emphasizing the primacy of domestic politics and social relations in the formation of German policy.

Williamson, Samuel R. Jr. *Austria-Hungary and the Origins of the First World War* (1991). Explores how the unspoken assumptions of the Habsburg monarchy drove it to a fatal war in 1914.

Imperialism

Cain, P. J., and A. G. Hopkins. *British Imperialism: Innovation and Expansion 1688–1914* (1993). Broad-ranging study asserting that the growth of financial and other services in the late nineteenth century vastly increased British colonial power. An important reinterpretation.

Headrick, Daniel R. *The Tools of Empire: Technology and European Imperialism in the Nineteenth Century* (1981). The role of gunboats, quinine, guns, and communications in nineteenth-century European expansion.

Hochschild, Adam. *King Leopold's Ghost: A Story of Greed, Terror, and Heroism in Colonial Africa* (1998). The horrific tale of imperialist abuses in the Congo.

Langer, William L. *The Diplomacy of Imperialism*, 2nd ed. (1951). Unsurpassed diplomatic history of the imperialist era. A classic.

Pakenham, Thomas. *The Scramble for Africa, 1876–1912* (1991). Broad narrative that encompasses the entire continent.

Porter, Andrew. *European Imperialism, 1860–1914* (1994). A relatively brief but thorough review of theories of imperialism with an excellent bibliography.

Robinson, Ronald E., and John Gallagher. *Africa and the Victorians: The Official Mind of Imperialism* (1981). Landmark work on the transformation of informal empire based on free trade to formal empire of the late nineteenth century. An extremely influential study.

Personalities

Jarausch, Konrad H. *The Enigmatic Chancellor: Bethmann Hollweg and the Hubris of Imperial Germany* (1973). Highly critical of the unrealistic thinking of the German upper classes in the years preceding World War I.

Kohut, Thomas. *Wilhelm II and the Germans: A Study in Leadership* (1991). Standard study of the impact of William II on German politics.

Marsh, Peter T. *Joseph Chamberlain: Entrepreneur in Politics* (1994). This voluminous biography is now the standard work.

CHAPTER 28

WAR AND REVOLUTION

The Menin Gate *Courtesy of Commonwealth War Graves Commission. Photo reproduced by kind permission of Marcus Taylor Photographs–England.*

August 1914	Great War erupts; Schlieffen plan fails; trench warfare in west; fluid but inconclusive front in east
May 1915	German submarine sinks *Lusitania*
early 1916	Battle of Verdun epitomizes bloody war of attrition
March 1917	Revolution topples Romanov dynasty
April 1917	United States enters war
November 1917	Bolsheviks seize power in Russia
January 1918	Woodrow Wilson announces Fourteen Points
March 1918	Treaty of Brest-Litovsk halts war on eastern front
September 1918	Breakthrough on Thessalonika front; Germans in full retreat on western front
November 9, 1918	Revolution in Germany; William II abdicates, flees to Holland
November 11, 1918	Armistice ends the Great War
1919	Treaty of Versailles imposed on Germany
1922	Greeks expelled from Anatolia

The most powerful monument in North America to the human cost of war is the Vietnam Veterans Memorial in Washington, D.C. Inscribed on two simple black granite walls are the names of more than fifty-eight thousand Americans who perished during the war in Southeast Asia. Every day, hundreds of people pass by "the Wall," many of them pausing, sometimes in tears, to see or touch the name of a person they remember.

The Menin Gate (previous page), in Ypres, Belgium, is similar to the Vietnam Veterans Memorial in one respect: On it are inscribed almost fifty-five thousand names—British soldiers who perished near Ypres over a thirty-four-month period from 1914 to 1917. Not far away, a military cemetery holds another fifty thousand named graves, these all German. Less than 10 miles distant stands a memorial engraved with the names of thirty-five thousand soldiers who were killed so violently that no trace of them large enough to bury was ever found. All of these young men perished in the Great War of 1914–1918. But they are just the beginning. The conflict exacted a staggering human cost: 743,000 British, 1,384,000 French, 1,800,000 German, 1,290,000 Austro-Hungarian, and 1,700,00 Russian combatants died, not to mention 1,000,000 Armenian civilians, close to 800,000 German noncombatants, and on and on.[1] Altogether almost 9 million young men lost their lives in the war, an average of fifty-six hundred deaths a day for more than four years. And these figures do not include another 5 million civilians. A memorial wall for World War I similar to the Vietnam Memorial would stretch more than 7½ miles.

Human beings were not the only casualties of the Great War. The four empires of central and eastern Europe—the Russian, German, Austro-Hungarian, and Ottoman Empires—expired as well. In their place came entirely new countries, such as Yugoslavia and Czechoslovakia, and restored or enlarged old ones, like Poland and Romania. The war dealt a final blow to the power of hereditary rulers, who in 1914 had still retained a considerable portion of their medieval prestige and authority. In Russia, revolutionary Marxists came to power, fundamentally reshaping European politics for the next seventy years. Finally, inadequate peace treaties, unstable economies, and unresolved animosities laid the foundation for an even worse legacy: Adolf Hitler and World War II. No wonder that many historians consider World War I the pivotal event of a tumultuous twentieth century.

TOTAL WAR

In the years preceding the outbreak of war in 1914, a kind of frenzy had taken over public life in Europe. The frantic buildup of arms, Darwinian rhetoric about a test of blood, and chauvinistic popular newspapers created an atmosphere of tension in which some saw war as almost a relief, a chance to settle frustrations once and for all. If there are lessons to be learned from history, however, one of them surely must be that the costs of acting on such all-or-nothing emotions are almost always very high. Despite the years of planning, the European powers went to war in 1914 with little consideration of the long-term consequences of their acts. They thought in terms of lashing out at enemies, of gaining territory, of victory—but not in terms of what would make a stable and prosperous Europe. When the war bogged down, they were forced to strain every muscle of their societies just to survive. The Great War became the first total war in European history.

---

[1] By contrast, Canada lost sixty thousand troops, the United States forty-eight thousand.

From "Short War" to Stalemate

The first indication that the war was not going to go as hoped was the failure of the carefully organized German offensive into France. The Schlieffen plan had calculated that German troops would sweep through Belgium unopposed, circle to the west of Paris, and pin the surprised French against the Swiss border. In the south, German troops facing the French across the Ardennes forest would hold the line, trusting to the success of the armies wheeling through France in the north.

Contrary to expectations, however, the Belgians stoutly resisted the German advance, especially at Liège, putting the plan four days behind schedule almost immediately. The Germans also had not calculated that the British would be able to land five army divisions and rush them to Mons. There they prevented the Germans from rounding the French flank and advancing to the west of Paris. When the German First Army turned south, the French responded with an unexpectedly strong counterattack along the Marne River, east of Paris. The fighting was so close to Paris that Parisian taxicabs participated in rushing troops to the front. In what became known as "the Miracle on the Marne," the French stopped the German advance. As that battle erupted, Helmuth von Moltke, chief of the German general staff, ordered his troops in the south to abandon their holding war and assault the French city of Nancy. In this way he committed himself to a peripheral battle at the cost of weakening his main thrust. Finally, the Germans had taken it for granted that the Russians would prove slow to mobilize and sluggish to attack, but in fact two Russian armies immediately invaded East Prussia.[2] Slightly more than one month into the war, therefore, the Schlieffen Plan had failed. In the west, the Germans fell back into defensive positions, their dreams of a speedy victory shattered (see Map 28-1).

Within months, lines of trenches—Germans on one side, English and French on the other—extended from Switzerland to the English Channel. In October and

---

[2] Schlieffen had warned that it was imperative not to weaken the right flank. In actuality, the German high command withdrew two divisions from that flank to send east against the Russians. Some historians have seen that as the reason for the failure of the Schlieffen Plan. Detailed research suggests, however, that it was the decision to move east rather than west of Paris that was fundamental to the defeat of the plan, not the withdrawal of the two divisions.

MAP 28-1

THE WESTERN AND ITALIAN FRONTS, 1914–1918

From the first month of the war until the last three or four months, the western front remained almost completely static. Millions of men lost their lives trying to break through, but usually made only minuscule and strategically insignificant gains.

Western Front
— Farthest German advance, 1914
— Front line during battle of Verdun, 1916
— Farthest German advance, spring 1918
— Armistice line, November 1918

Italian Front
— Farthest Italian advance against Austria-Hungary, 1915
— Farthest Austro-Hungarian advance against Italy, 1917

November, a new chief of the German General Staff, Erich von Falkenhayn, labored desperately to resume the German offensive by breaking through these trench lines. But his massive assaults near Ypres failed, at the cost of more than a hundred thousand casualties. This experience pushed Falkenhayn to a uniquely perceptive conclusion: The German army was "a broken instrument." In a report to Chancellor Bethmann-Hollweg, he argued that only by detaching France or England from the Triple Entente could Germany hope to prevail.

Bethmann hesitated to accept Falkenhayn's grim yet realistic assessment because in the east the Germans had routed the attacking Russians. Generals Paul von Hindenburg and Erich Ludendorff split the two brave but inept Russian armies invading East Prussia, crushing them at the battles of Tannenberg and the Masurian Lakes. Naturally, the German General Staff chose to emphasize these victories in the east rather than the failure of the offensive in the west.

Moltke paid for his mistakes in the west when Falkenhayn replaced him, and the German public adopted Hindenburg and Ludendorff as its two new heroes. Hindenburg was a retired general rushed back into service at the outbreak of war. Stolid, conservative, and honorable, he was convinced that Germany could win the war if only the civilian leaders would give him the resources he needed, which he constantly complained they were not doing. Ludendorff—mercurial, vain, and stubborn—went much

The German Military High Command Generals Hindenburg (left) and Ludendorff flank their emperor, William II, as they review war plans. As the war wore on, William II increasingly became a figurehead, and Ludendorff emerged as the dominant figure. This did not prevent Ludendorff from trying to blame Jews and socialists for losing the war, however. *Corbis / Bettmann–UPI.*

further. He believed that nothing short of German control of the economic and political assets of central and eastern Europe, including those in Russia, would satisfy German needs. The myth of invincibility that the early victories at Tannenberg and the Masurian Lakes gave to the Hindenburg/Ludendorff team permitted them to wrest power from the civilian government by 1917 and drive Germany toward disaster.[3]

Austria-Hungary, Germany's primary ally, also faced a two-front war. To the south, it felt obliged "to teach a lesson" to Serbia, where the war had begun. On August 12, 1914, Austrian armies began what they anticipated would be an easy march into Belgrade. To everyone's surprise, the Serbs not only pushed the Habsburg forces back but even had the temerity briefly to invade Austria-Hungary. The Austrians struck back, but after they seized the bulk of northern Serbia, their offensive collapsed. By the end of that year, the Serbs had cleared their country of foreign troops. The Austrians could not bring adequate force to bear in Serbia because they faced an invasion on a second front to the north, where four Russian armies pushed into Galicia. Despite strong resistance, the Austrians had to fall back there, too. By late September, they had abandoned Galicia to the Russians.

Mobilization for Total War

These setbacks came as a shock to the Central Powers.[4] The Russo-Japanese War of 1904–1905, which caused severe financial difficulties in Japan and ignited revolution in Russia, had convinced most Europeans that industrial countries could not sustain all-out war. The World War I adversaries felt confident that the coming struggle would be "a providential lightning flash that would clear the air." In Berlin and Vienna, troops marched off with cheers ringing in their ears and flowers tossed at their feet, while in London young men thronged recruiting offices in a rush to get at the Germans. The boys would be home before the leaves fell, it was said, or at the very latest by Christmas. By December 25, 1914, however, families across Europe had become painfully aware that their sons were not coming home soon and that many of them would never return at all.

Despite the formidable arms buildup preceding 1914, the extensive military planning undertaken in those years,

[3] Ludendorff was one of the very few high-ranking German officers who was not of noble origin (note the lack of a "von" before his last name). Hindenburg, of Junker background, provided the social status the team needed at the highest levels.

[4] In World War I, Germany and Austria were conventionally referred to as "the Central Powers," while the British/French/Russian side was often termed "the Allies." The term the *Triple Alliance* refers to Germany, Austria, and Italy prior to the war, while the *Entente Powers* are Britain, France, and Russia.

Off to War! German soldiers enthusiastically set out to settle accounts with the French in August 1914. Note the flowers in the rifle barrels and the switching of hats and helmets. It was going to be a nice little war. *Suddeutscher Verlag, Munich.*

and the strong presentiment of impending hostilities, the belief in a short war meant that no government had given more than cursory thought to sustaining a protracted conflict. Cranking out the phenomenal number of artillery shells demanded by the military posed a particularly urgent challenge. No longer simple metal balls, these projectiles had become precisely machined steel cases containing a fuse, high explosive TNT, and often hundreds of steel balls, an innovation of one Colonel Shrapnel. In September 1914, French commanding general Joffre informed his surprised government that he required an unbelievable seventy thousand of these sophisticated shells a day, and the numbers continued to mount.

Germany faced a unique munitions problem because it had imported almost all of its nitrates, essential to the production of explosives, from Chile. When the British navy cleared the seas of German merchant vessels by 1915 and established a blockade of Germany, the problem became acute. A new technology of nitrogen fixing solved the explosives difficulty for Germany—but the military failures of the first month of the campaign, coupled with the British blockade, presented the Central Powers with serious shortages, especially in food. Before the war, Germany had imported about one-third of its foodstuffs. Already in January 1915, the government took wheat production under its control, and in February Austria-Hungary followed suit. By June 1915, rationing had spread throughout Germany and waiting in line for hours in front of food stores became commonplace. One year later, the official ration for a worker in Vienna reached a dangerously mea-

ger 1,300 calories a day.[5] Working families, now headed by women, were reduced to scavenging and even begging. Over the course of the war, food shortages and other privations in Germany contributed to the deaths of the phenomenal number of almost eight hundred thousand civilians.

In Russia economic problems were as severe as those in Germany and Austria, but the tsarist government came up with few workable solutions. Its only real success was in the production of shells, where draconian but original methods of integrated production and procurement produced good results. The autocracy's main failure was its inability to grasp the needs of its civilian population. Used to a servile peasantry, Russian generals never quite understood the necessity of maintaining civilian morale or of putting the patriotic initiatives of its businessmen to good use. Disorganized and yet at the same time jealous of its privileges, the government refused to launch a national program of rationing despite frightening food shortages, and never established control over Russian labor markets. When a competent man found the energy and ability to organize a sector of the economy successfully, he was more likely than not to lose his position. For example, in 1916 the tsar replaced Russia's most successful organizer, A. A. Polivanov, because he had tried to involve public organizations

---

[5] A Burger King Whopper with medium fries and a small chocolate shake provides more than 1,300 calories. Of course, the Viennese poor were not eating hamburgers; they often subsisted on moldy potatoes, old cabbage, and scraps scavenged from garbage heaps.

THE HISTORICAL EVIDENCE

Horsemeat in Vienna

1918

As in Germany, the prolonged war made increasing demands on the citizens at home in Austria-Hungary. Anna Eisenmenger, whose prewar status was assured through her husband's work as a Vienna doctor, was responsible for feeding a family of four children, a son-in-law, a grandson, and an aunt. Toward the end of the war, her husband and one son had died, the son-in-law and two other sons were war invalids, and her daughter and aunt were sick from malnutrition. Eisenmenger resorted to hoarding food—an illegal act—bartering away her dead husband's tobacco, and did what was necessary to survive.

Ten dekagrammes [3.5 ounces] of horse-flesh per head are to be given out today for the week. The cavalry horses held in reserve by the military authorities are being slaughtered for lack of fodder, and the people of Vienna are for a change to get a few mouthfuls of meat of which they have so long been deprived. Horse-flesh! . . . My loathing of it is based, I believe, not on a physical but on a psychological prejudice.

I overcame my repugnance, rebuked myself for being sentimental, and left the house. A soft, steady rain was falling. . . . As I left the house before seven o'clock and the meat distribution did not begin until nine o'clock, I hoped to get well to the front of the queue. . . .

I estimated the crowd waiting here for a meagre midday meal at two thousand at least. Hundreds of women had spent the night here in order to be among the first and make sure of getting their bit of meat. . . . No one seemed to mind the rain, although many were already wet through. They passed the time chattering, and the theme was the familiar one: What have you had to eat? What are you going to eat? One could scense an atmosphere of mistrust in these conversations: they were all careful not to say too much or to betray anything that might get them into trouble.

At length the sale began. Slowly, infinitely slowly, we moved forward. The most determined, who had spent the night outside the gates of the hall, displayed their booty to the waiting crowd: a ragged, quite freshly slaughtered piece of meat with the characteristic yellow fat. [Others] alarmed those standing at the back by telling them that there was only a very small supply of meat and that not half the people waiting would get a share of it. The crowd became very uneasy and impatient, and before the police on guard could prevent it, those standing in front organized an attack on the hall. . . . Everyone seized whatever he could lay his hands on, and in a few moments all the eatables had vanished. In the confusion stands were overturned, and the police forced back the aggressors and closed the gates. The crowds waiting outside, many of whom had been there all night and were soaked through, angrily demanded their due, whereupon the mounted police made a little charge, provoking a wild panic and much screaming and cursing. At length I reached home, depressed and disgusted.

Source: From Anna Eisenmenger, *Blockade: The Diary of an Austrian Middle-Class Woman, 1914–1924,* trans. Winifred Ray (New York: Ray Long and Richard R. Smith, 1932), pp. 63–68.

in the mobilization effort. "He is simply a revolutionist," claimed the tsarina. Ironically, it was the Western democracies, not autocratic Russia, that imposed rigid rules for registering workers, prohibiting strikes, and regulating wages.

The French and British economies fared better than those in Germany and Russia. For one thing, neither suffered a blockade. Bread rationing did not start among the Allies until 1918, and caloric intake remained fairly high. A survey taken in 1918 showed that English workers were still getting about 3,000 calories a day, only a few percentage points down from 1914. In France, real wages fell only

about 20 percent during the war, making for hardship but not widespread privation.

Labor power, however, proved a difficult problem everywhere. In every warring country, military leaders demanded that all able-bodied men join the colors. Only belatedly did they realize the wisdom of retaining some workers at home to produce vital war materials. One solution was to bring women back into the workforce. In every country hundreds of thousands of women took up jobs first in war industries and then in almost every other job previously denied them. The Krupp works in Essen, Germany, for example, employed twelve thousand women, and all

Women Munitions Workers With the generals constantly crying for more men to send into the sausage grinder at the front, women stepped into jobs normally closed to them. In this poster (left), the government urges women to become munitions workers. This meant, among other things, undertaking the skilled work of turning brass cones for artillery shells, as the women are doing in the photograph on the right. Imagine how noisy this factory floor must have been. *Trustees of the Imperial War Museum, London.*

across Europe women took over the operation of skilled and semiskilled jobs, from operating heavy cranes to undertaking street repairs.

This innovation did not come without resistance. Unions, for example, feared the diminution of men's wages, and nationalists argued that women's main patriotic duty should be the repopulating of the realm. "The rearing of the child crop is the most vital to the nation of all its industries," said one British observer. In France in particular, war was seen as a masculine activity, an almost necessary act of restoring manhood after the humiliations of defeat by the Germans a generation earlier. Women, if they remained properly virginal, supplicating, nurturing, and obedient, could be nurses, caring for the heroes of the battlefield, but elsewhere they were perceived as a threat to the male domain. In part because of these feelings, common among women as well as men, full-scale female participation in European (and American) economies proved a passing wartime phenomenon. Not until World War II and after did women permanently enter the workforce in large numbers.

Every government eventually established economic agencies to coordinate its economy, to assign labor power, and to break bottlenecks. In Germany, industrialist Walter Rathenau, head of Germany's largest producer of electrical equipment, convinced a reluctant government that special

efforts were needed to organize Germany's raw materials. During the first year of the war he successfully organized German industry to counter the effects of the British blockade. In Britain, David Lloyd George, who became British prime minister in 1916, concentrated authority in the hands of five cabinet ministers. From this point on, the War Cabinet's conduct of Britain's war effort became increasingly authoritarian.

In Germany, the military took over directly. Hindenburg and Ludendorff had contended from the beginning that the war would be won in the east, the area of their greatest triumphs. They complained bitterly that civilian incompetence and lack of support was depriving Germany of its deserved victory. Chancellor Bethmann-Hollweg disagreed. No longer expecting victory by 1916, he thought Germany would have to seek peace. Ironically, however, Bethmann believed Germany could make peace only with the support of its two most popular soldiers. "The name Hindenburg," he wrote, "is a terror to our enemies; it electrifies our army and our people. . . . They would accept any peace covered by his name." In August 1916, therefore, he persuaded William II to name Hindenburg as chief of staff. Ludendorff became his alter ego as quartermaster general. Power in Germany now fell increasingly into the hands of Ludendorff, whose deceitfulness, vanity, and ambition knew no boundaries.

MAP 28-2
GERMAN WAR AIMS

Most of the nations involved developed war aims as the conflict dragged on, but none were so detailed or so specific as those elaborated by Germany. If the Central Powers had won the war, Germany intended to establish its firm domination over what it called *Mitteleuropa*, extending from eastern portions of France through Ukraine. Compare these geopolitical aims with those of Adolf Hitler during World War II. Abroad, Germany intended to augment its relatively small colonial empire at the expense of Belgium, France, Portugal, and perhaps even Great Britain so as to achieve its goal of Weltmacht.

The increasing influence of Ludendorff helped solidify German war aims. Most countries developed goals as the war progressed, often territorial or colonial, but none had as comprehensive a plan as the Germans. Although schemes proliferated throughout the war, from the very beginning the Reich's leaders planned to create a powerful *Mitteleuropa* (Central Europe), in which an expanded Germany would dominate a band of satellite states including Austria-Hungary and the Balkans. Economically, the Germans sought control of the French iron ore region of Longwy-Briey, which in 1913 produced 81 percent of French iron ore; economic domination of Ukraine, which was the most important industrial and grain producing region of the Russian Empire; and control of the sizable Romanian oil industry (see Map 28-2). Success, they hoped, would put them in the class of the United States as an invulnerable world power.

Efforts to consolidate, centralize, and organize vastly increased the state's participation in economic affairs in all of the combatant countries, and the patriotic rhetoric that accompanied it made that participation more acceptable to the public. Indeed, the legitimacy of government manipulation of the economy was one of the most lasting structural legacies of the Great War.

Despite the massive efforts to mobilize entire populations, little of the actual horror of war penetrated directly to the civilian world, because government censorship and propaganda conspired to paint a patriotic picture of heroic soldiers giving their all for God and country. Nevertheless, as the very term *home front* suggests, civilian life took on a new sense of threat and unease. Many suffered, but some profited, creating a strangely split society. Mourning for the dead became common, but sometimes widows were criticized for lowering morale by their "excessive" mourning and they often received a mere pittance from the state to sustain them. City lights were turned off at night as a precaution against bombs dropped from zeppelins (gas-filled airships) and the French parliament even banned absinthe (a traditional alcoholic drink), but war profiteers and well-paid officers enjoyed a frenzied nightlife, and the sales of perfume and lingerie boomed. Europeans, their stable pre-war lives turned upside down by war, never regained the confidence and sense of progress that characterized the late nineteenth century.

Trying to Outflank the Enemy

Confronted almost immediately by military impasse and unprecedented economic pressures, the two alliance systems cast about for ways to outflank their enemies. The biggest prize was Italy (see Map 27-3). The Italians had not entered the war in August 1914 because, as they accurately pointed out, the Triple Alliance obliged it to support Austria only if Austria were attacked. Some members of the government favored Germany as an ascendant power, but the dominant view was that Italy could use the war to gain territory around the Adriatic. Because Austria controlled areas such as the Trentino, Trieste, and Dalmatia, all of which had Italian populations, the Entente found it far easier to extend tempting promises to Italy than did the Central Powers. On April 15, 1915, the Italians signed the secret Treaty of London, which granted them territorial gains in northern Italy and around the Adriatic in return for joining in the fight against Germany and Austria. The Italians moved bravely to the front and lost some six hundred thousand young men during the war. Sadly for them, and for the political future of Italy, their sacrifice had little impact on the outcome.

In the Balkans, the two alliances competed for the allegiance of four countries—the Ottoman Empire, Bulgaria, Greece, and Romania. Istanbul had grown closer to Germany in the first years of the twentieth century. German officers had trained its army, and German merchants had gained a larger and larger share of its trade. The British hoped to keep the Ottomans at least neutral, so that supplies could flow easily to Russia through the Straits (the Bosphorus and the Dardenelles connecting the Black Sea to the Mediterranean). But in October 1914, the Ottomans foiled Britain's plans by declaring war on the Entente. The Ottoman entry helped to transform the European war into a global conflict, for it opened up battlefields in Persia (Iran), Syria, and Palestine.

The Germans gained the support of Bulgaria, primarily because they were able to offer the Bulgars Macedonia. Having lost Macedonia first in 1878 when the powers refused to accept the Treaty of San Stefano and then again in 1913 when its Balkan allies turned on it during the Second Balkan War, Bulgaria jumped at the chance to grab the disputed territory. In September 1915, it attacked

MAP 28-3
THE EASTERN FRONTS

Serbia from the south, while an Austro-German army struck from the north. This time the Serbs could not hold out, although the bulk of their army did escape through the wintry mountains of Albania to the Greek island of Corfu.

In Greece, King Constantine favored the Central Powers, whereas Prime Minister Eleutheros Venizelos, Greece's most renowned modern politician, favored the Entente. To settle the dilemma, in October 1915 the Allies landed an expeditionary force at Thessalonika and established a front there against Bulgaria and the Ottomans. Only in June 1917, after the pressure of an allied blockade and Venizelos's seizure of power in Athens, did Greece become a formal ally of the Entente.

Romania did its best to stay out of the war at first. Actually a signatory to the Triple Alliance from 1883, it too refused to enter on the side of the Central Powers, and in 1916 it declared for the Entente. The Germans promptly occupied most of the country and knocked Romania out of the war.

One final episode in the continental flanking efforts was the Gallipoli campaign. First Lord of the Admiralty Winston Churchill, among others, conceived the idea that

War: Myth vs. Reality Just as women were encouraged by posters to join the war effort, so were men. A powerful incentive was the propaganda campaign about the German thrust through neutral Belgium, which the British falsely claimed had been accompanied by rapes of nuns and similar atrocities. When the men got to the front, of course, life was considerably less heroic than the posters had suggested. *Trustees of the Imperial War Museum, London.*

the Royal Navy might sail from the Mediterranean Sea through the Straits to Istanbul and eliminate the Ottomans from the war. This move would both open the trade route to Russia and expose what Churchill in World War II called "the soft underbelly of Europe" (that is, the Balkans). The Royal Navy attempted to fight its way through the very narrow opening to the Straits, but Turkish fire sank three battleships and the navy did not renew its attack. Later it became known that a renewed attack on the Straits would have succeeded, for the Ottoman defenders were down to their last few armor-piercing shells. But the British, unaware of this weakness, and influenced by the army's lack of confidence in the navy, tried to seize the entry to the Straits by landing troops along the Gallipoli Peninsula. Once their forces had landed, however, a divided command and lack of initiative bogged them down in just the kind of trench warfare that characterized the

THE HISTORICAL EVIDENCE

French Troops Mutiny

June 1917

In the spring of 1917, after two and a half years of relentless slaughter on the western front, morale began to buckle in the French army. News of revolution in Russia may have helped trigger a series of mutinies, but the underlying cause was simply profound war-weariness. Only by a combination of harsh crackdowns and conciliatory promises was discipline restored, narrowly averting a general collapse of the French war effort. These extracts from a French officer's diary describe something of what happened.

1 June

The spirit of the troops is turning sour. There is talk of mutiny and of troops refusing to go to the lines. The "bad hats" amongst them are more vociferous.

3 June

All the companies are in a state of turmoil; the men are receiving letters from friends informing them of the present spirit and urging them not to march; the ringleaders are becoming insolent; others are trying to influence their comrades. My company does not escape this plague: a squad, under the sway of its corporal, refuses to fall in, the men claiming that they are ill. Just as we move to take them to the guardroom, they run off in the fields and insult the N.C.O.s. Some only return the following day.

I have five court-martialled, to get rid of the worst. Alas! that's just what many want—a motive to be court-martialled, so as to spend a year in prison; they are counting on some future amnesty and, during their stay in prison, they will be far from the Front. Once again, it will be the good who will go and get themselves killed and the scoundrels who will be protected.

In addition, a law has just increased the men's pay: first payment today. These men who are getting 20–30 francs rush to spend them on drink; drunkenness all along the line. Command becomes difficult.

5 June

I sit in judgement at the court-martial. What a procession of rogues! How stupid they seem in front of their judges. In their company they tried to be smart, insulted their superiors, tried to get their chums to desert; here they are now, sheepish, not daring to look up, full of repentance. . . .

The Army is becoming more and more a prey to this ill-feeling; those on leave on their return home from the front, are assailed by agitators who, going as far as uncoupling the trains, urge them not to return. I must go to Meaux to re-establish order.

Source: From Henry Desagneaux, *A French Soldier's War Diary* (Leeds, England: Elmsfield Press, 1975), pp. 38–40, as reprinted in Marilyn Shevin Coetzee and Frans Coetzee, eds., *World War I and European Society: A Sourcebook* (Lexington, Mass.: D. C. Heath, 1995), pp. 252–253.

---

western front.[6] The best the stymied British and French could do was to evacuate their troops a year later, a task they accomplished with far greater efficiency than they had the original landings.

The Trenches

The failure of the flanking efforts refocused the combatants' attention on the two original fronts: the trenches in the west and the war of movement in the east. The latter ultimately cost more lives and ranged over more territory, but the former has remained the most poignant symbol of the Great War's futility.

Once the Schlieffen Plan had failed, adversaries on the western front confronted each other from a wide variety of trenches, all dug according to detailed regulations. Usually the front lines consisted of a ditch about 6 feet deep and 4 or 5 feet wide. Men stood in these ditches for protection, rising on occasion to fire at the enemy similarly dug into the other side of "no-man's land." Small underground rooms provided space for sleeping and eating. As the war ground on, these rooms expanded, sometimes reaching as deep as 25 feet underground to provide protection against shelling. About 200 yards behind the front trench came

---

[6] It also did not help the British cause that when they had the opportunity to cut off the peninsula, their desultory efforts were met by troops under the very able command of Mustafa Kemal, later known as Atatürk, or Father of the Turks, the man who created the modern Turkish nation-state.

another of similar construction, and 400 yards behind that another, all connected by communications trenches and designed in a zigzag pattern to prevent a successful enemy attacker from firing down a long straight trench line.

Tens of thousands of young men endured life in these rat- and lice-infested hellholes—often soaked with rain, standing in mud up to their knees, or, at the other extreme, choking on dust or chlorine or phosgene gas, which became a common weapon by 1917. When the order to attack came, artillery would rain thousands of tons of shells on the enemy's trench system. With the enemy supposedly "softened up," the attacking troops, burdened with as much as 65 pounds of gear, would clamber over the top of their trenches, cut their way through the rolls of barbed wire that covered no-man's land, and advance toward the enemy trenches.

The idea behind these massive attacks was to break through to the rear, where freedom of movement would be restored, thus unlocking the standoff that trench warfare had created. But the hundreds of thousands of artillery shells that preceded each offensive projected most of their explosive energy upward, not downward into the deep living quarters. As soon as the barrage ended, the protected troops surfaced to mow down their attackers with machine guns.

Despite the suicidal futility of these frontal assaults, for two or three years neither side could conceive of an alternate strategy. Time and again, unimaginative and conventional commanders like British general Douglas Haig sent tens of thousands of men to their futile deaths attempting to break through the enemy's lines. The most horrendous battles of the war across these trenches became notorious for their unheard-of slaughter and fruitlessness. Early in 1916, for example, the Germans attempted to take the French stronghold of Verdun. For four months, they poured hundreds of thousands of troops into the effort, finally winning a few square miles at the insane cost of about 350,000 casualties. The French lost similar numbers. On July 1 that year, the British lost 60,000 men on just the first day of their assault along the Somme River. Willingness to shed blood was not an attribute only of the western generals. In two weeks in 1914, while advancing into Galicia, more than 500,000 Russians and Austrians lost their lives. General Alexei Brusilov commented: "Blood is flowing in endless streams, but there is no other way to fight. The more blood flows the better the results and the sooner the war will end."

For those who did not die, life in the trenches was a horrible experience: "At night, crouching in a shell-hole and filling it, the mud watches, like an enormous octopus. The victim arrives. It throws its poisonous slobber out at him, blinds him, closes round him, buries him. Hell is not fire, that would not be the ultimate in suffering. Hell is mud." A friend of the American-born British poet T. S. Eliot described the alternative to this hell in a letter of 1917:

The leprous earth, scattered with the swollen and blackened corpses of hundreds of young men. The appalling stench of rotten carrion. Mud like porridge, trenches like shallow and sloping cracks in the porridge—porridge that stinks in the sun. Swarms of flies and bluebottles clustering on pits of offal. Wounded men lying in the shell holes among the decaying corpses: helpless under the scorching sun and bitter nights, under repeated shelling. Men with bowels dropping out, lungs shot away, with blinded, smashed faces, or limbs blown into space. Men screaming and gibbering. Wounded men hanging in agony on the barbed wire, until a friendly spurt of liquid fire [from the newly invented flame thrower] shrivels them up like a fly in a candle.

In such an atmosphere of depression, fatigue, and trauma men became numbed, eyes lost their sparkle, and feelings became devalued. The man next to you is shot? You go on making your tea. As one British officer put it, "The inevitable conclusion that one comes to out here is that it is worse than useless to think about things."

New Technologies: Tanks, Airplanes, and Submarines

Technology provided one possible answer to the impasse of trench warfare. Perhaps new weapons could unhinge the "sausage grinder" that was eating up young men at a ferocious rate. And indeed, the war saw the invention of a host of new and fearsome devices, such as the depth charge, the flame thrower, and poison gas, as well as vast improvements in artillery. The invention with the most promise of revolutionizing trench warfare was the tank—but the tank's potential remained untapped, in part because of rigidity and lack of imagination among military commanders. Despite regular use after its first appearance in September 1916, the tank found only moderate favor with allied generals and had no lasting impact on the Great War. Airplanes played a more important role than tanks, proving themselves valuable for reconnaissance. Technical advances made it possible to synchronize machine gun fire through a rotating propeller blade and to carry and drop heavy bombs, but the small size of the planes and their lack of range limited their strategic value. Their main contribution was in romanticizing the war—phrases like *dog fight*, *aces*, and *the Red Baron* lent almost a chivalric overtone to death in the air.

The Germans had one especially formidable technological card to play: the submarine. Germans officers well understood the effects of cutting off a country's supply lines. In 1916 food shortages stemming from the British blockade led to rioting in both Austria-Hungary and Germany. Germany had only twenty-one primitive submarines (U-boats) when the war began, but the German General Staff nevertheless had declared the waters surrounding the

British Isles a war zone where they felt free to attack merchant ships. The United States, a neutral power but one of Britain's major suppliers, vigorously protested this interference with its shipping. When a German submarine sank the British liner *Lusitania* in May 1915, causing the loss of several hundred American lives, the uproar in the United States was so great that in order to preserve American neutrality the German government ordered its U-boat captains to limit their attacks to armed vessels.[7]

Ironically, given the role of the naval program in provoking the prewar arms race, Germany's surface fleet ventured into battle only once. In May 1916, it met a British fleet at Jutland in a battle much like what Tirpitz's "risk policy" (see Chapter 27) had foreseen: The German navy lost but dished out terrible losses to the British. But instead of intimidating the British, Jutland merely pushed them to intensify their blockade. The German fleet remained bottled up in port for the rest of the war.

By late 1916, therefore, the Hindenburg/Ludendorff team was looking for new solutions. Bethmann-Hollweg sought an end to hostilities. He had seen tentative negotiations with the Russians collapse in the fall, and in December 1916 he extended a peace feeler to the western Allies. When they rejected this initiative out of hand, Hindenburg and Ludendorff convinced William II that the only way to bring Britain to its knees was to sink any vessel that might be carrying goods to British ports. The General Staff knew that this action would probably bring the United States into the war, but they underestimated the potential impact of the Americans. They also overestimated their ability to prevent U.S. ships from crossing the Atlantic. One admiral assured the Kaiser that the British would sue for peace in six months. "I will give Your Majesty my word as an officer," he said, "that not one American will land on the continent."

At first the renewed submarine campaign racked up impressive results. In April 1917, the Germans sank 875,000 tons of shipping, and in the next month 590,000 tons. The British admiralty agonized over how to stop the hemorrhaging, which was on the verge of damaging the British ability to wage war. But in April, the United States followed through on its threat to treat unrestricted submarine warfare as intolerable provocation and declared war on Germany. At the same time, British prime minister Lloyd George forced a reluctant admiralty to begin using a convoy system, by which large numbers of vessels sailed together under the protection of an accompanying fleet. The convoy system proved an unqualified success, and British losses dropped dramatically. At the same time, use

---

[7] Despite its character as a passenger vessel, the *Lusitania* was in fact carrying munitions.

Prisoners of War Not every soldier died at the front. Many were taken prisoner, such as these German troops being marched through a French village to a prisoner-of-war camp late in the war. *U. S. Signal Corps, Photo No. 111-SC-13932 in the National Archives.*

of the newly invented depth charge—which destroys sub-marines by exploding near them underwater—depleted the German U-boat fleet. By the end of the year, the British were building more tonnage every month than the harried German submarines could sink. Worse for the Germans, the entry of the Americans assured the Allies of vast new resources, both in manpower and supplies.

Germany: Victory in the East, Defeat in the West

If German fortunes had taken a turn for the worse in the west, the opposite was true in the east. In March 1917, a spontaneous revolution toppled the Romanov dynasty, and in November of that year communist revolutionaries seized power from the provisional government (discussed in detail later in this chapter). Between March and November, the provisional Russian government tried to prosecute the war—even mounting one more major offensive—but when the communists seized power in November, they quickly sued for peace. Their armies disintegrating from desertions, revolution, and disaffection, the Russians no longer could prevent German forces from marching at will into their country. In March 1918, therefore, the new revolutionary government signed a peace treaty with the Germans at Brest-Litovsk.

Having won the war in the east, just as Hindenburg and Ludendorff had always hoped, the Germans now turned their attention westward. By 1918, however, the Central Powers were weaker than their victory over Russia implied. Food shortages, accentuated by the allied block-ade, remained acute. In Austria-Hungary, which required about 10 million tons of grain per year, production dropped to a mere 5.3 million tons. In January 1918, more than a million workers went on strike in Vienna and strikes erupted across Germany as well. The basic question now became this: Could Germany transfer enough forces from the eastern front to achieve a decisive breakthrough in the west before the home front collapsed and before the weight of American arms and troops could become deci-sive? In the spring of 1918, most western authorities believed that America's power would not reach its full potential until 1919.

At the same time, the Allies' war aims had become much clearer, due in good measure to the initiative of the American president, Woodrow Wilson. In January 1918, Wilson gave a speech to Congress in which he laid out fourteen principles on which peace should be established. The specifics are discussed later in this chapter, but under-lying Wilson's speech was his idea that the world should be made safe for democracy and that national self-determination should be a principle on which borders were drawn. Wilson's speech nudged Great Britain and France to accept the possibility of the demise of the Austro-Hungarian Empire, for example, but at the same time gave the impres-sion to some Germans that the Allies might be generous in the case of German defeat.

In March 1918, Ludendorff launched the offensive that he hoped would win the war in the west. Within two months, his troops had penetrated 40 miles in places, some of them within as many miles of Paris. Using a huge new gun, nicknamed Big Bertha, the Germans actually shelled the French capital. Despair gripped some Allied leaders. "I cannot exclude the possibility of disaster," wrote the secre-tary to the British war cabinet in his diary. But Ludendorff's troops were exhausted and the Germans could not keep their supply lines filled. When the Allies launched a coun-terattack on July 18, the Germans faltered. British, French, and American troops fought their way forward, mounting thrust after thrust. By September the German army was in steady retreat and little stood in the way of an Allied advance into Germany itself.

In the south, the quiescent Thessalonika front now erupted. Early in September, under the leadership of a new French general, British, French, and Serbian troops sud-denly broke through Bulgarian lines and advanced rapidly into the central Balkans. On September 30, the Bulgarians dropped out of the war. By the end of the next month, the Allied army had reached Belgrade and spread out toward Budapest in the north and the Adriatic Sea in the west. Under the pressure of this advance and the impending defeat of its German ally, the ancient Habsburg realm collapsed.

In Germany, Ludendorff fell apart also. Until almost the last minute, the General Staff had hidden the extent of the army's plight and had constantly predicted that victory was imminent.[8] On September 29, however, the distraught general informed a surprised emperor and government that Germany was beaten. When officials told William II that Wilson, now the linchpin of the peace negotiations, would not deal with an autocratic government, William an-nounced the establishment of a parliamentary regime. An offended Ludendorff quickly recovered his poise and insisted that Germany keep fighting. But the Allies relent-lessly advanced, buttressed by almost a million American troops and buoyed by the ten thousand more landing in Europe every day.

Ironically, it was sailors from the fleet that Admiral Tirpitz had hoped would secure Weltmacht for Germany who finally pushed the imperial regime over the edge early in November 1918. On November 3, sailors at Kiel refused orders to take their ships to sea. The mutiny spread quickly to other port cities, and on November 7 revolution broke out in Munich. By November 9, when the Kaiser finally

---

[8] Ludendorff's policy of hiding German failures until the very end meant that the German people would later be more receptive to Hitler's theory that the nation had been "stabbed in the back" by socialists and Jews at the end of World War I.

abdicated and fled to Holland, the red flag of revolution hung over eleven German cities. Friedrich Ebert, head of the Socialist party that held a majority in the Reichstag, took power in Berlin. He declared Germany a republic and agreed to an unconditional armistice. At 11:00 A.M. on the eleventh day of the eleventh month of 1918, the Great War at last came to an end.

THE RUSSIAN REVOLUTIONS

The outbreak of the Great War had united Russia momentarily, but the government's ineptness quickly dissipated public support. Russia's supply situation was almost as difficult as Germany's. With the Ottomans blocking the southern route and Germany occupying Poland, needed imports got through only in a trickle. By 1916 Russia had fewer locomotives in use than in 1914, and by 1917 only about half of Russia's blast furnaces were operating, and those far below capacity. The state rallied more than 15 million men to the colors—more than half of them were killed, wounded, or captured—but it made no effort to aid destitute peasant families. It even hindered private organizations that tried to help. In 1916 peasants began withholding grain from the market, and for the first time wages began to plummet. Serious food shortages led the chief of police in Petrograd to the "verge of despair."[9] The rigid tsarist government, clinging to its bureaucratic ways, turned a deaf ear to the popular despair. It retained an arbitrary and counterproductive pricing policy for grain and refused to contemplate political reforms that would tap the potential of Russian civil society. In December 1916 Grand Duke Paul asked Nicholas II to grant a true constitution. "The day of my coronation I took my oath to the absolute power," Nicholas replied. "I must leave this oath intact to my son."

1917: The February and October Revolutions

On March 8, 1917, parades celebrating Woman's Day marched through Petrograd.[10] The day before, the Putilov munitions works had gone on strike, putting many of its workers on the streets. After the parade, women began to gather at bread stores to complain about prices and lack of bread. Suddenly, without planning or forethought, thousands of people spontaneously thronged the center of the

---

[9] St. Petersburg had been renamed Petrograd to give it a Slavic rather than a Germanic ring.

[10] Because the Orthodox church did not reform its calendar in the sixteenth century as the Catholic church did, the Russian calendar was thirteen days behind the Western calendar in 1917. This is why the first Russian revolution is called the February Revolution, although it began on March 8 by the Western calendar, and the Bolshevik Revolution is called the October Revolution, although it started on November 7.

city. The next day, even more joined them, and on the third day the government called in reserve troops to clear the streets. Some troops fired, but others, instead of confronting the crowds, put down their guns and joined the people in what Leon Trotsky called a "process of molecular interpenetration." Overnight, the will to suppress the demonstrations collapsed. Officials fled into hiding, and the government simply melted away. On March 12, some of the leaders of the fourth Duma hurriedly met and declared themselves a provisional government. Three days later, Nicholas II, who was away at the front, abdicated in favor of his brother, who in turn also abdicated. Within the space of a week, without warning, the Romanov Dynasty, in power since 1613, disappeared. Nicholas II's phlegmatic reaction to his loss clearly demonstrated why he had not been the ruler Russia needed in this time of crisis. On the day of the initial outbreaks, he commented in his diary: "I greatly miss my half-hourly game of patience every evening. I shall take up dominoes in my spare time." The day after abdicating, he wrote: "I had a long sound sleep. Woke up beyond Dvinsk. Sunshine and frost. I read much of Julius Caesar."

The provisional government quickly assured the Allies that it would continue to prosecute the war, and resolved to hold a constituent assembly that would write a constitution for a new democratic state. But the new government faced enormous problems. The war was as unpopular and as draining as ever; peasant unrest cried out for land reform; and the economy threatened to collapse. Worse, it confronted a legitimate rival for power. The same day that the provisional government declared itself, a new Petrograd Soviet (Council) of Workers' and Soldiers' Deputies stepped forward to speak on behalf of the workers and peasants. Immediately the soviet issued Order Number 1, which decreed that military units should be run by elected committees and that officers could command only during actual combat. It followed with a Manifesto to the People of the World, which called for the workers of the world to unite for peace. This situation of "dual power," in which the provisional government controlled the state apparatus and the soviets gained the loyalty of the working class, persisted until the Bolshevik Revolution in November.

The term *Bolshevik* refers to the wing of the Social Democratic party controlled by Vladimir Ilich Lenin. Early in its clandestine history, the Russian Social Democratic party published a journal in western Europe called *Iskra*, or "Spark." At its Third Party Congress, held in London in 1903, Lenin's allies won an election to the editorial board of *Iskra*. From that time on, Lenin called his faction *Bolsheviks*, from the Russian word for "majority," and his Social Democratic opponents *Mensheviks*, from the word for "minority." In fact, the Mensheviks had far more members by the outbreak of World War I than the Bolsheviks, because they were the more open and more

Protesting Food Prices, Overthrowing the Tsar
The outbreak of revolution in Russia early in 1917 was neither anticipated nor planned. Many workers were out on strike in Petrograd when it broke out, but the catalyst was demonstrations by women seeking a lower price for bread. When troops refused to disperse the crowds, the government fell. The women in this picture are involved in a similar protest later in 1917. *Sovfoto / Eastfoto.*

democratic group. The Mensheviks educated workers, drew them into the party organization, and operated more or less democratically.

The Bolsheviks, driven by Lenin, were a professional party of underground revolutionaries. Lenin did not trust the workers. He believed that if they secured higher wages and shorter working hours from the capitalists, workers would forget about the main goal of socialist revolution. Consistent with the maximalist strain of the Russian revolutionary tradition, Lenin spurned liberal reforms and insisted on total change. The Bolsheviks did not aspire to represent the workers in some democratic sense. They intended to lead the proletariat in the direction that Lenin and his associates believed it should go. Undemocratic in organization, the Bolsheviks considered themselves the vanguard of the working class.

Neither the Bolsheviks nor the Mensheviks—not to mention the Social Revolutionaries, a peasant-oriented party that nevertheless used Marxist rhetoric—anticipated the February Revolution. But they all lurched into action immediately to take advantage of it. Most dramatic, Lenin returned from exile in Switzerland. Austrian and German authorities, believing that the revolutionary Lenin could destabilize their enemy, permitted him to return to Russia in April. Immediately after stepping off the train at Petrograd's Finland Station, Lenin denounced the provisional government, astounding his Bolshevik colleagues, including Joseph Stalin, who had expressed support for it. He also announced a radical program calling for socializing banks,

giving workers control over production and distribution of goods, dividing the land among the peasants, and liquidating the standing army and police. Quickly the Bolsheviks translated this rather intellectualized program into powerful slogans that the working class understood, such as "Land, Peace, Bread," and "Stop the War."

Lenin's program was only one of many political efforts that the suddenly open conditions of transition made possible in 1917. By May the provisional government admitted some moderate socialists, and in June another offensive put the final strain on the Russian military. Desertions rose astronomically, as peasant draftees simply started walking home—voting with their feet, as Lenin put it. This was not only because of their disgust with the war, but because spontaneous seizures of landlords' land were beginning, and village men wanted to go home to get their share. The provisional government, made up of liberals and moderate socialists, did not sanction these land seizures, but the more radical revolutionary parties did. By mid-1917 a veritable revolution was under way in the Russian countryside.

Early in July, Petrograd unions organized a massive demonstration against the war and the economic disaster facing the country, but the government managed to restore calm. The Bolsheviks judged the workers' outburst premature and participated only reluctantly in the July Days, as the demonstrations were called. Nevertheless, the provisional government used the occasion to arrest many of their leaders. Lenin went into hiding in Finland.

THE HISTORICAL EVIDENCE

Lenin's April Theses

April 1917

When the February Revolution broke out in Russia, Lenin was in Switzerland. The Germans, believing that Lenin would disrupt Russia's war effort, agreed to let him travel across Germany to St. Petersburg, where he arrived in April 1917. His Bolshevik colleagues, including Stalin, had supported the Provisional Government in the belief that it was the bourgeois revolution predicted by Karl Marx. Lenin shocked them by proclaiming war on the Provisional Government and forcing his militant opinion on the Bolsheviks. From that point on they worked diligently, and ultimately successfully, to seize power for themselves. Here is a shortened version of what became known as Lenin's April Theses.

1. The class-conscious proletariat can give its consent to a revolutionary war, which would really justify revolutionary defencism, only on conditions: (a) that the power pass to the proletariat and the poorest sections of the peasants aligned with the proletariat; (b) that all annexations be renounced in deed and not in word; (c) that a complete break be effected in actual fact with all capitalist interests. The most widespread campaign for this view must be organized in the army at the front. . . .

3. No support for the Provisional Government; the utter falsity of all its promises should be made clear, particularly of those relating to the renunciation of annexations. Exposure in place of the impermissible, illusion-breeding "demand" that *this* government, a government of capitalists, should *cease* to be an imperialist government. . . .

5. Not a parliamentary republic—to return to a parliamentary republic from the Soviets of Workers' Deputies would be a retrograde step—but a Republic of Soviets of Workers', Agricultural Laborers' and Peasants' Deputies throughout the country, from top to bottom.

    Abolition of the police, the army and the bureaucracy (i.e., the standing army to be replaced by the arming of the whole people).

    The salaries of all officials, all of whom are elective and displaceable at any time, not to exceed the average wage of a competent worker.

6. Confiscation of all landed estates.

    Nationalization of *all* lands in the country, the land to be disposed of by the local Soviets of Agricultural Laborers' and Peasants' Deputies. The setting up of a model farm on each of the large estates.

7. The immediate amalgamation of all banks in the country into a single national bank, and the institution of control over it by the Soviet of Workers' Deputies. . . .

9. Party tasks: [Among others, changing the party's name from the Social Democratic party to the Communist party].

Source: From Robert C. Tucker, ed. *The Lenin Anthology* (New York: Norton, 1975), pp. 296–298.

Shortly thereafter, Alexander Kerensky, a Social Revolutionary, became prime minister. Kerensky, along with many others, was deeply aware of the pattern of the French Revolution, in which moderates gave way to a reign of terror conducted by leftist radicals, who in turn were replaced by the military "man on horseback" (Napoleon). Kerensky believed that his government's success in putting down the July Days had turned back the threat from the left. Then, in September, General Lavr Kornilov—whom someone once characterized as a man with the heart of a lion and the brains of a sheep—tried unsuccessfully to march his troops into Petrograd and seize power. In Kerensky's mind, Kornilov's failure meant that the provisional government had survived the threat from the right as well, and was now on the way to elections, a constitutional convention, and stability. However, to combat Kornilov and the counterrevolutionary right, Kerensky had permitted the Petrograd soviet to arm military committees to protect the city and had released several Bolshevik leaders. By this time, the Bolsheviks, capitalizing on their simple slogans such as "Bread and Peace," had gained control of the Petrograd soviet. Now they began calling for "All Power to the Soviets," in other words, for the end of the provisional government and the creation of a revolutionary regime under the direction of Lenin and his vanguard party.

In October a meeting of workers' councils from all over the country (the All-Russian Congress of Soviets) was planned for Petrograd. Lenin secretly returned from

Finland and urged his colleagues to use the congress to seize power. In the meantime, Leon Trotsky, an inspired newcomer to the Bolshevik cause who had rushed back from his editor's job in the Bronx (New York) to join the revolution, was organizing a Military Revolutionary Committee in the Petrograd soviet. He found a willing audience for his revolutionary activism among the soldiers of the Petrograd garrison. By early November, he had neutralized the government's military forces in the capital.

On November 7, on the eve of the All-Russian Congress of Soviets, Kerensky's provisional government finally decided to close down the Bolshevik printing presses and suppress the movement. But the printers simply started up the presses again. Meanwhile, Trotsky's Red Guards moved out into the city. With the exception of a few military cadets in the former tsar's Winter Palace, Kerensky's disaffected troops offered little resistance to the Bolshevik workers and sailors, either in Petrograd or in the other cities across the country. The provisional government melted away with a suddenness and thoroughness matching that of the tsarist government eight months before.

When the Congress of Soviets convened, the Bolsheviks, who had a small majority, took over. The Mensheviks and other moderates protested vigorously, and many stalked out. As they left, Trotsky jeered, "You are pitiful isolated individuals; you are bankrupts; your role is played out. Go where you belong from now on—into the rubbish-can of history." When Lenin first appeared before the congress on the next day, he announced simply, "We shall now proceed to construct the socialist order." Immediately the Bolsheviks decreed the confiscation of state and church land without compensation, ordered the publication of all wartime secret treaties, and called for a general peace without annexations.

War, Communism, and Bolshevik Survival

Having seized power, the Bolsheviks were none too confident they could hold it. Lenin hoped to stay in control longer than the Paris Commune of 1871, which had lasted seventy-two days (see Chapter 24). Nevertheless, he did not leave the outcome to chance. He moved rapidly and ruthlessly to consolidate Bolshevik strength. From the beginning, his government made no pretense of balance. It contained only Bolsheviks and a few members of a radical splinter of the Social Revolutionary party. Within weeks he banned all non-Bolshevik newspapers and created the Extraordinary Commission for the Suppression of Counterrevolution, better known as the Cheka. This ominous organization was the forerunner of the notorious Soviet secret-police agencies, the NKVD and the KGB. These organs were to seek out and destroy all enemies of the working class—in practice, all enemies of the sole true representative of the working class, the Bolshevik party.

Lenin could not suppress the previously promised and widely anticipated elections to the Constituent Assembly, which took place three weeks after the Bolshevik seizure of power. These remarkably fair and widespread elections, the only ones of their kind held in Russia until 1989, produced a solid majority of moderate Social Revolutionaries. The Bolsheviks took about 25 percent of the seats, and other socialist and liberal parties split the rest. Because the Social Revolutionaries spoke primarily for the peasants, Lenin decided that they did not represent the true interests of the progressive class, the proletariat. When the delegates convened early in January for what they thought would be a constitutional convention, Lenin simply locked them out of their meeting hall after their first gathering and declared the convention dissolved. This event, which seems so crucial to us, passed almost unnoticed in Petrograd, not to mention in the country at large.

Lenin dealt with his second major problem, the war, with equal decisiveness. When the Soviet negotiators found it difficult to accept German terms, Trotsky proposed simply not negotiating. "Neither peace nor war," was his slogan. The German generals responded to this rhetoric by marching forward. By February, they were advancing into Russia at will. Even under this threat, Lenin had difficulty persuading his Central Committee to accept the German terms. Everyone knew that the people no longer supported the war, that Russia faced a hopeless military situation, and that the fledgling Soviet state was endangered. But when confronted with the loss of more than 1 million square miles of the old Russian Empire, about a quarter of its railroads, a third of its textile industry, almost 75 percent of its iron and steel industry, and 75 percent of its coal mines, a majority of Lenin's government favored continuing the war, even though their own party program had always advocated immediate peace. Some members hesitated also because they feared to betray their brothers in the German working class. Their unwillingness to budge suggests how difficult it is to make rational decisions in politics. Lenin's strengths as a politician were that he understood his main goal (saving the regime) and knew when to act (now). He insisted that without peace the Bolshevik experiment was doomed, and he threatened to resign. Even so, the party's Central Committee vote in favor of accepting the onerous peace terms was only 7 to 4, with 4 abstentions. The price was high, but Lenin was right. The Brest-Litovsk treaty gave the Bolsheviks the breathing space they needed.

Far from being secure, however, the Bolsheviks now faced another danger: civil war. With the collapse of central authority, many of Russia's national minority areas proclaimed their independence. The most important of these was Ukraine, which declared independence under German protection; but Armenia, Georgia, Azerbaijan, and the central Asian peoples all did the same. Lenin put Joseph Stalin, a Georgian but nevertheless a russianizing centralizer, in

Altering History These two photographs show Lenin agitating in Petrograd at the time of the Bolshevik Revolution. In the top photo, Leon Trotsky, one of the true heroes of the Bolshevik movement, is standing on the steps, obviously part of Lenin's group. *Hulton Getty/Liason Agency.* In the bottom photo, reproduced during Stalin's regime, the image of Trotsky, Stalin's greatest enemy, has been removed. *Sovfoto/Eastfoto.*

charge of nationality issues. Stalin defined national autonomy as a form in which "all power rests in the hands of workers and peasants," which of course meant in the hands of the vanguard party, the Bolsheviks. Using this formula as justification, armed forces whipped into shape by Trotsky, who proved to be a brilliant military organizer, invaded the national entities and suppressed their autonomous regimes (see Map 28-4).

The Bolsheviks also confronted opposition from officers and other armed remnants of the tsarist regime. Around Russia's borders, Bolshevism was not as popular or well known as it was among the urban working class. In 1918 generals of the tsarist army organized forces in these regions and launched assaults on the Bolsheviks. The Whites, as the oppositionists were called to contrast them with the Reds (Bolsheviks), never consolidated their

MAP 28-4
THE RUSSIAN CIVIL WAR,
1919–1921

Map legend:

- - - Soviet Russian border, 1921
—— Farthest western penetration of Red Army, 1920
—— Farthest German penetration 1918
→ Anti-Bolshevik attacks by Whites (1919–1920) and Poles (1920)
→ British/American attacks

Areas of core Bolshevik control
Red partisans
Areas controlled by interventionist powers
Areas of anti-Bolshevik guerrilla activity

leadership and fought disjointed—but bloody—campaigns. Occasionally, however, one of their number seriously threatened the regime. The struggle for the city of Tsaritsyn, a vital communications center, proved particularly fierce. Because Stalin played a role in that battle, the city later was renamed Stalingrad (and today, Volgograd). Although the wars between the Whites and the Reds are almost forgotten today, their fury claimed more lives than Russia lost in World War I itself.

Pressure came from outside as well. The Great War in Europe was still in progress when the Russian civil war broke out, and the western allies feared that Germany would seize abandoned Russian supplies. Some French and British leaders also harbored intense anti-Bolshevik sentiments. In 1918, therefore, the United States, Britain, France, and Japan all sent expeditionary forces to Russia. American forces in the Archangel region tended to protect supplies, but British and French forces in the south offered

active support to the Whites. When the armistice came in western Europe, the Allies kept their troops in Russia for another two to three years.

Finally, the Bolsheviks were plagued with internal problems. The Left Social Revolutionaries, who had initially supported Lenin's government, even organized an unsuccessful uprising in July 1918 and almost assassinated Lenin. But the most serious internal problem centered on the utter collapse of the economy. Peasants had seized land, with or without anyone's permission, and were farming it, but precious few manufactured goods were available to them. In retaliation, they withheld their grain, and the cities, where the proletariat lived, began to starve. The Bolsheviks resorted to harsh measures to feed the cities. They established committees of the poor in villages to seize grain from the more prosperous peasants, known as *kulaks*; they sent armed detachments out from the cities to take grain by force in what Lenin called a "crusade for bread";

THE HISTORICAL EVIDENCE

Revolutionary Art

March 1918

The Bolshevik Revolution affected all aspects of life, not just politics. In this document, published in March 1918 only a few months after the Bolshevik seizure of power, a group of avant-garde Russian writers known as "futurists" proclaim the liberation of art and its seizure by the people.

Decree No. 1 on the Democratization of Art (The hoarding of literature and the painting of streets)

Comrades and citizens, we, the leaders of Russian futurism—the revolutionary art of youth—declare:

1. From this day forward, with the abolition of tsardom, *the domicile of art* in the closets and sheds of human genius—palaces, galleries, salons, libraries, theaters—*is abrogated.*

2. In the name of the great march of equality for all, as far as culture is concerned, let the *Free Word* of creative personality be written on the corners of walls, fences, roofs, the streets of our cities and villages, on the backs of automobiles, carriages, streetcars, and on the clothes of all citizens.

3. Let *pictures* (colors) be thrown, like colored rainbows, across streets and squares, from house to house, delighting, ennobling the eye (taste) of the passer-by.

Artists and writers have the immediate duty to get hold of their pots of paint, and with their masterly brushes, to illuminate, to paint all the sides, foreheads, and chests of the cities, railway stations, and the ever-galloping herds of railway carriages.

From now on, let the citizen walking down the street enjoy at every moment the depths of thought of his great contemporaries, let him absorb the flowery gaudiness of this day's beautiful joy, let him listen to music—the melody, the roar, the buzz—of excellent composers everywhere.

Let the streets be a feast of art for all.

And if all this comes to pass, in accordance with our word, everyone who goes out into the street will grow to be a giant in wisdom, contemplating beauty instead of the present-day streets with their iron books (signboards), where every page has been written on their signs by greed, the lust for mammon, calculated meanness and low obtuseness, all of which soil the soul and offend the eye. "All art—to all the people!"

The initial pasting up of the poems and hanging of pictures will take place in Moscow on the day our journal is published.

Mayakovsky, Kamensky, Burliuk

Source: From Rex A. Wade, ed., *Documents of Soviet History*, vol. 1, *The Triumph of Bolshevism, 1917–1919* (Gulf Breeze, Fla.: Academic International Press, 1991), pp. 107–108.

---

and they created a barter system that tried to do away with money. A bitter struggle for survival ensued between the towns and the villages. By 1921 the land was producing only half what it had in 1913.

In industry, the picture was equally bad. At first the Bolsheviks encouraged workers to seize their workplaces, but when production plunged they realized that workers had no idea of how to run factories. To meet this problem, Lenin nationalized all industries, but the bureaucratic mechanisms also proved inadequate to the task. By 1921, steel production had dropped to 3 percent of prewar levels, and industrial production had fallen by 80 percent.

In light of all these problems, one might wonder how the Bolsheviks survived at all. They prevailed for several reasons. First, they eliminated their internal opponents quickly through terror. In February 1918, for example,

Lenin issued an order that revolutionary tribunals should shoot on the spot all "enemy agents, profiteers, marauders, hooligans, and counterrevolutionary agitators." The urban and rural poor, which on balance supported Bolshevism, proceeded to "loot the looters," thereby destroying the vestiges of the earlier order and intimidating (or killing) Bolshevik opponents. The Reds also operated on internal lines of communication. They controlled the central parts of the country, whereas their uncoordinated and contentious opponents attacked on the periphery. Further, they believed passionately in the rightness of their cause. Naturally, they wanted to stay in power, but tens of thousands of them fervently believed that they would not only build a new Russia, but a new world. In their view, revolution in Russia was only the first of the revolutions that soon would sweep Europe and replace a decadent capitalism with

Comrade Lenin Cleansing the World of Its Filth Soviet cartoonists loved to represent capitalism through images of fat men in black suits and top hats clutching bags of ill-gotten gains. Here, Lenin also sweeps away kings and priests. *The New York Public Library Picture Collection.*

honest and fair socialism. It would be a mistake to underestimate the energy that such beliefs can generate. It would also be a mistake to underestimate the attractiveness of the revolutionary situation to many tough and ruthless people who saw in the chaotic revolutionary conditions an uninhibited chance to grab power, wealth, or both.

Two other factors played crucial roles in the Bolsheviks' victory. First, they had a better program than their opponents. This does not mean that communism is better than capitalism, but that in the circumstances of the time they delivered a few basic things that many people wanted. They stopped the war, let the peasants seize land, and rooted out old oppressors. As the unknown, new men in charge, they seemed a good risk to people who knew all too well how bad the old rulers had been. The Bolsheviks may seem ruthless to us, and they were, but the Whites were just as ruthless, if not more so, and antisemitic besides. In a situation of complete chaos, the Bolsheviks seemed marginally the better bet to many people. Second, they rallied an outstanding group of leaders. Not only Lenin, Trotsky,

and Stalin, but dozens—even thousands—of able people found their way to the top of the Bolshevik hierarchy between 1917 and 1921. With no tradition or social barriers to stop them, able men (and a few women)—steeled by the uncompromising discipline of having participated in an underground revolutionary movement and promoted primarily on the basis of talent—directed the Bolshevik effort. No other political organization in Russia, and few in the history of the world, attracted so many capable leaders. Untiring, dedicated, and convinced that they were right, they drove the Bolsheviks to victory.

AFTERMATH OF WAR

The Russian Empire was not the only imperial state to disappear in 1918—the German, Habsburg, and Ottoman realms collapsed as well. Their downfall opened up a political vacuum hundreds of miles wide running from the Baltic Sea in the north to the Mediterranean Sea in the south. Into this void stepped six new countries and five restructured ones—the states of the Baltic, east-central Europe, and southeastern Europe.

New Countries in Eastern Europe

During most of the Great War, the Allies had no intention of destroying the Habsburg Empire and, until February 1917, no inkling of what was going to happen in Russia. Nevertheless, from the beginning, nationalist elements representing several east european peoples had advocated independence for their countries. In the three regions of Poland (divided among Austria, Prussia, and Russia), two quite distinct groupings emerged. Roman Dmowski, a nationalist who favored the Entente, fled to Paris, where he spent the war agitating on behalf of restoring Polish independence. By 1918 he had created the Polish National Committee and raised a Polish force that participated in some of the fighting on the western front. In this way he gained some leverage with the Allies. Józef Piłsudski, a Polish socialist and military officer, initially favored the Central Powers. He assembled a Polish volunteer force in Austrian Silesia. Both Russia and Germany considered Poland vital to their interests in central Europe, and both tried to win the Poles over. The Russians made various proclamations, but in November 1916 the Germans and the Austrians went so far as to declare an "independent" Poland. Poles immediately recognized the sham of this independence. "Do you imagine for one moment that you will win the nation's confidence by hanging Polish insignia on each of the fingers of the hand which is throttling Poland?" asked Piłsudski, whereupon the Germans promptly imprisoned him.

Before the Great War, Tomáš Garrigue Masaryk had been one of the most prominent public figures in Bohemia and Moravia, the Habsburg Czech lands. A professor of philosophy in Prague, Masaryk achieved a reputation

THE HISTORICAL EVIDENCE

Wilson's Fourteen Points

January 8, 1918

Early in 1918,President Woodrow Wilson outlined the war aims of the United States in an address to a joint session of Congress. In that speech, he provided fourteen points on which the peace should be based. They are given here in abbreviated form.

The program of the world's peace, therefore, is our program; and that program, the only possible program, as we see it, is this:

1. Open covenants of peace, openly arrived at.

2. Absolute freedom of navigation upon the seas, outside territorial waters, alike in peace and in war.

3. The removal, so far as possible, of all economic barriers.

4. Adequate guarantees given and taken that national armaments will be reduced to the lowest point consistent with domestic safety.

5. A free, open-minded, and absolutely impartial adjustment of all colonial claims.

6. The evacuation of all Russian territory and such a settlement of all questions affecting Russia as will secure the best and freest cooperation of the other nations of the world in obtaining for her an unhampered and unembarrassed opportunity for the independent determination of her own political development.

7. Belgium, the whole world will agree, must be evacuated and restored.

8. All French territory should be freed and the invaded portions restored, and the wrong done to France by Prussia in 1871 in the matter of Alsace-Lorraine should be righted.

9. A readjustment of the frontiers of Italy should be effected along clearly recognizable lines of nationality.

10. The peoples of Austria-Hungary should be accorded the freest opportunity of autonomous development.

11. Romania, Serbia, and Montenegro should be evacuated; occupied territories restored, Serbia accorded free and secure access to the sea; and the relations of the several Balkan states to one another determined by friendly counsel along historically established lines of allegiance and nationality.

12. The Turkish portions of the present Ottoman Empire should be assured a secure sovereignty, but the other nationalities should be assured an unmolested opportunity of autonomous development.

13. An independent Polish state should be erected which should include the territories inhabited by indisputably Polish populations, which should be assured a free and secure access to the sea.

14. A general association of nations must be formed under specific covenants for the purpose of affording mutual guarantees of political independence and territorial integrity to great and small states alike.

Source: From Arthur J. Link, ed., *The Papers of Woodrow Wilson*, vol. 45 (Princeton: Princeton University Press, 1984), pp. 536–538.

---

throughout Austria-Hungary as a political dissenter, a champion of democracy, a defender of women's rights,[11] and a foe of antisemitism. Controversial, he was still highly respected for his Czech patriotism. When the war broke out, Masaryk made his way to the western Allies, where he worked tirelessly for the creation of an entirely new state: Czechoslovakia. Despite disavowal by the west, which considered Czech problems an internal Austro-Hungarian matter, Masaryk and his Slovak associates created the Czechoslovak National Committee in 1916.

Only in the difficult year 1917 did the Allies begin to consider the possibility of an independent Poland and Czechoslovakia. The breakthrough came in January 1918, when, in a speech to a joint session of Congress, President Woodrow Wilson laid out the principles (the Fourteen Points) on which he hoped peace could be achieved. Wilson believed that the war offered a unique opportunity to establish "the principle of justice to all peoples and nationalities, and their right to live on equal terms of liberty and safety with one another." To accomplish that aim, he proposed creation of "a general association of nations . . . for the purpose of affording mutual guarantees of political independence and territorial integrity to great and small states alike." Wilson rejected the secret diplomacy that had

---

[11] Masaryk adopted his American wife's maiden name, Garrigue, as his own middle name—a highly unusual gesture at the time.

characterized the Allied relations during the war—such as the Treaty of London of 1915, by which the Allies gave Italy the Trentino and lands around the Adriatic. Agreements between states should be "open covenants openly arrived at," he proclaimed. A League of Nations would provide the mechanism for ensuring that these agreements maintained the peace. In addition, Wilson advocated a return to the practice of free trade, which had collapsed under mutual tariff barriers in the late 1890s, and, remembering the *Lusitania,* freedom of the seas.

For the east european nationalists, however, the most important parts of Wilson's speech were his support of an independent Poland with access to the sea and his advocacy of "the freest opportunity of autonomous development" for the peoples of Austria-Hungary. He did not use the phrase "self-determination of peoples" in this speech, but that was the principle that underlay his proposals. When Austria-Hungary collapsed, the way opened for Czech and Slovak delegations (these are two separate ethnic groups) to proclaim the independence of Czechoslovakia on October 28 and 29, 1918. Early in November, Piłsudski, released from jail, arrived in Warsaw, where he too established a provisional government.

In southeastern Europe another new country came into being. Almost immediately after war broke out between Serbia and Austria-Hungary, Serbia had proclaimed its main war aim as the creation of a new, larger state containing most of the South Slavs (or "Yugoslavs") living in the Balkans. At the same time, some Croatian and Slovenian politicians escaped from the Habsburg dominions and established the Yugoslav Committee, eventually headquartered in London. In 1917, the head of the Serbian government and the chairman of the Yugoslav

Committee met on the island of Corfu and decided to form a new state after the war. They left Corfu without agreeing on whether the new country should be a unitary or a federal state. The Serbs wanted the former; the Croats advocated the latter. Failure to solve that issue in the years that followed helped poison Serb-Croat relations and led directly to the eventual breakup of Yugoslavia in 1991. Nevertheless, when Austria-Hungary collapsed at the end of the war, delegates from various parts of the defunct empire hurriedly met in Belgrade. On November 30, 1918, they declared the independence of the Kingdom of the Serbs, Croats, and Slovenes (Yugoslavia) under the leadership of the Serbian king.[12]

The final East European beneficiary of the war was Romania. German troops had quickly overrun the country when Romania entered the war in 1916. Now, with Austria-Hungary splintering, the Romanian army reemerged to seize Transylvania. This territory had been under Habsburg political administration for two hundred years and Hungarian cultural domination since the Middle Ages, but the majority of its population was Romanian. Forcible seizure of Transylvania, along with other adjacent territories, more than doubled the size of Romania—and poisoned relations with all of its neighbors, particularly Hungary.

Revolution in Central Europe

In both Germany and the former Austria-Hungary, soldiers returning restless from the front, workers frustrated by the hardships of war, and left wing socialists inspired by the

---

[12] The country adopted the name Yugoslavia only in 1929.

Postwar Revolution: Defending Berlin
Germany endured considerable unrest during the first years after World War I. In March 1919, leftist revolutionaries staged an uprising in Berlin that right wing forces put down with considerable bloodshed. Here a group of revolutionaries take a position atop the Brandenburg Gate in the center of Berlin. *AKG London.*

THE HUMAN EXPERIENCE

Rosa Luxemburg, Polish and German Revolutionary

Small, frail, and slightly crippled from a childhood hip ailment, Rosa Luxemburg (1871–1919) questioned authority from her earliest youth. When she graduated from high school first in her class, authorities denied her the customary medal because of her "oppositional activities." Following the path of many other radical women, she moved to Zurich, where women were permitted to attend the university, and earned two doctorates, one in philosophy and one in law. In Switzerland she met some of the great figures of Russian socialism, including Lenin, and became a committed socialist. Her vivacity, intelligence, breadth of interest, and passion marked her as one of the leaders among the emigré revolutionaries.

After a short stay in France, in 1898 she contracted a false marriage to a German socialist in order to obtain German residency rights and settled in Berlin. There she immediately became involved in the great fight over revisionism that was raging within German socialism at the time.

Revisionism was the view that the economic and social situation had changed since Marx's time and that the best way to obtain benefits for the workers was not revolution but reform through participation in the political system. Luxemburg totally rejected this view (as did Lenin) and vigorously advocated a workers' revolution. The Russian revolution of 1905 only convinced her that revolutionary mass action was the key to overthrowing what she considered to be the bourgeois sham of parliamentary government.

The failure of the European socialist parties to oppose the Great War despite their promises to do so greatly disappointed Luxemburg. She and several colleagues formed the Spartacus League to overthrow the imperial regime, but spent most of the war in prison. Released late in 1918, she advocated giving power to the workers' councils that sprang up in the wake of Germany's defeat, although she insisted that the process of power transfer be strictly democratic. In January 1919, against her

advice and judgment, the tiny Spartacus League staged a revolt in an effort to seize power. Free Corps soldiers putting down the revolt seized Luxemburg and shot her.

Despite her lifelong radicalism, which superficially mirrored that of Lenin, Luxemburg consistently opposed the "pitiless" ultracentralism of the Bolsheviks. Lenin suspected spontaneity; Luxemburg respected the workers' creativity. As early as 1904 she accurately predicted that the principle of the vanguard party would lead to control by the central committee and eventually by a single leader, in whom all authority would become lodged. In her posthumously published assessment of the Russian Revolution, she stated the following: "Freedom only for supporters of the government, only for the members of one party—however numerous they may be—is no freedom at all. Freedom is always and exclusively freedom for the one who thinks differently." John Stuart Mill could not have expressed it better. ❖

Bolshevik Revolution stirred up revolutionary passions that the newly formed governments found almost impossible to handle. In Germany, the new government of socialist Friedrich Ebert, installed on November 9, exercised little direct control over the country. Ebert, however, accepted the support of the German army, which Ludendorff's replacement as supreme commander offered the government on its first day of existence. In December, when the Congress of Workers' Councils demanded that the old military system be replaced by a popular militia with elected officers, Ebert rejected the suggestion and reasserted his alliance with the army.[13] The generals authorized returning officers to organize volunteers into Free Corps (Freikorps) to provide security. Over the first four months of 1918, the Free Corps attracted thousands of disaffected officers and

soldiers. When a communist uprising broke out in Berlin in March 1919, the Free Corps put it down with great brutality, leaving fifteen hundred dead. They repeated the pattern in cities across Germany, finally completing the government's victory by smashing the Munich soviet in May 1919.

Friedrich Ebert has received unremitting criticism for allying his socialist government with the German military. Some historians argue that the Free Corps only confirmed the conservatism of the officer class, crushed the true revolutionary spirit, and left the country ripe for the appeals of Hitler's nazism ten years later. On the other hand, Ebert's survival ensured the success of the main revolutionary event that the Great War produced in Germany: the elimination of Hohenzollern authoritarianism and the creation of a parliamentary republic. A democrat at heart, Ebert knew that the Bolsheviks were a **totalitarian** party that threatened democracy in Germany. He held that democracy and the republic were more important than indulging

---

[13] In Russia this congress would have been called a Congress of Soviets, such as the one Trotsky and Lenin used on November 7, 1917.

THE HUMAN EXPERIENCE

Georges Clemenceau, French Politician

Clemenceau's nickname, "The Tiger," clearly suggests his most memorable characteristic: a combative and unsparing political style. Through most of his long career in French public life, Georges Clemenceau (1841–1929) made more enemies than friends. As a young delegate to the assembly in Bordeaux that had to accept German peace terms in 1871, he was among the few that held out against what he termed "shameful humiliation." In the 1870s and 1880s, as both a member of parliament and a newspaper editor, he was an acerbic critic of even his republican allies, not to mention conservatives and imperialists. Unwilling or unable to form governments himself, Clemenceau was adept at causing their fall, fashioning what one observer called "a career made of ruins."

Clemenceau learned his political style at the knee of his father, who considered Robespierre a hero and at one point had been sentenced to exile to Algeria for allegedly plotting against Napoleon III. Trained as a doctor, upon completion of his medical degree Clemenceau left for the United States, where he spent the years from 1865 to 1869. He taught for a while at a girls' school in Connecticut, where he married one of his students. The marriage did not last, but just as he maintained an aversion to Germany from his experiences in 1870 and 1871, so he retained a sympathy for America from his stay in the United States.

Crushed by his many opponents in the election of 1892, Clemenceau restored his reputation with his former republican friends by strongly supporting Alfred Dreyfus, the Jew falsely charged with treason. After election to the senate in 1904, in 1906 he became, for the first time, head of a government. During the Great War, Clemenceau strongly advocated government intervention to organize the country's resources and combated war weariness with a "will to victory." When he became premier in 1917, he applied a firm hand to France's military affairs, imposing a unified command, for example, in 1918. For these services, he became known in France as "the father of victory."

Clemenceau was not only a political man. He read the great writers of his day, most of whom he knew personally. He also appreciated music, and supported the impressionists. He particularly admired Claude Monet. After the Great War, Clemenceau persuaded Monet to paint a huge series of his water-lily paintings and got the French government to place them in the Orangerie in the Tuileries gardens, where visitors may observe them to this day.

Clemenceau is best known outside France through the acidic portrait that John Maynard Keynes, one of the twentieth century's greatest economists, wrote of him at the Paris peace negotiations. Keynes described how the worldly, witty, and cynical Clemenceau outmaneuvered a slower and less flexible Woodrow Wilson into giving the fierce old man what he wanted, which was a vindictive peace against Germany. According

---

in communist experiments, even if it meant allying with the military. In Russia, the Bolsheviks took over the military, leaving no organized elements to prevent their seizure of power. In Germany, Ebert used the military to preserve a fledgling democracy. He had no way of knowing that in less than fifteen years a native totalitarian regime would overwhelm the republic he saved.

Hungary's experience with revolution proved much more radical than Germany's. In the first place, the creation of Czechoslovakia, Yugoslavia, and an enlarged Romania shrank Hungary from its medieval borders to a small, ethnically homogeneous country, while leaving many Hungarians outside the new borders. As the war drew to a close, a prominent liberal politician, Mihály Károlyi, introduced universal suffrage, land reform, and democratization in Hungary. He hoped that by creating a liberal democratic regime, he could persuade the Allies to treat Hungary as a "new" state like Czechoslovakia, rather than as a defeated enemy. But when the Allies rejected this argument, a Bolshevik revolution led by Béla Kun seized power and held it for four months. Defeated in part by a Romanian invasion and in part by a rallying of conservative military forces, the Hungarian Soviet Republic collapsed in a sea of blood and a frenzy of retribution.

Waging Peace

If unrest, revolution, and civil war defined central and eastern Europe in late 1918 and early 1919, the politics of order dominated western Europe. As the leaders of the victorious Allies gathered in Paris in January 1919 for the to Keynes, Clemenceau "had one illusion—France; and one disillusion—mankind, including Frenchmen." But Keynes also pointed out that Clemenceau's vision was not to create a stable Europe for the future, but to "set the clock back and to undo what, since 1870, the progress of Germany had accomplished." His victory at Paris, therefore, ultimately proved a disaster for Europe. ❖

Negotiating the Peace Treaty Clemenceau, on the left, leaves the Versailles Palace with U.S. President Woodrow Wilson and British Prime Minister David Lloyd George. *Hulton Getty/Liaison Agency.*

peace conference, political leadership in Italy, Britain, and France all shifted noticeably toward the right. In Italy the Great War had damaged the moderate political forces of the center. The left, inspired by the Bolshevik Revolution, emerged from the war stronger than ever, but it was the right that dominated public discourse. Prodded by superpatriots who demanded that Italy seize not only the Trentino and Trieste but also the entire Dalmatian coast and Albania, Italian foreign minister Sidney Sonnino came to Paris with only one thought: Italy must get every square inch promised to it in the Treaty of London, plus as much more as he could manage.

In Britain, which held parliamentary elections late in 1918, Lloyd George, a Liberal, had to ally himself with the Conservatives to forge a majority government. Lloyd George was an audacious and witty Welsh politician

famous for the so-called people's budget he had put forward in 1909 as chancellor of the exchequer. His proposal to levy a capital gains tax on land sales created such resistance among landowners that it led to a parliamentary reform in 1911 that deprived the House of Lords of its last vestiges of real power. Having run the War Cabinet with vigor and skill in the final two years of the war, he had hoped to confine the 1918 electoral campaign to domestic issues, leaving himself a free hand in Paris, but the campaign quickly degenerated into shrill calls for a vindictive peace against Germany. Slogans such as "Hang the Kaiser" and demands to make the Germans "pay till the pips squeak," thrilled the electorate. Under new rules permitting all men over twenty-one and all women over thirty to vote, the expanded electorate gave this unrelenting policy a rousing endorsement.

Wilson: Loved by France
Prior to the Paris conference that wrote the peace treaties, U.S. President Woodrow Wilson traveled through Europe to a hero's welcome. His Fourteen Points had raised him above the pettiness of the wartime leaders in the public's mind, and they placed great hope in his ability to create a fair and lasting peace. The photograph shows the celebration and welcome Wilson received upon first landing in Brest, France. *The Granger Collection, New York.*

The main French participant in the peace negotiations was Georges Clemenceau, nicknamed "The Tiger." Clemenceau had started his political life as a radical, and as a journalist he was best known for his vigorous defense of Dreyfus. When he took power in 1917 at the age of seventy-six, he brought with him a vivid personal memory of the harsh peace terms that Germany had imposed on France in 1871. Now he had a chance to avenge that "shameful humiliation."

The only leader who brought a larger vision to Paris was American president Woodrow Wilson. As the war drew to a close, the Allies had reluctantly accepted his Fourteen Points as the basis for peace talks, except that they insisted on maintaining the blockade on Germany until they could determine how much monetary damages Germany would have to pay. But even in the United States, the idea of "open covenants openly arrived at" through deliberations in a League of Nations was not popular. The president's Democratic party lost control of the Congress to the Republicans in the off-year election of 1918. In the American system, this electoral defeat did not mean a change in government. Quite the contrary: It confirmed Wilson's determination to prevail. When he left for Europe in December 1918 he did not include a single Republican in his delegation.

Because Wilson seemed above the level of ordinary politics, European moderates placed great hopes in him. Germans in particular saw him as the great liberal who would ensure a fair peace. But when Wilson arrived in Paris in January 1919, after a triumphal visit to the Allied capitals, he quickly fell victim to the machinations of Clemenceau and the unwillingness of Lloyd George to anger his conservative partners back home. Wilson was not well equipped psychologically to deal with these world-weary men. A moralist, inexperienced in European intrigue, stubborn, and preachy, he ended up retreating on almost all of his Fourteen Points.

The main thing that Wilson wanted to achieve was the League of Nations. He believed that if such a league could be properly organized, it would provide a formal structure in which the European nations could work out their conflicting goals without resorting to war. By April 1919, he had obtained the agreement he wanted. Members, which included all of the thirty or so states that had joined in the Great War against the Central Powers, were to grant each other mutual protection against aggression, submit their disputes for adjudication, and assist the League's secretariat in coordinating disarmament, labor legislation, and similar policies. In a sense, the League extended and formalized the Concert of Europe from a hundred years earlier (see Chapter 21).

But to achieve agreement on the League, Wilson had to back down on other issues, although often Clemenceau helped him find principled justifications for doing so. Shocked Germans found that the treaty they were forced to sign contained nothing of the spirit of reconciliation that they had naively assumed Wilson would bring to the deliberations. Of course, defeated Germany lost all its colonies, which were placed under a mandate of the League of Nations and split up among the victors to administer. The Germans also had to give up Alsace and Lorraine, which they had taken from France in 1871, as well as any hopes of dominating Belgium and Luxembourg (see Map 28-5). Moreover, the Treaty of Versailles forced renunciation of Germany's short-lived domination of the east, achieved the previous year at Brest-Litovsk. The treaty even created a corridor through formerly German territory to permit newly independent Poland access to the sea. Only the denial of Danzig (Gdan´sk) to the Poles by making it a "free city" was a minor German success.

From this point, the Treaty of Versailles grew increasingly onerous and humiliating. The German military could

MAP 28-5

THE PARIS PEACE SETTLEMENT, 1919

The peace treaties of 1919 ratified the creation of a cordon of new states in central and eastern Europe and imposed territorial losses, both permanent and temporary, on Germany. Two impositions on Germany that had important consequences later were the demilitarized zone around the Rhine River and the Polish Corridor. The Polish-Soviet border was established separately in 1921 after a war between Poland and the Bolshevik regime.

994 CHAPTER 28 WAR AND REVOLUTION

not exceed one hundred thousand men, and conscription was forbidden. This small force was excluded entirely from an area running eastward from the French border to a point 30 miles beyond the Rhine River. Worse, the French were to occupy the industrial Saar region with its rich seams of coal, although a vote would be held after fifteen years to determine the region's final disposition. Then there were reparations. After handing over its entire navy and most of its railway stock at the time of the armistice, Germany had to pay $5 billion as a down payment on its obligation to reimburse the Allies for their losses during the war. The total amount would be determined later. Article 231 of the treaty justified all of these provisions. By this "war-guilt clause," Germany accepted responsibility "for causing all the loss and damage to which the Allied and Associated Governments and their nationals have been subjected as a consequence of the war imposed upon them by the aggression of Germany and her allies."

For a brief moment, some German military hotheads thought that they should resist signing such a humiliating treaty, but their position was hopeless. The hungry population was thoroughly tired of war; the armed forces had disintegrated; the economy, still blockaded, had collapsed; and the Allies were intransigent. Reluctantly, the Germans gave in. To rub in their defeat, the Allies made them sign the treaty in the same Hall of Mirrors of Louis XIV's palace in Versailles where the victorious Bismarck had proclaimed the German Empire in 1871(see Chapters 16 and 24).

While the peace negotiations unfolded in Paris without them, the Germans undertook to establish the legal basis of the new German republic. A constitutional convention convened in Weimar, the great poet Goethe's home city, in February 1919. By July the convention had written a new constitution. For the first time, Germans established a legal basis for a pluralist political system. But, as we shall see in Chapter 29, the troubled Weimar Republic, as it was called, would not survive.

The Treaty of Versailles was only one of five treaties written in Paris in 1919 and signed in various royal palaces outside the city. The Treaty of Trianon brought peace to Hungary; that of St. Germain to Austria; and Neuilly to Bulgaria. All of them reduced the size of the losers' armies and forced them to accept frustration of their territorial ambitions. For Hungary this meant abandoning millions of ethnic Hungarians in Transylvania, Yugoslavia, and Czechoslovakia; for Austria it meant giving up any idea of *Anschluss* (unification) with Germany; and for Bulgaria it meant giving up Macedonia for the third time in forty years.

The Treaty of Sèvres was the most problematic of the five treaties that ended the Great War. Ottoman entry into the war had stimulated British, French, and Russian efforts to divide Ottoman holdings among themselves. All three sent troops to the Middle East in order to make good their eventual claims. The Bolshevik Revolution removed Russia from the picture, but at the war's end the British and the French received mandates to administer Palestine and Syria respectively. The most dramatic and horrible event in this theater of the war was the massacre of approximately a million Armenian civilians by the Ottomans. Allegedly in order to prevent an uprising by the Christian Armenians, the Ottomans gathered up hundreds of thousands of men, women, and children living in eastern Turkey and marched them across wastelands, denying them food, water, and shelter, to the far reaches of their empire. The description of an American consular official was typical of foreign observers: "One of the most terrible sights ever seen in Aleppo was the arrival early in August 1915, of some 5,000 terribly emaciated, dirty, ragged and sick women and children. These people were the only survivors of the thrifty and well to do Armenian population of the province of Sivas, carefully estimated to have originally been over 300,000 souls!" Even today, the memory of this act of genocide, in which roughly one-third of all Armenians in the world perished, fuels an intense hatred of the Turks among Armenians.

In 1919 a weak and besieged Ottoman sultan signed the Treaty of Sèvres under heavy pressure from the victorious allies, but Turkish nationalists under the leadership of Mustapha Kemal, better known as Atatürk, revolted against his tottering regime. With Turkey in turmoil, inflamed nationalists in Greece rashly decided to invade the Anatolian peninsula with dreams of restoring a Hellenic empire. But Atatürk not only defeated this invasion, he pushed the Greeks into the sea at Smyrna, crushing their dreams of renewed glory. In 1923 Atatürk's new secular Republic of Turkey sealed the doom of the Ottoman regime by signing the Treaty of Lausanne, thus creating modern Turkey and finally formally ending the Great War.

ASSESSMENT

In some ways, the peace negotiations in Paris in 1919 paralleled those that took place one hundred years earlier at the Congress of Vienna (see Chapter 21). They both concluded lengthy and bitter European-wide struggles; they both were conducted by a few men representing the Great Powers; and they both produced peaces that profoundly influenced the future of Europe. Far more notable, however, are the contrasts between the two conferences. The negotiators who had met in Vienna brought with them the conviction that eighteenth-century balance-of-power politics no longer worked. At Vienna they adopted new principles intended to sustain the integrity of Europe on the basis of mutual agreement. The Concert of Europe system stabilized Europe for many years.

Except for Woodrow Wilson, the negotiators in Paris did not believe that the defining principles of the Century of Power—Realpolitik, nationalism, and imperialism—needed changing. The dominant figure at the negotiating table, Clemenceau, understood European politics in terms of an endless struggle between France and Germany in which Germany had won in 1871 and France in 1918. Germany had imposed a harsh peace on France in the first instance, and Bismarck had isolated France in the twenty years that followed. Now it was France's turn to make Germany's recovery as slow and as costly as possible. In Clemenceau's view, the only way to deal with Germans was to dictate to them with the backing of intimidating force. In contrast with the Congress of Vienna, where the victorious powers quickly admitted Talleyrand into their discussions, Germany had no representatives at the Paris negotiations.

Wilson managed to win limited acceptance for one of his new ideas, the principle of self-determination, but he failed to reassert freedom of the seas or to reestablish free trade. And, as we have seen, he could not produce a generous peace for Germany. His greatest accomplishment was the League of Nations, but even here his triumph was tempered by the fact that the United States Senate refused to ratify this innovation.

The League of Nations plan stipulated a council of five Great Powers (the United States, Great Britain, France, Italy, and Japan), delegates elected from smaller countries, and a World Court. Its most important feature was Article 10 of the Covenant, in which members pledged to "respect and preserve against external aggression the territorial integrity" of all other members. Most Americans probably favored joining the League, but some influential members of the Senate, both conservative Republicans and intransigent progressives, believed that Article 10 would limit American sovereignty and vigorously opposed ratifying the treaty. Instead of working out a reasonable compromise, which Senate leader Henry Cabot Lodge might have been willing to accept, Wilson dug in his heels and took the argument to the people, vigorously campaigning across the country for the League. After one particularly forceful speech, however, he collapsed with a stroke. For the last year and a half of his presidency, he lay incapacitated. Unwilling to compromise, he saw his own country reject his greatest accomplishment when the Senate failed to approve the Treaty of Versailles and the League of Nations that went with it. After providing the margin of victory in the Great War, the United States, arguably the most powerful country in the world by 1920, backed away from any responsibility in creating a stable peace. In significant measure, American unwillingness to play the international role its power and influence lay behind the collapse of Europe in World War II.

The ghosts that had haunted the Vienna Congress were Napoleonic militarism and the French Revolution. The specter at Paris was Bolshevism. But unlike in 1815,

The Cost of War   However the Great War began and whatever changes it wrought, for millions of men and women its consequence was quite simple: death.
Trustees of the Imperial War Museum, London.

when Napoleon had been defeated and sent to St. Helena, in 1919 the undefeated Lenin continued to trumpet the spread of the Bolshevik Revolution to the industrialized parts of Europe. The fear that revolution would sweep aside the European state structure was not entirely unfounded. Even while the Paris conference was going on, Béla Kun took control of Hungary, and leftist uprisings were being suppressed in Germany. Although neither Russia nor Bolshevism played a part in any of the peace settlements, anti-Bolshevism, as the renowned American social scientist Thorstein Veblen put it, provided the parchment on which the treaties were written.

CONCLUSION: OLD WINE IN OLD BOTTLES

As we shall see more fully in the coming chapters, the Treaty of Versailles did not work out as well as the Congress of Vienna. The vindictive peace imposed on Germany left Europe's largest nation and potentially most powerful economy frustrated, angry, and sullen. The exclusion of revolutionary Russia from the new concert of Europe and the failure of the United States to take up the responsibilities that its economic and industrial power implied left only Great Britain, France, and Italy to sustain European stability.

Rather than establishing new principles of international interaction, the settlements reinforced old ones. The lessons of the Great War that Woodrow Wilson wanted to teach—that the exercise of sheer power unmodified by notions of equity, autonomy, and law leads to catastrophe—were not yet learned. France wished to dominate Germany as Germany had dominated France. Great Britain wanted to keep its colonial empire intact and practice "splendid isolation" from the European continent. Russian autocracy found a more ruthless replacement in Soviet communism. In central and southeastern Europe, where major changes did take place, new states came into being with no political experience, weak economies, and virulent nationalistic feelings. It was said of the restored Bourbons early in the nineteenth century that during the French Revolution they had learned nothing and forgotten nothing. Much the same could be said of the politicians of Europe in 1919.

Selected Reading

Sources

Keynes, John Maynard. *The Economic Consequences of the Peace* (1919). The most famous, and most influential, analysis of the Treaty of Versailles, which includes vigorous portraits of Clemenceau and Wilson.

Lenin, Vladimir Ilich. *State and Revolution* (1917); and *What Is to Be Done?* (1902). Two of Lenin's most important theoretical works. The first contains his scheme for a new communist state based on Marx's interpretation of the Paris Commune. The second is prolix, polemical, and cranky, but nevertheless the classic statement of Bolshevik strategy.

Pankhurst, E. Sylvia. *The Home Front* (1987). Vivid memoir by a British radical detailing the appallingly callous treatment of the poor by the British government during World War I.

Pasternak, Boris. *Doctor Zhivago* (1958). Moving novel of vast sweep providing insight into the aftermath of the Russian revolutions.

Remarque, Erich Maria. *All Quiet on the Western Front* (1929). The greatest World War I novel. Required reading.

The Russian Revolution

Koenker, Diane P., William G. Rosenberg, and Ronald Grigor Suny. *Party, State, and Society in the Russian Civil War: Explorations in Social History* (1989). Excellent collection of articles indicating the more recent trends in the historiography of twentieth-century Russia.

Lincoln, W. Bruce. *In War's Dark Shadow: The Russians before the Great War* (1983); *Passage through Armageddon* (1986); and *Red Victory, a History of the Russian Civil War* (1989). Readable and authoritative narratives of the Russian experience in the early twentieth century.

Trotsky, Leon. *The Russian Revolution*, selected and edited by F. W. Dupee (1959). A rare instance of a great writer describing events in which he played a major shaping role.

Social and Economic Studies

Feldman, Gerald D. *Army, Industry, and Labor in Germany, 1914–1918* (1966). Detailed study of the German war effort on the home front.

Grieves, Keith. *The Politics of Manpower, 1914–1918* (1987). Shows how by the end of the war, Britain had achieved strict civilian control of its manpower.

Kocka, Jürgen. *Facing Total War: German Society, 1914–1918* (1984). Argues on the basis of moderate Marxism that class tension became sharper during the Great War. Controversial but stimulating.

Moyer, Laurence V. *Victory Must Be Ours: Germany in the Great War, 1914–1918* (1995). Vivid discussion of the hardships civilians faced, especially by the end of the war.

Williams, John. *The Other Battleground: The Home Fronts—Britain, France and Germany, 1914–1918* (1972). Readable comparative study full of interesting material.

Country Studies

Becker, Jean-Jacques. *The Great War and the French People* (1986). Concentrates on public opinion and why the French continued to accept the war.

Chickering, Roger. *Imperial Germany and the Great War, 1914-1918* (1998). A first-rate study of Germany's many difficulties during World War I.

Ferguson, Niall. *The Pity of War* (1999). Revisionist work arguing that Britain's vacillating prewar policies encouraged German aggression and that Europe would have been better off had Britain not entered the Great War.

Stevenson, David. *French War Aims against Germany, 1914–1919* (1982). A detailed study of French policy toward Germany showing that the high cost of retribution was not balanced by lasting results.

Thayer, John A. *Italy and the Great War: Politics and Culture, 1870–1915* (1964). Stimulating discussion of the meaning of postunification Italian history.

Personalities

Link, Arthur S. *Woodrow Wilson: Revolution, War, and Peace* (1979). A summary treatment of Wilson during the Great War by the author of the standard five-volume biography and editor of Wilson's papers.

Nettl, J. P. *Rosa Luxemburg*, 2 vols. (1966). Full-scale biography emphasizing the activism of one of the foremost left-wing (but not Leninist) revolutionaries in Germany.

Newhall, David S. *Clemenceau: A Life at War* (1991). Sympathetic but analytical biography of "The Tiger."

Versailles and the Postwar World

Fussell, Paul. *The Great War and Modern Memory* (1975). Brilliant analysis of how literature portrayed the Great War. The author presents "recognition scenes" in which he finds "our own buried lives."

Mayer, Arno J. *Politics and Diplomacy of Peacemaking: Containment and Counterrevolution at Versailles, 1918–1919* (1967). Detailed argument that fear of Bolshevism had an important influence on the peace deliberations of 1919.

Sharp, Alan. *The Versailles Settlement: Peacemaking in Paris, 1919* (1991). Relatively brief but solid treatment of the negotiations and their outcomes.

Smith, Daniel M. *The Great Departure: The United States and World War I, 1914–1920* (1965). Introductory survey of America's entry onto the world stage during World War I, arguing that Wilson's internationalism survived the Senate's rejection of the Versailles treaty.

THE INTERWAR SEARCH FOR SOLUTIONS

THE DESIRE FOR NORMALITY

The Search for International Security

Seeking Social Stability

Managing the Postwar Economies

THE SATISFIED POWERS

Great Britain: Labour and the Colonies

France: In Bismarck's Shadow

Central and Southeastern Europe:
Doomed Democracies

THE SOVIET UNION'S
PATHWAY OF REVOLUTION

THE REVISIONIST POWERS

Mussolini Brings Fascism to Italy

Weimar Germany Experiments with Democracy

COLLAPSE: THE DEPRESSION HITS

MODERNISM IN THE TWENTIES

CONCLUSION: WORLD WAR I
AS FAILURE

Pillars of Society *Gemalde von George Grosz, 1926. Öl auf Leinwand, 200 × 108 cm. Original; Staatliche Museen zu Berlin, Bildarchiv Preussischer Külterbesitz (bpk), Berlin, Nationalgaleria/ NG 4/57. Foto: Jörg P. Anders.*

*I*t is difficult to look back on the decade following World War I with any objectivity because we know what followed it: the Great Depression, Hitler, and World War II. People who were living through the decade did not know what was to come, of course, which is why some of the caricatures and paintings of George Grosz are so arresting. He painted *Pillars of Society,* shown opposite, in 1926, just when Germany was entering a short period of economic and political stability. And yet he vividly portrays a deeply disturbed political culture containing three ossified and ridiculous political tendencies—the right (with the swastika on the tie, and note the beer stein representing Hitler's so-called Beer Hall Putsch), the center (with the teacup on the head), and the left—posturing in front of the background forces of a leering judge and an angry soldier. A more vicious rendering of the forces threatening German and European social harmony is hard to imagine.

Grosz's work suggests the profound scars that the Great War inflicted on Europe. On many parts of the Continent, physical and demographic losses surpassed anything experienced since the Thirty Years' War three hundred years earlier. In 1919 a worldwide influenza epidemic swept away millions of people, many of them weakened by wartime privation. The French and British, their confidence shaken, found themselves deeply in debt to the United States. Frustrated Germans faced the humiliating defeat of their plans for Weltmacht (global power), while in central and southeastern Europe untested new countries struggled to establish democratic governments. The most devastated child of the Great War was Russia, which descended into a hellish civil war.

The victors in the Great War, particularly France and Britain, aspired to return to what they remembered as a peaceful and stable past. Parliamentary governments remained in power, but their goal became security—in the French case from renewed German aggression, and in the British case from threats to its economic leadership and its colonial empire. Memory of lives lost was so fresh that pacifism became a powerful public mood. The defeated countries, along with disgruntled and disillusioned Italy,

searched not for peace and stability, but to reverse the results of the war. In Germany and Hungary, revisions of the peace treaties became the driving force behind national politics. Italy had not lost the war, but its liberal government proved unable to contain the violence that engulfed the country in 1920 and 1921. Under the leadership of Benito Mussolini, Italian fascists replaced the impotent regime with a dictatorship they proudly described as totalitarian.

Soviet Russia was neither a victorious nor a revisionist power. It pursued its own revolutionary solutions under particularly chaotic circumstances. By the end of the 1920s, the communists under Stalin had imposed strict state control over all aspects of economic and social life and were launching a massive effort to transform the Soviet Union into an industrialized state as quickly as possible. Accusing the capitalist world of oppression and obsolescence, the Soviets claimed to be setting out on a new path to a better future.

Pacifism, revisionism, and revolution, not to mention fascism and communism, were poor foundations on which to build a stable international system. So were nationalism and imperialism—ideas left undiminished from the prewar period. Woodrow Wilson had hoped that the League of Nations would rise above these old ideas, but that fledgling organization began its life with several strikes against it. Without the United States, Germany, or Soviet Russia as original members, the League never became the foundation for a new Concert of Europe that Woodrow Wilson had hoped for. Few governments in the 1920s were willing to abandon nineteenth-century Realpolitik to the uncertainties of international collaboration.

Despite the extent of these problems and tensions, by the mid-1920s Europe had substantially rebalanced itself. Most economies had regained their prewar level of productivity; Germany had been admitted to the League of Nations; and reparations payments seemed under control. But at the end of the decade, disaster struck. A worldwide depression wiped out the modest economic gains of the late 1920s, calling into question the capacity of democratic governments and capitalism to cope with the problems of

Anti-European Feeling in Interwar America After World War I, unlike after World War II, the United States insisted that our European allies repay their wartime loans in full. Their inability to do so fueled isolationist resentments, as indicated in this cartoon in the *Detroit News* in the 1920s. *Courtesy of* Detroit News.

modernity. The consequences of that collapse—the rise of Hitler and World War II—are the subjects of Chapter 30. Here, in Chapter 29, we discuss the search for solutions in the 1920s that might have avoided that disastrous climax to the Century of Power.

THE DESIRE FOR NORMALITY

Every country wanted to return to what it considered "normal life" after the decidedly abnormal experiences of the Great War. But this proved, if not impossible, then very difficult. The war had not stopped urbanization, changes in the position of women and the family, expansion of information sources such as the radio, the mechanization of work, or hundreds of other disorienting developments that affected everyday life. The postwar world was not at all like the prewar world, so it was impossible simply to get back to some previous life. Indeed, critics of capitalism and liberalism on both the left (communism) and the right (fascism) claimed that it would be best not to re-create the old society, but to construct something entirely new. In this volatile situation, two needs seemed paramount—international security and domestic stability.

The Search for International Security

Every major power in 1920 perceived itself as insecure, including a significant non-European power: the United

States. The United States had been founded on principles growing out of the European experience. During the nineteenth century, it expanded across the North American continent, developing rapidly as an economic power. The United States entered into world affairs during the era of imperialism, and it became an integral player in European international relations by joining the Allies in World War I. Especially from this point on, therefore, developments in the United States become part of our story of Western civilization.

The United States was one of two countries that emerged from the Great War stronger than when it entered. (Japan was the other.) Nevertheless, the American public, steeped in a time-honored tradition of avoiding "entangling alliances," hesitated to assume international responsibilities corresponding to the country's strength. Having provided the decisive force that gave the Allies victory on the western front in 1918, the United States refused to maintain the active political engagement with European security arrangements that alone could have kept Germany from eventually reasserting itself. In the economic sphere, however, it was a different story. During the 1920s, American international investments grew seven times over. By the end of the decade, the United States controlled the finances of ten Latin American nations. Because the wartime Allies had borrowed large sums from the United States to support their war efforts, American economic policy played a key role in determining how Europe would recover. Instead of thinking in terms of long-term stability for Europe, as they would after World War II, in the 1920s the Americans insisted that Britain, France, and its other allies pay off their loans promptly, whatever the consequences. President Calvin Coolidge put it bluntly, "We hired them the money, didn't we?"

The emergence of the United States as a financial power seriously undermined the position of Great Britain, which reacted by trying to keep the value of the pound high. British statesmen knew that their country's power in the late nineteenth century derived from the invisible income generated by financial services, the success of which they attributed to stability of the pound. Therefore, during the 1920s Britain concentrated on restoring the value of the pound to its prewar level. As part of this effort, in 1926 the British government set the exchange rate of the pound artificially high, agreeing to buy and sell it for more than it was worth in other currencies. Here is a fictional example of what that means. Let us say that a widget can be bought in the United States for $4 and in Britain for £1, but the British government sets the exchange rate of the pound at $5. Obviously this will make it difficult for the British to export widgets, because a foreign purchaser can buy them for fewer dollars in the United States. When this consequence spreads through the entire economy, growth slows, investment declines, and unemployment increases. Mesmerized by a mythology of the pre-war pound, and absorbed with other domestic issues, the British proved only marginally interested in Continental problems, especially anything unfolding east of the Rhine River.

France, on the other hand, having experienced two German invasions in the preceding fifty years, took a lively interest in Continental affairs. The French had hoped that the British and the Americans would protect them against German aggression, but by 1921 that possibility had evaporated. The French devised four strategies to fill their security void.

First they strove to surround Germany with French allies in eastern Europe. The Bolshevik Revolution removed any possibility of re-creating the Franco-Russian alliance of 1894, so the French turned to Poland and Czechoslovakia. In 1921 and 1924, respectively, they signed a treaty of mutual protection with the former and a military alliance with the latter. Because Czechoslovakia had also allied with Romania and Yugoslavia for protection against Hungarian revisionism (forming the Little Entente), by 1927 France signed further agreements with these others as well (see Map 29-1). The French hoped that these agreements would establish a **cordon sanitaire** (or "containing wall") around Germany. The cordon sanitaire had an added benefit: It blocked the Soviet Union's access to central Europe.

As a second strategy, France insisted that the Germans strictly fulfill their obligation to pay for the damages caused by the Great War. German reparations would permit France to restore its financial stability without having to take the unpalatable step of raising taxes. A conference in 1921 set the amount to be paid, but the Germans had difficulty meeting the schedule. When they failed to make a payment in January 1923, the French invaded and seized Germany's most important and highly concentrated industrial and mining region, the Ruhr. By taking over approximately 80 percent of Germany's coal and steel industry, the French precipitated an economic crisis in Germany.

Because the invasion of the Ruhr so seriously destabilized Germany, the Allies agreed to a more realistic reparations schedule. A frustrated France now considered a third option: strengthening the League of Nations. In 1923 the French proposed that all members of the League be obligated to come to the assistance of any member that the League Council declared to be a victim of aggression. In 1924 they added a proposal that all disputes be sent to the International Court of Justice or to the League Council. Failure to do so would constitute "aggression." Had these proposals been adopted, they would have given the League real teeth. But Britain refused to promise to come to the aid of regions in which it had little interest, such as eastern Europe. As Prime Minister David Lloyd George had put it in 1921, "The British people felt that the populations in that quarter of Europe were unstable and excitable; they might start fighting at any time, and the rights and wrongs of the dispute might be very hard to disentangle."

When none of these strategies proved viable, the French turned late in the 1920s to a fourth option, building defensive fortifications against the possibility of a renewed German attack. They began constructing a series of massive bunkers and fortresses along the German border called the Maginot Line. In the final analysis, these fortifications proved of little use because they did not protect from attack through Belgium, whence the German *Blitzkrieg* (lightning war) would hit in 1940. Rather than increasing French security, they encouraged a passive attitude that contributed to France's rapid collapse in World War II.

Germany, meanwhile, faced an entirely different problem: finding a way back into the international community. Defeated in war, the Germans had survived a powerful surge of revolution in 1919 and established a democratic government, called the Weimar Republic (from the town in which its constitution had been written).[1] In contrast to the pacifist mood of Britain and France, feelings of anger and frustration coursed through the German public. All German political parties agreed that the "*Diktat* of Versailles" was unacceptable, even though in fact the reparations were probably manageable.

Two schools of thought predominated. The government generally pursued a policy of fulfilling the international

MAP 29-1
THE LITTLE ENTENTE AND THE CORDON SANITAIRE

---

[1] Weimar was chosen for this purpose because of its associations with the great poets Goethe and Schiller, both of whom had lived there for many years and had given the small city the aura of a shrine to Germany's humanistic traditions.

obligations Germany had agreed to in the Treaty of Versailles. Germany should continue to seek changes in the provisions of the treaty, advocates of this position argued, but in the meantime it should prove itself a good European citizen by paying its reparations regularly. Once Germany was economically strong again, it would be in a position to reenter the European community. Supporters of this policy also hoped that the plan would help Germany by splitting the Allies. If France benefited from reparations payments, then Britain would be sure to object. If reparations slowed and France and England could not repay their debts to the United States, then the United States would intervene. In any event, in a few years Germany would be strong again, and its burdens would lighten.

The "catastrophe" school of thought vigorously opposed fulfillment. Its supporters argued that Germany had no moral obligation to fulfill anything that was forced on it by the war. In 1914 Germany had merely overstepped when it sought Weltmacht before establishing its continental position. The goal, therefore, should be reestablishing the country's military might. Germany would renew its struggle for continental dominance from a position of strength. Because the Treaty of Versailles forbade Germany to rearm, champions of this position began to cultivate relations with the Soviet Union, Europe's other pariah state. German military officers, especially pilots and tank commanders, secretly trained in Soviet Russia throughout the 1920s in violation of the Versailles treaty.

The German foreign office, too, looked toward the Soviet Union as a way to end its isolation. In 1922, when attendees at an economic conference in Genoa spurned German foreign minister Walter Rathenau, he went off to nearby Rapallo and signed a separate agreement with the Soviets. This agreement, which actually had little long-range effect, nevertheless shocked France and Great Britain and provided part of the impetus behind the French invasion of the Ruhr.

Naturally, the Germans exploded with nationalistic outrage in response to the Ruhr invasion. The Weimar government stopped any pretense of reparations payments and adopted a policy of passive resistance. The French countered by bringing in foreign workers and trying to create an "independent" Rhineland. The Weimar regime then let inflation, which had reached epidemic proportions in 1922, spin completely out of control into hyperinflation. At the beginning of 1914, it took 4.21 marks to buy an American dollar; by the end of the war it took 7.43; by January 1922, a dollar was worth 191.81 marks. One year later, at the time of the French invasion, the mark stood at 17,972 to the dollar; by the end of 1923 it hit 4.2 *trillion*.

With the French organizing production in the Ruhr and their money totally useless, the Germans changed course. A coalition under the leadership of Gustav Stresemann took power in the fall of 1923 and introduced a new currency. An international reparations commission, meeting under the chairmanship of American banker

German Hyperinflation
The almost total worthlessness of the German Mark during the hyperinflation of 1923 led people to use the paper currency in frivolous ways. Here some boys make kites out of Mark notes. *Hulton Getty/Liaison Agency.*

Charles Dawes, produced a revised reparations schedule that Stresemann's government agreed to meet. The French withdrew, and Germany regained a measure of economic stability.

Stresemann now informed the allied governments that Germany was willing to accept its postwar boundaries with France and Belgium as permanent. A 1925 meeting in Locarno, Switzerland, confirmed this agreement—with Britain, France, Belgium, Germany, and Italy promising to submit any future disputes to arbitration. In western Europe, the Locarno treaty produced an audible sigh of relief. It appeared that the search for stability had ended at last with the reconciliation of the former enemies. One year later, in 1926, Germany entered the League of Nations with a seat on the League Council.

However, although Stresemann aimed to fulfill Germany's' postwar obligations in the west, he could not do the same in the east. The existence of the Polish corridor—a narrow strip of territory carved out of prewar German lands and awarded to Poland to provide that country access to the Baltic Sea—made it impossible for a German government to guarantee the new postwar borders of eastern Europe. The corridor separated the East Prussia region of Germany from the rest of Germany. Furthermore, 10 to 12 million Germans now lived in the new countries of eastern Europe, often in compact enclaves close to the German frontier. The lack of an eastern settlement at Locarno clearly signaled both the German unwillingness to compromise in the east and western Europe's relative indifference to the fate of eastern Europe.

Eastern Europe had preoccupied generals Hindenburg and Ludendorff during the Great War and remained a German fixation right up until 1945. The Soviet Union also considered eastern Europe, especially Poland, important to its security, but its isolation in the 1920s prevented it from playing a major role there. With the exception of the Rapallo agreement of 1922, the Soviet Union's most important foreign policy initiatives in the 1920s were taken by the local Moscow-led communist parties in each European country. The failure of Europe's socialist parties to follow through on their pacifist platforms in 1914 had spelled the ruin of the Second International Workingmen's Association. In 1919, in the midst of civil war, Lenin summoned left wing and internationalist European socialists to Moscow to institute a Third International. The resulting organization, the Communist International, or **Comintern,** was not to be a pluralist union of member socialist parties, as the Second International had been, but an arm of Soviet revolution. At first, socialist parties readily joined the Comintern, but at its second meeting in 1920 Lenin insisted that every party adhere to twenty-one points of doctrine. These points included accepting iron discipline imposed from Moscow, establishing an underground revolutionary organization, purging reformists and other "opportunists," calling themselves the

communist party, and "disorganizing" the armies in their respective countries.

Lenin's revolutionary demands fragmented the working-class movement of Europe. In almost every country, the formerly strong socialist parties split into two groups: a smaller but not inconsequential communist party that adhered to Moscow's line, and a larger social democratic party that continued its participation in ordinary politics. The two elements turned fiercely hostile. The communist parties hurled epithets at the socialists for betraying the revolution, undermining proletarian solidarity, and becoming "social fascists." The social democrats dismissed the communists as tools of Moscow, factionalists, and undemocratic extremists.

Lenin hoped that the Comintern would be able to act as a midwife to revolution in Europe. But the failure of communist uprisings in Hungary in 1919, Munich in 1921, and Bulgaria in 1923 shattered those dreams. In the late 1920s, the Comintern became a pawn for internal Soviet political struggles.

Seeking Social Stability

In the late nineteenth century, Europe had entered a **demographic transition** in which the high birthrates and death rates characteristic of agricultural societies gave way to the low birthrates and death rates of industrialized societies. In an agricultural society, annual birthrates average 40 to 50 per thousand members of the population and death rates 30 to 40 per thousand. The comparable figures in an industrialized society are 10 deaths and 12 births per thousand per year. But death rates usually drop first, so that during the transition, populations tend to grow rapidly.

The demographic transition did not take place evenly in twentieth-century Europe, and its impact varied. For example, German and French death rates had declined throughout the nineteenth century, but birthrates dropped only in the decades preceding World War I. The birthrates fell at about the same pace in both countries before the war, but the French decline started from a point far below that of Germany (21 births per thousand for the French versus 35 for the German). Between 1870 and 1930, therefore, the French population grew from 36 million to only 41 million, whereas Germany's population jumped from 41 million to 65 million (see Figure 29-1). During the interwar period, French fertility actually dropped below replacement levels. Frantic French nationalists insisted that women stay home and produce babies, but their pleas had little effect. France's tendency to rely on labor-intensive production methods exaggerated its labor shortages, inducing it to open the doors to foreign guest workers. By 1930, about 7 percent of the French population consisted of immigrant workers.

In Germany, by contrast, the postwar surplus of workers too young to have fought in the war concentrated

THE HISTORICAL EVIDENCE

Lenin's Twenty-One Conditions

1920

The Soviet Union tried to control leftist movements in Europe through the Communist International (Comintern), usually called the Third International, which was founded in 1919. In 1920, Lenin pushed twenty-one conditions for admission to the Comintern through its second congress. Controversy over their harsh revolutionary spirit split the socialist movement in Europe. The conditions can be compared in tone and intent to those put forward by Woodrow Wilson (see Chapter 28: The Historical Evidence, "Wilson's Fourteen Points"). The conditions are presented here in condensed form.

1. All propaganda and agitation must be of a genuinely communist character and in conformity with the program and decisions of the Communist International. The entire party press must be run by reliable communists.

2. Every organization must remove reformists and centrists from all responsible positions.

3. Communists can have no confidence in bourgeois legality. They are obliged everywhere to create a parallel illegal organization.

4. The obligation to spread communist ideas includes the special obligation to carry on systematic and energetic propaganda in the army.

5. Systematic and well-planned agitation must be carried on in the countryside.

6. Every party is obliged to bring home to the workers systematically that without the revolutionary overthrow of capitalism no "democratic" reorganization of the League of Nations will be able to prevent new imperialist wars.

7. Parties are obliged to recognize the necessity for a complete and absolute break with reformism.

8. Every party is obliged to expose the tricks and dodges of "its" imperialists in the colonies, [and] to support every colonial liberation movement.

9. Every party must carry on systematic and persistent communist activity inside the trade unions.

10. Every party is obliged to wage an unyielding struggle against the Amsterdam "International" of the yellow trade unions [the remnants of the Second International].

11. Parties are obliged to review the personnel of their parliamentary fractions and remove all unreliable elements.

12. Parties must be based on the principle of democratic centralism. The party will be able to fulfill its duty only if its organization is as centralized as possible [and] if iron discipline prevails.

13. Parties must from time to time undertake cleansing (re-registration) of the membership of the party in order to get rid of any petit-bourgeois elements which have crept in.

14. Every party is obliged to give unconditional support to any Soviet republic in its struggle against counter-revolutionary forces.

15. Parties are obliged to draw up a new communist program.

16. All the decisions of the congresses of the Communist International, as well as the decisions of its Executive Committee, are binding on all parties.

17. All parties must be called: the Communist party of such and such a country.

18. All leading party press organs are obliged to publish all important official documents of the Executive Committee of the Communist International.

19. All parties are obliged to hold a general congress as soon as possible.

20. Parties must see to it that not less than two-thirds of the members of their central committee consist of comrades who publicly and unambiguously advocated the entry of the party into the Communist International.

21. Those members of the party who reject in principle the conditions and theses put forward by the Communist International are to be expelled from the party.

Source: From Jane Degras, ed., *The Communist International, 1919–1943*, vol. 1, *1919–1922* (London: Oxford University Press, 1956), pp. 168–172.

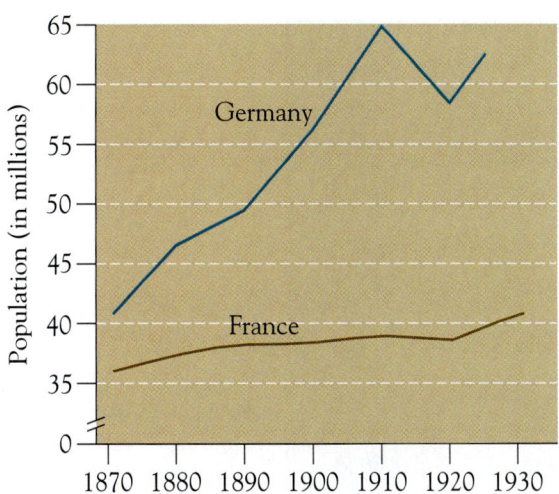

FIGURE 29-1

FRENCH AND GERMAN POPULATION GROWTH, 1870–1930

Source: Based on data from B. R. Mitchell's International Historical Statistics: Europe 1750–1993, *4th ed. London: Macmillan, 1998, table A1, p. 4.*

low wages, working women could not afford electrical appliances, preferred cozy homes to efficient ones, and had little time, money, or energy for late-night carousing. The popularity of fashion magazines and romantic films, however, did suggest a change in female leisure habits and aspirations.

Many governments responded to the changes wrought by industrialization by introducing new social security systems, or by adjusting the ones they already had. They added family allowances for children, medical insurance, and unemployment insurance to their accident insurance and old age pensions. By 1930 approximately half the population of central and western Europe were covered by some kind of a state insurance plan. Housing became another state concern. In 1919, Lloyd George campaigned with the slogan "Homes Fit for Heroes," and during the 1920s and 1930s local municipal councils built one-third of all new British housing. In Germany, the Weimar constitution assigned the state the responsibility of ensuring adequate shelter for its citizens. Half the new residential

public and governmental attention on "the youth problem." During the 1920s, approximately one German young person in two belonged to a youth club or organization, an unprecedented level of social participation in that country. The high level of youth activism provided a pool of engaged young people that would prove susceptible to extreme political movements when the Great Depression hit.

Demographic change had other striking implications. In the nineteenth century, large families had been common in Europe. By the interwar period, they were becoming the exception. In a sense, the relative scarcity of children increased their "value." The two-child family became the middle-class norm. Longer lives also became more common. Between 1900 and 1930, life expectancy at birth jumped by ten to fifteen years.

The combination of smaller families, the horrible losses of young men during the war, and the overall aging of the population unbalanced the social equation. With smaller families, women spent fewer years immersed in child care. With more time available for other pursuits, they began to seek paid jobs. Although the overall employment figures held steady, the number of women servants declined while the number of women in lower-level industrial and white-collar jobs (such as typist) increased. Magazines and film, an immensely popular new art form, portrayed the "new woman" of the 1920s either as an efficient housewife using newfangled electrical appliances such as stoves and washing machines or as a Charleston-dancing vamp. The phrase "the Roaring Twenties" captures that second characterization, with its implications of sexual license, dangerous living, and upper-class chic. In fact, most women fit neither stereotype. With long hours and

Europe's "New Woman" Two stylish French women discuss such things as where they will vacation and what exotic mountain cures to spend their money on. *Mary Evans Picture Library.*

Bauhaus-Designed Public Housing The Bauhaus school of architecture, founded by Walter Gropius, sought to eliminate the frivolous aspects of design and to make buildings that were scientifically functional. The results were rather cold, geometrically-shaped buildings, such as those in this public housing project. *Corbis/Bettman–UPI*

buildings constructed in Germany between 1924 and 1931 received assistance from a new housing rent tax.

Programs such as these stimulated architects to develop new ideas for urban development. In Germany, the Bauhaus School of Walter Gropius proved to be one of the most original, combining craftsmanship and artistic training into functional designs that greatly influenced architects throughout the world. "The ultimate, if distant, aim of the Bauhaus," the founding document of the school professed, "is the unified work of art—the great structure."

Managing the Postwar Economies

Despite the increased level of support for social programs, most European governments hesitated to intervene directly in the economy to promote economic growth. Reacting reflexively to short-term events and lacking economic sophistication each government nevertheless unconsciously influenced its country's economic health.

As we have seen, by overvaluing the pound the British made their exports more expensive and discouraged investment. Partly for this reason, British unemployment during the 1920s never dropped below 10 percent and the economy grew painfully slowly.

France, on the other hand, pursued an easy-money policy of inflation.[2] By devaluing the franc to about one-

fifth of its prewar level, the French boosted their economy. This decline in the value of the franc, when coupled with Soviet repudiation of tsarist debts, hit French investors hard. But after the key devaluation in 1926, France became more competitive internationally. By 1930 France's production was 40 percent above the 1913 level, the best performance in Europe.

Germany also pursued an inflationary policy during and just after the war, but the course of events there showed the dangers of the easy money strategy. Just after the war, the Weimar Republic spent more than it took in and printed money to make up the difference. For a few years, this policy stimulated economic growth, but, as we have seen, in 1922 and 1923 the government lost control of the money supply. Scholars still dispute whether the German hyperinflation had a positive or negative economic effect over the long run. By 1930 German industrial production ranked only slightly above that of 1913. But hyperinflation no doubt undermined middle-class confidence. Hardworking and frugal families found their savings wiped out in only a few months. The psychological damage wreaked by the collapse of German money paved the way for the radical solutions of the 1930s.

Faced with sluggish economies and declining international trade, governments everywhere moved to restrict imports through quotas, exchange controls, tariffs, and other means. The leader in protectionism was the United States, which enacted the restrictive Fordney-McCumber Tariff in 1922 and the even harsher Hawley-Smoot Tariff in 1930. Economically, these laws were grave mistakes.

---

[2] An "easy money" policy sets the value of the currency at a realistic rate, encourages lending, and promotes modest inflation.

They flew in the face of simultaneous insistence by the United States that its European debtors pay off their loans in full, because high tariffs made it difficult for these countries to earn the dollars they needed.

Protectionism constricted trade throughout the world in the 1920s, but nowhere did it have a worse effect than in eastern Europe. There small, competing nation-states replaced the large, economically integrated Austro-Hungarian Empire. With the exception of the industrialized areas of Czechoslovakia and Hungary, the Silesian portion of Poland, and the oil-rich region of Romania, the new east European countries all produced more or less the same agricultural products. Worse, most of them had serious conflicts with their neighbors. Czechs and Poles nursed a bitter grudge because Poland refused to accept the cession of a small industrial city that had gone to the Czechoslovakia in 1919. The Hungarians remained angered at all of their neighbors due to their huge losses under the Trianon Treaty. This dangerous combination—competition in similar products and nationalistic antagonisms—led to the raising of tariff barriers that impeded the normal development of these struggling economies.

Despite all the problems, by the middle of the decade industrial production in most European countries had almost returned to prewar levels. The mark, pound, and franc had stabilized, and slow economic growth had resumed. Unlike today, however, when growth is a preoccupation of all governments, only a few European businessmen consciously sought it in the interwar years, although they did continue to seek profits. "Taylorism" and "Fordism" were the watchwords of the more progressive industrialists. Before World War I, the American engineer Frederick Taylor had broken down production tasks into standardized units of work that could be timed, thus making it possible to measure each worker's efficiency. Rationalization, or making production more efficient through Taylor's methods, became a watchword of progressive industrialists. "Fordism" referred to the assembly-line and marketing techniques pioneered by the American carmaker Henry Ford. The assembly line reduced employees' work to discrete, repetitive tasks performed on pieces of equipment as they moved by on a production line. Using this method, along with innovative advertising strategies, Ford produced an automobile affordable by working people: the Model T. In consequence, the United States became the first country in which ordinary citizens owned automobiles—tens of millions of them by the 1930s. In France, André Citroën adopted Ford's methods to mass-produce automobiles, but he was the exception. Most European investors, more risk-averse than ever after the war because of the German inflation and the victory of Bolshevism, preferred to put their capital into government bonds, real estate, and equally safe investments. Domestic capital investment that might have stimulated growth remained sluggish through the 1920s.

Foreign competition, along with faulty fiscal policies and the reluctance to innovate, inhibited European economic growth in the 1920s. While Europe struggled to regain 1913 levels of production, the American economy more than doubled and the Japanese economy grew by 50 percent. These formidable newcomers reduced the German, French, and British share of international commerce from a little over one-third of world trade in 1913 to a little over one-quarter in 1925.

THE SATISFIED POWERS

Within the overall search for security and economic stability, three patterns of policies and innovations emerged. First there were the winners, the nations satisfied that they had found the determination and strength to defeat the Central Powers. Second, the Soviet Union constituted a category in its own right. It is difficult to say whether Russia ultimately won or lost the war with Germany, because once the Bolsheviks consolidated the October Revolution they pursued their radical path with only passing reference to the rest of Europe. Third were the revisionist states, the former Central Powers and Italy that smarted not only from the costs the war had imposed on them, but also, with the exception of Italy, from the humiliation of defeat.

Great Britain: Labour and the Colonies

During the 1920s, British internal politics revolved around the rise of the Labour party at the expense of the Liberal party.[3] In three elections—held in 1922, 1923, and 1924—Lloyd George's Liberals fell to third place in electoral strength, the Labour party gained temporary ascendancy, and finally the Conservative party under Stanley Baldwin took control. Labour's first government lasted only ten months, from January to November 1924, but it marked a sea change in British politics. British workers had the vote long before World War I, but Labour party representatives had entered Parliament only in 1906 with less than 5 percent of the vote. After the war, however, a newly confident working class rallied to the Labour banner, giving it one-third of the votes cast in the 1924 election. The Liberal party, on the other hand, dropped from nearly 50 percent of the votes in the 1906 election to less than 20 percent in 1924. Meanwhile, the Conservatives held steady at about 45 percent. The part of British society that activist liberalism had attracted early in the century took the Labour option by the mid-1920s.

Despite the Marxist rhetoric about class warfare of some local Labour figures, when the party achieved power

---

[3] Note that in Great Britain and Canada the spelling is *labour*, whereas in the United States it is *labor*. The British form is used when referring to the Labour party.

Coping with the British General Strike Many socialists, especially those known as syndicalists, believed that the workers' most powerful tool was a general strike to shut down all economic activity. In May 1926, the Trades Union Congress in Britain called such a strike for locked-out coal miners. But the strike was not revolutionary, and Stanley Baldwin's government weathered the storm in only nine days. In this photo, white-collar workers, unable to use the bus, commandeer other vehicles, such as trucks, for their ride to work. *The Granger Collection, New York.*

in 1924 it pursued a balanced policy that did not differ greatly from what late nineteenth-century liberals might have proposed. Its leader, Ramsay MacDonald, sought reconciliation with France and Germany, supported the League of Nations, and formally recognized the Soviet Union. At home, Labour raised unemployment benefits, eased requirements for pensions, and instituted subsidies for housing. But the Labour government did not have its own majority. It depended on Liberal support in Parliament. When that backing collapsed at the end of 1924, a red-baiting campaign by the Conservatives brought Baldwin back to power for the next five years.[4]

Baldwin's chancellor of the exchequer was Winston Churchill, who stood strongly behind the policy of overvaluing the pound. Resetting the value of the pound, along with other factors, such as obsolete technology, undercut the coal mining industry. In May 1926, when mine owners tried to close uneconomic pits and reposition the displaced workers elsewhere at lower wages, the miners struck. Three days later, the Trades Union Congress called a general strike in sympathy. For nine days, Britain shut down—the railroads stopped running, plants closed, and construction ground to a halt. But unlike St. Petersburg in 1905 or Germany in 1919, the strike was peaceful. When the government agreed to negotiate, the general strike ended, although the miners still refused to go back to work. After holding out for six months, the exhausted and impov-

erished miners had no choice but to return on the owners' terms.

After World War I, Britain was just as interested as ever in maintaining its colonial empire, although it did make some gestures at expanding self-rule. By 1926 it found a solution to dealing with the dominions (self-governing former colonies such as Australia, the Union of South Africa, and Canada) by granting them equality in the British Commonwealth of Nations. But the war had spawned profound unrest in other colonies. India, which had contributed some 1 million troops to the effort against Germany and Austria, remained the largest and most problematic colony. In 1917 the secretary of state for India had proclaimed the "gradual development of self-governing institutions" for the subcontinent, and the India Act of 1919 gave authority to regional legislatures. But the most important functions remained in the hands of British administrators. Disappointed Indian nationalists, under the leadership of pacifist Mohandas Gandhi, called *Mahatma* (or "Great Soul"), conducted massive independence campaigns of nonviolent civil disobedience through the 1920s and 1930s.

League of Nations mandates presented Britain with a different sort of colonial problem. The 1919 Paris peace conference had granted the League authority over the former German colonies, and it had passed this power over to the victor countries. In the Pacific, Japan took this opportunity to displace German and Russian influence in China, while France occupied Syria and Britain took over Palestine. In Palestine, British support of Jewish settlement stirred up continuous conflict. During the Great War, the

---

[4] *Red-baiting* refers to the tactic of destroying an opponent's reputation by falsely claiming he is a communist or sympathetic to communism.

British had encouraged Arabs to revolt against the Ottomans and the Germans by making vague promises of creating a "national home" for them. At the same time, in the Balfour Declaration of 1917, they agreed to create a Jewish homeland in Palestine. Because very few Jews, but about a million Arabs, then lived in Palestine (a predominantly Arab-populated land for centuries), the influx of tens of thousands of Jewish settlers in the interwar period ignited lasting tensions that conflicting British policies could not resolve.

World War I also had brought tensions in Ireland to a head. A revolutionary movement called Sinn Fein had urged the Irish not to support the British war effort. Sinn Fein had even sought German support for the Easter Uprising that broke out in 1916. The British crushed that revolt, but the event motivated Lloyd George to propose another Irish home-rule solution. Unionists, who had broken with Gladstone's Liberals in 1885 over this issue, defeated the proposal again, but Sinn Fein proceeded to set up its own shadow parliament in defiance of the British. When Sinn Fein's paramilitary arm, the Irish Republican Army (IRA), launched a campaign of terror, the British answered in kind. Close to fifteen hundred people perished in the ensuing struggle. Finally, Lloyd George pushed the Home Rule Act of 1920 through Parliament. It established two Irish legislatures: one for the six Ulster counties in the north, where Protestantism was strong, and one for the other twenty-six counties in which Catholics predominated. Ulster accepted the plan, but Sinn Fein did not. After a year of civil war in southern Ireland, Lloyd George finally worked out an agreement with Sinn Fein that created the Irish Free State, with dominion status. Under the leadership of the moderate William Cosgrave—and after 1932 under Sinn Fein leader Eamon de Valera—the Republic of Ireland gained complete independence by 1938. Only in 1998 did a negotiated settlement bring a tenuous peace to Ulster.

France: In Bismarck's Shadow

Like Britain, France saw its colonial empire expand after World War I. At the 1919 Paris peace conference, the French assumed administration of formerly German Togo and Cameroon in Africa, and formerly Ottoman Syria in the Middle East. Before the war, France's most important colonies had been Algeria, Equatorial and West Africa, and Indochina. Along with a variety of smaller communities, these regions had provided more than half a million combat troops for the French war effort. Algeria, France's oldest and most established colony, had already become part of metropolitan France. Its three departments (the local governing units) sent ten deputies to the National Assembly. In 1919 the French extended citizenship and electoral opportunities to Algerians and granted them a degree of local administration.

During the 1920s, Algeria seemed to prosper. In French Morocco, Syria, and Indochina, however, native nationalist movements vigorously opposed French rule, forcing the French to expend considerable resources in containing a series of revolts. Even though by 1929 colonial trade made up only 15 percent of French commerce, the French government remained as committed as ever to imperialism.

Domestic politics were more confused in France than in Britain. In the election of 1919, for example, instead of choosing between three main parties, as in Britain, the French gave more than 10 percent of the vote to each of five parties—two socialist, one centrist, and two rightist. During the 1920s, France had a series of twenty-one separate governments. Despite these superficial signs of disarray, French politics retained a decidedly centrist flavor. The parties of the left dissipated their strength in a mutually destructive struggle for the allegiance of the working class. At the beginning of the decade, when sympathizers with Lenin's Third International took over the Social Democratic party, a small minority of moderate socialists under Léon Blum split off. By the end of the decade, however, Moscow's insistence on abject obedience reduced the French Communist party to a relatively small cadre of loyalists, while Blum's Socialists grew to be France's largest political party. Thus both France and Britain experienced the growth of moderate political parties that appealed to the newly articulate and educated working class. On the right, a number of xenophobic, antisemitic, and royalist movements cropped up, but they lacked the mass appeal to affect normal politics.

Two figures—Raymond Poincaré and Aristide Briand—dominated French political life in the 1920s. The two men had distinctly different personalities. The rigid and honest Poincaré provided his own stamps for his personal mail, which he scrupulously separated out from his official correspondence. He also understood economics better than most French politicians, although this did not lessen his strong feeling that Germany should pay for France's postwar recovery. As prime minister from 1922 to 1924, Poincaré ordered the French occupation of the Ruhr. When this move did not produce the desired increase in German payments but led instead to adoption of the Dawes plan that lowered reparations, he changed strategy. Returning to power in 1926 for a three-year stint, Poincaré stabilized the French economy by raising taxes and revaluing the franc, prompting one Paris paper to call him "Poincaré the Well-Beloved."

The flexible and suave Briand was more difficult to classify. An anarchist in his youth, he later joined the socialists and finally moved toward the center, although with ill-defined party affiliation. Foreign minister from 1925 until 1932, Briand charmed Poincaré and the national assembly into approving a policy of reconciliation with Germany.

Central and Southeastern Europe: Doomed Democracies

French politics looked almost simplistic when compared to the political chaos of central and southeastern Europe. In their ethnic diversity, all the newly established countries of the region differed fundamentally from France and Great Britain. The postwar settlements in eastern Europe on the basis of "national self-determination" in fact had created only one homogeneous national state—Hungary—and even that nation lamented the millions of Hungarians whom the Treaty of Trianon had left in neighboring countries. Only about two-thirds of the residents of Poland were Polish. In Czechoslovakia about one-third of the population were neither Czechs nor Slovaks,[5] while in Yugoslavia the largest ethnic group, the Serbs, made up less than 45 percent of the country's population. Greece and Bulgaria, heirs to the Ottoman Empire, attacked the problem of their diversity directly. In the 1920s, as a result of the Treaty of Lausanne that finally ended the Great War for Turkey, about 1.3 million Greeks from Turkey were forcibly sent to Greece in exchange for almost four hundred thousand Turks. A smaller exchange took place between Greece and Bulgaria.

Because of eastern Europe's ethnic diversity, many of the region's new political parties formed along ethnic lines. In Yugoslavia, for example, only the Communists were able to draw votes throughout the country in the 1921 election. Most other parties, whether of the right or the left, prefaced their names with ethnic identifications, such as the Serbian Radical party or the Slovene Populist party. Nonethnic parties elsewhere in eastern Europe multiplied within several broad categories: Christian (Catholic) parties; peasant parties; communist and socialist parties; rightist and nationalist parties; centrist, more or less liberal parties; and a large "miscellaneous" category. By 1926, Poland's thirty-three ethnically oriented parties complemented twenty-six parties based on other criteria.

Eastern Europe's heavily agricultural economy made peasant parties especially important. These parties, of which the Croatian Peasant party and the Bulgarian Agrarian National Union were the most important, pursued populist programs that favored improving peasant life in the countryside rather than industrialization. The Bulgarian Alexander Stamboliski, who opposed his country's entry into the Great War on the side of the Central Powers, was the most flamboyant peasant leader. Coming to power at the end of the war, he introduced compulsory labor service, made cheap credit available, and forced peasants to take out crop insurance. To him the middle class was a "band of

parasites," "bloodsuckers," and "lice and bugs that we kill in order to live." Not surprisingly, therefore, Stamboliski forbade lawyers to practice while holding office, censored the bourgeois but not the peasant press, and reduced instruction at Sofia University. His extreme anti-urban policies—at one point he threatened to surround the capital of Sofia with his Orange Guards and starve the city out—finally led his opponents to organize a coup and to kill him sadistically in 1923.

Despite efforts to join together in a "Green International" that would combat the communist "Red International" (the Comintern), East European peasant parties such as Stamboliski's failed to introduce lasting reforms. With the exception of the Romanian Peasant party, which pursued balanced industrialization policies when it held power for a few years in the late 1920s, agrarian ideology left peasant leaders ill-equipped to deal with the problems of industrialization.

Inexperience with democracy, proliferation of political parties, gridlock in newly created parliaments, ethnic antagonisms, and economic weakness led many East Europeans to doubt the appropriateness of democracy for their circumstances. Only one country, Czechoslovakia, remained democratic well into the 1930s—but even there the political system has been called "managed democracy." Czechoslovakia was blessed with excellent political leadership that transcended the dominant personality of Tomáš Garrigue Masaryk. As the father of his country, Masaryk enjoyed unsurpassed prestige, but the five major parties in parliament provided a second major force in Czechoslovak politics. Instead of destructively competing with each other, these parties collaborated. The Czechoslovak electoral system made this cooperation possible. In Czechoslovakia, citizens voted not for individuals, but for parties. Each party then received seats in the parliament in proportion to its percentage of the vote. Because each party always decided to send its leadership to occupy its seats, parliament remained quite stable. The leaders of the five main parties met regularly. "We have agreed that we will agree," was their principle, which they put into effect by assigning certain ministries to certain parties, whatever the current coalition. A Social Democrat always got the ministry of transportation, for example. This cozy procedure did not preclude political infighting or changes in governments, but it did make Czechoslovakia the most politically stable country in eastern Europe. Czechoslovakia was the only east central European country that did not outlaw its Communist party, which continued to operate legally, but without much success, through the 1920s and 1930s.

Politics elsewhere had a less benign tone. In Poland, General Józef Piłsudski established the first postwar government, led Poland to victory over the invading Red Army in 1920, and saw through the writing of a new constitution in 1921. But Piłsudski then retired from public life to let the civilians take over. By the mid-1920s, bickering

---

[5] Czechs and Slovaks are also distinct ethnic groups, despite the insistence of Czech leaders like President Masaryk that "Czechoslovaks" were one people.

THE HISTORICAL EVIDENCE

Democracy as Compromise

1927

Czechoslovakia was one country in east-central Europe in which democracy flourished in the 1920s and 1930s. It was a managed democracy, with the main parties agreeing to split up duties among themselves, but there is no question that the country's leader, Tomáš Garrigue Masaryk, believed in the principles of democratic politics. In this selection, he answers the vociferous critics from the right who sought to undermine democracy in east-central Europe.

Democracy, say its opponents contemptuously, consists of perpetual compromise. Its partisans admit the impeachment, and take it as a compliment. Compromise, not of principles but of practice, is necessary in political life as in all fields of human activity. Even the [most extreme] extremists as, for example, Lenin when in power, make compromises. The policy of cultured and conscientious statesmen and parties is not, however, to reach a compromise between opposites but to carry out a program based on knowledge and on the understanding of history and of the situation of their State and nation in Europe and in the world. . . . For the maintenance and development of democracy the thought and cooperation of all are needed; and, as none is infallible, democracy, conceived as tolerant cooperation, signifies the acceptance of what is good no matter from what quarter it may come. What is hateful is the readiness of puny, short-sighted men, without aim or conviction, to make compromise an end in itself, to waver between opinion and opinion, to seek haltingly a middle course which usually runs from one wall to another.

I defend democracy, moreover, against dictatorial absolutism, whether the right to dictate be claimed by the proletariate [sic], the State or the Church. I know the argument that dictatorship is justified, since conscience and right, reason and science, are absolute; and I am not unfamiliar with talk about the dictatorship of "the heart." Logic, mathematics, and some moral maxims may be absolute, that is to say, not relative as they would be if all countries, parties and individuals had a special morality, mathematics and logic of their own; but there is a difference between the epistemological absolutism of theory, and practical, political absolutism. The most scientific policy depends upon experience and induction. It can claim no infallibility. It offers no eternal truths and can form no warrant for absolutism.

Source: From Thomas Garrigue Masaryk, *Making of a State* (New York: G. Allen & Irwin, London, 1927), pp. 466–467.

---

among the many political parties reduced Polish parliamentary life to chaos. In 1926, when the Polish currency collapsed, Piłsudski seized power himself. Originally a man of the left, Piłsudski was a curiously restrained dictator who retained the trappings of democracy. He operated on the principle of *sanacja* (or "regenerative cleansing"). By this he meant removing the army from political influences, professionalizing state service, and reducing injustice. These imprecise principles contrasted sharply with the more aggressive ideologies of fascism, nazism, and communism used by dictators in other parts of interwar Europe.

In Yugoslavia, the fundamental problem during the interwar years—the conflict between Serbs and Croats—was the same one that eventually led to the collapse of that country in 1991. Having won the Great War, the Serbs believed that the new Yugoslavia should be a centralized state run from Belgrade (the Serbian capital), and that

their southern Slavic brethren should adhere to it.[6] The Catholic Croats, on the other hand, fearful of domination by the Orthodox Serbs, wanted a federal state in which they had authority equal to that of the Serbs. In part because of political errors by the Croatian leadership, the constitution adopted in 1921 put the centralizing Serbian option in place, leading to endless controversy.

Even if Yugoslavia had achieved political harmony, however, its leaders would have faced stupendous problems. They had to integrate four legal systems from the pre-1914 era, introduce land reform into a bewildering variety of local conditions, reconcile several currencies, and unify armies whose officers only a short time before had been

---

[6] *Yugoslavia* means "land of the Southern Slavs." Linguistically, Slovene, Serbocroatian, and Macedonian are classified as South Slavic languages, as in Bulgarian.

enemies. And this is not to mention cultivating economic growth, which the Yugoslav government never found the time to consider. In 1929, King Alexander, fed up with bickering, abolished the 1921 constitution, reorganized parliament, and redrew the internal borders of the country on the basis of river watersheds rather than historic boundaries.

Romania, Bulgaria, and Greece also moved toward dictatorship in the interwar period, although somewhat later. King Carol of Romania established his domination late in the 1930s; a military conspiracy took power in Bulgaria in 1934; and in 1936 General Ioannis Metaxas seized power in Greece. In the three newly independent Baltic states—Estonia, Latvia, and Lithuania—dictatorships were also in place by the 1930s.

The replacement of democracy with dictatorship in eastern Europe during the interwar period suggests that a certain level of economic and ethnic stability is necessary for democracy to work. The east European effort was only a first approximation of democracy, installed by leaders inexperienced in the politics of accommodation and supported by populations unfamiliar with the hurly-burly of electoral politics. Their tentative efforts received scant outside support. Despite France's interest in creating the cordon sanitaire, French businessmen ignored eastern Europe. Great Britain had even less concern than France.

The Weimar Republic was either hostile, as in the case of Poland, or interested in helping its own minorities, as in the cases of Czechoslovakia and Romania. It had no intention of coming to the aid of weak regimes. The Soviet Union, of course, did its best through small communist parties to unhinge the bourgeois governments in the region. On their own, buffeted by nationalistic passions, economically weak, and soon to face an aggressive Germany, the democracies of eastern Europe had little chance of success.

THE SOVIET UNION'S PATHWAY OF REVOLUTION

The Soviet Union emerged from its civil war in worse shape than any European power. The Bolsheviks had eliminated their enemies, put down the nationalities, and chased out the bourgeoisie, but they had ruined the country in the process. Soviet Russia entered 1921 with industrial production almost at a halt, bread prices more than ten times higher than the previous year, and dire shortages of even the most basic necessities of life. Early in March, the sailors of the Kronstadt naval station near Petrograd, until then Lenin's most loyal supporters, rose in revolt, demanding "Soviets without Bolsheviks." Just a few days later, Lenin opened the Tenth Party Congress in Petrograd to assess the revolution.

NEP at Work: Moscow's Smolensk Street Market
Lenin's New Economic Policy freed up small businessmen (called in Russian *biznesmen*) to "truck, barter, and trade," as Adam Smith put it. Their activities created bustling markets, such as this one in Moscow in 1921, shortly after the policy was announced. *Hulton Getty/Liaison Agency.*

The Tenth Party Congress was one of the most important political meetings held in what was soon to become the Soviet Union, and the last one until 1989 that featured fairly open debate. The congress faced two major decisions: what to do about the economy and what to do about differences of opinion within the party. In the case of the economy, Lenin admitted that the revolution had pressed the nation too hard. The party was not strong enough yet to impose a purely socialist division of labor, as he put it. Accordingly, he called for a New Economic Policy, or NEP. Under the NEP, the state would still retain the "commanding heights" of the economy, the heavy industries and large enterprises, but it would permit private ownership of smaller enterprises and land, welcome foreign capital, and eliminate control over agricultural prices. Lenin's purpose was not to reintroduce free markets, which were incompatible with the party's aim of controlling society, but to grant breathing space in which Soviet Russia could recover. The idea worked. "NEPmen," as the entrepreneurs and salesmen who took advantage of the new rules were called, fanned out through the Soviet Union. By 1926 recovery had brought many forms of production back to something approaching prewar levels.

Differences of opinion within the party, which the Bolsheviks called fractionalism, posed a more difficult challenge at the Tenth Party Congress. Brutal suppression of the Kronstadt rebellion, which the Red Army put down almost within earshot of the congress, raised no objections about mistreating the working class. No Communist questioned that all opposition to the party must be stamped out. But what about opposition *within* the party? How far could a loyal party member go in criticizing the decisions of the Central Committee, for example?

The specific battle arose over how unions would be treated: Would they provide independent input in organizing the economy, or would they become "transmission belts" of party decisions? When Lenin's compromise proposal incorporating the latter position had been adopted, he exclaimed, "We have had enough of opposition." The congress thereupon adopted a resolution stating that "all class-conscious workers must clearly realize the perniciousness and impermissibility of fractionalism of any kind, because in practice fractionalism inevitably leads to the weakening of [the party's] work."

Henceforth, anyone who criticized the decisions of the Central Committee was to be expelled from the party. The new rule enormously strengthened the hand of those in power at the center. Because all party members accepted the premise that the party was always right, anyone with a differing view had no choice but to submit. Later, Stalin would make good use of these provisions introduced by Lenin.

The Soviet Union, or the Union of Soviet Socialist Republics (USSR), a "voluntary" federation of Russia and bolshevized republics from the borderlands of the old Russian Empire, officially came into being in 1922. But almost

Communist Leadership
Lenin (center) , Trotsky (left), and Lev Kamenev discuss strategy at the meeting of the Third International in 1920. Joseph Stalin later ousted both Trotsky and Kamenev. Trotsky was exiled and eventually murdered in Mexico by a Stalinist agent in 1940. Kamenev was shot after a show trial in 1936. *Sorfoto/Eastfoto*.

at the same time, Lenin suffered a debilitating stroke, and his ability to control fractionalism in the party waned rapidly. In 1924, before the new state could get on its feet, he died. Leon Trotsky seemed poised to assume Lenin's leading role. Trotsky, a splendid writer and brilliant organizer, had managed the revolt in Petrograd in October 1917, created the Red Army, and drove the communist troops to victory against the Whites. Few equaled him in oratorical skill, wit, or energy. But Trotsky had not become a member of the Bolshevik party until 1917. Moreover, he was a Jew in a land where antisemitism ran deep, and he was not a particularly good politician. He felt, probably correctly, that his was the revolution's greatest mind after Lenin and that the revolution would not have succeeded without him. Incapable of lobbying for a position he thought he deserved, he awaited the party's anointment.

Trotsky's implacable opponent was Joseph Stalin, almost in every way his opposite. A Georgian of lower-class birth, Stalin entered into revolutionary activity as a young man and by 1912 had come to Lenin's attention for his reliability rather than for his brains. In contrast to Trotsky, Stalin was almost invisible in 1917, emerging only after the revolution to become secretary of the Central Committee, a job that the other revolutionaries considered tedious and beneath their abilities.

Despite all this, Stalin was a master politician. Over the next few years, he pursued three main strategies that ultimately brought him supreme power. First, he wrapped the mantle of Lenin around himself. When Lenin died, Trotsky was vacationing far to the south and could not return in time for the funeral. Stalin delivered a eulogy to Lenin phrased in the reverent style of an Orthodox priest.[7] Lenin, whose embalmed body still lies in state in Red Square, became enshrined as the holy father of Soviet communism, the almost mythical leader in whose footsteps Stalin always claimed to be following. Once Stalin could pin ideas on Trotsky that were different from Lenin's, Trotsky was finished. "Trotskyism" was by definition not Leninism, and therefore it became unacceptable.

Second, Stalin invented a realizable goal for the new communist state: "Socialism in One Country." Marxists believed that the socialist revolution, once it came, would wash over all of Europe, and then the whole world. In 1919 and 1920, this was not a completely unrealistic hope. By 1924, however, it had become clear that the anticipated revolution would not materialize soon. Trotsky nevertheless held to his position of "permanent revolution," by which he meant constantly working to bring revolution to

Europe. Stalin's more realistic idea made Trotsky seem utopian and impractical.

As a third tactic, Stalin linked the other main figures of the leadership together in shifting alliances to rid the party of fractionalists, which by 1928 meant expelling Trotsky. En route to this victory over his main rival, and in the year or so that followed Trotsky's defeat, Stalin eliminated or weakened his opponents to such a degree that by 1930 he emerged as absolute ruler—the vanguard leader of the vanguard party.

Stalin's success did not derive solely from his thirst for power and his talent for politics. The Russian Revolution had devastated the old social order, replacing it with young and enthusiastic revolutionaries who, fired up from their victories, flooded the cities and the party. Often these men and women were able but uneducated. Nikita Khrushchev, for example, future leader of the Soviet Union, could not read until he attended a party school at age seventeen. Stalin was crude, but the new people, many of whom he installed in party jobs from his position as party secretary, embraced the lack of intellectualism that so appalled the other revolutionary leaders. A social revolution was under way, and in the eyes of its rising new administrators, Stalin was the right man to run it.

The weight of the Russian past helped Stalin, too. Russia had always been an autocracy, as was the Bolshevik party. With no experience in democracy and an aversion to ambiguity in public life, Russians felt uncomfortable with pluralism. Even the intellectuals yearned for a strong hand on the tiller. Nadezhda Mandelstam, wife of the great Russian poet Osip Mandelstam, put it this way:

> What we wanted was for the course of history to be made smooth, all the ruts and potholes to be removed. This longing prepared us, psychologically, for the appearance of the Wise Leaders. In our blindness we ourselves struggled to impose unanimity—because in every disagreement, in every difference of opinion, we saw the beginnings of new anarchy and chaos.

Stalin's consolidation of personal power did not solve Soviet economic problems, of course. In the middle to late 1920s, two developmental strategies reminiscent of earlier Russian programs emerged. The super-industrializers argued that the Soviet Union should concentrate on building heavy industry, while leaders such as Nikolai Bukharin argued that a prosperous peasantry held the key to development. Bukharin's plans would have required the party to permit tens of millions of quasi-independent producers a certain level of free choice in what to produce and market—something that a party committed to planning for a new socialist future could not allow. In 1927 Stalin asked his economic advisers to come up with a plan for Soviet industrial development over the next five years. The Five-Year Plan was a new idea in an era in which businesses

---

[7] As a young man, Stalin (then known by his original name, Dzhugashvili) was educated in a seminary for the Georgian Orthodox priesthood. He was expelled after he became involved in radical politics.

THE HISTORICAL EVIDENCE

Lenin's Testament and Stalin's Eulogy

December 1922, January 1924

Vladimir Ilich Lenin was the unquestioned leader of the Bolshevik Revolution, but he had a series of strokes that began in 1922 and finally caused his death in 1924. Joseph Stalin eventually replaced him by creating a cult of Leninism and making himself its leader. He was able to do this despite Lenin's preference for Trotsky and the fact that Lenin broke all personal relations with Stalin before his death. The first of these documents come from Lenin's "Testament," or notes that he wrote prior to his death, while the second is taken from Stalin's eulogy of Lenin. Note the traditional religious tone of the latter, designed to appeal to ordinary—and still religiously oriented—people.

Lenin's Testament

Comrade Stalin, having become Secretary General, has unlimited authority concentrated in his hands, and I am not sure whether he will always be capable of using that authority with sufficient caution. Comrade Trotsky, on the other hand, is distinguished not only by outstanding ability. He is personally perhaps the most capable man in the present Central Committee, but he has displayed excessive self-assurance and shown excessive preoccupation with the purely administrative side of the work.

Stalin is too rude and this defect, though quite tolerable in our midst and in dealings among us Communists, becomes intolerable in a General Secretary. That is why I suggest that the comrades think about a way of removing Stalin from that post and appointing another man in his stead who in all other respects differs from Comrade Stalin in having only one advantage, namely, that of being more tolerant, more loyal, more polite and more considerate to the comrades, less capricious, etc. This circumstance may appear to be a negligible detail. But I think that from the standpoint of safeguards against a split, it is a detail which can assume decisive importance.

Stalin's Eulogy of Lenin

Comrades, we Communists are people of a special cut. We have been cut out of peculiar stuff. . . . There is no loftier title than that of a member of the party, of which Comrade Lenin has been founder and leader. It is not given to everyone to be a member of such a party. It is not given to everyone to endure the hardships and storms that go with the membership of such a party. Sons of the working class, sons of misery and struggle, sons of incredible privation and heroic endeavour, these, above all, ought to be the members of such a party. . . .

In leaving us, Comrade Lenin ordained us to hold high and keep pure the great title of member of the party. We vow to thee, Comrade Lenin, that we shall honourably fulfill this thy commandment. . . .

In leaving us, Comrade Lenin ordained us to guard the unity of our party like the apple of our eye. We vow to thee, Comrade Lenin, that we shall fulfill honourably this thy commandment, too. . . .

In leaving us, Comrade Lenin ordained us to guard and strengthen the dictatorship of the proletariat. We vow to thee, Comrade Lenin, that without sparing our strength we shall honourably fulfill this thy commandment, too. . . .

In leaving us, Comrade Lenin ordained us to strengthen with all our might the alliance of workers and peasants. We vow to thee, Comrade Lenin, that we shall fulfill honourably this thy commandment, too. . . .

In leaving us, Comrade Lenin ordained us to strengthen and broaden the Union of the Republics. We vow to thee, Comrade Lenin, that we shall honourably fulfill this thy commandment, too. . . .

In leaving us, Comrade Lenin ordained us to keep faith with the principles of the Communist International. We vow to thee, Comrade Lenin, that we shall not spare our lives in the endeavour to strengthen and broaden the alliance of the workers of the whole world—the Communist International.

Sources: Lenin's testament is from Rex A. Wade and Alex G. Cummins, eds., *Documents of Soviet History*, vol. 2, *Triumph and Retreat, 1920–1922* (Gulf Breeze, Fla.: Academic International, 1991), pp. 438–439; Stalin's eulogy is from Isaac Deutscher, *Stalin: A Political Biography* (New York: Vintage, 1960), p. 270.

Propaganda of the Komsomol Shock Brigade Soviet propagandists used military metaphors to encourage intensive work during implementation of the five-year plans. A "shock brigade" was supposed to be an energetic and dedicated group of enthusiastic workers who encouraged others by eagerly fulfilling the plan. The Komsomol was the Soviet youth organization, to which all teenagers belonged. *The Granger Collection, New York.*

committed to the free market did almost no planning. It was also consistent with the communist idea, transmitted from the Enlightenment through Marx, that human reason could comprehend the world and change it. Finally, it promised to satisfy the Bolsheviks' desire to seize control of the Soviet Union and thrust it into the modern world.

The first Five-Year Plan, set in motion in 1928, emphasized heavy industry, not agriculture, for several reasons. First, the proletariat, the class of the future, worked in heavy industry, not on peasant farms in the countryside. Second, the concentration of mining, transportation, and production facilities in a relatively small number of enterprises made them more amenable to direction from the center than the widely dispersed individual peasants. Third, Stalin was deathly afraid of Soviet weakness in the face of what he perceived as growing capitalist strength and hostility. Peasants did not produce weapons; industry did.

Bukharin's push-from-the-bottom strategy never had a chance.

The combination of NEP followed by forced industrialization based on five-year plans inspired both leftists and technicians in western Europe and the United States. During the 1920s, thousands of French, British, American, and other specialists came to the Soviet Union to build the mines, railroads, and factories that they believed would transform the huge country into a modern society. Western intellectuals, discouraged by the pessimism engendered by the Great War and what they perceived as the pettiness of their own politicians and middle classes, also found inspiration in the Soviet Union's gigantic effort to pull itself up by its bootstraps. Many Europeans saw the Soviet Union as a vast new experiment in economic and social engineering that promised a better world.

At the same time that some westerners were growing fascinated with the Soviet Union, the party was eliminating the last vestiges of revolutionary spontaneity in Soviet culture. The revolutionary era and the first few years of the 1920s were fertile moments in Russian theater, art, and writing. Painters experimented with new perceptions of light; constructivist architects proposed vast projects utilizing modern materials such as concrete and steel in new ways; filmmakers devised new camera angles and fast cuts in their rapidly evolving art. But as the party solidified itself through the decade, it took control of more and more elements of the arts, shutting off historians who differed with official accounts, infiltrating and then controlling the Writer's Union, and purging poets who did not portray Soviet life positively enough. Not by coincidence, by the time Stalin had consolidated his dictatorship, the party had squeezed all the remaining life out of Soviet culture. The party supported only "socialist realists," those who wrote or painted uplifting narratives in which honest and hardworking proletarians following the example of good communists joyously built socialism. Originality brought suppression, exile, and death. The long path of stagnation, which would end in collapse sixty years later, had begun.

THE REVISIONIST POWERS

With the exception of the Soviet Union, which remained isolated, the winners of the Great War sought mainly to regain stability and avoid another war. The losers had far less pacific motivations. Humiliated by their losses and unwilling to accept them, Hungary, Bulgaria, and Germany all nursed grievances. The Treaty of Trianon had reduced the ancient lands of the Crown of St. Stephen to the small nation-state of Hungary. The Hungarian government, which remained conservative but not fascist well into World War II, refused to accept Trianon as final, using as its motto "No, No, Never." The Bulgarians had lost Macedonia for the third time in forty years. A terrorist organization called the Internal Macedonian Revolutionary

THE HUMAN EXPERIENCE

Atatürk (Mustafa Kemal), Turkish Statesman

Names such as Wilson, Lenin, Churchill, Mussolini, Stalin, Roosevelt, and Hitler are familiar to people with only a passing knowledge of twentieth-century history. Atatürk (1881–1938) was no less a commanding figure of this century than those better known men. His accomplishment was to turn the remnants of the Ottoman Empire, the Islamic state that at one point stretched from northern Africa to Persia and as far north as Budapest, into a modern nation-state.

Born in 1881 the son of an Ottoman officer, Mustafa received the name Kemal—meaning "The Perfect One"—in secondary school because of his skill in mathematics. Proceeding through the Ottoman system of military schools, he graduated near the top of his class from the General Staff College in Istanbul. As a rationalist, Kemal involved himself in oppositional activities even as a student. Sent to Thessalonika in 1907, he joined the Young Turk movement, which only two years later seized control of the weak Ottoman government. On poor personal terms with Enver Pasha, the leader of the Young Turk movement, Kemal found himself relegated in 1915 to an obscure command of the Ottoman forces on the Gallipoli Peninsula. His resolute actions in the face of the dawdling Allied invasion was instrumental in holding the Peninsula for the Ottomans.

With the Ottoman defeat in 1918, the Allies occupied Istanbul and began to partition the empire. On May 19, 1919, however, Kemal raised the standard of revolt. At first without funds or forces, he quickly found support in old army friends. By the end of that year, he had articulated a program and formed a provisional government in Ankara. Early in 1920, when Islamic radicals took over the rump Ottoman government, Kemal decided that rather than supporting the government against the Allies, his task was to overthrow the Islamic state and seize power himself. It took three more years to defeat the invading Greeks, who at one point had come within artillery sound of Ankara; to destroy, with the help of the Soviet Union, the fledgling Armenian state; to put down the Kurds; and to persuade the Allies to accept his government. On October 29, 1923, Kemal, now known as Atatürk, presided over the proclamation of the Turkish Republic.

Atatürk was as much a dictator as Mussolini or Franco. He ruled his country through a single party, which entered into every aspect of Turkish life. But Atatürk had a different goal. Instead of stagnation or aggression, he pursued change. Completely secular, Atatürk refused to seek the restoration of old Ottoman lands, concentrating instead on creating a Western-style nation-state. He changed from the Arabic to the Latin alphabet, closed Islamic institutions, emancipated women, adopted Western law codes, and traveled the country wearing his fedora (instead of the traditional fez) showing peasants how to write the new letters. Promiscuous, a heavy drinker, and, in his later years intolerant of opposition, he nevertheless laid the foundations for today's democratic Turkey. ❖

Archive Photos.

Organization (IMRO) disrupted and dominated Bulgarian politics for much of the interwar period.

Of the losers in the Great War, only Turkey did not want to revise the peace arrangements. The Ottoman Empire did not collapse instantaneously at the end of the war, as the Austro-Hungarian Empire did, although it faced nationalist rebellion, foreign occupation, and Greek aggression. The man who overcame these disabilities was Mustafa Kemal, known later as Atatürk, or "Father of the Turks." By defeating the Ottoman remnants, suppressing rebellions among the Armenians and Kurds, and driving the Greeks into the sea, this brilliant officer created the constitutional nation-state of Turkey by 1923. Rather than lust after the non-Turkish lands of the Ottoman Empire that had dropped away during the Great War, Atatürk concentrated on creating a secular national state. He abolished the sultanate and the caliphate and removed Islam as the state religion.[8] He reorganized the educational system to teach Turkish nationalism; took control of the national economy, even introducing a five-year plan in 1934; and transformed the status of women by permitting them to drop the veil and even to serve in parliament. Atatürk served as president until his death in 1938, putting Turkey on the path that led it to secular quasi-democracy after World War II.

Mussolini Brings Fascism to Italy

Atatürk was a dictator, but one who sought to instruct his people in the ways of parliamentary rule by law. Italy's Benito Mussolini was also a dictator, but he led his country in the opposite direction, away from the liberal state toward the one-party totalitarianism that came to characterize much of Europe by the end of the interwar era.

Italy lost six hundred thousand men in World War I and spent twice as much on the conflict as it had over the entire period since its initial unification in 1861. For this sacrifice, it received an important strategic gain: the security of its northern borders. The peace treaties extended Italy northward to the Brenner Pass, and the collapse of Austria-Hungary left Italy bordering France, a small Austria, a weak Yugoslavia, and a neutral Switzerland. Instead of being satisfied with this gain, however, Italian nationalists insisted on extending Italian interests around the Adriatic coast. In 1919 the romantic poet and quixotic adventurer Gabriele D'Annunzio briefly seized the Adriatic port of Fiume (today Rijeka, Croatia), backed by a group of disaffected soldiers, dissident socialists, and radical nationalists. D'Annunzio ruled his new "state" in the most melodramatic fashion, providing in his black uniforms, theatrical posturing, and unabashed profiteering a model for future Italian fascism, although his reign proved short-lived.

But nationalist outbursts were not the only problem confronting Italy after the Great War. Inflation, unemployment, and agricultural depression created a climate of tension. In its level of civil unrest, Italy did not differ greatly from Germany, but in Germany a socialist president used the power of a willing army to defeat the revolutionaries and establish a viable republic. No such political will existed in Italy. Three parties—the Liberals, the Catholic party, and the Socialists—initially enjoyed the most public support. However, Liberal political figures from the prewar and wartime periods were too immersed in their long-standing machinations to comprehend the dangers threatening their fragile state. Internal divisions also wracked the Catholic party.

The Socialists proved the most vigorous of the three main parties. Although they split into communist and social democratic sections over the question of adherence to the Third International, even the relatively moderate social democratic faction considered ideology more important than practical goals. When the Socialists won a plurality in the elections of 1919, for example, they used their new power not to form a government in cooperation with the Populists—which would have been a stabilizing step—but to make revolutionary gestures. Worker dissatisfaction with stubborn industrialists also drove the Italian Socialists to be less accommodating than their counterparts in France or Germany. When owners in the metallurgical industry locked workers out of their factories in 1920, the workers seized the plants. This action marked the high point of leftist activism, but it only reconfirmed middle-class fears of revolution.

The Liberals who dominated the government proved completely unable to calm Italy's postwar turmoil. When peasants seized land over the protests of the landowners and the courts, the state retroactively sanctioned the seizures. When the lockouts and subsequent strikes paralyzed industry, the police stood by. And when armed bands from the right attacked Socialists in the streets, the government took a stance of "nonintervention." Unable to curb violence, unwilling to take strong economic measures, and incapable of asserting themselves, both liberalism and parliamentary government lost the respect of the Italian people.

Into this chaotic political situation stepped a violent new force: gangs of activists led by Benito Mussolini. The son of a socialist blacksmith, Mussolini taught school as a young man but at the age of nineteen emigrated to Switzerland to avoid conscription. Living as a vagrant for two years, he returned to serve in the army and then took up journalism. Mussolini considered himself an intellectual. Well read in the radical literature of his day, he was a committed socialist who, as a youth, had admired his fellow exile in Switzerland, Lenin. But Mussolini was more of an adventurer than a revolutionary. He preferred the superficial to the profound. Brash efforts to become noticed marked his journalism more than did reasoned argument.

---

[8] In Islam, the caliph was the civic and religious successor of Muhammad. See Chapter 6.

THE HISTORICAL EVIDENCE

Mussolini on Totalitarianism

1935

When Benito Mussolini introduced the term totalitarianism, *he meant it in a positive sense, as an antiliberal, anticapitalist refreshing of European politics, a turning away from the principles of the French Revolution. In the second half of the twentieth century, after the catastrophes of World War II and the imposition of strict Stalinist rule on many East European countries, the term took on a much darker meaning. In the selection below, Mussolini presents his explanation of fascist totalitarianism.*

In the Fascist conception of history, man is man only by virtue of the spiritual process to which he contributes as a member of the family, the social group, the nation, and in function of history to which all nations bring their contribution. . . . Outside history man is a nonentity. Fascism is therefore opposed to all individualistic abstractions based on eighteenth century materialism; and it is opposed to all Jacobinistic utopias and innovations. . . .

Anti-individualistic, the Fascist conception of life stresses the importance of the State and accepts the individual only in so far as his interests coincide with those of the State, which stands for the conscience and the universal will of man as a historic entity. It is opposed to classical liberalism which arose as a reaction to absolutism and exhausted its historical function when the State became the expression of the conscience and will of the people.

Liberalism denied the State in the name of the individual; Fascism reasserts the rights of the State as expressing the real essence of the individual. And if liberty is to be the attribute of living men and not of abstract dummies invented by individualistic liberalism, then Fascism stands for liberty, and for the only liberty worth having, the liberty of the State and of the individual within the State. The Fascist conception of the State is all-embracing; outside of it no human or spiritual values can exist, much less have value. Thus understood, Fascism, is totalitarian, and the Fascist State—a synthesis and a unit inclusive of all values—interprets, develops, and potentiates the whole life of a people.

Source: From Benito Mussolini, *Fascism: Doctrine and Institutions* (Rome: Ardita Publishers, 1935), pp. 9–11.

In 1912 he became editor of *Avanti* (Forward), the main socialist newspaper in Italy. But when war came in 1914, he split from the socialists to advocate Italy's entrance into the war in his own paper, *Il Popolo d'Italia* (The Italian People). He titled his first article "Audacity," and chose two mottoes for the paper: "Who has iron has bread" and "Revolution is an idea which has found bayonets." Drafted again and wounded by a mortar explosion, Mussolini rose to the rank of corporal, just as Hitler did. After the war, Mussolini claimed that Italy had obtained far too little in return for its sacrifices. He also concluded that capitalism, contrary to his earlier belief, had a long future if it could be purified and returned to health. Assuming grandiose postures and exuding confidence that he would be Italy's savior, Mussolini turned to the right.

Mussolini's first *fasci di combattimento* ("battle groups") formed in Milan in 1919.[9] By early 1920, *squadristi* ("action squads") made up of restless former soldiers and outright thugs took to breaking up communist rallies, beating socialists, and even killing opponents. One of the mottoes of the squadristi was "I don't give a damn," a formula that empowered the most violent strata of the community. Carried by truck caravans and mobilized by telephone networks, fascist squads would converge on a town, beat up socialists, and flee. One of their favorite "treatments" was to force a victim to swallow a large amount of castor oil, which almost immediately produced a violent case of diarrhea. Socialists and communists answered in kind, but the fascists were better organized and usually had the tacit support of the authorities. In Bologna, a heavily socialist city, the shooting of a nationalist figure during fascist-inspired riots in November 1920 provoked a wave of assassinations and killings by fascist squads, who seized control of the city.

Violence proved seductive to the apprehensive middle class, especially its youth. In the year following the Bologna riots, the number of fasci grew from 88 to 834, and membership ballooned from twenty thousand to a quarter-million. Brutality seemed a cleansing purification in contrast to the ineffectiveness of formal politics. The fascists seized on this mood, justifying their violence as the only way to "save Italy from Bolshevism."

---

[9] The term *fascist* comes from these first units. *Fasces* are a bundle of rods bound up with an axe in the middle with its blade projecting outward. They were the symbol of authority of those who executed magistrates' decisions in ancient Rome. See Chapter 3.

Late in 1922, with tens of thousands of fascists meeting in Naples and calling for revolution, the Italian government asked King Victor Emmanuel III to sign the government's order declaring a state of emergency and calling for the arrest of the fascist leaders. The king refused. Instead, fearing a revolt in the army and possible civil war, he asked Mussolini to become prime minister. Twenty-five thousand of his black-shirted supporters marched jubilantly through Rome. Mussolini himself, waiting in Milan close to the Swiss border in case something went wrong, took a train to the capital.

With only thirty-six representatives in parliament and constituting a small minority among Italians, Mussolini and his party moved relatively slowly to consolidate their position—appointing twice as many nonfascists as fascists to his first government, for example. In 1923, however, he changed the electoral law so that the party or coalition with the largest number of votes, even if it was not a majority, would get an absolute majority of seats in the legislature. This system gave the fascists an overwhelming majority of seats in the election of 1924. When Giacomo Matteotti, leader of the oppositionist Socialist party, objected that the election was fraudulent, he disappeared. When he was shortly thereafter found murdered by fascist thugs, Mussolini faced a crisis. He responded in January 1925 by asserting his authority as the leader of fascism, and vowed to put down dissent by force if need be. Italy turned toward totalitarianism.

The word *totalitarian* refers to the claim by the state, or more likely by a dominant political party, that it has the right and duty to control all aspects of society, even those that go beyond the political. Totalitarians want to eradicate the separation between the state and civil society, and make all public behavior political. The communists undertook such a project in the Soviet Union as a reaction against capitalism. In Italy, the fascists claimed to be pursuing a third way between anarchic capitalism and coercive communism. Using words like *renew, restore, resurrect, remold,* and *heal,* they claimed to be halting an age of decline and decomposition in favor of a new dawn of civilization. Mussolini did not undertake this transformation out of ideological conviction, as did the Bolsheviks, for he had no set principles and was intellectually shallow. His thinking tended toward romantic vagueness, as in his definition of the fascist state:

> The fascist state is form, inner law, and discipline of the whole person. Its principle, the central inspiration of the human personality dwelling in the civic community, penetrates to the depths and settles in the heart of the man of action as well as of the thinker: as the spirit of the spirit.

Action allegedly took precedence over doctrine in Mussolini's state. "Our program is deeds," he explained. And in his first years, he was an activist leader. He restored the eight-hour workday, turned a budget deficit in the postal service into a surplus, and, as Europeans repeatedly pointed out, made the trains run on time (at least the express trains that tourists rode). By 1929, he even settled the differences between the Italian state and the Vatican. The Lateran Treaty of that year rewarded the church for its passive support by creating Vatican City and paying the pope an indemnity for the lands taken from him in 1870. In Catholic Italy, support of the church provided Mussolini with considerable legitimacy.

But as time wore on, the principal deeds that his regime accomplished amounted merely to carving out personal empires for his followers. Believing the motto plastered on kiosks all over Italy that "Mussolini is always right," *Il Duce* ("the Leader") made decisions after only the most cursory examination of the facts. In truth, Mussolini knew very little about what was going on in Italy, where corruption pervaded almost every act of the regime. At the beginning of World War II, for example, Mussolini was surprised to discover that the Italian army still used artillery left over from World War I, despite the billions of lire that had been sunk into rearmament. Industrialists prospered under Mussolini, but industrial production stagnated.

Nevertheless, for many years most Italians took pride in the energy of their young leader (he was only thirty-nine when he came to power) and accepted the turmoil that his followers unleashed. One reason was that Mussolini, whatever his other qualities, was a great showman. He was the first politician to put modern media fully to work for him. Moviegoers thrilled to newsreels showing Il Duce stripped to the waist and wielding a pitchfork in the "battle for wheat." Radio listeners heard crowds wildly cheering his speeches, and newspaper readers were treated to countless pictures of a martial Mussolini with his lower jaw aggressively jutting out. Reporters wrote convincingly of his phenomenal memory (he liked to memorize statistics and spit them back promptly to impress his ministers) and humble personality. But like Stalin, who cultivated the same modest image, Mussolini in fact was insanely egotistical.

Italians found this political theater amusing and attractive, and so did many Europeans. If the Soviet experience excited a number of western intellectuals because it rejected both liberalism and capitalism, just as many found Mussolini's fascism impressive because it rejected communism and liberalism without wholly embracing capitalism. Countless prominent writers, artists, and politicians (including Winston Churchill) made a pilgrimage to his massive office to meet the man who, as the fascist propaganda never failed to repeat, had "saved Italy from Bolshevism." During the 1920s, it seemed as if these two poles, the left and the right, each of which in its own way rejected the liberal state, comprised the wave of the future. The revolt of the masses in the competing and yet strangely similar forms of fascism and communism appeared to be out-competing the principles of pluralism and the politics of accommodation.

Il Duce Flaunts His Authority   Benito Mussolini loved show and display, even to the exclusion of reality. Here, speaking in Rome in the 1930s, he tosses off what he considers to be an appropriate authoritarian gesture. By contrast, Stalin, who exercised a far more ruthless control over his country than Mussolini did over Italy, assumed the pose of a modest and unassuming leader.   *The Granger Collection, New York.*

Weimar Germany Experiments with Democracy

Paradoxically, given what happened later in Germany, the Weimar Republic resisted the communist and fascist tides of the early postwar years. In the 1920s, Italy was a former democracy turning itself into an autocracy; Germany was a former aristocracy reshaping itself into a democracy. Until 1923, however, the republic's very survival remained in doubt. Three parties—the Social Democrats, the Center party, and the Democratic party—supported the republic, but together they did not constitute a majority in the new Reichstag. Their various opponents, each of whom also lacked a majority in the Reichstag, despised the republic. The Communists yearned for a revolutionary state, and the "national opposition" dreamed of the restoration of a militaristic monarchy. Many among the nation's elite also opposed the republic. Not a few university professors lectured that "democracy was an essentially non-German form of political organization, suitable for the materialistic Anglo-Saxons, but incompatible with the idealism of the Germanic race." Judges leaned over backwards to favor antirepublicans. For the 13 murders of which left wing activists were convicted in 1919 and 1920, the courts handed out eight death sentences and 176 years of prison time. By contrast, in the cases of 314 right wing murders, the courts levied one life sentence and a total of 31 years in prison.

The right operated under several articles of faith. First, it nurtured the legend that Germany had not lost the Great War on the battlefield but, as claimed by General Ludendorff—who mismanaged the last two years of the war—had been "stabbed in the back" by defeatist elements at home, such as liberals, moderates, socialists, and Jews. Second, authors on the right claimed that Germans did not bear any responsibility for starting the war; rather, they said it had justly defended itself against encirclement by jealous enemies. In taking this position, they tapped widely held resentments over the "war guilt clause" of the Versailles treaty (Article 234) that blamed Germany alone for the war. Third, prophets of violence, deeply affected by their experiences in the trenches, claimed that the "front experience" of comradeship, discipline, and readiness to sacrifice all for a great cause provided a better model for Germany than democracy, parliaments, and socialism. As in Italy, violence was the byword of right wing radicals. "War is a necessity and a release," wrote the radical theorist Ernst Jünger. "In it the true human being makes up in a drunken orgy for everything that he has been neglecting."

During the turbulent year of 1923, with the French occupying the Ruhr and the mark almost worthless, right wing forces, especially in Bavaria, increasingly thought in terms of emulating Mussolini's "march on Rome" with their own march on Berlin. Whatever plans they might have been hatching came to a head in November 1923 when General Ludendorff, always ready for extreme measures, and Adolf Hitler, leader of the minuscule National Socialist German Workers party, attempted to overthrow the Bavarian regional government. Unrepresentative of the dominant conservative forces in Bavaria, this "Beer Hall Putsch" in Munich not only failed—it undermined the right's half-formed plans to emulate Mussolini. When President Friedrich Ebert of the Weimar Republic heard of Hitler's attempt, he placed emergency powers in the hands of General Hans von Seeckt, commander of the army. In essence he put the question to Seeckt: Did the army intend to side with the republic, or with the revolutionaries? Seeckt chose the republic, and from 1924 until 1930 the threat from the right receded.

The year 1923 brought another stabilizing event: the entry into the government of Gustav Stresemann, the dominant figure in German politics until his death in 1929. With the country close to collapse, Stresemann and his colleagues had little choice but to resume a policy of fulfilling the conditions of the Versailles treaty, particularly reparations. At about the same time as the Beer Hall Putsch in Munich, Stresemann's government introduced a stable mark and worked out the Dawes Plan, which set reparations at a manageable level.[10] By the Locarno agreements and entry into the League of Nations, the German foreign minister restored Germany to a central position in the European system. Although Stresemann was not able to reach a comprehensive agreement with French foreign minister Briand for settling all outstanding Franco-German issues, the relatively accommodating policies of the two foreign ministers produced the most stable period of international relations of the interwar era. In Eastern issues, however, Stresemann was much less accommodating. He supported Germany's secret program of military cooperation with the Soviet Union, and worked actively to promote revision of the Versailles borders. Stresemann had been a rabid monarchist during the Great War, but in power he proved a flexible leader and a talented statesman when it came to relations with western Europe. His unwillingness to act with similar foresight and suppleness in eastern Europe helped lay the groundwork for German aggression there ten years after his death.

COLLAPSE: THE DEPRESSION HITS

The stabilization of the mark, when coupled with Stresemann's policy of fulfillment, turned Germany into a desirable area for investment, particularly for Americans. During the second half of the 1920s, a curious circular flow

of international capital evolved. The United States insisted that France, Britain, and Belgium repay their wartime debts. In turn, these countries based their repayments on receiving reparations from Germany. In order to pay the reparations, Germany borrowed money from the United States to improve its industrial capacity. In other words, American capital came to Germany, which paid its reparations, which then flowed back to the United States. This system worked for a while, but European dependency on American capital markets contained a grave weakness.

On October 24, 1929—Black Thursday—and in the month that followed, stock prices on the New York Stock Exchange suddenly collapsed. The "crash" did not necessarily herald the end of American prosperity, nor the beginning of a major economic downturn. But the U.S. economy, which had boomed during the 1920s, had several structural faults. For one thing, no federal deposit insurance existed to protect savings. When small banks failed, as some seven thousand of them did in the 1920s, they undermined the stability of the larger banks. Corporate structures were also unstable. Often complex holding companies depended on dividend payments flowing through several layers of paper corporations that produced nothing. When dividends at the bottom dried up, the hollow honeycombs of interlocking companies faced bankruptcy. Businessmen and economists lacked data about the economy, for little of the economic information that government agencies routinely provide to the public today existed at the time. Moreover, the prosperity of the 1920s had been narrowly based on the upper middle class, not on that of farmers and workers. During a downturn the middle class curbed its discretionary spending, and the economy weakened. Misinformation and outright fraud abounded in the unregulated stock market. Finally, a good deal of stock investment in 1929 was based on borrowed money. A run-up in stock prices had brought waves of speculators into the market. When prices fell, their inability to make good on the loans they used to buy stocks wiped them out and accentuated the crash.

At first Americans optimistically assumed that the recession the crash touched off would pass. Early in November 1929, President Herbert Hoover confidently predicted that "all evidence indicates that the worst effects of the crash upon unemployment will have been passed during the next sixty days." But a year later, in November and December 1930, a rash of bank failures spread from the small towns in the south and west to large banks in the northeast. At the end of the year the privately owned but psychologically important Bank of the United States failed. Still, early in 1931 it seemed that the worst was over. But it was not. Starting in June that year, a run on banks, as desperate depositors tried to withdraw their money, led to a complete collapse. By 1933, investment in the United States had dropped to 10 percent of its 1928 level, and the

---

[10] Named for Charles Dawes, the American financier who negotiated it and soon became vice-president of the United States.

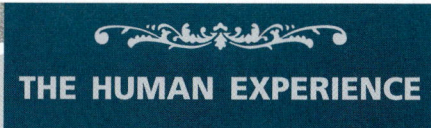

THE HUMAN EXPERIENCE

John Maynard Keynes, English Economist

England's most fascinating twentieth-century clique, if measured by the number of books and articles written about it, was the Bloomsbury group. Starting about 1905, a handful of friends, mostly Cambridge graduates who had been in the same secret society in college, along with their wives or lovers, took houses in the unfashionable Bloomsbury section of London. For the next twenty years, these writers, scholars, and artists constantly visited, gossiped, fell in and out of love with one another, and wrote. The novelists Virginia Wolff and E. M. Forster were part of the group, as was the artist Duncan Grant and the essayist Lytton Strachey. Not least among the group's members was John Maynard Keynes.

Keynes (1883–1946), the son of a successful Cambridge University administrator, received an impeccable upper-class education: Eton and King's College, Cambridge, where he excelled as a student. After a short term at the India Office, he returned at age twenty-six to King's College as a fellow, which meant lifetime employment as a scholar. Keynes quickly made his name as an economist and during World War I became an adviser to the government. His biting criticism of the Versailles settlement was only one of his jousts with British public policy after the war, when he emerged the country's most sought-after economic thinker. In 1926 he opposed Chancellor of the Exchequer Winston Churchill's decision to overvalue the pound. During World War II, Keynes was the main architect of the institutions, such as the International Monetary Fund, that today dominate international finance. Keynes's active participation in public affairs and his extensive writings on public policy were instrumental in turning the study of economics from the academic and theoretical discipline of his youth into the policy-oriented social science that it is today.

The question that intrigued Keynes throughout his life was how people make decisions under conditions of uncertainty. Given that one cannot know all the facts needed to make a fully rational decision, how do the ordinary mechanisms of economic interchange work? The most famous study to emerge from his highly technical work in pursuit of this question was *A General Theory of Employment, Interest, and Money* (1936), one of the most influential books written in the twentieth century. Among many compelling ideas put forward in the book was the notion of "liquidity preference." Simply put, Keynes suggested that the value of an asset is related to how easily the owner perceives it can be turned into cash. In other words, economic behavior is not entirely a question of supply and demand, but of confidence, perception, and anticipation as well.

As a young man, Keynes had pursued several homosexual love affairs, but in 1925, much to the scorn of his snobbish Bloomsbury colleagues, he married an uneducated but clever Russian ballerina, with whom he spent a happily married life. Keynes worked hard and though the watercolor here shows him relaxing, Keynes was not often seen doing so. In his spare time, he was a very successful investor, both on his own behalf and on behalf of his Bloomsbury friends. When asked near the end of his life whether he would have done anything differently, he answered that he regretted only not drinking more champagne and loving more beautiful women. ❖

The Granger Collection, New York.

unemployment rate stood at about 25 percent. The Great Depression had settled in.

What happened? Why did a cyclical downturn escalate into the worst economic disaster of the twentieth century? The main reason is that the U.S. government, along with those of other industrial countries, did almost everything wrong. At the time, political leaders and economists had only one model for understanding the crisis: the classical economics that had evolved since Adam Smith (see Chapter 20). By this theory, supply and demand would pull the economy out of any downturn. As soon as prices or wages sank low enough, buyers and employers would appear. Until then, conventional wisdom urged that budgets should be balanced, home industries protected by tariffs, trade deficits lowered by increasing exports, and the gold supply, which stood behind paper money, secured.

With hindsight, we now know that these were precisely the wrong things to do. In the 1930s, the English economist John Maynard Keynes (pronounced "canes") argued that during a severe depression no wage was low

enough to wipe out unemployment and no interest rate low enough to encourage investment. Market dynamics, he argued, related not just to supply and demand of goods or labor, but to the total amount of demand for capital, including government investment. The state had the power to increase *aggregate* demand by deficit spending—that is, by spending more than it received in taxes, and borrowing the rest through the sale of bonds. This borrowing would stimulate economic activity and pull the country out of depression. Conversely, Keynes argued, in times of prosperity the government should spend less than it takes in and buy back its bonds, thus slowing overheated growth. Keynes's ideas did not influence political leaders greatly in the 1930s, but they became almost an economic orthodoxy after World War II.

More recently, the American economist Milton Friedman offered a powerful theory of economic activity that has become almost as widely held as Keynesian notions. Friedman argued that the supply of money determines the growth or decline of an economy. (Thus his theory is called

Constructivist Art In the first few years after the Bolshevik Revolution many schools of avant garde art flourished in Russia. Vladimir Tatlin, for example, practiced "constructivist art," which sought to turn materials used in ordinary construction into art works that glorified the worker's revolution. He proposed this structure (shown in a later model) to celebrate a meeting of the Third International, but it was never actually built. *Hans Hammarskild/Moderna Museet.*

monetarism.) If governments keep the supply of money growing judiciously, they will stimulate stable growth. If they increase it too fast, they will trigger inflation; if they increase it too slowly, they will bring about recession or, in severe cases, even depression. Friedman argued that this is exactly what the United States government did in mid-1931. By acting to protect America's gold supply through conservative fiscal policies, the government killed the modest recovery of the first half of that year. Between 1929 and 1933, the money supply in the United States dropped by one-third, thus drying up liquidity, forcing bank failures, and ruining investment.

Whatever the reasons for the American collapse (and they are still debated by economists), it sent a shock of earthquake proportions through Europe. America's sudden reluctance to invest and its eagerness to call in its loans overstressed every economy dramatically. In 1931 the British finally had to devalue the pound and abandon the gold standard. Their already high unemployment rate jumped to more than 30 percent. In Germany production plummeted. By 1932 unemployment there had reached almost 30 percent. Searching for a way to increase its trade, salvage its banking system, and protect its investment capital, the German government proposed dropping tariff barriers with Austria, which would have been the correct step from an economic perspective. The French, who had so far escaped the most severe effects of the depression because of the soundness of the devalued franc, immediately objected. Still practicing the politics of power, they interpreted any step that brought Germany and Austria closer together as a threat to their dominant position in Europe. Partially as a consequence of France's intransigence, Creditanstalt, Austria's largest bank, soon collapsed. In 1932 a conference in Lausanne effectively ended reparations, in 1933 the United States essentially wrote off the European debts. But these moves came too late. Only ten years after the great inflation, Germany sank into severe economic depression, and the rest of Europe followed.

MODERNISM IN THE TWENTIES

The painting by George Grosz at the beginning of this chapter hints at the turmoil that swept the world of art and literature in the 1920s. We have already seen (Chapter 26) that it was during this period that modernists like Joyce and Proust hit their stride. But the shock of the Great War produced even more radical innovators, the most extreme of which was the Dada movement, founded in Zurich in 1917 at the height of the conflict. The point of Dada was that there was no point to anything. Poets mouthed nonsense syllables, painters assembled collages out of random materials, and satirists ridiculed every possible aspect of society. Less extreme, but still enormously energetic, were the futurist, constructivist, and rayonist schools of painting

Fritz Lang and the New Art of Filmmaking Motion pictures had an enormous impact on public sensibilities in the 1920s. Fritz Lang, an Austrian who fled the Nazis for Hollywood, was a master of visual composition. He produced many successful films, including his expressionist masterpiece *Metropolis*. In the 1980s, it was colorized and given a contemporary rock soundtrack. *The Granger Collection, New York.*

and sculpture, which tried to display sheer energy on their canvases or the dynamics of social movement in their sculptures. Somewhere in between were the surrealists, who, as their name implied, found ways to bend and transform realism into strange and confounding images.

On a popular level, the most characteristic art forms of the 1920s were graphics, film, and jazz. Professional artists turned their attention to magazine covers and advertising, bringing a new level of visual sophistication to formerly mundane endeavors. Motion pictures had been invented before the turn of the century, but they came into their own in the 1920s. Filmmakers like Sergei Eisenstein in Soviet Russia and Fritz Lang in Germany introduced new techniques that Hollywood quickly adopted. Stars like Charlie Chaplin became international celebrities, and investors built ornately decorated theaters to entice the crowds. American jazz, invented and popularized by African Americans, became enormously popular in Europe, where its pulsating rhythms seemed to liberate its listeners from stifling convention. Josephine Baker, a black American jazz singer who took up residence in Paris, became the most successful performer of her era, almost matching Chaplin in her fame.

Less obvious to the public, but no less important in its implications, were the innovations in the scientific world, particularly in physics. The discovery of radiation at the turn of the century had led the New Zealand-born English physicist Ernest Rutherford to propose a nuclear model of the atom. Building on this work, the Dane Niels Bohr suggested that energy of radiation was the product of a "jump" from one state to another. German physicist Werner Heisenberg constructed his principle of uncertainty on this idea: By measuring the position of an electron, which means introducing some form of energy into the system, we actually shift the situation we are trying to measure. We cannot know exactly where the electrons surrounding the nucleus of an atom are—only their statistical probabilities. To cap off these disturbing discoveries, the Czech mathematician Kurt Goedel showed that absolute proof of even so simple a system as arithmetic is impossible. Together, these discoveries, coupled with those of Max Planck, Albert Einstein, and many others, completely transformed our understanding of the physical world and laid the groundwork for the later unlocking of nuclear energy. These ideas and others, such as debate over the idea of an expanding universe, only added to the profound sense of disarray and confusion that peaked by the time of the Great Depression.

CONCLUSION: WORLD WAR I AS FAILURE

In a certain sense, World War I was an anachronism. As the European economies exploded in the second half of the nineteenth century, every industrialized country started to realize that international trade held the key to prosperity and power. However, the integrating tendency of the global trading system collided with the simultaneous flowering of nationalism. Whereas economic development called for lowering trade barriers and facilitating economic activity, nationalism demanded raising tariffs and seeking narrow economic advantage. The late nineteenth-century imperialist drive to create formal colonies suggested that the nationalist urge had more mobilizing power than did the desire for economic rationality.

On Austria-Hungary's part, World War I constituted an effort to eliminate a threatening nationalism on its borders; for Germany the Great War was a drive to defeat and dominate allegedly encircling neighbors. In both cases, leaders believed that the application of sheer power would solve both their internal and external problems. But the war showed that modern technology had rendered obsolete an old-fashioned victory of territorial occupation followed by a beneficial redrawing of borders. Once all the industrialized states became involved in the conflict, the strain of sustained war damaged every European combatant more than any possible fruits of victory could bring. Furthermore, the leaders of the Central Powers did not take into account the difficulty of maintaining their hold over conquered territories under the conditions of nationalism. This lesson was not as clear in World War I as it became later in the century. Nevertheless, the work of the Yugoslav Committee, the Czechoslovak Committee, and the Polish representatives showed that even if Germany and Austria-Hungary had prevailed on the battlefield, they would have had their hands full restraining the national aspirations of the subjugated peoples.

World War I, therefore, seemed to teach that the use of sheer power to establish direct physical control over the territory of alien peoples was no longer a rational goal. But the choices made after the Great War moved Europe precisely in the opposite direction. Instead of creating greater interlinkages, the European states reverted to confrontation. The Soviet Union interpreted World War I as proof that capitalism was in crisis and doomed to eventual collapse. Its leaders saw the liberal state as a worn out agent of bourgeois repression, not as a model for international development. Claiming that the free play of spontaneity characteristic of the market system produced isolated, atomized individuals, the Bolsheviks took complete control of all aspects of society. Their goal was to create "a new Soviet man," unalienated, fully conscious of his or her duties to society, and, not incidentally, controlled by the party. As a state, however, the Soviet Union had no interest in integration with other states, unless they accepted Soviet domination.

Italians traveled in a similar direction. Weary of the interminable political conflicts of the immediate postwar years, and contemptuous of their parliamentary government's inability to act, they too rejected the liberal state in favor of fascism. Ideologically vague, fascism, like Soviet communism, depended on the forcible conquest of society by a single violent element within it. In this way, both systems personified the Century of Power.

Even the democratic states, committed to constitutional and parliamentary government, refused to consider the possibility of working for a more integrated Europe. The French, smarting from the humiliations that Bismarck and his successors had heaped on them decades earlier, sought to turn the tables on Germany. Confronting Germany with the cordon sanitaire and keeping it weak through arms limitations and reparations, Clemenceau and Poincaré hoped to dominate European politics in the same way that Bismarck had done in his time. The British, focused on their colonies and their financial empire, withdrew from Continental affairs, except insofar as they concerned France and Germany. The main winner in the war, the United States, set itself apart even further. It not only withdrew into political isolation, but it pursued an economic policy that unbalanced European capital markets and made them vulnerable to the collapse that the depression finally brought.

In short, despite the many changes wrought by World War I, such as the creation of a democratic state in Germany, of new states in eastern Europe and of a Marxist state in Russia, most countries barely altered their approach to international affairs in the interwar period. The imperialist states, Britain and France, expanded their empires and ruled them with all the arrogance of prewar imperialism, although Britain did promise India eventual self-rule and created the Commonwealth. The new east European states imitated the Great Power politics that their leaders knew well from the late nineteenth century.

The continuation of these outdated policies reflected a general sense among Europeans that the golden years that preceded the war were far better than this uncertain present. Abandoning the confidence in progress that had marked the turn of the century, many Europeans now felt that the war had fatally undermined their hopes. Modernity suddenly seemed more a threat than a promise. Nowhere was this fear of modernity stronger than in Germany. There a deep craving for the rebirth of the mythic German community and for a restoration of confidence haunted public life. Unfortunately for Germany and the world, an evil presence waited in the wings that all too soon would take advantage of these phobias and fantasies.

Selected Reading

Sources
Kaes, Anton, Martin Jay, and Edward Dimendberg, eds. *The Weimar Republic Sourcebook* (1994).

General Works
Ambrosius, Gerold, and William H. Hubbard. *A Social and Economic History of Twentieth-Century Europe* (1989). Thematic history that sets forth the basic facts of its subjects with admirable clarity.

Berghahn, Volker R. *Modern Germany*, 2nd ed. (1987). This widely used paperback textbook contains a large number of useful statistical tables conveniently grouped at the back of the book.

Branson, Noreen. *Britain in the Nineteen Twenties* (1975). An engaging social history.

Wright, Gordon. *France in Modern Times: 1760 to the Present* (1960). Still a readable and valuable textbook.

The Soviet Union and Eastern Europe
Banac, Ivo. *The National Question in Yugoslavia: Origins, History, Politics* (1984). Original and stimulating history of the formation of Yugoslavia. Provides fundamental background to the wars of Yugoslav succession of the 1990s.

Fitzpatrick, Sheila. *The Russian Revolution, 1917–1932*, 2nd ed. (1974). An influential study showing the extent of the social revolution that was key in Stalin's rise to power.

Rothschild, Joseph. *East Central Europe between the Two World Wars* (1974). Standard political history of each of the East European countries.

Stites, Richard. *Revolutionary Dreams: Utopian Vision and Experimental Life in the Russian Revolution* (1989). Analyzes the richness of the early Soviet culture that Stalin killed.

Tucker, Robert. *Stalin as Revolutionary, 1879–1929* (1973). Provides a speculative but convincing psychological picture of a man to whom duplicity was second nature.

Economic Issues
Eichengreen, Barry. *Golden Fetters: The Gold Standard and the Great Depression, 1919–1939* (1992). Describes an arcane but fundamental issue in relatively accessible language.

Garraty, John A. *The Great Depression* (1986). Engagingly written popular history of the Depression in all the major countries.

Silverman, Dan P. *Reconstructing Europe after the Great War* (1982). How Britain and France, using the financial and monetary theories of their day, tried to cope with the economic consequences of a debilitating war.

Skidelsky, Robert. *John Maynard Keynes: Hopes Betrayed, 1883–1920* (1983); and *John Maynard Keynes: The Economist as Savior, 1920–1937* (1992). One reviewer put it this way: "a penetrating study, a moving love-story, a thought-provoking essay, and a kind of hymn to the role of creative imagination in social thought."

Weimar Germany and Mussolini's Italy

de Grazia, Victoria. *How Fascism Ruled Women: Italy, 1922–1945* (1992). How Mussolini's fascism promoted traditional women's roles in the name of building the nation-state.

Gay, Peter. *Weimar Culture: The Outsider as Insider* (1968). A rich essay on the intellectual and artistic life during Weimar, including the New Reality movement among others.

Mack Smith, Denis. *Mussolini* (1982). A thorough, knowledgeable, and quite damning biography of Mussolini.

Mommsen, Hans. *The Rise and Fall of Weimar Democracy* (1996). Balanced, magisterial study that is now the standard work on the Weimar Republic.

Nolte, Ernst. *The Three Faces of Fascism* (1965). Important book that explores the ideology of French, Italian, and German fascism.

Peukert, Detlev. *The Weimar Republic* (1992). Original, thorough, and provocative.

Sternhell, Zeev, with Mario Sznajder and Maia Asheri. *The Birth of Fascist Ideology* (1994). Controversial book arguing that fascism has deep roots in European civilization.

WORLD WAR II: THE CENTURY OF POWER BANKRUPT

Adolf Hitler
*Bundesarchiv
Plate #2-16-55.*

1929	Collectivization drive begins in Soviet Union	June 1940	France falls to German Blitzkrieg
1933	Hitler comes to power	Autumn 1940	Battle of Britain
1934	Kirov killed; purges begin in Soviet Union	June 1941	Germany invades Soviet Union
1935	Mussolini invades Ethiopia	December 1941	Japan attacks Pearl Harbor
March 1936	German troops occupy the demilitarized Rhineland	February 1943	Hitler's armies surrender at Stalingrad
Summer 1936	Spanish Civil War begins	September 1943	Italy surrenders
March 1938	*Anschluss*: Germany annexes Austria	June 1944	Western Allies land in France
September 1938	Western powers give Hitler the Sudetenland at Munich	August 1944	Warsaw Uprising begins
March 1939	Hitler seizes Bohemia; Britain and France guarantee Poland	November 1944	Warsaw Uprising crushed by Germans
September 1939	Germany invades Poland from the west, as Soviet Union invades from the east	April 1945	Roosevelt dies
		May 1945	Germany surrenders
		August 1945	Atomic bombs dropped on Hiroshima and Nagasaki
		September 1945	Japan surrenders

The debate over the origins of World War I began immediately after its end and continues even today. By contrast, few controversies cloud the origins of World War II. In Europe, Adolf Hitler consciously took his country into war in order to conquer territory and to eliminate what he considered his racial enemies. At the war's conclusion, unlike the situation in 1918, Germans could have no doubts that they had lost. After a slow start, the Allies, an unlikely coalition of capitalists and communists, utterly smashed Hitler's Third Reich and occupied a devastated Germany.[1] In Asia, a militarist Japan, seeking to extend its direct control over the western Pacific basin, attacked China and challenged the United States with its raid on Pearl Harbor. Four years later Japan too lay in ruins, crushed and occupied by U.S. troops.

World War I had left some Europeans craving peace, but it failed to diminish the forces of nationalism and imperialism. Continental rivalries continued to fester during the interwar period, and colonial empires emerged from the Great War seemingly stronger than ever. By contrast, Hitler's grab for power—twice as many people perished in the second great war as in the first, and property damage, forced migration, and economic disruption were far greater—soured Europeans on the traditional forms of international conflict. After World War II colonial empires collapsed and western Europe rejected the most blatant forms of nationalist competition.

In the decades preceding World War II, Realpolitik— the politics of power—was the standard principle of state behavior. Even with advances in democratic forms in Britain, the creation of a republic in France, and the creation of a socialist welfare state in Sweden, bald efforts to achieve domination through the exercise of power unrestrained by institutional constraints shaped the hundred years from 1848 until the devastating climax of World War II. The politics of accommodation and the principle of equity that emerged from Anglo-American experience and the French Revolution fell gradually into disrepute until both Nazis and communists specifically and emphatically rejected them. "The year 1789 is hereby eradicated from history," Adolf Hitler's propaganda chief pronounced in 1933 on the occasion of his master's accession to power.

But Germany's crushing defeat in 1945 discredited the politics of unconstrained power and reopened the door to the principles of equity and accommodation. Construction of the European Community in the 1950s, coupled with a Franco-German rapprochement in 1963, suggested that whatever its horrible cost, World War II had at least convinced many Europeans of the political bankruptcy of the Century of Power (1848–1945).

THE DESPERATE THIRTIES

The main theme of the 1930s was Hitler's march toward total war. But anxiety and violence marked the decade everywhere in Europe, and even in Asia. The Great Depression

---

[1] The first *Reich* (empire) was the Holy Roman Empire. The second was the German Empire founded by Bismarck in 1871 and supplanted by the Weimar Republic in 1919.

threw every developed country into social crisis, but the tension was not solely economic. Messy democratic processes did not seem fully capable of handling the tensions, whereas apparently dynamic programs of industrialization in the Soviet Union, military spending in Germany, and national enthusiasm in Italy seemed to minimize the effects of the Great Depression and to mobilize enthusiastic publics. In the long run, the democracies proved to be more resilient than those countries that experimented with communism, fascism, and nazism, but in the short run, it appeared to many that the democratic experiment was in danger.

The Democracies Face the Great Depression

The Great Depression began in the United States, and it was there that the most original, or at least the best known, efforts to cope with economic collapse took place. President Herbert Hoover's unwillingness to take drastic measures to stop the economic slide brought Franklin Delano Roosevelt to office in March 1933 at the depth of the economic crisis. In his inaugural address he argued that "the only thing we have to fear is fear itself," and immediately set to work by declaring a bank holiday[2] and bombarding Congress with reform bills. By 1935 his program to offer a "New Deal" to Americans had created many institutions that remain a basic part of American public life today, such as the federal insurance of small bank deposits, regulation of the securities industry, the Social Security pension plan, subsidies to farmers, administration of labor-management relations, and rural electrification. Many of these efforts were designed to maintain what was considered at that time a mature industrial economy, not to promote growth. Nevertheless, as long as Roosevelt spent money, the economy began to recover. When he cut back, however, recession returned, especially in the slump of 1937. Despite meeting with John Maynard Keynes, he never really accepted Keynes's view that recovery from the Great Depression would require huge deficit spending, so that by the start of World War II the United States still had 10 million unemployed and a substantially underutilized manufacturing capacity.

In Great Britain, the postwar efforts to maintain the value of the pound came to grief in 1931, when a run on the British gold supply led to the collapse of the government and the destruction at the polls of the Labour party that had been in power. As elsewhere, the ensuing British governments followed policies of strict economy, but the

Victims of the Depression   At the depth of the Great Depression, unemployment among German workers was about 25 percent. Here, exhausted and homeless workers pay a few pennies to sleep against a rope in a flophouse. This was called "sleeping on the line."   *Süddeutscher Verlag, Munich.*

cheaper pound created by going off the gold standard revived foreign trade, and lower interest rates stimulated housing starts. Nevertheless, by 1939 British unemployment had not dropped back to the already high level of 10 percent of a decade earlier.

France, in part because it had devalued the franc in 1928, managed to escape the Great Depression until 1931, but when the crisis hit it created one of the more chaotic political situations on the Continent. The coming to power of Hitler strengthened the French right, while the French left began to come together under Stalin's new policy of the "popular front," formed in 1935. In the previous year a rightist rally in Paris led to the deaths of fifteen demonstrators, and the contentious period that followed resulted in the election of France's first socialist (and first Jewish) prime minister, Léon Blum. Reversing the previous government's austerity program, Blum convinced industrialists to raise wages and attempted to introduce reforms looking a bit like Roosevelt's New Deal. But France's bitterly divided public could not agree, and the country approached 1939 with no clear national consensus.

The most sweeping and most successful democratic effort to cope with the darkening atmosphere of the 1930s took place in Sweden. The Great Depression hit Sweden hard initially, but in 1932 a government headed by the Social Democratic party came into office and introduced a comprehensive program of public works and agricultural subsidies that by 1939 had eliminated unemployment and raised wages. By pursuing a foreign policy program of strict neutrality, Sweden was able to keep itself on the sidelines of interwar conflicts. The success of the socialist programs and of the neutrality policy brought Sweden into the postwar era as the most thoroughly organized social welfare state in Europe.

---

[2] Unprecedented withdrawals by panicked depositors were forcing thousands of banks to fail. Roosevelt's "bank holiday" temporarily closed all banks until Treasury Department officials could examine their books. Financially sound banks were reopened; troubled banks were kept closed until they could be put on sound footing once again; and mismanaged banks were never reopened.

Stalinism and the Soviet Convulsion

In facing the Great Depression, the world's democracies had to cope with distressed publics and extremist parties who expressed their views publicly, with vigor, and in elections. This was not the case in the Soviet Union. There Communists claimed that Karl Marx had uniquely grasped the laws of human development, and that Lenin had provided the political formulas for translating those laws into effective action. For Communist party leaders, Marxism-Leninism was not merely one possibility among many sociopolitical theories. It was the only scientifically valid approach to transforming human society. They believed that through this "correct" understanding of the laws of history it would be possible for them to create something entirely new, unlike anything the world had ever seen. In the 1920s and 1930s, they set out to reengineer the human soul and construct "a new Soviet man" without inquiring whether the Soviet people were interested.

May Day, the Worker's Holiday   Soviet posters tended to emphasize happy workers building socialism. This one from the 1930s shows a happy male worker and a joyous female peasant combining to cry "Hoorah for the Proletarian Holiday, the First of May." The poster makes clear why the Soviets chose the hammer and sickle as their main symbol.   *Thomas P. Whitney Collection, Connecticut.*

In 1926, the New Economic Plan (NEP) came to an end, and the few consumer goods it had produced began to dry up. The following year, in the winter of 1927–1928, peasants began withholding grain. Why give the state grain, they reasoned, when there was nothing to buy in return? An enraged Stalin saw this as tantamount to sabotaging his plans for Soviet economic growth. He closed the open produce markets at which the peasants had sold their vegetables for cash and ordered the seizure of grain supplies. In 1929 he abruptly demanded that all peasants abandon their private farms and enroll in collective and state farms. Collective farms were huge enterprises to which the peasants "donated" their land and tools. Allegedly cooperatives in which the peasants freely participated, these huge enterprises were actually administered by bureaucrats following orders from Moscow.

Stalin called the collectivization drive "a test of our strength and their endurance." His chilling orders were that modestly prosperous peasants, called *kulaks*, were to be "eliminated as a class."[3] By 1938 almost all Russian peasants had been forced to give up their land and livestock to join collective farms, and the middle peasantry had indeed been eliminated. As many as 5 million of them had been deported to Siberia. Few ever returned. Additionally, Stalin intentionally allowed several million Ukrainian peasants to starve to death by ordering his administrators to take even the seed grain from their villages for export. Most of this suffering remained hidden from public view for a generation.

The main reason for Stalin's callous strategy was not economic, although he used that public justification, saying, for example, that the grain exports were needed to pay for imports of technology. Rather, gathering the peasantry into state-organized collective farms served the goal of simplifying central planning and political control, thus consolidating the party's—and Stalin's—authority. Economically, collectivization proved a disaster, in both the short and the long term. In the chaos of the transition, grain production dropped immediately, recovering only by the end of the decade. Livestock herds did not rebound until the 1950s. Poorly managed and listlessly farmed, collectives remained the Achilles heel of the Soviet Union until its disintegration in 1991.

Along with collectivization, Stalin pushed the analogous idea for rapid industrial development, the five-year plans mentioned in Chapter 29. As the system of centralized planning developed over the years, planning agencies imposed ever more detailed instructions for all aspects of economic activity throughout the country. No market mechanisms, which the Communists considered chaotic and irrational, would be allowed. The state—which in practice meant the

---

[3] *Kulak* means "fist," and it referred to moderately well off peasants who might have a cow when their neighbors had none. Quickly, however, it came to mean simply any opponent, or even a mere doubter, of collectivization.

Industrialization in Soviet Russia Despite the bleakness of this scene in a Crimean industrial plant in 1932, the Soviet five-year plans generated enormous enthusiasm not only among Russians but among many foreigners as well. The vision of a society pulling itself up by its own bootstraps was inspiring—until the failings of centralized planning became evident. *UPI/Corbis-Bettmann.*

party led by Stalin—would decide what society needed and direct the system to produce those things.

Despite falsified statistics, outright lying, economic irrationality, and enormous human suffering, the five-year plans accelerated Soviet heavy industrial production during the 1930s, perhaps as much as 12 to 14 percent annually.[4] But these numbers masked serious flaws. Stalin's excessive, even ludicrous, production targets, coupled with pressure to produce results whatever the cost, made the process hectic and brutal. Instead of encouraging innovation and initiative, the planners installed a suffocating administrative system. Business acumen became the ability to curry favor within the bureaucracy rather than to meet consumer needs, introduce products, or improve techniques. The state set prices administratively rather than competitively, creating wasteful inefficiencies and misallocation of resources. Failure to meet the plan's goals was considered treason. "Wreckers" might find themselves sent to a labor camp for dispatching a train ten minutes late, or for discussing a fish-breeding process with an unauthorized relative. Concentrated heavy industries were relatively easy to run by centralized planning, but the more dispersed sectors, such as light industry, housing, consumer goods, and agriculture, lagged far behind. In the end, the rigid centralized planning introduced under Stalin saddled the Soviet Union with a world-class heavy industry embedded in a Third World economy.

The dark side of collectivization and industrialization found a political parallel in Stalin's purges. This especially

horrifying chapter in Soviet history began in 1934, when an assassin, possibly encouraged by Stalin himself, shot and killed the party chief in Leningrad (today again known as St. Petersburg). Stalin immediately blamed "Trotskyites" and began arresting party members allegedly involved in antiparty activities. For the next five years, the Soviet Union endured a paroxysm of arrests and accusations unprecedented in European history. At first important party figures were targeted, but as the network of accusations spread, thousands, then hundreds of thousands, and finally millions of persons got caught up in the web of arrest, exile, and execution. Arrest constituted proof of counterrevolutionary activity. Being related to an arrested person, or simply failing to inform the authorities that one knew an arrested person, could land almost anybody in a frozen Siberian labor camp (called *gulags*, abbreviated from the Russian term for "state camps"). Prison cells burst at the seams, and labor camps overflowed with bewildered detainees, almost all of whom were in fact loyal citizens and sometimes even zealous party members. Estimates suggest that perhaps as many as 8 million persons were arrested, of which some 1 million perished. The Russian writer Isaac Babel lamented, "Today a man talks freely with his wife, at night, with the blankets pulled over his head."

Three pivotal trials in the years from 1936 to 1938 served as the centerpieces of the purges. In these proceedings, most of the old Bolshevik leaders—tortured by beatings, sleep deprivation, and threats to their families—confessed to outlandish crimes and treacheries. Chief prosecutor Andrei Vyshinski orchestrated the show trials like theatrical productions so as ensure the humiliation of former party leaders who had played any genuine role in the Lenin years. In the final bizarre act, Stalin ordered about

---

[4] One significant cost of this advance was enormous environmental damage. In their transformationist fervor, the Soviets saw concern for the environment as sentimental claptrap.

THE HUMAN EXPERIENCE

Evgeniia Ginzburg, Purged Soviet Writer

Evegniia Ginzburg with her son Vasilii Aksyonov, who became a prominent novelist.

At 4:00 A.M. on December 1, 1934, a curt telephone call summoned Communist party activist Evgeniia Ginzburg (1904–1977), a thirty-year-old teacher of literature, to party headquarters in her home city of Kazan. Later that same morning, Ginzburg was being asked about her responsibility for the murder of Sergei Kirov, head of the Leningrad party, which was the pretext for the beginning of the purges, and the loyal Ginzburg dutifully answered with the party slogans she had heard. But two months later, her former professor of literature visited her to apologize. He had been criticized for "certain errors in [his] treatment of the theory of permanent revolution [an idea associated with Trotsky]," and he was worried that her association with him

might harm her. "What rubbish," she thought. But that evening, the police arrested the professor and, almost immediately, party officials accused Ginzburg of not denouncing him. His arrest "proved" that he was a Trotskyite. Ginzburg resisted. Why me, she asked, when no one else denounced him? Was he really a Trotskyite?

For the next two years, Ginzburg tried to defend herself against the net of suspicion that closed around her. She even went to Moscow to protest, but to no avail. Her resistance only made the charges against her worse. In February 1937, the year that the purges hit full stride, the police asked her to come in for a chat of "forty minutes, perhaps an hour." Ten years later, she was released from the Siberian prison camps, and only nine years after that, in 1956, did she return to "the mainland," as the prisoners called it.

Transported to Moscow and housed in the infamous Butyrki prison after her initial arrest, Ginzburg was subjected to the "conveyor-belt" method of interrogation, in which the questioners come and go but the prisoner cannot rest. She had no information to give them because she had done nothing wrong. Finally a farcical seven-minute trial convicted her of counterrevolutionary terrorist activity (that is, knowing someone who had ideas analogous to those of Trotsky) and sentenced her to ten years' maximum isolation in

prison. Her first months of solitary confinement were difficult, but prison overcrowding forced authorities to give her a roommate, with whom she spent two years. In 1939, however, a general reshuffling ordered both of them to penal servitude in Kolyma in the farthest, coldest reaches of Siberia. Packed into cattle cars marked "special equipment," the prisoners slowly made their way across the Soviet Union to a transit camp. Stuffed into a rusted tramp steamer, Ginzburg then continued to Magadan, whence she entered the labor camps.

Ginzburg was resourceful. She suffered greatly from ill treatment, terrible diet, abuse, and cold (20 and 30 degrees below zero were normal in the winter). At the same time, she made friends and found ways to steer clear—at least much of the time—from jobs like felling trees in the frozen forest with inadequate tools. Eventually, she even fell in love with a prison doctor when she became a nurse.

In 1947 Ginzburg was released, but not freed. She moved a few miles into town and continued an extremely difficult existence until her rehabilitation in 1956 as part of Khrushchev's thaw. Her son, Vasilii Aksyonov, lived with her for a while in Magadan after 1947. Today he is one of Russia's most powerful novelists. Ginzburg's two books on her experiences are classics of prison literature. ❖

half of his officer corps shot, including all but four of his marshals, generals, and admirals.

Stalin purposely sent to their deaths more of his own citizens than any peacetime leader in European history. Despite the undoubted growth of heavy industry, his policies crippled agriculture, deprived the party of its experienced leaders, blanketed the country with a cloud of fear and suspicion, and decimated the military. Why? Part of the explanation lies in the character of Soviet communism.

Leninism provided a justification for authoritarian rule in the name of the proletariat. A centrally planned economy was probably unavoidable in the Soviet Union.

But rapid and destructive collectivization was not inevitable, nor were the purges. These sins must be laid at the feet of Stalin. The Soviet leader presented himself as both the modest servant of the state and the flawless leader. But these veneers hid a venomous hater and implacable opponent. A duplicitous schemer himself, Stalin believed everyone else wore a mask too, and that underneath even the most abject loyalty lurked a traitor. "Even wreckers can't spend all their time wrecking," he said, "or they won't survive." The brutality, the wanton use of force, and the abject, coerced confessions at the show trials all reflected Stalin's need to be right, to draw the mask of loyalty airtight. All dictators are driven by a deep need for control, but Stalin's relentless personal insecurity drove him far beyond any rational or productive measures.

Mussolini's Imperial Adventure

Mussolini was no Stalin. He and his party controlled the Italian economy, dominated the public arena, and dealt harshly with critics, but Mussolini confined his show to the drama of public life and did not indulge in mass confessions and packed labor camps. Nevertheless, by the time the Great Depression hit Italy almost ten years after his accession to power, Italian fascism had little to show for its vaunted policy of action. In 1932, Mussolini decided that Italy needed a diversion—as he put it, a demonstration to prove that it was "a fertile nation which has the pride and will to propagate its race over the face of the earth." He put Italy on a war footing and decided to add Ethiopia to his colonial holdings.

Italy had had designs on Ethiopia since the era of high imperialism, but a decisive defeat by Ethiopian forces in 1896 had thwarted those plans. After World War I, the Italians had assumed a "protective" (that is, menacing) stance toward the African country, and in October 1935, one year after manufacturing a phony crisis, Italian troops invaded Ethiopia. Mussolini characterized the attack as "a war of civilization and liberty, [and] a test of our virility." Much to the condescending amusement of other Europeans, the Italians at first had difficulty defeating the barefooted Ethiopian troops. By devoting some half-million men to the effort, however, Mussolini finally declared the annexation of Ethiopia completed by May 1936. "With the sword of Rome, civilization has triumphed over barbarism," he crowed.

The Ethiopian adventure revealed the weakness of the League of Nations. Almost immediately after the invasion, the League proclaimed Italy the aggressor, and within a month the League's council agreed to apply economic sanctions. But neither the French nor the British wished to alienate Italy entirely. By excluding coal and oil from the sanctions, they tacitly endorsed the Italian war effort. Because this was the first time an international organization had authorized sanctions in peacetime, forceful action could have constituted a step toward the international system of law that Woodrow Wilson had envisioned.[5] But the unwillingness of the powers to make any substantial com-

mitments in the face of such an obvious breach of the peace suggested that sanctions would remain a weak tool of international discipline.

The invasion of Ethiopia proved to be a disastrous strategic move for Italy, undercutting the postwar Italian policy of exerting influence in central Europe. Having secured its northern border by the peace settlement of 1919, Italy had pursued a protective policy toward the Austrian republic. In particular, it had taken a dim view of German interest in an *Anschluss*, or the unification of Austria and Germany. Austria never quite recovered from the collapse of the Habsburg Empire; the peace agreements had transformed it from the hub of a large multinational state into a small country with a huge capital, Vienna. Its prime minister in the early 1930s, Engelbert Dollfuss, was an authoritarian leader who secretly cooperated with Mussolini with an eye to turning Austria into a fascist state. In July 1934, a local Nazi paramilitary organization shot and killed Dollfuss during a coup attempt. In response, Mussolini mobilized four divisions and pledged to defend Austrian independence. Hitler backed off, disavowing the coup, and Italian security in the north was preserved. But the Ethiopian adventure, by putting so many troops into Africa, deprived Mussolini of the ability to protect Italian interests in the north. Ethiopia also proved to be a significant financial drain. Finally, and most importantly, the Ethiopian adventure cost Italy the support of France and Britain, forcing Mussolini to edge closer to Hitler. In October 1936, the two dictators signed a treaty creating what they called the Rome-Berlin Axis. From this moment on, Mussolini's Italy became increasingly subordinate to Hitler's Germany.

Civil War in Spain

During the nineteenth century, two political struggles had convulsed Spain. In the first, liberal and socialist republicans fought with conservative monarchists supported by the Catholic church, in the second, Catalans and Basques, neither of whom use Spanish as their native tongue, struggled for autonomy. In 1923, revolts in Catalonia and in Spain's North African colony of Morocco led to the seizure of power by General Miguel Primo de Rivera. Unable to generate the kind of following that Mussolini did in Italy, Primo de Rivera alienated not only the Spanish intelligentsia but even segments of the army. Economic collapse brought on by the Great Depression ended his regime in 1930. In its place, republicans and socialists came to power and promulgated a new constitution.

The republicans, dominated by the left, believed that the Catholic church was responsible for Spain's backwardness. Therefore their constitution separated the church and the state, nationalized church lands, and declared religious freedom. The republicans established state schools to replace church-run education, began to confiscate large estates, nationalized the railroads, introduced the eight-hour work

---

[5] In 1932 the League had branded Japan an aggressor in China, but had not applied sanctions.

MAP 30-1
THE SPANISH CIVIL WAR

day, and reduced the officer corps by half. They also granted Catalonia a charter of autonomy and began working on one for the Basques.

These changes were consistent with developments that had gradually been taking place elsewhere in Europe. But in Spain they came almost all at once, creating a pow-

erful backlash. In November 1933, a conservative Catholic majority was able to take advantage of popular anxiety and oust the left, but Catholic efforts to turn back republican reforms provoked even more unrest. Then in 1934 a strike by miners in the northeastern region of Asturias left three thousand dead, while a Catalan declaration of independence had to be put down by force. Finally, in the next-to-last swing of the pendulum, a coalition of socialists, communists, anarchists, nationalists, and moderate republicans joined together in what they called a Popular Front and won a decisive electoral victory in 1936 (see Map 30-1).

The nationalist right bitterly attacked the Popular Front, falsely claiming that the republic had fallen into communist hands. Answering the call of these nationalists, a group of officers led by General Francisco Franco decided to rid Spain of its republican reformers. In July 1936, Franco raised the standard of revolt in Spanish Morocco. Soon much of the army in Spain had rallied to his side. A cruel three-year struggle ensued, ending in 1939 with the collapse of the republic. Franco established a fascist-like dictatorship that lasted until his death in 1975.

Germany and Italy enthusiastically came to Franco's aid with tanks, antitank weapons, vehicles, and other supplies. The German Condor Legion contributed about a thousand airplanes, and Mussolini sent perhaps seventy-five thousand men to Spain over the course of the war. The Soviet Union countered these Nazi and fascist forces by financing some 35,000 to 40,000 volunteers on the side of

Picasso's *Guernica*   The ruthless attack on the Basque city of Guernica by German bombers during the Spanish Civil War horrified Europeans. Picasso's memorable painting of the event, rendered in black and white, hung for many years in the Museum of Modern Art in New York, but after the end of Francisco Franco's dictatorship, it returned to the Prado Museum in Madrid. Today, it is on display at the Museo Reina Sofía in Madrid, which built a new wall so that the painting could be shown in natural light.   © ARS, NY. *Museo Nacional Centro de Arted Reina Sofia, Madrid, Spain / Art Resource, NY.*

the republicans. The Soviets also sent about 900 tanks to Spain, which proved more effective in combat than the German tanks, along with a thousand airplanes and other substantial supplies. By 1937 Moscow communists had taken control of the republican resistance.

Nothing exercised public opinion in France and Britain in the 1930s more than the Spanish Civil War. Neither government wished to become involved in the conflict, in part because they perceived the republicans as being suspiciously communistic. The postwar ethic of pacifism remained strong in both countries.[6] In France, emotions ran especially high, because Léon Blum, the prime minister who supported nonintervention, was a socialist, and most people on the left believed that the democracies should act to counter fascism in Spain. Enthusiastic leftist volunteers from France, Britain, and even the United States flocked to fight on behalf of the republic.

The most haunting moment of the war came in April 1937, when 43 German aircraft from the Condor Legion dropped 50 tons of bombs on the undefended Basque town of Guernica and strafed the fleeing population, killing perhaps a thousand persons. This was the first time that aircraft had been used in such a brutal way. The massive destruction of World War II makes Guernica seem like a relatively modest tragedy now, but that is only because we have become inured to the horror of urban bombing. In the 1930s, death from the sky was something new. "No stretch of sky is nowadays devoid of menace," mourned the French historian Marc Bloch. Pablo Picasso commemorated the attack with perhaps his most famous painting, the black-and-white masterpiece titled simply *Guernica*.

HITLER AND THE COMING OF WAR

During the 1930s, political and military leaders in many industrial countries, chafing at what they considered the anarchy and chaos of liberalism and capitalism, established regimes of varying degrees of coercion and aggression. Many educated people who were neither fascists nor militarists sympathized with the rejection of constitutionalism, parliamentarianism, and the rule of law. Liberal irresolution in the face of violence convinced them that only extreme measures, either from the left or the right, could cure the maladies of societies in painful transition to mature industrialization. By the late 1930s, only France and Britain among the major European industrial states remained democracies, and in both countries many harbored doubts that this was the right course (see Map 30-2). Had Germany and Japan restrained their aggressiveness, their dictatorships might have enjoyed relatively long lives,

as similar regimes did in Spain and Portugal despite their flaws.[7]

But both Germany and Japan pushed beyond the normally elastic boundaries of international behavior. Germany provoked a general European war and invaded the Soviet Union; and Japan launched an Asian war and attacked the United States. Once those two vast powers were pulled into the conflict, the aggressor states had scant hope of fulfilling their overblown ambitions.

Hitler and His Party

Hitler came to power in 1933 legally, properly summoned to the chancellorship by the president of the Weimar Republic. Ever since the failure of his attempted coup d'état in Munich in 1923 (the Beer Hall Putsch), he had said he would take power only by legal means, and in the end he did so, albeit by a political deal rather than by election. But Hitler's entire political life was built on contempt for the norms of ordinary legality. Over the years, many contemporaries believed they could control him, that he would adhere to a program, that he could be satisfied diplomatically. They all failed to realize that Hitler had only one program: power without limit.

Much like Mussolini, whom he admired, Hitler discovered early that violence attracts. From the first years of his leadership of the National Socialist German Workers' party (the National Socialists, or Nazis), he always had physical force at his disposal. Early on, he could count on the *Sturmabteilung* (SA), the paramilitary Brown Shirts, to beat up Communists and Social Democrats. Later it was the *Schutz Staffeln* (SS) that systematically murdered Jews. The shiver of fear that Brown Shirt violence produced in the 1920s and 1930s thrilled many Germans. It gave them a feeling that something real was happening, led them to believe that the stress of change could be alleviated by striking out, and brought them into the Nazi camp.

Hitler supplemented his willingness to use violence with a crude political program. He believed that "the receptivity of the great masses is very limited, their intelligence is small, but their power of forgetting is enormous." With these cynical principles in mind, he relied on repetition of simple points unmodified by qualifications. The most basic of these was antisemitism. When Hitler joined the minuscule Nazi party in 1919, he quickly translated the crude Social Darwinism of authors such as Ernst Haeckel and Otto Weininger into a vicious code of ruthlessness.[8] "It is not by the principles of humanity that man lives or is able to preserve himself above the animal world," he wrote in *Mein Kampf* ("My Struggle"), "but solely by means of the

---

[6] The most famous instance of the pacifist climate in Britain came in February 1933, when the members of the Oxford Union, Britain's most important student organization, voted overwhelmingly that under no circumstances would they take up arms for king and country.

[7] In Spain, Franco's dictatorship endured until his death in 1975, while in Portugal António de Oliveira Salazar's regime, established in 1932, lasted until four years after his death in 1970.

[8] For Haeckel and Weininger, see Chapter 25.

**MAP 30-2
DEMOCRACY AND
DICTATORSHIP, JULY
1938**

most brutal struggle." In Hitler's view, the great historical contest, in which victory justified the use of any means, was not between classes, as Marx would have it. Nor was it between nations, although Hitler was a fervid German nationalist and sought to elevate Germany to the apex of European and even world power. Instead, the contest was between races—between the Aryans, which might loosely be translated as Germans and other "Nordics," and the Jews.

Hitler learned his antisemitism as a street artist in fin-de-siècle Vienna from the Christian Social movement of Karl Lueger, long-time mayor of that city (see Chapter 25). From a plethora of semiliterate tracts circulating in Vienna at the time, he "discovered" that the unclean Jew was the source of all evil in the world. In Hitler's mind, the Jew was a parasite, vampire, and despoiler of German maidens, as well as a contaminator of civilization. Hatred of Jews filled Hitler's mind from the beginning of his career to his dying day. When he returned to Munich after his service as a soldier in World War I ("the greatest and most unforgettable

time of my earthly existence"), one of his earliest political speeches—titled "Why Are We Antisemites?"—insisted on the "removal of the Jews from our nation." Only a few hours before his suicide in 1945, with Germany crashing down about him, he wrote:

> It is untrue that I, or anyone else in Germany, wanted the war in 1939. It was desired and instigated solely by those international statesmen who were either of Jewish descent or worked for Jewish interests. . . . Jewry, which is the real criminal of this murderous struggle, will be saddled with the responsibility. . . . Above all I charge the leaders of the nation . . . to merciless opposition to the universal poisoner of all peoples, international Jewry.

Hitler's other political slogans during the 1920s were as immoderate as his racial views. Germany, he complained, had been stabbed in the back by Jews and socialists at the end of World War I. In order to regain its rightful place in the world, it must not only throw off the shackles of Versailles, but create the conditions in which Aryans could exercise their rightful domination over the inferior races of Europe. Germany needed *Lebensraum* ("living space") for its people and resources for the flowering of its culture. East European countries like Poland and Ukraine provided the logical places for the expansion. Hitler was convinced that the populations of these lands were subhumans whose historic task was to serve German masters.

It is a shock to come across these ideas for the first time. Is it possible, one asks, that such crude and egoistic ideas could not only be spoken publicly, but could inspire a massive following in a civilized country? Hitler's racism tapped a sentiment already strong in modern Europe, but antisemitism existed elsewhere without leading to the Holocaust. In fact, prior to World War I, an observer might consider France, Romania, Austria, and Russia more overtly antisemitic than Germany. Why did Hitler's rhetoric inflame many ordinary Germans to the degree that they were willing to humiliate and kill Jews? Some suggest that a theme of aggression permeates Germany's modern history—that we can draw a line from Bismarck's destruction of the Concert of Europe through German war aims in World War I to Hitler. This theory does not account for the moderation of Weimar before the Great Depression, however, nor for the success of German democracy after World War II. Another suggestion argues that the idea of eliminating Jews from German society was so fundamental to German culture that when Hitler and his deputies legitimated acts against Jews, many ordinary Germans were perfectly willing to comply, even to the extent of killing Jews

with their own hands. Others have argued that Hitler succeeded because his regime embodied the ills of modernism, which include technologically enhanced violence and the ethic of self-interest.

Such questions to the side, Hitler rallied Germans in part through his magnetism as a public speaker. Had Hitler been a nervous or leaden orator, his mishmash of hateful commonplaces would have remained in the garbage heap where he found them. But Adolf Hitler was one of the great public speakers of modern times. Able to sense intuitively what his troubled audience wanted to hear, supremely confident in his ability to find just the right phrases that would touch each listener's emotional raw spot, a master of display, propaganda, and spectacle, and boldfaced in his ability to lie and accuse, Hitler thrilled his audiences and set them in motion. Rational argument was not what he was selling—excitement, movement, pride, power, hatred, and salvation were his messages, and no one has ever delivered them more effectively.

Crass though Hitler's political philosophy was, all observers concede that he was a superb and original politician, demonstrating perhaps that political talent does not require moral greatness. He knew when to act, and even more important, he knew how to wait, at least until World War II. He perceived the weaknesses of his enemies and found the right moment to move against them. At the same time, he gathered around himself a group of able assistants whose strange and evil talents he played off against each other to maintain his own power. The careless, foppish, sybaritic Hermann Goering was a loyal and at first even

Mesmerizing the Masses
One of Hitler's greatest assets was his immense talent as a public speaker. While he could, as a dictator, assemble huge crowds, such as this one at Tempelhof Field in Berlin in 1938, his passionate speaking style was hypnotic to many Germans. His effect was successful, not by compulsion, but because he struck sympathetic chords in their psyches by playing to their insecurities about the future and inciting their loyalty and patriotism. *Corbis/Bettmann*.

The "Aryan" Leaders An underground joke in Nazi Germany was that the ideal racial comrade was someone as slim as Goering, as blond as Hitler, as athletic as Goebbels (who had a club foot), and as handsome as Himmler. The four are shown together in Copenhagen. *UPI/Corbis-Bettmann.*

brilliant assistant. The clubfooted Joseph Goebbels created the most effective propaganda machine the world had yet seen. Heinrich Himmler, the mousy-looking fantasist, proved the perfect executor of Hitler's plan to rid Europe of its Jews. Around them swarmed thousands of others, carving out their areas of authority, their lesser reflections of Hitler's absolute power. And at the top, the *Führer* ("Leader") kept them all off balance, making sure that all the decisions in which he had an interest were in his hands.

Germans could not claim in January 1933 that they did not know what sort of man Hitler was. He had laid out his ideas clearly in *Mein Kampf* while serving a short prison sentence in 1924. In hundreds of campaign speeches, including many delivered over the new medium of radio, he relentlessly reduced all public issues to their simplest dimension, never hiding his contempt for the Weimar Republic, its institutions, and its principles. Still, Hitler understood that in the modern world, revolutions are made not against the state, but by using it. When he achieved power in 1933 and moved rapidly to solidify his position and to destroy the pluralistic institutions of German democracy, it should have been no surprise. But it was.

Weimar's Collapse

The gravediggers of the Weimar Republic were a group of conservative nationalist landowners, industrialists, and military officers gathered around General Kurt von Schleicher. Early in 1930, Schleicher had persuaded President Otto von Hindenburg, the popular but by now doddering and senile general elected to that office in 1925, to appoint Heinrich Brüning as chancellor. An intelligent and sincere leader of the Center party, Brüning did not possess a personality that could rally the nation in a time of crisis. His plan for restoring Germany's economic health, similar to those of the other democracies, was to lessen government expenditures and raise taxes. Today we know that these measures could not work, but Brüning insisted on putting them into effect even without the consent of the Reichstag. When the Reichstag responded with a vote of no confidence, Brüning, against the counsel of his civilian advisers, dissolved it in mid-1930 and called for new elections.

It is unclear why Brüning felt that a new election would produce a Reichstag more amenable to his austerity measures, when unemployment was rising rapidly and extreme parties were agitating in the streets. In any case, the Nazis reaped the most benefit from the September 1930 elections, increasing their representation in the Reichstag from 12 to 107 seats (see Figure 30-1). The Communists gained twenty-three seats, while the liberals lost heavily. Moderate conservatives barely held their own. The presence of the Nazis, virulently antisemitic, coarse, and opposed to the very idea of parliament, along with the increased representation of the equally antirepublican Communists, made the Reichstag—supposedly the bastion of Weimar democracy—its own worst enemy. During the next two years, Brüning ruled by special decree, without consulting the Reichstag. Austerity measures frustrated the electorate, the economy took an alarming dive, and unrest in the streets brought a rash of violent deaths. The Weimar Republic was coming unraveled.

In 1932 Hitler ran for president against the national hero Hindenburg. He lost, but he polled 13 million votes to Hindenburg's 18 million. Schleicher then convinced Hindenburg to replace Brüning with the foolish dilettante Franz von Papen. When the Nazis polled well in two further elections, Papen concluded that it was time for the conservative nationalists to make use of Hitler. But Hitler would not come into a cabinet just as a minister—he insisted on becoming chancellor. The overconfident Papen believed he could outmaneuver Hitler if the composition of the cabinet was right. Late in January 1933, he prevailed upon Hindenburg to appoint Hitler as chancellor. The new cabinet consisted of Papen, several strong right wing nationalists, and only two Nazis. "We have him framed in," remarked one of Papen's colleagues.

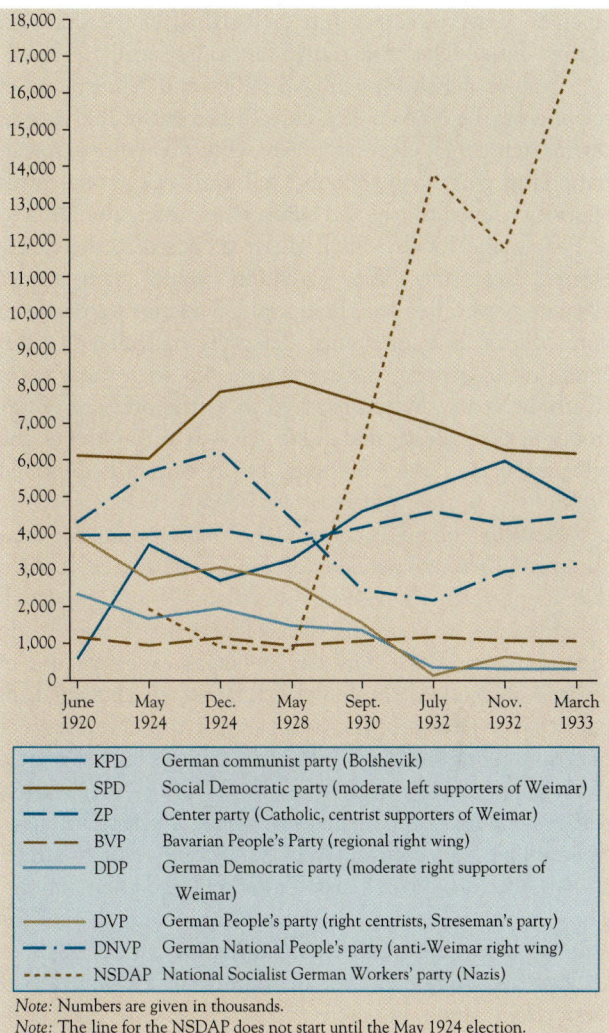

FIGURE 30-1
NAZI ELECTORAL RISE
Source: V. R. Berghahn, Modern Germany, 2nd. ed. (Cambridge: Cambridge University Press, 1987), p. 301.

The Hitler Revolution

Hitler's accession to power occurred in part because he knew how to wait for the right moment. Between 1930 and 1933, he resisted pressure from some members of his party to act. Once in power, however, he quickly threw off all restraints. As his first step he dissolved the Reichstag and called for immediate elections. Then he turned loose the Brown Shirts. Claiming to be "restoring public order," SA rowdies beat up socialists, smashed shop windows of Jews, and kidnapped for ransom anyone to whom they took a dislike. Shortly before the election, a fire, probably set by a mental incompetent with communist sympathies, gutted the Reichstag. The Nazis, blaming it on a Red plot, used this as an excuse to arrest four thousand Communist party members. Hitler then persuaded Hindenburg to sign an emergency decree suspending civil rights for the duration of the "crisis." The crisis turned out to last until 1945.

Despite massive torchlight rallies and harassment of opponents, the Nazis polled only 44 percent of the vote in the March 1933 election. Even with the help of other nationalist parties, this number fell short of the two-thirds majority needed to pass the Law for Removing the Distress of People and Reich, which Hitler proposed to the newly elected Reichstag. The legislation would grant Hitler absolute power. Because the Social Democrats were sure to vote against it (Communist delegates had already been carted off to prison), the swing votes lay with the Center (Catholic) party. When it caved in to the pressure of SA troops in the galleries and massed crowds in the streets, the bill passed, and the Reichstag, by its own act, deprived itself of any further influence on Hitler.

Now in complete control, the Nazis began to "synchronize" German public life. The civil service learned that henceforth "corpse-like obedience" was expected. Goering advised Prussian police officers that failure to do their duty would be punished, whereas excessive use of firearms would not. In July 1933, a decree abolished all political parties except the Nazi party, setting three years of imprisonment for anyone who tried to maintain or start a rival group. Every organization in Germany—from chess clubs to chambers of commerce to teachers' organizations—came under Nazi control. Workers lost the right to strike, and the Nazi German Labor Front replaced their unions. Those who objected to these measures found themselves sent to newly established concentration camps, such as Dachau, established outside of Munich in 1933. By 1939 more than three hundred thousand persons had been imprisoned as regime opponents.

While the party consolidated its power, Hitler concentrated his personal authority. Ernst Roehm, leader of the SA, was one roadblock to that end. Roehm believed that the SA should supplant the army as Nazism's military arm. "The SA is, and remains, Germany's destiny," he boasted in June 1934. Hitler had found the chaotic violence of the SA useful when he was out of power, but now that he controlled the state, he needed the support of the regular army, not a clamorous force of weekend bullies. Less than three weeks after Roehm's ill-timed assertion, and with the prior knowledge of top army officers, Hitler ordered him and several hundred of his associates and commanders killed during one bloody weekend. Shocking in its ferocity, but consistent with Hitler's drive for absolute power, the "night of the long knives" convinced the regular army generals that their position in Hitler's Third Reich was secure. After Hindenburg died in August 1934, they acquiesced when Hitler abolished the office of president and assumed the title of Führer. Elimination of the presidency removed the last possible center of independent power in the now completely Nazified state. As one Nazi theorist put it, "All pub-

lic power in the state as in the movement stems from the Führer's power. We must speak, not of state power, but of Führerpower."

The revolutionary restructuring of the country was painful—even fatal—to those whose organizations were decimated, whose jobs were taken over by party members, and who found themselves in opposition. But by 1935 Hitler's totalitarian thrust did not dissatisfy most Germans. One important reason was that Hitler's economic planners had pulled Germany out of the depression by unwittingly following a Keynesian strategy. The Nazi government spent billions of marks on public works, including the exciting *Autobahn* freeway system. Arms expenditures doubled between 1934 and 1936, and then increased even more rapidly. Germany also financed a growing trade deficit by borrowing money abroad.

These measures had an immediate effect. When Hitler took power in 1933, the German unemployment rate was about 25 percent among all workers and more than 40 percent among unionized workers. By 1936 the high level of aggregate investment had restored full employment. Real income increased only slowly, and many women were forced by economic circumstances to enter the workforce in low-paying and low-prestige jobs. But to many Germans who remembered the authoritarian era of William II as "the good old days," loss of their democracy did not seem such a high price to pay for a return to full employment.

Many others in German society, however, had less to be thankful for. Nazi racial theories extended not only to Jews, but to other categories of "undesirables" that might defile the Aryan race. These included the mentally defective, the handicapped, homosexuals, and the Roma (gypsies).[9] Eugenics, or the pseudo-science of producing "high-quality" offspring, had attracted popular attention throughout the developed world in the 1920s, but Nazi eugenicists pushed the theory of positive breeding to an extreme. In June 1933, immediately after coming to power, they ordered health workers to report clients with defects considered hereditary, such as deafness, schizophrenia, or manic depression, as well as mental and physical deformities. Panels of doctors who considered these reports usually recommended vasectomy for the men and tubal ligation for the women. More than three hundred thousand persons were sterilized between 1934 and 1939 through this process.[10] In time, Nazi racial cleansing became increasingly radical. By the end of the 1930s, sterilization gave way to euthanasia,

---

[9] The Roma (many of whom speak their own language called Romany) consider the term *gypsy* an ethnic slur because it links them to a slang word for cheating.

[10] For comparison, thirty state governments in the United States, with laws not too dissimilar to those in Germany, sterilized eleven thousand persons between 1900 and 1930.

by which almost one hundred thousand afflicted persons met their deaths. When the war broke out and death camps proliferated, Nazi doctors even conducted hideous medical "experiments" on selected prisoners.[11]

Nazi racial policies had a distinct effect on women. Following Weininger, Hitler believed that both sexes should pursue those endeavors for which nature best suited them—men the creative work; women the nurturing. The slogan *"Kinder, Küche, und Kirche"* ("Children, Kitchen, and Church") summed up the Nazi program. German women were to select genetically healthy mates and have as many children as possible. Paradoxically, while Nazi policy pushed women out of political life, it simultaneously offered them increased opportunities as educators, community organizers, health workers, and similar stereotypically feminine professions.

Jews suffered most from Hitler's racial theories. Two months after coming to power, the Nazis organized their first boycott of Jewish shops. "Germans Defend Yourselves!" posters blared. "Don't Buy from Jews!" The regime continually compressed the space in which Jews could act. Jewish civil servants were fired, lawyers barred from practice, doctors removed from the national health plan, children excluded from higher education, and civil rights denied. No level of pettiness was considered too extreme. Authorities renamed streets that had been named after German heroes of Jewish origin, and even banned Jews from owning carrier pigeons. "Aryans" began to take over Jewish businesses and to dismiss Jewish employees. On the night of November 9, 1938, mobs of rioters incited over the radio by Goebbels burned and dynamited synagogues, destroyed seven thousand Jewish businesses, murdered about a hundred Jews, and tormented thousands more. Authorities arrested thirty thousand Jewish men during and just after this *Kristallnacht* ("Crystal Night," after the broken glass). The government then required the Jewish community to remit a monstrous fine of one billion Reichsmarks and pay for the damages done by the Nazi thugs.

These outrages no longer derived from the medieval notion that Judaism was a religion and a culture, but rather from the "scientific" view that Jewishness was an undesirable genetic inheritance. In November 1935, authorities decreed that anyone with one Jewish grandparent was Jewish and therefore ineligible for citizenship. Jews so defined became merely "subjects of the state," forbidden to marry non-Jews or to have sexual intercourse with them. To the Nazis, no amount of cultural assimilation or religious conversion could wipe out the stain of racial impurity. The only way to rid Germany of the blemish would be to dispose of the Jews entirely.

---

[11] The Japanese conducted similar, even more bizarre, experiments on living persons, usually Chinese and Koreans.

Warning Off Jews   The street sign in this typical German small town says "Jews not wanted in this town." The signage, attitudes, and unmitigated display of open prejudice is, in many ways, reminiscent of those in America's southern streets and towns prior to the civil rights legislation in the 60s that banned such displays and provided greater protections to minorities.   *Hulton Getty/Liaison Agency.*

Many Jews fled persecution by emigrating. Albert Einstein was only the most prominent among the tens of thousands of Jews who left Germany and Austria in the 1930s. Many of these came to the United States, even though the American public strongly resisted admitting significant numbers of Jewish refugees. Nevertheless, the large number of European intellectuals and scientists that came from Europe to the United States in the 1930s and 1940s was one of the foundations of the postwar American emergence as the dominant global power. It lifted the United States from being an awkward provincial on the edge of European culture to intellectual leadership of Western civilization.

But most Jews refused to leave. They found it hard to believe what was happening to them. Jews were loyal Germans, after all. Some 35,000 of them had received decorations for bravery during the Great War, and most, with the exception of newly arrived refugees from eastern Europe, were well assimilated to German culture.

No German citizen could be unaware of the Nazi actions against these dedicated citizens, but few protested. Protestant and Catholic leaders, despite their justified fears of Hitler's anti-Christian views, never explicitly condemned the Nazi program of eliminating Jews from Germany, although they did protest, for example, Hitler's euthanasia schemes. Churches sometimes even distanced themselves from Jews who had converted to their faith, thereby accepting Nazi racial definitions. By its dehumanizing policies toward Jews, the regime successfully dissolved the bonds of sympathy that had held German society together. Fear played a part in this collapse of social cohesion—one could be sent to Dachau or worse for questioning the Nazis' racial policies. But in general, the police did not find it difficult to obtain information from citizens about Jews in hiding, and tens of thousands of Germans willingly occupied vacated Jewish flats or took over formerly Jewish businesses. Most Germans, more or less satisfied with the way Germany was developing under Hitler, decided simply to avert their gaze.

Germany Attacks Europe

Many Germans felt better about themselves under Hitler because of his aggressive foreign policy. For a country still smarting from losing the Great War, Hitler's successes in the 1930s generated a sense of pride and justification. Historians have long discussed Hitler's designs. Did he pursue a roughly outlined plan based on ridding Europe of Jews and seizing living space for Germans, ideas he outlined in *Mein Kampf*? Or did the chaotic decision making of his rule lead to a radicalization of the Nazi regime? It is not necessary to make an either-or decision on the matter. Hitler craved power, hated Jews, and sought conquest, but both he and his regime acted in an international context that permitted these ideas to mature into ever more extreme measures.

Hitler's first strategic priority after coming to power was to rearm. By disingenuously claiming that Germany would disarm completely if the other powers would do the same, Hitler made it seem that France and Britain were the ones standing in the way of peace in Europe. When the

other powers rejected his transparent ploy, Hitler withdrew from a disarmament conference that had been meeting since 1932. Soon, accusing the League of Nations of trying to keep Germany down, Hitler quit that organization too. A nationwide plebiscite overwhelmingly approved.

As his next step in these early diplomatic moves, Hitler signed a nonaggression treaty with Poland, thus breaching the French security system in eastern Europe. Freed from lingering international restrictions, in March 1935 Hitler renounced the disarmament clauses of the Treaty of Versailles and announced a rapid arms buildup.

As discussed in Chapter 29, French armies in 1923 invaded the Ruhr when Germany defaulted on reparations payments. But now, when Germany (having made no reparations payments since their suspension in 1931) repudiated the Versailles treaty and openly began to re-arm, France, Britain, and Italy did almost nothing. In 1935 their representatives met in the Italian lake resort of Stresa and declared their firm intention to support the Locarno agreements that guaranteed France's border. The League of Nations discussed what it might do the next time a power did not fulfill its obligations. But Hitler, sensing the deep longing for peace among the French and British public, calmed public opinion by speaking convincingly of his love of peace. At the same time he plucked Britain from the united front by offering it an advantageous naval treaty. Always mixing his aggressive moves with counterproposals stressing peace, Hitler kept the western powers off balance.

One country had changed its mind about Hitler, and that was the Soviet Union. Before 1933 Stalin had not considered Hitler and the Nazis a serious threat. Indeed, he had directed the Communist parties in Europe to attack the Social Democrats even more actively than they did the Nazis. After Hitler demonstrated his vigor, however, Stalin saw him in a new light. In 1935 the Comintern ordered Communist parties to stop their assaults on Social Democrats and to join them and others in an antifascist "popular front" to gain power through the electoral process. Such coalitions actually came to power briefly in Spain and France. Stalin also tried to shore up his security in eastern Europe by signing mutual-defense agreements with France and Czechoslovakia.

Such efforts did not impress Hitler. In March 1936, in his most daring move to date, he moved a contingent of German troops into the demilitarized zone of the Rhineland (see Map 30-3). According to the Locarno agreements, violating the Versailles treaty in this way justified a military response by France and its allies. Hitler's generals knew that they would have to withdraw if France mobilized to prevent the occupation, because France was still much stronger than Germany. But Hitler, observing the disarray and defeatism that characterized France in the 1930s, pushed ahead. Once again mixing velvet with iron, he simultaneously offered the western Europeans vague new arrangements that, he claimed, would guarantee the

**MAP 30-3
HITLER'S PEACETIME
GAINS**

Legend:
- Germany in 1935
- Rhineland, remilitarized 1936
- Saar, regained by plebiscite, 1936
- Austria, *Anschluss*, March 1938
- Sudetenland, annexed October 1938
- Bohemia and Moravia, German "protectorate" March 1939
- Memel, annexed March 1939
- Hungary in 1937
- Annexed by Hungary, fall 1938
- Annexed by Hungary, March 1939
- Slovakia, German satellite state, March 1939
- Annexed by Poland, fall 1938

peace. Hitler's gambit worked. The French, between governments, unable to agree on how to respond, and weakened by pacifism and bitter memories of the Great War, did nothing. Thus passed what many analysts believe was the last opportunity to stop Hitler short of a European war.

The occupation of the Rhineland particularly frightened governments in eastern and central Europe. If France was not willing to respond to an obvious and illegal threat to the security of its own borders, they asked themselves, how likely was it to defend its allies in eastern Europe? Capitalizing on this unease, Hitler introduced a creative economic policy to attract the east Europeans. The German economy still depended heavily on imports, despite the successes of crash programs to develop synthetics. Whereas west European businessmen dealt with east Europeans on the basis of normal business arrangements (full payment, market-rate loans), Hitler gave east European exporters preferential prices and cheap credit. Westerners scoffed that Germany paid in Marks, which the east Europeans could only spend in Germany. But the east Europeans, sunk in economic depression, were happy to find any outlet for their products. By the start of World War II, Germany was the most substantial trading partner of every eastern European country.

While occupying the Rhineland and attracting the nations of eastern Europe through his economic plan, Hitler turned his attention to Austria. Austria had posed a special problem for German nationalism since at least the revolutions of 1848—but as long as the Habsburg Empire survived, its chances of being included in greater Germany were slim. In 1931 France had stopped an Austro-German

customs union, and in 1934 Mussolini had forced Hitler to back off from an abortive Nazi coup in Vienna. But Hitler's successes of 1935 and 1936—and Mussolini's fateful decision to join rather than continue opposing him—now opened the way for unifying the two German-speaking lands (the *Anschluss*). Early in 1938 Hitler turned up the heat on Austria. He bullied the Austrian chancellor, demanded that he admit Nazis to his cabinet, and blatantly interfered in Austrian politics. When in March 1938 Hitler threatened to invade, the Austrian government capitulated, named a Nazi as chancellor, and invited German troops to enter the country. Enthusiastic crowds lined the streets to cheer Hitler's triumphal visit to Vienna, and the new Nazi government set about systematically enforcing the Führer's racial laws.

Hitler used force and pressure to subdue Austria, but he justified the act with a principle that Wilsonian liberals could readily understand—the right of national self-determination. Why should not German-speakers all live in the same country if they wished? But late in March 1938, he asserted that all the Germans living in the border regions of Czechoslovakia (the Sudetenland) should be included in Germany as well. The western powers balked. Britain put its fleet on alert, as the French did their army, and Hitler temporarily retreated. In September, however, he raised the issue again. The Czechoslovak government did everything it could to appease the Sudeten Germans, but the local Nazis, acting on Hitler's instructions, met each concession with more demands. The British prime minister Neville Chamberlain made two trips to visit Hitler in Germany, hoping to find a solution, but nothing

THE HISTORICAL EVIDENCE

Hitler's Plans for War

1937

In 1937, Adolf Hitler met with high-ranking officials and discussed his plans for going to war by at least 1943. The notes from that monologue are called the Hossbach Memorandum from the name of the underling who transcribed them. Cases 2 and 3, which called for absorbing Austria and Czechoslovakia, are not included here.

[Hitler] wished to explain to the gentlemen present his basic ideas concerning the opportunities for the development of our position in the field of foreign affairs and its requirements, and he asked, in the interests of a long-term German policy, that his exposition be regarded, in the event of his death, as his last will and testament.

The Führer then continued:

The aim of German policy was to make secure and to preserve the racial community [*Volksmasse*] and to enlarge it. It was therefore a question of space. . . .

Germany's problem could only be solved by means of force and this was never without attendant risk. The campaigns of Frederick the Great for Silesia and Bismarck's wars against Austria and France had involved unheard of risk, and the swiftness of the Prussian action in 1870 had kept Austria from entering the war. If one accepts as the basis of the following exposition the resort to force with its attendant risks, then there remain still to be answered the questions "when" and "how." In this matter there were three cases [*Fälle*] to be dealt with:

Case 1: Period 1943–1945

After this date only a change for the worse, from our point of view, could be expected.

The equipment of the army, navy, and Luftwaffe, as well as the formation of the officer corps, was nearly completed. Equipment and armament were modern; in further delay there lay the danger of their obsolescence. In particular, the secrecy of "special weapons" could not be preserved forever. The recruiting of reserves was limited to current age groups; further drafts from older untrained age groups were no longer available.

Our relative strength would decrease in relation to the rearmament which would by then have been carried out by the rest of the world. If we did not act by 1943–1945, any year could, in consequence of a lack of reserves, produce the food crisis, to cope with which the necessary foreign exchange was not available, and this must be regarded as a "waning point of the regime." Besides, the world was expecting our attack and was increasing its counter-measures from year to year. It was while the rest of the world was still preparing its defenses that we were obliged to take the offensive.

Nobody knew today what the situation would be in the years 1943–1945. One thing only was certain, that we could not wait longer.

On the one hand there was the great Wehrmacht, and the necessity of maintaining it at its present level, the aging of the movement and of its leaders; and on the other, the prospect of a lowering of the standard of living and of a limitation of the birth rate, which left no choice but to act. If the Führer was still living, it was his unalterable resolve to solve Germany's problem of space at the latest by 1943–1945.

Source: From "The Hossbach Memorandum," in Keith Eubank, ed., *World War II: Roots and Causes*, 2nd ed. (Lexington, Mass.: D.C. Heath, 1992), pp. 115–117; from *The Approach of War* by Christopher Thorne, pp. 35–50, 1967. Reprinted by permission of Macmillan Press, Ltd.

---

seemed to satisfy the Führer. Because Czechoslovakia had mutual defense treaties with both France and the Soviet Union, a European war appeared imminent.[12]

At the last minute, Chamberlain received an invitation to meet Hitler once again, this time in Munich in the presence of Mussolini and French premier Edouard Daladier. At the Munich conference late in September 1938, which neither Czechoslovakia nor the Soviet Union attended, Chamberlain and Daladier agreed to let Hitler annex about 10,000 square miles of Czechoslovak territory. Chamberlain stepped off the plane back in London with the agreement clutched in his hand. To a wildly cheering crowd and an approving nation, he reported that he had brought home "peace for our time."

The fatuousness of Chamberlain's remark has remained the most devastating symbol of what came to be called appeasement. For much of the rest of the century, political figures of all kinds often referred back to Munich when making their arguments about the need for this or

---

[12] The Soviet Union secretly mobilized ninety divisions in preparation for hostilities, but Poland and Romania would not grant permission for crossing their countries, and neither France nor Britain consulted the Soviets about the crisis.

"Respect" for Equals   The Hitler–Stalin Pact of August 1939 shocked the world, in good measure because Nazis and Communists had been bitter enemies for years. British cartoonist David Low takes the measure of the two dictators.   *1939, David Low.*

that intervention. Whatever stability arrangements such as the Locarno agreement had produced in interwar Europe depended on resolute action by France and Britain. Because these governments failed to counter German provocations between 1936 and 1938, the French and the British helped bring on World War II. Unwillingness to pay the lesser cost of standing up to Hitler led to the greater cost of World War II and the Holocaust. They acted in this way in part because neither the French nor the British believed that events in eastern Europe could harm them. As Chamberlain put it, the Czechoslovak crisis was "a quarrel in a far away country between people of whom we know nothing."

Stalin, unlike Chamberlain, was far from indifferent to eastern Europe. Russia had a long historical interest in the Slavic-speaking peoples who lived there, and Germany had invaded Russia through Polish lands in 1914. Stalin had his own interpretation of the West's indecision after Hitler came to power. In his view, the capitalist powers were not naively trying to maintain peace at any cost, but instead were seeking to push Hitler eastward into a region in which they knew the Soviet Union had a powerful interest. If communism and Nazism could be induced to destroy each other in eastern Europe, Stalin suspected, the capitalist states could pick up the pieces. Stalin decided to turn the tables on the West. An alliance with Hitler, he calculated, would forestall an attack on the Soviet Union and deflect Germany westward against the capitalists. After Munich, he began dropping broad hints that the Soviet Union might be willing to reach an agreement with Hitler if the price was right. In March 1939 he declared to a party congress that the Soviet Union would not allow itself "to be

drawn into conflicts by warmongers who are used to having others pull chestnuts out of the fire for them."

In that same month, Hitler decided that the Sudetenland was not enough. He occupied the rest of Bohemia and Moravia (which today constitute most of the Czech Republic) and set up a puppet regime in Slovakia. This time, he went beyond what his sympathizers could have argued were reasonable modifications of the vindictive Versailles treaty or a justifiable gathering of German-speaking peoples. Angered, and at the same time sobered, Chamberlain and the British drew their line in the sand. Stepping up their defense preparations, they announced that they would tolerate no more such acquisitions and called for a return of Czechoslovak sovereignty. Most important, they specifically guaranteed the integrity of Poland.

Britain had calculated correctly about Hitler's next target. In 1938 Hitler had laid before his advisers a general plan for the invasion of Poland, and in the spring of 1939 he directed his generals to ready themselves by the end of summer. All the demands, complaints, subterfuges, and justifications that began to stream out of Berlin in the summer of 1939 about righting the wrongs of Versailles and helping Germans in Danzig were but window dressing. Hitler had decided to seize Poland.

Despite his confidence in his own powers and in the weakness of France and England, Hitler realized that he was not yet strong enough to fight the Soviet Union, although he had always felt that his final struggle would be that same battle between Teuton and Slav that had animated imperial German ideologues before World War I. In August, as Hitler's military preparations neared completion, Stalin suddenly invited the Nazi foreign minister

MAP 30-4
GREATER GERMANY AND EASTERN EUROPE, 1939–1941

THE HISTORICAL EVIDENCE

The Fall of France

1940

Marc Bloch was France's most distinguished medieval historian in the 1930s. Bloch was born a Jew, but, as he put it, he was "above all, and quite simply, a Frenchman." After the fall of France in 1940, during which he served in the army, Bloch wrote a trenchant analysis of the disaster in which he devastatingly exposed the blunders of the government, the military, and the French middle class. But Bloch strove for "complete sincerity in word and thought," and he did not avoid placing a share of the blame on his own profession, as the selection below shows. Bloch joined the resistance and perished at the hands of a Nazi firing squad in 1944.

Many of us [among the professoriate] realized at a very early stage [in the post–World War I period] the nature of the abyss into which the diplomacy of Versailles and the Ruhr was threatening to plunge us. We knew perfectly well that it would have the double result of embroiling us with our former Allies and of keeping open and bleeding our ancient quarrel with an enemy who we had just, but only just, defeated. . . . Not being prophets we did not foresee the advent of the Nazis. But we did foresee that, in some form or other, though its precise nature was hidden from us, a German revival *would* come, that it would be embittered by rancorous memories to which our foolish ineptitude was daily adding, and that its explosion would be terrible. Had anyone asked us how we thought a second war would end we should, I doubt not, have answered that we hoped it would end in victory. But we should have been perfectly clear in our own minds that if the terrible storm broke again there was grave danger that the whole of European civilization might well suffer irremediable shipwreck. We did realize that in the Germany of that time there were

signs, however timid, of a new spirit of goodwill, of an attitude that was frankly pacific and honestly liberal. The only thing wanting was a gesture of encouragement on the part of our political leaders. We knew all that, and yet, from laziness, from cowardice, we let things take their course. We feared the opposition of the mob, the sarcasm of our friends, the ignorant mistrust of our masters. We dared not stand up in public and be the voice crying in the wilderness. It might have been just that, but at least we should have had the consolation of knowing that, whatever the outcome of its message, it had at least spoken aloud the faith that was in us. We preferred to lock ourselves into the fear-haunted tranquillity of our studies. May the young men forgive us the blood that is red upon our hands!

Source: From Marc Bloch, *Strange Defeat: A Statement of Evidence Written in 1940*, trans. Gerard Hopkins (London: Oxford University Press, 1949), pp. 171–172.

Joachim von Ribbentrop to Moscow. Even though the two powers had "poured buckets of filth" over each other for years, Stalin told Ribbentrop the time had come to cut a deal. The resultant Nazi-Soviet pact, signed on August 23 after hurried negotiations, stunned the world. A week later, on September 1, 1939, the German army (the *Wehrmacht*) swarmed into Poland. Britain, true to its guarantee of the spring, declared war on Germany, and France followed suit. Less noticed at the time, on September 17, as called for in a secret protocol to its agreement with Germany, the Soviet Union invaded Poland from the east.

Blitzkrieg

It took the Germans and the Soviets only a few weeks to destroy Poland (see Map 30-4). Goebbels' propaganda specialists had no difficulty portraying the Wehrmacht's tactics

of massive, fast-moving strikes by tanks supported by dive bombers as a new and devastating *Blitzkrieg* ("lightning war"). Hitler instructed his generals to destroy the Polish people, concentrating on the political and intellectual elites, and Stalin's occupying forces deported some 1.5 million educated Poles to Siberia in cattle cars. Both the Germans and the Russians aimed to eliminate the Poles as a historic people.

To Hitler's surprise, the now thoroughly aroused British refused to work out a peace following Poland's defeat. After several months of international inactivity, which some mindlessly called "the phony war" or "Sitzkrieg," Hitler occupied Denmark and Norway, and in May 1940 he attacked France through Belgium and the Netherlands. The French possessed almost double the armor tonnage of the Germans and more than twice the number of wheeled vehicles, but they lacked modern communications, a viable

Legend:
- Germany, German-occupied, and pro-German
- French boundary, 1939
- German occupied France
- German annexations, 1940
- Vichy France

GREAT BRITAIN
NETH.
GERMANY
BELGIUM
LUX.
Paris •
Demarcation line, 1940
SWITZ.
ATLANTIC OCEAN
Vichy •
FRANCE
ITALY
SPAIN
Mediterranean Sea

MAP 30-5
GERMAN-DOMINATED FRANCE

The Vichy regime controlled the French colonial empire, and the Germans occupied the rest of France in November 1943, though the Germans continued to administer southern France through the Vichy governmental apparatus. After the liberation, the Vichy leaders were tried and usually punished for treason.

strategy, and competent leadership. By June 14, German troops had occupied Paris and Germany's Blitzkrieg against France was complete. Hitler forced the French to sign their capitulation in the same railway car, set up in the same place, in which the Germans had signed the armistice of November 11, 1918. The agreement divided France into an occupied zone, with its center in Paris, and a satellite zone, administered by sympathetic French rightists led by General Philippe Pétain, French hero of the World War I battle of Verdun (see Map 30-5). This French ally of Germany became known as Vichy France, from the name of its capital city. Meanwhile, Stalin used the occasion of the French defeat to occupy the Baltic states of Latvia, Estonia, and Lithuania, which had been independent since World War I, and to snatch Bessarabia (today Moldova) from Romania.

The only success, if it could be called that, that the Allied forces scored in France was the British extrication of its army from what appeared to be certain destruction at Dunkirk. Nevertheless, France's collapse had left Britain completely isolated. In July 1940, Goering's air force (the *Luftwaffe*) began large-scale raids on British airfields and military installations, almost destroying the British capacity for air defense. The first potentially successful foreign invasion of the British Isles since 1066 seemed imminent.

Churchill Inspects the Blitz
Winston Churchill inspired the British people (and the world with his words, his deeds, and his concern for their survival). He often inspected ruins, as he is doing here in this bombed out church. *Reproduced from the Collections of the Library of Congress.*

But the Royal Air Force, though suffering serious losses, managed to hold its own by using the newly invented radar and by reading enemy messages with the German coding device Enigma, which they had secretly obtained in Poland in the 1930s. In August, in the incorrect—but widely held—opinion that massive bombing of urban centers would destroy civilian morale, the Luftwaffe shifted from bombing the strategically vital radar sites to bombing London and other British cities. This proved to be a crucial error. Not only did the Germans halt their raids on military targets a few weeks short of potentially gaining full air superiority, but their raids staunchly united the British public behind its bulldog of a new prime minister, Winston Churchill.

Churchill had entered Parliament for the first time in 1900 and had served in many governments since then. But during the 1930s, the Conservative leadership had shunned him. His firm conviction that German aggression was Britain's most serious threat flew in the face of Chamberlain's appeasement. When Chamberlain resigned in May 1940, however, Churchill's reputation as a fighter brought him to power. A fluent writer and dramatic speaker, Churchill used the radio and press to galvanize the British public behind him, even though, as he put it in his first speech to Parliament, he had "nothing to offer but blood, toil, tears, and sweat." In the dark hours following the evacuation of Dunkirk, when it appeared that Hitler might actually invade the British Isles, millions thrilled to hear him vow:

> We shall go on to the end. We shall fight in France, we shall fight on the seas and oceans, we shall fight . . . in the air, we shall defend our island, whatever the cost may be, we shall fight on the beaches, we shall fight on the landing grounds, we shall fight in the fields and in the streets, we shall fight in the hills; we shall never surrender.

During "the Blitz," as the British called the bombings of 1940, Churchill—trailed by reporters—was everywhere, viewing the bomb damage, visiting coastal batteries, always with a cigar in his mouth, always flashing his trademark "V for Victory" sign. Instead of becoming dispirited at their desperate situation, the British public enthusiastically rallied behind their leader. Churchill called it "their finest hour."

MAP 30-6
THE NAZI TIDE OF CONQUEST

Legend:
- U.S.S.R., September 1, 1939
- Soviet annexations, September 1, 1939– June 22, 1941
- Neutral states during World War II
- Germany, September 1, 1939
- German allies
- Pro-German states
- ✳ Major battles

It is not certain whether Hitler actually intended to invade Britain—although he planned for it as "Operation Sea Lion"—but in December 1940, by which time the raids on Britain had become costly, the Führer directed his generals to prepare for an invasion of the Soviet Union. The purpose of the invasion of the USSR was not to liberate the "human trash" that lived there, but to provide raw materials for Germans to consume and space for Germans to live. "There is no doubt that . . . many millions of people will be starved to death if we take out of the country the things we need," Goering's Economic Staff East wrote in May 1941. Goering himself ordered the taking of supplies anyway, knowing it could lead to the deaths of "tens of millions." The German soldier was to be "the carrier of a merciless racial concept." Special units assigned to kill Jews were attached to army units as the Wehrmacht swept forward.

Before the invasion, Hitler secured his flank in eastern Europe by buying off allies with favorable border adjustments (Bulgaria and Hungary), flattering rulers (Romania), playing to anti-Soviet passion (Finland), and crushing hesitant states militarily (Yugoslavia and Greece). On June 22, 1941, some 116 divisions containing 3 million German troops and a half-million troops from allied countries smashed across the border into the Soviet Union (see Map 30-6).

Many sources, from President Franklin D. Roosevelt to Stalin's own intelligence services, had warned of Hitler's impending attack, but Stalin stubbornly disregarded them. Until the day of the invasion, Soviet trains bearing supplies for their German ally continued to roll westward. Stalin rejected his commanders' requests to shift their troops back from indefensible border positions. When the attack came, the vulnerable Soviets fell back in complete disarray. Hitler's advance seemed limited only by the speed at which his troops and horses could march across the steppes.[13]

The German General Staff had expected to knock the Soviets out of the war in two months. Accordingly they had only supplied the troops with summer clothing. The rapid advance left very long supply lines, magnifying logistical problems. And Hitler made the strategic mistake of dispersing his forces, first toward the south and only later toward Moscow. By December 1941 the lightly clothed and poorly supplied Germans reached a point that today lies between the Moscow airport and the center of the city. Much of the Soviet government had already evacuated the

capital. Just at that desperate moment the Soviets counterattacked and an unusually harsh winter set in. German losses were heavy. Although by February 1942 the Germans had killed almost 3 million Soviet troops and taken another million prisoner, they had not defeated the Soviet Union.

"A Date Which Will Live in Infamy"

Almost precisely at the moment that the Soviets were stopping Hitler's armies short of Moscow, the Japanese launched their attack on the U.S. naval base at Pearl Harbor in Hawaii. Germany and Japan were allies, so when Germany invaded the Soviet Union, Japan contemplated renouncing a nonaggression pact that the Soviets had forced on them in 1939. Had the Japanese attacked the Soviet Union, there is no telling what the outcome might have been. But by this time, the Japanese were deeply committed to a campaign to conquer Southeast Asia, whose oil they desperately needed to keep their navy afloat. Rather than turning on the Soviets, they decided to concentrate on the obstacles that the United States had put in their way in the Pacific.

Many isolationist Americans did not want to be pulled into either the European or the Pacific war, but President Roosevelt understood the long-term dangers to the United States of Nazi and Japanese success. He moved first to assist those who were fighting Hitler. In March 1941, Roosevelt persuaded a reluctant Congress to pass the artfully named Lend-Lease Act, whereby the United States gave military equipment to Great Britain. In August he met with Winston Churchill and signed the Atlantic Charter, a statement of democratic and pluralistic principles, and in November he extended Lend-Lease to the beleaguered Soviet Union. Many Americans opposed these moves, especially the aid to the communist Soviet Union, because by Thanksgiving 1941, the need to protect of Lend-Lease convoys was drawing the United States into an undeclared naval war with Germany.

Direct American interests lay more in the Pacific than in Europe, however. The United States had seized the Philippines from Spain in 1898. The Japanese saw the U.S.-occupied Philippines as standing in the way of their conquest of Southeast Asia. When Hideki Tojo became prime minister in October 1941, he decided to cripple the American fleet in the Pacific with one blow.[14] With the surprise attack on Pearl Harbor on December 7 of that year—"a date which will live in infamy," as President Roosevelt called it in

---

[13] Despite the mythology of Tiger tanks and Stuka bombers, German supplies moved pirmarily by horse. Each infantry division required four to five thousand horses, creating significant logistical problems. For the Soviet invasion, the Germans used almost 750,000 horses, each requiring 20 pounds of feed a day.

[14] Tojo's name is given Western-style (given name first, family name second). In Japan, it would be reversed: Tojo Hideki.

THE HISTORICAL EVIDENCE

The Atlantic Charter

1941

In 1941, before the United States entered World War II, Winston Churchill and Franklin Roosevelt met at sea and concluded the Atlantic Charter, which set out the basic principles of the democracies. One can compare them to Wilson's Fourteen Points in Chapter 28 and to Hitler's Hossbach Memorandum earlier in this chapter.

Joint Declaration by the President and the Prime Minister: August 12, 1941

The President of the United States of America and the Prime Minister, Mr. Churchill, representing His Majesty's Government in the United Kingdom, being met together, deem it right to make known certain common principles in the national policies of their respective countries on which they base their hopes for a better future for the world.

First, their countries seek no aggrandisement, territorial or other.

Second, they desire to see no territorial changes that do not accord with the freely expressed wishes of the peoples concerned.

Third, they respect the right of all peoples to choose the form of government under which they will live: and they wish to see sovereign rights and self-government restored to those who have been forcibly deprived of them.

Fourth, they will endeavour, with due respect for their existing obligations, to further the enjoyment by all States, great or small, victor or vanquished, of access, on equal terms, to the trade and to the raw materials of the world which are needed for their economic prosperity.

Fifth, they desire to bring about the fullest collaboration between all nations in the economic field, with the object of securing for all improved labour standards, economic advancement, and social security.

Sixth, after the final destruction of the Nazi tyranny they hope to see established a peace which will afford to all nations the means of dwelling in safety within their own boundaries, which will afford assurance that all the men in all the lands may live out their lives in freedom from fear and want.

Seventh, such a peace should enable all men to traverse the high seas and oceans without hindrance.

Eighth, they believe that all the nations of the world, for realistic as well as spiritual reasons must come to the abandonment of the use of force. Since no future peace can be maintained if land, sea, or air armaments continue to be employed by nations which threaten, or may threaten, aggression outside of their frontiers, they believe, pending establishment of a wider and permanent system of general security, that the disarmament of such nations is essential. They will likewise aid and encourage all other practicable measures which will lighten for peace-loving peoples the crushing burden of armaments.

Source: From Winston S. Churchill, *The Grand Alliance* (Boston: Houghton Mifflin, 1950), pp. 443–444.

---

his request to Congress for a declaration of war—coupled with simultaneous assaults on American, British, and Dutch colonial forces elsewhere, the Japanese dealt the United States a heavy blow. During the first few months of the war, the Japanese progressed from one victory to another, conquering the Philippines, Indochina, Singapore, and much of what is today Indonesia.

Despite these initial triumphs, Japanese strategic thinking remained narrow and complacent. Tojo and his planners thought that by raising the cost of American participation in the war they would force the American democratic government, under pressure from a war-weary public, to cut its losses and make a deal with the Japanese, allowing them to keep much of their East Asian empire. Instead, Pearl Harbor jolted the sleeping industrial giant into action, uniting the nation behind its president and the war effort. It took time before the U.S. military buildup began to pay dividends, but no one could doubt the eventual outcome. In the long run, Japanese faith in their country's moral and spiritual superiority and in the bravery of its soldiers proved no match for the industrial might of the United States.

BANKRUPTCY OF THE CENTURY OF POWER

The high point of Nazi control of Europe came by mid-1942. What, one might ask, were the goals of this enormous military enterprise? Permanent subjugation of Europe to Germany would be the short answer. The Jews, not falling into the category of human beings in Nazi eyes, would be simply slaughtered. Slavs and other "inferior" peoples would become the labor force of Germany—about 7.5 million such slave workers were employed in Germany by the end of the war—while Aryan communities would be planted in the fertile regions of eastern Europe. The west Europeans, occupying a higher notch on the Nazi racial scale, would not be reduced to slavery, but they would still be subject to German control. And once the war was won, Hitler intended to attack the Christian churches of Germany, confiscate their property, and take over their schools. In the fall of 1942, this imposition of one people and one dictator on the rest of Europe by sheer force—a culmination of the Century of Power in a completely negative sense—did not seem outside the realm of possibility.

The Resistance Movements

The reactions to this monstrous German plan in the subjugated countries were many and varied. Some political figures became enthusiastic supporters of the ideals of Nazism. The name of one of them, Vidkun Quisling, who became the Nazi's puppet ruler in Norway, became synonymous with traitor. Almost every occupied country provided at least some enthusiastic members of the SS who entered vigorously into Nazi extermination plans. Others, like the Vichy government in France, were manned by conservatives and antisemites from the interwar period who believed that France's future lay with fascism and Nazism. Seeing themselves as "saving" France, they nevertheless pursued policies, such as rounding up Jews and sending them to their deaths, that closely followed Nazi plans.

At the other extreme, resistance movements sprang up in many countries, particularly in France, Poland, and Yugoslavia. After the war, a large number of French alleged that they were part of the resistance, or at least sympathetic to it. In fact, a relatively small number of people were involved. One of the reasons was that the most vigorous part of the resistance was Communist-led (at least after Hitler's invasion of the Soviet Union). The French also possessed a different kind of resistance, the Free French government and army in exile, led by General Charles de Gaulle. A tank commander during the German invasion, de Gaulle basically appointed himself the savior of France and organized a French force in exile. Prickly, proud, and patriotic, de Gaulle returned to France in 1944 at the head of the French forces and played a vital role in postwar French affairs.

In Poland, Communist influence in the resistance was slight, because Stalin had decimated the Polish Communist party in the 1930s. The Home Army, as it was called, had links to the Polish government in exile in London. Late in 1944, as the Red Army approached Warsaw, the Home Army staged an anti-German uprising, hoping to take control of the Polish capital before the Soviets arrived. But the Soviet armies stopped their advance, giving the Germans time to crush the uprising and, on Hitler's orders, to destroy the remaining parts of the city. When the Soviets finally arrived early in 1945, the city of a million persons was deserted, 90 percent destroyed.

The most spectacular resistance movement took place in Yugoslavia. The Germans and Italians had partitioned

The Passion of Resistance   In several places in Europe (notably France, Greece, and Yugoslavia) Communists proved to be the most dedicated resisters to Nazism. In this picture, a Yugoslav Partisan exhorts his countrymen to fight on just as he is about to be hanged by the Germans. *Yugoslav Information Service.*

THE HISTORICAL EVIDENCE

War in the East

1939–1944

These six excerpts are taken from the diary of a Polish doctor who survived World War II in eastern Poland. One condensed entry is given for each year of the war.

September 21, 1939: It was completely weird. This whole mass of people, seized with panic, were going ahead, without knowing where or why, and without any knowledge of where the exodus would end. Large numbers of passenger cars, several official limousines, all filthy and covered with mud, were trying to pass the truck and wagon convoys. Many people were hanging on to the roofs and fenders of the cars and trucks. Many of the vehicles had broken windshields and windows, damaged hoods or doors.

September 1, 1940: We are exhausted. Life is nerve shattering. We are living in uncertainty about what will happen to us, not in a month or a week, but in one hour. We live under the constant threat of search, arrest, beating, evacuation, and death, with the last one maybe not being the worst because of the treatment of prisoners in German prisons and camps.

October 4, 1941: Yesterday another transport of Soviet POWs, around 15,000, passed through. They all looked like skeletons, just shadows of human beings, barely moving. I have never in my life seen anything like this. Men were falling to the street; the stronger ones were carrying others, holding them up by their arms. They looked like starved animals, not like people. They were fighting for scraps of apples in the gutter, not paying any attention to the Germans who would beat them with rubber sticks.

October 21, 1942: From early morning until late at night we witnessed indescribable events. Armed SS soldiers, gendarmes, and "blue police"* ran through the city looking for Jews. The Jews were taken from their houses, barns, cellars, attics, and other hiding places. Pistol and gun shots were heard throughout the entire day. Sometimes hand grenades were thrown into the cellars. Jews were beaten and kicked; it made no difference whether they were men, women, or small children. All Jews will be shot.

October 10, 1943: I spent three days in Warsaw. There is much shooting on the streets. German gendarmes cruise the streets in open cars, carrying carbines and machine guns. Once, while I was riding the streetcar on Narutowicz Place, a shot was fired. Immediately all passengers lay down on the floor. It appears this is a daily routine and people are prepared for it.

July 26, 1944: At 8 A.M. a Russian officer arrived at the hospital. While talking with him I heard the cry, "Our boys are coming!" I left everything and ran to see for myself. From the direction of Blonie a group of approximately twenty young men approached; all were armed, in uniform, with red scarves around their necks and red and white arm bands on their left sleeves. The people went wild. They were crying, shouting, and throwing flowers.

Source: From Zygmunt Klukowski, *Diary from the Years of Occupation, 1939–1944*, trans. George Klukowski (Urbana: University of Illinois Press, 1993), pp. 16, 114, 173, 219, 284, 353.

*The "blue police" were members of local law enforcement who collaborated with the Nazis.

---

the country in 1941, permitting a rabid group of Croatian fascists called Ustashi to take power in the so-called Independent State of Croatia. The Ustashi put into effect a genocidal program of brutal killings and deportations to clear Croatia of racial "undesirables," such as Jews, Roma, Muslims, and—especially—Serbs. The Yugoslav government in exile also had its forces, primarily Serbs, called the Chetniks. But the most important movement was the Communist-led resistance, called the Partisans, under Josip Broz Tito. By advocating a nonnationalist program of "brotherhood and unity," the Partisans attracted many disgusted Croats, as well as others, to their movement, which was militarily

strong enough to hold down a number of German divisions right up through 1944. The bloody bitterness of the three-cornered struggle among Croat Ustashi, Serb Chetniks, and Tito's Partisans created long-lasting hatreds that Croatian and Serbian politicians brought back to the surface in 1991 to cause the breakup of Yugoslavia.

Home Fronts

Despite the experience of World War I, and despite what became the consuming nature of World War II, at first the warring countries did not put their economies in a wartime mode. Hitler, for example, believed that his Blitzkrieg war would make it possible to achieve quick victories and obtain enough booty to replenish combat losses. During the first two years of the war, in fact, he cut back arms production twice, once in 1940 after the fall of France, and again in the fall of 1941, when he believed Russia was defeated. Production of civilian goods actually increased during this time. Not until January 1942 did he order his able subordinate Albert Speer to take over arms production on a wartime basis. Despite being opposed by military leaders who sought to maintain their turf, Speer tripled production over the next two years, despite continued Allied air attacks.

In the Soviet Union, Stalin had begun shifting industrial facilities eastward beyond the Ural Mountains in 1938, so that by the time the war broke out more than a third of Soviet production of steel and coal was safe from German attack. As the Germans were overrunning Belarus and Ukraine in 1941, superhuman efforts transferred more than fifteen hundred other vital enterprises beyond the Urals as well, so that from 1942 onward, the Soviet Union was able to supply its huge armament needs successfully despite dramatic German advances.

Surprisingly, it was the British, not the authoritarian rulers, who were able to organize their economy most systematically. Despite their late start and great needs, the British government assumed, correctly as it turned out, that it would get better results over the long run by gradually increasing the calls on the population, relying on patriotism and civic pride. Winston Churchill's ability to evoke national enthusiasms in the face of hardship were instrumental in achieving this success. The "Dig for Victory" plan, for example, created 1.4 million plots (called "Victory Gardens" when they were introduced in the United States) that supplemented the threatened British food supply, while rationing limited consumption.

The two primary problems all the wartime economies faced were manpower and finances. Massive entry of women into the workforce alleviated the shortage of manpower. In Britain, for example, out of 2.8 million new workers during the war, 2.2 million were women, while in the Soviet Union the proportion of women in the workforce grew to more than 50 percent. The United States helped with the finances, through Lend-Lease to both Britain and Russia, and with a variety of loans and other devices. Germany took a different course. Although women entered the workforce there too, the most important new element was slave labor. Albert Speer wanted to use foreign workers in their native lands, and in fact about 7 million of them were, but the more "revolutionary" of Hitler's henchmen successfully argued on behalf of rounding up workers and bringing them to Germany. By mid-1944 about 20 percent of the German workforce were foreigners working under appalling conditions. As Himm-

ler put it in 1943, "Whether nations live in prosperity or starve to death interests me only insofar as we need them as slaves for our culture."

The key to the relative strength over time of the warring parties was the United States. In 1938, despite being the largest steel producer in the world by a significant margin, the United States was utilizing only about a third of its capacity and had about 10 million unemployed. When war came, the United States was able to vastly increase its production of military goods—producing one ship per day in the Kaiser shipyards, for example—whereas the other powers were already near capacity when the war started. This is not to say that the United States ever mobilized completely—it did not. Despite the success of advertising campaigns featuring "Rosie the Riveter," for example, a significantly lower percentage of women entered the workforce than in Britain and the Soviet Union. But American industrial strength so outweighed that of the rest of the world that its economic contributions to Allied victory were decisive.

Turning Points

In the Soviet Union, the German campaign of 1942 appeared to get off to a successful start. German troops advanced dramatically in the south, headed toward the rich oil fields on the Caspian Sea. But this time, instead of allowing itself to be surrounded and captured, the Red Army staged a fighting retreat. The farther the Germans advanced, the stiffer the Soviet resistance became. By the fall of 1942, plants relocated behind the Urals were not only producing more military supplies than Germany, but more technologically advanced tanks and aircraft as well. In September 1942, the fighting began to center on the psychologically and strategically vital city of Stalingrad (now called Volgograd), located at a crucial spot on the Volga River. Stalin ordered his men to stand and fight, and the city became consumed in vicious house-to-house combat. Meanwhile, Stalin's generals organized a vast pincer movement. In November they attacked the unsuspecting Germans on both flanks and enveloped the entire German Sixth Army. When Hitler refused to countenance an effort to break out of the encirclement, he sealed the German army's fate. On February 2, 1943, the 100,000 survivors of the once-powerful German force of 300,000 surrendered. Of these, only about 5,000 went back to Germany when released by the Soviets in 1955. The psychological effect of Stalingrad on both sides—positive for the Allies, negative for the Germans—carried even more weight than its physical and strategic costs.

Hitler experienced a second important defeat late in 1942. In his efforts against Great Britain, he had considered clearing the Mediterranean of British influence. Yet he was reluctant to emphasize this region, in part because it fell within Mussolini's sphere. Nevertheless, when the Italians failed to sustain effective operations against the British in North Africa, Hitler sent troops under General Erwin Rommel (the "Desert Fox") to Libya. By June 1942, Rommel had reached El Alamein in Egypt, only 70 miles from Alexandria. In October, however, the British launched a counterattack that drove Rommel into retreat, and in November Anglo-American troops led by General Dwight D. Eisenhower invaded French West Africa from the Atlantic. By May 1943, these two forces completed the defeat of the Italian and German armies in North Africa.

By mid-1943, it was apparent that despite the staggering price, the Allies were going to defeat Japan and Germany. In the Pacific, the Americans began a costly but effective strategy of "island hopping": in a series of bitter battles, they seized islands ever closer to Japan. In eastern Europe Soviet soldiers, increasingly well supplied, rolled back the German advances.[15] In the Mediterranean, Allied armies invaded Sicily and Italy, forcing Mussolini to resign. September brought Italy's surrender, although German forces took over, rescued Mussolini, and continued to fight.

From the early moments of the Soviet entry into the war, and especially after the Americans entered, Stalin clamored for a second front. The best the western Allies could do was to invade North Africa late in 1942. This was a concession by the Americans, who believed that all energy should be focused on an invasion through France. Churchill, hoping to keep the Soviet Union out of central Europe after the war, advocated an attack somewhere in the south, perhaps in the Balkans, but he could not sustain his view. In January 1943, Roosevelt and Churchill met in the Moroccan city of Casablanca and announced their plan to establish a second front against Germany by 1944. They adopted the American plan for a direct cross-Channel invasion rather than Churchill's strategically dubious scheme, and they made it clear that they would accept only unconditional surrender from the Germans. In December 1943, the British and American leaders met with Stalin in Teheran, Iran, where they settled on the broad lines of their advance into Europe and agreed not to negotiate a separate peace with Germany (see Map 30-7).

Closing in on Nazi Germany

By spring 1944, the Red Army had reached the USSR's approximate 1939 borders and stood poised to take the war into central and southeastern Europe. Up to this point, the main military contributions of the western Allies had been in North Africa and Italy, and in the air. The former

drained Germany, but could not be decisive. Despite massive raids by the British at nighttime and the Americans during daylight hours, bombing German cities and industries had surprisingly little effect on Nazi war production. After two years of raids, for example, the Germans were producing more fighter planes in mid-1944 than at any other time in the war. Also, as the British reaction to the Blitz had shown, the prewar belief that bombing would destroy civilian morale was mistaken. This is despite the horrific casualties inflicted by incendiary raids. In 1943, by dropping incendiary bombs for two days, Allied bombers created a firestorm over Hamburg that killed about 100,000 persons. For reasons still in dispute, Allied military leadership authorized another such raid on the strategically unimportant but beautiful city of Dresden late in the war that killed another 80,000 civilians.

The final blow to Germany came on June 6, 1944, when an invasion force of ultimately a million British, American, French, and other Allied troops landed in Normandy and opened the long-awaited second front. Hitler, who had long since taken command of every significant military operation, refused to believe that he was losing the war. He maintained faith in his secret weapons that came online late in 1944, such as a jet fighter and the V-2 ballistic missiles he fired at England. But these weapons were too few, too inaccurate, and too late. He even grasped at the frail hope that the death of Franklin Roosevelt in mid-April 1945 would split the Allies. But all was in vain. Forced at the end to recruit thirteen- and fourteen-year-olds, his cities in ruins, and the Red Army on the outskirts of Berlin, Hitler ordered the destruction of everything of value in Germany. Cornered in his underground bunker near the chancellery, this engineer of so much death at last took his own life.[16] The orders to destroy everything were not carried out, but on May 7, 1945, the Germans surrendered, and the war in Europe came to a shuddering end.

The Holocaust

As the war drew to a close in Europe, horrified Allied troops discovered the emaciated survivors of the death camps. The persecution of Jews had accelerated in intensity since the earliest days of Hitler's regime. Almost immediately after the invasion of Poland, however, the "racial mission" took a frightful new twist. Jews and Roma were shipped out of Germany in freight cars and gathered in Polish cities, where eastern Jews were also concentrated. German SS units, aided by Lithuanian, Ukrainian, and other volunteers, began moving Jews into highly restricted

---

[15] Until this point, the overwhelming majority of Soviet supplies were self-produced. Lend-lease supplies, especially motorized vehicles, started reaching the Soviet Union in massive quantities only early in 1944.

[16] Mussolini's fate was no better. Arrested by Italy's king, he escaped but was located and shot by members of the underground earlier in the spring of 1945. His body was taken to Milan, where it was hung by the heels for all to see.

MAP 30-7
THE LIBERATION OF EUROPE

ghettos, where the Nazis purposefully allowed the basic conditions of life to deteriorate rapidly. To administer these ghettos, the Germans established Councils of Jewish Elders, in which Jewish leaders, trying to save what they could, enforced the onerous rules. All Jewish economic and industrial assets, even small shops, were confiscated and given to new German owners. The Germans found every way possible to humiliate the Jews, setting fire to men's beards, making them desecrate holy objects, and forcing them to scrub streets with toothbrushes. Even these degradations paled before Germany's actions during the invasion of the Soviet Union, when special units sought out and killed all Jews they found, one by one, usually shooting them in the head after forcing them to dig their own graves. Hundreds of thousands died in these massacres, which all told took almost as many Jewish lives as the gas chambers. In one outrageous weekend, German forces killed 33,000 Jews at Babi Yar outside of Kiev.

THE HUMAN EXPERIENCE

Vladek Spiegelman, Holocaust Survivor

Vladek Spiegelman (1906–1982) was a Polish Jew who survived the Auschwitz death camp and came to live in the United States. Born before World War I in an industrial part of Poland, he married well and went into the textile business. Called into military service in 1939 to defend Poland from German attack, he found his way back to his home town of Sosnowiec after the defeat only with difficulty. After several narrow escapes from Germans rounding up Jews, Spiegelman and his household of twelve persons were forced into two and a half rooms in the Sosnowiec ghetto. Soon, the Gestapo (German Secret Police) called all Jews of the area to the center of town "to register." There authorities stamped valid permits into the passports of about ten thousand healthy workers, including Spiegelman and his wife Anja, and sent twenty thousand of the old, the sick, women with too many children, and others to the death camps.

Spiegelman and Anja started hiding in cellars, attics, and even garbage pits. Through a series of clever dealings and good luck, they were among the last surviving Jews of Sosnowiec. Finally, they heard of a scheme to smuggle Jews into Hungary, where they would be temporarily safe. But the smugglers betrayed them, and the Gestapo transported them to Auschwitz.

Spiegelman proved a good organizer, as the camp term went. His knowledge of English permitted him to survive initially when a Polish guard "hired" him to teach English. After two months, he was the only member of his original group who had not been sent to the gas chambers and furnaces. Next, his knowledge—or his ability to fake knowledge—of tinsmithing and shoemaking got him special treatment. He even managed to make contact with Anja, who was being held in Birkenau, the work camp nearby.

When the Soviet troops neared Auschwitz, the camp guards marched Spiegelman and thousands of other surviving prisoners almost 200 miles to Breslau (today Wrocław). A high proportion of the prisoners perished or were shot dead by the impatient guards during the ordeal. At Breslau, the Germans packed Spiegelman and hundreds of others into railcars so tightly that they could only stand, sealed the car without food or water, and left it on a siding. After about a week, the Germans returned, opened the car, and disposed of the corpses and filth. In time the few remaining survivors, Spiegelman among them, arrived at Dachau. After almost succumbing to typhus, he was exchanged for prisoners at the Swiss border, but in the chaos of the last days of the war his train never reached the border. Two separate German patrols, still intent on killing Jews, rounded up the wandering prisoners and prepared to shoot them, but the war ended and Spiegelman survived. Anja Spiegelman survived as well. After Vladek became a successful salesman in Sweden, the couple emigrated to the United States.

Almost every European Jew who lived through the Holocaust has a story similar to that of Vladek Spiegelman. Good luck, chance happenings, right choices at crucial moments, and skillful use of one's talents permitted some to survive. Yet for most of these, including Spiegelman, survival when 6 million others died remained a heavy burden for the rest of their lives. ❖

Separation for Death
The notorious entrance to Auschwitz. Here, Jews and others were herded out of trains and selected either for the gas chambers (left column for mainly women, children, and old men) or for labor in neighboring camps (right column mainly men). It is likely that those in the left column were dead within an hour of this picture being taken. *Sovfoto/Eastfoto.*

THE HISTORICAL EVIDENCE

The Pain of the Holocaust
1944–1945

It might seem bizarre to write a poem about the Holocaust, but Paul Celan's powerful "Deathfugue" has become perhaps the single best known postwar poem in Germany. Celan, who came from Bukovina (Romania), wrote in part to express the pain his mother suffered in the Holocaust. This rendition of "Deathfugue" is an English translation that slips into easily understood German at the end (der Tod means "death" in German; Margareta and Shulamith are English spellings; Margarete and Sulamith are German spellings).

Deathfugue

Black milk of daybreak we drink it at evening
we drink it at midday and morning we drink it at night
we drink and we drink
we shovel a grave in the air there you won't lie too
    cramped
A man lives in the house he plays with his vipers he writes
he writes when it grows dark to Deutschland your golden
    hair Margareta
he writes it and steps out of doors and the stars are all
    sparkling
      he whistles his hounds to come close
he whistles his Jews into rows has them shovel a grave in
    the ground
he commands us play up for the dance

Black milk of daybreak we drink you at night
we drink you at morning and midday we drink you at
    evening
we drink and we drink
A man lives in the house he plays with his vipers he writes
he writes when it grows dark to Deutschland your golden
    hair Margareta
Your ashen hair Shulamith we shovel a grave in the air
    there you won't lie too cramped

He shouts jab this earth deeper you lot there you others
    sing up and play
he grabs for the rod in his belt he swings it his eyes are so
    blue
jab your spades deeper you lot there you others play on for
    the dancing

Black milk of daybreak we drink you at night
we drink you at midday and morning we drink you at
    evening
we drink and we drink
a man lives in the house your goldenes Haar Margareta
your aschenes Haar Shulamith he plays with his vipers

He shouts play death more sweetly this Death is a master
    from Deutschland
he shouts scrape your strings darker you'll rise then as
    smoke to the sky
you'll have a grave then in the clouds there you won't lie
    too cramped

Black milk of daybreak we drink you at night
we drink you at midday Death is a master aus Deutschland
we drink you at evening and morning we drink and we
    drink
this Death is ein Meister aus Deutschland his eye it is blue
he shoots you with shot made of lead shoots you level and
    true
a man lives in the house your goldenes Haar Margarete
he looses his hounds on us grants us a grave in the air
he plays with his vipers and daydreams der Tod ist ein
    Meister aus Deutschland

dein goldenes Haar Margarete
dein aschenes Haar Sulamith

Source: From John Felstiner, *Paul Celan: Poet, Survivor, Jew* (New Haven, Conn.: Yale University Press, 1995), pp. 31–32.

Before the invasion of the Soviet Union, Heinrich Himmler, head of the SS, had ordered the expansion of the concentration camp at Auschwitz (in Polish: Oświęcim) into a massive extermination factory. "The Führer has given the order for a Final Solution of the Jewish Question," he told the camp commander. No documentation of an explicit order has been found, but none was needed. Nazi actions from 1940 on consistently supported the goal of "cleansing" Europe of all its Roma and Jews. A conference held at Wannsee in Berlin in January 1942 approved the plans for extermination camps. By the middle of 1942 death camps were operating in Chełmno, Treblinka,

Sobibór, Auschwitz, and elsewhere.[17] During the rest of the war, German bureaucrats, from Adolf Eichmann—the main administrator of the complex machinery needed to find, transport, and kill millions of people—down to locomotive drivers on the transport trains, performed their functions as if they were dealing with sacks of grain, indifferent to the grotesque inhumanity of their work.

The SS set about the task of mass killing with single-minded efficiency. After some experimentation, they settled on a deadly poison gas called Zyklon B, and built large "shower rooms" where this gas could snuff out the lives of scores of victims at once. German industry responded to the call for producing this gas, as well as for the ovens used to burn the constant stream of bodies. Those waiting to be killed worked in camp factories, such as the I. G. Farben plant in Birkenau, near Auschwitz. As the war wore on and Germany came under increasing pressure from bombing raids and military losses, the trains shipping Jews to Auschwitz and other death camps continued to have the highest priority, even over crucial military supplies. In the end, the Germans methodically organized and carried out the killing of some two-thirds of all Jews living in Europe in 1939—almost 6 million of them—and approximately the same proportion of the Roma population.

How much was known at the time about the systematic massacre of Jews? There is little question that most Germans, Poles, and others in the Nazi sphere knew what was happening. Even the Allies began to learn of the extent of the massacres in 1942. Today the Allied decision not to bomb the railroads leading to Auschwitz late in 1944, for example, remains controversial. Why did non-Jews in Germany not react? It is difficult to say what controls the human heart, but some possibilities are a deep-seated antisemitism that Hitler's regime unleashed (that is, many people approved of the elimination of Jews); the enormous tensions and brutality of the era, in which the norms of peacetime life disappeared; fear of reprisal from Nazi forces; and the desire to stay out of trouble.

It is difficult for us today to re-create the atmosphere of absolute control that the Nazis established in Europe, in which hundreds of thousands of troops and special forces shot or arrested whomever they wished. Numerous Jews found ways to avoid capture, but in the end not many could escape the brutal roundups. Nevertheless, Jewish resistance movements cropped up in the ghettos, and Jewish guerrilla forces emerged. Some even organized uprisings in the death camps, despite the near impossibility of obtaining good weapons and the certainty of failure. The most dramatic moment of defiance came in April and May

1943, when the Jewish resistance in the Warsaw Ghetto fought a losing battle with German troops for more than two weeks. "We all may perish in the struggle," the fighters proclaimed to the Poles of Warsaw, "but we will not surrender; like you, we breathe with desire for revenge for all the crimes of our common foe."

Bombing Japan into Submission

The defeat of Germany did not end World War II. The Japanese fought on. The tide of the Pacific war had changed quite early when in June 1942 a relatively small American fleet, whose codebreakers were able to read secret Japanese naval messages, had sunk four Japanese aircraft carriers in the battle of Midway. Japan never managed to replace the forces destroyed in the battle, and thereafter progressively lost command of the seas. This loss dealt a crucial blow to the Japanese, who depended heavily on imports. Indeed, cutting off Japan's sea-lanes was probably the single most important factor in bringing down Japan. Actually winning the war, however, required the Americans to invade island after island en route to an anticipated final assault on the Japanese homeland (see Map 30-8). In the first of these invasions, U.S. troops took Guadalcanal in August 1942; in the last they seized Okinawa in April 1945.

These victories allowed the United States to conduct massive air raids on Japan with the new long-range bomber, the B-29. Because of the inaccuracy of high-altitude bombing, the air force shifted to low altitude "carpet" bombing with incendiary explosives. On March 9 and 10, 1945, in the most destructive raid of World War II, reminiscent of the raids on Hamburg and Dresden, fire-bombs dropped from 334 B-29s burned out a 16-square-mile area of Tokyo, killing between eighty and a hundred thousand Japanese and obliterating much of the city's industry.

Despite these losses and the difficulty of importing raw materials, the Japanese continued to plan a powerful defense against the anticipated American invasion, the route of which they had correctly guessed. Experience with the determined, even fanatical, Japanese resistance at Iwo Jima and Okinawa had convinced American planners that opposition to an invasion of the Japanese homeland would be fierce. At Iwo Jima, for example, the Americans had lost six thousand dead and twenty-five thousand wounded subduing a force of only twenty thousand Japanese troops (of which only two hundred survived).

The United States had a powerful card up its sleeve, however, in the atomic bomb. In the late 1930s, a handful of European physicists had realized that an enormous amount of energy would be released very rapidly in a huge explosion if a substance could be made to emit more than one neutron for every neutron that bombarded it. Several

---

[17] More than ten thousand camps of various kinds (not all of which housed Jews and not all of which were death camps) have been identified. Controlling vast numbers of "socially dead" people was a basic ingredient of the Nazi system.

MAP 30-8
THE PACIFIC WAR

The Pacific theater of World War II differed substantially from the European theater due to the geography over which it was fought. Sea power and air power proved decisive in the American strategy of "island-hopping."

of these scientists had come to the United States fleeing fascism. These men feared that their able colleagues who remained in Europe would find a way to create a weapon for Hitler using this fission principle. They enlisted Albert Einstein to point this out to President Roosevelt, who immediately authorized building such a weapon. The Manhattan Project, as it was called, gathered a small army of physicists, mathematicians, engineers, and support staff in Los Alamos, New Mexico. In July 1945, they finally detonated their first explosive device. Its power, equivalent to 20,000 tons of high explosives, exceeded even their most optimistic projections.

Scientists and engineers can create new inventions, but deciding whether and how to use technology is a matter for the political process. Roosevelt had assumed that if the bomb was ready soon enough, he would use it against

Germany. By the time of the successful test, however, Roosevelt had died and the war in Europe was over. The decision whether to use the bomb against Japan was up to the new president, Harry S Truman. In July 1945, Stalin, Truman, and Churchill (replaced by Clement Atlee after a general election), met just outside of Berlin in Potsdam to work out postwar arrangements. As we will see in Part Six, they could not reach consensus, but they did agree to demand Japan's unconditional surrender. Their public announcement left the door open to Japanese moderates by hinting that Japan's emperor could remain on his throne. When the Japanese did not respond to the Potsdam conditions, Truman went ahead with the A-bomb. On August 6, 1945, an American plane named the *Enola Gay* dropped the first atomic weapon on Hiroshima, destroying the city, killing between sixty and eighty thousand people,

Atomic Destruction   The devastation at Hiroshima after the explosion of the first atomic bomb was almost beyond belief. Even had it not been destroyed, the city's lone ladder fire truck would have been of little use. The fire station was no more than a kilometer from ground zero. *Corbis/Bettmann.*

and wounding an equal number. Many of the wounded suffered radiation sickness and later died, and the genetic and other effects of the radiation haunted these cities for a generation.

The bombing of Hiroshima was a serious blow to the Japanese, but when the Soviets declared war and invaded Manchuria two days later, fulfilling their agreement with the Allies to enter the war against Japan three months after the European war ended, the Japanese realized that invasion of the home islands could well succeed. With the detonation of a second atomic bomb on Nagasaki the next day, the emperor forced his government to end the war. On September 2, Japanese military leaders signed the formal documents of surrender on the American battleship *Missouri* in Tokyo Bay.

CONCLUSION: THE END OF CONFIDENCE

The Century of Power ended in 1945 with Europe's confidence and sense of progress destroyed. One of the defining characteristics of modernity is its orientation to the future. Medieval Europeans looked back to the Roman Empire, the early Christian church, and the Garden of Eden as models of perfection. For early modern Europeans, adequate knowledge of the world had already been uncovered; the task of contemporary society was to uncover those truths in the glorious, but distant, past. Today, we believe that knowledge is accumulating, at least in the realms of science and technology. We do not consider ourselves poor copies of past cultures, but new and more complete societies than those that came before us. When we think about better communities, we conjure up imaginary future utopias.

This sense that the present is better than the past and that the future will be better still took a long time to replace the backward-looking vision, but it was never stronger in Europe than in the decades preceding World War I. At that time, Europeans nurtured a powerful feeling that they were participating in a unique phase of human history. City living was becoming healthier through the construction of systems for delivering pure water and carrying away sewage; most children attended public schools; mass literacy created a broad reading public; amazing inventions like electric motors, telephones, cinema, radio, automobiles, and airplanes not only spawned completely new industries but gave people the sense of living more

fully than humans had ever lived before. Imperialism in part reflected this enormous confidence. The belief that the rest of the world needed to be brought up to the West's level may have been presumptuous, but Europeans honestly felt and conscientiously pursued it. The ideal of progress inspired and motivated every developed society.

World War I bruised the idea of progress, but did not kill it. Indeed, those who stood for empowering the proletariat so that socialism could transcend capitalism and transform society called themselves *progressives*. Fascism and Nazism claimed that they were making completely new starts that would create healthy new societies. Imperial states even began to think in terms of how they might bring their colonies up the ladder to representative government and autonomy, if not full independence. Not every element in society shared in the optimism. Artists, for example, developed new styles that proclaimed the meaninglessness of modernity and mocked the pretensions of high culture. Nevertheless, almost everyone maintained a faith in the ability of technology to change the world for the better.

World War II utterly destroyed this confidence. What kind of a civilization was it that could send millions of innocent persons to death in Siberian prisons, murder millions more in purposefully designed death camps, and kill off other millions in raging warfare across the entire planet? Two unique events—the Holocaust and the dropping of the atomic bomb—powerfully reminded the people of Western civilization that modernity had not eliminated the uglier side of human nature. The death camps showed that underneath the facade of civilized behavior the ancient human potential for bestiality still lurked. The new bomb demonstrated that technology serves only those purposes that human decisions fashion for it. If the Holocaust revealed the frightening, dark side of modernity, the atomic bomb confirmed that technology is not always benign.

Could progress continue on the basis of optimistic Enlightenment rationality? After the devastating cataclysm of World War II, many did not think so. And yet, the most explosive era of economic growth the world had ever seen was about to take place; colonial empires were about to give way to independent states across the world; and western Europe was about to unite in an economic community in which French and German antagonisms would give way to cooperation. Why and how this new world came into being is the subject of the final section of this book.

Selected Reading

Sources

Ginzburg, Evgeniia. *Journey Into the Whirlwind* (1967).

Noakes, Jeremy, and Geoffrey Pridham, eds. *Nazism, 1919–1945. A Documentary Reader* (1974).

Riefenstahl, Leni, director. *The Triumph of the Will*. Perhaps the most famous documentary and propaganda film ever made, it depicts the Nazi party rally at Nuremberg in 1934.

General Works

Churchill, Winston. *The Second World War*, 6 vols. (1948–1953). Vividly written memoirs by a great stylist, not to mention inspirational leader of Britain during World War II.

Lash, Joseph P. *Roosevelt and Churchill, 1939–1941: The Partnership that Saved the West* (1976). Detailed narrative of how cordial relations developed between the two leaders before America's entry into the war.

Weinberg, Gerhard L. *A World at Arms: A Global History of World War II* (1994). A thousand-page history stressing the interrelation among the various theaters and the choices facing leaders.

Nazi Germany

Bracher, Karl Dietrich. *The German Dictatorship: The Origins, Structure, and Effects of National Socialism* (1971). An important political history that set the standard before the emergence of newer social history.

Broszat, Martin. *The Hitler State* (1981). Argues that power in Hitler's state was overlapping, inconsistent, and "polycratic." Undercuts conception of efficient totalitarianism.

Frei, Norbert. *National Socialist Rule in Germany: The Führer State, 1933–1945* (1993). A succinct internal history of the Third Reich from the moment Hitler fully consolidated his power in June 1934.

Goldhagen, Daniel Joseph. *Hitler's Willing Executioners: Ordinary Germans and the Holocaust* (1996). Controversial argument that the vast majority of Germans were antisemites who willingly participated in the Holocaust.

Herf, Jeffrey. *Reactionary Modernism: Technology, Culture, and Politics in Weimar and the Third Reich* (1984). Attacks the interesting question of how the Nazis could reject Enlightenment rationality and yet value technology.

Kershaw, Ian. *Hitler: 1889–1936: Hubris* (1999). The *New York Times* called this biography as "nearly definitive as anything we are likely to get."

—*The Nazi Dictatorship: Problems and Perspectives of Interpretation*, 3rd ed. (1993). Outstanding historiographical essay that discusses the vast literature on the Nazi era with clarity and vigor. The starting point for all further study.

Peukert, Detlev J. K. *Inside Nazi Germany: Conformity, Opposition, and Racism in Everyday Life* (1987). An original study arguing that the Nazi experience was an extreme demonstration of pathologies characteristic of modernity in general.

Europe at War

Bloch, Marc. *The Strange Defeat: A Statement of Evidence Written in 1940*, trans. Gerard Hopkins (1949). Influential essay by a famous medieval historian who joined the French resistance and paid for it with his life.

Burrin, Philippe. *France under the Germans: Collaboration and Compromise* (1997). Exhaustive account of how France accommodated itself to the German occupation, something that until recently the French did not talk about.

Paxton, R. O. *The Vichy Regime: Old Guard and New Order, 1940–1944* (1972). The standard history of the effort of the right to restructure France under the German occupation.

Weber, Eugen. *The Hollow Years: France in the 1930s* (1994). Convincing description of France's disarray, which left it almost helpless before the Germans in 1940.

Franco's Spain

Preston, Paul. *Franco: A Biography* (1995). Critical of the Spanish dictator, but the basic study of his life.

Thomas, Hugh. *The Spanish Civil War*, 3rd ed. (1977). Reliable, detailed, and accurate account, including several useful appendices.

Stalin and the Soviet Union

Conquest, Robert. *The Great Terror: Stalin's Purge of the Thirties* (1973). Readable, passionate, objective, amazing story of how Stalin killed millions of his most loyal citizens.

Fitzpatrick, Sheila. *Everyday Stalinism: Ordinary Life in Extraordinary Times, Soviet Russia in the 1930s* (1999). Fascinating discussion of how people actually lived under one of the most oppressive regimes of the twentieth century.

Tucker, Robert C. *Stalin in Power: The Revolution from Above, 1928–1941* (1990). Continuation of the most authoritative biography of Stalin.

The Holocaust

Bartov, Omer. *The Eastern Front, 1941–1945: German Troops and the Barbarization of Warfare* (1985). Shows the extent to which regular German army forces were involved in mistreating and massacring Jews and Slavic peoples during World War II.

Davidowicz, Lucy W. *The War against the Jews, 1933–1945* (1973). Somewhat dated, but still probably the best place to start in a massive Holocaust literature.

des Pres, Terrence. *The Survivor: An Anatomy of Life in the Death Camps* (1976). Original and even positive book about new meanings of heroism and community in a century in which death lost much of its meaning.

Levi, Primo. *Survival in Auschwitz: The Nazi Assault on Humanity* (1961). This harrowing and brilliantly written personal account remains in print in an inexpensive paperback edition.

Spiegelman, Art. *Maus I* (1986) and *Maus II* (1991). Pulitzer prize–winning story of Vladek Spiegelman, a Holocaust survivor, told in comic book form. A powerful tour de force.

Spielburg, Stephen, director. *Schindler's List*. Popular film portraying the Holocaust through the acts of one man who saved many Jews.

PART SIX

THE END OF THE EUROPEAN ERA

The Century of Power ended in emotional, political, and economic disaster for Europe. Bankrupt, destroyed, weakened; it looked to many as if what the nineteenth-century European proudly thought of as "civilization" had been destroyed. It had not, but it certainly was about to be transformed. Inside Europe, economies stimulated in the West by American aid and in the East by Soviet five-year plans suddenly began to prosper in the 1950s. The West Europeans, led by a small group of remarkable public servants, created an economic community—along with many other integrative structures—that completely changed the international structures on the Continent. France and Germany, bitter enemies for generations, emerged as the bulwarks of more or less cooperative relations.

It was outside Europe, however, that the most fundamental changes took place. Primary among them was the emergence of the United States as the replacement for Great Britain as the world economic powerhouse. Uninvaded, unbombed, and unmassacred, the Americans controlled about half of all world trade in the immediate postwar era, as their main rivals hunkered down to lick their war wounds. And, unlike what happened after World War I, this time the United States stepped forward to exert its influence not only in Europe but throughout the world. This influence came directly into conflict with the other European flanking power, the Soviet Union, especially in Asia. There, Chinese communists, who had gained widespread support for their resistance to the Japanese invaders before and during World War II, completed their seizure of power by 1949.

In other parts of Asia and in Africa, the postwar world saw equally dramatic change. In India, for example, where the Congress party had refused to support the British during the war, it quickly became apparent that independence was the only possible solution to colonialism. In 1948, the British handed over sovereignty to Hindu India and Islamic Pakistan. In Africa a similar process began. Nigeria, for example, which the British had thought would take at least a generation to prepare for independence, insisted upon and got it in 1960, although the country quickly collapsed into civil war. Elsewhere the transition to independence was even rougher. The French hung on for all their worth in Indochina (including Vietnam) and Algeria but were unable to prevent successful national liberation movements. In places like the Congo and Angola, the Belgians and the Portuguese did essentially nothing to prepare for local independence, but it came anyway. Suddenly, over a space of about only twenty years, almost the entire European colonial empire fell away into local hands. Usually the new countries based their initial steps toward independence on European legacies, such as socialism, Leninism, and nationalism. But no matter—Europe's five-hundred-year explosion into the world had ended.

The year 1945 had brought the end of one great twentieth-century experiment: right-wing extremism in the forms of fascism and Nazism. These movements explicitly rejected the Enlightenment notions of reason, popular sovereignty, and equity. But the close of the war did not end the second great twentieth-century experiment: Soviet socialism. In fact, in 1945 the Soviet Union appeared to be on the cusp of worldwide expansion, a view seemingly confirmed by the victory of the Chinese communists in 1949 and the leftist views of the majority of intellectuals throughout the world. However, Soviet strength proved illusory. In the 1970s and 1980s, the communist states of Europe and elsewhere found that their efforts to centrally plan their economies were not working. Their idealistic goal of freeing the human personality was being smothered under an increasingly false bureaucratic state. In the end, the technological revolution of the information age and their own efforts to reform from within led to the collapse of the Soviet Union and the East European regimes it supported. Thus, the second great experiment of the century—the effort to use reason to plan all aspects of social life—also failed.

The period from the end of World War II to the downfall of communism, from the end of the Nazi experiment to the end of the Leninist one, constitutes a well-bounded and coherent period of study. The two chapters in this final part of our book, therefore, discuss the various ways in which Europe coped with collapse, rebuilt itself, and even in many ways prospered during these forty-five years.

CHAPTER 31

NEW WORLD, NEW EUROPE

Triumph of the New York School   *Curt Marcus Gallery.*

1944	Bretton Woods agreements establish International Monetary Fund and other programs for postwar economic stability
April 1945	United Nations opens in San Francisco
November 1945	Nuremberg trials begin
March 1947	U.S. agrees to take over British responsibilities in Greece and Turkey
June 1947	Marshall Plan announced
September 1947	Cominform established
February 1948	Communist takeover in Czechoslovakia
June 1948	Soviets begin Berlin blockade
June 1948	Yugoslavia expelled from Cominform
1949	Federal Republic of Germany founded; German Democratic Republic founded; NATO established; Soviets end Berlin blockade; Mao's communists victorious in China

1950	North Korea invades South Korea
1953	Stalin dies, thaw begins
1955	Warsaw Pact created; Germany joins NATO; the State Treaty formally makes Austria a neutral power
1956	Soviets quash Hungarian Revolution
1957	Treaty of Rome establishes European Economic Community
1958	De Gaulle returns to power in France
1962	Algeria gains independence; first commercial passenger jet service; color TV comes into general use
1963	France and Germany sign Treaty of Friendship and Reconciliation

The ostensible subject of Mark Tansy's witty painting *Triumph of the New York School* (shown opposite) is the history of art. At the close of World War II, the center of innovation in painting shifted from the European continent, especially Paris, to New York, where the work of artists such as Jackson Pollock made the United States a new center of creativity. Tansy shows recognizable American artists and critics dressed in American military uniforms from World War II and looking rather like General MacArthur accepting the surrender of the Japanese, supervising the capitulation of a group of recognizable European artists, including Picasso, dressed in archaic-looking uniforms from World War I.

But Tansy's painting also makes a much broader and inclusive point: After the devastation and hatred of World War II, Europe temporarily collapsed and the United States emerged to the position of power and influence that its economic strength warranted. After World War I, the United States had held back, not signing the Treaty of Versailles and retreating into a form of diplomatic isolation. After World War II, however, the United States decided to enter world politics actively, taking the place of Europe as the dominant Western power.

One reason the United States reassessed its foreign policy was that the Soviet Union also took advantage of the European collapse to increase its influence in Europe and the world. By 1950, all of Eastern Europe had become communist, and so had China, the most populous state in the world. The contrast between the Marxist rhetoric of

revolution and the American rhetoric of democracy only made the contest between the two superpowers, as they were called, more intense. This rivalry led to competition and even warfare between the two powers and their surrogates (in Korea and Vietnam for example), but it did not lead to a major world war. The Cold War was cold instead of hot in part because both sides had nuclear weapons, and both knew that a direct conflict would be disastrous both for them and for humanity.

In Europe, as in the rest of the world, the Cold War fundamentally shaped events from 1945 to 1989. Spheres of influence staked out by communist states on the one side and noncommunist states on the other endured essentially unchanged for forty years. Winston Churchill coined the term "the Iron Curtain" to describe the completeness of the separation between East and West, and it was not just a metaphor—the Iron Curtain consisted of barbed wire, watchtowers, armed guards, and radio-jamming facilities that ran down the center of Europe. This stark division could occur in a continent formerly considered a single entity because the terrible destruction of World War II left the way open for the flanking powers of the United States and the Soviet Union to meet over the ravaged body of Europe.

The universal first reaction to the conclusion of World War II was joy. The agony had ended, the forces of aggression lay smashed, and the troops were heading home. But the second reaction, especially in Europe, was a stunned realization of the wreckage. Four times as many people had died as in World War I. Poland lost not only 3 million of its Jews in the Holocaust but 3 million other Poles as well. In the USSR, the figures reached almost unimaginable levels: from 12 to 20 million dead. The physical damage was equally devastating. In the U.S. occupation zone in Germany, more than three-quarters of all houses and bridges were ruined. The city of Warsaw, formerly inhabited by a million persons, lay in uninhabited rubble when the Red Army occupied it. French industrial production had collapsed to 35 percent of its prewar figure. It is no exaggeration to say that World War II temporarily destroyed Europe.

And yet, out of these ashes emerged a phoenix of recovery that dwarfed anything the world had ever seen. During the century and a half of industrialization that preceded World War II, the European economies had grown an unprecedented 225 percent. In only twenty-seven postwar years—from 1948 to 1975—they grew 250 percent. Mechanization, improved seed, fertilizers, protein-rich feed, and pesticides produced by conscious technological effort fueled an equivalent agricultural boom. Whereas in 1900 one German farmer could produce enough food for five persons, in 1980 a single farmer was feeding thirty-five Germans. The agricultural population of Europe, still 40 percent before the war, fell to 10 percent and less afterwards. Food surpluses replaced hunger as one of society's most volatile political issues.

As fewer and fewer farmers provided more and more food, cities became huge urban agglomerations that sprawled across the land, creating new styles of suburban living dependent on the automobile. Technologies of all kinds rewrote daily life. Antibiotics almost eliminated ancient diseases such as tuberculosis and syphilis and provided miracle cures for countless other hitherto untreatable afflictions. Television replaced the still new medium of radio as the mainstay of public information, and passenger jets opened the world to high-speed travel. Tens of thousands of newly developed chemical compounds became the basis of countless new products, while at the same time creating wholly new environmental problems.

In the political sphere, the threat of nuclear war made postwar politics almost as different from the politics of the previous century as the new technologies were from their predecessors. No German peace treaty concluded World War II in Europe. Instead, the two victorious flanking powers, the United States and the Soviet Union, divided the collapsed continent into spheres of influence, rigidly enforced by Stalin in the East and vigorously negotiated by the United States in the West.

Under cover of this Cold War between totalitarianism and pluralism, Europe experienced three fundamental changes: (1) French and German leaders agreed to end generations of bitter conflict; (2) this rapprochement made possible the creation of the European Economic Community (today known as the European Union), establishing a new kind of European equilibrium; and (3) Europe's five hundred years of colonial expansion came to a close. In all likelihood, none of these things would have happened unless Europe had disintegrated during World War II. In the first section of this chapter, therefore, we discuss collapse—the breakup of the wartime alliance, the loss of empire, the adherence of West Germany to the democratic alliance, and the emergence of the Cold War between the United States and the USSR. These events set the stage for creative reconstruction, which we discuss in the second section. The final section of the chapter argues that of all the changes that followed World War II, the most fundamental was rapid, sustained economic growth—the twentieth century's criterion of societal success.

THE CONSEQUENCES OF COLLAPSE

The most common experience of daily life is continuity. Individuals, and societies, become creatures of habit. We eat the same thing for breakfast, we take the same route to school, we sit in the same seat in class. Societies experience continuity not only because of such habitual behavior, but also because powerful social actors—the leaders, the dominant social groups, and the wealthy—have an interest in preserving their position. Societies do change, of course, but only against powerful pressures for sustaining whatever exists in the present. Europe in 1945, however, was not a normal society. Not only was the habitual life of almost every individual European thoroughly disrupted, but in many places the entire political and social structure of society was smashed, seemingly beyond repair. It was, as the Germans put it, *Stunde null*, or "zero hour." This catastrophe, this vacuum, presented enormous problems—how to rebuild, under which leaders, using what ideologies. But it also presented equally vast possibilities for innovation. The system that these complementary imperatives produced turned out to be unique in the long history of European development.

The Wartime Alliance

The wartime partnership among the victorious Allies was never an easy one. Stalin had allied himself with Hitler from 1939 to 1941, after all, and many in the West had felt deeply threatened by Soviet communism from its inception. But when Hitler invaded the Soviet Union, both British prime minister Winston Churchill and American president Franklin Delano Roosevelt set aside their differences with the Soviet regime and joined Stalin in a united effort to defeat Nazism. This cooperation did not mean, however, that the United States, Great Britain, and the Soviet Union pursued similar war aims.

President Roosevelt did not approach foreign affairs with the same hardheaded practicality as he did domestic politics. Wilsonian in his outlook, he and his State

Department detested territorial ambitions as the root cause of international conflict. Even before World War II broke out, Roosevelt had insisted in an off-the-record news conference that he would not conduct "political discussions" relating to "boundaries and territories. . . . We have not done it since Paris [1919] and there is no prospect of our doing it." Instead, Roosevelt cast American war aims as broad principles analogous to Wilson's Fourteen Points. In 1941 he and Churchill signed the Atlantic Charter, in which they advocated self-determination, equality of economic opportunity, friendly collaboration among the peoples of the world, and freedom from want and fear. To achieve these noble but vague goals, the two leaders hoped to establish an international organization that would prove

OURS... to fight for

Freedom of Speech   *Freedom of Worship*

Freedom from Want   *Freedom from Fear*

The Four Freedoms   In August 1941, Winston Churchill and Franklin Roosevelt signed the Atlantic Charter calling for self-determination of peoples, freedom of the seas, and other Wilsonian goals. In an effort to popularize the agreement, Roosevelt summed up its provisions as "Freedom of speech, freedom of religion, freedom from fear, and freedom from want." American painter Norman Rockwell depicted Roosevelt's characterization in a homey way in this propaganda poster. *National Archives Photo #44-PA-189.*

more effective than the League of Nations had been. In short, despite the reputation of Americans as practical problem solvers, Roosevelt's war aims were broadly ideological, an extension of Wilson's hope of making the world safe for democracy.

By contrast, Stalin pursued narrow, territorial war aims, despite the Soviet Union's reputation as a highly ideological state. Soviet goals had become apparent already in 1939 when the Red Army occupied eastern Poland in agreement with Hitler. Stalin then promptly incorporated the short-lived Baltic countries of Latvia, Lithuania, and Estonia into the Soviet state and seized strategic areas bordering on Leningrad (St. Petersburg) in a short but difficult war with Finland. In 1940 Soviet troops invaded Bessarabia, an area long claimed by the Russians but inhabited mostly by Romanian-speaking people, and added a similar territory, northern Bukovina. These actions moved the Soviet border some 200 miles to the west. When Hitler invaded the Soviet Union in 1941, therefore, the minimum Russian war aim became restoration of the Soviet Union's expanded borders at that time (see Map 31-1).

Great Britain went to war in 1939 to preserve the integrity of Poland's borders of that year, not those of 1941. Nevertheless, both Churchill and Roosevelt recognized that once the Red Army reoccupied the provinces of eastern Poland the Western Allies would be able to do little. At their conference in Tehran late in 1943, therefore, Roosevelt, Churchill, and Stalin agreed that the Soviet Union would retain eastern Poland and that Poland would be compensated with German territories. In other words, they moved Poland about 200 miles to the west.

The practical solution to the Polish border question sketched out at Tehran indicates the kind of sphere-of-influence arrangements that Churchill favored. The British prime minister found himself pulled by both Stalin and Roosevelt. Convinced of the rightness of the democratic form of government, and a great admirer of Roosevelt, he also appreciated geopolitical realities. When the Red Army reached the borders of Romania in the spring of 1944, Churchill initiated discussions concerning the postwar arrangements in southeastern Europe. Roosevelt reluctantly condoned these discussions but refused to commit himself. In October 1944, Churchill and Stalin, meeting in Moscow, finalized the levels of influence they would exercise in Eastern Europe. While Stalin was listening to a translation, Churchill wrote out various percentages on a piece of paper and shoved it over to Stalin. They were:

Romania: Russia 90%, the others, 10%
Greece: Great Britain (in accord with United States) 90%, Russia 10%
Yugoslavia: 50–50%
Hungary: 50–50%
Bulgaria: Russia 75%, the others 25%

MAP 31-1
SOVIET EXPANSION, 1939–1950

Shortly after the agreement with Hitler was signed in August 1939, the Soviet Union began a campaign of expansion into Eastern Europe. By the time Hitler invaded, the Soviets had seized substantial territories from Finland, Poland, and Romania, and had annexed Estonia, Latvia, and Lithuania. When the Red Army swept back through the region in 1945, Stalin added the Königsberg area (now Kaliningrad) and the small Ukrainian part of Czechoslovakia. By 1948, the Soviet satellite area included all the countries of Eastern Europe.

Stalin looked over the piece of paper and checked it off with his blue pencil. "After this there was a long silence," Churchill later wrote. "At length I said, 'Might it not be thought rather cynical if it seemed we have disposed of these issues, so fateful to millions of people, in such an off-hand manner? Let us burn the paper.' 'No, you keep it,' said Stalin."

As far as Churchill was concerned, Stalin kept his part of the bargain. Greek communists, the backbone of anti-German resistance in Greece, suddenly became amenable to compromise. Their militarily dominant underground movement put up only sporadic resistance to the British troops that landed late in 1944 in the wake of the German retreat. Over the next two years, the Soviets reaped the rewards of their side of the bargain by establishing servile pro-Soviet governments in Romania and Bulgaria.

As the discussions between Britain and the Soviet Union unfolded, the United States concentrated on the shape of the postwar economic system. Liberals in the United States wanted to avoid the destructive trade poli-

cies of interwar Europe. Realizing that the United States would come out of the war as the world's dominant economic power, they were convinced—as British liberals had been in a similar position in the nineteenth century—that free trade would not only stimulate world commerce but benefit their country as well. A viable world trading system needed stable currencies, such as had existed before World War I. In July 1944, therefore, representatives of the Allied states met at Bretton Woods, New Hampshire, and agreed to reestablish gold as the basis of currency. They also arranged to designate certain currencies, primarily the dollar, as reserve currencies that countries must hold to meet their international obligations, and to establish the International Monetary Fund to maintain monetary stability.

Later that year, representatives of the Allies met at Dumbarton Oaks, an estate in Washington, D.C., and concluded a basic agreement for establishing the United Nations. This reworking of Woodrow Wilson's scheme for instituting a rule of law in international affairs became a reality in April 1945. That month, the founding conference met in San

Francisco and finally, after several last-minute compromises, approved the UN Charter.

The climax of wartime negotiations came in February 1945 when Roosevelt, Churchill, and Stalin met in the Crimea at the tsar's old palace near **Yalta.** In retrospect, some have assessed this conference a critical failure of Western wartime policy, the moment when the democracies abandoned Eastern Europe to Stalin. But as we have seen, Poland's postwar borders had already been sketched in, and Churchill had already made his deal with Stalin concerning southeastern Europe. FDR came to Yalta with an agenda that had little to do with Eastern Europe. Most important, he wanted a Soviet commitment to enter the war against Japan. Roosevelt also needed Stalin's final approval for the United Nations. The American president got both of his wishes. Stalin promised to enter the war against Japan ninety days after the conclusion of the European war, and he agreed to the creation of the United Nations.

Yet Stalin had his own objectives at Yalta. Like Clemenceau after World War I, he sought heavy and prolonged reparations from Germany. Both Churchill and Roosevelt, however, seeing a democratic Germany as important to postwar stability, held out for more lenient treatment. Stalin also wanted Allied approval of the puppet regime he intended to install in Poland. Because the Red Army had occupied much of the country at this point, the only way for Roosevelt and Churchill to prevent a communist takeover would have been to go to war against the Soviet Union. With Hitler not yet defeated and the war still raging in the Pacific, such a turn of events was unthinkable. The best the three leaders could do was to paper over their differences with a vague statement on Polish unity.

The main time bomb at Yalta was a document produced by the United States Department of State titled the Declaration on Liberated Europe. Consistent with the Wilsonian thrust of American war aims, the Declaration called for the creation of interim governments in the liberated countries "broadly representative of all democratic elements." It also stipulated "free elections of governments responsive to the will of the people."

This formula contained a major flaw: It conflicted with the West's willingness to allow the Soviet Union to secure its western border. Recognizing that the Soviet Union had been invaded twice in one generation from Germany, the Allies agreed that the Soviets had a right to expect friendly governments in Eastern Europe. But no people of Eastern Europe, with the possible exception of the Bulgarians, would have freely elected a government friendly to the Soviet Union. This contradiction was insoluble. When the Declaration came up at Yalta, Stalin signed it as an inoffensive piece of window dressing. The State Department took the document more seriously, however, seeing it as an agreement to introduce the ideals enunciated by the Atlantic Charter into Eastern Europe. When instead the Soviets installed subservient regimes there, American conservatives in particular felt betrayed.

Yalta later became a symbol of the Cold War because the agreements signed there brought the long-standing contrast between the Western and Soviet systems into sharp focus. But neither Yalta nor any particular person was responsible for the Cold War. A great deal of ink has been spilled over this issue. According to the political left, the United States, by seeking to control world markets, provoked the Russians; the political right argues that the United States was only responding to Soviet aggression and trying to defend freedom. In truth, the destruction of Europe in 1945 provided a unique moment for both powers to assert their control over portions of the Continent. The two powers facing each other over the European void each defined themselves in highly ideological terms—the Soviet Union as the vanguard of world revolution, the Marxist-Leninist motherland of the future, and the United States as the paragon of democracy, combining the material success of capitalism with the principle of equity. With such highly charged differences, the wonder is not that conflict between the two systems colored world politics for forty years, but that the Cold War stayed cold.

Bringing Germany Back

Despite the differences that increasingly separated the United States and the Soviet Union as the war drew to a close, both sides agreed that Germany should lose some of its territory and that its Nazi leaders should be punished. For centuries German settlers had pushed eastward into central and southeastern Europe. During a few months in 1945, a massive population movement reversed those centuries of expansion. Germans from lands no longer to be considered part of the Reich, such as the Sudetenland, the Vojvodina (northern Yugoslavia), and western Poland, fled or were brutally evicted by invading troops. The Red Army in particular treated the German civilians with vicious hatred, wantonly killing and raping as they swept into Germany. The Czechs, Yugoslavs, and Poles joined in the retribution.[1] By 1950 Germany counted about 9 million expellees among its population; more than a million others died in the end-of-war chaos. Millions of other displaced persons from all over Europe filled resettlement camps in Italy and Germany in the months following the war. Many of them eventually found their way to North and South America, but many unlucky Soviet citizens were sent back to their native land, where a very large number were imprisoned or shot as traitors, even though in many cases their only "crime" was to have been captured while fighting the Nazis.

---

[1] This process at the end of World War II resembled the "ethnic cleansing" practiced in the former Yugoslavia in the 1990s. The eviction of millions of German civilians from east central Europe was widely supported on the grounds that local German populations had sympathized with and actively aided Nazi aggression.

Finding New Homes Poles suffered enormously during World War II, both from the Soviets, who seized eastern Poland, and from the Nazis. Both tried to eliminate Poland as a place and as a culture. The anxiety in the faces of these postwar Polish orphans, clothed by the American Red Cross and cared for by the Catholic church, reflects not only their own plight but that of millions of displaced survivors of the war. *Wide World Photos.*

In November 1945, an international court brought twenty-four surviving Nazi leaders to trial for crimes against humanity. Convened in the devastated city of Nuremberg, the site of the annual Nazi party conclaves and the place where some of the main anti-Jewish laws had been promulgated, the trial put a symbolic end to Nazism. After ten months of deliberation, the court found all but three of the accused guilty, and sentenced twelve men to death by hanging.[2] One of the important principles the court established was that simply following orders was not an adequate defense for crimes against humanity.

Soviet judges were part of the Nuremberg court, but Stalin's preferred method of justice was simply to kill off those he considered unreliable or threatening. In their zone of occupation, the Soviets imprisoned or shot thousands of those suspected of Nazi crimes or associations. The Western occupiers, on the other hand, wishing to establish notions of due process and individual guilt, undertook a massive review of personal histories. Scrutiny of millions of questionnaires led to the identification and punishment of some 1,700 Nazis as major offenders, 23,000 as offenders, and 150,500 as lesser offenders. The cumbersome process undermined the smooth running of business and government, and sometimes proved unfair. In 1951, by which time anticommunism seemed more important than settling

---

[2] Of the twenty-four indicted persons, one was never apprehended (Martin Bormann), two committed suicide, one was declared incompetent, three were acquitted, four received sentences from ten to twenty years, three received life sentences, and ten were hanged. Of the four main Nazi leaders, only Goering survived to be tried, and he committed suicide just after hearing his sentence to death by hanging.

old scores, a reinstatement act permitted many former Nazis to rejoin the civil service. By the early 1950s, half or more of government employees were former party members. Whatever the ethics of this fact, abandoning the pursuit of justice in favor of pragmatism prevented disgruntled Nazis from becoming a disruptive pressure group and in this way helped stabilize postwar Germany.

On the main issue, however—how to restore Germany as a political entity—the wartime Allies could not agree. In the summer of 1945, the Big Three met for the last time in the German city of Potsdam, with Harry S Truman replacing the deceased Roosevelt, and Labour party leader Clement Attlee, who had just won Britain's first postwar election, replacing Winston Churchill. In the most fateful decision of this meeting, the three leaders agreed to permit each of the occupying powers to take its reparations payments from its own occupation zone. The Western Allies, particularly the United States, confidently expected a free-market system to prevail in the postwar world, whereas the Soviet Union believed that only a centrally directed economy could rebuild Europe. This agreement thus ensured that as each occupying power organized its zone to extract reparations payments, Germany would develop as two distinct economies. Almost from the beginning, therefore, the Soviet zone and the Western zones of occupied Germany began drifting apart.

The opening of Soviet archives after 1991 has shown that Soviet leaders were far from united on how to deal with Germany. Their formal policy was to create a united but neutral Germany. But a harsh military commander introduced Stalinist devices into the Eastern zone. For example, he forced the surviving Social Democratic party to amalgamate with the Communist party of Germany to create the Socialist Unity Party (SED). By 1949, the Soviets turned their zone into a secure Stalinist satellite, the German Democratic Republic (GDR).

The Western Allies abandoned the idea of a single peace treaty for all of Germany even before the Soviets did. On January 1, 1947, the British and Americans combined the economies of their zones into what they called the Bizone, taking the first substantial step toward creating a West German state. At the same time they lifted all rationing and restrictions on trade. The new currency was a joint American-German scheme, but the freeing of trade was the unilateral brainchild of Ludwig Erhard, the German head of the economic committee of the Bizone. Erhard's move was daring in the climate of the day, when many believed that only a planned economy could deal with the tremendous postwar problems. Erhard acted on his own, without consulting General Lucius Clay, military governor of the American zone. When Clay confronted Erhard, he asked, "Herr Erhard, my advisors tell me that what you have done is a terrible mistake. What do you say to that?" "Herr general," Erhard replied, "pay no attention to them. My own advisors tell me the same thing." For

many years, the left decried Germany's failure to seize the opportunity to turn toward a managed economy. Today, most analysts consider Erhard's bold move the indispensable first step in Germany's miraculous economic recovery.

The currency reform, which clearly presaged the creation of a West German political entity, provoked the Soviets to respond. Berlin, like the rest of Germany, and like Austria and Vienna, had been divided into four occupation zones. Because the Soviet portion of occupied Germany surrounded the city, Western forces had to use specified highways, railroads, and canals to transport supplies to their parts of the city. With the announcement of the currency reform, the Soviets closed those routes in June 1948. The crisis that ensued was a defining moment. Should Western tanks push down the highways into Berlin? Might this mean war? Instead, the Western Allies began to supply their sectors of Berlin by plane. Many military leaders were not at all sure this would work, and it was entirely possible that the Soviets would fire on them. This almost surely would have precipitated a serious military confrontation. But the Soviets did not fire, and over the next eighteen months, until the Soviets relented, an airbridge of American and British planes landing every two minutes day and night supplied the Western sectors of Berlin with everything from vegetables to coal. By the time the Soviets lifted the embargo late in 1949, West Berlin had become a stronghold of pro-Western feeling. The Berlin Airlift set the tone for the Cold War in Europe: confrontation, but no actual hostilities.

Not entirely by coincidence, during the months of the Berlin Airlift, the Western Allies authorized the Germans to work out the legal structure for a new West German state. From September 1948 to March 1949, representatives of the eleven *Länder*, or German regions, wrote the Basic Law. They declined to term the document a *constitution*, because they saw it as a temporary arrangement pending the unification of all four occupation zones into one country. The Basic Law called the Federal Republic of Germany (FRG—West Germany) a "social state," but it left the structure of the economy—free market or socialist—to the future. The document included a number of provisions from former German practice, but was resolutely democratic in its procedures and in its guarantees of fundamental civil rights.

After approval by the Allies, West German elections held in August 1949 produced a small plurality for the Christian Democratic Union (CDU), the center-right party headed by Konrad Adenauer. Many Germans felt that a coalition uniting the CDU with the close second-place finisher, the German Social Democratic party (SPD), would provide the most broadly based leadership for rebuilding Germany. But Adenauer adamantly rejected this strategy. Adenauer, who had never collaborated with the Nazis, insisted that Germany's future lay with democracy and capitalism. Vigorously anticommunist and deeply suspicious of

THE HUMAN EXPERIENCE

Konrad Adenauer, West German Leader

Konrad Adenauer (1876–1967) lived most of his life in and around Cologne. Technically Cologne was part of Prussia, but culturally it was a Rhineland city, which meant that it looked more toward France and the West than did the Junkers who dominated the empire of Adenauer's youth. In his family life, Adenauer could easily have been mistaken for a Prussian. He was a strict disciplinarian, insisted on neatness and courtesy, and expected immediate compliance with his wishes. But in his political life, Adenauer was quite the opposite. He believed that the state should not dominate the individual, that Germany should not annex new territories, and that only rapprochement with France would secure Germany's future.

Adenauer came from a poor but not impoverished family. Through hard work and sacrifice (not eating meat on Sunday, for example—the only day the family would have been able to afford it) he and his father put aside enough money to send him to secondary school, after which he won a scholarship that permitted him to obtain a law degree. At age twenty-six he joined the firm of a man who headed the Center (Catholic) party of Cologne. Four years later his mentor permitted him to run for city council, and by 1917 he was lord mayor of Cologne.

Making his mark as mayor by reestablishing Cologne University, creating a greenbelt of parks and parkways circling the city, improving the Rhine's port facilities, and other

innovations, Adenauer entered into the national arena as speaker of the Prussian state council. His interests, however, remained primarily in the Rhine region. When Hitler became chancellor in 1933, Adenauer did what he could to hinder the Nazis, refusing to meet Hitler at the airport, for example, and removing swastikas from city property. The Nazis soon banished him from Cologne. Adenauer spent the next twelve years in internal exile, sometimes in hiding in a monastery or a mill, and in the end in prison. One week after Americans arrived in Cologne, they asked him to resume his post as mayor.

Cologne ended up in the British zone of occupation, and the British ousted Adenauer late in 1946, perhaps because they favored the socialists. This setback actually freed Adenauer to create a new party that brought together Catholics and Protestants: the Christian Democratic Union. By 1949 he had made himself head of that party, and therefore, after its victory in the first federal elections, he became the first head of the Federal Republic of Germany.

Adenauer was not interested in domestic issues. The man who got the credit for Germany's economic miracle was Ludwig Erhard, his minister of finance and successor as chancellor. Adenauer focused on Franco-German agreement. He had no tolerance for communism and was convinced that peaceful coexistence with totalitarianism was impossible. During his period in office West Germany broke relations with any country that recognized East Germany. Ambitious, cool, more than self-confident, and loving power, Adenauer nevertheless put Germany solidly on the track to democratic reintegration with Europe. ❖

Corbis-Bettmann.

the socialists, he held that a planned economy such as that advocated by the Social Democrats would stifle German recovery. Instead he envisioned a "social market economy" in which a safety net of social legislation would soften the harshest edges of market capitalism. Adenauer's coalition of parties of the center and right proved just strong enough to elect him chancellor by a razor-thin margin of one vote.[3]

It is impossible to exaggerate the significance of Adenauer's election. In 1949 West Germany could easily have turned to resentments similar to those that followed World War I. Had it done so, the history of Western Europe in the fifty years following World War II would have been dramatically less stable than it turned out to be. Adenauer advocated bringing Germany slowly but surely into the fold of democratic states by proving its commitment to democracy and to the market, thus pursuing Gustav Stresemann's interwar policy of fulfillment. Adenauer also believed that only German and French cooperation could guarantee European equilibrium. A prickly leader with strong views and an authoritarian bent, he set West Germany on a path that made it the most powerful—and perhaps the most democratic—country in Europe. Seventy-three years old at time of his initial election, he told his supporters he had the strength to last a year, perhaps two. In fact he held the office for fourteen years, longer than the entire existence of either the Weimar Republic or Hitler's Reich.

The Collapse of Empire

The cataclysmic end of World War II fatally weakened Europe's ability to contest its colonies' desire for freedom. Not surprisingly, Europeans and the peoples they encountered have always viewed colonialism in different lights. Europeans admitted that a primary purpose of their imperial adventures was "to become rich as all men desire to do," as Portuguese explorer Bartolomeu Dias put it in the late fifteenth century. But they also considered their expansion a civilizing mission, bringing God's word to "the heathen" in the sixteenth century and the virtues of liberalism and capitalism to the benighted natives in the nineteenth century. The former subjects of European imperialism, understandably, see events differently. With justification they point out the exploitation, the racism, the stultifying domination, and the hypocrisy of the imperial ethic. The Dual Revolution (French and Industrial) did not spread around the world by a process of passive cultural diffusion. Aggressive European adventurers, explorers, capitalists, missionaries, and politicians forced their way into the lives of millions of people at a high cost to indigenous traditions, religions, economies, and histories.

But the imperialists did not realize that their colonial structures contained the seeds of their own demise. The ideals of the French Revolution and, after 1917, of the Bolshevik Revolution attracted intellectuals everywhere. The first taught nationalism, equity, and social change, the second suggested a mechanism—the disciplined revolutionary party—for introducing those benefits. Out of the dozens of movements that proliferated to shake off European rule, a few major examples will have to suffice.

China was never a colony, although its military and political weakness left it open to despoliation in the nineteenth century. Paralyzed by its inability to change fast enough to fight off foreigners, and challenged at home by revolutionaries, the Chinese imperial government collapsed in 1911, more than two thousand years after the consolidation of the Han Dynasty. But it proved easier to overthrow the imperial regime than to establish a stable new one. Local strongmen defied the central government; a vigorous communist movement emerged; and the main nationalist party, the Guomindang, expended its energies trying to stay in power rather than by instituting reforms or countering its own corruption.

Japanese invasions in the 1930s only added to the Guomindang's problems. Under the leadership of Jiang Jieshi (Chiang Kai-shek), the nationalists fought back. The Communist party, which had fled to a remote area in 1934 to escape annihilation by Jiang, used Jiang's preoccupation with other problems to regroup. Mao Zedong, the communist leader, urged the party to reach the peasantry and organize every village. By "swimming among the masses," as Mao put it, and by maintaining steadfast opposition to any compromise with the Japanese, the communists came out of World War II as strong as the Guomindang. Invigorated by the support they received from the peasantry and inspired by the possibility of creating a new China, the communists won the civil war and in 1949 pushed the Guomindang off the mainland to Taiwan.

Like the victory of Lenin in Russia, Mao's triumph in China was possible only because of the disruption of a devastating war. Maoism combined European elements and Chinese adaptations into a new philosophy of revolution. It stressed the continuing nature of the revolutionary process, and emphasized revolutionary aims over the needs of the economy, education, or rational administration. For twenty-five years after the communist victory, China endured an often harrowing revolutionary upheaval that left it momentarily weak but changed forever.

India took another route to independence, one structured by centuries of European inroads and British administration. The British East India Company had united most of India under a single rule only in the first half of the nineteenth century. After putting down the Sepoy Rebellion of 1857–1859, the British government assumed rule from the company, and in the years that followed British administration became increasingly arbitrary. The Indians

---

[3] In parliamentary systems, such as those in West Germany and Great Britain, the parliament elects the prime minister (whose title is *chancellor* in Germany).

reacted in 1885 by forming the Indian National Congress, which by the turn of the century began to demand independence. Some Indians achieved a great deal in expanding educational and other opportunities for their people, but not until the Liberal party came to power in Britain during World War I did the British agree to begin devolution of power to the Indians themselves. Conservatives, including Winston Churchill, continued to oppose this step, while in India the conflict between Muslim and Hindu nationalists split the liberation movement. The enormous popularity of Mohandas Gandhi's program of nonviolent opposition and boycott proved that, despite their differences, both religious groups upheld the ideal of independence for India.

The Indian National Congress refused to support Britain in World War II unless India received full rights, and when the Labour party came to power in London in 1945 it moved quickly to hand over the final reins of authority. In 1947 India became an independent state. Because the Congress party was a strong movement even before the Bolshevik Revolution, it remained liberal in orientation and India has remained democratic since. But because Congress was a Hindu party, Indian Muslims felt they needed their own state, Pakistan. The two hundred thousand deaths that accompanied the independence of India and Pakistan were due to religious rioting that occurred as millions of Hindus and Muslims migrated into either one or the other new state. Pakistan itself split in 1971 when East Bengal formed the nation of Bangladesh.

Great Britain gave up its major colonies reluctantly, but at least with some degree of grace. Other colonial powers resisted more stubbornly. In Southeast Asia, for example, the French trained only a few Vietnamese in administration and fiercely resisted the liberation movement of Ho Chi Minh. When the French finally withdrew with ill grace after military defeat in 1954, they left a weakened country into which the United States soon was drawn as the French surrogate.

Letting go of Algeria was even more difficult for the French than Vietnam. Directly across the Mediterranean, this North African country contained about a million French settlers who were citizens of metropolitan France. The French did not permit the Algerians the opportunity to become French citizens until 1947, and instead economically subordinated the Algerians. These circumstances inevitably stimulated an Algerian independence movement. To combat the National Liberation Front (FLN), the French military turned to torture and the massacre of innocent civilians. It took General Charles de Gaulle to counter the French military and finally to let Algeria go in 1962. The episode, discussed more fully a little later in this chapter, created great bitterness among some elements of French society.

The least accommodating colonial power was the oldest: Portugal. The Portuguese empire, though not large by World War II, did include Angola. In this Southwest African country, the Portuguese ran all affairs themselves, refused to educate any Africans, and kept blacks trapped in low-income jobs. When the Portuguese left in 1975, taking all their administrative and economic expertise and possessions with them, Angola collapsed in chaos.

In general, new leaders elsewhere in Africa assumed that in order to enter the twentieth-century world they needed to follow the European example of creating nation-states. However, the borders of these states usually were inventions of the Europeans, and nationalism made little sense in countries that were home to many different ethnic groups. State socialism, which many African countries tried, turned out to be another wrong turn adopted from European experience. The combination of European exploitation and unwise adoption of European models helped doom Africa, despite the appearance of independent new states, to decades of slow development.

One new country appeared after World War II that was unique in its origins: Israel. The notion that Jews should have a state of their own appeared late in the nineteenth century in the form of Zionism. After World War I, Britain assumed a League of Nations mandate over Palestine and agreed, with much foot-dragging, that the Jews should have a homeland there. The Arab countries of the Middle East supported Palestinian opposition to this plan, but significant numbers of European Jews began moving to Palestine anyway, particularly after Hitler came to power.

At the conclusion of World War II, the horrendous Jewish losses in the Holocaust swung Western opinion, particularly in the United States, behind the idea of partitioning Palestine into a Jewish and an Arab state. The United Nations backed this solution in 1947. When the Arab states objected, warfare broke out between armed Jewish elements and the Arab League. By May 1948, the Jewish forces occupied their portion of Palestine, and more, and proclaimed the state of Israel, which both the Soviet Union and the United States quickly recognized. Deep antagonisms, however, prevented the creation of a counterpart Arab Palestinian state.

Of the European powers, only Great Britain gave any serious thought to how its colonies could sustain modern life without European tutelage. The ideas of the Century of Power, which had emphasized struggle, fitness, and superiority, left Europeans poorly equipped for a moment they thought never would come—Europe's removal from the international stage. Consequently, meeting the challenges of the Dual Revolution has been painful in much of the world. The tremors of the transition from colony to sovereignty oscillated political seismographs for thirty-five years after World War II.

The Flanking Powers Take Hold

The United States emerged from World War II incomparably the strongest power on earth. Its industry and infrastructure strengthened by the vast wartime effort, its level of personal savings at a record high, and its government in sole possession of atomic weaponry, the United States presented a vivid contrast to devastated Europe. In the years following the war, the United States turned out more than half of the world's industrial production. This unusual position of power did not necessarily mean that the United States would assume a more responsible role in international affairs than it did after World War I. It did ensure, however, that its policies would powerfully shape European and world affairs in the immediate postwar era.

As the war drew to a close, American policy makers realized that a postwar program akin to the wartime Lend-Lease Act would be needed to help Europe get back on its feet. The United Nations responded with the United Nations Relief and Rehabilitation Administration (UNRRA), which distributed about $4 billion worth of vitally needed food and supplies throughout Europe.[4] The United States contributed three-quarters of the UNRRA supplies. Congress stopped Lend-Lease itself, but during the next year and a half the United States extended more than $2 billion in loans to Europe through the World Bank, transferred billions of dollars worth of military equipment to friendly nations, contributed $2.75 billion to the International Monetary Fund, and loaned Britain $3.75 billion.

At the same time that these steps were establishing the U.S. economic position in Western Europe, the Soviet Union was consolidating its political hold on Eastern Europe. The passage of the Red Army through the region offered Stalin every opportunity to influence politics there, but East European dissatisfaction with the failures of democracy and capitalism in the interwar years had created a desire for change in the region as well. Nonetheless, Stalin acted most severely in Romania and Bulgaria, on the basis of his agreement with Churchill, and in Poland because of that country's strategic location between Germany and the Soviet Union. In Hungary and Czechoslovakia, strong but not dominant communist parties entered into coalition governments and Soviet troops withdrew.

Finland provides an apt study in the pragmatic quality of Stalin's policies toward Eastern Europe. This Nordic country had been part of the Russian Empire during the nineteenth century, and had even invaded the Soviet Union in 1941 as an ally of Hitler. Yet Soviet troops did not occupy the country. Instead, the Finns agreed to give the Soviets strategic military bases, ceded their most important mining region, and promised to support Soviet-Finnish friendship. Finland, blessed with able noncommunist leaders, saved its independence by giving the Soviets what they wanted.

Early in 1946 neither the Soviet Union nor the United States could predict the shape of their postwar relationship in Europe. Truman talked tough, but he expected to be able to bargain with the USSR. Stalin, sounding even more aggressive than Truman, behaved brutally in Poland and the Soviet occupation zone of Germany, but he counseled the powerful communist parties in France and Italy to avoid revolutionary adventures. As 1946 progressed, however, tensions increased. In February, Canadian investigators uncovered a Soviet spy ring, and Stalin gave a speech stressing the incompatibility of the capitalist and communist systems. In the same month, George Kennan, an experienced American diplomat stationed in Moscow, sent a long, influential telegram back to the State Department. He argued that Stalin required a hostile outside world to support his totalitarianism and therefore was incapable of reasonable behavior. In March, Winston Churchill, no longer in government but already an icon of British wartime resistance to Nazism, delivered a speech in the presence of President Truman suggesting that an "Iron Curtain" of communism had descended over Eastern Europe.

Soviet newspapers continually spoke of world revolution, condemned imperialist oppression, and held up the Soviet Union as the paragon of peaceful democracy. American counterparts spoke of communist aggression, free markets, and the need for free elections in Eastern Europe. Both sides felt convinced that the other was bent on world domination, and each could cite plentiful examples of the other's aggressive tendencies. The Soviets commanded the loyalty of communist parties around the world, and in China communist forces were poised to take over the globe's most populous country. The United States sent American carriers into the Mediterranean and established a sphere of influence in Iran. In occupied Japan, General Douglas MacArthur imposed a Western-style constitution and installed a democratic government, thus turning that former enemy into a Western ally.

The decisive point came in 1947. In February, Great Britain, its economy not yet recovered from the war despite the American loan, decided that it could no longer keep up its security commitments around the world. It informed the United States that it would no longer lend assistance to Turkey or help a right wing Greek government to prosecute the civil war that had broken out there in 1946. Truman and his advisers considered the communist revolt in Greece an especially serious instance of Stalinist aggression. They did not realize that the communists there received their support from Tito's Yugoslavia, not from Stalin. Nevertheless, on March 12, 1947, Truman went before Congress and requested that the United States aid Turkey and Greece. Truman saw the world split into two camps—one in which "life is based on the will of the majority," and the other in which it "is based on the will of a minority forcibly imposed upon the majority." Congress granted Truman's request. With this step, the United States

---

[4] To grasp the substantial size of the aid mentioned in this discussion, note that the U.S. gross national product in 1945 was $211.9 billion. In the year 2000 the GNP approached $9,000 billion. As a proportion of GNP, therefore, UNRRA aid would equal about $170 billion in 2000 terms.

THE HISTORICAL EVIDENCE

The World in Two Camps

1947

Early in 1947, Great Britain informed the United States that it could no longer support the conservative government of Greece against its communist insurgents. President Truman decided to step into the breach. The world was divided into two camps, he said, free and unfree, and it was the job of the United States to uphold the former. This was the decisive moment when the United States assumed the role of leadership that its economic strength after World War II implied. Later that year, Joseph Stalin called the communist parties of Europe together and, through his surrogate Andrei Zhdanov, laid out the Soviet view of two competing camps. Below are condensed excerpts from Truman's speech to Congress and Zhdanov's speech to the assembled communist leadership.

Harry S Truman to the United States Congress, March 1947

One of the primary objectives of the foreign policy of the United States is the creation of conditions in which we and other nations will be able to work out a way of life free from coercion. This was a fundamental issue in the war with Germany and Japan. Our victory was won over countries which sought to impose their will, and their way of life, upon other nations. The peoples of a number of countries of the world have recently had totalitarian regimes forced upon them against their will. At the present moment in world history nearly every nation must choose between alternative ways of life. The choice is too often not a free one. One way of life is based upon the will of the majority and is distinguished by free institutions, representative government, free elections, guarantees of individual liberty, freedom of speech and religion, and freedom from political oppression. The second way of life is based upon the will of a minority forcibly imposed upon the majority. It relies upon terror and oppression, a controlled press and radio, fixed elections, and the suppression of personal freedoms. I believe that it must be the policy of the United States to support free peoples who are resisting attempted subjugation by armed minorities or by outside pressures.

Andrei Zhdanov to a Meeting of European Communists, September 1947

Alarmed by the achievements of Socialism in the U.S.S.R., by the achievements of the new democracies, and by the postwar growth of the labor and democratic movement in all countries, the American reactionaries are disposed to take upon themselves the mission of "saviors" of the capitalist system from communism. The frank expansionist program of the United States is therefore highly reminiscent of the reckless program, which failed so ignominiously, of the fascist aggressors, who, as we know, also made a bid for world supremacy. A new alignment of political forces has arisen. The more the war recedes into the past, the more distinct become two major trends in postwar international policy, corresponding to the division of the political forces operating on the international arena into two major camps: the imperialist and antidemocratic camp, on the one hand, and the anti-imperialist and democratic camp, on the other. The cardinal purpose of the imperialist camp is to strengthen imperialism, to hatch a new imperialist war, to combat socialism and democracy and to support reactionary and antidemocratic profascist regimes and movements everywhere. The purpose of the [antifascist] camp is to resist the threat of new wars and imperialist expansion, to strengthen democracy and to extirpate the vestiges of fascism. Just as in the past the Munich policy untied the hands of the Nazi aggressors, so today concessions to the new course of the United States and the imperialist camp may encourage its inspirers to be even more insolent and aggressive. The Communist parties must therefore head the resistance to the plans of imperialist expansion and aggression along every line.

_____

Source: From Gale Stokes, ed., *From Stalinism to Pluralism*, 2nd ed. (New York: Oxford University Press, 1996), pp. 36, 39–40.

explicitly assumed the role of leadership that it had rejected in 1920.

Truman and his successors followed a policy called **containment.** George Kennan, now back in Washington, introduced the term in a 1947 article in the journal *Foreign* *Affairs*. The United States, he wrote, should follow a "policy of firm containment, designed to confront the Russians with unalterable counter-force at every point where they show signs of encroaching upon the interests of a peaceful and stable world." Although Kennan always claimed that containment should be achieved primarily by economic, political, and diplomatic means, it quickly turned into a military policy as well.

Stalin reacted to U.S. initiatives in September 1947 by calling together the European communist parties to create a new level of Soviet control, resulting in the Communist Information Bureau (or **Cominform**) At this meeting, Andrei Zhdanov, one of Stalin's most unpleasant and repressive henchmen, endorsed Truman's idea that the world was divided into two camps. But he defined them as the imperialist camp and the "antifascist and freedom-loving elements" led by the Soviet Union. Because the struggle between these two camps had moved to a new stage, Zhdanov instructed the parties of Eastern Europe to cease cooperating in their coalition governments. Accordingly, in February 1948, Communist in Czechoslovakia seized power in a coup d'état.

The Czechoslovak events, along with the Berlin blockade, unnerved both the Europeans and the United States. In April 1949, twelve Western countries, including the United States and Canada, created the **North Atlantic Treaty Organization (NATO),** a cooperative military alliance designed to deter the Soviet Union from invading Western Europe. The Soviet Union countered in 1955 by setting up the Warsaw Pact with its satellites. For the next thirty years these two military alliances confronted each other in the center of Europe.

EUROPE REBUILDS ITSELF

The events discussed so far were all heavily influenced by extra-European factors. Even the creation of the two new Germanies was more a reflection of power relations between the United States and the Soviet Union than it was of German initiatives. But very quickly after the dust had settled, the West European states reasserted themselves and began moving toward significantly changed relationships. The United States played an important role in these affairs, of course, through the Marshall Plan, NATO, and other devices. In the East, Stalin established a rigid dictatorship in central Europe that began to change only after his death in 1953.

A Look to the Left, a Turn to the Right

As colonies began to seek independence and Europe split into Eastern and a Western camps, normal political life began to reemerge. Immediately after the war, the parties of the left seemed to hold the upper hand. Even without the Stalinist imposition in Eastern Europe, dissatisfaction with the failures of the interwar years would have made socialist parties strong there. Large communist parties in Italy and France entered coalition governments, and in Great Britain, a Labour government took power promising to install a "socialist commonwealth." Every country in Europe engaged in at least some nationalization of formerly private enterprises. Under Clement Attlee, the British Labour government placed some 20 percent of the economy under the control of government boards and introduced a National Health Service to provide medical services to all citizens. Similar developments unfolded in France, Italy, and Czechoslovakia. These moves did not fulfill the hopes of most workers, however, because they usually did not give them any more say in running factories. The National Coal Board, for example, ran British mines more or less as the old owners had, and the Renault autoworks in France operated much the same under the government as it had under private ownership.

Britain was less successful in rebuilding its economy than the other major countries. The strains of war severely depleted British industry. Worse, invisible income from the colonies had shriveled, leaving Britain with few resources to pay for essential imports. By 1947 a strict rationing program prohibited all civilian driving, made using an electric heater in the summer a criminal offense, and slashed food rations to below the World War II level. In 1949, the government gave up trying to maintain the value of the British currency (the mistake of the interwar government) and devalued the pound from over $4.00 to $2.80. This realistic valuation made British goods more competitive, and slow recovery began. Even so, the British economy remained weak for a generation after World War II.

In France, the collaboration of the Vichy regime with Nazi Germany destroyed the antirepublican right, which had been a force in French politics for a century. Members of the resistance, who tended to be communists and socialists, took revenge on collaborators, and perhaps other enemies, in the days that followed liberation, and a court martial eventually convicted Marshal Pétain of treason. But the left faced a formidable obstacle to achieving power in the person of Charles de Gaulle. This former tank commander was a hardheaded but romantic patriot. He had vigorously opposed surrender to the Germans in 1941, but managed to escape to England. Asked upon his arrival about his mission, he replied, "I am not on a mission. I am here to save the honor of France." De Gaulle organized the Free French, an army that eventually numbered three hundred thousand men, and constantly badgered the Allies to increase French participation in the war effort. Among the first to enter liberated Paris in August 1944, he used his enormous prestige to become "dictator by consent." Establishing a government that included all non-fascist political opinions, he did not permit the left wing resistance leaders to assume control. A reestablished bureaucracy quickly restored a semblance of order to the devastated French economy.

At first it seemed that France would establish a stable new government on the basis of three major parties—the Communists, the Socialists, and the right-center party, the Popular Republican Movement. But when bickering intensified over the form of the new government—the public decisively rejected a return to the Third Republic—de Gaulle

THE HUMAN EXPERIENCE

Jean Monnet, Father of the European Community

Jean Monnet (1888–1979) never ran for elected office, was never a cabinet minister, and never held political power. He did not attend college, was a poor public speaker, rarely wrote anything himself, and was not especially wealthy. Nevertheless, Monnet is universally credited with being the spark behind the most original political invention of the twentieth century—the European Economic Community (today known as the European Union). He is a political category all to himself: the truly creative public servant.

Monnet spent his youth selling cognac abroad for his family business. When World War I started he immediately wangled an audience with the French prime minister through a relative and proposed unification of the British and French procurement services for the duration of the war. This

unprecedented—and successful— proposal was indicative of many cooperative ventures he was to make later. His work during the war led to appointment as deputy secretary general of the League of Nations, where he worked out an original plan that put Austria back on its feet. During the 1920s and 1930s, however, Monnet spent most of his time in the United States and China as an international banker. Monnet understood how American business worked, and he made lasting friendships with some of America's postwar leaders, including John Foster Dulles.

During World War II, Monnet represented French and British interests in Washington while at the same time playing a key role in unifying the Free French provisional government. When the war was over, his unmatched contacts, complete lack of

political ambition, and willingness to let others take credit opened essentially every important door to him in the Western world. Monnet was a practical man who had no time for grandiose schemes. His plan for the modernization of French industry, the Monnet Plan, eschewed end goals and theoretical justifications. He believed that the process itself, once set moving in the right direction, would produce its own results.

He used the same principle in proposing the European Coal and Steel Community to French prime minister Robert Schuman. As Schuman's declaration in 1950 put it, "Europe will not be conjured up at a stroke or by an overall design; it will be attained by concrete achievements generating a community of interests." Later Monnet characterized the European Community not as an institution or a thing, but as a process. The deepening and strengthening of the EC since its beginnings in 1957 has proved his judgment correct.

Monnet's strategy was to listen with intensity and comprehension to those with information and to speak with clarity and conviction to those with power. He did not try to be clever, did not speak down to anyone, and did not deceive—he used the same well-honed arguments with everyone. He polished these arguments by gathering intelligent and well-informed people around him and talking problems through until he emerged with his mind clear and objections contained. "Few men," François Valery remarked admiringly, "have enjoyed so little power and yet exerted so much influence." ❖

AP/Wide World Photos.

suddenly resigned in January 1946. Eventually a referendum approved a constitution creating the Fourth Republic, but its provisions restored many features of instability that had troubled prewar France. Between 1948 and 1958, the French experienced nineteen different governments. The

Communists, who lost their seats in the coalition government in March 1947, and a new party, the Rally of the French People, which de Gaulle founded in April of the same year, both opposed the Fourth Republic. To counter them, the Socialists allied with the parties of the right in shifting and ever-changing combinations to exclude the Communists and Gaullists from power for the next ten years.

By 1947 France had worked out the most extensive plan for postwar reconstruction achieved by any Western state. The architect of the plan, Jean Monnet, surely ranks as one of the most remarkable European political figures of the postwar era. Monnet was not impressed with grand schemes and ideology. His philosophy was to find a well-defined problem and solve it, regardless of who got the credit. He put together a small planning team; protected it from the bureaucrats; drew hundreds of businessmen, farmers, and labor leaders into the modernization discussions; obtained American support; and steered his plan to approval by early 1947. The Monnet Plan had its faults. It underestimated the amount of capital available, and it put off meeting the need for housing. But Monnet's idea that planners should facilitate collective decision making, not impose directives, energized French modernization without undermining the market economy. The economic plans produced by French governments from that time forward consisted primarily of broad national investment targets. This kind of indicative planning contrasted sharply with the detailed directives that Soviet-style centralized planning imposed on entire economies.

Events in Italy followed a similar path as in France, except that Italy had no de Gaulle. Instead, it had Alcide de Gasperi, leader of the Christian Democrats. De Gasperi's party won the first postwar election in 1946 but maintained a coalition government with the Communists and Socialists. The Communist party leadership wanted to demonstrate its ability to work in a democratic and constitutional state, and so was willing to make compromises. But after the Cold War heated up, de Gasperi, under pressure from both the Vatican and the Americans, dropped the Communists from the coalition in May 1948. This move completed the elimination of the Communist party from participation in Western governments. Because the exact opposite had occurred in Eastern Europe—the elimination of all except the Communist party—the political split between East and West became fixed for another generation.

Yugoslavia was an exception to this split, in significant measure because it was practically the only Marxist-Leninist regime that had arisen in Eastern Europe without Soviet sponsorship.[5] In 1945, Tito's Partisan movement emerged the victor in Yugoslavia's three-cornered civil war and established a communist state modeled in many ways on the Soviet Union. Until 1948, Yugoslavia was stoutly Stalinist. Tito put his enemies in prison, brutally settled scores with Serbian royalists and Croatian fascists who had lost the civil war, repressed nationalists and separatists of all ethnicities, installed central planning, and launched collective farming in some areas. Yugoslavia even shot down U.S. airplanes that strayed over its airspace and threatened war over control of the Italian port of Trieste. The world was shocked and amazed, therefore, when in June 1948 the Cominform ejected this militant Leninist state from the community of brotherly, socialist states. Stalin had excommunicated Yugoslavia. It quickly came to light that the Yugoslavs had complained to Stalin about heavy-handed Soviet interference in Yugoslav affairs. When Stalin accused the Yugoslavs of being Trotskyites, the worst calumny in the Soviet lexicon (and an utter absurdity), they shot back: "No matter how much each of us loves the land of socialism, the USSR, he can, in no case, love his own country less."

It took the Yugoslav communists a few years to recover from the Soviet economic blockade that followed separation. By that time, however, the West realized that Tito's maverick socialism might be an asset in the containment struggle and began to send aid. The Yugoslavs decided to differentiate themselves from Stalin's state-socialism by creating a new, non-Stalinist socialism they called *self-management*. According to this concept, all property would be socially owned (that is, technically owned by society at large rather than by the state or by any single owner) but run by the workers themselves. The theory attracted worldwide attention, but in actuality the League of Yugoslav Communists never relinquished its leading role in Yugoslav society. Nonetheless, in the 1960s Yugoslavia became the most open East European communist state.

The European Community

Early in 1947, European economies, though recovering, were still at a low ebb. The exceptionally harsh winter of 1946–1947 worsened the situation. In Berlin, more than two hundred people froze to death and people were paying 3 cents a night to escape the cold in railroad stations. In February 1947, former president Herbert Hoover reported that Germany was on the verge of starvation. American secretary of state George Marshall wanted to help, but in a way that would draw Europe together. He did not want states to get into a destructive competition with each other for U.S. aid. In June 1947, in a hastily arranged commencement speech at Harvard University, Marshall proposed the European Recovery program. Known as the **Marshall Plan**, it stipulated that the United States would provide generous help to the Europeans on the condition that they work out a joint plan for economic reconstruction.

In July 1947, seventeen countries—not including the Soviet Union and its satellites, which refused the invitation—met in Paris. They created the Organization for European Economic Cooperation (today the OECD—Organization for European Cooperation and Development) to coordinate plans to liberate trade and get Europe back

---

[5] The other such regime to win power on its own was that of Albania, but during and immediately after the war, the Albanian Communists were under Tito's influence, and the country seemed slated for eventual annexation by Yugoslavia.

Rebuilding and Resupplying Europe   The Marshall Plan not only sent money and goods such as locomotives and grain to Europe, but also provided resources such as sugar that helped European morale. In the end, the greatest contribution of the plan was in restoring European confidence.   *UPI/Corbis-Bettman.*

on its feet. Congress accepted Marshall's idea, and over the next four years the United States poured $13 billion of aid into Western Europe.[6] The Marshall Plan jump-started the European economies—growth rates during those four years reached 15 to 25 percent. Just as important, it reassured Europeans that America was not going to abandon them nor limit its aid to military and security matters.

[6] About $470 billion in 2000 terms, in proportion to the GNP.

The Marshall Plan fit well with the network of other schemes that created the postwar system of liberal capitalism. Stable currencies ensured by the Bretton Woods agreement and the International Monetary Fund (IMF), combined with a lowering of tariff barriers implemented by the General Agreement on Tariffs and Trade of 1947, produced a sixfold jump in world trade in manufactured goods between 1950 and 1970. The Council of Europe, founded in 1949, and the West European Union (WEU), founded in 1948, also proved useful over the years in promoting human rights.

These innovations encouraged creative thinking, especially on the question of how to reintegrate West Germany into Europe. In the late 1940s, the French had not yet decided on their policy toward Germany. Its leaders worried in particular over how the French steel industry, still considered the centerpiece of a modern economy, could compete with Germany, because the cheapest and best coking coal lay in the Ruhr. For the first five years after the war, the French devised several plans for controlling German resources. They insisted on and got restrictions on German steel production and created a satellite French regime in the Saar region. Some farsighted leaders, however, notably Jean Monnet, realized that in the long run France could not outcompete Germany in heavy industry, and that European stability would suffer if France and Germany got into a cutthroat economic competition. Monnet understood the interdependence of modern economies. "The nations of Europe are too circumscribed to give their people the prosperity made possible, and hence necessary, by modern conditions," he wrote in 1945. "Prosperity and vital social progress will remain elusive until the nations of Europe form a federation of a 'European entity' which will force them into a single economic unity." Rather than leave things to theory, Monnet's practical mind turned to coal and steel. Would these industries not provide an ideal foundation for German and French cooperation?

At a meeting of the foreign ministers of France, Britain, and the United States in September 1949, American secretary of state Dean Acheson asked French foreign minister Robert Schuman to propose a policy toward Germany for the three occupying powers at their next meeting in May 1950. This request put Schuman on the spot. France had to come up with a scheme for Germany. Only ten days before the crucial meeting, Monnet's team presented Schuman with a plan for pooling the German and French coal and steel industries. Schuman seized upon the idea. He hurried it through his cabinet, got Konrad Adenauer's approval, and announced it publicly before even well-informed people knew what was happening.

The Schuman Plan broke decisively with past French policy. Instead of trying to thwart Germany and compete with it directly, Monnet and Schuman proposed a true economic union of the coal and steel industries. The idea of a common market without tariffs and with free access to all parties was central to the plan, but its key achievement lay in the creation of a High Authority with the right to levy taxes and of a Court of Justice to adjudicate disputes. In other words, France and the other countries that joined the European Coal and Steel Community (ECSC) surrendered a bit of sovereignty in return for access to German coke, while Germany granted access to its raw materials in return for lifting restrictions on its production. The initial members of the community, which began operating in mid-1952 with Monnet as its director, included Belgium, the Netherlands, Luxembourg (the so-called Benelux countries), and Italy, along with France and the Federal Republic of Germany. Great Britain held aloof, still perceiving itself primarily as senior partner in the British Commonwealth and as enjoying a special relationship with the United States.

The Coal and Steel Community succeeded in part because it levied a turnover tax on coal and steel.[7] This revenue gave it the resources to retrain the workers displaced by the rapid decline in coal mining as oil and electricity became the dominant sources of power. The removal of tariff barriers triggered a boom in iron and steel. By 1958 employment in these industries had increased by eighty thousand while at the same time wages grew more than 20 percent. Best of all, there seemed to be little political backlash. The Coal and Steel Community, despite its interminable bureaucratic wrangling, foot dragging, and occasional bad press, seemed popular, and it was working.

The drive toward European integration received impetus from a completely unrelated event—the Korean War. In 1945 the Soviets had accepted the surrender of Japanese forces in North Korea and the United States had done the same in South Korea. In the years that followed, Korea split, just as Germany did, and both the Soviets and the Americans withdrew most of their troops. In June 1950, however, communist North Korea, after finally getting approval from Mao and a reluctant Stalin, invaded South Korea.

Coming so soon after the 1949 Chinese communist victory over the Guomindang and the establishment of a revolutionary regime in China, the invasion seemed to confirm America's worst fears that communism was inherently expansionist. Harry Truman leaped into action. Taking advantage of a temporary Soviet boycott of the United Nations Security Council, where the Soviet delegate had vetoed dozens of postwar measures, the United States got the council to authorize resistance to the invasion. UN forces, consisting primarily but not exclusively of American troops, battled their way northward as far as the Chi-

nese border (see Map 31-2). At this point the Chinese intervened, almost wiping out the United Nations troops. But the UN forces held, and in 1953 an armistice created the militarized border that still exists between the two Koreas. The Korean "police action" (Truman did not want to ask Congress to declare war) cost approximately 3 million lives, 54,000 of them American.

In Europe, American-led NATO provided the basic security against an invasion such as that in North Korea. But sound security arrangements would require German participation. This was a sticky issue. Only five years, after all, had passed since the defeat of Nazism, and Germany was once again becoming an economic powerhouse. One plan was to create a European Defense Community (EDC) in which the United States would not participate, but in mid-1954 the French assembly rejected this scheme because it meant German rearmament in a purely European setting. In 1955, the French permitted Germany to enter NATO, where American power could balance the German weight. These developments dashed the hopes of those who had envisioned a Europe free of American influence.

But Jean Monnet was not discouraged. Having resigned as head of the Coal and Steel Community, he formed an Action Committee comprising representatives of dozens of Europe's most important political institutions, including unions and political parties. Monnet concentrated his attention on a relatively small-scale but doable project: creating a European Atomic Energy Commission (Euratom). He wanted Europe to compete with the United States in what he believed would be the energy source of the future. In the meantime, Paul-Henri Spaak, the Belgian prime minister, developed a plan for a customs union among the six partners of the Coal and Steel Community. Monnet's Action Committee brought most of the important political elements in Europe on board, especially the German Social Democratic party. Until 1956, West German socialists had opposed European integration because they believed it would impede the unification of Germany. Spaak's and Monnet's joint efforts culminated with the Treaty of Rome, signed on March 25, 1957, when the six members of the Coal and Steel Community signed treaties establishing two new communities: Euratom and the **European Economic Community (EEC)**.[8]

The Commission of the European Economic Community, which took up its headquarters in Brussels, became the professional executive of the new organization. Its task

---

[7] A *turnover tax* is levied on a product at each stage of its progress toward final sale. A *value-added tax* is levied on the amount of value added to a product by each intermediate producer. A *sales tax* is imposed at the point of final sale. Sales taxes are common in North America, whereas turnover and value-added taxes are common in Europe.

[8] In 1967, administration of the European Coal and Steel Community, Euratom, and the European Economic Community were combined to create the European Community (EC). (Note that both the European Economic Community and the European Community are sometimes referred to as the Common Market.) In 1993 the European Community became the main pillar of the European Union.

MAP 31-2
THE KOREAN WAR

Although Korean borders ended up more or less where they had started, with Korea divided into a communist north and a noncommunist south, the war fluctuated enormously. At first, the South Korean troops, hastily reinforced by United Nations forces under General Douglas MacArthur, were pushed almost off the peninsula. The subsequent UN offensive reached nearly to the Chinese border, whereupon the Chinese army entered the war and pushed the UN troops back. It took two years to reach a settlement after these events.

Map labels:

CHINA

Manchuria

Sea of Japan

Chinese Communists cross Yalu River on November 26, 1950

Yalu R.

Chongjin

U.N. forces cross 38th parallel and push north to Yalu River

Hamhung

Hungnam

Pyongyang

NORTH KOREA

Withdrawal of U.N. forces and stabilization of defense area near 38th parallel (December 1950–April 1951)

Initial North Korean attack on June 25, 1950

38th Parallel

U.N. forces land at Inchon on September 15, 1950

Seoul

Inchon

U.N. forces after Inchon landing

Farthest advance of North Koreans. U.N. makes stand at Pusan Defense Perimeter, June–September 1950.

SOUTH KOREA

Pohang

Taegu

Pusan

Yellow Sea

JAPAN

North Korean forces
Chinese Communist forces
United Nations forces

---

was to prepare rules and regulations based on the decisions of the Council of Ministers, which was the law-adopting body. The Council of Ministers consisted of the appropriate representatives from each country (that is, transportation ministers would meet concerning transport, health ministers would meet on health issues, and so forth). The Court of Justice adjudicated violations of community regulations. The EEC's parliamentary committee, which eventually became the European Parliament meeting in Strasbourg, had only advisory power. Over the years, these agencies all changed in their importance and relationship to one another, but—perhaps most important—the court's decisions in its area of competence came to supersede national law. Thus, the EEC's vast number of regulations on everything from the size of trucks to the definition of mineral water have the force of law and are not mere intergovernmental agreements that can be broken on every pretext.

In today's European Community, a long-established institution, it is difficult to recall how original, creative, and unexpected it was in 1957. Four factors assisted its creation. First, American support and interest played a crucial role. Granted, the U.S. desire to counter the Soviets and to enhance its own trade drove American policy more than abstract principles—but nevertheless, starting with the Marshall Plan, the United States strongly supported European integration. Second, the separation of Eastern Europe under Soviet domination freed West Europeans from involvement in the ethnic politics of that region, a problem that surely would have complicated efforts to integrate. Third, postwar leaders felt a powerful new conviction that governments had to produce economic progress. The realization that political legitimacy rested on economic prosperity had not been common in the nineteenth century and was only vaguely sensed even in the interwar years. But after World War II, it burst into full bloom, motivating politicians to find new ways of assuring growth. The fourth and indispensable factor was leadership, not only by Monnet, Schuman, Spaak, and de Gasperi, but by Konrad Adenauer. From the beginning, Adenauer sought to bring Germany back to respectability by reintegrating his country with Europe. Reconciliation with France provided Adenauer with the pathway to European stability and German prosperity.

Formation of the European Economic Communities put in place the final major piece of the new international structure of postwar Western Europe (see Table 31-1). An alphabet soup of institutions—NATO, GATT, IMF, WEU,

TABLE 31-1

POSTWAR ECONOMIC ORGANIZATIONS

In the immediate postwar period a number of organizations were created to address the economic problems associated with rebuilding Europe. Some of these agencies and associations are still active today, while others merged, expanded, or otherwise adapted to changing conditions. Though by no means an exhaustive list, this table presents the major organizations discussed in this chapter.

Organization	Year Founded	Brief Description
International Monetary Fund (IMF)	1944	Created to stabilize international monetary rates and promote foreign exchange cooperation
World Bank	1945	Promotes economic development by facilitating capital investment in member states
General Agreement on Tariffs and Trade (GATT)	1948	Aimed at abolishing international trade quotas and reducing tariffs
European Coal and Steel Community (ECSC)	1951	Originally formed to unify the coal, iron, and steel industries of its six member nations.
European Atomic Energy Community (Euratom)	1957	Created to develop nuclear energy for peaceful uses.
European Economic Community (EEC)	1957	Outgrowth of the ECSC; created to remove economic barriers among member nations.
European Community (EC)	1967	Formed when ECSC, Euratom, and EEC merged to unify their administrative system.
European Union (EU)	1993	Outgrowth of the EC; reflects expanded membership (15 members in 2000) and scope of operations.
World Trade Organization (WTO)	1994	Outgrowth of GATT

the UN, EC, and more added over the years—provided dozens of negotiation venues in which countries could thrash out their problems. Today, it is no longer thinkable for a German politician like Bismarck to "wave a red rag in front of the Gallic bull" in order to provoke war. When disputes arise, Germany and France no longer produce Schlieffen Plans and build Maginot Lines. Armed with cellular phones and notebook computers, their negotiators hurry off to any one of the dozens of negotiating nodes that make up the European system and fight it out with paper and e-mail. Complaints about the complexity of the new "Eurocrat" rules and regulations, the futility and abstract quality of the endless GATT negotiations, and the lessening of national sovereignty can come only from those who have forgotten what the new European system replaced: the Century of Power, with its disastrous consequences.

The Communist World from Stalinism to Thaw

As Western Europe moved toward greater economic integration through voluntary agreements, the Soviet Union integrated Eastern Europe—except Yugoslavia and Albania—in a quite different way. As long as Stalin remained alive,

the countries of Eastern Europe became small replicas of the worst aspects of Soviet communism. Repressive governments nationalized property, eliminated opposition, reordered education, instituted centralized planned economies, and slavishly adulated the Soviet Union. In Czechoslovakia and Hungary, as well as in Bulgaria and Romania, vicious witch-hunts condemned loyal communists to death as "Titoist spies" and imprisoned tens of thousands of others in a bizarre replay of Stalin's purges of the 1930s.

Stalin also insisted that the East European economies join the socialist world economy, which meant reorienting their production and trade to fit Soviet needs. As part of this reorientation, the East European countries adopted a strategy of economic development that was not badly suited to their relative economic backwardness. Economies can grow in two ways: either though increasing inputs—labor or raw materials—or by raising efficiency. The latter method, which requires introducing new technology and entering into the world market, was not feasible under Stalin because he wanted to wall off the socialist economies. The socialist world adopted the alternative method. By bringing underemployed peasants and women

An Angry Khrushchev In 1960, during a tense time in Soviet-Western relations, Soviet leader Nikita Khrushchev gives an emotional speech at the plenary session of the United Nations in New York. At one point in the meetings he took off his shoe and pounded it on the table to object to a point with which he did not agree.

into medium-tech factories, East European countries rapidly expanded their economies in the 1950s. This growth was not as dramatic as that in the West, but the East European economies did grow, pulling the vast majority of women and peasants into the industrial workforce by the 1960s.

Early in 1953, Stalin died. Many Soviet citizens greeted the tyrant's death with tears and foreboding, having known nothing except his all-encompassing leadership for twenty-five years. The new leadership, a triumvirate out of which Nikita Khrushchev emerged as the dominant figure, greatly eased tensions in the Soviet Union. During the thaw that followed Stalin's death, Soviet leaders loosened censorship, released vast numbers of prisoners who had been swept up in the 1930s, and slightly modified centralized planning. In 1955 they also signed the State Treaty with Austria, withdrawing from central Europe and making Austria formally a neutral power.

In Eastern Europe, the thaw went further than the Soviet Union had planned. Early in 1956, Khrushchev delivered a lengthy speech to the Twentieth Party Congress in which he severely criticized Stalin for developing a "cult of personality." For the first time, Khrushchev detailed some of Stalin's crimes and the annihilation of not only his enemies but even loyal party members. Khrushchev added that Stalin had made many mistakes during World War II and yet insisted on taking sole credit for the victory. The

Soviet leader's speech, designed solely for important party members, quickly became known in the West and created a sensation, particularly in Poland and Hungary.

In Poland, the death of a Stalinist leader early in 1956 led to calls for reform and to rioting. In October of that year, the deepening crisis brought Khrushchev to Warsaw, where he acquiesced in the ascension to power of a national communist (rather than one trained primarily in Moscow). The change in Poland inspired both intellectuals and workers in Hungary. Late in October, strikes broke out there, and Imre Nagy, a reform-minded Communist party leader returned to power. Nagy asked the Soviet forces to leave, and they started to pull out. But when Nagy declared Hungary neutral and allowed noncommunist political parties to reconstitute themselves, the Soviet army came back shooting. In a short and vicious war, the Red Army reasserted Soviet control over Hungary. Nagy was soon hung.

The Hungarian revolutionaries harbored the naive hope that the West would come to their aid. Under President Dwight D. Eisenhower and his secretary of state John Foster Dulles, American foreign policy was hostile to the Soviet Union, and Dulles tried to line up every state he could in anti-Soviet alliances. Dulles sneered at "Finlandization" as a moral failure to commit fully to the anti-Soviet struggle. Some Americans, even many in government, had irresponsibly claimed to want to "roll back" communism. But these were empty words. In actuality, the West in no way wanted to risk a nuclear war over Hungary.

Complications arose when, at the height of the Hungarian Revolution, France and Britain attempted to seize the Suez Canal without consulting the United States. Suez had been the lifeline of European trade with Asia since its

Hungarians Revolt In October 1956, Soviet troops had started to pull out of Hungary, but when a new government tried to declare neutrality, they came back shooting. Before Soviet domination was reestablished, revolutionaries pulled this massive head of Stalin from its pedestal. *Corbis-Bettmann/UPI.*

THE HISTORICAL EVIDENCE

Khrushchev's Attack on Stalin's "Cult of the Individual"

February 1956

For the last twenty or more years of his life, Joseph Stalin ruled the Soviet Union with an iron fist. On the other hand, he was revered as the victorious leader of the Soviet Union over Hitler's Germany, and as someone elevated almost to the level of a god. Less than three years after he died, however, Nikita Khrushchev, the Soviet Union's new leader, stunned his colleagues with a speech in which he accused Stalin of creating a "cult of personality" around himself that had deviated from the true principles of Lenin, whose still valid principles, according to Khrushchev, Stalin had deformed. After going into detail to describe how Stalin falsely accused loyal party members and sent them to their deaths and how he had shown exceptionally poor leadership early in World War II, Khrushchev goes on in this excerpt to criticize Stalin's boundless vanity.

Comrades

The cult of the individual acquired such monstrous size chiefly because Stalin himself, using all conceivable methods, supported the glorification of his own person. This is supported by numerous facts. One of the most characteristic examples of Stalin's self-glorification and of his lack of even elementary modesty is the edition of his "Short Biography," which was published in 1948.

This book is an expression of the most dissolute flattery, an example of making a man into a godhead, of transforming him into an infallible sage "the greatest leader, sublime strategist of all times and nations." Finally, no other words could be found with which to lift Stalin up to the heavens.

We need not give here examples of the loathsome adulation filling this book. All we need to add is that they were approved and edited by Stalin personally and some of them were added in his own handwriting to the draft text of the book. . . .

[For example, in] the draft text of this book appeared the following sentence: "Stalin is the Lenin of today." This sentence appeared to Stalin to be too weak, so in his own handwriting, he changed it to read: "Stalin is the worthy continuer of Lenin's work, or, as it is said in our party, 'Stalin is the Lenin of today.'" You see how well it is said, not by the people but by Stalin himself.

Source: From Bertram D. Wolfe, *Khrushchev and Stalin's Ghost* (New York: Frederick A. Praeger, 1957), pp. 214–216.

---

opening in 1869, but in 1952 an Egyptian nationalist revolution with socialist tinges under the leadership of Gamal Abdel Nasser had seized power there. Early in 1956, the Egyptians adopted a constitution creating a socialist Arab state governed by a single party. Until then, Britain and the United States had been working with Egypt to control the Nile River's annual flooding by building a dam at Aswan. But John Foster Dulles decided that Egypt was becoming too socialist, and he cut off the aid. To raise money for the dam, Nasser nationalized the Suez Canal. This move provoked the British and French attack, which they coordinated with an Israeli assault on the Sinai Peninsula. It was a foolhardy venture. Neither the French nor the British had made appropriate preparations, as they soon discovered when the entire world, including President Eisenhower, denounced the effort and forced them to back down. The Suez fiasco amply demonstrated that the European ability to impose colonial decisions was finished. In the confusion, the revolution in Hungary was almost overlooked.

Despite the forceful Soviet intervention in Hungary, Khrushchev's foreign policy principle remained **peaceful coexistence,** a milder notion than Stalin's presumption that the West was plotting a decisive war against the Soviet Union. Khrushchev's main difficulty was keeping the communist movement united after the loss of its iron-fisted leader. He met his greatest defeat in China. There, Mao Zedong had his own definition of revolution. Mao stressed the ability of the ordinary person to revolutionize the land. In 1957 and 1958, the regime organized hundreds of thousands of people to build irrigation canals and to place small iron smelters in their yards. Party activists herded tens of millions of peasants into huge communes and oversaw massive urban construction projects. The Great Leap Forward proved a failure—the iron produced was useless, and agricultural production plummeted. But the contrast between Mao's aggressive revolutionary ideology and Khrushchev's post-Stalinist caution led to many controversies between the two communist giants. Finally, in 1960, the Soviets abruptly called home all their advisers and canceled economic assistance to China, and the rift between the two powers became public.

East Germany also presented Khrushchev with problems. From the time of the creation of the Germany Democratic Republic in 1949 until 1960, almost 3 million East Germans—about one-seventh of the country's population—had fled to the West. These emigrants were often among the most educated and skilled. By 1961 a thousand persons were leaving East Germany every day simply by taking the Berlin subway into the Western sectors. Suddenly, in August 1961, East German troops sealed off their zone of Berlin, at first with temporary fences but eventually with a high concrete wall backed by cleared fields, mines, and armed guards. The Berlin Wall worked, in the sense that it cut East German emigration dramatically, but it also became "a permanent, massive, anticommunist propaganda exhibition."

The most dangerous moment of the Khrushchev era came in 1962 when the Soviets attempted to place intermediate-range ballistic missiles in Cuba. When American intelligence discovered the effort, President John F. Kennedy ordered a quarantine of Cuba.[9] The tense days that followed were the closest the world has come to nuclear war. Finally, however, Khrushchev agreed to remove the missiles (the United States also removed some obsolete missiles from Turkey), and war was averted. The crisis actually improved U.S.-Soviet relations. Within a year, a "hot line" from Moscow to Washington permitted direct communication in times of tension. In Moscow, however, the Cuban missile crisis was the last straw in the minds of Khrushchev's conservative opponents. They saw him as an unstable enthusiast who rushed into grand schemes and then retreated when they failed or when he shifted his attention to something else. In 1964 Khrushchev returned from a vacation to discover that he had been sent into involuntary retirement by a collective leadership under Leonid Brezhnev, who dominated Soviet politics until his death in 1982.

The Last Great Frenchman

Charles de Gaulle—tall, proud, *French*—dominated West European political life in the 1960s. After a brief flurry of activity following his resignation in 1946, de Gaulle had retreated from public life and settled down in his country home just outside Paris. He had predicted that the Fourth Republic would be unstable, but as it stumbled from one government to another he remained silent.

The Algerian situation finally lured de Gaulle back to public life. After France's humiliating withdrawal from Indochina, smarting army officers vowed not to suffer the same fate in Algeria, where a revolt against French rule had been simmering since the end of World War II. As the French army's methods grew steadily more inhumane, its commanders started to usurp the government's power in Algeria. Stories of torture and atrocities committed against Algerians leaked out, and French public opinion began to turn against the army. Early in 1958, French pilots defied orders from Paris and bombed an Algerian village, killing many innocent civilians. When a new government intimated that it would begin negotiations with the Algerians, the most radical French civilians in Algeria united with the army there and seized control of Algiers. With sympathetic paratroopers landing in Corsica, a civil war like Franco's rebellion in Spain twenty years before loomed.

The army officers involved believed that if de Gaulle came to power, he would sympathize with their desire to keep Algeria under French control. Political leaders, on the other hand, believed that only "the General" could control the army. De Gaulle insisted on three conditions before he would assume power: that he command the army; that he have emergency powers for six months; and that France would adopt a new constitution featuring a strong president. When the National Assembly acceded to his demands, he returned. Within a few months, a referendum had passed a new constitution establishing the Fifth Republic. In a December election, the French public raised de Gaulle to president with almost 80 percent of the votes.

Soon after his initial assumption of power in June 1958, de Gaulle visited Algeria, where he encouraged his supporters with the ambiguous phrase "I have understood you." But it quickly became apparent that he intended to let Algeria go. In September 1959, he advanced the principle of self-determination, and in 1962 Algeria at last won its independence. The outcome so infuriated diehards that de Gaulle suffered approximately thirty attempts on his life during his ten-year presidency. In one of these incidents, just after the final agreement with Algeria, a would-be assassin riddled the president's car with fourteen bullets, but failed to hit him. Probably no other person in France could have released Algeria without precipitating civil war.

De Gaulle's political platform was old-fashioned and simple: the grandeur of France. Concentrating on continental affairs rather than on the Atlantic partners, he abandoned France's twentieth-century alliance with Britain in favor of friendship with Germany. During the de Gaulle era, the British applied twice for admission to the European Community, and both times de Gaulle vetoed their

---

[9] The action was called a "quarantine" because under international law a blockade is an act of war. The effect, however, was to set up an American blockade of Cuba by threatening to have the U.S. Navy stop and board all incoming Soviet-bloc ships.

Charles de Gaulle France's great postwar leader gestures to a political gathering. De Gaulle's uncompromising leadership of the Free French during World War II, his unquestioned patriotism, and his enormous popularity made it possible for him to survive coup attempts and pull the French out of Algeria. *AP/Wide World Photos*.

application, in part because he considered the British too close to the Americans. In January 1963, he and Konrad Adenauer, now in his late eighties, sealed fifteen years of French and German rapprochement with the Treaty of Friendship and Reconciliation.

De Gaulle's irritation with the American presence in Europe came to a head after he was reelected president for a seven-year term late in 1965.[10] He ordered NATO troops out of France and withdrew France from its military obligations to the alliance. He followed this with a trip to the Soviet Union to pursue his dream of a reconciled Europe, and he caustically criticized American involvement in Southeast Asia.

De Gaulle's notion of a French-led Europe contradicted the idea of supranational authority vested in the European Community. Yet his views did not prevent him

from using that institution to further French interests, particularly French agriculture. In France, farmers were more numerous and less technologically advanced than those in the Netherlands and in Germany. By early 1962, after some legendary negotiating sessions on this politically sensitive subject, the six EEC partners reached agreement on a Common Agricultural Policy (CAP). The centerpiece of the agreement was a mechanism for subsidizing farmers. The Common Agricultural Policy met its goal so thoroughly that Europe soon accumulated large surpluses of agricultural goods.

In other areas, however, de Gaulle vigorously opposed any measures that would limit French autonomy. In 1965, when the Commission of the European Community proposed using the weighted voting called for in the Treaty of Rome, the French representative simply walked out of the meetings, leaving an empty chair at France's appointed place in Brussels. Resolution of the empty chair crisis, as it was called, ensured that France—as well as the other members of the community—retained its veto, at least for the time being.

---

[10] He did not serve out the full term, however, resigning in 1969 when constitutional changes he had proposed were defeated at the polls.

GROWTH AND CHANGE

Despite French obstructions, the European Community provided the institutional setting for Europe's postwar economic miracle. Whereas after World War I the European economies sputtered and finally collapsed in depression, ten years after World War II prosperity had returned, and by the 1960s Europe was experiencing an economic boom. The boom had a fundamental impact on the lives of every citizen, not only in terms of increasing affluence, but in the structuring of leisure activity, the expectations citizens had of their state, and in the way artists and scientists looked at their rapidly changing world.

Economic Miracle in Europe

For most ordinary Europeans, economic and social change carried more weight than political shifts, except in the broad sense that political developments maintained the peace. Indeed, the postwar European economies grew so spectacularly that the phrase *economic miracle* is not unjustified. One example of what that term meant was the Candy Corporation, an Italian appliance maker. In 1947 Candy was producing one washing machine a day. In 1967 the company built one washing machine *every fifteen seconds*. In every continental country except Spain and Portugal, national product expanded at rates ranging from 4 to 8 percent per year from about 1947 to about 1965. Per capita wages increased accordingly. The same was true in Eastern Europe, although the growth rates were somewhat smaller and were concentrated in heavy industry. The specifics in each country differed. Germany, for example, benefited from the influx of refugees from the East who provided both cheap labor and, in the case of East German refugees, educated professionals. Italy used state involvement in industry to enhance the entrepreneurial skills of its manufacturing magnates. In France the Monnet Plan stimulated modernization. Yet overall growth was a product of several factors that all European countries had in common. First, wartime destruction created pent-up demand, especially in relatively backward regions. In 1951, for example, fewer than 8 percent of Italian households had a combination of electricity, running water, and an inside toilet. In Germany, apartments averaged only 540 square feet in area. If a family of three was lucky enough to have three rooms, the law required them to rent one of them to at least one and preferably two other persons. Second, the Marshall Plan not only pumped investment into Europe but also infused Europeans with hope. As George Kennan explained, "We felt that the psychological effect was four-fifths accomplished before the first supplies arrived." Third, the Korean War stimulated heavy industry, especially in Germany. With no military obligations of its own, Germany was able to use the agitated atmosphere of 1950 and 1951 to reestablish its traditional sectors of dominance, such as electrical goods and steel. Finally, the opening of markets occasioned by the Coal and Steel Community and then the European Community stimulated intra-European trade, forcing manufacturers in every country to compete. For example, the proportion of Italian goods exported to Common Market countries almost doubled from 23 percent in 1955 to more than 40 percent in 1965, and export volume expanded approximately fourfold.

Rapid enrichment meant new technologies that impacted the lives of every person. The automobile irrevocably changed lifestyles and forced every city and town in Europe to rethink its urban living patterns. In 1950 only five hundred thousand cars were on the road in West Germany. In 1980 the number hit 22 million. By the 1970s, the versatility and flexibility of transporting goods by truck made that form of shipping so widespread that railroads could survive only with substantial state subsidies. The stupendous outpouring of cars, trucks, and buses stimulated an investment in road networks and associated infrastructure that would have been considered lunatic if suggested in 1930. (That year, the German government had rejected a proposed Autobahn between Basel and Hamburg because it reckoned there never would be enough traffic to justify the expense. Today a sixteen-lane highway connects the two cities.)

The internal combustion engine took to the air, too. In 1958 the number of passengers crossing the Atlantic by airplane surpassed those going by ship. During the 1970s, travel by jet aircraft, invented only at the end of World War I, became routine for tourists and businesspeople alike. Tourists casually traveled halfway across the world for their vacations, and business became truly international. The developed countries went further, sending people into space, even placing them on the moon—notions rightly considered fantastical as recently as the 1930s.

Increased disposable income led to changes in leisure habits as well. One of the most widespread innovations of the economic miracle was television. Cafes and bars were the first to get the expensive devices, and people would gather there to watch shows or sports events. But by the middle of the 1960s, as TV became more affordable, families retired to their apartments to watch. Apartment buildings throughout Europe sprouted what looked like a living fungus of TV antennas. Today, people in developed countries spend several hours of every day watching television, often programs beamed instantaneously by satellite from faraway parts of the world. An entire citizenry can see the blood, hear the cries, and count the bodies as soldiers die in far-off places, significantly changing the political equation. Even without such dramatic subject matter, television and its companions in sound and picture reproduction—film, color photography, computer graphics—have made vivid images a part of everyday consciousness like never before.

If TV tended to isolate Europeans in their apartments, automobile ownership had the opposite effect. When the

Old and New In the 1960s, TV antennas sprouted like spring flowers over the Old World, signaling monumental change in leisure habits. *Keith Labbeth/Barnaby's Picture Library.*

hectic work pace of the 1940s and 1950s slackened, permanently employed persons commonly earned three or even four weeks of vacation a year. Tourism boomed. Between 1950 and 1980, annual tourist visits increased from 25 million to 285 million.

In medicine, the development of sulfa drugs and penicillin during the war set off equally unprecedented innovations. The discovery of the molecular structure of DNA in 1953 utterly transformed biology, while the introduction and widespread use of the birth control pill set off a revolution in sexual mores in the 1960s. The polio vaccine and the elimination of smallpox were only two of the most spectacular measures that transformed people's notions of disease, fate, and entitlement. Whereas in the past people believed illness struck through bad luck or punishment from God, in the postwar world people came to feel that they had a right to good health and that miracle drugs could provide it.

Surprisingly, these enormous changes did not exert much influence on the position of women in society. Despite the impact among intellectuals of Simone de Beauvoir's classic *The Second Sex* (1949), in the first twenty years after the war the proportion of women employed in France actually dropped below early twentieth-century levels. In Italy, most women remained housewives, although many took in piecework. France experienced a baby boom after the war, but in Italy the size of families declined slightly, and the traditional nuclear family of working husband, housewife, and children living together remained the norm. In Eastern Europe, most women were employed by the mid-1960s, but they still faced pressure to maintain households in the traditional manner.

The Welfare State

It comes as a bit of a surprise to learn that the term *welfare state* entered the English language only during World War II. One wonders what the purpose of the state might have been earlier if not the welfare of its citizens. This is especially so since one of the characteristics of industrialization has been the growth of legislation designed to protect and care for citizens. The early factory bills and child labor laws in England, Bismarck's unemployment and pension plans, French child care provisions, and Franklin Roosevelt's Social Security pension plan were all part of a growing webwork of government schemes designed to care for workers and citizens. Socialists in particular had long advocated a broad social safety network, and Sweden, for example, had begun creating one during the interwar period.

In June 1941, the Churchill government asked Sir William Beveridge to work up a plan to coordinate the great variety of British governmental agencies supervising social plans that had grown up over the years. Beveridge, disappointed because he wanted a more glamorous job, nevertheless produced a dynamic report in December 1942 that created a sensation in Britain. The Beveridge Report called for cooperation between the state and the individual, with both contributing to a comprehensive plan of family allowances, national health insurance, and unemployment insurance. Within a month an eager public snapped up a hundred thousand copies. Two years later, Beveridge produced a second report, this one calling for the government to pursue policies that would eliminate unemployment. When the Labour government came to power in 1945, it instituted as many of these ideas as Britain's weak economic condition after the war would permit.

"Cradle-to-grave" welfare plans such as that proposed by Beveridge became the norm in Europe after World War II. One of its results was population growth. Better health care, now routinely extended to all members of society, not just those who could afford it, lowered infant mortality and extended life expectancy. Payment plans that favored women who stayed at home augmented this tendency. Governments encouraged the spread of electricity, built highways, sponsored public housing, and legislated long vacations for workers. By the 1960s, when the economic boom reached its peak in most countries, ordinary people were sharing in the newly created wealth with a breadth never before experienced.

An important second element in the politics of the welfare state was the empowering of those who received the benefits. Workers struck to obtain further benefits;

To Banish Want   One of the surprising results of World War II, given the generally conservative style of prewar governments, was the vastly increased interest in social programs. The Beveridge plan of "cradle-to-grave" benefits for British workers became a reality in 1945 with the election of a Labour government.

politicians campaigned on the basis of stable retirement plans; and taxes rose to pay the costs. As long as economies expanded, the social safety net could be maintained and even expanded. But what would happen when governments became strapped for money? We have already seen how the Weimar Republic struggled in the Great Depression when it became unable to continue unemployment benefits just at the moment when they were most needed. Changes in the benefits structure, either in the case of a downturn or in order to stabilize growing expenditures, became increasingly difficult as the system took in more citizens. Therefore, every industrialized country adopted economic growth as its overriding societal goal. At the time of the Congress of Vienna, the term *legitimacy* referred to rulers. It meant that a prince was born to his office. In postwar Europe the legitimacy of governments came from their ability to produce, or at least to promise, industrial growth and the societal benefits that came with it.

The Divergence of Science and Culture

The second half of the twentieth century was the most technologically advanced era of human history, although it is certain that it will be far surpassed in the twenty-first century. Integral to the technology of the era is the sudden increase in the ability of science to describe the physical world. In a period of phenomenal change, three discoveries stand out: atomic fission, the transistor, and DNA. The first of these permitted the construction of nuclear weapons, whose presence (and residual radioactivity from early testing) continues to hang over the world today. The atomic structure of matter was scientifically confirmed only in the twentieth century, with the discovery of the proton, the neutron, and the electron, three of the basic building blocks of all matter. Late in the 1930s, German scientists discovered that if one bombarded the heaviest element known at that time, uranium, with neutrons, it would split into two other elements and release energy. At the same time, it would release more neutrons than were initially supplied to create the split. It was quickly realized that this phenomenon could lead to a chain reaction, in which each split provided the neutrons to activate the next split, the end result being a sudden and phenomenal release of energy (an explosion). Turning this theoretical insight into an actual weapon took an enormous amount of work and expense, but the fear that Germany might be producing such a weapon convinced President Roosevelt to authorize the Manhattan Project, which succeeded in creating a weapon by the end of World War II.

In the early postwar period, all the Great Powers realized that they would be vulnerable to attack if they did not possess this fearsome weapon, so well-intentioned efforts to internationalize atomic research failed. Instead, efforts escalated into creating a fusion bomb, in which an atomic bomb sets off a much bigger explosion in a form of hydrogen. By 1949 the Soviet Union had exploded its first atomic bomb, while the United States detonated its first hydrogen bomb in 1952. The original atomic bomb dropped on Hiroshima produced an explosion equivalent to that of about 10,000 tons of TNT; the largest hydrogen bomb, which the Soviet Union exploded in 1961, produced an explosion equivalent to almost 60 million tons of TNT. By the 1960s, all governments realized the long-term danger from radioactivity that these open-air tests represented. In 1963, the United States and the Soviet Union signed the Limited Test Ban Treaty, banning the testing of atomic weapons in the atmosphere, although it took until 1990 for the two countries to ratify treaties limiting the size of underground test explosions.

The scientific investigation of the atom initially held out hope of a vast new source of energy that could be turned to productive civilian uses, but the difficulty of disposing of wastes that would be radioactive for tens of thousands of years limited its practical use. France is the only country that has put atomic energy to widespread use. Whereas in Italy, for example, only a minuscule amount of electricity is produced by atomic generating plants, 75 percent of France's electrical energy comes from that source.

The transistor turned out to be far more significant for daily life than atomic energy. The basic invention that made the radio possible was the vacuum tube. This device, in which electrons come off a hot filament as in a lightbulb or a TV picture tube, had the disadvantages of generating heat, taking time to warm up, and wearing out. In 1947 a team of scientists at Bell Laboratories in the United States discovered that many of the functions performed by a tube could be undertaken by a specially designed piece of material they called a transistor. Rapid development of this device, especially the discovery that transistors could be made from cheap silicon, led in the late 1950s to the invention of the integrated circuit, in which many transistors were etched onto a single piece of silicon. The first such devices put about ten components on a small chip. Today, manufacturers squeeze tens of millions of components onto a 2-square-centimeter piece of silicon. The transistor—and its whole family of semiconductors—was what made the computer revolution possible.

The third great discovery was the molecular structure of DNA (deoxyribonucleic acid), the basic substance of heredity in all living things. This discovery depended on a number of previous ones, such as the discovery of how to get images of very small samples by shining X-rays off them. In 1953, an English biologist, Francis Crick, and an American researcher, James Watson, realized that the four proteins found in DNA were structured in a double helix— that is, pairs of proteins matched in certain sequences in a long string. They also saw how this string could duplicate itself, thus opening the way to a molecular understanding

Robert Rauschenberg, American Artistic Innovator
Rauschenberg's innovations in art in the early 1950s included making art from material objects, integrating photography into his paintings, and helping to develop "pop art." *Sam Falk*/New York Times/*Archive Photos.*

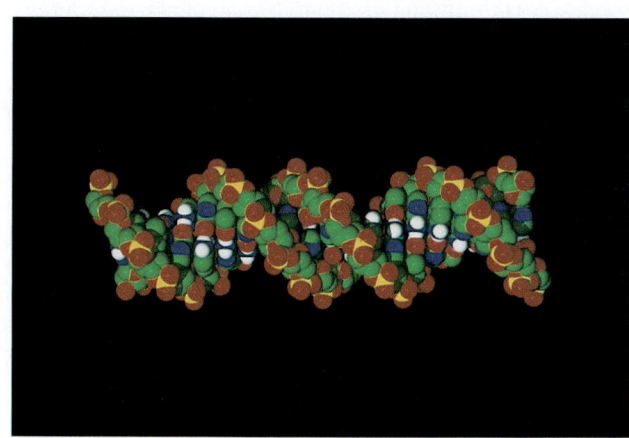

The Double Helix The discovery of DNA, which consists of two strands of proteins wound together in a shape called a double helix, has transformed our understanding of biological processes. By the 1990s DNA research had opened unprecedented new possibilities for genetic engineering, with both beneficial and frightening prospects. *Prof. D. Seddon and Dr. T. Evans, Queen's University, Belfast/Science Photo Library/Photo Researchers, Inc.*

of heredity. Their 900-word paper, published in the journal *Nature* in 1953, ended laconically. "It has not escaped our attention that the specific pairing we have postulated immediately suggests a possible copying mechanism for the genetic material." They were right. Their paper is one of the great classics of twentieth-century science and the basis of all biology today.

In contrast to these and other successes in understanding the physical world, the arts moved in a different direction—toward pluralism, even incoherence, as artists reacted against the mechanization of the world and the consumer society that seemed an integral part of it. Modernism, we can recall, undermined long-standing traditions in painting, writing, and music early in the twentieth century by scrapping the ideal of form, introducing new materials, and challenging the notion of meaning. This process continued apace after World War II, but with a difference.

Advertising Art
Advertising, usually thought of in terms of American commercialism, has been a common aspect of industrialization worldwide. In this advertisement for the Trabant automobile, advertisers in socialist East Germany played upon a romantic desire for elegance that is quite out of tune with the proletarian ethic. The advertisement is particularly ironic because by 1989 the clunky, pollution-spewing Trabant had become a symbol of East German industrial incompetence.

Now the center of activity became the United States, especially New York, as Mark Tansy's painting at the beginning of this chapter suggests. Jackson Pollock, the main artist of the abstract expressionist school, pushed painting even further than had the surrealists of the 1920s and 1930s by abandoning brushes and easels altogether. At his peak he laid canvas on the floor and swirled paint on it straight from the tube or can, using not only artist's oils but regular house paint and other materials as well. Then he would cut out a portion of the work he liked and mount it on a frame. Other artists moved toward collages made from random materials, outsized realistic representations of ordinary objects like soup cans and crushed automobiles, and eventually to simple piles of stone or similar materials.

In significant measure, this direction in the arts grew out of a sense that contemporary life was devaluing ordinary human relations. Artists mocked the pretensions of consumer society, which they saw as focused on ephemeral and trivial objects, pursued as an integral part of the drive of capitalism toward profit. Despite this sense of critique, however, the postwar era also saw the commercialization of art in two ways. First, some artists—represented by the major galleries in a few of the biggest cities and whose works were purchased by the famous museums—became very wealthy as the prices of their work escalated. And second, the inventive graphics that went with advertising brought a stunning array of new colors, images, and seductions to a vast public in both the print and the electronic media. Serious artists may have been social critics, but never before had so much stylish representation been seen by so many people.

CONCLUSION: *THE WEST TRANSFORMED*

Compared to what happened after World War I, the reconstitution of Europe after World War II was a remarkable success. The inability to write a peace treaty because of the division of Europe into Soviet and American spheres of influence had a serious deleterious effect on the countries under Soviet control, but in Western Europe it opened up the chance for innovations that eventually led to stability. Prior to 1945, international affairs were characterized by a tension between the interdependence of the world market system, which implied cooperative measures, and the aggressive defensiveness of nationalism, which led to conflict. During the 1930s, few political mechanisms matched the interlinked quality of capitalism. After World War II, however, West European states committed themselves to a vast new array of interdependent international organizations. The General Agreement of Tariffs and Trade, the International Monetary Fund, the World Bank, NATO, the United Nations, the West European Union, and, of course, the European Economic Community introduced the politics of accommodation to the international arena on a scale never before experienced.

The European Community also provided a vehicle for reintegrating West Germany into Europe. By including Germany in a joint venture with the other main powers, Germany's ambitions for the future became inextricably linked to the success of that cooperative institution. One of the most important functions of the European Community, therefore, was its contribution to security, even though it has no military arm. German and French prosperity came to depend on the smooth functioning of the European Community, a fact that essentially eliminated the likelihood of a return to old-fashioned German and French aggression.

New leaders pursuing a politics of accommodation emerged in most countries in the West soon after the war. In the East, however, Stalin remained in power long enough to establish regimes based on policies more characteristic of the Century of Power. The cost was high, but for a while at least it seemed that the economic gains might justify the price. In 1960 and 1961, the Soviets and their regimes in Eastern Europe were bursting with confidence. An exuberant memo from the Hungarian planning office in 1961 predicted that by 1980 growth would "not merely exempt our people wholly from problems of livelihood, but satisfy the harmonious physical and intellectual needs of man." The proposed level of consumption, these Hungarian communist officials reported, "will arrive at a standard of *saturation* on a society-wide scale."

The Hungarian bureaucrats were terribly wrong, of course, but so were West Europeans who thought that prosperity would go on forever. New cultural and intellectual currents led to widespread eruptions of protest in 1968, and during the 1970s radical changes in the price of oil sent economies reeling. How West Europeans reacted to this crisis by deepening the European Community and how East Europeans eventually threw off the stagnating weight of their communist regimes are the subjects of our next chapter.

Selected Reading

Sources

Fanon, Franz. *The Wretched of the Earth* (1963).

May, Ernest R. and Philip D. Zelikow, eds., *The Kennedy Tapes: Inside the White House During the Cuban Missile Crisis* (Cambridge, Mass.: Harvard University Press, 1997).

Solzhenitsyn, Aleksandr. *One Day in the Life of Ivan Denisovich* (1963). A fine prison camp novel that created a sensation when it appeared in the Soviet Union in 1962.

Stokes, Gale. *From Stalinism to Pluralism: A Documentary History of Eastern Europe since 1945*, 2nd ed. (1995).

Individual Countries

Bark, Dennis L., and David R. Gress. *A History of West Germany*, 2 vols., 2nd ed. (1993). Complete and positive analysis of West Germany's emergence as Europe's strongest power.

Brzezinski, Zbigniew. *The Soviet Bloc: Unity and Conflict*, rev. ed. (1961). Remains a basic text for the first two postwar decades.

Davidson, Basil. *The Black Man's Burden: Africa and the Curse of the Nation-State* (1992). How the imposition and adoption of the idea of nation-state disrupted Africa's development.

Elon, Amos. *The Israelis: Founders and Sons* (1971). Very readable popular history from early Zionism through the first twenty years of Israel's statehood.

Fulbrook, Mary. *The Divided Nation: A History of Germany, 1918–1990* (1991). Excellent interpretive history, and short.

Ginsborg, Paul. *A History of Contemporary Italy: Society and Politics, 1943–1988* (1990). The best single-volume history of postwar Italy.

Kuisel, Richard F. *Capitalism and the State in Modern France* (1981). Discusses the growth of the "conscious direction from above" of the twentieth-century French economy.

Morgan, Kenneth O. *The People's Peace: British History, 1945–1989* (1990). The best comprehensive introduction to postwar British history.

Rothschild, Joseph. *The Return to Diversity: A Political History of East Central Europe Since World War II*, 2nd ed. (1993). Especially strong on World War II and its aftermath up to 1968.

General

Dinan, Desmond. *Ever Closer Union? An Introduction to the European Community* (1994). The first book one should read on the history and functioning of the European Community.

Mazower, Mark. *Dark Continent: Europe's Twentieth Century* (1998). Interpretive study arguing that fascism and communism were not aberrations, but alternative attractions to many Europeans.

Milward, Alan S. *The European Rescue of the Nation-State* (1992). Revisionist study arguing that the European Union is a vehicle for sustaining the nation-state.

———. *The Reconstruction of Western Europe, 1945–1951* (1984). Argues that the new pattern of West European economic interdependence was not inevitable, did not grow out of ideas of European federalism, and was not a product of U.S.-European cooperation.

Personalities

Duchêne, François. *Jean Monnet: The First Statesman of Interdependence* (1994). A *New York Times* reviewer called this excellent biography "intelligently sympathetic but in no sense uncritical."

Prittie, Terence. *Konrad Adenauer, 1876–1967* (1972). Political biography by a well-informed journalist.

Williams, Charles. *The Last Great Frenchman* (1993). Excellent recent biography of Charles de Gaulle.

The Cold War

Gaddis, John Lewis. *The Long Peace: Inquiries into the History of the Cold War* (1987). Thoughtful reinterpretation of the Cold War by one of its most insightful and balanced historians.

McWilliams, Wayne C., and Harry Piotrowski. *The World since 1945: A History of International Relations*, 2nd ed. (1990). Handy text treatment.

Naimark, Norman M. *The Russians in Germany: A History of the Soviet Zone of Occupation, 1945–1949* (1995). Vivid discussion of the brutal Soviet occupation of eastern Germany.

Paterson, Thomas G. *On Every Front: The Making and Unmaking of the Cold War*, rev. ed. (1992). Thoughtful discussion.

CHAPTER 32

THE END OF THE EUROPEAN ERA

THE RADICAL SIXTIES

Old Left, New Left

The Vietnam War

May 1968

Reform and the Prague Spring

THE STUMBLING SEVENTIES

The Road to Helsinki

A Growing European Community

Economic Turmoil

Environmentalism

The New Feminism

THE DYNAMIC EIGHTIES

A Turn to the Right

Breakthrough to European Union

The Tired Socialist System

Antipolitics and Solidarity: Communism's
Loss of Legitimacy

Gorbachev and the Collapse of Communism

CONCLUSION: THE END OF
THE COLD WAR

Solidarity *Courtesy of the Smithsonian Institution Traveling Exhibition, from its exhibition "Art as Activist: Revolutionary Posters from Central and Eastern Europe."*

1954	French defeated, leave Vietnam
1965	Lyndon Johnson escalates Vietnam War
May 1968	Paris students stage strikes
August 1968	Soviets snuff out Prague Spring, institute Brezhnev Doctrine
1970	U.S. drops gold; Bretton Woods agreements collapse
1972	SALT I concluded
1973	Yom Kippur War; OPEC raises oil prices; Great Britain, Ireland, and Denmark join European Community
1975	Helsinki Accords accept postwar boundaries and human rights norms
1977	Czech antipoliticians issue Charter 77
1978	Karol Wojtyła elected Pope John Paul II
1979	SALT II resolved
1980	Workers form Solidarity movement in Poland
1981	Greece joins European Community
1985	Mikhail Gorbachev becomes leader of Soviet Union
1986	Spain and Portugal join European Community; Chernobyl nuclear disaster occurs
1989	Revolutions sweep through Eastern Europe
1991	Gorbachev resigns, Soviet Union collapses

Surely the most dramatic event of the past twenty-five years was the unexpected but total collapse of communism in Eastern Europe and the Soviet Union. A key moment in this process was the election in Poland on June 4, 1989. Against all expectations, the anticommunist Solidarity movement swept every available seat, and within the next six months communist regimes throughout Eastern Europe collapsed. In the election poster shown on the previous page, U.S. movie hero Gary Cooper strides purposefully to the election place with his Solidarity ballot, ready to oust the bandits. Two years after this election, the Soviet Union collapsed and the post–World War II era—and the twentieth century—came to a stunning close.

The first twenty years of the postwar period showed no signs of this eventual outcome, but were in many ways a time of success throughout the world. Rather than slipping back into the doldrums of depression, as many had feared, the economies of America, Japan, and Western Europe boomed. Eastern Europe, pursuing its own state-driven strategy of developing heavy industry, put ever-greater numbers of people to work and instituted a comprehensive social network that provided a decent if modest standard of living for its citizens. In other parts of the world, national liberation movements threw off European domination. New states established governments that superficially resembled the stable West European democracies, invited foreign investment, and created their own international diplomatic force in the Movement of Nonaligned States. In these and other ways they asserted their independence and aspirations for prosperity and respect.

The next twenty-five postwar years, by contrast, were much more varied. By the 1960s, as economic growth brought increasing affluence to Western Europe, the austerity and puritanism of the grim years immediately after World War II gave way to permissiveness, especially among the young. Protests against the U.S. military intervention in Vietnam fused the anticolonialism of the left with a youthful counterculture in both Europe and America. In 1968 this volatile mixture exploded in massive demonstrations in Paris and other European cities, while riots and assassinations haunted the United States. Eastern Europe, too, experienced the unrest of 1968. Student protests in Warsaw and Belgrade culminated in the Prague Spring, in which Czechoslovak communists sought to create "socialism with a human face."

The 1970s, on the other hand, became a decade of repression in Eastern Europe and a period of resignation and economic turmoil in Western Europe. Two alarming jumps in the price of oil dislocated the developed economies, causing simultaneous inflation and economic stagnation. In the Third World, the optimism of the first years of independence gave way to the realization that the economic problems of development were more difficult than anyone had imagined. Democracy proved equally problematic in many parts of the world. Populist dictatorships and even civil war became the norm.

During the 1980s, a decade of remarkable change, the pendulum continued to swing to the right. Throughout the world, the passion for state ownership and regulation that had characterized the early postwar years faded. Inspired by Margaret Thatcher's privatizing regime in Great Britain, governments sold off state-owned enterprises and deregulated business. Roused by this new enthusiasm for deregulation, the European Community adopted the Single Europe Act, which led in the 1990s to a widespread elimination of nontariff barriers and a fuller realization of the goals of the Treaty of Rome. Finally, and most surprisingly, the leadership of Mikhail Gorbachev in the Soviet Union, when coupled with the willingness of Poland and Hungary to experiment, led to the collapse of communism. In the ultimate act of privatization, the entire socialist system turned toward the market.

The years leading to the end of the European era, therefore, contained three phases roughly corresponding to the decades of the 1960s, the 1970s, and the 1980s. The dynamic first period ended in disillusion and rejection; the second decade was a relatively passive time of reaction and digestion; and the third period saw unexpected, fundamental change that brought the post-1945 era to a convincing close.

THE RADICAL SIXTIES

There is something special about the 1960s. Rock-n-roll, Elvis, the Beatles, John F. Kennedy, Che Guevara, Charles de Gaulle, Vietnam—they fascinate us or haunt us even today. The invention of the birth control pill led to sexual experimentation; miniskirts from Britain's Carnaby Street set a shocking new fashion; marijuana, which had long been a part of semi-illicit urban culture, temporarily replaced alcohol as the stimulant of choice among students; and advocates of much more powerful chemicals, such as LSD, urged the young to "tune in, turn on, and drop out." Every generation discovers sex, stimulation, and hope, but not usually with such open advocacy as the generation of the 1960s. And yet the world went its way.

Old Left, New Left

The European left emerged from World War II with the highest level of prestige and acceptance it had ever enjoyed. Bitterly opposed by the right throughout the nineteenth century and tainted by its links with the Soviet Union in the 1930s, leftists established their patriotic credentials by being the most vigorous underground oppositionists to Hitlerite regimes almost everywhere in occupied Europe. The Soviet Union's prestige stood at an all-time high, too, enhanced by the Soviet defeat of Nazi Germany. In the first year or two after the war, large communist parties in both France and Italy participated responsibly in coalition governments, while in Britain the Labour party took power by winning the first postwar election. Even in Eastern Europe, which quickly came under the Soviet thumb, sympathy for moderating the capitalist system ran high.

By 1948 the aggressive Stalinization of Eastern Europe and the clear division of Europe into East and West led the Italian and French coalitions to drop their communist partners, and in 1951 the Conservatives returned to power in Great Britain. A significant portion of the intellectual community, however, remained committed to the left, especially in France. European leftism took its lead from Paris in the first postwar decade, and Paris took its lead from the philosopher Jean-Paul Sartre, the most famous of the existentialists. The pessimistic Sartre held that human

beings are always creating unrealistic pictures of the world because they ascribe set characteristics to each other in the search for certainty. But certainty is impossible, because humans are not set, and therefore the effort ultimately is frustrating. Love is an acute version of this universal human difficulty. "Hell is other people," Sartre concluded in his play No Exit.

As a prisoner of war in 1941, Sartre had decided that a philosopher cannot remain indifferent to public events; he had to become "engaged." In the late 1940s and early 1950s, he and the majority of French intellectuals constructed a rhetoric of violence in support of Soviet communism. In the "struggle for peace," they attacked capitalists and their "running dog" defenders. Their abstract and intricate discussions did not seek primarily to understand the world, but to identify their opponents and to strike out at them. This attitude left them blind to the faults of Stalinism, which they defended even in the face of the East European purge trials during Stalin's last years. This "self-induced amnesia," as one critic calls it—or throwing in one's lot "with the people, with revolution and history," as Sartre put it—opened the traditional left to accusations of moral blindness.

The Soviet crushing of the Hungarian Revolution in 1956 disillusioned many older leftists, but at this very moment a new generation of critics began to replace them. The ideas of the old left were based on Marx—but the Marx experienced in the Soviet Union of the 1930s—but the new generation rejected Das Kapital, the main text of classical Marxism, and especially Engels's interpretations of it, and turned their attention to the writings of the young Marx. These writings had become widely known only after World War II. One of the issues the new left seized on was the concept of alienation. "The basic purpose of critical inquiry," one of the new left authors said, "is the discovery of those specific social institutions and structures that cripple human beings, arrest their development and impose on them patterns of simple, easily predictable, dull, stereotyped behavior." This particular critic was referring to communist governments in the Soviet Union and Eastern Europe, but leftists in Europe and America, also fascinated by the young Marx, argued that the analysis applied just as well, if not better, to the capitalist system. In their view, modern industrial society had alienated workers from the real, vital sources of human existence, and society had become filled with "one-dimensional" people, as one famous critic put it. This turn to a sociological critique of modern industrial society was truly international. One of the most famous publications of the movement came out of Zagreb, in Tito's Yugoslavia, and the most notorious, if not the most successful, student organization of the movement, Students for a Democratic Society (SDS), was a North American phenomenon.

The old leftists, both in Europe and the United States, could hardly turn their backs on what seemed to be a surge of interest in radicalism, but some of them had trouble accepting the new left's exuberance and unorthodox lifestyle. Old-line socialists and communists distrusted state power but accepted the necessity of having a state. They tended to think in class terms, to organize themselves in unions and political parties, and to live conventional lives. The new left rejected these established ways of opposition. They favored "self-managing" communities and cooperative producers, and scorned the big government they associated with a repressive state. Primarily middle-class students, who had never felt the pain of the Great Depression and who found postwar prosperity a bore, paid little attention to the rhetoric of class struggle, preferring to concentrate on individualism and what they considered the vibrant creative energy of Third World revolutionary movements. The old left accepted industrialization and productivity as positive aspects of modern life, albeit in need of socialist reorganization, but the new left rejected consumerism, advertising, and manipulation. And the new left devised decidedly unconventional tactics—its members occupied university buildings, demonstrated in the streets, and flaunted their sexuality, provoking conventional society in every way they could.

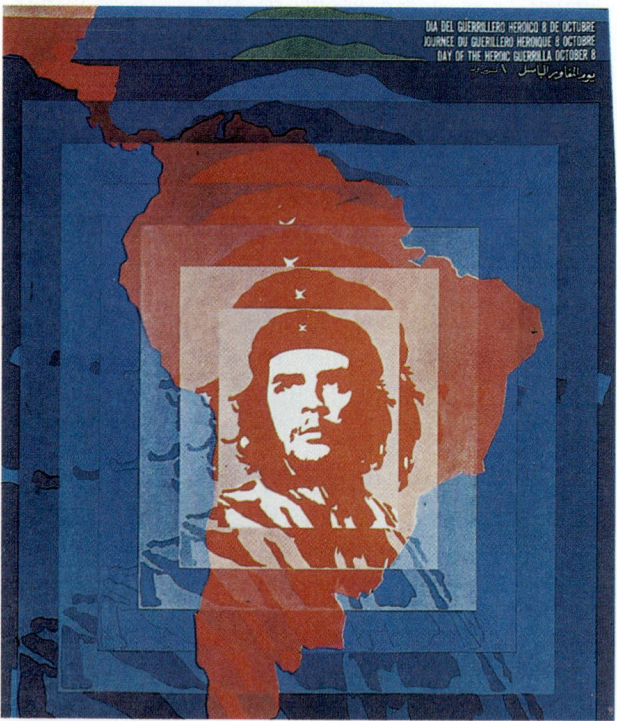

A Leftist Icon Che Guevara was one of the most popular revolutionaries of the New Left throughout the world. Born in Argentina, he joined the Cuban revolution of Fidel Castro and became a vigorous and articulate advocate of the revolutionary overthrow of American imperialism. His death in Bolivia in 1967 at the hands of government forces raised him to the status of an icon of resistance to oppression.

The Vietnam War

The issue that most agitated the new left, even in Europe, was the Vietnam War. This tragic disaster grew out of the U.S. policy of containment. In the 1950s, American policy makers believed that a worldwide organization directed from Moscow and Beijing was manipulating national liberation movements throughout the world. The North Korean invasion of South Korea, now known to have been primarily an initiative of Kim Il Sung that Stalin endorsed without enthusiasm, seemed to confirm that perception. The success in preventing North Korean seizure of the South seemed to suggest that the expanding monolith could be contained by military means. When the French had to leave Vietnam in 1954, only a year after the end of the Korean War, the United States undertook to support what it called the democratic forces in that country. In fact, the South Vietnamese government of the late 1950s and early 1960s was an autocratic regime that brutally suppressed opposition and forced tens of thousands of unwilling peasants to move from isolated villages into what it called strategic hamlets. The regime's tyrannical behavior drove thousands of angry peasants into armed opposition. As their movement (the Viet Minh, nicknamed the Viet Cong by American forces) gained strength, the United States gradually increased its support to the South Vietnamese government.

The critical moment came after the American presidential elections of 1964, which Democrat Lyndon Baines Johnson won partly by painting himself as a "dove" against the "hawk" Republican Barry Goldwater. After his landslide victory, Johnson and his advisers, convinced that the Viet Minh were the puppets of world communism and fearful of the political consequences of letting another country "fall" to the communists, changed their tune. Johnson got congressional approval to use all military means in Vietnam by falsely alleging that the North Vietnamese had attacked an American warship. From 1965 until 1973, when President Richard M. Nixon finally withdrew American troops from the war, the United States dropped more tonnage of bombs on Vietnam than it had on the Japanese and Germans together in World War II. It defoliated some 5 million acres of Vietnamese forests, destroyed hundreds of villages and many large cities, scarred tens of thousands of Vietnamese civilians with ghastly burns from napalm, which burns human flesh on contact, and contributed to the death of several million people.

The brutality of the war and the unwillingness of the American government to consider other approaches divided the United States like no issue since the Civil War. Mainstream America generally supported the war on the principles of anticommunism and patriotism. But millions of young Americans joined the new left in increasingly vigorous antiwar protests. Tens of thousands of young men burned their draft cards (the forms that men age eighteen and over had to carry to prove they were registered for conscription). Others fled to Canada to avoid serving in the military.

Adding to the ferment of change characteristic of the 1960s was the civil rights movement. Until World War II, African Americans, although technically free and equal following the Civil War, were treated as inferior citizens, lacking in many of the fundamental rights guaranteed by the U.S. Constitution. During World War II, racial discrimination was barred in American defense industries, and in 1948 President Harry S Truman outlawed racial segregation in the armed forces. At the same time, the National Association for the Advancement of Colored People (NAACP) began bringing suits arguing that "separate but equal" educational facilities were inherently discriminatory. In 1954, in the *Brown v. Board of Education* decision, the U.S. Supreme Court agreed.

Shortly thereafter, Rosa Parks, an African American in Montgomery, Alabama, refused to give up her seat to a white man on a public bus. Her courageous act began a series of protests, sit-ins, marches, and rallies that swept the American South for the next decade. This civil rights movement, led by Martin Luther King Jr., culminated in the Civil Rights Act of 1964, pushed through Congress by Lyndon B. Johnson after the assassination of President John F. Kennedy. After this, the civil rights movement, which had shown great solidarity during its often dangerous struggles, began to splinter, as the Vietnam War radicalized many African Americans. Riots in black ghettos in several U.S. cities indicated the frustration many African Americans felt at the resistance of whites to their liberation. The assassination of King in 1968 ended the initial phase of this postwar pursuit of the revolutionary goal of equity for African Americans.

The upheavals of the 1960s, especially the Vietnam War, left an emotional scar on the United States. For the first time in American history, veterans who had risked their lives and in some cases suffered grievous wounds, came home feeling judged and rejected for their participation. By the time of the final panicky withdrawal in 1975, many Americans considered the war to have been a colossal mistake. Defeat at such great expense cost the military much of the prestige it had enjoyed after World War II, and the policy of containment received a permanent black eye. On the other hand, a significant number of Americans rallied to the support of the military and remained vigorously anticommunist. They criticized the generation of the 1960s as unpatriotic, drug-ridden, and irresponsibly permissive. Even as late as 1992, presidential candidate Bill Clinton had to defend himself against angry accusations of lack of patriotism because he had opposed the Vietnam War in the 1960s. The passions aroused by this disastrous chapter in American history have not yet fully dissipated.

May 1968

Anti-Vietnam protests in the 1960s were not limited to the United States. During 1968 in particular, students in Japan, England, Germany, Italy, Spain, and even Yugoslavia went on strike, occupied buildings, and demanded better dormitories, classrooms, and professors. The outburst in France was the most massive. Protests and widespread strikes growing out of student unrest seemed as if they might topple Charles de Gaulle's government, even the Fifth Republic itself. De Gaulle had solved the Algerian problem by 1962, but as the 1960s wore on, his regime became less and less responsive to French problems. It hung on to power through a coalition arrangement, and barely survived three votes of confidence. Public frustration grew in part out of the regime's promulgation of unpopular economic rulings by decree rather than through the National Assembly. The events of May 1968, therefore, erupted in an already heated atmosphere.

Since World War II, the number of French college students had increased by a factor of 10, greatly diversifying the social background of the student body. Nevertheless, the French system of higher education remained geared to training the sons and daughters of the upper middle class. Only 30 percent of those who entered the university graduated, and many of these found it difficult to find employment. Crowded facilities forced students to listen to lectures broadcast over loudspeakers, and few ever encountered a professor on a personal basis.

Among the least attractive universities was a new campus in the outskirts of Paris at Nanterre. Overcrowded, ugly, and governed by a pettifogging university bureaucracy, Nanterre was also a center for a variety of fringe groups—Maoists, Trotskyites, left wing Catholics, and others—who opposed the Vietnam War. In May 1968, when the police arrested one of their number for participating in a protest bombing of the American Express Company, the campus burst into protest. In response, the authorities shut down the campus. When the students at the Sorbonne struck in sympathy, police waded in with nightsticks and tear gas, injuring dozens and arresting hundreds. As the nightly protests continued, and television broadcast vivid pictures of the police beating students, workers throughout France came out in sympathy strikes. Suddenly the word *participation* was on everyone's lips. The protesters' accusations that France was too rigid, too undemocratic, and too frustrated was reaching the broader public.

With millions protesting or on strike, the government seemed in danger. Momentarily panicked, de Gaulle and his family fled for a few hours to a French military base in Germany. But the old fighter gathered his wits, returned, and ordered fresh elections, changing the name of his party to Union for the Defense of the Republic. As had happened so often in the French past, the French public rallied behind a leader's call for law and order, and de Gaulle's

Paris, 1968 French police wade into student protesters during the mass student protests of May 1968. *AP/Wide World Photo.*

party won an overwhelming majority in the National Assembly. The strikes and protests petered out. Workers received raises and an increase in the minimum wage, and the government added students to university councils, promised to build more campuses, and introduced some decentralizing reforms.

The upheaval in France was noteworthy primarily because of its extent—it eventually involved most of the country. Elsewhere, nuclear disarmament protests, antiwar rallies, and occupation of university buildings exerted a local impact, created excitement, and left emotional scars. Yet they did not deflect government policies, except in the United States, where popular protest eventually helped persuade the U.S. government to get out of Vietnam. Disappointment at their lack of impact pushed a few radicals in the direction of violence in the 1970s. In the United States a group calling itself the Weathermen turned to bank robberies and bombings. In Germany and Italy the Red Army Faction and the Red Brigades took to assassination, kidnapping, bombing, and kneecapping (shooting right wing politicians and capitalists in the kneecap, thus permanently disabling them) in an effort to disrupt the societies they hated but were unable otherwise to reach.

Reform and the Prague Spring

The 1960s saw a bubbling up of ferment in Eastern Europe too, although within a more restricted arena than existed in the open societies of Western Europe and the United

States. At the governmental level, Stalin's death unfroze the glacial rigidity of the Soviet bloc. In 1960 the split between the communist parties of the Soviet Union and China came out in the open. In Eastern Europe, Romania and Albania took advantage of the split to go their own ways. Romania threw dust in the eyes of the Soviet Union by supporting China, refusing to go along with Khrushchev's plan for a unified East European economic system, and supporting Israel rather than the Soviets' Arab friends. Albania went even further, divorcing itself from the Soviet Union to become a staunch ally of China.

Less dramatic but more significant in the long run, János Kádár, communist leader of Hungary, stopped the brutal repression of those who had participated in the Hungarian Revolution of 1956. In 1962 he announced that "those who are not against us are with us." In other words, Kádár no longer expected energetic, public support for party rule, such as Stalin had required. Now, Hungarians could conduct a fairly free private life merely by not opposing the regime.

Stalin's departure also opened the door to revisionism within the East European communist parties.[1] Economists

---

[1] In the Marxist lexicon, *revisionism* referred to the position of the late nineteenth-century socialist Edward Bernstein, who argued that the working class could achieve its goals better through the political process than through revolution. Lenin and the Bolsheviks rejected this view. In the 1960s, East European Marxists trying to find new ways to make socialism work saw themselves as revisionists against Stalinism.

in particular searched for ways to introduce marketlike mechanisms that would improve the efficiency of the centrally planned economies. In Poland, the influential scholar Włodzimierz Brus proposed that indicative planning, such as that used in France, should replace directive planning. Instead of telling every factory exactly what to produce and under what conditions, Brus proposed that the state determine general guidelines and leave it up to the enterprises to meet those goals. Most important, in the Soviet Union itself, E. G. Liberman, an economist from Kharkov, proposed that enterprises increase their emphasis on profit, decentralize managerial decisions, and even charge a form of interest, which classical Marxism disdained. These revisions of Marxist economic doctrine had the greatest impact in Hungary, where in 1968 Kádár's regime introduced a decentralized and marketized form of socialism called the New Economic Mechanism (NEM).

Some of this ferment reached Czechoslovakia, primarily in the form of suggestions from writers and filmmakers for increased democratization. But during most of the 1960s, conservative leaders tending toward Stalinist solutions remained in power. Late in 1967 and early in 1968, however, the Slovak Alexander Dubček assumed control of the Czechoslovak Communist party apparatus. Encouraged by moderates, Dubček promised economic reform, took vague steps toward democratization, and relaxed censorship. The new freedom of expression let loose a torrent of excited commentary by the Czech intelligentsia. Some even went so far as to call for the creation of a second (socialist) party. The ferment seemed to be leading toward a much freer Czechoslovakia, as the West saw it, or a much weaker Communist party, as the Soviets saw it.

In 1964, the stolid, predictable Leonid Brezhnev had replaced the volatile Nikita Khrushchev as leader of the post-Stalinist Soviet Union. Khrushchev had opened up Soviet society somewhat: He had permitted publication of Aleksandr Solzhenitsyn's novel about the Soviet prison camps, *One Day in the Life of Ivan Denisovich*; had allowed discussion of Liberman's economic reforms; and even had visited a modern art exhibit, although he ordered it trashed. Brezhnev was not this imaginative. Shortly after coming to power, he allowed a limited experiment in economic reform, but his heart was not in it. By the mid-1960s, the Soviet and East European economies had put almost all their women and peasants to work. To continue to grow, they would have to increase efficiency. But efficiency required new technology, which would mean entering world markets, adopting Western accounting mechanisms, permitting foreign penetration of Soviet markets, and loosening up planning. These were steps Brezhnev and his colleagues were not willing to take. They firmly believed that the Communist party of the Soviet Union was the only true representative of the working class. To relax its social control, especially in response to market signals generated by the capitalist system, would be to betray the force of his-

tory, which, in their view, was leading them to socialist victory.

As the excitement in Czechoslovakia generated by Dubček's moderate policies mounted, Brezhnev's concern grew apace. The Prague Spring, as the newly open press called the reform discussions, seemed to threaten the party's ability to control affairs. Not incidentally, it also challenged the Soviet Union's capacity to dominate its satellites in Eastern Europe. After many consultations and warnings, Brezhnev decided to act. On August 24, 1968, troops of the Warsaw Pact countries (except for Romania, which held back) invaded Czechoslovakia. Within a year, Gustav Husák, also a Slovak, introduced a policy of "normalization." He dismissed half a million party members and purged all the intellectuals who had participated in the Prague Spring. Normalization was a civilized sort of violence. As one participant put it, "When bugging devices were installed in people's flats, it would be done without damage to the furniture." Professors, rather than being sent to prison, became window washers and boiler attendants. But normalization was violence nevertheless. Czechoslovakia, along with East Germany and Romania, became the most repressive state in Europe for the next twenty years.

In Western Europe, the upheavals of 1968 grew out of opposition to the Vietnam War, youthful boredom with the routines of satisfied regimes, and a powerful desire by young people for meaning and voice. But the protests had little lasting impact on the institutions of Western democracy. Instead they became symbols to be used in later political struggles, rather than inspirations for change. In Eastern Europe, however, Brezhnev's decision to put down the Prague Spring exerted a two-edged force on the Soviet system. On the one hand, it firmly reasserted the Soviet intention to maintain political control over Eastern Europe. The Brezhnev Doctrine, enunciated in the fall of 1968, stated that the "triumph of the socialist system in a country can be regarded as final. . . . The borders [of the socialist commonwealth] are stable and inviolable. . . . We advise all who are fond of encroaching on foreign borders to remember this well!" For the next twenty years, every Western observer believed that a strong Soviet Union would never give up its domination of Eastern Europe.

On the other hand, the turn against the Prague Spring had debilitating economic ramifications. The Soviet leadership chose not to modify strict centralized planning and not to enter directly into world markets. After the Prague Spring, every East European economy took a conservative turn. However, because of the inherent flaws in centralized planning—inaccurate pricing, inhibitions to innovation, tendency to shortages, indifference to consumers, and bureaucratic meddling—the socialist economies proved unable to provide their citizens with the one thing that legitimizes modern governments: economic prosperity. The Soviet Union and the more conservative of the East

European countries increasingly dropped to a Third World level in all but their military establishments. In trying to save socialism by crushing the Prague Spring, Brezhnev actually ensured its eventual collapse.

THE STUMBLING SEVENTIES

If the 1960s was a decade in which radicalism failed to dent West European pluralism, the decade of the 1970s had a decidedly rigid quality. The collapse of the Bretton Woods agreements that had provided stable exchange rates since World War II, a tenfold jump in oil prices provoked by crises in the Middle East, and a softening of Cold War attitudes sapped the confidence of Europeans and spawned malaise rather than activism. The inability of the United States to support both a war in Vietnam and the expanded social programs introduced by President Johnson undermined the economic hegemony it had enjoyed after 1945, while Germany's continued expansion and vigor elevated it to a new position of authority and power on the Continent.

The Road to Helsinki

When Konrad Adenauer reluctantly resigned as chancellor of the Federal Republic of Germany in 1963 at the age of 88, he was succeeded by his Christian Democratic colleague Ludwig Erhard, long-time minister of finance and acknowledged genius behind Germany's economic miracle. Erhard was a committed free-marketeer, a stance that had served Germany well in the palmy days of recovery. But in the mid-1960s, the German economy stumbled and Erhard's critics concluded that more government intervention along the lines suggested by John Maynard Keynes was needed. The Social Democratic party (SPD), cowed by its impotence in the 1950s, had dropped its residual Marxism and by the mid-1960s presented itself as the party that could provide new economic leadership. Neo-Nazi success in local elections so unnerved the Christian Democrats that they invited the Social Democrats into a coalition to protect the gains in democracy and stability that the far right threatened.

The Grand Coalition, which came to power in 1966, succeeded in renewing the economic boom. It worked out a compact between employers, unions, and government that ensured labor peace, and it emphasized exports. This latter policy contrasted with Brezhnev's decision to restrict Soviet exports. Instead, Germany tried to maximize its position in the world market. In the 1970s, the small economies of the Pacific rim—notably Taiwan, South Korea, and Singapore—made a similar decision to emphasize exports. Over the next two decades, countries that adopted this strategy grew much more rapidly than the Soviet-style economies.

The entry of the Social Democrats into the governmental coalition in West Germany bolstered their popularity to the extent that they won the election of 1969 and were able to form their own government under Willy Brandt. Almost immediately, Brandt, who had established his anticommunist credentials while mayor of West Berlin, announced his intention to improve relations with East Germany. In the 1950s, Konrad Adenauer had refused any dealings with the communist East. Now Brandt offered to accept the status quo in Eastern Europe and to regularize relations with East Germany. In 1970, he signed a treaty with Poland recognizing the borders that Stalin and Churchill had penciled in at Tehran in 1943 and that Adenauer had refused to accept as final. By 1973 he completed the arrangements with East Germany for full mutual recognition.

The Soviet Union welcomed Brandt's initiative, even replacing a doubtful East German leader with one more amenable to agreement. West Germans, however, greeted

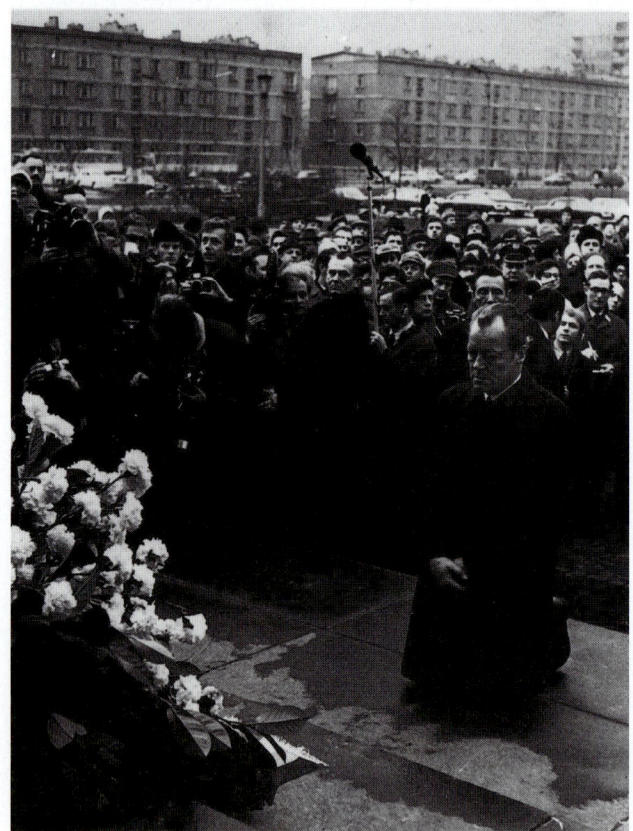

Paying Tribute West German Chancellor Willy Brandt's Ostpolitik transformed the calculus of European politics in the early 1970s. Here Brandt kneels in tribute to the Jewish martyrs of the Warsaw Ghetto, who rose in rebellion against the Nazis in 1943. The combination of reaching out to Poland and recognition of Jewish suffering moved many. *UPI/Corbis-Bettmann.*

THE HISTORICAL EVIDENCE

The Helsinki Accords

August 1, 1975

In Helsinki, Finland, in 1975, all the countries of Europe (except Albania) and the United States and Canada signed a major set of agreements on international security and human rights. The Helsinki Accords continued the process of defining rights and assumptions originally put onto the political agenda by the French and American Revolutions. A careful reader of these extracts will note that not all the principles are entirely consistent with one another.

The participating states regard as inviolable all one another's frontiers as well as the frontiers of all states in Europe, and therefore they will refrain now and in the future from assaulting these frontiers.

The participating states will respect the territorial integrity of each of the participating states.

The participating states will respect human rights and fundamental freedoms, including the freedom of thought, conscience, religion or belief, for all without distinction as to race, sex, language, or religion. They will promote and encourage the effective exercise of civil, political, economic, social, cultural, and other rights and freedoms, all of which derive from the inherent dignity of the human person and are essential for his free and full development.

Within this framework the participating states will recognize and respect the freedom of the individual to profess and practice, alone or in community with others, religion or belief acting in accordance with the dictates of his own conscience.

The participating states on whose territory national minorities exist will respect the right of persons belonging to such minorities to equality before the law, will afford them the full opportunity for the actual enjoyment of human rights and fundamental freedoms, and will, in this manner, protect their legitimate interests in this sphere.

They confirm the right of the individual to know and act upon his rights and duties in this field.

In the field of human rights and fundamental freedoms, the participating states will act in conformity with the purposes and principles of the Charter of the United Nations and with the Universal Declaration of Human Rights.

The participating states will respect the equal rights of peoples and their right to self-determination, acting at all times in conformity with the purposes and principles of the Charter of the United Nations and with the relevant norms of international law, including those relating to territorial integrity of states.

By virtue of the principle of equal rights and self-determination of peoples, all peoples always have the right, in full freedom, to determine, when and as they wish, their internal and external political status, without external interference, and to pursue as they wish their political, economic, social, and cultural development.

Source: Extracts from the Helsinki Accords, 1975, *Conference on Security and Cooperation in Europe: Part II*. Hearings before the Subcommittee on International Political and Military Affairs of the [House] Committee on International Relations (Washington, D.C.: U.S. Government Printing Office, 1975), pp. 122–124.

Brandt's opening to the East with mixed feelings. Many felt that his acceptance of the East German regime undermined the goal of German unity, while others distrusted any trafficking with the communists. Understanding that such a dramatic change in policy needed public support, Brandt called an election in 1971. When the SPD increased the number of its seats, he went ahead with his plans.

The United States approved of Brandt's *Ostpolitik* ("Eastern policy"), in part because it fit in with its own policy of opening to the Soviet Union. Late in 1969, the United States and the Soviet Union announced the beginning of disarmament talks. These discussions produced two important arms control agreements. The Strategic Arms

Limitation Treaties (SALT I and SALT II) of 1972 and 1979 limited and even reduced the vast arsenal of intercontinental ballistic missiles armed with nuclear warheads. These extraordinarily complex and technical negotiations fell under the general U.S. policy of *détente*, a French word meaning "easing" or "relaxation." The architects of détente, such as secretary of state Henry Kissinger, a close student of nineteenth-century Realpolitik, accepted the fact that the Soviet Union was not going to change its political system or give up its strategic interest in Eastern Europe. Even though, as we shall see later, the Soviet Union continued its buildup of strategic missiles during the 1970s and the United States answered in kind, Kissinger argued that the best solution was to find a way to live with Soviet reality.

Détente engendered a spirit of cooperation in European relations. Since the end of World War II, the Soviet Union had been seeking international recognition of its gains in Eastern Europe, especially the Oder-Neisse border between Poland and the German Democratic Republic. The success of Willy Brandt's Ostpolitik in legitimizing the German Democratic Republic opened the door to larger multinational negotiations on this subject and a broad range of other issues. In 1973 the Conference on Security and Cooperation in Europe (CSCE) convened, and in August 1975 the conferees signed the final accords in Helsinki. These agreements gave the Soviets the formal recognition of postwar borders they desired. For this reason, not everyone approved of the new agreements. Even though Republican president Richard Nixon began the negotiations for the United States, and Republican president Gerald Ford signed the agreements, conservatives throughout the Western world criticized Helsinki as a capitulation to communism.

But the accords also included a vital section on human rights. In this case it was the Soviet Union and the East European countries that agreed to a Western demand: They promised to guarantee a long list of specified human rights within their borders. This concession permitted Western leaders to undercut the left's high moral ground. Marxists had argued since the nineteenth century that capitalism exploited both workers at home and colonial peoples abroad. Because it was not hard to find examples of such exploitation, the West often found itself morally on the defensive. The Helsinki Accords, however, offered countless opportunities to show that the communists were not living up to their obligations to protect human rights. The Soviets countered by trying to redefine human rights not as freedom of speech or freedom of movement, but as economic rights, such as employment and medical care. The Helsinki Accords implanted the issue of human rights indelibly into international relations. At follow-up CSCE meetings, which reconvened periodically to assess progress in implementing the agreements, the West seized the ethical high ground and maintained it.[2] This change in moral positioning powerfully undermined the legitimacy of communist regimes in Eastern Europe.

A Growing European Community

Germany's creative foreign policy under Willy Brandt, coupled with its rapid recovery from a brief recession in 1965 and 1966, worried France and Great Britain, thus opening the door to Britain's admission to the European Community. After de Gaulle resigned in 1969, the French concluded that Britain might balance Germany's growing economic power. Britain also calculated that further integration of the EC would restrain a resurgent Germany. Once begun, negotiations proceeded quickly, and on January 1, 1973, Great Britain, along with its close trading partners Ireland and Denmark, joined the European Community.

Edward Heath, head of the governing Conservative party, led his country into the EC, but the British public remained reluctant. The Labour party officially opposed entry. British workers and employers did not feel themselves Europeans, and they resented the new rules and regulations elaborated by foreigners in Brussels. For example, the British had enjoyed cheap foodstuffs since the repeal of the Corn Laws in the nineteenth century (see Chapter 22). British farmers were efficient, and imports from the former colonies were inexpensive. The EC's Common Agricultural Policy, however, subsidized medium-sized family farms, thus increasing the cost of food. Most British did not understand why they should pay French and Danish farmers in order to make their own food more expensive.

Heath sought out EC membership nevertheless because of the weak condition of the British economy. Perhaps because Britain had been the first country to industrialize, it retained a Victorian style of doing business. Antiquated methods and outdated social attitudes put it at a competitive disadvantage with completely restructured Germany and Japan, not to mention with the United States. Labor unions held a narrow definition of self-interest and class conflict that contrasted sharply with postwar German practice of formalized cooperation between labor and management. Management was similarly hostile toward labor, while the upper classes continued to shun what they considered the grubby occupations of engineering and industrial management. These attitudes put a heavy drag on efforts to overcome the British fall from financial dominance after the war and to compete on the world stage. By the early 1970s, a majority of Conservatives believed that the bracing competition of the large European market would help stimulate the British economy.

But Great Britain entered the European Community grudgingly, and almost immediately began clamoring for renegotiation of its terms of membership. After interminable discussions that, as one observer remarked, "produced the minimum of results with a maximum of ill-will," some changes were made. But in 1979, Conservative party leader Margaret Thatcher came to power and raised a flood of further questions and complaints that dragged on until at least 1984. All in all, Britain proved an "awkward partner" in the European Community, as one author put it. Never really committed, constantly seeking redress, and always threatening in one way or another to leave, the British did not provide the balancing leadership that France had sought.

---

[2] Today the CSCE has been formalized into a permanent body, the Organization for Security and Cooperation in Europe (OSCE).

Disillusioned with the feckless British, the French turned to cooperation with the Germans. French president Valéry Giscard d'Estaing and German chancellor Helmut Schmidt (who replaced Brandt in 1974) developed a particularly close friendship. Nevertheless, they were not able to remove the many roadblocks that lay in the path of further integration.

Further enlargement of the European Community by the entry of Greece, Portugal, and Spain would not have been possible in the 1960s, because at that time all three countries were dictatorships. In Greece, a cabal of colonels had seized power in 1967; in Portugal António de Oliveira Salazar had ruled since the 1930s; and in Spain Francisco Franco's fascists remained in power. By 1975, however, all three countries had established democratic regimes. In Greece, a republican government returned to power in 1973 and brought Greece into the EC in 1981. In Spain and Portugal, the deaths of Franco and Salazar opened the door to membership later in the 1980s.

Spain experienced perhaps the most dramatic turnaround. A moderately large country of 38 million (in 1980), Spain had not played a major role in European affairs for three centuries. During the 1950s, however, Franco decided to abandon economic autarchy—although he maintained his dictatorship—and started to nudge Spain into the European economy. By the time of his death, Spain had undergone an economic transformation that resembled those of postwar Western Europe. Millions of peasants had moved to the cities, ordinary people owned automobiles and televisions, the birthrate had dropped, and gross national product had taken off.

King Juan Carlos I, chosen by Franco himself from the deposed Bourbon dynasty, provided the continuity and sage leadership that smoothed the political transition after Franco's death. He ensured the installation of a centrist government in 1976 that dampened Spanish extremists. At the same time, the Socialist Workers party, like all the postwar socialist parties in Europe, jettisoned its Marxist baggage and turned itself into a moderate political force. In 1982 it won a democratic election and led Spain into the European Community by 1986, the same year that Portugal also became a member. Today Spain, while still not reaching quite the level of the wealthiest members, has for the first time in its modern history prospered. It is now a respected and vital member of the international community.

Economic Turmoil

The malaise of the 1970s derived in large part from the recurrent economic shock waves rippling out from the collapse of the Bretton Woods currency exchange system and soaring oil prices. Until the late 1960s, the agreements made at Bretton Woods in 1944 had ensured liquidity during the postwar economic boom. Enough money

was available to finance investment, and it moved freely among the developed countries. The Bretton Woods system made this possible mainly through the convertibility of currencies, set exchange rates, help from the World Bank to permit countries to maintain reasonable balance of payments and foreign reserves, and an international system of management.[3]

In the late 1960s, the exchange rate regime collapsed. Most countries in the world by this time kept dollars as their reserve currency, but the United States, on the basis of the Bretton Woods agreements, pegged the dollar to gold. Because gold production lagged significantly behind world economic growth, the United States had to put extra dollars into the world trade system to maintain its liquidity. The United States did this by importing more goods than it exported. But this American trade deficit weakened confidence in the dollar. Not only did foreign accumulation of dollars exceed the value of the entire U.S. gold supply, but the excess of imports over exports undercut American industry. The enormous expenses of the Vietnam War only worsened matters. On the one hand, if the United States cut back on its spending and closed its trade deficit, growth of the world economy would slow. On the other hand, if it took steps to protect the American gold supply through restricting the money supply, it might bring on a depression, as similar government action had done in 1931.

In 1970 the United States decided to follow neither of these paths. President Nixon announced that the United States no longer would redeem its currency in gold, and thus removed the allegedly solid basis for the entire international monetary system. Soon almost every country was forced to abandon the "adjustable peg" through which it set its exchange rates. Currency exchange rates henceforth "floated," finding their own level. It turned out that the world economy was able to absorb this change, but between 1969 and 1974 uncertainty about the value of currencies inhibited investment and growth.

Just when the world economy had more or less weathered the collapse of the Bretton Woods exchange rate system, a new and more devastating shock struck: a tenfold increase in the price of oil. The major oil-producing regions of the Middle East had captured international attention from early in the twentieth century when oil replaced coal as the developed world's prime source of energy. After World War II, the United States in particular had taken a strong interest in the region, overthrowing a

---

[3] A currency is *convertible* when governments can exchange it for other currencies without hindrance. Countries whose currency is not convertible at the governmental level have difficulties participating freely in the world economy. Stable exchange rates among convertible currencies are desirable for world trade, although not necessarily for the interests of individual countries. None of the communist countries had a convertible currency.

democratically elected but leftist government in Iran in 1953, for example, to preserve that country's Western orientation. In the late 1950s, many of the Middle Eastern countries realized that their massive oil reserves gave them considerable international leverage. In 1960 these countries joined Nigeria and Venezuela (but not the United States nor the Soviet Union) in creating the Organization of Petroleum Exporting Countries (OPEC). The Muslim sheikdoms of the Arabian peninsula were the driving force behind OPEC.

In 1973, an outbreak of hostilities in the Middle East set the stage for trouble with OPEC. On Yom Kippur, the holiest Jewish holiday, Egypt attacked Israel, fearing that the Jewish state was about to escalate its conflict with the Arab states. It took the Israelis a few days to regain their balance, but soon they soundly defeated the Egyptians and the Syrians, who had joined in. Because the Soviet Union supported Egypt and the United States supported Israel, the Yom Kippur War pushed tensions between the superpowers to a dangerous level. The realization that Israeli-Egyptian conflict could have far-reaching consequences stimulated the United States to try to bring the two sides together. Despite a history of disruptive and frightening Arab terrorist attacks, such as the killing of eleven Israeli athletes and trainers at the 1972 Olympic Games, by 1979 American president Jimmy Carter succeeded in coaxing Egypt and Israel into signing a peace treaty.

Shortly after the Yom Kippur War, OPEC decided to turn off the oil spigot as a way to punish the West for aiding Israel. They stopped shipping oil to the United States and to the main European country of entry, the Netherlands. At the end of 1973, OPEC raised the price of oil by 70 percent, then by another 130 percent. By the end of the decade, the price of oil had gone from less than $3 per barrel to more than $30. This tremendous increase of the cost of the world's primary energy source had widespread repercussions. For a few months, consumers had to wait in lengthy lines at gas stations and suffer shortages of heating oil. Europe depended on Middle East oil for 63 percent of its energy. In the long run, the shock of higher prices finally stimulated industry and other consumers to take serious conservation measures. The search for oil also intensified. Discoveries along the northern slope of Alaska and in the North Sea off the British Isles yielded new reserves. France accelerated its atomic energy program, so that by the early 1980s some 75 percent of its electrical power came from that source.

The price hikes left the oil-producing countries suddenly awash in money. They invested a good portion of their petrodollars in the European banking system, which turned around and lent the new funds, sometimes on shaky terms, to Third World countries and to Eastern Europe. When these debts started to come due in the 1980s, most of the developing countries were unable to repay. The international debt crisis of the 1980s, in which various expedients had to be found to keep Third World countries afloat, was the culmination of the Yom Kippur War.

With the international exchange system in flux and the price of energy exploding, economies across the world faced hazardous times in the 1970s. The European Community, grappling with problems of British membership and its new and expensive common agricultural program, fared just as badly as the United States and Japan. Newspaper columnists spoke of "Europessimism," and pronounced the EC "Eurosclerotic." Nevertheless, not all the news was bad. The first direct elections to the European Parliament (see Chapter 31) took place in 1979, for example. Members of the European Parliament sit not by country, but by political persuasion (for example, conservative, liberal, Christian democrat, or socialist), thus symbolically suggesting a European rather than a national orientation. In the 1980s, the parliament became an increasingly important element in the European Community. By the end of the 1970s, the European Monetary System (EMS) had been created to take the place of the defunct Bretton Woods exchange system. Its operation was controversial, Great Britain never joined, and it did not lead to further monetary integration, as many had hoped, but it did stabilize currencies.

Environmentalism

If the 1970s was a period of economic turmoil and political adjustment, it was also a decade in which the environmentalist movement became firmly established in European and world politics. For several generations, the thrust of industrialization was growth and power, often glorified as progress. Inventions such as the railroad, the electric light, the automobile, and the airplane had given the impression that humans could conquer nature. Within this general viewpoint, however, the idea emerged in the late nineteenth century that nature should be respected, not just used. American president Theodore Roosevelt was one of the leaders of this conservation movement, which, while praising industrialization, nevertheless advocated acting responsibly to conserve natural resources. Others believed that humans too were natural beings, part of the physical world, not destined to somehow overwhelm it. The Scotland-born American naturalist John Muir argued that humans had to learn to live within nature, rather than conquering it.

After World War II, most Europeans were far more concerned with reconstructing their countries than with such issues. But in 1962, an American biologist, Rachel Carson, published *Silent Spring*, in which she showed the devastating effects of the chemical DDT (dichlorodiphenyltrichloroethane). DDT had been used indiscriminately since World War II as an insecticide, but Carson showed that in fact it was a biocide—that is, it had entered the food chain where it was killing not only insects, but substantial segments of the world's living species. Carson's

THE HISTORICAL EVIDENCE

Rachel Carson on DDT

1962

It is a rare book that has the impact of Rachel Carson's Silent Spring. *A best-seller in the United States, it was quickly translated into many languages and marks the beginning of modern environmentalism. In this selection, Carson discusses her main target, DDT.*

DDT (short for dichlorodiphenyltrichloroethane) was first synthesized by a German chemist in 1874, but its properties as an insecticide were not discovered until 1939. Almost immediately DDT was hailed as a means of stamping out insect-borne disease and winning the farmers' war against crop destroyers overnight. The discoverer, Paul Müller of Switzerland, won the Nobel Prize.

The Devastation of DDT The work of Rachel Carson revealed the effects of DDT on the environment. For example, it caused the shells of eggs to thin. Only one duckling has hatched out of these twelve contaminated eggs. *James Blair/NGS Image Collection.*

DDT is now so universally used [in 1962] that in most minds the product takes on the harmless aspect of the familiar. Perhaps the myth of the harmlessness of DDT rests on the fact that one of its first uses was the wartime dusting of many thousands of soldiers, refugees, and prisoners, to combat lice. It is widely believed that since so many people came into extremely intimate contact with DDT and suffered no immediate ill effects the chemical must certainly be innocent of harm. This understandable misconception arises from the fact that—unlike other chlorinated hydrocarbons—DDT *in powder form.* . . is absorbed slowly through the digestive tract; it may also be absorbed through the lungs. Once it has entered the body it is stored largely in organs rich in fatty substances (because DDT itself is fat-soluble) such as the adrenals, testes, or thyroid. Relatively large amounts are deposited in the liver, kidneys, and the fat of the large, protective mesenteries that enfold the intestines. . . .

The fatty storage depots act as biological magnifiers, so that an intake of as little as $\frac{1}{10}$ of 1 part per million in the diet results in storage of about 10 to 15 parts per million, an increase of one hundredfold or more. . . . One part in a million sounds like a very small amount—and so it is. But such substances are so potent that a minute quantity can bring about vast changes in the body. In animal experiments, 3 parts per million has been found to inhibit an essential enzyme in [the] heart muscle; only 5 parts per million has brought about necrosis or disintegration of liver cells; only 2.5 parts per million of the closely related chemicals dieldrin and chlordane did the same. . . .

All these facts—storage at even low levels, subsequent accumulation, and occurrence of liver damage at levels that may easily occur in normal diets—caused Food and Drug Administration scientists to declare as early as 1950 that it is "extremely likely the potential hazard of DDT has been underestimated." There has been no such parallel situation in medical history. No one yet knows what the ultimate consequences may be.

Source: Extracts from Rachel Carson, *Silent Spring* (New York: Houghton Mifflin, 1962), pp. 20–23.

Rachel Carson at Work Carson made her contribution not so much as a scientist but as an author. Her book, *Silent Spring,* shocked the world with its detailed and outraged discussions of the dangers of DDT and other man-made chemicals that were seriously upsetting the balance of nature. *Corbis/Underwood & Underwood.*

book, quickly translated into the world's major languages, became the founding document of a new movement: environmentalism. In 1970, American activists energized not only by environmentalism, but by antiwar sentiment and the civil rights movement, created the first Earth Day, which has since become a worldwide phenomenon. Later in the decade, the U.S. Congress enacted the Environmental Protection Act, the Clean Air Act, and the Clean Water Act, making environmentalism a public political issue from that time on.

Environmental groups formed in Western Europe too.[4] One of the most interesting groups, but one outside the populist mold of the environmental movement as a whole, was the Club of Rome. Reminiscent of Jean Monnet's Action Committee of the 1950s, this small organization of scientists and public officials from around the world published *The Limits to Growth* (1972). Through use of a com-

puter model of worldwide trends, this enormously popular and highly controversial book argued that industrialization could not continue to grow indefinitely without threatening the ability of the world to support life. "Sustainable growth" became the slogan of those who adhered to these ideas.

In almost every West European country, environmental activists began to enter politics in the 1970s, with greatest effect perhaps in the Federal Republic of Germany. There, at the end of the decade, a coalition of environmental and other groups created a new political party: the Greens. Opposition to nuclear power plants, which create long-lived, strongly radioactive waste products, motivated many of the Greens. Activists who had learned their nonviolent methods in the 1960s turned them into antinuclear protest marches and rallies in the 1970s. The Greens attracted not only antinuclear advocates and environmentalists, but protest groups of all kinds, including feminists, libertarians, gays and lesbians, and pacifists. By the end of the decade, the party was receiving about 8 percent of the vote in German elections.

The New Feminism

One aspect of the Green movement was feminism. Ecofeminists, as they started to be called in France in the 1970s, concentrated on issues that directly affected women, particularly in underdeveloped parts of the world. There women carry water and produce food, which makes them particularly affected by contaminated water, deforestation (which lessens the fuel available for cooking), and toxic household products. But ecofeminism was only one aspect of a broad feminist movement throughout the industrialized world following World War II. After World War I, women began to get the vote in many countries (although in some cantons in Switzerland not until the 1980s), but middle-class women retreated from the workplace they had occupied while the fighting had gone on. After World War II, however, middle-class women increasingly decided—or were forced by economic reality—to work. In part for this reason, they became increasingly active in the public sphere.

In 1949, Simone de Beauvoir, student and lover of Jean-Paul Sartre and a powerful intellectual figure in her own right, published *The Second Sex,* which became an instant classic. With wit and verve, de Beauvoir attacked the idea that women are the Other—complementing, serving, and reflecting the male, but never really equal to him. "How can a human being in woman's situation attain fulfillment?" she asked. Only "in terms of liberty," she answered.

Liberty in a practical form came to many women in 1960, when the American Food and Drug Administration approved public use of a birth control pill for women that prevented ovulation. The pill's introduction in Europe at

[4] In Eastern Europe and the Soviet Union, central planners not only took no account of environmental damage, but prohibited public discussion of the issue. As a result, for example, by the 1980s, 80 percent of the Vistula River, which runs through Poland, was too polluted even for *industrial* use.

about the same time gave women an unprecedented ability to choose whether to have children. With the widespread and increasingly open use of other contraceptives, public discussion of sex became much more open. Some feminists interpreted these events in terms of a woman's right to control her own body, an argument that led directly to bitter controversy over abortion. In 1974, for example, West Germany passed a law permitting abortion during the first three months of pregnancy, basing its decision on the rights of women. But shortly thereafter the German Constitutional Court declared this legislation incompatible with the need to protect life, and so abortion again became restricted in West Germany. In East Germany, on the other hand, and in most East European countries, where religious opposition was muted, abortions were freely available. The debate between a woman's right to choose and a fetus's right to live, often strongly influenced by religious beliefs, has continued with increasing bitterness to this day.

In related areas, a heightened level of awareness in the 1970s led to protection of raped and battered women. Police began to change the way they looked upon raped women, who came to be treated as victims of violence, rather than almost guilty of a transgression themselves. The first homes for battered women also appeared in the 1970s, and interest in the subject of incest began to show far more incidence of this family crime than anyone had suspected.

The new level of activism and awareness produced conflicts among the feminists themselves, as newly radicalized women scorned their older but seemingly less aggressive forebears. Disputes arose over whether women were equal with men, or should emphasize their differences from them. Were sexual relations private and personal, or were they subject to political and ideological norms? How should "consciousness raising" proceed? These and similar questions passed into the world of scholarship as well, at first as women's studies, but eventually as gender studies, which has proven to be one of the most original and stimulating innovations in historical writing of the last quarter-century. By the 1980s, women had not yet achieved parity in terms of salaries or numbers of public officials, but the level of public awareness of gender issues had been completely transformed.

THE DYNAMIC EIGHTIES

During the 1980s, most people still thought of themselves as living in a post–World War II era. The Cold War continued to shape the international atmosphere, with the United States spending ever more money on armaments and the Soviet Union getting bogged down in an armed attempt to impose communism in Afghanistan. In retrospect, however, we can see that many changes were preparing the way for a dramatic conclusion to the Cold War. Economically, the richest countries moved beyond indus-

trialism, as service industries powered by the computer gained dominance. Manufacturing industries, such as steel, found themselves buffeted by worldwide competition, forced to modernize and to lay off employees to survive. By contrast, the personal computer, invented only in 1978, not only spawned a totally new industry but dramatically changed information flows. The telegraph, daily newspaper, film, telephone, radio, and television had all vastly increased the amount of information available to the modern public, but the computer put an almost infinite amount of information instantaneously at people's fingertips and permitted manipulation of the data with unprecedented speed and flexibility. During the 1980s, these innovations changed the face of Western business, creating vast fortunes for its successful innovators. The silicon revolution—the fifth "industrial revolution" by one account—left the remnants of the first Industrial Revolution—the coal and steel industries—in the dust.

During the 1980s, the European Community removed many nontariff barriers to trade. Indeed, during this decade enthusiasm for cutting government regulation and limiting

Revenge of the Nerds Steve Jobs and Stephen Wozniak display a mock-up of their first Apple computer. They founded the company in 1977 with $1,300 raised when Jobs sold his VW van and Wozniak his programmable calculator. Six years later the company was listed by *Fortune* magazine as one of the 500 largest in the country. The age of the personal computer had begun. © *James Wilson/Woodfin Camp & Associates.*

state ownership swept the industrialized world. The postwar wave of nationalization petered out, as governments everywhere privatized industries that had become state-owned after the war. The Pacific Rim economies blossomed, and even communist China began extensive experimentation with private ownership.

By the end of the decade, a fundamental shift toward market economies took place even in Eastern Europe and the Soviet Union. In these regions the socialist regimes, almost without warning, collapsed. Unable to match the Western expenditure on arms, too regimented to compete with the individualistic, free-wheeling style of the computer age, and politically uncreative, the communist bloc fell further and further behind the West economically during the first half of the 1980s. In 1985 Mikhail Gorbachev came to power in the Soviet Union and attempted to reform the moribund socialism he found there. But his efforts failed. The fall of socialist regimes in 1989 and the disintegration of the Soviet Union two years later brought the postwar period to a startling end and opened a new era in European and world affairs.

A Turn to the Right

Two figures dominated Western politics in the 1980s: British prime minister Margaret Thatcher, elected in 1979, and American president Ronald Reagan, elected in 1980. Vigorously anticommunist and committed to free-market economics, these two conservatives shared the conviction that the growth of government in the postwar period was stifling individual initiative. The solution, they agreed, lay in so-called supply-side economics. Thatcher and Reagan believed that if taxes were lowered on the productive elements of society, successful businesses and entrepreneurs would respond by investing more in the economy, thus releasing a flood of economic growth that would "trickle down" to the rest of society. Reagan's solid victory in the 1980 election galvanized the U.S. Congress to lower federal income taxes in the following year, and Thatcher's disliked but respected chancellor, Nigel Lawson, did the same after her overwhelming reelection in 1983.

Both Reagan and Thatcher believed that labor unions hindered the free operation of markets. In the United States, Reagan reacted to a strike of air-traffic controllers in 1982 by firing them all, while Thatcher routed a year-long strike by British miners in 1984 and 1985 with a policy of resolute stonewalling. The other side of the union-bashing coin was the loosening of regulations on business. Reagan escalated the movement toward deregulation that had begun in the 1970s, and Thatcher sold off government enterprises amounting to some 5 percent of the British economy. Airlines and savings-and-loan associations saw marked deregulation in the United States, while in England the sale of British Air and Rolls Royce were only the

most visible devolutions of government ownership. In Thatcher's most significant privatization, government sold hundreds of thousands of council flats (that is, apartments built for working-class families by local government authorities with financial help from London). Having eased the housing problem after the war, the government now provided many working-class families with the same satisfactions of home ownership enjoyed by the middle class.

The Reagan-Thatcher revolution was not confined to the Anglo-American axis. Even France, where François Mitterrand became the country's first socialist president in 1981, turned toward neoconservative mechanisms. Initially Mitterrand implemented a traditional socialist program of raising the minimum wage, increasing family allowances, upping housing subsidies for the poor, raising pensions, and cutting the workweek. Instead of privatizing, he began acquiring enterprises, and he nationalized private banks. But these changes only worsened inflation, raised unemployment, and weakened the franc.[5] Just a year after taking office, Mitterrand did an about-face. In June 1982, he announced a freeze on wages and large cuts in public expenditure. By the mid-1980s France was cutting government, providing tax incentives, and imposing profitability demands on public enterprises like Renault. In Italy, too, "enterprise culture," as it was called there, dominated the middle and late 1980s.

The neoconservative revolution of the 1980s contained important paradoxes. Reagan the fiscal conservative found it easier to induce Congress to lower taxes than to cut government spending. During his presidency, government deficits soared to unprecedented heights. The United States went from being the world's main creditor country to being its largest debtor nation. Thatcher, the advocate of individualism, abolished many arms of local government, dominated formerly quasi-independent educational and professional organizations, and significantly expanded the power of the centralized government. Unleashing the profit motive also made life harsher. The U.S. stock market began a surge in 1982 that ever since has not faltered for long, and economic indicators bloomed in the late 1980s; but society paid the price in hostile corporate takeovers, the collapse of the tradition of lifetime employment in large firms, and a concentration of wealth in the hands of the affluent. "Trickle down" did not work. The richest 10 percent of the population considerably increased its share of the national wealth, while the share enjoyed by the lower 30 percent shrank. In the fifteen years from 1975 to

---

[5] According to the standard economic theory of the day, inflation and unemployment should be inversely related. As inflation goes up, unemployment should go down, and vice versa. When it did not work this way in many countries in the late 1970s and early 1980s, economists described the situation with the new term that combined the notions of stagnation and inflation: *stagflation*.

THE HUMAN EXPERIENCE

Margaret Roberts Thatcher, British Prime Minister

Margaret Thatcher (1925–) is the most prominent European woman of the twentieth century. She made her mark not merely by being Great Britain's first female prime minister, and one of the few women to lead a modern state of any kind, but by pursuing a clear-cut conservative program that shaped the course of European politics in the 1980s.

Thatcher's father was a strict Methodist. Parsimonious to a fault, he maintained an austere household, not installing hot water in the bathroom until after World War II, for example. In later life, Thatcher credited him for instilling her with proper values (she rarely mentions her mother). Having gained entry to

AP/Wide World Photos.

Oxford at the last minute, she immediately joined the student Conservative club there, rising by her fourth year to be its president. Upon graduating with a degree in chemistry, she took jobs with a plastics firm and then with a company in which she tested cake mixes. But her heart was in politics. The Conservative party was open to women in the postwar years, and she first ran for Parliament at the age of twenty-four, although this early bid was unsuccessful in a solidly Labour district.

In 1951 she married Denis Thatcher, owner of a chemical company. Freed from the necessity to earn a living that her own background had required, Mrs. Thatcher was able to study law, passing the bar in 1953. Over the next few years, she practiced law, gave birth to twins, and spent all of her spare time seeking a suitable place to run for Parliament. Already an accomplished politician, she had trouble convincing some Conservative clubs that a woman should get their nomination. In 1958, however, she outworked and outtalked two hundred applicants for a solid Conservative seat that had become available in Finchley. She represented Finchley for the next thirty years.

Working her way up through the party's hierarchy, she became party leader in 1975 and prime minister in 1979. The hallmark of Margaret Thatcher was her combative assurance. She reiterated time and again how she intended to give the country

back to the individuals. "We must always beware," she said, "of supposing that somehow we can get rid of our own moral duties by handing them over to the community." When Argentine troops seized the Falkland Islands in 1982, she ordered her military to throw them out by force, which they did, to the rousing cheers of the British public. When coal miners struck, she stonewalled them into defeat. These forceful acts earned her nickname "the Iron Lady."

But Margaret Thatcher also inspired her country, or at least a significant portion of it. When dissidents in the Conservative party disavowed her in 1990, she could— and did—look back on solid, if controversial, accomplishment. She privatized previously government-owned industry totaling about 5 percent of the British economy; she curbed the trade unions, which she thought had hobbled British industry; she created millions of new homeowners by selling off public housing; and she had presided over a significant revitalization of the British economy. Had the rich got richer and the poor poorer? Had she stood in the way of European unification? Had she turned loose a generation of self-serving nouveau riche? Margaret Thatcher greeted such criticisms with contempt and dismissal. Defiant, brazen, confident, tough, and able, Thatcher was Britain's most important statesman since Winston Churchill. ❖

1990, the average real income of American households (adjusted for inflation) actually declined, as lower-paying jobs proliferated. A single wage earner could no longer support a family. By the end of the period, middle-class women found that they were now in the position that working-class women had always faced—they *had* to work.

Breakthrough to European Union

The atmosphere of deregulation pushed the European Community toward reform. From 1979 to 1984, most of the public activity of the European Council—the semiannual meeting of the EC members' heads of state—focused on Margaret Thatcher's obsessive campaign to reduce the amount the British were paying for the privilege of membership. Tempers flared, accusations flew, and some believed the European Community was on the verge of collapse. But in July 1984, at the council meeting in Fontainebleau hosted by François Mitterrand, the participants finally reached an agreement that saved Britain some 15 billion dollars and satisfied Thatcher. At Fontainebleau the heads of state also decided to establish two temporary committees to investigate aspects of closer union. Normally, study committees are devices to avoid taking action, but in this case, the Fontainebleau committees produced a breakthrough.

As the fighting over the British contribution to the EC budget dragged on from 1979 to 1984, the prospects for a further lowering of European trade barriers had brightened on a number of fronts. In 1979, for example, in a key decision, the European Court ruled that foreign-made consumer products must be admitted to a member country if they were produced according to the rules and procedures of the country in which they were made. With this simple decision, EC member countries no longer needed to harmonize their production techniques—a laborious process that had been under way for twenty years with only modest results.

The United States also played a backhanded role in encouraging the Europeans to take a second look at their economic relations. Ronald Reagan had labeled the Soviet Union "the evil empire." When he came to power, he increased military spending and took a hard line against helping the Soviet and East European economies. He forbade participation of American companies in a projected natural gas pipeline that would bring Soviet gas to Western Europe, and tried to punish European firms that took up the slack. In the face of initiatives of this sort, many Europeans recalled how much economic influence America exerted on them, thus becoming more receptive to proposals for further economic cooperation among themselves.

In the European Parliament, Altiero Spinelli, an Italian member strongly in favor of creating a federal Europe, gathered a small group of like-minded members in the Crocodile Restaurant in Strasbourg to discuss possibilities. Soon the Crocodile Club, as it came to be called, outgrew the restaurant, and in 1981 Spinelli persuaded the European Parliament to establish the Committee on Institutional Affairs. Between 1980 and 1982, the parliament passed eight resolutions seeking reform. By early 1984, it had worked out a "Draft Treaty Establishing the European Union." This draft was not the document that became the Single Europe Act, but it indicated the breadth of interest in amending the Treaty of Rome.

The Single Europe Act that went into effect in 1987 expanded the power of the European Parliament and regulated voting on a number of issues by "qualified majority." In this latter procedure, each country received a number of votes in the Council of Ministers roughly related to its size.

Germany, France, Britain, and Italy were to have ten votes each, for example, whereas Luxembourg received only two. To pass, a resolution had to receive fifty-four out of the seventy-six available votes. In other words, twenty-three votes—the votes of two large countries and one small country, or of a number of small countries—would be enough to defeat a measure. This was a major change from the agreements made in the de Gaulle era (the Luxembourg Compromise of 1966). These arrangements had required that decisions be made "by consensus," which in practice had meant unanimously. The most sensitive issues, such as taxation, still required unanimity, but a host of lesser issues could now be decided by a qualified majority.

The Single Europe Act had another important feature: It called on member states to make 279 precisely specified changes. They included such technical and yet vital items as local procurement requirements, legal protection of biotechnological inventions, international rules on value-added taxes, and scores of similar arcane and thorny issues.

The negotiations leading up to the Single Europe Act, though heated, proceeded relatively quickly. When the act went into effect in the summer of 1987, the twelve members of the European Community committed themselves to completing the required changes by the end of 1992. Despite grave difficulties and the inability to agree on some eighteen important items, by January 1, 1993, the member states had reached a consensus on an overwhelming proportion of the proposed changes, and the European Union (EU) came into being.

The Single Europe Act stimulated further efforts toward cooperation. In December 1991, the European Council meeting at Maastricht in the Netherlands agreed to extend the powers of the European Community. It enhanced the position of the parliament, promised to work out a common foreign and security policy, and proposed creation of an Economic and Monetary Union (EMU) by 1999. Ratification of the Maastricht treaty proved more difficult than that of the Single Europe Act, although the proposal eventually squeaked through in every member country. The political sensitivity of creating a single European currency, which would eliminate the venerable mark, franc, lira, pound, and others, slowed agreement on monetary union, but the euro, as the new currency is called, nevertheless came into being in 1999. Creating an integrated security policy came afoul of the Wars of Yugoslav Succession in the early 1990s. Despite a full-scale review at an intergovernmental conference in Turin in 1996, the European Union has still to thoroughly coordinate its security pillar. The inability of the member states to synchronize their foreign policies, however, should not obscure the enormous progress made in the decade between 1984 and 1994 in fulfilling the promise of the Treaty of Rome. Today the existence of a powerful European Union, along with a host of other international institutions, provides a restraining force in European politics that makes the outbreak of catastrophic conflicts like World Wars I and II almost impossible.

The Tired Socialist System

As the European Community consolidated its open market, and as West European governments privatized formerly state-owned enterprises, the peoples of the Soviet Union and Eastern Europe remained in the grip of ossified regimes. In the Soviet Union, Leonid Brezhnev's regime of aging *apparatchiks* suppressed dissent, refused to change centralized planning, and continued to emphasize heavy industry over consumer goods.[6] Brezhnev, who ruled from 1964 until his death in 1982, nevertheless made two major contributions to Soviet development. He integrated the peasantry more fully than ever into Soviet life, and he strengthened the Soviet military.

Under most of Brezhnev's regime, the Soviet Union pursued a policy of détente with the United States. At the same time, it introduced medium-range nuclear missiles into Eastern Europe, built a "blue-water" navy (that is, one that could operate beyond Soviet coastal waters into the oceans of the world), and constructed an intercontinental ballistic missile force that rivaled that of the United States. President Jimmy Carter countered by agreeing to send intermediate-range cruise missiles to West European bases, a move stridently opposed by European peace movements. Ronald Reagan took an even more aggressive approach. He increased American expenditures on armaments and, in 1983, announced the Strategic Defense Initiative (SDI), popularly called Star Wars. This program, which underwent heavy criticism in the United States, promised to create a sophisticated missile system based on satellites and laser technologies. Star Wars was probably not technically feasible (at least on the scale planned by Reagan), but the possibility that the United States could outflank the Soviet Union technologically was real enough. At Brezhnev's death, the Soviets—having built a formidable war machine at great cost—found themselves facing even more costly technological improvements if they wanted to maintain military parity with the West. In some ways, Star Wars reminded one of the British decision to build the *Dreadnought* as an answer to German naval buildup in the first decade of the twentieth century (see Chapter 27), although the outcomes, fortunately, differed.

The gray dullness of the Brezhnev years had suffused Eastern Europe as well. Something vital had gone out of the socialist experiment in Eastern Europe after the crushing of the Prague Spring. The Brezhnev Doctrine seemed to extinguish all hope of change. "Real existing social-

ism," as several East European regimes called it, seemed implanted forever.

Antipolitics and Solidarity: Communism's Loss of Legitimacy

Opposition in the Soviet Union was extremely difficult, because the state quickly imprisoned anyone who overtly criticized, or even joked about, the regime. Nevertheless, in the 1960s a small dissident movement emerged there. Using clandestine resources, oppositionists published *The Chronicle of Current Events*, which brought to light examples of occasions in which Soviet authorities did not follow Soviet law but instead persecuted individuals. Daring students and writers copied poems and articles by hand and passed them on to friends. They called this form of publication *samizdat* ("self-publication") to contrast it with the official term *gosizdat* ("published by the state"). A tiny group even unfurled a flag in Red Square protesting the Warsaw Pact invasion of Czechoslovakia in 1968. But these efforts, heroic as they were, made little dent in the Soviet system, especially under the watchful eye of Brezhnev's secret police.

The repressions that followed the crushing of the Prague Spring posed a difficult question to thoughtful East Europeans: How could one live an authentic life knowing that sterile regimes protected from abroad dominated most aspects of the public arena? The Czech playwright Václav Havel provided one answer in his 1976 essay, "The Power of the Powerless." The post-Stalinist regimes must control every aspect of life, Havel wrote, because their ideology is false. This is why they react with such fury to those who do not conform. Even minor demonstrations that the system is false, such as not displaying a propaganda slogan in a shop window, threaten the entire rickety structure. The best way to counter the regime, therefore, is not to form opposition parties and movements, which merely reproduce in a different form the potentially oppressive mechanisms of modern politics, but simply to live in truth. Real life, Havel wrote, resides in the realm of the ethical, "the certainty that something makes sense." The alienation that one experiences in the totalitarian state is possible precisely because there actually is something in human beings to alienate: "Under the orderly surface of the life of lies, therefore, there slumbers the hidden sphere of life in its real aims." The power to find this authentic sphere even in the apparently hopeless conditions of "normalization" is what Havel called the power of the powerless.

Havel was only one of many who wrote in a similar vein. "Is not *honesty* in the final analysis the mortal enemy of totalitarianism?" asked a Romanian writer. Others suggested living "as if" one were free, or creating a civil society of nonpolitical associations. These authors feared traditional politics. They worried that if they tried to form

---

[6] *Apparatchik* is a derogatory term for bureaucrat in the Communist party apparatus.

an opposition political movement they would have to generate a program, win public support, and then, if successful, put the program into practice. But this would lead them into the same excesses as those they opposed. "My greatest nightmare," a Hungarian writer claimed, "is to have to tell millions of people what to do next." "By using force to storm the exiting Bastilles," a Polish essayist warned, "we shall unwittingly build new ones." Living in truth, in other words, meant being "antipolitical."

On January 1, 1977, a few Czech intellectuals distributed a document they called Charter 77. This declaration called on the Czechoslovak government to follow the obligation to protect human rights that it had agreed to by signing the Helsinki Accords and other international agreements. The group embodied the antipolitical spirit. "Charter 77 is not an organization," the originators wrote. "It has no rules, permanent bodies, or formal membership. It does not form the basis for any oppositional political activity. It does not aim to set out its own programs, but wishes to conduct a constructive dialogue by drawing attention to [the violation of] civil rights."

Antipolitics posed a fundamental threat to the communists. Revisionists in the 1960s had accepted the premise that socialism could be viable. The antipoliticians rejected it all—the state, the party, and even the vocabulary. Living in truth in this way took courage. It often meant losing one's job or even going to prison. Despite the small number of persons involved, however, the highly moral message of freedom expressed by the antipoliticians fundamentally undercut the legitimacy of the socialist regimes.

In 1976 a group of Polish intellectuals founded the Workers Defense Committee (KOR) to help workers imprisoned and fired in the widespread protests of that year. Their intent also was antipolitical—to provide a linkage between intellectuals and workers and to publicize injustice. But KOR helped foster an atmosphere of opposition in Poland that came to fruition in 1980. During the 1970s, the Polish government had tried to move away from the Stalinist strategy of a closed socialist system and to modernize by importing technology. Loans from foreign bankers were easy to get, owing to the surplus of petrodollars, but the corrupt centralized planning system failed to put the new capital to efficient use. In effect, the government borrowed money abroad and used it to raise workers' salaries, but without improving efficiency. This worked until about 1976, but after that the Polish economy began to decline, the debts came due, and unrest intensified.

Then, in 1978, a thunderbolt from the blue struck. The Polish cardinal Karol Wojtyła was elected Pope John Paul II, the first non-Italian pope in more than four hundred years. The news burst like a joyful bombshell over the Catholic Poles. When, the next year, John Paul visited his homeland, the communist government tried its best to discredit the visit. "The Pope is our enemy," an internal

memo said. "Due to his uncommon skills and great sense of humor [he] is dangerous because he charms everybody, especially journalists. We must strive at all costs to weaken the Church activities and undermine its authority in the society." But the pope's visit was a huge success. John Paul preached literally to millions of people, bringing Poles a sense of pride and engaging them in an elegant Polish that contrasted vividly with the stale bureaucratic language of the communist regime.

Social tensions in communist Poland often focused on food prices. Socialist regimes generally kept food prices low, but as time went by and the costs of production rose, the required subsidies reached an unsustainable magnitude. In 1980, the Polish government decided to increase some food prices. Just as they had in 1970 and 1976, when hit with similar hikes, factory workers all over the country came out on strike.

At the Lenin Shipyards in Gdańsk, the strike turned into a powerful demand for a union independent of Communist party control. The Communist party based its legitimacy on its claim to be the sole true representative of the working class, so the push for an independent union was in actuality a revolutionary demand. After failing to put down the strikes, the government finally agreed, although with much foot dragging, to recognize the new union, which took the name Solidarity. Under the leadership of Lech Wałęsa (pronounced "Va-WEN-sa"), Solidarity suddenly exploded into a nationwide movement of 10 million members. The organization tried to maintain its original antipolitical orientation—it claimed to be only a union with a work-related program. But any group 10 million strong does in fact have a claim on power, and that is what the Polish regime eventually could not abide. After getting its house in order by appointing General Wojciech Jaruzelski to head both the party and the state, the regime declared martial law late in 1981, imprisoned Wałęsa, and suppressed Solidarity by force.

Gorbachev and the Collapse of Communism

On the surface, the suppression of Solidarity seemed a replay of the Prague Spring without the intervention of Warsaw Pact troops. With Brezhnev in power, Solidarity leaders in jail, normalization still the policy in Czechoslovakia, and the megalomaniac Nicolae Ceauşescu in charge in Romania, Eastern Europe seemed doomed to eternal subservience to the Soviet model.

But appearances were deceiving. In Hungary János Kádár's regime decided in 1980 to democratize the Communist party somewhat and to bring Hungary closer to Western banking and trade practices. By the end of the decade, Hungary had become the most Westernized economy in Eastern Europe. In Poland itself, Jaruzelski failed to suppress the Solidarity spirit. Lech Wałęsa, released from jail in 1982, received the Nobel Peace Prize in 1984 and became a worldwide symbol of gallant resistance. Alternative schools and cultural organizations of all kinds flourished in Poland, and the number of university students joining the Communist party dropped to almost zero. Eventually, Jaruzelski expanded the sphere of "permissible pluralism," until by 1987 the American head of the human rights organization Helsinki Watch could call Poland the freest country in Eastern Europe.

The main change, however, came in the Soviet Union. After two feeble replacements for Brezhnev died in office, Mikhail Gorbachev came to power in 1985. Just fifty-four, Gorbachev was the harbinger of a new Soviet generation of intelligent, well-trained, and effective public servants. Well aware of the vigorous public image he and his sophisticated wife projected in comparison to the doddering Soviet leaders who had preceded him, Gorbachev traveled widely and achieved hearty public acclaim. He and his remarkable foreign secretary Eduard Shevardnadze took a much less confrontational attitude toward the West than their predecessors. They stopped nuclear testing and sought further disarmament agreements. They ended the Soviet intervention in Afghanistan, which had ground on since 1979, and they urged East-West cooperation in what Gorbachev called "our common European home."

Gorbachev understood that change was necessary at home, too. The costs of simply maintaining the status quo became crystal clear in 1986 when, during a botched experiment, a Soviet nuclear power plant near the town of Chernobyl blew up and emitted large amounts of radioactive matter into the atmosphere. At first the regime tried to hide or deny the accident, but when winds carried radiation into Europe and monitors picked it up, Gorbachev had to act, albeit slowly and hesitantly. In the meantime, tens of thousands of people had been contaminated, thirty-two of them fatally, and thousands of square miles had to be evacuated. The accident, the worst publicly acknowledged nuclear disaster, not only confirmed the fears of antinuclear activists around the world, but demonstrated both an alarming degree of Soviet technological incompetence and an equally alarming inability of the closed political system to cope with a devastating emergency.

Gorbachev knew that the Soviet economy was in trouble, that it could neither match the military spending of the United States nor provide acceptable living standards for its population. He hit on a threefold solution. First, he instituted a policy of *perestroika*, a Russian word meaning "restructuring." The word became well known in the West in the late 1980s. Gorbachev had no intention of dismantling socialism, but he did want to make it more efficient. However, he knew that the entrenched bureaucracies would not change their ways easily. Therefore, as the second element of his program, he tried to win the intelligentsia to his side through a policy of *glasnost*, or "openness." Starting about 1986, Soviet newspapers and television began modest and then more far-reaching political criticism; authors previously unpublished found their way into print; films rejected by the censors and gathering dust on shelves for years were finally released; the Soviet travel agency even began printing accurate tourist maps of Moscow, which it had never done in the past for fear of revealing some strategically significant data. Finally, pushed by the logic of perestroika and glasnost, Gorbachev sought to rally the people to his side with the third innovation of his program, *demokratsiya* ("democracy"). After televising a contentious meeting of the Central Committee in 1988, Gorbachev conducted competitive elections to the Supreme Soviet (national legislature). On May 25, 1989, an engrossed television audience witnessed the opening of the first freely elected Russian or Soviet legislature since the abortive Constitutional Assembly of January 1918.

With change pulsing through the Soviet Union, Gorbachev hoped the East European countries would change, too. Only two countries took advantage of the opening that Gorbachev offered them: Poland and Hungary. In Poland, General Jaruzelski finally accepted the fact that he would have to recognize Solidarity. By the time representatives of the party, the state, the church, and Solidarity sat down to roundtable discussions early in 1989, the deal was set: The state would recognize Solidarity, and Solidarity would agree to a minority participation in the government for an interim period, thus taking on partial responsibility for public affairs.

The final agreement, signed in April, called for an election to the Sejm—the Polish legislature—in which 65 percent of the seats were reserved for the Communist party and its satellite parties. Election to the other 35 percent of the seats would be open, as would the elections to a newly created Senate. Wałęsa thought his forces could win a significant number of the contested seats, but no one expected the actual outcome: Solidarity swept all but one contested seat in both the Senate and the Sejm. In some instances, even unopposed Communist party leaders lost their election bid when a majority of voters scratched their names off the ballot. Even Wałęsa was surprised. "I face the disaster of a good crop," he quipped. "Too much grain has ripened for me and I can't store it all in my granary."

Solidarity's overwhelming victory at the polls transformed the Polish political equation. How could the Communist party stay in power after such a resounding rejection? After two months of negotiation, and a clear indication by Gorbachev that he had no intention of intervening, the two sides reached a compromise: Jaruzelski would stay on as president, and a Solidarity activist would become prime minister. On August 24, 1989, Tadeusz Mazowiecki, the first noncommunist prime minister in Eastern Europe in almost forty years, took office. The sad-faced Mazowiecki was so overwhelmed that he fainted during the ceremonies. No wonder. The dramatic turn of events had left the entire world breathless.

"We Are One People"   In November 1989, an East German policeman reaches down from the now-obsolete Berlin Wall for a rose offered by a West German woman. One year later, the two Germanies were united after forty years of separation.   *Jacques Witt/Sipa Press.*

ple." By October, hundreds of thousands more were chanting on the streets of cities throughout East Germany. Now they shouted a new slogan: "We are one people." The demonstrators had given up not only on the communists, but on the German Democratic Republic as well. They wanted unification with the West.

Gorbachev was no help to the aged East German leadership. "Life punishes those who come too late," he remarked early in October, at the fortieth anniversary celebrations of the creation of the German Democratic Republic. The party tried to save itself, but it was indeed too late. On the evening of November 9, the East German politburo decided to simplify the visa requirements for visiting West Germany, But it worded its announcement so imprecisely that a rumor spread that the Berlin Wall was going to be opened. Crowds gathered, and just before midnight the confused guards started letting people through. Suddenly hundreds of thousands of ecstatic Germans poured through the wall to the West, and the German Democratic Republic collapsed. Within one year—almost instantaneously, as historical moments go—the GDR had reunited with West Germany, bringing to fruition the postwar dream of a single Germany.

The fall of the Berlin Wall thrilled millions, but more surprises were in store. The next day, Todor Zhivkov, the

November 24, 1989: Democracy Prevails   Václav Havel (right) hugs Alexander Dubček after receiving news that the entire Czech communist government had resigned.   *Corbis/Reuters.*

The elections in the Soviet Union and the unique change of government in Poland distracted the world momentarily from what was going on in Hungary. There, reformers had gained control of the Communist party and instituted their own roundtable discussions with the opposition; discussions that later enabled a conservative populist party to come to power.

More immediately, however, in March 1989 the Hungarian communists decided to open their borders. With wire cutters and bulldozers, they began dismantling the Iron Curtain—the heavily guarded border fortifications that had separated East from West for a generation. That summer, as Hungarian border guards winked, thousands of vacationing East Germans sneaked across the border into Austria en route to Germany. By September, the East German end-run through Hungary had become a flood, and the foundations of the East German regime began to tremble. Thousands of demonstrators appeared every Monday night on the streets of Leipzig chanting, "We are the peo-

THE HISTORICAL EVIDENCE

Václav Havel's New Year's Day Speech

January 1, 1990

After years of moral opposition to the communist government of Czechoslovakia, Václav Havel (1925–) became the country's president during the "Velvet Revolution" of 1989. This selection contains excerpts from his first speech. Notice the echoes not only of the "antipolitics" position of the dissidents of the 1970s and 1980s, but also of the views of the founder of the first Czechoslovak Republic Tomáš Garrigue Masaryk (see "Democracy as Compromise" section in Chapter 29).

Dear fellow citizens. For the past 40 years on this day you have heard my predecessors utter different variations on the same theme, about how our country is prospering, how many more billion tons of steel we have produced, how happy we all are, how much we trust our government, and what beautiful prospects lie ahead of us. I do not think you appointed me to this office for me, of all people, to lie to you.

Our country is not prospering. Whole sectors of industry are producing things in which no one is interested, while the things that we need are in short supply. The state, which calls itself a state of the working people, is humiliating and exploiting the workers. We have laid waste and soiled the rivers and the forests that our forefathers bequeathed to us, and we have the worst environment in the whole of Europe today.

But not even all of that is the most important thing. The worst thing is that we are living in a decayed moral environment. We have become morally ill, because we have become accustomed to saying one thing and thinking another. We have learned to not believe in anything, not to have consideration for one another, and only to look after ourselves. Notions such as love, friendship, compassion, humility, and forgiveness have lost their depth and dimension.

The previous regime, armed with its arrogant and intolerant ideology, denigrated man into a production force and nature into a production tool. It made talented people who were capable of managing their own affairs and making an enterprising living in their own country into cogs in some kind of monstrous, ramshackle, smelly machine whose purpose no one can understand.

When I talk about a decayed moral environment, I do not mean merely [our former leaders]. I mean all of us, because all of us have become accustomed to the totalitarian system, accepted it as an unalterable fact, and thereby kept it running. In other words, all of us are responsible, each to a different degree, for keeping the totalitarian machine running. None of us is merely a victim of it, because all of us helped to create it together.

Why do I mention this? It would be very unwise to see the sad legacy of the past 40 years as something alien to us, handed down to us by some distant relatives. On the contrary, we must accept this legacy as something that we have brought upon ourselves. If we can accept this, then we will understand that it is up to all of us to do something about it. We cannot lay all the blame on those who ruled us before, not only because this would not be true, but also because it could detract from the responsibility each of us now faces—the responsibility to act on our own initiative, freely, sensibly, and quickly.

Let us not delude ourselves: not even the best government, the best parliament, or the best president can do much on their own. Freedom and democracy, after all, mean that we all have a part to play and bear joint responsibility. If we can realize this, hope will return to our hearts.

Source: Condensed from *Federal Broadcasting Services, East Europe, 90–001* (Washington, D.C.: U.S. Government Printing Office, January 2, 1990).

---

leader of Bulgaria since 1954, resigned, and a reforming communist leadership turned Bulgaria in the direction of democracy. One week later, police overreaction to a student demonstration in Prague set off a nationwide series of protests in Czechoslovakia. Masses of people gathered in Wenceslas Square in central Prague, jangling their key chains, cheering Václav Havel and Alexander Dubček, and shouting "This is it!" and "Now is the time!" By the end of

the year, the "Velvet Revolution," so-called because of its lack of violence, had overthrown the Czechoslovak communist regime. Havel, almost straight from prison, became president. "I do not think you appointed me to this office for me, of all people, to lie to you," the new president said in his acceptance speech.

And then the last domino, Romania, came tumbling down. The hateful Nicolae and Elena Ceauşescu had ruled with the utmost brutality during the 1980s. Facing a debt crisis in 1980, Ceauşescu had decided to pay it off rather than restructure, but to do so he devastated the already weak Romanian economy. Food became scarce; people were allowed to burn only one 40-watt lightbulb per room; and central heating kept temperatures in apartment blocs at a frigid 55 degrees. A strict police regime stifled whatever opposition surfaced. In November 1989, with communism collapsing in the rest of the region, a subservient, even obsequious, party unanimously reelected the "giant of the Carpathians" as its leader. But in December, a protest over the reassignment of a Hungarian priest broke out in the regional center of Timişoara and sparked protests elsewhere.[7] When Ceauşescu tried to calm matters with force and then with a staged speech in Bucharest, he lost the support of the army. On December 25, 1989, a hastily convened irregular court convicted him and his wife of genocide and executed them. Reform communists, the only people in Romania with any political experience, assumed power and introduced democratic forms.

Gorbachev had hoped for change in Eastern Europe, but not to this extent. He envisioned reforms by vigorous young socialists, but not the complete replacement of socialist regimes with ones committed to free markets and democratic forms. Nevertheless, he did not intervene. Although the Soviets had almost four hundred thousand troops in Germany and a somewhat smaller number in Poland, to stem the tide of collapse they would have had to use Stalinesque levels of force. Having just extricated themselves from a disastrous war in Afghanistan, and seeking partnership with Western Europe, they could not use force without abandoning perestroika, glasnost, and demokratsiya.

The collapse of communism in Eastern Europe fatally weakened the Soviet Union and damaged Gorbachev. In August 1991, a group of military and secret service officers attempted to take advantage of Gorbachev's vacation to seize power and return to totalitarian ways. The wretchedly planned and badly executed coup failed, but it precipitated the eventual fragmenting of the Soviet Union itself. Gorbachev completely underestimated the strength of nationalism in the multinational Soviet state. He found it particularly unsettling in the Baltic republics (Latvia, Estonia, and Lithuania) which the Soviets had annexed in 1940. There, nationalist movements used the example of Eastern Europe to elect new leaders in 1990 and to insist that the Russian troops leave. The Baltic difficulties, which Gorbachev could not resolve even with force, tempted the other national groups—the Ukrainians, Georgians, Armenians, and others—to press their desires.

---

[7] A substantial Hungarian minority inhabits Transylvania and the western borderland of Romania, and it played a role in bringing down the chauvinistic Ceauşescu regime.

Adieu! As Soviet troops began boarding trains and heading back to the Soviet Union in 1989, a Hungarian artist wished them farewell: "Comrades Good-bye!" *Courtesy of the Smithsonian Institution Traveling Exhibition, from its exhibition "Art as Activist: Revolutionary Posters from Central and Eastern Europe."*

In addition to the ethnic difficulties, perestroika was destroying the old economy without replacing it with a viable new one. Soviet citizens suffered economic decline from an already low starting point. Worse, from Gorbachev's point of view, a challenger arose in the person of Boris Yeltsin. An enemy of Gorbachev since his expulsion from the Moscow party leadership in 1987, Yeltsin earned great public renown when, during the coup attempt of August 1991, he bravely stood atop a tank and called for resistance to the plotters. By the end of 1991, the republics of the Soviet Union had agreed to disband and to create a Commonwealth of Independent States. On Christmas Day 1991, two years to the day after Ceauşescu's execution, Gorbachev resigned and the Soviet Union went out of existence. He summed up his major contribution to the twentieth century with these words: "The totalitarian system that deprived the country of an opportunity to become successful and prosperous long ago has been eliminated."

The Last and the First
Mikhail Gorbachev (left) was the last head of the Soviet Union; Boris Yeltsin was elected president and prime minister of the new Russian Federation when the Soviet Union dissolved. Here, Yeltsin confronts Gorbachev as he addresses the Russian parliament in August 1991. *Corbis/ Reuters.*

CONCLUSION: THE END OF THE COLD WAR

The demise of communism in Eastern Europe and the fragmentation of the Soviet Union came as an enormous surprise. For a great power voluntarily to abandon its hegemony in a region of vast strategic importance and then completely disintegrate in peacetime was unprecedented. The failure had several immediate causes. In a society that had been closed for so long, Gorbachev's reform efforts confronted citizens with choices they never had to make before. Without experience with democracy, openness, or market economics, ordinary people became confused, resentful, and frustrated. Criminal elements forged to the forefront, and old ideas of Stalinism and the firm hand on the tiller resurfaced. American policy also pressured the Soviet Union. Relentless opposition to communism coupled with Reagan's increased military expenditures posed difficult decisions for the Soviet Union.

In Eastern Europe, economic failure and loss of political legitimacy were the primary causes of collapse. The centrally planned economies proved unable to navigate the constantly changing environment of world trade or to provide its citizens with adequate consumer goods. The Soviet Union shut its allies into a closed economic system conducted by relatively static planning criteria. By the 1980s, shortages that translated into long lines at shops, low-quality goods, and inadequate housing crippled the Soviet and East European economies.

Economic failure underlay the collapse of communism, but it was a sense of humiliation, the desire for freedom, and a need for authenticity that drew millions of East Europeans onto the streets in 1989. They wanted a better economic life, yes, but they also craved freedom, democracy, and respect. "Even if people never speak of it," Václav Havel wrote in a famous open letter to Czechoslovak party leader Gustav Husák in 1975, they "have a very acute appreciation of the price they have paid for outward peace and quiet: the permanent humiliation of their human dignity." Beneath the superficially calm and apparently strong surface of East European life during the 1970s and 1980s, support for the regimes rotted away. When the storm struck, the regimes collapsed like hollow reeds.

Selected Reading

Sources

de Beauvoir, Simone. *The Second Sex* (1974; originally published 1949).

Havel, Václav. *Open Letters: Selected Writings, 1965–1990* (1991).

Kundera, Milan. *Joke: The Definitive Version* (1993). Marvelous novel that Kundera claims is about love. Maybe so, but it is also a vivid portrait of Czechoslovakia under Stalinism and its descendants.

Smithsonian Institution. *Art as Activist: Revolutionary Posters from Central and Eastern Europe* (1992).

Torańska, Teresa. *"Them": Stalin's Polish Puppets* (1987). Interviews with Polish leaders of the 1940s and 1950s who continued to hold fiercely to the Stalinist cause.

International Affairs

Blacker, Coit D. *Reluctant Warriors: The United States, the Soviet Union, and Arms Control* (1987). Easy-to-follow narrative.

Colchester, Nicholas, and David Buchan. *Europower: The Essential Guide to Europe's Economic Transformation in 1992* (1990). Contains useful details about the complex processes that constitute the European Community.

Kovrig, Bennett. *Of Walls and Bridges: The United States and Eastern Europe* (1991). First-rate analysis arguing that the continuity of the U.S. policy of containment, coupled with flexibility in tactics, contributed fundamentally to the collapse of communism.

Marglin, Stephen A., and Juliet B. Schor. *The Golden Age of Capitalism: Reinterpreting the Postwar Experience* (1990). Several enlightening analyses of what lay behind the economic boom of the 1950s and 1960s, and what caused its moderation.

Williams, Allan M. *The European Community: The Contradictions of Integration*, 2nd ed. (1994). Useful text.

Williamson, John. *The Failure of World Monetary Reform, 1971–74* (1977). Monetary policy is notoriously technical, but this book explains the problem in accessible language.

Yergin, Daniel. *The Prize: The Epic Quest for Oil, Money, and Power* (1990). Fascinating book about oil as capitalism, a strategic commodity, and the energy basis of modern life.

The Collapse of Communism

Garton Ash, Timothy. *The Magic Lantern: The Revolution of '89 Witnessed in Warsaw, Budapest, Berlin and Prague* (1990); and *The Uses of Adversity: Essays on the Fate of Central Europe* (1989). Contemporary analyses by a journalist who knew the languages and the people who made the revolutions of 1989. Classics of their time.

Jarausch, Konrad H. *The Rush to German Unity* (1994). Detailed, authoritative discussion of German unification and its implications.

Kaiser, Robert G. *Why Gorbachev Happened: His Triumphs and His Failure* (1991). Political and personal history by a well-informed and long-time observer of the Soviet Union.

Stokes, Gale. *The Walls Came Tumbling Down: The Collapse of Communism in Eastern Europe* (1993). Readable account from 1968 stressing East European initiatives.

Individual Countries

Judt, Tony. *Past Imperfect: French Intellectuals, 1944–1956* (1992). Sophisticated analysis of the "moral amnesia" of apologists for Stalinism in postwar France.

Maxwell, Kenneth, and Steven Speigel. *The New Spain: From Isolation to Influence* (1994). Excellent brief overview of Spain's transition to a new position of respect in Europe.

Pérez-Díaz, Víctor M. *The Return of Civil Society: The Emergence of Democratic Spain* (1993). Interesting interpretation that puts the Spanish turn to democracy in a wider European context.

Robinson, Richard A. H. *Contemporary Portugal: A History* (1979). Introduction to the history of the Portuguese dictatorship (1926–1974) and the turn to democracy (1974–1978).

Williams, Karel, John Williams, and Dennis Thomas. *Why Are the British Bad at Manufacturing?* (1983). Lays Britain's problems at the foot of poor managerial control over labor and antagonistic state-business relations, among other things.

Personalities

Young, Hugo. *One of Us: A Biography of Margaret Thatcher* (1991). Balanced and readable.

NEW BEGINNINGS

Every ending in history is also a beginning. The periods and dates we identify, such as the Enlightenment or the year 2000, are human artifacts. In reality, time inexorably sweeps on, one second at a time, every moment a product of its past and at the same time pregnant with possibilities for the future. Still, some moments seem particularly significant. The collapse of communism between 1989 and 1991 is one such moment. It ended a number of periods in European history, but at the same time created a new situation that is still in the first stages of being worked out. The 1990s appear to constitute the first ten years of a new era in history, the main characteristics of which will only become clear in the future—possibly a distant future.

The most obvious period that ended in 1989 was the Cold War era. For a generation following the collapse of Europe in 1945, at the end of the Century of Power, the Soviet Union and the United States dominated world politics. The end of the communist regimes in Eastern Europe and, shortly thereafter, in the Soviet Union finished that relationship. The collapse of communism also ended the second of two great twentieth-century social and political experiments inspired by the French Revolution. Marxist communism carried to an extreme conclusion the Enlightenment idea that human beings could improve society by reorganizing it on the basis of reason. The Communist party claimed that it, and only it, truly understood human society and that therefore it had the right—even the duty—to reorganize society according to its own rules. The other failed twentieth-century experiment—fascism and Nazism—took the opposite tack by rejecting Enlightenment rationalism. In place of reason this approach emphasized emotion, blood, and soil. By 1945 the bankruptcy of this approach had become all too tragically clear.

One outgrowth of the French and American Revolutions, however, survived the collapse of fascism and the failure of communism: pluralism. This heir of the Enlightenment goes by many names—democracy, limited government, the open society, liberalism, the politics of accommodation, and constitutionalism are among them. Anarchic as democratic, liberal, or open societies seem, they possess one great asset that corresponds to the variety of human needs and experiences: Unlike fascism and communism, pluralist mechanisms are not based on the claim that there is one true understanding of the world. Fascist and communist systems offered final, irrefutable answers to humanity's problems. Pluralism, on the other hand, is not a

system. It makes no assertions about the ultimate good, nor does it provide final answers. Instead, as Jean Monnet said about the European Community, pluralism is a process. Democratic states have certain common institutions, such as parliaments, political parties, and rules about freedom of expression, but they differ greatly in specific organization and structure. Change in pluralist societies is never easy. Bitter struggles, corruption, injustice, cant and humbug, outrageous claims, class differences, and even failure haunt the democracies. But this is only to say that human beings are contentious. Pluralist societies permit a fuller range of human frailty to find public expression than did the totalitarian experiments of the twentieth century. But this seeming weakness lies behind pluralism's greatest strength—its ability to accommodate the vast variety of modern societies and to change. Communist and fascist regimes proved static, unable to cope with the rapid transformations of technological and social change. Whatever their other faults, pluralist systems have been able to reinvent themselves, slowly perhaps and sometimes painfully, but fruitfully.

This is not to say that pluralism has solved all of society's problems. Despite a spectacular rise in the general standard of living in industrialized countries, wrenching poverty still exists, particularly in the nonindustrial parts of the world. Indeed, the gap between the richer and the poorer segments of industrialized societies is growing, as is the gap between rich and poor nations. Pluralist regimes have only just begun to search out ways of controlling transnational problems such as pollution, the population explosion, and the reach of vast international conglomerates. And with the withering of the ideologies of the left, pluralist societies face a lack of principled criticism, a situation that in the long run could be seriously debilitating. But at the end of two hundred years of experience following the French Revolution (which began, conveniently enough, in 1789), it does seem that only some form of pluralism will be able to nourish creativity and sustain order in an industrializing world.

Apart from the Cold War, an even longer period has also ended: the European era. From the end of the fifteenth century to the end of the twentieth century, Europe exploded into the rest of the world, carrying its economic, political, and cultural institutions with it. After 1945, and especially after the political upheaval of 1989–1991, Europe's direct control over vast stretches of the world was finished. Europe's five hundred years of expansion are over—but those five hundred years completely restructured the planet. Today the world is organized politically in a system of states; the capitalist market system dominates almost all economic activity; the politics of accommodation has survived while more extreme manifestations of Enlightenment optimism have collapsed; and the ideal of equity or fairness inspires individuals and groups seeking their rights everywhere. But Europe itself is now only one of several large political and economic entities that face each other in a multipolar world. North America, South America, Southeast Asia, Japan, China, and, yes, perhaps in the future, even Russia, not to mention the Arab world

and Africa, all stand as powerful or potentially powerful players in the new world economic and political game.

In the new, powerful, and yet lessened Europe, two contradictory tendencies characterized the decade of the 1990s: the efforts to bring democracy to Eastern Europe and to unify the Continent into one economic and possibly even political entity, and the countervailing pressure of ethnic groups to create their own separate entities. The latter problem has received by far the most public attention.

In the summer of 1991, when the Soviet Union was in the final stages of its demise, the multinational federal state of Yugoslavia broke apart. In the case of the Soviet

MAP E/P-1
EASTERN EUROPE AFTER THE COLLAPSE OF COMMUNISM

Bosnian Serb Republic
Muslim–Croat Federation
Cease–fire line before the peace agreement
New interentity boundary

Union, the breakup was peaceful. There was some fighting in the Baltics, and later in some of the new republics, such as Georgia. Inside Russia itself, in Chechnya, a violent battle erupted. But in general, the breakup of the Soviet Union was as peaceful as one could expect for such a major event. (See Map E/P-1 for the new boundaries of Eastern Europe.)

Yugoslavia's breakup, however, was extremely violent. From its creation as a monarchy in 1918 and its reestablishment in 1945 as a socialist state, Yugoslavia had been beset by conflicts among its various peoples—Serbs, Croats, Slovenes, Bosnians, Albanians, and others. The strength, and the primary weakness, of nationalism is its claim that the nation is homogeneous, that the people are one. This claim is sustained by creating a sense of the Other—those who are not us. When advocated by politicians intent on sustaining their own power and increasing the power of their people, nationalism's almost inevitable result is conflict. Indeed, one of the main themes of European history in the past century and a half has been the violent effort of national entities to redraw state boundaries to include all of their own nation and exclude or subordinate all other peoples. The unification of Italy in the middle of the nineteenth century is an excellent example of this, as is the remapping of Poland after World War II.

In socialist Yugoslavia, the personal authority of its World War II leader, Josip Broz Tito, and the administrative grip of the League of Yugoslav Communists held that country together. But when socialism faltered, so did the country's unity. Pushed by a leader in Serbia who sought to establish his control over the country, in 1991 Slovenia and Croatia decided to secede from the federation. No Serbs lived in Slovenia, so it was able to go its way relatively easily. But because many Serbs lived in Croatia, its secession quickly led to an attack on Croatia by Serbia, allegedly to prevent Croatia from harming its Serbian residents. Within a year, a similar kind of outburst occurred in Bosnia, a multiethnic region inhabited not only by Orthodox Serbs and Catholic Croats, but by Muslim Bosnians too. The depredations of fanatical paramilitary volunteers who saw themselves engaged in a mission to cleanse regions of their ethnic enemies made the Wars of Yugoslav Succession exceptionally vicious and bloody. Several hundred thousand people perished and more than 2 million others were forced into exile as refugees.

The violence of the Yugoslav wars and the stubbornness of the Yugoslav leaders posed very difficult problems for both Europeans and Americans. Europeans, proud of being on the verge of fulfilling the Single Europe Act and having just reunited Germany, were shocked by the

The Balkan Wars, 1999 Serbian forces drove hundreds of thousands of ethnic Albanians out of the region of Kosovo. Here, in a scene reminiscent of the Holocaust, Albanians are crowded onto trains to be sent into involuntary exile. Unlike the Jews, however, most Albanians were able to return home after a few months under UN and NATO protection. *Agence France-Presse.*

outbreak of such violence so close to them. At the same time, they felt that it was a European problem, one they should be given a chance to solve without interference by the Americans. But the pluralist nature of the European Union and of NATO prevented Europe from acting in concert. French, British, and German interests often clashed, and it proved impossible to generate resolute action even in the face of genocide. Finally, when the United States did decide to act, primarily for fear of the collapse of its European interests, a shaky peace was established in Bosnia. The Dayton Accords, signed in 1995, established a multinational Bosnia—but one so divided by hatreds, monolithic ideas of national interests, and recent memories of grotesque atrocities that only a semipermanent force of NATO troops, including Americans, has been able to preserve a tense peace (see Map E/P-2).

Even more disastrous has been the outbreak of violence and ethnic cleansing in Kosovo, which is a province in the Yugoslav state of Serbia. Serbs consider Kosovo to be the ancient homeland of their national state, but by the 1990s the region was populated almost entirely by Albanians. In Serbia, the nationalist leader Slobodan Milošević came to power in 1987 vowing to make Kosovo an integral part of Serbia, despite its ethnic composition. At first,

Albanian leaders pursued a policy of nonviolence in the face of the strict controls Serbia placed on Kosovo, but in 1997 the Kosovo Liberation Army (KLA) emerged. The KLA opposed the Serbs through terrorist acts and sought to create an independent, or at least autonomous, Kosovo. Two irreconcilable issues were at stake here. The Serbs pointed out that the Helsinki Accords prohibited changing state boundaries by force and that Kosovo was legally a part of Serbia. The Albanians argued from the principle of self-determination of peoples that they had a right to choose their own—Albanian—government. The western powers sought to negotiate this difference, but when Milošević refused NATO began to bombard Serbia from the air in the spring of 1999. Milošević responded with a vast program of ethnic cleansing that mercilessly ejected hundreds of thousands of Albanians from Kosovo into the neighboring countries of Albania and Macedonia and killed thousands of others. After eleven weeks of punishing air strikes, Milošević relented and NATO troops occupied Kosovo, establishing an international protectorate there. In the long run, however, it appears that the only solution to the terrible events of the 1990s in the former Yugoslavia will be to redraw Balkan borders along ethnic lines. Only then will each of the Balkan peoples feel that they are authentic,

MAP E/P-2
YUGOSLAVIA'S CRISIS

autonomous nations, recognized by the other members of the state system as legitimate and therefore potentially willing to enter into the buffering mechanisms that have preserved stability in other parts of Europe since World War II. Exactly how to reach that point, just where such borders might be, what outside intervention will be needed, and how many people will die or be dispossessed of their homes in the process remains uncertain.

At the end of the 1990s, the violence in Kosovo overshadowed attempts to resolve creatively another long-standing ethnic conflict, the Protestant versus Catholic violence in Ulster, or Northern Ireland. Ulster has powerful historical overtones for the Catholic Irish, but for several centuries the majority of its population has been Protestant. When the Irish Free State came into being in 1922, Ulster refused to join. Since then an intractable struggle between Protestants sympathetic to and supported by Great Britain and Catholics partial to Ireland wracked Ulster. Irresponsible violence on the side of the underground Irish Republican Army (IRA) were matched by reckless political behavior among extreme Protestant elements. Finally, after three thousand deaths, forty thousand injuries, and the almost complete collapse of civility, negotiators reached an agreement in 1998. With overwhelming voter approval, Ireland dropped its claim to Ulster and a new government for Northern Ireland came into being that held a genuine possibility of balancing Catholic and Protestant interests (see Map E/P-3).

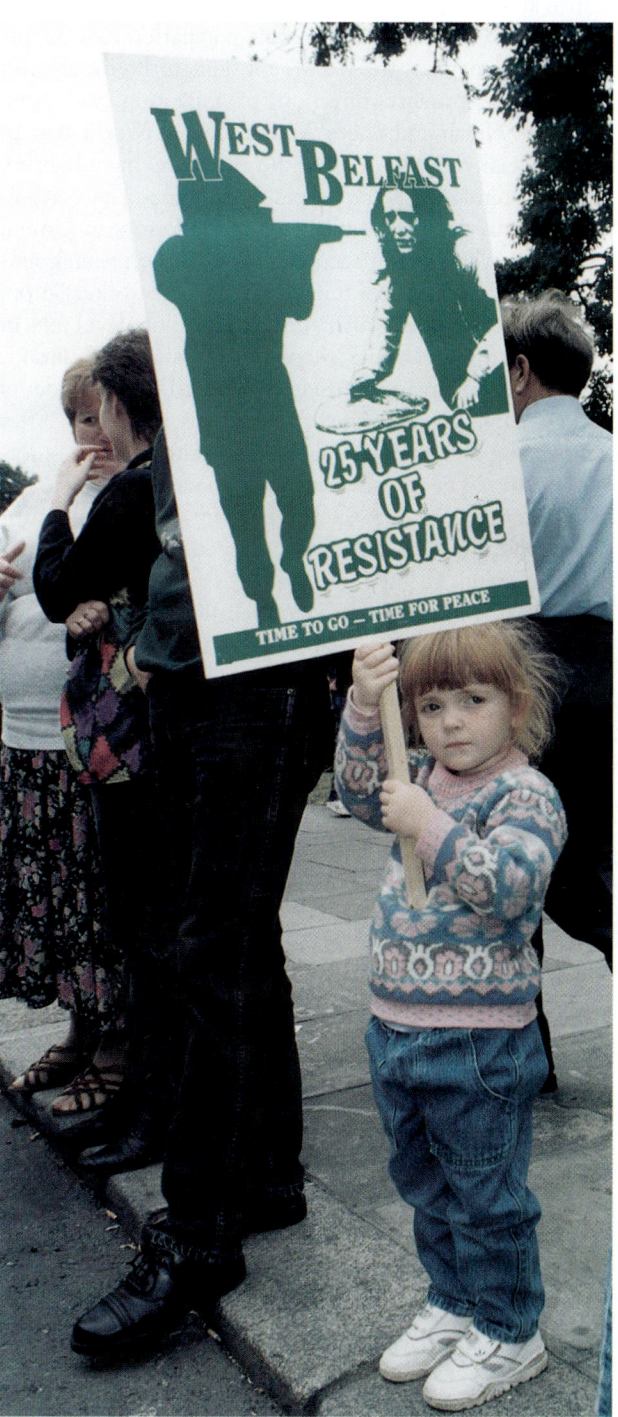

Peace for Ulster When Ireland achieved independence in 1922, six northern provinces remained part of the United Kingdom. There the activities of extremist Protestants and Catholics led to the deaths of thousands of people before a peace accord was reached in 1998. This child holds a sign pleading for peace in a stronghold of the Irish Republican Army, an underground terrorist group. Unfortunately, as this book goes to press, this accord may be unraveling. *Corbis/Oistin MacBride.*

MAP E/P-3
IRELAND AND NORTHERN IRELAND

The end of communism in Eastern Europe and the outbreak violence elsewhere intensified the flow of immigrants and refugees throughout Europe as the twentieth century drew to a close. Large-scale population movements are nothing new on the Continent, but in the nineteenth century the primary direction of migration was from Europe to North and South America. Since World War II, and especially in the 1990s, the direction has changed. Now the tendency is for people fleeing war or poverty to flow into the prosperous members of the European Union. During the years of the economic miracle, European countries invited hundreds of thousands of "guest workers" from southern Europe and North Africa to take low-level jobs in their booming economies. Many of them stayed. Today, for example, the largest concentration of Turks outside of Turkey, about four hundred thousand, is in Berlin. After the collapse of colonial empires, significant numbers of formerly colonial peoples, almost all of them people of color, found their way to Europe. The breakup of the communist system and the Wars of Yugoslav Succession have accentuated this trend, as millions of refugees seek ways to escape the terrors of war or to improve their life chances.

The influx of large numbers of non-Europeans has had a powerful impact on local politics. Right wing Populist movements have carved out a small but significant political presence with anti-immigrant programs. In Germany, bombings of apartments housing immigrants were a national scandal in the first half of the 1990s. And along the fringes of society, skinheads beat up Roma and other people they perceived as strangers in their midst. Since the coming of nationalism, European countries have not understood themselves as multicultural. Today, all of them are coping with the question of how to reconcile their national sensibilities with the presence of newcomers.

A hopeful sign in the sometimes frightening arena of nationalism has been the amelioration of antisemitism in Europe. The searing experience of the Holocaust underwent extensive discussion in the West in the postwar era, sensitizing European publics to the dangers of antisemitism. This new attitude has been transmitted to the emerging democracies of Eastern Europe. This does not mean that occasional outrages do not occur. But unlike in the 1930s, they are publicly condemned. East Europeans who for forty years had been outside the dialogue regarding antisemitism quickly found that they could not be respectable in the West if they tolerated it in their own countries.

In contrast to the disintegrating effects of national and ethnic violence, during the 1990s intra-European linkages deepened. The collapse of communism in Eastern Europe broached unexpected problems and opportunities. In Eastern Europe itself, the main thrust has been the effort to create viable democracies and working market economies in societies that for forty years had been under single-party rule and centralized planning. Whereas Margaret Thatcher

privatized 5 percent of the British economy in the 1980s, working in a well-established democracy, the East European countries have been faced with privatizing almost all of their economies at the same time they were trying to create democratic institutions and practices. Some countries have been more successful than others. Poland and Hungary have established vigorous democracies and growing economies, but the peaceful breakup of Czechoslovakia into two countries (the "Velvet Divorce," as it was called in reference to the "Velvet Revolution" of 1989) left a relatively prosperous Czech Republic and a temporarily retrograde Slovakia. In the Balkans, Romania and Bulgaria have faltered, and Albania, while reentering the international community from its previous complete isolation and abysmal poverty, has shown what collapse means in actual life.

All of the new countries of Eastern Europe, whatever their level of postcommunist success, have made vigorous efforts to enter into the web of regional and European institutions that provide stability for the Continent. During the Cold War era, security was closely connected with military preparedness. The North Atlantic Treaty Organization (NATO) came into being in 1949 specifically to counter any possible Soviet military thrust into Germany. By the time of the Soviet Union's collapse, however, European security had become primarily an economic and institutional issue rather than a military one. Today European security is protected by a vast alphabet soup of institutions, not limited just to the Continent. Some of the more important of the worldwide organizations include the International Monetary Fund (IMF), the United Nations (UN), the World Bank, and the World Trade Organization (WTO), while continental institutions include the West European Union (WEU), the Organization for Security and Cooperation in Europe (OSCE), the Organization for European Economic Cooperation (OEEC), NATO, and, of course, the European Union (EU). The goal of the East Europeans has been to enter as many of these organizations as possible. Most of them have been able to join most of the international organizations, but the crucial ones—NATO and the European Union—have been more difficult. In 1999, after lengthy discussion, Hungary, Poland, and the Czech Republic joined NATO, and at the same time the European Union opened discussions on potential membership with these countries plus Estonia, Slovenia, and Cyprus.

The great outliers in these negotiations have been the countries of the former Soviet Union, especially Ukraine and Russia. Ukraine is a large country populated by more than 50 million people that lies between Eastern Europe and Russia. Strategically very important for this reason, Ukraine has had great difficulty in establishing its economic viability and its democratic potential. Russia, on the other hand, after surviving an early period of turmoil,

"All in favor of joining NATO, say 'Aye.'"

Joining NATO With the collapse of the Iron Curtain, countries of Eastern Europe became candidates for inclusion in Western alliances such as NATO and the European Union. This cartoon suggests that they were more than eager to do so. In 1999 Poland, Hungary, and the Czech Republic entered NATO, but it was uncertain when other aspirants would be able to join. By the turn of the century, five countries had joined discussions for entry into the EU.   © The New Yorker *Collection, 1997. Al Ross from cartoonbank.com.*

achieved a modest amount of stability under the often erratic leadership of Boris Yeltsin. The problem for Russians is an old one—whether they really want to be part of the West. The more extreme Russian nationalists, such as the author Aleksandr Solzhenitsyn, would prefer to abandon the West for the traditions of Russian Orthodoxy, while some politically active nationalists attack democracy, liberalism, and the market vigorously. But most Russians are more realistic. For them, the problem is not how to abandon Europe, but how best to interact with it, and even more realistically, how to survive in a declining economy.

This question was part and parcel of Russian opinions about the expansion of NATO. Was expansion threatening to Russia's future security? What would it mean for Russia's place in Europe? Would apparent exclusion lead to conflict? In the West, similar questions emerged from the opposite side. Would expansion give ammunition to the nationalists that would lead to an undermining of Russian democracy? Wasn't the West drawing new lines along old principles of containment? In the end, NATO found a way to satisfy the Russians, at least temporarily, and to create a new kind of European partnership. Instead of taking Russia into NATO, an impossible event given Russia's size and stage of development, or simply ignoring it, which would increase tension, the two entities created a joint NATO-Russian council, which discusses issues of mutual interest. In this way Russia does not get a veto in NATO affairs, but

it does have input and in theory is treated as being equal to the entire alliance. The second round of NATO expansion will test whether this arrangement will continue to mollify the Russians.

A second aspect of European integration has been the internal development of the European Union itself. During the 1990s, the entry of three new countries (Austria, Finland, and Sweden) brought EU membership to fifteen. After the completion of so many of the Single Europe Act's provisions by January 1, 1993, including changing the name of the alliance to the European Union, the most surprising and potentially significant event of the 1990s was the creation of a new currency, the euro. Strongly pushed by Germany's chancellor Helmut Kohl, the euro came into being in 1999 and will become the sole currency in at least eleven European countries by 2002.

In the Western Hemisphere, countries are attempting to match the economic power of the European Union with economic unions of their own. In 1994 the United States and Canada extended their previous free trade arrangement by putting into effect the North American Free Trade Agreement (NAFTA) with Mexico. In South America, four countries of the Southern Cone (Brazil, Argentina, Paraguay, and Uruguay) formed the trading partnership Mercosul in 1991. By the end of the decade, the NAFTA and Mercosul countries were considering broadening their trade cooperation.

The Irony of Historical Memory In 1998, the post-Soviet Russian government exhumed the remains of Tsar Nicholas II and his family, all of whom had been killed by the Bolsheviks in 1918, and reburied them in the St. Peter and Paul Cathedral in St. Petersburg (known as Leningrad during the Soviet period). *AP Wide World/Pool.*

As these moves suggest, the most fundamental fact that faces not only Europe but every country today is the growing integration of the world economy. The ability to transfer funds instantaneously by electronic means, the availability of worldwide shipping networks, and the standardization of many kinds of commodities have lessened the localized character of even small-scale business. Huge international corporations no longer can be said to have a home base in a particular country. They, and the international elites who run them, are more and more difficult to regulate in a world system based on individual sovereign states. The problem is especially acute in areas such as labor relations and environmental costs, both of which are nationally regulated but have international repercussions.

Because of the intensification of worldwide competition, many industrialized states face difficulties meeting the costs of the extensive social programs extended to workers in the post–World War II period. Lower wages and lower social benefits in some countries made them attractive places for labor-intensive industries like textiles, while Asian Rim countries such as South Korea, Taiwan, and Singapore compete aggressively in high-tech and industrial goods. In the United States, these pressures came to a head during the 1980s, when the Reagan administration saw maintaining social benefits as less important than remaining economically competitive. First the American steel industry and then many other large corporations met the problem of relatively inefficient production by laying off substantial portions of their workforces, including even white-collar workers who previously had not faced downsizing. This, along with investment in new technologies, particularly electronics, produced greater efficiency and helped sustain economic growth in the United States through most of the 1990s. The cost to those people who lost their jobs, however, sometimes at an age at which it was difficult to find new work, was considerable.

Downsizing was more difficult to achieve in Europe because of laws protecting the worker. When a firm hires a worker in Germany, for example, it takes on a very substantial burden of extra costs associated with that worker— long paid vacations, high wages, health care, and various subsidies. Consequently, European firms tend to hire as few new workers as they can, perhaps farming out some of their work to new subsidiaries in Eastern Europe, where wages and benefits are lower. The result has been a consistently high level of unemployment throughout the 1990s, rising on occasion to as high as 20 percent in Spain, but consistently staying in the teens.

Quite naturally, European leaders look at the lower growth rates of their economies and the other problems they confront as serious issues demanding action. But from a larger perspective, issues more difficult than these relatively parochial concerns loom on the horizon. For example, all but one of the world's seventeen major fisheries are declining in output. The world is becoming warmer and the carbon dioxide levels in the atmosphere are increasing. Species are becoming extinct at a historically unprecedented rate. Despite reserves of oil and coal that appear good for several hundred years, it is increasingly understood that their supply is finite, especially as the developing economies seek to emulate the profligate ways of the rich economies. For these reasons, one of the more important international events of the 1990s was the United Nations Conference on Environment and Development held in Rio de Janeiro in 1992. Despite political squabbles and foot dragging, by 1996 some 117 governments had appointed commissions to develop strategies to deal with environmental issues.

One of the more surprising problems to emerge recently in Europe, given the dire predictions of the Club of Rome in the 1960s, is the imminent decline of European population. On a world-wide basis, population will continue to grow. Even if the average number of children borne by each woman in the world were to drop from the current rate of slightly under three children per lifetime to the strict replacement rate of 2.1, today's world population of about 6 billion people will reach 8.5 billion by 2150. But in Europe, population is about to decline.

In many of the most developed European countries the average number of children borne by each woman has dropped far below the 2.1 replacement rate. In Italy, it has reached 1.2 children per woman, the lowest ever recorded. When this lowered birth rate is coupled with increasing life spans, the result is a society in which proportionally fewer active workers are available to produce the wealth needed to support an ever larger number of inactive retirees on pensions.

A potentially even more fundamental issue, just coming into view, will test the ability of human beings to con-

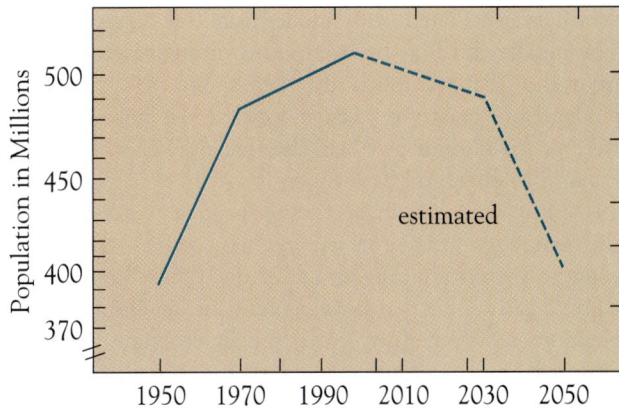

Population figures do not include the former Soviet Union.

FIGURE E/P-1
EUROPEAN POPULATION DECLINE

trol their destiny. For the first time in the several million years of hominid experience, it is becoming possible to make conscious choices about the direction of evolution. Rapid advances in understanding the role of genes and DNA have already made possible what one scientist calls "volitional evolution,"—that is, making choices about the genetic direction of the human race. Already, cures for genetically caused diseases are coming to the market and scientists are able to clone animals that are precise duplicates of the animal from which the genetic material is taken. Within a decade the human genome will have been entirely mapped. It will not be long before genetic evolution itself can be a conscious act, not simply a fact of nature. To say this will present profound intellectual and ethical issues is a prodigious understatement.

Just as it is impossible to understand the coming implications of genetic engineering, so it is equally difficult to make judgments about the state of Western cultural and spiritual life at the beginning of the new millennium. It would be easy to draw up lists of the writers, philosophers, artists, and religious leaders who have been active in the half-century since World War II and to offer capsule comments on their "contributions." The list would be long. But if our intent is to consider where Western civilization has come in our time and what future direction it might take, such a list would be of limited value. Singling out creative figures as "seminal" and "epoch-making" is a judgment that can only be made with considerable hindsight. How many great voices from antiquity, from the High Middle Ages, from the Renaissance, from the Enlightenment, from the Romantic era, truly speak to us today? And how many are known mainly or exclusively to scholars? It is likely that future generations will conduct a similar winnowing of the cultural history of our times, and they may well reach conclusions that would startle us.

The most recent major turning point in the West's cultural and spiritual life seems to have been the outburst of creativity associated with modernism (see Chapter 27). The middle third of the twentieth century, approximately from the 1930s through the 1960s, saw the climax of modernism's creativity carried forward the impulses that were set in motion by Nietzsche, Freud, Weber, Einstein, Picasso, Mahler, and Schoenberg between about 1880 and 1914. But we do not have the perspective to say whether the generation of creators who are now active—those who came to maturity during and after the 1960s—represent a truly creative further development of modernism, the beginnings of something entirely new, or simply the flagging energy of a cultural era whose inner spark has dimmed.

Still, the triumph of pluralism at the end of the twentieth century has meant a decline of ideological arrogance in the West, as well as a loss of faith in what once seemed immutable cultural standards. Modernism, much of which springs from Nietzsche's call to reevaluate all values, has in our own time spawned the school of thought known as post-modernism. This widespread academic and critical movement denies that any text (a work of art or a historical source) has intrinsic meaning and insists that meaning and value are imparted by the reader of that text. Does this imply that nothing has intrinsic meaning and that anything can "mean" anything we want it to? Debate over this question and many related issues escalated in North America in the 1990s into what was called the "culture wars." Both right and left wing protagonists hardened their positions into visions of "political correctness," each claiming to be more pluralist and open than the other. Although post-modernism seems to be losing some of its intellectual strength, exactly what cultural legacy it might leave, or what backlash it might generate, remains cloudy.

Religion offers another but related instance of the late twentieth-century West's embrace of pluralism. Among mainstream Protestants, debates inherited from the Reformation over free will and grace seem long-gone; ever since the Vatican II church council (1962–1965), Roman Catholicism has lost some of the rigidity that was born of the Counter Reformation and has embraced ecumenism and tolerance; religion has demonstrated remarkable recuperative power in the former Soviet Union and other areas once ruled by atheist Marxist-Leninist regimes; Jews and Christians regard one another with more understanding and forbearance than at any time since the first century A.D.; all the West's religious traditions now engage the world's other great faiths in constant dialogue. The con-

sensus that west Europeans and Americans have reached about the value of religious toleration intensifies the shock and disbelief with which they have responded to the blazing religious hatreds revealed by sectarian violence in Ulster and the Wars of Yugoslav Succession. Yet this openness and tolerance come at a time when religious affiliation in most west European countries (not the United States) has fallen to historically low levels, and when the papacy regards much of Europe as irreligious mission territory and seems to be reorienting Catholicism toward the Third World. Since religion has historically been one of the fundamental determinants of cultural identity, historians of the future may well regard these religious shifts as deeply significant.

The strains and tensions of contemporary life will certainly leave their mark on the West's ever-transforming culture. However Western society attacks or ameliorates its local problems of demography, unemployment, ethnic politics, and cultural pluralism, the old guidelines provided by the Cold War have disappeared. Entirely new problems sweeping across all boundaries will set the agenda of the future. In a sense, therefore, the year 2000 marks the beginning of a new age in the history of the West, and indeed in human history. The growing pains occasioned by the Dual Revolution (Industrial and French) are over, at least in the developed world. The Industrial Revolution has passed beyond the manufacturing stage of individually owned factories to an era of huge multinational corporations operating in every part of the world through electronic information networks. The provision of services and the transmittal of information now play a more significant role in the world economy than does the production of goods. World trade draws almost every country into contact and competition with almost every other country. Huge trading blocks in North America, Europe, and possibly even in Asia are realigning traditional economic relations. Politically, the disappearance of fascist and communist states has left the politics of accommodation as the most vigorous survivor of Enlightenment optimism. Whether pluralism is up to the stern tests that lie ahead is uncertain. But history is not over. Religious fundamentalism, nationalism, racism, degradation of the global biosphere, population growth, genetic engineering, and the grinding poverty of a majority of the world's inhabitants, not to mention the human propensity for violence, will provide more than enough grist for the angel of history's mill in the years to come.

Glossary

absolutism An ideology and a form of government that emerged in many European states in the seventeenth and eighteenth centuries. It called for strong monarchical rule and, where implemented, succeeded in undermining—and in some cases abolishing altogether—the ability of nobles and of corporate institutions (such as legislative and judicial bodies, churches, and municipal governments) to resist the implementation of royal degrees and policies (including taxation). Louis XIV of France, Frederick the Great of Prussia, and Peter the Great of Russia are good examples of absolute monarchs, although absolutism in theory has never been fully achieved in practice.

anthropomorphic Usually used to describe gods that are conceived of as having human characteristics (not all of them admirable and positive). The classic case of anthropomorphic gods are the Olympian divinities of ancient Greece and Rome: Zeus/Jupiter, Aphrodite/Venus, Ares/Mars, and so forth. The Judeo-Christian tradition holds (according to the Book of Genesis) that Yahweh created the human race "in his image and likeness"—a kind of anthropomorphism in reverse.

apocalyptic A term referring to the end of the world. The root word is the *Apocalypse*, the Greek title of the Book of Revelation, which is the last canonical book of the Christian New Testament dating from the late first century A.D., that set forth a prophetic vision of Jesus Christ coming on clouds of glory to destroy the sinful world and render the Last Judgment upon sinners. Apocalypticism—belief in a coming apocalypse—does not originate with Christianity, however. Ancient Persian Zoroastrianism, with its teaching that this world will end in a climactic struggle between Good and Evil, was probably the first expression of apocalypticism in Western civilization. Judaism developed a strong apocalyptic and messianic tradition beginning with the Babylonian Captivity, continuing in the Book of Daniel (second century B.C.), and culminating in the Pharisaic and Essene movements. Apocalypticism was a strong undercurrent in medieval and early modern Christianity because it provided an outlet for popular frustrations. Church and secular Christian leaders tried to keep apocalypticism under control—a difficult task, because ultimately Christianity is an apocalyptic faith, teaching that, in the fullness of time, Christ "will come again in glory to judge the living and the dead, and of his kingdom there will be no end" (to quote the Nicene Creed). In modern times, various revolutionary ideologies have typically displaced apocalypticism as an article of

vibrant faith, although twentieth-century cult movements seem to be reviving it successfully.

balance of power The conditions that exist among a group of states in which no one state is dominant over all the others; rather a rough equilibrium is sustained, such as on the Italian peninsula for forty years after the Peace of Lodí (1454). Medieval theory (but not always medieval practice) held that there should be a fixed hierarchy of states under the mantle of the Holy Roman Empire. This theory gave way in the sixteenth century to the goal of maintaining a balance of power among powers under shifting circumstances. The statesmen who negotiated at Westphalia (1648), Utrecht (1712), and Paris (1763) aimed at achieving such a balance, and much European diplomacy has been devoted to negotiating alliances that would preserve it.

bishop From a colloquial Greek word meaning "father." Latin-speaking Christians turned the word into *episcopus*, from which are derived such English words as *episcopal* (having to do with a bishop or bishops) and *Episcopalian* (a member of the Anglican communion in America, belonging to a church governed by bishops).

Bishops became important figures in the early Christian churches as these spiritual organizations developed firm hierarchical structures and confronted issues of heresy and discipline. When the Christian church entered into partnership with the Roman state, at the time of Emperor Constantine (early fourth century), bishops were transformed into officials of major authority, not only in the church but often also in secular society, and they were generally drawn from the upper social class. They retained this position throughout the Middle Ages and into the nineteenth century. Bishops in certain modern Christian denominations (Roman Catholicism, Episcopalianism or Anglicanism, and Methodism) and in Eastern Orthodoxy continue to exercise churchly responsibilities over a territorially defined jurisdiction, or *diocese*—a term, incidentally, that dates back to the later Roman Empire and originally meant an area of political jurisdiction.

bourgeoisie A word of French origin that literally means "people of the city." *Burg* is the medieval word for "city," its equivalents in German being *burg* and in English *burgh* or *borough*. An individual member of the bourgeoisie is a *bourgeois* (masculine, with the French feminine equivalent being *bourgeoisie*). These are also the adjective forms.

Originally, the term specifically referred to citizens of a city with defined privileges, such as the right to adopt orphans as wards. After the French Revolution, however, the term was used by Karl Marx to refer to those who owned the means of production (in contrast to the *proletariat*, or workers, who did not own the factories). Today the term often is used in a derogatory way and carries with it a meaning closer to "middle class;" see also *capitalism*.

Bronze Age A phase in the history of the Old World—nothing comparable to it occurred in the Western Hemisphere—that began sometime before 3000 B.C. when it was discovered that copper and tin could be melted down and combined to form a metallic alloy called bronze. Bronze is a fairly durable material, and until the Iron Age, which began in the Near East around 1200 B.C., it was the preferred metal for making weapons and tools. Making it depends, of course, on having access to copper and tin, and the latter especially is readily mined only in certain parts of the world, such as southern England. Long-range trade routes therefore had to be established to obtain it.

business cycles Refers to the cycles of boom and bust characteristic of early capitalism. High demand for goods leads to optimism, high prices, increased wages, and overpopulation. When the market is saturated, demand, prices, and wages fall, and pessimism sets in. Inflation is the mark of the upside; recession and depression of the downside. Today, governments in developed countries attempt to moderate the extremes of both ends of the cycle, and some policymakers dream of abolishing the business cycle, and even claim to have done so.

cameralism A school of eighteenth-century mercantilist thought (particularly strong in central Europe) that emphasized the needs of the community over the needs of the individual. Cameralist thinkers wrote tax and fiscal policies designed to encourage economic growth, but within an organic metaphor in which the entire initiative for policy came from the prince, not from the people. Cameralists assumed a traditional society in which each of the social orders (nobility, merchants, and peasants) had customary needs, and once those needs were met, the surplus should go to the prince for his own purposes.

capitalism The economic system based on the market in which wealth is regarded as something not to be simply hoarded or spent, but invested productively for future gain. Under capitalism, the most important economic decisions are made by private individuals in response to conditions of supply and demand.

Capitalism presupposes private property and the sanctity of contracts and requires for its successful functioning a government that upholds property and contract rights. Capitalism does not regard the acquisition of wealth as morally questionable and thus does not condemn the lending of money at interest (see also *usury*). Capitalism has been praised and blamed (according to the outlooks of competing ideologies) for everything from the rise of European global hegemony to the Scientific Revolution, from the Protestant Reformation to the French Revolution, and even from the liberation of humanity to the demise of the environment.

The debate over exactly when capitalism arose and how it became the dominant economic system of Western civilization is unsettled. Some historians see it in the earliest manifestations of a market economy in ancient times, while others deny its appearance until almost the eve of the Industrial Revolution. Elements of capitalism certainly existed in ancient times. However, constraints on such economic activities were also powerful in all premodern societies, and they have not disappeared entirely today. Among these constraints are religious and ethical condemnations of personal gain, social attitudes that place the highest value on community solidarity or on "unproductive" personal display, governmental insistence that the interests of the state take precedence over individual enterprise, and technological limits on how much increased productivity can be expected from infusions of capital. The story of the rise of capitalism in the Western world is a complex process involving the lessening of these constraints.

Most historians broadly agree that the development of capitalism owed much to efforts by late medieval merchants to gain control over the production and distribution of cloth (see *putting-out system*) and to organize banking and other credit institutions. Cultural and ethical constraints upon activities now labeled as "capitalistic" slowly declined in early modern Europe (fifteenth through eighteenth centuries). But only with the Industrial (or Energy) Revolution of the eighteenth and early nineteenth centuries did the technology appear that could fully benefit from capital investment to expand significantly the production of goods and services. It was the advent of such technology, together with the emergence in Western civilization of cultural attitudes sanctioning acquisitiveness in a market environment, that ushered in the fully developed capitalist system that flourishes today—as well as anti-capitalist ideologies such as Marxism.

capitalist See *capitalism*.

chauvinist A word originally referring to a Napoleonic-era French soldier, Nicholas Chauvin. Although he is now totally forgotten, his name lives on in many languages as a synonym for a rabid superpatriot, as well as in more recent forms, for example, *male chauvinist*.

cinquecento An Italian word meaning "the fifteen hundreds"; that is, the sixteenth century. The term is often used by historians of renaissance Italy to denote the period between 1501 and 1600.

civil law See *common law*.

civil society The wider network of connections—not just formal government, but also economic, social, and cultural interrelationships—that shapes interactions between individuals and groups in modern complex societies. The concept tends to emphasize those connections that are *not* subject to political rules or ideological controls. Recently, the notion was creatively developed by East European dissidents, such as Václav Havel in Czechoslovakia, in opposition to the communist regimes' efforts to dominate and shape every significant aspect of life; see also *totalitarianism*.

civilization An elusive, value-laden concept difficult to define accurately in a few words (this entire book is an attempt just to define *Western civilization*). However, a useful (though limited) definition of civilization is the combination of settled life (including but not exclusively *urban* life) and sufficient surpluses of food to enable elites and those who serve them to create traditions of religious, artistic, cultural, and political life. Although all civilizations share certain basic characteristics, the traditions they embody also have internal logics of their own. Once people of different cultural traditions come in contact with one another, interactions and cross-pollinations inevitably occur, making the history of civilization one of constant change.

class, social The division of people into different categories according to their relationship in the processes of producing goods and services. In this sense, social classes have existed even before the beginnings of civilization, whenever and wherever economic specialization has been practiced. However, most historians and many social scientists today believe that modern social classes—for example, the working class, the peasantry, the capitalist bourgeoisie—are products of the Industrial Revolution. Before the so-called Dual Revolution (the cumulative effect of the Industrial Revolution and the French Revolution), Europeans normally were classified and described according to their status: the privileges and rights they had and on whom they were dependent, rather than what their income or their job might be.

classical economics The notion brought forward most famously by Adam Smith that if all persons are left free to pursue their own self interests, the operation of the economic laws of supply and demand (the "unseen hand") will ensure that all products society needs will be produced, distributed, and consumed. The notion does not imply lack of government, however, because for the system to work properly, the state must control monopolies, maintain a sound currency, and enforce property rights and contracts.

Cominform In September 1947, in response to the Truman Doctrine and the Marshall Plan, Stalin formed the Communist Information Bureau (Cominform) of European Communist parties and gave the green light to the Czechoslovak and Hungarian Communist parties to seize power. After expelling Yugoslavia in 1948, the Cominform dissolved in the 1950s.

Comintern An abbreviation of the Communist International established by Lenin after the Bolshevik Revolution. The first International was founded by Karl Marx, Mikhail Bakunin and others in the 1860s. After its collapse, the socialist parties of many European countries founded the Second International Working Men's Association to coordinate socialist activities in Europe. By insisting that the members of the Third International adopt revolutionary Bolshevik norms, Lenin forced every European socialist to choose between revolution (Bolshevism) and reform (socialism). This resulted in the split of all European Socialist parties into two competing elements.

Commercial Revolution The cluster of institutional changes and innovations associated with the intensification of western European commerce during the High and Late Middle Ages. Such changes included replacing individual moneylenders with banking firms, turning letters of credit or currency exchange orders into checks and bank drafts, substituting permanent commercial firms for temporary partnerships, and standardizing the use of double-entry bookkeeping and of reckoning with Arabic rather than Roman numbers (which facilitated rapid and more accurate computation). Many of these changes represented the adaptation by west Europeans (especially Italians, Catalans, and Netherlanders) into business practices and institutions already familiar in the Byzantine and especially the Islamic worlds. Capitalism also, along with the Commercial Revolution, was taking shape in western Europe.

Precisely what chronological boundaries should be placed around the Commercial Revolution and the rise of capitalism are uncertain; historians prefer to think of them as processes rather than as specific events. As a process, the Commercial Revolution can be said to be still under way as business practices continue to respond to technological innovation and economic opportunity; see also *capitalism*.

common law The basis of the legal system of judge-based law that prevails today in England (not Scotland), Canada (outside Quebec) and most other countries of the British Commonwealth, and the United States. It originated in the legal practices of England in the centuries after the Norman Conquest of 1066. It is distinguished from the civil law system, which has its origins in Roman law, especially as codified under Justinian in the *Codex Juris Civilis*. However, it has been influenced by the civil law tradition, especially since the sixteenth century.

Common law is judge-made law based on precedent. The word *common* means that it was intended to be generally observed in England. The common law system became well established in England under Henry II in the twelfth century, before the revival of Roman (civil) law on the Continent had reached its full effectiveness. Under Edward I (1272–1307) trial by jury using common law became compulsory in all criminal cases. From Edward I's reign onward, statutes ("new" laws decreed by the king with the assent of Parliament) were added to the body of common law precedents. In the sixteenth and early seventeenth centuries, certain courts in England (such as the Court of Star Chamber) were set up outside the common-law tradition and used civil law in cases that the royal government claimed affected its prerogatives. These courts were abolished during the English Revolution, and the common-law tradition was reinforced by the popular commentaries of Sir Edward Coke (seventeenth century) and Sir William Blackstone (eighteenth century). These treatises, which defined and systematized common-law principles, had a great impact on Americans during the colonial and revolutionary periods, and they deeply influenced the development of legal doctrine in the United States. English law was extensively overhauled and modernized in the radically new conditions of nineteenth century life, but many of the traditions of the medieval common law were retained. Among these were the fundamental procedural principles guaranteeing defendants' basic rights.

communes, Commune The towns in central and northern Italy that gained de facto independence from emperors, kings, popes, and nobles beginning in the twelfth and thirteenth centuries. The essence of communal living was adherence to an oath of allegiance and mutual support that citizens of the city swore. Communal regimes endured in Italy until they were superseded by one-man or princely rule, which—depending on the city in question—occurred between the thirteenth and sixteenth centuries. Internally self-governing but not independent, communes also arose in the cities of medieval France, the Netherlands, and Germany during the High and Late Middle Ages.

The Commune of Paris was established by the working people of Paris in 1871 after the German victory in the Franco-German war of 1870–1871. The middle-class government of Adolph Thiers put down the communards with great bloodshed, thus reinforcing the social animosities that played an important role in French life. Karl Marx's brilliant but distorted analysis of the Paris Commune as an incipient socialist revolution gave V.I. Lenin much to draw upon as he theorized about the nature of the "dictatorship of the proletariat," which his Bolsheviks attempted to implement in Russia after the October Revolution.

In the 1960s, many young people of the New Left withdrew to "communes," in which they emulated the ideals of the nineteenth-century utopian socialists by giving up their commitment to private property.

Concert of Europe Term used after the Congress of Vienna (1815) to denote the general intention of the Great Powers to consult periodically among themselves and to prevent their own competition, actions by minor countries, or internal threats to international stability (such as revolutions) from causing a general war. The Concert of Europe functioned more or less as intended from the Congress of Vienna until the revolutions of 1848. Unlike later attempts at promoting international harmony, such as the League of Nations and the United Nations, the Concert of Europe had no charter or formal organization, nor a regular meetingplace.

condottieri Singular form: *condottiere;* Generals who recruited and commanded mercenary armies in return for money from Italian states. By the fifteenth century, the condottieri were exclusively Italians (rather than foreigners, as they had been earlier). A few succeeded in establishing themselves as princes.

conservatism An ideology that emerged in the nineteenth century, originally in reaction against the French Revolution and in opposition to liberalism. Historically, conservatives have ranged from reactionaries (opposed to all change and demanding the restoration of things as they once were) to moderates (who simply oppose hasty or ill-considered change). But the core of all conservative thinking is strong respect for tradition and the past. By the early twentieth century conservatives often accommodated themselves to the new political culture and adopted the former liberal position favoring laissez-faire economics, whereas liberals (especially in the United States) moved toward the old conservative predilection for a regulated and more paternalistic economy. During the Cold War, conservatives were strongly anti-Communist.

containment The general policy of the United States during the Cold War to "contain" communism within the boundaries that were current at around 1948. State department official George Kennan put the policy forward in an article in *Foreign Affairs* in 1947. The wars in Korea and Vietnam were conducted on the basis of this principle.

cordon sanitaire "Protective barrier" referring to the French government's policy of creating alliances with the new post-World War I countries of eastern Europe in order for both to surround Germany with French allies and to isolate western Europe from the bacillus of Soviet communism.

cosmopolitan A term created out of two Greek words, *cosmos* ("world" or "universe") and *polis* ("city-state"). It refers to a person or culture not rooted in a narrow, traditional mental environment, but open to the widest possible cultural influences. Specifically the word is often applied to Hellenistic society, in which Greeks left the confines of *poleis* (city-states) like Athens and took their chances in the "big world." By extension, the concept of cosmopolitanism can refer to the dynamic, sophisticated cultural interactions that occurred in the Babylonian and Persian empires of the ancient Near East, in the Roman Empire, in the medieval university world, in the eighteenth-century Enlightenment, and everywhere in modern Western civilization. The expression "rootless cosmopolitan" is sometimes pejoratively used by those who attack intellectuals for rejecting the supposedly bedrock truths of their culture and embracing "shallow" or "superficial" notions. The term has also been used as an invidious code word for *Jew*, as when Joseph Stalin denounced Jews as "rootless cosmopolitans" because of their alleged loyalty to Israel rather than to the Soviet Union and to his brand of Marxism-Leninism.

coup d'état A seizure of state power by a small group of conspirators (often military officers); contrasts with revolution, which implies a seizure of power by ideologues with a radical agenda for change. Typically, the leaders of a coup d'état lack the firm ideological commitment of the leaders of a revolution, and their efforts usually do not involve a thorough transformation of society.

Covenant God's agreement with his chosen people, the Hebrews, by which they acknowledged him as their Lord and sole God, and he promised to protect them.

dark age A general term useful in describing a period of profound economic regression, social upheaval, and cultural degeneration, with only fragmentary historical sources that survive. The classic concept of the Dark Ages once applied to all of medieval Europe, but this usage is now obsolete, rejected by historians who are well aware of the magnificent cultural flowering that the European Middle Ages produced. In a more acceptable sense, historians now apply the term to such periods as the disruption and turmoil in Greece and the Near East at the end of the Bronze Age (ca. 1200–800 B.C.) and the collapse of Roman authority in western Europe (ca. A.D. 500–700). Even so, the term should be used with caution.

deism The religious position held by most eighteenth-century philosophes that emphasizes a belief in God as the creator of a universe governed by natural laws (such as the law of universal gravitation that Newton had discovered). The Deists generally rejected doctrines that most Christians considered central (Christ's resurrection and miracles), along with other claims to religious truths based on divine revelation. They insisted instead on the reasonableness of the moral and ethical values shared, they thought, by all humanity, such as prohibitions against theft and murder and the necessity of kind and humane treatment of others. The Deists' strong support for religious toleration was highly influential.

demesne A French word, pronounced "duh-main," that describes two different kinds of medieval property. First, it refers to a medieval manor (see *manorialism*), which consisted of the lord's personal property, the parish church and its land, and the holdings of individual peasants, in addition to forests and pastures that were used in common by both the lord and the villagers. The lord's personal property was the *demesne*, and on it enserfed peasants were expected to perform labor services, typically for several days a week. Later, these duties were often transformed into monetary payments, enabling the lord to hire laborers to work the demesne, or else the lord simply rented out the demesne to tenants. Second, the *royal* demesne meant the estates owned by the king, whose net revenues helped support the royal government. These estates were typically scattered throughout a kingdom, although in France many were concentrated in the region called the Île de France, around Paris. Properly managing the royal demesne was a major concern for medieval monarchs. Ideally, kings were expected to "live of their own" (that is, support themselves out of their own estates' revenues), but this was seldom possible. When, as usually happened, demesne revenues were inadequate to meet expenses, taxes had to be imposed, which could lead to revolts and to demands from taxpaying subjects that they have a voice in how the money was to be spent.

demographic transition The differential created by low death rates and high birthrates in developing societies that creates a very large rate of population growth during a period of economic change. For instance, in nonindustrial societies, birthrates and death rates are high, in the range of forty to fifty per thousand persons per year. As modernization begins, the death rates begin to drop, but the birthrates do not start falling for a number of years. Eventually, in developed societies, the birthrates and death rates again come close, with the death rate often higher than the birthrate, somewhere below ten per thousand per year.

diaspora, Diaspora A dispersion of a people (defined religiously, ethnically, or racially) who retain a common identity and strong cultural links even though they are spread across a wide geographical space.

The term *Diaspora* was first applied to the ancient and medieval Jews who voluntarily or involuntarily left their homeland to inhabit the far reaches of the Mediterranean basin, Europe, and beyond. Recently the term has been used to describe the spread of African populations to the Western Hemisphere and to parts of the Islamic world as a result of the slave trade. It may also be applied to the global migrations of the Irish, the Armenians, the Chinese, and other peoples.

dowry In traditional societies, the property given by a father to his daughter at the time of her marriage. Typically the dowry was managed by the bride's husband, but it was to be returned to her male kinfolk if the marriage terminated. In some societies, wives maintained or secured control of the dowry.

Dual Revolution A term that refers to the enormous transformations wrought by the cumulative effect of the Industrial (or Energy) Revolution and the French Revolution, which occurred as separate clusters of events whose effects became increasingly intertwined. In this book, the concept of a dual revolution is also applied to medieval Europe, where the revival of a money economy and the rise of towns, together with the intensification of Christian piety and the assertion of papal power, combined for a broadly transforming effect.

Enclosure The act of taking over *common lands* (traditionally shared by an entire rural community) and establishing a private landholding in England (and parts of western Europe) between the sixteenth and eighteenth centuries. Usually the enclosed common lands had been used to pasture livestock. There is considerable debate among scholars about the extent to which such enclosures forced peasants off the land, but it is generally agreed that a willingness among those in authority (judges and members of Parliament) to permit enclosures was a sign that new attitudes toward property ownership were emerging.

Energy Revolution See *Industrial Revolution*.

Enlightenment The intellectual and cultural movement that swept across Europe and North America during the eighteenth century. Its leaders, the philosophes, believed they were bringing light to the world by overthrowing superstition, censorship, dogmatism, and despotism. Vigorous in their anticlericalism and advocacy of the Scientific Revolution and in the "idea of progress," they thought that freeing individuals to reason and express themselves without having to revere inherited, traditional authorities would lead to political, cultural, and social advance.

equity Fairness. The modern understanding of the principle of equality that was brought into public affairs by the French and American revolutions. People are in fact not equal, physically, socially, intellectually, or in other ways. Over the past two hundred years, however, the revolutionary ideal of equality has actually become expressed as the principle of equity: that everyone in society should be treated fairly.

Estate, estates Of medieval origin, the word means "status group" and referring to the privileges that defined each social group's rights and obligations. In general, these groups broke down into the aristocracy or nobility, the clergy, the merchants or townspeople, and the peasantry. The classic use of the term is in the French institution known as the Estates General, which between the Middle Ages and the early seventeenth century was periodically summoned by the kings of France to vote on taxes and approve other measures. The Estates General came to consist of three groups—clergy (First Estate), nobility (Second Estate), and the bourgeoisie and peasantry together (Third Estate). This medieval hierarchy broke down at the beginning of the French Revolution, in 1789, when Louis XVI summoned the Estates General for the first time in a century and a half to deal with the kingdom's impending bankruptcy. The Third Estate demanded that the whole socio-political hierarchy be scrapped and that a new National Assembly be formed, representing citizens regardless of their social status. With that, the system of estates collapsed in France. The same thing happened wherever the influence of the French Revolution thereafter made itself felt.

European Economic Community (EEC) An organization founded in 1957 by the Treaty of Rome signed by West Germany, France, Italy, and the Benelux countries, to eliminate trade barriers in Europe. Very successful in this task, the EEC eventually became part of the European Union, which by the year 2000 had grown to fifteen members.

Fertile Crescent The lands stretching in an arc from the Tigris-Euphrates Valley in Iraq to northern Syria and down to Palestine in which early civilization arose. The first extensive domestication of plants and animals took place in this area about ten thousand years ago, which led to the creation of the first large, imperial civilizations.

feudal See *feudalism*.

feudalism A complex and often-misused concept referring to the decentralization of power in a society, as in medieval Europe. Classic feudalism was that of medieval northwestern Europe in which the great lords held their lands by grants from a king to whom they owed military service, allegiance, and counsel. The greater lords in turn bestowed grants on their subordinates. The whole system was held together by reciprocal obligations and oaths. Roughly comparable feudalisms, such as among the ancient Kassites in Mesopotamia, in the Hittite kingdom, and in premodern Japan, have been detected by historians. The term is also used (incorrectly, in the opinion of the authors of this book) to denote any kind of society in which powerful landowners dominate poor peasants. In Marxist theory, feudalism is the stage of economic and social development that precedes capitalism.

feudal system See *feudalism*.

gentry In England, members of the landed class below the rank of peer—that is, those aristocrats who held seats in the House of Lords. Gentry thus included the younger sons of peers, as well as other prosperous landowners who did not have aristocratic titles. Being acknowledged as a member of the gentry generally meant having sufficient income from renting out rural property to be able to live comfortably without doing physical work or engaging in commerce. Members of the gentry were expected to be leaders in their parishes, and the more substantial ones often served as justices of the peace and as members of the House of Commons. The term is occasionally applied to lesser noble landowners elsewhere in Europe.

genus A category in the classification system used by biologists to describe all living things. Modern humans are biologically defined as follows: kingdom: animals; phylum: chordates; class: mammals; order: primates; suborder: *Anthropoidea*; superfamily: *Hominoide*; family: *Hominiae*; genus: *Homo*; species: *Homo sapiens*; subspecies: *Homo sapiens sapiens*. All hominids belong to the family *Hominidae*, of which the first genus to appear was *Australopithecus*.

geocentric Earth-centered, a term applied mainly to theories about the structure of the universe. Ancient and medieval western thinkers who sought to explain the universe almost invariably thought in geocentric terms, which corresponded to common sense (the sun and moon appear to rise and set while the earth stands still). Geocentrism did not necessarily mean that the earth was somehow sacred. Aristotelianism, for example, held that the earth was the "bottom" of Creation, a place of corruption and change, whereas the heavens above were perfect and changeless. But geocentrism did mean that the earth was the only place in creation where human beings existed, and it implied that the universe was something with large but still comprehensible bounds, all of which were under divine supervision.

Great Powers This term originally referred to the main negotiators at the Congress of Vienna: the United Kingdom, France, Prussia, Austria, and Russia. Although other states technically became Great Powers later in the nineteenth century (Italy and the Ottoman Empire, for example), these five states (or their successors) continued to dominate European politics until World War I.

guild, guilds An association of merchants, craftsmen, or artisans to which the authorities of a town have granted special privileges and to which a significant amount of internal self-regulation has been vested. Guilds arose in medieval Europe just as commerce was reviving and cities were acquiring charters of self-government. Merchants often formed the first guilds to bargain collectively with the authorities, but over time guilds subdivided and proliferated, especially in large towns with diverse economic interests. Guilds were the principle vehicles through which medieval and early modern townspeople exercised political power. Economically, the guilds wielded powerful influence over prices, working conditions, marketplace rules, standards of workmanship, and apprenticeship, usually with the explicit intention of restricting competition. Guilds also performed charitable activities, such as organizing and funding the funerals of deceased members, looking after the businesses of these deceased members, and assisting the members' widows to continue in the trade. Finally, the guilds played a significant role in members' religious lives by organizing devotions to a patron saint or doing acts of collective charity. In places of worship they often commissioned works of religious art. Early capitalism and the putting-out system undermined guilds, and the Industrial Revolution destroyed everything that guilds represented. Guilds were abolished in revolutionary France, and during the nineteenth century they virtually disappeared in Europe.

habeas corpus A writ (form of legal action in the common law of England) that, from the seventeenth century, was used to force royal officials to demonstrate promptly to a common law court that an individual's arrest and detention was based on law and not on an arbitrary decision. Its purpose has always been to protect personal liberty against the power of authority, such as when a person being held in prison without charges seeks either to be charged or released.

heliocentric A hypothesis of the universe, in which the earth, planets, and stars revolve around a fixed and perfect sun. To the thinkers of antiquity and the Middle Ages, such a system would have been staggeringly huge, the earth would have had to move at a literally dizzying pace, with possibly other "earths" existing out there and spinning along with us. For such reasons, heliocentrism was decisively rejected until Copernicus revived the concept in the sixteenth century; see also *geocentric*.

heresy An incorrect religious belief; a doctrinal principle that differs from that which is regarded by a particular culture, church organization, or society as orthodox, or "correct belief."

heretic Any person who holds incorrect religious views; see *heresy*.

heretical See *heresy*.

hermeticism A body of ideas believed in the late fifteenth and sixteenth centuries to have come from Hermes Trismegistus, who was supposedly an Egyptian high priest in Moses' time. Translated into Latin by Ficino and published after 1560, Hermetic writings center on the conviction that the human mind mirrors the entire universe. Thus an individual magus (natural magician) can gain power over nature through his understanding of its secret principles. Early in the seventeenth century, scholars showed that the Hermetic writings were actually products of Gnosticism (second and third centuries A.D.).

heterodoxy A Greek word meaning "different teaching;" heterodoxy often verges on heresy; see *orthodoxy*.

hieroglyphics The writing system used by ancient Egyptians (a rather comparable writing system was used by the pre-Columbian Mayans) that was thought by ancient Greeks to constitute an occult code. In hieroglyphics, each symbol has a syllabic equivalent. Egyptian hieroglyphics were deciphered in the early nineteenth century by a French scholar working with the famous Rosetta Stone (now in the British Museum).

historicism The positivist view as practiced by historians and legal scholars. Its practitioners believe that general interpretations grow out of detailed, factual, investigations of narrative history; see *positivism*.

Holocene The period in the earth's history in which we are now living. It began with the retreat of the continental ice sheets at the end of the last ice age, about ten to twelve thousand years ago.

hominid Modern human beings and earlier human-like creatures; see also *genus*.

humanism A term invented in the nineteenth century to describe the program of studies prescribed by teachers of the *studia humanitatis* (grammar, rhetoric, history, moral philosophy, poetry) that began in fifteenth-century Italy.

Secular in their emphasis on the nature, abilities, and potential of man, Renaissance humanists were however neither antireligious nor nonreligious. They energetically and passionately sought to recover completely and understand fully the texts of classical (especially Latin) antiquity, which had endured centuries of neglect. They also wanted to emulate the style of classical writers (Cicero, above all) and to apply the insights gained from their reading of ancient literature to contemporary debates. After the sixteenth century, humanism either decayed into pedantry and pedagogy or was transformed into specialized scholarship. Today, *humanism* (or secular humanism) is sometimes applied to an atheistic or agnostic belief in "human values" and the rejection of religion. But this current use of the term—whether in advocacy or in condemnation—has virtually nothing to do with Renaissance humanism.

humanist In Italian, *umanista*, arose in the medieval university community to describe a teacher of basic grammar and rhetoric, which were the first—and therefore the least prestigious—subjects that a student was expected to master before going on to such career-oriented studies as law and theology. With the onset of the Renaissance, the prestige of these subjects rose; see *humanism*.

ideology A body of visionary ideas that undergirds and motivates political activity and the language used to justify and explain the activity.

imperialism Originally used by the British to deride Napolean III, but today, refers to the expansion of European control over non-European peoples, especially in the late nineteenth and twentieth centuries.

Indo-Europeans An ancient group of peoples speaking a set of languages from which have descended many of the languages of modern Europe, the Caucasus, Iran, and India. Linguists believe that there was a parent language ("Proto-Indo-European"), spoken in the Indo-Europeans' homeland north of the Black Sea.

indulgence In the Late Middle Ages, with the church's permission and encouragement, Christians were allowed to purchase indulgences that promised the buyer a shorter time in purgatory. Indulgences could be granted for the performance of good deeds, such as venerating a saint's relics or donating gifts to the church. By the early sixteenth century, indulgences could be purchased as certified documents; out of this practice, a profitable business was created. Churchmen asserted that the saints had amassed a "treasury of grace" far beyond what they needed for salvation, and that the pope could draw upon this spiritual bank account in dispensing grace to the ordinary Christians who bought or otherwise earned indulgences.

The abuses of indulgence sellers prompted Martin Luther to question (in his famous Ninety-Five Theses) the whole idea of salvation by good works. Salvation, Luther insisted, came through faith alone, not through the purchasing of indulgences or the performance of other good "works." By refusing the papacy's demand that he cease raising such questions, Luther ignited the Protestant Reformation. The Council of Trent upheld the church's teaching on indulgences while it demanded reforms, such as substituting prayer, charity, and genuine repentance for the mechanical act of paying money.

Industrial Revolution A term that historians have long used to describe the enormous changes in technology that began in mid-eighteenth century Britain and transformed life everywhere they have reached. An alternative name now coming into use is *Energy Revolution*. The most important change that the Industrial/Energy Revolution brought about was the generating of power with new technologies—first the steam engine, later the harnessing of electricity, and then the widespread use of the internal combustion engine. Together with the French Revolution, which had an equivalently sweeping impact on political life, the Industrial/Energy Revolution produced the modern world in which we live.

intelligentsia Originally a Russian term used to refer to that educated stratum of society involved in working with the mind rather than the hands. In Europe, the intelligentsia (consisting of people such as writers, professors, artists, and public intellectuals) is assigned a respected role as social critic, whereas in North America its public presence is often confined to universities.

Iron Age The period in human history, beginning about 1200 B.C. and (properly speaking) not ending until the Industrial Revolution of modern times, in which iron metallurgy forms the basis of technology. It followed the Bronze Age.

joint-stock companies Whereas most business activity before the late sixteenth century was carried on by individuals or partnerships, companies organized in the sixteenth century began to spread the risks involved in business ventures across a wide range of investors. Joint-stock companies sold shares that could be traded, thus spreading risks still farther. England's first joint-stock company appeared in 1553, with the numbers of such enterprises growing slowly until late in the seventeenth century. Although speculative frenzies such as the South Sea Bubble occurred, the mobilization of investment capital that joint-stock companies facilitated portended the rise of modern capitalism in the form of stock markets.

knight Originally, the Germanic term *kneht,* from which the English "knight" derives, meaning a serving boy or lowly fighting man in the entourage of a mighty lord. (The related English word *knave* preserves the negative connotations of the original, and in modern German *Knecht* is a similarly invidious term for someone who does menial work.) During the Middle Ages the concept of knighthood gradually took on more dignity, greatly aided by the rise of chivalric ideals in literature, art, and social conventions. By the High Middle Ages, the great nobles boasted of their status as valiant knights. In French and German the very word *knight* was dropped in favor of *chevalier* (related to the French *cheval,* or "horse"; cf. *chivalry*) or *Ritter* (in German, "rider").

laissez-faire, or *laisser faire* To "leave it be"; the idea that markets are self-correcting and that government intervention is not only unnecessary but destructive. Laissez-faire is the classic prescription of capitalism for economic, social, and political policy, but it has seldom been applied consistently over a prolonged period owing to the protests of other interested groups, ranging from workers and consumers to government officials.

land bridge Between 15,000 and 50,000 years ago, lower sea levels exposed land that connected Siberia to Alaska and enabled the earliest human residents of North America to walk across from northeast Asia. Scholars debate over when the first hunter-gatherer bands arrived, but there is wide agreement that they did so by means of the land bridge.

levée en masse Mobilization of an entire population for war. First tried in the French Revolution, universal mobilization of a nation for war became common by World War II.

liberalism A primary ideology that emerged in early nineteenth-century Europe and the United States. Although agendas varied from one country to another, most liberals throughout the nineteenth century sought a reduction of state power (both in the political and the economic spheres) and an enlargement of individual freedom. In the twentieth century, liberalism radically changed its agenda, especially in the United States and to some extent in Great Britain. American liberalism now means advocating the use of state power to redistribute wealth more equitably, to promote the cause of hitherto-disadvantaged minorities, and to raise their economic status. Liberals traditionally seek to enlarge individual freedom. The older conception of liberalism lingers in modern Germany, France, Italy, and other west European countries, but liberal parties there tend to be small centrist or moderately right wing movements without mass followings.

liberty, liberties Considered a prerequisite of privilege prior to the eighteenth century (such as the "freedom" to hunt). After the Enlightenment, liberty (singular) was considered the condition necessary for popular sovereignty to operate effectively.

manor See *manorialism*.

manorialism In medieval western Europe, the *manor* was a central feature of rural society. It was a jurisdictional and economic unit consisting of one or more villages (or parts of villages) and the villagers' land, an individual lord's land (or demesne), and the forest and meadow land that everyone could use. The term *manorialism* refers to the complex social and economic relationships among lord, serfs, and (later) dues-paying peasant tenants. It should not be confused with the political relationships between lord and vassals known as *feudalism*.

Marshall Plan In 1947 the United States government realized that Europe remained economically devastated after World War II. In June of that year Secretary George C. Marshall proposed a plan that the United States undertake a massive program of loans and gifts to help get Europe back on its feet. The Marshall Plan was one of the important factors that made the European economic miracle of the 1950s possible.

Mass The central religious ceremony in Roman Catholicism and Orthodoxy, since the early centuries of Christianity. According to Catholic and Orthodox belief, Christ's sacrifice on Calvary is repeated when the priest celebrating Mass pronounces the words of consecration in the Eucharist: "This is my body" and "This is my blood." It was a core belief of all Protestants that Christ's redeeming sacrifice took place only once—on Calvary—and thus Protestants replaced the Mass with Communion (the Lord's Supper).

mercantilism The set of economic attitudes and related political policies practiced by almost all European states between the seventeenth and the late eighteenth centuries. The word was invented by nineteenth- and twentieth-century scholars and hence was not used by mercantilists themselves. Broadly speaking, mercantilism held that a country's prosperity depended upon its ability to attract and keep gold and silver within its borders and hence to deprive other states of gold and silver. To do this, a state must export more than it imports, must closely regulate trade to ensure that state interests are met, and must strive for self-sufficiency, either within its own borders or by establishing colonies that supply it with essential raw materials; see *cameralism*.

mercantilist See *mercantilism*.

metaphysics The branch of philosophy that inquires into such questions as the nature of being, the existence of God, and other matters that are outside the realm of physical reality. Literally it means "beyond [or after] physics," and received this name because the ancient editor of Aristotle's collected works placed the master's writings on this subject after those that dealt with physics. Aristotle's *Metaphysics* subsequently exerted a powerful influence on western, Islamic, and medieval Jewish philosophy and theology. Since the Enlightenment, the fundamental questions of metaphysics—God, immortality, and freedom of the will—have generally been regarded by western philosophers as beyond either proof or disproof.

middle class White-collar workers, professionals, certain types of merchants, investors, bankers, factory officials, and the like who achieved "respectability" through their participation in the Industrial Revolution. In the nineteenth century, the term and its equivalent in other lan-

guages, emerged to identify this one-fifth of the population; see also *bourgeoisie* and *capitalism*.

modernism Technically, a phase in the history of literature that occurred early in the twentieth century. However, the term has come to mean the entire family of changes associated with that time, such as the innovations in art (cubism) and the changes in science (relativity) that undermined the certainties of the nineteenth century.

modernist See *modernism*.

modernization A general term used to describe the overall process of adopting the political, economic, and social outcomes of the French and Industrial Revolutions. The term was widely used in the 1960s, but it has dropped out of favor because it implies that there is only one way to achieve these ends, the way followed in Europe. Thus many contemporary observers see the term as an aspect of Western imperialism or colonialism.

monolatry See *monotheism*.

monotheism The belief in one god (Judaism, Christianity, and Islam, for example), as opposed to *polytheism* (belief in many gods) and *monolatry* (worship of one god, although other gods exist). The first true monotheism to emerge in the ancient world was that of the Jews. Ancient Greek philosophers also tended to move in a monotheistic direction.

monotheist See *monotheism*.

nationalism An ideology claiming that "the People" consists of co-culturals; that is, those who share a common language, culture, or historical experience. The idea contrasts with "the Others," who are not readily recognizable as one of "Us." One of the basic thrusts of European history in the past two hundred years has been to consolidate state borders on the basis of national affiliations instead of on the basis of religion, affiliation to a ruler, or other criteria used prior to the French Revolution.

Neolithic The New Stone Age, from the Greek words *neo* (new) and *lithos* (stone). In many parts of the world, its onset coincided roughly with the retreat of the continental ice sheets at the end of the last ice age, about ten to twelve thousand years ago. In the Neolithic, tools and weapons continued to be made from stone, but they were ground or polished rather than simply chipped (as in the paleolithic, or Old Stone Age). The Neolithic Revolution began during the early stages of the Neolithic.

Neolithic Revolution A term given by anthropologists and historians to one of the most fundamental changes in human life: the discovery of agriculture, herding, metallurgy, and the development of settled village life rather than a hunting-gathering way of life. Whether the Old World's Neolithic Revolution originated once in the Old World and radiated out from that common center, or whether it occurred independently in different places, is much debated. All serious scholars, however, agree that the New World's Neolithic Revolution began independently. The first Neolithic Revolution is generally placed in the Near East, starting about 10000–9000 B.C.

New World Describes the two continents of the Western Hemisphere. The earliest use of the term dates back to the sixteenth century, when Europeans crossed the Atlantic Ocean and began to conquer and settle the Americas. In this sense the word is anachronistic: to the indigenous people of the Western Hemisphere, there was nothing new or discovered about the part of the world in which they lived. But the term continues to be valid from the standpoint of the evolution and dispersal of human beings. The human race and its hominid predecessors evolved in Africa and spread through Eurasia and even Australia long before the first human beings migrated across the Siberia-Alaska land bridge and settled the Americas.

nomadism See *nomads*.

nomads People whose way of life is based primarily on herding animals rather than on raising crops, although some nomadic groups do engage in agriculture on a limited scale. Nomads typically move over large areas, adjusting to seasonal conditions. The interactions—sometimes peaceful, sometimes aggressive, even exploitative—between nomadic and "settled" urban or agricultural peoples have been a major driving force in global history for thousands of years.

North Atlantic Treaty Organization (NATO) The post-World War II security organization founded in 1949 to rebuff any potential Soviet invasion of western Europe, to provide a way to re-arm Germany within controls, and to maintain an American presence on the European continent. Its purpose, as one official put it, was "to keep the Russians out, the Germans down, and the Americans in."

Observant Reformers during the fourteenth century who sprang up in all of the mendicant orders, including the Augustinian order that Luther later joined. The Observants stressed very strict observation of the monastic rules, and the growing criticism of the monks for the luxurious lives many of them lived was not directed at the Observant wings of the orders.

Old Paradigm In western thought, the set of beliefs (to which Aristotle and Ptolemy gave authoritative expression) about a geocentric universe and principles of physics that explained natural phenomena in qualita-

tive, not quantitative, terms. The Old Paradigm prevailed throughout the Middle Ages despite the steady accumulation of data that eventually undermined it; see also *paradigm*.

Old Stone Age See *Paleolithic*.

Old World The conventional term used to describe the continents of Africa, Europe, Asia (or Eurasia, as some prefer, lumping Europe and Asia together), and Australia, as opposed to the New World, or Western Hemisphere. Today, most authorities also use the term when referring to the origin and diffusion of hominids and the earliest human beings before they crossed the Siberia-Alaska land bridge to the Americas; see also *New World*.

oligarchy Government by a small group. *Oligarchy* is "government by the few," and *timocracy* is "government by the rich." Both are ancient Greek terms that appear to mean the same thing, and indeed they are so close that *timocracy* has become obsolete. Aristotle classified all governments into six types—three good and three bad. The good types were monarchy, aristocracy, and democracy; the bad types were "degenerate" forms: tyranny, oligarchy, and mob rule. The concept of oligarchy has survived into modern times, and the term usefully describes any political system in which the state is dominated by a relatively small class of powerful figures, such as landed aristocrats, merchants, capitalists, or members of a privileged ruling party like the post-Stalinist communists of the former Soviet Union.

orthodoxy A Greek word meaning "correct belief." Orthodoxy has meaning only in relation to *heresy* (formally condemned error), *heterodoxy* ("different teaching"), or *schism* (splitting the church). The concept of orthodoxy first arose in the course of debates in the early Christian church about the nature of Christ—whether or not he was divine, and how he was related to God the Father. Other early definitions of orthodoxy were advanced in the face of supposedly errant teachings about the validity of prophesy; that is, claiming to receive direct inspiration from God and the definition of who should be a member of the church (should it exclude sinners, including sinful clergy; should sacraments administered by sinful clergy be considered valid?) During the Middle Ages and the early modern period, church teachings (that is, orthodoxy) on these and other subjects became extremely complex and increasingly rigorous, with dissent condemned as heresy or schism.

The Orthodox church is the communion of Christian churches that claims to adhere to the teachings of the early medieval church councils, from which they see the medieval papacy as having deviated, culminating in the schism of 1054.

In modern Judaism, the Orthodox are Jews who continue to adhere rigorously to traditional practices and beliefs, in contrast to the Conservative and Reform movements that took shape in the nineteenth and twentieth centuries and have modified or abandoned certain aspects of Jewish practice.

pagan See *paganism*.

paganism A general term for all the polytheistic religions of the ancient Near Eastern and Greco-Roman worlds. For modern Western readers raised in the Judeo-Christian tradition, the word *paganism* has overtones of decadence or violence that need to be overlooked if one is to apply the term usefully to the religious life of pre-Christian Greece and Rome. A great many cults and belief systems can be described as pagan, encompassing primitive, orgiastic, patriotic, mystical, and philosophic approaches. There are signs that in Hellenistic and Roman times many pagans were coming to understand their gods as diverse reflections of a monotheistic deity. The Latin word *paganus*, from which the term derives, means a country person (compare the French word *paysan*, the Italian *paesano*, and the English *peasant*, all of which come from the same root).

Paleolithic The Old Stone Age, from the Greek words *paleo* (old) and *lithos* (stone). Anthropologists trace it back to the earliest *making* of stone tools (not simply throwing rocks as a weapon) by human beings or their biological ancestors. The stage ended when human beings began to fashion *polished* stone tools, rather than merely chipping them. The date when the Paleolithic ended and the Neolithic (New Stone Age) began varied tremendously, depending on the locale.

paradigm An explanatory model of how things work, ranging from a grammatical form to the mechanics of the universe. In recent decades historians of science have used the term to analyze basic changes in scientific theory. The Scientific Revolution, which began with Copernicus and culminated in Newton, destroyed the Old Paradigm and set in its place the New Paradigm, authoritatively summed up by Newtonian physics. In the twentieth century, with the advent of relativity and quantum theory, the Newtonian paradigm itself was subjected to extensive revision. So long as a particular paradigm is in use, students of nature usually have tried to explain new information in terms consistent with it. A "paradigm shift" occurs when scientists conclude that a new paradigm fits the available data better than the old one, see also *Old Paradigm*.

parish In Christianity, the district that is served by a single church and its priest. The spread of Christianity into rural areas during early medieval Europe occurred principally when bishops established churches on large manors (see *manorialism*), a process that was well advanced by the ninth century. A priest, usually a peasant from the locality who received instruction in Latin and Christian ritual, conducted worship services, administered the sacraments, and otherwise looked after the people's spiritual needs. He received a percentage of the manor's production (called the *tithe*) to support himself and maintain the church building. Towns and cities were also divided into parishes and took on administrative and charitable functions. Patronage over the appointment of parish priests was often a source of significant revenue to some secular or ecclesiastical lord.

In early modern times, the network of parishes was significantly strengthened by the Catholic Reformation (or Counter Reformation). Catholic parishes, for example, were instructed to maintain records of baptisms, marriages, and deaths that are (where they survive) a gold mine of information for demographic historians. In Protestant areas, parishes occupied a comparable position, playing an important role as conduits of information; high government or church officials could communicate through the local clergy to the ordinary, generally illiterate, population. By the sixteenth and seventeenth centuries in England, parishes were given legal responsibility to deal with the destitute or disabled (a responsibility they held until well into the nineteenth century). In eighteenth-century England, parishes became the unit of local government.

Parlement, parlements A French institution not to be confused with the English Parliament, although both had a similar linguistic origin in the French verb *parler*, meaning "to talk" or "to speak." In France, the *parlements* were royal courts of appeal, of which there were several; politically, the most important was the Parlement of Paris. Ever since the time of St. Louis IX in the thirteenth century, kings registered with the Parlement of Paris important laws that they had promulgated. Occasionally this or other parlements would formally refuse to register a law of which they disapproved, obliging the king to hold a *lit de justice* (literally, a "bed of justice") in which he would come to the Parlement, sit on a ceremonial chair, and personally order the law registered. Members of the parlements were not elected, but rather they inherited (or bought) their offices. As the sale of offices increased during the sixteenth century, the positions became essentially hereditary and thus a form of property; see *venality*. They were not legislators or representatives, but magistrates. The last significant action of the Parlement of Paris was to resist the reforms that the French royal government was pursuing in the 1780s in its attempt to head off bankruptcy and revitalize the monarchy. This resistance forced the king to resort to summoning the Estates General in 1788, with fatal consequences for the Old

Regime, and the French Revolution brought an end to the parlements.

patronage The dispensing of benefits—offices, honors, employment, and other such favors—to supporters and followers by a powerful personage or organization. The root word comes from the Latin *pater* ("father") and recalls the kind of influence that a Roman patrician (a member of an elite family in the early republic) or *paterfamilias* (the male head of an extended family) was expected to exercise on behalf of clients (dependents) and family members. Patronage usually includes a strong element of mutual obligation, or *quid pro quo*.

Patronage is also an important concept in cultural history, referring to the support that individuals, corporate bodies (guilds and churches), or governments (national, regional, or local) give to artists and writers. Historically, patrons have often exercised considerable influence over the works of art they helped produce. Cultural historians pay a great deal of attention to the effects of patronage on all the arts. In modern times, patronage has by no means ceased, although the marketplace has become an equally important source of support for the arts. Governments, private foundations, and businesses are among the most important sources of patronage today.

philosophes The writers and thinkers who led the Enlightenment campaign to reform European society and its institutions through the application of "reason," by which they meant the Scientific Revolution and its implications and consequences. The philosophes (a French word meaning *philosophers*), such as Montesquieu, Diderot, Voltaire, Rousseau, and Condorcet, were not professional, systematic philosophers. Most philosophes, but not all, were men, and although they were most numerous in France, other Europeans (such as Kant in Germany, Beccaria in Italy, and Hume in England) and North Americans (Jefferson and Franklin) made important contributions.

physiocrats Philosophes who regarded agriculture rather than trade as the key to national wealth in countries like France and England. They argued that governmental control of grain prices should be abolished in order to encourage farmers to increase production. Opposed to mercantilism, the physiocrats believed that economic growth required free markets.

polygyny A marriage system in which one male has several wives. Polygyny is a variety of *polygamy*, a marriage system in which spouses of either sex may have multiple partners. Polygyny was practiced by the powerful men of early Germanic society, and it survived for several centuries after northern Europe was nominally converted to Christianity. Its replacement by church-enforced monogamy was a key step in the evolution of the nuclear family (as opposed to the extended family), which had clearly emerged by A.D. 1000. Islam allowed polygyny, though husbands were limited to only four wives.

polytheism Belief in many gods; see *monotheism*.

popular sovereignty The principle whereby the people, or nation, rather than the king have the ultimate authority in the state; usually put into practice through elections.

positivism The notion, introduced by Auguste Comte, that nineteenth-century Europe was in a third stage of philosophical development, that of positive science. Comte believed that science properly pursued would answer the questions that had baffled metaphysicians for centuries. Sociology, the all-encompassing science of society, was the highest of such sciences for Comte. When generalized, the term means pursuing knowledge by the accumulation of data, which is then supposed to reveal its meaning without recourse to metaphysics.

predestination The Christian belief, based on such biblical texts as Matthew 20:23, Romans 8:28–30, and Ephesians 1:3–14, that God has chosen or "elected" some persons who are to be guided to salvation in heaven for eternity, and those not chosen presumably or explicitly are damned to hell. St. Augustine inclined toward accepting predestination, but the idea was not stressed in medieval Christianity. Instead, the medieval church emphasized that through the power of the sacraments and the intercession of the saints, salvation was available to all Christians who sincerely repented their sins; see also *indulgence*.

In the sixteenth century, Martin Luther revived Augustine's inclination toward predestination, but John Calvin made it a key principle of his theology that Christ died only for the elect and not for all persons. (Calvin himself regarded predestination as "this horrible decree," reflecting the unfathomable justice of God.) In conscious reaction against Protestant avowal of predestination, Counter Reformation Catholicism stressed the ability of individuals, by the exercise of their free will, to reject sin and accept the salvation that God offered to all. In Protestantism, first the influence of the Enlightenment and later the impact of nineteenth-century revivalism (which, like Catholicism, stressed free will in choosing God) brought about the virtual disappearance of predestination as a major theological position.

progress The idea, introduced during the Scientific Revolution, that human beings and their societies can aspire to and achieve continuing advances not only in social and moral but in material terms. The "idea of progress" rejected older views that denied the possibility of material progress, either because humankind was on a relentlessly downward path from the perfection of the Garden of Eden or because the best that could be hoped for was cyclical change (progress followed by decline, followed by progress again, and so on).

proletariat The working class; a term used especially in Marxism. The word derived from the ancient Roman class of poor men who owned virtually nothing but their labor.

prophets, prophecy Inspired men and women, thought to be vehicles through which God spoke directly to humanity. Among the ancient Hebrews, prophets played a major role in reshaping religion in the eighth through the sixth centuries B.C. In Islam, Muhammad is regarded as the last—the "Seal"—of the prophets, whose predecessors included Abraham and Moses, the Hebrew prophets, and Jesus.

proto-industrialization Before the Industrial Revolution drew workers into machine-filled factories beginning late in the eighteenth-century, some rural regions in Europe experienced the beginnings of industrial processes. In these areas, workers supported themselves partly by farming and partly by spinning or weaving textiles and performing other specialized tasks in their cottages; see *putting out system*.

providentialism The belief that events in history and nature are the direct result of God's intervention.

purgatory In Catholicism, the place where the souls of the dead who have been forgiven their mortal sins are obliged to expunge their burden of guilt before they are fit to enter heaven. Belief in purgatory spread in the eleventh century, in part as a grassroots phenomenon as priests sought to reassure the laity that the dead did not become lurking ghosts but were sent to a place of expiation. Purgatory, like hell, appealed to the medieval sense of justice: sooner or later, sin and guilt would be punished. By the Late Middle Ages, purgatory became central to the church's penetential system by which Christians were encouraged to do penance for sins that they or their loved ones had committed but been forgiven; see *indulgence*. The Protestant reformers rejected belief in purgatory, but it remains a vital part of Roman Catholicism.

putting out system A type of economic organization that arose in late medieval Europe and continued until the Industrial Revolution, in which a merchant capitalist distributed raw materials (wool, for example) to rural households and then collected and sold their output of finished or semi-finished goods. Sometimes the capitalist would also own the producers' machines (such as looms) and even their dwellings. The putting-out system dealt a heavy blow to urban guilds, but was replaced by the factory system of the Industrial Revolution.

quattrocento An Italian word meaning "the fourteen hundreds"; that is, the fifteenth century. The term is often used by historians of Renaissance Italy to denote the period between A.D. 1401 to 1500.

real wages Earnings calculated in relation to living costs, thus taking inflation into account. During inflationary periods, nominal wages (the money an employee is actually paid) increase, but if living costs rise faster, real wages fall.

Realpolitik A German term now often used in English to refer to a policy based on the realistic assessment and use of power. The term was first used in connection with Bismarck's diplomacy in the nineteenth century, but it had been practiced by statesmen since ancient times. In current North American parlance, it refers to political "hard ball."

Renaissance, renaissance In French, meaning "rebirth," refers above all to the new cultural energies that appeared in Italy in the late fourteenth and early fifteenth centuries, later spreading throughout Europe. The word was invented in the early nineteenth century by a French historian to characterize the "rebirth" of art and literature at the end of the Middle Ages, and in 1860 the great Swiss historian Jakob Burckhardt used the term in the title of his enormously influential book *The Civilization of the Renaissance in Italy*. Burckhardt argued that the Renaissance was a distinctive period of history marked by individualism, cultural creativity, ruthless statecraft, and the abandonment of austere medieval religiosity. Ever since, historians have debated Burckhardt's thesis, and have modified it in several important respects.

Since Burckhardt's time, renaissance has also been applied more broadly to a variety of historical periods marked by seeming cultural rebirths—the Northumbrian Renaissance of the seventh and early eighth centuries A.D.; the Carolingian Renaissance of Charlemagne's time; the Ottonian Renaissance around the year 1000. *The Renaissance of the 12th Century* (to quote the title of an American scholar's 1927 book), argues that during the High Middle Ages there was a sweeping revival of classical scholarship and artistic expressiveness rivaling that of Renaissance Italy. This proliferation of "renaissances" underscores the importance of not allowing abstract terms to dominate thinking about history.

revolution, revolutionary In contemporary usage, the term refers to a revolt (often violent) against an existing political structure that utilizes principles of radical reform that would be difficult to effect in normal times and this by consequence moves things forward with unusual rapidity. The term is also applied to any sweeping and fundamental change in economic organization, intellectual life, or technology, as exemplified by the

Commercial Revolution of the Middle Ages, the Scientific Revolution of the sixteenth through eighteenth centuries, and the Industrial (or Energy) Revolution that began in the eighteenth century.

Before the French Revolution, which in many ways serves as the prototype for all modern political and social revolutions, the word had entirely different connotations. Its root is the Latin verb *volere* ("to turn") and the prefix *re-* meaning "back." In other words, the original meaning was a turning back to a starting point, as a wheel revolves. It was in this sense that Copernicus spoke of the "revolutions of the celestial bodies" as they orbited the sun. Occasionally applied to politics (its use in a political context was uncommon), a revolution meant a return to some preexisting state or condition. In this sense English advocates of Parliamentary supremacy and limited monarchy spoke of "the Glorious Revolution" of 1688–1689 as "restoring" balance to the country's constitutional structure and Protestantism to the Church of England after the overthrow of the "tyrannical" and papist King James II. Whether the Glorious Revolution was in fact a simple act of restoration is another question entirely; the point is that the victorious revolutionaries thought of themselves not as effecting something new but of bringing back something old, tried, and true. The vast gulf that exists between the older and the modern connotations of the word suggests how deeply our views of the possibility of progress and of the desirability of change have altered over the past three hundred years.

romanticism A cultural attitude, with roots in eighteenth-century "sensibility," that came into focus in early nineteenth-century Europe. Romanticism stressed the primacy of feeling and intuition over rationalism and other aspects of the Enlightenment tradition. It exerted a powerful influence in early nineteenth-century European literature, music, and the fine arts, and in music it remained the dominant style until the early twentieth century. Romanticism deeply influenced nationalism as well, for it respected folk traditions, history, and the mystical ties that bound together people of a common culture. Romantics' political sympathies could range from reactionary conservatism to liberalism and extreme radicalism, but some romantics were totally apolitical. Some were drawn strongly to traditional religion, especially Roman Catholicism, and others went to the opposite extreme of rejecting organized religion and the Christian tradition entirely.

Sacraments, sacraments In Christianity, the rites that are believed to give special spiritual grace to the believer who receives them. Although formal church teachings about the nature of the sacraments developed only slowly, early Christians believed that baptism and the Eucharist (Holy Communion) were channels by which grace flowed from God to the believer. Baptism had been a purification rite practiced by Jews (such as the Essenes and John the Baptist) before the appearance of Christianity, and which Jesus himself underwent at the beginning of his ministry. Early Christians also believed that the Eucharist—the commemoration of Jesus' Last Supper—was a rite through which God continued to send them spiritual grace, a belief encouraged by Paul. As the concept of a Christian priesthood developed (it was in place by the third century), the belief arose that only a validly consecrated priest could bestow the sacraments. In the Middle Ages, faith in divine grace imparted by other sacraments also came into focus, and these beliefs were formally endorsed by the church in the twelfth and thirteenth centuries. Besides baptism and the Eucharist, these other sacraments were the ceremonies of confessing and being forgiven one's sins, confirmation, matrimony, holy orders (the ordination of a priest), and extreme unction (the last blessing of a dying person). The Reformation reverted to the early Christians' practice of recognizing only baptism and the Eucharist as sacraments, but the Roman Catholic church still affirms that there are seven sacraments; see *Mass* and *transubstantiation*.

Schlieffen Plan The plan put together by the chief of the German General Staff around 1900 that would permit Germany to pursue a two-front war. When World War I broke out, German armies swept through Belgium trying to outflank the French and obtain a quick victory, but the plan failed.

scholastic See *scholasticism*.

scholasticism The system of teaching and writing about philosophy and theology in medieval universities. Exponents of scholasticism, or the *scholastic method*, are often called "schoolmen." (Since there were no female teachers in the medieval universities, there were no "schoolwomen.") The scholastic approach was highly logical. It consisted of posing a question, marshaling arguments and authorities pro and con, and then arguing a conclusion. It was pioneered in the early twelfth century by Peter Abelard, and its greatest masters were St. Albert the Great (or Albertus Magnus) and St. Thomas Aquinas in the thirteenth century. Scholasticism continued to be a vigorous intellectual system in the fourteenth and fifteenth centuries. Although all scholastics were Christians (some making more concessions to Aristotle's pre-Christian opinions than others), scholasticism did not consist of a single theological or philosophical viewpoint. Some, for example, had far greater faith in the capacity of human reason to understand God and God's ways than did others. Common to all scholastics, however, was deductive reasoning—the drawing of conclusions from logical principles already established. When the opposite approach of inductive reasoning—that is, reasoning upward from empirical data—became established in the course of the seventeenth century, scholasticism went into decline. It lives on, however, in the "neo-Thomist" school of thought among late nineteenth- and twentieth-century Roman Catholic philosophers.

Scientific Revolution The new approach (emerging in the seventeenth century) to the study of nature that replaced scholastic ideas about nature. By the eighteenth century, it had come to be called the "new philosophy" and included controlled experimentation and the rendering of results in mathematical notation. Its most notable figure was Isaac Newton, who reduced the laws of motion to three simple formulae, thus replacing the medieval notions of essences and impetus characteristic of Aristotelian and scholastic physics. This period was revolutionary in the sense that it wrested the investigation of natural phenomena away from political and religious concerns and freed scientific exploration to go its own way with little or no interference from other social elements.

sect, sectarian Of or pertaining to any small religious group that is typically convinced it constitutes a "righteous remnant" of true believers who alone know and are doing God's bidding.

Historians of religion often distinguish between sectarian movements, which typically address themselves to a chosen few righteous people who alone know The Truth, and *churches*, which are broad (often aiming to be universal) institutions meant to lead as many people as possible in the path of righteousness. Sects and sectarian movements abound in every institutional religious system, for there are always people ready to believe that the original ideals of their faith have been betrayed by its leaders and that they alone constitute the "righteous remnant." Historically, some religious organizations, such as the medieval and early modern Christian church, have been quite intolerant of sectarianism, outlawing it as heresy. Other religious movements, including Buddhism and Hinduism, have tended to see such diversity as appropriate to the multiple paths by which individuals may reach the Divine.

serfdom A form of rural social and economic organization in which peasants have the right to cultivate a parcel of land and to pass this right on to their heirs, but in return are expected to remain on the holding, to render dues in either kind or money (or both), often to perform set labor services on the lord's demesne, to submit to the lord's court jurisdiction, and in general defer to and obey the lord; see *manorialism*. Serfs are generally distinguished from slaves (individuals considered the personal property of a master who can sell them and who often

wields the power of life and death over them). However, under extreme conditions (as in Russia and parts of eastern Europe in early modern times and as late as the mid-nineteenth century), serfs approached the condition of slavery in that they, too, could be sold apart from their land and even apart from other family members.

Serfdom arose in post-Carolingian Europe and reached its height in the West in the eleventh and twelfth centuries. But it often eroded as lords became more interested in extracting money instead of labor services from their villages. By the Late Middle Ages, it was disappearing in western Europe, although vestiges remained down to the time of the French Revolution. In eastern Europe, however, serfdom came into full focus later in the Middle Ages, and it was not abolished until the nineteenth century. Serfdom should be distinguished from *feudalism*, which refers to the formal bonds of mutual dependency that link an overlord (often a king) with his vassals (usually nobles).

serfs See *serfdom*.

Slavophile Literally, a "lover of Slavs"; those who speak a language of the Slavic family, such as Russian, Ukrainian, Polish, Czech, Serbian, Bulgarian, and the like. In nineteenth-century Russia, Slavophiles looked to the Russian past to assess public issues, in contrast to the Westerners, who looked to west European standards. The term is still used today to describe conservative, Orthodox, or nationalist thinkers in Russia.

Social Darwinism The turning of Darwin's scientific principles of evolution into theories of domination based on gender, race, and nations. A central slogan of late nineteenth-century social Darwinists was "the survival of the fittest," which they used to (falsely) argue that the domination of white, male Europeans both at home and in the colonies was justified.

socialism An ideal (in contrast to liberalism) that stresses the fact that every human being is a separate individual and that no human being can live and grow outside of a social group. Utopian socialism, which sought to establish small, special communities (see *utopia*), gave way during the nineteenth century to political socialism, which focused on mobilizing the working class either to revolution or to support reform political parties. Many of the aims of early socialists that seemed radical in the nineteenth century, such as unemployment insurance, labor unions, equality for women, and medical care for workers, are now ordinary, accepted aspects of modern life.

socialist See *socialism*.

statute In England, a new law that changes, supersedes, or adds to the existing body of law. Under Edward I (1272–1307), it became the practice for the king to enact statutes with the assent of Parliament. Some of the statutes of Edward's time were thought to restate common-law provisions. Together with the common law, statutory law is the basis of modern English and American jurisprudence.

Stone Age See *neolithic* and *paleolithic*.

subsistence economy Typically, an agriculturally-based economy in which the primary producers, usually peasants, consume almost all that they produce. Subsistence agriculturalists do not enter into market relationships except as required for the most minimal needs, such as salt or iron, and typically deal in barter rather than cash.

subsistence farming Living off of one's own agricultural production, as opposed to making a living by selling agricultural produce or other commodities on the market and purchasing needed goods for money.

tax farming A practice in which individuals, often high ranking financiers, acquire from the state the right to collect certain taxes. The tax farmer would provide to the government a prompt payment (assuring income for the state), while collecting a larger sum from the public to pay himself (almost always making a profit). Although tax farmers had to operate according to the laws of the realm, they often exceeded these rules, creating significant resentment. This practice was used heavily in Old Regime France.

theocracy A state or society directly ruled by priests. True theocracies are rare—in fact, no completely theocratic system has ever been created in Western civilization—although at times clergymen (such as Calvin in sixteenth-century Geneva) have wielded important influence in western societies.

theocratic See *theocracy*.

Torah In Judaism, the first five books of the Bible: Genesis, Exodus, Leviticus, Numbers, and Deuteronomy, whose author is traditionally thought to be Moses. Another technical name for the Torah is the *pentateuch*, a Greek word meaning "five books." The Torah contains the creation story, the saga of the early patriarchs, the Flood, the story of the Jews' bondage in Egypt, their deliverance by God through Moses, and the basic Jewish law codes. In modern Judaism, the Torah is the central focus of piety.

totalitarianism A political framework in which an individual or a party has the sole right to assert total control over society and to impose an all-encompassing ideology. Once it manages to seize power, a totalitarian party attempts to eliminate spontaneous behavior and places private organizations under its control.

Totalitarianism must be distinguished from *absolutism*, an ideology and political system characteristic of early modern Europe that claimed for the legitimate king the right to concentrate all political authority in his own hands and those of his officials. Absolutism had neither the ambition nor the means to impose anything like the kind of total control over the lives of its subjects that totalitarian ideologies demand. Only in the utopian prescriptions of such writers as Plato and Thomas More was anything like the degree of control over human beings envisioned that modern totalitarianism has required. Indeed, modern totalitarian regimes can be thought of as utopias that aim at the total transformation of human life. Nazi Germany, Stalinist Russia, Maoist China, and the communist regime in North Korea have all been examples of totalitarian "social engineering" that required an all-powerful dictatorship, the elimination or co-opting of all potentially competing elements of civil society, the constant use of propaganda and educational indoctrination to remold minds (particularly those of the young), and the ruthless application of terror against actual, potential, or imagined opponents.

The concept of modern totalitarianism was first advanced by Mussolini, who boasted that his Fascist dictatorship had achieved truly total control over Italy. In fact, the dictatorship of Mussolini and his Fascists was by no means as all-encompassing as he claimed. But Mussolini was correct in declaring that his movement and his regime were the antithesis of nineteenth-century liberalism and democracy. Hitler's Germany and Stalin's Soviet Union came much closer to the totalitarian ideal of unchallenged control for purposes of social re-engineering, and in the process, millions of people were murdered.

Between the late 1930s and the late 1960s liberal commentators in western Europe and the United States tended to conflate Nazism and Stalinism (if not all of Marxism-Leninism) into a single totalitarian model. This view lost favor as historians and political scientists uncovered evidence of the factionalism that lurked beneath the surface of these supposedly monolithic dictatorships, and it lost even more ground as post-Stalinist communism evolved into something not exactly benign but at least apparently oligarchic and conservative. Growing skepticism about traditional liberal, religious, and individualist values (which became widespread after the late 1960s) also contributed to the liberal commentators' view that harping on communism's totalitarian nature was merely Cold War propaganda. The downfall of the European Marxist-Leninist regimes in the late 1980s has, however, revived interest in the totalitarian mind-set as a tool of analysis.

transubstantiation In Christianity, the doctrine of the nature of the Eucharist (also known as Holy Communion or the Lord's Supper). Three of the Gospels (Matthew 26:26–28; Mark 14:22–24; Luke 22:17–20) related that at his parting meal before his crucifixion (the Last Supper) Jesus broke bread and shared a cup of wine with his apostles, saying "This is my body . . . This is my blood." In the early Christian community Jesus' words and his act of table fellowship were repeated as a central Christian ceremony, a practice endorsed by Paul (I Corinthians 12:23–26).

Historically, endless controversy has hinged on the meaning of Jesus' words, and in particular the verb *is*. Early Christians seem to have believed that Jesus was present among them when his words at the Last Supper were pronounced and bread and wine shared among the assembled believers. Whether this presence was believed by early Christians to be symbolic, spiritual, or physical (or whether they saw any difference between these kinds of presence) is difficult to determine on the basis of available evidence.

The use of the Latin word *transubstantiation* to describe Christ's "real presence" at the Mass under the "appearance" of bread and wine began early in the High Middle Ages, but this dating probably represents only the articulation of a belief long held by both Latin and Greek Christians. That Jesus was really present when the priest pronounced these consecrating words was generally accepted by the Orthodox church, and in the Latin-speaking Catholic church it was a position that was argued with growing conviction by high-medieval theologians. The Fourth Lateran Council (1215) endorsed transubstantiation as a position that theologians *could* hold, but it was not yet declared to be a position that they *must* hold. Meanwhile, however, medieval popular sentiment (represented both by laypeople and ordinary clergy) was fully on the side of transubstantiation. Much medieval piety focused on the firm belief that Jesus was physically present in the consecrated bread and wine.

The question of whether Christians must believe in transubstantiation came to a head in the Reformation. Aware that their high-medieval predecessors had debated the question, Protestant theologians reopened it as part of their effort to focus Christian faith on God's Word, not on miracles, priestly powers, or the Mass. Luther rejected transubstantiation but held to something rather close to it, a *consubstantiation*, which meant that the bread and wine continued to exist even though Christ was also really present through the believers' faith when the consecrating words were pronounced. Zwingli and later the Calvinists, however, interpreted the words "This is my body" to mean a symbolic rather than an actual, physical presence: "This *represents* my body." Christ, Zwingli and the Calvinists said, had actually sacrificed his body only once, on Calvary, and now he was in heaven, not physically present on the altar. The Council of Trent in the mid-sixteenth century decreed that belief in transubstantiation was binding on all Catholics, and that teaching it is still a central Roman Catholic doctrine. Most Protestant denominations today maintain positions closer to those of Luther or Calvin; see also *sacraments* and *Mass*.

trecento An Italian word meaning, "the thirteen hundreds"; that is, the fourteenth century. The term is often used by historians of Renaissance Italy to denote the period between 1301 and 1400.

tyranny In ancient Greece, any form of *illegitimate* one-man rule, as opposed to *legitimate* one-man rule (monarchy). Ancient Greek tyrants might or might not behave tyrannically, but they or their immediate predecessors had seized power illegally, and they held it without the sanction of law or custom. For Aristotle, tyranny meant the abusive rule of a single man whose aim was his own benefit, not the common good.

Historians apply the concept of tyranny as illegitimate one-man rule to the rise of the *signori* (singular: *signore*) in the medieval and Renaissance Italian city-republics. Signori supplanted the old commune, usually in a coup d'état. Like ancient tyrants, the signori might claim to act in the interests of the masses as opposed to the oligarchy whose rule they had overthrown, and such a claim might even have an element of truth. Nevertheless, the signorial regimes had taken power by extralegal means, and they had to be ready to use cunning or violence in order to maintain their power.

tyrant See *tyranny*.

usury Charging high interest on money lent to a borrower. Modern economic theory defines interest as the rent that one pays for the temporary use of someone else's money, or a rental that can be justified on the grounds that if the lender spent or invested the money rather than lending it, he or she could obtain something of value. The interest rate, therefore, is determined by the law of supply and demand.

Lending at interest was widespread in all the commercial societies of the ancient world, dating back to Sumer. Aristotle had doubts about whether lending at interest was morally acceptable. Money, he said, could not multiply of its own accord; why, then, should a lender have the right to demand repayment of a greater sum than he had lent? The Hebrew Bible (Deuteronomy 20:19–20) condemned usury as the uncharitable extraction of advantage from another's need. However, Deuteronomy apparently left the door open to charging interest if the debtor was not a "brother." Exactly how far this prohibition extended is unclear, although the prophets' attacks on the rich for "grinding the faces of the poor" leave little doubt that economic exploitation was part of life in ancient Israel.

Medieval Christianity followed both Deuteronomy and Aristotle in condemning usury as sinful, and church courts sometimes canceled debts on the grounds that they involved the payment of interest. (Islam also condemned usury as contrary to the charitable spirit that was expected to prevail in the *umma,* or Islamic community.) However, individuals' need for credit forced Christians, Jews, and Muslims to resort to various semi-legal subterfuges in order to borrow and lend at interest. These subterfuges, and the risks that lenders faced when borrowers might refuse to repay on the grounds that they were victims of usury, had the effect of driving interest rates higher than they might otherwise have been. In high-medieval Europe, many Christian theologians recognized these realities and allowed the charging of interest so long as rates were not "excessive." These rules seem to have meant in practice that merchants could borrow at the going market rate but that extracting interest from people in desperate need—to whom one should extend charity—was sinful. Essentially, this was the position of Protestant theologians of the sixteenth and seventeenth centuries. It is a historical myth that Protestantism gained middle-class adherents because it allowed them to charge interest whereas Catholicism forbade the practice. In fact, Luther and Calvin both tended to be more restrictive than contemporary Catholic authorities in what they defined as morally permissible economic practice.

In the western world, the full realization that interest rates should be determined by market conditions came only in the late seventeenth and eighteenth centuries. Since that time, the word *usury* has tended to disappear from public discourse except in populist (and Nazi) propaganda against banking in general and scapegoated Jews in particular. The term also applies today to clearly extortionate behavior, commonly called "loan-sharking," forcing people whom legitimate lenders (such as banks and credit card companies) do not consider creditworthy to make high interest payments on loans that are backed up by the threat of physical punishment or other force if payments are not made on schedule.

utopia Literally "no-place," a word coined from Greek roots by Thomas More in his classic book *Utopia* (1516). Utopias are ideal societies, invented by their creators to solve the problems that they see in the world around them. Plato's *Republic* (fourth century B.C.) is the first of the utopias created by Western thinkers, and all its successors (including More's) share common features: a critique of the muddled world in which we live, followed by a logical, rigid, often communistic, and usually despotic order of things in which we supposedly can live without further trouble. Actual attempts to construct utopian societies began in the nineteenth century, when socialist or religious enthusiasts sought to withdraw from the competitive world of industrial capitalism and build ideal communities free of corrupting materialism. Marx criticized utopian socialists (Saint Simon, Fourier, and Owen) on the grounds that their attempts were based on a false understanding of the world and not on the dialectical laws of history that he claimed to have uncovered.

venality The sale of judicial, administrative, financial, and other offices occurring widely in late medieval and early modern Europe. When the king offered an office for sale, the purchaser could use his own money or borrow from a moneylender. The king then annually paid the office-holder a small sum called a *rente,* perhaps 2 or 3 percent of the purchase price, which the officeholder could use to help pay off his debt. In France (and in other countries without a banking system), venalité proved an effective way for the king to mobilize capital for the use of the state, although the payment of rentes eventually became a serious financial burden. By early in the sixteenth century, many public offices in France were considered property that could be sold and inherited. Higher-ranking offices often brought immediate or eventual ennoblement.

Weltmacht A German term meaning "world power." At the end of the nineteenth century, many Germans felt that their country could not be truly great until it was able to articulate its power throughout the world as Britain did. This desire for Weltmacht contributed to the outbreak of World War I.

Yalta A resort in the Crimea (Russia/Soviet Union) where President Roosevelt, Marshall Stalin, and Prime Minister Churchill met in January 1945. Because this was the last meeting of the Big Three during World War II, the word became a symbol for the division of Europe. At the meeting, Stalin agreed to enter the war against Japan and to form a United Nations, while Roosevelt agreed to Soviet demands for reparations from Germany and for a transition government in Poland dominated by communists.

yeoman In medieval and early modern England, a farmer who stood at the top of the rural working population, but below the gentry on the social and political hierarchy. The word is of Middle English origin and simply means "the man." The English yeomanry emerged in the post-Black Death period, when some peasants who survived the epidemic managed to acquire (by purchase or by lease on favorable terms) substantial amounts of land, to emancipate themselves from serfdom, and to hire less fortunate rural people to work for them. Unlike gentry, yeomen farmers did physical work, but some of them managed to get their children into the ranks of the gentry by marriage, educated them at the university for careers in the church or the law, or sent them to cities to become skilled artisans or merchants.

Yiddish The German dialect that originated among medieval German Jews, whose descendants settled throughout eastern Europe.

$\mathscr{L}$iterary $\mathscr{C}$redits

Chapter 1

From *The Epic of Gilgamesh*, (pp. 110–112) rev. ed., trans. N. K. Sanders. (Penguin Classics 1960, 3rd. ed. 1972), Copyright © NK Saunders, 1960, 1964, 1972. Reproduced by permission of Penguin Books Ltd.

"Hammurabi's Code" from *Ancient Near Eastern Texts Relating to the Old Testament*. Ed. James B. Pritchard, trans. Theophile J. Meek. Copyright © 1950, 1955, 1969, renewed 1978 by Princeton University Press. Reprinted by permission of Princeton University Press.

"Judgment Seat" and "Akhenaten" from *Ancient Near Eastern Texts Relating to the Old Testament*. Ed. James B. Pritchard, 2nd ed. trans. John A. Wilson. Copyright © 1950, 1955, 1969, renewed 1978 by Princeton University Press. Reprinted by permission of Princeton University Press.

From the *New Oxford Annotated Bible*. Isaiah 36:1–2, 4–6; 37:1, 508, 14–20. Scripture quotations are from the New Revised Standard Version of the Bible. Copyright © 1989 by the division of Christian Education of the National Council of the Churches of Christ in the U.S.A. Used by permission. All rights reserved.

"Assyrian Siege" from *Ancient Near Eastern Texts Relating to the Old Testament*. Ed. James B. Pritchard, 2nd ed. trans. A. Lewis Oppenheim. Copyright © 1950, 1955, 1969, renewed 1978 by Princeton University Press. Reprinted by permission of Princeton University Press.

Chapter 2

"Hoplite" and "Solon" from *Greek Lyrics*, 2nd ed. trans. Richmond Lattimore. Copyright 1961 by University of Chicago Press. Used by permission of the publisher.

Chapter 3

From *Sappho of Lesbos: Her Works Restored*, trans. Beram Saklatvala. Copyright 1968 by Charles Skilton Ltd. Used by permission of Caversham Communications Ltd.

"Philosophers" and "Protagoras" from *Philosophers Speak for Themselves: From Thales to Plato*, ed. T. V. Smith. Copyright 1934 by University of Chicago Press. Used by permission of the publisher.

Excerpt by Plato from *The Last Days of Socrates* (pp. 61–62), rev. ed., trans. Hugh Tredennick. (Penguin Classics 1954, Second revised edition 1969) Copyright © Hugh Tredenick, 1954, 1959, 1969. Reproduced by permission of Penguin Books Ltd.

Excerpt by Aristotle from *The Politics* (pp. 245–246), trans. J. A. Sinclair. (Penguin Classics, 1962). Copyright © The Estate of J. A. Sinclair, 1962. Reproduced by permission of Penguin Books Ltd.

Chapter 4

"Cincinnatus" from Livy, *The Early History of Rome*, Books 1–5 of *The History of Rome from its Foundation* (pp. 213, 216), trans. Aubrey de Sélincourt. (Penguin Classics, 1960). Copyright © The Estate of Aubrey de Sélincourt, 1965. Reproduced by permission of Penguin Books Ltd.

From Cicero, *De Officiis*, Book 3, in *Selected Works* (pp. 166–167), rev. ed., trans. Michael Grant. (Penguin Classics 1960, second revised edition 1971) Copyright © Michael Grant 1960, 1965, 1971. Reproduced by permissiion of Penguin Books Ltd.

"Pliny" republilshed with permission of Columbia University Press, 562 W. 113th Street, New York, NY 10025. *Roman Civilization: Selected Readings*, ed. Naphthali Lewis and Meyer Reinhold, 1955. Reproduced by permission of the published via Copyright Clearance Center, Inc.

Chapter 5

Excerpt from "The Goddess Isis Intervenes" from *The Golden Ass: The Transformation of Lucius* translated by Robert Graves. Copyright © 1951 and copyright renewed © 1978 by Robert Graves. Reprinted by permission of Farrar, Straus and Giroux, LLC.

New Oxford Annotated Bible, Matthew 5:3–11, 38–45, 48, Romans 1:13–17; 2:1–5, 9–12; 3:1–2, 9; 5:1–5; 6:1–4, John 1:1–14. Scripture quotations are from the New Revised Standard Version of the Bible. Copyright © 1989 by the division of Christian Education of the National Council of the Churches of Christ in the U.S.A. Used by permission. All rights reserved.

"Thracian Village" republished with permission of Columbia University Press, 562 W. 113th Street, New York, NY 10025. *Roman Civilization: Selected Readings*, Naphthali Lewis and Meyer Rinehold, 1955. Reproduced by permission of the publisher via Copyright Clearance Center, Inc.

Chapter 6

"Vladimir" from *Harvard Studies and Notes in Philology and Literature, Volume 12* by Samuel H. Cross. Copyright © 1930 by the President and Fellows of Harvard College. Reprinted by permission of Harvard University Press.

Chapter 17

"Bodin" from *European Witchcraft*, E. William Monter, trans. and ed., pp. 52–53. Copyright © 1977 by McGraw-Hill. Reproduced with permission of The McGraw-Hill Companies.

Table 17-1 from *The Witch-Hunt in Early Modern Europe*, 2nd ed., Brian P. Levack, table 3, p. 314, 1995. Reprinted by permission of Pearson Education Limited.

"Galileo" from *Dialogue Concerning the Two Chief World Systems: The Ptolemaic and Copernican*, 2nd Revised Edition, by Galileo Galilei. Edited/translated by Stillman Drake, pp. 114–115. Copyright © 1952, 1962, 1967 Regents of the University of California

"Newton's Laws" from *Nature and Nature's Laws: Documents of the Scientific Revolution*, Marie Boas Hall, ed., pp. 271–272. Copyright © 1970 by Marie Boas Hall. HarperCollins Publishers, Inc.

Chapter 18

Table 18-1 adapted from Tables 6.1 and 6.2, *The European Demographic System, 1500–1820*, Michael W. Flinn, p. 82. © 1981 Johns Hopkins University Press. Reprinted by permission.

"Addison" from *Foundations of the Metaphysics of Morals, What is Enlightenment?* trans. Lewis White Beck, 1950. Reprinted by permission of Caroline H. Beck.

"Condorcet" from *Sketch for a Historical Picture of the Progress of the Human Mind* by Antoine-Nicolas de Condorcet, trans. June Barraclough, pp. 167–169, 173–176, 196–202, 1955, J. M. Dent Publishers. Reprinted by permission.

"Rousseau" from *The Confessions of Jean-Jacques Rousseau*, translated by J. M. Cohen, (Penguin Classics, 1953) pp. 362–363. Copyright © J. M. Cohen, 1953. Reproduced by permission of Penguin Books Ltd.

Chapter 19

"First Partition" and "Frederick" from *The Habsburg and Hohenzollern Dynasties in the Seventeenth and Eighteenth Centuries*, C. A. Macartney, ed., pp. 190–191, 345, © 1970. Reprinted by permission of Walker & Co.

Chapter 20

"Working Family" reprinted by permission from P. E. Razzell and R. W. Wainwright, *The Victorian Working Class: Selections from Letters to the Morning Chronicle*, pp. 295–297, Published by Frank Cass & Co. Ltd, 890–900 Eastern Avenue, Ilford, Essex, England, 1973.

Table 20-1 from *The Labouring Classes in Early Industrial England, 1750–1850*, John Rule, p. 89, 1986. Reprinted by permission of Pearson Education Limited.

Table 20-2 from *A Treatise on Indigence* by Patrick Colquhoun, 1806, reproduced in Harold Perkin's *The Origins of Modern English Society 1780–1880*, pp. 20–21, © 1969. Reprinted by permission of Routledge Ltd.

Chapter 21

"Jakob Walter" from *The Diary of a Napoleonic Soldier* by Jakob Walter, edited by Marc Raeff, pp. 41–42 and 85–87. Bantam/Doubleday/Dell Publishers.

Chapter 22

"Message to Siberia" from *The Poems, Prose, and Plays of Alexander Pushkin* by Alexander Pushkin, edited by A. Yarmolinsky, pp. 626–63. Copyright © 1936 and renewed 1964 by Random House, Inc. Reprinted by permission of Random House, Inc.

Chapter 23

"Middle Class" excerpts from *The Past Speaks*, 2nd ed., vol. 2, Walter Arenstein, ed., pp. 172, 178. Copyright © 1993 by Houghton Mifflin Company. Used with permission.

"Working Class" excerpts from *An Economic History of Modern Britain*, vol. 2 by J. H. Clapham, p. 24 as reprinted on p. 175 in *The Past Speaks*, 2nd ed., published by D. C. Heath, Inc., 1993. Reprinted with the permission of Cambridge University Press.

"Palacky" from "Letter Sent by Frantisek Palacky to Frankfurt" from *Slavonic & East European Review*, 26, 1948, p. 303–308. Reprinted by permission.

Chapter 25

"Domestic Servant" from *German Worker: Working Class Autobiographies from the Age of Industrialization*, Alfred Kelly, trans. and ed., pp. 140–141. Copyright © 1987 The Regents of the University of California.

Chapter 26

"Thus Spoke Zarathustra" by Friedrich Nietzsche from *The Portable Nietzsche* by Walter Kaufmann, editor, translated by Walter Kaufmann. Translation copyright 1954 by The Viking Press, renewed © 1982 by Viking Penguin Inc. Used by permission of Viking Penguin, a division of Penguin Putnam Inc.

Song "The Christmas Eve Revel of Beggars" from *Turn-Of-The-Century Cabaret*, pp. 38–39, by Harold B. Segel. Copyright © 1987 Columbia University Press. Reprinted with the permission of the publisher.

Chapter 28

"Mutiny" from *World War I and European Society: A Sourcebook*, Marilyn Shevin Coetzee and Frans Coetzee, pp. 252–253. Copyright © 1995 by Houghton Mifflin Company. Used with permission.

"Revolutionary Art" from *Documents of Soviet History, Vol I, The Triumph of Bolshevism, 1917–1919*, Rex A. Wade, Alex G. Cummins, eds., pp. 107–108, 1991. Academic International Press, Gulf Breeze, Fla. Reprinted by permission.

President Wilson's "14 Points" speech in *The Papers of Woodrow Wilson*, vol. 45, Arthur J. Link, ed., pp. 536–538. Copyright © 1984 by Princeton University Press. Reprinted by permission of Princeton University Press.

Chapter 29

"Lenin" from *The Communist International, 1919–1943*, Vol. 1 1919–1922, Jane Degras, ed., pp. 168–172, 1956. Reprinted by permission of Oxford University Press.

"Compromise" from *The Making of a State* by Thomas G. Masaryk, 1927, George Allen & Unwin, pp. 466–467. Reprinted by permission of Taylor & Francis.

"Testament" excerpt from *Documents of Soviet History, Vol. 2, Triumph and Retreat, 1920–1922*, Rex A. Wade, Alex G. Cummins, eds., pp. 438–439, 1991. Academic International Press. Reprinted by permission.

"Eulogy" excerpt from *Stalin: A Political Biography* by Isaac Deutscher. Copyright © 1949, 1966 by Oxford University Press. Reprinted by permission.

Chapter 30

"Hitler's Plans," The Hossbach Memorandum" from *The Approach of War* by Christopher Thorne, pp. 35–50, 1967. Reprinted by permission of Macmillan Press, Ltd.

"Fall of France" from *Strange Defeat: A Statement of Evidence Written in 1940* by Marc Bloch, trans. Gerard Hopkins, pp. 171–172, 1949, Oxford University Press Publishers.

"Atlantic Charter" from *The Grand Alliance* by Winston S. Churchill. pp. 443–444. Copyright 1950 by Houghton Mifflin Co., © renewed 1977 by Lady Spencer-Churchill, The Honourable Lady Sarah Audley, The Honourable Lady Soames. Reprinted by permission of Houghton Mifflin Co. All rights reserved.

"War in the East" from *Diary from the Years of Occupation, 1939–1944* by Zygmunt Klukowski, translated from the Polish by George Klukowski, pp. 16, 114, 173, 219, 284, 353. Copyright 1993 by Board of Trustees of the University of Illinois. Used with permission of the University of Illinois Press.

Poem "Death Fugue" from *Paul Celan: Poet Survivor, Jew* by John Felstiner, pp. 31–32. Copyright ©1995 John Felstiner. Published by Yale University Press. Reprinted by permission of the author.

Chapter 32

"DDT" from *Silent Spring* by Rachel Carson. Copyright © 1962 by Rachel L. Carson, renewed 1990 by Roger Christie. Reprinted by permission of Houghton Mifflin Company. All rights reserved.

Index

propaganda during, *974*
from "short war" to stalemate, 967–968
submarine warfare during, 976–978
tanks used in, 976
timeline on, 966
as total war, 966–979
and Treaty of Versailles, 989–996, *994,*
    1002, 1021, 1022
trench warfare during, 967–968,
    974–976, *974*
Wilson's Fourteen Points, 987–988, 990,
    1071
World War II
    aftermath of, 1030, 1070–1081,
        1096–1097
    Atlantic Charter and, 1052, 1053, 1071,
        1073
    Blitzkrieg (lightning war), 1001,
        1049–1052, 1056
    bombing of Japan, 1061–1064, *1062,*
        1063, 1094
    Casablanca conference and, 1057
    casualties of, 1052, 1057, 1063–1064,
        1069–1070
    closing in on Nazi Germany, 1057
    concluding comments on, 1064
    displaced persons following, 1073,
        1074
    Hitler's aggression and, 841
    Hitler's aggressions in peacetime before,
        841, 1044–1049, *1045, 1048*
    Hitler's war plans in 1937, 1046
    home fronts during, 1055–1056
    maps of, *1050, 1051, 1058*
    Nazi occupation of France, 1049–1050,
        1050
    in North Africa, 1057
    Nuremberg trials of Nazi war criminals
        after, 1074–1075, 1074n
    Pacific theater of, 1052–1053,
        1061–1064, *1062*
    painting on, *1068, 1069*
    partnership among Allies, 1070–1073
    Pearl Harbor attack during, 1052–1053,
        1062
    Potsdam conference and, 1063, 1075
    resistance movements during,
        1054–1055
    Roosevelt's Four Freedoms, 1071, *1071*

Teheran conference and, 1057, 1071
timeline on, 1030
turning points of, 1056–1057
U.S. entry into, 1052–1053
Yalta conference and, 1073
Worms, Concordat of, 289, 322
Wozniak, Stephen, *1113*
Wren, Christopher, 613
Writing systems
    alphabetic writing, 25, *25,* 25n, 27, 51,
        57, 58, 114, 200
    Carolingian minuscule, 234, *234*
    cuneiform, 9, *9,* 12, 38, 47
    Cyrillic alphabet, 200
    development of, xxx
    Greek alphabet, 51, 57, 58, 114
    hieroglyphics from ancient Egypt, 16,
        17, 47
    hieroglyphics of Maya civilization, 523
    invention of, xxix
    Islamic calligraphy, *206*
    Linear A and Linear B, 45, 47, 48, 50
    Merovingian script, *234*
    Slavic alphabet, 200
    of Sumeria, 6, 9, *9*
WTO. *See* World Trade Organization
    (WTO)
Württemberg, 818, 848, *850,* 852
Würm Glaciation, xxiv
Wycliffe, John, 411, 412, 413

Xeniades, 104
Xerxes, 66–67, 89

Yahweh, 29, 30, 31, 32, 39, 40, 56n, 103,
    163
Yahwist, 32n
Yalta conference, 1073
Yangtze, xxx
Yeltsin, Boris, 1122, *1123,* 1131
Yeomen, 537, 538
Yiddish, 895
Yom Kippur War, 1110
Yorkshire, 730, 730n
Young Ireland, 861
Young Italy, 801–802
Young Turks, 958, 1017
Young Woman Standing at a Virginal
    (Vermeer), 599

Ypres, *965,* 966, 968
Yucatán, 523, 525, 530
Yugoslavia
    breakup of, in 1991, 988, 1055,
        1126–1129, *1128,* 1134
    Communist party in, 1010, 1083
    creation of, 988, 989
    ethnic groups in, 1010, 1127–1128
    government of, in 1920s, 1011–1012,
        1018
    Hitler's invasion of, 1052
    Hungarians in, 992
    in Little Entente, 1001, *1001*
    meaning of term, 1011n
    resistance movement in, during World
        War II, 1054–1055
    Tito's dictatorship in, 1055, 1079, 1083,
        1101, 1127
    after World War II, 1083

Zacatecas, 526, 534
Zadar, 313
Zagreb, 924
Zagros Mountains, xxvi, 5, 6
Zama, battle of, 119
Zara, 313, 314
Zarathustra. *See* Zoroaster.
Zealot movement, 151
Zeespieghel (Blaeu), 636
Zeno, 104–105
Zeus, 52–54, *53,* 76–77, 87, 90, 103, 108,
    147, 158, 172
Zhdanov, Andrei, 1080, 1081
Zheng He, 514
Zhivkov, Todor, 1120–1121
Ziggurats, 8, 9, 12, 29
Zionism, 895
Žižka, Jan, 413
Zoffany, John, 659
Zola, Émile, 913, 914–915
Zollverein (free-trade zone), 818, 823
Zoroaster, 38–39, 444
Zoroastrianism, 38–39, 39n, 102, 204,
    301n
Zurich, 404, 477–478, *477,* 481, 652
Zwingli, Ulrich, 477–478, *477,* 480, 481,
    494, 504